Encyclopedia of Ukraine

Encyclopedia of

UKRAINE

VOLUME IV
Ph-Sr

Edited by
DANYLO HUSAR STRUK

under the auspices of
the Canadian Institute of Ukrainian Studies (University of Alberta),
the Shevchenko Scientific Society (Sarcelles, France), and
the Canadian Foundation for Ukrainian Studies

UNIVERSITY OF TORONTO PRESS INCORPORATED
Toronto Buffalo London

© University of Toronto Press Incorporated 1993
Toronto Buffalo London
Printed in Canada

ISBN 0-8020-3994-4
Collector's Edition: ISBN 0-8020-3009-2

Canadian Cataloguing in Publication Data
Main entry under title:
Encyclopedia of Ukraine

Revision of: Entsyklopediia ukraïnoznavstva.
Vols. 1–2 edited by Voldymyr Kubijovyč;
vols. 3–5 edited by Danylo Husar Struk.
Includes bibliographical references.
Contents: Map and gazetteer volume. –
V. 1. A–F – V. 2. G–K – V. 3. L–PF – V. 4. PH–SR – V. 5. ST–Z.
ISBN 0-8020-3994-4 (v. 4)

1. Ukraine – Dictionaries and encyclopedias.
2. Ukraine – Gazetteers.
I. Kubijovyč, V. (Volodymyr), 1900–85.
II. Struk, Danylo Husar, 1940–.
III. Canadian Institute of Ukrainian Studies.
IV. Naukove tovarystvo imeny Shevchenka.
V. Canadian Foundation for Ukrainian Studies.
VI. Title: Entsyklopediia ukraïnoznavstva.

DK508.E52213 1984 fol   947′.71′003   C84-099336-6

Volodymyr Kubijovyč, *Editor-in-Chief, volumes 1, 2*

Danylo Husar Struk, *Editor-in-Chief, volumes 3, 4, 5*

The publication of this volume

has been made possible in part

through a federal grant

in recognition of the contribution of Ukrainian pioneers

to the development of Canada.

EDITORIAL STAFF

P

Phanagoria. An ancient Greek colony on the Taman Peninsula at the site of present-day Sinna, Krasnodar krai, RF. It was founded in the middle of the 6th century BC by colonists from the Ionic city of Teos, and in the 5th century BC it became part of the *Bosporan Kingdom. Phanagoria flourished in the 5th to 2nd centuries and formed an independent state in the 1st century BC. Its inhabitants (Sindians, Maeotians, Sarmatians, and Greeks) engaged in agriculture, animal husbandry, fishing, various crafts, and trade with neighboring tribes and Mediterranean states. In the 4th century AD the city was razed by the Huns but was rebuilt by the end of the century. It died out in the 11th to 12th century. Excavations of Phanagoria began in the 19th century. More systematic digs conducted in the late 1930s and after the Second World War have uncovered the ruins of palaces, houses, wells, the city walls, a gymnasium, the acropolis, and the port.

Pharmacology. The science of drugs and their effect on or interaction with a living organism. In Kievan Rus' *Yevpraksiia Mstyslavna, the granddaughter of Volodymyr Monomakh, gathered information about medicaments and wrote the treatise *Mazi* (Salves). The preparation and administration of medicaments was largely in the hands of folk healers or sorcerers, of whom it was generally believed that they possessed magic powers (see *folk medicine). They prepared their concoctions mostly from *medicinal plants, infrequently from animal tissues, wine, or honey, and handed down their recipes shrouded in secrecy. After the Christianization of Ukraine the preparation of drugs was taken up by monasteries. Lviv pharmacists are mentioned in chronicles as early as the 14th century. By the 16th and 17th centuries handwritten books of remedies existed, called *travnyky, zeleinyky,* or *vertohrady*.

The first pharmacies in Left-Bank Ukraine were founded in major cities at the beginning of the 18th century by the decree of Peter I and were government-owned or privately operated. The Ukrainian obstetrician N. *Ambodyk-Maksymovych wrote an encyclopedic treatise on medical plants that is regarded as the first pharmacological textbook in the Russian Empire (1783). By the 19th century pharmacology was being taught in medical and veterinary institutes as well as at most universities. The foundations of experimental pharmacology in Ukraine were laid by V. Dybkovsky, H. Shkavera, O. *Cherkes, and Yu. Petrovsky.

After the 1917 Revolution the system of training pharmacologists resulted in the creation of related disciplines: pharmacy (the preparation and dispensation of drugs), pharmacognosy, pharmaceutical chemistry and technology, pharmacotherapy (the application of drugs in treating disease), toxicology (the study of drug poisoning), and veterinary pharmacology. Further evolution in pharmacology led to the establishment of its specialized subdivi-

sions: clinical pharmacology, immunopharmacology, chemotherapy, psychopharmacology, pharmacogenetics, and molecular and biochemical pharmacology. Research is conducted at the Kharkiv Chemico-pharmaceutical Research Institute and at the Kiev Scientific Research Institute of Pharmacology and Toxicology and in pharmacological laboratories at other medical and scientific research centers. The Scientific Pharmacological Society of Ukraine was founded in 1961 in Kiev and belonged to the All-Union Scientific Society of Pharmacologists. The collection *Farmakolohiia i toksykolohiia* is published in Kiev.

The Lviv Pharmacy Museum (on Rynok Square) is one of the city's oldest museums, with an exceptionally large collection of pharmaceutical items. It is located in the three-story premises of the original pharmacy (est 1735), and its collection includes scales, mortars, crucibles, manuscripts and incunabula, herbaria, and recipe books, totaling over 2,000 items.

In the diaspora, a department of pharmaceutics existed at the *Ukrainian Technical and Husbandry Institute in Munich in 1945–51.

P. Dzul

Pheasant (*Phasianus*; Ukrainian: *pantarka, fazan*). Birds of the family Phasianidae that are related to the quail, partridge, peacock, and jungle fowl. Pheasants are long-tailed birds of open woodlands and fields, where they nest on the ground and lead a sedentary life. They were naturalized in Ukraine and raised for hunting as excellent game birds. They inhabit the regions of Kiev, Kherson, Mykolaiv, the Crimea, and Transcarpathia.

Philadelphia. A city and port (1991 pop 1,585,000) in southeastern Pennsylvania, at the junction of the Delaware and Schuylkill rivers. It has been one of the main centers of Ukrainian settlement: 28,000 of its residents claimed Ukrainian origin in 1980 but other estimates have put this figure as high as 52,740.

Ukrainians from the Lemko region began to settle in Philadelphia in the 1880s. Later arrivals came from Transcarpathia and then from Galicia. They were attracted to the city by jobs in locomotive plants, steelworks, sugar refineries, railway transport, and port facilities. Women worked mostly as domestic help. The earliest organized community structure in the city was a Transcarpathian congregation which established the parish of the Holy Spirit in 1891. Galician immigrants, who were displeased by the Hungarian influence in the parish, soon organized their own St Michael's parish. With the coming of Bishop S. *Ortynsky, the city developed into a religious and educational center. The Cathedral of the Immaculate Conception was opened in 1908. National Prosvita conferences were held in Philadelphia in 1905 and 1909, and a network of reading rooms and Ukrainian schools was set up. The first branch of the Ukrainian National Association was es-

Ukrainian Catholic Cathedral of the Immaculate Conception in Philadelphia

tablished in 1905, and in 1909 the Society of Ruthenian-American Citizens was founded and housed in its own building. The Basilian order of nuns set up an orphanage in 1911. St Paul's Institute (Minor Seminary) was founded by Bishop K. Bohachevsky in 1925 (transferred to Stamford, Connecticut, 1933). The *Providence Association of Ukrainian Catholics established its head office in Philadelphia in 1914, and the Ruthenian Bank was founded in 1915 on Ortynsky's initiative. When the Greek Catholic exarchate was divided into separate Ukrainian and Byzantine Catholic (Transcarpathian) jurisdictions in 1924, the former established its seat in Philadelphia. In 1958 it was raised to the status of a metropoly. Archbishop I. *Teodorovych moved the seat of the Ukrainian Orthodox Church in the USA from Chicago to Philadelphia in 1925.

During the interwar period Philadelphia's Ukrainian community developed rapidly. In October 1922 the founding conference of the United Ukrainian Organizations in America was held in Philadelphia, and until 1930 its head office was located there. In July 1936 the Ukrainian Catholic Youth League staged a Ukrainian-American Olympiad there. By 1936 there were two Ukrainian Catholic churches, one Byzantine Catholic church, one Orthodox church, six community halls, a regular parish school, a girls' secondary school (both schools run by the Basilian nuns), six evening schools of Ukrainian language and culture, four library–reading rooms, three printing presses, and over a dozen women's youth, fraternal, sports, and choral organizations. The Catholic triweekly *Ameryka*, the Transcarpathian weekly *Rusyn*, the Orthodox journal *Dnipro*, the Catholic monthly *Misionar*, and the Russophile *Pravda* all came out in Philadelphia.

The founding of the *Ukrainian Congress Committee of America (UCCA) took place in 1940 in Philadelphia, which also is the site of the head office of the *United Ukrainian American Relief Committee since its establishment in 1944. In 1948 the *World Federation of Ukrainian Women's Organizations was founded in Philadelphia.

During the postwar years almost 6,000 Ukrainian refugees settled in Philadelphia. By 1981 the number of churches had increased to ten Catholic, three Orthodox,

two Evangelical-Baptist, and two Pentecostal. A host of new political, social, women's, veterans', professional, youth, and sports organizations appeared. The Trident sports club won six championships of the American Soccer League. Three financial institutions prospered: the Ukrainian Savings and Loan Association, the Self-Reliance Credit Union (est 1948), and the Trident Savings Association. Most of the local organizations were affiliated with the local branch of the UCCA till 1980, when the latter was split into two rival organizations. A number of national organizations had their head offices in Philadelphia, including the *Ukrainian National Women's League of America (1943–74), the *United Ukrainian War Veterans in America (1949–), the *Ukrainian Music Institute of America (1952–9), the *Ukrainian Patriarchal Society in the United States (1970–9), and the Saint Sophia Religious Association of Ukrainian Catholics (1977–). The main research and educational institutions in Philadelphia include *Manor Junior College (est 1947), the Ukrainian Art Studio (est 1952), the *Lypynsky East European Research Institute (est 1963), and a branch of the Ukrainian Catholic University (est 1977). The Ukrainian Educational and Cultural Center was established in 1980 to provide physical facilities for a wide range of community activities. It services over 40 organizations, including Saturday school, performing ensembles, professional groups, and youth organizations. In 1982 the UNR government-in-exile moved its head office to Philadelphia.

The city was home to the *Ukrainian Theater in Philadelphia (1949–57) and Teatr u Piatnytsiu (until 1974) under the direction of V. Blavatsky and V. Shasharovsky. In 1953 the Kobzar chorus, conducted by A. Rudnytsky, was founded. In the 1970s it was succeeded by the Prometheus chorus, under M. Dliaboha. A Ukrainian radio program has served the local community since 1939, followed by Blavatsky's Radio Hour (1951–), Holos Myrian (1971–), and the Ukrainian Hour (1973–).

Publications coming out of Philadelphia in the postwar period include the daily (since 1950) *Ameryka*, *Misionar*, and literary magazine *Kyiv* (1950–64); the quarterly *Ukraïns'ka knyha* (1971–82); the women's monthly *Nashe zhyttia* (1944–74); the Catholic weekly *Shliakh – The Way* (1940–); and the art magazine *Notatky z mystetstva* (1963–). Since the beginning of the century Philadelphia has been an important Ukrainian publishing center.

Economic prosperity has enabled Ukrainians to move to residential areas in the suburbs. A few old community centers have survived in the inner city, most notably the Catholic community in the Franklin Street vicinity. It encompasses a new cathedral designed by Yu. Yastremsky, several religious institutions, and a senior citizen's home.

BIBLIOGRAPHY
Shistdesiat' lit orhanizatsiinoho zhyttia ukraïntsiv u Filadel'fiï (Philadelphia 1944)
Zolotyi iuvilei ukraïns'koï hromady v Filadel'fiï (Philadelphia 1967)
Lushnycky, A. (ed.) *Ukrainians in Pennsylvania* (Philadelphia 1976)

V. Protsko, M. Labunka, V. Markus

Philanthropic Society for Publishing Generally Useful and Inexpensive Books (Blagotvoritelnoe obshchestvo izdaniia obshchepoleznykh i deshevykh knig). The Russian name adopted by the publishing society of the Ukrainian *Hromada in St Petersburg because of severe censorship. The society was founded in 1898 on the initiative of Gen M. Fedorovsky. It was headed first by D. *Mordovets, then by O. *Rusov, and later by P. *Stebnytsky, who initially, together with O. *Lototsky, conducted all of the society's activities. Among its members were hundreds of Ukrainians from various provinces. By 1917 the society had published 80 popular Ukrainian brochures (more than a million copies) on agriculture, hygiene, and, particularly, history. In 1904–5 the society addressed petitions to the supreme imperial institutions demanding the annulment of restrictions on Ukrainian publishing. Together with the auxiliary Shevchenko Society in St Petersburg, the society published the first complete edition of T. Shevchenko's *Kobzar in 1907.

Philately. See Ukraine-Philatelisten Verband, Ukrainian Philatelic and Numismatic Society, and Postage stamps.

Philipps, Tracy, b November 1890 in the United Kingdom, d 21 July 1959 in London. Journalist and international affairs expert. Educated at Oxford and Durham universities, Philipps was an enigmatic figure with connections to the British intelligence community. In addition to holding postings in East Africa and the Near East, he served as the British relief commissioner in Ukraine in 1921. Between the two world wars he was a foreign newspaper correspondent specializing in the Balkans and Eastern Europe. He came into contact with V. *Kaye-Kysilewsky in London during the 1930s, and in 1940 went to Canada, where he played an important role (together with Kaye-Kysilewsky and G. *Simpson) in establishing the *Ukrainian Canadian Committee (now Congress). In 1941–3 he was an adviser to the Canadian Department of War Services on European immigrant communities and their role in war industry. He was chief of planning, resettlement of displaced persons, United Nations Administration, in Washington and Germany in 1944–5. For a time (from 1939) he was married to L. *Kolessa, the daughter of O. *Kolessa. His writings included monographs and articles on zoology, Islam, ethnology, international affairs, and refugee and minority problems.

Philosophy. An intellectual discipline (literally, 'love of wisdom' in classical Greek) that, in the course of its history, has been variously defined as the study of the basic principles of being, the testing of the foundations of knowledge, the general guide to the good life, the analysis of basic scientific concepts and methods, and the examination of certain concepts of ordinary language. Unlike the specialized sciences, it does not have its own subject matter or distinctive method. Hence, only a vague definition, such as 'the critical and systematic reflection on questions of the greatest concern to man,' may be broad enough to cover the various forms assumed by philosophy.

Because it was adopted from other cultures to address certain pressing political or religious needs, philosophy in Ukraine has been preoccupied with practical rather than theoretical problems. The political calamities and attendant cultural disruptions in Ukraine's history account to a large extent for the lack of durable philosophical tradition in Ukraine and for the absence of a distinctively Ukrainian system or worldview. For this reason some important Ukrainian thinkers (eg, H. *Skovoroda) have been assigned mistakenly to Russia's more stable philosophical culture; others (P. *Yurkevych, V. *Lesevych) did in fact work in a non-Ukrainian tradition. Lacking its own philosophical literature and institutions, Ukrainian culture could be considered to have been incomplete during some periods of its development. At such times writers and poets rather than philosophers were the propagators of philosophical ideas and theories among the Ukrainian public.

Medieval period. The period from the adoption of Eastern Christianity to the Mongol invasion (10th–13th centuries) was marked by vigorous intellectual development. The assimilation of Byzantine culture was not passive, but an active rethinking that gave rise to original speculation. Because of a common literary language and alphabet, the work of Bulgarian translators and thinkers was readily transferable to Rus'. The ideas of Greek philosophers and the Church Fathers entered Rus' through Bulgarian translations of Greek collections or original Bulgarian compilations, including the *Izbornik of Sviatoslav (1073), Zlatostrui, Pchela (The Bee), the chronicles of John Malalas and Georgios Hamartolos, the Lives of ss Cyril and Methodius, the Hexaëmeron of Exarch John of Bulgaria, The Source of Knowledge of St John of Damascus, and apocrypha. The new, imported ideas, which themselves were not systematized and were often opposed, did not displace old popular beliefs, but were set alongside them. Thus, many conflicting answers to the same basic questions were found in different and even the same sources. Neither a single dogmatic scheme not a unified worldview was worked out.

Since political motives played a decisive role in the religious conversion of Rus', the emergent philosophical thought was focused on political rather than religious questions. Authors of the first original works produced in Rus' were not concerned much with personal salvation or the defense of Christian doctrine, but with a higher justification of the political order. Metropolitan Ilarion's *Slovo o zakoni i blahodati (Sermon on Law and Grace), the finest theoretical work written in Rus', shows how the Christianization of Rus' is the fulfillment of universal history. Grand Prince Volodymyr Monomakh's *Pouchenie ditiam (Instruction for [My] Children) and the Rus' chronicles portray the ideal prince, a combination of the pagan warrior and the fatherly Christian ruler. Besides these works, the sermons of Bishop Cyril of Turiv, the letters of Metropolitan Klym Smoliatych (reputedly the best philosopher in Rus'), and the writings of Nestor the Chronicler contain philosophical ideas, but fall far short of the kind of articulated, systematic thinking characteristic of scholasticism. The worldview expressed in the literature and folklore of Rus' was practical, optimistic, and life-asserting. The Church Fathers' Christian Neoplatonism reinforced the sense of divine presence in the world and the expectation of happiness in this life that were characteristic of the earlier pagan outlook. The sharp opposition between God and nature, as well as the spirit and the body, and its attendant rejection of the joys of this world was confined to a relatively narrow class of ascetic works.

The Mongol invasion of the mid-13th century began a long period of political turmoil and cultural decline in Rus'. For almost three centuries nothing significant was added to the Kievan intellectual heritage. As a mood of historical pessimism set in, people turned to religion and mysticism for comfort. In the mid-14th century Hesychasm, a form of monastic mysticism, spread from Bulgaria to Ukraine, and in the 15th century a rationalist sect of *Judaizers appeared in Kiev.

Renaissance period. Philosophical ideas and methods of argument gained a new importance in the period of religious struggle in Europe. At the end of the 15th century the ideas of *humanism were brought to Ukraine by foreign travelers and by Ukrainians studying at foreign universities. The *Reformation, which was carried into Galicia and Volhynia by rationalist sects, such as the *Socinians, was very different in origin and purpose from the humanist movement, yet their programs coincided and reinforced each other on many points: the extension of education and learning, the use of the vernacular, the right to individual opinion, and the need to return to the original sources and to reassess critically the traditions built on them. Protestant anticlericalism, public-mindedness, and national awareness had an important influence on the church *brotherhoods in Ukraine.

Although these two movements contributed to the cultural revival in Ukraine, it was the Counter-Reformation spearheaded by the *Jesuits that threatened the very existence of the Orthodox faith and Ukrainian culture and aroused the Ukrainian Orthodox nobility and burghers to vigorous organized action. At first the Orthodox adopted a defensive strategy: they turned inward toward their own Greco-Slavonic tradition and rejected anything belonging to the Latin-Polish tradition. Returning to the roots of their culture, they revived the use of Greek and Church Slavonic, translated the Bible, and studied patristic theology. The achievements of the Catholic West – scholastic theology, philosophy, and logic – were viewed with suspicion as a devilish ploy to lure believers away from the true faith. New institutions were set up toward the end of the 16th century to carry out this program: the Ostrih cultural center, consisting of the Ostrih Academy Press, a learned circle, and a string of brotherhoods modeled on the Lviv Dormition Brotherhood. The leading Orthodox proponents were I. *Vyshensky, V. Surazky, Kh. Filalet, H. Smotrytsky, Ostrozkyi Kliryk, Z. Kopystensky, K. Stavrovetsky, I. Kopynsky, and Y. Boretsky. To them philosophy was part of theology, and most of their ideas were derived from the same sources on which medieval thinkers had drawn – Pseudo-Dionysius, St John Chrysostom, St John of Damascus, and Exarch John of Bulgaria (see *Polemical literature).

This defensive strategy led to isolation from the larger society and from the dominant culture. Withdrawal from this world for the sake of another world did not appeal to the upper classes of the nobility, clergy, and burghers, who continued to drift away from the Orthodox faith and culture. The Orthodox countered by proposing to study and assimilate the tools (Latin, Polish, rhetoric, and logic) and ideas (scholasticism) of their rivals. This was a dangerous policy, for it diminished the differences between the competing cultures, but it was the only policy that offered some hope of success. The turn to scholasticism was a return to an outlived intellectual tradition, but it created the preconditions for the separation of philosophy from theology and the introduction of modern ideas into Ukraine. The chief proponents of the new strategy were M. Smotrytsky, K. *Sakovych, L. Zyzanii, and P. Mohyla. The Kievan Mohyla College (later Academy) was the leading institution to carry out this program.

In spite of royal prohibition, philosophy began to be taught at the Kievan Cave Monastery School (1631), and the practice was continued when the school was reorganized into the Kievan Mohyla College, later Academy (1632–1817). The philosophy courses, read in Latin, usually required three years and covered three main fields, logic, physics (natural philosophy), and metaphysics. Each instructor prepared his own course; hence, the courses differed significantly in content and style. Some of the professors who offered philosophy courses at the academy were Y. *Kononovych-Horbatsky (1639–42), I. *Gizel (1645–7), Y. *Krokovsky (1686–7), S. *Yavorsky (1691–3), I. Popovsky (1699), Y. Turoboisky (1702–4), Kh. Charnutsky (1704–5), T. *Prokopovych (1707–8), Y. Volchansky (1715–18), I. Levytsky (1723–5), I. Dubnevych (1725–6), A. *Dubnevych (1727–8), S. Kalynovsky (1729–30), S. Kuliabka (1735–9), M. *Kozachynsky (1741–5), H. *Konysky (1749), T. *Shcherbatsky (1751–3), and D. *Nashchynsky (1753–5).

The general character of these courses was syncretic – the result of blending elements of Christian Neoplatonism with Aristotelian doctrines. The academy's professors drew ideas freely from the ancient philosophers (mostly Aristotle and Plato, but also the Stoics and Ptolemy), the patristic tradition (Origen, St Basil the Great, St Augustine, Pseudo-Dionysius), medieval scholasticism (Albertus Magnus, Thomas Aquinas, J. Duns Scotus, and William of Ockham), and neoscholasticism (T. Cajetan, F. Suárez, P. Fonseca, L. de Molina, R. de Arriaga, and F. de Oviedo). They often criticized Thomas Aquinas, using the arguments of his scholastic opponents. Aristotle was quoted more than any other thinker but was not treated as an infallible authority. The logic course, which consisted of an introductory part called dialectic or minor logic and a more sophisticated part called major logic, was based on Aristotle's *Organon* and supplemented with refinements introduced by scholastic logicians. On the central problem discussed in logic – universals – the academy's professors rejected Platonism and accepted some version of Aristotelian realism. In natural philosophy they adopted Aristotelian hylomorphism, but tended to stress the ontological primacy of prime matter over form. Shcherbatsky was the first to proffer the Cartesian concept of matter instead of Aristotle's. While accepting creation the Kiev thinkers tended to minimize God's subsequent intervention in the natural world. This deistic tendency contrasted sharply with their Neoplatonist metaphysics, which emphasized God's immanence in nature. A growing interest in modern science and philosophy is evident in their discussion of Copernican, Galilean, and Cartesian theories (Shcherbatsky first adopted the heliocentric theory and Descartes's vortex theory) and the rejection of Aristotle's distinction between celestial and sublunar bodies (Prokopovych, Kozachynsky, Konysky, Shcherbatsky). Some added ethics treatises to their courses (Prokopovych, Kalynovsky, Kuliabka, Kozachynsky, Konysky, Shcherbatsky). They tended to reject a narrow, ascetic view of life and to assert the desirability of happiness in this as well as the next life and its attainability in an active, rationally governed life. In style the courses looked much like scholastic treatises: the chief problems of philosophy were discussed one by one by proposing a thesis, listing objections, and replying to the objections.

Modern period. During the second half of the 18th century the Kievan Mohyla Academy and the colleges in

Chernihiv, Pereiaslav, and Kharkiv were gradually reduced to mere seminaries. At the beginning of the 1760s the Kiev metropolitan ordered philosophy at the academy to be taught according to C. Baumeister's texts based on C. Wolff's system, and thus discouraged any individual originality and intellectual independence.

Ukraine's loss of the last vestiges of political autonomy under Catherine II and its swift cultural decline account for the weak impression that the Enlightenment made on Ukrainian thought. Without royal encouragement or interest and without vigorous institutions of higher learning independent of church control, the Enlightenment could not grow into a full-fledged movement. It is represented by a few individual thinkers, such as Ya. *Kozelsky, P. *Lodii, I. *Rizhsky, and J. *Schad, and propagandists, such as V. *Karazyn, H. *Vynsky, O. Palytsyn, and V. Kapnist. A conservative form of Enlightenment based on G. Leibniz's and C. Wolff's ideas was propagated by the higher schools; the more radical form articulated by F. Voltaire, J.-J. Rousseau, D. Diderot, C.-A. Helvétius, P.-H. Holbach, and Montesquieu was cultivated and propagated by small circles of educated nobles. Some Ukrainians (H. *Kozytsky, S. *Desnytsky, Kozelsky, I. Vanslov, Ya. Kostensky, H. *Poletyka, V. Ruban, and I. Tumansky) belonged to a society in St Petersburg (1768–83) that translated and published books by several French thinkers. *Kantianism was propagated by the German thinker L. Jacob, who was a professor at Kharkiv University (1807–9), and by Rev V. Dovhovych, a member of the Hungarian Academy of Sciences in Budapest. Kant's moral theory made a strong impression on Schad.

Grounding a doctrine of natural rights in an ahistorical concept of human nature, the enlightened thinkers proposed to realize these rights (to individual freedom, equality before the law, and enjoyment of property) by restructuring society. All of them were opposed to serfdom, but apart from Kozelsky and Karazyn they urged the restriction of landowners' rights rather than abolition. Karazyn and Lodii preferred constitutional monarchy while Kozelsky preferred a republic. Following Rousseau, Kozelsky advocated not merely equality before the law, but limits to economic disparity. All of them believed in peaceful social reform through education and the moral improvement of the monarch and small elite. Karazyn pointed also to the importance of scientific and technological development for social progress.

In its practical (moral and social) consequences the philosophy of H. *Skovoroda is very close to the teachings of the *Philosophes*, although it has no direct tie with the Enlightenment. It is rooted not in the new natural sciences, but in the humanist tradition going back to the ancient philosophers and in Christian Neoplatonism. In his writings Skovoroda denounced the injustice and exploitation he observed around him, and in practice he renounced this society by turning down a career in the church. His ideal society, which can be realized only by individual moral rebirth, is based on the fulfillment of each member's inner nature. In this context equality is the full (hence equal) realization by all individuals of their unequal potentialities.

A number of Ukrainians played an important role in the growth of mysticism in the 18th-century Russian Empire. This trend of thought paved the way for the Romantic worldview and German idealism.

The development of Ukrainian culture, particularly literature and art, in the 19th century was influenced decisively by German *romanticism. The Romantic outlook attained its fullest philosophical expression in the German idealists – J. Fichte, F. *Schelling, and G. Hegel – and it was those thinkers who had a determining influence on philosophical thought in Ukraine during the first half of the 19th century.

Fichte's ideas were introduced at Kharkiv University by J. Schad (1804) and were spread to other educational institutions by his students. The first translation of Fichte was done at Kharkiv by one of Schad's students in 1813. Schad also acquainted his students with some of Schelling's doctrines, and his successor to the university's chair of philosophy, A. Dudrovych (1818–30), absorbed Schelling's mystical spirit and taught Schellingian psychology. J. Kroneberg, who taught classical philosophy at Kharkiv University (1819–37), attempted to construct his own esthetic theory using Schelling's ideas. M. *Maksymovych, the first rector of Kiev University, formulated his ideas on nature under the impact of Schelling's and L. Oken's doctrines and was inspired in his later ethnographic work by Schelling's views. K. Zelenetsky, who tried to reconcile Schelling and Kant, and N. Kurliandtsev, who translated Schelling and H. Steffens, taught at the Richelieu Lyceum in Odessa in the first half of the century. P. Arsenev followed C. Carus in his psychology lectures at the Kiev Theological Academy and Kiev University in the 1840s and probably had some influence on the Cyril and Methodius Brotherhood. But the most influential German thinker was Hegel, whose system encompassed all the diverse trends within romanticism (moral, religious, esthetic) and subsumed them all under reason. Hegel's historicism and dialectic made a strong impression on O. *Novytsky, O. *Mykhnevych, and S. *Hohotsky. They not only adopted some of his ideas but also tried to apply his methods of interpretation. Hegel's theory of history influenced a number of historians, such as M. Lunin, who in turn influenced M. Kostomarov, and P. Pavlov, some literary historians such as A. Metlynsky and M. Kostyr, and the philosopher of law P. Redkyn (see *Hegelianism).

The Christian Romantic ideology of the *Cyril and Methodius Brotherhood is the finest example of a creative response by young Ukrainian intellectuals to new ideas from the West. As expressed in the *Knyhy bytiia ukraïns'koho narodu* (The Books of the Genesis of the Ukrainian People), their theory was a mixture of Enlightenment political ideals (equality, democracy, parliamentarism), pietist sentiment, and Romantic notions of historical providentialism and national messianism. A religiously colored faith in Ukraine's mission to unite the Slavs in a federation of free national republics inspired the writings of the leading Ukrainian writers of the mid-century and stimulated the growth of national consciousness.

As the prestige of the natural sciences rose, the Romantic Weltanschauung lost its credibility. But the ambition to unify all human experience in one all-embracing philosophical system remained strong throughout the second half of the century. P. *Yurkevych, probably the sharpest philosophical mind in Ukraine at the time, set out to reconcile idealism and materialism. Although he did not complete this project, his critique of materialism, interpretation of Platonism, and suggestions for an integrated concept of human nature were promising beginnings. A unified metaphysical system was worked out by A. Kozlov, who taught at Kiev University from 1876. Influenced by Leibniz, I. Kant, and A. Schopenhauer, he proposed a theory of critical spiritualism that admitted a multiplicity of spirits and denied the reality of matter. A similar system of 'synechiological spiritualism' was proposed later by A. *Giliarov, who viewed the universe as an infinite hierarchy of organisms.

Positivism was more popular among scientists than among philosophers in Ukraine. A Ukrainian positivist of particular note was V. *Lesevych. He accepted A. Comte's teachings at first, but later rejected them in favor of a stricter empiricism and worked out his own theory of knowledge, which was close to empiriocriticism. Some positivist ideas can be found in G. Chelpanov, who taught philosophy at Kiev University (1892–1906), P. *Linytsky, and N. Grot, who began his academic career at the Nizhen Lyceum and Odessa University (1883–6). All of them tried to make room for religious faith without weakening the authority of science. Following Kant they drew a clear line between knowledge and faith; they restricted the first to the realm of phenomena and accounted for it in empiriocritical terms. M. *Drahomanov developed his political and social theory in a positivist framework. The sociologist M. *Kovalevsky was influenced strongly by A. Comte, while B. *Kistiakovsky worked out a neo-Kantian foundation for the social sciences. F. *Zelenohorsky of Kharkiv University emphasized the importance of the inductive method without denying the role of deduction and imagination in scientific knowledge. *O. Potebnia's and D. *Ovsianiko-Kulikovsky's philosophy of language was based on associationist psychology.

After the First World War philosophy developed very differently in Western Ukraine under Polish rule, in Soviet Ukraine under the stifling restrictions of official ideology, and among Ukrainian émigrés. Denied their own university by the Polish authorities, Galicia's Ukrainians were unable to compete with the Poles in the quality of philosophical education and writing. Some philosophy was taught at the Lviv (Underground) Ukrainian University (eg, by S. *Balei) and at the Greek Catholic Theological Academy by Rev Y. *Slipy (scholasticism), M. *Konrad (ancient philosophy), and H. *Kostelnyk (epistemology). The Western Ukrainian and émigré proponents of different political ideologies, such as *conservatism, integral *nationalism, *socialism, and *Marxism, discussed, with varying sophistication and objectivity, the philosophical grounds of their outlook.

Soviet period. In Soviet Ukraine, for the first few years philosophical activity developed in a normal way: philosophers expressed their views freely, formed associations, and published their own journals. In 1922 the government dismissed some of its ideological opponents from their academic posts and banished them from the Ukrainian SSR, thus warning intellectual circles that it would no longer tolerate criticism of the official ideology. Gradually the regime imposed its control over ideas by dissolving all independent associations and publications and by establishing its own institutions for defining and propagating the approved ideology, *Marxism-Leninism. As political interference increased, philosophical debate degenerated quickly into servile dogmatism, invective, and denunciation. By 1931 all creative thinking on philosophical issues had been stifled.

The first philosophical institution in Ukraine set up by the Soviet regime was the Department of Marxism and Marxology in Kharkiv. It was established in the fall of 1921, and a year later it was reorganized into the Ukrainian Institute of Marxism, renamed the *Ukrainian Institute of Marxism-Leninism (UIML) in 1927. The institute had three divisions, each with three departments. The Philosophy-Sociology Division (chaired by S. *Semkovsky) consisted of the departments of Philosophy (headed by Semkovsky), Sociology (headed by V. *Yurynets), and, from 1928, Law (headed by Yu. Mazurenko). Members of the philosophy department included Ya. Bilyk, Z. Luzina, P. Demchuk, and T. Stepovy, who also lectured at other institutions in Kharkiv. Philosophical research was published in the institute's journal *Prapor marksyzmu* (1927–30). In 1927 the Ukrainian Society of Militant Materialists (later of Militant Materialists-Dialecticians) was organized at the institute. At the same time (from 1921) two departments of the Social-Economic Division of the VUAN – those of the History of Philosophy and Law (headed by A. *Giliarov) and Sociology (headed by S. Semkovsky) – functioned in Kiev. In 1931 they were replaced by the VUAN Philosophical Commission in Kharkiv, which was to prepare a philosophical dictionary. In 1926 the Kiev Scientific Research Department of Marxism-Leninism (headed by R. Levik and then O. Kamyshan) was set up under the VUAN. Its philosophical-sociological section (chaired by S. Semkovsky) formed special commissions devoted to scientific methodology, historical materialism, the sociology of law, the sociology of art, the methodology of the history of technology, and atheism. Leading associates of the department were V. Asmus, Ya. Rozanov, M. Perlin, O. Zahorulko, M. Nyrchuk, and V. Yurynets. In 1930 the department was turned into the Kiev branch of the UIML.

The UIML and the VUAN departments had two chief tasks: to articulate and propagate Marxism-Leninism and to train political specialists and propagandists for work in higher educational institutions. Besides translating the basic works of K. Marx, F. Engels, and V. Lenin and preparing anthologies and textbooks, their associates conducted prolonged discussions on the nature of philosophy, the place of the Hegelian dialectic in the physical world and the natural sciences, and the weight of Lenin's contribution to philosophy. Since dialectical materialism claimed to be both a scientific theory and a method of studying reality, its relation to the natural sciences and, particularly, the new theories of relativity and quantum mechanics aroused much interest (see *Philosophy of science). The third branch of philosophy to receive some attention was the history of philosophy, which was limited to the philosophical traditions from which Marxism-Leninism had sprung: B. Spinoza and the French materialists, Hegel and L. Feuerbach among the German philosophers, and N. Chernyshevsky, L. Tolstoi, and G. Plekhanov among the Russians. In 1930 P. Demchuk's book on Spinoza and V. Bon's book on 18th-century French materialism came out. Hegel's *Science of Logic* was translated in 1929. Although the philosophy department at the UIML had a special commission for the history of philosophy in Ukraine (chaired by S. Semkovsky), little was accomplished in this area. Only a collection of articles on H. Skovoroda (1923), some booklets, and a solid monograph on him by D. Bahalii (1926) were published.

The so-called philosophical discussion in Ukraine culminated at a conference in Kharkiv in January 1931, where accusations of nationalism, mechanism, and Menshevik idealism were directed at the leading figures of the philosophical establishment. Despite the absurdity of the charges, everyone admitted his 'errors' in a published self-criticism. The Party was thus able to call for a reorganization of the institutional system of research and the eradication of the vestiges of 'bourgeois science.' In June 1931 the UIML was converted by Party decree into the *All-Ukrainian Association of Marxist-Leninist Scientific Research Institutes (VUAMLIN). The UIML's three divisions were turned into three VUAMLIN institutes – Philosophy and Natural Science, Economics, and History – of the six that were created. Each institute had a three-year graduate program. The Institute of Philosophy and Natural Science (directed by R. Levik and then O. Vasileva, and A. Saradzhev) was divided into four sectors: dialectical materialism (including a section on the history of philosophy in Ukraine), historical materialism, natural science (with the Association of Natural Science), and antireligion. It published the journals *Prapor marksyzmu-leninizmu (1931–3), Pid markso-lenins'kym praporom (1934–6), and Za marksysts'ko-lenins'ke pryrodoznavstvo (1932–3). Among its leading associates were S. Semkovsky, V. Yurynets, T. Stepovy, O. Bervytsky, Ya. Bilyk, and V. Bon. So-called Red Professors institutes (est 1932) assumed the responsibility of training research and teaching cadres within each of the VUAMLIN institutes. At the Philosophy Institute of Red Professors (directed by S. Bludov and then O. Adrianov), V. Yurynets held the chair of dialectical materialism, T. Stepovy the chair of historical materialism, and O. Bervytsky the chair of the history of philosophy. In 1936 the separate institutes were merged into one Institute of Red Professors, with six departments. The philosophy department was chaired by A. Saradzhev and then Yu. Olman and M. Yushmanov. Philosophical research at the VUAMLIN had been long extinct by the time it was abolished in 1937. Many of the aforementioned leading thinkers perished in the terror of the 1930s.

After the Second World War research and teaching continued to be assigned to two distinct types of institution: research to institutes, and teaching to higher educational institutions, including universities. In 1946 the AN URSR (now ANU) *Institute of Philosophy was established in Kiev. It published Naukovi zapysky Instytutu filosofiï (1951–61, 7 vols) and the bimonthly Filosofs'ka dumka (est 1969), which in 1989 became the monthly Filosofs'ka i sotsiolohichna dumka. Another research body – the Department of Philosophy of the AN URSR Presidium – was established in early 1950. It was headed by M. *Omelianovsky and then M. Ovander and I. Holovakha. Since any new work in dialectical and historical materialism was ruled out by Stalin's treatment of the topic in the offical short course on the history of the Bolshevik party (1938), and since the methodology of the natural and social sciences remained an uncharted mine field, the history of philosophy in Ukraine became the most promising area in philosophy. A few monographs and numerous articles on the philosophical ideas of 19th-century scientists (M. Maksymovych, V. Danylevsky, and I. Mechnikov) and the so-called Russian and Ukrainian revolutionary democrats (A. Herzen, N. Chernyshevsky, N. Dobroliubov, D. Pisarev, T. Shevchenko, P. Myrny, I. Franko, M. Pavlyk, O. Terletsky, P. Hrabovsky, Lesia Ukrainka, and M. Kotsiubynsky) ap-

peared. In a crude and obvious manner their authors imposed a predictable interpretation on their subject: materialist, atheist, or social revolutionary. In the 1950s some work, which was equally tendentious, was done also on 17th- and 18th-century writers, such as I. Vyshensky, L. Baranovych, H. Skovoroda, and Ya. Kozelsky. Such studies proliferated in the 1960s; a collection of articles on the history of Ukrainian philosophy came out almost every year. The most important accomplishment of the period was the publication in 1961 of the first full and scholarly collection of Skovoroda's work. The Latin transcripts of philosophy courses taught at the Kievan Mohyla Academy began to be studied and translated, and excerpts appeared regularly in Filosofs'ka dumka. A Ukrainian translation of T. Prokopovych's courses was readied for publication, but appeared more than a decade later, in 1979–81. On the 250th anniversary of H. Skovoroda's birth a second, improved edition of his works (2 vols, 1973), a new biography by L. Makhnovets (1972), and several collections of articles on Skovoroda came out. The more important contributors in the field of Ukrainian philosophy were I. Ivano, D. *Ostrianyn, V. Dmytrychenko, A. *Brahinets, I. *Tabachnikov, V. Horsky, P. Manzenko, M. Rohovych, V. Yevdokymenko, and V. *Shynkaruk.

A wave of arrests throughout Ukraine in January 1972 launched a concerted campaign to suppress Ukrainian culture and language. At mid-year the Institute of Philosophy was purged: two of its associates, V. *Lisovy and Ye. *Proniuk, were imprisoned for criticizing the Party's policy, and a number of junior researchers and graduate students were expelled. The number and quality of the institute's publications declined: hardly anything was printed in Ukrainian, and the Ukrainian accomplishments had to be described as accomplishments of the three 'fraternal' (Russian, Ukrainian, Belarusian) peoples. The pace of publication picked up only in the 1980s. V. Nichyk's monograph on the philosophical tradition at the Kievan Mohyla Academy (1978) was followed by a series of related studies by Ya. Stratii (1981), I. Zakhara (1982), I. Paslavsky (1984), and V. Lytvynov (1984), and a catalogue of surviving transcripts of the rhetoric and philosophy courses at the academy (1982). The scope of research was broadened to include the medieval era, on which several collections of articles appeared (1983, 1987, 1988, 1990). Before his untimely death, Ivano finished his survey history of esthetics in Ukraine (1981) and his notable study of Skovoroda's thought (1983). Volumes 1 and 2 of the ANU multiauthor three-volume history of philosophy in Ukraine were published in 1987. The most significant recent achievement has been the publication of primary sources of Ukrainian thought of the 16th to 18th centuries in Standard Ukrainian translation: ethics courses at the Kievan Mohyla Academy (1987), the works of professors of brotherhood schools (1988), and H. Konysky's (1990) and S. Yavorsky's (1992) philosophy courses at the academy. Among the leading scholars in the field today are V. *Nichyk, M. Kashuba, V. Horsky, Ya. *Stratii, I. *Zakhara, V. *Lytvynov, I. Paslavsky, M. Luk, and A. *Pashuk.

Since 1972 the *Ukrainian Philosophical Society has promoted and co-ordinated philosophical studies in Ukraine.

Outside Ukraine. In the interwar period philosophy was taught in Prague at the Ukrainian Higher Pedagogical

Institute, at which the Skovoroda Philosophical Society (1925–30) was active, and at the Ukrainian Free University (UVU) by D. *Chyzhevsky, who established himself as the leading authority on the history of Ukrainian philosophy with his two monographs on philosophy in Ukraine, two books on Skovoroda, and a study of Hegel's influence in the Russian Empire. I. *Mirchuk, a historian of Ukrainian culture and philosophy, began his academic career at the UVU. M. *Shlemkevych, who completed his PH D under M. Schlick in Vienna, developed a philosophical genre of journalism dealing with fundamental psychological-cultural problems of Ukrainian society. After the Second World War Mirchuk continued his work on the history of philosophy. Some contributions were made by his colleagues at the UVU in Munich O. *Kulchytsky and V. *Yaniv. K. Mytrovych, a specialist in contemporary existentialism, has done some work on Skovoroda. Ye. Lashchyk, a professor of philosophy in the United States, has worked on V. Vynnychenko's 'concordism.' Among Ukrainian émigré scholars who have gained a world reputation are G. *Malantschuk, for his work on S. Kierkegaard's thought, and R. *Rozdolsky, for his interpretation of Marx's *Das Kapital*.

(For recent work in other fields of philosophy, see *Logic, *Marxism-Leninism, and *Philosophy of science).

BIBLIOGRAPHY

Chyzhevs'kyi, D. *Fil'osofiia na Ukraïni (sproba istoriografiï)* (Prague 1926; rev edn 1928)
– *Narysy z istoriï filosofiï na Ukraïni* (Prague 1931)
Ostrianyn, D; et al (eds). *Z istoriï suspil'no-politychnoï ta filosofs'koï dumky na Ukraïni* (Kiev 1956)
– *Z istoriï vitchyznianoï filosofs'koï ta suspil'no-politychnoï dumky* (Kiev 1959)
– *Z istoriï filosofs'koï dumky na Ukraïni* (Kiev 1963)
Ievdokymenko, V; et al (eds). *Borot'ba mizh materializmom ta idealizmom na Ukraïni v XIX st.* (Kiev 1964)
– *Z istoriï filosofs'koï dumky na Ukraïni* (Kiev 1965)
Ostrianyn, D.; et al (eds). *Narys istoriï filosofiï na Ukraïni* (Kiev 1966)
Ievdokymenko, V; et al (eds). *Z istoriï filosofiï na Ukraïni* (Kiev 1967)
– *Rozvytok filosofiï v Ukraïns'kii RSR* (Kiev 1968)
– *Z istoriï filosofiï ta sotsiolohiï na Ukraïni* (Kiev 1968)
Korchyns'ka, T.; Lavrova, O.; Proniuk, Ie. (comps). *Bibliohrafiia prats' Instytutu filosofiï AN URSR (1946–1967)* (Kiev 1969)
Oleksiuk, M. *Borot'ba filosofs'kykh techii na zakhidno-ukraïns'kykh zemliakh u 20–30-kh rokakh XX st.* (Lviv 1970)
Ostrianyn, D. *Rozvytok materialistychnoï filosofiï na Ukraïni* (Kiev 1971)
Ievdokymenko, V. (ed). *Filosofs'ka dumka na Ukraïni* (Kiev 1972)
Nichyk, V. (ed). *Vid Vyshens'koho do Skovorody* (Kiev 1972)
Nichik, V. *Iz istorii otechestvennoi filosofii kontsa XVII–nachala XVIII v.* (Kiev 1978)
Stratii, Ia. *Problemy naturfilosofii v filosofskoi mysli Ukrainy XVII v.* (Kiev 1981)
Shynkaruk, V.; et al (eds). *Filosofskaia mysl' v Kieve* (Kiev 1982)
Stratii, Ia.; Litvinov, V.; Andrushko, V. *Opisanie kursov filosofii i ritoriki professorov Kievo-Mogilianskoi akademii* (Kiev 1982)
Zakhara, I. *Bor'ba idei v filosofskoi mysli na Ukraine na rubezhe XVII–XVIII vv. (Stefan Iavorskii)* (Kiev 1982)
Gorskii, V. (ed). *U istokov obshchnosti filosofskikh kul'tur russkogo, ukrainskogo i bolgarskogo narodov: Sbornik nauchnykh trudov* (Kiev 1983)
Lytvynov, V. *Ideï rann'oho prosvitnytstva u filosofs'kii dumtsi Ukraïny* (Kiev 1984)
Paslavs'kyi, I. *Z istoriï rozvytku filosofs'kykh idei na Ukraïni v kintsi XVI–pershii tretyni XVII st.* (Kiev 1984)
Gorskii, V. (ed). *Chelovek i istoriia v srednevekovoi filosofskoi mysli russkogo, ukrainskogo i belorusskogo narodov: Sbornik nauchnykh trudov* (Kiev 1987)
Pamiatniki eticheskoi mysli na Ukraine XVII–pervoi poloviny XVIII st. Tr. M. Kashuba (Kiev 1987)
Shynkaruk, V.; et al (eds). *Istoriia filosofii na Ukraïni u 3 tomakh,* vols 1–2 (Kiev 1987)
Gorskii, V. *Filosofskie idei v kul'ture Kievskoi Rusi XI–nachala XII v.* (Kiev 1988)
Shynkaruk, V.; Nichyk, V.; Sukhov, A. (eds). *Pam'iatky brats'kykh shkil na Ukraïni: Kinets' XVI–pochatok XVII st: Teksty i doslidzhennia* (Kiev 1988)
Gorskii, V. (ed). *Slovo o polku Igoreve i mirovozrenie ego epokhi* (Kiev 1990)
Kashuba, M (ed). *Filosofiia Vidrodzhennia na Ukraïni* (Kiev 1990)
Luk, N. (ed). *Filosofskaia kul'tura Ukrainy i otechestvennaia obshchestvennaia mysl' XIX–XX v.v.* (Kiev 1990)

T. Zakydalsky

Philosophy of science. A branch of philosophy dealing with the distinctive nature of scientific knowledge – its logical structure, its relation to experience, and its growth. Formerly discussed among more general problems of epistemology, these questions received increasing attention in the 19th century and are accepted today as a separate field of philosophy.

In Ukraine the first contributions to the subject were made by scientists rather than philosophers. V. *Vernadsky tried to define the key features of science in his extended article on the scientific worldview (1902), and B. *Lichkov discussed the fundamental issues of the field in his books in Russian on the limits of knowledge in the natural sciences (1914) and on description and explanation in science (1919). During the early period of the Soviet regime, philosophers tried to define the relation of the new official ideology, *Marxism-Leninism, to the natural sciences instead of exploring the nature of scientific knowledge for its own sake. Nevertheless, many questions that belong to the philosophy of science were discussed, and some variety of views was tolerated until the early 1930s. In the 1920s a special commission on scientific methodology was set up within the philosophy department of the *Ukrainian Institute of Marxism-Leninism in Kharkiv to study the implications of dialectical materialism for the natural sciences. Besides the philosophers S. Semkovsky (chairman), V. Berkovych, P. Biliarchyk, P. Demchuk, V. Yurynets, T. Stepovy, R. Levik, and V. Chuchmarov, the commission's membership included prominent scientists, such as I. Sokoliansky, D. Tretiakov, O. Korshykov, A. Palladin, L. Pysarzhevsky, O. Goldman, D. Syntsov, and D. Grave. In Kiev a special commission on scientific methodology was set up within the VUAN Scientific Research Department of Marxism-Leninism in 1926.

The All-Union Conference on the Philosophical Problems of Science in 1958 marked a turning point in the history of the subject: by condemning the imposition of ideological dogma on science, it permitted the philosophy of science to develop independently of dialectical materialism. In 1962 a new Department for the Logic of Scientific Knowledge was set up at the AN URSR (now ANU) Institute of Philosophy. First chaired (1962–6) by the institute's director, P. *Kopnin, the department soon became one of the largest and most productive sections of the institute. Its first two collections of articles on logic and the methodology of science (ed P. Dyshlevy, 1964; ed M. Omelianovsky, 1967) and the multiauthor monograph on the logic of scientific research (ed P. Kopnin, 1965) outlined the department's research program. The nature of scientific theory has been analyzed in a multiauthor monograph (ed P. Dyshlevy, 1965) and in individual monographs by P. Kopnin (1963), M. Popovych (1966, 1971), V. Ryzhko (1975), V. Kuznetsov (1977), and V. Khramova (1984). The distinctive character of scientific explanation has been defined by M. Rozhenko (1970), E. Bystrytsky (1986), and N. Depenchuk, P. Dyshlevy, and N. Kyvenko (1981). Books by M. Vilnytsky (1965), P. Dyshlevy (ed, 1966), V. Khramova (1974), and V. Kyzyma (1976) dealt with the nature of scientific experiment and its role in theory confirmation. The problem of scientific discovery and growth has been discussed in a book by S. Krymsky (1974) and a collection of articles edited by M. Popovych (1983). The influence of general philosophical ideas in science has been explored by V. Chornovolenko (1970), S. Krymsky and V. Kuznetsov (1983), and L. Ozadovska (1989), and the problem of values in science has been approached from different perspectives by V. Zahorodnyk (1984), P. Yolon, S. Krymsky, and B. Parakhonsky (1989), and M. Burgin and V. Kuznetsov (1991). A number of collections have been devoted to the special methodological problems of biology (1966, 1968, 1970) and ecology (1974). In the 1960s many of the collections and monographs in the philosophy of science came out in Ukrainian. Since the abrupt change in policy at the beginning of the 1970s, all of the department's publications have been published only in Russian. Thus, in spite of its USSR-wide reputation as a leading philosophy of science center, except for a few individuals among its members, the department stands strangely aloof and alienated from Ukrainian intellectual life.

BIBLIOGRAPHY
Kopnin, P. *Gipoteza i poznanie deistvitel'nosti* (Kiev 1962)
Dyshlevyi, P. (ed). *Lohika i metodolohiia nauky* (Kiev 1964)
– (ed). *Pobudova naukovoï teoriï* (Kiev 1965)
Kopnin, P.; Popovich, M. (eds). *Logika nauchnogo issledovaniia* (Moscow 1965)
Vil'nyts'kyi, M. *Eksperyment v suchasnii nautsi* (Kiev 1965)
Popovych, M. *O filosofskom analize iazyka nauki* (Kiev 1966)
Omelianovs'kyi, M. (ed). *Lohika i metodolohiia nauky* (Kiev 1967)
Krymskii, S. *Nauchnoe znanie i printsipy ego transformatsii* (Kiev 1974)
Popovich, M. (ed). *Puti formirovaniia novogo znaniia v sovremennoi nauke* (Kiev 1983)
Bistritskii, E. *Nauchnoe poznanie i problema ponimaniia* (Kiev 1986)
Ozadovskaia, L. *Filosofsko-metodologicheskie reguliativy fizicheskogo znaniia* (Kiev 1989)
Burgin, M.; Kuznetsov, V. *Aksiologicheskie aspekty nauchnykh teorii* (Kiev 1991)

T. Zakydalsky

Photography. In 1841, four years after the invention of the daguerreotype, Professor J. Gleister began making daguerreotypes in Lviv. In Kiev the first daguerreotype portraits were made in December 1844 or in early 1845 by a Prussian, K. Shchodrovitsky. In 1858 in Odessa, Y. Mihursky, a graduate of the Richelieu Lyceum and a member of the Parisian photographic society, tried to form a society of amateur photographers but was unable to do so because of the opposition of Governor-General A. Stroganov. In 1863, however, he managed to establish an institute of photography, where he taught the theory and practice of the art. In 1859 O. Pokorsky-Zhoravko, a noble from Mglin, Chernihiv gubernia, and the Kievan photographer Chekhovych tried unsuccessfully to launch a

photography journal in Kiev. In 1852–3 the Englishman J. Bourne was invited to photograph the new bridge in Kiev. The 13 large prints he produced were the first calotypes made in Kiev. L. Plakhov, a graduate of the St Petersburg Academy of Arts, worked in various cities in Ukraine with a camera obscura. The English photographer R. Fenton documented the Crimean War in 1855. O. Ivanov from Kharkiv captured images of the Russian-Turkish War in the Balkans in 1877–8 and compiled an album of nearly 170 photos. The Odessa photographer M. Raul took many photos of daily life in Kiev, Poltava, Chernihiv, and Katerynoslav gubernias throughout the 1870s and received awards at the 1875 Paris Geographic Exhibition and the 1878 World Exposition. Nineteenth-century portrait photographers in Kiev included I. Hudovsky (three portraits of T. Shevchenko in 1859), V. Vysotsky, Y. Kordysh, and F. de Mezer; H. Chuhaievych specialized in urban scenes. Y. Khmilevsky from Poltava left a substantial collection of photos of the folkways of the Poltava region in the 1880s and 1890s, an album entitled *Gogol' na rodine* ([N.] Gogol in His Homeland, 1902), a collection of photos taken at the unveiling of the I. Kotliarevsky monument in Poltava in 1903, and a large series of photos of the Poltava Zemstvo building (1908–9). Ethnographic albums were also produced by Kh. Parfenenko. A. *Fedetsky, the first filmmaker and tricolor photographer in Ukraine, worked in Kharkiv from 1884 to 1902.

The first commercial photography studios in Ukraine were established in the early 1870s in Balta, Berdychiv, Bila Tserkva, Kamianets-Podilskyi, Korsun, Lypovets, Skvyra, Uman, Vinnytsia, Yampil, and other Ukrainian towns. On the eve of the First World War there were approx 70 commercial studios, 40 of them in Odessa, and 6 photographic-equipment stores in Kiev.

At the end of the 19th century, technological innovations facilitated the growth of photographic arts. In 1891 the Odessa Photographic Society (headed by M. Balikhov) was formed. By 1900 it had 192 members. It issued the periodicals *Vestnik Odesskogo fotograficheskogo obshchestva* (1912–14) and *Russkii fotograficheskii vestnik* (1915–16). Photography sections of branches of the Russian Technical Society were formed in Kharkiv (1891), Odessa (1897), and Kiev (1899). The Daguerre Society (1901–17) was established in Kiev by M. Bobyr, the author of *Khudozhnia fotografiia* (Art Photography, 1907), and others. In 1906–12 its president was M. *Petrov; he later lectured at the Kiev State Institute of Art and Institute of Cinematography.

The only school of photography in the Russian Empire, the Art and Craft Printing Workshop, was opened in Kiev in 1903. It was founded by V. *Kulzhenko. It was also in Kiev that the first international photo exhibition in the empire took place, in December 1908. It displayed over 500 works, including examples of X-ray photography. Kiev was also the venue for the Second Congress of Russian Photographers (1908) and an international salon of art photography (1911). Technical advances were made by V. Favorsky, a pioneer in microphotography, and in the 1910s the Kiev journal *Iskusstvo i pechatnoe delo* documented developments in color photography.

Ukrainians who wrote theoretical pieces on art photography included M. *Biliashivsky and I. *Trush. In 1914 Biliashivsky proposed that a systematic photographic census of Kiev be conducted. Articles on photography were published in Ukrainian periodicals (eg, H. Kovalenko's on domestic photography in *Literaturno-naukovyi vistnyk* [1899]), and photos of individuals were used as illustrations in works such as O. Shalatska's *Taiemnytsi mista Kyieva* (The Secrets of Kiev, 1904). Trush wrote about the relationship between painting and photography in 1905.

In Austrian-ruled Western Ukraine, Polish organizations, such as the Club of Photographic Art Amateurs in Lviv (1891–1903) and the Lviv Photographic Society (1903–14, 1924–39), were founded in Lviv, and a German Camera Club was created in Chernivtsi. Photography periodicals appeared in Lviv – *Przegląd Fotograficzny* (1895), *Kronika Fotograficzna* (1898–9), *Wiadomości Fotograficzne* (1903–6) and *Miesięcznik Fotograficzny* (1908–11). The pioneers of photography in Galicia were A. Karpiuk, V. *Shukhevych, and M. Petriv in Lviv; S. Dmokhovsky and Ye. Liubovych in Peremyshl; and F. Velychko in Stanyslaviv. Liubovych organized a photography club at the Peremyshl gymnasium in 1911. In 1912 the archeologist Ya. Pasternak called on photographers to document the ethnography and architecture (particularly wooden churches) of Galicia. At a combat photography exhibition held in Vienna in 1916, the Ukrainian Sich Riflemen's pavilion displayed photos of I. *Ivanets, M. *Uhryn-Bezhrishny, and others. In September 1918 the Riflemen's exhibit was brought to the National Museum in Lviv, becoming the first Western Ukrainian photographic exhibition.

In the interwar years of Soviet Ukraine the Kiev Photographic Institute enjoyed a brief existence, and in 1922 it organized an exposition. Original literature in Ukrainian emerged, the first example of which was L. *Skrypnyk's photographer's guide (1927). The photos of S. Arshenevsky, D. *Demutsky, M. Lishchynsky, D. Sotnyk, and P. Yezersky were landmarks of creative achievement, and periodicals such as *Foto-kino* (Kharkiv 1922–3) and *Foto – sotsbudivnytstvu* (Kharkiv 1928–34) popularized the art.

During the terror of the 1930s, Soviet Ukrainian photography suffered the same tragic fate as other branches of Ukrainian culture. The first All-Ukrainian Exhibition of Photographic Art was held in 1936, but its catalog was suppressed soon afterward. The first all-Union photography exhibit was brought to Kiev in 1938.

Photography continued to develop in interwar Western Ukraine and in the Ukrainian émigré community. In October 1920 a photography circle headed by O. Balytsky was established in the Ukrainian internment camp in Liberec, Bohemia, and it held a show within a year. In November 1930 the first general meeting of the Ukrainian Photographic Society was held in Lviv, and S. Dmokhovsky was chosen to head it. The society, which had 216 members in 1936, held regular exhibitions and published illustrated catalogs of works by Yu. Dorosh, R. Myrovych, O. *Mokh, and D. Figol and the journal *Svitlo i tin'* (1933–9), edited by S. Shchurat and O. Mokh. The Polish journals *Miesięcznik Fotograficzny* (1925–31), *Kamera Polska* (1932–3), and *Przegląd Fotograficzny* (1935–9) were also published in Lviv, and the second (1928) and sixth (1932) international photographic salons were held there. The Ukrainians L. Yanushevych and Ya. Shalabavka had commercial studios in Lviv.

In 1957 a photographers' section of the Union of Journalists of Ukraine was formed. The more prominent photojournalists include Ya. Davydzon, M. Kozlovsky, M. Melnyk, and H. Uhrynovych. Professional portrait

First issue of the new Ukrainian photography magazine, *Svitlo i tin'* (1991)

studios have been under the supervision of the Ministry of Consumer Services. Until the late 1980s the activity of amateur clubs was limited by government policy and the lack of equipment. Nonetheless, talented photo artists such as R. Baran, Ye. Derlemenko, I. Kostin (who documented the Chornobyl nuclear disaster), I. Kropyvnytsky, S. Marchenko, and V. Lysenko have left their mark. I. Honchar has amassed a large collection of ethnographic photographs from all parts of Ukraine. The first museum of photography in Ukraine was opened as a division of the *National Museum in Lviv.

S. Bilokin

Physical anthropology. The study of the physical characteristics of the human race with respect to origin, development, classification, and distribution. The subject can be subdivided into somatology and paleontology. The first describes and measures discrete bodily members, skin color, height and weight, blood type, and the structure of the internal organs (see *Races). The second deals with early human history on the basis of archeological evidence. The earliest information about the physical characteristics of Ukraine's inhabitants is in Herodotus' and Hippocrates' accounts of the Scythians. Medieval Byzantine and Arab authors, such as Procopius, Zacharias Rhetor, Ibn Dast or Ibn Rosta, and Ibn Fadlān, provided further data on Ukraine's population. Descriptions of Ukrainians are also found in the works of 17th- and 18th-century travelers. From impressionistic descriptions of the population of Kievan Rus' two anthropological types can be distinguished. The princes, knights, and merchants possessed mostly Nordic traits, whereas the general population consisted of short-headed Trypilians (or Armenoids).

According to archeological excavations the following anthropological types once inhabited Ukrainian territories: Neanderthal (Upper to Middle Paleolithic period), Mediterranean (Middle Paleolithic period), Cro-Magnon (Upper Paleolithic period), Lapponoid (Upper to late Paleolithic period), Southern Mediterranean with Negroid features (late Paleolithic to early Mesolithic period), Nordic Cro-Magnon (Neolithic and Eneolithic period), Armenoid (beginning of the Bronze Age), and Mediterranean (Bronze Age). The intermingling of these chief types led to the development of the East European or Sub-Nordic type (from the Lapponoid and Nordic types), the Adriatic or Dinaric type (from the Nordic and Armenoid types), and the Alpine type (from the Sub-Nordic and Dinaric types). The inhabitants of protohistoric and early historic Ukraine consisted of three main strata: people of the Trypilian culture, chiefly Armenoid in type; the Iranian (Sakian) people, chiefly Nordic and Mediterranean in type; and the Slavs, Nordic-Armenoid in type.

According to F. Vovk's findings at the beginning of the 20th century, the population of Ukraine can be divided into three anthropological belts: (1) the northern belt (southern Kursk, Chernihiv, northern Kiev, northern Volhynia, and Kholm regions); (2) the middle belt (southern Voronezh, Kharkiv, Poltava, and Kiev regions, northern Podilia, southern Volhynia, and eastern Galicia [excluding the Hutsul and Boiko regions]); and (3) the southern belt (Bačka [Yugoslavia], Transcarpathia, the southern Boiko and Hutsul regions, southern Podilia, and the Kherson, Zaporizhia, Tavriia, and Kuban regions). Most Ukrainians of the northern belt are of medium height, with fairly light hair and eyes, semiround heads with high foreheads, medium faces, and fairly wide noses, often snubbed. Ukrainians of the middle belt are mostly above medium height, with darker hair and eyes, round heads, high foreheads, medium-broad faces, narrow and straight noses. Most Ukrainians of the southern belt are tall with even darker hair and eyes, round heads, high foreheads, medium-broad and elongated faces, and narrow, mostly straight but sometimes curved and aquiline, noses.

Racial types	Territories
Adriatic; East European, dark and light	Regions of Kharkiv, southwestern Poltava, southwestern and northeastern Galicia; south and north Boiko region, Lemko region, Kholm region
Adriatic with an admixture of Armenoid Nordic	Hutsul region; north Podilia, Bačka, west Boiko, Kherson, and Odessa regions
Nordic with an admixture of Adriatic	Northern Kiev, Volhynia, Kuban
Adriatic, Mediterranean, dark Eastern European	Regions of Chernihiv, southern Voronezh, northeastern Poltava, central and southern Kiev, Katerynoslav, southern Podilia, central Galicia; central part of the Boiko region

In R. *Yendyk's findings this classification is modified and replaced by four territorial areas (see table). V. Diachenko's data (1965) suggest four central and one peripheral anthropological area.

BIBLIOGRAPHY
Volkov (Vovk), F. 'Antropologicheskie osobennosti ukrainskogo naroda,' *Ukrainskii narod v ego proshlom i nastoiashchem*, vol 2 (St Petersburg 1916)
Iendyk, R. *Antropolohichni prykmety ukraïns'koho narodu* (Lviv 1934)
Diachenko, V. *Antropolohichnyi sklad ukraïns'koho narodu* (Kiev 1965)

B. Medwidsky

Physical education (PE). The system of organized instruction in hygiene, calisthenics, and organized sports.
Western Ukraine to 1914. Until the early 20th century,

PE in Western Ukraine left much to be desired. For adults it was limited to sporadic training in hunting, swimming, rowing, skating, sledding, and fencing (training in the last was given by the Sich and Rus' student societies in Vienna and Graz, respectively). In elementary and secondary schools PE was usually taught by poorly qualified instructors. Instruction improved somewhat in the years immediately preceding the First World War, thanks to the efforts of the Sokil society and individual promoters of PE, such as I. Bobersky. At first, one to two school hours per week was devoted to PE. Eventually, extracurricular groups for tennis, track-and-field sports, hiking, swimming, skiing, sledding, and skating were organized. PE for girls and women, which had been neglected previously, began receiving some attention.

In 1887, using Czech examples, V. Lavrivsky drafted the first charter for a Ukrainian gymnastics society in Lviv. The Austrian authorities, however, did not permit a Ukrainian PE society to be set up until 1894. That year the *Sokil society was established in Lviv, and branches were soon founded throughout Galicia. The first Ukrainian exercise manual, by O. Popovych, was published in Chernivtsi in 1889; it was followed by I. Bobersky's books on games (2 vols, 1904–5) and soccer (1906), T. Franko's book on tennis, and O. Tysovsky's handbook for the Plast Ukrainian Youth Association (1913). During Bobersky's presidency (1908–14) the central Sokil society in Lviv purchased its own stadium and trained many PE instructors and teachers. Paramilitary riflemen's units were organized and trained in 1912–14 by S. Goruk as part of the program of the Sokil societies in Lviv, Drohobych, and other towns; they formed the nucleus of the *Ukrainian Sich Riflemen during the First World War.

PE in Galicia was also promoted by the *Sich society, founded by K. Trylovsky in 1900. Its branches in Galicia and Bukovyna operated independently until 1912, when they were integrated into the Ukrainian Sich Union.

Ukraine under tsarist rule. As in Western Ukraine, PE in Russian-ruled Ukraine was sporadic and amateurish. In the early 20th century, interest in PE increased with the introduction of a Sokil-style gymnastics program and track-and-field meets as part of the secondary-school curriculum, as well as of the scouting movement. There was, however, no organized Ukrainian PE movement before the 1917 Revolution, although a number of sports clubs were established in Kiev, Odessa, and other cities. During the First World War, gymnastics in the secondary schools was replaced by military drills.

During the revolutionary period of 1917–20, PE continued to be part of the secondary-school curriculum. Sports activities were organized by various Ukrainian youth and school clubs and by the first Ukrainian boy scout troops that appeared in Kiev, Chernihiv, Bila Tserkva, and other cities. The *Free Cossack movement also promoted PE among its ranks. As a result, semimilitary, semiathletic youth detachments fought on the side of the UNR in many parts of Ukraine.

Western Ukraine, 1918–44. Under Polish, Czechoslovak, and Rumanian rule, the development of Ukrainian PE organizations was to some extent obstructed by the authorities. In the Polish-ruled territories, PE in the schools improved considerably over what it had been under prewar Austrian rule. Besides calisthenics based on the Swedish, Danish, and German systems, the school programs included outdoor activities and games. Extracurricular sports, hiking, and camping activities were organized by Ukrainian groups such as the Plast Ukrainian Youth Association, branches of the revived Sokil and Sich societies, local branches of the Orly Catholic Association of Ukrainian Youth and the Union of Ukrainian Progressive Youth, and, after the Sich society was banned in 1924, the *Luh society. Many new Ukrainian sports societies were founded. In 1925 the sports section of Sokil central in Lviv, together with various sports societies, set up a central co-ordinating and planning agency, the *Ukrainian Sports Union (USS), which organized soccer tournaments, regional and provincial athletic competitions, PE courses, and training camps and introduced a general test culminating in a physical competence badge.

During the Second World War, PE in the German-occupied Generalgouvernement was co-ordinated by the Office of Physical Education of the Department for Youth Care of the Ukrainian Central Committee in Cracow. It organized a network of new clubs in the Lemko and Kholm regions. After the Germans occupied most of Ukraine, PE was able to develop only in Western Ukraine. In 1943 there were 124 PE societies there (including 22 in the Ternopil area, 16 in the Lviv region, 16 in the Stanyslaviv region, 13 in the Stryi region, 11 in the Peremyshl region, and 5 in the Kholm region) and 177 PE groups organized by Ukrainian educational societies, with a total membership of 11,000.

Soviet Ukraine. PE in Soviet Ukraine was part of the all-Soviet PE system. In the 1920s all existing sports organizations were quickly dissolved, and many of their leaders were persecuted. For most of the Soviet period, PE served the interests of the totalitarian state and was organized and controlled by it to prepare the masses for 'highly productive socialist labor' and for the defense of Soviet communism. All PE organizations and sports associations outside the school system created and controlled by the Communist Youth League or trade unions, themselves strictly subordinated to the Party and state. In 1918–19 the first PE teaching institutions were established, and PE became part of military training and the school curriculum. In the early 1920s special councils assumed control over PE on the local level. In 1930 centralized state control of PE in the USSR became official with the creation of the All-Union Council on Physical Culture, to which the existing Higher Council on Physical Culture of Ukraine was subordinated. In 1936 the All-Union Council was reorganized into the All-Union Committee on Physical Culture and Sports of the USSR Council of People's Commissars. Under this system all Komsomol and workers' sports organizations at educational institutions and industrial plants were subordinated to oblast councils of sports associations, and these are subordinated to councils of the central committees of the Komsomol or trade unions.

From 1931 Soviet PE was based on the so-called GTO (Ready for Labor and Defense of the USSR) mass fitness program introduced by the Komsomol. The revised program (1972) had five levels: (1) for children aged 10–13, (2) for adolescents aged 14–15, (3) for adolescents aged 16–18, (4) for men aged 19–39 and women 19–34, and (5) for men aged 40–60 and women 35–55. At each level certain physical testing was compulsory. All young people were taught and participated in cross-country running and skiing, in running obstacle courses, swimming, and gymnastics; other sports were elective. Testing reflected the

purpose of the program – to raise labor productivity and military readiness. According to official figures, approx 6.8 million people in Ukraine qualified for the GTO badge in 1982.

PE in nursery and elementary schools consisted of an approved program of lessons, exercises, and games. In elementary schools students were taught calisthenics and simple active games and were gradually introduced to gymnastics, track-and-field sports, swimming, skiing, and team sports. In Ukraine there were also over 800 'children's and youth sports schools,' at which more than 321,000 7- to 14-year-old children received preliminary training for future careers in sports. Selected for their athletic talents, the children usually specialized in one, two, or three of 43 sports. Those who went on received curricular and extracurricular training in sports proficiency schools (ages 16–18) and higher sports proficiency schools (ages 18 and over). Exceptionally promising children (ages 7–18) were sent to republican sports boarding schools (26 in the USSR), where they were trained to compete in the Olympic Games.

As sports contacts and competitions with the West increased after the Second World War, Soviet PE and sports training intensified. In 1959 the Committee on Physical Culture and Sports was replaced by the Union of Sports Societies and Organizations. Oblast, municipal, raion, and local PE councils supervised all existing *sports societies and clubs and physical-culture collectives at plants, factories, and collective and state farms. In 1981 there were in Ukraine approx 150,000 professional PE workers (65,000 of them with higher education) and 3,000 trainers, 2,500 registered referees, and over 315,000 GTO instructors. In 1987, training and sports facilities in the republic included 112,000 playing courts and fields, 13,600 gyms, 354 swimming pools, 600 skiing bases, 8,000 rifle ranges, 894 stadia, a swimming center in Kharkiv, and a rowing center in Kherson. PE instructors, trainers, referees, and coaches were educated at specialized secondary PE tekhnikums in Donetske, Dniprodzerzhynske, and Ivano-Frankivske; at PE departments of the Lutske, Mykolaiv, Odessa, Ternopil, Kharkiv, Cherkasy, Chernihiv, Luhanske, Vinnytsia, Zaporizhia, Kamianets-Podilskyi, and Kirovohrad pedagogical institutes; and at the *Kiev, *Lviv, and Dnipropetrovske institutes of physical culture. Sports medicine was taught at the Kiev Scientific Research Institute of the Medical Problems of Physical Culture (est 1969). Most recently, the Sokil society was revived in Lviv (1990).

Abroad. The Ukrainian interwar émigrés in Czechoslovakia had the best organized PE activities. These began in the internment camps and were continued by the Ukrainian Sokil and Sich unions abroad. PE was also part of the activities of the Sokil and Sich societies in the United States, Canada, and Argentina.

After the Second World War, refugees in Germany founded the *Ukrainian Council for Physical Culture in Augsburg (November 1945). Led by I. Lukiianenko, V. Blavatsky, I. Krasnyk, and S. Kikta, it introduced a physical fitness badge; organized skiing, volleyball, and basketball courses and a school for PE instructors in Mittenwald in 1947; and arranged soccer games and athletic competitions among sports clubs in the DP camps. PE among the postwar Ukrainian immigrants in North America, South America, and Australia has been part of the activities of Plast, the Ukrainian Youth Association, and the Ukrainian Democratic Youth Association. Competitions have been sponsored by the *Ukrainian Sports Federation of the United States and Canada.

BIBLIOGRAPHY

Chernova, Ie. *Rozvytok fizychnoï kul'tury i sportu v Ukraïns'kii RSR* (Kiev 1959)

Entsiklopedicheskii slovar' po fizicheskoi kul'ture i sportu, 3 vols (Moscow 1960)

Usykova, N. *Metodyka fizychnoho vykhovannia v shkoli* (Kiev 1960)

Samoukov, F.; et al (eds). *Fizicheskaia kul'tura i sport v SSSR* (Moscow 1967)

Shneidman, N. *The Soviet Road to Olympus: Theory and Practice of Soviet Physical Culture and Sport* (London and Henley 1979)

Riordan, J. *Soviet Sport: Background to the Olympics* (Oxford 1980)

E. Zharsky

Physical-Mechanical Institute of the Academy of Sciences of Ukraine (Fizyko-mekhanichnyi instytut ANU). A research institute in Lviv, founded in 1951 as the Institute of Mechanical Engineering and Automation and renamed in 1964. It has 21 departments, a special designs office, an experimental construction plant, and a graduate program. Its chief areas of research are the physicochemical mechanics of the brittle destruction of construction materials, metal corrosion and its prevention, the theory of the perception and processing of information for the purpose of simple image searching and recognition, the design of special systems and devices for investigating submarine and subterranean depths, nondestructive tests for the reliability of materials, and the automation of scientific experimentation. Among its notable scientists are H. Karpenko, K. Karandeev, V. Mykhailovsky, and H. Savin. The institute publishes the journal *Fiziko-khimicheskaia mekhanika materialov* and the collection *Otbor i peredacha informatsii*, both in Russian.

Physical-Technical Institute of the Academy of Sciences of Ukraine (Fizychno-tekhnichnyi instytut ANU). A research institute in Kharkiv established in 1928. Until 1938 it was called the Ukrainian Physical-Technical Institute and was under the jurisdiction of the Supreme Council of the National Economy and the People's Commissariat of Heavy Industry. It now has approx 2,500 employees in 14 departments; sections devoted to physical materials science, nuclear physics, and plasma physics; a technological design office; and an experimental plant. Its main fields of research are the behavior of electrons in the normal and superconducting state, methods of obtaining superpure metals, solid-state physics, and controlled nuclear fusion. The institute's accomplishments include the first induced nuclear transmutation in the USSR (1932), the production of liquid hydrogen (1931) and helium (1932), and the construction of the first three–co-ordinate radiolocator in the USSR (1938) and of the torsatron (1970). The directors of the institute have been I. Obreimov (1928–32), A. Leipunsky (1932–7), O. Shpetny (1937–44), K. Synelnykov (1944–65), V. Ivanov (1965–80), and V. Zelensky (since 1980). Many other noted scientists have worked at the institute, including L. Landau, G. Latyshev, L. Vereshchagin, L. Shubnikov, A. Walter, O. Akhiiezer, V. Bariakhtar, B. Lazarev, B. Verkin, O. Halkin, A. Prykhotko, V. Tolok, Ye. Borovyk, and O. Sytenko (see also *Physics).

BIBLIOGRAPHY

Ivanov, V. (ed). *50 let Khar'kovskomu fiziko-tekhnicheskomu institutu AN USSR* (Kiev 1978)

L. Onyshkevych

Physics. Originally 'physics' referred to the study of all aspects of nature. In the mid-19th century it was still synonymous with 'natural philosophy.' The earliest extant Ukrainian source on natural philosophy is the retelling of Aristotelian ideas in the *Izbornik of Sviatoslav (1073). In Ukraine attention was first devoted to quantitative problems in the Protestant schools, which appeared at the end of the 16th century (eg, Berestechko in Volhynia and Khmilnyk in Podilia). They produced mathematical and technical manuals for artisans and merchants, handwritten in the Ukrainian vernacular. Arithmetic and astronomy were taught in the *Ostrih Academy (est ca 1576), the first institution of higher learning in Ukraine. Considerable attention was devoted to the natural sciences in the *Kievan Mohyla Academy (est 1632). T. *Prokopovych's lectures on natural philosophy, physics, and mathematics at the academy were lucid treatments of much that was known on those subjects at the time.

From the 1730s, natural philosophy was taught at *Kharkiv College; in 1765 physics-related subjects, such as structural engineering, geodesy, and artillery and ballistics, became part of the curriculum; and in 1795, after the college merged with the Kharkiv Central Public College, physics was taught as a separate subject.

In the early 19th century, Kharkiv University was the center of physics research in Ukraine. The first professor of physics there was A. *Stojković (1805–13). T. *Osipovsky studied atmospheric optics and argued against the Kantian concept of space and time. His former student M. *Ostrohradsky was the first Ukrainian to contribute to the development of physics and mathematics on the international level. He copostulated the Gauss-Ostrohradsky theorem on the transformation of a volume integral into a surface integral, one of the cornerstones of continuum mechanics and electrodynamics, and solved a number of outstanding theoretical physics problems. In 1882 a Kharkiv University lecturer, M. *Pylchykov, investigating the polarization of light scattered by the atmosphere, found that blue light is scattered more than red, and corrected the prevailing view that the sky is blue because of air fluorescence. Fundamental discoveries in theoretical mechanics were made at the university in the last decade of the 19th century. By generalizing S. Kovalevska's 1889 theoretical studies of dynamical instabilities, A. *Liapunov provided a starting point for applied areas, such as radio technology and control theory. Recently, interest in his work was revived in studies of nonlinear dynamics and chaotic systems; the so-called Liapunov exponent is now an established indicator for determining if a motion is chaotic.

At Kiev University the basis for experimental physics research in Ukraine was laid by M. *Avenarius from 1866 on. Avenarius is best known for his discovery of the temperature dependence of the electromotive force of thermoelements (Avenarius's law) and for his systematic measurements of the critical temperatures of fluids. In 1884 the first chair of theoretical physics in Ukraine was founded at Kiev University. It was first held by N. *Shiller, who made important contributions to electrodynamics (highly regarded by J. Maxwell) and showed that differential equations describing the second law of thermodynamics contain an integrating factor that is a universal function of temperature. Shiller also founded the *Kiev Physics and Mathematics Society (1890); it played an important role in the development and popularization of physics in Ukraine.

Substantial contributions were also made by physicists working at the university in Odessa. There N. Umov introduced the concepts of energy density and the vector property of energy flow in 1874, and M. Pylchykov conducted the first measurements of radioactivity in Ukraine in 1900.

Soviet Ukraine

Kiev. From 1918 important work in mathematical physics, in particular on approximate integration of differential equations, was carried out in the Physical-Mathematical Division of the newly founded Ukrainian Academy of Sciences. Papers published in the 1920s in the academy's serials and subsequently abroad brought international recognition to those doing theoretical work in Ukraine. Of special significance was M. *Krylov and his student N. *Bogoliubov's (M. Boholiubov) development of modern nonlinear mechanics. Subsequently, Bogoliubov became world-renowned for his seminal contributions to statistical, nuclear, and particle physics and quantum-field theory.

The department of experimental physics organized in 1923 at the Kiev Polytechnical Institute by O. *Goldman was the first modern physics research center in Ukraine. Properties of dielectrics and semiconductors were investigated there. In 1929 the department was transformed into a multifaceted Physics Scientific Research Institute, which in 1936 was renamed the AN URSR (now ANU) *Institute of Physics. In 1927 Goldman started *Ukraïns'ki fizychni zapysky* (later *Fizychni zapysky*, 1926–41), the first Ukrainian serial devoted exclusively to physics. By that time Ukrainian physics and other scientific *terminology had been largely codified. *Fizychni zapysky* contributed substantially to the further development of physics terminology. In 1926 N. Morgulis established, as part of the department of physics at Kiev University, a laboratory for physical electronics, where experimental and theoretical work was conducted on the ionization of surfaces. In 1930 the laboratory became part of the Physics Scientific Research Institute.

Ten other ANU physics-related research establishments have been based in Kiev: the *Institute of Mechanics (est 1919); the Institute of Hydromechanics (est 1926); the Main *Astronomical Observatory (est 1944); the *Institute of Electrodynamics (est 1947); the *Institute of Metal Physics (est 1955); the *Institute of Semiconductors (est 1960), where theoretical and applied laser physics is studied; the *Institute of Geophysics (est 1960), which also develops and improves geophysical methods for discovering new mineral deposits; the *Institute of Technical Thermophysics (est 1947), which directs its efforts at investigating alternative and renewable energy sources; the *Institute of Theoretical Physics (est 1966); and the *Institute for Nuclear Research (est 1970). The last two institutes have in short order acquired international renown, the former for its research in quantum-field theory (O. Parasiuk, P. Fomin, V. Miransky, O. Parasiuk, G. Zinovev), nuclear and plasma theory (O. Sytenko, I. Simenoh, V. Kharchenko, I. Yakymenko), condensed-matter physics (V. Bariakhtar, I. Dziub), and quantum biophysics (O. Davydov, V. Hachok, E. Petrov, I. Ukrainsky), and the latter for its experimental facilities and a strong theoretical group (V. Strutynsky, V. Fushchych, D. Petryna of the Institute of Mathematics). Some of the other scientists who have contributed significantly to the advance of physical knowledge are V. Stryzhak (neutron physics at Kiev University, 1960–76), M.

Brodyn, I. Horban, A. Lubchenko, M. Shpak (optical properties of solids), and S. Pekar (polaron theory).

In 1990 the founding congress of the Ukrainian Physics Society was held in Kiev; V. Bariakhtar was elected president.

Kharkiv. In many respects, scientific research output from Kharkiv has rivaled and even surpassed Kiev's. In 1919 D. Rozhansky established a radio-physics laboratory at Kharkiv University, and in 1924–5 magnetrons for radio-wave generation were developed at the Kharkiv Institute of People's Education (KhINO) by A. Slutskin and D. Shteinberg. The All-Ukrainian Association of Physicists was founded at the KhINO in 1926; headed by ·A. Zhelekhivsky, it also had branches in Kiev (headed by O. Goldman), Dnipropetrovske (by A. Malinovsky), and Odessa (by E. Kirilov). A department of physics was founded at the KhINO in 1927; it was directed by D. Rozhansky. In 1928 the Ukrainian Physical-Technical Institute (UPTI) was established. It developed rapidly into a major physics center for the entire USSR. The vigorous development of experimental nuclear physics at the institute was exemplified by the 400-KeV electrostatic accelerator brought on-line in 1932 and by the 3.5-MeV facility made operational in 1937 (the most powerful in Europe at the time). Soviet heavy-water production was first achieved there by A. Brodsky in 1934. Major contributions were also made to theoretical and experimental nuclear, high-energy, plasma, low-temperature, and solid-state physics. Important discoveries were made in the areas of antiferromagnetism, ideal diamagnetism of semiconductors, nuclear magnetism, dynamics of magnetic moments, interacting spin waves (magnons), and magnetoacoustic resonance.

In 1938 the UPTI was renamed the AN URSR *Physical-Technical Institute (PTI). Today substantive theoretical work on supersymmetry is conducted there (D. Volkov). Salient postwar experimental achievements are exemplified by the bringing on-line in 1964 of a 2-GeV electron accelerator (K. Synelnykov, I. Hrishaiev), and by the breakthroughs in high-frequency and turbulent-plasma heating and in the confinement and control of thermonuclear plasma (Ya. Fainberg). Research in advanced fusion technology is pursued with the torsatron SATURN (1970, the world's first) and the Uragan 1–3 series of stellarators (V. Tolok).

Notable scientists have been associated at one time or another with the UPTI and PTI. In 1932 A. Leipunsky, K. Synelnykov, A. Walter, and G. Latyshev were the first in the USSR to induce the disintegration of a stable nucleus (lithium) by means of accelerated protons. Leipunsky became internationally known in 1934 while working in England in E. Rutherford's laboratory; there he obtained the first experimental evidence for the existence of the neutrino. In 1930, while working at the UPTI, the Russian physicist V. Fock became well known in the atomic and nuclear physics community for his contribution to the Hartree-Fock self-consistent field approximation. The 1962 Nobel Prize winner L. Landau headed the UPTI theoretical department in 1932–7. His imprint has been strongly felt there to the present day. There he and his student E. Lifshits wrote the landmark ten-volume *Course of Theoretical Physics*, which is still used world-wide. I. Pomeranchuk, author of the Pomeranchuk theorem, worked at the PTI, as did O. Akhiiezer and O. Sytenko, who are known for their theory of plasma fluctuations, I. Lifshits (theory of metals), M. Asbel and E. Kahner, who discovered cyclotron resonance in metals, and V. Zelensky (materials science).

In 1960 the Physical-Technical Institute of Low Temperatures was founded as a PTI offshoot, where fundamental and applied investigations have been conducted in superconductivity, the electronic properties of solids, the molecular physics of heat exchange, macromolecules, and cryogenics (see L. *Shubnikov). Physics research has also been conducted at Kharkiv University; the Kharkiv Polytechnical (formerly Technological) Institute; the Kharkiv Astronomical Observatory; and the ANU *Institute of Radio Physics and Electronics (est 1955), known for the discovery of the 10.4-Hz acoustic laser. A recent outgrowth of the latter institute is the Radio Astronomy Institute (est 1986), directed by S. Braude. It has operated the decameter-band radio telescope UTR-2, the largest in the world (in 1989) in the 10- to 25-MHz range, which has located some 60 new discrete decameter sources. The UTR-2 is the main component of the new system of four decameter-band interferometers (dubbed URAN, an acronym for Ukrainian Radiointerferometers of the ANU) with baseline lengths of between 40 and 900 km.

Lviv. Under Austrian rule, pioneering work was done at Lviv University in 1900–13 by Prof M. Smoluchowski on the theory of fluctuations. He contributed greatly to a microscopic understanding of the second law of thermodynamics. Under Polish rule, in 1935–6 L. Infeld worked there on general relativity and nonlinear electrodynamics. In the early 1960s strong spectroscopy and solid-state research groups were formed at Lviv University under the direction of A. Glauberman, and Ukrainian textbooks on quantum mechanics and atomic physics were written. It was also at Lviv University that O. Vlokh discovered the phenomenon of electrogyration, and I. Stasiuk provided a theoretical explanation for it. In the 1970s and 1980s major research in statistical condensed-matter physics was carried out at the Lviv branch of the ANU Institute of Theoretical Physics (since 1991 a separate ANU institute) under the guidance of I. *Yukhnovsky. Yukhnovsky's school developed the collective-variable method for the study of electrolytes (the first microscopic treatment including all interparticle forces), was the first to model successfully second-order phase transitions in several areas of physics, and obtained significant results in the theory of metals and in crystal optics.

Physics research was also conducted by the All-Union Scientific Research Institute of the Metrology of Measuring and Control Systems (est 1977); the Lviv Astronomical Observatory (research in astrometry, solar physics, and theoretical astrophysics); the Lviv Polytechnical Institute, where the school of V. Milianchuk has worked on atomic spectroscopy, quantum electrodynamics, and general quantum-field theory; and the ANU Institute for Applied Problems in Mechanics and Mathematics (est 1978).

Odessa. As a professor (1918–??) at the Odessa Polytechnical Institute, the Soviet physicist L. Mandelshtam made substantive contributions to the theory of and experiments on light scattering from crystals (Raman scattering, Brillouin-Mandelshtam scattering). In 1926 a State Physics Scientific Research Institute was founded. There a group under E. Kirilov investigated photochemical and photoelectric reactions in the photographic process and obtained new and extensive data on the photoelectric effect in semiconductors and on the luminescence of dyes and crystals. In 1933 the institute became part of Odessa University. In the late 1940s V. Fedoseev and D. Polishchuk conducted work at the university on evaporation, burning, and gas dynamics of liquid and solid fuels, which found applications in jet engines and rocket motors. Physics research is also done at the *Odessa Astronomical Observatory (est 1871), which operates five reflector and five refractor telescopes, a URAN-4 radio telescope (since 1981), and a synchronized satellite-tracking facility in co-ordination with additional observation stations in Kiev, Lviv, and Uzhhorod; the Odessa Electrotechnical Institute of Communications (est 1930); the Odessa Hydrometeorological Institute (est 1932); the Odessa Institute of Navy Engineers (est 1930); and the Odessa Technological Institute of the Refrigeration Industry (since 1970).

The Crimea. There are two important physics-related research institutions in the Crimea: the *Crimean Astrophysical Observatory (est 1945) near Bakhchesarai, with Europe's largest reflector telescope, a 22-m radio telescope, and a solar telescope (with which A. Severny discovered rapid solar pulsations), and whose research laboratories developed a solar telescope for the SALUT space laboratory and have collaborated with Canadian astrophysicists on very long baseline high-precision interferometry (ASTRON); and the ANU *Marine Hydrophysical Oceanographic Institute, based in Symferopil since 1963.

Donetske. At the ANU Physical-Technical Institute (est 1965), an offshoot of the ANU Physical-Technical Institute of Low Temperatures in Kharkiv, the main thrust of research has been in materials science (the effects of high pressures and intense magnetic fields at low temperatures on the magnetic and electronic properties of solids). O. *Halkin, director of the institute from its inception until 1982, V. Bariakhtar, and K. *Tolpyho are largely credited with establishing and maintaining the high scientific level. Among its significant achievements are the discovery of an intermediate state in ferromagnetics and the determination that the transition from fragility to plasticity constitutes a phase transition linked to the number of mobile dislocations. Applied physics research on nonlinear systems is conducted at the ANU *Institute of Applied Mathematics and Mechanics (est 1970).

Dnipropetrovske. Notable physics research dates back to G. Kurdiumov's school on phase transitions in metals at the Dnipropetrovske Physical-Technical Institute (1932–44). The ANU Institute of Technical Mechanics (est 1980) specializes in the dynamics of complex mechanical and hydromechanical systems. Of note is its research on high-speed transportation involving magnetic levitation. Dnipropetrovske University (est 1918) has an applied physics research laboratory.

Poltava. Since 1926 the Poltava Gravimetric Observatory has carried out high-precision measurement of the precession and nutation of the earth's rotational axis and of the tides of the earth's mantle and crust.

Chernivtsi. Research has been conducted at a branch of the ANU Institute of Semiconductors (interesting results on narrow-band semiconductors have been obtained by K. Tovstiuk), at Chernivtsi University (theoretical solid-state physics), and at a branch of the Lviv-based Institute for Applied Problems in Mechanics and Mathematics.

Uzhhorod. Research in theoretical high-energy physics, axiomatic quantum-field theory (Y. Lomsadze), and experimental atomic physics (J. Zapesochny) has been carried out at Uzhhorod University and at a branch of the ANU Institute for Nuclear Research.

Serials. Physics research has been published in Ukraine mostly in VUAN and ANU serials: *Protokoly zasidan' Fizychno-matematychnoho viddilu Ukraïns'koï akademiï nauk u Kyievi* (1918–19); *Dopovidi Akademiï nauk Ukraïns'koï RSR, Seriia 'A'* (since 1918); *Zapysky Fizychno-matematychnoho viddilu* (1923–31); *Trudy Fizychno-matematychnoho viddilu* (1923–9); *Zbirnyk prats' Instytutu tekhnichnoï mekhaniky* (1926–9); *Fizychni zapysky* (1932–41); *Physikalische Zeitschrift der Sowjetunion* (1932–8), published by the ANU Physical-Technical Institute in Kharkiv in German and English; *Visti Instytutu hidrolohiï* (1938, 1940); *Visti Instytutu hidrolohiï i hidrotekhniky* (1948–51, 1963); *Izvestiia Instituta gidrologii i gidrotekhniki* (1951, 1953–6, 1959–63); *Zapysky Kafedry matematychnoï fizyky* (1937–9); *Dopovidi Viddilu fizyko-khimichnykh i matematychnykh nauk* (1944); *Trudy Instituta fiziki* (1951–6); **Ukraïns'kyi fizychnyi zhurnal* (1956–78 and since 1989), *Ukrainskii fizicheskii zhurnal* (1978–88), *Fiziko-khimicheskaia mekhanika materialov* (since 1965), *Fizika nizkikh temperatur* (since 1975), *Visnyk Kyïvs'koho universytetu: Seriia fizyky* (since 1962), *Visnyk Lvivs'koho universytetu: Seriia fizyky* (since 1962), *Fizika mnogochastichnykh sistem* (since 1972), and *Fizika, khimiia i mekhanika materialov* (since 1988). Starting in the 1930s Ukrainian physics periodicals came under strong government pressure to publish in Russian (see **Russification). The premier Ukrainian physics journal, *Ukraïns'kyi fizychnyi zhurnal*, which appeared in Ukrainian until 1972, had a parallel Russian edition from 1972 until 1978, and from 1978 was published in Russian only. Since 1989 this journal has published contributions in Ukrainian, Russian, and English.

BIBLIOGRAPHY
Khramov, Iu. *Fizyky: Dovidnyk* (Kiev 1974)
Shul'ha, M. *Khronolohichnyi dovidnyk vitchyznianoï fizyky* (Kiev 1980)
Azarov, A.; et al (eds). *Istoriia Akademiï nauk Ukraïns'koï RSR* (Kiev 1982)
Khramov, Iu. *Fiziki: Biograficheskii spravochnik* (Moscow 1983)
– *Biografia fiziki: Khronologicheskii spravochnik* (Kiev 1983)
O. Bilaniuk, M. Horbatsch

Physiology. A discipline that employs anatomical, chemical, and physical means to inquire into the causes and mechanisms of the activities of all living things, particularly healthy humans. The first centers to study physiology in Ukraine were established in Kiev, Odessa, Kharkiv, and Lviv at their respective universities in the first half of the 19th century. In the second half of the 19th century departments of physiology were established at existing veterinary and agronomy institutes. Among the Ukrainian scientists active in the field of physiology were M. Biletsky, V. *Danylevsky, G. *Folbort, O. *Nahorny, Ye. *Prykhodkova, V. *Nikitin, and I. Shchelkov (in Kharkiv); V. *Bets, V. *Chahovets, O. *Bohomolets, A. *Yemchenko, A. *Walter, and D. *Vorontsov (in Kiev); and B. Babkin, P. *Spiro, and B. Verigo (in Odessa). The first journal of physiology in the Russian Empire was published by the brothers O. and V. Danylevsky in Kharkiv (1888–91).

Because of the human impact on the environment and the important question of world ecology, comparative physiology is regarded as one of the most pressing problems of our time on both medical and economic levels. The Ukrainian Society of Physiologists, Biochemists, and Pharmacologists was founded in 1929, and split into three independent societies in 1961, including the Ukrainian Physiological Society (UFT). By 1984 the latter had 15 city chapters and 1,345 members. Physiological research in Ukraine is also conducted at the ANU *Institute of Physiology, co-ordinated by the UFT and the ANU Scientific Council for Problems of Animal and Human Physiology. Journals published in Ukraine include *Fiziologicheskii zhurnal* (since 1955) and *Neirofiziologiia*.

BIBLIOGRAPHY
Vorontsov, D.; Nikitin, V.; Sierkov, P. *Narysy z istoriï fiziolohiï na Ukraïni* (Kiev 1959)
Kostiuk, P. *Fiziologiia tsentral'noi nervovoi sistemy* (Kiev 1977)
Obshchaia fiziologiia nervovoi sistemy (Lviv 1979)
Chastnaia fiziologiia nervovoi sistemy (Lviv 1983)
Nikitin, V. *Istoricheskii ocherk razvitiia fiziologii cheloveka i zhivotnykh* (Kharkiv 1983)
P. Dzul

Phytogeography. The study of the geographical distribution of plants. Like many other sciences, it developed into a formal science during the 18th century, although some elements of plant geography appeared in ancient writings. The botanical-geographical regionalization of Ukrainian flora has been studied by P. Pallas, S. Korzynsky, A. Kryshtofovych, M. Maksymovych, N. Vavilov, M. Popov, M. Klokov, M. Kotov, Ye. Lavrenko, and others.

Piarists (*piiary*). The popular name of the Order of Poor Clerics Regular of the Mother of God of the Pious Schools, a congregation of priest-teachers established in 1597 in Rome by J. Calasanctius to provide free education for children. Piarists first appeared in the Polish-Lithuanian Commonwealth in 1682. They rapidly established a host of colleges, which they operated in competition with the Jesuits, particularly after the school reforms of 1754. In Polish-controlled Right-Bank Ukraine the Piarists maintained monasteries and schools in Kholm, Zolochiv, Lviv, Mezhyhiria, and other locations. The order was liquidated in Russian-controlled territories in 1832, following the Polish uprising.

Piasetsky, Andrii [Pjasec'kyj, Andrij], b 27 August 1909 in Reklynets, Zhovkva county, Galicia, d 25 November 1942 in Lviv. Forester, community figure, and an active member of Plast. A graduate in forestry engineering from the Lviv Polytechnical Institute, he was appointed inspector of forests in the Lviv archdiocese by Metropolitan A. Sheptytsky in 1935. Before the Second World War he purchased 150 ha of forests in Lozyna, near Yaniv (Horodok county), for a Ukrainian forestry research station. During the Soviet occupation he taught in the forestry department of the Lviv Polytechnical Institute (1939–41). In 1941 he was a member of the Ukrainian State Administration in Lviv. During the German occupation he published a work on the building and biological development of Ukrainian forests (1942), founded and ran a forestry institute, and acquired the Yaniv research station for it. He was arrested and shot by the Gestapo.

Piatakov, Georgii (Yurii) [Pjatakov, Georgij (Jurij)], b 6 August 1890 in Horodyshche, Cherkasy county, Kiev gubernia, d January 1937. Russian Bolshevik revolutionary and Soviet leader. After the February Revolution Piatakov headed the Kiev Bolshevik Committee and represented it in the Central Rada. Although he opposed the Rada's separatist policies, for tactical purposes he co-operated with it and even sat on the Little Rada (August–November 1917). In September 1917 he became the chairman of the Kiev Council of Workers' Deputies, and after the Bolshevik coup he was called to Petrograd to oversee the State Bank. In April 1918, after returning to Ukraine, he became the first chairman of the Organizational Bureau of the newly founded CP(B)U and the CC secretary. To gain Ukrainian support for the Bolsheviks, he promoted, contrary to his principles, CP(B)U autonomy vis-à-vis the Russian Party. When the peasant uprising he had organized failed, Moscow loyalists (the Katerynoslav group) took control of the CP(B)U, and in September 1918 Piatakov was replaced as CC secretary. After the German retreat from Ukraine Piatakov headed the Soviet *Provisional Workers' and Peasants' Government of Ukraine (November 1918 to January 1919) and implemented some ultraleft social and economic policies. While he demanded military and political autonomy from Moscow, he waged war against the UNR Directory and an ideological struggle against the *Borotbists. In January 1919 he was replaced as head of the government by V. Lenin's supporter, Kh. Rakovsky.

From 1920 Piatakov supported L. *Trotsky's positions. As director of the mining industry in the Urals (1920) and the Donbas (1921) he restored order and production by 'militarizing' and thenceforth was considered a leading Soviet administrator and economic expert. A key figure in Soviet economic debates of the mid-1920s, Piatakov elaborated a five-year plan for capital accumulation that provided for the accelerated industrialization of Ukraine instead of the Urals.

After the defeat of the Left Opposition in 1927, Piatakov was removed from the USSR Supreme Council of the National Economy (VSNKh) and expelled from the Party. He recanted and in 1929 was readmitted into the Party and appointed chairman of the State Bank in Moscow. As a member of the VSNKh and deputy commissar of heavy industry, he was responsible for much of the industrial success of the Second Five-Year Plan. In the fall of 1936 he was arrested. At the second Moscow show trial of the 'anti-Soviet Trotskyist center' in January 1937, Piatakov 'confessed' to heading a 'Ukrainian Trotskyist center' whose goal was Ukraine's secession from the USSR. He was executed with 12 codefendants immediately after the trial.

V. Holubnychy, R. Senkus

Piatakov, Leonid [Pjatakov], b 4 October 1888 in Horodyshche, Cherkasy county, Kiev gubernia, d ca 7 January 1918 in Kiev. Bolshevik revolutionary; brother of G. *Piatakov. A graduate of the Kiev Polytechnical Institute (1908), he joined the Bolsheviks in 1915. After the February Revolution he helped organize the Red Guard in Kiev and was a member of the Kiev Bolshevik Committee, the Executive Committee of the Kiev Council of Workers' Deputies, and, briefly, the Central Rada. In December 1917 he was elected a candidate member of the Chief Committee of Social Democracy in Ukraine (the supreme Bolshevik body in Right-Bank Ukraine) and a member of the Bolshevik All-Ukrainian Central Executive Committee.

Piatnytska Church. See Good Friday, Church of.

Piatnytsky, Ihor [P'jatnyts'kyj], b 5 November 1910 in Kiev. Analytical chemist. A graduate of Kiev University (1937), he taught there and became a professor and chairman of the analytical chemistry department in 1960. He published over 80 papers on the reaction of metal complexes with oxyacids and their use in analytical chemistry, on the characterization of complexes derived from fatty acids and metal cations, and on their extractive behavior. He coauthored three textbooks on analytical chemistry, including *Analytical Chemistry of Cobalt* (English trans 1969).

Piatnytsky, Ivan [P'jatnyc'kyj], b 1856, d ? Church historian. A graduate of the St Petersburg Theological Seminary, in the 1890s he lectured at the Mahiliou Theological Academy (in Belarus) and edited the Mahiliou eparchial organ. He is the author of a history of sectarianism in the Russian Orthodox church (1884), *Ocherk istorii kievskoi mitropolii v period vremeni otdel'nogo ee sushchestvovaniia ot mitropolii moskovskoi, 1459–1686* (A Brief History of Kiev Metropoly during the Period of Its Separation from Moscow Metropoly in 1459–1686, 1891), and other works. He also edited and published the sermons of H. Konysky (1892).

Piatnytsky, Porfyrii [P'jatnyc'kyj, Porfyrij], b 15 September 1859 in Riga, d 30 December 1940 in Kiev. Geologist. After graduating from Kharkiv University (1896) he lectured there (1903–20) and served as rector (1918–20) of the university. He worked as a geologist in Krasnodar (1920–2), Moscow (1922–6), and Leningrad (1926–32) before returning to Ukraine in 1932 to become a research associate at the Ukrainian Geological Administration and the AN URSR (now ANU) Institute of Geological Sciences (from 1938). His major research interests included Precambrian crystalline schists of Ukraine, particularly of the Kryvyi Rih Iron-ore Basin.

Piatnytsky, Serhii [P'jatnyc'kyj, Serhij], b 15 March 1905 in Kharkiv gubernia, d 2 May 1971 in Kharkiv. Silviculturist; corresponding member of the All-Union Academy of Agricultural Sciences. He graduated from the Kharkiv Agricultural Institute (1925), and from 1934 he headed the selection department at the Ukrainian Scientific Research Institute of Forest Management and Agroforest Amelioration in Kharkiv. From 1949 he was also a professor at the Kharkiv Agricultural Institute. He wrote on the theoretical foundations of agroforest amelioration, silviculture, and forest selection and genetics and developed new varieties of oak trees able to survive in a steppe environment.

Piatykhatky [P'jatyxatky]. V-14. A city (1989 pop 21,600) and raion center in Dnipropetrovske oblast. The town arose ca 1886 as a railway junction and attained city status in 1938. It is now an industrial and communications center with railway servicing enterprises, a clothes factory, and a food industry.

Pich. See Stove.

Picheta, Volodymyr [Pičeta] (Vladimir), b 22 October 1878 in Poltava, d 23 June 1947 in Moscow. Historian and

Volodymyr Picheta

Slavist of Serbian and Ukrainian descent; full member of the Academy of Sciences of the Belorussian SSR from 1928 and of the USSR from 1946. A graduate of Moscow University (1901), he taught in secondary schools in Moscow (1901–2, 1905–10), Korostyshiv (1902–3), and Katerynoslav (1903–5) and was a member of the Katerynoslav Learned Archival Commission. He was a privatdocent at Moscow University (1910–11) and then taught at Moscow's School of Higher Courses for Women and Practical Academy of Commercial Sciences. He received his PH D in 1918.

Under Soviet rule Picheta was a lecturer and professor at Moscow University (1918–21) and the first rector of the Belarusian University in Minsk (1921–30). He was arrested by the OGPU in September 1930, tried on fabricated charges of belonging to counterrevolutionary and Belarusian bourgeois nationalist organizations, and exiled in August 1931 to Viatka. He was released in 1934 after E. Beneš, then Czechoslovakia's foreign minister, told J. Stalin he wanted to meet Picheta while he visited Moscow. Picheta then taught at two Voronezh institutes (1934–6) before returning to Moscow to become a senior associate of the USSR academy's Institute of History (1937), a professor at Moscow's university and pedagogical institute (1938), a corresponding member of the academy and chairman of the Institute of History's Sector of Slavic Studies (1939), and chairman of the department of the history of the Western and Southern Slavs at Moscow University (1943). From 1946 he was one of two deputy directors of the academy's Institute of Slavic Studies.

Picheta's works in Slavic history include a historical survey of the Slavs (1914) and monographs on Bulgaria's struggle for national unification (1915), the agrarian reform of King Sigismund II Augustus in the Lithuanian-Ruthenian state (master's and doctoral diss, 2 vols, 1917; 2nd edn 1958), Russian historiography (1922), the beginnings of industrialization and the disintegration of the serf economy in Russia (1923), peasant wars in Russia (1923), the history of Belarus (1924), the history of agriculture and land ownership in Belarus to the late 16th century (1927), principal moments in the history of Western Ukraine and western Belarus (1940), the history of Bohemia (1947), and 15th- and 16th-century Belarus and Lithuania (1961). Some of his studies were published in *Letopis' Ekaterinoslavskoi uchenoi arkhivnoi komissii*, *Ukraïns'kyi naukovyi zbirnyk* (1915), *Ukrainskaia zhizn'* (1915, 1917), and VUAN collections. He wrote numerous articles on the history of the Cossack period, a brochure about the 17th- to 18th-century Cossack state in Ukraine (1945), and a survey of

Ukrainian history (1947). A bibliography of his works was published in Minsk in 1978.

A. Zhukovsky

Pid markso-lenins'kym praporom. See *Prapor marksyzmu-leninizmu.*

Pid praporom leninizmu (Under the Flag of Leninism). A semimonthly journal of political propaganda and agitation published by the CC CPU in Kiev in 1941 and from 1944 to 1991. Its previous names were *Na dopomohu ahitatoru* (1941) and *Bloknot ahitatora* (1944–69). A Russian-language version of the journal, *Pod znamenem leninizma*, was published from 1953. In 1980 the circulation of the Russian edition was 229,000, and of the Ukrainian edition, 230,000.

Piddubny, Hryhorii [Piddubnyj, Hryhorij] (real surname: Tovmachiv), b 1882 in Tetleha, Pryluka county, Poltava gubernia, d 3 November 1937 in the Solovets Islands. Journalist, writer, and political activist. He emigrated to Austria before the First World War and returned to Ukraine in 1917. After joining the Ukrainian Party of Socialist Revolutionaries he coedited its organ *Trudova respublika* (1918–19). In 1919–20 he belonged to the External Group of the Ukrainian Communist party in Vienna and contributed to its weekly *Nova doba*. Then he worked for Soviet intelligence and as a correspondent of the Kiev daily *Proletars'ka pravda*. In 1928 he returned to Ukraine, and in 1935 he was imprisoned in the Solovets Islands. His writings include political and historical works, such as *Za Radians'ku Ukraïnu* (For Soviet Ukraine, 1921) and *Bukovyna: Ïi mynule i suchasne* (Bukovyna: Past and Present, 1928), short stories, and translations of A. Chekhov, G. Sand, and H.G. Wells.

Ivan Piddubny   Volodymyr Pidhaietsky

Piddubny, Ivan [Piddubnyj], b 8 October 1871 in Krasenivka, Zolotonosha county, Poltava gubernia, d 8 August 1949 in Yeiske, Krasnodar krai, RSFSR. Wrestler. From 1898 he performed as a strongman and wrestler in circuses that toured the Russian Empire and, later, the USSR. In 1905–9 he won six world championships in professional wrestling. In 1926–7 he fought in the United States. In his 40-year career he did not lose a single championship fight, and he became known around the world as the 'champion of champions.' A museum in his honor was opened in Yeiske in 1971.

Piddubyk-Sushchevsky, Petro [Piddubyk-Suščev-s'kyj], b 1756 in the Chernihiv region, d 4 September 1811 in Chernihiv. Orthopedist and traumatologist. A graduate of Chernihiv College and the medico-surgical school at the St Petersburg Military Hospital, he served as an army medic and in 1788 obtained the rank of staff physician. From 1797 he worked on the Little Russia Medical Board.

Pidhaichyky Yustynovi. A multi-occupational archeological site near Pidhaichyky, Terebovlia raion, Ternopil oblast. Excavations by W. Demetrikiewicz in 1900 uncovered a Neolithic stone burial vault, a Trypilian settlement, a cache of Roman coins from the 1st to 2nd century, and a 4th- to 5th-century early Slavic burial ground.

Pidhaietsky, Volodymyr [Pidhajec'kyj], b 23 July 1889 in Kamianets-Podilskyi, Podilia gubernia, d 3 November 1937. Hygienist and civic leader. He was a member of the Central Rada in 1917–18, a professor of occupational hygiene at the Kiev Medical Institute (1921–30), director of the Institute of Physical Culture in Kiev, and a senior research associate of the All-Ukrainian Academy of Sciences. Accused of being a member of the *Union for the Liberation of Ukraine, he was sentenced in 1930 to eight years' confinement and three years' deprivation of personal rights. In October 1937 an NKVD tribunal sentenced him to death. The Ukrainian SSR Supreme Court rehabilitated him in 1989.

Bohdan Pidhainy   Semen Pidhainy

Pidhainy, Bohdan [Pidhajnyj], b 2 January 1906 in Polonychna, Kaminka-Strumylova county, Galicia, d 1 September 1980 in Toronto. Mechanical engineer and political and civic activist. A graduate of the Danzig Polytechnic, he joined the Ukrainian Military Organization and in the 1930s became operations chief in the home executive of the OUN in Galicia. He was sentenced in 1935 to life in prison in connection with B. *Pieracki's assassination and in 1936 to 15 years as a member of the OUN Home Executive. During the Second World War he took part in the eastward march of the OUN expeditionary groups and in the operations of the Division Galizien. Later he was interned as a POW in Rimini, and served on the executive of the OUN (Bandera faction). After emigrating to Canada in 1956, he became a member of the Political Council of the OUN Abroad and Canadian president of the Brotherhood of Former Soldiers of the First Ukrainian Division of the Ukrainian National Army.

Pidhainy, Leonyd [Pidhajnyj], b 1899 in Yabluniv, Kaniv county, Kiev gubernia, d 15 December 1950 in Kiev. Literary scholar and critic. From 1931 to 1941 he was a docent at the Kiev Institute of People's Education (Kiev University from 1934). He was first published in 1928. His monographs are *Lesia Ukraïnka* (1929), *Literaturnye kommentarii k proizvedeniiam M. Kotsiubinskogo* (Literary Commentaries on the Works of M. Kotsiubynsky, 1931), *Franko i Zolia* (Franko and Zola, 1936), and *Lesia Ukraïnka* (1941).

Pidhainy, Oleh [Pidhajnyj], b 1933 in Kharkiv. Historian; son of S. *Pidhainy. He graduated from McGill University in Montreal (1962) and taught at Auburn University in Alabama. He has published works on the history of Ukraine in 1917–20, including *The Formation of the Ukrainian Republic* (1966) and *The Ukrainian Republic in the Great East-European Revolution: A Bibliography* (coeditor, 2 pts, 1971, 1975).

Pidhainy, Semen [Pidhajnyj], b 17 April 1907 in Novominska Stanytsia, Kuban, d 14 November 1965 in Toronto. Historian, writer, civic and political activist. A graduate of the Kiev Institute of People's Education and the Kharkiv Scientific Research Institute of Material Culture, he worked at the Museum of Slobidska Ukraine and the Kharkiv Institute of People's Education and was a research associate of the All-Ukrainian Academy of Sciences. From 1933 to 1941 he was an inmate of Soviet labor camps, mostly in the Solovets Islands. He fled from the USSR in 1943 and emigrated to Canada in 1949. He was deputy secretary of the Ukrainian Revolutionary Democratic party and a member of the Ukrainian National Council. He organized and headed the *Ukrainian Association of Victims of Russian Communist Terror and the World Federation of Ukrainian Former Political Prisoners and Victims of the Soviet Regime. He wrote a number of works on Soviet terror, including *Ukraïns'ka inteligentsiia na Solovkakh* (The Ukrainian Intelligentsia in the Solovets Islands, 1947) and *Nedostriliani* (Those Left Unshot, 2 vols, 1949; Eng trans *Islands of Death* 1953), and edited *The Black Deeds of the Kremlin: A White Book* (2 vols, 1953). He also published the *New Review*.

Pidhaitsi [Pidhajci]. IV-6. A city (1973 pop 3,277) on the Koropets River in Berezhany raion, Ternopil oblast. The town is first mentioned in historical sources in 1463. It was granted the rights of Magdeburg law in 1539. When Podilia was annexed by Poland, the town became part of Halych county in Rus' voivodeship. It was owned by the Buczacki and then the Potocki magnate family. In the 17th century it was the site of many battles among the Cossacks, Poles, and Turks and Tatars. The Tatars destroyed Pidhaitsi in 1667 and again in 1675. After the partition of Poland in 1772, the town came under Austrian rule. In 1919 it was acquired by Poland, and in 1939, by the Ukrainian SSR. Today Pidhaitsi has a canning, a mixed-feed, and a metalworking factory. Its historical monuments are a Roman Catholic church built in the Renaissance style in 1634, the Dormition Church, built in the 1650s, and the remnants of a castle from the 16th and 17th centuries.

BIBLIOGRAPHY
Hunczak, T. (ed). *Pidhaiets'ka zemlia* (New York–Paris–Sydney–Toronto 1980)

Mariika Pidhirianka

Pidhirianka, Mariika [Pidhirjanka, Marijka] (pseud of Mariia Lenert), b 29 March 1881 in Bili Oslavy, Nadvirna county, Galicia, d 20 May 1963 in Rudno (now part of Lviv). Writer and teacher; wife of A. *Dombrovsky. A teacher from 1900, in the 1920s and early 1930s she taught in Transcarpathia. From 1902 until the Second World War her poetry, stories, fables, and plays appeared in Galician, Transcarpathian, and émigré periodicals and children's magazines, primers, and chrestomathies. She is the author of the poetry collections *Vidhuky dushi* (Echoes of the Soul, 1908) and *Zbirnychok virshiv dlia ditei* (A Small Collection of Verse for Children, 1920); the plays *Son na mohyli* (A Dream at the Grave, 1916), *Vertep* (1921), and *V chuzhim pir'iu* (In Someone Else's Feathers, 1922); the narrative poem *Maty-stradnytsia* (The Mother-Martyr, 1922, 1929; repr in *Duklia*, 1984, no. 1); and three books of poetry, folklore, and translated literature for schoolchildren, *Lastivochka* (The Little Swallow, 1925–7). Her Ukrainian translation of *Robinson Crusoe* (1925) was widely read in Western Ukraine. Three collections of her poetry for children appeared posthumously, in 1970, 1978, and 1981.

Pidhiriany settlement. A multi-occupational archeological site near Pidhiriany, Terebovlia raion, Ternopil oblast. Excavated by W. Demetrikiewicz (1899) and by Ya. *Pasternak (1931, 1937), it yielded the remains of a *Trypilian settlement, late *Bronze and *Iron Age burials (the latter containing Daco-Thracian pottery fragments), a 2nd- to 3rd-century AD burial ground (containing mainly cremated bodies), and a Rus' settlement.

Pidhirny, Mykola [Pidhirnyj] (Podgorny), b 18 February 1903 in Karlivka, Kostiantynohrad county, Poltava gubernia, d 11 January 1983 in Moscow. Soviet official and Party leader. A graduate of the Kiev Technological Institute of the Food Industry (1930), he worked as an engineer at sugar refineries in Ukraine and rose to the position of deputy people's commissar of the food industry in Ukraine (1939–40, 1944–6) and the USSR (1940–2). At the same time (1944–6) he oversaw the *resettlement of Ukrainians from the bo derlands retained by Poland. After serving as permanent representative of the Ukrainian Council of Ministers in Moscow (1946–50) he advanced quickly in the Party from the positions of first (1950–3) and second (1953–7) secretary of the CPU Kharkiv Oblast Committee to those of second (1953–7) and first (1957–63)

secretary of the CC CPU. In spite of Pidhirny's failure to increase farm production N. Khrushchev promoted him to the Presidium of the CC CPSU (1960–77) and to the office of secretary of the CC CPSU (1963–5). After helping L. Brezhnev to overthrow N. Khrushchev Pidhirny was removed from the center of power by being appointed chairman of the Presidium of the USSR Supreme Soviet (1965) and member of the CC CPSU Politburo (1966). In 1977 he was retired from those positions.

Pidhirny, Volodymyr [Pidhirnyj], b 4 October 1928 in Verkhnobohdanivka, Luhanske okruha. Composer and pedagogue. After graduating from the Kharkiv Conservatory (1956) he began lecturing at the Kharkiv Art Institute. His works include a symphony (1956), chamber pieces, vocal works, and songs for children.

Samiilo Pidhirsky

Pidhirsky, Samiilo [Pidhirs'kyj, Samijlo], b 20 September 1888 in Liublyntsi, Kovel county, Volhynia gubernia, d 1945. Lawyer and civic and political leader. After graduating from St Petersburg University (1914) he practiced law in Kiev and founded a society of Ukrainian lawyers. A year later he moved to Zhytomyr, where he was active in local government and was elected president of the gubernial zemstvo and the Volhynian Prosvita society. In 1917 he edited *Hromadianyn*, the first Ukrainian newspaper in Volhynia, and then *Volyns'ka hazeta* (1918–19) and *Hromada* (1920) in Lutske. A radical populist by conviction, he was a member of the Central Rada and of the Labor Congress in Kiev. In 1922 he was elected to the Polish Sejm, where he served as chairman of the Ukrainian Parliamentary Representation. He also acted as defense counsel in many political trials. At the end of the Second World War Pidhirsky was executed by the Soviets.

Pidhirtsi [Pidhirci]. IV-5. A village (1972 pop 1,400) in Zolochiv raion, Lviv oblast. It is first mentioned, as Plisnesk or Plisnysk, in chronicles in 1188 and 1233. The town's ruins – a complex of ramparts and moats covering nearly 160 ha – are the largest and finest of old Rus' fortifications to survive. In the 12th and 13th centuries Plisnesk was one of the largest cities of the Halych and Galician-Volhynian principalities and an important trade center. It was destroyed in 1241 by the Mongols, and had disappeared by the mid-15th century. The village of Pidhirtsi was founded close by. It is first mentioned in historical documents in 1432. The Polish grand hetman S. Koniecpolski built a fortified Renaissance palace there in 1635–40. Besides the palace a number of architectural

Pidhirtsi palace (17th century)

monuments, including a Basilian monastery from 1659 and an Orthodox church from 1726, have been preserved.

Pidhirtsi settlement. A settlement of the 5th to 4th century BC near Pidhirtsi, Obukhiv raion, Kiev oblast. Excavations in 1950 unearthed an early *Iron Age settlement where weaving, bronze casting, and iron working were well developed. A hoard of artistic bronze objects from the same era and a cache of objects of Caucasian origin ca 9th to 8th century BC were found nearby.

Borys Pidhoretsky

Pidhoretsky, Borys [Pidhorec'kyj], b 6 April 1873 in Lubni, Poltava gubernia, d 19 February 1919 in Moscow. Composer, music critic, folklorist, pedagogue, and conductor. He graduated from the Warsaw Institute of Music, and from 1900 lived in Moscow, working as a teacher and studying composition with A. Ilinsky. In 1912 he was sent by the Russian Geographical Society's ethnomusicological commission to study folk music in Ukraine, where he collected over 120 folk songs. From 1915 he taught choral singing at the Moscow Conservatory and was a music critic for several newspapers, among them *Golos Moskvy* and *Izvestiia*. His works include the operas *Kupal'na iskra* (The Kupalo Spark, 1901) and *Poor Liza* (1916); choral pieces; and music to words of T. Shevchenko, I. Franko, and Ye. Hrebinka. His biography, by K. Cherpukhova (1968), and

a collection of his writings on musical themes (1970) were published in Kiev.

Pidhorny, Anatolii [Pidhornyj, Anatolij], b 5 April 1932 in Andrushivka, Kiev oblast. Mechanics and machine scientist; corresponding member of the AN URSR (now ANU) since 1973. He studied and taught at the Kharkiv Polytechnical Institute. He headed the Kharkiv branch of the ANU Institute of Thermodynamics (from 1971) and became director of the ANU Institute for Problems of Machine Building (in 1972). His main contributions are in the fields of dynamics and the strength of machines. He has developed mathematical methods of solving nonlinear equations in the theory of plastic deformation and creep, which helped in the understanding of failure mechanisms in loaded structures. He has worked also on methods of hydrogen utilization in engines.

Pidhoroddia. A multi-occupational site near Pidhoroddia, Rohatyn raion, Ivano-Frankivske oblast. Excavated intermittently from 1882 to 1951, the site yielded the remains of a Neolithic settlement, several early Slavic settlements, a large number of Roman coins, the foundations of six medieval churches, and the remains of boyar and merchant homes, which at one time made up a suburb of princely *Halych.

Pidhorodetsky, Vasyl [Pidhorodec'kyj, Vasyl'], b 1926. Freedom fighter and political prisoner. A soldier in the UPA, he was captured in 1951 and sentenced to 25 years in Siberian labor camps. In 1955 he was one of the organizers of the prisoners' revolt in the Taishet camp, for which he was sentenced to an additional 15 years in 1956. He continued to participate in the strikes and protests of the political prisoners, and in 1975 he renounced his Soviet citizenship. In the late 1960s or early 1970s he was transferred to a camp in Perm oblast. He was released in 1981, but was once again arrested and incarcerated in 1982–3 and 1984–5.

Pidhorodne. V-16. A city (1966 pop 16,500) on the Kilchen River in Dnipropetrovske raion. The earliest settlement arose at the beginning of the 17th century through the merging of several Cossack homesteads. In 1688 a fortress was built to protect the village from Tatar raids. After the destruction of the Zaporozhian Sich (1775) the Cossacks of Pidhorodne served in the Katerynoslav Cossack Army. After its abolition in 1796, many of them emigrated to the Kuban. Today, near the suburbs of Dnipropetrovske, the city is known for its fruit growing and hothouse farming.

Pidkarpats'ka Rus' (Subcarpathian Ruthenia). A monthly journal of regional studies and pedagogy, published by the Pedagogical Society of Subcarpathian Ruthenia in Uzhhorod from 1923 to 1936. Until 1935 it was called *Podkarpatska Rus'*. The chief editors were P. Yatsko, V. Hadzhega, and A. Shtefan, but the de facto editor was I. *Pankevych. The journal published source materials on the history, literature, geography, and economics of Transcarpathia and many articles on local folklore, ethnography, and dialectology, written mostly by village teachers and students. The main contributors were Pankevych, A. Voloshyn, M. Lelekach, O. Markush, L. Demian, and I. Kondratovych.

Pidkarpatskii holos (Subcarpathian Voice). A weekly newspaper published by the Ukrainian Social Democratic party in Drohobych in 1907–11. Edited by S. Vityk, it was the first Ukrainian-language newspaper in the city. It published articles on the workers' movement in Galicia and abroad, political commentary, and valuable descriptions of the lives of workers in Drohobych. It was succeeded by the weekly *Holos Pidkarpattia* (1911–13).

Pidkomorskyi **court.** A type of land court in medieval Poland, the Grand Duchy of Lithuania, and Right-Bank Ukraine. *Pidkomorski* courts were based on the Second (1566) and Third (1588) *Lithuanian Statute, and functioned in Ukraine until 1654. Initially they consisted of representatives of each of the sides in a land dispute, but eventually they were reduced to a single judge (*pidkomorii*) appointed by the king. The judge could choose an assistant. They were closely connected with the *land courts and their verdicts could be appealed to the *marshal-commissioner courts. After a one-century interval these courts were re-established by Hetman K. Rozumovsky in 1763. Each regiment of the Hetman state set up its own court, consisting of the *pidkomorii, komornyk*, and scribe, who were elected by the landowners and regimental *starshyna*. The courts were again abolished, by Catherine II, in 1783, and again re-established in 1796. Renamed boundary courts in 1834, they continued to function until 1840.

Ivan Pidkova

Pidkova, Ivan (Moldavian: Potcoavă, Ioan), b ?, d 16 June 1578 in Lviv. Cossack otaman and Moldavian hospodar. In 1577 Pidkova and Otaman Ya. Shakh led a force of 1,200 Zaporozhian Cossacks into Turkish-controlled Moldavia, defeated the forces of Hospodar Peter Şchiopul, and occupied Iaşi on 29 December. There Pidkova was proclaimed the new hospodar, but soon thereafter the Cossacks were forced to retreat to Ukraine by the Turkish-Wallachian army. Pidkova was seized through treachery in Nemyriv by J. Zbaraski, the voivode of Bratslav. He was executed by order of King Stephen Báthory. His exploits were glorified in Cossack songs, and he is the hero of T. Shevchenko's narrative poem 'Ivan Pidkova' (1840) and two novels by the Rumanian writer M. Sadoveanu, Şoimii (The Victors, 1904) and Nicoară Potcoavă (1952).

Pidliashia. See Podlachia.

Pidliute [Pidljute]. A village under the jurisdiction of the Osmoloda rural council, in Rozhniativ raion, Ivano-Frankivske oblast. The village is situated on the Limnytsia River in the heart of the Gorgany Mountains. Before 1939 it was the site of a small health resort with sulfur-iodic mineral springs, the summer residence of the Greek Catholic metropolitan, and the camping grounds of the *Plast Ukrainian Youth Association.

Valeriian Pidmohylny   Ivan Pidoplichko

Pidmohylny, Valeriian [Pidmohyl'nyj, Valerijan], b 2 February 1901 in Chapli, Katerynoslav county, d 3 November 1937 in the Solovets Islands. Writer and translator. He graduated from high school in Katerynoslav in 1918 and then continued his studies at Kiev University. In 1921 he began working with various publishing houses and joined the editorial board of *Zhyttia i revoliutsiia*. The first of his stories to be published were 'Vania' and 'Haidamaky' (Haidamakas), which appeared in 1919 in *Sich*, a journal in Katerynoslav. He also contributed to the almanac *Vyr revoliutsiï* (1921). He was a member of the literary organization Lanka (see *MARS). His published collections of stories include *Tvory* (Works, vol 1, 1920), *V epidemichnomu baratsi* (In the Quarantine Ward, 1922), *Povstantsi i ynshi opovidannia* (The Insurgents and Other Stories, 1923), *Viis'kovyi litun* (Army Pilot, 1924), and *Problema khliba* (The Problem of Bread, 1927, 1930). He also wrote the novelette *Ostap Shaptala* (1922). Pidmohylny's early works focus on various pre- and postrevolutionary realities, such as the famine of 1920–1. His most notable work is the novel *Misto* (The City, 1928), one theme of which captures the relationship between the city and the village against the backdrop of the New Economic Policy. His last published work was *Nevelychka drama* (A Little Drama), a novel about people in the 'era of socialist reconstruction,' which was serialized in *Zhyttia i revoliutsiia* in 1930 but first released separately in Paris in 1956. It appeared in translation as *A Little Touch of Drama* (trans by G.S.N. and M. Luckyj, 1972). Pidmohylny's translations, particularly those of the works of H. de Balzac, D. Diderot, A. France, G. de Maupassant, and Stendhal, significantly influenced the development of Ukrainian literature in the 1920s. Pidmohylny's early works were subjected to severe official criticism. Some were even attacked for 'romanticizing Makhnovism' (A. Khvylia). The novel *Misto* was also denounced. Pidmohylny was expelled from his editorial position in 1930 and was arrested in 1934. He was incarcerated in various prisons and concentration camps until he was shot, along with many other Ukrainian writers. He was rehabilitated in 1956. *Misto* and some other stories were republished in Ukraine in 1989. A selection of stories, including some previously never published, appeared in 1991 as *Istoriia pani Ïvhy* (The Story of Mrs Ivha).

B. Kravtsiv

Pidoima (Lever). An organization that represented Ukrainian landholders in the *Drohobych-Boryslav Industrial Region and negotiated royalties paid by the government for extracting oil and gas from their land. Centered in Drohobych, the organization was founded in 1917 but began to function only in 1923, when it was recognized by the Polish government. From then until 1939, Ukrainian landholders were paid almost 10 million dollars in royalties. Pidoima collected a commission of 1 percent, which it used for its own needs and to support Ukrainian cultural and social causes. The directors of the organization were V. *Ilnytsky, M. Terletsky, R. Savoika, and S. Sasyk. V. Patslavsky and then P. Ilkiv headed the advisory board.

Pidoplichko, Ivan [Pidopličko], b 2 August 1905 in Kozatske, Zvenyhorodka county, Kiev gubernia, d 20 June 1975 in Kiev. Zoologist and paleontologist; full member of the AN URSR (now ANU) from 1967. A graduate of the Leningrad Institute of Applied Zoology and Phytopathology (1927), he was a longtime associate of the ANU Institute of Zoology (department head in 1935–41 and 1947–73 and director in 1965–73), a lecturer and professor at Kiev University (1939–59), associate editor of *Ukraïns'ka radians'ka entsyklopediia* (The Ukrainian Soviet Encyclopedia, 1958–67), and director of the ANU Central Scientific Museum of Natural History (1973–5). Pidoplichko took part in research excavations at several late Paleolithic sites, notably in Mezhyrich and Mizyn, and wrote *Materialy do vyvchennia mynulykh faun URSR* (Materials for the Study of Past Fauna of the Ukrainian SSR, 2 vols, 1938, 1956), *Korotka istoriia Zemli* (A Short History of Earth, 1958), and *Okhorona pryrody na Ukraïni* (Protecting Nature in Ukraine, 1958).

Pidoplichko, Mykola [Pidopličko], b 3 April 1904 in Kozatske, Zvenyhorodka county, Kiev gubernia, d 27

Mykola Pidoplichko   Yaroslav Pidstryhach

March 1975 in Kiev. Botanist and mycologist; corresponding member of the AN URSR (now ANU) from 1957. He completed study at the Kiev Institute of People's Education (1929) and then worked at the ANU Institute of Microbiology and Virology, where he founded and directed the mycology division (from 1933). He wrote over 100 works dealing with the systemization and flora of fungi, including the world's first field guide to fungi (1938), and compiled Ukrainian mycological terminology.

Pidpaly, Volodymyr [Pidpalyj], b 13 May 1936 in Lazirky, Orzhytsia raion, Poltava oblast, d 24 November 1973 in Kiev. Poet of the *shestydesiatnyky. After graduating from Kiev University (1962) he worked as an editor at the Dnipro and Radianskyi Pysmennyk publishing houses. He began publishing in 1958 and wrote the collections *Zelena hilka* (The Green Branch, 1964), *Povesinnia* (After Spring, 1964), *Trydtsiate lito* (The Thirtieth Summer, 1967), *V dorohu – za lastivkamy* (On the Way – After Swallows, 1968), and *Vyshnevyi tsvit* (Cherry Blossoms, 1970). His collections *Syni troiandy* (Blue Roses, 1979) and *Poeziï* (Poems, 1982, 1986) were published posthumously.

Pidriz, Apollinarii (Podrez), b 30 November 1852 in Kupianka county, Kharkiv gubernia, d 22 November 1900 in Kharkiv. Surgeon and urologist. A graduate of Kharkiv University (1875), he was a lecturer (from 1884) and professor (from 1887) at the university. He wrote over 50 works on field surgery, heart surgery, urology, and bone and joint tuberculosis, including the first urology textbook in Russian. He was the first in the Russian Empire to perform a spleen removal operation (1887) and to remove a foreign body from the heart (1897).

Pidstryhach, Yaroslav [Pidstryhač, Jaroslav] (Podstrygach), b 25 May 1928 in Samostrily, Rivne county, Volhynia voivodeship. Mechanics scientist; full member of the AN URSR (now ANU) since 1972. He graduated from Lviv University (1951) and worked at the ANU Institute of Physical Mechanics. He headed the Lviv branch of the ANU Institute of Mathematics (1972–8) and became director of the ANU Institute of Applied Problems in Mechanics and Mathematics (in 1978). He made contributions in theoretical mechanics, particularly in the field of the thermomechanics of amorphous solids, and in hydroacoustics. His mathematical models of the deformation of solids under stress are widely used in engineering design.

Pidsudky. Members of *land courts in the 14th to 18th centuries in the Grand Duchy of Lithuania, Poland, and the Hetman state. *Pidsudky* were elected by the nobility of a county in Lithuania and Poland and by the officers of a regiment in the Hetman state, and were confirmed by the king or hetman.

Pidsukha, Oleksander [Pidsuxa], b 16 October 1918 in Nizhylovychi, Radomyshl county, Kiev gubernia, d 1990. Socialist-realist writer. He graduated from the Kharkiv Pedagogical Institute of Foreign Languages (1939), and after the Second World War he taught at the Donetske Industrial and Kiev Pedagogical institutes. He was managing editor of the journal *Dnipro* (1953–8) and then editor in charge of novels at the Dnipro publishing house. From 1973 to 1979 he headed the *Ukraïna Society for Cultural Relations with Ukrainians Abroad. Between 1948 and 1980 he published many poetry collections, the novel in verse *Polis'ka trylohiia* (Polisian Trilogy, 1962), the prose collection *Vich-na-vich: Nevyhadani istorii* (Face to Face: Uncontrived Histories, 1962), the four-play collection *Komu kuiut' zozuli* (For Whom the Cuckoos Cry, 1973), and the plays *Nespodivana pisnia* (Unexpected Song, 1973), and *Zhyvy, Krutoiare* (Live, Krutoiar, 1975). A two-volume edition of his selected works was published in 1978.

Pidsusidky. See Landless peasants.

Pidtychenko, Mariia [Pidtyčenko, Marija], b 6 June 1912 in Chornohlazivka, Pavlohrad county, Katerynoslav gubernia. Pedagogue; full member of the USSR Academy of Pedagogical Sciences from 1968. After graduating from Kharkiv University in 1934, she taught at various educational institutions in Dnipropetrovske, where she held several important Party positions. In 1956–70 she was rector of and from 1970 a professor-consultant at the *Kiev Pedagogical Institute. She is the author of works dealing with the socialization of young people in a communist spirit.

Pidvolochyske or **Pidvolochysk** [Pidvoločys'ke or Pidvoločys'k]. IV-7. A town smt (1986 pop 8,300) on the Zbruch River and a raion center in Ternopil oblast. The town is on the site of an ancient settlement dating from the 3rd and 4th centuries AD. In the 15th century two villages, both called Volochyshche, arose on opposite banks of the Zbruch. One of them, mentioned in documents in 1463, was renamed Pidvolochyske in the mid-17th century. A road linking Pidvolochyske with Ternopil was built in 1786, and contributed to the growth of the local economy. After the partition of Poland in 1772, the town was acquired by Austria. In 1919–39 it was under Polish rule. Today the town has a plastics factory and food industry.

Pidvysotsky, Kost [Pidvysoc'kyj, Kost'], b 28 June 1851 in Korzhova, Pidhaitsi county, Galicia, d 12 June 1904 in Medukha, Stanslaviv county, Galicia. Actor, stage director, and dramatist. He acted in O. Bachynsky's troupe (1875–81 and 1882–5) and acted and directed in the Ruska Besida Theater (1881–2, 1886–9, 1893–7, and 1900–2), in M. Kropyvnytsky's and M. Starytsky's troupes (1889–92), and in M. Yaroshenko's and O. Sukhodolsky's troupes (1898–1902). As a director Pidvysotsky first staged I. Franko's *Ukradene shchastia* (Stolen Happiness), in which he acted the part of Mykola, and staged M. Kropyvnytsky's *Nevol'nyk* (The Captive), I. Karpenko-Kary's *Burlaka* (The Vagabond), and M. Arkas's opera *Kateryna*. He wrote the comedy *Pidshyvanets'* (The Impostor, 1888) and adaptations of J. Korzeniowski's *Pomsta hutsula* (A Hutsul's Revenge, 1893) and *Hal'ka* (1899, based on W. Wolski; music by S. Moniuszko).

Pidvysotsky, Volodymyr [Pidvysoc'kyj], b 5 June 1857 in Maksymivka, Borzna county, Chernihiv gubernia, d 4 February 1913 in St Petersburg. Pathologist, microbiologist, and endocrinologist. A graduate of Kiev University (1884), he was a professor at Kiev (1887–1900) and Odessa (1900–5) universities and directed the Institute of Experimental Medicine in St Petersburg (1905–13). His publications dealt with the microscopic structure of the pancreas,

Volodymyr Pidvysotsky   Fedir Pigido

regeneration, and the etiology of malignant tumors. He wrote one of the first textbooks in general and experimental pathology (1891–4, 1905). Among his followers were I. Savchenko, O. Bohomolets, L. Tarasevych, F. Omelchenko, D. Zabolotny, and S. Shchasny.

Pieracki, Bronisław, b 28 May 1895 at Gorlice, d 15 June 1934 in Warsaw. Polish politician and government official. One of the leading activists of the *Sanacja regime, he headed the Nonparty Bloc of Co-operation with the Government. He supported 'strong-arm' tactics with respect to national minorities and the introduction of the so-called active policy with regard to the Ukrainians. In 1930 he directed the *Pacification in Lviv and then (as minister of the interior) was responsible for similar actions in Lisko county in 1931 and in Volhynia and Polisia in 1932. In 1931 he made some concessions in economics and education to the Ukrainian minority. In June of that year he held several meetings with UNDO leaders and Metropolitan A. Sheptytsky. He was assassinated by H. Matseiko, an OUN follower. The assassination was used by the Polish government to justify the creation of a concentration camp for political prisoners at Bereza Kartuzka. The organizers of the assassination, with the exception of Matseiko, who managed to escape, were tried from September 1935 to January 1936 at the so-called Warsaw OUN Trial. A study of the trial by Z. Knysh appeared in Toronto (2 vols, 1986).

Pietros, Mount. One of the higher peaks (elevation, 2,020 m) in the Ukrainian Carpathian Mountains. It is located in the northwestern part of the Chornohora Massif. Its slopes, marked by glacial deposits, are covered with brush, forests, and upland meadows. The mountain is a popular tourist site.

Pigido, Fedir (Pihida), b 18 September 1888 in Stoiky, Kiev county, Kiev gubernia, d 11 November 1962 in Munich. Economist, publicist, and civic and political activist. After graduating from an industrial institute in 1921, he worked in various building-materials concerns in Ukraine. He became active in politics only after emigrating to Germany in 1944: in 1949 he joined the Ukrainian Revolutionary Democratic party (URDP) and was admitted to its Central Committee, and in 1953 he represented a faction of the URDP on the Ukrainian National Council. From 1957 he served as vice-president, press and information secretary, and finance secretary in the council's executive. In addition to articles in *Ukraïns'ki visti*, *Prometei*, and *Nashi pozytsiï* he wrote a number of books, such as *8,000,000* (1951), *The Stalin Famine* (1954), and *Materials Concerning Ukrainian-Jewish Relations during the Years of the Revolution, 1917–1921* (1956).

Pihrov, Kostiantyn (Pigrov, Konstantin), b 7 November 1876 in Malaia Dzhalga, Stavropol gubernia, d 22 December 1962 in Odessa. Choir conductor and pedagogue. In 1901 he completed his studies in conducting with the St Petersburg court kapelle and began working in various cities as a pedagogue and conductor of church choirs. In 1920 he started teaching choral conducting at the school which later became the Odessa Conservatory. In 1930 he founded an independent Moldavian choral ensemble that in 1936 became the Doina Choir. His students included the conductors A. Avdiievsky, M. Hrynyshyn, Ye. Dushchenko, and D. Zahretsky. He is the author of textbooks on choral conducting (1956) and solfeggio (1970).

Yerotei Pihuliak

Yustyn Pihuliak (self-portrait, 1885)

Pihuliak, Yerotei [Pihuljak, Jerotej] (Pihuleak, Hierotheus), b 1851 in Novi Mamaivtsi, Chernivtsi county, Bukovyna, d 1924 in Chernivtsi. Political and civic figure. He was one of the leaders of Bukovyna's Ukrainian populist movement and National Democratic party. As a member of the Bukovynian provincial diet (1890–1918), the Austrian parliament (1898–1918), and Bukovyna's Provincial Executive and School Council he defended the interests of the Ukrainian community and Orthodox church. Thanks to his efforts Bukovyna's Ukrainian Orthodox were granted religious equality with the Rumanians on the eve of the First World War. Pihuliak was elected the first president of the People's Home society in Chernivtsi (1884) and president of the Ruska Besida (1884) and Ruska Rada (1885) societies there. He participated in the Ukrainian takeover in Bukovyna in November 1918. He contributed articles on cultural and religious affairs to Bukovyna's Ukrainian and German press and wrote two brochures in German on the religious question (1909, 1914), as well as some poetry and prose.

Pihuliak, Yustyn [Pihuljak, Justyn], b 1845 in Novi Mamaivtsi (now Novosilka), Bukovyna, d 2 June 1919 in Chernivtsi. Painter; brother of Ye. *Pihuliak. After gradu-

ating from the Vienna Academy of Arts in 1874, he taught painting at the Higher Realschule in Chernivtsi until 1906. He did genre paintings (eg, *Hutsuls, Bukovynian Girl, Love and Fidelity*), landscapes, paintings inspired by T. Shevchenko's poems, and portraits of Yu. Fedkovych (1886), I. Vorobkevych (1887), Shevchenko (1889), and O. Kobylianska (1916).

Pike perch (*Lucioperca* or *Stizostedion*; Ukrainian: *sudak*). A genus of fish resembling the pike that belongs to the Percidae family. Pike perch have greenish gray, small-scaled bodies up to 130 cm in length; they weigh 12–20 kg. The common pike perch (*L.* or *S. lucioperca*) is the largest and most commercially important perch species in Europe; a minimum catch size has been established at 35–40 cm for the *fishing industry. In Ukraine pike perch inhabit the Black Sea and the Sea of Azov and occasionally enter the waters of the Dnieper and Buh rivers. Common pike perch are also cultivated in fisheries and stocked in natural and man-made lakes. Other species found in Ukraine are the European pike perch or zander (*L.* or *S. marina*; Ukrainian: *sudak morskyi*) and the smaller Volga pike perch (*L.* or *S. volgensis*).

Pikhno, Dmitrii [Pixno, Dmitrij], b 13 January 1853 near Chyhyryn, Kiev gubernia, d 11 August 1913 in Kiev. Economist, statistician, publisher, and politician. After graduating from Kiev University (1874) he taught economics and law there (1877–1902). He was an adviser to the Russian Ministry of Finance and a member of the State Council from 1907. As an economist he was a follower of the English classical school and a believer in market competition and the capitalist rationalization of industry and agriculture. His theories and research were summarized in several monographs and articles. From 1878 he was the publisher of the reactionary monarchist and anti-Ukrainian newspaper *Kievlianin*, the leader of the Union of the Russian People in Kiev, and a member of the *Kiev Club of Russian Nationalists.

Pilger, Martin-Heinrich (Pilher, Fedir), b 5 June 1761 in Wetzlar, Germany, d 25 April 1828 in Kharkiv. German veterinarian. A graduate of Erlangen University (1779), he was one of the first professors of veterinary medicine in Ukraine, where he headed the veterinary department at Kharkiv University (from 1806). In 1817 he established *Ukrainskii domovod*, the first veterinary journal in the Russian Empire. He wrote *Systematisches Handbuch der theoretisch-praktischen Veterinärwissenschaft* (2 vols, 1801–3).

Pilgrimage. Travel to sacred places became fairly common among Ukrainians after the introduction of Christianity and has remained a prominent public manifestation of faith. Individual pilgrimages to the Holy Land from Ukraine were known to have taken place as early as the 11th century (eg, by Hegumen Varlaam in 1062). *Danylo, the hegumen of a Chernihiv monastery, left an account of the pilgrimage he made in 1106–8, and St Anthony of the Caves traveled to Mount Athos in the early 12th century. The shrines of Rome and the relics of St Nicholas in Bari, Italy, also attracted pilgrims from Ukraine. Such treks became so common that some churchmen even warned against the exaggeration of their spiritual significance. Pilgrimages to the Holy Land, especially

*Jerusalem, continued despite the fall of Constantinople, and accounts of these trips were widely read in Ukraine. Particularly valuable descriptions of pilgrimages in the 18th century were left by V. *Hryhorovych-Barsky and the monk Serapion of the Motronynskyi Trinity Monastery.

The most popular pilgrimage destinations in Ukraine have been the many churches and monasteries in Kiev, particularly the *Kievan Cave Monastery. Although the Soviet authorities actively discouraged pilgrimages, ruined many shrines, and turned others into museums, factories, or administrative buildings, this repression did not stem the annual flow of thousands of pilgrims. The greatest flow of pilgrims occurred on days of particular celebration at the shrines, such as the feast of Yov Zalizo (10 September [28 August OS]) and the festival of the Dormition (28 August [15 August OS]) in Pochaiv. Pilgrimages to the *Pochaiv Monastery began in the 18th century, and it remains the second most popular destination, although it too had been subjected to depredations under Soviet rule. In Galicia the more prominent holy sites are Zarvanytsia in Podilia, Hoshiv in the Carpathian foothills, and the Krekhiv Monastery in the Buh region. Others include Chernecha Hora, near Mukachiv, in Transcarpathia, and Suceava and Khreshchatyk in Bukovyna. In the 1930s in Turkovychi, in the Kholm region, some Ukrainian Orthodox pilgrimages became national, patriotic demonstrations against Polish persecution. In recent times, particularly during the celebrations of the millennium of the Christianization of Rus'-Ukraine, many pilgrims gathered around the monument to St Volodymyr the Great in Kiev, and in Galicia large gatherings were held at the Church of the Three Saints in Hrushiv, in the Boiko region near Drohobych, where people were said to have witnessed apparitions of Mary. Emigré Ukrainians (esp Catholics) frequently travel on pilgrimages to Rome and Lourdes, France, the site of the Dormition Church for pilgrims.

Pilhuk, Ivan [Pil'huk], b 20 December 1899 in Reshetylivka, Poltava county, d 18 July 1984 in Kiev. Literary scholar and writer. From 1932 he lectured on the history of Ukrainian literature in institutions of higher learning, and from 1948 he was a professor at the Kiev Pedagogical Institute. He is the author of a series of textbooks for high schools and philological faculties. Pilhuk began to publish his work in 1929. He produced the collections of short stories *Sutsil'ni lany* (Undivided Grainfields, 1931), *Nazustrich strumovi Dniprohesu* (Welcoming the Current of the Dnieper Hydroelectric Station, 1932), and *Atanas Kyrylo Fedorovych Peichov* (1932). His major scholarly works are on Yu. Fedkovych (1943), I. Kotliarevsky (1943, 1954), M. Kotsiubynsky (1950), T. Shevchenko (1950, 1951, 1954, 1958, 1961, 1965), S. Rudansky (1956), and M. Kropyvnytsky (1960). He is also the author of the novels *Hrozovyi ranok* (Stormy Morning, 1968) and *Povii, vitre* (Blow, Wind, 1969).

Pillipiw, Ivan. See Pylypiv, Ivan.

Piłsudski, Józef, b 5 December 1867 in Zulavas, Švenčionys county, Lithuania, d 12 May 1935 in Warsaw. Polish military leader and statesman. Before coming to power Piłsudski had advocated the dismemberment of the Russian Empire and an East-European federation of Poland, Ukraine, Lithuania, and Belarus. Although his scheme re-served a dominant role for Poland, it did not receive much Polish public support. Consequently, after coming to power, Piłsudski actively backed Polish revanchist territorial claims to Western Ukraine. In April 1919 he sent J. *Haller's army into Galicia (see *Ukrainian-Polish War in Galicia). To counter the Red Army offensive against Poland he concluded the Treaty of *Warsaw with the UNR government in April 1920. After the allied Polish-UNR forces were forced to retreat from Ukraine and Belarus, he organized a successful counteroffensive in which the UNR Army played a major role (see *Ukrainian-Soviet War). Piłsudski's signing of the Peace Treaty of *Riga, which partitioned Ukraine and Belarus between Poland and Soviet Russia, put an end to his dreams of East European 'federalism.'

Resistance to the Polish occupation of Galicia and Volhynia continued after the war: in September 1921 S. Fedak, a member of the Ukrainian Military Organization, tried to assassinate Piłsudski. With the election of the new Polish president, G. Narutowicz, in December 1922, Piłsudski remained chief of the Polish General Staff. When a right-wing government took power in May 1923, he retired. Disturbed by the political and economic chaos in Poland, he came out of retirement in May 1926 to lead a military coup d'état. Thenceforth Piłsudski, as defense minister, controlled Poland, while preserving the trappings of parliamentary rule. Western Ukrainians remained suspicious of Piłsudski's new regime, supported as it was by the conservative Polish nobility in Western Ukraine. Although some of Piłsudski's closest associates (eg, T. Hołówko, P. Dunin-Borkowski) sympathized with Western Ukrainians, and his government subsidized the UNR government-in-exile, nothing was done to stem Polonization and the administration's anti-Ukrainian policies in Western Ukraine. The Ukrainian-Polish conflict grew steadily and assumed mass proportions in the 1930 *Pacification of Galicia. In September 1934 Piłsudski proposed an agreement protecting Poland's national minorities, but his foreign minister, J. Beck, would not endorse it. The political unrest that followed Piłsudski's death considerably weakened the Polish state. (See also *Poland.)

BIBLIOGRAPHY
Piłsudski, J. *Pisma zbiorowe*, 10 vols (Warsaw 1937–8)
Rothschild, J. *Piłsudski's Coup d'Etat* (New York 1966)
Dziewanowski, M. *Joseph Piłsudski: A European Federalist, 1918–1922* (Stanford, Calif 1969)

B. Budurowycz

Mariia Piltser

Piltser, Mariia [Pil'cer, Marija], b 27 November 1912 in Nyzhnia Hrabivnytsia, Transcarpathia, d 21 March 1976 in Uzhhorod. Stage actress; wife of H. Ihnatovych. She studied drama in Uzhhorod (1934–6) and then worked as an actress in the National Drama Theater in Prague (1936–7). From 1946 she was the leading actress and one of the founders of the Transcarpathian Ukrainian Music and Drama Theater in Uzhhorod.

Pinchuk, Vadym [Pinčuk], b 28 December 1930 in Poltava. Oncologist; corresponding member of the AN URSR (now ANU) since 1973. A graduate of the Kiev Medical Institute (1954), he was the first deputy director (1971, director since 1979) of the ANU Institute for Problems of Oncology. His publications deal with the mechanisms of carcinogenesis.

Pine (*Pinus*; Ukrainian: *sosna*). A genus of the family *Pinaceae*, normally tall evergreen conifers (up to 50 m high) and occasionally spreading shrubs. Pines occupy about 2.5 million ha of land in Ukraine, 34 percent of all forest land. Predominantly pine forests are widely spread in the forest and forest-steppe belts and in the mountain forest zones of Ukraine (Polisia and the Buh and Sian valleys). Pines rarely grow in the steppe zone. Of the nine species of *Pinus* found in Ukraine, the most prevalent is the common or Scots pine (*P. silvestris*). The trees live hundreds of years and require full sun and clean air. Pinewood is used for making masts, poles, interior construction lumber, furniture, plywood, and paper, and is burned as fuel. Pine yields a gum used in the production of turpentine, pitch, tar, and resin. Pine needles yield vitamin C and essential oils. Mountain pine (*P. mugo*) is used as a cover for rocky spills, to strengthen steep slopes, to prevent washouts and landslides, and to protect against flash floods. Chalk pine (*P. cretaceae*) is found along the Donets River; European cedar pine (*P. cembra*) and *juniper grow in the Carpathian Mountains; and *P. pallasiana*, *P. stankeviczi*, *P. zerovii*, and *P. rostellata* are common on the Crimean peninsula.

Pinot-Rudakevych, Yaroslav [Rudakevyč, Jaroslav], b 22 June 1910 in Zakomaria, Zalochiv county, Galicia. Stage actor. He began his theatrical career in Y. Stadnyk's troupe (1931–3) and then worked in the Zahrava Theater (1933–8), the Kotliarevsky Theater (1938–9), the Lesia Ukrainka Theater (1939–41), and the Lviv Opera Theater (1941–4). Having fled from Ukraine during the Second World War, he acted in the Ensemble of Ukrainian Actors in West Germany (1945–9) and, after emigrating to the United States, in the Ukrainian Theater in Philadelphia (from 1963).

Pinsk. See Pynske.

Pinzel, Johann (Pinsel, Pincel, Pintsel), b and d ? Eighteenth-century sculptor. In the 1750s and 1760s he worked in Galicia. The most famous of his surviving works are the rococo stone statues of SS Louis, Athanasius, and George on the façade of St George's Cathedral in Lviv (1759–61) and the wood statues of the side altars in the Roman Catholic church in Monastyryska (1761). The stone carvings on the façade of the Buchach town hall, the figures and bas-reliefs in the Buchach Holy Protectress Church, and the sculpted church decorations in Horodets are attributed to him. He carved several crucifixions, the most interesting

Johann Pinzel: *St Felix Holding a Child* (painted wood, 1760s)

of which was in St Martin's Roman Catholic Church in Lviv.

Pioneer Organization of Ukraine (Pionerska orhanizatsiia Ukrainy). A communist mass organization in Soviet Ukraine for children aged 10 to 15. It was an integral part of the All-Union Pioneer Organization; its direction was assigned by the CPSU to the All-Union Communist Youth League (Komsomol). The Republican Council of the All-Union Pioneer Organization formed the leadership of the organization in Ukraine, under the control of the *Communist Youth League of Ukraine.

The precursors of the Pioneer organization were youth groups established in 1920–1 by various CP(B)U branches, such as the Children's International in Kiev and the Soviet of Children's Deputies in Katerynoslav. In addition groups of Young Communist Scouts or Young Communists were organized in many cities in Ukraine. Modeled on the Boy Scouts organization, they were disbanded by a 1919 decree of the Second All-Russian Congress of the Komsomol. Because those diverse children's groups often did not address the political priorities of the communist leadership, in 1922 the Komsomol called for the fusion of all children's and youth groups into a single organization. In Ukraine the organization was called Yunyi Spartak

(Young Spartacus), and published a newspaper by that name. Under the leadership of the Komsomol its groups participated in the rebuilding of the ruined economy, in spreading atheist propaganda, and in helping the large number of orphans left homeless by the Ukrainian-Soviet War. In July 1922 the CC of the Komsomol of Ukraine approved the statute of a new children's organization, and in January 1923 it created the Central Bureau of the Communist Children's Movement, with bureaus at the gubernial level. In 1924 the Yunyi Spartak groups were renamed Young Pioneers, and a centralized organizational structure was established, with 360,000 members in Ukraine. The First All-Ukrainian Rally of Young Pioneers took place in Kharkiv in 1929. That year the organization had 550,000 members.

Following the April 1932 resolution of the CC of the All-Union Communist party, which criticized the Pioneer organizations for their tendency to merge completely with the schools, the Pioneers were given responsibility for intensifying school discipline and actively promoting industrialization and collectivization. Between 1930 and 1940, Pioneers were encouraged to co-operate with the police and the *NKVD in exposing 'enemies of the people' and reporting their parents' opposition to collectivization. Military defense training was also introduced in Pioneer groups. During the Second World War many Pioneers were active in the Soviet underground and war effort. Following the Soviet occupation of Western Ukraine in 1939, the Pioneer organization was established there. (In the 1920s and 1930s there existed a small illegal organization called the Red Pioneers of Western Ukraine. In 1938 it was dissolved by the Comintern, together with its parent organization, the *Communist Party of Western Ukraine.)

All schoolchildren of appropriate age were eligible to join their local Pioneer organization at their school or apartment building, and virtually all did so. Entrants took the Pioneer oath, observed Pioneer laws, and wore a red Pioneer neckerchief, the three corners of which represented the unity of the Pioneers, the Komsomol, and the Party. Pioneers held regular meetings to discuss organizational matters and films, books, and other subjects; they also paraded on numerous occasions, visited local places of communist or military significance, formed honorary guards at war memorials, and attended summer camps. Military rituals were widely used, especially from the 1960s, to develop positive identification with Soviet state symbols and to foster Soviet patriotism. Although Pioneers were eligible to join the Komsomol upon reaching the age of 14, a significant number of them chose not to do so. Most children, prior to joining the Pioneers, were members of the Young Octobrists (Zhovteniata), an affiliated organization for children aged seven to nine.

The Ukrainian Pioneers had their own newspapers (*Zirka and the Russian *Iunyi leninets), journals (*Pioneriia and, for younger children, *Barvinok and *Maliatko), daily radio program ('Pioner Ukrainy'), and television program ('Vpered, orliata').

In the 1980s, Pioneer membership declined (in 1981 there were some four million members). In 1986 there were over 3.5 million Pioneers in Ukraine. That year the Pioneer organization ran 16,700 summer camps. With the erosion of communist power an increasingly large number of parents (especially in the western oblasts) refused to enroll their children in the Pioneer organization. The Pio-

neers' militarism and veneration of Soviet state symbols were criticized, and the organization was enjoined to focus more on pedagogical and humanistic goals. With the dissolution of the USSR and the disbanding of the CPU the Pioneer organizations ceased to function, although they were not officially liquidated. Many of their functions were taken over by newly formed youth organizations.

I. Bakalo, D. Goshko, B. Krawchenko

Pioneer palaces and houses (*palatsy i budynky pioneriv i shkoliariv*). Centers of extramural education and activities for schoolchildren in Soviet Ukraine. They were under the jurisdiction of the various republican ministries of education in the USSR. The first such palace was opened in Moscow in 1923–4. In Ukraine the role of the palaces was filled by children's clubs in the 1920s, and the first Pioneer palaces were opened only in 1934–5 in Kharkiv, Kiev, Poltava, and Donetske. Palaces existed in almost all urban centers. They operated under the supervision of the appropriate organs of public education, the Communist Komsomol Youth League, and the Pioneer organization. Their primary function was to support the school system, to inculcate communist values, and to prepare children for membership in the Pioneers and, eventually, the Komsomol. The Pioneer palaces organized classes in industrial arts, art, and physical education and sports and organized trips and tours. They hosted large concerts and celebrations, sporting meets, artistic competitions, and meetings with important or interesting citizens. Children's choirs, orchestras, dance and drama troupes, and the like were based at palaces. The largest Pioneer palace in Ukraine was in Kiev. In 1980 there were 804 Pioneer palaces and houses in the Ukrainian SSR, 135 more than in 1959. They served a total of 573,000 children. In 1987 there were 820 palaces and houses, which served 935,000 children.

Pioneriia (Pioneering). A monthly children's magazine published by the Communist Youth League of Ukraine and the *Pioneer Organization of Ukraine from 1931 to 1992. It succeeded the magazines *Chervoni kvity* and *Bil'shovycheniata*. It appeared in Kharkiv until the outset of the Second World War and was renewed in March 1950 in Kiev in parallel Ukrainian and Russian editions. *Pioneriia* included articles on the lives of Pioneers and schoolchildren and on artistic and popular-science topics, games, songs, riddles, and so on. Each year one issue of the magazine was prepared by children.

Piontek, Liutsiana, b 1899 in Lubni, Poltava gubernia, d 25 September 1937. Ukrainian writer of Jewish descent; wife of I. *Kulyk. She lived in Canada with her husband (1924–7), where she took part in Ukrainian community life and belonged to the Canadian branch of the proletarian writers' group *Hart. Upon her return to Ukraine in 1927 she joined the All-Ukrainian Association of Proletarian Writers. Her first published work appeared in 1917. Her works were printed in the Kharkiv journals *Hart* and *Chervonyi shliakh*. She also published collections of verse, *Tykhym dysonansom* (In Quiet Dissonance, 1927), and of short stories, *Balaklava* (1929). She was arrested during the Stalinist terror and eventually shot.

Piotrków Trybunalski (Ukrainian: Petrykiv). A city (1989 pop 80,500) and voivodeship center in Poland. In 1921 it was the site of an internment camp for soldiers of the UNR Army. As in other internment camps, the Ukrainian administration in Piotrków organized cultural and educational programs, including literacy, foreign language, and history classes, a students' club, and a choir.

Pip Ivan. V-5. One of the highest Carpathian peaks (elevation, 2,022 m) in Ukraine, located in the southeastern part of the Chornohora mountain group. The slopes are covered with mixed-fir forest to approx 1,200 m and then with fir to approx 1,550 m. Above that point pines and green alders, brush, and subalpine vegetation can be found.

Pipeline transportation. Pipeline transportation is the most modern and economical way to transport gases, liquids, and slurries from the source to the point of processing or consumption. The transportation system consists of many complex components, such as pipelines, reservoirs, compressor stations, controls, and pumping stations. The pipeline network has three major parts: (1) the main lines, to carry the material over long distances; (2) the local lines, to collect the material and deliver it from the source to the main lines and then to distribute it from the main lines; and (3) the internal lines, to carry the material for short distances within a city, enterprise, or building. Pipeline transportation is operational all year round and is nonpolluting.

In Ukraine the first pipeline was built in 1924 to carry natural gas from Dashava to Stryi (14 km). In 1940 the line was extended to Lviv (72 km), and in 1948 to Kiev. At that time it was the longest gas pipeline in Europe. In 1951 the Dashava line reached Moscow: 851 km of it ran through Ukrainian territory. Another 477 km of pipeline were added as feeders to more than 20 Ukrainian cities along its route.

With the exploitation of the *Shebelynka gas fields in the mid-1950s, three gas lines were constructed: the first reached Kharkiv and was extended later to Briansk (RF) and joined to the Dashava–Moscow line; the second ran to Kiev via Dykanka and then to Western Ukraine; and the third ran to Dnipropetrovske, Kryvyi Rih, and Izmail. Besides those major lines, shorter lines, such as the Shebelynka–Belgorod (RF) and the Shebelynka–Slovianske, were built.

In the 1960s, additional gas pipelines were built from the Subcarpathian deposits at Stryi and Bilche-Volytsia to Minsk, Belarus (approx 665 km), and to Poland. In 1967 a main line was laid from Dolyna to Šala, Czechoslovakia. In 1966–70, 8,700 km of new gas line were built in Ukraine, including the long Yefremivka–Kiev–Kamianka-Buzka and the Dykanka–Kryvyi Rih lines.

In the 1970s two international gas lines were laid through Ukraine: the Soiuz line, originating at Orenburg and stretching to Chop, Transcarpathia oblast (annual capacity: 28 billion cu m), and the Urengoi–Uzhhorod line, carrying gas from western Siberia to several European countries (annual capacity: 32 billion cu m).

In the 1940s and 1950s, when significant petroleum deposits were discovered in western Ukraine at Dolyna, Oriv, and Bytkiv, in Poltava oblast at Hlynske, and in Chernihiv oblast at Leliaky, Hnidyntsi, and Kachanivka, oil pipelines were laid from Dolyna to Drohobych (80 km)

Basic indexes of pipeline transportation in Ukraine, 1960–86

Category	1960	1970	1980	1986
1. Length of main lines (in 1,000 km)				
Gas	9.8	10.9	18.6	24.0
Oil	–	1.2	2.0	3.0
2. Output of oil and oil products (in billion Tkm)*	0.1	11.2	54.6	56.5
3. Volume of oil and oil products (in million t)	1.3	22.4	101.6	124.2
4. Average trip distance per t (in km)	76.9	500.0	537.4	454.9
5. Share of oil pipeline output in total transportation output (percentage)	0.05	1.8	7.0	6.0

*Tkm = tonnes per kilometer.

and from Hnidyntsi to Kremenchuk (approx 200 km) and to Michurinsk (RF). Most oil lines, including the Kremenchuk–Kiev (330 km), Kremenchuk–Cherkasy (260 km), Kherson–Rozdilna (340 km), Lysychanske–Mariiupil–Berdianske (300 km), and Drohobych–Stryi (30 km) lines, transport both oil and oil products. In 1981–5 work began on the longest petroleum pipeline, from Lysychanske to the Crimean Peninsula. Several branch lines will serve the neighboring industrial centers.

All pipelines were under the control of the central government and were built according to Union plans. Some matters, such as personnel, the regulation of flow, and timetables, were in the hands of local management. In recent years pipeline transportation growth has been spectacular: output in tons per kilometer grew fivefold between 1970 and 1986. Although the volume of goods carried by pipeline is rising faster than in other modes of transportation, its share of the total volume transported is low, because relatively few substances can be transported by pipeline. Basic indexes of pipeline transportation are given in the table.

E. Bej

Piradov, Volodymyr, b 14 February 1892 in Warsaw, d 20 April 1954 in Kiev. Opera conductor. He graduated from the Tbilisi music school and from 1914 worked in the opera theaters of Tbilisi, Baku, Minsk, and Moscow. In 1936–41 he was a conductor at the Kiev Theater of Opera and Ballet, and in 1950–4 its main conductor. In 1944–7 he conducted the Kharkiv Opera. From 1950 he also served as a professor at the Kiev Conservatory. The K. Dankevych opera *Bohdan Khmel'nyts'kyi* was his last work, mounted by the Kiev Opera in 1953.

Pirogov, Nikolai, b 25 November 1810 in Moscow, d 5 December 1881 in Vyshnia, Vinnytsia county, Podilia gubernia. Russian surgeon, anatomist, educator, and civic figure; corresponding member of the Russian Academy of Sciences from 1847. A graduate of Moscow (1828) and Dorpat (1832) universities, he was a professor of surgery at the latter (1836–40) and then a professor at the hospital surgery clinic at the St Petersburg Medico-Surgical Academy (1841–56). During the Crimean War (1853–6) he made a classic description of hemorrhagic and traumatic shock and proposed a conservative management of gunshot fractures of extremities. As superintendent of the Odessa (1856–8) and Kiev (1858–61) school districts he expanded the school system, initiated the founding of Odessa University, and encouraged the opening of Sunday schools in the Kiev district and the use of Ukrainian in them. He opposed early specialization and discrimination based on class or nationality and was released from his post because of his liberal educational policy. From 1866 he lived on his estate in Vyshnia, and there he worked as a consultant on military medicine and surgery during the Franco-Prussian (1870–1) and Russo-Turkish (1877–8) wars. He wrote on anesthesia, the foundations of bone and plastic surgery, and surgical technique. Pirogov's estate was converted into a museum in 1947, and his collected works were published in Moscow (8 vols, 1957–62). The medical institutes in Odessa and Vinnytsia were named after him.

BIBLIOGRAPHY
Mohylevs'kyi, B. *Zhyttia Pyrohova* (Kiev 1953)
Aronova, F.; et al. *N.I. Pirogov na Ukraine: Bibliograficheskii ukazatel' literatury* (Kiev 1961)

Hryhorii Pisetsky

Pisetsky, Hryhorii [Pisec'kyj, Hryhorij], b 12 February 1907 in Korniv, Horodenka county, d 20 July 1930 near Bibrka, Galicia. Nationalist revolutionary; member of the Ukrainian Military Organization and of *Plast. He participated in an expropriation raid on a Polish postal wagon, in which he was killed. His unintended participation in the raid while wearing the Plast uniform gave Polish authorities a pretext for banning the organization in Polish-ruled Galicia.

Pishchane [Piščane]. A village in Zolotonosha raion, Cherkasy oblast near which remains of a Black Sea merchant were buried. Discovered by chance in 1960–1, the find revealed that the individual was buried in a dugout canoe and with 15 pieces of bronze. From the bronze items, many of them vessels for storing and serving wine, the burial is dated late 6th to early 5th century BC.

Pishchanka [Piščanka]. V-9. A town smt (1986 pop 6,400) and raion center in Vinnytsia oblast. It was first mentioned in historical documents in 1734, under the name Pishchana. In 1784 it was renamed. At the Second Partition of Poland in 1793, the town was acquired by Russia. It became part of Yampil county in Podilia gubernia. Until the early 19th century it was owned by the Lubomirski family. Today the town has a food industry and a limestone quarry.

Piskivka. III-10. A town smt (1986 pop 7,700) in Borodianka raion, Kiev oblast. Piskivka was founded at the beginning of the 17th century. In 1760 a foundry was built there. Today the town has a forest industry and a glass factory.

Kostiantyn Piskorsky: *Kozak-Mamai* (watercolor, 1920)

Piskorsky, Kostiantyn [Piskors'kyj, Kostjantyn], b 18 May 1892 in Kiev, d 9 March 1922 in Kiev. Painter; son of V. *Piskorsky. In 1919–20 he studied under H. *Narbut. His paintings (mostly watercolors) evolved from flatly rendered, simplified, natural forms to abstract compositions. They ranged from bold, stylized ornamental forms, highly reduced symbolist images, and geometricized landscapes marked by repetitions of figurative patterns (eg, *Forest Fire*, 1919) to nonrepresentational geometric paintings (eg, *White World*, 1919). His works are preserved at the Archive-Museum of Literature and Art in Kiev.

Piskorsky, Volodymyr (Vladimir) [Piskors'kyj], b 10 August 1867 in Odessa, d 16 August 1910 in Kazan, Russia. Historian; father of K. *Piskorsky. He studied at Kiev University (1896–90) under I. Luchytsky and was a privatdocent there (1893–5) and a professor of world history at the Nizhen Historical-Philological Institute (1895–1906) and Kazan University (1906–10). A specialist in the history of medieval Spain, Portugal, and Italy, he wrote monographs in Russian on the Castilian Cortes in 1188–1520 (master's thesis, 1897; Spanish trans 1930, 1977), F. Ferrucio and his era (1891), the meaning and origin of the six 'bad customs' in Catalonia (1899; Spanish trans 1929), and serfdom in medieval Catalonia (doctoral diss, 1901). He is also the coauthor of a Russian-language history of Spain and Portugal (2nd rev edn 1909).

Piskunov, Fortunat, b and d ? Ukrainian lexicographer and ethnographer of the second half of the 19th century. He compiled the 8,000-word Ukrainian-Russian *Slovnytsia ukraïns'koï (abo iuhovo-rus'koï) movy* (Dictionary of the Ukrainian [or South Ruthenian] Language, 1873), and its revised, 15,000-word second edition, *Slovnyk zhyvoï narodneï, pis'mennoï i aktovoï movy rus'kykh iuhivshchan Rossiis'koï i Avstriis'ko-Vengers'koï tsesariï* (Dictionary of the Current Folk, Literary, and Chancery Language of the Ruthenian Southerners of the Russian and Austro-Hungarian Empires, 1882), much of it taken from M. Zakrevsky's 1861 dictionary of 'Little Russian' idioms. The lexicon was printed in a Cyrillic phonetic orthography but in the order of the letters in the Latin alphabet (ie, *a, b, c, d, e, je, f, g* [in the Latin grapheme], *h, x*, etc) and consisted of many archaisms, little-used dialectal words, garbled loanwords, and even Piskunov's neologisms (eg, *bylynar* 'botanist', *vsedijma* 'history', *hojnyk* 'surgeon', *hnita* 'print'). Many of the definitions were incorrect. In their time the two editions of the dictionary were sharply criticized and rejected by B. *Hrinchenko and K. Sheikovsky, and today they have only a historical value. Piskunov also published *Chaika* (The Seagull, 1876), an album of Ukrainian songs, dumas, tales, fables, and poems (including several of his own); a collection of articles about T. Shevchenko (1878); and a posthumous edition of Ya. Kukharenko's works (1880).

Pislanets' pravdy (Messenger of Truth). An evangelical Baptist journal published bimonthly in Łódź (1927–31) and then Rava Ruska (to 1939). It was edited by S. Bilynsky and then V. Peretiatko, and in 1930 it appeared in a pressrun of 1,000 copies. The journal was renewed in the United States in 1949 as the organ of the All-Ukrainian Evangelical Baptist Fellowship. It was published in Chester, Pennsylvania (ed L. Zhabko-Potapovych), and later, from 1966, in Evanston, Illinois (ed O. Harbuziuk).

Pisniachevsky, Dmytro [Pisnjačevs'kyj], b 22 January 1898 in Podilia gubernia, d 12 January 1966 in Paris. Economist and co-operative leader. He left Ukraine in 1920 and lived as an émigré in Poland, Czechoslovakia, and France (from 1927). Until 1939 he was the representative in France of the *Audit Union of Ukrainian Co-operatives. He wrote articles on economic and co-operative topics for the Ukrainian, French, and Czech press. He also wrote the monograph *Vid kapitalizmu do kooperatyzmu* (From Capitalism to Co-operativism, 1945).

Viktor Pisniachevsky

Pisniachevsky, Viktor [Pisnjačevs'kyj], b 1883 in Podilia gubernia, d 11 October 1933 in Bratislava, Czechoslovakia. Physician, journalist, and civic leader. As a student at the Military Medical Academy in St Petersburg he took part in organizing the Ukrainian caucus in the First State Duma and in founding and editing its organ *Ridna sprava – Dums'ki visti* (1907). Under the pseudonym A. Horlenko he contributed to the Kiev daily *Rada*. While working as a physician and lecturer at Odessa University, he founded and edited the Russian-language daily *Odesskii listok* in 1917 and *Molodaia Ukraina* in 1918. In the following two years he published and edited the weekly *Volia* in Vienna. Having exhausted his financial resources he moved to Bratislava and confined himself to practicing medicine. Besides articles on political and social issues he wrote several dozen scientific articles on medicine.

Pisochyn [Pisočyn]. IV-17. A town smt (1986 pop 12,400) on the Udy River in Kharkiv raion, Kharkiv oblast. It was founded in 1732. Today it lies just outside Kharkiv on the Kharkiv–Kiev highway and railway line. Its factories produce furniture, rubber toys, and metal goods.

Pisotsky, Anatol. See Richytsky, Andrii.

Pit-Grave culture. A Copper–Bronze Age culture of the late 3rd to early 2nd millennium BC that existed along the Dnieper River, in the steppe region, in the Crimea, near the Danube Estuary, and in locations east of Ukraine (up to the Urals). Sites have been excavated since the mid-19th century, and the culture was classified by V. *Gorodtsov in the early 20th century. This culture took its name from pit graves used for burials in family or clan kurhans. Corpses were covered with red ocher and laid either in a supine position or on their sides with flexed legs. Grave goods included egg-shaped pottery containing food, stone, bone, and copper implements, weapons, and adornments. The culture's major economic occupation was animal husbandry, with agriculture, hunting, and fishing of secondary importance. Excavations at Pit-Grave sites also revealed primitive carts that were pulled by oxen and stelae bearing images of humans. The people of this culture usually lived in surface dwellings in fortified settlements. They had contacts with tribes in northern Caucasia and with Trypilian tribes in Ukraine. Significant culture sites include the *Mykhailivka settlement and *Storozhova Mohyla.

Pitschmann, Josef, b 1758 in Trieste, Italy, d 1 September 1834 in Kremianets, Volhynia gubernia. German painter. He graduated from the Vienna Academy of Art and became a member of it in 1787. After working as a portraitist in Lviv (1794–1806) he settled in Kremianets and taught painting at the lyceum there. He produced over 500 portraits, including ones of King Stanislaus II Augustus Poniatowski (ca 1792), T. Czacki, and Counts J. and F. Tarnowski, and many paintings on mythological and biblical themes, such as *Adam and Eve in Paradise*, *Sleeping Nymph and Satyr*, and *Achilles over Patroclus's Corpse*.

Pitted-Comb Pottery culture. A Neolithic archeological culture which existed in northeastern Ukraine during the mid-4th to 3rd millennium BC. It was first studied in the early 20th century by V. *Gorodtsov, M. *Rudynsky, and others. The people of this culture generally settled along river banks or terraces near lakes. Their major defining feature was slightly oval pottery decorated in the upper portions (and occasionally on the inside near the crown) with bands of pit marks and combed lines. The pottery was usually well-fired and thin-walled. The culture was adept with microlithic and macrolithic flint technology. Studies at sites have revealed a variety of implements, including axes, chisels, cutters, arrowheads, and awls. Several epochs of the culture have been identified. Scholars believe that the Pitted-Comb culture may have been a predecessor of the *Marianivka culture.

Pittsburgh. The second-largest city in Pennsylvania and the center of Allegheny County. The population in 1980 was 423,938 (metropolitan area, 2.3 million). An estimated 34,000 Ukrainians live in the greater Pittsburgh area.
　The first Ukrainian immigrants to the city were four

St George's Ukrainian Catholic Church in Pittsburgh

young men from the Lemko region, who arrived in 1878. More emigrants followed in the 1880s and 1890s, most of them from the Lemko village of Hanchova and Klymkivka of Gorlice county, Galicia. The first Ukrainian church in Pittsburgh, the Ruthenian Greek Catholic Church of St John the Baptist, was established in 1891. It is now known as St John the Baptist Ukrainian Catholic Church. Other Ukrainian churches include a second St John the Baptist church (1900), St George's Ukrainian Catholic Church (1918), and St Volodymyr's Ukrainian Orthodox Church (1926), which served as a cultural and social center during the depression years. In 1903 the Ukrainian Presbyterians also established a church, which was later incorporated into the presbytery of Pittsburgh.

The earliest secular organizations to appear were mutual aid and fraternal associations. The first and oldest fraternal organization was the *Ukrainian National Association, whose Branch 53 was organized in 1888 and officially established in 1892. Today the local branches of the larger fraternal associations include four branches of the Ukrainian National Association, three branches of the *Ukrainian Fraternal Association (1911), and three branches of the *Providence Association (1912). In 1914 the Pittsburgh Ukrainians organized a fraternal benefit and insurance association, the *Ukrainian National Aid Association of America (UNAAA). The UNAAA, with its headquarters in Pittsburgh in 1921–81, publishes the newspaper Ukraïns'ke narodne slovo. In 1910 the Ukrainian Bookstore (Knyharnia Novostei) was opened. The Ukrainian Beneficial Union was organized in the south side in 1919, and moved in 1962 to a new location, where it be-

came known as the Ukrainian Home. In 1974 the Self-Reliance Association of American Ukrainians of Western Pennsylvania was affiliated with the Ukrainian Home. The Ukrainian women of Pittsburgh are organized into the Ukrainian Women's League (Branch 27), the Ukrainian Gold Cross, and numerous church sisterhoods.

The first Ukrainian school was organized in 1895 at St John the Baptist Church. In the late 1920s a Ukrainian school was established by St Volodymyr's Ukrainian Orthodox Church. In 1933 an all-day school was instituted at St John the Baptist Church, and in the 1970s a Saturday Ukrainian heritage school was founded in the city. The first youth organization, Zaporizska Sich, originated in 1908 and endured throughout the First World War. Since 1930 the University of Pittsburgh has had an active Ukrainian Club, which initiated the monthly Trident (later the club became the League of Ukrainian Catholics). During the 1940s, branches of the Ukrainian Catholic Youth League and the Ukrainian Orthodox League were formed. Drama and choir ensembles of note include the Western Pennsylvania Regional Choir. Among the early newspapers to appear in Pittsburgh were Amerikanskaia Rus' (1909–14), Rusyn (1911–17), and the weekly Soiuz (1911–15), which in time became affiliated with the Ukrainian Presbyterian Movement in Pittsburgh and then the Ukrainian Evangelical Alliance of North America.

In the post–Second World War era approx 3,500 new immigrants came to Pittsburgh. This influx helped launch numerous organizations, including the Organization for the Defense of Four Freedoms for Ukraine, the United Ukrainian-American Organizations of Western Pennsylvania, the Ukrainian Youth Association of America, the Ukrainian-American Citizens' Club, the Ukrainian Theological Society, the Ukrainian Students' Organization of Michnovsky, the Ukrainian Beneficial Society, and the Pittsburgh Ukrainian Festival Committee.

Pittsburgh is also the home of two Ukrainian art and book stores, Dniester (1946) and Howerla (1956); two general-interest Sunday Ukrainian radio programs; and two Ukrainian religious programs (Baptist and Catholic).

A. Lushnycky

Pittsburgh metropoly. A Byzantine rite Catholic church province in the United States that primarily consists of emigrants (and their descendants) from the Transcarpathia region (Hajdudorog, Mukachiv, and Prešov eparchies) and Yugoslavia (Križevci eparchy). In general the members of the church do not consider themselves to be Ukrainian and have a weakly developed sense of their national origin, most viewing themselves as Ruthenians (Rusyns). Although initially united with Galician Ukrainians in a single Greek Catholic church in the United States (the first bishop, S. *Ortynsky), the priests and leading activists of the community demanded a separate eparchy after 1916. It was granted them by the Vatican in 1924, with the creation of the Pittsburgh exarchate under Bishop V. *Takach. The exarchate was reconstituted as an eparchy in 1963, when another eparchy centered in Passaic, New Jersey, was formed. In 1969 Pittsburgh eparchy was raised to the status of an archeparchy and metropolitan see, and a new eparchy in Parma, Ohio, was formed. Finally, in 1981 a fourth eparchy was established in Van Nuys, California.

The Pittsburgh metropoly has approx 80 priests and

153,000 faithful. Bishop Takach was succeeded by D. Ivancho (1948–54), N. Elko (1954–67), S. Kotsisko [Kocisko] (1968; from 1969 to 1991 as metropolitan), and metropolitan T. Dolinay (since 1991). Passaic eparchy, headed by Bishops S. Kotsisko (1963–8) and M. Dudyk (since 1968), has approx 115 priests and 87,000 faithful. Parma eparchy, headed by Bishops E. Mihalik (1969–84) and A. Pataki (since 1984), has approx 60 priests and 26,000 faithful. Van Nuys eparchy, headed by Bishop T. Dolinay (1981–1991), and G. Kuzma (since 1991), has approx 25 priests and 9,000 faithful.

The metropoly maintains the Cyril and Methodius Seminary in Pittsburgh to train priests for all of the eparchies. The official organ of Pittsburgh eparchy in 1924–55 was the monthly *Nebesnaia tsaritsa. Since then the church's official paper has been the weekly *Byzantine Catholic World, while the official paper of Passaic eparchy has been The Eastern Catholic Life (since 1964). Several monastic orders are active in the metropoly.

Although most of the church's adherents identify themselves as Ruthenians, Rusyns, or Carpatho-Rusyns, there are also some Hungarian and Slovak faithful. In general the church has been subjected to strong Latinizing (all parishes have adopted the Gregorian calendar) and Americanizing influences (English has been used widely in liturgies since 1964). In 1963 a special commission was established to standardize observances and to translate liturgical books into English. The Pittsburgh metropoly maintains no formal relationship with the *Ukrainian Catholic church. Dissension over the Latinization of the church, especially the introduction of compulsory celibacy, led several parishes and priests to leave the church and create the separate American Carpatho-Russian Orthodox Greek Catholic church in 1937.

BIBLIOGRAPHY
Pekar, A. Our Past and Present: Historical Outline of the Byzantine Ruthenian Metropolitan Province (Pittsburgh 1974)
W. Lencyk, A. Pekar

Pitukhivka settlement. A village and archeological site in Ochakiv raion, Mykolaiv oblast. Excavations in 1940–50 revealed a 4th- to 3rd-century BC Scythian settlement containing fine examples of metalwork. Nearby on the Boh Estuary a 2nd-century BC to 4th-century AD town was unearthed. Its spacious houses were solidly built with stone foundations and walls of unbaked brick.

Bohdan Piurko

Piurko, Bohdan [Pjurko], b 4 July 1906 in Nemyriv, Rava Ruska county, Galicia, d 23 October 1953 in Detroit. Conductor and teacher. He studied with V. Barvinsky at the Lysenko Higher Institute of Music in Lviv, and then graduated from the Prague Conservatory in 1930. He was concertmaster at the Kiev Opera Theatre in 1930–2 and director of the Music Institute and Boian choir in Drohobych from 1933. He emigrated after the Second World War, conducted the Ukrainian Opera Ensemble in Germany in 1947–9, and then settled in Detroit, where he worked as a teacher.

Pius IX (secular name: Giovanni Maria Mastai-Ferretti), b 13 May 1792 in Senigallia, Italy, d 7 February 1878 in Rome. Pope of the Catholic church in 1846–78. During his lengthy tenure he elevated the Galician metropolitan M. *Levytsky to the rank of cardinal (1856), founded the *Congregation for Eastern Churches (1862), enacted a *concordat regulating relations between Ukrainian and Polish Catholics in Galicia, established canonical chapters (capitula) in Lviv and Peremyshl eparchies (1867), and protested the liquidation of the Ukrainian Catholic church in the Kholm and Podlachia regions by the Russian authorities (1864–75).

Pius X (secular name: Giuseppe Melchiorre Sarto), b 2 June 1835 in Riese, Italy, d 20 August 1914 in Rome. Pope of the Catholic church in 1903–14. He appointed Ukrainian bishops for the United States (1907) and Canada (1912) and granted Metropolitan A. *Sheptytsky authority over Ukrainian and Belarusian territories formerly within the jurisdiction of the Kievan metropoly (liquidated by the Russian government in 1839).

Pius XI (secular name: Ambrogio Damiano Achille Ratti), b 31 May 1857 in Desio, Italy, d 10 February 1939 in Rome. Pope of the Catholic church in 1922–39. As papal nuncio in Poland (1919–21) he intervened against Polish assaults on the Ukrainian Catholic church following the occupation of Galicia. Later he oversaw the conclusion (1925) of a concordat to regulate relations between Ukrainian and Polish Catholics in Galicia; this agreement, however, did not extend to Volhynia, and the Ukrainian hierarchy had no authority there. He also sought to shore up the Ukrainian church hierarchy in Czechoslovakia, Rumania, Canada, Brazil, and the United States. Other initiatives during his papacy included the building of *St Josaphat's Ukrainian Pontifical College in Rome (1931), the transfer of the Basilian order's administrative center to Rome and the addition of Hungary and Rumania to its jurisdictions, and the establishment of a pontifical commission for the codification of Eastern rite canon law (1935).

Pius XII (secular name: Eugenio Pacelli], b 2 March 1876 in Rome, d 9 October 1958 in Castel Gandolfo. Pope of the Catholic church in 1939–58. He issued an encyclical to the Catholic church in 1946 on the occasion of the 350th anniversary of the Church Union of Berestia in which he protested Soviet repressions against the Ukrainian Catholic church. In the postwar period he helped Ukrainian refugees and the *Division Galizien and worked to prevent their forcible repatriation to the USSR. He created metropolies for the Ukrainian Catholic church in Canada (1956) and the United States as well as exarchates in Great Britain, Brazil, and Australia (in 1958).

Pivdendiprobudm (full name: Derzhavnyi instytut po proektuvanniu pidpryiemstv promyslovosti budivelnykh materialiv pivdennykh raioniv krainy, or State Institute for the Design of Enterprises of the Building-Materials Industry in the Southern Regions of the Country). A planning office of the Chief Administration of Scientific Research and Design Organizations of the former USSR Ministry of the Building-Materials Industry, located in Kiev. Founded in 1944, the office designed factories and other enterprises of the *building-materials industry, including mineral enrichment factories and mines. It also studied problems of production planning and plans for the rationalization of production. The institute has 17 departments and a branch in Kharkiv.

Pivdendipronaftoprovid (full name: Derzhavnyi instytut po proektuvanniu naftoprovodiv, naftoprodukto-provodiv i naftobaz, or State Institute for the Design of Oil Pipelines, Oil Products Pipelines, and Oil Storage Bases). A design office of the former USSR Ministry of the Petroleum Industry, founded in 1972 in Kiev. Organized in 21 departments with 7 subdepartments, the office planned and designed oil pipelines and other facilities of the oil industry in Ukraine.

Pivdendiprosklo (full name: Derzhavnyi instytut po proektuvanniu pidpryiemstv sklianoi promyslovosti, or State Institute for the Design of Enterprises of the Glass Industry). A planning office of the Chief Administration of Scientific Research and Design Organizations of the former USSR Ministry of the Building-Materials Industry, located in Kiev. It was founded in 1960 as a branch of Diprosklo in Leningrad, and assumed its current name in 1975. The institute designed factories and other enterprises for the glass industry and prepared plans for remodeling, reconstructing, and upgrading existing facilities. It also designed systems for improving production.

Pivdenna pravda (Southern Truth). A daily newspaper of the Mykolaiv oblast and city CPU committees and soviets. It began publication in Mykolaiv in Russian in 1917 as *Proletarskoe znamia*. After several name changes it became *Krasnyi Nikolaev* in 1921. From 1930 it was published in Ukrainian as *Chervonyi Mykolaiv*, *Shliakh industrializatsii* (1930–7), and *Bil'shovyts'kyi shliakh* (1937–41, 1943–4), and *Pivdenna pravda* (1944–91). From 1959 it appeared also in a parallel Russian edition, *Iuzhnaia pravda*.

Pivdenne. IV-17. A city (1989 pop 10,400) in Kharkiv raion, Kharkiv oblast. The city was formed in 1963 by the amalgamation of the towns of Komarivka, founded in the 17th century, and Pivdenne, founded in 1906, and was granted city status. Its yards service the railway industry, and its factories manufacture plastic goods and textiles. There are some health resorts on its outskirts.

Pivnichne siaivo (Northern Lights). A miscellany of literature and art, five issues of which were published in Edmonton from 1964 to 1971 by Ya. *Slavutych.

Pivustav **script.** A Cyrillic script used in East and South Slavic manuscripts from the 13th century on and in early Cyrillic printed books. It was freer and more minuscule than the older *ustav script, the letters were quite often slanted and more irregular, and spacing was unequal. Abbreviations, superscripts, accents, and aspirates were used more frequently. The *pivustav* evolved in the second half of the 15th century into the *skoropys* script – the foundation of unified 19th-century Cyrillic handwriting – which omitted the etymological jers, the *jus* vowel (ѫ), Greek letters, and accents and aspirates; had more rounded letters with ascending and descending strokes; and was more cursive. Forms of the *skoropys* varied according to chancery school and local tradition, particularly in the 16th and 17th centuries.

Serhii Plachynda   Mykola Plakhotniuk

Plachynda, Serhii [Plačynda, Serhij], b 18 June 1928 on Shevchenkove *khutir*, near present-day Kirovohrad. Writer, journalist, and literary critic. He graduated from Kiev University (1953), did graduate work at the Institute of Literature of the AN URSR (now ANU), and worked for the paper *Literaturna Ukraïna* (contributing editor) and the Molod publishing house. He is the author of the novels *Tania Solomakha* (1959), *Syn'ooka sestra* (Blue-Eyed Sister, 1962), *De lany shyrokopoli* (Where the Broad Fields, 1963), *Duma pro liudynu* (Duma about a Person, 1974), *Stepova saha* (Steppe Saga, 1977), *Vziaty na sebe* (To Take upon Oneself, 1981), *Shuhaï* (The Shuhais, 1986), and *Revuchyi* (The Roaring [Dnieper], 1988). He has also written the historical prose collections *Neopalyma kupyna* (The Burning Bush, coauthor, 1968) and *Kyïvs'ki fresky* (Kievan Frescoes, 1982), several collections of essays, a collection of fairy tales (1967), two books about the works of Yu. Yanovsky (1957, 1969), a book about O. Dovzhenko (1964), the biographical novels *Oleksandr Dovzhenko* (1980) and *Iurii Ianovs'kyi* (1986), and a biography of P. Zhytetsky (1987).

Plague (*chuma*). An infectious, often fatal disease caused by the microbe *Pasteurella pestis*. There are two main forms: (1) the bubonic plague, characterized by swollen glands in the groin, armpit, or neck, which is transmitted by fleas from rodents to humans and kills 50–80 percent of the infected victims within 10 days; and (2) the rare pneumonic plague, which is transmitted directly from human to human and kills all infected victims within 3 days. Before the exact cause was identified in 1894, the various forms of plague were treated as different diseases.

Reports of plague epidemics in Ukraine date from as early as the 11th century: in 1090 over 10,000 people in Kiev died of plague within two weeks. The Black Death that killed off a quarter of Europe's population in the mid-14th century was brought to the Crimea in 1346 and then through Poland to Ukraine and Russia in 1351; it killed off all the inhabitants of Pereiaslav. There were widespread epidemics affecting Ukraine and Russia in 1414, 1420, and 1423. Epidemics broke out in Kiev in 1630, in Right-Bank Ukraine in 1654, 1709–12, 1738–9, and 1770–2, in Southern Ukraine in 1783–4, and in Volhynia in 1798. In the 19th century plague was imported to Odessa from Turkey and Persia (1812–13, 1828–30, 1837) and to Ukraine from Russia (1878 and 1896). The last outbreaks occurred in Odessa in 1901–2 and 1910.

One of first detailed clinical accounts of the disease in the Russian Empire was written by D. *Samoilovych. He also proposed treatment methods and preventive measures, which were tested in his fieldwork. D. *Zabolotny did extensive research on the disease and proposed a hypothesis about the natural breeding grounds of plague. At the beginning of the 20th century several scientists, among them V. Vysokovych, I. Mechnikov, and M. Hamaliia, devoted some attention to plague.

BIBLIOGRAPHY
Zabolotnyi, D. *Chuma* (St Petersburg 1907)
Alexander, J. *Bubonic Plague in Early Modern Russia: Public Health and Urban Disaster* (Baltimore 1980)

H. Schultz

Plai (Mountain Path). A regional-studies and hiking society, founded in Lviv in 1924. Until 1939 it also had branches in Peremyshl, Sambir, Stryi, and Ternopil. In 1931, after the Polish authorities banned the Plast scouting organization, two sports sections, Plai and Chernyk, were set up as part of the Lviv society to carry on Plast activities. The society published a special page in the Lviv paper *Novyi chas* in 1925 (ed I. Krypiakevych) and the 1930s (ed Ye. Pelensky); its own magazine, *Nasha bat'kivshchyna* (1937–9); and hiking guides to the Opir i Stryi valleys by Ye. Pelensky and the Lemko Beskyd by Yu. Tarnovych. The presidents of Plai were S. Starosolsky, D. Korenets, and K. Pankivsky.

Plakhotniuk, Mykola [Plaxotnjuk], b 8 May 1936 in Fosforit, Shchigry raion, Kursk oblast. Dissident. A physician working near Kiev, he published an article in the samvydav journal *Ukraïns'kyi visnyk* (no. 2, 1970) defending several political prisoners and analyzing Russification in Dnipropetrovske. For this he lost his position at the Kiev Medical Institute. He was arrested in January 1972 for his involvement in *Ukraïns'kyi visnyk* and sentenced in November to an indefinite term in psychiatric prisons in Dnipropetrovske, Kazan, and Smila. After being released in March 1981, he was rearrested in September and sentenced in 1982 to four years in labor camps. He was released soon afterward.

Plaksii, Borys [Plaksij], b 21 August 1937 in Smila, now in Cherkasy oblast. Painter and sculptor. He studied at the Dnipropetrovske Art School and graduated from the Kiev State Art Institute (1965). In the 1960s, together with A. Horska and V. Zaretsky, he created decorative murals for various restaurants and buildings in Kiev. Because of his

Borys Plaksii: sculpture in the Mykhailo Kotsiubynsky Memorial Museum in Chernihiv

unorthodox depictions and because he signed a political petition in 1968, he was denied membership in the Union of Artists. His murals at the Khreshchatyi Yar café, which depicted historical events and contemporary writers in a powerful, expressionist manner, were destroyed by the authorities in 1971. Plaksii survived by ghost-painting for officially recognized artists, painting portraits on commission, and working in Siberia. His oils are distinguished by a dark palette and tragic subject matter. They include *Shackles* (1971), *He Who Is Coming* (1973), *Female Friends* (1981), *Chornobyl* (1986), *Anathema* (1989), and *Pain* (1990). Plaksii's murals and many wood sculptures can be found at the Mykhailo Kotsiubynsky Memorial Museum in Chernihiv. Over half of his more than 1,000 works are in private collections. The first solo exhibition of his works was held in Toronto in 1991.

Plaksii, Oleksandr [Plaksij], b 13 August 1911 in Kursk, Russia. Theatrical designer. In 1936 he completed study at the Kharkiv Art Institute (pupil of O. Khvostenko-Khvostov and S. Prokhorov). He worked in the Kharkiv Young Spectator's Theater (1937–40) and then in the Chernivtsi Oblast Ukrainian Music and Drama Theater (from 1947 as principal designer). His notable designs were for the Chernivtsi Theater's productions of O. Korniichuk's *Zahybel' eskadry* (The Destruction of the Squadron), M. Andriievych's *Lesia*, and B. Brecht's *Mutter Courage und ihre Kinder*.

Plamenytsky, Anatolii [Plamenyc'kyj, Anatolij], b 19 November 1920 in Yagodnoe, Orenburg gubernia, d 10 September 1982 in Kiev. Painter. A graduate of the Kiev State Art Institute (1953), he taught there from 1963. He did genre paintings, portraits, and landscapes, such as *Evening* (1957), *Rain* (1960), *Mother* (1961), and *Election Day* (1971).

Planning. See Economic planning, Five-year plan, and State Planning Committee of the Ukrainian SSR.

Plant cultivation. See Crop cultivation.

Plant physiology. The processes governing the life of plants: the ways they absorb water and minerals, the ways they grow, develop, and bear fruit, photosynthetic processes, respiration, biosynthesis and storage of the necessary substances, and so on. Knowledge of plant physiology provides a basis for the rational planting of crops, their acclimatization, and the maintenance of proper ecological balance.

The founder of the Ukrainian school of plant physiologists was Ye. *Votchal, who investigated the relationship between photosynthesis and water metabolism. His students and followers include V. *Zalensky (who studied water balance regulation in plants), V. Kolkunov (who studied the correlation between the anatomic structure of beet roots and their sugar content), and V. *Liubymenko (who discovered that the chlorophyll present in chloroplast is bound to proteins and does not exist in a free state). Other Ukrainian plant physiologists include M. *Kholodny (auxins), A. Nychypurovych (the composition of the organic substances produced by a plant and its relationship to the conditions of photosynthesis), Y. *Baranetsky (the water regimen of plants and their resistance to drought), D. *Hrodzinsky (plant biophysics), R. Butenko (the physiology of plant morphogenesis), A. *Manoryk, F. *Matskov, A. *Okanenko, K. Sytnyk, and A. *Zaikevych.

The principal center for plant physiology studies in Ukraine has been the AN URSR (now ANU) Institute of Plant Physiology in Kiev. It has published the journal *Fiziologiia i biokhimiia kul'turnykh rastenii* since 1969.

I. Masnyk

Plantain (*Plantago*; Ukrainian: *podorozhnyk*). A plant of the family Plantaginacae, a perennial grass with a rosette of leaves and leafless stalks bearing a terminal spike of small flowers, usually found in temperate zones. In Ukraine it grows in meadows, in steppes, among weeds, and along country roads. The most common species are the greater plantago (*P. major*), the hoary plantago (*P. media*), and the ribwort (*P. lanceolata*). Widely used in folk medicine to treat cuts and boils and to stop bleeding, the plants were also used as laxatives and expectorants, as agents to improve digestion, and as a treatment for gastritis and enteritis.

Plast Ukrainian Youth Association (Plast, Orhanizatsiia ukrainskoi molodi). A Ukrainian scouting organization, based on universal Scout principles adapted to the needs and interests of Ukrainian young people. Its main goals include nurturing skills (particularly camping and outdoor activities), developing moral character and leadership qualities, and fostering a sense of Ukrainian patri-

Emblem of the Plast Ukrainian Youth Association

otism among its members. The organizational name Plast is derived from the Ukrainian word *plastun*, a scout of the Zaporozhian Cossacks.

History to 1945. Ukrainian scouting organizations emerged almost simultaneously in both the Russian and the Austro-Hungarian empires not long after Lord Baden-Powell introduced the scouting concept to the world in 1907. After the struggle for Ukraine's independence, however, they survived only in Western Ukraine. In the Ukrainian SSR scouting was suppressed and replaced by the Pioneer and Komsomol organizations.

The driving force behind scouting in Western Ukraine was O. *Tysovsky, the founder of Plast. In 1911 he formed an extracurricular scouting group at the Academic Gymnasium of Lviv, where he was a teacher. Similar groups were formed concurrently by P. *Franko and I. *Chmola. The Plast scouting movement spread quickly to other cities and towns. By 1913 an organizational framework had begun to evolve, and two organizational handbooks had been published, Tysovsky's *Plast* and Franko's *Plastovi hry i zabavy* (Plast Games and Activities). With the outbreak of the First World War Plast activities decreased considerably, as many older members volunteered for military duty with the *Sich Riflemen and later the *Ukrainian Galician Army. In 1915 a girls' Plast organization arose.

Scouting groups emerged in Russian-controlled Ukraine as early as 1909 and included up to 50,000 adherents by 1917. The activity was initially unstructured, but it started to organize according to the Baden-Powell model with an institutional base when officials of the Kiev educational district, led by a Russian, A. Anokhin, began promoting scouting as an extracurricular program. Specifically Ukrainian scouting troops were first formed in 1917, when Ye. *Slabchenko organized a scouting troop in Bila Tserkva. Similar groups were formed shortly thereafter in Kaniv, Kiev, Katerynoslav, Vinnytsia, and other locations. After the establishment of Soviet rule in Ukraine, these groups were disbanded. In some locations (Kiev, Odessa, Chernihiv) former scout leaders re-established their troops nominally as 'young Communist' scout groups, but these were judged by the authorities to be apolitical and were disbanded. The socializing of young people carried out by scouting was eventually taken over by the *Pioneer Organization of Ukraine.

After the First World War Plast entered its most active phase in Western Ukraine. For a short period (1918–20) Plast activities were carried out under the auspices of the legally sanctioned *Ukrainian National Society for Child and Adolescent Care. By 1920–1 Plast had resumed operations under its own name. It soon developed a network of groups affiliated with secondary schools in Galicia and with *Prosvita societies in Volhynia. A highly successful Plast movement was started in Transcarpathia in 1921, but it remained independent of the Plast mainstream. The organization's core group, Ulad plastovoho yunatstva, or UPYu, for 12- to 18-year-olds (equivalent to Scouts and Guides), was supplemented with Ulad plastovoho novatstva, or UPN, for 7- to 12-year-olds (equivalent to Cubs and Brownies) in 1924; with Ulad starshykh plastuniv, or USP, for 18- to 30-year-olds (Rovers), in 1924–5; and with Ulad plastovykh senioriv, or UPS, for those over 30 years of age (Senior Scouts), in 1930. Organizational journals began to be published, including *Molode zhyttia, which also had a general circulation. Special courses for training group leaders were organized, and an organizational handbook, Zhyttia v Plasti (Life in Plast), was prepared by Tysovsky in 1921. Support materials for group leaders often appeared in specialty publications, such as *Plastovyi shliakh, Plastovyi provid, and Ukraïns'kyi Plast. Organizers were designated to provide assistance in forming new groups. Finally, an economic co-operative was formed under the Plast name.

Plast members and Metropolitan Andrei Sheptytsky

Plast failed to develop in Bukovyna during the interwar period because of the suppression of Ukrainian cultural activities by the Rumanian authorities. Some furtive attempts were made in the early 1930s to establish semilegal Plast groups at a number of secondary schools and gymnasiums, and individuals and clubs maintained ties with Plast in Galicia.

By 1930 Plast had developed a wide-ranging organizational structure, with over 6,000 members in 10 regional districts, and was able to sponsor diverse programs, including a series of highly successful summer camps, for young people. Even more significant, Plast was becoming a popular movement with support emerging from beyond urban educational circles and slowly developing among the working class and at the village level throughout Western Ukraine. It had developed a definite group ethos, part of which included a strong Ukrainian consciousness. Concern about Plast's growing influence on Ukrainian young people, as well as the tendency for nationalist organizations to recruit Plast members after they left the ranks, led the Polish government to bar the organization from forming in state schools (1924), from operating in Volhynia (1928), and finally from operating altogether in Polish-controlled territory (1930). With most of its assets confiscated, its publications banned, and a number of its leading members arrested, Plast was forced underground. Throughout the 1930s it operated illegally or through other bodies, such as the *Ukrainian Hygienic Society (in organizing summer camps) and the *Plai hiking society, and thus managed to maintain certain aspects of its program. More routine Plast activities were continued in Transcarpathia (until it was occupied by Hungary in 1939) and in individual Central and Western European cities in which Plast units had been formed. The latter were organized into the Prague-based Union of Ukrainian Plast Emigrants, or SUPE, in 1931.

In October 1939 under German occupation, M. Ivanenko revived Plast in Sianik (Sanok), but soon thereafter the German authorities ordered the organization to disband. Still, during the Second World War Ukrainian scouting activities in Western Ukraine continued to be carried out through other agencies, the *Ukrainian Youth Educational Societies. The Soviet occupation of Western Ukraine in 1944 brought an end to all Plast activity there.

Development in the West. Plast re-established itself in the West after the Second World War. The groundwork for the new wave of activity was laid in 1945–8 in the *displaced persons' camps of Germany. In October 1945 a gathering in Karlsfeld (near Munich) revived SUPE and developed general guidelines for conducting organizational activity in the camps. Plast attracted a membership of approx 4,800, renewed programs, and resumed its publishing activity (*Iunak, Plastovyi shliakh, *Hotuis'). Subsequent gatherings in 1947 and 1948 established more formal organizational structures (specifically the Plast International Council, or HPR, and the International Executive, or HPB) and guidelines for developing Plast branches (stanytsi) in the West. After the mass resettlement of displaced Ukrainians in 1948–52, Plast branches were established in Australia, Argentina, Canada, Great Britain, Germany, and the United States. The First National Plast Conference was held in Toronto in 1949. In 1954 the first Conference of Ukrainian Plast Organizations, or KUPO (which replaced SUPE), was organized in order to elect new members to the HPR and HPB. Since that time KUPO elections have taken place every three years.

The HPB co-ordinates the program and gives directives to Plast National Executives, which in turn direct their respective local branches. Methodological training for scouting leaders is also governed by the HPB. Training of scoutmasters for the UPN is organized by Orlynnyi kruh. Notable members include L. Bachynsky, T. Bilostotsky, T. Samotulka, A. Horokhovych, L. Khraplyva, and Ye. Hoidysh. Training of leaders of the UPYu is carried out by Lisova shkola (for males) and Shkola bulavnykh (for females). Notable organizers of Lisova shkola have included M. Rakovsky, Yu. Kryzhanivsky, and P. Sodol. Organizers of Shkola bulavnykh have included O. Kuzmovych, T. Boiko, and D. Horbachevska. Specialty camps have been organized by specific kurini (companies) of USP and UPS: the kurin Pershi stezhi, for example, organizes the Stezhky kultury (Paths of Culture) camp; the Burlaky (Vagabonds) specialize in ski and mountain-climbing camps; and the Chornomortsi (males) and Chornomorski khvyli (females) organize special water-sports camps. In 1991 there were 27 different *kurini* of USP and UPS: *Kurin im. Tysovskykh, Ti shcho hrebli rvut, Lisovi Chorty, Kharakternyky, Chervona Kalyna, Zakarpattsi, Kurin im. A. Voinarovskoho, Kurin im. H. Orlyka, Chornomortsi, Dubova Kora, Burlaky, Pershi Stezhi, Chota Krylatykh, Khrestonostsi, Buryverkhy, Karpatski Vovky, Khmelnychenky, Chortopolokhy, Kniahyni, Verkhovynky, Siromantsi, Blyskavky, Vovkulaky, Stepovi Vidmy, Braty Movgli, Shostokryli,* and *Pobratymy*; as well as three that are still waiting registration, *Spartanky, Chornomorski khvyli,* and *Lisovi Mavky.*

1957 Plast jamboree at the Plast camp near Grafton, Ontario

The titular head of the whole Plast movement is the *Nachalnyi Plastun* (Head Scout). To date, two have been elected, S. *Levytsky (1947–62) and Yu. *Starosolsky (1972–91).

In 1990 Plast was legally restored in Ukraine as the Plast Ukrainian Scout Association; it is currently active in the cities of Kiev, Lutske, Lviv, Ternopil, and Zhytomyr. The movement is spreading rapidly to other cities and towns. Plast has been restored also among Ukrainians in Poland and in the Prešov region of Slovakia.

Plast in the diaspora has remained active to the present day. Activities include weekly meetings of UPN and UPYu, lectures, sports events and competitions, hikes and tours, and winter and summer camps. In August 1991 Plast was still independent of the International Scouting Organization and other national scouting movements.

Yu. Starosolsky

Plastovyi shliakh (Plast Way). An ideological and programmatic journal of the *Plast Ukrainian Youth Association. The first three issues appeared in Lviv in 1930 under the editorship of S. *Levytsky. The journal stopped appearing when Plast was outlawed by the Polish government in that year, but it was renewed in Munich in 1950. Four issues appeared there until 1954. Since 1966 the journal has been published in Toronto. In Germany and Canada the journal has been edited by an editorial board, members of which have been L. Onyshkevych, A. Horokhovych, O. Kuzmovych, Yu. Piasetsky, O. Tarnavsky, and V. Sokhanivsky. *Plastovyi shliakh* publishes articles on Ukrainian émigré community life, on political, historical, and cultural topics, and, especially, on the ideals and activities of Plast.

Plastun (Scout). The first Ukrainian scouting journal in Transcarpathia, published in Uzhhorod in 1923–31 and Sevliush (now Vynohradiv) in 1934–5. In 1923–7 *Plastun–Junák–Cserkesz* appeared in Ukrainian, Czech, and Hungarian one to six times a year as the joint publication of the three national scouting associations in the Czechoslovak Republic. From 1928 *Plastun* appeared eight times a year as the independent organ of the Plast Ukrainian scouting organization. It was edited by O. Vakhnianyn (1923–4), L. Bachynsky (1924–9), Yu. Revai (1929–32), and A. Voron (1934–5). Among the contributors were S. Cherkasenko, V. Grendzha-Donsky, V. Pachovsky, M. Pidhirianka, B. Zaklynsky, and Yu. Borshosh-Kumiatsky.

Plateau landscape. One of several landscape types in Ukraine, characterized by wide plains dotted with hills and dissected by deep valleys formed by water erosion. It is found in the *Podolian, *Volhynia-Kholm, and *Pokutian-Bessarabian uplands as well as the *Roztochia region.

Platonov, Khariton, b 1842 in Vorona, Yaroslavl gubernia, Russia, d 5 September 1907. Painter. A graduate of the St Petersburg Academy of Arts (1870), he was elected its full member in 1893. He lived in Kiev from 1879 and taught at the *Kiev Drawing School (1880–1900). In his work he was close to the *Peredvizhniki. He produced genre paintings, such as *Beggar* (1874), *Servant Girl* (1887), *Little Nurse* (1881), and *Berries for Sale* (1888), and also painted a portrait of the kobzar O. Veresai (1885).

Platonov, Kostiantyn, b 30 October 1877 in Kharkiv, d 8 August 1969 in Kharkiv. Psychoneurologist. A graduate of Kharkiv University (1904), he worked in V. Bekhterev's psychiatric clinic in St Petersburg (1909–12), Kharkiv University (1919–28, from 1921 the Kharkiv Medical Institute), and the Kharkiv Railway Psychoneurological Clinic. From 1920 he conducted research at the Ukrainian Psychoneurological Scientific Research Institute. The founder of the Kharkiv school of psychotherapists, he published works dealing with the treatment of neuroses using hypnosis, and with painless childbirth. His *Slovo iak fiziolohichnyi i likuval'nyi faktor* (The Word as a Physiological and Therapeutic Factor, 1957) has been translated into many languages.

Plaviuk, Mykola [Plavjuk], b 5 June 1925 in Rusiv, Sniatyn county, Galicia. Economist and political leader. He

Mykola Plaviuk

joined the OUN during the war and fought in its partisan units. After the war he studied economics at the University of Munich and was an executive member of the Central Union of Ukrainian Students (1947–9). After emigrating to Canada in 1949, he was active in the *Zarevo Ukrainian Student Association and the *Ukrainian National Federation. As president of the latter organization (1956–66) he played a key role in organizing the *World Congress of Free Ukrainians and served as its general secretary (1967–9), vice-president (1973–8), and president (1978–81). At the same time he was vice-president of the Ukrainian Canadian Committee (now Congress, 1966–71). The head of the OUN Melnyk faction since 1979, he was elected vice-president of the *Government-in-exile of the Ukrainian National Republic in June 1989 and served as its last president (1990–92).

Pleiada (Pleiad). A literary group established in 1888 by Lesia Ukrainka and her brother, M. Kosach, in Kiev. It was modeled on the French school of poetry the Pléiade. Its members included M. Bykovska, H. Hryhorenko, M. Komarov, A. Krymsky, V. Samiilenko, M. Slavinsky, L. Starytska-Cherniakhivska, I. Steshenko, and Ye. Tymchenko. Their meetings took place in various homes and were attended by M. Lysenko, P. Kosach, K. Mykhalchuk, M. Starytsky, and others. The group also held literary evenings and contests and translated the works of non-Ukrainian authors, such as H. Heine, Dante, P. de Béranger, Molière, and V. Korolenko. The members prepared three collections for publication, 'Vesna' (Kiev), 'Desna' (Chernihiv), and 'Spilka' (Odessa), but all three were banned by the Russian censor. Pleiada was active until 1893.

Ilarion Pleshchynsky: *The Shevchenko Memorial Preserve in Kaniv* (pencil, 1937)

Pleshchynsky, Ilarion [Pleščyns'kyj], b 28 April 1892 in Dokshitsy, Vitsebsk gubernia, Belarus, d 6 February 1961 in Kiev. Graphic artist. After graduating from the Kazan Art Institute (1921) he moved to Kiev and taught at the Kiev State Art Institute (1925–34, 1944–61) and the Kiev Civil-Engineering Institute (1934–44). His works consist of prints depicting landscapes, posters, and book illustrations. He produced many series of etchings and drawings, such as 'Boats on the Dnieper' (1925), 'Kiev: Landscapes on the Dnieper's Banks' (1927), 'Dnieper Motifs' (1947–61), and 'Ukrainian Landscapes' (1935–9). A book about him was published in Kiev in 1964.

Pleshkan, Olha [Pleškan, Ol'ha], b 15 June 1898 in Chortovets, Horodenka county, Galicia, d ? Painter. She studied at the Novakivsky Art School in Lviv (1925–32) and exhibited her works at shows organized by the Ukrainian Society of Friends of Art. She painted landscapes, portraits, and genre paintings, such as *Self-Portrait* (1928), *Apple Tree in V. Stefanyk's Orchard* (1927), *Washerwoman* (1932), *Corn Cleaning* (1961), and *View of Tulova* (1963).

Pleshkevych, Omelian [Pleškevyč, Omeljan], b 1897 in Makovysko, Jarosław county, Galicia, d 7 July 1960 in Chicago. Conductor. In 1931–7 he conducted the Banduryst male student choir in Lviv, and in 1937–44 the St George's Cathedral choir and Surma male choir. He continued as conductor of the émigré Surma choir in Germany (1945–9) and Chicago (1951–4), helping to make it one of the most important Ukrainian choral ensembles in the United States. He also arranged a number of UPA songs.

Archimandrite Yelysei Pletenetsky

Pletenetsky, Yelysei [Pletenec'kyj, Jelysej], b 1550 in Pletenytsi, near Zolovchiv, Lviv region, d 29 October 1624 in Kiev. Orthodox churchman and cultural leader. He was archimandrite of a monastery in the Pynske region (1595–99) and participated in the church sobor of Berestia (1596). He then became archimandrite of the Kievan Cave Monastery (1599–1624) and secured the right of stauropegion for it. With the assistance of the Cossacks and Hetman P. *Sahaidachny he reclaimed the monastery's valuables that had been given to the Uniates by the Polish king Sigismund III in 1614. He sought to reform monastic life, organized a women's monastery near the Cave Monastery, and restored the Church of the Caves. He also established a hospital for the poor at the monastery.

Pletenetsky attracted a group of notable church and cultural figures at the monastery, including P. and S. Berynda, Y. Borotsky, H. Dorofeievych, Z. Kopystensky, T. Zemka, and L. Zyzanii. He also founded the *Kievan Cave Monastery Press, wrote introductions to many of its earliest publications, and established a paper factory in Radomyshl to provide paper for it. His introductions were published in Kh. Titov's *Materiialy dlia istoriï knyzhnoï spravy na Vkraïni v XVI–XVIII vv.* (Materials for the History of Publishing in Ukraine in the 16th–18th centuries, 1924).

Mykola and Oleksander Plevako

Plevako, Mykola, b 9 December 1890 in Dvorichna, Kupianka county, Kharkiv gubernia, d 25 May 1941 in Vishneva raion, Kazakhstan. Literary scholar and bibliographer. He studied under M. Sumtsov at Kharkiv University, from which he graduated in 1916. He was a professor of Ukrainian literary history at the Kamianets-Podilskyi Ukrainian State University (1919–21), a professor at the Kharkiv Institute of People's Education (from 1921), and director of the bibliography cabinet of the Taras Shevchenko Scientific Research Institute in Kharkiv (1926–33). In 1938 he was exiled to Kazakhstan, where he died in unknown circumstances.

Plevako published studies of L. Hlibov and M. Shashkevych, *Zhyttia ta pratsia B. Hrinchenka* (The Life and Work of B. Hrinchenko, 1911), *O stile i iazyke povesti G.F. Kvitky 'Marusia'* (The Style and Language of H. Kvitka's Novelette *Marusia*, 1916), *Shevchenkiv shchodennyk* (Shevchenko's Diary, 1924), *Shevchenko i krytyka* (Shevchenko and Criticism, 1924), *Shevchenko v tsyfrakh* (Shevchenko in Numbers, 1926), and other works. He edited a number of readers, including *Khrestomatiia po ukraïns'kii literaturi* (An Anthology of Ukrainian Literature, coedited by M. Sumtsov, 1918) and *Khrestomatiia novoï ukraïns'koï literatury* (An Anthology of Modern Ukrainian Literature, 2 vols, 1923, 1926; includes biographies and comprehensive bibliographies of 75 writers, from I. Kotliarevsky to M. Khvylovy). He also edited *Tvory L. Hlibova* (The Works of L. Hlibov, 1927, with I. Kapustiansky) and T. Shevchenko's *Kobzar* (1930, with Ya. Aizenshtok). His *Bio-bibliohrafichnyi slovnyk ukraïns'kykh pys'mennykiv* (Biobibliographical Dictionary of Ukrainian Writers), which he worked on for 10 years (1924–34), has been lost. A compilation of his works was published posthumously, *Mykola Plevako: Statti, rozvidky, i bio-bibliohrafichni materiialy* (Mykola Plevako: Articles, Studies, and Biobibliographic Materials, 1961).

I. Koshelivets

Plevako, Oleksander, b 9 May 1899 in Dvorichna, Kupianka county, Kharkiv gubernia, d 14 February 1990 in Kamianske (former Dniprodzerzhynske), Dnipropetrovske oblast. Economic historian; brother of M. and P. Plevako. After graduating from the Kiev Institute of the National Economy in 1922, he worked as a research associate of the VUAN and in 1925–7 published lengthy articles on the history of the sugar industry in Ukraine. He was arrested in 1928 and exiled to the Urals and Siberia. After returning to Ukraine he wrote short stories about animals, which came out in four collections (1960, 1964, 1969, and 1978). In 1954 he was rehabilitated.

Petro Plevako   Paul Plishka

Plevako, Petro, b 21 December 1888 in Dvorichna, Kupianka county, Kharkiv gubernia, d 4 February 1986 in Paris. Political, civic, and church leader; brother of M. *Plevako. A legal assistant of M. Mikhnovsky, he became a member of the Central Committee of the Ukrainian Party of Socialist Revolutionaries and of the Central Rada. He was appointed department director in the UNR Ministry of Roads and vice-chairman of the Ukrainian Committee of Railwaymen (1918–19). After emigrating to Vienna in 1919 and then to Paris in 1925, he was active in émigré affairs. In 1953 he became a member of the Metropolitan's Council of the Ukrainian Autocephalous Orthodox church in Europe, and for many years he was chairman of the board of directors of the Petliura Library in Paris. He published his brother's works in 1961.

Pliatsko, Hryhorii [Pljacko, Hryhorij], b 14 April 1928 in Ostrovok (Ostriv), Sokal county, Galicia. Mechanics scientist. He graduated from the Lviv Polytechnical Institute (1950) and worked at the AN URSR (now ANU) Physical-Mechanical Institute (from 1957) and the Lviv branch of the Institute of Mathematics (since 1973, and since 1975 as department head). He has made contributions in the fields of thermal conductivity and thermoelasticity and in various areas of solid state physics. He has studied and developed theoretical models of the behavior of solids under conditions in which very high energy flows through them.

Plisetsky, Marko [Plisec'kyj], b 14 January 1909 in Chernihiv. Literary scholar and folklorist. A graduate of Kiev University (1937), he worked in journalism and publishing and lectured at Kiev University and other higher schools. A specialist in Ukrainian and Russian folklore studies, particularly in the development of the Slavic folk epos, he wrote a book on Ukrainian lyrical folk poetry (1941), on dumas and historical songs (1944), and on the ties between Russian and Ukrainian epos (1963).

Plishka, Paul [Pliška], b 28 August 1941 in Old Forge, Pennsylvania. American opera and concert singer (bass) of Ukrainian descent. He studied under A. Bohajian and at Montclair State College. Plishka's lyrical singing bass extends easily into the baritone range. In 1967 he made his New York Metropolitan Opera (Met) debut as the Monk in A. Ponchielli's *La Gioconda*. Plishka's main roles include Sarastro, Figaro, and Leporello in W. Mozart's *Die Zauberflöte*, *Le Nozze di Figaro*, and *Don Giovanni*; Colline in G. Puccini's *La Bohème*; Oroveso and Sir George in V. Bellini's *Norma* and *I Puritani*; Ramfis and Procida in G. Verdi's *Aida* and *I Vespri siciliani*; Mephistopheles in C. Gounod's *Faust*; Varlaam and Pimen in M. Mussorgsky's *Boris Godunov*; and Prince Gremin in P. Tchaikovsky's *Eugene Onegin*. Altogether he has sung more than 40 roles at the Met. Plishka performed leading parts in recordings of Bellini's *Norma* and *I Puritani*, G. Puccini's *Turandot*, Massenet's *Le Cid*, and G. Donizetti's *Gemma di Vergy*. He has been a guest performer at the opera houses of Chicago, San Francisco, Dallas, and Philadelphia; since 1974 he has toured major European theaters, including Milan's La Scala, the Vienna State Opera, the Paris Grand Opera, and Covent Garden. He is frequently heard in the United States as a concert soloist with leading symphony orchestras, performing works by C. Monteverdi, D. Scarlatti, F. Schubert, R. Schumann, S. Rachmaninoff, and J. Niles. In 1978–9 Plishka included in his recitals Ukrainian art songs and folk song settings by M. Lysenko (texts by T. Shevchenko), V. Barvinsky, K. Stetsenko, L. Revutsky, M. Verykivsky, M. Fomenko, and I. Sonevytsky. He recorded an album titled *Songs of Ukraine*.

R. Savytsky

Plisnesk. A fortified Rus' settlement located on the banks of the Buh River near Pidhirtsi, Brody raion, Lviv oblast, and excavated in 1880–3 and 1940–54. Mentioned in medieval chronicles and in *Slovo o polku Ihorevi* as an important center of the Principality of *Galicia-Volhynia, Plisnesk was founded in the 7th to 8th century as an unfortified settlement. By the 11th century it had grown into a major trading center (with a total area of 160 ha) surrounded by moats and walls with towers. Its inhabitants engaged in metalworking, weaving, jewelry and pottery making, and woodworking. The town was sacked by the Mongols in 1241 and it never recovered. It disappeared completely in the 14th century.

Pliuiko, Serhii [Pljujko, Serhij], b 20 November 1887 in Dykanka, Poltava county, d ? A professor of zootechnology and dean of the Kamianets-Podilskyi Agricultural Institute (from 1923), he was arrested by the GPU during the early 1930s and sentenced to a five-year term of hard labor on the White Sea Canal. Although his subsequent fate cannot be confirmed, it is believed that he was given a second term after his sentence was completed, and that he died in a Soviet prison camp.

Pliukfelder, Rudolf [Pljukfel'der, Rudol'f], b 6 September 1928 in Novorlivka, Shakhtarske raion, Donetske oblast. Light-heavyweight weight lifter. He won the 1964 Olympic gold medal in his class; the world championship in 1959 and 1961; and the European championship in 1959, 1960, and 1961. He set 13 world records in weight lifting. At the end of the 1970s he was the trainer of the USSR weight-lifting team.

Leonid Pliushch

Pliushch, Leonid [Pliušč] (Pliouchtch), b 26 April 1939 in Naryn, Kirgizia. Ukrainian mathematician, dissident, and literary critic. He completed his studies at the University of Kiev with a degree in mathematics in 1963 and worked at the Institute of Cybernetics of the AN URSR (now ANU) until 1968. In 1969 he joined the Initiating Group for the Defense of Human Rights. He was dismissed from his job in 1969 and arrested in 1972 for writing articles and signing letters of protest against the violation of human rights. He was declared mentally ill and incarcerated in the Dnipropetrovske psychiatric prison. Pressure from various groups in the West, most notably from French mathematicians, led to his release and his summary expulsion from the Soviet Union to France in 1976, where he has resided since then. In 1977 his autobiography appeared, *Na karnavali istoriï* (At the Carnival of History; also in English as *History's Carnival*, and in French, Italian, and German translations). Fascinated by the Tartu structuralist school (Iu. Lotman) and the Moscow mythologists (V. Ivanov), Pliushch turned to the study of literature. His approach to literature, somewhat influenced also by M. Bakhtin's notions of the 'carnival,' permits free-ranging associative interpretations. He made his debut as a literary scholar and critic with an insightful study of T. Shevchenko as mythologizer, *Ekzod Tarasa Shevchenka: Navkolo 'Moskalevoï krynytsi' dvanadtsiat' stattiv* (Taras Shevchenko's Exodus: Twelve Essays apropos 'The Soldier's Well,' 1987). This was followed by a similarly stimulating examination of the most influential writer of the 1920s, M. *Khvylovy, in *Ioho taiemnytsia* (His Secret, 1990). Pliushch is active in the External Representation of the Ukrainian Helsinki Union and publishes in various Ukrainian and Russian newspapers and journals on literary and political subjects.

D.H. Struk

Pliushch, Oleksii [Pljušč, Oleksij] (pseuds: O. Dafnenko, O. Dafne-Hederenko, Smutnenko), b 25 May 1887 in Olenivka, Borzna county, Chernihiv gubernia, d 26 May 1907. Writer. He studied at the Nizhen Historical-Philological Institute. From 1905 his populist stories, poems, and plays appeared in Ukrainian literary miscellanies and periodicals. His collected works (2 vols, 1911, 1912) and novelette *Velykyi v malim i malyi u velykim* (The Great in the Small and the Small in the Great, 1930) were published posthumously. A selection of his works appeared as *Spovid'* (The Confession, 1991).

Pliushch, Pavlo [Pljušč], b 31 December 1896 in Volodkova Divytsia, Nizhen county, Chernihiv gubernia, d 4 March 1975 in Kiev. Linguist and pedagogue. After graduating from the Nizhen Pedagogical Institute (1923) and the Dnipropetrovske Institute of Social Education (1931) he completed his graduate studies under A. Krymsky and from 1937 taught Ukrainian at Kiev University, where he became head of the Ukrainian language department (1955). He published over 100 works, including a collection of exercises in syntax and punctuation (with O. Sarnatsky, 1938; 8th edn 1954); his doctoral dissertation on the history of the Ukrainian language (1958); books on I. Kotliarevsky's humorous linguistic devices in *Eneïda* (1959) and on the language of T. Shevchenko's *Kobzar* (1964); a history of the Ukrainian literary language (1971); and articles on the history, periodization, and development of the Ukrainian language and on the language and style of the Peresopnytsia Gospel, M. Kotsiubynsky, I. Tobilevych, and V. Stefanyk.

Vasyl Pliushch   Vladyslav Ploshevsky

Pliushch, Vasyl [Pljušč, Vasyl'], b 10 January 1903 in Warsaw, d 16 November 1976 in Munich. Physician and political figure; full member of the Shevchenko Scientific Society. A graduate of the Kiev Medical Institute (1928), he directed an interraion tuberculosis dispensary in Rivne and conducted research at the Odessa Scientific Research Institute for Tuberculosis. He began to work as a specialist in tuberculosis at the Ukrainian Scientific Research Institute for Tuberculosis in Kiev in 1932 and at the Kiev Institute for the Upgrading of Physicians. In 1938 he helped organize the Ukrainian Scientific Society of Phthisiatrists and became its first scientific secretary. During the Soviet occupation of Western Ukraine he was sent as a tuberculosis inspector to Lviv, where he implemented a plan for a network of dispensaries and organized and directed the Lviv Tuberculosis Institute. A postwar refugee, he worked in West Germany and was president (1951–3) of the Supreme Council of the *Central Representation of the Ukrainian Emigration in Germany, and founder and pres-

ident of the Association for the Liberation of Ukraine abroad. His scientific publications include papers and monographs, such as *Klinika gematogenno-disseminirovannogo tuberkuleza legkikh* (Clinic of Hematogenetically Dissemi-nated Lung Tuberculosis, 1938) and *Narysy z istoriï ukraïns'koï medychnoï nauky ta osvity* (Outlines of the History of Ukrainian Medical Science and Education, 2 vols, 1970, 1983). He contributed medical articles to *Entsyklopediia ukraïnoznavstva* (Encyclopedia of Ukraine, 10 vols, 1955–84) and wrote publicistic articles in Ukrainian, English, and German.

Pliushch, Yefrem [Pljušč, Jefrem], 1872–? Civil engineer and specialist in bridge and rail construction. During the rule of Hetman P. Skoropadsky he served as an inspector of roads in the Ministry of Transportation, and in 1919 he was director of railroads for the UNR government. After the war he worked as a railway construction engineer in Poland. A prolific inventor, he developed new construction methods, among them methods of building concrete structures under water, laying rail lines over swamps, and preventing derailing on bridges.

Plokhii, Serhii [Ploxij, Serhij], b 23 May 1957 in Gorky (now Nizhnii Novgorod), Russia. Ukrainian historian. He graduated from Dnipropetrovske University (1980) and received his doctorate in history from Kiev University (1990). He has headed the department of general history at Dnipropetrovske University (as a professor from 1990) and directed a study of German and Mennonite settlements in Southern Ukraine. Since 1992 he has been head of a department in the ANU Institute of Ukrainian Archeography in Kiev. Among his published works are *Osvoboditel'naia voina ukrainskogo naroda v latinoiazychnoi istoriografii serediny XVII v.* (The Liberation War of the Ukrainian People in the Latin-Language Historiography of the Mid-17th Century, 1983) and *Papstvo i Ukraina: Politika rimskoi kurii na ukrainskikh zemliakh (XVI–XVII vv.)* (The Papacy and Ukraine: The Policy of the Roman Curia in Ukrainian Lands [16th–17th Centuries], 1989).

Plokhynsky, Mykhailo [Ploxyns'kyj, Myxajlo], b 1864 in Kursk gubernia, d 1906 in Kharkiv. Historian and archivist. He graduated from Kharkiv University, taught history at a Kharkiv gymnasium, and managed the archive of the Kharkiv Historical-Philological Society (1888–97). In its *Sbornik Khar'kovskogo istoriko-filologicheskogo obshchestva* he published studies on the social history of Left-Bank Ukraine, trapping and hunting, Hetman I. Mazepa as a Russian gentry landowner, and T. Kaplonsky's voyage to Italy in the late 17th century. He also wrote monographs on the archives of Chernihiv gubernia (1899) and on Greeks, Gypsies, and Georgians in Old Little Russia (1905).

Ploshchansky, Venedykt [Ploščans'kyj], b 1834, d 1902. Galician historian and publicist; corresponding member of the Moscow Archeological Society from 1874. He was the last editor of the Lviv Russophile newspaper *Slovo* (1871–87). In 1882 he was a codefendant in the Lviv trial of Russophile leaders accused of treason. In 1887 he emigrated to the Russian Empire and worked in the Vilnius Commission for the Analysis of Ancient Documents and as a government censor. He wrote articles about Galician towns and villages (published mostly in the collections of the Halytsko-Ruska Matytsia society), books about several Galician villages (1872) and the history of the Kholm region according to archival documents and other sources (2 vols, 1899, 1901), an account of the 1882 trial (1892), and a study of the acts of the 16th- and 17th-century Kholm courts (1895).

Ploshevsky, Vladyslav [Plošev'skyj] (Płoszewski, Władysław), b 1853 in Nyzhankovychi, Peremyshl county, Galicia, d 29 January 1892 in Lviv. Actor and scenery designer of Polish origin. He began his career in the Lviv Polish Theater (1873) and then was a leading actor in the Ruska Besida Theater (1874–80, 1882–3, and 1886–92). He also designed scenery for those theaters' productions. He played Peter the Great in Y. Barvinsky's *Pavlo Polubotok* and sang Gaspar in R. Planquette's *Les Cloches de Corneville*. His acting talents, particularly his natural pathos in tragedies, were praised by I. Pelekh and M. Yatskiv. After his portrayal of Franz Moor in F. von Schiller's *Die Räuber* he became insane; he died days later.

Plotkin, Hryhorii, b 22 December 1917 in Odessa, d 9 February 1986 in Kiev. Socialist-realist writer of Jewish origin. From 1936 to 1941 he headed the Odessa branch of the Writers' Union of Ukraine. He began publishing in 1931. He wrote over 10 poetry collections, a novelette in verse about the Decembrists, *Visnyky svobody* (Heralds of Liberty, 1955), publicistic accounts of his travels to Israel (1959) and India (1963), over 10 plays, opera librettos, and documentary-film scripts. A two-volume edition of his selected poetry and plays was published in 1987.

Plotnikov, Vladimir, b 19 May 1873 in Orel, Russia, d 11 September 1947 in Kiev. Physical chemist; full VUAN/ AN URSR (now ANU) member from 1920 and corresponding member of the USSR Academy of Sciences from 1932. A graduate of Moscow University (1895), he worked at the Kiev Polytechnical Institute (1899–1941), from 1910 as a professor, and directed the ANU Institute of Chemistry (1931–41) and the Laboratory of Nonaqueous Solutions of the ANU Institute of General and Inorganic Chemistry (1945–7). Plotnikov's research focused on inorganic chemistry, notably of aluminum salts and complexes, and on nonaqueous electrochemistry. He established the close relationship between electrolytic dissociation and complex formation in solutions; was the first to obtain aluminum at room temperature through electrolysis in nonaqueous solvents; and introduced an original theory of electrochemical resonance to account for electrochemical conductivity.

Plow (*pluh*). The most important farm implement for working the soil in preparation for planting. The first plow was no more than a digging stick pushed or pulled to break the surface of the ground. In Ukrainian territories the plow evolved over many centuries through the same stages as in other countries. During the 1st millennium BC and the first few centuries AD the wooden plow (Ukrainian *ralo*) was widely used among the East Slavs. It consisted of a wooden draft beam, to which a draft animal was tied, a wooden (later iron-tipped) share beam, which cut into the soil, and a tail handle, which the plowman used to control the motion of the plow. Unlike later types of plow

the wooden plow merely cut the earth without turning it over or breaking it up. The furrow it produced was symmetrical, narrow, and shallow. Because of its lightness and the shallow incision it made the wooden plow could be drawn by one or two oxen or horses.

The true plow, which is characterized by its ability to undercut and overturn the soil, appeared in Ukraine only at the end of the 17th century. In addition to an iron share it possessed an asymmetrical moldboard which turned the soil over and pushed it to one side. The addition of wheels made for heavier plows that were capable of working the heavier and deeper chernozem of the steppe.

The introduction of the tractor made still larger and heavier plows possible. The first serial plows in the USSR were built in Odessa in 1925. Today plows of different construction – disk, chisel, rotary, combination – are adapted to various soils and special functions.

Members of the Pluh writers' association in Kharkiv (1923)

Pluh. An all-Ukrainian peasant writers' union based in Kharkiv, with branches throughout Ukraine, founded in 1922 by H. *Koliada, A. *Paniv, S. *Pylypenko, I. *Senchenko, and I. *Shevchenko. Other members included S. Bozhko, D. Humenna, H. Epik, A. Hai-Holovko, I. Kyrylenko, O. Kopylenko, V. Mynko, P. Panch, V. Mysyk, P. Usenko, and N. Zabila. Its stated aim was to 'educate its members and the broad peasant masses in the spirit of proletarian revolution and to draw them into active creative work in this vein.' With that goal in mind, its chief ideologue, Pylypenko, made an orientation to the masses the principal objective for the whole organization. His doing so resulted in sharp polemical exchanges with M. Khvylovy in the *Literary Discussion of 1925–8. Khvylovy was harshly critical of the organization's provincialism and simplistic didacticism. In the course of the discussions many members left Pluh. Usenko, along with other Komsomol writers, departed to form Molodniak. A. Dyky, Kyrylenko, Zabila, and others joined the All-Ukrainian Association of Proletarian Writers. In 1931, in connection with the new collectivization drive, the organization changed its name to the Proletarian Collective-Farm Writers' Union. A year later, by decree of the Central Committee of the Communist Party (Bolshevik) of Ukraine, issued on 23 April 1932, the union was dissolved. Its leaders were either shot or imprisoned (Bozhko, Epik, V. Gzhytsky, Paniv, Pylypenko, and others). Its official organ was the journal *Pluzhanyn*, renamed *Pluh* in 1928.

I. Koshelivets

First almanac of *Pluh* (1924)

Pluh (Plow). A monthly journal of literature and the arts of the *Pluh writers' association. It was published in Kharkiv and edited by S. *Pylypenko, I. Senchenko, A. Holovko, I. Kyrylenko, D. Zahul, and others. It was established in 1925 as *Pluzhanyn*, but its name was changed to *Pluh* in 1928, and as such it was known until 1932. In 1933 its last two issues appeared, as *Kolhospna Ukraïna*. *Pluh* is also the name of a collection of essays, writings and statutes of Pluh, edited by Pylypenko, which was issued in 1922. Pluh also issued three almanacs bearing the same title (1924–7, edited by Pylypenko). They included M. Yashek's bibliographical index of the Literary Discussion of 1925–8 and another bibliography, 'Pluzhans'ka tvorchist'' (The Works of Pluh).

Plum, European (*Prunus domestica*; Ukrainian: *slyva domashnia*). A fruit plant of the family Rosaceae that grows as a tree or shrub. Plums grow in all regions of Ukraine, especially the Podilia, Pokutia, Transcarpathia, Kharkiv, and Kiev regions, and account for 15.5 percent of all fruit trees planted in Ukraine (or 50 million trees).

Pluzhanyn. See *Pluh*.

Yevhen Pluzhnyk

Pluzhnyk, Yevhen [Plužnyk, Jevhen], b 26 December 1898 in Kantemyrivka, Bohuchar county, Voronezh gubernia, d 2 February 1936 in the Solovets Islands. Writer. In the years 1923–8 he belonged to the Kiev writers' groups *Aspys and Lanka (see *MARS) and contributed poetry to several Soviet Ukrainian journals. During his life-time he published only two poetry collections, *Dni* (Days) in 1926 and *Rannia osin'* (Early Autumn) in 1927; a third, *Rivnovaha* (Equilibrium), first appeared posthumously in an émigré edition in Augsburg in 1948. He also wrote the novel *Neduha* (Illness, 1928), which was banned from circulation shortly after its publication. Two of his plays, *Profesor Sukhorab* and *U dvori na peredmisti* (In the Courtyard in the Suburb), appeared in *Zhyttia i revoliutsiia* in 1929; a drama in verse, 'Shkidnyky' (Wreckers), was never published. He also translated Russian literature into Ukrainian and compiled (with V. Pidmohylny) a dictionary of Ukrainian official phraseology (1926) and (with V. Atamaniuk and F. Yakubovsky) an anthology of Ukrainian poetry (1930–2).

Although Pluzhnyk was one of the finest Ukrainian poets of the 1920s (he has been compared to R.M. Rilke), Party criticism was hostile to his contemplative, laconic, and frequently gloomy lyricism and depiction of revolutionary atrocities and Soviet reality. After his novel was banned from circulation, he published very little. In December 1934 he was arrested together with many other Ukrainian figures, and in March 1935 he was sentenced by a military tribunal to death by firing squad. The verdict was commuted to 10 years' imprisonment in the Solovets Islands in the White Sea, where he soon died of the tuberculosis that had afflicted him since 1926. He was rehabilitated posthumously in 1956, and editions of his collected poems were published in Kiev in 1966 and 1988. An uncensored edition appeared in Munich in 1979.

R. Senkus

Plyhunov, Oleksandr (Pligunov, Alexandr), b 26 May 1904 in Verkhnie, Starobilske county, Kharkiv gubernia, d 26 October 1975 in Kiev. Chemist. After graduating from the Kiev Polytechnical Institute (1930) he worked there and became a professor and rector (1943–52, 1955–72). His research dealt with optimizing technological processes and using novel resources for producing cement and other construction materials.

Plykhanenko, Sava [Plyxanenko], b ?, d 1768 in Kodnia, Zhytomyr region. Peasant leader during the *Koliivshchyna rebellion. In the spring of 1768 he organized peasants in and around the village of Malopolovetske, near Fastiv (Khvastiv), into a haidamaka contingent. Under his leadership and with the help of the Zaporozhian Cossacks the rebels fought in the Bila Tserkva district. Plykhanenko was captured and executed by Polish forces.

Pneumoconiosis. A disease of the lungs caused by the habitual inhalation of inorganic, organic, or chemical irritants. It is an occupational disease, and in Ukraine an overwhelming number of cases are found in the Donbas and Kryvyi Rih regions, where there is an extraordinary concentration of mining and heavy industry. The least severe forms of pneumoconiosis occur when coal dust is inhaled by coal workers (anthracosis or black lung disease); iron dust by welders and hematite and magnesite by miners (siderosis); and tin, barium chromate, and clay by miners. The inhalation of dust containing silicon is far more serious in effect and is widespread among those with occupations in mining, sandblasting, and pottery making. Known as silicosis, it is the most common form of pneumoconiosis. The generally old, dilapidated, and poorly ventilated condition of factories and mines in Ukraine increases the frequency of its occurrence. The Kiev Scientific Research Institute of Tuberculosis and Pulmonary Surgery (founded in Kharkiv in 1922 on the basis of a local tuberculosis clinic and moved to Kiev in 1930) works on problems pertaining to cases of pneumoconiosis, silicosis, and other lung diseases from the Donbas and Kryvyi Rih regions. The solutions lie not only in the treatment of those who already have the disease, but even more in the elimination of the heavy *pollution which now plagues Ukraine.

P. Dzul

Po, Lina (pseud of Polina Horenshtein), b 18 January 1899 in Katerynoslav (now Dnipropetrovske), d 26 November 1948 in Moscow. Sculptor and dancer. She studied sculpture at E. Blokh's studio in Kharkiv and at the Higher Artistic and Technical Workshop in Moscow (1920–4). At the same time she studied ballet in Moscow, and from 1924 she performed in Kiev. In 1934 she lost her eyesight, and from then on she devoted herself to sculpture. Her work consists of plasticine and clay statuettes on dance themes (eg, *Dance Suite* [1937], *Dance with a Scarf* [1937], and *Dances of the Peoples of the USSR* [1946–7]), portraits, and thematic scenes.

Poale Zion (Workers of Zion). A moderate Jewish socialist movement that originated in Ukraine (Katerynoslav, Odessa, and Poltava), Vilnius, and Vitsebsk at the beginning of the 20th century and spread to the Austrian Empire, Britain, the United States, Palestine, and Argentina. Although it did not advocate Ukrainian independence, Poale Zion maintained strong contacts with Ukrainian activists, particularly with the Ukrainian Social Democratic Workers' party, and later entered the Central Rada and the UNR Directory. Some of its members, such as S. *Goldelman, were strong supporters of the Ukrainian national movement. The party split into factions after the October Revolution and was banned by the Soviet government in 1928.

Pobedonostsev, Konstantin [Pobedonoscev], b 2 June 1827 in Moscow, d 23 March 1907 in St Petersburg. Russian government official and chief procurator of the *Holy Synod. After graduating from the Moscow School of Jurisprudence (1846) he worked in the civil service and was a professor of civil law at Moscow University (1859–65). Over time he was granted the posts of senator (from 1868), member of the Council of State (from 1872), and lay director (procurator) of the Holy Synod of the Russian Orthodox church (1880–1905). He also had considerable influence as a personal adviser to Emperor Alexander III, particularly after the assassination of Alexander II in 1881.

Pobedonostsev was a relentless propagator of the concepts of a state based on Orthodoxy, autocracy, and Russian identity. He played a central role in the campaign launched during the 1880s to Russify the empire's Baltic holdings and in efforts to contain the Poles and Polish influences. He instigated the conversion of Uniates in the Kholm region to Russian Orthodoxy in 1875 and established numerous restrictions on Greek and Roman Catholics. He did not allow Russian sermons in Roman Catholic churches or the translation of the Bible into Ukrainian. He also supported anti-Semitic legislation that restricted the social mobility and access to education of Jews and continued their confinement within the *Pale of Settlement.

Pobedonostsev harbored aspirations for the annexation of Galicia and Transcarpathia, believing the predominantly Uniate Ukrainian inhabitants there to be Orthodox Russians who would have been part of the empire and church if not for centuries of Polish and Catholic oppression. He arranged for generous subsidies to *Russophile currents in both regions and maintained personal contacts with figures such as I. Naumovych and A. Dobriansky. He caused the Holy Synod to underwrite Russian Orthodox mission work among Ukrainian immigrants in Canada and the United States, in the belief that inroads there would assist similar efforts in Western Ukraine. A collection of his ideological essays was published in Moscow in 1896 as *Moskovskii sbornik* (Moscow Collection; trans edn pub as *Reflections of a Russian Statesman*, 1965).

BIBLIOGRAPHY
Byrnes, R. *Pobedonostsev: His Life and Thought* (Bloomington, Ill–London 1968)

A. Makuch

Poberezny, Paul [Poberežnyj, Pavlo], b 14 September 1921 in Fort Leavenworth, Kansas. American pilot and aviation promoter, of Ukrainian descent; member of the Society of Experimental Test Pilots (1978), the Fédération Aéronautique Internationale, and the Wisconsin Air National Guard Hall of Fame (1988). The son of Ukrainian immigrants from Galicia, he became the only person in the US armed forces to attain all seven aviation wings before retiring at the rank of colonel in 1970. During his flying career Poberezny piloted 378 types of flying craft, accumulated 29,000 hours of flight time, and designed and built 13 different airplanes. In 1953 he founded the Experimental Aircraft Association (EAA), which promotes amateur aircraft building and sport aviation. In 1991 the EAA numbered over 125,000 members in 100 countries. Poberezny also initiated the EAA's international Fly-In Convention in Oshkosh, Wisconsin, the largest event of its kind in the world (1 million people and 13,000 aircraft annually). The publisher of five EAA monthly magazines and numerous technical manuals, Poberezny received the US Federal Aviation Administration Award for Extraordinary Service (1972) and the first-ever Charles A. Lindbergh Award for lifetime contribution to aviation (1990).

Pobodailo, Stepan [Pobodajlo] (Podobailo), b ? in the Chernihiv region, d 1654. Cossack officer. He served in the private forces of A. Kysil until 1648 and then joined B. Khmelnytsky's forces, with which he took part in numerous battles, as captain (1651) and colonel (1651–4) of Chernihiv regiment and as the hetman's deputy for Left-Bank Ukraine (1652). He was an opponent of the Treaty of Bila Tserkva. He fought Polish-Lithuanian forces in the Chernihiv region in 1652, and he participated in negotiations for the Pereiaslav Treaty of 1654. He was killed during the Belarusian campaign at Stare Bykhovo and was buried in the Trinity–St Elijah's Monastery in Chernihiv (the restoration of which he had funded).

Pobut (Way of Life). An organ of the *Ethnographic Society, published in Kiev in 1928–30 (seven issues altogether). It contained reports on the society's activities and ethnographic expeditions and articles on ethnographic methodology and Ukrainian folk culture. The journal was edited by a committee that included O. Malynka, A. Onyshchuk, and N. Malecha.

Pobuzke [Pobuz'ke]. V-11. A town smt (1986 pop 7,000) on the Boh River in Holovanivske raion, Kirovohrad oblast. The town was founded in 1959. It produces building materials and fruit conserves.

Pochaiv [Počajiv]. III-6. A city (1989 pop 11,000) in Kremenets raion, Ternopil oblast. It is first mentioned in historical documents in 1450 and was known as Yerofeivka until the 16th century. In that century an Orthodox monastery was founded there, and at the beginning of the 17th century the monastery acquired a printing press. In 1795 Pochaiv was annexed by Russia. Its monastery was raised to the status of *lavra* in 1833. In the interwar period the town belonged to Poland, and since 1939 it has been part of Ukraine. In 1978 it was granted city status. Its main industry is food processing. Pochaiv's architectural monuments include the monastery complex and the wooden Church of the Holy Protectress, from 1643.

Pochaiv Monastery (Pochaivska lavra). The largest monastery in Volhynia, and the second largest men's monastery in Ukraine, after the Kievan Cave Monastery. Initially called the Pochaiv Dormition Monastery, it was founded, according to some accounts, by monks who fled from the Kievan Cave Monastery at the time of the Tatar invasion of 1240. The first written mention of it dates to 1527. In 1597, the noblewoman A. Hoiska donated a large estate to the monastery, as well as a miracle-working icon that had been brought to Volhynia by a Greek metropolitan in 1559. The cloister flourished during the tenure of Hegumen St Yov *Zalizo in the early 17th century. In 1649 F. and Ya. Domashevsky funded the construction of the monastery's Holy Trinity Church. In 1675 the monastery was attacked by Turks and Tatars but was reputedly

Fedir and Yavdokha Domashevsky, benefactors of the Pochaiv Monastery (1649)

saved by an apparition of the Mother of God; this event has been immortalized in many songs, including 'Oi ziishla zoria vecherovaia' (Oh the Evening Star Appeared). In 1713 the monastery officially joined the Uniate church and became a center of the Basilian monastic order, which developed it into an important cultural and publishing center and founded the *Pochaiv Monastery Press in 1730. In 1771–83, the Holy Trinity Church was demolished and replaced by the Dormition Cathedral, funded by M. Potocki.

In 1831, the Russian government gave the monastery to the Russian Orthodox church on the pretext that its monks supported the Polish Insurrection of 1830–1. It also raised its status to that of a *lavra*. In 1833–41 the monastery was the see of the bishop of Volhynia, and after that its archimandrites were named Bishop of Ostrih. In the late 19th century an icon painting workshop and a historical museum were established, and many buildings were rebuilt or expanded. In the 18th to 19th centuries the monks of the monastery developed a distinctive style of liturgical singing. A number of hermitages were controlled by the monastery.

In the 20th century, under the Volhynian archbishop A. *Khrapovitsky, the Pochaiv Monastery became a strategic center of Russification, reactionaryism, and anti-Ukrainianism. The archimandrite V. Maksymenko was an influential supporter of the *Black Hundreds movement and of publications such as *Pochaevskii listok*. During the interwar period, its archimandrite was the metropolitan of Warsaw of the Polish Autocephalous Orthodox church, but now he is the bishop of Lviv and Ternopil. After western Volhynia was incorporated into the Ukrainian SSR following the war, the Pochaiv area was annexed to Ternopil oblast, and the hierarch of Lviv-Ternopil served as archimandrite. The monastery lost its estates, falling victim to the antireligious policies of the Soviet regime. The number of monks declined sharply, from 200 in 1939 to 74 in 1959 and approx 12 in 1970. Nonetheless, efforts by the Soviet authorities to close the monastery outright in 1964 were met by protests of local Ukrainians and of the international community. The monastery remained open, but many of its artifacts were confiscated and housed in the Pochaiv Museum of Atheism, located at the monastery.

Before the revolution, the Pochaiv Monastery was a popular destination for religious pilgrims, tens of thousands of whom came to celebrate the feasts of the Dormition (28 August) and of St Yov Zalizo (10 September). Among its most revered artifacts are a 'footprint' of the Mother of God, a miracle-working icon, and the relics of St Yov.

Architecturally, the Pochaiv Monastery appears as a complex of buildings uniquely adapted to the natural environment. The buildings are set on a cliffside, rising to a three-story terrace with a parapet. The terrace is the site of the central Dormition Cathedral, built in 1771–83 in the Rococo style by the Silesian architect G. Hoffman. The vast cathedral (it can accommodate 6,000 people) has eight large and seven smaller cupolas, and two large arches at the front. The sculptures within were created by M. Poleiovsky (1781–6), and the fresco on the dome was rendered by P. Preniatytsky. L. *Dolynsky painted the icons for the iconostasis, the 'Miracle of Christ' cycle, and 50 other smaller works, all in the classical style, and L. and I. Bernakevych crafted the engravings for the church. The cathedral suffered a fire in 1869, and only four of Dolyn-

The Dormition Cathedral (1771–91) at the Pochaiv Monastery

sky's works were saved, but the original appearance of the interior has been preserved in a drawing by T. Shevchenko (1846). The cathedral was renovated in 1876 by local icon painters. Other buildings in the Pochaiv Monastery complex include the monks' cells (1771–80), which surround the cathedral, the bishop's residence (1825), built in the classical style, and a large bell tower (1861–71). The Trinity Church, constructed in 1910–13 after a design by A. Shchusev, was built in the Novgorod style of the 12th to 13th centuries, and differs markedly from other structures in the complex.

BIBLIOGRAPHY
Khoinatskii, A. Pochaevskaia uspenskaia lavra: Istoricheskoe opisanie (Pochaiv 1897)
Antonovych, S. Korotkyi istorychnyi narys Pochaïvs'koï uspins'koï lavry (Kremianets, 1938; San Andres, Argentina 1961)
Ilarion (Ohiienko, I.). Fortetsia pravoslaviia na Volyni: Sviata Pochaïvs'ka lavra (Winnipeg 1961)
Dubylko, I. Pochaïvs'kyi manastyr v istoriï nashoho narodu (Winnipeg 1986)

Pochaiv Monastery Press (Pochaivska drukarnia). An important early press in Ukraine, established at the Pochaiv Monastery in 1730 after it became a Basilian monastic center. Granted royal charters in 1732 and 1736, the press was subsidized by Bishop T. Rudnytsky-Liubienitsky of Lutske. Between 1731 and 1800 it published over 355 books, most of them liturgical ones, but also didactic, theological, and polemical works, literary works in Polish and Latin, collections of documents on Ukrainian church history, primers, textbooks, and educational works. Some of its editions – eg, *Narodovishchanie* (1756), a collection of catechismal and didactic literature, and *Bohohlasnyk* (1790), a collection of poems and religious songs – were among the highest achievements of Ukrainian publishing and literature of the time.

The press's publications were known for their artistic ornamentation and the quality of their paper and print. Many were printed in the so-called Pochaiv cursive, a typeface based on Ukrainian calligraphy of the 16th to 18th centuries. Illustrations and engravings were done by well-known artists, such as N. Zubrytsky, A. and Y. Hochemsky, A. Holota, and F. Strilbytsky.

After the Pochaiv Monastery was taken over by the Russian Orthodox church in 1831, the press continued printing religious and secular books, including several on the history of Volhynia. It printed the eparchial newspaper of Volhynia gubernia (1867–1915) and the reactionary newspaper *Pochaevskii listok*, later a major organ of the Union of the Russian People. The press was closed down in 1918, and part of its equipment was moved to Kiev and thence to Moscow and finally Warsaw.

BIBLIOGRAPHY
Tikhovskii, Iu. 'Mnimaia tipografiia Pochaevskago monastyria (s kontsa XVI do I-i chetverti XVIII v.), KS, 1895, nos 7–9
Svientsits'kyi, I. Pochatky knyhopechatannia na zemliakh Ukraïny (Lviv 1924)
Ohiienko, I. Istoriia ukraïns'koho drukarstva: Istorychno-bibliohrafichnyi ohliad ukraïns'koho drukarstva XV–XVII v.v. (Lviv 1925; Winnipeg 1983)
Boiko, M. Knyhodrukuvannia v Pochaievi i Kremiantsi ta mandrivni drukari (Bloomington, Ind 1980)
Zapasko, Ia.; Isaievych, Ia. Pam'iatky knyzhkovoho mystetstva: Kataloh starodrukiv, vydanykh na Ukraïni, vol 2, pts 1–2 (Lviv 1984)
B. Kravtsiv

Pochapy settlement. A multilayered archeological site near Pochapy, Zolochiv raion, Lviv oblast. The site was excavated by Ya. *Pasternak and T. Sulimirski in 1931–2. Paleolithic flint remains, traces of a Mesolithic settlement, an early Bronze Age burial site, and indications of an early Iron Age settlement were found there.

Pochasky, Sofronii [Počas'kyj, Sofronij] (secular name: Stefan), b and d ? Church activist, pedagogue, and writer of the first half of the 17th century. He studied at the Kiev Epiphany Brotherhood School and possibly abroad before becoming a preacher at the Kievan Cave Monastery and a professor of rhetoric at the monastery school (1631–2). He was a professor at and rector of (1638–40) the Kievan Mohyla College (later Academy) and cofounded an Orthodox school in Iaşi (Moldavia). From 1640 until his death he was hegumen of the Three Hierarchs Monastery in Iaşi. He edited and published a collection of panegyric poems by the students of the Kievan Mohyla College, entitled *Eucharisterion* ... (1632), dedicated to Metropolitan P. *Mohyla

Pochatkova shkola (Primary School). A pedagogical organ of the Ukrainian Ministry of Education, published monthly in Kiev since 1969. The journal addresses questions of the organization of education and upbringing in primary schools and contains materials to aid teachers, educational administrators, and parents. It also prints articles about artists, authors, and composers whose works are studied in the elementary school program. In 1982 it appeared in a pressrun of 82,000.

Pochep [Počep]. I-14. A town (1959 pop 15,700) on the Sudost River and a raion center in Briansk oblast, RF. It was first mentioned in historical documents in the 15th century. In 1503 it was transferred from Lithuanian to Muscovite control, and in 1616, to Polish control. From the mid-17th century it was a company center of Starodub regiment in the Hetman state. In 1686 it came under Russian rule, and during the 19th century it was a trading town in Mglin county, Chernihiv gubernia. In 1917 it became a county center. According to the census of 1926, Ukrainians accounted for 11.7 percent of the population in Pochep county.

Pochynok, Tymotei [Počynok, Tymotej], b 26 February 1885 in Uhryn, Chortkiv county, Galicia, d 3 November 1962 in Detroit. Pioneer of the Ukrainian socialist movement in the United States. Influenced by the writings of M. Drahomanov, he supported the *Ukrainian Radical party in his youth. He emigrated to the United States in 1908. The following year he organized a Ukrainian branch of the Socialist party and the Volia society in Scranton, Pennsylvania. After moving to Detroit in 1910, he set up another branch there. The Ukrainian Federation of the Socialist Party (est 1912) appointed him editor of its paper *Robitnyk* in 1914. A consistent defender of Ukrainian independence, Pochynok resigned from the federation when it assumed a communist orientation in 1917. He joined the Federation of Ukrainians in the United States and then Oborona Ukrainy (1923). In 1930 he began to publish the paper *Pora* (later called *Ukraïns'ka hromads'ka pora*), which supported the policies of the Ukrainian Radical party. After the dissolution of Oborona Ukrainy in the 1940s, he joined the Ukrainian Free Society of America.

Pochynok, Viktor [Počynok], b 1 May 1915 in Kiev. Organic chemist. After graduating from Kiev University (1939) he worked there and became a professor (1962) and chairman of the monomers and polymers department (1963). His work on heterocyclics, polymers, and monomers was directed at the chemistry of photographic processes (in particular at silver-free photographic emulsions) and biologically active polymers. He discovered the azido-tetrazole tautomerism and was the first to introduce long chain-substituted aromatic triazenes as alkylating agents.

Poděbrady. A city (1985 pop 15,000) in Czechoslovakia on the Laba River approx 50 km east of Prague. The city was the site of the *Ukrainian Husbandry Academy (UHA, 1922–35) and the *Ukrainian Technical and Husbandry Institute (1932–45). In 1926 there were 800 Ukrainians there. It also served as a center for 52 Ukrainian organizations, of which 38 were connected to the UHA. Among the latter were the Academic Hromada of the UHA, the Community of Students of the UHA, an academic choir of 50 singers, a writers' group, a drama group that staged over 30 productions, a bandurist association, and a sporting club. The Academic Hromada published a journal, *Nasha hromada*. Poděbrady was the center for the *League of Ukrainian Nationalists (headed by M. Stsiborsky) in 1925–9. Local branches of the Plast Ukrainian Youth Association and Sokil were also active there.

Poderviansky, Serhii [Poderv'jans'kyj, Serhij], b 15 July 1916 in Kiev. Painter. After graduating from the Leningrad Institute of Painting, Sculpture, and Architecture (1952) he began teaching at the Kiev State Institute of Art. His watercolor and tempera works consist of portraits and genre paintings, such as *Valia* (1958), *Abandoned* (1961), *Behind a Living Wall* (1965), and *In the Days of Occupation* (1980), and posters.

Podgorny, Nikolai. See Pidhirny, Mykola.

Podil district in Kiev (lithograph, 1862)

Podil (originally Podoliie, or 'lower part'). The northern part of the old city of Kiev, situated on the lower terrace of the Dnieper's right bank between the mouth of the Pochaina River and the slopes of the Starokyivska, Zamkova, Khorevytsia, and Shchekavytsia hills. During the Princely era, beginning in the 9th century, Podil was the heart of commerce and artisanry in Kiev. Separate districts of potters, pitch makers, and tanners and the town's harbor and customs house were located there. At the center was a large marketplace, Torzhyshche. After the sack of Kiev's upper town by the Mongols in 1240, Podil became the central part of Kiev. In the 16th century the town hall, the *Kiev Epiphany Brotherhood and its monastery and school, and the *Kievan Mohyla Academy were built there, and from 1798 the annual *Kiev Contract Fair was held there. Much of Podil was destroyed in the great fire of 1811, but the district was rebuilt, and new streets were created. In the 19th and early 20th centuries Podil was the main commercial district of Kiev. Today it is located in Kiev's Podilskyi raion.

Mykhailo Podilchak

Podilchak, Mykhailo [Podil'čak, Myxajlo], b 14 August 1919 in Korovytsia, Liubachiv county, Galicia. Surgeon. A graduate of Prague University (1942), he worked at a pediatric surgery clinic in Lviv and was a professor at the Lviv Medical Institute and from 1961 head of the hospital surgery department. His more than 170 publications include *Vplyv mikrobnoï infektsiï na rak* (The Influence of Microbe Infection on Cancer, 1950) and *Khronicheskoe vospalenie i opukholevyi rost* (Chronic Inflammation and Tumor Growth, 1965).

Podilia (Podolia). A historical-geographical upland region of southwestern Ukraine, consisting of the western part of the forest-steppe belt. Podilia is bounded in the southwest by the Dniester River, beyond which lie the Pokutian-Bessarabian Upland and Subcarpathia. To the north it overlaps with the historical region of Volhynia, where the Podolian Upland descends to Little Polisia and Polisia. In the west it is bounded by the Vereshytsia River, beyond which lies the Sian Lowland. To the east Podilia passes imperceptibly into the Dnieper Upland, with the Boh River serving as part of the demarcation line, and in the southeast it descends gradually toward the Black Sea Lowland and is delimited by the Yahorlyk and the Kodyma rivers. The Podilia region thus coincides with the Podolian Upland, which occupies an area of approx 60,000 sq km.

The name Podilia has been known since the mid-14th century, but it did not originally refer to the aforementioned geographical region or to a single administrative-territorial unit. It usually meant the land between two left-bank tributaries of the Dniester, the Strypa River in the west and the Murafa River in the southeast, and the Boh River in the east, an area of approx 40,000 sq km. Podilia voivodeship, established at the beginning of the 15th century, encompassed only the central part of Podilia. During the Polish-Lithuanian Commonwealth Podilia was understood to include not only Podilia voivodeship but also Bratslav voivodeship and the northeastern part of Rus' voivodeship. Its southern and southeastern areas, however, remained unsettled, and the border between the commonwealth and the Ottoman Empire marked by the Kodyma and the Syniukha rivers was only conventional. In the 19th century eastern Podilia often meant Podilia gubernia, which consisted approximately of the former Podilia and Bratslav voivodeships, whereas western Podilia meant the eastern part of Galicia. At the beginning of the 20th century the name Podilia was applied to lands as far west as the Zolota River. Today Podilia encompasses Ternopil oblast (although the Kremianets area historically belonged to Volhynia), almost the whole of Khmelnytskyi and Vinnytsia oblasts, and small parts of Lviv and Ivano-Frankivske oblasts.

The history of Podilia was strongly influenced by its proximity to the steppe, for centuries the source of nomadic raids. For a long time much of Podilia was under the control of the Pechenegs, Cumans, and Tatars. From the mid-15th century Podilia was the favorite target of Tatar raids. When they diminished, the fertile region attracted Polish colonists from the northwest, who filled the political power vacuum.

Physical geography. Structurally, Podilia is connected to the following tectonic regions: the western slope of the *Ukrainian Crystalline Shield, the *Volhynia-Podilia Plate, and the Galician-Volhynian Depression. The Precambrian foundation of Podilia is exposed in the east by the Boh River, which has eroded the thin Tertiary deposits. To the southwest the shield dips (down to 6,000 m) below Paleozoic deposits of Silurian limestones and sandstones and Devonian red Terebovlia sandstones, marls, and dolomites, which constitute the bedrock of 'Paleozoic Podilia' between the Zolota Lypa and the Murafa. Jurassic deposits appear on the surface only in western Podilia along the Dniester. Thick deposits of Cretaceous chalk and marl (exposed in western Podilia and in deep ravines) and of middle Miocene sands, sandstones, marls, and limestones are found throughout Podilia. They are covered with layers of Quaternary clays, silts, and loess (up to 20 m thick).

Podilia is a plateau dissected by valleys that has an elevation of 300–400 m above sea level. The region may be differentiated into a number of landscapes according to geological formation, elevation, distance from the baseline of erosion (for most of Podilia, the Dniester), and tectonic movement. The highest part of Podilia is its northern rim, known as the *Holohory-Kremianets Ridge, approx 350–470 m above sea level (Kamula, 473 m). From there elevations drop sharply (150–200 m) to Little Polisia. The western part of Podilia, west of the upper reaches of the Zolota Lypa, the Koropets, and the mouth of the Strypa, is known as Opilia Upland. With elevations ranging from 350 to 470 m, Opilia has a foundation of soft gray Cretaceous marl, which was eroded vertically and laterally by rivers to produce a hilly landscape. East of Opilia, Podilia is divided from the northwest to the southeast by a low ridge, the *Tovtry, into western and eastern Podilia. Western Podilia consists of the Ternopil Plain in the north and the gullied fringe along the Dniester in the south. The Ternopil Plain is characterized by relatively flat interfluves and broad, often swampy river valleys (now containing many artificial ponds) in the soft chalk bedrock. Farther south, as the rivers cut into the Devonian sandstones and then into the Silurian shales, their profile becomes steeper, white water and waterfalls appear, and the valleys turn into deep ravines. The deepest and most spectacular ravine is that of the Dniester: it is carved approx 100–150 m below the adjacent uplands, sometimes in a straight line but more frequently in tightly twisting meanders. The upland between the ravines is a gently undulating plateau. Wherever chalk deposits come close to the surface along the Dniester, karst phenomena abound – sink holes, temporarily or permanently filled with water, and caves, notably at Bilche Zolote and Kryvche.

The mostly featureless plain of Podilia proper is interrupted by the Tovtry or Medobory. East of them lies eastern Podilia, of which the northern and southern parts are different. The northern part, which encompasses the headwaters of the tributaries of the Prypiat and the Dniester rivers as well as the drainage basin of the upper Boh River, resembles the Ternopil Plain. Reaching 360 m above sea level, the upland consists of broad intervalley crests rising slightly above broad, often swampy and ponded valleys. The highest elevations occur along the watersheds between the Prypiat drainage basin to the north and the Dniester and the Boh drainage basins to the south and between the Boh and the Dniester drainage basins. The southern fringe of eastern Podilia is a continuation of the Dniester region, a zone of ravines and gullies

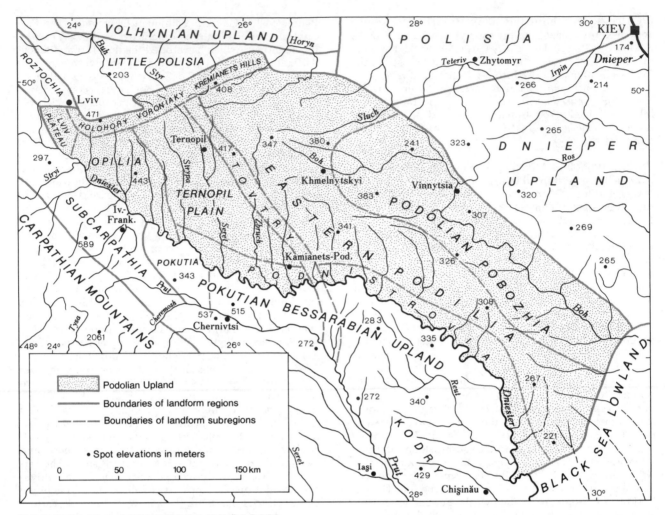

PODILIA'S LANDFORM REGIONS

flanking the northern bank of the Dniester River. Near Yampil the deep Dniester Gorge exposes the granite foundation of the Ukrainian Crystalline Shield.

The easternmost part of Podilia, often called the Podolian Pobozhia region, is a transition zone between Podilia and the Dnieper Upland, from a plateau to a granitic landscape. Elevations there reach 300 m above sea level, and the rivers cut deep ravines and valleys (500–570 m), especially to the south.

The climate of Podilia is temperate continental. The continentality increases from the northwest to the southeast, as is evident in the increasing annual temperature range, from 23°°C in Opilia to 25.5°C in the east. The number of days with temperatures above 15°C also increases, from 100 in the west to 120 in the southeast. The greatest precipitation occurs in Opilia and along the northern rim, where it exceeds 700 mm per year, and along the Tovtry, and the lowest, along the southern slopes, where it is approx 475 mm. Most of the precipitation occurs in the summer, often in the form of downpours. There is a marked difference in temperature between northern and southern Podilia: whereas in Ternopil the average January temperature is –5.5°C, in Zalishchyky (100 km south, on the Dniester), it is –4.7°C; and the corresponding average July temperatures are 18.3°C and 19.4°C. The growing season is

203 and 215 days. The warmest areas are the sheltered, south-facing slopes in the Dniester Gorge.

The river network of Podilia is fairly dense. The densest drainage network consists of the numerous south-flowing streams that empty into the Dniester River. The drainage system of the Boh River Basin and the network contributing to the Prypiat River are less dense. Only the Dniester River can be navigated by shallow-water rivercraft. The hydroelectric potential of the rivers has not been fully exploited. In the south the rivers provide some water for irrigation.

The most common soils in Podilia are (1) the moderately fertile gray and light gray podzolized soils on loess, mostly in the southeast, (2) the hilly, fertile degraded chernozems and dark gray podzolized soils on loess, mostly in the west, and (3) the highly fertile, low-humus typical chernozems on loess, mostly in the northeast. The soil types are frequently interspersed among one another, especially in the deeply sculpted and therefore highly varied Dniester region.

The vegetation of Podilia is influenced by its transitional location, between the Carpathian Mountains in the southwest, Polisia in the north, and the steppe in the south, and by its special morphology and soils. Most of Podilia belongs to the forest-steppe belt. Forests cover less than 10 percent of the region: substantial tracts are found only in the Tovtry, in the Dniester Gorge and its tributaries, and along the Boh River. The distribution limits of a number of eastern and western plant species run through Podilia. The eastern limits of the beech, yew, fir, and spruce lie in western Podilia. The most common trees found in central and eastern Podilia, therefore, are the oak and hornbeam, with admixtures of ash, maple, elm, and cherry. By human intervention mixed oak groves are being replaced by uniform woods of hornbeam. The underbrush is dominated by hazel, snowball tree, buckthorn, and red bilberry. Some of the eastern species, such as the common maple, do not penetrate farther west. A peculiar vegetation complex is found in the ravines of Podilia and on the rock outcrops and detritus. The meadow steppes of Podilia are fully cultivated. At the end of the 19th century, the last remnant of the steppe, between the Seret and the Strypa rivers, was known as the Pantalykha Steppe. It contained a great variety of herbs and broad-leaved grasses typical of the meadow-steppe, including the lungwort, nettle, and madder.

The transitional nature of Podilia also determines its fauna. The more densely forested western part is inhabited by the fox, the rabbit, two kinds of marten, the squirrel, and the now-rare wolf and boar. Valuable fur-bearing animals, such as the mink and otter, lived along the rivers. Among forest birds the goldeneye, and in the meadows the partridge and quail, were common. In western Podilia near Subcarpathia the typical animals were the ermine, weasel, wildcat, boar, and muskrat; among the ungulates, the chamois and deer; in wet areas, the salamander; and among the birds, the bullfinch. The peripheral location of western Podilia was suited to some West European fauna, including certain varieties of bat, vole, and insect. At the same time some steppe fauna, such as the mole-rat, polecat, field vole, gopher, steppe lark, black-headed yellowhammer, and, less frequently, the bustard, the steppe snake, the green lizard, the boa, and a variety of mollusks, insects (including beetles), and spiders, intruded into Podilia. In the southeast most of the steppe fauna was adapted to wide open spaces and a rather dry climate. As farming spread, so did various mice, field voles, and other small rodents, as well as various insect pests.

Prehistory. The oldest traces of human habitation in Ukraine are found in Podilia and the Crimea. The site at Luka-Vrublivetska belongs to the Acheulean culture (400,000–100,000 years ago) of the Lower Paleolithic Period. From that time Podilia was continuously inhabited, by Neanderthal humans of the Mousterian culture of the Lower Paleolithic Period, by Cro-Magnon humans of the Aurignacian, Solutrean, and Magdalenian cultures of the Upper Paleolithic Period, and finally by humans of the Campignian culture of the Mesolithic Period.

History. According to Herodotus the forest-steppe belt, including Podilia, was inhabited by Scythian farmers, whose way of life differed from that of Scythian nomads in the steppe. Beginning in the 2nd century BC the Scythian nomads were displaced by the Sarmatians, who often raided the Podolian settlements. At the end of the 1st millennium BC the warlike Venedi and the Celtic Bastarnae crossed Podilia, but neither left a significant cultural impact on its population, which continued to grow grain and sell its surplus to the Greek colonies on the Black Sea and the Roman merchants in Dacia. From the 1st to the 4th century the Cherniakhiv culture prevailed in the Ukrainian forest-steppe belt, including Podilia. The early Slavic tribes, known as the *Antes in Byzantine sources, were the most likely bearers of that culture. They survived the invasion of the Goths (4th century) and the Huns (5th century) and finally collapsed under the onslaught of the Avars (7th century).

According to the Primary Chronicle Podilia was settled by several Ukrainian tribes: the Ulychians (along the Boh River), the Tivertsians (along the Middle and Lower Dniester River), the White Croatians (in Subcarpathia, in the southwest), and the Dulibians (in the northwest along the Buh River). During the reign of Princes Oleh and Ihor Podilia became part of the Kievan state. At the same time the southern part of Podilia was seized by the Pechenegs, who forced the Ulychians and the Tivertsians to move north. As Kiev's power waned, it lost interest in eastern Podilia, and the region became a marchland of Galicia. The Tatar Burundai's campaign against Galicia (1259) sealed Podilia's fate for a century. Western Podilia along with Galicia remained under the Romanovych dynasty, and middle and eastern Podilia was administered directly by the Tatars of the Golden Horde.

Under Lithuanian-Polish rule. The political situation changed radically in the mid-14th century. The Lithuanian grand duke Algirdas defeated the Tatars at Syni Vody (1363), captured middle Podilia, and granted it as a fiefdom to his relatives, the Koriiatovych family. The new masters built fortified towns, including Smotrych, Bakota, and Kamianets-Podilskyi. After the death of the last Galician prince, Yurii II Boleslav, Casimir III annexed Galicia (1349) and western Podilia (1366), which was integrated with Poland in 1387. The conflict between Poland and the Lithuanian grand duke Vytautas over middle Podilia and its principal town, Kamianets-Podilskyi, led to the expulsion of F. Koriiatovych in 1393. Vytautas kept eastern Podilia (the Bratslav and Vinnytsia regions) and ceded middle Podilia to Jagiełło of Poland (1395) but later reclaimed it (1411). After the duke's death the pro-Polish gentry of middle Podilia declared it Polish and turned it into *Podilia voivodeship. Western Podilia was incorporated into *Rus' voivodeship.

Polonization in Podilia was promoted not only by the Polish administration but also by the Roman Catholic church, which established a diocese in Kamianets-Podilskyi. Ukrainians became a minority among the nobility, and eventually only the petty gentry, who served in the borderland forts, remained Ukrainian. Meanwhile the population of Podilia grew, because the fertile soil and the relatively undemanding corvée attracted peasants. The towns attracted mainly Poles and Jews as well as some Germans and Armenians.

After 1430 only eastern Podilia, with the towns of Bratslav and Vinnytsia, remained under Lithuania. The Poles made every effort to annex that part and succeeded in doing so in the Union of Lublin (1569). From then, Polish magnates swarmed into eastern Podilia, where they set up enormous estates and seized key administrative positions. Eastern Podilia became *Bratslav voivodeship.

Crimean Tatar raids, which began in the second half of the 15th century, crippled Podilia's developing economy. The Crimean Horde regarded Podilia not only as an object of prey but also as a gateway, via the Kuchmanskyi Route and the Black Route, to the more populous lands of Vol-

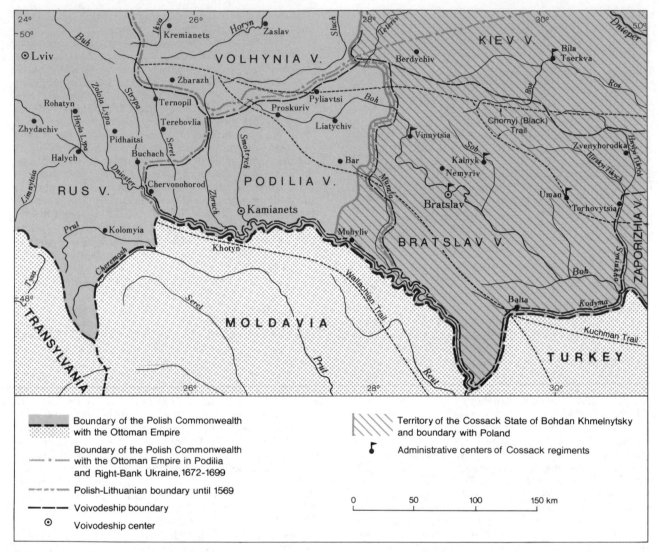

PODILIA, 16TH AND 17TH CENTURIES

hynia, Galicia, Kholm, and Poland proper. At the beginning of the 16th century southeastern Podilia became deserted, and the advances in colonization made during the 15th century were lost. Colonization resumed in the mid-16th century. As the demand for grain rose in Western Europe, the large landowners in Podilia developed commercial farming and raised the corvée obligations of the peasants. The *Cossacks and the alienated Ukrainian burghers came to the defense of the peasantry. The Cossack state set up by B. Khmelnytsky encompassed only a part of Podilia; namely, Bratslav and Kalnyk regiments. When Poland and Muscovy divided Ukraine into the Right-Bank and Left-Bank hetmanates in 1667, Podilia became part of Right-Bank Ukraine. Hetman P. Doroshenko's attempt to reunify Left-Bank and Right-Bank Ukraine with Turkey's help ended with Turkey's annexation of Podilia voivodeship (1672). Although Doroshenko retained control of the Bratslav region, continuous warfare, Tatar raids, and Turkish oppression caused mass migration into Left-Bank Ukraine. In 1699 Podilia was taken by Poland. In 1712, after an unsuccessful rebellion, the Cos-

sack regiments were disbanded. In the first half of the 18th century Podilia was colonized intensively. Peasants, mostly from Rus' voivodeship and Volhynia but also from Left-Bank Ukraine, Moldavia, and Poland proper, poured into the depopulated territory. By the mid-18th century Podilia voivodeship had the highest population density in the Polish Commonwealth. Although Tatar raids had ceased, there was no lasting peace in the region. National and religious oppression along with increasing corvée provoked the so-called *haidamaka uprisings against the Polish nobility. Centered in the southern part of the Kiev region and the southeastern part of the Bratslav region, theyencompassed all of eastern Podilia.

The modern period. With the First Partition of Poland (1772) western Podilia, east to the Zbruch River, was annexed by Austria, and with the Second Partition (1793) eastern Podilia was transferred to Russia. A portion of Austrian-ruled Podilia (Ternopil and Zalishchyky counties) was held briefly (1809–15) by Russia. After the division each part of Podilia developed differently. In eastern Podilia the intensification of serfdom gave rise to peasant

PODILIA, 1861–1917

discontent and U. *Karmaliuk's revolts. Kamianets-Podilskyi became the administrative center of *Podilia gubernia and *Podilia eparchy. The Ukrainian national and cultural movement developed slowly in Podilia, mainly at the end of the 19th century. Its centers were Kamianets-Podilskyi and Vinnytsia. Social and economic progress in the gubernia was also slow: a zemstvo was set up only in 1911

In western Podilia, as in all Galicia, the Polish population continued to increase and to dominate the administration of the land. Nevertheless western Podilia, along with the rest of Galicia and Bukovyna, became the base of the modern Ukrainian national and political movement. Because of their proximity to Lviv the towns of western Podilia (Ternopil, Berezhany, Buchach, and Chortkiv) did not develop into great cultural and political centers.

During the struggle for Ukrainian independence (1917–20) Podilia was a battleground for the Ukrainian, Polish, Russian, and Bolshevik armies. In the interwar period western Podilia was ruled by Poland and was known as Ternopil voivodeship. Eastern Podilia, meanwhile, was part of the Ukrainian SSR. After the Second World War all Podilia became part of the Ukrainian SSR. It consisted of three oblasts: Ternopil, Khmelnytskyi (formerly Proskuriv), and Vinnytsia. It remains one of the most agricultural and least industrialized regions of Ukraine.

Population. Since the middle of the 18th century Podilia, together with Pokutia and Subcarpathia, has been the most densely populated part of Ukraine. Today those regions as well as lowland Transcarpathia have the highest rural population densities. In 1860 western Podilia was settled more densely (63 persons/sq km) than eastern Podilia (43 persons/sq km), but eventually the gap narrowed (in 1897 the figures were 96 and 75, and in 1932, 99 and 98). With a low level of urbanization (approx 10 percent) Podilia, especially its western part, was one of the most land-hungry regions of Ukraine. The peasants of western Podilia responded to the problem of employment with mass emigration (over 200,000 people between 1890 and 1913) to the New World and a reduced rate of natural increase. Emigration from eastern Podilia was smaller, partly because there was local employment in the sugar industry. Sizable population losses occurred in eastern Podilia during collectivization and in all of Podilia during the Second World War (1940–6). By 1959 the population of Podilia was still 14.5 percent smaller than in 1926. The process of urbanization was slower there than anywhere else in Ukraine. The changes in the composition and density of the population in the three Podilia oblasts (Ternopil, Khmelnytskyi, and Vinnytsia) are given in table 1. Podilia's migration balance has continued to be negative. In the six years from 1963 to 1968 the region's natural in-

Traditional dress of Podilia

crease was 210,000, and its net population increase only 20,000. Despite a positive natural increase the population of Podilia has declined since 1970. Population distribution, expressed as rural population density, does not vary greatly from one raion to another. Rural population densities range from 50 to 80 persons per sq km but usually lie between 60 and 70.

The settlements in Podilia are concentrated along rivers in the valleys or wide canyons, and the interfluves of the plateau are occupied by cropland. Only where the ravines are too narrow to accommodate them are villages built along the rim of the plateau.

Before industries developed, the towns of Podilia were administrative and trading centers. The smaller towns en-

TABLE 1
Population changes in Podilia, 1926–89

Year	Total population (1,000s)	Density/ sq km	Urban population (1,000s)	% of total	Rural population (1,000s)	Density/ sq km
1926	5,690	93.4	690	12.1	5,000	82.1
1959	4,840	79.5	850	17.6	3,990	65.5
1970	4,900	80.5	1,240	25.3	3,660	60.1
1989	4,628	76.0	2,057	44.4	2,571	42.2

gaged in local trade and services for farming. Now all the more important towns of Podilia have industries, but in comparison to other parts of Ukraine they are relatively small. In 1989 only four cities had over 100,000 residents: Vinnytsia (374,000), Khmelnytskyi (237,000), Ternopil (205,000), and Kamianets-Podilskyi (102,000). In Opilia, the westernmost part of Podilia, the smaller towns (1980 population estimates) include Berezhany (13,500), Bibrka (3,100), Khodoriv (10,000), Monastyryska (5,100), Peremyshliany (4,100), Pidhaitsi (3,300), and Rohatyn (5,500). The southwestern gullied part includes the towns of Borshchiv (8,600), Buchach (11,400), Chortkiv (20,000), Kopychyntsi (7,500), Terebovlia (10,700), and Zalishchyky (8,400), and the flat northern part of western Podilia includes Ternopil, Zalistsi (2,200), Zbarazh (8,400), and Zboriv (3,900). On the northwestern rim are Brody (13,500), Kremianets (20,500), and Zolochiv (13,100). The more important economic and cultural centers are Ternopil, Berezhany, Buchach, Chortkiv, and Kremianets. In eastern Podilia, along the Dniester, the main center is Kamianets-Podilskyi; it is followed by Mohyliv-Podilskyi (26,000), Yampil (8,000), and Rybnytsia (32,300, in Moldova). The northern plain of eastern Podilia is dominated by Khmelnytskyi and, to a lesser extent, by Starokostiantyniv (22,000). On the northern border with Volhynia are Iziaslav (14,700), the rail hub Shepetivka (39,100), and Polonne (22,400). Along the Boh River Vinnytsia predominates among the small towns, such as Liatychiv (or Letychiv, 9,100), Lityn (5,300), Tulchyn (14,300), Bratslav (4,400), Bar (13,500), Khmilnyk (18,500), Derazhnia (7,900), Medzhybizh (2,800), the important railway hub Zhmerynka (36,200), and a smaller hub, Vapniarka (7,500). To the southeast are located Bershad (11,400), Balta (20,000, although in the mid-19th century it was, after Kamianets-Podilskyi, the second-largest town in Podilia), Kotovske (34,300), and Ananiv (18,900).

In past centuries there was a steady flow of Poles (particularly in the first half of the 18th century) and Jews into Podilia. The Jews constituted a majority in most of the towns. The Poles were concentrated in the north, on both sides of the Zbruch River. Some of the Poles living among the Ukrainians became linguistically assimilated and retained only their Roman Catholic faith.

During the 19th and 20th centuries interethnic relations evolved very differently in western (under Austria and Poland) and eastern Podilia (under Russia and in the Ukrainian SSR). In the eastern region the Polish and Roman Catholic element was deprived of government support and reinforcements from the west, and began to succumb to Ukrainization and, in the cities, to a degree of Russification. Most Roman Catholics were Ukrainian-speaking (in 1926, 50 percent; by 1959, up to 85 percent). The proportion of Jews in the population grew until the end of the 19th century and then began to decline. Russians were a small minority (7 percent in towns and cities, 1 percent in the villages). In southern Podilia along the Dniester (within today's Moldova) some 50,000 Moldavians were concentrated in one area. As a result of the Second World War the Jewish population fell drastically, the Polish element declined, and the Russian element increased substantially (see table 2).

In western Podilia for two centuries, particularly after the mid-19th century, the proportion of Poles increased at the expense of Ukrainians. There was a continuous flow of

TABLE 2
Ethnic composition of Khmelnytskyi and Vinnytsia
oblasts, 1897–1989 (percentages)

Nationality	1897	1926	1959	1979	1989
Ukrainian	75.3	85.1	91.3	91.4	92.4
Jewish	12.3	7.8	1.8	1.3	1.0
Polish*	8.8	3.7	2.4	1.5	1.1
Russian	2.3	1.7	4.4	5.2	4.9
Other	1.3	1.7	0.1	0.6	0.6

*Including Ukrainian-speaking Roman Catholics

Poles from the western (Polish) part of Galicia to the towns dominated by a Polish administration and to farmlands sold off by Polish landowners. Emigration to the New World, which drew proportionally more Ukrainians than Poles, and the Polonization of Ukrainians through conversion from the Uniate (Greek Catholic) faith to Roman Catholicism were less significant. The changes in the composition of the population according to religion are shown in table 3. The greatest loss of Ukrainians occurred in a zone extending from Lviv to the Zbruch River, where the Poles and the Ukrainian-speaking Roman Catholics represented about one-third of the population. Most of the residents in the towns of western Podilia were Jewish; in number they were followed by Poles or Ukrainians. By contrast, in eastern Podilia one-half of the urban population was Ukrainian, over one-third was Jewish, and an insignificant proportion was Polish. As a result of the Second World War the ethnic composition of western Podilia changed dramatically, and today it resembles that of eastern Podilia. In Ternopil oblast the ethnic composition for 1959 and 1979 indicates the persistent growth of the Ukrainian element: Ukrainians made up 90.2 and 96.6 percent, Russians, 2.5 and 2.2 percent, Poles, 2.2 and 0.9 percent, and Jews and others, 5.1 and 0.3 percent.

TABLE 3
Religious affiliation in western Podilia, 1857–1931 (percentages)

Religion	1857	1880	1900	1910	1921	1931
Uniate	63.0	62.0	61.0	60.3	59.2	54.9
Roman Catholic	25.4	24.1	26.6	28.4	32.2	37.2
Jewish	10.9	13.3	11.9	11.2	8.3	7.7
Other	0.7	0.6	0.5	0.1	0.3	0.2

Economy. Agriculture has always been the foundation of the Podilian economy. In the 1920s nearly 80 percent of the population was employed in farming and less than 10 percent worked in the trades and industry. Until the mid-1930s only the food industry, consisting of the sugar industry and liquor distilling, was developed. The sugar industry was limited to eastern Podilia, because Czech competition and Polish competition after the war blocked its growth in western Podilia. During the Soviet period industrializaion was speeded up, but Podilia remains one of the least industrialized regions in Ukraine.

Agriculture. Most of the land in Podilia is tilled (72 percent). The rest is devoted to hayfields, meadows and pastures (7 percent), orchards and berry plantings (3 percent), and forests (nearly 15 percent). The sown area in the three

oblasts of Podilia in 1987 totaled 4,187,000 ha, of which 2,014,000 ha (48.1 percent) were devoted to grain. As in the rest of Ukraine the share of the grain area has declined, from about 75 percent in the 1920s, and the share of land given to industrial crops (especially in Galician Podilia) and fodder crops has increased. Sugar beet is Podilia's predominant industrial crop; it occupies 489,000 ha (88 percent of all industrial-crop land, or 12 percent of all crop land) and represents 23 percent of the sugar-beet area in Ukraine. The sugar-beet area has increased by almost two and a half times since 1940 (especially in western Podilia). Other industrial crops include sunflower (50,000 ha, mostly in Vinnytsia oblast), rape, tobacco, hemp, aromatic oil seeds, and medicinal herbs. The area of feed crops has increased by 2.45 times since 1940; it amounted to some 1,305,000 ha, or 31.2 percent of the sown area, in 1987. Besides perennial and annual grasses, corn and other feed crops are raised. The sown area in potatoes and vegetables has declined from 424,000 ha in 1940 to 314,000 ha (7.5 percent of the sown area), a reflection of the falling demand for potatoes. After Southern Ukraine Podilia is the second most important fruit-farming region in Ukraine. Orchards in Podilia occupy over 200,00 ha, and vineyards, over 5,000 ha. The most common fruit trees are apple, plum, pear, cherry, morello cherry, apricot, peach, and walnut.

In animal husbandry the leading branches are dairy and beef farming and hog raising (see table 4).

TABLE 4
Livestock and livestock products in Podilia in 1975

		Land productivity	
		Per 100 ha of agricultural land	% of Ukraine's
Livestock (head)			
Cattle	3,157,000	67.5	12.1
of which cows	1,207,000	25.8	12.2
Hogs	2,950,000	63.0	12.8
Sheep and goats	713,000	15.2	6.7
Products (t)			
Meat and fat	471,000	10.10	12.1
Pork only	235,000	5.00	13.4
Milk	2,733,000	58.40	11.6
Wool	1,800	0.04	5.7

Podilia produces commercial surpluses of sugar beets, which are processed locally, fruits, and animal products. There is little regional specialization in agriculture, but the region south of Ternopil is known for its tobacco, and the regions along the Dniester in eastern Podilia, to the south of Khmelnytskyi and to the southwest of Vinnytsia, are known for their fruits and vegetables.

Industry. Podilia lags considerably behind other parts of Ukraine in industrial development. Its main industry is food processing, which accounts for about 60 percent of the value of its industrial output; food processing is followed by machine building and metalworking (15 percent), light industry (13 percent), and the building-materials industry (6 percent). The dominant branch of the food industry in Podilia is sugar refining (39 enterprises in Vinnytsia oblast alone); in 1987 that branch produced some 2.1 million t, or 28 percent of Ukraine's output of sugar. Liquor distilling is another important branch. Its raw materials are molasses (a by-product of the sugar industry), potatoes, and grain. Over 30 enterprises in the region produce alcohol. Their subsidiary operations include the production of feed yeast and vitamins. The largest distilleries are located in Bar and Kalynivka, in Vinnytsia oblast. The meat-processing industry is highly developed. Large meat packing plants are located in the three oblast centers. The dairy industry, which produces 42,000 t of butter per year (14 percent of the republic's total), is widely distributed. Its largest plant is in Horodok. The largest urban (fluid milk) dairies are located in the oblast centers. Podilia contributes about 12 percent of the republic's canned fruits and vegetables. Oil pressing, flour milling, baking, confectionery manufacturing, brewing, and tobacco processing are mostly of regional or local significance.

The machine-building and metalworking industries arose in Podilia mostly in the 1950s and 1960s, along with related electrotechnical and chemical industries, and continue to grow in importance. Their main products are electrotechnical equipment, tractor assemblies and bearings, equipment for sugar refineries, transformer substation equipment, foundry equipment, and sheet-metal presses, tractor parts, electrical equipment, and agricultural machinery. The Vinnytsia Chemical Plant, which produces granulated superphosphate with manganese, was one of the largest fertilizer plants in the Soviet Union. Podilia's light industry manufactures textiles, garments, and footwear. Its textile plants produce nearly 12 percent of the cotton cloth and 7 percent of the woolen cloth manufactured in Ukraine.

The building-materials industry includes the quarrying and finishing of granite and marble blocks, the mining and processing of limestone and chalk, brick-making, and tile manufacturing. Wood, mostly from Polisia, is used to make cellulose and paper in Poninka and paper in Slavuta, Polonne, and Rososha. Altogether the industry contributes nearly 23 percent of Ukraine's paper production.

The fuel and power industries of Podilia depend on coal, petroleum products, and natural gas brought in from the Donbas, Subcarpathia, and Shebelynka respectively. Electricity is generated principally at small thermal stations in Vinnytsia, Mohyliv-Podilskyi, Khmelnytskyi, Kamianets-Podilskyi, Shepetivka, Ternopil, and Kremianets, but their output has not met the needs of the region. It is supplemented by the new Ladyzhyn thermal-electric station on the Boh River, the Dniester Hydroelectric Station, and the Khmelnytskyi Nuclear Power Station. Most of the power from Ladyzhyn and the other new generating stations is slated for export to Hungary, Rumania, and Bulgaria.

Transport. Railways, which carry up to nine-tenths of the freight, are Podilia's most important means of transportation. Podilia has 2,542 km of track, about 11.5 percent of the republic's network, and a density of 42 km per 1,000 sq km, or 112 percent of the mean density of Ukraine. A three-pronged trunk line forms the skeleton of the railway system: it joins Lviv with Odessa through Ternopil and Khmelnytskyi and branches off at Zhmerynka through Vinnytsia to Kiev. The other major lines that pass through Podilia and are connected to the trunk are: Zhmerynka–Mohyliv–Podilskyi–Chernivtsi, Koziatyn–Shepetivka–Rivne, Shepetivka–Ternopil–Chortkiv–Chernivtsi, and Korosten–Shepetivka–Khmelnytskyi–Kamianets-Podilskyi. The most important railroad junctions are Zhmerynka, Koziatyn, Shepetivka, and Vapniarka as well as the major cities of Ternopil, Khmelnytskyi, and Vinnytsia. Highways are of less importance, although they are necessary for truck transport, which serves agriculture and the food-processing industries. Podilia has 22,800 km of roads, of which 16,300 km are hard surface. Those figures represent 14 percent and 12 percent of the republic's road networks respectively. The principal highway from Kiev and Zhytomyr to Chernivtsi crosses Podilia running through Vinnytsia, Khmelnytskyi, and Kamianets-Podilskyi. Several other major highways cross Podilia from west to east – Kremianets–Koziatyn, Lviv–Ternopil–Khmelnytskyi–Vinnytsia–Uman, Ivano-Frankivske–Buchach–Chortkiv–Dunaivtsi–Mohyliv-Podilskyi – and from north to south – Lutske–Kremianets–Ternopil–Chortkiv–Zalishchyky–Chernivtsi and Novohrad-Volynskyi–Shepetivka–Khmelnytskyi.

Three major gas trunk lines cross Podilia from east to west. The Dashava–Kiev–Moscow line supplies natural gas to Khmelnytskyi, Vinnytsia, and other towns in Podilia. The newer pipelines, such as the Soiuz line (1978), from the southern Urals to Czechoslovakia, and the Urengoi–Czechoslovakia line (1983–4), are used exclusively for exporting gas. (See *Pipeline transportation.)

Transport on the Boh River is negligible, and on the Dniester River, limited. Recent completion of the Dniester Hydroelectric Complex has extended navigation on the Dniester.

BIBLIOGRAPHY

Marczyński, W. *Statystyczne, topograficzne i historyczne opisanie gubernii Podolskiej*, 4 vols (Vilnius 1820–2)

Molchanovskii, N. *Ocherk izvestii o Podols'koi zemle do 1434 goda* (Kiev 1885)

Batiushkov, P. *Podoliia: Istoricheskoe opisanie* (St Petersburg 1891)

Janusz, B. *Zabytki przedhistoryczne Podola galicyjskiego* (Lviv 1918)

Białkowski, L. *Podole w XVI wieku* (Warsaw 1920)

Sitsins'kyi, Ie. *Narysy z istoriï Podillia*, 1 (Vinnytsia 1927)

Chyzhov, M. *Ukraïns'kyi lisostep* (Kiev 1961)

Serczyk, W. *Gospodarstwo magnackie w wojewodstwie podolskim w drugiej polowie XVIII wieku* (Wrocław 1965)

Shliakhamy zolotoho Podillia, 3 vols (Philadelphia 1960, 1970, 1983)

V. Kubijovyč, I. Stebelsky, M. Zhdan

Podilia Church Historical-Archeological Society (Podilske tserkovne istorychno-arkheolohichne tovarystvo). A scholarly society established in 1903 in Kamianets-Podilskyi. Its forerunner, the Podilia Eparchial Historical-Statistical Committee (est 1865), published several volumes of *Trudy* (12 vols, 1876–1916) containing valuable historical, statistical, geographic, and ethnographic studies of Podilia and Podilia eparchy's parishes and monasteries. Under its permanent president, Rev Yu. Sitsinsky, the society ran the Kamianets-Podilskyi Church Museum of Antiquities (now the Kamianets-Podilskyi Historical Museum and Preserve). In 1919 it was amalgamated with the Podilia Society. The society was forced to dissolve in late 1920. It was replaced by the Kamianets-Podilskyi Committee for the Protection of Ancient, Artistic, and Natural Monuments, under the direction of P. Klymenko, and, in 1925, by the VUAN-affiliated Kamianets-Podilskyi Scientific Society, headed by V. Chuhai, O. Polonsky, Sitsinsky, and V. Zborovets. The latter society was abolished in the early 1930s, and many of its 70 members suffered Stalinist repression.

Podilia eparchy. An Orthodox eparchy comprising the territory of Podilia gubernia, with its see in Kamianets-Podilskyi. It was established in 1795, after the partitions of Poland, out of territory that had formerly belonged to the eparchy of Kiev and then Halych. Initially the see was in Bratslav, so afterward the eparchy was often referred to as Podilia-Bratslav eparchy. At the turn of the 20th century the eparchy had almost 1,700 parishes and 5 men's and 5 women's monasteries. In 1917, in addition to the titular bishop, the eparchy had two vicar bishops (in Vinnytsia and Balta). The Podilia Church Historical-Archeological Society published several volumes of materials on the history of the eparchy, and Yu. Sitsinsky published several histories and descriptions of the eparchy in the 19th and early 20th centuries. The eparchial organ, *Podol'skie eparkhial'nye vedomosti*, appeared from 1863 to 1917.

In the 1920s the *Ukrainian Autocephalous Orthodox church established a church okruha in Podilia, which, under Bishop I. *Teodorovych, was for some time the largest eparchy in the church. Part of the Podilia eparchy was included in the Khmelnytskyi eparchy created by the Russian Orthodox church after 1945.

Podilia gubernia. An administrative-territorial unit created in Russian-ruled Right-Bank Ukraine in 1797 out of 7 counties of Podilia vicegerency, 9 counties of Bratslav vicegerency, and 4 counties (3 in part) of Voznesenske vicegerency. Its territory (42,017 sq km) was subdivided into 12 counties: Balta, Bratslav, Haisyn, Kamianets-Podilskyi, Letychiv, Lityn, Mohyliv-Podilskyi, Olhopil, Proskuriv, Vinnytsia, Nova Ushytsia, and Yampil. The capital was Kamianets-Podilskyi. In 1811 the gubernia had 1,297,800 inhabitants. In 1897 it had 3,018,300, of whom only 7.5 percent were urban. Ukrainians constituted 80.2 percent of the total population but only 1 percent of the urban population. The major ethnic minorities were Jews (12.2 percent), Russians (3.3), Poles (2.3), and Rumanians (0.9). The gubernia was an economically backward, predominantly agricultural region. Its main industry was sugar refining. In 1914 only 8.8 percent of the population was urban. The gubernia was devastated during the First World War and Ukrainian-Soviet War and suffered many human losses. In 1923, 11.5 percent of its 3,457,000 inhabitants were urban; 31 percent of the urban population was Ukrainian, 55 percent was Jewish, and 9 percent was Russian. That year the counties were replaced by Haisyn, Kamianets-Podilskyi, Mohyliv-Podilskyi, Proskuriv, Tulchyn, and Vinnytsia okruhas, and in 1925 the gubernia was abolished.

Podilia regiment. See Mohyliv-Podilskyi regiment.

Podilia vicegerency. An administrative territory in Right-Bank Ukraine, set up in 1783 after the partition of Poland. It consisted of the former Podilia voivodeship, and its administrative center was Mohyliv-Podilskyi. In 1797 the vicegerency was abolished, and its territory was divided between Podilia and Volhynia gubernias.

Podilia voivodeship. An administrative territory formed under Polish rule in the mid-15th century. It incorporated most of western Podilia and consisted of Kamianets, Letychiv, and Chervonohorod counties. Its administrative center was Kamianets-Podilskyi. The Poles were expelled from the territory for a brief period during the Cossack-Polish War (1648–57) and the Turkish occupation (1672–99). During the partitions of Poland the voivodeship was divided between Austria, which annexed Chervonohorod county in 1772, and Russia, which took the rest of the territory in 1793.

Podilian dialects. The eastern group of the *southwestern dialects, bordering on the *South Volhynian dialects to the north, the *steppe dialects to the east, the *Dniester dialects to the west, and the *Bukovyna-Pokutia dialects to the southwest. They are used on the territories of what are today the southern parts of Khmelnytskyi and Vinnytsia oblasts, the northern part of Odessa oblast, the northwestern part of Mykolaiv oblast, and the western part of Kirovohrad oblast. The eastern Podilian dialects share common traits with the South Volhynian dialects, while the western dialects are most akin to the Dniester dialects, particularly in morphology.

In the Podilian dialects the pronunciation of consonants before *i* (from *ō*) is hard (except in the east where, eg, Standard Ukrainian [SU] *stil* 'table' is pronounced *s't'il/s'c'il*; and in sing fem adjectives in the dat and loc cases and in pl adjectives in the nom case, eg, *čórn'i koróvi, čórn'i kón'i* [SU *čórnij koróvi, čórni kóni*] 'to/on the black cow, black horses'). The pronunciation of unstressed *o, e, u* is raised to *u, y, i*, particularly before a syllable with (unstressed) *u, i* (eg, *bujités'a, pišít, vis'íl'a* [SU *bojítsja, pyšít', vesíllja*] 'you are afraid [pl], write [pl imperative], wedding'). Some typical pronunciations are *mn'áso* (SU *m'jáso*) 'meat', *rýbl'ačyi* (SU *rýbjačyj*) 'fishy', *rímnyj* (SU *rívnyj*) 'straight', *pýsan'a* (SU *pysánnja*) 'writing', *fist* (SU *xvist*) 'tail', *lóška* (SU *lóžka*) 'spoon', *zorá* (SU *zorjá*) 'star'. A prothetic *h-* is used, eg, *hyndýk* (SU *indýk*) 'turkey' (except in the west, where a prothetic *v-* is used instead, eg, *vóstryj* [SU *hóstryj*] 'sharp', and partly in the east, where SU *ískra* 'spark' is pronounced *ýskra*). There are Western Ukrainian–type pronunciations and stress; eg, *xustyný* (SU *xustýny*) 'kerchiefs', *jamý* (SU *jámy*) 'pits', *čýtan'a* (SU *čytánnja*) 'reading', *xódžu/xód'u* (SU *xodžú*) 'I go', *byrém* (SU *beremó*) 'we take', *byréty* (SU *bereté*) 'you take', *pjéty* (SU *p'jeté*) 'you drink'. In nouns there is a definite influence of the hard nominal declension on the soft; eg, *kon'óvi* (SU *konévi*) 'horse' dative, *nožóm* (SU *nožém*) 'with a knife', *pál'c'om* (SU *pál'cem*) 'with a finger', *pól'om* (SU *pólem*) 'field' instrumental, *tyl'óm* (SU *teljám*) 'cal' instrumental, *na čórnim/-omu kon'óvi/zyml'í* (SU *na čórnomu koní/zemlí*) 'on the black horse/earth', *c'óju zyml'óju* (SU *cijéju zemléju*) 'with this black earth', *móju t'ín'uju* (SU *mojéju tínnju*) 'with my shadow', *píčuju* (SU *píččju*) 'with the stove', *d'ityj* (SU *ditéj*) 'of the children'. In the Vinnytsia region forms such as *na pál'c'ox, v dýn'ox* (SU *na pál'cjax, v dýnjax*) 'on the fingers, in the melons' are used, and the dual form of feminine and neuter nouns, eg, *dvi s'c'in'í, jábluc'i* (SU *stíny, jábluka*) 'two walls, two apples', has been preserved. Adjectives are only of the hard type (eg, *sýnyj* [SU *sýnij*] 'blue'), except in the east, where the soft type prevails in adjectives in which the stress is on the stem (eg, *čórn'ij, sývij, l'úc'k'ij* [SU *čórnyj, sývyj, ljúds'kyj*] 'black, gray, human'), and where the suffix forming the comparative degree of adjectives is *-iščyj* (SU *-išyj*), eg, *bil'íščyj* 'whiter'. In pronoun declension there are forms such as *mohó, mój i, móju* (SU *móho, mojéji, mojéju*) 'of my (masc, neut), of my (fem), with my (fem)', *jakýs'* (SU *jakýjs'*) 'some sort of' (masc), *totá, toté* (SU *ta/te*) 'that' (fem, neut), *sys'á, sysé* (SU *cja, ce*) 'this' (fem, neut).

Some typical verbal forms are *pyktý* (SU *pektý*) 'to bake', *falýtys'a* or (in the east) *falýtys'* (SU *xvalýtysja*) 'to boast, be proud of', *xódžu* or (in the east and southeast) *xód'u, xódyt/ xódy, xód'at* (SU *xodžú, xódyt', xódjat'*) 'I walk, he walks, they walk', *nysém* (SU *nesemó*) 'we carry', *xod'ím* (SU *xodí-m[o]*) 'let's go', *xodít* (SU *xodít'*) 'you go' (imp), *robýüjem, robýüjes', robýlys'mo, robýlys'te* (SU *ja robýv, ty robýv, my robýly, vy robýly*) 'I made, you (sing) made, we made, you (pl) made', *búdu robýü* (SU *búdu robýty*) 'I will make', *ja s'a zabúü* (SU *ja zabúvsja*) 'I forgot', gerunds such as *xódžyn'a* (SU *xódžennja*) 'walking', and participles such as *zróbl'anyj* (SU *zróblenyj*) 'made' and (in the east) *kúpynyj, výkosynyj* (SU *kúplenyj, výkošenyj*) 'bought, mown'.

In the southwest along the Dniester, the influence of the Pokutia and Dniester dialects is evident in pronoun forms, eg, *t'i/t'a* (SU *tebé*) 'you' accusative, and in the partial retention of soft-type endings in nouns; eg, *xlópec, xlópcevy/xlópcovy, xlópca* (SU *xlópec', xlópcevi, xlópcja*) 'boy' nominative, dative, accusative, *na zymlý/k'inc'í/pól'u* (SU *na zemlí/kincí/póli*) 'on the land/end/field', *v hrúdex* (SU *v hrúdjax*) 'in the chest', *toü doróhoü* (SU *tóju doróhoju*) 'that road' instrumental (in the northwest, *tom doróhom/zeml'óm/kós't'om* [SU *tóju doróhoju/zemléju/kístju*] 'that road/land/bone' instr).

Elements of the Podilian dialects, particularly lexical ones, can be found in the works of writers such as A. Svydnytsky, S. Rudansky, M. Kotsiubynsky, H. Zhurba, M. Stelmakh, and Ye. Hutsalo. Articles on the dialects have been written by H. Holoskevych, V. Ostrokovsky, A. Sorochan, V. Zborovets, B. Yatsymyrsky, Ye. Rudnytsky, M. Khrashchevsky, Ye. Hrytsak, O. Melnychuk, I. Hrytsiutenko, A. Derdiuk, T. Babina, A. Ocheretny, H. Pelykh, L. Tereshko, and K. Batsenko.

O. Horbach

Podil's'ka volia (Podilian Freedom). A weekly and later semiweekly newspaper published in Vinnytsia from July 1917 to 1918. It was nonpartisan but supported the Central Rada. The editor was D. Markovych.

Podil's'ke slovo (Podilian Word). A weekly and later semimonthly newspaper published from January 1909 to 1912 in Ternopil. It was edited by P. Chubaty and then Y. Kovalsky, who was also the publisher.

Podil's'kyi holos (Podilian Voice). A newspaper published semimonthly, then weekly, and from 1906 monthly in Ternopil from January 1904 to 1908. The organ of the Ternopil People's Organization, it was edited and published by S. Holubovych and O. Postryhach.

Podil's'kyi holos (Podilian Voice). A semimonthly newspaper published in Ternopil in 1928–30 by S. Baran. Edited by V. Bachynsky, it printed articles on politics, popular enlightenment, and farming and supported the Ukrainian National Democratic Alliance. In 1930 it had a pressrun of 1,200.

Podkarpatska Rus'. See *Pidkarpats'ka Rus'.*

Podlachia (Ukrainian: Pidliashshia; Polish: Podlasie). A historical-geographical region along the middle stretch of the Buh (Bug) River between the Kholm region in the south and the Narva River (the Belarus border) in the north and between Mazovia in the west and Volhynia and Polisia in the east. A part of the region consists of the Podlachian Lowland.

The Ukrainian name is derived from the word *liakh* 'Pole' and means 'near Poland,' whereas the Polish name is derived from *las* 'forest,' and means 'near the forest.' The name was first used in 1520 to designate Podlachia voivodeship, which extended at that time as far north as the sources of the Borba River. In the 19th century the name was applied generally to the part south of the Buh River and within the Kingdom of Poland. The northern part of Podlachia, approx 2,700 sq km, constituted Bielsk county in Hrodna gubernia. Southern Podlachia was often assigned to the Kholm region, because it lay within Kholm eparchy and (from 1912) within Kholm gubernia. The region had an area of approx 5,350 sq km and included Biała Podlaska, Volodava, and Kostiantyniv counties.

Because of its peripheral location Podlachia did not develop strong ties with other parts of Ukraine or a sharp sense of national identity. In the northern part the national distinctions between Ukrainians and Belarusians did not crystallize. Podlachia's proximity to the Polish heartland facilitated Polish expansion into the region. Flanked by Prussia on one side and the marshlands of Polisia on the other, Podlachia served as a corridor between Poland and Lithuania (the Warsaw–Vilnius route), Belarus, and Russia.

Physical geography. The geological foundation of the region consists of white chalk, which comes to the surface only near Melnyk and Volodava, in the Buh River Valley. The chalk is overlain with thick layers of glacial and alluvial deposits and here and there with thin Paleogene deposits. The landscape is typically a uniform plain. The Bielsk, Dorohychyn, and Siedlce-Janów uplands, which reach an elevation of 200 m, are separated by broad river valleys formed by meltwaters and covered with thick alluvial deposits. The rivers are sluggish and lined with marshes. The highest parts of the region consist of terminal moraines: a northern belt runs from Siedlce through Melnyk to Vysoke, and a southern belt, from Lubartów to Volodava. Southeastern Podlachia, west of Volodava, with its marshes, peat bogs, sandy soils, and numerous small lakes, resembles Polisia in landscape and is known as Volodava Polisia. The most varied topography in all Podlachia is found in the Buh Valley, which cuts deeply (up to 80 m) into the elevated plains. Podlachian soils are poor, mostly gray loamy or gray sandy soils and sometimes bog soils. The rivers draining the region, the Buh with its tributaries (the Volodavka, the Krzna, the Mukhavets, the Nurets, the Narva, and the Lisna) and the Vepr (or Wieprz), empty into the Vistula River.

Podlachia has a transitional climate between a continental and an oceanic one. Winters are mild (the average January temperature is between −3.5 and −4.5°C), and summers are cool (the average July temperature is between 18 and 18.5°C). The spring and the fall are long. Temperatures dip below the freezing point for 60 to 80 days of the year, and snow cover lasts for 80 to 100 days. The annual precipitation is approx 500 to 600 mm. The vegetation is typical of the northern forest belt, although

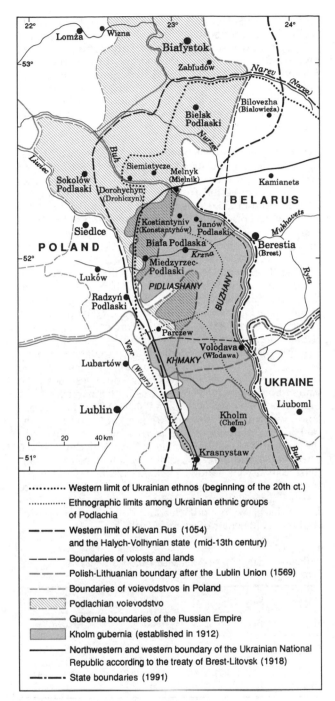

Western limit of Ukrainian ethnos (beginning of the 20th ct.)

.... Ethnographic limits among Ukrainian ethnic groups of Podlachia

——— Western limit of Kievan Rus (1054) and the Halych-Volhynian state (mid-13th century)

– – – Boundaries of volosts and lands

–·–·– Polish-Lithuanian boundary after the Lublin Union (1569)

– – – Boundaries of voievodstvos in Poland

▨ Podlachian voievodstvo

——— Gubernia boundaries of the Russian Empire

▓ Kholm gubernia (established in 1912)

——— Northwestern and western boundary of the Ukrainian National Republic according to the treaty of Brest-Litovsk (1918)

—·—· State boundaries (1991)

PODLACHIA

the southwestern part of Podlachia borders on the Central European forest belt. The eastern limit of the beech, spruce, larch, and hornbeam and the southwestern limit of the fir run through Podlachia.

History. The earliest signs of human habitation in Podlachia date back to the Upper Paleolithic and Mesolithic periods. In the Neolithic Period the region was occupied by carriers of the Pitted-Comb Pottery culture and the Buh culture. During the Bronze Age it was invaded from the west by bearers of the Lusatian culture and then,

toward the end of the Iron Age, by the Venedi. Later evidence of cremation shows that by the beginning of the modern era Podlachia was settled by Slavs from the Dnieper region. It can be assumed that by the 3rd century the region was being crossed by the Goths en route to the Dnieper region. The earliest signs of trade between Podlachia and the Kiev region date back to the 4th century.

In the 9th and 10th centuries most of the territory was settled by the Derevlianians. The Drehovichians occupied the land to the north beyond the Narva River, and the Dulibians, probably the land to the south. By that time a major trade route from Poland and the Baltic countries to Ukraine and the Near East ran through Podlachia.

The medieval period. In the 10th century Podlachia became a part of Kievan Rus'; it constituted the western portion of Berestia land and then the separate Dorohychyn land. It was annexed to Volhynia principality in the 11th century and then to Turiv-Pynske principality (1088–1157). In 1238 Prince Danylo Romanovych added it to Halych principality. Until 1340 it belonged to the Principality of Galicia-Volhynia. The border between the Kievan state (Volhynia principality) and the Polish state (Mazovia principality) ran west of Briansk and Dorohychyn-Międzyrzec territories and remained stable during the period. Mazovian attempts to annex the region succeeded only for a brief period in the 1230s. Because of their security from Tatar raids and their lively trade with the Poles and the Teutonic Knights, Dorohychyn and Berestia lands played an important role in the Galician-Volhynian state in the 13th and 14th centuries. They served as launching sites of Danylo Romanovych's and his successors' campaigns against the Yatvingians. In 1253 Danylo's coronation took place in Dorohychyn. Podlachia was one of the most heavily populated regions of Ukraine at that time.

As the Galician-Volhynian state declined, the Lithuanian grand duke Gediminas occupied the Berestia region, in 1320, and then Kęstutis annexed all Podlachia, which he passed on to his son, Vytautas. During the territorial struggle between Lithuania and Poland Dorohychyn land came under Mazovian rule only briefly, in 1391–2 and 1440–3. Polish influence in the region was nevertheless strong. The influx of Polish colonists, particularly of the petty gentry, began in the second half of the 14th century. By the 15th century the local wealthy nobility of Ukrainian origin had been Polonized, and the petty gentry had lost its influence. In 1501 Polish law was introduced for the Polish gentry in the north (Bielsk land), and in 1516 it was extended to all the gentry in Dorohychyn land. In 1516 Grand Duke Sigismund restricted the right to stand for election to the land and city courts to Catholic inhabitants of the region. Latin replaced Ruthenian as the official language in the Ukrainian territories of the Grand Duchy of Lithuania. In 1520 Podlachia, consisting of the lands of Dorohychyn, Bielsk, and Berestia, was established as a separate voivodeship with its center in Dorohychyn. In 1566 Berestia land was amalgamated with Turiv-Pynske land into the new Berestia-Lithuanian voivodeship, and in 1569 the remaining Podlachian territory was divided into Dorohychyn, Bielsk, and Melnyk lands and incorporated into Poland. Podlachia, particularly Dorohychyn land, prospered in the 15th and 16th centuries, because the Cracow–Vilnius and Warsaw–Vilnius trade routes merged there. The Polish offensive against the Ruthenian faith and the Orthodox clergy persisted even after the Church Union of Berestia in 1596.

During B. Khmelnytsky's uprising the Cossacks briefly captured southern Podlachia, in 1648. Col M. Krychevsky was a native of the region. In 1657 Col A. Zhdanovych's Cossack force, which took part in a joint Ukrainian-Swedish-Transylvanian campaign against Poland, operated in Podlachia.

19th and 20th centuries. After the partition of Poland in 1795, southern Podlachia (up to the Buh River) was annexed by Austria, the northern part by Prussia, and the Berestia region by Russia. During the Napoleonic Wars the northern part was transferred to Russia, and the southern part to the Grand Duchy of Warsaw and then, in 1815, to the Congress Kingdom of Poland. In 1842 the northern part (Bielsk county and the Berestia region) was assigned to Hrodna gubernia, and the southern part ended up in Warsaw general gubernia. The two regions developed very differently.

The history of southern Podlachia was closely linked with that of the *Kholm region. The two regions even became known by one name, Kholm Rus', Transbuh Rus', or simply Kholm region. Both were subjected to the same oppression by the Poles. In 1829 the Uniate Kholm eparchy was removed from the jurisdiction of Halych metropoly and subjected to long-term Latinization. The linguistic Polonization of the clergy and local population gathered momentum. The abolition of the Uniate and the imposition of the Orthodox church by the Russian authorities in 1874 only reinforced the Polonization process, because most Uniates clung to Catholicism and, after the edict of toleration (17 April 1905), adopted the Roman Catholic faith. In 1905–8 the Orthodox church in Podlachia lost 58 percent of its members (compared to 22 percent in the Kholm region). Thus a *Kalakut* community arose in Podlachia. To limit Polish influence Kholm gubernia was set up in 1912 out of those parts of Podlachia and the Kholm region where Ukrainians constituted a majority. The end of the 19th century marked the beginning of the Ukrainian national revival in Podlachia, particularly among young teachers.

During the First World War Ukrainians in Podlachia suffered heavy losses. In 1915 over 80 percent of them were evacuated by the retreating Russians. For Ukrainians left behind under the German occupation, the *Union for the Liberation of Ukraine organized at the beginning of 1917 a string of Ukrainian schools taught by POWs from the Bluecoats. The Ukrainian Hromada, a central organization for Podlachia, and the Ukrainian School Council were set up in Biała. In June 1917 the first Ukrainian newspaper in Podlachia, *Ridne slovo*, appeared. From early 1918 the cultural work continued under the leadership of O. Skoropys-Yoltukhovsky and V. Dmytriiuk and spread to the Berestia and Pynske regions.

According to the terms of the Peace Treaty of Brest-Litovsk all Kholm gubernia was to belong to the UNR, but by the end of 1918 that region had been occupied by the Poles. Podlachia was subsequently incorporated into Lublin (Biała, Kostiantyniv, Volodava, and Radzyń counties) and Białystok (Bielsk county) voivodeships. The Berestia region became part of Polisia voivodeship. In 1918–23 only some of the evacuated Ukrainians returned. Ukrainian political and cultural life in Podlachia revived in spite of Polish interference. Some Ukrainian candidates were elected to the Sejm and Senate in 1922. The Ridna Khata society headed the educational and cultural movement. In the 1930s, however, all Ukrainian activities were banned by the authorities. They resumed only in 1939–44, when Podlachia became part of the Generalgouvernement. Under the German occupation Ukrainian mutual aid committees, schools, co-operatives, cultural societies, and churches were organized. The major centers of Ukrainian life were Biała and Volodava.

The northern part of Podlachia (Bielsk county) did not experience the change in national consciousness or the religious strife that occurred in the south in the 19th and 20th centuries. In the 1830s the Ukrainian and Belarusian population converted from the Uniate to the Orthodox faith without much opposition and escaped Polonization. There were no Ukrainian organizations there, however. Only in 1941–4, when northern Podlachia became a part of the German Reich, was a branch of the Ukrainian National Alliance formed in Bielsk.

After the Second World War Podlachia was restored to Poland and was divided among Lublin, Warsaw, and Białystok voivodeships. Most Ukrainians were resettled in the Soviet Union or in the newly acquired lands in western or northern Poland. (For 20th-century history see also *Kholm region and *Kholm eparchy.)

Population. In 1931 Podlachia's population density was 46 people per sq km (45 in 1964). Then, as now, the highest density was in the fertile southwest near the Kholm border, and the lowest was in the marshy area of Bilovezha Forest and Volodava Polisia. Most of the population was rural: in 1931 only 15 percent (in 1964, 20 percent) of the population was urban. The larger towns in the central and southern regions are Volodava, Biała, Międzyrzec, and Parczew, and the smaller ones are Vyshnytsi, Slaviatychi, Janów, Kostiantyniv, and Terespil. In the north Bielsk, Melnyk, Dorohychyn, and Semiatycze are the larger settlements. The city of Brest (Berestia), on the border between Podlachia and Polisia, can be considered the main center of eastern Podlachia.

TABLE 1
Orthodox inhabitants of Podlachia, 1905–31 (thousands; percentage of total inhabitants in parentheses)

	County		
Year	Biała Podlaska	Volodava	Radzyń*
1905	69.0 (57.0)	71.4 (58.0)	52.2 (32.0)
1908	27.7 (23.2)	46.5 (37.5)	6.1 (3.8)
1921	12.0 (14.2)	22.5 (26.8)	2.9 (1.4)
1931	18.1 (15.6)	30.6 (27.0)	3.1 (1.4)

*Including parts of Siedlce and Sokołów

TABLE 2
Religious composition of Podlachia, 1905–31 (thousands; percentage of total in parentheses)

Year	Roman Catholics	Orthodox and Greek Catholics
1905	140 (34.3)	194 (47.5)
1908	256 (62.5)	79 (19.3)
1921	232 (72.5)	37 (11.6)
1931	280 (71.9)	52 (13.3)

At the beginning of the 20th century almost half (47.5 percent) of Podlachia's population was Greek Catholic or Orthodox. Roman Catholics accounted for a third (34.3 percent), and Jews for a sixth (16.8 percent). Resettlement and government policy brought about a dramatic change. By 1931 the Uniates and Orthodox constituted only 13.3 percent of the population, Roman Catholics, 71.9 percent, and Jews, 13.8 percent (see table 2). The predominantly Ukrainian territory shifted 20 to 30 km east of the Puhachiv–Parchiv–Międzyrzec–Dorohychyn line. Until 1945, Ukrainians formed a majority only in a narrow strip along the Buh River. West of that strip lay a mixed zone, with a Polish and *Kalakut* majority, and then a zone containing only small islands of Ukrainians. In southern Podlachia (excluding the western zone) the ethnic composition was 20.4 percent Ukrainians, 29.2 percent *Kalakuty*, 35 percent Poles, and 13.7 percent Jews.

In northern Podlachia no comparable religious or demographic shift was experienced. In Bielsk county the ethnic mix of the population remained about the same as in 1931: Ukrainians, 70.9 percent, Poles, 21.5 percent, and Jews, 6.5 percent.

Before the Second World War the Ukrainian population of Podlachia could be divided into three main groups, the Podlachians proper (*Pidliashany*), the Buhians (*Buzhany*), and the Khmaks (*Khmaky*). The first group inhabited the northwestern part of the region and were distinguished by their somber dress and manner. The second occupied a wide strip of land on the west bank of the Buh River and were noted for their tall stature, light features, and love for elaborate dress, music, and dancing. The Khmaks settled the southwestern part of Podlachia around Volodava and were known for their archaic dress. Their name was derived from their use of -*khmo* instead of -*s'mo* for the past tense ending of 'to be' (eg, *bulyxmo* instead of *bulys'mo* 'we were').

Economy. Before the Second World War Podlachia was an agricultural region, in which almost 80 percent of the population was occupied in farming. Some industrial development began to occur outside the Ukrainian parts of the region. The towns engaged in trade and the crafts.

The old forests of Podlachia survived only in the northeastern part around Bilovezha Forest. In general only small pockets of forest are left. Much of the southeastern region (Volodava Polisia) consists of wasteland and hayfields. Arable land accounts for 47 percent of the land area, forests, for 23 percent, meadows and pastures, for 21 percent, and other land, for 9 percent. The main crops are rye (42 percent of the seeded area), potatoes (17 percent), oats (14 percent), animal feed (12 percent), wheat (7 percent), and barley (4 percent). The region produces a surplus of pork and dairy products.

BIBLIOGRAPHY

Batiushkov, P. *Kholmskaia Rus'* (St Petersburg 1887)
Karetnikov, S. *Kholmskaia guberniia* (Lubny 1913)
Korduba, M. *Pivnichno-zakhidna Ukraïna* (Vienna 1917)
– *Istoriia Kholmshchyny i Pidliashshia* (Cracow 1941)
Pasternak, Ie. *Narys istoriï Kholmshchyny i Pidliashshia: Novishi chasy* (Winnipeg 1968)
Martyniuk, M. (ed). *Nadbuzhanshchyna*, 1 (New York 1986)
V. Kubijovyč

Podlachian dialects. The westernmost group of the *Polisian dialects, spoken by the inhabitants of Podlachia and a small number of pockets in the Kholm region. East of the Buh and Lisna rivers they merge with the western Polisian dialects. During the past century their territory has drastically decreased, particularly in southern Podlachia, and has been transformed into linguistic islands in a Polish environment. Intense Polonization pressures resulted in the emergence of several transitional mixed Ukrainian-Polish dialects, which have gradually become Polish ones. The mixed dialects in the vicinity of Siemiatycze and Bielsk Podlaski, for example, absorbed *mazurzenie*, ie, the Polish dialectal substitution of dental stops and affricates for alveolar stops and affricates (eg, *káze, súsyt, xóce, sadzáje* [SU *káže, súšyt', xóče, sadžáje*] 'he says, he dries, he wants, he seats'), the Polish change of *t', d'* into *c', dz'* (eg, *nedz'íel'a* [SU *nedilja*] 'Sunday'), and forms without *l'* after labials before once iotated vowels (eg, *kupjú, kúpjat* [SU *kupljú, kúpljat'*] 'I/they will buy').

North of the Narew River certain typical Ukrainian features (eg, hard consonants before *e, i*) have given way to Belarusian ones, such as palatalization and sporadic *dzekan'e* (eg, *ós'en', n'e xóču, kos'íc'i* [SU *ósin', ne xóču, kosýty*] 'autumn, I don't want, to mow'). Others – diphthongs with *o, e, ě*, a softened *c'* – have been retained (eg, *s'íeno, mied, pryv'uoz, p'játn'ic'a* [SU *sino, med, pryviz, p'jatnycja*] 'hay, honey, I transported, Friday'). The influence of the *South Volhynian dialects is evident in the Buh valley. Under the impact of Polish, hard dentals before *e* and *i* did not develop in the western and northwestern dialectal belts (eg, *pól'e, hovorýl'i, zobáčyt'i, s'élam'i* [SU *póle, hovorýly, zobáčyty, sélamy*] 'field, they said, to see, villages' instr). In the west and north the diphthongs *uo, ue, uy, uÿ, ÿy, ie* from *ō, ē, ě* appear in a stressed position (eg, *hnuoj, zam'juol, s'ieno, jačm'ien'* [SU *hnij, zamív, síno, jačmín'*] 'manure, he swept, hay, barley'). In the southeast they have been simplified into *ÿ, ÿe* (eg, *hnÿj, sobjé* [SU *hnij, sobí* 'manure, to myself') and, in the unstressed position, *u, y/i* (eg, *pudrusl'í, jáščurka, pópyl, žýncy* [SU *pidroslý, jáščirka, pópil, žínci*] 'grew-up, lizard, ashes, to the woman'). In the west, *e, i* appear in place of *'a* from *ę* in an unstressed position (eg, *pametáju, kolódz'iz'a* [SU *pam'jatáju, kolódjazja*] 'I remember, of the well'). Unstressed *o, e* are articulated high as *u, y* (eg, *purubýÿ* [SU *porobýv*] 'I made'). The groups *ky, gy, hy, xy*, are articulated high as *k'i, g'i, h'i, x'i* (eg, *kolosk'í, x'ítry* [SU *koloský, xýtryj*] 'grain stalks, sly'), and the unstressed groups *ča, ža, ša, r'a* are articulated as *č'ja...* around Biała Podlaska (eg, *š'jápka* [SU *šápka*] 'hat') and as *č'e* in the south (eg, *č'es* [SU *čas*] 'time'). Sporadically *e* changes into *'o* (eg, *viet'or, byróza, ukrad'óny* [SU *víter, beréza, ukrádenyj*] 'wind, birch, stolen'). Initial *o-, i-* are preceded by a prothetic *h-* (eg, *hórut, hínyj* [SU *orjút', ínej*] 'they plow, frost'). The soft *r'* became hard (eg, *výradyÿ* [SU *výrjadyv*] 'he equipped'), the cluster *st'* is pronounced *s'c'* (eg, *šers'c', s'c'iény* [SU *šerst', stíny*] '[animal] hair, walls').

Declension forms are of the type *kon'óm* (SU *koném*) 'with a horse', *kón'um* (SU *kónjam*) 'to the horses', *na kón'ux* (SU *na kónjax*) 'on the horses', *zeml'óju* (SU *zemléju*) 'with the earth', *na muludómu kun'óvy* (SU *na molodómu koní*) 'on a young horse', *tel'át'a* (SU *teljáty*) 'of the calf', *tel'át'ovy* (SU *teljati*) 'to the calf', *tel'át'om* (SU *teljám*) 'with the calf', *mórovy* (SU *mórju*) 'to the sea', *noč'iéj* (SU *nočéj*) 'of the nights'. In certain nominal cases both hard and soft masculine, feminine, and neuter nouns, in which the stress is on the stem, have the same endings; eg, *nóhi, zéml'i* (SU *nóhy, zémli*) 'legs, lands', *zuby, kóny* (SU *zúby, kóni*) 'teeth, horses', *na koróvy, v néby* (SU *na koróvi, v nébi*) 'on the cow, in the sky'. Dual forms are also present; eg, *2 ukn'í, styn'í, pól'i, kon'íe* (SU *2 vikná, stiný, pólja, kóni*) '2 windows, walls, fields, horses'. In adjectives, long forms are used; eg, *molodý, -ája, -úju, -óje, -ýji* (SU *molodýj, -á, -ú, -é, -í*) 'young' masculine and feminine nominative singular, feminine accusative singular, neuter nominative singular, nominative plural. Short forms are used when the stress is on the root; eg, *žýtny, -na, -ne, -ny* (SU *žýtnij, -nja, -nje, -ni*) 'rye' masculine, feminine, neuter nominative singular, nominative plural. *Naš* 'our' has both long and short forms; eg, *náša/-aja* feminine nominative, *nášu/-uju* feminine accusative, *náše/-oje* neuter nominative. Pronouns have forms such as *ton, tája, téje, týji, vsen'* (SU *toj, ta, te, ti, uvés'*) 'that one' masculine, feminine, neuter singular, 'those ones', 'all'. Postprepositional third-person forms omit *n-*, eg, *v jóho, na jýj, z jímy* (SU *v n'óho, na níj, z nýmy*) 'in him, on her, with them'. The influence of soft-type endings is evident in possessive and demonstrative pronouns; eg, *méji, téji, méju, téju* (SU *mojéji, tijéji, mojéju, tijéjú*) 'of my, of that, with my, with that' feminine.

In conjugation, forms such as *napečý* (SU *napekty*) 'to bake' and infinitives ending in *-ie*, eg, *itíe, pečýe* 'to go, to bake' in the northwest along the Buh are, perhaps, evidence of a Yatvingian substratum. Typical verbal forms are *xódyt, budút', pytájec'c'a, žn'íem, id'íete, púojd'um, búd'omo, búdu/máju nočovát'i, kupývem, kupýves', kupýl'is'-mo* (SU *xódyt', búdut', pytájetsja, žnemó, ideté, pídemo, búdemo, búdu/máju nočuváty, ja kupýv, ty kupýv, my kupýly*) 'he walks, they will be, he asks, we reap, you (pl) go, we will go, we will be, I will be spending/am supposed to spend the night, I (masc) bought, you (masc sing) bought, we bought'. In the northwest the reflexive particle *-sja* is used separately from the verb.

The lexicon of the Podlachian dialects has many Polonisms, as well as expressions unknown elsewhere that are etymologically identical with Polish ones; eg, *knjážyč* 'the moon', *divosnúby* 'matchmaking'. The dialects have been studied by M. Yanchuk, I. Bessaraba, J. Polívka, P. Rastorguev, I. Zilynsky, W. Kuraszkiewicz, Ja. Tarnacki, M. Lesiv (Łesiów), and G. Vinokur.

O. Horbach

Podolchak, Ihor [Podol'čak], b 9 April 1962 in Lviv. Artist. He graduated from the Lviv Institute of Applied and Decorative Arts in 1984. His graphic works have received recognition at international expositions in Spain (1988) and Canada (1989). He won second prize at the International Ex Libris Exhibition in Germany (1987) and the Johnson Graphic Prize in the United States (1990). He has exhibited in group shows since 1985 and has had one-man shows in Łódź, Poland (1988); Cadaqués, Spain, Paris, and London (1990); and Lviv, Haifa, and Moscow (1991).

Podoliak, Borys. See Kostiuk, Hryhorii.

Podoliaka, Ivan [Podoljaka], b and d ? Haidamaka leader from Kropyvna, Pereiaslav regiment. During the 1730s he worked at the Zaporozhian Sich, and in the late 1740s he joined a haidamaka rebel group that was active in the Smila, Chyhyryn, and Cherkasy districts. After forming his own rebel detachment in 1750, he conducted raids in the Hornostaipil, Chornobyl, and Khabne districts, and even as far as Radomyshl. He was captured by a Polish punitive expedition and handed over to the tsarist authorities; his further fate is unknown.

Podolian Upland or **Podolian Plateau**. An upland in the *Podilia region of southwestern Ukraine on the left bank of the Dniester River. Elongated in shape, the upland has declining elevations along its length from 380 to 320 m in the northwest and from 220 to 130 m in the southeast. Its relatively flat surface is dissected by many parallel, canyonlike valleys joining the Dniester River valley to the south. The upland is underlain by limestones, marls, sandstones, and shales, and in its eastern part by granites and gneisses covered with layers of loess. As a result of intensive erosion its northern rim is a hilly escarpment, rising to over 400 m. The Dniester side is deeply incised by rivers, and the changing base levels of erosion are reflected in a series of steplike terraces. Once covered by a varied forest-steppe vegetation, the surface of the Podolian Upland is now extensively cultivated. Together with the Volhynia-Kholm Upland to the west-northwest, it forms the Volhynia-Podilia Upland.

Podolianochka. A group dance for girls, accompanied with song. Traditionally a spring rite, the dance was performed by girls in a circle with one girl in the middle. While the girls in the circle sang, the 'Podolian girl' in the middle illustrated the song by mimicry or gesture. Then she chose someone else to be in the middle. The dance music is in 4/4 time with an extra beat at the end of each stanza. The *podolianochka* melody has been used by L. Revutsky and A. Kos-Anatolsky in their compositions.

Podolinsky, Andrei [Podolinskij, Andrej] (Podolynsky, Andrii), b 13 July 1806 in Kiev, d 16 January 1886 in Kiev. Russian Romantic poet of Ukrainian descent; father of S. Podolynsky. In the 1820s his long poems, particularly 'Div i Peri' (Div and Peri) and 'Smert' Peri' (Peri's Death), and the novelette in verse *Borskii* were well received by Russian critics and readers. From 1839 to 1854 he did not publish. By the 1860s he was considered old-fashioned. His posthumously published novelette *Zmei* (The Dragon) is based on Ukrainian folkways and folklore. Editions of his works were published in 1837, 1885, and 1936.

Podolinsky, Sergei. See Podolynsky, Serhii.

Podolynsky, Mykhailo [Podolyns'kyj, Myxajlo], b 1844 in Dolyna county, Galicia, d 1894. Publicist, translator, and community activist; son of V. *Podolynsky. He was a founder and leader (1868–9) of the Sich student society in Vienna. He taught in gymnasiums in Lviv and Brody and contributed to the newspapers *Pravda, Dilo*, and *Zoria*. He wrote pedagogical essays, literary and art criticism, travelogs, and translations of Russian, Italian, and French works.

Podolynsky, Serhii [Podolyns'kyj, Serhij] (Podolinsky, Sergei), b 31 July 1850 in Yaroslavka, Zvenyhorod county, Kiev gubernia, d 12 July 1891 in Kiev. Socialist theoretician and activist, and physician. Podolynsky studied science and medicine in Kiev, Paris, Zurich, and Breslau (now Wrocław). He published a number of works on medical topics, including a long study titled *Zhyttia i zdorovia liudei na Ukraïni* (The Life and Health of People in

Ukraine, 1879). He worked as a physician in Ukraine in the mid-1870s, but in 1878 he settled in Montpellier, France, where he continued to practice medicine and also lectured at the famous Montpellier medical school. In the early 1870s he became involved both with the Russian populist P. Lavrov's *Vpered!* group and with the *Hromada of Kiev, particularly with the Hromada's most radical members, the socialist M. *Drahomanov and the Marxist M. *Ziber. To the end of his active life Podolynsky combined a revolutionary socialist perspective with devotion to the Ukrainian nation.

In 1875 he broke with the Russian Lavrovists over the national question and spoke of the formation of a separate 'Ukrainian social-democratic party.' In the same year he wrote two brochures that were the first works in the Ukrainian language to advocate socialism, *Parova mashyna* (The Steam Engine) and *Pro bidnist'* (On Poverty). Podolynsky produced more popular socialist literature in Ukrainian over the next few years as well as some longer tracts on agrarian problems and the development of Ukrainian industry. He co-operated closely with Drahomanov and his journal *Hromada*, to which he contributed several articles and of which he formally became coeditor in 1881. He was also involved in the international socialist movement, contributed to German-, Italian-, and especially French-language socialist journals, and reported on international socialist affairs in *Vpered!* and *Hromada*.

Podolynsky made an important contribution to theory in his article 'Socialism, or Human Labor and the Unity of Physical Forces,' which was published in several versions and four languages in 1880–3. Although the theory was rejected by F. Engels and then long forgotten, it came to light again in the 1970s and 1980s. The Ukrainian dissident M. *Rudenko drew on Podolynsky's ideas for his *Ekonomichni monolohy* (Economic Monologues). Podolynsky has also come to be regarded as a precursor of energy economics or socioenergetics. His activities were cut short in January 1882 when he suffered a mental collapse, from which he never recovered.

BIBLIOGRAPHY
Mytsiuk, O. *Ukraïns'kyi ekonomist-hromadivets' S.A. Podolins'kyi* (Lviv 1933)
Martínes, A; Naredo, J. 'A Marxist Precursor of Energy Economics: Podolinsky,' *Journal of Peasant Studies*, 9, no. 2 (January 1982)
Podolyns'kyi, S. *Vybrani tvory*, ed R. Serbyn (Montreal 1990)
Zlupko, S. *Serhii Podolyns'kyi – Vchenyi, myslytel', revoliutsioner* (Lviv 1990)
J.-P. Himka

Podolynsky, Vasyl [Podolyns'kyj, Vasyl'], b 14 or 15 January 1815 in Bilych, Sambir circle, d 24 August 1876 in Maniv, Lisko county, Galicia. Priest and publicist; father of M. *Podolynsky. As a student at the Greek Catholic Theological Seminary in Lviv (1837–41) he belonged to the Polish clandestine Union of Sons of the Homeland. He was ordained in 1843, and served as a priest in Vetlyn, Peremyshl circle. During the Revolution of 1848 he published in Sianik a Polish brochure, *Słowo przestrogi* (A Word of Warning), in which he analyzed the pro-Polish, pro-Russian, pro-Austrian, and pro-Ukrainian political orientations among Galicia's Ukrainians, defended the use of Ukrainian as a separate language, and substantiated the idea of an independent, united Ukrainian state and

a federation of free Slavic peoples. The brochure influenced the politics of the *Supreme Ruthenian Council. Podolynsky was arrested while on his way to join the Hungarian revolutionaries. After the revolution he was persecuted by the church hierarchy. He was a pastor in Maniv from 1852, and he established an elementary school there in 1859.

Podushko, Zinovii [Poduško, Zinovij], b 29 October 1887 in Ocheretyne, Izium county, Kharkiv gubernia, d 3 March 1963 in Łódź, Poland. Painter. A graduate of the Kiev Art School (1911) and St Petersburg Academy of Arts (1917), from 1919 he lived in Poland. In Łódź he worked as a scenery designer for local theaters and as a draftsman for the city planning bureau. His early works were exhibited in Lviv, Cracow, Warsaw, and Lublin. He was known for his many realist oil landscapes, such as *Sunset*, *Evening in the Steppe*. Most of them perished during the Second World War.

Podvezko, Mykhailo [Podvez'ko, Myxajlo] (Podvesko), b 14 November 1901 in Riabushky, Lebedyn county, Kharkiv gubernia, d ? Lexicographer. A graduate of the Ukrainian Institute of Linguistic Education in Kharkiv (1935), he taught in secondary and postsecondary schools in Kiev until 1941. From 1945 he worked as an editor and lexicographer. He compiled the first Soviet English-Ukrainian dictionaries (50,000 words, 1948; 25,000 words, 1955; 65,000 words, with M. Balla, 1974) and, with the help of K. Hryhorenko, the first Soviet Ukrainian-English dictionary (60,000 words, 1952; rev edn 1957).

Podvorniak, Mykhailo [Podvornjak, Myxajlo], b 24 December 1911 in Khotovytsia, Kremianets county, Volhynia gubernia. Writer. A postwar refugee, he settled in Winnipeg in 1949. There he has edited the Baptist monthly *Khrystyians'kyi visnyk* and been secretary of the Research Institute of Volyn. He is the author of the story collections *Na shliakhu zhyttia* (On Life's Road, 2 vols, 1951, 1953), *Zelenyi hai* (The Green Grove, 1959), *Bozhyi spokii* (Divine Tranquility, 1966), *Vidpavshi* (Those Who Fell Away, 1968), *Zapashnist' polia* (The Field's Fragrance, 1971), *Zolota osin'* (Golden Autumn, 1974), *Daleki berehy* (Distant Shores, 1975), *Odnoho dnia* (One Day, 1977), and *Stezhky i dorohy* (Paths and Roads, 1981); the novels *Nedospivana pisnia* (The Unfinished Song, 1967), *Brat i sestra* (Brother and Sister, 1979), and *Persha liubov* (First Love, 1986); and the memoirs *Daleka doroha* (The Long Road, 1963), *Nebesnyi dim* (The Celestial Abode, 1965), and *Viter z Volyni* (Wind from Volhynia, 1981). He has also translated Russian religious literature into Ukrainian.

Pody (aka *pady*, *zapadyny*, or *chapli*). Flat-bottomed depressions commonly found in Ukraine on the loessial plains of the forest-steppe and steppe zones. They are circular, oval, or elongated in form and range from 0.2 to 10 km across and 0.5 to 17 m in depth. They are particularly numerous between the Dnieper and the Molochna rivers and also between the Dnieper and the Boh rivers. In the spring *pody* collect meltwater and frequently form seasonal lakes. They thereupon accumulate a greater quantity of moisture and support rich meadows for use as pastures or hayfields. One of the larger *pody* contains part of the Askaniia-Nova Nature Reserve.

The origins of *pody* in Ukraine have been associated with various processes. P. Tutkovsky considered that they were formed by means of wind deflation. M. Dmytriiev associated their genesis with karst phenomena in the underlying Pontic Sea limestones that caused a subsidence of the surface loess. V. Bondarchuk, however, correlated their formation with the late Pliocene epoch surface of the area, after the Pontic Sea had receded but before the accumulation of loess. Expanding on that idea P. Zamorii considered the large *pody* as remnants of bays from the receding sea; the smaller ones he accounted for as loessial subsidence that resulted from differentiated leaching or loessial karst. A. Mulika suggested a mix of the aforementioned factors and added that some *pody* were actually dried-up lakes.

Related to the *pody* are small depressions in the loessial plains known as *bliudtsia*. Common in nearly all of the steppe and forest-steppe zones of Ukraine, they are often considered to be small *pody*. They range from a few meters to several hundred meters across and may be from 0.5 to 4 m deep.

I. Stebelsky

Podzhio, Aleksandr [Podžio] (Poggio), b 8 May 1798, d 18 June 1873 in Voronky, Kozelets county, Chernihiv gubernia. Russian nobleman and Decembrist of Italian origin; son of an early architect of Odessa. He became a member of the Northern Society in 1821 while serving as an officer in the Preobrazhenskii Regiment. In 1823 he retired as a reserve colonel of the Dnieper Regiment and moved to his mother's estate in Kiev gubernia. There he joined the *Southern Society and became a close associate of P. *Pestel. After the revolt of the Chernihiv Regiment failed, Podzhio was arrested, tried for treason, and sentenced to death. The verdict was commuted to 20 years of hard labor in Siberia. After his release in 1859, he lived abroad (mostly in Switzerland) for several years and became a close friend of A. Herzen. Podzhio's memoirs of the Decembrist movement were published in 1930.

Podzhio, Borys [Podžio], b 1875? d 1920. UNR Army general. A brigadier general in the Russian army, in 1917 he commanded a division. Upon joining the UNR Army he was assigned to command a division in the Second Ukrainian Corps. In 1918 he commanded the Third Kherson Corps, and in 1919, briefly, the Zaporozhian Corps.

Poetics (from Greek *poietike*). The term, in its broadest sense, refers to works on the theory of literature and esthetics, the first such being Aristotle's renowned treatise *Poetics*. More specifically, poetics embraces that segment of literary studies which is concerned with the structure of a work of literature, its language, its tropes, and so on. In its narrowest sense the term is used to describe a work devoted to the nature and laws of poetry.

In Ukraine the heyday of poetics occurred in the 17th and 18th centuries and was closely tied to developments in education and the curriculum of the *Kievan Mohyla Academy. At the academy poetics, together with rhetoric and philosophy, was a compulsory subject taught in Latin. It was not customary to publish the texts for the courses, but as many as 15 exist in manuscript form, mainly from the end of the 17th century. The first such manuscript, *Liber artis poëticae ... anno Domini 1637*, is dated five years after the establishment of the academy. Even earlier, some rules of versification were included in the grammars of L. Zyzanii (1596) and M. Smotrytsky (1619). Both Zyzanii and Smotrytsky, as well as all of the later school poetics, tried to impose Greek and Latin versification rules on Ukrainian verse. Not until the poetics of M. Dovhalevsky (1736) and H. Slomynsky (1744–5) was any attention given to contemporary Ukrainian verse. Another important work of the 18th century was the *De arte poëtica libri tres ...* of T. Prokopovych, written in 1705–6 but published only in 1786 by H. Konysky, as a textbook.

In the 19th century no new poetics were written, but interest in the subject appears toward the later part of the century, in some works of O. Potebnia, M. Drahomanov, and I. Franko and especially in K. Luchakovsky's *Nacherk stylistyky, poetyky i retoryky* (Outline of Stylistics, Poetics, and Rhetoric, 1894), which was part of the high school curriculum in Galicia at that time. A renewed interest in the more narrow sense of poetics occurred in the 20th century, during the 1920s; several works appeared in the new Soviet Ukraine: S. Haievsky's *Teoriia poeziï* (Theory of Poetry, 1921), B. Yakubsky's *Nauka virshuvannia* (Study of Versification, 1922), D. Zahul's *Poetyka* (Poetics, 1923), and B. Navrotsky's *Mova ta poeziia* (Language and Poetry, 1925). Other more broadly defined works on poetics also appeared: H. Maifet's collection *Teoriia literatury* (Theory of Literature, 2 vols, 1931–2), M. Yohansen's *Iak buduiet'sia opovidannia* (How a Story Is Constructed, 1928), and several works on various aspects of creativity by such scholars as M. Zerov and P. Fylypovych. Western Ukraine also saw a revival in the study of poetics, in such works as V. Dombrovsky's *Ukraïns'ka stylistyka i rytmika* (Ukrainian Stylistics and Rhythmics, 1923), M. Rudnytsky's *Mizh ideieiu i formoiu* (Between the Idea and the Form, 1932), and several works by F. Kolessa. Work on poetics continued among émigrés after the Second World War: S. Hordynsky's *Ukraïns'kyi virsh* (The Ukrainian Poem, 1947), I. Koshelivets's *Narysy z teoriï literatury* (Outlines of the Theory of Literature, 1954), and I. Kachurovsky's *Strofika* (Strophes, 1967), *Fonika* (Phonics, 1984), and *Narys komparatyvnoï metryky* (Outline of Comparative Metrics, 1985).

Work on poetics became revitalized in Ukraine in the 1960s, when several studies appeared: V. Kovalevsky's *Rytmichni zasoby ukraïns'koho literaturnoho virsha* (The Rhythmic Devices of Ukrainian Literary Verse, 1960) and *Ryma* (Rhyme, 1965), H. Sydorenko's *Virshuvannia v ukraïns'kii literaturi* (Versification in Ukrainian Literature, 1962), and P. Volynsky's *Osnovy teoriï literatury* (Fundamentals of the Theory of Literature, 1962). Structuralist theory found its proponent in the work of M. Laslo-Kutsiuk in Rumania, in *Pytannia ukraïns'koï poetyky* (Studies of Ukrainian Poetics, 1974).

BIBLIOGRAPHY
Petrov, N. 'O slovesnykh naukakh i literaturnykh zaniatiiakh v Kievskoi akademii ot nachala ee do preobrazovaniia v 1819 godu,' TKDA, 1866, nos 7, 11–12; 1867, no. 1; 1868, no. 3
Syvokin', H. *Davni ukraïns'ki poetyky* (Kharkiv 1960)
Krekoten', V. 'Kyïvs'ka poetyka,' in *Literaturna spadshchyna Kyïvs'koï Rusi i ukraïns'ka literatura XVI–XVIII st.*, ed O. Myshanych (Kiev 1981)
Sulyma, M. 'Teoriia virshuvannia na Ukraïni v XVI–XVII st. (Sproba opysu i rekonstruktsiï),' in *Literaturna spadshchyna Kyïvs'koï Rusi i ukraïns'ka literatura XVI–XVIII st.*, ed O. Myshanych (Kiev 1981)

I. Kachurovsky, D.H. Struk

Poetry (from Greek *poiesis*, meaning creativity). In its original sense the term 'poetry' is synonymous with creative artistic literature. In a stricter and more conventional sense 'poetry' refers to that genre of literature which is written in verse as opposed to *prose. Although poetry is a highly developed genre in classical and modern Ukrainian literature, it nonetheless shares general outlines of development with all Ukrainian literature, especially in the first two periods, the Kievan and the Cossack (see *Literature for periodization).

The Kievan period. Like all of the other literary genres poetry was at first imported in translations together with liturgical material. It consisted mainly of Byzantine and Old Bulgarian hymns as well as poetic introductions to the Gospels, such as 'Pokhvala tsariu Symeonu' in the *Izbornik* of Sviatoslav of 1073, or the prologue to the didactic Gospel of K. Preslavsky, the so-called 'alphabet prayer.' Those and other church-related poems (introductions, praises, alphabet poems – the latter often used to teach the Slavonic alphabet) as well as numerous Byzantine liturgical hymns played an important role in the formation of original Ukrainian poetry. Such hymns were compiled in menaia, triodia, octoechos, and psalters and had a profound influence on poetic perception. The translated corpus of hymns served as a source for the imagery, comparisons, and epithets in the literary monuments of the period. The first known original Ukrainian poem is the song of praise to SS Boris and Hlib from the chronicle *Povist' vremennykh lit*. The work, written by an anonymous author (some say Metropolitan Ioann I), is poetically similar to various Byzantine hymns of praise, and its verse elements are derived from a syntactical parallelism based on the repetition of the word 'rejoice.' Similar syntactic versification is found in another original work, 'Slovo v novu nediliu po Pastsi' (A Word on the First Sunday after Easter, ca 1170), by the noteworthy 12th-century sermonizer Bishop Cyril of Turiv. Many translated texts lost their graphic designation of verse and were written out in proselike lines, but there seems little doubt that the old Rus' scribes and translators were familiar with Greek poetics and the rules governing the structure of hymns. It is not surprising, therefore, that quite complicated poetic forms have been found, where lines of various syllables exist, and where no rhyme is present. The unifying poetic structure emanates from a contextual semantic line, syntactic parallelism, and various other poetic or rhetorical devices. Such free nonsyllabic verse is derived from Byzantine models, the original of which go back to biblical verse. A sample of such a semantically structured poem is found in *Moleniie Danyla Zatochnyka* (Supplication of Daniel the Exile, end of the 12th or beginning of the 13th century), in the anonymous 'Slovo pro pohybel' rus'koï zemli' (The Tale of Disintegration of the Rus' Lands, ca 13th to 14th century), and in the anonymous 'Slovo o Lazarevim voskresinni' (Tale of Lazarus's Resurrection). In the multisyllabic line and the recitative nature of those poems there is much similarity to various samples of folk poetry.

Both the Byzantine and the native folk influence found their reflection in the most outstanding poetic work of the Kievan period, the epic poem *Slovo o polku Ihorevi* (The Tale of Ihor's Campaign, ca 1187). I. *Franko pointed out (1907) that the versificatory underpinnings of the epic and other 'slovos' were based on church hymns, and at the same time coincided with the syllabic and syntactic structures found in folk songs. His claim that there existed a 'retinue-chivalrous' (*druzhynno-lytsars'ka*) school of poetry to which all those and many nonexistent works belong is unverifiable precisely owing to the paucity of existing examples. As with other genres there are no samples of poetry from the 14th and 15th centuries.

The Cossack period. Although there are some poems from the beginning of the 16th century (eg, P. *Rusyn's songs from 1509), most of the poetry begins in the second half of the century, since it is closely tied to the establishment of *brotherhood schools. As the numerous extant copies of *poetics attest, versification was a compulsory subject in the schools, and all pupils were taught poetic models based first and foremost on Polish syllabic verse and even on ancient Greek and Latin models (eg, M. Smotrytsky's *Gramatiki* ...). The other major influence on early Ukrainian poetry was the poetic structure inherent in folk songs – a syllabic versification with determined ictuses, and thereby readily congenial to both the syllabic verse imported from Poland and the individual modulations which later became the basis for the emergence of the tonic principle of versification. The 'school poetry,' as the vast production of the period is called, although often imitative and stilted, varies in the language used (Latin, Polish, Old Ukrainian, or Church Slavonic) and can be roughly divided into three groups: (1) strict school-type poems, written in accordance with poetic rules, often in Latin, Polish, or Church Slavonic, as well as various trick-poems, acrostics, and the like; (2) poems that took their cue from folk poetry and even became part of the folk repertoire (some poems by H. *Skovoroda and S. Klymovsky's 'Ïkhav kozak za Dunai' [The Cossack Rode beyond the Danube], which was made eternal by L. van Beethoven's variations on the song); and (3) humorous and satiric poems and travesties. Into the first group fall the Latin hexameters of Klymovych, S. Pekalid, and H. Vyshnevsky as well as the Old Ukrainian, Polish, and Church Slavonic syllabic verses of L. Baranovych, M. Smotrytsky, O. Mytura, K. Sakovych, and S. Pochasky. Interesting are A. Kalnofoisky, the author of *Teraturhima* (1638), for his epitaphs written in Polish, I. Maksymovych for his 25,000-line hymn to the Virgin (*Bohorodytse Divo* [Virgin Mother of God, 1707]), and T. *Prokopovych for the sheer variety of his creativity.

The poets belonging to the second group are more stimulating in that they pushed the confines of school poetics to the limits and thus paved the way for the poetry which was to follow in the 19th century. Skovoroda is the best known and most gifted of the group. Interesting verses with a syllabic structure approaching folk styles are found among the poems of I. Velychkovsky, I. Pashkovsky, Z. Dziubarevych, and, especially, K. *Stavrovetsky-Tranquillon (*Perlo mnohotsinnoie* [A Priceless Pearl, 1646]), who uses lines of irregular syllables close to those of folk *dumas. P. *Berynda's use of poetic dialogue in 1611 is expanded further by S. Divovych in 'Razhovor Velikorossii s Malorossiei' (The Conversation of Great Russia with Little Russia, 1762). The most notable works of the third group are, for their sheer number (369), the opinionated poems of K. Zynoviev, written sometime at the beginning of the 18th century; the Polish verses of D. Bratkovsky; the satiric poems of the monk Yakiv; and the facile and loquacious verses of I. Nekrashevych.

Although no major poet emerged, and few of the poets have any consistency in their writings, many wrote poetry which could fit all three of the aforementioned categories. Poetry was more an adjunct of an educated man than a creative art; hence, it was used for various purposes – religious, polemical, humorous, and as a means of expressing gratitude (the numerous panegyrics, heraldic poems, and epigrams). Few works were published, and many remained in manuscript form; they are unknown except to specialists in the period. A notable place is occupied by the folk *dumas composed during the period; their influence on later Romantic poets was profound.

The vernacular period. Classicism with its strict dicta on use of language, together with the nascent tonic versification in Russia, contributed to the birth and the nature of vernacular Ukrainian poetry. I. *Kotliarevsky wrote a travesty of Virgil's *Aeneid* in contemporary spoken Ukrainian and composed the *Eneïda* in a 10-line strophe of four-foot iambs, thereby giving a start to syllabo-tonic metrics in Ukrainian literature. Two poets who still wrote within the classicist dicta were P. *Hulak-Artemovsky, with his translations and travesties, and Ye. *Hrebinka, who wrote versified fables (*Malorossiiskie prikazki* [Little Russian Proverbs, 1834]). Other poets of the first half of the 19th century were already under the influence of romanticism, the tenets of which were highly propitious to the development of literature in the vernacular and to an intensification of the influence of folk poetry. Members of the *Kharkiv Romantic School, most notably L. *Borovykovsky, with his ballads, and A. *Metlynsky, full of nostalgia for the heroic past of the Cossacks and pessimism for the future, were soon followed by a more ideological group in Kiev, the *Cyril and Methodius Brotherhood.

By far the greatest poet of that group and the greatest poet in Ukrainian literature, T. *Shevchenko, led Ukrainian poetry firmly out of travesty and burlesque and established its canons by skillfully blending the popular *kolomyika* syllabic structure (two lines of 4 + 4 + 6 syllables, variously rhymed) and other folk syllabic structures with a tonic system of various metric feet. Overshadowed by Shevchenko but more conscious of his poetic role was M. *Kulish, who experimented with language (the conscious introduction of Church Slavonic into the vernacular) and with structure (the attempt to domesticate various ancient and canonical strophes). Another prominent member of the Kiev group was the historian M. *Kostomarov, who wrote historical ballads under the pseudonym Yeremiia Halka.

The symbiotic relationship between folk poetry and literary creation is seen in the works of several poets whose poems have entered the folk-song repertoire: S. Pysarevsky ('De ty brodysh moia dole?' [Where Do You Wander, My Fate?]), M. Petrenko ('Dyvlius' ia na nebo' [I Gaze at the Sky]), K. Dumytrashko ('Chornii brovy, karii ochi' [Black Eyebrows, Hazel Eyes]), and P. Nishchynsky ('Zakuvala ta syva zozulia' [The Gray Cuckoo Has Called]), to name just the most famous. Poetry played a key role in spreading the vernacular to other parts of Ukraine. The *Ruthenian Triad of I. Vahylevych, Ya. Holovatsky, and M. *Shaskevych (the most gifted poet of the three) introduced the vernacular to Galicia in their *Rusalka Dnistrovaia* (Dniester Nymph, 1837). Yu. *Fedkovych's ballads and soldier poems did the same for Bukovyna (first collection in 1862), and O. *Dukhnovych's poems for

Transcarpathia. Other poets of note in the first half of the 19th century were the Galician A. *Mohylnytsky, S. *Vorobkevych, V. *Mova, the sensitive lyricist L. *Hlibov, and S. *Rudansky, known chiefly for his collection of verse based on folk humor and wisdom, *Spivomovky*.

The second half of the century saw a decline in poetry, partly because of the overwhelming weight of Shevchenko's influence, which encouraged a proliferation of epigones, but mainly because of the dominance of realism and naturalism, the esthetic programs of which lent themselves to prose. No small part in the decline of the quality of poetry and of literary activity in general was played by the tsarist prohibitions of Ukrainian letters, the Valuev circular (see P. *Valuev) and the *Ems Ukase. What poetry appeared was mainly directed to the advancement of the struggle of the downtrodden – the peasant, the artisan, the worker, or the Ukrainian people in general. A major part of the poetic output by such populist writers as Ya. Shchoholiv, B. *Hrinchenko, P. *Hrabovsky, and I. Manzhura consisted of rather standard quatrains with regular meters and rhymes, devoted thematically to 'realistic' depiction of the difficult conditions, and of exhortations to persevere and to struggle for a better future. Somewhat more lyrical were the poems of V. Shchurat, S. Yarychevsky, M. Kichura, and the feminist U. Kravchenko.

The unfavorable climate for poetry was overcome by Franko and Lesia *Ukrainka. Franko's mastery of form and wealth of themes (from revolutionary hymns such as 'Ne pora ...' [It Is Not Time Now ...] to the exquisite personal lyricism in *Ziv'iale lystia* [Withered Leaves, 1896]) greatly advanced the development of Ukrainian poetry. Similarly, Lesia Ukrainka enhanced the Ukrainian poetic tradition by her poetic dramas, in which she skillfully domesticated world themes and revealed a masterful command of iambic pentameter.

The influences of Western *symbolism, supported by similar developments in Russia and in Poland, gave rise toward the end of the century to a new esthetic perception. M. *Vorony launched Ukrainian modernism by issuing a manifesto (1901) calling for 'broader esthetic horizons' and publishing an almanac, *Z nad khmar i dolyn* (From above the Clouds and from Valleys, 1903), which attempted, with little success, to publish only 'modern' works.

Neither Vorony's poetry nor that of other modernist poets was exceptional. Such poets as P. *Karmansky, V. *Pachovsky, S. Tverdokhlib, O. Lutsky, S. Charnetsky (all part of *Moloda Muza in Lviv) and K. *Alchevska, M. Sribliansky (Mykyta *Shapoval), who contributed to the modernist journal *Ukraïns'ka khata*, pursued the idea of 'art for art's sake,' often embraced the *fin-de-siècle* despair in pessimistic outpourings, and, in general, greatly expanded the borders of the acceptable in Ukrainian poetry. M. *Cherniavsky, a poet from an older generation, V. *Samiilenko, with his satiric verse, and A. *Krymsky, with his exoticism, all contributed to the revival of lyrical poetry. Symbolism, especially P. Verlaine's notion of 'music above all else,' found many adherents, especially O. *Oles, by far the most popular lyricist of the time, and H. *Chuprynka. Poetry also expanded into prose in the miniatures of M. *Yatskiv and in some works of poetic prose by O. Kobylianska ('Bytva' [The Battle]), V. Stefanyk ('Moie slovo' [My Word] and 'Moia doroha' [My Road]), and M. Kotsiubynsky ('Intermezzo').

The literary renaissance of the 1920s was all-embracing, but poetry was a dominant genre. P. *Tychyna's unique poetic expression, a revitalized, skillfully structured folk idiom imbued with contemporary symbols and tropes, placed Ukrainian poetry on the first truly new course since Shevchenko. Out of the hundreds of poets who appeared, many were excellent, but none were as influential with respect to the development of Ukrainian poetry as Tychyna. The poetry of other symbolists, such as Ya. *Savchenko, O. *Slisarenko, M. *Tereshchenko, D. *Zahul, and V. *Svidzinsky, was close to Tychyna's. More unconventional poetry was written by the proponents of *futurism M. *Semenko, G. *Shkurupii, and O. *Vlyzko. Deriving from futurism but original and forceful was the poetry of M. *Bazhan. French Parnassian poetry influenced several poets, including M. *Zerov, M. *Rylsky, M. *Drai-Khmara, P. *Fylypovych, and Yu. *Klen, who were unofficially united in the group of *Neoclassicists. More traditional and without a specific 'ism' was the poetry of V. *Blakytny, V. *Polishchuk, V. *Chumak, D. *Falkivsky, M. *Yohansen, and Ye. *Pluzhnyk. Lyrical, prolific, and popular was the poet V. *Sosiura. The mass phenomenon in the literature of the period did not bypass poetry, and there were multitudes of 'poets' who wrote contemporary verses singing the praises of the proletariat. Better examples of such poetry can be found in the works of T. Masenko and V. Mysyk. But the renaissance was short-lived. Few of the many poets and writers managed to survive the terror of the 1930s and the difficult years that followed until the death of J. Stalin. Some, such as T. *Osmachka, I. *Bahriany, and V. *Barka, not only survived but managed to emigrate and thus provide a continuity between the poetry of the 1920s and that of later decades.

Western Ukraine in the interwar period produced one major poet, B.I. *Antonych. Whereas Tychyna brought a fresh new sound to Ukrainian poetry, Antonych refurbished its imagery. During and immediately after the struggle for national independence, certain poets wrote poetry celebrating the movement and exploits of the *Sich Riflemen. Much of it was written in the genre of folk songs, by R. *Kupchynsky, L. Lepky, Yu. Shkrumeliak, and others. Other poets in Western Ukraine grouped themselves around various journals according to ideological or esthetic conviction. Antonych was the main poet of the Catholic journal Dzvony. The pro-Soviet Novi shliakhy and Vikna featured A. *Kolomyiets and V. *Bobynsky. Bobynsky and O. Babii also wrote for *Mytusa, and S. *Hordynsky and V. *Lesych contributed to Nazustrich, both of which journals espoused art above ideology. The majority of poets were in the nationalist camp and grouped themselves around *Vistnyk, whether in Lviv (eg, B. *Kravtsiv), Prague (eg, Yu. Darahan, O. *Liaturynska, L. *Mosendz, O. *Stefanovych, O. *Olzhych, and O. *Teliha), or Warsaw (eg, Yu. *Lypa, N. *Livytska-Kholodna, and Ye. *Malaniuk). Their poetry, often written in regular meters and strophes and employing heroic imagery, was aimed chiefly at furthering the struggle for national liberation. Somewhat apart geographically but not ideologically or in matters of form were the poets of Transcarpathian Ukraine, among whom the most noted were V. *Grendzha-Donsky, I. *Irliavsky, and A. *Harasevych.

Rylsky, Bazhan, and Tychyna were the few great poets who survived the purges and continued writing through the artistically barren years of the 1940s and 1950s. They were joined by other, younger poets, such as A. *Malyshko, P. *Voronko, O. Pidsukha, R. *Bratun, and D. *Pavlychko, whose talents could not always develop freely in the difficult political circumstances. Through the 1940s and 1950s they, like everyone else, wrote what was demanded and expected of them by the Party. Rarely did their verse have anything to do with poetry. Others, from both Soviet and Western Ukraine, such as Osmachka, Bahriany, Barka, Klen, Malaniuk, Mosendz, Kravtsiv, Lesych, Liaturynska, Hordynsky, and M. *Orest, emigrated and continued to write after the Second World War. Some new poets appeared during the literary heyday that took place after the war in the displaced persons' camps. Poets such as Ya. *Slavutych, L. *Lyman, P. *Karpenko-Krynytsia, and H. *Cherin remained true both thematically and stylistically to the nationalistic poetry of the preceding generation. Somewhat different were the symbolistic and hermetic poetry of O. *Zuievsky, the philosophical sonnets of O. *Tarnavsky, and the introspective lyricism of B. *Oleksandriv and V. *Skorupsky. All continued to write after resettling outside of Europe, mostly in Canada (Slavutych, Zuievsky, Oleskandriv, Skorupsky, and others) or the United States (Tarnavsky, Cherin, Lyman, Hordynsky, and others). There are Ukrainian poets in every country to which Ukrainians emigrated. In Australia the best known are Z. Kohut, P. Vakulenko, and V. Onufriienko; in Great Britain, B. Bora, H. Mazurenko, and A. Lehit; in France, M. Kalytovska; in Germany, E. *Andiievska, I. *Kachurovsky, and the more recent émigré from Ukraine, M. Fishbein; and in Belgium, R. Baboval.

When the émigrés resettled in North America after the Second World War, they found a poetic tradition cultivated by the earlier émigrés, especially in Canada. Most of the poetry written in the first half of the 20th century consisted of folksy verses expressing longing for the homeland and the hardships of pioneer life. Such were the poems of P. Bozhyk, S. Palamariuk, T. *Fedyk, and others. More imbued with interwar nationalism were the poems of V. Kudryk, M. Gowda, I. Novosad, T. Kroiter, and, later, M. *Mandryka. (For fuller lists see *Canada.)

A major shift in Ukrainian poetry occurred in the late 1950s. After the death of Stalin in 1953 and the 'de-Stalinization' speech by N. Khrushchev at the 20th Party Congress in February 1956, literature, expecially poetry, revived. The so-called *shestydesiatnyky were able to overcome the destruction wrought by Stalinism for three decades and proceeded with the development of poetry where it had left off in the 1920s. A vitality and freshness permeates their lyricism. More than 60 new poets appeared; others, such as Pavlychko, were able to show their real talent for the first time. The foremost poets of that generation were L. *Kostenko, I. *Drach, V. *Korotych, M. *Vinhranovsky, and V. *Symonenko. Although new repressions occurred in the 1970s, a second generation of poets managed to appear. Among them the most noted were I. *Kalynets, V. *Stus, V. *Holoborodko, and I. *Zhylenko. Kalynets gave promise of moving Ukrainian poetry, as Tychyna had done before him, onto a new plane, in his synthesis of elemental Ukrainian spirituality and modern versification, but the repressions of L. Brezhnev prevented his doing so. The almost-official poet of Ukraine of the 1980s was B. *Oliinyk, although Drach, Pavlychko, and Kostenko retained their prominence. Some younger poets who showed promise in the 1980s were V. Zatulyviter, O. Slonovska, S. Yovenko, N. Davydovska, N. Bilotserkivets, and M. Barandii.

Almost simultaneously with the appearance of the *shestedysiatnyky* a modernization occurred in Ukrainian poetry outside of Ukraine. The *New York Group embraced younger poets who rejected the nationalist poetry of their predecessors and were searching for a new synthesis and expression capable of absorbing their peculiar situation as permanent émigrés. Their methods varied, from the surrealism of Andiievska to the depoetizations of G. *Tarnawsky, the sensuality of B. *Boychuk, the exoticism of V. Vovk, the intellectualism of B. *Rubchak, and the estrangement of P. Kylyna (*Warren).

A decade later the Prague Spring also brought a revival in the poetry of Ukrainians living in Czechoslovakia, most notably that of S. *Makara and S. *Hostyniak. Of interest also is the poetry of P. Romaniuk in Rumania.

Despite various political intrusions the writing of poetry continues to be the major Ukrainian literary activity. Among the émigrés there are many versifiers but few poets. There is some promise, however, in the youngest generation, namely, M. Revakovych, L. Gavur, and Dzhaveh [A. Wynnyckyj] in North America. In Ukraine in the late 1980s a most interesting phenomenon was the appearance of new poetic groupings, such as the avant-garde Bu-Ba-Bu, with the satiric, often parodic verses of V. Neborak, Yu. Andrukhovych, and O. Irvanets; LuHoSad, embracing the neofuturistic wordplay of I. Luchuk, N. Honchar, and R. Sadlovsky; and Propala Hramota, composed of the equally verbally daring and playful poets of Kiev O. Semenchenko (pseud: Semen Lybon), Yu. Lysenko (pseud: Yurko Pozaiak), and V. Lapkin (pseud: Viktor Nedostup). Under the new conditions of literary freedom some poets of previous generations were finally published (eg, M. *Vorobiov and T. *Melnychuk). Among the many younger poets of interest who appeared in the 1980s are V. Herasymiuk, I. Malkovych, I. Rymaruk, L. Taran, O. Lysheha, and O. Zabushko.

BIBLIOGRAPHY
Lepkyi, B. *Struny: Antol'ogiia ukraïns'koï poeziï* (Berlin 1922)
Kravtsiv, B. (ed). *Obirvani struny: Antolohiia poeziï poliahlykh, rozstrilianykh, zamuchenykh i zaslanykh, 1920–1945* (New York 1955)
Stel'makh, M.; Synytsia, I. (eds). *Narodna liryka* (Kiev 1956)
Derzhavyn, V. (ed). *Antolohiia ukraïns'koï poeziï* (London 1957)
Sydorenko, H. *Virshuvannia v ukraïns'kii literaturi* (Kiev 1962)
Andrusyshen, C.H.; Kirkconnell, W. (eds). *The Ukrainian Poets, 1189–1962* (Toronto 1963)
Mykytas', V.; Rudlovchak, O. (eds). *Poety Zakarpattia: Antolohiia zakarpatoukraïns'koï poeziï (XVI st.–1945 r.)* (Prešov 1965)
Kravtsiv, B. (ed). *Shistdesiat poetiv shistdesiatykh rokiv* (New York 1967)
Mishchenko, L. (ed). *Trydtsiat' ukraïns'kykh poetes: Antolohiia* (Kiev 1968)
Polishchuk, F. (ed). *Ukraïns'ka narodna poetychna tvorchist': Khrestomatiia* (Kiev 1968)
Boichuk, B.; Rubchak, B. (eds). *Koordynaty: Antolohiia suchasnoï ukraïns'koï poeziï na zakhodi*, 2 vols (Munich 1969)
Hrytsai, M. *Davnia ukraïns'ka poeziia* (Kiev 1972)
Dobrians'kyi, A. (ed). *Ukraïns'kyi sonet: Antolohiia* (Kiev 1976)
Slavutych, Ia. *Ukraïns'ka poeziia v Kanadi* (Edmonton 1976)
Ukraïns'ki poety v Avstraliï: Z-pid evkaliptiv: Poeziï (Melbourne 1976)
Mykytas', V. (ed). *Ukraïns'ka poeziia: Kinets' XVI–pochatok XVIII st.* (Kiev 1978)
Krekoten', V. (ed). *Apollonova liutnia: Kyïvs'ki poety XVII–XVIII st.* (Kiev 1982)
Antolohiia ukraïns'koï poeziï, 4 vols (Kiev 1984–6)
Sulyma, M. *Ukraïns'ke virshuvannia kintsia XVI–pochatku XVII st.* (Kiev 1985)
Struk, D.H. 'Ukraïns'ka radians'ka poeziia v 1984 rotsi,' *Suchasnist'*, 1986, no. 4
Rymaruk, I. (ed). *Visimdesiatnyky: Antolohiia novoï ukraïns'koï poeziï* (Edmonton 1990)

D.H. Struk

Pogodin, Mikhail, b 22 November 1800 in Moscow, d 20 December 1875 in Moscow. Russian historian, philologist, and journalist; corresponding member of the Russian Academy of Sciences from 1841. He graduated from Moscow University (1823) and taught there from 1826 to 1844. He advocated the *Normanist theory and opposed M. Kachenovsky's theory of the Khazar origin of Rus'. Pogodin published the nationalist journals *Moskovskii vestnik* (1827–30) and *Moskvitianin* (1841–56). During the reign of Nicholas I he developed and defended the reactionary theory of official nationality. Pogodin was an ideologue of tsarist *Pan-Slavism and the spiritual mentor of Galician *Russophiles (eg, D. Zubrytsky). He visited Lviv in 1835 and 1839–40, after which a 'Pogodin colony' was established there. From 1844 he worked for the Ministry of Education.

In three articles (1856–7) on the language of ancient Rus' Pogodin argued that before the Mongol invasion the Dnieper River Basin was inhabited by Russians, that Ukrainians (migrants from Subcarpathia) did not settle in the evacuated territories until the 16th century, and that the Cossacks were a separate Slavic-Turkic tribe. His views (later echoed by A. *Sobolevsky) provoked a debate, in which they were proved unfounded and unscholarly by prominent historians (M. Maksymovych, V. Antonovych, M. Vladimirsky-Budanov, M. Dashkevych, M. Hrushevsky) and philologists (O. Kotliarevsky, P. Zhytetsky, V. Jagić, A. Krymsky). Pogodin did pioneering research on the Rus' chronicles. He wrote books on Nestor the Chronicler and the origin of the Rus' chronicles (his PHD diss, 1839), the Norman period of Russian history (1859), and pre-Mongol Rus' history (3 vols, 1871), and studies, notes, and lectures on pre-Mongol Rus' (7 vols, 1846–57). His letters to M. Maksymovych were published in 1882, and a biography of him and his works were published by N. Barsukov (22 vols, 1888–1910).

Pogrom. In its widest meaning the term refers to a violent attack on the persons and property of any weaker ethnic, religious, or national group by members of a dominant group. The measures taken against the Ukrainian population during the Russian occupation of Galicia in 1914–15, for instance, sometimes figured as the 'Galician pogroms' in contemporary accounts. In its most common sense, however, the term 'pogrom' refers to the attacks accompanied by looting and bloodshed against the *Jews of the Russian Empire in the late 19th and early 20th centuries. More precisely the term refers to three waves of widespread assault on the Jewish population that occurred in 1881–4, 1903–6, and 1918–21 as offshoots of larger crises in the Russian Empire as a whole. The first disturbances of the sort actually occurred in 1859, following the Crimean War (1853–6), and in 1871 in Odessa, when Greeks and Jews clashed over the grain trade.

The first major series of pogroms took place after members of *Narodnaia Volia assassinated Alexander II on 13 March 1881. The attacks began in Yelysavethrad at the end of April and spread to the gubernias of Chernihiv, Katerynoslav, Kherson, Kiev, Odessa, Poltava, and Tavriia in early May. In July and August they flared anew in Poltava and Chernihiv provinces. Pogroms also took place in Warsaw, Balta, and several towns of Belarus and Lithuania. Pogrom activity largely ceased after a decree issued by the new interior minister, D. Tolstoi, on 21 June 1882, although there were isolated outbreaks in the spring of 1883 in Rostov and Katerynoslav and in the summer of 1884 in Nizhnii Novgorod.

In Ukraine the attacks were carried out largely by urban dwellers, mainly seasonal workers in factories, railways, and ports who had migrated from Russia. They did not spread to the villages in a significant way. Destruction and looting of property and beatings were characteristic of the pogroms. A relatively small number of people were killed. The pogroms had an electrifying effect on the Jewish population and provided an impetus for the *Zionist movement as well as emigration to the New World. Ironically the imperial Russian government responded to the attacks by instituting further legislative restrictions on the Jews within and outside the *Pale of Settlement and expelling Jews en masse from Moscow in 1891–2. A common explanation offered for that wave of pogroms has been that a spontaneous uprising resulted from rumors that Jews had been instrumental in the tsar's assassination. A more likely explanation is that alienated (and commonly migrant) workers were venting personal and economic frustration. The attacks were not officially condoned, although the imperial authorities showed their duplicity by failing to maintain public order.

The pogroms of 1903–6 had a different character. Faced with growing unrest (see *Revolution of 1905) and hoping to divert discontent arising from the empire's losses in the Russo-Japanese War, the imperial authorities granted reactionary newspapers and ultraconservative loyalist groups known as *Black Hundreds a free hand to agitate against 'Jewish machinations' as the cause of the social upheavals of the time. The pogroms followed as an intensification of that campaign. The first in a series of attacks occurred in Chişinău (Kishinev), in Bessarabia, during Passover in 1903, and the next in Homel, in Belarus, in September. In the fall of 1904 army recruits and local rabble perpetrated a series of pogroms in Ukraine, in Oleksandriia, Rivne, Smila, and elsewhere. As the revolutionary movement gained strength in 1905, the attacks intensified. In February a pogrom took place in Teodosiia, in April in Melitopil, and in May in Zhytomyr. The severest pogroms followed the proclamation of the October Manifesto, particularly in the first week of November 1905, when the non-Jewish intelligentsia was also attacked. In Ukraine major pogroms occurred in Kamianets-Podilskyi, Katerynoslav, Kiev, Kremenchuk, Mykolaiv, Odessa, Romen, Chernihiv, Symferopil, and Yelysavethrad. Altogether about 700 pogroms were recorded. The scope of the attacks went beyond the wholesale destruction of property seen in 1881–2, to include rape and the killing of several hundred Jews. Again the most prominent participants were industrial and railway workers, small shopkeepers, and artisans. Peasants mostly joined in order to loot property. The second wave of pogroms intensified the desire of Jews to emigrate from the Russian Empire.

The last wave of pogroms took place in connection with the Revolution of 1917 and the chaos that accompanied the *Ukrainian-Soviet War of 1917–21. Those pogroms far exceeded the earlier outbreaks in both size and severity. According to somewhat conservative (but wide-ranging) estimates made in the 1920s by N. Gergel, 887 major pogroms and 349 less severe attacks against Jews took place in Ukraine in 1918–20 and resulted in the death of 31,071 people and the injury of tens of thousands of others. Other estimates have put the number of dead as high as 60,000. The Gergel figures put the annual figure for pogroms at 80 in 1918, 934 in 1919, and 178 in 1920. Most (80 percent) were perpetrated in Right-Bank Ukraine, where the majority of the Jewish population in the Russian Empire lived. The pogroms began with the slaughter of Jews by Bolshevik units in the spring of 1918 in Hlukhiv and Novhorod-Siverskyi. In time, however, the Red Army was able to restore military discipline (and curb pogrom activity) among its troops, and it eventually established itself in the minds of Jews as the only force capable of protecting them. The Army of the UNR, under the command of S. *Petliura, was unable to control its troops in the same manner. A decree from Petliura in January 1919 to stem a growing wave of violence was ineffectual, and several of his commanders carried out a series of violent attacks against Jews in Berdychiv, Gvardiiske, Zhytomyr, (particularly) Proskuriv, and other locations. In spite of petitions from Jewish representatives Petliura remained silent on the pogrom issue until April. By that time Jewish leaders had lost faith in the Directory. Gergel's figures attributed 40 percent of the pogroms carried out in 1918–20 (355) to Directory troops, as well as nearly 54 percent of the resulting deaths (16,706). Various independent leaders of the *partisan movement in Ukraine (known commonly as otamans) also perpetrated pogroms (estimated at 28.8 percent of the total number of pogroms, and 26 percent of the total mortalities). They included otamans N. Hryhoriiv (who led the bloodiest of the pogroms), Anhel, and D. Terpylo (Zeleny). The Russian Volunteer Army commanded by Gen A. Denikin, often inspired by a Black Hundreds ideology, perpetrated numerous pogroms. In Ukraine alone it was responsible for 183 pogroms (20.6 percent of that country's total) and an estimated 5,235 deaths (nearly 17 percent). Its largest action took place in Khvastiv in September 1919 and claimed approx 1,500 lives.

Because the majority of Jews within the Russian Empire lived in Ukraine, the majority of pogroms in the Russian Empire were perpetrated there. Their number and intensity there has given rise to the assumption that they were carried out by the local population, and to a stereotypical image of the Ukrainian as an inherently anti-Semitic *pogromchik*. The notion became particularly widespread in the West as a result of the public sensation caused in France by the *Schwartzbard Trial, which followed the assassination of Petliura in Paris in 1926. Petliura was assassinated by a Bessarabian Jew on the grounds that Petliura personally was responsbile for the horrors of the pogroms in Ukraine.

BIBLIOGRAPHY

Heifetz, E. *The Slaughter of the Jews in the Ukraine in 1919* (New York 1921)

Krasnyi-Admoni, G.Ia. (ed). *Materialy dlia istorii antievreiskikh pogromov v Rossii*, vol 2, *Vos'midesiatyie gody (15 aprelia 1881 g.–29 fevralia 1882 g.)* (Petrograd–Moscow 1923)

Tcherikower, E. *Antisemitizm i pogromy na Ukraine 1917–1918 gg. (K istorii ukrainsko-evreiskikh otnoshenii)* (Berlin 1923)

Rybynsʹkyi, V.P. 'Protyievreisʹkyi rukh r. 1881-ho na Ukraïni,' *Zbirnyk pratsʹ Ievreisʹkoï istorychno-arkheohrafichnoï komisiï* (Vseukraïnsʹka akademiia nauk, *Zbirnyk Istorychno-filolohichnoho viddilu*, 73), vol 2 (1929)

Tcherikower, E. *Di ukrainer pogromen in yor 1919* (New York 1965)

Hunczak, T. 'A Reappraisal of Symon Petliura and Ukrainian-Jewish Relations, 1917–1921,' *Jewish Social Studies*, 31 (1969)

Szajkowski, Z. 'A Reappraisal of Symon Petliura and Ukrainian-Jewish Relations, 1917–1921: A Rebuttal,' *Jewish Social Studies*, 31 (1969)

Dubnow, S.M. *History of the Jews in Russia and Poland from the Earliest Times to the Present Day*, 3 vols (Philadelphia 1916–20; new edn, New York 1975)

Szajkowski, Z. *An Illustrated Sourcebook of Russian Antisemitism, 1881–1978* (New York 1980)

Pritsak, O. 'The Pogroms of 1881,' *HUS*, 11, no. 1/2 (June 1987)
                                                            P. Potichnyj

Pohlmann, Friedrich, b 1805, d 16 August 1870 in Lviv. Scenery designer of German origin. He was the first designer in the Ruska Besida Theater, for which he created scenery for the productions of *Marusia* (1864, based on H. Kvitka-Osnovianenko), T. Shevchenko's *Nazar Stodolia* (1865), and H. Yakymovych's *Roksoliana* (1865). In 1842–70 he worked in F. Skarbek's Polish theater in Lviv.

Mykhailo Pohoretsky   Oleksii Pohorielov (Aleksei Pogorelov)

Pohoretsky, Mykhailo [Pohorecʹkyj, Myxajlo] (Pohorecky, Michael), b 21 December 1899 in Hadynkivtsi, Kopychyntsi county, Galicia, d 26 July 1964 in Winnipeg. Journalist. A former officer in the *Ukrainian Sich Riflemen, he studied in Lviv at the underground university and at the Ukrainian Free University. Pohoretsky emigrated to Canada in 1927 and edited *Zakhidni visti* in Edmonton with V. *Kaye-Kysilewsky before establishing *Novyi shliakh* and serving as its longtime editor (1930–54, 1960–4). He was a founding member of the *Ukrainian National Federation and its president in 1936. For many years he was on the presidium of the Ukrainian Canadian Committee (now Congress).

Pohorielov, Oleksii [Pohorjelov, Oleksij] (Pogorelov, Aleksei), b 3 March 1919 in Korocha,   rsk gubernia, Russia. Mathematician; full member of the AN URSR (now ANU) since 1961 and of the USSR (now Russian) Academy of Sciences since 1976. After completing his studies at the Military-Aviation Academy in 1945, he worked at the Central Aerohydrodynamics Institute (1945–7) and then at Kharkiv University (professor from 1950). He also headed a department at the ANU Physical-Technical Institute of Low Temperatures in Kharkiv (since 1960) and the Northeast Scientific Center of the ANU (1978–81). Pohorielov's fundamental and lasting contributions are in the field of geometry in large. V. Drinfeld, one of the scholars from Pohorielov's school, was awarded the Fields Medal in 1990. He solved completely a number of outstanding problems, including the classical problem of the unique determination of a convex surface by its internal metric, the external regularity of convex surfaces with regular internal metric, the celebrated Hilbert's fourth problem, the Minkowski multidimensional problem, and the problem of Weil concerning the isometric immersion in the large of a two-dimensional Riemannian manifold into a three-dimensional one. He developed the nonlinear theory of elastic shells and obtained fundamental results regarding such difficult problems as the regularity of convex surfaces under various conditions and infidecimal bending of convex surfaces. His work has had a great impact on the theory of partial differential equations.

                                                            W. Petryshyn

Pohorilivka archeological site. A late Neolithic (mid to late 3rd millennium BC) site near Pohorilivka, Krolevets raion, Sumy oblast. Excavations since the 1920s have revealed a variety of hunting and fishing utensils and remains of pottery decorated by pitting and combing.

Pohost (Russian: *pogost*). An administrative term, dating from the time of Kievan Rusʹ, denoting a territorial unit that usually encompassed a rural community. Under the Hetman state (17th–18th centuries) in Starodub regiment a resettled colony of Russian Old Believers was called a *pohost*. In other regions during the 15th to 17th centuries, particularly Novgorod, a *pogost* signified a village with a church and cemetery or simply a rural cemetery. The term was used in the latter sense in folk literature at the end of the 19th century.

Pohrebennyk, Fedir, b 29 June 1929 in Rozhniv, Stanyslaviv county, Galicia. Literary scholar. He completed a degree in literature at Chernivtsi University and since 1959 has worked at the Institute of Literature of the AN URSR (now ANU). Except for some articles on T. Shevchenko, Pohrebennyk has concentrated on the turn-of-the-century writers from his native region. He coedited *Pysʹmennyky Bukovyny* (Writers of Bukovyna, 1958) and edited a book on M. Cheremshyna (1975) and a book on O. Kobylianska (1982). He wrote *Osyp Makovei: Krytyko-biohrafichnyi narys* (Osyp Makovei: A Critical-Biographic Sketch, 1960). The majority of his works, however, are devoted to V. *Stefanyk: besides the three-volume collection of Stefanyk's works, which he coedited with V. Lesyn in 1964, he edited *Spivetsʹ znedolenoho selianstva* (The Singer of the Unfortunate Peasantry, 1974) and wrote *Vasylʹ Stefanyk u slovʹiansʹkykh literaturakh* (Vasyl Stefanyk in Slavic Literatures, 1976), *Vasylʹ Stefanyk: Seminariï* (Vasyl Stefanyk: Seminars, 1979), and his doctoral study, *Storinky zhyttia i tvorchosti Vasylia Stefanyka* (Pages from the Life and Creativity of Vasyl Stefanyk, 1980). Pohrebennyk's approach, like that of the majority of Soviet literary scholars, avoided the ideological pitfalls of interpretive reading and concentrated on biographical details.

                                                            D.H. Struk

Pohrebinsky, Solomon [Pohrebins'kyj], b 19 March 1924 in Kiev. Computer scientist. He graduated from the Kiev Polytechnical Institute (1949) and worked at the AN URSR (now ANU) institutes of Exact Mechanics and Computing Technology (1949–56), Mathematics (1956–7), and Cybernetics (since 1957). His main contributions are in the field of computer theory. He was a member of the teams which designed the earliest Soviet computers, including the *MEOM and MIR.

Pohrebniak, Petro [Pohrebnjak], b 10 July 1900 in Volokhiv Yar, Chuhuiv county, Kharkiv gubernia, d 25 July 1976 in Kiev. Forester and soil scientist; full member of the AN URSR (now ANU) from 1948. He graduated from the Kharkiv Agricultural Institute (1924) and worked for the Ukrainian Scientific Research Institute of Forest Management and Agroforest Amelioration (1931–3). He was a department head at the Kiev Institute of Forest Management (1933–41), taught at Kiev University (1944–56), headed the ANU Institute of Forestry (1945–56), and served as vice-president of the ANU and chairman of its Economic Production Studies Committee (1948–50). He was an acting department head of the Central Republican Botanical Garden (1956–60) and the geography division of the ANU, and of the Institute of Botany (from 1964). Pohrebniak's major scholarly interests included forest typology and the physiology of trees and shrubs, forest hydrology, plant ecology, forest soil study, and forestation techniques in sandy soils. He undertook pioneering work in the field of phytoecology and is known for his classifications of soil systems, particularly his articulation of the idea of a soil continuum. He wrote numerous works, including *Osnovy lesnoi tipologii* (The Foundations of Forest Typology, 1955) and a book coauthored with N. Remezov and translated as *Forest Soil Science* (1969). He also served as head of the Ukrainian Society for the Protection of Nature in 1950–62.

Pohrebniak, Yakym [Pohrebnjak, Jakym], b ? in Nova Vodolaha, in the Kharkiv region, d ? Eighteenth-century master builder. He built cruciform wooden churches with pyramidal roofs, including the five-cupola churches in Merefa and Artemivka (1761, destroyed by the Soviets) and the largest wooden structure in Ukraine of the 18th century – the Trinity Cathedral in Novomoskovske, with nine frames and nine cupolas almost 65 m in height (1773–8).

Pohrebyshche [Pohrebyšče]. IV-10. A city (1989 pop 11,700) on the Ros River and a raion center in Vinnytsia oblast. In the 12th century the town of Rokytnia stood at the site. After its destruction by the Tatars in 1240, the new settlement was called Pohrebyshche. At the beginning of the 16th century it came under Polish rule. In the 1580s a fortress was built there, and in 1595 it was captured by rebellious peasants and Cossacks. The town's inhabitants took part in B. Khmelnytsky's uprising, and in 1648 Pohrebyshche became a company center in Bratslav regiment. By the Treaty of Andrusovo (1667) it was ceded to Poland, and after the partition of Poland in 1793, to Russia. It attained city status in 1984. Today it produces sugar, powdered milk, animal feed, reinforced concrete, brick, and construction materials.

Pohribniak, Mykola [Pohribnjak], b 5 December 1885 in Kozatske, Zvenyhorodka county, Kiev gubernia, d 30 May 1965 in Dnipropetrovske. Painter and graphic artist. He studied under O. Slastion at the Myrhorod Applied Arts School (1903–8) and later taught at the Dnipropetrovske Art School. His work consists of genre paintings and landscapes, such as *After the Rain* (1912), *In the Kiev Region* (1913), *Evening* (1937), and *Snowstorm* (1945), and illustrations for children's books and school texts. He amassed a large collection of Ukrainian decorative designs.

Pohribny, Mykola [Pohribnyj], b 13 May 1920 in Mochalyshche, Kozelets county, Chernihiv gubernia. Lexicographer. A graduate of the Zaporizhia Pedagogical Institute, he taught secondary school and worked as a radio announcer. He compiled the first dictionary of stresses in Standard Ukrainian (1959, 1964), an orthoepic dictionary (1984), and a dictionary of proper names (unpublished). His studies of current usage are published in the methodological collection *Teleradiovisnyk Ukraïny* (Television-Radio Herald of Ukraine), and his column on norms appears in the radio magazine *Slovo*.

Poiarkov, Yurii [Pojarkov, Jurij], b 10 February 1937 in Kharkiv. One of the best volleyball players in the history of the sport. He played on more winning teams of world, Olympic, and European championships than any other male player. A regular player on the Kharkiv Burevisnyk team, he played on the USSR teams that won the 1964 and 1968 Olympic gold medals, the 1972 bronze medal, the 1960 and 1962 world championships, and the 1967 and 1971 European championships.

Poida, Dmytro [Pojda], b 3 November 1908 in Borodaivski Khutory, Verkhnodniprovske county, Katerynoslav gubernia. Soviet Ukrainian historian. He graduated from the Kharkiv Pedagogical Institute (1936), and from 1937 he taught in Dnipropetrovske at the higher CP school, the Mining Institute, and (from 1965) the university, as head of the department of the history of the USSR and the Ukrainian SSR. He wrote *Krest'ianskoe dvizhenie na Pravoberezhnoi Ukraine v poreformennyi period (1866–1900 gg.)* (The Peasant Movement in Right-Bank Ukraine in the Post-Reform Period [1866–1900], 1960) and *Z istoriï borot'by ukraïns'koho selianstva proty dukhivnytstva v dorevoliutsiinyi chas* (On the History of the Struggle of Ukrainian Peasants against the Clergy in the Prerevolutionary Period, 1961).

Pokalchuk, Volodymyr [Pokal'čuk], b 1 July 1897 in Velyka Fosnia, Ovruch county, Volhynia gubernia, d 5 January 1985 in Lutske. Philologist and teacher; father of Yu. Pokalchuk. During the 1920s he studied at the Kiev Institute of People's Education (1923–8) and was active there in the Group for the Culture of the Ukrainian Word (HuKUS). In 1928 he began postgraduate studies under M. Zerov at the Taras Shevchenko Scientific Research Institute. His book reviews and articles on 19th-century Ukrainian writers were published in *Zhyttia i revoliutsiia*. Pokalchuk was one of the many Ukrainian intellectuals arrested by the GPU in 1930 in preparation for the show trial of the so-called *Union for the Liberation of Ukraine. He was released from a Kiev prison in 1932 but was barred from pursuing a scholarly career. After a few years he was allowed to teach, and lectured at the pedagogical institutes in Poltava and Kremianets (1939–41). After the Second World War he taught at the Lutske Pedagogical Institute and researched the dialects, ethnography, and regional history of Volhynia. Until his retirement in 1980, he suffered occasional persecution by the Soviet authorities, including dismissal from the Lutske institute for one year.

Pokalchuk, Yurii [Pokal'čuk, Jurij], b 24 January 1941 in Kremianets, Ternopil oblast. Writer, literary scholar, and translator; son of V. *Pokalchuk. He graduated from Leningrad University (1964) and did graduate work at the AN URSR (now ANU) Institute of Literature. After receiving a candidate's degree in 1969, he worked as a scholarly associate of the institute (until 1977) and wrote books about postwar American literature (1972) and contemporary Latin American prose (1978). He began writing fiction in 1965 and is the author of the prose collections *Khto ty?* (Who Are You?, 1979), *Kol'orovi melodii* (Colored Melodies, 1984), *Velykyi i malyi* (The Big and the Small, 1986), and *Kava z Matagal'py* (Coffee from Matagalpa, 1987) and of the novels *I zaraz, i zavzhdy ...* (Now and Forever, 1981), *Shablia i strila* (The Sword and the Arrow, 1988), and *Moderat* (1990).

Pokhodenko, Vitalii [Poxodenko, Vitalij], b 9 January 1936 in Komunarske, Luhanske oblast. Physical chemist; AN URSR (now ANU) corresponding member since 1973 and full member since 1985. After graduating from Kiev University (1958) he joined the ANU Institute of Physical Chemistry and became its deputy director in 1971 and director in 1983. He has studied the effects of structure on the spectral properties, kinetics, and mechanism of free radical reactions; determined the electronic structure of various free radicals, proving the radical mechanism of many reactions; discovered a new reaction type involving single electron transfers; and determined the effect of a reagent's electronic structure on free radical redox reactions.

Pokhodnia, Ihor [Poxodnja], b 24 January 1927 in Moscow. Ukrainian metallurgist; full member of the AN URSR (now ANU) since 1976. He graduated from the Kiev Polytechnical Institute (1949) and since 1952 has worked at the ANU Institute of Electric Welding. In 1970 he became chief academic secretary of the ANU. He headed the developmental effort in the area of vacuum welding, which was later successfully used in space, particularly during the flight of the satellite Soiuz-6.

***Pokhozhi* peasants** (*pokhozhi seliany*). A category of formally free peasants who lived on and utilized state-owned lands in the 14th- to 16th-century Lithuanian-Ruthenian state. In exchange they paid tribute or taxes in cash or kind and fulfilled basic agricultural and labor obligations to the state (eg, plowing and harvesting land on the grand duke's estates and around castles, delivering hay and wood to castles, building roads, bridges, and fortifications, hunting and fishing for the grand duke). Those obligations were collectively called *tiahlo* ('draft,' from the use of draft animals; thence the term *tiahlo* peasants). The *pokhozhi* ('mobile') peasants had the right to move to other places. Their personal property, and their inheritance rights, which were regulated by customary law, were diminished over time. *Pokhozhi* peasants who moved onto lands owned by feudal lords, or who lived on lands granted by the grand duke to such lords, no longer had obligations to the state, but paid quitrents to and performed corvée for the lords. Their freedom to leave was subject to restrictive loan agreements with the lord and excessive penalties for breaking their contracts. After 10 years they became *nepokhozhi* peasants; that is, they lost their freedom to move and were partially enserfed.

Dmytro Pokhylevych

Pokhylevych, Dmytro [Poxylevyč], b 22 September 1897 in Vodotni, Zhytomyr county, Volhynia gubernia, d 29 May 1974 in Lviv. Historian. A graduate of the Kiev Institute of People's Education (1924), he taught in postsecondary institutes in Ukraine and Russia. From 1946 he was in charge of medieval history at Lviv University, and in 1952–73 he chaired the department of South and West Slavic history there. Pokhylevych wrote numerous articles, mainly on agrarian relations and the history of the peasantry of Ukraine, Belarus, Lithuania, and Poland, and monographs on the 16th- to 18th-century Belarusian and Lithuanian peasantry (1957), Poland in the feudal era (1965), and the Belarusian and Lithuanian peasantry in the second half of the 18th century (1966).

Pokhylevych, Lavrentii [Poxylevyč, Lavrentij], b 1816, d 1893. Regional historian. He worked as a clerk in the Kiev Consistory and wrote books in Russian on tales about the populated places of Kiev gubernia (1864) and the populated places of Kiev and Radomyshl counties (1887). They contain a wealth of topographic, statistical, economic, religious, ethnographic, and historical information, not all of which is accurate.

Pokhytonov, Ivan [Poxytonov], b 8 February 1850 in Motronivka, Oleksandriia county, Kherson gubernia, d 12 December 1923 in Liège or Brussels. Painter; full member of the St Petersburg Academy of Arts from 1904. From 1876 he lived in France and Belgium and was influenced by the Barbizon school. In 1891 he joined the *Society of South Russian Artists. In 1903–5 he worked in Belarus, and in 1905 he became a member of the *Peredvizhniki society. In 1913 he returned to the Kherson region. From 1919 he lived as an émigré in Belgium. He is known for his small but masterly landscapes, including many of Ukraine, such as *Peasant Wedding, In the Reeds, Winter Dusk, Potato Gathering, Evening in Ukraine,* and *Harvest.* A catalog of his works was published in Moscow in 1963.

Ivan Pokhytonov: *Winter Dusk in Ukraine* (oil, 1886)

Pokotylivka. IV-17. A town smt (1986 pop 10,800) in Kharkiv raion, Kharkiv oblast. The town was formed in the 1959 by the amalgamation of two villages, Karachivka and Pokotylivka. Many of its residents work in Kharkiv, which is only 8 km away. Pokotylivka has a fruit-canning factory and a reforestation station.

Pokotylo, Mykhailo, b 21 June 1906 in Borshna, Pryluka county, Poltava gubernia, d 1 September 1971 in Kiev. Stage and film actor and director. He studied in the Kiev (1927–8) and Kharkiv (1928–30) music and drama institutes and then worked in the Kharkiv Chervonozavodskyi Ukrainian Drama Theater (1931–3), the Kharkiv Ukrainian Drama Theater (1934–61), and the Kiev Ukrainian Drama Theater (1961–71). He acted in the films *Pedahohichna poema* (A Pedagogical Poem, 1955, based on A. Makarenko's novel) and *Shel'menko-denshchyk* (Shelmenko the Orderly, 1957, based on H. Kvitka-Osnovianenko's comedy).

Pokrovsk. See Engels.

Pokrovske [Pokrovs'ke]. VI-17. A town smt (1986 pop 11,900) on the Vovcha River and a raion center in Dnipropetrovske oblast. It developed out of a Cossack homestead (est in 1760) into a military settlement. Today it has a food industry.

Pokrovsky, Andrii [Pokrovs'kyj, Andrij], b and d ? Navy admiral. A vice-admiral in the Russian navy during the First World War, in 1918 he served the UNR as commander of Black Sea ports and was promoted to admiral by the Hetman government. In November–December 1918 he was minister of the navy in the Hetman government of S. Gerbel.

Pokrovsky, Mikhail, b 29 August 1868 in Moscow, d 10 April 1932 in Moscow. Russian Marxist historian. Pokrovsky studied at Moscow University (1887–91) under P. Vinogradov and V. *Kliuchevsky. A member of the Bolshevik party from 1905, he was an important organizer of Soviet historical scholarship after the revolution until the Stalin period. He headed the Institute of Red Professors and edited the journal *Krasnyi arkhiv*. One of his major works, *Russkaia istoriia s drevneishikh vremen* (A History of Russia from the Earliest Times, 5 vols, 1910–13), had a long chapter titled 'The Struggle for Ukraine.' It interpreted Ukrainian history from the 16th through the 18th century as essentially social strivings under the guise of national or national-religious struggle. The chapter was omitted from the authorized English translation, *A History of Russia*, prepared by J.D. Clarkson and M.R.M. Griffiths in 1931. Pokrovsky's work was marked by an absence of Russian nationalism. He respected the historiographical contributions of M. *Kostomarov and M. *Hrushevsky and considered that Ukraine had been in a colonial relationship to tsarist Russia. Pokrovsky's historical methods had a major influence on the Ukrainian Marxist historian M. *Yavorsky. A collection of Pokrovsky's articles on Ukraine, edited by M. Popov, was published in Kiev in 1935. A critical edition of Pokrovsky's selected works appeared in Moscow in 1965–7. R. Szporluk edited a collection of Pokrovsky's articles in English translation in 1970.

J.-P. Himka

Pokrovsky, Mykola [Pokrovs'kyj], b 28 October 1901 in Tulchyn, Bratslav county, Podilia gubernia, d 16 July 1985 in Odessa. Opera conductor. A graduate of the Kiev Institute of Music and Drama (1925), Pokrovsky studied under M. Leontovych. In 1924–6 he was music director of the Berezil theater and then conducted opera in Odessa (1926–33, 1944–75), Kharkiv (1934–40, 1941–4), and Lviv (1940–1). He premiered B. Yanovsky's *The Black Sea Duma* (1929), V. Kostenko's *Karmeliuk* (1930), and K. Dankevych's *Bohdan Khmelnytsky* (1951). From 1947 he taught at the Odessa Conservatory.

Pokrovsky, Vasilii [Pokrovskij, Vasilij], b 1839 near Kaluga, Russia, d 31 January 1877 in Kiev. Russian physician. A graduate of the St Petersburg Medico-Surgical Academy (1861), from 1867 he was a professor at Kiev University, where he taught in the fields of pediatrics, skin diseases, otolaryngology, and nervous and psychic disorders. He was also director of the internal medicine clinic at the Kiev Military Hospital; he died directing efforts to control an outbreak of typhus in Kiev.

Pokrovsky, Yosyp [Pokrovs'kyj, Josyp], b 5 September 1868 in Hlukhiv county, Chernihiv gubernia, d 14 May 1920 in Moscow. Legal scholar. After graduating from the law faculty of Kiev University and the seminar on Roman law at Berlin University, he lectured at Yurev (now Tartu) (1894–6), Kiev (1896–1902), St Petersburg (1902–17), and Moscow (1918–20) universities. A specialist in Roman and civil law, Pokrovsky accepted the concept of natural law and defended the absolute freedom of the individual. His chief books are *Pravo i fakt v rimskom prave* (Law and Fact in Roman Law, 1898) and *Osnovatel'nye problemy grazhdanskogo prava* (Fundamental Problems of Civil Law, 1917).

Pokukhovne. A tax on liquor sales under the Hetmanate. It was introduced during B. Khmelnytsky's uprising (1648–57) and was collected from innkeepers according to the number of casks (*kufy*) sold. Monasteries and certain estates were exempted from the tax. The income generated was divided among the regimental *starshyna*. The tax was abolished in the 1780s, when the tsarist regime reorganized the administrative system in Ukraine.

Pokutia (Rumanian: Pokucia). A historical-geographic upland region bounded by the Dniester River and the Podolian Upland to the north, the Prut River and Subcarpathia to the south, the Stanyslaviv Depression to the west, and the Kitsman Depression and the Sovytsia River to the east. Extending up to 100 km from east to west and 25–40 km from north to south, Pokutia covers about 3,000 sq km and has a population of about 400,000. Users of the Pokutian dialects (see *Bukovyna-Pokutia dialects) also inhabit a portion of Subcarpathia. Because of their presence there, the term Pokutia has been used to refer to the entire southeastern corner of Galicia between historic Hungary to the southwest and Moldavia to the southeast. Occasionally the term even included a part of Bukovyna.

Physical geography. Pokutia is the northwestern part of the Pokutian-Bessarabian Upland. Tectonically, it is the southwestern branch of the Ukrainian Crystalline Shield. The old Paleozoic sedimentaries lie far below the Miocene marls, limestones, shales, and gypsum, which in turn are covered by thick layers of loess. At the end of the Tertiary period Pokutia was a flat lowland crossed by the meandering Dniester River. At the end of the Pliocene and the beginning of the Pleistocene epoch an uplift caused the Dniester and the Prut to cut deeply into the sediments, thereby setting off subsequent erosion by their tributaries and the dissection of the Prut-Dniester interfluve. At that time a relative downwarping formed the Stanyslaviv Depression and caused the Bystrytsia River to change direction and to flow into the Dniester instead of the Prut.

Today Pokutia is a gently undulating plain sloping to the southeast. Elevations range from 300 to 350 m above sea level. In general the western part is more dissected than the eastern part. The landscape is divided into a number of alternating rises and shallow basins. Widespread gypsum deposits account for the abundance of karst features, such as sink holes, dolines, caves, karst lakes, disappearing rivers, and bare gypsum cliffs, particularly in the Tovmach-Horodenka Basin.

The Dniester region, a narrow (10–15 km) band along the right bank of the Dniester River, has a different landscape. It is as deeply dissected as the opposite bank on the Podilia side. In the south the long Kolomyia-Chernivtsi Depression forms a terraced alluvial lowland along the Prut River.

The river network of Pokutia has a radial character. Short rivers flow northward into the Dniester River, longer ones flow southward into the Prut River, and a few join Bystrytsia (tributary of the Dniester) to the west. The network is poorly developed because of the karst landscape. The rivers are short, shallow, and deeply incised in the soft, relatively soluble rock.

The climate of Pokutia is temperate continental: the average annual temperature ranges from 6.9°C to 7.6°C, the average January temperature, from –4.8°C to –5.1°C, and the average July temperature, from 18.2°C to 18.8°C. The number of days with temperatures above 15°C ranges from 96 to 110. Precipitation is adequate to fairly abundant, from 550 to 640 mm per year, depending on the elevation of the region. Soils are mostly podzolized chernozems (with up to 4 percent humus). In western Pokutia there are also gray forest podzolized soils (1–3 percent humus). The natural vegetation is typical of the Central European broad-leaved forest zone and the East European forest-steppe. Very little of Pokutia's original vegetation has survived. The forests have been reduced to barely 10 percent of the land area in western Pokutia and 7 percent in the east. The forests usually consist of hornbeam and oak, and the groves along the rivers, of alder. Remnants of steppe vegetation include wormwood, esparto grass, thistle, and sage.

History. Greek and Roman accounts of widespread Slavic settlement have been confirmed by archeological finds in Pokutia. In the 4th and 5th centuries the Slavs of Pokutia were members of the Antes tribal alliance, in the 6th and 7th centuries, of the Dulebian alliance, and in the 8th and 9th centuries, of the Tivertsian alliance. In the 10th century Pokutia was part of Kievan Rus', and after the *Liubech congress of princes it became part of the Halych principality. Although it was sparsely settled, there were some towns, such as Sniatyn (known since 1158) and Kolomyia (since 1240), in the region. In the second half of the 14th century Poland annexed Galicia, including Pokutia, which was claimed by the emerging principality of Moldavia. The name Pokutia was first mentioned in 1395 in a Moldavian charter, and again in a 15th-century Polish chronicle by J. Dlugosz. In 1388, for a loan of 3,000 gold coins Jagiełło of Poland placed Pokutia under the administration of the Moldavian voivode P. Muşat. *Stephen III of Moldavia (1457–1504) led two campaigns to Pokutia (1498, 1502) and pushed the Poles back beyond the Bystrytsia. His son, Bogdan III (1504–17), disclaimed Pokutia and then occupied it briefly, in 1509–10. Voivode P. Rareş's attempts to recapture Pokutia (1531, 1535) failed. The last Moldavian attempt to seize Pokutia was made by John the Terrible in 1572. The Moldavian-Polish wars caused the local population much suffering. Many Pokutians were captured and resettled in Moldavia and Bukovyna, where they strengthened the Ukrainian element.

Along with western Ukraine Pokutia remained under Polish rule until 1772, when it became part of the Austrian Empire. In the 17th to 19th centuries the Ukrainian *opryshoks were active in the region. When the Austrian Empire collapsed, most of Pokutia became part of the Western Ukrainian National Republic (1919). Except for the eastern extremity (east of Sniatyn), which was taken by Rumania, Pokutia was occupied by Poland in 1919–39 and then incorporated into Soviet Ukraine. Most of its territory lies in Ivano-Frankivske oblast. The eastern part lies in Chernivtsi oblast.

Population. Along with Subcarpathia Pokutia belongs to the most densely populated part of Ukraine. The average density approaches 130 people per sq km, and the rural density, 100 people per sq km. The highest densities occur in southern Pokutia along the Prut River. Less than 30 percent of the population is urban. Cities such as Ivano-Frankivske and Chernivtsi lie outside the region. The Pokutian cities of Kolomyia (1989 pop 63,000), Sniatyn (7,300), and Zabolotiv (4,200) are all located on the Prut River. The former county towns of Horodenka (8,100) and Tovmach (5,100) and the urban-type settlements of Obertyn (3,700), Hvizdets (1,500), and Otynia (3,900) are located in the upland.

At the end of the 18th century Pokutia was inhabited by Ukrainians, who constituted nearly 90 percent of the population, some Jews, and a small number of Poles and Armenians. With time more Poles settled in the region, especially in the 1920s and 1930s. A small number of Germans lived in Kolomyia and its vicinity. In 1939, Ukrainians constituted 74 percent of Pokutia's population, Poles, 9 percent, Ukrainian-speaking Roman Catholics, 7 percent, and Jews, 9 percent. In the 1990s Ukrainians account for 97 percent, Russians, 2 percent, Poles, less than 1 percent, and Jews, 0.2 percent of the population.

Economy. Pokutia was and remains predominantly agricultural. Nearly 76 percent of the land is cultivated, 9 percent is hayfield and pasture, and 9 percent is forest. The sown area is distributed approximately as follows: grains occupy 44 percent, including some 20 percent occupied by wheat, 10 percent by corn, 7 percent by barley, 4 percent by rye, 2 percent by oats, and 1 percent by millet and buckwheat; potatoes and vegetables together take up 15 percent; technical crops another 14 percent, including 10 percent occupied by sugar beets; and feed crops, the remaining 27 percent. The area devoted to corn, sugar beets, and tobacco increases toward the east. Livestock husbandry is concentrated on meat and milk production.

Industry does not play an important role in the region. Only Kolomyia, the largest city, has a broad base of light industries (cotton textiles, knitting, clothing, curtain-making, and footwear), food processing (meat packing, meat canning, dairying, grist milling, distilling), woodworking (furniture and paper manufacturing), and agricultural machine building. Traditional handicrafts are maintained, such as wood carving, embroidery, and kilim weaving. Other towns have a food industry: sugar refining in Kostryzhivka and dairying (butter, cheese, and milk products) in Horodenka and Sniatyn. The deposits of phosphorites, gypsum, and limestone have not been exploited on a large scale by the chemical or building-materials industries.

BIBLIOGRAPHY
Korduba, M. 'Moldavs'ko-pol's'ka hranytsia na Pokutiu do smerty Stefana Velykoho,' *Naukovyi zbirnyk prysviachenyi profesorovy Mykhailovy Hrushevs'komu* (Lviv 1906)
Czyżewski, J.; Koczwara, M.; Zglinicka, A. *Pokucie* (Lviv 1931)
Kvitkovs'kyi, D.; Bryndzan, T.; Zhukovs'kyi, A. (eds). *Bukovyna, ïï mynule i suchasne* (Paris–Philadelphia–Detroit 1956)
Koinov, M. *Pryroda Stanyslavivs'koï oblasti* (Lviv 1960)
Istoriia mist i sil Ukraïns'koï RSR: Ivano-Frankivs'ka oblast' (Kiev 1971)
V. Kubijovyč, M. Kovaliuk, I. Stebelsky, A. Zhukovsky

Pokutian dialects. See Bukovyna-Pokutia dialects.

Pokutian-Bessarabian Upland. The southwesternmost section of the Ukrainian uplands, situated between the Prut River and the Stanyslaviv Depression to the west, the Dniester River (bordering on the Podolian Upland) to the east, and the Black Sea Lowland to the south. It lies on the southwestern border of the Ukrainian Crystalline Shield. Paleozoic and Upper Mesozoic strata are found in the upland only in the Dniester Valley. The rest of it consists of middle Miocene strata (Pokutian clay, gypsum, and limestone) covered by strata of later Miocene (sands, limestone, and clay). In the south the latter are covered with layers of Pliocene sand and clay. The entire upland is covered by a deposit of loess up to 30 m in depth.

The average elevation of the upland is 300–400 m; the upland forms an undulating plateau that is dissected by valleys and ravines and bears certain characteristics of foothills. It is commonly divided into (from north to south) the Pokutian Upland, the Berdo-Horodyshche Elevation, the Khotyn-Soroky Divide, the Beltsi (Bălţi) Plain, and the Kodry Hills. The northern and northeastern sections of the upland are settled by Ukrainians, and the rest by Rumanians. The region was formerly a part of Galicia, Bukovyna, and Bessarabia, but now it forms parts of Ivano-Frankivske and Chernivtsi oblasts and Moldova.

The Pokutian Upland is a plateau (elevation 300–350 m) with karst features and few intersections. The Berdo-Horodyshche Elevation in northern Bukovyna is covered with beech forest and rises to over 516 m in places. It extends into the Khotyn-Soroky Divide (also known as the Khotyn or Khotyn-Sadhorod Elevation), the watershed between the Dniester and the Prut rivers, which descend from 460 m near Khotyn to 300 m in the southeast. The Rumanian portions of the upland have a few pockets of Ukrainian settlement.

V. Kubijovyč

Pokutian-Bukovynian Carpathians. See Hutsul Beskyd.

Pokuts'ke slovo (Pokutian Word). A semimonthly newspaper published in Stanyslaviv (now Ivano-Frankivske) and then Kolomyia in 1926–7 by the Ukrainian Socialist Radical party (see *Ukrainian Radical party).

Pokuts'kyi vistnyk (Pokutia Herald). An organ of the Kolomyia regional council of the Ukrainian National Rada. It was published twice and then three times a week from November 1918 to May 1919 and was edited by Ya. Navchuk and, after the fourth issue, O. Karashkevych.

Oleksander Pol

Pol, Oleksander [Pol'], b 1 September 1832 in Malooleksandrivske, Verkhnodniprovske county, Katerynoslav guberniia, d 7 August 1890 in Katerynoslav. Entrepreneur and collector of historical artifacts. The grandson of a German settler, Pol recognized the potential of the *Kryvyi Rih Iron-ore Basin deposits and played an important role in their development. His true passion, however, was regional history – possibly because his mother was Hetman P. Polubotok's granddaughter. After finishing law studies at Dorpat (now Tartu) University, he travelled throughout the Katerynoslav region, learning its history, taking part in archeological digs, and collecting artifacts. He pursued this hobby to the point of near financial ruin. Eventually he gathered a collection of 5,000 artifacts from prehistoric to Cossack times, estimated to be worth 200,000 rubles. After his death, Pol's collection was donated to the Katerynoslav Museum of Antiquities, which was subsequently named in his honor; it is now the *Dnipropetrovske Historical Museum.

Pol, Wincenty, b 20 April 1807 in Lublin, d 2 December 1872 in Cracow. Polish Romantic poet, geographer, ethnographer, and founder of the anthropogeographic method in ethnography. After graduating from Lviv University in 1827, he lectured at Vilnius University (1830–2). In 1849 he became the holder of the first chair of geography in Poland at Cracow University. He was the first professor in Poland to give a course in general ethnography. His books about his travels in Ukraine (1835), the philosophy and proverbs of the people in Poland (1836), episodes from his life and travels (1846), the northern slopes of the Carpathians (1851), and the natural environment of northeastern Europe (1851) contain much information about Ukrainian folklore and folkways. He also wrote a book on the Hutsuls (1847) and published a collection of Ukrainian songs in German translation (1853). Many of his manuscripts have been preserved at the Tatry Museum in Zakopane and Cracow University. Some of them, including several articles on the Hutsuls, Lemkos, and Boikos, were published in *Wincenty Pol: Prace z etnografii północnych stoków Karpat* (Wincenty Pol: Works in the Ethnography of the Northern Slopes of the Carpathians, 1966).

Poland. A country extending south to the Sudety and western Carpathian mountains, which separate the area of Polish settlement from that of the Czechs and Slovaks and the Polish state from the Bohemian and Hungarian kingdoms (as of 1526 the Habsburg monarchy, as of 1918 Czechoslovakia), north to the Baltic sea, west to Prussia (as of 1871 Germany, as of 1949 the German Democratic Republic, as of 1991 Germany), east to Ukraine and Belarus, and northeast to Lithuania and Eastern Prussia (as of 1945 Kaliningrad oblast of the RSFSR, as of 1992 the Russian Federation). The ethnic and state borders of Poland have remained stable in the south; in the north Poland did not always extend to its natural boundary, the Baltic. Poland's western and eastern borders underwent great changes over the centuries. A Polish state existed from the mid-10th century until 1795; it was restored in 1918, dismantled in 1939, and restored once again in 1945. The Polish state incorporated Ukrainian ethnic territory from the middle of the 14th century, when it annexed the Principality of Galicia. In 1569 it acquired a major part of Ukraine, from Lithuania. In the mid-17th century it lost Left-Bank Ukraine to the Hetman state (which was subsequently subsumed by the Russian Empire), and in the late 18th century it lost Galicia to Austria and the remainder of its Ukrainian holdings to Russia. As restored after the First World War, Poland included much of Western Ukraine (Galicia, Volhynia, Polisia); as restored after the Second World War, it included only part of the westernmost extensions of Ukrainian ethnic territory.

History. Both Poland and Ukraine emerged as political entities at approximately the same time in the 9th and 10th centuries. The relationship between Poland and *Kievan Rus' was marked by occasional military intervention as each party pursued its own aims or threw its support to a feuding faction in the neighboring state as well as by routine dynastic marriages formed for purposes of achieving diplomatic security. Each faced ongoing warfare with external foes (the Germans and the steppe nomads respectively) that made all-out hostilities between them (aimed at territorial aggrandizement) an unlikely prospect. The two powers lived in a state of approximate equilibrium (although Rus' remained the greater power), and for nearly 300 years the borders dividing them did not change significantly.

The Mongol invasion in the mid-13th century devastated the Ukrainian principalities of Rus', which already faced serious problems due to internecine strife. The Grand Duchy of *Lithuania was soon able to incorporate large tracts of Ukrainian territory into its realm and establish a joint *Lithuanian-Ruthenian state. Poland was held off by the continued existence of the Principality of *Galicia-Volhynia. With the demise of that principality in 1340, the Polish king Casimir III the Great initiated an extended period of territorial expansion eastward, taking most of the principality by 1349. Poland's acquisitions in Ukraine subsequently were realized through more peaceable means. The Union of *Krevo (1385), which established a dynastic link between the Lithuanian grand duke Jagiełło and the Polish queen Jadwiga, allowed Poland to extend its cultural and political influence into the affairs of the Lithuanian state as well as to consolidate its control over Galicia and expand into Podilia. For several centuries the *history of Ukraine, particularly that of *Galicia, was inextricably bound to that of Poland. The growing influence of Poland resulted finally in the Union of *Lublin (1569), which united Poland and Lithuania into a single Commonwealth (Rzeczpospolita). In practical terms the union was dominated by the Poles, who now took direct control over most of Ukraine.

The Polish influence on Ukraine was profound. Most of the Ukrainian nobles, granted equal rights with their Polish counterparts, were quickly Polonized, and Ukraine was thus bereft of its own social elite. The last vestiges of the Rus' state disappeared as the Ukrainian lands were divided into six voivodeships, or provinces. Large tracts of land were granted to Polish nobles, who established sizable estates (*filvarky*) that could produce effectively for the booming European grain trade. Some of the largest estates (latifundia) in the Commonwealth were situated in Ukraine. Greater demands were placed on the Ukrainian peasantry, which was being reduced to serfdom. The religious tolerance in the Commonwealth, phenomenal for its times, also had an impact in Ukraine, as the Reformation period saw the influence of Protestant groups, such as the Socinians and Lutherans, spread into Ukraine through Poland. Nevertheless pressure was put on the predominantly Orthodox population of Ukraine to convert to Catholicism, and it resulted indirectly in the establishment of the *Ukrainian Catholic church by the Union of *Berestia (1596). At the same time Ukraine experienced a tremendous revival. Theological and secular education, literature, and the fine arts all began to flourish, and printing was introduced. The ideas of the Renaissance began to work their way into Ukraine through Poland as the 'Golden Age' of 16th-century Polish culture left its mark.

The situation in Ukraine under Polish rule became increasingly more volatile in the first half of the 17th century as socioeconomic, religious, and national tensions grew. The most obvious sources of dissatisfaction lay with the peasantry, which historically had not been tied to manor-style economies; the Orthodox, who were relegated to a

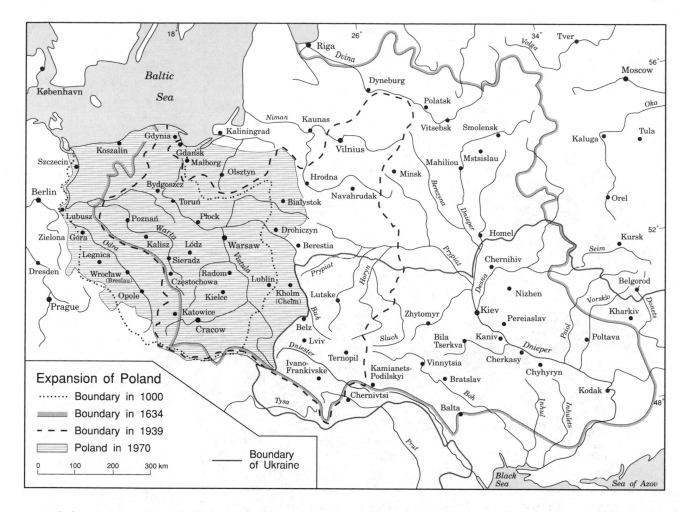

Expansion of Poland

········· Boundary in 1000

▦ Boundary in 1634

— — — Boundary in 1939

▨ Poland in 1970

—— Boundary of Ukraine

0   100   200   300 km

second-class status within the Commonwealth; and the *Cossacks, who defended the borderlands of the Polish state against Crimean Tatar and Turkish attack but were granted few of the privileges of a military class. The Cossacks were regarded as troublesome and problematic by the ruling elite of the Commonwealth, and constant attempts were made to control them. Tensions peaked in 1648, when a full-scale uprising led by B. *Khmelnytsky erupted in Ukraine and engulfed the Commonwealth in the *Cossack-Polish War.

The uprising represented a fundamental turning point. Ukraine might have re-entered the Polish state on the basis of equality within a tripartite Commonwealth (that was an option favored by Khmelnytsky and others), but the instability of the times prevented even a serious discussion of the possibility. Unable to assert full independence alone, Khmelnytsky turned to the Russian tsar Aleksei Mikhailovich for assistance and concluded the *Pereiaslav Treaty of 1654 with the Russians. That treaty set in motion the gradual process by which most of Ukraine moved from the Polish sphere of influence into the Russian. An attempt was made to abrogate the Pereiaslav agreement with the Treaty of *Hadiache (1658), which would have brought Ukraine back into the Commonwealth as an autonomous administrative unit. Ultimately approved by the Commonwealth diet, the agreement was opposed by a large segment of the Cossacks, who did not wish to return to the Polish sphere of

influence. At the same time the Russians invaded Ukraine, and their invasion signaled the start of a period of protracted fighting and political instability known as the *Ruin. Turkey even entered the fray by occupying a large section of the Right-Bank region. A preliminary agreement to resolve the situation was made between Poland and Russia in 1667 with the Treaty of *Andrusovo. The division of Ukraine into Right and Left banks was confirmed (with a provision for Moscow's control of Kiev) in the *Eternal Peace of 1686.

Poland had regained full control of Right-Bank Ukraine by 1714, after an extended period of occupation of the region by Ottoman forces and Cossacks. The largely devastated region once again saw the return of large estates and increased corvée obligations for the peasantry, of which the consequence was a series of *haidamaka uprisings. The Polish Commonwealth, by now rendered largely ineffectual because of the weakness of its elected kings and the chaotic state of its parliament, was forced to rely on Russian assistance in quelling the worst of the uprisings. The Russian intervention in Poland's internal affairs culminated in that country's active role in the partitioning of Poland (1772, 1793, and 1795), whereby Russia acquired all of Poland's Ukrainian possessions other than Galicia and Bukovyna (which were annexed by the Austrian Empire).

Russian Empire, 1795–1917. For some time after Poland's incorporation into the Russian Empire the Ukrainian

POLAND'S GROWTH IN THE 15TH-18TH CENTURIES

lands west of the Dnieper were treated as Polish territory. The socioeconomic order inherited from Poland, with its domination by Polish magnates and gentry, remained intact, and serfdom became even more intensive. The Russian monarchs Paul I (1796–1801) and Alexander I (1801–25) preserved the hegemony of the Polish nobility in the region. Polish culture and education in Volhynia and Right-Bank Ukraine developed more dynamically under tsarist rule than it had under Poland owing to the establishment of the *Kremianets Lyceum and the Vilnius (Wilno) School District, which co-ordinated Polish cultural self-government in Russia throughout the formerly Polish territories.

The *Polish Insurrection of 1830–1, the leadership of which called for the restitution of Poland in its boundaries of 1772, was primarily based in the *Congress Kingdom of Poland, but Polish gentry and clergy from Ukraine also participated. Gen J. Dwernicki's campaign of April 1831 failed to spread the insurrection to Podilia and Volhynia. Punitive policies implemented by the Russian government in Ukrainian territories after the suppression of the insurrection included the liquidation of Polish educational institutions and the removal of many Poles from the local administration. Nevertheless the Polish nobility's economic domination was unaffected, and its cultural he-

gemony, though weakened, was not eradicated.

With the defeat of the 1831 insurrection Polish political life became centered in the emigration, particularly in Paris. Two broad currents developed: a conservative one headed by Prince A. *Czartoryski, who sought the fulfillment of Polish aspirations primarily through the aid of some foreign power, and a democratic one, which urged another insurrection that would aim for social reform as well as Polish independence and thereby attract popular support. Both currents essentially considered the Ukrainian question an internal Polish one, but each in its own way also contributed to the development of the Ukrainian national revival. Czartoryski fostered various schemes aimed at enlisting Ukrainian support, including the creation of a Cossack legion in Turkey during the *Crimean War (which fought under the command of M. *Czajkowski). The democrats founded conspiratorial groups in Right-Bank Ukraine that aimed at the restoration of Poland to its boundaries of 1772 and the establishment of an egalitarian social order in which serfdom was abolished. The most significant of the groups were connected with the Association of the Polis   People (Stowarzyszenie Ludu Polskiego), led in Ukraine in 1835–8 by S. Konarski. The groups, which sometimes wrote revolutionary literature in the Ukrainian language and appealed to Cossack

Map legend:
- Boundaries of Poland in 1768
- Boundaries between Polish Crown and Lithuanian Principality
- State boundaries after partitions of 1772, 1793 and 1795
- Boundaries of Ukraine in 1991
- Other state boundaries

Partitions of Poland

	Russia	Austria	Prussia
1st Partition			
2nd Partition			
3rd Partition			

traditions, spurred the development of a Ukrainian political consciousness.

Russia's defeat in the Crimean War of 1853–6 saw a resurgence of Polish political activity in Ukraine. Polish young people founded secret patriotic societies, particularly in Kiev. The movement in Poland and Ukraine culminated in the *Polish Insurrection of 1863–4, in which Poles from Ukraine played a prominent part. Partisan warfare encompassed the Right Bank and Volhynia. The brutal and systematic repressions that followed the defeat of the insurrection (as well as the abolition of serfdom prior to the insurrection in 1861) destroyed Polish hegemony in Ukrainian lands under Russian rule. Although Poles continued to be active in Ukrainian political life (Polish socialists organized workers' circles in Ukraine in the 1870s, for example), the real revival of Polish political life was toward the end of the 19th century and particularly after 1905. Of the various Polish political currents only the Polish Socialist party declared its support for the Ukrainian movement.

The commercial agreements of Russia with Austria and Prussia in 1818 included Right-Bank Ukraine in the Polish customs territory, and the tariff of 1819 separated Right-Bank Ukraine and the Congress Kingdom from the rest of the Russian Empire. The Right Bank remained an important market for the Polish textile industry, even after the abolition of the Polish-Russian customs border in 1850. With the construction of railroads commercial relations between the Congress Kingdom and Ukraine expanded considerably. In 1895 Ukraine began to export iron ore to Poland; it became the main raw material for Polish metallurgy. Ukraine also exported to Poland rails, agricultural machines, grain, flour, cattle, salt, sugar, tobacco, flax, and wool. From Poland Ukraine imported woolen and cotton textiles, paper, chemical products, soap, and leather. Ukrainian and Polish coal competed intensively for the central Russian market. Poland maintained a favorable balance of trade vis-à-vis the rest of the Russian Empire.

Austrian Empire, 1772–1918. After its third partition in 1795, Poland ceased to exist as a political polity. The mainstay of Polish national consciousness remained until the 20th century with its nobility, the *szlachta*, and the geographical center of hope for a national revival became those Polish territories within the Austrian Empire, specifically the Crownland of Galicia, which Austria acquired from Poland in 1772. Galicia, however, consisted of two historically and ethnically distinct regions: the west, which was largely Polish, formed from the former Cracow and Sandomierz voivodeships, and the east, which was largely Ukrainian, formed from the former Rus' voivodeship (originally the Prinicipality of Halych), with parts of the Belz, Volhynia, and Podilia voivodeships. Galicia also became a focal point of Ukrainian national aspirations during the 19th century.

Until the mid-19th century no specifically contentious issues emerged between the Ukrainians and the Poles in Galicia. Only with the respective national revivals of the two nations did antagonism begin to grow. In 1848, Ukrainians started organizing themselves politically (with the *Supreme Ruthenian Council), achieving recognition as a separate people, and demanding a division of Galicia into two crownlands along ethnic lines. The Poles maintained, however, that, historically, Galicia in its entirety belonged to Poland. They established the pro-Polish *Ruthenian

Congress, which published the newspaper *Dnewnyk Ruskij* and worked to counter Ukrainian claims.

The subsequent political realignment of the Austrian Empire exacerbated Polish-Ukrainian tensions. The appointment of A. Gołuchowski as governor of Galicia in 1849 (his tenure lasted until 1875, with only minor interruptions) heralded a political understanding between the central government and the Poles that the Poles would, by and large, have control of the Galician provincial administration. Such control was solidified after the reorganization of the empire into a dual monarchy in 1867. The perception among Poles that Galicia was the most likely base for a Polish national revival grew after the failure of the Polish Insurrection of 1863–4. For Ukrainians, after the *Ems Ukase banned Ukrainian publications in the Russian Empire, the center of Ukrainian national life moved to Galicia – now called the 'Piedmont' of Ukraine. Until the outbreak of the First World War both Ukrainians and Poles maintained aspirations for statehood and took many steps toward that goal within their respective territories under Austro-Hungarian rule. In some cases the efforts of the one were mirrored by those of the other (for example, in the creation of sporting or paramilitary groups as the precursors of a national army).

20th century. With the end of hostilities in 1918 and the collapse of the Habsburg Empire Poland moved to reestablish its historical state, as much as possible in accordance with its pre-1772 borders. The effort brought Poland into conflict with Ukrainians, who had proclaimed the *Western Ukrainian National Republic (centered around the territory of Galicia). The rival territorial ambitions finally erupted in the *Ukrainian-Polish War in Galicia (1918–19), which commenced with the *November Uprising in Lviv. Poland benefited in its efforts because of Entente fears of a Bolshevik offensive westward: on 28 June 1919 the Supreme Council of the Paris Peace Conference allowed Poland to occupy all of eastern Galicia (subject to a review of its international status).

After the Ukrainian Galician Army was pushed out of Galicia in the summer of 1919, the newly restored Polish state occupied the region. On 18 March 1921 Poland, Soviet Russia, and Soviet Ukraine signed the Peace Treaty of *Riga, which ended the Soviet-Polish War and established the Soviet-Polish border. The agreement ceded Galicia as well as Polisia and western Volhynia (formerly within the Russian Empire) to Poland. On 15 March 1923 the *Conference of Ambassadors also recognized that border. Ukrainians protested with a mass demonstration in front of St George's Cathedral in Lviv on 24 March 1923. Galicia, Polisia, and Volhynia remained within the boundaries of the Polish state until September 1939, when Poland was divided between Germany and the Soviet Union.

In order to win recognition of Poland's eastern boundaries by the Council of Ambassadors, the Polish Sejm had passed a law on 26 September 1922 which provided for autonomous government for Galicia, prohibited Polish colonization there, and projected the establishment of a Ukrainian university; those remained paper declarations. On 28 June 1919 Poland had agreed at Versailles to respect the national and religious rights of its national minorities, but it unilaterally repudiated that agreement, which it had never honored, on 13 September 1934.

When the former socialist Marshal J. *Piłsudski took power in a coup in May 1926 and established the *Sanacja

CHANGES IN THE UKRAINIAN-POLISH BOUNDARY

regime, the national minorities looked forward to an improvement in their situation. In fact Piłsudski and his successors continued the previous governments' policies of denationalization and Polonization.

The rights of the Ukrainian language in the administration, the judiciary system, and the school system were severely restricted, and in Kholm region and Podlachia even the minimal legal norms existing in Galicia, Volhynia, and Polisia were bypassed. Most Ukrainian-language schools that had existed from Austrian times were changed into bilingual Polish-Ukrainian schools, and in the Kholm region and Podlachia only Polish-language schools existed. Not only did the Polish government prevent the establishment of a Ukrainian university, but it closed down all the Ukrainian-language chairs that had existed at Lviv University under Austrian rule.

The Orthodox church in Poland was completely dependent on a government which tried to Polonize it and convert Orthodox Christians to Roman Catholicism. Orthodox churches in the Kholm region and Podlachia were destroyed en masse in 1938, and in Volhynia (notably the village of *Hrynky) there were instances of forcible conversion from Orthodoxy to Roman Catholicism. Another Polish initiative was the *neounion campaign, which sought to spread Eastern rite Christianity (under Latin rite jurisdiction) among Ukrainians outside Galicia.

In spite of agrarian overpopulation the Polish government and voluntary associations implemented a program of colonization in Western Ukraine by Poles. In 1920–3, state lands in Volhynia and Polisia were distributed to Polish veterans, most of whom were not even peasants. During implementation of the land reform some great estates were subdivided in Western Ukraine (so called 'parcelation'), but most of the 800,000 ha thus obtained were sold to Poles.

The Polish state pursued a policy of 'divide and rule' in Ukrainian territories, and established the *Sokal border as part of that effort. In the Kholm region and Podlachia it denied local Ukrainians any cultural rights whatsoever. In Polisia it tried to cultivate a purely local, non-Ukrainian consciousness by encouraging the population to define itself only as *tuteishi*, or 'people who live here.' In Volhynia it sought out local Ukrainian leaders willing to collaborate with the Polish authorities (they helped to establish the *Volhynian Ukrainian Alliance), and in particular it sought to isolate Ukrainian institutions there from contacts with their Galician counterparts. In Galicia, where Ukrainian national consciousness was most intense, the authorities tried overtly to curb Ukrainian political, social, cultural, and economic activities; they also made efforts to divide Ukrainians there by supporting the otherwise moribund *Russophiles, by encouraging the formation of separate national identities for *Lemkos and *Hutsuls, and by seeking to draw Roman Catholic Ukrainians (*latynnyky) and Ukrainian *petty gentry into the Polish nation.

The failure of the interwar Polish state to accommodate Ukrainian interests in even the slightest way helped to provoke a militant backlash. In the 1920s the *Ukrainian Military Organization carried out a number of sabotage actions against the regime, and in the 1930s its work was continued on an even broader scale by the *Organization of Ukrainian Nationalists. The Polish government attempted to cow its Ukrainian population by carrying out the *Pacification in 1930. That action prompted the Ukrainian political mainstream to attempt a rapprochement with the government – the so-called *Normalization. But it proved to be a fiasco. Ukrainians by and large remained extremely dissatisfied with the Polish regime.

After Poland was once again divided, in September 1939, that time by Germany and the Soviet Union, most of the Ukrainian territories of the interwar Polish state fell under Soviet control in 1939–41, with a small westerly strip remaining in the Generalgouvernement. In 1941 the remainder fell to the Germans. Throughout the war Poland maintained the recovery of eastern Galicia as one of its territorial imperatives. That goal proved a stumbling block for effective co-operation between Ukrainian resistance forces and the underground *Polish Home Army.

With the reoccupation of Western Ukrainian lands in 1944 and the establishment of a Soviet satellite regime in Poland after the Second World War, Poland's relationship to Ukraine changed fundamentally. The borders between the two states were re-established, and a subsequent resettlement of populations between the two states, in which Ukrainians in Poland were moved to the Ukrainian SSR and Poles in the Ukrainian SSR moved to Poland, was completed in 1947 with *Operation Wisła, which cleared the Polish-Ukrainian borderland area of most Ukrainians.

The extensive Ukrainianization of Galicia in the postwar era and the specter of a common foe, the Russian-dominated Soviet Union, resulted in improved relations between Ukraine and Poland after 1945. Official relations were conducted largely under the rubric of Eastern Bloc institutions and state-sanctioned cultural exchanges. On a more informal level political dissenters found a common cause, and Poland, with a somewhat more relaxed political atmosphere, served as a conduit for (among other things) political ideas and literature to Ukraine. Poland was the first state to recognize Ukrainian independence after the referendum of 1 December 1991.

Ukrainians in Poland. Although many Ukrainians lived within Polish national territory before the 20th century, relatively few of them were located within ethnic Polish lands. A substantial number of Ukrainians lived in the borderland Lemko, Sian, Podlachia, and Kholm regions, but only approx 20,000 lived in Poland proper. Many of that group left Poland during the First World War. They were replaced in the interwar period with a very different type of Ukrainian community. After the Second World War the nature of the Ukrainian presence in Poland again changed drastically.

Pre–1914. Within the Polish territories of the Austro-Hungarian Empire *Cracow was the only city with a large concentration of Ukrainians. A Ukrainian Catholic parish had been established there in the late 18th century, and by 1910 there were approx 1,500 Ukrainians living in the city. Within Polish territories under the Russian Empire *Warsaw was the main center. Even within the Rzeczpospolita the city attracted a substantial number of Ukrainian gentry, merchants, and Cossacks. In 1721 a Ukrainian Basilian monastery was established there. By the early 20th century there were some 5,000 to 10,000 Ukrainians living there. Many were civil servants, members of the Russian imperial bureaucracy, or students at Warsaw University and other postsecondary institutions. Smaller numbers of Ukrainians lived in Lublin and Siedlce, the administrative centers of the Kholm region and Podlachia. On the eve of the First World War there were up to 50,000 Ukrainians living in Poland proper (not including the Kholm region). The majority of those left in 1915 during the general Russian evacuation before the advancing German and Austro-Hungarian armies.

Interwar era. A new Ukrainian community emerged in Poland in the interwar period. With the final defeat of the UNR Army approx 30,000 Ukrainians, mostly military personnel, remained or were interned in Poland. Camps were situated in *Kalisz, Łańcut, *Szczepiórno, Piotrków, *Strzałków, *Tarnów, *Wadowice, and other locations until 1923. Thereafter most of the internees left for France or Czechoslovakia, but a group remained and settled throughout the country. Poland became a major center of Ukrainian émigré political activity until 1939, and Warsaw emerged as an important cultural center. Poland served as the home base of the UNR government-in-exile until 1923, and Ukrainians pressed their case for independence through bodies such as the Warsaw-centered *Promethean movement. Important scholastic work was undertaken by the *Ukrainian Scientific Institute in Warsaw and other bodies. By the late 1930s there were about 20,000 Ukrainians living in central Poland, of whom most were in Warsaw (ca 3,000), Cracow (ca 2,000), and smaller centers, such as Katowice, Kielce, Łódź, *Lublin, *Poznań, Radom, and Rzeszów. That number included political émigrés, students, and several thousand professionals and laborers who had migrated from Western Ukraine to central Poland in search of employment.

During the early part of the Second World War (1939–41) the number of Ukrainians in Poland increased dramatically as a result of the influx of refugees from the Bolshevik-occupied territories to the German-controlled Generalgouvernement. Cracow became the new hub of Ukrainian life, with a community numbering approx 3,000 (compared to Warsaw's 5,000 and Lublin's 1,000). Ukrainian community life became more vibrant as a result of the work of the *Ukrainian Central Committee. After the Germans occupied Western Ukraine, a substantial number of the refugees returned there.

Post–Second World War. Ukrainian life in Poland changed completely in the postwar period. Most Ukrainians who lived in central Poland left for the West before it was occupied by Soviet forces in 1944–5, and most of those remaining were resettled in ethnic Ukrainian territory as a result of the final alignment of borders between the Polish People's Republic (PPR) and the Ukrainian SSR. Approx 500,000 Ukrainians living in the PPR were resettled in the Ukrainian SSR. Nevertheless a substantial Ukrainian minority remained within the newly drawn Polish border in northwestern Galicia, the Sian region, Podlachia, and particularly the Lemko region, which was controlled by the UPA in 1946–7. In April–July 1947 the Polish government mounted Operation Wisła, a wholesale forced deportation of Ukrainians from their ethnographic territory. They were resettled in the so-called regained lands (Ziemie Odzyskane), the former territories of eastern and northern Germany and East Prussia acquired by Poland after the Second World War. A very small number of Ukrainians managed to stay in Ukrainian ethnographic territory, mostly in Podlachia.

The hostility afforded Ukrainians as individuals was also evident in official and general societal attitudes toward them (there was a general refusal to recognize Ukrainians in Poland as a distinct national minority) and made it extremely difficult for Ukrainians to organize and present their demands. Only in 1956, after a liberalization of the communist regime, were Ukrainians granted certain rights and allowed to form their own organization,

the *Ukrainian Social and Cultural Society (USKT; since 1990 the Alliance of Ukrainians in Poland [OUP]).

In spite of numerous petitions by the resettled Ukrainians the Polish government continued to enforce a ban on their return to their former homelands. In 1957–8 up to 11,000 requested permission to resettle. Approx 2,000 to 3,000 managed to do so (mainly back to the Lemko region), but at their own risk. Ironically, large sections of the Lemko region continued to be sparsely settled (in the 1960s there were 27 inhabitants/sq km, whereas in 1939 there had been 70), and the Boiko region remained virtually depopulated.

The exact number and distribution of the Ukrainian population in postwar Poland can only be estimated, as census figures did not record information regarding ethnic background or language use. Official estimates put the total number of Ukrainians at 180,000; unofficial figures commonly range as high as 300,000. The largest single concentration of Ukrainians is found in the Olsztyn voivodeship, in northern Poland, where they number 50,000 to 60,000 and constitute approx 6 percent of the region's population. Other major areas of Ukrainian settlement in Poland include the voivodeships of Koszalin in the northwest (30,000), Wrocław in the west (approx 20,000), Szczecin in the west (over 10,000), and Zielona Góra in the west (approx 10,000). Another 2,000 live in the south-central voivodeship of Opole.

The Lemko region, the Sian region, and northwestern Galicia are now part of Nowy Sącz, Krosno, and Peremyshl voivodeships. The Lemko region was inhabited by about 10,000 Ukrainians in the 1960s, and in some districts (such as Komańcza, Mokre, and Morochów) they even constitute a majority. In the Sian region a substantial number of Ukrainians live in the Peremyshl (in the city and in Ukrainian villages, such as Pozdiacz and Kalników) and Jarosław districts. There were approx 20,000 Ukrainians in what are now Zamość, Kholm, Biała Podlaska, and Białystok voivodeships, mainly in the Biała Podlaska and Volodova regions of Podlachia, particularly in the area of Siemiatycze, Bielsk Podlaski, and Hainivka (Hajnówka). They are officially considered Belarusians, however. Relatively few Ukrainians live in central Poland, and those who do live in cities.

Nearly 90 percent of Ukrainians lived in rural areas in the 1960s. Since then there has been a degree of urbanization. The largest urban concentrations of Ukrainians are in Cracow, Legnica, Lublin, Peremyshl, Szczecin, Warsaw, and Wrocław.

Conditions for community life. In 1956, Ukrainians were permitted to form the OUP, the single Ukrainian institution allowed to educate and encourage cultural activity among Ukrainians. It also served as a representative body and assisted the authorities in deciding questions regarding the Ukrainian minority in Poland. Its headquarters were in Warsaw. It was under the direct control of the Polish Communist party (formally named the Polish United Workers' party) and the government and was a semiofficial organization. In 1958 it was given authority over 8 voivodeship and 34 district administrations, which oversaw 270 communities, of which some were in cities and some in the countryside. Its membership was 7,000. In 1970 the OUP had 5 voivodeship executives, 14 district administrations, 205 groups, and 4,750 members.

The Ukrainian community, however, faced considerable hostility from virtually all segments of Polish society, particularly Poles resettled from the Ukrainian SSR. Local officials were commonly the ones who immediately made community work difficult among Ukrainians, although the upper reaches of the Polish government also fomented hatred and distrust of Ukrainians by issuing publications and films about the 'bestial acts' of the UPA and the 'Banderites' (using that term in a specifically pejorative manner), the 'collaboration' of Ukrainians with the Nazis, and the alleged participation of Ukrainians in the suppression of the Warsaw Uprising of 1944.

Many Ukrainians, particularly those in cities, concealed their national identity. The loss of a traditional territorial base, their wide dispersal, and the small size of the intelligentsia resulted in widespread denationalization among Ukrainians, particularly the younger generation. The situation was exacerbated by the policy of Russification within the USSR and the total indifference of the government of the Ukrainian SSR to the fate of Ukrainians in Poland; Ukrainian diplomatic representation in Poland, visits by official or semiofficial delegations, and the sponsorship of summer camps for Ukrainian children in Poland or of instructional sessions for teachers were all either minimal or nonexistent.

Church life. Ukrainians in Poland adhere to the Ukrainian Catholic and Orthodox faiths in roughly equal numbers. Both traditional churches have been beset with a wide range of problems in the post–Second World War period. In the immediate postwar period the *Ukrainian Catholic church was not formally liquidated as it was in the Ukrainian SSR at the Lviv Sobor of 1946. Its institutional structure, however, was effectively dismantled with the deportation of its spiritual head, Bishop Y. Kotsylovsky of Peremyshl, and other priests to the USSR. After Operation Wisła the church hierarchy was physically eliminated. Many priests were incarcerated in the Jaworzno prison. Those priests remaining free were forbidden to practice in their rite. Pope Pius XII responded to those developments by rejecting the dissolution of the Ukrainian Catholic church in Poland. He appointed A. Hlond (primate of Poland) and then (after Hlond's death) S. Wyszyński (archbishop and later primate) as ordinary of the Eastern rite Catholics in Poland.

Wyszyński, himself imprisoned by the Polish authorities in 1953–6, was incapable of assisting the Ukrainian church: he recommended that Eastern rite priests save themselves by converting to the Latin rite. It was in that spirit that the Basilian monastery in Warsaw converted to the Latin rite. Meanwhile the Polish (Roman Catholic) church proceeded with numerous claims on the properties of the paralyzed Ukrainian Catholic church. After the liberalization of 1956, Ukrainian Catholics were finally allowed liturgies in their own rite but not separate parishes: they could maintain only priests who would be subservient to a Roman Catholic hierarchy. In some instances (one notable example being in Katowice under Bishop H. Bednorz) the arrangement worked well, and the local hierarch actively promoted the development of the Ukrainian church; in many, however, problems arose through both misunderstandings and deep-rooted prejudices. Some church communities converted to Orthodoxy. By 1977 the Ukrainian Catholic church, however, had developed a network of 77 centers. Several religious orders have been formed since the 1950s, and in 1969 an Eastern rite theo-

logical seminary was established in Lublin. In 1989 I. Martyniak was consecrated the first Ukrainian Catholic bishop in Poland, and in 1991 he assumed the re-established see of Peremyshl. Estimates of the number of Greek Catholics in Poland range as high as 400,000, although many Ukrainians have identified themselves as Roman Catholics in order to avoid harassment.

The *Polish Autocephalous Orthodox church (PAOC) emerged in the 1920s as a body serving the needs of the approx four million Ukrainian, Belarusian, and (to a lesser extent) Russian and Polish adherents of Orthodoxy. The majority of them were located in the areas of interwar Poland that had been in the Russian Empire (notably the Kholm region). In the interwar era the PAOC maintained a strong Ukrainophile current, and during the Second World War PAOC bishops played an important role in the establishment of the Ukrainian Autocephalous Orthodox church. Nevertheless a strong Russophile current existed within the church hierarchy. The Poles maintained their efforts to convert the Orthodox population to Catholicism, in some cases by force and in general through the launching of the neounion campaign.

After the Second World War the PAOC, under pressure from the Soviet authorities, lost its independence. In 1945 Metropolitan D. *Valedinsky was removed from his post; it was filled in 1951 by a Russian Orthodox hierarch. More significant, the 1924 *Tomos* issued by the Patriarch of Constantinople, which provided the PAOC with its autocephaly, was revoked in 1948 by the Patriarch of Moscow, who now brought the church under his jurisdiction. Since then the Russian language has occupied a more prominent position in ecclesiastical affairs, and much of the Ukrainian character of the church has been muted. At present the PAOC has approx 500,000 faithful (primarily Ukrainians and Belarusians) and is centered in Białystok voivodeship, with smaller concentrations in the other voivodeships.

The Ukrainian Millennium choir from Koszalin, Poland (artistic director and conductor: Yaroslav Poliansky)

Schools, education, press, publishing houses. After the liberalization of 1956 the Polish educational administration, in association with the OUP, began introducing Ukrainian language courses in elementary schools. Since then primary education in Ukrainian has been available in schools numbering from two to nine (reaching a maximum of 583 pupils in 1960–1). Ukrainian was also introduced as a subject and taught in as many as 152 schools (1958–9) and to as many as 2,711 pupils (1963–4). Ukrainian-language education was also introduced into two secondary schools (Legnica and Górowo Iławskie). A department of Ukrainian philology was established at Warsaw University in 1953, and for a period university-level Ukrainian courses were offered in Szczecin (1957–65) and Olsztyn (1965–7). Ukrainian has also been taught at the pedagogical institute in Bartoszice. The proportion of Ukrainian students receiving instruction in their native language has been very low, and the number of fully qualified Ukrainian teachers assigned to Ukrainian classes has also been small (commonly the authorities refused to appoint them to schools where Ukrainian courses are offered).

Extracurricular education is weakly developed. The OUP organized about 18 clubs and 60 independent choir, drama, and dance groups, with a membership of about 600. In 1967, the OUP began organizing annual festivals of Ukrainian music and song (first held in Sianik [Sanok]). In 1959 a section of the OUP devoted to the preservation and development of Lemko culture was formed.

The only Ukrainian newspaper in Poland is the weekly *Nashe slovo* (est 1956), which is published by the central administration of the OUP along with its supplements *Lemkivs'ke slovo* and *Svitanok* (for children) and the monthly journal *Nasha kul'tura* (from 1958). *Nasha kul'tura* provides some information about cultural life in what was Soviet Ukraine and in the diaspora. Since 1957 the OUP has also published the almanac *Ukraïns'kyi kalendar*, in a pressrun of 9,000. In the 1980s the students of Ukrainian philology at Warsaw University began to publish an irregular journal named *Zustrichi*, which over time has expanded its format and begun to address broad issues of community concern. The respective Ukrainian religious dominations now publish Orthodox (since 1986) and Catholic (since 1987) church almanacs in Ukrainian.

In Olsztyn and Rzeszów weekly Ukrainian radio programs are transmitted regionally; in the 1960s and 1970s programs existed in Koszalin and Lublin. There are few titles pubished in Ukrainian other than the almanacs and texts for elementary schools issued by the OUP. The demand for Ukrainian publications was only partially satisfied by Soviet Ukrainian production.

Literature, art, and scholarship. The Ukrainian poets in Poland include Ya. Dudra, Ya. Hudemchuk, O. Lapsky, I. Reit, Ye. Samokhvalenko, O. Zhabsky, and I. Zlatokudr. The prose writers include H. Boichuk, D. Halytsky, S. Kozak, K. Kuzyk, I. Sheliuk, and A. Serednytsky (Verba). An anthology of works by those authors was published by the OUP in 1964 as *Homin* (Echo). The Ukrainian artists in Poland include J. *Nowosielski and V. Savuliak (who were professors at the art academy in Cracow), *Nykyfor, L. Gets, A. Mentukh, V. Pankiv, H. Petsukh, Z. Podushko, M. Smerek, V. Vaskivsky, and T. Venhrynovych. Other noted cultural figures include S. Cherhoniak, Ya. Konstantynovych, and V. Hodys, who are art scholars; T. Demchuk, a theater critic; Ya. *Poliansky, a composer of music and organizer of choirs; and D. Denysenko, A. Matsihanovska, M. Shchutska, and O. Tabachnyk, Ukrainian actors who appeared on the Polish stage.

Centers of Ukrainian scholarship in Poland are the Ukrainian departments (language and literature) at the Institute of Slavic Studies of the Polish Academy of Sciences, the department of Ukrainian philology at Warsaw University, and departments of Slavic studies at other universities. Among Ukrainian scholars in Poland are the historians A. Serednytsky and Ya. Yurkevych; the linguists and literary scholars M. Lesiv, S. Kozak, V. Mokry, and W. Witkowski; the psychologists S. *Balei and V. Shevchuk; and the musicologist J. *Chomiński.

BIBLIOGRAPHY

Dragomanov, M. *Istoricheskaia Pol'sha i velikorusskaia demokratiia* (Geneva 1881)

Jabłonowski, A. *Pisma*, vol 1, *Ziemie Ruskie Rzeczypospolitej* (Warsaw 1910); vol 2, *Kresy Ukrainne* (1910); vol 3, *Ukraina* (1911); vol 4, *Wołyń, Podole i Ruś Czerwona* (1911)

Halecki, O. *Dzieje Unii Jagiellońskiej*, 2 vols (Cracow 1919–20)

Wojnarowskyj, T. *Das Schicksal des ukrainischen Volkes unter polnischer Herrschaft* (Vienna 1921)

Wasilewski, L. *Ukraińska sprawa narodowa w jej rozwoju historycznym* (Warsaw 1925)

Sprawy Narodowościowe (Warsaw 1927–39)

Kutschabsky, W. *Die Westukraine im Kampfe mit Polen und dem Bolschewismus in den Jahren 1918–1923* (Berlin 1934)

Bocheński, A.; Łoś, S.; Bączkowski, W. *Problem polsko-ukraiński w Ziemi Czerwieńskiej* (Warsaw 1938)

Żółtowski, A. *Border of Europe: A Study of the Polish Eastern Provinces* (London 1950)

Rhode, G. *Die Ostgrenze Polens: Politische Entwicklung, kulturelle Bedeutung und geistige Auswirkung*, vol 1, *Im Mittelalter bis zum Jahre 1401* (Cologne–Graz 1955)

Lewyćkyj, B. *Warszawa-Kijów: Informacja o stosunkach politycznych, gospodarczych i kulturalnych w latach 1945–1957: Dokumenty*, no. 4 (Paris 1958)

Verves, H. *Holovni problemy ukraïns'ko-pol's'kykh literaturnykh vzaiemyn XIX st.* (Kiev 1958)

Horak, S. *Poland and Her National Minorities, 1919–1939: A Case Study* (New York–Washington–Hollywood 1961)

Kubijovyč, V. *Western Ukraine within Poland, 1920–1939 (Ethnic Relationships)* (Chicago 1963)

Perdenia, J. *Stanowisko Rzeczypospolitej szlacheckiej wobec sprawy Ukrainy na przełomie XVII–XVIII w.* (Wrocław–Warsaw–Cracow 1963)

Ripetskyj, S. *Ukrainian-Polish Diplomatic Struggle, 1918–1923* (Chicago 1963)

Włodarski, B. *Polska i Ruś 1194–1340* (Warsaw 1966)

Hornowa, E. *Ukraiński obóz postępowy i jego współpraca z polską lewicą społeczną w Galicji 1876–1895* (Wrocław–Warsaw–Cracow 1968)

Demkovych-Dobrians'kyi, M. *Ukraïns'ko-pol's'ki stosunky u XIX st.* (Munich 1969)

Deruga, A. *Polityka wschodnia Polski wobec ziem Litwy, Białorusi i Ukrainy (1918–1919)* (Warsaw 1969)

Podraza, A. (ed.) *Kraków-Kijów: Szkice z dziejów stosunków polsko-ukraińskich* (Cracow 1969)

Szcześniak, A.B.; Szota, W.Z. *Droga do nikąd: Działalność Organizacji Ukraińskich Nacjonalistów i jej likwidacja w Polsce* (Warsaw 1973)

Kozak, S.; Jakóbiec, M. (eds) *Z dziejów stosunków literackich polsko-ukraińskich* (Wrocław–Warsaw–Cracow–Gdańsk 1974)

Kwilecki, A. *Łemkowie: Zagadnienie migracji i asymilacji* (Warsaw 1974)

Chojnowski, A. *Koncepcje polityki narodowościowej rządów polskich w latach 1921–1939* (Wrocław 1979)

Papierzyńska-Turek, M. *Sprawa ukraińska w Drugiej Rzeczypospolitej 1922–1926* (Cracow 1979)

Potichnyj, P. (ed). *Poland and Ukraine: Past and Present* (Edmonton 1980)

Piotrkiewicz, T. *Kwestia ukraińska w Polsce w koncepcjach piłsudczyzny 1926–1930* (Warsaw 1981)

Hunczak, T. (ed). *Ukraine and Poland in Documents, 1918–1922*, 2 vols (New York–Paris–Sydney–Toronto 1983)

Beauvois, D. *Le noble, le serf, et le révizor: La noblesse polonaise entre le tsarisme et les masses ukrainiennes (1831–1863)* (Paris 1985)

Sysyn, F.E. *Between Poland and the Ukraine: The Dilemma of Adam Kysil, 1600–1653* (Cambridge Mass 1985)
Torzecki, R. *Kwestia ukraińska w Polsce w latach 1923–1929* (Cracow 1989)
Trukhan, M. *Ukraïntsi v Pol'shchi pislia druhoï svitovoï viiny, 1944–84* (New York–Paris–Sydney–Toronto 1990)
   B. Kravtsiv, V. Kubijovyč, O. Ohloblyn, I.L. Rudnytsky, M. Zhdan

Polatsk principality. A principality founded in the 10th century on the territory of present-day northern Belarus, inhabited by the Slavic Polochanians (*Krivichians). The capital was Polatsk. Other important towns were Minsk, Vitsebsk, Iziaslav, Drutsk, Lahoisk, Lukoml, Svislach, Braslau, and Barysau. The principality's economic importance derived from its connection via the West Dvina and the Neman rivers to the centers of Baltic trade. Grand Prince Volodymyr the Great of Kiev conquered the principality in the late 10th century, killed its ruler, Rogvolod (Rahvolod), and married Rogvolod's daughter, *Rohnida (Rahneda, Rogned). The principality's population was subsequently Christianized, and a bishopric was established in Polatsk. Volodymyr and Rohnida's son, Iziaslav, inherited the principality. Iziaslav's son, Briachyslav (Brachyslau, 1001–44), attained independence from Kiev in 1023, but struggle for control of the principality with Kiev continued. Briachyslav's son, Vseslav (Usiaslau, 1044–1101), began a war with Kiev in 1065, but he was routed by Iziaslav Yaroslavych and imprisoned in Kiev. In 1068 Kiev's inhabitants rebelled against Iziaslav and installed Vseslav on the Kievan throne, but a year later Vseslav was forced to abandon Kiev by the forces of Iziaslav and his cousin Bolesław II of Poland and to return to Polatsk. Thereafter Polatsk principality remained independent of Kiev. Internecine struggles among Vseslav's six sons arose after his death, however, and the principality was consequently divided among them and their many sons into feuding appanages. *Mstyslav I Volodymyrovych was the last Kievan grand prince to attempt to annex the principality. He conquered it in 1130, but soon thereafter it regained its independence. In the second half of the 12th century the principality came under the domination of the northern Rus' princes of Smolensk. In the 13th century it suffered invasions by the Livonian Knights and the Grand Duchy of Lithuania, which asserted its political control over Polatsk and annexed it in 1307. Under Lithuanian rule the principality retained a measure of autonomy until 1385.

BIBLIOGRAPHY
Danilevich, V. *Ocherk istorii Polotskoi zemli do kontsa XIV stoletiia* (Kiev 1896)
Alekseev, L. *Polotskaia zemlia (ocherki istorii severnoi Belorussii) v IX–XIII vv.* (Moscow 1966)
Shtykhov, G. *Goroda Polotskoi zemli (IX–XIII vv.)* (Minsk 1978)
   M. Zhdan

Polcha-Mizoch Upland. A rolling upland located in Volhynia between the Styr and the Horyn rivers. The upland consists of Cretaceous and Tertiary strata with Devonian outcrops and has a maximum elevation of 342 m. It is dissected by the tributaries of the Ikva and the Horyn rivers, and its terrain is somewhat reminiscent of foothills.

Poleiovsky, Matvii [Polejovs'kyj, Matvij], b ca 1720, d ca 1800. Sculptor; brother of P. *Poleiovsky. He created the rococo sculptures in the Franciscan church in Peremyshl (1760–6), the main altar figures in the Roman Catholic cathedral in Lviv (1766–70) and in the church of the Pauline monks in Volodava (ca 1776), and many statues at the Pochaiv Monastery (1790–4).

Poleiovsky, Petro [Polejovs'kyj], b ?, d ca 1780. Architect; brother of M. *Poleiovsky. He worked in Poland and Ukraine. His chief works include the reconstructed Roman Catholic cathedral in Lviv (1765–76) and the Dormition Cathedral in Pochaiv (1771–83, with three other architects).

Polek, Johann, b 27 February 1843 in Bautsch (Budišov nad Budišovkou), Moravia, d 10 January 1920 in Vienna. Austrian historian and bibliographer. He studied at Vienna University (1865–8; PH D, 1871) and was custodian (1882–1900) and director (1900–13) of the Chernivtsi University library, a member of the board of trustees of the Bukovynian Provincial Museum, and a member of the editorial board of *Jahrbuch des Bukowiner Landesmuseums*. From 1913 he lived in Vienna. Together with F.A. Wickenhauser and R.F. Kaindl Polek pioneered the Austrian study of Bukovynian history, ethnography, and bibliography. His works include *Die Erwerbung der Bukowina durch Österreich* (1889) and articles, mostly in the *Jahrbuch*, titled 'Die Anfänge des Volksschulwesens in der Bukowina' (1891), 'Repertorium der landeskundlichen Literatur der Bukowina' (1892), 'Ortschaftenverzeichnis aus der Bukowina aus dem Jahre 1775' (1893), 'Die Lipowaner in der Bukowina' (1894–97), 'Josefs II. Reisen nach Galizien und der Bukowina und ihre Bedeutung für letztere Provinz' (1895), 'Religion und Kirchenwesen in der Bukowina' (1898), 'Die Vereinigung der Bukowina mit Galizien im Jahre 1786' (1901), and 'Die Zigeuner in der Bukowina' (1905–6). Polek is also the author of chapters in the volume *Bukowina* of *Die österreichisch-ungarische Monarchie in Wort und Bild* (1899).

Polemical literature. Publicistic and literary writings on religious and church issues and on national politics. In Ukraine and Belarus polemical literature dates back to the religious denominational struggles of the 16th and 17th centuries, especially those in conjunction with the 1596 Church Union of *Berestia, but also those that were part of the general European processes of the Reformation and the Counter-Reformation. Polemical writings were written in Old Ukrainian and in Old Polish, rarely in Church Slavonic. The stormy religious and political polemics were initiated by the Polish Jesuits P. *Skarga and B. *Herbest, who harshly criticized the institutional and spiritual 'vices' of the Orthodox church. In *O jedności kościoła Bożego pod jednym pasterzem* (On the Unity of God's Church under One Shepherd, 1577) Skarga outlined the ideological basis and the program of a church union. In response the Orthodox published H. *Smotrytsky's book (1587), which was composed of two treatises, 'Kliuch tsarstva nebesnoho ...' (The Key to the Heavenly Kingdom ...) and 'Kalendar rymskyi novyi' (The New Roman Calendar). Also written in reply was V. Surazky's *Knyzhytsia u shosty viddilakh: O edynoi ystynnoi pravoslavnoi viri* (A Book in Six Parts: On the Only True and Orthodox Faith, 1588). Those works defended the dogmas of the Eastern church and simultaneously criticized Catholic teachings, the deeds of the Roman popes, and the new Gregorian calendar. Along with the Ostrih polemicists, I. *Vyshensky, the most outstanding publicist in Ukrainian literature, stepped into the fray against the Catholics. Another active Orthodox polemicist was S. *Zyzanii, who was the author of the *Malyi katekhizys* (The Short Catechism, 1596) and other polemical works.

The development of polemical literature was notably influenced by the letters and epistles of Prince K. *Ostrozky, who opposed the church union. I. *Potii, a leading Uniate polemicist, wrote many theological and polemical works, including the well-known *Antiryzis* (Antidiscourse), published in Vilnius in Old Ukrainian in 1599 and in Polish in 1600. Further polemics between the Catholics and the Orthodox were sparked by the publication of Skarga's treatise 'Synod brzeski i jego obrona' (The Berestia Synod and Its Defense, 1596), published after the Uniate synod in Berestia and translated and published by Potii in Old Ukrainian in 1597. The writings of Potii also played a significant role. The Orthodox replied to the attack with a series of writings, the more important of which are the brochure 'Ekthesis' (1597), about the Orthodox Synod in Berestia; *Apokrisis* (1597), purportedly written by the Protestant M. Broniewski under the pseudonym K. *Filalet; 'Otpys na lyst ... Potiia' (Reply to the Letter ... of Potii, 1598–9) by *Ostrozkyi Kliryk; the anonymous pamphlet *Perestoroha* (A Warning, ca 1606); the theological and polemical lecture *Palinodiia*, written by Z. Kopystensky in 1621; and the pamphlet *Antidot ...* (Antidote ..., 1629) by A. Muzhylovsky.

M. *Smotrytsky, the author of *Trenos ...* (Threnody ..., 1610) and other polemical treatises, played a prominent role. He first directed his polemics against the Catholics (the Uniates) but then changed his allegiance to the Uniate church, in 1627, and figured prominently once again as the author of several treatises against the Orthodox. On the side of the Uniates were L. Krewza-Rzewuski, Y. Rutsky, and A. Seliava, who polemicized against the Orthodox after the synods in Berestia. In the early 1640s, following a brief interval of peace, the polemical battle intensified owing to the appearance of the writings of K. *Sakovych, especially his treatise *Epanorthosis, albo perspektiwa ...* (Epanorthosis, or Perspectives ..., 1642). The Orthodox replied with 'Lithos abo kamien ...' (Litos, or Stone ..., 1644), of a collective authorship, although P. *Mohyla is regarded as its main author and initiator.

In the second half of the 17th century Orthodox and Uniate polemical literature took on a more theological nature and concerned itself with disagreements on matters of dogma or theology. A sharper tone characterizes the writings of the Vilnius Jesuit P. Boima, *Stara wiara* (The Old Faith, 1668), and the Uniate T. Rutka, *Goliat swoim mieczem porażony ...* (Goliath Wounded by His Own Sword ..., 1689). Orthodox writers replied in kind, particularly L. *Baranovych, in his treatise *Nowa miara starej wiary* (A New Measure for the Old Faith, 1676), and I. *Galiatovsky, who also initiated polemical writings concerned with Judaism and Islam (*Łabędź ...* [The Swan ..., 1679] and *Alkoran Machometów* [The Muslims' Koran, 1683]). Putting aside the rancor of the polemicists, the harsh words, the rebukes and the slander, the manipulation of texts and facts to one's advantage, polemical literature produced a legacy of many fine works. The writings hold an important place in the church and political history of their period as well as in the history of Ukrainian literature.

BIBLIOGRAPHY
Pamiatniki polemicheskoi literatury v Zapadnoi Rusi, 3 vols (St Petersburg 1878–1903), in the series Russkaia istoricheskaia biblioteka, vols 4, 7, 9
Zavitnevich, V. *Palinodiia Zakharii Kopistenskogo i ee mesto v istorii zapadnorusskoi polemiki XVI i XVII vv.* (Warsaw 1883)
Petrov, N. 'Zapadnorusskie polemicheskie sochineniia XVI veka,' *Trudy Kievskoi dukhovnoi akademii*, 1894, nos 2–4
Studyns'kyi, K. *Pam'iatky polemichnoho pys'menstva kin. XVI i pochatku XVII v.*, vol 1 (Lviv 1906)
Vozniak, M. *Istoriia ukraïns'koï literatury*, vol 2 (Lviv 1921; repr, The Hague–Paris 1970)
Vishenskii, I. *Sochineniia* (Moscow–Leningrad 1955)
Zahaiko, P. *Ukraïns'ki pys'mennyky polemisty kintsia XVI–pochatku XVII st. v borot'bi proty Vatykanu i uniï* (Kiev 1957)
Vyshens'kyi, I. *Tvory* (Kiev 1959)
Galiatovs'kyi, I. *Kliuch rozuminnia* (Kiev 1985)
Ukraïns'ka literatura XVII st. (Kiev 1987)
M. Ivanek, I. Korovytsky, B. Kravtsiv

Poles in Ukraine. The first Poles in Ukraine were probably merchants engaged in transit trade with the Orient. Others began arriving in the retinues of Polish princesses who married Rus' nobles. A larger contingent was made up of prisoners of war, who were commonly assigned places of settlement. The first such group were taken by Yaroslav the Wise in his campaign against Poland in 1030–1 and placed in the Ros region. They became farmers and assimilated with the local population. By the early 12th century the needs of the numerous Polish settlers in Rus' (and the desire of the Vatican to expand the influence of the Roman Church) had given rise to the establishment of a Catholic mission in Kiev. It remained open until 1233. The greatest number of Poles, however, were concentrated in the borderlands of the Kievan state – Galicia, Volhynia, the Kholm region, and Podlachia. They played a substantial role in the development of those regions, particularly after the Tatar invasion of 1240–1. They even formed a significant element in the courts of Galician and Volhynian princes. The strongest Polish presence in the Galician-Volhynian state came during the reign of the last Ukrainian prince, Yurii II Boleslav.

1340–1569. Many Poles came to Ukraine after the demise of the Galician-Volhynian state and the takeover of Galicia, western Podilia, and the Kholm and Belz regions by King Casimir III. In order to secure Poland's hold on the territories, Casimir and his successors confiscated the estates of Ukrainian boyars and granted generous domains to their Polish counterparts. Among the Polish nobility given holdings in Galicia and Volhynia were the Habdank, Odrowąż, Pakosław, Tarnowski, Herburt, Buczacki, Potocki, Jazłowiecki, Lanckoroński, and Sieniawski families. Villages were often given to Polish nobles on a military tenure basis. Many new villages were established and populated with relocated Ukrainian and Polish peasants. Existing cities were expanded, and most of them were granted *Magdeburg law. New towns and cities were developed, and German, Polish, and Armenian craftsmen and merchants were enticed to settle there. Voluntary immigrants, particularly from Little Poland, were attracted by the sparsely populated land, fertile soil, warmer climate, and wide range of fauna found in Galicia. They were also given incentives, such as exemptions from taxes and corvée duties.

Most of the Ukrainian boyar families, including the Churyla, Kyrdei, Strus, Volodyiovsky, and Yarmolynsky, were quickly Polonized. By the 16th century the urban communities of Germans, Armenians, and (in part) Ukrainians were also Polonized. In contrast the Polish peasantry, who lived among the Ukrainian population, were largely Ukrainianized. Ultimately nationality came to be identified through religious affiliation, Roman Catholicism with the Poles and Orthodoxy (and later Greek Catholicism) with the Ukrainians. A comparable situation existed in *Podlachia, where a considerable number of petty gentry had resettled from neighboring Mazovia.

Polish influence in the region became stronger still after the establishment in Halych in 1375 of a Roman Catholic archdiocese, which was moved to Lviv in 1412. Dioceses were also introduced in Peremyshl, Kholm, and Volodymyr-Volynskyi (moved to Lutske in 1428). The Latin rite clergy and monastic orders were also granted substantial estates. The Polish element was weaker in Volhynia and the Kiev and Bratslav regions, which had been annexed by the Grand Duchy of Lithuania. But various restrictions notwithstanding, some Poles established themselves there by buying or leasing lands. They generally maintained cordial relations with the surrounding population. In the 15th century, Polish Catholic bishoprics were formed in Kiev and Kamianets-Podilskyi. In the same period the colonization (both Ukrainian and Polish) of those regions and Podilia was halted and even rolled back because of the increasing frequency of Tatar attacks. A line of defensive fortifications was built to stem the attacks; the fortifications were, in part, inhabited by Poles.

While the Ukrainian political and economic situation generally was becoming weaker, Polish life and culture was developing vibrantly in major Ukrainian centers, such as Lviv, Peremyshl, Jarosław, and Kamianets-Podilskyi. The estates of Polish magnates also became the focus of cultural and artistic development. Among the leading Polish writers and cultural figures who emerged in Ukraine (some of them of Ukrainian background) were Grzegorz (Hryhorii) of Sianik (1407–77), one of the first Polish humanists and poets and a Catholic archbishop of Lviv; Grzegorz (Hryhorii) of Sambir (literary pseudonyms, Roxolanus and Ruthenus) a panegyrist and educator; the humanist Paweł of Krosno (also known as Pavlo Rusyn, d 1517), a writer and teacher of classical literature at Cracow University; and M. *Rej, a writer and Calvinist polemicist who was one of the founders of Polish literature. Those who belonged to the first Ukrainian school in Polish literature include S. Orzechowski (1513–66), a writer and polemicist who initially defended the Orthodox in Ukrainian lands, and S.F. Klonowicz (1545–1602), one of the first writers to deal with Ukrainian themes in Polish (*Roxolania*, 1584).

1569–1700. As a result of the annexation of Volhynia and the Bratslav and Kiev regions by Poland following the Union of *Lublin, Polish magnates and noblemen began settling in Right-Bank Ukraine. They were lured by fertile lands and a sparse population: in 1572 the population density of central Poland stood at 16 persons/sq km, of the Rus' and Belz voivodeships, at 9 persons/sq km, and of Volhynia and Podilia, at 6.4 persons/sq km. The Kiev region had less than half the density of Volhynia and Podilia. The colonization of Left-Bank Ukraine did not begin until the late 16th and early 17th centuries.

The colonization campaign was started in earnest by King *Stephen Báthory, who decreed that the 'wastelands'

in Podilia, Bratslav, and Volhynia voivodeships be distributed in perpetuity to Polish magnates and the nobility. The policy was given further impetus under *Sigismund III Vasa. Among the beneficiaries were the Jabłonowski, Kalinowski, Koniecpolski, Potocki, Sieniawski, Zamoyski, and Żółkiewski families. In taking control of their new holdings the magnates settled them with serfs, estate managers (commonly from the petty gentry), and leaseholder–tavern keepers (often Jews). In 1619 the Chernihiv region, acquired by Poland in 1618, was parceled out in reward for military service largely to settlers from central Poland. In the 1630s and 1640s officers from the Grand Duchy of Lithuania were granted holdings in the Siversk region.

A number of so-called kinglets were created in Ukraine in the period as large tracts of land were consolidated into latifundia as a result of petitions to the king or Sejm, purchase for a nominal price, or seizure by force. Peasants were induced to settle there by the promise of 'freedoms,' specifically an exemption (for 20–30 years) from serfdom. Most of those settlers were Ukrainian peasants fleeing from northwestern Ukraine and Galicia, although peasants from central Poland also joined in. A significant number of those from central Poland later became Cossacks and even led Cossack armies, particularly in the early days of the movement. The private armies of magnates were made up largely of Poles, particularly the petty gentry. The magnates themselves were the unchallenged rulers of their domains and had considerable influence on the conduct of Polish internal and external affairs. Two magnates from Ukraine became Polish kings (*Michael Korybut Wiśniowiecki, 1669–73, and *Jan III Sobieski, 1674–96), and others (S. *Czarniecki, S. *Żółkiewski) were important political and military leaders. The Polish estates in Galicia and Volhynia were more numerous than those in central Ukraine, but they tended to be much smaller. One of the largest estates in Ukraine was owned by J. Wiśniowiecki, who ruled (in the 1640s) over 38,000 households and 230,000 subjects.

The Roman Catholic church began to expand its influence in Ukraine considerably, largely through the work of monastic orders, particularly the Polish *Jesuits. The Jesuit schools attracted not only Polish magnates and nobility but also the wealthier and more talented Ukrainians, who thus were frequently assimilated to Polish culture and converted to the Catholic faith.

The spread of education and the growth of general economic prosperity were accompanied by a remarkable flowering of Polish culture, notably in architecture, painting, and engraving. In Ukraine Polish spiritual and cultural life was concentrated in (although not limited to) Galicia. The writers S. Szymonowicz, S. *Twardowski, and S. *Zimorowicz; the historians B. *Paprocki and J. *Zimorowicz; and the bishop of Kiev, J. Wereszczyński (Y. *Vereshchynsky), all lived in Ukraine. In the 17th and 18th centuries a number of ornate fortified castles were built there, together with magnate estates that housed large art collections, libraries, and archives. Polish centers in Ukraine rivaled, and in some cases even surpassed, their counterparts in central Poland.

Polish political and economic expansion eastward into Ukraine was slowed in the early 17th century by a series of Cossack uprisings and then brought to a standstill in 1648 by the Khmelnytsky uprising. The attacks on landlords resulted in an exodus of Poles from Left-Bank Ukraine and the eastern reaches of Right-Bank Ukraine. Some magnates, including such Polonized Ukrainian families as the Wiśniowiecki and Zasławski, fought the uprising with their own armies and inflicted widespread retribution on local populations, thereby increasing the hostility of the peasantry toward themselves.

A number of landowners, some of them even Polonized Ukrainian gentry, remained in central Ukraine and participated in the war against Poland in 1648–57. Several thereafter secured high positions in the Cossack state. Some Polish noblemen began returning to Ukraine in the last years of the Cossack-Polish War and during the tenure of Hetmans I. *Vyhovsky (particularly after the signing of the Treaty of *Hadiache) and P. *Teteria. The influx was halted once again during the period of the *Ruin, when Cossack and peasant attacks resulted in the death of a number of Polish nobles. At the end of the hostilities, however, *Right-Bank Ukraine retained its Polish orientation. The Polish presence in Left-Bank Ukraine, however, was virtually eliminated. Nevertheless the Polish influence on Ukrainian culture remained widespread until the middle of the 18th century, as Polish continued to be taught and books to be published in Polish by the printing houses of Kiev, Novhorod-Siverskyi, and Chernihiv.

18th century. After years of devastation due to ongoing fighting during the Ruin and massive depopulation due to large-scale migration to Left-Bank Ukraine, Right-Bank Ukraine saw a new wave of Polish colonization at the beginning of the 18th century. Magnates began returning to their former estates or settling new lands. They established latifundia with separate administrations and armies that occasionally numbered 4,000 to 5,000. The latifundia were settled by the landless gentry (as tenants) as well as by peasants and burghers from other Polish territories. This massive wave of colonization in Podilia and the Kiev and Bratslav regions was stemmed in part by the popular rebellions, known as the *haidamaka uprisings, that broke out in response to religious and social oppression, the re-enserfment of the population, and the suppression of the Orthodox church. The uprisings, which culminated in the Koliivshchyna rebellion of 1768, destabilized the region and resulted in the death of many Polish landlords and their stewards.

During a period of uninterrupted rule in the 17th and 18th centuries, the local Polish population grew in size and importance in Galicia, the Kholm region, Podlachia, and Volhynia. At that time the Polish educational system in Western Ukrainian territories reached its broadest state of development, largely through the work of the Jesuits. After the order was abolished in 1773, the educational system in Volhynia and Right-Bank Ukraine was administered by the Polish Commission of National Education, which transferred control of some Jesuit schools and colleges to the *Basilian order. Access to those schools was restricted to those of noble birth, and the students were educated to conform to Polish ways (although instruction in Old Church Slavonic was provided). The schools of the *Piarists raised pupils to be Polish patriots, as did branches of the Cracow Academy.

Polish printing houses also contributed to general Polonization. They were run privately in various centers as well as by the Jesuits in Lviv and Peremyshl, the Basilians in Pochaiv, the Dominicans in Lutske, and the Carmelites in Berdychiv. Most printing houses, especially those of the Jesuits, had substantial libraries. The estates of magnates became cultural centers in the 18th century, especially those of the Jabłonowski, Wiśniowiecki, Potocki, Sanguszko, Rzewuski, Ostrozky, and Lubomirski families.

A number of leaders of the Polish Commonwealth in the 18th century originated from Ukrainian territories, public figures with names such as Branicki, Czartoryski, Jabłonowski, Lubomirski, Potocki, Rzewuski, and Wiśniowiecki. Most of the leaders of the Confederation of Bar (such as A. Krasiński, the bishop of Kamianets-Podilskyi) and the *Torhovytsia Confederacy (S. Potocki, K. Branicki, S. Rzewuski) were from Ukraine, as were many of the participants in the Four-Year Sejm (1788–92). The hero of the rebellion of 1794, T. Kościuszko, was from Volhynia.

Among notable Poles from Ukraine were the philosopher, educator, and coauthor of the Polish constitution of 3 May 1791 H. Kołłątaj, the historian T. Czacki, the historian and bishop of Lutske A. Naruszewicz, and the writer and reformer I. Krasicki.

Russian Empire, 1795–1917. The Ukrainian lands annexed by the Russian Empire after the partitions of Poland in 1793–5 (Volhynia, Podilia, and the Kiev region) were home to approx 240,000 Roman Catholics, who constituted 11–12 percent of the total population. Another 60,000 lived in the Kholm region, Podlachia, and Polisia. Most of the Roman Catholic population were Poles with the exception of those peasants and petty nobles who became Ukrainianized through the years and became part of the *latynnyky.

Polish magnates and aristocrats maintained their estate privileges and even increased their power over serfs. Polish landowners prospered economically as the latifundia in Right-Bank Ukraine played a leading role in the production and export of grain (mainly wheat). Polish culture continued to dominate its Ukrainian counterpart in the region, even under Russian control, and the *Kremianets Lyceum (est 1805) became a leading center of Polish education and culture. Polish was the official language of education, administration, and the courts. The predominantly Polish Roman Catholic church went about its affairs without harassment, even though its largely Ukrainian Greek Catholic counterpart came under close official scrutiny. Poles were also allowed to settle and acquire estates in Kiev, the Left Bank, and Southern Ukraine without restriction.

The Polish elite consisted of a small contingent of magnates; they were followed in size by middle and lesser landowners, and a large number of petty gentry. Commonly impoverished, the petty gentry on the magnates' estates paid cash rents. They also provided the cadres for service as estate managers, administrators, and the like. Most of the magnates were loyal to the Russian Empire, even after the Polish insurrections. They readily identified with the Russian gentry, and many moved to St Petersburg. The middle nobility was left as the local bulwark of Polish patriotism aiming to restore Poland to its pre-1772 borders. About half of the Poles in Ukraine were immigrants who had arrived in the first half of the 18th century and settled among Ukrainians or, more rarely, in separate hamlets. Relatively few Poles lived in urban areas.

The enterprises established by the Branicki, Czartoryski, Lubomirski, Potocki, and Sanguszko families made the Right Bank the most industrially developed region in

Ukraine until the mid-19th century. Their prosperity enabled the Polish estate owners to weather the reactions to the failed insurrections of 1830–1 and 1863, including the confiscation of the assets of the participants and a discriminatory land policy. It also helped tide them over through to the reforms of 1861. In fact the Polish landowners maintained considerable economic strength and influence until the outbreak of the Revolution of 1917.

But the privileges afforded the Polish nobility in Right-Bank Ukraine were rolled back during the 19th century, and their domination of the Right Bank was diminished. After the *Polish Insurrection of 1830–1, thousands of participants were exiled to the Kuban and the Urals, and their properties were seized. Their serfs became state peasants. Among the exiles was S. Konarski, who returned in 1835 and organized the Society of the Polish People in Ukraine, an underground group that was later uncovered, and of which 200 members were arrested. The Kremianets Lyceum was closed down, and its library was transferred to Kiev for use by the newly formed Kiev University. The initial intention of the new academic body was to assist in the Russification of Ukraine.

A relaxation in Russian policy after the Crimean War resulted in renewed activity among Polish secret societies, such as the Trojnicki Union (among whose organizers was V. *Antonovych). By 1861 the Polish political movement had developed to the point that it could organize patriotic demonstrations in Kiev, Zhytomyr, and Berdychiv. Memorandums were addressed to the Russian authorities demanding agrarian reforms, the establishment of Polish schools in Podilia, the teaching of Polish at Kiev University, and (by certain figures in Podilia) even the return of Right-Bank territories to the administrative realm of the Congress Kingdom of Poland.

In the first half of the 19th century some currents of Ukrainophilism appeared among Poles as well as a territorial Polish-Ukrainian patriotism that sought to merge the nascent Ukrainian movement with efforts to create a new, possibly federative, Polish Commonwealth. In the 1820s W. Rzewuski organized on his estate a camp modeled on the Zaporozhian Sich as well as a school for lirnyks. The poet T. *Padura, whose Ukrainian-language dumas urged an uprising against Russia, stayed there for a time. A number of Polish writers were active in Right-Bank Ukraine, including J. *Słowacki, the poets of the *Ukrainian school in Polish literature (A. Malczewski, B. Zaleski, S. Goszczyński, and others), M.*Czajkowski (pseud: Sadyk Pasza), A. Feliński, J. Korzeniowski, H. Rzewuski, L. Sowiński, and the historian M. Grabowski. J. Kraszewski's work, like that of others, dealt with Ukrainian themes.

During the Crimean War Czajkowski, emulating the traditions of Hetman P. Doroshenko, organized a Cossack detachment to support the Turks. In the late 1850s a group of Polonized Ukrainian noblemen created the populist *khlopoman movement. It was led by Antonovych, and sought a return to the Ukrainian folk life. The members' quest took them to the point that in 1863 Antonovych and several close associates (T. *Rylsky, B. *Poznansky, and others) renounced any support for Polish claims to non-Polish territories and adopted an openly Ukrainian national perspective. Most Polish circles, even Ukrainophiles, were incapable of such a radical break with the ethos of their social traditions.

On the eve of the *Polish Insurrection of 1863 there were 471,000 Roman Catholics in Right-Bank Ukraine, constituting 9 percent of the total population. The failure of the rebellion resulted in harsh repercussions and a significant decline in Polish political and cultural influence. In addition to numerous executions, deportations, and confiscations or forcible sales (to non-Poles) of assets there was a total ban on the Polish spoken and printed word (even in Roman Catholic religious instruction) and the abolition of all Polish associations and organizations. Polish landowners by and large were forced to relinquish their political and cultural activities and concentrate strictly on economic undertakings. The Polish clergy diminished in size and was also forced to limit its field of action. Even the zemstvo system of municipal self-administration was not introduced into the Right-Bank gubernias for nearly half a century because of imperial mistrust of the Poles. Advances in agriculture in the 1870s in Ukraine gave the Poles a foothold for their limited reascent to strength, first economically and then culturally and even politically.

From the 1870s the distribution and social structure of the Polish population in Ukraine underwent substantial changes. The Poles' rate of natural increase fell behind that of other segments of the population. In Volhynia (1901 statistics) Roman Catholics registered a natural growth rate of 18 percent, compared to 21 percent for the Orthodox. The same trend was evident in Podilia (14 and 17 percent respectively) and in the Kiev region (11 and 17 percent). Assimilation and immigration also came into play. As Ukraine became more industrialized in the later part of the century, a new wave of Poles from central Poland arrived. A growing number of professionals and industrial workers gravitated to the cities. With the abolition of serfdom Polish peasants came to Volhynian Polisia seeking lands being distributed through parcelation. A substantial number of dispossessed Poles from Right-Bank Ukraine and recent arrivals from Poland proper settled in larger cities, such as Kiev, Odessa, Kharkiv, and Mykolaiv. The extent of the influx was not clear in official statistics as population gains were offset by the linguistic and religious assimilation of Polish peasants who had settled on Ukrainian territories. Imperial law also required that all children of mixed marriages be baptized in the Orthodox church.

Table 1 gives the number of Roman Catholics (among whom there were a small number of Germans and Czechs) and Polish speakers in the Ukrainian gubernias according to the census of 1897.

TABLE 1
Roman Catholics and Polish speakers in the Right-Bank Ukrainian gubernias, 1897 (thousands; percentage of the total population in parentheses)

Gubernia	Roman Catholics	Polish speakers
Volhynia	291 (10.0)	185 (6.2)
Podilia	261 (8.7)	72 (2.3)
Kiev	104 (2.9)	68 (3.4)

A large percentage of (linguistic) Poles were urban dwellers. In 1897, 30.3 percent of all Poles in Ukraine lived in cities. Kiev had the largest concentration of Poles, and their number there increased rapidly. There were 10,400 Poles in the city (8.2 percent of its total population) in

1874, 16,700 (6.8 percent) in 1897, and 44,400 (9.8 percent) in 1909. In Right-Bank Ukraine they settled in Berdychiv, Kamianets-Podilskyi, and Zhytomyr; in Southern Ukraine they lived in Katerynoslav (13,000), Kherson, Mykolaiv, and Odessa (in 1914, 26,000); and in Slobidska Ukraine they had their largest concentration in Kharkiv (6,000). According to Russian governmental statistics for 1909, there were 424,000 Poles living in the three Right-Bank gubernias (3.8 percent of the total population). Church statistics for 1909 provide a figure of 802,000 Roman Catholics (6.3 percent of the total) in the same territories. Officially the numbers of Roman Catholics and Poles in Russian-controlled Ukraine outside of the Right Bank were as given in table 2.

TABLE 2
Roman Catholics and Poles in the Ukrainian territories of the Russian Empire outside the Right Bank, 1909 (thousands; percentage of the total population in parentheses)

Gubernia/region	Roman Catholics	Poles
Hrodna and Minsk (Ukrainian regions)	130 (11.0)	100 (8.5)
Kholm region and Podlachia	371 (44.0)	201 (24.0)
Other Ukrainian regions	230 (0.9)	180 (0.7)

The most significant concentration of Roman Catholics in the Right-Bank region was found in a strip generally 80–100 km wide running north from Kamianets-Podilskyi to Novohrad-Volynskyi and then curving eastward past Lutske. There the Poles constituted up to 20 percent or more of the local population. Imperial Russian figures note that there were 1,390,000 Roman Catholics and 809,000 Poles in the Ukrainian gubernias in 1914.

Polish landowning magnates continued to exert considerable influence. Russian statistics for 1909 note that in the Right Bank they controlled 2,306,000 desiatins (2,540,000 ha) of land, representing 46 percent of all private holdings and 15.4 percent of the entire area of the three Ukrainian gubernias. Combined with the holdings of smaller-scale landowners, the figure for Polish-controlled lands stood at nearly 3 million ha. The Poles were leaders in the development of sugar refining in Right-Bank Ukraine, and Polish factories (primarily in Kiev) supplied machinery and supplies for refineries. Other skilled Poles worked in distilleries, breweries, smelters, mines, and glassworks. Poles also constituted a sizable contingent among those engaged as independent craftsmen and in the free professions.

Polish economic, cultural, and political life became more active in the late 19th century owing in part to the relaxing of tsarist controls. Three main currents of Polish political thought in Ukraine emerged: conservative, represented by the large landowners, whose press organs were the weeklies *Kraj* (published in St Petersburg) and *Kresy* (published in Kiev); national democratic, represented by R. Dmowski's National League and *Przegląd Wszechpolski*; and socialist, represented by the Polish Socialist party's (PPS) underground paper *Robotnik*, published in Kiev in 1901–2. The *Ukrainian Socialist party was modeled on its Polish counterpart and led by a Polonized Ukrainian, B.

*Yaroshevsky, before eventually joining with the Revolutionary Ukrainian party.

Polish conservatives considered the Ukrainian question an internal Russian matter, and the national democrats denied that Ukrainians had legitimate national aspirations. Only the leaders of the PPS expressed any support for the Ukrainian movement, and they did so cautiously. In exception to the general lack of support was the formation of a group of 'Ukrainians of Polish culture,' or 'Roman Catholic Ukrainians,' led by V. *Lypynsky. Other members included L. Siedlecki, F. *Volska, and Y. Yurkevych. Their press organ was the biweekly *Przegląd Krajowy*, published in Kiev in 1909. Lypynsky and his associates adopted a Ukrainian national and even independentist platform. Others who switched from Polish to Ukrainian nationality included M. *Tyshkevych and J. *Tokarzewski-Karaszewicz. Ukrainophilism and territorial patriotism also continued to manifest itself in Right-Bank Ukraine.

Polish political and community life intensified after the Revolution of 1905. In Kiev the Ogniwo club and the gymnastic club Sokół were established. The first Polish daily, *Dziennik Kijowski*, which had a national-democratic orientation, began publication through the efforts of a group of Polish landowners. Other Polish periodicals issued in Kiev included *Nasza Przyszłość*, the literary weekly *Kłosy Ukraińskie*, and the socio-political weekly *Przedświt*. Ukrainian-Polish literary co-operation resulted in the publishing of the bilingual journal *Novorichnyk avtoriv pol's'kykh i ukraïns'kykh* in 1908. In 1906 Poles in Ukraine elected five representatives to the First State Duma and three to the State Council. Polish parliamentarians co-operated with the Ukrainian caucus and in the Autonomists' Union (formed at Polish initiative). Poles exercised considerable influence in the administrations of municipal governments and of gubernial and district zemstvos, after they were established in the Right-Bank gubernias in 1911.

In addition to underground schools several Polish educational groups were active in Ukraine before 1905, notably the Society for Popular Education (est 1897) and the Society for National Education (est 1904). After 1905 Oświata and other educational organizations could operate legally. A network of private Polish schools was established and overseen by the Polska Macierz Szkolna society. By 1917 the group had 103 schools, with an enrollment of 8,880.

Polish literary, musical, and artistic activity grew considerably from the mid-19th to the early 20th centuries in centers such as Kiev, Zhytomyr, Berdychiv, Kamianets-Podilskyi, and certain landowners' estates. A number of important figures in Polish culture either lived or worked in Ukraine, including the poet T.T. Jeż (Z. Miłkowski) and the writer L. *Sowiński; the painters H. Siemiradzki and W. Kotarbiński; and the composers and musicians J. Zarębski, I. Paderewski, and K. Szymanowski. J. Conrad (J. Korzeniowski) was born in Ukraine, where he lived until his parents were exiled for revolutionary activity. Polish stagecraft was much in evidence in Kiev, where in 1911 F. Rychłowski organized a permanent dramatic theater. It became particularly successful after many leading Polish actors joined it in 1916–18. L. Idzikowski established a bookstore and publishing house in Kiev (1857–1920s) that issued over 200 titles by Polish authors, mainly those who lived in or were active in Ukraine. It also became a major publisher of music by Ukrainian (M. Lysenko) and Polish composers.

Polish scholars who were born or lived in Ukraine included E. *Rulikowski and T. Stecki (regional studies); L. Białkowski, F. Gawroński, A. *Jabłonowski, T. Michalski, and A. Rolle (history); J. *Talko-Hryncewicz (anthropology); J. Bartoszewicz (economics); H. Ułaszyn (Slavic studies); and W. Klinger (classical philology). Ukrainian scholars of Polish background included A. *Skalkovsky (history), K. Bolsunovsky (numismatics and archeology), and V. *Horodetsky (architecture).

Poles in Ukraine generally maintained their own distinct communities even though they generally were fluent in Ukrainian and Russian. Large Polish landowners and their attendant administrators tended to regard Ukrainian peasants as a lower caste and treated them with a fair amount of contempt. In cities Poles lived in their own ghettos, and their contact with Ukrainians was minimal. The relations between Poles and the imperial authorities were usually restrained.

Although the Poles were usually either unsupportive of (even antagonistic to) or neutral to Ukrainian political and national strivings, they played a significant and overall positive role in the development of Ukraine in the 19th and early 20th centuries. The substantial Polish presence in Right-Bank Ukraine served as a counterpoint to Russian political domination and cultural Russification. Although neither the Russians nor the Poles would concede that Ukrainians should be treated as equals, the tension between the two helped to crystallize a conviction among Ukrainians that they were culturally and politically distinct. Moreover, certain people raised in a Polish cultural milieu (V. Antonovych, V. Lypynsky, T. Rylsky, and others) contributed significantly to the formation of the modern Ukrainian nation.

Galicia, 1772–1918. In 1914 there were 1,240,000 Roman Catholics living in eastern *Galicia (including the Lemko region, but not the ethnic Polish borderland districts), where they constituted 23.1 percent of the total population. About two-thirds of them were ethnic Poles, and most of the rest were *latynnyky*. About 25 percent of Roman Catholics (virtually all of them Poles) lived in cities, compared to 8 percent of Greek Catholics. Such differences were also common in the respective occupational profiles. In 1910 fewer Roman Catholics were engaged in agriculture than Greek Catholics (68 compared to 90 percent), and more were active in industry (16 compared to 3 percent), trade and transport (8.5 compared to 2.5 percent), and the civil service and free professions (7.5 compared to 4.5 percent).

Changes in ethnic and religious demography reflected a growth in the number of Roman Catholics. They constituted 21.4 percent of the total Galician population in 1857 (Greek Catholics, 66.5 percent), 22.2 percent in 1880 (Greek Catholics, 63.4 percent), 23.5 percent in 1900 (Greek Catholics, 62.8 percent), and 25.3 percent in 1910 (Greek Catholics, 61.7 percent; the figures do not include the Lemko region, but include the Polish border districts). The rise was due largely to the eastward migrations of people from central Poland (35,000 in 1891–1900). Other possible factors were the greater number of Galician Ukrainians emigrating to North and South America and the Polonization of Ukrainians, Germans, and Jews, particularly in large cities. The highest concentrations of Poles lived in large pockets around Lviv, Mostyska, Sambir, and Ternopil and in a swath of territory reaching from Peremyshl and Sambir in the west to the Zbruch River in the east.

The core of the Polish community in Galicia was composed of the landowners, civil servants, professionals, industrial workers, and other urban elements. The reforms of *Joseph II of Austria limited the powers of Polish magnates and nobles over the peasantry, but after Joseph's death in 1790 they began taking control of the local bureaucratic apparatus. Poles were able to influence the Austrian administration by lobbying senior Austrian officials on the one hand and by filling lower-echelon positions with Polish petty noblemen on the other. Poles became the ruling elite of municipal governments and of the Galician Estates Diet (1817–45). A number of former royal Austro-Hungarian estates in Galicia were sold to Polish magnates, who thus increased their holdings.

Polish revolutionary democrats contributed considerably to the awakening of national consciousness among the Galician clerical intelligentsia in the 1830s and 1840s. Activists such as K. Cięglewicz and M. Popel circulated propaganda in Ukrainian and sought to disseminate it among Greek Catholic peasants and students in seminaries. The events of 1848–9, however, underlined the deep divisions between Ukrainians and Poles.

The appointment of Count A. Gołuchowski as governor of Galicia in 1849 and a political understanding reached with the Austrian government in 1867 consolidated the Poles' status as the ruling group in Galicia. They now dominated the crownland's bureaucracy; by the early 20th century virtually all upper-rank civil servants and county heads were Poles. In 1912 there were 112 Poles with senior positions in the central Viennese administration, compared to only 5 Ukrainians.

Poles also owned much of the land in Galicia. In 1892 the holdings of large landowners, virtually all of whom were Poles, constituted 43 percent of the total landholdings. Polish settlements also expanded in eastern Galicia as the result of a sustained colonization effort. In 1852–1912, Polish immigrants from the western part of the crownland received 237,000 ha of land earmarked for parcelation in eastern Galicia, in comparison to 38,000 ha given to Ukrainians. Gymnasiums and postsecondary educational institutions were also predominantly Polish in character. The postsecondary institutions were all Polish, and there were 39 Polish state gymnasiums in eastern Galicia, compared to 3 Ukrainian.

The antagonism between Poles and Ukrainians was further exacerbated by the almost universal anti-Ukrainian stance of the major Polish political parties in the late 19th and early 20th centuries. The most influential Polish party of the 1870s and 1880s, the Cracow-based group of western Galician conservatives commonly known as the *Stańczyk* group (Ukrainian: *stanchyky*), controlled the higher offices of the crownland and many senior posts in the Viennese government; one of their number was always appointed Austrian minister for Galicia, and some of them managed to become premier. In 1907 they formed the National Right party. The leading figures of the group included K. *Badeni, L. Biliński (Austrian minister of finance), M. *Bobrzyński, and A. Potocki. Another group of Polish conservatives, based in Lviv, included D. Abrahamowicz, W. Dzieduszycki, Gołuchowski, and K. Grocholski. That group was particularly vociferous in combating Ukrainian interests (even more so than the Cracow group). In the early 20th century the liberal-nationalist National Democratic party, popularly known as the *En-*

decja, was a chauvinistic group; it supported Russia in its foreign policy, and its members therefore were often considered Russophiles. Its ideologist was R. *Dmowski, and its leaders were S. Głąbiński, S. *Grabski, A. Skarbek, and others, who published the daily *Słowo Polskie*. The group influenced such large community organizations as Sokół and the Society for Public Schools.

The Polish political faction most receptive to Ukrainian political aspirations was the socialist camp, which worked closely with its Ukrainian counterpart. Its leaders included I. Daszyński, H. Diamand, H. Lieberman, and B. Limanowski. Polish and Ukrainian socialists also collaborated within unions to which members of both groups belonged.

On the eve of the First World War the Polish political world in Galicia was divided into two camps. On the one hand were the Cracow conservatives and democratic groups (liberals, socialists, and populists), and on the other, the Podolians and the National Democrats. The former group eventually managed to reach a comprehensive Ukrainian-Polish rapprochement, which was never put into practice owing to the outbreak of the First World War.

Along with political power came disproportionate benefits to Polish cultural concerns. In 1902, 333,050 crowns were dispensed for Polish cultural aims by the Galician provincial diet; Ukrainians were issued 35,900 crowns. Lviv continued to be an important center of Polish political and cultural life, at times more important than Cracow and even Warsaw. Alongside the university and the polytechnical school were a number of Polish scholarly institutions, including the *Ossolineum, the Polish Historical Society, the Polish Society of Naturalists, and various libraries, museums, theaters, book clubs, and journal reading clubs. Peremyshl, Stanyslaviv, Ternopil, and other centers also boasted considerable Polish cultural activity.

Many Poles of eastern Galicia (including a substantial number of immigrants from central Poland and Right-Bank Ukraine) influenced the development of Ukrainian cultural, academic, and political life. Among them were the writers A. Fredro, Z. Kaczkowski, J. Lam, K. Ujejski, T. *Zaborowski, and J. *Zachariasiewicz (who frequently touched on Ukrainian matters and themes in their works); the literary scholars A. Brückner, W. Feldman, J. Kleiner, and M. Mochnacki; the painters and sculptors A. Grottger, J. *Kossak, and K. *Sichulski; the composers and musicians J. Gall, H. Jarecki, and M. Sołtys; many actors who performed at the Lviv Theater; the historians A. Bielowski, F. *Bujak, W. *Łoziński, A. *Prochaska, and K. Szajnocha; the economists L. Caro and S. Szczepanowski; the statistician J. Buzek; and the geographer E. *Romer.

Central Ukraine, 1917–20. After the outbreak of the First World War (particularly in 1915) there was a large influx of Polish refugees from territories occupied by the Central Powers. Most of them settled in Kiev; by 1917 their number in that city had reached 42,800 (or 9.5 percent of the city's total population). The Polish Society for Relief of Victims of War (with about 50 branches) and the Central Civilian Committee were established to assist them.

After the February Revolution of 1917 a number of Polish political and community organizations were established, including the Polish Executive Committee in Ruthenia (PKW), headed by J. Bartoszewicz. Polish national democrats and landowners were the dominant forces in

that organization, whose leaders also included J. Zdziechowski.

In July 1917 an all-Ukrainian congress of Poles was convened in Kiev. It split into two groups after a democratic faction, influenced by the PPS and the Polish Army Organization, seceded. The PPS itself later split into left and right factions. The mainstream Polish group, the Polish Democratic Center party, was led by such figures as S. *Stempowski, R. Knoll, and M. *Mickiewicz. Both Polish political camps were receptive to the Ukrainian national revival, but the PKW opposed the Central Rada's policies. Therefore, on 24 July 1917, only representatives of the Democratic Center party joined the Central (20 deputies) and Little Radas (W. Matuszewski and W. Rudnicki). Mickiewicz served as one of the advisers on nationality affairs to the General Secretariat, and after the Third Universal (20 November 1917) he was appointed head of the newly formed Ministry of Polish Affairs. The Central Rada's radical agrarian policies alienated many Poles from the cause of Ukrainian statehood.

In accordance with legislation on personal national autonomy passed on 24 January 1918 the Polish minority in Ukraine had the right to establish a separate national union with rights of autonomy. The projected elections for its first congress, however, never took place (as war with invading Soviet forces broke out). Most Poles in Ukraine continued to support the PKW and shunned the UNR's Ministry of Polish Affairs because it was left-wing. Despite the adverse conditions the ministry had some achievements in the fields of education, social services, and the defense of Polish interests. The Polish educational organization, Związek Macierzy Polskiej, was also active in 1917–18.

All nationality ministries were abolished after the Hetman coup, and Polish schools were placed under the jurisdiction of the Ukrainian Ministry of Education. P. Skoropadsky's support of the interests of Polish landowners garnered him their loyalty, however. During his regime the PKW continued to be active.

In 1917–18 there were over 1,300 Polish schools in Ukraine, with 84,000 pupils and 1,800 teachers. There were 13 secondary schools in Kiev, 2 in Zhytomyr, and 2 in Odessa. In November 1917 the Polish University College was established in Kiev, with L. Janowski as its first rector. In 1917–18 it had an enrollment of 718.

In 1919 the chaos in Ukraine and the occupation of most of its territory by Bolshevik forces set in motion a massive Polish emigration to the newly established Polish state. The conclusion of the subsequent Soviet-Polish War and the signing of the Peace Treaty of *Riga precluded the possibility of a return to Ukraine for many Polish landowners and members of the intelligentsia and prompted the emigration of many of those who had remained. Some of the new emigrants assumed senior positions in the Polish government and maintained relations with associations of refugees from Ukraine.

Ukrainian SSR, 1920–1930s. According to the census of 1926 there were 476,400 Poles in Soviet Ukraine (1.6 percent of the total population). Of those, 230,400 (48.4 percent) listed Ukrainian as their mother tongue (15.7 percent in the cities, 56.9 percent in rural areas). They were probably *latynnyky*. A large majority (86 percent) of the Poles in Ukraine (408,000) lived in territories that had belonged to the Polish state until the late 18th century. Their distribution remained similar to the distribution recorded in 1897. They were most highly concentrated in Volhynia (Zhytomyr) and Proskuriv okruhas, where they formed 12.5 percent and 10.2 percent of the respective total populations. The only region with a Polish majority was Marchlewski raion (*Dovbysh), where 69.2 percent of the people were Poles by nationality, and approx 33 percent, Poles by language. There were also small Polish communities in the steppe regions. A large number of Poles lived in larger urban centers, such as Kiev (13,700, or 2.7 percent of the population), Odessa (11,600), Kharkiv (7,000), Kherson (4,500), and Dnipropetrovske (4,000).

The process of assimilation of the Polish peasantry in Right-Bank Ukraine continued, as the data of the 1897 and 1926 censuses testify. In general the category of Roman Catholic included those who gave Polish as their nationality, that is, both true Poles and *latynnyky*. That means that the Polish community in Ukraine contracted by 38 percent in 30 years (1897–1926). The percentage of the Polish population in cities also declined, from 3.1 percent of Ukraine's urban population to 1.9 percent. In 1897, 30 percent of Ukraine's Poles lived in cities; in 1926, 15 percent. Prior to the revolution their social distribution was different from that of Ukrainians. By 1926 it had become the same. The community suffered far more than after the revolts of 1830–1 and 1863–4. It became a small minority, and its elite virtually ceased to exist.

In the 1920s Poles in the Ukrainian SSR were regarded and treated as a distinct national minority. Under the Bolshevik regime, however, Polish political, community, and cultural organizations either were abolished or dissolved themselves, and schools were brought under the control of the Soviet educational system. Of the political parties only some cells of the left wing of the Polish Democratic Center party remained, and they were co-opted by the CP(B)U. The CP(B)U maintained Polish bureaus in the Central Committee as well as in municipal and oblast committees. In the 1920s those bureaus oversaw Polish community life in the Ukrainian SSR. Nationality councils were also established in areas where Poles were concentrated (139 in May 1927). A total of six courts presided over cases in Polish.

On 1 January 1927 there were 281 Polish labor schools (134 in 1936). In 1928, 38 Polish books were published in Ukraine; in 1934, 63. There were 17 newspapers published in Polish, including the daily *Sierp* (renamed *Głos Radziecki* in 1935). The People's Commissariat of Education of the Ukrainian SSR had a Polish Central Bureau. In Kiev there was also the Central Polish Library and a Polish department in the State Publishing House. In 1931 the Institute of Polish Proletarian Culture was established at the All-Ukrainian Academy of Sciences. It did not manage to undertake any serious work, however, because it was liquidated soon thereafter. The Polish section of the Kiev Central Historical Archive met a similar fate.

In the early 1930s, relations between Poland and the USSR worsened. In late 1933 P. *Postyshev declared that an 'underground' Polish Army Organization had been uncovered. He accused Polish members of the CP(B)U of being leaders of the organization and had them shot as spies. Thereafter Marchlewski raion was liquidated. Senior party and government members in the Ukrainian SSR of Polish or Polish-Jewish background (including F. *Kon, J. Kosior, and S. *Kosior) made virtually no effort in the sphere of Polish affairs.

Ukrainian territories under Poland, 1919–39. The course of ethnic relations was different in every region of Western Ukraine. In Galicia, despite pressures exerted by the local Polish population and those who arrived seeking parceled land, the percentage of Roman Catholics rose only from 24 to 25 percent (Polish statistics cite 30 percent). The small growth was due to the larger rate of natural population increase among Greek Catholics, a reduced rate of emigration to the Western Hemisphere, and a reduced rate of migration from central Poland (the Poles there gravitated more to cities in Silesia, in the Poznań region, and along the Baltic Sea coast). Many senior Polish officials, scholars, activists, artists, and others left Lviv for Warsaw, Poznań, and Vilnius.

In western Volhynia and Polisia Poles and *latynnyky* constituted 9 and 4.5 percent respectively of the population in 1897. Their numbers doubled in the interwar period owing to a strong influx of Poles into the cities (particularly as administrators) and to rural areas (military personnel and parcelation recipients). In the Kholm region and Podlachia the number of Ukrainians diminished because many former Uniates (since Uniatism had been outlawed in 1875–6) and Orthodox converted to Roman Catholicism (and became known as *kalakuty*). In addition only a portion of the Poles who had been evacuated eastward during the First World War (in 1915) returned to the region.

In Galicia in 1931, agriculture occupied 69.9 percent of Roman Catholics (88.1 percent of Greek Catholics); industry, 11 percent (5.8 percent of Greek Catholics); trade, 5.8 percent (1.5 percent of Greek Catholics); the civil service, 5.6 percent (1.2 percent of Greek Catholics); and other activities, 7.7 percent (3.4 percent of Greek Catholics).

Lviv continued to be the focus of considerable Polish activity in scholarship and culture. Less important, but active nevertheless, were Peremyshl, Stanyslaviv, Lutske, Ternopil, Brest, and other locales. Poles continued their pre-eminence in publishing. In 1929, of 313 periodicals issued in the eastern voivodeships of Poland (including German and Jewish publications) only 77 were Ukrainian. Of the 16 dailies, only 2 were Ukrainian.

Polish writers active in the region included M. Jastrun, K. Makuszyński, J. Parandowski, L. Staff, and S. Vincenz. Those active in music included L. Bronarski, A. Sołtys, and T. Szeligowski; in linguistics, J. Janów, J. Kuryłowicz, and T. *Lehr-Spławiński; in ethnography, A. *Fiszer; in law, A. Halban; in geology, W. Rogala and W. *Teisseyre; in botany, S. Kulczyński; in anthropology, J. Czekanowski; in mathematics, S. *Banach and K. Bartel; and in chemistry, I. Mościcki (later the president of Poland).

Among Polish cultural figures born in Right-Bank Ukraine (outside Galicia) were the writers M. Choromański, J. Iwaszkiewicz, Z. Kossak-Szczucka, J. *Łobodowski, and W. *Słobodnik; the composers M. Kondracki and K. Szymanowski; and the architect T. Tolwinski. Polish political leaders active in Western Ukraine included H. *Józewski, J. Wołoszynowski, and W. Biernacki-Kostek.

Everyday relations between Ukrainians and Poles in the Western Ukrainian districts varied. In general, relations between Ukrainian peasants and *latynnyky* were good and neighborly, particularly with those Poles who had settled there long before. There was, however, hostility to newcomers from the city, such as teachers and police, forestry department, and manorial officials. Contacts between the Ukrainian and Polish rural intelligentsia were mostly official. Ethnic relations in the cities also tended to be official, regardless of social standing.

After 1939. After the Soviet occupation of Western Ukraine in 1939, Polish influence in that region declined immediately. Large and middle-sized Polish estates were liquidated, and many Polish colonists and administration officials were deported. A large number of refugees from German-occupied Poland arrived in Lviv, including Communist leaders, such as W. Gomułka and Z. Kliszko. There was a Polish theater of drama and satire in the city as well as a number of Polish-language newspapers and journals.

After the new border was established between the Ukrainian SSR and Poland (on 16 August 1945), a massive exchange of borderland population ensued. In 1946 virtually all Poles were deported from Western Ukraine to territories recently acquired by Poland from Germany (the so-called regained lands). Large numbers of Ukrainians were moved from borderland regions into newly opened lands. Many of the Ukrainians who had remained in Ukrainian ethnic territory ceded to Poland (northwestern Galicia and the Lemko, Kholm, and Sian regions) were deported westward by the Polish authorities. As a result the ethnic boundaries between Ukrainian and Polish areas of settlement came to correspond roughly with the political borders, and the Polish element in Ukraine was reduced to a relatively insignificant minority.

According to the census of 1959 there were 363,000 Poles and *latynnyky* in the Ukrainian SSR, representing 0.9 percent of the total population. In 1933 there had been 2,100,000 (or 5 percent of the total) within the same boundaries (inclusive of Western Ukraine). In 1959 only 68,000 Poles in Ukraine spoke Polish (19 percent), whereas 69 percent spoke Ukrainian, and 12 percent (mostly urban dwellers) spoke Russian. Of the 1,570,000 Poles and *latynnyky* who had lived in Western Ukraine (21.9 percent of the local population) only 37,000 remained. The majority of Poles (approx 209,000, representing 57 percent of the total Polish population of Ukraine) lived in Right-Bank Ukraine, from which fewer had been resettled; only 23,700 of them spoke Polish. They were concentrated in Zhytomyr (103,000) and Khmelnytskyi (70,000) oblasts. Approx 45 percent of Poles lived in cities, and 55 percent in the countryside. About 15,000 lived in Lviv, and 8,400 in Kiev.

By 1970 the number of Poles in Ukraine had dropped to 295,000, or 0.6 percent of the total population; in 1989 the figure stood at 219,000 (0.4 percent).

Polish academic institutions, including libraries and museums, were all merged with Ukrainian ones. Only some were permitted to transfer to Poland, among them the Ossolineum. Polish community and cultural organizations ceased to exist. A few Roman Catholic parishes and schools continued to be active, mainly in Lviv.

(See *Poland for bibliography.)

B. Kravtsiv, V. Kubijovyč, O. Ohloblyn, I.L. Rudnytsky

Poletyka. A family of Cossack *starshyna* in Left-Bank Ukraine (possibly of Right-Bank origin). The founder was Ivan, a Cossack of Lubni regiment in 1649. His descendant Pavlo was a fellow of the banner in Lubni regiment who died in the 1709 Battle of Poltava. Pavlo's son, Andrii (1692–1773), was mayor of Romen (1727–9) and a fellow of the banner and fellow of the standard (1749–57) in Lubni regiment. Andrii had five sons, among them Andrii *Poletyka, Hryhorii *Poletyka, and Ivan *Poletyka. In the 18th and 19th centuries Hryhorii's son, Vasyl *Poletyka, Ivan's sons, Mykhailo *Poletyka and Petro *Poletyka, and their cousin, Hryhorii *Poletyka, were civic and cultural fig-

ures. Their descendant Volodymyr (1886–?) was a zemstvo official, marshal of the nobility in Myrhorod county, and senior secretary of the Hetman government's mission in Vienna in 1918–19.

Andrii Poletyka   Hryhorii Poletyka

Poletyka, Andrii, b ca 1739–41?, d ca 1798. Civic figure; brother of H. and I. *Poletyka. In 1758 he became a chancellor in the Hetman state's General Military Chancellery. He was appointed a notable military fellow in 1763 and a fellow of the standard in 1767. Later, as marshal of the nobility in Romen county (1784, 1797–8) and of all Chernihiv gubernia (1785–8), he was an advocate of granting imperial noble status and privileges to the largest number of Cossack *starshyna*. From 1787 he had the rank of court counsel in the Russian imperial civil service. Poletyka's diary of Catherine II's visit to Kiev in 1787 was published in *Pamiatnaia knizhka Kievskoi gubernii na 1858 g.* (Memorial Book of Kiev Gubernia for 1858).

Poletyka, Hryhorii, b 1725 in Romen, Lubni regiment, d 8 December 1784 in St Petersburg. Civic leader and writer; brother of I. *Poletyka. He completed his studies at the Kievan Mohyla Academy (1745) and then worked in St Petersburg as a translator of Latin and German works.

Poletyka entered Ukrainian public life as the replacement for the Lubni regimental representative to Catherine II's Legislative Council of 1767–9. He emerged as a leading proponent of Ukrainian interests at the landmark gathering following the sudden resignation of K. Rozumovsky. Poletyka articulated a view of Ukraine ruled as a gentry democracy in the manner of the Polish Commonwealth. His views differed markedly from those of Rozumovsky regarding the restoration of the Cossack institutions that had been abolished in 1764 and the role of the hetman in Ukrainian society. The viability of his arguments and the passion of his defence of Ukrainian autonomy won him the support of Ukrainian delegates at the council. Catherine's administrative changes in Ukraine disregarded the positions of Poletyka and the petitions of hundreds of Ukrainians. Nevertheless the exercise had brought forth a clear articulation of perceived rights, and it played an important role in the development of a Ukrainian historical consciousness in modern times.

In addition to items submitted to the Legislative Council Poletyka prepared works regarding the origins of the Kievan Mohyla Academy and the development of education in Russia, as well as Russian translations of Aristotle and a six-language dictionary (Russian, Greek, Latin, French, German, and English). Some historians credit him (or him and his son, Vasyl) with writing *Istoriia Rusov* (History of the Rus' People).

BIBLIOGRAPHY
Kohut, Z. *Russian Centralism and Ukrainian Autonomy: Imperial Absorption of the Hetmanate, 1760s–1830s* (Cambridge, Mass 1988)
V. Omelchenko

Poletyka, Hryhorii, b ca 1735, d 1798. Historian and diplomat; cousin of A., H., and I. *Poletyka. He graduated from the Kievan Mohyla Academy, Moscow Academy, and St Petersburg University. He served as translator in the Russian College of Foreign Affairs (1755–62), secretary of the Russian legation at the royal court of the Holy Roman Empire (from 1762), and adviser to the Russian embassy in Vienna (from 1770). He translated Latin works and wrote an article about the Zaporozhian Cossacks, which was published in *Wiener Taschenkalender zum Nutzen und Vergnügen* (1788). In 1777 Joseph II granted him Austrian noble status.

Poletyka, Ivan, b 29 August 1726 in Romen, Lubni regiment, d 3 May 1783 in Vasylkiv, Kiev gubernia. Physician; brother of H. *Poletyka. A graduate of the Kievan Mohyla Academy (1746), he studied at the Kiel Medical Academy in Germany (1746–52) and wrote his doctoral dissertation at Leiden University on hereditary diseases (1754). He taught at the Kiel Academy (1754–6) and then went to Russia to direct the St Petersburg Military Hospital and teach at its medical school (1756–9). His quarrelsome character led to his demotion, and he was transferred to Ukraine and placed in charge of the Border Quarantine Service in Vasylkiv (1763–83). His publications dealt with infectious diseases.

Poletyka, Mykhailo, b 28 September 1768, d 17 December 1824. Philosopher; son of I. *Poletyka and brother of P. *Poletyka. A graduate of the First Cadet Corps, he served as secretary to Empress Maria Fedorovna. After retiring from service in 1807, he wrote *Essais philosophiques sur l'homme, ses principaux rapports et sa destinée, fondés sur l'expérience et la raison, suivis d'observations sur le beau*, which was published anonymously in Halle (1818) and again in St Petersburg (1822).

Poletyka, Petro (Pierre de Poletica), b 27 August 1778 in Vasylkiv, near Kiev, d 7 February 1849 in St Petersburg. Career diplomat; son of I. *Poletyka and brother of M. *Poletyka. In 1798 he became a translator in the Russian College of Foreign Affairs. Later he served as a chancellor in the Russian diplomatic missions in Stockholm (1802–3) and Naples (1803–5), adviser to the missions in Philadelphia (1809–11), Rio de Janeiro (1811–12), Madrid (1812–14), and London (1816–17), and Russian special envoy and minister plenipotentiary in the United States (1818–22). He was the minister who negotiated and signed the 1824 Russian-US agreement regarding the Russian American Company and the Russian-US (1824) and Russian-British (1825) conventions on trade, fishing, and navigation in the Pacific. In 1825 he was appointed a privy councillor and senator. Poletyka is the author of *A Sketch of the Internal Conditions of the United States and Their Political Relations with Europe* (Baltimore 1826). Excerpts from his memoirs

of 1778–1849 were published in *Russkii arkhiv* (vol 3, 1885). He was elected a member of the American Philosophical Society in Philadelphia in 1822. A mountain on the British Columbia–Alaska border was named after Poletyka in 1923, and M. Hutsuliak's book about him was published in Vancouver in 1967.

Vasyl Poletyka   Liudmyla Polevska

Poletyka, Vasyl, b 1765 in St Petersburg, d 1845 in Korovyntsi, Romen county, Poltava gubernia. Historian and civic figure; son of H. *Poletyka the elder. After studying at Vilnius University he served in the Russian army (1786–90), from which he retired with the rank of second major to his estate in Korovyntsi. In 1802 and 1805–12 he was marshal of the nobility in Romen county. His study of the history of ancient Egypt and the Assyrians, Medes, and Persians was published in St Petersburg in 1788, and a few of his shorter works were printed in various publications of the period. He collected many materials for a history of Ukraine he planned to write. According to O. Lazarevsky, V. Horlenko, L. Maikov, E. Borschak, and other scholars Poletyka was the author, alone or with his father, of *Istoriia Rusov*.

Polevska, Liudmyla [Polevs'ka, Ljudmyla] (née Tymoshenko), b 1893 in Kharkiv, d 19 December 1975 in New York. Cellist and teacher; spouse of M. Polevsky. She studied cello at the Kharkiv and Moscow conservatories and then performed as a soloist with the Kiev, Kharkiv, and Moscow philharmonic orchestras under S. Rachmaninoff, S. Koussevitzky, and others. She was a member (with her husband) of the Ukrainian State Trio (Kharkiv) from 1926, and also a professor of cello at the Kharkiv Conservatory in 1928–41. A postwar émigré, from 1952 she was a faculty member of the Ukrainian Music Institute of America in New York. She appeared as a soloist in Western Europe, Canada, and the United States.

Polevska, Zoia [Polevs'ka, Zoja], b 1925 in Kharkiv. Concert cellist; daughter of L. Polevska and M. Polevsky. She studied at the Kharkiv Conservatory in the class of her mother and graduated from the Vienna Academy of Music (*Meisterschule*). She then concertized successfully and extensively throughout Europe and appeared as soloist with the Vienna Philharmonic under W. Furtwängler. She was also a soloist with the Radio Italiano Orchestra and in

Zoia Polevska   Mykola Polevsky

numerous other radio recitals. Since the 1950s she has performed in Canada and the United States. Her repertoire includes J.S. Bach, A. Vivaldi, G. Frescobaldi, A. Dvořák, P. Tchaikovsky, G. Fauré, M. Ravel, and L. Revutsky.

Polevsky, Mykola, b 27 December 1894 in Gori, Georgia, d 4 January 1969 in New York. Pianist and teacher. A student of S. Rachmaninoff, he graduated in 1918 from the Moscow Conservatory. From 1919 he taught piano and lectured on musicological subjects at the Kharkiv Conservatory, as professor during 1928–41. From 1926 he was also a member of the Kharkiv-based Ukrainian State Trio, which championed an extensive Ukrainian chamber repertoire. He subsequently taught at the Vienna (1943–5) and Rome conservatories, and from 1952 was a faculty member of the Ukrainian Music Institute of America in New York and Philadelphia. Among his students were noted pianists and teachers, including L. Sahalov, Z. Chernevska, L. Ostrin, G. Oransky, and V. Sechkin.

Polferov, Yakov [Polfjorov, Jakov], b 13 April 1891 in Ilinskaia stanitsa, Krasnodar krai, d 30 September 1966 in Kharkiv. Musicologist and conductor. After graduating from the St Petersburg Conservatory in 1911, he studied composition at the Odessa Conservatory. He worked as a conductor at various theaters in St Petersburg and other cities, lectured at the Odessa Conservatory (1918–21), directed a music tekhnikum in Petrograd (1921–4), and edited the journal *Ezhenedel'nik petrogradskikh gosudarstvennykh akademicheskikh teatrov* (1922–3). From 1924 he lived in Kharkiv, where he served as rector of the Music and Drama Institute (1924–5), artistic director of Ukrainian radio broadcasting (1927–9), and head of the music department of the Kharkiv State Library. His scholarly works include *Zvukovi i muzychni elementy v tvorakh ukraïns'kykh prozaïkiv* (Sound and Musical Elements in the Works of Ukrainian Prose Writers, 1929), *Orhanika* (Organ Music, 1930), and a bibliographic reference book, *Rosiis'ka muzyka 19 ta 20 stolit'* (Russian Music of the 19th and 20th Centuries, 1935).

Poliakov, Illia [Poljakov, Illja], b 16 September 1905 in Kharkiv, d 4 November 1976 in Kiev. Biologist; corresponding member of the AN URSR (now ANU) from 1948. A graduate of the Kharkiv Institute of People's Education (1926), he was a department head at Kharkiv University (1932–48) and worked at the ANU Institute of Genetics and Selection (1947–56). He was later associate director and director (from 1968) of the Ukrainian Scientific Research Institute of Plant Cultivation, Selection, and Genetics. He wrote on experimental botany, Darwinism, and the history and theoretical problems of biology and obtained significant results in the fertilization of flowering plants.

Poliakov, Mykola [Poljakov], b 18 May 1903 in Katerynoslav (now Dnipropetrovske). Mining scientist and geologist; full member of the AN URSR (now ANU) since 1967. He studied and taught at the Dnipropetrovske Mining Institute and worked at the ANU Institute of Mining (from 1945). He headed the Dnipropetrovske branch of the ANU Institute of Mechanics (from 1962) and became director of the ANU Institute of Geotechnical Mechanics (1967–75). He was involved in the development of new technology for mining the extensive deposits of manganese ore and brown coal in Ukraine, and in the reconstruction of the Ukrainian mining industry after the Second World War.

Poliakov, Petro [Poljakov], b 15 November 1907 in Odessa, d 5 October 1973 in Kiev. Composer, conductor, and pedagogue. A graduate (1931) of the Lysenko Music and Drama Institute, he studied composition with B. Liatoshynsky and conducting with V. Berdiaiev. He then served as conductor and artistic director of the Kiev Radio Orchestra (1933–53), the Ukrainian State Symphony Orchestra (1953–6), and the Kiev Theater of Musical Comedy (1956–61). His works include the musical comedy *Koho ia kokhaiu?* (Whom Do I Love?, 1959); the cantata *Zhyvy Ukraino* (Long Live Ukraine, 1942); symphonic suites; music for radio and film; orchestrations of works by M. Lysenko, K. Stetsenko, P. Sokalsky, and others; and editions of M. Kropyvnytsky's stage music. He taught at the Kiev Conservatory (1951–8).

Poliana [Poljana]. V-3. A town smt (1986 pop 3,500) in Svaliava raion, Transcarpathia oblast. It is first mentioned in historical documents in the 12th century. Poliana is a balneological health resort with two sanatoriums that are open all year. The mineral waters provided by its four springs are used to treat chronic gastritis, ulcers, and liver and kidney ailments.

Polianians (*poliany*). A Slavic tribe (a tribal alliance, according to M. Braichevsky) that lived on the right bank of the middle reaches of the Dnieper River, between the tributaries Ros and Irpin. They are mentioned in the earliest, undated section of the Rus' Primary Chronicle as living in the Kievan hills alongside the *Varangian route to the Greeks. The last mention of them is under the year 944, where they are referred to as among Prince Ihor's warriors. Their name is derived from the fields (*polia*) they inhabited. The location of the Polianians' territory at the intersection of important trade routes contributed to their economic and cultural development as organizers of the Kievan state. In the 9th and 10th centuries they were already known as the Rus', a name that was soon applied to all the tribes that made up *Kievan Rus'. The Polianians' principal city was Kiev. Other important centers were Bilhorod, Bohuslav, Vyshhorod, and Zvenyhorod. Archeological evidence and the chronicles indicate that the Polianians engaged in agriculture (they used the hoe and plow), animal husbandry, hunting, beekeeping, and fishing and were skilled artisans. The chronicles state that they were socioeconomically more advanced than the neighboring Slavic tribes.

BIBLIOGRAPHY
Hrushevs'kyi, M. *Istoriia Ukraïny-Rusy*, vol 1 (Lviv 1904; Kiev 1913; New York 1954)
Tret'iakov, P. *Vostochnoslavianskie plemena*, 2nd edn (Moscow 1953)
Bibikov, S. (ed). *Narysy starodavn'oï istoriï Ukraïns'koï RSR* (Kiev 1959)
Mezentseva, H. *Kanivs'ke poselennia polian* (Kiev 1965)
Rusanova, I. *Kurgany polian X–XII vv.* (Moscow 1966)
Braichevs'kyi, M. *Pokhodzhennia Rusi* (Kiev 1968)

A. Zhukovsky

Polianovka Peace Treaty. A treaty ending the Polish-Muscovite War of 1632–4, concluded on 4 June 1634 at the Polianovka River in the Smolensk region. The Polish-Lithuanian Commonwealth agreed to remove its forces from Muscovite territory, and King Władysław IV Vasa renounced his claim to the Muscovite throne in exchange for 20,000 rubles. Muscovy relinquished its claim to most of the lands, including the Chernihiv and Novhorod-Siverskyi regions, that it had been forced to cede to the Commonwealth by the Deulin Treaty of 1618.

Polianska-Karpenko, Olha [Poljans'ka], b 1869 in Novocherkassk, Don Cossack region, d 1943. Stage actress and singer (contralto). She worked in the troupes of M. Kropyvnytsky (1884–8 and 1894–8), M. Sadovsky (1888–93), and O. Suslov and P. Saksahansky (1898–1905) and in Sadovsky's Theater (1906–14), the Society of Ukrainian Actors (1915–16), the Ukrainian National Theater (1917–18), the State People's Theater (1918–19), and the Shevchenko First Theater of the Ukrainian Soviet Republic. In 1925 she retired from the stage. Among her roles were Lymerykha in P. Myrny's *Lymerivna* (The Saddler's Daughter) and Hordylia in M. Starytsky's *Tsyhanka Aza* (The Gypsy Aza).

Poliansky, Fedir (Teodor) [Poljans'kyj], b ?, d after 1783 in Lviv. Bell founder. His best-known works are the clock bell in the tower of the Kamianets-Podilskyi city hall (1753) and the Kyrylo Bell at the Dormition Church in Lviv (1783). He also cast the bells for churches in Shchyrets (1753), Susidovychi (1759), Turynka (1761), and Krakovets, in the Lviv region; Kozyna (1759) and Mykhailivka (1764), in the Peremyshl region; the Peremyshl cathedral (1766); and the Bernardine (1743), Carmelite (1753), Franciscan (1769), and Armenian (1782) churches in Lviv.

Poliansky, Oleksander [Poljans'kyj], b 1890 in Veriatsia, now in Vynohradiv raion, Transcarpathia, d 1952 in Prague. Pedagogue and political activist. He was a member of the Ukrainian Social Democratic party and head of the Prosvita society in Mukachiv. He was also a founding member of the Teachers' Hromada of Subcarpathian Ruthenia and editor of the monthly *Uchytel's'kyi holos* (1929–39). Poliansky wrote textbooks for elementary schools and cofounded the literary almanac *Trembita*.

Poliansky, Toma [Poljans'kyj], b 1794 in Bartne, Sianik circle, Galicia, d 11 November 1869 in Peremyshl. Greek Catholic bishop. He graduated from the Greek Catholic Theological Seminary in Lviv (1818) and then served as prefect there (1820–9) and completed a D TH at Lviv University (1826). He was canon of Peremyshl eparchy before being consecrated bishop of Peremyshl in 1860. He played a key role in the negotiations with the Vatican that led to the establishment of the Concordat of 1863 guaranteeing the equality of the Byzantine and Roman rites in Galicia. Polansky also served as a deputy to the Galician and Viennese diets (1861–8).

Poliansky, Toma [Poljans'kyj], b 1822 in Felshtyn, Sambir circle, Galicia, d 3 June 1886 in Peremyshl. Greek Catholic priest, pedagogue, and political activist. He studied theology in Vienna and was ordained in 1845. In 1846 he began to teach religion at the Peremyshl gymnasium. From 1847 he also served in the Peremyshl cathedral, and he was the first priest to deliver a sermon in Ukrainian there (previously only Polish had been used). During the Revolution of 1848–9 he campaigned for Ukrainian rights in Galicia and wrote an open letter calling for the increased use of Ukrainian and equal rights for Ukrainian schools and other institutions. He also served as secretary of the Ruthenian Congress in Peremyshl. In 1859 he was a member of the commission working for the adoption of the Latin alphabet for Ukrainian (see *Alphabet war). From the 1850s he worked as a school inspector or director of gymnasiums in Rzeszów and Peremyshl. He was elected a deputy to the Galician Diet in 1867 and to the Viennese parliament in 1868, where he served on the education commission. Gradually Poliansky adopted a Russophile position and withdrew from Ukrainian affairs.

Yaroslav Poliansky

Poliansky, Yaroslav [Poljans'kyj, Jaroslav], b 15 August 1930 in Poliany, Nowy Sącz county, Galicia. Conductor, composer, folklorist, and community activist. He was deported to western Poland along with his family in 1947. He studied at the Chopin Academy of Music in Warsaw (1961–6) and in Kiev and Lviv (1964). In 1972 he founded the *Zhuravli men's choir, and he served as its conductor until 1982. In 1977 he established a Ukrainian chamber choir at the Church of the Basilian Order in Warsaw, and since 1987 he has conducted the Ukrainian Millenium youth choir. He has written many compositions on works by Ukrainian poets in Poland, including Ya. Hudemchuk, O. Lapsky, V. Nazaruk, I. Reit, and Ye. Samokhvalenko; scored more than 200 arrangements of folk songs; transcribed over 5,000 Ukrainian (primarily Lemko) folk songs, over 800 of which have been published in *Nashe slovo*; and written scholarly studies on choral conducting and Lemko music.

Yurii Poliansky

Poliansky, Yurii [Poljans'kyj, Jurij], b 6 March 1892 in Zhovtantsi, Zhovkva county, Galicia, d 19 July 1975 in Buenos Aires. Geologist and geographer; member of the Shevchenko Scientific Society from 1927 and honorary member of the Argentine Geological Society. He graduated from Lviv University in 1914. During the First World War he served in the Austrian army and then joined the Ukrainian Galician Army as an artillery officer. After the war he taught at the Academic Gymnasium of Lviv (1920–30), worked at the State Geological Institute (1927–8), and, at the same time, completed his doctoral dissertation on the morphology of Podilia (pub in *Zbirnyk Matematychno-pryrodopysno-likars'koï sektsiï NTSh*, 1929). In the 1930s he taught anthropology at the Greek Catholic Theological Academy in Lviv. During the first Soviet and German occupation of Western Ukraine (1939–44) he taught at Lviv University and was director of the reorganized Natural Science Museum of the AN URSR (now ANU). After fleeing to Austria and Germany, where he taught at the Ukrainian Free University (1945–7), he emigrated to Argentina. There he worked as a geologist and taught geology at the state university in Buenos Aires (1956–67). In the 1920s and 1930s he published several studies of the geology and archeology of Galician Podilia, many of them in the serial publications of the Shevchenko Scientific Society. He also prepared a geological map of southern Polisia (1934) and general geological surveys of Ukraine. In Argentina he wrote several articles on the geology of Argentina.

S. Trofimenko

Polianych, B. See Luzhnytsky, Hryhorii.

Police (*politsiia, zhandarmeriia, militsiia*). A branch of the state responsible for keeping civil order and ensuring the security of citizens. Under totalitarian regimes the police, especially the branch responsible for state security, are able to violate civil rights with impunity because there is no rule of law.

The autocratic tsarist regime, ever fearful of political opposition, developed a complex police structure. In 1697 Peter I created a central *prikaz* (agency) and chancellery in Preobrazhenskoe, near Moscow, that served as a political police directorate. Its work was aided by a network of government agents known as *fiskaly*, who specialized in surveillance and informing. Peter I also instituted a higher security organization, the Chancellery for Secret Investigation. Those police organizations played a major role in rooting out 'Mazepists' after the defeat of Hetman I. *Mazepa at the Battle of Poltava in 1709.

The police structure of the Russian Empire underwent several reorganizations. At the beginning of the 20th cen-

tury there existed a Police Department and a Gendarmery Corps subordinated to the minister of internal affairs. At the gubernia level the highest representative of police authority was the governor; at the county level the highest authority was the *ispravnik. From 1826 the gendarmes served as antiriot troops in the cities and as a posse in rural areas and were given wide-ranging political powers of summary arrest, trial, and exile of persons suspected of political offenses. In 1881 Sections for the Protection of Public Security and Order (known as the *Okhrana) were created to serve as a secret police. The Okhrana had rights to enter without warrant, to deport persons to Siberia without trial, to carry out surveillance of anyone, and, in important cases, to impose the death penalty without trial. It actively persecuted the Ukrainian national movement.

In Western Ukraine under Austrian rule, police were subordinated to the Ministry of Internal Affairs. In Galicia and Bukovyna the highest local police authority was the viceroy. In Lviv and Chernivtsi there existed police commissions, to which the commissions in smaller towns were subordinated. A gendarmery organized along military principles served as a security service. The gendarmery, especially in the Hungarian parts of the Austro-Hungarian Empire, actively persecuted the Ukrainian national movement.

After the Revolution of 1917 the police, gendarmery, and Okhrana were abolished and replaced with a militia (*militsiia*). Police functions were performed by municipal and rural county militias under the Central Rada and the UNR Directory, and by the *National Guard under the Hetman government. In 1917–18, units of *Free Cossacks also patrolled villages and protected them from attacks by bands. In 1919 a battalion for the Protection of the Republican Order also performed policing duties, and in 1920 the UNR organized a gendarmery in the territories it controlled.

In the Western Ukrainian National Republic (ZUNR) the police was organized on the Austrian model. The main police force was the State Gendarmery Corps, whose structure underwent several reorganizations during 1918–19. In 1919 the corps had 23 units, staffed by 31 senior officers, 1,000 professional gendarmes, 400 trainees, and 3,000 militiamen. In July 1919, after the ZUNR forces and government were forced to retreat into central Ukraine, the corps was renamed the People's Guard. Its eight units served as a state security service and as an auxiliary force of the Ukrainian Galician Army (see also *Field gendarmery).

In interwar Western Ukraine under Polish rule, the state police was under the jurisdiction of the Ministry of Internal Affairs and was organized along the lines of the Austrian gendarmery. It persecuted most manifestations of Ukrainian national and cultural life. In interwar Transcarpathia under Czechoslovak rule, the police and gendarmery were also organized along Austrian lines. In Bukovyna under Rumanian rule, the rural gendarmery had public security and criminal investigation functions. There was also a political police.

The German police apparatus in Ukraine under the Nazi occupation during the Second World War was complex and all-pervasive. It consisted of the Sipo (*Sicherheitspolizei*), the SS security police; the SD (*Sicherheitsdienst*), the SS security and intelligence service, which controlled the notorious *Einsatzgruppen*; the *Gestapo (state security police); and the Kripo (criminal police). Those police formations had sweeping powers and carried out mass repression. *Schutzmannschaften* – local militias and auxiliary police units under German supervision – were created in the Reichskommissariat Ukraine; in Galicia they were called the *Ukrainian Auxiliary Police.

In Soviet Ukraine the functions of the tsarist regular police were assumed by the so-called militia, established in Ukraine in February 1919 by the Council of People's Commissars. From 1931 it was controlled by the *GPU, and later, by the *NKVD, *MGB, and *MVD. The militia's main tasks have been criminal investigation and prevention, for which they have had powers to demand identification, to enter buildings, and to arrest; the maintenance of public order; the enforcement of the internal *passport system; licensing the possession of firearms, explosives, and photocopiers; and traffic control, including the administration, licensing, and inspection of motor vehicles. Militia departments have consisted of uniformed police, criminal detectives, a passport section, a state automobile inspection unit, and a prosecuting section, which acts when investigation is not undertaken by the State Procurator's Office or the KGB. The MVD also maintained its own infantry units, which were called upon to quell serious outbreaks of protest or disorder. In 1990 the strength of the MVD infantry in the USSR was increased from 36,000 to 350,000, the additions coming from among soldiers withdrawn from Eastern Europe and Afghanistan. A special transportation unit was subordinated to both the regular militia and the appropriate state transportation organization. The political administration within the militia was the major vehicle of Party control. *Narodni druzhyny*, civilian volunteer detachments that patrolled communities, helped the militia maintain public order and combat drunkenness. In the M. Gorbachev period the militia was criticized for its history of human rights abuses and suppression of legitimate public protest, and calls were made for the disbanding of its political administration. In 1990 the USSR Supreme Soviet considered adopting a new law on the militia, which was to provide the first comprehensive legislative framework for the operation of the police. Although according to Ukraine's 1990 proclamation of sovereignty the militia was to come under the control of the government of Ukraine, it and the MVD remained under the central control of Moscow until the demise of the USSR in late 1991.

The *KGB and its forerunners, the *Cheka, GPU, NKVD, and MGB, were the state security police and the main organizations of Soviet intelligence and espionage. They also commanded special troops for quelling domestic disturbances and guarding borders. The Soviet security or secret police was the primary instrument of totalitarian social control through mass *terror from 1918 until the mid-1950s and of the persecution of internal opposition and the *dissident movement in the post-Stalin period. From 1930 it also ran the notorious network of Soviet *concentration camps. In the late 1980s the KGB initiated a public relations campaign to try to distance itself from its sordid past and to convince the population that it was now a reformed organization operating within the law. With the rise of the democratic and national movement in the USSR, however, calls for the abolition of the KGB were increasingly heard, and it was outlawed together with the Party in 1991. It was not liquidated, but transformed into the National Security Service (Sluzhba Natsionalnoi Bezpeky, or SNB).

BIBLIOGRAPHY
Wolin, S.; Slusser, R. (eds). *The Soviet Secret Police* (New York 1957)
Zahorski, A. *Centralne instytucje policyjne w Polsce w dobie rozbiorów* (Warsaw 1959)
Monas, S. *The Third Section: Police and Society in Russia under Nicholas I* (Cambridge, Mass 1961)
Conquest, R. (ed). *The Soviet Police System* (London 1968)
Squire, P. *The Third Department: The Establishment and Practices of the Political Police in the Russia of Nicholas I* (Cambridge 1968)
Hingley, R. *The Russian Secret Police: Muscovite, Imperial Russian, and Soviet Political Security Operations, 1565–1970* (London 1970)
Deriabin, P. *Watchdogs of Terror: Russian Bodyguards from the Tsars to the Commissars* (New Rochelle, NY 1972)
Levytsky, B. *The Uses of Terror: The Soviet Secret Police, 1917–1970* (New York 1972)
Knight, A.M. *The KGB: Police and Politics in the Soviet Union* (London 1988)
I. Kozak, B. Krawchenko

Polikarp. An early 13th-century writer and monk at the Kievan Cave Monastery. His writings about various Kievan monks constituted the basis of the *Kievan Cave Patericon.

Polikarpov, Gennadii, b 16 August 1929 in Bolshaia Glushitsa, Samara oblast, Russia. Hydrobiologist; full member of the AN URSR (now ANU) since 1990. A graduate of Saratov University (1952), he worked at the ANU Institute of the Biology of Southern Seas (from 1956, as department head from 1963) and the International Laboratory of Marine Radioactivity in Monaco (1975–9). His 1964 monograph was published in English as *Radioecology of Aquatic Organisms* (1966).

Polinska, Vira [Polins'ka], b 13 October 1913 in Irkutsk, Siberia. Stage actress. She completed study at the Kiev Theater Institute (1936) and then worked in the Zaporizhia Ukrainian Drama Theater (from 1944 the Lviv Ukrainian Drama Theater). Her repertoire has varied from world classics to contemporary Ukrainian plays.

Polish Autocephalous Orthodox church (PAOC). Following the Peace Treaty of Riga (1921), some 4 million Orthodox believers, including about 2.5 million Ukrainians, found themselves in the newly established Polish state. They lived primarily in Belarusian and Ukrainian (Volhynia, the Polisia and Kholm regions) territories that had been part of the Russian Empire and where the only church permitted had been the Russian Orthodox church. In January 1922 the Polish government issued an order recognizing the Orthodox church and placing it under the authority of the state. At the same time a Ukrainian, Yu. *Yaroshevsky, was appointed metropolitan and exarch by the patriarch of Moscow. When Yaroshevsky began to reject the authority of the Moscow patriarch, he was assassinated by a Russian monk. Nonetheless, his successor, D. *Valedinsky, continued to work for the *autocephaly of the Polish Orthodox church, which was finally granted by the patriarch of Constantinople in his *Tomos* of 1924.

From that time the PAOC was independent of the canonical authority of the Moscow patriarch and claimed the right to administer its internal affairs. The church was divided into five eparchies – Warsaw-Kholm, Polisia, Volhynia, Hrodna, and Vilnius – and the Council of Bishops (Synod) became the highest authority in the church. Administrative affairs were the responsibility of the Holy Synod, headed by the metropolitan. In practice, however, the church was controlled by the Polish Ministry of Confessions and Education. The authorities did not permit the convening of a sobor, and instead promulgated two decrees in 1938 – the Internal Statutes of the POAC and the Presidential Decree on the Relations of the State to the Polish Orthodox Church – which defined the nature of the church and its organization. The government reserved the right to review all ecclesiastical appointments (ensuring that two Poles were consecrated as bishops) and insisted on the introduction of Polish as the official language of the church. The government also destroyed Ukrainian churches in the Kholm region and supported efforts by the Roman Catholic church forcibly to convert Orthodox believers. At the same time the PAOC was influenced by Russophile elements in the leadership, who sought to Russify church life despite the preponderance of Ukrainian and Belarusian believers.

These obstacles notwithstanding, some aspects of Ukrainian Orthodoxy thrived in the PAOC. The vernacular was used for sermons and the Ukrainian pronunciation of Church Slavonic for services in Ukrainian regions, and two Ukrainian hierarchs were consecrated (P. *Sikorsky and O. *Hromadsky). Moreover, Ukrainian scholars (O. Lototsky, V. Bidnov, D. Doroshenko, I. Ohiienko) taught at the Faculty of Theology at Warsaw University, several Ukrainian religious journals were published (*Tserkva i narid, Dukhovnyi siiach, Za sobornist'*, and *Shliakh*), and groups such as the *Mohyla Society researched and popularized the Ukrainian Orthodox rite.

During the Second World War, bishops of the PAOC played an important role in the re-establishment of the *Ukrainian Autocephlous Orthodox church (UAOC). Metropolitan Valedinsky sanctioned the organization of the church and appointed Bishop Sikorsky as the UAOC administrator in the *Reichskommissariat Ukraine. At the same time he consecrated I. Ohiienko and P. Vydybida-Rudenko as bishops for Ukrainian territories (the Kholm and Lemko regions) in the *Generalgouvernement. Under their leadership new statutes stressing the Ukrainian character of the church were adopted, and much was done to introduce Ukrainian religious practices. At the end of the war all the Ukrainian hierarchs and most prominent clergy and lay leaders of the church fled to the West. Valedinsky was removed from his post in 1945 under Soviet pressure and replaced in 1951 by M. Oksiiuk of the Russian Orthodox church. In 1948 the Moscow patriarch annulled the 1924 *Tomos* of the patriarch of Constantinople granting autocephaly and replaced it with his own grant reasserting Moscow's control over the PAOC.

Today the PAOC unites about 500,000 faithful, primarily Ukrainians and Belarusians, as well as a small number of Russians, Poles, and others. Nearly 70 percent of them live in Białystok voivodeship, and slightly under 10 percent reside in other voivodeships (ie, in territories that were part of interwar Poland). Others live in the western and northern voivodeships to which they were forcibly moved from the Kholm, Podlachia, and Lemko regions after the war. Most Orthodox Ukrainians live in northern Podlachia in Białystok voivodeship (where they are often considered Belarusian); others are dispersed throughout Poland (communities are found in the Biała Podlaska, Kholm, Krosno, Nowy Sącz, Olsztyn, Suwałki, and Zamość voivodeships).

The metropoly, with its see in Warsaw, has been successively headed by M. Oksiiuk, T. Szreter, S. Rudyk, and (since 1970) V. Doroshkevych. Its highest authority is the Synod of Bishops, which consists of the metropolitan and all active bishops. The metropoly is divided into six eparchies: Warsaw-Bielsk (the archeparchy headed by the metropolitan, with 98 parishes), Lublin-Kholm (carved in 1988 out of the Warsaw-Bielsk archeparchy, with its see in Lublin), Białystok-Gdańsk (47 parishes), Łódź-Poznań (15 parishes), Wrocław-Szczecin (45 parishes), and Peremyshl-Nowy Sącz (17 parishes, est 1983 with its seat in Sianik). In total, the PAOC has some 250 parishes, 350 churches, and 300 priests, most of whom are graduates of the theological seminaries in Warsaw and Jabłeczna or the Orthodox section of the Christian Theological Academy in Warsaw. The PAOC has two monasteries for men, the *Yablochyn St Onuphrius's Monastery (Biała Podlaska voivodeship) and the Suprasl St Mary's Monastery (Białystok voivodeship), and one monastery for women, SS Martha and Mary (Białyskok voivodeship).

The church leadership is often hostile toward Ukrainian or Belarusian national causes, and as recently as 1990 Metropolitan Doroshkevych denounced the goal of Ukrainian independence. The official language of the church is Polish, but Russian is frequently used in administration (this has led to charges that the PAOC is purposely Russifying or Polonizing its Ukrainian followers). The monthly *Tserkovnyi vestnik* (est 1954) appears in Russian, but the annual *Pravoslavnyi kalendar* has some material in Ukrainian and Belarusian, as well as in the Lemko dialect. In 1961 and 1968–77 P. Domanchuk edited the Ukrainian-language *Tserkovnyi kalendar*, which was revived in 1985 as a publication of the new Peremyshl–Nowy Sącz eparchy.

Liturgies are conducted in Old Church Slavonic with Russian, sometimes Ukrainian or Belarusian, pronunciation. Sermons are usually delivered in Ukrainian or Belarusian. Relations with Polish Catholic chauvinists and the Polish regime are often strained. Many Orthodox churches – unique historical, artistic, and architectural artifacts graced by valuable icons – have been destroyed in areas from which the Orthodox were deported after the war. The regime continues to hinder the PAOC's development and places restrictions on its activity.

BIBLIOGRAPHY
Kupranets', O. *Pravoslavna tserkva v mizhvoiennii Pol'shchi, 1918–1939* (Rome 1974)
Sorokowski, A. *Ukrainian Catholics and Orthodox in Poland and Czechoslovakia* (Cambridge, Mass 1988)
Papierzyńska-Turek, M. *Między tradycję a rzeczywistością: Państwo wobec prawosławia 1918–1938* (Warsaw 1989)
I. Korovytsky, M. Trukhan

Polish Historical Society (Polskie Towarzystwo Historyczne). A scholarly society in Austrian-ruled Galicia, established in 1886 by Polish historians in Lviv. Until 1924 it was called the Historical Society. The society's first presidents – K. Liske (1886–91), T. Wojciechowski (1891–1914), L. Finkel (1914–23), S. Zakrzewski (1923–32, 1934–6), F. Bujak (1932–4, 1936–7), L. Kolankowski (1937–47) – were professors at Lviv University, and until 1939 Lviv was the society's hub and executive seat. Under Austrian rule its membership (mostly Poles in Galicia) grew from 216 to 314 in 1895, but then dropped to 264 in 1905 and 163 in 1906. From 1890, circles were founded in many Galician towns, such as Drohobych, Sniatyn, Ternopil, Buchach, and Chortkiv, and in Poland, notably in Cracow (est 1902; 124 members in 1914). In interwar Poland and in Ukraine under Polish rule the society adopted a national mandate, and in 1924 it adopted its current name. Its membership grew from 423 in 1923 to 1,329 in 1933. Branches with at least 20 members each were founded in Warsaw (1925), Vilnius (1925), Poznań (1925), Cracow (1925), Lviv (1925), Lublin (1927), Lódź (1927), Peremyshl (1928), Katowice (1929), Kielce (1933), Brest, Hrodna, and, after the Second World War, other Polish cities. Since 1950 the society has been centered in Warsaw. The society has sponsored the second (Lviv, 1890), third (Cracow, 1900), fourth (Poznań, 1925), fifth (Warsaw, 1930), sixth (Vilnius, 1935), and subsequent congresses (every five years since 1948) of Polish historians. Its serials *Kwartalnik Historyczny* (Lviv 1887–39; Cracow 1947–50; Warsaw since 1950) and *Ziemia Czerwieńska* (Lviv 1935–9) contain many studies, reviews, and other materials pertaining to Ukrainian history.

Polish Home Army (Polish: Armija Krajowa [AK]). The main partisan organization in Poland during the Second World War. It emerged as a coalition of anti-German underground groups called the Union of Armed Resistance. In 1941 it became affiliated with the Polish government in London, and eventually it was renamed. The AK carried out extensive intelligence and sabotage operations in Poland. In the spring of 1944 it organized a general military uprising (code name: Burza) against the Germans in advance of the Red Army offensive into Western Ukraine and Poland. When the Red Army arrived, many of the AK leaders were jailed or executed, while rank-and-file members were pressed into pro-Soviet military service. The organization was disbanded in 1945 but resurfaced in 1947 as the Freedom and Independence movement. In spite of their having a common enemy, the Home Army did not collaborate with the Ukrainian resistance forces. Its partisans terrorized Ukrainian villages in the Kholm region and attacked Samooborona units and UPA forces. AK ambitions to restore Polish rule in Galicia could not but arouse Ukrainian hostility. Relations between the UPA and the reconstituted AK improved after the Soviet occupation of Poland, and several joint Polish-Ukrainian operations were carried out against the Soviets.

BIBLIOGRAPHY
Korbonski, S. *The Polish Underground State* (New York 1978)
Bor-Komorowski, T. *The Secret Army* (Nashville 1984)
                                                A. Makuch

Polish Insurrection of 1830–1. An armed Polish revolt against Russian rule which encompassed the Kingdom of Poland, Lithuania, Belarus, and Right-Bank Ukraine. The insurrection broke out in Warsaw on 29 November 1830 (hence it is often called the November Insurrection) and lasted until October 1831. Although the immediate cause of the outbreak was a reaction to reports that Emperor Nicholas I was planning to dispatch Polish troops to fight a rebellion in France, it quickly escalated into an effort to restore a Polish state within its pre-partition borders (inclusive of Right-Bank Ukraine and Galicia).

The insurrection spread to Right-Bank Ukraine in April and May 1831. Leaders of the revolt in Volhynia gubernia included Gen. J. Dwernicki, K. Różycki, and S. Worcell (deputy to the Sejm from Volhynia); B. Kołyszko led 5,000 insurgents in Podilia and Kiev gubernias. The insurgents

were composed almost exclusively of the Polish gentry. They hoped that the Ukrainian population would support them, but both the Orthodox clergy and the Ukrainian peasantry were indifferent or hostile to the revolt. The lack of popular support sealed the fate of the insurrection in the Right Bank, where it was defeated by tsarist forces in May. Although the insurrection did not spread to Galicia, Poles there helped equip the insurgents, and some Galician Poles fought as volunteers.

In the aftermath of the insurrection's suppression the tsarist authorities took measures to eliminate Polish influence in the Right-Bank region. They confiscated the estates of nobles who had participated in the insurrection, liquidated the Polish educational system, founded 'Russian' institutions (such as Kiev University), and abolished the Uniate church in Belarus and the Right-Bank (1839). The radical Polish gentry responded to the defeat of the insurrection and to the tsarist government's repressive policies by forming conspiratorial groups to prepare a new insurrection. Such groups existed in both the Right Bank and Galicia, where they sometimes developed a pro-Ukrainian character and, in Galicia, even won adherents among Greek Catholic seminarians.

BIBLIOGRAPHY
Łepkowski, T. 'Społeczne i narodowe aspekty powstania 1831 roku na Ukrainie,' *Kwartalnik Historyczny*, 64, no. 6 (1957)
                                                J.-P. Himka

Polish Insurrection of 1863–4. An armed uprising against Russian rule that sought independence for Poland and social reforms. It began in Warsaw in January 1863 and was centered in the Congress Kingdom of Poland and Lithuania, with relatively minor activity in Right-Bank Ukraine beginning in early May. Poles living in Austrian-ruled Galicia and Prussia supported the revolt, organized volunteer detachments, and gave financial aid to the insurgents. Despite some successes the Poles were never able to form a regular army; their military activities were largely uncoordinated, and the insurgents generally fought in small, partisan detachments. By mid-1864 the rebellion had died out, although some military engagements continued into 1865.

Support for the uprising was strong among Poles in Right-Bank Ukraine, who were largely from the nobility. But appeals to Polish patriotism could not sway the largely peasant Ukrainian population to join the revolt. In an attempt to gain Ukrainian support the Polish provisional government issued two proclamations in Ukrainian shortly after the insurrection began, 'Zolota hramota' and 'Ruskyi narode!' In them the provisional government made some national and cultural concessions and promised more favorable emancipation terms to the peasantry than the tsarist government had offered. The attempts were on the whole unsuccessful: most peasants continued to associate the Poles with the lords and the system of serfdom. The Ukrainian intelligentsia largely refused to cooperate, for it could not accept the program to re-establish the borders of the old Polish Commonwealth. Already on the eve of the insurrection a small group of young, largely Kiev University students (known as *khlopomany*), many of whom were Polonized descendants of the old Ukrainian nobility, had split from the Polish secret societies of Kiev (which were in favor of the insurrection) to join the Ukrainian national movement. All the same a small number of Ukrainian peasants and intellectuals supported the rebellion.

The repercussions of the insurrection and its failure were immense. Russian chauvinists, led by M. Katkov, took advantage of the tense circumstances to frighten the government and to discredit liberals and radicals, who were largely sympathetic, at least initially, to Polish claims for more autonomy. Peasant disturbances and the rise in discontent among the radical intelligentsia further frightened the regime. Those factors served to strengthen conservative, chauvinistic, and reactionary tendencies in Russian government and society. They also hastened the decline of Polish influence in the Right Bank and, consequently, of the ties of that region to ethnic Poland. During and following the insurrection the regime determined to extend the practice it had begun after the failed insurrection of 1830–1 of weakening Polish influence in the Right Bank and to Russify the region thoroughly.

The insurrection had repercussions on the nascent Ukrainian national movement. Despite its general antipathy toward the Poles the Ukrainian movement was called a 'Polish intrigue' and labeled 'separatist,' and some Ukrainian activists were accused of fomenting discontent among the peasantry. Those sorts of charges contributed to the issuing of the Valuev circular of 1863, which forbade publication of popular religious and educational texts in Ukrainian, and the repression of individual Ukrainian activists. The Uniate church, which had been banned in Right-Bank Ukraine following the 1830–1 Polish insurrection, was abolished in the Kholm and Podlachia regions in 1875 after an extended period of persecutions that began in the aftermath of the insurrection.

BIBLIOGRAPHY
Rawita-Gawroński, F. *Rok 1863 na Rusi* (Lviv 1909)
Marakhov, G. *Pol'skoe vosstanie 1863 g. na Pravoberezhnoi Ukraine* (Kiev 1967)
– (ed). *Suspil'no-politychni rukhy na Ukraïni v 1856–1864 rr.*, 2 vols (Kiev–Moscow–Wrocław 1963–4)

B. Klid

Polish Liquidation Commission (Polska Komisja Likwidacyjna, or PKL). A Polish provisional government established in Cracow on 28 October 1918 on the initiative of Polish deputies to the Austrian national parliament in Vienna. The commission created a civil administration, security forces, and an army; it claimed to be the supreme authority over all historical Polish lands in the Austrian realm, but in reality it governed only western Galicia. The socialists in the commission tried to achieve a compromise with the Ukrainians regarding power-sharing, and on 1 November 1918 a local Polish-Ukrainian agreement was signed in Peremyshl. As a result of the outbreak of armed combat, it was never realized.

The majority of the commission members treated Eastern Galicia as part of the Polish state and demanded that the government in Warsaw provide intensive armed aid for Poles there. After the departure of the Ukrainian forces from Lviv the city was ruled by the Temporary Governing Committee (Tymczasowy Komitet Rządzący, or TKR), from 23 November 1918. The committee annulled all the Ukrainian acts and embarked upon repressions of the members of the *Ukrainian National Rada who stayed behind in Lviv. On 10 January the PKL and TKR merged into the Governing Commission for Galicia, Cieszyn Silesia,

Orava, and Spiš (48 members). The Warsaw government treated it as an autonomous organ which had partial legislative competence. As eastern Galicia was taken over by Polish forces, the commission organized the administration but had no power regarding foreign policy and military matters. On 26 March 1919 the commission was dissolved, and its functions were taken over by the general delegate of the government in Galicia (K. Gałecki).

A. Chojnowski

Polish language in Ukraine. The influence of Ukrainian on the development of standard Polish came from Poles who settled in Ukraine from the 14th century on and from Polonized Ukrainians. This process, which began with the medieval linguistic contacts of Galicia with Little Poland and of Volhynia and Podlachia with Mazovia, intensified after the 1596 Union of *Lublin, when the influence of the Polish nobility and burghers in Ukraine began to rise. The Polonized Ukrainian nobles and magnates introduced into their speech phonetical, lexical, and grammatical Ukrainianisms. Consequently, literary Polish differs from all Polish dialects in phonology (eg, the disappearance of the phoneme $\mathring{a} < \bar{a}$ in the 17th century) or from most of them (eg, the absence of *mazurzenie*, and attempts until the 1930s to eliminate the 'vulgar' pronunciation of *ł* as *u* and certain stresses). During the period of greatest Ukrainian (and Belarusian) linguistic influences (16th–19th centuries), Ukrainian grammatical features that were limited to particular times and authors or that have endured (the nominal endings *-ów* and *-am*, the pluperfect, the object in the accusative case after a negative predicate, the patronymic suffixes *-owicz* and *-ewicz*, and truncated verbal forms, eg, *depczę* 'I trample'), as well as lexical borrowings and semantic equivalents, were absorbed into the Polish language.

The language of the Poles living in Ukraine in the 19th and 20th centuries (excluding the Ukrainian dialects of the so-called *latynnyky*) can be divided into three distinct sociolinguistic layers. (1) The educated Polish nobility, clergy, *intelligentsia, and civil servants developed a characteristic pronunciation. The vowel *ą* became denasalized (eg, *chódzo* instead of *chodzą* 'they walk'). Differentiation of the consonants *h:x* occurred, and *l'* was used instead of *l*. Typical pronunciations were *svuj* instead of *sfuj* for *swój* 'one's own', *nog'e* for *nogę* 'leg' accusative singular, *xl'ip* for *chleb* 'bread', *ml'iko* for *mleko* 'milk', and, in Right-Bank Ukraine, *kreu* instead of *kref* for *krew* 'blood', *ržyka* for *rzeka* 'river', and *mogłem* for *mugem/mukem* 'I could'. Many lexical Ukrainianisms and common Ukrainian-Polish lexemes were used. (2) The lower urban strata developed a similar pronunciation, as well as many slang words. Particularly in Lviv, the typical pronunciation of unstressed *o, e* was *u, y/i*, and of stressed *o–ŭo* (light diphthongization), as in adjacent Ukrainian dialects. (3) Polish peasants who settled in Galicia and Podilia also developed their own speech. Only the dialects spoken around Komarne (15th–16th centuries) and Zaliztsi (17th century) in Galicia have been systematically studied. As a result of centuries-old bilingualism the dialects absorbed Ukrainian features in their phonetics (eg, the absence of *mazurzenie* – the Mazovian dialectal substitution of dentals for postdentals [*č, ž, š* > *c, z, s*], the hardening of soft labials, prothetic sounds before initial vowels, the change $\bar{o} > y$ [eg, *vyn* instead of *on* 'he']), morphology (eg, types of endings in nominal declension, -*mo*/-*mu* ending of 1st per pl verbs [eg, *muśimo* instead of *musimy* (cf Ukrainian *musymo*) 'we must']), and syntax (eg, the absence of special endings indicating male persons in the nom case of pl adjectives and in verbs). The Polish peasant dialects of Podlachia and the Kholm region developed out of the Polonization of originally Ukrainian villages (see *Podlachian dialects).

Many Polish writers who were born or lived in Ukraine phonetically assimilated Ukrainian words and phrases in their writings (eg, M. Rej, S. Orzechowski, S. Szymonowic, J. Zimorowicz, S. Trembecki, H. Rzewuski, J. Słowacki, J. Zaleski, A. Malczewski, S. Goszczyński, J. Korzeniowski, M. Grabowski, M. Czajkowski, Z. Miłkowski, J. Kraszewski, A. Fredro, W. Łoziński, J. Lam, K. Ujejski, J. Parandowski, and J. Iwaszkiewicz). Others (eg, W. Potocki, H. Sienkiewicz) used Ukrainianisms for local color in their works on Ukrainian-Polish themes. (See also *Poles in Ukraine.)

BIBLIOGRAPHY

Kremer, A. 'Słowniczek prowincjonalizmów podolskich, ułożony w Kamieńcu Podolskim w r. 1863,' *Rocznik T-wa Naukowego Uniwersytetu Krakowskiego*, 18 (1870)

Kurka, A. *Słownik mowy złodziejskiej*, 3 edns (Lviv 1896, 1899, 1907)

Estreicher, K. *Szwargot więzienny* (Cracow 1903)

Harhala, W. 'Gwara polska okolic Komarna,' *Lud Słowiański*, IIA, 156–77 (Cracow 1931)

Hrabec, S. *Elementy kresowe w języku niektórych pisarzy polskich XVI i XVII w.* (Toruń 1950)

– 'O polskiej gwarze wsi Duliby w b. powiecie buczackim,' *Rozprawy Komisji Językowej Łódzkiego Towarzystwa Naukowego*, 3 (1955)

Dejna, K. 'Gwara Milna,' *Rozprawy Komisji Językowej Łódzkiego Towarzystwa Naukowego*, I, 1, vol 4 (Łódź 1959)

Verenich, V. (ed). *Polskie govory v SSSR*, I–II (Minsk 1973)

Kurzowa, S. *Elementy kresowe w języku powieści powojennej* (Warsaw 1975)

Rieger, J.; Verenich, V. (eds). *Studia nad polszczyzną kresową*, I–VI (1982–91) (vol VI provides a bibliography)

Czyżewski, F. *Atlas gwar polskich i ukraińskich okolic Włodawy* (Lublin 1986)

O. Horbach

Polish law. From the 15th century to the partitions of Poland, and in the interwar period of the 20th century, Ukrainian territories under Polish rule were governed by Polish law. The law was introduced in the 1430s in Rus' and Podilia voivodeships and parts of Bratslav voivodeship, and from 1501 in the Kholm region. It was used along with older laws, such as *Rus', Armenian, *Wallachian, and *Germanic law. The Jewish community, meanwhile, had its own system. The sources for Polish law were primarily customary law and, later, written statutes. There were many attempts to codify the law, but the first comprehensive effort was made by Casimir III the Great. His Wiślica Statute of 1347 was translated partly into Ukrainian and was used mostly in Western Ukraine. A second, superior code, called the Łaski Statute, was ratified by the Sejm in 1506. In 1522 the Sejm decided to have all customary laws codified, but this project was later reduced to codifying only private, criminal, and procedural law. A special commission prepared the so-called Correctura Irium, but the Sejm rejected it (1534). The Constitution of 1791 reformed political law and provided for the publication of a new legal code, but this was not carried out be-

cause of the partitioning of Poland. Thus, Poland had been governed only by statutes and, apart from procedural law, lacked any legal codes. Various territories had their own provincial statutes, which they defended jealously.

The fundamental characteristics of Polish law were reliance on custom, unevenness, particularism, and insufficient codification. The guiding legislative principle was the protection of the privileges of the nobility and the interests of the state and the church; the Catholic hierarchy was particularly influential. Until the 16th century the legal system was distinctively Polish, with few borrowings from foreign sources. Then, many elements of Roman law were adopted. It was only at the end of the 18th century that some modern ideas from Western Europe were imported into Polish law.

After the partitions of Poland, Polish law was replaced by Austrian and Prussian law, the Napoleonic Code in the Kingdom of Poland, and the *Lithuanian Statute, which was more sophisticated than any of the Polish projects. The statute remained in force in Right-Bank Ukraine until 1840, when it was replaced by Russian law.

During the Polish occupation of Western Ukraine in 1919–39, the former Austrian and Russian laws were gradually replaced by new Polish laws: the constitutions of 1921 and 1935, the law on the justice system (1928), the law on criminal and civil procedure (1930), a criminal code (1932), and part of a civil code (1933). The development of the Polish law in this period was marked by an increasing tendency toward authoritarianism. Compared with the liberal Constitution of 1921, the Constitution of 1935 was restrictive: it limited the rights of civil society, abolished juries in criminal trials, and introduced emergency courts (1932) and concentration camps (1934).

Polish Second Corps. An Allied military formation during the Second World War. It comprised approx 45,000 Polish nationals, including some 2,000 Ukrainians who had been interned in Soviet prisons or labor camps following the 1939 partition of Poland. The Soviet government agreed to set up this force during negotiations with the London-based Polish government-in-exile in August 1941. Gen W. *Anders was chosen as commander. After many delays and prolonged political wrangling, the corps was assigned, finally, to the British army and in 1942 sent to northern Iran. By the end of 1943 it had joined the British forces in the Italian campaign, and it distinguished itself in the Battle of Monte Cassino (11–12 May 1944). Many of its veterans later emigrated to the West.

Polishchuk, Klym [Poliščuk] (pseuds: Volyniak, K. Lavrynovych, Ivan Mecheslavenko, O. Cherednychenko, and others), b 25 November 1891 in Krasnopil, Zhytomyr county, Volhynia gubernia, d 1937? Writer. He studied at the St Petersburg Academy of Arts (1909–12) and then worked for the Volhynia gubernia zemstvo. During the Revolution of 1917 he worked as an editor of *Ukraïns'kyi holos* and *Narodna volia* and as a member of the editorial boards of *Narodna sprava*, *Mystetstvo*, and other periodicals. In 1919 he joined the symbolist group *Muzahet. In 1920 he moved to Galicia, where most of his works were published. He returned to Kiev in 1925. Polishchuk was arrested in 1935 and imprisoned in the Solovets Islands in the White Sea; he was last heard from in 1937. He began writing poetry early in his life, and his first poems ap-

Klym Polishchuk   Valeriian Polishchuk

peared without his knowledge in the paper *Volyn'*. He published his first story in 1909. In 1913 he published a collection of Ukrainian songs. Most of his stories and his three novels are about the revolutionary years in Ukraine. Polishchuk was a prolific writer, with numerous collections of short stories, such as *Daleki zori* (Distant Stars, 1914), *Sered mohyl i ruïn* (Among Graves and Ruins, 1918), *Tini mynuloho: Volyns'ki legendy* (Shadows of the Past: Volhynian Legends, 1919), *Vesele v sumnomu* (The Joyful in the Sad, 1921), *Zhmenia zemli: Halyts'ki legendy* (A Handful of Earth: Galician Legends, 1921), *Zoloti zerniatka* (Golden Kernels, 1921), *Skarby vikiv: Ukraïns'ki legendy* (Treasures of the Ages: Ukrainian Legends, 1921), *Anhel's'kyi lyst* (The Angel's Letter, 1923), and *Zhertva* (The Sacrifice, 1923). He also wrote the novels *Otaman Zelenyi* (1922), *Svit chervonyi* (The Red World, 1923), and *Huliaipil's'kyi 'bat'-ko'* (The Huliai Pole 'Father,' 2 vols, 1925); the poetry collections *Spivy v poliakh* (Singing in the Fields, 1917), *Poeziï* (Poems, 1919), and *Zvukolirnist'* (Sound-Lyricalness, 1921); the drama *Trivozhni* [sic] *dni* (Turbulent Days, 1924); and memoirs about literary life in Kiev in 1919, *Z vyru revoliutsiï* (From the Vortex of the Revolution, 1925).

R. Senkus

Polishchuk, Petro [Poliščuk], b 23 December 1913 in Nosivtsi, Ternopil county, Galicia, d 17 June 1987 in Zürich. Educator and Jungian psychoanalyst. From 1933 he studied law at Lviv University and helped edit *Iuni druzi*. In 1937 he worked in Tsentrobank. During the first Soviet occupation of Western Ukraine he was in charge of the youth section of the Ukrainian Central Committee in Cracow. Following his arrest by the Gestapo in 1941, the rest of his war years were spent in concentration camps. After the war he worked for the Ukrainian Medical-Charitable Service in Munich (1945), the Ukrainian Relief Committee in Rome (1945–8), and the Shevchenko Scientific Society in France. He also served as general secretary of the Union of Ukrainian Workers in France. Upon graduating from the Jung Institute in Zürich (1967) he practiced psychotherapy and lectured at that institution.

Polishchuk, Valeriian [Poliščuk, Valerijan] (pseuds: Vasyl Sontsetsvit, Mykyta Volokyta), b 1 October 1897 in Bilche, Dubno county, Volhynia gubernia, d 11 November 1937 on Solovets Islands. Writer and literary critic and theorist. His first published work appeared in 1918. In 1923

he joined Hart and in 1925 in Kharkiv he founded the organization *Avanhard, which advanced a program of constructivist dynamism (or spiralism) and relied heavily on Russian (I. Selvinsky), Western European (E. Wergarn), and American (W. Whitman) avant-garde literature. Polishchuk aimed to sing the praises of modern civilization and its technological revolution. He wrote poetry, prose, and children's literature. Initially he wrote historical fiction, such as *Skazannia davnieie pro te, iak Ol'ha Korosten' spalyla* (An Ancient Account of How Olha Burned *Korosten, 1919), but then he began to praise the Bolshevik regime and the world communist revolution. His communism is most evident in pieces such as *Lenin* (1922), *Duma pro Barmashykhu* (A Duma about a Barmash Woman, 1922), *Zhmutok chervonoho* (A Shred of Red, 1924), *Evropa na vul'kani* (Europe on a Volcano, 1925), *Metalevyi tembr* (The Metal Timbre, 1928), and *Elektrychni zahravy* (Electric Dawns, 1929). In his theoretical writings he conceived of the idea of *khvyliady*, or 'wave cycles,' a form of free verse used in his works. Polishchuk was arrested in the 1930s, and died in a prison camp. He was posthumously rehabilitated, in the late 1950s. Editions of his selected works were published in 1960 and 1987.

I. Koshelivets

Polishchuk, Vasyl [Poliščuk, Vasyl'], b 25 May 1918 in Mikhailovskoe, now in Novosibirsk oblast, Russia, d 19 July 1979 in Uzhhorod. Writer and journalist. He graduated from the Communist Institute of Journalism in Kharkiv (1940) and the Higher Party School of the Central Committee of the CPSU in Moscow (1955). He worked on the editorial board of the oblast newspapers *Chervone Zaporizhzhia* and *Radians'ke Zakarpattia* and was a correspondent for *Pravda Ukrainy*, covering Transcarpathia. He published prose, including *Dzveniat' strumochky* (The Burbling Brooks, 1958), *Zustrinemos' na Menchuli* (We Will Meet on the Menchul, 1959), *Entuziiasty* (The Enthusiasts, 1964), *Kazky karpats'koho lisu* (Tales of the Carpathian Forest, 1968), and *Lisova povist'* (The Forest Story, 1971).

Polishchuk, Vitalii [Poliščuk, Vitalij], b 6 April 1931 in Kiev. Metallurgist. He graduated from the Kiev Polytechnical Institute (1954) and has worked at the AN URSR (now ANU) Institute for Problems of Casting (since 1958). He specializes in the area of metal casting, and his main contributions are in applications of magnetohydrodynamics to the casting process.

Polisia (Polish: Polesie). A physical-geographical region of lowlands and mixed forests lying between the Belarusian Upland to the north, the Volhynia-Kholm Upland and the Dnieper Upland to the south, the Buh River and Podlachia to the west, and the Dnieper Lowland to the east. Polisia is a large, flat lowland covered with glacial, fluvioglacial, and alluvial deposits. Low river gradients and shallow groundwater levels account for extensive marshes. Large areas are occupied by sands. The entire region is well forested.

Boundaries. Under the broad definition Polisia covers a territory of over 200,000 sq km. Under the narrow definition, which excludes Chernihiv Polisia, Little Polisia, and Volodava Polisia, Polisia proper occupies about 160,000 sq km (see map). Unlike its northern boundary, Polisia's southern boundary is sharply defined. It extends from Kholm in the west through Volodymyr-Volynskyi,

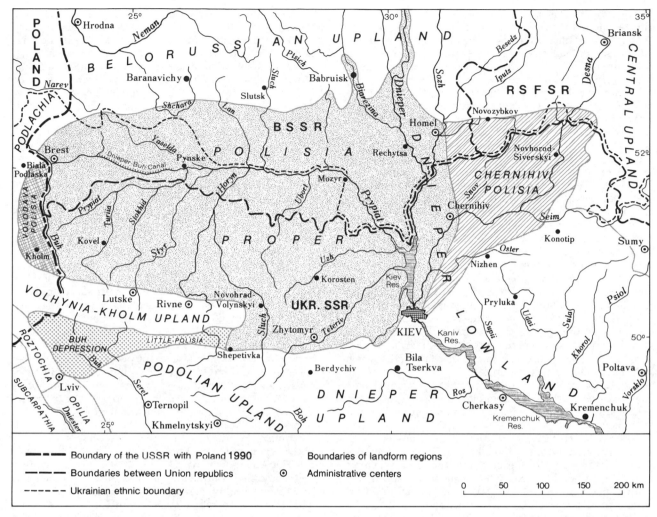

Boundary of the USSR with Poland 1990
Boundaries between Union republics
Ukrainian ethnic boundary

Boundaries of landform regions
Administrative centers

0   50   100   150   200 km

POLISIA

Lutske, Rivne, and Korets. East of Korets the southern boundary shifts southward to Shepetivka and then continues through Zhytomyr to Kiev. On the left bank of the Dnieper the southern boundary of Chernihiv Polisia runs through Nizhen, Komarivka, Baturyn, Krolevets, and Hlukhiv but is not as sharply defined.

The Ukrainian-Belarusian ethnic border crosses Polisia from west to east approx along the line Pruzhany–Bereza Kartuzka–Vyhonivske Lake, down the Bobryk and along the Prypiat to Mozyr, south to the Slovechna River and east along the Ukrainian-Belarusian border to the Dnieper, and then north along the Dnieper. In the west the political-administrative border between Ukraine and Belarus does not correspond to the ethnic border, because the Soviet regime ceded the northwestern portion of Ukrainian ethnic territory (approx 27,000 sq km) to the Belorussian SSR.

Today Ukrainian Polisia is defined as Ukraine's forest belt (including Little Polisia and Chernihiv Polisia), which covers approx 100,000 sq km. Ukrainian Polisia encompasses most of Volhynia and Rivne oblasts, about two-thirds of Zhytomyr oblast, the northern third of Kiev oblast, and the Ukrainian-settled parts of Brest oblast (over one-half) and Homel oblast (about one-sixth) in Belarus.

Geology and geomorphology. The oldest geostructural region of Polisia is the northwestern part of the Ukrainian Crystalline Shield, which is most prominent in Zhytomyr oblast. The region consists of Precambrian rocks, whereas the adjacent Ovruch Ridge is built mostly of quartzites and Proterozoic pyrophyllitic schists. The Precambrian foundation supports thin deposits from the Cretaceous and Paleocene periods here and there and a thin Quarternary overburden almost everywhere. The northwestern part of Polisia consists of the Brest Depression, which is filled to some 2,500 m with old Paleozoic, Jurassic, Cretaceous, and Tertiary sedimentaries, covered with a layer of Quarternary deposits. It is separated from the Prypiat Trough by the Polisia Arch, built on Precambrian and Devonian deposits. The arch runs northward toward the Belarusian Anticline and comes to the surface at several points. In earlier geological periods it separated two large troughs, the North Ukrainian from the Mazovian.

Continental glaciers, which twice covered parts of Polisia, left stretches of ground and terminal moraines with erratics (boulders), thus smoothing out the preceding stream-eroded relief. Meltwaters carrying large quantities of sand and silt were joined by renewed small rivers that flowed to the north. The Styr-Slovechna spillway was formed along the edge of the glacier and carried the meltwaters to the Dnieper River. As the glacier receded to the Mozyr stage, the Prypiat River resumed its function and took up the waters of the Buh River, which was still blocked by the ice sheet to the northwest. Thus, the wide Old Buh–Prypiat spillway was formed. Glacial meltwaters and river waters washed away the moraines, which now occupy only small areas, and formed large lakes, because the flow of the Prypiat River was impaired by terminal moraines and the Ukrainian Crystalline Shield. The subsidence of Polisia's axis also led to widespread ponding. After the Prypiat broke through the terminal moraines between Mozyr and Yurevychi, the Polisian lakes were partially drained, and turned mostly into swamps. But the Prypiat lacked the power to remove the sands and alluviums that filled its valley, for the Buh River was captured by the Vistula, the base level of erosion of which, with the emergence of the Baltic Sea, was lower than that of the Dnieper. Consequently, large areas of Polisia, both valleys and interfluvial lowlands, remained covered with marshes and sands. The fluctuation of glacial and interglacial periods, the epeirogenic movements, such as the subsidence of Polisia's axis and the isostatic recovery and rise of its southern rim, and the alternation of erosion and accumulation resulted in the appearance of terraces in the river valleys. There are also small pockets of loess which belong to the Quaternary deposits.

Generally Polisia is a uniform lowland plain, broken here and there by a few higher elevations, hills, or ridges of glacial, fluvioglacial, eolian, or denudational origin and by valleys.

The axial part of Polisia is the broad, low floodplain that extends along both sides of the Prypiat River and its tributaries. Its relief does not exceed 5 m, and its width varies from 5 to 35 km. Flooded by meltwaters each spring, the bottomlands consist of thick layers of alluvial deposits, mud, sand, and peat. The river terraces are low there, rising to 7 m above the bottomlands, but to the south their relief increases to 15 m or more. The alluvial-outwash deposits in Little Polisia between Shepetivka and Zhytomyr and along the lower Teteriv River, and the outwash plain along the Ubort River, are related to those alluvial-accumulation lowlands.

A Polisia landscape

The southern, elevated part of Polisia, as well as Kiev Polisia, is less swampy. The swamps alternate with dry land, and the valleys are lightly incised. Those denudational plains are covered with a thin layer of outwash sands. In the southwest the relief of Volhynian Polisia is broken occasionally by chalk ridges. To the northeast the lowland is disrupted here and there by long and narrow ridges up to 60 m above the plain, including the Ovruch and Ozeriany ridges.

Another kind of elevation consists of hills of terminal moraines. The best example of the formation is the Volhynian moraine ridge, which extends from the west through Liuboml, Kovel, Dubrovytsia, and Stolyn to the northeast. Small moraines occur on the Mozyr and Chornobyl 'islands.'

Large areas of Polisia are covered with sand dunes, wind-blown sands, and blowouts. In some places the sand dunes form chains or entire dune fields. On wide sandy plains and floodplains the sand dunes stand out as the highest points of relief and are called mountains by the local inhabitants. They were formed at the end of the Pleistocene Epoch, when large quantities of sand accumulated in front of the terminal moraines under conditions of a dry climate and prevailing easterly winds. Many of them were later partially covered by marshes and peat bogs. Sand dunes influence not only the landscape but also the river network and the way of life of the people. Lowland rivers can penetrate dune fields only with great difficulty. Because they are rarely flooded, dunes have long served as sites for settlement and roads. In more recent times the dunes were cleared for plowland and were quickly turned into a sandy wasteland by the wind.

Climate. Polisia has a temperate continental climate with a warm and humid summer and a mild, cloudy winter. The Atlantic air mass dominates during the winter, and a modified continental air mass prevails in the summer. Continentality increases from west to east. The average annual temperature varies from 6.5°C to 7.5°C; the average January temperature decreases from –4°C in the west to –7°C in the east, and the minimum temperature drops from –32°C to –39°C. Summer temperatures are nearly the same: the average temperature is 18°C in the northwest and 19°C in the southeast. The frost-free period is 170 days in the northeast and 180 days in the southwest. The annual precipitation varies from 600 to 650 mm, although in any year it may vary from 300 to 950 mm. The maximum is obtained in June and July, when heavy rains and even downpours are frequent. The snow cover lasts from 90 to 100 days, and its depth varies from 15 cm in the west to 30 cm in the east. Fogs occur often – 60 to 70 days per year, mostly from October to January.

Water resources. Polisia is well supplied with water. It has a dense network of rivers, lakes, and marshes and large reserves of groundwater. Nearly all of Polisia lies within the Dnieper drainage basin. Only a small western segment is drained by the Buh, which flows into the Vistula. The main artery of Polisia is the Prypiat River. Its system is asymmetric: the northern tributaries (the Pyna, the Yaselda, the Lan, the Sluch, and the Ptsich) are short and small in volume, whereas the southern tributaries (the Turiia, the Stokhid, the Styr, the Horyn, the Stvyha, the Ubort, the Slovechna, the Zholon, and the Uzh) are mostly long and voluminous. The Teteriv and the Irpin are direct tributaries of the Dnieper. Polisia is rich in groundwater, which is found at various levels according to the geological structure. Quarternary deposits contain shallow groundwater. The best potable water in Kiev Polisia is obtained from Paleocene deposits, and in Volhynia, from Cretaceous deposits.

Polisia, especially its western part, contains more lakes (nearly 550) and ponds (nearly 1,000) than any other region of Ukraine. The largest lake in Polisia, Chervone (area, 38.5 sq km; maximum depth, 9 m), formerly known as Kniazhe and Zhyd, belongs to Belarus. In Ukrainian Polisia the largest lakes are Svytiaz (area, 27.5 sq km; maximum depth, 58 m) and Vyhonivske (area, 26.5 sq km; depth, 2.7 m). About one-third of Polisia is covered with bogs and marshes. The flat terrain, the shallow depth of the groundwater, and the low gradient of the rivers account for the poor drainage. The marshes are concentrated along the Prypiat and the Horyn rivers.

Soils. Nearly 70 percent of Polisia is covered with podzolic soils. Their natural fertility is low and proportional to their clay content. The least fertile sandy podzols are most common, the more fertile sandy loams cover the interfluves, and the most fertile loams cover small areas in Volhynian and Zhytomyr Polisia. Muck and bog soils occupy 15 percent of Polisia, mostly river valleys and depressions. With melioration they become the most fertile soils in Polisia. The most fertile natural soils are the rendzina soils, which occur on the chalk and marl deposits of Volhynian Polisia, the gray forest soils, which form 'islands' in the loessial loam deposits near Ovruch, Zhytomyr, Novohrad-Volynskyi, and Mozyr, and tiny areas of degraded chernozems on the border between Polisia and the forest-steppe.

Vegetation. Polisia belongs to the mixed forest subzone of the East European broad-leaved forest zone. In the past the whole of Polisia was completely covered with forest and marshland. As a result of deforestation, mostly in the second half of the 19th century, and the growth of swamps, forests now occupy scarcely one-third of the land area. Plowland accounts for over one-quarter of the land, and hayfields, pastures, and meadows for about one-fifth. Generally the forests alternate with the marshes. The most widespread tree is the pine (*Pinus silvestris*, 58 percent); it is followed by the oak (*Quercus robur*, 15 percent), birch (*Betula verrucosa*, 12 percent), and black alder (*Alnus glutinosa*). Small areas are occupied by the aspen (*Populus tremula*), hornbeam (*Carpinus betulus*), and rare silver fir (*Abies alba*), only in northern and Volhynian Polisia.

Marshy forest near the Lva River in Polisia

The wetlands vegetation displays pronounced differentiation. The greatest variety occurs on the lowland swamps enriched with mineral salts. The prevalent plants belong to the sedge complex, the hypnum mosses-sedge complex (some with willow and birch brush), and the cereal-sedge-hypnum mosses complex. The vegetation of the upland bogs is considerably poorer: it consists of various kinds of peat (notably sphagnum), scattered dwarf pines, and shrub containing heather, bilberry, and several grasses. A considerable area is occupied by meadows, either floodplains or deforested tracts.

Fauna. Part of the Eurasian forest zone, Polisia contains a richer complex of fauna than the forest-steppe or the steppe of Ukraine. Among the forests of Polisia the richest fauna is found in the mixed forests, which contain the lynx, wolf, forest marten, chamois, fox, squirrel, weasel, ermine, wild boar, and bear and are visited by the elk (*Alces alces*, now very rare) from the marshy forest.

The rivers support the valuable fur-bearing beaver (in the nature preserves), otter, and mink. Two other fur-bearing animals were successfully introduced, the muskrat and the nutria. The most common waterfowl species are ducks, snipes, black-headed gulls, mallards, bank swallows, and blue kingfishers. The rivers are full of various species of the carp family, such as the carp, gardon, chub, bream, roach, tench, and crucian carp, as well as the pike, sheatfish, loach, perch, and ruff. The eel from the Baltic Basin has entered the Prypiat river system through canals.

In the 17th century bison and aurochs still inhabited Polisia; in the 18th century, the flying squirrel; and in the 19th century, numerous wolverines, bears, and elk. Overhunting, the impact of human activities, and the reduction of the natural habitat have contributed to the extinction of some species or their displacement to the north.

History. Evidence of human habitation in Polisia dates back to the Upper Paleolithic Period (10,000–8000 BC). Considerably more evidence from the Mesolithic Period (8000–5000 BC) has been found on sand dunes along the rivers.

In the 9th century Polisia was inhabited, according to the Primary Chronicle, by the following tribes: along both sides of the Buh River to the Yaselda in the north lived the Dulibians (later known as the Volhynians); to the southeast and south of the Prypiat River were the Derevlianians (their main towns, Iskorosten and Ovruch); and to the north along the Prypiat were the Drehovichians (main towns, Turiv and Mozyr). Thus the Yaselda–Prypiat line, which now forms the ethnic border between Ukrainians and Belarusians, marked off tribal territories long ago.

In the 10th century Polisia became part of the Kievan state. *Turiv-Pynske principality, which occupied the central part of Polisia, became part of Kievan Rus' at the end of the 10th century and regained independence at the beginning of the 12th. A century later it was divided into a number of small principalities, Pynske, Turiv, Dorohobuzh, Peresopnytsia, Davyd-Horodok, and others, which were dominated alternately by Kiev and Volhynia principalities. Eastern Polisia belonged to Kiev principality, southwestern Polisia to Volhynia principality, and the Brest land to Turiv-Pynske principality and later to Volhynia principality. After the Tatar invasion almost the whole of Polisia became part of the Principality of Galicia-Volhynia. At the beginning of the 14th century northern and Prypiat Polisia were annexed by the Lithuanian grand duke Gediminas. After the collapse of the Galician-Volhynian state the whole of Polisia became part of Lithuania. In the middle of the 15th century most of Polisia was administered by the Olelkovych princes of Kiev. From 1519 the Pynske land belonged to Queen Bona, the wife of the Polish king Sigismund I. She settled it with Polish peasants and petty gentry and made the first major attempt to drain the Polisian marshes. After the Union of Lublin (1569) Polisia was divided: the northern part remained in the Grand Duchy of Lithuania (all of Brest, part of Minsk, and slices of Novhorod voivodeships), whereas the southern part was acquired by Poland (parts of Kiev and Volhynia voivodeships and the Kholm land). The major cities and the more populated parts of those territories, with the exception of Brest, were located beyond Polisia or on its periphery. Polisia gained importance in Ukraine's history during the Tatar conquest of the forest-steppe in the 13th century and the Crimean Tatar raids after the mid-15th century. A large proportion of the Ukrainian population of the forest-steppe sought refuge in Polisia, which was less vulnerable to attack.

After the partitions of Poland the whole of Polisia was incorporated into the Russian Empire. The southern part was assigned to Volhynia and Kiev gubernias (which formed a part of the Southwestern krai), and the central and northern parts were incorporated into Hrodna and Minsk gubernias (part of the Western krai). A large part of Ukrainian Polisia was thereby incorporated into gubernias with a Belarusian majority. Polisia was the most neglected and poorest part of Ukrainian territories within the Russian Empire. Conditions improved somewhat when the I. Zhilinsky expedition drained some parts of the region, although its work was confined mostly to state and nobles' estates. Railroads brought a significant improvement in Polisia's economy.

According to the Peace Treaty of Brest-Litovsk the whole of Ukrainian Polisia became part of the Ukrainian state. In 1917–18 the same Ukrainian national movement encompassed western Polisia and Podlachia. It was spearheaded by the Bluecoats Regiment and the Ukrainian administration. The Prosvita society, with its head office in Brest, organized 150 reading rooms. Ukrainian schools, co-operatives, and the newspaper *Ridne slovo* were established. The Peace Treaty of Riga resulted in the partition of Polisia between Poland and the USSR. Almost the whole of eastern Polisia, settled by Ukrainians, became part of the Ukrainian SSR. Only a small portion of it around Mozyr (6,400 sq km) was made part of the Belorussian SSR. Most of western Polisia, which was acquired by Poland, was formed into Polisia voivodeship, with its center in Brest; its southern part was joined to Volhynia voivodeship.

Taking advantage of the low level of national consciousness among both Ukrainian and Belarusian Polisians, the Polish administration tried to Polonize them and to increase the Polish population in the region, which in 1920 accounted for under 5 percent of the total. Poland did not recognize Ukrainians or Belarusians in Polisia but set up the artificial category of 'local people' (*tuteshni*). In the 1931 census 62.4 percent of the inhabitants were registered as speakers of the 'local language,' 6.7 percent as Belarusian, and only 4.8 percent as Ukrainian. Moreover, the Ukrainian language in Polisia received no recognition.

Polish was the only language taught in schools, and eventually it became the official language of the Orthodox church. No Ukrainian political, social, or cultural life was permitted: Ukrainian institutions, such as the Brest Prosvita and Ukrainian schools, were closed down. All Ukrainian activities were strictly controlled by the local administration, the police, and, in border counties, the military. The policy was enforced from 1932 by Voivode W. Barnacki-Kostek. In 1920–31 about 40,000 Poles, mostly colonists and military settlers, were resettled on former Russian nobles' estates and state lands. In the years just before the Second World War the authorities attempted to Polonize and Catholicize the petty Orthodox gentry in Polisia. The 'Polish Holland' that was to be created on drained wetlands was to attract a new influx of Polish peasants, but the plan was defeated by the Polish general staff, who wanted to use Polisia as a buffer zone with the USSR.

In September 1939 western Polisia was occupied by the Soviet Army. Only a small part of the former Polisia voivodeship (7,200 sq km) settled by Ukrainians was attached to the Ukrainian SSR; most of it (20,500 sq km) was assigned to the Belorussian SSR. The partition occurred according to the 'will' of the people's deputies of western Belarus, expressed by their convention in Białystok on 28 October 1939. The demands of rural delegations to oblast centers in Brest and Pynske for union with the Ukrainian SSR were of no avail. Belarusian, or even Russian, was imposed as the language of instruction in schools, which the local population had started to Ukrainize. In the first months of the German occupation (summer 1941) Ukrainian life in Polisia revived, only to be stifled by the Nazis. Taking advantage of the swampy, wooded terrain the Ukrainian resistance became active, in the form of the *Polisian Sich, which later became part of the Ukrainian Insurgent Army. Soviet partisan groups also operated in the region.

After the Soviets reoccupied Polisia, the previous borders were renewed. The Ukrainians (approx 800,000), who live compactly in Brest oblast and on the southern fringe of Homel oblast, are officially considered Belarusian. Ukrainian has not been recognized in the government or schools and is not used in print. Ukrainians in Belarus are threatened with assimilation to the Belarusian culture in the rural areas and to the Russian culture in the cities.

Population. The distribution of the population and the way of life were strongly affected by the geographical conditions in Polisia. Its inaccessible terrain protected the inhabitants from invasion and isolated them from foreign influences. Polisian people retained the ancient wooden

A village in Volhynian Polisia

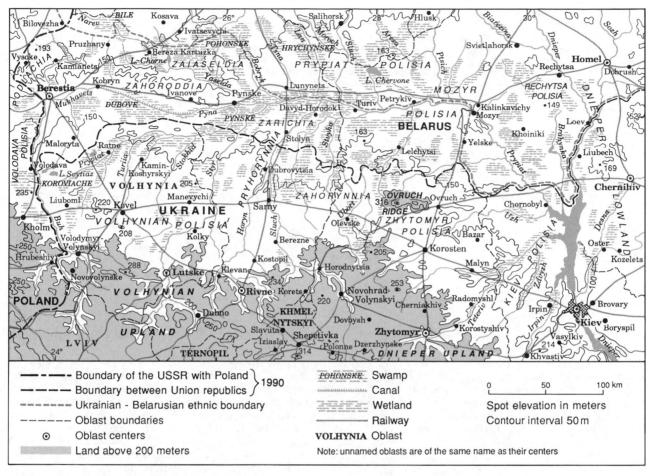

- —·—·—·— Boundary of the USSR with Poland ⎫
- — — — — Boundary between Union republics ⎬ 1990
- - - - - - - Ukrainian - Belarusian ethnic boundary ⎭
- — — — — Oblast boundaries
- ⊙ Oblast centers
- Land above 200 meters

- *POHONSKE* Swamp
- Canal
- Wetland
- Railway
- **VOLHYNIA** Oblast

0   50   100 km

Spot elevation in meters
Contour interval 50 m

Note: unnamed oblasts are of the same name as their centers

UKRAINIAN POLISIA

architecture, the ancient dress with traces from the Princely era, and a rich store of customs, traditions, and folklore, which are closely related in content and style with those of the rest of Ukraine. The people preserved many carols with ancient themes and old ritual songs, some of which have been adopted by the Belarusians. Since the end of the 19th century, however, the accelerated pace of change, improved transportation, the two world wars, and, especially, Soviet integration policies have forced out the ancient forms.

Because of their isolation the inhabitants of Polisia never had a strong sense of national identity. They always felt and continue to feel that they are different from their neighbors the Poles, Russians, and Jews, and usually referred to themselves as 'locals' (*tuteshni*), 'simple folk' (*prosti*), or 'Orthodox' (*pravoslavni*). The names *polishchuk* and *pynchuk*, derived from place-names, were usually used by outsiders. The distinction between Ukrainian and Belarusian Polisians is not settled but can be drawn more or less along the linguistic border. The Polisians themselves recognize the difference in the hard and soft pronunciation of similar words (eg, the Ukrainian *khodyty* or *khodity*, and the Belarusian *khadzity* 'to walk') and distinguish Ukrainians from Belarusians without any difficulty. Ukrainian Polisians called the Belarusians *lytvyny* or *lytsvyny* (Lithuanians) and sometimes *hedyky* or, pejora-

tively, *lapatsony*. The Belarusians, in turn, called the Ukrainians *hiduni* or *hetuni*. The Ukrainians of Polisia regarded themselves as different from the Belarusians and the Ukrainians of Volhynia and the Kiev region. Their pilgrimages to the Kievan Cave Monastery and especially to the Pochaiv Monastery in Volhynia contributed to that sense of affinity.

There is no agreement on the demarcation of Ukrainians from Belarusians in Polisia. The Russian census of 1897 recognized the inhabitants of Brest and Kobryn counties, in Hrodna gubernia, as Ukrainians but regarded the people of Pynske and Mozyr counties as Belarusians, although specialists on Polisia, such as K. Mykhalchuk, E. Karsky, D. Shendryk, and M. Dovnar-Zapolsky, clearly claimed that they were Ukrainian. The Soviet censuses of 1926 and 1959 took the border between the two republics as the Ukrainian-Belarusian demarcation line. The Polish censuses of 1921 and 1931 treated the nationality and language questions quite arbitrarily: the 1921 census, for example, 'discovered' a sizable Polish population in Kobryn county, which disappeared from the 1931 census by its being merged with the 'locals.' There were marked differences between the Ukrainians and Belarusians of Polisia in their folklore, dress, anthropological features, and psychology. The differences in their economic life and material culture were considerably smaller. Furthermore, the

Land use and population density by natural region in Polisia, 1931

Natural region	Area (1,000 sq km)	Land use (% of area)				Population	
		Plowland	Hayfields & pastures	Forests	Other	Total (1,000s)	Density (persons/sq km)
Dry Polisia	54.5	36	18	33	13	2,778	51
Zahorodia	6.5	37	35	15	13	369	57
Volhynian Polisia	13.7	33	23	28	16	694	51
Western	4.7	39	33	13	15	256	54
Eastern	9.0	30	19	35	16	438	49
Crystalline Shield	24.7	33.5	12.5	41	13	1,167	47
Western	11.0	17	13	52.5	17.5	317	29
Eastern	13.7	46.5	12.5	31.5	9.5	850	60
Kiev Polisia	9.6	44	14	32	10	548	57
Marshy Polisia	51.0	18	24	33	25	1,321	26
Zarichia	15.9	20	33	24	23	495	31
North Polisia	14.0	13	24	38	25	267	19
Zahorynia	7.2	12	17	37	34	78	11
Mozyr Polisia	13.9	26	18	35	21	81	35
All Polisia	105.5	27	21	33	19	4,099	39

line of ethnic demarcation is not always sharp: there are transitional dialects as well as 'islands' of Belarusian settlers on Ukrainian territories. Nor is the Ukrainian population ethnically homogeneous: it is divided into a number of tribes distinguished by geographical conditions (history, and distance from developed Ukrainian lands and from Belarus). Those tribal differences have not been studied and are quickly disappearing.

Because of its poverty Polisia did not attract foreigners. By the 1860s no more than 20 percent of the population consisted of Jews, Poles, Ukrainian-speaking Roman Catholics, and a few Russians, concentrated in the cities. Among the Ukrainians the petty gentry constituted a separate group. After the abolition of serfdom the landowners in southern Polisia sold off some of their land to Polish and German colonists. The proportion of Ukrainians in Ukrainian Polisia declined to 71 percent, the Jews made up 15 percent (the highest in all Ukrainian lands), the Poles and Roman Catholics, 7 percent, the Russians, 4 percent, and the Germans, 3 percent. As a result of the hostilities during 1914–20 and postwar adjustments the share of the Jewish population declined to 13 percent, and the German and Russian, to 2 percent each, whereas the Polish and Roman Catholic increased to 9 percent in western Polisia and declined in eastern Polisia, and the Ukrainian increased to 74 percent. As a result of the Second World War and the population exchange between the USSR and Germany, the Germans were no longer registered (in the 1959 census), the Jews declined to 2 percent, and the Poles, to 2.5 percent (only 1 percent in western and 3–4 percent in eastern Ukrainian Polisia), whereas the Russians increased to 5 percent, and the Ukrainians, to 90.5 percent. Belarusians numbered less than 0.4 percent in 1959.

Polisia, especially its marshy part, is the least populated region of Ukraine. The population density in Ukrainian Polisia is 43 persons per sq km, and in rural areas as low as 25 (in 1987). In the early 1930s the population density in dry Polisia was 51 persons per sq km; in marshy Polisia it was 26. In dry Polisia plowland occupied 36 percent of the land area, hayfields and pastures, 18 percent, and forests,

33 percent. In marshy Polisia, by contrast, the corresponding figures were 18, 24, and 33 percent (see the table).

A unique pattern of temporary settlement arose in marshy, forested Polisia. With their arable land scattered on small 'islands' remote from the village, the farmers moved there for the spring fieldwork and the harvesting and lived there in primitive shelters. Haying required a stay of two to three weeks. The harvest was brought in when the marshes froze over, and the snow made sleigh transportation possible. Shepherds and fishermen spent even longer periods away from the village. As the population grew, groupings of seasonal shelters developed into permanent settlements.

The population of Ukrainian Polisia grew rapidly in the decades before the First World War. From 1856 to 1914 it increased by 180 percent. The increase was a result not only of natural growth but also of the heavy influx of Ukrainians, Poles, Germans, and Belarusians, who bought up partitioned estates. At the same time nearly one-third of the forests were cleared for farming. After the war the population continued to grow rapidly: in western Polisia, despite some emigration overseas, it increased by 51 percent in 1921–31, as a result of a high rate of natural increase (2.6 percent), the return of wartime evacuees, and the influx of Polish colonists. During the Second World War the population dynamics in Polisia was the same as in other parts of Ukraine. By 1956 the population of Polisia had reached its 1939 level. Because jobs were scarce, people left Polisia in 1963–8. Polisia's net population increase amounted to only 35 percent of the natural increase. The population of Ukrainian Polisia was estimated at 4.5 million in 1970 and at almost 4.7 million in 1987.

Polisia had and still has the lowest level of urbanization in Ukraine: in 1914 scarcely 10 percent of its population was urban, and in 1989, under 50 percent. In the same period the urbanization of Ukraine as a whole rose from 34 to 67 percent. Urban centers developed only in dry Polisia or on the dry 'islands' of marshy Polisia. Lacking large manufacturing enterprises, the cities of Polisia until the 1930s were dependent on trade, crafts, and administrative jobs. Jews comprised 60 percent of their population. To-day all the larger cities have manufacturing enterprises.

Economy. For centuries most inhabitants of Polisia lived off the forest and wetlands resources. Farming was important economically only in dry Polisia. The forests supported beekeeping and pitch-, potash-, and charcoal-making. Wood was the basic material for various implements, from plow to bastshoes. Flax, hemp, and wool were the raw materials for cloth-making, and clay was the basis for pottery. Even iron was smelted locally from bog ores, using charcoal. Forest products, such as furs, honey, potash, pitch, tar, and lumber, were exported.

Agriculture in Polisia had a number of distinctive features: deep furrows were used to drain the soil, haystacks were raised on poles, and grain was dried on separate, high palings. In the second half of the 19th century the plow replaced the hooked plow (*sokha*) and wooden plow (*ralo*). In dry Polisia the tiny, scattered parcels of farmland began to be consolidated before 1914. After the war the process was accelerated in western Polisia. In eastern Polisia collectivization resulted in consolidation on a large scale. The main crops in Polisia were rye (41 percent of the sown area), potatoes (16 percent), oats (13 percent), buckwheat (6 percent), barley (6 percent), and millet (3 percent). Among technical crops the most important was flax; hemp and hops were less important. The grain yields averaged only 7–10 centners per ha and the potato, 70–100.

Forest products were Polisia's most valuable exports. Lumber became an important export at the end of the 18th century, when the canals connecting Polisia to the Baltic Sea were completed, and even more so when the railways were built in the 1880s.

Polisia was one of the poorest agrarian regions of Ukraine. Although its peasants had more land than the peasants of the forest-steppe, the soil was poor, and the yields low. Farming, especially in wet Polisia, was primitive and backward and had little connection with the markets. It produced a small surplus in cattle and forest products (mushrooms, berries). Home-manufactured goods were seldom marketed, except for clay pottery from Horodnytsia and baskets from Khliaby. The forest industry provided many jobs. Other industries were poorly developed and along with trade were controlled by foreigners. Many peasants emigrated to Asia (from eastern Polisia) or to America (from western Polisia). The inflow of Polish colonists into western Polisia under the Polish regime only added to the hardships of the Ukrainian peasants.

Industry is still relatively weak in Polisia, although it has grown considerably since the 1960s. Most of it is involved in processing local agricultural, forest, and mineral raw materials. The food industry accounts for the largest share of the gross production. Its main branches include alcohol distilling, butter- and cheese-making (Kovel, Radomyshl, Olevske), meat packing (Kovel, Brest, Pynske, Kobryn, Sarny), fruit canning (Ovruch, Zhytomyr), grain milling, and brewing. The lumber, woodworking, furniture, and paper industries are widespread. Their main plants are in Pynske, Kobryn, Kovel, Kyvertsi, Tsuman, Orzhiv, and Kostopil. Prefabricated houses are manufactured in Kostopil and Irpin. Furniture factories are found in Malyn, Zhytomyr, Kostopil, and Brest; paper plants, in Malyn, Korostyshiv, Myropil, Poninka, Chyzhivka, Slavuta, and Mokvyn; wood-chemicals plants, in Korosten, Ovruch, and Slavuta; and a match factory, in Pynske.

Light industry in Polisia includes the linen manufacturing complex in Zhytomyr (the largest in the former USSR) and a similar one in Rivne; smaller linen plants in Kovel, Korostyshiv, Novohrad-Volynskyi, Yemilchyne, and Ovruch; sewing factories in Zhytomyr, Korosten, Novo-hrad-Volynskyi, Rivne, Lutske, Kovel, Brest, Kobryn, and Pynske; cotton-textiles factories in Brest and Korostyshiv; and leather footwear factories in Zhytomyr, Lutske, and Brest.

The machine-building and metalworking industries have been established in Polisia since the 1960s. Their more important enterprises include agricultural machinery plants in Kovel, Rozhyshche, Rivne, Zdolbuniv, and Novohrad-Volynskyi; the tractor factory at Olevske; the automobile plant in Lutske; the electrotechnical factories in Brest, Lutske, and Rivne; the instrument-making factories in Lutske and Zhytomyr; the chemical machinery and highway machinery plants in Korosten; and a boat-building plant in Pynske. The chemical industry is also new to Polisia. Its representative enterprises are the fertilizer plant in Rivne, the petroleum refinery in Mozyr, the petrochemical refinery and the synthetic-fiber factory in Zhytomyr, the plastics plants in Lutske and Mozyr, and the paint and dye factories in Pynske.

Various building materials are mined and processed in Polisia: pink granites and black labradorites, kaolin (for ceramics, tiles) and quartzites (for glass), and basalts on the Horyn River. Bricks and tiles are manufactured from clay in many towns, and cement from marl in Zdolbuniv. Because of the abundance of kaolin the porcelain and faience industries in Polisia are more developed than in other regions of Ukraine. Their major enterprises are located in Baranivka, Horodnytsia, Korosten, and Dovbysh. The glass industry, with a large plant in Zhytomyr, is based on local deposits of quartzite sands.

Energy for Polisia's industries comes from imported coal and oil (some from Rechytsa, in Belarusian Polisia) and from the unified electric grid, which encompasses some power plants in Polisia: the Chornobyl (at Prypiat) and the Rivne (at Kuznetsovsk) atomic power stations and the thermal power stations in Zhytomyr, Novohrad-Volynskyi, Korosten, Bereza, and Mozyr.

Polisia has the lowest density of roads and railways in all Ukraine. In 1880–5 a railway line from Homel to Brest through Kalinkavichy and Pynske was built. In 1902 a second parallel line through southern Polisia, Kiev–Korosten–Sarny–Kovel–Kholm, was added. Of the two perpendicular lines, which connect Volhynia with the Belarusian Upland, the first was built in 1885 from Baranavichy through Lunynets and Sarny to Rivne, the other during the First World War from Zhlobin through Kalinkavichy, Mozyr, Korosten, and Zhytomyr to Berdychiv and Shepetivka. During the Soviet period the lines Chernihiv–Ovruch and Khvastiv–Zhytomyr–Novohrad-Volynskyi were built. Many narrow-gauge lines, built mostly during the First World War, are used for moving timber and cordwood. The major railway junctions are Brest, Lunynets, Kalinkavichy, Zhytomyr, Korosten, Sarny, and Kovel. Most all-weather roads in Polisia were built during the Soviet period. The main east–west highways are the Kiev–Brest highway (Kiev–Zhytomyr–Novohrad-Volynskyi–Rivne–Lutske–Kovel–Brest) and the Brest–Homel highway through Pynske and Kalinkavichy. The major north–south highways are the Kiev–Chernihiv–Homel stretch of the Odessa–St Petersburg highway, which essentially bypasses Polisia in the east, and the Zhytomyr–Korosten–Ovruch–Mozyr–Babruisk stretch of the Vinnytsia–Minsk highway. An all-weather road connects Rivne with Pynske through Sarny and Stolyn, and a perpendicular all-weather road from Kholm to Kiev follows the railway line through Kovel, Sarny, Korosten, and Malyn. The waterways in Polisia are an important part of the transport network. Navigable routes include the Dnieper, the Prypiat (and its tributaries), the Styr, and the Horyn rivers, and the Dnieper–Buh Canal. Many other rivers are used for rafting timber.

BIBLIOGRAPHY

Zhilinskii, I. *Ocherk rabot Zapadnoi ekspeditsii po osusheniiu bolot (1873–1898)* (St Petersburg 1899)
Tutkovskii, P. *Ortograficheskii ocherk Tsentral'nogo i Iuzhnogo Poles'ia* (Moscow 1913)
Kubijowicz, W. 'Rozmieszczenie ludności na Polesiu,' in *Sprawozdanie Krakowskiego Koła Geografów* (Cracow 1925)
Mondalski, W. *Polesie* (Brest 1927)
Prace Biura Meljoracji Polesia (Brest 1929–33)
Kysilevs'ka, O. *Po ridnomu kraiu: Polissia* (Kolomyia 1935)
Narysy pro pryrodu i sil's'ke hospodarstvo Polissia (Kiev 1955)
Odrach, F. *Nashe Polissia* (Winnipeg 1955)
Zapadnoe Poles'e USSR (Kiev 1956)
Povarnitsyn, V. *Lisy Ukraïns'koho Polissia* (Kiev 1959)

Korzhuev, S. *Rel'ef Pripiatskogo Poles'ia* (Moscow 1960)
Marynych, O. *Ukraïns'ke Polissia: Fizyko-heohrafichnyi narys* (Kiev 1962)
Marinich, A. *Geomorfologiia Iuzhnogo Poles'ia* (Kiev 1963)
Bondarchik, V. (ed). *Poles'e: Material'naia kul'tura* (Kiev 1988)

V. Kubijovyč, I. Stebelsky, I. Sydoruk-Pauls

Polisia Nature Reserve (Poliskyi zapovidnyk). A state nature reserve set up in 1968 to preserve the characteristic landscape, vegetation, and animal species of Polisia. It covers 20,100 ha of land in Olevske and Ovruch raions of Zhytomyr oblast. Its forests and wetlands are inhabited by species such as the lynx, moose, beaver, forest marten, black stork, and hazel grouse. The reserve's research laboratories, museum, and administrative offices are located in Selezivka.

Polisian dialects. The Polisian dialects constitute, together with the *Podlachian dialects in northwestern Ukraine, the archaic group of the *northern dialects spoken north of the Kholm–Kiev–Putyvl line. As a result of the unequal northward spread of Ukrainian phonetic traits (ie, hard consonants before *e, i*) and the expansion of Belarusian traits to the south and southeast (ie, *akan'e* [pronunciation of unstressed *o* as *a*, eg, *nahá* (Standard

POLISIA'S LINGUISTIC BOUNDARIES

Ukrainian [SU] *nohá*) 'leg'] and *dzekan'e* [eg, *dziéci*, cf SU *díty* 'children'), a belt of transitional (in places, mixed) Ukrainian-Belarusian dialects developed.

The main feature of the dialects is the use of diphthongs (*uo, ÿö, uy, ie*) or the vowels *u, ÿ* (*y* in the south) in place of *o* and *e* before the lost *jer, and also in place of a stressed *e*, and the use of *o, e, e/y* in unstressed positions (eg, *duom – domký* [SU *dim – dimký*] 'house – little houses', *jačmién' – pópel* [SU *jačmin' – pópil*] 'barley – ashes', *miésec – mysec'íe* [SU *mísjac' – misjací*] 'moon – moons'). Dual reflexiveness is characteristic of *ę* and *ja-*, alternating with *'a, ja-* in a stressed position and *e, je-* in an unstressed position (eg, *pjat' – petá* [SU *p'jat' – p'jatá*] 'five – heel', *jak – jek'í* [SU *jak – jakýj*] 'as – which', particularly in the east).

The Polisian dialects are divided into (1) the eastern, or Left-Bank/Chernihiv, dialects (EPD), east of the Dnieper River; (2) the middle, or Right-Bank, dialects (MPD), between the Dnieper and Horyn rivers; and (3) the western, or Volhynian, dialects (WPD), between the Horyn and Buh/Lisna rivers. Most of them share the following traits: (1) traces of the semipalatalized pronunciation of several consonants before *i, e* (eg, *d'éǔka, pl'éten'* [SU *dívka, pletín'*] 'girl, wattle' in the EPD, *sv'et* [SU *svit*] 'world' in the MPD), particularly of the sibilants *č, ž, š* (eg, *š'est', mež'éju* [SU *šist', mežéju*] 'six, along the boundary'), and, in the MPD, in the form of *j* before a stressed *a* (eg, *žjába, čjas, šjápka* [SU *žába, čas, šápka*] 'frog, time, hat'); (2) a hard *r* (eg, *zorá* [SU *zorjá*] 'star') and, except in most WPD, a hard *c* (eg, *úlyca, zájec, tancovát'* [SU *vúlycja, zájac, tancjuváty*] 'street, hare, to dance', and, in the north EPD, *ž'en'ícca* [SU *ženýtsja*] 'to marry'); (3) aphaeresis of the initial vowel in a word following a preposition ending in a vowel (eg, *do dnohó* [SU *do odnohó*] 'to one'); (4) eastern-Ukrainian stress types in word formation (eg, *začíska* [SU *záčiska*] 'hairdo') and in verbs (eg, *xvaljú: xvályš* [SU *xvaljú: xvályš*] 'I praise: you praise', *(po)nestý, (po)neslá, (po)nesló, (po)neslý* 'to carry, she/it/they carried', *nošú: prynóšu, prynósyty* [SU *nošú: prynóšu, prynósyty*] 'I carry: I bring, to bring', cf WPD *nesémo, neséte* [SU *nesemó, neseté*] 'we/you [pl] carry'); (5) no stress shift in pronouns after prepositions (eg, *do mené, pry sobí, do tohó* [SU *do méne, pry sóbi, do tóho*] 'to me, with oneself, to that'); (6) a weaker morphological use of stress in juxtaposing plural and singular nouns, particularly in the EPD (eg, *xáty, xátam, xátax* [SU *xatý, xatám, xatáx*] 'houses' nom, dat, loc); (7) noun forms of the type *žyt't'é, pysán'n'e* (SU *žyttjá, pysánnja*) 'life, writing'; (8) the ending *-u* in the dative singular of masculine and neuter nouns (eg, *brátu, kon'ú* [SU *brátovi, konévi*] 'brother, horse'), and, in the WPD, also *-ovy* (eg, *xlópc'ovy/xlópc'u* [SU *xlópcevi*] 'boy'); (9) the use of the collective-plural ending *-á* in the nominative plural of some masculine nouns, particularly in the EPD (eg, *xolodá* [SU *xolodý*] 'cold weather'); (10) the ending *-(an)e* in the nominative plural of other nouns (eg, *sel'áne, l'úde* [SU *seljány, ljúdy*] 'peasants, people'); (11) frequent use (less so in the WPD) of the ending *-éj* in the genitive plural of nouns (eg, *xlehéj, storožéj, poléj, xatéj* [SU *xlibív, storožív, polív, xat*] 'breads, guards, fields, houses'); (12) long forms of adjectives and pronouns (eg *tája, nášaja, molodája* [SU *ta, náša, molodá*] 'that, our, young' fem), in the WPD mostly in adjectives only with stressed endings; (13) the loss of *-j* (except in the WPD) in the nominative singular masculine adjectives (eg, *vesély, l'iétn'i* [SU *vesélyj, lítnij*] 'happy, summery'; (14) postprepositional forms of the personal pronoun without the prothetic *n-* (eg, *do její, na jýj* [SU *do néji, na níj*] 'to her, on her'), as well as old plural

forms of the type *t'ix, t'im, t'imy* (SU *tyx, tym, tymy*) 'those' genitive, dative, instrumental; (15) in verbs, infinitives ending in *-ovaty* (*-ovat'* in the EPD, *-ovat'/-ovat* in the MPD), second person imperative plural ending in *-ite* (eg, *nes'iéte, xod'iéte* [SU *nesít', xodít'*] 'carry, walk'), and two forms of the future tense, eg, *búdu robýty/-ýt'* and *robýtymu* 'will do' (particularly in the MPD and WPD, in which the form *máju robýty* 'I am supposed to do' is also used); (16) sporadic use in certain expressions of a soft *n* after *y/i* (eg, *pín'a, slýn'a* [SU *pína, slýna*] 'foam, saliva').

The EPD north of the Desna River have retained archaic diphthong forms and some phonetic features similar to Belarusian (semipalatalized consonants before *e* and *y* [also from *ы*, which can sound like *i*]). The southern Desna dialects use sporadic *akan'e* (eg, *nášaha, kan'óm* [SU *nášoho, koném*] 'of our, with a horse') and a palatalized *č'*. In conjugation endings of the third person singular and plural, *e* influences *y/ji* in verbs with the stress on the root (eg, *xóde, xód'ut'* [SU *xódyt', xódjat'*] 'he walks, they walk'). In the southeast there are dual forms for feminine nouns in the instrumental singular in which the stress is on the root (eg, *xátoju/xátoj* 'with a house'), pronominal forms such as *sej, s'ája, séje* (SU *cej, cja, ce*) 'this' masculine, feminine, neuter, and a number of lexical features.

In the MPD the following forms are more frequent: *pójes, predút'/predút* (SU *pójas, prjadút'*) 'belt, they spin [yarn]'; *akan'e* (eg, *vadá* [SU *vodá*] 'water'), including the syncopated pronunciation of unstressed *a* as *o* (eg, *storúxa* [SU *starúxa*] 'old woman'); a hard *-t'* in verbal endings (eg, *róbyt'/róbyt, robýt'/robýt* [SU *róbyt, robýty*] 'he does, to do'; endings in the instrumental singular of the type *kon'óm, dušóju* [SU *koném, dušéju*] 'horse, soul'; differentiation of *tej/ toj* (SU *toj/vin*) 'that one, he'; constructions of the type *ja berú serpá, mení bolýt' holová* (SU *ja berú serp, u méne bolýt' holová*) 'I take the sickle, I have a headache'; lexical parallels with south Belarusian dialects; and mostly monophthongized diphthongs (eg, *vuz* [SU *viz*] 'wagon', but *pjýena, obyéd* [SU *pína, obíd*] 'foam, dinner').

The distinctive features of the WPD are the labial-labial (and labial-dental) pronunciation of postvocal *v* (eg, *dav*, not *daǔ* [SU *dav*] 'I gave'); prothetic consonants (eg, *húlyc'a, hynáčyj* [SU *vúlytsja, inákšyj*] 'street, different'); hard consonants before unstressed *-y* from *-ѣ* (thence forms of fem nouns in the dat-loc such as *xáty, klúny* [SU *xáti, klúni*] 'house, threshing barn', and of nouns in the nom pl such as *kóny* [SU *kóni*] 'horses'); the influence of soft pronominal endings on feminine singular adjectives in which the stress is on the root (eg, *méji, bíleji, bíleju* [SU *mojéji, bíloji, bíloju*] 'of my, of white, with white'); endings of feminine nouns in the instrumental singular of the type *t'ín'n'u, mýšju, kostéju* (SU *tínnju, mýšeju, kístju*) 'shadow, mouse, bone'; endings of neuter singular nouns of the type *tel'á, -áta, -átovy, -átom, -áty/-átovy* (SU *teljá, -játy, -játi, -jám, -játi*) 'calf' nominative, genitive, dative, instrumental, locative, or *v uxóvy* (SU *u vúsi*) 'in the ear'; endings of masculine and neuter nouns in the dative and locative plural of the type *-am/-om* and *-ax/ox* (particularly in the northeast, eg, *na vozáx/-óx, vozám/-óm* 'on the wagons, to the wagons'); verbal forms of the type *bíxčy, pečý* (SU *bíhty, pektý*) 'to run, to bake'; adverbs of degree of the type *horíej, dályj* (SU *hírše, dál'še*) 'worse, farther'; the prefix *ny-* (eg, *nyxtó* [SU *nixtó*] 'nobody'); the suffixal particle of indefiniteness *-s'a* (eg, *kotrýjs'a* [SU *kotrýjs'*] 'some'; and lexical connections with the Podlachian and Volhynian dialects.

Traits of the EPD can be found in the works of I. Nekrashevych, P. Kulish, B. Hrinchenko, P. Tychyna, and other writers. The Polisian dialects have been studied by V. Hantsov, P. Hladky, V. Kaminsky, E. Karsky, W. Kuraszkiewicz, O. Kurylo, P. Lysenko, T. Nazarova, L. Ossowski, P. Popov, P. Rastorguev, S. Smal-Stotsky, J. Pauls, O. Syniavsky, J. Tarnacki, Yu. Vynohradsky, and others.

BIBLIOGRAPHY
Tarnacki, J. *Studia porównawcze nad geografią wyrazów (Polesie – Mazowsze)* (Warsaw 1939)
Dyialektalahichny atlas belaruskai movy (Minsk 1963)
Leksika Poles'ia: Materialy dlia polesskogo dialekticheskogo slovaria (Moscow 1968)
Poles'ie (lingvistika, arkheologiia, toponimika) (Moscow 1968)
Lysenko, P. *Slovnyk polis'kykh hovoriv* (Kiev 1974)
Nykonchuk, M. *Materialy do leksychnoho atlasu ukraïns'koï movy (Pravoberezhne Polissia)* (Kiev 1979)
Atlas ukraïns'koï movy v tr'okh tomakh, vol 1, *Polissia, serednia Naddniprianshchyna i sumizhni zemli*, ed I. Matviias (Kiev 1984)

O. Horbach

Polisian Sich (Poliska sich). A Ukrainian insurgent formation, organized in June 1941 by T. *Borovets under the aegis of the UNR government-in-exile. Its earliest anti-Soviet activities in Sarny county consisted of attacking NKVD jails and Red Army mobilization centers and capturing arms and ammunition. In July 1941 the Sich was recognized by the German authorities as a local militia, whose primary mission was to clear Polisia of the remnants of the Soviet army before they regrouped into partisan detachments. In August Borovets obtained the support of the OUN (Melnyk faction) and, assisted by a cadre of UNR Army officers, expanded his force to several thousand men. The Sich's chief of staff was P. Smorodsky, a lieutenant colonel of the UNR Army. After defeating a Soviet force at Olevske on 21 August, Borovets established his headquarters there. With the elimination of the Soviet partisan threat, the Germans forced the Polisian Sich to demobilize (15 November 1941). In March 1942 Borovets reactivated it, this time as an anti-Nazi insurgent force, and renamed it the Ukrainian Insurgent Army (UPA). The five-company army began its anti-Nazi activities in late April 1942. Its best-known operation took place at Shepetivka on 19 August. In the autumn of 1942 Borovets signed an armistice with Soviet partisans, but failed to reach an agreement with the Germans, and hostilities with the Soviet partisans and the Germans resumed in February 1943. By that time, partisan units controlled by the OUN (Bandera faction) had become the dominant Ukrainian force. The two Ukrainian insurgent forces shared a common name, the UPA, without merging into one army. The steady loss of men to the rival UPA and the decline in peasant support prompted Borovets to rename his force the Ukrainian People's Revolutionary Army. On 18 August 1943 the force was surrounded and disarmed by the UPA. Borovets and his staff escaped and remained active until November 1943.

BIBLIOGRAPHY
Borovets', T. *Armiia bez derzhavy: Slava i trahediia ukraïns'koho povstans'koho rukhu* (Winnipeg 1981)

P. Sodol

Poliske [Polis'ke]. II-10. A town smt (1986 pop 11,300) on the Uzh River and a raion center in Kiev oblast. The town, which is first mentioned in historical documents in 1415, was called Khabne until 1958. In the 16th century it was owned by King Sigismund I of Poland. When Right-Bank Ukraine was acquired by the Russian Empire in 1793, Khabne became part of Radomyshl county, Kiev gubernia. At the beginning of the 19th century the town belonged to the Radziwiłł family, who built a cloth factory there in 1809. Today the town manufactures textiles as well as furniture, hemp, lumber, and building materials.

Poliszczuk, Orest [Poliščuk], b 7 January 1942 in Lviv. Painter, graphic artist, and sculptor. A refugee in the United States since 1949, he studied at the University of Maryland. Since 1960 he has taught at Montgomery College in Rockville, Maryland. Solo exhibitions of his works have been held in Detroit (1975, 1979), New York (1976), Toronto (1978), Baltimore (1980), and Rockville (1982).

Politburo (abbreviation for *Politychne biuro*). The top policy-making body of the CC CPSU and of the central committees of the republican organizations of the Party. The first Politburo of the CC CP(B)U was set up on 6 March 1919. In Ukraine it was called the Bureau of the CC CPU (1952–3), the Presidium of the CC CPU (1953–66), and then by its original name of Politburo. Until its dissolution in the wake of the M. Gorbachev reforms, the Politburo consisted of 10 to 11 full (voting) and 3 to 7 candidate members, who were elected by the CC CPU. These were secretaries of the CC, the head of the Presidium of the Supreme Soviet, the president of the Council of Ministers and some of his deputies, the commander of the Kiev Military District, and sometimes several first secretaries of oblast Party committees. The body was controlled directly by the Politburo of the CC CPSU and oversaw all political work in Ukraine. It worked closely with the *Secretariat of the CC CPU, which was responsible for organizational matters, and there was usually some overlap in their membership.

Political commissar (*politychnyi komisar*). The political representative of the Communist party in the Soviet armed forces. Political commissars began to be appointed at the higher levels of the army in 1918 and at units smaller than a battalion (where they were called *politruky*) at the end of 1919. These officers came under the chief political administrations of the army and navy, and functioned as representatives of the Communist party conducting propaganda and ensuring that Party policy was followed. Until 1924 the commissars and *politruky*, who usually lacked military competence, were equal in rank to the military commander of the unit and could even veto his orders. This state of affairs caused much tension in the armed forces, because professional officers resented heavy-handed political interference. Then a system of unitary command was adopted, and the commissars were subordinated to the military commanders. In 1937–40, following the massive purges that swept the military in the mid-1930s, and again in 1941–2, following the Soviet entry into the Second World War, political commissars were restored to the rank of co-commander. In October 1942 the unitary command system was reinstated, and the political officers were redesignated deputies to the commanding officers (*zampolity*). After the Second World War political commissars were recruited from among serving officers and were men of superior ability and achievement. They were given a military rank but were exempt from normal military activities.

Political crime. A violation of the law for a political reason. Faced with oppressive foreign regimes which ruled out any legal form of opposition, Ukrainians were forced to resort sometimes to illegal means in the struggle for their national, political, and social rights.

In the Princely era, such political crimes were recognized as treason and conspiracy against the state and public order. Under the influence of Western law the criminal law of the Grand Duchy of Lithuania recognized certain political crimes, of which the most important were (1) crimes against the duke's authority, such as lèse-majesté, treason, and conspiracy; (2) military crimes, such as desertion and collaboration; and (3) crimes against the social order, such as counterfeiting documents and currency. Usually, political crimes were punished severely, by death, corporal punishment, confiscation of property, or imprisonment.

The Cossack state built on the tradition of Lithuanian law and, under the influence of Western and Russian legislation, expanded the list of political crimes and the forms of punishment. The third section of the Code of Laws of 1743 includes political crimes, such as killing, injuring, or insulting a foreign diplomat.

The law on political crimes in the countries that ruled Ukrainian territories in the 18th to 20th centuries reflected the political and ideological profile of their regimes. Under some regimes (the Russian, for example), simple membership in Ukrainian parties or participation in the Ukrainian national movement was considered a political crime and punished by judicial or administrative means.

Soviet law and judicial and administrative practice recognized a wide range of political crimes. During the struggle for Ukraine's independence and the first years of Soviet rule in Ukraine, a large number of decrees and laws on political crimes were enforced. Most political crimes were described as 'counterrevolutionary,' and they were punished severely by judicial and extrajudicial process. Political crimes were handled by revolutionary and military-revolutionary tribunals and by the Cheka.

The Criminal Code of the Ukrainian SSR of 1927 classified political crimes into counterrevolutionary crimes and crimes against administrative order. The revised code of 1960 listed as 'especially dangerous crimes against the state' (arts 56–65) treason, espionage, terrorism, wrecking, sabotage, and anti-Soviet propaganda. 'Other crimes against the state' (arts 66–80) included the following: violation of national and racial equality, divulging of state secrets, banditry, smuggling, mass disorder, evasion of call-up for military service, evasion of mobilization, evasion of wartime services and of payment of taxes, illegal exit from and entry into the USSR, infringement of international air regulations, infringement of regulations governing traffic and operation in transport, damaging of communications and means of transport, preparation and issuing of counterfeit money or securities, infringement of currency regulations, and failure to report crimes against the state (the latter is especially characteristic of Soviet law). For 11 different crimes the maximum punishment was death. Some types of political crime (eg, treason, anti-Soviet propaganda, and membership in anti-Soviet organizations) were not clearly defined and were open to arbitrary interpretation. According to the criminal law of Ukraine, political crimes came under Union jurisdiction, and the law on crimes against the state, passed by the USSR Supreme Soviet, was included in the Criminal Code of the Ukrainian SSR.

The concept of crimes against the state was much broader in the USSR than in Western democracies; it included even some economic crimes. In the Soviet Union and in Ukraine only some political trials were widely publicized – the show trials. Most were held in camera, although this practice was contrary to the procedural law on publicity. (See also *Political prisoners and *Concentration camps.)

V. Markus

Political economy. A social science dealing with the theoretical foundations of *economic studies. It is based on ethical, normative, or methodological principles that define schools, doctrines, and currents in economic thought and reflect particular economic interests (eg, national, class, state, private-sector, consumer, or trade-union). In Ukraine the origins of political economy (PE) can be traced back to the first written comments on economic problems found in medieval religious teachings (ie, the church's views on money and usury) and to the earliest legal documents of Kievan Rus', which reflect economic activity and establish norms for it (eg, *Ruskaia Pravda*).

Political economy as a discipline, however, begins in Ukraine with the physiocratic school which developed there in the early 19th century, later than it did in Western Europe (in Russia proper, it barely developed at all). Ukrainian physiocrats, such as V. Karazyn, differed from their Western counterparts by their radical critique of serfdom. They were simultaneously influenced by the classical school of PE, which reached Ukraine in the early 19th century. The first Russian translation of A. Smith's *Wealth of Nations* was done by the Chernihiv vice-governor N. Politkovsky and published in 1802–6. The first abridged Ukrainian translation, by O. Mykhalevych, was not published until 1913.

For many years Kharkiv University was the center of classical PE in Ukraine and in the Russian Empire. The German scholar L.H. von Jacob, a disciple of Smith, J.B. Say, and J. Bentham, was the first professor of PE there (1806–10) and in Ukraine in general. One of his successors, T. Stepanov (1832–47), wrote the first PE textbook (2 vols, 1844, 1848, in Russian) using the concepts of D. Ricardo and Smith. It was at Kharkiv that S. Pakhman wrote one of the first theoretical works on stock companies (1861); K. Gattenberger convincingly criticized the historical school, by proving that it added nothing to the classical approach; N. Kossovsky tried to develop a theory of liberal socialism based on the PE of Smith and Ricardo; and, in the early 20th century, P. Fomin and A. Volsky elaborated the foundations for a syndicate economy.

A second center of classical PE developed at Kiev University under I. Vernadsky (1846–50) and N. Bunge (1850–80). Bunge and his pupil H. Tsekhanovetsky (at Kiev in 1859–72 and at Kharkiv in 1873–98) advocated capitalism, the industrialization of Ukraine, and the development of cheap bank credit. In their writings on the steel and sugar industries and the railways, they emphasized the superiority of free trade and competition. It was at Kiev University that M. *Ziber translated into Russian Ricardo's *Principles of Political Economy and Taxation* in 1873 and published works on J.S. Mill and J.K. Rodbertus; and A. Antonovych wrote a book on the theory of value (1877) and a PE textbook (1886). In the early 20th century a 'Kievan school' of Russian PE (D. Pikhno, A. Bilimovich, V. Zheleznev) arose. Although it was politically reactionary, it advocated freedom of competition and of enterprises.

At Odessa University L. Fedorovych, the professor of economics (1884–1905), published books on the theory of monetary and credit circulation (1888) and the history of PE before Smith (1900).

In the early 20th century a capitalist PE prevailed among Ukraine's agrarian theorists (V. Kosynsky, P. Liashchenko, Yu. Meiendorf, and others). The peculiar Germano-Russian PE school that arose in the 19th century in St Petersburg and Moscow (like the Russian Slavophiles, populists, and utopian socialists) were hostile to liberalism and rejected capitalist competition as incompatible with conditions prevailing in the Russian Empire. In contrast, because industrial and agricultural capitalism were being developed much more intensively in Ukraine than elsewhere in the empire, most economists there and those who had left Ukraine for St Petersburg or Moscow (M. Baluhiansky, Vernadsky, Bunge, I. Yanzhul, and others) were antietatist and advocated economic freedom and competition. In the late 19th and early 20th centuries socialist and Marxist thought became widespread in the Russian Empire and there engendered widely accepted predictions of an inevitable general crisis and the demise of capitalism. At the same time, however, M. *Tuhan-Baranovsky developed the classical principles of Ricardo and Say. An opponent of the views of V. Lenin and R. Luxemburg, he proposed his own theory of the market (1898), according to which capitalism could continue evolving without economic crises as long as there was a rational division of resources, because the cyclical decrease in popular consumption would be compensated for by the growth of productive capital investments by the private sector and the state. To some extent Tuhan-Baranovsky's views anticipated the modern theories of planned and regulated capitalism.

The Romantic, historical, and institutional schools of PE had virtually no adherents in Ukraine, nor did F. List's nationalist school. In ethnic Russia, however, those schools were widespread (eg, S. Witte's nationalism).

Ukrainian *socialism differed substantially from its ethnic Russian counterpart in that it was influenced primarily by French rather than German thinkers. For example, Ukrainian socialist M. Drahomanov considered himself a disciple of P.-J. Proudhon, while Tuhan-Baranovsky wrote favorably about him. The evolution of Ukrainian socialist PE from Drahomanov's communalism to Tuhan-Baranovsky's co-operativism and market socialism (and even to the Workers' Opposition in the CP(B)U in the 1920s) was marked by the retention of programmatic traits, such as (1) the socialization, but not *nationalization, of property; (2) democratic self-management by socialist enterprises (peasant *hromady*, artels, co-operatives, worker-controlled factories); and (3) free market relations among socialist enterprises. Even as late as the 1920s Ukrainian thinkers did not advocate centralized state planning – which distinguished them from Russian socialist thinkers. The economic theory of co-operation, which was first elaborated in the Russian Empire by Ziber (1869) and was further developed by Ye. *Slutsky and others in Ukraine, was characteristic of Ukrainian socialist PE. It was refined by Tuhan-Baranovsky in his program for a 'co-operative society' (1918), which influenced even Lenin's thinking. Finally, Ukrainian socialist PE was primarily ethical, not materialist. For Ukrainian political economists, such as S. *Podolynsky, M. *Levytsky, Ziber (in his early

works), and, in Austrian-ruled Galicia, I. Franko and V. Navrotsky, the central concerns were the well-being of the masses, poverty, health care, and social security, not the development of productive forces as with Russian thinkers.

Until the late 1920s, Marxist PE was disproportionately weaker in Ukraine than was liberal or non-Marxist socialist PE. Although Ziber was recognized (even by K. Marx) as the first Marxist economist in the Russian Empire, he, along with Podolynsky, Yu. Bachynsky, and other Ukrainian Marxists, belonged to the school of 'legal Marxism' or 'economism' (to which Tuhan-Baranovsky was assigned later), which believed in the evolution of socioeconomic relations and opposed *populism and *Leninism.

The Austrian psychological school of PE, the theory of marginal utility, marginalism, and mathematical economics were introduced in Ukraine in the late 19th century. Tuhan-Baranovsky was the first to popularize the Austrian school in the Russian Empire (1890). His own attempt at synthesis of the theories of labor surplus and marginal utility, later proved to be incorrect, was mathematically substantiated in Kiev by N. Stoliarov. In Odessa R. Orzhentsky elaborated a theory of marginalism well before the Russian economist V. Dmitriev did. British and American neoclassical PE came too late to become widespread in Ukraine. (It did gain some currency in Soviet Russia during the period of the *New Economic Policy.) In contrast, the works of Kiev's Slutsky on the consumption function (1915), the rational behavior of consumers, and cyclical processes were published in Italian, German, and English, and influenced British neoclassical economists (J. Hicks, R. Allen) and American econometricians (eg, K. Arrow, G. Debreu, H. Houthakker) from the 1930s on.

In the second half of the 19th century *statistics began to develop in Ukraine. By the beginning of the 20th century a unique Ukrainian school of territorial (regional) econometrics had evolved, decades ahead of similar schools in other multinational states. Distinguished by its methodology of constructing and differentiating Ukraine's territorial economic balances from the statistical indicators for the Russian Empire as a whole, the school arose from M. *Yasnopolsky, M. Porsh, and P. Maltsiv's estimates of the imperial revenues and expenditures in Ukraine and was developed further in the 1920s by the Soviet Ukrainian economists M. Shafir and V. Dobrohaiev. Supplementary statistical research on Ukraine's external trade balance (by H. Kryvchenko, M. Shrah, K. Kobersky, and others) and *national income (by Myshkis and, in relation to the USSR as a whole, L. Litoshenko) showed that Ukraine was financially exploited by the tsarist and Soviet centralized systems of taxation. On the basis of these studies and the Marxist-Leninist theory of imperialism, M. *Volobuiev concluded that Ukraine had been and continued to be a Russian colony. Consequently he was repressed and vilified by the Stalinist regime as the founder of a Ukrainian nationalist PE.

In the 1920s and 1930s certain Soviet Ukrainian economists (V. Akulenko, Ya. Dimanshtein, I. Lando) analyzed Ukraine's development and growth. They showed that the productivity of labor and capital in Ukraine was higher than in central and eastern Russia, and that it was therefore necessary to give Ukraine priority in Soviet economic planning. A certain continuation of that view was evident in the analytical studies of the effectiveness of capital investments done by Soviet economists of the 1960s.

Dogmatic Stalinist PE dates from 1930, when a postsecondary textbook of PE edited by B. Radzikovsky was published in Kharkiv. Soon afterward the textbook was banned as 'Bukharinist' and withdrawn from circulation. No other textbook was available until 1954. Since the 1930s instruction in PE has been primitive. With minor changes, distorted presentations, particularly of the PE of Soviet socialism, remained normative in Soviet economics. Since the 1960s the number of critical studies of contemporary Western PE published in Kiev has grown considerably, but their scholarly value has been little. No synthetic monograph on the history of Ukrainian PE has appeared. Articles on Ukrainian PE have been published in two collections (1956, 1961), the monthly *Ekonomika Radians'koï Ukraïny*, Kiev University's bimonthly *Pytannia politychnoï ekonomiï*, and the annual *Istoriia narodnoho hospodarstva ta ekonomichnoï dumky Ukraïns'koï RSR* (since 1970).

Analyses by émigré economists (Ye. Glovinsky, K. Kononenko, D. Solovei, M. Vasyliv, B. Wynar, V. Holubnychy, Z. Melnyk, V. Bandera, I. Koropeckyj, M. Maksudov) of compulsory Soviet *agricultural and *grain procurements and the export of agricultural products and raw materials from Ukraine to Russia, particularly during the period of *War Communism and the artificial *famine of 1932–3, laid the foundations for a new, mostly Western, school of Ukrainian PE, whose members also consider Ukraine a Russian economic colony. Another émigré scholar, R. *Rozdolsky, made a major contribution to the methodological reconsideration of Marx's economic theory in the 1950s and 1960s.

BIBLIOGRAPHY
Shymonovych, I. *Istoriia politychnoï ekonomiï (Skorochenyi kurs liektsii)* (Lviv 1923)
Virnyk, D. (ed). *Narysy z istoriï ekonomichnoï dumky na Ukraïni* (Kiev 1956)
Teplyts'kyi, V.; Korniichuk, L.; Shablii, Ie. (eds). *Z istoriï ekonomichnoï dumky na Ukraïni* (Kiev 1961)
Vynar, B. *Materiialy do istoriï ekonomichnykh doslidiv na emigratsiï (1919–1964)* (Munich 1965)
Sorokovs'ka, S. *Istoriia ekonomichnoï dumky na Ukraïni (IX–pochatok XX st.): Bibliohrafichnyi pokazhchyk* (Kiev 1968)
Zlupko, S. *Ekonomichna dumka na Ukraïni: Narysy istoriï ekonomichnoï dumky na zakhidnoukraïns'kykh zemliakh u druhii polovyni XIX st.* (Lviv 1969)
Gritsai, S. *Razvitie ekonomicheskoi mysli po agrarnomu voprosu na Ukraine v perekhodnyi period ot kapitalizma k sotsializmu* (Kharkiv 1970)
Vynar, B. *Rozvytok ekonomichnoï dumky u Kyïvs'kii Rusi* (New York and Munich 1974)
Koropeckyj, I. (ed). *Selected Contributions of Ukrainian Scholars to Economics* (Cambridge, Mass 1984)

V. Holubnychy

Political prisoners. Persons imprisoned for their political beliefs or activities or for committing a *political crime. Imprisonment for political reasons is a modern phenomenon connected to the introduction of criminal and criminal-procedure codes, state courts, and limitations on monarchical absolutism. The first such political prisoners in Ukraine were incarcerated under Austrian rule in the early 19th century and under Russian rule in the later 19th century. Up to that time, particularly during the period of unchecked absolutism, the concept of political prisoner was unclear, and imprisonment and *exile were matters of the monarch's discretion rather than consequences of proven guilt. P. *Polubotok, P. *Kalnyshevsky, and other representatives of the Cossack *starshyna* became political prisoners by tsarist fiat. T. Shevchenko was exiled as a result not of a judicial process but of an administrative decision. Political trials and an increase in the number of political prisoners often occur after 'illegal' means are used to combat a government. Political trials were rare in Ukraine prior to 1914.

Ukrainian SSR. From the beginning of Soviet rule, the authorities and their terroristic apparat sought to liquidate or isolate persons they did not trust because of their social origins or because of their attitudes to the state's economic and cultural plans. Such people were considered counterrevolutionaries and 'wreckers.' Rarely were people repressed for actions that were truly contraventions of state laws. In fact most Soviet political prisoners did not violate any law.

In 1918 the *Cheka was established in Russia to combat political crime, and the first revolutionary tribunals were set up. Their enemy was anyone who opposed Soviet rule or was a potential opponent. The definition of the 'enemy' changed as the Soviet state evolved, and in the 1930s it subsumed even the social class that ostensibly supported the Soviet regime, the poor peasantry. The Cheka was succeeded in 1922 by the *GPU, which was replaced in 1934 by the *NKVD.

In 1934 J. Stalin's decrees 'On the Investigation and Examination of Cases of Terrorist Organizations and Terrorist Actions against the Workers of Soviet Power' and 'On the Examination of Actions of Counterrevolutionary Sabotage and Diversions' were included in the criminal-procedure codes of all Soviet republics. Those decrees allowed the trial and sentencing of persons 24 hours after their being officially accused, or in absentia. No provisions were made for appeals, and death sentences were carried out immediately. Such trials were conducted by oblast courts or military tribunals. All that was required as proof of guilt was a coerced confession or the secret testimony of a state operative. Trials were conducted without the accused's being allowed even the most elementary rights and without the participation of either a prosecutor (the court itself had that function) or a defense counsel. The prosecution had unlimited rights to re-examine earlier trials and to 'correct' verdicts that had been handed down. Consequently, political prisoners in the 1920s and 1930s were often reincarcerated for the very same 'offense,' and Soviet concentration camps were soon filled with innocent people or those whose offenses were trivial.

Ukrainian political prisoners in camps included both those who actively opposed the Soviet regime and those whom the Bolsheviks simply disliked or distrusted: peasants or agronomists opposed to collectivization, religious leaders, priests, believers, writers, artists, soldiers who were captured by or surrendered to the Germans during the Second World War, anyone suspected of having nationalist views, and, after 1944, members or supporters (however marginal) of the Organization of Ukrainian Nationalists or the Ukrainian Insurgent Army.

Although political trials took place in the Ukrainian SSR from its inception, it has been impossible to obtain reliable information about most of them because they were secret or closed. The actual number of such trials has never been determined. Until recently the only available information was drawn from the testimonies and reminiscences of émigrés about the persecution of the Ukrainian Autocephalous Orthodox church in the 1920s; the trials of the alleged members of the *Union for the Liberation of Ukraine in 1930; the trials of D. *Falkivsky, H. *Kosynka, A. *Krushelnytsky and his sons, and O. *Vlyzko in December 1934; the *Trial of the 59 in January 1941; and samvydav accounts of the trials of members of the *dissident movement of the 1960s and 1970s.

After the 20th CPSU Congress in 1956, N. Khrushchev declared that there would no longer be political prisoners, and that only those who truly committed crimes against the state would remain in *labor camps. In fact, however, far from everyone imprisoned under J. Stalin was freed, and in the ensuing years the number of political prisoners grew as the dissident movement gained momentum. In the 1950s, 1960s, and 1970s they included not only members of underground nationalist organizations but also those who publicly defended Ukrainian language rights and spoke out against Russification and political and religious persecution. From the 1960s on most political prisoners were charged with 'malicious hooliganism' or fabricated criminal offenses. The concept of political prisoner thus remained fluid, and it was not defined in the criminal code. The investigation of all 'political' cases was conducted by the *KGB, and the courts were subordinated to it. Thus, one could say that anyone whose case was handled by the KGB was a political prisoner. Many trials continued to be held in camera or with a 'selected' audience.

In April 1991 over 1,100 former political prisoners gathered in Lviv to form the Association of Ukrainian Political Prisoners. I. Hubka was elected chairman of the new organization. In June 1991 the First World Congress of [former] Ukrainian Political Prisoners was held in Kiev. Attended by some 1,000 participants from Ukraine and the West, it elected as its head the president of the recently created All-Ukrainian Society of the [Politically] Repressed, Ye. Proniuk.

The brutal treatment of political prisoners has been documented in the writings of former prisoners, such as V. Moroz, P. Grigorenko, L. Pliushch, M. Osadchy, S. Pidhainy, D. Shumuk, H. Kostiuk, and L. Kopelev. The most comprehensive account is provided by A. Solzhenitsyn in *The Gulag Archipelago*.

Western Ukraine. In interwar Ukraine under Polish rule, the first political prisoners were former active participants in the Ukrainian-Polish War of 1918–19, civic and community leaders, and members of the underground *Ukrainian Military Organization (UVO) and *Communist Party of Western Ukraine (KPZU). During the *Pacification of Galicia in 1930, many members of legal Ukrainian political parties were imprisoned. In the 1930s many members of the KPZU and OUN were tried and imprisoned. Hundreds of OUN members were confined in the *Bereza Kartuzka concentration camp in 1934–9. Altogether in the interwar period, there were some 1,000 Ukrainian political prisoners under Polish rule. Several dozen were executed.

Persons accused of political crimes were tried by jury in Galicia and by regular courts in northwestern Ukraine until 1939. Extraordinary and emergency courts were convened in some cases, as, for instance, in the trials of V. *Bilas and D. *Danylyshyn in 1932. Membership in the

UVO and OUN was punishable by up to several years of imprisonment, and from the mid-1930s by up to 15 years.

Political prisoners organized their own hierarchically structured communities in the Polish prisons and camps. They maintained internal communications, conducted political training, and co-ordinated activity (eg, hunger strikes and demands for Ukrainian newspapers, the rights to correspond, privacy, separate cells, and indictments written in Ukrainian). Such communities were illegal, but prison authorities knew about them and often negotiated directly with their leaders. Those who were sentenced to longer terms were sent to prisons in Poland proper (eg, in Tarnów, Rawicz, Wronki, Katowice, and Siedlce), where they were placed in cells with common criminals.

Political prisoners in Rumanian prisons in the interwar period were mostly OUN members, but there were also some members of some public Ukrainian organizations.

In Transcarpathia political prisoners became a widespread phenomenon during the Hungarian occupation of 1939–44, and hundreds of people were interned in concentration camps without trial. In 1942 in Mukachiv, a military tribunal sentenced in camera over 150 OUN members to terms in the Sátoraljaújhely and Vác prisons. Many Communist underground members and partisans were also imprisoned.

During the Second World War hundreds of OUN members were imprisoned in German concentration camps, notably in *Oświęcim (Auschwitz) and *Sachsenhausen.

A. Bilynsky, M. Prokop

Political sections. Local organs under the CC CPSU intended to enforce Party discipline and central control over particularly important or strategic institutions and bodies. They were established first in the Red Army in the second half of 1918. In 1933 political sections were established at machine-tractor stations (MTS) and at state farms to further Party control in the countryside. In 1934 the political sections at the MTS were reorganized into regular Party committees and merged with the raion Party committees. In 1940 the political sections at state farms were also abolished. They were renewed in 1941–3 to tighten central control during the war. From 1933 to 1956 political sections also functioned in institutions of the transportation industry.

In Ukraine political sections at MTS and state farms played an important role in the *collectivization of agriculture and the famine of 1932–3. Starting in January 1933 thousands of Party members from Russia or the Russified cities of Ukraine were assigned to political sections in the countryside to organize grain requisitions and press the peasants into collective farms. Many of them were armed, and they used violence with complete impunity. After the Second World War political sections were established at MTS throughout Western Ukraine. They were placed under the jurisdiction of the political department of Ukraine's Ministry of Agriculture, and their purpose was to speed up collectivization in the newly acquired territories. In 1953 political sections at MTS and state farms in the USSR were abolished.

Politkovsky, Fedir [Politkovs'kyj], b 1756 in Chernihiv regiment, d 25 July 1809 in Moscow. Physician and scientist. A graduate in philosophy and medicine of Moscow University (1778), he defended a doctoral dissertation at Leiden University on putrefaction (1781) and studied natural science and clinical medicine in Paris. From 1784 he lectured on natural history at Moscow University, and in 1802 he was appointed to the chair of applied medicine and chemistry. He was also director of the university's museum of natural history. He was one of the first medical theorists to propose that most diseases were caused by external factors. He introduced a new method for examining patients and collecting case histories.

Politvydav Ukrainy. A publishing house of political literature in Soviet Ukraine. Founded in Kharkiv in 1922 as the Proletar publishing house, it was located in Kiev from 1934 and had several names before assuming its present one in 1964. It published collections of official Party and government documents; books by Party leaders and prominent Communists; works on the history of the CPSU and CPU; works in Marxist–Leninist theory, philosophy, 'scientific' atheism, politics, economics, law, and sociology; books reflecting the Party line on the history of Soviet Ukraine and the USSR; and Ukrainian-language editions of the collected works of V. Lenin (55 vols) and K. Marx and F. Engels (50 vols). It released over half of all political and socioeconomic books published in the Ukrainian SSR.

Polityka (Politics). A semimonthly political journal published in Lviv from October 1925 to March 1926 by V. Paneiko. Edited by S. Tomashivsky, it propagated conciliatory relations between Poles and Ukrainians in Western Ukraine, criticized extremists in both camps, and supported the Ukrainian National Democratic Alliance. Among its contributors were V. Bachynsky, Rev T. Halushchynsky, I. Krypiakevych, V. Kuchabsky, and O. Nazaruk.

Poliuta, Heorhii (Yurii) [Poljuta, Heorhij], b 1820 in Hrodna, Belarus, d 27 April 1897 in Kharkiv. Veterinary pharmacologist. A graduate in pharmacology of the Vilnius Medico-Surgical Academy (1839) and the veterinary school (1844) and medical faculty (1849) of Kharkiv University, he taught pharmacology and internal medicine at the Kharkiv Veterinary School (1851–9) and the Kharkiv Veterinary Institute (1859–81). He wrote a textbook in veterinary pharmacology (1878) and was a member of the Kharkiv, Warsaw, Vilnius, and Viatka medical societies and the Paris Botanical Society.

Polivanova, Galina, b 1 April 1929 in Krasne Selo, near Leningrad. Opera singer (lyric soprano). She graduated from the Odessa Conservatory (1953; student of I. Raichenko) and then was a soloist of the Odessa Theater of Opera and Ballet. Her operatic roles included the nameparts in G. Puccini's *Madame Butterfly* and G. Verdi's *Aida*, and Oksana in S. Hulak-Artemovsky's *Zaporozhian Cossack beyond the Danube.* Since 1977 she has headed the vocal department at the Odessa Conservatory.

Polívka, Jiří, b 6 March 1858 in Enns, Austria, d 21 March 1933 in Prague. Czech philologist and founder of comparative Slavic folklore studies, member of the Shevchenko Scientific Society from 1914, the All-Ukrainian Academy of Sciences from 1924, and the Prosvita society in Uzhhorod. After studying at Prague, Zagreb, and Vienna (PH D, 1882) universities he taught at Prague University. Having visited the Russian Empire in 1889–90, he became interested in Ukrainian affairs and began to corre-

spond with I. Franko, M. Hrushevsky, V. Hnatiuk, and V. Shcherbakivsky. His comparative studies of Slavic folktales, such as *Anmerkungen zu den Kinder- und Hausmärchen der Brüder Grimm* (5 vols, 1913–32), *Výber ruských pohádek* (A Selection of Ruthenian Tales, 3 vols, 1924–5), *Slovanské pohádky* (Slavic Tales, vol 1, 1932), and *Lidové povídky slovanské* (Slavic Folk Stories, 2 vols, 1929, 1939), show his wide knowledge of Ukrainian folktales. His *Soupis slovenských rozprávok* (Catalog of Slavic Tales, 5 vols, 1923–31) included Ukrainian tales from Transcarpathia. As secretary of the Czechoslovak Ethnographic Society and president of the State Folk Songs Institute he played an important role in collecting Ukrainian folklore and ethnographic material in Transcarpathia and eastern Slovakia. His articles appeared in Kiev, Lviv, and Uzhhorod periodicals, and his reviews of publications in Ukrainian folklore were printed in German and Czech journals.

Polka. A Bohemian folk pair dance that originated in the middle of the 19th century and spread throughout Europe. Its music is quick and has two beats to a bar. In Ukraine it took on some national characteristics in music and choreography and often was named according to places where a variant was popular: 'Poltavska,' 'Poliska,' 'Sanzhary,' 'Pleskach,' and the like.

Poll tax (Russian: *podushnaia podat'*). The basic form of direct taxation in the Russian Empire during the 18th and 19th centuries. It was levied on every male (*dusha* 'soul'), except members of the nobility, clergy, and government administration. The poll tax was introduced by Peter I in 1724 and was extended to Slobidska Ukraine in 1776, to Left-Bank Ukraine in 1783, and to Right-Bank Ukraine in 1796. In 1863 urban residents and tradesmen were exempted from the tax, and only the peasantry was left subject to it. The tax was rescinded in Ukraine and European Russia in 1887.

Pollution. The contamination of the environment, including air, water, and land, with undesirable amounts of material or energy. Such contamination originates from human activities that create waste products. An industrial and intensively farmed republic, Ukraine contains some of the most polluted landscapes in Eastern Europe. Pollution became evident in Ukraine with industrial development in the 19th century. The Soviet drive for rapid industrial development during much of the 20th century greatly intensified pollution at the expense of the environment and society.

Air pollution is especially severe in many of the heavily industrialized cities and towns of southeastern Ukraine, notably in Kharkiv, Luhanske, Donetske, Dnipropetrovske, and Zaporizhia oblasts. Coal-using industries, such as metallurgical coke-chemical plants, steel mills, and thermal power plants, are major point-sources of high levels of uncontrolled emissions of sulfur dioxide, dust, unburned hydrocarbons, and other harmful substances. In particular the air quality in the cities of Dnipropetrovske, Dniprodzerzhynske, Kryvyi Rih, Mariiupil, and Zaporizhia is reported to be among the worst in the entire former USSR. Farther to the east the atmosphere over the cities of Lysychanske and Siverskodonetske has the highest phenol and formaldehyde concentration of any city in the former USSR. Lead-zinc smelting in Kostiantynivka pro-

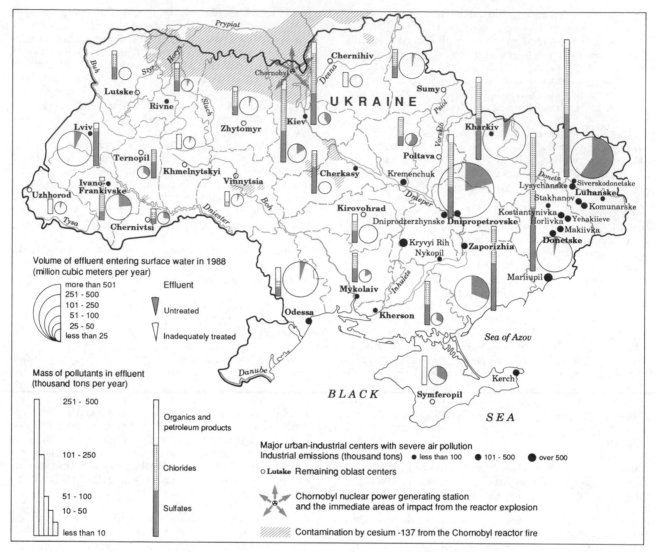

Volume of effluent entering surface water in 1988
(million cubic meters per year)

more than 501
251 - 500
101 - 250
51 - 100
25 - 50
less than 25

Effluent

Untreated

Inadequately treated

Mass of pollutants in effluent
(thousand tons per year)

251 - 500

101 - 250

51 - 100

10 - 50

less than 10

Organics and
petroleum products

Chlorides

Sulfates

Major urban-industrial centers with severe air pollution
Industrial emissions (thousand tons)   ● less than 100   ● 101 - 500   ● over 500

○ Lutske   Remaining oblast centers

Chornobyl nuclear power generating station
and the immediate areas of impact from the reactor explosion

Contamination by cesium -137 from the Chornobyl reactor fire

POLLUTION

duces the largest emissions of heavy metals and their subsequent precipitation and pollution of soils. In what used to be the USSR three Ukrainian cities, Kremenchuk, Rivne, and Cherkasy, rank among the worst 15 cities with regard to increased incidence of human illness, presumably related to air pollution. Other Ukrainian cities with major chronic air pollution problems include Donetske, Kiev, Komunarske, Makiivka, and Odessa.

Despite official claims that approximately 75 percent of all harmful substances potentially discharged from stationary point-sources in Ukraine are being intercepted and neutralized, uncontrolled or poorly controlled smokestacks dot the republic's industrial landscape and make the claims seem far too optimistic.

Over one-third of the emissions into the atmosphere originate from automobile transport. That source, which attains overwhelming proportions in cities with little industry, such as Uzhhorod (91 percent), Yalta, Poltava, and Khmelnytskyi (88 percent each), is aggravated by the use of leaded gasoline and inefficient engines as well as a lack of catalytic converters.

Almost all surface waters of Ukraine belong to the Black Sea and the Sea of Azov drainage basins. The high population density, heavy industrial development, and relatively low freshwater endowment of those basins, and the low governmental priority placed upon environmental protection until very recently, have given rise to chronic and serious levels of water pollution throughout Ukraine. Although a reported 81 percent of Ukraine's industrial water needs are being met by recirculating water-supply systems, in 1988 over 18.7 billion cu m of waste water were being discharged into bodies of surface water in the republic, over 2.6 billion cu m of which were highly polluted. Of those highly polluted waters, 2.145 billion cu m received inadequate purification, and the remaining 489 million cu m were discharged without any treatment whatsoever.

According to Goskompriroda (the Soviet State Committee on the Environment) the Dniester and the Danube are included among the most polluted bodies of water in the territory of the former Soviet Union. Hundreds of small rivers supply water for three-quarters of the villages and half of Ukraine's cities. Widespread fear is growing in Ukraine that a substantial fraction of those water arteries are so polluted as to pose fatal health risks to the people who depend on them. Recent published accounts indicate that serious chronic water pollution levels exist along many stretches of the Azov and Black Sea coasts and estuaries, including many of the popular resort beaches in the Crimea. Groundwater pollution by industrial waste is another major problem in the Crimea. Severe pollution of the Dniester, the Inhulets, and the Donets, as well as the Dnieper and (especially since the 1986 Chornobyl accident) its tributaries, the Prypiat and the Desna, has been acknowledged. About one-half of the chemical fertilizers, herbicides, and pesticides applied in the fields are washed off into rivers. Moreover, surface runoff from industrial territories is highly contaminated and has been reported to be equivalent to 6–12 percent of the surface runoff in Donetske and Kharkiv oblasts. Finally, municipalities and industries still discharge untreated or inadequately treated waste water.

One of the areas suffering most from serious and chronic coastal water pollution is the Sea of Azov. That shallow and previously biologically rich and commercially productive body of water has experienced serious problems of industrial and municipal waste-water contamination and increased levels of salinity since the early 1970s. A primary cause of the sea's ecological deterioration has been the diversion for purposes of irrigation (up to 80 percent) of fresh, but not necessarily pure, water inflow from the Don and the Kuban rivers. As a result the sea's salinity has increased by more than 40 percent since the 1950s. Combined with pollution that increase has resulted in a dramatic drop in fish catches (by 60–90 percent). Despite repeated warnings and special government antipollution resolutions, the conditions in the Sea of Azov continue to deteriorate. Swimming beaches have now been closed along the entire shoreline in Donetske oblast.

Contamination by various radioactive isotopes, such as cesium-137, iodine-131, strontium-90, plutonium-239, and plutonium-240, from the Chornobyl nuclear accident have affected the air, land, and water of Ukraine and vast areas beyond it. Recorded but unreported radiation levels in Kiev a few days after the accident exceeded the maximum allowable levels by a hundredfold. Press reports claim that significant numbers of deaths by radiation sickness and elevated levels of spontaneous abortions, stillbirths, and birth defects and highly elevated rates of childhood leukemia have occurred in the affected areas. Those claims and other concerns are being researched by a host of scientists and medical professionals from Ukraine and other countries. Recent detailed field studies indicate that significant areas of agricultural and forest lands of Ukraine, Belarus, and Russia will remain unsafe for human occupancy and food production for upwards of eight thousand years. Nevertheless, thousands of people who were evacuated after the accident have returned to live and farm in these highly contaminated regions. Thus, the Chornobyl region, in fact, has become something of a living laboratory for the study of nuclear contamination.

BIBLIOGRAPHY

Muntian, V. *Pravova okhorona pryrody URSR* (Kiev 1973)
Volgyes, I. (ed). *Environmental Deterioration in the Soviet Union and Eastern Europe* (New York 1974)
ZumBrunnen, C. 'Water Pollution,' in *The Ukraine within the USSR: An Economic Balance Sheet*, ed I. Koropeckyj (New York 1977)
Ukraïna na hrani ekolohichnoï katastrofy: Dovidnyk, 2nd edn (Toronto 1990)

C. ZumBrunnen

Polohy. VI-17. A city (1989 pop 24,300) on the Konka River and a raion center in Zaporizhia oblast. It arose at the end of the 19th century as a workers' settlement during the construction of a railway line. In 1928–37 the town was called Chubarivka. It was granted city status in 1938. Polohy is a railway junction, and many of its enterprises service the railway. It also has a building-materials plant, a feed factory, an oil-extraction plant, and a metal-stamping plant.

Polohy kaolin and refractory-clay deposit (Polohivske rodovyshche kaoliniv i vohnetryvkykh hlyn). A deposit located on the banks of the Konka River in Polohy raion, Zaporizhia oblast. It covers an area 30 km in length and 5 km in width. The kaolin and clay are found in seams that are 1.5–15 m wide and 3–25 m deep. The estimated extractable reserves are 11 million t of kaolin and 44 million t of refractory clay (1981). The deposit was discovered in 1891 and surveyed in the 1950s. The clay is used to manufacture refractory and ceramic products.

Polonisms. Borrowings from the Polish language. They are found in Ukrainian phonetics (the sporadic Western Ukrainian pronunciation of *ŭ* instead of *l*), morphology (eg, *dobre, zle* instead of *dobri, zli* 'good, evil' pl, the southwestern dialectal form *tom dóbrom rukóm* [SU *tóju dóbroju rukóju*] 'with that good hand'), syntax (eg, the Western Ukrainian *rozxódyt'sja o xátu* [SU *jdét'sja pro xátu*] 'it concerns the house'), semantics (eg, *místo/hórod* 'town'), and, in a narrower sense, vocabulary, particularly as loanwords and calques in the 16th to 17th and 19th to 20th centuries. The number and character of Polonisms differed in the various Ukrainian dialects and periods of development of literary Ukrainian. They were absorbed through the printed medium from literary Polish (especially as calques by educated bilingual speakers) and through personal contacts with the politically and culturally dominant Poles (and, to a lesser extent, Polish agricultural colonies) in Galicia in the 14th to 20th centuries, in Right-Bank Ukraine and Volhynia in the 16th to 18th centuries, and in Left-Bank Ukraine in the 16th and 17th centuries.

The extent of Polish influence on the Ukrainian dialects varied with the time a given region spent under Polish political and cultural domination. The largest number of lexical Polonisms is found in the northern *Lemko dialects, where, as early as the 14th and 15th centuries, *-an-/-am-* replaced the Polish nasal vowels *ǫ, ę* [eg, *gámba, pljantátysia* (Polish [P] *gęba, plątać się*) 'mouth (vulgar), to get tangled'], and *Sian and *Podlachian-Kholm dialects; in those dialects many Ukrainian sound substitutions for Polish lexemes also developed (eg, *vórha, četyrdésjat, ton, kolotýtysja, hadáty* [P *warga, czterdzieści, ten, kłócić się, gadać*] 'lip, forty, this, to argue, to talk'). Polonisms were also used in dialects to mystify vulgarisms (eg, the curse *psjakrev* [P *psiakrew*] 'dog's blood!' [ie, 'damn']). Traces of class- and religious-based Polonisms are evident in certain dialects; the largest number is found in the speech of the Podilian *latynnyky (eg, *popjélec'* [P *popielec*] 'Ash Wednesday') and Subcarpathian petty gentry (eg, *vášec'* [P *Waszeć* 'Your

Grace') suburban and small-town artisans and merchants (eg, *pidogónnja, korčmar* [P *podogonie, karzmarz*] 'crupper, innkeeper'). A particularly high percentage of Polonisms developed in the urban argot and slang of Western Ukraine (eg, *žlob* [P *żłób*] 'unpleasant/stupid person').

In literary Ukrainian the earliest Polonisms were social and political terms used in Galicia and Volhynia (eg, *kmet', zemjane, potreba* [P *kmieć, ziemianie, potrzeba*] 'peasant, landed nobility, need'). Their number increased considerably in the period of the Lithuanian-Ruthenian state and until the second half of the 17th century, particularly in publicistic literature and in chancery documents. In the literary and official language of the 17th century, phonetic Polonisms assumed the stylistic function of Church Slavonicisms – to create word forms different from those used by commoners (eg, *bronjú, krvávyj* [P *bronię, krwawy*] 'I defend, bloody'); perhaps the poetic use of certain Polonisms in songs (eg, *zlóto, gréčnyj* [P *złoto, grzeczny*] 'gold, polite') is a remnant of that use. In 19th- and 20th-century literary Ukrainian many Polish scientific and journalistic calques (eg, *parystokopýtnyj, obnjáty katédru* [P *parzystokopytny, objąć katedrę*] 'cloven-hoofed, to take up a [university] chair') superseded Church Slavonic and Latin terms; many of the calques were taken from Latin or German (eg, *vplyv, lystonósha* [P *wpływ, listonosz* from the German *Einfluss, Briefträger*] 'influence, mailman'). Most German, Latin, Italian, and French and some Czech loanwords entered literary Ukrainian and the dialects via Polish (eg, *lýcar, ratúš(a), cex, vuxnál', pljáška, kóštuváty* [P *rycerz, ratusz, cech, hufnal, flaszka, kosztować*] 'knight, town hall, guild, horseshoe nail, bottle, to cost' from the German *Ritter, Rathaus, Zeche, Hufnagel, Flasche, kosten; rácija, krókis, burják, kólir* [P *racja, krokus, burak, kolor*] 'reason, crocus, beet, color' from the Latin *ratio, crocus, borago, color; škarpétka* [P *skarpetka*] 'sock' from Italian *scarpa; etažérka* [P *etażerka*] 'bookshelf' from French *étagère; vlásnyj, bráma* [P *własny, brama*] 'one's own, gate' from Czech *vlastní, bráma*).

Polonisms can be recognized by the phonetic features distinguishing them from words of Ukrainian origin, especially by stress (eg, *xlópec', krílyk, vydélka, kovádlo, skárha, partáč, sejm, léps'kyj, nikčémnyj, krévnyj, zvómpyty, pónčyk, ks'ondz, pýsar* [P *chłopiec, królik, widelec, kowadło, skarga, partacz, łebski, nikczemny, krewny, zwątpić, pączek, ksiądz, pisarz* 'boy, rabbit, fork, anvil, grievance, tinker, parliament, fine, despicable, relative, to despair, doughnut, priest, scribe/writer'). They should be distinguished from common Polish-Ukrainian lexemes in the Western Ukrainian dialects (eg, *zdumítysja, nadaražátysja, xovstáty, dídyč, perejá* 'to be astonished, to laugh/scoff at, to whip, heir, row of houses').

Western Ukrainian purists waged a struggle against the use of non-calque Polonisms and tried to eliminate the use of old eastern-Ukrainian Polonisms (eg, *doščéntu, dopíru, závše* [P *do szczętu, dopiero, zawsze*] 'totally, just now, always'). In the 1930s there was an official campaign in Soviet Ukraine to expurgate Polish calques that entered the Ukrainian language in the 19th and 20th centuries. They were replaced by Russianisms or by loanword equivalents that had entered the Russian language (eg, *bihún* [P *biegun*] was replaced by the Russian *póljus* [from the Greek *polos*] 'pole'). In contemporary Standard Ukrainian most Polonisms that were absorbed centuries ago and are used in the Left-Bank dialects have been retained (eg, *pévnyj, mic', obicjáty, gedz', kepkuváty, pánstvo* [P *pewny,*

moc, obiecać, giez, kiepkować, państwo 'certain, strength/power, to promise, gadfly, to deride/mock, Mr and Mrs/ladies and gentlemen').

Polonisms in the Ukrainian language have been studied by P. Rastorguev, I. Ohiienko, I. Zilynsky, A. Martel, Z. Stieber, K. Dejna, J. Tarnacki, R. Richhardt, G.Y. Shevelov, L. Humetska, M. Khudash, F. Tkach, V. Witkowski, F. Nepyivoda, D. Hrynchyshyn, V. Akulenko, M. Łesiów (Lesiv), T. Hołyńska-Baranowa, T. Lehr-Spławiński, O. Horbach, M. Onyshkevych, V. Anichenko, and V. Rusanivsky.

BIBLIOGRAPHY
Richhardt, R. *Polnische Lehnwörter im Ukrainischen* (Berlin 1957)
Horbatsch, O. 'Polnische Lehnwörter in den ukrainischen Mundarten,' in *Slavistische Studien zum VI. Internationalen Slavistenkongress in Prag 1968*, ed E. Koschmieder and M. Braun (Munich 1968)
Shevelov, G.Y. 'On Lexical Polonisms in Literary Ukrainian,' in *For Wiktor Weintraub: Essays in Polish Literature, Language, and History Presented on the Occasion of His 65th Birthday*, ed V. Erlich et al (The Hague–Paris 1975)
Strumins'kyj, B. 'Ukrainian between Old Bulgarian, Polish, and Russian,' *Journal of Ukrainian Graduate Studies*, 3, no. 2 (1978)

O. Horbach

The Transfiguration Church in Polonne (1612)

Polonne. III-8. A city (1989 pop 21,700) on the Khomora River and a raion center in Khmelnytskyi oblast. It is first mentioned in historical documents in 996, when Prince Volodymyr the Great granted it to the Church of the Tithes. In the second half of the 12th century a fortress was built there by the Kievan princes to defend the settlement against nomadic raids. In the 13th century the town was attacked by the Tatars. Kievan and Volhynian princes competed for Polonne before it became part of the Principality of Galicia-Volhynia. In the second half of the 14th century it was annexed by Lithuania. It received the rights of Magdeburg law in the 16th century. After the Union of Lublin in 1569, it was acquired by Poland, and in 1648 it was seized by the Cossacks and local peasants. It was recaptured by the Poles, and remained under their rule until the partition of Poland in 1793. Under Russian rule it was part of Novohrad-Volynskyi county, Volhynia gubernia. The town became a center of the porcelain industry in Ukraine and has a museum based on a porcelain factory built in 1889. Today Polonne continues to produce porcelain and decorative ceramics, as well as bricks and building materials.

Nataliia Polonska-Vasylenko

Simeon Polotsky

Polonska-Vasylenko, Nataliia [Polons'ka-Vasylenko, Natalija], b 12 February 1884 in Kharkiv, d 8 June 1973 in Dornstadt, near Ulm, Germany. Historian and archeologist; full member of the Historical Society of Nestor the Chronicler from 1912, the Tavriia Learned Archival Commission from 1916, the Shevchenko Scientific Society from 1947, and the Ukrainian Free Academy of Sciences from 1948; daughter of D. *Menshov and wife of M. *Vasylenko and O. *Morhun. A graduate of the Kiev school of Higher Courses for Women and Kiev University (1913), she was a privatdocent at the university (1916–20) and director of its archeological museum. Under Soviet rule she was a professor at the Kiev Institutes of Geography, Archeology (1918–25), and Art (1927–30) and a research associate at the VUAN (1924–33), the Kiev Central Archive of Old Documents (1925–7), and the AN URSR (now ANU, 1937–41). In 1940 she defended her doctorate and became a professor at Kiev University (1940–1). During the Nazi occupation she directed the Kiev Central Archive of Old Documents (1942–3). As an émigré she was a professor at the Ukrainian Free University (UVU) in Prague (1944–5) and Munich (1945–73; dean of its philosophy faculty from 1966) and at the Theological Academy of the Ukrainian Autocephalous Orthodox church in Munich (1946–52). From 1965 she was vice-president of the Ukrainian Historical Association.

Polonska-Vasylenko is the author of numerous studies in Ukrainian archeology and history and of reminiscences about Ukrainian civic figures and scholars. They include a Russian cultural history atlas (3 vols, 1913–14); booklets on Kiev during the reigns of Princes Volodymyr the Great and Yaroslav the Wise (1944) and the theory of the Third Rome in 18th- and 19th-century Russia (1952); a history of the VUAN and AN URSR (2 vols, 1955, 1958); a monograph (her revised doctoral diss) titled *The Settlement of the Southern Ukraine (1750–1775)* (vol 4–5 [1955] of *The Annals of the Ukrainian Academy of Arts and Sciences in the US*); a book-length article on Soviet Ukrainian historical scholarship in the 1920s and Stalinist repression of Ukrainian historians (*Zapysky NTSh*, vol 173 [1962]); a book on the historical foundations of the Ukrainian Autocephalous Orthodox church (1964); booklets titled *Ukraine-Rus' and Western Europe in 10th–13th Centuries* [sic] (1964) and *Two Conceptions of the History of Ukraine and Russia* (1968); many studies on

the history of the 18th-century Zaporizhia and Southern Ukraine, 14 of which were republished as *Zaporizhzhia XVIII stolittia ta ioho spadshchyna* (The 18th-Century Zaporizhia and Its Legacy, 2 vols, 1965, 1967); a book about Ukraine's prominent women (1969); and a general history of Ukraine (2 vols, 1972, 1976), which appeared in an abridged German translation as *Geschichte der Ukraine von den Anfängen bis 1923* (1988). The fullest bibliographies of her works appear in I. Gerus-Tarnavetska's booklet *Nataliia Polons'ka* (1974) and in *Jahrbuch der Ukrainekunde* (1987).

A. Zhukovsky

Polonsky, Fedir [Polons'kyj], b 27 February 1887 in Reshetylivka, Poltava county, Poltava gubernia, d ? Geologist and mining engineer. In the 1920s he headed the Department of Useful Minerals at the Ukrainian Scientific Research Institute of Geology and oversaw the VUAN Geology Cabinet. He compiled *Slovnyk pryrodnychoï terminolohiï* (Dictionary of Natural Science Terminology, 1928). He was arrested during the Stalinist terror and in 1937 was sent to Siberian labor camps, where he disappeared.

Polonsky, Yoanikii [Polons'kyj, Joanikij], b 1742 in Polonne, Volhynia, d 7 February 1819 in Kamianets-Podilskyi. Orthodox churchman. He studied at the Kievan Mohyla Academy and then taught in theological seminaries and served as rector of the Smolensk Theological Seminary. He was consecrated as the first bishop of Bratslav-Podilia (1795). In 1797 he founded the eparchial seminary in Sharhorod, which in 1806 was transferred to Kamianets. He was elevated to the rank of archbishop in 1801.

Polonyk, Vasyl, b 13 February 1930 in Pryvillia, Izium okruha. Sculptor. He studied at the Voroshylovhrad Art School (1945–50) and under M. Lysenko at the Kiev State Art Institute (1950–6). He has sculpted statues and portraits, such as *At the Mine Face* (1956), *Miner* (1961), *Sapper* (1965), *Female Construction Worker* (1967), and *Portrait of a Worker* (1970), and the Victory monument in Dmytrivka (1976) in the socialist realist style.

Polonynian Beskyd. The highest and most compact section of the Ukrainian *Carpathian Mountains. Running northwest to southeast in a ridge situated between the Inner Carpathian Valley and Maramureş Basin on the southwest and the Middle Carpathian Depression to the northeast, the Polonynian Beskyd reaches heights of over 2,000 m. It connects with the Low Beskyd in the northwest and the East Bukovynian Beskyd in the southeast.

Polotniuk, Daryna. See Vilde, Iryna.

Polotsky, Simeon [Polockij] (secular name: Samuil Petrovsky-Sitnianovich), b December 1629 in Polatsk, Belarus, d 4 September 1680 in Moscow. Churchman and writer; originator of Russian syllabic verse and a pioneering educational and cultural westernizer in Russia. He graduated from the Kievan Mohyla College (1651–2) and also studied at the Vilnius Jesuit college. After taking monastic vows at the Polatsk Epiphany Monastery in 1656, he became a teacher at the brotherhood school there. Having moved to Moscow in 1663, he taught Latin at the Zaikono-spasskii Monastery school from 1665. As a teacher, court poet, and homilist in Moscow he was an erudite representative of Belarusian and Ukrainian culture and of Kievan scholarship. Applying what he had read and studied in Kiev, he wrote many works; they include the scholastic polemical tract *Zhezl" pravleniia* ... (Scepter of Rule ..., 1667), the compendium of knowledge *Venets very kafolicheskoi* (The Crown of the Catholic Faith, 1670), the encyclopedic primer in verse *Vertograd" mnogotsvetnyi* (The Multiflorous Orchard, 1678), the large panegyrical poetry collection *Rifmologion* (1680), a versified translation of the Psalms of David (1680), two volumes of homilies (1681, 1683), and two of the first Russian school dramas. His collected works were published in Moscow in 1953.

Polous, Fedir, b and d ? Zaporozhian Cossack leader. He led a garrison of registered Cossacks at Khortytsia Island and directed their campaign at Budzhak against the Turks. He joined S. Nalyvaiko and M. Shaula in battling Polish-Lithuanian forces in 1594–6, and they advanced as far as Mozyr, in Belarus. In 1597–8 Polous was the Zaporozhian otaman; his further fate is unknown.

Polovets, Semen [Polovec'] (Połowiec), b and d ? Cossack officer. He was colonel of Bila Tserkva regiment (intermittently in 1653–8) and a supporter of I. Vyhovsky. He served as an envoy to Moscow in 1655. He later became a general quartermaster under P. Teteria (ca 1664), an envoy of the Korsun Council to Turkey (1669), and a general judge under P. Doroshenko (ca 1671). Polovets's daughter, Anna (the widow of S. Frydrykevych, colonel of Bila Tserkva regiment in 1664), married Hetman I. Mazepa ca 1668–9.

Polovko, Ivan, b 12 July 1886 in Ichnia, Borzna county, Chernihiv gubernia, d 24 April 1967 in Kiev. Meteorologist and climatologist. He graduated from Kiev University (1912) and remained there to teach and conduct scientific work. He was instrumental in establishing the first meteorological service in Ukraine and worked in the Hydrometeorological Service of the Ukrainian SSR (1919–57). He contributed significantly to the study of climate in Ukraine, as well as of actinometry, thermal systems in the air and ground, and ground radioactivity.

Polovtsians. See Cumans.

Polovy, Vasyl [Pol'ovyj, Vasyl'], b 22 April 1936 in Kryvyi Rih. Painter. Expelled from the Leningrad Institute of Applied Art in 1963 for 'avant-gardism,' he found work as a muralist in Moscow, where he became a member of the Union of Artists and began using Ukrainian themes in his still lifes, landscapes, and figural compositions (eg, *Carolers* [1968] and *Wedding Train* [1968]). He moved to Lviv in 1970. In 1980 he was expelled from the Union of Artists for his religious beliefs. He was reinstated in 1988, but emigrated to the United States in 1990.

Polovyk [Pol'ovyk]. A minor deity in charge of the fields in Ukrainian folk mythology. He was portrayed as a demon of human form, covered with hair, with large claws, calflike ears, a tail, and batlike wings. He lived in holes, ravines, or open grave pits. During harvest festivals a sheaf of uncut wheat twisted into a 'beard' symbolizing future harvests was left in the cleared fields to appease *Polovyk*.

Poloz, Mykhailo (Polozov), b 1890, d 3 November 1937 on Solovets Islands. Political figure. A leading member of the Ukrainian Party of Socialist Revolutionaries, in 1917 he sat on the Central Rada and served as its representative at the war ministry of the Provisional Government. In 1918 he attended the Peace Conference in Brest-Litovsk with the Ukrainian delegation and helped organize an abortive left Socialist-Revolutionary coup against the Central Rada. An advocate of collaboration with the Bolsheviks, he joined Kh. Rakovsky's government in 1919 and served as chairman of the Supreme Council of the People's Economy. As one of the founders of the Ukrainian Communist party (of Borotbists), he opposed its dissolution and absorption in the CP(B)U. On V. Lenin's recommendation he was appointed representative of the Soviet Ukrainian government to the Russian Soviet government, and then served as Ukraine's people's commissar of finance. He was elected to the CC CP(B)U in 1927 and 1930. He was arrested for allegedly belonging to the Ukrainian Nationalist Organization (1930) and tried for plotting with the Bukharin opposition to separate Ukraine from the USSR. He was imprisoned in the Solovets Islands in 1934 and shot a few years later.

Polozhii, Heorhii [Položij, Heorhij], b 23 April 1914 in the Transbaikal region, Russia, d 26 November 1968 in Kiev. Mathematician; corresponding member of the AN URSR (now ANU) from 1967. After completing his studies at Saratov University (1937), he taught there and at Kiev University (1949–68). He obtained important results in the theory of functions of complex variables, approximation theory and numerical methods, mathematical physics, applied mathematics, elasticity, and the theory of filtration. In 1962–6 he developed the theory of the new class of (p,q)-analytic functions and the domain of its application. He also proposed a method for summary representation of numerical solutions of problems in mathematical physics.

Polozov, Viacheslav, b 1952 in Mariiupil, Donetske oblast. Opera singer (dramatic tenor). He was the principal soloist of the Minsk Opera and appeared as a guest performer at the Bolshoi and Kiev opera and ballet theaters. In Italy he appeared at La Scala, the Arena di Verona, and the Opera Roma. After defecting from the Soviet Union he made his American debut (the summer of 1986) in a concert performance of G. Puccini's *Tosca* with the Pittsburgh Symphony. Since then he has performed in New York, Washington, DC, Chicago, and San Francisco opera theaters. His debut with the Metropolitan Opera (January 1987) was in the part of Pinkerton in G. Puccini's *Madame Butterfly*.

Poltava, Leonid, b 24 August 1921 in Poltava gubernia, d 19 April 1990 in New York. Writer. As a postwar émigré he lived in Germany, Paris, Madrid, and the United States (from 1958). He directed the Ukrainian section of Spanish National Radio (1952–3) and was an editor of émigré periodicals, such as *Ukraïns'ki visti, Ukraïnets'-Chas, Svoboda, Vyzvol'nyi shliakh, Krylati,* and *Ukraïns'ke narodne slovo.* He is the author of the poetry collections *Za muramy Berlinu* (Behind the Walls of Berlin, 1946), *Zhovti karuseli* (Yellow Carousels, 1948), *Ukraïns'ki baliady* (Ukrainian Ballads, 1952), *Ryms'ki sonety* (Roman Sonnets, 1958), *Bila trava*

Leonid Poltava   Petro Poltava

(White Grass, 1963), *Valtorna* (1972), *Iz espans'koho zshytka* (From a Spanish Notebook, 1978), *Smak sontsia* (A Taste of Sun, 1981), and *Poemy* (Poems, 1983); the epic poem *Eneïda moderna ...* (The Modern Aeneid ..., 1955); the plays *Choho shumliat' duby* (Why the Oaks Rustle, 1950) and *Zametil'* (The Blizzard, 1967); the story collection *U vyshnevii kraïni* (In the Cherry Land, 1952); the adventure novella *Chy ziide zavtra sontse?* (Will the Sun Rise Tomorrow?, 1955); the historical novel *1709* (1960); several longer poems ('Slovo pro Ukraïnu' [A Word about Ukraine, 1970]) and poems and stories for children; four opera librettos; and a study of the image of S. Bandera in literature and art (1979). He edited the poetry anthology *Slovo i zbroia* (The Word and Arms, 1968) and an anthology of articles and poetry about Kiev (1984).

Poltava, Petro (nom de guerre of Petro Fedun), b 1919 in Brody county, d 23 December 1951 in Stanyslaviv oblast. UPA political officer and OUN publicist. He served on the National Executive of the youth wing of the OUN (Bandera faction) and on the editorial board of *Iunak* (1941–3). Then he was chief of political education for UPA-West (1944–6), chief political officer of UPA (1946–9), chief of the press bureau of the Ukrainian Supreme Liberation Council (UHVR), vice-chairman of its General Secretariat (1950–1), and member of the OUN leadership (1948–51). His articles on the national state, the concept of an independent Ukraine, and the battle plan for Ukrainian independence make him one of the leading ideologists of the UPA. A selection of his works was published under the title *Zbirnyk pidpil'nykh pysan'* (Collection of Underground Writings, 1959). He was awarded the highest UPA decorations: the Gold Cross of Combat Merit and the Medal for Combat in Extreme Circumstances.

Poltava. IV-15. A city (1990 pop 317,000) on the right bank of the Vorskla River and the administrative center of Poltava oblast. It is also a major industrial and communications center.

History to 1914. The archeological evidence shows that the city site was inhabited as early as the 7th or 6th century BC. The city is first mentioned, as Ltava, in the Hypatian Chronicle under the year 1174. In 1240 it was captured by the Tatars, and from the second half of the 14th century it belonged to the Grand Duchy of Lithuania. After a long si-

lence its name appears in a charter of Grand Duke Vytautas in 1430. In 1569 Poltava became part of the Polish Commonwealth. In the Hetman state set up by B. Khmelnytsky it served as a regimental center (1648–1775) and flourished as a trading town. It obtained the rights of *Magdeburg law in the 17th century. The town suffered losses in 1658, when its colonel, M. Pushkar, rebelled against Hetman I. Vyhovsky, and in the 1690s, when it was attacked by the Crimean Tatars. During the Russian-Swedish War (1708–9) it withstood the two-month siege by Swedish and Ukrainian forces and witnessed the allies' defeat by Peter I on 8 July 1709. With the abolition of the Hetman state Poltava became a county center of New Russia gubernia (1775–83), Katerynoslav vicegerency (1784–95), and Little Russia gubernia (1796–1802). Then, for over a century, it served as the administrative center of Poltava gubernia.

Poltava in the 18th century (painting by Angelstein)

At the end of the 18th century Poltava covered a flat plateau that descended abruptly to the Vorskla River and was dissected by several ravines. In the southeastern corner of the plateau stood a fortress, the earthworks and moats of which encircled the administrative buildings, cathedral, and other churches. The Monastery of the Elevation of the Cross was built in 1650 by Pushkar outside the town walls. In 1798–9 Poltava's population reached 7,200.

Cathedral of the Elevation of the Cross (1689–1709) in Poltava

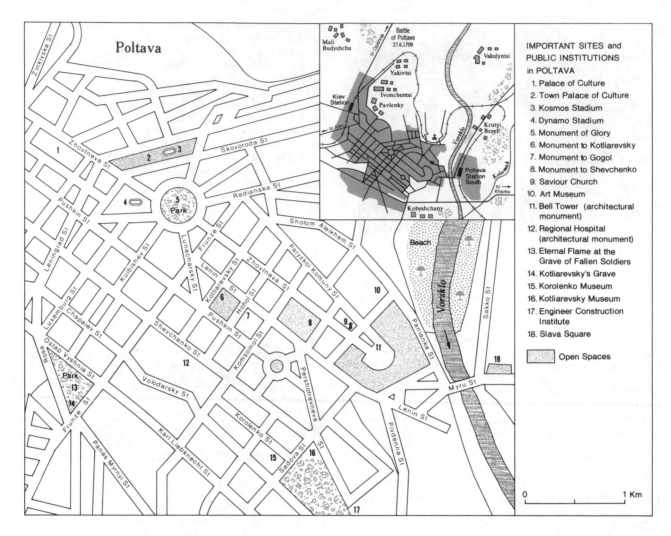

Poltava

IMPORTANT SITES and
PUBLIC INSTITUTIONS
in POLTAVA

1. Palace of Culture
2. Town Palace of Culture
3. Kosmos Stadium
4. Dynamo Stadium
5. Monument of Glory
6. Monument to Kotliarevsky
7. Monument to Gogol
8. Monument to Shevchenko
9. Saviour Church
10. Art Museum
11. Bell Tower (architectural monument)
12. Regional Hospital (architectural monument)
13. Eternal Flame at the Grave of Fallen Soldiers
14. Kotliarevsky's Grave
15. Korolenko Museum
16. Kotliarevsky Museum
17. Engineer Construction Institute
18. Slava Square

Open Spaces

0   1 Km

In the 19th century Poltava, as the gubernia capital and the seat of the governor-general of Little Russia, was completely rebuilt according to a general plan approved by the imperial government in St Petersburg on 10 February 1803. The old fortifications were leveled, and the new town was designed around Kruhla Square, a circular plaza 345 m in diameter. Eight streets radiated at equal angles from the square to the other districts. At the center of the square the Column of Glory was erected in 1811 to commemorate the Russian victory over the Swedish-Ukrainian allies. The main avenue of the town was Oleksandrivska Street (later Radianska). In the 1830s the central square was planted with trees and converted into a public park. The establishment of Poltava eparchy in 1803 contributed to the town's importance, although the bishop's seat was not transferred from Pereiaslav to Poltava until 1847. Prince A. Kurakin, the governor-general of Little Russia, fostered the town's growth.

A textile (woolen-cloth) industry was established in the town by German families, who settled there in 1808. In 1852 the St Elijah Fair, one of the largest wool and horse fairs in Ukraine, was transferred to Poltava from Romen. In 1863 alone, 16.9 million rubles' worth of goods was sold at the fair. New railways built in the 1870s and 1890s provided a stimulus to the town's economy. Toward the end of the 19th century, however, competition from Kharkiv undercut Poltava's economic position. It became a provincial administrative-commercial town with manufacturing limited mostly to cottage industry. The more important branches were food processing (brewing, dairying, flour milling, and tobacco processing) and light industry (hosiery-making). The larger enterprises employed only about 2,000 people. The population grew quite rapidly, from 8,000 in 1802 to 15,500 in 1858, 29,500 in 1863, 53,700 in 1897, and 60,100 in 1902. Despite its population growth and physical expansion, at the beginning of the 20th century Poltava was still a semirural town. In 1882 scarcely 9.4 percent of the buildings were stone, and in 1910 barely 8 percent of the roads were hard surface. The houses in the low-lying suburbs, mostly Cossack homesteads, were completely rural in character. At the end of the 19th and the beginning of the 20th century, a number of graceful, mostly public, buildings, such as the Poltava Zemstvo Building (1903–7), were constructed.

Cultural and political life. In the last quarter of the 18th century Poltava began to develop into an important cultural center. The sons of some regimental officers (Paskevych, Hnidych, and others) studied at German universities. In the 1770s P. Paskevych, a fellow of the standard, opened a bookstore and sold Russian and other foreign publications. The Poltava Slavonic Seminary (1770–80) contributed to the town's cultural life. In the first quarter of the 19th century Poltava continued to develop, and its culture became increasingly Ukrainian. The Ukrainian autonomists, including V. *Kapnist and V. *Lukashevych, were active in the local Masonic lodge, which called itself Love of Truth, and in the *Little Russian Secret Society. D. *Bantysh-Kamensky wrote his *Istoriia Maloi Rossii* (A History of Little Russia, 1822) in Poltava. In the 1840s the local members of the Cyril and Methodius Brotherhood, such as V. Bilozersky, Yu. Andruzky, and D. Pylchykiv, spread its ideas in the region. In 1861 a hromada of about 60 members, including D. Pylchykiv, O. Konysky, V. Loboda, V. Kulyk, M. Zhuchenko, and Ye. Myloradovych, arose in Poltava. It conducted educational and cultural work until the authorities launched their reactionary policies against Ukrainian culture in 1863.

In the 19th century Poltava was an important educational center: a gymnasium was opened (1805), an institute for the daughters of the nobility and a clerical school (1818), a cadet school (1840), and a theological seminary (1797–1819 and 1862–1917). Many Ukrainian cultural figures graduated from the town's schools: M. Drahomanov, M. Ostrohradsky, L. Hlibov, and M. Starytsky were graduates of its gymnasium, and V. Hohol-Yanovsky, O. Bodiansky, L. Borovykovsky, and S. Petliura attended its seminary. N. Gogol studied at the Poltava county school in 1818–19. Later in the century, the Poltava Gubernia Zemstvo played a leading cultural and scientific role: it published over 110 scholarly volumes on the Poltava region, including a collection of materials for assessing the land in the gubernia, a collection of economic statistics, and a series of yearbooks. In 1891 the zemstvo administration established a museum. From 1903 the Poltava Gubernia Learned Archival Commission took the lead in organizing research on the region.

Poltava played a prominent role in the Ukrainian literary renaissance of the 19th century. The writers I. *Kotliarevsky, Borovykovsky, Starytsky (1850s), Konysky, and P. Myrny (1871–1920) and the Russian writer of Ukrainian

Ivan Kotliarevsky's home in Poltava (now a state preserve)

origin V. Korolenko (1903–21) lived and worked in Poltava. In 1838 the weekly *Poltavskie vedomosti* and in 1863 *Poltavskie eparkhialnye vedomosti* began to appear there. After the Revolution of 1905 the Ukrainian weekly *Ridnyi krai* was published by H. Markevych, who established himself as a publisher in Poltava.

Poltava has a long theatrical tradition. One of the first theaters in Ukraine was built there in 1808. Kotliarevsky wrote and staged his plays there in 1818–21. The first professional performances of his plays were done in Poltava by O. Kalynovsky and J. Stein's touring company and involved the actors M. Shchepkin and K. Nalotova. Then K. Solenyk performed in Poltava with Stein's and L. Mlotkovsky's companies. The famous troups of M. Kropyvnytsky, M. Sadovsky, and P. Saksahansky, with stars such as M. Zankovetska, H. Zatyrkevych-Karpynska, I. Tobilevych, and M. Sadovska, visited Poltava. In 1906 Sadovsky organized a company and prepared a repertoire in Poltava for his first permanent theater, which he set up in Kiev in 1907.

In the early 19th century, concerts in Poltava were performed by serf orchestras and choirs. The composers A. Jedlička (from 1848) and P. Shchurovsky (early 1870s) worked there. In the 19th century the sculptor L. Pozen and at the beginning of the 20th century the painters M. Yaroshenko, S. Vasylkivsky, V. Krychevsky, P. Martynovych, and M. Havrylko lived and worked in Poltava.

By the early 20th century the Ukrainian movement was well entrenched in Poltava. The dedication of the Kotliarevsky monument on 30 August 1903 drew to Poltava representatives of the national movement from all parts of Ukraine. In 1906 the Prosvita society was set up. In 1900 a circle of the Revolutionary Ukrainian party was formed in Poltava. Later the Society of Ukrainian Progressives (TUP) was active there.

History after 1914. During the brief period of Ukrainian independence Poltava was an important locus of Ukrainian political and cultural activity. In May 1917 TUP organized a conference of 600 delegates from the Poltava region. A. Livytsky was appointed the UNR gubernia commissioner, and V. Andriievsky, education commissioner. *Vistnyk Poltavs'koho huberniial'noho komitetu* was published in Ukrainian and Russian.

Under the Soviet regime Poltava became an okruha (1925–30), a county (1930–7), and finally an oblast center. During the Second World War it suffered extensive destruction, particularly in 1943, but it was rebuilt in the late 1940s and early 1950s. In 1957 a plan of development for the city was worked out. The city is built up more densely than before: it covers an area of 8,341 ha, of which 2,543 ha are open space and 5,100 are built up. New building ensembles have appeared near Teatralna and Pryvokzalna squares. New residential districts have been developed in the northwest near the Kiev–Kharkiv highway, in the northeast near the Poltava battlefield, and in the valley along the Vorskla River. The city was divided into three administrative raions.

Poltava's population grew from 60,100 in 1912 to 92,600 in 1926, 128,500 in 1939, 143,100 in 1953, and 220,000 in 1970. Of the larger cities in Ukraine Poltava has the highest percentage of Ukrainians. In 1926, 68.3 percent of its residents were Ukrainian, 20.1 percent were Jewish, and 8.9 percent were Russian. In 1959, 80 percent were Ukrainian, 15 percent were Russian, and 3 percent were Jewish.

The population growth can be attributed largely to the change in the structure of Poltava's economy: since the end of the 1920s, industrial development has been emphasized. Today 34.8 percent of the city's jobs are in industry, 11.1 percent are in transportation, and 8.3 percent are in construction. There are over 50 large industrial enterprises in Poltava. The largest branch is the food industry, which accounts for 40 percent of the industrial output. It includes an oil-, lard-, and meat-processing complex, a poultry packing complex, flour mills, and a confectionery factory. Light industry, which includes a cotton-spinning plant, a sewing factory, a knitwear and glove factory, an embroidery factory, and a leather footwear factory, accounts for about 20 percent of the industrial output. About 25 percent of the output is produced by the machine-building and metalworking industries, which include a locomotive repair yard, machine building for chemical industry, a turbine plant, an electrical machinery factory, an engine foundry, and a meat and dairy machinery plant. The chemical industry produces glass and plastics. The building-materials industry and the printing industry are also important in the local economy.

Education and culture. The Ukrainian Learned Society for the Study and Preservation of Historical and Artistic Monuments of the Poltava Region was founded in 1919. It managed to publish the first volume of its proceedings. In the 1920s it was reorganized into the Poltava Scientific Society of the All-Ukrainian Academy of Sciences; its membership included N. Mirza-Avakiants, V. Shcherbakivsky, D. Solovei, M. Rudynsky, V. Shchepotiev, P. Klepatsky, and M. Buzhynsky. Owing to the efforts of the Prosvita society and the support of D. Bahalii, M. Sumtsov, and other faculty members of Kharkiv University, the historical-philological faculty was set up in 1918. In 1920 it was merged with the Pedagogical Institute (the former Teachers' Institute) to form the Poltava Institute of People's Education, which in 1934 was turned into the Poltava Pedagogical Institute. The Soviet pedagogue A. *Makarenko worked in Poltava in 1914–20. Today Poltava has four higher educational institutions besides the pedagogical institute: a civil-engineering institute, an agricultural institute, a co-operative institute, and a medical stomatological institute. There are 11 special secondary schools and 9 vocational schools. The chief research institutes are the Poltava Gravimetric Observatory, the Poltava Agricultural Research Station, and the Poltava Scientific Research Institute of Hog Raising.

The city supports two theaters (the Ukrainian Music and Drama Theater and the puppet theater), a philharmonic orchestra, and six music schools. It has six major museums: the Regional Studies Museum, the Art Museum, the Museum of the Battle of Poltava, and the Kotliarevsky, Korolenko, and Myrny literary memorial museums.

Architecture. A small proportion of the city's historical monuments have been preserved. Only the baroque cathedral (1689–1709) and its four-tier bell tower (1786, restored in 1954–5) remain of the Monastery of the Elevation of the Cross. Of the churches that were once within the town fortifications, only the wooden Transfiguration Church (1705–9), in a stone encasing, and the bell tower (1801) of the destroyed town cathedral (1748–70) survive. The building ensemble on Kruhla Square designed by A. Zakharov in 1805–11 is a fine example of classicism. It includes the residences of the governor-general, governor

A modern residential district in Poltava

(now the building of the oblast trade unions), and vice-governor, the gubernia office building (now the building of the oblast executive committee), the nobles' assembly building (now the Kotliarevsky Cinema), designed by M. Onyshchenko, and the municipal hospital, built by M. Amvrosimov. The Column of Glory at the center of the square was built by T. de Tomon and sculpted by F. Shchedrin. All those buildings were heavily damaged in 1943 and restored in 1950. The building of the Poltava Gubernia Zemstvo (now of the Poltava Regional Studies Museum), designed by V. Krychevsky in 1903–7, painted by S. Vasylkivsky, and ornamented by P. Yukhymenko, embodies the traditional forms of Ukrainian folk architecture. Modern ensembles have been built on Pryvokzalna, Teatralna, and Dzerzhynsky squares. One of the better examples of contemporary styles is the Ukrainian Music and Drama Theater (1952–7), designed by O. Malyshenko and O. Kralova. The more important monuments in Poltava are those to Kotliarevsky (1903, by L. Pozen), Gogol (1915, by L. Pozen), Myrny (1951, by M. Vronsky and O. Oliinyk), and T. Shevchenko (1926, by I. Kavaleridze).

Poltava is one of the greenest cities in Ukraine. Its largest park is Petrovsky. Since 1960 the city has been supplied with natural gas. Its public transportation system uses buses and streetcars.

BIBLIOGRAPHY
Buchnevich, V. *Zapiski o Poltave i ee pamiatnikakh* (Poltava 1902)
Pavlovskii, I. *Poltava v nachale XIX veka* (Kiev 1902)
Rudyns'kyi, M. *Arkhitekturne oblychchia Poltavy* (Poltava 1918)
Andriievs'kyi, V. *Z mynuloho: 1917 rik na Poltavshchyni* (Berlin 1921; 2nd edn, New York 1963)
Ihnatin, I.; Vainhort, L. *Poltava* (Kiev 1966)
Poltavi 800 rokiv, 1174–1974 (Kiev 1974)
Solovei, D. *Rozhrom Poltavy* (Winnipeg 1974)

V. Kubijovyč

Poltava, Battle of. The turning point in the Great Northern War (1700–21) between Sweden and Russia. When Hetman I. *Mazepa learned that Tsar *Peter I intended to abolish the autonomy of the Hetmanate, he began secret negotiations with *Charles XII of Sweden to ensure that Ukraine would not be annexed by Poland in the event of a Swedish victory. After the main Swedish army entered Ukraine, Mazepa openly sided with Charles against Peter.

Because of the harsh winter of 1708–9 and a series of military defeats the situation of the Swedish army in Ukraine became precarious. The assistance Charles expected from Turkey and the Crimean Khanate did not materialize, and the Polish army of King Stanislaus I Leszczyński and a Swedish corps were forced to remain in

Battle of Poltava (18th-century engraving)

Poland to fight the supporters of Augustus II. Charles's only success at that time was enlisting the support of Otaman K. *Hordiienko and his army of 8,000 Zaporozhian Cossacks in April 1709. Semiencircled by the Russians, Charles chose not to retreat to Volhynia (as his generals counseled) but to advance to the Vorskla River and thence on to Moscow via Kharkiv and Kursk. Several fortified cities on the way encumbered Charles's advance. One such city was Poltava, situated at the intersection of important routes to Southern, Right-Bank, and Slobidska Ukraine and the Don region. It was defended by a garrison of 4,300 Russian soldiers and 2,600 Ukrainian volunteers commanded by Gen A. Kelin.

In early May 1709, on Mazepa's advice, Charles decided to capture Poltava. Having failed to take it by storm, he besieged and bombarded the hungry city. Peter arrived to relieve Poltava and decided his army of 42,500 soldiers and 102 cannons would attack the Swedes on 10 July. Cossack forces loyal to Peter under the command of Hetman I. Skoropadksy cut off possible Swedish retreat to the Dnieper between Pereiaslav and Kremenchuk. Charles had 31,000 men but only 4 cannons; 6,000 of his soldiers were engaged in maintaining the siege or guarding the Vorskla rear. Mazepa's small force was held in reserve to protect the Swedish western flank and ensure that Kelin would not attack from the fortress.

When Charles learned, during the night of 7 July, that a Kalmyk army of 40,000 would arrive to reinforce the Russians in two days, he decided to act first and destroy the Russian encampment in a lightning blow. At 5 AM on 8 July the Swedish infantry advanced on Russian positions but was repelled by cavalry. The Swedish cavalry successfully engaged its counterpart but was forced to retreat under heavy fire. The Swedish infantry attacked once more and captured two Russian redoubts, but failed to hold them. As the Swedes attempted to bypass the redoubts, Prince A. Menshikov's troops encircled them and inflicted heavy casualties. Fifty to seventy meters from Russian positions the Swedes met a hail of deadly artillery fire. Panic ensued in their ranks, but they managed to retreat into the nearby Budyshcha forest, where Charles was able, with considerable difficulty, to restore order.

At around 9 AM, having regrouped their forces, both Peter and Charles ordered their troops to advance. Intense Russian artillery fire again created chaos in the Swedish ranks, their center buckled, and a disorderly retreat ensued to the Swedish encampment, which by then had been captured by Russian forces. By 11 AM the Swedes had been routed. Over 9,300 died, and nearly 2,900 were taken prisoner, including Field Marshal K.-G. Rehnskjold and the first minister, C. Piper. The Russian army suffered 1,345 dead and 3,290 wounded. Swedish units that were not captured were led by Gen A.L. Lewenhaupt along the Vorskla River to Perevolochna, whence Charles, Mazepa, and Hordiienko and a contingent of 3,000 Swedes and Cossacks crossed the Dnieper and fled into Turkish-occupied territory. Lewenhaupt's army of 16,000 was forced to capitulate and surrender to Menshikov. According to the fifth provision of the capitulation agreement Cossacks under Swedish command were handed over to the Russians. Most of them were executed on the spot, and the rest were exiled to Siberia.

The Battle of Poltava resulted in Russian military rule in the Hetmanate and increasing curtailment of its autonomy. The Museum of the History of the Battle of Poltava was opened at the battle site in 1950.

BIBLIOGRAPHY

Adlerfelt, G. *The Military History of Charles XII, King of Sweden, Written by the Express Order of His Majesty*, 3 vols (London 1740)

Iunakov, N. 'Severnaia voina: Kampaniia 1708–1709 gg.,' *Trudy Imperatorskago Russkago voenno-istoricheskago obshchestva*, vols 2 and 4 (St Petersburg 1909)

Beskrovnyi, L.; et al (eds). *Poltava: K 250-letiiu Poltavskogo srazheniia: Sbornik statei* (Moscow 1959)

Diadychenko, V. (ed). *250 rokiv Poltavs'koï bytvy (1709–1959): Zbirnyk statei* (Kiev 1959)

Grekov, M.; Koroliuk, V. (eds). *Poltavskaia pobeda: Iz istorii mezhdunarodnykh otnoshenii nakanune i posle Poltavy* (Moscow 1959)

T. Mackiw

Poltava Agricultural Institute (Poltavskyi silsko-hospodarskyi instytut). An institution of higher learning, under the jurisdiction of the Ministry of Agriculture. Founded in 1920 on the basis of a horticultural tekhnikum, the institute has departments of agronomy, zoology-engineering, economics, and the mechanization of agriculture, a correspondence school, and a preparatory section for foreign students. It also maintains an experimental farm, encompassing 3,161 ha, where high-quality plant strains are developed for collective farms in Poltava oblast, and a livestock-breeding station. The library has 325,000 volumes. The student enrollment in 1986–7 was over 4,000. The institute has published scholarly works in both Ukrainian and Russian and grants advanced graduate degrees.

Poltava Agricultural Research Station (Poltavska derzhavna oblasna silsko-hospodarska doslidna stantsiia). One of the oldest agricultural research stations in Ukraine. It was formed in 1956 on the basis of the Poltava Experimental Field (established in 1884), the Poltava Agricultural Research Station (1910), the Ukrainian Scientific Research Institute of Fodder Crops (1931), and the Ukrainian branch of the All-Union Scientific Research Institute of Fodder Crops (1938). The station has developed new techniques for farming and animal husbandry and conducted experiments in selection. Considerable emphasis has been placed on improving feed crops. In the 1950s the station covered 4,200 ha.

Poltava Art Museum

Poltava Art Museum (Poltavskyi khudozhnii muzei). A museum in Poltava, established in 1919. Until 1940 it was called the Poltava Picture Gallery. Originally it consisted of 60 paintings by M. *Yaroshenko and the nationalized private collections of the Kochubei, Galagan, Kapnist, and Repnin families. The museum is housed in a building built in 1912 and designed by P. Aloshyn. During the Second World War over 25,000 objects were removed by the Nazis. Today the museum's departments of 16th- to 19th-century European art, 17th- to early 20th-century Ukrainian and Russian art, and Soviet art contain over 8,000 works, including ones by painters such as J.-B. Greuze, E. Delacroix, L. Cranach, P. Lely, G. van Eyck, V. Borovykovsky, D. Levytsky, O. Orlovsky, P. Levchenko, M. Yaroshenko, S. Vasylkivsky, I. Repin, O. Slastion, I. Hrabar, M. Burachek, F. Krychevsky, M. Hlushchenko, K. Bilokur, N. Onatsky, M. Derehus, O. Shovkunenko, and T. Yablonska.

Poltava Chervonyi Perets Theater (Poltavskyi ukrainskyi peresuvnyi teatr satyry Chervonyi perets). A touring theater established in 1929. Its repertoire consisted of Russian comedy plays and of satirical sketches, songs, and dances united in programs such as *Vohon' po boliachkakh* (Fire on Sore Spots) and *Dovbneiu po holovi* (Clubbed on the Head). Chervonyi Perets toured the Poltava, Kharkiv, and Sumy regions until 1941.

Poltava Civil-Engineering Institute (Poltavskyi inzhenerno-budivelnyi instytut). An institution of higher learning, under the jurisdiction of the Ministry of Higher and Specialized Secondary Education, founded in 1930 on the basis of the agricultural construction engineering faculty of the Poltava Agricultural Institute. The institute has faculties of industrial and civil construction, agricultural construction, sanitation engineering, architecture, and technology, and a correspondence school. The library has over 370,000 volumes. The student enrollment in 1986–7 was 5,000.

Poltava Co-operative Institute (Poltavskyi kooperatyvnyi instytut). An institution of higher learning, under the jurisdiction of the Central Union of Consumers' Societies, founded in 1974. The institute has departments of economics, trade, procurement, and engineering technology. The library has 280,000 volumes. In 1985–6 the student enrollment was 5,000.

Poltava eparchy. An Orthodox eparchy created at the turn of the 18th century. It comprised the territory of Poltava gubernia, much of which had formerly been a part of *Pereiaslav eparchy (hence, the eparchy was also known as Poltava-Pereiaslav eparchy). *Poltavskie eparkhial'nye vedomosti* was the official eparchial organ from 1863 to 1917. At the turn of the 20th century Poltava-Pereiaslav eparchy had over 1,100 parishes and 4 men's and 5 women's monasteries. In 1917, in addition to the titular bishop, the eparchy had one vicar bishop (in Pryluka). In the 1920s Poltava was the center of a church okruha of the Ukrainian Autocephalous Orthodox church. An eparchy was re-established there during the Second World War, under Bishop I. Huba.

Poltava Free Theater (Poltavskyi vilnyi teatr). A theater organized in Poltava in 1817 with a partial cast of the Kharkiv Russian professional troupe of J. Stein and Y. Kalinovsky. Its artistic director was I. *Kotliarevsky. P. Barsov was stage director, and among the actors were M. Shchepkin, K. Nalotova, and I. Ugarov. There being little Ukrainian theatrical repertoire at the time, the theater performed Russian works with only scant Ukrainian reference, such as S. Davidov's *Dneprovskaia rusalka* (The Dnieper Nymph) and the opera-vaudevilles *Udacha ot neudachi* (Fortune from Misfortune) by P. Semenov and *Kazak-stikhotvorets* (The Cossack Poet) by A. Shakhovskoi. Exasperated by the distorted Ukrainian language used by Shakhovskoi, I. Kotliarevsky wrote the plays *Natalka Poltavka* (Natalka from Poltava) and *Moskal'-charivnyk* (The Muscovite-Sorcerer) in 1819 and so founded Ukrainian drama. The Poltava Free Theater was active until 1821.

Poltava Gravimetric Observatory (Poltavska hravimetrychna observatoriia). A research institution founded in Poltava in 1926. Originally it was funded by the Ukrainian Supreme Chamber of Weights and Measures, and conducted studies of the force of gravity in 500 Ukrainian locales. In 1936 it came under the jurisdiction of the AN URSR (now ANU), and since 1964 it has been part of the Institute of Geophysics. The observatory has a staff of approx 60 in two departments and four laboratories, who study the earth's rotation and gravity and the physics of its core and mantle. It operates two zenith telescopes, an AVR-2 refractor, and a prism astrolabe and publishes in Russian a serial devoted to the earth's rotation and tidal deformations. The observatory has been directed by O. (A.) Orlov (1926–34, 1939–51), Z. Aksenteva (1951–69), and M. Panchenko.

Poltava gubernia. An administrative-territorial unit created in Russian-ruled Left-Bank Ukraine in 1802 after the abolition of *Little Russia gubernia. Its territory

(45,894 sq km) was subdivided into 15 counties: Hadiache, Khorol, Kobeliaky, Kostiantynohrad, Kremenchuk, Lokhvytsia, Lubni, Myrhorod, Pereiaslav, Pyriatyn, Poltava, Pryluka, Romen, Zinkiv, and Zolotonosha. In 1803 the gubernia had 1,343,000 inhabitants. A predominantly agricultural, economically backward region, 90 percent of its 2,778,151 inhabitants were peasants in 1897 and 93.6 percent were Ukrainian. The main ethnic minorities were Jews (3.7 percent), Russians (2.4 percent), and Germans (0.7 percent). The gubernia's main commercial centers were Poltava, Kremenchuk, and Romen. The major nonagrarian occupations were brewing, distilling, wine making, flour and lumber milling, sugar refining, and tobacco processing. Because of rural poverty, nearly 200,000 peasants emigrated from the gubernia to Siberia and the Far East in the years 1906–12. As a result of the deaths and emigration that occurred during the First World War and Ukrainian-Soviet War and the transfer of Pereiaslav county to Kiev gubernia in 1920, the gubernia's population dropped from 3,792,100 (only 10.6 percent urban) in early 1914 to 3,566,800 in 1924. In 1924, only 12 percent of the population was urban; 68 percent of the urban population was Ukrainian, 25 percent was Jewish, and 5 percent was Russian. That year the counties were replaced by the seven okruhas of Krasnohrad (formerly Kostiantynohrad), Kremenchuk, Lubni, Poltava, Pryluka, Romen, and Zolotonosha, and in 1925 the gubernia was abolished.

Poltava Gubernia Learned Archival Commission (Poltavska huberniialna vchena arkhivna komisiia). An institution founded in Poltava in 1903 to research the archeology, history, ethnography, and culture of Poltava gubernia and to protect ancient monuments there. Funded by membership dues and the Poltava Gubernia Zemstvo, it soon broadened its scope to include Kharkiv and Kamianets-Podilskyi gubernias and became an important center of Ukrainian regional studies. Its members (eg, I. Pavlovsky, L. Padalka, V. Parkhomenko, V. Vasylenko, V. Modzalevsky, M. Makarenko, V. Shchepotiev, O. Slastion, V. Myloradovych, V. Shcherbakivsky, M. Rudynsky, P. Klepatsky, H. Kovalenko, V. Buchnevych, I. Zaretsky, M. Astriab, I. Zubkovsky, P. Hniedych) produced many monographs and articles. The commission itself published their research and documentary and archival materials in its serial *Trudy Poltavskoi uchenoi arkhivnoi komissii* (15 vols, 1905–17). Separately it published Buchnevych's book on Poltava and its monuments (1902); Pavlovsky's book on 19th-century Poltava (1907), biographical dictionary of the scholars and writers of Poltava gubernia (1912; supplement 1913), and description of Poltava gubernia's archives (1915); the records of the 17th-century Poltava municipal government (ed Modzalevsky, 3 vols, 1911–14); a systematic index to the journal *Kievskaia starina* (1911); Zubkovsky's history of Myrhorod (1912); Padalka's books on the history of Poltava eparchy (1914) and the Poltava region and its colonization (1914); materials on the oral folk literature of Romen county compiled by Hniedych (4 vols, 1915–16); and Makarenko's book on the fortified settlements and kurhans in Poltava gubernia (1917). It operated its own library, initiated the creation of a museum of church antiquities in Poltava, and in 1909 opened the Museum of the Battle of Poltava (the director was Pavlovsky). In 1918 the commission was succeeded by the Ukrainian Scientific Society for the Research and Protection of Monuments of Antiquity and Art in the Poltava Region, which published one volume of *Zapysky* (1919). In 1922 it was renamed the VUAN Poltava Scientific Society, and under that name it published another volume of *Zapysky* (1928). In the early 1930s many of its 70 members were repressed, and the society was abolished.

R. Senkus

Poltava Medical Stomatological Institute (Poltavskyi medychnyi stomatolohichnyi instytut). Established in 1931 as the Kharkiv Medical Stomatological Institute on the basis of the *stomatology faculty of the *Kharkiv Medical Institute, it was relocated and renamed in 1967. Under the Ukrainian SSR Ministry of Health, in 1987 it had medical dental faculties and over 5,000 students. Its library houses 240,000 volumes. Among its prominent scholars during the Kharkiv period were V. *Vorobiov and V. *Danylevsky.

Poltava oblast. An administrative region (1990 pop 1,757,000) along the Dnieper River, formed on 22 September 1937. It covers an area of 28,800 sq km and is divided into 25 raions, 15 cities, 21 towns (smt), and 410 rural councils. The capital is *Poltava.

Physical geography. The oblast lies on a plain sloping in a southwestern direction from the Poltava Plateau (170–202 m high) in the northeast toward the Dnieper River in the south. Most of the plain consists of the Dnieper Lowland (elevation, 60–100 m), which is dissected by river valleys and ravines. The main rivers are the Sula, the Psol, and the Vorskla, which flow southward to the Dnieper. The climate is moderate continental, with an average January temperature of –6.8°C and July temperature of 20.9°C. The annual precipitation is 430–500 mm. In the south the oblast is bounded by the Kremenchuk and Dniprodzerzhynske reservoirs.

Low and moderate humus chornozems account for 65 percent of the oblast's soils. Saline chernozems, gray loess, and bog soils are common in the southern parts, and gray podzolized soils line the river valleys. The oblast lies at the southern edge of the forest-steppe belt. Forests, consisting mainly of oak, ash, elm, and maple, cover 7.1 percent of the land area.

History. The territory of Poltava oblast was settled as early as the Paleolithic Period. In the 10th and 11th centuries it belonged to Kievan Rus' and in the 11th to 13th centuries to Pereiaslav principality. The Tatars controlled the region from the mid-13th century. In the 14th century it was annexed by the Grand Duchy of Lithuania. As part of the Hetman state (1648–1775) it was divided into Myrhorod, Poltava, and Lubni regiments. Under Russian rule the territory was part of Little Russia gubernia (1775–83, 1796–1802), Katerynoslav vicegerency (1784–95), and Poltava gubernia (1803–1925).

Population. The population of the oblast is predominantly Ukrainian (91.3 percent in 1970 and 87.9 percent in 1989). The main minorities are the Russians (7.2 and 10.2 percent) and the Jews. The population density is over 60 persons per sq km: the highest density (approx 93/sq km) is in Poltava and Karlivka raions, and the lowest (40/sq km), in Hlobyne, Mashivka, and Kotelva raions. In 1989, 57 percent of the population was urban. The largest cities are Poltava, Kremenchuk, Lubni, Myrhorod, and Komsomolske.

Industry. The oblast's main industries are machine building and metalworking (34.2 percent of the industrial output), food processing (24.9 percent), fuel (18.3 percent), light industry (7.6 percent), and ferrous metallurgy (5.1 percent). The largest machine-building enterprises are in Poltava (turbines, electric motors, and chemical, meat-packing, and dairy machinery), Kremenchuk (motor vehicles and railway cars), Lubni (machine tools and adding machines), and Karlivka (food-processing machinery). The main branches of the food industry are meat packing (Poltava, Kremenchuk, Lubni, Myrhorod, Pyriatyn, and Hadiache), sugar refining (Lokhvytsia and Kobeliaky), dairying (Poltava and Kremenchuk), fruit canning (Poltava, Myrhorod, and Pyriatyn), vegetable oil and lard (Poltava), distilling (Lokhvytsia), and tobacco products (Kremenchuk). Oil refining is concentrated in Kremenchuk, and there is a large chemical and pharmaceutical plant in Lubni. The largest factories of light industry are in Poltava (cotton spinning, knitwear, and footwear) and Kremenchuk (knitwear). Ferrous metallurgy is concentrated in Kremenchuk. The building-materials industry is well developed in Poltava, Kremenchuk, Lubni, Lokhvytsia, and Kobeliaky. The oblast is well known for its handicrafts: pottery and ceramics (in Opishnia and Myrhorod), kilim weaving (in Poltava and Myrhorod), and embroidery (in Poltava and Reshetylivka).

Agriculture. In 1983 there were 391 collective farms and 73 state farms in the oblast. Of the 2,193,000 ha of farmland in the oblast, 85.6 percent was cultivated, 6.8 percent was hayfield, and 6.6 percent was pasture. Almost 41,000 ha were irrigated, and 37,000 ha were drained. The main crops are grains, such as winter wheat, barley, and corn; industrial crops, such as sugar beets and sunflowers; vegetables and melons; and feed crops. Fruit orchards are commonly found on farms, and vegetable gardening is popular near the large cities. The oblast also supplies 14 percent of the herbs grown in Ukraine. Animal husbandry concentrates primarily on the raising of beef and dairy cattle and swine; in 1990 it produced 225,000 t of meat. Secondary enterprises in that branch include poultry and rabbit raising, beekeeping, and fishing. The total value of the oblast's agricultural output in 1990 was 2,625,900,000 rubles (at 1983 prices) or 5.4 percent of Ukraine's total.

Transportation. In 1989 there were 853 km of railroad in the oblast. The main railway lines are the Kiev–Poltava–Kharkiv, Kiev–Poltava–Donetske, Bakhmach–Romodan–Kremenchuk, and Poltava–Kremenchuk–Odessa. Poltava, Kremenchuk, Romodan, and Hrebinka are the main rail junctions. There are 7,900 km of highways, of which 6,600 are paved. The main highways crossing the oblast are the Kiev–Kharkiv, Kiev–Sumy, Poltava–Kremenchuk, Poltava–Dnipropetrovske, Kremenchuk–Cherkasy, Poltava–Hadiache, and Rozbyshivka–Kremenchuk–Khorol–Myrhorod. River transport on the Dnieper and the Sula (navigable for 146 km) is an economical means of freight transportation. Kremenchuk is the largest river port. The Shebelynka–Kremenchuk–Odessa gas pipeline and the Kremenchuk–Kherson oil pipeline run through the oblast. The main airport is in Poltava.

Poltava Pedagogical Institute (Poltavskyi pedahohichnyi instytut im. V.H. Korolenka). An institution of higher learning, under the jurisdiction of the Ministry of Education, that prepares teachers for the elementary and secondary school system. Founded in 1914 as a teachers' institute, in 1919 it was transformed into a pedagogical institute. It became an institute of people's education in 1921 and was progressively Ukrainized. In 1925 there were 267 students and 32 lecturers. In 1930 it was transformed into an institute of social training, and finally, in 1933, it again became a pedagogical institute. The institute has (1981) six faculties – philology, history, physics-mathematics, natural sciences, pedagogy, and general technical arts – a library with over 380,000 volumes, and a total student enrollment (1986–7) of 5,140.

Poltava regiment (Poltavskyi polk). A military and administrative-territorial unit of the Hetman state in 1648–1775. Originally the regiment had 6 companies, 3 in Poltava and 1 each in Kobeliaky, Balakliia, and Bahachka. By October 1649 it had grown to 19 companies: 3 each in Poltava and Hadiache, 2 in Burky, and 1 each in Bahachka, Balakliia, Kobeliaky, Kovalivka, Kuzemyne, Liutenka, Lukomlia, Opishnia, Rashivka, Vepryk, and Zinkiv. In 1654 there were 19 cities and towns in the regiment. Because of territorial changes, the creation of new regiments, and the interregimental transfer of companies the number of companies in Poltava regiment changed to 14 in 1660, 20 in 1667, and 25 in the 1670s. In the 1670s the regiment's population grew considerably because of the influx of refugees from Right-Bank Ukraine fleeing from Turkish and Crimean Tatar depredations. In the 18th century the number of companies remained stable, at 18 or 19: 2 in Poltava (3 from the 1730s), and 1 each in Bilyky, Budyshcha, Keleberda, Kobeliaky, Kyshynka, Kytaihorod, Maiachka, Nekhvoroshcha, Novi Sanzhary, Orly, Perevolochna, Reshetylivka, Sokolets, Stara Samara, Stari Sanzhary, and Tsarychanka. The regiment had a male population of 13,244 (6,497 Cossacks) in 1649, 13,839 (5,135 Cossacks) in 1721, and 76,499 (12,982 Cossacks) in 1764.

Poltava regiment was the first regiment of the Hetmanate to be abolished. In 1764 most of its companies were disbanded, their Cossacks were transformed into four Russian *lancer regiments, and their territory became part of *New Russia gubernia. The remaining 5 companies (3 in Poltava, 1 each in Budyshcha and Reshetylivka) were abolished in 1775 and also incorporated into New Russia gubernia. Notable colonels of the regiment were M. *Pushkar (1648–58, with interruptions), F. *Zhuchenko (1659–61, 1670–2, 1679–80, 1686–91), P. Hertsyk (1675–7, 1683–6, 1692–5), I. *Iskra (1696–1700), I. Levenets (1701–9, 1725–9), V. Kochubei (1729–43), and A. Horlenko (1743–74).

A. Zhukovsky

Poltava region. A historical-geographic territory in Left-Bank Ukraine. The region is bounded to the southwest by the Dnieper River, to the northeast by the Central Upland and Slobidska Ukraine, to the south by the Dnipropetrovske region (in Steppe Ukraine), and to the north by the Chernihiv region (coinciding with the edge of the forest-steppe and forest zones). Until the 1770s it was part of the Hetmanate, and in the 19th and early 20th centuries it corresponded roughly with the territory of *Poltava gubernia. It included 45,900 sq km (with 3 million inhabitants) of Poltava gubernia, and currently includes 29,000 sq km (1.7 million inhabitants) of *Poltava oblast as well as parts of Cherkasy, Chernihiv, Kharkiv, Kiev, and Sumy oblasts.

Physical geography. The Poltava region lies in the southern section of the forest-steppe reaches of the Dnieper Lowland. It is an undulating plain that descends to the Dnieper from an elevation of 170–200 m in the northeast to 60–100 m in the southwest. Its major rivers include the Dnieper and its tributaries, the Psol, the Sula, and the Vorskla. Its soils are mainly chernozem, although near the Dnieper podzolized chernozem as well as solonchak and solonetzic soils can be found. The region's natural steppe flora has largely disappeared and been supplanted by cultivation. Its forests are mainly oak, but also contain stands of ash, maple, elm, and hornbeam. On the sandy terraces formed by rivers there are also pine, birch, and alder. The climate is continental, with average January temperatures of −5.5° to −7.5° C and July temperatures of 20.9° to 21.7° C. The average annual precipitation is 430–560 mm, and the average growing season is 168 days.

Typical landscape in the Poltava region

The region has deposits of iron ore (in the Kremenchuk district), natural gas and petroleum, peat, clay, and stone suitable for construction. There are also sources of mineral water in the Myrhorod region.

History. At one time the Poltava and Chernihiv regions were the territory of the Siverianians. After the reign of Yaroslav the Wise the Poltava region became part of Pereiaslav principality, which came under the control of the Golden Horde in 1240. In 1360 Lithuania established its hegemony over the area, and then Poland (after the Union of Lublin) incorporated it into Kiev voivodeship. Waves of attacks by Polovtsians and then by Tatars depopulated the region. Resettlement began in the 15th century and reached the Sula River before it halted again in the 16th century. It resumed in the early 17th century, at which time it reached the Vorskla and the Orel rivers.

Under the Cossack Hetman state the territory was divided into Poltava, Pereiaslav, Myrhorod, Lubni, Pryluka, and (partially) Kiev regiments. After the abolition of the regimental system the region became part of Kiev, Chernihiv, and Katerynoslav vicegerencies and New Russia gubernia. After 1796 it was briefly in Little Russia gubernia. Poltava gubernia was formed in 1802, and existed until 1925. In 1914 the gubernia had 15 districts, with an area of 45,893 sq km.

Throughout the 19th century and until 1914 the population of the region increased steadily, particularly after the abolition of serfdom. In 1851 it stood at 1,669,000; by 1897 it had reached 2,778,000, an increase of 67 percent; and in 1914, it was 3,790,000 (36.5 percent higher than the previous level and more than double the 1851 figure). Its natural growth rate was one of the highest in Ukraine and in the Russian Empire. In 1887–97 it stood as 18.8 per 1,000 inhabitants (48.3 births and 29.5 deaths).

At the same time migration out of the region was more substantial than in any other Ukrainian gubernia; it proceeded at about a third of the rate of natural growth. It was prompted mainly by severe rural overpopulation and a lack of industry. Initially most emigrants headed for Southern Ukraine and the Kuban, then, to eastern Transcaucasia, and from the late 19th century, beyond the Urals to Siberia and the Far East. By 1897 an estimated 443,000 people (representing approx 16 percent of the region's remaining population) had left. In 1897–1914 over 360,000 more people left (about 22 percent of all emigrants from the nine Ukrainian gubernias). Another 100,000 to 200,000 Poltavians worked seasonally outside the region as agricultural laborers or as miners in the Donbas. The names of certain settlements in Subcaucasia and Asia (Poltava, Poltavka, Novopoltava) bear witness to the presence there of Ukrainians from the Poltava region.

In 1897 approx 90 percent of the population of the Poltava region was rural. The largest cities were Kremenchuk (pop 58,600), Poltava (the gubernial center, 53,000), Romen (22,500), and Pryluka (19,100). The district towns included Hadiache, Lubni, Myrhorod, Pereiaslav, Pyriatyn, and Zolotonosha. The region had the highest proportion (93 percent) of Ukrainians of all Ukrainian territories. The minority groups included Jews (4 percent, mainly in Kremenchuk and Poltava), Russians (2.6 percent, mainly in the cities and some towns of Kostitantynohrad county), and Germans (0.2 percent). In all of the cities except Kremenchuk Ukrainians consituted a majority of the population.

Three-quarters of the gross domestic product of the region was tied to agriculture, and it supported 90 percent of the population. After the abolition of serfdom peasants owned 50 percent of the land, and landowners controlled 47 percent. Although peasants gradually bought up most of the arable land, population growth offset their gains. In 1877 the average size of a private holding was 10.9 desiatins; in 1905 it was 9.6. In 1910 there were 450,000 agricultural households in the region, of which 23,900 were landless and 189,200 had very little land (less than 3 desiatins). It is estimated that on the eve of the First World War 47.3 percent of households in the Poltava region could not subsist on the revenues and produce generated by the land they controlled.

Agricultural methods in the region were outdated (most farmers used the three-field system). Seventy-five percent of the territory's area was under cultivation. Peasants plowed 75 percent of their holdings, and the larger landowners plowed 57 percent of theirs. Grains were the dominant crop, although tobacco was also raised extensively (the Poltava and Chernihiv regions being major tobacco producers in the Russian Empire in the 19th century). In 1913, 27.1 percent of the land was used for growing spring wheat, 25.8 percent for rye, 13.7 percent for barley, 13.4 percent for oats, 5.3 percent for winter wheat, 3.1 percent for millet, 3 percent for potatoes, 1.1 percent for hemp, 1.1 percent for sugar beets, and 0.5 percent for flax. The average grain yield per harvest in 1883–1900 was 7–8 centners per ha. Through the efforts of zemstvos in introducing new methods, yields increased steadily, and by 1913 they ranged from 10.7 to 12.7 centners per ha. Zemstvos also set up breeding stations for the improvement of livestock strains (particularly cattle). Peasant livestock, however, was both quantitatively (in 1913 there were 14 horses, 22 cattle, 20 sheep, and 13 pigs per 100 inhabitants) and qualitatively deficient. Nevertheless the region enjoyed a large agricultural surplus (about 25 percent of its grain production, less for livestock).

Local industry was geared primarily to the refining of raw materials to satisfy the needs of the local population. Enterprises were small and employed a total of about 40,000 people (1913). Eighty-five percent of industrial production of the area was connected with foods (milling, various oils, distilling, brewing, sugar refining, etc). Kremenchuk and Poltava were the principal centers. Local crafts were highly developed (about 6,000 establishments) and included pottery (in Opishnia), basket-weaving, carpet-weaving, embroidery (Reshetylivka, Dihtiari), tanning, and woodworking. Zemstvo administrations encouraged the development of such craftsmanship through special schools, courses, and workshops and the work of itinerant instructors. In 1913 zemstvos spent 419,000 rubles on such a program in the Poltava region (49.7 percent of the total zemstvo expenditures in the field for the nine Ukrainian gubernias).

The Poltava region played an important role in the history of the Ukrainian people in the 19th and early 20th centuries. From 1825 it took the lead in Ukrainian civic affairs away from the Chernihiv region, which had been the culturally and politically dominant region of the Hetmanate in the 18th and early 19th centuries. Several factors played a role in the change. The geography of the region made it particularly suitable for agricultural development. The colonization of Southern Ukraine, the growth of trade routes to the Black Sea and Sea of Azov, and the shift of marketplaces southward in the early 19th century accelerated the region's rise to economic pre-eminence. The economic security and estate privileges enjoyed by the larger landowners and the presence of a number of Cossack officers' families afforded them the independence to preserve Ukrainian traditions in ideology and everyday life and to preserve the Ukrainian character of the people who lived on their estates.

The fact that the headquarters of the Russian imperial administration for Left-Bank Ukraine (the Little Russian general governorship) was in Poltava from 1800 until the 1830s also came into play. Some of its leading officials, including Princes A. Kurakin and N. *Repnin, were sympathetic to Ukrainians and assisted the local gentry in furthering their careers and in securing local social and political influence. The leading Ukrainian noblemen of the imperial establishment either had landholdings or served as administrators in the Poltava region. Their position helped to cushion the region from the anti-Ukrainian campaign waged by the imperial authorities in the late 19th century.

In addition to Poltava itself the regional cultural and political centers included cities such as Hadiache, Lubni, Myrhorod, and Pryluka as well as the estates of nobles in Kybyntsi (D. *Troshchynsky), Obukhivka (V. *Kapnist and his heirs), Khomutets (*Muravev-Apostol family), Yahotyn (Repnin family, formerly of the *Rozumovskys), Trostianets (*Skoropadsky family), Sokyryntsi (*Galagan family), and Kachanivka (*Tarnovsky family). The society of these families proved to be receptive to the ideas of T. *Shevchenko and the *Cyril and Methodius Brotherhood. It also helped to establish the Ukrainophile nature of the region's zemstvo administration, which until 1917 was perhaps the most nationally conscious and active body in community and cultural life in central and eastern Ukraine.

Many notable 19th- and 20th-century Ukrainian cultural and political figures were born or were active in the Poltava region. They include the scholars D. Bantysh-Kamensky, P. Chubynsky, M. Drahomanov, V. Horlenko, V. Lesevych, I. Luchytsky, M. Makarenko, M. Maksymovych, M. Markevych, M. Nomys, M. Ostrohradsky, I. *Pavlovsky (who focused much of his work on the Poltava region in particular), O. Potebnia, V. Shchepotiev, Ya. Shulhyn, M. Storozhenko, and M. Tuhan-Baranovsky; the writers B. Antonenko-Davydovych, P. Biletsky-Nosenko, M. Drai-Khmara, N. Gogol, L. Hlibov, V. Hohol-Yanovsky, Ye. Hrebinka, V. Kapnist, V. Korolenko, I. Kotliarevsky, Lesia Ukrainka, A. Metlynsky, P. Myrny, O. Pchilka, V. Samiilenko, M. Starytsky, O. Storozhenko, A. Teslenko, O. Vyshnia, and L. Yanovska; the composers V. Borovykovsky and M. Lysenko; the kobza players O. Slastion and O. Veresai; the religious activists P. Levytsky and O. Yareshchenko; and the political activists O. Markovych, B. Martos, M. Mikhnovsky, S. Petliura, M. Porsh, and O. Shlikhter.

After the Revolution of 1917 the Poltava region was vitally important to the new Ukrainian state. Many of the state's governmental leaders (A. Livytsky, Martos, Petliura, Porsh) were born there and became active there. In 1917 the Ukrainian Democratic Agrarian party was formed in the region. Other local political activists of the period included V. Lypynsky, Mikhnovsky, and S. and V. Shemet.

After the transition to centralized Soviet rule the Poltava region no longer played the special role it had held in Ukrainian affairs. In 1925, upon the abolition of the gubernias, the region was divided into five okruhas (Poltava, Kremenchuk, Lubni, Pryluka, and Romen). In 1932 it was divided between Kiev and Kharkiv oblasts. In 1937 Poltava oblast was established and divided into 25 districts. It incorporated approx 62 percent of the area of the former Poltava gubernia. (See *Poltava oblast.)

BIBLIOGRAPHY
Lazarevskii, A. 'Poltavshchina v XVII v.,' KS, 1891, no. 9
Padalka, L. Proshloe Poltavskoi territorii i ee zaselenie (Poltava 1914)
Andriievs'kyi, V. Z mynuloho: 1917 r. na Poltavshchyni (Berlin 1921)
Liatoshyns'kyi, M. Istorychnyi narys terytoriial'noho skladu Poltavshchyny (Kiev 1929)

V. Kubijovyč, O. Ohloblyn

Poltava Regional Studies Museum (Poltavskyi kraieznavchyi muzei). One of the oldest and richest museums in Ukraine, established in 1891 as the Poltava Zemstvo Natural Science and History Museum and renamed the

Poltava Regional Studies Museum

Poltava Gubernia Zemstvo Museum in 1893. In 1905 it acquired K. Skarzhynska's valuable collection of manuscripts, books, and historical documents. Later the museum was housed in part of the famous zemstvo building designed in the Ukrainian Moderne style by V. *Krychevsky and built in 1903–6. Decorated on the inside by S. Vasylkivsky and M. Samokysh, it was destroyed during the Second World War and rebuilt in the 1960s. In 1920, reorganized into the Central Proletarian Museum of the Poltava Region, it took over the museum, library, and archives of the former Poltava eparchial depository of antiquities, part of the collection of the Poltava Theological Seminary, and many valuable objects from local churches and monasteries. Renamed the Poltava State Museum in the 1920s (directed by N. Onatsky in 1933–7), it got its present name in the late 1940s, when its collections were rebuilt. The museum has departments of natural science (based originally on V. *Dokuchaev's chernozem collections), prerevolutionary history, and Soviet history. The Chornukhy and Dykanka historical-regional museums and the Mate Zalka Literary-Memorial Museum in Bilyky, Kobeliaky raion, are its departments, and the Panas Myrny, Vladimir Korolenko, and Ivan Kotliarevsky literary memorial museums in Poltava, the Lokhvytsia and Myrhorod regional museums, and the David Guramishvili Literary Memorial Museum in Myrhorod are its branches. (In 1986 there were plans to open Anton Makarenko, Yurii Kondratiuk, and Sydir Kovpak memorial museums and a ceramics museum in Opishnia as new departments.) The museum contains over 180,000 objects, including some of the most valuable collections in Ukraine of archeological objects, historical documents and manuscript books, kilims, folk dress, embroidery, and carvings, Opishnia ceramics, and weapons; a permanent exhibition of the Poltava region's folkways and folk art; and a diorama of the Poltava region's animal world. A large collection of articles about the history of the museum and its holdings was published in 1928, and guidebooks to the museum were published in 1915 and 1978.

Poltava Scientific Research Institute of Hog Raising (Poltavskyi naukovo-doslidnyi instytut svynarstva). The major center co-ordinating research in *hog raising in Ukraine. It was founded in 1930 on the basis of the animal husbandry section of the Poltava Agricultural Research Station and was under the jurisdiction of the All-Union Academy of Agricultural Sciences. In 1982 it had seven departments and three laboratories. The institute develops new hog breeds (including the Myrhorod hog), feeds, medicines, and farming techniques. It also offers graduate courses in hog raising and qualification upgrading programs, and publishes the scientific collection *Svynarstvo* (Hog Raising).

Poltava Ukrainian Drama Society. See Poltava Zhovten Theater.

Poltava Ukrainian Music and Drama Theater

Poltava Ukrainian Music and Drama Theater (Poltavskyi ukrainskyi muzychno-dramatychnyi teatr im. M. Hoholia). A theater founded in 1936 on the basis of the former Kharkiv Komsomol Ukrainian Music and Drama Theater, which itself emerged from an opera studio. Its first artistic director was V. Skliarenko, and among the actors were Ye. Khutorna, Ye. Zolotarenko, V. Varetska, and P. Kolesnyk. During the Second World War the theater was located in Zirianovsk, in Kazahkstan; it returned to Poltava in 1944. In 1969 the theater celebrated the bicentenary of I. Kotliarevsky's birth by staging an adaptation of his *Eneïda* (Aeneid). In 1987 its artistic director was V. Miroshnychenko, and V. Herashchenko was its principal stage designer.

Poltava Zhovten Theater (Teatr Zhovten u Poltavi). Originally the Poltava Ukrainian Drama Society, established in 1914 to popularize classical Ukrainian drama among workers and peasants. It was a touring theater in 1917–24, serving the oblast and local Soviet army divisions. In 1924 it was reorganized into the Rukh Theater and toured the Donbas. In the fall of 1924 a group of its actors under H. Vanchenko formed the Zhovten Theater, which was active until 1925.

Ivan Poltavets-Ostrianytsia

Poltavets-Ostrianytsia, Ivan [Poltavec'-Ostrjanycja], b 26 September 1890 in Subotiv, Chyhyryn county, Kiev gubernia, d 1957. Military and political activist. A graduate of the cadet school in Chuhuiv (1912), he served in the Russian army during the First World War. After the Revolution of 1917 he was one of the organizers of the Free Cossacks, and in April 1918 he became general chancellor in the Hetman government. From 1919 he lived in Munich, where he founded the *Ukrainian Free Cossacks (initially as the Ukrainian National Cossack Union) and published the paper *Ukraïns'kyi kozak* (1923–4). He tried to obtain German financial support for his organization by claiming to represent 150,000 members in Ukraine and abroad but was regarded as an opportunist and adventurer. He consorted with the Nazis and supported A. Hitler even before the unsuccessful 1923 Beer Hall Putsch.

Poltavochka. A folk dance similar to the polka. It originated in the Poltava region.

Poltavska. The former name of Krasnoarmeiskaia Stanitsa, Krasnodar krai, the Kuban. Almost all its inhabitants perished in the famine of 1932–3. The survivors were later deported.

Poltavs'kyi kooperator (Poltava Co-operator). A semimonthly organ of the Poltava Association of Consumer Co-operatives, published in Poltava in 1918–22. It contained articles on political, cultural, social, and economic developments, and reports on co-operative affairs.

Poltavs'kyi selianyn (Poltava Peasant). A semimonthly popular agricultural journal published in Poltava in 1925–9 by the Poltava Agricultural Research Station. It was edited by O. Tutkevych. In 1930 it was called *Za nove selo*.

Poltoratsky, Marko [Poltorac'kyj], b 28 April 1729 in Sosnytsia, Chernihiv regiment, d 24 April 1795 in St Petersburg. Singer (baritone) and choir conductor. After studying at the Latin School in Chernihiv and the Kiev Bursa he was recruited as a singer for the imperial court by O. Rozumovsky and brought to St Petersburg in 1745. He became a member of the court choir in 1746 and later its conductor (from 1753) and director (1763–95). His debut in 1750 with the Italian opera company, imported to the Russian court in 1730, marked the first time a non-Italian appeared on stage with the troupe, and is commonly regarded as the beginning of 'Russian' opera. He contin-

ued to appear as a soloist in Italian operas until 1770. His students included M. Berezovsky and D. Bortniansky.

Poltoratsky, Oleksii [Poltorac'kyj, Oleksij], b 1 December 1905 in Chernihiv, d 15 March 1977 in Kiev. Writer, publicist, and critic. He graduated from the Kiev Institute of People's Education in 1926. Together with M. Semenko he edited the Kharkiv futurist journal *Nova generatsiia* from 1927 to 1930. After the war he was editor in chief of *Ukraïna* (1948–52), *Vitchyzna* (1948–52), and *Vsesvit* (1958–71). As a theoretician of Ukrainian futurism in the 1920s he was often harshly attacked by official criticism until he conformed to the Party line. His *Literaturni zasoby* (Literary Devices, 1929) was one of the first vulgarizations of the sociological method in Ukrainian literary criticism. In the 1930s he published a few travelogues, including *Ostanni dni burkhaniv* (The Last Days of the Storms, 1930) and *Ataka na Gobi* (Attack on the Gobi, 1936). He also wrote a few stories about N. Gogol (1941, 1954, 1957), which were in line with the official interpretation of Ukrainian-Russian friendship. After the Second World War he published a number of essays concerning his travels outside the USSR, as well as the war novel *Liudy idut' u vohon'* (People Go into the Fire, 1965). He abetted the KGB's quest for the destruction of Ukrainian culture by writing pamphlets against Ukrainian political émigrés (eg, *Ukraïns'ki burzhuazni natsionalisty – nailiutishi vorohy ukraïns'koho narodu* [Ukrainian Bourgeois Nationalists, the Fiercest Enemies of the Ukrainian People, 1953]), apologia for Russification and for the repression of defenders of Ukrainian culture, and attacks on dissidents, such as S. Karavansky, V. Chornovil, and I. Dziuba.

I. Koshelivets

Poltva Land Drainage and Melioration System. An aqueduct system covering 2,800 ha around the Poltva River near Lviv. It drains the floodplains of the Poltva and carries treated sewage from Lviv. The water is used for irrigating and fertilizing the land.

Polubotok. A family of Cossack *starshyna* in the Chernihiv region, probably of burgher origin. Yarema (Ieremiia) Polubotok was a member of Chernihiv's *magistrat* in 1637–42, and Artem was a burgher there in the mid-17th century. Artem's son was Leontii *Polubotok, and his son was Pavlo *Polubotok. For most of I. Mazepa's hetmancy Leontii and Pavlo, who had been removed from their military-administrative posts, concentrated on developing trade and industry (glassworks, mining) on their estates. Pavlo's sons, Yakiv (d 15 April 1734 in Brody, Galicia) and Andrii (d 28 November 1744), were fellows of the standard from 1726 and 1728 respectively, as was Pavlo's grandson, Vasyl (d 29 June 1768), from 1752. In the 18th century the Polubotoks were the wealthiest *starshyna* family in the Left-Bank Hetman state, where they owned 3,200 peasant households. The last male Polubotok died in the second half of the 18th century, and the family's properties were inherited by the *Myloradovych and Lashkevych families.

Polubotok, Leontii, b ?, d ca 1695. Cossack officer; father of P. *Polubotok. He was a supporter (and an indirect relation) of I. Samoilovych. He served as Chernihiv regimental chancellor (1668), company captain (1671–2), general standard-bearer (1672–7), and general osaul (1678–81); later he became colonel of Pereiaslav regiment (1683–7 and 1689–90). Polubotok was one of a number of *starshyna* officers opposed to I. Mazepa's increasingly unilateral exercise of power during the 1680s, and he was a major player in an intrigue against the hetman which involved the Crimean khan. After his plans were exposed in 1688, Polubotok was forced to resign his commission, but he retained his freedom under the protection of Muscovy and spent his remaining days on his estate.

Hetman Pavlo Polubotok

Polubotok, Pavlo, b ca 1660, d 29 December 1724 in St Petersburg. Cossack statesman; son of L. *Polubotok. A graduate of the Kievan Mohyla College (1679), he became a *notable military fellow in 1689. Because of his involvement in Cossack *starshyna* conspiracies against Hetman I. Mazepa, he was barred from government positions until 1706, when he was appointed colonel of Chernihiv regiment. After Mazepa's defeat at the Battle of Poltava in 1709 and flight abroad, Polubotok submitted his candidacy for the position of hetman, but Emperor Peter I did not trust him and supported I. Skoropadsky's candidacy instead. In compensation Polubotok was given many properties (including the town of Liubech and over 2,000 peasant households) in the Hetmanate and Slobidska Ukraine, which gift made him the wealthiest member of the Cossack *starshyna*. After Skoropadsky's death in 1722, Polubotok became acting hetman. Peter, however, forbade the election of a new hetman and created the *Little Russian Collegium to rule in the Hetmanate in place of the General Military Chancellery. Polubotok's repeated appeals to Peter to abolish the collegium, fully restore the *starshyna*'s privileges, and allow the election of a new hetman, coupled with D. Apostol's submission of the *Kolomak Petitions, angered the emperor and resulted in the arrest of Polubotok and his closest associates in November 1723. Polubotok was imprisoned in St Petersburg's Peter and Paul Fortress, where he died a year later, and his properties were confiscated and redistributed.

Polubotok had an abiding interest in Ukrainian history and wrote a chronicle describing the events of 1452–1715, which was included in the diary of his son-in-law, Ya. *Markovych. His defense of Ukrainian (albeit *starshyna*) rights and his tragic fate made him a hero in the eyes of his contemporaries and subsequent generations of Ukrainians. He was lionized in *Istoriia Rusov* and by such early 19th-century Ukrainian historians as D. Bantysh-Kamensky and M. Markevych. In 1917 the Ukrainian Central Rada named the *Polubotok Regiment in his honor. Pop-

ulist (O. Lazarevsky, A. Yefymenko) and Soviet historians, however, have presented him in a harsh light by concentrating on his personal ambitions and overt class interests. V. Modzalevsky and M. Vasylenko have offered a more objective assessment. Non-Soviet 20th-century Ukrainian historians, though admitting that he was primarily a spokesman for the Cossack elite and its privileges, have viewed Polubotok as a defender of the principles of Ukrainian autonomy articulated in the Pereiaslav Treaty of 1654.

Polubotok has been depicted in T. Shevchenko's poems 'Son' (Dream) and 'Velykyi l'okh' (Great Vault) and in K. Burevii's historical drama *Pavlo Polubotok*. His great wealth and traditional popularity gave rise in the 1860s to the legend that he had deposited a massive amount of gold in Lloyd's Bank in London. The legend caused a stir before the outbreak of the First World War and still reappears occasionally in the press.

BIBLIOGRAPHY
Miloradovich, G. 'Opis' imushchestv Polubotka,' *Chteniia v Moskovskom obshchestve istorii i drevnostei*, 1862, no. 3
Lazarevskii, A. 'Pavel Polubotok: Ocherk iz istorii Malorossii XVIII veka,' *RA*, 1880, no. 1
Modzalevskii, V. *Pavel Polubotok* (St Petersburg 1905)

O. Ohloblyn

Polubotok Regiment (Polk im. hetmana P. Polubotka). A Ukrainian military unit which sprang up spontaneously in June 1917 at the Russian army distribution depot in Kiev. Its elected commander was Lt Romanenko. The Central Rada attempted unsuccessfully to send the regiment out of Kiev to the front. During the night of 17–18 July 1917 the regiment, on its own initiative and without informing the Central Rada or the Ukrainian Military Committee, tried to take control of Kiev by driving out representatives of the Russian Provisional Government. The action was not supported by the Central Rada, which allowed Russian troops in Kiev to disarm the regiment and send it on 27 July to the combat zone. Some of its soldiers were arrested and imprisoned for several months. The episode remains controversial and unclear.

Poludenny, Mykola [Poludennyj], b 10 April 1938 in Dnipropetrovske. Opera singer (baritone). A graduate of the Kiev Conservatory (1961), he sang as a soloist with the Kuibysheve (1966–74) and Dnipropetrovske opera theaters. His repertoire spans over 30 roles, including the name-parts in A. Rubinstein's *The Demon*, P. Tchaikovsky's *Eugene Onegin*, G. Verdi's *Rigoletto*, and W. Mozart's *Don Giovanni*, and Figaro in G. Rossini's *The Barber of Seville*, Koshovy in Yu. Meitus's *The Young Guard*, and Babushkin in L. Kolodub's *Dnieper Rapids*.

Poluektov, Nikolai, b 13 October 1910 in Odessa, d 15 April 1986 in Odessa. Analytical chemist; AN URSR (now ANU) full member from 1972. A graduate of the Odessa Medical-Analytical Institute (1931), he worked at the Odessa Rare Metals Institute (1932–41, 1945–58), headed the Odessa laboratories of the ANU Institute of General and Inorganic Chemistry (1958–77), and from 1977 headed a department at the new ANU Physical-Chemical Institute in Odessa. His research dealt with physical-chemical methods of determining rare elements by flame photometry, atomic absorption, and spectrophotometric and luminescence techniques. He also studied the chemistry and spectroscopy of lanthanide complexes and introduced several novel organic reagents for their detection and determination. His monograph *Techniques in Flame Photometric Analysis* (1961) was published in English translation.

Polyclinic. A *clinic with multiple services or departments, in which many types of diseases are treated, and preventive *public health measures are organized. Usually associated with a *hospital, equipped with x-ray apparatus, and designed to be the primary clinical resource for the population, polyclinics attended to over 80 percent of the medical complaints in the former Soviet Union. There may be separate polyclinics for children, students, women, or adults, and they may be divided by medical field or occupation. In 1980 there were over 8,000 clinics and polyclinics in Ukraine.

Polygraphic industry. See Printing industry.

Polymetallic ores. Ores which combine a basic metal, such as lead or zinc, with others, such as silver, gold, cadmium, and so forth. They are found in Ukraine most commonly in the Donbas, in the southeastern and southern reaches of the Ukrainian Crystalline Shield, and in Transcarpathia and Subcarpathia.

Polyphonic singing (Ukrainian: *partesnyi spiv*, from the Latin *partes*, parts, voices). A form of a cappella church singing prevalent in Ukraine in the 16th to 18th centuries. Works for polyphonic singing were composed for 4 to 12 voices, in some instances even for more than 20. The most widespread form was the polyphonic concerto, in which a full choir (*tutti*) alternated with individual voices of the choir or groups within it. The form developed in Kiev and spread to other Ukrainian cities, such as Lviv, Lutske, and Ostrih. The compositions of M. *Dyletsky, S. Pekalytsky, and others who wrote works for polyphonic singing were in the repertoire of many choirs.

Polytechnical education (*politekhnichna osvita*). Instruction in the basics of science and technology, particularly in their practical application to industry and agriculture. Introductory polytechnical education was said to be fundamental to the Soviet general education schools, and was implemented through classroom instruction, visits to agricultural and industrial enterprises, and practical experience developed in school workshops. The mandate of polytechnical education is to familiarize students with the theory and practice of the main sectors of production and to provide a medium in which students can become proficient in the use of basic equipment and tools. This kind of education differs from vocational education in that no attempt is made to prepare pupils for any particular occupation. Polytechnical education was considered to be a central component of the Marxist-Leninist theory of education, as set forth in the 1919 Eighth Congress of the CPSU.

In the early years of Soviet rule the Ukrainian People's Commissariat of Education placed little emphasis on polytechnical education in general education schools; instead it focused on professional and social education in the *seven-year schools. Ukrainian educational authorities argued that polytechnical education was a utopian ideal, given the economic devastation and ruin of the re-

public. They maintained that the path to an eventual polytechnical education system lay in specific professional and vocational training. In 1928, however, a Plenum of the CPSU Central Committee decreed the unification of the system of technical education, and the Ukrainian People's Commissariat of Education introduced a differentiated seven-year school: in rural areas it entailed agricultural training, and in urban centers, experience in factories. Hence, schools for collective-farm youth (see *Schools for peasant youth) and *factory seven-year schools were established. In 1930–1 the 1,088 schools for collective-farm youth accounted for 53.4 percent of rural schools, and the 900 factory seven-year schools represented 78 percent of all urban seven-year schools in Ukraine. In general, however, the combination of schooling and industry retained a purely formal character: polytechnical education in elementary and secondary schools consisted only of basic industrial arts and home economics, components which were entirely removed from the regular schooling process.

In 1937 industrial instruction in the schools was terminated, school workshops were closed, and polytechnical education was essentially discontinued. Following the Nineteenth Congress of the CPSU (October 1952) industrial training courses were reintroduced into the school curriculum. Under N. Khrushchev an attempt was made to unify general and polytechnical education with industry (as outlined in the December 1958 law 'On the strengthening of the ties between school and life, and on the further development of public education in the country'). The new scheme introduced a massive polytechnical component into the curriculum, with practical orientation of subject matter, the teaching of manual skills, involvement of pupils in the production processes and manual jobs, and the creation of direct school-enterprise links. To accommodate the extra activities the complete secondary education program was extended by one year (from 10 to 11), and work activities were added to the school holiday period. The reform met with considerable opposition from educators, parents, and enterprise managers, and schoolchildren failed to develop an interest in the program. Financial and administrative difficulties as well as a shortage of equipment contributed further to the failure of the program. In November 1966 a new law on the general school system, which downplayed the polytechnization of education, was enacted. Subsequently a December 1977 education decree, which strongly emphasized the need for a 'link with life' (in order to meet the growing labor shortage), represented a move toward the greater development of vocational schools rather than a move toward polytechnical education.

The difficulties encountered in the polytechnization of the general schools were again addressed by the 1985 school reform, which emphasized the need to acquaint pupils, in theory and practice, with all the main branches of production. In 1988, however, a report to the CPSU Central Committee noted that little progress had been made in this endeavor. Instead of polytechnical education, schools were providing primitive vocational training in highly inadequate school facilities.

More advanced polytechnical instruction is conducted through polytechnical and industrial institutes, higher-level educational establishments which train engineers for various industrial enterprises, and other institutions of higher learning. In 1984 there were 6 polytechnical institutes and 2 industrial institutes, and 44 other technical institutions of higher learning in Ukraine.

BIBLIOGRAPHY
Riappo, Ia. *Narodnia osvita na Ukraïni za desiat' rokiv revoliutsiï* (Kharkiv 1927)
Siropolko, S. *Narodnia osvita na Soviets'kii Ukraïni* (Warsaw 1934)
Tomiak, J.J. *Soviet Education in the 1980s* (New York 1983)
I. Bakalo, N. Freeland, B. Krawchenko

Polyvaniv Yar settlement. A fortified Trypilian settlement of the mid-3rd to early 2nd millennium BC near near Polyvaniv Yar, Kelmentsi raion, Chernivtsi oblast. Excavations in 1949–51 by T. *Passek revealed the remains of surface and semi-pit dwellings, flint workshops, a variety of tools, copper items, earthenware cult statues of women, and tableware decorated with designs in red, white, and black.

Pomeranchuk, Isaak [Pomerančuk] (Pomeranczuk, Izaak), b 20 May 1913 in Warsaw, d 14 December 1966 in Moscow. Theoretical physicist; full member of the USSR Academy of Sciences from 1964. A graduate of the Leningrad Polytechnical Institute (1936), he began his scientific career in 1935 in Kharkiv at the AN URSR (now ANU) Physical-Technical Institute under the tutelage of L. *Landau and in co-operation with O. *Akhiiezer. In the two years Pomeranchuk spent in Kharkiv, he made breakthrough contributions to the theory of the scattering of light by light and on the role of electron-electron interactions in the resistivity of pure metals at low temperatures. In 1937 he followed Landau to Moscow and went on to become one of the most productive and internationally known Soviet physicists.

Pomeranian culture. An archeological culture of the 6th to 2nd century BC found in eastern Poland and adjacent borderlands in Ukraine and Belarus. The people of this culture lived in unfortified settlements in surface and semi-pit dwellings with post construction. Their major activities were agriculture and animal husbandry. They practiced a distinctive burial rite of placing cremated remains into earthenware urns decorated with facial images. The urns were placed usually into stone vaults in the ground and not covered with a kurhan. Scholars believe the Pomeranian culture to have been an early Slavic grouping.

Pomichna [Pomična]. V-12. A city (1989 pop 13,200) in Dobrovelychkivka raion, Kirovohrad oblast. It originated as a workers' settlement in 1868 during the construction of a railway line. It received city status in 1957. Most of its inhabitants work in enterprises servicing the railway and in farming. It produces building materials and canned fruits.

Pomology. See Orcharding and fruit farming.

Pomynky. Commemorative rites for a deceased person held by his or her relatives and connected with a church requiem (*panakhyda* or *parastas*). One form of *pomynky*, the *tryzna*, was observed in Ukraine and among other Slavs into the 10th century. It was held right after the burial and consisted of warrior games and contests followed by a banquet. The custom of the commemorative meal was condemned by the church because of the pagan elements in it, but it became well established among the common people and, known as *tryzna, stypa, parastas, umerlyny,* and *komashnia,* exists to this day. Usually the funeral meal takes place right after the burial at the home of the deceased or at the grave. The 40th day after death (*sorochyny, shestyny*) is observed with special solemnity: a *panakhyda* is conducted in church or at home, and then the guests are hosted generously. The dead are commemorated also on specific days during the year, particularly on *provody* (the Tuesday of St Thomas's Week, right after Easter, or the first Sunday after Easter). After the liturgy everyone goes (sometimes in procession) to the cemetery, where each family symbolically shares the blessed Easter meal with its deceased members. In more recent times, especially in towns, the funeral meal has become an occasion for speeches, funeral dirges, and expressions of condolence. The Soviet authorities attempted to substitute a 'day of community remembrance' for the folk and church *pomynky.* On this day the relatives and friends of the deceased go in procession to the cemetery, make speeches, and decorate the grave.

B. Medwidsky

Mykola Ponedilok

Ponedilok, Mykola, b 24 September 1922 in Novomyrhorod, Yelysavethrad county, Kherson gubernia, d 25 January 1976 in New York. Writer. Having been displaced by the Second World War, Ponedilok found himself in Germany in 1943 and the United States in 1949. Although his literary career began in 1947 with the publication of a short story, he devoted himself at first to writing and translating dramas for the V. Blavatsky and Y. Hirniak theaters in DP camps. He translated the *Antigone* and *Médée* of J. Anouilh and some farces by J. Priestley and wrote *Znedoleni* (The Misfortunate), *Liaitenant Fliaiev* (Lieutenant Fliaiev), and *A my tuiu chervonu kalynu ...* (And We Will [Raise] That Red Viburnum ..., 1957). Ponedilok's forte as well as his fame, however, was in humor and satire. His short stories and feuilletons about émigré life and life under the Soviet regime were tinged with lyricism and filled with a good-natured love for his characters in particular and humanity in general. They appeared in the collections *Vitaminy* (Vitamins, 1957), *Sobornyi borshch* (Pan-Ukrainian Borshch, 1960), and *Smishni sl'ozyny* (Funny Tears, 1966; Eng trans 1982). Progressively, however, humor and satire gave way to nostalgia, and Ponedilok wrote lyrical reminiscences of his lost native land and youth. He began the trend with *Hovoryt' lyshe* *pole* (Only the Field Speaks, 1962) and continued it with *Zorepad* (Shooting Stars, 1969), *Riatuite moiu dushu!* (Save My Soul!, 1973), and the posthumous *Dyvo v resheti* (A Marvel in the Sieve, 1977).

D.H. Struk

Poniatenko, Prokip [Ponjatenko], b 1880 in Poltava, d ? Civic and political activist. He was active in the Poltava and Katerynodar branches of the Revolutionary Ukrainian party and an editor of its Lviv publications (1905) and the journal *Vil'na Ukraïna* in St Petersburg (1906). In 1917, under the Central Rada, he served as UNR consul in Katerynodar. Under the UNR Directory he was a member of the diplomatic mission to Warsaw (1919–20). His fate after his return to the Kuban in 1920 is unknown.

Poniatowski, Stanisław. See Stanislaus II Augustus Poniatowski.

Rev Petro Poniatyshyn

Poniatyshyn, Petro [Ponjatyšyn], b 15 July 1877 in Semeniv, Terebovlia county, Galicia, d 4 February 1960 in Skokie, Illinois. Ukrainian Catholic church and community leader in the United States. Upon ordination (1902) he emigrated to the United States and became involved in Ukrainian religious and civic life there. After the death of Bishop S. Ortynsky he was appointed administrator of the Greek Catholic diocese in the United States (1916–24). During the First World War he chaired the *Ukrainian National Committee (1918–22) and organized support for the independence struggle in Ukraine and relief for Ukrainian war victims. His articles appeared in almanacs and collections published by the Ukrainian National Association.

Poninka. III-8. A town smt (1981 pop 8,700) in Polonne raion, Khmelnytskyi oblast. It was founded in the 18th century. Its cardboard and paper factory, which was established in 1858, is the largest of its kind in Ukraine.

Ponomarenko, Anatolii, b 2 February 1922 in Katerynopil, Zvenyhorodka county, Kiev gubernia. Scenery designer and graphic artist. A graduate of the Kiev Art School (1946), he has designed scenery for the Kiev Artistic Film Studio, the Kiev Young Spectator's Theater, and the Kiev Ukrainian Drama Theater; books, such as the Ukrainian translation of J. Reed's *Ten Days that Shook the World* (1958) and T. Shevchenko's works in three volumes (1963); and the Ukrainian section of the USSR pavilion at Expo '67 in Montreal.

Ponomarenko, Yevhen, b 9 March 1909 in Kherson. Actor. He began his theatrical career in the Odessa Derzhdrama studio in 1926 (pupil of L. Hakkebush and V. Vasylko), and he stayed with the theater until 1936, when he joined the Kiev Ukrainian Drama Theater. He played over 100 roles on stage and in films; he had a large creative range in the contemporary Ukrainian and non-Ukrainian repertoire. His biography by L. Sydorenko appeared in Kiev in 1979.

Ponomarev, Stepan, b 15 August 1828 in Konotip, Chernihiv gubernia, d 13 November 1913 in Konotip. Philologist and bibliographer; corresponding member of the Russian Academy of Sciences. He graduated from Kiev University (1852) and became a teacher in Poltava and in Konotip (from 1872). Using S. Zhelezniak and 41 other known pseudonyms, he contributed to *Kievskaia starina*, *Kievlianin*, and many Russian scholarly journals and newspapers, in which he published articles about, bibliographic guides to, and the correspondence of various Ukrainian and Russian scholars and writers, including T. Shevchenko, M. Maksymovych, L. Borovykovsky, O. Lazarevsky, and N. Gogol. He compiled biobibliographic dictionaries of Ukrainian writers born in Kiev, Poltava, Volhynia, Podilia, and Chernihiv gubernias; only the one for Chernihiv gubernia, *Zemliaki* (Countrymen, 1898), was published. Among his many other works are a booklet on Maksymovych (1872), books of materials for the biography of Metropolitan E. Bolkhovitinov (1867) and for a dictionary of pseudonyms (1881), biobibliographic dictionaries of Bolkhovitinov and Archbishop F. Gumilevsky, a volume of Gogol's letters to Maksymovych (1877), and a bibliography of works about Gogol (1882). A complete bibliography of his 688 works (1913) and a volume of letters written to him (1915) have been published.

Pontic Kingdom (Pontus). A Hellenized Persian state in northeastern Anatolia founded ca 364–302 BC. It reached its zenith under its last king, Mithridates VI Eupator (ca 115–63 BC), who annexed the *Bosporan Kingdom (107 BC) and the *ancient states on the northern Black Sea coast. Pontus became a Roman province in the 1st century AD.

Ponyrka, Denys, b 1746 in Poloshky, Hlukhiv county, Chernihiv gubernia, d ca 1790. Physician. A graduate of the Kievan Mohyla Academy (1766) and the Moscow Medico-Surgical School (1771), he received a doctoral degree from Strasburg University (1780) and then worked at the St Petersburg Admiralty Hospital and at the Border Quarantine Service in Vasylkiv (1783–9). His publications dealt with the treatment of syphilis, smallpox, and the plague.

Ponyzia [Ponyzzja]. According to the Galician-Volhynian chronicle, a land in the middle Dniester Basin. Some historians believe that it extended from southern Galicia to the Black Sea (P. Hrytsak), others limit it to central Podilia along the Dniester (I. Krypiakevych), and Soviet historians define it as the territory between the Boh and the Dniester rivers. It is likely that Ponyzia already belonged to Halych principality during the reign of Yaroslav Osmomysl. It was definitely part of that principality during the reign of Mstyslav Mstyslavych, who ceded Galicia in 1227 to his son-in-law, Prince Andrew of Hungary, but remained ruler of Ponyzia. As the power of Halych waned, it lost control of Ponyzia.

Ponyzia's population consisted primarily of settlers from Galicia engaged in farming, fishing, and river transportation from Galicia to the Black Sea. Semisedentary *Chorni Klobuky and *Cumans who had come as mercenaries of Galician princes also lived there. The region's main towns were Ushytsia (its original center), Bakota (which became the center), Kamianets-Podilskyi, Kaliius, Onut, and Vasyliv. After the Mongol invasion of 1239–41 Ponyzia was dominated by the Tatars. Beginning in the late 13th century its name no longer appears in historical sources. In the 14th century *Podilia emerged as the name of the region that encompasses the former Ponyzia. (For a bibliography, see *Galicia-Volhynia, Principality of.)

Poor Cossacks. See *Holota*.

Popadia [Popadja]. V-4. A peak (elevation, 1,740 m) in the Gorgany Mountains of Transcarpathia oblast. Situated near the sources of the Limnytsia and the Teresva rivers, the mountain is marked by deposits of fallen rock. It is covered with fir and fir-beech forests on its lower elevations and brush in its upper reaches.

Zorian Popadiuk

Stepan Popel

Popadiuk, Zorian [Popadjuk, Zorjan], b 21 April 1953 in Sambir, Lviv oblast. Dissident. A student at Lviv University, he was arrested in March 1973 and sentenced to seven years' imprisonment and five years' exile for his human rights activities and for editing an unofficial student journal, *Prohres*. He served his term in the Vladimir prison and in labor camps in the Mordovian ASSR, where he participated in hunger strikes and other protests in defense of prisoners' rights. Exiled to Yakutia in 1980 and Kazakhstan in 1981, he was arrested there in September 1982 and sentenced in March 1983 to 10 more years in labor camps and 5 years' exile. He was released in the spring of 1987. That year he became a founding member of the Ukrainian Initiative Group for the Release of Prisoners of Conscience.

Popasna. V-19, DB II-4. A city (1989 pop 31,100) and raion center in Luhanske oblast. It arose in 1878 when the Donetske railway was being built. In 1938 it was granted city status. Today Popasna is a railway junction and industrial city. Most of its machine-building and metalworking industry serves the railway. It also has a glass plant and a sewing factory.

Popel, Antin [Popel'] (Popiel, Antoni), b 1865 in Szczakowa, Poland, d 1910 in Lviv. Sculptor. A graduate of the Cracow School of Fine Art (1884) and the Vienna Academy of Art (1888), he taught painting and sculpture at the Lviv Polytechnic and worked as a sculptor. He sculpted some of the decorative statues at the Lviv Opera Theater, the composition *Justice* for the Palace of Justice in Lviv, and several monuments, including the A. Mickiewicz monument in Lviv (with M. Parashchuk, 1905–6), the J. Korzeniowski monument in Brody, and the T. Kościuszko monument in Washington, DC.

Popel, Markel [Popel'], b 1825, d 1900. Russophile church figure. As a Greek Catholic priest in Galicia, he published religious textbooks, edited the newspaper *Nedilia*, and taught catechism in Ternopil and Lviv. In 1867 he arrived in Kholm with other Russophile clergymen from Galicia. There he lectured in liturgics and served as pastor of the Kholm cathedral. In 1871 he became administrator of the *Kholm eparchy. Popel favored the conversion of the Uniates to Orthodoxy. In May 1875 he headed a delegation to the tsar that petitioned for the transfer of 120 parishes in the eparchy to the Orthodox church. For this he was consecrated bishop of Lublin; later he served as bishop of Podilia and then of Polatsk and Vitsebsk. From 1889 he was also a member of the Holy Synod of the Russian Orthodox church.

Popel, Mykhailo [Popel', Myxajlo] (Popiel, Michał), b 1817 in Kulchytsi, Sambir circle, Galicia, d 1903 probably in Sambir. Polonized Galician Uniate petty noble and politician. He studied at the Sambir gymnasium, and in 1836 he was leader of a clandestine circle of Ukrainian students there. He wrote, in mixed Polish and Ukrainian, an anti-Austrian, anti-*szlachta*, pro-Polish-independence poem, 'Rusyn na praznyku' (A Ruthenian at the [Religious] Festival), which was circulated and hand-copied (and published in *Zhytie i slovo* in 1896). In 1837 Popel and 18 other members of the circle were arrested and put on trial. Popel was imprisoned from December 1839 to August 1843. During the Revolution of 1848 he joined the Polonophile *Ruthenian Congress, organized the National Guard in Sambir, and published the pamphlet *Adzov k bratiam* (Appeal to [My] Brothers), calling for Polish-Ukrainian solidarity to fight Austrian and tsarist oppression. That year he was elected to the first Austrian parliament, where he spoke out for the abolition of serfdom without cash indemnity payments to the landlords. He also advocated abolishing all the peasantry's traditional rights to forests and pastures. From 1853 he practiced law in Sambir; he served as the town's mayor (1861–7) and a member of the Galician Diet (1867–82) and the Sambir County Council (1867–73, 1879–90). In the diet he opposed the notion of the national equality of Poles and Ukrainians, on the ground that they were two branches of one nation, and he objected to the claims of the Uniate clergy to represent the Ruthenians.

Popel, Stepan [Popel'], b 15 August 1907 in Komarnyky, Turka county, Galicia, d 27 December 1987 in Fargo, North Dakota. Chess champion and philologist. He graduated from Lviv University (M PHIL, 1931; M JUR, 1938), taught French and Latin in a Lviv gymnasium (1930–9), and was a professor at the Lviv Pedagogical Institute (1939–41) and Lviv Technical Institute (1941–4). He was personal secretary to Metropolitan A. *Sheptytsky (1929–44). In 1928 he won the Galician chess tournament in Lviv and became the champion of Lviv (1930) and Ukraine (1944). He wrote *Pochatky shakhista* (Beginnings of a Chess Player, 1943). As a postwar refugee in France (1946–55) Popel won first prize in 14 of the 18 international Western European chess tournaments in which he took part, and was a three-time champion of Paris and four-time champion of England. After emigrating to the United States in 1956, he was a chess champion in the states of Michigan, Minnesota, Illinois, Nebraska, and North Dakota (five times).

Popilnia [Popil'nja]. IV-10. A town smt (1986 pop 5,700) and raion center in Zhytomyr oblast. It arose in the 1860s during the construction of a railway line. It has a stone quarry, an asphalt factory, and a food industry.

Rev Oleksander Popiv

Popiv, Oleksander, b 24 August 1891 in Kupievakha, Kharkiv gubernia, d 6 May 1958 in Fort Wayne, Indiana. Pedagogue, literary scholar, and church activist. A graduate in history and philology of Kharkiv University (1915), he was a lecturer in pedagogy there (1918–25) and then a professor and dean of the Faculty of Social Education of the Kharkiv Institute of People's Education (1925–33), head of its department of pedagogy (1925–9), and director of the Ukrainian Scientific Research Institute of Pedagogy (1926–30). In 1933 he was arrested and expelled from all of his posts. He was ordained a priest of the Ukrainian Autocephalous Orthodox church (UAOC) by Archbishop N. Abramovych in 1943 and made pastor of St Andrew's Cathedral in Kiev. He fled to Lviv in 1944, then to Prague, and finally to Germany, where he was a refugee in Aschaffenburg (1945–8) and Leipheim (1949–50). In 1950 he emigrated to the United States, where he was curate of parishes in Hamtramck, Michigan (1950–2), and Fort Wayne (1952–8).

Popiv was one of the founders of the *Ukrainian Autocephalous Orthodox Church (Conciliar), which split from the UAOC in 1948, and in the United States he served on the church's council. He also helped found and edited (to 1954) its organ, *Pravoslavnyi ukraïnets'*. In the 1920s he published studies in pedagogy, Ukrainian literary studies,

and a series of Ukrainian classics, and edited the journal *Ridna shkola*.

Popko, Hryhorii, b 1852 in Timashevka Stanytsia, the Kuban, d 1883 near Nerchinsk, Transbaikal oblast, Siberia. Populist revolutionary. He studied at a seminary in Stavropil (1870), an agricultural school in Moscow (1874), and the University of Odessa, where he met and worked with Ye. Zaslavsky. In 1876 he represented Odessa at the gathering of Lavrovist populists in Paris, and he traveled to Lviv, Vienna, and Geneva before returning to Ukraine. He later became involved with V. *Osinsky and the terrorist actions of the (Southern) Executive Committee of the Russian Socialist Revolutionary party. Popko assassinated the adjutant of the Kiev police, Baron Geiking, in May 1878, and was sentenced to hard labor for life.

Popko, Ivan, b 1819, d 1893. Historian and ethnographer. After graduating from the Moscow Theological Academy in 1841, he joined the Black Sea Cossacks and eventually attained the rank of lieutenant general. He wrote several books on the Cossacks, including *Statisticheskoe opisanie Chernomorskogo voiska* (A Statistical Description of the Black Sea Host, 1840) and *Chernomorskie kazaki v ikh grazhdanskom i voennom bytu* (The Black Sea Cossacks in Their Civilian and Military Life, 1858).

Poplar (*Populus*; Ukrainian: *topolia, osyka, osokir*). A rapid-growing, deciduous tree of the family Salicaceae, valued for its pulp, shade, and beauty. Many species of poplar are known, and found in the temperate zone of the Northern Hemisphere. In Ukraine three species grow wild – the European aspen (*P. tremula*; Ukrainian: *osyka*), the black poplar (*P. nigra*; Ukrainian: *osokir*), and the white poplar (*P. alba*; Ukrainian: *topolia*) – on the floodplains of large rivers, along lakefronts, in dried-up riverbeds, or as protective screens along roads and fields. Some poplars are cultivated as ornamentals; pollution-resistant *P. italica*, *P. deltoides*, and *P. balsamifera* provide green foliage in cities. The wood is light, soft, and easily worked, and is used in the manufacture of paper, matches, plywood, and packing crates, in construction, and in the production of rayon. Poplars figure frequently in Ukrainian folk songs and literary works.

Poplechnyk. A personally free but *landless peasant in the Lithuanian-Ruthenian state during the 14th to 16th centuries. The social status of *poplechnyky* was similar to that of the later *state peasants. They lived on the estates of the grand duke and paid monetary taxes or performed various feudal obligations in exchange for the use of arable plots. When the estates were granted to feudal lords (see *feudalism), the *poplechnyky* there became enserfed.

Popluzhne (from *pluh* 'plow'). The oldest form of land tax in Kievan Rus', based on a unit of plowed land. Payment was made in kind.

Popov, Fedir, b 13 March 1857 in Kharkiv, d 19 January 1921 in Kharkiv. Veterinary toxicologist. A graduate of the Kharkiv Veterinary Institute, he taught there, as a professor from 1913. At the institute he set up the first chair of forensic veterinary medicine and toxicology in the Russian Empire and wrote the only textbook in the field before the revolution, *Kratkii kurs sudovoi veterinarii dlia* *studentov i vrachei* (A Short Course in Forensic Veterinary Science for Students and Physicians, 1907).

Mykhailo Popov: *The Day Is Mine, the Age Is Mine* (oil, 1989)

Popov, Mykhailo, b 15 September 1946 on the *khutir* Yahly, near Kharkiv. Painter. He graduated from the Kharkiv Industrial Design Institute in 1976. At first he painted only watercolors, mostly of landscapes (eg, *Pale Blue Sakhalin*, 1979). Since the early 1980s he has worked in oils and painted figures in an expressionist manner. Popov finds inspiration in nature and Ukrainian folklore. He transforms reality into extraordinary images defying rationalization, using rich and intense colors and fluid and spontaneous brush strokes that convey his enjoyment of the medium (eg, *The Years of Youth Have Passed*, 1990). People and animals exist in harmony in his canvases, which are colorfully lush and rhythmically vibrant (eg, *Cuckoo Birds*, 1989). Popov's first solo exhibition was held in Kharkiv in 1986, and the second in Toronto in 1990.

Popov, Nikolai, b 5 January 1891 in Kutaisi, Georgia, d 10 February 1938. Russian Bolshevik leader, propagandist, and historian. He was active in Kharkiv and Moscow as a Menshevik revolutionary from 1906. He was arrested in 1911 and exiled to Siberia in 1912. He joined the Bolshevik party in 1919 and served in Ukraine as deputy editor and editor of the Bolshevik daily, *Kommunist* (Kharkiv and Kiev 1920–1), as CP(B)U first secretary of Kharkiv gubernia (1921–3), and as the chief of the CP(B)U Agitation Department. He was promoted to the CC CP(B)U and became editor of its organ, *Komunist* (1925–8). From 1928 he worked in Moscow as a senior CP propagandist, member of the Executive Committee of the Comintern and the CC of the Communist Party of Western Ukraine, and later also editor of *Pravda*. He returned to Ukraine in 1933 with P. Postyshev to serve as CC CP(B)U secretary in charge of propaganda and the press, as well as a Politburo candidate (1933–6) and member (1936–7). Popov wrote official histories of the Bolshevik party in the Soviet Union (1926; 15th edn 1933; English trans 1934) and in Ukraine (1928; 5th edn 1933), a book on Soviet nationality policy (1927), and booklets on the October Revolution in Ukraine (1927, 1934). He also edited collections of writings on Ukraine by M. Pokrovsky (1935) and V. Lenin (1936). Although he was a major Stalinist critic of M. Skrypnyk, M. Khvylovy,

V. Yurynets, and the Ukrainian national-Communists and intelligentsia in general and thus facilitated the Stalinist terror and purges in Ukraine, he himself was arrested with other CP(B)U leaders in June 1937, accused of being a member of a fascist conspiracy, and executed.

Popov, Nikolai, b 7 August 1927 in Yastrebovka, Kursk oblast, Russia. Printmaker. He studied at the Kiev State Art Institute (1950–6) and has taught there since in 1961. He has produced over 20 print series, such as 'Motifs from T. Shevchenko's *Kobzar*' (1961–4), 'Years of the Occupation' (1961–8), 'My Childhood' (1970–2), 'Skovoroda' (1972), and 'Winter Sedniv' (1977–80).

Popov, Oleksander, b 24 October 1885 in Tulchyn, Bratslav county, Podilia gubernia, d ? In the 1920s he was a professor at the Kiev Agricultural Institute and an associate of the VUAN. He wrote articles on Ukrainian foreign trade, including Ukrainian economic relations with Russia, and the history of Ukrainian industry. He was arrested in the terror of the 1930s, and disappeared.

Pavlo Popov

Popov, Pavlo, b 28 July 1890 in Mykolaivka, Putyvl county, Kursk gubernia, Russia, d 4 April 1971 in Kiev. Literary scholar, fine arts scholar, and folklorist. He graduated from the historical-philological faculty at Kiev University (1916). From 1934 he was a professor at Kiev University and a corresponding member of the AN URSR (now ANU). Among his scholarly works are *Drukarstvo, ioho pochatok i poshyrennia v Evropi* (Printing: Its Beginnings and Growth in Europe, 1925), *Materiialy do slovnyka ukraïns'kykh graveriv* (Materials for a Dictionary of Ukrainian Engravers, 1926), *Pro deiaki pytannia teoriï narodnopoetychnoï tvorchosty* (On Some Theoretical Issues of Folk Poetry, 1955), *Hryhorii Skovoroda: Zhyttia i tvorchist'* (Hryhorii Skovoroda: His Life and Works, 1960), *Shevchenko i Kyïvs'kyi universytet* (Shevchenko and Kiev University, 1964), and *M. Kostomarov iak folkl'oryst i etnohraf* (M. Kostomarov as Folklorist and Ethnographer, 1968).

Popov, Valentyn, b 16 April 1894 in Rylsk, Kursk gubernia, Russia, d ? Geographer and climatologist. He headed the department of agricultural meteorology at the Mliiv Orcharding Research Station (1921–30) and worked at the Ukrainian Scientific Research Institute of Orcharding (1931–41). After the war he taught at Kiev University, where he was appointed professor in 1949. He specialized in the moisture content of different soils and agroclimatic and physical regionalization in Ukraine. He invented a type of vaporizer that was widely used in meteorological stations in the Soviet Union and other countries.

Popov, Yevgenii, b 8 March 1899 in Putyvl, Kursk gubernia, Russia, d 9 June 1961 in Moscow. Psychiatrist; full member of the USSR Academy of Medical Sciences (AMN SSSR) from 1957. A graduate of the Kharkiv Medical Institute (1924), he taught at the Kharkiv (1934–8, 1943–51) and Moscow (1951–60) medical institutes and directed a psychiatric clinic in Kharkiv (1932–41). In 1961 he was appointed research director of the AMN SSSR Institute of Psychiatry. He proposed a new theory of hallucination and a biological conception of schizophrenia.

Popova, Lidiia, b 17 February 1925 in Kharkiv. Art scholar and critic. A graduate of Moscow University (1947), she has specialized in the history of Ukrainian art. She has written books on S. Svitoslavsky (1955) and L. Zhemchuzhnikov (1961) and is the coauthor of books on Soviet Ukrainian art of the 1920s and 1930s (1966), T. Yablonska (1968), and Soviet Ukrainian satire (1971).

Popova, Liubov, b 24 February 1925 in Minusinsk, Krasnoiarsk krai, RSFSR. Opera singer (mezzo-soprano). In 1950 she graduated from the Kharkiv Music School. From 1948 she appeared as a soloist with the Kharkiv Theater of Opera and Ballet. Her main roles include Odarka in S. Hulak-Artemovsky's *Zaporozhian Cossack beyond the Danube,* the Mother in M. Arkas's *Kateryna,* Stekha and Solomiia in K. Dankevych's *Nazar Stodolia* and *Bohdan Khmelnytsky,* the Countess and Olga in P. Tchaikovsky's *Queen of Spades* and *Eugene Onegin,* Carmen in G. Bizet's *Carmen,* and Amneris in G. Verdi's *Aida.*

Matthew Popovich

Popovich, Matthew [Popovyč, Matvij] (Popowich), b 1890 in Lubianky, Zbarazh county, Galicia, d 19 August 1943 in Grimsby, Ontario. Communist leader and journalist. He emigrated to the United States in 1910 and then to Canada in 1911. He became involved with the Ukrainian Social Democratic party of Canada and its newspaper *Robochyi narod.* In 1919 he took part in organizing the Winnipeg General Strike. He played an important role in the formation of the *Ukrainian Labour-Farmer Temple Association (ULFTA) and the Workers' Benevolent Association and was a founding member of the Communist Party of Canada (CPC). He served on the executive of the ULFTA

and was a member of the Central Committee of the CPC, for which he edited the Ukrainian-language journal *Za bil'shovyzatsiiu.* Popovich was arrested with other CPC leaders in 1931 under the provisions of the Criminal Code of Canada and was imprisoned for over two years. In 1940, while in failing health, he was again interned, under the War Measures Act; he was virtually an invalid when released.

Popovsky, Ivan [Popovs'kyj], b and d ? 18th-century singer (bass). He sang at the court of Hetman I. Skoropadsky in Hlukhiv before he was appointed precentor of the singing kapelle at the royal court in St Petersburg in 1714. He came to Ukraine in 1718 to recruit singers for his kapelle. In 1725 he copied a collection of 18th-century church hymns; his text has been preserved to this day.

Popovtsy. See Old Believers.

Popovych, Dmytro [Popovyč], b 7 November 1899 in Velyki Komiaty, Transcarpathia, d 3 October 1968 in Khust, Transcarpathia oblast. Greek Catholic priest, educator, and civic leader. After completing his theological studies in Budapest he served as a catechist in Khust, edited religious periodicals, and wrote a number of religious textbooks. He took part in the populist movement and opposed communist and Russophile influences in Transcarpathia. In 1938–9 he was principal of the Ukrainian Greek Catholic gymnasium in Khust and president of the Society of Ukrainian Greek Catholic Priests. In 1949 he was arrested (for a second time) by the Soviets and sentenced to 25 years of hard labor. He returned to Khust in 1956, crippled after years in the mines of Irkutsk.

Ilko Popovych

Popovych, Ilko [Popovyč, Il'ko], b 1883 in Chernivtsi, d 1 July 1955 in Munich. Engineer and civic and political leader; son of Omelian *Popovych. He was an organizer of Sich societies and, from 1906, of the Ukrainian Radical party in Bukovyna. He helped edit the party's paper *Hromadianyn* in Chernivtsi (1909–10). When Ukrainians took control of Bukovyna in November 1918, he served briefly as military commander of Chernivtsi and then fled from the invading Rumanian troops to Galicia. There he became a member of the Ukrainian National Rada, and in 1919 he attended the Labor Congress in Kiev. In the interwar period he lived in Galicia, where he was a member of the Central Committee of the Ukrainian Socialist Radical party. He was arrested and deported during the first Soviet occupation of Galicia. He emigrated to Germany after the Second World War, where he served as acting president of the Ukrainian National Council.

Popovych, Ivan [Popovyč], b ? in Khodorkiv, Pavoloch regiment, d 1663. Cossack officer. He was a distinguished veteran of the Cossack-Polish War, particularly the battle for Homel (1651). He served as acting colonel of Pavoloch regiment in 1663. He opposed the pro-Polish policies of the Right-Bank hetman, P. Teteria, and was arrested early in 1663 for organizing a rebellion. Fearing the potential repercussions of executing Popovych, Teteria allowed him to leave the Cossacks quietly and enter the priesthood. Popovych, however, sparked a rebellion a few months later and took over Pavoloch. When the city was besieged by Polish forces, he was captured, tortured, and executed.

Popovych, Matvii. See Popovich, Matthew.

Myroslav Popovych   Oksana Popovych

Popovych, Myroslav [Popovyč], b 12 April 1930. Philosopher. A graduate of Kiev University, he has been a senior researcher at the AN URSR (now ANU) Institute of Philosophy since 1963, a doctor since 1967, and chairman of the institute's Department for the Logic of Scientific Knowledge since 1969. In December 1986 he was elected president of the Ukrainian Branch of the USSR Philosophical Society. He has written books in Russian on the philosophical analysis of scientific language (1966), in which he reviews the development of syntactic and semantic methods of analysis in order to clarify the relation of theory to reality; on the philosophical questions of semantics (1975); and on the development of logical ideas in a cultural-historical context (1979). He has also edited several books on the logic of scientific methodology and research. He cultivated an interest in the general history of ideas and has published articles on writers such as F. Dostoevsky and N. Gogol and a book on the worldview of the ancient Slavs (1985). In Ukrainian he has published a defense of Marxist materialism (1964), a biographical novel about H. Skovoroda (with I. Drach and S. Krymsky, 1984), and a novel with an essay about N. Gogol (1989). Since 1989 he has been active in the leading organs of the Popular Movement of Ukraine (Rukh).

Popovych, Oksana [Popovyč], b 2 February 1926 in Horodenka, Galicia. Freedom fighter, human rights activist, and political prisoner. She was incarcerated in labor camps in the Soviet Arctic in 1944–54 for her participation in the resistance in Western Ukraine during the Second World War. After her release she organized aid to Ukrainian political prisoners and was active in the Ukrainian human rights movement. She was rearrested in October 1974, and in February 1975 she became the first woman prisoner of conscience tried by the Soviet authorities during International Women's Year. Despite the fact that she was handicapped as a result of her previous imprisonment, she was sentenced to eight years in labor camps in the Mordovian ASSR and five years' exile. In the camps she vigorously protested against her treatment and that of other political prisoners, and in February 1979 she joined the *Ukrainian Helsinki Group. She was released from Siberian exile in 1987.

Popovych, Oleksander [Popovyč] (pen name: Rudolf Oskar von Waldburg), b 1828, d 1867. Orthodox priest and Bukovynian civic activist and writer; father of Omelian *Popovych. He contributed poetry, short stories, novels, and ethnographic studies to German newspapers and journals. His fiction portrayed mostly the life of Ukrainians in Bukovyna.

Popovych, Oleksander [Popovyč], b 1879 in Chernivtsi, Bukovyna, d 1 November 1936 in Drohobych, Galicia. Bukovynian pedagogue and translator; son of Omelian Popovych. He translated into German works by T. Shevchenko, M. Vovchok, I. Franko, and other Ukrainian writers and wrote the article 'Deutsche Art im Spiegel ukrainischer Dichtung' in *Ostdeutsche Monatshefte* (Berlin 1927, no. 12). With V. Kushnir he coedited the book *Taras Schewtschenko, der grösste Dichter der Ukraine* (1914), which included his translations of Shevchenko's works.

Popovych, Oleksander [Popovyč], b 1895, d 29 January 1918 near Kruty, Nizhen county, Chernihiv gubernia. Civic figure. During the First World War he was a student leader in Kiev and a peasant organizer in the Kiev region. He belonged to the Ukrainian Party of Socialist Revolutionaries. As the Bolsheviks invaded Ukraine at the beginning of 1918, he helped organize the Student Kurin, and he died in its ranks at Kruty.

Omelian Popovych

Popovych, Omelian [Popovyč, Omeljan], b 18 August 1856 in Vatra Dornei, Bukovyna, d 22 March 1930 in Zalishchyky, Galicia. Community activist, pedagogue, and publicist. He graduated (1876) from the teachers' college in Chernivtsi and then taught in the city until 1892. He was the commissioner of elementary schools for the Bukovynian Provincial School Board in 1895–1906. Popovych was designated as the first provincial inspector of Ukrainian elementary schools and teachers' colleges in Bukovyna in 1906, and remained at this post until 1912.

Popovych was a leading Ukrainian civic figure in Bukovyna. He was the long-standing secretary (from 1878) and then head of Ruska Besida and was involved in Ruska Shkola, Narodnyi Dim, and other societies. He served as a coeditor or editor of the newspaper *Bukovyna (1885–92), the Biblioteka dlia molodezhy, selian i mishchan (Library for Youths, Peasants, and Burghers, 1885–94), later Lastivka (Swallow) series, and the almanacs (1885–1918) of Ruska Besida. A member of the Bukovynian Diet in 1911–18, Popovych emerged in October 1918 as head of the Ukrainian Regional Committee, and then as president of the short-lived Ukrainian Bukovynian state. He was also the Bukovynian representative and then a vice-president of the *Ukrainian National Rada of the Western Ukrainian National Republic and head of its school commission. After the occupation of Bukovyna by Rumanian forces late in 1918, Popovych emigrated to Galicia, where he was an inspector of elementary schools and teachers' colleges for the Ridna Shkola society.

Popovych wrote a number of readers and grammars, most notable among which were *Hramatyka dlia shkil narodnykh* (A Grammar for Elementary Schools, 3 vols, 1893–4) and *Ruthenisches Sprachbuch für Mittelschulen* (3 vols, 1897–1902). In the 1920s he wrote four Ukrainian grammar texts for Galician schools, which were approved by the Polish educational authorities. He edited *Gesetz und Verordnungsblatt für bukowiner Schulwesen* and headed the Ukrainian section of *Bukowiner Schule*. He wrote numerous articles on pedagogy and literature, published the poetry collections *Bukovyna* (1875) and *Dumka* (Thought, 1886), and translated various works. He compiled the *Rus'ko-nimets'kyi slovar* (Ruthenian-German Dictionary, 1904), whose second edition appeared in 1911 under the title *Ruthenisch-deutsches Wörterbuch*, with 25,000 entries. His memoirs, *Vidrodzhennia Bukovyny* (The Rebirth of Bukovyna), were published in 1933.

A. Zhukovsky

Popovych, Orest (Popovyč), b 18 January 1933 in Lviv. Chemistry professor and chess player. A postwar refugee in the United States since 1949, he graduated from Rutgers University (B SC, 1955) and the Massachusetts Institute of Technology (PH D, 1959). Since 1963 he has taught at Brooklyn College. He became a US chess master in 1957 and a senior master in 1972 and was ranked 13th in the United States. He won the 1959, 1961, 1965, and 1986 New Jersey state championships; the 1984 Atlantic Open Tournament; and five tournaments of the Ukrainian Sports Federation of the USA and Canada.

Popovych, Pavlo [Popovyč], b 5 October 1930 in Uzyn, Bila Tserkva raion (now in Kiev oblast). Astronaut and pilot. He studied at the Soviet Military Aviation School and the Air Force Engineering Academy. He was appointed general-major in the Soviet Air Force and joined the first group of prospective cosmonauts in 1960. Popovych flew in Vostok-4 from 12 to 15 August 1962. He was the first Ukrainian in space, the fourth person in orbital spaceflight, and a member of the first group flight of satellites, together with A. Nikolaev in Vostok-3. From 3 to 19 July

Pavlo Popovych

1974 Popovych commanded the spacecraft Soiuz-14, which docked successfully with the space station Saliut-3. Popovych is active among Ukrainians living in Moscow and heads the Ukrainian Slavutych Society there.

Popovych, Vasyl [Popovyč, Vasyl'], b 12 September 1796 in Velyki Komiaty, Ugocsa komitat, Transcarpathia, d 19 October 1864. Greek Catholic bishop. In 1820, after obtaining a PH D in philosophy from the University of Pest, he became a priest and secretary to the bishop of Prešov, H. Tarkovych. In 1837 he was consecrated bishop of Mukachiv eparchy, following a six-year vacancy. His attempts to undo the Latinizing work of his Rumanian predecessor, A. Pocsy, led to a renewal of national and religious life in the eparchy, including the revival of Eastern rite observances and the use of the Ukrainian language by the clergy. He also improved education in the eparchy, launched an extensive renovation and building program, took steps to ensure the material well-being of the clergy, and sought to provide each parish with trained cantors and an adequate supply of liturgical books. Popovych became increasingly conservative and Magyarophile, after the defeat of the Hungarians (whom he supported) in the Revolution of 1848–9.

Popovych, Volodymyr [Popovyč], b 7 December 1922 in Vilshany, Peremyshl county, Galicia. Doctor and community leader in Belgium. He studied at Lviv (1942–4) and Leuven (1945–50) universities. In 1951–86 he headed the Ukrainian Relief Committee (UDK) in Belgium and edited its *Visti* (1972–89). A collector of Ukrainian art, he is also author of the catalogs *Sofiia Zarytska* (1967), *Mykhailo Andriienko* (1969), *Gregor Kruk – Plastik* (Hryhorii Kruk – Sculptor, 1969), *Mariia Dol'nyts'ka* (1978), and with S. Hordynsky, *Halyna Mazepa* (1982); and of articles about Ukrainian artists in journals such as *Notatky z mystetstva*, *Suchasnist'*, and *Avangard*.

Popovych, Yevhen [Popovyč, Jevhen], b 25 June 1930 in Mezhyrich, Cherkasy okruha. Writer and translator. He graduated from the philological faculty of Kiev University (1956) and then worked in the fields of publishing and editing. He has translated works of German authors into Ukrainian, including those of H.E. Lessing, E.T.A. Hoffmann, H. Heine, F. Herschteker, T. Mann, E.M. Remarque, M. Frisch, H. Hesse, and M. von der Grün.

Popovych-Boiarska, Klementyna [Popovyč-Bojars'-ka], b 3 February 1863 in Veldizh (now Shevchenkove), Stryi circle, Galicia, d 7 May 1945 in Babyntsi, Borshchiv raion, Ternopil oblast. Galician writer and elementary school teacher. She was active in the Galician women's movement. In the 1890s and 1900s she taught in Bukovyna. Beginning in the 1880s her poems and stories about the Galician intelligentsia and about women appeared in *Zoria*, *Dilo*, and *Literaturno-naukovyi vistnyk*, in Galician women's periodicals, in *Pershyi vinok*, and in other literary anthologies and miscellanies. She also wrote reminiscences about I. Franko and N. Kobrynska and an ethnographic study of Ukrainian embroidery. Her poems were republished in a 1968 Kiev anthology of 30 Ukrainian women poets.

Poppy (*Papaver*; Ukrainian: *mak*). Annual and perennial plants of the family Papaveraceae, with lobed or dissected leaves, nodding buds on solitary stalks, and four- to six-petaled bright-colored or white flowers. The fruit is a rounded capsule containing many small seeds used for food, in baking, flavoring food, and for its oil. In Ukraine the opium poppy (*P. somniferum*), cultivated for its seeds and oil, was used in the past by Ukrainian peasants to keep their infants pacified while they worked in the fields. Poppy seeds are edible; they contain 45–55 percent high-quality oil and up to 20 percent protein. The high-quality oil is used in the confectionery and canning industries, in the production of perfume, and in the manufacture of paints. Poppy-seed cakes are valuable fodder for livestock. Ukraine was the leading producer of poppy seeds in the former USSR; optimal seed harvests have reached 2 t per ha. Two varieties of poppy, Voronezh 1042 and Novynka 198, are especially popular. A wild variety, *P. rhoeas* (Ukrainian: *mak dykyi, samosii*), grows as a weed among many crops in Ukraine.

Popular Movement of Ukraine (Narodnyi rukh Ukrainy), popularly known as Rukh (the Movement). The most important noncommunist, grass-roots organization created in Ukraine during the period under M. Gorbachev. It was initially called the Popular Movement of Ukraine for Restructuring (*perebudova*; Russian: *perestroika*). Its initiative group was formed in November 1988 and published the Rukh draft program in February 1989.

Rukh's stated main objectives were the full attainment of human, political, and religious rights and freedoms; the moral rejuvenation of society; the democratization of Soviet society and the Soviet state; the political and economic sovereignty of Ukraine; constitutional reform; economic renewal; social justice; environmental safety and protection (including the shutdown of all nuclear reactors in Ukraine); the restructuring and improvement of social security and the public health system; the protection of the Ukrainian language and minority rights; and world peace.

The CPU media campaign against Rukh that lasted until September 1989 merely served to increase Rukh's popularity and membership. Rukh succeeded in becoming an umbrella organization uniting almost all *neformaly* and new political *parties in Ukraine. It gained the support of the revived Ukrainian Catholic and Ukrainian Autocephalous Orthodox churches and most members of the Writers' Union of Ukraine (writers and intellectuals have played leading roles in Rukh). Rukh sponsored many ini-

tiatives designed to break the power monopoly of the CPU, including an independent Ukrainian Communist party, the Yednist free trade union (which held its founding congress in February 1990 in Kharkiv), the Union of Free Journalists, and the Ukrainian Olympic Committee.

The first national Rukh congress was held in Kiev in September 1989. It was attended by 1,109 delegates, representing 280,000 registered, dues-paying members in branches throughout Ukraine, a delegation from the Polish Solidarity movement led by A. Michnik, representations from the Baltic states, Belarus, Moldova, the Transcaucasian peoples, and Moscow, and three observers from Ukrainian communities in the West. Elected to senior leadership positions were I. *Drach, chairman; S. Konev, first vice-chairman; V. *Yavorivsky, vice-chairman in charge of the 81-member Council of [Regional] Representatives; V. Cherniak, vice-chairman in charge of the 93-member Council of Collegiums, which co-ordinates, through commissions, the development and implementation of the political, juridical, social, economic, cultural, scientific, educational, and ecological objectives of Rukh as stated in its program and decided by the congress; and M. *Horyn, vice-chairman in charge of the Secretariat, the executive and administrative organ in Kiev that implements the decisions of the Rukh congress and councils, and chairman of the Great Council, a body consisting of the aforementioned officers and the members of the Councils of Collegiums and Representatives, which meets at least three times a year and supervises and determines Rukh's activity in between its national congresses.

After the congress Rukh concentrated its efforts on the campaign for the March 1990 elections to the Supreme Soviet of Ukraine. In September and October 1989, together with members of the Ukrainian Club of Deputies in the USSR Congress of People's Deputies, Rukh co-ordinated public demands for a more democratic electoral law in Ukraine.

By 1990 Rukh had become the largest public organization in Ukraine, with an estimated 5 million supporters and over 50 different periodicals. On 21 January 1990 it sponsored the successful 500-km chain of people linking hands from Kiev to Lviv and on to Ivano-Frankivske in

Part of the human chain linking Lviv and Kiev on 21 January 1990 that was organized by the Popular Movement of Ukraine to commemorate the 1919 proclamation of Ukraine's independence

commemoration of the 1918 and 1919 proclamations of Ukrainian independence and the union of Western and central Ukraine. In February 1990 the first issue of *Narodna hazeta*, the chief Rukh organ, appeared in a pressrun of 10,000 copies.

Although the CPU ensured that Rukh was unable to register as an organization in time to field its own candidates for the Supreme Soviet elections, candidates supporting Rukh formed a Democratic Bloc to contest 30 percent of the seats. In June 1990 the elected pro-Rukh candidates and those representing the 'democratic' wing of the CPU (who later left the CPU and formed the Ukrainian Democratic Party of Renewal, in December 1990) jointly constituted the People's Council – the opposition to the CPU, representing 35 percent of the seats in the Supreme Soviet. The People's Council was instrumental in the adoption of the 16 July 1990 declaration of Ukrainian sovereignty by the Supreme Soviet. In September 1990 a joint Rukh–People's Council press center began operating in Kiev.

The October 1990 second national Rukh congress in Kiev was attended by over 2,125 delegates, representing nearly 633,000 members and 44 civic and political organizations. The congress adopted the full independence of Ukraine as the chief goal of Rukh and disallowed the membership of Communists. Elected to the senior leadership were Drach, chairman; Horyn, first vice-chairman in charge of the Political Council (the body in charge of political policy and strategy); O. Lavrynovych, vice-chairman in charge of agitation and propaganda; M. Porovsky, head of the Co-ordinating Council; I. Zaiets, head of the Council of Collegiums; O. Burakhovsky, head of the Council of Nationalities; and V. Burlakov, head of the Secretariat. In the fall of 1991 Rukh played a key role in promoting the 'yes' vote in the 1 December referendum on Ukrainian independence.

The creation of a Rukh faction headed by Horyn in the Ukrainian parliament was officially declared on 8 February 1992. The third national Rukh congress (held from 28 February to 1 March 1992), which was attended by 800 delegates, reflected factional divisions within the movement and acute differences over political strategy and orientation. A compromise was reached by electing the factional leaders V. *Chornovil, Drach, and Horyn as co-chairmen of Rukh. At the fourth congress (4–6 December 1992) Rukh was transformed into a political party headed by Chornovil.

BIBLIOGRAPHY
Ustanovchyi z'izd Narodnoho rukhu Ukraïny za perebudovu. Special issue of *Suchasnist'*, December 1989
Joukovsky, A.; Popowycz, J. (eds). *Matériaux du Congrès constitutif du Mouvement National d'Ukraine pour la restructuration – ROUKh* (Paris 1990)

T. Kuzio, R. Senkus

Population genetics. The study of the genetic structure and dynamics of the genetic makeup of populations, including changes in the genotype and in the frequency of individual genes, the nature of crossings within a population, interpopulation migrations, and natural and random fluctuations. A study of genes in animal populations provides information on past migrations, evolutionary relationships, the extent of mixing among different species, and methods of adaptation to the environment. It is a relatively recent science, whose pioneering steps in the USSR were made in the 1920s and 1930s by S. Chetverikov. The biologist I. *Shmalhauzen postulated that from the evolutionary standpoint genetic heterogeneity is a peculiar 'mobilization reserve' used by populations during gradual or sudden changes in environmental conditions.

Population of Ukraine. Ukraine's territory has been inhabited by humans since the Paleolithic period (see *History of Ukraine). The East Slavic tribal groups living there developed in the 8th and 9th centuries AD into a proto-Ukrainian people, out of which the *Ukrainians evolved in the 14th and 15th centuries. By the 16th century they constituted a modern, independent ethnos in the Dnieper and Dniester basins. The consolidation and unification of the ethnos took place in struggle against Polish-Lithuanian and Hungarian feudalism and Tatar-Turkish invasions. In the 17th century the ethnos began evolving into a nation. The evolution sharply decelerated after the partition of Ukraine between Poland and Russia by the 1667 Treaty of Andrusovo and again after the defeat in 1708–9 of Hetman I. Mazepa's attempts to establish a more independent Hetman state.

The regrouping of the Ukrainian ethnic territories as a result of the 18th-century Russo-Turkish wars and partitions of the Polish Commonwealth created favorable conditions for the development and the formation of a modern Ukrainian nation. The landmarks in the process were the emancipation of the peasantry in Western Ukraine in 1848 and the abolition of serfdom in Russian-ruled Ukraine in 1861, and the consequent industrial transformations and rise of an independent Ukrainian literature, standard language, and nationally conscious intelligentsia. In the years 1920–85, however, the process of national consolidation was substantially retarded, because the area of compact habitation by the Ukrainians was subjugated by the Soviet totalitarian state, which actively pursued a policy of *Russification and engaged in various forms of genocide.

Ukraine's population can be determined for the 17th century and later. In 1629 it was between five and six million. In the feudal period population growth was hampered by frequent, devastating wars, epidemics, and famines. The Ukrainian people suffered particularly great population losses as a result of Crimean Tatar raids and Turkish military invasions, during which many captives were taken and sold into *slavery or transformed into *janissaries. Ya. Dashkevych has estimated that from the 15th to the mid-17th century approx 2 to 2.5 million Ukrainians were killed or taken from Ukraine as slaves. As a result Ukraine's urban and rural social-class structure lost its most intellectually developed inhabitants, that is, the requisite potential for the development of a more socially and economically advanced population and for the transformation of the Ukrainian ethnos into a nation.

In 1764–74 Ukraine had over eight million inhabitants. A significant contribution to the development of the nation was made by the colonization of *Slobidska Ukraine in the 17th century and of *Southern Ukraine and the *Kuban in the 18th century. As a result of that colonization the *territory of compact habitation by the Ukrainians was considerably enlarged. By 1870 the present territory of Ukraine had a population of 18.7 million. As a market economy developed in the following years, the population grew rapidly, to reach 28.4 million in 1897 and 35.2

million in 1913. At the same time rural overpopulation induced mass *emigration. In the years 1896–1914, 1.6 million inhabitants of the nine Russian-ruled gubernias emigrated to the Siberian, Central Asian, and Far Eastern regions of the Russian Empire. Emigration from Austrian- and Hungarian-ruled Western Ukraine to the New World was also significant; it totaled 413,000 in the years 1895–1913. In the interwar period an additional 196,500 Ukrainian political refugees and economic emigrants left Ukraine.

In the late 19th and early 20th centuries Ukraine's demographic development was distinguished by high fertility and mortality rates. According to R. Kuczynski, at the end of the 19th century Ukraine had the highest fertility rate in Europe – an average of 7.5 children per woman. According to M. Ptukha's calculations, in 1896–7 life expectancy at birth in Ukraine was 36 years for males and 37 years for females. Such indicators were characteristic of a population with a traditional way of life, that is, marriage at an early age, practically no use of birth control, high infant mortality, and a rapid generational shift.

Global changes in the development of Ukraine's population have occurred in the 20th century. They were brought about by a demographic revolution – the shift from high fertility and mortality rates and underdeveloped demographic relations to low rates and regulated demographic relations – and by extraordinary, cataclysmic events that significantly altered the normal course of demographic processes.

During the years of the Ukrainian-Soviet War (1918–20) mortality in Ukraine was greater than during the First World War. Large subsequent losses were caused by the famine that ravaged Southern Ukraine in 1921–2 and by various *epidemics that occurred after the collapse of the health-protection system during the Ukrainian-Soviet War. The total population losses between 1914 and the early 1920s in Ukraine, both direct and indirect (ie, the number of children not born because of the death of potential marriage partners or because of the temporary decline in marriages caused by military mobilization), have been estimated at between three and four million.

In the mid-1920s a significant change in Soviet Ukraine's demographic development began. The aggregate birthrate kept steadily decreasing from a high of 5.2 children per woman in 1926. In 1926–7 life expectancy was 44 years for males and 48 years for women – an increase over the preceding 30 years of 8 years for males and 11 years for females. The figures for the population's age structure in the 1926 Soviet census indicate that the social convulsions of the 1920s brought about a break in Ukraine's demographic development. There was a significant gap in the 5–9 age cohort; its number was lower by 366,000 persons than that of the 10–14 age cohort. Those two cohorts most reflected the disastrous consequences of the First World War, the Ukrainian-Soviet War, and the social transformations of the 1920s. The scale of the impact of those events is reflected in the change in the mortality rate in interwar Soviet Ukraine. According to A. Khomenko, the mortality rate was 26.7 per 1,000 inhabitants in 1914, 31.9 in 1915, 36.1 in 1916, 27.5 in 1917, 28.9 in 1918, 38.5 in 1919, 40.3 in 1920, 28.8 in 1921, and 35.2 in 1922.

After 1926, demographic transformations in Soviet Ukraine affected the evolution of the age structure. The profound social convulsions during the period under J.

Stalin acutely disturbed normal demographic processes. The change in population size after 1926 was caused by evolutionary factors and crises and was reflected in the change in the age structure (the significant decline in the number of children and the increase in the demographic weight of the elderly) and its substantial deformation. The period of the New Economic Policy of the 1920s had been characterized by a high fertility rate and a decline in the mortality rate in Soviet Ukraine. During the Stalinist period of forced collectivization and industrialization, which began in 1929, the fertility rate decreased substantially. The demographic decline rapidly turned into a demographic cataclysm, caused by the mass deportation of Ukrainian peasants (see *Kulaks) to other parts of the USSR, the totalitarian state's man-made *famine of 1932–3, and the political repression and destruction of hundreds of thousands of Ukrainian citizens, primarily members of the nationally conscious intelligentsia, during the *terror of the 1930s. The total losses of interwar Soviet Ukraine's demographic potential caused solely by the Stalinist social convulsions of the late 1920s and the 1930s numbered approx seven to nine million persons.

In the 1940s Ukraine again suffered huge population losses as a result of the large-scale Soviet deportation of Western Ukrainians to Siberia in 1940–1, the deaths wrought by the German-Soviet War of 1941–5, the migration of conscripted laborers, *Ostarbeiter, and political refugees to the West, postwar population transfers between Ukraine and Poland, the famine of 1947, and the organized 'voluntary resettlement' of Ukrainian peasants in Siberia and the Soviet Far East. Those losses continued into the 1950s, when many Ukrainians were resettled in Kazakhstan's virgin lands.

Ukraine's losses totaled 8.8 million persons in the period 1939–59 and anywhere from 15.8 to 17 million in the period 1929–59. The demographic cataclysms of the first half of the 20th century seriously distorted both the quantitative and qualitative indicators of Ukraine's demographic reproductivity and age structure, and hindered the republic's social and economic development. The capacity to reproduce a social-class structure declined following the destruction and deportation of the intelligentsia class in Ukraine. The absence of an actively creative segment of society resulted in socioeconomic and political retardation and helped accelerate the growth of the power of the bureaucracy and military-industrial complex. The immense population losses substantially reduced the population's labor potential, facilitated the economic coercion and exploitation of the remaining labor force, sharply reduced Ukraine's demographic potential, retarded urbanization processes within the Ukrainian ethnos, and accelerated the in-migration of Russians and other non-Ukrainians.

National composition. The dynamics of Ukraine's national composition have reflected not only changes in the socioeconomic conditions affecting demographic reproductivity, but also changes in political borders and migration patterns (including the deportation of Ukrainians, Poles, Germans, and Crimean Tatars and the mass emigration of Jews) and the consequences of the demographic cataclysms. After the Second World War the various ethnic groups inhabiting Ukraine quickly attained the same birthrate. Consequently, postwar changes in the national composition have occurred mainly as a result of the

TABLE 1
Ukraine's population, 1897–1991*

Year	Total (millions)	Urban (%)	Rural (%)
1897	28.4	16	84
1914	37.4	–	–
1926	37.7	19	81
1937	28.4	–	–
1940	42.2	34	66
1950	36.6	35	65
1959	41.9	46	54
1970	47.1	55	45
1979	49.8	61	39
1989	51.7	67	33
1991	51.9	68	32

* Within the political borders of corresponding years

TABLE 2
Indicators of the natural growth of Ukraine's real and stable populations, 1897–1989

	Rates of natural growth					
	BR*	DR*	NI*	GR*	NR*	LEW (yr)
1897						
Real	50.3	27.6	22.7	3.66		36.85
Stable	50.7	27.3	23.4		2.01	
1926						
Real	41.2	17.9	23.3	2.48		47.5
Stable	37.5	20.4	17.1		1.64	
1939						
Real	27.3	14.3	13.0	1.89		54.2
Stable	27.5	16.0	11.5		1.38	
1959						
Real	21.0	7.2	13.8	1.12		72.5
Stable	15.0	13.0	2.0		1.05	
1970						
Real	15.2	8.8	6.4	1.00		74.2
Stable	12.9	14.2	–1.3		0.96	
1979						
Real	14.7	11.1	3.6	0.96		74.1
Stable	12.1	14.9	–2.8		0.93	
1989						
Real	13.3	11.6	1.7	1.14		75.2
Stable	12.8	14.3	–1.5		0.99	

BR = birth rate, DR = death rate, NI = natural increase, GR = gross reproduction ratio (the number of females born per number of women of reproductive age), NR = net reproduction ratio (the number of females born who survive to reproductive age [20 years] per number of women of reproductive age), LEW = life expectancy of women at birth
*In 1,000s

changes in ethnic identification and through *migration. The regional distribution of the ethnic Ukrainian population in Ukraine is unequal. Its demographic weight is highest in the western oblasts but significantly lower in several southern oblasts and in the Donbas. On the whole, however, ethnic Ukrainians make up the majority of Ukraine's population (72.7 percent in 1989). In 1989 there were 44.2 million Ukrainians in the USSR, 84.7 percent of them in Ukraine.

Until the 20th century, ethnic Ukrainians constituted minorities in Ukraine's towns. In 1897 they constituted only 32.5 percent of the urban population of the territory that became interwar Soviet Ukraine. Their share of the urban population rose to 46 percent in 1926, and they were recognized as the majority in their cities – 58.1 percent – for the first time only in the 1939 Soviet census. Since 1939 the ethnic Ukrainian share of the urban population in Soviet Ukraine has grown very slowly. In 1959, 61.5 percent of city dwellers were Ukrainian; in 1970, 63.0 percent; in 1979, 64.1 percent; and in 1989, 65.8 percent.

Only in 1965 did Ukraine's population become predominantly urban. Because of the intensive influx of nonindigenous, primarily Russian, migrants into Ukraine's urban centers, however, the weight of urban inhabitants within the ethnic Ukrainian population has grown much more slowly than that within the population in general. Thus the urbanization of the Ukrainian nation had been substantially delayed. It was not until the 1970s that the ethnic Ukrainians themselves became predominantly urban. In 1979, 53 percent of them were urban inhabitants; at the same time 86.4 percent of the Russians in Ukraine were urban inhabitants. By 1989 the urbanization indicator for Ukrainians had risen to 60.3 percent, compared to 87.6 percent for Russians.

In 1989 Ukraine had between 51.4 and 51.7 million inhabitants, which number made it the sixth most populous country in Europe. Its population is now characterized by low fertility and mortality levels, insignificant growth, a positive migratory balance through interrepublic exchange, nuclear families with few children, and high mobility. Analyses indicate that population reproductivity with a net coefficient close to one and an age structure close to the structure of a stable population with a zero coefficient of natural increase is being replaced by reduced reproductivity, in which generations of mothers are not being replaced by generations of daughters. The present state arose as a result of the steady maintenance of an aggregate birth coefficient at fewer than two children per woman and an increase in deaths since 1986. In 1989, life expectancy at birth in Ukraine was 66.1 years for males and 75.2 for females; those are significantly lower indicators than the corresponding indicators in the advanced Western countries. In other words, in the late 1980s Ukraine entered a prolonged period of yet another demographic crisis, the consequences and duration of which are difficult to ascertain. At the same time it is evident that a reduced mortality rate is not likely to occur in the future, given the effects of the Chornobyl nuclear accident, the ecological destruction of many of Ukraine's regions, and the consequent contamination of the food chain and food products.

Population registers and censuses. Medieval chronicles indicate that in 9th- and 10th-century Kievan Rus' various units, such as the *dym and pluh (ralo), were applied, according to the level of socioeconomic development, to calculate the size of family properties for taxation purposes. Those calculations testify to the significant influence of the Byzantine taxation system and in several cases were directly adopted from it. Data before the 15th century do not, however, exist. From the 16th century on, large-scale enumerations of peasant properties were conducted in Polish- and Lithuanian-ruled Ukraine. The development of productive forces and population growth brought about a new form of census taking based on household property rather than the land occupied.

The first national statistics were gathered during the Cossack-Polish War of 1648–57. The earliest extant example is the 1649 Zboriv Register of Ukrainian Cossacks, which enumerated all adult Cossack warriors and family heads able to bear arms at their own expense. In 1666 the Muscovite administration in Left-Bank Ukraine conducted a property enumeration of 'commoners' (urban merchants and craftsmen, as well as peasants) for purposes of imposing taxes that would directly enter the tsar's treasury. The census was incomplete: it did not include commoners living on monastery-owned lands or on lands set aside for the support of the hetman. The first mixed household census in Ukraine, which registered not only properties but also adult males, Cossacks, commoners, and representatives of several other population categories, was conducted in Slobidska Ukraine in 1732. A similar census was conducted in the Left-Bank Hetman state in 1763. From 1782 to 1857, censuses of males and females were conducted for *poll tax purposes in Russian-ruled Ukraine. The first all-Russian imperial one-day census took place in 1897. Succeeding all-Soviet censuses were conducted in 1926, 1937, 1939, 1959, 1979, and 1989. In the 20th century other specialized censuses of individual population categories were conducted in the Russian Empire and the USSR, including Ukraine: the 1916–17 all-Russian agricultural census, the 1923 Soviet census of the urban population, and the 1931 all-Union enumeration of the Soviet urban population.

In the Western Ukrainian lands not ruled by Russia the first census was conducted in 1818 by the Austrian state. One-day population censuses in the Austro-Hungarian Empire were conducted in 1857, 1869, 1880, 1890, 1900, and 1910. In the interwar period the population of Western Ukraine was enumerated in the Polish censuses of 1921 and 1931, the Czechoslovak censuses of 1921 and 1930, and the Rumanian censuses of 1920 and 1930. During the Second World War, in 1941 the Hungarians enumerated the population of Transcarpathia and the occupying Rumanians conducted a census of Transnistria, and in 1943 the Germans conducted censuses in the Distrikt Galizien of the Generalgouvernement and in the occupied Ukrainian oblasts of the Reichskommissariat Ukraine, except those directly abutting the German-Soviet front.

The mass registration of marriages, births, baptisms, and deaths in Ukraine has taken place since 1646, when Metropolitan P. Mohyla of Kiev made *church registers compulsory. His initiative, however, was neglected during the succeeding upheavals of the 17th century. The church register of the Orthodox population in Right-Bank and Western Ukraine was revived by Bishop Y. Shumliansky of Lviv. Under Hetman I. Mazepa such registers were introduced in the parishes of his capital, Baturyn, in the early years of the 18th century. In Russian-ruled Left-Bank and Slobidska Ukraine they were introduced in 1722.

Throughout Ukraine's history demographic data have been used as an object of political insinuation and economic struggle, and under Soviet rule they were subject to official falsification. The 1666 census of the population of Left-Bank Ukraine, for example, was one of the causes of the popular uprising against the tsarist administration there, because the inhabitants feared that the census would be used to implement a tax increase. The enumeration of 1782 gave impetus to the mass flight of peasants and Cossacks to the southern borderlands. And the 1931 all-Union enumeration of the Soviet urban population was used to deny city status to dozens of urban settlements in Ukraine and thus the guarantee of food coupons to their inhabitants, who were thereby condemned to hunger.

For nearly six decades the Communist party denied the existence of the man-made famine of 1932–3 and its millions of victims. Because the 1937 Soviet census indicated a population decline in the USSR in general and in Ukraine and Kazakhstan in particular, the Stalinist regime annulled it, banned publication of its results for many decades, and repressed its organizers as 'enemies of the state.' Because the 1939 census also showed a population decline, its data were falsified by the directors of state statistics, and publication of the data was initially restricted to newspaper notices. To cover up the massive Soviet population losses of the Second World War the first postwar census was postponed until January 1959. Beginning with the Soviet censuses of the 1930s, national-composition data for individual republics and regions were repeatedly falsified. Thus, in the 1939 census the Ukrainian population of the Don region, the Kuban, and Stavropol krai almost entirely 'disappeared,' to hide the fact that countless Ukrainians there had died during the 1932–3 famine or been deported as kulaks to Siberia. The chief reason, however, for the decline in the number of Ukrainians in those and several other regions was the decision of the local authorities to falsify national-composition data. Thus, many Ukrainians living in Belarus's Brest oblast 'disappeared' because they were registered en masse as Belarusians in the 1959 census. In Crimea oblast the practice of 'de-Ukrainianizing' the population survived until the 1989 census.

Population studies. The first population data about Ukraine's regions were provided in statistical-geographic descriptions written by 18th-century Ukrainian, Russian, and foreign authors. The first demographic studies of Ukraine were written by the 18th-century scholars F. Tumansky, M. Antonovsky, A. Rigelman, and Ya. Ruban. In the first half of the 19th century interest in the reproductivity of individual social groups, primarily the peasantry, grew. V. Karazyn published the first study of that phenomenon in 1820. D. Zhuravsky developed the first schema for the study of population reproductivity; N. Bunge elaborated the concept of the demographic crisis of the peasantry in the Russian Empire; O. Roslavsky-Petrovsky drew attention to the need to study the movement of the population according to its social indicators without limiting research to the general number of births and deaths; and I. Vernadsky initiated the study of national composition and the history of the interdisciplinary problems of political economy and demography. In the second half of the 19th century the leading demographers of Ukraine were M. Ziber, S. Podolynsky, T. Rylsky, V. Rapatsky, and V. Navrotsky. I. Franko played a notable role by showing, in several articles on emigration from Galicia, the interconnectedness of mortality, fertility, and the quality of the population with economic (including property and distribution) relations and living standards. Important contributions were made by specialists on public health, such as I. Barzhitsky, I. Pantiukhov, T. Makovetsky, P. Diatroptov, and O. Korchak-Chepurkivsky. Concrete general demographic research was limited to regional, local, and municipal studies (eg, by A. Skalkovsky, O. Rusov, and A. Borynevych).

The most politically significant research was on the national composition of Ukraine and of its individual social groups. Pioneers in the area were V. Barvinsky, S. Dnistriansky, V. Okhrymovych, Rusov, and M. Porsh.

A new stage in *demography began after the creation of the VUAN Demographic Institute (headed by M. Ptukha) in 1919, the *Central Statistical Administration (headed by A. Khomenko) in 1920, and a demographic center under the jurisdiction of the People's Commissariat of Public Health. As a result of their work Ukraine led the way in Soviet demographic research and was a major contributor on the international level. Studies in the field of historical demography were conducted by VUAN scholars (eg, M. Hrushevsky, M. Ptukha, O. Baranovych, P. Klymenko, V. Romanovsky, I. Lebedynsky). In the late 1930s, however, the Stalinist state banned all demographic research and suppressed many of its practitioners. Demography in Ukraine was not revived until the 1960s. Since that time important empirical studies have been conducted, and many works by the pioneers of Soviet Ukrainian demography have been published. Beginning in the 1970s, however, Marxist-Leninist dogma began playing an excessive role in the demographic research of certain scholarly collectives. They began elaborating the concept of the 'self-reproductivity' of the population and a corresponding 'law of population,' which in the late 1980s was 'replaced' by the concept of the 'socialist self-reproductivity' of the population. Such theories have hampered the development of demography as a science. In the early 1990s a new revival of demography began in Ukraine. The field's parameters have been substantially broadened, the understanding of the mechanism of demographic processes has improved, the population indicators during the cataclysms of the 1930s and 1940s have been reconstructed, and Ukrainian and Western scholars have begun collaborating on the major scholarly and practical questions of Ukraine's population.

(See also *National composition, *Social stratification, and *Urbanization.)

BIBLIOGRAPHY

Kordouba, M. *Le Territoire et la population de l'Ukraine: Contribution géographique et statistique* (Bern 1919)

Masiutyn, Iu. 'Profesiina statystyka v Rosiï ta na Ukraïni,' *Demohrafichnyi zbirnyk*, 7 (1930)

Smal'-Stots'kyi, R. (ed). *Ukraïns'ka liudnist' SSSR* (Warsaw 1931)

Ptukha, M. *Ocherki po statistike naseleniia* (Moscow 1960)

Korchak-Chepurkovskii, Iu. *Izbrannye demograficheskie issledovaniia* (Moscow 1970)

Ptukha, M. *Vybrani pratsi* (Kiev 1971)

Prociuk, S. 'Human Losses in the Ukraine in World War I and II,' *AUA*, 13 (1973–7)

Lewis, R.; Rowland, R.; Clem, R. *Nationality and Population Change in Russia and the USSR: An Evaluation of Census Data, 1897–1970* (New York, Washington, and London 1976)

Zhuchenko, V. (ed). *Demograficheskoe razvitie Ukrainskoi SSR (1959–1970 gg.)* (Kiev 1977)

Chinn, J. 'Changing Demographic Characteristics of the Population of the Ukraine,' *AUA*, 14 (1978–80)

Korchak-Chepurkivs'kyi, Iu. 'Smertnist' naselennia,' *Demohrafichni doslidzhennia*, no. 5 (1980)

Bruk, S.; Kabuzan, V. 'Chislennost'' i rasselenie ukrainskogo etnosa v XVIII–nachale XX v.,' *Sovetskaia etnografiia*, 1981, no. 5

Serbyn, R.; Krawchenko, B. (eds). *Famine in Ukraine, 1932–1933* (Edmonton 1986)

Steshenko, V. (ed). *Demograficheskoe razvitie Ukrainskoi SSR (1970–1979 gg.)* (Kiev 1987)

Kozlov, V. *The Peoples of the Soviet Union* (London and Bloomington, Ind 1988)

Libanova, E.; Palii, O. 'Tryvalist' zhyttia naselennia Ukraïny: Analiz suchasnykh tendentsii,' *Visnyk Akademiï nauk Ukraïns'koï RSR*, 1989, no. 9

Naulko, V.; Chorna, N. 'Dynamika chysel'nosti i rozmishchennia ukraïntsiv u sviti (XVIII–XX st.),' *NTE*, 1990, no. 5

Ryan, M. (comp and trans). *Contemporary Soviet Society: A Statistical Handbook* (Aldershot, England, and Brookfield, Vt 1990)

Pirozhkov, S. 'Iaki zh nashi liuds'ki vtraty?' *Visnyk Akademiï nauk Ukraïns'koï RSR*, 1991, no. 1

A. Perkovsky, S. Pirozhkov

Populism, Russian and Ukrainian. Ukrainian and Russian populism (*narodnytstvo* in Ukrainian; *narodnichestvo* in Russian) had certain common traits. Ukrainian and Russian populists idealized the people (*narod*), which, practically speaking, meant the peasantry. Populists believed that their theories reflected the interests of the peasantry, and that it was their duty to try to help them. Neither Russian nor Ukrainian ideologues developed a doctrine to which all populists of either nationality adhered; within both ideologies and movements there were various trends, sometimes similar, at other times opposed, to one another. Neither was successful in forming modern political parties, although the Ukrainian populist M. *Drahomanov is considered to be the father of the peasant-based *Ukrainian Radical party of Galicia. Therefore both Ukrainian and Russian populism were essentially ideologies and movements of the intelligentsia.

Classic Ukrainian and Russian populism began to crystallize following the *Crimean War during the reign of the Russian tsar Alexander II, when the Russian government began enacting fundamental reforms to prepare the groundwork for the modernization of Russia. The relaxation of censorship allowed society to express itself more freely. Discussion of the reform program was at times acrimonious, especially over the terms of the emancipation of the peasantry from serfdom. In that debate the Russian radicals A. *Herzen and N. *Chernyshevsky laid the intellectual foundations of Russian populism; for Ukrainian populists the intellectual heritage of the *Cyril and Methodius Brotherhood, especially of M. *Kostomarov and T. *Shevchenko, was of primary importance. The era of classical populism came to a close around the beginning of the 20th century, with the birth of modern political parties, many of which were rooted in the populist tradition.

The main tenets of Ukrainian populism were federalism, the emancipation of the peasantry, and the recognition of the cultural distinctiveness of the Ukrainian people (as initially espoused by the Cyrillo-Methodians, especially Kostomarov). Study of the Cossacks induced romantic visions of rebellions against landlords and national oppressors and of the existence of a Cossack republic based on equality and brotherhood. Those ideas, reinforced by the fiery poetry of Shevchenko, inspired a younger generation of Ukrainophiles (see *Ukrainophilism), some of whom were also influenced by Western European utopian socialists as well as Herzen, Chernyshevsky, and the anarchist M. Bakunin.

Russian populism, as ideology, was socially more radical and utopian than Ukrainian populism. Idealizing peasant traditions, especially communal farming, Russian populist thinkers came to believe that the *obshchina* (peasant commune) could serve as the foundation of a future socialist Russia. By modernizing and building on the commune, Russia could bypass capitalist development and move directly to the next, higher stage, socialism. That belief served as the populists' solution to economic backwardness; the proposed reorganization of society would also end economic injustice and the exploitation of the peasantry.

The Ukrainian populist movement began with the return of the old Cyrillo-Methodians from exile, the appearance of the *khlopoman movement, and the organization of *hromadas in the late 1850s. The Cyrillo-Methodians were the first to formulate a populist political platform based on social and national emancipation, albeit couched in religious and romantic terms. The organization was broken up by the authorities in 1847, and its leading members were exiled. In Kiev V. *Antonovych, leader of the *khlopomany*, issued a typically populist manifesto, 'Moia ispoved'' (My Confession), published in *Osnova in 1862. In it he called on the Polish lords to renounce their privileges and work for the benefit of the people among whom they lived, the Ukrainian peasantry. The *khlopomany* eventually merged with other young Ukrainians to form the *Hromada of Kiev. Hromadas were organized in several cities at that time. Members, both liberals and radicals, organized *Sunday schools to teach literacy to peasants and workers, supported and contributed to Ukrainian populist journals, and promoted Ukrainian scholarship. Some became involved in revolutionary activities, although the dominant trend was for peaceful change. Ukrainian populists were generally known by their contemporaries as Ukrainophiles, and the Ukrainian populist movement has been called national populist. The most prominent among them were Antonovych and Drahomanov, both of whom came to represent two basic trends within the movement; cautious (even apolitical) cultural work (Antonovych) and radical (activist) socialism (Drahomanov).

The fact that Ukrainian populists were involved primarily in cultural work did not protect them from repressions. Ukrainian populists were accused of being separatists, of supporting the Poles, of fomenting discontent among the peasantry, and of socialism. Some were exiled, and the Sunday schools were closed, but the biggest blow was the enactment of P. *Valuev's circular in 1863, which forbade the publication of popular, educational, and religious literature in the Ukrainian language. An assassination attempt on the tsar in 1866 reinforced the reactionary tendencies of the government. In those conditions the hromadas became less active, but scholarly work proceeded.

The early 1870s were especially fruitful for Ukrainian scholarship. The period also saw the renewal of hromadas. Ukrainian populists in Kiev, many of whom were also scholars, helped found the *Southwestern Branch of the Imperial Russian Geographic Society in 1873 and developed it into an unofficial Ukrainian academy of sciences. By late 1874 they had gained control of the newspaper *Kievskii telegraf. Also in 1874, Ukrainophiles organized and hosted the Third Archeological Congress in Kiev, which devoted much of its program to Ukrainian topics. Closer ties were established with Western Ukrainian populists in the early 1870s, and cultural activists from central

and eastern Ukraine helped to found the Shevchenko (later Scientific) Society and published their uncensored articles in the organ of the Galician national populists, *Pravda.

The Ukrainophiles suffered major setbacks during a reaction in 1875–6. Drahomanov was removed from his position at Kiev University and forbidden to teach in Ukraine; the Southwestern Branch was disbanded, and its organizer, P. *Chubynsky, was exiled; *Kievskii telegraf* was shut down. The most crippling blow, however, was the proclamation of the *Ems Ukase by the tsar in May 1876, which forbade (with few exceptions) the printing of all Ukrainian-language material in the Russian Empire and its importation.

A Russian revolutionary populist movement had also activated itself by the 1870s. In all its phases the Russian movement was well represented in Ukraine as part of a general all-Russian current. Nevertheless it had its own distinctiveness in Ukraine, where objective conditions were different than in Russia. In addressing the national question some Russian populists felt that national differences would be resolved by reorganizing the empire according to federal principles. Yet the federalist concept was weakly developed, and most Russian populists did not consider the national question important. The language issue was likewise not openly addressed, although some revolutionary propaganda work was conducted in Ukrainian.

The revolutionary populist movement in Ukraine was also particularly strong. The *Kharkiv-Kiev Secret Society, founded in 1856, was one of the first revolutionary populist groups established in the Russian Empire. One of its founders, P. *Yefymenko, was a well-known Ukrainophile. Ukraine was one of the regions of intense activity on the part of the 'going to the people' movement of 1874–5. The first working-class organization in the Russian Empire, the *South Russian Union of Workers, was founded by revolutionary populists in Odessa. That city was a center of intense activity on the part of populist groups, as well as Kiev and Kharkiv. The Bakuninist trend in revolutionary populism, as exemplified by the *Southern Rebels, was particularly strong in Ukraine. *Narodnaia Volia was also very active there.

In certain instances there was co-operation between hromada members and Russian groups; some members of the revolutionary groups had strong ties with or were among the radical members of hromadas. A. Zheliabov had attended meetings of the Odessa Hromada. The radical Ukrainophile S. *Podolynsky helped establish Lavrov's émigré journal, *Vpered*, an important organ of Russian revolutionary populism. He later argued that Ukrainians needed to establish their own socialist party. Attempts were made to establish Ukrainian revolutionary groups. V. Malovany of the Odessa Hromada was arrested and exiled for attempting to establish a Ukrainian social-revolutionary party in the early 1880s.

An attempt to form an émigré Ukrainian radical or socialist center was made by Drahomanov. After he was removed as a professor, Drahomanov emigrated. In Geneva he was joined by Podolynsky, and M. *Ziber. With the financial support of the Kiev Hromada and later of Podolynsky Drahomanov established a Ukrainian printing press and published a radical Ukrainophile journal called *Hromada. The journal was smuggled into Ukraine, where it had some influence among radical Ukrainophiles. Drahomanov initially maintained close ties with Russian revolutionaries, although a few years after emigrating he came to condemn their terrorism, centralism, and disregard of the national question.

Whereas Drahomanov was deeply involved, at least initially after emigrating, in radical politics, the Kiev Hromada was becoming more cautious. The government's repressive policies acted to reinforce those in favor of retrenchment and strictly apolitical, cultural work. Following Alexander II's assassination in 1881 by Narodnaia Volia members, repression intensified. By the mid-1880s the Kiev Hromada had decided to break with Drahomanov and cease subsidizing him. Drahomanov criticized their action and maintained that it was precisely such apoliticism that caused many young radicals to forsake the struggle for Ukrainian rights and join the Russian movement instead.

The hromadas thus limited themselves primarily to cultural work. In 1882 the Kiev Hromada was instrumental in founding *Kievskaia starina*, which became an important journal of Ukrainian studies. Significant work was done on various projects, such as a Ukrainian dictionary, completed by B. *Hrinchenko as *Slovar ukraïns'koï movy* (1907–9).

Populist ideals had a profound impact on Ukrainian literature in the second half of the 19th century. Early populist trends were most clearly represented by Shevchenko and M. Vovchok. By the end of the 1870s P. Myrny and I. Nechui-Levytsky had written some of their most important works, and I. Franko had made his literary debut; in the 1880s M. Kotsiubynsky and the poet P. Hrabovsky began their literary careers. Despite the ban on the Ukrainian language Ukrainian literature had become established in its own right by the 1880s, that is, during the period when it was most evidently populist in orientation. Populist writers began to examine new, previously unexplored, themes in Ukrainian literature, such as the role of the intelligentsia and the women's question, in addition to the well-worn theme of the fate of village folk. To avoid censorship writers from Russian-ruled Ukraine published extensively in Galicia. Ukrainian theater, also populist in orientation, was established with the formation in 1882 of the first Ukrainian professional troupe in the Russian empire, by M. Kropyvnytsky.

Populist ideas had a great influence on Ukrainian historiography. The most important early Ukrainian populist historian was Kostomarov, but Antonovych, as founder of the Kiev school of populist historiography, had a great impact as well. In addition to making his own contributions he influenced a whole generation of historians, including M. Hrushevsky and D. Bahalii. Ukrainian populist historians emphasized the role of common folk and popular institutions in their works, wrote much on the Cossacks and haidamaka uprisings, and promoted regional studies. To a large degree theirs was a natural response to the stateless condition of the Ukrainian nation as well as to the statist and official schools in Russian historiography.

BIBLIOGRAPHY

Okhrymovych, Iu. *Rozvytok ukraïns'koï natsional'no-politychnoï dumky* (Lviv–Kiev 1922; repr, New York 1965)
Iavors'kyi, M. *Narysy z istoriï revoliutsiinoï borot'by na Ukraïni*, 2 vols (Kharkiv 1927–8)
Iastrebov, F. *Revoliutsionnye demokraty na Ukraine: Vtoraia polovina 50-kh–nachalo 60-kh godov XIX st.* (Kiev 1960)
Katrenko, A. 'Revoliutsiine narodnytstvo 70-kh–pochatku 80-kh rokiv XIX st. na Ukraïni v istoriohrafiï radians'koho periodu,' *Istorychni dzherela ta ïkh vykorystannia*, no. 3 (1968)
Ionescu, G.; Gellern, E. (eds). *Populism: Its Meaning and National Characteristics* (London 1969)
Rud'ko, M. *Revoliutsiini narodnyky na Ukraïni (70-ti roku XIX st.)* (Kiev 1973)
Voloshchenko, A. *Narysy z istoriï suspil'no-politychnoho rukhu na Ukraïni v 70-kh–na pochatku 80-kh rokiv XIX st.* (Kiev 1974)
Canovan, M. *Populism* (New York 1981)

B. Klid

Populism, Western Ukrainian. A cultural and then political movement initiated in the 1860s by the young Ukrainian intelligentsia in Galicia (known commonly as *narodovtsi*, or populists). It arose in counterpoint to the clerical conservatism of the older intelligentsia, who had become disillusioned with the possibility of independent Ukrainian national development after the failure of efforts to secure full national emancipation and had begun to orient itself increasingly (both culturally and politically) to Russia (see *Old Ruthenians and *Russophiles).

The *narodovtsi* sought to help Ukrainians better themselves through their own resources. They identified themselves with Ukrainians in the Russian Empire and insisted on the use of vernacular Ukrainian in literature and education. Their movement, deeply influenced by the writings of T. Shevchenko, M. Shashkevych, P. Kulish, M. Kostomarov, M. Vovchok, and others, built on the traditions of the Ukrainian national revival of the 1830s and 1840s as represented by the *Cyril and Methodius Brotherhood in Kiev, the *Ruthenian Triad, and the *Supreme Ruthenian Council in Lviv.

Ukrainophiles in the Russian Empire had a determining influence in the establishment and development of the populist movement in Galicia, particularly the *khlopomany of the 1850s, who propagated the idea of unity with the common folk and working among them. In the early stages of the movement contacts with Ukrainian students and the works of Ukrainian writers in the Russian Empire had a significant impact on it.

The populist movement in Galicia initially included students, teachers, writers, and young clergymen. The earliest focus of its activity was literary, and many of its activists organized themselves around journals. Because of a shortage of funds, those publications (including *Vechernytsi*, *Meta*, *Nyva*, and *Rusalka*) commonly died out and were then revived under new names. The *narodovtsi* also established contacts with the young Ukrainian intelligentsia in central Ukraine that was grouped around *hromadas, and organized similar bodies (largely composed of students) in Berezhany, Drohobych, Kolomyia, Lviv, Peremyshl, Sambir, Stanyslaviv, and Ternopil. Some older community leaders and writers, including I. Borysykevych, S. Kachala, Yu. Lavrivsky, K. Ustiianovych, and S. Vorobkevych, joined them. The younger generation of writers active in the movement included K. Horbal, K. Klymkovych, and V. Shashkevych; O. Partytsky and D. Taniachkevych served as the principal ideologues and organizers of the early hromadas.

The proscription of the Ukrainian printed word by the Russian authorities in 1863 and 1876 forced certain writers, including M. *Drahomanov, O. Konysky, P. Kulish, I. Nechui-Levytsky, and M. Starytsky, to publish their works in Galicia. Their doing so stimulated literary and scholarly activity among the populists there, and in 1867 the literary journal *Pravda* was established as the main voice of the populists (until *Dilo* emerged in 1880).

The populists took advantage of the new Austrian constitution by forming a number of new organizations, including the Ruska (later *Ukrainska) Besida society (1861) and an attendant full-time theater (1864) and the *Prosvita society (1868), whose branches and reading rooms played a critical role in the Ukrainian national movement. In 1873, financial backers from central Ukraine helped to establish the Shevchenko Literary Society, which in 1893 was renamed the *Shevchenko Scientific Society. Those community and scholarly organizations helped to shape a new populist national identity, worldview, and political outlook among Western Ukrainians. The ideas of *Drahomanov were particularly influential, although not everyone in the populist movement agreed with his offerings. The crystallization of a populist viewpoint was further aided by the *Sich student society of Vienna (est 1868), which acted as a conduit for transmitting Western European ideas to Galicia.

The poor showing of the largely Russophile Ruthenian Council in the Viennese parliamentary elections of 1879 (it elected only three delegates) prompted the populists to participate more directly in politics. Their activity initially took the form of publishing political newspapers for the peasantry (*Bat'kivshchyna*, from 1879) and the intelligentsia (*Dilo*, from 1880). In 1880 the populists organized the first Ukrainian all-people's meeting in Lviv, at which various addresses on political and economic themes were delivered. In 1885 they established their own political organization, the *People's Council, which soon became the strongest Ukrainian party in Galicia. The leading populists of the period included O. Barvinsky and his brother, V. Barvinsky (editor of *Dilo*), the economist V. Navrotsky, D. Hladylovych, O. Ohonovsky, Yu. Romanchuk (editor of *Bat'kivshchyna*), and the composer A. Vakhnianyn.

In the course of its evolution the populist movement lost its element of social radicalism and dropped its opposition to the Greek Catholic hierarchy; eventually it became quite conservative, loyal to the Austrian government, and dominated by the clergy. The shift was a result of the aging of its membership and its co-operation with clerics who had broken with the Russophiles. A new radical populist movement arose in reaction. That group, which looked to Drahomanov as a mentor, included I. *Franko, T. *Okunevsky, M. *Pavlyk, and O. *Terletsky. It finally established definite structures in 1890 with the creation of the *Ukrainian Radical party and the newspaper *Narod*.

In 1890 the Austrian government, in conjunction with the Polish provincial administration of Galicia, attempted to appease Ukrainian cultural and political demands by establishing the *New Era policy. The populists in particular were courted for their support. Although the New Era provided some concessions, it lacked substance and was largely unpopular among the Ukrainian people. Opposed by such leading populists as Ye. Olesnytsky, the New Era lasted only until 1894. That year a schism emerged in the populist contingent of parliamentary delegates between a progovernment faction led by O. Barvinsky and A. Vakhnianyn and an opposition faction led by Yu. Romanchuk. In 1899 the majority of populists joined with the right wing of the Ukrainian Radical party to form the *National Democratic party. O. Barvinsky's faction, centered around the offices of the newspaper *Ruslan*, continued to support New Era policies and later formed the Catholic Ruthenian People's Union (later the *Christian Social Movement).

Influenced by its counterpart in Galicia, the populist movement in Bukovyna emerged initially in literature. In 1869 O. Fedkovych came out in favor of using the Ukrainian vernacular, as did the brothers H. and S. Vorobkevych. In the mid-1880s the populists overcame the influence of local Russophiles and took control of leading community organizations, such as Ruska Besida (1884) and the Ruthenian Council (1885). The newspaper *Bukovyna* was formed in 1885 as the voice of the local populists, who included Fedkovych, Ye. Pihuliak, O. Popovych, I. Tyminsky, and V. Volian. A schism among populists did not occur in Bukovyna until after 1900, when they broke off into the National Democratic party, the Radical Party, and the Social Democratic party.

Ukrainian populism was slowest to develop in Transcarpathia, where it was initiated in the 1880s by L. Csopey in literature and language education. It became more widespread in the 20th century as a result of the efforts of A. Voloshyn, H. Strypsky, and Yu. Zhatkovych. The Ukrainian national revival in Transcarpathia in the 1920s and 1930s was marked largely by a populist ideology.

BIBLIOGRAPHY
Terlets'kyi, O. *Moskvofily i narodovtsi v 1870-ykh rr.* (Lviv 1902)
Barvins'kyi, O. *Spohady z moho zhyttia*, 2 vols (Lviv 1912–13)
Levyts'kyi, K. *Istoriia politychnoï dumky halyts'kykh ukraïntsiv 1848–1914* (Lviv 1926)
Olesnyts'kyi, E. *Storinky z moho zhyttia*, 2 vols (Lviv 1935)
Sokhots'kyi, I. *Budivnychi novitn'oï derzhavnosty v Halychyni* (New York 1961)

V. Lev, I. Vytanovych

Poputchik (Russian for 'fellow traveler'; Ukrainian: *poputnyk*). A term in early Soviet literature for those writers who were neither Party members nor actively involved in imposing Soviet rule yet were sympathetic to some degree of co-operation. In Ukraine *poputchiki* were usually writers who did not belong to the 'proletarian' literary organizations (such as Hart, later the All-Ukrainian Association of Proletarian Writers). At first the term *poputchiki* even included writers in futuristic literary organizations, such as Fliamingo (1919), the *Association of Panfuturists (1922–5), *Nova Generatsiia (1927–31), and *Avanhard (1926–9). As *poputchiki*, however, those writers were often politically inconsistent, in that some eventually moved to the extreme left wing, such as the onetime theoretician of Ukrainian futurism O. *Poltoratsky. At first the most typical of the *poputchiki* were the writers belonging to Kiev literary circles who grouped around the journal *Knyhar* (1917–20) and then around the Kiev publishing house Slovo (out of whom the group of *Neoclassicists emerged). The Kiev writers in the group Lanka (1924–6, renamed *MARS in 1926) can also be classed as *poputchiki*. A few literary critics were *poputchiki*, such as B. *Yakubsky, A. *Lebid, O. *Doroshkevych, H. *Maifet, and M. *Dolengo, who mainly grouped around the journals *Chervonyi shliakh*, *Zhyttia i revoliutsiia*, and, later, *Literaturnyi iarmarok*. In the 1930s the majority of the *poputchiki* were arrested and deported to labor camps, where they died (M. Zerov, P. Fylypovych, M. Drai-Khmara, H. Kosynka, Ye. Pluzhnyk, D. Falkivsky, H. Brasiuk, B. Teneta, and others). Some died during the Second World War in German labor camps (Ya. Kachura); others, after years of leading a wretched existence in exile, were rehabilitated (B. Antonenko-Davydovych). The most vocal critics against the *poputchiki* were V. Koriak, D. Zahul, Ya. Savchenko, O. Poltoratsky, and B. Kovalenko. The writers' organization *Vaplite worked with the *poputchiki* and defended them, and later some *poputchiki* joined Vaplite. The term *poputchik* was officially discarded after the Party's decree in 1932 that all writers should unite in a single Writers' Union of Ukraine.

M. Stepovy

Pora. See *Ukraïns'ka hromads'ka pora*.

Poraiko, Vasyl [Porajko, Vasyl'], b 12 November 1888 in Ustia, Sniatyn county, Galicia, d 25 November 1937. Soviet political figure. During the First World War he was captured and deported by the Russians to Astrakhan, where he joined the Bolsheviks. Upon returing to Galicia he became a member of the CP(B)U and commander in chief of the Red Ukrainian Galician Army (March–August 1920). He served on the All-Ukrainian Central Executive Committee (1920–5) and then held important posts in the Ukrainian government – chief procurator, commissar of justice (1927–30), and deputy head of the Council of People's Commissars (1930–7). At the same time he was a member of the Organizational Bureau of the CP(B)U. He was arrested in August 1937 during the purge of the Ukrainian government and Party and shot a few months later.

Porcelain and china industry. A branch of the fine ceramics industry manufacturing household and artistic porcelain, faience and *majolica, and laboratory, medical, insulation, radio, and sanitary porcelain. Good-quality plastic and refractory white clays, kaolins, feldspar, and quartz are mixed to form porcelain paste. The pottery formed from the paste is fired at different temperatures and with different additives to produce white hard porcelain (at a temperature of up to 1,400°C), soft porcelain (1,300–1,350°C), and special porcelain (above 1,450°C), which is impervious to water and gas. Porcelain or china is usually finished with a transparent glaze and decorated with ceramic paints. For faience more clay and less feldspar is used, and the ware is porous and of a light cream color. It is usually covered with a colored glaze.

Ukraine provides favorable conditions for the development of the porcelain and china industry. Deposits of the best sorts of kaolin are found mostly in the Ukrainian Crystalline Shield, and the porcelain and china factories are therefore located mostly in that belt, particularly in the Zhytomyr region. The industry began to develop in Ukraine in the first half of the 18th century. The first china and faience factories in Ukraine were set up by Polish magnates to compete with foreign imports. Such factories appeared in Biała Podlaska, in Podlachia (1738–42), Zhovkva, in Galicia, and Chudniv, in Volhynia. All of them were managed by German craftsmen. J. Czartoryski established a large factory in Korets (1783–1832), which became famous for its china and faience. It was managed by craftsmen from Sèvres, the brothers F. and M. Maser. Until 1790 it manufactured faience, and afterward, china as well. In 1793 about 1,000 workers and 73 painters were employed at the factory, which was run by Sobinski. Its monthly output was 20,000 units of domestic, decorative, and pharmaceutical ware. At first its products imitated the rococo and Empire styles of the china manufactured in Meissen, Sèvres, and Vienna. Eventually, original motifs appeared on the Korets china. Blue in all its shades was the most frequently used color. In 1815 polychromatic ornamentation was introduced, consisting mainly of vegetative motifs derived from the local flora; miniature landscapes of French design but taken sometimes from the local region; and transparent incisions. Count Zamoyski's factory in Tomaszow, in the Kholm region (1795–1834 and 1842–96), produced ware that was popular in Ukraine, Poland, Hungary, and Moldavia. It was decorated by M. Maser and, beginning in 1842, by Wendler. The factory produced 20,000 pieces annually. From 1806 it produced china mostly in the Empire style. One of the largest china and earthenware factories (at first 100 workers, then 500) was located in Baranivka on the estates of the Walewski family from 1802. The factory was owned by F. Maser and the members of his family and, from 1895, by the Hrypari family. It manufactured mostly household china that was decorated with polychromatic and sometimes monochromatic floral designs and, from the 1820s, with miniature landscapes. The yellow color was one of the factory's inventions. Smaller china and faience factories were located in Horodets, Emelchyn, Dovbysh, Kamianyi Brid, Polonne, Romaniv, Patsykiv, and Korosten.

Beyond Volhynia a large earthenware factory was located near Kiev, the *Mezhyhiria Faience Factory (1798–1874). The influence of Ukrainian folk art is evident in the forms and decorations of its products. A. Myklashevsky owned a china factory in the village of Volokytyne, in the Chernihiv region (1839–62). Its products consisted mostly of expensive dining sets, sculptures emulating French models, and Empire fireplaces in the baroque style with a touch of Ukrainian folklore.

In the second half of the 19th century the porcelain and china industry in Ukraine declined, mostly because of foreign competition. By 1895 there were only eight porcelain factories in Ukraine, employing 430 workers and producing 75,000 rubles' worth of goods. In 1913 there were 9 enterprises, compared to 27 in Russia. The largest faience factory, established in 1887, was located in Budy, near Kharkiv. It employed over 1,000 wage and salary workers. In 1913 it produced 11 million units of various earthenware.

After the 1917 Revolution the porcelain and china factories in Ukraine were nationalized, and at the beginning of the 1920s they resumed production. Eventually most of them were rebuilt, and most of the manual labor was mechanized. Production increased dramatically: the largest factory in Budy had turned out 44 million items by 1940. At first the porcelain and china factories used the old patterns. With time they adopted some standard patterns for mass production. Besides household china, the factories in Baranivka, Dovbysh, and, particularly, Horodets produced statuettes of animals and of Soviet life designed mostly by the craftsmen Yu. Havryliuk and R. Marchuk. In 1929–41 vegetative motifs instead of geometric folk ornamentation were increasingly used to decorate tea sets. Mechanized methods of decoration with hackneyed scenes of Soviet life designed by such artists as M. Kotenko and V. Panashchatenko were adopted.

After the Second World War and the collapse of the industry in 1941–4, it was rebuilt; by the beginning of the 1950s it had reached the 1940 level of production. New techniques and technology were introduced, production was expanded, new factories were built, and the assortment of products was increased. The main porcelain and china factories are located in Kiev, Baranivka, Horodets, and Korosten. The Kiev Experimental Ceramic and Artistic Plant (est 1945) does research on the technology of porcelain making. New porcelain designs are invented there for the porcelain factories in Ukraine. The Kiev factory applied the motifs of Ukrainian folk wall-painting to the decoration of china. Artists such as O. Sorokin, O. Zhnykrup, S. Bolzan, O. Rapai-Markish, H. Moldavan, and V. Shcherbyna specialize in table sculpture. The porcelain factory in Baranivka has the largest assortment of goods. The decoration process is mechanized. The most common ornament is floral, based on Ukrainian folk art. Its porcelain figures depict characters from Ukrainian literature and folktales and representatives of social groups in folk costumes. About 20 painters under the direction of M. Kryvorukova and sculptors under the direction of V. Pokosovska and D. Hoch were employed at the plant. In 1976, 39.4 million articles were produced. The Horodets Porcelain Factory specializes in tea sets, table sets, and decorative china. Its production in 1968 was 18 million pieces of china. The factory in Korosten specializes in dining sets, drinking china, and jugs. Since 1960 it has also produced statuettes. Its chief artist was H. Malytsky, and its chief sculptor was T. Tokarenko. At the Polonne factory the chief artist was P. Ivanchenko, and at the Dovbysh factory, O. Yarosh. Both factories specialize in tea sets, gift mugs, cups, and toy dining sets. The *Budy Faience Factory is the largest and most modern porcelain plant in the former Soviet Union. Besides dishes the factory manufactures medical, sanitary, and decorative faience. In 1976 there were 16 porcelain and china factories in Ukraine. The factories at Slovianske, Pervomaiske, and Olevske made porcelain insulators. Ukraine's output of household china and porcelain was 6,000 t in 1940, 7,400 t in 1950, 21,700 t in 1960, 39,500 t in 1970, and 57,900 t in 1979. Ukraine's output accounted for about 30 percent of the USSR output. Some of it was exported to the other Soviet republics and beyond the Soviet Union. Nevertheless, there is an acute shortage of household china in Ukraine.

Ceramic artists are trained at the Odessa Industrial Arts School, the Myrhorod Ceramics Tekhnikum, and the Lviv Institute of Applied and Decorative Arts.

BIBLIOGRAPHY
Lysin, B. 'Proizvodstvo keramicheskikh izdelei Iugo-Zapadnoi Rossii,' *Vestnik tekhnologii khimicheskikh i stroitel'nykh materialov*, no. 3 (Kiev 1911)
Smolichev, P. 'Do istorii portselianovoho vyrobnytstva na Chernihivshchyni,' in *Iuvileinyi zbirnyk na poshanu M.S. Hrushevs'koho*, 1 (Kiev 1928)
Ohloblyn, O. 'Do istorii portselianovo-faiansovoi promyslovosti na Ukraïni,' *Pratsi Komisiï sotsiial'no-ekonomichnoï istoriï Ukraïny*, 1 (Kiev 1932)
Sichyns'kyi, V. *Ukraïns'ka portseliana* (Philadelphia 1952)
Dolinskii, L. *Ukrainskii khudozhnii farfor* (Kiev 1963)
Farfor, faians, maiolika (Kiev 1970)

V. Kubijovyč, O. Ohloblyn

Porfirev, Vladimir [Porfirjev], b 8 July 1899 in Viatka, Russia, d 30 January 1982 in Kiev. Geologist; full member of the AN URSR (now ANU) from 1957. He graduated from the Leningrad Geological Institute in 1926. He then worked in geological institutes in Leningrad and in 1938 joined the ANU Institute of Geological Sciences. He served as chairman of its petroleum department (1944–50) and became director of the ANU institutes of the Geology and Geochemistry of Fossil Fuels (1951–63) and of Geological Sciences (1963–8). He conducted petroleum explorations in Central Asia, Caucasia, and Ukraine, especially in the Dnipropetrovske-Donetske and Carpathian regions, and published extensively on the origin of fossil fuels. He proposed theories on the origins of petroleum, ozocerite, and coal.

Porohy (Rapids). A monthly magazine of literature and art, published in Buenos Aires in 1949–57 (a total of 79 issues). Edited by A. Halan and I. Kachurovsky, it published works and translations by Ukrainian émigré writers. Among the contributors were K. Buldyn, L. Poltava, M. Sytnyk, M. Orest, V. Derzhavyn, V. Chaplenko, Ye. Onatsky, and O. Drahomanova.

Porokhivsky, K. See Zyblikevych, Yevhen.

Porpoise (Ukrainian: *morska svynia, delfin*). A marine mammal of the order Cetacea, suborder Odontoceti, which also includes the whale (Ukrainian: *kyt*). The porpoise (family Delphinidae) is the only cetacean found in Ukrainian waters, in the Black Sea and Sea of Azov. It grows to up to 2 m in length and weighs about 90 kg. Previously important commercially, it was hunted for its meat, skin, and oil. Since 1965 hunting for porpoises has been banned.

Mykola Porsh

Porsh, Mykola [Porš], b 19 October 1879 in Lubni, Poltava gubernia, d 16 April 1944 in Berlin. Economist and civic figure of German-Jewish descent and a leading member of the *Revolutionary Ukrainian party and of the *Ukrainian Social Democratic Workers' party. In the late 1890s he conducted revolutionary work in the Lubni region, and from 1904 he worked in the political underground in Kiev and Nizhen. During the revolutionary period he was a member of the Central Rada and its Little Rada. In January 1918 he was appointed UNR minister of defense and labor. After serving as UNR envoy to Germany in 1919–20, he stayed abroad and turned away from political activity. His studies of Ukraine's agrarian and economic problems demonstrated, by an examination of issues such as land use and ownership, the labor market, and Russian state budget policies, how Ukraine was exploited by Russia. Methodologically, Porsh was one of the first economists to separate the statistical data on Ukraine from the data on the Russian Empire. Under the pseudonym Hordiienko he engaged in polemics with P. Struve on the question of Ukraine's national economy. He also translated K. Marx's *Zur Kritik der politischen Ökonomie* into Ukrainian (1923).

Port Arthur. See Thunder Bay.

Portraiture. The artistic depiction of one or more particular persons. The oldest form of secular art in Ukraine, it dates back to the 4th-century BC portraits found in burial sights in Chersonese Taurica. Medieval examples are the depictions of Grand Prince Yaroslav the Wise and his family (1044) in the frescoes of the St Sophia Cathedral in Kiev and the depictions of Grand Prince Sviatoslav II Yaroslavych and his family in the illuminations of the *Izbornik* of Sviatoslav (1073). Prince Yaropolk Iziaslavych and his wife, Kunigunde-Irina, are shown in the Trier Psalter (1078–87).

Although portraiture did not emerge as a separate genre until the 16th century, its existence may be traced back to the canonical renderings of SS Anthony and Theodosius of the Caves in the *Holy Protectress of the Caves* icon (ca 1288), where they have been given individualized features. In the late 15th and early 16th centuries the rendering of icon countenances became more realistic as a result of Renaissance influences (eg, the *Krasiv Mother of God*). In the 17th century, realistic portrayals of patrons were part of the composition of icons, such as the *Crucifixion*, with a portrait of L. Svichka, by Y. Ivanovych, the *Holy Protectress*, with a portrait of Hetman B. Khmelnytsky, and the fresco *Supplication* (1644–6), with Metropolitan P. Mohyla, in the Transfiguration Church in the Berestove district of Kiev.

Late 16th- to 18th-century religious and secular portraits at first had some characteristics of the icon, such as flattened forms, static frontal composition, and hieratic figural representation. With time, under the influence of Renaissance painting, they became three-dimensional and were painted with a linear and aerial perspective. Many portraits of patrons of shrines and churches were painted and displayed inside churches. In one of the earliest surviving portraits of this type, that of J. Herburt (ca 1578), only the face and hands show signs of modeling. The later portrait of K. Korniakt (1630s) is more three-dimensional, but its composition is static. A portrait of T. Palii (ca 1711), however, is rendered rather flatly and hieratically, her garments decoratively silhouetted against a shallow backdrop.

Memorial portraits of members of the upper classes were painted on wood or metal and attached to the lids of their coffins. One of the most sensitive and beautifully modeled was that of V. Lanhysh (1635), found in the Lviv Dormition Brotherhood's portrait collection. Thought to be by M. Petrakhnovych, it was painted in oils on a metal oval. Portraits were also painted on banners used at funerals; the one of K. Korniakt (1603) is an outstanding example. Small votive pictures with unsophisticated portrayals of deceased individuals, such as F. Stefanyk (1618), S. Komarnytsky (1654), and I. Vysotsky (1677), were also popular.

The rich also commissioned sculptural depictions of deceased family members, which were set atop tombstones; notable cemetery sculptures were those of K. Ostrozky (1579), O. Lahodovsky (1573), the Syniavsky family (ca 1573–1642) in Berezhany, K. Romultova (1572) in Drohobych, and A. Kysil (1653) in Nyzkynychi, Volhynia.

Secular portraits of nobles, Cossack and peasant leaders, and rich burghers gained currency in the 16th century and grew in popularity through the 17th and 18th centuries. A portrait of the Polish king Stefan Batory (ca 1578) painted by the Lviv guild artist V. Stefanovsky during the king's visit to Lviv was a realistic depiction without the pomposity and idealization prevalent in portraits of that time. A special type of portrait painting developed in Ukraine, the *parsunnyi* (from the Latin *persona*), depicting notable figures in rich attire and formal poses against a background reaffirming their official status; included in this category are portraits of K. Zbarazky (1620s), Hetman I. Samoilovych (1674), M. Myklashevsky (ca 1700), V. Darahan (1760s), and H. Hamaliia (1750s).

During the baroque period of the late 17th and early 18th centuries many official portraits of Cossack hetmans, including B. Khmelnytsky, I. Mazepa, I. Skoropadsky, D. Apostol, and P. Polubotok, were painted depicting the regalia of office. Church leaders were also well represented in portraiture (eg, I. Krokovsky, 1718; D. Postovsky, 1752). Family portraits mirrored social and historical changes in their composition and the manner in which the subjects were painted. The portrait of Col S. Sulyma and his wife (1754), for example, depicts them in the elaborate dress of Cossack leaders, whereas that of their son and his wife (1780s) portrays them as typical courtiers.

Until the 18th century, artists rarely signed their works. Of the few names of portraitists that are known, F. *Senkovych, M. *Petrakhnovych, *Vasyl of Lviv, I. *Rutkovych, O. *Lianytsky, Master Samuil, and Master Andrii deserve mention. The development of regional styles gave rise to the Kievan, Galician, and Volhynian schools of portrait painting. Portraits were also made by engravers, such as L. and O. *Tarasevych (K. Klokotsky, 1685), I. *Shchyrsky (V. Yasynsky, 1707), O. Irkliivsky, and H. *Levytsky (portrait of R. Zaborovsky, 1739). L. Tarasevych was the most prominent portraitist of royalty and nobility (eg, *Princess Sofiia Alekseevna*, 1689; *K.-S. Radziwiłł*, 1692). D. Galakhovsky was the author of the engraving of I. Mazepa printed in a scholarly tract.

The tsarist abolition of Ukrainian autonomy in the 18th century coincided with the establishment of the St Petersburg Academy of Arts (1758), which attracted many Ukrainian artists. D. *Levytsky of Kiev became a professor at the academy and the greatest portraitist in the Russian Empire of his time. V. *Borovykovsky, another outstanding portraitist, also worked in St Petersburg in the classical, academic manner favored by the imperial court. In the 19th century many portraits were painted in Ukraine by trainees of the academy (V. Tropinin, A. *Mokrytsky, K. *Pavlov, H. *Vasko) and of guild workshops (H. Hanetsky, H. Kushliansky) as well as by self-taught artists (M. Dyrov, I. Sliusarenko) and amateurs (O. Berdiaev, H. *Psol). Among the many portraits painted, *Portrait of My Wife* (1835) by Mokrytsky and *Portrait of a Young Man* (1847) by Vasko stand out. Portraits were also painted by wandering artists (P. Orlov, K. Yushkevych-Stakhovsky) and by artists who were formers serfs, such as D. Maliarenko, I. *Shapovalenko, P. Zaitsev, I. Zasidatel, and T.

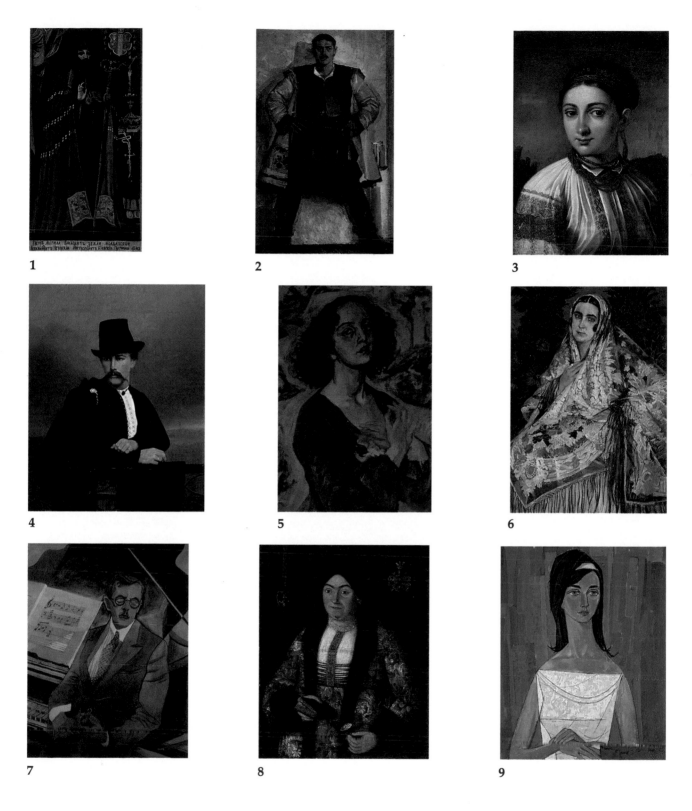

PORTRAITURE 1) Anonymous: *Petro Mohyla, Metropolitan of Kiev and Halych (1574–1647)* (oil, 18th century; Kiev Museum of Ukrainian Art). 2) F. Krychevsky: *Self-Portrait* (oil, 1937; Kiev Museum of Ukrainian Art). 3) V. Tropinin: *Girl from Podilia* (oil, 1804–12; Kiev Museum of Ukrainian Art). 4) A. Horonovych: *Vasyl Tarnovsky* (oil, 19th century; Kiev Museum of Ukrainian Art). 5) O. Novakivsky: *Halyna Holubovska* (oil, ca 1905; courtesy of M. Mushynka). 6) O. Shovkunenko: *Fadiieva* (oil on wood, 1922; Kiev Museum of Ukrainian Art). (Photographs 1–5 courtesy of the Winnipeg Art Gallery.) 7) A. Petrytsky: *Kozytsky* (watercolor and India ink on paper, 1931; Kiev Museum of Ukrainian Art). 8) Anonymous: *Paraska Vasylivna Sulyma* (oil, 1750s; Kiev Museum of Ukrainian Art). 9) M. Levytsky: *Oksana* (oil, 1964; courtesy of O. Struk).

*Shevchenko, whose contribution to the Ukrainian art has often been underrated. Shevchenko's portraits displayed a broad social range of subjects, from peasants (*The Kazakh Girl*, 1856) to nobility (*Princess E. Keikuatova*, 1847), and sensitive three-dimensional modeling with light. He painted over 150 portraits, 43 of them self-portraits.

Portraits remained popular throughout the 19th century. They were done by most artists, including M. Murashko (*Portrait of M. Ge*, 1906), M. Kuznetsov (*Portrait of P. Tchaikovsky*, 1893), M. Pymonenko (*Portrait of the Wife in Green Dress*, 1893), H. Tsyss (*V. Mahdenko*, 1910), and K. Kostandi (*Portrait of M. Kniazeva*, 1898). P. Martynovych created strong images of Ukrainian peasants (*H. Honchar, Portrait*, 1870s), and S. Vasylkivsky specialized in historical portraits, including ones of B. Khmelnytsky, P. Mohyla, and I. Gonta. Women artists who painted portraits included M. *Raievska-Ivanova (*Self-Portrait*, 1866) and M. *Bashkirtseva (*Portrait of a Parisienne*, 1883), who worked mostly in France.

In the 20th century, artists have created portraits in a variety of styles. O. *Murashko, famous for his *Girl in a Red Hat* (1902–3), experimented with impressionist light effects (*Zhorzh and Oleksandra Murashko*, 1904–8; *Portrait of a Peasant Family*, 1914). F. *Krychevsky's interest in impressionism, postimpressionism, and cubo-futurism can be seen in his *Girl in Pale Blue* (1904), *H. Pavlutsky* (1922), and *P. Krychevska* (1926) respectively. In the 1930s he turned to more realistic depictions (*Happy Dairymaids*, 1937). M. *Zhuk painted a variety of portraits, including some with cubist analysis of space (*P. Tychyna*, 1919). Among the followers of M. Boichuk, O. *Pavlenko devoted considerable time to self-portraits and portraits of women (*Mariika*, 1920; *Self-Portrait*, 1925, 1930, 1970). A. *Petrytsky, who explored cubo-futurism, deserves special mention for creating, between 1928 and 1933, 150 portraits of Ukrainian cultural figures; tragically, most disappeared or were destroyed during the Stalinist terror.

With the imposition of *socialist realism by the Soviet regime in the early 1930s, all open explorations in modernism came to a standstill. Thenceforth most portraits created in Soviet Ukraine portrayed Party leaders, revolutionary figures, and workers, peasants, and soldiers in an idealized manner. Among the more versatile portraitists working within the framework of socialist realism were O. *Shovkunenko (*M. Rylsky*, 1944–5), V. *Kostetsky (*P. Voronko*, 1945), and the graphic artist V. *Kasiian (a series of etchings of V. Lenin, 1947; and the often-reproduced portrait of T. Shevchenko, 1960). M. *Bozhii painted several portraits of Lenin and of Shevchenko.

In Western Ukraine under Austro-Hungarian and Polish interwar rule, portraitists painted in the styles popular in Western Europe. I. *Trush painted prominent Ukrainian writers, such as I. Franko (1897), V. Stefanyk (1897), and Lesia Ukrainka (1900). The best-known portraitist in Lviv was O. *Novakivsky, who painted numerous portraits in a modified impressionist (*Portrait of My Wife*, 1906) and later an expressionist manner (*Self-Portrait*, 1927; *O. Dovbush*, 1931). O. *Kulchytska also used an impressionist palette in her early works (*Portrait of My Sister Olha*, 1912). In 1920 she rendered a series of linocut portraits of Ukrainian literary figures.

After Western Ukraine became part of the USSR in 1944, artists were required to produce socialist-realist portraits (eg, V. Manastyrsky's *Highlander*, 1949). During the Khrushchev cultural thaw, however, many Lviv artists returned to exploring a variety of figural styles. Portraits of women in Hutsul dress have been painted by V. *Manastyrsky (*Marichka*, 1973) and H. *Smolsky (*The Fiancée*, 1960). M. *Selska has painted several portraits in a semiabstract manner, using flattened areas of color and heavy textures (*R. Selsky*, 1968). D. Dovboshynsky has worked with heavy impasto and vibrant hues (*R. Turyn*, 1984); V. *Patyk's portraits have been rendered in an expressionist manner (*Woman from Rusiv*, 1971). Of the younger artists L. *Medvid has painted portraits in a superrealistic manner without any details (*Portrait of My Wife*, 1968; *S. Liudkevych*, 1980).

Of the portrait painters in Transcarpathia, A. *Erdeli painted *Young Woman* (1940) and *Engaged Couple* (1953) in bold, vibrant colors and with the subjects wearing folk dress, as did A. *Kotska (*Highland Woman*, 1956, 1970).

In Soviet Ukraine from the 1930s, most sculptural portraits were of Communist party leaders, revolutionaries, and workers rendered in a heroic, idealized manner (P. *Ulianov's *October Hero*, 1931; I. Yakunin's *V. Lenin*, 1968). Busts and full-length figures of writers and artists have also been popular (I. Severa's *I. Franko*, 1947; E. *Mysko's *Portrait of a Young Architect*, 1972). Most were commissioned for public display. Officially favored sculptors included M. *Lysenko, I. *Znoba, Ya. *Chaika, I. *Severa, H. *Kalchenko, Yu. *Synkevych, H. Redko, and D. *Krvavych.

Not all postwar Soviet Ukrainian artists adhered strictly to socialist realism, however. In sculpture M. Hrytsiuk modeled sensitive and intimate portraits (*Rostropovich; Valia*, 1969), and in painting O. Zalyvakha chose subjects not sanctioned officially (*Hetman Kalnyshevsky*, 1964) and a manner of depiction labeled as formalist.

In Kiev I. *Marchuk turned to portraiture in the 1980s and painted several starkly modeled, intimate portraits against fantastically rendered backgrounds (*S. Pavlychko*, 1982) and neutral settings (*R. Selsky*, 1982). One of the more impressive portraitists of a classical style is B. *Plaksii. Among the Kiev women artists T. *Yablonska, V. Vyrodova-Gotie, and V. Kuleba-Barynova have painted portraits of children and adults.

Ukrainian portraitists also worked outside their homeland. M. *Parashchuk, a sculptor who modeled expressive busts of V. Stefanyk and S. Liudkevych in 1906 while still in Lviv, worked in Sofia, Bulgaria, from 1922. The world-renowned sculptor A. *Archipenko left Kiev in 1908 and worked thereafter in France, Germany, and the United States. He created several busts of Shevchenko as well as portraits of his wife, Angelica. V. *Masiutyn, who lived in Berlin from 1921, created 63 medallions of Ukrainian political and cultural leaders and busts of P. Doroshenko and I. Mazepa. H. *Kruk, who worked in postwar Munich, modeled and carved memorable heads of children (*Portrait of Peter*) and intimate portraits of his contemporaries (*A. Zhuk, V. Kubijovyč*, and *V. Yaniv*).

Several postwar émigré artists in North America have devoted considerable time to painting portraits in a variety of figurative styles: J. *Hnizdovsky (*K. Antonovych*, 1972), M. *Dmytrenko (*Romtsia Savchuk*, 1966), P. *Andrusiv (*The Painter's Wife*, 1955), P. *Mehyk (*The Sculptor V. Simiantsev*, 1978), L. *Hutsaliuk (*Renata*, 1958) in the United States, and K. *Antonovych (*Woman from Bukovyna*, 1956), M. *Levytsky (*Self-Portrait*, 1948, 1951, 1960), and A.

Babych (*Vera*, 1979) in Canada. L. Molodozhanyn (Mol), who settled in Winnipeg, gained an international reputation for his sculptural portraits of famous people. Emigré sculptors who have worked in the United States are M. *Chereshnovsky (*Y. Hirniak, Lesia Ukrainka*), S. *Lytvynenko (*E. Andiievska*, 1962), and V. *Simiantsev (*Prof. A. Shtefan*, 1948).

Among the postwar generation of artists of Ukrainian origin born in North America, portraiture has been central to the work of L. Bodnar-Balahutrak, who paints close-up likenesses in a photorealist manner (*The Madonna Complex*, 1981).

BIBLIOGRAPHY

Holubets', M. *Ukraïns'ke maliarstvo XVI–XVII stolit' pid pokrovom Stavropihiï* (Lviv 1920)

Shcherbakivs'kyi, D; Ernst, F. *Ukraïns'kyi portret: Vystavka ukraïns'koho portretu XVII–XX st.* (Kiev 1925)

Ovsiichuk, V. *L'vivs'kyi portret XVI–XVIII st.: Kataloh vystavky* (Kiev 1967)

Bilets'kyi, P. *Ukraïns'kyi portretnyi zhyvopys XVII–XVIII st.* (Kiev 1969)

Ruban, V. *Ukraïns'kyi radians'kyi portretnyi zhyvopys* (Kiev 1977)

Zholtovs'kyi, P. *Ukraïns'kyi zhyvopys XVII–XVIII st.* (Kiev 1978)

Ruban, V. *Portret u tvorchosti ukraïns'kykh zhyvopystsiv* (Kiev 1979)

Beletskii, P. *Ukrainskaia portretnaia zhivopis' XVII–XVIII vv.* (Leningrad 1981)

Ruban, V. *Ukraïns'kyi portretnyi zhyvopys pershoï polovyny XIX st.* (Kiev 1984)

– *Ukraïns'kyi portretnyi zhyvopys druhoï polovyny XIX–pochatku XX stolittia* (Kiev 1986)

– *Zabytye imena: Rasskazy ob ukrainskikh khudozhnikakh XIX–nachala XX veka* (Kiev 1990)

– (ed). *Anatol' Petryts'kyi: Portrety suchasnykiv: Al'bom* (Kiev 1991)

V. Ruban, D. Zelska-Darewych

Posad. The trading and manufacturing district of a town in Kievan Rus'. Such districts were usually located outside the town walls; hence, the *posad* was a suburb. Since fortified towns were built as a rule on higher ground, the suburbs were below (*pod*) them and were known as *podil* (pl *podoly*). In the 13th century *posad* became the prevalent term in northeastern Rus'; gradually it was extended to whole towns that were inhabited mostly by merchants and tradesmen. By the end of the 18th century, when the difference between the merchant and the artisan classes became sharper, the term *posad* ceased to be used of town districts. It was brought to Ukraine from Russia in the second half of the 17th century to designate certain kinds of settlements and was used mostly in Starodub and Nizhen regiments, Slobidska Ukraine, and Southern Ukraine.

Poshtuchne (from *shtuka*, from German *Stück* 'piece'). A tax in kind imposed on state peasants under Lithuanian, Polish, and Moldavian rule from the 14th to 17th centuries. It was proportional (from 1:10 to 1:30) to the number of cattle or meters of woven cloth owned by a family.

Poshyvailo [Pošyvajlo]. A family of ceramicists from Opishnia, Poltava oblast. The first renowned potter in the family was Taras, who lived in the second half of the 19th and in the early 20th century. His works consisted of enameled pots, bowls, cups, and pans. His wife, Kylyna (?–1930), was known for her ceramic toys, and their son, Nykyfor (b late 1880s, d October 1936), specialized in enameled dishware. Nykyfor's son, Havrylo (b 7 April 1909), has made functional earthenware and small decorative pieces, which were painted with floral or animal designs by his wife, Yevdokhiia (b 14 March 1910). Their son, Mykola (b 27 May 1930), besides plates, toys, ashtrays, and candle holders, has produced sculptural compositions, such as *Farmer* (1974) and *Natalka and Petro* (1974). The family's work has been displayed in France, Belgium, and Bulgaria and can be found in museums in Kiev, Poltava, and Vilnius.

Posiada, Ivan [Posjada], b 9 April 1823 in Zinkiv, Poltava gubernia, d 24 October 1894 in Korostyshiv, Radomyshl county, Kiev gubernia. Pedagogue and political activist. A student in the philosophy faculty of Kiev University from 1843, in 1846 he joined the *Cyril and Methodius Brotherhood. When this society was suppressed by the authorities in 1847, he was arrested and exiled to Kazan, where he finished his university studies. Afterward he worked in the state administration and in schools in Russia before being allowed to return to Ukraine in 1869 as director of the Korostyshiv Teachers' Seminary (until 1879).

Poslannyk (Messenger). A semimonthly Catholic journal published in Berezhany, Lviv, Ternopil, and Peremyshl in 1889–1911. The publisher and editor was Rev L. Dzhulynsky; he was assisted at various times by Yu. Nasalsky and L. Nesterovych. Dzhulynsky also published the *Knyzhochky myssiiny book series.

Pospielov, Volodymyr [Pospjelov] (Pospelov, Vladimir), b 22 March 1872 in Bogoroditsk, Tula gubernia, Russia, d 1 February 1949 in Kiev. Zoologist and entomologist; full member of the AN URSR (now ANU) from 1939. After graduating from Moscow University (1896), he worked at the Moscow (1896–1904), Voronezh (1913–20), and Leningrad (1930–40) agricultural institutes and the Kiev Entomological Station (1904–13), taught at Saratov (1927–30) and Kiev (1944–5) universities, and headed the laboratory at the All-Union Institute of Plant Conservation (1929–40). He became a member of the ANU presidium in 1939 and director of the ANU Institute of Entomology and Phytopathology in 1946. He initiated the creation of the first plant quarantine service in the USSR, pursued ecologically safe methods of biological and chemical control of agricultural pests, and discovered the infertility of butterflies in certain ecological conditions.

Pospolyti. The general name for the majority of the peasant population in the Hetman state and in Slobidska Ukraine in the 17th and 18th centuries. Initially, under Polish rule, the name also included city dwellers – in general, all non-nobles; during the Hetman state it included all non-Cossacks. Single men often joined the Cossack host and married men took up farming. The *pospolyti* did no military duty, except in emergencies. They supported the Cossack host by paying taxes and providing services, such as road maintenance, fortification construction, and troop quartering. There was no sharp division between the Cossacks and *pospolyti*: the richer peasants could readily acquire Cossack privileges, and the poorer Cossacks could become farmers. The *pospolyti* fell into several groups, depending on whose land they inhabited, and what their relations and obligations were to the local administration or landowners: peasants inhabiting free military villages (under the hetman's administration); *ratushni* peasants (under the administration of the local company and town councils); rank peasants (living on lands ceded for temporary rule to the *starshyna* for military service rendered); monastery peasants; and peasants living on lands owned outright by the Cossack *starshyna*. The obligation of the *pospolyti* peasants varied from monetary taxes to taxes in kind to various duties. The burden of those increased with time. A certain subgroup of the *pospolyti* was formed by the *landless peasants. The *pospolyti* were enserfed in 1783.

Possessional peasants (*posesiini seliany*). That category of peasants in the Russian Empire who during the 18th and 19th centuries were attached to factories and could not be separated from specified industrial enterprises. The category emerged in response to the need for a labor force to serve developing manufacturing enterprises. An imperial decree issued on 7 January 1736 legally bound to enterprises those workers who had been trained in specialized skills, and who had been laboring in them at the time the law was enacted. Thus, possessional peasants were considered the property of a manufacturing firm as opposed to a particular landowner. In Ukraine possessional peasants were usually employed in sugar-processing plants. In the 19th century, owners of manufacturing firms steadily replaced possessional peasants with hired workers. By 1840, legislation had abolished possessional relations, and the laws leading to the emancipation of serfdom in 1861–3 abandoned the category altogether.

Postage stamps. Shortly after the first stamps for the prepayment of letter postage were issued in Great Britain (1840), postage stamps appeared in Ukrainian territories under Austro-Hungarian rule (1850) and Russian rule (1857). In 1864, laws were promulgated in the Russian Empire allowing for zemstvo or local issues. From their appearance in 1865 until their discontinuance in 1917, a total of about 790 zemstvo stamps were issued in Ukraine at 39 locations.

The first definitive stamps issued by an independent Ukrainian government were the five-value *shah* issues. The 10- and 20-*shah* stamps were designed by A. Sereda and the 30-, 40-, and 50-*shah* stamps by the noted Ukrainian graphic artist H. Narbut. Authorized by the government of the UNR, the stamp set was released on 18 July 1918 by the government of the Ukrainian State under Hetman P. Skoropadsky. All *shah* postage stamps were issued imperforate. They were widely used for postage in Ukraine until the end of 1920. Three months earlier (18 April 1918) a five-value set of *currency stamps was printed and released from the same plates as the *shah* issues. The currency stamps (perforated 11½ and printed on card stock) were used in place of coins owing to the shortage of metals and were inscribed on the reverse with a trident and words in Ukrainian that translate as 'circulates in lieu of coins.' The stamps were neither intended nor authorized for postal purposes.

After the proclamation of Ukraine's independence in January 1918, the postage stamps of tsarist Russia remained valid for postal use. In order to minimize Russian influence, provide postage stamps in more denomina-

tions, and save treasury funds, the Ministry of Postal and Telegraph Services issued an order on 20 August 1918 'to overprint with the national emblem of the Ukrainian State (ie, the trident) all postage stamps of Russian origin, which are at the present time used for postage in the territory of Ukraine.' The first trident overprints on postage stamps appeared in circulation even before the official decree, on 8 August 1918; on postal cards they date from 16 July 1918. After 1 October 1918 all Russian stamps without the overprint became invalid. Ukrainian territory at that time was divided into the postal districts of Kiev, Poltava, Katerynoslav, Kharkiv, Odessa, and Podilia. In order to comply with the overprint directive, each postal district prepared one or more overprinting devices. The trident overprint provisionals thus prepared were of different size, color, and form in each of the districts. To date, researchers have identified about 60 overprints, including some produced by local postal authorities. In addition to trident overprints on tsarist stamps, trident overprints also appeared on 8 August 1919 in Zhmerynka on stamps issued by the 1917 Russian Provisional Government.

Provisional trident overprints remained in use for some time after the withdrawal of the Directory of the UNR. The latest authenticated date of usage is on an Odessa postal card from Pryvilne (near Mykolaiv) to Kharkiv, dated 8 February 1926. Forgeries of provisional trident postage stamps began to appear in southern Ukraine toward the end of 1918. Later, counterfeits were produced by speculators outside the borders of Ukraine who forged overprints and postal cancels and created nonexistent values.

Realizing the need for a wider range of postal values, Postal and Telegraph Services of the Ukrainian State set about preparing a second definitive issue. Made up of values greater than 50 *shahy*, it was to replace the trident overprint provisionals and supplement the first five *shah* values. The stamps of the second issue were printed in Kiev during the fall of 1918. When the supply of the high-value trident overprint provisionals was exhausted in Volhynia and Podilia, the Ministry of Posts released only the 20-*hryvnia* value to ease the shortage. No other values of the second definitive set were ever placed in postal use. By the time the 20-*hryvnia* stamps became available in January 1919, the Hetman government, which had authorized their production, had been replaced by that of the UNR. At that time 100 *shah* equaled one *hryvnia*, and two *hryvni* equaled one *karbovanets* (ruble). Because of the high value of the 20-*hryvnia* stamp, its use was limited to the prepayment of postal money orders, particularly those for very high sums.

On 27 August 1920 the Government-in-exile of the UNR, meeting in the Polish city of Tarnów, resolved to replace all existing postage stamps then in use on Ukrainian territories with a new 14-stamp definitive issue containing values from 1 to 200 *hryvni*. Designed and printed by the Military Geographical Institute in Vienna, the beautiful stamp set, now known as the Vienna Issue, was never circulated despite published reports claiming otherwise. Some stamps of the Vienna Issue were overprinted, in anticipation of a military expedition into Ukraine in 1923, but the mission was not carried out, and the stamps (approx 300,000 sets) were never used for postal purposes. The Government-in-exile of the UNR also issued several stamps (labels) in 1935 (designed by P. Kholodny), com-

Postage stamps. 1st row: UNR *shah* issues; 2nd row: five examples of trident overprints and the 20-*hryvnia* stamp of the Ukrainian State (Hetman government); 3rd row: five values of the UNR Vienna Issue; 4th row: the Ukrainian SSR famine relief set; 5th row: the Western Ukrainian National Republic's Lviv octagonal overprint, Kolomyia 50-*sotyk* registration stamp, and stamps from the 3rd and 4th Stanyslaviv issues; 6th row: Carpatho-Ukraine's overprinted 3-*korona* Czechoslovakian stamp, UNC overprint, and UNC definitive memorating the 10th anniversary of the assassination of S. Petliura and the 950th anniversary of Christianity in Ukraine, as well as a 1939 stamp commemorating the 60th birthday of President A. Livytsky.

In June 1923 the government of the Ukrainian SSR issued a set of four semipostal stamps in Ukrainian, *Ukraïna v borotbi z holodom* (Ukraine Battles the Famine), *Selianyn obezzbroiuie smert'* (The Peasant Disarms Death), *Portret T. Shevchenka* (Portrait of T. Shevchenko), and *Dopomoha holoduiuchym* (Aid to the Starving); the surcharge on the stamps was intended for famine victims. Designed by O. Makarenko and B. Porai-Koshyts, the set circulated briefly in six cities from 25 June to 15 July 1923 and remained the only postal issue ever released by the government of the Ukrainian SSR.

After seceding from the Austro-Hungarian Empire (1 November 1918) the Western Ukrainian National Republic (ZUNR) issued stamps as overprints of Austrian issues. The first stamps, with an octagonal overprint showing a Galician lion emblem and the full name of the ZUNR, appeared in Lviv on 20 November 1918; subsequent stamps were produced in Kolomyia, and a series of four issues was released in Stanyslaviv. Two additional stamp sets, printed for the ZUNR in Vienna, became available after the Polish occupation of Galicia (July 1919) but never entered postal circulation.

The first regular airmail service anywhere in the world was the Vienna–Cracow–Lviv line, which functioned from 31 March to 11 October 1918. An extension of the line to Kiev via Proskuriv (from late June 1918) made the route the world's first 'international' airmail line. Another service, the Budapest–Vienna–Cracow–Lviv line, functioned briefly from 4 July to 23 July 1918, and a few letters from Budapest were also carried as far as Kiev. For both of those *postal services, special airmail stamps were issued by the overprinting of existing Austrian postal designs with *Flugpost* and of Hungarian stamps with *Repülö Posta*.

During the interwar period the various regions of Western Ukraine were occupied by Poland, Rumania, and Czechoslovakia. The stamps issued by those states often depicted Ukrainian images and landmarks, such as the Pidhirtsi castle, the Lviv Polytechnical Institute, the Khotyn fortress, and Bukovynian folk motifs.

In 1941 Germany overprinted its 18-stamp definitive set with the single-line black overprint *Ukraine* for use in the Reichskommissariat Ukraine. The overprints were in postal circulation until late 1944, when those Ukrainian territories were recaptured by Soviet troops. Attempts were also made by local Ukrainian authorities under the German occupation to issue postage stamps. Local stamps appearing in Sarny, Horokhiv, and Kamianets-Podilskyi were soon banned by the German authorities.

On the day Carpatho-Ukraine declared its independence from Czechoslovakia (15 March 1939), it issued a single stamp, consisting of the overprint *Karpatska Ukraina* on the 3-koruna Czechoslovak stamp depicting a wooden church in Yasinia. After Carpatho-Ukraine's short-lived independence the territory was administered by Hungary, during which time Hungarian stamps were used. By the fall of 1944 the eastern provinces of Carpatho-Ukraine were being administered by Czechoslovakia, and in the areas to the west the Ukrainian National Committee (UNC) had taken control. Both jurisdictions issued overprinted Hungarian stamps and the UNC released a series of defin-

itive issues in 1945. After the Second World War the Ukrainian POW camp in Rimini, Italy, and the DP camps in Germany organized their own postal services, issued postage stamps and stationery, and prepared their own cancellations. Semipostals and commemoratives were also issued to generate revenue for camp administrations. Definitive issues were released by the Rimini (1946), Regensburg (1947), and Bayreuth (1948) camps.

The only stamps used in the Ukrainian SSR were those of the USSR. A Shevchenko series was issued in 1939; a large Ukrainian-language series was issued in 1954 to commemorate the tricentenary of the 'reunification' of Ukraine with Russia; and other series with Ukrainian themes were periodically released, including poets and writers, scenery, folk art, industrial plants, and cultural landmarks. After the dissolution of the USSR, the newly re-established Ukraine issued provisional stamps (consisting of meter mail markings on white paper) for several months in 1992. Ukraine's first commemorative stamps were issued in March of that year (500 years of Ukrainian Cossackdom, 100 years of Ukrainian settlement in Canada, and the M. Lysenko anniversary) and a definitive series honoring H. Narbut in May. Local trident overprints on Soviet stamps appeared in Kiev during March–April.

The first two postage stamps released in newly independent Ukraine in 1992

In the diaspora the Ukrainian National Council continued to issue stamps (more properly termed labels), souvenir sheets, and postal stationery through the 1970s. Postage stamps featuring Ukrainian themes have also been issued by countries with an émigré Ukrainian community. The Canadian government, for example, issued stamps to commemorate the millennium of Christianity in Ukraine (a Byzantine icon, 1988) and the centenary of Ukrainian immigration to Canada (paintings by W. Kurelek, 1991). Semipostal and souvenir stamps and postal stationery have also been issued by Ukrainian organizations in the diaspora, such as the Plast scouting association. The *Ukraine-Philatelisten Verband in Berlin has promoted Ukrainian philately since 1920. The *Ukrainian Philatelic and Numismatic Society is based in the United States; it publishes the semiannual journal *Ukraïns'kyi filatelist/Ukrainian Philatelist*, as well as a bimonthly newsletter, *Trident/Visnyk*.

Postage stamps issued in Ukraine in 1992, including a USSR stamp overprinted with a trident

BIBLIOGRAPHY

Kotyk, E. 'On the History of the Stamps of the Western Ukraine,' *Ukrains'kyi filatelist*, 3, no. 4 (1953)

Roberts, C. *The Trident Issues of the Ukraine*, 5 vols (Ilminster, England 1953–66)

Alekseev, A. *Hovoriat' marky* (Kharkiv 1961)

Baillie, I. *Ukraine: The Shagiv Issues* (Bristol 1963)

Seichter, R. *Sonder-Katalog Ukraine (1918–1920)*, 3rd rev edn (Soltau, West Germany 1966)

Bulat, J. *Illustrated Postage Stamp History of Western Ukrainian Republic 1918–19* (Yonkers, NY 1973)

Fessak, B. *Ukrainian DP Camp, POW Camp, Government in Exile, and National Council Issues* (Washington, DC 1992)

I. Kuzych-Berezovsky

Postal services. Little is known of the earliest postal services on the territory of present-day Ukraine. In the 1st millennium BC, letters were carried between Greece and the Greek city-states on the Black Sea littoral, and traders carried messages up and down the Dnieper River. The Scythian kings used mounted messengers. The first recorded organized mail service in Ukraine dates from the 13th century AD, during the period of Kievan Rus', when mounted messengers conveyed letters among the rulers, princes, noblemen, and traders. The system continued until the 15th century, when the messengers were known as *putni* boyars since they were minor noblemen who chose that type of service rather than carrying arms for the prince.

A regular postal service in the modern sense was established in Western Ukraine in 1629 by the Italian R. Bandinelli. The service connected the city of Lviv with Poland; regular weekly mail deliveries were made by mounted postmen known as *kursory*. The Cossacks in Ukraine at various times during their history had their own messenger system. Certain sources report that Hetman B. Khmelnytsky's minister of the treasury, O. Atamanenko, organized a wide-ranging system of mails; that a formal postal service was established in 1669 by Hetman D. Mnohohrishny, which connected such cities as Kiev, Nizhyn, and Baturyn; and that messages were sent by the otaman of the Zaporozhian Sich, I. Sirko, to Hetman P. Doroshenko in 1675.

In 1674 the Russians, as part of the process of annexing Ukraine to Muscovy, began establishing a separate postal service of their own in Ukraine. The system linked Kiev with Moscow and was financed primarily out of the Ukrainian state treasury. By 1768 the Russian governors of New Russia and Kiev vicegerencies had established an elaborate system of mounted messengers. The Zaporozhian Sich was required to establish a network of messenger lines (by 1775 amounting to eight separate lines of communication), with hundreds of messenger stations, horses, and trained Cossack couriers at the ready.

During the Cossack era an interesting 'telegraph' system was set up on the borderlands between Ukraine and Crimean Tatar lands, consisting of a line of tall towers (*khvyhury*) manned by sentinels. Pitch barrels on the towers were set ablaze if a Tatar raiding party was sighted. By 1723 the whole southern frontier was dotted with the towers, spaced every 200–300 m. Another informal messenger service during the period of Cossack wars with the Poles and Russians (16th–18th centuries) was the network of kobzars who carried messages from village to village throughout the occupied portions of Ukraine.

By the mid-18th century regular mail services had been established almost everywhere in Ukraine, and gradually they became a monopoly of the occupying powers. The first postage stamps appeared in Western Ukraine (under Austria) in 1850 and in Eastern Ukraine (under Russia) in 1857. In Left-Bank Ukraine a system of semiautonomous zemstvo local mails came into being in 1865, which ran their own local post offices and issued their own postage stamps – the first postage stamps made in Ukraine (see *Postage stamps).

The independent Ukrainian government of 1917–20 established the *All-Ukrainian Postal-Telegraph Union, which became a member of the worldwide Universal Postal Union (UPU) in 1918. The ministers of postal and telegraph services in independent Ukraine were M. Shapoval (January 1918), H. Sydorenko (spring of 1918), V. Kuliabko-Koretsky (during the Hetman government), I. Shtefan (spring of 1919), I. Palyvoda (summer of 1919), and I. Kosenko (1920). The Western Ukrainian National Republic had its own mail system (minister of posts, O. Pisetsky) until it voluntarily merged with the UNR. Both governments issued postage stamps, and in June 1918 an airmail service was established between Austria and Ukraine (Vienna–Cracow–Lviv–Proskuriv–Kiev). It was the first regular and the first international airmail service in the world. Carpatho-Ukraine, during its brief existence in 1939, issued its own stamp. The Ukrainian Insurgent Army had its own postal service. Various local mail services were briefly in operation during the interwar and Second World War periods; local mail services were also established in various postwar Ukrainian refugee and POW camps.

1

2

3

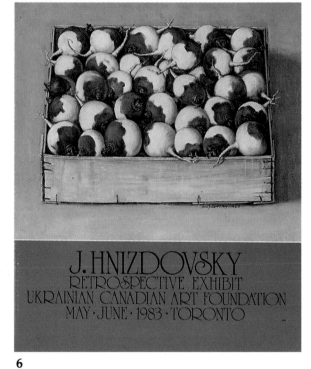

4

5

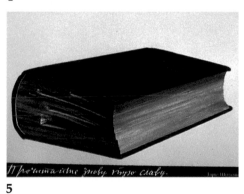

6

POSTERS 1) L. Palii: *Plast Week* (1976). 2) H. Horobievska: *Live Ukraine; the Soviet State* (1967). 3) A. Strakhov: *Let Us Complete the Coal Five-Year Plan in Three Years* (1931). 4) Y. Prokofiev: *Ozhyvut' hetmany …* (The Hetmans Will Come Alive …, 1989). 5) V. Shostia: *Prochytaite znovu tuiu slavu!* (T. Shevchenko: Read Again That Glory, 1988). 6) V. Buczko: *Jacques Hnizdovsky Exhibition* (1983).

The postal service of the Ukrainian SSR at first operated autonomously and issued its own stamps. In the early 1920s the service was subordinated to the All-Union Soviet Post, although it remained a separate member of the UPU. With the dissolution of the USSR, Ukraine once again has an independent postal service.

L. Onyshkevych

Postel, Oleksander [Postel'], b 1 May 1904 in Odessa, d 19 January 1989 in Odessa. Painter and printmaker. He studied at the Odessa Art Institute (1920–9) and taught at various art schools in Odessa (1931–67). In the 1920s he was a member of the Association of Revolutionary Art of Ukraine. He created paintings, such as *Odessa Environs* (1939), *Sun in a Halo* (1948), and *The Snow Has Melted* (1955), and print series, such as 'Uzbekistan Landscapes' (1942–5), 'Seasons of the Year' (1956–60), 'Odessa Landscapes' (1945–70), and 'Flowers' (1965–6). He also illustrated books and designed film sets.

Poster. An art form that emerged in the latter part of the 19th century, mainly as a result of advances in lithography. Although posters have been used mainly for advertising purposes, there are strong links between their design and developments in modern art. Many prominent artists, including H. de Toulouse-Lautrec, P. Picasso, and H. Matisse, have designed them. Posters were first used as propaganda tools during the First World War, and they have been widely used in this way by the Soviet, Nazi, and other totalitarian regimes.

The first Ukrainian-language posters in Ukraine appeared after the February Revolution of 1917. The prominent Ukrainian artists H. Narbut and M. Boichuk designed posters promoting the commemoration of T. Shevchenko in 1920. Both incorporated Ukrainian graphic and folk-art traditions into their designs. Narbut also developed a new typeface based on a synthesis of old Ukrainian engravings and modern simplification. In the 1920s, avant-garde artists, such as V. Yermilov, B. Sylkin, and O. Khvostenko-Khvostov, created bold poster designs promoting communism and the proletariat. Film posters were designed by O. Dovzhenko, M. Ivasiuk, I. Litynsky, O. Syrotenko, K. Bolotov, and other artists. A. Marenkov designed posters denouncing nationalist leaders, such as S. Petliura ('The Hireling Petliura Sold Ukraine to [His] Polish Masters,' 1920). Other posters glorified the Soviet regime and warned against famine ('Famine Is Threatening the Soviet Republics ...,' 1920). Posters exalting the Red Army and the Bolshevik Revolution were common and continued to be used extensively by the Communist party to promote its ideology and goals and to glorify its leaders. Hackneyed slogans often accompanied stereotypical images, as in A. Strakhov's 'Let Us Fulfill the Coal Five-Year Plan in Three' (1931). During the Second World War well-known graphic artists, such as V. Kasiian, O. Dovhal, K. Ahnit-Stedzevsky, and V. Fatalchuk, were asked to design posters promoting the Soviet war effort against Nazi Germany. In 1944 V. Lytvynenko produced the poster 'Ukraine Is Free!' showing a map of Western Ukraine in red behind a striding Red Army soldier.

During the cultural thaw after Stalin's death, particularly in the early 1960s, the officially promoted folklorization of all Ukrainian art also affected poster design. T. Liashchuk designed posters using highly stylized ethno-

graphic elements (eg, 'Soviet Ukraine, May You Be Glorified from Generation to Generation,' 1967). Poster design was stimulated by various competitions sponsored by the Union of Artists of Ukraine.

In interwar Western Ukraine, posters designed in the 1930s were more varied than in Soviet Ukraine because artists were able to make use of the latest trends in art. Their works were not mass-produced, however, because most were designed for use by private enterprises or community organizations.

Ukrainian émigré artists, especially after the Second World War, have produced posters to mark anniversaries and celebrate events. Some of the more interesting ones have been designed by V. Tsymbal in Argentina, M. Levytsky in Canada, and J. Hnizdovsky in the United States. V. Bednarsky has designed several posters for the World Congress of Free Ukrainians, and the World Federation of Ukrainian Women's Organizations has commissioned several artists to produce posters marking its activities. V. Buchko of Toronto has designed a number of art exhibition posters, using reproductions of paintings by J. Hnizdovsky, A. Solomukha, F. Humeniuk, and V. Makarenko.

Many innovative, often satirical posters appeared in Soviet Ukraine in the late 1980s, in the period of glasnost and perestroika. They satirized the Soviet system, warned of ecological and cultural disasters, and promoted various organizations, such as the Ukrainian Language Society, Zelenyi Svit, and the Popular Movement of Ukraine, and the ideal of Ukrainian independence.

BIBLIOGRAPHY
Khmuryi, V. *Ukraïns'kyi revoliutsiinyi plakat* (Kharkiv 1932)
Butnyk-Sivers'kyi, B.; Kozhukhov, A. (comps). *Ukraïns'kyi radians'kyi plakat* (Kiev 1957)
Lashkul, Z. *Ukrainskii sovetskii plakat v gody Velikoi Otechestvennoi voiny (1941–1945)* (Kiev 1962)
Skliars'ka, M. (ed). *Ukraïns'kyi radians'kyi plakat* (Kiev 1971)
Vladych, L. (ed). *The Ukrainian Political Poster* (Kiev 1981)
Zolotoverkhova, I. *Ukraïns'kyi radians'kyi kinoplakat 20–30-kh rokiv* (Kiev 1983)
Vladych, L. *Maistry plakata: Tvorchi portrety ukraïns'kykh radians'kykh khudozhnykiv-plakatystiv* (Kiev 1989)

D. Zelska-Darewych

Posternak, Stepan, b 9 May 1880 in Stepanivka, Nizhen county, Chernihiv gubernia, d ? Pedagogue, library scientist, and bibliographer. He headed the history of Ukrainian education section of the Educational and Pedagogical Commission of the All-Ukrainian Academy of Sciences (VUAN) and was secretary of the VUAN Commission for the Compilation of an Encyclopedic Dictionary in 1921–2. He then served as director of the National Library of Ukraine in 1923–9 and coedited its periodicals *Bibliotechnyi zbirnyk* and *Zhurnal bibliotekoznavstva ta bibliohrafiï*. He wrote *Vsenarodna biblioteka Ukraïny* (The National Library of Ukraine, 1923), *Z istoriï osvitn'oho rukhu na Ukraïni za chasy revoliutsiï 1917–19* (From the History of the Educational Movement in Ukraine during the Time of Revolution, 1917–19, 1920), and articles on the theory of bibliography and library science. He fell out of favor in the early 1930s and was persecuted by the authorities. His ultimate fate is unknown.

Postnikov, Ivan, b 10 September 1906 in Ershovo, Kostroma gubernia, Russia, d 7 August 1990. Russian electrical engineer; corresponding member of the AN URSR (now ANU) from 1967. He graduated from the Leningrad Polytechnical Institute and taught at the Kiev Polytechnical Institute (from 1950). He worked at the ANU Institute of Electric Technology and headed the ANU Institute of Electrodynamics (from 1963). His technical contributions were in the theory, design, and applications of electric machinery.

Postnikov, Vladimir, b 1844, d 1908. Russian economist and statistician. He worked for the Ministries of Agriculture and State Domains and published several major studies of agriculture in the Russian Empire, including *Iuzhno-russkoe krest'ianskoe khoziaistvo* (South-Russian Peasant Economy, 1891), which is rich in factual information on agriculture in the Ukrainian steppe gubernias. He advocated the large-scale use of machinery in agriculture and predicted the emergence of commercial farming in the empire, especially in Southern Ukraine.

Petro Postoliuk   Antin Postolovsky

Postoliuk, Petro [Postoljuk], b 10 July 1894 in Storonybaby, Zolochiv county, Galicia, d 27 September 1978 in Newark, New Jersey. Civic activist and publisher. He enlisted in the Legion of Ukrainian Sich Riflemen in 1914 and fought in its ranks until 1920. After completing his university studies in Vienna (1923) he worked as a manager in I. Tyktor's Ukrainska Presa publishing house and as a director of the *Chervona Kalyna publishing co-operative, which he had founded with a group of veterans. He was also a member of the board of directors of the Izmarahd publishing house in Lviv. During the Second World War he was a director of the Ukrainske Vydavnytstvo publishers in Cracow. After emigrating to the United States in 1949, he revived the Chervona Kalyna publishing house there and served as its president until the end of his life. He also worked with the Svoboda Press.

Postolovsky, Antin [Postolovs'kyj], b 1889 in eastern Podilia gubernia, d 1990. Civic and military leader. He was active in the Ukrainian Party of Socialist Revolutionaries. In November 1917 he was elected to the All-Ukrainian Council of Military Deputies, and then served as secretary of the Central Rada and as a member of its Little Rada (1917–18). A postwar refugee, he emigrated to Argentina in 1949.

Postup (Kolomyia)

Postup (Progress). A weekly newspaper for peasants, published from January 1903 to December 1905 in Kolomyia by O. Kulchytsky. Edited by V. Bachynsky, it contained popular articles on history, science, hygiene, medicine, politics, and prose and poetry.

Postup (Progress). A Catholic monthly journal of literature, culture, and philosophy, published in Lviv from 1921 to 1930. Until 1927 it was a 'student herald' funded by Bishop H. Khomyshyn. Thereafter it was directed at a more general readership, supported the conservative hetmanite movement, and was funded by Metropolitan A. Sheptytsky and edited by O. Mokh, H. Luzhnytsky, and I. Hladylovych.

Postup (Progress). A monthly pro-Soviet journal for students, published in Prague from December 1931 to March 1933. Initiated by the Transcarpathian Regional Committee of the Czechoslovak Communist party, it was published by P. Dobrovsky, often in double and triple issues, and edited by I. Horvat and M. Tsuperiak. It contained articles on political and economic developments in Transcarpathia, criticized the 'bourgeois' circles there, and reprinted works by Soviet Ukrainian and other writers.

Postup (Progress). A weekly organ of the Winnipeg archeparchy of the Ukrainian Catholic church in Canada, published since February 1959. It contains articles on religious, cultural, and historical topics and reports on church affairs in Canada, Ukraine, and elsewhere. Since 1960 the paper has included a separate English-language section, and since 1968 it has published the supplement *Mii pryiatel'* for children. The first editor of *Postup*, R. Danylevych, was succeeded by S. Izhyk in 1962.

Postyshev, Pavel [Postyšev], b 18 September 1887 in Ivanovo-Voznesensk, Vladimir gubernia, Russia, d 26 February 1939 in Kuibyshev, Russia. Communist party functionary. In 1923 he was recalled from the Far Eastern Republic to oversee organizational work on the Party's Kiev gubernia committee, and a year later he was elected secretary of the committee. By the end of 1925 he had become secretary of the CC CP(B)U. Then he became a member of its Politburo and Organizational Bureau (1926–30). As secretary of the Kharkiv district and city Party committees he played a leading role in the purge of Trotskyists and Ukrainian national-Communists and in the industrialization and collectivization campaigns in the Kharkiv region. From July 1930 he was secretary of the CC of the All-Union Communist Party (Bolshevik) in charge of propaganda and organization. In January 1933 he was

Pavel Postyshev

sent back to Ukraine as J. Stalin's personal representative, accompanied by thousands of political cadres from Russia. He was immediately elected second secretary of the CC CP(B)U and first secretary of the Kharkiv city and oblast Party organizations. From July 1934 to January 1937 he was in charge of the Kiev oblast Party organization. As second secretary he was the real power in Ukraine, overshadowing S. *Kosior, the first secretary. During the manmade *famine in Ukraine Postyshev's mission was to eliminate all opposition to collectivization and the forcible requisition of grain and to crush the Communists who defended Ukrainization and the republic's economic, political, and cultural rights. He oversaw a major *Russification drive in Ukraine: the Ukrainian intelligentsia was decimated, and scores of Ukrainian cultural and educational institutions were closed. In the mass purge of the CP(B)U (1933–4) some 100,000 members were expelled from the Party, many of whom were subsequently arrested on trumped-up charges and executed. In the 1930s Postyshev became popularly known as the 'hangman of Ukraine.' Having acquired a taste for power Postyshev began to develop his own cult of personality and to consolidate his position in the republic by making some concessions to Ukrainian national sentiments in 1935–6. This development raised Stalin's suspicions. In 1937 Postyshev was removed from Ukraine and appointed first secretary of the Kuibyshev Oblast Party Committee. He was arrested in January 1938, executed a year later, and rehabilitated in 1956.

K. Hohol, B. Krawchenko

Potapenko, Ignatii, b December 1856 in Fedorivka, Kherson gubernia, d 17 May 1929 in Leningrad. Russian writer of Ukrainian descent. He studied at the Odessa Theological Seminary, Odessa University, and the St Petersburg Conservatory. His frequently humorous stories, which depicted Ukrainian folkways and peasant life, appeared in many Russian periodicals from 1881 on. He also wrote novels about the rural intelligentsia and clergy (*Na deistvitel'noi sluzhbe* [In Real Service, 1890; Ukrainian trans by A. Borkovsky serialized in *Zoria* in 1897], *Ne geroi* [Not a Hero, 1891], and *Otstuplenie* [The Retreat, 1915]) and several plays. Some of his works were translated into Ukrainian by M. Kotsiubynsky, O. Makovei, and H. Kovalenko.

Potapenko, Viacheslav (pseuds: V. Bezbrezhny, Chornomor), b 2 January 1864 in Veselyi Kut, Odessa county, Kherson gubernia, d 20 October 1942 in Krasnodar, Kuban. Writer and actor. From 1883 to 1890 he performed in M. Kropyvnytsky's and M. Sadovsky's theater troupes, and from 1890 he worked as a director in M. Vasyliev-Sviatoshenko's troupe. From 1888 his peasant stories appeared in *Zoria, Literaturno-naukovyi vistnyk,* and other periodicals. I. Franko likened his talent to that of M. Kotsiubynsky and considered his story 'Na novi hnizda' (To New Nests, 1899) one of the best stories depicting peasant emigration. Potapenko also wrote about 40 plays, including *Za druha* (For a Friend, 1887, written with M. Starytsky). From 1904 he lived in Katerynodar (Krasnodar), where he published the newspaper *Novaia zaria.*

Potapova, Olena, b 16 February 1930 in Samara (Kuibyshev), Russia. Ballerina. In 1948 she completed study in the choreography studio at the Kiev Theater of Opera and Ballet. She danced there as a soloist until 1976 and performed the title parts in K. Dankevych's *Lileia* and A. Svechnikov's *Marusia Bohuslavka.* In 1977 she became the theater's ballet master.

Potash industry. Potash is made by washing wood ashes with water and evaporating the resulting solution. The process produces various potassium compounds, chiefly crude potassium carbonate, which are used extensively in making soap, glass, and paint, for cleaning wool, and for coloring and bleaching cloth.

Potash was made in Ukraine in the medieval period and became widespread beginning in the 16th century. Wood was burned in piles (called *budy*) wherever large stands of forest were found. The first major center of the potash industry was the Polisia region, where Polish and Ukrainian magnates produced potash (as well as charcoal, tar, and other products) for export to Western Europe. Potash making spread throughout Volhynia, the Kiev region, the Chernihiv region (in the 17th and 18th centuries), and the Carpathian Mountains. It was common in the Hetman state, where it was controlled by the hetman, the *starshyna,* and monasteries. Eventually merchants, wealthy Cossacks, and local potash producers (called *budnyky*) became active in the industry. From the 18th century the Russian government tried to control the industry with the help of Russian merchants by restricting the production and export of potash. From then on it was used primarily in the domestic glass industry.

The potash industry declined drastically in the 19th century. The number of workers involved in potash production in Volhynia, for example, fell from 804 in 1795 to 279 in 1859. In the second half of the century the industry was completely displaced by other modern industries. Unfortunately the wanton burning of wood to produce potash almost completely destroyed the forest resources of Ukraine, especially in the forest-steppe belt.

Potato (*Solanum tuberosum*; Ukrainian: *kartoplia,* also *barabolia* or *bulba*). A plant the edible tuber of which is a major food crop of the world. Potatoes were first cultivated in the northwestern reaches of South America and were introduced into Europe in the late 16th century. They made their way into Ukraine in the late 17th and early 18th centuries via Poland. The potato remained a novelty in Ukraine – a garden crop eaten mainly as a snack by burghers or the Cossack *starshyna* – until the large-scale immigration of Germans into Ukraine starting in the 1760s. Then the potato became a field crop eaten as a staple by all social classes, including the peasantry, and eventually a key ingredient in Ukrainian traditional *foods. By the mid-19th century the potato rivaled bread as a mainstay of the Ukrainian peasant diet. Shrinking plot sizes and the use of potatoes as fodder and in alcohol distillation made the potato an attractive crop for peasant agriculture. The amount sown grew dramatically in the late 19th century and by 1913 had reached 1.1 million ha (3.9 percent of arable land) in Russian-ruled Ukraine.

The most common areas in Ukraine for potato cultivation include southern Polisia, the forest-steppe belt, and the Carpathian and Transcarpathia regions, where approx 20 percent of arable land is used for their cultivation. In 1978, 1.7 million ha were sown and yielded 24.1 million t of potatoes. The Ukrainian Scientific Research Institute of Potato Cultivation in Nemishaieve (Borodianske raion, Kiev oblast) was established by R. *Shekhaiev in 1968 on the basis of the local selection research station (est 1932). It publishes the periodical *Kartopliarstvo* (19 issues by 1988) and manages two research stations, in Polisia and Chernihiv.

BIBLIOGRAPHY
Hordiienko, H. *Istoriia kul'turnykh roslyn* (Munich 1970)

Potebnia, Andrii [Potebnja, Andrij], b 31 August 1838 in Perekopivka, Romen county, Poltava gubernia, d 4 March 1863 near Piaszczysta Skała, Cracow circle, western Galicia. Political activist and revolutionary; brother of O. *Potebnia. While studying at the Cadet Corps in St Petersburg (1856) he came in contact with Polish revolutionary democrats. He obtained a commission with the Schlüsselburg Regiment and was stationed in Poland, where he formed the underground Committee of Russian Officers in Poland (1861) that linked up with the clandestine revolutionary organization Zemlia i Volia (1862). Potebnia was mortally wounded while taking part in the Polish insurrection. A biography of him (with bibliography) was published in Kiev in 1957.

Potebnia, Andrii [Potebnja, Andrij], b 23 May 1870 in Kharkiv, d 7 March 1919. Botanist; son of O. *Potebnia. After working at the *Nikita Botanical Garden, he lectured at Kharkiv University (from 1903) and led the phytopathology department at the Kharkiv Oblast Agricultural Research Station (from 1913). His research centered on the biology, morphology, and systemization of parasitic fungi (especially ascomycetes).

Potebnia, Oleksander (Aleksandr) [Potebnja], b 22 September 1835 on his family's *khutir* near Havrylivka (now Hryshyne), Romen county, Poltava gubernia, d 11 December 1891 in Kharkiv. Linguist, folklorist, and literary scholar; from 1875 a corresponding member of the Russian Imperial Academy of Sciences; brother of A. Potebnia and father of A. and O. Potebnia. He studied law, history, and philology at Kharkiv University (PH D, 1874). In the early 1860s he was active in the Ukrainophile Kharkiv Hromada, wrote a Ukrainian primer for Sunday schools, and took part in folklore expeditions in Poltava

Oleksander Potebnia

and Okhtyrka counties. In 1874 he was appointed professor of Russian language and literature at Kharkiv University. He also presided over the *Kharkiv Historical-Philological Society (1877–90) and was a member of the Czech Scientific Society (from 1887). In the 1880s he edited collections of H. Kvitka-Osnovianenko's, P. Hulak-Artemovsky's, and I. Manzhura's works and began a Ukrainian translation of Homer's *Odyssey*.

As a linguist Potebnia specialized in four areas: the philosophy of language, the historical phonetics of the East Slavic languages, etymology, and Slavic historical syntax. His major works on the philosophy of language are *Mysl' i iazyk* (Thought and Language, 5 edns, 1862, 1892, 1913, 1922, 1926); *O sviazi nekotorykh predstavlenii v iazyke* (On the Relation among Some Representations in Language, 1864); his doctoral dissertation, *Iz zapisok po russkoi grammatike* (From Notes on Russian Grammar, vol 1, 1874; repr 1958); and the posthumously published 'Iazyk i narodnost'' (Language and Nationality, in *Vestnik Evropy*, 1895). He was particularly interested in the relations among language, thought, and reality. Language for him was primarily the means by which the mind ordered the influx of impressions and stimuli. Words carry not only a meaning, but also the past experience of the individual and the nation, through which all new experience is filtered. Thus a word usually has three aspects: an external form, a meaning, and an internal form. It is through the internal form that the objective world is subjectivized. In many cases the internal form is rooted in myth and, hence, acts as a bridge between language and folklore (with its symbols). These ideas constitute the framework of Potebnia's master's thesis, *O nekotorykh simvolakh v slavianskoi narodnoi poezii* (On Some Symbols in Slavic Folk Poetry, 1860; expanded edn 1914), and his monumental work *Obiasneniia malorusskikh i srodnykh narodnykh pesen* (Explanations of Little Russian and Related Folk Songs, 2 vols, 1883, 1887). With time the consciousness of a word's internal form fades, and one of the tasks of literature is to restore this consciousness. According to this theory, literature is a hierarchy of genres; the simplest ones (the proverb, riddle, and fable) directly recall or renew the word's internal form, and the other genres do so in a more complicated, sometimes hardly detectable, way through a complex system of subjective (in poetry) or seemingly objective (in the novel) images. Potebnia's principal works on this subject were published posthumously: *Iz lektsii po teorii slovesnosti: Basnia, poslovitsa, pogovorka* (From Lectures on the Theory of Literature: The Fable, the Adage, the Proverb, 1894; repr 1970; Ukrainian trans 1930), *Iz zapi-*

sok po teorii slovesnosti: Poeziia i proza, tropy i figury, myshle-nie poeticheskoe i mificheskoe, prilozheniia (From Notes on the Theory of Literature: Poetry and Prose, Tropes and Figures, Poetic and Mythical Thought, Addenda, 1905; repr 1970), and 'Chernovyia zametki ... o L.N. Tolstom i F.M. Dostoevskom' (Preliminary Remarks ... on L. Tolstoy and F. Dostoevsky) in *Voprosy teorii i psikhologii tvorchestva* (vol 5 [1914]). Regarding language as an individual's or a nation's only possible means of perceiving the world and of thinking, Potebnia protested vehemently against denationalization in general and the Russification of Ukrainians in particular, and equated this process with spiritual and intellectual disintegration. Potebnia's philosophy of language is rooted in W. Humboldt's romantic idealism, but he was also influenced by J. Herbart's and H. Lotze's associative psychology, and particularly by H. Steinthal's psycholinguistic writings.

Potebnia viewed the history of a language as the history of its dialects and used the concept of phonetic law, although he often tried to find a psychological basis for the concept. He recognized the existence of a proto-Rus' language, but located the beginning of its disintegration into dialects back in prehistoric times. He made many discoveries in Ukrainian historical phonetics, such as the primordial *dž* < *dj* alteration, the so-called second pleophony, and the conditions for the alternation *e:o*. He was the first to propose the theory that diphthongs were a transitional stage between Old Ukrainian *o, e, ѣ* and Modern Ukrainian *i*.

As an etymologist, Potebnia paid much attention to semantic development and the history of words against an expansive historical, folkloric, and psychological background. His major etymological writings were collected in *K istorii zvukov russkago iazyka* (Toward a History of the Sounds in the Russian Language, vols 2–4, 1880–1, 1883). His annotations to *The Tale of Ihor's Campaign* (1878; repr 1914) are a brilliant synthesis of the etymological, folkloristic, and historical approaches.

From the 1870s Potebnia concentrated on the study of the historical syntax of the Slavic languages against a comparative Indo-European background. His *Iz zapisok po russkoi grammatike* contains his writings on predicate forms and the participle (vol 2, 1874; rev edn 1888; repr 1958), the noun and the adjective (vol 3, 1899; repr 1968), and the verb and indeclinable words (vol 4, 1941; rev edn 1978). Before his work the field of Slavic historical syntax consisted mostly of inventories of constructions collected from literary monuments of various periods. He revised it to create a broadly drawn picture of category and construction changes tied to changes in ways of thinking, by integrating historical, dialectal, and folkloric materials. His comparative analysis uncovered remnants of prehistoric syntax in later constructions and reinterpretations of archaic constructions in later syntactic systems; that is, it demonstrated the historical character of syntactic categories and parts of speech. A. Budilovich equated Potebnia's contribution to the field of historical syntax with C. Darwin's contribution to the study of the origin of species.

Potebnia was far ahead of his contemporaries and not very popular during his lifetime. In the field of historical syntax his only immediate followers were A. Popov and, to a certain extent, D. *Ovsianiko-Kulikovsky (in his outline of Russian syntax). His ideas on literature were adopted as a theoretical framework by the 'Kharkiv school' (B.

Lezin, V. Khartsiev, A. Gornfeld, T. Rainov, O. Vetukhiv, and others) grouped around the serial *Voprosy teorii i psikhologii tvorchestva* (8 vols, 1907–23). They also had a significant impact on the esthetics of the Russian Symbolists (particularly A. Bely) and an indirect influence on the Ukrainian Symbolists. In 1945 the AN URSR (now ANU) Institute of Linguistics was named after Potebnia. Collections of his works on accentology (1973) and esthetics and poetics (1976, 1985) have been published.

BIBLIOGRAPHY
Chekhovych, K. *Oleksander Potebnia: Ukraïns'kyi myslytel'-lingvist* (Warsaw 1931)
Shevelov, G.Y. 'Alexander Potebnja as a Linguist,' *AUA*, 5, nos 2–3 (1956)
Bilodid, I.; et al (eds). *O.O. Potebnia i deiaki pytannia suchasnoï slavistyky* (Kharkiv 1962)
Tsiluiko, K.; et al (eds). *Oleksandr Opanasovych Potebnia: Iuvileinyi zbirnyk do 125-richchia z dnia narodzhennia* (Kiev 1962)
Franchuk, V. *Oleksandr Opanasovych Potebnia* (Kiev 1975; rev edn, Kiev 1985)
Presniakov, O. *A.A. Potebnia i russkoe literaturovedenie kontsa XIX–nachala XX veka* (Saratov 1978)
– *Poetika poznaniia i tvorchestva: Teoriia slovesnosti A.A. Potebni* (Moscow 1980)
Izhakevych, H.; et al (eds). *Potebnians'ki chytannia* (Kiev 1981)
Franchuk, V. (ed). *Naukova spadshchyna O.O. Potebni i suchasna filolohiia: Do 150-richchia z dnia narodzhennia O.O. Potebni; Zbirnyk naukovykh prats'* (Kiev 1985)
Fizer, J. *Alexander A. Potebnja's Psycholinguistic Theory of Literature: A Metacritical Inquiry* (Cambridge, Mass 1986)

G.Y. Shevelov

Potebnia, Oleksander [Potebnja], b 24 December 1868 in Kharkiv, d 16 November 1935 in Kharkiv. Scientist in the field of electric technology; son of O. *Potebnia. He graduated from the Kharkiv Technological Institute (1900) and taught in Tomsk and Kharkiv. He was a professor at the Kharkiv Electrotechnical Institute from 1923. He served as a consultant under *GOELRO during the planning of the major electrification of Ukraine, particularly for the Dnieper Hydroelectric Station at Zaporizhia, and made technical contributions in the field of electric machinery theory.

Potelych. See Potylych.

Potelych Church of the Holy Ghost (Tserkva sv. Dukha). A monument of 16th-century Ukrainian wooden architecture in Potelych (aka Potylych; now in Nesterov raion, Lviv oblast). A typical Boiko church, it consists of three frames with a tiered pyramidal top (built in the 18th century) over the central frame. The interior walls of the nave and the southern wall of the vestibule were decorated with religious paintings done in the 1620s to 1640s by masters of a single school. The artists applied tempera directly to the walls and did not adhere closely to the traditional rules: they added a 'national' flavor to some of the scenes by replacing SS Constantine and Helen with Prince Volodymyr the Great and Princess Olha, and depicting warriors as Cossacks and the Pharisees as Galician Jews of the period. The paintings are preserved in the National Museum in Lviv and have been described in monographs by L. Miliaieva (1969, 1971).

Potemkin, Grigorii, b 24 September 1739 in Chizhevo, near Smolensk, Russia, d 16 October 1791 near Iaşi. Rus-

Potelych Church of the Holy Ghost

sian general, count, and statesman. As the former lover, trusted adviser, and favorite of Empress Catherine II he was appointed supreme commander of New Russia in 1774, governor-general of New Russia, Azov, and Astrakhan gubernias in 1776, and viceroy in 1777. He oversaw the suppression of the Pugachev rebellion in 1774, the destruction of the *Zaporozhian Sich in 1775, and the annexation of the *Crimea and Georgia in 1783. For his achievements he received the title of prince of Tavriia (1783) and the 'grand hetmancy' of the Katerynoslav and Black Sea Cossack armies (1790). From 1774 until his death Potemkin had unlimited power in the territories under his rule and was the most influential man in the Russian Empire. In *Southern Ukraine and the Crimea he implemented a broad program of Ukrainian, Russian, and foreign (Serbian, Greek, German, Vlach) peasant and gentry colonization and urban development so as to transform those regions into well-populated and economically powerful parts of the Russian Empire. He founded the cities of Katerynoslav (now *Dnipropetrovske), *Kherson, *Mykolaiv, *Mariiupil, and *Sevastopil, supervised the development of the *Black Sea Fleet, encouraged mineral exploration (particularly in the Donets Basin), and established schools and presses.

N. Polonska-Vasylenko

Potemkin (full name: *Kniaz Potemkin Tavricheskii* [Prince Potemkin of Tavriia]). A battleship of the Russian Black Sea Fleet, built in 1904 and named after Prince G. Potemkin, aboard which a famous mutiny occurred during the *Revolution of 1905. On 27 June, while on maneuvers in Tendriv Bay, the ship's sailors – most of them

Ukrainians – refused to eat borsch made with rotten meat. When the ship's commander ordered the guards to shoot 30 of the suspected instigators of the insubordination, the outraged sailors shot him and 6 other officers and arrested the remaining officers. They then proclaimed their ship on the side of the people against tsarist despotism and elected a 15-man revolutionary committee headed by P. Matiushenko. The mutiny spread to the nearby torpedo boat 267, after which both ships made for Odessa, where an armed workers' rebellion had erupted on 26 June in response to the mass arrest and shooting of over 1,000 general strikers and rioters by the police.

On 30 June the crews of 12 warships of the Black Sea Fleet sent from Symferopil to apprehend the *Potemkin* expressed solidarity with the *Potemkin* upon arrival. The sailors of the battleship *Georgii Pobedonosets* arrested their officers and remained with the *Potemkin* until a petty officer ran their ship aground in Odessa harbor. The *Potemkin* and 267 then set course for the Rumanian port of Constanţa. On 1 July the *Potemkin*'s sailors were refused fuel and provisions in Constanţa, and on 3 July they issued appeals to 'the civilized world' and 'all European states' explaining why they had rebelled against tsarist autocracy. The 267 surrendered in Sevastopil, and the *Potemkin* returned to Constanţa. There on 8 July the sailors surrendered their ship. The *Potemkin* was returned to Sevastopil, where it was disarmed and renamed the *Panteleimon*. A major manifestation of military opposition to tsarist rule, the *Potemkin* mutiny has been the subject of many Soviet books and memoirs and a famous film by S. Eisenstein.

R. Senkus

Peter Potichnyj   Metropolitan Ipatii Potii

Potichnyj, Peter (Petro), b 2 June 1930 in Pavlokoma, Brzozów county, Galicia. Political scientist. Potichnyj left Ukraine with a westward-bound company of the *Ukrainian Insurgent Army (UPA). He emigrated to the United States in the 1950s and served with the US forces in Korea. He studied at Temple (BA, 1958) and Columbia (MA, 1961; PH D, 1966) universities. Since 1964 he has taught political science at McMaster University in Hamilton, Ontario, and since 1985 he has been a consultant to Heilongjiang University in Harbin, China. He is the author of *Soviet Agricultural Trade Unions, 1917–70* (1972), a coauthor of *The Ukraine and the Czechoslovak Crisis* (1970) and *Jewish-Ukrainian Relations: Two Solitudes* (1983, 1987), the editor of several collections of articles on the USSR and Soviet Ukraine, and a coeditor of the multivolume *Litopys Ukraïns'koï povstans'koï armiï* (Chronicle of the Ukrainian Insurgent Army, 18 vols, 1976–90) and *Political Thought of the Ukrainian Underground, 1943–51* (1986).

Potii, Ipatii [Potij, Ipatij] (secular name: Adam), b 12 April 1541 in Rozhanka, Podlachia region, d 1613. Churchman and Uniate metropolitan of Kiev. The son of a nobleman, he was raised at the Polish royal court, and attended a Calvinist school run by the Lithuanian chancellor A. Radziwiłł. After attending Cracow University he entered the service of King Sigismund II August. He then served in Brest as a zemstvo judge, tax collector, and castellan and senator.

Potii was continually involved in religious affairs. Having adopted Calvinism under the influence of Radziwiłł, he reconverted to Orthodoxy in 1574. At the initiative of Prince K. Ostrozky he was made bishop of Volodymyr and Brest in 1593. As bishop he began formal negotiations with Roman Catholic representatives, and in 1595 he was sent to Rome, with K. Terletsky, as a representative of the church in Ukraine, to set forth its confession of faith before Pope Clement VIII. They returned to lead the sobor that culminated in the Church Union of *Berestia. After the proclamation of the union Potii was one of its leading supporters, both in defending it against Orthodox opposition and in seeking equal rights with Roman Catholics in the Polish-Lithuanian Commonwealth. After the death of Metropolitan M. Rahoza in 1599, Potii became the second Uniate metropolitan of Kiev and Halych (1600–13).

Potii was a noted polemicist and wrote in Ukrainian, Polish, and Latin. Several anonymous works have been attributed to him, including *Uniia, al'bo vyklad predneishykh artykulov ...* (The Union, or an Exposition of the Articles ..., 1595) on the terms of the Union of Berestia, *Antirysis* (Anti-Discourse, 1599; Polish trans 1600), *Oborona ś. Synodu Florentskiego ...* (A Defense of the Council of Florence ..., 1603), and *Harmoniia, al'bo sohlasie very ...* (Harmony, or the Agreement of Faiths ..., 1608). He also founded a theological seminary in Vilnius and a Greek Catholic school in Brest.

BIBLIOGRAPHY
Chubatyi, M. *Mytropolyt Ipatii Potii, apostol tserkovnoï iednosty: V 300-litnii iuvilei ioho smerty* (Lviv 1914)
Savyts'kyi, I. *Ipatii Potii, ep. Volodymyrs'kyi i mytr. Kyïvs'kyi: Iuvileina knyha v 300-litni rokovyny m. I. Potiia* (Lviv 1914)
W. Lencyk, I. Nazarko

Potiienko, Vasyl [Potijenko, Vasyl'], b 9 April 1898 in Sosnytsia, Chernihiv gubernia, d 12 April 1945 in Weimar, Germany. *Ukrainian Autocephalous Orthodox church (UAOC) activist. He studied at Kiev University and was ordained as an archdeacon. In 1924–6 he headed the *All-Ukrainian Orthodox Church Council and assisted in organizing 20 UAOC parishes in the Sosnytsia region. He was imprisoned briefly by the Soviet authorities in 1926, and then rearrested in 1934 and exiled for five years. He returned to Ukraine after serving his term. In 1941–3 he was an organizer of the renewed UAOC in Slobidska Ukraine and headed the church's administrative offices in Kharkiv. He emigrated to the West in 1943. He was killed during a bombing raid.

Potochyska settlement. A multi-occupational archeological site near Potochyska (Potochyshche), Horodenka raion, Ivano-Frankivske oblast. Excavations ca 1880 yielded the remains of a Trypilian culture village, a stone Nordic burial vault, a cache of 1st-century BC bronze items, and Thracian ceramics.

Potocki. A Polish noble family. It originated in the 14th century in the Cracow region; its name derives from the village of Złoty Potok, near Częstochowa. The family became prominent in the late 16th and early 17th centuries as a result of the patronage of Chancellor J. Zamoyski and King Sigismund III Vasa and dynastic ties with the Movilă family of Moldavian hospodars. In that period the Potockis became owners of many towns (eg, Brody, Krystynopil, Nemyriv, Stanyslaviv, Zbarazh), hundreds of villages, and huge latifundia in Galicia, Podilia, and Right-Bank Ukraine. Thenceforth they were one of the wealthiest and most influential magnate families in the Polish Commonwealth.

The Potockis played a significant role in Ukrainian history as Polish starostas (eg, of Belz, Halych, Kolomyia, Mostyska, Sambir, Sniatyn, Vinnytsia), voivodes, and military leaders. Jakub (b ca 1554, d 26 January 1613 in Smolensk) was castellan of Kamianets-Podilskyi from 1609 and voivode of Bratslav voivodeship from 1611. His brother, Jan (b ca 1552, d 22 or 25 April 1611), was general of the lands of Podilia from 1592 and voivode of Bratslav voivodeship from 1608; he led an army into Moldavia in 1607 to help his brother-in-law, C. Movilă, ascend the Moldavian throne. Jakub's son Mikołaj *Potocki was grand hetman of the Polish royal army; he suppressed the 1637–8 rebellions led by P. Pavliuk and D. Hunia and commanded the Polish army during the Cossack-Polish War of 1648–57. Mikołaj's brother Stanisław (b 1607, d 20 March 1647) was a cavalry colonel and the Polish commissioner for Cossack affairs. Another brother, Andrzej (d before 19 May 1663 in Lviv), was royal quartermaster from 1655 and voivode of Bratslav voivodeship; he commanded the Polish cavalry that aided Hetman I. Vyhovsky in 1658–60. Mikołaj's son, Stefan (b ca 1624, d 19 May 1648), was starosta of Nizhen and a military commander during the Battle of Zhovti Vody. Jakub and Jan's nephew, Stanisław Rewera *Potocki, was grand hetman in 1654–67. His son, Andrzej (d 30 August 1691 in Stanyslaviv), was voivode of Kiev voivodeship (1668–8) and grand hetman (1684–92); he founded the town of Stanyslaviv (now Ivano-Frankivske) in 1662, defeated the Crimean Tatars at Kalush in 1675, regained a large part of Podilia from Turkey in 1683, and participated in the unsuccessful Moldavian campaigns of Jan III Sobieski in 1684–5. Andrzej's son, Józef (d 17 May 1751), was voivode of Kiev voivodeship (1702–9) and grand hetman (1735–43); he suppressed the 1703 popular rebellion led by S. *Palii. Józef's son Stanisław (b 1698 near Stanyslaviv, d 8 February 1760) was in charge of defending the Commonwealth's border with the Ottoman Empire from 1738, fortified Stanyslaviv and Kamianets-Podilskyi, and was voivode of Kiev voivodeship in 1744–6. His brother, Franciszek Salezy (b 1700, d 22 October 1772 in Krystynopil), was voivode of Volhynia voivodeship from 1755 and Kiev voivodeship from 1756; he owned 70 towns and several hundred villages. Franciszek's son, Stanisław Szczęsny (b 1751 in Krystynopil, d before 15 March 1805 in Tulchyn), was voivode of Rus' voivodeship (1782–8), general of the royal artillery (1788–92), and marshal of the *Torhovytsia Confederacy (1792).

A few Potockis played a role in the economic life of Ukraine. Wincenty (?–1825), the royal chamberlain and a lieutenant general from 1773, applied modern management methods to the numerous enterprises he created in Nemyriv. Antoni Protazy (aka Prot, b 11 September 1761, d 1801), a Warsaw banker and the owner of Chudniv, organized several factories in the village of Makhnivka, near Berdychiv, directed the Polish Black Sea Trading Company, and ran an import-export business in Russian-ruled Kherson.

Under Austrian rule three Potockis distinguished themselves in Galician politics: Count Adam (b 24 February 1822, d 15 June 1872), a proponent of Polish-Ukrainian co-operation, Galician autonomy, and the transformation of the Austrian Empire into a federated state; Count Alfred (b 29 July 1822, d 18 May 1889), the Austrian minister of agriculture (1867–70), prime minister (1870–1), and viceroy of Galicia (1875–83); and his son, Andrzej *Potocki, the viceroy of Galicia (1903–8).

A. Zhukovsky

Potocki, Andrzej, b 10 June 1861 in Krzeszowice, Cracow circle, western Galicia, d 12 April 1908 in Lviv. Polish count and conservative politician. He was one of the wealthiest land, mine, and factory owners in Galicia as well as the Russian-ruled Kholm region and Podilia and Kiev gubernias. He was a former Austrian diplomat, and from 1890 he held various public offices in Cracow. In 1895 he was elected a member of the Austrian parliament and the Galician Diet. Potocki became an influential member of the Austrian Reichsrat (from 1901) and marshal of the Galician Diet (1901–3). In the aftermath of the 1902 *peasant strikes in Galicia he was appointed Austrian viceroy of Galicia (1903) with the support of other large Polish landowners. Potocki was hostile to the Ukrainian peasants and hindered their attempts at emigration. He used the police to suppress public manifestations of solidarity with the Revolution of 1905 in the Russian Empire. He was an opponent of electoral reforms, and during the 1907–8 electoral campaigns he spoke out against the Ukrainian Radicals, Social Democrats, and National Democrats and supported the conservative Russophiles. Under Potocki's authoritarian rule the Polish-controlled Galician government's corruption, electoral abuses, and police repression (especially during the 1906 peasant strikes and 1907–8 elections) were aimed at maintaining Polish superiority. He was assassinated by the student M. *Sichynsky.

Potocki, Jan, b 8 March 1761 in Pykiv, near Vinnytsia, Podilia voivodeship, d 2 December 1815 in Uladivka, Lityn county, Podilia gubernia. Polish count, historian, geographer, and writer. A pioneer in Slavic archeology, he was one of the first to propound the autochthonous theory of the origin of the Slavic peoples. His major works were published in French: *Essai sur l'histoire universelle et recherches sur la Sarmatie* (4 vols, 1789–92), *Chroniques, mémoires et recherches pour servir à l'histoire de tous les peuples slaves* (2 vols, 1793), *Voyage dans quelques parties de la Basse Saxe pour la recherche des antiquités slaves* (1795), *Fragments historiques et géographiques sur la Scythie, la Sarmatie et les Slaves* (4

vols, 1796), *Histoire primitive des peuples de la Russie* (1802), *Histoire ancienne du gouvernement de Cherson* (1804), *Histoire ancienne du gouvernement de Podolie* (1805), and *Atlas archéologique de la Russie européenne* (1805; 3rd edn 1829). He also wrote accounts of his voyages, a collection of six one-act plays, and a fantasy novel, *Manuscrit trouvé à Saragosse* (pub 1958).

Potocki, Mikołaj, b 1594, d 20 November 1651 in Khmilnyk, Podilia. Polish magnate and military leader in Ukraine. He was captured by the Turks during the 1620 Battle of Cecora but was released in 1621. A colonel from 1624, he commanded Polish troops in battles with the Crimean Tatars, the Zaporozhian Cossacks (eg, the 1625 Battle of Kurukove, the 1630 Battle of Pereiaslav), and, in 1626–9, the Swedes. He was appointed general of the Polish forces in Podilia, starosta of Liatychiv, and full crown secretary in 1633; starosta of Nizhen and voivode of Bratslav voivodeship in 1636; field hetman (deputy commander in chief) of the Polish royal army in 1637; starosta of Oster after 1642; starosta of Cherkasy before 1643; and starosta of Bar, castellan of Cracow, and grand hetman (commander in chief) of the Polish royal army in 1646. He commanded the Polish army that fought and suppressed the Cossack-peasant uprisings led by P. Pavliuk, K. Skydan, D. Hunia, and Ya. Ostrianyn in 1637–8. For his achievements the king awarded him with huge latifundia in Ukraine. During the Cossack-Polish War of 1648 Potocki's army was defeated at the Battle of *Korsun, and he was captured by the Cossacks. Hetman B. Khmelnytsky handed him over to the Crimean khan, who released him in 1650. In 1651 Potocki commanded the Polish army during the Battle of *Berestechko and negotiated the Treaty of *Bila Tserkva with Khmelnytsky. He died soon afterward.

A. Zhukovsky

Potocki, Stanisław Rewera, b 1579, d 27 February 1667 in Pidhaitsi, Galicia. Polish magnate and military leader. He was appointed chamberlain of Podilia in 1621, castellan of Kamianets-Podilskyi in 1628, voivode of Bratslav voivodeship in 1631, voivode of Podilia voivodeship in 1636, field hetman (deputy commander in chief) of the Polish royal army in 1652, voivode of Kiev voivodeship in 1653, grand hetman (commander in chief) of the army in 1654, and voivode of Cracow voivodeship in 1658. He commanded the Polish troops that fought against the Cossack rebellion led by T. Fedorovych in 1630 and in the battle against the Crimean Tatars at Kamianets-Podilskyi in 1633, and troops during the Cossack-Polish War, in the battles of Zboriv, Berestechko, and Bila Tserkva. Under his supreme command the Polish army fought the Cossacks and Muscovites in the Battle of *Okhmativ in 1655 and the Muscovites in the Battle of Chudniv in 1660. Among the towns he owned were Kytaihorod and Panivtsi, in Podilia, and Pidhaitsi, in Galicia. He was starosta of Halych from 1627, Bar from 1651, and Dolyna from 1659.

Potocki, Wacław, b 1621 in Wola Łużańska, near Gorlice, western Galicia, d July 1696 in neighboring Łużna. Polish noble; poet. He took part in Polish campaigns against the Cossacks in Ukraine in 1638 and 1651. Motifs from Ukrainian folklore can be found in his collections of emblematic and epigrammatic, anecdotal, and humorous poems *Poczet herbów szlachty Korony Polskiey ...* (Enumeration of Crests of the Nobility of the Polish Crown, 1696) and *Ogród fraszek* (Garden of Trifles, pub 1907). In his epic poem *Transakcyja wojny chocimskiej* (The Transaction of the Khotyn War, 1670; pub 1850) he portrayed sympathetically the participation of the Cossacks under Hetman P. Sahaidachny in the 1621 Battle of Khotyn against the Turks.

Pottery. See Ceramics.

Poturaev, Valentin, b 18 January 1922 in Gustomoi, Lgov county, Kursk gubernia, Russia. Mechanics scientist; AN URSR (now ANU) corresponding member from 1976 and full member from 1979. A graduate of the Dnipropetrovske Institute of Railway-Transport Engineers (1948), he worked at the Dnipropetrovske Mining Institute (1953–74), where he served as prorector (1962–72) and rector (1972–3). In 1967 he became a department head at the ANU Institute of Geotechnical Mechanics, and in 1975 he was appointed the institute's director. Poturaev has made contributions in the areas of the stability of heavy-mining machinery, mining mechanics, vibration calculations in heavy machinery, and the damping of vibrations in machines with heavy loading. He developed mathematical methods of assessing the effects of and predicting behavior under heavy loading of machine components constructed of rubber.

Fedir Potushniak

Potushniak, Fedir [Potušnjak] (pseuds: Teodor Berehovsky, F. Vilshytsky, F. Pasichnyk), b 27 February 1910 in Osii, Bereg komitat, Transcarpathia, d 12 February 1960 in Uzhhorod. Writer, ethnographer, and archeologist. He graduated from Prague University in 1937 and worked as a village teacher in Transcarpathia. From 1941 to 1944 he edited the publications of the Subcarpathian Scientific Society. From 1946 he taught archeology, ethnography, and Czech at Uzhhorod University. His modernist poetry appeared in Transcarpathian periodicals from 1928. He is the author of the poetry collections *Daleki vohni* (Distant Fires, 1934), *Khvylyny vichnosty* (Moments of Eternity, 1936), *Tainmychi vechory* (Mysterious Evenings, 1938), *Mozhlyvosti* (Possibilities, 1939), *Na bilykh skalakh* (On the White Cliffs, 1942), *Krystaly* (Crystals, 1943), and *Terezy vichnosty* (The Scales of Eternity, 1944); the realistic prose collections *Zemlia* (Land, 1938), *Opovidannia* (Stories, 1943), *Hrikh* (A Sin, 1944), *V dolyni syn'oï riky* (In the Valley of the Blue River, 1957), *Maty-zemlia* (Mother Earth, 1962), and *Chest' rodu* (The Clan's Honor, 1973); a novel about interwar

Transcarpathia, *Povin'* (The Flood, 1959; pt 3, 1965); a monograph on archeological finds from the Bronze and Iron ages in Transcarpathia (1958); and many articles on the Transcarpathian language, folklore, archeology, and other subjects. A collection of his works was published in 1980.

R. Senkus

Potylych or **Potelych** [Potylyč or Potelyč]. III-4. A former Galician town, now a village (1968 pop 2,950) in Nesterov raion, Lviv oblast. In 1498 it was granted Magdeburg law. The zenith of Potylych's development occurred in the 16th and 17th centuries, when it was noted for its pottery and glassworks. Notable examples of wooden church architecture in Potylych are the *Potelych Church of the Holy Ghost, the fortified Trinity Church (built 1593), and the Church of the Nativity of the Mother of God (1607). The latter two churches were destroyed during the Second World War, but 50 works of religious art from all three churches are preserved at the National Museum in Lviv.

Poucheniie ditiam (Instruction for [My] Children). An original literary work written by Grand Prince *Volodymyr Monomakh of Kiev ca 1117. Several incomplete parts of it were preserved in the Laurentian redaction of the Primary Chronicle; certain scholars consider them to be individual works. The *Poucheniie* is an example of the didactic genre that was widespread in medieval literature, and is the first autobiographical narrative in Old Ukrainian literature by a grand prince. It consists of a religious and moral introduction with many scriptural quotations, a section dealing with the duties and obligations of a ruler, and a section describing the author's own life as an illustration of those duties and obligations. In setting an example for his sons the erudite Volodymyr portrays himself as the embodiment of the idea of a unitary Rus' state, a brave warrior, an ethical and just Christian ruler, and a learned man. His psychological characterizations, colorful expressions, and imagery are outstanding features of the work. The text, written in a combination of Church Slavonic and the vernacular, was first published in St Petersburg in 1793.

Poultry farming. The raising of chickens, geese, ducks, turkeys, and other fowl for eggs, meat, feathers, and down. Poultry farming is one of the most efficient branches of *animal husbandry. It gives a high output of nutritious food for relatively little investment in labor and feed. Poultry farming has always been practiced throughout Ukraine, especially in Galicia, on the Right Bank, and in the Kuban. Prior to the collectivization of agriculture, poultry farming provided peasants with a good return, and even the poorest households could afford to keep fowl. Before the First World War there were some 70 million poultry in Ukraine, although there was little intensive poultry farming. Eggs, meat, and down were commonly exported: before 1914 the Ukrainian gubernias of the Russian Empire exported almost 70 million eggs annually, almost a half of the empire's egg export. Eggs were also exported from Galicia (30 million in 1929–30).

After the collectivization of agriculture most poultry farming in Ukraine was still practiced by individual peasants, and most eggs, meat, and down were sold privately.

TABLE 1
Number of poultry in Ukraine, 1960–83 (in millions)

	1960	1975	1983
Total	135.1	185.3	246.0
On private farms	103.6	99.5	106.0
On collective farms	25.8	42.1	51.0
On state farms	5.7	43.7	89.0

TABLE 2
Number of eggs produced in Ukraine, 1960–87 (in millions)

	1960	1970	1980	1987
Total	7,103	9,141	13,695	16,266
On private farms	6,122	5,696	5,963	6,000
On collective farms	726	1,854	2,381	2,330
On state farms	255	1,591	5,351	7,936

In recent years the government has made intensive, large-scale poultry farming by specialized state farms a priority. Table 1 summarizes changes in the number and distribution of poultry in Ukraine and illustrates the increased importance of state poultry farming. In 1971 there were 52.2 million chickens (including 30.2 million layers), 237,000 geese, 3.8 million ducks, and 237,000 turkeys in Ukraine, accounting for 24 percent of all the poultry in the former USSR. Since then the significance of chickens has increased relative to that of other poultry.

The importance of poultry as a food source is summarized in table 2. The table also underscores the growing importance of state farms in egg production. The total production of poultry meat increased from 255,000 t in 1960 to 673,000 t in 1987. The greatest problem facing the industry is lack of feed.

Various hybrid breeds of poultry are farmed in Ukraine. The Ukrainian Scientific Research Institute of Poultry Farming, established in 1932 and currently located in Birky, Kharkiv oblast, develops new breeds of poultry and new techniques for poultry farming.

Povarennykh, Aleksandr [Povarennyx], b 3 February 1915 in Petrograd, d 4 March 1986 in Kiev. Geologist; full member of the AN URSR (now ANU) from 1973. He graduated from the Central Asian Industrial Institute in Tashkent (1940) and taught at the Kryvyi Rih Mining Institute (1949–60). Then he chaired a department of the ANU Institute of Geological Sciences (1960–9) and worked at the ANU Institute of the Geochemistry and Physics of Minerals. His major works deal with the chemistry of crystals and minerals, the history of mineralogy, and the philosophy of science. He is the author of *Kristallokhimicheskaia klassifikatsiia mineral'nykh vidov* (The Crystallochemical Classification of Mineral Types, 1966).

Povarnitsyn, Vladimir [Povarnicyn], b 27 July 1899 in Viatka, Russia, d 21 October 1962 in Kiev. Botanist; corresponding member of the AN URSR (now ANU) from 1948. After completing studies at the Leningrad Forestry Institute (1925) he worked in Leningrad at the Forestry Technology Academy (1925–35) and the university (1935–7) and in Krasnoiarsk at the Siberian Forestry Technical School (1937–45). He then moved to Kiev. From 1945 he

headed the forestry and dendrology departments at the Ukrainian Agricultural Academy and worked for the ANU Institute of Botany. Povarnitsyn's major research interests included forest typology and classification, the acclimatization of tree species, and geobotanical regionalization. He undertook several research expeditions to Western Ukraine, edited *Roslynnist' Zakarpats'koï oblasti URSR* (The Vegetation of the Transcarpathia Oblast of the Ukrainian SSR, 1954), and wrote *Lisy Ukraïns'koho Polissia* (The Forests of Ukrainian Polisia, 1959).

Povazhenko, Ivan [Považenko], b 4 August 1901 in Boiarka, Zvenyhorodka county, Kiev gubernia. Veterinary surgeon. A graduate of the Kiev Zootechnical-Veterinary Institute (1925) and the Kiev Medical Institute (1930), in 1937 he was appointed head of the surgery department of the Kiev Veterinary Institute (now a faculty of the Ukrainian Agricultural Academy). He wrote *Osnovnye voprosy veterinarnoi voenno-polevoi khirurgii* (Fundamental Questions of Veterinary Military-Field Surgery, 1944) and *Obshchaia veterinarnaiia khirurgiia* (General Veterinary Surgery, 1961).

Povist' o Akiri premudrom (The Tale of Akir the All-Wise). An Assyro-Babylonian didactic tale taken from *The Thousand and One Nights* and translated in Kiev from Greek in the 11th century, during the reign of Grand Prince Yaroslav the Wise. Many of the expressions and proverbs found in it became part of Ukrainian oral folklore. A. Grigorev's monograph about the tale appeared in Moscow in 1913.

Povist' vremennykh lit (The Tale of Bygone Years). A chronicle of events in Kievan Rus' in the 12th century, under the editorship (in the opinion of most scholars) of *Nestor the Chronicler. A valuable historical source and an excellent example of medieval Rus' literature, it begins with an account of the Flood and Noah's division of the world among his sons; then it proceeds to a description of the dispersal of the Slavic tribes in Eastern and Central Europe and a recounting of the apocryphal sermon of St Andrew on the banks of the Dnieper. The history of Kiev and the *Polianians is central to the narrative. After an account of the founding of Kiev by Kyi, Shchek, Khoryv, and their sister, Lybed, the chronicle deals with the question of who first ruled Rus'; it ascribes the origin of Rus' to the summoning of the *Varangians and the establishment of the *Riurykide dynasty. Subsequent events in Rus' history are described in annal form to the year 1110.

The *Povist'* is based on earlier Kievan and Novgorodian *chronicles, mainly the Primary Chronicle written (possibly by the monk *Nykon) at the Kievan Cave Monastery, in which events are described to 1093. It draws on contemporary Byzantine chronicles, such as that of Georgios Harmatolos, and includes the texts of Rus'-Byzantine treaties of 907, 912, and 972. Folk legends, such as the accounts of Princess Olha's revenge on the Derevlianians, Kozhemiaka's defeat of a Pecheneg champion, and the 997 Pecheneg siege, are recounted.

Three redactions of the *Povist'* were compiled. The first, now-inextant redaction was completed in 1113 by Nestor the Chronicler, who edited the Primary Chronicle and supplemented it with descriptions of events of the late 11th and early 12th centuries. The detailed account of the

Kievan Cave Monastery in the years 1094–1110 supports the view that Nestor was the chronicle's compiler. The redaction provides eyewitness accounts of internecine conflicts among the sons of Grand Prince Yaroslav the Wise, the blinding of Prince Vasylko of Terebovlia in 1097, and the Liubech, Vytychiv, and Dolobske congresses of princes.

The second redaction was completed in 1116, at the behest of Grand Prince Volodymyr Monomakh, at the Vydubychi Monastery by the hegumen *Sylvestr. Sylvestr added, among other things, Monomakh's speech at the Dolobske congress of princes in 1103. The redaction was preserved in the later *Laurentian Chronicle and *Radziwiłł Chronicle. The third redaction was composed in 1118 at the Kievan Cave Monastery by an unknown author. The text focuses on the events pertinent to the Monomakhovych line (Volodymyr Monomakh, his father, Vsevolod Yaroslavych, and his son, Mstyslav I Volodymyrovych the Great). The redaction was preserved in the *Hypatian Chronicle of ca 1425.

The central idea of the *Povist'* is the unity of the Rus' land and state, as symbolized by the Riurykide dynasty in Kiev. The *Povist'* served as the basis of most later Rus' chronicles (eg, the *Kiev Chronicle and the *Galician-Volhynian Chronicle). Until the 16th century all of them began with the text of the *Povist'*. The language of the *Povist'* is a combination of Old Church Slavonic and the contemporary Rus' vernacular.

The *Povist'* has been translated and published in French (by L. Leger, 1884), Swedish (by A. Norrback, 1919), German (by R. Trautmann, 1931; and D. Chyzhevsky, 1969), Rumanian (by G. Popa-Lisseanu, 1935), Russian (by D. Likhachev and B. Romanov, 1950), English (by S.H. Cross and O.P. Sherbowitz-Wetzor, 1953), Czech (by K. Erben, 1954), Polish (by F. Sielicki, 1968), and Ukrainian (by V. Blyznets, 1982; L. Makhnovets, 1990; and V. Yaremenko, 1990).

BIBLIOGRAPHY
Shakhmatov, A. *O nachal'nom Kievskom letopisnom svode* (Moscow 1897)
Polnoe sobranie russkikh letopisei, vol 2, *Ipat'evskaia letopis'*, ed A. Shakhmatov, 2nd edn (St Petersburg 1908)
Shakhmatov, A. *Razyskaniia o drevneishikh letopisnykh svodakh* (St Petersburg 1908)
Povest' vremennykh let, vol 1, *Vvodnaia chast', tekst, primechaniia*, ed A. Shakhmatov (Petrograd 1916)
Povest' vremennykh let, ed D. Likhachev, 2 pts (Moscow and Leningrad 1950)
The Russian Primary Chronicle: Laurentian Text, trans and ed S.H. Cross and O.P. Sherbowitz-Wetzor (Cambridge, Mass [1953])
Aleshkovskii, M. *Povest' vremennykh let: Sud'ba literaturnogo proizvedeniia v drevnei Rusi* (Moscow 1971)
Müller, L. (ed). *Handbuch zur Nestorchronik*, 3 vols (Munich 1977–9)
Tvorogov, O. (ed). *Pamiatniki literatury Drevnei Rusi: Nachalo russkoi literatury, XI–nachalo XII veka: Povest' vremennykh let* (Moscow 1978)
Pritsak, O. *On the Writing of History of Kievan Rus'* (Cambridge, Mass 1988)
Litopys rus'kyi za Ipats'kym spyskom, trans and ed L. Makhnovets' (Kiev 1990)
Povist' vrem'ianykh lit: Litopys (za Ipats'kym spyskom), trans and ed V. Iaremenko (Kiev 1990)

A. Zhukovsky

Povit. see County.

Povkh, Ivan [Povx], b 11 November 1909 in Myropillia, Sudzha county, Kursk gubernia, Russia. Scientist in the fields of mechanics and hydromechanics; corresponding member of the AN URSR (now ANU) since 1961. He graduated from the Leningrad Industrial (now Polytechnical) Institute (1936). He worked at the ANU institutes of Mining and Ferrous Metals in Donetske (1961–4) and held a chair at Donetske University (from 1964). His main contributions are in the fields of physical hydrodynamics, aerohydrodynamics, turbine design, ore purification, and the theory of friction.

Povoroznyk, Hnat, b 25 December 1895 in Zhovtantsi, Zhovkva county, Galicia, d 25 January 1979 in Hamilton, Ontario. Businessman and community activist. During the war he served in the Ukrainian Galician Army. In 1927 he emigrated to Canada, where he established Essex Packers in southern Ontario. He was active in the Ukrainian War Veterans' Association of Canada and the Ukrainian National Federation. He was president of the Novyi Shliakh publishers and a generous patron of Ukrainian organizations.

Povstanets' (Insurgent). A journal published by the Supreme Command of the UPA for its soldiers. The first issue appeared in November 1944 and contained on its cover page the 'Oath of a UPA Soldier.' Planned as a 16-page monthly, it sometimes came out in 24-page bimonthly issues. The editor was Capt M. Duzhy (1944–5). The last issue appeared in August–September 1946.

Oleksa Povstenko

Povstenko, Oleksa, b 25 February 1902 in Khashchova, Haisyn county, Podilia gubernia, d 15 January 1973 in Washington, DC. Architect and art scholar; member of the Ukrainian Academy of Arts and Sciences in the USA. A graduate of the Volhynian Industrial Polytechnic (1927), he completed his studies at the Kharkiv Institute of Industrial Construction, taught at the Kharkiv Construction Tekhnikum and Civil-Engineering Institute, and worked as an architectural engineer and, from 1935, an architect for the People's Commissariat of Education in Kiev. During the German occupation (1941–3) he directed the *St Sophia Museum in Kiev. A postwar émigré, he settled in the United States in 1950 and worked in the architecture department of the Capitol in Washington. He designed a number of residential and public buildings, including the Kharkiv Pedagogical Institute, the Kharkiv Astronomical Observatory, and the Holy Trinity Cathedral in Winnipeg

(1949, codesigner). He compiled a dictionary of Ukrainian architectural terminology (1939–41) and wrote books on the historical maps of Kiev (1946, with P. Kurinny), the history of Ukrainian art (1948), and Kiev's history and architecture (1954) and *The Cathedral of St. Sophia in Kiev* (1954).

Powder metallurgy. See Metallurgy.

Leonid Pozen: the monument to Ivan Kotliarevsky in Poltava (1903)

Pozen, Leonid, b 22 July 1849 in Obolon, Khorol county, Poltava gubernia, d 8 January 1921 in Petrograd. Sculptor; full member of the St Petersburg Academy of Arts from 1894. He began exhibiting his work in 1880 and joined the *Peredvizhniki society in 1891. His numerous small-scale compositions depicted the folkways and history of the Ukrainian people. They include *Kobzar* (1883), *Beggar* (1886), *Zaporozhian Scout* (1887), and *Plowed Field in Ukraine* (1897). He also sculpted portraits (eg, of M. Yaroshenko) and the monuments to I. Kotliarevsky (1896–1902) and N. Gogol (1913–15) in Poltava. P. Vladych's monograph about Pozen was published in Kiev in 1961.

Pozharna Balka settlement. An early 7th- to 5th-century BC Scythian settlement near Pozharna Balka, Poltava raion. Excavations in 1949 uncovered several ash pits, the bones of domesticated animals, the remains of a fireplace in a surface dwelling, large amounts of ceramic tableware, and a variety of tools.

Pozharsky, Petro [Požars'kyj], b 2 February 1878 in Hvozdiv, Kiev county, d ? Economist and co-operative leader. He contributed to the co-operative newspapers *Slovo* (1907–9) and *Nasha kooperatsiia* (1913–14). In 1917–18 he was a delegate to the Central Rada and an organizer of the Ukrainian Central Co-operative Committee. He also helped organize and direct the Tsentral agricultural co-operative. A professor of co-operative studies in the 1920s at the Kiev Co-operative Institute, he was arrested in connection with the trial of the *Union for the Liberation of Ukraine in 1929, and his subsequent fate is unknown. Pozharsky wrote *Narysy z istoriï ukraïns'koï kooperatsiï* (Outlines from the History of Ukrainian Co-operation, 1919) and articles on the history and theory of the Ukrainian co-operative movement.

Pozharsky, Serhii [Požars'kyj, Serhij], b 1900, d 1970 in Moscow. Graphic artist. In the early 1920s he studied under V. Krychevsky, M. Boichuk, and H. Narbut at the Ukrainian State Academy of Art in Kiev and then worked mostly in Russia. He specialized in book graphics, using a Narbutesque style. His work was displayed at the 1932 exhibition of Ukrainian graphic art organized in Lviv by the Association of Independent Ukrainian Artists.

Pozmogov, Anatolii, b 16 April 1921 in Tashkent, Uzbek SSR. Roentgenologist and oncologist. A graduate of the Tashkent Medical Institute (1943), he was prorector and head of the roentgenology and radiology department of the Kiev Medical Institute (1963–6), assistant director of the Kiev Scientific Research Institute of Experimental and Clinical Oncology (1966–71), and director of the Kiev Roentgenological-Radiological and Oncological Scientific Research Institute (from 1971). His most important works deal with the X-ray diagnosis of tumors.

Poznań. A provincial capital and industrial center (1989 pop 589,000) in western Poland. A small Ukrainian community has existed in Poznań since the 1920s. In the interwar period it consisted of about 300 émigrés from central and eastern Ukraine, who established a branch of the Ukrainian Central Committee; about 100 students, with their own organizations; and some Ukrainians from Galicia. In 1940–5 a branch of the Ukrainian National Alliance in Germany was active in the city. After the war a branch of the Ukrainian Social and Cultural Society and an Orthodox parish attended by Ukrainians were established there.

Poznanska, Mariia [Poznans'ka, Marija], b 15 July 1917 in Petrashivka (now Haivoron), Tarashcha county, Kiev gubernia. Children's poet. She graduated from the Kiev Pedagogical Institute in 1949. Since 1946 she has published over 30 collections of poetry for children. An illustrated edition of her selected works, *Zhorzhyny tsvitut'* (The Dahlias Are Blooming), was published in 1987.

Poznansky, Borys [Poznans'kyj], b 7 May 1841 in Starodub, Chernihiv gubernia, d 27 September 1906. Ethnographer and civic figure. As a student at Kiev University (1859–61) he belonged to a *khlopoman circle. Later he was a member of the Old Hromada of Kiev. For several years he worked among the peasants of the Kaniv and Katerynoslav regions to raise their educational level and studied their traditions and folklore. In 1865 he was arrested and exiled to the Voronezh region, where he continued his ethnographic research among the Ukrainian inhabitants. He contributed ethnographic and historical materials and fiction to Ukrainian journals, such as *Osnova*, *Kievskaia starina*, and *Zoria*. His major contribution was a study of Ukrainian dress (1905).

Pozychaniuk, Yosyp [Pozyčanjuk, Josyp] (noms de guerre: Shakhai, Shuhai), b 1911 near Dashiv, Lypovets county, Kiev gubernia, d 21 December 1944 in Yushkivtsi, near Zhydachiv, Galicia. Writer and nationalist revolutionary. During the Second World War he organized detachments of the Ukrainian Insurgent Army (UPA) in central Ukraine, edited the UPA newspapers *Za Ukraïnu* and *Za ukraïns'ku derzhavu*, and was chief of the political education section of the UPA Supreme Command in Volhynia, under the command of Lt Col R. Shukhevych. In November 1943 he took part in the First Conference of Subjugated Peoples, and in June 1944 he was elected to the *Ukrainian Supreme Liberation Council and was appointed head of the Information Bureau at its First Grand Assembly. He is the author of many short stories about the UPA and life under Soviet rule (published in underground and émigré periodicals) and of an internal UPA memorandum about tactics vis-à-vis the Russian people (1944). He died in battle against Soviet security forces.

Praca (Work). A Polish socialist newspaper published in Lviv from July 1878 to 1892. Founded and edited by J. Daniluk and Z. Mańkowski, it was at first intended for the printers and other artisans of Lviv. Under the influence of M. Pavlyk and especially I. *Franko, who was one of the most frequent contributors to the paper and its leading theoretician, *Praca* tried to appeal to a broader readership of proletarians and peasants. It advocated political freedoms, printed the first socialist program in Galicia, and promoted co-operation among Polish, Ukrainian, and Jewish socialists there. Frequently censored by the authorities – over half of its issues in 1881–3 were confiscated – *Praca* appeared irregularly until 1890, when it became a semimonthly.

Prach, Ivan [Prač] (Práč, Johann Gottfried), b ca 1750 in Silesia, d ca 1818 in St Petersburg. Composer, pianist, teacher, and ethnographer. A Czech by birth, he moved to St Petersburg in the late 1770s to teach piano. He became one of the first collectors and arrangers of Russian and Ukrainian folk songs, and published the landmark *Sobranie russkikh narodnykh pesen s ikh golosami* (A Collection of Russian Folk Songs with Vocal Parts) in 1790 (with subsequent editions in 1806, 1815, and 1896). This work, containing Ukrainian folk songs in separate sections subtitled 'Songs of Little Russia,' interpreted folk music in a Western style rather than using traditional harmonies, and provided subsequent Russian composers (including P. Tchaikovsky, M. Mussorgsky, and N. Rimsky-Korsakov) with a source of musical themes for their works. L. van Beethoven, who owned a copy of the 2nd edition, used the melody of S. Klymovsky's song 'The Cossack Rode beyond the Danube' in two of his chamber works.

Prague. The capital of and largest city in Czechoslovakia (1989 pop 1,211,000), situated on the Vltava River. It is an important center for interaction between Slavs, and home to approx 3,000 Ukrainians.

Trade relations between the city and Ukrainian territo-

ries were established in the 10th century along a route that originated in central Europe, passed through Prague, and then went on to Cracow, Kiev, and, eventually, Asia. In the 11th century, Prague established direct relations with Kievan Rus'. In the 14th century, Ukrainian students began traveling to Prague to study at Charles University (est 1348), and many of them quartered in a residence established in the late 14th century for Lithuanian, Belarusian, and Ukrainian students. F. Skoryna's Ruthenian Bible, which drew upon the earlier Czech Bible, was published in Prague in 1517–20 and had a profound effect on cultural life in Ukraine. O. Khlopytsky, an emissary of the Zaporozhian Sich, visited Prague in 1594–5.

During the Czech national revival in the early 19th century, there were scholars and writers in Prague who took an active interest in Ukraine; of note were F. Čelakovský, J. Dobrovský, K. Havliček-Borovský, J. Koubek, P. Šafařík, and K. Zap. Translations of Ukrainian literary works appeared in literary and academic periodicals, as did articles on Ukrainian culture and customs, particularly those written by Ya. Holovatsky and I. Vahylevych. The presence of O. Bodiansky (1837–8) and I. Sreznevsky (1839–41) in Prague greatly spurred the growth of local interest in Ukraine, as did the participation of a delegation from Galicia at the *Slavic Congress of 1848. In the 1850s and 1860s a number of Ukrainian cultural and political activists visited Prague, such as V. Bernatovych, I. Bilozersky, O. Bodiansky, M. Kostomarov, P. Kulish, M. Lysenko, M. Maksymovych, and O. Potebnia. The gifts and parcels of books they had been sending from Ukraine for some time served as the basis for the rich Ukrainian collections in local libraries. In 1876 a two-volume edition of T. Shevchenko's works that included previously censored poems was published in the city through the efforts of O. Rusov. I. Franko made several significant presentations at the first Congress of Progressive Slavic Youth, held in May 1891. F. Řehoř, who lived in the city from 1891, established a substantial Ukrainian collection at the Prague Museum with his generous donations of Ukrainian books and folk art items. I. Horbachevsky and I. Puliui, two eminent Ukrainian scholars, taught in postsecondary institutions in the city.

Ukrainian students studying in Prague established a hromada (1902); O. Bochkovsky, I. Bryk, and L. Hankevych were active members. At the outbreak of the First World War many Ukrainian refugees came to Prague. A primary school was opened for their children in the nearby town of Nusle. The UNR government maintained a mission, headed by M. Slavinsky, to the newly established Czechoslovak Republic in Prague, which later became a legation. It was superseded by an embassy of the Ukrainian SSR, headed by M. Levytsky.

Prague became the most important center of Ukrainian émigré cultural and political life in the 1920s, following a major influx of Ukrainian immigrants in 1920–1. It retained this position into the 1930s, even though a section of the emigration (particularly students) left the city. Many UNR officials and military figures settled in Prague; among them were A. Makarenko, M. and I. Omelianovych-Pavlenko, V. Petriv, S. Shelukhyn, F. Shvets, and A. Yakovliv. Other political activists to arrive were members of the Ukrainian Social Democratic Workers' party (O. Bochkovsky, P. Fedenko, B. Matiushenko, and Isaak Mazepa) and an important group of Socialist Revolutionaries (N. Hryhoriiv and Mykyta Shapoval), which published the journal *Trudova Ukraïna*. Prague was the birthplace of the Ukrainian nationalist movement. The Group of Ukrainian National Youth, led by S. Nyzhankivsky and Yu. Vassyian, was centered there, as was the League of Ukrainian Nationalists. The second conference of Ukrainian nationalists took place in Prague in 1928. Sovietophile elements gathered in the city in the 1920s around the T. Shevchenko reading room, the Association of Citizens of the Ukrainian SSR, and the Zhovtneve Kolo literary association.

The Prague-based *Ukrainian Citizens' Committee oversaw the interests of Ukrainian émigrés in 1921–5. Many Ukrainian academic organizations were centered in Prague, the *Ukrainian Academic Committee, the *Ukrainian Scholarly Association, the *Ukrainian Historical-Philological Society (est 1923), the Ukrainian Pedagogical Society, and the *Ukrainian Society of Bibliophiles. Local museums and archives included the *Museum of Ukraine's Struggle for Independence (1925–45, then 1945–8 as the Ukrainian Museum) and the Ukrainian Cabinet of History. Local Ukrainian secondary and postsecondary schools consisted of the *Ukrainian Free University (1921–45), the *Ukrainian Higher Pedagogical Institute (1923–33), the *Ukrainian Studio of Plastic Art (1923–45), and the Ukrainian Real Gymnasium (1925–7). The youth association Plast and the Union of Ukrainian Plast Emigrés were also active in the city. The Ukrainian Academic Hromada was founded in 1919 as an organization of Ukrainian students; by March 1924 it had 1,255 members. There was also a wide range of other student and professional organizations. The *Central Union of Ukrainian Students was located there in 1922–35, and it held several congresses and two academic conferences in the city. Prague was also the residence of many Ukrainian writers (O. Babii, M. Chyrsky, Yu. Darahan, M. Irchan, I. Irliavsky, I. Krushelnytsky, O. Liaturynska, Ye. Malaniuk, I. Narizhna, O. Oles, O. Olzhych, A. Pavliuk, U. Samchuk, O. Stefanovych, and O. Teliha), artists (M. Brynsky, M. Butovych, V. Kasiian, V. Khmeliuk, I. Kulets, R. Lisovsky, H. Mazepa, and V. Sichynsky), and scholars (D. Antonovych, L. Biletsky, D. Chyzhevsky, S. Dnistriansky, D. Doroshenko, O. Kolessa, I. Panas, I. Pankevych, S. Rudnytsky, S. Rusova, S. Siropolko, S. Smal-Stotsky, A. Yakovliv, and I. Zilynsky).

Prague was also an important Ukrainian publishing center; the Siiach (1924–33), Proboiem (1939–43), Kolos, Yu. Tyshchenko, and Ye. Vorony publishing houses were active there. Periodicals published in Prague included *Nova Ukraïna* (1922–8), *Students'kyi visnyk* (1923–31), *Rozbudova natsiï* (1928–34), *Proboiem* (1933–43), *Nastup* (biweekly, 1934–44), and *Ukraïns'ka diisnist'* (biweekly, 1940–5).

Ukrainian émigré scholars maintained healthy relations with their Czech counterparts, and their works were printed in Czech academic journals. From 1926 Ukrainian language and literature were taught at Charles University. The visits of Ukrainian writers and artists in the 1920s also stimulated interest in Ukrainian creative work: O. Dosvitny, V. Polishchuk, and P. Tychyna in 1925; M. Boichuk, L. Kurbas, and V. Sedliar in 1927; O. Kobylianska, O. Kopylenko, A. Liubchenko, and V. Pidmohylny in 1928; and O. Dovzhenko in 1930.

During the Second World War a large number of Ukrainians arrived from Transcarpathia as well as Western Ukraine to enroll in Prague's schools. In mid-1939 the government of Carpatho-Ukraine, led by A. *Voloshyn, moved to Prague. In 1944 a large contingent of scholars from central Ukraine reached the city.

With the arrival of Soviet armies in 1945, the number of Ukrainians in the city declined sharply, since most had fled to Germany. Others came, however, including soldiers from Czech units in the Soviet Army and students from Prešov. Nevertheless, Ukrainian organizations and institutions were disbanded and closed. The last to go were the Ukrainian Museum (1948) and I. Kulets's painters' school (1952). In 1946–8 the Russophile journals *Kostér* and *Karpats'kaia zvezda* came out. Currently there is only a small group of independent artists and a choir led by O. Prykhodko and P. Shchurovska-Rosinevych active in the city. In 1968 the Greek Catholic parish was reopened. The Czechoslovak Autocephalous Orthodox church metropoly is centered in Prague.

Prague has also become an important translation center for Ukrainian literature. Since the war nearly 300 titles have been translated and published, and the Czech artists' union has a section devoted to translation of Ukrainian literature, headed by R. Hůlka and M. Marčanová. Charles University had a department of Ukrainian language and literature, headed by I. *Zilynsky and I. *Pankevych, where Z. Genyk-Berezovska, J. Moravec, and V. Židlický worked. A Ukrainian language-instruction textbook for Czechs was published in Prague, as were a number of texts on Ukrainian literature (including anthologies) and history. The Slavic Library in Prague, which contains nearly 50,000 Ukrainian titles, is an important storehouse of Ukrainian culture. Its holdings include valuable religious manuscripts, such as the *Apostol* by I. Fedorovych, P. Mohyla's *Trebnyk*, and the Ostrih Bible. The city's archives also contain many valuable Ukrainian materials. The celebrations of T. Shevchenko's anniversaries in 1951, 1961, and 1989, with their attendant exhibitions, were of cultural importance, as was a Franko festival held in 1956, at which a commemorative plaque was unveiled. Today in Prague there is an association of Ukrainians in the Czech Republic headed by B. Zilynsky, and a Ukrainian student club at the university.

BIBLIOGRAPHY
Halahan, M. *Desiat' rokiv Ukraïns'koï hromady v ChSR: Ohliad zhyttia i chynnosty (1927–37)* (Prague 1938)
Antonovych, M. *20 rokiv Ukraïns'koï akademichnoï hromady v Prazi* (Prague 1941)
Narizhnyi, S. *Ukraïns'ka emigratsiia* (Prague 1942)

O. Zilynsky

Prakhov, Adrian [Praxov, Adrian], b 16 March 1846 in Mstsislau, Belarus, d 14 May 1916 in Yalta, Crimea. Art scholar, archeologist, and critic. A graduate of St Petersburg University (1867), he taught art history and theory there (1873–87, 1897–1914) and at the St Petersburg Academy of Arts (1875–87) and Kiev University (1887–97). He wrote studies on ancient Egyptian and Greek art, the artistic masterpieces of Kievan Rus', medieval church architecture in Volhynia (1886), and T. Shevchenko's artworks, and served as art editor for the journals *Pchela* (1875–8) and *Khudozhestvennyia sokrovishcha Rossii* (1904–7). Having discovered the 12th-century frescoes of St Cyril's Church in Kiev in 1881–2, he invited M. Vrubel to restore them, and he oversaw the construction and interior deco-

Adrian Prakhov   Bishop Ivan Prashko

ration work of *St Volodymyr's Cathedral in Kiev (1895–6).

Prapor (Flag). A publishing house in Kharkiv. It was established in 1945 as the Kharkiv Oblast Book-Journal-Newspaper Publishing House and assumed its present name in 1964. It publishes the journal *Prapor, prose, poetry, and works on historical, political, scientific, arts, and economic topics. In the period 1971–5 it issued 505 titles.

Prapor (Flag). A monthly journal for Ukrainian Catholic priests published in Peremyshl in 1897–1900. It was edited by T. Kormosh.

Prapor (Flag). A pedagogical journal published semimonthly (1908–9) and then three times a month (1910–12), briefly in Lviv and then in Kolomyia. It was concerned primarily with organizing Ukrainian elementary-school teachers in Galicia and publishing teaching materials, curricula, and book and journal reviews. *Prapor* was edited by L. Lototsky, I. Petryshyn, M. Baran, and Ye. Kulchytsky.

Prapor (Flag). A bimonthly Catholic paper published in Curitiba (nos 1–21) and Prudentópolis (nos 22–5), Brazil, from January 1910 to early 1911. It was edited by S. Petrytsky and K. Gutkovsky.

Prapor (Flag). A literary and publicistic monthly of the Writers' Union of Ukraine, published in Kharkiv since January 1956. Its contributors are mostly writers and critics living in eastern Ukraine. The journal regularly published translations of literature from the other Soviet republics. From 1959 to 1971 it serialized a Russian-Ukrainian phraseological dictionary compiled by I. Vyrhan and M. Pylynsky and edited by M. Nakonechny. Its chief editors have been Yu. *Shovkoplias, Yu. Makhnenko, M. Okan, N. Cherchenko, Yu. Stadnychenko, and, since 1981, I. Maslov. The journal's name was changed to *Berezil'* in 1991.

Prapor komunizmu (Flag of Communism). An illegal underground organ of the Central Committee of the *Communist Party of Western Ukraine, published in Lviv in 1932 (a total of four issues). It succeeded *Komunistychnyi prapor* (1930–1).

Prapor marksyzmu-leninizmu (Flag of Marxism-Leninism). The first Ukrainian philosophical journal, published from 1927 in Kharkiv by the *Ukrainian Institute of Marxism-Leninism and then by the *All-Ukrainian Association of Marxist-Leninist Scientific Research Institutes (VUAMLIN). Until the end of 1930 (nos 1–14) it was called *Prapor marksyzmu*. Then it was renamed *Prapor marksyzmu-leninizmu* (1931–3, 14 issues). In 1934 the journal was merged with *Ekonomist-marksyst* and renamed *Pid markso-lenins'kym praporom* (Under the Marxist-Leninist Flag, 14 issues, 1934–6). In 1935–6 it was published in Kiev. The journal served as a vehicle for the development of Marxist-Leninist thought, and published articles on the history and relation of Marxist-Leninist thought to current developments in science, literature, art, and social life. Its editorial board included M. Skrypnyk, M. Popov, V. Yurynets, M. Yavorsky, and Yu. Mazurkevych. After M. Skrypnyk's suicide in 1933, the journal was denounced by Stalinist critics, and all members of its editorial board suffered political persecution.

Prapor peremohy (Flag of Victory). A newspaper of Luhanske oblast's CPU Committee and Soviet, published five days a week in Luhanske from February 1946. Its pressrun was increased from 25,000 in 1960 to 50,000 in 1970 and 60,000 in 1980; in respective years the pressrun of its Russian-language equivalent, *Voroshilovgradskaia pravda*, was increased from 53,000 to 205,000 and 252,000.

Prashko, Ivan [Praško], b 1 May 1914 in Zbarazh, Galicia. Ukrainian Catholic bishop; full member of the Shevchenko Scientific Society since 1965. After being ordained in 1939 and completing theological studies in Rome and a dissertation on the Uniate church in the 17th century (1944), he did pastoral work in Italy. He was sent to Australia in 1950 and has been active there in establishing churches and community organizations. He was consecrated a bishop in 1958 and served as exarch until 1982, when he was elevated to the office of bishop of Australia, New Zealand, and Oceania. Upon retirement in 1993 he was replaced by Bishop P. Stasiuk.

Pratsia (Work). A semimonthly newspaper published in Chernivtsi from April to December 1897 (a total of 17 issues). Edited by V. *Budzynovsky, it supported the Ukrainian Radical party and was merged with that party's paper in Lviv, *Hromads'kyi holos*. V. *Stefanyk published some of his earliest stories in *Pratsia*.

Pratsia (Work). An irregular organ of the clandestine *Revolutionary Ukrainian party. Published in Lviv in 1904 (10 issues) and 1905 (4 issues) as a successor to *Dobra novyna* (1903–4), it was edited by Ye. Holitsynsky and K. Holitsynska, and then by D. Antonovych and M. Porsh, and smuggled into Russian-ruled Ukraine.

Pratsia (Work). A bimonthly organ of the Foreign Group of the clandestine Ukrainian Social Democratic Workers' party. It was published in Lviv in 1909–10 and smuggled into Russian-ruled Ukraine. The editors were D. Dontsov, V. Doroshenko, A. Zhuk, and V. Sadovsky.

Pratsia (Work; in local transcription: *Pracia*). A Brazilian-Ukrainian newspaper published by the Basilian fathers in

Prudentópolis since 1912. Initially a fortnightly, it became a weekly in 1915. It carried mainly regional news and religious articles. It was closed down by the Brazilian authorities in 1917–19 and 1940–6. Annual almanacs have been published (with interruptions) by the paper since 1919. In 1966 it added a regular children's section. The pressrun has been estimated at approx 1,700 in the 1930s and 2,300 to 3,000 in the postwar period. *Pratsia* editors have included O. Martynets, Y. Martynets, M. Nychka, I. Vihorynsky, K. Korchagin, V. Burko, and V. Zinko.

Pratsia (Work). A semimonthly organ of the Ukrainian Social Democratic party (USDP) in Galicia, published in 1914 in Lviv by P. Buniak and edited by I. Kushnir and V. Temnytsky. Issues of the journal were frequently censored and confiscated by the authorities. Another journal with the same title was published in Vienna in 1918 by S. Vityk and other supporters of the left faction of the USDP.

Pratsia (Work). A weekly organ of the *Ukrainian Party of Labor (1927–32) and the Ukrainian Peasant Alliance (1933–4), a front organization of *Sel-Rob. Published in Lviv and edited by R. Skazynsky (to 1930) and A. Maletsky, it initially supported Ye. Petrushevych but later became pro-Soviet, for which stance it was eventually closed down by the Polish authorities. Its circulation in 1930 was 1,500.

Pratsiuiucha molod' (Working Youth). An organ for Transcarpathian youth sponsored by the Communist Party of Czechoslovakia. The first issue was published in Prague in November 1926. From the second issue (December 1926) it was published monthly to February 1927 and then biweekly by I. Mondiuk in Uzhhorod. The managing editors were A. Zapototsky (1926), E. Klima (1926–8), M. Zhupnyk (1928–9), and, from October 1929, O. Borkaniuk, who moved it to Mukachiv. The journal was censored by the authorities, the editors were persecuted and even imprisoned, and publication from 1931 on was infrequent. Many issues were confiscated, and in 1934 the journal was closed down.

Prava, po kotorym suditsia malorossiiskii narod. See Code of Laws of 1743.

Pravda (Truth). A literary, scholarly, and political journal published in Lviv three times a month in 1867, four times a month in 1868–70, semimonthly in 1872–8 (in 1878 it also issued a miscellany in 2 vols), monthly in 1879, as a miscellany in 1880 (1 vol) and 1884 (1 vol, ed V. Barvinsky and I. Franko), and again as a monthly in 1888–93 and a semimonthly in 1894–6. It was initiated by intellectuals in Lviv and elsewhere in Galicia, but was funded by the writers P. Kulish and O. Konysky from Russian-ruled Ukraine. Until the establishment of the newspaper *Dilo in 1880, *Pravda* was the main organ of the Galician populists and the most important journal of the time. Its contributors included many writers and scholars in both Austrian- and Russian-ruled Ukraine, among them O. Ohonovsky, I. Franko, O. Partytsky, I. Verkhratsky, O. and V. Barvinsky, Yu. Fedkovych, S. Vorobkevych, V. Navrotsky, M. Podolynsky, O. Terletsky, O. Konysky, P. Kulish, H. Barvinok, Marko Vovchok, P. Myrny, M. Starytsky, I. Karpenko-Kary, I. Nechui-Levytsky, S. Rudansky, and O. Storozhenko. In this period the chief editors of the journal were I. Mykyta, A. Vakhnianyn (1869–70), O. Ohonovsky (1872–6), L. Lukashevych (1876), and V. Barvinsky (1876–9). Beginning in the early 1870s it was openly criticized by M. Drahomanov, a regular contributor, who in 1873 submitted an open letter on behalf of 76 noted Ukrainians in the Russian Empire complaining about the conservative orientation of the journal. An index to the first volumes appeared in the 1884 issue.

After a four-year interruption *Pravda* resumed publication in 1888 on the initiative of V. Antonovych and O. Konysky. In the 1890s it was the chief organ of the populist right and supported the politics of the *New Era. The publishers were Ye. Olesnytsky (1888), I. Stronsky (1889), P. Kyrchiv (1890–1), and A. Berezynsky (1891–6), but the main force behind it was O. Barvinsky. *Pravda* strongly criticized the Russophiles and the new Ukrainian Radical party; it engaged in spirited polemics with the leaders of that party, I. Franko and M. Pavlyk, who until then had co-operated closely with it. Literary contributors in this period included B. Hrinchenko, M. Kotsiubynsky, A. Krymsky, M. Komarov, O. Makovei, and Yu. Romanchuk.

Pravda (Truth). An organ of the Russian Brotherhood Organization of America, a Russophile organization whose members are primarily immigrants from Transcarpathia and their descendants. It has appeared since 1902, at first semiweekly, then weekly, and now monthly. *Pravda* has been published in New York, Olyphant, and (now) Philadelphia. The language of the paper is mostly English, with some Russian.

Pravda (Truth). A monthly organ of the clandestine Ukrainian Social Democratic *Spilka, edited by P. Tuchapsky and P. Kanivets. It was published in Lviv in early 1905 and smuggled into Russian-ruled Ukraine. In the summer of 1905 it was printed for a brief time in Russian by an underground press in Odessa.

Pravda (Truth). A daily Russian-language organ of the CC CPSU. It appeared from May 1912 to July 1914 and from March 1917 (with frequent interruptions and under different names) in Petrograd. Since March 1918 it has been published in Moscow. Some of its early editorial board members and contributors were Ukrainian Communists, such as M. Skrypnyk and Yu. Kotsiubynsky, especially in the so-called preconference Party discussions. With J. Stalin's consolidation of power the paper became the normative organ of the CC CPSU: its materials reflected the official line of the Politburo on all issues, both domestic and foreign. Its articles on the nationality question in the USSR and on Ukrainian affairs were no exception. Printed from matrices prepared in Moscow and flown to the major cities, the paper often reached the newsstands before the local papers. For these reasons *Pravda* enjoyed wide circulation, over 11 million in 1981. In Ukraine it was an important instrument of Russification. Under perestroika, *Pravda's* circulation declined drastically, as the Party lost its authority in society. Suspended briefly in 1991, it resumed publication as a newspaper of conservative orientation.

Pravda (Truth). A weekly newspaper of literary, cultural, and community affairs published in Lviv in 1927–39. It supported the Ukrainian Christian Organization and was edited by V. Yatsenko, A. Lototsky, and R. Haiduk. A supplement for children, *Vinochok*, was published in 1932–7. In 1930 *Pravda* appeared in a pressrun of 5,000 copies. Its popularity grew, mainly because of its lively style and illustrations, and by 1939 it had over 30,000 subscribers.

Pravda (Truth). A Ukrainian-language organ of the Rumanian Agrarian party, published irregularly in Chernivtsi in 1930–6. It printed sharp attacks on the Ukrainian national movement in Rumanian-ruled Bukovyna and on prominent Ukrainian leaders and institutions there. The editor was H. Andriiashchuk.

Pravda (Truth). A farmer-worker newspaper in Canada. It appeared weekly and then semimonthly in Winnipeg from February 1936, and then continued as a weekly in Toronto from 1938 to June 1940 under the title *Vpered*. It was published by breakaway members of the Ukrainian Labour-Farmer Temple Association, including D. Lobai, M. Khvalyboha, T. Kobzei, and N. Handziuk. Although the paper retained its socialist perspective and supported the Co-operative Commonwealth Federation (CCF) in Canadian politics, it openly criticized Soviet policies and gradually moved toward a compromise with Ukrainian nationalist organizations in Canada. The chief editor of both *Pravda* and *Vpered* was D. *Lobai.

Pravda i volia

Pravda i volia (Truth and Liberty). A newspaper published weekly and then semimonthly in Winnipeg from January 1929 to early 1932. Initially the organ of the Ukrainian People's Home and then of the Ukrainian Labor Alliance in Canada, it published articles on political affairs and the labor movement. Although socialist in profile and perspective, the paper criticized Stalinism and the USSR and especially the pro-communist Ukrainian Labour-Farmer Temple Association. The editor of *Pravda i volia* was M. *Mandryka. Contributors included D. Hunkevych, N. Baran, S. Kovbel, and such leading members of the Ukrainian Party of Socialist Revolutionaries in Europe as N. Hryhoriiv, S. Borodaievsky, and S. Dovhal.

Pravda Ukrainy (Truth of Ukraine). A daily Russian-language organ of the CC CPU and the Ukrainian Supreme Soviet and Council of Ministers until 1992. It began to appear in Kiev in January 1938 as *Sovetskaia Ukraina*. During the Second World War it was published in Kharkiv, Moscow, Saratov, and Luhanske. In 1944 it was renamed, and returned to Kiev. The paper is a parallel edition to the Ukrainian-language *Radians'ka Ukraïna*, although not all articles appear in both versions. In practice *Pravda Ukrainy* contains more articles on the economy, science, and technology than its more propagandistic-ideological counterpart. Both papers, however, are inferior in content and style to such central papers as *Pravda* and *Izvestiia*. The paper's pressrun increased from some 300,000 copies in 1950 to 477,000 in 1970 and 550,000 in 1975, and fell to 220,000 in 1991.

Pravdych-Nemynsky, Volodymyr [Pravdyč-Nemyns'kyj], b 1879 in Kiev, d 17 May 1952 in Moscow. Physiologist. After graduating from Kiev University with degrees in physics and mathematics (1907) and medicine (1917) he became a lecturer of physiology there. He also worked for the VUAN (1923–9) and with the Institute of Health Care for Mothers and Children (1929–49), and directed the physiology and EEG laboratory at the USSR Academy of Medical Sciences. Much of his research was devoted to electroencephalography.

Pravnychyi vistnyk (Legal Herald). A quarterly published in Lviv in 1910–13 by the *Society of Ukrainian Lawyers. It was edited by S. Dnistriansky, and its contributors included V. Verhanovsky, M. Voloshyn, H. Hankevych, D. Nasada, T. Voinarovsky-Stolobut, Ye. Erlikh, and M. Liskevych.

Pravoslavna Volyn' (Orthodox Volhynia). An official publication of the Volhynian Orthodox eparchial council, edited by V. *Bidnov. The decision to publish this Ukrainian-language successor to *Volynskie eparkhial'nye vedomosti* was made at a church council in Pochaiv in October 1921. It started to appear in 1922 in Kremianets, but soon ran into trouble for supporting the Ukrainianization of the church. Bidnov was transferred out of Kremianets, and publication ceased soon after.

Pravoslavnaia Bukovina

Pravoslavnaia Bukovina (Orthodox Bukovyna). A Russophile newspaper published semimonthly from March 1893 to 1905, initially in Vienna but after the first few issues in Chernivtsi. The successor to *Russka pravda*, it published attacks on the Ukrainian national movement and its leaders in Western Ukraine. It devoted considerable attention to the Orthodox church in Bukovyna; promoted the growth of Russophile organizations, such as the Russian People's Home and the Society of Russian Women in Bukovyna; and supported the politics of tsarist Russia. The paper's publisher and longtime editor was K. Kozaryshchuk.

Pravoslavnaia Rus' (Orthodox Rus'). A weekly organ of the Russophile Narodnaia Rada society in Bukovyna. Published in Chernivtsi from February 1909 to July 1910 (a total of 71 issues) by Rev K. Bohatyrets and edited by A. Olshevsky and then K. Smerechynsky, it attacked the Ukrainian national movement and its leaders in Bukovyna and Galicia and strongly criticized Ukrainian 'separatists' in the Russian Empire. It also reported extensively on political developments in Eastern Europe. When the Austro-Hungarian authorities cracked down on the Russophile movement and forced the newspaper to cease publication, it was replaced by *Russkaia pravda.

Pravoslavnyi rus'kyi kalendar (Orthodox Ruthenian Calendar). An annual almanac of the *Ruska Besida society in Bukovyna, published from 1874 to 1918 in Chernivtsi. From the 1890s it appeared as *Bukovyns'kyi pravoslavnyi kalendar* or *Iliustrovanyi bukovyns'kyi pravoslavnyi kalendar*. It contained poetry, prose, and much information on the history of Bukovyna and especially the Orthodox church there. The editors included S. and H. Vorobkevych, Ye. Kalytovsky, and O. Popovych. In 1890 it had a pressrun of 1,500.

Pravoslavnyi ukraïnets' (Orthodox Ukrainian). A nonperiodic organ of the Ukrainian Autocephalous Orthodox Church (UAOC) (Conciliar) in the United States. Published in Chicago since 1952, it includes church news and accounts of the UAOC in the 1920s.

Pravoslavnyi visnyk (Orthodox Herald). The only official Ukrainian-language publication of the Russian Orthodox church. It appeared in Lviv from 1946 as a monthly, initially as *Eparkhiial'nyi visnyk* (Eparchial Herald). Edited by Rev H. *Kostelnyk and other advocates of the submission of the Ukrainian Catholic church to Russian Orthodox control, it was distributed until 1963 in Western Ukraine only. It then ceased publication until 1968, when it was revived in Lviv. In 1971 it was moved to Kiev and put out by Kiev metropoly as the official organ of the Ukrainian exarchate, since 1990 the Ukrainian Orthodox church. The publication is popular in tone and, unlike the organ of the Moscow patriarchate, publishes little of a scholarly nature.

Pravoslavnyi visnyk. See *Visnyk*.

Precentor (*diak*). A layman in Ukrainian Orthodox and Catholic churches whose function is to assist in church services. In the Orthodox church precentors are also called psalmists (*psalomshchyky*). Their duties include reading responses and singing (during the Divine Liturgy and other services), directing the church choir, and assisting the priest in the fulfillment of his pastoral duties. Sometimes precentors have the privilege of wearing a surplice during church services. This custom is no longer practiced in the Catholic church.

In Kievan Rus' precentors were considered *church people. From the beginning they were supported materially by their parishes, and their position was defined by local common law; thus the precentor was more dependent on the people than was the priest. Precentors usually lived in the church buildings, were allowed to farm a portion (approx one-third to one-half) of the church lands, and were entitled to one-third of the customary payments made by parish members. In Russian-ruled Ukraine these norms were regulated by the church reforms of 1869 and 1885. In some areas precentors received an annual income (*rokivshchyna*), paid either in cash or in goods, from each parish family. The better precentors were sometimes ordained as deacons or priests, particularly during the period when theological training was lax. In the 18th century these priests were known as 'little precentors' (*diachky*) in Galicia.

In some areas, mainly in Russian-ruled Ukraine, precentors had some seminary training or attended a *brotherhood school, but little is known of their specialized training. In the 17th and 18th centuries many Cossacks became precentors, and a special school for them was established at the monastery school of the Zaporozhian Sich. In the 19th and 20th centuries there were special courses for Orthodox and Greek Catholic precentors at eparchial chancelleries and monasteries, which usually lasted two or three years but sometimes only several months. Practice in church singing and church rites were emphasized, but brief courses in dogma, church history, and pastoral theology were also taught. These courses were under the authority of the local bishops, and in some places there were boarding schools for the students. There was a precentors' school at the Orthodox metropolitan's residence in Chernivtsi. In 1817 an institute for training Greek Catholic precentors was established in Peremyshl; graduates were also qualified to teach catechism. The institute's director was Rev I. *Mohylnytsky. A similar school existed in Lviv, and qualified precentors were trained at the Greek Catholic seminary in Uzhhorod. In all cases this training was concluded with formal examinations conducted by special eparchial commissions, and graduates received diplomas; smaller and poorer parishes, however, had a large number of amateur peasant precentors. Especially in Western Ukraine, the number of qualified precentors increased steadily, and by the 1930s more than 60 percent of them had diplomas.

A special function of the early precentors was the teaching of reading and writing. As early as the 11th century they were teaching children on an elementary level, either privately or in church-affiliated schools. Precentor-teachers in the 14th to 18th centuries were called *dydaskaly* (pedagogues) or *bakaliari* (tutors). During the 16th and 17th centuries *Itinerant tutors were widely known throughout Ukraine. These were usually former students of the Kievan Mohyla Academy or other colleges who taught the children of priests, Cossack officers, or burghers. They were also known for their carousing and were facetiously dubbed *pyvorizy* (beer guzzlers); many sang songs and composed verses satirizing the church and other institutions. A Russian order of 1782 abolished the itinerant tutors; thereafter they had to remain in one place and fulfill their church duties there. Until the end of the 19th century most teachers in *parochial schools were precentors; their schools operated in parallel with the state schools established at the end of the 18th century.

The shortage of teachers in Western Ukraine led the

government to allow precentors to teach in elementary church schools. Many nobles, however, opposed popular education even in this primitive form and pressed precentors into military service, despite a 1788 decree exempting precentor-teachers from such service. In the first half of the 19th century the elementary education of Ukrainians under Austria-Hungary (especially in Transcarpathia) still depended almost exclusively on the priest and the precentor-teacher. The precentors also did beneficial social work in the villages. Since many were among the best-educated peasants, they were usually the village scribes, and they maintained the parish register; they also organized choirs and made other contributions to cultural and educational life.

In Galicia there was a separate professional organization, the Precentors' Mutual-Aid Society, based in Lviv. The society, headed for many years by Revs Ye. Dutkevych and V. Lonchyna, published the journal *Diakivs'ki vidomosti* (1923–39). The first vocational publication for Galician precentors was *Diakivs'kyi hlas* (Precentor's Voice, 1895–1910), later *Holos diakiv* (Voice of the Precentors, 1910–14), published in Stanyslaviv (Ivano-Frankivske). In Bukovyna the Orthodox precentors published *Diakivs'ki vidomosti* (Precentors' News) from 1910 to 1914. In the United States, the Society of Ukrainian Greek-Catholic Precentor-Teachers of America was founded in 1913, and in 1918–19 it published the journal *Ridna shkola*.

Today most church parishes outside Ukraine have their own precentor, but there are no formal organizations for precentor training or affiliation.

A. Zhukovsky

Prechtl, Joseph, b 1737 in Vienna, d 1799 in Brailiv, Vinnytsia county, Podilia gubernia. Painter. He studied at the Vienna Academy of Arts and in 1757 entered a Trinitarian monastery in Berestechko, Volhynia. His works include frescoes in the Roman Catholic church in Brailiv, paintings in St John's Cathedral in Kamianets-Podilskyi, frescoes and 16 paintings in the Trinitarian church in Berestechko, paintings in a Roman Catholic church in Stanyslaviv, and murals in the Czacki palace in Boremel, Volhynia.

Predslavych, Leonyd [Predslavyč], b 1897, d 25 March 1960 in Kharkiv. Stage director, writer, and actor. He was an actor in Molodyi Teatr and Kyidramte (1917–21) and then organized and directed workers' and peasants' theaters in Odessa (1924), Yelysavethrad (1926), and Kharkiv (1927) and published *Peresuvnyi robitnycho-selians'kyi teatr* (Touring Workers' and Peasants' Theater) in 1928. In 1945–50 he directed in the Transcarpathian Ukrainian Music and Drama Theater. He adapted I. Franko's *Boryslavs'ki opovidannia* (The Boryslav Stories, 1956) and wrote the libretto to K. Dankevych's opera *Nazar Stodolia* (1959).

Preschool education (*doshkilne vykhovannia*). Formal preschool education was first offered in Ukraine in the 19th century. In earlier times children of what would now be considered preschool age were sometimes communally cared for by monasteries and other institutions. In the 19th century, preschool education was provided by local *zemstvo authorities, the church, and private individuals and societies. These last two groups offered preschool educa-

tional facilities for various reasons. Owners of large estates provided preschool care in order to free women for fieldwork during peak times; philanthropic societies offered preschool care for working-class and peasant children; urban middle-class activists organized preschool education for their own children; Ukrainian groups provided Ukrainian preschool education as part of the separate Ukrainian social infrastructure they were building.

The first nursery in Russian-ruled Ukraine, opened in Poltava in 1839, offered care from 7 AM to 9 PM to children two years old and older. In other cities similar institutions were established by local zemstvo authorities. Like their counterparts in the rest of Europe, these first nurseries were run as charities and were more concerned with providing rudimentary child-care than with offering a structured educational program. The first private nursery school in Ukraine was opened in 1872 in Kiev by S. *Rusova, a prominent preschool education activist. Ukrainian supporters of the pedagogical theories of F. Froebel and M. Montessori, who formed the Froebel Kiev Pedagogical Society in 1908 in Kiev, established private nurseries based on Froebel and Montessori techniques. Societies for the protection of the poor opened people's nurseries, which provided care for children of the lower classes and were maintained chiefly through charitable donations. Preschool teachers were trained at the Froebel Pedagogical Institute and the Froebel Courses in Kiev and through similar classes in Kharkiv. Because most urban nurseries in Russian-ruled Ukraine operated in Russian, members of the Ukrainian intelligentsia organized private schools in the homes of Ukrainian families, including the *Lysenko and the *Starytsky family homes. In 1917 the Children's House society was formed in Kiev, and established the first formal Ukrainian nursery in that city, with Rusova as its director. In that year for the first time, Ukrainian classes were offered at the Froebel Pedagogical Institute in Kiev. In 1916 there were 47 nurseries in Russian-ruled Ukraine (16 percent of the 288 nursery schools in imperial Russia). Between 1917 and 1919, nurseries were opened throughout Ukraine which were funded by local governments. Teachers applied Froebel and Montessori techniques and the suggestions contained in *Poradnyk*, a handbook for preschool teachers published in 1919 by the children's division of the UNR Ministry of Education, headed by Rusova. Important preschool education activists in this period include Rusova, O. Petrushevska, E. Panych, N. Krasina, L. Dovbnia, I. Chechil, M. Sheiko, O. Idiiasevych, L. Kepkalo, O. Doroshenko, and M. Yurkevych.

Under Soviet rule the number of nursery schools in central and eastern Ukraine increased. The provision of daycare was fundamental in the Bolshevik attempt to incorporate women into the work force and to create alternatives to the traditional family. In 1924 there were 136 nurseries in Ukraine, which cared for 6,000 children; in 1928 there were 431, with 17,836 children; in 1936 there were 4,609, with 216,000 children; in 1940 there were 3,384 nurseries, with 10,827 teachers and 172,208 children. Nursery teachers were trained at preschool education faculties at pedagogical institutes in Kiev, Poltava, Odessa, and Kharkiv.

By the end of the 1920s a policy of Russification had been imposed on the education system in Ukraine; it extended to preschool education (see *Education). A journal devoted to preschool education, *Za komunistychne vykhovannia doshkil'nyka* (1931–41), was published in Soviet Ukraine in the interwar period by the Commissariat of Education. The journal was a tribunal for the Stalinist forces, which purged those educators in Ukraine who had created an independent education system and advocated Ukrainization in the early years of Soviet rule.

The original idea for organizing a community association which would promote and support day-care centers was voiced by N. Kobrynska in the 1880s; in 1893 she published a model set of bylaws for such a society in *Nasha dolia*, an almanac she edited and published in Stryi. There had been initial opposition to the day-care centers owing to fear that they would supplant the family as the primary care-giver for children. Women promoting child-care were accused of destroying the family. But the arguments for day-care in Galicia were bolstered by the fact that child mortality in the eastern part of the Habsburg Empire was second only to that in the Russian Empire. Children were most at risk during harvest, when mothers, along with other adults, left them in charge of other children. Some clergy supported the women and defended day-care centers for children and the education such centers would provide. Rev K. *Seletsky established the first Ukrainian official day-care center in 1892, in Zhuzhil, Sokal county. The day-care centers fostered the use of Ukrainian, helped alleviate malnutrition, and came to be seen as a means of strengthening the Ukrainian nation physically and intellectually. The first urban nursery was opened in Lviv in 1902 by the Ruska Zakhoronka society (later renamed *Ukrainska Zakhoronka). The Ukrainian Pedagogical society (see *Ridna Shkola society), in conjunction with local groups, organized seasonal nurseries in villages to provide care for children during seeding and harvest. The Women's Hromada and the *Myronosytsi sisterhood established the first nursery in Bukovyna in 1896, in Chernivtsi, and later founded other nurseries throughout the province. By 1914, in Chernivtsi alone there were four nurseries.

In response to the government's Polonization policies in Western Ukraine after the First World War, the Ukrainian Nursery society extended its work beyond Lviv. The Ridna Shkola society, working in co-operation with *Prosvita, organized a network of seasonal nurseries in rural Galicia. In 1936–7, 29,885 children were being cared for at 768 seasonal nurseries affiliated with Ridna Shkola. Almost all of the children cared for during the two to four months that these nurseries operated were of peasant origin. Ridna Shkola established the nurseries with the dual purpose of ensuring that young children were not left alone during peak farming periods and of fostering literacy and patriotism. Nurseries were usually housed in Prosvita reading rooms and libraries or in buildings belonging to Ukrainian co-operatives, because government permission was often denied to groups wishing to open Ukrainian nurseries.

Before the outbreak of the Second World War 16 permanent nurseries, providing care for 500 children, existed in Galicia. Preschool educational theorists in Galicia included I. Blazhkevych, K. Malytska, N. Selezinka, S. Fedorchak, M. Pasternak, P. Bilaniuk, S. Kondar, Ya. Kondar, S. Rakova, I. Pavlykovska, and M. Dontsova. Prominent preschool educators included M. Yavorska, M. Hanushchakova, M. Kozlovska, Iu. Mytsyk-Teslia, and E. Vyniarska.

In Volhynia the dismantling of the Ukrainian school system by the Polish government hampered the development of nurseries. Even so, in the 1930s several permanent nurseries operated by Ukrainian societies existed in the region. In Transcarpathia nurseries prospered under Czechoslovak rule. By 1931 there were 102 nurseries, of which 45 were Ukrainian, and by 1938 the number had risen to 252, of which 132 were Ukrainian.

During the Soviet occupation of Western Ukraine in 1939–40, civic societies, such as the Ukrainian Zakhoronka and Ridna Shkola, were closed, and all nurseries were brought under the jurisdiction of the Soviet authorities. During the German occupation of Western Ukraine in 1941–4, the *Ukrainian Central Committee took over responsibility for preschool education in all of the Ukrainian territories of the *Generalgouvernement. In the summer of 1943 there were 241 permanent nurseries, which cared for 13,875 children, and 1,696 seasonal nurseries, which cared for 114,091 children. Courses to train preschool teachers were also organized – 3 classes for preschool education instructors, with 300 students, and 160 classes for preschool teachers, with 4,500 students.

After the Second World War the Soviet system of preschool education was established in all of Ukraine. The system consists of three types of institutions which provide preschool care: *iasla*, providing care for children from 2–3 months to 3 years old (established in 1959); *sadky*, providing care for children from 3 to 7 years old; and *iasla-sadky*, providing care for children from 2–3 months to 7 years old. Seasonal preschool care is organized in rural areas, and some summer camps accept preschool children. Preschool institutions provide care for 9, 10, 12, or 24 hours of the day.

Preschool education methodology is overseen by the central scholarly-methodological bureau of the Ministry of Education of Ukraine and administered by the oblast and raion branches of the ministry. The Ministry of Education has published the journal *Doshkil'ne vykhovannia since 1951.

In 1990, 2,428,000 children, of whom 23 percent were rural residents, were cared for, at 24,500 nurseries, of which 51 percent were rural.

In 1979 a decree of the Ministry of Education of the Ukrainian SSR made Russian-language instruction obligatory for all children cared for at nurseries beginning at age five. Such instruction is no longer obligatory, but until 1991 there were no laws requiring nurseries to instruct children in Ukrainian. In 1987 in Ukraine, only one-quarter of the children receiving public preschool care were cared for in nominally Ukrainian-language institutions. In Kiev in 1987, although 201 of the 730 kindergartens in the city were officially considered to be Ukrainian-language kindergartens, instruction was not provided exclusively in Ukrainian at a single one of these schools. In response the T. Shevchenko Ukrainian Language Society was established, to foster and safeguard the Ukrainian language in the educational institutions of Ukraine.

In 1990 in Ukraine, according to official data, 182,000 children were on nursery school waiting lists. This figure does not include children whose parents have been forced by the shortage of nurseries to make other arrangements for them and are no longer applying for public preschool care. Nurseries are overcrowded and unsanitary, and as a consequence children cared for at nurseries are often ill. In

1987, 167,000 children were cared for at nurseries which were overcrowded according to government norms.

The first Ukrainian preschool organized outside of Ukraine was established in the United States before the First World War, by Bishop S. *Ortynsky. Early nurseries in Canada and in the United States were often run by nuns. Today Ukrainian preschool education exists in Canada, the United States, Germany, France, Belgium, Austria, Brazil, Argentina, and Australia. In Canada the provision of *Ukrainian bilingual education through the public school system has improved the level and availability of Ukrainian preschool education.

BIBLIOGRAPHY
Doroshenko, O. *Dytiachyi sadok* (Kiev 1922)
Rusova, S. *Novi metody doshkil'noho vykhovannia* (Prague 1927)
Iasin'chuk, L. *Ukraïns'ke doshkillia* (Lviv 1936)
Kerivnytstvo doshkil'nym zakladom (Kiev 1977)
Titarenko, T. *Rol' doshkol'nogo vospitaniia v formirovanii lichnosti* (Kiev 1977)
Valsiner, J. *The Childhood of the Soviet Citizen: Socialization of Loyalty* (Ottawa 1984)
    C. Freeland, M. Pasternakova, L. Petrushevska, M. Yurkevych

Preservation of historical and cultural monuments. To ensure the preservation of the representative and outstanding cultural objects of a given nation or people, state and public measures are often enacted. The process commonly requires the identification of such objects, their designation as having a special legal status, their restoration and ongoing conservation, and an interpretation of their cultural or historical significance for a broader public. To a certain extent those functions are carried out by museums and archives. In a more specific sense the status of a historical or cultural monument is usually attributed to public buildings, cultural objects, and sites with particular significance to the country or region in which they are located. *Architecture plays an especially prominent role.

The preservation of historical and cultural monuments over the course of centuries is a difficult feat even under ideal circumstances. The situation in Ukraine was complicated first by numerous wars and invasions, such as the ongoing Tatar attacks, the *Cossack-Polish War and the *Ruin, and the German invasion and occupation during the Second World War. A second difficulty was posed by centuries of Russian rule, which resulted in the destruction of key sites of Ukrainian Cossack history, including the hetman's capital at *Baturyn and the *Zaporozhian Sich, as well as the removal of many national treasures to St Petersburg and Moscow. Finally, the establishment of Bolshevik power in Ukraine proved extremely damaging as the Soviet regime consciously and deliberately destroyed numerous Ukrainian cultural monuments.

No systematic efforts at preservation were made in Ukraine until the late 17th and early 18th centuries. At that time Hetman I. Mazepa restored approx 20 churches, and other patrons followed his example. As Ukraine became increasingly integrated into the Russian Empire, it began to be influenced by imperial laws and trends regarding historical preservation. The earliest of those was invoked by Peter I, who established restrictions on the demolition of structures constructed before the 18th century. Throughout the 19th century Ukraine, and other parts of the Russian Empire, witnessed a phenomenal in-

crease of interest in the study of antiquities and regional history. New bodies, such as the *Odessa Society of History and Antiquities and the *Kiev Archeographic Commission, were formed. The work carried out by such associations helped to establish basic schemes of history and to underscore the significance of specific cultural monuments in various regions. The Third Archeological Congress, held in Kiev in 1874, dealt extensively with Ukrainian matters. A notable event at the gathering was M. *Levchenko's widely publicized address which focused on the devastation of Ukrainian cultural artifacts. Among the others who disseminated such information were Ye. Kuzmin, G. Lukomsky, and V. Riznychenko. In 1910 the *Kiev Society for the Preservation of Ancient and Artistic Monuments was formed. Its members were active in various parts of Ukraine, where they studied and preserved monuments of Ukrainian antiquity.

The preservation of monuments became a national question during the Ukrainian struggle for independence and the construction of a nation-state. In May 1917, at the initiative of I. *Svientsitsky, the Ukrainian Committee for the Protection of Historical Monuments was formed under the direction of M. Biliashivsky. In late 1917, matters of preservation and attendant staff were taken over by the Ministry of Education. Under the Hetman government monuments were the responsibility of the General Administration of Artistic Affairs and National Culture, headed by P. Doroshenko.

After the establishment of a Soviet regime in Ukraine in 1919, all national and community institutions were abolished, and responsibility for matters of preservation was assumed by the All-Ukrainian Committee for the Protection of Ancient and Artistic Monuments (Vukopmys). Although headed by obscure and inexperienced Party functionaries, the committee's staff included notable figures, such as Biliashivsky, F. Ernst, Yu. Mykhailiv, A. Sereda, and D. Shcherbakivsky. The staff rescued numerous valuable collections and individual artifacts during a general process of state nationalization and expropriation. Their work was limited, however, by the committee's overall mandate, which was to concentrate less on actual preservation work than on acquisition and inventory. No immediate measures were enacted to stop the indiscriminate destruction of historical treasures or their export. Owing to a general outcry, a moratorium on the exporting of artifacts of historical value was declared in 1924, but it was rescinded in 1926.

In spite of such difficulties in the 1920s, some concrete measures were taken to ensure the preservation of major cultural artifacts. In 1924 the territory of the ancient Greek colony at *Olbia was declared a national treasure, and in 1925 the grave site of T. Shevchenko was established as a state preserve. On 16 June 1926 landmark legislation, 'Regarding Monuments of Culture and Nature,' was enacted. It contained a comprehensive outline of institutions and measures for preservation. The territory of Ukraine was divided into four inspectorates, headed by S. Dlozhevsky, Ernst, P. Kozar, and S. Taranushenko (V. Dubrovsky was to be chief inspector). In that period the *Kievan Cave Monastery (1926), the Carmelite Monastery in Berdychiv (1928), the fortress in Kamianets-Podilskyi (1928), and the Ostrozky castle in Starokostiantyniv (1929) were declared state historical-cultural preserves.

The Ukrainian Committee for the Protection of Cultural

Monuments, headed by a staunch Communist, I. Kulyk, was struck by the People's Commissariat for Education in 1929. Twelve district preservation commissions were established, which were to be staffed by 121 volunteer associates. The potential activity of the group was stemmed by the political ramifications of the show trial of the so-called *Union for the Liberation of Ukraine and the growing entrenchment of Stalinism in Ukraine. The wholesale destruction of the Ukrainian intelligentsia that began in 1929 rendered the preservation of historical sites highly unlikely. The 1930s saw major losses of Ukrainian cultural monuments. Numerous churches were either sacked or closed down and left to the elements, and the estates of Ukrainian notables, such as the Muravevs and D. Troshchynsky, suffered a comparable fate. One of the most notorious actions was the leveling of a series of notable architectural monuments in Kiev in 1933–4, including some of the churches restored by P. Mohyla, ostensibly for the purpose of providing room for the relocation of the government of the Ukrainian SSR from Kharkiv to Kiev.

The battles of the Second World War caused extensive damage to much of Ukraine; moreover, Ukrainian museums and art collections were savaged by the Nazi occupiers.

No specific relief was afforded to Ukrainian cultural monuments in the immediate postwar period, notwithstanding simultaneous all-Union and republican decrees on 30 December 1948 regarding 'the improvement of the protection of cultural artifacts on the territory of the Ukrainian SSR.' The regeneration of Ukrainian scholarly activity in the 1950s helped to establish a new base for preservation activity. Not until the 1960s, however, were any substantive results seen. On 28 August 1965 the Council of Ministers of the Ukrainian SSR passed a resolution allowing for the establishment of the *Ukrainian Society for the Protection of Historical and Cultural Monuments (the founding meeting took place in December 1966). The increase in serious efforts to preserve artifacts and monuments in the years following is attributable to the society's longtime head, P. *Tronko, the deputy leader of the Council of Ministers at that time. On 21 July 1965 the Council of Ministers ratified a list of monuments designated as under state protection. This list included 115 artistic, 117 historical, and 142 archeological items. On 20 February 1967 the council stated that those artifacts were in a state of unacceptable deterioration; that conclusion was considered grounds for a reaffirmation of the aforementioned society's statutes in June 1967. But in spite of those measures (and additional legislation in the 1970s), an attitude of official neglect toward Ukrainian cultural monuments was maintained.

The postwar period also saw the growth of efforts by the Soviet regime to buttress its position by creating a host of official 'cultural' monuments commemorating its history. In 1955–8 three resolutions were passed by the Central Committee of the CPU and the Council of Ministers of the Ukrainian SSR calling for the placing of plaques celebrating the achievements of the regime throughout Ukraine. Thirteen were to commemorate events of the Revolution of 1905–7, 78 were to mark the victory of Bolshevism of 1917–20, and 4 were to note the history of the CPU. A resolution passed by the Central Committee and the council on 28 February 1968 called for a massive campaign of distribution of plaques, plates, stones, monuments, and the

like; oblast legislative and executive councils were held responsible for its success.

The muted hostility of Soviet state institutions toward the protection of Ukrainian cultural monuments created a situation in which most of the work was carried out by voluntary societies and amateur enthusiasts, such as I. *Honchar, O. *Kompan, and O. Sylyn. It also rendered cultural activism in the realm of Ukrainian historical preservation a subtle form of political opposition. An additional problem was afforded by the fact that the political climate in the USSR did not allow preservation work to be carried out in all areas of Ukrainian history. Some fields, such as Kievan Rus' and medieval Ukraine, could be dealt with within a politically acceptable framework. Others, notably the Ukrainian Cossack past, were regarded as suspect and as a result were seriously neglected. Those dealing with Ukrainian's struggle for independence were strictly taboo. With the gradual disintegration of the Soviet regime from the mid-1980s, a phenomenal upsurge of interest in Ukrainian historical preservation took place, particularly with respect to Cossackdom and the struggle for independence.

BIBLIOGRAPHY

Zakonodavstvo pro pam'iatnyky istoriï ta kul'tury: Zbirnyk normatyvnykh aktiv (Kiev 1970)

Kashka, M. *S'ohodni i zavtra okhorony pam'iatok Ukraïny* (Kiev 1986)

S. Bilokin

Presniakov, Aleksandr [Presnjakov], b 3 May 1870 in Odessa, Kherson gubernia, d 30 September 1929 in Leningrad. Russian historian; corresponding member of the USSR Academy of Sciences from 1920. He graduated from St Petersburg University and taught there from 1907 (professor from 1918). His *Kniazhoe pravo v drevnei Rusi* (Princely Law in Ancient Rus', 1909) remains one of the foremost works in the history of Kievan Rus'. His major work is considered to be *Obrazovanie Velikorusskogo gosudarstva* (PH D diss, 1918; English trans as *The Formation of the Great Russian State*, 1970). He also wrote important monographs on the tsardom of Muscovy (1918; English trans 1978), Alexander I (1923), Nicholas I (1925; English trans 1974), and the Decembrist revolt (1926). Presniakov was one of the few Russian historians to give some credit to M. Hrushevsky's critique of the traditional scheme of Russian history and to accept to some degree the notion of the independent evolution of Ukrainian history. An edition of his lectures on Russian history (2 vols, 1938–9) was published posthumously.

Prešov (Ukrainian: Priashiv). A city (1989 pop 85,000) in eastern Slovakia, situated on the Torysa River, with approx 2,000 Ukrainian inhabitants. In 1935 its population was 22,000, of whom 2,500 were Ukrainians. A transit point for trade between Galicia and Hungary from the Middle Ages on, it was mentioned in a document of 1247 as an important city. It later became the center of the Sáros (Šariš) komitat. Although not within Ukrainian ethnographic territory, the city has developed as a Ukrainian center. In 1816 it became the capital of a Greek Catholic eparchy, of which the first bishop was H. Tarkovych. The city's cultural significance for Ukrainians grew in 1850, with the establishment of the Prešov Literary Society by

O. *Dukhnovych. Active until 1853, the group had 72 members and published nine books (including textbooks and three issues of the almanac *Pozdravlenie rusynov*, 1850–2). The John the Baptist Society, a charitable and educational organization, was founded in the city in 1862. A hostile attitude toward minorities by local authorities and the prevailing Russophilism or Magyarophilism of the local intelligentsia (particularly among the clergy) retarded Ukrainian cultural growth for decades. It was given new impetus only when the Prešov region joined Czechoslovakia in 1919. Nevertheless, because no administrative ties were established with Ukrainian regions of Transcarpathia, cultural development continued to proceed slowly. There were a number of Russophile organizations and institutions active in the city, including the Russian People's Council, the Russian People's Home, the Russian Club, the Russian Museum, the Dukhnovych Society (est 1933), the Union of Russian Women, and the Union of Russian Teachers.

View of Prešov, with the monument to Oleksander Dukhnovych to the right (1933)

Russophile newspapers included the clerical *Russkoe slovo* (1924–39), *Narodnaia gazeta* (1924–35), and *Russkaia narodnaia gazeta* (1937–8). *Slovo naroda* was published in Ukrainian in 1931–2 and edited by I. Nevytska.

A Greek Catholic theological seminary (est 1880), teacher's college (1895), and gymnasium (est 1936) were also active. A Ukrainian radio program began broadcasting locally in 1934 and has continued serving the region to this day.

In 1945 Prešov was recognized as the offical center of the Ukrainian population in Czechoslovakia, and the Ukrainian People's Council of the Prešov Region was established there. The new body sponsored several publications, including the newspaper *Priashivshchyna*. In 1946 the *Prešov Ukrainian National Theater, which has staged over 300 productions in Ukrainian and Russian, was established. In 1951 the *Cultural Association of Ukrainian Workers was formed, and succeeded the Ukrainian People's Council. After the Velvet Revolution in 1990, it changed its name to Union of Ruthenian-Ukrainians of Czechoslovakia. In 1951 *Priashivshchyna* was replaced by the weekly *Nove zhyttia*, the illustrated monthly *Druzhno vpered*, and the literary quarterly (now a bimonthly) *Duklia*. In 1952 a Ukrainian branch of the Slovak Writers' Union was established in Prešov. A department of Ukrai-

nian language and literature at the Prešov division of Košice University, an Orthodox theological seminary, a Ukrainian elementary and primary school, and the Duklia Ukrainian Folk Ensemble are also found there. Greater numbers of Ukrainians have entered Prešov's intelligentsia in recent years. Since 1950 the city has been the center of an Orthodox bishopric, and in 1969 it became an ordinariate of the revived Greek Catholic church. The Ukrainian department of the Slovak pedagogical publishing house annually publishes 12 to 15 Ukrainian works of literature or scholarship and a comparable number of textbooks. The local Ukrainian intelligentsia was particularly active in the latter 1960s, but after the 1968 invasion by the Soviet Union a number were dismissed from their posts, including Yu. Bacha, Ye. Biss, I. Matsynsky, M. Mushynka, P. Murashko, and Y. Shelepets. Most were rehabilitated in 1990. In 1989 the Ukrainian gymnasium was renamed the Shevchenko Gymnasium.

In the 1960s to 1980s, a number of conferences on the works of O. Dukhnovych, I. Franko, F. Lazoryk, I. Pankevych, I. Pavlovych, T. Shevchenko, and other Ukrainian cultural figures were held in the city. An academic society in Prešov is affiliated with the Union of Ruthenian-Ukrainians of Czechoslovakia. Ukrainian departments are situated at the regional pedagogical institute and the Pedagogical Research Institute.

Ukrainian editions of the monthly (Orthodox) *Zapovit Kyryla i Mefodiia* and (Greek Catholic) *Blahovisnyk* are published along with the Slovak versions. (See also *Prešov region.)

M. Mushynka, O. Zilynsky

Prešov eparchy. A Byzantine rite Catholic eparchy in western Transcarpathia, with its see in Prešov, now located in eastern Czechoslovakia. Prešov eparchy was proposed in 1816 by the Austrian emperor Francis Joseph I and was formally erected by Pope Pius VII in 1818. Encompassing 194 parishes with approx 150,000 faithful, it consisted of the Košice Greek Catholic vicariate (est 1787) of Mukachiv eparchy. The eparchy's bishops have included H. Tarkovych (1821–41), Y. Gaganets (1843–75), N. Tovt (1876–82), I. Valii (1883–1911), S. Novak (1913–20), D. Niaradi (1922–7, as apostolic administrator), P. Goidych (1927–60), and suffragan V. Hopko (1947–76). Among the institutions established in Prešov were an eparchial seminary (est 1880), a seminary for precentors and teachers (1895), and a Greek Catholic gymnasium (1936). Most religious orders active in the eparchy – the Redemptorists, the Basilians, and the Sisters Servants of Mary Immaculate – were established under Bishop Goidych; the Basilian Sisters were active there from 1922.

Several major swings in national orientation have marked the history of Prešov eparchy. By the turn of the century many of the clergy, in particular the hierarchy, displayed a marked Magyarophilism and favored the Latinization of the church. In reaction the Russophiles of the region launched a concerted effort to establish a (Russian) Orthodox church in Transcarpathia, which they hoped would lead most of the Prešov parishes away from Greek Catholicism. Under Bishops Niaradi and Goidych, however, the church stressed its Ukrainian and eastern character and successfully countered most of the Russophile efforts.

During the Second World War, Prešov eparchy gained

jurisdiction over several new areas, and by 1948 it included Prešov eparchy proper (143,000), the Mukachiv administration (80,600), and the Czech and Moravian administrations (68,400), for a total of 292,600 faithful. On 28 April 1950 the eparchy was forcibly converted by Communist authorities to Orthodoxy at the so-called Prešov Sobor. This action was accompanied by the formal liquidation of the Greek Catholic church, the closing of monasteries, the arrest of both bishops, and the arrest and imprisonment in labor camps of most of the clergy. Authority over the eparchy was claimed by the patriarch of Moscow, who established four administrative jurisdictions in Czechoslovakia: the archeparchy of Prague and the eparchies of Brno-Olomouc, Michalovce (including parts of the Mukachiv administration), and Prešov (virtually intact territorially). On 23 November 1951 these were united into the Autocephalous Orthodox Church of Czechoslovakia, and E. Vorontsov, a Russian, was placed at the head of the church by the Moscow patriarch. Since 1964 the church has been led by the Transcarpathian-born D. Fylyp.

In 1968, during the Prague Spring, the government allowed the restoration of the Greek Catholic church in Czechoslovakia. In Prešov eparchy 204 of 246 churches and 69 priests returned to Eastern rite Catholicism. Bishop Hopko, who had assumed leadership of the eparchy after Goidych's death in 1960, returned to Prešov to assume his post. A struggle for control over the eparchy erupted, however, between Slovak and Ukrainian Greek Catholics. One of the Slovaks, I. Hirka, emerged as administrator of the eparchy in 1969 and launched a campaign for the Slovakization of the eparchy, in which effort he was supported by the Slovak authorities. In response many Ukrainian Catholic and even some Slovak villages returned to the Orthodox church, where the Church Slavonic language was used, and the Eastern rite adhered to. Hirka was ordained bishop in 1990. Today the bishop of Prešov eparchy does not retain any formal ties to the *Ukrainian Catholic church and does not participate in the church's synods.

BIBLIOGRAPHY
Pekar, A. *Narys istoriï tserkvy Zakarpattia* (Rome 1967)
– *Historic Background of the Eparchy of Prjashev* (Pittsburg 1968)
Kubiniy, J. *The History of the Prjašiv Eparchy* (Rome 1970)
Duchnovič, A. *The History of the Eparchy of Prjašev* (Rome 1971)
Sabol, S. *Holhota Hreko-Katolyc'koï Tserkvy v Chekhoslovachchyni* (Toronto 1978)

A. Pekar

Prešov Literary Society (Priashevskoe literaturnoe zavedenie). An organization established by O. *Dukhnovych, with the aim of publishing books in the Transcarpathian dialect and raising the educational level of Transcarpathia's Ukrainian population. It functioned semilegally from 1850 to 1853 out of Dukhnovych's home in Prešov. Its several dozen members were from the local nationally conscious literati (eg, A. and V. Dobriansky, A. Baludiansky, A. Popovych, M. Nod, O. Homichkov, O. Pavlovych, H. Sholtys, M. Mykhalych, I. Vyslotsky, P. Yanovych, A. Rubii, O. Labants, A. Yankura, A. Fedorovych, A. Kryher-Dobrianska, T. Podhaietska, M. Nevytska, I. Churhovych); there were a few Czech and Slovak sympathizers among them (eg, J. Moravčik). The society issued 12 publications, including the first Transcarpathian

Ukrainian schoolbooks, calendars, and two literary miscellanies, and the first published Transcarpathian Ukrainian play, Dukhnovych's *Dobroditel' prevyshaiet bohatstvo* (A Philanthropist Transcends Wealth, 1850). Under its auspices Dukhnovych collected materials in the region for a future national museum and organized the recording of folklore. In 1853 the society failed to receive support from the local church hierarchy, and finally it was banned by the Austrian government, which considered its activities subversive.

Prešov Mountains. See Slanské Mountains.

Prešov region (Priashivshchyna). An area within the northeastern part of Slovakia inhabited by Ukrainians. The region has never had a distinct legal or administrative status, so the term Prešov region – also Prešov Rus' – is encountered only in writings about the area. The name derives from the city of *Prešov (Ukrainian: Priashiv), which since the early 19th century has been the religious and cultural center for the region's Ukrainians. The alternate term, Prešov Rus', reflects the fact that until the second half of the 20th century the East Slavic population there referred to itself exclusively by the historic name Ruthenian (Rusyn), or by its regional variant, Rusnak.

At present the Prešov region is administratively part of Slovakia. The part of Slovakia inhabited by Ukrainians consists of about 300 villages located within the northernmost portions of the counties (Slovak: *okresy*) of Stará L'ubovňa, Bardejov, Svydnyk (Svidník), Prešov, and, in particular, Humenné. Before 1918 the area made up the northernmost portions of the historical Hungarian komitats (*megye*) of Spiš (Hungarian: Szepes), Šariš (Sáros), Zemplin (Zemplén), and southwestern Už (Ung). According to official Czechoslovak census data Ukrainians form a majority in none of the present-day counties. In 1991, 32,400 inhabitants in the Prešov region designated their national identity as Ruthenian (Rusyn) or Ukrainian, although unofficial sources estimate their number could be as high as 130,000 to 140,000.

The Ukrainians inhabit a small strip of territory that somewhat resembles an irregular triangle bounded by the crests of the Carpathians in the north. Starting from the west at a point in the valley of the Poprad River, the Prešov region gradually widens in an eastward direction until it reaches as far south as the outskirts of Uzhhorod, near the border with Ukraine.

The Prešov region forms an ethnographic unit with the *Lemko region on the adjacent northern slopes of the Carpathian crests. Scholars therefore often refer to the Prešov region as the southern Lemko region. The region's inhabitants, however, have never, with rare exceptions, designated themselves Lemkos, and their political separation from the north (which eventually fell under Polish control) has allowed them to follow a distinct historical development.

Geography and climate. The Prešov region makes up about 3,500 sq km of territory. It sits in some of the lowest elevations of the Carpathians within the Lower Beskyd and Western Beskyd ranges; most of the Ukrainian villages are situated only 450–900 m above sea level. The generally low Beskyd ranges (highest 1,289 m) are broken by several passes – Tylych (683 m), Duklia (502 m), Lupków (657 m), Ruskyi (797 m) – which historically have played

Languages spoken circa 1960

Ukrainian

Slovak

Hungarian

Polish

International boundary

PREŠOV REGION

an important role in the movement of people and goods to and from Poland.

Several river valleys connect the region southward into the Slovak lowland and the Hungarian plain. The major rivers, the upper reaches of which flow southward through the Prešov region toward the Tysa, include (from west to east) the Poprad (which unlike the others flows northward) and the Hornád, the Torysa, the Toplia, the Laborets, the Ondava, and the Chirokha. The north–south flow of the rivers has until recently made it easier for Ukrainians to reach Slovak-inhabited towns at the southern end of their several valleys than to reach the valleys immediately to the east or west inhabited by their fellow Ukrainians.

The climate is basically continental, although somewhat warmer than in the neighboring Transcarpathian region to the east. At lower elevations the temperature averages 21°C (July) to –3°C (January), with an annual rainfall of 580 mm. At higher elevations the temperature averages drop to 14°C (July) and –8°C (January), with rainfall increasing to 1,100 mm annually. The Prešov region today remains an agricultural and pastoral land which, owing to the mountainous and forested terrain, at best affords a subsistence-level economy. Lumbering is the only other viable economic pursuit.

Early history. There is much disagreement concerning the early history of the Prešov region and of the Ukrainians (Ruthenians) living south of the Carpathian Mountains. Archeological evidence suggests that the region was already inhabited during the late Stone Age. From the 3rd century BC to the 5th century AD a series of peoples – Celts, Dacians, Goths, Huns, and Avars – passed through, set-

tling there briefly and leaving behind remnants of their way of life. Linguistic and archeological evidence indicates that by the 6th or 7th century AD the region's inhabitants were Slavs, although there is no consensus on whether they were West Slavs ('ancestors' of the Slovaks) or East Slavs (*White Croatians, 'ancestors' of the Ruthenians [Ukrainians]). It seems that the first permanent settlers in the Prešov region arrived from north of the Carpathians sometime between the 6th and 11th centuries, which date would suggest that they were East Slavs. Slovak scholars contend, however, that there was a continuous settlement of West Slavs from the 7th century, and that the ancestors of the Ukrainian-Ruthenians did not arrive in the area until their migration from Galicia beginning in the 14th century (a view also held by Hungarian scholars). It has also been debated whether the Prešov region received Christianity in the Byzantine form from the Bulgarian Empire in the 9th century or from Kievan Rus' in the 11th century. What is certain is that the first parishes in the Prešov region, for which there are documents beginning only in the 14th century, were initially under the jurisdiction of the Orthodox bishop of Peremyshl and then (after the 15th century) the bishop of Mukachiv.

Throughout its early history the Prešov region was a sparsely settled border area between the Hungarian Kingdom to the south and the Kievan Rus' principality of Galicia to the north. In the 11th and 12th centuries the Hungarian kings pushed northward toward the crest of the Carpathians and even beyond, into parts of Galicia, where they ruled intermittently until the end of the 14th century. To ensure their control of that northern border region the Hungarian kings granted, during the 14th century, large tracts of land to princes (mostly from southern Italy and therefore related to Hungary's new ruling House of Anjou), such as the Drugeth family in Zemplin county and the Perényi family in Šariš county. Thus from the 12th century until 1918 the Prešov region was to remain within the political and socioeconomic framework of the Hungarian Kingdom.

The first consistent documentation about the Prešov region dates from the 14th century, thereby coinciding with the increasing settlement of the area. Ukrainian colonization came from two directions, southeast and north. The colonization from the southeast was related to the movement of *Vlachs (Wallachians) northward and westward through the Carpathians. By the time they reached Transcarpathia, the Wallachians had assimilated with the local population. When they moved farther westward into the Prešov region, they were for the most part ethnically Ukrainians, even though they retained the name Wallachians. The colonization from the north consisted of Ukrainian peasants who fled the spread of the feudal system in Galicia. The heaviest immigration from the north dates from the 16th century, when many new villages in the Prešov region were established. Peasants were attracted to the sparsely settled Prešov region because of the special privileges granted to new colonists, including limited taxes and duties, a certain degree of self-rule and judicial authority over minor crimes, and the right to buy and sell land.

The 16th and 17th centuries. Hungarian control over the Prešov region increased during the 16th century, after Hungary's Christian princes were forced to retreat to the northern part of the kingdom in the wake of their defeat at Ottoman hands in 1526. As a result the feudal duties required of Ukrainian peasants and Wallachian shepherds increased. The princes themselves were soon embroiled in a dynastic struggle for the Hungarian crown.

The Hungarian rivalries assumed a religious dimension in the second half of the century, when the Reformation pitted Hungarian Protestant princes in Transylvania against Catholic princes in the rest of the non-Ottoman-ruled kingdom. The Orthodox Ukrainians found themselves caught in the middle. The Prešov region came under Catholic Habsburg control, and Transcarpathia, including the Orthodox eparchial see of Mukachiv, came under Protestant Transylvania. The Ukrainians in the Prešov region were now cut off from their brethren just to the east. The situation strengthened their contact northward with the diocese of Peremyshl, from which Orthodox church books, icons, and other religious materials now came in greater numbers. The contact grew after 1596, when the Uniate (Greek Catholic) church came into being in Ukraine. Following that example, Prince G. Drugeth III (d 1620) of Humenné, who owned numerous villages in the Prešov region, tried in 1614 to introduce a church union on his lands. As part of his effort he established the Jesuit College in Humenné (1613), the first secondary school for the Prešov region. Although Drugeth's efforts failed, his desires were realized with the *Uzhhorod Union of 1646. Backed by pro-Habsburg Hungarian rule, the union took hold in the Prešov region, and most of the Orthodox Ukrainian villages there became Uniate. Among the exceptions were a few villages that became Protestant (Lutheran and Calvinist). The Protestant presence, however, was short-lived. By the mid-18th century all the Ukrainian villages had become Uniate (later Greek Catholic); they remained so, with few exceptions, until 1918.

Dynastic and religious wars between pro- and anti-Habsburg forces broke out in the wake of the Uzhhorod union and ravaged the Prešov region. The Ukrainians in the region sometimes joined in the military conflicts, most notably in the last of the major anti-Habsburg revolts, led by F. Rákóczi. With the restoration of order (and Habsburg rule) came an increase in the feudal dues imposed on the peasantry. Many Ukrainian peasants fled to southern Hungary (in the Bačka-Vojvodina region of present-day Serbia), to Slovak territory farther west, or across the mountains northward to Galicia. In Šariš and Zemplin counties as many as one-third of the villages were deserted by the beginning of the 18th century.

The renewal of Habsburg authority. The marked decline in the number of Ukrainian inhabitants in the Prešov region was made up for during the 18th century by natural demographic increases that resulted from political stability and economic prosperity under Habsburg rule as well as new immigration from Galicia, especially after the 1730s. Since local Hungarian landlords were anxious to repopulate their villages in the Prešov region, they welcomed the newcomers with reduced taxes and other temporary privileges. The period also saw an influx of Galician Jews, who were often contracted by the lords to collect rents, tolls, and other duties and granted the right to brew and sell liquor.

The 18th century also witnessed an improvement in the status of the Uniate clergy following an imperial decree of 1692 that had freed them from all duties previously owed to local landlords. Before long the priests themselves became village landlords.

The prosperity of the 18th century encouraged significant cultural development. Numerous churches were constructed throughout the Prešov region; those built entirely of wood still represent some of the finest achievements of Ukrainian church architecture. The first publications for Ukrainians also date from the period, including the *Bukvar* (Primer, 1770) attributed to Bishop I. *Bradach. Elementary schools were established at the rural monasteries of Bukovská Hôrka and Krásny Brod, the latter including an advanced philosophical and theological school, where monks such as A. Kotsak prepared grammars and other texts that in part used the local Ukrainian (Ruthenian) vernacular. The second half of the 18th century also saw the appearance of the first histories of Ukrainians, the most extensive being a three-volume work by Y. *Bazylovych, a native of the Prešov region.

In 1771, under Bishop Bradach, the Habsburgs granted the eparchy of Mukachiv equal status with the Roman Catholic church and accepted a change in the name of the church from Uniate to Greek Catholic. In 1787 the Mukachiv eparchy established a vicariate for Greek Catholics in the Prešov region with a seat in Košice (in 1805 it was transferred to Prešov). Finally, in 1815 an Austrian imperial decree, confirmed three years later by the Apostolic See, raised the Prešov vicariate to the status of an independent eparchy. The new eparchy under its first bishop, H. Tarkovych, consisted of 193 parishes, with 149,000 faithful. With the creation of the eparchy Ukrainians in the Prešov region were for the first time made jurisdictionally distinct from their brethren just to the east in Transcarpathia, who remained within the eparchy of Mukachiv. That development also brought about the rise of Prešov as the region's cultural center and the establishment of an eparchial library, a cathedral church, an episcopal residence, and, eventually, a seminary (1880) and teacher's college (1895).

The Greek Catholic church remained the only choice for Ukrainians of the Prešov region who wished to pursue a career other than agriculture. For those few who obtained an education but wished to enter secular professions without having to become assimilated to the increasingly dominant Hungarian culture of the kingdom in which they lived, one possibility was emigration abroad. By the beginning of the 19th century Ukrainians had begun to emigrate eastward from the Prešov region, some to neighboring Galicia, but most to the Russian Empire, where they were to become leading figures in the recently reformed tsarist educational system – M. *Baluhiansky, P. *Lodii, and I. *Orlai. Only Orlai continued to maintain contact with his homeland. He published a history of the Carpatho-Ruthenians (1804), which contended that Hungary's 'Russians' were related to other 'Russians,' especially those living in Little Russia (Ukraine).

The socioeconomic structure in the Prešov region changed little during the first half of the 19th century. Nor did the national consciousness of the Ukrainians in the region (and in Transcarpathia) manifest itself in the same manner as among their Slavic neighbors during what was a general period of national awakening. They had no newspapers, no cultural organizations, and no standard language. Their secular intelligentsia emigrated abroad (mostly to the Russian Empire), and the few Greek Catholic clergymen who thought in national terms expressed at best vague ideas of unity with Russia. Most, nevertheless, adapted to the new conditions in Hungary, where a vibrant Hungarian national movement called upon all its citizens – of whatever ethnolinguistic background – to learn Magyar and to adopt it as the cultured medium for communication. That state of affairs made the growth of Ukrainian national life that began with the Revolution of 1848 all the more remarkable.

The national awakening and decline. With the outbreak of the *Revolution of 1848–9 in the Habsburg monarchy the Greek Catholic clergy and seminarians in the Prešov region immediately expressed support for Hungary. In sharp contrast to them, the secular leader A. *Dobriansky formulated a political program calling for the unity of Ukrainians in Hungary with their brethren north of the mountains in Galicia. He then played an important role in the suppression of the Hungarian revolt as Austrian liaison with the Russian army, which Tsar Nicholas I sent in response to Vienna's request for aid. After Hungary was defeated in August 1849, the kingdom was reorganized under direct Austrian military control. Dobriansky became administrator of the Uzhhorod civil district (Uzh, Bereg, Ugocsa, and Maramureş counties), where he implemented policies for Ukrainian national autonomy. Ukrainians in the Prešov region demanded to be united with the 'Rusyn' Uzhhorod district, but that ambition was not realized before the district was abolished in March 1850.

More lasting than political gains were the cultural achievements of the Ukrainians of Hungary. Again, they were associated with an activist from the Prešov region,

the Greek Catholic priest O. *Dukhnovych. In 1850 he organized the first Ukrainian cultural organization in the region, the *Prešov Literary Society. In 1862 he worked with Dobriansky to establish the Society of St John the Baptist in Prešov, whose purpose was to educate young people in a national spirit. Dukhnovych also wrote several histories of his people and newspaper accounts of their current affairs.

Despite the achievements of Dobriansky and Dukhnovych in stimulating the political and cultural renaissance of their people, the majority of the Greek Catholic clergy and young seminarians remained immune to the Slavic aspects of their culture. They preferred to speak Magyar, to adopt Magyar mannerisms, and to strive to be loyal citizens of Hungary – even at the expense of surrendering their national identity.

The political changes that resulted from the 1867 *Ausgleich* that created the Austro-Hungarian dual monarchy had a profound effect on Ukrainian life in the Prešov region. The Magyars now had full control over all national minorities living in Hungary, including (1870) approx 450,000 Ukrainians (18 percent of whom lived in the Prešov region). Magyarone Ukrainians had little difficulty in adjusting to the new situation. Dukhnovych and his generation, however, were now in a more tenuous position. Their situation was exacerbated by the fact that they had never resolved the question of a standard literary language (often resorting to a jargonish *yazychiie* viewed as superior to the 'peasant vulgarism' of vernacular speech) and the closely related problem of national identity. Increasingly they began to identify with the Russian nationality as a way of preventing the disappearance of their people and became *Russophiles.

By the 1870s no Ukrainian institutions or publications remained in the Prešov region. Literary production continued, although local writers were forced to work in isolation and to publish whenever possible in Uzhhorod or in Lviv in neighboring Galicia. Of the best-known Ukrainian writers in Hungary of that period four were natives of the Prešov region: O. Pavlovych, A. *Kralytsky, Yu. Stavrovsky-Popradov, and I. Danylovych-Korytniansky. All were Greek Catholic priests, who through their poetry, prose, and plays tried to instill pride and patriotism by describing the physical beauties of their Carpathian homeland and the supposed greatness of its historical past. Their message, however, was for the most part not in the vernacular speech of the local populace, but in the *yazychiie.*

More problematic for the survival of Ukrainians was the fact that the educational system was not producing any new cadres of leaders with some form of national consciousness. The few secondary schools in Prešov were administered by the Greek Catholic church, and all taught exclusively in Magyar. At the lower level there were elementary schools sponsored by the church, village, or state, where students received at least rudimentary training in the Cyrillic alphabet and therefore some exposure to their native culture. That situation was to change rapidly, however. In 1874 the Prešov region had 237 elementary schools using some form of Ukrainian; three decades later, in 1906, that number had decreased to only 23, with 68 more offering Ukrainian-Magyar bilingual instruction.

Those decades saw the economic situation of the Prešov region decline substantially, as farm holdings diminished in size owing to a growing population, and the need for agricultural laborers decreased owing to mechanization. Those factors forced Ukrainians to emigrate, in particular to the United States. The first few individuals left in the late 1870s, and by 1914 an estimated 150,000 Ukrainians had left Hungary, approx half of them from the Prešov region. The departing emigrants not only helped to relieve the immediate pressures on the local economy but also contributed to it by means of the remittances they forwarded from the New World. Some later returned home to buy up as much land as possible.

The Hungarian authorities maintained and intensified their policy of Magyarization in the early 20th century. All Greek Catholics were now considered 'Magyars of the Greek Catholic faith,' and people were compelled to Magyarize their family and given names. A new school law took effect in 1907, as a result of which the 68 Magyar-Ukrainian bilingual schools in the Prešov region were fully Magyarized by 1912, and the number of schools using some form of Ukrainian declined from 23 to 9. The government's policy was more often than not implemented by local Magyarone teachers, priests, and officials of Ukrainian background. Foremost in such efforts was the Magyarone Greek Catholic bishop of the Prešov eparchy, I. Novak, who in 1915 introduced the Latin alphabet into school and liturgical texts and dropped the traditional Julian calendar in favor of the Gregorian.

At the time of the First World War Ukrainian national life in the Prešov region had reached its lowest point. There were no secondary schools and only a few elementary schools where the native language was used; there were no national institutions, and the only publication was a weekly (*Nase otecsesctvo*, 1916–19) written in a Magyar-based Latin alphabet and devoid of Ukrainian patriotism. Finally, the hierarchy and many priests in the Greek Catholic church, as well as the secular and lay intelligentsia, had been completely Magyarized.

The impact of the First World War. In the months immediately following the end of the war the implications of the contemporary political upheavals for Ukrainians living south of the Carpathians were unclear. The first movement toward change came from Ruthenian immigrants living in the United States. Under the leadership of a young Ruthenian-American lawyer, H. Zhatkovych, the *American National Council of Uhro-Rusins was established in the summer of 1918. By the end of the year its members were actively pursuing efforts to incorporate their European homeland into the new Czechoslovakian state as an autonomous region. Meanwhile Ukrainians in the Transcarpathian region began holding a series of meetings (councils) to discuss their political future. The first was the *Ruthenian People's Council in Stará Ľubovňa, held on 8 November 1918. The gathering concluded that continued life under Hungary was unacceptable, but it could reach no consensus on an alternative. When a group of Ukrainians met in Uzhhorod on 9 November 1918 and pledged their loyalty to Hungary, the Ruthenian People's Council reconvened in Prešov. Several months of contradictory political activity followed: national councils were convened farther east in Subcarpathia, and called for union with Ukraine; the Hungarian government (republican and communist) attempted to restore its rule in the area; and the Carpatho-Ruthenian–American delegation arrived with its proposal for union with Czechoslovakia. The developments culminated on 8

May 1919, when some 200 Ukrainian delegates met in Uzhhorod to form the *Central Ruthenian People's Council. The council unequivocally endorsed the option of autonomy within a Czecho-Slovak state, albeit at the cost of dropping plans for union with the Lemkos to the north.

The establishment of the territory of *Subcarpathian Ruthenia (Czech: Podkarpatská Rus) created a 'temporary' boundary along the Uzh River, which left Ukrainians of the Prešov region separated administratively from their brethren farther east for the first time. Within a decade the boundary, with slight changes, became permanent. The Prešov region remained outside Subcarpathian Ruthenia and under Slovak administration.

The interwar years. Ukrainian life in Czechoslovakia experienced a notable renaissance during the interwar era. The Hungarian authorities had had an active policy of assimilation, but the Slavic state was generally sympathetic to the Ukrainians' language and culture. The situation did not entirely hold for the Ukrainians of the Prešov region, however, for whereas their kinfolk in Subcarpathian Ruthenia were established as one of the state nationalities, in the Prešov region they constituted only a national minority with no political or administrative autonomy.

The political status of the Prešov region remained uncertain until 1928. All Ukrainian leaders had maintained from the earliest negotiations with Czechoslovak leaders in the United States and Europe that the Ukrainian-inhabited Prešov region would have to become part of an autonomous Subcarpathian Ruthenia. Slovak leaders, however, remained completely opposed. The question of unification with their brethren to the east became the basic goal of the Russophile *Ruthenian People's party, established in 1921 in Prešov by the brothers K., N., and A. *Beskyd. The matter was finally resolved in 1928, when the national parliament passed a law dividing the Czechoslovak Republic into four provinces (Bohemia, Moravia-Silesia, Slovakia, and Subcarpathian Ruthenia) and making permanent with only slight changes the formerly temporary boundary between Slovakia and Subcarpathian Ruthenia. Despite that decision the Ruthenian People's party and its organs, *Rus'* (Prešov 1921–3) and *Narodnaia gazeta* (Prešov 1924–36), continued in vain to demand unification.

Separated from Subcarpathian Ruthenia, the Ukrainians of the Prešov region were subject to the policies of a Slovak administration unsympathetic to them. The Slovakization of the school system began in 1922, when the minister of education in Bratislava adopted a policy whereby Greek Catholic elementary schools that had taught in Magyar before 1919 should now use Slovak. In spite of guarantees in the Czechoslovak constitution that (theoretically) required at least 237 elementary schools to provide Ruthenian-Ukrainian vernacular instruction, only 95 elementary schools in the Prešov region were doing so in 1923–4. Slovak authorities defended that state of affairs by citing census statistics. But the statistics had been manipulated by local officials who had urged Ruthenian Ukrainians to identify themselves as 'Czechoslovaks' on census questionnaires and thereby caused a drop in the number of Ukrainians officially noted as such, from 111,280 (1910) to 85,628 (1921). The resulting census dispute added to the friction between Slovaks and Ukrainians that continued to grow (especially among political leaders) throughout the interwar period.

The economic situation of the Ukrainian population deteriorated as well. Eastern Slovakia, particularly the Prešov region, remained one of the most underdeveloped sections of Czechoslovakia. Lumber mills in about a dozen locations (the largest being Medzilaborce and Udavské) employed only approx 3.3 percent of the work force in 1930. The vast majority of the Ukrainians (89.6 percent in 1939) remained agriculturalists. Their already precarious situation worsened in the 1930s as a result of a bad harvest in 1931–2, coupled with the Depression. The ensuing bankruptcies and foreclosures prompted several significant disturbances and strengthened the support of antigovernment political parties.

Despite serious political and economic problems there were notable social and cultural developments in the Prešov region during the period. Continued protests by the Ruthenian People's party and the Prešov Greek Catholic eparchy resulted in an increase in the number of schools teaching in some variant of the local dialect of Ukrainian, so that by 1938 there were a total of 168 of such elementary schools and 43 others in which some Ruthenian-Ukrainian was taught. A gymnasium (albeit Russian-language) was opened in Prešov in 1936.

The Orthodox church began making greater inroads in the region during the interwar era. Pro-Orthodox sentiment had arisen in the area for the first time in centuries in the 1890s, as an outgrowth of Russophile tendencies and a response to tsarist propaganda and the return of emigrants from the United States (who had converted during their sojourn abroad). It had been kept in check, however, by the Hungarian authorities. Now, from a base in the village of Ladomirová, near Svydnyk, the church grew to include 18 parishes, with more than 9,000 adherents, by 1935. The initial success of the Orthodox movement was in part related to a crisis in the Greek Catholic eparchy of Prešov resulting from the earlier Magyarone sympathies of Bishop Novak and other church hierarchs. The growing shift of Greek Catholics to Orthodoxy was stemmed somewhat by Bishop D. Niaradi, the church's apostolic administrator in 1922–7. The situation of the Greek Catholic church finally stabilized with the appointment of a new bishop, P. *Goidych, who provided the active leadership needed to revive it.

The greater freedom of Ukrainians under Czechoslovak than under Hungarian rule made possible a broader discussion concerning national identity. The residents of the region, having had no experience comparable to the blossoming of Ukrainian civic culture in Galicia during the 19th century or to the cathartic Revolution of 1917 in central Ukraine, largely rejected a Ukrainophile orientation. The local intelligentsia urged the people instead to identify themselves as Ruthenians (*Rusyny* or Rusyns). Characteristically that orientation was manifested in one of two forms, Russian or regional, although it was often difficult to distinguish between the two, as both groups claimed they were Carpatho-Ruthenians (*karpatorusskii*) maintaining the tradition of 19th-century leaders such as Dukhnovych and Dobriansky. The Russophiles were initially represented by A. Beskyd and his supporters in the Ruthenian People's party, who demanded the introduction of the Russian language into local schools and touted the notion of one 'Russian' people 'from the Poprad River to the Pacific Ocean.' The regional Ruthenian orientation was

represented by the Greek Catholic hierarchy and by the Prešov branch of the *Dukhnovych Society. Their views commonly appeared in the unofficial organ of the Greek Catholic eparchy, *Russkoe slovo* (Prešov 1924–38). They were marked by a strong attachment to local culture and institutions as well as to the language used in the area, one of the *Transcarpathian dialects that they regarded virtually as a separate Subcarpathian Ruthenian language.

In 1930 D. Zubrytsky and I. Nevytska set up in Prešov a branch of the Ukrainianophile Prosvita society, which was also based in Uzhhorod. The group published a few issues of a Ukrainian-language newspaper, *Slovo naroda* (Prešov 1931–2), but failed to develop a broad network of village affiliates.

A modest renaissance in literature also took place in the Prešov region during the interwar years. The older generation, best represented by I. Kyzak, was joined by new writers, such as I. Nevytska, D. Zubrytsky, F. Lazoryk, A. Farynych, and M. Horniak. Several other natives of the Prešov region, such as the poet S. *Sabol and the playwright P. Fedor, lived and published in nearby Subcarpathian Ruthenia. Among the most prolific scholars at the time was N. Beskyd. With the exception of Nevytska, Zubrytsky, and Sabol, most other representatives of the intelligentsia of the Prešov region wrote in Russian and for the most part supported a Russophile national orientation.

The decade of international crises, 1938–48. Following the signing of the *Munich Agreement in September 1938 the state of Czechoslovakia was redrawn and transformed into a federal republic. As a result both Slovakia and Subcarpathian Ruthenia received their long-awaited autonomy. In October the Ukrainians of the Prešov region, now living in an autonomous Slovakia, formed a national council led by parliamentary deputies I. Peshchak and P. Zhydovsky. The council called for greater autonomy for the Prešov region and its eventual incorporation into Subcarpathian Ruthenia. The Subcarpathian autonomous government in Uzhhorod included Peshchak as a state secretary representing the Prešov region.

In early November the Ukrainophile A. *Voloshyn became head of the government of *Carpatho-Ukraine. Voloshyn's government demanded union with the Prešov region, but the local population and their predominantly Russophile leaders now rejected association with what they considered an alien 'Ukrainian' government. On 22 November the national council in Prešov voted against unification with Carpatho-Ukraine. Instead it urged participation in the December elections to the Slovak Diet. The issue of unification soon proved a moot point. On 15 March 1939 Hitler made Bohemia and Moravia protectorates of the Third Reich, Slovakia became an independent state allied to Germany, and Hungary forcibly annexed Carpatho-Ukraine as well as a section of eastern Slovakia that included 36 Ukrainian villages (20,000 people) from the Prešov region.

For the duration of the war most of the Prešov region was under the control of a state governed by Slovaks in Bratislava. The government aimed to Slovakize all aspects of the country and targeted the Ukrainians of the Prešov region, since immediately after the Munich crisis they had expressed a desire to unite with Subcarpathian Ruthenia. The national council was banned, and the activity of the Dukhnovych Society restricted. Ukrainians were allowed three deputies to the Slovak Diet, and they were expected to support the government's policy. One newspaper was permitted to operate. Only the Greek Catholic church under Bishop Goidych was able to defend the national interests of the Prešov region's Ukrainians; he did so particularly by assuming responsibility for teaching in elementary schools.

The Ukrainians were among the first in Slovakia to organize an underground resistance, the Carpatho-Ruthenian Autonomous Union for National Liberation (Karpatorusskii Avtonomnyi Soiuz Natsionalnogo Osvobozhdeniia, or KRASNO). They also received assurances from the underground Slovak National Council that the restored state would be 'a fraternal republic of three equal nations' – Czechs, Slovaks, and Carpatho-Ruthenians. Almost immediately after the withdrawal of German troops village and town councils were formed throughout the Prešov region. On 1 March 1945 their representatives met in Prešov to form the *Ukrainian People's Council of the Prešov Region. That was the first time that the name Ukrainian had been used in the title of an organization in the Prešov region. The People's Council also reiterated the long-standing desire for unification with their Transcarpathian brethren, who had been calling for 'unification with the Soviet Union' since November 1944. That decision worried the Slovak leaders, who urged Ukrainians in the Prešov region to remain within Czechoslovakia. To that end they guaranteed full rights for the Prešov region Ukrainians as a national minority. By May 1945 the Prešov council finally declared its intention to support the new Czechoslovak government headed by the pre-1938 president, E. *Beneš, but only on the condition that political and cultural autonomy be granted. On 26 June 1945 the area of Transcarpathian Ukraine became part of Soviet Ukraine, and the Ukrainians of the Prešov region were left territorially divided from their Transcarpathian brethren.

According to an agreement on population transfers signed in July 1946 between Czechoslovakia and the Soviet Union, Prešov region Ukrainians were given a chance to emigrate to the Ukrainian SSR if they wished to. More than 8,000 local Ukrainians did so, largely for economic reasons. They settled mainly near Rivne in lands abandoned by Volhynian Czechs who had gone to Bohemia.

The Communist party emerged as the strongest political group in postwar Czechoslovakia. In the Prešov region the Communists obtained 45.9 percent of the vote in the open elections of 1946. Communists also dominated the Ukrainian People's Council, which continued to demand that it be recognized as a political body representing Ukrainians. The demand was rejected by the Slovak National Council in 1947, and the rejection highlighted the fact that Ukrainians would have no special autonomous or corporate political status in the restored Czechoslovak republic. The People's Council was more successful in matters of culture: it sponsored the Ukrainian National Theater, a publishing house, an office for schools, a youth organization, and the influential newspaper *Priashevshchina* (1945–52). In spite of the People's Council's Ukrainian name, much of its business was conducted in Russian.

1948 to 1968. In 1948 the plurality of Czech political life was replaced by communist domination. Major political and social transformations were then undertaken, three of which were to have a profound impact on the Ukrainians in the Prešov region: collectivization, de-Catholicization, and Ukrainianization. Those occurred more or less simultaneously between 1949 and 1953. By 1960 an average of only 63 percent of the farmland in the Prešov region was collectivized. The process of de-Catholicization went much more quickly. The Greek Catholic church was liquidated at a church council in Prešov on 28 April 1950, and all 239 former Greek Catholic parishes, as well as 20 Orthodox parishes, were reorganized into the Orthodox eparchies of Prešov and Michalovce within the Russian Orthodox Patriarchate of Moscow. In November 1951 the two Prešov region eparchies became part of the newly created Autocephalous Orthodox church of Czechoslovakia.

The question of national identity was also settled by administrative fiat. Following the Soviet model in Transcarpathia, the regime decided to promote a Ukrainian identity and cultural orientation. Standard Ukrainian was introduced in schools as a subject in 1949. In June 1952 the Slovak Communist party in Bratislava decreed that Ukrainian should be used in all schools of the Prešov region, and the following year it became the language of instruction for all subjects. The local Russophile intelligentsia were compelled to Ukrainianize or lose their positions, and the local population was expected to identify itself as Ukrainian. Most of the new postwar organizations, whether or not they were Russophile in orientation, were liquidated between 1949 and 1952, including the People's Council.

In 1951 a new nonpolitical and acceptably socialist organization was created, the *Cultural Association of Ukrainian Workers (KSUT). It became the dominant representative association for Ukrainians in Czechoslovakia, until it was succeeded in 1990 by the Union of Ruthenian-Ukrainians of Czechoslovakia. The KSUT sponsored a variety of publications, organized lectures throughout the Prešov region, supported (by 1963) 242 local folk ensembles, and sponsored annual drama, sport, and folk festivals, the largest of which has been held annually since 1956 in Svydnyk. The Czechoslovak government also provided funds to establish the *Svydnyk Museum of Ukrainian Culture (1956), a department of Ukrainian language and literature at Šafárik University in Prešov, and the *Duklia Ukrainian Folk Ensemble as part of the Ukrainian National Theater in Prešov.

While the Prešov region's Russophile intelligentsia was adjusting to the new cultural order, some Ukrainian activists from Transcarpathian Ukraine, such as I. *Hryts-Duda and V. *Grendzha-Donsky, helped to fill the gap. Also of importance were Ukrainian scholars from Prague, among them I. *Pankevych and I. and O. *Zilynsky. Former Russophiles from Subcarpathian Ruthenia who were active in the Prešov region's cultural organizations included F. *Ivanchov, Y. *Kostiuk, O. Liubymov, and O. *Rudlovchak. Several younger Prešov region intellectuals were sent to Kiev to supplement their Ukrainian education. Since the 1960s the Prešov region has had a growing number of talented native-born Ukrainian leaders. They include belletrists and publicists, such as Yu. *Bacha, V. *Datsei, S. *Hostyniak, F. *Lazoryk, I. *Matsynsky, M. *Shmaida, and V. *Zozuliak; the theatrical director I. Ivancho; and scholars, such as the linguists P. Bunganych, V. *Latta, M. *Shtets, the literary historians F. *Kovach and A. Shlepetsky, the historians I. Baitsura, A. Kovach, M.

Rychalka, O. Stavrovsky, and I. Vanat, the ethnographers M. *Mushynka and M. Hyriak, and the musicologist Yu. Tsymbora.

Despite the continued and substantial funding by the Czechoslovak government for the cultural development of the Ukrainian minority, considerable assimilation (to the Slovak nationality) has taken place. Some scholars believe the assimilation is the result of the local population's unwillingness to accept a Ukrainian identity seemingly imposed upon it by external forces. The response is most graphically revealed in the census figures (Prešov inhabitants were asked to identify themselves as Rusnak/Russian/Rusyn/Ukrainian or Hungarian/Czech/Slovak) and school statistics. The census data reveal a decline in the number of people who identify themselves as Ukrainians in the 20th century despite a natural increase in their numbers (from 88,010 in 1880 to 111,280 in 1910 and 37,179 in 1980).

The number of schools teaching Ukrainian (including the regional Transcarpathian dialect) declined during the period 1948–66 from 275 to 68 elementary schools, from 41 to 3 municipal schools, and from 4 to 1 gymnasiums. In many cases Slovak instruction replaced Ukrainian.

The Prague Spring and after. During the political thaw under the regime of A. Dubček, Ukrainians began raising the issue of their status within the country. In March 1968 the KSUT called for a national congress to reconstitute the People's Council, and the newspaper *Nove zhyttia* burst forth with a series of articles demanding political, economic, and cultural autonomy for Ukrainians. The discussion regarding territorial autonomy for the Prešov region that was raised in the debate, however, overstepped the bounds that the Party would tolerate, and the proposed national congress was abruptly called off by the authorities. Greater success was realized in religious affairs when the Greek Catholic church was again legalized, in June 1968. It failed, however, to assume its historic role as a unifying force for Ukrainian interests when it became embroiled in disputes with the Orthodox church over property division and with the church's Slovak clergy over language and leadership issues. Other demands centered on the old question of national identity. Meetings, letters, and newspaper articles reflected a popular desire to do away with the 'artificial' Ukrainian orientation of the 'little band of intellectuals' and return to 'our own' schools and cultural leaders. The people were once again officially referred to as Ruthenians – which term had been forbidden since the introduction of Ukrainianization in 1952 – and the proposed national council was to be called the Council of Czechoslovak Ruthenians (Rada Chekhoslovatskykh Rusyniv).

The discussions and plans for change were cut short on 21 August 1968 when the invasion of more than half a million Warsaw Pact troops led by the Soviet Union put an end to the Prague Spring. The shock of external intervention was compounded for Ukrainians of the Prešov region by the protracted Catholic-Orthodox religious struggle and an increasingly hostile attitude toward them on the part of the Slovaks, who were openly critical of their political and cultural demands and even accused Ukrainians of collaboration with the Soviets.

In those circumstances Ukrainian villagers often tried to demonstrate their loyalty by demanding Slovak schools. By 1970 there was only one elementary school using Ukrainian exclusively and 29 with some degree of instruction. That year only 42,146 (out of a potential 130,000 to 140,000) Ukrainians identified themselves as such in the census, in spite of a campaign to do so by the Ukrainian intelligentsia. Beginning in 1970 a policy of 'political consolidation' removed supporters of the Prague Spring from the Communist party. Many also lost their jobs, among them the more vocal leaders in the Prešov region. Supporters were also expelled from the Ukrainian Writers' Union and forbidden to publish for periods of time that in some cases lasted two decades. Nonetheless, belletristic and scholarly books and serial publications have continued to appear, and Ukrainian cultural institutions, such as KSUT, the museum in Svydnyk, and the university department in Prešov, maintain about the same level of activity with even greater financial backing than they had before 1968.

Since the Second World War there have been substantial socioeconomic developments in the Prešov region, with the establishment of a communications system, the building of new roads, and the setting up of several industrial enterprises. The development has drastically changed the region's social structure. By 1970 only 30.1 percent of Ukrainians were engaged in agriculture and forestry, and another 24.3 percent in nonindustrial pursuits (probably related to agriculture) whereas 27 percent worked in industry, 9.9 percent in the building trades, 4.5 percent in stores and restaurants, and 2.9 percent in transport. In spite of such improvements the average income of Ukrainians in 1968 was almost three-fifths of the all-Czechoslovak average. The discrepancy has spurred many young people to emigrate to Slovak cities in the eastern part of the country, or westward to the industrial regions of northern Moravia, where wages are much higher; their migration has caused labor shortages on the farms and turned many Ukrainian villages into little more than havens for older people.

That state of affairs has raised some questions about the future of Ukrainians in the Prešov region as a group. For many years assimilation was staved off by the area's economic backwardness and geographic isolation. Social and economic mobility has now altered the physical base of Ukrainian life and increasingly brought younger Ukrainians into the mainstream of a largely Slovak world. Slovakization is further facilitated by the advent of television that is exclusively in Czech or Slovak, the similarity in language and religion between the two groups, and increasing interethnic marriage in which Slovak becomes the dominant medium of the household.

Czechoslovakia's Velvet Revolution of November 1989 profoundly changed life throughout the country, including the Prešov region. Communist rule came to an end and pluralism was rapidly implemented in political, cultural, religious, and economic affairs. Since that time the Ukrainian intelligentsia of the Prešov region has split into two factions, each with its own organization and publications. Those who eschew the name Ukrainian and insist on calling themselves by the historical name Ruthenian formed the Ruthenian Renaissance society (Rusynska Obroda) in March 1990. It began publishing its own newspaper (*Narodny novynky*) and magazine (*Rusyn*) using the local Ruthenian dialect of Ukrainian. Together with the newly created World Congress of Ruthenians (established in March 1991) it promotes the idea that the population of the Prešov region together with that of the neighboring Lemko region and Transcarpathia comprise a 'distinct fourth' East Slavic nationality. The Oleksander Dukhnovych Theater (formerly the *Prešov Ukrainian National Theater) has joined the Ruthenian Renaissance Society's orientation and now stages plays in the local dialect of Ukrainian. The Union of Ruthenian-Ukrainians of Czechoslovakia (SRUCh), since February 1990 the successor of KSUT, continues to publish in Ukrainian and to favor a Ukrainian self-identification and closer ties with the newly independent Ukraine. The factiousness which effectively splits the Ukrainian minority in the Prešov region has been recognized and supported since 1990 by the Czecho-Slovak federal and the Slovak republic governments.

BIBLIOGRAPHY
Hnatiuk, V. 'Slovaky chy rusyny? Prychynok do vyiasnennia sporu pro natsionalnist' zakhidnykh rusyniv,' ZNTSh, 42 (1900)
Húsek, J. Národopisná hranice mezi Slováky a Karpatorusy (Bratislava 1925)
Halaga, O.R. Slovanské osídlenie Potisia a východoslovenskí gréckokatolíci (Košice 1947)
Shlepetskii, A. (ed). Priashevshchina: Istoriko-literaturnyi sbornik (Prague 1948)
Haraksim, L. K sociálnym a kúlturnym dejinám Ukrajincov na Slovensku do roku 1867 (Bratislava 1961)
Varsik, B. Osídlenie košickej kotliny, 3 vols (Bratislava 1964–77)
Bajcura, I. Ukrajinská otázka v ČSSR (Košice 1967)
Stavrovs'kyi, O. Slovats'ko-pol'sko-ukraïns'ke prykordonnia do 18-ho stolittia (Bratislava–Prešov 1967)
Kubinyi, J. The History of Prjašiv Eparchy (Rome 1970)
Vanat, I. Narysy novitnoï istoriï ukraïntsiv Skhidnoï Slovachchyny, 2 vols (Bratislava–Prešov 1979, 1985)
Rudlovchak, O. Bilia dzherel suchasnosti: Rozvidky, statti, narysy (Bratislava–Prešov 1981)
Magocsi, P.R. The Rusyn–Ukrainians of Czechoslovakia: An Historical Survey (Vienna 1983)
Pekar, A.B. The History of the Church in Carpathian Rus' (New York 1992)

P.R. Magocsi

Scene from a performance of Ivan Franko's Ukradene shchastia (Stolen Happiness) at the Prešov Ukrainian National Theater

Prešov Ukrainian National Theater (Ukrainskyi natsionalnyi teatr). A professional musical-drama *touring theater organized in 1946 for the Ukrainian minority in Czechoslovakia. Also known as the Ukrainian People's Theater, in 1957 it became a drama theater, and in 1961 a resident theater. Since its first production, of M. Starytsky's Oi ne khody, Hrytsiu ... (Don't Go to the Party, Hryts ...) in 1946, the Ukrainian National Theater has staged over 300 plays. Its repertoire spans the works of local Ukrainian authors, classical Ukrainian dramatists, Czech and Slovak authors, and world classical dramatists as well as the works of modern Western, Eastern European, and Soviet dramatists. Yu. Sherehii, V. Bavoliar, Yu. Felbaba, and Ya. Sysak have worked as directors, and M. and T. Symko, Y. and M. Korba, Yu. Yakub, and A. Lutsyk as actors. Since 1985 its artistic director has been I. Ivancho. In 1990 it was renamed the Dukhnovych Theater.

BIBLIOGRAPHY
Ukraïns'kyi natsional'nyi teatr na sluzhbi narodu (Prešov 1976)

Press, Iryna, b 10 March 1939 in Kharkiv. Champion hurdler and pentathlete. She won Olympic gold medals in the women's 80-m hurdles in 1960 and in the pentathlon (world and Olympic record) in 1964, and set 12 world records in the women's 80-m hurdles. She has lived in Leningrad and Moscow since the late 1950s, and has received a candidate's degree in pedagogy.

Press, Tamara, b 10 May 1937 in Kharkiv. Women's shot put and discus champion. She was the 1958 European discus champion, won Olympic gold medals in the shot put (1960 and 1964) and discus throw (1964), and set a total of 11 world records in the shot put (1959–68) and discus throw (1960–7). She lives in St Petersburg and has received a candidate's degree in pedagogy.

Press. The development of the Ukrainian press is closely connected to that of organized Ukrainian cultural, economic, and nation-building activity and political thought. In general, until the end of the first half of the 19th century in Austrian-ruled Ukraine and 1905 in Russian-ruled Ukraine, conditions were such that a Ukrainian-language press could not freely develop. Ukrainian-language periodicals were established through the efforts of individual Ukrainians, and despite inadequate financing, a limited readership, and constant *censorship and administrative restrictions, they grew in number, content, and circulation, gradually encompassing all facets of national life.

Western Ukraine. The first periodical published in Ukraine was a French-language weekly in Austrian-ruled Lviv, *Gazette de Léopol (1776). The first daily newspapers were published in Polish in Lviv: Dziennik patryjotycznykch polityków (1792–3, 1794–8), edited by the Ukrainian Rev M. Harasevych, and Gazeta Lwowska (1811–1918), which became a state-owned paper in 1847 and from 1890 carried a Ukrainian-language supplement, *Narodna chasopys.

During the Revolution of 1848–9, the first Ukrainian-language papers in Western Ukraine – *Zoria halytska (1848–57), the pro-Polish *Dnewnyk Ruskij (1848), the Russophile Novyny (1849) and *Pchola (1849), and the Austrian government's *Halycho-ruskii vistnyk (1849–50) – were founded in Lviv. The first Ukrainian women's periodical, Lada, was published in Lviv in 1853 (15 issues).

With the introduction of the 1860 Austrian constitution, the Western Ukrainian press was able to develop much more freely. Between 1862 and 1866 the Galician *populists in Lviv published the journals *Vechernytsi, *Meta,

*Nyva, and *Rusalka; then they put out *Pravda (1867–80, 1884, 1888–96), a journal that assumed a national importance, and the semiweekly Osnova (1870–2). The *Russophiles also issued their own periodicals, notably the paper *Slovo (1861–87) in Lviv and the journal *Nauka (1872–1902) in Kolomyia. Other periodicals also appeared, such as the satirical magazine *Strakhopud (1863–8, 1872–3, 1880–2, 1886–93), the agricultural-economic papers *Nedilia (1865–6) and *Hospodar (1869–72), the women's semimonthly *Rusalka (1868–70), the children's magazine *Lastivka (1869–81), the religious semimonthly *Ruskii Sion (1871–83), the student journal *Druh (1874–7), and the educational gazette *Hazeta shkol'na (1875–9). Outside Lviv the first Ukrainian-language periodical in Galicia was *Holos narodnyi (1865–8) in Kolomyia. In Bukovyna the first Ukrainian periodical was the weekly Bukovynskaia zoria, published by I. Hlibovytsky in Chernivtsi in 1870 (16 issues).

With the imposition of the *Ems Ukase in 1876 in Russian-ruled Ukraine, moderate and conservative Ukrainian-language newspapers in Galicia and Bukovyna – notably *Bat'kivshchyna (1879–96), *Dilo (1880–1939), *Svoboda (1897–1919, 1922–39), *Ruslan (1897–14), *Narodne slovo (1907–11), and *Nove slovo (1912–14) in Lviv, and *Bukovyna (1885–1918), *Ruska rada (1898–1908), and *Narodnyi holos (1909–14) in Chernivtsi – fulfilled the role of 'national' organs. At the same time they were forced to compete with a persistent Russophile press – eg, *Russkaia rada (1871–1912) in Kolomyia; *Prolom (1880–2), *Vistnyk Narodnoho doma (1882–1924), Novyi prolom (1883–7), Chervonaia Rus' (1888–91), *Russkoe slovo (1890–1914), *Halytskaia Rus' (1891–2), *Halychanyn (1893–1913), *Zhivaia mysl' (1902–5), *Prikarpatskaia Rus' (1909–15, 1918–20), and Holos naroda (1909–14) in Lviv; *Russka pravda (1888–92) in Vienna; and *Pravoslavnaia Bukovina (1893–1905), Bukovynski vidomosty (1895–1909), *Pravoslavnaia Rus' (1909–10), and *Russkaia pravda (1910–14) in Chernivtsi. In Hungarian-ruled Transcarpathia the press either was Russophile – eg, *Karpat (1873–86) and *Listok (1885–1903) in Uzhhorod – or reflected a regional identity using the Transcarpathian dialect – eg, *Nauka (1897–1914) in Uzhhorod and Nedilia (1898–1918) in Budapest.

In the late 1870s, under the influence of M. *Drahomanov's ideas, the Galician populists split into moderates and socialists, and the first Ukrainian socialist miscellanies – I. Franko and M. Pavlyk's *Hromads'kyi druh, *Dzvin, and *Molot in Lviv in 1878, and Drahomanov's influential *Hromada (1878–82) in Geneva – were published. Franko edited the first socialist monthly, *S'vit (1881–2), but it was only after the creation of the *Ukrainian Radical party (URP) in 1890 that a truly viable Ukrainian radical and socialist press appeared in Galicia and Bukovyna: the URP organs *Narod (1890–5), *Hromads'kyi holos (1892–1939), *Khliborob (1891–5), *Radykal (1895–6), Narodna sprava (1907–10), and *Hromadianyn (1909–11), and the *Ukrainian Social Democratic party (USDP) organs *Volia (1900–7), *Zemlia i volia (1906–13, 1919–20, 1922–4), *Chervonyi prapor (1906–7), Borba (1908–14), *Nash holos (1910–11), and *Vpered (1911–13, 1918–24). In addition, organs of the underground *Revolutionary Ukrainian party and *Ukrainian Social Democratic Workers' party (USDRP) in Russian-ruled Ukraine – *Haslo (1902–3), *Pratsia (1904–6), *Selianyn (1903–6), *Pratsia (1909–10), *Robitnyk (1910), and *Nash holos (1910–11) – were printed in Chernivtsi or Lviv and smuggled into Russian-ruled Ukraine.

The first Ukrainian-language academic periodicals were published in Lviv: the Halytsko-Ruska Matytsia society's Naukovyi sbornyk (1865–8) and the Shevchenko Scientific Society's (NTSh) *Zapysky Naukovoho tovarystva im. Shevchenka (est 1892) and *Chasopys pravnycha (1889–1906, 1912). The first major Ukrainian literary-cultural and scholarly journals were also published there: the NTSh's *Zoria (1880–97), which became a pan-Ukrainian literary forum in the 1890s, and I. Franko's more radical *Zhytie i slovo (1894–7). The latter two journals ceased publication to allow M. Hrushevsky to establish *Literaturno-naukovyi vistnyk, a journal published in Lviv (1898–1906), then in Kiev (1907–14), and again in Lviv (1922–32) that until 1919 played a seminal role in the development of Ukrainian literature. Also published in Lviv were the pedagogical periodicals Uchytel' (1889–1914) and Nasha shkola (1909–14, 1916–18); the modernist journals *Ruska khata (1905–6), *S'vit (1906–7), and Buduchyna (1909–10); the first Ukrainian arts magazine, Artystychnyi vistnyk (1905–7); the progressive women's paper *Meta (1908); the legal journal *Pravnychyi vistnyk (1910–13); the first Ukrainian sports papers, Sokil's'ki visty (1909–10) and *Visty z Zaporozha (1910–14); the first Ukrainian-language medical journal, *Zdorovlie (1912–14); and the popular cultural magazine *Iliustrovana Ukraïna (1913–14). Many other periodicals were also published (see *Agricultural periodicals, *Children's magazines, *Economic press, *Humoristic and satiric press, *Legal press, *Pedagogical periodicals, *Religious press, *Student press, and *Women's press).

Russian-ruled Ukraine. The first periodicals in Russian-ruled Ukraine were published in Russian in the cultural and academic center, Kharkiv: the weekly magazine Khar'kovskii ezhenedel'nik (1812), the cultural-cum-scholarly journals *Ukrainskii vestnik (1816–19) and *Ukrainskii zhurnal (1824–5), the satirical magazine *Khar'kovskii Demokrit (1816), the agricultural magazine *Ukrainskii domovod (1817), and the weekly newspaper *Khar'kovskie izvestiia (1817–23). Others appeared in French and Russian in Odessa: the biweekly newspapers Messager de la Russie méridionale (1820) and Vestnik Iuzhnoi Rossii (1821), the semiweekly paper Journal d'Odessa (1824–81), and the semiweekly (from 1864 daily) *Odesskii vestnik (1827–94).

Elsewhere in Russian-ruled Ukraine, it took nearly two decades for the first periodicals to appear. In Kiev the first was the contract-fair paper Kievskie ob"iavleniia (1835–8). From 1838 official Russian-language newspapers titled Gubernskie vedomosti were published weekly and later more often (eg, daily in Kharkiv from 1874) in every gubernial capital.

Although some Ukrainian prose and poetry appeared in the Kharkiv periodicals in 1817, thereafter the publication of Ukrainian-language belles lettres was limited to nonserial miscellanies (see *Almanacs). Nearly half a century passed before Ukrainian materials reappeared in a periodical published in the Russian Empire – the literary and scholarly monthly *Osnova (1861–2) in St Petersburg. Despite its brevity Osnova had a decisive impact on the development of a Ukrainian national consciousness in both the Russian and the Austrian empires. After its suppression the only periodical to publish material in the Ukrainian language in the Russian Empire was L. Hlibov's briefly published weekly, *Chernigovskii listok (Chernihiv, 1861–3). The first Ukrainian newspaper – in spirit though not in language – was *Kievskii telegraf (1859–76), the unofficial organ of the *Hromada of Kiev. Repeatedly denounced by the Russian tsarist paper *Kievlianin (1864–1919), it was shut down in 1876, the year that the *Ems Ukase forbade all printing in Ukrainian in the Russian Empire. During the next three decades the journal *Kievskaia starina (1882–1907) was the only periodical promoting Ukrainian culture and Ukrainian studies in Russian-ruled Ukraine.

From the 1860s on, Eparkhial'nye vedomosti, official newspapers of the Russian Orthodox church, were published semimonthly and later more frequently in every eparchial see. No legal newspapers in Russian-ruled Ukraine – including dailies founded in Kiev, Mykolaiv, Kharkiv, Katerynoslav, Odessa, Zhytomyr, Kamianets-Podilskyi, and Yelysavethrad from the 1860s on – were allowed to print independent political accounts and editorials; instead they reprinted news provided by the official St Petersburg press.

Scholars and scientists were able to contribute to Russian-language academic periodicals published in Ukraine, including the Imperial Agricultural Society of Southern Russia's Zapiski (est 1832), *Zapiski Imperatorskogo Odesskogo obshchestva istorii i drevnostei (est 1844), and *Zapiski Imperatorskogo Novorossiiskogo universiteta (est 1853) in Odessa; *Trudy Kievskoi dukhovnoi akademii (est 1860) and Kievskie universitetskie izvestiia (est 1861) in Kiev; the Zapiski published by branches of the Imperial Russian Technical Society in Kiev (from 1871), Kharkiv (from 1881), and Odessa (from 1885); and *Zapiski Imperatorskogo Khar'kovskogo universiteta (est 1874) in Kharkiv.

During the Russian Revolution of 1905–6, restrictions and censorship were relaxed, and the Ukrainian-language press flourished. The first periodical to appear was the newspaper *Khliborob in Lubni, five issues of which were published briefly in 1905 before it was shut down. Many periodicals were published in Kiev, among them the influential dailies *Hromads'ka dumka (1905–6) and *Rada (1906–14); the literary monthlies *Nova hromada (1906), *Ukraïns'ka khata (1909–14), *Dzvin (1913–14), and *Siaivo (1913–14); the satirical weekly *Shershen' (1906); the children's magazine *Moloda Ukraïna (1908–12, 1914); the weekly papers *Slovo (1907–9), Selo (1909–11), *Zasiv (1911–12), and *Maiak (1913–14); the scholarly *Zapysky Ukraïns'koho naukovoho tovarystva u Kyievi (1908–13); the pedagogical monthly *Svitlo (1910–14); and the semimonthly co-operative magazine Nasha kooperatsiia (1913–14). Thirty-odd Ukrainian-language periodicals were published elsewhere. Notable were the weekly *Ridnyi krai (1905–12, 1914–16) in Poltava, Kiev, and Hadiache; the farmers' weekly *Svitova zirnytsia (1906–13) in Mohyliv-Podilskyi, Penkivka (Podilia gubernia), and Kiev; the beekeeping magazine Ukraïns'ke bzhil'nytstvo (1906–10) in St Petersburg and Kiev; the illustrated semimonthly *Dniprovi khvyli (1910–13) in Katerynoslav; and the weekly *Snip (1912–13) in Kharkiv. Plagued with financial difficulties and subjected to official bans, restrictions, and new strict censorship laws, most periodicals were short-lived.

Outside Ukraine to 1914. The first Ukrainian-language periodicals outside Ukraine were published in Vienna by the Austrian government – *Vistnyk (1850–66), Vistnyk zakonov derzhavnykh i pravytel'stva (1854–8), and Vistnyk zakonov derzhavnykh dlia korolevstv i kraev ... (1872–1916). At the turn of the 20th century, Ukrainians published in Vienna two German-language periodicals – *Ruthenische Revue (1903–5) and *Ukrainische Rundschau (1905–15) – to inform the Western public about the Ukrainian question.

The first periodical to serve Transcarpathia's Ruthenians was a religious weekly published in Budapest, *Tserkovnaia gazeta (1856–8). Later another weekly, Nedilia (1898–1918), was published there.

In the Russian Empire, after the aforementioned Osnova (1861–2), the first Ukrainian-language periodicals outside Ukraine, *Ukrainskii vestnik (1906), Nasha Duma (1907), and *Ridna sprava – Dums'ki visty (1907), were published in St Petersburg as the organs of the Ukrainian caucus in the Russian State Duma. The USDRP monthly *Vil'na Ukraïna (1906) was also published there. A short-lived weekly, *Zoria (1906), and an influential Russian-language monthly dealing with Ukraine, *Ukrainskaia zhizn' (1912–17), were published in Moscow.

The immigrant press in the New World. Overseas the first wave of immigrants from Western Ukraine established their own periodicals. In the United States the first Ukrainian newspaper, *Ameryka (1886–90), was published in Shenandoah, Pennsylvania. The first major paper, the Ruthenian (now Ukrainian) National Association's *Svoboda, was founded in New York City in 1893 and has remained the most important Ukrainian newspaper in the United States. Other papers were founded in the 1900s and 1910s, among them the still extant *Narodna volia (est 1911) in Olyphant, Pennsylvania (now in Scranton), and *Ameryka (est 1912) in New Britain, Connecticut (now in Philadelphia).

In Canada the first Ukrainian newspaper, *Kanadiiskyi farmer, supported by the Canadian Liberal party, was founded in Winnipeg in 1903. It was followed by a similar but short-lived paper, Slovo (1904–5), supported by the Conservative party. A still-extant weekly, *Ukraïns'kyi holos, was founded in Winnipeg in 1910. Many other newspapers with differing political and religious views were published in the United States and Canada between 1907 and 1914 and in the interwar years. The first Ukrainian newspaper in Brazil, *Zoria, was published in Curitiba in 1907–10.

TABLE 1
Newspapers published in Ukrainian in selected years, 1848–1913

	1848	1861	1881	1890	1900	1906	1913
Within Russian Empire	–	1	–	1	1	17	19
Outside Russian Empire	2	3	28	32	39	80	122
Total	2	4	28	33	40	97	141

In 1913, 141 Ukrainian-language periodicals were published throughout the world. Only 19 of them were in the Russian Empire, as compared to 234 periodicals in Polish, 13 in Yiddish, and 21 in Armenian. At the same time, in Russian-ruled Ukraine 226 Russian periodicals were published. Eighty Ukrainian periodicals were published in Austria-Hungary: 66 in Galicia, 8 in Bukovyna, 2 in Transcarpathia, and 4 in Vienna or Budapest. Although publications of the Ukrainian press at home and abroad grew in number, there was not often a corresponding rise in quality. Of the newspapers published there were only three dailies and very few weeklies, and their editors for the most part lacked professional training. Most periodicals were financially unstable: few had private benefactors, none had state or municipal subsidies, and all had little advertising revenue and a limited readership.

1914–17. The First World War was catastrophic for the Ukrainian press. The tsarist authorities banned and closed down most Ukrainian-language periodicals the day after Russia entered the war, and on 3 January 1915 all Ukrainian publications were prohibited within the Kiev Military District. Only *Ridnyi krai*, published in 1915–16 in Hadiache by O. Pchilka, was allowed to appear in the **yaryzhka* alphabet. The literary monthly **Osnova*, published by A. Nikovsky in Odessa in 1915, was shut down after three issues, and other periodicals in Russian-ruled Ukraine that began legal publication in 1915 and 1916 met with the same fate. The only surviving sanctioned Ukrainophile organ in the Russian Empire was *Ukrainskaia zhizn'* in Moscow. In these circumstances only clandestine publications, such as *Borot'ba* of the *Ukrainian Party of Socialist Revolutionaries (UPSR) and the Ukrainian Radical Democratic Association's *Vil'na dumka*, were circulated secretly in Kiev in 1915.

During the Russian military occupation of Galicia and Bukovyna, all Ukrainian publications there were closed down and banned, and only Russophile and Polish ones were allowed. Following the Russian retreat from Lviv in June 1915, however, the Western Ukrainian press was revived (eg, the new paper **Ukraïns'ke slovo* [1915–18] and **Shliakhy* [1913–18], which became an organ of the Ukrainian Sich Riflemen). Propaganda promoting the Ukrainian cause was disseminated in newspapers published by the Austrian government for Ukrainian soldiers serving in the Austrian army in **Vidrodzhennia Ukraïny* (1918), and for Ukrainian soldiers interned by the Russian army in Austrian POW camps in the Russian-language *Nedelia* (1916–18). The newspapers *Dilo*, *Svoboda*, and *Bukovyna* were published in Vienna during the war. There they played an important part in Ukrainian journalism, as did the separatist newspaper **Vistnyk Soiuza vyzvolennia Ukraïny* (1914–18) of the *Union for the Liberation of Ukraine (SVU). The SVU also published **Ukrainische Nachrichten* (1914–18) in Vienna and *La *Revue ukrainienne* (1915, 1917) in Lausanne, and it laid the groundwork for newspapers published in POW camps holding Ukrainians in Austria and Germany, such as **Prosvitnyi lystok* (1915–16) and *Hromads'ka dumka* (1917–18) in Wetzlar, *Rozvaha* (1915–18) in Freistadt, **Rozsvit* (1916–18) in Rastatt, and **Vil'ne slovo* (1916–18) and *Selianyn* in Salzwedel.

A few other Ukrainian periodicals were published in other languages to disseminate information about Ukraine and the Ukrainian cause: the General (later Supreme) Ukrainian Council's **Ukrainische Korrespondenz* (1914–18) in Vienna, the monthly *L'*Ukraine* (1915–20) in Lausanne, and the government-sponsored *Negyilya* and **Ukránia* (1916–17) in Budapest.

1917–20. The February Revolution in Russia, the collapse of Austria-Hungary, and the establishment of Ukrainian statehood created favorable conditions for the development of the Ukrainian press. Several partisan dailies came into being in Kiev in March and April 1917, notably **Nova rada* (1917–19), **Robitnycha hazeta* (1917–19), **Narodnia volia* (1917–19), and **Borot'ba* (1917–20). Later the dailies *Hromads'ke slovo* (1917) and *Promin'* (1917), the nonpartisan daily **Vidrodzhennia* (1918), and the semiofficial organ of the UNR Directory **Trybuna* (1918–19) appeared, as well as *Trudova respublyka* (1918) and many

other Ukrainian, Russian, Jewish, and Polish newspapers.

Ukrainian newspapers published in gubernial and county centers in 1917 and 1918 were also predominantly partisan, a reflection of the political division of Ukrainian society. Thus, for example, the USDRP published *Robitnyk* in Kharkiv, *Holos robitnyka* and *Nasha sprava* in Katerynoslav, *Vil'nyi holos* in Poltava, and *Borot'ba* in Kamianets-Podilskyi; the UPSR published *Rukh* in Kharkiv, *Sotsiialist-revoliutsioner* in Poltava, and *Zemlia i volia* in Katerynoslav; the Union of Autonomists-Federalists published *Vil'na Ukraïna* in Uman; and the Ukrainian Party of Socialists-Independentists published *Samostiinyk* in Kiev and, later, the daily *Ukraïna*. The Peasant Union, Prosvita societies, co-operative associations, and gubernial people's councils (former zemstvos) also published a great number of newspapers.

In Kiev new literary, scholarly, and art journals appeared: **Knyhar* (1917–20), **Teatral'ni visty* (1917), the revived *Literaturno-naukovyi vistnyk* (1917–19, transferred from Moscow to Kiev in 1918), *Universal'nyi zhurnal* (1918), **Nashe mynule* (1918–19), **Mystetstvo* (1919–20), **Muzahet* (1919), and the satirical *Gedz'*, *Rep'iakhy*, and *Budiak*.

Specialized and professional periodicals also appeared, most of them in Kiev: eg, in education, *Vil'na ukraïns'ka shkola*, *Osvita* (Kamianets-Podilskyi), and *Nova shkola* (Poltava); for children, *Sterno*, *Kameniar*, *Voloshky*, and *Iunak* (Pereiaslav); for women, *Zhinochyi vistnyk*; the military periodical *Ukraïns'ka viis'kova sprava*; the medical semimonthly *Ukraïns'ki medychni visty*; the legal journal **Zakon i pravo*; and the Zemstvo Union's organ *Vistnyk hromads'koï agronomiï*.

A number of official publications appeared in Kiev under the Central Rada, the Hetman government, and the UNR Directory: **Visty z Ukraïns'koï Tsentral'noï Rady*, **Vistnyk Heneral'noho Sekretariiatu Ukraïns'koï Narodn'oï Respubliky*, and bulletins of various government ministries, bureaus, and trade unions. Under the Hetman government, the monthly **Viis'kovo-naukovyi vistnyk Heneral'noho shtabu* was published. After the Directory abandoned Kiev, some of its publications came out in Vinnytsia and Kamianets-Podilskyi, and new newspapers also sprang up there, eg, **Nova Ukraïna*, **Respublikans'ki visty*, **Zhyttia Podillia*, *Trudova Ukraïna*, *Trudovyi shliakh*, **Nash shliakh*, and *Slovo*.

In the 1918–19 Western Ukrainian National Republic, 59 Ukrainian-language periodicals were published. After the Polish occupation of Lviv in November 1918, a new daily, *Ukraïns'kyi holos*, appeared in Ternopil as the organ of the State Secretariat. The Ukrainian-held city of Stanyslaviv (today Ivano-Frankivske) served as the main center of Ukrainian publishing, however. Published there were *Svoboda* (moved from Lviv as the organ of the National Committee), **Narod*, **Republyka*, **Nove zhyttia*, *Volia*, *Respublykanets'*, and nine other papers. Other weekly and less frequent papers were published in county centers.

Over 20 Bolshevik Russian-language newspapers were published in Ukraine in 1917–18. The most important were *Donetskii proletarii*, *Proletarii*, and *Kommunist* in Kharkiv; *Proletarskaia mysl'* in Kiev; *Odesskii kommunist* in Odessa; and *Zvezda* in Katerynoslav. The only Bolshevik paper published in Ukrainian at that time was *Vistnyk Ukraïns'koï Narodnoï Respubliky* (Kharkiv and Kiev, January–March 1918), the organ of the Central Executive Committee of the All-Ukrainian Soviet of Workers', Soldiers', and Peasants' Deputies.

Ukrainian newspapers were also published in 1917 and 1918 in other parts of the Russian Empire: *Promin' (1916–17) in Moscow, Ukraïns'ki visty Zakavkazu and Ukraïns'ka Narodnia Respublika in Tbilisi, Ukraïns'ka amurs'ka sprava in Blagoveshchensk, Zasiv in Harbin, Ukraïnets' na Zelenomu Klyni in Vladivostok, Khvylia Ukraïny in Khabarovsk, Ukraïnets' na Sybiri in Omsk, Chornomorets' in Katerynodar, Ukraïns'kyi holos in Riga, Pratsia i volia in Voronezh, and Chornomors'ka rada and Chornomors'kyi ukraïnets' in Novorossiisk.

The growth of the Ukrainian press during the 1917–20 struggle for independence was much greater than that of education, scholarship, or even book publishing. Although only 10 Ukrainian-language periodicals had appeared in Russian-ruled Ukraine in 1916, after the February Revolution of 1917 there were 106. By 1918 their number had reached a maximum of 218, and then it dropped to 173 in 1919 and 79 in 1920. Despite paper shortages, newspapers were printed in large quantities. The chaos in transportation and communications provided the impetus for establishing numerous newspapers and journals in the provinces. From 1917 until 1919 most periodicals appeared fairly regularly. In 1919, however, because of the Ukrainian-Soviet and Ukrainian-Polish wars, they were often forced to change location and to suspend publication. Although functioning primarily as a source of information, the Ukrainian press of this period was also an important factor in the formation of political opinion, particularly in the countryside, where there was a shortage of books and schools.

The UNR Ministry of Propaganda, the State Press Bureau, and the Ukrainian Telegraph Agency, the latter two of which were established in May 1918 by the Hetman government and headed by D. Dontsov (by V. Kalynovych under the UNR Directory), played an important part in the development of the press. The Hetman government's Ministry of International Affairs published a weekly bulletin on the foreign press, Vistnyk zakordonnoï presy, in Kiev in 1918. Ukrainian *press and information bureaus were active abroad in 1918–20. They were attached to the Ukrainian legations in Berlin, Paris, London, Rome, Washington, Prague, Copenhagen, and Vienna and published information bulletins. The Ukrainian governments also sponsored foreign-language journals, such as Die *Ukraine in Berlin (1918–26), *Ukrainische Blätter in Vienna (1918), L'Ukraine in Lausanne (1919), France et Ukraine in Paris (1920), La Voce dell Ukraina in Rome (1919), and newspapers published in Greek in Athens and in Bulgarian in Sofia (1919–20).

Soviet Ukraine, 1919–41. The first major Bolshevik dailies in Ukrainian were *Bil'shovyk (1919–25) in Kiev, *Visti VUTsVK (1920–34) in Kharkiv and Kiev (1934–41), and Selians'ka bidnota (est 1920) in Kharkiv. Important communist newspapers and journals were *Visti TsK Komunistychnoï partiï (bil'shovykiv) Ukraïny (est 1921) in Kharkiv and, in Russian, Kommunist (est 1918 in Moscow and published in Kharkiv from 1919), the CC CP(B)U journal Kommunist (1920–1), and Proletarskaia pravda (1917–24) and Kievskii proletarii (1920–31) in Kiev. Upon establishing their control over Ukraine the Bolsheviks gradually discontinued all noncommunist publications in 1919–20. A temporary respite was granted only to their allies, the *Borotbists and *Ukrainian Communist party, who were allowed to continue publishing their organs Borot'ba and Trudove zhyttia in Kiev, Chervonyi prapor (1919–24) in Kiev and later Kharkiv, and Chervonyi shliakh in Kamianets-Podilskyi. In 1920, of 151 periodicals published in Soviet Ukraine, only 82 were in Ukrainian. By 1922 there were no noncommunist periodicals in Ukraine, and only 69 Ukrainian-language publications.

With the introduction of the policy of *Ukrainization in 1923, a new stage began in the development of the Ukrainian press. For the first time in Ukrainian history, the majority of newspapers and journals in Ukraine, even outside Kiev and Kharkiv (eg, in Odessa and Katerynoslav), were published in Ukrainian. The number of periodicals increased significantly. The literary rather than political press played the leading role in Soviet Ukrainian intellectual life, after V. Blakytny, the editor in chief of Visti VUTsVK, introduced the supplement Kul'tura i pobut and published therein M. Khvylovy's polemics on literature and culture, and the major literary-political monthly *Chervonyi shliakh (1923–36) was begun in Kharkiv.

The Soviet Ukrainian political press was controlled by Moscow, and served primarily as a tool of Party propaganda, often criticizing and condemning the literary journals for their 'nationalist deviations.' The newspapers of this period with the largest circulation were the republican dailies Kommunist (published in Ukrainian from 1926) and Visti VUTsVK. Other major dailies were *Proletars'ka pravda (1924–43) and Kievskii proletarii (1925–31) in Kiev, Khar'kovskii proletarii (1924–30) in Kharkiv, Izvestiia (1920–9) and *Chornomors'ka komuna (est 1929) in Odessa, the republican Komsomol paper Komsomolets' Ukraïny (1925–43), the republican trade-union papers *Proletarii (1923–35) and *Robitnycha hazeta Proletar (1926–32), Diktatura truda (1920–32) in Staline (now Donetske), Zvezda (1917–29) in Dnipropetrovske, and the organs of the Ukrainian Military District Chervona Armiia (1926–38) and Oborona. Newspapers for the peasants, with their own distinctive character, appeared during this period, eg, *Selians'ka pravda (1921–5) and *Radians'ke selo (1924–32). In general the Soviet Ukrainian newspapers of this time were not yet carbon copies of their Russian counterparts. They devoted attention to Ukrainian topics and issues in both Soviet and Western Ukraine; their focus, however, was usually determined by the Party line.

Party control over the *literary and art journals was also quite firm, but not complete. Even Chervonyi shliakh sometimes published veiled critiques of the regime. A new major literary monthly, *Zhyttia i revoliutsiia (1925–33) in Kiev, was less communist in orientation and solicited contributions from various writers' groups, including *MARS and the *Neoclassicists. It also devoted much attention to the promotion of Ukrainian traditions and cultural ties with the West. Another seminal journal was the bimonthly *Vaplite (1926–7), published by M. Khvylovy's coterie. After it was forced by the Party to close in 1927, direct criticism of the Party and of Soviet life was no longer possible; and the contributors to Vaplite's successor, the innovative monthly *Literaturnyi iarmarok (1928–30), employed Aesopian language to express their anti-Stalinist views.

Other important literary journals published during the Ukrainization period were: in Kharkiv, the Futurists' Gong komunkul'ta (1924) and *Nova generatsiia (1927–30), the Pluh association's *Pluzhanyn* (1925–7) and *Pluh (1925–33), the Sovietophile Western Ukrainian émigré writers' **Zakhidnia Ukraïna* (1927–33), the journal of the All-Ukrainian Association of Proletarian Writers (VUSPP) *Hart (1927–32), the Prolitfront group's *Prolitfront (1930), and the popular **Universal'nyi zhurnal* (1928–9); in Kiev, the Komsomol journal *Molodniak (1927–37) and the popular semimonthly *Nova hromada (1923–33); in Odessa, *Shkval (1924–33) and *Metalevi dni* (1930–3); in Dnipropetrovske, *Zoria (1925–34); and in Artemivske and then Luhanske, *Zaboi (1923–32).

There were a few periodicals devoted exclusively to literary criticism and literature studies. They included the bibliographical journals *Knyha* (1923–4) and *Nova knyha (1924–5), the scholarly bimonthly **Literaturnyi arkhiv* (1930–1), and the Marxist journal *Krytyka* (1928–32), renamed *Za markso-lenins'ku krytyku* (1932–5) and **Literaturna krytyka* (1935–40).

Ukrainian scholarly and scientific periodicals flourished in the 1920s and early 1930s. Most were published by the All-Ukrainian *Academy of Sciences in Kiev, including the journal of Ukrainian studies *Ukraïna (1924–33), edited by M. Hrushevsky. New periodicals in the arts were published in the 1920s and 1930s: **Shliakhy mystetstva* (1921–3), *Nove mystetstvo (1925–8), **Radians'ke mystetstvo* (1928–32), **Mystets'ka trybuna* (1930–1), and *Maliarstvo i skul'ptura* (1935–9), renamed **Obrazotvorche mystetstvo* (1939–41). New *music journals were also published, as were theater periodicals, such as *Teatr–Muzyka–Kino* (1925–7), *Sil's'kyi teatr* (1926–30), renamed *Masovyi teatr (1931–3), and *Radians'kyi teatr* (1929–31), and film periodicals, such as *Kino (1925–33) and *Radians'ke kino* (1935–8).

Popular illustrated magazines in this period were *Hlobus (1923–35), *Znannia (1923–35), *Vsesvit (1925–34), *Dekada* (est 1930, merged with *Vsesvit* in 1933), the atheist *Bezvirnyk (1925–35), *Molodyi bil'shovyk* (1925–33), *Selians'kyi zhurnal* (1929–31), and, for women, *Komunarka Ukraïny* (1920–34) and *Selianka Ukraïny* (1924–31), renamed **Kolhospnytsia Ukraïny* (1931–41). There were numerous publications for children in the 1920s and 1930s. Among the more important were *Chervoni kvity (1923–31), *Bil'shovycheniata* (1924–31), *Oktiabr'skie vskhody* (1924–30), *Tuk-tuk (1929–35), *Pioneriia (1931–41), *Vesela bryhada (1931–7), *Zhovtenia (1928–41), and, for 'activist children,' *Na roboti* (1930–3). Among satirical magazines the semimonthly **Chervonyi perets'* (1927–34) was notable.

During the Stalinist terror of the 1930s most Ukrainian scholarly and literary periodicals were abolished. Scholarly institutions and editorial staffs were thoroughly purged in the early 1930s, and trusted Party members – usually nonprofessional dilettantes in journalism and literature – were appointed chief editors. Nearly all non-newspaper periodical publications in Soviet Ukraine were discontinued in 1933–4, and Ukrainian magazines published elsewhere in the USSR (eg, *Chervonu huzelu* in Rostov, *Novym shliakhom* in Krasnodar, and *Sotsiialistychna perebudova* in the Far East) were closed down.

The mid-1930s marked the beginning of the total centralization of the press. An extensive network of raion newspapers, factory and plant broadsheets, and organs of political departments of machine-tractor stations and state farms was established. By 1940 there were 1,672 newspapers with a combined single pressrun of 6.9 million copies. Because of strict censorship, however, they provided little information about what was really happening in Ukraine or abroad. Instead they served as propaganda tools aimed at increasing labor productivity and fostering a love for Russia, Stalin, and the Party. Most newspapers were one-page sheets; 85 percent of them were printed in Ukrainian in 1930, 84.9 percent in 1933, and 80 percent in 1934, as compared to 10 percent printed in Russian in 1933, 15.8 percent in 1934, and over 22 percent in 1940. *Komunist* and *Visti* had the largest circulations, approx 305,000 and 375,000 respectively. More than 50 newspapers were published in each of Kiev, Kharkiv, and Odessa.

The Ukrainization policy was abandoned during the terror, and *Russification of the press ensued; it affected not only Ukrainian periodicals but also those in Polish, Yiddish, Bulgarian, and Greek, most of which were suspended. By 1938 the number of Russian-language newspapers and magazines in Ukraine had increased substantially. A new republican newspaper, *Sovetskaia Ukraina* (now *Pravda Ukrainy*), and new oblast dailies in Russian were introduced.

After the Soviet occupation of Galicia, Volhynia (1939), and Bukovyna (1940) all existing Ukrainian periodicals there were closed down. New Soviet periodicals were introduced, eg, the daily **Vil'na Ukraïna* (est 1939) and the magazine *Literatura i mystetstvo* (1940–1) in Lviv, the daily **Radians'ka Bukovyna* (est 1940) in Chernivtsi, and 15 oblast and 49 raion newspapers.

Western Ukraine, 1918–39. In Polish-occupied Lviv the authorities prohibited the revival of *Dilo*. The publisher circumvented the ban by bringing out the paper under the titles *Ukraïns'ka dumka*, *Hromads'ka dumka*, *Ukraïns'kyi vistnyk*, *Hromads'kyi vistnyk*, and *Svoboda* until 1923, when permission to publish *Dilo* was granted. It remained the leading Ukrainian daily in interwar Western Ukraine.

Under Polish rule Ukrainian periodicals were plagued by official prohibitions, strict censorship, confiscations of entire pressruns, the imposition of strict fines on and the imprisonment of editors, and financial instability. Conditions were particularly difficult for periodicals published in Volhynia, the Kholm region, Polisia, and Podlachia, which were artificially separated from Galicia by the so-called Sokal border. In 1930 new censorship regulations effectively abolished freedom of speech in those regions. Nonetheless many periodicals did appear. Newspapers published in Lutske, the primary publications center, included *Ukraïns'ke zhyttia* (1922–4); **Selians'ka dolia* (1923–4) and *Nash shliakh* (1924–5), organs of the Ukrainian Social Democratic Club in the Polish Sejm; *Hromada (1924–6) and **Ukraïns'ka hromada* (1926–9), organs of the *Ukrainian National Democratic Alliance (UNDO); and the pro-UNDO **Volyns'ka nedilia* (1928–34) and *Nova doba* (1936). Another pro-UNDO paper, *Narid (1926–8), was published in Warsaw and distributed in Volhynia. Several Sovietophile, pro-communist papers were published in Kholm, among them *Nashe zhyttia (1920, 1922–8), *Nove zhyttia (1928–30), and **Selians'kyi shliakh* (1927–8). The weekly *Nove selo (1930–9) was published in Lviv but distributed primarily in Volhynia. Papers subsidized by and supportive of the Polish government and its policies included *Dosvitnia zoria* (1923–7) in Volodymyr-Volynskyi; *Dzvin* (1923–7) in Rivne; **Ukraïns'ka nyva*, originally published in Warsaw (1926–8) and then moved to Lutske (1929–36); and *Volyns'ke slovo* (1937–9) in Lutske.

One of the first magazines published in Volhynia was the Orthodox semimonthly *Pravoslavna Volyn'* (1922) in Kremianets. Most magazines were published in Lutske, eg, the agricultural-cum-civic semimonthly *Sil's'kyi svit* (1929–31) and monthlies *Nova skyba* (1933–5) and *Ridnyi kolos* (1933–9), the popular Orthodox monthlies *Za sobornist'* (1932–5) and *Shliakh* (1937–9), and the Sel-Rob monthly *Postup* (1929–30). Orthodox magazines – *Na varti* (1924–6), *Ridna tserkva* (1927–8), and *Dukhovnyi siiach* (1928–31) – were published by the Orthodox Consistory in Volodymyr-Volynskyi. Another, *Tserkva i narid* (1935–8), was published in Kremianets. Other popular Orthodox bi-weeklies, *Dukhovna besida* (1924–5) and *Nasha besida* (1926–7), were published in Warsaw and distributed in Volhynia, as was the illustrated weekly *Nash svit* (1924–5), later published in Lutske (1935–6). The children's semi-monthly *Sonechko* (1936–9) was published in Rivne.

Conditions were more favorable, although also constrained, in Galicia. All Ukrainian political parties there had their own organs. The USDP revived *Vpered* (1918–24), which served as a national newspaper while *Dilo* was banned and was later itself banned, and *Zemlia i volia* (1919–20, 1922–4). It also published the semimonthly *Sotsiialistychna dumka* (1921–4), the monthly *Nova kul'tura* (1923–4), and the semimonthly *Svit* (1925–9). The UNDO continued publishing the weekly *Svoboda* until 1939. It was supported by the journal *Polityka* (1925–6). The Ukrainian Socialist Radical party revived the weekly *Hromads'kyi holos* (1921–39) and published the journals *Proty khvyl'* (1928–9) and *Zhyve slovo* (1939) in Lviv. The radical nationalist *Ukrainian Party of National Work published the semimonthly *Zahrava* (1923–4). The monarchist nationalist weekly *Ukraïns'kyi holos* (1919–32) in Peremyshl became an OUN organ in 1929. The OUN also published the Lviv weeklies *Nash klych* (1933), *Visty* (1933–4), *Holos natsiï* (1936–7), and *Holos* (1937–9). The *Ukrainian Labor party had *Nash prapor* (1923–4) and *Prapor* (1924). The Ukrainian People's Labor party had *Ukraïns'ka rada* (1924–5) and *Rada* (1925–34). In 1927 *Rada* became the organ of the *Ukrainian Party of Labor, which also published *Pratsia* (1927–34) until 1933, when it became an organ of the clandestine Communist Party of Western Ukraine (KPZU). Other pro-OUN papers were *Ridnyi grunt* (1935–7) and *Frontom* (1936–7) in Lviv, *Proryv* (1936–7) in Peremyshl, *Homin baseinu* (1937) and *Homin kraiu* (1937–8) in Drohobych, and *Avangard* (1937–8) in Kolomyia. The moderate nationalist *Front of National Unity published the daily *Ukraïns'ki visty* (1935–9), the weekly *Bat'kivshchyna* (1934–9), and the quarterly *Peremoha* (1933–9). Conservative Catholic and nationalist views were expressed in *Nova zoria* (1926–39) in Lviv and *Beskyd* (1928–33) and *Ukraïns'kyi Beskyd* (1933–9) in Peremyshl. The weekly *Meta* (1931–9) represented a more liberal Catholic outlook. Galician supporters of the het-manite movement published the monthly *Khliborobs'kyi shliakh* (1932–5). A pro-Polish conciliatory viewpoint was represented by *Ridnyi krai* (1920–3) and *Selianyn* (1929–34). The Sovietophile and pro-communist press was particularly strong in the 1920s; it published the newspapers *Svitlo* (1925–8), *Syla* (1930–2), *Nasha zemlia* (1930–2), *Sel'-Rob* (1927–32), and the clandestine *Volia naroda* (1921–8) and *Zemlia i volia* (1925–9). Russophile newspa-

pers, eg, *Zemlia i volia* (1928–39) and the moribund *Russkii golos* (1922–39), had a declining influence.

Nonpartisan newspapers included the family weekly *Nedilia* (1928–39); the daily *Chas* (1931–2), edited by M. Holubets; and particularly the newspapers and magazines *Novyi chas* (1923–39), *Narodna sprava* (1928–39), *Nash prapor* (1932–9), and *Nash lemko* (1934–9), published by I. *Tyktor's publishing house, *Ukrainska Presa.

Much of the women's press also developed along partisan lines. Notable periodicals were the pro-UNDO *Zhinocha dolia* (1925–39), the organ of the *Union of Ukrainian Women *Zhinka* (1935–8), the radical *Zhinochyi holos* (1931–9), and the housekeeping magazine *Nova khata* (1925–39).

Ukrainian literary, art, and scholarly periodicals reached a high level of development in interwar Galicia. The first literary journal to appear in Lviv after the First World War was *Mytusa* (1922). *Literaturno-naukovyi vistnyk* was re-established in 1922. Edited by D. *Dontsov, it united all outstanding Western Ukrainian and émigré writers and even published Soviet contributions. After being renamed *Vistnyk* in 1933, it served until 1939 as the main forum for Dontsov's integral nationalist ideology and exerted considerable influence on the views of the 1930s generation in Western Ukraine and abroad. The magazines *Dazhboh* (1932–5), *Obriï* (1936–7), and *Naperedodni* (1937–8) were ideologically akin to *Vistnyk*. Catholic writers contributed to *Dzvony* (1931–9). The semimonthly *Nazustrich* (1934–8) was an important moderate magazine. Marxist and Sovietophile writers contributed to the monthlies *Nova kul'tura* (1923–6), which was renamed *Kul'tura* (1927–31), and *Vikna* (1927–32), *Novi shliakhy* (1929–32), and *Krytyka* (1933). Notable journals in the arts were *Ukraïns'ke mystetstvo* (1926) and the avant-garde *Mystetstvo* (1932–6), the music journal *Ukraïns'ka muzyka* (1937–9), the photography journal *Svitlo i tin'* (1933–9), and the theater journals *Teatral'ne mystetstvo* (1922–4) and *Masovyi teatr* (1930–2).

A number of scholarly periodicals were published in Lviv: the theology and church history quarterly *Bohoslo-viia* (1923–39), the cultural history magazine *Stara Ukraïna* (1924–5), the Slavic studies journal *Slovo* (1936–8), the journal of Ukrainian studies *S'ohochasne i mynule* (1939), the jurisprudence quarterly *Zhyttia i pravo*, and the bibliographical monthly *Ukraïns'ka knyha* (1937–9). The widely read monthly magazine *Litopys Chervonoï kalyny* (1929–39) was devoted to the history of the Ukrainian Sich Riflemen and the Ukrainian Galician Army. Other popular magazines were the Prosvita society's monthly *Zhyttia i znannia* (1927–39) and the regional studies magazines *Litopys Boikivshchyny* (1931–9) and *Nasha bat'kivshchyna* (1937–9).

The religious press also flourished in Western Ukraine. Notable Catholic periodicals were the quarterly *Dobryi pastyr* (1931–9) in Stanyslaviv, the quarterly *Katolyts'ka aktsiia* (1934–9) in Lviv, the Basilian monthly *Misionar* (est 1897) in Zhovkva, *Sivach* (1936–9), and the very popular weekly (circulation 85,000) *Khrystos nasha syla* (1936–9) in Lviv. The co-operative press and agricultural periodicals were also popular. Particularly so were the weekly *Hospodars'ko-kooperatyvnyi chasopys* (1921–44), the magazine *Sil's'kyi hospodar* (1926–39, 1940–4), the theoretical monthly of the Ukrainian co-operative movement *Ko-*

operatyvna respublyka (1928–39), the educational monthly *Kooperatyvna rodyna* (1934–9), and the dairyman's monthly *Kooperatyvne molocharstvo* (1926–39). Several *pedagogical periodicals were also published. Adult education was promoted in the Prosvita society's revived *Pys'mo z Prosvity* (1921–2) and *Narodna prosvita* (1923–7), and in *Samoosvitnyk* (1937–9).

Children's magazines were popular in interwar Western Ukraine, especially because the regime restricted the activities of Ukrainian schools. The most important were *Svit dytyny* (1919–39); *Moloda Ukraïna* (1923–6), for teenagers; *Dzvinochok* (1931–9); the Catholic *Nash pryiatel'* (1922–39); the Plast scouting organization's *Molode zhyttia* (1921–30); and, following the prohibition of Plast, the monthly *Vohni* (1931–8). Notable student periodicals were the Union of Ukrainian Nationalist Youth's *Smoloskypy* (1927–8); the Catholic *Postup* (1921–30), *Ukraïns'ke iunatstvo* (1933–9), and *Lytsarstvo Presviatoi Divy Mariï* (1936–9); and the Union of Progressive Youth's *Kameniari* (1932–9). With the political ascendance of the OUN in the 1930s, the centralist student organs *Students'kyi shliakh* (1931–4) and *Students'kyi vistnyk* (1935–9) promoted its ideology. Periodicals promoting sports and an athletic lifestyle were *Visty z Luhu* (1926–39), *Sokil's'ki visty* (1928–38), *Sportovi visty* (1931), *Hotovi* (1934–5), *Sport* (1936–7), and *Zmah* (1937–9).

Altogether, in the years 1918–39, 834 Ukrainian periodicals and 138 calendar-almanacs were published under Polish rule. Despite adverse political conditions they improved considerably, grew stronger financially, and became more popular and varied in political orientation and subject matter. Some newspapers and magazines reached relatively high circulation figures. The number of dailies increased from one to three. Weeklies were the most widespread publications, and their largest readership was in rural areas. But the absence of a Ukrainian press agency and the shortage of professionally trained journalists contributed to shortcomings in the Ukrainian press, such as inadequate news coverage and an excess of patriotic zeal, by comparison with the numerous Polish papers and the Jewish daily *Chwila*.

Conditions were highly unfavorable in Rumanian-ruled Bukovyna. The only Ukrainian daily there was *Chas* (1928–40) in Chernivtsi. Other newspapers were the Social Democratic *Volia naroda* (1919–21), *Robitnyk* (1919–23), *Vpered* (1923), *Hromada* (1923), and *Zemlia i volia* (1927); the Sovietophile *Narod* (1923); the *Ukrainian National party's *Ridnyi krai* (1926–30) and *Rada* (1934–8); and the pro-OUN *Samostiinist'* (1934–7). The Rumanian regime was supported in *Khliborobs'ka pravda* (1924–38) and *Pravda* (1930–6). Other, short-lived newspapers were *Narodnyi holos* (1921, 1923), *Zoria* (1923–5), *Zemlia* (1925–6), *Narod* (1926), and *Narodnia syla* (1932–4). Journals published were the pro-OUN literary monthly *Samostiina dumka* (1931–7), which had many émigré contributors; the student literary monthly *Promin'* (1921–3); and *Ukraïns'ka lastivka* (1933–9), for children. Only 10 Ukrainian periodicals were published in Bukovyna in 1936. Bessarabia had no Ukrainian periodicals.

In Transcarpathia, Czechoslovakia's democratic government did not hinder the development of the Ukrainian press. Overcoming the region's underdeveloped national consciousness, the press, gradually displacing Russophile

periodicals, became stronger and more influential; it numbered 23 periodicals by 1936. The leading Ukrainophile newspaper was the revived weekly *Nauka* (1919–22), which was renamed *Svoboda* (1922–38) as the organ of the Christian People's party, and then *Nova svoboda* (1938–9) as the daily of the Ukrainian National Alliance in Carpatho-Ukraine. Other important papers were the semiofficial *Rusyn* (1920–3), the Ruthenian Agrarian party's *Rus'ka nyva* (1921–4), the Subcarpathian Social Democratic party's *Narod* (1920–1) and *Vpered* (1922–38), the Czechoslovak Agrarian party's *Selo* (1920–4) and *Zemlia i volia* (1934–8), the independent *Ukraïns'ke slovo* (1932–8), the 'Rusynophile' *Nedilia* (1935–44), and the pro-OUN *Narodnia syla* (1936–8) and *Nastup* (1938–9). The Russophile papers *Russkaia zemlia* (1919–38), *Russkii vestnik* (1923–38), and *Karpatorusskii golos* (1932–4, 1938–44); the communist *Karpats'ka pravda* (1920–33, 1935–8); and lesser Ukrainophile, Russophile, and Magyarophile papers also appeared. The most important paper in the Prešov region was *Russkoe slovo* (1924–39). Other important periodicals in Transcarpathia were the Sovietophile monthly *Nasha zemlia* (1927–9); the ethnographic-pedagogical journal *Pidkarpats'ka Rus'* (1923–36); the pedagogical periodicals *Uchytel'* (1920–36), *Zoria* (1921–31), *Narodnaia shkola* (1921–38), *Uchytel'skyi holos* (1930–8), and *Nasha shkola* (1935–8); the Mukachiv Prosvita society's *Svitlo* (1933–8); the religious monthlies *Dushpastyr* (1923–41) and *Blahovistnyk* (1921–44, 1946–9); the children's magazines *Pchilka* (1923–34) and *Nash ridnyi krai* (1922–38); and the scouting journal *Plastun* (1923–31, 1934–7).

In interwar Transcarpathia 62 periodicals were published in Ukrainian, 25 in the *yazychiie*, 39 in Russian, 34 in Hungarian, 13 in Czech, and 4 in Yiddish. In 1938–9 in Carpatho-Ukraine, there were 11 Ukrainian periodicals, 3 Russian, 1 Czech, and 1 Czech-Ukrainian.

The émigré press in Europe, 1920–40. The development of the Ukrainian press in interwar Western and Central Europe was connected directly to the mass emigration from Soviet-occupied Ukraine. Under the difficult conditions of émigré life, publications were widely dispersed and short-lived. They still managed, however, to exert considerable influence on developments in foreign-occupied Western and Soviet Ukraine, which they reached through both legal and illegal means.

The main centers of the Ukrainian émigré press were Berlin, Warsaw, Prague, and Paris. Published in Berlin were *Nove slovo* (1920), the organ of the Ukrainian People's party; *Ukraïns'ke slovo* (1921–3), a pro-hetmanite weekly and then daily; and the weekly *Litopys polityky, pys'menstva i mystetstva* (1923–4). The newspaper *Ukraïns'kyi prapor* was published in Vienna (1919–23) and then in Berlin (1923–32); it represented the views of the Government-in-exile of the Western Ukrainian National Republic. Also published in Vienna were the UPSR's *Boritesia – poborete!* (1920–2), the Sovietophile monthly *Nova hromada* (1923–4), the Foreign Group of the Ukrainian Communist party's journal *Nova doba* (1920–1), and the nonpartisan *Volia* (1919–21). Published in Prague were *Sotsiialistychna dumka* (1921–3) of the Ukrainian Socialist Democratic Workers' party and *Trudova Ukraïna* (1932–9) of the UPSR. In Warsaw, Ye. Lukasevych, with the help of the Government-in-exile of the UNR, published the daily *Ukraïns'ka trybuna* (1921–2). The semiofficial weekly of the UNR government-in-exile *Tryzub* (1925–40), the Sovietophile semimonthly, later weekly, *Ukraïns'ki visty (1926–9), and the nationalist weekly *Ukraïns'ke slovo (est 1933) were published in Paris.

Publications for covert distribution in Western Ukraine included the newspaper of the underground *Ukrainian Military Organization, *Surma, in Berlin (1927–8) and in Kaunas, Lithuania (1928–34); the ideological organ of the OUN, *Rozbudova natsiï (1928–34) in Prague; and the KPZU organ *Nasha pravda in Vienna (1921–3) and Czechoslovakia (after 1934).

The literary journals Na perelomi (1920) and Vyzvolennia (1923) were published in Vienna. The most prominent and influential literary and political journal, *Nova Ukraïna (1922–8), was published in Prague, as were a number of scholarly serials and the student journals Ukraïns'kyi student (1920–4) and *Students'kyi visnyk (1923–31), the organ of the *Central Union of Ukrainian Students. A literary and arts bimonthly, *My (1933–9), was published in Warsaw, as were I. Ohiienko's scholarly-literary *Nasha kul'tura (1935–7) and philological *Ridna mova (1933–6). Military affairs were the subject of the journal *Tabor, published in Kalisz (1923–4, 1927–30) and in Warsaw (1930–9).

New Ukrainian *press and information bureaus abroad published many periodicals in several Western languages, to inform the European public about the Ukrainian question. Altogether, 55 émigré periodicals – 6 newspapers and 49 journals – were published in Europe in 1936. Two others appeared in Manchuria. By 1939 the number had dropped to 37.

Non-Soviet newspapers published in Ukraine during the Second World War

The Second World War. Following the Soviet occupation of Western Ukraine in 1939, all Ukrainian periodicals were closed down, and many journalists were repressed. Only in the Nazi-occupied Generalgouvernement in Poland and abroad could the Ukrainian 'national' press function. The new Ukrainske Vydavnytstvo publishing house in Cracow published the daily *Krakivs'ki visti (1940–5) and a weekly version, the monthly Iliustrovani visti (1940–1), and the weekly Kholms'ka zemlia (1942–4). These newspapers were distributed mainly in the Ukrainian parts of the Generalgouvernement – the Lemko, Sian, Kholm, and Podlachia regions – and in Galicia after the expansion of the Generalgouvernement in 1941. In Cracow and later in Lviv, Ukrainske Vydavnytstvo also published a magazine for teenagers, *Doroha (1940–4), the literary magazine *Vechirnia hodyna (1942–4), the popular monthly *Nashi dni (1941–4), the co-operative monthly Sil's'kyi hospodar (1940–4), and the children's magazine Mali druzi (1940–4). After the Nazi authorities banned the new Lviv daily Ukraïns'ki shchodenni visti (1941), *L'viv-s'ki visti (1941–4) served as the official daily in Galicia. A weekly, *Ridna zemlia (1941–4), was also published. These

newspapers were not allowed to circulate outside the Generalgouvernement.

The early phase of the German occupation of central and eastern Ukraine in 1941 saw a great upsurge in nationalist publishing activity. Soviet newspapers had ceased publication or were banned, and new newspapers were founded in virtually every oblast and raion center. After the creation of the *Reichskommissariat Ukraine and the transfer of power to Nazi civilian authorities, however, they were either shut down or turned into provincial and local Nazi organs, which were strictly controlled and censored. The editors of the nationalist Kiev daily *Ukraïns'ke slovo (1941) and literary magazine *Litavry (1941), for example, were arrested and later executed, and Ukraïns'ke slovo became the pro-Nazi *Nove ukraïns'ke slovo (1941–3). The initially independent weekly Volyn' (1941–4) in Rivne was curtailed (see *Volyn). Greater freedom of publication was allowed in areas close to the battlefront. Kharkiv, for example, had the nationalist daily *Nova Ukraïna (1941–3) and the literary journal Ukraïns'kyi zasiv (1942–3).

No Ukrainian press was allowed in Rumanian-occupied *Transnistria. The weekly *Nashe zhyttia (1940–4), however, was published in Bucharest. Most Ukrainian periodicals published in Nazi-occupied Europe, including Warsaw and Paris, were suspended. Those allowed to continue publishing in Berlin and Prague, including *Ukraïns'kyi visnyk (1936–45), *Ukraïns'ka diisnist' (1939–45), Natsiia v pokhodi (1939–41), *Proboiem (1933–43), and *Nastup (1937–44), were banned in the Generalgouvernement and Reichskommissariat Ukraine.

The millions of Ukrainian laborers, Ostarbeiter, and prisoners of war in Germany proper were served by several state-controlled periodicals: the biweekly *Holos (1940–5), which had a circulation of 250,000 in 1944; the weeklies *Ukraïnets' (1942–5), *Visti (1942–5), *Na shakhti (1942–5), *Zemlia (1942–5), and *Nova doba (1941–5); and the magazine Dozvillia (1942–5). Ukrainian units in the German forces – the Ukrainian Liberation Army and the Division Galizien – had their own newspapers, Ukraïns'kyi dobrovolets' (1942–5), Za Ukraïnu (1943), and Do peremohy (1943–5). Altogether, over 300 Ukrainian periodicals, most of them local papers, were published in German-occupied Ukraine and Europe. The only truly free Ukrainian press during the Second World War consisted of 20-odd clandestine political, military, children's, and satirical publications of the OUN (eg, *Ideia i chyn [1942–6]), the Ukrainian Insurgent Army (eg, Do zbroï and Vil'na Ukraïna), and the Ukrainian Supreme Liberation Council.

During the German occupation several Soviet Ukrainian newspapers and journals, eg, Radians'ka Ukraïna, Pravda Ukraïny, and Literatura i mystetstvo, were evacuated and published in Bashkiria or in Moscow. A number of Soviet underground and partisan papers and bulletins were distributed in German-occupied Ukraine during the war.

Soviet Ukraine since 1945. The postwar Soviet Ukrainian press continued developing according to the parameters set in 1938: centralization, Party control, and Russification. The press remained basically a tool of the Communist party, although some concessions to Ukrainian patriotism were made, and new Ukrainian-language periodicals were introduced during a short period of relative liberalization in 1945–6 and during a longer period after Stalin's death in 1954. Newspapers – usually limited to four pages per issue – were not allowed to give readers objective information about external or domestic developments, but merely reprinted official statements and accounts. Articles and reviews were censored to ensure conformity with the Party line. All sanctioned periodicals were official publications of the Party, the government, Komsomol, individual ministries, trade unions, or other state or public organizations. The entire press was until around 1990 under the jurisdiction of the Department of Propaganda and Agitation of the CC CPU and the Press Committee of the Council of Ministers of the Ukrainian SSR. Party and government press editors in chief acted as censors and were appointed exclusively from among loyal Party members and trained at special journalism schools run by the Party.

In the last years under Stalin, in the late 1940s and early 1950s, many Ukrainian-language periodicals were discontinued. At the same time Russian-language equivalents of certain Ukrainian-language newspapers and journals were established. Usually they were allotted larger pressruns than their Ukrainian counterparts; their greater availability and, therefore, greater popularity served as a justification for discontinuing the Ukrainian-language editions. After Stalin's death many new newspapers – including republican and Komsomol oblast ones – and academic, scientific, and cultural journals and other serials were established. Many of the latter in the pure, applied, technical, and medical sciences, however, were published only in Russian. Between 1950 and 1960 the number of Ukrainian-language journals increased from 27 to 54, while Russian-language journals increased from 5 to 26. From late 1959 on, existing separate Ukrainian- and Russian-language Party newspapers in oblast centers were amalgamated, and single newspapers that were published in parallel Ukrainian and Russian editions thereby created. In 1962 it became possible for someone living outside Ukraine in the USSR to subscribe to republican-level periodicals, something that until then had not been allowed.

Because of Soviet nationality policy, in which Russification had been the key component, the Ukrainian-language press was not accorded the same status or privileges as the Russian-language press in Ukraine. In 1959 the population of Soviet Ukraine was 77 percent Ukrainian and 17 percent Russian. Between 1954 and 1960, however, the combined pressrun of Ukrainian-language journals doubled, whereas that of Russian-language journals increased 2.5 times while being allotted over 36 times the number of printed sheets. The number of Ukrainian-language newspapers increased from 784 to 814, while Russian-language newspapers increased from 226 to 378; their combined pressruns increased 168 percent and 154 percent respectively. In 1965 the combined pressrun of Ukrainian-language newspapers was 72 percent of the single-issue total and 71 percent of the annual total in Ukraine, while that of Russian-language newspapers was 27 and 28 percent respectively.

The situation of the Ukrainian-language press worsened in the 1970s and 1980s. As a result of official all-Soviet policies, the number of Ukrainian-language journals increased from 54 in 1960 to 63 in 1970 and then dropped to 51 in 1988, while Russian-language journals in Ukraine increased from 26 in 1960 to 39 in 1970, 44 in 1975, and 55 in 1988. The number of Ukrainian-language newspapers

Postwar Soviet Ukrainian newspapers, journals, and magazines

(excluding collective-farm papers) increased from 919 in 1959 to 1,261 in 1988, while Russian-language newspapers increased from 381 in 1959 to 520 (29 percent) in 1988. From the mid-1970s on, many Ukrainian and other non-Russian periodicals in the USSR were not granted annual increases in their pressruns or subscription allotments, and by 1980 most of them had circulations that had declined in absolute terms from their 1975 levels. Between 1969 and 1980 the percentage of journals published in Russian by the AN URSR (now ANU) increased from 19 to 76.2, while the proportion of the Ukrainian-language journals decreased accordingly, and had fallen to 16.3 percent by 1989. By 1984 the pressruns of most Ukrainian-language literary and scholarly journals were nearly half of what they were in 1975. In 1988 the combined pressrun of the Ukrainian-language newspapers was 66 percent of the single-issue total and 64 percent of the annual total in Ukraine, while that of the Russian-language papers was 33.4 and 35 percent respectively.

This discrimination was even more apparent when statistics for the Russian and Ukrainian populations of the USSR are compared with those of the Soviet press. In 1989 the USSR population was 50.8 percent Russian and 15.4 percent Ukrainian. In 1988, however, 65.7 percent of all Soviet newspapers were published in Russian, but only 14.7 percent (1,261 newspapers) were published in Ukrainian. The pressruns of the Russian-language newspapers comprised 79.6 percent of the single-issue total and 83.5 percent of the annual Soviet total, while Ukrainian-language papers comprised 7.4 percent and 6.0 percent respectively. Although millions of Ukrainians – over 6.7

TABLE 2
Newspapers published in Ukraine in selected years, 1955–90, by language (excluding collective-farm publications)

Year	All newspapers	Ukrainian	Russian	Others
1955	1,192	972	205	15
1960	1,206	814	378	14
1965	1,104	742	353	9
1970	1,347	936	400	11
1975	1,266	878	377	11
1980	1,274	874	389	11
1985	1,367	910	445	12
1990	1,476	991	473	12

million in 1989 (11 million, according to V. Kubijovyč) – lived in other Soviet republics, not one Ukrainian-language periodical was published in the USSR outside Ukraine.

Newspapers. In 1980, 19 Ukrainian republic-level newspapers for the general public or for specific occupational or social groups were published. Not one was a daily. (The only daily in the entire USSR was *Pravda* in Moscow.) Five came out six times a week; 2, five times a week; 3, three times a week; 4, twice a week; and 5, once a week. Their total single printing was nearly 8.1 million copies, approximately the same as that of a single edition of an average all-Union daily newspaper. Their circulation ranged from 380,000 for a paper published three times a week to 4.1 million for a weekly. The republican newspapers were: the CC CPU, Supreme Soviet, and Council of Ministers or-

gans *Radians'ka Ukraïna* (est 1926, called *Komunist* until 1943 and *Demokratychna Ukraïna* since 1991) and its Russian counterpart, *Pravda Ukrainy* (est 1938, called *Sovetskaia Ukraina* until 1944); the CC CPU papers *Robitnycha hazeta* (est 1957), *Rabochaia gazeta* (in Russian, est 1957), and *Sil's'ki visti* (est 1924, called *Radians'ke selo* until 1933, then *Kolhospne selo* until 1939 and in 1949–65); the Komsomol's *Molod' Ukraïny* (est 1925, called *Komsomolets' Ukraïny* until 1943) and *Komsomol'skoe znamia* (in Russian, est 1938, called *Stalinskoe plemia* until 1956); the Writers' Union of Ukraine's *Literaturna Ukraïna* (est 1927, called *Literaturna hazeta* until 1962); the Ministry of Culture's *Kul'tura i zhyttia* (est 1945, called *Radians'ke mystetstvo* until 1955, then *Radians'ka kul'tura* until 1965); the Ministry of Education's *Radians'ka osvita* (est 1940, renamed *Osvita* in 1991); the Pioneer Organization's *Zirka* (est 1943) and *Iunyi leninets* (in Russian, est 1922, called *Iunyi Spartak* until 1923 and *Iunyi pioner* in 1938–41); the Physical Culture and Sport Committee's *Sportyvna hazeta* (est 1934, called *Radians'kyi sport* until 1964); the Voluntary Society for Assistance to the Army, Air Force, and Navy's *Patriot Bat'kivshchyny* (est 1939); the State Publishing, Printing, and Book Trade Affairs Committee's *Druh chytacha* (est 1960); the Ukraina Society's *News from Ukraine* and *Visti z Ukraïny* (est 1960); the Ukrainian Hearing Society's *Nashe zhyttia* (est 1967); the Ministry of Internal Affairs' *Radians'kyi militsioner* (est 1955) and *Sovetskii militsioner* (in Russian, est 1974), now replaced by *Militseis'kii kur'ier*; and the Chief River Fleet Administration's *Vodnyk* (est 1919).

The number of oblast newspapers grew from 53 in 1950 to 78 in 1990. In 1975, 37 were oblast Party committee and

TABLE 3
Daily pressrun and annual circulation of newspapers published in Ukraine in selected years, 1955–90, by language

Year	Total daily pressrun (thousands)				Annual circulation (millions)			Copies (per 100 population)
	Total	Ukrainian	Russian	Other	Total	Ukrainian	Russian	
1955	5,593	3,801	1,764	28	1,078.7	699.8	372.2	2,747
1960	10,408	7,547	2,803	58	1,624.4	1,103.7	509.9	3,825
1965	13,521	9,952	3,503	66	2,077.3	1,478.4	584.7	4,603
1970	20,560	14,304	6,141	115	3,478.5	2,345.5	1,110.8	7,382
1975	24,344	16,347	7,861	136	4,447.5	2,895.9	1,524.5	9,099
1980	23,654	15,659	7,867	128	4,497.4	2,914.9	1,556.5	9,003
1985	23,016	15,307	7,577	132	4,437.9	2,893.8	1,517.4	8,726
1990	24,919	16,519	8,262	138	4,652.1	2,965.0	1,660.3	8,974

TABLE 4
Newspapers and bulletins in various categories published in Ukraine in 1990, with pressrun and circulation figures (including collective-farm publications)

Category	Number	Copies printed (thousands)	Average copies printed per title (thousands)	Annual circulation (millions)	% of all titles	% of all copies printed	% of total annual circulation
Republic	19	8,185	431	1,612.9	1.1	32.8	34.7
Oblast	78	6,007	77	1,330.1	4.3	24.1	28.6
City	153	4,797	31	1,011.8	8.6	19.3	21.7
Raion	442	4,441	10	627.1	24.7	17.8	13.5
Institutional	784	1,252	2	65.4	43.9	5.0	1.4
Collective farm	311	237	1	4.8	17.4	1.0	0.1
Total	1,787	24,919	–	4,652.1	100.0	100.0	100.0

soviet organs, and 25 were Komsomol committee organs. They resembled the republican newspapers in form and content, but also covered oblast affairs and local news. None could be sent abroad. Thirteen came out six times a week; 27, five times a week; 30, three times a week; 1, twice a week; and 1, once a week. Their total single printing was nearly 7.3 million.

The oblast Party newspapers were published in parallel Ukrainian and Russian editions in Crimea, Dnipropetrovske, Donetske, Luhanske, Lviv, Mykolaiv, Odessa, Transcarpathia, and Zaporizhia oblasts. In 1980 the pressruns of the Russian editions were substantially higher than those of the Ukrainian in the most populous and urbanized oblasts of Ukraine – Donetske (by 614 percent), Luhanske (by 417 percent), Odessa (by 299 percent in 1975), Dnipropetrovske (by 219 percent), Zaporizhia (by 215 percent), and Kharkiv (by 212 percent). The oblast papers with the five largest single-issue pressruns were published in Russian: *Sotsialisticheskii Donbass* (362,00 copies) in Donetske, *Krymskaia pravda* (280,000) in Symferopil, *Industrial'noe Zaporozh'e* (257,00) in Zaporizhia, *Voroshilovgradskaia pravda* (250,000) in Voroshylovhrad (Luhanske), and *Znamia kommunizma* (236,000) in Odessa. The next largest was the Ukrainian-language *Vil'na Ukraïna* (230,500) in Lviv. The papers with the smallest pressruns were, with the exception of the Hungarian-language *Karpati igaz szo* (38,000) in Uzhhorod and the Moldavian-language *Zorile Bucovinei* (26,000) in Chernivtsi, the Ukrainian-language editions in Donetske (59,000), Voroshylovhrad (60,000), and Kharkiv (62,000).

In 1980, 23 of the 26 oblast Komsomol papers were published in Ukrainian three times a week. Only those in Crimea and Donetske oblasts were published in Russian, and the latter, *Komsomolets Donbassa*, was the only one published five times a week. The Komsomol paper of Transcarpathia oblast also appeared in a parallel Hungarian-language edition.

The number of 'city' newspapers – organs of Party committees in municipalities officially classified as cities (*mista*) – grew from 55 in 1950 to 60 in 1960, 80 in 1970, 108 in 1980, and 153 in 1990. Their news coverage was limited to their own cities, and they are not sold outside them or available abroad. In 1980, 40 of the 108 city papers were in Russian; they were published in Voroshylovhrad (11 of 13 city papers), Dnipropetrovske (2 of 8), Donetske (14 of 19), the Crimea (all 7), Odessa (4 of 5), Kharkiv (1 of 5), and Sumy (1 of 5) oblasts. In 1980, 62 of the city papers appeared four times a week; 29, three times a week; 11, five times a week; and 6, six times a week. Those published two or three times a week had single-issue pressruns in the 10,000 to 30,000 range. Thirteen papers published five or six times a week – eight of them in Russian – had much higher pressruns. They were *Vechernii Donetsk* (230,000 copies in 1980) in Donetske, *Vechirnii Kyïv* (200,000) in Kiev, *Dnepr vechernii* (162,900; formerly the Ukrainian-language *Dnipro vechirnii* [1972–6]) in Dnipropetrovske, *Prapor komunizmu* (133,000) in Kiev (renamed *Kyïvs'kyi visnyk* in 1990), *Vecherniaia Odessa* (123,000) in Odessa, *Chervonyi hirnyk* (116,000) in Kryvyi Rih, *Priazovskii rabochii* (107,000) in Zhdanov (Mariiupil), *Makeevskii rabochii* (85,000) in Makiivka, *Vechirnii Kharkiv* (84,000) in Kharkiv, *Slava Sevastopolia* (75,000) in Sevastopil, *Kochegarka* (64,500) in Horlivka, *Dzerzhynets'* (53,000) in Dniprodzerzhynske, and *Kerchenskii rabochii* (41,500) in Kerch. Two oblasts, Chernivtsi and Ternopil, did not have any city papers, but only oblast and raion organs. Only Kiev had two city papers, both appearing in a Ukrainian and a Russian version.

Raion newspapers were published by the Party committee in each raion. Usually two pages long, they contained materials of interest to the Party organization and some local news, and were not available outside the raion. Most appear three times a week in a pressrun of approx 5,000 to 20,000 copies. In 1980, of the 480 raion papers in Ukraine, 58 were published in Russian: all 14 raion papers in Crimea oblast, 12 of 19 in Donetske oblast, 12 of 19 in Voroshylovhrad oblast, 9 of 27 in Odessa oblast, 4 of 18 in Sumy oblast, 3 of 18 in Zaporizhia oblast, 3 of 27 in Kharkiv oblast, and 1 of 22 in Chernihiv oblast. Three of 13 raion papers in Chernivtsi oblast and one in Odessa oblast appeared in Moldavian, and 3 of 16 in Transcarpathia oblast appeared in Hungarian.

Collective-farm bulletins were also published in Ukraine, mostly as monthlies. Their number grew from 146 in 1956 to 2,203 in 1959, and then declined to 2,074 in 1960, 1,271 in 1970, 763 in 1975, and 311 in 1990. Like the bulletins (781 in 1988) of individual local industrial enterprises and higher educational institutions, they were not listed in official registers of the Soviet press.

Moscow's all-Union Russian-language newspapers were distributed widely in Ukraine, where they were telexed and printed in Kiev, Kharkiv, and other cities. In 1962, for example, when the 934 Soviet Ukrainian newspapers had a combined single-issue pressrun of over 10 million copies, an additional 10 million copies of the all-Union papers were also circulated daily in Ukraine.

Newspapers were published in every raion of Ukraine. In terms of their combined single-issue pressrun, however, in 1988 the top five producers were the city of Kiev, with 35.6 percent; Donetske oblast, with 7.3 percent; Dnipropetrovske oblast, with 4.9 percent; Lviv oblast, with 4.0 percent; and Odessa oblast, with 3.9 percent.

In 1988, 4.1 percent of all non-newspaper periodicals in the USSR were published in Ukraine. Of the 107 Soviet Ukrainian journals – 7.5 percent of all journals published in the USSR – 1 was a weekly, 3 were semimonthlies, 61 were monthlies, 1 was a semiquarterly, 39 were bimonthlies, and 2 were quarterlies.

Journals and serials. *Literary journals constituted the journal category with the largest combined pressrun; in 1988 there were nine with a combined pressrun of over 55.5 million copies, or 32 percent of the total pressrun of all non-newspaper periodicals published in Ukraine. The journals were the Writers' Union's monthlies *Vitchyzna, *Dnipro, *Vsesvit, *Kyïv, and, in Russian, *Raduga (formerly *Sovetskaia Ukraina* [1951–63]) in Kiev, *Prapor (renamed *Berezil'* in 1990) in Kharkiv, *Zhovten' (renamed *Dzvin* in 1990) in Lviv, *Donbas in Donetske, and the Komsomol's monthly *Ranok (formerly *Zmina* [1953–65]) in Kiev.

Journals dealing with politics, society, and the economy had the second largest combined pressrun; in 1988 there were 21 such journals with a combined pressrun of over 47.1 million copies, or 27.3 percent of the total pressrun of all non-newspaper periodicals. The major political journals were published by the CC CPU in parallel Ukrainian and Russian editions: the ideological monthly *Komunist Ukraïny/Kommunist Ukrainy* and the agitation and propaganda biweekly *Pid praporom leninizmu/Pod znamenem leninizmu* (formerly *Bloknot ahitatora* [1944–69]), renamed *Polityka i chas/Politika i vremia* in 1991.

TABLE 5
Annual circulation of periodicals and journals in Ukraine in selected years, 1955–1990, by language

Year	All periodical publications			Journals			Copies (per 100 population)
	Total	Ukrainian	Russian	Total	Ukrainian	Russian	
1955	22,983	19,153	3,773	12,398	11,417	981	59
1960	44,809	37,775	6,918	22,769	20,832	1,937	106
1965	77,710	67,588	10,122	53,393	49,782	3,611	172
1970	187,321	167,347	19,929	144,953	125,864	19,044	398
1975	222,981	202,291	20,623	177,710	157,322	20,328	456
1980	211,442	193,373	17,830	174,412	156,751	17,433	423
1985	169,767	151,309	18,218	140,254	122,209	17,818	334
1990	165,706	149,622	15,884	139,366	123,514	15,652	320

In 1988 the remaining pressrun of all non-newspaper periodicals was divided among the 5 children's magazines (15 percent); the Republican Council of Trade Unions and Writers' Union's monthly for women, *Radians'ka zhinka (renamed Zhinka in 1991; 15 percent); 6 journals dealing with culture or education (3.9 percent); 5 devoted to the arts (3.1 percent); 4 journals for young people (1.8 percent), the most important of which was the monthly *Znannia ta pratsia (renamed Nauka-fantastyka in 1990); the organ of the Russian Orthodox church in Ukraine, *Pravoslavnyi visnyk, and a monthly of atheist propaganda, *Liudyna i svit (formerly Voiovnychyi ateist [1960–4], 1.2 percent in 1965); 5 agricultural journals (0.7 percent; see *Agricultural periodicals); 20 technical journals (0.6 percent); the only sports magazine, the monthly *Start (formerly Fizkul'tura i sport [1957–65], 0.6 percent); 7 *medical journals (0.3 percent); 1 each in linguistics and literature studies (0.2 percent); and 25 natural science journals (0.1 percent).

The ANU has published a monthly informational journal, *Visnyk Akademiï nauk Ukraïns'koï RSR. It also published several academic journals in the humanities and social sciences: the history monthly *Ukraïns'kyi istorychnyi zhurnal; the literature studies monthly *Radians'ke literaturoznavstvo (renamed Slovo i chas in 1990); the jurisprudence monthly *Radians'ke pravo (renamed Pravo Ukraïny in 1991) – the most widely distributed ANU journal – copublished with the Ministry of Justice and Supreme Court; the economics monthly *Ekonomika Radians'koï Ukraïny (renamed Ekonomika Ukraïny in 1991) and its Russian parallel, Ekonomika Sovetskoi Ukrainy (Ekonomika Ukrainy); the folklore, folk art, and ethnography bimonthly *Narodna tvorchist' ta etnohrafiia; the linguistics bimonthly *Movoznavstvo; and the philosophy bimonthly Filosofs'ka dumka, which in 1989 became the philosophy and sociology monthly Filosofs'ka i sotsiolohichna dumka, also published in a parallel Russian edition, Filosofskaia i sotsiologicheskaia mysl'. An annual (now semiannual) serial, Nauka i kul'tura: Ukraïna, has been copublished since 1967 by the ANU and the Znannia Society. Znannia has also published three popular monthlies, *Nauka i suspil'stvo (formerly Nauka i zhyttia [1951–65]), the aforementioned Liudyna i svit, and Trybuna lektora (renamed Trybuna in 1990).

Journals published by Ukraine's governmental bodies have included the weekly organ *Vidomosti Verkhovnoï Rady URSR (renamed Vidomosti Verkhovnoï Rady Ukraïny in 1991), which also appeared in a parallel Russian edition; the Ministry of Culture's cultural-educational monthly,

*Sotsialistychna kul'tura (renamed Ukraïns'ka kul'tura in 1991), and, since 1970, bimonthlies devoted to Ukrainian art, music, and theater, *Obrazotvorche mystetstvo (formerly *Mystetstvo [1954–69]), *Muzyka, and *Ukraïns'kyi teatr; four pedagogical monthlies in Ukrainian – *Radians'ka shkola (renamed *Ridna shkola in 1991), *Doshkil'ne vykhovannia, *Ukraïns'ka mova i literatura v shkoli, and *Pochatkova shkola – and a bimonthly in Russian, Russkii iazyk i literatura v shkolakh USSR (est 1976; renamed Russkii iazyk i literatura v srednikh uchebnykh zavedeniakh USSR in 1984), published by the Ministry of Education; and a monthly devoted to film, *Novyny kinoekranu, published by the State Cinematographic Committee and the Union of Cinematographers.

Among technical and scientific journals, most were published by the institutes and divisions of the ANU. Since the late 1970s only two of them, *Dopovidi Akademiï nauk Ukraïns'koï RSR (renamed Dopovidi Akademiï nauk Ukraïny in 1991) and the botany bimonthly *Ukraïns'kyi botanichnyi zhurnal, had been published in Ukrainian. In 1990, ANU journals published in Russian were the monthlies Avtomaticheskaia svarka, Fizika nizkikh temperatur, Poroshkovaia metallurgiia, Prikladnaia mekhanika, Problemy prochnosti, Ukrainskii fizicheskii zhurnal, and Ukrainskii khimicheskii zhurnal; the bimonthlies Avtomatika, Biopolimery i kletka, Eksperimental'naia onkologiia, Elektronnoe modelirovanie, Fiziko-khimicheskaia mekhanika materialov, Fiziologicheskii zhurnal, Fiziologiia i biokhimiia kul'turnykh rastenii, Geofizicheskii zhurnal, Geologicheskii zhurnal, Gidrobiologicheskii zhurnal, Khimicheskaia tekhnologiia, Khimiia i tekhnologiia vody, Kibernetika, Kinematika i fizika nebesnykh tel, Metallofizika, Mikrobiologicheskii zhurnal, Mineralogicheskii zhurnal, Morskoi gidrofizicheskii zhurnal, Neirofiziologiia, Promyshlennaia teplotekhnika, Sverkhtverdye materialy, Teoreticheskaia i eksperimental'naia khimiia, Tekhnicheskaia elektrodinamika, Tsitologiia i genetika, Ukrainskii biokhimicheskii zhurnal, Ukrainskii matematicheskii zhurnal, Upravliaiushchie sistemy i mashiny, and Vestnik zoologii; and the quarterlies Kriobiologiia and Problemy spetsial'noi elektrometallurgii.

Also published in Russian were the State Construction Committee and Union of Architects' monthly Stroitel'stvo i arkhitektura (originally also published in Ukrainian as Arkhitektura i budivnytstvo [1953–7] and Budivnytstvo i arkhitektura [1957–9]); the Ministry of the Coal Industry's monthly Ugol' Ukrainy; and the Ministry of Health Protection's monthlies Vrachebnoe delo and Klinicheskaia khirurgiia, semiquarterly Oftal'mologicheskii zhurnal, and bimonthly Zhurnal ushnykh, nosovykh i gorlovykh boleznei. The only medical journals published in Ukrainian have been the latter ministry's bimonthlies *Pediatriia, akusherstvo i hinekolohiia* and *Farmatsevtychnyi zhurnal.*

Several important Ukrainian journals were not readily available outside the USSR: *Ridna pryroda*, the State Committee for Environmental Protection's quarterly; *Arkhivy Ukraïny*, the Chief Archival Administration's bimonthly; *bibliographic journals published by the Book Chamber of the Ukrainian SSR; *Zhurnalist Ukraïny*, the monthly of the Union of Journalists; and *Pam'iatky Ukraïny*, the quarterly of the Ukrainian Society for the Protection of Historical and Cultural Monuments.

In 1975 the journals with the 10 largest annual press-runs were *Perets'*, an illustrated biweekly of humor and satire (68,400,000 copies); *Radians'ka zhinka* (22,768,700); *Ukraïna*, the only weekly and a popular illustrated political, cultural, and literary magazine (17,284,800); *Barvinok*, the Komsomol's literary monthly for children, published in parallel Ukrainian and Russian editions (16,517,900); *Pid praporom leninizmu/Pod znamenem leninizma* (11,-946,200); *Maliatko*, the Komsomol's illustrated monthly for preschoolers (9,432,000); *Pioneriia*, the Komsomol's illustrated monthly for children, published in parallel Ukrainian and Russian editions (3,840,200); *Komunist Ukraïny/Kommunist Ukrainy* (2,451,600); *Ranok* (2,040,000); and *Liudyna i svit* (2,022,300).

Of the 208 non-newspaper periodicals published in Ukraine in 1988, 188 (90 percent) were published in Kiev, 9 in Kharkiv, 6 in Odessa, 2 in Lviv, and 1 each in Dnipropetrovske, Donetske, and Sumy.

Most recent times. With the introduction of glasnost and perestroika in 1985, Party control of the press gradually diminished. As a result the 'blank spots' in the Soviet past and present – repression, terror, collectivization, destruction of the kulaks, the 1932–3 famine in Ukraine, the Party purges, the physical annihilation of almost an entire generation of Ukrainian intelligentsia, the Second World War, the postwar famine, the suppression of dissent in the postwar period, Russification, national and religious oppression, and current social and economic ills – were openly discussed, and opinions and writings that were or would previously have been banned or suppressed were published. Many journalists and editors resigned from the CPU, and in October 1990 an independent union of journalists was founded. Hundreds of 'unofficial' periodicals – including organs of political groups and parties opposed to the CPSU and advocating its abolition, the dissolution of the USSR, and independence for its republics – were founded, particularly after a law guaranteeing freedom of

TABLE 6
Periodical publications in Ukraine in selected years, 1955–90, by language (excluding newspapers)

Year	All periodical publications	Ukrainian		Russian	
		Journals	Others	Journals	Others
1955	245	34	81	12	115
1960	369	54	138	26	148
1965	256	49	59	29	119
1970	523	63	123	39	297
1975	185	63	45	44	28
1980	198	50	51	50	42
1985	206	51	50	55	45
1990	185	56	41	60	27

TABLE 7
Periodicals published in Ukraine in 1990 by subject (excluding newspapers)

Subject or type	Number	Quantity (1,000s)	% of total
Politics, society, and economics	32	45,228	17.3
including atheism and religion	(2)	(834)	(1.1)
Natural sciences, mathematics	30	992	16.2
Technology	34	1,133	18.4
Agriculture	6	3,867	3.3
Medicine	7	489	3.8
Physical culture, sports	1	1,398	0.5
Culture, education, scholarship	48	28,845	25.9
Linguistics, literary studies	2	80	1.1
Literature	11	53,185	6.0
Children's literature	5	21,937	2.7
Art (history and criticism)	8	8,534	4.3
General interest	1	18	0.5
Periodicals for youth	(4)	(3,815)	(2.2)
Periodicals for women	(1)	(25,874)	(0.5)
Total	185	165,706	100.0

NOTE: Figures in parentheses are not included in the total.

speech, the press, and other mass media and abolishing censorship was introduced in the fall of 1990. The new law did not permit advocating the violent overthrow of the Soviet state, war, racism, national and religious intolerance, hatred, any form of violence, criminal activity, or immorality, or revealing state secrets.

Most of the new alternatives to the communist press in Ukraine were 4- to 12-page monthly papers with press-runs of 1,000 to 10,000 copies. Some were printed in the Baltic republics because of the shortage of paper and the lack of access to printing presses in Ukraine. At least 10 'thick' journals appeared.

The main rival of the CPU, the umbrella organization *Popular Movement of Ukraine – or Rukh – has published over 50 periodicals since its founding congress in September 1989. Twelve, including Rukh's central organ *Narodna hazeta, Ohliadach, Ekspres novyny*, and *Svit* (formerly *Visnyk Rukhu*), were published in Kiev; 22, in other central, southern, and eastern Ukrainian cities, including 3 in Kharkiv (*Slobids'ka Ukraïna, Na spolokh, Visti – Vil'na presa*); and 15 in western Ukraine, including 4 in Lviv (*Viche, Vybory, Iednist', Zaspiv*) and 2 in Ivano-Frankivske (*Halychyna, Poklyk*). Pro-Rukh periodicals have also been published by Ukrainians living or studying in Moscow (*Pora*), Riga (*Trybuna, Dzherelo*), Vilnius (*Prolisok*), and Tallinn (*Struny*).

The independentist Ukrainian Republican party (URP, called in 1988–90 the Ukrainian Helsinki Association – the successor to the *Ukrainian Helsinki Group) has published over 25 periodicals. Foremost among them have been the 'thick' journal *Ukraïns'kyi visnyk* (est 1987, continuing a *samvydav journal circulated in 1970–4); its chief organ, *Samostiina Ukraïna* (formerly *Holos vidrodzhennia*); and *Tsentral'na rada* and *Na ruïni* in Kiev, *Volia* in Chernihiv, *Lvivs'ki novyny* and *Respublikanets'* in Lviv, and *Ternystyi shliakh* in Ternopil. The URP has also published 4 other periodicals in Kiev, 2 others in Chernihiv, and 1 other in Lviv, as well as 2 organs in Ivano-Frankivske and in Kherson, 1 each in Lutske, Rivne, Chernivtsi, Kamianets-Podilskyi, Kharkiv, Kherson, Zaporizhia, Dnipropetrov-

Some of the new newspapers published in Ukraine in 1992

ske, and Cherkasy; and *Ukrainskii vopros* and *Natsional'nyi vopros*, in Russian, in Moscow.

Other new political organs have been the Lviv Social Democratic Organization's *Reforma* and *Al'ternatyva* in Lviv; *Demokratychnyi vybir* and, in Russian, *Demokraticheskii vybor* of the Democratic Platform in the CPU; the Ukrainian Democratic party's *Holos* in Kiev; the Ukrainian Christian Democratic party's *Voskresinnia* in Ivano-Frankivske and *Za viru i voliu* in Ternopil; the Ukrainian National party's *Visnyk* in Lviv; the Ukrainian Popular Democratic League's *Nezalezhnist'* in Kiev; the Lviv Electors' Club's *Vyborche pravo*; the Ukrainian Independence and Statehood party's *Poklyk voli* and *Samostiinist'* in Lviv; the nonpartisan nationalist *Zoloti vorota* in Kiev; the Radical Group's *Za i proty* in Lviv; the Social Democratic Federation of Ukraine's Russian-language papers *Sotsial demokrat Ukrainy* and *Osvobozhdenie* and journal *Dialog* in Kiev; the Ukrainian Peasant Democratic party's *Zemlia i volia* in Lviv; and the anarcho-syndicalist *Nabat* in Russian in Kharkiv.

Over 30 new periodicals for young people and students have appeared, mostly in Lviv or Kiev. The URP-affiliated Association of Independent Ukrainian Youth (SNUM) has published *Molodyi natsionalist* in Lviv, *Smoloskyp* in Chernivtsi, *Surma* in Stryi, and several other organs. A more integral-nationalist splinter group, SNUM-Nationalists, took over *Zamkova hora* from SNUM and has also published the journal *Rada* in Kiev and a few other periodicals. The pro-OUN Association of Ukrainian Youth has published organs in Chernivtsi, Kosiv, and Kharkiv.

Other notable alternative periodicals are the Ukrainian Association of Independent Creative Intelligentsia's literary journals *Kafedra* and *Ievshan zillia* in Lviv, *Karby hir* in Ivano-Frankivske, *Porohy* in Dnipropetrovske, and *Snip* in

Kharkiv; the All-Ukrainian Prosvita Society's (formerly Ukrainian Language Society) papers *Slovo* in Kiev and *Prosvita* in Lviv; the Ukrainian Autocephalous Orthodox church's *Nasha vira* in Kiev and *Svitlo viry* in Lutske; the Ukrainian Ecological Association's *Zelenyi svit* in Kiev; the *Lev Society's *Postup* and children's magazine *Svit dytyny* in Lviv; the *Memorial society's *Dzvin* in Ternopil and *Poklyk sumlinnia* in Lviv; the Ternopil Vertep society's *Posvit*; the independent papers *Vil'ne slovo* in Kiev, *Ukrains'kyi chas* in Dnipropetrovske and Lviv, *L'vivs'kyi visnyk*, *Nova doba*, and *Zhyttia i pratsia* in Lviv, and *Al'ternatyva* in Pavlohrad; the Ukrainian Independent Press Agency's *Polityka*, *Perspektyva*, and, in Russian, *Puti* in Kiev; the Kiev student Hromada's *Dzvin* (1988–9); the Lviv Student Brotherhood's paper *Bratstvo* and journal *Vikno*; the independent (formerly SNUM) nationalist youth paper *Moloda Ukraïna* in Lviv; and the Kiev Ukrainian Student Association's paper *Svoboda*.

Some of the new newspapers published in Ukraine in 1992

More frequently published alternative newspapers were established in 1990. They include the Lviv Oblast Council's *Za vil'nu Ukraïnu* (over 345,000 copies 3 times a week in 1992) and weekly *Frankova krynytsia*; Lviv oblast's paper *Moloda Halychyna* (until 1990 the Komsomol paper *Lenins'ka molod'*, 232,000 copies 3 times a week in 1992); the Lviv City Council's evening paper *Ratusha* (20,000 copies 3 times a week); and the Ukrainian Culture Fund's weekly *Zapovit* (50,000 copies) in Ternopil. Since 1991 the Ukrainian Supreme Council has published an official organ, *Holos Ukraïny*, 5 times a week in both Ukrainian and Russian editions (363,000 copies in 1992).

In 1992 there were 2,263 registered newspapers (290 republic-level) and 346 registered journals (262 republic-level) in Ukraine.

In 1992 the most widely circulated national newspapers in Ukraine were *Sil's'ki visti* (2,268,000 copies 5 times a week); *Nezavisimost'* (1,323,000 copies 1 to 4 times a week); *Molod' Ukraïny* (713,000 copies 3 times a week); *Holos Ukraïny*; *Robitnycha hazeta/Rabochaia gazeta* (300,000 copies 3 times a week); *Sportyvna hazeta* (243,000 copies 3 times a week); *Pravda Ukrainy* (220,000 copies 5 times a week); *Osvita* (164,000 copies once a week); *Demokratychna Ukraïna* (112,000 copies 3 times a week; and *Literaturna Ukraïna* (105,000 copies once a week). Influential regional newspapers were *Vechirnii Kyïv/Vechernii Kiev* (546,000 copies 5 times a week); Lviv's *Za vil'nu Ukraïnu* (345,000 copies 3 times a week) and *Moloda Halychyna* (232,000 copies 3 times a week); Ternopil's *Zakhidna Ukraïna* (100,000 copies once a week); and Ivano-Frankivske's *Halychyna* (134,000 copies 3 times a week).

Other new notable newspapers include Kiev's *Khreshchatyk* (5 issues per week), *Kyïvs'ka pravda* (3 issues per week), and weekly *Andriivs'kyi uzviz, Dilova Ukraïna/Delovaia Ukraina, Rada, Ukraïna-Business, Finansovyi Kyïv,* and *Fortune*; Lviv's *Vysokyi zamok* (3 issues per week), *Dilo* (semiweekly), and *Post-Postup* (weekly); Dnipropetrovske's biweekly *Vil'na dumka*; Ternopil's *Vil'ne zhyttia* (5 times a week) and semiweekly *Ternopil' vechirnii*; Uzhhorod's *Novyny Zakarpattia* (3 to 4 issues per week); and Rivne's weekly *Rivne*. New journals include the Volhynian cultural quarterly *Volyn'* (Lutske); the bimonthly *Kyïvs'ka starovyna*; the bibliological bimonthly *Knyzhnyk*; the Lviv monthlies *Literaturno-naukovyi visnyk* and *Litopys Chervonoï kalyny*; the Kiev monthlies *Dilove zhyttia Ukraïny/Delovaia zhizn' Ukrainy, Bytyi shliakh, Nova heneratsiia, Polityka i chas/Politika i vremia, Trybuna, Tryzub,* and *Viche/Veche*; the children's monthly *Soniashnyk*; and the Ternopil bimonthly *Ternopil'*.

The postwar émigrés and refugees. After the Second World War the approx 200,000 Ukrainian refugees and émigrés in the non-Soviet occupation zones of Germany and Austria, as well as soldiers of the Ukrainian National Army (UNA) interned by the British near Rimini, Italy, began publishing their own newspapers, bulletins, and journals. In the years 1945–50 at least 327 noncommunist periodicals reflecting a wide spectrum of partisan opinion and interests appeared, two-thirds of them in the US zone in Bavaria. They included mimeographed bulletins in 19 displaced persons camps; 17 intercamp papers, 5 dealing with resettlement issues; and 18 church, 20 student, 14 literary, 13 organizational, 11 women's, 11 humorous, 11 satirical, 21 Plast, 6 OUN (Bandera faction), 4 OUN (Melnyk faction), 5 Ukrainian Youth Association (SUM), 4 Ukrainian Revolutionary Democratic party (URDP), 3 hetmanite, 3 health, 3 sports, 2 socialist, 25 specialized, and many unclassified periodicals, with a total combined pressrun of 15 million copies. Many of the periodicals were mimeographed. The largest number appeared in the years 1946–8, before the German currency reform and the mass emigration of the majority of the refugees.

In the US zone only the semiweekly and later weekly paper *Ukraïns'ki visti* (Neu-Ulm, 1945–78), the weekly papers **Chas* (Fürth, 1945–9), **Nashe zhyttia* (Augsburg, 1945–8), **Nedilia* (Schweinfurt, Aschaffenburg, and Augsburg, 1945–56), and *Na chuzhyni* (Vilsbiburg, 1947–8), the semiweekly paper **Ukraïns'ka trybuna* (Munich, 1946–9), the Plast magazines *Plastun* (Augsburg, 1945–7) and **Molode zhyttia* (Munich, 1946–50), the literary-cultural journal **Orlyk* (Berchtesgaden, 1946–8), and the illustrated magazine **Pu-hu* (Augsburg, 1947–50) received publishing licenses from the military government and free paper from the International Refugee Organization. The hundreds of other periodicals were sublicensed or published as supplements by them, or mimeographed on paper bought on the black market.

Widely read periodicals published in the US zone were, in addition to the aforementioned, the weeklies **Slovo* (Regensburg, 1945–6), *Khrystyians'kyi shliakh* (Munich, Karlsfeld, and Mittenwald, 1945–7), and *Ukraïns'ka dumka*

Ukrainian émigré journals published in Germany in 1945–50

Ukrainian émigré newspapers published in postwar Germany

(Augsburg, 1946–8); the OUN journals **Vyzvol'na polityka* (Munich, 1946–9), *Za samostiinist'* (Munich, 1946–8), *Nasha dumka* (Munich, 1947–8), and **Surma* (Munich, 1949); the URDP journal *Nashi pozytsiï* (Neu-Ulm, 1945–9); the Hetmanite journal *Ukraïns'kyi litopys* (Augsburg, 1946–8); the military journal *Do zbroï* (Munich 1946–5) and the literary almanacs of **MUR* (Munich, 1946–7) and the literary-cultural journals *Ridne slovo* (Munich, 1945–6), **Zahrava* (Augsburg, 1946), and **Arka* (Munich, 1947–8); the women's magazine *Hromadianka* (Augsburg, 1946–50); the SUM journal **Avangard* (Munich, 1946–51); the satirical biweeklies

Đzhak (Ellwangen, 1946), *Komar-izhak* (Munich, 1946–9), and *Lys Mykyta* (Munich, 1947–9); the children's monthly *Mali druzi* (Augsburg, 1947–8); the political journal *Problemy* (Munich, 1946–8); and the religious weekly *Khrystyians'kyi holos* (Munich, est 1949).

Notable periodicals in the more controlled and censored British zone were the mimeographed camp dailies *Biuleten' taboru im. M. Lysenka* (Hannover, 1945–7), *Radionovyny* (Braunschweig, 1945–7), and *Ostanni visti* (Heidenau, 1947–8); the printed weeklies *Luna* (Heidenau, 1946), *Nasha poshta* (Heidenau, 1946–7), *Ukraïns'ke slovo* (Blomberg, 1948–9), and *Ranok* (1948–51); the journal *Na chuzhyni* (Korigen, 1946–8); and the scholarly-literary magazine *Ukraïna i svit* (Hannover, 1949–69). In Austria there were the camp daily *Taborovi visti* (Landeck, 1945–7); the weekly papers *Ostanni novyny* (Salzburg, 1945–9), *Nedil'ni visti* (Landeck, 1945–7), *Novi dni* (Salzburg, 1945–8), and *Promin'* (Salzburg, 1946–9); the satirical weekly *Proty shersty* (Landeck, 1946–7); and the literary-cultural journals *Kerma* (Salzburg, 1946–7), *Zveno* (Innsbruck, 1946–7), and *Litavry* (Salzburg, 1947). At the POW camp near Rimini, Italy, the daily *Zhyttia v tabori* (1945–6), the weekly *Bat'kivshchyna* (1945–7), and five other camp periodicals appeared.

Because of the mass emigration of Ukrainian refugees to other Western countries, by 1951 there were only 7 newspapers and 16 other periodicals in West *Germany, and none in Austria. Dozens of Ukrainian newspapers and journals and hundreds of bulletins have been established in the new host countries since the late 1940s, how-

Some of the Ukrainian magazines published in Canada in the postwar period

ever, primarily in the *United States and *Canada but also in *Australia, *Great Britain, *France, *Belgium, *Argentina, and *Brazil. They have reflected the political, religious, organizational, institutional, and occupational diversity, growth, and decline of the organized Ukrainian communities in those countries.

(See also *Agricultural periodicals, *Bibliographic journals, *Children's magazines, *Co-operative press, *Economic press, *Humoristic and satiric press, *Legal press, *Literary journals, *Medical journals, *Music journals, *Pedagogical periodicals, *Religious press, *Student press, *Technical journals, and *Women's press. For information on the few Ukrainian-language periodicals published in postwar Eastern Europe, see *Poland, *Prešov region, *Rumania, and *Yugoslavia.)

Some of the Ukrainian newspapers published in the West since the Second World War

BIBLIOGRAPHY

Lisovskii, N. *Russkaia periodicheskaia pechat', 1703–1900 g. (Bibliografiia i graficheskiia tablitsy)* (Petrograd 1915)

Kuzelia, Z. *Z kul'turnoho zhyttia Ukraïny* (Salzwedel 1918)

Kalynovych, I. *Ukraïns'ka presa i vydavnytstva za 1923 rik* (Lviv–Kiev 1924)

Ihnatiienko, V. *Ukraïns'ka presa (1816–1923 rr.) (Istoryko-bibliohrafichnyi etiud)* (Kharkiv 1926)

Gorodetskii, B. *Periodika Kubansko-Chernomorskogo kraia, 1863–1925* (Krasnodar 1927)

Otamanovs'kyi, V. (ed). *Chasopysy Podillia: Istorychno-bibliohrafichnyi zbirnyk z nahody 150-littia pershoï hazety na Ukraïni (1776–1926) ta 10-littia isnuvannia USRR* (Vinnytsia 1927–8)

Ihnatiienko, V. *Bibliohrafiia ukraïns'koï presy, 1816–1916* (Kiev 1930; repr, State College, Penn 1968)

Chyzh, Ia. 'Piv stolittia ukraïns'koï presy v Amerytsi,' *Kalendar Ukraïns'koho robitnychoho soiuza na rik 1939* (Scranton, Penn)

Zlenko, P. 'Periodychni vydannia Naddniprianshchyny v 1918 rotsi,' *Ukraïns'ka knyha*, 1938, nos 6–7

Zhyvotko, A. *Presa Karpats'koï Ukraïny* (Prague 1940)
– *Istoriia ukraïns'koï presy* (Regensburg 1946)

Myshuha, L.; Drahan, A. (eds). *Iuvileinyi al'manakh 'Svobody,' 1893–1953* (Jersey City)

Martynets', V. 'Ukraïns'ka natsionalistychna presa,' in *Orhanizatsiia ukraïns'kykh natsionalistiv 1929–1954* ([Paris] 1955)

Bahrych, M.; Mazus, D.; Ruban, H. (comps). *Periodychni vydannia URSR, 1918–1950. Zhurnaly: Bibliohrafichnyi pokazhchyk* (Kharkiv 1956)

Kravchuk, P. *P'iatdesiat rokiv sluzhinnia narodu: Do istoriï ukraïns'koï narodnoï presy v Kanadi* (Toronto 1957)

Beliaeva, L.; Zinov'eva, M.; Nikiforov, M. *Bibliografiia periodicheskikh izdanii Rossii, 1910–1916*, 3 vols (Leningrad 1958–60)

Shcherbak, A. *Pershi kroky: Z istoriï radians'koï literatury ta presy na Ukraïni (1917–1920 rr.)* (Kiev 1958; 2d edn, 1967)

Dei, O. *Ukraïns'ka revoliutsiino-demokratychna zhurnalistyka: Problema, vynyknennia i stanovlennia* (Kiev 1959)

Fedchenko, P. *Materialy z istoriï ukraïns'koï zhurnalistyky*, vol 1, *Persha polovyna XIX st.* (Kiev 1959)

Doroshenko, V. (comp). 'Ukraïns'ka presa u vil'nomu sviti v rokakh 1961 i 1962,' *Svoboda, 1893–1963: Al'manakh na rik 1963* (Jersey City)

Periodychni vydannia URSR, 1918–1960. Hazety: Bibliohrafichnyi dovidnyk (Kharkiv 1965)

Radion, S. 'Bibliohrafichnyi ohliad: Presovi vydannia (hazety, biuleteni, kalendari i inshe),' in *Ukraïntsi v Avstraliï: Materiialy do istoriï poselennia ukraïntsiv v Avstraliï* (Melbourne 1966)

Fedyns'kyi, O. *Bibliohrafichnyi pokazhchyk ukraïns'koï presy poza mezhamy Ukraïny za 1966 rik* (Cleveland 1967)

Ruban, V. *I v trudi i v boiu ... (50 rokiv ukraïns'koï radians'koï presy)* (Kiev 1967)

Fedchenko, P. *Presa ta ïï poperednyky: Istoriia zarodzhennia i osnovni zakonomirnosti rozvytku* (Kiev 1969)

Boiko, M. *Bibliohrafiia periodyky Volyni* (Bloomington 1970)

Puzyr'ova, O.; Dmytriiev, O.; Dovhalenko, Iu. (comps). *Kataloh dorevoliutsiinykh hazet, shcho vydavalysia na Ukraïni (1822–1916): Publikatsiï fondu TsNB URSR* (Kiev 1971; repr, Edmonton 1988)

Oleksiuk, M. *Prohresyvna presa Zakhidnoï Ukraïny v borot'bi na zakhyst SRSR (20–30-ti roky)* (Kiev 1973)

Ternopil's'kyi, Iu. [Lukasevych, L.]. *Ukraïns'ka presa z perspektyvy 150-littia (Statystychno istorychnyi narys)* (Jersey City 1974)

Fedyns'kyi, O. *Bibliohrafichnyi pokazhchyk ukraïns'koï presy poza mezhamy Ukraïny: Richnyk VII–IX za 1972–1974 roky* (Cleveland, Ohio 1975)

Chaikovs'kyi, I. *Ukraïns'ki periodychni vydannia v druhii svitovii viini, 1939–1945*, ed M. Kravchuk (Philadelphia 1976)

Kmiecik, Z.; Myślinski, J.; et al. *Prasa polska w latach 1864–1918* (Warsaw 1976)

Nyzovyi, M.; et al (comps). *Presa Ukraïns'koï RSR, 1918–1975: Naukovo-statystychnyi dovidnyk* (Kharkiv 1976)

Borovyk, M. *Ukraïns'ko-kanads'ka presa ta ïï znachennia dlia ukraïns'koï menshyny v Kanadi* (Munich 1977)

Holiiat, R. 'Istoriia ukraïns'koï presy v Amerytsi,' *Al'manakh Ukraïns'koho narodnoho soiuzu 1978* (Jersey City)

Pakhucha, L.; Luk'ianchuk, O.; Sira, I. (comps). *Hazety Radians'koï Ukraïny, 1917–1920 rr. (Za materialamy hazetnykh fondiv TsNB AN URSR): Bibliohrafichnyi pokazhchyk* (Kiev 1979; repr Edmonton 1988)

Paczkowski, A. *Prasa polska w latach 1918–1939* (Warsaw 1980)

Pakhucha, L.; Luk'ianchuk, O.; Sira, I. (comps). *Hazety Radians'koï Ukraïny, 1921–1925 rr. (Za materialamy hazetnykh fondiv TsNB URSR* (Kiev 1981; repr, Edmonton 1988)

Notkowski, A. *Polska prasa prowincjonal'na Drugiej Rzeczypospolitej (1918–1939)* (Warsaw–Łódź 1982)

Letopis' periodicheskikh i prodolzhaiushchikhsia izdanii, 1976–1980: Gosudarstvennyi bibliograficheskii ukazatel' SSSR, 2 vols (Moscow 1983, 1985)

Il'nyts'kyi, R. 'Ukraïns'ka presa taborovoï doby,' *Suchasnist'*, 1984, no. 5

Misiło, E. 'Prasa ukraińska w Polsce (1918–1939),' *Kwartalnik Historii Prasy Polskiej*, 23, no. 4 (1984)

Pakhucha, L.; Luk'ianchuk, O.; Sira, I. (comps). *Hazety Radians'koï Ukraïny 1926–1929 rr. u fondakh TsNB URSR: Kataloh* (Kiev 1985; repr, Edmonton 1988)

Wynar, L. 'The Ukrainian Press in the United States: Past and Present Developments,' *Ethnic Forum: Journal of Ethnic Studies and Ethnic Bibliography*, 5, nos 1–2 (1985)

– *Guide to the American Ethnic Press: Slavic and East European Newspapers and Periodicals* (Kent, Ohio 1986)

Misiło, E. 'Prasa Zachodnio-Ukraińskiej Republiki Ludowej: Zarys bibliograficzny,' *Kwartalnik Historii Prasy Polskiej*, 26, no. 2 (1987)

Sydorenko, O. (comp). *Ukraïnomovna presa Rosiï, 1905–1907 rr.: Anotovanyi pokazhchyk periodychnykh vydan'* (Kiev 1987)

Narizhnyi, S. 'Ukraïns'ka presa,' in *Ukraïns'ka kul'tura*, ed D. Antonovych (Munich 1988)

Sydorenko, O. (comp). *Nezdiisneni vydannia: Anotovanyi pokazhchyk nerealizovanykh proektiv ukraïnomovnykh periodychnykh orhaniv* (Kiev 1990)

Borysenko, T.; Zavarzina, O.; Zalizniuk, O. (comps). *Vydannia politychnykh partii, rukhiv, samodiial'nykh hromads'kykh ob'iednan' i tovarystv v Ukraïni, 1989–1990 rr.: Kataloh (Za materialamy hazetnykh fondiv TsNB im. V.I. Vernads'koho AN URSR* (Edmonton 1991)

Kataloh respublikans'kykh, oblasnykh ta mis'kykh hazet Ukraïns'koï RSR (1985–1980) (Edmonton 1991)

Misylo, Ie. *Bibliohrafiia ukraïns'koï presy u Pol'shchi (1918–1939) i Zakhidn'o-Ukraïns'kii Narodnii Respublitsi (1918–1919)* (Edmonton 1991)

B. Kravtsiv, R. Senkus

Press and information bureaus abroad. In the second half of the 19th century, Ukrainian émigrés (M. *Drahomanov and his Geneva circle), Galician and Bukovynian parliamentarians in Vienna, and I. Franko and other Galician publicists began informing the Western press and public about Ukrainian affairs, the national oppression of the Ukrainians, and the goals of the Ukrainian national movement. In the Russian Empire, members of the St Petersburg Ukrainian Hromada and later the State Duma, particularly M. Kostomarov, P. Kulish, D. Mordovets, O. Lototsky, P. Stebnytsky, M. Mohyliansky, M. Hrushevsky, O. Salikovsky, M. Slavinsky, S. Petliura, P. Chyzhevsky, V. Shemet, and I. Shrah, played a similar role by contributing articles to influential Russian publications and later issuing their own periodicals, such as *Ukrainskii vestnik* (1906) in St Petersburg and *Ukrainskaia zhizn'* (1912–17) in Moscow.

From 1900 to 1920 the principal foreign center of information about Ukraine was Vienna. There R. *Sembratovych edited the Ukrainian affairs journals *X-Strahlen* (1901–2) and *Ruthenische Revue* (1903–5), and V. *Kushnir edited *Ukrainische Rundschau* (1906–14). In 1907 Kushnir established the first independent Ukrainian press bureau in Vienna. Elsewhere in Europe similar efforts were made by Ya. *Fedorchuk in Geneva and Paris, V. *Stepankivsky and G. *Raffalovich in London, O. Bochkovsky in Prague, and L. Drahomanova and her husband, I. Shishmanov, in Sofia. In 1912 a short-lived Ukrainian Information Committee was initiated by A. *Zhuk in Lviv.

During the First World War the *General Ukrainian Council in Vienna published in German the information weeklies *Ukrainisches Korrespondenzblatt* (1914–16) and *Ukrainische Korrespondenz* (1917–18). The Vienna-based *Union for the Liberation of Ukraine (SVU) published

Ukrainische Nachrichten (1914–18) and *Ukrainische Blätter* (1916–18) in Vienna, *La Revue Ukrainienne* (1915–17) in Lausanne, Switzerland, and pro-Ukrainian propaganda in 11 European languages. Also in Lausanne, Stepankivsky organized a Ukrainian Bureau and published *L'Ukraine* (1915–20) and, irregularly, *The Ukraine*. The bureau disseminated the latest news about Ukraine, which it received from I. Nimchuk and I. Krevetsky, who worked for the Press Bureau of the Austrian Ministry of War. In Berlin a Ukrainian Press Bureau was organized by D. Dontsov and funded by the Ukrainian Parliamentary Representation; it published *Nachrichten des Ukrainischen Pressbüros* and political brochures in 1914–16. In 1916 Dontsov moved to Bern, Switzerland, where until March 1917 he headed the Bureau of Nationalities of Russia and published in German, French, and English the bulletin *Korrespondenz der Nationalitäten Russlands*, funded by V. Stepankivsky. In Budapest H. Strypsky published, in cooperation with the SVU, the Hungarian-language monthly *Ukránia* (1916–17). In the United States two organizations – the Ukrainian National Council (later Committee) and the Federation of Ukrainians – published a number of information bulletins and brochures.

After the creation of the Ukrainian Central Rada in 1917, and particularly after the proclamation of Ukrainian independence in January 1918, information services became the responsibility of government agencies, notably of Ukrainian consulates and missions abroad, which were allotted funds for this purpose from the state budget. In addition a private Ukrainian press bureau functioned in Vienna under the direction of V. Biberovych and M. Bardakh briefly in 1917. The 1918 Hetman government's Ministry of Internal Affairs established a Ukrainian Telegraph Agency (UTA) and State Press Bureau; headed by D. Dontsov, the UTA systematically published press bulletins in various European languages. In Vienna in 1918, V. Kalynovych published *Ukrainische Blätter*, and late that year the UNR Directory established a Ukrainian Press Service (UPS) there. Headed by V. Bryndzan and O. Kushchak, the UPS was financed initially by the Western Ukrainian National Republic (ZUNR) mission in Vienna and in 1919–20 by the UNR mission. It was the main Ukrainian information agency in Europe at the time. In addition press bureaus attached to UNR missions in London, Sofia, The Hague, Copenhagen, Berlin, Budapest, Helsinki, Paris, Bern, Lausanne, Athens, and New York issued bulletins in the official languages of their host countries. Particularly comprehensive press and information activities were conducted by the UNR and ZUNR delegations at the Paris Peace Conference, to countervail the Polish and Russian émigré lobbies there.

In the interwar period the Government-in-exile of the ZUNR established a press bureau in Vienna; headed by V. Biberovych, it functioned from early 1920 to March 1923. Until 1939 the *Government-in-exile of the UNR conducted an intensive information campaign through its various representatives employed by foreign press agencies (eg, M. Kovalevsky, M. Yeremiiv) and through its missions, primarily that in Paris, which subsidized the periodicals *L'Europe orientale* (1919–20), *France et L'Ukraine* (1920), *Prométhée* (1924–38), *L'Ukraine nouvelle* (1927–9), *Bulletin du Bureau de Presse ukrainienne* (1934–9), *La *Revue de Prométhée* (1938–40), and other publications. In Switzerland M. Yeremiiv's *Ofinor agency issued press bulletins

A bulletin published by the Ukrainian Press Service in Geneva (1930)

in German, French, and Ukrainian in Geneva (1928–44); in French (1929–39) and Spanish (1932–6) in Paris; and in Italian in Rome (1929–43). In Berlin a government-supported *German-Ukrainian Society published the journal *Die *Ukraine* (1918–26). Other news and information periodicals were also published there: *Deutsch-Ukrainische Zeitung* (1920), edited by H. Kliuk; *Osteuropäische Korrespondenz* (1926–34), edited by Z. Kuzelia and R. Jary; and *Ukrainische Kulturberichte* (1933–40), published by the Ukrainian Scientific Institute in Berlin. In London the Ukrainian Bureau, headed by V. Kaye-Kysilewsky, published several bulletins from 1930 to 1939, and a group of hetmanite supporters published the bulletin *The Investigator* (1932–4), edited by V. Korostovets. In Prague *Ukraïns'ka korespondentsiia* (1930–1) and *Ukrajina* published information in Czech, and M. *Hekhter wrote on Ukrainian affairs in the journals *Prager Presse* (1921–38) and *Slavische Rundschau* (1929–40). In Warsaw the Ukrainian question in Poland was illuminated in *Natio* (1926–7), a monthly edited by P. Lysiak and published in English, French, German, and Polish, and in the weekly *Biuletyn Polsko-Ukraiński* (1932–8) and monthly *Problemy Europy Wschodniej* (1939), edited by W. Bączkowski.

In the 1930s the OUN developed its own press and information network in Europe. Its *Ukrainian Press Service in Berlin published the bulletin *Ukrainischer Pressedienst*, edited by M. Seleshko (1931–4) and V. Stakhiv (1937–41). In New York City the OUN ran a Ukrainian Press Service from 1938 to 1941 under the direction of Ye. Skotsko. It also issued *Bulletin d'informations ukrainiennes* (ed M. Kushnir) in Geneva, a bulletin in English (ed Ye. Liakhovych [1933–5] and S. Davidovich [1938–9]) in London, and bulletins in other languages in Rome, Prague, Kaunas, Paris, Vienna, and Madrid.

Since the Second World War, information about Ukraine has been disseminated in the West by various Ukrainian political and community organizations in Western Europe and the New World. Information in several languages has been released by the Munich-based Ukrainian Supreme Liberation Council (UHVR) and Ukrainian National Council. English-language news and analyses of developments in Ukraine have been published in Jersey City, New Jersey, in the Ukrainian National Association's *Ukrainian Weekly* (est 1933); in New York City in the Ukrainian Congress Committee of America's *Ukrainian Quarterly* (est 1944) and biweekly *Ukrainian Bulletin* (1951–70), in the *Prolog Research Corporation's *Digest of the Soviet Ukrainian Press* (1957–77) and *Prolog* (1957–61), and, in the early 1980s, in the *Herald of Repression in Ukraine* (ed N. Svitlychna) of the External Representation of the Ukrainian Helsinki Group; in Munich in the Anti-Bolshevik Bloc of Nations' ABN *Correspondence* (est 1950) and the quarterly *Problems of the Peoples of the USSR* of the League for the Liberation of Ukraine; in London in the Association of Ukrainians in Great Britain's *Ukrainian Review* (est 1954) and, in the mid-1980s, in the Prolog-funded *Focus on Ukraine* and *Soviet Nationality Survey*; in Baltimore, Maryland, in the *Smoloskyp information service's *Smoloskyp* (est 1974); and in Toronto in the World Congress of Free Ukrainians' *Ukrainian Newsletter* (est 1980). In the late 1980s the London-based Ukrainian Press Agency, directed by T. Kuzio, issued press releases about developments in Ukraine. Information has appeared in German in *Ukraine in Vergangenheit und Gegenwart* (1952–7, 1962–8) in Munich; in Portuguese in *Boletim informativo* (1946–9), a monthly published in Curitiba, Brazil, by a UHVR-affiliated Ukrainian Press Service; in Spanish in *Ucrania Libre*, published in the 1950s by a Ukrainian Information Bureau in Buenos Aires, and in a Spanish version of *Smoloskyp* (est 1975); in Italian in *Ucraina* (1954–6, ed V. Fedoronchuk) and in press releases issued by a Ukrainian Press Bureau (est 1985) monitoring religious affairs in Ukraine, in Rome; and in French in *L'Est européen* (est 1960), *Echoes d'Ukraine* (1962–9), *Bulletin Franco–Ukrainien* (1959–70), and *Echanges: Revue franco-ukrainienne* (est 1971) in Paris.

Notable non-Ukrainian institutions that have issued information on and analyses of developments in Ukraine are *Radio Liberty and the *Institute for the Study of the USSR in Munich, Vatican Radio, and Keston College in England.

V. Markus

Press Office of the Supreme Command of the Ukrainian Galician Army (Presova kvatyra Nachalnoi komandy UHA). A press and information department that from January 1919 to January 1920 organized education and entertainment for the soldiers of the Ukrainian Galician Army (UHA) and civilians and publicized the army's activities and the cause of Ukrainian independence. Headed by I. Erdenberger, I. Herasymovych, and, from November 1919, O. Levytsky, it published the newspapers *Kozats'kyi holos* (68 issues, 1919–20) and *Strilets'*, the al-

manac *Ukraïns'kyi prapor*, pamphlets, and leaflets and organized lectures, plays, concerts, public meetings, and libraries on wheels. The office had information bureaus in the three UHA corps and representatives in all the brigades. UHA officers attached to the press office included writers and journalists, such as I. Krevetsky, V. Pachovsky, R. Kovshevych, R. Kupchynsky, L. Lepky, and V. Bobynsky.

Ivan Bobersky at the Press Office of the Ukrainian Sich Riflemen in Sosniv in 1916. From left: Osyp Kurylas, Lev Lepky, Mykhailo Haivoronsky, Roman Kupchynsky, Bobersky, Ivan Ivanets

Press Office of the Ukrainian Sich Riflemen (Presova kvartyra Ukrainskykh Sichovykh Striltsiv). The information department of the Ukrainian Sich Riflemen (USS). Established in the fall of 1914, it published prose, poetry, manuals, and songbooks for the USS; the newspaper *Vistnyk Presovoï kvatyry*; the humor magazines *Samokhotnyk* (35 issues, 1915–19) and *Samopal* (1916, 10 issues); and an almanac (1917). The office's first heads were T. Melen and O. Nazaruk. They were succeeded by I. Ivanets, who headed its work at the front (1916–18), and M. Uhryn-Bezhrishny, who directed the work at headquarters. Many writers, artists, and musicians were attached as USS to the office, among them L. Lepky, R. Kupchynsky, M. Haivoronsky, A. Babiuk (M. Irchan), L. Lutsiv, L. Gets, Yu. Butsmaniuk, M. Havrylko, M. Holubets, and O. Kurylas. The office also maintained a written and photographic chronicle of the USS, and organized education for the soldiers.

Pretvych, Yov [Pretvyč, Jov], b ?, d (probably) 29 October 1571. Architect, military engineer, and builder. One of the outstanding Ukrainian Renaissance architects, he worked on various castles and fortifications, notably in Cracow and Vilnius. He is particularly famous for his complete reconstruction of the fortress at Kamianets-Podilskyi, where he rebuilt and strengthened the defensive walls and five of the main towers, and erected many new structures, including the so-called Polish gate system with towers and other fortifications.

Pretwicz, Bernard, b ca 1500, d ca 1563. Silesian noble and Polish military figure. From 1525 he served King Sigismund I as an envoy in Europe. As the Polish cavalry commander in Podilia from 1538 and starosta of Bar (1540–51) Pretwicz became famous for his defense of the Polish Commonwealth's steppe frontier in Ukraine. His force of Polish cavalry and registered Cossacks fought Tatar raiders in Podilia and Right-Bank Ukraine; it defeated them 70 times, and 3 times (1541, 1542, 1545) it attacked the Ottoman fortress in Ochakiv. His troops released many Tatar captives and took many horses and prisoners. In his apologia (pub 1866) presented to the Polish Sejm in 1550, Pretwicz reported on the border war and defended himself against the sultan's grievances. He was relieved of his command and appointed starosta of Terebovlia in 1552.

Priashevshchina (The Prešov Region). A semiweekly (1945) and then weekly organ of the pro-Soviet Ukrainian People's Council of the Prešov Region, published in Prešov from March 1945 to August 1951. It was supported primarily by Russophiles and appeared mostly in Russian, although some articles and feuilletons and humor were published in the Prešov dialect, especially after 1949. The paper contained pro-communist articles on political and community affairs in the Prešov region. The chief editors were I. Pieshchak and F. Lazoryk.

Přibik, Josyf (Pryibik, Yosyp), b 11 March 1855 in Příbram, Bohemia, d 20 October 1937 in Odessa. Conductor, composer, and pedagogue of Bohemian descent. After graduating from the Prague Piano Academy (1875), he moved to Smolensk (1878) to teach at the Russian Musical Society school. He subsequently worked as an opera conductor (1880–94) in Kharkiv, Lviv, Kiev, Moscow, and Tbilisi before becoming principal conductor of the Odessa Opera (1894–1937). From 1919 he served as a professor at the Odessa Conservatory. His works include eight one-act operas, symphonic and vocal pieces, and articles on music theory.

Prices. The amounts of money for which things are exchanged. From 1917 the Soviet government in Ukraine implemented price-stabilizing policies as an integral part of economic planning. During the period of War Communism hyperinflation made the currency worthless. Transactions between state enterprises were made on the basis of bookkeeping entries. Food was requisitioned from the peasantry by the government, and workers were paid in kind. The *New Economic Policy announced in 1921 restored private trade and monetary transactions. Hyperinflation continued because of the dearth of goods on the market. To control the situation the *chervonets*, backed by gold, was introduced in 1922 alongside the rapidly depreciating *radznak*, which was abolished in early 1924. In autumn 1923 the so-called Scissors Crisis occurred as a result of falling agricultural prices and rising industrial prices. Based on an index of 100 for 1 November 1923, wholesale industrial prices in Kharkiv reached 4740.6 by 1 March 1924. State-enforced selling of industrial products eventually brought about price stability.

During the late 1920s price controls were used increasingly as an instrument of economic policy. State enterprises and co-operatives were required to undercut prices found in the private retail sector. That measure led only to shortages, speculation, and the payment of low grain prices by the state to the peasants. With the onset of collectivization and the First *Five-year Plan the private sector was eliminated, the peasantry was forced to sell its produce to the state at fixed prices, and price controls were imposed on all goods. In Ukraine in 1928 the price paid by the state for wheat was set at 8.05 *karbovantsi* per 100 kilograms. It remained fixed until 1935, when a 10 percent increase was allowed. From 1928 to 1940 economic policy emphasized industrialization at the expense of price stability. A turnover tax was introduced in 1930, and thereafter price increases became a function of increases in tax. Different prices were introduced for the same commodity: retail prices for goods sold by ration coupons, state 'commercial' prices for goods sold by special authorization at higher prices, and market prices found in quasi-legal bazaars and the black market. Prices in state and co-operative stores were eventually raised to obviate the need for rationing.

The immediate postwar period saw a return to the system found in the early 1930s. Large subsidies kept industrial prices down, rationing and high 'commercial' prices emerged, and eventually rationing, which had been preceded by large price increases, was abolished. Price reductions were introduced between 1947 and 1954, but the measure resulted only in large-scale shortages. After 1954 the Soviet government embarked on a rigid policy of price stabilization, which halted inflation and resulted in continual shortages in state stores and in a flourishing black market. Although officially denied, some degree of inflation continued, because factories replaced low-priced old products with slightly modified higher-priced new products.

Price formation was highly centralized, and prices were set by the USSR State Planning Committee (Gosplan) and its affiliated section, the State Committee on Prices. Factory wholesale prices were determined by the average cost of production plus a certain profit margin (usually 3–5 percent). Industrial wholesale prices were prices at which goods were transferred to users outside the industry, and they included a turnover tax. Retail prices were also set by the state, and included a turnover tax. In practice prices were set quite arbitrarily. Many industrial and agricultural products were heavily subsidized, and many industries operated at a continuous loss. Bread and meat prices did not change for decades, whereas vodka prices went up by large jumps. There were also regional price differences, although the differences within a republic were small. It has been calculated that food prices in Ukraine were 13 percent lower than the Union average. Arbitrary prices were also a means of achieving capital transfers between republics. Ukraine, as an exporter of predominantly low-priced raw materials and semiprocessed goods, such as grain, coal, and metal products, and an importer of high-priced finished products, such as machinery, manufactures, and textiles, effectively exported its national income regardless of its interrepublican trade balance.

Complete price revisions, such as the 1967 and 1982 changes, were political decisions. From 1987 price reform reduced the number of commodity prices fixed by the Central State Planning Committee and delegated more responsibility to territorial boards and self-financing enterprises. Large-scale price reform based on market supply and demand was actively discussed and continually delayed until the decline of the USSR in 1991.

B. Somchynsky

Priiatel' ditei (Children's Friend). An illustrated magazine for children, edited and published in 1881–3 in Kolomyia monthly and then semimonthly (a total of 25 issues) by I. Trembytsky.

Prikarpatskaia Rus' (Subcarpathian Ruthenia). A Russophile daily newspaper published in Lviv in 1909–15 by the Russian People's Organization and edited by S. Labensky. Renewed after the First World War (December 1918 to December 1920) as the organ of the *Russian Executive Committee under the editorship of K. Valnytsky, it supported the White forces in the Russian Civil War and welcomed Hetman P. Skoropadsky's proclamation of Ukraine's federation with Russia. Falling circulation caused the newspaper to close; it was succeeded by *Volia narodu*.

Prikaz. A Russian term for a government office or chancellery, from the Russian word for order or command. In the 16th, 17th, and early 18th centuries *prikazy* were agencies of the Muscovite central government. Each *prikaz* had specific responsibilities and its own budget and staff. Their number was not constant; altogether there were 80 of them. Each *prikaz* was headed by a *sudia* (judge) appointed, usually from among the boyars, by the tsar. Day-to-day operations were conducted by *diaki* (secretaries), *podiachie* (undersecretaries), and their support staff. *Prikazy* that dealt with Ukrainian matters were the Foreign Office (Posolskii prikaz); the *Little Russian Office; the War Office (Razriadnyi prikaz), which supervised the towns of the Hetman state where Muscovite garrisons were stationed; and the Office of Great Russia (Prikaz Velikoi Rossii), which supervised the administration of Slobidska Ukraine's regiments in 1687–1700. In 1718–20 Emperor Peter I replaced the *prikazy* with fewer but more efficient *kollegii* (collegiums) modeled on Swedish counterparts (see *Little Russian Collegium).

Primary Chronicle. See *Povist' vremennykh lit*.

Primary education. See Education and Elementary schools.

Primary party organizations (PPO). The lowest units in the structure of the CPSU. Their major goal was to recruit new members and to ensure adherence to Party policy at every level of economic activity. They were formed in places of employment, such as factories, collective farms, institutions, military units, and schools, or in specific housing districts or settlements. Until 1939 these organizations were referred to as 'cells.' At an annual meeting members elected a secretary and deputy. If a PPO had more than 15 members, a larger bureau was elected to run its day-to-day affairs. If there were more than 150 members, full-time Party workers were hired. A PPO was required to hold monthly meetings. The minimum size of a PPO was 3 members. In factories with over 50 Party members PPOs could be established in individual departments. In factories with over 300 Party members, or in some cases over 100 members, a Party committee could be formed to co-ordinate the work of the PPOs in the departments. In all instances smaller Party groups could be formed in the various work brigades. Funding for a PPO was provided by the CPU. In 1986 there were 70,900 PPOs in Ukraine, with an average membership of 107 per PPO.

Primitive art. Pictures by artists without professional training who work in a way that differs from the traditional or avant-garde with respect to manner of depiction and techniques of paint application. Such pictures show an idiosyncratic naïveté in the treatment and depiction of the subject matter and the use of the medium. Icons on glass popular from the late 18th to the early 20th centuries in Western Ukraine are charming examples of primitive art, as are folk icons on panels created by artists who took inspiration from professionally painted models. The most prominent Ukrainian primitive artist is *Nykyfor, who rendered churches, other buildings, saints, and people in captivating compositions. Others whose work was influenced by Ukrainian folk art and ornamentation include K. *Bilokur, who painted flower fantasies, and M. *Pryimachenko and H. *Sobachko-Shostak, both of whom portrayed fantastic creatures and plant motifs in vivid colors. Of the Ukrainian primitive artists working outside their homeland, D. *Stryjek in Canada has received the greatest recognition.

Primore krai. See Far East.

Primorsko-Akhtarsk [Primorsko-Axtarsk] (Ukrainian: Prymorsko-Akhtarske). VII-19. A port city (1974 pop 28,000) on the Sea of Azov and a raion center in Krasnodar krai, RF. According to the Soviet census of 1926, Ukrainians accounted for 64.5 percent of the city's population.

Prince (*kniaz*). The title of the ruler among many Slavic peoples. In medieval Ukraine the first princes were the rulers of the various Slavic *tribes. Their authority was usually restricted to military defense of the tribal territory and a few administrative and judicial functions. The various lands, districts, and village communities had their own organs of self-government. After the establishment of the *Riurykide dynasty and the creation of the Kievan Rus' state in the 9th century, the authority of the prince gradually increased and became more monarchical in nature. Most of the East Slavic lands came under the rule of the so-called grand prince of Kiev. In the late 11th century the Kievan state began breaking up into separate independent principalities. Thenceforth the various Rus' princes were no longer the sole bearers of executive power, but ruled alongside the *Boyar Council and the popular assembly, or *viche. The prince had supreme military, legislative, and judicial authority within his principality. He collected taxes and tribute from the population and represented it at various congresses of princes (*snemy*).

The order of princely succession was complex. The guiding principle was genealogical seniority, according to which the oldest member of the dynasty ascended the Kievan throne, and the younger members, according to their age and place on the genealogical tree, became the rulers of various appanages that were themselves ranked hierarchically. All Riurykides had the right to rule a principality, and in the event of the death of one of the senior princes they acquired a higher-ranking appanage. At the

1097 *Liubech congress of princes genealogical seniority was abandoned in favor of the principle of primogeniture. Both principles, however, were at times disregarded by the *viche*, which elected another prince as their ruler after expelling (and even killing) a prince who had neglected his responsibilities or abused his office. Often the principles were violated by the more powerful princes themselves, who would seize the thrones of their weaker counterparts.

In addition to princes who ruled there were also servitor (*sluzhebni*) princes, who did not inherit domains, or were forced to cede the ones they had, and entered the service of ruling princes. After the Mongol-Tatar invasion the princes' role was dramatically reduced. The khan of the Golden Horde influenced succession to the various thrones by conferring his patent (*iarlyk*) only on princes who were sufficiently obeisant and brought him tribute. After the annexation of most of Ukraine by the Grand Duchy of Lithuania in the 14th century, the Ukrainian princes became its vassals. In the 15th and 16th centuries they gradually ceased being rulers and became influential landowning magnates who retained only a few of their ancient privileges, such as the right to maintain a small, private military force (*korohva*). Essentially, however, they became the upper echelon of the Lithuanian-Ruthenian landed nobility.

BIBLIOGRAPHY
Sergeevich, V. *Veche i kniaz'* (Moscow 1867)
Vladimirskii-Budanov, M. *Obzor istorii russkago prava* (Kiev 1907)
Presniakov, A. *Kniazhee pravo v drevnei Rusi* (St Petersburg 1909)
Rapov, O. *Kniazheskiie vladeniia na Rusi v X–pervoi polovine XIII v.* (Moscow 1977)

L. Okinshevych

Princely era (*kniazha doba*). The term used by non–Soviet Ukrainian historians, and some Russian historians, to designate a 500-year period in the Middle Ages when the East Slavic *princes held political power over the territory of present-day Ukraine. The princely era encompasses (1) the period from the creation of the independent *Kievan Rus' state in the 9th century to its disintegration after the Mongol-Tatar invasion of 1240, and (2) the contiguous period of the independent Principality of *Galicia-Volhynia, which disintegrated after the death of its last prince, Yurii II Boleslav, in 1340.

Most modern non–Soviet Ukrainian historians have adhered to M. *Hrushevsky's scheme of Eastern Slav history, in which the princely era is treated as an integral part of Ukrainian history. According to Hrushevsky 'the Kievan [Rus'] state, law, and culture were the creation of a single nationality – the Ukrainian-Rus' [nationality]' and 'the Kievan period merged with the Galician-Volhynian period in the 13th century.' Most Russian and some Western

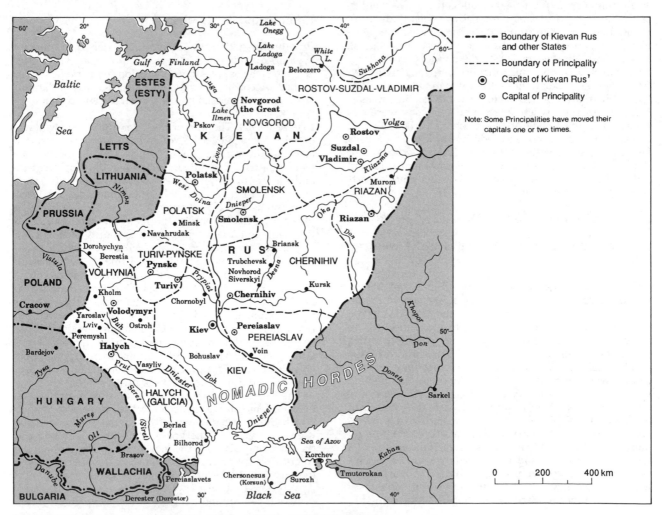

PRINCELY ERA IN THE 11TH–13TH CENTURIES

historians have viewed the era as belonging solely to Russian history. The term 'princely era' was not used at all in Soviet historiography. Instead Soviet historians used the term 'period of feudalism' and propounded the officially sanctioned view that an 'ancient Rus' people' and the 'ancient Rus' state' were the cradle of three 'fraternal' peoples, the Russians, Ukrainians, and Belarusians. Ukrainian historians in the West have rejected the appropriation of the princely era by Russian historians and the Soviet fraternal peoples theory, viewing it as a veiled version of the Russian imperialist interpretation.

A. Zhukovsky

Printing. The earliest books printed in the Ukrainian redaction of Church Slavonic and in the Cyrillic alphabet in general – the Orthodox hymnal *Oktoikh* (Octoechos) and *Chasoslovets'* (Horologion) – were produced in 1491 by S. Fiol, a Franconian expatriate in Cracow. These were followed by liturgical books produced in the Lithuanian-Ruthenian state by short-lived presses on Belarusian territory, such as F. Skoryna's in Vilno (now Vilnius in Lithuania, 1525), I. Fedorovych and P. Mstislavets's in Zabludove (now Zabłudów in Poland, 1568–70), and V. Tsiapinsky's itinerant press (ca 1565–70).

The first press on Ukrainian ethnic territory was founded by I. *Fedorovych in Lviv (1573–4). Its equipment and assets were used to found the *Lviv Dormition Brotherhood Press (1591–1788), which played a key role in the history of early Ukrainian printing. Thereafter Lviv remained a major printing center. Established there were Polish (1592–1602, 1670–3, 1684–93), Calvinist (1608–11), and Armenian (1616–18) presses; Cyrillic presses owned by Y. Sheliha (1618–20, 1626–36), M. *Slozka (1638–67), Bishop A. *Zhelyborsky (1644–6), and Bishop Y. *Shumliansky at St George's Cathedral (1687–8); a press at the Polish Jesuit college (1642–1773); and the Polish presses of P. Golczewski (1735–51), J. Filipowicz (1753–67), and the Szlichtyn family (1755–85). Under Austrian rule the Piller family press (1772 to 19th century) printed books in Latin, Gothic, Hebrew, Greek, and Cyrillic. Other early Cyrillic presses in Galicia were Bishop H. Balaban's *Striatyn Press (1602–6), his press in Krylos (1605–6), Y. Sheliha's press in Dobromyl (1611–17), P. *Liutkovych-Telytsia's press in Uhortsi (1617–21), and the *Univ Monastery press (1648–1770), founded by Bishop Zhelyborsky. A Jewish press founded by U. Foebus Halewy operated in Zhovkva (1693–1782); smaller ones existed in Sambir and Turka.

Printing in Volhynia began after Fedorovych entered the service of Prince K. Ostrozky and founded what became the important *Ostrih Press (1577–1612). Other Cyrillic presses were founded by Prince Ostrozky at the *Derman Monastery (1602–5); by K. *Stavrovetsky in Rokhmaniv (1618–19); by P. Liutkovych-Telytsia in Chetvertnia (1624–5), Lutske (1625–8), and Chorna (1629); and at the Epiphany Monastery in Kremianets (1637–8). Later the important *Pochaiv Monastery Press (1730–1918) was founded.

In Right-Bank Ukraine the Polish Protestant Panivtsi Press (1608–11) functioned briefly in Podilia. In Kiev, printing began with the founding of the *Kievan Cave Monastery Press (1615–1918). It remained the largest press in Ukraine until the mid-19th century. Other presses in Kiev were founded by T. *Verbytsky (1624–8) and S. Sobol (1628–31). In 1787 a press was founded at the Kiev-

an Mohyla Academy; later it became the press of the Kiev Theological Academy.

In Left-Bank Ukraine the first presses were those of K. Stavrovetsky in Chernihiv (1646) and Archbishop L. Baranovych in Novhorod-Siverskyi (1674–9), which was moved to Chernihiv and became the important *Chernihiv printing press (it was later housed, until 1785, at the *Trinity–St Elijah Monastery).

In 1720 Tsar Peter I subordinated the presses in Kiev and Chernihiv to the Russian Orthodox church and forbade the printing of all but church books sanctioned by church censors in St Petersburg. From 1721 all books printed in Ukraine were strictly controlled and censored by the Holy Synod, and all Ukrainianisms were consequently banned in imprints of liturgical texts. Secular printeries founded in the second half of the 18th century printed mostly tsarist decrees and government instructions and Russian books of minor importance. Under tsarist rule a Polish-Russian press operated at the Carmelite monastery in Berdychiv (1760–1840). Gubernial government presses were founded in Kremenchuk (1765, 1788–9, 1791), Zhytomyr (1783–1918), Katerynoslav (1793–1918), Kharkiv (1793–1918), Chernihiv (1797–1918), Mykolaiv (1797–1918), Kamianets-Podilskyi (1798–1918), Kiev (1799–1918), and, in 1807, all other gubernial capitals. Jewish presses were founded in several Volhynian and Podilian towns, and Polish presses existed in Yaryshiv (1790–2), Minkivtsi (1792–1829), Mohyliv (1797), Yaniv (1812–20), and Kamianets-Podilskyi (1811–49) in Podilia.

In the early 19th century, metal and mechanical printing was introduced into Ukraine, and the modern *printing industry evolved there. A Museum of Book Printing was opened in Lviv in 1977.

BIBLIOGRAPHY
Ohiienko, I. *Istoriia ukraïns'koho drukarstva: Istorychno-bibliohrafichnyi ohliad ukraïns'koho drukarstva XV–XVIII vv.* (Lviv 1925; Winnipeg 1983)
Popov, M. (ed). *Knyha i drukarstvo na Ukraïni* (Kiev 1965)
Zapasko, Ia.; Isaievych, Ia. *Pam'iatky knyzhkovoho mystetstva: Kataloh starodrukiv vydanykh na Ukraïni*, 3 vols (Lviv 1981, 1984)
Zimmer, S. *The Beginning of Cyrillic Printing, Cracow, 1491: From the Orthodox Past in Poland* (New York 1983)

Ya. Isaievych, R. Senkus

Printing industry. A branch of industry that produces various types of printed goods: books, newspapers, journals, maps, posters, tickets, brochures, and so forth. Under the official Soviet system of economic classification the printing industry includes printing enterprises and manufacturing associations, typesetters, bookbinders, and enterprises that produce printing equipment and dyes. Printing as a modern industry emerged in the early 19th century with the development of new printing processes. (For the early history of the industry, see *Publishers and publishing and *Printing.)

The invention of lithography in the 1790s marked an important turning point in the printing industry, as it was cheaper than old-style printing methods and made better prints (see *Graphic art). The first lithographic press in Ukraine was established in Lviv in 1822; soon afterward such presses were set up in Kiev (1828), Odessa, Kharkiv, and elsewhere. The introduction of automated rotary printing presses in the second half of the 19th century made possible a rapid increase in the speed and ease of printing. The presses were developed primarily to meet the demands of newspaper publishing. Wide-circulation newspapers were published for almost every gubernia in the Russian Empire after the 1860s. In addition there were several eparchial newspapers, some privately owned papers, journals, and other publications (see *Press). Most of those publications appeared in Russian, because of the official ban on the Ukrainian language. The ban especially hindered the development of *book publishing in Ukraine. By 1897 there were 22 printing houses in Kiev, 55 in Odessa, 27 in Kharkiv gubernia, 36 in Poltava gubernia, and 27 in Volhynia gubernia. In Galicia the number of presses increased from 25 in 1851 to 85 in 1890; most of them were located in Lviv. At that time hardly any printing machinery or equipment was produced in Ukraine, and everything was imported from abroad (mostly Germany). Innovations such as monotype, linotype, and offset printing also came from Western Europe or the United States. In 1917 in Kiev there were 154 printing houses, employing over 1,700 workers. They owned 14 rotary, 182 offset and flatbed, 35 lithographic, and 152 cast presses, and 9 linotypes and 5 monotypes.

In the 1920s literacy spread rapidly throughout the country, and the Communist party placed great emphasis on the development of printing, primarily for the purpose of agitation and propaganda. At the beginning of 1922 there were 230 printing enterprises, employing over 12,000 people, in Ukraine. By 1932 every raion (390 altogether) had a printing press, and oblast capitals and other major cities had several. The major printing enterprises were concentrated in Kharkiv, the capital of Ukraine at the time. They included the Dzerzhinsky, Blakytny, and Komunist printing houses, which specialized in newspaper printing, and the Frunze factory, which concentrated on journals and books. Other large printing houses were in Kiev, Kremenchuk, Luhanske, Donetske, and Odessa. The larger presses were administered by the republican authorities; smaller ones were under oblast, city, raion, or other administration. On the eve of the Second World War there were some 140 small printing houses in Lviv and many in other cities of Western Ukraine. Those privately owned presses were nationalized by the Soviet regime after the occupation of Western Ukraine. By 1940 throughout the Ukrainian SSR there were 885 printing houses, including 30 republican, 24 oblast, 58 city, 743 raion, and 30 other presses. In total some 20,000 workers were employed in the industry. In 1941, printing establishments in Ukraine contained 250 linotypes, 9 monotypes, and 1,041 flatbed, 45 newspaper rotary, 2 book rotary, and 12 offset presses.

The printing industry continued to expand after the Second World War. Kiev emerged as its most important center. Printing technology improved, and greater capacity was concentrated in fewer printing houses. In 1970 there were 857 printing houses in Ukraine – 27 republican, 18 oblast, 9 Party, 104 city, and 408 raion presses – employing some 35,000 workers. Those enterprises operated 1,639 typesetting machines (monotypes, linotypes, etc), and 28 book rotary, 206 newspaper rotary, 2,828 flatbed, and 267 offset presses. In recent years the concentration of printing facilities has continued, as has the increase in capacity. In 1984, 544 enterprises of the printing industry came under the authority of the Ukrainian SSR State Committee for Publishing, Printing, and Book Trade: 23 under republican, 11 under oblast, 90 under city, and 420 under raion jurisdiction. Other presses were under the direct control of the Communist party or government ministries or agencies. In general, however, the industry was still much more poorly developed than in other parts of the USSR; in 1967, for example, per capita book production in Ukraine was 33 percent of that in the RSFSR, and per capita newspaper production was 57 percent. The industry was highly centralized. The mass production of Russian-language publications served to further Russification in Ukraine. The postwar trends in the three main branches of the industry, book, newspaper, and journal printing, are summarized in the table. But the capacity of the printing industry has increased. In general a relatively small number of mostly political and propagandistic works were printed in very large pressruns.

The printing of books, journals, newspapers, and bulletins in Ukraine, 1960–87

	1960	1970	1980	1987
Book titles	7,889	8,133	9,061	8,134
Pressrun (in millions)	113	122	145	167
in Ukrainian	79	92	92	73
Periodical titles	369	523	198	219
Pressrun (in millions) including circulation	45	187	211	181
of Ukrainian titles	38	167	193	161
Newspaper and bulletin titles	3,280	2,618	1,737	1,784
Annual circulation (in millions)	1,624	3,478	4,497	4,718

The largest printing facilities today are the Demokratychna (formerly Radianska) Ukraina Printing Complex in Kiev, which has printed the publications of the *Radianska Ukraina publishing house and many other periodicals; the Kiev Polihrafknyha Manufacturing Association, whose 12 printing houses (including 6 in Kiev) print books, especially colored and illustrated books; the Kharkiv Frunze Book Factory, which specializes in textbooks; and the Lviv Atas Manufacturing Association, which concentrates on children's books. The Zoria and Polihrafist manufacturing associations print mostly packaging and labeling materials and writing paper.

Printing and typesetting machinery was built in the USSR from the 1920s. The first linotype was made in Leningrad in 1930. Increasingly the industry has adopted offset technology. By 1983 some 46 percent of the output of enterprises under the State Committee for Publishing was being done on offset printing presses. The development of phototypesetting and the adoption of computers in the printing industry has been very slow in comparison with Western Europe and North America.

The problems of the printing industry are studied at the *Ukrainian Scientific Research Institute of the Printing Industry. Technical personnel are trained at the *Ukrainian Printing Institute in Lviv.

BIBLIOGRAPHY
Mashtalir, R.; Kovba, Zh.; Feller, M. *Rozvytok polihrafiï na Ukraïni* (Lviv 1974)

B. Balan, V. Holubnychy

Printmaking (*estamp, stankova graviura*). The process and art of imprinting or stamping an engraved image onto paper, cloth, or leather. Unlike engravings or lithographs, prints are not necessarily made to be printed in books but are works of art that exist independently of textual material. In practice early Ukrainian artists did not make this distinction. They often glued prints into books, and some reprinted illustrations on loose sheets and hung them as prints. Modern prints are individually signed by the artist in pencil and are printed in small quantities (usually 25 to 100 copies). According to established tradition some engravers often carve their name or initial in the bottom right-hand corner of the engraving block.

Early Ukrainian wood engravings of the 16th century are not prints in the strict sense of the word, because they were all printed in books. They could, however, function as prints (eg, the picture of the Evangelist Luke in the *Apostol* printed in Lviv in 1574). The first prints executed on individual sheets of paper were the early-17th-century portrayals of the four Evangelists printed by P. Berynda at the Striatyn Press. During the 17th and 18th centuries prints of folk icons and folk drawings became popular throughout Ukrainian society because they were much less expensive than paintings or painted icons.

Professional printmaking of the 17th and 18th centuries holds a special place in Ukrainian art. At that time it was developed more fully than painting, sculpture, or graphic art. Not only religious but also secular portrait, landscape, and still-life printmaking developed fully. Synthetic genres particular to the art of printmaking were created – the address of welcome, the thesis frontispiece, the calendar of saints, the genealogical tree, and the heraldic crest. Ukrainian printmaking generated variations of European styles (Renaissance, baroque, rococo, classical, and Romantic). The print styles spread to other art forms. Thus printmaking was the innovator among the art forms. The greatest printmakers of the Cossack era were *Illia, *Prokopii, D. *Sinkevych, N. *Zubrytsky, O. and L. *Tarasevych, I. *Shchyrsky, I. *Myhura, A. *Kozachkivsky, H. *Levytsky, D. *Haliakhovsky, and Ya. Konchakivsky.

During the 19th century printmaking underwent great changes. The technique of engraving was perfected, and lithography was introduced. Prints acquired characteristics of painting, because painters desired to popularize their works by 'translating' them into graphic art. The secularization of art had a negative effect on printmaking: it reduced its subject matter and diluted the force of its spiritual expressiveness and the unique national character achieved during the preceding centuries. Only T. *Shevchenko can be included among those artists who raised the level of printmaking, in both subject matter and technique. Many foreign masters of printmaking worked in Ukraine during the 19th century.

Ukrainian printmaking was reborn in the 20th century in the works of original graphic artists, such as O. *Kulchytska, V. *Zauze, H. *Narbut, M. *Zhuk, L. *Levytsky, V. *Kasiian, and M. *Derehus. Emigré graphic artists also made their contributions. The most famous is J. *Hnizdovsky, who made his best prints in postwar New York. Postwar printmakers in Soviet Ukraine have worked mostly in the linocut (eg, H. Yakutovych, V. *Kutkin, I. Batechko, and H. Malakov) and in plastic (M. Stratilat and V. Lopata). The art of miniature printmaking in

the *bookplate has become popular, and there is continued interest in the traditional techniques of engraving, such as woodcut, copper engraving, watermarking, and *lithography (O. Danchenko, O. *Fishchenko, and V. *Lytvynenko).

BIBLIOGRAPHY
Turchenko, Iu. *Ukraïns'kyi estamp* (Kiev 1964)
Stepovyk, D. *Ukraïns'ka hrafika XVI–XVII stolit': Evoliutsiia obraznoï systemy* (Kiev 1982)

D. Stepovyk

Pripisnye **peasants** (*prypysni seliany*). Literally, 'assigned peasants,' referring to a large segment of the state peasantry who, during the 18th and until the mid-19th century, lived on crownlands and were assigned to work in state or private enterprises in lieu of paying quitrent or a poll tax. In Ukraine the *pripisnye* peasants were usually employed in state rather than private industries, often in those oriented to manufacturing and river transport. During the late 18th century the state gradually began to cease the practice of assigning peasants to factories, and by 1822 in Ukraine the *pripisnye* peasants had been redesignated as 'indispensable workers' and incorporated into the category of *possessional peasants; the latter category disappeared with the emancipation of the serfs in 1861–3.

Prisoner of war camps. Camps interning persons captured by a belligerent power during war. Until the beginning of the 20th century there were no effective multilateral agreements regulating prisoner of war (POW) camps. Serious attempts to forge such agreements were made at the First and Second Hague peace conventions of 1899 and 1907. The 1929 Geneva Convention of Land Warfare elaborated on the principle of protecting the welfare of POWs. That pact was signed by, among others, Germany, but not the USSR.

During the First World War Ukrainians were held in camps in Germany, Austria-Hungary, Russia, and Italy. Approx 300,000 of the 1.4 million prisoners from the Russian Empire held in German camps in October 1918 are said to have been Ukrainian. Through the intervention of the *Union for the Liberation of Ukraine some 50,000 Ukrainian prisoners were shifted to three special camps (*Rastatt, *Salzwedel, and *Wetzlar); from those, two Ukrainian divisions, the so-called *Bluecoats, were later created. An estimated 200,000 Ukrainians were among the 1.1 million Russian army personnel held as prisoners in Austria-Hungary. The *Graycoats division was formed from Ukrainian POWs interned at the Freistadt camp in 1918.

There were about 120,000 Ukrainians among the 1.7 million or so POWs from Austria-Hungary in the Russian Empire. Although Russia was a signatory to the Hague conventions, the camps spread across the empire are said to have been the worst of all POW camps during the First World War. Generally, prisoners of Slavic origin were put in camps in the European parts of the empire, and those of other origins were interned in the most distant regions. Prisoners were engaged in various types of labor, but very soon POW camps became recruiting bases for armies in the later stages of the war and during the revolution. The Czechoslovak Legion, for instance, initiated under the auspices of the Russian government and the Czechoslovak National Council, was formed in Ukraine from POWs.

Both the Whites and the Bolsheviks drafted remaining POWs into their armies. The Sich Riflemen was also a unit created from former POWs.

In Italy some 40,000 to 60,000 Ukrainians who had fought in the Austro-Hungarian army were interned in POW camps on the island of Asinara and near Cassino and Arquata. Attempts in 1919 by delegates of the Western Ukrainian National Republic to have them repatriated proved fruitless. They were freed only in 1921.

In Poland up to 100,000 Ukrainians were interned in POW camps in 1919–20 following the Polish occupation of Galicia. Many of them were soldiers of the Ukrainian Galician Army (UHA) and of the forces of the Ukrainian National Republic. They were incarcerated in camps at Strzałków, Brest, Wadowice, and Dąbie. About 15,000 of those prisoners died from poor nourishment and unsanitary conditions. The majority of the survivors were freed in 1920. Soldiers of the UHA were also interned in Rumania during 1919. During the Ukrainian Revolution of 1917–21 Ukrainian combatants were interned in camps across Russia. Among them was the camp of Kozhukhov, near Moscow.

Between 1939 and 1945 hundreds of thousands of Ukrainians serving in the Polish, the Soviet, and other armies were interned. After the Hungarian occupation of Transcarpathia in 1939, several hundred members of the Carpathian Sich were interned in camps in Dryva (near Khust) and Varju-Lapos (near Nyiregyháza). When the Germans advanced into Poland in 1939, approx 700,000 officers and soldiers from the Polish army were captured and interned, among them 60,000 to 70,000 Ukrainians. The 1929 Geneva Convention was generally observed by the Germans in the case of those prisoners, and from 1940 many of the inmates were freed and allowed to return home or to work in the factories of the Reich. A number of Ukrainians were among those Polish combatants captured and interned by the Red Army during the Soviet invasion of Poland in 1939.

The largest capture of enemy soldiers in history took place during the German invasion of the Soviet Union in 1941. An estimated 1.3 million Ukrainians were among the 3.6 million Soviet POWs held by the Germans in 1941. The Soviets, who had not formally ratified either the 1899 or the 1907 Hague convention or signed the Geneva Convention of 1929, considered Soviet POWs traitors and rejected International Red Cross overtures to assist them. Soviet POWs were therefore outside the protection of international law and at the mercy of captors, who considered them 'subhuman.' Scattered across camps from Ukraine itself to the region of Lorraine (annexed by Germany), many of the Ukrainian Soviet POWs perished as a result of the inhuman treatment they suffered. The treatment of Soviet POWs often depended upon the attitudes of German district commanders, and thus the fate of prisoners varied from camp to camp. For instance, whereas in the POW camp located in Jarosław Ukrainian inmates were set free very quickly, at Ban-St-Jean in the Moselle department of France, the vast majority of the approx 24,000 inmates perished during the course of the war owing to multiple privations, or even as a result of having been buried alive. Famine, disease, and mass executions were the rule in other camps where Ukrainians were interned (Khyriv, Kholm, and elsewhere).

The Germans did not have a well-defined or preconceived policy toward Soviet POWs. For a while, particularly in August–October 1941, a number of Ukrainians were released from some camps, especially those in Right-Bank Ukraine, and put to labor in German-occupied Ukraine. But the releases ceased in November 1941. Ukrainian POWs were also interned in *concentration camps along with other inmates targeted for destruction. From the spring of 1942 the treatment of many POWs improved, when the Germans began to use them in larger numbers for labor in the war economy.

Few Ukrainian POWs were able to escape; some of those who did were aided by compatriots living in the vicinity of the camps. The Germans discouraged local Ukrainians, at gunpoint, from visiting or coming to the aid of inmates. That, along with the atrocities committed in the camps, contributed to the stiffening of anti-Nazi sentiment among the Ukrainian people. Altogether some 5.8 million Soviets were captured by the Germans between 1941 and 1945. According to a German report of 1 May 1944, of the 5,160,000 Soviet POWs interned to that date 1,981,000 had perished in the camps, 818,000 had been released to civilian or military status, 67,000 had escaped, and 1,241,000 were 'unaccounted for' (disappeared or killed). Some 875,000 of the surviving 1,053,000 inmates were engaged in construction and other labor. Toward the end of the war a number of Ukrainians were among the POWs drafted into German armies. Because the Kremlin never acknowledged formally the surrender and desertion of Red Army soldiers, the crimes committed in the POW camps have largely gone unpunished, even though the death of the Soviet POWs constitutes one of the largest wholesale murders of the Second World War.

Those Ukrainians who served in Allied (specifically US or Canadian) or Axis military formations and fell into enemy hands generally shared the fate of their captured colleagues in those armies in enemy camps.

In 1945–7 some 10,000 members of the *Division Galizien were interned by the British in POW camps near Bellaria and Rimini, in Italy. In some cases Ukrainians published their own periodicals in POW camps. *Chervona Ukraïna*, for instance, was published by Ukrainian POWs in Hungary between March and August 1919, and the weekly *Nova doba* by Soviet Ukrainian POWs in Berlin in 1941–5. The Ukrainian SSR was among the signatories of the 1949 Geneva Convention on POWs.

BIBLIOGRAPHY
Lozyns'kyi, M. (ed). *Krivava knyha*, 2 vols (Vienna 1919, 1921)
Golovina, N. *The Russian Army in the World War* (New Haven 1931)
Flory, W. *Prisoners of War* (Washington 1942)
Kamenetsky, I. *Hitler's Occupation of Ukraine (1941–1944): A Study of Totalitarian Imperialism* (Milwaukee 1956)
Williamson, S; Pastor, P. (eds). *Essays on World War I: Origins and Prisoners of War* (New York 1983)
Boshyk, Y. (ed). *Ukraine during World War II: History and Its Aftermath* (Edmonton 1986)
Hirschfeld, G. (ed). *The Policies of Genocide: Jews and Soviet Prisoners of War in Nazi Germany* (London 1986)
                                                    S. Cipko, L. Shankovsky

Prisons. See Penitentiary system.

Pritsak, Omeljan [Pricak], b 7 April 1919 in Luka (now Ozerne), Sambir county, Galicia. Historian; member of the Shevchenko Scientific Society since 1951, the Ukrainian

Omeljan Pritsak

Academy of Arts and Sciences, and foreign member of the AN URSR (now ANU) since 1990. He studied at Lviv University (1940), the ANU Institute of History (under A. Krymsky), and the universities of Berlin (1943) and Göttingen (PH D, 1948). He taught at the University of Hamburg (as a professor from 1957) before moving to the United States in 1961. Since 1964 he has been a professor at Harvard University and the first holder of the Hrushevsky Chair of Ukrainian History. In 1967 he proposed the establishment of a center for Ukrainian studies in the United States, which proposal led to the formation of the *Harvard Ukrainian Research Institute in 1973, with Pritsak as its first director (a position he held until 1989). Pritsak's interest in incorporating Arabic, Turkish, and Persian sources into Ukrainian historiography led him to specialize in Oriental studies. His scholarly work has focused on a reinterpretation of the origins of Kievan Rus' using Oriental, Scandinavian, and other source materials. To that end he has worked on the compilation of a six-part magnum opus, *The Origin of Rus'*, the first volume (*Old Scandinavian Sources Other Than the Sagas*) of which was published in 1981. In 1991 he became the first director of the new ANU Institute of Oriental Studies in Kiev. Two festschrifts in his honor, *Eucharisterion* and *Adelphotes*, were published by the Harvard Ukrainian Research Institute in 1979–80 (2 vols) and 1990.

Private enterprise. Production and service enterprises under private, not state, control and ownership. Private enterprise has existed in Ukraine since medieval times. It was not uncommon for the boyars of Kievan Rus', unlike the landowning nobility of Western Europe, to engage in trade. Besides a substantial merchant class there were many skilled craftsmen producing goods for the domestic market. About 50 trades were practiced in Kiev, including carpentry, blacksmithing, pottery, and leather working. Under Polish-Lithuanian rule during the 14th through 16th centuries, private enterprise flourished in the towns of Western Ukraine. Lviv supported 14 different *guilds and 500 master craftsmen. As discrimination against Ukrainians grew stronger in the towns, private enterprises became increasingly dominated by minorities, such as Germans, Jews, Poles, and Armenians.

In Cossack times the *starshyna* and the gentry engaged in milling, distilling, glass manufacturing, and ironworking, and monasteries were involved in paper manufacturing. Manufacturing enterprises were small; they usually employed 15 to 20 workers and were located mostly on the owner's estates in the countryside. Towns continued to be centers for the trades. Large manufacturing enterprises were owned by the imperial government.

During the 19th century discriminatory tariff policies on the part of the tsarist government were detrimental to native Ukrainian capital. In 1900, for example, out of 93 enterprises in Kiev only 6 were owned by Ukrainians. Private enterprise was largely stimulated by foreign investment. In the 1840s and 1850s Polish landlords introduced large-scale capitalist farming and sugar refineries in southwestern Ukraine. In 1857–77 a liberal customs policy encouraged German entrepreneurs to invest in agricultural machinery assembly plants. With the abolition of serfdom in 1861 a mass of cheap labor was made available for capitalist enterprises. From 1880 Ukraine experienced an industrial boom: foreign capital, mostly French and Belgian, flowed into Ukraine to set up large-scale coal, iron and steel, rail, and sugar-refining companies. The industrial development was concentrated in the Kryvyi Rih and the Donbas regions. Foreign ownership was exercised directly or through industrial investment banks nominally controlled by large *cartels and syndicates.

After the 1917 Revolution the Soviet regime in Ukraine nationalized the large-scale private enterprises. Under the *New Economic Policy in the 1920s, private manufacturing enterprises were permitted, but they were restricted mostly to light industry, and employed fewer than 20 workers each. Although nearly a quarter of the factories in the mid-1920s were privately owned, their share in the gross output was only 8.7 percent, and their share of the work force was only 2.5 percent. In Ukraine the private sector played a marginally more significant role than in other regions of the former USSR because of the importance of flour milling, which was largely in private hands. With the introduction of restrictive credit and labor policies in the summer of 1926, the private sector declined rapidly. In 1926–7 only 11.9 percent of the factories were private. They employed 0.8 percent of the work force and produced 2.3 percent of the gross output. Under the First Five-year Plan all private enterprises were nationalized.

In recent years, as a result of the crisis in the Soviet economy, the private sector has been allowed to re-emerge. Its role, however, has been severely circumscribed by law and bureaucratic interference. Until 1990 the term 'private enterprise' was avoided, and private businesses were called 'co-operatives.' In 1989 there were 13,534 such co-operatives, employing 248,000 people and producing goods and services valued at 900 million rubles. Further privatization plans were announced in 1990 but were not realized prior to the dissolution of the USSR.

BIBLIOGRAPHY
Dereviankin, T. (ed). *Istoriia narodnoho hospodarstva Ukraïns'koï RSR*, 3 vols (Kiev 1983–7)

B. Somchynsky

Private plot (*prysadybne hospodarstvo*). A small piece of land with a cottage and farm buildings allotted in the Soviet system to collective farmers, workers, and office workers in rural areas for their private use. Farming on private plots was carried out by means of individual labor and initiative, and added significantly to the overall agricultural output. It was an important source of foodstuffs and supplementary income for the farmer and an additional source of food supplies for the cities. Although private farming did not fit into the socialist economic model, it became solidly established in the USSR. In spite of many attempts to abolish it, private farming grew in importance.

In 1918 V. Lenin nationalized all landholdings. Legally, land became the property of society and could not be sold or exchanged. The forced collectivization of 1929–33 was to put an end to all private farming. It was only when the agricultural system approached collapse that J. Stalin permitted small plots of land (usually one-sixth of a hectare) to be allotted to farmers, provided they still worked on collective farms. The decision was viewed as a temporary palliative and concession to the peasants.

After the Second World War attempts were made to abolish private plots, but economic difficulties and international tensions were not conducive to the eradication of this vestige of 'capitalism.' N. Krushchev's attempt in the early 1950s to create 'agrocities' and to transform peasants into state workers was a failure. Except for the brief thaw in 1956–9, Soviet agriculture fared poorly. Beset by bad weather, poor harvests, and bureaucratic mismanagement, it could not afford to abolish private plots. During his regime L. Brezhnev did not try to do away with private plots. The 1977 Constitution sanctioned supplementary private farming as a derivative form of socialist property. Article 13 stated that personal property is based on one's labor, and that the right to possess a private plot is based on one's individual toil. The article required that citizens make rational use of the allotted land, and that collective farms provide the necessary assistance.

The legal status and the size of private plots were defined in Paragraph 42 of the Collective-Farm Statute Model (1969) and by decrees of the Union and republican governments. The size of the plot, including the cottage, could not exceed 0.5 ha and in the irrigated regions 0.2 ha. The actual size of the plot was to be determined by the collective-farm assembly according to one's work record and the size of one's family. If one left the collective, the plot was to be reduced to an area adjacent to the house. According to Article 77 of the Land Code of the Ukrainian SSR, plots could be allotted to state-farm and office workers in the rural areas. Recently, plots of 0.15 ha had become accessible to urban residents, who unlike rural residents were charged a minimal rent and required to pay for various services. At the end of the 1980s the size of the Ukrainian household plot was between 0.3 and 0.5 ha, depending on the size and location of the collective farm,

TABLE 1
Cultivated land, excluding pastures or meadows, allotted to different users (in million ha)

	USSR[1]		Ukraine	
	1978	1987	1973	1987
All enterprises	214.90	240.00	33.48	34.3
Socialized sector[2]	208.75	221.25	31.43	32.2
Private sector	6.15	8.75	2.05	2.1
Share of private sector (percentage)	2.86	3.65	6.1	5.8
Average size of private plot (in ha)	0.32	0.38	0.4	0.46

[1]USSR figures include reserve or fallow land.
[2]Includes collective farms, state farms, and other state enterprises.

its work force, soil, and fertility, and other factors. The share of land allotted to private farming is given in table 1.

In most cases private farming has proved to be much more productive than collective farming. Its share in the agricultural output exceeds its share of the cultivated land by several factors (see table 2). In table 2 only major crops, for which there are published data, are shown. Some vegetables, such as onions, garlic, and parsley, are produced mostly by the private sector and do not normally appear in statistical yearbooks. They are constantly in demand, since the socialized sector delivers an inferior product and distribution service. Depending upon the season, prices on the farmer's market can be three or even four times higher than in the state stores.

As the Ukrainian economy is restructured following independence, the system of private plots is expected to be replaced, eventually, with the private ownership of land.

E. Bej

Private property. The property belonging to an individual, a family, or a legal entity, not to a state or local government. The owner of private property has the right to possess and dispose of it freely by selling, trading, renting or mortgaging it, or giving it away.

Before the Revolution of 1917 there were various forms of private property in Ukraine, including individual, joint, collective, and co-operative. Furthermore there was municipal, communal, and state property; 70 percent of the railways were owned by the state.

TABLE 2
Output of selected farm products in Ukraine, 1973 and 1983 (percentage of total in parentheses)

	Socialized sector		Private sector	
	1973	1983	1973	1983
Meat (in 1,000 t)	1,782.0 (62.5)	2,438.0 (66.3)	1,068.0 (37.5)	1,239.0 (33.7)
Milk (in million t)	12.5 (67.8)	16.5 (74.0)	6.2 (33.2)	5.8 (26.0)
Eggs (in million t)	3,506.0 (39.1)	9,979.0 (61.9)	5,696.0 (61.9)	6,143.0 (38.1)
Wool (in 1,000 t)	23.6 (95.2)	26.3 (93.6)	1.2 (4.8)	1.8 (6.4)
Potatoes (in 1,000 t)	7,894.0 (33.3)	6,060.0 (29.2)	15,830.0 (66.7)	14,670.0 (70.8)
Vegetables (in 1,000 t)	6,221.0 (75.7)	5,315.0 (75.5)	1,992.0 (24.3)	1,723.0 (24.5)
Fodder (in 1,000 t)	22,300.0 (79.8)	18,805.0 (82.2)	5,634.0 (20.2)	4,068.0 (17.8)
Fruits (in 1,000 t)	1,490.0 (45.6)	1,524.0 (45.2)	1,775.0 (54.4)	1,846.0 (54.8)
Grapes (in 1,000 t)	1,035.0 (82.5)	594.0 (78.1)	219.0 (17.5)	167.0 (21.9)

The concentration of property in the hands of a small number of private owners resulted in a highly uneven distribution of wealth and income. The propertyless class was much larger in Ukraine than in Western Europe, and its size was one of the principal reasons for the eventual revolution.

Legislation introduced by the Central Rada and the Directory (1917–19) placed some limits on private property, particularly in land, and socialized it. After a brief period of virtually total nationalization of all property under *War Communism and another brief *New Economic Policy (NEP) period, permanent forms of property were introduced in the Ukrainian SSR and the entire USSR, during 1929–32.

Soviet jurists denied that any form of private property existed in the Soviet Union but conceded that there was 'personal property.' It consisted of consumer items and objects of personal use, such as clothes, housing, furniture, livestock, motor vehicles, money, copyrights, and patents that belonged to a person or a person's family. All such property had to be acquired through personal labor. Personal property was permitted by the constitutions of the USSR and the Ukrainian SSR and was protected by law. The Criminal Code of the Ukrainian SSR provided punishment of 1 to 6 years' imprisonment for theft and burglary, 3 to 12 years' imprisonment for robbery, and a half to 1 year's imprisonment for the arbitrary seizure, purchase, or sale of land. Despite protestations there was no fundamental difference between 'personal' and private property. Under Soviet law personal property could be bought and sold, inherited, and rented. There were open markets in the cities and villages, where various things could be purchased, including some means of production. The so-called collective-farm market, which was officially sanctioned, sold produce grown on *private plots. Every larger city also had a *tovkuchka* or flea market, where used goods were sold. There was also a semilegal black market, on which virtually everything was bought and sold, including construction materials, fuel, precision instruments, foreign currency, bank drafts, and almost any items generally in short supply. There was a rural black market also, where livestock, grain, agricultural produce, and farm machinery were sold. There are no data on the dimensions of those free markets.

Many laws outlawed or regulated the free markets, but they were ineffective. Soviet law did not recognize private ownership of land. Collective farms gave members private plots of land, but they were for 'personal use' and could not be sold. People could sell their houses and their movable belongings, however, because they were considered to be personal property. In cities the municipal government granted lots for the construction of new private houses, which were limited by law to five rooms or 60 sq m, regardless of family size. A family could have no more than one such house and one dacha. When a private house was sold, the house became the personal property of the new owner, but the lot was only transferred to his or her use. In 1940, 49.6 percent of the urban housing in Ukraine was personal property, in 1960, 50.0 percent, and in 1969, 43.2 percent. Rural housing was almost exclusively personal property.

About 450 million rubles per year was invested by the population in private housing in the 1960s. Families in the rural areas were also allowed to own livestock. Money was always an important category of personal property.

Savings were kept in banks or converted into government bonds that usually yielded 2–3 percent annually.

The right of inheritance, as contrary to the principles of Marxism, was initially abolished in the Ukrainian SSR by the decree of 21 March 1919, but it was reintroduced in 1922 under the NEP as long as the inheritance did not exceed 10,000 rubles in value (amounts in excess were prohibitively taxed). In 1926 the value limit on inheritance was abolished, and on 14 March 1945 an all-Union law removed all limits from inheritance.

The sum of personal property increased as the standard of living rose. Ukraine's new law on property, adopted on 7 February 1991, did not extend the right of private ownership to land. It stated, however, for the first time in Soviet history, that private ownership is equal to all other types of ownership, and that the state will support all types of ownership. Furthermore, it expanded private ownership to include not only private dwellings, personal belongings, and livestock but also the means of production, the results of any production, means of transport, stocks, and any other valuable possessions.

BIBLIOGRAPHY
Khalfina, R. *Pravo lichnoi sobstvennosti* (Moscow 1964)
Hordon, M. *Radians'ke tsyvil'ne pravo*, no. 2 (Kharkiv 1966)
Vil'nians'kyi, S. *Radians'ke tsyvil'ne pravo*, no. 1 (Kharkiv 1966)
V. Holubnychy, O. Rohach

Privet (*Ligustrum*; Ukrainian: *byriuchyna*). An evergreen or deciduous plant of the family Oleaceae that grows as a shrub or small tree. In Ukraine the common privet (*L. vulgare*), a shrub with shiny leaves, white flowers, and black berries, grows wild in the southern forest-steppe, in the steppe, and in Transcarpathia. It is cultivated all over Ukraine, in hedges, in screens, and as an ornamental plant in parks. It is also used to protect fields and ravines from erosion. The wood is strong and suitable for turning. The berries are used in the manufacture of dyes. Glossy privet (*L. lucidum*) is cultivated in the Crimea and around the Black Sea.

Prizes and awards. In Ukraine, as elsewhere in the world, persons who have made prominent scientific, scholarly, cultural, technological, and economic contributions have been rewarded with various monetary awards, citations, *orders, medals, and honorific titles. Under the tsarist regime monetary awards were granted by the state for economic achievements. Beginning in 1866, for example, 3,000 rubles were awarded for every steam locomotive made in the empire from domestic materials. From 1831 the Imperial Academy of Sciences granted monetary prizes from private endowments and donations, including the annual 1,420-ruble P. Demidov Prize (1831–65) for contributions to Russian scholarly literature; the S. Uvarov Prize (est 1855) for works in Russian language, literature, and history; the triannual T. Ber Prize for contributions in the biological sciences; the 500-ruble G. Gelmersen Prize (est 1879), awarded every five years for contributions to imperial geology, paleontology, or physical geography (by other than full members); the A. Pushkin Prize (est 1881) for works on the history of Russian literature and language, Russian belles lettres, or literary criticism; the triannual 150- to 800-ruble D. Tolstoi Prize (est 1882) for privately published works in all fields; the triannual 1,000-ruble A.(O.) Kotliarevsky Prize (est 1883) for works in Slavic philology and archeology published in Russian; and the 1,000-ruble M. Lomonosov Prize for works in Russian or Slavic philology and history.

Under the Soviet regime prizes and awards in Ukraine were granted by state bodies and official institutions on the recommendation of selection committees. The highest Soviet award was the Lenin Prize (granted in 1926–35 and from 1957). From 1967, 25 such prizes in science and technology and 6 in literature, art, and architecture were awarded biannually by the USSR Council of Ministers. Their recipients (laureates) each received 10,000 rubles. In 1967 the USSR Council of Ministers also began awarding annual USSR State Prizes worth 5,000 rubles each: 50 in science and technology, 10 in literature, art, and architecture, and (since 1974) 25 for exemplary contributions to the Soviet economy by workers and farmers (see *Socialist competition).

In 1969 the Ukrainian SSR Council of Ministers began awarding annual Ukrainian SSR State Prizes worth 2,500 rubles each: 17 in science and technology (2 of which were awarded from 1972 to authors of secondary or postsecondary textbooks), and (jointly with the Ukrainian Republican Council of Trade Unions) 2 (from 1974) to 4 (from 1977) to leaders in 'socialist competition' or for prominent labor achievements. In addition, 8 T. Shevchenko State Prizes (established in 1961 as the Shevchenko Republican Prize and renamed in 1969) were awarded, one each in the fields of literature, fine art, music, theater, cinematography, architecture, performance, and (since 1980) journalism.

In addition to state prizes Ukrainian scholars and scientists have been eligible for prizes awarded by the AN URSR (now ANU) presidium: since 1946, the O. Bohomolets Prize (physiology and theoretical medicine); since 1964, the M. Krylov Prize (mathematics, mathematical physics, and theoretical cybernetics), Ye. Paton Prize (metallurgy), L. Pysarzhevsky Prize (chemistry and chemical technology), and V. Yuriev Prize (genetics and advancements in agricultural science); since 1967, the D. Zabolotny Prize (microbiology, virology, epidemiology, and zoology); since 1972, the O. Dynnyk Prize (mechanics and machine building), M. Kholodny Prize (botany and plant physiology), D. Manuilsky Prize (history, philosophy, political science, and law), O. Shlikhter Prize (economics), and V. Vernadsky Prize (geology, geochemistry, geophysics, and hydrophysics); since 1973, the O.(A.) Palladin Prize (biochemistry and molecular biology); since 1974, the H. Proskura Prize (energetics) and K. Synelnykov Prize (physics); since 1976, the S. Lebedev Prize (computer technology); since 1977, the M. Yanhel Prize (applied and technical mechanics); since 1979, the I. Franko Prize (philology, ethnography, and art history); since 1980, the L. Symyrenko Prize (orcharding); and since 1982, the V. Hlushkov Prize (cybernetics and computer science). Each prize has been awarded to one laureate per year and has a monetary value of 1,200 rubles.

Various literary prizes have been awarded in Ukraine besides the coveted Shevchenko State Prize. The Ukrainian Council of Ministers established the Lesia Ukrainka Prize (best works for children) in 1971 (awarded jointly with the CC CPU), the M. Rylsky Prize (best translations of foreign works into Ukrainian) in 1972, and the P. Tychyna Prize (best works depicting the friendship and unity of the Soviet peoples) and the Republican Prize (best works in socialist-realist theory) in 1973. The Writers' Union of Ukraine established the A. Holovko Prize (best novel) in 1979. With the paper *Literaturna Ukraïna* it established the V. Sosiura Prize (best poetry collection, long poem, or substantial selection of poetry in a periodical) in 1982; with the journal *Vitchyzna*, the Yu. Yanovsky Prize (best short prose) also in 1982; and, with the Radianskyi Pysmennyk publishing house, the Ostap Vyshnia Prize (best humorous or satirical work) in 1983. The Communist Youth League of Ukraine established the N. Ostrovsky Prize (literature, art, architecture, performance) in 1958 and awarded it every two years from 1968. It also established four annual prizes: with the Molod publishing house, the P. Usenko Prize (best works on Komsomol themes) in 1976; with the journal *Barvinok*, the O. Kopylenko Prize (best didactic art works or book illustrations for students and youths) in 1978; with the journal *Pioneriia*, the M. Trublaini Prize (best literary works or illustrations for children) in 1979; and, with the journal *Dnipro*, the A. Malyshko Prize (best prose, poetry, publicism, or literary criticism) in 1982. The Union of Journalists of Ukraine also sponsored a literary award, the Ya. Halan Prize, from 1964 (for the most antinationalist works).

A notable feature of the granting of awards and prizes in Ukraine (and throughout the USSR), particularly in nonscientific fields, was the consideration afforded 'politically correct' recipients. With the political changes of the late 1980s, awards in Ukraine began to be granted to persons who previously had been shunned because of the nature of their work or views. Also, new prizes were named in honor of hitherto-ignored personalities: the V. Symonenko Prize (from 1987, for the best book of poetry by a young author) and the V. Stus Prize from the Writers' Union of Ukraine; and the V. Vynnychenko Prize (two awards for charitable work by an individual or group in the field of Ukrainian literature or theater, one given in Ukraine and the second outside its borders) and the M. Hrushevsky Prize (for work in Ukrainian history, folklore, or ethnography) from 1991 by the Ukrainian Culture Fund.

In North America various literary prizes and scholarships have been awarded by Ukrainian community organizations and scholarly bodies for many years. Only since the early 1980s, however, have such awards been granted on a regular basis. The most notable ones are the 5,000-dollar Antonovych prizes, two of which have been awarded each year since 1982 by the O. and T. Antonovych Foundation in Washington, DC, for the best Ukrainian literary work and best work in Ukrainian studies, and the M. Cenko Prize in Ukrainian bibliography. Since 1981 the Canadian Foundation for Ukrainian Studies has awarded the 5,000-dollar Award for Scholarly Excellence in Ukrainian Studies to several scholars.

Prnjavor. A town (1961 pop 2,800) in Banja Luka county, Bosnia. With its 1,100 Ukrainian inhabitants and strategic location near a cluster of Ukrainian villages, it has been the chief Ukrainian center of Bosnia. The bulk of Ukrainian immigrants came there in 1897–1914. A Greek Catholic parish was founded in Prnjavor in 1900, and the Church of the Transfiguration was built in 1912. In 1942 about half of the town's Ukrainian inhabitants moved to the Srem and Bačka regions. The Shevchenko Cultural and Educational Society maintained a children's choir and an active drama group.

Problems of the Peoples of the USSR. A quarterly organ of the League for the Liberation of the Peoples of the USSR (the *Paris Bloc), published in Munich in 1958–67. It contained articles on the history of the USSR and reports and analyses of current developments, particularly in national relations in the USSR, and studies of the interaction between communism and nationalism in other countries, especially in Africa and Asia. The contributors were Soviet émigrés, reporters, political commentators, and scholars, including R. Pipes, R. Conquest, H. Seton-Watson, W. Leonhard, and W. Laquer. Among the Ukrainian contributors were F. Haienko, Ye. Glovinsky, V. Borysenko, B. and P. Fedenko, M. Dobriansky-Demkovych, I. Koshelivets, O. Yurchenko, and S. Dovhal (the editor).

Problemy (Problems). A monthly journal of politics, edited and published in Munich from 1946 to March 1948 (a total of 14 issues) by M. Dobriansky-Demkovych.

Proboiem

Proboiem ([Let's] Force Through). A monthly journal published in Prague from December 1933 to January 1944 and edited by S. Rosokha. The organ of the *Union of Subcarpathian Ukrainian Students, it fostered Ukrainian national consciousness among Transcarpathian students. From 1939 it was an overtly nationalist literary and scholarly journal. Contributors included prominent writers and critics. The Proboiem publishing house also issued some 40 books in several series. The publishing house and journal were closed by the Nazi occupational authorities.

Procedural law. See Civil procedure and Criminal procedure.

Proch, Don [Proč], b 5 May 1943 in Asessippi, Manitoba. Ukrainian-Canadian sculptor, assemblage artist, and printmaker. His fiberglass masks and sculptures have established him as one of Canada's most innovative artists. The masks are three-dimensional objects covered by two-dimensional drawings that are a depiction in themselves and a feature of the sculptural composition (eg, *Prairie Hunting Mask* [1976] and *Wild Bill Lobchuk Back Forties Mask* [1976]). His drawings are usually of the prairie landscape, to which Proch has a strong attachment. His first

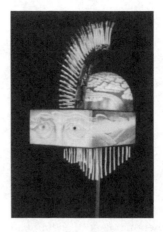

Don Proch: *Mask* (mixed media)

solo show was held in 1972 in Winnipeg. Proch's works have also been exhibited in Montreal, Windsor, Paris (1973), London, and Brussels (1984–5). Although there are no obviously Ukrainian images in his works, Proch has been credited with incorporating Ukrainian cultural traditions, such as the decorating of Ukrainian Easter eggs, into his space-age masks and thereby transcending the traditions to create complex, universal images.

Prochaska, Antoni, b 23 March 1852 in Zalishchyky Mali, Chortkiv circle, Galicia, d 23 September 1930 in Lviv. Polish historian; member of the Polish Academy of Learning from 1891. He was a specialist in the history of the 14th- and 15th-century Polish-Lithuanian Commonwealth. From 1878 he was a curator in the Lviv archives. His writings include works about the Union of Berestia (1896), the Polish king Władysław Jagiełło (2 vols, 1908), and the Lithuanian grand duke Vytautas (1914).

Prociuk, Stephen. See Protsiuk, Stepan.

Procko, Bohdan, b 18 July 1922 in Rychyhiv, Rudky county, Galicia. Historian. A graduate of Columbia University (MA, 1946) and the University of Ottawa (PH D, 1964), he has taught history at Villanova University since 1949. He has written several works on the history of the Ukrainian Catholic church and Ukrainians in America, including *Ukrainian Catholics in America: A History* (1982).

Proclamation of Ukrainian statehood, 1941 (Akt 30-oho chervnia). In the wake of Germany's attack on the Soviet Union on 22 June 1941, several members of the Bandera faction of the recently split *Organization of Ukrainian Nationalists (OUN[B]) set out to proclaim a Ukrainian state in Lviv. They put into motion a bold plan to force the German government to commit itself to an independent Ukraine. It was their hope the Germans would take what they perceived to be a rational course of action and ally themselves with the 'enslaved' nations of the USSR; alternately, a proclamation of statehood could provide a rallying point for national resistance in the event that Germany should turn against the interests of the Ukrainian people. Their actions have been assessed as brilliant or reckless (even foolish) by supporters of Ukrainian aspirations for independence. The Soviet authorities (especially after regaining control of Western Ukraine) painted them in the blackest terms as the perfidious undertakings of evil collaborators riding on the coattails of the Nazis.

S. *Bandera's lieutenant, Ya. *Stetsko, entered Lviv on the same day as the Germans, 30 June 1941, and began the task of state-building. A group of 50 to 200 Lviv residents (estimates vary) came to a hastily arranged evening meeting to hear what the OUN 'émigrés' from Cracow had to report, only to witness Stetsko declare: 'By the will of the Ukrainian people the OUN, under the direction of Stepan Bandera, proclaims the creation of a Ukrainian state.' What is believed to be the original of several versions of the proclamation went on to say that this Western Ukrainian government would submit to a national government yet to be created (in Kiev), and that it would co-operate with Germany in its struggle against Moscow's occupation of Ukraine.

The OUN(B) 'Akt 30-oho chervnia' (Act of 30 June), as the proclamation has come to be known, was followed by a decree by Bandera appointing Stetsko as head of state. In that way the OUN(B) executed its plan as a rapid series of what it hoped would become faits accomplis that took both the Germans and the Ukrainians by surprise. That course of action, in fact, was based on a practical consideration, for if the Gestapo had been warned of the possibility, it likely would have stopped the entire affair.

The OUN(B)'s coup was in harnessing a significant, albeit short-lived, legitimacy for its 'Akt.' Stetsko could intimate that the foundation for his government had already been laid in Cracow on 22 June 1941 through the OUN(B)'s efforts at consolidating the émigré community in a *Ukrainian National Committee. The split in the OUN's ranks did not immediately undermine Stetsko's position, since the Soviet occupation of Galicia had kept Lviv residents largely ignorant of that development. Ironically, it was the 'Akt' itself which attracted attention to the matter by highlighting that there was an OUN under Bandera; Lviv residents knew only of an OUN under A. *Melnyk (OUN[M]). More important, the evidence suggesting a German-OUN(B) agreement (where there was none) was overwhelming. The OUN(B)'s confident and unprecedented public appearances, the fact that its volunteer unit Nachtigall (see *Legion of Ukrainian Nationalists), dressed in German uniforms, was leading the German army into Lviv, the greetings of a German officer at the proclamation itself, and the OUN's peaceable control of Lviv radio for some three days after the German arrival all contributed to the impression that there was such an agreement. Doubts even among the skeptics dissipated when Stetsko and Nachtigall's chaplain, I. Hrynokh, had an audience at the residence of Metropolitan A. *Sheptytsky and procured his blessing as well as his immense authority for the OUN(B)'s imminent 'Akt.' Hrynokh spoke at the proclamation on behalf of the Ukrainian soldiers in Nachtigall and read over Lviv radio Sheptytsky's pastoral letter, which exhorted the nation to support Stetsko's government. The inaction of the German army in establishing a civil administration, and the fact that spontaneously formed Ukrainian administrations were at first tolerated, strengthened the illusion of German approval. Various Ukrainian bodies pledged their allegiance to Stetsko's government, and the proclamation was joyously repeated at mass gatherings all over Western Ukraine.

Stetsko's government was effectively paralyzed when he was quietly ushered to Berlin for 'discussions' on 12 July 1941, although public perception did not immediately recognize the significance of the move. Shrewdly, the Germans did not begin their mass arrests of OUN(B) members until mid-September, by which time most of Ukraine had been easily occupied.

During his brief tenure the 29-year-old Stetsko controlled no significant forces and was unable to bring in outside (non-OUN[B]) expertise to his administration. Much of the Lviv leadership had denied him their co-operation on three grounds: that the OUN first had to mend its internal split; that neither the international nor the internal situation justified the risks of such a proclamation in the absence of knowledge of Germany's plans for Ukraine; and that there was concern about what was perceived as the amorality of OUN(B) behaviour. The last objection was based on false or misleading OUN(B) claims about its relationship with the Germans, about the nature of its consolidation of Ukrainian émigrés, about internal OUN difficulties, and about the consent of Lviv leaders to positions in Stetsko's administration. The OUN(B) quickly lost its credibility, and a non-OUN(B) council to deal with the Germans was formed. Even Metropolitan Sheptytsky publicly withdrew his support. In spite of those setbacks and pressure from the Germans, the OUN(B) leadership resisted all demands to revoke the 'Akt.' Their resistance was a key element in the subsequent arrest of the OUN(B) leaders by the Nazis, as well as of prominent OUN(M) figures, who themselves had been considering making a proclamation of Ukrainian statehood in Kiev.

BIBLIOGRAPHY
Lysyi, V. 'Do istoriï 30 chervnia,' Vil'na Ukraïna, no. 11 (1956)
Pankivs'kyi, K. Vid derzavy do komitetu (New York–Toronto 1957)
Rosliak, M. 'Do istoriï 30 chervnia 1941 r.,' Vil'na Ukraïna, no. 14 (1957)
Stets'ko, Ia. Trydsiatoho chervnia 1941 (Toronto 1967)
Kosyk, V. L'Allemagne national-socialiste et L'Ukraine (Paris 1986)
                                                          M. Savaryn

Procopius of Caesarea (Prokopii Kesariisky, b ca 490–507 in Caesarea, Palestine, d after 562. Byzantine historian, whose writings are valued as a source for 6th-century geography and history. He chronicled the campaigns of the Byzantine emperor Justinian against Persia, the Vandals, and the Goths, and he described the great plague of 542 in Constantinople. His work *Secret History* also included information about the nomad tribes of Caucasia, among them the Antes.

Procurator's office (*prokuratura*). The state body that investigates crimes, prosecutes criminals, and oversees the execution of sentences. The procurators (usually called public prosecutors in English) emerged in Western Europe in the 18th century as a result of liberal demands to ensure the procedural rights of the accused. The inquisitorial process, in which the court conducted the investigation, trial, and punishment, gave way in the British system to the separation of the prosecutorial and judicial functions. The near equality of the prosecutor with the attorney for the accused was eventually established, as a legal principle throughout Western Europe, as well as in Ukrainian territories under Austrian, Russian, and Polish rule, before their annexation by the USSR.

The procurator's office in the Ukrainian SSR differed in some ways from its counterparts in other countries. Abolished immediately after the Bolshevik seizure of power, the institution was re-established in 1922. In recent times the office functioned according to the Law on the Procurator's Office of the USSR (1979) and articles 162–5 of the Constitution of the Ukrainian SSR. It was part of a centralized, all-Union system that was headed by the general procurator of the USSR, appointed for seven years by the USSR Supreme Soviet. He appointed republican procurators for five-year terms; these procurators were responsible to the general procurator. Thus, unlike the courts, Ukraine's procuracy was a Union, not a republican, institution. The major responsibility of the procurator's office was to 'oversee the precise implementation of law' and to practice 'socialist legality.' Because the meaning of 'socialist legality' was relative and dependent upon the current policy of the Party and state, the procurator's interpretation of the law had a decisive influence on the courts, especially in political cases.

In a broad sense, the procurator's office combined the functions of a Western district attorney, inspector of prisons, attorney general, and ombudsman. It supervised criminal investigations, authorized arrests, prosecuted offenders, and supervised prisons. To ensure that all government institutions, as well as individuals, adhered to the law, the procurator's office reviewed the laws, decrees, and orders of the administrative organs (except the Supreme Soviet of the USSR and the USSR Council of Ministers) and even the decisions of public and co-operative organizations. The office could appeal verdicts to higher courts; it could even appeal to the Supreme Court of the USSR, while the defendant could appeal only to the republican supreme court. The office could also interfere in civil cases, supporting one side against the other, if it believed that doing so would serve the public interest. An individual who had been wronged or libeled by an official or administrative organ could turn to the procurator's office for redress. Such cases were decided by the procurator in secret, and the decision was not subject to appeal. Thus, Soviet citizens could not defend their rights themselves but were dependent on the procurator's protection.

Yu. Starosolsky

Prodamet (full name: Obshchestvo dlia prodazhi izdelii russkikh metallurgicheskikh zavodov, or Society for the Sale of Products of Russian Metallurgical Factories). A cartel controlled by a group of European banks that ran the largest industrial monopoly in the Russian Empire. The plan to organize Prodamet was first devised in 1901 at the 16th Conference of Mining Industrialists of Southern Russia in Kharkiv, and official approval was granted in July 1902. The cartel consisted of 12 of the largest metallurgical companies in Ukraine, with total capital reserves of almost 175 million rubles, including the Donets-Yurev, Providence, Briansk-Oleksandrivkse, South Dnieper, and Huta-Bankova iron and steel works. Those companies were in turn owned by French (Crédit Lyonnais, Banque de Paris et des Pays-Bas, Société Générale pour l'Industrie en Russie), Belgian (Société Générale de Belgique, Crédit Général à Liège, Nagelmäckers et Fils), German (Deutsche Bank, Bank für Handel und Industrie, Dresdner Bank), and Russian (Azov-Don, Russian-Asiatic, Russian Foreign Trade, and Russian Commercial) banks. The French interests controlled 52 percent of Prodamet's capital, the Belgian, 23 percent, the German, 17 percent, and the Russian,

8 percent. Although the central office of Prodamet was located in St Petersburg and most of its operations were conducted from Kharkiv, the key decisions were made in Paris by its major shareholders through the so-called Paris Committee.

In 1902–5 Prodamet established a monopoly on the distribution of sheet iron, steel rails, pipes, railway ties, beams, and axles in Ukraine. In 1908 it began to expand its monopoly on metal products into the Baltic region, Moscow, and the Congress Kingdom of Poland. By 1913 it had overcome its major competitor, the large Krovlia syndicate of Ural iron and steel manufacturers, and established its monopoly throughout the empire. It controlled over 85 percent of the metals market in the Russian Empire. Prodamet accepted orders for metal products from Russian and foreign consumers and divided them among its members. It set prices and ordered certain factories to specialize in order to limit competition. The main goal of its policies was to stabilize and modernize metals production. From 1902 to 1912 it paid its members an average of 13 percent on their investment, and the rest of its profits was used to modernize production. At the same time Prodamet waged a continuous struggle with the *Produgol and *Prodarud syndicates. Eventually Prodamet emerged as a single, vertically integrated monopoly of iron-ore, coal, and metals producers throughout the Russian Empire. It was even able to gain control over the Truboprodazh syndicate and German metalworking plants in Ukraine, and became an all-encompassing monopoly in heavy industry. After 1911 internal bickering among members of the monopoly over the division of orders and dividends was stopped only through the intervention of the Paris Committee. From then on Prodamet concentrated on raising prices by limiting production.

The tsarist government became displeased with Prodamet's tactics, which raised the cost of railway construction and arms production. Its attempts to regulate the industry, however, had little success, and Prodamet continued to raise prices during the war. Only in 1915 did the government impose some control on the metallurgical industry. In January 1918 the new Soviet regime in Russia nationalized Prodamet. In Ukraine the syndicate retained legal ownership of its properties for a year longer.

BIBLIOGRAPHY
Lauwick, M. L'Industrie dans la Russie Méridionale, sa situation, son avenir (Brussels 1907)
Tsyperovich, G. Sindikaty i tresty v Rossii (Moscow 1919)
Tsukernik, A. Sindikat 'Prodamet': Istoriko-ekonomicheskii ocherk, 1902–iiul' 1914 g. (Moscow 1958)
Monopolii v metallurgicheskoi promyshlennosti Rossii, 1900–1917: Dokumenty i materialy (Moscow–Leningrad 1963)
Portal, R. La Russie industrielle de 1800 à 1914 (Paris 1966)
Crisp, O. Studies in the Russian Economy before 1914 (London 1976)
V. Holubnychy

Prodan, Kornii, b 11 September 1888 in Huliai Pole, Oleksandrivske county, Katerynoslav gubernia, d 15 June 1973 in Calgary. Agronomist and community activist; member of the Shevchenko Scientific Society and the Ukrainian Academy of Arts and Sciences. After emigrating to Canada in 1907, he completed teachers' college and worked as a teacher. Upon graduating from the agricultural faculty of the University of Manitoba (1921), he worked for the Ministry of Agriculture in Manitoba until

Kornii Prodan

Rev Vasyl Prodan

1957. He was a leading member of the Ukrainian People's Home and the Prosvita Institute in Winnipeg and president of the *Saint Raphael's Ukrainian Immigrants' Welfare Association of Canada for many years. He contributed articles on practical farming to Ukrainian papers in Canada and Western Ukraine and wrote a number of brochures on agriculture.

Prodan, Vasyl, b 29 January 1809 in Sukhoverkhiv, Bukovyna, d 16 December 1882 in Lashkivka, Bukovyna. Bukovynian civic, cultural, and church activist, writer, Orthodox priest, and Russophile. A priest at the cathedral church in Chernivtsi, he headed the *Ruska Besida in Bukovyna (1869–78) and the political society *Ruska Rada (1870). He wrote many panegyrics in the vernacular, including 'Stykh posviachen Evheniiu Hakmanu' (Verse Dedicated to Yevhen Hakman) and 'Oda na posviachenie tserkvy v Chernovtsiakh' (Ode on the Occasion of the Consecration of a Church in Chernivtsi). He also published a collection of poems, *Stykhy* (Verses).

Prodarud (full name: Obshchestvo dlia prodazhi rud yuga Rossii, or Society for the Sale of Ores from the South of Russia). A cartel of iron-ore producers in the Kryvyi Rih region and one of the largest monopolies in Ukraine and the Russian Empire. It was formed in 1908 by the eight largest mining companies, which produced 80 percent of the iron ore, to control ore prices. Financed by French, Belgian, and Russian capital, the cartel waged a fierce struggle against *Prodamet. In 1913–15 Prodarud fell apart, and its members were forced to submit to the Prodamet cartel and join in a single, vertically integrated monopoly of iron-ore, coal, and metal producers.

Prodazha. A monetary penalty imposed in Kievan Rus' on people not punished with a *vyra or *potok* for the killing of a slave or for a transgression against a freeman's property or liberty. The amounts and types of these fines were listed in *Ruskaia Pravda* as ranging from 1 to 12 *hryvni.*

Producer co-operative. See Artel.

Production brigade (*vyrobnycha bryhada*). A group of workers in the Soviet system who worked together and shared responsibility for a single production assignment. The brigadier, who in addition to the usual job led the bri-

gade, received extra pay for doing so. The purpose of the brigade system was to divide labor and responsibilities more rationally and to improve productivity. There were two types of brigades in the USSR: specialized brigades, in which workers of the same trade worked at similar jobs, and integrated brigades, in which workers of different trades worked at different jobs on a single project. Both forms of brigade could involve shift work. The brigade was paid according to its contract with an enterprise: a part of its earnings depended on the number of hours worked and the skill level, and a part on the result of the collective effort.

Production brigades became popular in the USSR in the late 1970s and were modeled on the brigades of the Volga Automobile Plant. They averaged 100 to 300 members each and were credited with increasing productivity by 15–20 percent and wages by 7–8 percent. Although they were generally popular with workers, especially the highly skilled workers, they were often opposed by the more traditional ministries and enterprises.

Production conference (*vyrobnycha narada*). A formal organizational unit of workers and managers in Soviet enterprises. The purpose of such bodies was to increase worker and community involvement in industrial management, improve labor discipline, and raise productivity. They were introduced in the 1920s, but almost all were dissolved under J. Stalin's regime. In the late 1950s, production conferences were set up in all enterprises and offices with over 300 employees. They were administered by trade-union committees and the Party. They met at least four times a year and could rule on a wide range of issues, but in practice they did little but rubber-stamp management decisions. In 1977 almost 21,000 of the total 130,000 production conferences in the USSR were located in Ukraine.

Produgol (full name: Obshchestvo dlia torgovli mineralnym toplivom Donetskogo basseina, or Society for the Trade in Mineral Fuel of the Donets Basin). A cartel of coal producers and one of the largest industrial syndicates in Ukraine and the Russian Empire. It was established in May 1904 by 11 of the largest coal producers in the Donets Basin, all of which were owned by French or Belgian capitalists. By 1910 the cartel had 24 members and produced 75 percent of all the coal mined in the basin. The administration of Produgol was located in St Petersburg, but real control was exercised by the Paris Committee, which represented the major foreign shareholders. Produgol accepted orders for coal and distributed them among its members, rationalizing the entire delivery system and lowering costs for its members. From the outset it practiced the typical monopolistic tactics of raising prices and limiting production: between 1904 and 1914 the price it charged per pood (16.38 kg) increased from 7 to 17 kopecks. In that period the average return on investment for its members was 17 percent. Produgol also reached an agreement with the Dombrowa coal cartel in Poland that prevented it from competing in the Donets Basin, and acquired control over two coal-producing cartels based in Siberia.

The artificial 'coal famine' of 1911–12, engineered by Produgol, angered the leaders of the *Prodamet metallurgical cartel, the main consumers of Donets Basin coal. In

1911 they established in Paris l'Union Minière et Métallurgique de Russie, which was to acquire coal mines in the Donets region and iron mines in the Kryvyi Rih region for Prodamet and organize the vertical integration of the metallurgical industry in Ukraine. The action greatly undermined Produgol's position. By 1914 its share of coal production in the Donets Basin had fallen to 54 percent. That same year the Russian government launched court proceedings against the syndicate for corrupting officials. The case was dropped after intercessions by the French government. Finally, in January 1914 six members withdrew from Produgol because of internal dissension. At the end of 1915 Produgol was formally dissolved. Its affairs in Paris were taken over by l'Union Minière du Sud de la Russie, which as late as the mid-1920s attempted to acquire mining concessions from the Soviet government.

BIBLIOGRAPHY
Fomin, P. Sindikaty i tresty (Kharkiv 1919)
Shpolianskii, D. Monopolii ugol'no-metallurgicheskoi promyshlennosti iuga Rossii v nachale xx veka (Moscow 1953)
McKay, J. Pioneers for Profit: Foreign Entrepreneurship and Russian Industrialization, 1885–1913 (Chicago–London 1970)
Crisp, O. Studies in the Russian Economy before 1914 (London 1976)
V. Holubnychy

Profesiini visty (Professional News). An unofficial trade-union paper of the Communist Party of Western Ukraine, published biweekly in Lviv from December 1926 to September 1928 (a total of 28 issues). The editor was A. Hoshovsky. The Polish authorities confiscated most of the issues and in the end closed down the paper.

Profesional'nyi vistnyk (Professional Herald). A semimonthly trade-union newspaper published by the Ukrainian Social Democratic party in Lviv in 1920–1. It was edited by A. Chernetsky and I. Kushnir.

Professional and vocational education (*profesiina osvita*).

The acquisition of specialized knowledge and skills required for entry into specific professions or occupations, obtained through educational institutions or training programs. In modern society, professional education (such as law, medicine, engineering) is acquired at institutions of higher learning, and entry into such establishments demands complete secondary education; vocational training is obtained either in specialized secondary schools, technical schools, or vocational schools or through apprenticeship programs.

The first institutions to offer vocational education in Ukraine were the artisan schools organized in the mid-16th century by guild organizations of the Orthodox *brotherhoods in Lviv, Kiev, and Peremyshl. In Russian-ruled Ukraine, by 1716 the so-called *tsyferni* (numbers) schools had been established in provincial capitals to train scribes, assistants to master shipbuilders, architects, and apothecaries. The origins of professional education in Ukraine date back to the 18th century, with the establishment of theological seminaries and institutions such as the medical-surgical school in Yelysavethrad (now Kirovohrad). Toward the end of the 18th century the first agricultural schools were established. In 1839 a veterinary school was founded in Kharkiv. Further development occurred with the establishment of universities – Kharkiv (1805) and Kiev (1834) – and of *lyceums, which emerged as cen-

ters of *higher education (legal, pedagogical, and medical training in particular).

A network of professional schools began to develop in the 1860s with the abolition of serfdom, the rise of the *zemstvo schools, and the development of trade and industry. Professional and vocational education became the concern of district and gubernia zemstvos, some ministries, and private individuals and societies. An important role was played by Western European industrialists, who developed Ukraine's industry, and who brought with them their own engineers, technicians, and skilled workers, from whom the local population acquired knowledge and skills. The organization of professional schools was decreed by a law enacted in 1869. Regulations passed in 1888 divided technical-industrial schools into three groups: (1) secondary technical schools, with a 4-year program for the training of technicians, (2) lower technical schools, with a 3-year program for training master craftsmen and tradesmen, and (3) trade schools, with a 3-year program for preparing skilled workers.

Between 1870 and 1890 *Realschulen had supplementary classes of applied mechanical and chemical studies, and had commerce departments which offered specialized secondary education. Toward the end of the 19th century important professional schools were founded, such as the Kharkiv Technological Institute (1885), the Kiev Polytechnical Institute (1898), and the Katerynoslav Higher Mining School (1899).

Prior to the Revolution of 1917 there were 16 higher professional schools (including 4 technical, 3 medical, 3 pedagogical, and 2 commercial), 125 secondary professional schools (including 66 commercial, 23 pedagogical, 11 art, 9 theological, and 6 agricultural), and 535 lower schools (369 trade and industrial, 54 agricultural, 34 pedagogical, 30 theological, 21 commercial, 16 medical, and 11 art). As a rule professional and vocational education was poorly developed in Russian-ruled Ukraine in comparison with Western Europe. The tsarist regime stymied the development of the country's productive forces and paid little attention to the establishment of a network of professional and vocational schools in Ukraine.

During the revolutionary period of 1917–20 efforts were made to Ukrainianize professional and vocational education, since all instruction had hitherto been conducted in Russian. Plans were also made by the educational authorities of the Ukrainian National Republic to organize trade schools with 1- or 2-year programs, and 4- or 5-year professional education programs at universities and institutes. Two new universities were founded (at Kamianets-Podilskyi and Katerynoslav) which offered some professional educational programs.

With the establishment of Soviet rule in Ukraine, professional and vocational education was reorganized. In the 1920s the professional school became the standard secondary school, offering 2-, and, later, 3- and 4-year programs. The following types of professional schools existed: industrial-technical, agricultural, socioeconomic, medical, art, artisan-industrial, construction, and transport. Survey data for November 1929 show that there were 678 professional schools in Ukraine, with an enrollment of 88,200 students. The most numerous were agricultural schools (249 schools, with 27,000 students) and industrial-technical schools (157 schools, with 26,000 students). Professional schools were established to train a skilled work force and prepare students for higher education.

Vocational training of skilled industrial workers was conducted in the factory apprenticeship schools. Established in 1920, these schools offered 3- and 4-year programs of technical training and general education to 14- and 15-year-olds who worked in factories and plants, and who had completed four grades of elementary education. In 1929 there were 201 such schools, with 30,000 students. In the 1930s the program of study was reduced to one and a half or two years. Similar schools existed for rural young people who worked on state farms (see *Schools for peasant youth).

Higher education was also reorganized. In 1920, universities were abolished and replaced by *institutes (agricultural, industrial-technical, socioeconomic, medical, pedagogical, art, and transport) which offered professional education programs that encompassed all facets of production (theory, economics, management, and practical skills). Technical colleges or *tekhnikums were established on the basis of former secondary technical schools and Realschulen and were designed to train specialists in narrow, practical technical fields. In 1928 there were 38 institutes, with 33,400 students, and 126 tekhnikums, with 26,900 students.

In 1929 the All-Union Supreme Council of the Economy ordered all levels of Ukraine's education system to be reorganized along Russian lines. Whereas in the 1920s Ukrainian had increasingly become the language of instruction in institutions of professional and vocational education, in the 1930s the trend was reversed, in favor of Russian-language instruction. In 1931, tekhnikums were reduced to the status of secondary schools. By 1933 some professional schools had been transformed into schools that offered *secondary special education; others had been liquidated.

In 1934 *Kharkiv, *Kiev, *Odessa, and *Dnipropetrovske universities were re-established. Tekhnikums were charged with the preparation of specialists at the intermediate level, and institutions of higher education (institutes and universities) were to offer advanced qualifications. Institutions of higher technical education with a three- or four-year program were organized in larger industrial enterprises. Under the impact of rapid industrialization the number of institutions of higher learning grew from 42 in 1929 to 173 in 1940. The student population increased from 40,900 to 196,800, and most students were trained in narrow, highly specialized technical fields.

With the approach of the war the supply of labor from the tekhnikums and factory apprenticeship schools was deemed insufficient, and in 1940 the Main Administration of the State Labor Reserve was established with its own schools. All vocational training schools below the level of tekhnikums were placed under the jurisdiction of this highly centralized institution (see *Labor reserve schools). In 1959 the labor reserve schools were transformed into urban and rural *vocational-technical schools, and the whole system of vocational training was transferred to the jurisdiction of a state committee of the Ukrainian SSR Council of Ministers.

Under N. Khrushchev an attempt was made to unify secondary general education with rudimentary vocational education, in a system of specialized secondary and higher education offering practical experience of production processes in enterprises. The attempt failed, and in 1964 professional and vocational training was again reorganized.

In Western Ukraine under Austrian rule, in the 19th century professional and vocational education was poorly developed, and both the authorities and the Ukrainian community focused on the development of the general education school system. *Lviv and *Chernivtsi universities offered professional education, although few Ukrainians were enrolled there because of discriminatory policies. The *Lviv Polytechnical Institute was founded in 1844, and there were veterinary, agricultural, and forestry schools in Lviv as well. There were practically no public vocational schools with Ukrainian as the language of instruction, and only one private secondary-level trade school, operated by the *Prosvita society in Lviv. There was also a Prosvita agricultural school of lower rank in Mylovannia.

In Western Ukraine under Polish rule, professional and vocational education contined to be weak. The most highly developed professional schools were institutions offering pedagogical training. Professional education organized by the Galician land board was poorly developed; there were only a few schools at the secondary level (eg, commercial art and trade schools in Lviv) and a few more of lower rank (primarily vocational schools). Polish was the language of instruction.

In 1937–8 there were 146 secondary vocational schools (91 in Galicia and 55 in Volhynia), with 22,000 students (17,300 and 4,700 respectively). The number of Ukrainian students attending these schools was negligible because the transition from rural elementary to professional and secondary schools was difficult. In Galicia the Ukrainian community gradually developed private professional schools – four secondary and eight lower schools. In the Lviv school district, out of 154 secondary and lower vocational schools only 13 were Ukrainian-language institutions; out of 97 schools offering supplementary vocational instruction 5 gave instruction in the Ukrainian language, and all were private institutions. Various community organizations, such as *Ridna Shkola and Prosvita, offered short-term vocational courses. During the Second World War, under the *Generalgouvernement, professional and vocational education expanded owing to Ukrainian community efforts. There were 330 professional schools, with 81,885 students. In 1941–2, higher education programs were organized in the fields of medicine, veterinary science, pharmacy, technology, agronomy, and forestry.

In Bukovyna, under Rumanian rule, there were few opportunities for professional and vocational education. In 1927 all Ukrainian-language schools were closed. Transcarpathia, under Czechoslovak rule, was in a better situation. In 1938 there were 5 teachers' seminaries (4 with Ukrainian as the language of instruction) and 3 secondary vocational schools (all Ukrainian, including the Trade Academy in Mukachiv), 9 lower vocational schools (of which 8 were Ukrainian), and 151 supplementary vocational schools (113 Ukrainian).

In contemporary Ukraine lower-grade vocational education is provided in vocational-technical schools, which, beginning in 1969, have gradually been transformed into institutions of secondary education offering general education as well as instruction in a specific trade. Full-time and part-time programs are offered that vary from one to three years. In 1986 there were 1,100 such schools, with 742,000 students. Institutions of *secondary special education provide middle-grade vocational or semiprofessional education (for the training of technicians, paramedics, and the like). In 1987–8 there were 734 specialized secondary schools, with 800,600 students (of whom 524,300 were in full-time day programs). Schools specializing in commerce and business had 106,800 students in 1987–8; machine-building and -equipment secondary special schools had 102,200 students.

Various institutions of higher education train specialists with advanced qualifications. In 1987–8 there were 146 such establishments in Ukraine, with 852,300 students, of whom 454,500 were in full-time day programs. The largest number of students, 321,300, were in industrial and construction institutes, and 248,800 were enrolled in pedagogical institutes.

Institutions of professional and vocational education were under the jurisdiction of various all-Union ministries in Moscow or of ministries in Kiev. The number of students admitted to these institutions in any given year is determined according to a plan. Graduates are given employment by the appropriate ministry and normally must work at the designated position for three years. In some years up to 18 percent of Ukraine's graduates were given jobs in the USSR outside Ukraine. In recent years there has been much discussion of the quality of vocational and professional education, its failure to keep pace with technological and scientific progress, and its emphasis on narrow specialization. The extreme *Russification of this sector of education and the lack of opportunity to study in the West have also been criticized. In 1987 only 25 percent of the courses in institutions of professional and technical education were taught in Ukrainian, and there were virtually no textbooks written in the language. Since 1988, however, the use of Ukrainian has slowly expanded.

Institutions of professional and vocational education were also organized by Ukrainian émigrés in Czechoslovakia – notably, the *Ukrainian Husbandry Academy, the *Ukrainian Higher Pedagogical Institute, and the *Ukrainian Studio of Plastic Arts. After the Second World War professional and vocational programs were organized for the large number of Ukrainian refugees in various *displaced persons camps in Germany and Austria. In Germany, in 1947–8 there were 26 professional schools and courses, with 1,163 students, and in Austria, 8 secondary professional schools and 140 professional courses of various types.

BIBLIOGRAPHY
Riappo, Ia. *Systema narodnoï osvity na Ukraïni* (Kharkiv 1926)
Siropolko, S. *Narodna osvita na Soviets'kii Ukraïni* (Warsaw 1934)
– *Istoriiu osvity na Ukraïni* (Lviv 1937)
De Witt, N. *Education and Professional Employment in the USSR* (Washington 1961)
Veselov, A. *Professional'no-tekhnicheskoe obrazovanie v SSSR* (Moscow 1961)
Pennar, J.; Bakalo, I.; Beredey, G. (eds). *Modernization and Diversity in Soviet Education with Special Reference to Nationality Groups* (New York 1971)
Matthews, M. *Education in the Soviet Union* (London 1982)
I. Bakalo, B. Krawchenko

Program music. Instrumental music, composed around a particular theme from literature, history, or nature, that is used to tell a story or illustrate an ideal. Notable examples of program music by Ukrainian composers include the symphonic poem *Taras Shevchenko* by K. Dankevych,

Dusha poeta (The Soul of a Poet) by A. Shtoharenko, the piano cycle *Liubov* (Love) by V. Barvinsky, and the symphonic *Hutsulian Pictures* by L. Kolodub.

Vasyl Prokhoda   Semen Prokhorov (self-portrait, 1895)

Prokhoda, Vasyl [Proxoda, Vasyl'], b 6 January 1891 near Pavlivka in the Kuban, d 8 December 1971 in Denver. Military and public figure. While serving as a lieutenant in the Russian army he was captured in the Carpathians, in 1915, and interned in POW camps in Bohemia. There he was active in the Ukrainianization movement. After returning home in 1918, he served as staff captain in the UNR Army's Graycoats Division (fall 1918), the Third Iron Rifle Division (spring 1919), and the Fourth Gray Brigade (summer 1919). After internment by the Poles he emigrated (1922) to Czechoslovakia and studied and then taught forestry (1927–33) at the Ukrainian Husbandry Academy in Poděbrady. He headed the Ukrainian Agrarian Society and edited its irregular organ, *Selo*; headed the Society of Former Ukrainian Military Officers in Czechoslovakia; and wrote a booklet about S. Petliura (1930). In January 1945 he was arrested by the NKVD, and he spent ten years in Soviet prisons and concentration camps. He was repatriated to Czechoslovakia in 1956 and emigrated to the United States in 1965. His memoirs are titled *Zapysky nepokirlyvoho* (Memoirs of an Indocile, 2 vols, Toronto 1967, Neu-Ulm 1972).

Prokhorov, Semen [Proxorov], b 11 February 1873 in Maloiaroslavets, Kaluga gubernia, Russia, d 23 July 1948 in Kharkiv. Painter. After graduating from the Moscow School of Painting, Sculpture, and Architecture (1904) he studied under I. Repin at the St Petersburg Academy of Arts (1904–9) and lectured at the Kharkiv Art School (1913–22) and Art Institute (1922–48). In the 1920s he took part in the exhibitions of the Association of Revolutionary Art of Ukraine and the Association of Artists of Red Ukraine. He painted portraits, landscapes, and genre paintings, such as *Sick Child* (1909), the cycle 'In the Colony' (1915–18), *Boy in a Hat, Golden Autumn* (1921), *Female Harvesters* (1922–3), *The Women's Department* (1929), *Orphans*, and *Village Commune* (1929).

Prokipchak, Ivan [Prokipčak], b 6 January 1917 in Medzilaborce, eastern Slovakia. Writer, teacher, and civic figure in the *Prešov region. He graduated from the teachers' seminary in Prešov (1935) and worked as a village school teacher until the Second World War. He lost his position as ideological secretary in Prešov and the right to teach during the Stalinist purge of 1951. He was later reinstated, and became director of the Duklia Ukrainian Folk Ensemble (1953–7), head of the Humenné District People's Council (1957–61) and the Cultural Association of Ukrainian Workers in Czechoslovakia (1971–80), and a deputy to the Slovak National Council (1972–6). He is the author of the story collections *Ranok* (Morning, 1955), *Borot'ba pochynaiet'sia* (The Struggle Is Beginning, 1956), and *Vyboïny* (Potholes, 1965) and of stories and publicistic articles in the Ukrainian press in Czechoslovakia. Yu. Kundrat's book about him appeared in 1977.

Prokofev, Aleksandr [Prokof'ev], b 2 December 1900 in Kobona, St Petersburg gubernia, Russia, d 18 October 1971 in Leningrad. Russian poet. He often wrote on Ukrainian subjects, and he translated T. Shevchenko, I. Franko, Lesia Ukrainka, P. Tychyna, M. Rylsky, and A. Malyshko into Russian. Prokofev's book of verse has been published in Ukrainian as *Vybrana liryka* (Selected Lyric Verse, 1960).

Prokofiev, Sergei [Prokof'ev, Sergej], b 7 December 1874 in Morshansk, Tambov gubernia, Russia, d 14 January 1944 in Kiev. Civil engineer. He graduated from the St Petersburg Institute of Road Engineers (1899). From 1908 he taught at the Kiev Polytechnical Institute, where he was a professor from 1922. He was instrumental in the construction of the first reinforced-concrete bridges in the Russian Empire and started the first course on reinforced concrete. Prokofiev was a pioneer in the field of reinforced concrete. His scientific works dealt with the technology, particulars, and applications of reinforced concrete, stress calculations, and related areas.

Prokofiev, Sergei [Prokof'ev, Sergej], b 23 April 1891 in Sontsivka, Bakhmut county, Katerynoslav gubernia, d 5 March 1953 in Moscow. Russian composer. He was exposed to Ukrainian folk songs while growing up, and motifs from these songs are prevalent in a number of his works, including the ballet *On the Dnieper* (1930), the opera *Semen Kotko* (1939), and sound tracks to the films *Partyzany v stepakh Ukraïny* (Partisans on the Steppes of Ukraine, 1942) and *Kotovs'kii* (1942).

Prokop, Myroslav (pseud: M. Vyrovy), b 1913 in Peremyshl, Galicia. Lawyer, political activist, and publicist. For his activity in the OUN he was imprisoned by the Poles in 1933–7. Upon his release he edited (1938–9) the student journal *Students'kyi visnyk* in Lviv and contributed (1939–41) to the publications of the Ukrainian Press Service in London. In 1942 he belonged to the home executive of the OUN (Bandera faction) in Kiev and then to its leadership (1943–4). He helped edit the underground OUN organ *Ideia i chyn* (1942–4). He was a founder of the *Ukrainian Supreme Liberation Council (UHVR) and a member of its presidium, and vice-president of the External Representation of the UHVR. After emigrating to the United States in 1949, he served as vice-president of the *Prolog Research Corporation and an editor of *Digest of the Soviet Ukrainian Press* (1957–77) and *Suchasnist'* (1967–). In addition to contributing articles to the Ukrainian press and entries to *Entsyklopediia ukraïnoznavstva* (Encyclopedia of Ukraine, 1955–84) he wrote *Ukraïna i ukraïns'ka polityka Moskvy* (Ukraine and Moscow's Ukrainian Policy, 1956; repr 1981).

Prokopchak, Petro [Prokopčak] (Prokop), b 12 November 1903 in Vapenne, Gorlice county, Galicia, d 31 October 1981 in Toronto. Communist leader and journalist. After emigrating to Canada in 1926, he worked in the mines and joined the Ukrainian Labour-Farmer Temple Association and the Communist Party of Canada. In the early 1930s he studied journalism in Kharkiv and then edited *Robitnytsia*, *Ukraïns'ki robitnychi visti*, *Narodna hazeta*, *Ukraïns'ke zhyttia*, and *Zhyttia i slovo* in Canada. He was interned during the Second World War (1940–2) under Defence of Canada regulations. In 1946 he was elected national secretary and in 1972 president of the *Association of United Ukrainian Canadians. At the same time he sat on the board of directors of the Workers' Benevolent Association.

Hryhorii Prokopchuk

Prokopchuk, Hryhorii [Prokopčuk, Hryhorij] (Prokoptschuk, Gregor), b 1909 in Galicia, d 25 October 1972 in Munich. Emigré historian, publicist, and publisher in West Germany. He received a doctorate from Munich University in 1942 for the dissertation 'Die österreichische Kirchenpolitik in der Westukraine während der Regierungszeit Maria Theresa, 1772–1780.' He founded the Baturyn Ukrainian student society in Munich in 1939 and was a research associate of the East European Institute in Cracow in 1942–4. In the postwar period he was a central figure in the *German-Ukrainian Society in Munich and its publishing house Ukraine. He edited and contributed articles on Ukrainian church history and culture to the society's journal *Ukraine in Vergangenheit und Gegenwart* (1952–68), and he wrote *Das ukrainische Lwiw-Lemberg: Kultur-politische Betrachtung* (1954), *Der Metropolit Andreas Graf Scheptyćkyj: Leben und Wirken des grössten Förderers der Kirchenunion* (1955; rev edn 1967), *Ukrainer in München* (1958), *Ukrainer in der Bundesrepublik* (1959), and *Deutsch-Ukrainische Gesellschaft, 1918–1968* (1968).

Prokopchyts, Yevstafii [Prokopčyc', Jevstafij], b 1806, d 1856. Educator, philologist, and civic and political leader. In 1848, while teaching at a gymnasium in Stanyslaviv, he was elected to the Austrian parliament. That year he was appointed principal of the new Ternopil German Gymnasium. Under pseudonyms such as I. Kolosowicz and ein Rusin he wrote poetry, articles on political issues, and linguistic studies. He was a strong promoter of Ukrainian education.

Prokopenko, Oleksii, b 19 November 1925 in Auly, now in Krynychky raion, Dnipropetrovske oblast. Cinematographer. He graduated from the State Institute of Cinema Arts in Moscow (1955) and then participated in the production of *Ivanna* (1960), *Lisova pisnia* (The Forest Song, 1961), *Sofiia Hrushko* (1972), *Poïzd nadzvychainoho pryznachennia* (A Train of a Singular Assignment, 1980), and the telefilm *Istoriia odnoï liubovy* (The Story of One Love, 1981).

Prokopii [Prokopij], b and d ? Wood engraver of the mid-17th century. He did illustrations for the publications of the Kievan Cave Monastery Press, including *Apokalipsys* (Apocalypse, 1646–62) and the first editions of the Kievan Cave Patericon (1661 and 1678). The illustrations to the latter were also issued as separate prints.

Prokopovych, Borys [Prokopovyč], b 13 July 1929 in Kutriv, Dubno county, Volhynia voivodeship, d 19 February 1980 in Poltava. Stage director and actor. In 1953 he completed study at the Kharkiv Theater Institute. He worked as a stage director and actor in the Poltava Ukrainian Music and Drama Theater, and from 1965 was its artistic director.

Prokopovych, Petro [Prokopovyč], b 10 July 1775 in Mytchenky, near Baturyn, Nizhen regiment, d 3 April 1850 in Palchyky, Chernihiv gubernia. Apiarist. He completed study at the Kievan Mohyla Academy and then served in the army (1794–8) before retiring to his estate and concentrating on beekeeping. Prokopovych gained considerable expertise in his field and established apiculture as a branch of agricultural science. He invented the frame hive in 1814, a marked improvement in beekeeping technology, and was the first in the world to obtain clear comb honey without destroying bees. He established the first scientific beekeeping school in Eastern Europe (which trained nearly 600 apiarists in 1828–74) and developed the first nomenclature for modern beekeeping in Eastern Europe. Prokopovych planned to purchase a printing press to publish his lectures in Ukrainian but was prevented from doing so by the tsarist authorities. A number of his essays were published in Russian scientific journals, and a collection of his lectures in Russian was published posthumously (later translated into German, French, and Polish).

Prokopovych, Sava [Prokopovyč], b ?, d 1701. Member of the Cossack *starshyna*; progenitor of the *Savych family. He was captain of Voronizh company in Nizhen regiment (1669), a signatory of the *Hlukhiv Articles, Hetman D. Mnohohrishny's envoy in Moscow (1669), and chancellor of Pereiaslav regiment (1671). He was appointed general chancellor (1672–87) and general judge (1687–1701) of the Hetman state. He took part in the *starshyna*'s overthrow of Hetman I. Samoilovych in 1687.

Prokopovych, Teofan [Prokopovyč] (secular name: Eleazar), b 18 June 1681 in Kiev, d 19 September 1736 in St Petersburg. Orthodox archbishop, writer, scholar, and philosopher. He graduated from the Kievan Mohyla Academy in 1696 and continued his education in Lithuania, Poland, and at the St Athanasius Greek College in Rome. In 1704 he returned to the Mohyla Academy to teach poetics, rhetoric, philosophy, and theology. He also served as prefect from 1708 and rector in 1711–16. He gained prominence as a writer and as a supporter of Hetman I. *Mazepa. His most famous work, *Vladimir*, is ded-

icated to the hetman, whom he depicted as the figure of the Grand Prince of Kiev. Prokopovych also praised Mazepa in his sermons and propounded Kiev as the second Jerusalem. Following Mazepa's unsuccessful revolt against Tsar Peter I in 1709, however, Prokopovych denounced him and expressed his complete allegiance to Peter. He participated in the campaign to vilify Mazepa, calling him 'the one filled with the Devil's spirit' and 'the new Judas.' From then he became a favorite of Peter's and was rewarded with several promotions. He was called to St Petersburg to be a preacher and adviser to the tsar, was consecrated bishop (1718) and then archbishop (1720) of Pskov, was appointed vice-president of the new *Holy Synod in 1721, and finally was made archbishop of Novgorod in 1725.

In the 1720s Prokopovych played a crucial role in the reform of the Russian Orthodox church. He supported the liquidation of the position of patriarch and the creation of the Holy Synod under the direct authority of the tsar. In 1721 he wrote the *Dukhovnyi reglament*, a reform statute under which the church was transformed into a state bureaucracy. He was also one of the major theorists of Russian autocracy. These positions brought him into conflict with the traditional church establishment and the boyars, who succeeded in isolating him from Russian political and cultural life after Peter's death.

Teofan Prokopovych and his book on poetics (1786)

Prokopovych's most notable contribution to Ukrainian literature was the drama *Vladimir* (1705). Although filled with Old Church Slavonic expressions, it is innovative in its use of dialogue and varied patterns of verse. His other poetic works include a panegyric on the Battle of Poltava in Ukrainian, German, and Latin; various elegies; and other works. He wrote an authoritative textbook on poetics, *De arte poetica* ..., which was influenced more by classical poetics than by prevailing baroque theory. In this he introduced the use of the hexameter and developed the epigram and other poetic forms. After his departure to St Petersburg, Prokopovych lost contact with Ukrainian literary development. His subsequent works were all in Russian and often devoted to praising Peter and his imperial reforms.

He wrote many theological works in Latin and Old Church Slavonic. His course notes on theology from the Kievan Academy were published as *Chistianae orthodoxae theologiae in Academia Kijoviensi* (5 vols, 1773–5) and *Com-*

pendium sacrae orthodoxae theologiae (1802). His theology showed the influence of Protestant theologians and his conscious departure from the Catholic influences that earlier predominated at the academy. His *Philosophia peripatetica* is a philosophical text that embraces logic, natural philosophy, mathematics, and ethics. In it he set out the ideas of Descartes, Locke, Bacon, Hobbes, and Spinoza and supported the theories of Galileo, Kepler, and Copernicus. He also introduced the teaching of mathematics and geometry into the curriculum of the Kievan Academy. His text on rhetoric, *De arte rhetorica libri X* (which appeared in Ukrainian translation as *Pro rytorychne mystetstvo*, 1979), criticized the baroque style in speeches, sermons, and panegyrics and argued for the dominance of content over form.

Most of Prokopovych's historical writings deal with the reign of Peter I. The most important of these is *Istoriia imperatora Petra Velykogo ot rozhdeniia ego do Poltavskoi batalii* (The History of Emperor Peter the Great from His Birth to the Battle of Poltava, 1788).

The most complete collections of his works appeared in 1961 (ed I. Eremin) and in 3 vols in 1979–81 (published in Ukrainian translation by the AN URSR [now ANU]). A bibliography of his works, compiled by J. Cracraft, appeared in *Oxford Slavonic Papers* (1975).

BIBLIOGRAPHY
Samarin, Iu. *Stefan Iavorskii i Feofan Prokopovich kak propovedniki* (Moscow 1844)
Chistovich, I. *Feofan Prokopovich i ego vremia* (Petersburg 1868)
Šerech, J. [Shevelov, G.]. 'On Teofan Prokopovič as Writer and Preacher in His Kiev Period,' *Harvard Slavic Studies*, 2 (1954)
Härtel, H-J. *Byzantinisches Erbe und Orthodoxie bei Feofan Prokopovič* (Würzburg 1970)
Nichik, V. *Feofan Prokopovich* (Moscow 1977)
Cracraft, J. 'Feofan Prokopovich and the Kievan Academy,' in *Russian Orthodoxy under the Old Regime*, ed R. Nichols and T. Stavron (Minneapolis 1978)
– 'Prokopovyč's Kiev Period Reconsidered,' *HUS*, 2, no. 2 (June 1978)
Avtukhovych, T. 'Kyïvs'kyi period tvorchosti Feofana Prokopovycha i barokko,' in *Ukraïns'ke literaturne barokko: Zbirnyk naukovykh prats'* (Kiev 1987)

I. Korovytsky, A. Zhukovsky

Viacheslav Prokopovych

Prokopovych, Viacheslav [Prokopovyč, V'jačeslav] (pseud: S. Volokh), b 10 June 1881 in Kiev, d 7 June 1942 in Besancourt, near Paris. Political leader, pedagogue, publicist, and historian. After graduating in history and philology from Kiev University (studying under V. An-

tonovych), he taught history at a Kiev state gymnasium. He was released for 'Ukrainophilism,' taught briefly at a private gymnasium, and then served as a librarian in the Kievan Local Museum. From 1905 he was active in the Ukrainian Radical Democratic party and from 1908 in the Society of Ukrainian Progressives (TUP). He edited the pedagogical journal *Svitlo* and published articles in the Ukrainian press (particularly in *Rada*). A member of the Central Committee of the Ukrainian Party of Socialist Federalists, he became a representative to the Ukrainian Central Rada in 1917 and then a member of its executive council. He served as minister of education in the cabinet of the UNR *Holubovych government (January–April 1918), and under the Hetman government he worked in the offices of the Kiev gubernial zemstvo. After the arrest of S. Petliura, he became the head of the National Zemstvo Administration. He remained in Kiev until May 1920. In May–October 1920 he was the head of the UNR Council of National Ministers, and in early 1921 he was the minister of education in a cabinet led by A. Livytsky. He emigrated to Poland and stayed in internment camps in Tarnów, Kalisz, and Szczepiórno. He arrived in Paris in 1924, and worked closely with S. Petliura. After the latter's death, he once again headed the UNR *government-in-exile's Council of National Ministers (1926–39). In October 1939–May 1940, he was the head of the UNR Directory and deputy to the Supreme Otaman of the UNR, in Paris. Pokopovych edited and wrote for the weekly *Tryzub* in Paris in 1925–9 and was one of the initiators (and a director) of the Petliura Library in that city.

A. Zhukovsky

Prokopovych-Antonsky, Antin [Prokopovyč-Antons'kyj], b 28 January 1762 in Chernihiv regiment, d 18 July 1848 in Moscow. Naturalist and pedagogue; full member of the Imperial Russian Academy of Sciences from 1813. He graduated from the Kievan Mohyla Academy (1782) and Moscow University (1786) and taught natural science at the Moscow University Boarding School for the Nobility (1787–1802) and then held the chair of agriculture and mineralogy at the university (1804–28). He served as director of the boarding school (1818–24) and was elected rector of the university three times (1818–26). At the same time he presided over the Society of Lovers of Russian Literature at the university and oversaw the first department of the Imperial Moscow Society of Agriculture. He edited a number of journals: *Detskie chteniia dlia serdtsa i razuma* (1785), *Magazin natural'noi istorii, fiziki i khimii* (1788–90, a supplement to *Moskovskie vedemosti*), and *Zemledel'cheskii zhurnal* (1823–45).

Proletar. See Politvydav Ukrainy.

Proletar (Proletarian). A newspaper published by the Galician Regional Bureau of the Siberian Bureau of the Communist Party in Omsk, Siberia, in 1920 (a total of 13 issues). It was aimed at Galician POWs in the city.

Proletariat. See Working class.

Proletarii (Proletarian). A Russian-language daily organ of the CC CP(B)U and the All-Ukrainian Council of Trade Unions, published in Kharkiv in 1923–35 and briefly in Kiev in 1935. Until 1924 it appeared as a supplement to the newspaper *Komunist*. In 1926–7 it was called *Vseukrainskii proletarii*.

Proletars'ka pravda (Proletarian Truth). A daily organ of the Kiev Gubernia (then Oblast) Party Committee, published in 1921–41. It was published in Russian as *Proletarskaia pravda* until 1925, when it merged with *Bil'shovyk* and switched to Ukrainian. Previous organs of the Kiev Gubernia Party Committee, including *Kievskii kommunist* (1918–19) and *Kommunist* (1919–21), were also published in Russian. Under its longtime editor, S. Shchupak, the newspaper played a role in the Ukrainization movement of the 1920s. It was succeeded by **Kyïvs'ka pravda*.

Proletkult (Ukrainian acronym for *proletarska kul'tura* 'proletarian culture'). A leftist mass movement in the immediate postrevolutionary period, which originated in Russia in 1917 and was carried over into Ukraine. Proletkult's theoreticians (including A. Bogdanov and V. Pletnev) were opposed to classical traditions; they considered them bourgeois and inimical to the proletariat. They believed that a 'purely proletarian' culture was to be created 'in the laboratory.' Driven by an imperative to educate the masses in the new form of culture, the organizers established a system of reading groups and workshops in literature, drama, and the visual arts. Their mass and largely nonartistic nature fostered the production of meager works by dilettantes and graphomaniacs. V. Lenin recognized that such production could result in a general cultural breakdown, and came out against the Proletkult in 1920. Nevertheless it continued to be active, particularly in Ukraine, where it led the assault on Ukrainian culture. Initially it worked under the auspices of the People's Commissariat of Education and the All-Ukrainian Organizational Bureau of the Proletkult, which in 1922 briefly issued a Russian-language monthly, *Zoria griadushchego*. Many of the leading activists of the movement in Ukraine were Russians (eg, A. Gastev, G. Petnikov) and were among those opposed to Ukrainization. Proletkult's orientation to the masses was similar to that of the organizations Pluh and Hart; it differed, however, in its national orientation. The *Neoclassicists (led by M. Zerov) and members of *Vaplite (led by M. Khvylovy) opposed the Proletkult's mass orientation and its members' ignorance. Their opposition was reflected in the *Literary Discussion of 1925–8, although by that time the Proletkult was in decline.

I. Koshelivets

Prolitfront (Proletarskyi literaturnyi front [Proletarian Literary Front]). A Ukrainian literary organization founded in Kharkiv by M. *Khvylovy, other former members of *Vaplite, members of *Molodniak, and members of other literary organizations. It was active from April 1930 to January 1931, when it was pressured by the All-Ukrainian Association of Proletarian Writers (VUSPP) to disband. It was the last attempt of the Vaplite group to take a collective stand for the right of writers to belong to organizations other than the VUSPP, which sought a monopoly on the entire Ukrainian literary world. Among its members were Khvylovy, P. Tychyna, M. Kulish, O. Vyshnia, Yu. Yanovsky, O. Dosvitnii, I. Senchenko, P. Panch, I. Dniprovsky, H. Epik, H. Kostiuk, V. Mysyk, M. Yalovy, L. Kvitko, and I. Momot. Prolitfront issued no direct statements of opposition, but it rejected from the VUSPP's adopted method of 'proletarian realism.' Like Vaplite it sought to unite the best in Ukrainian literature and create a free environment for its development. Prolitfront also issued an official organ of the same name. Its fall was brought about by increasing political and cultural centralism and increasing disunity among Ukrainian Communists.

Prolitfront (acronym for Proletarian Literary Front). A monthly literary journal, the official organ of an organization of the same name. It was published from April to December 1930 (eight issues) in Kharkiv. It was the vehicle for the works of M. Khvylovy, P. Tychyna, M. Kulish, O. Vyshnia, Yu. Yanovsky, O. Dosvitnii, I. Senchenko. P. Panch, I. Dniprovsky, H. Epik, H. Kostiuk, V. Mysyk, M. Yalovy, L. Kvitko, I. Momot, and others.

Prolog. An Old Ukrainian expanded version of the Greek Synaxarion, which is a collection of lives of the saints for every day of the year. The name is derived from the introduction (*prólogos*) to the Synaxarion, which was translated into Church Slavonic in the early 12th century. *Prolog* is three times larger than its prototype; it includes additional lives of Slavic and Rus' saints (eg, SS Borys and Hlib and Theodosius of the Caves) and other religious and edifying material taken from Byzantine religious and secular sources, the Patericons, and the Rus' Primary Chronicle. Two Ukrainian redactions exist. The first dates from the early 13th century. The second is believed to have been the work of Cyril of Turiv. *Prolog* was used widely as a book of knowledge and served as the foundation for didactic literature in Rus'. M. *Petrov's book about it was published in Kiev in 1875.

Prolog Research Corporation (Proloh). A research and publishing association set up in New York in 1952 by members of the *Ukrainian Supreme Liberation Council (M. Lebed, M. Prokop, Yu. Lopatynsky, B. Chaikivsky, and others) to monitor and report on political, economic, and cultural developments in Soviet Ukraine. It published an English-language quarterly, *Prologue* (1957–61), under the editorship of L. Shankovsky, and a monthly, *Digest of the Soviet Ukrainian Press* (1957–77). It has assisted the Suchasnist Ukrainian Society for International Studies in producing the periodical *Suchasnist' and has published over 200 books in Ukrainian and 5 in Russian on Ukraine's political and literary history, contemporary writing, and the dissident movement. The association was reorganized into a corporation in 1968. Its directors have been M. Lebed (1952–73), M. Prokop (1973–79), R. Kupchynsky (1979–91), and P. Sodol (since 1991).

Prolom (Breach). A biweekly Russophile journal published in Lviv in 1881 (15 issues) and 1882 (22 issues) by Y.(O.) Markov. It was edited by Markov and O. Avdykovsky (1881, nos 1–15), V. Lutsyk (1882, no. 2), I. Yavdyk (1882, nos 3–12), and S. Labash (1892, no. 13). A supplementary newspaper, *Viche*, accompanied each issue. In 1883 Markov replaced *Prolom* with a semiweekly newspaper, **Novyi prolom*.

Prombank. A bank founded in Lviv in 1936 by a group of activists from the *Union of Ukrainian Merchants and

Entrepreneurs to promote the development of Ukrainian industry and trade. The bank encouraged small investors to open accounts and used its reserves to provide primarily short-term credit. It helped finance several enterprises in Lviv, a nail factory in Vynnyky, a gravel operation in Sarny, and other businesses. Prombank had branches or representatives in 20 cities and towns in Galicia and Volhynia. Its membership increased quickly, from 815 in 1937 to 1,550 in 1938, and total deposits increased from 407,000 zlotys to 627,000 zlotys. The bank's board of directors was headed by Ya. Skopliak and included A. Milianych, its founder, R. Mytsyk, and V. Yatsyshyn. When Soviet forces occupied Galicia in 1939, Prombank was dissolved, and its assets were seized by the State Bank of the USSR.

Prometei (Prometheus). An émigré publishing house owned and operated by R. *Paladiichuk in Augsburg and Neu-Ulm, Germany, from 1947 to 1951. It published six literary works (including two fairy-tales for children) by I. *Bahriany, Yu. Kosach's *Enei i zhyttia inshykh* (Aeneas and the Lives of Others), U. Samchuk's *Iunist' Vasylia Sheremety* (The Youth of Vasyl Sheremeta), historical and political works by Isaak *Mazepa (5 vols), S. Pidhainy's memoirs of Ukrainian political prisoners in the Soviet concentration camps in the Solovets Islands, O. Han's biography of M. Khvylovy, and I. Ševčenko's Ukrainian translation of G. Orwell's *Animal Farm*.

Map issued by the Promethean movement

Promethean movement. A political movement of opposition to the Soviet government, named after the mythical god Prometheus (a symbol of the struggle of all enslaved nations for freedom), that emerged in Europe in the 1920s among émigré communities of nations under Soviet rule. It was formed as the Promethean League of Nations Subjugated by Moscow (commonly known as the Promethean League) in 1925 after a conference of representatives of various governments-in-exile and national committees based in Paris, Warsaw, Bucharest, Istanbul, Helsinki, and Prague. Its headquarters was set up in Warsaw. The league's first executive included president R. *Smal-Stotsky of Ukraine and two vice-presidents, W. Mustapha Bei of Azerbaidzhan and J. Salakaya of Georgia. The league consisted of Azerbaidzhani, Buriat, Cau-

casian Mountain Peoples', Crimean Tatar, Don Cossack, Georgian, Idel-Ural Tatar, Ingrian, Kazakh, Kirghiz, Komi, Kuban Cossack, Mari, Mordovian, Tadzhik, Turkmen, and Ukrainian representatives. Armenians and Belarusians were not represented. The league claimed to speak for up to 80 million people. Its most concrete undertaking was a campaign to block the admission of the USSR into the League of Nations. In connection with this campaign it sent memorandums and other materials to all attending delegations. The Promethean League's representative in Geneva was M. Livytsky. The league sponsored a congress in Warsaw in 1935 which was attended by 200 delegates and specialists in the nationalities question in their respective countries.

Much of the Promethean movement's activity consisted of advocacy work. It was carried out mainly by local clubs through lectures, meetings, and informative gatherings aimed at acquainting the participants with the movement's struggle. Local chapters also published periodicals, such as the French-language *Prométhée* (1926–8) and *Revue de Prométhée* (1938–40). Journals in other languages were also published, and articles for publication in the press, books, and brochures were written by Promethean supporters.

Paris and Warsaw were the main centers of Promethean activity. Paris was an important publishing center and served as the headquarters for the allied Friendship Committee of the Peoples of Caucasia, Turkestan, and Ukraine and the France-Orient organization (which had a Ukrainian section), both of which were organized under the auspices of Prince J. Tokarzewski-Karaszewicz. The leading activists among the Ukrainians were M. Kovalsky, I. Kosenko, V. Prokopovych, and O. and R. Shulhyn.

In Warsaw the movement benefited from the financial and administrative support of government and semigovernmental agencies, military officials, and supporters of J. Piłsudski. The Oriental Institute in Warsaw (S. Siedlecki, director; O. Gurka, secretary) was the main base for the movement, and many scholars and professionals associated with it worked there. A youth circle formed around the institute published *Wschód (L'Orient)* under the editorship of W. Bączkowski. The Polish Institute of Nationalities Research, the Ukrainian Scientific Institute in Warsaw, and the *Biuletyń Polsko-Ukraiński* were also havens for movement supporters, as was the Institute of Eastern Europe in Vilnius (V. Bielgorski, director). Other Polish proponents of the movement included A. Bocheński, T. Hołowko, M. Handelsman, S. Poniatowski, S. Stempowski, and L. Wasilewski. Leading activists among the Ukrainians included S. Baziak, L. Chykalenko, T. Olesiiuk, V. Salsky (head of the Ukrainian section), P. Shandruk, R. Smal-Stotsky (long-standing head of the Prometei club), P. Suliatynsky (of the Kuban), and V. Zmiienko.

Secondary centers of the league's activity were Berlin, Harbin, Helsinki, Istanbul, Prague, and Teheran. In 1932–7 the Prometei club was active in Harbin, and in 1933 it published a collection of articles in Ukrainian, Georgian, Turkic-Tatar, and Polish. Local activists were I. Paslavsky and I. Svit. There was also a Promethean group in Shanghai, formed by refugees from Manchuria and Soviet territory.

After the Second World War certain ideas of the Promethean movement were perpetuated by organizations such as the *Anti-Bolshevik Bloc of Nations, the *Paris Bloc, and the Federation of Former Central and East European Veterans.

A. Zhukovsky

Prométhée

Prométhée. A French-language journal published in Paris monthly from 1926 to 1936 and then quarterly to 1938 (a total of 137 issues). The organ of the *Promethean movement, it promoted the national aspirations of the Ukrainians and the Caucasian and Turkic peoples in the USSR and contained much information on political and cultural developments there. Its contributors included many prominent Ukrainian, Armenian, Georgian, and other émigrés. The chief editor was the Georgian Zh. Gvazava, and the Ukrainian section was edited by M. Shulhyn and then I. Kosenko. *Prométhée* was succeeded by *Revue de Prométhée*.

Promin (Ray). A publishing house in Dnipropetrovske, established in 1954. It was called the Dnipropetrovske Book-Journal-Newspaper Publishing House until 1964. It has published political propaganda, prose, poetry, children's books, technical literature, and especially books on regional history and tourist guides in both Ukrainian and Russian. In the years 1966–75 it issued 1,057 titles with a combined pressrun of 13.4 million copies. In 1990 the publishing house was renamed Sich.

Promin' (Vashkivtsi)

Promin' (Ray). A pedagogical journal for Ukrainian teachers in Bukovyna and Galicia, published semimonthly in Vashkivtsi, Bukovyna, in 1904–7. Founded and edited by I. *Herasymovych, assisted by I. Karbulytsky, the journal published articles on pedagogical topics, on the history of Ukrainian education, on culture and literature, and on general political and social issues. The journal also supported the establishment of the Ukrainian Teachers' Mutual Aid Society.

Promin' (Ray). A weekly newspaper of literary, cultural, and community affairs, published in Moscow from December 1916 until early 1917, when it was closed by the Russian authorities. It was edited by L. Solohub with the close co-operation of V. Vynnychenko. Among the contributors were O. Lototsky, L. Abramovych, M. Hrushevsky, S. Yefremov, D. Doroshenko, O. Oles, O.

Salikovsky, P. Stebnytsky, P. Tychyna, M. Filiansky, and H. Chuprynka.

Promin' (Ray). A literary monthly published in Chernivtsi from 1921 to 1923 under the editorship of I. Pihuliak. Among its contributors were O. Kobylianska, O. Makovei, M. Marfiievych, O. Vilshyna, O. Hrytsai, F. Dudko, K. Polishchuk, H. Orlivna, O. Oles, A. Pavliuk, O. Zaduma, V. Limnychenko (Melnyk), A. Voloshchak, D. Makohon, V. Zalozetsky-Sas, M. Pidhirianka, M. Nyzhankivska, L. Myroniuk, and O. Shevchukevych. It ceased publication after Pihuliak's emigration and because of the pressures of Rumanian censorship.

Promin' (Ray). An illustrated monthly children's magazine published in Winnipeg from January 1927 to 1930. It contained stories, poetry, songs, and games and was especially intended to raise the national consciousness of Ukrainian children. The magazine was edited by S. *Doroshchuk. Contributors included O. Darkovych and D. Hunkevych.

Promin' (Ray). A newspaper for displaced persons, published in Salzburg, Austria, from September 1946 to April 1949 and then in Munich to September 1949 (a total of 96 issues). It was edited by Ye. Lazor.

Promin' (Ray). The monthly organ of the *Ukrainian Women's Association of Canada, published in Winnipeg since January 1960. The journal publishes articles on women's issues, culture, child rearing, and political and historical topics. It also contains some belles lettres and news of the association and its members. Its longtime editor was N. *Kohuska.

Pronchenko, Mykhailo [Prončenko, Myxajlo], b 1902 in Apostolove, near Kryvyi Rih, Kherson gubernia, d April 1942 in Kryvyi Rih. Poet and community figure. He began publishing in 1927, with the collection *Zdobuvaiu nadra* (I Conquer the Earth's Interior). He was arrested in 1933 and imprisoned for over five years in a labor camp in the Soviet Far East. During the Nazi occupation he edited the nationalist weekly *Dzvin* in Kryvyi Rih from October to December 1941 and published the patriotic poetry collection *Kobza* (1941). He was arrested in January 1942 and executed by the Gestapo. I. *Bahriany's novel *Rozhrom* (The Rout) was dedicated to the memory of Pronchenko.

Proniuk, Yevhen [Pronjuk, Jevhen], b 26 September 1936 in Khomiakivka, Kolomyia county, Galicia. Philosopher and dissident. He grew up in Karaganda oblast in Kazakhstan, to which his family was deported in 1947. After studying philosophy at Kiev University as a correspondence student (1957–62) he worked as a researcher and bibliographer at the AN URSR (now ANU) Institute of Philosophy and wrote a candidate of sciences' dissertation on O. Terletsky (1965). Between 1964 and 1972 he wrote a number of articles on 19th-century Ukrainian thought and socialism, particularly in Galicia, and was one of three compilers of the bibliography of the works of the Institute of Philosophy (1969), a guide which was organized according to his scheme. For helping V. *Lisovy prepare an open letter to the CC CPSU criticizing its policies, and for distributing the letter, he was arrested in July

Yevhen Proniuk

1972. In November 1973 he was sentenced to seven years in labor camps in Perm oblast and Vladimir prison and five years' internal exile for anti-Soviet agitation and propaganda. Ill with tuberculosis, Proniuk barely survived his long term. After his release in 1984 he was permitted to work in Kiev only at menial jobs. In June 1989 he was elected president of the Society of Politically Repressed Ukrainians at its founding congress, and in 1990 he was elected to the co-ordinating council of the *Memorial Society and to the Kiev City Council.

Proniv, Danylo, b 1923 in Hrabivka, Kalush county, Galicia. Neurologist. A graduate of the Lviv Medical Institute (1951), he worked there as an intern, taught at the Kiev Institute for the Upgrading of Physicians, and headed the neurology department at the Lviv Medical Institute (from 1963). He has published works on vascular diseases of the nervous system and nerve regeneration.

Propaganda. See Agitation and propaganda.

Propination (*propinatsiia*; Polish: *propinacje*). The right to manufacture and distribute or sell alcohol and alcoholic beverages (derived from the Latin *propinare* 'to drink to one's health'). In theory a sovereign ruler always had the authority to regulate the production and sale of alcohol; in practice the exercise of that authority has depended on circumstances, especially on the power actually at the disposal of the ruler.

In Kievan Rus' and subsequently in Muscovy until the late 15th or early 16th century, it was the practice of the boyars to make specific amounts of mead, wine, kvass, and beer for special occasions. Others could brew privately for similar occasions on payment of a fee to the overlord and on condition that the drinks be used for domestic consumption only.

By the late 15th century most Ukrainian lands were under the joint control of the Kingdom of Poland and the Grand Duchy of Lithuania. In 1496 the sovereign granted to the nobility the exclusive right to manufacture and sell spirits. That propination right included the sole right of the manor lords to operate taverns on their estates. Over time the interpretation of the propination right was broadened so that estate owners could use alcoholic beverages as a form of payment for peasant labor. Records of estates in the 18th century show that serfs were required to purchase set quantities of alcohol as part of their obligations to manor lords. Further, peasants were forbidden to buy alcohol from any other source.

The propination privilege provided the landlords with substantial incomes, especially from the 18th century on. As the export of grain declined in significance, the Polish nobility turned increasingly to distilling as an inexpensive and profitable means of disposing of surplus grain. The king of Poland reconfirmed the nobility's propination right in 1768; it continued in Right-Bank Ukraine and in Austrian Galicia after the partitions of Poland.

In Left-Bank Ukraine the Cossack *starshyna* acquired many of the rights of the nobility after the collapse of Polish rule. Where the tsarist state was able to exert its authority, Russian regulations applied: distilling was in private hands except on crownland property, but the tsar regulated trade in alcohol. Peter I encouraged merchants to engage in the distilling industry, but in 1754 the landowning gentry were granted a monopoly over alcohol production on contract to supply the crown. Stills belonging to merchants were to be sold to the gentry or destroyed. The predominance of the gentry in the distilling industry was reinforced in the late 18th century when the Russian Empire expanded to the southern steppes and the gentry had exclusive distilling rights there.

In 1801 there were 19,067 stills in the Ukrainian lands under tsarist rule. Small local stills were the norm, but during the first half of the 19th century the economics of the distilling industry made practicable consolidation and the use of larger stills. By 1860 the number of stills had been reduced to 4,437. In Right-Bank Ukraine the nobility continued domestic distillation for the inn (*korchma*) and drink-house (*shynok*) on their estates. Russian regulations and sales were only gradually extended to those lands.

Changes were made in the alcohol production and marketing systems during the reform era of the 1860s. The notoriously corrupt liquor tax-farming system was abolished in 1863. Instead an excise tax on production was collected by state officials even in the Ukrainian lands, where the landlords continued their rights of production and retailing. Retailers had to pay a license fee. The tsarist government took away the right of the Polish nobles to sell alcohol on their estates as punishment for their involvement in the Polish Insurrection of 1863–4. They were, however, allowed to sell alcoholic beverages to the towns and cities. Between 1894 and 1902 the tsarist state progressively implemented monopolistic control of all aspects of the alcohol trade, thereby ensuring not only the effective regulation of retail outlets and better quality control, but also an increase in crown revenues. The previous owners of monopoly rights were compensated. Those measures effectively ended the historical propination right in the Ukrainian lands of the Russian Empire.

In Western Ukraine (eastern Galicia) the Habsburg rulers initially attempted to ease the lot of the peasantry by limiting certain manorial rights. By a decree of 1775, manor lords could no longer force peasants to buy alcohol exclusively from them or their taverns, and by a decree of 1789 anyone, regardless of social status, who built a decent tavern could retail alcoholic beverages. Neither decree was strenuously enforced, and the latter, which represented a challenge to the nobles' propination right, was rescinded in 1815. The 1775 decree was reconfirmed in 1848. The abolition of the peasants' compulsory labor for the manor lords was not accompanied, however, by an abrogation of the propination right.

During the first half of the 19th century, potatoes had replaced grain in the distillation process, and larger and more efficient units had taken the place of small stills. In 1867 the right to rule on propination in Galicia was transferred from the central government in Vienna to the provincial administration. It passed a law in 1875 that was to end the exclusive right of landlords to produce and sell alcoholic beverages in the villages, which (until 1848) had formed part of their estates. Nonmanorial 'concessioned' taverns could thereafter operate in the villages, and anyone who could pay a 2,000-gulden fee and had the other necessary capital could operate a distillery or brewery, or, for a fee of 100 gulden, a mead winery. The nobility retained the propination right in part until 1910, however, for holders of the right could continue to operate one tavern in the community in which their estate was located, and they could maintain their distilleries and breweries as before. In addition they were to receive redemption payments as compensation for the loss of a proprietary right. Those were to come from a special 'redemption fund' composed of levies on tavern-keepers, fines for drunkenness, and the like. In 1890, in reaction to an increased excise tax on vodka imposed by the Austrian government, the nobility, through the Galician Diet, voted themselves a higher redemption payment (62 million guldens) and lengthened the term for its payment to 1916. It was only then that that lucrative right came to an end.

BIBLIOGRAPHY
Burszta, J. *Społeczeństwo i karczma: Propinacja, karczma i sprawa alkoholizmu w społeczeństwie polskim XIX wieku* (Warsaw 1951)
Smith, R.; Christian, D. *Bread & Salt: A Social and Economic History of Food and Drink in Russia* (Cambridge, Mass 1984)
S. Hryniuk

Prose. The plain speech of humankind. As a literary genre prose includes all forms of literary expression not metrically versified or designed for theatrical presentation. Literary prose is distinct from poetry and drama.

Ukrainian prose literature first appeared after the Christianization of Rus' in 988 and the adoption of Church Slavonic as a written language. The earliest works of Ukrainian prose literature, written in that language, were liturgical and other religious books either copied from those of the previously Christianized Balkan and Moravian Slavs or newly translated in Constantinople or Kiev from Byzantine Greek sources. Liturgical works included full texts or selections of the Gospels (eg, the oldest dated monument of Rus' literature, the Ostromir Gospel, ca 1056–7) and the Acts of the Apostles. In Kievan Rus', from the 10th to 14th centuries, the Old Testament was known mostly through translations of the *Paremeinik* (selected quotations used in the liturgy) and the Pentateuch and Octateuch. Instruction books for divine services and church ceremonies were also available, as were hagiographic lives of the saints and sermons in various collections and anthologies. Translated secular literature included the Byzantine chronicles of John Malalas, Georgius Hamartolus, and Georgius Sincellus; collections of scientific knowledge, such as the *Shestydnevi* (Hexamerons) of Basil the Great and of John the Exarch, and the anonymous *Fiziolog*; and miscellanies, such as Maximus's *Pchela* (The Bee) and the *izborniki*, such as the *Izbornik* of Sviatoslav of 1073 and 1076. Translated prose tales also circulated, including the *Aleksandriia* (legends about Alexander the Great), *Devheniieve diianiie* (The Deeds of Degenis), *Varlaam i Ioasaf* (Barlaam and Josaphat), *Povist' o Akiri Pre-*

mudrom (The Tale of Akir the Wise), and *Povist' pro Indiiske tsarstvo* (The Tale of the Indian Kingdom).

The original literary prose in Kievan Rus' was small in quantity and heavily influenced by Byzantine sources in its forms and substance. The most important prose works of Kievan Rus' were the annalistic chronicles, **Povist' vremennykh lit* and the Galician-Volhynian Chronicle. Also significant were sermons, such as those of Theodosius, Ilarion, and Cyril of Turiv; original hagiographic literature, such as the lives of ss Borys and Hlib or of St Theodosius and the works contained in the *Paterik* of the Kievan Cave Monastery; original tales, which appear in the text of the chronicles; and works such as *Zhytiie i khozhdeniie Danyla, rus'koï zemli ihumena* (The Life and Pilgrimage of Danylo, Abbot of Rus', ca 1100), Volodymyr Monomakh's *Poucheniie ditiam* (An Instruction for [My] Children, ca 1117), and various prayers, letters, and supplications, such as the *Moleniie Danyla Zatochnyka* (Supplication of Daniel the Exile, ca 12th or 13th century).

After the break in Ukrainian cultural development caused by the Mongol invasion of the 13th century, Ukrainian literary prose reappeared along with the general resurgence of culture in the second half of the 16th century. The resurgence was characterized by the influence of Renaissance, Reformation, and Counter-Reformation ideas from Western Europe and by growing religious and national awareness among Orthodox Ukrainians under pressure from Polish Catholicism. The 16th century witnessed a renewed interest in the genres of translated prose that were popular in Rus', as in the Ostrih Bible of 1581 (a complete and verified Slavonic text), the Peresopnytsia and other Gospels that appeared between 1556 and 1600, various sermons, and secular works and collections, among them *Velyke zertsalo* (The Great Mirror) and the *Rymski diiannia* (Gesta Romanorum). Original works, such as the sermons of L. Baranovych and D. Tuptalo's collection of saints' lives, were also popular in the 17th century.

The most important genre of Ukrainian prose in the second half of the 16th and first half of the 17th centuries was **polemical literature. The subject of the polemic was the religious and cultural struggle between Catholicism (both Latin and Uniate) and Orthodoxy. The rhetorical works on both sides of the debate were highly charged philippics written in Old Ukrainian, Church Slavonic, or Polish. On the Orthodox side the outstanding polemicist was I. *Vyshensky, a monk who lived on Mount Athos, and whose works consist of sermons and letters to his countrymen. Other Orthodox polemicists were Z. Kopystensky, H. Smotrytsky, L. Zyzanii, and, later, I. Galiatovsky and M. Andrella. Another important figure in the polemic, M. *Smotrytsky, began as a defender of Orthodoxy but later converted to Catholicism. The outstanding Uniate polemicist was I. Potii. Many works written anonymously or pseudonymously have not been definitively attributed to specific authors, among them *Apokrisis*, *Perestoroha*, and *Poslaniie do latyn*. P. Skarga and B. Herbest were Polish Jesuits who participated in the polemic.

After the establishment of the *Kievan Mohyla Academy and the Cossack-Polish War Ukrainian prose was enriched with historical writing and scholarship. History appeared in the form of the so-called Cossack chronicles, among them the Samovydets, Hrabianka, and Velychko chronicles, which give accounts of the Cossack wars, and the *Synopsis*, which was composed at the Kievan Cave Monastery. Scholarship from the 17th and 18th centuries covered a wide range of topics: linguistics, as in M. Smotrytsky's Slavonic grammar and P. Berynda's Slavonic dictionary; theology, as in the treatises of K. Stavrovetsky-Tranquillon and H. Dometsky; philosophy, as in the Latin treatises of I. Gizel and T. Prokopovych; and various other works, usually derived from Western sources and often produced as textbooks for the Kievan Mohyla Academy, on rhetoric, poetics, science, and mathematics written by a variety of authors in Church Slavonic, Old Ukrainian, or Latin. Ukrainian philosophical prose culminated with the work of H. Skovoroda at the end of the 18th century. His original treatises and dialogues, as well as his fables, were written in the bookish language of the time. *Istoriia Rusov, an influential early 19th-century history of Ukraine, bridged the gap between the traditions of the Cossack chronicles and the literature of the emerging Ukrainian national revival.

Cultural secularization and national self-consciousness dramatically changed the Ukrainian cultural landscape at the beginning of the 19th century. Modern Ukrainian prose did not develop as rapidly or as richly as poetry, but it made a clean break with the past in adopting a modern system of belletristic genres and in abandoning the bookish language of the 18th century in favor of the modern forms of either Ukrainian or Russian. Many writers of the first half of the 19th century, among them H. *Kvitka-Osnovianenko, Ye. Hrebinka, N. Gogol, P. *Kulish, and T. Shevchenko, chose to write prose in Russian. The unqualified choice of Ukrainian as the language of prose literature occurred in the second half of the century.

Kvitka-Osnovianenko was the first major figure in modern Ukrainian prose. His short stories combined elements of burlesque classicism and moralizing sentimentalism with lengthy and abundant descriptions of ethnographic detail, such descriptions as would become a feature of Ukrainian prose throughout the 19th century. The first novel in Ukrainian, written in 1845–6, was Kulish's Chorna rada (The Black Council), a historical novel influenced by Sir Walter Scott, on the subject of the Cossack past, which Gogol and Kulish had already pursued in Russian novels. Kulish was also instrumental in promoting the Ukrainian works of M. *Vovchok, whose emotional, abolitionist short stories describe the horrors of serfdom and the cruel fate of women. A number of her stories were published in the journal Osnova, edited by Kulish and published in St Petersburg in 1861–2. Osnova also published ethnographic stories by lesser figures, such as H. Barvinok and P. Kuzmenko.

The tsarist government's Valuev circular (1863; see P. *Valuev) and *Ems Ukase (1876) were particularly heavy blows for Ukrainian prose because they closed off the possibility of publishing, except in Western Ukraine. Some works remained unknown to the general public, among them A. Svydnytsky's realist novel Liuboratski (The Liuboratsky Family), written in the 1860s but not published in its entirety until 1901. Because of the prohibition the realist period in Ukrainian prose was an assortment of individual writers rather than a cohesive literary movement.

The last quarter of the century was dominated by the large presence of I. *Nechui-Levytsky, the author of over 50 stories and novels (Nechui-Levytsky, like most 19th-century authors, called all his long works povisti [tales]). A descriptive realist with a focus on social and national issues, Nechui-Levytsky set himself the task of describing contemporary Ukraine in the abundance of its social, cultural, ethnic, and geographic types. His contemporary and fellow realist P. *Myrny wrote a number of stories and novels focusing on social issues. Other writers in eastern Ukraine, such as O. Konysky, B. Hrinchenko, and O. Pchilka, were largely ethnographic realists who depicted populist social issues. M. Starytsky wrote novels and short stories in Russian on themes from Ukrainian history. In Western Ukraine, under Austria-Hungary, the major figure was I. *Franko, whose prose works, heavily influenced by Western European naturalists, particularly E. Zola, focus on the misery and victimization of workers and peasants under changing economic conditions. Among other prose writers in Western Ukraine were Yu. Fedkovych, a late Romantic, and O. *Kobylianska, a modernist who focused on the psychology of the new woman.

The 20th century brought major changes to Ukrainian prose. Cultural, national, and political ferment created an atmosphere that allowed literature to develop as an organic system. Modernist esthetics challenged the prevailing realist canon in a lively and productive assault. As government restraints were lifted, Ukrainian prose acquired a new readership with new interests.

The major figure of 20th-century prose has been M. *Kotsiubynsky. In his modernist works Kotsiubynsky concentrated on the psychology of his heroes, usually exceptional persons, through subjective narration, an impressionistic descriptive technique, and a poetic, lyrical style. Many of his works depict social conditions at the time of the Revolution of 1905. Kotsiubynsky's influence on subsequent Ukrainian prose, particularly the short story in the 1920s, was overwhelming. A different direction in prose was charted by V. *Vynnychenko, the most popular Ukrainian writer in the 1910s and 1920s. Vynnychenko practiced a form of psychological realism similar to that of G. de Maupassant and D.H. Lawrence. His short stories and novels often focus on the loss of human dignity under the weight of oppressive social stratification and on the personal dilemma of sexual morality. In Western Ukraine the first half of the century was dominated by the novellas of V. *Stefanyk, who depicted the tragedy of human existence in an extremely laconic style, and the less successful stories of L. Martovych and M. Cheremshyna.

The 1920s was a period of unprecedented growth and development for Ukrainian prose in Soviet Ukraine. After a few years of tentative efforts, between 1923 and 1927 the Ukrainian short story underwent a burst of creativity. Hundreds of new writers, not all of them highly skilled, appeared. After 1927 much of the energy turned from the short story to the novel. The generic and stylistic profile of the period was, for the first time in the history of Ukrainian literature, heterogeneous in the characteristically modern manner. The prose genres included every imaginable form: adventure stories, thrillers, science fiction, historical stories, travel stories, erotica, melodrama, biographies, humorous feuilletons, experimental novels, poems in prose, and so on. The styles included those of neoromanticism, ethnographic realism, psychological realism, and modernism of various stripes. Although many works still centered on Ukrainian village life, others dealt with newer subjects, such as industrialization, prostitution, and life in Central Asia.

In the early years of the decade the characteristic genre was the highly lyrical and melodramatic short story, often about the turbulent events of the revolution and civil war and their effects on an individual's psychology. The focus was usually on the incompatibility of the individual's personal values with the demands placed on him or her by the new ideology. Among the outstanding practitioners of the genre were M. *Khvylovy, H. *Kosynka, B. Antonenko-Davydovych, A. Holovko, M. Ivchenko, and A. Liubchenko. Major novelists in the second half of the decade, V. *Pidmohylny and V. *Petrov (Domontovych) wrote intellectual novels using psychological realism. Their works, particularly Pidmohylny's outstanding novel *Misto* (The City), examined philosophical questions about humanity in the 20th century against the backdrop of Soviet reality. Yu. *Yanovsky wrote romantic idylls set in contemporary times; O. Dosvitny, travel novels set in exotic places; Yu. *Smolych, adventure novels; and G. Shkurupii and M. Yohansen, experimental novels. Among the most popular novels were those of V. Vynnychenko, even though their author lived abroad and was considered an ideological enemy. O. Vyshnia was a popular humorist. Other writers, such as P. Panch and I. Le, wrote novels that reflected the values and ideology of the Communist party. Their weak and artificial works anticipated the prescribed style of the Stalin era, *socialist realism.

The massive campaign of the early 1930s against the Ukrainian nation and its culture brought the growth and development of Ukrainian prose to an abrupt halt. Most writers were either silenced or destroyed. Those who continued to write were forced to adopt the official style of socialist realism, a poorly defined concept that amounted to glorification of the Soviet Union, its ideology, its defenders and heroes, and its way of life, while prohibiting psychological, especially Freudian, characterization, philosophical speculation, and formal experimentation. The Second World War introduced new enemies and a military backdrop, but otherwise Ukrainian prose changed little.

The general thaw in Soviet Ukraine in the late 1950s and 1960s brought a renewal in the prose genres. New writers, such as O. *Honchar and P. Zahrebelny, produced works that did not challenge the rules of socialist realism but gently expanded and humanized them. What was new in their works was often a return to the traditions of the early decades of the 20th century, as in O. *Dovzhenko's small autobiographical masterpiece *Zacharovana Desna* (The Enchanted Desna). In the 1970s, under renewed ideological pressure, Ukrainian prose developed slowly. Young writers who had first appeared in the 1960s continued to experiment tentatively with new techniques and new subjects. In the novels and stories of Hryhir *Tiutiunnyk, V. Drozd, A. Dimarov, and Valerii *Shevchuk human values and the mundane struggles of human existence replaced state ideology as the guiding principle. The trend continued through the 1980s. Since 1991 there has been a slow but steady stream of original and interesting works in a variety of genres and styles from both new and established writers. In the emigration Ukrainian prose is scant and weak: U. *Samchuk continued the realistic tradition, and E. *Andiievska endeavored to write complex surrealistic novels.

The study of Ukrainian prose is poorly developed, a reflection of that genre's subordinate position relative to poetry. There is no general history of Ukrainian prose or of the Ukrainian novel or short story. Most existing special-ized studies, such as M. Levchenko's *Vyprobuvannia istoriieiu* (Trial by History, 1970) on the prerevolutionary novel or I. Hrytsiutenko's *Estetychna funktsiia khudozhn'oho slova* (The Esthetic Function of the Artistic Word, 1972), about 16th- and 17th-century prose, are limited in scope, methodologically unsound, and ideologically biased.

BIBLIOGRAPHY
Derkach, B. *Perekladna ukraïns'ka povist' XVII–XVIII stolit'* (Kiev 1960)
Holubieva, Z. *Ukraïns'kyi radians'kyi roman 20-kh rokiv* (Kharkiv 1967)
Kyryliuk, Ie.; et al. (eds). *Istoriia ukraïns'koï literatury u vos'my tomakh* (Kiev 1967–71)
Čyževs'kyj, D. *A History of Ukrainian Literature* (Littleton, Colo 1975)
Mishchuk, R. *Ukraïns'ka opovidna proza 50–60-kh rokiv XIX st.* (Kiev 1978)
Denysiuk, I. *Rozvytok ukraïns'koï maloï prozy XIX–pochatku XX st.* (Kiev 1981)
Vlasenko, V. *Ukraïns'kyi dozhovtnevyi roman* (Kiev 1983)
M. Tarnawsky

Prosiana [Prosjana]. V-17. A town smt (1986 pop 6,700) in Pokrovske raion, Dnipropetrovske oblast. A workers' settlement was established there in 1882 during the construction of the Donetske railway line. The first fire-brick factory was built in 1894 to exploit the local kaolin deposits. Today Prosiana has the largest refractory-products manufacturing complex in Europe and two kaolin enrichment plants.

Prosiana kaolin deposit. A kaolin deposit located in Pokrovske raion, Dnipropetrovske oblast. It covers an area of approx 80 sq km, and its estimated recoverable reserves are 88.7 million t (1982). The kaolin is found in seams 0.1–61.5 m thick at a depth of 14–23 m. The field has been known since 1894. The kaolin is mined and processed for use in the chemical, ceramic, paper, and other industries.

Heorhii Proskura

Proskura, Heorhii (Yurii), b 28 April 1876 in Smila, Cherkasy county, Kiev gubernia, d 30 September 1958 in Kharkiv. Scientist in the fields of hydromechanics, marine construction, and aviation; full member of the AN URSR (now ANU) from 1929. He graduated from the Moscow Higher Technical School (1901) and taught at the Kharkiv Technological Institute (from 1902), where he introduced one of the first courses on the theory of aviation. From 1945 he was director of the ANU Laboratory of High-Speed

Machines and Mechanisms (now the Institute for Problems of Machine Building). He made important contributions in the areas of hydrodynamics, turbines, wind tunnels, and the modeling of fluid flow and was instrumental in the design and construction of major hydraulic works in the USSR, including the Moscow Canal. In 1974 a scientific prize in the area of energy research was established in his name by the ANU. Proskura's selected works were published in Kiev in 1972, and a biography of him was published there in 1979.

Proskura, Olha, b 31 May 1904 in Kiev, d 2 May 1978 in Kiev. Urologist. A graduate of the Kiev Medical Institute (1928), she taught at the Kiev Institute for the Upgrading of Physicians and headed its urology department (1953–69), and was chief urologist at the Ministry of Health of the Ukrainian SSR. Her main publications deal with urologic reconstructive surgery.

Proskuriv. See Khmelnytskyi.

Proskurivna, Mariia (pseud of Mariia Semenko), b 15 June 1863 in Kybyntsi, Myrhorod county, Poltava gubernia, d 19 October 1945 in Kiev. Writer; mother of M. *Semenko. She contributed her first Vovchokesque stories about the peasantry (some of them autobiographical) to the prerevolutionary weekly *Ridnyi krai*. Her stories *Od sina do solomy* (From Hay to Straw, 1913) and *Pani pysarka* (Madame Scribe, 1914) and novella *Uliasia* (1913) were published separately. In the mid-1920s several of her stories appeared in the Soviet Ukrainian press.

Prostitution. Promiscuous sexual activity performed in exchange for money or valuables. Prostitution has existed in Ukraine, as in other countries, since the earliest times. Its large-scale growth began in the 18th century as a result of the creation of large standing armies, urban development, and the increased circulation of money.

In Russian-ruled Ukraine attempts by the state to combat prostitution were spurred by the spread of *venereal diseases, which infected a large number of troops. In 1843 a certain toleration of prostitution was legislated. Brothels and individual prostitutes had to register with a medical-police commission. The regulation of prostitution was rife with corruption, however, and it has been estimated that only a third of the prostitutes actually registered with the authorities.

An 1890 study of female prostitution in the Russian Empire serves as the most complete source of information to date, though it is in some respects inaccurate. Central statistical data collected in 1889 showed that there were 912 brothels, with 6,121 prostitutes, in European Russia. Russian-ruled Ukraine accounted for 157 brothels and 1,349 prostitutes. There were 6,826 registered prostitutes in European Russia, 802 of them in Ukraine. Prostitution in Ukraine was limited to the large centers, especially the port cities (one-third of the prostitutes in Ukraine were located in Kherson gubernia). The average age of prostitutes was 22, and over a third were infected with syphilis or other venereal diseases. The majority of women who became prostitutes did so before the age of 18, and almost a quarter started before they were 16. Three-quarters of prostitutes were from poor families, almost 90 percent were illiterate, and over 90 percent were orphans. A prostitute in a brothel charged 20 kopecks to 1 ruble per customer and had 3 to 10 visitors per day. (A well-paid worker in metallurgy earned 3 rubles a day.) Almost 20 percent of the women concerned had been raped before becoming prostitutes. Two-thirds of all brothel keepers were Jewish by nationality. Because the vast majority of Ukrainian women were peasants and were tied to traditional rural, agrarian life, only a small proportion of prostitutes were Ukrainian. According to 1897 census data, 75 percent of the female population of Ukraine was Ukrainian, but less than a quarter of the total number of prostitutes were of that nationality. Almost 50 percent were Russian, and some 20 percent were Jewish. There were fewer than 100 male prostitutes in Ukraine.

In Western Ukraine under Austrian rule, as a result of Empress Maria Theresa's energetic struggle against prostitution, in 1774 all brothels were closed down, and solicitation in taverns was prohibited. Consequently, prostitutes took to the streets, and the incidence of venereal diseases increased. Although only individual prostitution was allowed, illegal brothels existed in most large towns. Because prostitution in Western Ukraine, as in the Russian-ruled regions, was concentrated in urban centers, it involved relatively few Ukrainians, who were overwhelmingly an agrarian people.

When the Bolsheviks assumed power in Russia in 1917, they abolished all regulations prohibiting prostitution. Instead of imposing administrative measures against prostitutes, the Bolsheviks emphasized rehabilitation programs in the early years of their rule. In 1919 the Commission to Combat Prostitution was created by the People's Commissariat of Public Health. In 1920 the first camps for the rehabilitation of female speculators, pickpockets, and prostitutes were established. The CP(B)U Women's Sections (established in 1920) also took up the struggle against prostitution. Because of the economic crisis, however, prostitution continued to develop. In response, in 1922 the Interdepartmental Commission to Combat Prostitution was created in the USSR, and branches were opened in Soviet Ukraine. It established a network of centers (called prophylactoria) for the rehabilitation and retraining of former prostitutes. One of the largest such centers in Ukraine was in Dnipropetrovske. Although formally the commission was not to use administrative measures to combat prostitution, in practice prostitutes were forcibly confined in the centers.

In the 1920s prostitution was substantially reduced from what it had been during the prerevolutionary period. Changes in family and marriage law, and laws and policies designed to promote women's equality, played an important role in the reduction, as did the acceptance of freer sexual relations that gained currency as part of the revolutionary struggle against the 'old' morality. The shortage of housing and difficulties in getting hotel rooms also served to limit prostitution. The high rate of unemployment among certain categories of women, however, continued to push women into prostitution. Under early Soviet rule the social composition of prostitutes changed dramatically. Women from the former privileged classes (merchants, nobility, the petite bourgeoisie) formed almost 43 percent of prostitutes according to 1926 data; women of working-class origin formed only 14 percent; and peasant women, especially those who had entered domestic service, formed 43 percent. Prostitutes from the former privileged classes often established liaisons with members of the new Soviet elite and were often used by the secret police as spies and informers.

In 1932, during the First Five-Year Plan, the Stalinist regime announced that industrialization policies had liquidated female unemployment, which was considered to be the root cause of prostitution, and that prostitution had ceased to exist in the USSR. Thenceforth, until recently, officials claimed that prostitution in the USSR was not a significant social phenomenon, and that only isolated incidents of such 'social parasitism' occurred. In reality prostitution continued to exist, and the security police often procured prostitutes for members of the Soviet elite. Soviet legislation established criminal responsibility for drawing minors into prostitution, for procuring a prostitute, for maintaining dens of vice, and for spreading venereal disease. The Criminal Code of the Ukrainian SSR and other Soviet republics carried no penalty for the sale of one's body, however. Most women arrested for prostitution were charged with currency offences – a frequent occurrence, given that 'hard-currency' prostitution in cities visited by Western tourists was and remains widespread. Homosexual prostitution was rare because until very recently homosexuality was a criminal offense.

Under the policy of glasnost officials finally admitted that prostitution had plagued Soviet society for many decades. In 1987 prostitution was made an offense, punishable by fines of up to 200 rubles, and apprehended prostitutes were subjected to a compulsory medical examination for venereal diseases. Prostitution continues to be widespread in Ukraine, especially in the large cities and resort areas (eg, the Crimea). Hard-currency prostitution is common in Kiev and in Odessa and other port cities. The majority of prostitutes are streetwalkers. A small minority work as call girls, catering to important diplomats and foreigners. In the past the KGB often used them for entrapment. Recent studies have shown that the majority of prostitutes are 30 years old or younger. Seventy percent of hard-currency prostitutes are under 30, but 86 percent of the street and train-station 'ruble' prostitutes are over 35. Twenty-six percent of the hard-currency prostitutes are daytime blue-collar workers, 25 percent are white-collar employees, and 7 percent are students; 38 percent do not have other jobs. About 50 percent are divorced, 26 percent are married, and 23 percent have children. Between 1987 and 1990 administrative sanctions were imposed on some 5,000 prostitutes, but had little effect. As elsewhere, most of what a prostitute earns is taken by her pimp, who pays expenses, including bribes to policemen. The spread of AIDS has heightened concern about prostitution and its moral, medical, and social impact.

BIBLIOGRAPHY
Statistika Rossiiskoi Imperii, vol 13, *Prostitutsiia* (St Petersburg 1890)
Chirkov, P. *Reshenie zhenskogo voprosa v SSSR (1917–1937 gg.)* (Moscow 1978)
Stern, M.; with Stern, A. *Sex in the USSR* (New York 1980)
Stites, R. 'Prostitute and Society in Pre-Revolutionary Russia,' *Jahrbücher für Geschichte Osteuropas*, 31 (1983)
Stevenson Sanjian, A. 'Prostitution, the Press, and Agenda-Building in the Soviet Policy Process,' in *Soviet Social Problems*, ed A. Jones, W.D. Connor, and D.E. Powell (Boulder, Colo, and Oxford 1991)

B. Krawchenko

Prosvita (Enlightenment). A monthly organ of the Prosvita society, published in Lviv in 1936–9. It was intended for Prosvita society supporters who were fostering literacy and enlightenment among the Ukrainian peasantry. The journal contained reading exercises, articles on hygiene, education, and culture, and instructions on how to administer choirs and other local organizations. Its editor was I. *Bryk.

Prosvita societies (Enlightenment societies). Ukrainian community organizations active in Ukraine from the late 1860s to the 1940s and in other countries from the early 20th century. Prosvita societies were first established in Galicia and became most developed there. Initially they had a general educational purpose and incorporated only the intelligentsia, but over time they assumed a mass character and diversified into a number of areas of activity. In several instances they laid the groundwork for the establishment of economic co-operatives, educational societies, and other groups that were instrumental in the Ukrainian national movement. In central and eastern Ukraine the development of Prosvita societies was stymied by political hostility to the Ukrainian populist ideals that underpinned their work. Nevertheless, the small number of Prosvitas established after the Revolution of 1905 had a substantial impact on the development of Ukrainian national consciousness. The ground swell of support for the movement following the Revolution of 1917 indicated that the societies probably would have developed a mass character if they had not been suppressed by the Soviet regime early in the 1920s. In other parts of the Russian Empire Prosvita societies provided a key focal point for community activity. Prosvita societies also developed in Europe and the Americas, and although they were vital community institutions, they never assumed the same mass character as the Galician Prosvita.

Galicia. The first Prosvita society was founded in Lviv on 8 December 1868 by a group of young populists who were unhappy with the conservatism and increasing Russophilism of the *Halytsko-Ruska Matytsia. The idea of the new society was proposed by S. *Kachala. The first constitution defined Prosvita as a learned society, whose purpose was to 'know and edify the people.' Besides 'promoting the moral, material, and political edification of the people' it was to 'collect and publish all the fruits of oral folk literature.' The original membership (72) was limited to a small circle of the intelligentsia. In the new constitution of 1870 the society's mandate was narrowed down to that of 'promoting education among the Ruthenian (Ukrainian) people' by means of popular publications in the vernacular and the organization of county committees, which eventually developed into branches. Prosvita's research function was transferred to the Shevchenko Society, which in 1893 was reorganized into the *Shevchenko Scientific Society. To increase membership, the constitution was amended in 1876: the admission fee was abolished, annual dues were reduced drastically, and all members received a free popular booklet each month. With these changes Prosvita started to become a truly popular organization. The first presidents of Prosvita were A. *Vakhnianyn (1868–70), Yu. *Lavrivsky (1870–3), V. *Fedorovych (1873–7), and O. *Ohonovsky (1877–94).

Prosvita devoted considerable attention to the development of Ukrainian schools. It demanded from the govern-

Building of the Prosvita society in Lviv

care of Prosvita. They had no organizational ties among themselves, however, nor with the center in Lviv. Yet it was largely through Prosvita's initiative that the popular paper *Bat'kivshchyna* (1879) and the populist political organization the People's Council (1885) were established. The main rival to the avowedly Ukrainophile Prosvita was the *Kachkovsky Society, a cultural-educational association established in 1874 by Galician Russophiles.

As more and more peasants joined the society, its structure was reshaped, and its goals were expanded. The revised constitution of 1891 provided for the establishment of autonomous rural reading societies tied to the central society in Lviv through county branches; a multitude of unconnected reading rooms would thereby be converted into a single network covering all of Galicia. Between 1891 and 1914 the number of reading rooms within Prosvita increased from 5 to 2,944, and the number of branches from 7 to 77, 3 of which (Sianik, Jasło, and Nowy Sącz) were in the Lemko region. In 1914, 75 percent of the cities, towns, and villages in Galicia had a reading room, and 20 percent of the province's Ukrainian population belonged to Prosvita (for growth in membership see the table).

At that time also the society assumed an activist posture and added the task of 'raising the welfare of the Ukrainian people' to its general educational purpose. Its new program called for the establishment of economic institutions, such as credit unions, stores, farm co-operatives, dairies, and warehouses, in association with reading rooms. The society became involved in improving farming methods, organizing agricultural courses, and publishing agronomic literature. From 1906 a special agricultural-industrial commission at the head office supervised its economic activities. By 1912 the Prosvita reading rooms had 540 stores, 339 small credit unions, and 121 warehouses. Its work in the area of economic life culminated with the First Educational-Economic Congress, held in February 1909 to commemorate the 40th anniversary of the society. As Ukrainian involvement in the economy expanded and became diversified, Prosvita transferred some of its economic functions to specialized central organizations, such as the Provincial Audit Union (later the *Audit Union of Ukrainian Co-operatives), *Maslosoiuz, and *Silskyi Hospodar. It continued to play a role in economic education by maintaining itinerant farming in-

ment that Ukrainian schools be established and that Ukrainian be taught in the schools. It petitioned the government to establish a chair of Ukrainian history at Lviv University. It fought for equal rights for the Ukrainian language in the educational system. It published Ukrainian textbooks, not only for Galicia but also for Bukovyna and Hungary. In 1881 Prosvita's educational activities led to the establishment of the Ruthenian Pedagogical Society (later *Ridna Shkola).

The absence of local cells was Prosvita's major shortcoming in its early period. Outside Lviv educational work among the people was conducted by reading rooms, some of which were inspired or aided by the Prosvita society. In 1881–5 there were 320 reading rooms in Galicia under the

The growth of Prosvita in Galicia, 1869–1939

Year	Prosvita branches	Reading room centrals	Local reading rooms	Members (1,000s)	Libraries	Titles published	Pressrun (1,000s)	Buildings
1869	–	–	–	–	–	4	20	–
1875	–	–	–	–	–	6	83	–
1880	4	–	–	1.5	–	6	23	–
1890	4	–	–	4.8	–	8	50	–
1895	14	42	233	7.9	843	9	45	34
1900	22	76	924	13.4	1,248	9	83	75
1905	35	100	1,550	19.0	1,753	8	120	118
1910	60	114	2,355	–	2,290	16	111	310
1914	77	197	2,944	36.5	2,664	16	150	504
1920	73	–	0,882	–	–	8	35	–
1925	81	121	2,020	6.9	978	10	48	395
1930	87	207	3,110	14.8	2,215	24	95	912
1935	83	275	3,071	31.1	2,915	16	129	1,301
1939	83	360	3,075	–	2,988	–	–	1,475

The Galician Prosvita society's agricultural school in Mylovannia

structors and publishing popular economic literature. It set up and financed a commercial school in Lviv, a women's domestic school in Uhertsi Vyniavski (1912–18), and a farming school in Mylovannia (1912–39). Furthermore, the society granted scholarships to students of agronomy, dairying, and domestic management and sent its best scholarship holders abroad to study (40 in 1907–14).

Prosvita's involvement in book publishing began in 1869, when it released *Zoria* (Star), a reader for peasants. Then similar readers and popular brochures about temperance brotherhoods, community banks, and warehouses began coming out, albeit irregularly. With the help of government grants the society published 17 textbooks for the lower Ukrainian gymnasium grades in 1871–6. From 1877 the society began printing monthly booklets, which members received free of charge. In a 50-year period (1868–1918) 348 popular booklets, including 305 monthly booklets (1877–1914), totaling 2,941,115 copies were published; of these, 88 were devoted to fiction, 52 to history and geography, 42 to economics and trade, 22 to science and medicine, 22 to legal issues, 11 to religion and military affairs, and 20 to biography. Another 41 were anual almanacs, and the remainder dealt with miscellaneous topics. The Ruska (later Ukrainska) pysmennist (Ruthenian [Ukrainian] Literature) series (1904–28) contained 28 volumes (over 170,000 copies) of Ukrainian classics. Eight books (23,000 copies) were issued in the Hospodarska biblioteka (Farming Library) series (1907–27). The Prosvitni lystky (Prosvita Leaflets) series consisted of 60 pamphlets (190,450 copies), mostly reprints of articles in Prosvita's almanacs and in *Pys'mo z Prosvity*. An additional 44 publications (183,606 copies) came out after 1909. The society published the educational and cultural magazines *Pys'mo z Prosvity* (1877–9, 1907–14) and *Chytal'nia* (1894–6). The editors of these various publications included O. Partytsky, V. Shashkevych, Yu. Tselevych, Yu. Fedkovych, I. Franko, A. Vakhnianyn, V Lukych-Levytsky, P. Ohonovsky, K. Pankivsky, K. Levytsky, O. Borkovsky, V. Biletsky, Ya. Vesolovsky, H. Khotkevych, Yu. Balytsky, and F. Fedortsiv. By 1914 over half the reading rooms had their own libraries, consisting largely of Prosvita's publications.

In the three-tiered structure of the Prosvita society the chief executive council in Lviv co-ordinated the work of the branches, which in turn assumed responsibility (from

Cover of early publications published by the Prosvita society in Lviv

1891) for the local reading rooms in their counties. The head office in Lviv, directed for many years by A. Skorodynsky and then by A. Hapiak, provided the branches with materials, organizers, examiners (particularly auditors), and lecturers. To manage the large organizational network, it relied on help from a number of commissions, particularly publishing, economic, and educational-organizational, which were formed in 1906–8. From 1869 the central Prosvita in Lviv maintained a library which received donations and book contributions, particularly from eastern Ukraine. In 1909, after transferring its most valuable collections to the Shevchenko Scientific Society, it was reorganized into a public lending library (16,900 volumes in 1935). An archive and museum set up at the Lviv Prosvita in 1869 was eventually donated to the Shevchenko Scientific Society and the National Museum. The central society organized a series of all-Ukrainian events, such as the Educational-Economic Congress in 1909 and the centennial of T. Shevchenko's birth in 1914. From 1895 it owned its own building in the heart of the city.

Prosvita derived its income from membership dues (202,000 out of a total income of 793,000 kronen between 1868 and 1907), subsidies from the provincial and central governments, individual donations, and profits from its own operations, such as publishing. The subsidies from the Galician Diet were small and were often cut off because of Polish opposition. From 1908 they were increased, particularly to support the society's economic program. From 1870 to 1914 the Galician government donated 190,000 kronen to Prosvita for publishing and 173,000 kronen (1906–14) for economic operations. The Vienna government provided 42,000 kronen in 1906–9 for economic projects. Prosvita's first patron was its president, V. Fedorovych, who donated 24,000 kronen in 1875. Eventually a number of foundations for specific purposes were set up. Many of them provided scholarships for young people, among them the foundations of Rev S. Kachala, Count M. Tyshkevych, Rev S. Novosad (120,000 kronen for secondary-school scholarships), Rev I. Zalutsky, and S. Dubrovsky. M. Maletsky left his estate in Uhertsi Vyniavski for a women's school. In 1869–1907 Prosvita's income totaled 793,000 kronen and its expenses, 791,000.

Until 1914 the Prosvita society was the most important Ukrainian mass organization in Galicia. Its activities encompassed almost all aspects of the nation's life, and it gave birth to various cultural, political, economic, farming, and sports organizations and societies which eventually became independent entities. Its reading rooms were the chief Ukrainian community organizations in the countryside and the focal points for the establishment of savings unions, co-operative stores, Silskyi Hospodar circles, and kindergartens. In short, Prosvita played a central role in the growth of national consciousness among the Ukrainian population and in the improvement of its standard of living: without its work the restoration of Ukrainian statehood in Galicia in 1918 would have been impossible. Prosvita also served as a model for the Bukovynian educational and cultural organization Ruska Besida, the Prosvita society in the Dnieper region (est 1905), and the Prosvitas of the emigrants in the New World, with whom the Lviv-based society maintained contact.

The First World War inflicted heavy losses on the society: its buildings, equipment, and libraries suffered extensive damage, and most of its reading rooms were closed. Until 1921 the Polish authorities refused to allow them to be restored. Accordingly, in 1920 there were only 882 reading rooms in 73 branches. At the same time the society found itself in a financial crisis, as its holdings, which in 1914 were worth 352,000 kronen, had suffered from devaluation, and government subsidies had stopped altogether. It was only in 1924, when a new constitution was approved by the Polish authorities, that reading rooms began to be reopened on a wide scale. The Polish government continued to harbor reservations about Prosvita's work: during the Polish *Pacification (1930) many Prosvita reading rooms were damaged or destroyed, and in 1936 one branch and 135 reading rooms were dissolved by the authorities. The society was also forbidden to expand its activities into the so-called northwestern lands (Volhynia, Podlachia, and the Kholm region). In the early 1930s its reading rooms in the western Lemko region were closed down.

In spite of government opposition the number of reading rooms increased steadily: by 1939 there were 3,075 reading rooms and 360,000 members in Prosvita (85 percent of Ukrainian settlements in Galicia had a reading room, and the membership incorporated 15 percent of the adult population). Almost 50 percent of the reading rooms owned their own premises. The highest percentage of the Ukrainian population enrolled in Prosvita was in Ternopil, Zbarazh, Skalat, and Sokal counties. In some villages

Members of the Galician Prosvita society's chief executive and auditing commission in 1936

there were also Young Prosvitas, which recruited young men and women. In the 1930s there were a lending library, a bookbinding shop, and a bookstore at the head office in Lviv.

The paragraph on economic activities was dropped from Prosvita's new constitution of 1924. Henceforth the society's work was restricted to the educational field, to which the presidents M. *Halushchynsky (1923–31) and I. *Bryk (1932–9) devoted most of their attention. Increasingly the work was carried out by full-time professional staff at the head office and at most of the branches, and even among groups of neighboring reading rooms. The policy on educational work was set by the Second Prosvita Congress in September 1929. Besides managing the usual affairs of the organization, in 1935–7 the head office organized 1,932 literacy courses, 112 courses for executive members of reading rooms, 37 courses for play directors, 26 courses for choir conductors, 8 courses for leaders of Young Prosvitas, and 11 general educational courses. In the second half of the 1930s the staff of the head office numbered several dozen. V. Mudry, S. Shakh, and M. Duzhy were the key theoreticians and managers of educational work, besides the presidents, the secretaries, and the other members of the executive, such as K. Malytska. Branch inspectors and secretaries, such as S. Magalias, P. Petryk, M. Brylynsky, V. Haftkovych, and M. Kushnir, provided support for the head office.

Because of financial difficulties Prosvita did not publish in the same quantities as before the First World War, but its publications improved in content and design. Besides continuing the Ruska pysmennist series, it published 8 books (31,500 copies) in the Zahalna biblioteka (General Library) series (1919–28), including M. Vozniak's Istoriia ukraïns'koï literatury (History of Ukrainian Literature, 3 vols, 1920–4) and Ukraïns'ki narodni dumy (Ukrainian Folk Dumas, 1920) under the editorship of F. Kolessa. By 1938, 22 works of popular scholarship, by such authors as M. Vozniak, M. Holubets, V. Doroshenko, Kolessa, I. Krypiakevych, V. Kubijovyč, I. Rakovsky, S. Rudnytsky, S. Siropolko, and O. Terletsky, had come out in the Uchitesia, braty moi (Learn, My Brothers) series. The Narodna biblioteka (Popular Library) series (1919–28), which replaced the monthly booklets, contained 38 books (203,000 copies), including calendars. Ten books (48,000 copies) came out in the Istorychna Biblioteka (Historical Library)

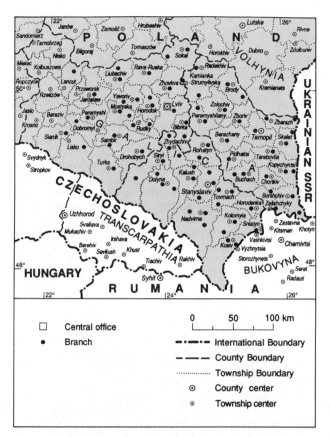

THE PROSVITA SOCIETY IN INTER-WAR GALICIA

series. Another 53 booklets (157,000 copies) came out, mostly reprints of articles in *Zhyttia i znannia*.

Prosvita published over 600 books (3,995,000 copies) during its lifetime: 477 books, booklets, and leaflets (3,479,000 copies) in 1869–1918; and 126 titles (516,000 copies) in 1919–28.

In the interwar era Prosvita's periodical publications included the renewed *Pys'mo z Prosvity* (1921–2), which was reorganized into a magazine for extramural education titled *Narodnia prosvita* (1923–7), the monthly *Prosvita* (1936–9), the popular *Zhyttia i znannia* (1927–39), and the specialized magazines *Amators'kyi poradnyk* (1925–7) and *Bibliotechnyi poradnyk* (1925–6). The editors of Prosvita books and magazines included V. Doroshenko, F. Fedortsiv, S. Shakh, V. Mudry, O. Terletsky, and V. Simovych.

The number of reading-room libraries increased from 2,664 in 1914 to 3,209 (with 688,186 books) in 1936. To expand the holdings of local libraries Prosvita organized a system of book purchasing and distribution. In 1924 the head office introduced traveling libraries (49 by 1935), which served the poorest communities and particularly the villages without reading rooms. The branch offices conducted similar activities. The branch libraries were usually lending libraries and often included special collections on extramural education and amateur theater.

In the interwar period Prosvita depended on membership dues, profits from its publications and cultural events, and individual donations for its budget. A fund-raising drive known as Dar Prosviti (A Gift to Prosvita) was held in December of each year on the anniversary of the society's founding. Substantial financial aid also came from emigrants in the New World, who sometimes financed entire libraries or buildings to house reading rooms.

In spite of government interference the Galician Prosvita made some contribution to the cultural and educational life in the northwestern lands. It provided advice and supplied books to the reading rooms there. Prosvita's ties with emigrant communities were also strong.

With the Soviet occupation of Galicia in 1939, Prosvita's entire network was dismantled, and some of its libraries were destroyed. In the Lemko and Sian regions, which were under the German occupation, hundreds of reading rooms sprang up, some of them as revivals of the societies which had been closed down by the Poles in the 1930s. When the Germans captured eastern Galicia in 1941, they permitted reading rooms to be revived, but only under the auspices of officially recognized *Ukrainian educational societies.

Central and eastern Ukraine. The success of the Galician Prosvita attracted wide interest among Ukrainian circles in central Ukraine. Activists and writers from this region of Ukraine, including I. Nechui-Levytsky, S. Rusova, Kh. Alchevska, D. Doroshenko, M. Levytsky, and B. and M. Hrinchenko, enlisted as secret (anonymous) members of Prosvita, supported it financially, and sent their works for publication in its magazines and book series. It served as an example for the Vik publishing house, established in Kiev in 1895, and the Philanthropic Society for Publishing Generally Useful and Inexpensive Books in St Petersburg in 1898.

The first educational societies, which were called Prosvita after the Galician reading rooms, arose only after the 1905 Revolution. First among them was the Prosvita formed on 8 October 1905 in Katerynoslav, which had a membership of 400, including D. Yavornytsky, V. Bidnov, Ye. Vyrovy, D. and N. Doroshenko, P. Narizhny, S. Lypkivsky, H. Denysenko, and L. Bidnova. It established branches in Manuilivka, Diivka, Perepyna, Hupalivka, and a number of other villages. Its activities consisted of organizing reading rooms, arranging various celebrations, concerts, plays, lectures, and evenings, and selling subscriptions to Ukrainian papers, magazines, and books. In 1914 it was closed down for 'promoting separatism,' but it continued to operate as the Ukrainian branch of the Russian Scientific Society. The rural reading rooms survived until 1916.

A second Prosvita was founded in Odessa on 30 October 1905 by I. Lutsenko, M. Komarov, I. Lypa, S. Shelukhyn, A. Nikovsky, and M. Slabchenko. This unique club of Ukrainian intelligentsia organized lectures and discussions, literary-musical evenings every Saturday, and plays every Sunday. Through its efforts O. Hrushevsky began to lecture in Ukrainian on Ukrainian history at the university in 1906, the paper *Narodnia sprava* appeared, and two popular books were published. The society maintained a library and reading room, bookstore, museum, and choir until the authorities closed it down in 1908.

In May 1906 a Prosvita society was founded in Kiev by B. Hrinchenko, H. Kovalenko, M. Lysenko, F. Krasytsky, F. Matushevsky, and M. Starytsky with the support of Lesia Ukrainka, S. Yefremov, and D. Durdukivsky. Since it was prohibited from establishing branches, the society limited its activities, such as lectures, public readings, concerts, and plays, to the city and its suburbs. Laying down broad plans for educational work and publishing and setting up special committees for different activities, the Kiev society assumed a leading role among the Prosvitas. It gave particular weight to publishing and within five years printed 34 books (163,760 copies) for the common people. Its reading-room library contained over 10,000 volumes, mostly in Ukrainian studies. By 1909 its membership had reached 625, but in 1910 the authorities dissolved the society by administrative order.

From 1906 Prosvitas sprang up in other centers, including Kamianets-Podilskyi, Zhytomyr, Chernihiv, Mykolaiv, and Melitopil. In the Kuban Prosvitas appeared in Katerynodar, Temriuk, and Maikop. Prosvitas were organized also in Novocherkassk (Don region), Baku (Caucasia), and Vladivostok (Far East). The authorities withheld approval of Prosvitas in Poltava and Kharkiv gubernias. Prosvitas in other gubernias were rarely allowed to set up branches. All Prosvita societies were closed down in 1910–11. Although there were only about 40 short-lived Prosvitas, including branches, in eastern Ukraine, they made a significant contribution to the growth of national consciousness.

With the outbreak of the Revolution of 1917, Prosvitas sprang up spontaneously in Ukrainian towns and villages. By the summer of 1917 a dense network covered eastern Ukraine. The revived Kiev Prosvita assumed the leading role in the movement, and on 20 September 1917 it convened the First All-Ukrainian Conference of Prosvitas, which set up the All-Ukrainian Association of Prosvitas and the Central Bureau for co-ordinating the activities of rural societies and county associations. Many Prosvitas arose in the Far East and the Kuban. Within a short time thousands of Prosvita societies were established, and almost every town and larger village in Ukraine had a reading room. In 1917–22 the reading rooms were centers of Ukrainian national life. The new Soviet regime viewed the Prosvitas as centers of Ukrainian national resistance. In July 1920 the Central Executive Committee of the CP(B)U passed a resolution to take control of the Prosvitas and incorporate them into state structures. This measure proved unsuccessful, and the Prosvitas continued to expand their influence, with the number of societies growing in 1921 from approx 4,000 to 4,500 with a total membership of 400,000. In February 1922 a meeting of the Ukrainian gubernial departments decided to destroy the Prosvitas and initiated measures to force their closure. As a result only 573 Prosvita branches were still operational in 1923, and these were converted into 'Soviet' Prosvitas, *village centers, or reading houses. The Prosvitas in the Kuban, the Far East, and throughout the RSFSR were abolished also. Of the Far East Prosvitas only the one in Harbin survived until 1945.

With the German occupation of Ukraine in 1941 Prosvitas began to appear, often at the initiative of the OUN expeditionary groups, but as the administration passed into the hands of the German civil authorities, they dissolved themselves to avoid repression or were suppressed. The Prosvita in Kharkiv, with the president V. Dubrovsky, the vice-president Z. Sapitska, and such members as B. Porai-Koshyts, O. Popov, D. Solovei, and F. Bulbenko, was reg-istered officially as an organization for mutual aid, particularly for food supplies, but went far beyond these activities to become the focus of Ukrainian civic life in the city (1941–3). It organized an exhibition of documents and memorabilia of Soviet terror, titled 'Away with Bolshevism.'

Northwestern Ukraine. At the beginning of the 20th century there were active Prosvitas in Siedlce, Hrubeshiv, and Kobyliaky (in Biała Podlaska county) and in the Kremianets region of Volhynia. In 1916–18, during the Austrian-German occupation of Volhynia, the Ukrainian popular educational movement began to expand there as a result of the presence of the Ukrainian Sich Riflemen and the Bluecoats and Graycoats divisions. The Prosvita established in Brest in 1918, headed by V. Dmytriiuk and V. Krynytsky, organized about 100 reading rooms in the villages and towns of Polisia. It was closed down by the Polish authorities in 1919 and revived in 1923, but eventually most of its reading rooms were closed down, and the rest disintegrated.

In the Kholm region and Podlachia the *Ridna Khata society served as a regional counterpart to Prosvita. It had almost 125 branches by the time it was banned (1930) by the Polish authorities. The Prosvita in Lutske, established in 1918, had 134 branches by 1932, when it was banned. Its membership included I. Vlasovsky, Ye. Petrytsky (a longtime president), V. Ostrovsky, O. Levchanivska, and M. Maslov. On its initiative two educational conferences were convened in Lutske. They resolved to set up a Volhynian Prosvita, which would cover the entire region, but the Polish government did not give consent. The Lutske Prosvita organized courses in Ukrainian studies and workshops on co-operative management. Other county Prosvitas maintained similar programs. The most active were in Kremianets, Rivne, Kovel, Dubno, Horokhiv, Volodymyr-Volynskyi, Ostrih, Kostopil, Liuboml, and Oleksandriia. From the late 1920s the Polish authorities systematically closed down Prosvita branch offices and reading rooms in Volhynia and Polisia, until all 600 had been removed. The Prosvitas in the northwestern lands tried to maintain close contacts with the Prosvita society in Lviv, and in 1932–3 they started to establish Ridna Khata societies in Volhynia. These were disbanded in 1937–9. In the summer and fall of 1941, after the German occupation of Volhynia, a string of Prosvitas sprang up. These too were soon banned.

Transcarpathia. Prosvita was formally constituted in Transcarpathia only in the interwar era. It had some antecedents. In 1896 the Greek Catholic Reading Room, based on the constitution of the Lviv Prosvita and closely associated with it, was founded by Rev O. Shtefan in Skotarske. It was the first of several semilegal reading rooms and circles established after 1900, in villages such as Velyki Veretsky, Holubyne, Lypcha, Rakhiv, Stroine, and Yasinia. Commonly they received Prosvita's publications from Lviv and distributed them in spite of restrictions and prohibitions by the Hungarian authorities.

Prosvita was formally established in Uzhhorod in 1920, and subsequently its network spread throughout Transcarpathia. By 1923 it had four branches in county centers and 82 reading rooms, 30 drama groups, and 12 choirs in towns and villages. In 1934 there were 10 branches (including Prešov and Bratislava), 230 reading rooms, 146 theater groups, 21 orchestras, 98 choirs, and 47 sports groups. The membership reached 15,337. By the time it was dissolved in 1939, the Transcarpathian Prosvita had published over 200 books and brochures, almanacs, and an annual collection for Carpatho-Ukrainian studies, *Naukovyi zbirnyk* (14 vols, 1922–38). In 1925 *Prosvita*, a scientific-literary and economic monthly, came out for a brief period. The central society in Uzhhorod maintained the Ruthenian Theater of the Prosvita Society, directed by M. Sadovsky and then O. Zaharov, the Nova Stsena national theater (1934–9), directed by Yu. Sherehii, and the Ruthenian National Chorus, conducted by O. Prykhodko. The village choirs were usually conducted by Prykhodko's students, among whom were A. Mino, Yu. Paliukh, F. Povkhan, I. Tymkanych, and F. Shymanovsky. A. Kist taught courses in folk dancing, and I. Romanenko organized orchestras. The larger branches and reading rooms owned their own buildings. The head office in Uzhhorod (built in 1926) also housed an ethnographic museum, the offices of various organizations, an editing office, and a library of 10,000 volumes (based on H. Strypsky's private collection). The leading figures were Yu. and M. Brashchaiko, Rev A. Voloshyn, Rev V. Hadzhega, Rev V. Zheltvai, A. Shtefan, P. Yatsko, S. Klochurak, and Rev K. Fedelesh. The Prešov branch was managed by Rev E. Biharii and I. Nevytska. Annual conferences took place in various parts of Transcarpathia. The largest of them was the all-Prosvita conference of 1937 in Uzhhorod, attended by over 12,000 participants. Prosvita's chief competitor was the Russophile *Dukhnovych Society (est 1923). The Hungarian authorities banned Prosvita in 1939 and confiscated its property. Its archive and part of its library were destroyed, and the remainder of its assets (along with all the property of the head office, its branches, and reading rooms) was transferred to the Subcarpathian Scientific Society.

Europe. In 1919, after the downfall of Austria-Hungary, the Ukrainians in the Bačka and Srem regions (of Yugoslavia) founded the *Ruthenian People's Enlightenment Society in Novi Sad. It had a number of branches and a broad program that included publishing. Its activities were banned by the Hungarians, who occupied Bačka in April 1941. In 1923 a Prosvita society was established in Zagreb on the model of the Lviv one. It had branches and representations in Slavonia, Bosnia, and Belgrade. It published an irregular bulletin that eventually became *Vistnyk Ukraïns'koho tovarystva Prosvita v Zahrebi* (1936–9) and maintained contacts with Prosvita in Lviv. After Croatia declared independence in 1941, the Zagreb Prosvita transferred its functions to the Ukrainian Representation, the only functioning Ukrainian organization there, which paid little attention to educational work. After 1944 neither organization could resume its work, under the communist regime.

The first Prosvita outside Ukraine's ethnographic territory was the society established in Cracow in 1894 as a reading room under the Lviv Prosvita. In 1923 it became a branch of the Lviv society. A Prosvita operated in Vienna from 1908 to 1918. During the First World War there were Prosvita societies in Ukrainian refugee camps and in some POW camps for soldiers of the Russian army in Germany and Austria. In Czechoslovakia the Ukrainian Labor Battalion in Brno had a Prosvita (1922–3), and the societies in Bratislava and Prešov were tied to the Prosvita in Uzhhorod.

In France Prosvita societies arose among emigrant workers and were organized along the lines of Galician reading rooms. In the interwar period such reading rooms functioned in Versailles, Lyon, Metz, Orléans, Strasbourg, and Soissons. In 1932 there were 75 Prosvitas registered with the Ukrainian National Union in France.

North and South America. Popular educational societies modeled on the Lviv Prosvita were established among the Ukrainian emigrants in the New World. Eventually most of them were incorporated into various organizations, although their programs and activities were obviously influenced by the Lviv society. Separate Prosvita societies developed only in Argentina, Paraguay, Uruguay, and several Canadian centers.

The first Prosvita society in the United States was established in Shenandoah, Pennsylvania, in 1887. Other communities followed suit and also formed popular educational societies. From 1896 Rev A. Bonezevsky led a campaign to develop a Prosvita-like association in the United States. The idea was pursued seriously by a group of Ukrainophile priests known as the American Circle after Bonezevsky's death in 1903, when they established a Prosvita-style press (Slovo) using moneys the priest had left in his will for this purpose. The venture folded in 1906 because of a lack of support, but it was revived under a different name for one more year. In 1909 the idea of an American Prosvita society was discussed at the All-People's Enlightenment Conference, held in Philadelphia. With the powerful backing of Bishop S. *Ortynsky the gathering launched an American Prosvita. The new group had an auspicious beginning, but it was scuttled in the heated dispute that broke out between Ortynsky and the Ukrainian National Association (UNA) in 1910. The UNA launched its own attempt at a Prosvita-style organization in 1912, when it formed the Enlightenment Committee. This group also enjoyed some initial success but failed to develop a Prosvita structure. Some UNA locals maintained the Prosvita name, and the general aims of Prosvita were pursued independently by various Ukrainian-American associations, but the society itself never took root. In the interwar period the Lviv Prosvita maintained contacts with Ukrainians in the United States and published three issues of *Amerykans'kyi prosvitianyn* to recruit members from among them.

Even though a large number of popular educational associations developed among Ukrainians in Canada along Prosvita lines, the society itself failed to take root there also. The first Ukrainian-Canadian reading society was established in Winnipeg, in 1899, and by the early 1920s such societies were widespread throughout the country. In the period after the First World War many of them were housed in community centers, which commonly referred to themselves as people's homes (*narodni domy*). These groups usually developed formal or informal ties with the national religious or ideological structures which were established in Canada in the 1920s and 1930s, and were not organized into Prosvita affiliates. Nevertheless, they functioned much as Prosvita societies, and 35 of the 116 educational societies in Canada in 1935 referred to themselves as Prosvitas. The most significant Ukrainian educational societies which were organized as Prosvitas were located in Winnipeg and Port Arthur–Fort William (Thunder Bay), and the people's homes in Edmonton and Toronto operated much along the lines of Prosvitas. An attempt was made (under the auspices of the Ukrainian Self-Reliance League) to establish a *Union of Ukrainian Community Centres of Canada that would have served many of the functions of a central Prosvita organization, but the group failed to develop as anticipated.

The first Prosvita society in South America arose in Curitiba, Brazil, in 1902. Until 1914 educational organizations there bore various names, including Prosvita. After they merged into the Ukrainian Union in 1922 (later the *Union for Agricultural Education), they ceased to act as independent societies.

In Argentina the first Prosvita society was founded in 1910 in Apostoles. Others arose only in the 1920s. In 1924 the Ukrainian Central Prosvita Society was formed in Buenos Aires, and it became the head office for all the Prosvitas in Argentina. Before the Second World War branches were situated in Dock Sud, Valentin Alciua, Chaco, Tres Capones, and other centers. After the war the Prosvita society received a major influx of new members from among recent immigrants and was reoriented politically into a group supporting the Bandera faction of the OUN. New branches were also formed in Lavallon, Vila Caraça, San Martin, and other locations. In 1971 Prosvita had 15 branches and 1,226 members. Each branch had its own building, Ukrainian school, and secondary school. The society maintains a dance group and a banduryst kapelle and publishes *Ukraïns'ke slovo* (since 1928), almanacs, and books.

In Paraguay educational societies began forming in the late 1920s and led to the establishment of a Prosvita society in Encarnación in 1937. By 1945 it had 10 branches. After the Second World War it developed a youth section, branches of which were later reconstituted as Ukrainian Youth Association groups. In the 1980s Prosvita in Paraguay maintained a central office in Encarnación and had five branches.

In Uruguay a Prosvita society was established in Montevideo in 1934 as a branch of the Buenos Aires Prosvita.

BIBLIOGRAPHY
Lozyns'kyi, M. *Sorok lit diial'nosty 'Pros'vity'* (Lviv 1908)
Bryk, I.; Kotsiuba, M. (eds). *Pershyi ukraïns'kyi prosvitno-ekonomichnyi kongres* (Lviv 1910)
Shakh, S. *Populiarna istoriia tovarystva 'Prosvita' u L'vovi* (Lviv 1932)
Doroshenko, V. *'Prosvita': Ïï zasnuvannia i pratsia* (Philadelphia 1959)
Pers'kyi, S.; Volynets', S.; Hospodyn, S. *Narys istoriï matirnoho tovarystva 'Prosvity' i ohliad prosvitnykh tovarystv u Kanadi* (Winnipeg 1968)
                    B. Kravtsiv, M. Borovsky, V. Markus, A. Shtefan

Prosvitnyi lystok (Educational Bulletin). A newspaper for Ukrainian soldiers of the Russian army interned by the Germans in the First World War. It was published in 1915–16 at the Wetzlar POW camp in Germany three times per month, and was later absorbed by *Hromads'ka dumka*.

Proterozoic era. See Geology of Ukraine.

'Protestacja' (Protestation). A memorandum written in Polish in the spring of 1621 by Metropolitan Y. Boretsky of Kiev and M. Smotrynsky and sent in the name of the Orthodox hierarchy and clergy of the Polish Commonwealth to King Sigismund III Vasa. The memorandum defended the historic rights of the Orthodox church and especially the legitimacy of the hierarchs consecrated by Patriarch Theophanes of Jerusalem in 1620, stressed the positive role of the Cossacks as defenders of the Orthodox church, and criticized Metropolitan Y. Rutsky and the Uniate hierarchy. It was circulated widely in manuscript throughout Ukraine and Belarus. The text was first published, with annotations by P. Zhukovich, in *Stati po slavianovedeniiu*, vol 3, 1909.

Protestantism. A major branch of Christianity established in the 16th century as a result of the *Reformation. Protestantism emerged in the 16th century in opposition to the dogma and institutional practices of the Catholic church and quickly spread throughout the western, northern, and central reaches of Europe as well as into Eastern Europe. Incorporating the teachings of theologians such as M. Luther, J. Calvin, H. Zwingli, and T. Müntzer, Protestantism rejected the ritualism, entrenched dogmatism, and authoritarianism of the Catholic church in favor of the concept of grace through faith, the involvement of the laity in church affairs, and a personal understanding of the Bible. The movement quickly spawned a number of new churches, among them the Anglican, Lutheran, Baptist, Presbyterian, and Methodist. For the history of Protestantism in Ukraine see *Evangelical Christians, *Socinians, *Baptists, *Adventists, *Lutherans, *Mennonites, and *Stundists. Some Ukrainians in *Canada and the *United States also joined Protestant or Protestant-inspired churches, such as the *Independent Greek Church.

Protofis. See Union of Industry, Trade, Finance, and Agriculture.

Viktor Protopopov

Protopopov, Viktor, b 22 October 1880 in Yurky, Kobeliaky county, Poltava gubernia, d 29 November 1957 in Kiev. Psychiatrist; full member of the AN URSR (now ANU) from 1945. A graduate of the St Petersburg Military Medical Academy (1906), he worked there until 1921 and then served as a professor at Perm University and at the Kharkiv Medical Institute (1923–44). He was director of the Institute of Clinical Psychiatry and Social Psychohygiene (1926–9) and of the psychiatric clinic of the Psychoneurological Institute in Kharkiv (1932–41), taught at the Kiev Institute for the Upgrading of Physicians (1944–57), and headed the psychiatry department of the ANU Institute of Physiology (from 1944). He was chief psychiatrist and president of the Scientific Council of the Ukrainian SSR Ministry of Health. He introduced the pathophysiological approach to psychiatry, applied I. Pavlov's theories in psychiatry, proposed new methods for treating schizophrenia and manic depression, and was one of the first psychiatrists in the USSR to use hypnosis as therapy. His collected works were published in Kiev (1961).

Protsenko, Havrylo [Procenko], b and d ? Kievan engraver and silversmith of the first half of the 19th century. A member and president (1828–9) of the Kiev goldsmiths' guild, in 1840 he was elected an honorary citizen of Kiev. He did the engravings *Council of the Kievan Cave Saints* (1820–1), *St Gregory* (1822) in the Kievan Cave Liturgicon (1832), and *John the Theologian* (1827). Together with F. Korobka he made silver articles for the Kievan Cave Monastery.

Protsenko, Volodymyr [Procenko], b 4 January 1942 in Mariiupil, Donetske oblast. Mathematician. After completing his studies at the Berdianske Pedagogical Institute, he taught at the Kharkiv Agricultural Institute (1964–72) and then at the Kharkiv Aviation Institute. His main contributions are in the theory and application of R-functions.

Protsiuk, Stepan [Procjuk] (Prociuk, Stephen), b 3 January 1916 in Chocen, Czechoslovakia, d 12 October 1984 in New York. Mechanical engineer and economist; member of the Ukrainian Academy of Arts and Sciences. He studied and worked at the Lviv Polytechnical Institute and emigrated in 1943, first to Austria, then to Australia, and then, in 1957, to the United States. He published numerous studies and articles about the development of technology, transport, and energy in Ukraine and other parts of the USSR. Among his most important contributions are studies of the Kakhivka Hydroelectric Station, the economic development of Siberia, the economic reconstruction of Ukraine after the Second World War, the Ukrainian aircraft industry, Ukrainian contributions to space sciences, the organization of research and development in Soviet Ukraine, and Ukrainian scientific and technical publishing. He was active in the Ukrainian Engineers' Society of America and was editor of *Visti ukraïns'kykh inzheneriv* for many years. He contributed entries to *Entsyklopediia ukraïnoznavstva* (Encyclopedia of Ukraine, 1955–84) and the *Encyclopedia of Ukraine* (1984–93).

Protsyshyn, Zhyhmont [Procyšyn, Žyhmont] (pseud: Pavlo Mariichyn), b 1910 in Kavsko, Stryi county, Galicia, d 1945 in Belgium. Galician writer and journalist. As a student at Cracow University he began contributing to the Lviv daily *Dilo*. In 1929 he was arrested by the Polish authorities and tried in Lviv with several others for belonging to the Ukrainian Military Organization and distributing its organ *Surma*, but he was acquitted. In the late 1930s he coedited, with B. Kravtsiv, the OUN political weekly *Holos natsii*. He wrote stories about the plight of political prisoners and the prose collection *Molode pokolinnia* (The Young Generation, 1933), the copies of which were confiscated by the authorities. During the German occupation he was deputy director of the Lviv District Committee of the Ukrainian Service to the Fatherland, an organization that recruited and trained students as a labor force for the German war effort. For a brief period after the war he was a professor of Slavic studies at Ghent University and contributed political articles to the Belgian press.

Proty khvyl'! (Against the Currents). A monthly journal of socialist thought and political affairs, published in Lviv in 1928–9. It was closely allied with the Ukrainian Radical party and was edited by prominent leaders of the party, such as M. Stakhiv, K. Kobersky, and O. Pavliv-Bilozersky.

Proverbs (*prykazky, prypovidky, pryslivia*). Brief, pithy popular maxims which are often rhymed and easily remembered. Dating back to prehistoric times, they typically express a universal concept through a concrete image, often with a dash of humor. Proverbs are part of the oral rather than the literary tradition.

Proverbs deal with various aspects of life and are said to constitute an encyclopedia of popular wisdom. Their principal themes are nature, farming, flora and fauna, domestic life, human nature, family and social relations, customs, folk wisdom, religion, and morality. In content and form they are similar to adages, folk metaphors, puns, and fables. Because of their simple structure they can be memorized easily. Usually they consist of two symmetrical sections that rhyme.

Proverbs can be found in the literary monuments of Kievan Rus', such as the *Izbornik* of Sviatoslav, the Primary Chronicle, and *Slovo o polku Ihorevi* (The Tale of Ihor's Campaign). The first written collections of Ukrainian proverbs did not appear until the late 17th century. These were *Povisty ili poslovitsy vsenarodniia po alfavytu* (Most Common Sayings or Proverbs in Alphabetical Order) and Klymentii's *Prypovisty, abo tezh prysloviia, pospolitye* (Proverbs or Sayings of the Common People). I. Yuhasevych-Skliarsky's collection of 370 Transcarpathian Ukrainian proverbs, published in 1809, was unique in its time. The first printed collection, of 618 Ukrainian proverbs, was V. Smyrnytsky's *Malorosiiskiia poslovitsy i pogovorki* (Little Russian Proverbs and Sayings, 1834), published in Kharkiv. The second was *Halyts'ki prypovidky i zahadky* (Galician Proverbs and Riddles, 1841), published in Lviv (2,715 items). The best collection of proverbs in the 19th century was M. *Nomys's *Ukrains'ki prykazky, pryslivia i take inshe* (Ukrainian Sayings, Proverbs, and the Like, 1864), published in St Petersburg (14,339 items). To this day I. Franko's collection of over 30,000 items, *Halyts'ko-rus'ki narodni prypovidky* (Galician-Ruthenian Folk Proverbs, 6 vols, 1901–10), has not been surpassed.

Collections of proverbs published during the Soviet period include large sections of so-called Soviet proverbs and sayings, about love of the people, the Communist party, the Soviet order, Marxist-Leninist ideology, and 'enemies of the people.' Most of these sayings are artificial: they were devised at the behest of Party authorities and have nothing to do with the people. The collections often fail to meet the basic criteria of scholarship. The first scholarly collection, *Prysliv'ia ta prykazky* (Proverbs and Sayings, vol 1, 1989), edited by M. Paziak, deals with sayings about nature and man's economic activities. The first bibliographic guide to Ukrainian proverbs was *Paremiologiia Ukrainy* (Paroemiology of Ukraine, 2 vols, 3,342 items, 1982–3), edited by A. Bushui and A. Ivchenko. Virtually all Ukrainian writers from I. Vyshensky and H. Skovoroda to the poets of the 1980s have used proverbs in their works.

BIBLIOGRAPHY
Paziak, M. *Ukraïns'ki prysliv'ia ta prykazky* (Kiev 1984)
*Folkl'ornyi zbirnyk Matviia Nomysa: Do sto-dvadtsiatyrichchia per-
shoho vydannia, 1864–1984* (South Bound Brook, 1985)
M. Mushynka

Flag of the Providence Association

Original charter (1914) of the Providence Association

**Providence Association of Ukrainian Catholics in
America** (Soiuz ukraintsiv katolykiv Provydinnia). A fraternal benefit and insurance association founded by Bishop S. *Ortynsky in 1912 for the purpose of providing
moral support and material aid to Ukrainian immigrants.
Ortynsky had earlier desired to create a Catholic fraternal
institution and had attempted to do so by proposing a
change to the constitution of the Ruthenian National Association (later the *Ukrainian National Association) that
would give it an explicitly (Catholic) confessional rather
than secular character. Strong opposition to his initiative
convinced the bishop to abandon this approach and to set
up a separate body. The Providence Association's founding conference took place in New York after a number of
priests and some lay members resigned from the Ruthenian National Association. The first Providence branches
arose in New York, Newark, Jersey City, and Yonkers. By
1914, when its head office was moved to Philadelphia, the
association had about 600 members. By 1971 Providence
had 212 branches with a membership of 18,700 and assets
of 6.8 million dollars, and by 1989 it had 213 branches with
almost 18,000 members and assets of about 12 million dollars. Besides helping the families of its members, the association sponsored Ukrainian nurseries and schools in
Galicia, Ukrainian eparchies in the United States and Argentina, Ukrainian seminaries and schools in the United
States, and various cultural events. It was a founder and
presidium member of the Ukrainian Congress Committee

of America (UCCA) until 1982, when it withdrew its participation in the UCCA in order to remain neutral in its dispute with the Ukrainian American Coordinating Council.
Since 1912 it has published the paper *Ameryka*, and since
1918 an annual *Kalendar*. It has also published some valuable monographs, such as H. Luzhnytsky's *Ukraïns'ka
tserkva mizh skhodom i zakhodom* (The Ukrainian Church between East and West, 1954) and S. Hordynsky's *The Ukrainian Icon of the 12th to 18th Centuries* (1973). The presidents
of Providence have been Revs Ye. Barysh (1912), M. Pidhoretsky (1912–16), P. Poniatyshyn (1916), V. Dovhovych
(1916–18), M. Kuziv (1919–21), I. Ortynsky (1922–9), A.
Lotovych (1930–41), V. Bilynsky (1942–57), R. Lobodych
(1958–9), R. Sukhy (1959–61), S. Tykhansky (1962–5), M.
Kharyna (1966–78), R. Moskal (1978–82), S. Chomko
(1982–6), and M. Kanavan (1986–90). The association's history is presented in jubilee books published in 1974 (60th
anniversary) and 1987 (75th anniversary).

Provincial School Union (Kraiovyi shkilnyi soiuz). An
organization founded in 1910 in Lviv by representatives
of several Ukrainian political parties and principal community organizations to co-ordinate and administer
Ukrainian private education in Galicia. Its primary concern was secondary education. M. *Hrushevsky and I.
*Kyveliuk served as presidents of the union, and L. Salo
served as director. The union suspended activity with the
onset of the First World War and eventually disbanded, in
1920. On many occasions the union worked together with
the Ukrainian Pedagogical Society (see *Ridna Shkola).

Provisional Committee for Investigating Antiquities in the City of Kiev (Vremennyi komitet dlia izyskaniia drevnostei v gorode Kieve). A committee formed in 1835 to undertake archeological studies in Kiev. Under the leadership of M. *Maksymovych, the rector of Kiev University, the committee searched for Rus' sites in Kiev and undertook studies of St Michael's Golden-Domed and St Cyril's monasteries, St Michael's church, and the grounds of St Sophia Cathedral. The committee was composed largely of academics, including V. Tsykh, S. Ornatsky, A. Petrov, I. Daniłowicz, and M. Berlynsky. As a direct result of its work, an archeological museum was established at Kiev University in 1837. More significantly, the committee's activity laid the groundwork for a lasting vehicle for archeological investigation in Ukrainian lands: when it was dismantled in 1845, an expanded version of its mandate was transferred to the *Kiev Archeographic Commission.

Provisional Government (Vremennoe pravitelstvo). The Russian government from the *February Revolution (15 March 1917) to the *October Revolution (7 November 1917), composed of members of the Constitutional Democratic, Russian Socialist Revolutionary, Octobrist, and Russian Social Democratic Workers' (Mensheviks) parties. The Provisional Government favored continuing the war with the Central Powers and tried to maintain the unity of the Russian Empire in the new democratic Russian republic against the autonomist and separatist aspirations of the non-Russian nationalities. It attempted to introduce reforms gradually and faced opposition from the revolutionary wing of Russian social democracy, the Bolsheviks.

The Provisional Government established gubernial (and county) executive committees chosen by the local zemstvo assemblies and revolutionary committees. They were headed by gubernial commissars. Many Ukrainians were chosen for those local administrative positions in Ukraine. The Provisional Government appointed D. Doroshenko krai commissioner of the occupied regions of Galicia and Bukovyna; he, in turn, appointed I. Kraskovsky gubernial commissioner of the Ternopil region and O. Lototsky gubernial commissioner of Bukovyna. In Ukraine a dual governing structure was agreed to in principle, in which the Provisional Government was to share power with the *Central Rada (unlike the situation in most of the former empire, where the soviets were contesting for power). The Provisional Government attempted to limit the competency of the Rada, however, and a mutually acceptable solution of power sharing was never worked out.

Prince G. Lvov headed the Provisional Government until 20 July; after a period of crisis, A. *Kerensky assumed the leadership of a coalition government on 6 August and remained head of the government until its demise. At first the Provisional Government took a negative view of the Central Rada's demand for the national-territorial autonomy of Ukraine, and the Central Rada defied it in its First Universal (see *Universals of the Central Rada) and by the establishment of an autonomous Ukrainian government, the *General Secretariat of the Central Rada. But since the Provisional Government was threatened by increasing revolutionary unrest throughout the country, it decided to come to terms with the Rada. On 11 July the Provisional Government ministers Kerensky, M. Tereshchenko, and I.

Tseretelli came to Kiev and negotiated a compromise: the Provisional Government would recognize the General Secretariat as the supreme organ of government in most of Ukraine, and the Rada and General Secretariat, recognizing the Provisional Government, would refrain from a unilateral implementation of autonomy and would co-opt members of national minorities in Ukraine. The agreement was codified in the Rada's Second Universal. The Provisional Government did not agree with the Statute of the Higher Administration of Ukraine drafted by the Rada, and instead issued its own Instruction (17 August), which limited the rights of both the Rada and its General Secretariat. The Provisional Government, however, did not even hold to the Instruction, but hindered the Rada and the General Secretariat from establishing their authority in Ukraine.

Of the members of the Provisional Government the Georgian Tseretelli was the most sympathetic to Ukrainian demands, and the Constitutional Democrats were the most ill disposed. The minister Tereshchenko, though of Ukrainian nationality, showed little sympathy for the Ukrainian cause. A delegation from the General Secretariat was in Petrograd in November to settle differences with the Provisional Government when the Bolsheviks took power.

BIBLIOGRAPHY
Stojko, W. 'Ukrainian National Aspirations and the Russian Provisional Government,' in *The Ukraine, 1917–1921: A Study in Revolution*, ed. T. Hunczak (Cambridge, Mass 1977)

J.-P. Himka

Provisional Workers' and Peasants' Government of Ukraine (Tymchasovyi robitnycho-selianskyi uriad Ukrainy). The second Bolshevik attempt to form a Soviet administration in Ukraine. Set up on 20 November 1918 in Kursk Russia by the CC of the Russian Communist Party (Bolshevik), the new government was announced on 28 November. The CC of the CP(B)U had no say in its creation. Its first head, G. *Piatakov, was replaced on 29 November by Kh. *Rakovsky, an even stronger opponent of Ukrainian independence. The chief positions in the government were held by Russians who were anti-Ukrainian: foreign affairs by Rakovsky; national economy by G. Piatakov, E. Kviring, and M. Rukhymovych; propaganda by Artem; military affairs by N. Podvoisky and V. Mezhlauk; and internal affairs by V. Averin and K. Voroshilov. Ukrainians received secondary appointments: V. Zatonsky, education; O. Khmelnytsky, justice; M. Skrypnyk, state control; A. Zharko, communications; and Yu. Kotsiubynsky and E. Shchadenko, members of the Revolutionary Military Council. In January 1919 this government was established in Kharkiv by the Red Army. Its immediate task was to supply Russia with bread during the winter of 1918–19 and then to replace the Hetman regime with the Soviet one. In early March the Third All Ukrainian Congress of Soviets, called by the provisional government, changed its name to the Workers' and Peasants' Government of the Ukrainian SSR and adopted the First Constitution of Soviet Ukraine, which copied closely the RSFSR Constitution.

O. Skrypnyk

Provody. Memorial services for the deceased that were held during the so-called *Mavka* week immediately after

Easter. They were usually held on the Sunday or Monday following Easter. In some cases they were held on Holy Thursday. In Bukovyna they took place on the Saturday following Easter; in Galicia, on the Friday or Saturday following Easter. Participants gathered at the cemetery, bringing Easter eggs, bread, bowls of food, and liquor or wine. After a commemoration service they ate a meal at the graves, where they left some of the food and drink for the dead. In some regions the *provody* concluded with games and dancing. The first Monday after Pentecost, when the **rusalky* were conducted away from the village and the sown fields, was also known as *provody*.

Prozorov, Hryhorii, b 1803 in the Chernihiv region, d 20 January 1885 in St Petersburg. Physician. A graduate of the Chernihiv Seminary (1821) and the St Petersburg Medico-Surgical Academy (1825), he obtained a doctorate in medicine and surgery (1836), was a professor of veterinary science at the academy (1836–63), and introduced the first course on zoonoses. His numerous publications include papers on zoonoses, horse colic, scarlet fever, and syphilis; a collection of materials on the history of the academy; and textbooks on veterinary obstetrics and horse diseases. He created a scholarship fund for students from the Chernihiv region attending the academy.

Prozumenshchikova, Galina [Prozumenščikova], b 26 November 1948 in Sevastopil, Crimea. Champion swimmer. She was the first Soviet swimmer to win an Olympic gold medal, in the 1964 women's 200-m breaststroke. She won two silver medals in the women's 100-m breaststroke and two bronze medals in the women's 200-m breaststroke in the 1968 and 1972 Olympic Games, was the European champion in the 1966 women's 200-m breaststroke and the 1970 200-m and 100-m breaststroke, set five world records in 1964–6, and was a USSR champion 15 times (1963–73). Since 1968 she has lived in Moscow.

Ukrainian Catholic church in Prudentópolis

Prudentópolis. A town (1987 pop 51,7000) with an area of 2,395 sq km, located in the state of **Paraná* in Brazil. The population is estimated to be 75 percent Ukrainian and 20 percent Polish; the town has one of the major concentrations of Slavs in South America and is one of the largest centers of Ukrainian immigration on that continent. Ukrainian immigrants began to arrive in the late 1890s in São João de Capanema, today Prudentópolis. From the beginning it became the center of the Ukrainian Catholic church. By 1897 a parish had already been founded, with 5,250 members, by S. Kizyma of the Basilian order. A chapel was ready in 1898, and in 1904 a new church had been built, which was later replaced by an even larger one. St Josaphat parish now comprises a number of churches and chapels from the neighboring areas.

A number of church organizations exist, such as the Sisters of the Sacred Heart of Jesus (from 1899), which has branches in Brazil, Argentina (Oberá), and Paraguay (Encarnación). The nuns are trained by the Basilian Fathers, and often they participate in other nonreligious organizations in addition to teaching at local schools and directing one of the state schools (where Ukrainian is taught as an optional subject). Also located in Prudentópolis are the Internato S. Olga (administered by the St Olha Association of the Ukrainian Catechists of the Sacred Heart of Jesus); the Seminário São José; and the printing house of the Basilian Fathers, which publishes *Pratsia* and *Ukraïns'kyi misionar*. A local radio station transmits Ukrainian programs in Portuguese and Ukrainian. A large number of secular Ukrainian organizations are also active there.

BIBLIOGRAPHY
Borushenko, O.; et al. *Arquivos de Prudentópolis* (Curitiba 1971)
N. Kerechuk

Prudky, Nykon [Prudkyj], b 5 April 1890 in Kaniv, Kiev gubernia, d 8 December 1982 in Cherkasy. Banduryst. He learned to play the bandura as a teenager, from the kobzars and lirnyks who frequented the markets of Kiev. In the 1920s he wandered through the villages of the Kaniv region, and in 1928–32 he became curator of the museum at T. Shevchenko's grave in Kaniv. Later he directed an amateur bandura ensemble in Cherkasy. His repertoire consisted of over 100 songs, many of which were dedicated to Shevchenko and were Prudky's own compositions.

Prusianowski, Jan, b 1818 in Podorozhnia, Lityn county, Podilia gubernia, d 9 December 1892 in Zhytomyr, Volhynia gubernia. Polish writer and folklorist. After being expelled from Kiev University for revolutionary activity he completed his studies at Kazan and eventually established a law practice in Zhytomyr (1850–80). His collection *Z podań ludu i z obcéj mowy* (From Folk Legends and from General Speech, 1856) contained some Ukrainian materials, and his collection of Ukrainian proverbs appeared in *Biblioteka Warszawska* (1862–3).

Prut River. A major waterway in southwestern Ukraine that eventually flows into the Danube. It is 910 km long (nearly 240 km are in Ukraine) and drains a basin area of 27,500 sq km (approx 8,000 sq km in Ukraine). Its source is near Mt Hoverlia, and it flows through the Carpathians, Subcarpathia, and the Pokutian-Bessarabian and Moldavian uplands. The river is the demarcation point for a short section of the Ukrainian-Rumanian border and the length of the Rumanian-Moldovan border. The first section of the Prut (to Deliatyn) flows through narrow mountain valleys and is marked by rapids and waterfalls (near

Bridge across the Prut River near Yaremche (engraving)

Yaremche). From that point the river widens, although it still has a considerable drop. Fed by rain and meltwater, the Prut freezes over lightly from January to March. The river is used for log rafting. Major centers along its banks include Deliatyn, Kolomyia, Sniatyn, and Chernivtsi. Its tributaries in Ukraine include the Pistynka, the Rybnytsia, and the Cheremosh.

Prut Treaty of 1711. A Russo-Turkish treaty concluded on 22 July 1711 at the Prut River near Iaşi, where the Russian army, led into Moldavia by Emperor Peter I, was encircled by a superior Ottoman force. The treaty's provisions were unfavorable to Russia. In exchange for being allowed to withdraw peacefully from Moldavia Peter agreed to return the recently conquered city of Azov (Oziv) and to destroy the newly constructed Russian fortresses of Tahanrih (Taganrog), Kamianyi Zaton, and Novobogoroditskaia, near the mouth of the Samara River, and others on the Don and the Dniester rivers. He was also forced to agree not to interfere in Polish affairs and to guarantee safe passage to King Charles XII during the king's return to Sweden. Disputes over alleged violations of the treaty resulted in the signing of other accords on 16 April 1712 and 24 April 1713, which obligated Russia to withdraw its armies from Right-Bank Ukraine.

Pruzhany [Pružany]. I-5. A town (1979 pop 7,600) in western Polisia on the Mukhavets River, in Berestia oblast, Belarus. It is on the border of Ukrainian ethnic territory.

Prybylovych, Stepan [Prybylovyč], b ? in Yaroslav, Galicia, d ca 1726 in St Petersburg. Theologian and philosopher. A monk at the Kievan Cave Monastery from ca 1693, he served as a preacher and philosophy lecturer at the Moscow Theological Academy in 1707–10. In 1711 he returned to Kiev and became hegumen of the Kievan Cave Zmiiv Monastery (1713–16). Accused of heresy and Protestant sympathies, he was tried (1717–18) in St Petersburg and banished to a monastery. Prybylovych wrote the unpublished works 'Summulae logicales' (1708), 'Tractatus phisicus' (1710), and an anti-Uniate polemical tract in Russian (1720). He died at the Aleksandr Nevsky Monastery.

Prychodko, Andrii [Pryxod'ko, Andrij], b 18 July 1951 in Toronto. Painter. He has lived and worked in France and Switzerland since 1970. Prychodko has exhibited in Canada, Italy, Switzerland, and France. He combines calligraphic signs and symbols with geometric forms in a flattened space (eg, *Tower*, 1982). Since 1983 he has painted on canvas, using acrylics, tempera, and pastels. He is a sensitive colorist who uses unusual combinations of calm and intense hues and spontaneous and controlled brush strokes (*Horse Trading*, 1983–5).

Prychodko, Nicholas. See Prykhodko, Mykola.

Roman Prydatkevych

Prydatkevych, Roman [Prydatkevyč], b 1 June 1895 in Żywiec, near Cracow, d 17 November 1980 in Owensboro, Kentucky. Violinist, composer, and pedagogue; full member of the Shevchenko Scientific Society from 1963. He studied at the Lysenko Higher Institute of Music in Lviv and at the Vienna Academy of Music, before serving in the Austrian army and the Ukrainian Galician Army, and then teaching music in Odessa (1920–2). He continued his musical studies in Berlin and New York, and from 1930 he played in concerts throughout the United States and Canada, with a mainly Ukrainian repertoire. He organized the Ukrainian Trio, the Ukrainian Music Appreciation Society (with H. Pavlovsky), and the New York–based Ukrainian Conservatory (with M. Haivoronsky), which he directed in 1924–9. In 1946 he became a professor of music at Murray State University in Kentucky. His compositions were written primarily for violin and orchestra and include four symphonies, the *Ukrainian Suite* for chamber orchestra, works for violin and piano such as the *Hutsul Suite*, two rhapsodies, and a sonata. They have been performed by orchestras in Denver, Rochester, Detroit, and other cities by such noted conductors as L. Stokowski, F. Fennel, and H. Hanson. His style is modern romantic, with frequent references to Ukrainian folk music.

Pryhara, Andrii, b 27 June 1836 in Kobeliaky county, Poltava gubernia, d 1 July 1875 in Kiev. Legal scholar. After graduating from the universities of Kharkiv and Kiev (MA, 1868) he taught state law at Odessa University. A strong believer in decentralization, he wrote a monograph on the legal status of burghers in Russia under Peter I (1868) and worked on a doctoral dissertation on federal states. He was also interested in the nationality question and the relation of Ukrainian and Russian cultures. Pryhara was active in the *Prosvita movement in Ukraine.

Mariia Pryhara   Roma Pryima-Bohachevska

Pryhara, Mariia, b 20 February 1908 in Moscow, d 8 September 1983 in Kiev. Writer. From the 1920s she lived in Kiev, where she graduated from the Institute of People's Education (1930). She began to publish her work in 1924, and from 1928 she wrote mainly for children. Her first books of children's verse, *Vesna na seli* (Spring in the Village) and *Dytiachyi sadok* (The Children's Nursery), were published in 1929. During the decades that followed, Pryhara was one of the leading writers for children and published many books, including *Shkoliari* (Schoolchildren, 1951), *Kazky* (Stories, 1956), *Rostemo zavziati* (We Grow Up Determined, 1959), *My liubymo sontse i vesnu* (We Love the Sun and Springtime, 1960), *Kozak Holota* (1966), and *Ruchaï* (Brooklets, 1968). She also wrote the historical novelette *Mykhailyk – dzhura kozats'kyi* (Mykhailyk, the Cossack Page, 1974), *Kalytochka* (The Little Leather Purse, 1974), and collections of poetry for adults, and she translated from Polish into Ukrainian. An edition of her selected works (2 vols) was published in 1978.

Pryhodii, Mykhailo [Pryhodij, Myxajlo], b 31 July 1922 in Berezivka, Horodnia county, Chernihiv gubernia. Literary scholar. He graduated from Lviv University in 1949. He has taught at postsecondary schools and worked at the AN URSR (now ANU) Institute of Literature and, from 1970, the CC CPU Institute of the History of the Party. He has written books on M. Gorky as a Soviet publicist (1958), the interaction of the various Soviet literatures (1966), the dialectic of the rapprochement of literatures (1970), V. Lenin and the problem of the creation of a Soviet literature (1970), the all-Union consolidation of literatures (1972), the fraternal unification of the artistic cultures of the Soviet peoples (1976), the Leninist conception of the 'Partyness' of literature (1985), and other subjects.

Pryima, Fedir [Pryjma], b 8 February 1909 in Akhtanizovska, Kuban. Literary scholar. He graduated from the Krasnodar Pedagogical Institute (1932) and worked as a senior associate at the Institute of Russian Literature of the Academy of Science of the USSR in Leningrad. Among his works are articles about T. Shevchenko in journals and Shevchenko studies collections; Russian books on I. Franko, (1956), Shevchenko and 19th-century Russian literature (1961; for which he was awarded the Lenin Prize in 1964), and *Slovo o polku Ihorevi* (The Tale of Ihor's Campaign) in Russian literary history of the first third of the 19th century (1980); and a Ukrainian book on Shevchenko and the Russian liberation movement (1966).

Pryima, Ivan [Pryjma], b 1867 in Selyska, Bibrka county, Galicia, d June 1921 in Kharkiv. Educator and civic leader. After graduating from Lviv University he taught secondary school in Peremyshl, Kitsman, and Chernivtsi. Then he served as principal of the Ukrainian gymnasiums in Horodenka (1910–12) and Yavoriv (1912–15). Having been deported east as a hostage by the Russians in 1915, he was freed after a few months, and settled in Poltava. There he directed the Ukrainian gymnasium and played a leading role in organizing the Ukrainian community and advocating the Ukrainization of local institutions. A member of the Committee for Ukraine's Liberation, he was arrested and transferred to Kharkiv, where he died of typhus in a prison hospital.

Pryima-Bohachevska, Roma [Pryjma-Bohačevska], b 3 March 1927 in Peremyshl, Galicia (now in Poland). Ballerina and modern dance choreographer. A pupil of J. Dalcroze (Lviv) and H. Kreutzberg (Vienna), she worked in the Lviv Opera Theater (1939–44) and was the soloist dancer in the Innsbruck Theater (1947–9) and in R. Sorell's troupe in Montreal (1949–51). In 1951 she settled in New York, and from 1964 led her own ballet school there. Her dance compositions include *Strakhittia viiny* (The Horrors of War), *Chaika* (The Seagull), and *Icon*. She also staged *Cinderella* (1967) and *Kvit paporoti* (The Fern Flower, 1971).

Mariia Pryimachenko: *Halia and a Cossack* (gouache, 1967)

Pryimachenko, Mariia [Pryjmačenko, Marija], b 30 December 1908 in Bolotnia, Radomyshl county, Kiev gubernia. Famous folk painter. She has lived in Bolotnia (now in the Chornobyl nuclear accident zone) throughout her life and has done over 500 primitive paintings, murals, illustrations to verses and children's stories, and ceramic decorations. Distinguished by their vivid colors, they include the painting series 'Bolotnia's Animals' (1935–41), 'For People's Enjoyment' (1960–6), and the recent 'Chornobyl Cycle'; murals, such as *Peahen* (1936), *Cossack Grave* (1962), and *Bears in the Apiary* (1965); and illustrations to several children's poetry books by M. Stelmakh. Her works have been displayed at Soviet and international exhibitions. Albums of her paintings were published in 1971 and 1985.

ART 1) O. Slastion: *Send-off to the Sich* (oil, 1889; Kharkiv Art Museum). 2) R. Selsky: *Fishing Nets* (oil, 1966; Lviv Art Gallery).
3) R. Romanyshyn: *Barrier* (mixed media on paper, 1991; courtesy of D. Zelska-Darewych). 4) A. Solomukha: *Les masques et la pomme* (mixed media, 1984; private collection). 5) A. Prychodko: *Window* (mixed media on metal and linen, 1985). 6) M. Pryimachenko: *Peacock amid Hop Vines* (gouache, 1965).

Ivanna Pryima-Shmerykovska   Mykola Prykhodko

Pryima-Shmerykovska, Ivanna [Pryjma-Šmerykovs'ka], b 19 January 1898 in Nadvirna, Galicia, d 19 January 1982 in New York. Pianist, singer (mezzo-soprano), and pedagogue. A graduate of the Lviv Conservatory (1920), she continued her studies in Paris and then concertized in Lviv, Warsaw, and Cracow. She taught singing at the Lviv Conservatory from 1937 and was concertmaster at the Lviv Opera in 1942–3. She emigrated to the West after the Second World War, and in 1951–9 taught at the Ukrainian Music Institute in New York. Upon retirement, she became the music director of a school in Palm Beach, Florida.

Pryimak, Borys [Pryjmak], b 11 June 1909 in Novocherkassk, Don Cossack region. Architect. After graduating from the Kharkiv Art Institute in 1930, he worked for planning agencies in Kharkiv and participated in drafting reconstruction plans for Zaporizhia, Kryvyi Rih, Mariiupil, and Tbilisi (1930–6). From 1946 he worked in Kiev, and he became its chief architect (1955–73). From 1966 he also taught at the Kiev State Art Institute. He took part in drafting the general reconstruction plan for Kiev and the plans for rebuilding the Khreshchatyk; helped design many buildings in Kiev, including the Ministry of Communications (1950–5), the Main Post Office (1952–6), the Moskva Hotel (1959–66), and the metro stations Zavod Bilshovyk (1962–3), Nyvky (1971), Zhovtneva (1971), and Chervona Ploshcha (1976); designed several monuments; and wrote articles on architecture.

Prykarpats'ka pravda (Subcarpathian Truth). An organ of Ivano-Frankivske (formerly Stanyslaviv) oblast's CPU Committee and Soviet until the end of 1991, published five times a week in Ivano-Frankivske from April 1944. The paper's pressrun was increased from 27,000 in 1950 to 145,000 in 1970 and 186,000 in 1980.

Prykhodko, Antin [Pryxod'ko], b 1892, d ? Political figure. In 1917 he represented the Ukrainian Party of Socialist Revolutionaries in the Central Rada. Afterward he was one of the leading Borotbists and, from 1920, a member of the CP(B)U. In the 1920s he held several important portfolios in the Soviet Ukrainian government, including those of deputy people's commissar of education and of justice. He perished in the late 1930s, during the Stalinist terror.

Prykhodko, Hryhorii [Pryxod'ko, Hryhorij], b 20 December 1937 in Oleksandropil, Synelnykove raion, Dnipropetrovske oblast. Dissident and political prisoner. He was arrested in December 1973 in Kaluga, Russia, and sentenced, for writing and distributing an anti-Soviet leaflet, to five years in labor camps in the Mordovian ASSR, and in the Vladimir prison near Moscow. In November 1975 he renounced his Soviet citizenship. He was rearrested in July 1980 and sentenced to 10 years in camps and 5 years' exile. In the camps he participated in prisoners' protests and signed numerous declarations and open letters. After being released in the fall of 1987, he settled in Lviv, where he led the radical nationalist Ukrainian National party until 1991. In early 1989 he began publishing an unofficial newspaper, *Ukraïns'kyi chas*.

Prykhodko, Maryna [Pryxod'ko], b 1927 in Prague. Poet and translator; daughter of T. *Olesiiuk. For taking part in the Warsaw Uprising she was imprisoned in a Nazi concentration camp. Since 1949 she has lived in the United States. She began publishing in the 1950s and has written modernistic and experimental poetry. Her collection *Potoibich mostu* (On the Other Side of the Bridge) appeared in 1967. She has also translated into Ukrainian poems by J. Tuwim, R.M. Rilke, M. Lermontov, M. Tsvetaeva, and other poets.

Prykhodko, Mykola [Pryxod'ko] (Prychodko, Nicholas), b 23 December 1904 in Chapaievka, Zolotonosha county, Poltava gubernia, d 19 February 1980 in Niagara Falls, Ontario. Writer and community figure. After studing in Kiev in the pedagogical and polytechnic institutes and at the university (docent, 1935) and teaching in high schools and the Polytechnic Institute, he was arrested by the NKVD and sent to a labor camp in Siberia in 1938. He returned to Ukraine in 1941 and emigrated to Canada in 1948, where he worked as a research engineer with Massey-Ferguson and wrote extensively about his experiences. His works include *Na rozdorizhzhiakh smerty* (At the Crossroads of Death, 1949), which was translated as *One of 15 Million* (1952); *Ia proshu slova* (I Ask to Speak, 1949); and *Dalekymy dorohamy* (Along Distant Paths, 1961), which was translated as *Stormy Road to Freedom* (1968) and reprinted as *Good-bye Siberia* (1976).

Prykhodko, Nadiia [Pryxod'ko, Nadija], b 27 March 1926 in Hoholiv, Brovary raion, Kiev oblast, d 24 March 1980. Poet. She wrote the poetry collections *Divocha pisnia* (A Maiden's Song, 1958), *Ranok v horakh* (Morning in the Mountains, 1960), *Zoriana balada* (A Stellar Ballad, 1972), and *Prolisok* (The Clearing, 1975) and five books of poetry for children.

Prykhodko, Petro [Pryxod'ko], b 13 January 1908 in Verbky, Pavlohrad county, Katerynoslav gubernia, d 11 January 1970 in Kiev. Literary scholar. He graduated from the pedagogical institute in Kherson in 1935 and completed graduate work at the Science Research Institute of Pedagogy of the Ukrainian SSR in 1938. From 1945 to 1962 he was a senior associate of the Shevchenko studies department of the Institute of Literature of the AN URSR (now ANU). He wrote books on the study of T. Shevchenko in secondary schools (1939), about Shevchenko's long poem *Son* (A Dream, 1957), and about Shevchenko and Ukrainian romanticism (1963), and articles on Shevchenko's poetry. He helped to prepare a guidebook to places in Ukraine pertaining to Shevchenko (1957) and was coeditor of the 1957 (vol 6) and 1963 (vol 1) editions of Shevchenko's works, the 1952–3 (vol 2) edition of I. Kotliarevsky's works, and the 1955–6 (vol 1) and 1964–7 (vols 1, 3, 6) editions of M. Vovchok's works.

Viktor Prykhodko

Antonina Prykhotko

Prykhodko, Viktor [Pryxod'ko], b 31 January 1886 in Kniazhpil, Kamianets-Podilskyi county, Podilia gubernia, d 6 February 1982 in New York. Lawyer and civic and cultural figure. After graduating from the law faculty of Kiev University (1912) he worked as court investigator at the Podilia circuit court. As head of the education department of the Podilia zemstvo in 1917, he Ukrainianized the gubernia's public school system. In 1918 and 1919 he was elected president of the gubernial zemstvo. After leaving Ukraine in 1920, he served in the UNR government-in-exile and was a lecturer at the Ukrainian Husbandry Academy in Poděbrady. In 1929 he proposed to convene an All-Ukrainian National Congress and to introduce a national tax among émigrés. In 1949 he emigrated to the United States, and thereafter he worked at the head office of the Ukrainian Congress Committee of America, for 10 years. Besides contributing articles to the Ukrainian press he published his memoirs as *Pid sontsem Podillia* (Under Podilia's Sun, 1927; repr 1931 and 1948).

Prykhodko, Yevhen [Pryxod'ko, Jevhen], b 24 December 1901 in Yarmolyntsi, Proskuriv county, Podilia gubernia, d 4 August 1965 in New York. Geologist and civic figure. He studied in Kamianets-Podilskyi and at the Faculty of Law of Kharkiv University. He was arrested and sentenced to death by Bolshevik forces in 1919. He was freed through the intercession of his friends, and left for Czechoslovakia, where he studied geodesy at the Prague Polytechnical Institute. He later emigrated to the United States and became the US representative of the Ukrainian National Rada's executive branch.

Prykhodkova, Yelyzaveta [Pryxod'kova, Jelyzaveta], b 19 August 1892 in Kharkiv, d 12 August 1975 in Kharkiv. Physiologist; corresponding member of the AN URSR (now ANU) from 1951. She graduated from the Women's Medical Institute in Kharkiv (1918) and worked there, as a department head from 1946, and at the Ukrainian Scientific

Research Institute for Experimental Endocrinology (1919–48). She researched organ, tissue, and internal secretion gland extracts, the adaptive trophic role of the nervous system, and the stimulative effect of acetylcholine.

Prykhotko, Antonina [Pryxot'ko], b 26 April 1906 in Piatigorsk, Stavropol krai, Subcaucasia. Physicist; AN URSR (now ANU) full member since 1964. A graduate of the Leningrad Polytechnical Institute (1930), until 1941 she worked at the ANU Physical-Technical Institute in Kharkiv. There she investigated spectra of solid oxygen, nitrogen, methane, and other gases at temperatures close to absolute zero and contributed to the understanding of corresponding crystalline structures. From 1944 until her retirement she worked at the ANU Institute of Physics in Kiev, where she also served as director (1965–70). There she contributed to the understanding of the role of excitons in molecular crystals, discovered and investigated the exciton luminescence of these crystals, and collaborated in research that led to the discovery of biexcitons and polyexcitons.

Prykhylny, Amvrosii [Pryxyl'nyj, Amvrosij], b ? in Italy, d 1641. Architect of Italian origin. P. di *Barbone's assistant from 1588, he became a member of the Lviv builders' guild in 1591 and was elected often to its presidency. He took part in the construction of the *Dormition Church in Lviv (1591–1631) and the buildings of the Lviv Dormition Brotherhood. After P. Romanus's death he completed the Bernardine church in Lviv (1630). He also built his own residence in Lviv and collaborated in building St Lazarus's Roman Catholic Church in Lviv, the Ostrozky family's castle in Stare Selo, near Lviv, and the Roman Catholic church in Zhovkva (1605). His style is a blend of the Italian Renaissance with indigenous architectural motifs.

Pryliuk, Dmytro [Pryljuk], b 8 November 1918 in Bozhykivtsi, Letychiv county, Podilia gubernia, d 22 September 1987. Writer and journalist. He graduated from the journalism institute in Kharkiv in 1941, worked as editor of the newspapers of Poltava, Kiev, and Vinnytsia oblasts, and of the CC CPU daily *Kolhospne selo*, and became dean of the journalism faculty and director of the chair of the theory and practice of the Soviet press at Kiev University (1965–82). Most of his literary works deal with contemporary Ukrainian rural life. He is the author of the essay collections *Uroky* (Lessons, 1956) and *Selo na nashii Ukraïni* (The Village in Our Ukraine, 1961); the short novels *Selo, a v n'omu liudy* (A Village, and in It Are People, 1976) and *Zemnosyly* (Earthly Powers, 1979); the novels *De ty, dole?* (Where Are You, Fate?, 1971), *Povnokolossia* (Full Ears of Grain, 1977), and, a trilogy, *Vidhomin* (The Echo, 1979–83); three books of humor and feuilletons; two books of ballads; two story collections; and three books on the theory and practice of journalism.

Pryluka or **Pryluky**. III-13. A city (1989 pop 72,000) on the Udai River and a raion center in Chernihiv oblast. It was first mentioned, as a fortress, in the Hypatian Chronicle under the year 1092. From 1362 Pryluka belonged to the Grand Duchy of Lithuania, and from 1569, to the Polish Commonwealth. After B. Khmelnytsky's uprising it became a regiment center of the Hetman state (1654–1781)

St Nicholas's Church in Pryluka (1720)

and then a county center of Chernihiv vicegerency (1781–1802) and Poltava gubernia (1802–1925). It was granted the rights of *Magdeburg law in 1783. Before the industrialization drive of the 1930s Pryluka's main occupations were farming and tobacco processing. Today the city is an industrial and communications (railway) center. Its chief industries are machine building, chemicals and building-materials manufacturing, woodworking, textile manufacturing, and food processing. Its architectural monuments of the baroque period include the Cathedral of the Transfiguration (1705–16), the regiment treasury (1708), the Church of the Savior (1717), St Nicholas's Church (1720), and the Church of the Nativity (18th century).

Pryluka regiment. An administrative territory and military formation of the Hetman state. It was formed in 1648 at the outbreak of B. Khmelnytsky's uprising but was soon greatly reduced in size. In 1649 it had 20 companies, with a total of 2,100 registered Cossacks. It suffered heavy losses in M. Pushkar's revolt and the Cossack-Muscovite War (1657–9). In the 1720s it consisted of only eight companies, with 3,300 Cossacks and 7,000 peasants. By the end of the century the regiment had 11 companies and a population of 69,200, including 10,900 elect Cossacks and 9,700 Cossack helpers. A number of its colonels served on the general officer staff of the Hetmanate, and one of them, P. *Doroshenko (1657–9), became hetman of Right-Bank Ukraine. The regiment also spawned two traitors, whom Peter I rewarded for their treason with a colonelcy: I. Nos (1708–14), who led the Russians into Hetman I. Mazepa's capital, Baturyn, and H. *Galagan (1714–39), who helped them capture the Sich.

Prymak, Fedir, b 23 April 1899 in Tatarivka (now Sofiivka), Nizhen county, Chernihiv gubernia, d 9 September 1981 in Kiev. Internal medicine specialist. A graduate of the Kiev Medical Institute (1924, doctorate 1936), he served as a professor and head of the internal medicine department at the Lviv Medical Institute (1940–1) and as head of the Department of the Propaedeutics for Internal Diseases at the Kiev Medical Institute (1952–73). Among his publications are works on tuberculosis, angiology, hypertonia, wound sepsis, and hypoxia.

Prymak, Thomas [Pryjmak, Toma], b 10 April 1948 in Winnipeg. Historian. Since graduating from the University of Toronto (PH D, 1984) he has taught at the universities of Saskatchewan, Toronto, and McMaster. He is the author of *Mykhailo Hrushevsky: The Politics of National Culture* (1987) and *Maple Leaf and Trident: The Ukrainian Canadians during the Second World War* (1988).

Prymorske [Prymors'ke]. VII-17. A city (1989 pop 13,500) on the Obytochna River and a raion center in Zaporizhia oblast. In 1821 the village of Obytochne was converted into the town of Nohaiske. In spite of its potential as a port, it did not develop; by 1896 its population was only 4,100. In 1964 it was renamed, and in 1967 it was granted city status. Most of its inhabitants are occupied in agriculture; only 19 percent work in industry. The main industries are metalworking and building-materials manufacturing.

Prymorske [Prymors'ke]. VI-18. A town smt (1986 pop 10,800) on the Kalmiius River near Mariiupil, Donetske oblast. It was founded as a Greek colony called Sartana in 1780. In 1938 it attained smt status, and in 1946 it was renamed. Today it is administered by the council of Illich raion of Mariiupil city.

Prymorskyi [Prymors'kyj]. VIII-16. A town smt (1982 pop 12,800) on Teodosiia Bay near Teodosiia, Crimea oblast. It was founded in 1952 and is administered by the Teodosiia municipal council.

Prypiat [Prypjat']. II-11. A city (1986 pop 45,000) on the Prypiat River in Chornobyl raion, Kiev oblast. It was founded in 1979 to house the workers of the adjacent Chornobyl nuclear power station. Prypiat was granted city status in 1980. On the morning of 27 April 1986, following the nuclear accident at the station the day before, the city was evacuated. Since then it has been turned into a ghost town.

Prypiat River [Prypjat']. The major right-bank tributary of the Dnieper River. It is 761 km long (the second-longest tributary of the Dnieper, next to the Desna) and drains a basin area of 121,000 sq km (the largest in the Dnieper watershed). Most of it passes through Ukrainian ethnographic territory and its borderland in Belarus. Its upper reaches (185 km) and lower reaches (80 km) as well as 57 percent of its basin are in Ukraine (nearly 75 percent is in Ukrainian ethnographic territory). The river flows slowly, meandering through wide floodplains, frequently breaking into and rejoining branches. In its upper course it is 30–40 m wide, in the middle, 200–250 m wide, and in the lower, 200–500 m wide. The large homogeneous floodplain of the river consists of oxbows, marshes, bush, and coppice. The river freezes in mid-December and thaws in late March. Its average annual discharge is 14.5 cu km, 60 percent of its flow coming in the spring. Spring floods last well into the summer. Its principal tributaries include (right bank) the Horyn, the Slovechna, the Stokhid, the Stvyha, the Styr, the Ubort, the Uzh, the Vyzhivka, the Turia, and the Zholon rivers, and (left bank) the Lan, the Pyna, the Ptsich, the Sluch, and the Yaselda rivers. The Prypiat is connected to the Vistula River by the Dnieper-Buh Canal. It is used for shipping, log rafting, and water supply. The river contains a wide variety of fish (pike, carp, perch, catfish, bream, and others). The main centers along the river include Pynske, Petrykiv, Mozyr, and Chornobyl.

Prypkhan, Roman [Prypxan], b 6 September 1919 in Stanyslaviv, Galicia. Psychiatrist. After completing his medical studies at Poznań, Lviv, and Vienna (MD, 1943) universities he specialized in surgery at the Regensburg International Refugee Organization Hospital (1946–8). He emigrated to Venezuela (1948); there he was a professor of psychopathology at Carabobo University, opened his own psychiatric clinic, and was president of the central Ukrainian organization in Venezuela (1956–8). His scientific publications include papers on balantidiasis, chronic schizophrenia, and the drug treatment of mental illnesses.

Prysetsky, Ivan [Prysec'kyj], b 1854, d 1911. Civic activist in the Poltava region. He collaborated with V. *Malovany and Ye. Borysov on the draft of a social and political program, which was published by M. Drahomanov as *Volnyi soiuz/Vil'na spilka* (A Free Union, 1884). He was arrested upon returning from abroad in 1883 and exiled to Siberia. He later served as a Ukrainian caucus member in the First Russian State Duma.

Hryhorii Pryshedko: *In the Cosmic Orchestra* (1971)

Pryshedko, Hryhorii [Pryšed'ko, Hryhorij], b 9 June 1927 in Dnipropetrovske, d 21 August 1978 in Kiev. Mosaicist and painter. A graduate of the Dnipropetrovske Art School (1951), together with his wife, H. *Zubchenko, he created the large-scale wall mosaics in Kiev at the ANU Sports Palace, the ANU instututes of Roentgenology and Oncology Nuclear Research, and Cybernetics. Most of the mosaics are stylized and incorporate folk-art motifs.

Prystai, Oleksa [Prystaj], b 1863 in Truskavets, Drohobych county, Galicia, d 17 January 1944 in Slowsburg, New York. Catholic priest and writer. In 1907 he emigrated to the United States, where he did missionary work among Ukrainian coal miners. He wrote the memoirs Z

Truskavtsia u svit khmaroderiv (From Truskavets to the World of Skyscrapers, 1933).

Khoma Prystupa

Prystupa, Khoma (Toma), b 3 November 1895 in Zadviria, Peremyshliany county, Galicia, d mid-1930s. Volhynian Communist politician. An agronomist educated in Kiev, he worked in Lutske, was active in the Spilka cooperative and the Prosvita society, and edited the Lutske newspaper *Ukraïns'ke zhyttia* (1922–4). In 1922–7 he served as a deputy from Volhynia voivodeship to the Polish Sejm. In 1924 he left the independentist Ukrainian Parliamentary Representation and joined the *Ukrainian Social Democratic party, which was controlled by the underground *Communist Party of Western Ukraine (KPZU). That same year he was elected to the CC KPZU. In 1927 he emigrated to Soviet Ukraine, where he joined the CP(B)U and worked at the People's Commissariat of Industry. He disappeared in the Stalinist terror.

Pryvillia [Pryvillja]. IV-19. A city (1989 pop 11,800) on the Donets River in Lysychanske raion, Luhanske oblast. It is administered by the Lysychanske city council. It was founded in 1695 by runaway serfs and was first called Asesorske. Then it was known as Piata Rota and Pryvilne; it became Pryvillia in 1938. In 1963 it was granted city status. Its economy depends on its coal mine and enrichment plant.

Pryvilne. A multi-occupational site near the present-day village of Pryvilne, Chervonoarmiiske raion, Zaporizhia oblast. Excavated in 1929, the site produced evidence of a Neolithic camping ground and a 3rd- to 5th-century *Cherniakiv culture settlement.

Przegląd Krajowy (Homeland Review). A Polish semimonthly political, literary, and scholarly journal published in Kiev in 1909 (a total of 14 issues) by a coalition of Polonized Ukrainian and Polish gentry in Right-Bank Ukraine. It promoted Polish-Ukrainian rapprochement and recognized the territorial and democratic demands of the Ukrainian national movement. The publisher was L. Radziejowski and the de facto editor was V. Lypynsky, who was assisted by B. Yaroshevsky and Yu. Yankovsky. Among the contributors were L. Wasilewski, S. Yefremov, V. Domanytsky, and B. Lepky.

Przemyśl. See Peremyshl.

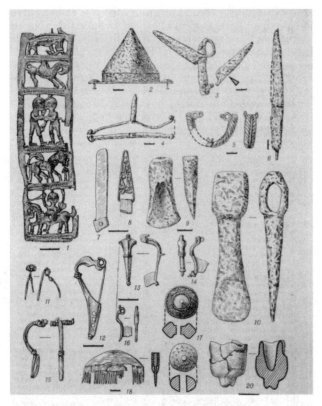

Artifacts of the Przeworsk culture

Przeworsk culture. A prehistoric culture of the 1st century BC to 4th century AD found in central and southern Poland as well as parts of western Ukraine. It is named after an archeological site in Poland. The people of this culture engaged primarily in agriculture and animal husbandry, although they were also adept at ironworking and pottery (they began using wheels in the 3rd century). They established settlements along rivers and lived in surface dwellings with hearths or ovens inside and storage pits outside. Trade with the Romans brought them coins, bronze, glass, red lacquered tableware, and personal adornments. The common burial practice was cremation, with remains placed into pits or urns. The influence of this culture was felt in Ukraine mainly along the Sian and Buh river routes. Most scholars believe that the people of the Przeworsk culture were the proto-Slavic *Venedi.

Przyłęcki, Stanisław, b 1805 in Arekhauka, Vitsebsk gubernia, Belarus, d 1 August 1866 in Wilanów, Poland. Polish librarian, bibliographer, and historian. He studied at Lviv University and was custodian of the Ossolineum Institute library in Lviv (1832–7), librarian of G. Pawlikowski's library in Medyka, near Peremyshl (1839–44), secretary of the Galician Husbandry Society in Lviv (1845–62), and editor of its weekly *Pamiętnik Gospodarski* and its serial *Rozprawy* (29 vols, 1846–61). He compiled Polish bibliographies, wrote works on bibliology and library science, and published many works he found in various archives, including a volume of materials on 17th-century Ukrainian affairs, *Ukrainne sprawy* (1842), and, for the first time, W. Potocki's epic poem *Wojna Chocimska* (The Khotyn War, 1850). From 1862 he was librarian of A. Potocki's library in Wilanów.

Psalms. The sacred songs, hymns, and laments collected in the *Psalter. After the Christianization of Ukraine they were cited in literary works (from the 11th century), used in teaching, sung in unison by alternating choirs or read during liturgies, and read at funeral services. Various free musical and poetic renditions of the Psalms (by anonymous authors and by D. Tuptalo) became widespread in Ukraine from the 16th century and were published in collections (eg, *Bohohlasnyk* [1790]). As 'spiritual songs' they remained part of the *lirnyks' repertoire until the 20th century. Parodies of them were composed and performed by *itinerant tutors in the 17th and 18th centuries and by students living in bursas in the 19th century. H. Skovoroda, P. Hulak-Artemovsky, T. Shevchenko, P. Kulish, S. Rudansky, I. Franko, and other 18th- and 19th-century poets imitated or paraphrased the Psalms. The Psalms were translated by M. Maksymovych (1859). They have been set to music by M. Dyletsky, A. Vedel, M. Berezovsky, D. Bortniansky, M. Leontovych, O. Koshyts, M. Haivoronsky, P. Kozytsky, and other Ukrainian composers.

Psalter (*psaltyr*). A collection of 150 lyrical poems and hymns (Psalms) that constitutes an important book of the Old Testament. The Psalms are widely used in the liturgies of the Christian churches, including the Ukrainian church. They were first translated into Church Slavonic by SS Cyril and Methodius and were disseminated through Ukraine after the adoption of Christianity. The earliest renditions of the Psalter were particularly notable for their ambiguous passages and outcries against the Jewish faith. By the 11th century the Psalter was being used in fortunetelling, with expository passages commonly accompanying each Psalm (in a 'speculative' or *hadatelnyi* tone) advising people how to act in various situations. The Psalter was a popular work and one of the first items to be published in Ukrainian and Belarusian by F. Skoryna (1517), I. Fedorovych (1570), and others.

For centuries the Psalter was used as a school text. It was also used for reading over the dead or infirm. It has been a common source of quotation in Ukrainian literature from as early as the 11th century up to modern times.

In the 20th century, new translations of the Psalms have been attempted by several authors, including I. Puliui (1903, using Hebrew sources), A. Bachynsky (1903), Ya. Levytsky (1925), M. Kobryn (1936), I. Ohiienko (1962), and I. Khomenko (1963).

Pshenychny, Borys [Pšenyčnyj], b 24 April 1937 in Kiev. Mathematician; corresponding member of the AN URSR (now ANU) since 1985. Since graduating from Lviv University (1959) he has worked for the ANU Institute of Cybernetics. His research contributions are in the fields of mathematical programming, theory of differential games, computational methods of optimization, and theory of optimal control.

Pshepiurska-Ovcharenko, Mariia [Pšepjurs'ka-Ovčarenko, Marija], b 19 June 1909 in Tarnawka, Przeworsk county, Galicia. Slavic philologist; member of the Shevchenko Scientific Society since 1952 and the Ukrainian Academy of Arts and Sciences in the US. A graduate of the universities of Cracow (M PHIL, 1934) and Prague (PH D, 1945), she taught Ukrainian in gymnasiums in Peremyshl (1934) and Lviv (1934–9). From 1939 to 1941 she was an as-

Mariia Pshepiurska-Ovcharenko

Yaroslav Pstrak (self-portrait, 1913)

sociate of the Lviv branch of the AN URSR (now ANU) Institute of Linguistics and taught at the Lviv Teachers' and Medical institutes. She taught at Ukrainian DP camps in Bavaria (1945–9). After emigrating to the United States (1949) she taught at various colleges and at the Ukrainian Catholic University in Rome. She is the author of a book on the *Sian dialects (1938), a Ukrainian school reader (3 edns, 1955, 1959, 1962), the booklet *Gogol (Hohol) and Osmachka* (1969), and articles on Ukrainian language and literature.

Pshepiursky, Andrii [Pšepjurs'kyj, Andrij], b December 1874 in Yavoriv, Galicia, d 1947 in Stariava, Mostyska county, Galicia. Greek Catholic priest and civic leader. After completing his studies at the Peremyshl Seminary (1901) he served as parish priest in Tarnavka and as chaplain (1915–17) in the Ukrainian Sich Riflemen. He was appointed to Stariava parish in 1925 and organized a Prosvita circle, a co-operative, and a Luh sports club in the Mostyska region. He was active in the Ukrainian National Democratic Alliance and sat on its Central Committee.

Pshysh River [Pšyš]. A left-bank tributary of the Kuban River. It is 253 km long and drains a basin area of 2,000 sq km. It flows along the northern slope of the Caucasus Mountains. At the start of its course it is a narrow river flowing through a deep valley, but it broadens when it reaches the Kuban Lowland.

Psol, Hlafira [Ps'ol] (married name: Dunina-Borkovska), b 24 October 1823 in Psolivka, Myrhorod county, Poltava gubernia, d 26 April 1886. Self-taught painter; sister of O. *Psol. In 1843 she met T. Shevchenko in Yahotyn and received his advice on painting. She did portraits of N. Repnin, V. Repnina (1839), and Shevchenko.

Psol, Oleksandra [Ps'ol], b 1817 in Psolivka (now Psilske), Myrhorod county, Poltava gubernia, d 27 October 1887 in Moscow. Poet; sister of H. *Psol. She lived and studied in Yahotyn, with the family of N. Repnin, where she met T. Shevchenko (1843–4). She later corresponded with him and sent him her poetry when he was in exile. Shevchenko favorably judged some of her early poetry (eg, 'Sviachena voda' [Holy Water]). Her poetic cycle 'Try

sl'ozy divchyny' (Three Tears of a Girl) was published in the almanac *Khata* (1960). The cycle included the poems 'Zaplakala Ukraïna' (Ukraine Began to Cry), 'Oi, koly b ia holos soloveika mala' (Oh, If I Had the Voice of a Nightingale), and 'Viie viter nad Kyievom' (The Wind Blows over Kiev). Her poetry is marked by patriotic motifs (eg, protests over the dissolution of the Cyril and Methodius Brotherhood). One poem, 'Ne pytai ty moïkh pisen'' (Don't Ask My Songs), was erroneously attributed to Shevchenko and was published in some editions of his *Kobzar*.

The Psol River valley

Psol River [Ps'ol] (also Psel and Pslo). A left-bank tributary of the Dnieper River. It is 717 km long and drains a basin area of 22,800 sq km. It originates along the western edge of the Central Upland in Kursk and Belgorod oblasts and passes through Sumy and Poltava oblasts before emptying into the Dnieper's Dniprodzerzhynske Reservoir, near Kremenchuk. The river valley is fairly wide (10–15 km) in its lower reaches, and its right bank tends to be higher than its left. The Psol freezes over from late November to mid-March. The major centers along the river include Oboian, Sumy, and Hadiache. Its major tributaries in Ukraine include the Hrun-Tashan (left bank) and the Khorol (right bank) rivers.

Pstrak, Yaroslav, b 24 March 1878 in Hvizdets, Kolomyia county, Galicia, d 1916 in Kharkiv. Painter and graphic artist. He studied at the Cracow and Munich (1895–9) academies of art. From 1900 he lived in Lviv and Pokutia. He did paintings with biblical subjects, such as *Christ on the Mount of Olives* (1900), *Moses, Last Supper,* and *Christ with Angels*; many portraits, landscapes, and genre paintings, particularly of the Hutsuls, such as *Hutsul Girl with a Candle, Quarrier* (1904), *Vengeance* (1907), and *On a Summer Day*; and historical canvases, such as *Cossack with a Captured Janissary* and *Oleksa Dovbush.* He illustrated I. Franko's *Zakhar Berkut* (1902), A. Krushelnytsky's reader (1905), N. Gogol's *Taras Bul'ba* (1907), and the satirical magazines *Komar, Osa,* and *Zerkalo* (1900–8). A book about Pstrak by M. Figol was published in Kiev in 1966.

Pstruch, Mysail [Pstruč, Mysajil], b and d ? Orthodox metropolitan. The archbishop of Smolensk (1445–74), he was elevated to the office of metropolitan of Kiev (1475–80) without the consent of the Patriarch of Constantinople. At around the same time, the patriarch appointed his own metropolitan, Spyridon, who was turned away when he set off to assume his post, and ended his years in Muscovy. Pstruch is known for a letter he wrote to Pope Sixtus IV in 1476 that praised the pontiff lavishly, suggested a desire for closer co-operation between Catholics and Orthodox Christians, and then pointedly criticized the Catholic clergy for its infringements on the rights of the local Orthodox population. A slightly modified version of the letter was presented in 1605 by the Uniate metropolitan I. Potii as evidence of a long-standing desire by the Orthodox population to unite with Rome.

Psychiatric hospitals, special. The main difference between regular and special psychiatric hospitals (Ukrainian slang: *psykhushky*) is that the former fell under the jurisdiction of the Ministry of Health whereas the latter were under the direct jurisdiction of the *MVD. In the special psychiatric hospitals (SPH) security factors were given priority over medical considerations, and instances of abuse of *psychiatry for political purposes were common. A person could be sentenced, without right of appeal, to 'compulsory psychiatric treatment' for 'anti-Soviet agitation and propaganda' (Article 70 of the USSR), 'circulation of fabrications known to be false which defame the Soviet state and social system' (Article 190-1), 'betrayal of the Fatherland' (Article 64), or 'illegally leaving the country and illegally entering the USSR' (Article 83).

As late as the 1980s there were SPH operating in the USSR, with two new SPH known to have been established in 1972 (see table). The most notorious SPH was the Sichevka. Female patients consigned to involuntary psychiatric treatment were invariably taken to Kazan. One SPH was located in Ukraine, in Dnipropetrovske; like most others it was housed in a former prison. Until the mid-1950s SPH were officially classified as prison institutions or places of detention. They were surrounded by walls as well as barbed wire and guarded by military personnel with dogs. Personnel, including hospital directors, heads of departments, and many of the psychiatrists (who were not obliged to tell their full names to the inmates or their relatives), were officers in the MVD. Many sanitary orderlies were convicts recruited from the penitentiary system, and they were granted the authority to maintain discipline among patients.

The patients of the SPH were committed there by the

Special psychiatric hospitals in the former USSR

Conventional name	Town or city	Oblast	Republic
Alma-Ata SPH	Talgar	Alma-Ata	Kazakhstan
Arsenalnaia* SPH	Leningrad	–	Russia
Blagoveshchensk SPH	Blagoveshchensk	Amur	Russia
Cherniakhovsk* SPH	Cherniakhovsk	Kaliningrad	Russia
Dnepropetrovsk* SPH	Dnipropetrovske	–	Ukraine
Kazan* SPH	Kazan	–	Tatar ASSR
Kzyl-Orda SPH	Kzyl-Orda	–	Kazakhstan
Minsk SPH	Minsk	–	Belorussia
Mahiliou SPH	Mahiliou	–	Belorussia
Orel* SPH	Orel	–	Russia
Smolensk SPH	Smolensk	–	Russia
Sichevka* SPH	Sichevka	Smolensk	Russia
Tashkent SPH	Tashkent	–	Tadzhikistan
Volgograd SPH	Dvorianskoe	Volgograd	Russia

*Major SPH

courts, but there was no legal code governing conditions of detention, nor any set limit on the length of a person's confinement, as there is for prisons. Biannual commissions composed of the administration and medical staff of the SPH recommended a person's release or transfer to another institution, which then was considered by the courts. Abuses often occurred at the time of release, with either the extension of compulsory confinement or the reservation of the right to re-examine without warrant at any time and to recommend further treatment. The anonymity of the psychiatrists and the irrefutability of their decisions, the administration of potent drugs, such as sulfadiazine, haloperidol, and insulin, not for medical purposes but as a form of punishment, and almost total isolation from society – either singly or in combination, these factors have abetted violations of the *human rights of inmates in the system of SPH in the USSR.

A partial list of Ukrainians who underwent involuntary psychiatric treatment in SPH includes P. *Grigorenko, L. *Pliushch, V. and V. Rybak, V. Kolyshenko, V. Tiurychev, Y. *Terelia, M. Valkov, V. *Ruban, I. Medvedev, I. Marynchenko, L. Biloborodov, V. Kaliuzhny, V. Zinoviev, M. Hershkan, V. Khailo, K. Striltsev, V. Spynenko, P. *Skochok, M. Ozerny, I. *Lytvynov, A. Mykhailenko, V. Kolomiitsev, D. Kutsil, V. Lutskiv, V. Polynok (Poliinyk), A. *Lupynis, V. *Rafalsky, Yu. Osmanov, I. Khomiak, V. *Klebanov, M. Breslavsky, O. Bondarenko, O. Borovsky, O. Cherep, V. Dmytrenko, F. Dvoretsky, I. Hreshchuk, O. Ivanytsky, M. Klishch, A. Kochby, V. Korol, O. Nozhak, I. Osadchuk, V. Siry, F. Sydenko, V. Synyhovsky, I. Steba, M. Yakubenko, A. Yavorsky, and Kalush (first name unknown).

The psychiatrists S. Gluzman of Kiev and A. Koriagin of Kharkiv were arrested, sentenced, and incarcerated in corrective labor camps for resisting the practice of declaring dissidents mentally ill. Following the nuclear explosion at the Chornobyl Atomic Energy Station in 1986, some protesters were sent to SPH for 'radiophobia.'

The International Independent Research Center of Psychiatry in Moscow, established in 1988 under the aegis of the International Human Rights Association (later becoming independent), in two years reviewed the cases of 2,000 persons sentenced to penal psychiatry and obtained the release and *rehabilitation of many of them. The center experienced repressions and harassment, especially from the KGB, and was officially shut down in early 1991 after M. Gorbachev granted special powers to the KGB to investigate organizations.

A decree concerning the conditions and procedure for psychiatric treatment was ratified by the Presidium of the Supreme Soviet and came into effect in March 1988. The All-Union Society of Psychiatrists and Addictologists was reinstated in 1989 as a member of the World Psychiatric Association after resigning to avoid expulsion in 1983. As of 1989 not a single SPH had been closed down, and the practice of abusing psychology for political purposes in the SPH did not cease until the demise of the USSR.

BIBLIOGRAPHY
Abuse of Psychiatry for Political Repression in the Soviet Union (New York 1973)
Grigorenko, P. Mysli sumasshedshego (Amsterdam 1973)
Amnesty International. 'Special Psychiatric Hospitals,' in Prisoners of Conscience in the USSR: Their Treatment and Conditions (London 1975)
Bloch, S.; Reddaway, P. Psychiatric Terror: How Soviet Psychiatry Is Used to Suppress Dissent (New York 1977)
Fireside, H. Soviet Psychoprisons (New York 1979)
Bloch, S.; Reddaway, P. Soviet Psychiatric Abuse: The Shadow over World Psychiatry (London 1984)
                                                            P. Dzul

Psychiatry. A branch of medicine that deals with disorders of thought, feeling, and behavior (see also *Psychology). The first research on psychiatry in the Russian Empire was done by Ukrainians in the second half of the 18th century – K. Yahelsky, N. Kviatkovsky, M. Kozlovsky, S. Uspensky, and O. *Maslovsky. The first textbook on psychiatry was published in Kharkiv by P. *Butkovsky in 1834. The first journal of psychiatry, Arkhiv psikhiatrii, nevrologii i sudebnoi psikhopatologii, was published by P. *Kovalevsky in Kharkiv in 1883. The journal Voprosy nervno-psikhicheskoi meditsiny was published in Kiev (1896–1905). In the 20th century, departments of psychiatry were established in Kiev (P. *Nechai, V. Hakkebush), Odessa (Ye. Shevalov), and Dnipropetrovske (D. Frank) universities. Ukrainian scientists active in the field included Ye. Kopystynsky, O. *Yushchenko, V. *Protopopov, T. Yudin, Ya. Frumkin, and N. Tatarenko. In the 1920s, psychoneurological institutes were founded in Kharkiv (1921), Kiev (1922), and Odessa (1930). The journal Sovremennaia psikhonevrologiia, later renamed Sovetskaia psikhiatriia, was published from 1925, first in Kiev and later in Kharkiv. At present working in the field of psychiatry in Ukraine are the Scientific Research Institute of Neurology and Psychiatry in Kharkiv and the Department of Psychiatry and Pathology of the Central Nervous System at the ANU *Institute of Physiology in Kiev. Departments of psychiatry and neurology also exist at all medical institutes, including those for the upgrading of physicians. Psychiatry in the former USSR was divided into independent branches of child, judicial, army, labor, narcotics, organizational, and geriatric psychology, among others. Research had been co-ordinated by the USSR Academy of Medical Sciences and by the Ukrainian SSR Ministry of Health.

The Ukrainian Society of Psychiatrists and Neurologists was part of the All-Union Society of Psychiatrists and Neurologists, which belonged to the World Psychiatric Association (WPA) until 1983. In 1983 the All-Union Society of Psychiatrists and Neurologists resigned from the WPA to avoid expulsion for political abuse of psychiatry in its special *psychiatric hospitals in the former USSR.

Despite being reinstated in the WPA in 1989, the All-Union Society of Psychiatrists and Addictologists (renamed in 1988) was firmly opposed to any kind of reform of psychiatry in the former USSR and was still headed by the old guard of Soviet psychiatrists (including G. Morozov, M. Vartanian, N. Zharikov, and A. Churkin).

BIBLIOGRAPHY
Protopopov, V.; Polishchuk, I. 'Rozvytok psykhiatrii v URSR,' in Dosiahnennia okhorony zdorov'ia v URSR (Kiev 1958)
Frumkin, Ia.; Voronkov, H.; Shevchuk, I. Psikhiatriia (Kiev 1977)
Cohen, D. Soviet Psychiatry (1989)
                                                            P. Dzul

Psychology. In Ukraine psychology was an integral part of the study of *philosophy beginning in the Princely era; it did not constitute a scientific discipline in itself until the mid-19th century. In his theological and philosophical works Nicephorus, a 12th-century Kievan metropolitan, set out a conception of the dual (corporeal and spiritual) nature of a human being, analyzed the basic principles of will, emotion, and intellect, and examined the function of the five sensory faculties. Such theological and philosophical thinking about psychological problems disappeared after the Mongol invasions of the mid-13th century. The question of the dualism of human nature was taken up again in the 16th century in the philosophical works of I. Vyshensky. At the Kievan Mohyla College (later the Kievan Mohyla Academy) a course in psychology was taught by I. Gizel. L. Baranovych and I. Galiatovsky wrote on psychology with reference to the philosophical works of Aristotle. Reviews (by P. Pelekh) of the Latin text of psychology lectures at the academy (17th–18th centuries) suggest that the professors were knowledgeable in contemporary psychological theory. T. Prokopovych was an adherent of the theory of human duality. H. Skovoroda's philosophical system stressed the need to 'discover oneself.' Devoting considerable attention to the 'microcosmos' of individuals and their earthly concerns, he broke with the categorical monistic conception of the invisible spiritual and the visible corporeal.

In Ukraine the first psychophysical parallelism in psychology appeared in the works of Ya. Kozelsky, who taught that the actions of the human spirit are connected to the neurophysiological structure of the organism. He defended sensualism and sought to prove that knowledge is derived from the senses. The sensualism of I. Rizhsky continued the materialist trend in philosophy. Believing in the indissolubility of the sensory and rational elements, without which it is impossible to grasp the essence of phenomena, he investigated the influence of the material world on human consciousness. P. Lodii held similar sensualist convictions and sought to prove the spirit's dependence on the body (the psychic on the physical). More traditional views of the primacy of the psyche prevailed in the teachings of I. Hrynevych, O. *Novytsky, and P. Yurkevych at Kiev University. In opposition to H. Skovoroda's idealistic rationalism, Yurkevych stressed the importance of the emotional components in mental development and pedagogy.

In his textbook *Rukovodstvo k opytnoi psikhologii* (A Guide to Experimental Psychology, 1840) Novytsky, a proponent of psychophysical dualism, set out the neurophysiological basis of memory and focused on the active role of attention in perceptions. Severe restrictions placed on philosophical studies in Russian imperial universities in 1850 halted the development of psychological sciences. Novytsky's successors were I. Skvortsov (from 1850), S. Hohotsky (1851–86), and O. Kozlov (1876–87), who returned to the concept of rational psychology as a philosophical discipline. In *Mysl' i iazyk* (Thought and Language, 1862) O. Potebnia examined the interaction of thought and language from a psycholinguistic point of view and claimed that concepts cannot be formulated without words and that 'consciousness cannot be conjured out of nothing.'

Experimental psychology in Ukraine was initiated by the famous physiologist I. Sechenov, who worked at Odessa University (1871–6). He had a profound influence on subsequent research in reflexology. In the 1880s his successor, P. *Kovalevsky, established the first psychological research laboratory in Ukraine, at Kharkiv University's clinic of psychic and nervous diseases. N. *Lange established a similar laboratory at Odessa University in 1895. Lange sought to reconcile traditional psychophysical dualism with reflexology.

G. Chelpanov, a Russian philosopher and a professor at Kiev University (1892–1907), was the first to conduct psychological seminars and practical workshops with students. He set up the first experimental laboratory in Kiev and collected much valuable psychological data. V. *Zenkovsky followed in Chelpanov's footsteps and sought to reconcile idealistic views on the nature of the psyche with experiential learning. I. *Sikorsky, one of the first in the world to apply experimental methods in researching child psychology, laid the groundwork for the field of developmental psychology.

In Western Ukraine before the Second World War, psychological studies were associated with the work of Polish scholars at Lviv University, particularly K. Twardowski, who established the first psychological laboratory there in 1901. The most notable of his Ukrainian students was S. *Balei. He published the first Ukrainian textbook on psychology in Western Ukraine, as well as numerous articles on developmental psychology and a psychological study of T. Shevchenko's work.

In the first few decades after the imposition of Soviet rule in Ukraine, psychology was subjected to rigid Party control, and developed exclusively as a branch of reflexology. The new definition entailed a shift from the tradition of idealism in psychology to materialism, imposed as the new orthodox science. General psychology began to disappear from the curriculum in schools, even as an area of research. In the Ukrainian SSR the center of studies in reflexology was the Ukrainian Scientific Research Institute of Pedagogy in Kharkiv. Its leading academician was V. *Protopopov, who considered psychology to be a superfluous discipline, although he acknowledged the existence of a 'subjective element of the personality.' The Kharkiv psychiatrist Ye. Popov and defectologist I. Sokoliansky completely denied the existence of a human psyche and consciousness and proposed that they were accumulated reflexological sets of the individual. O.

Zaluzhny expanded on that proposition to formulate a theory of the 'reflexology of collectives' on the basis that 'all social life is a reflex.' The journal *Ukraïns'kyi visnyk refleksolohiï ta eksperymental'noï pedahohiky* was published in Kharkiv in 1925–30. Psychologists in Ukraine were also interested in various aspects of educational psychology, mostly dealing with the problems of memory processes and the relationship between learning and maturation. Leading researchers of that time included P. *Zinchenko, who did pioneering work in perception, processing, and memory and established a psychological laboratory devoted to the investigation of memory; and O. *Zaporozhets, who did educational, psychological, and physiological research on the optimum chronological age for symbolic and abstract learning.

In Kiev a pedagogical institute was established by the psychiatrist A. *Volodymyrsky. He was one of the first in Ukraine to initiate experimental studies of psychological anomalies in children. K. Mokulsky taught reflexology at the Kiev Institute of People's Education.

In the 1930s there was a reaction against the unilateral mechanistic conception of humans as passive organisms whose behavior is determined by their physiology and environment. Reflexology was condemned as 'a vulgar attempt to biologize social phenomena.' Soviet psychologists, however, continued to maintain the primacy of physiology, recognizing only that the autonomy of the psyche was a characteristic of 'highly organized matter' which operated according to its own laws. Renewed emphasis was placed on the consciousness and on individual responsibility for behavior, in opposition to the previously held view of the complete modification of behavior by the environment. The approaches remained materialistic, however, in that they continued to deny the presence of an unchangeable soul and stressed the dynamic evolution of consciousness as a product of nature and history. In that regard psychology was hampered by its links to dialectical materialism and utilitarian considerations of social policy.

The return from reflexology to general psychology was argued by the noted psychological historian H. *Kostiuk, the director of the Institute of Psychology of the Ukrainian SSR in Kiev (from 1945) and head of the Ukrainian branch of the All-Union Association of Psychologists. From a position of materialistic monism he sought to explain consciousness as one of the characteristics of matter in the higher stages of development. He also supported the viewpoint that historical development determines the ontogenesis of human personality by biological and social means. D. Elkin, a department head at Odessa University from 1930, stressed the individuality of consciousness that is inherent in a physical subject.

Specialized research institutes were initially established in Kharkiv, including the Psychoneurological Scientific Research Institute (reorganized in 1937), the psychology division of the Scientific Research Institute of Pedagogy of the People's Commissariat of Education of the Ukrainian SSR, the Institute of Labor, and the Scientific Research Institute of Defectology. In those institutions attention was focused primarily on diseases or congenital defects that had a direct or indirect effect on the psyche.

Kiev began to gain importance as a research center in psychology in the 1940s. The first autonomous academic department of psychology was established in Kiev (1944). In 1945 the Institute of Psychology of the Ukrainian SSR was formed in Kiev to co-ordinate the work of Ukrainian researchers. The institute had departments of general psychology, child psychology, educational and polytechnic education psychology, professional development psychology, and special psychology. It published *Naukovi zapysky*, various thematic collections of works, and popular works. In 1959 a Ukrainian section of the Association of Soviet Psychologists at the Academy of Pedagogical Sciences of the RSFSR (later of the USSR) was established.

The most developed disciplines came to be child psychology and developmental psychology as well as the history of psychology (Kostiuk, V. Voitko, A. Hubko). Scientists in those fields included L. Balatska, P. Chamata (who edited a psychology text for pedagogical schools, 1954), T. Kosma (at the department of psychology at Kharkiv University, 1931–5), Kostiuk, O. Leontev, D. Nikolenko, and N. Vovchyk-Blakytna, as well as Zaporozhets and P. Zinchenko. Kostiuk and O. *Raievsky (head of the department of psychology at Kiev University from 1945) studied the philosophical and physiological bases of psychology. Raievsky also researched the history of psychology with P. Pelekh and the psychology of language with M. Zhinkin. Ye. Milerian researched the psychology of labor.

In Ukraine there was also an early interest in zoopsychology, among such researchers as Balei and M. Pargamin. The conceptual anthropomorphization of animals and mechanistic reflexological theories held that there were only quantitative differences between the psyches of animals and humans. Later theories proposed by A. Khilchenko, N. Ladygina-Kots, V. Protopopov, and H. Rohinsky held that animal psyches were established only biologically, whereas human consciousness was molded socially as well.

Of more specialized areas of research, the most notable include studies of the perception of time, particularly the influence of experience on the subjective deformation of perception of time (D. Elkin, T. Kozina, and V. Yaroshchuk), the psychology of mathematical problem solving (Yu. Moshbytsia), and the psychology of technical construction (B. Baieva). The formation of worldviews and individual self-awareness was researched by Chamata (1956). Raievsky studied the relation between the emergence of consciousness in early humans and its dependence on the physical environment, particularly social class.

Emigré Ukrainian psychology was initially centered in Prague, where Ya. Yarema, a professor at the Ukrainian Higher Pedagogical Institute, studied the problem of psychometry in schools and published a textbook on pedagogical psychology. O. Ivanov worked at the Psychotechnical Institute of the Masaryk Academy and as a lecturer (until 1945) at the Ukrainian Free University (UVU). Psychology gained importance as a discipline at the UVU after it was moved to Munich, where O. *Kulchytsky headed the department of psychology (from 1946). Kulchytsky believed in holistic psychology and pedagogical characterology. M. *Mishchenko taught experimental psychology at the UVU in 1946–9. In 1955 V. *Yaniv became director of its department in psychology. Yaniv studied the psychology of prisoners and the social trends among Ukrainians. The Munich school focused on the psychological characteristics of Ukrainians (ethnopsychology) and organized a number of thematic conferences with non-

Ukrainian scholars (Munich, 1953; Leuven, 1954). H. *Vashchenko also worked in the field of ethnopsychology (he published a survey of reflexological studies in the Ukrainian SSR), as did D. Chyzhevsky and I. Mirchuk. In the United States, B. *Tsymbalisty studied problems involving geometrical and optical illusions and was a director of psychology programs at the Jamesburg State Home for delinquents. I. Holowinsky published in the areas of mental retardation, learning disorders, and the history of psychology.

In the 1970s and 1980s in the Ukrainian SSR, developments in psychology continued to be hampered by Russification and Party control. The publications of psychologists were not allowed to deviate from official dogma, and doctoral degree programs in psychology at Soviet universities were approved only in 1968. Ukrainian psychologists were obliged to publish their papers in the Russian-language journals *Voprosy psikhologii* (est 1955) and *Defektologiia*; the Ukrainian-language pedagogical journal *Radians'ka shkola* (from 1945) contained articles of a descriptive, nonempirical nature.

The Institute of Psychology of the Ukrainian SSR expanded its mandate to include the area of programmed instruction, and established a laboratory to study the methodology of psychological research (1973). Ukrainian psychologists also continued their studies in perception and memory (H. Sereda, N. Venger, T. Zinchenko, V. Zinchenko), developmental psychology (L. Venger, Zaporozhets), personality psychology, and the history of psychology (Kostiuk). In 1988 Kostiuk's collected psychological works were published in Kiev. H. Sereda proposed the unity of short-term and long-term memory mechanisms (1970). T. Zinchenko formulated information processing and information search models, and V. Zinchenko suggested a functional model of information transformation in which memory mechanisms are arranged in a hierarchical sequence (1971). V. Zinchenko continues to publish in the area of developmental psychology (1991).

N. Venger investigated the perceptual characteristics of preschool children (ages 5–7). Venger distinguished between the sensory and intellectual aspects of the assimilation and systematization of the external properties of objects (1970). Soviet psychologists used a qualitative approach in assessing and evaluating cognitive skills, as opposed to the standardized quantitative psychometric tests accepted in the West. They rejected the idea that it is possible to measure intellectual potential independently of the conditions of experience and education. As well, there was a reluctance to acknowledge the existence of behavioral disorders with a primarily social etiology, such as social and emotional maladjustment and juvenile delinquency.

BIBLIOGRAPHY

Bauer, R. *The New Man in Soviet Psychology* (Cambridge, Mass 1952)

Kostiuk, H. (ed). *Psykholohiia* (Kiev 1955)

Kultschytzkyj, A. *Die Marxistisch-sowjetische Konzeption des Menschen im Lichte der westlichen Psychologie* (Munich 1956)

Vaščenko, H. 'Die materialistische Konzeption des Sowjetmenschen,' in *Proceedings of the Historical-Philological Section of the Shevchenko Scientific Society*, vol 2 (New York 1957)

Chamata, P. 'Psykholohichna nauka v URSR za 40 rr.,' *Naukovi zapysky Kyïvs'koho pedahohichnoho instytutu*, 28 (1958)

Chamata, P.; Opryshko, K.; Skrypchenko, O. *Bibliohrafichnyi dovidnyk prats' z psykholohiï za 40 rr. (1917–1957)* (Kiev 1958)

Narysy z istoriï vitchyznianoï psykholohiï kintsia XIX *i pochatku* XX *st.*
   (Kiev 1959)
Brozek, J.; Slobin, D. *Psychology in the* USSR: *An Historical Perspective* (White Plains, NY 1972)
Kostiuk, H. 'Razvitie pedagogicheskoi psikhologii v Ukrainskoi
   SSR,' *Voprosy psikhologii*, 1972, no. 5
Holowinsky, I. 'Contemporary Psychology in the Ukrainian SSR,'
   American Psychologist, 1978, no. 2
Hubko, A. 'Rol' Kievo-Mogilianskoi akademii v zarodzhenii
   psikhologicheskoi nauki na Ukraine,' *Voprosy psikhologii*, 1980,
   no. 1
Valsiner, J. *Developmental Psychology in the Soviet Union* (Bloomington, Ind 1988)

V. Yaniv

Mykhailo Ptukha

Ptukha, Mykhailo [Ptuxa, Myxajlo], b 7 November 1884 in Oster, Chernihiv gubernia, d 3 October 1961 in Kiev. Pioneering demographer and statistician; full member of the VUAN from 1920 and corresponding member of the USSR Academy of Sciences from 1943. While a gymnasium student he worked during the summers for the statistics section of the Chernihiv zemstvo bureau. He studied at St Petersburg University (1906–10) and abroad, notably in Berlin (1910–12) and London (1914–15). In 1913 he began teaching statistics at St Petersburg University. Ptukha moved to Kiev in 1918. In 1919 he organized the VUAN Demographic Institute (renamed the AN URSR [now ANU] Institute of Demography and Health Statistics in 1934), which he headed until its absorption by the ANU Institute of Economics in 1938. Ptukha organized the latter institute's statistical section and headed it from 1940 to 1950. From 1944 to 1950 he also headed the ANU Section of Social Sciences and was a member of the ANU presidium. In 1929 he was elected a member of the International Statistical Institute.

Ptukha founded the Ukrainian school of demographers. The Demographic Institute he headed was the first research center on demographic statistics in the world and trained many prominent scholars. Ptukha wrote numerous articles and reports and 11 books, including ones on the theory of population and mortality statistics (1916, master's diss), the marriage index (1922), the population of Kiev gubernia (1925), mortality in Russia and Ukraine (1928), D. Zhuravsky (1951), and the history of statistics in the Russian Empire (2 vols, 1955, 1959). A collection of his writings on population statistics was published in Moscow in 1960, and an edition of his selected works appeared in Kiev in 1971.

Ptushynsky, Yurii [Ptušyns'kyj, Jurij], b 29 November 1927 in Kiev. Physicist; AN URSR (now ANU) corresponding member since 1978. A graduate of Kiev University (1951), in 1954 he joined the ANU Institute of Physics, where since 1970 he has been deputy director and department head. An expert in surface physics, he has contributed substantially to the understanding of the electronic aspects of adsorption and desorption and of galvanomagnetic phenomena in thin metal films.

Public education. See Education and Extramural education.

Public expenditure. The total moneys spent by the state on Ukraine's territory or on Ukraine's behalf. The budgetary expenses of the central state (tsarist or Soviet) included transportation, communications, and defense. Funds spent directly in Ukraine were distributed among various levels of government, institutions, and enterprises.

Prior to 1917 the tsarist government did not record expenditures for Ukraine as a separate budgetary item. Economists such as M. *Yasnopolsky, M. *Porsh, P. Maltsiv, V. Dobrohaiev, and M. *Volobuiev estimated the size of Ukraine's budgetary expenditures and the net balance of receipts over expenses. The imperial government consistently collected more taxes from Ukraine than it spent on the country. Government expenditures were concentrated in the administrative center of Kiev and in the Black Sea ports of the navy. At the beginning of the 20th century Ukraine contributed on average 20 percent of the imperial revenues and received only 13 percent of the expenditures. In absolute terms the yearly negative balance has been estimated at 50 to 210 million rubles. In 1913 state expenditures in Ukraine were 584 million rubles, state revenues 649 million, and the negative balance 62.6 million rubles.

The first Soviet Ukrainian government did not have a separate budget and was subject to the budgetary policies of the Russian SFSR. The first formal budget was established for the year 1923–4. From then the budgetary system was divided between expenditures by the Union commissariats and ministries on the territory of Ukraine and the republican state budget. Furthermore the expenditures of the republican state budget were divided between ministries under joint Union-republican supervision and those under exclusive republican authority.

Initially, in the mid-1920s, 40 percent of the republican budget was spent on educational and social needs, and a large part of the investment in the economy came from the Union budget. The First Five-Year Plan saw a large increase in capital investment, although the share of investment funds under republican (including local government) control declined from 28 to 18 percent. Approx 43 percent of all expenditure in Ukraine was devoted to financing industrial projects (excluding transportation and communication). During that period republican expenditures amounted to 1.7 billion rubles, and Union expenditures in Ukraine totaled 11.8 billion rubles. Nevertheless the net budgetary surplus of revenues over expenditures accumulated by the Union government has been estimated at 5 billion rubles, or 23.2 percent of revenues raised in Ukraine by all levels of government (local, republican, and all-Union).

The 1932 reform, which emphasized direct sector control of the economy, increased the power of the Union commissariats in Ukraine. The republican budget continued to play a minor role in financing Ukraine's needs. In 1937, republican expenditures amounted to only 3.8 percent of the total USSR state expenditures. In 1957 N. Khrushchev reformed the system of economic administration and replaced ministries with regional economic councils. The system increased somewhat Ukraine's control over economic expenditures, and as a result Ukraine's share of the total USSR state expenditures had increased by 1960 to 10.3 percent. In 1959–61 average state (republican and Union) expenditures in Ukraine were 85.8 billion rubles, whereas state revenues were 125.9 billion. Thus the negative balance for Ukraine was 40.1 billion rubles. In 1959–70 the excess of budgetary receipts over expenditures in Ukraine was about 33.6 percent. In other words, the central government in Moscow retained for its purposes 90.1 billion rubles of the revenues it collected in Ukraine. Data for budgetary transfers in later years are not available.

In 1970 the republican government's expenditures in Ukraine amounted to 13.3 billion rubles, or 8.7 percent of the total Union budget. In 1988 Ukraine's state expenditures were 34.4 billion rubles, of which 47 percent was spent on the economy, and 50.8 percent on social and cultural needs. Ukraine's budget that year represented 8.5 percent of the Union budget. In 1990 Ukraine proclaimed its economic sovereignty, thereby claiming full control over all revenues and expenditures in the republic.

BIBLIOGRAPHY
Natsional'nyi dokhid Ukraïns'koï RSR (Kiev 1963)
Melnyk, Z. Soviet Capital Formation: Ukraine, 1928–1932 (Munich 1965)
Koropeckyj, I. (ed). The Ukraine within the USSR: An Economic Balance Sheet (New York 1977)
Gosudarstvennyi biudzhet SSSR 1981–1985 (Moscow 1987)
                                                    B. Somchynsky

Public health. During the pre-Christian era in Ukraine, *folk medicine, *medicinal plants, and primitive psychotherapy in the form of therapeutic suggestion were applied as health care services, and with time, specialists appeared such as midwives (baby povytukhy), bonesetters (kostopravy), and diviners (vorozhbyty). The development of health care in Kievan Rus' was greatly influenced by Byzantine-Christian medicine. Physicians from Byzantium and Western Europe began arriving in Ukraine in the 11th century. The *Kievan Cave Patericon provides information about the activities of local, Greek, Armenian, and other physicians, and payment to physicians is mentioned in *Ruskaia Pravda.

During the Princely era, care for the sick and aged was the responsibility of the churches and *monasteries. In addition, some care for the infirm was provided by *brotherhoods or by municipalities in the 16th and 17th centuries. A tsyrulnyk, or phlebotomist, was able to provide a variety of primitive health care services, including bloodletting and treatment of wounds and venereal diseases. Guilds of tsyrulnyky existed in most medieval Ukrainian cities. The Zaporozhian Cossack army had its own hospitals in Trakhtemyriv (from the end of the 16th century) and in the Mezhyhiria Transfiguration Monastery (in the 17th century). Therapy typically consisted of the application of old folk remedies. Obstetric care was provided by midwives. Healers (znakhari) applied the knowledge of medicinal plants acquired from their forefathers. Ukrainian manuscripts of the 18th century show that the use of leeches for bloodletting was prevalent. A bloodletters' guild existed in Kiev until 1834, and these tsyrulnyky practiced in villages until the 1870s, even after government injunctions made the practice of bloodletting illegal.

When scientific *medicine began to develop in Europe in the 19th century, and measures in sanitation and *hygiene began to be adopted, Ukraine was divided between the Russian and Austrian empires and was thus subject to their public health laws and regulations.

Ukraine under the Russian Empire. Health care services were divided among various ministries and did not come under the jurisdiction of a single ministry devoted to public health until 1916. *Sanitary-epidemiological measures, alimentary and industrial hygiene, and the network of medical institutions were inadequate and unevenly distributed, and most hospitals and infirmaries were located in the cities. Medical help for the general population was hopelessly lacking, and sanitary-rehabilitative care remained in private hands.

In 1911 there were 3,933 medical doctors in Ukraine. In 1915 there were 5,000 intermediary medical personnel and 28,500 hospital beds in 617 gubernial and county hospitals, 21 city hospitals, 202 factory hospitals, 47 Jewish hospitals, 4 church-run hospitals, 26 charity hospitals, 4 hospitals run by the Red Cross, 66 private hospitals, 17 university clinics, 15 railroad hospitals, 68 prison hospitals, and 58 hospitals run by various other institutions and organizations. There were also 22 psychiatric institutions and 291 clinics. The system of health care was best organized in the large urban centers, particularly Kiev, Kharkiv, and Odessa, where there were highly qualified personnel and well-equipped clinical facilities at the university medical faculties, in addition to good private institutions. City administrations had departments devoted to health care, as well as medical-sanitary councils that managed city hospitals and sanitary conditions in the urban centers, and combated epidemics.

The only recourse for the rural population was to the zemstvo doctors in those gubernias where zemstvos existed (see *Zemstvo medicine). The zemstvo clinics generally consisted of a doctor, a midwife, and a *feldsher and were supplemented by various outposts staffed by amateurs, who served under difficult conditions. In the event of a plague epidemiological doctors were sent in. Medical societies educated civilians about sanitation and hygiene and practiced some preventive medicine, particularly smallpox vaccination. Zemstvo doctors also provided general education and conducted scientific research on health in the Ukrainian countryside by compiling lists of epidemic diseases and describing working and general living conditions. Medical assistance was provided by volunteer organizations, such as the Red Cross and the Tuberculosis League, which operated 14 cloisters and 5 sanatoriums before the revolution. Community initiatives resulted in the creation of a network of *Pasteur stations for inoculation against rabies, which was then widely prevalent. In a period of 25 years of activity at the Kharkiv Pasteur Institute (from 1887), 32,800 people brought in from outlying provinces were inoculated.

Western Ukraine under Austria-Hungary. Public

health was overseen by the health department of the Ministry of the Interior, and in Galicia it was in the hands of the local parliaments. The first health care ministry in Austria was established in 1917 (headed by the Ukrainian I. Horbachevsky). Medical assistance was generally provided in cities, on the basis of payment for services rendered, by private doctors operating under the auspices of local and state medical foundations. For poorer segments of the population there were hospitals funded by municipalities and charitable organizations. Sanitary-rehabilitation measures were in private hands. Although sanitary conditions and means of combating epidemics were somewhat better developed within the boundaries of Austria-Hungary than in the Russian Empire, the poor living conditions and poor *nutrition of the rural population resulted in a high mortality rate, particularly among children. Ukrainian doctors active in providing general health care included Ye. Ozarkevych, S. Drymalyk, and I. Kurovets. In 1912 the *Ukrainian Physicians' Society was established in Lviv; it issued the monthly publication *Zdorovlia.

The period of Ukrainian national revival. In 1917, under the rule of the Central Rada, the People's Commission for Public Health was set up. After the declaration of independence it became the Department of Public Health, and during the period of the Hetman government, the Ministry of Public Health, headed by Yu. Liubynsky.

In the Western Ukrainian National Republic the State Secretariat for Public Health was headed by I. Kurovets. The medical services of the Ukrainian Galician Army were directed by R. Bilas and then T. Burachynsky. Throughout the liberation struggles the Ukrainian government maintained a health ministry; it was headed at various times by D. Odryna, O. Bilous, and S. Stempowski.

Interwar Soviet Ukraine. During the first years of the Bolshevik occupation, health care services deteriorated catastrophically in the anarchic conditions. The breakdown of the medical and sanitation network compounded by the war brought about a rise in the death rate as a result of malnutrition, *typhus, venereal disease, and *tuberculosis. Conditions did not begin to improve until the NEP period. A tripartite health care system was then installed. First, the state health care apparatus consisted of various foundations under the authority of the Ukrainian SSR People's Commissariat of Public Health, with provincial, regional, and district divisions of health services. These medical services, concentrated in the rural regions, instituted measures of preventive medicine by combating epidemics and improving sanitary conditions. Second, workers' medicine was developed by the establishment of workers' treasuries for the institution of health insurance for urban workers and civil servants. Third, volunteer associations, such as the Ukrainian Red Cross, the Tuberculosis League, Jewish assistance organizations, and a network of private doctors, instituted private and co-operative medical foundations (such as the polyclinic of medical professionals in Kharkiv). Thus the general network of medical institutions and services was slowly restored, as were the various scientific research institutes. In 1928 there were 5 sanitary-bacteriological, 1 protozoan, 2 radiological, and 3 psychoneurological institutes, and 1 for internal medicine, 1 for orthopedic and traumatological research, 1 for workers' medicine, 1 for experimental

pharmacology, and 3 clinics for postgraduate training in the Ukrainian SSR.

The Soviet government placed particular emphasis on preventive medicine. Wide social and sanitary legal provisions were set, including mandatory two-week holidays, pregnancy leave, prohibition of child labor, work norms for minors and women, health insurance, employment insurance and protection, additional rations in dangerous industries, statutes concerning the cleanliness of land, water, and air, and directives concerning nutrition, living conditions, community hygiene, and so on. An institute was established for the training of doctors in housing, community, nutritional, scholastic, and professional hygiene; epidemiologists and pediatricians were trained; and a network of dispensaries were built, as were day and night workers' clinics, nutritional dining halls, tuberculosis and *venereal disease clinics, dispensaries for minors, and consultation boards for pregnant women. Emphasis was also placed on the construction of sanatoriums.

Even so, the program did not produce the desired results, in some measure because the training of general practitioners and the building of general hospitals were neglected, and because the *standard of living and living conditions remained poor. There was no perceptible decline in the population's susceptibility to disease, there was a constant shortage of beds in hospitals, and doctors were overloaded with patients. According to official statistics there was 1 doctor for every 7,400 inhabitants in the rural areas in 1928, and 1 hospital bed for every 1,900 rural inhabitants in 1927. Medical specialists were particularly rare in rural areas. The one surgeon of the Kamianets-Podilskyi district was responsible for 160,000 people; the one in the Konotop district, for 200,000; and in the Romen district, for 225,000.

The bankruptcy of a health care policy devoted primarily to preventive medicine forced the government to reorient the system toward therapy and to begin constructing hospitals. The reorientation was implemented at the beginning of Stalin's dictatorship through bureaucratization and the centralization of all power in Moscow.

Interwar Western Ukraine. In Poland the Ministry of Health had divisions in the voievodship administrations, complemented by local physicians, workers' and civil servants' treasuries, and a network of privately owned medical installations and private practitioners, as well as various benevolent associations, notably religious community organizations. The health care system was more efficiently organized than in Austria-Hungary. There were a state employment insurance agency, certain kinds of social insurance, and pensions. Medical insurance programs financed a network of adequately equipped installations, including polyclinics, hospitals, and sanatoriums. In the non-Polish regions of Galicia, Volhynia, and Polisia, however, the conditions were measurably worse. There there was a shortage of medical institutions and a high incidence of tuberculosis, syphilis, and other contagious diseases. Ya. Hynylevych compiled statistics concerning the high infant mortality, which in some years reached 30 percent.

A concerted effort to bring health care to the population was undertaken by the *Ukrainian Hygienic Society in Lviv, *Narodnia Lichnytsia, the *Ukrainian National Society for Child and Adolescent Care, and *Vidrodzhennia. There were also an antitubercular dispensary (est by M.

*Panchyshyn), a bacteriological laboratory, and health co-operatives in Remeniv (Lviv county), Bodnariv (Stanyslaviv county), and Tsebliv (Sokal county), initiated by I. Fur in the late 1930s. The Shevchenko Scientific Society's Medical Commission published *Likars'kyi vistnyk* in conjunction with the Ukrainian Physicians' Society. In outlying regions the peasants were also served by itinerant practitioners, such as V. Bilozor, V. Hankivsky, and T. *Vorobets.

In Transcarpathia under Czechoslovakia, general and workers' insurance was common, and medical care for the peasantry was adequate, but the scarcity of Ukrainian doctors in the region curtailed the possibilities of community action in health care. I. Rykhlo published *Likars'ka komora*. In Bukovyna under Rumania, organized medical care for the Ukrainian population was primitive and only partly accommodated by private and individual practitioners.

Soviet Ukraine, 1945 to the 1960s. The German-Soviet War damaged the public health system in Ukraine. Soviet statistics show that in the Ukrainian SSR there were 160,993 beds available (33,649 doctors) in 1940, 144,512 (21,441) in 1945, and 194,223 (48,626) in 1950.

The health care system was headed by the Ministry of Health of the USSR (MOZ). Its counterpart in the Ukrainian SSR was subservient to it, with oblast and raion representation. The medical sections of all levels of this administration figured prominently in the setting of policy. Sanitation affairs came under the jurisdiction of the State Sanitation Inspectorate. In the MOZ there were subgroupings, such as the Medical Scientific Research Institutes Administration, the Administration for Institutions of Higher Education in Medicine, the Administration for Sanatoriums and Health Resorts, and the State Medical Publications Office. A number of medical installations were under the control of the Ministry for State Security (including Special *psychiatric hospitals), the Ministry of the Armed Forces, the Ministry of Defense, the Ministry of Internal Affairs, and the Ministry of Communications. Various ministries also operated their own medical services (so-called *spetslikarni*), which cared for Party and state functionaries.

Soviet affairs of public health were predicated on the system of state control, with an emphasis on preventive medicine, its application in the industrial workplace, the ensuring of readiness for work, and the differentiation of service for various levels of society (optimal service for Party members and state functionaries). Full state control and centralization of health care services were in tandem with the continuing bureaucratization of society. The growth of medical cadres was a focus for the Soviet government, but the distribution of the doctors was skewed, tending toward concentration in the large urban centers. Women figured prominently in the profession and constituted 68 percent of its ranks (1964). In total there were 871,000 medical personnel in Ukraine in 1966, but the low proportion of doctors in this figure resulted in inadequate medical care in up to 80 percent of cases.

The provision of beds in *hospitals, *clinics, and *polyclinics was also uneven, the urban areas being favored, as well as institutions that serviced visitors from the rest of the Soviet Union, such as the Crimea. With 44.8 beds per 10,000 pop in 1966, the Ukrainian SSR lagged behind world averages (West Germany, 108; France, 131; Japan, 124).

There was a relatively large number of beds for psychiatric hospitals, but few in comparison with the United States.

The field of balneology and climatology saw considerable development. In 1966 there were 447 sanatoriums, with a total capacity of 100,400. These extensive facilities were mainly used by visitors to Ukraine, however. A large proportion were also reserved for tuberculosis patients and for children. (See *Health resorts and sanatoriums.)

Health care for mothers and children was highly developed, a reflection of the policies of massive induction of women into the workplace and child rearing by the state apart from the family. (See *Obstetrics and *Pediatrics.) *Sanitation education and the basics of hygiene were taught in regular schools, in the industrial workplace, in special health-oriented universities in cities, and in instructive seminars given by doctors in rural areas.

The considerable development of a network of medical installations and the upkeep of approx 100,000 doctors and over 700,000 intermediary medical personnel was made possible only by the extraordinarily low wages set by the MOZ. The average monthly wage of a doctor ranged from 100 to 150 rubles; intermediary medical personnel earned an average of 76 rubles. In comparison, the average for most workers and civil servants was 95 rubles per month. The yearly salaries of all doctors in the Ukrainian SSR totaled approx 150 million rubles, whereas in West Germany the cost of maintaining a smaller number of doctors (94,500) was over 3 billion DM, and in the United States, even higher.

Soviet Ukraine since the 1960s. Life expectancy at birth in the Soviet Union had risen by nearly six years in the 1950s and early 1960s, and the country had undergone rapid improvements in public health services. But progress in reducing mortality virtually halted during the 1960s, and by the early 1970s life expectancy was actually falling. Nearly every age group (except teen-agers) had higher death rates in 1975 than in 1960. Measured by the health of its people, the USSR in 1981 was no longer a developed nation, even though caloric intake, educational attainment, and the ratio of doctors to population seemed to be higher than in Western Europe. Life expectancy had dropped by six years, and infant mortality had tripled.

Among the possible factors contributing to the deteriorating health conditions were (1) the stress accompanying modern industrialization, introduced at a faster pace in the Soviet Union than in the West; (2) air *pollution, the misuse and abuse of pesticides and fertilizers, the careless release of industrial waste and heavy metals into the waters, and the radiation emitted from poorly constructed or only partially safeguarded nuclear facilities; (3) excessive cigarette smoking, affecting particularly the incidence of respiratory diseases; (4) the monotonous diet, traditionally high in animal fats; and (5) a sharp rise in the consumption of alcohol, estimated in 1980 to be more than 70 percent higher in Eastern Europe than in Western Europe and more than twice as high as in the United States or Sweden (the cutbacks instituted by M. Gorbachev's restraint program in 1986–7 were swiftly compensated for by the escalating production of *samohon* 'moonshine'). Although it would have been theoretically possible for properly framed and implemented state social policies to mitigate the deterioration in health conditions, the problems rooted in the very concept of 'free' health care in the centralized system of the USSR had resulted in a health crisis by the 1980s. Even the relatively high ratios of medical personnel and hospital beds to population seemed to be inversely related to the quality of the health care services provided.

Statistically, public health care in the Soviet Union appeared impressive. The administration expressed concern for public health, announced new advances in medical research and technology, and reported on national decisions to update, modernize, and add to medical facilities. These plans were often not realized, however, because of shortages in materials, funds, and manpower, or simply because of poor planning. There was also too much emphasis on expanding rather than maintaining and upgrading existing facilities.

Because Soviet public health services were financed directly and virtually entirely by the state, the policies governing the services were determined not by the consumers but according to political priorities, which often ran directly contrary to the needs of consumers. Health care expenditures were not easily budgeted or accounted for because they were usually grouped together with pensions, disability outlays, and research and construction costs. Being low on the Soviet government's list of priorities, public health services were the first to be affected when cutbacks were required – the so-called *zalyshkovyi* (leftover) principle of budgeting. The proportion of the country's GNP spent on health care continually dropped (estimated at 9.8 percent in 1955, 7.5 percent in 1977, and less than 5 percent in 1990), and auxiliary medical institutions were repeatedly neglected, while official statistics presented an image of rising expenditures and uninterrupted technological advances (eg, new housing projects with inadequate sewage-disposal facilities or new factories that did not comply with the proper safety standards).

Even the most dedicated and qualified doctors could not provide an effective service without the minimum in supplies, equipment, and medications. The shortages also served to reinforce the rampant practice of *blat* 'payment under the table.' In 1990 Ukraine had 32 percent of the multiple-use syringes, 7 percent of the multiple-use injection needles, 21 percent of the disposable syringes, and 8 percent of the laryngoscopes it needed. These shortages, combined with the absence of a system of industrial sterilization for medical tools and preparations, as well as repeated cases of patients being infected with blood-transmitted diseases in Soviet hospitals, have resulted in a mass phobia of inoculations and a concomitant increase in infectious diseases. Moreover, the health of Ukraine's population has been endangered by a serious drop in immunity due to ecological catastrophes and social demoralization, identified by Ukrainian immunologists as 'Increased Immune Fatigue Syndrome.'

In 1990 a diphtheria epidemic affected the entire republic and killed 18 people. Each year in Ukraine there are 90,000 cases of viral hepatitis (including 16,000 cases of hepatitis B), 20 congenital disorders per 1,000 newborns, more than 1 million abortions and 40,000 miscarriages (reported), and 14,000 children born with congenital disorders. Influenza, not yet under control, kills tens of thousands of babies each year, and rickets is common. Eighty percent of all 18-year-olds had chronic diseases.

The devastating crisis in public health services in Ukraine has served to illustrate many of the weaknesses of the wider social and economic system of which it was a part.

BIBLIOGRAPHY

Duplenko, K. (ed). *Materialy do istoriï rozvytku okhorony zdorov'ia na Ukraïni* (Kiev 1957)

Maistrakh, O. *Orhanizatsiia okhorony zdorov'ia* (Kiev 1957)

Pliushch, V. 'Korotka istoriia okhorony zdorov'ia v Ukraïni,' in *Ukraïns'kyi zbirnyk Instytutu dlia vyvchennia SSSR*, 9 (Munich 1957)

Shupyk, P. (ed). *Osiahnennia okhorony zdorov'ia v Ukraïns'kii RSR* (Kiev 1958)

Okhorona zdorov'ia URSR (Kiev 1963)

Riaboshenko, O. *Okhorona zdorov'ia naselennia zakhidnykh oblastei Ukraïny* (Kiev 1963)

Burenkov, S. *Medicine and Health Care in the USSR* (New York 1985)

Miskiewicz, S. 'Faltering Health Services,' in *Social and Economic Rights in the Soviet Bloc* (New Brunswick, NJ 1987)

V. Pliushch, O. Maryniak

Public libraries and reading rooms (*narodni biblioteky i chytalni*). Centers founded in the 19th and first half of the 20th centuries, primarily by community rather than government organizations, which provided access to books and newspapers for a public largely deprived of these resources. The educational work done in public libraries and reading rooms, which were regularly the venues of literacy drives, often had a political character. In 1913 in all of Ukraine (within present boundaries) there were 3,153 mass circulation public libraries, with 1,917,000 volumes; of these, 414 libraries (894,000 volumes) were located in urban centers, and 2,739 libraries (1,023,000 volumes) in rural areas.

Public libraries and reading rooms were most widespread in Galicia, where independent social organizations flourished. There were approximately 400 reading rooms in Galicia in the mid-1880s, and over 3,000 by 1939. Reading rooms had a particularly marked effect on rural society. Most rural reading rooms were founded by political organizations led by the urban intelligentsia, which sought grass-roots support in the villages. In the 1880s the Russophile *Kachkovsky Society was the most active in establishing rural reading rooms. As the Ukrainian national current came to dominate the political life of Galicia, the Ukrainian *Prosvita society took the lead in organizing reading rooms. Of the 3,244 reading rooms operating in 1914, 2,944 were associated with Prosvita, and 300 with the Kachkovsky Society. In that year Prosvita also operated 2,664 public libraries.

Because of reading rooms, reading in the villages became a part of adult life and not an activity confined to the schoolhouse. Prosvita's reading rooms are closely associated with the rise of national consciousness in rural Galicia. Newspapers would be read aloud in reading rooms, urban intelligentsia would visit and give talks, and election strategy would be discussed. The 197,000 people who were members of Prosvita's reading rooms in 1914 were the basis of a burgeoning popular movement. In some ways reading rooms conformed to the usual pattern of social relations in the village: 60.5 percent of reading-room presidents were priests, in keeping with the traditional leading role of the clergy in rural life, and men were the main participants in reading room activities. In other ways reading rooms challenged the old order. The founding of a reading room was a major event, complete with a concert, speeches, and the shooting of rifles or mortars, and reading rooms quickly became a center of village life, threatening the focal role the tavern had traditionally played. Closely connected with the Ukrainian co-operative movement, reading rooms challenged economic relations in the village as well. The gentry and village notables, supported by the government, sometimes opposed the founding of reading rooms.

In Bukovyna the *Ruska Besida society organized reading rooms; in 1914 there were 150 in the province. In interwar Transcarpathia, public libraries run by the Czechoslovak state satisfied much of the population's need for literature; in addition, the *Dukhnovych and Prosvita societies organized reading rooms.

Public libraries and reading rooms in Russian-ruled Ukraine were not as widespread as and played a more narrowly educational role than their counterparts in Western Ukraine. Three types of public libraries existed in imperial Russia, public, community, and free. Of these only the free libraries did not charge patrons for borrowing books. Rural libraries were established principally by zemstvo authorities and co-operatives. Urban libraries were founded and funded by city dumas, educational and literacy societies, and philanthropic patrons. The first public library in Ukraine was established by the city government in Odessa in 1829. It was followed by municipal public libraries in Kherson (1872), Chernihiv (1877), Kharkiv (1886), and Katerynoslav (1887). In Kharkiv the first free library was opened in 1891, and by 1896 there were three more. By the 1890s there were five free libraries in Kiev, two of them founded by the *Kiev Literacy Society and three by the city council. There were two free libraries in Odessa at the turn of the century. In 1897 there were 141 public libraries in Russian-ruled Ukraine, most of them set up by local zemstvos in villages. Between a quarter and a half of the patrons of urban public libraries were factory workers or tradespeople, and roughly half of the library users were children. To make literature more accessible to workers, libraries were often set up at factory sites and in traveling railcars. The materials public libraries were permitted to circulate were severely restricted: only 9.5 percent of those books passed by the censor for the general public were permitted in public libraries. The 1890 Law on Free Public Reading Rooms and the Supervision of Them placed additional limitations on free libraries. From then on they could be opened only with the governor's permission, were directly under government control, could circulate only Russian-language religious and educational material, and could be summarily closed. In the 20th century the number of public libraries and reading rooms has grown significantly. There were 684 public libraries and reading rooms, with combined holdings of 542,800 volumes, in 1911 in Kharkiv gubernia, and 322 public libraries and reading rooms, with combined holdings of 141,000 volumes, in 1912 in Chernihiv gubernia. Only 3–6 percent of these materials were in Ukrainian. The restrictive law of 1890 was modified in the aftermath of the 1905 Revolution. As a result the Prosvita society began organizing Ukrainian public libraries and reading rooms, but it had minimal success, and its efforts were frequently thwarted by the state. In Russian-ruled Ukraine in 1913 (within pre-1939 boundaries) there were 2,340 public libraries, containing 1,770,000 volumes; of these, 359 libraries (845,000 volumes) were located in ur-

ban centers, and 1,981 (925,000 volumes) in rural areas.

During the struggle for Ukrainian independence (1917–20) public libraries and reading rooms were established and co-ordinated by the Prosvita society and closely affiliated with the co-operative movement. Under Soviet rule they were reorganized first into political education buildings, then into public libraries called *reading houses, and later into libraries in *people's homes, village halls, and collective-farm, state-farm, and factory clubhouses. The number of public libraries increased from 5,154 in 1924 to 10,275 in 1933. Ukrainian-language books, however, accounted for only 2.3 percent of general library holdings (in 1929), despite measures to increase the acquisition of such materials. In 1940 in all of Ukraine, including the Western Ukrainian territories occupied in 1939, there were 22,297 public libraries, with combined holdings of 41 million volumes. In 1960 there were 32,600 public libraries, with holdings of 196 million volumes. By 1970 the number of libraries had decreased to 27,600, but holdings had increased to 292 million volumes. This trend has continued, with totals in 1980 of 26,200 libraries and 371 million volumes, and in 1988 of 25,800 libraries and 421 million volumes. In the same period (1970–88) the number of public libraries throughout the USSR increased from 128,000 to 133,700, and the number of books and journals from 1.363 billion to 2.154 billion (an increase of 57 percent for the USSR as a whole, as compared to 44 percent for Ukraine). In recent years public complaints about the shortage of Ukrainian-language books in public libraries have resurfaced: in 1988 fully 61 percent of all literary holdings were Russian books and journals, and only 38 percent were Ukrainian. (See also *Libraries.)

BIBLIOGRAPHY
Kizichenko, V. Kul'turno-osvitnii riven' robitnychoho klasu Ukraïny naperedodni revoliutsiï 1905–1907 rr. (Kiev 1972)
Narodna osvita, nauka i kul'tura v Ukraïns'kii RSR: Statystychnyi zbirnyk (Kiev 1973)
Himka, J.P. Galician Villagers and the Ukrainian National Movement in the Nineteenth Century (Edmonton 1988)

C. Freeland, B. Krawchenko

Public opinion. The collection through questionnaires of individual opinions on issues of public policy. The sample group questioned is generally quite large, and their opinions are interpreted as representing the entire population of a region or country.

In the USSR the study of public opinion was not allowed to develop freely. Opinion studies that were carried out were designed to show virtually unanimous support for state policies and to serve as a tool of agitation and propaganda. The study of public opinion was concentrated in the centers of various CPSU committees in Moscow and some institutes of the USSR Academy of Sciences.

The democratization of Soviet society in the late 1980s revived interest in the study of public opinion. The Soviet government itself recognized the need for the establishment of a professional research center that would provide it with information and analyses about public views, and in 1988 the All-Union Center for the Study of Public Opinion on Social and Economic Questions was established by the Central Council of Trade Unions and the USSR State Committee on Labor. Headed by T. Zaslavskaia, the center had two branches in Ukraine, in Kiev and Lviv.

Public opinion is also being studied by the recently

founded Institute of Sociology of the AN URSR (now ANU), Kiev University's Center for the Study of Political Psychology, and sociological laboratories at Kharkiv, Lviv, and Odessa universities and the Dnipropetrovske Chemical-Technological Institute. Since the late 1980s the academy's journal *Filosofs'ka i sotsiolohichna dumka* has regularly published results of public opinion research, and many public organizations and newspapers have conducted their own public opinion surveys. Although some of the surveys lack methodological rigor, they cover a wide range of topics hitherto considered taboo.

BIBLIOGRAPHY
Shlapentokh, V. *Soviet Public Opinion and Ideology: Mythology and Pragmatism in Interaction* (New York 1986)

N. Chernysh

Public readings. The reading of popular books to audiences of illiterate or semiliterate people, practiced in the Russian Empire in the 19th century as a form of *extramural education. The materials read were literary works, historical or geographical studies, essays on science or religion, and practical guides to farming, co-operative enterprise, or hygiene. In Ukraine the first public readings were organized in Poltava in 1861. They were prohibited by the authorities and were revived only in the 1870s. They became particularly popular in Kiev and Kharkiv. From 1882 they were organized by a special commission in Kiev. In rural areas they were organized by zemstvos. By the end of the 19th century public readings were widespread and popular. They were conducted only in Russian and were closely monitored by the authorities. After 1906 readers were permitted to recount the substance of books in their own words, and occasionally works of Ukrainian writers were read. Public readings were also a common activity of popular educational societies (most notably *Prosvita) in Western Ukraine.

Public Relief Committee of Ukrainian Emigrants in Rumania (Hromadsko-dopomohovyi komitet ukrainskykh emigrantiv v Rumunii). An organization of émigrés from the central and eastern regions of Ukraine after the First World War. It was founded in 1923 in Bucharest and had local branches in Braşov, Vatra Dornei, Chişinău, Piatra-Neamt, and Tolmadjiv. The president was K. Matsiievych, and the most active members were D. Heredot, I. Havryliuk, V. Trepke, and H. Porokhivsky. The committee was active until the Second World War.

Publishers and publishing. Publishing began in Ukraine soon after the emergence of printing and became active in periods of cultural and national renaissance. The more noted publishers of the late 16th and the 17th centuries included Prince K. *Ostrozky (from the early 1580s), the *Lviv Dormition Brotherhood (from 1586), Bishop H. *Balaban and F. Balaban in Striatyn, M. *Slozka in Lviv, the *Kievan Cave Monastery (from 1617), S. Sobol in Kiev, Archbishop L. *Baranovych in Novhorod-Siverskyi (from 1674), and the Univ Monastery (1660–1770). In the 18th century, Ukrainian publishing houses declined because of bans imposed by the Russian government.

When the Ukrainian national movement revived in the early 19th century, the few Ukrainian books published were produced by Russian houses or through the offices of individual Ukrainian sponsors. These included the

works of P. Hulak-Artemovsky and H. Kvitka-Osnovianenko, as well as a number of almanacs of the romantics in the 1830s and 1840s. They appeared mainly in Kharkiv. When the Cyril and Methodius Brotherhood was disbanded in 1847, there was a further crackdown, but publishing resumed in the early 1860s (with the publishing activity of P. Kulish, O. Konysky, and others). The Valuev circular of 1863 and the *Ems Ukase of 1876 made it virtually impossible for anything to be published in Ukrainian within the Russian Empire. Apart from individual exceptions, works by Ukrainian authors were published elsewhere, mostly in Austrian-ruled Lviv and by other émigré publishing houses, such as M. Drahomanov's Ukrainian Press in Geneva.

In Austrian-ruled Galicia there were no government proscriptions to contend with. The first sporadic attempts at publishing occurred in the 1830s (the works of M. Levytsky, M. Luchkai, M. Shashkevych). The Halytsko-Ruska Matytsia publishing house was established in 1848. The Prosvita society began to publish in 1877, and the Russophile Kachkovsky Society in 1874. The 1860s to 1880s saw the emergence of full-time periodicals (such as *Pravda*, *Dilo*, *Hazeta shkol'na*), as well as of publishing houses of various political parties, the Ridna Shkola society, the Basilian monastic order in Zhovkva (in 1895), and so on. Textbooks were published by the Knyzhky Shkilni press, Prosvita, the Shevchenko Scientific Society (NTSh), and other publishers. Publication series began to be issued, such as the Dribna biblioteka (Little Library) series (1877–81), edited by I. Franko; the Biblioteka naiznametnishykh povistei (Library of the Greatest Stories; 1881–1900) of *Dilo*; the Rus'ka istorychna biblioteka (Ruthenian Historical Library, 1886–1904); Ya. Orenshtain's Zahal'na biblioteka (General Library, 1903–18); F. Fedortsiv's Novitnia biblioteka (New Library, 1912–23); D. Nykolyshyn's *Zahalna Knyhozbirnia (General Book Collection, 1914–33); and the NTSh's Ukraïnsko-rus'ka biblioteka (Ukrainian-Ruthenian Library).

In Bukovyna the Ruska Besida Society published the Biblioteka dlia molodezhy, selian i mishchanstva (Library for Young People, Peasants, and Burghers) series and other items. In the 1900s a number of similar series were issued. The Ukrainska Shkola society published textbooks.

In Transcarpathian Ukraine publishing efforts were more limited. They were initiated in 1850 by O. Dukhnovych through the Prešov Literary Society and later continued by the Society of St Basil the Great (1864–1902).

The *Ukrainian-Ruthenian Publishing Company, established in 1899 under the direction of M. Hrushevsky, I. Franko, and V. Hnatiuk, played an important part in Galician publishing in the early 20th century. It issued many scholarly and popular works and in 1905 took over the publication of the *Literaturno-naukovyi vistnyk*. The NTSh was also active at this time; it issued approx 1,200 titles with reproductions.

After a long period of prohibition, the pressure of censorship in Russian-ruled Ukraine began to lighten in the late 1890s. Literature as well as popular works began to appear. On the initiative of B. Hrinchenko and with funding from I. Cherevatenko, the publishing house in Chernihiv issued close to 50 titles with pressruns of 5,000 to 10,000 in the years 1894–1909. In 1895 O. Lototsky, S. Yefremov, V. Domanytsky, and others established the *Vik publishing house in Kiev. Although it was subjected to Russian censorship, the Vik house managed to put out 140 titles in 560,000 copies (mainly reprintings of Ukrainian classics) by 1914. Other ventures included *Kievskaia starina* and operations in Odessa, Kharkiv, St Petersburg (the Philanthropic Society for Publishing Generally Useful and Inexpensive Books), and elsewhere. After the Revolution of 1905, a number of publishing houses were opened in Kiev, notably Chas, Krynytsia, Ranok, Dzvin, Nasha Kooperatsiia, and Lan. The Ukrainske Vydavnytstvo was opened in Katerynoslav; Dnister began operations in Kamianets-Podilskyi. Books were also put out by the Kiev and Katerynoslav branches of Prosvita, the Ukrainian Scientific Society in Kiev, and various co-operatives, zemstvos, and private publishers.

Ukrainian publishing was interrupted by the First World War, the repressions of the Russian imperial government, and persecution (in Galicia) by the occupying forces of the Russian army. It resumed in Western Ukraine toward the end of the war, largely through the efforts of the *Union for the Liberation of Ukraine and Mykola Zalizniak in Vienna.

The Revolution of 1917 revived publishing in Kiev and other cities in spite of adverse economic conditions. Individual publishers established themselves (A. Kashchenko, E. Cherepovsky, and others), as well as community and co-operative operations, such as Chas, Vik, Dzvin, Krynytsia, the Ukrainian Co-operative Publishing Union, the All-Ukrainian Teachers' Publishing Company, Dniprosoiuz, Siaivo, Rukh (Kharkiv), and *Ukrainske Vydavnytstvo in Katerynoslav. The Ukrainian-Soviet War of 1919–20 markedly limited publishing activity, although in Right-Bank Ukraine (mainly in Kamianets-Podilskyi) the ministries of the Ukrainian National Republic continued to issue books and periodicals.

After the Bolshevik occupation in 1920, all Ukrainian publishing houses were closed. Then, during the period of Ukrainization and of the New Economic Policy, publishing expanded dramatically. By the 1930s the many new operations had managed to produce a large number of titles of new and old Ukrainian literature, scholarly publications, textbooks, dictionaries, and so on. Work in the 1920s was concentrated in the State Publishing House of Ukraine (DVU, 1919–30) and in the co-operatives Knyhospilka, Rukh, Chervonyi Shliakh (Kharkiv), Slovo (Kiev), Siaivo, and Kultura. Specialized publications were issued by Radianskyi Selianyn, Ukrainskyi Robitnyk, Naukova Dumka, the press of the People's Commissariat of Justice, the VUAN, and other presses. In 1930, as a result of increasing government pressure, Soviet Ukraine's publishing industry was largely reorganized. The DVU was turned into the State Publishing Alliance of Ukraine (DVOU); it included the specialized presses Literatura i Mystetstvo (books on literature and art), Radianska Shkola (textbooks), Molodyi Bilshovyk (books for young people), Ukrainskyi Robitnyk (books for workers), and Na Varti (military publications). In 1934 DVOU was itself dissolved, and the entire network of Soviet Ukrainian publishing houses was handed over to the central state publishing operation in Moscow.

In 1920–39 in Galicia, under Polish occupation, the principal publishing firms were those of I. Tyktor, M. Taranko, M. Matchak, R. Paladiichuk, Ridna Shkola, Chervona Kalyna, *Dilo*, the NTSh, Bystrytsia, *Vistnyk*, and co-opera-

tives, such as the Audit Union of Ukrainian Co-operatives, Silskyi Hospodar, Maslosoiuz, and the temperance society Vidrodzhennia. In Bukovyna the conditions of Rumanian occupation proved limiting; Yu. Hlynka's Publishing Company was the most active. In Czechoslovak-ruled Transcarpathia the Prosvita society, the Teachers' Society of Subcarpathian Ruthenia, the Teachers' Hromada, and other societies issued publications. In interwar Bohemia, Ukrainian émigré academic and professional societies and organizations published their own periodicals; the Ukrainian Civic Publishing Fund and individuals such as V. Koroliv-Stary, M. Omelchenko, and S. Rosokha had their own publishing houses in Prague. Other active émigré firms included Ukrainske Slovo (Berlin, 1921–4), Ya. Orenshtain's Ukrainska Nakladnia (Berlin–Leipzig, 1919–32), and a number in Warsaw, including Nasha Kultura, Variah, and the Ukrainian Scientific Institute.

During the Second World War, when publishing in Ukraine was largely paralyzed, the most active houses were Ukrainske Vydavnytstvo in Cracow and Lviv, those of the Ukrainian National Alliance and *Holos* in Germany, and *Proboiem* and Yu. Tyshchenko's operation in Czechoslovakia.

After the war there was a brief period (1946–50) of resurgence in publishing, conducted by émigré individuals and organizations in the displaced persons camps. Subsequently the more notable publishers have been the NTSh; the Ukrainian Academy of Arts and Sciences in the US; Molode Zhyttia, and Dniprova Khvylia in Munich; the Basilian presses in Rome, Toronto, and Prudentopolis; the Ukrainian National Association and Svoboda Press in Jersey City; Yu. Tkach (Bayda Books) in Australia; O. Mokh's Dobra Knyzhka press in Toronto; the Prolog Research Corporation in New York; Smoloskyp in Baltimore and Toronto; the Slovo Association of Ukrainian Writers in Exile in New York and Toronto; M. Denysiuk in Buenos Aires; M. Kots in Philadelphia; the Ukrainian Publishers Limited in London; *Suchasnist'* in Munich and New York; *Ukraïns'ki visti* in Neu-Ulm and Detroit; the First Ukrainian Press in Paris; the Trident Press and I. Tyktor in Winnipeg; and *Novi dni* in Toronto. English-language scholarly works have been published by the Ukrainian Academic Press (Littleton, Colorado), the Harvard Ukrainian Research Institute, the Canadian Institute of Ukrainian Studies (Edmonton), and the Ukrainian Language Education Centre (Edmonton).

In postwar Soviet Ukraine the main publishers were the State Publishing House for Literature (Derzhlitvydav), Dnipro and Radianskyi Pysmennyk (belles lettres), Mystetstvo (art books), Molod (young people's books), Vyshcha Shkola (postsecondary textbooks and monographs), Radianska Shkola (textbooks and pedagogical literature), the Ukrainska Radianska Entsyklopediia press (encyclopedias), Tekhnika (technical books), Urozhai (agricultural books), Muzychna Ukraina (music books), Veselka (children's literature), Zdorovia (medical and health books), Politvydav Ukrainy (political propaganda), Radianska Ukraina (the publishing house of the CC CPU), Naukova Dumka (scientific publications), the Kiev, Kharkiv, and Lviv university presses, and several oblast houses (eg, Kameniar in Lviv, Tavriia in Symferopil, Karpaty in Uzhhorod). Through the administration of the Ministry of Culture of the Ukrainian SSR that co-ordinated all publishing, from 1949 all presses were subordinated to the Chief Administration of the Printing Industry, Publishing, and Book Trade of the USSR Council of Ministers in Moscow. After Ukraine gained independence in 1991 many of the aforementioned institutions continued to function, some of them under new names.

(See also *Book publishing and *Press.)

BIBLIOGRAPHY

Chepyha, I. *Ukraïns'ki vydavnytstva u Vidni* (Vienna 1916)
Kuzelia, Z. 'Ukraïns'ki vydavnytstva,' in his *Z kul'turnoho zhyttia Ukraïny* (Salzwedel 1918)
Kozachenko, A. 'Knyzhkova produktsiia USRR (1923–1926),' *Bibliolohichni visti*, 1927, no. 2
Simovych, V. 'Vydavnycha sprava na Bukovyni v ostannim desiatylitti (1918–1928),' *Knyhar* (Prague), 1928, nos 1–2
Kozachenko, A. *10 rokiv knyzhkovoï produktsiï Radians'koï Ukraïny* (Kharkiv 1929)
Masiukevych, M. 'Vydavnytstva i presa v pidsoviets'kii Ukraïni,' *Visti Ukraïns'koho naukovoho instytutu* (Berlin), 1937, no. 1
Tyshchenko-Siryi, Iu. *Z istoriï vydavnychoï i knyhars'koï spravy v Ukraïni* (Prague 1940)
Bykovs'kyi, L. 'Nash vydavnychyi doribok na chuzhyni za 1945–1956 roky,' *Vyzvol'nyi shliakh*, 1956, no. 12
– 'Ukraïns'ki naukovi vydavnytstva na emigratsiï (1945–1950),' *Vyzvol'nyi shliakh*, 1958, no. 11
Dei, A. 'Izdatel'stva ukrainskoi knigi v XIX–nachale XX vekov,' *Kniga: Issledovaniia i materialy*, 10 (1965)
Hnatiuk, D. *Knyhovydavnycha sprava na Ukraïni v pisliavoienni roky* (Kiev 1965)
Bryl', M. 'Heohrafiia rozmishchennia knyhovydavnychoï spravy i knyhotorhovel'noï merezhi v Ukraïns'kii RSR,' *Ukraïns'kyi istoryko-heografichnyi zbirnyk*, 2 (Kiev 1972)
Reva, N. 'Suchasni ukraïns'ki vydavnytstva, shcho vypuskaiut' literaturno-khudozhni vydannia,' in his *Bibliohrafiia ukraïns'koï khudozhn'oï literatury ta literaturoznavstva* (Kiev 1979)
Maruniak, V. 'Vydavnycha diial'nist' ukraïns'koï emigratsiï v ChSR/Protektorati v 1900–1945 rr.,' in *Symbolae in honorem Volodymyri Janiw* (Munich 1983)
Skrypnyk, T. 'Stanovlennia vydavnychoï systemy v Ukraïns'kii RSR,' in *Teoriia ta istoriia radians'koï knyhy na Ukraïni: Zbirnyk naukovykh prats'* (Kiev 1983)
Gol'denberg, L.; et al (comps). *Kniga i knizhnoe delo v Ukrainskoi SSR: Sbornik dokumentov i materialov*, 2 vols (Kiev 1985–6)
R. Senkus

Puchkivska, Nadiia [Pučkivs'ka, Nadija], b 25 May 1908 in Smolensk, Russia. Ophthalmologist; full member of the USSR Academy of Medical Sciences since 1971; daughter of O. *Puchkivsky. A graduate of the Kiev Medical Institute (1930), from 1946 she worked at the Odessa Scientific Research Institute of Eye Diseases and Tissue Therapy (from 1956 as its director). Her chief publications deal with cornea transplants, the treatment of severe eye burns, the application of laser beams in ophthalmology, and the organization of ophthalmological care for the public. From 1956 she edited the journal *Oftal'mologicheskii zhurnal*. She was a member (6th–10th assemblies) and deputy chairman (7th–8th assemblies) of the Ukrainian SSR Supreme Soviet, and a member of the International Ophthalmological Academy (from 1975).

Puchkivsky, Oleksandr [Pučkivs'kyj], b 17 June 1881 in Baturyn, Konotip county, Chernihiv gubernia, d 14 February 1942. Otolaryngologist. A graduate of the St Petersburg Military Medical Academy (1905), he taught at Odessa University, the Odessa Medical Institute, and the Kiev Medical Institute (from 1922), where he organized a department of otolaryngology. Accused of belonging to the *Union for the Liberation of Ukraine, he was sentenced to long imprisonment. His publications dealt with rhinoscleroma, tuberculosis of the larynx, and the history of otolaryngology, and he wrote the first Ukrainian textbook in the field of otolaryngology.

Pud. See Weights and measures.

Pu-hu. An illustrated weekly magazine for displaced persons, published, with interruptions, in Augsburg, Germany, from March 1947 to 1951 and in 1954 by V. Charnetsky.

Volodymyr Pukhalsky   Heorhii (Yurii) Pukhov

Pukhalsky, Volodymyr [Puxal's'kyj], b 2 April 1848 in Minsk, d 23 February 1933 in Kiev. Teacher, pianist, and composer. In 1874 he graduated from the St Petersburg Conservatory, and in 1876 he was appointed director of the Russian Musical Society's school in Kiev. From 1913 he was a professor of piano at the Kiev Conservatory (in 1913–14 its first director) and at its successor, the *Lysenko Music and Drama Institute. He also performed as a pianist in St Petersburg, Kiev, and Odessa. His students included V. Horowitz, A. Brailowsky, and K. Mykhailov. Among his main works are the opera *Valeria* (1923), the symphonic *Little Russian Fantasy* (1882), a piano concerto (1881; the first such work for modern piano in Ukrainian music), works for piano solo, and the *Liturgy of St John Chrysostom* for choir.

Pukhov, Heorhii (Yurii) [Puxov, Heorhij], b 23 August 1916 in Sarapul, Viatka gubernia, Russia. Scientist in the fields of electrotechnical theory, computational sciences, and applied mathematics; full member of the AN URSR (now ANU) since 1967. He graduated from the Tomsk Polytechnical Institute and taught at the universities of Lviv, Tomsk, Tahanrih, and Kiev (1944–59). He worked at the ANU institutes of Cybernetics (1959–70) and Electrodynamics (1971–80) and has been director of the ANU Institute for Problems of Modeling in Energetics (since 1981). In 1978 he became a member of the ANU presidium. His main scientific contributions are in the analysis and synthesis of complex electrical machinery and processes, and the theory of electric machines. He developed new methods of designing analog and hybrid electronic computers and created the theoretical basis for quasi-analog modeling.

Pułaski, Kazimierz, b 19 January 1845 in Borushkivtsi, Zhytomyr county, Volhynia gubernia, d 5 January 1926 in Poznań, Poland. Polish historian and heraldic scholar. He studied at Prague and Vienna universities. From the mid-1870s to 1918 he owned an estate in Zavadyntsi, Podilia gubernia, wrote reports on Podilia for *Gazeta Warszawska*, and contributed articles about the history and archeology of Podilia to Polish periodicals. His *Stosunki z Mendli-Girejem, Chanem Tatarów Perekopskich, 1469–1515: Akta i listy* (Relations with Mengli-Girei, Khan of the Perekop Tatars, 1469–1515: Documents and Letters, 1881), *Szkice i poszukiwania historyczne* (Historical Sketches and Explorations, 4 vols, 1887, 1898, 1906, 1909), and *Kronika polskich rodów szlacheckich Podola, Wołynia, i Ukrainy* (Chronicle of Polish Noble Families of Podilia, Volhynia, and Ukraine, 1911) contain a wealth of information on the history of the early Cossack period.

Pulemet Lake. II-4. A lake in northwestern Volhynia oblast. The lake is approx 6 km long and up to 3.6 km wide, with a surface area of 16.3 sq km. Its deepest point is 19 m. Its southern shores are sandy, and its northern ones marshy. Straits join Pulemet with Luka and Svytiaz lakes.

Ivan Puliui

Puliui, Ivan [Puljuj] (Puluj, Jan), b 2 February 1845 in Hrymaliv, Ternopil circle, Galicia, d 31 January 1918 in Prague. Physicist, electrical engineer, inventor, translator, and community figure. He studied theology (1864–9) and physics (1869–72) at Vienna University and received a PHD in physics from Strassbourg University (1877). He taught physics at the Naval Academy in Fiume (1873–5) and at Vienna University (1877–83). From 1884 to 1916 he was a professor of experimental physics and electric technology at the Prague Polytechnical Institute, where he served as rector (1899–1900) and the first dean of the electric technology faculty (from 1902). Puliui made major contributions in the fields of electrical discharges in gases, molecular physics, cathode rays, and the technology of alternating electrical currents. While working with a cathode-ray tube of his own invention (widely known at the time as the 'Puluj tube'), he observed and recorded on film 'mysterious invisible rays' several years prior to W. Roentgen's observation, but he published his results only after Roentgen published his. Puliui also created many inventions in the fields of thermal measurements, electric incandescent lamps, and telemetry; and he wrote, in German, over 50 technical and scientific books and papers and approx 30 articles and brochures on the Ukrainian question. He translated into Ukrainian the Gospels (1871) and the entire New Testament (1880), with P. *Kulish. These translations and his translations, with I. Nechui-Levytsky, of the Old Testament became part of the Ukrainian Bible published by the British Bible Society in 1903. Puliui also translated and published in Vienna the first colloquial Ukrainian prayer book (1871). He was active in Ukrainian community life in Vienna and Prague, particularly in various relief committees. In 1865 he founded the Society of Ukrainian Theologians in Vienna, which in 1868 was transformed into the *Sich student society. A collection of articles about him was published by the Shevchenko Scientific Society in 1928, and Yu. Hryvniak's biography of him was published in London in 1971.

L. Onyshkevych

Pulo. A copper coin that circulated in Galicia in the 14th and 15th centuries. It was coined by Casimir III, his successor Louis I of Hungary, and Louis's viceroy in Galicia, Władysław of Opole. The fact that the coin was used in Galicia but not in Poland proper underscores the relative autonomy of Galicia at the time. The *pulo* also circulated in the 15th century in Muscovy, Tver, Novgorod, and other Russian principalities to the north and west.

Pumpkin. See Squash.

PUN. See Organization of Ukrainian Nationalists.

Punctuation. The use of spacing and conventional signs to clarify the construction, syntax, rhythm, and intonation of a sentence. In medieval Old Ukrainian writing, the punctuation used was that of Byzantine Greek (the comma, raised period, three and four points, cross, and, rarely, question mark [;]). Words in the oldest texts were not written separately, initial and final syllables were sometimes marked by acute and grave accents, and a stressed vowel was marked by an aspirate. The punctuation marks and their functions in Modern Ukrainian have much in common with German and other European languages. Their use became widespread after the introduction of printing and followed the practice of the great 15th- and 16th-century Italian and French printers. They include the period (Ukrainian: *krapka*), comma (*protynka, koma*), exclamation mark (*znak oklyku*), question mark (*znak pytannia*), colon (*dvokrapka*), semicolon (*serednyk*), hyphen (*rozdilka, defis*), dash (*ryska, tyre*), parentheses (*duzhky*), quotation marks (*lapky*), and virgule (*skisna ryska*). Paragraphs are indented, letter spacing and italics are used for emphasis, ellipses are marked by three periods or asterisks, and German quotation marks or French guillemets are used to indicate direct speech. A dash is often used in place of the verb 'is/are' (eg, *My – ukraïntsi*. 'We are Ukrainians.'), and apostrophes are used in words between labials and iotated vowels (eg, *zv'iazok* 'contact'). The rules of comma use with subordinate, restrictive, and nonrestrictive clauses are more rigid in Ukrainian than in English. In the names of most institutions and organizations (except supreme governmental bodies) and in book titles, only the first letter of the first word is capitalized.

BIBLIOGRAPHY
Hruns'kyi, M.; Myronenko, M. *Rozdilovi znaky* (Kharkiv–Kiev 1929)
Korovyts'kyi, I. 'Rozdilovi znaky v ukraïns'kii movi,' *Ridna mova* (Warsaw), 1934, nos 2–3
Bulakhovs'kyi, L. *Ukraïns'ka punktuatsiia* (Kiev–Lviv 1943)
Tsiluiko, K. (ed). *Ukraïns'kyi pravopys*, 2nd rev edn (Kiev 1960)
Buriachok, A.; Palamarchuk, L.; Rusanivs'kyi, V.; Tots'ka, N. *Dovidnyk z ukraïns'koho pravopysu*, 2nd rev edn (Kiev 1973)
Holovashchuk, S. *Slovnyk-dovidnyk z pravopysu ta slovo-vzhyvannia* (Kiev 1989)
Ditel', O. (ed.) *Ukraïns'kyi pravopys*, 3rd rev edn (Kiev 1990)
R. Senkus

Pavlo Pundii Yurii Pundyk

Pundii, Pavlo [Pundij] (Pundy), b 14 April 1922 in Kosiv, Chortkiv county, Galicia. Physician, publicist, and bibliographer. He studied at the Lviv Medical Institute and Erlangen University (MD, 1949). After emigrating to the United States in 1950, he established himself as an industrial physician in Chicago, managed the medical archives and library of the Ukrainian Medical Association of North America (from 1977), and edited the collection *Ukraïns'kyi medychnyi arkhiv* (Ukrainian Medical Archives, 10 vols, 1980–6). With M. Boiko he compiled and edited *Vyznachni ukraïns'ki likari zakhidn'oï Ukraïny i diaspory* (Distinguished Ukrainian Physicians of Western Ukraine and the Diaspora, 3 vols, 1987–8).

Pundyk, Yurii, b 4 November 1918 in Pechyrna, Kremianets county, Volhynia, d 28 October 1973 in Hibbing, Minnesota. Educator and political activist. A graduate of the Kremianets Seminary, he fled Ukraine in 1944 and served on the executive of the OUN in Austria and Germany (1945–9). He was also executive secretary of the Ukrainian Refugee Relief Committee in Salzburg (1945–6) and editor of the weekly *Promin'* (1947–9). After settling in the United States (1949) he completed his education at the University of Minnesota (MA, 1955) and taught economics at Hibbing State Junior College. He held various executive posts in the Organization for the Rebirth of Ukraine, contributed articles to *Samostiina Ukraïna*, *Novyi shliakh*, and *Ukraïns'ke slovo*, and wrote *Ukraïns'kyi natsionalizm* (Ukrainian Nationalism, 1966). A collection of his articles, *U polum'ï druzhn'oho slova* (In the Flame of a Friendly Word), appeared in 1983.

Puppet theater. From the end of 16th until the mid-19th century puppet theaters in Ukraine existed almost exclusively in *vertep* form. After the establishment of Soviet rule oblast-level puppet theaters were registered in Kiev (from 1929 as a separate theater, founded with the help of O. Solomarsky); Vinnytsia (1937); Kharkiv, Dnipropetrovske, Poltava, and Voroshylovhrad (1939); Symferopil, Zhytomyr, Stanyslaviv (now Ivano-Frankivske), and Odessa (1945); Lviv (1946); Donetske (1958); Khmelnytskyi, Kirovohrad, Mykolaiv, and Cherkasy (1970); Zaporizhia and Kherson (1971); Sumy and Rivne (1975); Chernihiv and Lutske (1976); Kryvyi Rih (1977); Ternopil (1980); and Chernivtsi and Uzhhorod (1981). Along with *young spectator's theaters, puppet theaters are dedicated to performing for children, although they stage some productions for adults. Most puppet theaters use hand puppets operated by actors hidden behind a curtain, rather than marionettes operated by strings. Their repertoire includes *Farbovanyi lys* (The Painted Fox), based on I. Franko; Yu. Chepovetsky's *Mysheniatko Mytsyk* (Mytsyk the Mouse), *Dobryi Khorton* (The Good Khorton), and *Ia – kurchatko, ty – kurchatko* (I'm a Chick, You're a Chick, coauthored by H. Usach); Usach's *Kotyhoroshko* (The Pea Roller) and *Veselkova kazka* (A Rainbow Tale); B. Yanker's *Bila troianda* (A White Rose); Ye. Radaban's *Malenka feia* (A Small Fairy); A. Shyian's *Ivasyk-Telesyk*; B. Chaly's *Barvinok za synim morem* (A Periwinkle beyond the Blue Sea); *The Mermaid* and *The Steadfast Tin Soldier*, based on H.C. Andersen; and *Puss 'n Boots*, based on C. Perrault. The repertoire for adults includes *Joseph Shveik against Francis Joseph*, an adaptation of J. Hašek's novel, I. Shtok's *The Divine Comedy* produced by the *Kiev Puppet Theater, and S. Hulak-Artemovsky's *Zaporozhian Cossack beyond the Danube*, produced by the Kharkiv Puppet Theater. Until recently the repertoire of puppet theaters also included plays which propagated the ideology of the CP and the Komsomol. In 1979 a drama workshop for puppet theaters was opened under Yu. Chepovetsky.

BIBLIOGRAPHY
Chepovets'kyi, Iu. 'Malyi hliadach i lial'ka,' *Ukraïns'kyi teatr*, 1973, no. 3
Motsar, T. 'Shcho pokazuiut' lial'ky,' *Ukraïns'kyi teatr*, 1986, no. 2
V. Revutsky

Purges (*chystky*). Periodic membership reviews in the Communist party and other institutions of the USSR for the purpose of 'cleansing' them of unworthy or undesirable members, such as careerists, dissolute individuals, criminals, and political opponents. From 1933 to J. Stalin's death, those purged were usually arrested.

The first large-scale purge of the Russian Communist Party (Bolshevik) (RCP[B]) was authorized by the Eighth Congress in March 1919. Almost half the Party membership was expelled in the reregistration process. Another reregistration, conducted in 1920, removed mostly adherents of T. Sapronov's Democratic Centralist opposition. A 'verification' of the Party membership, proclaimed by the Central Committee in July 1921, led to the expulsion of 186,386 of the 730,000 RCP(B) members in the next three months. In the CP(B)U 22.5 percent of the members were expelled according to official sources, and about 50 percent, including most of the former *Borotbists, according to M. Skrypnyk. The Party census of 1922 supports the latter estimate. Lesser purges of RCP(B) and CP(B)U nonproduction cells and village cells were carried out in 1924 and 1925 respectively, but no figures are available. Followers of L. Trotsky (see *Left Opposition) were expelled in

1923–4, and of G. Zinoviev in 1926–7, without any formal purges. Following the Fifteenth Congress of the All-Russian Communist Party (Bolshevik) (VKP[B]; 1927), about 1,500 oppositionists who refused to recant their views were expelled.

Beginning with the Shakhty show trial of so-called bourgeois specialists in the spring of 1928, various types of 'class enemy' were purged from industrial, educational, art, and academic institutions. In Ukraine the show trial of the *Union for the Liberation of Ukraine (1930) led to the arrest of thousands of so-called bourgeois nationalist scholars, clergy, teachers, and intelligentsia. In general, show trials attempted to define the nature of the 'enemy' to be sought out on a wide scale.

The Sixteenth VKP(B) Conference, in April 1929, ordered another major purge, which was connected with the forced *collectivization of agriculture. Its main target, the so-called *Right Opposition, included N. Bukharin's supporters and those who, like him, lacked the required enthusiasm for dispossessing *kulaks and forcing peasants into collective farms. Of 129,200 reviewed CP(B)U members and candidates in industrial centers, 9 percent were expelled and 13 percent were fined; of 35,800 reviewed rural CP(B)U members and candidates, 16 percent were expelled and 16 percent were fined. In the winter of 1929–30 the state apparatus was purged also: 164,000 of 1.5 million employees reviewed throughout the USSR were dismissed.

The next major purge was carried out in 1933–4. The guidelines of April 1933 targeted six categories for exclusion: (1) class enemies; (2) double-dealers; (3) violators of Party discipline; (4) traitors who had joined the class enemy; (5) careerists, self-seekers, and bureaucrats; and (6) moral degenerates. Two trials helped define the 'enemy': the Kotov case, which dealt with a former Party secretary from the Kuban who had advanced local farmers more than the prescribed amount of food, and the case of 75 agricultural officials who, supposedly, had organized 'wrecking' on collective farms in Ukraine, Belarus, and north Caucasia. In subsequent months various 'Ukrainian nationalist conspiracies' were also 'exposed.' Of approx 3.5 million VKP(B) members and candidates, over 800,000 were purged in 1933, and 340,000 in 1935, for a total of 32.6 percent; out of 267,900 CP(B)U members and candidates, only 51,700 (19.3 percent) were purged. In Ukraine the 1933–4 purge was supervised by P. *Postyshev and was directed on the one hand against adherents of *national communism and M. Skrypnyk, and on the other against district and collective-farm officials who were too lenient in seizing food from the peasantry at the height of the man-made famine. Skrypnyk committed suicide, and most of his supporters were arrested as alleged members of the Ukrainian Military Organization (UVO). In Ukraine's 496 raions, 237 raion committee secretaries, 249 raion executive committee chairmen, and 158 raion control commission chairmen had been replaced by November 1933. At the same time 3,000 collective-farm chairmen and Party secretaries were dismissed. The final figures are not available but must have been much higher. Those who lost their posts were usually arrested.

After S. Kirov's assassination on 1 December 1934, the purges changed from a periodic expulsion ritual to a continuous bloody hunt for 'enemies of the people,' which lasted about four years and is known as the Great Purge or the *Yezhov terror. Because Kirov's assassin had used forged Party documents, the Central Committee ordered,

on 13 May 1935, all Party documents to be verified. Figures on exclusions from the Party after 1933 are not available. The purge was marked by three show trials in Moscow, which 'exposed' an all-embracing terrorist conspiracy headed by L. Trotsky and involving virtually all the top Party leaders of V. Lenin's day. In the atmosphere of universal suspicion, Stalin destroyed the existing Party leadership and replaced it with one dependent completely on him.

As second secretary of the CP(B)U and candidate of the VKP(B) Politburo, Postyshev protected the Ukrainian leadership from the purge for several months. When a certain Nikolenko denounced some of the CP(B)U leaders, she was expelled, and then reinstated by Stalin. In March 1937 Postyshev was transferred from Ukraine, and after about a year he disappeared. With his transfer a purge of the oblast and raion Party organizations began. It claimed two-thirds of the oblast and one-third of the raion secretaries.

On 30 August 1937, following a series of attacks on the CP(B)U leadership in the Moscow press, a special mission consisting of N. Yezhov, V. Molotov, and N. Khrushchev came to Kiev. Special mobile NKVD squads were sent from Moscow, and military units stationed in Ukraine were replaced by troops from Siberia. Molotov demanded that the CC of the CP(B)U remove all three of its secretaries, S. Kosior, M. Khataevich, and N. Popov; the head of state, H. Petrovsky; and the head of government, P. Liubchenko; and appoint Khrushchev first secretary. The CC refused, and Liubchenko committed suicide. The plenum of the CC of the CP(B)U was reconvened in Moscow, where some of its members were arrested immediately. Within a year the entire CP(B)U Politburo, Organizational Bureau, Secretariat, and Central Control Commission were arrested. Only 3 of the 102 CC members survived. All oblast Party secretaries in Ukraine were removed, and many raion secretaries, raion executive committee chairmen, industrial managers, directors of scholarly institutions, and prominent writers were arrested. As commissars appeared and disappeared, Party and state authority collapsed, and for several months the Ukrainian SSR was an NKVD fief.

In January 1938 Khrushchev and D. Korotchenko were appointed first secretary of the CP(B)U and chairman of the Ukrainian Council of People's Commissars respectively. Between February and June the 12 new oblast secretaries and the new government were replaced again. The Party was reconstructed from the ground up. CP(B)U membership declined by 37 percent, from 453,500 in January 1934 to 285,800 in May 1938. The figure includes not only arrested but also transferred personnel.

In 1938 the *Communist Party of Western Ukraine was accused of serving the Polish 'fascist' government and was abolished. Those of its leaders who were in the Soviet Union were executed as Polish spies. When Stalin annexed Western Ukraine a year later, there were hardly any local Communists to put in power. By early 1940 mass repressions had begun, and with the outbreak of the German-Soviet War in June 1941, large numbers of political prisoners were executed by the Soviets in Western Ukraine and in labor camps.

Immediately after the Second World War the CP(B)U was purged again. In some oblast organizations over 80 percent of Party members were expelled. Over half the CP(B)U's 'leading workers' were dismissed between May 1945 and August 1946, including 38 percent of Party secretaries, 64 percent of regional executive committee chairmen, and about two-thirds of machine-tractor-station directors. In the postwar A. Zhdanov period a number of Ukrainian cultural figures were purged. The so-called Doctors' Plot of 1952 and some circumstantial evidence indicate that at the time of his death Stalin was planning another great purge.

Since Stalin's death there were no Party purges comparable to the earlier ones, but there were waves of arrests and repressions of Ukrainian cultural and political activists. The first wave of trials, in 1965–6, coincided more or less with similar trials in Moscow. The trials aroused protests in Moscow and Kiev and failed to stop the growth of the *dissident movement. The second wave of repressions, in 1972, was far more extensive and cruel. Widespread arrests of national and human rights activists began in January. After P. Shelest's dismissal from the CPU leadership, in May, thousands of arrests and searches were carried out, educational and academic institutions were thoroughly purged, some writers and journalists were forbidden to publish, and several journals were discontinued. By October the purge had reached the Party, and several Shelest supporters were removed. An exchange of Party cards in 1973–4 resulted in the exclusion of 37,000 CPU members (1.5 percent of the January 1973 membership).

BIBLIOGRAPHY
Popov, M. *Narys istoriï Komunistychnoï partiï (bil'shovykiv) Ukraïny* (Kharkiv 1928)
Dmytryshyn, B. *Moscow and the Ukraine, 1918–1953: A Study of Russian Bolshevik Nationality Policy* (New York 1956)
Kostiuk, H. *Stalinist Rule in the Ukraine: A Study in the Decade of Mass Terror, 1929–1939* (London 1960)
Shapiro, L. *The Communist Party of the Soviet Union* (New York 1960; 2nd rev edn 1970)
Conquest, R. *The Great Terror: Stalin's Purge of the Thirties* (New York 1968)

J. Mace

Purism. A normative tendency in language policy aimed at eliminating from use foreign borrowings in vocabulary, word formation, and syntax, and replacing them with neologisms or colloquial constructions. It arises in societies that strive to throw off alien cultural and linguistic impositions during periods of national revival and struggle for national independence. Excessive purism impoverishes the stylistic richness of a language and creates superfluous lexical doublets, thereby increasing the distance between the literary language and the vernacular. In their struggle against the impact of *Polonisms, Ukrainian purists relied in the 17th and 18th centuries on Church Slavonicisms and in the 19th and 20th centuries on neologisms (particularly terminological ones) and German, Czech, and even Polish calques. In the 1920s Ukrainian purists in Soviet Ukraine (Ye. Tymchenko, O. Kurylo, S. Smerechynsky, M. Sulyma, A. Krymsky, and others) reacted similarly to Russianisms. During the Stalinist terror of the 1930s, the purists were condemned as 'Ukrainian bourgeois nationalists in language' and repressed. After Stalin's death moderate 'puristic' views were expressed in the Soviet Ukrainian monthly *Ukraïns'ka mova i literatura v shkoli*, in the collection *Pro kul'turu movy* (On the Culture of Language, 1964), and in the serials *Pytannia movnoï kul'tury* (1967–) and *Kul'tura slova* (41 issues by 1991). Purism has also been advocated in columns on language in

various émigré periodicals and by linguists such as I. *Ohiienko (in *Ridna mova*) and J. *Rudnyckyj (in *Slovo na storozhi*).

BIBLIOGRAPHY
Wexler, P. *Purism and Language: A Study in Modern Ukrainian and Belorussian Nationalism (1840–1967)* (Bloomington 1974)

O. Horbach

Pushcha-Vodytsia

Pushcha-Vodytsia [Pušča-Vodycja]. A town smt (1982 pop 7,200) in Podilskyi raion on the northwestern outskirts of Kiev. In the medieval period the forested area was a hunting ground of the princes. In 1893 the Kiev city council set up the cottage district of Pushcha-Vodytsia, and in 1904 the first tuberculosis sanatorium was built there. A streetcar line was laid from the city to the district in 1909. Today the town has about 40 sanatoriums, rest homes, and camping grounds and a wooded park covering more than 40 ha.

Pushkar, Martyn [Puškar], b ?, d 11 June 1658 near Poltava. Cossack leader. From 1648 he was colonel of Poltava regiment. After B. Khmelnytsky's death in 1657, Pushkar, being one of the senior colonels in the Hetman state, was considered a candidate for the hetmancy, but I. *Vyhovsky was elected instead. That personal slight, coupled with his opposition to Vyhovsky's pro-Polish leanings and alliance with the Crimean Tatars, prompted Pushkar to form a coalition against Vyhovsky with the anti-*starshy-*

na Zaporozhian Cossacks led by Otaman Ya. Barabash. Pushkar received the support of the entire Poltava regiment and many other Cossacks who were opposed to Vyhovsky's policies and his appointment of foreigners to the *starshyna*. In November 1657 a Cossack-peasant rebellion against Vyhovsky led by Pushkar and Barabash erupted in the Poltava region. Vyhovsky's army and his Tatar allies crushed the rebellion and razed Poltava in June 1658, killing Pushkar and 8,000 to 15,000 of his supporters in battle. Barabash was captured later and executed.

BIBLIOGRAPHY

Korenets', D. 'Povstannie Martyna Pushkaria,' *Naukovyi zbirnyk prys'viachenyi profesorovy Mykhailovy Hrushevs'komu* ... (Lviv 1906)

Stetsiuk, K. *Narodni rukhy na Livoberezhnii i Slobids'kii Ukraïni v 50–70-kh rokakh* XVII *st.* (Kiev 1960)

Pushkar, Mykola [Puškar], b 30 October 1894 in Holovchyntsi, Zalishchyky county, Galicia, d ? Slavic philologist. A graduate of Prague University (PH D, 1925), he studied education at Warsaw University and then taught in gymnasiums in Yavoriv, Łańcut, Rzeszów, Lviv, and Horodok. In 1940–1 and from 1945 to 1974 he taught at Lviv University, chairing its department of Slavic philology in 1950–6. A comparative linguist, he is the author of articles on pedagogy and the Ukrainian, Slovak, and Czech languages; a book of lectures on Standard Czech (3 parts, 1963); and books on the palatalization of Ukrainian consonants (1932), and on Czech historical phonetics (2 parts, 1965) and historical morphology (2 parts, 1970, 1972).

Pushkar, Mykola [Puškar], b 3 August 1930. Cryobiologist; corresponding member of the AN URSR (now ANU) since 1978 and member of the American Society of Cryobiologists. A graduate of the Dnipropetrovske Medical Institute (1954), he worked in the area of organized medicine and medical education and researched the effect of extreme cold temperatures on human organs and tissues. He was one of the founders and the first director of the ANU Institute for Problems of Cryobiology and Cryomedicine (1972–83). Since 1983 he has headed the division of low-temperature conservation at the institute, where he has worked on cryomicroscopy and theoretical and experimental models of cryobiological processes. He is the author of numerous scientific works, including 9 monographs and over 40 inventions.

Stefaniia Pushkar

Pushkar, Stefaniia [Puškar, Stefanija] (née Ortynsky), b 9 January 1901 in Chornoriky, Krosno county, Galicia, d 11 April 1988 in Philadelphia. Industrial engineer and civic leader; wife of V. *Pushkar. She was director of the Ukrainske Narodne Mystetstvo co-operative (1929–39 and 1941–4) and helped found the journal *Nova khata*. After emigrating to the United States in 1947, she was active in the Ukrainian National Women's League of America as a member of its executive and as president (1966–71), as well as in the World Federation of Ukrainian Women's Organizations as vice-president.

Pushkar, Volodymyr [Puškar], b 9 August 1907 in Peremyshl. Civic and co-operative leader; husband of S. *Pushkar. In 1941–4 he was deputy director of finance at the *Ukrainian Central Committee. After emigrating to the United States in 1947, he helped found a number of financial institutions, such as the Self-Reliance Association of American Ukrainians, Self-Reliance credit unions, and the Ukrainian Economic Advisory Association. He served as secretary and then as vice-president (1959–65) of the Providence Association of Ukrainian Catholics in America, was an executive member of the Ukrainian Congress Committee of America, and headed (1969–74) the Ukrainian Patriarchal World Federation.

Pushkari. A village in Novhorod-Siverskyi raion, Chernihiv oblast, near which Paleolithic and Mesolithic camping grounds were excavated in 1932–3 by M. *Rudynsky and in 1937–9 by P. Boryskovsky. Pushkari I revealed the remains of a semi-pit dwelling which was reinforced by mammoth bone and linked together three round living areas, each with its own fireplace. Pushkari VII contained a large number of flint tools from the Mesolithic Period.

Pushkin, Aleksandr [Puškin], b 6 June 1799 in Moscow, d 10 November 1837 in St Petersburg. Russian poet, playwright, and prose writer. Pushkin maintained close relations with the Ukrainians M. Markevych, M. Maksymovych, D. Bantysh-Kamensky, and O. Somov and helped N. Gogol to establish himself in Russian literature. He maintained an interest in Ukrainian folklore, and his book collection included *Opyt sobraniia drevnikh malorossiiskikh pesnei* (An Attempted Collection of Old Little Russian Songs, 1819) by M. Tsertelev, *Malorossiiskie pesni* (Little Russian Songs, 1827) and *Ukrainskie narodnye pesni* (Ukrainian Folk Songs, 1834) by M. Maksymovych, and *Zaporozhskaia starina* (Zaporizhia Antiquities, 1833) by I. Sreznevsky. Nonetheless, Ukrainian folk imagery was virtually absent from his writing. His stay in Ukraine during his exile from Russia in 1820–4 (Katerynoslav, Odessa, Kamianky, near Bila Tserkva, and, for a visit, Kiev) did little to acquaint Pushkin with the Ukrainian national movement. Pushkin attempted to influence K. Ryleev to rework his poem 'Voinarovskii' to reflect the Russian nationalist spirit. He wrote his collection of notes 'Istoriia Petra' (History of Peter) in a similar vein, including a subjective Russian interpretation of the Swedish-Moscovite-Ukrainian war of 1708–9.

Pushkin wrote the poem 'Poltava,' which was highly praised by Tsar Nicholas I. Being under investigation at the time, he had followed the tsar's suggestions and thus demonstrated his loyalty to the official ideology. The purpose of 'Poltava' was to prove the 'historical correctness' of the destruction of Ukrainian statehood and the building of the Russian Empire. Peter I is extolled as in an ode where was Hetman I. Mazepa is portrayed melodramatically and described as 'sly,' 'cruel,' 'cunning,' 'cold,' 'destructive,' 'wily,' and 'a snake.' P. Kulish, who was influenced by Pushkin's imperialistic Great Russian ideology as much as by his poetic style, stressed Pushkin's importance for Ukrainian literature. Shevchenko, however, in his poem 'Son' (The Dream) passionately contradicted Pushkin's apotheosis of St Petersburg in 'Mednyi vsadnik' (The Bronze Horseman). The works of Pushkin were first translated into Ukrainian in 1829 by L. Borovykovsky. The best prerevolutionary translations are by Borovykovsky, M. Starytsky, I. Franko, and M. Vorony. Of the postrevolutionary translators the most noteworthy are P. Fylypovych, M. Zerov, M. Rylsky, M. Bazhan, M. Tereshchenko, and N. Zabila.

Yu. Boiko

Pushyk, Stepan [Pušyk], b 26 January 1944 in Viktoriv, Halych raion, Ivano-Frankivske oblast. Writer. He graduated from the Ivano-Frankivske Pedagogical Institute (1964) and Gorky Institute of Literature in Moscow (1972), and is the author of four poetry collections and several books of children's verse. He has gained renown for his novels *Pero zolotoho ptakha* (Quill of the Golden Bird, 1978) and *Strazh-hora* (1981), for which he was awarded the Shevchenko State Prize for literature in 1990. An edition of the two novels and 21 of his stories was published in 1988. Pushyk is also the author of a book about Ivano-Frankivske oblast (1984), a collection of song lyrics (1985), and a collection of literary and folkloristic essays, *Daraby plyvut' u lehendu* (Rafts Float into Legend, 1990). He received the Shevchenko Prize in 1990 for his novel *Halyts'-ka brama* (The Halych Gate).

Puskova, Olha, b 1857 in Kiev, d 1911 in Odessa. Opera singer (contralto). A graduate of the Moscow Conservatory (1874), she studied voice under M. Viardot-Garcia in Paris. She sang as a soloist with the Kiev (1874–6, 1878–9) and Kharkiv (1876–7) operas, and then gave concerts and taught music in Kiev, Katerynoslav, and Odessa. Her main roles were Vania in M. Glinka's *Ivan Susanin*, Basmanova in P. Tchaikovsky's *Oprichnik* (a role written especially for her), and Azucena in G. Verdi's *Il Trovatore*.

Pustomyty. IV-4. A town smt (1986 pop 7,900) on the Stavchanka River and a raion center in Lviv oblast. It is first mentioned in 1441 in the Lviv court records. Lying on a busy trade route, it became a royal tariff post. After the partition of Poland in 1772, Pustomyty belonged to Austria. Taking advantage of its natural sulfur springs, the local landowner set up a spa in 1880. In 1919 the town was annexed by Poland, and in 1939, by the USSR. At the beginning of the 20th century lime enterprises were set up. In the 1950s an asphalt and a reinforced-concrete plant were constructed. Besides building materials Pustomyty manufactures mineral fertilizer.

Pustoviit, Havrylo [Pustovijt], b 26 July 1900 in Mezhyrich, Kaniv county, Kiev gubernia, d 20 March 1947 in Kiev. Graphic artist. He studied at the Kiev Art School (1916–18) and the Kiev State Art Institute (1923–30) under

Havrylo Pustoviit: *Grape Harvest in Moldavia* (color lithograph, 1937)

M. Boichuk, I. Pleshchynsky, and S. Nalepinska. From 1930 to 1934 he taught at the Ukrainian Printing Institute in Kharkiv. He designed covers for Ukrainian translations of J. London's *Iron Heel* (1928) and E. Remarque's *All Quiet on the Western Front* (1929) and illustrated editons of T. Shevchenko's *Naimychka* (The Hired Girl, 1938), M. Kotsiubynsky's stories, M. Bazhan's *Danylo Halyts'kyi* (Danylo of Halych, 1942), and I. Franko's *Zakhar Berkut* (1946). He did a number of lithograph series, including 'Landscapes of Caucasia' (1935) and 'The Industrial Dnieper' (1937), and drawing series, such as 'Lviv' (1939–41) and 'The Hutsul Region' (1939–41). In 1941–2 he drew many portraits, including ones of Yu. Yanovsky, V. Sosiura, O. Dovzhenko, I. Le, and A. Malyshko.

Pustovoit, Vasyl [Pustovojt, Vasyl'], b 14 January 1886 in Taranivka, Zmiiv county, Kharkiv gubernia, d 11 October 1972 in Krasnodar. Selection scientist; full member of the USSR Academy of Sciences from 1964 and of the All-Union Academy of Agricultural Sciences from 1956. A graduate of the Kharkiv agricultural school (1907) and the Kuban Agricultural Institute (1926), he was a lecturer at the Kuban agricultural tekhnikum (1908–24) and head of the department of genetics, selection, and seed cultivation at the agricultural institute (1926–30). He founded an experimental farm at the Kuban tekhnikum (1912) that was the basis for the All-Union Scientific Research Institute of Oil Cultures (est 1932), at which he headed the selection and oil seed cultivation division and the sunflower selection laboratory. He created 20 varieties of sunflower with a high oil yield (up to 57 percent in dry seeds), including Peredovyk (Leader) and VNIIMK 8883 and 6540.

Pustynky settlement. A *Bronze Age settlement on the Dnieper River near Pustynky, Chernihiv raion. An estimated 200–250 people – practicing mainly agriculture and animal husbandry – lived in this settlement of the 13th to 12th century BC. Excavations in 1964–7 revealed the remains of dwelling, agricultural, and religious structures, ceramic items, and stone and bone tools. A burial ground with cremated remains was located nearby.

Put' prosveshcheniia. See *Shliakh osvity.*

Putiatyn, Viktor [Putjatyn], b 12 September 1941 in Kharkiv. Champion fencer. He was a member of the USSR men's foil teams that won gold medals at the 1965, 1966, 1969, and 1970 world fencing championships and the 1968 and 1972 Olympic silver medals, and was a Ukrainian and USSR champion many times. In 1981 he was elected a member of the Executive Committee of the International Fencing Federation.

Putna Gospel (Putnianske yevanheliie). An Old Ukrainian manuscript transcribed in the *ustav* from a Macedonian Glagolitic original by two copyists (folios 1–48, 49–146) in the second half of the 13th century, somewhere in southern Galicia or southwestern Volhynia. It was preserved at the Putna Monastery in northern Bukovyna. The text has many Ukrainian phonetic features similar to those of the *Halych Gospel of 1266–1301. It was published and analyzed by O. Kaluzhniatsky under the title *Evangeliarium Putnanum* (1888).

Putni **boyars**. The lower category of *boyar military servitors in the Lithuanian-Ruthenian state. They had the same privileges as the *pantsyrni* boyars. In the 15th and 16th centuries they occupied a social position between the state peasants and the petty nobility. By the end of the 16th century most of them had been absorbed by those groups or, in Ukraine, become *registered Cossacks. In some localities in Right-Bank Ukraine, however, *putni* boyars could be still found in the 18th century.

Putyliv or **Putyla**. VI-6. A town smt (1986 pop 2,900) in the Putylivka River Valley and a raion center in Chernivtsi oblast. It was first mentioned in historical documents in 1501 under its original name, Putyliv. At that time it was under Moldavian rule. In 1774 Bukovyna along with Putyliv was annexed by Austria. From the end of the 18th century the town was called Putyla-Storonets, and in 1920 it was renamed Putyla by the Rumanians. It was annexed by the USSR in 1940. Its main industries are forestry, woodworking, and wool processing. Yu. *Fedkovych's homestead in Putyliv, where he was born, has been converted into a literary memorial museum.

Putyvl or **Putyvel** [Putyvl' or Putyvel']. II-14. A town (1989 pop 19,100) on the Seim River and a raion center in Sumy oblast. It was first mentioned, as a fortress, in the Hypatian Chronicle under the year 1146. Putyvl was established in 988 at the crossroads of several trade routes. From the 12th century until 1523 Putyvl was the center of an appanage principality, which was part of Kievan Rus', the Grand Duchy of Lithuania (1356–1503), and Muscovy. The town, which is described in *Slovo o polku Ihorevi*, withstood a Cuman siege in 1186. In 1239 it was destroyed by Batu's horde. In 1618 it was captured by Hetman P. Sahaidachny. As Slobidska Ukraine became colonized in the 17th century, Putyvl lost its strategic importance. In the 19th century it was a county center of Kursk gubernia. In 1926 it became part of the Ukrainian SSR. Today its main industries are food processing and tourism. It produces canned fruits, butter, powdered milk, and mixed feed. In 1988 Putyvl was declared a historical and cultural reserve. Its architectural monuments include the fortified complex of Movchanskyi Monastery, built in the 1570s, with its Cathedral of the Nativity of the Theotokos (1630–6) and Transfiguration Church (1666–7), the building complex of the Transfiguration Monastery (1617–1707) with its cathedral, the main gate surmounted by the Annunciation Church (1693–7), St Nicholas's Church (1735–7), and the Church of the Resurrection (1758). Only the last two are designed in the Ukrainian baroque style. Artistic monu-

St Nicholas's Church (1735–7) in Putyvl

ments of the 17th and 18th centuries include the sculpture of Jesus in a dungeon, some icons by local masters, an image of the Madonna in gold and silver on white satin, a shroud with an image of Christ (1666), the bookbindings of the gospel, and a church bell.

Puza, Yevhen, b 2 February 1880 in the Bačka region, d 13 December 1922 in Uzhhorod, Transcarpathia. Political and military figure. He studied at the military technical academy in Prague and worked at the Military Cartography Institute and as a government notary in Vienna. With the fall of Austria-Hungary he became deputy leader of the *Ruthenian People's Council in L'ubovňa (1918) and its delegate to the Ukrainian National Council in Stanyslaviv. In 1919–20 he was a major in the Ukrainian Galician Army, and in 1920 he was a member of the Directory of Subcarpathian Ruthenia in Prague. After moving to Uzhhorod he edited *Narod* and *Vpered* and founded Prosvita society chapters in the Hutsul region.

Puzyna, Kostiantyn, b 1790 in the Poltava district, d 1850 in Vydubychi Monastery near Kiev. Poet. He concluded his studies at the St Petersburg Theological Academy (1814) and taught at the theological seminary in Vologda. In 1822 he joined a monastic order and adopted the religious name Filadelf. Puzyna wrote in Ukrainian and Russian and maintained that Ukrainians should not forsake their native tongue, even if they lived in distant St Petersburg. Most of his poetry was written in St Petersburg. It includes poems in genres popular in his day, such as name-day greetings in verse and verses of condolence. Burlesque in style, Puzyna's poems have a democratic theme, in particular the poem 'Oda – malorossiiskii krest'ianyn' (An Ode: The Little Russian Peasant), in which the poet defends the peasant against the misrule of the gentry.

Puzyr. A family of potters. Musii (1812–95) opened a workshop in Radychiv, Chernihiv gubernia, in 1842. His sons, Lavrentii (1845–1917) and Hryhorii (ca 1850–1930), learned from and worked with him. Eventually Lavrentii set up his own shop in Novhorod-Siverskyi. The Puzyrs produced decorative and consumer earthenware decorated with plant motifs and horizontal bands.

Puzyrkov, Viktor, b 4 October 1918 in Katerynoslav. Painter. He studied at the Kiev State Art Institute (1938–46) and has taught there since 1948. He is known for his seascapes and socialist-realist battle scenes, including *The Undefeated* (1946), *Black Sea Sailors* (1947), *Soldiers* (1972), and *Kiev: 1942* (1974). He also painted the triptych *Lesia Ukrainka* (1979).

Puzytsky, Antin [Puzyc'kyj], b 1880, d 1945. Senior army officer. As a colonel of the Russian army during the First World War, he was captured by the Austrians, in 1917. In 1918 he served as a regimental commander of the Graycoats Division and from December 1918 he commanded the division. He was promoted to brigadier general of the UNR Army. In the interwar years he lived in Poland and contributed to Ukrainian military journals.

Pykulychi [Pykulyči]. A village in Peremyshl county, Galicia, which in 1919–21 was the site of a Polish internment camp. Initially, Ukrainian civilians from Galicia (approx 1,920 people in 1919) and then soldiers of the UNR Army and the Ukrainian Galician Army were interned there by the Poles.

Pylchykov, Dmytro [Pyl'čykov], b 7 November 1821 in Kherson gubernia, d 17 October 1893 in Kharkiv. Educator

Dmytro Pylchykov   Mykola Pylchykov

and civic leader; father of M. *Pylchykov. After graduating from Kiev University (1843) he lectured at the Poltava Cadet Corps (1846–64). In 1846 he became acquainted with T. Shevchenko and joined the Cyril and Methodius Brotherhood. An avid Ukrainophile and active member of the Poltava Hromada, he helped organize Sunday schools in Poltava in 1859–62. He maintained ties with M. Drahomanov abroad and with Galician cultural and civic leaders. In 1873 he visited Lviv and became a patron of the Shevchenko Scientific Society.

Pylchykov, Mykola [Pyl'čykov], b 21 May 1857 in Poltava, d 19 May 1908 in Kharkiv. Pioneering experimental physicist and instrument designer; son of D. *Pylchykov. After graduating from Kharkiv University in 1880 he taught there and became a professor in 1889. Later he was a professor at the university in Odessa (1894–1902) and at the Kharkiv Technological Institute (1902–8). Throughout his career he was an active researcher in the fields of optics, geomagnetism, radioactivity, X-rays, and radio control and guidance. In 1893 he researched the *Kursk Magnetic Anomaly.

Pyliankevych, Oleksander [Pyljankevyč], b 16 March 1933 in Korosten, Kiev oblast, d 13 November 1989 in Kiev. Materials scientist; corresponding member of the AN URSR (now ANU) from 1976. He graduated from the Kiev Polytechnic Institute (1955) and worked at the ANU Institute for Problems of Materials Science, as assistant director from 1968. A specialist in electron microscopy, he studied, in particular, the molecular structure of boron nitride, using that material to develop a new superhard material. He also worked in the area of metal thin-films, in which he studied the mechanisms of nucleation and structure formation.

Pyliavtsi, Battle of. A major battle of the *Cossack-Polish War. It took place on 21–24 September 1648 near the Podilian village of Pyliavtsi, now Pyliava, in Stara Syniava raion, Khmelnytskyi oblast. The battle pitted the 100,000-strong Cossack-peasant army led by Hetman B. Khmelnytsky and colonels such as I. Bohun and M. Kryvonis and a force of 3,000 to 4,000 Budzhak Tatars against a Polish levy en masse of 32,000 nobles, over 100,000 servitors, and 8,000 German mercenaries led by the magnates D. Zasławski, M. Ostroróg, and A. Koniecpolski. Khmelnytsky split the Polish army by sending a large force directly into its midst. Tatar cavalry forays created confusion, and Khmelnytsky's remaining troops surrounded the Poles and attacked them with musket fire. The Polish army was routed and fled in disarray, leaving behind its artillery, ammunition, and supplies. After the victory Khmelnytsky's army gained control of Podilia and Volhynia and moved on to Lviv and Zamość. News of the Polish defeat was a catalyst for the spread of anti-Polish insurgency in Galicia.

Pylynska, Mariia [Pylyns'ka, Marija], b 18 October 1898 in Kamianets-Podilskyi, d 16 December 1976. Teacher and translator; wife of I. *Dniprovsky. She graduated from the teachers' seminary in 1917, and in the 1920s she worked as a teacher, an orphanage director, and a translator for the Radio and Telegraph Agency of Ukraine. From 1928 she was a Ukrainian translator of Russian literature. In the

1960s she prepared a Russian-Ukrainian phraseological dictionary with I. Vyrhan, which was published in the journal *Prapor*.

Pylypchuk, Pylyp [Pylypčuk], b 1869 in Volhynia, d 1940 in Kholm. Engineer and civic and political leader. In the 1900s he was active in the Ukrainian community in St Petersburg. In 1917–18 he lectured on theoretical mechanics at the Kiev Polytechnical Institute, and in 1919 he was in charge of the Dnieper River route system. At the same time he served as UNR communications minister in V. Chekhivsky's and S. Ostapenko's cabinets. In mid-1919 he was appointed chief of the UNR negotiations mission to Warsaw. He remained there and served briefly as prime minister of the UNR government-in-exile (1921–2). He was appointed a professor at the Lviv (Underground) Ukrainian Higher Polytechnical School (1922–5). From 1927 he worked in Lutske as a municipal engineer. There he founded and headed the Lesia Ukrainka Society.

Pylypchuk, Vasyl [Pylypčuk, Vasyl'], b 1871, d 17 February 1941 in Liubsha, Zhydachiv county, Galicia. Community leader and beekeeper. After graduating from the Greek Catholic Theological Seminary in Lviv he served as a parish priest. He set up a large, successful apiary, contributed to the monthly *Ukraïns'kyi pasichnyk*, and wrote *Pidruchnyk pasichnytstva* (A Handbook on Beekeeping, 1913; 2nd rev edn 1930). He organized local credit unions, dairy co-operatives, and Prosvita reading rooms.

Pylypenko, Anatolii, b 3 May 1914 in Kyrylivka (now Shevchenkove), Zvenyhorodka county, Kiev gubernia. Analytical chemist; AN URSR (now ANU) full member since 1972. A graduate of the Kiev Industrial (now Polytechnical) Institute (1936), he worked at the Kiev Technological Institute of Silicates (1939–41), headed the Laboratory of the Central Research Institute of Building Materials of the Ministry of the Building Materials Industry (1944–6), taught at Kiev University (from 1964), worked at the ANU Institute of General and Inorganic Chemistry (1968–75), and directed the ANU Institute of Colloidal Chemistry and Hydrochemistry (1975–). Pylypenko's research covers the use of complexing agents in inorganic analysis, the complex formation between metal ions and organic or inorganic ligands, and their analytical utilization. He established a classification system for organic reagents used in analytical chemistry and developed photometric and luminescence-based methods for the determination of rare elements.

Pylypenko, Borys, b ca 1892 in Chernihiv gubernia, d 3 November 1937 on Solovets Islands. Historian, ethnographer, and art historian. He was an associate of the Chernihiv Historical Museum in the 1920s. He then headed the history department at the All-Ukrainian Historical Museum in Kiev (1928–33) and the fieldwork of the joint museum-VUAN Polisian Historical-Economic Expedition (1932). He was arrested during the Stalinist terror of 1933 in Ukraine and was most likely shot.

Pylypenko, Mykhailo, b 8 October 1888 in Nosachiv, Cherkasy county, Kiev gubernia, d 27 July 1952 in Kiev. Actor. He completed theatrical studies at the Lysenko Music and Drama Institute in Kiev (1919) and then worked in the Shevchenko First Theater of the Ukrainian Soviet Republic (1919–20), the Kiev Operetta Theater (1934–5), and the Kiev Ukrainian Drama Theater (1921–52). He played comic and character roles and was known for his recitations of humorous and satirical stories.

Pylypenko, Nataliia (née Komilevska; married name: Khodymchuk), b 26 August 1898 in the Chernihiv region, d 27 October 1973 in New York. Stage actress and director. In 1918 she joined Molodyi Teatr; then she acted in the Shevchenko First Theater of the Ukrainian Soviet Republic (1919–21) and in Berezil (1922–34). She was expelled from the cast in 1934 as a result of the arrest of her husband, and she returned to theatrical activities only as an émigré in Paris, where she led a Ukrainian troupe (1948–57). Her memoirs are titled *Zhyttia v teatri* (Life in the Theater, 1968).

Serhii Pylypenko   Ivan Pylypiv

Pylypenko, Serhii, b 22 July 1891 in Kiev, d 3 March 1934. Writer and journalist. He was active in the Ukrainian Party of Socialist Revolutionaries in 1917–18 and then joined the Ukrainian Communist party. In the early 1920s he edited a number of newspapers, among them *Selians'ka pravda*. He published several collections of stories: *Baikivnytsia* (The Storyteller, 1922), *Baiky* (Stories, 1927), *Svyni na dubi* (Pigs on the Oak, 1932), and others. His writing is secondary to his role in literary and scholarly organizations, however. He founded *Pluh and edited its publications. He took an active role in the *Literary Discussion of 1925–8, in which he came out against M. *Khvylovy. In addition he was director of the *Taras Shevchenko Scientific Research Institute in Kharkiv (1926–33) and sat on the boards of directors of the Knyhospilka publishing house and the State Publishing House of Ukraine. In 1933 he was arrested, accused of belonging to a counterrevolutionary Ukrainian organization, and sentenced by a NKVD tribunal to be shot. In 1957 a military tribunal found no ground for his arrest, and he was posthumously rehabilitated.

Pylypenko, Viktor, b 15 November 1935 in Zaporizhia. Machine scientist; full member of the AN URSR (now ANU) since 1982. He graduated from Dnipropetrovske University (1959) and has worked at the ANU Institute of Technical Mechanics since 1966, as director since 1980. He has made scientific contributions in machine design, dynamic calculations in complex hydromechanical systems, and mathematical models for cavitating oscillations in pumping systems.

Pylypenko's Hill. A fortified settlement of the 3rd century BC to 1st century AD, 4 km south of Kaniv, Cherkasy oblast, on the right bank of the Dnieper. Excavations in 1948 and 1966–70 revealed 44 small, deeply set rectangular dwellings arranged in rows. Other remains found include local and Greek ceramic tableware, iron slag, crucibles for pouring bronze jewelry, and iron, bronze, and glass items. The settlement was a significant center of the *Zarubyntsi culture.

Pylypiv, Ivan (Pylypiw, Pillipiw; né Pylypivsky), b 7 July 1859 in Nebyliv, Kalush county, Galicia, d 10 October 1936 near North Bank, Alberta. Pioneer settler. Pylypiv, along with W. *Eleniak, another peasant from Nebyliv, has been regarded as the first Ukrainian to come to Canada; he arrived in 1891 to investigate the suitability of the country for settlement. After returning to Galicia early in 1892 for his family, he was arrested by the Austrian authorities on charges of sedition and inciting people to emigrate, and spent four months in jail. He returned to Canada in 1893 and took out his first homestead near Bruderheim, Alberta, before settling in Alberta's Edna-Star colony in 1894. Pylypiv acquired growing stature among Ukrainian Canadians after his death, once an article by I. Bobersky in the 1937 almanac of *Kanadiis'kyi farmer* established him and Eleniak as the first Ukrainians in Canada. Pylypiv's home was moved to the *Ukrainian Cultural Heritage Village near Edmonton in the 1970s and has been restored as a historical monument.

Pylyshenko, Volodymyr [Pylyšenko] (pseud: Mirko), b 28 July 1934 in Volodymyr-Volynskyi. Painter. A refugee, Pylyshenko emigrated to the United States after the Second World War and completed his studies at the Rochester Institute of Technology (MFA, 1963). Since 1963 he has been a professor of drawing and painting at the State University of New York at Brockport. He has exhibited his figurative and expressionistic oils and prints since 1963.

Pylyshyn, Zenon [Pylyšyn], b 25 August 1937 in Montreal. Psychologist; specialist in cognitive science. A graduate of McGill University (B ENG, 1959) and the University of Saskatchewan (1961; PH D, 1963), he joined the faculty of the University of Western Ontario in 1966 and was appointed director of its Centre for Cognitive Science in 1981. Since 1984 he has been a fellow of the Canadian Institute for Advanced Research and national director of its program in artificial intelligence and robotics. He was a founding member and board member of the Canadian Society for Computational Studies of Intelligence and of the International Cognitive Science Association, of which he was president in 1986. He has done experimental research on short-term memory, computer analysis of text, machine vision, computer models of human visual attention and perceptual-motor co-ordination, and the role of imagery in reasoning. He has written over 60 articles and book chapters, and 4 books, including *Computation and Cognition: Toward a Foundation for Cognitive Science* (1984).

Pymenova, Nina, b 27 December 1888 in Pułtusk, Poland, d 14 April 1941 in Kiev. Geologist and paleobotanist. She graduated from the Higher Courses for Women in St Petersburg (1910) and then taught secondary school in Warsaw, Moscow, and Kiev. She became a research associate of the geology chair at the VUAN (1924) and of the Institute of Geological Sciences (1926). At the same time she taught paleontology at Kiev University. Her main works deal with the plant fossils and the stratigraphy of Cretaceous, Paleogene, and Neogene deposits in Ukraine.

Mykola Pymonenko

Pymonenko, Mykola, b 9 March 1862 in Priorka (a suburb of Kiev), d 26 March 1912 in Kiev. Prominent Ukrainian realist painter; son-in-law of V. *Orlovsky; full member of the St Petersburg Academy of Arts from 1904. After studying at the *Kiev Drawing School (1878–82) and the St Petersburg Academy of Arts (1882–4) he taught at the Kiev Drawing School (1884–1900) and *Kiev Art School (1900–6). He took part in the exhibitions of the *Society of South Russian Artists (1891–6) and *Peredvizhniki society (from 1893) and became a member of the latter society in 1899. In 1909 he was elected a member of the Paris International Association of Arts and Literatures. Pymonenko produced over 700 genre scenes, landscapes, and portraits, many of which were reproduced as postcards. They include *Wedding in Kiev Gubernia* (1891), *At the Well* (1894), *Kiev Flower Seller* (1897), *At the Market* (1898), *Victim of Fanaticism* (1899), *Trial of One's Own (Horse Thief)* (1900), *Before the Storm* (1906), *Hay Gathering in Ukraine* (1907), *Rivals: At the Well* (1908), *Hopak* (1908; bought by the Louvre), and *Paschal Matins* (1910). Pymonenko also created illustrations for several of T. Shevchenko's narrative poems, and in the 1890s he took part in painting the murals in *St Volodymyr's Cathedral in Kiev. Books about him have been written by Ya. Zatenatsky (1955) and P. Hovdia (1957), and an album of his works was published in Kiev in 1983.

Pyna River. A left-bank tributary of the Prypiat River. It is 88 km long. It originates in marshland and then develops into a connecting waterway for the Dnieper–Buh Canal before joining the Prypiat near Pynske. Its entire course is in the Polisian area of Belarus. The river is regulated by dams.

Pynchuky. The name of the inhabitants of the Pynske region of Polisia. Sometimes the term is applied to all natives of Polisia (*polishchuky*), to whom the *pynchuky* are culturally related. Together with that of the Podlachians, the dialect of the *pynchuky* belongs to the western Polisian subgroup of northern Ukrainian dialects.

The Jesuit college and church in Pynske

Pynske or **Pinsk.** I-7. A city in Polisia (1990 pop 122,000), the center of the Pynske region and a raion center in Brest oblast (Belarus), situated at the confluence of the Pyna and the Prypiat rivers, on the eastern (dry) boundary of the Polisian swamps. The environs were first settled in the Neolithic age, and artifacts of the *Zarubyntsi culture have been unearthed there. The city was first mentioned in a chronicle under the year 1097 as Pynesk. During the Princely era it was the capital of the Turiv-Pynske principality and from the late 12th century, of the Pynske principality. It was annexed by Lithuania, and in 1569 became part of the Polish state. In 1581 it was granted the rights of *Magdeburg law. In the 16th and early 17th centuries it was an important trading and cultural center (an Orthodox and then Uniate bishopric, the site of a Jesuit college). It went into a period of decline until the late 18th century, when waterways were developed. Between 1793 and 1917 it was part of the Russian Empire and a county center of Minsk gubernia. It was a trading center for bread, fat, and wood products and later a center of the lumber and woodworking industry. In the late 19th century it attracted a large Jewish community, which came to constitute most of its population (1897, 28,000). In 1920–39 the city was controlled by Poland. By 1931 its population had reached 31,700. It was annexed by the Soviet Union in 1939 and assigned to the Belorussian SSR even though the population

in the surrounding area is predominantly Ukrainian.

Today local industry is varied: it includes furniture, shoe, weaving, match-making, and linen and hemp factories. There are also a foundry, a crane repair plant, a ship repair plant, food-processing plants, and a river port. Of cultural interest are a regional studies museum, a baroque Polish church and Jesuit college (17th century), and a Catholic cathedral (16th–18th centuries).

Pynske Congregation (Pynska kongregatsiia). An Orthodox sobor held from 15 June to 2 July 1791 in Pynske. In the late 18th century the Orthodox eparchy in Polish-ruled Belarus and Ukraine was subordinated to the Russian *Holy Synod, and its subordinate status gave St Petersburg a pretext for interfering in the internal affairs of the Polish Commonwealth. To inhibit such interference the Polish Sejm proclaimed religious freedom in 1790 and guaranteed government assistance to the Commonwealth's Orthodox faithful. The Pynske Congregation was convened to formalize the new arrangement. It was attended by 96 delegates drawn from the clergy, nobility, and bourgeoisie. The Commonwealth's only Orthodox bishop, V. Sadkovsky, could not attend because he was in prison. Archimandrite I. Balanovsky of the Motronynskyi Trinity Monastery was elected director of the congregation.

The congregation adopted rules regarding the structure of the Orthodox church in the Commonwealth that proscribed ties with the Russian Holy Synod and renewed the jurisdiction of the Patriarch of Constantinople. It also endorsed a new hierarchy consisting of a metropolitan and three bishops. A sobor held every four years was to be the church's legislative authority, and executive authority was to be vested in the metropolitan's Consistory in Pynske. Hegumen S. Palmovsky was elected chairman of the Consistory. Resolutions essentially proclaiming the autocephaly of the Orthodox church were adopted. The Sejm ratified the congregation's decisions on 16 May 1792. None of them were implemented, however, because of the 1793 and 1795 partitions of Poland and the resulting annexation of the Belarusian and Ukrainian territories by the Russian Empire.

BIBLIOGRAPHY
Smoleński, W. *Ostatni rok sejmu Wielkiego* (Cracow 1897)
Bidnov, V. *Pravoslavnaia Tserkov' v Pol'she i Litve (po Volumina legum)* (Katerynoslav 1908)
Vlasovs'kyi, I. *Narys istoriï Ukraïns'koï Pravoslavnoï Tserkvy*, vol 3 (New York and Bound Brook, NJ 1957)
                                    I. Korovytsky, A. Zhukovsky

Pynske region. A historical territory in the upper reaches of the Prypiat River in Polisia. Until the late 12th century it was part of *Turiv-Pynske principality, but later it constituted an appanage of Pynske principality dominated by the princes of Kiev and Volodymyr-Volynskyi. The rulers of Pynske principality included the brothers Yaroslav (1183) and Yaropolk (1190) Yaroslavych and their descendants, Volodymyr (1206–7), Rostyslav (1228–32), Mykhailo (1228), Teodor (1262), and Yurii (d 1289). In the mid-13th century the principality recognized the overlordship of King Danylo Romanovych of Galicia-Volhynia, and ca 1318 it was annexed by the Lithuanian grand duke Gediminas. From 1471 to 1521 it was governed by the *Olelkovych family of Lithuanian-Ruthenian princes of Kiev. Thenceforth it was under Polish rule. During the Cossack-Polish War the principality's nobles officially joined the Hetman state on 20 June 1657, and created *Pynske-Turiv regiment.

Pynske-Turiv regiment. An administrative territory and military formation of the Hetman state. It was established in 1657, when the Ukrainian Cossacks expelled the Polish landowners from Belarusian territory. The regiment was dissolved in the middle of 1659, when Polish forces recaptured the region. The commanders of the regiment were Cols I. Hrusha (1657) and K. Vyhovsky (1657–9).

Pyntia (Pinta), b and d ? Leader, perhaps of Rumanian origin, of a band of Transcarpathian *opryshoks from 1701. The rebels participated in the Kuruc peasant revolt of 1703, which overran Berehove, Mukachiv, Khust, and Uzhhorod before it was suppressed. Pyntia's band fled across the Carpathians to Polish-ruled Pokutia, where together with I. *Pysklyvy's band it attacked the nobles and usurers of Kolomyia and its vicinity.

Pypin, Aleksandr, b 6 April 1833 in Saratov, d 9 December 1904 in St Petersburg. Russian Slavist and cultural historian; full member of the Russian Academy of Sciences from 1898 and the Shevchenko Scientific Society from 1903. He studied under I. Sreznevsky at St Petersburg University and was a professor there in 1860–1. Both he and M. *Kostomarov resigned as professors in protest against the tsarist oppression of the student movement. Pypin played an important editorial role in the progressive journals *Sovremennik* and *Vestnik Evropy*, in which he published his reviews of Ukrainian literature. He wrote nearly 1,200 works. He discussed the development of Ukrainian literature and ethnography in his pioneering histories of ancient Russian tales (master's thesis, 1857), Slavic literatures (coauthor, V. Spasovich, 1865; 2 vols, 1879, 1881), Russian ethnography (4 vols, 1890–2; vol 3 is devoted to Ukrainian ethnography), and Russian literature (4 vols, 1898–9). Pypin also wrote articles about T. Shevchenko; he considered him one of the best Slavic poets and a talented realist prose writer. His 1890 *Vestnik Evropy* review of O. *Ohonovsky's history of Ruthenian literature, in which Pypin disagreed that Ukrainian literature has its origins in Kievan Rus' and that it evolved independently of Russian literature, elicited a lively polemic in which Ohonovsky, I. Nechui-Levytsky, M. Komarov, K. Mykhalchuk, M. Drahomanov, I. Franko (with whom Pypin corresponded), and other scholars took part. Information regarding Ukraine can be found in his books on the social (1871) and religious (1916) movements during the reign of Alexander I and on Russian Freemasonry (1916). His reminiscences were published in 1910.

R. Senkus

Pyriatyn [Pyrjatyn]. III-13. A city (1989 pop 20,500) on the Udai River and a raion center in Poltava oblast. It was first mentioned in the Hypatian Chronicle under the year 1155. From the mid-14th century it belonged to the Grand Duchy of Lithuania, and from 1569, to the Polish Commonwealth. It was granted the rights of *Magdeburg law in 1592. Under the Hetman state (1648–1781) Pyriatyn belonged to Kropyvna and Lubni regiments. Then, for over

a century, it was a county center in Poltava gubernia. Today the city is an industrial center with a metalworking, building-materials, woodworking, and food industry. Its architectural monuments include the Cathedral of Christ's Nativity (1781) and a hospital building designed by N. Amvrosimov in the early 19th century.

Mykola Pyrohiv

Pyrohiv, Mykola, b 28 March 1875 in Chernihiv, d March 1961 in Blacktown, Australia. Physician, educator, and army officer; grandson of N. *Pirogov. After graduating from the St Petersburg Military Medical Academy he served in Kovel as an army doctor. During the First World War he was chief physician at the Military Surgical Hospital in Kiev and principal of the Fourth Coeducational Ukrainian Gymnasium, which he had organized. He commanded a regiment in the Zaporozhian Corps in the UNR Army in 1919 and a battalion in the First Zaporozhian Rifle Division in 1920. He received the rank of colonel. After returning to Kovel in 1921, he practiced medicine and was active in the Prosvita Society and the Ukrainbank. In 1922 he was elected to the Polish Sejm, where he served as vice-president of the *Ukrainian Parliamentary Representation. After the war he emigrated to Australia (1951).

Pyrohoshcha Church of the Mother of God (Tserkva Bohorodytsi Pyrohoshchi, aka Soborna tserkva Uspinnia presv. Bohorodytsi). A church built in the Byzantine style in the Podil district of Kiev in 1132–6 during the reign of Prince Mstyslav I Volodymyrovych the Great. The short church consisted of three naves and apses covered by one dome. The walls were decorated with frescoes, and the floor was laid with glazed and mosaic tiles. The first building of the Kievan princes to be erected entirely of brick instead of stone, in the medieval period it was the main church of the Podil's merchants and tradesmen and housed an orphanage, a hospital for the poor, and the municipal archives. In 1613–33, when the St Sophia Cathedral was the seat of the Uniate Kiev metropoly, the church served as the cathedral of the Orthodox metropolitans. It was reconstructed several times: in 1613–14 by the Italian architect S. Bracci, in the 1770s in the baroque style by I. Hryhorovych-Barsky, and in 1811 in the neoclassical style by A. Melensky. In 1778 it acquired one of the finest rococo iconostases in Ukraine. In 1835 its five-level belfry was dismantled, and a new one was built in the Empire style above the main entrance. In 1935 the church was de-

Pyrohoshcha Church of the Mother of God

stroyed by the Soviet authorities so that a public square could be expanded. In the latter half of the 1970s the foundations of the old church were excavated, and the question of rebuilding the church in its original form was raised.

Pyrola (Ukrainian: *hrushanka*). Perennial grasses of the family Pyrolaceae. In Ukraine *P. rotundifolia* and *P. minor* grow in the forest zone in mossy, coniferous, and mixed forests. They are occasionally grown as decorative ground covers in shady areas of parks. Extracts of *P. chimaphila umbellata* were used to treat urinary bladder infections.

Pysanka. See Easter egg.

Heorhii Pysarenko

Lev Pysarzhevsky

Pysarenko, Heorhii (Yurii), b 12 November 1910 in Poltava. Scientist in the field of mechanics and strength of materials; full member of the AN URSR (now ANU) since 1964 and of the International Academy of Astronautics since 1977. He graduated from the Gorkii Industrial Institute (1936) and worked at the ANU Institute of Mechanics (1939–51) and the ANU Institute for Problems of Materials Science (1951–66). He was director of the ANU Institute for Problems of the Strength of Materials (1966–88) and taught at the Kiev Polytechnical Institute. He also served as the first scientific secretary (1962–6) and vice-president (1970–8) of the ANU. His main scientific contributions are in the field of mechanical vibrations and in various areas of the theoretical study of the strength of materials.

Pysarenko, Leonid, b 10 March 1907 in Znamianka, Oleksandriia county, Kherson gubernia, d 23 January 1979 in Kiev. Scenery designer. In 1931–6 he studied at the Kharkiv Arts Institute (pupil of B. Kosariv). Then he designed scenery (mostly monumentalist) for over 80 drama, opera, and ballet productions in Kiev, Lviv, Kharkiv, and Zaporizhia. He also created the panel *Science* in the House of Culture in Sutysky, Tyvriv raion, Vinnytsia oblast (1965).

Pysarevsky, Leonid. See Zymny, Leonid.

Pysarevsky, Stepan [Pysarevs'kyj] (pseud: Stetsko Shereperia), b 1780s, d 3 February 1839 in Vovchanske, Slobidska Ukraine. Writer. He studied at Kharkiv College and served as a priest in Kharkiv, Bohodukhiv, and Vovchanske. He began to publish in 1813. Pysarevsky set some of his poems to music, and they became popular folk songs ('Za Neman' idu' [I'm Going beyond the Neman], 'De ty brodysh moia dole?' [Where Are You Roaming, My Fate?]). He contributed to the almanacs *Snip* and *Lastivka*. He wrote an operetta, *Kupala na Ivana* (On St John's Eve, 1840), which I. Ozarkevych reworked and retitled *Vesillia, abo Nad tsyhana Shmahaila nema rozumnishoho* (The Wedding, or There's No One Smarter Than Shmahailo the Gypsy), and for which M. Verbytsky composed the music.

Pysarzhevsky, Lev [Pysarževs'kyj], b 13 February 1874 in Kishinev, Bessarabia, d 23 March 1938 in Dnipropetrovske. Inorganic and physical chemist; VUAN/AN URSR (now ANU) full member from 1925; corresponding member of the USSR Academy of Sciences from 1928 and full member from 1930. A graduate of the university in Odessa (1896; M SC, 1903), he was a professor at Yurev (Tartu) University (1904–8), the Kiev Polytechnical Institute (1908–11), and the Katerynoslav (now Dnipropetrovske) Mining (1913–30) and Chemical Technology (1930–2) institutes. He cofounded and directed the Ukrainian Physical-Chemical Institute in Dnipropetrovske (1927–34), the Tbilisi Chemical Research Institute (1929–31), and the ANU Institute of Physical Chemistry in Kiev (1934–8), which is named in his honor. Pysarzhevsky studied the structure and properties of peroxides and peracids, the influence of solvents on chemical equilibria, the free energy of reactions, and electronic concepts of chemistry in all their ramifications. His work played a significant role in establishing the current views on the nature of chemical bonding and chemical reaction mechanisms, with particular emphasis on the electronic theory of heterogeneous catalysis. He wrote over 90 papers, monographs, and textbooks. His book on elementary chemistry (1926) introduced a holistic view of chemistry from the standpoint of electronic interactions. Editions of his selected works were published in 1936, 1955, and 1956. Since 1964 the ANU has awarded the Pysarzhevsky Prize for outstanding contributions to chemistry or chemical technology. A biography, by K. Yatsymrsky and R. Kostrova, was published in Kiev in 1979.

S. Trofimenko

Pysemsky, Hryhorii [Pysems'kyj, Hryhorij], b 7 February 1862 in Pyriatyn, Poltava gubernia, d 25 July 1937 in Kiev. Obstetrician and gynecologist. A graduate of Kiev University (1888), he served as a lecturer at Kiev University (1905–13); professor at Moscow Univeristy (1913–15), the Kiev Medical Institute (1921–30), and the Kiev Institute for the Upgrading of Physicians (1930–7); and scientific director of the Kiev Institute for the Protection of Maternity and Childhood (1930–7). He organized the first consultation office for pregnant women in Kiev and presided over the Ukrainian and the Kiev scientific societies of obstetricians and gynecologists. He wrote over 70 works dealing with the innervation of the womb, problems of operative gynecology and oncology, postnatal complications, and the organization of obstetric aid.

Pysh, Symeon [Pyž], b 14 February 1894 in Vapenne, Gorlice county, Galicia, d 10 June 1957 in Yonkers, New York. Lemko activist. After spending most of the First World War in an Austrian internment camp and an Italian POW camp, he studied law at Charles University in Prague (PH D, 1922). He emigrated to the United States in 1923 and became editor of *Pravda*, the weekly organ of the Russian Brotherhood Organization. He helped found the *Lemko Association and in 1934 was appointed editor of its newspaper *Lemko* in Cleveland and then *Karpats'ka Rus'* in Yonkers. His *Short History of Carpatho-Russia*, originally printed in 1938, appeared in English translation in 1973.

Pyshkin, Borys [Pyškin], b 3 September 1893 in Kazan, Russia, d 29 January 1970 in Kiev. Scientist in the field of hydrotechnology; corresponding member of the AN URSR (now ANU) from 1951. He graduated form the Moscow Agricultural Academy (1924), worked at the ANU Institute of Hydrology and Hydrotechnology (from 1948, now the Institute of Hydromechanics), and taught at Kiev University (from 1962). He contributed to research on the mathematical modeling of dynamics of large bodies of water, processes of wave formation, erosion by waves on shores and shore structures, and methods of preventing wave-caused erosion.

Pysklyvy, Ivan [Pysklyvyj], b ? in Dovhopillia, Pokutia, d 1705 in Stanyslaviv. Leader of a band of *opryshoks in the Hutsul region from 1701. In 1703 the band attacked the nobles and usurers in the town of Kolomyia and the villages of Otynia, Bereziv, Vorona, Zabolotiv, and Nezvysko, and in 1704 it joined *Pyntia's band to attack Kosiv. Pysklyvy was captured by the Poles and executed.

Pysmenna, Larysa [Pys'menna], b 11 February 1914 in Chopovychi, Radomyshl county, Kiev gubernia. Writer. She worked as head of the literature editorial office at the

Larysa Pysmenna

Veselka publishing house. She began publishing in 1931 and has written numerous books of stories and fables for children, including *Iak u Chubasyka smikh ukraly* (How Chubasyk Had His Laughter Stolen, 1965), *Charivnyk na tonkykh nizhkakh* (A Sorcerer on Thin Little Legs, 1972), *Skarb vovchoï krynytsi* (The Treasure of the Vovcha Spring, 1975), *Ne za synimy moriamy* (Not beyond Blue Seas, 1980), and *Tysiacha vikon i odyn zhuravel'* (A Thousand Windows and One Crane, 1984). Pysmenna has also written prose for teenagers and young adults: such collections as *Khochete prozhyty dvisti rokiv?* (Do You Want to Live 200 Years?, 1972), *Nenapysanyi portret* (The Unpainted Portrait, 1979), and *Lina* (1983), and the novels *Zlochyn Nadiï Polishchuk* (The Crime of Nadiia Polishchuk, 1964), *Palats bez stin* (A Palace without Walls, 1965), *Zhyvi zustrichaiut' svitanok* (The Living Greet the Dawn, 1969), and *Bat'ko* (Father, 1978). She was awarded the Lesia Ukrainka Prize in 1984. A book of her reminiscences, *Choho ne znav erudyt* (What the Erudite One Did Not Know), was published in 1989.

Pysmenny, Oleksii [Pys'mennyj, Oleksij], b and d ? Haidamaka leader of Polish origin. He organized a rebel detachment of Zaporozhians during the 1750 haidamaka uprising. The group was active in Right-Bank Ukraine until it was broken up during a skirmish with a Polish punitive expedition near the town of Vilshana. Pysmenny's further fate is unknown.

Pys'mo do hromady (Letter to the Community). A political and literary newspaper for peasants, published in Lviv and edited by S. Shekhovych. A single issue appeared in 1863. The newspaper reappeared as a semimonthly in August 1864 (1864–5 and 1867–8; a total of 90 issues). It contained popular educational and religious articles, community news, and belles lettres by writers such as H. Barvinok, M. Vovchok, S. Rudansky, L. Hlibov, I. Naumovych, and M. Ustyianovych.

Pys'mo z Prosvity (Writing from Prosvita). The title of three organs of the *Prosvita society in Lviv. All of them contained practical information and advice on farming and animal husbandry, reports on the activities of the Prosvita society throughout Galicia, poetry, and prose. The first appeared monthly from October 1877 to May 1879 and was edited by A. Vakhnianyn and, from 1878, O. Partytsky. In 1894 Prosvita took over publication of the semimonthly *Chytal'nia* (est 1893) from the Dnister insurance company and published it as *Chytal'nia – Pys'mo z Prosvity* until the end of 1896, under the editorship of K. Pankivsky. In 1907–8 *Pys'mo z Prosvity* reappeared as a monthly edited by Ya. Vesolovsky and then H. Khotkevych. From 1909 to 1914 it was a semimonthly edited by Yu. Balytsky. Publication was interrupted by the First World War, although an issue edited by V. Lukych appeared in 1916. From December 1921 to the end of 1922 the periodical was a semimonthly edited by V. Doroshenko.

Pyvorizy. See Itinerant tutors.

Pyvovariv, Mykola, b ?, d 1935 in Vinnytsia. Church figure. He was a bishop of the Ukrainian Autocephalous Orthodox church (UAOC) in Kamianets-Podilskyi from 1922. From 1924 he headed the Active Church of Christ, a dissident faction of the church, before returning to good standing with the UAOC in 1927. Pyvovariv was arrested in 1929, together with 45 other priests and believers, and imprisoned in Siberia. He was released in 1934 because of illness, and he returned to Ukraine and died shortly thereafter.

Hryhorii Pyvovarov:
Portrait of Oleksander Dovzhenko (bronze, 1940)

Pyvovarov, Hryhorii, b 22 March 1908 in Lokhvytsia, Poltava gubernia, d 15 May 1942 in Kerch, Crimea. Sculptor. He studied at the Kiev State Art Institute (1926–31) and was a member of the Union of Young Artists of Ukraine (1928–31). He scupted plaster portraits of T. Shevchenko (1936), I. Franko (1939), and O. Dovzhenko (1940); collaborated with Yu. Bilostotsky and E. Fridman on the multifigural compositions *Socialist Agriculture* and *Socialist Industry* for the Ukrainian pavilion at the Exhibition of the Achievements of the National Economy in Moscow (1937); and created granite monuments to Komsomol heroes in Trypilia (1934–6), to Soviet heroes of the stratosphere in Donetske (1938), and to M. Shchors in Shchors (1939).

Pyziur, Eugene [Pyzjur, Jevhen], b 16 April 1917 in Belzets, Rava Ruska county, Galicia, d 13 March 1980 in St Louis, Missouri. Political scientist and community figure; full member of the Ukrainian Academy of Arts and Sciences in the US and member of the Shevchenko Scientific Society. He studied law at the Universities of Lviv (1936–9) and Vienna (1942–5). While in Vienna, he headed the *Sich student society (1943–4) and *Nationalist Organization of Ukrainian Students in Germany (1944). As a postwar refugee in Germany he was a member of the executive of the *Central Union of Ukrainian Students (1945–8) and editor of its *Students'kyi visnyk,* and he continued his studies at the Ukrainian Free University in Munich (1947–8; LLD, 1949). After emigrating to the United States, he studied political philosophy at Columbia University (1954) and the University of Notre Dame (1957–8; PH D, 1961). In 1961 he joined the Department of Political Science at St Louis University, and from 1965 he was also an associate and editor of the *Lypynsky East European Research Institute in Philadelphia. Pyziur is the author of *The Doctrine of Anarchism of Michael A. Bakunin* (1955) and articles in Ukrainian émigré and American periodicals on Soviet agricultural policy (1952), D. Chyzhevsky (1955), the ideas of B. Kistiakovsky (1958), M. Drahomanov (1966), and M. Katkov (1967), T. Shevchenko and E. Burke (1980), Soviet nationality policy, and Marxist ideology.

Giacomo Quarenghi: architectural rendering of the new Transfiguration Cathedral in Novhorod-Siverskyi (ca 1790)

Quarenghi, Giacomo, b 20 or 21 September 1744 in Valle-Imania, near Bergamo, Italy, d 2 March 1817 in St Petersburg. Italian architect. From 1780 he worked in the Russian Empire, where he built palaces and public buildings in the Empire style in St Petersburg and Peterhof. In Ukraine he built the cathedral of the Novhorod-Siverskyi Transfiguration Monastery (1796), the cathedral in Kremenchuk (1790s), and Count P. Zavadovsky's palace in Lialychi, Chernihiv gubernia (1780s to 1790s). The Ukrainian architect A. Melensky was taught by Quarenghi.

Quarrying. A branch of the *building-materials industry that mines and processes sand, blocks, gravel, and stone slabs. These products are used in the construction, road-building, and other industries. In Ukraine most quarries are located in the *Ukrainian Crystalline Shield. Quarrying has been practiced in Ukraine for centuries, but it emerged as a major industry only in the 20th century. From 1940 to 1980 the total output of quarries in Ukraine increased from 3.2 million sq m to approx 170 million sq m. The major products of the industry are gravel, stone, and *granite, which is used as decorative facing.

Quince (*Cydonia oblonga*; Ukrainian: *aiva zvychaina*). A fruit tree of the family Rosaceae, native to the Crimea, Iran, and Turkey. In Ukraine it is also cultivated in the south, in Transcarpathia, and in Chernivtsi oblast. It grows in a dwarf form and a tall form. Several Ukrainian varieties exist. The aromatic fruit is sweetish sour and contains 5–15 percent sugars, approx 1 percent organic acids, and less than 1 percent pectin. It is processed for consumption as preserves, jelly, compote, marmalade, and candied peels. Quince is often used as a stock for the grafting of *pear.

Quitrent. Feudal rent paid in kind or money by landless peasants, townspeople, and other free persons for the use of royal-, state-, church-, and gentry-owned farmlands, pastures, forests, ponds, hunting places, mills, shops, and other properties in perpetuity. Quitrent replaced *tribute as the main form of peasant exploitation in the late Middle Ages. In Polish- and Lithuanian-ruled Ukraine from the 14th century, peasant households paid quitrents in grain, honey, furs, livestock, food, and money. They had several names: *chynsh* (from German *Zins*, from Latin *census*), *podymne* (quitrent paid by each *dym*), *diaklo*, *serebshchyna* (from *serebro* 'silver,' quitrent in silver coins), *ordynshchyna* (from *orda* 'horde,' originally tribute paid to the Golden Horde), *poholovshchyna* (from *holova* 'head,' a form of poll tax), and *povolovshchyna* (from *vil* 'ox,' quitrent in livestock). Their amounts were regulated by a *chynsh* law and custom and varied from place to place. After the *voloka* land reform of 1557 and the imposition of *serfdom the use of quitrents declined and was replaced by the more oppressive corvée. *Chynsh* was revived on the vast colonized estates of the Polish magnates in Right-Bank Ukraine in the late 17th century. Economic relations based on *chynsh* law were maintained in the Polish-dominated territories annexed by the Russian Empire.

In Russian gubernias where the soil was poor, more peasants (60 percent in the mid-19th century) paid quitrent (called *obrok*) than performed corvée. From 1724 the tsarist state imposed an *obrok* tax on state peasants in addition to the *poll tax. In the black-earth Ukrainian gubernias, the *obrok* tax was paid by most state peasants (44 percent of all peasants in 1860). Only a small minority (1.2 percent in 1858) of the gentry-owned serfs paid cash *obrok* to their owners; the vast majority performed corvée instead. After the abolition of serfdom in the Russian Empire in 1861, peasants continued paying *obrok* for the land they received until it was replaced by *redemption payments in 1886. In Western Ukraine the emancipated peasants paid *chynsh* for *servitudes until the 1939 Soviet occupation.

R. Senkus

R

Rabbit (*Oryctolagus cuniculus*; Ukrainian: *kril*, also *zaiats* or *zaiets*). The Old World rabbit, also known as the European or true rabbit. Along with the cottontail rabbit (*Sylvilagus*) and other genera, it belongs to the family Leporidae (rabbits and *hare) of timid and swift, long-eared, small gnawing mammals. The ancestor of the domestic rabbit, the gregarious Old World rabbit is found in the wild in southwestern Ukraine. It is widely hunted for its flesh and fur; in some places it is exterminated as a serious agricultural pest. Domestic rabbits, of which there are many breeds and varieties, are kept as pets and as fur, meat, and laboratory animals. Research on *rabbit breeding is co-ordinated by the Scientific Research Institute of Animal Husbandry of the Forest-Steppe and Polisia, in Kharkiv. The rabbit is a popular character in *children's folklore.

Rabbit breeding. A branch of *animal husbandry that raises rabbits for meat, fur, and down and for use as scientific laboratory animals. Because rabbits require relatively little attention and feed, multiply quickly, and yield high-quality meat and fur, their breeding is economically efficient and profitable. In Ukraine up to 90 percent of all rabbits are raised privately by peasants and workers. Large-scale commercial rabbit breeding was introduced only in the late 1920s, and today there are about 500 rabbit farms, primarily in the Crimea but also in Cherkasy and Kherson oblasts. Production of rabbit meat, which is concentrated in Poltava and Cherkasy oblasts, increased from 37,000 t in 1960 to 67,000 t in 1987. In 1961, 26.4 million pelts were produced in Ukraine (45 percent of the entire USSR production). In 1985 about 10.6 million rabbits were bred in Ukraine. (See also *Rabbit.)

Yuliian Rabii

Rabii, Yuliian [Rabij, Julijan], b 5 January 1894 in Sambir, Galicia, d 17 November 1982 in Utica, New York. Lawyer and civic leader. He acted as defense counsel at many political trials and founded various local organizations, such as the Sokil sports club, the Knyzhka library, a branch of the Lysenko Music Society in Lviv, the Boian singing society, and the Banduryst wind orchestra. In 1944 he fled from Ukraine to Germany, and in 1951 he emigrated to the United States. He contributed many articles to the Ukrainian press based on his recollections and wrote the monograph *Sambirs'ka Bohorodytsia* (The Sambir Mother of God, 1970).

Rabotnik (Worker). The first legal Bolshevik newspaper in Ukraine. Two issues appeared in Russian in Kiev in June 1906, before the newspaper was closed down by the authorities.

Rabynovych, Zinovii [Rabynovyč, Zinovij], b 1 August 1918 in Kiev. Computer scientist. He graduated from the Kiev Polytechnical Institute (1941) and worked in industry, at the AN URSR (now ANU), and, from 1957, at the ANU Institute of Cybernetics as a department head. His main contributions are in the field of the theory of digital computers. He was one of the creators and the main designer of the first Soviet digital computer (the *MEOM).

Race (*rasa*). A biological grouping of a breeding population of individuals with certain genetically transmitted characteristics. It is not the uniformity but the comparative frequency of the appearance of inherited characteristics which defines a population as a racial group. The idea of race is statistical in principle in that it describes the characteristics of a population and not necessarily its individual members, and the diversity within a racial group is enormous. The markers used in identifying various races of humans are skin color, eye cast, hair form and bone structure, blood type, and so on. At present three general racial groups are recognized: the Mongoloid race, the Caucasoid race, and the Negroid race.

In broad terms Ukrainians are of the Caucasoid or Europoid race, with a wide range of skin color, from pale alabaster white to shades of brown. Eyes vary from the northern light blue to the dark brown to black of the Mediterranean inhabitants. The hair is usually soft, straight or wavy, its color ranging from light blond to raven black. The structure of the nose varies from high and narrow to broad and snub; the lips are usually thin. Both sexes have relatively large amounts of body hair, and men grow heavy beards. Although typically Slavic in general, Ukrainians show a wide range of the aforementioned characteristics as a result of the centuries of turmoil and the influence of nomadic nations in their ethnic territory (see *Physical anthropology).

More precisely, the current structure of the Ukrainian population reflects the following distribution of racial formations: (1) the Nordic–sub-Nordic race, found in the territory of Podlachia, Polisia, Volhynia, and Zhytomyr, and then down towards the southern Kiev, Poltava, and Dnipropetrovske regions, with some islands in Ivano-

Frankivske oblast and in the Prut River basin; (2) the Dinaric race, predominant in Subcarpathia and Transcarpathia, western and central Galicia, Podilia, and the Kholm region, with some penetration into Kiev oblast (Alpinian traces are found in some Transcarpathian zones, in the Podilia and Kiev regions; and definite Armenoid characteristics appear along the crests of the Carpathian Mountains in the area inhabited by Hutsuls, down to Bukovyna); (3) the Alpinian-Lappanoid race, predominant in the Kharkiv, Poltava, Sumy, and Chernihiv regions; (4) the sub-Lappanoid races, characteristics of which are found in the Donbas and southern steppe zones, with some Alpinian admixtures; (5) the Mediterranean race, which appears in the territory between the Prut and Dniester rivers, south to Zalishchyky. These five groups are the results of complex processes which began in prehistoric times with the *Trypilian culture. (See also *Anthropological studies.)

I. Masnyk

Rachmaninoff, Sergei [Raxmaninov, Sergej], b 1 April 1873 in Oneg, Novgorod gubernia, d 28 March 1943 in Beverly Hills, California. Russian composer, pianist, and conductor. He studied at the St Petersburg Conservatory in the theory and harmony class of Ukrainian musicologist O. Rubets (1882–5) and frequently appeared as pianist and conductor in Kiev, Kharkiv, and Odessa before emigrating to the United States after the revolution. Several of his works contain conspicuous Ukrainian elements; they include a setting of the Ukrainian folk song 'Choboty' (Boots) for mixed chorus a cappella (1899), a fragment for vocal quartet titled 'Mazeppa' (ca 1890, lyrics based on Pushkin), the symphonic poem *Prince Rostyslav* (1891), and transcriptions of Mussorgsky's 'Hopak' dance from *Sorochyntsi Fair*. He also composed three songs for solo voice with piano to Russian versions of poems by T. Shevchenko – 'The Days Pass By' or 'Duma,' 'Soldier's Wife,' and 'Again I Am Alone.' Some of his works are influenced by or contain ancient ritualistic chants of the Kievan Cave Monastery, among them the *Third Piano Concerto* (First Movement, opening theme), the *Sacred Liturgy of St John Chrysostom* (1910), and *Vespers Service* (1915).

Rachynsky, Andrii [Račyns'kyj, Andrij], b 24 November 1724 in Velyki Mosty, Sokal county, Galicia, d 1794 in Novhorod-Siverskyi. Composer and conductor. He studied at the Collegium in Lviv, where he also conducted the archbishop's kapelle for three years. In 1753 he started working at the court of Hetman K. Rozumovsky, where he founded the Hlukhiv Music Library and introduced Italian music in Left-Bank Ukraine. In 1761–2 he became a chamber musician at the court of Peter III, and in 1763 he was made captain of the Novhorod-Siverskyi company. During the next 30 years he made numerous trips throughout Ukraine recruiting promising young singers for court service. His works include the sacred vocal concertos *Raduitesia Bohu, pomoshchnyku nashemu* (Rejoice in God, Our Helper) and *Vozliubykh Tia, Hospody* (Loving Thee, O Lord).

Rachynsky, Havrylo [Račyns'kyj], b 1777 in Novhorod-Siverskyi, d 11 April 1843 in Novhorod-Siverskyi. Composer, violinist, guitarist, and pedagogue; son of A. Rachynsky. At an early age he was taught to play the vio-

lin by his father. In 1789–95 he probably studied with A. Vedel at the Kiev Academy, and in 1795–7 he studied in Moscow, where he subsequently taught advanced music until 1805. Beginning in 1808 he concertized throughout Ukraine. He was one of the first Ukrainian musicians to embark on a career as a concert artist. From 1823 to 1840 he lived in Moscow. His works consist mostly of songs, romances, variations, and arrangements of Ukrainian folk songs. His best-known set of variations is on the song 'Viiut' vitry, viiut' buini' (The Wild Winds Blow).

Rada. The Ukrainian term (equivalent to council) for a representative state governing body or the leading body of a party, organization, or institution. The term has been used since the medieval period: it was applied to the Boyar Council in Kievan Rus' and the Council of Lords in the Grand Duchy of Lithuania. The Cossack host and state had radas: the Sich Council, the General Military Council, and the Council of Officers.

The representative national congress of the people of Galicia in 1848 was called the Supreme Ruthenian Council, and the political representation of Ukrainians in Austria in 1914 was known as the Supreme Ukrainian Council. After the Revolution of 1917 the highest representative bodies and government agencies in Ukraine were the Central Rada and the Ukrainian National Rada.

All-Ukrainian councils of peasants', workers', and soldiers' deputies were formed in Kiev in 1917 to represent certain segments of the population, and in December 1917 they convened the All-Ukrainian Congress of Workers', Soldiers', and Peasants' Deputies. The Peasant Association–Ukrainian Party of Socialist Revolutionaries bloc set up its own radas in volosts, counties, and villages in 1918–19 as organs of local government. In Transcarpathia in 1918–19 local people's radas and the Central Ruthenian People's Council were formed to decide the fate of the region. A similar body, the American Ruthenian National Council, was organized by émigrés in the United States.

In the civic and legal context a rada is a representative body. Some examples include the National Council of Ukrainian Women, the Ukrainian National Council (émigré political center), and the Ukrainian Supreme Liberation Council. The State Popular Council and the Council of the Republic were conceived in 1920–1 as advisory bodies of the UNR government, which was run by the Council of National Ministers.

In 1917–18 the Bolsheviks used the abbreviated form Rada instead of Central Rada in their official documents and press. They called their own regime and its governing organs 'soviet' at first. Only in 1919 did they begin to use the Ukrainian term rada and its adjective *radianskyi* for their ruling organs. They applied the adjectives *radivskyi* and *radivtsi* to the Central Rada. Since 1920 the Ukrainian term rada has been generally accepted as the name for *soviets at every level. On 6 January 1919 Soviet Ukraine adopted the official name of the Ukrainska Sotsialistychna Radianska Respublika. Yet in other languages the term was commonly translated from the Russian as, for example, Soviet Ukraine or L'Ukraine soviétique. In Western Ukraine (before 1945) and among Ukrainians abroad the terms Soviet and *sovietskyi* were preferred to rada and *radianskyi* in identifying Soviet Ukrainian institutions, because they imply the non-Ukrainian origin of the institutions.

O. Ohloblyn, M. Stakhiv

Rada, pt 1 (1883)

Rada (Council). A Ukrainian almanac edited and published by M. Starytsky in two volumes in Kiev in 1883–4. It included poetry by Starytsky, Chaichenko (B. Hrinchenko), Bobenko (A. Bibik), M. Sadovsky, Khrushch (O. Afanasiev-Chuzhbynsky), Ya. Shchoholiv, P. Ratai (P. Kulish), and others; I. Nechui-Levytsky's famous novelette 'Mykola Dzheria'; the first two of four parts of P. Myrny's classic realist novel 'Poviia' (Loose Woman); stories by O. Pchilka, D. Mordovtsev, Bobenko, Hnat Kary (I. Tobilevych), Lopukh (A. Hrabenko), H. Barvinok, P. Myrny, and T. Alatonchenko; Starytsky's drama 'Ne sudylos'' (It Was Not Destined); V. Vasylenko's article on peasant associations; a demonological sketch by H. Desiatyn (H. Lukianov); and M. Komarov's pioneering bibliography of Ukrainian literature (1798–1883) with addenda.

The editors of *Rada* in 1908. Sitting, from left: O. Kuzmynsky, Spyrydon Cherkasenko, Leonyd Pakharevsky, Yevhen Chykalenko, Hryhorii Sherstiuk, Serhii Yefremov, Fedir Matushevsky; standing: Maksym Hekhter, Prokip Poniatenko, Mykola Vorony, Metodii Pavlovsky, P. Hai, P. Sabaldyr, S. Panasenko, Oleksander Oles

Rada (Council). A political and cultural newspaper published in Kiev from September 1906 to August 1914. In that period it was the only Ukrainian-language daily in tsarist-ruled Ukraine. *Rada* succeeded the banned daily *Hromads'ka dumka*. It was published by B. Hrinchenko and, from 1907, by Ye. Chykalenko, who provided most of the funding. Some capital investment came from V. Symyrenko, V. Leontovych, P. Stebnytsky, M. Komarov, P. Pelekhin, and L. Zhebunov. Although officially nonpartisan, from 1908 *Rada* reflected the political views of the *Society of Ukrainian Progressives, to which Chykalenko and

many of the contributors belonged. Its chief editors were F. Matushevsky, M. Pavlovsky (1907–13), and A. Nikovsky. The editorial secretaries were S. Petliura, V. Koroliv-Stary, and P. Sabaldyr (Maiorsky). From 1907 the paper also had several section editors: D. Doroshenko (to 1909, developments in Ukraine), L. Starytska-Cherniakhivska (developments in the Russian Empire), M. Lozynsky (foreign developments), H. Sherstiuk (education), M. Hekhter (socioeconomic affairs), and B.-V. Yaroshevsky and occasionally V. Lypynsky (developments in Poland). Its prominent contributors were H. Chuprynka, P. Chyzhevsky, V. Domanytsky, V. Doroshenko, S. Drahomanov, V. Durdukivsky, I. Dzhydzhora, I. Franko, M. Hrinchenko, M. Hrushevsky, P. Kapelhorodsky, H. Kovalenko, M. Kotsiubynsky, M. Levytsky, O. Lototsky, I. Lypa, Ya. Mamontov, O. Oles, L. Padalka, V. Pisniachevsky, M. Porsh, V. Prokopovych, O. Rusov, V. Samiilenko, S. Shelukhyn, K. Shyrotsky, V. Stepankivsky, H. Stepura, M. Trotsky, Yu. Tyshchenko, S. Vasylchenko, M. Vorony, V. Vynnychenko, A. Yakovliv, and A. Zhuk. By providing news from all the Ukrainian lands and responding to all political and cultural developments, *Rada* played a key role in the crystallization of a nationally conscious Ukrainian intelligentsia. Because of persistent tsarist interference and persecution as well as frequent fines and confiscations of issues, it was able to print only 3,000 to 5,000 copies and had no more than 2,000 subscribers. Three days after the Russian Empire entered the First World War, the paper was shut down. It was revived after the February Revolution under the title *Nova rada*.

V. Pavlovsky

Rada (Council). A newspaper published weekly, semi-weekly, and then three times a month in Lviv from August 1925 to 1934. It succeeded *Nash prapor* (1923–4), *Prapor* (1924), and *Ukraïns'ka rada* (1924–5) as the organ of the 'Independent Group' in the *Ukrainian Labor party. Soon afterward it became an organ of the *Ukrainian National Democratic Alliance. From 1927 it was the organ of the Sovietophile *Ukrainian Party of Labor and reported favorably on nation-building efforts in the Ukrainian SSR. It was edited by H. Myketei, V. Budzynovsky (1927–30), and L. Petrushevych. In 1930 *Rada* had a pressrun of 1,500.

Rada (Council). A weekly newspaper published, with interruptions, from January 1934 to the end of 1935 and from early 1937 to February 1938 in Chernivtsi. It carried regular reports on Ukrainian life in Western and Soviet Ukraine and abroad, devoted considerable attention to international affairs, and supported the *Ukrainian National party in Bukovyna. The editor and main contributor was Yu. Serbyniuk.

Rada of State Secretaries of the Western Ukrainian National Republic. See State Secretariat of the Western Ukrainian National Republic.

Rădăuți (Ukrainian: Radivtsi). VI-6. A town (1965 pop 18,800) on the Topliţa River in Rumania. It is one of the oldest towns in Bukovyna: references to it in historical documents begin in the 14th century. The western part of Rădăuți county is part of Ukrainian ethnic territory. In 1930 over 26,000 Ukrainians lived in the county, where they accounted for 16 percent of the population.

Radchenko, Andrii [Radčenko, Andrij], b 30 October 1887 in Parafiivka, Pryluka county, Poltava gubernia, d 20 January 1938. Bolshevik revolutionary and Soviet official. In 1912 he left the Mensheviks, whom he had supported from 1904, and joined the Bolsheviks. In 1917–18 he chaired the Druzhkivka Council of Workers' and Soldiers' Deputies in the Donbas and then did political work in the Red Army. From 1920 he worked in the Party and the trade unions and rose to the position of secretary of the Donetske Gubernia Party Committee (by 1924), chairman of the All-Ukrainian Trade Union Council (1925–8), and vice-chairman of the All-Union Central Trade Union Council. During this time he was a member of the CC and Politburo of the CP(B)U. He disappeared in Stalin's purges of the late 1930s.

Radchenko, Klavdiia [Radčenko, Klavdija], b 14 December 1929 in Bila Tserkva. Opera singer (lyric soprano). After graduating from the Kiev Conservatory in 1956, she joined the Kiev Theater of Opera and Ballet as a soloist. She has appeared as Oksana in S. Hulak-Artemovsky's *Zaporozhian Cossack beyond the Danube*, Natalka in M. Lysenko's *Natalka from Poltava*, Tatiana in P. Tchaikovsky's *Eugene Onegin*, Eurydice in C. Gluck's *Orpheus and Eurydice*, Marguerite in C. Gounod's *Faust*, Halia in K. Dankevych's *Nazar Stodolia*, and Mylana in H. Maiboroda's *Mylana*. She sang in concerts as well as in opera.

Radchenko, Oleksander [Radčenko], b 20 August 1894 in Lokhvytsia, Poltava gubernia, d 20 January 1975 in Lviv. Composer, conductor, and pedagogue. After studying at the Odessa Music School and conservatory (1911) he was an army concertmaster (1913–23). He subsequently (1923–30) organized and conducted independent orchestras in Odessa before becoming the music director of the Ukrainian State Theater of Drama in Zaporizhia (1931–41) and Lviv (1944–60). He composed incidental music to almost 500 plays, including T. Shevchenko's *Haidamaky*, M. Kropyvnytsky's *Nevol'nyk* (The Slave), M. Starytsky's *Marusia Bohuslavka*, and W. Shakespeare's *Othello* and *King Lear*. His other works include military marches, symphonic and choral pieces, and arrangements of Ukrainian folk songs.

Radchenko, Petro [Radčenko], b 14 July 1902 in Kiev, d 19 July 1942 in Kiev. Writer. He worked as a teacher and book editor, as managing secretary of the Kiev Komsomol journal *Molodyi bil'shovyk*, and, in the late 1930s, as a secretary and department head of the paper *Literaturna hazeta*. A member of the writers' organizations Molodniak and the All-Ukrainian Association of Proletarian Writers, he began publishing stories in 1925 and produced the novelettes *Skrypka* (The Violin, 1928) and *Zalizni shory* (Iron Blinders, 1932; 2nd edn 1955) and the story collection *Chornyi khlib* (Black Bread, 1931). A Soviet partisan during the Second World War, he was tortured to death by the Gestapo.

Radchenko, Serhii [Radčenko, Serhij], b 16 October 1880 in Konotip, Chernihiv gubernia, d 13 September 1942. Hygienist. A graduate of Kiev University (1907), he worked in factories and zemstvos in the Kiev region. He served as director of the county health department in Bila Tserkva (1920–4), a research associate of the Kiev Medical Institute (1924–9), and head of its social hygiene department (1929–41). His publications dealt with the history of *zemstvo medicine in Ukraine, the problems of providing health care for peasants, and sanitation education.

Radchenko, Viktor [Radčenko], b 24 December 1907 in Kiev, d 31 January 1961 in Kiev. Cameraman. He completed study at the Kiev Institute of Fine Arts (1930) and the Kiev Institute of Cinema (1932). In 1931 he began to produce popular science films at the Kiev Artistic Film Studio, some of which received awards at world cinema festivals in Karlovy Vary (Czechoslovakia, 1948) and Montevideo (Uruguay, 1957).

Radchuk, Fedir [Radčuk], b 2 January 1899 in Okunyn, Volodymyr-Volynskyi county, Volhynia gubernia, d 2 October 1986 in Kharkiv. Stage and film character actor. He completed study in the drama school at the Kiev Society of Folk Theater and Art (1921) and then worked in the Shevchenko First Theater of the Ukrainian Soviet Republic (1921–2) and Berezil (1922–34, from 1935 the Kharkiv Ukrainian Drama Theater). He also appeared in the films *Fata morgana* (1931) and *Kyianka* (The Kiev Girl, 1958).

Radekhiv [Radexiv]. III-5. A city (1989 pop 8,900) and raion center in Lviv oblast. It was first mentioned in historical documents in 1493, when it was under Polish rule. It was granted the rights of *Magdeburg law in 1752. After the partition of Poland in 1772, Radekhiv belonged to Austria, was ruled by Poland (1919–39), and finally became part of the Ukrainian SSR (1939). Radekhiv has a building-materials factory, a dairy, and a brewery.

Radians'ka Bukovyna (Soviet Bukovyna). An organ of Chernivtsi oblast's CPU Committee and Soviet, published five times a week in Chernivtsi in 1940–1 and from 1944. In 1980 it had a pressrun of 136,000.

Radians'ka Donechchyna (Soviet Donets Region). An organ of Donetske oblast's CPU Committee and Soviet, published five times a week in Donetske from July 1944. Until December 1945 it was called *Sotsialistychnyi Donbas*. In 1980 it had a pressrun of 59,000 copies. Its Russian-language parallel, *Sotsialisticheskii Donbass*, had a much larger pressrun.

Radians'ka kul'tura. See *Kul'tura i zhyttia*.

Radians'ka literatura. See *Vitchyzna*.

Radians'ka muzyka (Soviet Music). A music journal published in Kiev by the Union of Composers of Ukraine. A successor to the music journal *Muzyka*, it came out as a monthly in 1933–4 and a bimonthly in 1936–41. A total of 54 issues appeared. Its editors were A. Olkhovsky and O. Bilokopytov. The journal served as the ideological standard of the composers' union and tended to deal more with propaganda than with art.

Radians'ka osvita (Soviet Education). A popular pedagogical monthly and the organ of the People's Commissariat of Education of Ukraine and the Ukrainian Bureau of the Central Committee of Educational Workers. It was published in Kharkiv from 1923 under the formal editorship of the commissar of education – V. Zatonsky, then O. Shumsky, and finally M. Skrypnyk. It served as a popular forum for the discussion of educational issues and played an important role in the Ukrainization of Ukrainian schools. In 1931 it merged with *Za politekhnichnu osvitu* to form *Politekhnichna shkola* (1932–4).

Radians'ka osvita (Soviet Education). A pedagogical and professional newspaper for teachers and educators, published twice a week in Kiev. Established in 1940, it was an organ of the People's Commissariat of Education of Ukraine and of the Central Committee of the Professional Union of Workers in Primary and Secondary Schools. In 1960 it became the organ of the Ministry of Education of Ukraine, the Ministry of Higher and Specialized Secondary Education of Ukraine, and the Ukrainian Republican Committee of Professional Workers in Educa-tion and Science. It publishes news about social-political events and highlights professional and pedagogical developments. Since 1992 it has been called *Osvita* and appears weekly.

Radianska Shkola (Soviet School). A publishing house established in 1919 as a subsection of the All-Ukrainian Publishing House in Kharkiv. In 1923 it was reorganized, placed under the jurisdiction of the People's Commissariat (later Ministry) of Education, and renamed Shliakh Osvity. It acquired its name in 1930. In 1934 it was moved to Kiev. The press supplies general and specialized textbooks, methodological guides for teachers, reference works and dictionaries, pedagogical journals and monographs, and books for children in Ukrainian. It also issues books and periodicals in Russian, Hungarian, Polish, Moldavian, English, German, and French. Periodicals published include the journals *Radians'ka shkola, Pochatkova shkola, Doshkil'ne vykhovannia, Ukraïns'ka mova i literatura v shkoli*, and *Russkii iazyk i literatura v shkolakh USSR*, and the newspaper *Radians'ka osvita*. The press maintains editorial offices in Kharkiv, Lviv, Uzhhorod, and Chernivtsi. The largest publishing house in Ukraine, in the years 1966–75 it published 5,068 titles with a total pressrun of nearly 431 million copies. In 1978 it published 435 titles with a pressrun of 74.8 million copies.

Radians'ka shkola (Soviet School). A monthly pedagogical journal published by the Ministry of Education of Ukraine. It was founded in 1945 in place of **Shliakh osvity* (later *Komunistychna osvita*). The journal was devoted to articles on education administration, pedagogy, psychology, teaching methods and communist upbringing, professional training, and comparative education. In 1992 the journal was renamed *Ridna shkola*.

Radianska Ukraina (Soviet Ukraine). A publishing conglomerate of the CC CPU in Kiev, established in 1943. Its many printing plants produced 11 republican newspapers and 10 journals of the CPU and Komsomol, Kiev editions of 17 newspapers of the CC CPSU and USSR government in Moscow, 22 other journals, and specialized Russian-language publications for distribution in Ukraine.

Radians'ka Ukraïna (Soviet Ukraine). A daily (six days a week) organ of the CC CPU and the Supreme Soviet and Council of Ministers of the Ukrainian SSR. It first appeared in Kharkiv in 1919 as *Kommunist*, the Russian-language organ of the Central Executive Committee of the CP(B)U and Kharkiv gubernia (later okruha) Party Committee. From June 1926 the paper was published in Ukrainian as *Komunist*. It reached the height of its popularity during the *Ukrainization period of the latter half of the 1920s, when it and **Visti VUTsVK* were the leading political newspapers in the Ukrainian SSR. Edited by the former Borotbists M. **Liubchenko and T. **Taran, it published articles by Soviet Ukrainian journalists and writers (eg, P. Panch, M. Irchan, I. Mykytenko), leading Party and government officials in Ukraine, and Communist leaders in other republics and abroad. Under Stalinist rule, however, the paper was little more than a propaganda tool of the state. In 1930–2 it appeared seven days a week (359 or 360 issues a year), and it reached a circulation of 450,000 in 1932. It was used to push the collectivization drive and the First Five-Year Plan. In 1934 it was transferred to Kiev when that city was made the republic's capital. Later its editorial staff and correspondents were severely repressed; many, including Liubchenko and Taran, were imprisoned or shot. In 1938 A. Chekaniuk became editor, and he served in that capacity until 1943. In 1938 a parallel Russian-language version of the paper, *Sovetskaia Ukraina* (now **Pravda Ukrainy*), was established.

After *Visti VUTsVK* ceased publication in 1941, *Komunist* assumed its function as the organ of the Supreme Soviet. During the Second World War the paper was published in Voroshylovrad, Saratov, Moscow, and Kharkiv. It acquired its *Radians'ka Ukraïna* name in February 1943 and returned to Kiev in 1944. The paper's pressrun rose from 400,000 in 1950 to 560,000 in 1977; from then it remained at approx 555,000. By contrast the pressruns of the Moscow papers *Pravda* and *Izvestiia* increased dramatically, in practice displacing republican organs such as *Radians'ka Ukraïna* as the main source of information for Ukrainian readers. The central papers were larger (six pages vs four for the Ukrainian papers), distributed more effectively in Ukraine, and of a higher professional and intellectual quality. Unlike them, *Radians'ka Ukraïna* did not have foreign correspondents, and devoted little attention to international affairs. In general the paper was politically conservative, even by Soviet standards. Despite the changes brought about by M. Gorbachev and his glasnost policy, *Radians'ka Ukraïna* changed little. It continued to publish scurrilous attacks on Ukrainian 'bourgeois nationalists' abroad and in Ukraine and did little to further reform or liberalization. While the Russian-language *Pravda Ukrainy* devoted some attention to the economy, science, and technology, *Radians'ka Ukraïna* published considerably more propagandistic and ideological articles.

In 1970 the paper employed some 95 journalists, including 60 so-called creative contributors. Thirty-five of these contributors worked in the editorial office; the rest were employed as correspondents. The editors were part of the **nomenklatura* of the CC CPSU and not of the Ukrainian Party; central control over the paper was thus ensured. After the demise of the USSR in 1991, *Radians'ka Ukraïna* was renamed *Demokratychna Ukraïna*.

R. Szporluk

Radians'ka Ukraïna (Soviet Ukraine). A monthly journal of the All-Ukrainian Central Executive Committee

(1921–38) and the Presidium of the Supreme Soviet (1938–9) of the Ukrainian SSR, published weekly and then semimonthly in Kharkiv (1921–36) and Kiev (1936–9). It appeared in 1921 in Russian as the committee's *Biulleten'*. From 1924 it appeared in Ukrainian as *Biuleten'*, and in July 1925 it was renamed *Radians'ka Ukraïna*. It published reports on the activities of the Soviet Ukrainian government and official institutions. In 1939 only four issues appeared.

Radians'ka Ukraïna. See *Literaturna krytyka*.

Radians'ka Volyn' (Soviet Volhynia). An organ of Volhynia oblast's CPU Committee and Soviet until 1991, published five times a week in Lutske. It first appeared from September 1939, after the USSR annexed western Volhynia, until 1940 as *Vil'na pratsia*. The newspaper was not published during the 1941–3 German occupation of Lutske. In 1980 it had a pressrun of 162,000.

Radians'ka Volyn'. See *Radians'ka Zhytomyrshchyna*.

Radians'ka zhinka (Soviet Woman). A republican monthly women's magazine published from 1946 in Kiev by the Writers' Union of Ukraine and the Ukrainian Republican Council of Trade Unions. In addition to propagandistic articles about the achievements of Soviet Ukrainian women in cultural, scholarly, and political life, *Radians'ka zhinka* published articles on child rearing, home economics, health care, and culture, and prose and poetry. Special attention was devoted to international affairs and the peace movement. In 1984 it had a pressrun of 2,052,800, the second largest of all magazines and journals published in Ukraine. In 1992 the magazine was renamed *Zhinka*.

Radians'ka Zhytomyrshchyna (Soviet Zhytomyr Region). An organ of Zhytomyr oblast's CP Committee and Soviet until 1991, published five times a week in Zhytomyr. It first appeared in Russian in March 1919 as *Izvestiia*, of the Volhynia Gubernia Military-Revolutionary Committee. From January 1921 it appeared three times a week in Ukrainian as *Visti*, but in July it reverted to Russian under the title *Volynskii proletarii*. From August 1924 it was again published in Ukrainian, as *Radians'ka Volyn'* and then *Chervone Polissia* (October 1937 to June 1941). The newspaper was not published during the 1941–3 German occupation. It resumed publication in January 1944 as *Radians'ka Zhytomyrshchyna*. In 1980 it had a pressrun of 133,000.

Radians'ke literaturoznavstvo. See *Slovo i chas*.

Radians'ke mystetstvo (Soviet Art). A magazine published in Kiev in 1928–32 (a total of 78 issues). From 1930 it was the organ of the Kiev municipal trade union council and Komsomol committee. It devoted particular attention to Ukrainian theater and the work of Ukrainian cultural clubs. The editor was K. Kravchenko.

Radians'ke mystetstvo (Soviet Art). A weekly organ of the Committee for Artistic Affairs and the Administration for Cinematographic Affairs of the Council of Ministers of the Ukrainian SSR, published in Kiev in 1945–54 (a total of 506 issues). Edited by Yu. Kostiuk, O. Borshchahivsky, and others, it appeared in a pressrun of 15,000 and contained propagandistic articles on art and cinema. It was succeeded by *Radians'ka kul'tura*, later renamed *Kul'tura i zhyttia*.

Radians'ke Podillia (Soviet Podilia). An organ of the CPU committees and soviets of Kamianets-Podilskyi oblast (1944–54) and Khmelnytskyi oblast (1954–91), published five times a week in Khmelnytskyi (formerly Proskuriv). It succeeded *Chervonyi kordon*, the Party organ of Kamianets-Podilskyi okruha (1924–37) and oblast (1937–41), published in Kamianets-Podilskyi. In 1980 the paper had a pressrun of 126,000.

Radians'ke pravo (Soviet Law). A monthly organ of Ukraine's Ministry of Justice, procurator's office, and Supreme Court and of the AN URSR (now ANU) Institute of State and Law. Published in Kiev since 1958 as the continuation of *Revoliutsiine pravo*, it is the only legal journal in Ukraine. It contains articles on political affairs, legal history, and Soviet legal theory and practice. It also publishes some official legal pronouncements and documents, book reviews, and bibliographies of legal publications. In recent years the pressrun of the journal has declined considerably, from 64,000 in 1975 to 49,000 in 1980 and 31,940 in 1990. The editors have included V. Zaichuk, D. Panasiuk, and Yu. Verbenko. In 1992 it was renamed *Pravo Ukraïny*.

Radians'ke selo (Soviet Village). A newspaper for peasants. It was published weekly from June 1924 in Kiev as the organ of Kiev gubernia's CP Committee, for the peasants of Right-Bank Ukraine. In November 1925 the paper was moved to Kharkiv and merged with *Selians'ka pravda* to become the CC CP(B)U organ for Ukraine's peasantry. Published three times a week under the editorship of S. Pylypenko, it became the most popular newspaper in Soviet Ukraine, with a pressrun of 250,600 in 1929. It contained articles on cultural affairs, prose, poetry, humor (eg, by O. Vyshnia), political news, and stories of interest to its peasant readers. In January 1933 the paper was renamed *Kolhospne selo*. After it was closed down in December 1934, no republic-level newspaper for the Ukrainian peasantry was published until 1939 (see *Sil's'ki visti*).

Radians'ke Zakarpattia (Soviet Transcarpathia). A literary-arts compendium published in Uzhhorod in 1947–57 and continued in 1958–9 as *Karpaty*. It contained Ukrainian- and Russian-language works by Transcarpathian writers, folklore materials, and articles on the history and culture of Transcarpathia. Some of its 25 issues also appeared in Hungarian.

Radians'kyi arkhiv (Soviet Archive). A journal of the Central Archival Administration of the Ukrainian SSR published in Kharkiv in 1931–2 as the successor to *Arkhivna sprava*. It contained specialized articles on archival affairs in Ukraine as well as surveys of archival collections. Six issues appeared before it was merged with the administration's newsletter to form *Arkhiv Radians'koi Ukraïny*.

Radians'kyi knyhar (Soviet Bookman). A journal published semimonthly in 1929–30 and then every ten days to the end of 1932 in Kharkiv by the All-Ukrainian Council of Congresses of Publishing Houses and Book Trade Organizations. A total of 101 issues appeared. It provided information on publishing and the book trade in Soviet Ukraine and promoted the distribution of Ukrainian books. It also published the supplements *Rekomendatsiini spysky* (Recommended Lists) and *Knyzhkovi novyny* (Book News) in 1929 and *Biuleten' na knyzhkovo-zhurnal'nu produktsiiu URSR* (Bulletin of Book and Journal Production of the Ukrainian SSR) in 1932.

Radians'kyi kredyt (Soviet Credit). A monthly journal devoted to agricultural finances in Soviet Ukraine, published in Kharkiv in 1927–8 (18 issues in all). It was edited by V. Bohutsky and published by the Ukrainian Agricultural Bank. In mid-1928 the journal was merged with *Kooperovane selo* (formerly *Sil's'kyi hospodar*) to form *Kooperovana hromada* (1928–30).

Radians'kyi L'viv. See *Zhovten'*.

Radians'kyi myslyvets' ta rybalka (Soviet Hunter and Fisherman). A weekly organ of the All-Ukrainian Association of Hunters and Fishermen, published in Kharkiv in 1927–30. It contained articles on hunting and fishing, Ukraine's fauna, and the association's activities. It had a pressrun of 12,000 in 1929.

Radianskyi Pysmennyk (Soviet Writer). The publishing house of the *Writers' Union of Ukraine (SPU). It was established as the Radianska Literatura publishing house in Kharkiv in 1933. It was moved to Kiev in 1934 and renamed in 1939. It has published prose, poetry, literary criticism, and anthologies, primarily by SPU members, as well as translations of foreign literature, several book series, the SPU organ *Literaturna Ukraïna*, and the SPU journals *Vitchyzna*, *Vsesvit*, *Kyïv*, and *Raduga*. In the years 1966–75 it published 1,271 titles with a combined pressrun of nearly 31.8 million copies. In 1987 the chief editor was V. Bilenko.

Radianskyi Selianyn (Soviet Peasant). A publishing house of the People's Commissariat of Land Affairs in Kharkiv. Between 1925 and 1930 it published for mass distribution popular and scientific literature on farming in Ukrainian and Russian, and periodicals such as *Radians'kyi selianyn*, *Visnyk sadivnytstva, vynohradarstva ta horodnytstva*, and *Veterynarne dilo*. In 1930 the enterprise became part of the State Publishing Alliance of Ukraine.

Radians'kyi selianyn (Soviet Peasant). A popular agricultural semimonthly journal of the Peoples' Commissariat of Land Affairs of the Ukrainian SSR, published in Kharkiv in 1924–31 (a total of 162 issues). The journal provided practical advice on farming and promoted the elimination of illiteracy. From 1926 it included a monthly almanac as a supplement. In 1929 it had a pressrun of 11,000.

Radians'kyi selianyn (Soviet Peasant). A newspaper of the CC CP(B)U, published nine times a month from April 1945 and 13 times a month from 1946 to August 1949 in Kiev. It was distributed among the peasants of the newly acquired territories of Western Ukraine and had a pressrun of 45,000 to 50,000. It was merged with *Kolhospnyk Ukraïny* to form *Kolhospne selo* (now *Sil's'ki visti*).

Radians'kyi sport. See *Sportyvna hazeta*.

Radians'kyi teatr. See *Masovyi teatr*.

Radicalism. In its most general sense radicalism (from the Latin *radix* 'root') is the striving for fundamental change. Usually the term has a narrower meaning in politics. Although there can be right-wing or nationalist radicalism, the term is more often used in connection with movements on the left of the political spectrum. In the context of Ukrainian history radicalism refers to a brand of agrarian socialism that emerged in Galicia in the late 19th century and survived there until the Second World War.

The ideological inspiration for radicalism came from the political thinker M. *Drahomanov and was embodied in the *Ukrainian Radical party (est 1890) in Galicia. Before the party was founded, 'radicals' generally had referred to themselves as 'socialists' or 'progressives.' V. *Budzynovsky claimed that he originally proposed the name for the party because the founders of the party were called 'radicals' by representatives of the traditional Ukrainian movement in Galicia. Soon, however, the term 'radicalism' began to take on a new and more specific meaning. Immediately after the party announced its existence, Polish and Austrian social democrats urged it to change its name to 'socialist' or 'social democratic,' adopt a Marxist program, and join the Second Socialist International. Marxist ideas were soon adopted by a number of the younger members of the Radical party. The party leadership, particularly M. *Pavlyk and I. *Franko, however, wanted to distinguish their party, its program, and its name from those of the social democrats. They argued that Marxism was suitable for Western European socialists, whose countries had an industrial proletariat. The Ukrainians, however, were a predominantly peasant people, and Drahomanov's political theories suited them much more than K. Marx's. Franko and Pavlyk elaborated the theory of radicalism as an agrarian, peasant-oriented form of socialism and claimed kinship with the Serbian Radical party, which was also an agrarian socialist party in a largely peasant society. Their view ultimately prevailed in the party, and the discontented minority left the Radicals in 1899 to form the *Ukrainian Social Democratic party. Anticlericalism was one of the distinctive characteristics of radicalism. Ukrainian radicalism also had a pronounced anticlericalism.

Radicalism was pre-eminently a Galician phenomenon, but it had resonances elsewhere in Ukraine. A radical party of the Galician type was founded in Bukovyna in 1906. A more distant relation was the *Ukrainian Radical party, formed in Kiev late in 1904, which soon dissolved and in 1908 was replaced by the *Society of Ukrainian Progressives. Ideologically the Kievan radicals had little in common with their Galician counterparts. In 1926 the Galician Radical party united with the *Ukrainian Party of Socialist Revolutionaries in Volhynia and Polisia to form the Ukrainian Socialist Radical party. In practice, however, the Galician branch of the party carried on the traditions of radicalism, and the Volhynian-Polisian branch continued as a socialist revolutionary organization. After the Second World War there was little room for radicalism in Ukraine. Aside from the Communist monopoly in political life, the traditional Ukrainian peasantry, in whose interests the radicals had claimed to work, had been transformed into collective-farm workers, and the Ukrainian Catholic church, which had been the target of radical criticism, was abolished in 1946.

BIBLIOGRAPHY
Franko, I. *Radykaly i radykalizm* (Lviv 1896)
Himka, J.-P. *Socialism in Galicia: The Emergence of Polish Socialism and Ukrainian Radicalism (1860–1890)* (Cambridge 1983)
J.-P. Himka

Radimichians (*radymychi*; Belarusian: *radzimichy*). A Slavic tribe that lived in the watershed of the Dnieper, the Sozh, and the Desna rivers from the 9th to 12th centuries. Their principal towns were Homel, Vshchizh, and Chechersk. Until the mid-9th century the Radimichians paid tribute to the Khazars. Grand Prince Oleh of Kiev joined them to the Kievan state in 885, and they took part in the Rus' campaign against Byzantium in 911. They did not, however, become formally part of Kievan Rus' until 984, when they were conquered by Volodymyr the Great. After the death of Yaroslav the Wise the western Radimichian lands came under the rule of Smolensk principality, and those in the east became part of Chernihiv principality. The Radimichians are last mentioned in the Rus' chronicles under the year 1169. Together with the *Krivichians and *Drehovichians they are the ancestors of the Belarusians.

BIBLIOGRAPHY
Ribakou, B. *Radzimichy* (Minsk 1922)
Tret'iakov, P. *Vostochnoslavianskie plemena* (Moscow 1953)

Radio. Radio broadcasting in Soviet Ukraine and in the USSR as a whole served the interests of the Communist state and Party. All news, arts, and public information broadcasts were subordinated to the aims of official internal and external propaganda. Their planning and subject matter were determined by all-Union and republican CPSU departments of propaganda and agitation and delegated by them to broadcasting committees of the Councils of Ministers of the USSR and Ukrainian SSR. Control was also exercised by designated organs of Soviet state censorship such as the Chief Administration for Literature and Publishing (Glavlit) and the KGB.

In Ukraine radiotelegraph communication was introduced in the Kherson area in 1902. The first broadcasts began once a week in Kharkiv, with low-level transmitters, in November 1924, four years after 4-kW radio stations began operating in Moscow, Leningrad, and Kazan. In 1925 the construction of the first high-powered stations was begun in Kharkiv and Kiev by the Moscow Joint-Stock Company for Radio Communications, the Radio Society of Ukraine was created, and local associations of radio enthusiasts arose. By 1928 there were radio stations in Kiev, Odessa, Dnipropetrovske, Donetske, and nine other Ukrainian cities. The Kharkiv station RV 4, which began operating in 1927, was the fourth most powerful in the USSR. In 1941 the most powerful long-wave radio station was in the Soviet Ukrainian capital, Kiev (RV 84); it transmitted propaganda outside the USSR.

A radio network in Ukraine was begun in 1928 under the direction of the People's Commissariat of Post and Telegraphy of the USSR. It used a relay system that transmitted signals by wire to loudspeakers. The wireless receiver system common in most other countries was rarely used, and such receivers were produced only in small quantities, mainly for government and Party institutions and personnel. Their number began increasing toward the end of the 1930s, when jamming of foreign radio broadcasts was perfected and the production of radios that could receive only Soviet broadcasts became possible. Until recent times the main system of radio broadcasting in the USSR, particularly in urban workers' districts and in the villages, still used wired transmitters and receivers. In 1940 there were 1,047,000 point-to-point wired receivers in Ukraine, 137,200 of them in rural areas. There were only 255,400 radio sets, mostly in the cities, which had to be registered with the militia.

In August 1930 an all-Ukrainian government radio center in Kharkiv, with a subordinate center in the Moldavian ASSR and a network of local transmission stations, was established. In 1933 the All-Ukrainian Radio Administration was renamed the All-Ukrainian Committee of Radio-Network Development and Broadcasting of the Council of People's Commissars of the Ukrainian SSR. In 1938 its name was shortened to Ukrainian Radio Committee (URC). The URC received information on an ongoing basis from the *Radio and Telegraph Agency of Ukraine. In the 1930s there also existed a Committee for the Support of Radio-Network Development and Amateur Radio Communications of the Komsomol CC. The committees published the journal *Radio (1930–5, 1938–41).

At first, broadcasting in the Ukrainian SSR was dominated by Moscow radio. Transmissions in Ukrainian were limited in both time and subject matter. In the late 1920s and early 1930s, 70 percent of such programs were devoted to political education and agitation. The programming of the Kharkiv center, aside from 'radio gazettes' for workers, peasants, the Komsomol, Pioneers, the Jewish community, and Esperantists, consisted of speeches, discussions, news, and Party congress and conference reports. Of 18 hours of daily broadcasting, only 3 to 4 were devoted to literary and cultural topics. In the latter half of the 1930s, music, literary, drama, and special programs for children were added. Thirty to 40 percent of broadcast time was occupied by the compulsory transmission of Moscow broadcasts and news in the Russian language (12 times a day).

During the Second World War most civilian Soviet radio stations were destroyed, and the population was served by official broadcasts of the Nazi occupation or by Moscow radio (the station Soviet Ukraine) and the mobile Soviet army station Dnipro and Soviet partisan station Partyzanka. In 1941–4 official Soviet broadcasts were transmitted in Ukrainian from the Taras Shevchenko station in Saratov, Russia, where the equipment of Ukraine's radio stations and the URC had been evacuated.

After the war the reconstruction of stations and broadcasting and network development came under the jurisdiction of the Committee for Radio Broadcasting, renamed in 1950 the Committee for Radio and Television Broadcasting, of the Council of Ministers of the Ukrainian SSR. From February 1957 this committee had its own network called Hovoryt Kyiv (This Is Kiev Speaking). From 1947 it was also a member of the International Organization of Radio Broadcasting and Television in the Soviet-

Radio relay centers, reception points, and equipment in Ukraine and the USSR, 1950 to 1984–7

	1950	1960	1965	1970	1984–7
Radio relay centers					
In Ukraine	3,055	5,870	5,462	4,657	3,403
In rural areas	1,910	3,655	3,168	–	–
In the USSR	18,911	39,033	34,206	35,145	–
Radio reception points (in 1,000s)					
In Ukraine	1,482	7,203	8,356	10,267	24,000
In rural areas	334	4,418.5	4,850	4,970	–
In the USSR	9,685	30,837	35,638	46,193	–
Radio receivers (in 1,000s)					
In Ukraine (40 in 1928)	528	4,431	6,571	8,157	13,948
In rural areas	158	1,101	1,535	1,889	–
In the USSR	3,643	27,811	32,828	48,575	–
Production of radio equipment in Ukraine (in 1,000s)					
Receivers and radio-phonographs	8.5	231.2	553	673	–
Loudspeakers	165	899	700	1,648	–

bloc countries (based in Prague from 1950). In 1965 there were over 50 powerful shortwave, long-wave, and ultra-shortwave stations in Ukraine.

The relay transmitting system still predominates in Ukraine. In 1965 there was one radio per 6.9 persons (in rural areas, one per 14.4), compared to one per 1.2 persons in the United States. For a very long time radios made in the USSR could not receive broadcasts of wavelengths shorter than 25 m and were thereby prevented from receiving most foreign broadcasts. In the postwar period, radio broadcasting in Ukraine has increased considerably. In 1965 there was an average of 30 hours of programming in Ukrainian per day. In addition to 10 daily news programs provided by the Kiev center, 24 oblast radio committees broadcast lectures, discussions, advice, information, music, literary programs, and special programs for children and teen-agers. In 1984 Kiev Radio broadcast 7.5 hours of programming in Ukrainian and foreign languages to 70 countries. In the 1980s there were three republican radio networks. Network One was broadcast via reception stations and points to mass audiences; 20 to 25 percent of its time was devoted to local Party and economic issues, and the remaining time was taken up by transmissions from Moscow. Networks Two and Three were transmitted to people in urban areas with their own radios, and devoted more attention to Ukrainian topics, literature, and art. Apart from the weekly program 'Hovoryt i pokazuie Ukraina' (Ukraine Tells and Shows) there was no other Ukrainian-language radio journal.

Radio technology has been taught and researched at the Odessa Electrotechnical Institute of Communications, the Kharkiv Institute of Radioelectronics, the AN URSR (now ANU) Institute of Radio Physics and Electronics, and the Kiev Polytechnical Institute. Amateur radio clubs and groups were monitored by the All-Union *Voluntary Society for Assistance to the Army, Air Force, and Navy. In 1961 there were 220 clubs, over 24,000 enthusiasts, and over 2,500 amateur stations. Until the 1980s, great expense was devoted to the jamming of foreign broadcasts; as a result it was particularly difficult to receive these transmissions in large cities.

In interwar Western Ukraine under Polish rule, all broadcasting was state-controlled. All radios had to be registered, and their owners had to pay monthly user fees. Ukrainian-language programs did not exist until the 1930s, when Lviv Radio sporadically broadcast short (15–30 minutes) programs whose content was limited by official censors. On Sundays and holy days liturgies were broadcast from Ukrainian churches. In the Czechoslovak Republic, Ukrainian-language programs were broadcast in the 1930s to the population of Transcarpathia twice a week (from 1934 five times a week) for 15 minutes from Košice. Radio Prague began daily news broadcasts to Transcarpathia in 1934. During the existence of the Carpatho-Ukrainian state in 1938–9, Ukrainian-language programs were broadcast from Banská Bystrica in Slovakia, and in early 1939 a shortwave station existed in Khust.

During the 1939–41 Soviet rule, the population of Western Ukraine was served by new Soviet radio stations established in Lviv, Stanyslaviv (now Ivano-Frankivske), and Ternopil. During the 1941–4 German occupation of Western Ukraine a German-controlled station in Lviv broadcast 30-minute censored programs and propaganda in Ukrainian three times a week.

In the postwar period Ukrainian-language programs have been broadcast daily by Czechoslovak Radio in Prešov since 1948 (11.5 hours per week in 1988), weekly by several radio stations in Poland since the 1960s, and weekly in the Bačka dialect from Novi Sad in Serbia since 1949. In the West, Ukrainian-language programs have been broadcast to Ukraine daily by *Voice of America in Washington, *Radio Canada International in Montreal, *Radio Liberty in Munich, and Vatican Radio. Ukrainian community programs have also been broadcast by radio stations in Rome, Madrid, and other European cities and in cities in Brazil, Argentina, the United States, and Canada, where there are large Ukrainian communities. Most have been half-hour or hour-long weekly programs, although there have been some daily programs (eg, in Edmonton, Winnipeg, and Toronto).

Radio. A popular journal for amateur radio operators and technicians, published in Kharkiv in 1930–5 and in

Kiev in 1935 and 1938–41. It appeared semimonthly to mid-1933 and then monthly. It was an organ of the All-Ukrainian Radio Administration in 1930–2 and the Komsomol CC and Council of People's Commissars' committees for broadcasting and radio affairs thereafter.

Radio and Telegraph Agency of Ukraine (Radiotelehrafichne ahenstvo Ukrainy, or RATAU). The official news agency of the Council of Ministers (formerly People's Commissars) of the Ukrainian SSR. It was founded in April 1921 in Kharkiv on the basis of Ukrosta, the All-Ukrainian Bureau of the Russian Telegraph Agency, founded in January 1920, which in turn was based on the Bureau of the Ukrainian Press (December 1918 to August 1919). Initially RATAU was to collect and disseminate information about developments in the USSR and abroad, to provide a news service for Ukrainian press and radio, and to inform the Soviet and foreign public about the work of the Soviet Ukrainian government. It was also supposed to exchange reports with foreign press agencies and to establish bureaus and a network of correspondents at diplomatic and foreign trade offices of the Ukrainian SSR. With the formation of the Telegraph Agency of the USSR (TASS) in 1925, RATAU lost many of its functions. Located in Kiev since 1934, it was limited almost exclusively to collecting and disseminating news of Soviet Ukrainian internal affairs and of the Ukrainian delegation at the United Nations. A constituent member of TASS from 1971, RATAU has had correspondents in every oblast of Ukraine and separate bureaus in Lviv, Odessa, Donetske, and Kharkiv. In May 1990 RATAU was renamed the Ukrainian Information Agency (Ukrinform) and was placed under the directorship of V. Burlai. It has a staff of approx 500, including a correspondent in New York City. In 1990 it served 970 newspapers and 230 television and radio stations and other bodies. It is now independent of TASS.

Radio Canada International. The international service of the Canadian Broadcasting Corporation, based in Montreal. Established in 1952 as the Voice of Canada, it broadcasts domestic and international news, information, and commentaries from a Canadian perspective. Since 1986 it has transmitted one hour a day in Ukrainian to listeners in the USSR and its successor states, Eastern Europe, and elsewhere in the world. A special transmitter broadcasts to Ukrainians living in the Far East. Under the terms of a protocol signed between Canada and the USSR, transmissions were not jammed by the Soviets. The first head of the Ukrainian section was G. Panchuk. He was succeeded by B. Veselovsky, O. Bachynsky, R. Olynyk (R. Rakhmanny), Ya. Harchun, and R. Pitt. In 1989 the Ukrainian section had five full-time announcer-producers and several freelance contributors across Canada.

Radio Liberty (RL). A radio service established in 1953 and financed by the US government (initially through the *American Committee of Liberation and then through the United States Information Agency) to provide Soviet listeners with nonpartisan, uncensored news, information, and commentary about the outside world and developments in the USSR; to propagate democratic principles as later outlined in the United Nations Universal Declaration of Human Rights; and to promote the right of national self-determination in the Soviet Union. Its headquarters

are in Munich, where 1,000 of its approx 1,750 employees are based. RL transmits 24 hours a day in 19 different languages of the former USSR. A daily 1.5-hour Ukrainian service has broadcast news, a chronicle of Ukrainian affairs, press summaries, commentaries on developments in the Soviet Union and abroad, information on Ukrainian history, literary reviews, religious programs, interviews, and materials from Ukrainian samvydav and about the dissident movement. The broadcasts were denounced as anti-Soviet by the Soviet authorities, and until 1988 they were jammed. RL also has a well-developed research department, whose staff has provided much information and analysis on political, economic, and social developments in Ukraine. This research is summarized in regular publications and research reports. In the mid-1980s the research department was merged with that of Radio Free Europe, a similar institution that broadcasts to the countries of the Soviet bloc. The Ukrainian broadcast service has been headed by M. Kovalsky, M. Dobriansky, M. Diakovsky, I. Basarab, A. Romashko (pseud of V. Kubryk), A. Kaminsky, B. Nahaylo, and R. Kupchinsky. Research staff members who have written extensively on Ukrainian subjects include R. Solchanyk, D. Marples, K. Mihalisko, and B. Nahaylo. In 1992 RL opened an office in Kiev.

Radio technology. Radio technological research in Ukraine originated with M. *Pylchykov at Odessa University and the Kharkiv Technological Institute, M. Umov at Odessa University, and D. *Rozhansky at Kharkiv University. Pylchykov oversaw the installation of a research radio station at the Kherson lighthouse and did experiments in radiotelecontrol. In 1906 M. Bonch-Bruevich in Kiev invented an original radio transmitter. In the 1920s, radio-technological research was conducted by M. Papaleksi at the Odessa Polytechnical Institute (in the areas of radiotelegraphy, radio communications with submarines, and telecontrol) and by V. *Ohiievsky at the Kiev Polytechnical Institute. In 1924 in Kharkiv Ohiievsky set up the first radio station in Ukraine. Scientists at Kharkiv University, and then at Lviv University and other higher educational institutions, developed interest and research in the field.

Today radio technology research is conducted by the ANU (formerly AN URSR) *Physical-Technical Institute in Kharkiv, the ANU *Institute of Radio Physics and Electronics in Kharkiv, and the Kiev Institute of Radio-technological Problems. A. *Slutskin, S. *Braude, I. Truten, and H. Levin studied powerful superfrequency generators and the theory of the magnetron. S. *Tetelbaum and O. *Usykov investigated the remote transmission of energy over long distances, new modulation methods, television, radiolocation, the electronics of superfrequencies, and the phase method of generating radio waves. V. *Lashkarov and S. *Pekar developed the theory and technology of semiconductors, electron diffraction, and the kinetics of photoconduction. O. *Kotelnykov devoted attention to the technology of weak currents, electrodynamics, and the theory of long lines. At the Institute of Radio Physics and Electronics Braude researched the reflection of radio waves from meteor tracks and other problems of radio astronomy. Along with I. *Ostrovsky, I. Turgenev, and A. Men he also contributed to understanding of the propagation of radio waves in the troposphere and to the development of radio oceanography. V. *Marchenko and V. *Shestopalov studied the diffraction of radio waves, and N. *Morgulis specialized in electron emission. New research methods in nonlinear mechanics, quantum field theory, and quantum radio technology developed by N. *Bogoliubov, M. *Krylov, and A. Chernets were useful in the development of theoretical radio technology. The quarterly *Radiotekhnika* and the interdepartmental collection *Radiotekhnik* were devoted to problems of radio technology. Some articles in the field appeared in the journal *Radio* (1930–41).

L. Onyshkevych

Radiobiology. The science devoted to the investigation of the effects of ionizing radiation on living organisms. It covers the range of electromagnetic waves from radio waves, through infrared, visible, and ultraviolet spectra and X rays, to high-energy gamma quanta and subatomic particles that are capable of penetrating living organisms. Irreversible changes are often the cumulative effect of multiple low-dose exposures. H. Chench was the first to use radium for therapeutic purposes in Ukraine, in 1916. The first institutions where radiotherapy was practiced were the Kharkiv Roentgenologic Institute and similar institutes in Kiev and Odessa around 1924. Noted Ukrainian radiobiologists include O. *Krontovsky, O. *Horodetsky, P. Berezhansky, M. Mahat, R. *Kavetsky, B. Kyrychynsky, M. Zaiko, S. Nikitin, M. Lypkan, S. Pokrovsky, and the early radiotherapists I. *Shevchenko, O. Shramenko, H. Perevertun, Ya. Porokhovnyk, and D. Dubovy.

The catastrophic explosion at the Chornobyl Atomic Electric Station in Ukraine on 26 April 1986 exposed millions of Ukrainians, Belarusians, Poles, Russians, and Scandinavians to excessive radiation and reinforced concern about the dangers of overexposure. The number of officially reported victims was suspiciously low; it took the Soviet government over two and a half years to acknowledge that the early fatalities numbered in the hundreds. As a result of the Chornobyl disaster the Center for Radiobiological Research was established in Kiev to co-ordinate a USSR-wide effort in this field. Its efficacy has yet to be established.

I. Masnyk

Radion, Stepan, b 24 July 1912 in Sylne, Lutske county, Volhynia gubernia. Journalist and writer. After emigrating to Australia in 1949, he completed his studies at the Australian School of Journalism (1954). In addition to publishing numerous articles in the Ukrainian press, he prepared a history of the Shevchenko Scientific Society in Australia (1976), a dictionary of Ukrainian surnames in Australia (1981), a list of Ukrainian-Australian graduates (1982), and a six-part bibliography of Ukrainian publications in Australia (1975–87).

Radish (*Raphanus*; Ukrainian: *redka*). An annual or biennial plant of the carrot family Brassicaceae, grown for its succulent root, which usually has red or pink skin and white meat. Most radishes have small roots (up to 20 g); Japanese late field varieties have roots that weigh up to 1 kg. Spring varieties, the leaves of which are suitable for salads, are perishable; larger winter varieties keep well in storage. In Ukraine radish (*R. sativus*) is cultivated principally in the central regions in sandy loams. Radish root is a low-calorie source of bulk food and is usually eaten raw; it contains 1–2 percent each of proteins, carbohydrates, and sugars, and up to 25–30 mg per 100 g of vitamin C.

In addition to the cultivated radish a wild variety (*R. raphanistrum*) grows as a weed, and a white radish (*R. candidus*) grows in Polisia and the northern forest-steppe region. Radishes play a role in Ukrainian folk beliefs; a long root, for example, presages a long winter.

Radkevych, Arsen [Radkevyč], b 1759, d 1821. Basilian priest and professor. A rector (1797 and 1804) of the theological faculty at Lviv University, he taught Hebrew, Greek, and hermeneutics in both of its divisions, the Studium Ruthenum (for Eastern rite theology) and the Studium Latinum (for Roman Catholic theology). From 1818 he was the protohegumen of the Basilian order in Galicia.

Radomyselsky, Izrail [Radomysel's'kyj, Izrajil'], b 6 May 1914 in Zhytomyr, Volhynia gubernia, d 29 January 1986 in Kiev. Metallurgist. He graduated from the Kiev Polytechnical Institute (1939) and worked in Kiev and Novosibirsk, at the AN URSR (now ANU) Institute of Ferrous Metallurgy (1948–55), and at the ANU Institute for Problems of Materials Science (from 1955). A specialist in powder metallurgy, he researched the renewal of metal oxides, wear resistance, and the design and preparation of metal powders with predetermined characteristics.

Radomyshl [Radomyšl']. III-10. A town (1989 pop 16,800) on the Teteriv River and a raion center in Zhytomyr oblast. Until 1946 it was known as Radomysl. It was first mentioned, as Michesk, in the chronicles under the year 1150. In 1362 it came under Lithuanian rule, and in 1390 it is referred to in a historical document as Mytsko. In 1569 it became part of the Polish Commonwealth, and from then it was called Radomyshl. At the beginning of the 17th century Ukraine's first paper factory was established there. For half a century the town was the residence of the Uniate bishops of Kiev (1746–95). With the partition of Poland in 1793, it was transferred to Russia, and became a county center of Volhynia (1795) and then Kiev (1797–1925) gubernias. Today Radomyshl has machine-building, flax-processing, brick-making, canning, and furniture factories, a dairy, a bakery, and a brewery. It has a regional museum and a natural science museum.

Radomyshl camp site. A late Paleolithic campground located near Radomyshl, Zhytomyr oblast. Excavations in 1957–9 and 1963–5 by I. *Shovkoplias uncovered the remains of five small tentlike surface dwellings whose walls were supported by mammoth bones. Other discoveries included a large pit filled with mammoth and other animal bones, flint tools, and a work area for shaping flint pieces.

Raduga (Rainbow). A Russian-language monthly journal published in Kiev since 1963 by the Writers' Union of Ukraine. It was preceded by the monthly *Krasnoe slovo* (Kharkiv, 1927–32), the monthly *Litstroi* (Kharkiv, 1933), the monthly (Kharkiv, 1934) and bimonthly (Kiev, 1935–7) *Sovetskaia literatura*, and the quarterly (1948–50) and monthly (1951–63) *Sovetskaia Ukraina*. *Raduga* contains works by Russian-language authors living in Ukraine and translations from Ukrainian. It has served mainly to further Russification in Ukraine.

Radvanka settlement. A settlement of the 9th to 8th century BC discovered in 1950 in Uzhhorod, Transcarpathia oblast. Excavations revealed the remains of semi-pit dwellings, pottery fragments, and the bones of domestic and wild animals. Traces of a late Paleolithic occupation were also noted at Radvanka.

Radvansky, Anatol [Radvans'kyj, Anatol'], b 23 March 1913 in Brody, Galicia, d 29 May 1991 in Philadelphia. Stage actor and singer (baritone). He worked in the Sadovsky Ukrainian Drama Theater (1931–3), the Zahrava Theater (1933–5), the Tobilevych Theater (1936–8), the Lesia Ukrainka Theater (1939–41), and the Lviv Opera Theater (1941–4). After fleeing from the Soviet advance he acted in the Ensemble of Ukrainian Actors in Germany; he continued with the ensemble after emigrating to the United States (1945–57). He retired from the stage in 1957.

Radykal (Radical). A semimonthly political journal published in Lviv from October 1895. It was edited by V. Budzynovsky, and supported the Ukrainian Radical party. Among the contributors were L. Trubatsky and V. Shchurat. In 1896 *Radykal* merged with **Zhytie i slovo*.

Radylovsky, Yurii [Radylovs'kyj, Jurij] (Radyvylivsky), b and d ? Painter of the mid-18th century in Kamianets-Podilskyi. In Dubno he did several portraits of Prince Lubomirski and his wife (1743). In 1749, with his student L. Dolynsky, he painted icons for the iconostasis of St George's Cathedral in Lviv.

Radysh, Myroslav [Radyš], b 21 October 1910 in Ilyntsi, Sniatyn county, Galicia, d 7 June 1956 in New York. Painter and scenery designer. A graduate of the Poznań Art School (1938), from 1940 he was chief designer at the Lviv Opera Theater. In 1942–4 he participated in exhibitions organized by the Labor Association of Ukrainian Pictorial Artists. A postwar émigré, he worked as a painter and scenery designer for the Ensemble of Ukrainian Actors in Augsburg, Germany. In 1950 he settled in the United States, where he participated in Ukrainian group shows and had solo shows in New York (1952, 1953) and Philadelphia (1954). Radysh painted portraits, still lifes, and landscapes, such as *Madonna* (1948), *Brooklyn Bridge* (1951), *Blue Landscape* (1954), *Mother and Child* (1954), *By the River* (1955), and *Factory Smokestacks* (1956). His impressionist style evolved toward an ever-greater emphasis on color. A book about him was published by his wife in 1966.

Radyvylovsky, Antin (Antonii) [Radyvylovs'kyj], b ?, d 20 December 1688 in Kiev. Churchman and writer. During the 1640s he studied at the Kievan Mohyla Academy, and after graduating he was tonsured and became a noted preacher in various Kievan churches. He was at the Kievan Cave Monastery from 1656 until 1683, when he became hegumen of St Nicholas's Monastery in Kiev. He is the author of two collections of sermons printed at the Kievan Cave Monastery Press: *Ohorodok Marii Bohorodytsi* ... (The Garden of Mary Mother of God ..., 1676), which included sermons for important feast days and about various saints, including SS Anthony and Theodosius of the Caves and Volodymyr the Great, and *Vinets Khristov z propovidii nedelnykh* ... (A Garland for Christ from Sunday Sermons ..., 1688), which included sermons for all Sundays. These sermons, which were written in a bookish Ukrainian close to the vernacular, are excellent examples of baroque oratory prose. In some of them Radyvylovsky touched on contemporary issues, such as the hard life of peasants and women. Some of his themes and parables were drawn from such popular anthologies as *Rym'ski diiannia* (Roman Acts) and *Velyke zertsalo* (The Great Mirror).

BIBLIOGRAPHY
Markovskii, M. *Antonii Radivilovskii, iuzhnorusskii propovednik* XVII *v.* (Kiev 1894)

Myroslav Radysh: *Study*

Janusz Radziejowski

Radziejowski, Janusz, b 3 June 1925 in Kiev. Polish historian. He was educated at the Higher School of Economics and Statistics in Moscow (1949–54) and worked for the Soviet census bureau, where he compiled information about nationality groups in the USSR. Following the rehabilitation of his father (who had perished in the Stalinist purges) in 1959, Radziejowski moved to Warsaw and worked at the Institute of Party History (to 1970) and the Institute of Scientific Policy, Technological Progress, and Higher Education. In 1970 he received a PH D in history from Warsaw University. He has written articles on Polish-Ukrainian relations and on the impact of collectivization on Ukraine. The monograph *The Communist Party of Western Ukraine, 1919–1929* (1983) is a revised translation of his work in Polish (1976).

Radziievsky, Mykola [Radzijevs'kyj], b 27 November 1884 in Yerky, Zvenyhorodka county, Kiev gubernia, d 27 May 1965 in Khmelnytskyi. Composer and conductor. He studied composition with S. Taneev at the Moscow Conservatory, served as an executive member of the Leontovych Music Society, and then worked as an opera conductor in Moscow and Kiev. During the 1920s he organized and conducted an experimental orchestra of folk instruments, known by the acronym MIK. After 1945 he was conductor and music director of the Vinnytsia and Khmelnytskyi theaters of music and drama. His works include the overtures *Sahaidachnyi* and *Fantastic Poem*; chamber and choral pieces; and songs to poems by H. Skovoroda, T. Shevchenko, I. Franko, and M. Rylsky.

Radziievsky, Oleksii [Radzijevs'kyj, Oleksij], b 14 April 1864 in Vasylkiv, Kiev gubernia, d 22 September 1934 in Kiev. Surgeon and urologist; nephew of I. *Nechui-Levytsky. A graduate of Kiev University (1890), he worked there and was a professor at the Higher Courses for Women (1903–20) and the Kiev Medical Institute (1921–30). His publications dealt with operative surgery, the urological treatment of patients with prostatic hypertrophy (particularly surgical treatment of prostatic hypertrophy and uremia), and bacteriology.

Radziviliv. See Chervonoarmiiske.

Radziwiłł (Radzivil; Lithuanian: Radvilas). A Lithuanian magnate family in the 15th- to 16th-century Lithuanian-Ruthenian state and the 16th- to 18th-century Polish-Lithuanian Commonwealth. The progenitor was the Lithuanian noble Radvilas Astikas. In the 16th century the Radziwiłłs established links through marriage with the Jagiellon, the Hohenzollern, and other European royal dynasties and became the only Lithuanian family to receive the title of princes of the Holy Roman Empire (1547). The family owned thousands of rural estates as well as castles and towns, many of them in Volhynia and Kiev voivodeships. It also had its own private army with some 6,000 soldiers. Twenty-two of its members held high military and political offices (grand hetman, grand chancellor, voivode) in the Grand Duchy of Lithuania.

Several Radziwiłłs were directly involved in Ukrainian history. Albrycht-Stanisław (b 1 July 1593 in Olyka, Volhynia, d 12 November 1636 in Gdańsk) was the Lithuanian grand chancellor from 1623. His *Memoriale rerum gestarum in Polonia, 1632–1656* (4 vols, 1968–74; Polish trans: *Pamiętnik o dziejach w Polsce*, 3 vols, 1980) contains valuable observations and information about the Cossack-Polish War. Janusz (b 2 December 1612, d 31 December 1655) was the Lithuanian field hetman (1646–54) and grand hetman (1654–5) during the Cossack-Polish War. He fought the invading Cossacks in Belarus in 1649, defeated them at Loev on 6 July 1651, and captured Kiev on

4 August 1651, after which he exacted harsh retributions against its inhabitants. In 1654 his army was defeated by the allied Cossack and Muscovite forces. Janusz's son, Bogusław (b 3 May 1620, d 31 December 1669), was the Lithuanian equerry from 1646. During the later part of the Cossack-Polish War he made a pact with Sweden and in 1656 requested that Hetman B. Khmelnytsky take his domain of Slutsk principality under his protection. In 1657–65 Bogusław was the governor of ducal Prussia and an ally of Sweden against King Jan II Casimir Vasa. He donated the *Radziwiłł Chronicle to a library in Königsberg. His autobiography was published in Warsaw in 1979. Karol Stanisław (b 27 February 1734, d 21 November 1790) was a leader of the Confederation of *Bar in 1768.

L. Wynar, A. Zhukovsky

Radziwiłł Chronicle (Radzivilivskyi litopys), aka Königsberg Chronicle. A late 15th-century illustrated compilation of medieval Rus' chronicles, including *Povist' vremennykh lit* in the Sylvestrian redaction of 1116 and excerpts from other chronicles of 1112–1206 in southern (Ukraine) and northern (Russia) Rus'. The manuscript is a copy of a 13th-century compilation. In the 17th century it was owned by the Lithuanian prince J. Radziwiłł (hence its name), and his son donated it to the Königsberg library. It remained there until 1758, when the city was occupied by the Russians during the Seven Years' War, and the manuscript was taken to the library of the Russian Academy of Sciences in St Petersburg. Of particular value in the chronicle are its 617 color miniatures. Although they show the marked influence of Western graphic art, they are most likely copies of earlier miniatures. The first, incomplete printing of the chronicle was published in St Petersburg in 1767. A full photomechanical edition appeared in 1902. The chronicle has been studied by A. Shakhmatov, N. Kondakov, V. Sizov, M. Artamonov, and the Ukrainian linguist V. Hantsov.

Volodymyr Radzykevych

Radzykevych, Volodymyr [Radzykevyč], b 17 October 1886 in Vyshenka, Horodok county, Galicia, d 14 September 1966 in Cleveland, Ohio. Pedagogue, literary scholar, and writer. In 1908 he completed philological studies at Lviv University and became a teacher at the Academic Gymnasium of Lviv (1908–39). He was also a founder of and a teacher at the Second Ukrainian Gymnasium in Lviv (1941–4), and from 1945 to 1950 he taught at various gymnasiums in DP camps in Germany. He was a member of the Shevchenko Scientific Society from 1932, head of the

Teachers' Hromada (1929–39), and, from 1950, an active member of the Association of Ukrainian Writers for Young People in Cleveland. Under the pseudonym Vuiko Vlodko he wrote poems, plays, and historical tales for children. Most famous, and republished several times, was his verse adventure *Pryhody Iurchyka kucheriavoho* (Adventures of Curly George). As a literary scholar Radzykevych wrote articles for *Zapysky NTSh* and a monograph on P. Svientsitsky (1911). His most important work was *Istoriia ukraïns'koï literatury* (History of Ukrainian Literature), a widely used text for secondary schools which was published in Lviv in 1922, reissued there in 1937 and 1942, published in 1947 in Germany, and published in 1955–6 in the United States.

D.H. Struk

Radzykevych, Yuliian [Radzykevyč, Julijan], b 4 July 1900 in Vyshenka Mala, Horodok county, Galicia, d 1968 in Springfield, Massachusetts. Physician, civic leader, and writer; brother of V. *Radzykevych. He served as an artillery officer in the Ukrainian Galician Army and then studied medicine at the Lviv (Underground) Ukrainian University and Prague University (MD, 1927). He practiced medicine in Sudova Vyshnia and headed the county committee of the Ukrainian National Democratic Alliance. During the Second World War he organized and directed a hospital and provided medical aid to the Ukrainian Insurgent Army. He emigrated via Austria to the United States (1949), where he became director of a tuberculosis hospital. Besides many short stories he wrote the historical novels *Polkovnyk Danylo Nechai* (Colonel Danylo Nechai, 2 vols, 1961), *Polum'ia* (The Flame, 1963), and *Zoloto i krov* (Gold and Blood, 1967).

Radzykhovsky, Borys [Radzyxovs'kyj], b 6 August 1909 in Novooleksiivka, Oleshky county, Tavriia gubernia, d 17 February 1975 in Chernivtsi. Ophthalmologist. A graduate of the Dnipropetrovske Medical Institute (1932), he headed the Department of Eye Diseases at the Chernivtsi Medical Institute (1945–75). His publications deal with the treatment of trachoma, roentgenological methods of locating foreign objects in the eye, and the construction of ophthalmological instruments.

Valentyna Radzymovska   Yevhen Radzymovsky

Radzymovska, Valentyna [Radzymovs'ka], b 13 October 1886 in Lubni, Poltava gubernia, d 22 December 1953 in Champaign, Illinois. Physiologist and biochemist; member of the Shevchenko Scientific Society from 1950.

She studied in St Petersburg and graduated from Kiev University (1913). She taught at the Kiev Medical Institute (from 1924) and the Kiev Institute of People's Education (1924–9). Her major research areas included biochemistry, pathophysiology, and tuberculosis. A member of the Revolutionary Ukrainian and the Ukrainian Social Democratic parties, she was arrested in 1929 and released after one year. She was a professor at the Melitopil Pedagogical Institute (1939–41) and headed departments of several medical research institutes in Kiev. She was a professor at the Lviv Medical Institute (1941–3), and after the Second World War she taught at the Ukrainian Technical and Husbandry Institute in Munich (1947–50) and then emigrated to the United States (1950). A biography has been written by I. Rozhin (1968).

Radzymovsky, Yevhen [Radzymovs'kyj, Jevhen] (Radzimovsky, Eugene), b 4 December 1905 in Severynivka, Tarashcha county, Kiev gubernia. Mechanical engineer; full member of the Shevchenko Scientific Society; son of V. Radzymovska. A graduate of the Kiev Polytechnical Institute (1927), he lectured there (1930–41), headed its hoisting-machine development department, and was an associate of the AN URSR (now ANU) Institute of Mechanics. A postwar refugee, he taught in Munich at the International University (1944–7) and the Ukrainian Technical Institute (1946–9). After emigrating to the United States in 1950, he taught mechanical engineering at the University of Illinois; worked as an industrial consultant specializing in machine design, lubrication, engineering mechanics, and stress analysis; and wrote *Lubrication of Bearings: Theoretical Principles and Design* (1959).

Radzyń Podlaski (Ukrainian: Radyn). II-3. A town (1989 pop 15,600) on the Biała River in Biała Podlaska voivodeship, Poland. It was founded in 1468 and was originally known as Kozirynek. In 1905 there were 33,600 Ukrainians of the Orthodox faith in Radzyń county, representing one-third of the population. By 1931 there were only about 2,000 of them left, the rest having converted to Roman Catholicism.

Raevsky, Mikhail, b 18 July 1811 in Arzamas, Nizhnii-Novgorod gubernia, Russia, d 2 May 1884 in Vienna. Russian diplomat and foreign service agent. He graduated from the St Petersburg Theological Academy (1833). He served as a chaplain at the Russian embassy in Stockholm and an agent of the tsarist Ministry of External Affairs and the Russian Synod there, and in 1842 he was transferred to the Russian embassy in Vienna. Raevsky was a proponent of Pan-Slavism; he facilitated contacts between Slavic intellectuals in the Russian Empire and their counterparts in Austria-Hungary, Serbia, and Bulgaria. Through him the tsarist regime funded many Slavic scholarly, social, and religious institutions in Galicia, Bukovyna, and Transcarpathia. In the late 1860s he recruited teachers, among them Western Ukrainian Russophiles, for Russian classical gymnasiums. He was a corresponding member of the Odessa Society of History and Antiquities (1848), a representative of Moscow's Slavic Philanthropic Committee (from 1860), and a founding member of the Dukhnovych Society in Prešov (1863). A biography of Raevsky, by K. Ustyianovych, was published in Lviv in 1884, and a volume of his correspondence was published in Moscow in 1975.

Rafalovych, Artem [Rafalovyč], b 25 November 1816 in Podilia gubernia, d 15 May 1851 in St Petersburg. Physician and traveler. He completed his medical studies at Berlin University and obtained a doctoral degree at Dorpat University (1838). In 1840 he was appointed a professor of forensic medicine at the Richelieu Lyceum in Odessa. As a senior member of a research expedition on the plague, he visited Turkey, Syria, Palestine, Egypt, Tunis, and Algeria (1846–8) and recorded valuable ethnographic and geographic information. He was elected a full member of the Imperial Russian Geographic Society and was appointed to the Medical Council of the Ministry of Internal Affairs (1850). His publications include medico-statistical surveys of Odessa, an account of his travels, a study of syphilis, and an introduction to forensic medicine.

Viktor Rafalsky

Rafalsky, Viktor [Rafal's'kyj], b 1919 in the Rivne region of Volhynia. Dissident and political prisoner. An author of unpublished short stories, novels, and plays, he was committed to Soviet psychiatric prisons in Leningrad, Dnipropetrovske, and Lviv for 24 years, for belonging to a clandestine Marxist group (1954–9), writing anti-Soviet prose (1962–5), and possessing anti-Soviet literature (1968–83). When he was finally released, in the winter of 1987, he was pronounced sane.

Rafes, Moisei, b 1883 in Minsk, Belarus, d 1942. Jewish-Russian revolutionary. A wig-maker by profession, he was a leading member of the social democratic Jewish Workers' *Bund from 1903, and after the February Revolution of 1917 he represented it in the Ukrainian Central Rada and Little Rada. In July 1917 he was appointed general secretary of state control, and he went with V. Vynnychenko and Kh. Baranovsky to Moscow to present the *Statute of the Higher Administration of Ukraine to the Russian Provisional Government. In November 1917 he became a member of the *Committee for the Defense of the Revolution in Ukraine. In January 1918 he voted against adopting the Fourth Universal that proclaimed the UNR as an independent state. He was critical of the UNR law on *national-personal autonomy, and he spoke out against the creation of a national army. In March 1918 he voted against the UNR's signing a separate peace treaty with the Central Powers at Brest-Litovsk. He was imprisoned under the Hetman government. At the Ukrainian Labor Congress in January 1919, Rafes voiced the Bund's support for rule by revolutionary councils, argued for a UNR Directory–Soviet Russian military alliance against the

Whites and the Allied intervention, and condemned the Directory for its war with the Bolsheviks and its inability to prevent pogroms against the Jews. In March 1919 he joined the Bolshevik party, and in December he was elected deputy chairman of the CP(B)U in Kiev gubernia. Rafes served as a leader of the Jewish Section in the Bolshevik Central Executive Committee and as a Red Army commissar. After the civil war ended, he directed the agitprop section of the Comintern Secretariat in Moscow and worked for the Comintern in China. Under Stalin he was removed from the Comintern, and worked in the Soviet film industry. He wrote memoirs about Ukraine in 1918 (1919) and books about the Bund in Ukraine in 1917–19 (1920), the national question (1921), the history of the Bund (1923), and the Chinese revolution (1927). He was arrested during the Stalinist purges, and probably died in a concentration camp.

R. Senkus

Raffalovich, George (pseud: Bedwin Sands), b 1880 in Cannes, France, d 17 May 1958 in New Orleans, Louisiana. Journalist and novelist. Ancestors on his father's side were Jews from Ukraine. A British citizen from 1906, he lived in London. He was honorary secretary of the so-called Ukraine Committee (1913–14); wrote over a dozen articles on the Ukrainian question for English journals (eg, The *New Age, Outlook, Contemporary Review*, and The *Commentator*) and the book *The Ukraine: Reprint of a Lecture Delivered on Ukrainian History and Present-Day Political Problems* (1914); translated and published a long article by M. Hrushevsky as *The Historical Evolution of the Ukrainian Problem* (1915); and edited the collection *The Russians in Galicia*, which was published by the Ukrainian National Council in New York in 1916. The best-informed observer of Ukrainian affairs in Great Britain in his day, he did much to try to influence British public opinion and gain support for the Ukrainian independence movement. After being accused of pro-German sympathies, he was forced to leave Britain. He moved to the United States, where he taught French and Slavic history at several universities. An account of his life and a bibliography of his writings by O. Kravcheniuk appeared in *Suchasnist'* (1963, no. 9).

Raguzinsky (Vladislavić), Savva [Raguzinskij], b ca 1660–70 in Dubrovnik or Hercegnovi, Dalmatia, d 18 or 28 June 1738 in St Petersburg. Serbian noble and businessman; prince of Illyria from 1711. During the hetmancy of I. Mazepa he leased the import-duty operations in the Hetmanate and exported Ukrainian potash. In 1710 Peter I awarded Raguzinsky large estates confiscated from the émigré *starshyna* supporters of Mazepa. Ca 1728–31 near Velyka Topal, Starodub regiment, he opened the first sail- and linen-cloth factory in Left-Bank Ukraine. The inheritors of Raguzinsky's Ukrainian estates, his nephews G. and M. Vladislavich, married daughters of the Cossack *starshyna* and continued operating his businesses in Ukraine. In 1770 Catherine II awarded their estates to Count P. Rumiantsev.

Rahoza, Mykhailo (Rohoza), b 1540 in Volhynia, d 1599. Metropolitan of Kiev. In 1576 he entered a monastery in Minsk and in 1579 became its archimandrite. He was appointed metropolitan of Kiev by the king of Poland and was consecrated by Patriarch Jeremiah II of Constantinople in August 1589 in Vilnius. He supported the

Church Union of *Berestia; he dispatched Bishops I. Potii and K. Terletsky to Rome to complete the negotiations, and he signed the act of union in 1596. For this he was opposed by the Orthodox brotherhoods and some of the Orthodox clergy and nobility, led by Prince K. Ostrozky.

Mariia Raievska-Ivanova (self-portrait, 1866)

Raievska-Ivanova, Mariia [Rajevs'ka-Ivanova, Marija], b 1840 in Havrylivka, Kharkiv gubernia, d 1912 in Kharkiv. Painter and educator; the first woman in the Russian Empire to be granted the title of artist by the St Petersburg Academy of Arts (1868). She studied painting in Dresden. She founded the *Kharkiv Painting School (1869) and later wrote a handbook on drawing for home and school (1879). Her oils and watercolors were influenced by the academic style – *Self-Portrait* (1866), *Death of a Peasant in Ukraine* (1868), and *Girl by a Fence*, for example.

Raievsky, Arkadii [Rajevs'kyj, Arkadij] (Raevsky), b 1848 in Voronezh, Russia, d 28 November 1916 in Kharkiv. Veterinarian and educator. A graduate of the Medico-Surgical Academy in St Petersburg (1871), he taught there from 1875 (as professor from 1879). In 1884 he became a professor at and the director of the Kharkiv Veterinary Institute, where he founded a veterinary-bacteriological station for developing vaccines, a zoohygienic laboratory, and courses for upgrading zemstvo veterinarians. One of the first organizers of veterinary education in the Russian Empire, in the 1870s he wrote *Patologicheskaia anatomiia i gistologiia domashnikh zhivotnykh* (Pathological

Anatomy and Histology of Domestic Animals) and *Rukovodstvo k izucheniiu infektsionnykh boleznei domashnikh zhivotnykh* (A Guide to the Study of Infectious Diseases of Domestic Animals).

Raievsky, Borys [Rajevs'kyj] (Rajewsky, Boris), b 19 July 1893 in Chyhyryn, Kiev gubernia, d 22 November 1974 in Frankfurt am Main. Biophysicist. A graduate of Kiev University, he became a docent (1929) and a professor (1934) at Frankfurt University. Concurrently he worked at the Max Planck Biophysics Institute in Frankfurt and served as its director (1937–66). As rector of Frankfurt University in the difficult postwar years, he played an important role in its reconstruction. His research dealt primarily with the biological effects of ionizing radiation, ultrasound, and nonionizing electro-magnetic radiation. He provided expert input into the process of establishing radiation protection standards.

Raievsky, Oleksander [Rajevs'kyj], b 4 February 1872 in Kharkiv, d 23 June 1924 in Moscow. Engineer. He graduated from the Kharkiv Institute of Technology (1895), worked as a specialist in locomotive design at the Kharkiv Locomotive-Building Factory (from 1900), and was a professor at the Petrograd Polytechnical Institute (from 1920). He was a pioneer in the development of locomotives in the Russian Empire and designed various early models of locomotive, including the first Soviet-built M-series locomotive. He developed methods for the calculation of loading parameters in locomotives.

Raievsky, Oleksandr [Rajevs'kyj], b 21 August 1891 in Kiev, d 14 September 1971 in Kiev. Psychologist. A graduate of Kiev University (1917), he taught psychology there (as a professor from 1925) and became chairman of the psychology department (from 1945). He worked in the Scientific Research Institute of Psychology of the Ukrainian SSR (1945–59). He published about 80 works dealing with methodological problems of teaching psychology, the psychology of language and thought, and the history of psychology, and wrote *Psikhologiia rechi v sovetskoi psikhologicheskoi nauke za 40 let (1917–1957)* (The Psychology of Language in Soviet Psychological Science over 40 Years [1917–1957], 1958).

Raievsky, Petro [Rajevs'kyj], b 1847 in Boryspil, Pereiaslav county, Poltava gubernia, d 20 January 1886 in Kiev. Writer and ethnographer. He graduated from the Lublin Progymnasium in 1867. He took part in P. *Chubynsky's ethnographic expedition in Ukraine and worked for three years as a functionary of the Chernihiv surveying service. From 1875 he lived in Boryspil and devoted himself to writing. He contributed regularly to the daily *Kievlianin*, in which he published over 40 novelettes, stories, and true accounts of the peasantry of Chernihiv gubernia and life in Kiev and, from 1877, the folkways, folklore, and demonology of Volhynian Polisia. His prose appeared separately as *Stseny iz'' malorusskago narodnago byta* (Scenes from Little Russian Folkways, 5 edns, 1871–86), *Epizody iz zhizni malorussov''* (Episodes from the Life of the Little Russians, 1872), and *Novyia stseny i razskazy iz'' malorusskago byta* (New Scenes and Stories from Little Russian Folkways, 1883). An epigone of N. Gogol, Raievsky used a half-Russian, half-Ukrainian vernacular in his works. Although many of them lack artistic merit, they are a valuable source of information about the Ukrainian peasantry and their social and economic relations with the Russian and Polish nobility and clergy and Jewish taverners.

Raievsky, Serhii [Rajevs'kyj, Serhij], b 8 October 1905 in Faivka, Novhorod-Siverskyi county, Chernihiv gubernia. Art scholar. A graduate of the Kiev State Art Institute (1930), he was director of the Gallery of T. Shevchenko's Paintings in Kharkiv (1935–6). He wrote many scholarly and popular articles on Ukrainian painting, particularly on Shevchenko's artistic work, and published a number of books, including *Plakat A. Strakhova* (A. Strakhov's Posters, 1936) and *Zhyttia i tvorchist' khudozhnyka Tarasa Shevchenka* (The Life and Work of the Artist Taras Shevchenko, 1939).

Raiffeisen credit co-operative. A form of rural *credit union, first organized by W. Raiffeisen in Germany in the mid-19th century. The first such union in Russian-ruled Ukraine was founded in Ivanivka, Pryluka county, Poltava gubernia, in 1895, following the adoption of a new law on credit co-operatives. The unions were popular with Ukrainian peasants, who had little money. By 1915 there were 1,978 Raiffeisen credit unions in the nine Ukrainian gubernias of the Russian Empire, 176 in the Kuban, and several hundred more in predominantly Ukrainian regions of Bessarabia and other neighboring gubernias. In 1914 those institutions had 1,754,000 members, total assets of over 130 million rubles, and outstanding loans of over 117 million rubles. The unions were dissolved by the Bolshevik regime.

In Galicia most Ukrainian Raiffeisen credit unions were under the control of the *Patrons of Agricultural Associations (est 1899). Before the First World War another 33 were under the Audit Union of Ukrainian Co-operatives (RSUK). After the war the RSUK devoted considerable attention to activating Ukrainian Raiffeisen credit unions, and by 1938 there were over 500 individual offices. Most of them provided long-term loans to peasants and peasant co-operatives. They worked closely with the Ukrainbank credit unions, which served urban dwellers, and the Tsentrobank, which functioned as the overall co-ordinating body for Ukrainian credit co-operatives in the interwar period. All of the Raiffeisen credit co-operatives were abolished in 1939, when Soviet forces occupied Western Ukraine.

Raihorodka hoard. A cache of late *Bronze Age bronze items found in 1926 on the banks of the Aidar River near Raihorodka, Novoaidar raion, Luhanske oblast. Among the items found were six sickles, the head of a mace, two sections of a sword, pins, and brass ingots. The pieces are characteristic of the *Sabatynivka and *Noua cultures, making Raihorodka an unusual discovery because of its location far to the east of the center of these cultures.

Raiky fortified settlement. A Rus' fortress town on the Hnylopiat River near Raiky, Berdychiv raion, Zhytomyr oblast. It was excavated in 1929–35 by T. *Molchanivsky and in 1946–7 by V. Honcharov. Raiky was one of a series of fortified outposts along the steppe frontier of Kievan Rus'. It occupied a territory of 1.25 ha and was surrounded by a deep (7 m) moat and earthen walls with towers. Excavations revealed the remains of 52 dwellings and a variety of tools used in agriculture, iron production (from local ore deposits), metalworking, jewelry making, and ceramic production. The town was destroyed in 1241 by the Mongols; the remains of those who died defending the settlement were found in the stronghold.

Rail, water (*Rallus aquaticus*; Ukrainian: *pastushok*). A slender marsh bird, 11–45 cm in length, belonging to the family Rallidae. Rails are fast runners and good swimmers and divers, but poor fliers. The water rail is the only species represented in Ukraine; it has a long, reddish bill. Under Ukrainian climatic conditions it is a migratory bird inhabiting reed thickets and brush. It is considered an excellent game bird but has no other commercial value.

Railroad transportation. In Ukraine railroads are a major mode of transportation. Because the natural waterways lie from north to south, the east–west traffic must be borne by land transportation, in which railways played the dominant role. The lower cost of railroad building and maintenance gives them an advantage over motor vehicle transport. Ukraine's railroad network was developed by the imperial powers that controlled its territories and served the interest of the imperial economies, not Ukraine's economy.

The first railroad line in Ukraine, built in 1861, connected Lviv, Cracow, and Vienna. Later the line was extended southward toward Chernivtsi, in Bukovyna (1866), and eastward to Brody and Pidvolochyska (1867–71). By the turn of the century nine lines had spread rapidly from Lviv, the largest rail center in Western Ukraine. The other main junctions, with five lines each, were Stanyslaviv, Stryi, and Ternopil. The first railroad in Russian-ruled Ukraine was built in 1865. It ran from Balta to Odessa. In 1868 it was extended to Yelysavethrad and from there through Kremenchuk to Kiev (1872). By then Kiev had been connected by rail to Moscow (1869). In the 1870s the Moscow–Kursk–Kharkiv line was extended south to Lozova, and then branched out to Rostov-na-Donu and Sevastopil. In 1870 Kiev was connected with Odessa through Zhmerynka and with Moscow through Konotip. In 1880 to 1890 numerous trunk lines were constructed to connect the Donets coal region with the Kryvyi Rih Iron-ore Basin and the newly established heavy-industry complexes at Katerynoslav and Oleksandrivske (now Zaporizhia). By 1914 several other main lines, including the Mykolaiv–Bakhmach, Kiev–Donbas, Kiev–Warsaw, and Fastiv–Katerynoslav, were built. The railways in central and eastern Ukraine carried mostly wheat to the seaports for export and raw materials to the rapidly growing industry in the Dnieper region and in Russia. By 1913 Ukraine had approx 15,600 km of rails, some of them double-track trunk lines. Lines were built without any general plans, so that some important cities, such as Radomyshl, Bobrynets, and Pereiaslav, were left without rail service. The physical plant, rolling stock, and carrying capacity of the railways were well below European standards. The Ukrainian-Soviet War (1917–21) destroyed much of the railroad network in Ukraine.

In the interwar period the Soviet regime built some lines that had been planned before the war, including the Kharkiv–Dnipropetrovske–Kherson, Khvastiv–Novohrad-Volynskyi–Zhytomyr, Chernihiv–Horodnytsia, and Pavlohrad–Hryshyne lines and several short links in the Vinnytsia and Kiev regions serving the sugar industry. A number of short lines in the heavily industrialized Dnieper-Donets region were opened to relieve congestion on the

Electrified railroad lines
Other railroad lines
Railroad lines planned
or under construction
Boundary of Ukraine

0   250   500 km

RAILROAD TRANSPORTATION IN UKRAINE

trunk lines, such as Fedorivka–Snihurivka in the Kherson region, Vesele–Dniprorudne in the Zaporizhia region, Dolynska–Pomichna in the Kirovohrad region, Novomoskovske–Dniprodzerzhynske in the Dnipropetrovske region, and Horlivka–Ocheretyne in the Donetske region. Many of the new lines had a special purpose and were restricted to a certain industry or enterprise. Altogether about 4,000 km of track were added to Ukraine's network. During the Second World War over 9,200 km of track were destroyed. Ukraine's railways returned to their prewar capacity only in 1948. No new lines were built; instead some old ones in the heavily populated areas of Western Ukraine were shut down. To stimulate trade with Western Europe the Lutske–Ustyluh line has been rebuilt recently.

For a country of its size Ukraine's railroad network is inadequate. At present the two major junctions in Ukraine are Kharkiv and Lviv, with eight railroad lines each. Kiev, Bakhmach, Kupianka, Yasynuvata, Krasnoarmiiske, Korosten, Kovel, Shepetivka, Stryi, Ternopil, and Pomichna are five-line junctions. Many other important junctions are small towns, such as Koziatyn, or even villages, such as Hrebinka and Romodan. The republic's capital, Kiev, has only one terminal, which until 1933 was a wooden structure. Another terminal is planned in Bykivnia, just outside the city. Kharkiv has three terminals; Lviv, Odessa, Poltava, and Dnipropetrovske have two terminals each.

Since the 1950s the railway network had been expand-

ed and improved. Many trunk lines have been double-tracked, and approx 7,800 km have been electrified. With the exception of some local lines, all lines use either electric or diesel power. Lines linking Ukraine with other republics of the former USSR and international lines, such as the Kiev–Lviv–Chop, Koziatyn–Kovel, and Lviv–Odessa lines, are double-track and electrified. The heavily used Kiev–Konotip trunk line is being rebuilt into a three-track main line. Modern tracks consisting of heavier rail (R-100 instead of R-50 or R-75), a solid ballast-type bed, concrete ties, and deep side ditches for drainage have a higher load capacity. Containers and longer cars with eight instead of four axles have been introduced. More powerful locomotives make it possible to pull heavier loads at higher speeds. By European standards train speeds are still quite low: the technical speed is approx 55 km/hr, and sectional speed is 45 km/hr. Most locomotives used in Ukraine are built at its own locomotive works (see *Locomotive industry). Major repair shops are located in Luhanske, Popasna, Dnipropetrovske, Odessa, Lviv, and Stryi.

With minimal capital outlays Soviet railroads were run to the point of exhaustion. Whereas Western railroads require sizable government subsidies, Soviet railroads were profitable with an index of efficiency between 0.75 and 0.85.

The Ukrainian system suffers less from obsolete or outdated rolling stock than from managerial incompetence. Infrequent train runs, empty freight runs, poor traffic dis-

TABLE 1
Output of Ukrainian railroad directorates, 1965–87

Directorate	Network (in 1,000 km)	Category of activity						
		A	B	C	D	E	F	G
Donets	2.9	12.8	2.7	2.5	40	15	35	10
Lviv	4.5	19.8	1.6	1.3	18	13	28	41
Odessa	4.2	18.5	2.5	2.2	15	30	15	40
Dnieper	3.2	14.1	2.5	2.3	35	28	24	13
Southern	3.6	9.2	nd	4.3	10	18	6	66
Southwestern	4.7	20.7	2.7	4.0	12	23	12	53

A = percentage of Ukrainian network.
B = percentage of the former USSR freight output.
C = percentage of the former USSR passenger output.
D = percentage of Ukraine's exports to countries within and outside the former USSR.
E = percentage of Ukraine's imports from countries within and outside the former USSR.
F = percentage of Ukraine's local traffic.
G = percentage of Ukraine's transit traffic (transport of goods not produced or sorted in Ukraine).

TABLE 2
Railroad transportation: basic indexes, 1940–86

Category	1940	1970	1980	1986
1. Length of network (in 1,000 km)	20.1	22.06	22.55	22.72
including electrified lines	0.2	5.3	7.1	7.4
2. Industrial rail (in 1,000 km)	nd	20.5	24.8	25.7
3. Density				
(km per 1,000 sq km)	33.3	36.5	37.4	37.6
(km per 10,000 people)	4.9	4.7	4.5	4.5
Freight traffic				
4. Output (in billion Tkm[1])	71.9	380.2	469.3	506.3
5. Volume (in million t)	200.0	794.7	981.1	1,042.9
Coal	nd	229.0	247.0	243.0
Ores	nd	112.0	132.0	132.0
Chemical products	nd	192.0	261.0	267.0
Other products	nd	262.0	341.0	367.0
Container haul (in 1,000 t)	–	–	6,953.0	10,567.0
Packaged haul (in 1,000 t)	–	–	38,565.0	53,435.0
6. Density of haul (in million Tkm)	3.6	17.2	20.8	22.3
(for the former USSR)	(4.3)	(18.5)	(24.3)	(26.3)
7. Average trip distance per t of haul (in km)	359.5	458.4	478.0	485.4
(for the former USSR)	(695.0)	(861.0)	(923.0)	(945.0)
Passenger traffic				
8. Output (in billion Pkm[2])	16.4	42.1	60.1	68.3
9. Volume (in million passengers)	242.6	506.4	648.9	635.5
10. Density of haul (in million Pkm)	0.8	1.8	2.5	3.0
(for the former USSR)	(1.0)	(2.0)	(2.4)	(2.8)
11. Average trip distance of 1 passenger (in km)	67.6	83.1	92.6	107.5
(for the former USSR)	(73.0)	(82.0)	(84.0)	(92.0)
Percentage of railway output relative to Ukraine's transportation output				
12. Freight	–	62.2	60.7	56.2
13. Passenger	–	43.8	38.9	39.8

[1]Tkm = tonnes per kilometer.
[2]Pkm = passengers per kilometer.

tribution, and lower locomotive working time are the main sources of inefficiency. Suburban traffic has its own problems. The major one is the irregularity of traffic.

Ukraine was divided into six railroad directorates: Donets, Dnieper, Southern, Lviv, Southwestern, and Odessa. The directorates enjoy some autonomy in planning and regulating rail traffic and services, but capital

for the construction of new railroads and basic improvements was controlled by the central government in Moscow.

Table 1 shows that traffic density was distributed unevenly. The Donets railroad had the highest traffic density in the USSR network. The Dnieper railroad was export-oriented, with freight density much higher than the network's average. The Southern railroad was plagued with great irregularities of traffic flow; it had a high percentage of empty runs. The Southwestern railroad had a significant transit traffic, but its freight flow was close to equilibrium level. The Lviv railroad was a transit-type directorate with traffic irregularities close to the former Union average. The Odessa railroad was known for its large share of imports and a traffic irregularity close to 50 percent.

E. Bej

Railroad-car industry. A branch of the machine-building industry that builds and repairs passenger and freight cars used in railroad transportation. Before the 1917 Revolution railroad cars were manufactured in five factories, in Kiev, Katerynoslav, Mykolaiv, Kharkiv, and Horlivka. In 1900 their output accounted for only 4 percent of all the railroad cars produced in the Russian Empire. Today, unlike the *locomotive industry, the railroad-car industry in Ukraine remains underdeveloped. The only major plants producing railroad cars are in Kriukiv (the *Kriukiv Freight-Car Plant) and Dniprodzerzhynske, and their output is limited to freight cars. No passenger cars are produced in Ukraine. Railroad cars are repaired in most major railroad centers in Ukraine. The largest is located in Darnytsia, a suburb of Kiev. Other major depots are in Popasna, Luhanske oblast, and in Dnipropetrovske.

Raion. An administrative-territorial unit established in the Ukrainian SSR in 1923. It was part of the conversion from the territorial system of gubernias, counties, and volosts to okruhas (consolidated into oblasts in 1932), raions, and rural soviets. In size the raions were smaller than counties but larger than volosts. In 1923 there were 706 set up in the Ukrainian SSR, where they replaced 1,989 volosts. The number and size of the raions changed constantly: there were 666 in 1925, 383 in 1930, 500 in 1938, 786 in 1956 (including those in Western Ukraine and the Crimea), and 604 in 1961. Another reorganization, in 1962, reduced their number to 251, but the number rose to 394 in 1965, 447 in 1966, 475 in 1968, 476 in 1970, and 481 in 1990. Cities with a population of over 100,000 are also divided into raions. There were 90 city raions in 1970 and 120 in 1990.

The raion council was one of the organs of the government system. It was elected for two years, and appointed an executive committee, which had its own bureaucracy. The raion executive oversaw rural and town (smt) soviets, and city councils of the smaller cities, and was responsible to higher administrative authorities and to the raion soviet. Because the executive committee had to make decisions and take action in all areas under the soviet's jurisdiction, the raion soviet was reduced to the status of a supplementary organ of the administrative system. The executive was supposed to convene the soviet at least six times annually to inform it about the state of the raion, but that was rarely done. In addition, the sessions of the soviet, which were usually brief, did not permit in-depth discussion. Standing commissions advising the executive were more influential than the soviet. Nonelected individuals could be named to the commissions. Raion jurisdiction was fairly limited and local. It had hardly any control over industry and dealt mostly with agricultural, co-operative, community, and cultural affairs. (See also *Soviet.)

The true source of local authority at the raion level was the raion committee of the CPU, which issued directives to both the soviet and its executive committee.

A. Bilynsky

Raion people's court. See People's court.

Rais, Emmanuel [Rajs], b 1909 in Khotyn, Bessarabia, d 27 January 1981 in Paris. Literary critic and translator of Jewish origin. He studied law and literature at Bucharest and Paris universities (1934–40) and earned a PH D from the Sorbonne (1972). He specialized in the study of lyric poetry and published many studies of French, Russian, and Ukrainian literature. His interest in Ukrainian poetry began in the mid-1950s; thereafter he published a number of articles on the works of E. Andiievska, M. Drai-Khmara, V. Svidzinsky, various émigré poets, and poets in the Ukrainian SSR (particularly the *shestydesiatnyky) in Ukraïns'ka literaturna hazeta and Suchasnist'. He also wrote articles of general interest on esthetics and philosophy. He edited and wrote the introduction to a collection of Ukrainian poetry in French translation, L'Ukraine, cette inconnue (1967).

Raitsa (from Polish *rajca*). A member of the municipal *magistrat. At first each magistrat had 4 to 8 elected raitsi (aka ratmany, radnyky), but with time their number increased to 12 and even 24, and they were appointed for life by the viit, starosta, or voivode. The raitsi ran the municipal administration, civil court, economy, and police. In Austrian-ruled Western Ukraine they and the magistrat were abolished in 1780, but in Russian-ruled Ukraine they survived until the judicial reform of 1864.

Rak, Liudmyla, b 1909. Linguist. An associate of the AN URSR (now ANU) Institute of Linguistics, she was a coauthor of a Ukrainian orthographic school dictionary (1936) and a Russian-Ukrainian agricultural dictionary (1963), and wrote articles on the dialectal features of the village of Kodnia in the Zhytomyr region and on the lexical-morphemic features, hyperbole, and synonyms in folk dumas.

Rak, Yaroslav, b 29 July 1908 in Vynnyky, Lviv county, Galicia, d 8 November 1989 in Maplewood, New Jersey. Lawyer, youth leader, and political activist. In the 1930s he was active in the Ukrainian Sports Union in Lviv and president of the Ukrainian Students' Sports Club. An OUN member, he was tried for participating in the 1934 assassination of B. Pieracki. In 1939–40 he headed the youth department of the Ukrainian Central Committee in Cracow, and in 1941–4 he was imprisoned in the Auschwitz concentration camp. After the Second World War he was in charge of the youth department of the Central Representation of the Ukrainian Emigration in Germany (1945–8) and was a member of the executive of the *Plast Ukrainian Youth Association (1945–53). Later he emigrated to the United States, where he continued to work with youth and in education.

Rakhiv [Raxiv]. V-5. A city (1989 pop 15,800) on the Tysa River and a raion center in Transcarpathia oblast. It was first mentioned in historical documents in 1447. Lying on the trade route between Galicia and Transylvania, Moldavia, and Hungary, the town was a major livestock trading center in the 17th and 18th centuries. In 1920 Rakhiv was transferred from Hungary to Czechoslovakia, and in 1945 it was annexed to the Ukrainian SSR. It acquired city status in 1958. Most of its inhabitants work in industry, producing forest products, cardboard, and vegetable oil.

Rakhiv Mountains. See Hutsul Alps.

Rakhlin, Natan [Raxlin], b 10 January 1906 in Snovske (now Shchors), Horodnia county, Chernihiv gubernia, d 28 June 1979 in Kazan (buried in Kiev). Orchestral conductor. He studied at the Kiev Conservatory (1923–7) and the Lysenko Music and Drama Institute and then served (1937–62, with brief interruptions) as the main conductor of the State Symphony Orchestra of the Ukrainian SSR. In 1941–5 he was also the main conductor of the State Symphony Orchestra of the USSR in Moscow. He premiered B. Liatoshynsky's *Third Symphony*, V. Kossenko's *Heroic Overture*, and works by V. Homoliaka, H. Maiboroda, and L. Kolodub. He was the first to record scores by M. Kolachevsky, V. Kosenko, V. Sokalsky, L. Revutsky, B. Liatoshynsky, A. Shtoharenko, and others for the Melodiya label. From 1939 he also taught at the Kiev Conservatory.

Roman Rakhmanny   Ivan Rakovsky

Rakhmanny, Roman [Raxmannyj] (pseud of Roman Olynyk [Olijnyk]), b 26 December 1918 in Lviv. Journalist and political analyst. As a postwar émigré in Germany he worked as an editor of Ukrainian newspapers, such as *Chas* and *Ukraïns'ka trybuna*. After emigrating to Canada in 1948, he was chief editor of *Homin Ukraïny* (1949–51). From 1959 to 1984 he worked as a producer for the Ukrainian section of Radio Canada International, and he served as section head from 1975. He defended his PH D dissertation at McGill University in 1962 and taught courses in Ukrainian studies there for several years. Rakhmanny is the author of hundreds of articles and essays on Ukrainian topics in émigré Ukrainian, Canadian, American, and Western European newspapers and periodicals. These essays range over the fields of politics, literature, and history and have appeared in several collections, including *Krov i chornylo* (Blood and Ink, 1960), *Na p'iatdesiatii paraleli* (On the Fiftieth Parallel, 1969), *Vohni samostiinoï Ukraïny* (Flames of an Independent Ukraine, 1978), *In Defense of the Ukrainian Cause* (1979), and *Ukraïna atomnoho viku* (Ukraine in the Atomic Age, 2 vols, 1987, 1988).

Rákóczi, György I, b 8 June 1593, d 11 October 1648 in Sárospatak, Transylvania. Prince of Transylvania from 1630; father of György II Rákóczi. From 1644 he was a leader of the anti-Habsburg coalition in the Thirty Years' War, and in 1645 he annexed part of Transcarpathia. After the death of King Władysław IV Vasa in 1648, Rákóczi was a candidate for the Polish throne. To that end he solicited support from Hetman B. Khmelnytsky through Yu. Nemyrych. Khmelnytsky wrote a letter promising military support to Rákóczi, but the hetman's delegation, headed by I. Vyhovsky, that took the letter to Transylvania did not arrive until after Rákóczi's death.

Rákóczi, György II, b 30 January 1621 in Sárospatak, Transylvania, d 7 January 1660 in Nagyvárad (now Oradea), Transylvania. Prince of Transylvania from 1648; son of György I *Rákóczi. He continued his father's relations with Hetman B. Khmelnytsky until Khmelnytsky's military intervention in Moldavia in 1652. Rákóczi then broke with Khmelnytsky and joined the side of Wallachia and Poland against Ukraine. In 1654, however, he resumed diplomatic relations with Khmelnytsky, and in 1656 he entered into an anti-Polish coalition with Transylvania, Ukraine, and Sweden. In 1657 Rákóczi's army captured a large part of Poland, including Cracow and Warsaw, with the help of Swedish and Ukrainian forces. He quickly proved not to be an able military or political leader, however, and Khmelnytsky withdrew his troops (commanded by Col A. Zhdanovych) to Ukraine. Abandoned by his allies, Rákóczi was surrounded by the Poles on 23 July 1657 and forced to surrender near Chornyi Ostriv, in Podilia.

Rakovets burial site. A *Cherniakhiv culture burial ground of the 3rd to 4th century near Rakovets, Zbarazh raion, Ternopil oblast. Excavations in 1962–3 revealed 18 burials, some of which were cremations. Items of interest discovered included two cylindrical earthenware goblets with solar and lunar designs on them and a stone idol.

Rakovsky, Ivan [Rakovs'kyj], b 5 March 1815 in Stavne, Transcarpathia, d 3 December 1885 in Iza, Transcarpathia. Russophile Greek Catholic clergyman and publicist. He studied at the Uzhhorod Theological Seminary and was ordained in 1839. His work in Uzhhorod (1844–50) as vice-rector of the theological seminary and lecturer at the teachers' seminary led to a position in Budapest (1850–9) as a translator and editor of a government bulletin for the peoples of the Hungarian crownland. During this period he developed his contacts with Galician Russophiles and published the newspapers *Tserkovnaia gazeta* (1856–8) and *Tserkovnyi viestnik dlia rusynov avstriiskoi derzhavy* (1858). He became a leading figure in the *Society of St Basil the Great and wrote arithmetic, geometry, and Russian language textbooks. He believed that Russian should be the language of Transcarpathia, and his writings generally used a standard Russian rather than *yazychiie. In 1871 a Magyarophile element took over the St Basil society and ousted Rakovsky from the leadership. He then largely removed himself from public life.

Rakovsky, Ivan [Rakovs'kyj], b 24 August 1874 in Protesy, Zhydachiv county, Galicia, d 1 March 1949 in Newark, New Jersey. Anthropologist, zoologist, pedagogue, and civic leader; honorary member of the Shevchenko Scientific Society (NTSh, full member from 1903). As a student he helped found the *Academic Hromada and served as its first president. He graduated from Lviv University (1896; PH D, 1903) and taught secondary school in Kolomyia. In 1903–5 he took part in F. *Vovk's anthropological expeditions to the Carpathians (Lemko, Boiko, and Hutsul regions) and Podilia. In Lviv (1908) he cofounded the Teacher's Hromada and was active in the NTSh (as secretary to the president, M. Hrushevsky) as well as in the Prosvita and Vidrodzhennia societies. After the First World War Rakovsky was one of the founders of the *Lviv (Underground) Ukrainian University, where he taught anthropology and zoology (1921–5). In 1925, in an essay he wrote with S. Rudenko, he developed a theory (contrary to Vovk's) that the Ukrainian population consisted not of one racial (Dinaric) type but of at least six European racial types (although with the Dinaric type predominant). He was editor in chief of *Ukraïns'ka zahal'na entsyklopediia* (The Ukrainian General Encyclopedia, 1930–5). Twice he was elected president of the NTSh, first in Lviv (1935–9) and then in Germany (1946–9). After the Second World War he emigrated to Germany, and then in 1948 to the United States. His publications include articles in zoology and on the anthropology of Ukrainians, science textbooks, and popular works on science, such as *Novyi svitohliad s'ohochasnoï nauky* (The New Worldview of Contemporary Science, 1947).

Khristian Rakovsky   Rev Yosyp Rakovsky

Rakovsky, Khristian [Rakovs'kyj, Xrystyjan], b 1 August 1873 in Gradets, Bulgaria (then part of the Ottoman Empire), d 11 September 1941. Political activist and Soviet Ukrainian state figure. Active in the pre-1914 Bulgarian and Rumanian socialist movements, Rakovsky opposed participation in the First World War and served on the Central Bureau of the antiwar Revolutionary Balkan Social Democratic Labor Federation (est 1915). In 1918 he joined the Bolshevik party and served as chairman of the Supreme Autonomous Collegium established in Odessa to suppress counterrevolution in Ukraine and Rumania. He was also a member of the Central Executive Committee of Soviets of the Rumanian Front, Black Sea Fleet, and Odessa Military District (RUMChEROD) and participated in Soviet diplomatic delegations to Hetman P. Skoropadsky's government and to Germany. From January 1919 until July 1923, with interruptions, he headed the Soviet Ukrainian government. He opposed Ukrainian 'particularism' in the name of internationalism, and went so far as

to question the existence of a distinct Ukrainian nationality. By the end of 1921, however, he had changed his views; he insisted on greater sensitivity with regard to the Ukrainian national question and also sought to expand the political and economic autonomy of the Ukrainian SSR. At the 12th congress of the Russian Communist party in April 1923, he sharply criticized J. Stalin's position on the national question. After being removed from the Ukrainian leadership he served as USSR ambassador to Britain (1923–5) and France (1925–7). Having been expelled from France for revolutionary activity, he returned to Ukraine in the fall of 1927 and spent a month organizing the *Left Opposition there. In December 1927, at the 15th congress of the Russian Communist party, he was expelled from the party, and a month later he was exiled to Astrakhan. From 1929 he was the recognized leader of the Left Opposition within the USSR. In February 1934 he submitted to party discipline and was allowed to return to Moscow, where he directed the scientific research institutes of the Commissariat of Health. In the fall of 1937 he was arrested as a spy, and in March 1938 he was sentenced to 20 years' imprisonment. He was shot in a Soviet prison.

BIBLIOGRAPHY
Conte, F. *Un révolutionnaire-diplomate: Christian Rakovski, l'Union soviétique, et l'Europe (1922–1941)* (Paris 1978)
Rakovsky, C. *Selected Writings on Opposition in the USSR, 1923–30*, ed G. Fagan (London 1980)
Conte, F. *Christian Rakovski (1873–1941): A Political Biography* (Boulder, Colo 1989)

J.-P. Himka

Rakovsky, Mykhailo [Rakovs'kyj, Myxajlo], b 20 April 1916 in Yelets, Orel gubernia, Russia. Soviet Ukrainian historian. After graduating from the Moscow Pedagogical Institute he did political work in the Red Army (1939–50). From 1951 he taught at Odessa University, and in 1968 he became a professor and the head of the department of the history of the USSR. His specializations included the revolutionary period in Southern Ukraine and primary source materials for the study of Soviet history.

Rakovsky, Yosyp [Rakovs'kyj, Josyp], b 6 October 1870, d 16 November 1944 in Lviv. Agronomist, educator, and pioneer of civic agronomy in Galicia. After graduating from the Greek Catholic Theological Seminary in Lviv he studied agronomy at Dubliany and worked as an agronomist and teacher of natural science and agronomy in teachers' seminaries in Sokal, Zalishchyky, and Stanyslaviv. He organized Prosvita reading rooms, co-operatives, and branches of *Silskyi Hospodar. For many years he was president of Silskyi Hospodar in Stanyslaviv. In 1909 he helped organize the First Educational-Economic Congress in Lviv. He contributed articles to economic journals and wrote several popular booklets on farming.

Rakushka, Roman [Rakuška] (Romanovsky), b 1622 in Nizhen, d 1703. Member of the Cossack *starshyna* and Orthodox priest. He was inspector general of the Hetman state's treasury and treasurer of Nizhen regiment in 1654–5, captain of Nizhen company in 1658–63, judge of Nizhen regiment in 1659, and general treasurer of the Hetman state under Hetman I. Briukhovetsky in 1663–8. After clashing with Hetman I. Mnohohrishny he moved to Right-Bank Ukraine, was ordained, and in 1668–75 served as an archpriest in Bratslav. In 1670 he was Metropolitan Y. Tukalsky-Neliubovych's envoy to the Patriarch of Constantinople. In 1676 he returned to Left-Bank Ukraine and settled in Starodub, where he served as pastor of St Nicholas's Church. According to many historians (eg, M. Hrushevsky, K. Kharlampovych, D. Doroshenko, O. Ohloblyn, M. Petrovsky, V. Romanovsky, M. Marchenko, Ya. Dzyra) Rakushka is the author of the *Samovydets Chronicle.

BIBLIOGRAPHY
Modzalevs'kyi, V. 'Pershyi viis'kovyi pidskarbii (1663–1669) Roman Rakushka (Narys ioho zhyttia ta diial'nosty),' ZIFV, 1, 2–3 (1919, 1922)
Petrovs'kyi, M. 'Do pytannia pro pevnist' vidomostei Litopystsia Samovydtsia i pro avtora litopysu (Romana Rakushku-Romanovs'koho),' Zapysky Nizhens'koho instytutu narodnoï osvity, 6 (1926)

Ralston, William, b 4 April 1828 in London, d 6 August 1889 in London. English scholar; corresponding member of the Russian Imperial Academy of Sciences from 1885. One of the first English scholars to specialize in Russian studies, from 1853 he worked at the British Museum. Ukrainian ethnographic and historical material is found in his *Songs of the Russian People as Illustrative of Slavonic Mythology and Russian Social Life* (1872), his lectures *Early Russian History* (1874), and his translation *Russian Folk Tales* (1878). He published reviews of V. Antonovych and M. Drahomanov's collection of Ukrainian historical songs and I. Rudchenko's collection of chumak songs.

Raltsi. A tribute in kind or money paid at Christmas and Easter by Cossacks, peasants, and burghers to the regimental and company Cossack *starshyna*, the municipal *magistrat*, and landed gentry in the Hetman state. Legally it was held to be voluntary, but in reality it was compulsory. In the 1720s Hetman I. Skoropadsky tried to abolish the tribute, but it lasted in Left-Bank Ukraine until the 1780s and in Kiev until the 1820s.

Rank estates (*rangovi maietnosti*). Landed estates in the Hetman state awarded to *Cossack *starshyna* by the hetman for the duration of their commission in return for their service and costs incurred by them in the course of service. They were introduced by Hetman B. Khmelnytsky after 1654 and were distributed out of the land fund created by the confiscation of holdings of Polish landowners and the Catholic church. Military or free lands were also used. Larger rank estates (*volosti*) were granted to hetmans by the tsar. All rank estates were administered by the General Military Chancellery, but their size was not standardized according to rank until 1732. At that time it was established that the general quartermaster was to receive an estate with 400 peasant households; the general justice and general treasurer, one with 300 households; and so on. Russian officials in Ukraine were also given estates (eg, P. Rumiantsev, president of the Little Russian Collegium). In the 18th century the number of rank estates awarded increased rapidly. Holders attempted to transform them into hereditary property, but only a few senior officials who were granted estates by the tsar succeeded. In 1764, 48 persons held 116 rank estates, with a total of 2,791 peasant households in the nine regiments of the Hetman state. After the abolition of the Hetmanate in the 1780s, most of the estates became the private property of their holders and their descendants, who received Russian noble status.

BIBLIOGRAPHY
Miakotin, V. Ocherki sotsial'noi istorii Ukrainy v XVII–XVIII vv., vol 1, fasc 2 (Prague 1926)
Diadychenko, V.A. Narysy suspil'no-politychnoho ustroiu Livoberezhnoï Ukraïny kintsia XVII–pochatku XVIII st. (Kiev 1959)
                                                            A. Zhukovsky

Rank peasants (*rangovi seliany, rangovi pospolyti*). Peasants who lived on rank estates in the Hetman state and Slobidska Ukraine in the 17th and 18th centuries. They were obligated to perform various duties for the estate holder, including tilling, harvesting, hay mowing, and timber cutting, and had to pay rent in agricultural products. Their duties were increasingly onerous and by the 18th century they approached the conditions of serfdom. After the abolition of the autonomy of Left-Bank Ukraine on 14 May 1783, most rank peasants became serfs, and the minority became *state peasants.

Ranks, military. See Military ranks.

Ranks, Table of (Russian: *tabel o rangakh*) A system for establishing equivalences in rank among the branches of service in the Imperial Russian military, civil, and court bureaucracies and for defining the hierarchy of offices and the ladder of promotion. The system was established by Tsar Peter I in January 1722, and existed (with several major modifications) until November 1917. The intent of the table was to facilitate the development of a professional and competent service elite for the state.

Initially there were 14 ranks defined in the table in ascending order. The table did not include the lowest functionaries in the bureaucracy or noncommissioned soldiers and seamen. The lowest or 14th rank was adjutant in the army, ship commissary in the navy, and collegial registrar in the civil service; the highest or 1st rank was field marshal, admiral general, and chancellor. At first everyone whose rank was in the table was considered to have noble status, and everyone in the 10th rank in the military or the 8th rank in the civil service achieved hereditary noble status. Because too many people were considered to be gaining noble status, by the mid-19th century only civil servants above the 5th rank and military officers above the 7th rank were being granted hereditary nobility, and only those above the 10th rank achieved personal nobility.

In the 17th and 18th centuries the Hetman state developed its own system of estates. In order to preserve its rights and autonomy in response to greater Russian influence and interference in its internal affairs, the Cossack *starshyna* sent formal requests in 1733, 1742, 1756, 1763, and 1767 that Moscow recognize the legitimacy of the various Cossack titles and offices. Moreover, in 1756 Hetman K. Rozumovsky presented Moscow with a Ukrainian table of ranks that consisted of 12 classes, without the *hetman and *acting hetman.

Beginning in the 1760s, in order to undermine the independence of the Hetman state and to attract the support of individual Cossack officers, Catherine II often granted Ukrainians ranks from the Russian table. When the Cossack regiments were reformed as regular Russian army units in 1783, the officers were given ranks from the Rus-

Hetman K. Rozumovsky's Table of Ranks, 1756, with a list of all 'Little Russian' (Ukrainian) ranks*

Rank	Office
	Hetman
	Acting hetman
1st	General quartermaster
2nd	General judge; General treasurer
3rd	General chancellor; General flag-bearer; General osaul; General standard-bearer
4th	Colonel
5th	Fellow of the standard; Osaul of the General Artillery; Colonel of mercenary cavalry regiment; Secretary of the General Military Court; Senior chancellor of the General Military Chancellery
6th	General Artillery flag-bearer; Regimental judge; Quartermaster of mercenary cavalry regiment
7th	Regimental secretary, osaul, and flag-bearer; Translator of the General Military Chancellery
8th	Captain; Chancellor of the General Military Chancellery; Otaman of the General Artillery; Osaul, flag-bearer, and secretary of mercenary cavalry regiment
9th	Fellow of the banner; Regimental court secretary; Captain of the hetman's personal guard; Otaman of company city; Captain of mercenary cavalry
10th	Otaman of the hetman's personal guard; Company osaul, flag-bearer, and secretary; Regimental chancellor; Regimental artillery flag-bearer and otaman; Mercenary company officer
11th	Kurin otaman; Mayor (horodnychyi) of company city; Village otaman
12th	Cossack; Guard; Member of the hetman's guard (zholdak); Mercenary cavalryman (kompaniiets); Artilleryman (pushkar)

*According to D. Miller (1892)

sian army table. The process was not governed by strict rules, and the granting of a rank to a person depended not so much on his previous position as on his particular accomplishments, abilities, and support for the Russian administration. From 1784 all Ukrainian titles were officially prohibited. With the proclamation of the new Charter of the Nobility in 1785, many of the restrictions keeping the *starshyna* from entering the system of the Russian *nobility were removed. With the introduction of the Russian judicial system in 1796, Ukrainian administrative positions were redefined according to an equivalent in the Table of Ranks (eg, *general judge was equivalent to the 4th rank, county chancellor to the 10th rank, and *voznyi* to the 14th rank).

BIBLIOGRAPHY
Miller, D. 'Ocherki iz istorii i iuridicheskogo byta staroi Malorossii: Prevrashchenie kozatskoi starshiny v dvorianstvo,' *KS*, 1892, nos 1–4
Kohut, Z.E. *Russian Centralism and Ukrainian Autonomy: Imperial Absorption of the Hetmanate, 1760s–1830s* (Cambridge, Mass 1988)

O. Sereda

Ranks and degrees, academic. In the former Ukrainian SSR the granting of academic rank and degrees was tightly controlled by the central authorities in Moscow. Students of postsecondary institutions (known commonly by the acronym VUZ), including universities, and scientific research institutes wrote major course essays (*kursovi roboty*), and in the last year of their program they defended a thesis (*dyplomna robota*) before a committee. Those who intended to work as scholars could write a candidate's dissertation under the supervision of an academic adviser. Upon completion they could work in their field and go on to complete a doctoral dissertation. Candidate's dissertations were limited to 150 pages (180–195 pages in the humanities), and doctoral dissertations to 300 pages (360–390 pages in the humanities). The general thrust of a candidate's dissertation also had to appear in published articles. The results of the public defense of a dissertation before a special council of the VUZ or scientific research institute were submitted to the All-Union Higher Attestation Commission (VAK), whose presidium usually then granted a diploma certifying that the applicant had secured the rank of a candidate of sciences. Doctoral students were expected to publish a monograph that set out a new direction in research. The monograph was printed in a run of 100 and distributed to relevant institutions. The applicant then had to secure the opinions of one reviewer and two or more opponents.

The system sought to establish a single and hermetic organism of Soviet scholarship and science, monolithic in terms of ideology and language. In rare cases linguists and literary scholars were permitted to defend their dissertations in their native tongue, but all documents submitted to the VAK had to be in Russian. The Ukrainian VAK in Kharkiv was dissolved in the early 1930s.

Those who were granted their rank or degrees worked in a scientific research institute or taught in VUZs. They then passed through the academic *nomenklatura of junior, senior, leading, and chief academic worker. In other cases scholars were given the rank of assistant, docent, or professor. The latter two were conferred by the VAK upon the recommendation of VUZ councils. The title of professor was given only to scholars with doctoratates, and they were entitled to appointment, election, and re-election as department heads or institute directors.

The ranks were determined by the presidium of the Academy of Sciences of Ukraine, which also determined salary levels. The character and direction of Soviet academic studies were determined by the leadership of the Academy of Sciences of the USSR and the republics (selected from various academic institutions), which was under the control of the central committees of the Communist party. The resolution of the Council of Ministers of the USSR 'On the Determination of Academic Appellations,' adopted on 29 March 1945 and revised on 20 February 1956, provided for the ranks of corresponding member, academician, and honorary academician in the academies of sciences.

Specialists were trained at the various VUZs in accordance with a similar planning procedure. Professionals and scholars were then assigned to maintain cadres and to disseminate Soviet conceptions of the construction and functioning of society.

S. Bilokin

Ranok (Morning). A publishing house in Kiev owned and operated by O. *Kovalenko and I. Samonenko. Between 1906 and 1908 it issued 18 literary and political pamphlets with a combined pressrun of some 40,000 copies.

Ranok (Morning). An organ of the *Independent Greek church, published in Winnipeg from April 1905 and edited by I. Bodrug. It first appeared monthly; then, after a brief interruption, semimonthly (1907–10); and finally weekly. *Ranok* contained articles on religion written from a Presbyterian perspective and often sharply polemical in tone; covered general developments in Ukraine and Canada; and printed satire, prose, and poetry. In 1920 it merged with *Kanadyiets'* to form *Kanadiis'kyi ranok*.

Ranok (Morning). A weekly and later irregular organ of the Union of Hetmanites, published in Heidenau, West Germany, from October 1948 to July 1951. It published articles on political and community affairs and engaged in vigorous polemics with other émigré newspapers. The editor was I. Marchenko.

Ranok (Morning). An illustrated journal of literature and political, cultural, and current affairs, published monthly in Kiev since 1953. Until July 1965 it was called *Zmina*, and until 1991 it was published by the Komsomol. In the 1960s and early 1970s *Ranok* served as an important forum for the better writers of the postwar generation, among them H. Tiutiunnyk, V. Shevchuk, I. Dziuba, Ye. Hutsalo, I. Drach, M. Synhaivsky, M. Vinhranovsky, Ye. Sverstiuk, V. Didenko, and V. Korotych. Its popularity at that time is reflected in the fact that its pressrun was increased from 71,100 in 1960 to 170,000 in 1975. By 1984 it had been reduced to 113,000.

Rapai-Markish, Olha [Rapaj-Markiš, Ol'ha], b 1 August 1929 in Kharkiv. Ceramist. A graduate of the Kiev State Art Institute (1956), where she studied under M. Helman, she has done the 'Circus' series of porcelain statuettes and a series of female porcelain figures in Ukrainian folk costumes; numerous porcelain compositions, such as *Hopak* (1958–9), *Lovers* (1959–60), and *Wedding* (1968); and ceramic wall panels, reliefs, and anthropomorphic vases. She created the reliefs at the Trade Building in Kiev (1967) and the interior decorations of the Chornomorka Sanatorium in Odessa (1969).

Rape (*Brassica napus*; Ukrainian: *ripak*). An annual *oil plant of the mustard family Cruciferae, cultivated for thousands of years and at present unknown in its wild state. In Ukraine rape is planted in Polisia and in the Carpathian Mountains. It grows to 30 cm or more in height and has smooth, bluish green foilage, distinctive pale yellow flowers, and a long, usually thin taproot. A variety of rape known as swede is grown for its enlarged edible root (*brukva*), which is used for human and cattle consumption (see *Turnip). Rapeseeds contain as much as 40–50 percent colza oil, used as fuel, in cooking, and in the production of margarine, soap, and synthetic rubber (see *Vegetable-oil industry). Oil cake, high in protein, makes valuable cattle fodder.

Rarahovsky, Dmytro [Rarahovs'kyj], b 4 November 1878 in Slyvky, Kalush county, Galicia, d January 1957 in Edmonton. One of the first Ukrainian-Canadian poets. After emigrating to Canada in 1903, he contributed to *Chervonyi prapor*, *Robochyi narod*, *Ukraïns'ki robitnychi visti*, and other Ukrainian-Canadian left-wing newspapers. He was active in the Ukrainian Social Democratic Party of Canada and the Ukrainian Labor-Farmer Temple Association. The *kolomyika*-like poems in his two collections, *Robitnychi pisni* (Workers' Songs, 1908) and *Ukraïns'ki robitnychi pisni* (Ukrainian Workers' Songs, 1945), reflect the experiences and views of Ukrainian immigrants in Canada.

Rare metals. According to normal classifications, rare metals include beryllium, germanium, yttrium, zirconium, niobium, molybdenum, ruthenium, cadmium, stibnite, lanthanum, cerium, hafnium, tungsten, rhenium, uranium, and so on. Some precious metals – silver and gold, for example – are also rare. Many of those metals are used in the metallurgical industry to strengthen steel and iron, and in the electronics industry, especially in making television screens.

In Ukraine silver (usually amalgams) is found almost equally in ankerite and cinnabar. Silver is also found in some hydrothermal deposits in Transcarpathia. Overall, however, estimated reserves are small, and there is little chance they can be commercially exploited. Some gold was found in the late 1960s and early 1970s in Precambrian metamorphic deposits and in alluvials of the early Paleogene in the Dnieper Basin. Gold concentrations reached 37 g per t, and individual nuggets reached diameters of 0.2–2.5 mm.

Zirconium and germanium are found in Precambrian deposits of the Ukrainian Crystalline Shield, especially in quartz and feldspar. The concentration of germanium averages 1.7–4 g per t. Molybdenum and tungsten have been discovered in greisen zones in Volhynia and in hydrothermal formations in Transcarpathia. Rich uranium deposits (containing uranium ores of U_3O_8 with an admixture of ThO_2) are found in the vicinity of Zhovti Vody in the Kryvyi Rih region. The largest uranium- and plutonium-processing facility in the former USSR has been built there. Uranium from that area is used at the Chornobyl Nuclear Power Station.

In recent years celestite, boracite, and monazite trappings containing varying concentrations of yttrium, lanthanum, cerium, neodymium, and other rare metals have been discovered. Traces of those metals, as well as of niobium and zirconium, have also been found in Ukrainian deposits of ilmenite. Industrial exploitation of rare metal ores was begun in the area of the Samotkan ilmenite deposit in Dnipropetrovske oblast. The Mariiupil Rare Metals Administration was established in 1946 to direct the exploitation of deposits in that region. Chances are good that rare metals can be extracted from the iron-cobalt-nickel deposits of the Dnieper Basin and the Zavallia region, in Kirovohrad oblast. Refining of some rare metals is done in Dnipropetrovske and Kirovohrad oblasts and the Crimea.

Ukraine lacks several important rare metals, such as cerium, antimony, and beryllium, and does not have the technology to use them in steel and iron refining. Their unavailability limits the development of Ukraine's metallurgical and electronics industries and, especially, its machine-building and nuclear reactor industries. Developments in the exploitation and refining of rare metals will have important implications for the economy of Ukraine.

BIBLIOGRAPHY
Belevtsev, Ia. (ed). *Problemy metallogenii Ukrainy* (Kiev 1964)
Redkie i redkozemel'nye elementy v tekhnike (Kiev 1964)
S. Protsiuk

Rashevsky, Ivan [Raševs'kyj], b 1849 in Chuhuiv, Zmiiv county, Kharkiv gubernia, d 1921 in Chernihiv. Painter and sculptor. After graduating from the law faculty of Kiev University he studied painting in St Petersburg. He painted landscapes and genre scenes such as *On the Desna* (1889) and *On the Feast of the Transfiguration* (1900). He sculpted models for a monument to T. Shevchenko in Chernihiv (1921). Most of his works perished during the Second World War.

Rashkiv settlements. A series of early Slavic settlements along the Dniester River near Rashkiv, Khotyn raion, Chernivtsi oblast. Excavations at three settlements in the 1970s revealed a large number of rectangular semi-pit dwellings: 81 at Rashkiv I (late 7th–9th century), 8 at Rashkiv II (5th–7th century), and 91 at Rashkiv III (5th–7th century). Cherniakhiv culture pottery remains were unearthed at sites II and III, while Rashkiv I contained wheel-thrown items. Iron, bronze, bone, and flint artifacts were common to all the sites. The study of this settlement complex provided a clear picture of life in the Middle Dniester area in the latter half of the 1st millennium.

Raskolnik. See Old Believer.

Rašković, Srđan, b 20 December 1952 in Split, Croatia. Serbian writer, translator, and literary scholar. Besides his own literary works he has translated into Serbian from Ukrainian, Russian, and Belarusian. His translations have appeared in numerous journals as well as in separate editions, namely *Povest plamenih godina* (translation and annotation of O. *Dovzhenko's *Povist' polum'ianykh lit* [The Tale of Fiery Years], 1978) and *Skitska baba* (Scythian Woman; an annotated translation of poems by L. *Kostenko, 1981). He has also contributed articles to the *Encyclopedia of Ukraine* and Yugoslav encyclopedias.

Rasp, Karl-Wilhelm, b 16 November 1805 in Plana, Austria (now in Czechoslovakia), d 9 April 1874 in Lviv. Austrian historian and archivist. He was educated at Prague and Vienna universities, and he served as an official of the Lviv *magistrat* (from 1831) and as curator of the Lviv municipal archives (1861–72). Rasp wrote a comprehensive history of Lviv (1870) based on primary sources and assisted in the publication of *Akta grodzkie i ziemskie*.

Rasprava. Rural court for state peasants. *Raspravy* were introduced in Left-Bank Ukraine and Slobidska Ukraine in 1782–92, after the dismantling of the Cossack judicial system. Each gubernia had a higher *rasprava* that handled appeals against the decisions of the lower, local, courts.

Rastatt. A town (1979 pop 37,000) in Germany, and the site of a German POW camp in 1915–18. Many Ukrainians were interned there. As in other German POW camps, the *Union for the Liberation of Ukraine conducted classes (up to grade six), maintained a Ukrainian library and drama group, and published the magazine *Rozsvit*. A Sich society was organized there, and the first units of the *Bluecoats sprang up in the camp. A book describing the

Monument to the Ukrainians who died in the Rastatt POW camp (sculptor Mykhailo Parashchuk)

Ukrainian cultural and educational activities in Rastatt was published by O. Terletsky in 1919, and a memorial erected to the Ukrainian prisoners who died there was designed by M. Parashchuk.

Rastorguev, Pavel, b 1 July 1881 in Starodub, Chernihiv gubernia, d 21 March 1959 in Novozybkov, Briansk oblast, Russia. Belarusian linguist. A graduate of the Hlukhiv Teachers' Institute (1901) and Moscow University (1908). A specialist on the Belarusian dialects of the Briansk, Chernihiv, Homel, and Smolensk regions, he published an important book on the Seversk (Siverianian) Belarusian dialect (1927). In his many articles he dealt with themes such as the dialectal traits of the 18th-century Starodub regiment (1928), the Polish and Belarusian influence on the Ukrainian dialects in the former Siedlce gubernia (1929), and the Ukrainian features in the dialects of western Briansk oblast (1948). In 1927 he prepared and published the results of a 1903–4 survey of dialects in Chernihiv gubernia. His dialectal dictionary of the western Briansk region, which was ready for publication in 1954, came out only in 1973.

Rastrelli, Bartolomeo Francesco, b 1700 in Paris, d 1771 in St Petersburg. Architect of Italian origin. Having arrived in St Petersburg in 1716 with his father, C. Rastrelli, who did many sculptures for Emperor Peter I, he was appointed court architect in 1730. His renovations of the Great Palace in Peterhof (1747–52; now Petrodvorets), the Catherinian Palace in Tsarskoe Selo (1752–7), the Winter Palace (1754–62), M. Vorontsov's palace (1749–57), and S. Stroganov's palace (1752–4) in St Petersburg are the finest examples of late baroque architecture. He designed two outstanding buildings in Kiev, *St Andrew's Church (1747–53) and the *Mariinskyi Palace (1752–5).

RATAU. See Radio and Telegraph Agency of Ukraine.

Ratensky, Petro [Ratens'kyj], b ? in Ratne, Volhynia, d 21 December 1326 in Moscow. Churchman and painter. As a monk in Dvorets, in the Lviv region, he painted icons and donated them to various churches in Ukraine and abroad. A number of icons of the Theotokos, including those at the Dormition Cathedral in Volodymyr-Volynskyi, the St Sophia Cathedral in Novgorod, the Dormition Cathedral in the Moscow Kremlin, and the Krekhiv monastery, have been attributed to him. In 1308–26 he served as metropolitan of Kiev and all Rus' while residing in Moscow. He was canonized by the Orthodox church in 1340.

Ratmyrov, Andrii (real surname: Tymkivsky), b 14 October 1884 in Yelysavethrad, Kherson gubernia, d 26 February 1967 in Uzhhorod. Stage actor and director. In 1908 he completed study at the University of Odessa. Then he worked in the Russian troupe there, the Ukrainian National Theater in Kiev (1917–18), the State People's Theater (1918–19), and various other regional theaters (1930–5). He was exiled before the Second World War. Upon his return to Ukraine he worked in the Kiev Oblast (1943–7), the Kirovohrad Ukrainian (1947–9), and the Transcarpathian Ukrainian Music and Drama theaters (1949–59).

Ratmyrova, Olena, b 1869 in Novokhopersk, Voronezh gubernia, d 1927 in Novocherkassk, Rostov oblast, RSFSR. Stage actress and singer (mezzo-soprano). She worked in M. Sadovsky's troupe (1888–93) and M. Kropyvnytsky's troupe (1894–1900) and led her own troupe in 1900–1. In 1908–14 she also sang in opera theaters in Kiev, Kharkiv, and Odessa.

Ratne. II-5. A town smt (1986 pop 5,500) on the Prypiat River and a raion center in Volhynia oblast. It was first mentioned in historical records in the early 13th century, as a fortified outpost of the Principality of Galicia-Volhynia. It changed hands several times in the 14th century before it was finally surrendered by Lithuania to Poland in 1433. In 1440 it was granted the rights of *Magdeburg law. After the partition of Poland in 1795, the town was acquired by Russia, and became a trading center in Kovel county, Volhynia gubernia. In 1921 it was acquired by Poland, and in 1939 it was annexed by the USSR. Most of its inhabitants work in industry. It has a large wood-chemicals plant.

Ratusha or **ratush.** Derived from the German *Rathaus* (city hall), the terms were used in Ukraine to denote both a certain type of municipal government and the city hall building. From the 14th to 17th centuries towns in Ukraine that did not have the rights of *Magdeburg law were called *ratushni* and were governed by a *viit* and one or two *burmistry*. Those officials were not independent, but were responsible to the local lord or the local representative of the state, such as the starosta.

Ratusha or *ratush* also denoted the building of the municipal government, which usually had one tall tower and stood at the center of the town or city. Such buildings first appeared in Ukraine in the 14th century. The oldest architectural monuments of the kind in Ukraine are in Staryi Sambir (1668), Buchach (1751), and Kamianets-Podilskyi (1754). Kharkiv, Poltava, Lviv, and Chernivtsi have some fine examples of 19th-century city halls.

Rava Brigade of the Ukrainian Galician Army (Ravska [6] brygada UHA). A unit of the First Corps of the UHA, formed in January 1919 from units of the Rava Ruska Group. It consisted of three infantry battalions, an artillery regiment, and a cavalry troop and had a total strength of approx 2,800 men. Its commanders were Capt V. Stafiniak and, later, Capt Yu. *Holovinsky. The brigade distinguished itself during the Chortkiv offensive in June 1919 and in battles for Kiev in August 1919. In February 1920 it was reorganized into the Sixth Regiment of the Red Ukrainian Galician Army. After separating from the Red Army, the regiment was disarmed, and its members were imprisoned by the Poles.

Rava-Ruska [Rava-Rus'ka]. III-4. A city (1989 pop 8,800) on the Rata River in Nesterov raion, Lviv oblast. It is first mentioned in historical documents in 1455, when it was under Polish rule. In the early 17th century it obtained the rights of *Magdeburg law. A church brotherhood arose there in 1707. After the partition of Poland in 1772, the town belonged to Austria. It began to grow when two railway lines were laid through it in 1887, and it had reached a population of 9,000 by 1900. In the interwar period Rava-Ruska was ruled by Poland, and then became part of the Ukrainian SSR. Today it is an industrial and transportation center. Its main industry is food processing.

Raven (*Corvus corax*; Ukrainian: *kruk, voron*). A bird of the family Corvidae, 60–65 cm in length, shiny black in color. Ravens are ubiquitous, though not numerous, omnivorous birds. They are found all through Ukraine. In Ukrainian folklore they represent a bad omen, especially if heard cawing in the morning.

Ravliuk, Mykola [Ravljuk], b 1881 in Orelets, Sniatyn county, Galicia, d 1933 in Chernivtsi. Pedagogue. He graduated from Chernivtsi University in 1908 and became a teacher of Ukrainian and Latin at the Kitsman Gymnasium. During the First World War he was captured by Russian forces and was a POW in Tashkent. From 1920 he taught at the gymnasium in Chernivtsi. Among Ravliuk's works are *Diieprykmetnyky i diiepryslivnyky v ukraïns'kii movi* (Participles and Gerunds in the Ukrainian Language, 1912), *Pro diieprykmetnyky i diiepryslivnyky u tvorakh H. Kvitky-Osnovianenka, M. Vovchka, Yu. Fed'kovycha i V. Stefanyka* (Participles and Gerunds in the Works of H. Kvitka-Osnovianenko, M. Vovchok, Yu. Fedkovych, and V. Stefanyk, 1911–12), and a reader for first- and second-year gymnasium (1924).

Ravych, Dmytro [Ravyč], b 25 November 1901 in Sribne, Pryluka county, Poltava gubernia, d 4 June 1942 in

Dmytro Ravych

Vienna. Engineer, musicologist, and student leader. He was an assistant at the *Ukrainian Higher Pedagogical Institute in Prague and longtime head of the *Ukrainian Academic Hromada in Prague. From 1939 he was head of the *Central Union of Ukrainian Students.

Ivan Ravych: chalice for blessing water (1720)

Ravych, Ivan [Ravyč], b 1677 in Kiev, d 1762. Master goldsmith. While working in his own studio in Kiev's Podil district, he was active in civil affairs and served as a court magistrate and city councilor. He produced chalices, cups, goblets, silver book jackets, icon screens, candelabras, plates, and arks decorated with rococo acanthus, cartouches, thematic compositions, and medallions. His patrons were monasteries, bishops, hetmans, Cossack officers, and Russian nobles. Over 60 of his works have survived; most of them are in the Historical Museum of the Ukrainian SSR in Kiev.

Ravytsky, Mykola [Ravyc'kyj], b 29 January 1921 in Sorochanove, Yelysavethrad county, Kherson gubernia. Stage director. In 1950 he completed study at the Kiev Institute of Theater Arts (pupil of V. Nelli and V. Vilner). He was a director of Ukrainian Music and Drama theaters in Ivano-Frankivske (1950–8), Kherson (1958–70), and Zaporizhia (1970–3) and of the Kiev Young Spectator's Theater (1975–9). He served as head of the Theater Administration in the USSR Ministry of Culture (1973–5). In 1979 he was named stage and administrative director of the Kiev Druzhba Theater.

Rawita, Franciszek. See Gawroński, Franciszek.

Razhba, Yakiv [Ražba, Jakiv], b 29 August 1904 in Kremenchuk, Poltava gubernia. Sculptor. He studied under B. Kratko and L. Blokh at the Kharkiv Art Institute (1924–9). He sculpted the decorative reliefs in the Dnipropetrovske Workers' Theater (1936–7), the grave monument of D. Guramishvili in Myrhorod (1949), the monument to the victims of the Second World War in Kotelva (1981), compositions on themes from the works of T. Shevchenko

Yakiv Razhba: *From the Field* (plaster high relief inside the Workers' Theater in Dnipropetrovske, 1937)

(*Poplar*, 1957) and Lesia Ukrainka, (*Lily*, 1957) and socialist realist compositions such as *Partisan* (1968)

Razumovsky. See Rozumovsky.

Reading house (*khata-chytalnia*). A rural cultural-educational institution founded in the initial years of Soviet rule in Ukraine. Reading houses replaced *Prosvita-affiliated reading rooms, which were disbanded by the Soviet regime. Reading houses had libraries and were venues of political agitation, literacy classes, training in new farm techniques, and concerts and plays, often staged by local amateur groups. They were often the center for village Party and Komsomol organizations. In 1927 there were 6,203 reading houses in Soviet Ukraine. In the early 1950s reading houses were transformed into collective-farm clubs and *palaces of culture. By the 1960s reading houses remained only in a few isolated areas.

Realism. A term that usually refers to art that is representational and depicts the visible material world as closely as possible. It may also be used to designate the opposite of stylized or abstract art or simply to describe a work of art that portrays not the beautiful and idealized, but the common, unconventional, or ugly. As a 19th-century art movement it is usually associated in painting with the work of French artists, such as G. Courbet, even though it found independent expression in other countries, including Ukraine.

Realism became popular in Russian-ruled Ukraine through the efforts of the *Peredvizhniki, a group of artists established in 1870 in St Petersburg that promoted enlightenment through traveling exhibitions of pictures portraying the conditions of contemporary life, particularly of the peasants, and depicting landscapes. Style was relegated to a minor role, and socially relevant subject matter was of major importance. Several prominent Ukrainianborn artists were members of or exhibited with the Peredvizhniki (eg, N. Ge, I. Repin, K. Kostandi, S. Vasylkivsky).

In 19th-century Western Ukraine I. *Trush, A. *Manastyrsky, and M. *Ivasiuk painted realistic depictions of mundane subjects, often with peasant themes and ethnographic elements. Realistic works produced with an impressionist palette and brush strokes were created by F. *Krychevsky, M. *Kozyk, P. *Volokidin, I. *Shulha, O. *Kulchytska, and others.

A type of realism known as *socialist realism was forced on all art and artists in the USSR, including Soviet Ukraine, in the early 1930s, and remained the only officially sanctioned method until the late 1980s. Demanding politically correct content, naturalistic rendering, and adherence to Marxist-Leninist esthetics and to the dictates of the Communist party, it resulted in many stereotypical depictions of Communist heroes and leaders and happy workers and peasants. The more interesting socialist-realist artists in Ukraine were M. *Bozhii, O. *Lopukhov, S. *Hryhoriev, O. *Shovkunenko, and T. *Yablonska.

A variety of socialist realism known as the 'severe style' appeared in the USSR after the death of J. Stalin. Its adherents portrayed the ordinary aspects of life instead of idealized and heroic socialist-realist subjects. L. *Medvid depicted the unpleasant and perturbing side of life in paintings such as *First Collective Farms in the Lviv Region* (1972).

A new kind of realism known as photorealism or hyperrealism developed in the West in 1970s. It has had an impact on the work of artists in Ukraine, such as S. Bazylev and S. Geta, who have used precisely rendered close-up views and photographic images. It can also be seen in the work of L. Bodnar-Balahutrak in the United States and in the superrealist figural compositions of N. *Husar amd M. Stefura in Canada. J. *Hnizdovsky depicted selected objects and figures in a meticulously rendered realist manner.

(For realism in literature, see *Drama, *Literature, and *Prose.)

D. Zelska-Darewych

Realschule (*realne uchylyshche*). A secondary school with a six- or seven-year program of study, established in imperial Russia by the conservative education minister Count D. Tolstoi's Realschule Statute of 1872. The curriculum of the Realschule was pioneered in Western Europe. Emphasis was placed on natural sciences, modern languages, and the application of technical knowledge, whereas in *gymnasiums emphasis was placed on Latin and Greek. Although there had been schools in Ukraine which provided practical training from the beginning of the 19th century, such as the Chernihiv Trade School (est 1804), it was not until 1864, when the Russian education minister, Count Golovin, established the eight-year realgymnasium, that 'real' studies in imperial Russia were taught in an academic rather than a purely vocational context. In 1872 the classical education obtained at gymnasiums was made the only conduit to university. Realgymnasiums, which taught natural sciences and modern

languages instead of Latin and Greek, were replaced by Realschulen. Social mobility through education was restricted, and the modern or 'real' curriculum was relegated to second-class status. Realschule students, more likely to be from the lower classes than their gymnasium counterparts, were considered politically volatile and given a narrowly technical education which barred them from entering university and many other postsecondary institutions. The drop-out rate in Realschulen was higher than that in gymnasiums, where a diploma promised academic advancement. In 1879, 20 percent of Realschule students dropped out, compared with 15 percent of gymnasium students. Central government funding of Realschule corresponded to their inferior status, and local *zemstvos were compelled to provide much of the support. In 1885 there were 75 Realschulen in the European part of the Russian Empire, with 14,722 students; 19 of these schools and 4,345 of the students were in Ukraine.

In 1888 time devoted to vocational training in Realschulen was decreased, and a special grade was added to prepare students for higher specialized education. Realschule graduates were given the right to enter all postsecondary technical and agricultural institutes and the physics, mathematical, and medical faculties of universities. Commercial schools, established by the Ministry of Finance in 1896, began to rival Realschulen and gymnasiums. They offered a general rather than a narrowly classical or vocational education, greater scope for local control, limited coeducation, and no class restrictions or quotas on the admission of Jews. By 1913–14, 51,632 students were enrolled in commercial schools, only 40 percent fewer than the 80,800 pupils of the more entrenched Realschulen, and a third as many as studied at boys' gymnasiums. In 1915 graduates of Realschulen were granted the right to enter all university faculties.

In Austrian-ruled Ukraine 'real' studies were taught in both realgymnasiums and Realschulen. Graduates of the eight-year realgymnasiums could enter any school of higher learning; graduates of the seven-year Realschule could enter all institutions of higher learning except universities. In 1906 there were 20 realgymnasiums and Realschulen in Galicia and Bukovyna.

After the October Revolution of 1917, Soviet education reforms abolished Realschulen. (See *Education.)

C. Freeland

Rebet, Dariia (née Tsisyk), b 26 February 1913 in Kitsman, Bukovyna, d 5 January 1992 in Munich. Political leader and publicist; wife of L. *Rebet. She studied law at Lviv and Lublin universities. As a young woman she joined the clandestine Ukrainian Military Organization and its successor, the OUN. In the 1930s she was OUN youth representative and headed the OUN women's groups of the OUN Stryi district executive and the OUN organization in the Stryi district (1933–4). In 1935–8 she was a member of the OUN Home Executive in Western Ukraine responsible for liaison with the émigré Leadership of Ukrainian Nationalists. In 1939 she spent six months in a Polish prison. In 1941 she became a member of the Cracow-based OUN (Bandera faction) Home Executive, headed by R. Shukhevych. During the German occupation of Lviv she worked in the OUN educational and propaganda sectors. She was a delegate at the OUN Third Extraordinary Congress in 1943, and in 1944 she was a member of the OUN

Dariia Rebet Lev Rebet

Preparatory Commission, which organized the *Ukrainian Supreme Liberation Council (UHVR). She was elected to the first UHVR presidium and was the author of the first UHVR statute. While living as a postwar émigré in Germany she was a member of the UHVR Representation Abroad. When the émigré Bandera faction split in 1956, she joined the new OUN (Abroad) and was elected to its Political Council, which she headed from 1979. Rebet was active in Ukrainian émigré women's organizations and was a delegate to the First World Congress of Ukrainian Women in Philadelphia in 1948. She was a member of the editorial boards of Suchasna Ukraïna, Suchasnist', and Ukraïns'kyi samostiinyk and edited a collection of articles about the Ukrainian Women's Alliance in Germany (1980). She was the author of articles dealing with the OUN ideology, program, and history, Ukrainian liberation politics, the UHVR, Soviet affairs, Ukrainian émigré community concerns, and educational issues.

Rebet, Lev, b 3 March 1912 in Stryi, Galicia, d 12 October 1957 in Munich. Political leader and publicist; husband of D. *Rebet. He received a master's degree in law from Lviv University (1938) and a doctorate from the Ukrainian Free University in Munich (1947), where he taught state law from 1948 and became a professor in 1954. He joined the clandestine Ukrainian Military Organization in 1927. From 1930 he headed the OUN organization in the Stryi district, and in 1935–8 he headed the OUN Home Executive in Western Ukraine. In the 1930s he was repeatedly arrested by the Poles, and he spent two and a half years in Polish prisons in Stryi and Lviv. During the OUN split in 1940 he sided with the Bandera faction. In 1941 he was second vice-president of the short-lived *Ukrainian State Administration in Lviv and headed it after its president, Ya. Stetsko, was arrested by the Germans. Rebet was himself arrested in September 1941 and sent to the Auschwitz concentration camp. He was released in 1944, and fled to the West.

In 1945 he became chief judge of the émigré Bandera faction and took part in secret talks in Vienna and Munich with representatives of the OUN, headed by R. Shukhevych in Ukraine. In 1952 he became a member of the Foreign Representation of the *Ukrainian Supreme Liberation Council and head of its Council of Representatives. In 1953–4 he headed the collegium charged with reorganizing the émigré Bandera faction along guidelines received from the OUN leadership in Ukraine. After S. Ban-

dera resigned from the collegium in February 1954, Rebet became head of a separate faction which in 1956 began to call itself OUN (Abroad). He was assassinated by a Soviet agent (see *Stashynsky trial).

Rebet contributed to postwar Ukrainian periodicals in West Germany, such as Ukraïns'ka trybuna, Chas, and Suchasna Ukraïna, and was editor in chief of *Ukraïns'kyi samostiinyk (1955–7). He wrote programmatic documents for the OUN and articles on the question of the nation and the state, émigré issues, and Soviet affairs. His major works are a booklet on the formation of the Ukrainian nation (1951), a monograph on the theory of the nation (1955), and a posthumously published book about the OUN (1964).

A. Zhukovsky

Reboshapka, Ivan [Rebošapka] (Riaboshapka, Reboşapcă), b 29 May 1935 in Dărmăneşti, Suceava district, Rumania. Folklorist, pedagogue, and translator. A graduate of Bucharest University (1960), he is a professor of Ukrainian literature, language, and folklore there. His primary interests are Ukrainian folklore in Rumania and Rumanian-Ukrainian folklore ties. He has prepared Curs de folklor literar ucrainean (A Course in Ukrainian Literary Folklore, 1977); 14 textbooks in Ukrainian language and literature for secondary schools; several folklore collections (in Ukrainian), including Narodni spivanky (Folk Songs, 1969), Oi u sadu-vynohradu (In the Vineyard, 1971), Vidhomin vikiv (Echo of the Ages, 1974), Olens'kyi tsvit (Oleander Bloom, 1976), and Narod skazhe – iak zav'iazhe (Popular Sayings Are Apt, 1976); and some theoretical studies of folklore, such as Narodzhennia symvolu: Aspekty vzaiemodiï obriadu ta obriadovoï poeziï (The Birth of a Symbol: Aspects of the Interaction of Ritual and Ritual Poetry, 1975). He has translated Ukrainian textbooks, folklore collections, and literature (O. Vyshnia, M. Pryhara, and V. Nestaiko) into Rumanian.

Rebro, Petro, b 19 May 1932 in Bilotserkivka, Kuibysheve raion, Zaporizhia oblast. Writer. He graduated from the Zaporizhia Pedagogical Institute (1953) and has worked as a newspaper and book editor in Zaporizhia. Since 1955 he has published collections of lyrical and satirical poetry, documentary novelettes, travel essays, and books of poetry for children. An edition of his selected poetry appeared in 1982.

Rebryk, Bohdan, b 30 June 1938 in Pavlykivka, Kalush county, Galicia. Dissident and political prisoner. A

Bohdan Rebryk

teacher by profession, he was imprisoned in a labor camp in 1967–70 for his pro-Ukrainian views. He was rearrested in May 1974, and sentenced in March 1975 to seven years in special-regime labor camps in the Mordovian ASSR and Perm oblast and three years' exile in Kazakhstan. In February 1979 he joined the *Ukrainian Helsinki Group. He wrote several open letters of protest, notably to AFL-CIO president G. Meany, to D. Milner in Great Britain, and to 'progressive' Ukrainians in Canada and the United States. He was released in 1984. Since 1988 he has edited *Karby hir*, an unofficial literary journal in Ivano-Frankivske.

Rechmedin, Valentyn [Rečmedin], b 12 February 1916 in Andrushivka, Lypovets county, Kiev gubernia, d 6 June 1986 in Kiev. Writer and editor. He was an editor of *Kul'-tura i zhyttia* and assistant editor of *Vitchyzna* in Kiev. He wrote the novels *Na verkhovyni* (In the Highland, 1951), *Koly zakypala krov* (When the Blood Boiled, 1958), *Vesniani hrozy* (Spring Storms, 1961), *Tvii pobratym* (Your Loyal Friend, 1962), *Synu, khodim zi mnoiu* (Son, Come with Me, 1965), *Divchyna v ternovomu vinku* (A Girl with a Crown of Thorns, 1967), *Vohon' bat'kovykh ran* (The Fire of a Father's Wounds, 1969), *Narodzhennia Afrodity* (The Birth of Aphrodite, 1974), *Pora piznikh dorih* (A Time of Late Roads, 1975), *Za vesnoiu vesna* (After Spring Comes Spring, 1979), and *Navpereimy doli* (Crossing Destiny's Path, 1983).

Reclus, Jean-Jacques Elisée, b 15 March 1830 in Saint-Foy-la-Grande, Gironde, France, d 4 July 1905 in Turnhout, Belgium. French geographer and political theorist. A graduate of Brussels University and a member of the First International from 1865, he was exiled permanently from France in 1871 because of his involvement in the Paris Commune. He lived in Italy, Switzerland, and Belgium, where he taught in universities. His major scholarly work was the 19-volume *Nouvelle géographie universelle* (1876–94). In the fifth volume a substantial section with the heading 'Russia in Europe' dealt with Ukraine. Reclus recognized Ukraine as a distinct geographical and historical entity. Much of his information about Ukraine was derived from the writings of M. *Drahomanov, whom he knew personally.

Recorded music. The first Ukrainian recordings appeared in 1900, when two German Gramophone Co recording experts, F. Gaisberg and S. Darby, visited St Petersburg and recorded at least five Ukrainian songs by soprano P. Havryltseva-Khmara. Most Ukrainian records in the Russian Empire were on the Gramophone, Pathé, Xenophone, Favorite, Syrena, and Beka labels. Kiev-based Extraphone issued (ca 1910) songs performed by O. Petliash (accompanied on the piano by M. Lysenko) and Ukrainian Christmas songs sung by the Kiev University Student Chorus directed by O. Koshyts. Around the same time Ukrainian singers, such as M. Brochenko, T. Piddubny, P. Platonov, I. Hryhorovych, M. Shvets, A. Hvozdetska, A. Kramska, L. Lypkivska (Lipkowska), M. Mikhailova, E. Petrenko, and E. Zarnytska, were recording in the Russian Empire. Choruses were also engaged in recording activity. The growth of these endeavors can be illustrated by the 1914 Gramophone-Zonophone catalog, which shows 306 Ukrainian titles with 366 recordings, or the 1916 Pathé catalog, which shows 193 and 238 respectively.

With the introduction of the electric recording process in the USSR (1929), Ukrainian soloists, such as I. Patorzhynsky, M. Lytvynenko-Volhemut, M. Mykysha, M. Hryshko, M. Donets, O. Petrusenko, and Z. Haidai, became committed to discs. Choruses that were recorded included DUMKA and the State Exemplary Banduryst Kapelle. Starting in the late 1940s a younger generation of vocalists (among them I. Kozlovsky, D. Hnatiuk, B. Hmyria, P. Karmaliuk, and B. Rudenko) as well as vocal and instrumental ensembles appeared on disc.

Companies like Gramophone and Pathé also had the largest share of the Austro-Hungarian market. Gramophone conducted four recording expeditions to Lviv between 1904 and 1908. The Pathé brothers operated in Vienna, where they recorded tenor R. Lubinetsky and basses O. Nosalevych and O. Nyzankivsky between 1910 and 1913.

With the large influx of immigrants from Eastern Europe into the United States and Canada before the First World War, American companies such as Columbia and Victor saw an opportunity to market millions of ethnic records. Around 1908 these firms began to issue foreign-language records, mostly copies of European originals. By the Second World War Columbia had issued approx 550 records labeled Ukrainian, Ruthenian, Lemko-Russian, and Carpatho-Russian, while Victor had produced approx 200 of the same. A conservative estimate of Ukrainian recordings on the Odeon/Okeh label (1920s and 1930s) comes to more than 120 discs. In 1922–4 the Ukrainian National Chorus under the direction of O. Koshyts recorded 26 folk songs as arranged by Ukrainian composers on another American label, Brunswick. By the 1940s at least 900 Ukrainian records had been produced in the United States, in performances ranging from S. Krushelnytska's Ukrainian songs to typical village bands with exceptionally talented fiddlers, such as P. Humeniuk and J. Pizio.

In the 1930s the Polish company Syrena-Electro marketed 73 records, most notably with the Surma Chorus of Lviv (26 records). At the same time in Germany tenor C. Andrijenko (K. Chichka-Andriienko) recorded Ukrainian and Italian material on the Telefunken label.

After the Second World War most American companies dropped the ethnic record-producing business, leaving small ethnic bookstores, artistic groups, and private entrepreneurs to take over the task. In the late 1940s and early 1950s these private entrepreneurs reissued some pre–Second World War Ukrainian recordings culled from American and Soviet sources. The Stinson company was the most prominent among them. The Surma bookstore in New York did the same thing on its Surma, Fortuna, and Boian labels, later producing some original material. Also in New York, the Arka bookstore began to produce original Ukrainian recordings under the Arka label. These consisted largely of entertainment and popular music, as well as choral issues (the DUMKA and Kobzar choruses, conducted by L. Krushelnytsky and A. Rudnytsky respectively) and recordings of such soloists as M. Starytsky, Ye. Mozhova, I. Orlovska-Fomenko, M. Minsky, and V. Tysiak. They were issued on 78 RPM or early LP formats. A number of Ukrainian vocalists, among them tenor O. Rusnak, were issued by the Chwyli Dnistra label (Cleveland). The RCA Victor custom department produced four albums of the Ukrainian Bandurist Chorus (Detroit) starting in 1950.

In Canada the largest producer of Ukrainian records was Arka (Toronto), which featured entertainment and popular music. There were also active labels in Montreal and Edmonton. The Ukraina Chorus of Montreal under the direction of N. Horodovenko recorded (1951) an album of six records with Ukrainian titles.

In Argentina RCA Victor issued Ukrainian records by sopranos T. Lykholay and E. Saprun and tenor O. Khlebych. The Boyan label in that country issued recordings of choral music. The Australian Cosmopolitan label produced recordings of the Ukrainian National Choir, with soloists W. Rykhtowsky, A. Hai, and Z. Moroz. In Great Britain the Burlaka chorus made a number of successful recordings in the early 1950s on the Oriole label.

The list of singers who recorded in the 78 RPM and early LP periods also includes S. Krushelnytska on Gramophone (1902), Typewriter (Warsaw 1902), Fonotipia (Milan 1906–10), and Columbia (United States 1928); I. Alchevsky on Gramophone (1903); O. Myshuha on Gramophone and Zonophone (1911); M. Menzinsky on Gramophone (1910–11) and HMV; O. Rusnak (Gerlach) on HMV/Electrola (1932–3); M. Sokil-Rudnytsky on Asch (New York 1940), the first such album in North America featuring professional settings; Ye. Zarytska on London (1949), Decca (1948, 1957), and other labels; H. Shandrovsky on Okeh, Victor, and Columbia (1920s–1930s); and M. Holynsky on Muza (Canada 1950s).

The LP era (mono and stereo). Ukrainian music first appeared on LP in the West on the album *Chants d'Ukraine* (Songs of Ukraine), recorded by Ye. Zarytska with G. Favaretto at the piano (Paris, Columbia 1956). It consisted of folk song arrangements by nine Ukrainian composers of the 20th century. Noted Soviet releases in 1954 included the opera *Bohdan Khmelnytsky* by K. Dankevych and L. Revutsky's *Symphony no. 2* as conducted by N. Rakhlin.

The first stereo LP was recorded in 1959 by Ye. Zarytska (New York, Urania) and consisted of Ukrainian folk songs. Although the USSR began to issue stereo LPS in 1960, Ukrainian repertoire using this technology was not recorded until the 1970s. Both vocal and instrumental music were produced in some quantity, with a strong preference for the folk genre. Piano works now appeared on stereo LPS, making available music ranging from D. Bortniansky through M. Lysenko to S. Liudkevych, L. Revutsky, V. Kosenko, and B. Liatoshynsky, as recorded by M. Krushelnytska, R. Lysenko, V. Sechkin, M. Stepanenko, Ye. Rzhanov, and others.

In 1981 German pianist M. Grill produced the first stereo LP of piano music by a Ukrainian composer (V. Barvinsky) recorded in the West. Also active in the West were pianists V. Baley, T. Bohdanska, Ye. Masliuk, D. Karanovych, J. Osinchuk, R. Rudnytsky, C. Saurer-Smith, M. Shlemkevych-Savytsky, A. Slobodianik, and R. Savytsky. Violinists recording in the West included E. Gratovich, O. Krysa, A. Lysy, Yu. Mazurkevych, and S. Staryk. Outstanding recordings have been produced both in and outside Ukraine by such singers as Y. Hoshuliak, A. Kocherha, S. Kopchak, I. Malaniuk, Yu. Mazurok, P. Plishka, and A. Solovianenko. Major recorded choruses include the Ukrainian Bandurist Chorus (Detroit), the State Banduryst Kapelle of the Ukrainian SSR, the Bukovynian Ensemble, the Verovka State Chorus, the Kiev Chamber Choir, the O. Koshyts Choir (Winnipeg), and the Byz-

antine Choir (Utrecht). Among the conductors who have recorded in the West are V. Bozhyk, A. Hnatyshyn, I. Kovaliv, H. Kytasty, G. Oransky, L. Turkevych, and I. Zadorozhny.

Operas recorded in the USSR include those by D. Bortniansky, M. Lysenko, S. Hulak-Artemovsky, M. Arkas, H. Maiboroda, and M. Verykivsky. These are commonly performed by the Kiev Theater of Opera and Ballet. Much recording is done of the orchestral repertoire of such composers as L. Revutsky, B. Liatoshynsky, L. Kolodub, and L. Hrabovsky. Outstanding Soviet Ukrainian conductors being recorded include I. Blazhkov, M. Kolessa, V. Kozhukhar, N. Rakhlin, V. Tolba, and S. Turchak. The orchestra most often recorded is the State Symphony Orchestra of the Ukrainian SSR (Kiev). Also committed to discs is chamber music by D. Bortniansky, M. Lysenko, V. Barvinsky, V. Kosenko, B. Liatoshynsky, and M. Skoryk, performed by such ensembles as the Lysenko and the Leontovych quartets.

Cantatas composed by L. Revutsky and S. Liudkevych to words by T. Shevchenko have been recorded. The latter's *Caucasus* and *Testament* were recorded by the Trembita chorus (Lviv) under M. Kolessa's direction.

The absence of any record-producing facilities in Ukraine, other than some recording studios in Kiev (without complementary pressing plants), has led to a situation in which only a limited number of Ukrainian issues are released. Only a handful of Ukrainian works have ever been granted a second recording, among them L. Revutsky's *Symphony no. 2*, B. Liatoshynsky's *Symphony no. 3*, and the operas *Kateryna* and *Taras Bulba* by M. Arkas and M. Lysenko respectively. At present most Ukrainian classics are still not available in stereo from Melodiya, even popular operas such as *Zaporozhian Cossack beyond the Danube* and *Natalka from Poltava*. Moreover, significant operatic works ranging from M. Lysenko's *Nocturne* to B. Liatoshynsky's *The Golden Ring* have never been recorded (even in mono). Although the complete choral works of M. Leontovych were recorded, the majority of choral and art songs from M. Lysenko to V. Barvinsky still wait their turn.

Popular and dance music has recently been issued by such ensembles as Kobza (Kiev), Smerichka and Vatra (both in Lviv), Chervona Ruta (Chernivtsi), Rushnychok and Cheremshyna (both in Montreal), Burya (Toronto), Nichna Melodiia (Rochester), and Iskra (New York). Recording kobzars and bandurysts in Ukraine include F. Zharko, H. Menkush, and K. Novytsky, and in the West, Z. Shtokalko, V. Lutsiv, V. Mishalow, and H. and Yu. Kytasty.

Digital technology. The first digital LPS and cassettes of Ukrainian music were issued by the choir Musicus Bortnianskii (Toronto 1985–90), featuring recordings of D. Bortniansky's 35 a capella sacred concertos. Almost simultaneously the same Bortniansky cycle was recorded digitally by the Millennium Choir (V. Kolesnyk, conductor) and released in 1989. The Ukrainian Bandurist Chorus (Detroit), conducted by V. Kolesnyk, issued the album *Christmas Night* (1987) – the first digital stereo LP featuring Ukrainian carols. Music by Ukrainian composers, performed by violinist E. Gratovich and pianist S. Golomon, was issued in 1989 digitally on LP, cassette, and CD. *Kvitka – Two Colors* by K. Tsisyk became the first CD of Ukrainian solo songs (Clinton Recordings, 1989). M. Leontovych's 'Shchedryk,' known commonly as 'Carol of the Bells,' is also available on CD in several recordings by American musicians.

BIBLIOGRAPHY
Kataloh ukraïns'kykh kruzhkiv – Syrena-Elektro (Warsaw nd)
Katalog-zakaznik gramplastinok (Moscow 1966)
Soviet Long-Playing Gramophone Records: Ukrainian Music (Moscow 1969; in Ukrainian and English)
Bennet, J. (comp). *Melodiya: A Soviet Russian L.P. Discography* (London 1981)
Spottswood, R. *Ethnic Music on Records: A Discography of Commercial Ethnic Recordings Produced in the United States 1893–1942* (Urbana 1990)
                                                S. Maksymiuk, R. Savytsky

Recruitment. See Military service.

Recruits' and soldiers' songs. A subclass of lyrical songs about the life of recruits and soldiers. In Russian-ruled Ukraine they began to appear at the end of the 18th century, when Catherine II abolished the voluntary Cossack forces and replaced them with long-term conscript (up to 25 years) military service. In Austrian-ruled Ukraine they arose at the end of the 18th century, when Maria Theresa introduced compulsory service for those between the ages of 17 and 40. These songs developed from old Cossack songs and contain references to different historical periods. Their basic themes are the recruitment process (drafting, induction, desertion, capture, purchasing one's freedom); the parting with one's family, homeland, and sweetheart; the soldier's life (hardships, homesickness, and loneliness); time off duty; war (marches, battles, death or crippling); and the return to civilian life (greeting one's family and friends). The songs were composed by the soldiers or by peasants, particularly women and girls. Their treatment of the soldier's experiences is more realistic than romantic. Allegory, symbolism, and psychological parallelism are widely used. The melodies usually have a marching tempo. Recruits' and soldiers' songs of Russian-ruled Ukraine are generally many-voiced. The songs in Western Ukraine are related closely in melody and theme to the songs of other Western or Southern Slavs, who served with Ukrainians in the Austrian army.

The themes of recruit's and soldiers' songs often appear in Ukrainian literature, especially in the works of T. Shevchenko, Yu. Fedkovych, S. Vorobkevych, and O. Makovei, and some recruit's and soldiers' songs have been based on Shevchenko's, S. Rudansky's, and Fedkovych's verses. The best-known musical arrangements of Ukrainian recruits' and soldiers' songs have been those by S. Liudkevych, L. Revutsky, M. Leontovych, F. Kolessa, and V. Kosenko. These songs have inspired compositions not only by Ukrainian composers, such as M. Arkas, Revutsky, M. Verbytsky, and Kolessa, but also by non-Ukrainians, such as J. Haydn, J.S. Bach, and L. van Beethoven.

BIBLIOGRAPHY
Ioanidi, A.; Pravdiuk, O. (comps). *Rekruts'ki ta soldats'ki pisni* (Kiev 1974)
                                                M. Mushynka

Red Army. See Soviet Army.

Red Cossacks (Chervone kozatstvo Ukrainy). A Bolshevik military formation that was active in Ukraine in 1918–20 and is considered to be the first regular Soviet Ukrainian fighting unit. The first regiment of the Red Cossacks was formed on 10 January 1918 as the Bolshevik counterpart of the UNR's *Free Cossacks. Its commander was V. Prymakov. The Red Cossacks fought on the Soviet side in the *Ukrainian-Soviet War. Besides the UNR Army, they fought the Central Powers, the Don Cossacks, N. *Hryhoriiv's partisans, and A. *Denikin's and P. *Wrangel's armies.

Red Cross Society of the Ukrainian SSR. See Ukrainian Red Cross.

Red corner (*chervonyi kutok*). A type of cultural-educational club in the USSR under the auspices of the Communist party, trade-union, and Komsomol organizations. Red corners were found in the workplace, in student and worker dormitories, on state and collective farms, and at other enterprises. They carried out mass political agitation, disseminated technical and agricultural propaganda, held meetings, and organized cultural events for workers.

Red Rus'. See Chervona Rus'.

Red Steppe cattle (*Chervona stepova khudoba*). One of the most productive breeds of dairy *great horned cattle, developed in Ukraine in the early 19th century by selective crossing of imported breeds (mostly Ostfriesland) with local Red and Gray Steppe cattle. In the late 19th century the breed was improved by crossing Red Steppe cows with Dutch, Angelu, Wilstermarsh, and other bulls, and a selective breeding program was established in the 1920s. Red Steppe cattle are lean and strong, the bulls weighing approx 1,000 kg and the cows weighing 420–540 kg. Annual milk yield is 4,000–4,500 kg, with 3.6–3.8 percent fat content. Red Steppe cattle are distributed and raised primarily in Ukraine and other regions of the former USSR (see *Cattle raising).

Red Ukrainian Galician Army (Chervona Ukrainska Halytska Armiia [ChUHA]). The official name of the *Ukrainian Galician Army (UHA) after its forced absorption into the Red Army in February 1920. By December 1919 the 20,000-strong UHA stationed in eastern Podilia and northwestern Kherson gubernia was reduced to 5,000 active men by a typhus epidemic. The army began negotiations with the advancing Red Army and on 12 February 1920 agreed to become an autonomous part of the Red Army, on the condition that it would fight on the Polish front. Gen O. *Mykytka, the commander of the UHA, and Gen G. *Ziritz, his chief of staff, were deported to Moscow and executed. Under V. Zatonsky's direction the Bolsheviks reorganized the UHA into three brigades and assigned them to different Soviet divisions. The commanders of the brigades were Lt Col A. Bizanz, Capt Yu. Holovinsky, and Capt O. Stanimir. The Bolshevik interference and propaganda aroused much hostility among the rank and file. In mid-April 1920, shortly before the Polish invasion of Ukraine, the Second and Third brigades of the ChUHA deserted the Red Army. Soon afterward they were surrounded by the Poles, and surrendered. The Bolsheviks retaliated by executing many Galician soldiers and officers left in the rear. The First Brigade continued to fight as part of the Tarashcha Division against the invading Polish army. The Poles defeated it at Makhnivka and then let most of the soldiers return home interned the officers.

BIBLIOGRAPHY
Hirniak, N. *Ostannii akt trahediï Ukraïns'koï halyts'koï armiï* (Perth Amboy, NJ 1960)

A. Makuch

Rededia, b ?, d 1022. Prince of the Kasogians (now called the Cherkess Caucasian mountain people). In a war against the prince of Tmutorokan, Mstyslav Volodymyrovych, Rededia proposed single combat between the leaders in order to spare the armies, and he lost the duel. The incident is noted in the epic *Slovo o polku Ihorevi* (The Tale of Ihor's Campaign).

Redeemer's Voice. See *Holos Spasytelia.*

Redemption payments. Annual payments imposed on the peasants of the Russian Empire after the abolition of serfdom in 1861 and the introduction of *land reforms. On state-owned lands, from 1866 the emancipated *state peasants paid to the state a monetary *quitrent based on their total incomes instead of the value of the allotments they received. In Ukraine 28 percent of the gentry-owned land was set aside for purchase by the former proprietary serfs at grossly inflated prices (the equivalent of 16.66 years' quitrent). Because the peasants did not have the money to purchase their allotments, the state intervened and advanced the gentry 75–80 percent of the price in cash and interest-bearing bonds, after which the peasants redeemed their allotments by assuming 49-year mortgages from the state at 6 percent annual interest. Payments by the peasants to the gentry for the remaining 20–25 percent were in the form of monetary quitrent or corvée-like services on the remaining gentry-owned lands. Titles to the allotments were entrusted to the *obshchina* instead of to individual peasants to ensure collective responsibility for payments. The peasants in Right-Bank Ukraine were able to redeem land at market value and even received reductions because the state needed their support after the Polish Insurrection of 1863–4. In Left-Bank and Southern Ukraine, however, the payments were 40 percent higher. Laws imposed compulsory 49-year-term redemption payments on all peasants on gentry-owned lands in January 1882 (effective January 1883) and on state-owned lands in June 1886. Most peasants were too poor, too indebted, and too burdened with various taxes to make regular or full redemption payments, and the state deferred and even canceled certain arrears in 1881, 1884, 1896, and 1899. In the wake of the massive peasant disturbances that occurred in 1902 (in Kharkiv and Poltava gubernias) and during the Revolution of 1905–6 the government was forced to reduce the redemption payments and finally to abolish them in January 1907. By then the peasants in the nine Ukrainian gubernias had paid out 382 million rubles in payments (of a total 503 million rubles assessed) for land valued at 128 million rubles.

R. Senkus

Redemptorist Fathers (formally, the Congregation of the Most Holy Redeemer). An order of Catholic priests and monks founded in 1732 by A. de Liguori in Scala (near

The metropolitan's palace in Univ, Galicia, the first Redemptorist Fathers' residence in Ukraine

Naples), Italy. Established as an order of evangelists and practicing clergymen, it spread throughout Europe in the late 18th century and by the 1970s had over 7,400 members. In 1913 Metropolitan A. *Sheptytsky and P. Murray, the head of the order, reached an agreement (approved by the Vatican's Congregation for the Propagation of the Faith) by which Belgian Redemptorists who had been working in Saskatchewan were brought to Galicia and converted to the Eastern rite. They formed a Ukrainian branch of the order, centered near Lviv. Mission houses were opened in Stanyslaviv (now Ivano-Frankivske), Kovel (in Volhynia), Lviv (the residence of its protohegumen), and Ternopil. By the Second World War there were almost 100 members of the order in Galicia and another 24 in Transcarpathia (in Mykhailivtsi and Khust). The first Ukrainian Redemptorist house in Canada was established in Yorkton (Saskatchewan), under the direction of Rev A. *Delaere in 1913. Other centers opened in Wynyard and Ituna (Saskatchewan); Roblin (Manitoba), where the order runs a boarding school; Toronto; and Winnipeg (the residence of the protohegumen). The major center remained Yorkton, where a religious publishing house and the journals *Holos Spasytelia* and *Logos* were established. In the United States there are 60 monks (1987) in missions in Newark and in Washington. Several Ukrainian Catholic bishops have belonged to the order, including metropolitans M. Hermaniuk and V. Sterniuk and bishops V. Malanchuk, V. Velychkovsky, M. Hrynchyshyn, and F. Kurchaba.

W. Lencyk, V. Malanchuk

Redens, Stanislav, b ?, d 1938. Bolshevik and Soviet security official of Polish origin married to J. Stalin's wife's sister. He served as F. Dzerzhinsky's secretary (from 1918). In 1919–21 and 1928–33 he directed the operations of the Cheka and the GPU in Ukraine, the Crimea, and the Caucasus. He was particularly vindictive against supporters of S. Petliura and the Ukrainian Autocephalous Orthodox church. From 1933 to 1938 he headed the Moscow NKVD; then he was demoted to Kazakhstan, arrested, and executed (later rehabilitated by N. Khrushchev).

Redin, Egor, b 14 November 1863 in Starshee, Dmitriev county, Kursk gubernia, Russia, d 10 May 1908 in

Kharkiv. Art historian and archeologist. A graduate of Odessa University, from 1893 he taught art history at Kharkiv University, directed the Kharkiv Museum of Fine Arts, and belonged to the Kharkiv Historical-Philological Society and the Moscow Archeological Society (full member from 1902). Redin researched the archeological remains of early Christianity, the art and architecture of Kievan Rus' and the Italian Renaissance, and Kharkiv's artistic monuments. He compiled the seven catalogues of the 12th All-Russian Archeological Congress, held in Kharkiv (in 1902), and prepared the album of its exhibition (1903). His chief works deal with the Kievan St Sophia Cathedral's mosaics and fresco paintings (1889, with D. Ainalov), the mosaics of Ravenna's churches (1896), and the church antiquities of Kharkiv (1905).

Redkyn, Petro [Red'kyn] (Redkin, Petr), b 16 October 1808 in Romen, Poltava gubernia, d 19 March 1891 in St Petersburg. Philosopher of law and pedagogue. Educated at Moscow, Dorpat, and Berlin universities, he was awarded an LL D degree by St Petersburg University in 1835 and was appointed a professor of law at Moscow University. He was dismissed in 1848 for his liberal views. He served in the Department of Appanages (1848–82) and later chaired the St Petersburg Pedagogical Society (1860–74) and became a professor of law at (1863–78) and rector of (1873–6) St Petersburg University. From 1882 he was a member of the State Council. Redkyn's early views on the nature and development of law were influenced strongly by G. Hegel. In 1841 he published in *Moskvitianin* the first Russian study of Hegel's dialectical logic. Keeping abreast of Western trends, he turned to positivism (A. Comte) in the 1860s, but he retained some Hegelian habits of thought. He was one of the founders and president (1860–74) of the St Petersburg Pedagogical Society and contributed articles to *Uchitel'* (1861–70). In the 1880s he wrote a seven-volume work consisting of a collection of his lectures on the history of the philosophy of law in relation to the history of philosophy in general (1889–91).

Reed, common (*Phragmites communis* or *australis*; Ukrainian: o*cheret zvychainyi*). A large aquatic grass of the family Poaceae that grows along lakeshores, in marshy areas, in forests, or in sites with nearby ground water. The common or water reed is the only reed found in Ukraine. It grows up to 9 m tall. Dense thickets, covering about 110,000 ha, are found in the Dnieper, Dniester, and Danube rivers as they approach the Black Sea. Reeds tolerate salt water. They have been used for centuries as thatching and construction material, in basketry, and in the manufacture of coarse paper, pens, and musical instruments; they are also used as litter for livestock and as fuel. Young reed plants are eaten by cattle and horses, and they are a valuable food source for muskrat, nutria, elk, and deer.

Reedgrass (*Calamagrostis*; Ukrainian: o*cheretnyk, kunychnyk*). A perennial grass, also known as bluejoint, belonging to the Poaceae family. Ten species can be found in Ukraine, the most common being a surface reedgrass (*C. epigeios*) which grows in meadows, sands, and fallow fields throughout Ukraine and a reedy reedgrass (*C. arundinacea*) which grows in the shady forests of Polisia.

Reformation. A religious, political, and social movement that had as its precursor J. Hus and the Hussites in late 15th-century Bohemia. It is usually considered to have originated with M. Luther and with the spread of *Protestantism in Germany and other countries in northern, central, and eastern Europe in the 16th century. The Reformation was directed against the Catholic church's dogma, feudal structure, and economic and political domination. Its adherents introduced the use of the national vernaculars not only in the Protestant churches but also in many European literatures, thereby strengthening national consciousness and national cultural development. The Reformation cut across social, national, and state boundaries and frequently caused bitter religious conflicts and wars.

Reformational ideas were introduced into Ukraine by students returning from their studies in Bohemia and Germany and by Hussite and German colonists in the Polish-Lithuanian Commonwealth. By the 16th century the ideas had become popular among many noble families (eg, *Radziwiłł, *Sapieha, and *Nemyrych) in the Commonwealth. After the 1569 Union of *Lublin reformational congregations were established in Ukraine (63 in Rus' and Belz voivodeships, 27 in Volhynia, 6 in Podilia, and 7 in the Kiev and Bratslav regions). Although the Reformation did not affect all of Ukrainian territory or society, it helped to mobilize the Orthodox nobility, burghers, Cossacks, and clergy against the Catholic offensive, particularly after the 1596 Church Union of Berestia, and to imbue their Ruthenian (ie, Ukrainian-Belarusian) Orthodox faith with elements of a nascent national consciousness. The leader of the Orthodox opposition to the church union, Prince K. *Ostrozky, favored rapprochement with the Protestants, and joint Orthodox-Protestant conferences were held in 1595, 1596, and, in Vilnius, 1599. In 1632 Archimandrite P. Mohyla and Hetman K. Radziwiłł of Lithuania organized an Orthodox-Protestant coalition against the Catholic-Uniate majority in the Polish Sejm, thereby helping to bring about the restoration of the legal status of the Orthodox church in the Commonwealth.

The Reformation had a marked influence on Ukrainian religious-cultural life. Czech Protestant translations of the Bible were already being used in Ukraine in the 15th century, and in the late 16th century, Ruthenian translations of the Scriptures based primarily on Protestant texts (eg, V. Nehalevsky's translation of part of the New Testament [1581] and V. Tsiapinsky's translation of the Gospel) were published and used privately and during liturgies. Use of the vernacular became widespread in homiletics and religious polemics. Thus, under the influence of the Reformation a bookish Ruthenian language gained currency in writing, alongside the traditional Church Slavonic and the Polish favored by the social elite. Even Catholic publications began appearing in Ruthenian (eg, a catechism published in 1585), and bilingual editions of works (Polish-Ruthenian) were published.

A number of reformational schools were founded in Ukraine, including Calvinist ones in Panivtsi, in Podilia, and Ostrih and Berestechko, in Volhynia, and *Socinian schools in Kyselyn, Hoshcha, Cherniakhiv, and Liubar, in Volhynia. Their quality of education often surpassed that of the Catholic schools, and they attracted many Ukrainian and Belarusian students.

The Reformation reinforced the Ukrainian church's tradition of conciliar rule, as is particularly evident in the work of the 16th- and 17th-century church *brotherhoods. The brethren read from the Scriptures at meetings and at home, monitored each other's conduct, supervised church affairs, and controlled the actions of priests and bishops, to the point of declaring some of them 'enemies of truth' (eg, in the 1588 statute of the Lviv Dormition Brotherhood). Consequently the Orthodox bishops protested against the extent of lay involvement and control in church affairs. The reformational tendencies in the Orthodox congregations prompted many bishops to accept the union with the Roman church.

The Reformation influenced the growth of national consciousness in Ukraine and political mobilization among Cossacks. In the first half of the 17th century they became the vanguard in Ukrainian society; they presented increasingly greater opposition to Polish rule in Ukraine and openly supported the Orthodox church in its struggle against the Catholic onslaught. In their search for allies against Poland the Cossacks repeatedly turned to Protestant states, such as Sweden, Transylvania, and Brandenburg.

The influence and successes of the Reformation did not endure in Ukraine, however. Its link to Protestantism placed it between two warring camps, Catholic Poland and Orthodox Ukraine, both of which grew increasingly antagonistic not only to each other but also to reformational currents. The Polish Catholic church (largely the *Jesuits) waged a successful Counter-Reformation against Protestantism, and the Orthodox church became hostile to Protestants in general and to the Antitrinitarian and other radical Protestant currents popular among the Right-Bank nobility in particular. Consequently the Reformation was deprived of a social base, and the Ukrainian uprising of the mid-17th century under Hetman B. Khmelnytsky opened the way for the penetration of other cultural and political currents (eg, the baroque). Most of the reformational communities in Ukraine ceased to exist around that time.

BIBLIOGRAPHY
Krasinski, V. Historical Sketch of the Rise, Progress, and Decline of the Reformation in Poland ..., 2 vols (London 1838, 1840)
Bukowski, J. Dzieje Reformacyi w Polsce od wejścia jej do Polski aż do jej upadku, 2 vols (Cracow 1883, 1886)
Liubovich, N. Istoriia Reformatsii v Pol'she: Kal'vinisty i antitrinitarii (Po neizdannym istochnikam) (Warsaw 1883)
Hrushevs'kyi, M. Kul'turno-natsional'nyi rukh na Ukraïni v XVI–XVII vitsi (Kiev and Lviv 1912)
Fox, P. The Reformation in Poland: Some Social and Economic Aspects (Baltimore 1924)
Savych, A. Narysy z istoriï kul'turnykh rukhiv na Vkraïni ta Bilorusi v XVI–XVIII v. (Kiev 1929)
Kot, S. La Réforme dans le Grand Duché de Lithuanie: Facteur d'occidentalisation culturelle (Brussels 1953)
Koch, H. Ukraine und Protestantismus (Munich 1954)
Jobert, A. De Luther à Mohila: La Pologne dans la crise de Chrétienté, 1517–1648 (Paris 1974)
Williams, G. 'Protestants in the Ukraine during the Period of the Polish-Lithuanian Commonwealth,' HUS 2 (1978), nos. 1, 2
Nichyk, V.; Lytvynov, V.; Stratii, Ia. Humanistychni i reformatsiini ideï na Ukraïni (XVI–pochatok XVII st.) (Kiev 1990)
Hryniv, Ie. (ed). Sekuliaryzatsiia dukhovnoho zhyttia na Ukraïni v epokhu humanizmu i Reformatsiï: Zbirnyk naukovykh prats' (Kiev 1991)

I. Korovytsky

Sergei Reformatsky

Reformatsky, Sergei [Reformatskij, Sergej], b 1 April 1860 in Borisoglebsk (now in Ivanovo oblast), Russia, d 27 December 1934 in Moscow. Organic chemist; corresponding member of the USSR Academy of Sciences from 1929. A graduate of Kazan University (1882), he studied at Heidelberg and Leipzig universities and was a professor at Kiev University (1891–1934) and the Kiev Polytechnical Institute (1898–1907). He is regarded as the founder of the Kiev school of organic chemists. Reformatsky's research dealt primarily with organometallic synthesis. He studied (1882) the reduction of tertiary alcohols to isostructural hydrocarbons, but is best known for his discovery (1887) of beta-oxyacid synthesis through the action of zinc and complex esters on aldehydes (the Reformatsky reaction). This reaction was extended to unsaturated systems, and it later permitted the synthesis of vitamin A. Reformatsky's textbook on organic chemistry went through 17 editions between 1893 and 1930.

Refractory clays. See Clays.

Refractory-materials industry. An industry that processes refractory clays and materials, which are used primarily in making ovens for the metallurgical and glass industries, and equipment and parts for various high-technology industries. The most important feature of such materials is their ability to withstand high temperatures. Ukraine is rich in refractory *clays. They have been used since ancient times. In Ukraine the first specialized refractory-materials factories were built in *Chasiv Yar (1887), the site of the largest refractory-clay deposit in the former USSR, and Krasnohorivka (1896), both in the Donets Basin. In 1913, 326,000 t of refractory materials were produced in Russian-ruled Ukraine; the total for the entire empire was 582,000.

Since the 1920s, and especially since the Second World War, the industry has developed into an important part of the economy. Total production of refractory materials reached 1.2 million t in 1940, 2.8 million t in 1960, and 3.6 million t in 1970. The industry's output began to drop in the 1970s. It fell to 3.3 million t in 1980 and 3.1 million in 1987. The greatest decline was in the production of fireclay, which is made by baking *kaolin; whereas 1.9 million t were produced in 1960 and 2.6 million t in 1970, by 1987 the figure was only 1.9 million t. Production of Dinas bricks (made from silica) fell from 347,000 t in 1960 to 269,900 t in 1970, and has remained steady since then at just under 300,000 t per year (294,900 t in 1987). Meanwhile production of magnesite increased from 532,000 (1960) to 730,000 (1970) and 840,000 (1987). Today the largest refractory-materials factories are in Chasiv Yar, Siverske, Dokuchaievske, and Krasnoarmiiske.

Regalia. Emblems, symbols, or paraphernalia of power or office. Archeological finds in Ukraine show that stone maces and axes were used as signs of power in the Stone Age. In the Princely era family coats of arms served as regalia, those of a princely house usually including a *trident of some kind. Standards (*bunchuky*) and flags were used widely, but the *bulava* was rare.

In the Cossack period flags, *bulavy*, *bunchuky*, seals, *litavry*, bugles, and staffs with silver balls signified various offices of the Zaporozhian Sich and the Cossack state. The *bulava* was used by the hetman, and the *pernach* by colonels, from the 16th century. B. Khmelnytsky received a silver *bulava* from the king of Poland, the Turkish sultan, and the Russian tsar. The *bulava* was also a sign of the Zaporozhian otaman's authority. From the Zaporozhian Sich it was passed on to the Kuban Cossacks, and was used by them until Soviet power was established in the Kuban.

The *bunchuk*, a distinctive standard of Turkish origin, consisted of a wooden staff with a decorative metal head, to which tasseled cords and one or more bundles of horsehair were attached. According to Cossack tradition, in 1578 Stephen Bathory presented the Cossack hetman with a *bunchuk* and other regalia. The *bunchuky* carried by hetmans had red horsetails and white-and-black cords.

Cossack banners were usually made of carmine cloth with images of saints, crosses, and coats of arms embroidered on them. They were carried on each side of the hetman or otaman at the head of the Cossack army. The *litavry* were large copper kettledrums used for announcing various solemn events. The Russian tsars presented the Cossack hetmans and the Zaporozhian Host with various regalia.

In the Ukrainian church the chief regalia are the miter, panagia, and crosier. The miter has been used since the 11th century. Shaped at first like a crown, it evolved to a high, pointed hat with enamel medallions on the sides. Originally worn by bishops, by the end of the 12th century the miter was bestowed on archimandrites and distinguished clergymen. The panagia is a round metal icon of the Holy Mother on a chain that is worn on the breast by Orthodox prelates and archimandrites of stauropegion monasteries. The crosier (*posokh* or *zhezl*) is presented to a hierarch at his consecration. It is topped with a metal cross.

M. Miller

Regensburg. A city (1989 est pop 119,000) in Bavaria, Germany, and the site in 1945–9 of the largest Ukrainian DP camp in Germany. At its peak (1947) the workers' district of Ganghofersiedlung housed almost 5,000 Ukrainian and 1,000 non-Ukrainian refugees and *displaced persons. With a population from all regions of Ukraine and of all occupations, the camp formed a microcosm of Ukrainian society. Its governing bodies were elected by the residents. The administration was headed first by V. Zaiats and then by A. Artymovych (1946), Ya. Serbyn (1946–8), and P. Balei (1948–). A wide range of institutions and or-

View of the Regensburg DP camp (1947)

ganizations was set up: a Ukrainian Catholic parish headed by Rev O. Sharanevych and later by Ye. Haidukevych; a Ukrainian Orthodox parish under Rev V. Shevchuk; a school system, consisting of a kindergarten, elementary and secondary schools, vocational courses in home economics, radio mechanics, driving, and photography, and the Ukrainian Technical and Husbandry Institute; the Plast and SUM Ukrainian youth associations and the Sich sports club; cultural and social organizations, such as a church choir conducted by I. Kurylenko, a drama group and orchestra led by I. Povaliachek, a music school, and the Ensemble of Ukrainian Actors directed by V. Blavatsky (1947–9); a medical and social service; camp-run tailor, barber, toy, leather-ware, jewelry, and ceramics workshops; the Ukrainske Mystetstvo co-operative; some private enterprises; and political blocs, which competed in camp elections. Several periodicals were published there: the weekly *Slovo* (1945–6), edited by S. Dovhal; *Ukraïns'ke slovo* (1946–7), edited by Yu. Tarnovych; *Visnyk oseli* (1947–?), edited by I. Durbak; and *Weekly Information Bulletin* (1946). A number of private and co-operative publishers published literary and scientific works and practical manuals.

BIBLIOGRAPHY
Kushnir, O. (ed). *Regensburg: Statti-spohady-dokumenty* (New York 1985)

Regiment (*polk*). During the Princely era any separate military unit or expedition that a prince or his vicegerent commanded in time of war was known as a *polk* (eg, as in the epic *Slovo o polku Ihorevi* [The Tale of (Prince) Ihor's Campaign]). In 14th- and 15th-century Lithuanian-ruled Ukraine military units raised by the inhabitants of towns and lands to repel Tatar attacks were also known as *polky*. In the late 16th century under Polish rule, the first regiments of *registered Cossacks were formed and named after the towns where their colonel and chancellery were located. Before the 1648–57 Cossack-Polish War six such regiments were based in Bila Tserkva, Cherkasy, Chyhyryn, Kaniv, Korsun, and Pereiaslav. Earlier, from 1625 to 1638, there was also a Myrhorod Cossack Regiment.

In the Cossack *Hetman state the regiment was not only a military but also an administrative-territorial unit (see *Company system and *Regimental system). It also had *mercenary regiments of cavalry and infantry (*Serdiuk regiments). An analogous system existed in Russian-controlled *Slobidska Ukraine, where in the late 17th century five Cossack regiments defended the southern frontier of the Russian Empire from the Crimean and Nogay Tatars. In 1764 and the 1770s the Russian regime created *lancer regiments in the newly annexed region of New Russia, to which they recruited Cossacks from the Poltava and Myrhorod regiments and Russian and foreign colonists. In the early 1780s the tsarist regime abolished the Cossack regimental system, and in 1784 it replaced it with the Little Russian Cavalry of 10 carabineer regiments as part of the Russian imperial army. Each regiment had 10 squadrons, which were initially organized by territory and commanded by Ukrainian officers. Since that time Russian imperial, Ukrainian (1917–21), and Soviet *military formations have been organized along the lines of other European armed forces.

A. Zhukovsky

Regimental court (*polkovyi sud*). A criminal and civil court with jurisdiction in the territory of a given regiment of the Hetman state in the 17th and 18th centuries. It was composed of the regimental *starshyna* and was headed by the regimental judge. It served also as a military court.

Regimental system. The administrative, territorial, military, and judicial structure of the 17th- to 18th-century *Hetman state and *Slobidska Ukraine. Under Hetman

B. Khmelnytsky there were initially 22 regiments, which were named after towns where their headquarters were located. Their colonels and other officers (*starshyna*) had jurisdiction over both the Cossacks and the civilian population in their territories. The colonels belonged to the hetman's *Council of Officers. Before 1648 they had been appointed by the Polish government. Hetman Khmelnytsky, however, frequently appointed colonels personally. From the hetmancy of I. Samoilovych to that of I. Mazepa they were elected by a regimental council in the presence of the hetman's representatives, who greatly influenced the choice of candidate. The hetman confirmed all appointments after the consent of the Council of Officers. The election of colonels persisted longest in the southern Hetmanate (in Poltava regiment). After 1709 Peter I and other Russian tsars appointed or dismissed colonels by fiat, and often chose Russians, Moldavians, Serbs, and other foreigners. Hetman D. Apostol's government had the right only to recommend candidates to the tsar.

The regimental colonel was assisted by his senior staff, which included a quartermaster, a justice, a chancellor, one or two *osauls, and one or two flag-bearers. A regimental council of officers served as an advisory body to

REGIMENTS

the colonel. The regimental chancellery was initially only a secretarial apparatus, but in the 18th century it served as a collegial administrative body that included the colonel and other regimental officers. The *regimental court settled criminal and some civil cases in the territory of the regiment. It was presided over by the regimental judge except in grave criminal cases, when the colonel himself took over. The regiments were divided into companies commanded by captains. Chernihiv regiment had the fewest companies (7), and Bratslav, the most (22). (See also *Company system.)

From 1650 to 1653 there were 17 regiments in the Hetman state. Ten were in Right-Bank Ukraine: Bratslav, Bila Tserkva, Cherkasy, Chyhyryn, Kaniv, Vinnytsia (aka Kalnyk), Kiev, Korsun, Pavoloch, and Uman. Cherkasy, Chyhyryn, Kaniv, and Kiev regiments also had adjacent territories in Left-Bank Ukraine. Seven regiments were in the Left Bank: Chernihiv, Kropyvna (divided between Lubni and Pereiaslav regiments in 1658), Myrhorod, Nizhen, Pereiaslav, Poltava, and Pryluka.

In the 1670s and 1680s the Right-Bank regiments collapsed after Polish rule in the region was restored. From the 1680s Col S. *Palii of Khvastiv ruled the territory of the lapsed Bila Tserkva regiment. In 1702 he restored the regiments of Bila Tserkva (the new headquarters of the Right-Bank Cossacks), Bohuslav, Bratslav, and Korsun. In 1704 they were supplemented by new Chyhyryn, Mohyliv-Podilskyi, and Uman regiments. The seven regiments were active until 1712, when, in accordance with a Russo-Polish treaty, many of their Cossacks were transferred to the Left Bank.

In the Left-Bank Hetman state three new regiments, Lubni, Hadiache, and Starodub, were formed in the late 1650s and early 1660s, and the total was thereby brought to 10. The regimental system survived there until the tsarist abolition of the Hetman state in the 1780s. It was replaced by Russian administrative-territorial *vice-gerencies and courts and 10 regiments of Russian light (after 1784, carabineer) cavalry known as the Little Russian Cavalry.

In Russian-ruled Slobidska Ukraine five autonomous Cossack regiments – Izium, Kharkiv, Okhtyrka, Ostrohozke (aka Rybinsk), and Sumy – were created in the 1650s. They were subordinated to the Russian military governor of Belgorod and the Razriadnyi prikaz in Moscow, and in 1765 they were abolished and transformed into five Russian hussar regiments.

Altogether there were 51 Cossack regiments in 17th- and 18th-century Ukraine: the *Belorussian (aka Chavusy and Mahiliou, 1654–9), Bila Tserkva (1648–74, 1702–12), Bohuslav (1685–1712), Borzna (1648–9, 1654–5), Brahin (1648–9), Bratslav (1648–85, 1690–1712), Chechelnyk (1650, 1673), Cherkasy (1648–76), Chernihiv (1648–1783), Chornobyl (1649, 1651), Chyhyryn (1648–83, 1704–11), Hadiache (1648–9, 1672–1782), Ichnia (1648–9), Irkliiv (1648–9, 1658–63), Izium (1685–1765), Hlukhiv (1663–5), Kaniv (1648–78), *Kharkiv (1659–1765), Khvastiv (1651, 1685–1702), *Kiev (1648–1782), Korsun (1648–1712), Kremenchuk (1661–3), Kropyvna (1649–58), *Lubni (1648–9, 1658–1782), Lysianka (1648–9, 1657–9, 1664–6, 1674), *Mohyliv-Podilskyi (1648–9, 1656–76), *Myrhorod (1648–1782), *Nizhen (1648–1782), Novhorod-Siverskyi (1653–4, 1668), *Okhtyrka (1655–1765), *Ostrohozke (1652–1765), Ovruch (1648–9, 1657–66), *Pavoloch (1650 to ca 1674),

*Pereiaslav (1648–1782), *Poltava (1648–1775), *Pryluka (1648–1782), Sosnytsia (1648–9, 1663–8), *Starodub (1663–1782), *Sumy (1648–1765), Torhovytsia (1664–76), Turiv-Pynske (1657–9), *Uman (1648–86, 1704–12), *Vinnytsia (aka Kalnyk, 1648–78), Zhyvotiv (ca 1649 to ca 1664), *Zinkiv (1662–72), *Zviahel (1648–9, 1657–8), Ladyzhyn, Mliiv, Dymer, Medvedyn, and Kamianets-Podilskyi (dates of the last four are unavailable).

BIBLIOGRAPHY

Slabchenko, M.D. *Malorusskii polk v administrativnom otnoshenii* (Odessa 1909)

Diadychenko, V. *Narysy suspil'no-politychnoho ustroiu Livoberezhnoï Ukraïny kintsia XVII–pochatku XVIII st.* (Kiev 1959)

Gajecky, G. *The Cossack Administration of the Hetmanate*, 2 vols (Cambridge, Mass 1978)

A. Zhukovsky

Regina. The capital (1986 pop 175,000) and commercial center of Saskatchewan, with a Ukrainian population (1981) of 14,455. Ukrainians, mainly laborers or railway workers, began to settle in Regina in the mid-1890s. In 1909 the provincial government set up the Training School for Teachers for Foreign-Speaking Communities there, which by 1914 had graduated about 100 Ukrainian teachers. By 1911 there were about 500 Ukrainians in Regina, most of them from Bukovyna. The political association

St Basil's, the first Ukrainian Catholic church (1928) in Regina

Ukraine (est 1914) merged in 1917 with the local branch of the Ukrainian Socialist Democratic party (est 1914) to form the Ukrainian Workers' Association. When this organization took on a pro-communist profile, its nationalist members left and formed the Prosvita society, in 1921. The remaining members went on to establish a local of the Ukrainian Labour-Farmer Temple Association. The Ukrainian Orthodox parish of the Descent of the Holy Ghost (est 1924) built its first church in 1928 and a larger one in 1960. St Basil's Ukrainian Catholic parish (est 1925) consecrated its church in 1929 and a new church in 1960. A branch of the Ukrainian National Federation, organized in 1933 by the Prosvita Institute and the Ukrainian War Veterans' Association, ran a Ukrainian school and a cultural program. The University of Regina began to offer Ukrainian language courses in 1966 and Ukrainian literature courses in 1971. In the 1991 census, only 2,285 inhabitants of Regina stated Ukrainian was their mother tongue.

Regional economic councils (*rady narodnoho hospodarstva* or *radnarhospy*; Russian: *sovnarkhozy*). Territorial bodies for economic planning and management, which operated in the USSR in 1918–31 and 1957–64. The first local economic councils in Ukraine were set up in January 1918 by the Southern Economic Council of the Donets–Kryvyi Rih Basin to manage the nationalized enterprises under the jurisdiction of the Supreme Council for the National Economy of the RSFSR. Under *War Communism there was constant conflict between the economic councils and *workers' control organizations. During the NEP period the local economic councils were abolished, and branch trusts, syndicates, and associations were set up. When the USSR was established, the Supreme Council for the National Economy of Ukraine was renamed the Ukrainian Council for the National Economy and subordinated to the Supreme Council for the National Economy of the USSR. It operated under the chairmanship of V. *Holubovych until 1931. In 1932–4 the supreme economic councils, trusts, and syndicates were dissolved, and Union and Union-republican people's commissariats for the various branches of the economy were set up. In 1946 they were replaced by ministries.

In May 1957, after most of the economic ministries had been abolished, territorial councils were formed to administer the economic regions (see *Economic regionalization). In Ukraine 14 regional economic councils were set up, and almost all industrial enterprises, except for military ones, were placed under their control. Their task was to implement the plans drawn up by the USSR and the Ukrainian state planning committees, draft the plans for enterprises, monitor their fulfillment, distribute the cadres and the funded production, and manage the communications among enterprises. The councils developed local loyalty; that is, they gave priority to the interests of their own regions above the interests of other regions or republics. In 1960 a republican Ukrainian Council for the National Economy, headed by M. *Sobol, was established. In 1962 the economic councils were centralized and consolidated; their number in Ukraine was reduced to seven, and the Council for the National Economy of the USSR was formed. At the same time the state planning committees were restricted to long-range planning, and the Ukrainian and USSR councils for the national economy were entrust-

ed with the drafting and implementation of the yearly plans. When N. Khrushchev was ousted in 1964, all the regional economic councils were abolished, and the centralized branch system under ministries, which was similar to the system under J. Stalin, was restored. The former functions of the state planning committees were also restored, but the importance of the republican planning fell considerably.

V. Holubnychy

Regional economics. A branch of economics dealing with the role of geographic location and space in the allocation of productive resources. It combines the methods of political economy, geography, and statistics. With regard to Ukraine the key objectives are to analyze the efficiency of industrial location, capital investments, interregional and foreign trade, transfers of capital and labor, and the effectiveness of regional planning and administration.

During the 19th and early 20th centuries Ukrainian territories under Russian and Austrian rule were divided into districts for purposes of administration, taxation, and military strategy. Regional specialization increased during industrialization in the latter part of the 19th century. Thanks to its rich natural resources, the southeastern forest-steppe region became the base of the coal, metallurgical, and chemical industries and, later, of the rail, shipbuilding, and construction industries. The steppe region became a major exporter of grain to Europe.

Western Ukrainian territories under Austria (Galicia, Bukovyna, Transcarpathia, and the Lemko regions) were industrially underdeveloped and overpopulated. Their condition gave rise to extensive emigration.

Geographic studies of the Russian Empire by P. Semenov-Tian-Shansky, D. Mendeleev, and A. Rikhter viewed Ukraine as a distinct entity that was subdivided further into various regions. Although the imperial economy had one tariff-free market and monetary and fiscal systems, major regions, such as Ukraine, Poland, and the Baltic, developed integrated economies in their own right. Inadequate long-distance highways and railroads could not overcome the advantages of local river transportation. Regionalism was also promoted by foreign investors: French and Belgian capital favored Ukraine, German investment gravitated toward Poland and Finland, and Russian private capital controlled the Urals, Siberia, and Central Asia. Up to the First World War Ukraine developed as a cohesive economy that specialized in certain products and traded with other regions of the empire and European countries.

The federal constitution of the USSR as well as practical considerations permitted the Ukrainian SSR to enjoy limited economic autonomy. The planning and management of local consumer industries as well as the administration of educational and social services came under the republic's jurisdiction. The republic's government retained 16.4 percent of the turnover tax collected in Ukraine in 1950, 27.7 percent of the tax in 1960, 27.2 percent in 1970, and 54.8 percent in 1980. The branch or sectoral approach to economic management, however, gave the Union ministries in Moscow decisive control over the largest and most important industries.

In 1957–65 the USSR was divided into self-managed macroregions under the jurisdiction of *regional economic councils. Since most economic activities became subordinated to the republic's Council of Ministers, more attention was paid to regional criteria in planning, budgeting, and management.

In the 1980s Ukraine was divided into three economic macroregions of the USSR subordinated directly to Moscow: (1) the Donets-Dnieper region, encompassing 8 oblasts, with cities such as Donetske, Kharkiv, Dnipropetrovske, and Zaporizhia, and accounting for over half of Ukraine's industrial and a third of its agricultural output; (2) the Southwestern region, encompassing 13 oblasts, 7 of which were annexed during the Second World War, including the cities of Kiev, Lviv, Lutse, Uzhhorod, and Chernivtsi, and accounting for over half of Ukraine's agricultural and a third of its industrial production; and (3) the Southern region, consisting of 4 oblasts, with the major port cities of Odessa, Mykolaiv, and Sevastopil. In addition to shipping and shipbuilding, the region has large machine-building, food-processing, and textile industries, and a well-diversified agriculture. The Crimea is a health-resort and tourist area.

Statistics comparing Ukraine with other Soviet republics were widely published but often misinterpreted. The Union government claimed to pursue a Leninist policy of regional economic equalization aimed at eliminating the causes of conflict among the nationalities. But wide regional differences in economic development had persisted. Thus, the standard of living, wage rates, and capital investment in Ukraine during the 1970s and 1980s lagged behind those in the RSFSR and the Baltic states. There are also considerable disparities among the regions within Ukraine. Pockets of underdevelopment and overpopulation persist in Western Ukraine, and the concentration of industry in the *Donets Basin exceeds what is ecologically safe.

Foreign trade and Ukraine's international specialization also fall within the scope of spatial analysis. As a result of Moscow's policies favoring the development of the eastern regions of the USSR, trade between Ukraine and Russia has been diminishing; Ukraine's export of metals to Russia, for example, dropped from 60 percent of the total production in 1940 to 24 percent in 1960 and 12 percent in 1970. At the same time Ukraine used more of its own output and traded more with Belarus, the Baltic states, and Eastern Europe.

Soviet regional development was shaped by Moscow's tendency toward a centralized planned system and the struggle of the republics for a more efficient and cohesive development of their regions. The losses of capital reflected in Ukraine's annual budgets and balances of payments constituted a form of exploitation.

Research in Soviet regional economics has been conducted by K. Vobly, M. Palamarchuk, L. Koretsky, P. Voloboi, V. Popovkin, I. Panko, and O. Koroid in the USSR and by V. Holubnychy, I. Koropeckyj, B. Wynar, Z. Melnyk, and V. Bandera in the United States.

(See also *Industry and *Economic regionalization.)

BIBLIOGRAPHY

Koropeckyj, I. Location Problems in Soviet Industry before World War II: The Case of the Ukraine (Chapel Hill 1971)

Bandera, V.; Melnyk, Z. (eds). The Soviet Economy in Regional Perspective (New York 1973)

Palamarchuk, M. Ekonomichna heohrafiia Ukrainskoï SSR (Kiev 1975)

Koropeckyj, I.; Schroeder, G. (eds). Economics of Soviet Regions (New York 1981)

Koropeckyj, I. (ed). Selected Works of Vsevolod Holubnychy: Soviet Regional Economics (Edmonton 1982)

V. Bandera

Regional studies. The study of a given part of a country, such as a province, county, or town, from many standpoints – geographic, historical, ethnographic, economic, botanical, zoological, agricultural, and so on. In the USSR regional studies are conducted by regional museums, societies, and clubs which rely heavily on local support and are associated closely with educational programs in the local schools.

Before the 1917 Revolution various central and local government and zemstvo institutions, learned societies, and individuals collected and published regional lore and infor-mation. In the 1850s the Commission for the Description of the Gubernias of the Kiev School District at Kiev University developed a wide program of regional studies. The short-lived *Southwestern Branch of the Imperial Russian Geographic Society made major contributions to regional studies. The Moscow Society of Naturalists sent research expeditions to Ukraine to study its flora and fauna. The Polish Society of Regional Studies in Warsaw, which published the periodical Ziemia, included Right-Bank and Western Ukraine in its range of interest. A number of historical societies were active in regional studies: the *Kiev Archeographic Commission, the *archival commissions of Tavriia, Chernihiv, Poltava, Katerynoslav, Kiev, and Kherson gubernias, the *Odessa Society of History and Antiquities, the Nizhen Historical-Philological Society, and the *Kharkiv Historical-Philological Society. Naturalists' societies at universities collected and studied the flora and fauna in their regions, and statistics departments of gubernial zemstvos collected economic data on their gubernias. The *Shevchenko Scientific Society in Lviv encouraged regional studies in Galicia.

In the 1920s regional studies in Soviet Ukraine developed rapidly. The Regional Studies Commission of the All-Ukrainian Academy of Sciences (est 1922) had a student section and subcommissions in Kharkiv and Odessa. The Cabinet for the Study of Podilia (est 1924) in Vinnytsia collaborated with the commission. Regional studies were conducted also by the *Agricultural Scientific Committee of Ukraine; the Ukrainian Committee of Regional Studies in Kharkiv, which published 28 issues of the monthly Kraieznavstno (1927–30); and the *Central Statistical Administration of the Council of Ministers of the Ukrainian SSR and its branches. Much work was done on the local level by scientific and learned societies, museums, and clubs, some of which published their own regional periodicals. The *Kiev Society of Naturalists published studies of regional flora and fauna in journals and collections. In 1920 the Odessa Regional Studies Commission began to publish Visnyk kraieznavstva. The Cabinet for the Study of Podilia issued 23 works in regional studies, and the Kamianets-Podilskyi District Committee for Regional Studies published two volumes of the collection Kamianechchyna (The Kamianets Region). Vsia Odeshchyna (All the Odessa Region) and collections of materials about the Vinnytsia, Uman, and Mykolaiv regions came out. Several committees of the All-Ukrainian Academy of Sciences, such as the commissions on Kiev, Right-Bank Ukraine, Southern Ukraine, Left-Bank Ukraine, and Western Ukraine, and the Historical Geography Commission, were involved in regional studies. During this period there were almost a hundred regional studies organizations in Soviet Ukraine.

In the 1930s regional studies institutions were dissolved, and the discipline was suppressed. The Regional Studies Commission was abolished in the reorganization of the Academy of Sciences. Leading scholars and museum workers were repressed. In 1937 the authorities declared that central and local regional studies institutes were superfluous. When local societies and clubs were disbanded, only museums carried on some regional research, but because of staff shortages (under 200 museum workers) the results were insignificant.

After the Second World War regional studies in Ukraine were revived and were subordinated to the needs of economic planning and political propaganda. Surveys of local resources and studies of their efficient exploitation were stressed, and local heroes of the Revolution and the Second World War were glorified. Over 50 special *regional studies museums are active in the field. They include large oblast museums, such as the Vinnytsia, Zhytomyr, Transcarpathia, Crimea, Donetske, and Chernivtsi museums, and many raion, school, and collective-farm museums. Regional studies publications began to appear in significant pressruns only at the end of the 1950s. They included books on specific oblasts, tourist guidebooks, maps, and the journal *Kraieznavstvo v shkoli*. Local regional studies clubs were set up in libraries, museums, organizations, and schools, but for many years there was no central Ukrainian institution or journal devoted to regional studies. A republican center for regional studies was established within the AN URSR (now ANU) Institute of History only in the mid-1970s. The institute prepared the 26-volume *Istoriia mist i sil Ukraïns'koï RSR* (History of Cities and Villages of the Ukrainian SSR, 1967–74). In the late 1980s many independent societies and clubs devoted to studies of their regions sprang up.

During the interwar period in Western Ukraine, the Plai society in Lviv organized walking tours and published regional materials in its magazine *Nasha bat'kivshchyna* (1937–9). The *Boikivshchyna society, with its important museum and journal, was a leading center of regional studies. Regional studies museums were opened in Sianik (for the Lemko region), Yavoriv, Kolomyia, and Uzhhorod. The collection *Karpats'ka Ukraïna* (Carpathian Ukraine, 1939) and Yu. Tarnovych's works on the Lemko region were important contributions to the field.

Outside Ukraine regional studies are conducted by the *Research Institute of Volyn. A series of regional collections has been published by the Shevchenko Scientific Society in collaboration with ad hoc regional committees. It includes works on Bukovyna, Podilia, and the Peremyshl, Stanyslaviv, Buchach, Zbarazh, Horodenka, Terebovlia, Drohobych, Uhniv, Zolochiv, Sian, Lemko, Stryi, and Buh regions.

B. Medwidsky

Regional studies museums. Cultural, educational, and scientific institutions that collect, preserve, exhibit, and study monuments of a region's natural, archeological, ethnic, artistic, and political development. In Ukraine museums of regional history appeared in the 19th century: in Mykolaiv (1806), Odessa (1825), Kerch (1826), Kiev (1835), Katerynoslav (1849), Chernivtsi (1863), Symferopil (1887),

Kherson (1890), Poltava (1891), Lviv (1893), and Chernihiv (1897). Their basic collections consisted of artifacts from archeological excavations; those were supplemented gradually with historical, ethnographic, natural, and artistic materials. The first founders of such museums were O. Pol, O. *Lazarevsky, F. Gumilevsky, and D. *Yavornytsky. During a period of official suppression of Ukrainian culture the regional museums reminded people of Ukraine's rich historical legacy.

After 1917–18 new regional studies museums were organized from the collections of various associations, church communities, and private individuals, such as V. Tazhovsky, the *Khanenko brothers, V. Shavynsky, and P. Pototsky. They developed rapidly in the 1920s, as a result of the intensive work of the Regional Studies Commission of the All-Ukrainian Academy of Sciences (est in 1922) and the Ukrainian Committee of Regional Studies in Kharkiv. In the 1930s many of them became inactive, and some were closed down. During the Second World War many museum exhibits were destroyed or shipped out of Ukraine.

The Volhynian Regional Studies Museum in Lutske

Regional studies museums are divided into two main groups: state museums, which are fully government-supported, and community museums, which are funded by a local community and are housed on factory premises, in collective-farm buildings, or in schools. The latter group are run by volunteers who are concerned about the preservation of cultural monuments. In 1983 there were 52 state regional studies museums. The more important ones are the *Poltava, *Rivne, *Kherson, *Luhanske, *Ivano-Frankivske, Cherkasy (est 1918, four branches, 75,000 exhibits), *Zaporizhia, *Transcarpathian, *Zhytomyr, Khmelnytskyi (est 1925, four branches, 57,000 exhibits), Crimea (est 1899, two branches, 56,000 exhibits), Odessa (est 1955, seven branches, 50,000 exhibits), and *Vinnytsia regional studies museums. In the Soviet period the exhibition in each of them was organized according to a prescribed format and was usually divided into the following departments: natural history, ethnography, prerevolutionary history, history of the Soviet period, and the contemporary period. Most of the materials were of recent origin: they dealt with the founding of local communist organizations; the local people's involvement in the revolution, the Civil War, and the First and Second world wars; workers and products of the local industries; production statistics and graphs; improvements in living standards; the local writers, artists, and press. There were few materials of national significance; most of them were ethnographic. Religious artifacts were used for atheistic propaganda. The commentary of the guides was screened by higher authorities and was given in Russian. Ukrainian was used occasionally only in some museums in Western Ukraine. Regional museums were treated as an important medium of ideological propaganda. Each museum was staffed by several dozen specialists. Apart from guides to exhibits very little was published by the museums.

Community-run regional studies museums began to appear in the 1940s and 1950s and were organized by amateur groups. In 1959 there were approximately 200 such museums. In the late 1960s the authorities threw their support behind local initiatives and set up a broad regional studies museums program. By 1965 there were up to 1,000 regional museums in Ukraine. In 1965 the Ministry of Culture in Moscow issued a special decree on the organization and activities of community museums in the USSR. Besides general there were specialized (historical, literary, theater, art) regional museums. The museums in Opishna, Velyki Sorochyntsi, and Marianivka in Poltava oblast, Velykyi Khodachkiv in Ternopil oblast, and Serednie Vodiane in Transcarpathia have specialized in folk costume and embroidery; those in Yavoriv and Sosnivka in Lviv oblast and Petrykivka in Dnipropetrovske oblast have dealt with folk decorative art. Regional studies museums in schools were regulated by a specific statute on school museums issued by the USSR Ministry of Education in 1974. By 1983 there were nearly 6,000 community museums in Ukraine. Most of them were small amateur expositions in community buildings, dealing with the history of particular villages, towns, factories, and firms, or with military or production heroes. The museums have conducted valuable ethnographic studies of various territories. They have preserved implements and costumes that have been dis-appearing from everyday use because of technological progress, such as hand mills, mortars, weapons from different periods, ceramic and wooden dishes, folk costumes, embroidery, footwear, coins, manuscripts, and old books. Some of the museums have reconstructions of the interior of peasant cottages. State museum staff and specialists from various cultural, scientific, and educational institutions often have acted as consultants to community museums. Churches and abandoned cottages often have been converted into museum facilities. Some 49 community museums in Ukraine have been housed in churches in 1978. In the late 1980s some of these churches have been returned to their religious communities.

Open-air community museums are becoming increasingly popular. In the late 1960s and early 1970s over 10 such museums were established in Transcarpathia, in Antonivka, Zubivka, Osii, Petrivka, and elsewhere. In the late 1980s independent associations or clubs of amateurs interested in Ukrainian history have sprung up at the museums. Many private collections amassed by enthusiasts of national culture, such as I. Honchar in Kiev, could be counted as regional studies museums.

Ukrainian regional studies museums exist also outside Ukraine. A number of museums were established after the Second World War: the *Svydnyk Museum of Ukrainian Culture in Czechoslovakia, the museums of Ruthenian culture in Ruski Krstur and Petrovci in Yugoslavia, the Museum of Lemko Culture in Zyndranowe, Gorlice, and Bielanka in Poland. In Alberta the *Ukrainian Cultural Heritage Village collects and studies materials on the life of Ukrainians in Canada.

M. Mushynka

Regionalization, economic. The territorial subdivision of a larger economically integrated territory, such as a country, a bloc, or the world, into constituent parts that commonly differ from one another in economic specialization or the division of labor. The beginnings of economic regionalization of Ukraine may be traced to the end of the 18th century, when in both the Russian and the Austrian empires descriptions of Ukrainian lands were written and projects for their economic regionalization undertaken for the purpose of taxation or for military-strategic planning. The first scientific contributions to economic regionalization were geographical studies of the Russian Empire by P. Semenov-Tian-Shanskiy (1880), D. Mendeleev (1893), A. Rikhter (1898), and others, which involved the subdivision of Ukraine (among other parts of the Russian Empire) into natural-economic regions. More specialized schemes for agricultural regionalization of the European part of the Russian Empire (which also included Ukraine) were made at the end of the 19th century by the Russian agricultural economists A. Fortunatov (1896), A. Chelintsev (1910) and A. Skvortsov (1914). A most innovative study of spatial distribution of Russian government income and expenditures was made by the Ukrainian economist M. Yasnopolsky (1891–97), who started the first school of territorial financial econometrics. The industrial regionalization of Ukraine was studied by S. Podolynsky (1880). Important works involving the economic regionalization of Ukraine were written by P. Fomin (1914), I. Feshchenko-Chopivsky (1918), and K. Vobly (in several editions from 1919).

Industrialization in the last quarter of the 19th and the beginning of the 20th centuries developed by sectors in specific regions. Agricultural-machine building emerged in Southern and Central Ukraine; sugar-beet processing and refining in the forest-steppe; coal mining, metallurgy, and chemical and metal fabricating in the Donets-Dnieper region; and food processing throughout Ukraine. Heavy-machine building (ships, locomotives) developed in the Black Sea ports and near the Donbas. Agricultural regional specialization progressed with commercial development. The livestock raising in the steppe in the early 19th century gave way to grain production, which was geared to export via Black Sea ports to Western Europe. Sugar-beet production gained commercial prominence in the Right-Bank forest-steppe. The western Ukrainian lands under Austria constituted an economic hinterland for that empire; they remained a distinct underdeveloped agrarian region (although small pockets of intensive agriculture catered to local urban markets).

ECONOMIC REGIONALIZATION OF UKRAINE

In conjunction with the nationalization of the economy and the introduction of state planning, economic regionalization became a tool for the planning and implementing of state policies for centralized management of the national economy during the Soviet period. A struggle developed between the government in Moscow, which aimed to establish its undisputed control over all the economic regions of the USSR, and the republics and other territorial-administrative units, which wanted to preserve or even broaden their prerogatives for autonomous economic decision-making.

The struggle around the economic regionalization of the Ukrainian SSR began in 1920–1. With the support of some leaders of the Russian Communist party (such as F. Artem, M. Kalinin, J. Stalin, and G. Zinovev) and scientific establishments and commissions (such as the Commission for the Study of Productive Forces, affiliated with the Academy of Sciences of the USSR), a number of prospectuses (such as those by I. Aleksandrov, G. Krzhizhanovsky, M. Vladimirsky) proposed the subdivision of Ukraine into three or two administrative units. Those projects limited the Ukrainian SSR mostly to the Right-Bank forest-steppe, and excluded from it all the industrial regions (the Kharkiv region, the Donbas, the Dnieper Industrial Region, and the Black Sea littoral with its ports) because those areas were not dominated by the Ukrainian proletariat. The projects represented the renewal of the concept of Russian proletarian territories, such as the

Donets–Kryvyi Rih and the Odessa soviet republics, which had arisen in those areas in 1918–19. Ukrainian national-communists countered those projects with the argument that a nonproletarian agrarian Ukrainian SSR would not be viable. They proposed to bring the Soviet government to the population by retaining Ukraine intact and by subdividing it into several dozen urban-centered economic-administrative provinces and several hundred regions, united in a centralized Ukrainian SSR. Despite the opposition of the RSFSR, the executive committee of the Ukrainian SSR declared (October 1922) the proposal as the basic principle for the economic-administrative regionalization of Ukraine. The proposal was successfully defended by the Ukrainian delegation (M. Poloz and others) in Moscow, and the 12th Congress of the Russian Communist party adopted it as a basic principle that was extended (1924–9) throughout the USSR. Nevertheless, in February 1924 the Ukrainian SSR lost the eastern Donbas (the predominantly Ukrainian Shakhty and Tahanrih okruhas) to the RSFSR. That measure of reorganization disrupted the integrity of the Donbas economic region but provided an urban-industrial component for the largely rural Don region. In 1931–2 the okruhas of Ukraine were replaced by the larger oblasts, whose party organs were subordinated to both Kiev and Moscow. That centralization remained a major factor in the administration and planning of local industry, agriculture, and cultural activities.

The formation of economic regions in industry and agriculture, both in Ukraine and in the USSR as a whole, proceeded during the NEP as it did before the revolution. Until 1923 in the Ukrainian SSR there were 19 territorial-branch industrial trusts and a number of syndicates and associations. Until 1929 control over those trusts was vested in the hands of the government of the Ukrainian SSR, which also restricted their competition with the trusts of the RSFSR. With the establishment in 1932–4 of centralized all-Union and Union-republican commissariats (since 1946, ministries) for various branches of industry, the existing economic region-forming processes were significantly altered. First, enterprises were subdivided and subordinated to various government organs or Party authorities responsible either directly to Moscow or through Kiev to Moscow. Second, a policy was initiated which involved the planned reallocation of resources and the accelerated development of some economic regions at the cost of the neglect or exploitation of others.

In the First Five-Year Plan, targets were set for the entire USSR within the framework of 24 economic regions. The Second Five-Year Plan involved 32 economic regions, and the Third Five-Year Plan, 19. The national economy of the Ukrainian SSR was planned as a republican unit, but within that framework special plans were designated for the Donbas, for the Kryvyi Rih area, and so forth. From 1930 the eastern regions of the USSR (the Urals, Siberia, Kazakhstan, and northern RSFSR) were designated for accelerated development mostly at the expense of Ukraine. Since the capital and human resources were not returned to Ukraine, they were not loans, nor was there a repayment of interest for lost time. Their shift from Ukraine constituted an outright economic exploitation of the republic. Approximate estimates for the periods 1928–40 and 1950–70 suggest that the capital transfers from Ukraine alone to other regions of the USSR amounted to about 135 billion rubles (1961 valuation). Since capital invested in the eastern regions yielded 20–25 percent lower recoupment than in the Ukrainian SSR, the economic loss was suffered not only by Ukraine but also by the Soviet economy as a whole. Advantages accrued only to the regions that received the investments.

The acceleration of the development of the eastern regions during Stalin's rule was motivated by the needs of strategic defense and, after the war, by an inflated evaluation of the regions' natural-resource base. The main theoretical supporters of the development of the eastern regions were the leaders of the Council for the Study of the Productive Forces of the USSR of the Academy of Sciences of the USSR and the State Planning Committee of the USSR (Gosplan SSSR). The State Planning Committee of Ukraine (Derzhplan URSR) and the Council for the Study of the Productive Resources of Ukraine were among the agencies opposed to such plans. Both Stalin and, after his death, the leadership of the Communist party consistently supported a policy of developing the eastern regions. During the entire period approx 40–50 percent of all capital allocations were invested there.

The economic regionalization of Ukraine was in fact part of the economic regionalization of the USSR as a whole. During the period of highly centralized planning, economic regions had no prerogatives. They served Moscow as convenient spatial units for the purpose of planning output and accounting for performance. Already during the last two prewar five-year plans the economic regionalization of the USSR was being geared to military-strategic plans. In the first postwar decade the USSR five-year plans distinguished 13 large economic regions (with Ukraine and Moldavia combined into one such region). Within that framework the State Planning Agency of the Ukrainian SSR subdivided Ukraine in 1956 into seven economic regions for the purpose of its own planning: Donbas, Dnieper, Left-Bank, Right-Bank, Western, Polisia, and Southwest.

A brief change occurred after Stalin's death when N. Khrushchev attempted to decentralize industry and construction according to the territorial principle (1957–64). The entire USSR was subdivided into 105 economic-administrative regions, called *regional economic councils, with some managerial and planning prerogatives. Within the Ukrainian SSR there were 11 such units. The administration of so many units directly from Moscow proved somewhat unwieldy. Their self-administration, however, was viewed as a threat to central control. Above all, military considerations (nuclear warfare) prompted their subordination in 1961 to 17 (and in 1963 to 18) large economic regions of the USSR. The regional economic councils too were reduced in number, to 47, so within the Ukrainian SSR there were 7 in 1962.

With the demise of Khrushchev and the return to centralized management in 1965 under L. Brezhnev, the regional economic councils were abolished, although the large economic regions were retained. Two principles formed the basis of the large economic regionalization – economic self-sufficiency of each region in the event of war, and the continued ability to develop the eastern regions during peace. Each large economic region had a planning commission and a council for co-ordination, subordinated directly to Moscow. Three large economic regions constituted the Ukrainian SSR from 1961, the Donets-Dnieper, the Southwest, and the South (see the table). In the 1970s, proposals were even raised to limit the signif-

Economic regions of Ukraine after 1961

Region	Subregion	Oblast
Donets-Dnieper	Donets	Donetske
		Luhanske
	Dnieper	Dnipopetrovske
		Zaporizhia
		Kirovohrad
	Kharkiv	Kharkiv
		Poltava
		Sumy
Southwest	Kiev	Kiev
		Zhytomyr
		Cherkasy
		Chernihiv
	Podilia	Vinnytsia
		Khmelnytskyi
		Ternopil
		Chernivtsi
	Lviv	Lviv
		Volhynia
		Rivne
		Ivano-Frankivske
		Transcarpathia
South		Odessa
		Mykolaiv
		Kherson
		Crimea

icance of the republics and to transform the economic regions into autonomous units of the USSR. By contrast, in Ukraine, as in other republics, the directors of the Derzhplan URSR (F. Khyliuk, P. Rozenko) demanded integrated planning of the entire national economy of the Ukrainian SSR and the reporting of Union enterprises to the republic's government.

Despite its unequal regional development Ukraine retained a specific presence within the economy of the USSR. Nevertheless, Ukraine's share in the economy of the USSR had declined as a result of the growth of the economy of central Russia and the eastern regions since the Second World War. Notably, the economic interaction between Ukraine and Russia had lost its previous significance. The shipment of metal from Ukraine to Russia, for example, declined from 60 percent of the production of the Ukrainian SSR in 1940 to 24 percent in 1960 and only 10 percent in 1970. Similarly the shipment of coal from the Donbas to Russia declined from 30 percent of production to 14 percent and 12 percent respectively.

At the same time Ukraine's external economic relations have diversified, with a growing share of interaction with Belarus and the Baltic republics, the Eastern European countries of the Council for Mutual Economic Assistance (CMEA), and, more recently, with the countries of Western Europe, North Africa, and Japan. Now politically independent and situated between Russia, Eastern Europe, and the Black Sea–Mediterranean basin, Ukraine has all the requirements for emerging as an independent economic power.

BIBLIOGRAPHY
Aleksandrov, I. Osnovy khoziastvennogo raionirovaniia SSSR (Moscow 1924)
Butsenko, A. K voprosu raionirovaniia Ukrainy (Kharkiv 1925)
Voblyi, K. (ed). Narysy ekonomichnoï heohrafiï Radians'koï Ukraïny, 2 vols (Kiev 1949, 1952)
Alampiev, P. Ekonomicheskoe raionirovanie SSSR, 2 vols (Moscow 1959, 1963)
Kugukalo, I.; Koretskii, L.; Velichko, I. Ob ekonomicheskom raionirovanii Ukrainskoi SSR (Leningrad 1959)
Obshchaia metodika razrabotki general'noi skhemy razmeshcheniia proizvoditel'nykh sil SSSR na 1971–1980 gg. (Moscow 1966)
Korets'kyi, L.; Palamarchuk, M. Heohrafiia promyslovosti URSR (Kiev 1967)
Voloboi, P.; Popovkin, V. Problemy terytorial'noï spetsializatsiï i kompleksnoho rozvytku narodnoho hospodarstva URSR (Kiev 1972)
Bandera, V.; Melnyk, Z. The Soviet Economy in Regional Perspective (New York 1973)
Koropeckyj, I. The Ukraine within the USSR: An Economic Balance Sheet (New York 1977)
Palamarchuk, M. Ekonomicheskaia geografiia Ukrainskoi SSR (Kiev 1977)
Korets'kyi, L. 'Ekonomichne raionuvannia,' in Heohrafichna entsyklopediia Ukraïny, vol 1 (Kiev 1989)
V. Holubnychy, I. Stebelsky

Regionalization, physical-geographic. A territorial subdivision of the surface of a country or territory into parts that differ from one another in their natural properties. The physical-geographic regionalization of Ukraine is hampered by the fact that, with the exception of a few mountainous areas, variation in relief is small. Consequently the physical-geographic regionalization of Ukraine must incorporate other components of the landscape, such as drainage basin, soils, and vegetation.

The first attempts at physical-geographic regionalization of Ukrainian lands in the early 20th century were associated with the regionalization of European Russia (by V. Dokuchaev and G. Tanfilev) and of historical Poland (by E. Romer). They had a general character. More precise physical-geographic regionalization of Ukraine was accomplished in the 1920s by B. Lichkov, who delineated seven regions, and by P. Tutkovsky, who distinguished seven landscape types. The physical-geographic regionalization by S. *Rudnytsky was considerably more comprehensive and placed all Ukrainian lands in 25 regions on the basis of geomorphological criteria. That regionalization has retained its significance to the present day.

More recent physical-geographic regionalization includes that of K. *Vobly (1945), who subdivided the Ukrainian SSR into the Polisia, the forest-steppe, and the steppe zones, and the mountain zone of the Carpathians and the Subcaucasus, and within those zones distinguished nine regions. Beginning in 1957 physical-geographic regionalization was revitalized by the Ministry of Higher and Secondary Special Education of Ukraine for agricultural purposes. Among the schemes formulated was one for the agroclimatic regionalization of Ukraine, which appeared in Atlas sil's'koho hospodarstva Ukraïns'koï RSR (Agricultural Atlas of the Ukrainian SSR, 1958) and involved the division of the territory into five zones (forest, forest-steppe, steppe, Carpathians, and Crimean Mountains) and 25 regions. The partition of the republic's territory into five zones became standard practice for subsequent physical-geographic regionalization.

The subdivision of the five zones into varying numbers of smaller regions was commonly undertaken on the basis of geomorphological criteria. A 1962 physical-geographic regionalization by V. Popov, A. Lanko, O. Marynych, and O. Poryvkina, for example, featured the five zones subdivided into 47 regions and 28 subregions. Later Marynych (1969), in the Ukraine volume of an all-Union regional geography series, formulated a simplified physical-geographic regionalization that included the same five zones but only 22 regions. In a 1969 university geography textbook Lanko, Marynych, and M. Shcherban provided a physical-geographic regionalization consisting of the five zones described previously, but subdivided into eight provinces and 50 regions. Lanko, Marynych, Popov, Poryvkina, and N. Syrota, in the 1972 Ukraine and Moldavia volume of an all-Union series on natural conditions and physical resources, presented a scheme of physical-geographic regionalization consisting of the five zones subdivided into 18 provinces and 56 regions. In a 1982 university textbook on the physical geography of Ukraine, Marynych, Lanko, Shcherban, and P. Shyshchenko revised that scheme and subdivided the five zones into 53 regions. The most recent physical-geographic regionalization was done by Marynych, H. Parkhomenko, and V. Pashchenko in a 1990 text that subdivided the Ukrainian SSR into two mountain 'countries' and three lowland 'zones.' In that scheme the steppe zone was further differentiated into three 'subzones,' and then the forest-steppe and the steppe zones divided into provinces. Finally, both the 'countries' and the subunits of the 'zones' were subdivided into 57 regions.

In addition to those general schemes of the physical-geographic regionalization of the Ukrainian SSR, there were various regionalizations that involved the use of a single set of criteria. One example is P. Tsys's 1962 text on the geomorphology of Ukraine, which involved only geomorphological criteria and resulted in the subdivision of the republic into 18 provinces, 10 subprovinces, and 109 regions. A subsequent geomorphological regionalization by Yu. Grubrin (1972) provided for 11 provinces and 107 regions. Similar examples can be found for agroclimatic regionalization, agro-soil regionalization, geobotanical regionalization, and the like.

BIBLIOGRAPHY

Dokuchaev, V. *Zony prirody i klassifikatsiia pochv* (St Petersburg 1900)
Lichkov, B. *Estestvennye raiony Ukrainy* (Kiev 1922)
Tutkovs'kyi, P. *Pryrodna raionizatsiia Ukraïny* (Kiev 1922)
Rudnyts'kyi, S. *Osnovy zemleznannia Ukraïny*, vol 1 (Lviv 1924)
Atlas sil's'koho hospodarstva Ukraïns'koï RSR (Kiev 1958)
Trudy Nauchnogo soveshchaniia po priorodno-geograficheskomu raionirovaniiu Ukrainskoi SSR (Kiev 1961)
Popov, V.; Lan'ko, A.; Marinich, A.; Poryvkina, O. 'Fiziko-geograficheskoe raionirovanie,' in *Atlas Ukrainskoi SSR i Moldavskoi SSR* (Kiev 1962)
Tsys', P. *Heomorfolohiia URSR* (Lviv 1962)
Lan'ko, A.; Marynych, O.; Shcherban', M. *Fizychna heohrafiia Ukraïns'koï RSR* (Kiev 1969)
Grubrin, Iu. 'Geomorfologicheskoe raionirovanie,' in *Prirodnye usloviia i estestvennye resursy SSSR: Ukraina i Moldaviia* (Moscow 1972)
Lan'ko, A.; Marinich, A.; Popov, V.; Poryvkina, O.; Sirota, N. 'Prirodnoe raionirovanie,' in *Prirodnye usloviia i estestvennye resursy SSSR: Ukraina i Moldaviia* (Moscow 1972)
Marynych, O.; Lan'ko, A.; Shcherban', M.; Shyshchenko, P. *Fizychna heohrafiia Ukraïns'koï RSR* (Kiev 1982)

V. Kubijovyč, I. Stebelsky

Regions of Ukraine. The regions of Ukraine derive their characteristics from a diverse complex of physical-geographic and human factors, including natural phe-nomena (topography, vegetation, climate) and human characteristics (population, political-administrative borders, economic indicators). The most permanent features over the centuries of human record are *landforms. They influence the drainage patterns, the climate, the flora, the density of population, and the economy. The most noticeable feature, difference in altitude, is pronounced only where the mountains begin, or where the uplands are marked off by deep valleys or escarpments. In some places, as in the northern lowland, the swamps of Polisia become the prevalent feature; in others, as in the southern plains of Ukraine, the transition from the forest-steppe to the steppe vegetation and a drier climate become the main factors of regional differentiation. Ukraine can thus be divided into four major natural units: the northern, the middle, the southern, and the mountainous. The northern belt, commonly known as Polisia, is a sparsely populated territory of postglacial landscapes, forests, and swamps. The middle belt is a territory of erosive loess landscapes. It has a temperate, subhumid climate and degraded chernozem and chernozem soils that developed under a natural forest-steppe vegetation. Possessing excellent conditions for agriculture, the middle belt supports arable farmland and is densely populated. The southern belt differs from the middle belt in its warmer, semiarid climate. Its chernozem and chestnut soils developed under the steppe flora, which until recently was grazed by herds of wild or domesticated ungulates. At present it is largely plowed where some crops enjoy supplemental irrigation, but it is less densely peopled than the middle belt, except in the industrial areas. The Carpathian Mountains, the Crimean Mountains, and the Caucasus, along with their respective foothills and submontane depressions, constitute separate small units.

HISTORICAL REGIONS OF UKRAINE

The differentiation of Ukrainian national territory on the basis of human characteristics can involve matters of ethnography. The cultural attributes of Ukrainians, which have evolved in conjunction with their use of the environment and interrelations with their neighbours, include subtle differences in language (dialects), music, beliefs, and social behaviour, as well as in elements of material culture, such as house types and styles in clothing, embroidery, pottery, and the like. Such characteristics are best preserved in isolated locations with minimum immigration, such as swampy Polisia or the secluded valleys of the Carpathian Mountains. V. Horlenko recognized six ethnographic regions and several subregions of Ukraine. The Polisia or northern region (which corresponds closely to the physical-geographic region of Polisia) possesses autochthons with archaic cultural traits. It may be subdivided into three subregions, the left-bank region or Chernihiv Polisia, the central region or Kievan Polisia (northwest of Kiev), and the western region or Volhynian Polisia. The Carpathian ethnographic region is the most complex region of all. It includes not only the Carpathian Mountains but also the Tysa Lowland in Transcarpathia and the Dniester Valley in Subcarpathia, extends northward to Roztochchia, and includes the western end of the Podolian Upland. The region shares borders with the Poles, Slovaks, Hungarians, and Rumanians, peoples with whom the Ukrainians of the region have had lengthy interactions. In the mountains there still exist three distinct Ukrainian ethnographic groups (from the southeast to the west, respectively), the Hutsuls, the Boikos, and the Lemkos. The remaining regions, by contrast, are more homogeneous and similar to one another. The Podolian ethnographic region corresponds to the central and eastern parts of the Podolian Upland. The central or Dnieper ethnographic region extends south of Kiev along both sides of the Dnieper to Kirovohrad in the south and Poltava in the east. It is the Ukrainian heartland and was the locus of the most vigorous development of the Ukrainian nationality from the 15th and 16th centuries. Slobidska Ukraine, the fifth major ethnographic region, was settled in the 17th century by Ukrainian Cossacks as military servitors on the Muscovite steppe frontier, and thus experienced a long period of Russian-Ukrainian interaction. The territory extends in an arc from Sumy through Kharkiv and eastward, with a strip in the RF south of Lgov and Belgorod that broadens into a wedge south of Voronezh to Novokhopersk and south to Morozovsk in Rostov oblast. Finally, the southern or steppe ethnographic region is large and not clearly differentiated. It corresponds approximately to the steppe belt. The region was settled only in the 18th century, by Ukrainian farmers who, more than in other regions, were influenced by the commerce and urban way of life of the Russians (throughout the belt), and by interaction with them and with the Germans (in the west, center, and east), the Rumanians (in the west), the Bulgarians (in the west and center), the Greeks (in the east), and the Caucasian peoples (in the Kuban).

Distinct regional Ukrainian identities have developed among segments of the population that have been isolated from the mass of the Ukrainian people by historical circumstance. The most obvious examples are the populations of Transcarpathia (which existed as a unit under the Kingdom of Hungary, Transylvania, Hungary of the Austro-Hungarian Empire, and Czechoslovakia), Galicia (under the Kingdom of Poland, Austria, and then Poland again), Bukovyna (under Rumania), Kholm and Podlachia (both mostly under Poland), Polisia (under Lithuania and then Russia, Poland, and Belarus), Slobidska Ukraine (under Muscovy, the Russian Empire, and the RSFSR), and the Kuban and the eastern Subcaucasus (under the Russian Empire and the RSFSR). The groups affected by regionalism constitute approx one-fifth of the Ukrainian population; the rather undifferentiated mass of Central Ukrainians form the remaining four-fifths.

Taking into consideration the historical past of Ukraine, the regional differences of the population, its present distribution, and economic conditions, V. Kubijovyč divided Ukraine into 14 historical-geographic regions. Although Transcarpathia and the Crimea are smaller, they are singled out as separate regions because of their historical and geographical individuality. Similarly, the Kholm area and Podlachia and Bukovyna are regarded as separate regions. Polisia is divided among the Volhynian, Kiev, and Chernihiv regions, because its residents tended to interact (culturally and economically) with the more densely populated and more economically developed centers. The center of each region is based on the potential possibilities of development. (See also *Administrative territorial division.)

BIBLIOGRAPHY
Tutkovs'kyi, P. *Pryrodne raionuvannia Ukraïny* (Kiev 1922)
Rudnyts'kyi, S. *Osnovy zemleznannia Ukraïny*, 1 (Lviv 1924)
Kubiiovych, V. *Heohrafiia ukraïns'kykh i sumezhnykh zemel'* (Cracow–Lviv 1943)
Tsys', P. *Heomorfolohiia URSR* (Lviv 1962)
Pistun, M.; Shypovych, Ie. (eds). *Heohrafiia Ukraïns'koï RSR* (Kiev 1982)
Horlenko, V. 'Etnohrafichne raionuvannia,' in *Heohrafichna entsyklopediia Ukraïny*, vol 1 (Kiev 1989)

I. Stebelsky

Registered Cossacks (*reiestrovi kozaky*). *Cossacks who were accepted into the special Cossack units of the Polish-Lithuanian Commonwealth army and were enrolled in a special register (hence the term). The first effort to secure the Cossacks' military services was made in 1524 by King Sigismund I, who assigned S. Polozovych and K. Kmytych the task of setting up a Cossack unit in the royal army. Because the crown lacked sufficient funds to pay the Cossacks for their services, the plan was not realized, and similar efforts by O. *Dashkevych, the starosta of Cherkasy, in 1533 and again by Sigismund in 1541 also failed. Whereas the starostas in Ukraine wanted to organize Cossack units primarily for more effective defense of the Commonwealth's frontier against Tatar attacks, the kings wanted them for the purpose of controlling the Zaporozhian Cossacks and restraining their anti-Crimean Tatar and anti-Turkish campaigns and raids.

The creation of a registered Cossack force was first decreed on 2 June 1572 by King Sigismund II Augustus, who ordered the grand hetman of the army, J. Jazłowiecki, to hire and register 300 of the wealthiest Cossacks. Thenceforth nonregistered Cossacks were accorded a semilegal status. The registered Cossacks were officially outside the jurisdiction of the local authorities and were placed under the command of a government-appointed elder (*starshyi*), the first of whom was the Polish noble J. Badowski. In 1578 King Stephen Báthory allowed the register to be increased to 600 Cossacks, and appointed Prince *Michał Korybut Wiśniowiecki as their elder. The registered Cossacks were exempted from taxation and granted the right to own land and the privilege of self-government under an appointed member of the *starshyna*. They had their own standards, kettledrums, and other insignia; were paid in cash and clothing; and were given ownership of the town of Trakhtemyriv and its monastery to house their winter quarters, arsenal, and hospital. The Commonwealth government officially named the registered Cossacks the Zaporozhian Army to underscore the fact that it considered the actual *Zaporozhian Host a legal nonentity. The registered Cossacks were obligated to serve in central Ukraine and, when ordered to do so by the government, set up garrisons beyond the Dnieper Rapids.

The efforts of Stephen Báthory and his successors to control the growth of Cossack society through registration proved futile. From the late 16th century on, its consolidation occurred in two centers, the Zaporozhian Sich and Trakhtemyriv. The Sich became the hearth of revolutionary independence, and Trakhtemyriv was the headquarters of the privileged, conservative, registered Cossack elite. After the Cossack rebellions of the 1580s in Ukraine, the Commonwealth government decreed an increase in the register to 1,000 on 25 June 1590 and turned over the Kremenchuk fortress to the registered Cossacks. During the Commonwealth's wars with Muscovy and the Ottoman Empire the register was increased to 10,000, in 1618. The 1619 *Rostavytsia Treaty reduced it to 3,000, but in 1620 it was again increased, that time to 20,000.

The 1625 *Kurukove Treaty set the register at 6,000 and granted the registered Cossacks the right to elect their own hetman, subject to approval by the king. Under the provisions of the *Pereiaslav Treaty of 1630 the register was expanded to 8,000. In 1638, after the suppression of the rebellions led by P. Pavliuk and K. Skydan, in which registered Cossacks had joined the rebel side, the register was reduced to 6,000 and then 5,000, the registered Cossacks lost the right to elect their own *starshyna* and have their own court system, the hetman was replaced by an appointed commissioner subordinated to the Polish grand hetman, and Cossacks excluded from the register were enserfed. After the outbreak of the Cossack-Polish War in 1648, the registered Cossacks mostly sided with Hetman B. Khmelnytsky and played an instrumental role in subsequent Polish defeats. Under Khmelnytsky the Cossack register was replaced by the *komput*, and the former registered Cossacks were designated *town Cossacks. The Poles' attempts at reducing the register to 40,000 in the 1649 Treaty of *Zboriv and then 20,000 in the 1651 Treaty of *Bila Tserkva proved unenforceable, and Khmelnytsky increased it to 50,000 and then 60,000 in 1654. The term 'registered Cossacks' was not used after 1660.

Prominent leaders of the registered Cossacks included S. *Kishka, K. *Kosynsky, P. *Sahaidachny, Ya. *Borodavka, M. *Doroshenko, H. *Chorny, and I. *Karaimovych. In 1875 O. Bodiansky published the detailed register of the entire Zaporozhian Host compiled after the Treaty of Zboriv.

BIBLIOGRAPHY

Iakovliv, A. 'Z istoriï reiestratsiï ukraïns'kykh kozakiv,' *Ukraïna*, 1 (1907)

Kryp'iakevych, I. 'Kozachchyna i Batoriievi vil'nosti,' *Zherela do istoriï Ukraïny-Rusy*, vol 8 (Lviv 1908)

Golobutskii, V. *Zaporozhskoe kazachestvo* (Kiev 1957)

Vynar, L. 'Pochatky ukraïns'koho reiestrovoho kozatstva,' UI, no. 2–3 (1964)

L. Wynar

Rehabilitation. A Soviet legal practice by which a previously condemned person was cleared, often posthumously, of the crimes attributed to him or her and was restored officially to full civilian status. The procedure was one of the key methods by which the Soviet regime tried to reclaim public confidence and legitimacy after having destroyed, through execution, imprisonment, deportation, and exile, millions of innocent people. The wide-scale use of extralegal procedures and the gross violations of judicial processes that took place under J. Stalin's regime eventually had to be admitted and condemned by the Party, and the stigma of guilt, which justified continued discrimination against the victims of repression and their families, had to be removed.

In Soviet Ukraine rehabilitation began soon after Stalin's death. Several family members of repressed Ukrainian leaders, such as S. Kosior, were released from the labor camps. The first group of Stalin's victims who profited from the milder climate in 1953 was the Soviet partisan group. Its members were repressed in 1944 for acting without proper clearance from the Soviet partisan staff in Ukraine. Until 1956 the process of rehabilitation was conducted in silence, with no announcements in the press. At the 20th Party Congress (1956) A. Mikoyan and N. Khrushchev praised some Party leaders in Ukraine who had been repressed by Stalin, but there was little interest in rehabilitating them. Only in 1958–9 was N. Khrushchev's secret speech echoed in the press by a few references to prominent Ukrainian victims of Stalinist *terror.

The 22nd Congress of the CPSU (1961) persuaded the Ukrainian leaders to adopt a bolder policy on rehabilitation. During the congress M. Pidhirny exposed L. Kaganovich's role in the purge of 1947, and three months later he drew public attention to M. Skrypnyk. It was not until 1962 that Skrypnyk was cleared of 'bourgeois nationalism,' and he was so cleared in the context of an attack on Stalin's nationality policy. The use of rehabilitation for political purposes was typical of the late Khrushchev period. The Ukrainian press participated in the anti-Stalin campaign of 1963–4. The publication of information about V. Zatonsky was an important step. But the disclosures continued to be unreliable and incomplete. Although many victims were mentioned, their ultimate fate remained a secret. Ukrainian victims received less attention than victims from other national groups. After 1963 a number of Ukrainian leaders of the 1930s, such as E. Veger, M. Maiorov, K. Sukhomlyn, P. Liubchenko, and A. Medvedev, were rehabilitated. In the 1970s the anti-Stalin campaign was curtailed, yet the names of prominent victims continued to appear, M. Chuvirin and V. Stroganov, for example. The second edition of *Ukraïns'ka radians'ka entsyklopediia* (Ukrainian Soviet Encyclopedia, 1977–85) contained information about many rehabilitated leaders without explaining how they perished.

The rehabilitation of victims who were not Party members was a more delicate problem. In the 1950s most labor-camp inmates who had been involved in the postwar national movements were not released, let alone rehabilitated. The new category of victims, the prisoners of conscience of Khrushchev's and L. Brezhnev's regimes, had not been rehabilitated by 1991. Under M. Gorbachev's policy of glasnost the amount of information about Stalinist and later repressions increased dramatically, but the range of rehabilitation categories grew slowly.

BIBLIOGRAPHY
Goudoever, A. van. *The Limits of Destalinization: Political Rehabilitation in the Soviet Union* (London–New York 1986)

A. van Goudoever

Rehabilitation medicine. In its medico-social aspect, rehabilitation is a system of knowledge and methods directed to the maximum compensatory adaptive function and independence of physically disabled individuals. Rehabilitative techniques have specific characteristics at various stages of treatment: in-hospital, outpatient, and sanatorium. In the former USSR rehabilitation medicine was not a separate specialty. Rehabilitation therapies were developed in the various individual specialties, particularly in neurology, neurosurgery, and orthopedics. In Ukraine rehabilitation units are associated with the larger hospitals in Kiev, Lviv, Donetske, Dnipropetrovske, Kharkiv, Odessa, Saky, Slovianske, and Yalta.

The first department of rehabilitation in a medical education institute in the USSR was established in 1969 at the *Kiev Institute for the Upgrading of Physicians, under the directorship of L. Pelekh. Over 500 physicians from Ukraine and from other Soviet republics were trained yearly in the department, which has been instrumental in developing new methods of rehabilitative therapy for patients with neurological and neurosurgical conditions such as stroke, head injury, hemiplegia, and radiculitis. Research is conducted in the use of electrostimulation and manual therapeutics for paralytic conditions. The department has also developed a model for providing rehabilitative care in rural communities. In early 1991 the Department of Rehabilitation Medicine organized the first course in electromyography in the former USSR.

BIBLIOGRAPHY
Maryniak, O.; Ovcharenko, A.; Pelekh, L.; Palamarchuk, L. 'Rehabilitation in the Rural Community in Ukraine: A Pilot Project,' *International Disability Studies*, vol 13, no. 2 (1991)

O. Maryniak, A. Ovcharenko

Rehman, Antoni, b 15 May 1840 in Cracow, Poland, d 12 January 1917 in Lviv. He was appointed a professor of geography at Lviv University in 1882. He conducted several botanical expeditions to southern Africa, the Crimea, and Podilia. His two-volume survey *Ziemie dawnej Polski i sąsiednich krajów słowiańskich* (Lands of Ancient Poland and the Adjoining Slavic Territories, 1895, 1904) served for many years as an important reference work about Ukraine's geography and flora.

Řehoř, František, b 16 December 1857 in Stěžery, Bohemia, d 6 October 1899 in Prague. Czech ethnographer and folklorist; honorary member of the Prosvita society from 1895. While living in Galicia (1877–90) he contributed articles to the Czech press about the traditions and lore of the Ukrainian people and wrote over 160 entries on Ukrainian subjects for *Ottův slovník naučný*. He was acquainted with many Ukrainian scholars and writers, such as I. Franko, M. Pavlyk, V. Shukhevych, and O. Kobylianska. He donated his Czech-language library to the Prosvita society in Lviv and his ethnographic collection to the Prague Industrial Museum, which later transferred it to the ethnography department of the Czech National Museum.

Reich Food Office. See German Labor Front.

Reichskommissariat Ukraine (RKU). An administrative unit that included most of the Ukrainian territory under civilian rule during the German occupation of 1941–4. It was one of the four commissariats that A. *Rosenberg, head of the Ministry for the Occupied Eastern Territories, planned to establish. On 20 April 1941 A. *Hitler instructed him to prepare a plan for the political restructuring of the European portion of the USSR following its occupation. According to the plan the RKU was to constitute a territory independent of Russia with a temporary Ukrainian government under German political, economic, and military control. Hitler appointed Rosenberg minister for the occupied territories on 17 July 1941 but did not sanction the formation of a Ukrainian government. In order to weaken Ukrainian aspirations to independence he excluded several territories from the proposed Reichskommissariat. Galicia was annexed to the Generalgouvernement, and northern Bukovyna and Transnistria were given to Rumania. The Volhynian town of Rivne, not Kiev, was made the capital of the RKU.

The RKU, officially established on 1 September 1941, was made up of Volhynia, Polisia, Right-Bank Ukraine, and part of the Poltava region. Following the advance of German forces the remainder of the Poltava region and Dnipropetrovske, Zaporizhia, and Kherson oblasts were annexed to the RKU on 2 September 1942, and the rest of Left-Bank Ukraine remained under military rule. The territory of the RKU comprised 339,275 sq km, with a population of approximately 17 million.

In practice the administration of the RKU was directed not by Rosenberg but by E. *Koch, whom Hitler appointed Reichskommissar of Ukraine without consulting Rosenberg. Koch, who described himself as 'a brutal dog,' represented Nazi policy at its most ruthless. No Nazi official did more than Koch to antagonize Ukrainians. Owing to his good connections with Hitler's secretary, M. Bormann, Koch was able to neutralize most of Rosenberg's instructions. Among the RKU's most prominent officials were Koch's deputy and follower, P. Dargel, and their opponent A. Frauenfeld, *Generalkommissar* of Tavriia.

A number of important departments operating in the RKU were subordinate to the central authorities in Berlin. Among them were the police, under H. Himmler; H. Göring's Four-Year Plan and Economic Executive Staff East, which managed heavy industry and resource extraction; the mobilization of labor for work in Germany, under the direction of F. Sauckel; propaganda, under J. Goebbels; and transport and communications, directed by ministries in Berlin.

In administrative terms the RKU was divided into *Generalbezirke* headed by *Generalkommissäre* appointed by Hitler; the latter were subdivided into *Kreise*, each made up of four raions, headed by *Gebietskommissäre* appointed by Rosenberg. Larger towns were administered by *Stadtkommissäre*, and raion centers had German police stations and

REICHSKOMMISSARIAT UKRAINE

Landwirtschaftsführer, who were in charge of agriculture. Local administration consisted of raion officials and village elders, all subordinate to *Gebietskommissäre*. The mayors of larger towns were under the authority of *Stadtkommissäre*. The *Ukrainian auxiliary police, recruited by raion heads and mayors of larger towns, was subordinate to the German police and the civil administration of the RKU.

Soviet criminal law was abolished in the RKU and replaced by German law. In civil cases German legal norms (rather than laws) were to be applied, but customary law and the instructions of German administrators were also used. Both German and local (*vlasnokraiovi*) courts existed in the RKU. In centers administered by *Generalkommissäre* there were German courts of first instance for civil and criminal cases involving German citizens and *Volksdeutsche*. The German Supreme Court (Deutsches Obergericht) had its seat in Rivne. Attached to every German court was a so-called special court consisting of a judge and two jurors (who did not necessarily have legal training), which adjudicated cases that threatened the interests of the Reich, such as attacks on German administrators and murders of *Reichsdeutsche*. Such crimes bore statutory death penalties. Sentences imposed by the German Supreme Court and special courts could not be appealed. When an immediate threat to security and public order was involved, cases could be tried by summary courts

(*Standesgerichte*) convened by the *Generalkommissar* or his representatives. Once confirmed by the *Generalkommissar*, their verdicts were not subject to appeal.

Owing to Koch's delaying tactics, it was not until the spring of 1942 that local courts (*kraiove sudivnytstvo*) were established to deal with civil and minor criminal cases (major cases were tried by German courts). Many cases were adjudicated by *Gebietskommissäre*, who handed down administrative decisions. The insignificant number of tribunals accessible to the non-German inhabitants of the RKU did not provide sufficient legal protection, especially to the rural population. More important, the destructive policies of Koch and Himmler were not subject to the RKU's official norms (see *Nazi war crimes in Ukraine).

Property rights were not formally established. Following the abolition of Soviet law the German administration stood for private ownership in principle and criticized the collective-farm system. Nevertheless the system remained basically unaltered in the RKU. Koch and the officials of the German food and agriculture ministry believed that collective farms facilitated the exploitation of Ukrainian peasants for Germany's benefit. Not until the German defeat at Stalingrad did Rosenberg propose the reprivatization of collective-farm property by means of a statute dated 3 June 1943, but it was largely boycotted by Koch and limited by partisan activity, as well as by the German retreat. Barely 10 percent of the land intended for distribution was actually allotted to the peasants.

Industry and commerce were mobilized to serve Göring's Four-Year Plan. A law regulating commercial and industrial property ownership was to be enacted after the war; for the duration, property was considered basically nationalized. Industrial concerns were administered by German firms and entrepreneurs (an arrangement known as *Treuhandverwaltung*), and German commercial monopolies were established to produce for Germany's needs and distribute consumer goods to the working population of the RKU. The only exception was the All-Ukrainian Association of Consumer Co-operative Organizations, which was left in Ukrainian hands out of practical considerations, although its organizational structure above the raion level was turned into a German commercial institution at the end of 1942. All taxes levied under Soviet rule remained in force, and a Central Bank of Issue for Ukraine was established in March 1942.

Hitler never clarified the administrative norms that were to prevail in the RKU or the legal status of its population. The national feelings of Ukrainians in the RKU were to be encouraged insofar as they divided Ukrainians and Russians and eliminated the danger of a combined anti-German front. Such motives lay behind measures such as the introduction of the Ukrainian language along with German in the RKU to the exclusion of Russian and the minting of the *karbovanets* instead of the ruble. A particular measure taken for the purpose of fanning anti-Soviet sentiment was the investigation of the *Vinnytsia Massacre. In other respects the Nazis weakened and retarded elements of national consciousness that might have led Ukrainians to demand independence. General education was limited to four grades of primary school, and higher education was restricted to narrowly specialized vocational courses. Cultural institutions, such as the Prosvita society, libraries, museums, theaters, scholarly bodies, and publishing houses, were closed; the press was placed under German control and held to a lower standard. The population's capacity for physical survival was undermined in various ways: food supplies were cut; medical services were reduced (to check the 'biological power of the Ukrainians,' in Koch's words); Ukrainian *Ostarbeiter and POWs were physically abused; and various strata of the population were decimated for actual or supposed support of the partisan movement. It was in Koch's immediate area, Volhynia, that his brutal methods prompted the formation of the *Ukrainian Insurgent Army in 1942; he was also opposed by *Soviet partisans in Ukraine.

A German colony, the RKU constituted an important part of Hitler's *Lebensraum* and was completely deprived of autonomy or international status. Nazi plans called for the postwar unification of the RKU with the territory of the German Reich; most Ukrainians (considered unfit for Germanization) were to be resettled beyond the Urals to make room for German colonists. In fact Hitler was unable to inspire many Germans to colonize Ukraine. Despite ambitious plans only a few villages were cleared of their Ukrainian inhabitants and populated with Germans (both groups were resettled under duress). Those experiments were profoundly resented by the local population, which saw them as portents of German postwar intentions. Resettlement was also prevented by the German retreat and then by the formal liquidation of the RKU on 10 November 1944.

BIBLIOGRAPHY
Forostiv'kyi, L. *Kyïv pid vorozhymy okupatsiiamy* (Buenos Aires 1952)
Bräutigam, O. *Überblick über die Besetzten Ostgebiete während des zweiten Weltkrieges* (Tübingen 1954)
Herzog, R. *Grundzüge der deutschen Besatzungsverwaltung in der Ost- und Südeuropäischen Ländern während des zweiten Weltkrieges* (Tübingen 1955)
Moritz, G. *Gerichtsbarkeit in den von Deutschland besetzten Gebieten, 1939–1945* (Tübingen 1955)
Ilnytzkyj, R. *Deutschland und die Ukraine 1934–1945*, 2 vols (Munich 1955–6)
Kamenetsky, I. *Hitler's Occupation of Ukraine (1941–1944): A Study of Totalitarian Imperialism* (Milwaukee 1956)
– *Secret Nazi Plans for Eastern Europe: A Study of Lebensraum Policies* (New York 1961)
Dallin, A. *German Rule in Russia, 1941–1945: A Study of Occupation Policies*, 2nd edn (Boulder, Colo 1981)
Mulligan, T. *The Politics of Illusion and Empire: German Occupation Policy in the Soviet Union, 1942–1943* (New York 1988)
I. Kamenetsky, M. Yurkevich

Reichsnährstand. See German Labor Front.

Reichsrat. See Parliament.

Reikhel, Mykhailo [Rejxel', Myxajlo], b 1880, d 1956. Soviet jurist and statesman. A former Menshevik and a lawyer by profession, under Soviet rule he was Ukrainian SSR people's commissar of labor (1920), chairman of the Little Council of People's Commissars (1921–6), and deputy people's commissar of justice and deputy general procurator (1922–6). From 1926 he served on the Chief Concession Committee in Moscow and as a Soviet diplomat, and from 1938 he taught state and civil law. He wrote books on the constitutional relations of the Soviet republics (1925) and Soviet family law (1942), edited a compendium on Soviet federalism (1930), and contributed many articles to Soviet law journals.

Reims Gospel (Reimske yevanheliie). One of the oldest extant Church Slavonic literary monuments. It consists of (1) parts of the Gospels (the last 16 of 35 folios) in Cyrillic, which the Holy Roman emperor Charles IV acquired somewhere in Hungary and presented to the Emmaus Monastery in Prague; and (2) 31 folios of readings from the Gospels and Epistles transcribed in the Glagolitic alphabet from a Croatian original by a Czech monk at the Emmaus Monastery in 1395 for use in Roman Catholic services. The entire codex was taken to Istanbul, most likely by Hussites after the Emmaus Monastery burned down in 1421. There it was bought by Cardinal Charles of Lorraine and presented to the cathedral in Reims, France, where it was preserved from 1574 and later given to the Reims Municipal Library. In 1793 the gems inlaid in its cover were plundered. The gospel is legendary: it has been said that French monarchs used it during their coronation oaths, and that the Cyrillic text was first read from it by Tsar Peter I in 1717 or by a Russian emissary in 1728. A facsimile edition of the gospel was first published by S. de Sacy in Paris in two volumes in 1843. The text, together with that of the Ostromir Gospel and a parallel Polish translation, was published by V. Hanka in Prague in 1846. An 1852 edition of the text with a Latin translation was funded by Tsar Nicholas I and published in Paris. A fourth edition of the text was published by L. Léger in Reims in

1899. Its language was studied by P. Rakovsky-Biliarsky (1847), who believed the Cyrillic parts were a 14th-century Rumanian copy of a Serbo-Croatian original, and by A. Sobolevsky (1887), who claimed they were of 11th- or 12th-century East Slavic origin. The text, along with a history of the scholarship, was published by L. Zhukovskaia in Moscow in 1978.

O. Horbach

Lev Reinarovych

Reinarovych, Lev [Rejnarovyč] (Rejnarovycz), b 14 January 1914 in Kniazhpil, Dobromyl county, Galicia, d 31 January 1987 in New York. Opera singer (baritone). A graduate of the Lysenko Higher Institute of Music in Lviv, from 1941 he was a soloist at the Lviv Opera Theater and from 1946 a member of B. Piurko's Ukrainian Opera Ensemble in Germany. After emigrating to the United States he appeared on stage in New York and other cities and on television. His operatic roles included Scarpia in G. Puccini's *Tosca*, Escamillo in G. Bizet's *Carmen*, Karas in S. Hulak-Artemovsky's *Zaporozhian Cossack beyond the Danube*, and Henry I in A. Rudnytsky's *Anna Yaroslavna*.

Reinforced-concrete industry. A branch of the *building-materials industry that produces reinforced-concrete structural members and components for almost every branch of the construction industry. Its chief products are columns, beams, frames, panels, plates, tubes, and poles. About 35 percent of the total volume of the USSR reinforced-concrete production (1970) consisted of cast reinforced-concrete members (nonstandard or very heavy parts). The use of precast reinforced-concrete products in construction allows a considerable gain in labor efficiency and product quality. By 1978 the USSR was producing over 130 million cu m of precast structural members, including over 23 million produced by Ukraine. A substantial part of the production consisted of large panels for housing, manufactured by plants in Kiev, Kharkiv, Donetske, Odessa, and Dnipropetrovske. The largest precast products plant in Ukraine is the Kremenchuk Experimental Plant of Modular Housing Construction. The first plant-building complexes in the USSR, which manufactured and assembled reinforced-concrete structural parts for industrial plants, were set up in Brovary, near Kiev, Donetske, Zaporizhia, Dnipropetrovske, Lviv, and Berdianske. The Kiev Reinforced-Concrete Products Plant No. 5 supplies preschool institutions and administrative offices with special products. The Kakhivka, Novomoskovske, and Artsyz plants supply reinforced-concrete parts to the hydrotechnological building industry. Research on the re-

inforced-concrete production process and the application of reinforced-concrete products in the construction industry is conducted at the *Scientific Research Institute of Building Systems and the State Institute for the Development and Design of Civil Residential Construction and Enterprises of the Construction Industry.

Reinfuss, Roman, b 27 May 1910 in Przeworsk, Poland. Polish ethnographer specializing in Western Ukraine. A graduate of Cracow University (PH D, 1946), he lectured on ethnography at Wrocław (1946–9), Lublin, and Cracow universities. From 1946 he headed the research workshop of folk art at the Art Institute of the Polish Academy of Sciences, which he founded. He organized the first systematic research on folk culture in Poland and devoted considerable attention to the Lemko region. In 1960 he organized a research workshop of folk art and a folk architecture museum in Sianik. He has published over 30 ethnographic studies of the Lemkos and Boikos, including articles in *Wierchy* (vol 14, 1936), *Prace i materialy etnograficzne* (vol 7, 1948), and *Etnografia polska* (1961).

Reipolsky, Ivan [Rejpol's'kyj], b 1789, d 3 October 1863 in Kharkiv. Physician. A graduate of Kharkiv College (1810) and the Moscow Medico-Surgical Academy (1814), he served as a military doctor and from 1823 taught pathology, internal medicine, and botany at Kharkiv University. He helped to fight cholera in Kharkiv and Kursk and described various types of poisoning, including lead poisoning. In 1823 he wrote a veterinary handbook.

Rej, Mikołaj, b 4 February 1505 in Zhuravno, near Zhydachiv, Galicia, d 4 November 1569 in Rejowiec, in the Kholm region. Polish writer and moralist, and Calvinist polemicist. His prose works were marked by their folksy and simple style and the use of many Ukrainian loanwords. They were very popular in Ukraine and an important influence on the baroque literature of the 16th and 17th centuries, especially the *didactic gospels.

Rekanovsky, Petro [Rekanovs'kyj], b ca 1800, d after 1865 in Kiev. Theater director and actor. He began his career in Kiev in A. Lenkavsky's troupe and then led his own Ukrainian-Russian-Polish troupe in Kiev (1834–5, 1836–7, 1840–2, 1843), Chernihiv (1837), and Mykolaiv (1837–40). He played Vybornyi in I. Kotliarevsky's *Natalka Poltavka* (Natalka from Poltava).

Reklinsky, Ivan [Reklins'kyj], b and d ? Late-17th- to early-18th-century wood engraver at the Kievan Cave Monastery Press. He engraved the title pages of A. Radyvylovsky's *Vinets Khrystov* (Christ's Wreath, 1688) and a Liturgicon (1692) and the illustrations of Christ and the bookmen in *Vinets Khrystov*, of the pharaoh's drowning in the Psalter of 1690, of the Theotokos with the Archangels Michael and Gabriel and of Christ with the Holy Mother and John the Evangelist in the Acathistus of 1693, and of King David in the Psalter of 1708.

Reklinsky, Vasyl [Reklins'kyj, Vasyl'], b and d ? Painter of the 18th century. He painted the iconostases in the cathedral at the Monastery of the Exultation of the Holy Cross in Poltava (1727) and in St Nicholas's Cathedral in Nizhen (1734).

Religiino-naukovyi vistnyk (Religious-Scholarly Messenger). An irregular journal of theology and church history published by the Orthodox Brotherhood of St Mary the Protectress in the internment camps for soldiers of the Army of the UNR in Aleksandrów Kujawski and then Szczepiórno, Poland. It appeared from March 1921 to 1923 under the editorship of P. Bilon.

Religious funds. Funds established in the Habsburg Empire in the 1780s by Emperor Joseph II out of assets confiscated from churches and monasteries. They covered the expenditures mainly of the Catholic church, but also of the Orthodox church in Bukovyna. The funds provided for the needs of the eparchies and the chapters of cathedral clergy, and for the education and supplemental income of the clergy. For a brief time there was a single fund administered by a special imperial council; later, separate funds were established for each crownland. In Western Ukraine there were religious funds for Galicia and Bukovyna; Transcarpathia was eligible for the Hungarian religious fund.

In Galicia the fund was quickly dispensed and largely wasted because of the sale of church objects for excessively low prices, and because of the corruption of its administrators. The central government eventually ended up subsidizing the fund annually to cover expenditures.

The religious fund for Bukovyna was large and well run. It was gathered from 14 monasteries and consisted largely of forests, arable land, and fish ponds, totaling over 200,000 ha or almost 20 percent of all of the crownland. It was administered by the Orthodox metropoly in Chernivtsi and gave support to monasteries, schools, and parishes. It provided funds for the construction of the metropolitan's residence (now the main campus of Chernivtsi University) and a large cathedral. It also financed a number of secondary schools, a theological institute, and the theology faculty at Chernivtsi University from 1875.

After the dissolution of the Austro-Hungarian Empire, the landholdings in the religious funds were divided among Austria, Hungary, Poland, Czechoslovakia, Rumania, and Yugoslavia. In Rumania the fund remained in the jurisdiction of the Bukovynian metropolitan's consistory, and the state reserved the right to review its activities.

Religious holidays. See Church holidays.

Religious music. See Church music.

Religious press. Orthodox, Catholic, and Evangelical serials and periodicals devoted to theology, spirituality, and religious affairs.

Orthodox press. The Russian Orthodox press of the 19th and early 20th centuries in Russian-ruled Ukraine was exclusively Russian in language and tsarist in spirit. Each eparchy had an official organ, *Eparkhial'nye vedomosti*, which published official announcements, sermons, articles on theological and church topics, and some articles on local history and ethnography. These semimonthly periodicals were established in Odessa (Kherson eparchy) in 1860, Kiev and Chernihiv in 1861, Kamianets-Podilskyi (Podilia eparchy) in 1862, Poltava in 1863, Kharkiv and Kremianets (Volhynia eparchy) in 1867, Symferopil (Tavriia eparchy) in 1869, Katerynoslav in 1872, and

Kholm (Kholm–Warsaw eparchy) in 1877. The main religious scholarly journal was *Trudy Kievskoi dukhovnoi akademii* (est 1860). Others were the monthly *Dukhovnyi vestnik* (1862–7) in Kharkiv and the Kharkiv Theological Seminary's weekly and then semimonthly *Dukhovnyi dnevnik* (1864–5) and semimonthly *Vera i razum* (1884–1917). In Kiev the weekly *Rukovodstvo dlia sels'kikh pastyrei* (est 1860) of the Kiev Theological Seminary and the monthly *Propovedchiskii listok* (1882–) helped priests prepare sermons. Other religious periodicals were the weekly *Voskresnoe chtenie* (est 1837) in Kiev; the semimonthly *Blagovest* in Kharkiv (1883–8) and Nizhen (from 1889); the semimonthly *Nastavleniia i utesheniia Sviatoi Very Khristianskoi* (est 1887) of the St Andrew Skete on Mt Athos, published in Odessa; and the weekly *Pochaevskii listok* (est 1887), the political-religious organ of the reactionary Union of the Russian Peoples published by the Pochaiv Monastery Press. Part of *Kholmskaia Rus'* (1912–17), the daily organ of the Kholm Brotherhood of the Holy Mother of God, appeared in Ukrainian.

After the establishment of the Ukrainian Central Rada in 1917, the first short-lived religious periodicals appeared in Ukrainian: the UNR Ministry of Religious Affairs weekly *Vira ta derzhava* (1918) and daily *Slovo* (from October 1918), and *Kyivs'kyi pravoslavnyi vistnyk* in Kiev; *Pravoslavnaia Volyn'* (1917–21), the organ of Volhynia eparchy, which appeared primarily in Russian but published sermons in Ukrainian, and *Svitets'* (ed N. Abramovych) in Zhytomyr; and *Tserkovnyi vistnyk* (1918) in Zaporizhia. In the early Soviet period the official organ of the Ukrainian Autocephalous Orthodox church was *Tserkva i zhyttia* (Kharkiv, 1927–8). Other religious journals were *Ukraïns'kyi pravoslavnyi blahovisnyk* (1925–32?), of the Russian Orthodox Patriarchal church in Ukraine, and *Tserkovni visti* (1927), of the so-called Renovationist church. The religious press was almost entirely suppressed during the Stalinist terror of the 1930s. From then in Soviet Ukraine (and from 1945 in annexed Western Ukraine) the only permitted religious journals were the Moscow patriarchate's *Zhurnal Moskovskoi patriarkhii* (est 1931) and *Pravoslavnyi visnyk* (est 1946), the organ of the Ukrainian exarchate of the Russian Orthodox church. These journals were allotted very small pressruns, and their readers were held in great suspicion by the authorities. In contrast, *antireligious propaganda was fostered by the regime from the early 1920s, and several journals were published by the state to promote atheism, such as *Bezvirnyk* (1925–35), *Voiovnychyi ateïst* (1960–4), and its successor, *Liudyna i svit* (est 1965).

The Orthodox church in interwar Poland, especially in Volhynia and Warsaw, enjoyed greater freedom than in the USSR. Published in Ukrainian were *Pravoslavna Volyn'* (1922) and *Tserkva i narid* (1935–8) in Kremianets; *Na varti* (1924–6), *Ridna tserkva* (1927–8), and *Dukhovnyi siiach* (1927–31) in Volodymyr-Volynskyi; *Dukhovna besida* (1924–5) and *Nasha besida* (1926–7) in Warsaw; and *Za sobornist'* (1932–5) and *Shliakh* (1937–9) in Lutske. The Polish scholarly serial of the Faculty of Orthodox Theology at Warsaw University, *Elpis* (1926–37), published some materials in Ukrainian. In Warsaw the metropolitan see published the weekly *Pravoslavnyi selianyn* (1932–5) and, for children, the monthly *Dytyna* (1936–8) as supplements to its Russian-language paper, *Slovo*. The irregular *Religiino-naukovyi vistnyk* was published in the internment camps for soldiers of the UNR Army in Aleksandrów Kujawski (1921), Szczepiórno (1922), and Skalmierzyce (1923).

In interwar Transcarpathia Orthodox periodicals were Russophile and appeared in Russian. They were *Russkii pravoslavnyi vestnik* (1921–2, 1935) in Uzhhorod, which supported the Russian Orthodox Church in Exile; *Tserkovnaia pravda* (1925), *Pravoslavnaia Karpatskaia Rus'* (1928–30), and *Pravoslavnaia Rus'* (1931–9); *Pravoslavnyi karpatorusskii vestnik* (1935–8), the organ of Mukachiv and Prešov eparchies; and *Russkoe slovo* (1936) in Prešov. After the Second World War *Svet Pravoslaviia* appeared in Russian before switching to Ukrainian as *Holos Pravoslaviia* in 1958. Since 1958 *Zapovit sv. Kyryla i Mefodiia* has appeared in Ukrainian as the official organ of the Orthodox church in Czechoslovakia.

Each of the major jurisdictions of the émigré Ukrainian Orthodox church has had its own regular organs. The Ukrainian Orthodox Church in the USA has published *Dnipro (1922–50), *Ukraïns'ke pravoslavne slovo (since 1950), *Ukrainian Orthodox Word (since 1967), and the annual *Ukraïns'kyi pravoslavnyi kalendar* (since 1951). The Ukrainian Orthodox Church of America has published the bilingual *Ukrainian Orthodox Herald since 1935. The organs of the Ukrainian Autocephalous Orthodox Church (Conciliar) have been *Pravoslavnyi ukraïnets' (est 1952) and *Tserkva i zhyttia (1957–77). The organ of the Ukrainian Autocephalous Orthodox Church in Exile was the quarterly *Zhyttia i tserkva* (1956–67). Many parishes, local brotherhoods, and the Ukrainian Orthodox Youth Society have also published their own bulletins and magazines.

In Canada the earliest Orthodox periodicals – *Pravoslaviie* (1907–8) in Winnipeg, *Pravoslavnyi rusin* (1911–13) in Mundare, Alberta, and *Kanadiiskaia pravoslavnaia Rus' (1916–17) in Winnipeg – attempted to cultivate Russophile sympathies among Ukrainian immigrants, especially Orthodox settlers from Bukovyna. The first Ukrainian-language periodical was *Pravoslavnyi vistnyk* (est 1924), now *Visnyk, the organ of the Ukrainian Orthodox Church of Canada (UOCC). A pro-autocephaly faction led by V. Svystun published the bulletin *Ridna tserkva* (1935–40) in Winnipeg. After the Second World War the UOCC also published several popular journals of theology and church history edited primarily by Metropolitan Ilarion (I. Ohiienko), such as *Tserkva i narid (1949–51), *Nasha kul'tura (1951–3), *Vira i kul'tura (since 1953), and the annual calendar-almanac *Ridna nyva.*

After the Second World War Orthodox periodicals emerged in other Western countries to which Ukrainian refugees had emigrated: the irregular *Dzvin* (est 1950) in Buenos Aires; *Ukraïns'ka pravoslavna nyva* (1953–74) in Brazil; the quarterly *Vidomosti Heneral'noho tserkovnoho upravlinnia UAPTs u Velykii Britaniï* (est 1950) in Great Britain; *Tserkovnyi visnyk* (1945–6), *Tserkva i zhyttia* (1946), *Bohoslovs'kyi visnyk* (1948–9), and the quarterly *Ridna tserkva* (1952–88) in Germany; and *Nash holos* (est 1952), *Pratsia i zhyttia* (est 1966), and *Ukraïns'ka pravoslavna informatsiina sluzhba* (est 1962) in Australia. Most have been organs of the Ukrainian Autocephalous Orthodox church.

Catholic press. In Western Ukraine the first Ukrainian Catholic periodical was *Poucheniia tserkovnyia* (1853–4), a supplement to *Zoria halytska. The first separate Catholic publications were *Tserkovnaia gazeta (1856–8) and *Tserkovnyi vistnyk dlia rusynov Avstriiskoi derzhavy* (1858) in Budapest; both displayed Russophile tendencies and were closed by the Hungarian authorities. Another simi-

lar journal was *Sion, tserkov', shkola*, a biweekly supplement (1858–9) to *Vistnyk in Vienna.

The first Ukrainophile periodical was the semimonthly *Ruskii Sion (1871–85) in Lviv. Populist priests published *Druh naroda (1876), *Rus' (1885–7), *Myr (1885–7), *Dushpastyr (1887–98), and *Nyva (1904–39) in Lviv and *Prapor (1897–1900) in Peremyshl. Scholarly journals from that period included the quarterly *Bohoslovskii vistnyk* (1900–3) and the Russophile *Tserkovnyi vostok* (1911–14) in Lviv. Students at the Greek Catholic Theological Seminary in Lviv published the quarterly *Katolyts'kyi vskhid (1904–7). The official organs of the Peremyshl Consistory (1874–8) and *Vistnyk of the Peremyshl (1889–1918), Stanyslaviv (1886–1939), and Lviv (1889–1944) eparchies initially appeared in the artificial *yazychiie or *etymological spelling. They contained church news, sermons, and articles on theological and historical topics.

The last quarter of the 19th century saw a rapid growth in popular Catholic religious periodicals, such as *Slovo Bozhe (1879–81) in Lviv; *Kyryl i Metodii (1886) in Jarosław; *Poslannyk (1889–1911) in Berezhany, Lviv, Peremyshl, and Ternopil; and *Misionar (1897–1944) and, for children, *Malyi misionarchyk (1903–14, 1920) in Zhovkva. The political and social journals *Ruslan (1897–1914) and *Osnova (1906–13) in Lviv also supported the Catholic church and devoted attention to religious issues.

In the interwar period *Misionar and *Nyva continued to appear, and several new periodicals were published, especially for children and youths. These included *Nash pryiatel' (1922–39), *Postup (1921–31), *Ukraïns'ke iunatstvo (1933–9), *Lytsarstvo Presviatoï Bohorodytsi* (1935–9), and *Katolyts'ka aktsiia (1934–9). The journal *Dzvony (1931–9) published prose, poetry, and articles by Catholic writers; the journals *Bohosloviia (1923–39), *Analecta Ordinis S. Basilii Magni (1924–39), and *Dobryi pastyr (1931–9) published scholarly works. The monthly *Sivach* (1936–9) was dedicated to homiletics and catechism. Newspapers with a Catholic orientation were *Nova zoria (1926–39), *Pravda (1927–39), *Beskyd (1928–33), *Ukraïns'kyi Beskyd (1933–9), *Meta (1931–9), and *Khrystos nasha syla* (1933–9).

After the Soviet occupation and annexation of Western Ukraine all Catholic periodicals there were closed. Since that time *Khronika Katolyts'koï tserkvy na Ukraïni and some other publications have been circulated as samvydav. After the official reinstatement of the Ukrainian Catholic church in Ukraine, the magazine *Vira bat'kiv* began to appear in Lviv (1990).

In Uzhhorod, Transcarpathia, the Russophile Society of St Basil the Great published the religious, cultural, and political periodicals *Svit (1867–71), *Karpat (1873–86), *Nauka (1897–1912, 1918–22), and, in Hungarian, *Görök Katholikus Szemle (1899–1918). The journal *Listok (1885–1903) was similar in content and orientation. The Basilian Fathers published *Svitlo (1913–14, 1926) for children. In the interwar period *Dushpastyr (1921–41) was the monthly organ of Mukachiv and Prešov eparchies. Other periodicals in this period were the monthly *Da priidet Tsarstvie Tvoe* (1928–38), the Russian-language organ of the Society of the Sacred Heart of Jesus in Prešov, and the Basilian monthly *Blahovistnyk (1921–39, 1946–9). Since 1968 *Blahovestnik, the monthly eparchial organ for Uniate Catholics in Czechoslovakia, has been published in Prešov.

The official organ of the Greek Catholic *Križevci eparchy in Yugoslavia has been *Visnyk Kryzhevats'koï eparkhiï.*

In the United States the forerunners of the Ukrainian

Catholic press were the newspaper *Ameryka (1886–90) in Shenandoah and *Tserkovnaia nauka* (1903) in Johnstown, Pennsylvania. The first official church organs were *Dushpastyr* (1908–14), Bishop S. Ortynsky's monthly in New York and then Philadelphia and New Britain, Connecticut; the Basilian monthly *Ukraïns'kyi misionar (est 1917) and the weekly *Katolyts'kyi provid* (1927–8) in Philadelphia; and *Nebesnaia tsaritsa (1927–55), the organ of the Byzantine Ruthenian Greek Catholic Diocese of Pittsburgh. *Ameryka, a Catholic newspaper published five times a week by the Providence Association of Ukrainian Catholics in America, has appeared in Philadelphia since 1912, and the weekly *Shliakh has appeared there since 1940. Catholic periodicals founded in the postwar period include *Kovcheh (1946–56) in Stamford, Connecticut; the *Byzantine Catholic World* (est 1956) in Pittsburgh; the weekly *Nova zoria (est 1965) in Chicago; *Eastern Catholic Rite* (est 1965) in Passaic; the quarterly *Myrianyn* (1967–79) in Chicago; the Ukrainian Patriarchal World Federation monthly *Patriiarkhat (formerly *Za patriiarkhat*, est 1967) in Philadelphia; the biweekly *Tserkovnyi visnyk (est 1968) in Chicago; and the literary and scholarly quarterly *Dzvony* (1977–9) in Detroit.

In Canada the first Ukrainian Catholic paper, *Kanadyis'kyi rusyn*, appeared in Winnipeg in 1911; from 1919 to 1931 it was called *Kanadiis'kyi ukraïnets'. The Redemptorist monthly *Holos Spasytelia has been published in Yorkton, Saskatchewan, since 1923, and the Basilian monthly *Svitlo has been published since 1938 in Mundare, Alberta, and then Toronto. The newspapers *Ukraïns'ki visti (est 1932) in Edmonton, *Nasha meta (est 1949) in Toronto, and *Postup (est 1959) in Winnipeg serve as eparchial organs. Other periodicals were founded in the postwar period: the monthly *Mii pryiatel' (est 1949) for children in Winnipeg; *Lohos (1950–83), a theological quarterly, published in Waterford, Ontario, and then Yorkton; the scholarly quarterly *Zhyttia i slovo* (1948–9) in Toronto; the monthly *Ekleziia* (1951–64) in Montreal; the Basilian magazine *Beacon* (est 1966) in Toronto; *Za ridnu tserkvu* (1966–75), the bimonthly bulletin of the Committees for the Defense of the Rite, Traditions, and Language of the Ukrainian Catholic Church in the USA and Canada, published in Toronto; and *Pravda* (1969–75), a bimonthly journal published by O. *Mokh in Toronto. Many Catholic parishes and national and local lay organizations in Canada and the United States have issued their own newsletters and bulletins.

Ukrainian Catholic periodicals have also been published in other countries. They include *Misionar (1911–16), *Pratsia (est 1912), and *Ukraïns'kyi misionar u Brazyliï* (est 1935) in Brazil; *Zhyttia (est 1948), *Visnyk Apostol's'koho ekzarkhatu* (est 1968), and *Nazareth* (est 1973) in Argentina; *Tserkva i zhyttia (est 1960) in Australia; *Visnyk Ukraïns'koï Hreko-Katolyts'koï Tserkvy v Zakhidnii Evropi* (1940, 1945–52) and *Slidamy maloï sviatoï (est 1948) in France; *Khrytyians'kyi shliakh* (1946–7), *Khrystos naoha syla* (1946–9), and *Khrystyians'kyi holos (est 1949) in Germany; *Holos Khrysta Cholovikoliubtsia* (est 1947) in Belgium; and the quarterly *Nasha tserkva* (1953 to mid-1960s) in Great Britain. The revived theological-scholarly journals *Analecta Ordinis S. Basilii Magni (since 1949) and *Bohosloviia (since 1962), the irregular bulletin *Visti z Rymu* (est 1963), and *Blahovisnyk, the theological organ (est 1965) of metropolitans Y. Slipy and M. Liubachivsky, have been published in Rome.

Evangelical press. In interwar Galicia the Ukrainian Evangelical Reformed church published *Vira i nauka (1926–30, 1933–9), *Ukraïns'ka reformatsiia (1929–31), and *Siiach (1932–3), and the Ukrainian Evangelical Church of the Augsburg Confession published *Stiah (1932–9), *Novyi svit* (1934) for children, and *Prozry!* (1931–9) in Stanyslaviv. Baptists outside Galicia, including immigrants in North America, were served by the monthly *Pislanets' pravdy (1927–39). The Pentecostal church in Volhynia published the monthlies *Budivnychyi Tserkvy* (1936–9) and *Ievanhel's'kyi holos* (1936–9). In Soviet Ukraine, in the 1920s the Russian-language journal *Baptist Ukrainy* published some articles in Ukrainian. Since 1945 Evangelical Christians in Ukraine have been served primarily by the Russian-language bimonthly *Bratskii vestnik* in Moscow.

In the West the greatest number of Ukrainian Evangelical periodicals have been published in Canada. They include the Presbyterian biweekly *Ranok (1905–20) in Winnipeg and monthlies *Nashe slovo* (1933–5) in Oshawa, Ontario, and *Ievanhel's'ka pravda (1940–79) in Toronto; the Baptist weeklies *Domashnii pryiatel'* (1909–11) and *S'vidok pravdy* (1911–25) in Toronto, the bimonthly *Khrystyians'kyi visnyk* (est 1942) in Winnipeg, and the quarterly *Ukraïns'ka nyva (1947–66) in Saskatoon; the Methodist weekly *Kanadyiets' (1912–20) in Edmonton; the United church's weekly *Kanadiis'kyi ranok (1920–61) in Winnipeg; the Ukrainian Bible Student Association's bimonthly *Zorinnia novoï doby i vistnyk prysutnosty Khrysta* (est 1937) in Winnipeg; the Ukrainian Independent Reformed church's bimonthly *Slovo* (1950–5) in Toronto; the Pentecostal monthly *Ievanhelyst* (1957–71) and quarterly *Ievanhel's'kyi holos* (est 1967) in Toronto; and the Ukrainian Evangelical Alliance of North America's monthly and then quarterly *Ievanhel's'kyi ranok (est 1961) in Toronto. Several other short-lived periodicals have also appeared.

In the United States the first Evangelical organ was the Presbyterian weekly *Soiuz in New York (1908–11) and Pittsburgh (1912–21). The Pentecostal bimonthly *Ievanhel's'kyi palomnyk* (est 1941) has been published in New York, and the former Galician Baptist *Pislanets' pravdy* has been published in Chester, Pennsylvania, and then Chicago since 1947. The Watch Tower and Bible Tract Society in the United States has published *Vartova bashta* and *Probudys'* in Brooklyn for Ukrainian Jehovah's Witnesses. In Argentina the Pentecostal quarterly *Ievanhels'kyi holos* (1958–61) and Baptist quarterly/semiannual *Ievanhels'ka zirka* (est 1953) have appeared. Baptist periodicals published in other Western countries include the quarterly *Dobra novyna* (est 1967) in Australia; the quarterly *Khrystyianyn* and then *Visnyk spasinnia* (est 1951) in Great Britain; and *Dorohu pravdy* (1946–9), *Holos pravdy* (1954–60), and the quarterly *Nove zhyttia* (est 1963) in Germany.

The postwar émigré, non-Christian *Ukrainian Native Faith church has published in Canada the monthlies *Samobutnia Ukraïna* (est 1967) and *Novi skryzhali* (est 1972).

BIBLIOGRAPHY

Krevets'kyi, I. 'Ukraïns'ka katolyts'ka presa: Istorychno-bibliohrafichnyi ohliad v 75-littia ïï isnuvannia,' *Kanadiis'kyi ukraïnets'*, 1929, nos 45–6
Doroshenko, V. 'Ukraïns'ka ievanhel's'ka presa (v rr. 1945–1952 po tsei bik zaliznoï zaslony),' *Kanadiis'kyi ranok*, 1 July 1952
– 'Pokaznyk ukraïns'koï katolyts'koï presy v ZDA,' *Shliakh* 1952, nos 32–3
Vaida, M. 'Ukraïns'ka katolyts'ka presa v ZDA,' *Ameryka*, 25 February 1953

Doroshenko, V. 'Ukraïns'ka katolyts'ka presa v Kanadi v rokakh 1945–62,' *Nasha meta*, 14 July to 5 August 1962

Mokh, O. 'Narysy z istoriï ukraïns'koï katolyts'koï presy,' *Pravda* (Toronto), 1975, nos 1–2

V. Borovsky, I. Korovytsky

Rembalovych, Ivan [Rembalovyč], b 1891, d 21 July 1944 near Brody, Galicia. Army officer. In 1917 he was a delegate to the First, Second, and Third all-Ukrainian military congresses in Kiev. He served as chief of communications in the Zaporozhian Corps (1918–19) and in the First Zaporozhian Rifle Division (1920) of the UNR Army. He participated in the First and Second winter campaigns. He attained the rank of lieutenant colonel in the UNR Army. He joined the Division Galizien in 1943 and was killed in the Battle of Brody.

Remeslo, Vasyl, b 10 February 1907 in Teplivka, Pyriatyn county, Poltava gubernia, d 4 September 1983 in Kiev. Agricultural scientist; full member of the USSR Academy of Sciences from 1974 and of the All-Union Academy of Agricultural Sciences from 1964. He completed study at the Maslivka Institute of Selection and Seed Cultivation (1928). In 1968 he became director of the Myronivka Institute of Wheat Selection and Seed Cultivation. Remeslo developed selection methods that led to the production of various strains of wheat that today are in worldwide use. He is also credited with creating 17 varieties of winter wheat.

Yevhen Remez

Remez, Yevhen, b 17 February 1896 in Mstsislau, Mahiliou gubernia, Belarus, d 30 August 1975 in Kiev. Mathematician; corresponding member of the AN URSR (now ANU) from 1939. A graduate of the Kiev Institute of People's Education (1924), he taught at various institutions in Kiev, including the pedagogical institute (1933–55) and university (1935–8), and worked at the ANU Institute of Mathematics (1935–75). Remez made basic contributions to the constructive theory of functions and to approximation analysis. He developed a new numerical method, known as the Remez algorithm, of constructing with a prescribed degree of exactness a polynomial of the best Chebychev approximation for a given continuous function. Later, he constructed a similar algorithm for the rational approximation of a continuous function defined on a request. He also extended the characterization theory of Chebychev and Markov and used it to obtain approximate solutions of differential equations.

Renaissance. A new age in European civilization that started in Italy in the 14th century and culminated in the 16th century. It was marked by the revival of learning, art, and architecture and by the upsurge of *humanism, *philosophy, vernacular literature, and *printing.

In the visual arts and architecture the term Renaissance refers to the style that replaced the prevailing *Gothic style of the Middle Ages. Based on a deliberate return to the art and architecture of classical antiquity, it reached Ukraine in the early 16th century and was popular there until the mid-17th century. It became most widespread in Galicia (particularly in Lviv), where it was introduced by Italian and Swiss architects employed by local magnates, burghers, and church brotherhoods. Its development paralleled that of *cities and towns and their expanding political and economic roles.

Renaissance synagogue in Brody (early 17th century)

Some of the earliest examples of the Renaissance style in Ukraine are the Epiphany Church in Ostrih (rebuilt in 1521) and the synagogue in Sataniv (1532). In secular architecture its influences can be seen in the application of classical systems of articulation of walls and in the harmonious proportions of the rebuilt castles in Kamianets-Podilskyi (1541–4), Stare Selo and Olesko in Lviv oblast, and Berezhany (1554) in Ternopil oblast.

The city of Lviv was reconstructed in the Renaissance style after the fire of 1527. The most interesting examples of surviving Renaissance architecture there are three private residences in Rynok Square: the Hepner building (1540), at no. 28; the *Black Building (1577), at no. 4; and the *Korniakt building (1580), at no 6. Rusticated stones and pilasters were used in the Black Building; the Korniakt building is a smooth masonry construction with pedimented windows in the upper floors and the only inner-courtyard arcaded loggia in Ukraine. Other examples of Renaissance architecture in Lviv are the buildings of the *Dormition Church; the Kampian family chapel, completed in 1619 by P. Romanus; the Boim family chapel (1609–11), which has an elaborately carved entablature and a façade profusely decorated with carved ornaments and relief figures that hide the underlying classical structure; and the Roman Catholic Bernardine Church (1600–30), built by Romanus and A. Prykhylny, which incorporates baroque elements and is thus an example of a transitional building.

The Renaissance had less impact on Ukrainian architecture outside Galicia, because there was little new masonry construction at the time. As old churches were rebuilt,

Renaissance castle in Stare Selo near Lviv (16th to mid-17th century)

some elements of the late Renaissance were used, but most of these buildings have not survived or were later altered. St Elijah's Church (1653) in Subotiv, funded by Hetman B. Khmelnytsky, combined the northern Renaissance style with baroque elements.

During the Renaissance sculpture flourished. In Lviv it may be seen in the ornamental and relief carvings of the Black Building, the Korniakt residence, and the Korniakt and Boim chapels. Their portals and windows are framed with columns and pilasters with elaborately carved plant motifs. The frieze on the exterior walls of the Dormition Church has a variety of carved rosettes, sunflowers, grapevines, and figures in the metopes, as does the Kampian Chapel. The façade of the Boim Chapel is covered with relief carvings executed by a group of craftsmen headed by H. Scholtz; it included J. Pfister, later one of the best-known sculptors in Lviv.

Iconostases were constructed with classical orders and carved plant motifs. The oldest surviving iconostasis, from the Dormition Church (1630) in Lviv, is now in the church in Velyki Hrybovychi, Nesterov raion, Lviv oblast. The iconostasis of the Church of Good Friday in Lviv is another beautiful example of intricate late Renaissance carving in Ukraine.

Memorial tombs were decorated with sculptures of figures in armor reclining or semireclining in traditional Renaissance architectural settings similar to those found in northern Italian tombs. Examples include the tombs of Prince K. Ostrozky (1579), at the Kievan Cave Monastery; of M. Herburt, in the Roman Catholic cathedral in Lviv, by the Nuremberg master P. Lackenwolf; of O. Lahodovsky (1573), in Univ; of the Syniavsky family (ca 1573–1642), in Berezhany, by J. Pfister; and of K. Ramultova, in Drohobych.

In book decoration geometric designs gave way to three-dimensional plant motifs. The *Peresopnytsia Gospel (1555–61) echoes some aspects of Italian Renaissance ornamentation. The engravings in the Lviv *Apostol* (1574), particularly the rendering of the Apostle Luke, are a combination of German Renaissance traditions and Ukrainian-Byzantine influences. In the early 17th century the center of engraving shifted from the presses in Lviv and Ostrih to the *Kievan Cave Monastery Press. It became famous not only for its religious publications but also for its illustrations of historical themes, portraits, and town plans. The gradual shift from Byzantine iconography and stylization to more realistic representation may be seen in

Renaissance portrait of Kostiantyn Korniakt, Jr (17th century)

the wood engravings in K. Sakovych's book of verses (1622), published on the occasion of the death of Hetman P. Sahaidachny.

In painting changes came about gradually. Icons lost some of their flatness and stylization and were painted with more realistic rendering of facial features and with localized landscapes (eg, the icon *Transfiguration* from Yabluniv, Kosiv raion, Ivano-Frankivske oblast). In the icon *Kiss of Judas* from the 'Passion of Christ' cycle in the Dormition Church in Lviv, the features of the apostles are individualized, and the figures are more three-dimensional. Portraits of patrons appeared alongside depictions of religious personages (eg, that of P. Mohyla in the fresco *Supplication* [1644–6] in the Transfiguration Church in the Berestove district of Kiev). Portraits of patrons and their family members without figures of saints came into existence with the rise of rich burghers. In the portrait of the Pochaiv patron A. Hoiska (ca 1597) the previous static representation and flattened rendering of the figure have given way to a more softly modeled head. Memorial portraits of patrons were usually done on dark backgrounds, and attention was concentrated on the modeling of faces (eg, the portraits of J. Herburt [1578] and K. Korniakt [1603]). Secular portraits of the ruling aristocracy and of the rich also gained in popularity. The portraits of K. Zbarazky and K. and O. Korniakt (early 17th century) are full-length formal depictions.

The Renaissance style left its imprint on the furniture of the time and in the decorative arts, particularly in the more realistic rendering of plant motifs. The Easter shroud (1655) from the Kievan Cave Monastery, with its embroidered silver and gold floral borders, is a fine example of the decorative art of the period.

BIBLIOGRAPHY
Miliaieva, L.; Lohvyn, H. *Ukraïns'ke mystetstvo XIV–pershoï polovyny XVII st.* (Kiev 1963)

D. Zelska-Darewych

Reni. VIII-9. A city (1989 pop 23,900) on the Danube River and a raion center in Odessa oblast. Reni is first mentioned in historical documents in 1548, as part of the Moldavian principality. In 1621 it was annexed by Turkey and renamed Tomarovo. It was captured twice by Russia (1769, 1790) and then assigned to Russia by the Treaty of Bucharest (1812). After handing it over to Moldavia in 1856, Russia recaptured it in 1877–8. From 1918 to 1940 the city was under Rumania. Reni is a river port. Most of its inhabitants are occupied in the transportation industry. It also has some fish-processing and meat-processing plants.

Renovationist church (Russian: *obnovlentsy*). The popular name of a reform movement in the Russian Orthodox church during the 1920s and 1930s. The church emerged in Russia when reform-minded Russian Orthodox clerics proclaimed a dissident 'Living church' in 1922 and established a Renovationist (Synodal) church the following year. The church hoped to take over the jurisdiction of the Patriarchal Russian Orthodox church, which faced a major crisis following the arrest of its spiritual head, Tikhon, in 1922. It rejected traditional episcopal authority and was especially critical of the monastic clergy. It had the backing of the Soviet authorities, who saw it as a means of countering the resistance of the Patriarchal church to the fledgling regime. The Renovationist church started losing political support after 1927, when the Patriarchal church reached an understanding with the government; it was devastated by the antireligion campaign of 1929–41 in the USSR and liquidated in 1943. The Renovationist church actively sought to establish itself in Ukraine during the 1920s (see *Living church), with mixed results.

Repatriation. The act of returning people or restoring cultural objects or documents to their country of origin. People returning to their country of origin usually are those who have resided either temporarily or permanently in other countries (commonly in situations involving armed conflicts); they may be repatriated either by their own free will or forcibly by a political power.

In 1921 Poland broke off relations with the Directory of the Ukrainian National Republic and concluded the Peace Treaty of *Riga with the Ukrainian SSR and the Russian SFSR. One of the provisions of the preliminary agreement in 1920, which later became part of the treaty, involved the repatriation of the former soldiers of the Army of the UNR (then interned in camps in Poland) to the Ukrainian SSR. It was to be a voluntary repatriation, and most internees resisted it. Soviet representatives undertook intensive agitation in the camps to induce the internees to return home by promising them a pardon and the return of citizenship rights. A number of them did return.

The greatest repatriation of Ukrainians took place in the period immediately following the Second *World War. It was part of a larger effort by the victorious Allies to return home the estimated 5.6 to 8.4 million Eastern Europeans who were displaced during the Nazi occupation or other phases of the war. Most found themselves in the various countries of central, northern, and western Europe, with the largest numbers in Germany and Austria. The total number included approximately 2.8 million persons taken by the Nazis from their homes as forced laborers to work in the German war industry (the so-called *Ostarbeiter, or Eastern workers). The majority of them (2.2 million) were from Ukraine. Another category were the POWs, including former soldiers of the Red Army who were captured by the Germans. Altogether they numbered around three million people. Other categories were survivors of the German concentration camps (totaling over 200,000) and refugees who fled their homes before the westward advance of the Red Army. The *displaced persons represented a variety of Eastern European nationalities.

The main solution to the problem of displaced people offered by the Allies was repatriation. As the armies of the Allies advanced, they repatriated large numbers of persons on their conquered territories. In 1943 the Allies established the United Nations Relief and Rehabilitation Administration (UNRRA); it began its work in 1944. Its function was the repatriation of all persons displaced by the war. UNRRA worked under the direction of the American-controlled Supreme Headquarters of the Allied Expeditionary Force, which provided an official definition of a displaced person (DP). The legal basis for Eastern European repatriation was established in February 1945 at the *Yalta Conference, when the Western Allies signed an agreement with the Soviet Union which guaranteed repatriation of all Soviet nationals. The term was understood, particularly by the Soviets, to mean (if necessary) forcible repatriation.

By mid-1945 the Soviets had repatriated approx three million people from their areas of occupation. By the fall

Ukrainians at the Regensburg DP camp protesting Allied repatriation actions (1946)

of 1945 an additional 2.2 (or more) million persons had been transferred to areas of Soviet control, when the Western Allies pulled back from German territory previously designated as part of the Soviet zone. Most of the people concerned had to be moved by force. Of the total number of approximately 5.2 million repatriates, around 3 million were former military personnel and 2 million were civilians. The civilians included many of the Ukrainians who had been brought to Germany and Austria by the Nazis as conscript laborers.

The zeal with which the Soviet authorities pursued repatriation may be explained in several ways. One of the foremost reasons was a desire to punish those who had neglected their duty to the 'Soviet homeland' and assisted the Nazis, whether as actual collaborators, POWs, or forced laborers. That motivation involved not only retribution but also the upholding of the principle of mandatory service to the state on the part of Soviet citizens. The need for workers in the process of postwar reconstruction was also a factor. Finally, the Soviet authorities probably feared that their international reputation would be severely damaged by the revelations concerning life under the Soviet regime that would likely surface if a large number of their ex-nationals were living in the West, particularly Ukrainians; the Soviet authorities were especially vigilant in pursuing their repatriation. The apprehensions of refugees facing the prospect of returning to the Soviet Union were based in part on a distaste or even open disdain for the regime and in large measure on the fear of retribution by the Soviet authorities for crimes real or imagined. The worst fears of many repatriates were later realized: approx 300,000 of them were executed upon their return to their homeland, and about 2.5 million were sentenced to labor camps for periods ranging from 3 to 25 years (a 10-year term being the most common). About half of those sentenced to labor camps did not survive their imprisonment. The attitude of the Allied powers in the entire affair was based on several things: ignorance, a desire not to antagonize the Soviet Union (especially at a time when not all Allied POWs in Soviet-controlled territories had been repatriated), and a determination to clear up the refugee situation (which involved substantial expense and major logistical problems) as quickly as possible.

The repatriation process faced one of its major difficulties with the refusal of refugees in the zones occupied by the Western Allies to be returned. Initially the Soviets insisted on their mandatory repatriation in accord with the Yalta Agreement without regard to the wishes of the DPs involved. The Allies did not immediately question that interpretation of the agreement, and assisted the Soviets in the process. The Soviets established a number of repatriation mission teams in the zones occupied by the Allies. Those units engaged both in making appeals to the refugees to persuade them to go home and in organizing convoys to remove refugees from their camps, often by trickery and force. Few refugees had doubts about the treatment they would receive, as numerous incidents testify. Many committed suicide rather than leave. Some jumped off transport trucks or trains either in a bid to escape or in order to commit suicide. Incidents of violence occurred, as Soviet repatriation agents were attacked, or as designated returnees rioted. The most violent incidents took place in the camps of Hersfeld, Kempten, Hanau, Füssen, and Passau.

As the Americans became increasingly aware of the na-

ture of Soviet repatriation and the reasons for the refugees' resistance, they stopped assisting the Soviets in their efforts. A number of limitations on who should be repatriated were established. They specified that 'Soviet citizens' meant only those who were Soviet nationals before the outbreak of the war, and thus effectively excluded Ukrainians, Poles, and Balts from the regions annexed by the Soviet Union in 1939 or later. By the fall of 1945 most American generals were objecting to the use of force in repatriation, and in December 1945, soon after Gen D. Eisenhower was appointed the army chief of staff, the Americans exempted the remaining displaced Soviet civilians from forced repatriation altogether. The Americans also accepted the McNarney-Clark directive, which narrowly specified which former military personnel could be repatriated by force. The British remained more willing than the Americans to assist the Soviets with their repatriation efforts even though their top-level administrators and military were aware of the consequences of such actions. But half a year later they too refused to allow repatriation by force. Isolated incidents of forced repatriation by the Soviets still continued, however, until the middle of 1947, and, in spite of the US State Department's declaration in that year that the Yalta Agreement was no longer in effect, the last Soviet repatriation team did not leave Western Europe until March 1949.

It has been estimated that in addition to the roughly two million Ukrainians who had been repatriated to the Soviet Union by mid-1945, 40,000 to 60,000 more refugees were repatriated after that. By the end of 1947, when UNRRA ceased its operation, and the International Refugee Organization came into existence with the mandate of resettling rather than repatriating refugees, there were close to one million refugees of all nationalities left in Western Europe (including approx 250,000 Ukrainians).

Ukrainian-Canadian and Ukrainian-American organizations played a role in the effort to stop forcible repatriation of the refugees. Both the Ukrainian Canadian Committee (now Congress) and the Ukrainian American Congress Committee conducted advocacy campaigns, and the London-based *Ukrainian Canadian Servicemen's Association in England intervened on behalf of the Ukrainians stranded in Italy. Later those associations established relief organizations which provided substantial help for the resettlement of Ukrainian DPs to the United States, Canada, England, and Australia.

The term repatriation is also sometimes applied to the transfer of populations that took place in Western Ukraine at the end of the Second World War and in the immediate postwar period as a result of border adjustments between Poland and the Soviet Union. The settlement included provisions for a transfer of populations, and between 1944 and 1947 about one million Poles, including Jews and Ukrainians who presented themselves as Poles, were moved across the new border to Poland. In return about 520,000 Ukrainians were transferred, mostly by force, by the Soviet-directed Polish army from the Polish side of the border to the Ukrainian SSR. The process involved some violent incidents, most notably in the village of Zavadka Morokhivska, Sianik county, in 1946. Another postwar population transfer occurred in the 1950s, when 6,000 to 8,000 Ukrainians from the Prešov region of Czechoslovakia, who had been moved to the Ukrainian SSR immediately after the war, were allowed to return to Czechoslovakia.

BIBLIOGRAPHY
Dushnyck, W.; Gibbons, W.J. *Refugees Are People: The Plight of Europe's Displaced Persons* (New York 1947)
Dushnyck, W. *Death and Devastation on the Curzon Line: The Story of the Deportations from Ukraine* (New York 1948)
Proudfoot, M.J. *European Refugees, 1939–52: A Study in Forced Population Movement* (London 1956)
Epstein, J. *Operation Keelhaul: The Story of Forced Repatriation from 1944 to the Present* (Old Greenwich, Conn 1973)
Tolstoy, N. *Victims of Yalta* (London 1978)
Elliott, M.R. *Pawns of Yalta: Soviet Refugees and America's Role in Their Repatriation* (Urbana 1982)
Maruniak, V. *Ukraïns'ka emigratsiia v Nimechchyni i Avstriï po druhii svitovii viini* (Munich 1985)

W. Isajiw

Repen, Mykola, b 18 December 1884 in Hryniv, Bibrka county, Galicia, d ? Editor and political activist. An active member of the *Ukrainian Radical party and an organizer of Sich societies, he emigrated to the United States in 1914. While working in steel mills he used his free time to set up a branch of the Ukrainian Fraternal Association and establish a drama group in Cleveland. He edited *Ukraïns'ka hazeta* in New York (1919), *Narodne slovo* in Pittsburgh (1920–1), *Lys Mykyta* in New York (1921–2), and *Narodna volia* in Scranton (1923–4). In 1925 he returned to Hryniv and again became active in the Radical party.

Ilia Repin: *The Zaporozhian Cossacks Write a Letter to the Turkish Sultan* (oil, 1880–91)

Repin, Ilia, b 5 August 1844 in Chuhuiv, Zmiiv county, Kharkiv gubernia, d 29 September 1930 in Kuokkala, Finland. Painter; full member of the St Petersburg Academy of Arts from 1893. He studied in St Petersburg under I. Kramskoi at the Drawing School of the Society for the Support of Artists (1863–4) and then at the Academy of Arts (1864–71), which granted him a scholarship to study in Italy and France (1873–6). He joined the *Peredvizhniki society in 1878 and the Mir Iskusstva group in 1890. For many years he lived in St Petersburg and served as a professor (1894–1907) at and the rector (1898–9) of the Academy of Arts, where his students included the Ukrainian painters M. Pymonenko, O. Murashko, F. Krasytsky, and S. Prokhorov. From 1900 Repin lived in Kuokkala. A good part of his work consists of genre paintings. Some of the works show his attachment to Ukraine, its people, and its history, among them the famous painting *The Zaporozhian Cossacks Write a Letter to the Turkish Sultan* (1880–91), *Evening Party* (1881), *Haidamakas* (1898–1917), *Cossack in the Steppe, Black Sea Freebooters* (1908), and *Hopak* (1926–30,

unfinished). He painted many portraits of Russian and Ukrainian cultural figures, including M. Murashko (1877), A. Kuindzhi (1877), M. Kostomarov (1880, 1886), I. Kramskoi (1882), V. Tarnovsky (1880), S. Tarnovska (1880), T. Shevchenko (1888), and D. Bahalii (1906); did illustrations for editions of N. Gogol's *Taras Bul'ba* (1872) and *Sorochinskaia iarmarka* (Sorochyntsi Fair, 1882) and for his friend D. Yavornytsky's *Zaporozh'e v ostatkakh stariny i predaniiakh naroda* (The Zaporizhia in the Remnants of Antiquity and the Legends of the People, 1888); submitted four drawings in the competition for the design of Shevchenko's monument in Kiev (1910–14); and sketched many Ukrainian landscapes and inhabitants. Although Repin was a realist, his rich colors and restless lines often produce an almost expressionistic effect. Some of his paintings show the influence of impressionism and symbolism.

BIBLIOGRAPHY
Butnik-Siverskii, B. (ed). *Repin i Ukraina: Pis'ma deiatelei ukrainskoi kul'tury i iskusstva k Repinu, 1896–1927* (Kiev 1962)
Bielichko, Iu. *Ukraïna v tvorchosti I. Iu. Riepina* (Kiev 1963)
Grabar, I. *Repin*, 2nd rev edn, 2 vols (Moscow 1963–4)
Parker, F.; Parker, S. *Russia on Canvas: Ilya Repin* (University Park–London 1980)
Sternin, G.; et al. *Ilya Repin: Painting, Graphic Arts* (Leningrad 1985)
Kridl Valkenier, E. *Ilya Repin and the World of Russian Art* (New York 1990)

S. Hordynsky

Repnin, Nikolai (né Volkonsky), b 1778, d 18 January 1845 in Yahotyn, Pyriatyn county, Poltava gubernia. Political and military leader in the Russian Empire; descendant of the Chernihiv line of the Riurykide dynasty; husband of K. Rozumovsky's granddaughter. During the Napoleonic occupation he was governor-general of Saxony (1813–14). Later he served as governor-general of Little Russia, which consisted of Poltava and Chernihiv gubernias, in Left-Bank Ukraine (1816–34), and was a member of the State Council. He sympathized with Ukrainian autonomists, kept in close contact with I. *Kotliarevsky and the Poltava circle, and defended Ukrainian interests before the Russian government. He drew up a plan for the reinstatement of the Cossack regimental system. Repnin assisted D. Bantysh-Kamensky in writing *Istoriia Maloi Rossii ...* (A History of Little Russia ..., 4 vols, 1822), and it has been speculated that he was the author of the anonymous historical exposition *Istoriia Rusov*. His political leanings (his brother was the Decembrist S. Volkonsky) and his wide popularity in Ukraine made Tsar Nicholas I suspicious, particularly in the light of the 1830–1 Polish uprisings and the 1832 conspiracy of Georgian autonomists. Repnin was removed from the governor-generalship, and left the empire. In 1842 he returned to live out his days on his estate in Yahotyn, where he was visited by T. *Shevchenko in 1843–4. He was buried in the Hustynia Trinity Monastery near Pryluka.

O. Ohloblyn

Repnina, Varvara, b 31 July 1808 in Moscow, d 9 December 1891 in Moscow. Russian princess and writer; daughter of N. *Repnin. While growing up in Poltava, she knew N. Gogol, and later she wrote memoirs of him. In the 1840s she lived on her father's estate in Yahotyn, in Poltava gubernia. She fell in love with T. Shevchenko, who was a guest there in 1843–4. Shevchenko dedicated his Russian poem 'Trizna' (The Funeral Feast) to her and painted two portraits of her. Repnina promoted Shevchenko's artistic career, and during his exile she corresponded with him (until forbidden to do so in 1850) and tried to get the authorities to ease his situation. From the early 1850s she lived in Moscow. She depicted her relationship with Shevchenko in an early unfinished novel, 'Devochka' (A Girl), in which he is a central figure; excerpts of it were published in 1916. Her memoirs and an article about him appeared in *Russkii arkhiv*. M. Vozniak's book about Shevchenko and Repnina appeared in Lviv in 1925.

Repnin-Fomin, Flor [Rjepnin-Fomin], b 1778 in Cherkassk-na-Donu, Don region, d 1857. Painter. After graduating from the St Petersburg Academy of Arts (1802) he taught at the Katerynoslav Gymnasium (1804–15) and Kharkiv University (1815–38). His work consists of thematic paintings and portraits, including *Eviction from the Temple* (1800), *The Death of Socrates* (1802), *The Escape of the Holy Family to Egypt* (1802), and *The Death of Hostomysl* (1804).

Repriev, Oleksandr [Reprjev] (Reprev, Aleksandr), b 26 August 1853 near Suzdal, Vladimir gubernia, Russia, d 21 June 1930. Pathologist; one of the founders of endocrinology in Ukraine. A graduate of the Medico-Surgical Academy in St Petersburg (1878), he taught at Tomsk (1891–5) and Kharkiv (1895–1924) universities and at the same time worked at the Kharkiv Veterinary Institute and the Higher Courses for Women. His publications deal with metabolism during pregnancy, internal secretion glands, and problems of radiobiology and oncology. He wrote *Osnovy obshchei i eksperimental'noi patologii* (Foundations of General and Experimental Pathology, 1911).

Repta, Vasyl (monastic name: Volodymyr), b 1841 in Banyliv on the Cheremosh, Bukovyna, d January 1926 in Chernivtsi. Orthodox metropolitan and pedagogue. He graduated from the theological institute in Chernivtsi and then continued his studies in Vienna, Munich, Bonn, and Zurich before becoming a professor of theology at Chernivtsi University (from 1875). He was consecrated bishop of Rădăuţi (1898–1902) and then metropolitan of Bukovyna (1902–25). Although he initially considered himself a Ukrainian (having organized the first Shevchenko memorial festival in Chernivtsi in 1864), from the 1870s he supported the Rumanianization of the Bukovynian metropolitanate and opposed granting Ukrainians equal religious rights in Bukovyna. In November 1918, with his approval, the Rumanian authorities dismissed the Ukrainian members of the consistory and closed down the two academic chairs in the theological faculty of Chernivtsi University where instruction was provided in Ukrainian.

Republyka (Republic). An official daily of the Western Ukrainian National Republic, published in Stanyslaviv (now Ivano-Frankivske) from February to May 1919 (a total of 94 issues). It was edited by I. Krevetsky with the assistance of V. Doroshenko, M. Strutynsky, and M. Yevshan. Members of the editorial board included K. Levytsky, M. Hrushevsky, S. Vytvytsky, and L. Myshuha.

Research Institute of Volyn (Instytut doslidiv Volyni). An émigré institution established in Winnipeg in 1951 to conduct and publish research on the history and culture of Volhynia. Its directors have been Yu. Mulyk-Lutsyk (1951–2, 1954–6), A. Shumovsky (1952–4), M. Borovsky (1956–68), and S. Radchuk (since 1969). Metropolitan N. Abramovych was an honorary president, and Metropolitan I. Ohiienko was an honorary head of its council. In 1961 the institute had 17 full scholarly members, 20 scholarly members, and 46 corresponding members, most of them in North America. By 1989 the institute had published 15 volumes of *Litopys Volyni* (Chronicle of Volhynia, starting in 1953) and 60 books and brochures, including I. Levkovych's survey history of Volhynia to 1914 (1953); S. Kylymnyk's monograph on Ukrainian calendric folk customs (5 vols, 1955–63); Metropolitan Ohiienko's books on the Pochaiv Monastery (1961), the life of A. Matsiievych (1964), and Ukrainian pre-Christian beliefs (1965) and his dictionary of T. Shevchenko's language (1961); P. Shumovsky's book on the history of Ostrih (1964); Ye. Pasternak's history of the Kholm region and Podlachia (1968); O. Tsynkalovsky's geographic dictionary of Volhynia and Volhynian Polisia (2 vols, 1984, 1986); and the memoirs of L. Bykovsky, U. Samchuk, M. Hutsuliak, T. Borovets, M. Podvorniak, O. Semmo, H. Stetsiuk, and M. Dubylko. The institute's publications have been financed by branches of the *Society of Volyn in Winnipeg, Toronto, New York, Cleveland, Germany, and England.

Research Society for Ukrainian Terminology (Naukovo-doslidne tovarystvo ukrainskoi terminolohii). An institution established in New York City in 1971. The society has published a new Ukrainian orthographic dictionary (ed J.B. Rudnyckyj and K. Tserkevych, 1979), a Ukrainian language reference book (ed K. Tserkevych and V. Pavlovsky, 1982), and the memoirs of Yu. Movchan (2 vols, 1982, 1984), I. Desiak (1984), and O. Kaniuka (1984). It has also republished I. Ohiienko's dictionary of words not used in literary Ukrainian (1973), P. Derkach's short dictionary of Ukrainian synonyms (ed V. Volkov, N. Pazuniak, and K. Tserkevych, 1975), B. Antonenko-Davydovych's *Iak my hovorymo (i iak treba hovoryty)* (How We Speak [and How We Should Speak], 1980), D. Humenna's novel *Dity chumats'koho shliakhu* (Children of the Milky Way, 1983), and the Russian-Ukrainian legal dictionary edited by A. Krymsky (rev edn, ed K. Tserkevych and V. Pavlovsky, 1984).

Reservoir. See Water reservoir.

Resettlement. Relocation to a new place of residence either in an organized manner or by individual families. Resettlement means the same thing as *migration but is an older term, widely used in the late 19th and early 20th centuries to refer to the agrarian mass emigration from Russian-ruled Ukraine to the east, particularly the colonization of *Siberia, *Kazakhstan, and the *Far East, and from Western Ukraine under Austria-Hungary to the *United States, *Canada, *Brazil, and *Argentina.

During collectivization (1929–30) the Soviet regime forcibly deported and resettled hundreds of thousands of so-called *kulaks from Ukraine to the northern regions of Russia and the Urals. In the 1940s, following the occupation of Western Ukraine by the Soviet authorities, large-scale deportations of Ukrainians to remote regions of Russia and Siberia also took place. After the Second World War nearly 500,000 Ukrainian inhabitants of the *Sian, *Kholm, and *Lemko regions were forcibly resettled in western and northern Poland or in Soviet Ukraine, and *Poles living in Ukraine were resettled in Poland (see *Operation Wisła). In the 1950s, voluntary resettlement to the Asian regions of the USSR was encouraged in connection with the opening up of the so-called virgin lands. Settlers received financial assistance for the move. Resettlement for the purpose of working in one or another area of industry or construction was called *organized recruitment of workers. In the 1950s and 1960s organized recruitment was responsible for the relocation of a significant portion of the labor force, but from the 1970s its importance decreased. (See also *Migrant workers.)

BIBLIOGRAPHY
Buhai, M. 'Deportatsiï naselennia z Ukraïny v 30–50-ti roky,' *UIZh*, 1990, nos 10–11
Trukhan, M. *Ukraïntsi v Pol'shchi pislia druhoï svitovoï viiny, 1944–1984* (New York, Paris, Sydney, and Toronto 1990)

Reshetar, John [Rešetar], b 14 July 1924 in Minneapolis. Political scientist. He graduated from Harvard University (1946; PH D, 1950). He taught at Princeton, Harvard, and the University of Pennsylvania before joining the faculty of the University of Washington in Seattle in 1957. A specialist in Ukrainian and Soviet affairs, he has written *The Ukrainian Revolution, 1917–1920: A Study in Nationalism* (1952), *A Concise History of the Communist Party of the Soviet Union* (1960), and *The Soviet Polity: Government and Politics in the Soviet Union* (1971).

Reshetylivka [Rešetylivka]. IV-15. A town smt (1986 pop 8,800) on the Hovtva River and a raion center in Poltava oblast. It was first mentioned in historical documents in 1638. Under the Hetman state it was a company center of Poltava regiment (1648–1775). In 1696 the town was destroyed by the Tatars. In 1709 Peter I signed the *Reshetylivka Articles there. In the 19th century the town belonged to Poltava county in Poltava gubernia and became known for its folk handicrafts. Today its factories specialize in traditional kilims, woven cloths, embroidered shirts, blouses, tablecloths, napkins, and *rushnyky*.

Reshetylivka Articles of 1709. A 14-point petition submitted by Hetman I. *Skoropadsky to Tsar Peter I in Reshetylivka (Poltava region) on 17 July 1709. Its aim was to obtain an elaboration of the rights and freedoms of the Ukrainian Hetmanate that had been outlined in the tsar's manifesto of 1 November 1708, as well as to address certain issues related to contemporary events and circumstances. In reply Peter issued an ukase on 31 July 1709 in Kiev, in which he reiterated his guarantees of Hetmanate autonomy and confirmed in principle the rights and freedoms and military order as set out in articles submitted by previous hetmans, most notably B. *Khmelnytsky. Nevertheless, the provisions of the petition limited Ukraine's autonomy, in that Russian commanders were placed in key posts of the Cossack armies, Russian garrisons in Ukrainian cities were expanded, and Russians assumed control of the collection of taxes. The matter of the petition (not the ukase) was raised once again in 1710, but it was not resolved then or later. Peter I had decided to continue limiting the autonomy of the Hetmanate and did not wish to be restricted by concrete promises or commitments.

Rev Stepan Reshetylo

Reshetylo, Stepan [Rešetylo], b 26 January 1889 in Uhniv, Galicia, d 26 December 1950 in Dawson, Pennsylvania. Basilian priest. He joined the Basilian order in 1905 and was ordained in 1915, and then became master of novices at the Krekhiv Monastery. He was sent to Transcarpathia in 1924, following a reform of the Basilian order there. Together with other monks from Galicia he created the St Josaphat Missionary Society and carried out major educational and missionary activity. In 1929–30 he was hegumen of the Basilian monastery in Warsaw, and in 1931–5, protohegumen for the order in Galicia. He returned to Transcarpathia in 1935 and served as personal secretary to Bishop D. *Niaradi (1938–9). After the Second World War he moved to the United States.

Resistance. See Partisan movement in Ukraine, 1918–22; Polisian Sich; Soviet partisans in Ukraine, 1941–5; and Ukrainian Insurgent Army.

Respublikans'ki visty (Republican News). A weekly newspaper published in Vinnytsia and then Kamianets-Podilskyi in 1919–20. It supported the Directory of the UNR.

Restoration. In architecture and art, the process of bringing a work as close to its original state as possible. It is a craft, like conservation, which demands great skill, awareness of materials, and knowledge of art history. Although restoration has been carried out since antiquity, its theoretical basis was formulated in the 19th century. Restoration includes the preservation of the original, the reconstruction of missing or damaged parts, and the total reconstruction of destroyed objects. Current restorational practice utilizes the scientific discoveries of fields such as chemistry, optics, and radiology.

Much of the restoration funded by the Cossack *starshyna* and hetmans in the 17th and 18th centuries was, in fact, rebuilding (eg, the baroque cupolas of the St Sophia Cathedral in Kiev). Restoration initiated by Metropolitan P. Mohyla ca 1633 was continued under Metropolitan S. Kosov between 1647 and 1657 and was finished in the baroque style under the patronage of Hetman I. Mazepa. The restoration of original frescoes in the 19th century resulted in their being painted over with oils.

In Soviet Ukraine no restoration of churches was done in the 1930s; instead, many churches were destroyed. The State Scientific Research Restoration Workshop established by the Soviet Ukrainian government in 1938 received jurisdiction over paintings, sculpture, and other objects of art. Its branches in Kiev, Kharkiv, Lviv, and Odessa service over 327 museums in Ukraine. The *Ukrainian Society for the Protection of Historical and Cultural Monuments is also involved in restoration, but on an amateur level. Since 1951 restoration of architectural monuments has been under the jurisdiction of the republican restoration institute and workshops of the State Committee for Construction (Derzhbud), which have branches in Kiev, Lviv, Chernihiv, Odessa, and the Crimea. They restored the buildings of the Kievan Cave Monastery, the St Sophia Cathedral, and the Vydubychi Monastery in Kiev as well as the medieval churches in Chernihiv. The castle in Olesko, Lviv oblast, was restored in the 1970s and now houses part of the Lviv Art Gallery's collection of Renaissance and baroque paintings, sculpture, and furniture.

The general state of restoration in Ukraine however, is not good. A material base, equipment, and qualified personnel are lacking. Restoration is taught only at the Kiev State Art Institute, and as a profession it does not have legal status in Ukraine. No enterprise in Ukraine manufactures restoration equipment or necessary materials, and restorers are forced to make do with what is available (including dangerous and toxic substances) in their work. The resulting low technical level of restoration affects the quality of work in general. The situation is further complicated by the fact that many of Ukraine's museums are housed not in specially built structures but in adapted buildings. There objects are often stored without proper temperature and humidity controls and their deterioration is thereby accelerated.

BIBLIOGRAPHY
Svientsits'kyi, I. Konservatsiia i restavratsiia istorychnykh pam'iatok tserkovnoho mystetstva (Lviv 1932)

D. Zelska-Darewych

Retail trade. The sale of goods or commodities in small quantities to the ultimate consumer. During the medieval period retail trade in Ukraine was limited. The peasantry relied on home industry for household necessities, and retail trade was restricted to the towns, where tradesmen and traveling salesmen provided manufactured goods to noble families, monasteries, and members of the emerging merchant class. When the towns in Ukraine grew in the 14th century, retail trade expanded. It was promoted by regularly scheduled *fairs, at which products from the countryside were exchanged for finished goods produced by foreign and local craftsmen. Large fairs were held in the major towns, and small fairs and markets in smaller towns and villages. In the 19th century the number of markets and retail shops in Ukraine increased sharply, from 3,662 to 15,089 shops between 1825 and 1861.

Discriminatory religious and economic policies by foreign governments in Ukraine kept most of the trade in the hands of non-Ukrainians (Poles, Jews, Germans, and Russians). The enserfment of the Ukrainian peasantry restricted its opportunities to engage in trade. After the abolition of serfdom in Russian-ruled Ukraine in 1861, retail trade assumed greater importance in the economic life of the countryside there. In the 30 years following the reform the number of large and medium fairs increased from 351 to 897, with a trade turnover of more than 80 million rubles. Whereas earlier the fairs had been held mostly in towns, in the second half of the 19th century they were mostly vil-

Distribution of retail trade enterprises by sector, 1923–4 to 1930 (percentages)

Year	State		Co-operative		Private	
	Urban	Rural	Urban	Rural	Urban	Rural
1923–4	16.7	3.8	15.1	43.1	68.2	53.1
1925–6	17.5	4.4	31.7	57.7	50.8	37.9
1927–8	11.3	5.9	50.7	72.6	38.0	21.5
1930	15.4	11.6	79.2	87.,0	5.4	1.4

lage fairs. For the first time goods manufactured in towns became widely available in the countryside. In urban centers, stores, shops, and kiosks replaced fairs as the dominant retail outlets. By 1913 Ukraine had 34,000 retail stores and hundreds of thousands of small shops and kiosks. Nevertheless, the spending power of the population remained low compared to that in other European countries and Russian cities such as St Petersburg and Moscow. In 1913, for example, per capita consumer spending in Moscow was 202 rubles, whereas in Ukraine it was 35–37 rubles. In gubernias such as Podilia, Chernihiv, and Volhynia, per capita spending was as low as 15–17 rubles.

The First World War and War Communism, with its policy of forced grain requisition, devastated the Ukrainian economy. With the introduction of the *New Economic Policy in 1921, private retail trade was encouraged, and grew rapidly. Up to a half of the consumer goods manufactured in Soviet factories were distributed by private retailers. Within a few years, however, the Soviet authorities had begun to support co-operative and state retail enterprises and to use both economic and administrative measures to restrict the private retail sector, first in the countryside and then in the towns (see the table).

In the 1930s Soviet Ukrainian retail trade was organized into three sectors, state, co-operative, and collective-farm. Whereas co-operative retail trade remained dominant in the countryside, consumer co-operatives were taken over and centralized by the state retail system. By 1935 consumer co-operatives accounted for only 4.7 percent of retail trade outlets. Until 1957 retail trade was regulated by the USSR Ministry of Internal Trade. Then its functions were assumed by republican ministries. From the 1930s, retail trade, including prices, quantity, and selection of goods, was controlled by the state. Private retail trade was limited to the output of *private plots. From 1987 private trade in other goods, such as clothing and repair services, was permitted, but a private retail network was barely developed. In 1988 total retail trade turnover in Ukraine amounted to 62,442 million rubles, or 16.6 percent of the USSR retail trade turnover. Retail trade in the USSR was characterized by extremely poor service, high levels of corruption, and an inadequate supply and assortment of consumer goods and services.

B. Somchynsky

Revai, Fedir [Revaj], b 1888, d 1945. Transcarpathian political and civic leader; brother of Yu. *Revai. He was a member of the chief executive of the Prosvita society in Uzhhorod and a deputy of the Czechoslovak Social Democratic party to the Provincial Assembly of Subcarpathian Ruthenia (1928–35). In 1937 he was expelled from the party because of his Ukrainian nationalism. He was a copublisher of the paper *Nova svoboda* (1938–9). In January 1939 he was elected president of the *Ukrainian National Alliance, and in March, deputy speaker of the Diet of Carpatho-Ukraine. At the same time he served as director of the Carpatho-Ukrainian state press in Khust. He was persecuted by the Hungarian authorities (1939–44) and then arrested and deported by the Soviet secret police. He perished in a Soviet prison.

Yuliian Revai   Omelian Reviuk

Revai, Yuliian [Revaj, Julijan], b 26 June 1899 in Mircha, Ung komitat, Transcarpathia, d 30 April 1979 in New York. Educator and noted Transcarpathian political leader; brother of F. *Revai. He was a founder and president of the Teachers' Hromada of Subcarpathian Ruthenia, secretary of the Pedagogical Society of Subcarpathian Ruthenia, chief leader of Plast for Transcarpathia, editor of *Uchytel'* (1924–35) and publisher of *Do peremohy* (1935–8), and an executive member of the Prosvita society in Uzhhorod. A member of the Transcarpathian branch of the Czechoslovak Social Democratic party, he was elected to parliament (1935–9) and was one of the authors of the bill granting autonomy to Carpatho-Ukraine. As vice-president of the Central Ruthenian People's Council he was also a founder of the Ukrainian National Alliance and was elected on its slate to the Diet of *Carpatho-Ukraine, where he was appointed minister of communications and public works (October 1938) and minister of health and social welfare (November 1938 to March 1939). With the declaration of an independent Carpatho-Ukrainian state on 15 March 1939, Revai was appointed prime minister and minister of foreign affairs. After fleeing the subsequent Hungarian invasion he sought support in Vienna, Berlin, and Bratislava for ending Hungarian repressions in Carpatho-Ukraine, and aiding Ukrainian refugees. In 1945 he was arrested by the Soviets in Prague but managed to escape to the American zone of Germany, where he served on the executive of the Central Representation of the Ukrainian Emigration in Germany. After emigrating to the United States in 1948, he served as executive director of the Ukrainian Congress Committee of America (1949–57), president of the Self-Reliance Association of American Ukrainians and the Self-Reliance Federal Credit Union, president of the Carpatho-Ukrainian Research Center, and director of the Ukrainian Institute of America. He was one of the founders and an executive member of the World Congress of Free Ukrainians.

Revakovych, Tyt [Revakovyč], b 1846, d 14 October 1919 in Lviv. Judge, civic leader, and founding member of the *Shevchenko Scientific Society in 1873. A councilor of the provincial court in Lviv, he was active in the Prosvita society as its legal adviser, an organizer, and the president of its Lviv county branch (1914–18). He was also president of the St Raphael Galician and Bukovynian Emigrant Aid Society. He published literary studies in *Zapysky NTSh* and contributed articles to the Ukrainian press.

Revenko, Tymofii, b 20 February 1919 in Novorossiisk, Kuban. Orthopedist and traumatologist; member of the Scientific Council of the USSR Academy of Medical Sciences from 1976. A graduate of the Kharkiv Medical Institute (1949), he worked at the Ukrainian Scientific Research Institute of Traumatology and Orthopedics in Kharkiv, directed the Donetske Scientific Research Institute of Traumatology and Orthopedics (from 1957), and was vice-president of the Ukrainian Scientific Society of Traumatologists and Orthopedists (1959). His chief publications deal with problems of trauma prevention, reconstructive operations of the large joints, and new operating methods and instruments.

Reviuk, Omelian [Revjuk, Omeljan] (Revyuk, Emil), b 1887 in Pererisl, Nadvirna county, Galicia, d 21 February 1972 in New York. Civic activist and journalist. After emigrating to Canada (1912) and then the United States he helped found the Federation of Ukrainians in the United States. While working as associate (1920–6) and chief editor (1926–33) of the daily *Svoboda* he served as president of the United Ukrainian Organizations in America (1927–39). In addition to articles on Ukrainian immigration to the United States he wrote a pamphlet, *Ukraine and the Ukrainians* (1920), and edited a collection of materials on the 1930 Pacification campaign titled *Polish Atrocities in Ukraine* (1931).

Reviziia. A periodic population census taken in the Russian Empire to determine who should pay the *poll tax and take part in military service (peasants, townspeople, tradesmen, and others). The *reviziia* was introduced at the beginning of the 18th century, when the *household tax was changed to the poll tax. It also counted as a general census of the majority of the population (*revizki dushi*), including those who did not have to pay taxes (the clergy, discharged soldiers and their families, and so forth) and women (in the sixth *reviziia*). The nobility and government officials were not polled in most of the *revizii*, and the regular army, the navy, and foreigners were polled in none. Some *revizii* registered as much as 95 percent of the population. The Russian Empire conducted 10 *revizii*, in 1719, 1744, 1763, 1782, 1795, 1811, 1815, 1833, 1850, 1857; from 1782 on *revizii* were also conducted in Ukraine (except for Slobidska Ukraine, where they began earlier). Each *reviziia* lasted several years. Information recorded in the census rosters (*revizki kazky*) included marital status, age during the previous and current *revizii*, and any births, deaths, and changes of ownership since the last *reviziia*, as well as nationality (during the 18th century). The *revizii* are a valuable source of data on the number, distribution, and composition of the population of Ukraine. *Revizii* during the Hetmanate have been studied by P. Klymenko.

A. Zhukovsky

Revizorchuk, Antin [Revizorčuk], b ? in Krasnopillia, in the Hutsul region, d ca 1835. Opryshok leader. In the 1820s he deserted from the Austrian army and joined M. *Shtoliuk's band of opryshoks. After Shtoliuk's capture and execution in 1830, Revizorchuk headed the band, which attacked the estates of Polish nobles and usurers in the Hutsul region. He was captured by Austrian troops and executed. Folk legends about him were used by J. *Korzeniowski in his drama *Karpaccy górale* (Carpathian Highlanders, 1843).

Revkom. See Revolutionary committee.

Revna River. A left-bank tributary of the Snov River. It is 81 km long and drains a basin area of 1,660 sq km. The river starts in Brianske oblast and then cuts across the northern tip of Chernihiv oblast. Its width varies from 5–10 m to 20–40 m. The river is fed by snow and groundwater and is used for domestic water supply.

Revoliutsiia i natsional'nosti (Revolution and Nationalities). A monthly Russian-language journal of the Soviet of Nationalities of the USSR Central Executive Committee, published in Moscow in 1930–7. An important source of information on developments in Soviet Ukraine, it succeeded *Zhizn' natsional'nostei* (1921–4).

Revoliutsiine pravo (Revolutionary Law). A law journal of the People's Commissariat of Justice of the Ukrainian SSR, published 10 to 18 times a year in Kharkiv (1931–6) and semimonthly in Kiev (1937–41). A total of 173 issues appeared. It succeeded *Chervone pravo* and the semimonthly *Visnyk radians'koï iustytsiï* (1922–3).

Revolution of 1848–9 in the Habsburg monarchy.
The unsuccessful democratic revolution that encompassed much of Europe in 1848–9, which broke out also in the Habsburg monarchy, including the Ukrainian territories. Inspired by a republican revolution in Paris in February 1848, demonstrations broke out in Vienna in March. By mid-month, under pressure from the people, Emperor Ferdinand I had dismissed his reactionary adviser K. Metternich, authorized the formation of a national guard, and promised to establish a parliament. The news of those revolutionary events reached the Ukrainian territories of Galicia, Bukovyna, and Transcarpathia on the weekend of 18–19 March. Immediately crowds gathered in the squares of Lviv, where Polish democrats circulated a petition calling for civil rights and the abolition of serfdom. In Chernivtsi mobs attacked the unpopular mayor and police commissioner. In the small, largely Magyarized towns of Transcarpathia the population gathered to read and discuss the 12 demands put forward by radical Hungarian activists in Pest. Thus began a period of revolutionary development that did not come to an end until the Hungarian revolutionary army surrendered to Austrian imperial and Russian forces on 13 August 1849.

Prior to the revolution there had been a Ukrainian national revival in Galicia and Transcarpathia, but the movement had been entirely cultural. With the outbreak of the revolution, however, the Ukrainian question became a political question. The first representative Ukrainian political organization was founded in Lviv on 2 May 1848, the *Supreme Ruthenian Council (HRR). It was established as a counterweight to the Galician Poles' National Council (Rada Narodowa) and saw as its chief purpose the defense of the Ukrainian nationality against Polish domination. The Poles attempted to thwart the HRR by establishing the rival, pro-Polish *Ruthenian Congress in late May, but that organization had little influence in Ukrainian society.

The major political goal advocated by Ukrainians during the revolution was the creation of a predominantly Ukrainian crownland within the Habsburg monarchy. The Galicians, in particular the HRR, took the lead. The HRR gathered 200,000 signatures on a petition calling for the division of Galicia into separate Ukrainian and Polish provinces (Eastern Galicia was largely Ukrainian, western Galicia largely Polish). Some Transcarpathian Ukrainians, notably A. *Dobriansky and O. *Dukhnovych, sought to have Transcarpathia joined to Ukrainian Galicia, and petitioned the emperor to that effect in January 1849. In 1848 Bukovyna was still part of Galicia. Rumanian politicians hoped, however, to detach it and eventually unite it with other Rumanian-inhabited territories. The status of Bukovyna was debated in the Austrian Reichstag. The Ukrainian deputies from Bukovyna as well as the HRR sought to keep Bukovyna, or at least Ukrainian-inhabited northern Bukovyna, attached to Ukrainian Galicia. Although the relatively underdeveloped Ukrainian movements in Transcarpathia and Bukovyna were as yet unclear on the point, the Ukrainians of Galicia repeatedly emphasized in their publications that the Ukrainians of the Habsburg monarchy were part of the same distinct Ukrainian nation that could be found in Ukraine in the Russian Empire.

In June 1848, Ukrainians participated in the *Slavic Congress in Prague. Three delegates from the HRR sought to defend Ukrainian interests against Polish pretensions, and also to work out a basis for co-operation with the Poles. No Transcarpathian Ukrainians attended the congress, but the Slovak delegation called for the protection of their national rights in the face of Hungarian chauvinism.

Also in June 1848 the Ukrainians of Galicia and Bukovyna participated in the first parliamentary elections ever held on Ukrainian territory, the elections to the constituent Austrian Reichstag. Altogether 30 Ukrainians were elected (of 383 deputies in total). The Ukrainians of Galicia organized a Ukrainian National Guard (fall of 1848) as well as the volunteer *Ruthenian Battalion of Mountain Riflemen (winter of 1849) to combat Hungarian insurgents. Throughout the revolution the vast majority of Ukrainians remained loyal to the emperor.

The revolution accelerated Ukrainian cultural development. The first Ukrainian-language newspaper, *Zoria halytska*, began to appear in Lviv on 15 May 1848, and several more Ukrainian periodicals were founded within a year. In October 1848 Lviv hosted a *Congress of Ruthenian Scholars attended by over a hundred delegates. The congress formally established the *Halytsko-Ruska Matytsia, a Ukrainian literary and educational society that had existed informally for several months.

The Ukrainian movement made rapid progress during the revolution because the revolution emancipated and politicized the peasantry, who constituted the vast majority of the Ukrainian nation. As early as 22 April 1848, earlier than anywhere else in Austria, the governor of Galicia, F. Stadion, abolished serfdom. Even though Bukovyna was still administratively part of Galicia, the early abolition of serfdom did not apply to it. That unfavorable separate treatment provoked unrest among the Bukovynian peasantry which continued even after serfdom was abolished there on 9 August 1848 (retroactive to 1 July). The abolition of serfdom still left many questions of vital interest to the peasantry unresolved (notably, the question of compensation to landlords for the abolition of compulsory labor and other feudal rents and the status of the traditional rights of peasant communities to forests and pastures); the peasantry therefore took an active interest in politics during the revolution. In the elections to the Austrian Reichstag in June 1848, Ukrainian peasants tended to elect fellow peasants to represent their interests. Sixteen of the 25 Ukrainian deputies from Galicia were peasants, as were all 5 from Bukovyna. One of the Bukovynian deputies was L. *Kobylytsia, who had led a peasant uprising in the mid-1840s. After the Reichstag was temporarily dispersed in October 1848, Kobylytsia returned to his village and organized an armed rebellion. In Transcarpathia serfdom was largely abolished by the Hungarian revolutionary government on 18 March 1848. In 1848-9 Ukrainian peasants refused to perform labor on seignorial estates and seized much property disputed between landlords and peasants. In the summer of 1849 the Western Ukrainian countryside was placed under military occupation so that order would be restored.

The end of the revolutionary period, May–September 1849, saw the appearance of Russian troops in Western Ukraine, brought in to subdue the Hungarian insurgent army. The Russians passed through Bukovyna on their way in and through Bukovyna and Galicia on their way out. They stayed longest in Transcarpathia, where Dobriansky was assigned to them as a liaison. The presence of the Russian military in Transcarpathia in 1849 is considered an important moment in the genesis of Russophilism in the region.

The revolution had been defeated by the fall of 1849, and many of the achievements of the revolutionary years were undone. The Austrian government dissolved the Reichstag in March 1849, the HRR was dissolved in 1851, and the Ukrainian periodical press declined through the 1850s until it almost disappeared. The peasants remained emancipated, but on terms much less favorable than they had hoped for. The rebirth of constitutional government in the 1860s restored some of the gains of 1848 in Galicia and Bukovyna, including a Ukrainian periodical press and Ukrainian representation in a parliament.

BIBLIOGRAPHY
Vozniak, M. Iak probudylosia ukraïns'ke narodnie zhyttia v Halychyni za Avstriï (Lviv 1924)
Danylak, M. Halyts'ki, bukovyns'ki, zakarpats'ki ukraïntsi v revoliutsiï 1848–1849 rokiv (Bratislava 1972)
Wagner, R. Die Revolutionsjahre 1848/49 im Königreich Galizien-Lodomerien (einschliesslich Bukowina): Dokumente aus österreichischer Zeit (Munich 1983)
Kozik, J. The Ukrainian National Movement in Galicia: 1815–1849 (Edmonton 1986)

J.-P. Himka

Revolution of 1905. A period of revolutionary unrest and radical reform in the Russian Empire in 1905–7. The revolution broke out on 22 January 1905, when the tsarist authorities opened fire on a peaceful demonstration of workers in St Petersburg. During the next few weeks workers throughout the empire went on strike, including those in the Ukrainian cities of Katerynoslav, Kharkiv, Kiev, Mykolaiv, and Odessa. By mid-April some 810,000 workers had gone on strike in the empire, 170,000 of them in Ukraine. The strike movement reached its peak in the fall of 1905 and continued, with declining intensity, into 1907. Strikes in Kharkiv and elsewhere escalated into armed confrontations between workers and representatives of the state. In the fall of 1905, workers' councils or soviets (radas) began to appear in Katerynoslav, Kiev, Luhanske, Mariiupil, Mykolaiv, Odessa, Oleksandrivske, Yuzivka, and other Ukrainian cities.

The revolution spread to the military, particularly the *Black Sea Fleet. In June 1905 the crew of the battleship *Potemkin in Odessa harbor mutinied; one of the chief leaders of the mutiny was the Ukrainian P. Matiushenko, and another prominent mutineer was O. *Kovalenko, who had been a founder of the Revolutionary Ukrainian party. In November 1905 the crew of the cruiser Ochakov, off Sevastopil, also mutinied.

Peasant unrest was a characteristic feature of the revolution in Ukraine. A wave of agricultural laborers' strikes engulfed Right-Bank Ukraine in the spring and summer of 1905, 1906, and, to a lesser extent, 1907. Among Ukrainian political parties the most active in support of the peasant movement was the Ukrainian Social Democratic *Spilka.

In the face of widespread social unrest Tsar Nicholas II made concessions to the people in a manifesto of 30 October 1905. Among other things, the October manifesto established a limited parliament, the State *Duma, in which Ukrainians participated in 1906–17 (see *Ukrainian caucus in the Russian State Duma). The manifesto also promised fundamental civil rights, including freedom of the press and freedom of association, which did much to accelerate the development of the Ukrainian movement in the Russian Empire. Even before the tsar's manifesto, in March 1905, the Academy of Sciences in St Petersburg had declared that the Ukrainian language was not a dialect of Russian but an independent Slavic language, and recommended that the restrictions placed on it by P. *Valuev's circular and the *Ems Ukase be lifted. In the wake of the October manifesto Ukrainian newspapers and journals began to appear in Kharkiv, Kiev, Lubni, Odessa, Poltava, and elsewhere. In 1906, 18 Ukrainian periodicals appeared. The most important periodical of the era was the daily newspaper *Hromads'ka dumka, which was succeeded by the daily *Rada. The fortunes of the Ukrainian periodical press waned with those of the revolution. Beginning in late 1906 the interference of the authorities substantially limited Ukrainian-language publication. Although some attempts were made during the revolution to introduce the Ukrainian language into educational institutions, those attempts were immediately thwarted by the Russian government.

The revolution witnessed the proliferation of Ukrainian voluntary associations. Branches of the adult educational and cultural society *Prosvita were established in Kiev, Odessa, and about a dozen other cities; numerous branches were also established in villages. Few, however, survived the reactionary period that began in 1907. Several hundred Ukrainian co-operatives also appeared in 1905–7. Various other musical, dramatic, and educational clubs emerged during the revolution in Ukraine.

To fight the revolution the Russian government and reactionaries stirred up an extreme Russian nationalism that was antisocialist, anti-Semitic, and anti-Ukrainian. The nationalists, known as *Black Hundreds, organized *pogroms against Jews and against supporters of the revolution. Moderate Ukrainian politicians condemned the anti-Jewish pogroms in their organ *Ukrainskii vestnik*; revolutionary Ukrainian activists, especially members of the *Ukrainian Social Democratic Workers' party, organized self-defense units to combat the pogromists.

BIBLIOGRAPHY
Revoliutsiia 1905–1907 gg. na Ukraine: Sbornik dokumentov i materialov, 2 vols in 3 pts (Kiev 1955)
Revoliutsiina borot'ba trudiashchykh Ukraïny v 1905–1907 rr. (Kiev 1980)
Edelman, R. *Proletarian Peasants: The Revolution of 1905 in Russia's Southwest* (Ithaca, NY–London 1987)

J.-P. Himka

Revolution of 1917. See February Revolution of 1917 and October Revolution of 1917.

Revolutionary committee (*revoliutsiinyi komitet*, or *revkom*). A temporary body of local government set up by the Bolsheviks during the revolutionary period (1918–20). Introduced in October 1917 in Russia, such committees were assigned the task of preparing an uprising against the Provisional Government. In Ukraine the committees appeared from late October to November 1917, in Kharkiv, Kiev, and the Donbas. The revolutionary committees worked closely with the local soviets and Red Guards and sometimes served as local police forces for the *revolutionary tribunals. The *revkomy* often dealt brutally with 'class enemies' and opponents of Soviet rule. In December 1919 the All-Ukrainian Revolutionary Committee was created to co-ordinate Bolshevik activity throughout Ukraine and organize the Red Army. The body was also supported by the Borotbists. As the Party consolidated its power and introduced Soviet rule, the revolutionary committees were disbanded. Because of strong resistance to the Soviets, in Ukraine some *revkomy* continued to operate until mid-1921.

Revolutionary committees were created also by other parties. In December 1918 the *Borotbists organized military-revolutionary committees to overthrow the UNR Directory, and an *All-Ukrainian Revolutionary Committee was created by the Ukrainian Social Democratic Workers' party in Right-Bank Ukraine in 1919 to fight the Bolsheviks.

Revolutionary tribunal (*revoliutsiinyi trybunal* or *revtrybunal*). An extraordinary judicial institution created by the Bolshevik authorities in Russia and then in other republics. In Ukraine the revolutionary tribunals were established by a decree of the Soviet government issued in Kharkiv on 4 January 1918. In early 1919 they served as organs of local Bolshevik revolutionary committees. On 15 April 1919 the Supreme Revolutionary Tribunal was set up under the All-Ukrainian Central Executive Committee to deal with particularly important cases. The tribunals tried individuals considered to be enemies of Soviet rule ('counterrevolutionaries') or class enemies, and employed illegal and brutal methods of investigation and punishment. The only criterion of judgment was the interest of the revolution. The judges and executors of the sentences were members of the Cheka. The revolutionary tribunals were abolished in 1922, when the court system of Soviet Ukraine was reformed.

Revolutionary Ukrainian party (*Revoliutsiina ukrainska partiia*, or RUP). The first mass Ukrainian revolutionary party in Russian-ruled Ukraine, established on 11 February 1900 by the then Kharkiv Student Hromada leaders P. Andriievsky, D. Antonovych, B. Kaminsky, Yu. Kollard, O. Kovalenko, L. Matsiievych, D. Poznansky, and M. Rusov. RUP was the culmination of earlier attempts at creating a Ukrainian political organization in a society whose intelligentsia was by and large apolitical, and whose Ukrainophile activity was limited to the cultural sphere. Its political antecedents were the *Brotherhood of Taras (est 1891) and the first 'Ukrainian Social Democracy' group (est 1896 in Kiev), headed by I. Steshenko and Lesia Ukrainka.

Mykola Mikhnovsky's *Samostiina Ukraïna* (Independent Ukraine, 1900), the first RUP publication

Initially RUP based its politics on a speech delivered by a sympathizer, M. *Mikhnovsky, at public commemorations of T. Shevchenko in Poltava and Kharkiv in March 1900; the speech was solicited by the founding members and published as the first RUP brochure under the title *Samostiina Ukraïna* (Independent Ukraine, 1900). Mikhnovsky called for 'a single, unitary, indivisible, free, independent Ukraine from the Carpathians to the Caucasus and the immediate goal of the 'restoration ... of rights defined in the Pereiaslav [Ukrainian-Muscovite treaty] constitution of 1654 and the dissemination of its authority throughout the entire territory of the Ukrainian people in Russia.'

The first RUP members were nationally conscious students at various schools in Ukraine and elsewhere in the Russian Empire. In June 1901 they met for the first time at the clandestine third Ukrainian student conference in Poltava. At the first RUP congress in December 1902 the six existing RUP 'free communities' – based in the cities of Kharkiv, Poltava, Kiev, Nizhen (the Chernihiv Community), Lubni, and Katerynodar, in the Kuban (the Black Sea Community) – and smaller groups in Romen, Pryluka, St Petersburg, Odessa, and Moscow were united in one organization. The congress elected an RUP Central Committee (Antonovych, Ye. Holitsynsky [replaced by V. Vynnychenko], V. Kozynenko, and M. Tkachenko) based in Kiev, and a Foreign Committee (directed by Vynnychenko and Antonovych) and Publications Committee, both of which were to be based in Austrian-ruled Lviv and Chernivtsi.

Initially RUP advocated the use of political terrorism and armed struggle against the tsarist regime and the large landowners. By 1902 it had moved away from revolutionary nationalism toward an agrarian Marxism that emphasized both national and social liberation. Its members concentrated on politicizing the Ukrainian peasantry and rural proletariat, organizing peasant groups, strikes, and boycotts in Kiev, Chernihiv, Poltava, and Kharkiv gubernias, and disseminating revolutionary literature written in Ukrainian, such as its monthly organs *Haslo (1902–3), *Selianyn (1903–6), Dobra novyna (1903), and *Pratsia (1904–6), 38 brochures and books (including translations of the socialist writings of A. Bebel, P. Lafargue, F. Lassalle, W. Liebknecht, and K. Kautsky), and many proclamations. To that end it co-operated with non-Ukrainian parties in Ukraine, such as the Russian Socialist Revolutionary party, Jewish Workers' Bund, Russian Social Democratic Workers' party (RSDWP), and Polish Socialist party. Most of the RUP publications were printed in Austrian-ruled Chernivtsi and Lviv and smuggled in with the aid of the *Ukrainian Social Democratic party there; some leaflets were printed by underground presses in Russian-ruled Ukraine.

In 1903 RUP repudiated the extreme nationalism of *Samostiina Ukraïna* and adopted a draft program based on the principles, goals, and tactics of international social democracy (ie, the German Social Democratic party's Erfurt Program). For practical reasons the call for an independent Ukraine was replaced by one for Ukraine's full national-territorial autonomy within a federated, democratic Russia. Also that year the small *Ukrainian Socialist party in Right-Bank Ukraine fused (for six months) with RUP, many RUP members were arrested, and others fled to Lviv, where M. Melenevsky became the head of the Foreign Committee.

In 1904 M. Porsh became the new party leader. Under him RUP shifted its focus away from the peasantry to the ethnic Ukrainian urban proletariat, adopted organizational principles of 'democratic centralism,' theoretical training, and strict conspiracy, recruited many new students, workers, and peasants, and expanded its influence to Right-Bank and Southern Ukraine and the Kuban. Holitsynsky represented RUP at the Socialist International Congress in Amsterdam in August; after RSDWP delegates protested against the participation of a separate Ukrainian delegation, he was forced to join their delegation. In December 1904, at the second RUP congress in Lviv, ideological and tactical differences among Porsh, Antonovych, Melenevsky, and Vynnychenko, especially regarding the national question and the need for Ukrainian independence, split the party. In January 1905 an orthodox Marxist minority faction headed by Melenevsky united with the RSDWP as the autonomous Ukrainian Social Democratic *Spilka. During the Revolution of 1905 RUP members organized workers' and peasants' strikes and boycotts. At the third RUP congress in December 1905, the remaining national-autonomist members renamed their party the *Ukrainian Social Democratic Workers' party.

Although it had many adherents and a mass appeal, RUP had only 116 known members. Another 75 have been identified as possible members, and there were many unidentified members. In addition to those already mentioned, the members who later played important roles in Ukrainian political, cultural, and scholarly life were K. Bezkrovny, V. Chekhivsky, D. Dontsov, D. and V. Doroshenko, M. Halahan, M. Hekhter, H. Ivanytsky, H. Kova-

lenko, M. Kovalsky, P. Krat, M. Livytska, A. Livytsky, I. Lychko, S. Manzhula, B. Matiushenko, Isaak Mazepa, S. and V. Mazurenko, O. Mytsiuk, O. Nazariiv, S. Petliura, P. Poniatenko, N. Romanovych-Tkachenko, I. Rotar, I. Rudychiv, I. Severyn, Mykyta Shapoval, O. Skoropys-Yoltukhovsky, O. Sokolovsky, O. Stepanenko, V. Stepankivsky, M. Trotsky, S. Tymoshenko, Yu. Tyshchenko, S. Veselovsky, M. Vorony, L. Yurkevych, and Andrii and Anna Zhuk.

BIBLIOGRAPHY
Doroshenko, V. *Ukraïnstvo v Rossiï: Noviishi chasy: Pam'iatkova knyzhka* SVU (Vienna 1917)
– *Revoliutsiina Ukraïns'ka Partiia (RUP) (1900–1905 rr.): Narys z istoriï ukraïns'koï sotsiial-demokratychnoï partiï* (Lviv 1921)
Hermaize, O. *Narysy z istoriï revoliutsiinoho rukhu na Ukraïni*, vol 1, *Revoliutsiina Ukraïns'ka Partiia* (Kiev 1926)
Kollard, Iu. *Spohady iunats'kykh dniv, 1897–1906: Ukraïns'ka students'ka hromada v Kharkovi i Revoliutsiina Ukraïns'ka Partiia (RUP)* (Toronto 1972)
Boshyk, G. 'The Rise of Ukrainian Political Parties in Russia, 1900–1907: With Special Reference to Social Democracy,' D Phil diss, Oxford University, 1981
                                                    A. Zhukovsky

Revue de Prométhée, La. A French-language bimonthly journal dedicated to the national question in the USSR and Eastern Europe, edited by O. Shulhyn with the assistance of M. Kovalsky and published in 1938–40 in Paris (a total of nine issues). It succeeded *Prométhée as the major organ of the *Promethean movement. In addition to printing articles on political affairs, the journal devoted attention to the culture and history of the non-Russian peoples under Soviet domination, especially the Ukrainians.

Revue des études slaves. A scholarly journal published by the Institute of Slavic Studies at the University of Paris since 1921. It contains articles on Slavic history, literature, linguistics, and culture, including numerous works on Ukrainian topics and extensive bibliographies and reviews of works in Slavic studies. Surveys of Soviet, émigré, and French books and articles in Ukrainian studies have been compiled by A. Mazon, A. Martel, B. Unbegaun, E. Borschak, and M. Scherrer. An index to the first 34 volumes was published in 1949.

Revue ukrainienne, La. A French-language monthly organ of the *Union for the Liberation of Ukraine published in Lausanne, Switzerland, in 1915–17 (a total of nine issues) to inform the Western powers about the Ukrainian question and garner popular support for Ukrainian independence. It was published initially in a pressrun of 7,000 copies and was widely distributed, but the events of the First World War made it impossible for the effort to be kept up. The editor was A. Zelib and then E. Batchinsky, assisted by A. Zhuk.

Revusky, Abraham [Revuc'kyj, Avraam] (Revutsky), b 8 February 1889 in Smila, Cherkasy county, Kiev gubernia, d 8 February 1946 in Yonkers, New York. Journalist and Zionist leader. He grew up in Palestine and studied at the universities of Odessa and Vienna. A member of the *Poale Zion party and a regular contributor to the Russian and Yiddish press, in 1917–18 he was a leader of the Jewish community in Odessa. In 1918 he was the Poale Zion representative to the Central Rada, and in January–February 1919 he served as the minister of Jewish affairs in the UNR *Council of National Ministers; he left that post in protest over the UNR Directory's negotiations with the Entente powers. In 1920 Revusky returned to Palestine, but in 1921 was expelled by the British. In 1925 he emigrated from Western Europe to the United States, where he was active in Zionist politics and the Jewish press. His memoirs of the revolutionary period, *In di Shvere Teg oyf Ukraine* (In the Difficult Days of Ukraine), were published in 1924.

Dmytro Revutsky   Lev Revutsky

Revutsky, Dmytro [Revuc'kyj], b 5 April 1881 in Irzhavets, Pryluka county, Poltava gubernia, d 29 December 1941 in Kiev. Musicologist and folklorist; brother of L. *Revutsky. After graduating from Kiev University (1906) he was a gymnasium teacher until 1918, when he helped to establish and began lecturing at the Kiev *Lysenko Music and Drama Institute. From 1923 he also served as a research associate with the VUAN Commission of Ethnography. Charges of 'bourgeois nationalism' in 1932 led to dismissal from his posts. Only in 1938 was he restored to an official position, as a senior research associate at the AN URSR (now ANU) Institute of Folklore. Having missed the evacuation of scholars from Kiev before its occupation by Nazi forces in 1941, Revutsky continued his academic work under the German regime. Both he and his wife were murdered not long thereafter, probably by Soviet agents.

Revutsky compiled a three-volume collection of Ukrainian folk songs under the name *Zoloti kliuchi* (The Golden Keys, 1926–9) and wrote a variety of articles on topics related to Ukrainian ethnomusicology.

Revutsky, Lev [Revuc'kyj], b 20 February 1889 in Irzhavets, Pryluka county, Poltava gubernia, d 30 March 1977 in Kiev. Composer, teacher, music activist; brother of D. *Revutsky; full member of the AN URSR (now ANU) from 1957. He entered Kiev University in 1907 and began legal studies in 1908. At the same time he studied music, and he graduated from the Kiev Conservatory in 1916. He had studied with M. Lysenko, H. Liubomyrsky, H. Khodorovsky, and R. Glière. His *First Symphony* is one of the compositions of this period. After teaching music for several years in the Pryluka area and being appointed in 1924 to the *Lysenko Music and Drama Institute in Kiev, he reached the height of his composing career. Following a restructuring of music education and the closing of the

Lysenko Institute in 1934, Revutsky began lecturing at the Kiev Conservatory. That same year he was severely criticized by the authorities for his *Second Piano Concerto*. He subsequently focused his energies in the area of teaching, his composing now consisting largely of editing his previous works or generating occasional pieces for state consumption. He was appointed a professor at the conservatory and headed the *Union of Composers of Ukraine (1944–8). He also supervised the editing of the complete works of M. *Lysenko in the 1950s and served on the editorial board of *Ukraïns'ka radians'ka entsyklopediia* (The Ukrainian Soviet Encyclopedia) in 1958–68.

The list of Revutsky's pupils, which includes M. Dremliuha, V. Homoliaka, H. Zhukovsky, Yu. and P. Maiboroda, V. Kyreiko, A. Kolomyiets, O. Znosko-Borovsky, V. Rozhdestvensky, and L. Hrabovsky, testifies to the strong influence he exerted on the development of music in Ukraine. His compositions were innovative and continued the trend of the Ukrainian national school into the Soviet era. His two symphonies (1920, revised in 1957; and 1926, revised in 1940 and 1970), which showed his keen ear for orchestral color, were notable developments in Ukrainian music. His chamber and piano works (preludes for piano, works for violin and cello with piano) displayed a fresh musical language and technical skill. His best vocal works include the cantata *Khustyna* (The Kerchief, 1923; revised and orchestrated in 1944) and his anthologies of folk song arrangements for voice with piano, such as *Sonechko* (Little Sun, 1925–6), *Kozats'ki pisni* (Cossack Songs, 1926), and *Halyts'ki pisni* (Galician Songs, 1926–8). Among his other vocal compositions are four quartets and works for choir with orchestra, such as *Pro Karmeliuka* (About Karmeliuk, 1925). Revutsky also edited two versions of M. Lysenko's opera *Taras Bul'ba* (1937 and 1955).

BIBLIOGRAPHY
Sheffer, T. *L.M. Revuts'kyi* (Kiev 1958, 1982)
Klyn, V. *L. Revuts'kyi: Kompozytor-piianist* (Kiev 1972)
Bialik, M. *L.N. Revutskii: Monografiia* (Leningrad 1979)
Kuzyk, V. (ed). *Lev Nikolaievich Revutskii: Statti, vospominaniia* (Kiev 1989)
Lisets'kyi, S. *Lev Mykolaiovych Revuts'kyi* (Kiev 1989)
                                                      A. Rudnytsky

Valeriian Revutsky

Revutsky, Valeriian [Revuc'kyj, Valerijan], b 14 June 1911 in Irzhavets, Pryluka county, Poltava gubernia. Theater scholar and critic; son of D. *Revutsky. He graduated from the Moscow Theater Institute (1941) and the University of Toronto (1957). He taught at the Kiev Conservatory (1941–2), was artistic director of the Grono Young Spectator's Theater in Kiev (1942), and worked at the theater school of the Lviv Institute of Folk Culture (1943–4). Revutsky arrived in Canada in 1950 and taught at the University of British Columbia (1960–76). He is the author of *Piat' velykykh avtoriv ukraïns'koï stseny* (Five Great Authors of the Ukrainian Stage, 1955), *P'iesy Mykoly Kulisha* (The Plays of Mykola Kulish, 1956), *Neskoreni berezil'tsi: Iosyp Hirniak i Olympiia Dobrovol's'ka* (Undefeated Berezil Actors: Yosyp Hirniak and Olimpiia Dobrovolska, 1985), and numerous articles in *Entsyklopediia ukraïnoznavstva* (1949–84), *Ukraine: A Concise Encyclopaedia* (1971), and the *Encyclopedia of Ukraine*. He also edited a volume on Les Kurbas (1989).

Revutsky, Yevhen [Revuc'kyj, Jevhen], b 1 June 1919 in Ichnia, Borzna county, Chernihiv gubernia. Internal medicine specialist; son of L. *Revutsky. A graduate of the Kiev Medical Institute (1947), he worked at the AN URSR (now ANU) Institute of Physiology (1954–67), chaired the Department of Diagnostics and Internal Medicine of the Institute of Experimental and Clinical Oncology of the Ministry of Health of the Ukrainian SSR, was deputy director of research at the Ukrainian Scientific Research Institute of Cardiology (from 1970), and was head of the internal medicine department at the Kiev Medical Institute (from 1973). His publications deal with problems of gastroenterology, clinical oncology, and cardiology.

Rewakowicz, Henryk (Revakovych), b 18 January 1837 in Sokolniki, near Tarnobrzeg, Poland, d November 1907 in Lviv. Polish political activist of Ukrainian origin. He had left-wing democratic views. He was editor of the daily newspaper *Kurier Lwowski* (1887–1907) and president (1897–1907) of the populist political party Stronnictwo Ludowe.

Rezana. A monetary unit of Kievan Rus', worth one-fiftieth of a *hryvnia* (see *Currency and coins).

Rezanov, Vladimir. See Riezanov, Volodymyr.

Rhapsody. A composition in an indefinite form, usually based upon epic or national melodies. In the original Greek the term referred to the recitation of portions of an epic poem. In the works of F. Liszt, A. Dvořák, and others the form is an instrumental fantasia generally employing folk or national themes. In Ukrainian music M. Lysenko wrote two rhapsodies for piano solo; and orchestral works of this type include S. Liudkevych's *Striletska rapsodiia* (The Sich-Rifleman Rhapsody, now known as the *Galician Rhapsody*), V. Barvinsky's *Ukrainian Rhapsody*, M. Verykivsky's *Lemko Rhapsody* and *Transcarpathian Rhapsody*, H. Maiboroda's *Hutsulian Rhapsody*, and L. Kolodub's *Ukrainian Carpathian Rhapsody*. S. Liapunov wrote a *Ukrainian Rhapsody* for piano and orchestra (1907).

Rhetoric (from Greek *rhetorikè téchne*, Latin *ars rhetorica*). The study of the methodology of constructing texts (oral and written) the objective of which is to persuade listeners or readers or to influence their emotions and behavior.

The main corpus of rhetorical theory was formulated in antiquity, when two basic schools of rhetoric existed: the Greek, which was theoretical and reflective, and the Latin, which was pragmatic and normative. From those a third school developed, the Byzantine, which devoted more attention to the question of esthetics and to the role of rhetoric in teaching. That school also laid the basis on which the rhetorical trends of the Renaissance and baroque periods developed. The break with the classical schools of rhetoric came only in the second half of the 19th century. No modern school of rhetoric traces its development directly from classical rhetoric. Of modern schools, the most important are the French and the American schools.

The development of rhetoric in Ukraine is closely tied to the emergence of the rhetorical theory of the Renaissance and baroque periods. There were only a few Ukrainian pieces of accomplished rhetorical prose written during the Middle Ages, such as the works of Cyril of Turiv and Metropolitan Ilarion. Ukrainian rhetoric from the 17th and 18th centuries can be divided into two areas, rhetoric as a subject in schools and religious oratory prose. The writers of oratory prose were S. Orikhovsky (who wrote in Latin), L. Baranovych, I. Galiatovsky, A. Radyvylovsky, T. *Prokopovych, and S. Yavorsky. The earliest surviving course of rhetorical theory, dated 1635, is *Orator Mohileanus Marci Tullii Ciceronis apparatissimis partitionibus excultus* (1635–6), written by Y. *Kononovych-Horbatsky. The most prominent theoretician of the art of rhetoric was Prokopovych, who lectured in rhetoric in the Kievan Mohyla Academy in 1706. The study of rhetoric declined in Ukraine in the 19th century owing, on the one hand, to the decline of the education system and, on the other, to the rise of romanticism, which substituted artistic individualism for the normativism of rhetoric. Recently an interest in reviving the study of rhetoric has been noted in Ukraine.

BIBLIOGRAPHY
Prokopovych, F. 'Pro rytorychne mystetstvo ...,' in his *Filosofs'ki tvory*, vol 1 (Kiev 1979)
Prokopovič, F. 'De Arte Rhetorica, Libri X, Kijovie, 1706,' commentary by R. Lachmann, ed B. Uhlenbruch, *Slavistishe Forschungen* 27/II and *Rhetorica Slavica*, vol 2 (Köln–Vienna 1981)
Stratii, Ia.; Litvinov, V.; Andrushko, V. *Opisanie kursov filosofii i ritoriki professorov Kievo-Mogilianskoi akademii* (Kiev 1982)
Masliuk, V. *Latynomovni poetyky i rytoryky XVII–pershoï polovyny XVIII stolittia ta ikh rol' u rozvytku teoriï literatury na Ukraïni* (Kiev 1983)
Stabryka, S. (ed). *Rzymska krytyka i teoria literatury: Wybór* (Wroclaw–Warsaw 1983)

M. Ivanek

Rhododendron. A woody plant (genus: *Rhododendron*; Ukrainian: *berdulets*) of the family Ericaceae. There are hundreds of species worldwide; most are evergreen, and the deciduous ones are commonly called azaleas. Many are cultivated as ornamentals. In Ukraine the only native rhododendron (*R. kochi*), a shrub with deep violet-lilac flowers, grows in the East Carpathians on the rocky slopes of subalpine and alpine ranges (elevations to 2,000 m). Whole islands of rhododendron exist in Polisia on the azalea preserve near Tomashhorod. Rhododendron honey is often toxic.

Rhubarb (*Rheum*; Ukrainian: *revin*). Hardy perennial plants of the family Polygonaceae, grown for their large, succulent leaf stalks and for medicine. Of the approx 30 species known worldwide, three – *R. undulatum*, *R. compactum*, and the garden rhubarb *R. rhaponticum* – are cultivated in Ukraine. The leaf stalks contain up to 2.5 percent sugars and 3.5 percent organic acids and vitamin C, as well as minerals. Rhubarb is used to make compotes, jelly, jam, wine, and aperitifs. The powdered roots of *R. palmatum* are used in *folk medicine as laxatives.

Riabchenko, Serhii [Rjabčenko, Serhij], b 22 October 1940 in Dnipropetrovske. Physicist. After graduating from Dnipropetrovske University (1962) he joined the AN URSR (now ANU) Institute of Physics in Kiev, where since 1983 he has headed the Laboratory of Physics of Magnetic Phenomena. Since 1987 he has also been a professor of physics at Kiev University. His principal contributions are in the fields of semiconductor magneto-optics and magnetic resonance.

Riabchuk, Mykola [Rjabčuk], b 27 September 1953 in Lutske, Volhynia oblast. Critic, poet, and translator. He graduated from the Lviv Polytechnical Institute (1977), has worked as an editor for the journal *Vsesvit* (deputy chief editor from 1991), and became literary editor of *Suchasnist'* in 1992. His insightful literary criticism and political commentaries have appeared in Ukrainian and Russian journals and separately as the collection *Potreba slova* (The Need for a Word, 1985). A collection of his poetry, *Zyma u L'vovi* (Winter in Lviv), was published in 1988. He has also translated Polish, Russian, and Slovak literature into Ukrainian.

Riabchynska, Yuliia [Rjabčyns'ka, Julija], b 26 January 1947 in Odessa, d 13 January 1973. Champion canoeist. She was a member the USSR women's team that won a gold medal in the kayak fours at the 1971 world championships, and she herself won the 1972 Olympic gold medal in the women's 500-m kayak singles and the 1971 Ukrainian and USSR championships.

Riabinin, Nikolai [Rjabinin, Nikolaj], b 31 July 1919 in Krasnoe, Kostroma gubernia, Russia, d 9 March 1992 in Kharkiv. Sculptor; corresponding member of the USSR Academy of Arts since 1973. He studied art in Moscow (1941–4), graduated from the Kiev State Art Institute (1945), and taught at the Lviv Institute of Applied and Decorative Arts (1947–56) and the Kharkiv Art Institute (1956–66). He has sculpted many busts, and portraits in the socialist realist manner, including *Oleksa Dovbush* (with V. Skolozdra, 1950–1), *T. Shevchenko and I. Aldridge* (1952), *Africa Awakens* (1957), *Fidel Castro* (1960–3), *Mother* (1967), and *M. Kybalchych* (1971).

Riabinin-Skliarevsky, Oleksander [Rjabinin-Skljarevs'kyj], b 23 May 1878 in the Odessa region, d ? Historian and archivist. He worked at the Odessa Historical Archives and in the history section of the VUAN. He published a number of studies on the history of Ukraine in the 18th to 19th centuries and articles in *Ukraïna* (1924–30) on the Odessa Hromada (1926), I. Kotliarevsky and the Zaporozhian Cossacks (1926), the Kiev Hromada (1927), the Ukrainian revolutionary movement of the 1870s and 1880s (1927), Ukrainian themes in A. Pushkin's poem 'Poltava' (1928), and the end of the Danubian Sich (1929). He was arrested and sent to a concentration camp in 1934; his subsequent fate is unknown.

Riabko, Pavlo [Rjabko] (Riabkov), b 29 June 1848 in Kherson, d 28 December 1926 in Zinoviivske (now Kirovohrad). Civic activist and ethnographer. He graduated

from a land surveying course at the Kherson gymnasium (1868). In 1877–8 he took an active part in the populist movement in Odessa, Kherson, and Yelysavethrad county, and then he moved to Kiev. In 1879–84 he was exiled to Serednokolimsk (in Yakutia, Siberia). After his release he worked in zemstvo statistical offices in Kherson (1884–92) and Yelysavethrad (1892–1901). Having been dismissed for aiding starving peasants in Kherson gubernia, he went abroad and studied at the Russian Higher School of Social Sciences in Paris (est by M. Kovalevsky). In 1904 Riabko participated in an ethnographic-anthropological expedition, led by F. Vovk and I. Franko, to the Boiko and Hutsul regions and Bukovyna; his descriptions were published in *Etnograficheskoe obozrenie*. He researched the way of life and customs of Ukrainian chumaks and fisherman in the Kherson region, and cofounded the local museum of regional studies in Yelysavethrad (1917). He also wrote memoirs of I. Franko and V. Korolenko.

Riabokliach, Ivan [Rjabokljač], b 8 November 1914 in Pivtsi, Kaniv county, Kiev gubernia. Writer. From 1933 he worked as a journalist in the Donbas and translated Russian literature into Ukrainian. He wrote the novel *Zolototysiachnyk* (The Centaury, 1948), for which he received the Stalin State Prize in 1949; the story collections *Zhaivoronky* (Larks, 1957), *Chaiky* (The Gulls, 1960), and *Antoniv Hai* (1967); the historical-biographical plays *Persha ...* (The First, 1969, about I. Kotliarevsky) and *Mariia Zan'kovets'ka* (1971); and the dramas *Shliakhy i stezhynky* (Roads and Trails, 1958), *Na peredn'omu kraï* (On the Leading Edge, 1961), and *Zhyva voda* (Live Water, 1962). An edition of his selected stories appeared in 1984.

Riabov, Ivan [Rjabov], b 25 July 1897 in Goritsy, Moscow gubernia, d 2 June 1984 in Yalta. Horticulturist. A graduate of the Petrine Agricultural Academy (1921), he worked at the *Nikita Botanical Garden (1923–77). He developed 14 peach and 10 cherry varieties.

Riabov, Oleh [Rjabov], b 23 December 1932 in Kremenchuk, Kharkiv (now Poltava) oblast. Conductor. Afer graduating from the Kiev Conservatory in 1960, he was appointed conductor at the Kiev Theater of Opera and Ballet. In 1966–71 he conducted at the Bolshoi Theater in Moscow. His best performances include the operas *Rigoletto* by G. Verdi, *Lucia di Lammermoor* by G. Donizetti, *Eugene Onegin* by P. Tchaikovsky, and *Nazar Stodolia* by K. Dankevych and the ballets *Swan Lake* and *The Nutcracker* by P. Tchaikovsky, *Romeo and Juliet* by S. Prokofiev, and *The Lily* by K. Dankevych.

Riabov, Oleksii [Rjabov, Oleksij], b 17 March 1899 in Kharkiv, d 18 December 1955 in Kiev. Composer and conductor. After graduating from the Kharkiv Conservatory (1918), he conducted symphony orchestras (1919–29) in Ostrih, Kharkiv, and Armavir (Krasnodar krai). He later became music director, conductor, and composer-in-residence of the Kharkiv Theater of Musical Comedy (1929–41) and the Kiev Theater of Musical Comedy (1941–55). He wrote 25 operettas for the two theaters and is considered the creator of the Soviet Ukrainian operetta. His most popular works are *Sorochyntsi Fair* (1936), *May Night* (1937), and *The Wedding in Malynivka* (1938). His works also include a symphony (1921), a violin concerto (1919), cantatas, and chamber pieces.

Mykola Riabovol   Vera Rich

Riabovol, Mykola [Rjabovol], b 17 December 1883 in Dinska Stanytsia, Kuban, d 28 June 1919 in Rostov-na-Donu. Kuban Ukrainian political leader. He graduated from the Kiev Polytechnical Institute. He served as director of the Kuban–Black Sea railroad co-operative (1911–14) and president of the Kuban Co-operative Credit Union (1918–19). He was head of the Cossack Military Council and its successor, the Kuban Territorial Council (1917–19). Riabovol favored land reform and the creation of independent political entities out of the former Russian Empire, views that placed him in opposition to the Russian Volunteer Army, which had established its base of operation in the Kuban region. He was assassinated while attending a conference called to determine relations among the Don, Terek, and Kuban Cossack hosts, as well as with A. Denikin's army. An investigation suggested that Denikin's army was responsible for the murder.

Riappo, Yan, b 11 April 1880 in what is now Vyru oblast, Estonia, d 14 April 1958 in Tallinn, Estonia. Pedagogue. He graduated from St Petersburg University in 1909 with a degree in history, philosophy, and Eastern languages. In 1921–8 he was deputy people's commissar of education of the Ukrainian SSR and played a leading role in developing Ukraine's independent public education system, known as the Hrynko-Riappo system (see *Unified labor school). In 1922–7 he was editor of the journal *Shliakh osvity. In 1928–38 he worked in industry, and in 1938–48 in public education in Ukraine and Russia. Riappo's books include *Reforma vysshei shkoly na Ukraine v gody revoliutsii, 1920–24* (Reforms of the Higher School in the Years of the Revolution, 1920–24, 1925) and *Systema narodn'oï osvity na Ukraïni* (The Elementary School System in Ukraine, 1926).

Rice (*Oryza sativa*; Ukrainian: *ryzh* or *rys*). Annual and perennial plants of the family Gramineae, cultivated for their starchy grain. Rice is the principal cereal crop of most of the world's population; its origins have been traced by N. Vavilov to India in approx 3000 BC. Rice was introduced in Ukraine in the 1930s. A large area is now planted annually; in the 1970s, 32,000 ha were under rice cultivation in the Black Sea area and the Danube and Boh river deltas, and an additional 140,000 ha in the Kuban region with a yield of up to 5 t of grain per ha. Varieties have been developed which grow with intermittent flooding or periodic watering rather than continuous flooding. The most common varieties in Ukraine are Dubivsky 129, Vros 5123, Uzros 2842, and Zeravshanika 427 and 2586-1.

Rich, Vera, b 24 April 1936 in London. English poet and translator; general secretary of the Anglo-Ukrainian Society in the 1950s and 1960s. Her poetry on Ukrainian themes appeared in her collections *Outlines* (1960) and *Portents and Images* (1963). She has published her own poems, translations of Ukrainian poetry (by T. Shevchenko, I. Franko, Lesia Ukrainka, Hetman I. Mazepa, M. Shashkevych, the Neoclassicists, O. Teliha, E. Andiievska, and others), and a few articles in *Ukrainian Review* and *Ukrainian Quarterly*. Published separately have been her translations *Song of Darkness: Poems by Taras Shevchenko* (1961), *Lesya Ukrainka: Selected Works* (1968), *The Medvedev Papers* (1971), and an anthology of Belarusian poetry (1971).

Armand-Emmanuel du Plessis   Arsen Richynsky
de Richelieu

Richelieu, Armand-Emmanuel du Plessis, duc de, b 25 September 1766 in Paris, d 17 May 1822 in Paris. French nobleman and statesman. He joined the Russian army in 1790 to fight the Turks at Izmail, and with the outbreak of the French Revolution he fought alongside the royalists (1793–4). He settled in Russia in 1795 and became governor of Odessa in 1803 and governor-general of so-called *New Russia (Katerynoslav, Kherson, and Tavriia gubernias, plus Bessarabia gubernia from 1812) in 1805. He contributed significantly to the development of commerce, trade, and agriculture in the region and oversaw the transformation of Odessa from a village into a modern city. He encouraged the in-migration of Germans, Bulgarians, Greeks, and Jews and helped to defend the population against the plague (1812). In 1814 Richelieu returned to France, where he served as minister of foreign affairs (1815–18) and prime minister (1820–1). The *Richelieu Lyceum in Odessa (est 1817) was named after him, and a monument, by I. Martos, was erected in Odessa in his honor in 1828.

Richelieu Lyceum (Rishelivskyi litsei). A private institution of learning, founded in 1817 in Odessa. It was named in honor of the former governor-general of New Russia, A.-E. *Richelieu. Students were drawn primarily from the aristocracy and wealthy merchant families. French was the only language of instruction until 1820, when a number of Russian pedagogues became affiliated with the lyceum and began to teach classes in Russian as well. Until 1837 the lyceum operated as a *gymnasium. Its eight-year program emphasized philosophy and juridical-political studies and precluded technical or professional specialization. Under I. *Orlai (the lyceum's director in 1826–9) teaching methods were modernized, and departments of mathematics, physics, chemistry, biology, geography, and history were established. A pedagogical institute was also formed as a branch of the lyceum. Its function was to prepare pedagogical cadres for district and commercial schools. In 1837 the lyceum's status rose to that of an institution of *higher education. At that time also an Eastern languages institute was established to train translators for military departments. In 1842 agricultural and natural science sections were added, and the institute's mandate became the preparation of government officials for various departments. By 1848 the lyceum had a seven-year gymnasium preparatory school affiliated with it. Under the influence of N. *Pirogov, who became head of the Odessa school district in 1856, the lyceum became the basis for the New Russia University (see *Odessa University), established in 1865. The institute's library collection subsequently developed into the Odessa Library. It was one of the most important libraries in Russian-ruled Ukraine, with a collection of 314,000 volumes in 1915.

N. Freeland

Richka [Rička]. V-5. A village (1972 pop 2,400) on the Richka River in Kosiv raion, Ivano-Frankivske oblast. It was first mentioned in historical documents in 1735. It has long been a center for Carpathian folk art, especially decorative woodcarving, burning, and inlay. The town has a museum of Hutsul folk art.

Richynsky, Arsen [Ričyns'kyj], b 1892 in the Volhynia region, d 1941? Orthodox church activist and physician. He completed studies at the Volhynian Theological Seminary and then at the medical faculty of Warsaw University. After graduating in 1916, he established a medical practice in Volhynia and became a strong proponent of the Ukrainianization of the Orthodox church in the region; after the Revolution of 1917 he advocated the transfer of its jurisdiction from the Moscow patriarch to the Ukrainian Autocephalous Orthodox church. To further these goals in the interwar period, he financed, published, and edited several publications, including *Nova doroha*, *Na varti, Ridna tserkva*, and *Nashe bratstvo*. In June 1927 Richynsky organized a major gathering of Volhynia eparchy's laity in Lutske to discuss church matters. He headed the 'Church Committee,' elected at the gathering, that coordinated the implementation of resolutions. The committee was dissolved in the summer of 1928 by Polish authorities concerned about its growing militancy. Richynsky's activities also brought him into conflict with the Russophile hierarchy of the Polish Autocephalous Orthodox church, and he was excommunicated in April 1929 (he was permitted to rejoin the church a year later). In 1939 he was jailed in the Bereza Kartuzka concentration camp by Polish authorities. When the Red Army occupied Volhynia, he was arrested and sent to a labor camp, in 1940 or 1941, from which he never returned. Richynsky is the author of *Problemy ukraïns'koï relihiinoï svidomosti* (Problems of Ukrainian Religious Consciousness, 1933).

Richytsky, Andrii [Ričyc'kyj, Andrij] (pseud of Anatolii Pisotsky), b 1890 in Richytsia, Radomyshl county, Kiev gubernia, d 1934 in Bashtanka, now in Mykolaiv oblast. Political leader, publicist, and literary critic. After the February Revolution he was a member of the Ukrainian Social Democratic Workers' party, a representative in the Ukrainian Central Rada (1917–18) and a member of its Little Rada, and the chief ideologue of the *Ukrainian Social Democratic Workers' party (Independentists; 1919) and the *Ukrainian Communist party (UKP, 1920–5). He coedited the UKP organ *Chervonyi prapor*, in which he criticized the CP(B)U as a party of Russian occupation. In 1920 he was elected a member of the *All-Ukrainian Central Executive Committee. After the Comintern abolished the UKP in 1925, Richytsky joined the CP(B)U and was elected a candidate member of its CC. He directed the statistical division of the co-operative *Ukrainbank and then was editor in chief of the *State Publishing House of Ukraine (DVU). From the second half of the 1920s he was also a professor at the Ukrainian Institute of Marxism-Leninism and headed the Commission of Shevchenko Studies at the *Taras Shevchenko Scientific Research Institute. Richytsky was a major interpreter and popularizer of M. *Skrypnyk's Ukrainization policies. Although he had been an official critic of the views of O. Shumsky, M. Volobuiev, M. Hrushevsky, M. Khvylovy, and the émigré V. Vynnychenko, after Skrypnyk's suicide in 1933 he himself was denounced in the Party press as an apologist for Vynnychenko and for allowing the DVU to publish large runs of Vynnychenko's works, labeled a spy and a traitor, and then arrested in Bashtanka, where he was tried on fabricated charges of 'overfulfilling' grain requisition quotas in famine-stricken villages and shot.

Richytsky wrote a book about T. Shevchenko and his works from a sociological Marxist approach (1923; 2nd edn 1925), a collection of articles criticizing Vynnychenko as a writer and politician (1928), a refutation of Volobuiev's views (1928), a booklet about the Central Rada (1928), a monograph on the foundations of Ukrainian studies (1929), an interpretation of Skrypnyk as a theoretician of the national question (1929), a biography of K. Marx (1929), and a booklet on the national question in the light of the directives of the 16th congress of the Bolshevik party (1931). He also edited the first Ukrainian edition of Marx's *Kapital* (1927–9). After his repression all of his works were banned in Soviet Ukraine.

V. Holubnychy, A. Zhukovsky

Riddle (*zahadka*). A mystifying or puzzling question that is posed as a game and answered by guessing. Most folk riddles are aphoristic expressions in which the subject to be identified is depicted by a mere metaphor. Some are nonmetaphorical; they consist of a partial description of the subject that is to be identified. Riddles are the simplest form of folklore.

In the past, when most of the Ukrainian population was illiterate, riddles played an important role in the life of the peasants. A person's knowledge of riddles and ability to solve them was accepted as an indication of his or her intelligence. A candidate to a bachelors' group was often required to answer publicly a series of riddles before he was accepted. At a wedding the best man or the master of ceremonies answered riddles for the groom. Riddles were among the games played by young people at evening gatherings and at collectively undertaken tasks. In the Middle Ages a correct answer to a riddle sometimes saved a condemned man from death. In ancient times riddles were believed to have magical powers. During courtship, for example, a suitor would address the family of the courted girl in riddles to deceive the evil spirits. Riddles are an important component of spells, carols, *rusalka* and wedding songs, funeral rituals, tales, legends, and anecdotes. In some folk works riddles play the dominant role. In their aphoristic character some riddles come close to being sayings or proverbs. Riddles appear throughout Ukrainian literature, from the works of H. Skovoroda, I. Kotliarevsky, and T. Shevchenko to those of current authors.

Riddles began to be studied as a separate folklore genre only in the 19th century. Collections of varying size were published by M. Luchkai (1830), H. Ilkevych (1841), I. Holovatsky (1847), M. Zakrevsky (1861), M. Nomys (1864), and P. Chubynsky (1877). The first collection devoted only to riddles was *Malorosiiskie ta galitskie zagadki* (Little Russian and Galician Riddles, 1851), which was compiled and edited by O. Sementovsky and contained 380 items. The most comprehensive collection, consisting of 3,805 riddles, was compiled by I. Berezovsky (1962), who also wrote the best study of riddles. O. Voropai's collection came out in London in 1955, and N. Varkhol's collection of riddles recorded by Ukrainians in eastern Slovakia appeared in Prešov in 1985. The riddle genre continues to develop. New riddles about various features of modern life are being invented constantly.

M. Mushynka

Ridna Khata (Native Home). A cultural and educational society in the Kholm region and Podlachia established in Kholm in 1920. Ridna Khata was modeled on the *Prosvita society in Lviv, which was not permitted to expand its organization into the so-called northwestern Ukrainian lands. It was banned by the Polish authorities in 1921 but continued to operate semisecretly until 1922. That year it was registered as the Ridna Khata Ruthenian Charitable Society, a name which allowed it to emphasize its charitable profile and deflect attention from its cultural-educational purpose, and which downplayed (before officialdom) the fact that it was a Ukrainian organization. The head office was located in Kholm, where the society owned its own building and boasted a semiprofessional theater (directed by D. Krykh), a choir, and a co-operative bookstore called Buh. Its branches operated libraries, reading rooms, amateur drama groups and choirs, co-operatives, and Ukrainian languages classes. By 1927 there were 90 branches, and by 1930 approx 125, most of them in Volodava (33), Hrubeshiv (32), Kholm (20), and Tomaszów (20) counties. The other counties in the region had two to six branches. The leading members of Ridna Khata were A. and P. Vasynchuk, Ya. Voitiuk, S. Liubarsky, S. Makivka, I. Pasternak, O. Rochniak, and K. Soshynsky (its permanent secretary). By the end of the 1920s members of the left faction of Sel-Rob, led by S. Makivka, gained control of the society. This development allowed the Polish authorities to dissolve the group under the pretext that it had become a communist front organization.

During its 10-year existence the Ridna Khata society strengthened Ukrainian national consciousness in the Kholm region and Podlachia. After the partition of Poland in 1939, the organization revived, and the number of branches quickly exceeded the 1930 figure. In 1940 the association was banned, and its branches were converted into *Ukrainian educational societies by the authorities of the Generalgouvernement.

Ridna mova (Native Language). A popular monthly journal published in Warsaw in 1933–6 and then Zhovkva to 1939 (a total of 94 issues). Edited by I. *Ohiienko, it was devoted to standardizing Ukrainian *orthography and grammar and advocated the adoption of the academic 'Kharkiv orthography' of 1927 by Ukrainians outside the USSR. It published articles on the language of contemporary Ukrainian writers, etymology, word formation, phraseology, syntax, and dialectology, and a separate book series. In response to its harsh criticism of Russification policies in Soviet Ukraine, the journal was attacked by the Kiev linguistic journal *Movoznavstvo*. *Ridna mova* was also reproached by some Western Ukrainians for its *purism.

Ridna pryroda (Native Nature). A quarterly bulletin of the State Committee for Environmental Protection of Ukraine, the Ukrainian Society of Hunters and Fishermen, and the Ukrainian Society for Nature Conservation. Published in Kiev since 1971, it contains articles on *environmental protection and ecology in Ukraine.

Ridna shkola (Native School). A monthly journal published in Jersey City, New Jersey, from January 1918 to April 1919 by the Society of Greek Catholic Precentors-Teachers in America. It was intended to raise the educational and cultural level of Ukrainian immigrants in the United States. The editor was D. *Andreiko.

Ridna shkola (Native School). An organ of the Ridna Shkola society, published in Lviv. It first appeared in 1927 (six issues), and was renewed in 1932–9 as a semimonthly. It published teaching materials and articles on pedagogy and the history and current status of Ukrainian education. *Ridna shkola* was edited by M. Strutynsky, I. Herasymovych (1933–6), and M. Terletsky.

Ridna shkola (Native School). A cultural and educational magazine of the *Ukrainian Teachers' Federation of Canada, published monthly in Toronto from April 1956 to March 1960. V. Lutsiv was the managing editor. From late 1962 he briefly published a magazine of the same name in Stamford, Connecticut.

Ridna shkola (Native School). An educational journal published quarterly, then every two months, and now three times a year by the school council of the Ukrainian Congress Committee of America and the Ukrainian Teachers' Federation of Canada (1966–7). It has been published in New York since 1964. *Ridna shkola* contains articles on the council's activities, on the teaching of Ukrainian, and on pedagogy, and book reviews. The journal's editors have included E. Zharsky, P. Andriienko-Danchuk, and Ye. Fedorenko.

Ridna Shkola society. The popular name of the Ruthenian (later Ukrainian) Pedagogical Society (Ruske Pedahohichne Tovarystvo), established in Lviv in 1881 to promote Ukrainian-language education. It was active in Galicia (later in Volhynia) until the Second World War. The society was founded (as the Ruthenian Pedagogical

Members of the chief executive of the Ruthenian Pedagogical Society (later Ridna Shkola society). Sitting, from left: A. Pidliashetsky, Andrii Alyskevych, Rev Ivan Chapelsky, Konstantyna Malytska, Rev Demian Lopatynsky; standing: Osyp Yaniv, Sakhryn, Mykhailo Rybachek, M. Moroz, S. Gerusynsky, M. Kots

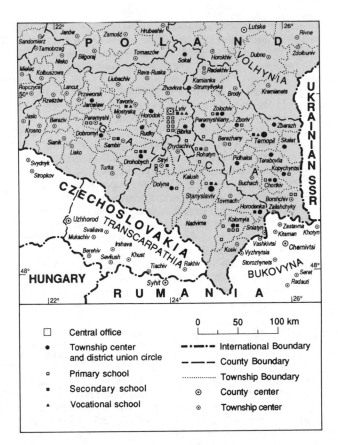

□	Central office	
●	Township center and district union circle	
◻	Primary school	
◼	Secondary school	
▲	Vocational school	

—··—··—	International Boundary
— — —	County Boundary
··············	Township Boundary
⊙	County center
⊚	Township center

0   50   100 km

RIDNA SHKOLA SOCIETY

Society) in an attempt to redress the weakness of Ukrainian educational institutions in Galicia in the late 19th century. After an initial program of petitioning the government for broader Ukrainian educational access and sensitizing the Ukrainian population at large about educational matters, the society began sponsoring its own educational ventures. It established student *bursas for village youths studying at institutes of secondary education (by 1905 there were 4 bursas in Lviv and 16 in other larger centers). Its publishing house, *Biblioteka dlia Molodi, printed children's books and popular editions of fictional and semiacademic works. Ridna Shkola also published the children's journal *Dzvinok (1892–1914) and school primers and textbooks. It dealt with the professional concerns of teachers before the establishment of the *Ukrainian Teachers' Mutual Aid Society in 1905 and published the journal *Uchytel' (1889–1914). The society did not sponsor private schools of its own until 1898, when it opened a school for girls in Lviv. A teachers' seminary for girls in Lviv (1903) with a training school attached to it (in 1907) and primary schools in villages (from 1906) followed. In purely organizational terms the group saw a steady growth, from 83 members in 1881 to 943 in 1900 and to approx 3,000, with 33 branches, in 1906.

In 1912 the group changed its formal name from the Ruthenian to the Ukrainian Pedagogical Society (UPS). It also decentralized its structure, thereby becoming a federation of largely autonomous regional pedagogical councils. In the years preceding the First World War the UPS concentrated its efforts on opening new schools (secondary schools, preparatory courses for rural youths seeking to attend a *gymnasium, and teachers' seminaries), starting literacy courses, forming libraries, expanding the bursa network (26 were established in 1907–14), and publishing. By 1914 the society was the sponsor of 18 elementary schools, 38 preparatory courses, and 7 gymnasiums. Its membership had grown to 4,814, organized in 59 branches. Lobbying of government institutions was instrumental in increasing the number of Ukrainian public schools (by 1914 there were 2,510 elementary schools, 6 gymnasiums, and 10 bilingual secondary seminaries providing Ukrainian-language education in Galicia). Some of the outstanding figures involved with the UPS before 1918 were V. Ilnytsky, I. Chapelsky, O. Barvinsky, E. Kharkevych, O.

Makarushka, T. Voinarovsky, A. Vakhnianyn, H. Vretsona, R. Zaklynsky, K. Malytska, K. Pankivsky, Yu. Romanchuk, O. Stefanovych, and V. Shukhevych.

Immediately after the First World War the UPS faced an openly hostile Polish government intent on eliminating Ukrainian-language education. The number of Ukrainian-language schools in eastern Galicia had fallen to 352. In 1924 the society's circumstances improved somewhat following constitutional changes. It was even granted permission to organize in Volhynia and other Ukrainian territories annexed by Poland. In 1926 'Ridna Shkola' was formally added to the UPS name, although the group had been popularly known as such for several years. At the same time the organizational structure was tightened, with the Lviv headquarters overlooking a network of branches whose work was co-ordinated by county councils (*povitovi soiuzy*). By 1939 Ridna Shkola had 2,074 branches, with 105,000 members.

During this period Ridna Shkola became a central agency for the establishment of private Ukrainian educational institutions. By 1938 it was running 33 primary schools (6,100 students), 23 general education secondary schools (2,500 students), and 15 technical schools (1,500 students).

Ridna Shkola also sponsored educational classes for adults, concerts, and theatrical productions, as well as classes in a variety of areas (eg, Ukrainian studies, teacher upgrading, basic literacy, cooking). Local branches ran small lending libraries (653 in 1937, with a total of 72,207 books and 17,097 registered users). The organization's publishing activity continued (specifically from 1932, with the illustrated journal *Ridna shkola* and its own publishing house), although it was considerably less than in the pre-1914 era. The organization also operated two bookstores.

Among the main figures in Ridna Shkola during the interwar period (in addition to a number of the pre-1914 activists) were O. Terletsky, I. Kokorudz, M. Zaiachkivsky, D. Korenets, I. Herasymovych, O. Kysilevska, M. Konovalets, O. Popovych, M. Terletsky, and L. Yasinchuk.

The Ridna Shkola society was liquidated following the Soviet occupation of Western Ukraine in 1939. Most of its assets were transferred to the *Ukrainian educational societies during the 1941–4 German occupation.

Organizations comparable to (and sometimes named after) Ridna Shkola were formed outside of Ukraine, in Europe and in North America, to co-ordinate private part-time Ukrainian education. These groups were not formally affiliated with Ridna Shkola, although they provided the central organization with funds raised through donation campaigns. Some of these groups have remained active to this day.

BIBLIOGRAPHY
Yasinchuk, L. *P'iatdesiat lit Ridnoï Shkoly, 1881–1931* (Lviv 1931)
V. Kubijovyč

Ridna sprava – Dums'ki visti ([Our] Native Cause – Duma News). A semiweekly organ of the *Ukrainian caucus in the Second Russian State Duma, published from April to June 1907 (a total of 12 issues) in St Petersburg. It was officially edited by M. Khotovytsky and then S. Nechytailo, but the de facto editor was V. Domanytsky. *Ridna sprava* published reports on debates in the Duma, commented on political developments, and supported the idea of Ukrainian autonomy. Unlike *Ukrainskii vestnik*, the journal of the Ukrainian caucus in the first Duma, *Ridna sprava* was published in Ukrainian, probably in an attempt to reach a broader Ukrainian peasant audience.

Ridna tserkva (Native Church). A religious journal and the organ of the Ukrainian Autocephalous Orthodox church (UAOC) in Western Europe. It appeared bimonthly from September 1952 to 1957 and then quarterly to the end of 1988 (a total of 156 issues). It was published in Landshut (1952–70) and Neu-Ulm (1970–88), West Germany. The journal was founded and edited by Archbishop A. Dubliansky. Its contributors included Dubliansky, Metropolitan N. Abramovych, Yu. Boiko, D. Burko (D. Sviatohirsky), P. Dubytsky, S. Fostun, M. Haiuk, M. Hiltaichuk, A. Koval, F. Luhovenko, Yu. Perkhorovych, I. Vlasovsky, N. Polonska-Vasylenko, Z. Sokoliuk, and I. Stus.

Ridna tserkva published pastoral letters of the UAOC hierarchy, sermons, religious articles, and materials on church history. It featured a comprehensive chronicle of events in the life of the Ukrainian Orthodox church, in the diaspora with particular emphasis on the UAOC. It also carried reviews and bibliographies of publications on church affairs, as well as some religious poetry.

Ridna zemlia (Native Land). A weekly newspaper for 'peasants and workers' in the Distrikt Galizien of the *Generalgouvernement, published by the German occupational authorities in Lviv from August 1941 to May 1944. The newspaper was edited by Yu. Tarnovych with the assistance of M. Pasika, H. Sirko-Skhidny, and B. Romanenchuk. Separate editions containing additional information about more local affairs were published for the various counties of Galicia. These appeared as *Volia Pokuttia* (1941–3), *Holos Sambirshchyny* (1942–4), *Stanyslavivs'ke slovo* (1942–4), *Ternopils'kyi holos* (1942–4), *Chortivks'ka dumka* (1943), and *Holos Pidkarpattia* (1943). As the Red Army approached Galicia in 1944, *Ridna zemlia* was published daily to inform the population about events, in a pressrun of 100,000. It was distributed free of charge throughout the countryside.

Ridne slovo (Native Word). A weekly newspaper published by members of the *Bluecoats Division and the Ukrainian Hromada in Biała Podlaska, from June 1917 to December 1918 in Biała Podlaska and then to February 1919 in Brest. It was edited by M. Solovii and A. Savchuk. The newspaper disseminated the views of the *Union for the Liberation of Ukraine. Its press also published some popular-educational books and pamphlets.

Ridne slovo (Native Word). The first Ukrainian newspaper in Yugoslavia, published from the spring of 1933 to 1941 by Rev M. Firak, the Greek Catholic curate in Piškorevci and then Ruski Krstur, in the Bačka region of Serbia. He was assisted by Revs F. Didovych and Zh. Slyzh. The paper was printed in Djakovo (1933–4), Osijek (1934–6), Derventa (1936–7), and Ruski Krstur (1937–41). It appeared, in literary Ukrainian, monthly until August 1935, then semimonthly until the first issue in 1940, and thenceforth three times a month. The paper published news and information about Ukraine, Yugoslavia, its Ukrainian community, and the world, as well as popular articles on Ukrainian history, culture, and education. Its press also issued annual calendar-almanacs and popular-educational literature.

Last meeting of the editorial boad of *Ridnyi krai* (Poltava, 1907). Sitting, from left: Hryhorii Kovalenko, Panas Myrny, Lesia Ukrainka, Olena Pchilka, Mykola Dmytriiev; standing: Leonyd Pakharevsky and Hryhorii Sherstiuk

Ridnyi krai (Native Land). The second Ukrainian-language newspaper established in Russian-ruled Ukraine. The initiator and first editor was M. *Dmytriiev, and the first publisher was H. Markevych. It was published weekly in Poltava from 6 January 1906 until May 1907, when it was closed down by the tsarist authorities because of Dmytriiev's political activity. It was renewed in October in Kiev by O. *Pchilka, who published it there weekly, three times a week from 1910 and then irregularly from 1913 until it was closed down again during the general crackdown against the Ukrainian press after the outbreak of the First World War. It was renewed again in Hadiache in 1915–16 by Pchilka, who circumvented the laws prohibiting publication in Ukrainian by printing the paper in the *yaryzhka alphabet. Ridnyi krai covered political, economic, and cultural developments and published prose, poetry, and articles on farming, the co-operative movement, history, literature, ethnography, and education. The children's magazine *Moloda Ukraïna was published as a monthly supplement to Ridnyi krai.

Ridnyi krai (Native Land). A daily newspaper published in Lviv in 1920–3 as the organ of the Ukrainian Agrarian Union and then the *Ukrainian Agrarian party. It was funded by the Polish regime and espoused active co-operation with it, thereby earning it great enmity in Ukrainian nationalist circles. The newspaper was founded and edited by S. *Tverdokhlib. After his assassination in 1922 it was edited by M. *Yatskiv. The paper's general line was continued by Pravo narodu (1923), the weekly organ of the Ukrainian People's party (Ilkiv faction), published in Kolomyia.

Ridnyi krai (Native Land). A weekly newspaper published in Chernivtsi in 1926–30 (a total of 201 issues). Edited by L. Kohut, it supported the Ukrainian National party in Rumania and promoted the Silskyi Hospodar society. Among the contributors were Yu. Serbyniuk, I. Stryisky, H. Skehar, V. Simenovych, S. Smal-Stotsky, M. Korduba, and S. Siropolko. In 1930 the paper merged with *Chas.

Rieger, Janusz, b 20 September 1934 in Cracow. Polish linguist. Rieger studied at the Jagellonian University in Cracow (MA, 1955) and at the Polish Academy of Sciences (PH D, 1967). He has taught at various universities in Poland and since 1988 has been a professor at the Catholic University in Lublin. Rieger's specialization is Slavic (esp Ukrainian) dialectology, and he has worked in the areas of Slavic onomastics and Polish-Ukrainian linguistic relations. He is the author and coauthor of 15 books and numerous articles; among them the linguistic atlas of the Boiko dialects (vols 1–6, 1980–6), which he edited and compiled, is of special importance to Ukrainian linguistics.

Riezanov, Volodymyr [Rjezanov] (Rezanov, Vladimir), b 9 September 1867 in Liubache, Oboian county, Kursk gubernia, d 31 December 1936 in Nizhen, Chernihiv oblast. Literary scholar; corresponding member of the Academy of Sciences of the USSR from 1923; VUAN associate. He graduated from the Bezborodko Historical-Philological Institute (1890, see *Nizhen Lyceum), where he taught from 1899 and became a professor in 1910. In 1934 he was purged from his position. Riezanov wrote 70 works on the history of Ukrainian, Russian, and world literature. His studies on the history of Jesuit religious drama and the Ukrainian school drama that arose on its foundation are based on extensive use of primary sources. They include books on the history of Russian drama (1907), an accompanying volume of texts of 17th- and 18th-century school plays (1910), and books on 17th- and 18th-century school plays and Jesuit theater (1910), on Jesuit theater (1910), and on school dramas in Polish-Lithuanian colleges (1916). His Drama ukraïns'ka: Starovynnyi teatr ukraïns'kyi (Ukrainian Drama: Old Ukrainian Theater, vols 1, 3–6, 1926–9) is a fundamental scholarly work and collection of primary sources on the subject. He also wrote Do istoriï literaturnykh styliv: Poetyka renesansu na tereni Ukraïny i Rosiï (Toward a History of Literary Styles: Renaissance Poetics in the Territory of Ukraine and Russia, 1931).

R. Senkus

Rieznyk, Borys [Rjeznyk], b 5 January 1929 in Kholodna Balka, Odessa okruha. Pediatrician. A graduate of the Odessa Medical Institute (1950), he worked at the Donetske Medical Institute (1956–72, as professor from 1966) and chaired the Department of Faculty and Hospital Pediatrics at the Odessa Medical Institute. He has published numerous papers on juvenile hematology, infectious diseases, and meningitis, the use of pharmacotherapy and electrocardiography in pediatrics, and the influence of vaccines on children's health.

Rieznykov, Oleksandr [Rjeznykov], b 12 November 1939 in Odessa. Endocrinologist and pathophysiologist. A graduate of the Odessa Medical Institute (1962), in 1965 he began to work in the pathophysiological laboratory of the Kiev Scientific Research Institute of Endocrinology and Metabolism. In 1973 he became director of the institute's Laboratory for the Neurohormonal Regulation of Reproduction. His chief publications deal with the physiology, biochemistry, and pathology of adrenal and sexual glands, the neuroendocrine regulation of reproduction and sexual development, and the application of new diagnostic and therapeutic methods in public health and animal husbandry.

Riga. The capital (1989 pop 915,000) of Latvia and one of the main ports of the Baltic Sea. The Ukrainian community in Riga dates from the 19th century. After Latvia won its independence in 1918, the UNR maintained an embassy (headed by V. Kedrovsky) in Riga, and the Western Ukrainian National Republic sent a delegation under K. Levytsky there. In October 1920 Poland signed a peace agreement in Riga with Soviet Russia and Ukraine, and then the Peace Treaty of Riga, on 18 March 1921. In 1933 the Latvian-Ukrainian Society was founded. In the 1970s approx 25,300 residents of Riga were of Ukrainian origin. Of these, 12,000 gave Ukrainian as their mother tongue. (See also *Latvia.)

Riga, Peace Treaty of. A convention, signed on 18 March 1921, between the Polish government and the governments of the Russian Socialist Federal Soviet Republic (RSFSR) and the Ukrainian Socialist Soviet Republic, ending the Polish-Soviet War of 1919–20. The peace negotiations commenced on 17 August 1920 in Minsk, and from 21 September 1920 they were conducted in Riga. The Polish delegation was headed by J. Dąbski; the Russian, by K. Danishevsky (Minsk) and A. Joffe (Riga); and the Ukrainian, by D. Manuilsky, E. Kviring, and Yu. Kotsiubynsky. The delegations of the Ukrainian National Republic, headed by A. Livytsky, and the Western Ukrainian National Republic, headed by K. Levytsky, were not admitted to the negotiations: Ukraine had, in effect, already been divided in principle between the emerging Soviet state (the Ukrainian SSR) and Poland (eastern Galicia).

On 12 October 1920 both sides signed the preliminary treaty, and on 2 November 1920 they exchanged preliminary documents. Nonetheless the Polish armies remained on the territories to the east of the provisionally delineated Polish-Soviet frontier, where they were protecting the UNR troops of S. Petliura, which were engaged in combat against the Bolsheviks in the regions of Berdychiv, Zhytomyr, Mohyliv, and Kamianets-Podilskyi. Not until 14 November 1920 was a protocol that compelled the Polish side to withdraw its armed forces signed. The final editing of the text of the treaty lasted from mid-November 1920 until the beginning of March 1921.

The Riga treaty is composed of 26 articles. In Article 2 both sides recognized the independence of Ukraine and Belarus (in accordance with the principle of the self-determination of nations) and established the line of frontiers. The Poles received a considerable piece of territory east of the *Curzon Line, which had been designated earlier by the Allies as the border between Poland and Ukraine. In the subsequent articles both sides bound themselves to recognize the other's sovereignty and to refrain from spreading hostile propaganda and from harboring in their territories organizations which would pursue activities directed against the other party (Article 5). The Poles in Russia and Ukraine and the Ukrainians and Russians in Poland received a guarantee of their cultural, linguistic and religious rights (Article 7). Furthermore the Riga Treaty regulated the questions of citizenship, war reparations (from which both sides resigned), the repatriation of the population, the principles of the transit of commodities, and the relocation of state, self-government, and private property.

In Article 11 Soviet Russia bound itself to return to Poland all art collections, archives, and libraries that had been removed from Poland after 1772, as well as (Article 13) to pay 30 million rubles in gold as Poland's share of the assets of the former Russian Empire. Finally, the treaty foresaw (Article 24) the establishment of diplomatic relations.

The treaty was ratified by the Polish Sejm on 15 April 1921 and by the Russian and Ukrainian soviets on 14 and 17 April, and the ratification documents were exchanged in Minsk on 3 May. It remained valid until 17 September 1939, when the Red Army occupied Western Belarus and Western Ukraine.

BIBLIOGRAPHY
Dąbski, J. Pokój ryski (Warsaw 1931)
Wandycz, P. Soviet-Polish Relations, 1917–1921 (Cambridge, Mass 1969)
Hunchak, T. (ed). Ukraïns'ka revoliutsiia: Dokumenty, 1919–1921 (New York 1984)
Kumaniecki, J. Pokój polsko-radziecki, 1921 (Warsaw 1985)
                                    B. Budurowicz, A. Chojnowski

Rigelman, Aleksandr [Rigel'man], b 1720 in St Petersburg, d 3 November 1789 in Andriivka, Chernihiv region. Historian, military engineer, and topographer; descendant of a German aristocratic family that settled in Russia in the 1730s. He studied at the Cadet Corps in St Petersburg (1738) and was stationed in Zaporizhia (1741–3) to work on the demarcation of the Russian-Turkish border.

Then he drew plans for Ukrainian cities (1745–8) and built fortified lines extending through Southern Ukraine, along the Azov Sea coast, and around the periphery of Kiev (1747–9). In the 1750s and 1760s he worked in the Don region, where he built the St Dimitrii Fortress (now Rostovna-Donu). After his retirement in 1782, he settled on his Ukrainian wife's (née Lyzohub) estate, where he died.

Rigelman produced a number of historical studies, focusing mainly on Ukraine and the Don region, most of which were published in the 19th century. They included *Istoriia ili povestvovanie o Donskikh kazakakh* (The History or Account of the Don Cossacks; written in 1778, pub in 1846) and *Letopisnoe povestvovanie o Maloi Rossii i ee narode i kazakakh voobshche* (A Chronicle Account of Little Russia and Its People and the Cossacks in General; written in 4 pts in 1785–6, pub by O. Bodiansky in *Chteniia Moskovskogo obshchestva istorii i drevnostei*, nos 5–9 [1847], and separately). He also wrote a five-part supplement to the chronicle that included a description of the life and customs of the Zaporozhian Cossacks and an ethnographic description of the Ukrainian people, with 28 drawings by T. Kalynsky of Ukrainian types in traditional costumes.

BIBLIOGRAPHY
Iershov, A. ' "Letopisnoe povestvovanie" O. Rigel'mana,' Zapysky Nizhyns'koho instytutu narodnoï osvity, vol 7 (1927)
Dzyra, Ia. 'Dzherel'na osnova pratsi O. Rihel'mana z istorii Ukraïny,' in Istoriohrafichni doslidzhennia v Ukraïns'kii RSR, 2nd edn (Kiev 1969)
                                    O. Ohloblyn

Rigelman, Nikolai [Rigel'man], b 1817 in Chernihiv gubernia, d 2 June 1888. Historian, publicist, and Slavophile civic leader; grandson of A. *Rigelman. He headed the Kiev Slavic Benevolent Society, supported Russophile societies in Lviv, and worked closely with the *Cyril and Methodius Brotherhood (to the point where he himself was questioned during the inquiry). He became acquainted with T. *Shevchenko in 1840 and came to aid him financially in 1857. He was a director of elementary schools in Kiev gubernia and a member of the Kiev Archeographic Commission; together with I. Samchevsky he edited the chronicle of S. Velychko, which was published by the commission (vols 1–4, 1848–64). Rigelman wrote many publicistic works on Slavic and *Slavophile issues of his time. He approached the Ukrainian issue from the viewpoint of conservative Slavophilism. Having access to government archives, Rigelman wrote about Shevchenko's testimony in the Cyril and Methodius Brotherhood trial ('Dopros T.G. Shevchenka v 1847 g.' [The Interrogation of T. Shevchenko in 1847], *Kievskaia starina*, 1902, no. 2).

Right of national self-determination. See Self-determination.

Right Opposition. A faction that emerged in the All-Union Communist Party (Bolshevik) in the mid-1920s under the leadership of N. Bukharin, M. Tomsky, and A. Rykov. It supported the *New Economic Policy, lower taxes for the peasantry, and other 'liberal' policies. It opposed the *Left Opposition headed by L. Trotsky, which called for rapid industrialization and collectivization. Unlike the Left Opposition, the Right Opposition was a relatively loose and small group. It seems to have had few followers among the CP(B)U leadership, who supported J. Stalin's plans for rapid, large-scale industrialization. Nonetheless, after the defeat of the Right Opposition a major Party and government purge was launched in Ukraine. Besides Party members many workers of the agricultural commissariat, the Ukrainian Peasant Bank, and the co-operative movement were dismissed and arrested. This purge paved the way for the severe collectivization drive and ultimately for the man-made famine of 1932–3.

Right-Bank Ukraine (Pravoberezhna Ukraina, Pravoberezhzhia). A historical, geographic, and administrative region consisting of the Ukrainian lands west of the Dnieper River, south of the Prypiat marshes, north of the steppes, and east of the upper Boh and the Sluch rivers. The Right-Bank Cossack administration included five core regiments (Chyhyryn, Cherkasy, Korsun, Kaniv, Bila Tserkva) and four frontier regiments (Uman, Bratslav, Kalnyk-Vinnytsia, Pavoloch). Under Polish control the region formed the voivodeships of Kiev (without the city and its environs) and Bratslav as well as portions of Volhynia and Podilia. Under imperial Russian rule in the early 19th century, the Right Bank was renamed the *Southwestern land. Right-Bank Ukraine today encompasses the oblasts of Vinnytsia, Zhytomyr, northern Kirovohrad, and (west of the Dnieper) Kiev and Cherkasy.

Right-Bank Ukraine developed under the Cossacks as an important political, cultural, and economic region. Fol-

lowing the death of Hetman B. *Khmelnytsky in 1657, it was devastated and depopulated during the *Ruin as a result of prolonged fighting among the Cossacks, Poland, Muscovy, and Turkey. The destruction was aggravated by the instability of the Cossack structure itself, which was split in 1660 when the Left-Bank regiments rejected the leadership of Yu. Khmelnytsky and elected their own hetman (Ya. Somko). Their action initiated the political division of Ukraine into Left and Right Banks, which acquired significance in international affairs with the Polish-Muscovite Treaty of *Andrusovo, by which Muscovy and Poland ratified their respective spheres of influence along the Dnieper River: Muscovy received *Left-Bank Ukraine plus Kiev with its environs, and Poland received Right-Bank Ukraine.

The treaty ended the pro-Polish orientation of successive Right-Bank Cossack leaders and initiated nearly a half-century of chaos in the Right Bank. Hetman P. *Doroshenko rejected both Muscovite and Polish interference and unified both banks (1668) under his leadership. His achievement, however, was short-lived, and he was forced to return to the Right Bank, at which time Muscovy restored its influence in the Left Bank. Doroshenko then turned to Turkey for assistance (the result being the Peace Treaty of *Buchach) and embroiled the region in a succession of maneuvers for control. In 1676 the Left-Bank hetman I. *Samoilovych defeated Doroshenko and briefly united both banks under his hetmanship. Pressed by

RIGHT-BANK UKRAINE IN THE 17TH AND 18TH CENTURIES

Turkish forces, Samoilovych attempted in 1678 to remove the Right-Bank population to Left-Bank and Slobidska Ukraine. The Treaty of *Bakhchesarai (1681) delineated the Dnieper River as the boundary between the Ottoman and Muscovite empires, with the southern Right Bank a vacant neutral zone. The *Eternal Peace Treaty between Muscovy and Poland (1686) confirmed the previous Treaty of Andrusovo, whereby Poland retained the Right Bank. Ukraine was now completely partitioned among its three neighbors.

In 1685, as protection against Tatar raids, the Polish king Jan III Sobieski established Cossack regiments in Bratslav, Bohuslav, Korsun, and Khvastiv, but under a royally appointed hetman and officers. Some Cossacks also served as mercenaries in the magnates' armies.

By the terms of the Treaty of Carlowitz (1699) Poland regained control of the Right Bank from Turkey. That year the Cossack administration was formally abolished in the Right Bank, but a Cossack uprising in 1700–3, led by Col S. *Palii, briefly overthrew Polish rule in the Right Bank; the Left-Bank hetman I. Mazepa took advantage of the confusion to unite both banks under his rule. By the Treaty of Prut (1711), however, Right-Bank Ukraine was returned to Poland. The Cossacks were then completely suppressed.

Because continual warfare had destroyed the towns and villages and depopulated the Right Bank, the Polish and Polonized Ukrainian magnates upon their return offered incentives to the peasantry of northwestern Ukraine, especially Volhynia, to resettle the Right Bank. Peasants were promised 15 to 20 years of exemptions from corvée and other obligations. When the concessions ended, and the obligations of serfdom were imposed, spontaneous anti-Polish peasant *haidamaka uprisings swept the Right Bank, in 1734, 1750, and 1768 (see also *Koliivshchyna).

By the Third Partition of Poland (1795) Right-Bank Ukraine was annexed by the Russian Empire. That territorial acquisition brought a substantial number of Jews into the imperial realm for the first time; the Russian authorities responded by establishing the *Pale of Settlement, which restricted Jewish settlement to the Right-Bank regions and other areas removed from the heartland of the empire.

Several distinctive features and structures of Right-Bank Ukraine persisted until the Revolution of 1917. One was the extensive influence of the Right-Bank *Poles in Ukraine. As well, vast tracts of land in the region were worked as large estates known as latifundia. The latifundia system hampered the growth of towns and a Ukrainian urban middle class. Towns were populated predominantly by Jewish merchants and artisans.

In the early 19th century the tsarist administration allowed a Polish school system to function in the Right Bank, under the supervision of the University of Vilnius. The school system included an institution of higher education, *Kremianets Lyceum. After the Right-Bank gentry took part in the *Polish Insurrection of 1830–1, however, the tsarist authorities abolished the Polish educational system in the Right Bank. Some representatives of the Polish gentry in the early 19th century contributed to the development of the nascent Ukrainian movement in the Right Bank by writing literature on Ukrainian themes (see *Ukrainian school in Polish literature) and conducting ethnographic research on the Ukrainian peasantry.

On the eve of the *Polish Insurrection of 1863–4, some students from the Polonized Ukrainian gentry, including V. *Antonovych, broke with Polish society and returned to their Ukrainian roots. Known as the *khlopomany (lovers of the peasantry), they contributed much to the development of the Ukrainian national awakening in the Right Bank.

A. Beniuk

Rii (Swarm). A Transcarpathian organization of beekeepers, founded in 1924 in Uzhhorod to promote modern beekeeping. It organized a commercial apiary, beekeeping courses, and exhibitions and published the journal *Pidkarpats'ke pcholiarstvo* (1923–5). The association was active until 1930.

Rii Provincial Beekeeper's Alliance (Kraiove pasichnytske obiednannia Rii). A co-operative organization of beekeepers, established in Lviv in 1926 by Ye. Arkhypenko. It represented beekeepers throughout Western Ukraine, encouraged the use of modern equipment and hives, and provided inexpensive sugar for the bees. Rii also organized the sale of honey produced by its members. Its workshop built hives, and the organization maintained model apiaries near Lviv and in Perehinsko, in Gorgany. It also operated stores in Lviv and Łódź. From 1928 it was assisted by the Silskyi Hospodar society. In 1938 its membership was 1,370, and its honey revenue was 60,800 zlotys. Rii was closed during the first Soviet occupation in 1939–40, but renewed its activities under the German occupation of Galicia (1941–4). During the war it also operated in the Kholm region. Rii was directed by M. *Borovsky (1928–37) and R. *Holod (1937–9); other leaders included A. Adamchuk and S. Yatsura. Its monthly organ was the journal *Ukraïns'kyi pasichnyk*.

Rika River (also Velyka Rika). A right-bank tributary of the Tysa River that flows for 92 km through Transcarpathia oblast and drains a basin area of 1,130 sq km. Formed by the confluence of the Pryslip and the Torunka rivers, the Rika has a deep valley in its upper reaches. A hydroelectric station is situated on the river near the city of Khust. The river is also used for industry and water supply.

Rikhter, Anatolii [Rixter, Anatolij], b 24 March 1930 in Beltsi, Bessarabia, Rumania. Ukrainian opera singer (bass). After graduating from the Kiev Conservatory in 1960, he joined the Odessa Opera and Ballet Theater as a soloist. He appeared as Karas in S. Hulak-Artemovsky's *Zaporozhian Cossack beyond the Danube*, Taras in M. Lysenko's *Taras Bulba*, Boris in M. Mussorgsky's *Boris Godunov*, and the General in H. Maiboroda's *Arsenal*.

Rilke, Rainer Maria, b 4 December 1875 in Prague, d 29 December 1926 in Val-Mont, Switzerland. Austro-German poet, acclaimed especially for his collections *Duineser Elegien* (1923) and *Die Sonette an Orpheus* (1923). His poetry, characterized by a subtle and dense symbolism and by its profoundly philosophical reflection on self and world, influenced the development of literary modernism, not least in Ukraine.

Rilke's journeys to the Russian Empire in the spring of 1899 and summer of 1900 were an early and formative experience. The second took him south from Moscow to Ukraine, where he visited Kiev, Kaniv (T. Shevchenko's grave on Chernecha hill), and Poltava. Rilke is known to have been interested at the time in the early, thematically Ukrainian stories of N. Gogol, and to have acquired a copy of Shevchenko's *Kobzar* in Russian translation. He did not, however, clearly distinguish between Russia and Ukraine, and his responses to what he saw in Russia and Ukraine were strongly influenced by the turn-of-the-century myth of the simple and god-seeking 'Russian soul.'

Thematic echoes of the Ukrainian journey can be found in 'Das Buch von der Pilgerschaft,' which forms the second part of *Das Stunden-Buch* (1905); in 'Karl der Zwölfte von Schweden reitet in der Ukraine' and 'Sturm,' both in *Buch der Bilder* (1902); and in two prose works from *Geschichten vom lieben Gott* (1900), 'Wie der alte Timofei singend starb' and 'Das Lied von der Gerechtigkeit.' Rilke also translated the medieval epic *Slovo o polku Ihorevi* (The Tale of Ihor's Campaign, 1902–4).

A selection of Rilke's poems was translated into Ukrainian by B. Kravtsiv: *Rechi i obrazy* (Objects and Images, 1947). Other translators have included M. Zerov, M. Yohansen, O. Lutsky, Yu. Lypa, Yu. Klen, L. Mosendz, M. Orest, M. Bazhan, L. Pervomaisky, O. Zuievsky, and V. Stus.

BIBLIOGRAPHY
Pelens'kyi, Ie. *Rainer Mariia Ril'ke i Ukraïna* (Lviv 1935)
Izars'kyi, O. *Ril'ke na Ukraïni* (Phildalephia–Kiev 1952)
Nahirnyi, M. 'Tvorchist' Rainera Mariï Ril'ke v rakursi ukraïns'koï tematyky,' *Ukraïns'ke literaturoznavstvo*, no. 45 (1985)
                                             B. Kravtsiv, M. Pavlyshyn

Rillia (Ploughed Field). A semimonthly newspaper for peasants published in Kiev from 1910 until it was closed down in the tsarist campaign against the Ukrainian press that followed the outbreak of the First World War. It was renewed as a co-operative organ by the Ukrainskyi Agronom society in October 1917 and published until sometime in 1918. The newspaper offered practical advice on farming and the co-operative management of agriculture. The editors were A. Avramenko (1910–14), A. Ternychenko (1913–14), and I. Prykhozhenko and K. Osmak (1917–18). In 1914 *Rillia* had 2,000 subscribers.

Internees of the Rimini POW camp during the blessing of their flag

Rimini. A city (1971 pop 121,000) on the Adriatic coast in northern Italy, and the site of British POW camps at the end of the Second World War. About 10,000 soldiers of the *Division Galizien, who surrendered to the British in Austria in May 1945, were interned first in Camp No. 5C at

Bellaria (June–October 1945) and then in Camp No. 1B at Miramare (October 1945 to June 1947). The Soviet repatriation mission persuaded about 900 (8.5 percent) of the prisoners to return home. The camps were placed under the command of Col M. Krat (June–August 1945), Maj S. Yaskevych (August–February 1946 and May 1946 to May 1947), and Lt Col R. Dolynsky (February–May 1946) and their staffs. The soldiers were divided into eight regiments and a special unit consisting of staff workers, a sanitary company, and the military police. Of 9,310 prisoners in May 1946, 288 were officers; 822, junior officers; and 8,200, soldiers. A high standard of discipline and morale was maintained in the camp throughout its existence.

Four Ukrainian Catholic chaplains (Revs E. Korduba, O. Babii, O. Markevych, and M. Ratushynsky) and one Orthodox chaplain (Rev Y. Skakalsky) served the religious needs of the internees. Health care was provided by a staff of 16 physicians under the supervision of Drs B. Dziubanovsky, B. Rozdilsky, L. Miroshnychenko, and, finally, R. Turko. The cultural and educational department under V. Malets, Yu. Kruk-Drozdovsky, B. Pidhainy, and, finally, Ya. Lytvyn oversaw a rich cultural program, consisting of concerts by the Burlaka (conductor S. Huminilovych) and Slavuta (conductor Ya. Havryliak) choirs and the Bandura camp orchestra (conductor O. Holovatsky), film shows, cabarets, and plays in the camp theater. Its school section, headed by Capt O. Vynnytsky and then Lt Ya. Kulytsky, ran elementary and secondary courses, a commercial and pedagogical college, and a one-year technical, farming, and forestry program. The camp press included a daily bulletin, *Zhyttia v tabori*; a weekly paper, *Bat'kivshchyna*; a biweekly paper, *Iunats'kyi zryv*; a satirical biweekly, *Osa*; a sports paper, *Na starti*; and the literary and art journals *Nash shliakh* and *Hrono*. An art circle, a literary club, and Prosvita reading rooms were also active.

The camps were visited by Ukrainian leaders from the United States and Canada, including V. Kushnir, V. Galan, and A. Hlynka. The Ukrainian Relief Committee in Rome, headed by Bishop I. Buchko, was particularly active in helping the internees. In 1947 the internees were transported to England, where they were later released.

BIBLIOGRAPHY
Budnyi, V. (ed). *Rimini, 1945–1947* (New York 1979)
Veryha, V. *Pid sontsem Italiï* (Toronto 1984)

Rimsky-Korsakov, Nikolai [Rimskij-Korsakov, Nikolaj], b 18 March 1844 in Tikhvin, d 21 June 1908 near Luga, Russia. Russian composer and conductor. He wrote two operas on Ukrainian subjects based on tales by N. Gogol, *May Night* (1878) and *Christmas Eve* (1894–5), and composed the opera *Tale of Tsar Saltan* (1899–1900), based on Pushkin's tale about fictitious personages from Ukraine's medieval period. His other works include a *Ukrainian Fantasia* for orchestra, arrangements of ancient chants of the Klevan Cave Monastery for male choir a cappella, and *Song about Oleh the Fated* for male chorus, soloists, and orchestra (1899), based on Pushkin's poem about the Kievan Rus' ruler.

Rio Grande do Sul. The most southerly state of Brazil (1990 pop 9,163,200), bordering on Santa Catrina to the north and Uruguay to the south, with an area of 280,674 sq km. Its climate is subtropical. Its capital is Porto Alegre. The fourth-largest Ukrainian community of Brazil (est pop, near 10,000) lives in the state. The first wave of settlement, consisting of approx 200 families, arrived from Galicia in 1895–9. A second influx occurred after 1907, when immigrants who had worked on the São-Paulo–Rio Grande Railway settled in places such as Guarni, Campinas, Iguí, Jaguari, and Erechim. After the Second World War more Ukrainians settled in the state, particularly its capital. The isolation of the state from the heartland of Ukrainian life in Brazil has resulted in a slow and somewhat truncated development of church and community structures. (See *Brazil.)

Ripai, Andrii [Ripaj, Andrij], b 1829 in Ulych-Kryve, Uzhok county, Transcarpathia, d 1914. Pedagogue. He taught at and for a period of time was director of the teachers' seminary in Uzhhorod. He edited the first Transcarpathian pedagogical journal, *Uchytel'* (Uzhhorod 1867), and was the author of a booklet on farming and cattle breeding (1864) for peasants.

Ripetsky, Myroslav [Ripec'kyj], b 13 June 1889 in Sambir, Galicia, d 29 April 1974 in Chrzanowo, Suwałki voivodeship, Poland. Ukrainian Catholic priest, community figure, and writer. He was made canon (1927) and dean (1939) by Bishop Y. Kotsylovsky. In June 1947 Ripetsky was deported with many other residents of Lisky, Sokal county, to northeastern Poland. There he organized a chapel (in Chrzanowo) and was for many years the only Ukrainian Catholic pastor in Warmia diocese. He contributed many articles to *Nova zoria*, *Pravda*, and *Ukraïns'kyi beskyd*, and wrote 38 brochures, mostly on topics in Ukrainian church, secular, and cultural history. He was mitred by Cardinal Y. Slipy in 1966.

Nestor Ripetsky

Stepan Ripetsky

Ripetsky, Nestor [Ripec'kyj] (pseuds: Bohdar Zharsky, Vsevolod Lystvych), b 19 April 1919 in Sokal, Galicia, d 19 March 1974 in Toronto. Writer and journalist. In Galicia he contributed to the daily *Dilo* and other papers and was an editor of the journals *Svit pered namy* (1934) and *Na hrani* (1935), the weekly *Stanyslavivs'ki visti* (1936), and the Sokal daily *Ukraïns'ki visti* (1941). A postwar refugee, he lived from 1948 in Winnipeg and from 1950 in Toronto. He directed a Ukrainian radio program in Winnipeg; in Toronto he was an editor of the literary and art monthly *Pace* (1954–6) and later headed the Ukrainian Journalists' Association of Canada and the World Federation of Ukrainian

Journalists. He wrote the poetry collections *Kucheriavi dni* (Billowy Days, 1936), *Shliakh pilihryma* (The Pilgrim's Road, 1937), *Tryvoha* (Trepidation, 1939), and *Povorot* (The Return, 1941); a collection of renderings of Japanese poetry, *Pisni dalekykh ostroviv* (Songs of Distant Islands, 1940); the plays *Ukraïna v krovi* (Ukraine in Blood, 1938) and *Halia* (1947); the publicistic books *Dumky na vitri* (Thoughts in the Wind, 1941) and *Khvyli shukaiut' berehiv* (Waves Seeking Shores, 1954); the story collections *Troiandy v krovi* (Roses in Blood, 1946) and *R 33* (1967); and the novelette *Sontse skhodyt' iz zakhodu (Istoriia maizhe pravdyva)* (The Sun Rises in the West [An Almost True Story], 1954).

Ripetsky, Stepan [Ripec'kyj], b 22 December 1894 in Sambir, Galicia, d 2 October 1986 in Ridgewood, New Jersey. Civic and political figure and publicist; son of T. *Ripetsky. He completed law studies in Lviv and Prague and served as an officer in the Ukrainian Sich Riflemen during the First World War. Later he was head of the Ukrainian Academic Hromada (1921), a lecturer in sociology at the Ukrainian Pedagogical Institute in Prague, and a member of the Foreign Delegation of the Ukrainian Party of Socialist Revolutionaries. In 1926 he returned to Galicia, where he was an executive member of the Ukrainian Socialist Radical party until 1939. He was arrested and interned by the Germans in 1943, and in postwar Germany he served as an executive member of the Ukrainian Socialist party and a representative member of the Ukrainian National Rada. After moving to the United States in 1949, he edited the journal *Vil'na Ukraïna* and wrote and edited several books concerning the struggle for statehood in Western Ukraine, including *Za voliu Ukraïny* (For the Freedom of Ukraine, 1967).

Ripetsky, Teodor [Ripec'kyj], b 1861, d 1901. Priest and community activist. He was the initiator of the *Ryznytsia church goods trade association and established a shelter for the widows and orphans of priests in Sambir. Among his works on historical and religious topics were *Illiustrovannaia narodnaia istoriia Rusi* (The Illustrated Popular History of Rus', 1890) and *Vybrani zhyttia sviatykh* (A Selection of Saints' Lives, 1890).

Ripetsky, Vsevolod [Ripec'kyj], b 1884 in Sambir, Galicia, d July 1919 near Solotvyna, Nadvirna county, Galicia. Student and political activist; son of T. *Ripetsky. He attended the gymnasium in Sambir and studied law in Lviv. A member of the Ukrainian Social Democratic party, he was politically active in the Sambir and Drohobych regions and was an advocate of electoral reforms in 1907. In 1918–19 he served as county commissioner of Turka county (for the Western Province of the UNR). He was executed without a trial by Polish soldiers (along with M. *Martynets, I. Siletsky, and Siletsky's son, Stepan, and son-in-law, V. Padokh).

Ripko, Oleksii, b 25 December 1907 in Okhtyrka, Kharkiv gubernia, d 7 March 1983 in Lviv. Theater director. He began working in theaters in 1929, and in 1934 he completed the stage direction course at the Kharkiv Music and Drama Institute (pupil of B. Tiahno). In 1935–55 he worked in Ukrainian theaters in Kharkiv, Sumy, Ternopil, and Okhtyrka. In 1956–83 he was a director in the Lviv Ukrainian Drama Theater. He staged approx 150 plays in all.

Ripky. II-12. A town smt (1986 pop 6,700) and raion center in Chernihiv oblast. It is first mentioned in historical documents in 1607. Its inhabitants took part in B. Khmelnytsky's uprising in 1648 and then belonged to Chernihiv regiment in the Hetman state. Under Russian rule the town belonged to Chernihiv vicegerency (1782–95), Little Russia gubernia (1796–1802), and Chernihiv gubernia (1802–1925). In the second half of the 17th century its iron-ore deposits began to be mined, and in the 18th century a ceramics industry began to develop there. Today Ripky has a woodworking and a building-materials industry.

Ripniv settlements. Three Slavic settlements of the 3rd to 11th century located near Ripniv, Buzke raion, Lviv oblast. Intermittent excavations during 1954–64 uncovered the remains of semi-pit and surface dwellings (commonly with clay ovens), hand built and wheel thrown pottery, three blacksmith furnaces, kilns, and iron, bronze, bone, and glass objects. The walls of a number of dwellings from the 6th to 7th centuries were faced with wood.

Rishko, Mykola [Riško], b 1907 in Drahove, near Khust, Transcarpathia, d ? Writer. He began publishing poetry in the Transcarpathian dialect in the 1920s in Prešov. A postwar Soviet citizen, he is the author of the poetry collections *Hirs'ki vatry* (Mountain Bonfires, 1936), *Zahraly struny* (The Strings Began Playing, 1960), *Rozmova z matir'iu* (A Talk with Mother, 1973), and *Povernennia* (The Return, 1980) and the prose collections *Vtecha z temriavy* (Flight from Darkness, 1964) and *Krasa virnosti* (The Beauty of Loyalty, 1983).

Ritter, Pavlo, b 5 April 1872 in Chutove, Poltava county, d 17 April 1939. Literary scholar, linguist-Sanskritologist, and translator. He graduated from Kharkiv University (1894), where he taught from 1897, became a professor in 1921, and became head of the chair of linguistics in 1922. One of the founders of the *All-Ukrainian Learned Association of Oriental Studies and its organ *Skhidnyi svit*, he contributed many entries on Indian literature to the Russian prerevolutionary Granat encyclopedia, translated numerous Sanskrit literary works into Russian, and translated works by Kalidasa and R. Tagore and Vedic hymns into Ukrainian. After being arrested during the Stalinist terror in 1938, he went mad and died in prison. A collection of biographical and bibliographic materials about him was published in 1966.

Ritter von Rittersberg, Ludwig (Ritter z Rittersberku, Ludvík), b 19 November 1809 in Prague, d 6 June 1858 in Vršovice, Bohemia. Czech writer, journalist, and composer. He studied music in Lviv. Among his writings are descriptions of Galicia and tales about the Hutsuls. In his *Gedanken über slavischen Gesang* (1843) and elsewhere he wrote that Podilia was the cradle of the Slavic song and that the *kolomyika* was the prototype.

Rittikh, Aleksandr [Rittix], b 1831, d ? Russian cartographer, ethnographer, and statistician. After graduating from the Nikolai Engineering Academy and the General Staff Academy in St Petersburg, Rittikh served as a career officer in the Russian army (1862–94). He prepared the first detailed ethnographic maps and statistical tables of the territories in the Russian Empire. Some of them, including the maps of the Slavic peoples (1874), European Russia (1875), the Russian state (1878), Kharkiv gubernia (1879), and the Slavic world (1885), contained information on the national composition of Ukraine.

Ritual songs (*obriadovi pisni*). Folk songs that accompanied important changes in a person's life and the seasonal cycles in farming. Calendric ritual songs include *carols or *koliadky* and *shchedrivky* (on Christmas and Epiphany), Shrovetide songs, *vesnianky-hahilky* and *ryndzivky* (on Easter), *rusalka* and *tsarynni* songs (on the Rosalia), St Peter's day songs, haymowers' and rakers' songs, Kupalo songs, *harvest songs, *vechernytsi* songs, and songs to St Nicholas. The ritual songs of family life include christening songs, *wedding songs, and funeral hymns and *laments. At one time ritual songs were believed to possess magical powers: they could ensure a bountiful harvest and the well-being of the persons mentioned in them. Eventually they lost their magical meaning and were regarded simply as entertaining or expressive. All ritual songs contain some ancient pagan elements mixed with more recent, mostly Christian, elements. The majority of them are tied to ritual acts, games, dances, and customs.

After the Bolshevik Revolution attempts were made to integrate ritual songs with newly created civic celebrations and rituals. There were also attempts to create artificial new songs praising 'the happy Soviet life' and thanking the Party, V. Lenin, or J. Stalin for it. These songs did not catch on and did not become part of daily life. In the last few years there has been a marked revival of traditional rituals and songs, particularly of carols and wedding songs.

Ukrainian ritual songs have been collected and studied by J. Lasycki, H. Kalynovsky, P. Chubynsky, Ya. Holovatsky, I. Franko, V. Hnatiuk, O. Potebnia, M. Hrushevsky, V. Petrov, K. Koperzhynsky, F. Kolessa, K. Kvitka, Z. Kuzelia, O. Dei, V. Hoshovsky, and O. Zilynsky.

BIBLIOGRAPHY
Dei, O. *Narodno-pisenni zhanry* (Kiev 1979; 2nd edn, 1983)
M. Mushynka

Riuryk [Rjuryk] (Rurik, Riurik), b ?, d 879 in Novgorod, in northern Rus'. According to the Primary Chronicle Riuryk was a Varangian chieftain who was invited to rule Novgorod in 862, and whose brothers, Sineus and Truvor, were invited to rule Beloozero and Izborsk respectively. Within two years both his brothers were dead, and Riuryk annexed their realms, thereby becoming the ruler of the northern Slavic (Slovene and Krivichian) and Finnish (Meria, Chud, and Ves) tribes and territories. According to the Hypatian Chronicle Riuryk ruled in Ladoga before seizing Novgorod in 862, and he suppressed an anti-Varangian uprising there in 869.

An early 12th-century Rus' chronicler's explanation of the emergence of the ruling dynasty of Kievan Rus' as the 'coming of the Varangians led by Riuryk, his brothers, and his host' has served as the basis of the *Norman theory of the origin of Rus'. Later Riuryk's son (or grandson), *Ihor, became the prince of a separate Kievan realm to the south and annexed some of the northern tribes to his state, thereby beginning the ruling *Riurykide dynasty of Kievan Rus'.

Some historians (eg, A. Shakhmatov) have accepted the Primary Chronicle's account of Riuryk and believe him to have been an actual historical figure; they have, however, rejected the story of his two brothers. Other historians (eg, D. Likhachev) believe that Riuryk was a legendary or semilegendary figure. Still others (eg, B. Beliaev, P. Kovalevsky, O. Pritsak) believe that Riuryk of Novgorod was the same person as Hroerekr (Rorik), the 9th-century Norse king of Jutland and Frisia, and that widespread myths about him inspired the chroniclers' account of Riuryk as the progenitor of the Riurykide dynasty.

BIBLIOGRAPHY
Shakhmatov, A. *Razyskaniia o drevneishikh letopisnykh svodakh* (St Petersburg 1908)
Perfets'kyi, E. 'Peremyshl's'kyi litopysnyi kodeks pershoï redaktsiï v skladi khroniky Iana Dlugosha (Opovidannia pro Riuryka, Syneusa i Truvora v skladi zvodu 1100 roku),' *ZNTSh*, 147 (1927), 149 (1928), 151 (1931)
Beliaev, N. 'Rorik of Jutland and Rurik of the Russian Chronicles,' *Saga Book of the Viking Society for Northern Research*, 10 (1928–9)

A. Zhukovsky

Riuryk Rostyslavych [Rjuryk Rostyslavyč], b ?, d 1092. Rus' prince; great-grandson of Yaroslav the Wise. The western frontiers of Rus' were governed by the Rostyslavych brothers Riuryk, Volodar, and Vasylko possibly as early as 1077. After the death of Rostyslav Volodymyrovych in 1084, Riuryk remained in Volodymyr-Volynskyi with his brother Vasylko, as princes-in-exile at the court of Yaropolk Iziaslavych, and in 1086 Riuryk became prince of Peremyshl. That year, according to the Primary Chronicle, Riuryk's secret servant Neradets fled to Peremyshl after killing Yaropolk. Riuryk probably hoped to receive the rule of Volodymyr-Volynskyi, but the Kievan prince Vsevolod Yaroslavych granted it to Davyd Ihorevych. After Riuryk died, the rule of Peremyshl passed to his brother Volodar.

Riuryk Rostyslavych [Rjuryk Rostyslavyč], b ca 1140, d 19 April 1212 (other sources state 1211, 1214, or 1215) in Chernihiv. Kievan Rus' prince; grandson of Mstyslav I Volodymyrovych. He governed an independent Derevlianian province in the 1160s, and his son, Volodymyr, replaced him when he went to rule Ovruch in 1168. He later ruled in Novgorod and Kiev for brief periods in 1173 and 1181. Following the death of Sviatoslav III Vsevolodovych in 1194, Riuryk became prince of Kiev, which he ruled until 1210 (with interruptions). A falling out with members of the Olhovych dynasty and, later, with Roman Mstyslavych caused Riuryk to seek an alliance with the Cumans. In 1210 he was forced to abdicate the Kievan throne to Vsevolod Sviatoslavych Chermny; he governed in Chernihiv for the remainder of his life.

Riurykide dynasty (Riurykovych; Russian and Belarusian: Riurikovich). The ruling princely dynasty of *Kievan Rus', descended from Prince *Ihor of Kiev, who according to the Primary Chronicle was the son of the Varangian *Riuryk. The separation of certain Rus' lands and growing independence of individual principalities from the Kievan center resulted in the creation of some 15 (and later more) autonomous Riurykide houses, which were denoted genealogically either by the name of the principality they controlled or by the name of their founder.

Ukrainian branches of the Riurykide dynasty were the Monomakhovych house of Kiev and Volhynia, descended from *Volodymyr Monomakh; the *Romanovych house of Galicia-Volhynia, descended from *Roman Mstyslavych; the Rostyslavych house of Galicia, descended from *Rostyslav Volodymyrovych; the *Olhovych house of Chernihiv and Novhorod-Siverskyi, descended from *Oleh Sviatoslavych; and the Turiv-Pynske house, descended from *Iziaslav Yaroslavych. One of the houses, descended from Prince *Yurii Dolgorukii, the youngest son of Volodymyr Monomakh, became the family of the grand princes of Vladimir-Suzdal and then of the grand princes and tsars of Muscovy. The last Riurykide tsar, Fedor I Ivanovich, died without heirs in 1598. The Belarusian Riurykides included the Polatsk house, descended from *Iziaslav Volodymyrovych and his grandson, Vseslav, which became autonomous in the 11th century; and the Smolensk house, descended from *Rostyslav Mstyslavych, Monomakh's grandson. The descendants of the various houses, particularly those of Belarus and Chernihiv–Novhorod-Siverskyi, were many, and they maintained their patrimonial appanages until they became servitor princes of the Grand Duchy of Lithuania or Muscovy. A number of junior families lost their princely titles at that time.

Riurykide families who managed to preserve their princely status in the Russian Empire until the 20th century include the Bariatinskys, Dolgorukovs, Gorchakovs, Obolenskys, Repnins, Shcherbatovs, and Volkonskys, descended from the Chernihiv house; the Drutsky-Liubetskys, Drutsky-Sokolynskys, Sviatopolk-Mirskys, and *Sviatopolk-Chetvertynskys, descended from the Galician-Volhynian house; the Kropotkins and Viazemskys, descended from the Smolensk house; and many other families of various Russian houses.

BIBLIOGRAPHY
Dolgorukov, P. *Rossiiskaia rodoslovnaia kniga*, pt 1 (Moscow 1855)
Vlas'ev, G. *Potomstvo Riurika: Materialy dlia sostavleniia rodoslovii*, 3 pts (St Petersburg 1906–7)
Baumgarten, N. *Généalogies et mariages occidentaux des Rurikides russes du Xe au XIIIe siècle* (Rome 1928) – *Généalogie des branches régnantes des Rurikides du XIIIe au XVIe siècle* (Rome 1934)

O. Ohloblyn

Riv River. A right-bank tributary of the Boh River. It is 104 km long and drains a basin area of 1,160 sq km. It originates in the Podolian Upland and flows through Khmelnytskyi and Vinnytsia oblasts. The river is used for irrigation, water supply, and fishing.

Rivenky or **Rovenky** [Riven'ky]. V-20, DB III-6. A city (1990 pop 58,300) in Luhanske oblast. It was founded as a Cossack settlement in 1705 and was first known as Osynovyi Rovenok or simply Rovenok. From the 1730s to the 1760s it was a defensive outpost on the Ukrainian line and was called Katerynivka. From 1793 it was the sloboda Orlovo-Rovenetska or Rovenky. It was granted city status in 1934. Today it is an industrial center with seven coal mines and a footwear factory.

River transportation. A mode of transportation using natural and man-made waterways. Before railways were built, rivers offered the chief means of transportation in Ukraine, which has a dense river network and conditions favorable to river navigation. There are approx 3,000 rivers over 10 km long and 116 rivers over 100 km long in Ukraine. Owing to rainfall levels and the gentle slope of

TABLE 1
Ukraine's major rivers

	Total length (km)	Within Ukraine (km)	Navigable length (km)
Dnieper	2,285	981	981
Dniester	1,362	1,362	500
Boh	792	806	105
Desna	1,126	591	535
Donets	1,053	672	none
Danube	2,960	174	174
Horyn	659	659	250
Samara	311	320	80
Prypiat	748	261	85

the land, many of the rivers have a water flow large enough and slow enough for easy navigation (for the main navigable rivers see table 1). River transportion is the cheapest mode of transportation, but it is slow and not always available. River traffic is interrupted by the long, cold winters in Ukraine and by low water levels in the summer, particularly in the southern regions.

The first steamboats appeared on the Dnieper River in 1823, and a regular passenger service was established between Kremenchuk and Pinsk in 1850. The Russian Steamshipping and Trading Society (ROPIT), established in 1857, dominated the freight traffic on the lower Dnieper and along the seacoast. By 1894, 79 of the 280 steamships on the river were owned by ROPIT. In 1913 the Dnieper commercial fleet did not exceed 400 small vessels, and the

TABLE 2
Inland 'seas' of the Greater Dnieper system

'Sea' (reservoir)	Area (sq km)	Depth (m)
Kiev	922	4–14.5
Kaniv	675	3.9–21
Kremenchuk	2,250	6–20
Dniprodzerzhynske	567	4.3 (avg)
Kakhivka	2,155	8.5–24
Zaporizhia	410	8–53

TABLE 3
Transportation and irrigation canals

Canal	Length (km)
Dnieper-Donbas	500.0
Dnieper–Kryvyi Rih	42.5
North Crimean	412.6
Kakhivka	130.0
Saky	30.0
Donets-Donbas	131.6
Dnieper-Inhulets	83.0

freight volume of river transportation was a mere 1.7 million t. After the revolution two river directorates were established, the Upper-Dnieper directorate in Kiev and the Lower-Dnieper Directorate in Kherson. In 1957 jurisdiction over river transportation and boat registration was transferred to the Ukrainian government, but investment

TABLE 4
Basic indexes of river transportation, 1940–86

Category	1940	1970	1980	1986
1. Length of network (in 1,000 km)	3.2	4.8	4.9	5.0
2. Length of canals (in 1,000 km)	0.1	1.8	2.2	2.4
Freight traffic				
3. Output (in billion Tkm[1])	1.1	6.1	10.7	12.7
4. Volume (in million t)	4.6	27.3	51.3	58.5
including:				
(a) container hauls (in 1,000 t)	–	–.	480.0	524.0
(b) packaged goods (in 1,000 t)	–	–	274.0	271.0
5. Average trip distance per t of haul (km)	239.1	223.4	208.0	217.1
6. Average density of haul per km of network (in 1,000 Tkm)	343.8	1,270.8	2,183.7	2,540.0
7. Cost of 10 Tkm (in kopecks)	–	2.77	2.99	3.1
Passenger traffic				
8. Output (in million Pkm[2])	356.0	495.0	557.0	600.0
9. Volume (in million passengers)	6.8	21.4	24.8	21.0
10. Average trip distance per passenger (in km)	52.3	23.1	22.5	23.8
11. Average density of haul per km of network (in 1,000 passengers)	112.3	103.1	113.7	100.0
12. Cost of 10 Pkm (in kopecks)	–	17.9	29.67	28.98
13. Percentage of river to total transport output				
(a) freight	1.4	1.0	1.4	1.4
(b) passenger	–	0.5	0.4	0.4

[1]Tkm = tons per km.
[2]Pkm = passengers per km.

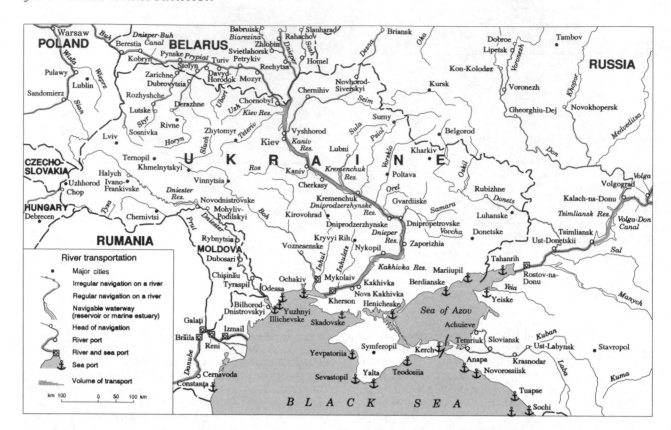

and production targets continued to be controlled by the Central State Planning Committee.

During the Soviet period some important changes took place in Ukraine's river transportation: the number and the engine power of vessels increased; new port facilities were built, and existing ones enlarged; navigation barriers, such as the Dnieper and Boh rapids, were virtually removed; the Greater Dnieper project was completed; and the course of the Dniester, Boh, Desna, and Seim rivers was changed.

The Greater Dnieper project consists of 5 giant, artificial 'seas,', 6 hydroelectric stations with dams, 3 major canals, and several irrigation systems. The basic indexes of the so-called 'seas' are shown in table 2. The canals serve two purposes, shipping and irrigation. Some branches of irrigation canals are closed to boat traffic. Connecting canals accommodate semilarge vessels and barges. Their productive capacity depends on the water level. The indexes of artificial canals are shown in table 3. There are similar plans for the Dniester, Boh, Desna, and Donets rivers.

Ukrainian rivers are relatively poor in port facilities. Before the 1970s the major ports on the Dnieper River were Kiev, Kremenchuk, Dnipropetrovske, Zaporizhia, and Kherson. Since then Chornobyl, Kaniv, Cherkasy, Dniprodzerzhynske, Nykopil, and Beryslav-Kakhivka have been added. The main ports on the Boh are Mykolaiv and Voznesenske. On the lower Dniester River there are two ports, Bilhorod and Ovidiopil. Ukraine has two major ports on the Danube River, Izmail and Reni, and a third, Ust Dunaiske, is under construction. The Donets has no major ports, but Izium, Rubizhne, and Lysychanske have loading and unloading facilities.

River vessels and barges are mostly built of metal.

Voshkod-type ships with a maximum capacity of 5,000 t are equipped with computers, and their traffic is generally programmed. On the Dnieper passengers are carried in comfortable liners and high-speed hydrofoils. The industry's passenger volume has declined slowly, and its freight volume has increased, but its share of the transportation output has remained fairly stable over the last four decades (see table 4).

E. Bej

Rivers. Courses of flowing water in well-defined channels, usually growing in volume between the source and the point of entry into a sea, a lake, or another river. Streams or rivulets are smaller, with the volumes involved not being closely defined.

The rivers of Ukraine generally flow southward into the Black Sea or the Sea of Azov. The notable exceptions are in the northwest, where the prevalent flow is northward into the *Prypiat, a tributary of the *Dnieper, or into the *Vistula (Wisła), which flows through Poland into the Baltic Sea. Nevertheless over 90 percent of the territory of Ukraine is situated in the Black Sea–Sea of Azov drainage basin. That area is drained by major rivers, such as the *Tysa, the *Prut, and the *Seret, by way of the *Danube; the *Dniester, the *Boh, and the Dnieper, together with its major tributaries, the Prypiat and the *Desna; the *Don with the Donets and its tributary, the *Oskil (Oskol in Russian); and the *Kuban. The remaining Ukrainian territory belongs to the Baltic Sea drainage basin, which incorporates the right-bank tributaries of the Vistula, the Buh, the *Vepr, and the *Sian. With the exception of the Carpathians, the divides between the Black Sea and the Baltic Sea drainage basins and between the major river basins usually follow low elevations. That allows the rivers of various drainage basins to be connected with canals for river-barge navigation between the Baltic and the Black seas.

There are approx 30,000 rivers crossing Ukrainian ethnographic territory. Of that number about 23,000 are in Ukraine. With a combined length of nearly 180,000 km, most are small; in Ukraine there are 117 rivers the watercourses of which exceed 100 km, but only 13 that are longer than 500 km (they are noted in table 1). The characteristics of rivers, such as the density of the river network as well as the volume and the seasonality of the flow, depend on factors such as climate, geology, relief, vegetation, and human modifications of the landscape.

River characteristics. River networks or drainage densities vary throughout Ukraine. They are highest in the mountainous regions, where the greatest annual precipitation occurs; there they attain nearly 1.1 km of watercourse per sq km of territory. Drainage densities decline to

TABLE 1
Area of river basin, length of channel, and mean annual surface runoff for major rivers of Ukraine

River	Area of drainage basin (sq km)	Length of channel (km)	Mean annual surface runoff (L/S per sq km)	(mm)
I *Rivers draining into the Black Sea and the Sea of Azov*				
A				
Dnieper	510,000	2,285	3.2	102
Prypiat	114,300	748	3.8	120
Horyn	27,650	659	3.3	105
Sluch	13,900	451	3.5	108
Desna	88,900	1,126	3.9	123
Psol	22,800	692	2.4	75
Samara	22,600	311	0.8	27
Sula	18,100	310	2.3	72
Teteriv	15,300	385	3.0	92
Vorsklo	14,700	452	2.1	68
Inhulets	14,460	549	0.7	21
Ros	12,575	346	2.2	72
B				
Dniester	72,000	1,362	5.0	157
C				
Boh	63,700	792	1.5	47
Syniukha	16,752	111	1.7	54
D Tributaries of the Danube				
Prut	27,000	845	2.4	78
Tysa	150,000	1,410	1.3	42
E Tributaries of the Don				
Donets	98,900	1,053	1.6	51
Oskil	14,680	436	2.9	95
F				
Kuban	61,500	910	6.5	203
II *Rivers draining into the Baltic Sea*				
Tributaries of the Vistula				
Buh	73,470	813	3.7	117
Sian	16,730	444	6.0	188

about 0.6 km/sq km in Subcarpathia, the Tysa Lowland, and Subcaucasia, and to 0.5 km/sq km in the uplands of Roztochia, Podilia, and Donets, where porous limestone provides for better underground drainage. In general the river network becomes less dense to the south and east in keeping with the declining precipitation. Low drainage densities (less than 0.1 km/sq km) occur between the lower Desna and the upper reaches of the *Oster and between the *Trubizh and the *Supii. There are no rivers (except for a few seasonal intermittent streams) between the lower Dnieper and the Molochna.

Rivers are fed by rainfall, snowmelt, groundwater, and glaciers. In Ukraine rainfall accounts for nearly 75 percent of the total precipitation. The greater proportion of rainfall evaporates from the surface or infiltrates the soil, and only a small portion provides for surface runoff into the rivers (less than 10 percent in the plains, although it can reach up to 50 percent in the mountains). In the steppe zone nearly all the rainfall evaporates or seeps into the soil. The rivers of the plains are fed mainly by melting snow. Groundwater feeds rivers throughout the year. The mountain glaciers of the Caucasus provide water for the Kuban and other rivers. In general the main source of water for the mountain rivers is rainfall. In the plains the rivers are fed mainly by snowmelt, 50–80 percent; groundwater contributes an additional 10–20 percent.

For Ukraine as a whole the mean annual surface runoff amounts to 14 percent of the atmospheric precipitation (in Ukraine representing approx 85 mm of river discharge of approx 600 mm). The mean annual surface runoff varies not only among the river basins (see table 1) but also within the river basins themselves, according to the hydrological conditions. The highest runoff (in liters per second per sq km or L/S/sq km) is 75 (2,340 mm) in the Caucasus, 35 (1,100 mm) in the Carpathians, and 15 (470 mm) in the Crimean Mountains. For the Ukrainian uplands and lowlands the mean annual surface runoff ranges from 1 to 4 L/S/sq km (30–130 mm). In the steppe it diminishes to a range of 0.5 to 1 L/S/sq km (16–30 mm). In the nonmountainous areas there is a gradient of decreasing runoff from north to south in keeping with precipitation. High anomalies occur on uplands, where higher precipitation and better drainage contribute to higher runoff. Low anomalies are found in the lowlands north of Lutske and east of Kiev, the former associated with karst (where porous limestone absorbs much of the precipitation), and the latter with bogs (where impeded drainage reduces runoff). In the mountains runoff increases with higher elevation.

Stream flow varies considerably from year to year. In dry years, for example, the large rivers of Ukraine discharge from three-quarters to less than one-half of their flow in normal years (see table 2). Over a monthly period greater variations occur. The Boh River, for example, with a mean March runoff of 20.7 mm, discharged only 3.6 mm in March 1921, but 81 mm in March 1922. Even greater variations are experienced by smaller streams.

Seasonal variation in the flow of rivers is considerable and is closely related to the amount of surface water available. Both the highest availability of surface water and the highest flows occur in the spring, when the snow melts. The spring flow accounts for 50–80 percent of the total annual discharge of the major rivers and for nearly all the annual discharge of the small, intermittent streams of the steppes. The lowest availability of surface water occurs in

TABLE 2
Variation of flow among selected large rivers of Ukraine

River	Area of drainage basin (sq km)	Annual surface runoff (mm, and as % of average year)		
		Average year	Dry year	Very dry year
Dnieper	510,000	102 (100)	84 (83)	63 (62)
Prypiat	114,300	120 (100)	87 (72)	60 (49)
Desna	88,900	123 (100)	100 (81)	72 (59)
Dniester	72,000	157 (100)	94 (60)	68 (43)
Boh	63,700	47 (100)	35 (74)	20 (43)
Psol	22,800	75 (100)	61 (81)	39 (53)

the winter, when only occasional thaws release snowmelt, and the lowest flows tend to occur during the warm, dry weather of the late summer and early fall, when the lowest quantities of water are available through both surface run-off and groundwater seepage. Spring floods or high flows in small streams last for 10 to 15 days, whereas large rivers may sustain high flows for 30 to 45 days. In addition to spring peak flows, summer floods associated with downpours are particularly common in the mountain streams of the Caucasus and Carpathian regions. The Kuban River hydrograph, however, reveals four seasonal high flows: two in the spring (in February, when the snow melts in the lower part of the drainage basin, and in April, when the snow melts in the mountains), one in the summer (through June and July, associated with the surface melting of the glaciers), and one in the fall (caused by increased precipitation in October). In the Tysa River Basin, winter floods are not uncommon; they are associated with the thaws triggered by the incursions of cyclonic storms from the Mediterranean.

Before the construction of the Kiev Reservoir particularly large spring floods occurred in the Dnieper River north of Kiev, where waters from snowmelt converged from both the Prypiat and the Desna. Spring floods in the broad, flat Prypiat floodplain occur regularly. Spring floods in the northward-flowing Sian and Buh and in the upper part of the Dniester are caused by early and rapid melting of the snow in the upper part of the river basins, while the frozen middle stretches of the rivers overflow with ice jams. Near the mouths of the Dnieper, the Danube, the Boh, and the Kuban considerable flooding and fluctuation in water level occur in conjunction with the wind's pushing of seawater up against the windward shore (setup) or as a backwash following the offshore wind's withdrawing of it (seiche).

The winter regime of the rivers begins with the formation of ice on the surface. The freeze-up occurs earliest in the northeast (the upper Desna River Basin) at the end of November and progressively expands southward. Freeze-up along the Dnieper comes later; it reaches Kiev by 21 December and Kherson by 28 December. The less voluminous Boh River experiences somewhat earlier freeze-ups, at Vinnytsia by 6 December and at Voznesenske by 11 December. The upper reaches of the Dniester in Subcarpathia begin to freeze up in mid-December, but lower down near Zalishchyky the river does not freeze over until the end of December. Further east at Dubosari, freeze-up sets in by 20 December. The Kuban and the Tysa rivers do not attain a stable ice cover, and the ice cover on the Sian and the Buh rivers is often disrupted by thaws.

The breakup of ice in the spring begins in the south and advances northward. The mean dates for the Dnieper are 3 March at Kherson, 15 March at Zaporizhia, and 24 March at Kiev. For the Boh River they are 7 March at Voznesenske and 21 March at Vinnytsia. On the Dniester ice begins to break up at Zalishchyky (4 March) before it does so at Dubosari (9 March), with ice jam flooding often the result. The problem is even more severe on the northward-flowing Sian and Buh rivers. Mountain streams, which begin the breakup of ice from downstream, are spared the worst ice jam flooding. On average the rivers are ice-covered in northern Ukraine for nearly 3.5 months; in the south the ice cover lasts 2.5 months or less.

Rivers carry considerable material in suspension and solution, the quantity depending on the velocity of the current and the geology of the terrain. Mountain streams transport the largest quantity of suspended material, especially during floods, when they are capable of rolling stones and small boulders along their beds. Slow-flowing rivers in the lowlands carry the least material. Rivers almost always carry very small particles (mostly clay and silt) in suspension, which make the water appear muddy. The clearest rivers of Ukraine are found in Polisia, where small particles in suspension do not exceed 50 g/cu m; the muddiest are the mountain streams in flood and the full-fed tributaries of the middle stretch of the Dniester, which may carry up to 1,000 g/cu m. In other rivers the concentration of particles in suspension generally varies from 150 to 500 g/cu m.

The concentration of dissolved minerals in river waters of northern Ukraine varies from 200 to 500 mg/L. That concentration increases to the south and east, where there is an increasing presence of soluble minerals in sedimentary rocks and an increasing soil salinity; it attains the highest values (nearly 2,000 mg/L) in the Donets Basin and in rivers between the Danube and the Dniester. The lowest concentrations (below 100 mg/L) are found in the fast-flowing Carpathian mountain streams.

Regional characteristics of rivers. Ukraine may be subdivided into 11 regions according to hydrological factors and the nature of the rivers: Polisia, the Volhynia-Kholm Upland, the Podolian Upland, the Dnieper Upland, the Dnieper Lowland, the Donets Ridge, the southwestern margin of the Central Upland, the Black Sea Lowland, the Crimean Mountains, the Carpathians and Subcarpathia, and the Western Caucasus and Subcaucasia. Polisia is drained by the Dnieper (north of Kiev), the Prypiat, the Desna, and the Buh rivers. The mean annual precipitation is 500–600 mm, and the mean annual runoff, 100–120 mm (20 percent). River gradients are gentle (about 0.5 m/km), and the river currents are slow. River valleys are wide, and their low and swampy banks are inundated each year by the spring floods. Ice covers the rivers, on average, 3.5 months, with longer duration in the east than the west.

The Volhynia-Kholm Upland is drained by the Vepr, the Buh, and the right-bank (southern) tributaries of the Prypiat – the *Stokhid, the *Styr with its tributary, the *Ikva, and the *Horyn with its tributary, the *Sluch. The mean annual precipitation is 500–700 mm, and the mean annual runoff, 100–150 mm (20 percent). River gradients in the south exceed 1 m/km but decline to the north. River valleys are wide and frequently swampy and experience floods in the spring. The duration of the ice cover varies from 3 months in the west to 3.5 months in the east.

The Podolian Upland is drained by the left-bank (north-

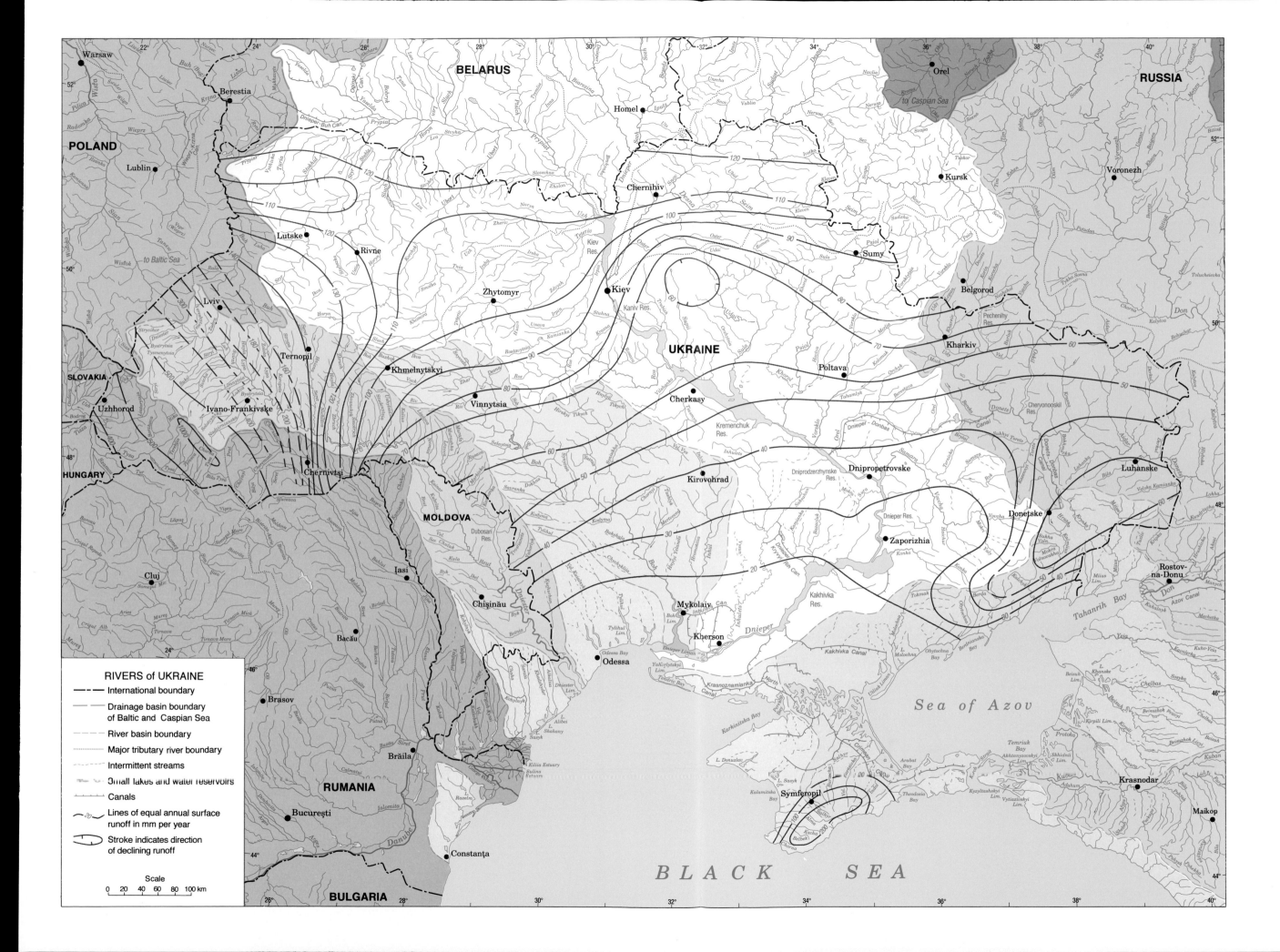

BELARUS

POLAND

RUSSIA

Warsaw

Berestia

Lublin

Homel

Orel

Voronezh

Kursk

Chernihiv

Lutske

Rivne

Kiev Res.

Sumy

Belgorod

Lviv

Zhytomyr

Kiev

Kaniv Res.

UKRAINE

Kharkiv

Pecheniny Res.

Ternopil

Khmelnytskyi

Vinnytsia

Cherkasy

Poltava

SLOVAKIA

Uzhhorod

Ivano-Frankivske

Kremenchuk Res.

Chernonooskil Res.

HUNGARY

Chernivtsi

Dniprodzerzhynske Res.

Dnipropetrovske

Luhanske

Kirovohrad

MOLDOVA

Dubosari Res.

Dnieper – Donbas Canal

Dnieper Res.

Donetske

Iasi

Zaporizhia

Rostov-na-Donu

Cluj

Bacău

Chişinău

Kakhivka Res.

Mykolaiv

Kherson

Dnieper

Tahanrih Bay

Brasov

Odessa Bay

Odessa

Krasnamianka Canal

Kakhivka Canal

Sea of Azov

Brăila

Krasnodar

RUMANIA

Bucureşti

Kiliia Estuary

Sulina Estuary

Symferopil

Maikop

Danube

Constanţa

BULGARIA

B L A C K   S E A

ern) tributaries of the Dniester and the right-bank (western) tributaries of the Boh. The mean annual precipitation declines from 700 mm in the west to 450 mm in the southeast, and the range of the mean annual runoff is even greater, from 200 mm (30 percent) in the west to 40 mm (10 percent) in the southeast. The density of the river network varies from 0.4 to 0.5 km/sq km. In the upper reaches of the rivers the gradient is shallow (about 1 m/km), and the valleys are wide and swampy in places. In the middle reaches the gradient becomes steeper, and the river valleys become narrow and deep, most notably in the Dniester's middle reaches. In the southwestern extremity of the Ukrainian Crystalline Shield the riverbeds are stony. Spring floods are common, and the Dniester also experiences summer floods. The ice cover lasts about 3 months.

The Dnieper Upland is drained by the right-bank (western) tributaries of the Dnieper (the *Teteriv, the *Irpin, the *Ros, the *Tiasmyn, and the upper *Inhulets) and the left-bank (eastern) tributaries of the Boh (the *Sob, the *Syniukha, and the upper *Inhul). The mean annual precipitation is 450–550 mm, and the mean annual runoff diminishes from 100 mm (20 percent) in the northwest to 30 mm (6 percent) in the southeast. River gradients are approx 2 m/km. Rivers in the Ukrainian Crystalline Shield are stony and have rapids. The deep river valleys are canyonlike in their upper reaches. Floods occur in the spring. The ice cover lasts for three months, although the period is shorter by one to two weeks in the south.

The Dnieper Lowland is drained by the left-bank (eastern) tributaries of the Dnieper: the *Sula, the *Psol, the *Vorskla, the *Orel, and the *Samara. The mean annual precipitation decreases from 550 mm in the north to 450 mm in the south, and the mean annual runoff declines from 120 mm (22 percent) to 40 mm (9 percent) in the same direction. Riverbeds are well graded, with a drop of 1 m/km. The river valleys are broad with gently sloping banks. High water levels occur in the spring. The ice cover period ranges from 3.5 months in the north to only 2 months in the south.

The Donets Ridge, bounded by the Donets River to the north, is drained by the right-bank (southwestern) tributaries of the Donets, the *Miius, and the *Kalmiius that flow into the Sea of Azov, and the upper reaches of two left-bank (eastern) tributaries of the Dnieper, the *Vovcha and the Samara. The mean annual precipitation is approx 500 mm, and the mean annual runoff, approx 50 mm (10 percent). The gradient of the Donets is only 0.5 m/km; the gradients of the other rivers are 1 m/km or more. The river valleys are deep, and the right bank of the Donets is considerably higher than the left bank. High water occurs in the spring, and the ice cover lasts about 3 months.

The southwestern margin of the Central Upland is drained by the upper reaches of the left-bank (eastern) tributaries of the Dnieper (the Desna with its tributary, the *Seim, the Psol, and the Vorskla), the upper reaches of the Donets and its left-bank (eastern) tributaries (the Oskil, the *Aidar, and the Derkul), and the right-bank (western) tributaries of the Don (notably the Chorna Kalytva). The mean annual precipitation is 400–500 mm, with runoff decreasing from 120 mm (24 percent) in the north to 60 mm (15 percent) or less in the south. River gradients are approx 2 m/km. River valleys are deep, with the right banks higher than the left banks. Floods occur in the spring, and the ice cover lasts about 3.5 months.

The Black Sea Lowland is drained by the lower reaches of the Dniester, the Boh, the Dnieper, and other smaller rivers flowing into the Black Sea and the Sea of Azov. To the south and east small intermittent streams drain the Crimean Lowland and small, though mostly permanent, streams drain the Kuban Lowland into the Sea of Azov. The mean annual precipitation ranges between 270 and 400 mm (up to 500 mm in the Kuban Lowland); the mean annual runoff, occurring mostly in the spring, is less than 25 mm (6 percent or less) in the dry steppe and up to to 50 mm (10 percent) in the Kuban Lowland. In the summer nearly all the water evaporates, and small streams and middle-sized rivers, such as the Malyi Kuialnyk, the Velykyi Kuialnyk, and the Tylihul, tend to dry up. Lacking sufficient power such rivers flow into coastal terminal lakes, which are cut off from the sea by shoreline bars. River valleys are broad with low banks and floodplains overgrown with reeds. The ice cover is not always stable; it lasts up to 2.5 months.

The Crimean Mountains obtain 400–1,000 mm of mean annual precipitation, mostly in the late fall and the winter. A large proportion of the rainfall is absorbed by the porous limestones (underground drainage); there is left a mean annual runoff of 20–200 mm (5–20 percent). The short mountain streams form deep, narrow gorges. Those flowing north onto the Crimean Lowland become intermittent and assume characteristics common to the smaller rivers of the Black Sea Lowland.

The Carpathians and Subcarpathia are drained to the north by the right-bank tributaries of the upper Vistula (the Dunajec, the Wisłoka, and the Sian) and by the Dniester headwaters, including its left-bank tributary, the *Stryvihor, and its many right-bank tributaries, such as the *Bystrytsia, the *Stryi, the *Svicha, the *Limnytsia, the *Bystrytsia Solotvynska, and the Bystrytsia Nadvirnianska. To the south the Carpathians are drained by the Tysa with its right-bank tributaries, the Teresva, the *Tereblia, the *Rika, the *Borzhava, the *Liatorytsia, the *Uzh, the *Laborets, and the *Ondava with its tributary, the Toplia. To the east the Carpathians are drained by the headwaters of the left-bank tributaries of the Danube, the Seret and the Prut. The mean annual precipitation varies widely, from 700 mm in the foothills to 1,500 mm at the highest mountain elevations. The mean annual runoff also varies, in keeping with the elevation, from 350 to 750 mm (50 percent or more). River density is 1.1 km/sq km. Gradients are very steep, 60–70 m/km, in the upper reaches but decline to 5–10 m/km in the lower reaches. River valleys in the mountains are relatively narrow and deep (600–800 m), in the foothills, less so (150–250 m). Summer flash floods are not uncommon. The ice cover varies from 2.5 to 4 months, according to the elevation. Almost every winter the ice cover in the foothills is interrupted by thaws. The middle reaches of the Tysa lack a permanent ice cover in winter. Rivers carry a large quantity of material in suspension, but not in solution.

The Western Subcaucasus is drained by the Kuban and its left-bank (southern) tributaries, the *Zelenchuk Malyi, the Zelenchuk Velykyi, the *Laba, the *Bila, and the *Pshysh. The mean annual precipitation increases from 500 mm in the lower reaches of the Kuban to 1,000 mm in the foothills and 2,400 mm in the Caucasus Mountains. Runoff in the mountains attains or exceeds 50 percent of the precipitation; in the lowland it remains at 10 percent. Rivers are fed by rainfall, snow, and glaciers. Valleys in the mountains are deep and narrow; in the lowland they are wide, with gentle slopes. An ice cover does not form every year.

In the past, rivers provided settlements with water supply, transportation, and fishing. Recently river transport and river fisheries have declined in significance, and the role played by rivers in municipal and industrial water supply, irrigation, drainage, the removal of sewage and industrial effluents, and the generation of hydroelectric power has increased. Rivers also serve as sites for outdoor recreation and as routes for tourism, but with increasing *pollution the quality of their waters and hence their value for municipal, industrial, and recreational uses have declined.

BIBLIOGRAPHY
Ohiievs'kyi, A. *Hidrolohiia* (Kharkiv–Kiev 1933)
Davydov, L. *Gidrografiia SSSR (Vody sushi)*, 2 vols (Leningrad 1953, 1955)
Chyppynh, H.; Lysenko K. *Richnyi ta minimal'nyi stik na terytorii Ukraïny* (Kiev 1959)
Hidrolohichni rozrakhunky dlia richok Ukraïny (Kiev 1962)
Shvets' H. *Kharakterystyka vodnosti richok Ukrainy* (Kiev 1964)
L'vovich, M. *Reki SSSR* (Moscow 1971)
Priroda Ukrainskoi SSR: Moria i vnutrennie vody (Kiev 1987)
                                                    I. Stebelsky, I. Tesla

Rivna. A Carpathian mountain group in the Polonynian Beskyds in Transcarpathia oblast. Situated between the Turiia and the Uzh rivers, the massif contains peaks reaching as high as 1,479 m. The mountains are quite wide and, except in the northern section, have gently rising slopes covered with meadows and mixed beech forest. Above 1,100 m the meadows are used for summer grazing.

The Rivne gymnasium, built in the 1870s

Rivne (aka Rovno). III-7. A city (1990 pop 233,000) on the Ustia River and the administrative center of Rivne oblast. The town developed out of a settlement around a fortress in the Principality of Galicia-Volhynia. It is first mentioned in historical documents in 1282, as the site of a battle between the Polish prince Leszek Czarny and the Lithuanian noble Vitenas. In the second half of the 14th century it became part of the Grand Duchy of Lithuania, and by the end of the century it had been granted the rights of *Magdeburg law. Because of its convenient location on the Kiev–Volodymyr trade route the town pros-

pered as a commercial center. In 1518–1621 it was owned by the Ostrozky family. With the Union of Lublin (1569) Rivne became part of the Polish Commonwealth. With the partitioning of Poland in 1793 it was annexed by Russia and was made a county center of Volhynia gubernia (from 1797).

Toward the end of the 19th century Rivne developed from a small administrative and trading town into a major railway junction on the Odessa–Warsaw (1873), Lviv–Zdolbuniv–Rivne, and Rivne–Lunynets–Vilnius–St Petersburg lines. Its population jumped from 6,300 in 1870 to 24,600 in 1897 and 33,700 in 1911. From the 1890s over half the population was Jewish.

In 1917–19 the city was controlled intermittently by the UNR government. It was awarded to Poland by the Treaty of Riga in 1921. Rivne was occupied by Soviet forces in 1939 and set up as the center of a new oblast. In 1941 it was captured by the Germans and turned into the administrative center for *Reichskommissariat Ukraine. In November 1941 and July 1942 respectively the Germans killed approx 18,000 and 5,000 local Jews. Soviet troops reoccupied Rivne in 1944.

Since the 1950s Rivne has developed rapidly as an industrial center. Its main industries are machine building (tractor assemblies, high-power equipment) and metalworking, building-materials manufacturing, construction, light industry (linen manufacturing), and food processing (meat packing, fruit canning, and confectionery). Rivne remains an important railway junction. It has seven special secondary schools, eight vocational schools, and three higher educational institutions, including a pedagogical institute, an institute of water management, and an institute of culture. The city supports a music and drama theater and a puppet theater, a philharmonic orchestra, and five museums. It had two oblast papers, *Chervonyi prapor* and *Zmina*. Now its city paper is the weekly *Rivne*. Its chief architectural monuments are the Dormition Church and belfry (1756) and the gymnasium building (1839).

Rivne Azot Manufacturing Consortium (Rovenske vyrobnyche obiednannia Azot). A consortium formed in 1975 on the basis of the Rivne Chemical Complex, built in 1965–9 on the outskirts of Rivne. It has three manufacturing facilities, which produce ammonia, ammonium nitrate, dry ice, unconcentrated nitric acid, sulfuric and phosphoric acids, ammonium sulfate, and other chemicals.

Rivne Institute of Culture (Rivenskyi instytut kultury). An institution of postsecondary education in Rivne, administered by the Ukrainian Ministry of Culture. It was founded in 1979 on the basis of the Rivne cultural-educational faculty of the Kiev Institute of Culture (est 1970). In 1986–7 the institute had faculties of cultural education and library science, 16 departments, and a library with over 93,000 volumes. Approx 1,600 students studied there, half of them full-time.

Rivne Linen Complex (Rovenskyi lonokombinat). A linen factory in Rivne, built in 1959–65. The factory produces canvas and tarpaulin for packaging and bags, tablecloth and bedding linen, linen for clothing, textiles for shirts and blouses, and other products. In the 1970s the complex employed over 2,000 workers.

The Kozatski Mohyly Museum and Preserve (formerly
St George's Church [1910–14]) in Pliasheva in Rivne oblast

Rivne oblast. An administrative territory in northwestern Ukraine, established on 4 December 1939. It has an area of 20,100 sq km and a population of 1,173,300 (1990). About 62 percent of the population is urban. Its ethnic composition is 93.3 percent Ukrainian and 4.6 percent Russian. The oblast is divided into 15 raions, 10 cities, 18 towns (smt), and 319 village councils. The largest cities are Rivne (the capital), Dubno, Zdolbuniv, Kostopil, and Sarny.

The oblast lies in Polisia, a marshy lowland rich in rivers and lakes. The Volhynian Upland reaches the southwestern corner of the oblast. The climate is moderate continental, with an average January temperature of –5°C and an average July temperature of 18°C. The frost-free period lasts 163 days, and the annual precipitation is 600–700 mm. The oblast's rich flora and fauna are protected in 11 nature preserves.

Under the Soviet regime the oblast was industrialized rapidly. The main branches of its industry are the food industry, which accounts for about 30 percent of the industrial output, light industry (22 percent), the machine-building and metalworking industries (17 percent), the woodworking and paper industries (10 percent), the chemical industry (9 percent), and the building-materials industry (8 percent). The main products of the food industry are sugar (refined mostly in Dubno, Korets, Mizoch, and Ostrih), meat (in Dubno and Rivne), and canning (in Demydivka, Dubno, Ostrozhets, Ostrih, Mezhyrich, and Chervonoarmiiske). The light industry produces textiles and footwear; the largest textile factories are in Rivne. The machine-building and metalworking industries are concentrated in Rivne, Kostopil, and Dubno. The woodworking industry is widely distributed: there are a house-building complex in Kostopil, a woodworking complex in Orzhiv, and furniture factories in Dubno, Kostopil, Ostrih, Rivne, Sarny, and Chervonoarmiiske. There is a large paper mill in Pershotravneve. The largest chemical plant is in Rivne. The oblast is rich in building materials, such as lime and granite.

In 1990 the agricultural output of Rivne oblast was worth 1,339,400,000 rubles or 2.7 percent of that of Ukraine. The area of its arable land is about 929,000 ha

(1988). Of that area 670,000 ha are cultivated, 122,000 ha are in hayfields, and 125,000 are in pasture. The sown area is devoted to feed crops (35 percent); they are followed by winter wheat (14 percent), barley (13 percent), potatoes (12 percent), and sugar beets (8 percent).

Railways are the chief means of freight transport. The oblast has 611 km of track (1982). It is crossed by the Kiev–Kovel–Brest, Brest–Rivne–Vinnytsia–Odessa, St Petersburg–Lviv, and several other trunk lines. The main railway junctions are Zdolbuniv, Rivne, and Sarny. The highway network consists of 5,600 km of road, 3,600 of which are hard surface. The main highways running through the oblast are Kiev–Warsaw, Kiev–Rivne–Dubno–Lviv, Brest–Lutske–Dubno–Ternopil–Chernivtsi, Kiev–Sarny–Kovel, and Rivne–Sarny–Pynske. Rivne is served by an airport.

Rivne Pedagogical Institute (Rivenskyi pedahohichnyi instytut). An institution of higher learning under the jurisdiction of the Ministry of Education of Ukraine. Founded in 1940 as a *teachers' institute, it became a pedagogical institute in 1953. In 1986–7 the institute had five faculties – physics-mathematics, philology, early childhood education, music education, and industrial arts – and an enrollment of 4,700. Its library contains over 322,000 volumes.

Rivne Regional Studies Museum (Rivenskyi oblasnyi kraieznavchyi muzei). A museum located in Rivne, founded in 1906 by W. Okięcki of the Rivne Agricultural Society. It had departments of natural science, archeology, numismatics, and ethnography, and underwent an expansion of its collections, and the addition of a fifth department, of books and manuscripts, in 1910. The museum was destroyed and pillaged during both world wars and was a natural history museum during the interwar Polish occupation. During the Soviet period the museum had departments of natural science, prerevolutionary history, and Soviet social history. In 1975 it was relocated to a new building. Subordinated to it were the *Kozatski Mohyly Museum and Preserve, the Rivne Museum of Atheism, the Sarny, Berezne, and Mlyniv regional studies museums, the Korets Historical Museum, and the Nikolai Ostrovsky and Mykola Kuznetsov memorial rooms, as well as the Dubno Regional Studies Museum. In 1982 the museum had approx 130,000 artifacts in its collections. A guidebook to the museum was published in Russian in 1982.

Rivne Ukrainian Music and Drama Theater (Rivenskyi ukrainskyi muzychno-dramatychnyi teatr). A theater founded in 1939 on the basis of the Melitopil Ukrainian Music and Drama Theater. It premiered W. Shakespeare's *King Lear* in Ukrainian in 1956. Its repertoire has consisted mostly of contemporary Soviet plays. In 1987 its principal stage director was Ya. Babii.

Rizhsky, Ivan [Rižskij], b 19 September 1759 in Riga, Latvia, d 27 March 1811 in Kharkiv. Russian classical and literary scholar and philosopher; member of the Imperial Russian Academy of Sciences from 1803 and the first rector of Kharkiv University (1805–7, 1808–11). He was educated and taught in St Petersburg. There he published two books on ancient Roman religion (1784) and politics (1786), two widely used textbooks on logic (1790) and rhetoric (1796; 2nd edn [1805] and 3rd edn [1822]: Kharkiv), and a translation of P. Pallas's physical and topographic description of the Crimea (1795). In Kharkiv he was a professor of literature and published an introduction to the study of literature (1806) and one of the first Russian books on poetics (1811). He was influenced by the writings of the encyclopedists and Voltaire.

Volodymyr Riznychenko

Riznychenko, Volodymyr [Riznyčenko], b 18 October 1870 in Velentiiv *khutir*, Nizhen county, Chernihiv gubernia, d 1 April 1932 in Kiev. Geologist; full member of the VUAN from 1929. After graduating from Kharkiv University (1896), until 1916 he took part in geological expeditions to study the Asian mountain ranges of Tarbagataj, Tien Shan, and Altai. His subsequent scientific work dealt exclusively with Ukraine and included the study of the stratigraphy and tectonics of Right-Bank Ukraine (particularly the Kaniv Hills). He also studied hydrogeological conditions in Volhynia and published extensively in the areas of general, dynamic, and regional geology, hydrogeology, geography, and archeology. In 1930–2 he became director of the VUAN Geological Institute. He was also a poet and cartoonist.

Rizol, Mykola [Rizol'], b 19 December 1919 in Katerynoslav. Accordionist and educator. In 1951 he graduated from the Kiev Conservatory. He developed a theory of five-finger application for the accordion and wrote a manual on the subject (1977). He organized an accordion quartet at the Kiev Philharmonic Orchestra in 1939 and served as its artistic director and a member. His compositions for accordion include a concerto for accordion and orchestra, arrangements of folk songs, and short pieces.

Rizun (nom de guerre of Vasyl Andrusiak), b 1914 in Sniatyn county, d 24 February 1946 in the Chornyi Lis forest, near Stanyslaviv. UPA field commander. In 1941 he became active in the anti-Nazi underground and rose to OUN leader in the Sniatyn-Kolomyia area. In June 1943 he helped organize the first UPA units in Galicia, which were known as the Ukrainian People's Self-Defense, and in the following month he established a base of operations in Chornyi Lis. By November 1943 Rizun was commanding a company, and thereafter, several companies. In the second half of 1944 he organized new UPA companies and co-ordinated combat operations in the Chornyi Lis area. In January 1945 he was appointed commander of the Stanyslaviv Tactical Sector, which consisted of five combat battalions. Killed in battle with MVD troops, Rizun was

promoted posthumously to colonel and awarded the highest UPA decorations for bravery: the Gold Cross of Combat Merit First Class and the Gold Cross of Combat Merit Second Class.

Rklytsky, Mykhailo [Rklyc'kyj, Myxajlo], b 22 September 1864 in Pohrebky, Novhorod-Siverskyi county, Chernihiv gubernia, d ? Historian and statistician. He studied law at Kharkiv University. He was exiled to Siberia in 1888 for his involvement in a revolutionary populist group. After his return to Ukraine he worked as an attorney in Novhorod-Siverskyi and as secretary of the Poltava gubernia zemstvo administration (from 1898) and director of its statistical bureau (from 1902). In publications of the Chernihiv and Poltava zemstvos he published articles on the history of Novhorod-Siverskyi, literacy in Novhorod-Siverskyi county, peasant libraries and landholdings in Poltava gubernia, and the Cossacks in Zolotonosha, Poltava, and Zinkiv counties according to the Rumiantsev census. He also wrote a statistical guide to the Russian 'South' (1910) and stories which were published in *Russkiia vedomosti*, *Russkoe bogatstvo*, and *Zhurnal dlia vsekh*. His reminiscences about P. Hrabovsky were published in the VUAN collection *Literatura* (1928).

Ro, Lev, b 2 November 1883 in Novosaratovka, St Petersburg gubernia, d 14 September 1957 in Kiev. Horticulturist. He taught and did research on the biology and selection of fruit plants in Uman, Poltava, Mliiv, and Symferopil. He developed a pear and 12 types of apples that were adopted as standard varieties in Ukraine.

Roads and highways. Hard-surface (cement or asphalt) or unpaved thoroughfares used by automobiles, buses, or trucks. Compared to those in Western Europe and similarly settled parts of North America Ukraine's road and highway network is not dense; and compared to the adjoining republics, Ukraine's road and highway density is only slightly higher than Belarus's and slightly lower than Moldova's. Ukraine's highway density relative to its population, however, is lower than Belarus's, about the same

TABLE 1
Highway networks of selected republics, 1986

Republic	Category						
	A	B	C	D	E	F	G
Ukraine	603.7	209.2	34.7	149.5	24.8	4.1	2.9
Belarus	207.6	51.0	24.6	42.4	20.4	5.1	4.2
Moldova	33.7	12.3	36.5	9.5	28.2	2.9	2.3
Lithuania	65.2	29.2	44.8	20.9	32.1	8.0	5.7
Latvia	64.5	20.3	31.5	18.1	28.1	7.7	6.8
Estonia	45.1	27.0	60.0	14.7	32.6	17.4	9.4

A = territory (in 1,000 sq km).
B = all paved highways, including ones used exclusively by certain agencies (in 1,000 km).
C = highway density (per 100 sq km), or B/A.
D = paved highways for general public use (in 1,000 km).
E = general highway density (per 100 sq km), or D/A.
F = highway density per unit of population (1,000 people), or B/pop.
G = general highway density per unit of population (1,000 people), or D/pop.

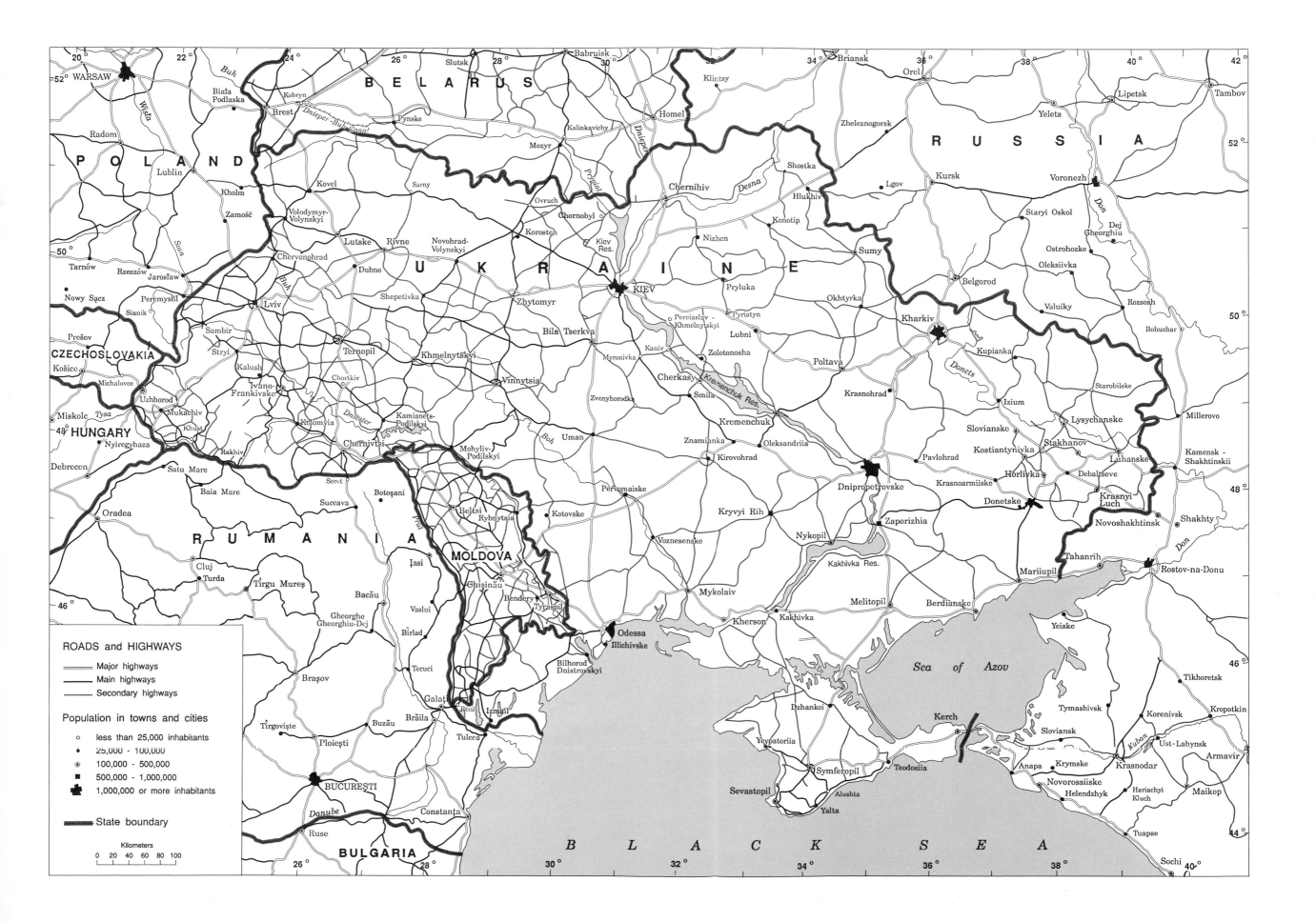

as Russia's (3.2 km/1,000 people), and higher than Moldova's (see table 1).

The road and highway network of Ukraine has inherited two distinct patterns that developed under the Austro-Hungarian and Russian empires respectively. A dense network of roads and highways was developed in the Austrian crownlands, and today the highest densities are found in precisely those regions – in declining order, Chernivtsi (formerly Bukovyna), Ternopil, Lviv, and Ivano-Frankivske oblasts (formerly Galicia). Lower densities of roads and highways were developed in the Russian Empire, particularly in the less-populated rural regions, such as the steppe (now Kherson, Mykolaiv, Kirovohrad, and Luhanske oblasts) and Polisia (now Chernihiv, Zhytomyr, Rivne, and Volhynia oblasts). Nodal patterns were more clearly established for the economic-administrative centers of Lviv, Chernivtsi, and Ternopil. In the Russian Empire they were less clearly developed for Kiev, Kharkiv, Odessa, Dnipropetrovske, and Donetske, and that remains largely true today (see table 2).

The network of roads and highways in Ukraine was classified according to a hierarchy common to the entire USSR. At the top were the main highways of all-Union status; they were followed by other highways of all-Union status, highways of republican status, and, finally, roads of local status. The main highways had a strategic value. They formed a major node at Moscow, from which they radiated in all directions, linking the largest cities in the USSR, including Kiev, Odessa, and Kharkiv. The other highways of all-Union status joined intermediate-sized cities in Ukraine. Highways of republican significance joined small cities and towns and served as feeders into large cities. Local roads served villages and towns and fed into highways.

Hard-surface roads in 1940 accounted for only one-tenth of the road kilometers. The number of paved highways increased slowly. After 1970 the share of paved roads doubled each decade. By 1987 the share of paved roads and highways had reached 91.6 percent (see table 3). Road and highway improvement was related closely to the growth of the automobile industry. Even so, road use increased much more rapidly than did the length of paved highways: from 1940 to 1987 the load-distance trucked increased by a factor of 43, and the passenger-distance bused, by a factor of 315, whereas the length of paved roads increased by only a factor of 5.

TABLE 2
Highway distribution among oblasts

Density range (km/100 sq km)	Oblasts
35.8–30.1	Ivano-Frankivske, Lviv, Khmelnytskyi, Chernivtsi, Ternopil. Similar to Italy and Estonia
29.4–25.8	Vinnytsia, Donetske, Kiev, Transcarpathia. Similar to countries in southeastern Europe, such as Bulgaria
25.4–23.5	Cherkasy, Crimea, Dnipropetrovske
23.0–15.8	Kherson, Mykolaiv, Kirovohrad, Luhanske, Chernihiv, Kharkiv,. Zaporizhia, Odessa, Poltava, Rivne, Sumy, Volhynia, and Zhytomyr

From 1940 to 1987 the total length of the road network declined by 107,500 km (see table 3). The difference consisted mostly of unpaved roads, which could not be justified economically. At the same time paved roads and highways increased, by 120,200 km, but they are generally in poor condition, and accidents and breakdowns are frequent. Hence, road transportation is expensive. In general the cost of trucking in Ukraine is 35 percent of the value of the cargo, whereas in most countries in Western Europe it does not exceed 10 percent.

TABLE 3
The road and highway network and its utilization in Ukraine, 1940–87

Indicator	1940	1960	1970	1980	1987
Length of roads and highways (in 1,000 km)	270.7	236.2	223.5	163.2	163.2
Paved (in 1,000 km)	29.3	47.4	90.8	133.7	149.5
Share of roads paved (%)	10.8	20.1	40.6	81.9	91.6

Research on roads and highways is conducted by the Scientific Research Institute of Motor Vehicle Transport in Kiev, which has branches in Dnipropetrovske, Lviv, Odessa, and Symferopil.

BIBLIOGRAPHY
Stolbovoi, V. *Transport Ukrainskoi SSR* (Kiev 1971)
Povyshenie effektivnosti raboty transporta Ukrainskoi SSR (Kiev 1979)
I. Stebelsky, B. Wynar

Robitfak. See Workers' faculties.

Robitnycha hazeta (Workers' Gazette). A central organ of the *Ukrainian Social Democratic Workers'* party published daily (with interruptions) from April 1917 to sometime in 1919 in Kiev, Vinnytsia, and finally Kamianets-Podilskyi. It was edited by V. Vynnychenko and then by an editorial board headed by Isaak Mazepa. The newspaper fostered the development of Ukrainian national consciousness among Ukraine's working class and is an important primary source on Ukraine during the revolutionary period. It had a circulation of approx 15,000.

Robitnycha hazeta (Workers' Gazette). A newspaper published six times a week in Kiev since January 1957. Until 1962 it was the organ of the Ukrainian Republican Council of Trade Unions; since then there has been no republican Ukrainian trade union organ. In 1962–91 it was an organ of the CC CPU. In the 1960s it was a vocal proponent of Ukrainian economic and cultural autonomy and supported the more liberal policies of CPU First Secretary P. Shelest; it also published articles and letters criticizing policies restricting the development of the Ukrainian-language press and the use of Ukrainian in general. After Shelest's removal from power a purge was conducted at the paper, and several journalists and editors were removed from their positions. A Russian-language edition of the paper has been published as *Rabochaia gazeta*. Because of the official policy of Russification, in 1960 the Ukrainian edition had a pressrun of only 40,000 copies, while the Russian edition's was 85,000; by 1980 the gap had widened, with the two editions having pressruns of 95,000 and 385,000 respectively. In 1992 it began to appear only three times a week and had a pressrun of 300,000 in each language edition.

Robitnycha hazeta Proletar (Workers' Gazette Proletarian). A daily organ of the All-Ukrainian Council of Trade Unions and, from November 1929, the CC CP(B)U, published in Kharkiv from November 1926 to March 1932. A mass-circulation paper intended primarily for urban workers, it printed *Terpuh* (1927–9), *Industriializatsiia, ratsionalizatsiia, vynakhidstvo* (1927–8), *Fizkul'turna Ukraïna* (1929), and other supplements. In 1929 the paper had a daily pressrun of 63,300.

Robitnycha osvita (Workers' Education). A monthly organ of the Komsomol CC and Central Council of Educational Workers of the People's Commissariat of Education (from 1928), the Central Council of Workers' Education of the Supreme Council of the National Economy (from 1931), and the People's Commissariat of Heavy Industry (1932), published in Kharkiv from January 1927 to April 1932.

Robitnyche slovo (Workers' Word). A socialist weekly newspaper published in Toronto from June 1916 to September 1918, when it was closed down by the Canadian government. It succeeded the semimonthly *Svidoma syla* (est June 1915) and continued the same numbering scheme. It was published by members of the *Ukrainian Social Democratic Party (USDP) of Canada who were in opposition to the party's executive. *Robitnyche slovo* aimed to raise the class consciousness of Ukrainian immigrant workers in Canada; informed its readers about developments in Ukraine, especially after the February Revolution of 1917; and polemicized with the more radical, pro-Bolshevik *Robochyi narod*, the official USDP organ. Over time it became a less partisan educational journal for workers and farmers. The editor of both *Svidoma syla* and *Robitnyche slovo* was I. Stefanitsky, and H. Mak, P. Krat, and D. Borysko were associate editors.

Robitnychi visty (Workers' News). A semimonthly and later irregular Trotskyist newspaper published in Toronto from November 1933 to March 1938. It covered news of interest to Ukrainian workers and farmers in North America and from July 1936 included a regular section on literary developments in both Soviet and Western Ukraine. *Robitnychi visty* commented extensively on political developments in Ukraine and criticized Stalinist policies in the USSR and the Canadian Communist movement. It was formally allied with the Fourth International and even printed a letter of greetings from L. Trotsky. The editors were V. Bosovych, M. Oleniuk, and N. Oliinyk.

Robitnyk (Worker). A semimonthly newspaper published briefly in 1897 in Lviv (a total of four issues) by a group of social democrats who split from the Ukrainian Radical party. Edited by M. Hankevych (pseud I. Hlynchak), it was published in the Latin script and promoted better relations between Ukrainian and Polish social democrats in Galicia.

Robitnyk (Worker). A central organ of the Ukrainian Social Democratic Workers' party, published and edited in 1910 in Lviv by I. Skulsky.

Robitnyk (Worker). A radical socialist newspaper founded in Detroit in 1914; from 1915 the organ of the newly formed Ukrainian Federation of the Socialist Party of America. The newspaper appeared three times a month in Detroit in 1914 and then weekly (1915–17), and daily in Cleveland; it was often interrupted, and several times it was suppressed by US authorities. From December 1918 to January 1920 it was published in New York City. *Robitnyk* was edited by T. Pochynok, M. Sichynsky, M. Tsehlynsky, E. Kruk, and, from April 1918, an editorial board consisting of H. Lehun, P. Ladan, D. Moisa, and I. Selsky. At first it was concerned mainly with organizing the Ukrainian socialist movement in the United States and was particularly anticlerical and anti-Habsburg. After the February Revolution of 1917 it devoted considerable attention to developments in Ukraine, and initially it supported the Central Rada and the Ukrainian Social Democratic Workers' party there. Eventually it became pro-Bolshevik, and from September 1919 it was the official organ of the newly formed Ukrainian Federation of the Communist Party in America. *Robitnyk* was succeeded in 1920 by *Ukraïns'ki shchodenni visty* (later *Ukraïns'ki visti*).

Robitnyk (Worker). An organ of the Ukrainian section of the International Social Democratic Party of Bukovyna, published weekly (with several interruptions) in Chernivtsi in 1919–23. It was edited by V. Rusnak. *Robitnyk* was succeeded by *Borot'ba* (1925–8), a Sovietophile weekly edited by I. Stasiuk, S. Halytsky, I. Mykhailovych, T. Kozak, and Rusnak. Both papers were severely censored by the Rumanian authorities, and the editors were persecuted.

Robitnytsia (Working Woman). An organ of the Women's Section of the *Ukrainian Labour-Farmer Temple Association, published biweekly from 15 March 1924 to July 1937 (except 1932, when it appeared monthly) in Winnipeg. It was created through the merger of two other monthlies published in Winnipeg, *Holos pratsi* (Voice of Labor), established in April 1922 and edited by M. Popovich and M. Shatulsky, and *Holos robitnytsi* (Voice of the Working Woman), established in January 1923 and also edited by M. Popovich. *Robitnytsia* focused on education and child rearing, on the role of women in the class struggle, and on the growth of the Communist women's movement in Canada. It invariably supported Soviet policies in Ukraine and criticized Polish rule in Western Ukraine. In 1929 the newspaper had a circulation of approximately 6,800. Its editors were all men: M. Irchan (1924–9), M. Lenartovych (1929–32), P. Prokopchak (1933–6), and P. Chaikivsky and P. Lysets.

Robochyi narod (*Robuchyi narod, Robotchyi narod*; Working People). A newspaper established in Winnipeg in May 1909 by Ukrainians active in the Socialist Party of Canada. The successor to *Chervonyi prapor*, it appeared monthly (1909–10), biweekly (1910–11), three times a month (1911), weekly (1911–15), and again monthly (1915–18). From September 1910 the paper was the official organ of the *Federation of Ukrainian Social Democrats in Canada. Steadily adopting more radical positions, it published the first Ukrainian translation of K. Marx and M. Engels's *Communist Manifesto* to appear in Canada (1915) and several articles by V. Lenin, advocated Canada's withdrawal from the First World War, and by 1918 was decidedly pro-Bolshevik. In 1917 it had approximately 3,000 subscribers.

Its editors were M. Stechishin (1909–12), I. Navizivsky (1912–13), Ye. Hutsailo (who came from Bukovyna to edit the paper in 1913–14), I. Stefanitsky (1914), P. Krat (1914–15), D. Lobai (1915–16), and M. Popovich (1916–18). *Robochyi narod* was banned and closed down by the Canadian government in late September 1918. It was succeeded in 1919 by *Ukraïns'ki robitnychi visti*.

Bishop Andrii Roboretsky

Roboretsky, Andrii [Roborec'kyj, Andrij] (Andrew Roborecky), b 12 December 1910 in Mosty Velyki, Zhovkva county, Galicia, d 23 October 1982 in Toronto. Ukrainian Catholic bishop. After emigrating to Canada with his parents in 1913, Roboretsky was ordained in 1934 and appointed auxiliary bishop to Bishop V. Ladyka in 1948. In 1951 he headed the Saskatoon exarchate, and in 1956 he was appointed bishop of the newly created eparchy of Saskatoon. He was prominent in the creation of the *Sheptytsky Institute in Saskatoon and took part in the Second Vatican Council.

Robselkor. An acronym for *robitnychyi i selianskyi korespondent* (workers' and peasants' correspondent). The *robselkor* movement was initiated by the Bolshevik party in the early years of Soviet rule. This network of local correspondents loyal to the Soviet regime has played an important role in Communist agitation and propaganda. In the early 1920s many *robselkory* who denounced the 'anti-Soviet' activities of their neighbors were murdered. The authorities, in their turn, used these crimes to justify state repression and terror. The all-Union press in Moscow acted as patron of the *robselkor* movement, and local newspapers published many articles by these often semiliterate or poorly educated correspondents. In Soviet Ukraine there were regular okruha and oblast *robselkor* conferences throughout the interwar period, and the journal *Robsel'kor* was published for them. Since the Second World War, use by newspapers of *robselkor* correspondence has declined. In the 1960s, however, there were still over 400,000 *robselkory* in Ukraine.

Robsel'kor (Workers' and Peasants' Correspondent). An organ of the *robselkor* movement, published in Kharkiv (1928–34) and Kiev (1934–41); established in May 1928 by the merger of the monthlies *Robkor Ukraïny* (1927–8) and *Sel'kor Ukraïny* (1926–8). It contained reports from worker and peasant correspondents throughout Soviet Ukraine and was an important instrument in the agitation and propaganda work of the CP(B)U. *Robsel'kor* was published monthly (1927–8, 1933–4), semimonthly (1929–30, 1934–

41), three times a month (1931–3), and monthly (1933–4). The editor was I. Sazonov.

St Josaphat's Ukrainian Catholic Church in Rochester

Rochester. A city (1980 pop 242,000; metropolitan pop 972,000) on Lake Ontario in northwestern New York State. Founded at the beginning of the 19th century, it has developed from a flour-milling town into a manufacturing center for specialized precision equipment. In 1980 there were between 5,800 (official) and 8,860 (estimated) Ukrainian residents in the area. The first Ukrainian immigrants, who began to arrive in 1901, came mostly from the Rohatyn region, Galicia. By 1908 a group of Ukrainian Catholics had set up St Josaphat's Brotherhood, which formed the core of the first Ukrainian parish. Several local fraternal associations arose to help newcomers and to support Ukrainian institutions in the homeland: the Free Cossack Society (1909), the Zaporozhian Sich Society (1913), the Sisterhood of the Birth of the Virgin Mary (1916), and the Ivan Franko Society (1923). By the mid-1930s there were about 3,000 Ukrainians and 16 Ukrainian organizations in the city. With the influx of new immigrants after the Second World War, the Ukrainian community grew, and new organizations sprang up (52 by 1990). Another Catholic parish (1958) and an Orthodox parish (1950) were set up. The Ukrainian Heritage Center was established in 1983 at St Josaphat's Church to preserve and display samples of Ukrainian folk arts and crafts.

Rocket. A missile propelled by the reaction resulting from the rearward discharge of gases liberated by combustion. Crude rockets have been used for centuries as fireworks, signaling devices, and incendiary devices by the military. There is some evidence in the chronicles that the Cossacks used small rockets filled with gunpowder to create chaos and panic in Tatar encampments. In the 19th century a number of Ukrainians experimented with rockets and proposed technical improvements or new applications for them. In 1815 O. *Zasiadko, an artillery officer from Hadiache, began experimental work on rockets for military use. In the latter half of the century the revolutionary M. *Kybalchych was interested in the theory of jet propulsion, and in 1881 he outlined a design for a jet-propelled aircraft. The first Ukrainian scientist to treat the rocket as a vehicle for *space travel was Yu. *Kondratiuk (real name: O. Sharhei). By 1921 he had calculated the escape velocity of a space vehicle and the amount of fuel needed to attain that velocity, and designed a four-stage rocket. The three aforementioned Ukrainian scientists have craters on the far side of the moon named for them. S. *Korolov was a member of the Jet Propulsion Research Group set up in Moscow in 1932, and later he was the chief designer of the first earth satellite and the rocket that lifted it into earth orbit in 1957.

Rocky Caucasus Range (Skelystyi khrebet). A frontal ridge along the northern slope of the Great Caucasus Range. Stretching from the Bila River in the west to the upper reaches of the Terek in the east, the ridge is 330 km long with peaks ranging in height from 1,200–1,700 m in the west to up to 3,000 m in the east (Mount Karakaia is the tallest point, at 3,646 m). The ridge is situated in the central and western parts of the Caucasus Mountains. The range is a cuesta with a sharp southern slope and gentle northern one. It consists largely of hard limestone and has karst features. A number of rivers, including the Kuban, dissect it into several plateaus. The ridge's southern slopes are covered with mountain steppes and meadows, and broad-leaved forests grow along the northern slopes to approx 1,800 m.

Rococo. An architectural and decorative style that emerged in France in the early 18th century. It replaced the plasticity of the *baroque and was characterized by light, graceful decoration, trivial subject matter, and small-scale sculpture. In decoration the open shell (*rocaille* in French) motif became popular. Rococo was used in church architecture throughout Ukraine, but because baroque influences were strong the two styles were often intermingled. Examples of the rococo style in Ukraine are *St Andrew's Church (1747–53) in Kiev; the Church of the Nativity of the Mother of God (1752–63) in Kozelets, Chernihiv gubernia; the Roman Catholic churches of the Dominican order in Lviv (1747–64) and Ternopil (1745–9); *St George's Cathedral (1745–70) in Lviv; the Dormition Church at the Pochaiv Monastery (1771–83) in Volhynia; and the city hall (1751) in Buchach, Galicia.

Rococo influences in Ukrainian sculpture can be seen particularly in iconostases, where carved shell motifs and interlace patterns replaced grapevines and acanthus foliage, often without structural logic (eg, the Royal Gates in St George's Cathedral in Lviv). The iconostases of St Andrew's Church in Kiev and the church of the Mhar Transfiguration Monastery (1762–5) in Poltava gubernia have delicately carved rococo surface decorations. Three-dimensional carved heads of angels with wings were used to decorate St Andrew's Church in Kiev. In religious painting the rococo style had little impact because of the strong hold of the baroque. A few still lifes, intimate in scale, appeared for the first time, however, and rococo de-

The rococo iconostasis of St Andrew's Church in Kiev

sign and decoration left a mark on furniture produced in Hlukhiv and Nizhen in Chernihiv gubernia and in Olesko in Galicia. Furniture tended to be light, small, and curvilinear, with gold gilding over white. Porcelain with rococo motifs was manufactured in Korets and Volokytyne in Chernihiv gubernia.

D. Zelska-Darewych

Rocznik Wołyński (Volhynian Yearbook). A Polish-language yearbook of the Volhynian branch of the Union of Polish Teachers, published in Rivne in 1930–9 (a total of 8 issues). It contained popular-scholarly articles on the history, culture, and geography of Volhynia and useful bibliographies of Volhyniana. The editor was J. Hoffman.

Rod. A major Slavic deity, the creator of the world and ruler of the heavens and rain. The cult of Rod and the *rozhanytsia* (the Fates) associated with him came under severe attack from the church in 11th-century Rus'. According to B. Rybakov the cult displaced the ancient cult of the Mother, which prevailed under the matriarchal system, and preceded the warrior cult of Perun. The Western Slavs knew Rod by the name of *Sviatovyt.

Rodakove. V-20, DB II-6. A town smt (1986 pop 7,400) in Slovianoserbske raion, Luhanske oblast. It was founded as a workers' settlement in 1878 during the construction of the Debaltseve–Luhanske railway line. By 1912 it was an important railway junction. There is a kurhan from the Bronze Age near the town.

Roden (reconstruction by H. Mezentseva)

Roden or **Rodnia** [Roden' or Rodnja]. A fortified city on the hill called *Kniazha Hora, near the mouth of the Ros River, south of *Kaniv. According to archeological excavations Roden was founded in the 7th or 8th century. It is mentioned in the Primary Chronicle in 980 as the place where the Kievan prince Volodymyr the Great besieged his brother, Yaropolk I Sviatoslavych. Roden reached its economic and cultural zenith in the 11th and 12th centuries, when it was no longer simply a fortress against nomadic attacks, but also an important center of artisanship and trade. It consisted of a central castle with trade and market districts, encircled by fortified walls and moats. Excavations have unearthed wooden and clay dwellings, work implements, weapons (spear- and arrowheads, swords, sabers), and ornaments (diadems, rings, bracelets, earrings). Roden was destroyed during the Tatar invasions of the 1240s and was not rebuilt. Excavations on the site of the city were conducted by M. Biliashivsky in 1891 and by an expedition from Kiev University in 1958–65.

Rodimyi listok

Rodimyi listok (Native Page). A Russophile semimonthly newspaper published in Chernivtsi from January 1879 to January 1882 (a total of 73 issues). It published news, belles lettres, and especially articles on Slavic ethnography and culture. The editor was M. Ohonovsky; the newspaper was closed down when he was arrested during an Austro-Hungarian crackdown against Russophiles suspected of treason.

Rodionov, Sergei, b 26 September 1898 in Zagorsk, Russia, d 2 May 1961 in Kiev. Geologist; member of the AN URSR (now ANU) from 1951. After graduating from the Dnipropetrovske Mining Institute in 1929, he held various teaching and administrative positions in Kryvyi Rih and Kiev. He joined the ANU Institute of Geological Sciences in 1938 and became department chairman at Kiev University (1945–52). Rodionov's research dealt with problems of petrography in the Ukrainian tectonic plate and the distribution patterns of Precambrian deposits in Ukraine. He was one of the first to study the numerous magnetic anomalies around the Kryvyi Rih deposits, and his publications have provided a theoretical basis for effective mineral exploration around the iron-ore zones.

Rodynske [Rodyns'ke]. V-18, DB III-2. A city (1989 pop 15,700) in Donetske oblast, administered by the Krasnoarmiiske municipal council. It was set up in 1950, when two coal mines were opened. In 1962 it was granted city status. Besides the mines it has a coal enrichment plant.

Rodzevych, Serhii [Rodzevyč, Serhij], b 28 August 1888 in Lódź, Poland, d 29 January 1942. Literary scholar. He graduated from Kiev University (1913) and taught in Kiev's secondary schools before becoming a professor at Kiev University in 1935. He wrote articles on T. Shevchenko's early poems, on modern Polish poetry, and on European writers, such as I. Turgenev, N. Gogol, J. Tuwim, J. London, E. Zola, R. Roland, A. France, and L. Aragon, and introductions to Ukrainian translations of works by W. Shakespeare, Voltaire, H. de Balzac, and D. Diderot. In the years 1928–31 he published 10 review articles on new Ukrainian translations of foreign literature in the journal *Zhyttia i revoliutsiia*. He stopped publishing during the Stalinist terror of the 1930s.

Rodzianko [Rodzjanko]. A family line of Cossack officers and nobility of the Poltava and Katerynoslav regions in the 18th to 20th centuries. It was established by Vasyl Rodzianko (1652–1734), a captain of Khorol regiment (1701–4) and *oboznyi* (quartermaster) of Myrhorod regiment (1723–34). The captaincy of Khorol regiment was passed on to his sons, Stepan and Ivan Rodzianko, and grandsons, Yeremii and Ivan Rodzianko (until 1768). Stepan (1687–1736) and Yeremii Rodzianko were also *obozni* of Myrhorod regiment (1735–6 and 1767–9 respectively), and Ivan Rodzianko (d 1751) was also colonel of Hadiache regiment. Their descendants maintained estates and official positions in the Poltava region until the 20th century. In the 1780s, though, a branch of the family settled in the Katerynoslav region, where it was Russified and came to control large estates in Novomoskovske county (eg, Mykhailo *Rodzianko).

The Rodzianko family was related to the Lesevych, Domykovsky, Obolonsky, Ostrohradsky, and Starytsky (including M. Starytsky and L. Starytska-Cherniakhivska) families. Semen Rodzianko (1782–1808?) was a poet and a member of the Friendship Literary Society in Moscow (1801–4). Arkadii Rodzianko (1793–1846) belonged to the Society of Lovers of Literature, Scholarship, and the Arts (1825) and wrote verse in Ukrainian and Russian (he was also a friend of A. Pushkin and T. Shevchenko). His brother, Platon Rodzianko (1802–?), was representative (*predvodytel*) of the nobility in Khorol county, Poltava gubernia.

Valerian Rodzianko (1846–1904) was a member of the Ukrainian (Little Russian) Hromada in Moscow in the 1860s (he was among those arrested in 1866), and later he worked as a court functionary in Kharkiv. Serhii Rodzianko (b 1866) was commissioner of the Central Rada in the Kholm region in 1917–18, and he kept his position under the Hetman government.

O. Ohloblyn

Rodzianko, Mykhailo [Rodzjanko, Myxajlo] (Mikhail), b 1859 in Katerynoslav gubernia, d 24 January 1924 in Yugoslavia. Large landowner and political leader. He was marshal of the nobility for Novomoskovske county (1886–96), chairman of the executive of the Katerynoslav gubernia zemstvo (1900–6), member of the State Council (1906–7), deputy from the Katerynoslav region in the Third and Fourth state dumas (1907–17), and president of the State Duma (1911–17). He was one of the leading members of the Octoberist party and was opposed to Ukrainian national aspirations. An advocate of a constitutional monarchy of the British type, he was associated with Russian antigovernment circles, which during the First World War tried to get rid of G. Rasputin and prepared a 'revolution from above.' In March 1917 he chaired the Provisional Committee of the Duma members, which assumed supreme power from Nicholas II, but was blocked from any position in the Provisional Government that succeeded it. In 1920, serving for a short period in A. Denikin's Volunteer Army, he emigrated to Yugoslavia. His memoirs, *Krushenie imperii*, came out in 1924 and have appeared in several English editions as *The Reign of Rasputin: An Empire's Collapse.*

Rodzin, Mykola, b 28 March 1924 in Novoselivka, Kharkiv okruha, d 2 March 1978 in Dnipropetrovske. Printmaker. A graduate of the Kharkiv Art Institute (1955), he did several series of etchings, including 'Industrial Motifs' (1955), 'Kakhivka Hydroelectric Station' (1956–7), 'Across Ukraine' (1963), and 'My Land' (1966–7); the triptych *Preservation of the Sevastopil Panorama* (1967–70); and various prints.

Roe deer (*Capreolus capreolus*; Ukrainian: *kozulia*). A small (100 cm tall at the shoulder), nimble, almost tailless deer of the family Cervidae that inhabits lightly forested zones of Ukraine in the Carpathian and Crimean mountains and in Polisia. Its coat is reddish brown in summer and grayish brown in winter. The roe deer is hunted commercially for its meat, hide, and antlers. In the 1970s its population in Ukraine exceeded 125,000. It is a protected species; approx 10 percent of the roe deer population is allowed to be taken annually.

Roentgenology. That branch of medicine which studies X rays, their effect on the human organism, and their use in the discovery, diagnosis, and treatment of disease. In Ukraine roentgenology was slow to develop. At the beginning of the 20th century two journals were published, *Rentgenovskii vestnik* (1907–9) in Odessa and *Izvestiia Kievskoi rentgenovskoi komissii* (1915–17) in Kiev. Scientific research institutes of roentgenology were created in Kharkiv and Kiev in 1920. The first departments of roentgenology were established in 1923–4 at the Kharkiv and Odessa medical institutes and at the Odessa Institute for the Upgrading of Physicians; others followed at the Kiev (1927), Kharkiv (1928), and Donetske (1932) medical institutes and at the Kiev Institute for the Upgrading of Physicians (1936). Pioneers in roentgenology in Ukraine included S. Hryhoriv, S. (Yu.) Teslenko, M. Isachenko, M. Afanasiev, F. Bohatyrchuk, V. Diachenko, and A. Lemberg; Ya. Shyk wrote a medical roentgenology textbook and edited the journal *Eksperymental'na ta klinychna renthenolohiia*, published in 1931. Today the Kiev Roentgeno-Radiological and Oncological Scientific Research Institute is the leader in research and practical work in Ukraine.

BIBLIOGRAPHY
Pozmogov, A. 'Razvitie rentgenologii v USSR za gody sovetskoi vlasti,' *Vestnik rentgenologii i radiologii*, 1972, no. 6

P. Dzul

Rogoza, Aleksandr, b 1869 in Kiev gubernia, d 1919. Army general. A regular officer in the Russian army, during the First World War he commanded the Fourth Russian Army and was promoted to major general. In 1918 he served as defense minister in the Hetman government of F. Lyzohub. He was killed by the Cheka.

Rogulia, Petro [Rogulja], b ? in the Poltava region, d ? Icon and portrait painter of the 18th century. He studied under T. Pavlovsky at the Kievan Cave Monastery Icon Painting Studio. His works include icons in the Holy Trinity Monastery cathedral in Okhtyrka (1744) and the Church of the Holy Protectress in Kotelva (1749).

Rogulsky, Ivan [Rogul's'kyj], b 1892 in Holobutiv, Stryi county, Galicia, d 1934. Senior officer of the Sich Riflemen. In 1914 he volunteered to serve in the Legion of Ukrainian Sich Riflemen, and by 1916 he was promoted to lieutenant and commanded a mortar platoon. After internment by the Russians (1916–17) he joined the Sich Riflemen Battalion in Kiev (January 1918). He became regimental (December 1918) and division (July 1919) commander in the Corps of Sich Riflemen and rose to the rank of colonel. He stayed in Soviet Ukraine after 1920. In the 1930s he was arrested and executed by the Cheka.

Mykola Rogutsky   Ivan Rohach

Rogutsky, Mykola [Roguc'kyj], b 31 July 1886 in Kupnovychi, Rudky county, Galicia, d 26 June 1941 in Sambir, Galicia. Civic and political organizer. A farmer by occupation, he was a leading activist and longtime vice-president (from 1924) of the Ukrainian Radical party. He was elected deputy to the Polish Sejm (1928–30) and was arrested a number of times by the Polish authorities for his political activities. On the eve of the Soviet retreat from Western Ukraine he was arrested by the NKVD and tortured to death.

Rohach, Ivan [Rohač], b 1913 in Velykyi Bereznyi, Transcarpathia, d 1942. Journalist and political figure. In the 1930s he was a leader of the OUN in Transcarpathia, and in 1938–9, of the paramilitary *Ukrainian National Defense and *Carpathian Sich there. He was also secretary to the president of the 1938–9 Carpatho-Ukrainian state, A. Voloshyn, and editor of *Nova svoboda* (1938). In 1941 Rohach commanded an OUN (Melnyk faction) Expeditionary Group in central Ukraine and was managing editor of the nationalist newspaper *Ukraïns'ke slovo* in Kiev. He was arrested by the Gestapo in December 1941 and killed by them in 1942, together with his sister, Anna.

Rohachevsky, Ivan [Rohačevs'kyj]. Early 18th-century archpriest in Lokhvytsia, Lubni regiment. He was arrested in 1712 and exiled to the Solovets Islands together with others loyal to Hetman I. *Mazepa. Later he obtained permission to teach at a newly founded school in Arkhangelsk, and in the 1720s he returned to Ukraine. There he joined the commission that prepared the Code of Laws of 1743.

Rohalevsky, Ilarion [Rohalevs'kyj], b ? in Minsk, Belarus, d 1739. Orthodox church hierarch. He studied at the Kievan Mohyla Academy and then served as a military chaplain before becoming archimandrite of the Mhar Transfiguration (1722–8) and Moscow Donskoi (1728–32) monasteries. He was consecrated archbishop of Kazan (1732) and then of Chernihiv (1735). A close associate of T. *Prokopovych, he established schools for newly baptized children, notably Kazan Tatars. He improved the education of the clergy and opposed tsarist limitations on the Ukrainian church, particularly restrictions on monasteries' acquisition of land. This opposition led to his arrest. He was confined to the Kievan Cave Monastery in 1738 and died en route to his trial in St Petersburg. He was buried in Tver.

Rohalyk camp site. An early Mesolithic camping ground located in the *khutir* Rohalyk, now part of Petrivka, Stanychno-Luhanske raion, Luhanske oblast. Excavations in 1927–36 unearthed the remains of fire pits that burned coal or charcoal, flint tools, bone objects, and pendants of crayfish shells and fish spines.

Rohan [Rohan']. IV-17. A town smt (1986 pop 5,200) on the Rohan River in Kharkiv raion, Kharkiv oblast. It was first mentioned in historical documents in 1736. At the end of the 19th century a paper factory, which is still operating, was built there. The town lies on the Kharkiv–Rostov-na-Donu highway. An experimental farm of the Kharkiv Agricultural Institute is located in Rohan.

The iconostasis of the Church of the Holy Spirit in Rohatyn

Rohatyn. IV-5. A city (1989 pop 8,500) on the Hnyla Lypa River and a raion center in Ivano-Frankivske oblast. It was first mentioned in historical documents in the 12th century. In 1415, under Polish rule, it was granted the rights of *Magdeburg law, and subsequently it developed into an important trading and manufacturing town. In 1520 the famous *Roksoliana was captured there by the Crimean Tatars and sold to the Turkish sultan. In the 16th century a renowned school of icon painting arose in Rohatyn, and in the 1580s an Orthodox brotherhood, which obtained stauropegion, was founded. After the partition of Poland in 1772, Rohatyn was annexed by Austria, and became a county center. A Ukrainian gymnasium was established there in 1909, and a minor theological seminary in 1931. During the interwar period the town was under Polish rule. In 1939 it became part of Soviet Ukraine and was grated city status. Today it is an important highway junction; 26 percent of its inhabitants work in the transportation industry. Its chief architectural monuments are the stone Church of the Nativity of the Theotokos (end of the 14th century), the remnants of the town walls and gate from the 13th and 14th centuries, the wooden Church of the Holy Spirit (1644–5) with its magnificent iconostasis (1647–50), the ruins of the Dominican monastery (1614), a Roman Catholic church in the Renaissance style (1666), and the wooden St Nicholas's Church (1729).

Rohatynets, Yurii [Rohatynec', Jurij], b ? in Rohatyn, Galicia, d 1608 in Lviv, Galicia. Religious activist. He was a wealthy burgher of Lviv and a leading member of the Lviv Dormition Brotherhood (coauthor of the statutes of its school). He maintained good relations with Prince K.

*Ostrozky and I. *Potii. Although he defended Ukrainian Orthodoxy in letters to the Lviv (1596) and Vilnius (1599) brotherhoods, he advocated moderation in religious polemics. In 1604 I. *Vyshensky spoke out against Rohatynets's wealth. Some scholars (including I. Franko in *Z dziejów synodu brzeskiego 1596 r.* [From the History of the Berestia Synod of 1596, 1895], and Ya. Isaievych) attribute the authorship of the anti-Uniate pamphlet *Perestoroha* to Rohatynets, but many others (eg, P. Yaremenko) dispute that claim.

Rohnida (Rogneda, Ragnheiôr), b ?, d 1000. Princess of Polatsk (Polotsk); daughter of Rogvolod (Rogvald). In 980 *Volodymyr the Great captured the *Polatsk principality and took Rohnida for his wife. They had four sons, *Iziaslav Volodymyrovych, *Mstyslav I Volodymyrovych, *Yaroslav the Wise, and Vsevolod (d 995), and two daughters, one of whom was Predslava (d after 1015). Volodymyr built the city of Iziaslav in the Polatsk land for his son Iziaslav, who ruled there with Rohnida until 988. A lake in the region was reportedly called Lake Rohnida. Rohnida also governed a town called Lybed near Kiev. The Primary Chronicle's description of Rohnida's marriage to Volodymyr was used by T. Shevchenko in his poem 'Tsari' (Princes).

Opanas Rohovych

Rohovych, Opanas [Rohovyč], b 30 January 1812 in Rohivli *khutir*, Starodub county, Chernihiv gubernia, d 1878 in Kiev. Botanist and paleontologist. He completed study at Kiev University (1838). He was director of its botanical gardens (from 1852) and a professor of botany there (1853–68). He gathered substantial amounts of information during research expeditions he undertook throughout Ukraine, and he prepared the first fundamental catalog of the flora of Polisia and the forest-steppe region. He also cultivated a herbarium of 10,000 plants (which he donated to the university) and compiled entries for a dictionary of folk colloquial terms for plants in Ukraine that was never published.

Rohoza, Mykhailo. See Rahoza, Mykhailo.

Rohrbach, Paul, b 1869 in Ostsee, Courland (now Latvia), d 19 July 1956 in Munich. Baptist theologian, historian of Eastern Europe, and publicist of Baltic German origin. He studied history and geography at Dorpat University and then moved to Berlin, where in March 1918, together with A. Schmidt, he founded the *German-Ukrainian Society and its organ, *Die Ukraine.* In a series of books, articles, and brochures beginning in 1914, Rohrbach expounded on the threat of Russian expansionism and argued that Ukraine was nationally and culturally distinct from Russia, and that world powers should support Ukrainian independence. His position won him great popularity among Ukrainians; he was awarded an honorary doctorate from the Ukrainian Free University and named honorary president (1952–6) of the renewed German-Ukrainian Society.

Roik, Vira [Rojik], b 25 April 1911 in Lubni, Poltava gubernia. Master embroiderer. Since 1952 she has lived and worked in Symferopil. She studied the stylistic peculiarities of Ukrainian embroidery of the different regions and created her own distinctive designs. Her works include embroideries for ceremonial *rushnyky, such as *Roosters* (1960), *Volhynian* (1971), *Grapes* (1973), and *Poltavian* (1977); decorative panels, such as *Dear Sun* (1981); and portraits.

Roiter, Volodymyr [Rojter], b 26 July 1903 in Nyzhnodniprovske (now part of Dnipropetrovske), d 8 August 1973 in Kiev. Physical chemist; AN URSR (now ANU) full member from 1961. A graduate of the Dnipropetrovske Institute of People's Education (1926), from 1929 to his death he worked at the ANU Institute of Physical Chemistry and taught at postsecondary schools in Dnipropetrovske (from 1934 as a professor). Roiter's research encompassed kinetics, catalysis, and electrochemistry. He studied the mechanisms of industrial processes such as ammonia synthesis, carbon monoxide conversion, and selective oxidations of hydrogen sulfide and of acetylene. He was one of the founders of macrokinetics, a new area of physical chemistry dealing with material transfer in fixed-bed catalytic reactors, and wrote a monograph on the theory of kinetics and catalysis (1962, 1971).

Rokachevsky, Opanas [Rokačevs'kyj], b 1830 in Kiev, d 25 January 1901 in Kiev. Painter; full member of the St Petersburg Academy of Arts from 1860. After studying at the St Petersburg Academy of Arts (1852–7) he returned to Kiev and from 1860 headed the painting school at the Kievan Cave Monastery. His portraits display typical features of *academism. They include portraits of Count A. Tolstoi (1852), Rokachevsky's daughter (1860), a peasant woman, and a student (1880).

Roksolany fortified settlement. An ancient (6th–3rd century BC) Greek city-state on the Dniester Estuary near Roksolany, Ovidiopil raion, Odessa oblast. Excavations since 1957 have unearthed the remains of dwellings with stone foundations and brick walls, tools, coins, amphoras, and black lacquered tableware. Researchers at Roksolany believe that it is the Greek colony Nikhonion mentioned by some ancient writers.

Roksoliana [Roksoljana] (née Nastia Lisovska), b 1505 in Rohatyn, Galicia, d 15 April 1558 (other sources cite 1561) in Istanbul. Ukrainian wife of the Ottoman sultan Süleyman I Canuni. She was captured by Crimean Tatars in 1520 and sold into slavery. In Süleyman's harem she was given the name Roksoliana. Captivated by her personality and intelligence, the sultan made her his only wife, and he frequently consulted her regarding matters of state. A dis-

Roksoliana (16th-century portrait by an unknown artist)

trict in old Istanbul retains the name Khurrem ('laughing one'), Süleyman's pet name for Roksoliana. Their sons, Selim and Bayezid, were rivals to the throne, and Roksoliana eventually maneuvered the elder, Selim, into the position of heir apparent. Roksoliana became a legendary figure among Ukrainians and the subject of an opera by D. Sichynsky (1908), a play by H. Yakymovych (1869), and literary works by O. Nazaruk (1930), M. Lazorsky (1965), and P. Zahrebelny (1980).

Rokytne. IV-11. A town smt (1986 pop 14,200) on the Ros River and a raion center in Kiev oblast. It is first mentioned in historical documents in 1590. During B. Khmelnytsky's uprising in 1648 Rokytne threw off Polish rule and became a company center of Bila Tserkva regiment. In the 1670s it was destroyed by the Tatars and resettled by its Polish owner. After the partition of Poland in 1793, the town was annexed by Russia and assigned to Vasylkiv county, Kiev gubernia. It attained smt status in 1957. Most of its inhabitants are employed in the food industry, but some work in its asphalt factory and two granite quarries.

Rokytne. II-8. A town smt (1986 pop 6,900) and a raion center in Rivne oblast. It was founded in 1888 by a Belgian firm that built a glass factory there to exploit the local sand deposits. The settlement, known as Okhotnykove until 1922, belonged to Ovruch county, Volhynia gubernia. In the interwar period Rokytne was under the Polish regime. Today its main employers are an aggregate plant and a glass factory.

Rokytne. III-16. A village and raion center in Belgorod oblast, RF. According to the Soviet census of 1926, Ukrainians accounted for 49.1 percent of the volost population.

Mykola Rokytsky: *Apple Tree* (tempera, 1923)

Opanas Rokachevsky: *Portrait of a Woman* (oil, 1860)

Rokytsky, Mykola [Rokyc'kyj], b 19 April 1901 in Zarichia, Kovel county, Volhynia gubernia, d 11 February 1944 in Kiev. Painter and designer. In 1927 he graduated from the Kiev State Art Institute, where he studied under M. *Boichuk. In the 1920s he was a member of the *Association of Revolutionary Art of Ukraine. His easel paintings include *Apple Trees* (1925), the cycle 'Blast Furnace Shop' (1929), and *Defense of Luhanske* (1932). He is best known for his frescoes, such as *Shift Change* at the Kiev State Art Institute (1927) and *Harvest Celebration* (with O. Myzin) at the Peasant Sanatorium in Odessa (1928). His early works were influenced by postimpressionist trends. He was accused of formalism and stylization by Stalinist critics, and in the 1930s he painted socialist-realist works, such as *Funeral of a Comrade in Arms* (1935), and designed tapestries and carpets.

Rokyty. A Carpathian mountain group located in the Hutsul Beskyd in Ivano-Frankivske oblast. Nearly 25 km long, the formation consists of a series of low and middle-sized peaks (Makivka, Rokyta Velyka, Rokyta Mala, and others). The peaks of the mountains and their approaches are generally bare. The mountains are a popular tourist site.

Roland. See Legion of Ukrainian Nationalists.

Yakiv Roll

Roll, Yakiv, b 2 November 1887 in Luhanske, Sloviano-serbske county, Katerynoslav gubernia, d 3 November 1961 in Kiev. Botanist and hydrobiologist; corresponding member of the AN URSR (now ANU) from 1939. A graduate of Kharkiv University (1913), he taught and worked at the Kharkiv Agricultural Institute (1920–34), the Kiev Hydro-biological Station (1934–59; from 1939 director of the ANU Institute of Hydrobiology), the Kiev Forest Management Institute (1930–59), and Kiev University (1945–53). His research centered on the flora of freshwater algae and the phytoplankton of rivers in Ukraine.

Rolle, Antoni Józef (pseud: Dr Antoni J.), b 1830 in Henrykivka (now Rolia), near Sharhorod, Mohyliv county, Podilia gubernia, d 21 January 1894 in Kamianets-Podilskyi, Podilia gubernia. Historian and doctor; son of a Polonized French immigrant. He completed his studies in Kiev (1855) and worked as a doctor in Kamianets-Podilskyi (from 1861). He wrote a series of essays and semificitional works about Right-Bank Ukraine during the 16th to 19th centuries, using documents he sought out in the archives of H. Lubomirski's estate. His major work was *Zameczki podolskie na kresach multańskich* (Podilian Fortresses on the Borders of the Muntenia Region, 3 vols, 1869). A number of his stories appeared in *Kievskaia starina* in translation.

Roller, common (*Coracias garrulus*; Ukrainian: *raksha, syvoraksha*). Colorful migratory birds of the family Coracidae, found from southern Europe to western Asia. Common rollers are 25–40 cm long and have vivid blue wings. In northern Ukraine they nest in tree hollows and in southern Ukraine, in ground holes, on cliffs, and on riverbanks. They are also known as Eurasian rollers. They feed on large insects, locusts, and lizards, thereby providing a service to agriculture.

Roman, b ?, d 1361. Metropolitan. After the death of Metropolitan Theognostos of Kiev in 1353, a struggle for control over Kiev metropoly began between Muscovy and Lithuania. The Lithuanian prince Algirdas, supported by the princes of Tver, dispatched Roman to Constantinople to be consecrated. Theognostos, however, had earlier appointed Aleksei, archbishop of Vladimir, as his successor. The Patriarch of Constantinople resolved the conflict by installing Roman as metropolitan of Lithuania and Volhynia in 1354, with his see in Navahrudak. His jurisdiction was extended to include the eparchies of Halych, Kholm, Lutske, Peremyshl, Polatsk and Turiv, and Volodymyr (but not Kiev or any eastern or northern eparchies). Both Algirdas and Roman were dissatisfied with this solution and attempted to win control over the rest of the metropoly. Roman also attempted to have the see of the metropolitan of Kiev and all Rus' moved from Moscow back to Kiev. Upon his arrival in Kiev (which remained in Algirdas's jurisdiction) Roman proclaimed himself metropolitan. He died suddenly shortly thereafter.

Roman, Mykhailo, b 11 November 1930 in Kobylnice, Bardejov county, Slovakia. Literary scholar in the Prešov region. He worked as an elementary school teacher (1950–2) and as a school inspector (1953). He graduated from Kiev University (1958) and has taught Ukrainian literature at Šafařík University in Prešov since 1958, where he became a professor in 1980. He was elected secretary (1977) and, later, head of the Ukrainian branch of the Slovak Writers' Union. A regular contributor to *Duklia* and a member of its editorial board, he is the author of books on Soviet literature in Slovakia in the 1930s (1964, in Russian), interwar Slovak translations of Soviet Russian literature (1970, in Slovak), Slovak-Ukrainian cultural and literary relations (1971), F. Lazoryk (1974), F. Ivanchov (1976), Ukrainian literature in Czechoslovakia since 1945 (1979), and Ukrainian writers in Czechoslovakia (1989). An edition of his selected literary criticism and studies appeared in 1987.

Roman. A Ukrainian folk dance that is meant to depict conditions before and during a windstorm. It is performed by several groups of three couples each. The tempo (2/4 time) is slow at the beginning but increases steadily to one of intense speed. The *roman* was popular in the Kiev region.

Roman Danylovych [Danylovyč], b ?, d 1258. Rus' prince; third of Danylo Romanovych's five sons. He married the heiress of the Austrian throne, Gertrude Babenberg, after the death of the last member of the Babenberg dynasty, Friedrich II. He ruled Austria briefly (1252) and resided in Himberg, near Vienna. Ca 1254 the Lithuanian duke Mindaugas granted him the rule of *Chorna Rus' (including Navahrudak, Slonim, and Vaukavysk). In 1258 the Tatar leader *Burundai forced Roman, along with *Vasylko Romanovych (prince of Volhynia) and other Ukrainian princes, to join a campaign against Lithuania, and he was killed in battle.

Roman Ihorevych [Ihorevyč], b ?, d September 1211 in Halych. Kievan Rus' prince; son of the hero of *Slovo o polku Ihorevi* (The Tale of Ihor's Campaign), Ihor Sviatoslavych. Around 1205–6 he was elevated to the rule of Zvenyhorod by Galician boyars. He launched a campaign of territorial expansion in 1207 and fought his brother Volodymyr for the rule of Halych. After being forced out once by Hungarian forces he returned and sought to strengthen his power by eliminating rivals and enemies. In 1208–9 he killed approx 500 boyars, thereby prompting others to call upon the Hungarian king, Andrew II, for aid. Roman was again ousted from Halych and was captured by the Hungarians. The boyars purchased the custody of him and his brother Sviatoslav and hanged them.

Roman Mstyslavych [Mstyslavyč] (Romanko), b after 1160, d 14 October 1205 in Zawichost, on the Wisła River in Poland. Rus' prince; son of Mstyslav Iziaslavych and Agnieszka (daughter of the Polish prince Bolesław Krzywousty). When his father died he was bequeathed the Volodymyr-Volynskyi principality (1170). After the death in 1199 of the last Halych prince, Volodymyr Yaroslavych of the Rostyslavych dynasty, Roman united Galicia and Volhynia and created the powerful principality of *Galicia-Volhynia. An able political and military leader, he brought the restive boyars to heel and cultivated the support of the burghers. He waged two successful campaigns against the Cumans, in 1201–2 and 1203–4, from which he returned with many rescued captives. In 1204 he captured Kiev and thus became the most powerful of all the Rus' princes. He played an active role in the political affairs of neighboring states, such as Poland, Hungary, Byzantium, Lithuania, and Germany. Roman died in the Battle of Zawichost after he was ambushed by the Poles. He was described by a contemporary chronicler as a 'grand prince, the sole ruler of all Rus', who conquered the pagans and wisely adhered to the commandments of God.' He founded the *Romanovych dynasty (1199–1340).

Romanchenko, Ivan [Romančenko], b 16 March 1894 in Kishinev, Bessarabia, d 3 April 1977 in Lviv. Literary historian and bibliographer. He graduated from the Odessa Institute of People's Education (1928) and taught Ukrainian literature there and at the Odessa Music and Drama Institute (1930–6) and at postsecondary institutes in Nizhen (1938–9), Lviv (1939–41, 1945–55), Drohobych, and Kremianets. He was also a learned secretary of the Pushkin Committee and the Gorky Archive and a senior scholarly associate of the Institute of World Literature in Moscow of the Academy of Sciences of the USSR (1956–8) and worked at the Institute of Social Sciences of the AN URSR (now ANU) in Lviv. From 1928 he published many works, including articles on T. Shevchenko, M. Kostomarov, P. Kulish, I. Franko, and other Ukrainian writers, and numerous articles and a book (1964, with D. Zaslavsky) on M. *Drahomanov. He was also one of the compilers of a Russian bibliographic guide to Shevchenko (1941), and he edited the 1970 edition of Drahomanov's selected works. Ye.

Kravchenko's bibliography of Romanchenko's works was published in Lviv in 1968.

Romanchenko, Mykola [Romančenko], b 29 August 1921 in Romaniv, Novohrad-Volynskyi county, Volhynia gubernia. Writer. He graduated from the Ukrainian Communist Institute of Journalism in Kharkiv (1940) and has been deputy head and secretary responsible for the Lviv branch of the Writers' Union of Ukraine and chief editor (1966–8) of its journal *Zhovten'*. Since 1956 he has published a number of collections of poetry, the novelette *Zakhmarnyi harnizon* (The Garrison beyond the Clouds, 1966), and a book of essays, memoirs, and travel notes. An edition of his selected poetry appeared in 1981.

Romanchenko, Trokhym [Romančenko, Troxym] (pseuds: Mykola Hrytsenko, Katerynoslavets, Trokhym R., Roman Trokhymenko), b 4 August 1880 in Poltava, d 11 June 1930 in Dnipropetrovske. Writer and ethnographer. A self-educated worker, for many years he was curator of the Katerynoslav (later Dnipropetrovske) Historical Museum and was active in the Katerynoslav Prosvita society. From 1905 he published poetry, stories, and ethnographic articles in literary miscellanies and journals. A small collection of his poems appeared in 1916, and a book of folk songs collected and transcribed by him was published in Kiev in 1980.

Tyt Romanchuk: *Back from the Journey* (1898)

Romanchuk, Tyt [Romančuk], b 1865 in Lviv, d 1911 in Lovran, Croatia. Painter and graphic artist. He studied at a technical school in Lviv and S. Grocholski's private studio in Munich and then worked as a caricaturist and illustrator in Lviv. He illustrated *Zerkalo* (1882), the Prosvita society's almanac, and M. Arkas's history of Ukraine (1912). His impressionist paintings include landscapes (*Forest Clearing*, 1890), portraits (*Yu. Fedkovych*, 1891), and genre paintings (*At the Watering Hole*, 1893).

Romanchuk, Yuliian [Romančuk, Julijan] (Romanczuk, Julian; pseud: U.S. Postupyshyn), b 24 February 1842 in Krylos, Stanyslaviv circle, Galicia, d 22 April 1932 in Lviv. Galician politician, community leader, journalist, scholar, and publisher; full member of the Shevchenko

Yuliian Romanchuk   Bohdan Romanenchuk

Scientific Society (NTSh) from 1909; father of T. *Romanchuk. He graduated from Lviv University and taught classics at a German gymnasium (1863–8) and at the Ukrainian Academic Gymnasium (1868–1900) in Lviv. He was elected to the Galician Diet (1883–95) and headed its Ruthenian Club (1889–95) and the populist *People's Council (1885–99). A leading representative of Western Ukrainian *populism, he spearheaded the campaign in the diet for Ukrainian autonomy, gymnasiums, and teachers' seminaries. In 1890 he was one of the architects of the so-called *New Era in Austrian, Polish, and Ukrainian political co-operation, but with its failure in 1894 he led the Ukrainian opposition to it. For nearly three decades Romanchuk was a member of the Austrian Reichsrat (1891–7, 1901–18). He headed the Ukrainian Parliamentary Club (1901–10, 1916–17), served as its vice-president from 1910, and in 1905 was the only non-Jewish deputy who spoke in favor of a Jewish curia and equal rights for Jews.

Romanchuk was a founding member and the first leader (1899–1907) of the *National Democratic party. During the First World War he was chairman of the Vienna-based Ukrainian Relief Committee and *Ukrainian Cultural Council. After Austria's defeat he served in the *Ukrainian National Rada (October 1918 to June 1919) of the Western Ukrainian National Republic; on 10 November 1918 he swore in the members of its State Secretariat. On 14 March 1923, after the Conference of Ambassadors sanctioned Poland's occupation of Western Ukraine, he presided over the oath of loyalty to Ukrainian statehood, which thousands of Ukrainians took during the rally in St George's Square in Lviv.

Romanchuk was a distinguished activist in the Galician Ukrainian community. He was a founding member of the NTSh, the *Prosvita society (president in 1896–1906), the Ridna Shkola society, and the *Teachers' Hromada (president in 1912–15) in Lviv and was elected an honorary member of the last three organizations. He contributed to the Lviv gazettes Slovo and Pravda (which he helped edit in the 1870s); he was the founder (1879), publisher, and actual chief editor (until 1887) of the Lviv populist gazette *Bat'kivshchyna; and he cofounded and contributed regularly to *Dilo, Lviv's major Ukrainian newspaper from 1880, and Vienna's *Ruthenische Revue (1903–5) and *Ukrainische Rundschau (1905–14). He edited many Prosvita almanacs and monthly booklets, and from 1871 he compiled Ukrainian readers for elementary and junior high schools in Galicia. He introduced, with O. Barvinsky, the phonetic orthography in schoolbooks in 1890 and in Prosvita publications in 1899. He edited and published in Lviv editions of T. Shevchenko's selected poetry (2 vols, 1894–5), poetry (1902), works (1907, 1912), and Kobzar (1914), and he wrote several articles on Shevchenko and his poetry, literary criticism, and the brochure Die Ruthenen und ihre Gegner in Galizien (1902). He initiated many Prosvita society publications and founded the library of Ukrainian classics *Rus'ka Pys'mennist', the first 27 volumes of which he edited (1904–20).

Romanchuk actively maintained contact with Ukrainian writers and political and community leaders in Russian-ruled Ukraine. In 1903 he spoke on behalf of Galicia's Ukrainians at the unveiling of I. Kotliarevsky's monument in Poltava. As a senior statesman and the de facto leader (together with Ye. Olesnytsky and K. Levytsky) of Galicia's Ukrainians in 1900–10, he was widely respected by the Ukrainian public.

I. Sokhotsky

Romanchych, Hanka [Romančyč], b 14 February 1907 in Kosiw (near Dauphin), Manitoba, d 14 October 1984 in St Catharines, Ontario. Home economist and community figure. As an employee of the Ministry of Agriculture, she toured the Ukrainian districts of Alberta from the late 1920s and lectured on topics related to home economics. During the Depression of the 1930s she organized rural women's circles, which produced handicrafts for sale. With the founding of the Ukrainian Women's Association of Canada (SUK) she became its first secretary and a founder of the Ukrainian Museum of Canada, for which she collected articles in Canada and Ukraine. She participated in international women's conferences, such as the First Congress of Ukrainian Women in Stanyslaviv (1934), a League of Nations panel on the status of women in Canada (1936), and the International Conference of Women's Councils (1947). In 1945–51 she was vice-president of SUK.

Romanenchuk, Bohdan [Romanenčuk], b 23 February 1906 in Voskresintsi, Kolomyia county, Galicia, d 9 January 1989 in Philadelphia. Literary scholar and critic. He emigrated to Austria in 1944 and then to the United States. He was a professor of Russian language and literature at Niagara University in 1965–80. Romanenchuk published and edited the literary journal *Kyiv (1950–61) and was the compiler and editor of the unfinished literary encyclopedia Azbukovnyk: Korotka ensyklopedia ukraïns'koï literatury (A Primer: A Short Encyclopedia of Ukrainian Literature, 2 vols, 1966, 1975). He also edited the bibliographic journal Ukraïns'ka knyha (1971–81). His works include Ukraïns'ke pys'menstvo: Stara doba (Ukrainian Writing: The Old Period, 1946), Z zhyttia i tvorchosty Nataliï Kobryns'koï (From the Life and Works of Nataliia Kobrynska, 1951), and Bibliohrafiia vydan' ukraïns'koï emigratsiinoï literatury, 1945–1970 (A Bibliography of Ukrainian Emigré Literature, 1945–70, 1974).

Romanenko, Illia, b 2 August 1909 in Maidanivka, Kiev county, Kiev gubernia, d 28 October 1982 in Kiev. Economist and agronomist; corresponding member of the All-Union Academy of Agricultural Sciences from 1956. A graduate of the Kiev Zootechnical Institute (1932), he worked at various research and teaching institutes in

Kiev. He directed the Ukrainian Scientific Research Institute of the Economics and Organization of Agriculture (1955–66) and headed the Department of Economics at the Ukrainian Agricultural Academy (1966–77). He wrote over 150 works, including the monographs *Sil's'ke hospodarstvo Ukraïns'koï RSR* (The Agriculture of the Ukrainian SSR, 1958), *Ekonomicheskaia effektivnost' intensivnykh sistem zemledeliia* (The Economic Efficiency of Intensive Systems of Land Use, 1963), and several works on animal husbandry in Ukraine.

Romanenko, Ivan, b 1794, d 1854. Kobzar and lirnyk who lived in Borzna and then Brytan, Chernihiv gubernia. His dumas, including those about a Cossack's departure, the orphaned and hapless Fedir, the Cossack Holota, Ivas Konovchenko, and Udovychenko, were written down by M. Bilozersky and published by A. Metlynsky (1854).

Romanenko, Oleksander, b 23 June 1901 in Odessa, d 4 September 1992 in Kiev. Stage and film actor and singer (bass); husband of I. *Steshenko. He began his theatrical career in 1922 in the touring Franko New Drama Theater (1924–5) and then worked in the State Podilian Ukrainian Drama Theater, Berezil (1926–33), and the Kiev Ukrainian Drama Theater (1934–57). He acted in the films *Suvori dni* (Grim Days, 1933) and *Polumia hnivu* (Flames of Rage, 1955).

Romanenko, Vitalii, b 13 July 1927 in Rusaniv, Brovary raion, Kiev oblast. Marksman. He won the 1954 world championship in the running-deer competition (world record) and the 1956 Olympic gold medal in the same event, and was a member of USSR teams that won world shooting championships in 1954, 1958, 1961, and 1962 and European championships in 1955 and 1959. He was the USSR shooting champion 11 times.

Romanenko, Yurii, b 1 August 1944 in Koltubanovskii, Orenburg oblast, RSFSR. Ukrainian pilot and astronaut. He graduated from the Chernihiv Higher Aviation School of Pilots (1966) and became an astronaut in 1970. He was commander of the Soiuz-26 space flight from 10 December 1977 to 16 March 1978. With H. Hrechko also on board, the Soiuz-26 docked with the Saliut-6 space station, and later with the Soiuz-27, Soiuz-28, and Progress-1 satellites. Romanenko returned on the Soiuz-27 spacecraft. He has flown two more space missions: on the Soiuz-38, with the Cuban astronaut A. Tamaio Mendes in 1980, and on the Soiuz TM-2 in 1987.

Romanesque. A style that became popular in European art and architecture in the 11th century and prevailed in western Europe until the end of the 12th century. In Ukraine the Romanesque style at first interacted with the dominant Byzantine style of construction, and it was not until the 13th century that it took hold there, primarily in western Ukraine. Adopting the style involved a change of building materials from brick and mortar to cut stone, which was readily available in the western regions. Of the churches built in the Romanesque style in western Ukraine, only St Panteleimon's Church in Halych has survived. Its western portal is marked by two pilasters and alternating columns, is covered by a semicircular vault, and recedes in concentrically narrowing arches typical of the style. The exteriors of its apses are marked by decorative blind arcades. In secular Romanesque architecture only remnants of towers have survived. The one in Kamianets-Podilskyi is round with several stories of Romanesque window openings and a well-developed cornice. Some elements of Romanesque influence can also be seen in Chernihiv, particularly in the church of the Yeletskyi Dormition Monastery.

In sculpture, which was for the most part engaged with relief and subordinated to architecture, natural forms were freely adapted to linear designs, with distortions and stylizations the result. In the St Panteleimon's Church in Halych the friezes are carved with acanthus foliage, and the capitals combine interlace patterns with foliage. No examples of Romanesque murals have survived. There are, however, Romanesque elements in the illuminations of the *Trier Psalter (11th century).

D. Zelska-Darewych

Romania. See Rumania.

Romaniuk, Anatol [Romanjuk, Anatol'] (Romaniuc, Anatole), b 28 February 1924 in Zarozhany, Khotyn county, Bukovyna. Demographer. He graduated from the University of Louvain (PH D, 1967). He then served as chief of the Demographic Bureau in Zaire (1953–60), a professor at the Universities of Ottawa (1964–80) and Montreal (1969–72), and a division director at Statistics Canada (since 1968). He is a coauthor of *The Demography of Tropical Africa* (1968), the editor of *Population Estimation Methods, Canada* (1987) and the author of *Fertility in Canada: From Baby-Boom to Baby-Bust* (1987) and of many articles on fertility in Africa.

Archbishop Vasyl (Volodymyr) Romaniuk

Romaniuk, Vasyl [Romanjuk, Vasyl'], b 9 December 1925. Human rights activist and political prisoner, and Orthodox archbishop. He was accused of participating in the Ukrainian resistance and imprisoned in labor camps in the Urals and Kolyma in 1944–53. In 1958 he was allowed to return to Ukraine. In 1959 he was rehabilitated. He took correspondence courses from the Moscow Theological Seminary and was ordained in 1964, and served in Kosmach, Kosiv raion, Ivano-Frankivske oblast. He was arrested in January 1972 and sentenced to seven years in special-regime labor camps in the Mordovian ASSR and five years' exile in the Yakut ASSR for his active defense of human and religious rights. In the camps he went on a hunger strike in 1975 and joined the *Ukrainian Helsinki Group in February 1979. After his release in 1981, he was not allowed to do pastoral work until 1984, when he resumed his priestly duties in Pistyn, Kostiv raion. In 1990 he was consecrated Archbishop Volodymyr of the revived Ukrainian Autocephalous Orthodox church, with special responsibility for eastern Ukraine. A collection of Romaniuk's letters, appeals, essays, and materials relating to his case, *A Voice in the Wilderness*, was published in English translation in 1980.

Oleh Romaniv

Romaniv, Oleh, b 21 March 1928 in Sokal, Galicia. Materials scientist. After graduating from the Lviv Polytechnical Institute (1950) he supervised the planning and coordination of power station networks in Lviv. Since 1956 he has worked at the AN URSR (now ANU) Physical Mechanics Institute (until 1964 the Institute of Machine Building and Automation) in Lviv, and in 1977 he became its deputy director. His research has dealt with the thermomechanical strengthening of materials, fractography, and the mechanism of metal corrosion. In 1989 Romaniv was elected president of the revived *Shevchenko Scientific Society in Lviv.

Romaniv. See Dzerzhynske.

Romanivska, Mariia [Romanivs'ka, Marija], b 28 July 1901 in Yerky, Myrhorod county, Poltava gubernia, d 21 September 1983 in Kiev. Writer and teacher. She graduated from the Zinkiv gymnasium and worked as a teacher and later for the newspaper *Visti VUTsVK*. She is the author of the prose collections *Murashyna peremoha* (The Ant's Victory, 1927), *Bolotna solov'ikha* (The Mud Hen–Nightingale, 1959), and *Naprovesni* (In Early Spring, 1927), the play *Nezhyt' leitenanta Shvainera* (Lieutenant Schweiner's Cold, 1941), the novelettes *Mariika* (1930), *Vysokyi lit* (The High Flight, 1950), and *Chervonyi tiul'pan* (The Red Tulip, 1956), and the novel *Liubov i myr* (Love and Peace, 1966).

Romankiv, Liubomyr (Lubomyr), b 17 April 1931 in Zhovkva, Galicia. Materials scientist and chemical engineer; member of the Shevchenko Scientific Society and IBM fellow since 1986. He graduated from the University of Alberta (1955) and the Massachusetts Institute of Technology (PH D, 1962). He was the head of the Plast International Executive (1976–84) and an active member of the World Congress of Free Ukrainians. He is a senior scientist and manager of electrochemistry and device fabrication at the IBM Thomas J. Watson Research Center in Yorktown Heights, New York. Among his patented inventions and technical advances are microfabrication technology for thin-film magnetic heads in high-performance disk and tape systems and laser-enhanced electrochemical processing. He has published numerous scientific papers and book chapters.

Roman-Kosh [Roman-Koš]. IX–15. The highest elevation in the Crimean Mountains. Situated in the Babuhan Yaila massif, the peak has a height of 1,545 m. Its top portion is bare, and its slopes are covered mainly with mountain meadow vegetation. It consists primarily of limestones. The mountain is located within the Crimean Game Preserve.

Romanov. A dynasty of tsars that ruled Russia and the Russian Empire from 1613 to 1917. With the ending of the *Riurykide dynasty in 1598 (its male side died out), Muscovy entered a period of widespread unrest that lasted until 1613, when Mikhail Fedorovich (1613–45), the son of the Patriarch of Moscow (a Romanov by birth), was elected tsar. His successors to the Russian throne were his son, Aleksei Mikhailovich (1645–76); his grandsons, Fedor Alekseievich (1676–82), Ivan V (1682–82), and *Peter I (1682–1725); *Catherine I (Peter I's second wife, 1725–7); *Peter II (Peter I's grandson, 1727–30), with whom the male side of the line died out; *Anna Ivanovna, Ivan V's daughter (1730–40); Ivan VI, great-grandson of Ivan V (1740–1); and *Elizabeth I (daughter of Peter I, 1741–61), with whom the female side of the line died out. Elizabeth's successors continued to use the dynastic name, although they were actually members of a German lineage. They included *Peter III, the son of Peter I's daughter, Anna, and Karl Friedrich, duke of Holstein-Gottorp (1761–2); Catherine II, the wife of Peter III and a princess of Anhalt-Zerbst by birth (1762–96), and their son, Paul I (1796–1801); Paul's sons, *Alexander I (1801–25) and *Nicholas I (1825–55); *Alexander II (son of Nicholas, 1855–81), his son, *Alexander III (1881–94), and his grandson, *Nicholas II (1894–1917), who abdicated the throne following the *February Revolution in 1917. In 1918, after the Bolsheviks seized power, Nicholas was murdered along with the members of his family. Many other members of the Romanov family were killed in 1918–19, although some managed to emigrate to Western Europe or the United States.

Romanova, Odarka (pseuds: Odarka, O. Romanenko). Late 19th- and early 20th-century writer. She lived in Kiev, where she was part of the milieu of the Starytsky, Lysenko, and Kosach families and belonged to the literary circle *Pleiada. From 1887 her poems and stories were published in the journals *Zoria* and *Literaturno-naukovyi vistnyk* and in several literary miscellanies. She is the author of the collection *Pisni, dumky, legendy* (Songs, Thoughts, Legends, 1896) and of fables, many of which appeared in the Lviv children's biweekly *Dzvinok*.

Romanovsky, Oleksii [Romanovs'kyj, Oleksij], b 18 February 1918 in Talova Balka, Oleksandriia county, Kherson gubernia. Literary scholar and politician. He graduated from the Kiev Pedagogical Institute (1951) and the CC CPSU Academy of Social Sciences (1958) and became scholarly secretary of the Institute of Literature of the AN

URSR (now ANU). A former secretary of the Kiev City Committee of the CPU, in 1964 and again in 1977 he was appointed rector of the Kiev Pedagogical Institute of Foreign Languages, and later, rector of the Kiev Pedagogical Institute. From 1973 to 1977 he was minister of culture of the Ukrainian SSR, and in 1976 he was elected to the Auditing Commission of the CC CPU.

Romanovsky, Viktor [Romanovs'kyj], b 16 or 18 January 1890 in Hlukhiv, Chernihiv gubernia, d 10 February 1971 in Stavropol, RF. Historian, archeographer, and archivist. He studied at Kiev University (1909–14) under M. Dovnar-Zapolsky, lectured there (1914) and at the Kiev Archeological Institute (1918), and was deputy director (1914–21) and director (1921–31) of the *Kiev Central Archive of Old Documents. He was also active in the VUAN as a member of the Commission for the Study of the History of Western-Ruthenian and Ukrainian Law and the Commission for the Study of the Socioeconomic History of 18th- and 19th-Century Ukraine, and secretary (1929) and director (1930–4) of the Archeographic Commission; and was an associate of the Scientific Research Institute of the History of Ukrainian Culture in Kharkiv. Romanovsky was arrested during the Stalinist terror in 1934 and imprisoned in a labor camp in Kazakhstan. After his release he lectured at the Karaganda Teachers' Institute (1940–7) and then chaired the history department at the Stavropol Pedagogical Institute.

Romanovsky wrote several articles on 17th- and 18th-century Ukrainian history, a book about the pioneering printer I. Fedorovych (1925), a book of essays in archival studies (1927), and a critical evaluation of the 1666 population census in Left-Bank Ukraine and its organization (1967). He edited the VUAN publication of the 1666 census books (1931). His doctoral dissertation (1947) on the state economy of Ukraine in the second half of the 17th century remains unpublished, as does his compilation of the codex of charters granting Magdeburg law to 16th- to 18th-century Ukrainian cities.

A. Zhukovsky

Romanovych [Romanovyč]. A branch of the *Riurykide dynasty, descended from *Roman Mstyslavych, that ruled the Principality of Galicia-Volhynia from 1200 to 1340. Its most noted members were the princes *Danylo Romanovych, *Lev Danylovych, *Yurii Lvovych, *Andrii Yuriiovych, *Lev Yuriiovych, and *Yurii II Boleslav.

Romanovych, Marko [Romanovyč], b 13 December 1904 in Sniatyn, Galicia, d 8 December 1958 in Grimsby, Ontario. Basilian priest. He was ordained in 1930 and came to Canada in 1933 to teach at the Basilian novitiate in Mundare, Alberta. In 1938 he founded the journal *Svitlo, which he edited until 1943, when he moved to Grimsby with the relocated novitiate. He was also the initiator of the Missionary Sisters of Christian Charity, a community established in 1946.

Romanovych, Teofila [Romanovyč] (real surname: Rozhankivska), b 16 May 1842 in Dovhopillia, near Putyliv, Bukovyna, d 16 January 1924 in Chernivtsi, Bukovyna. Actress and theater director. She began her career as an actress in the Ruska Besida Theater (1867–73), where she played character roles. In 1873 she led her own touring company. In 1874–80, as administrative director of the Ruska Besida Theater, she enlarged its repertoire and improved its artistic level by recruiting many talented actors and directors. In 1880–2 she led her own troupe, and in 1883–5, the amateur theater in Chernivtsi.

Romanovych-Slavatynsky, Oleksander [Romanovyč-Slavatyns'kyj], b 14 July 1832 in Voitove, Pereiaslav county, Poltava gubernia, d 7 September 1910. Legal scholar. After graduating from the law faculty of Kiev University (1855) he taught at a gymnasium and prepared his MA thesis on the introduction of gubernial administration in Russia (1859). In 1862 he returned from Western Europe, where for two years he had studied law in London, Heidelberg, and Paris, and began to teach Russian and foreign law at Kiev University. He wrote a textbook on state law (1872), the fundamental *Dvorianstvo v Rossii ot nachala XVIII v. do otmeny krepostnogo prava* (The Nobility of Russia from the Beginning of the 18th Century to the Abolition of Serfdom, 1870), and biographies of M. Ivanyshev (1876) and M. Speransky (1873). His memoirs were serialized in *Vestnik Evropy* in 1903.

Natalia Romanovych-Tkachenko   Gen Joseph Romanow

Romanovych-Tkachenko, Natalia [Romanovyč-Tkačenko, Natalja], b 1884 in Skvyra, Kiev gubernia, d 1933 in Kiev. Prose writer. In 1905 she started to publish short stories in *Literaturna-naukovyi vistnyk*, and later she went on to publish the trilogy *Mandrivnytsia* (The Wanderer) and her notes of travels to Galicia (1917–18). She was a member of the writers' group Pluh, and from 1923 she contributed to the journal *Chervonyi shliakh*. The published collections of her short stories include *Zhyttia liuds'ke* (Human Life, 1918), *Nespodivanyi zemletrus* (The Unexpected Earthquake, 1928), *Chebrets' zillia* (Wild Thyme, 1928), and *Zin'kova zirka* (Zinko's Star, 1929). Also published was the book *Nas klychut' hudky: Zapysky revoliutsionerky 900-ykh rr.* (The Sirens Are Calling Us: Notes of a Revolutionary of the 1900s, 1931).

Romanow, Joseph [Romaniv, Yosyp], b 3 May 1921 in Saskatoon. General of the Canadian Armed Forces. After serving as a pilot of the Royal Canadian Air Force (RCAF) in Europe (1944–6) he completed his education at the University of Saskatchewan (1950), the Cranfield Institute of Technology (England, 1957), and the National Defence

College of Armed Forces (1971). Advancing quickly in the air force he served as section head at Air Materiel Command (1951–5); commanding officer of the RCAF quality control laboratory in Ottawa (1957–8); chief technical officer, senior staff officer, and chief of staff at Air Transport Command (1961–70); deputy chief of staff at NATO headquarters in Germany (1971–4); and director general of manpower and organization at National Defence headquarters in Ottawa (1974–). He is an active member of the Ukrainian Catholic church and the Ukrainian Canadian Servicemen's Association and a frequent speaker at Ukrainian community events.

Premier Roy Romanow

Romanow, Roy [Romaniv, Roman], b 12 August 1939 in Saskatoon. Lawyer and politician. Educated at the University of Saskatchewan (LL D, 1964), Romanow was first elected to the Saskatchewan legislature in 1967 as the New Democratic party member for Saskatoon–Riversdale. He was re-elected in 1971, 1975, and 1978; defeated in 1982; and re-elected in 1986. He was deputy premier and attorney general of Saskatchewan (1971–82) and minister of intergovernmental affairs (1979–82). In 1981 he played a pivotal role in federal-provincial negotiations on the patriation of the Canadian Constitution and the creation of the Canadian Charter of Rights and Freedoms. He was chosen as party leader in 1987 and elected premier of the province in October 1991.

Romans. During its eastward expansion in the 1st century BC, the Roman Empire seized the southern and eastern coasts of the Black Sea. It successfully waged war against the *Pontic Kingdom and annexed its vassal states, the *Bosporan Kingdom and the Hellenic *ancient states on the northern Black Sea coast. Roman control there was entrenched after the defeat of a rebellion in 48 BC led by Pharnaces II, the son of the last Pontic king, Mithridates IV Eupator. Julius Caesar appointed a ruler for the Bosporan Kingdom, and Roman garrisons were stationed in every Hellenic colony. Roman control in the region was frequently interrupted by invasions of various steppe nomadic peoples, but it was consolidated after Trajan conquered Dacia in 106 AD, strengthened the Roman garrisons, and built a series of fortifications (see *Trajan's Walls). In the 2nd and 3rd centuries *Chersonese Taurica was the center of the Roman army and navy in the Crimea. Rome's control did not extend far beyond the coastal cities

and colonies, however, and its domination of the northern Pontic littoral ended during the great migration of peoples and the arrival of the *Goths in the late 3rd century. In 271 AD Roman legions were withdrawn south of the Danube.

During their rule in what is today Ukraine, the Romans established economic and cultural contacts with the neighboring *Scythians, *Sarmatians, and tribes of the *Zarubyntsi culture. The coastal cities were thriving centers where agricultural products from the Ukrainian territories were traded for Roman-imported weapons, jewelry, textiles, ceramics, and other goods. Many Roman merchants settled there and traveled into the Ukrainian hinterland. Roman coins have been found in over 1,000 locations in Ukraine, and 137 large hoards have been discovered there, evidence that the Roman silver denarius was a principal currency in Ukraine in the 2nd to 5th centuries. Archeologists' discoveries of Roman artifacts of daily use, luxury items, and pagan idols indicate that the Romans influenced the material culture and religious worldview of Ukraine's ancient inhabitants.

Pliny, Ovid, Tacitus, Ammianus Marcellinus, and Justinian are among the Roman writers and historians who wrote about the peoples of Eastern Europe. Ukrainian scholars who have written about the Romans include M. Drahomanov (an 1869 study on the historical significance of the Roman Empire and Tacitus), I. Franko, I. Sharanevych, O. Partytsky (in his 1881 history of ancient Galicia), M. Sonevytsky, M. Smishko, M. Braichevsky, and M. Miller.

BIBLIOGRAPHY

Smiszko, M. *Kultury wczesnego okresu cesarstwa rzymskiego w Małopolsce Wschodniej* (Lviv 1932)
Majewski, K. *Importy rzymskie na ziemiach słowiańskich* (Wrocław 1949)
Braichevs'kyi, M. 'Arkheolohichni svidchennia uchasti skhidnykh slov'ian u politychnykh podiiakh ryms'koï istoriï II–IV st. n.e.,' *Arkheolohiia*, 8 (1953)
Kallistov, D. *Pivnichne Prychornomoria v antychnu epokhu* (Kiev 1953)
Braichevs'kyi, M. *Ryms'ka moneta na terytoriï Ukraïny* (Kiev 1959)
Chaplygina, N. *Naselenie Dnestrovsko-Karpatskikh zemel' i Rim v I–nachale III v. n. e.* (Kishinev 1990)

A. Zhukovsky

Romanticism. An artistic and ideological movement in literature, art, and music and a world view which arose toward the end of the 18th century in Germany, England, and France. In the beginning of the 19th century it spread to Russia, Poland, and Austria, and in the mid-19th century it encompassed other countries of Europe as well as North and South America. Romanticism, which appeared after the French Revolution in an environment of growing absolutism at the turn of the 19th century, was a reaction against the rationalism of the Enlightenment and the stilted forms, schemata, and canons of *classicism and, at times, sentimentalism. Paramount features of romanticism were idealism, a belief in the natural goodness of the individual person, and, hence, the cult of feeling as opposed to reason; a predilection for the more 'primitive' expressions of human creativity as being closer to the fundamental goodness of the person and, hence, an enthusiasm for folk art, poetry, and songs; a belief in the perfectibility of the individual person and, hence, a predilection for change and the espousal of 'striving' as a mode of behavior; and a search for historical consciousness and an intensified learning of history (historicism), coupled at times with an escape from surrounding reality into an idealized past or future or into a world of fantasy. The Romantic world view fostered its own style and gave rise to specific genres of literature: ballads, lyrical songs, romances, and historical novels and dramas.

Certain elements of romanticism, especially those which emphasized the value of the folk, such as J. *Herder's notion of the importance of folklore in the development of literature, encouraged a resurgence of interest in folklore and history. The study of both resulted in a general reawakening of Slavic peoples, including the Ukrainians. The first manifestations of the influence of romanticism in Ukraine were the publications in St Petersburg of O. Pavlovsky's *Grammatika malorossiiskogo narechiia* (The Grammar of the Little Russian Dialect) in 1818 and of N. *Tsertelev's *Opyt sobraniia starinnykh malorossiiskikh pesnei* (An Attempt at Collecting Ancient Little Russian Songs) in 1819 – a collection remarkable not only for the songs but, more important, for its emphasis on the rich and unique nature of Ukrainian folk songs. Appreciation of Ukrainian folk songs was strengthened by the publication in Moscow in 1827 of M. *Maksymovych's collection *Malorossiiskie pesni* (Little Russian Songs). In literature the precursor of Ukrainian romanticism was P. *Hulak-Artemovsky. His ballads, like Ukrainian romanticism in general, were less a protest against the rather insignificant classical movement in Ukraine than a reaction against the prevalent concept that only burlesque and travesties could be written in the 'peasant' vernacular – the adjective aptly describes the status of the Ukrainian language in the Russian Empire at the beginning of the 19th century.

Also influential in the development of Ukrainian romanticism were the so-called 'Ukrainian schools' in Russian and Polish literature. In Russian literature the leading members of the 'Ukrainian school' were not only Russians (K. Ryleev, F. Bulgarin) enthralled by the exotic nature of things Ukrainian (nature, history, folk mores, and folklore) but also Ukrainians who wrote in Russian (O. *Somov, M. *Markevych, Ye. *Hrebinka, and, foremost among them, N. *Gogol). In Polish literature the 'Ukrainian school,' with its fascination with Ukrainian 'exotic' themes, consisted of writers such as A. Malczewski, J.B. Zaleski, and S. Goszczyński.

The interest in folklore and history spawned by romanticism in Ukraine produced a wealth of material: collections of folk songs by Maksymovych (1827, 1834, 1849), compilations of historical songs and *dumas by I. *Sreznevsky in *Zaporozhskaia starina* (1833–80), a gathering of oral folk literature by P. Lukashevych (1836), and numerous publications of historical monuments and works, by D. *Bantysh-Kamensky, M. Markevych, O. *Bodiansky, A. *Skalkovsky, and others.

The first locus of Ukrainian romanticism was the *Kharkiv Romantic School. The group was centered around Sreznevsky and consisted of poets such as L. *Borovykovsky, A. *Metlynsky, M. *Kostomarov, M. *Petrenko, and O. *Korsun. It published two miscellanies, *Ukrainskii al'manakh* (1831) and *Zaporozhskaia starina*.

Contemporaneously with the Kharkiv Romantic School appeared the *Ruthenian Triad in Galicia. It consisted of I. *Vahylevych, Ya. *Holovatsky, and, primarily, M. *Shash-

kevych and was most noted for the publication of the almanac *Rusalka Dnistrovaia* (The Dniester Nymph, 1836). The romanticism of the Ruthenian Triad lay in its promulgation of the folk language (ie, Ukrainian) in opposition to the prevalent *yazychiie. The followers of the triad's program were such Galician authors as M. *Ustyianovych and A. *Mohylnytsky, as well as O. *Dukhnovych in Transcarpathia.

The second phase of Ukrainian romanticism, which had a more pronounced national and political program that resulted in a greater variety of literary works, occurred in the late 1830s and early 1840s in Kiev. The Kievan group consisted of Maksymovych, P. *Kulish, T. *Shevchenko, and the former members of the Kharkiv Romantic School Metlynsky and Kostomarov, who moved to Kiev. The group's philosophical and ideological focus came from the *Cyril and Methodius Brotherhood, whose Christian-Romantic program, expressed in *Knyhy bytiia ukraïns'koho narodu* (Books of the Genesis of the Ukrainian People), had been inspired by Kostomarov, and manifested itself most artistically in the messianic poetry of Shevchenko. Other expressions of that phase of Ukrainian romanticism can be found in the almanacs and miscellanies *Kievlianin* (1840, 1841, 1850), *Lastivka* (1841), *Snip* (1841), *Molodyk* (1843, 1844), and *Iuzhno-russkii sbornik* (1848). Other writers tied to the Kievan group of Romantics were V. *Zabila from Chernihiv, O. *Afanasiev-Chuzhbynsky from Poltava, and the poet and editor Bodiansky, who lived in Moscow.

The third phase of Ukrainian romanticism centered around the journal *Osnova* (1861–2), published in St Petersburg by the former members of the Cyril and Methodius Brotherhood V. *Bilozersky, Kostomarov, and Kulish. Also part of that late Romantic phase are authors such as O. *Storozhenko, with his fantastic stories full of the more gory and Gothic folkloric motifs, poets such as Ya. *Shchoholev, and the Bukovynian bard Yu. *Fedkovych.

The poetry of Ukrainian romanticism can be divided, in general, into two streams: national-patriotic lyricism, based in the majority of the Ukrainian Romantic poets on an idealization of the heroic Cossack past, and subjective personal lyricism, found to a lesser degree in all of the poets but predominantly in such authors as Petrenko, Zabila, and Shchoholev. The Ukrainian Romantic movement differs from the Russian in the historicism of its epic genre, its idealization of the past, and its predilection for the songlike structure, with motifs of national as opposed to personal longing. Ukrainian romanticism is more akin to Polish romanticism.

Having discovered the importance of folk poetry and folk art in the development and growth of literature, and the importance of historical monuments and research for the development of national consciousness, Ukrainian romanticism also contributed to the independence of the Ukrainian literary language and to the perfection of poetic tropes. Nonetheless the Romantic poets, having chosen the ballad and the lyrical poem as the prime mode of expression, did little in other genres. The exceptions were the early epic poems by Shevchenko, the single historical novel *Chorna rada* (The Black Council) by Kulish, and the valiant attempts at historical dramas by Kostomarov. But Ukrainian themes in the works of the Russian and Polish Romantics did much to popularize Ukraine, its culture and history, in the Western world.

Romanticism gave way in the second half of the 19th century to realism, with its naturalistic method and populist philosophy. Yet elements of romanticism began to appear again in the first decades of the 20th century, during the height of *modernism. That 'neoromanticism' is characterized by a return to folklore as the source of inspiration (eg, M. Kotsiubynsky's *Tini zabutykh predkiv* [Shadows of Forgotten Ancestors, 1911], Lesia Ukrainka's *Lisova pisnia* [The Forest Song, 1911], H. Khotkevych's *Kaminna dusha* [The Soul of Stone, 1911]), or to the personification of nature as a self-willed participant in human life (O. Kobylianska's story 'Bytva' [Battle]). A type of neoromanticism also appeared in the Ukrainian literature of the 1920s in the poetic works of the so-called neo-Romantics M. Bazhan, O. Vlyzko, D. Falkivsky, and V. Sosiura; in the prose of Yu. Yanovsky; and in the concept of 'vitaism' (vitalized romanticism) of M. *Khvylovy.

The ideas, themes, and subjects of romanticism had a profound influence on art toward the end of the 18th and the beginning of the 19th centuries in Western Europe and in the Slavic countries neighboring on Ukraine. In Ukraine romanticism had its effect on the art of non-Ukrainians living in Ukraine, such as the Russian V. Tropinin, the Armenian I. Aivazovsky, and the Poles J. Kossak and A. Grottger. The influence of romanticism can also be seen in the early paintings of Shevchenko and K. Trutovsky, as well as in the works of the Ukrainian artists I. Soshenko, A. Mokrytsky, O. Slastion, M. Ivasiuk, S. Vasylkivsky, M. Pymonenko, and A. Zhdakha, among others.

Romantic influences in Ukrainian music, however, were meager and can be seen only in the works of some composers in the second half of the 19th century, such as S. Hulak-Artemovsky, M. Lysenko, V. Matiuk, P. Vorobkevych, and A. Vakhnianyn, especially in their compositions to the words of Romantic poets. In theater the influence of romanticism was very small. Ukrainian historical plays did not achieve prominence, and only a Romantic sentimentality can be seen in the standard repertoire of ethnographic realism. Thus Ukrainian romanticism was predominantly a poetic phenomenon, the importance of which lies first and foremost in its contribution to the reawakening of Ukrainian national consciousness through the recaptured and idealized heroic past and rich and unique folkloric heritage.

BIBLIOGRAPHY

Shamrai, A. 'Do pochatkiv romantyzmu,' *Ukraïna*, 1929, nos 10–11

Čiževskij, D. *On Romanticism in Slavic Literature* (The Hague 1957)

Kotsiubyns'ka, M. 'Poetyka Shevchenka i ukraïns'kyi romantyzm,' in *Zbirnyk Shostoï naukovoï shevchenkivs'koï konferentsiï* (Kiev 1958)

Prykhod'ko, P. *Shevchenko i ukraïns'kyi romantyzm 30–50-kh rr. XIX st.* (Kiev 1963)

Volyns'kyi, P. *Ukraïns'kyi romantyzm u zv'iazku z rozvytkom romantyzmu v slov'ians'kykh literaturakh* (Kiev 1963)

Kyrchiv, R. *Ukraïnika v pol's'kykh al'manakhakh doby romantyzmu* (Kiev 1965)

Shevel'ov, Iu. 'Z istoriï ukraïns'koho romantyzmu,' in *Orbis Scriptus: Dimitrij Tschizevskij zum 70 Geburtstag* (Munich 1966)

Ukraïns'ki poety romantyky 20–40-kh rokiv XIX st. (Kiev 1968)

Guliaev, N. (ed). *Voprosy romantizma v sovetskom literaturovedenii: Bibliograficheskii ukazatel'* (Kazan 1970)

Kyryliuk, Ie. *Ukraïns'kyi romantyzm u typolohichnomu zistavlenni z literaturamy zakhidno- i pivdennoslov'ians'kykh narodiv: Persha polovyna XIX st.* (Kiev 1973)

Kozak, S. *U źródeł romantyzmu i nowoczesnej myśli społecznej na Ukrainie* (Wroclaw–Warsaw–Cracow–Gdansk 1978)

Komarynets', T. *Ideino-estetychni osnovy ukraïns'koho romantyzmu* (Lviv 1983)

Kovaliv, Iu. *Romantychna styl'ova techiia v ukraïns'kii radians'kii poeziï 20–30-kh rokiv* (Kiev 1988)

Naienko, M. *Romantychnyi epos: Liryko-romantychna styl'ova techiia v ukraïns'kii radians'kii prozi* (Kiev 1988)

B. Kravtsiv, D.H. Struk

Romanus, Paolo (Pavlo Rymlianyn), b ? in Rome, d 1618 in Lviv. Italian architect. His name first appears in Lviv guild records in 1585. He built various buildings in Lviv and took part in the construction of Lviv's Dormition (1591–8), Bernardine (1606–30), and Benedictine churches and Kampian Chapel. He creatively adapted the Italian Renaissance style to local traditions and needs.

Mykhailo Romanyshyn: *Shepherd* (fragment, 1968)

Romanyshyn, Mykhailo [Romanyšyn, Myxajlo], b 16 August 1933 in Velykyi Bereznyi, Transcarpathia. Painter. After graduating from the Uzhhorod School of Applied Art (1953), where he studied under A. Erdeli, Y. Bokshai, and F. Manailo, he studied under K. Trokhymenko and H. Melikhov at the Kiev State Art Institute (1954–60). His work consists of genre paintings in the socialist realist manner such as *Logger* (1963) and *Labor Festival* (1975), and landscapes, such as *Moonlit Night: Kiev* (1980). An album of his works was published in 1979. Romanyshyn is director of the Kiev Museum of Ukrainian Art.

Romanyshyn, Oleh [Romanyšyn], b 7 October 1941 in Lviv. Journalist. After emigrating to Argentina (1949) and then Canada (1960) he completed his studies in Hispanic and Slavic studies at the University of Toronto (PH D, 1979). Since 1981 he has been editor of the newspaper *Homin Ukraïny*. His writings include articles on literary, historical, and political issues, in émigré Ukrainian and Canadian publications. In 1990 he was elected president of the *Canadian League for Ukraine's Liberation.

Roman Romanyshyn: *Hunter* (from the Carpathian Easter Eggs series, mixed media, 1987)

Romanyshyn, Roman [Romanyšyn], b 13 July 1957 in Tovmach, Ivano-Frankivske oblast. Painter and graphic artist. He graduated from the Lviv Institute of Applied and Decorative Arts (1982). A prolific and inventive artist, he attracted attention through his use of an unusual, wax-resistant method of achieving a pattern of white lines in his early watercolors. Romanyshyn has continued experimenting in mixed media with techniques based on Ukrainian (particularly Boiko) Easter egg decoration, icon painting, and folk painting on glass. His work is dominated by sophisticated, symbolic images rooted in Ukrainian mythology, folklore, literature, and history (eg, the diptych *Two Looks into the Well*, 1987). Solo exhibitions of his works have been held in Lviv (1990), Kiev (1991), and Toronto (1991).

Romanytsky, Borys [Romanyts'kyj], b 31 March 1891 in Chornobai, Zolotonosha county, Poltava gubernia, d 24 August 1988 in Lviv. Actor, director, and public figure. He completed study at the Lysenko Music and Drama School in Kiev (in 1915) and joined the Society of Ukrainian Actors. From 1918 he worked in the People's Theater, and in 1922 he became one of the founders and the artistic director (until 1948) of the Zankovetska Theater (see *Lviv Ukrainian Drama Theater). Romanytsky's creative activi-

Borys Romanytsky

ty spanned nearly 300 roles and 70 productions. In his repertoire were such important roles as Pototsky in I. Karpenko-Kary's *Sava Chalyi*, Vyhovsky in L. Dmyterko's *Naviky razom* (Forever Together), and the title roles in the M. Starytsky and O. Korniichuk versions of *Bohdan Khmel'nyts'kyi*, K. Gutzkow's *Uriel Acosta*, and W. Shakespeare's *Othello* (his was the first Ukrainian interpretation of this last role). A versatile actor, he was equally successful in both heroic and character roles. He played Karl and Franz in F. Schiller's *Die Räuber*, Stepan and Koval in M. Kropyvnytsky's *Nevol'nyk* (The Captive), Panas and Tsokul in I. Karpenko-Kary's *Naimychka* (The Servant Girl), and Koshkin and Shvandia in K. Trenev's *Liubov' Iarovaia*. Romanytsky was also a director in *Saksahansky's troupe, most effective with realistic-psychological dramas, such as I. Franko's *Ukradene shchastia* (Stolen Happiness, 1922, 1940, and 1949). He was a member of the Lviv municipal and oblast governments and a cofounder of the Ukrainian Theatrical Society. Romanytsky is the author of *Ukraïns'kyi teatr u mynylomy i suchasnomu* (Ukrainian Theater in the Past and Present, 1950). A biography, by B. Zavadka, was published in Kiev in 1978.

V. Revutsky

Rome. See Italy and Vatican.

View of the center of Romen, from the opposite bank of the Sula River, with the Cathedral of the Holy Spirit in the background

Romen or **Romny.** III-14. A city (1989 pop 57,000) at the junction of the Romen and the Sula rivers and a raion center in Sumy oblast. It was first mentioned, as a border fortress of Kievan Rus', in the Laurentian Chronicle under the year 1096. From the mid-14th century it belonged to the Grand Duchy of Lithuania, and from the beginning of the 17th century, to the Polish Commonwealth. After B. Khmelnytsky's uprising it became a company center of Myrhorod (1648–58) and later Lubni regiment (1658–1782). With the abolition of the Hetman state the town became part of Chernihiv vicegerency, and in 1783 it obtained the rights of *Magdeburg law. In 1802 it became a county center in Poltava gubernia. In the 19th century Romen was a prosperous trading town, and until 1852 the home of one of Ukraine's largest annual fairs. Today the city is an industrial center with a machine-building, a building-materials, and a food-processing industry. Its architectural monuments include the wooden St George's Church (1730), the stone Cathedral of the Holy Spirit (1742–6), and the Assumption Church with its belfry (1753–97). The remains of the *Monastyryshche settlement are nearby.

Romen Drainage System. A canal network covering 14,100 ha of the floodlands of the Romen and the Torhovytsia rivers in Sumy and Chernihiv oblasts. It was constructed in 1933 and rebuilt in 1954. The total length of the pipes and canals is 517.3 km.

Romen geese

Romen goose (*romenska poroda husei*). A popular breed of domestic *goose in Ukraine; its name derives from the city of Romen, in Sumy oblast. Most Romen geese have one or two folds on the abdomen and no wattle on the head. Their plumage is gray, white, or mottled. Romen geese are bred in Chernihiv, Sumy, Poltava, Kiev, Kharkiv, Luhanske, Kherson, and Odessa oblasts. Ganders reach 5–7 kg in weight, geese, 5–6 kg. They are readily force-fed, and yield fatty, juicy, highly caloric meat.

Romen River. A right-bank tributary of the Sula River. It is 121 km long and drains a basin area of 1,660 sq km. It originates in east central Sumy oblast and cuts into Chernihiv oblast, where it briefly bends back to join the Sula at Romen. Its waters are used for irrigation and domestic consumption.

Romen-Borshcheve culture. A medieval culture whose typology is based on Slavic fortified frontier settlements of the 8th to 10th centuries located in the upper reaches of the Desna, Seim, Sula, Psol, and Vorskla rivers. The distinctive features of this culture include the physical location of settlements for defensive purposes, semi-pit houses with clay or stone stoves, hand-built pottery, and crematory funeral practices. Its people (mainly *Siverianians) engaged in agriculture and practiced well-developed trades, including metallurgy. Notable examples of this culture's settlements include *Monastyryshche (near Romen) and the *Novotroitske fortified settlement.

Mykhailo Romensky   Bishop Teodor Yurii Romzha

Romensky, Mykhailo [Romens'kyj, Myxajlo], b 20 November 1887 in Kursk, Russia, d 21 November 1971 in Kiev. Opera singer (bass). He studied with L. Donskoi at the Moscow Conservatory (1913–16) and then appeared as a soloist with theaters in Rostov-na-Donu (1920–34), Kharkiv (1934–42), and Kiev (1942–58) in operas by M. Lysenko, S. Hulak-Artemovsky, M. Glinka, A. Dargomyzhsky, K. Dankevych, and C. Gounod. In recital he performed vocal chamber music and Ukrainian folk songs. In 1947–52 he taught singing at the Kiev Conservatory.

Romer, Eugeniusz, b 3 February 1871 in Lviv, d 28 January 1954 in Cracow. Polish geographer and cartographer; member of the Polish Academy of Learning and the Polish Academy of Sciences. He graduated from Lviv University (PH D, 1894) and was professor there (1911–31). He wrote a number of synthetic works on the borders, morphology, and climate of Poland. In his works he treated Western and Right-Bank Ukraine as an integral part of Poland on the ground that until 1772 they were part of the Polish Commonwealth. He did so in *Geograficzno-statystyczny atlas Polski* (Polish Geographical-Statistical Atlas, 1916), which was used as an authoritative source for establishing the borders of Poland in 1919–21. Romer served as a consultant on borders to the Polish government at the Paris Peace Conference. His attitude toward Ukraine and Ukrainians was hostile.

Romny. See Romen.

Romodan route. An ancient north–south trade route that traversed Left-Bank Ukraine, through Romen, Lokhvytsia, Lubni, and Kremenchuk, as part of the route from Russia to the Crimea. It avoided larger settlements and sandy expanses and crossed relatively few rivers. Until the construction of railway lines in the 1860s to 1880s, the Romodan route was one of the most important of the routes used by the Left-Bank *chumaks in their journeys to the Crimea for salt. In the 19th century it was also used for driving herds from Ukraine to the central gubernias of the Russian Empire.

Romzha, Teodor Yurii [Romža, Teodor Jurij], b 14 April 1911 in Velykyi Bychkiv, Transcarpathia, d 1 November 1947 in Mukachiv. Ukrainian Catholic bishop. He studied philosophy and theology in Rome at the Collegium Russicum, and was ordained in 1936. He served as a parish priest in Berezove, Transcarpathia, and a priest and professor of philosophy at the Uzhhorod Seminary (from 1939). In 1944 he was consecrated as an assistant bishop to Bishop M. Dudash and administrator of Mukachiv eparchy. He was assassinated when he opposed the liquidation of his eparchy and refused to co-operate with the Soviet authorities.

Rook (*Corvus frugilegus*; Ukrainian: *haivoron, hrak*). An Old World gregarious bird of the family Corvidae, growing to up to 45 cm in length, similar to a carrion *crow except with white skin at the base of the sharp bill. In Ukraine rooks are found year round, nesting in colonies in high trees. They feed on agricultural and forest pest insects, but they may also dig up planted seedlings.

Rooster (*piven* or *kohut*). The rooster was a common figure in Ukrainian folk literature and mythology. It was seen as the summoner and symbol of the sun. Transplanted into the Christian context, the rooster became a symbol of faith; hence, in Ukraine roadside crosses were often decorated with images of roosters. It was also accepted as an image of the independent farmer in Ukrainian folk sayings. The rooster was believed to protect farm animals from evil powers. It was used in folk fortune-telling practices and as a sacrificial bird in wedding and house-building rites.

Ropska, Oleksandra [Rops'ka], b 23 April 1897 in Shyriaievo, Voronezh gubernia, Russia, d 20 April 1957 in Kiev. Opera singer (mezzo-soprano). A graduate of the Saratov Conservatory (1919), she began singing in Poltava, and then worked with the opera theaters of Odessa (1926–7), Kharkiv (1927–8), and Kiev (1928–57), with which she appeared in operas by M. Lysenko, N. Rimsky-Korsakov, P. Tchaikovsky, and G. Verdi. She taught singing at the Kiev Conservatory (from 1944).

Ros region (Porossia). A historical-geographic region located between the Ros and the Stuhna rivers south of Kiev (today the southern part of Kiev oblast and northern tip of Cherkasy oblast). Ros was settled originally by the Polianians, and developed into a frontier area of the Rus' empire. A number of fortified towns were established there in the 10th century, among them Bohuslav, Korsun, Kaniv, and Yuriv (later Bila Tserkva). War captives, among them many Poles, were settled in the region to pro-

vide a frontline force against attacks by steppe nomads. In the 12th century, Pechenegs and Turks began settling in the region and mixing with the local population. The area was overrun by the Tatars in the 13th century, and its fortresses sacked. All references to Ros as a distinctive region then ceased.

The Ros River

Ros River [Ros']. A right-bank tributary of the Dnieper River. It is 346 km long and drains a basin area of 12,575 sq km. It originates in the Dnieper Upland and flows through Vinnytsia, Kiev, and Cherkasy oblasts. There are several small hydroelectric stations on the river and water from it is used for irrigation. The major centers on the river include Bila Tserkva, Bohuslav, and Korsun-Shevchenkivskyi.

Rosalia (Rusallia, Troitsia, Zeleni sviata). A summer feast held 50 days after Easter, and associated with the pagan cult of the dead and the *rusalky. The name 'Rusallia' is derived from the ancient Roman festival of the roses (23 May), which reached Ukraine via the southern Slavs and was incorporated into its pagan calendar as a fertility festival.

The first mention of Rosalia on Ukrainian territory is in the Primary Chronicle under 1067. On the eve of the feast, houses were adorned with green branches and linden or maple leaves. In church the floor was covered with fragrant grasses, including wormwood. On the feast day itself green branches were set up in the fields to protect the growing grain from thunder and evil spirits and to ensure fertility. For this reason the festival is also known as Zeleni sviata 'Green Feast.' In some regions the young people walked about the fields with torches, cracking whips and firing guns into the air to drive away evil spirits. For several days young men and women met in the fields, usually between villages, for games that were frequently erotic and were condemned by churchmen as 'demonic.' The young women collected food and carried a decorated tree into the woods or to a stream, where for days and nights they entertained and frolicked with the young men. The Rosalia was a youth festival from which adults (with the exception of young childless wives) were barred. In some regions this pagan festival survived into the 20th century.

In the 17th and 18th centuries mass pilgrimages to certain monasteries in Western Ukraine took place during this season. Foreigners called them 'girl markets' because many young couples met and married during the pilgrimages. In such a way the church legitimized folk traditions of pagan origin. In eastern Ukraine, particularly in the Poltava region, a personified Topolia ('poplar') was led through the village. In Volhynia the figure was known as Lialia ('doll'), and in Polisia, as Kusta. The favorite rites included dressing girls up as *rusalky*, wreath weaving, dancing *rusalka* group dances, and singing *rusalka* songs. A bachelor who fancied a girl planted a *mai* (a green birch) in her yard. In the Prešov region this custom is still practiced. Until the 18th century, in Western Ukraine the bachelors of a village elected a 'rusalka' reeve, who ran the village for three days.

Rites honoring the dead were an integral part of the Rosalia. In Volhynia a seven-course commemorative feast was held on Rosalia Saturday. According to folk belief the souls of the departed (called *rusalky*) came out of their graves on this day. To win their favor, food and drink were placed on the graves. The *rusalky* were believed to leave the streams on Rosalia Thursday (called *rusalchyn* or *mavskyi* Easter) and to spend a week in the forests and fields looking for foolhardy bachelors, whom they tickled to death. In some localities Rosalia week concluded with *rusalka* games or a *rusalka* farewell procession.

Various rituals were conducted to protect livestock from spells cast by witches; smoke from herbs was directed at animals, for example, and wreaths or green branches were hung on the horns of cattle.

Today in and outside Ukraine the Rosalia is closely associated with remembrance of the soldiers who fell in the struggle for Ukrainian independence.

BIBLIOGRAPHY
Maksimovich, M. *Dni i mesiatsy ukrainskogo selianina* (Kiev 1858)
Kylymnyk, S. *Ukraïns'kyi rik u narodnikh zvychaiakh v istorychnomu osvitlenni*, vol 4 (Winnipeg 1957)
Dei, O. *Ihry ta pisni: Vesniano-litnia poeziia trudovoho roku* (Kiev 1963)
Voropai, O. *Zvychaï nashoho narodu*, vol 2 (Munich 1966)
                                                                M. Mushynka

Rosava River. A left-bank tributary of the Ros River. It is 90 km long and drains a basin area of 1,720 sq km. It flows through Kiev and Cherkasy oblasts, and its waters are used for industry and domestic consumption. Kaharlyk and Myronivka are located on the river.

Rosdolsky, Roman. See Rozdolsky, Roman.

Rose (*Rosa*; Ukrainian: *rozha, roza, troianda*). A perennial shrub or vine plant of the family Rosaceae, with a prickly stem and fragrant flowers of many colors. Almost universally distributed and widely cultivated, roses are valuable flowers in decorative horticulture. Attar of rose (esp *R. damascena*) is used in perfume production. Herbal tea and preserves are made from the hips and petals of the *sweetbrier (R. eglanteria)*, the prairie rose (*R. setigera*), and *R. rugosa*. Rose hips contain vitamin C and they were widely used in folk medicine. Roses play an important role in Ukrainian folk songs and poetry as symbols of love and beauty. Many roses are maintained in the Nikita and Odessa botanical gardens as well as in the Central Republican Botanical Garden of the AN URSR (now ANU) in Kiev. Among the various Ukrainian hybrid roses are the Ukrainka, Kateryna, Nikita Pink, Vesnianka, Natalka, Red Ukraina, and Marusia.

Rosenberg, Alfred, b 12 January 1893 in Revel (now Tallinn), Estonia, d 16 October 1946 in Nuremberg. Nazi ideologist of Baltic German origin. He grew up in tsarist-ruled Estonia and studied architecture at Moscow University. He fled from Russia in 1917, joined the nascent Nazi party in Munich in 1919, became editor of its organ, *Völkischer Beobachter*, in 1923, and briefly led the party in 1923–4 after the failed Munich Putsch. Rosenberg was the leading Nazi ideologue and cultural propagandist. He expanded on A. *Hitler's *Lebensraum* ideas in his *Der Zukunftsweg einer deutschen Aussenpolitik* (1927), in which he urged the conquest of Poland and the USSR, and he expounded on Nazi racist, anti-Christian, and German-superiority theories in *Der Mythus des XX Jahrhunderts* (1934). As chief of the Nazi Department of Foreign Affairs from 1933, he had discussions with representatives of the Ukrainian Scientific Institute in Berlin and the OUN leadership there. After the 1941 invasion of the USSR he was the largely powerless Reichsminister of the occupied eastern territories, including the *Reichskommissariat Ukraine. His attempts to persuade H. *Himmler and E. *Koch, the Reichskommissar of Ukraine, to scale down their brutal extermination policies were unsuccessful. Although Hitler accepted Rosenberg's proposal for the partitioning of the USSR, he rejected his idea of gaining the support of non-Russians by allowing them quasi-autonomy and separate armed forces. Rosenberg was tried as a war criminal at the Nuremberg trials and hanged.

Roshchybiuk [Roščybjuk]. A family of master potters from Staryi Kosiv, Kosiv raion, Ivano-Frankivske oblast. It includes Hanna (b 17 November 1903 in Staryi Kosiv, d 29 January 1981 in Kolomyia), the sister of P. *Tsvilyk; her husband, Mykhailo (b 12 March 1903 in Kolomyia, d 20 January 1972 in Kolomyia); and their daughters, Orysia Kozak, Stefaniia Voloshchuk, and Rozaliia Iliuk, who have worked in the shops of the Artistic Fund of the Ukrainian SSR and made decorative plates, vases, candlesticks, and cups.

Roshchynsky, Petro [Roščyns'kyj], b 1890 in Hlukhiv, Chernihiv gubernia, d 23 February 1943. Physician and civic leader in Volhynia. A graduate of the medical faculty of Moscow University (1916), he served as a doctor in the UNR Army and after the war practiced medicine in Kostopil, Rivne, Kholm, Lviv, and Kremianets. He was persecuted by the Polish authorities for his Ukrainian activism and imprisoned in the Bereza Kartuzka concentration camp. During the German occupation he and his wife, Hanna (née Strutynska), and nephew, Yu. Cherkavsky, were executed by the Gestapo.

Roshkevych, Olha [Roškevyč, Ol'ha] (married name: Ozarkevych), b 1855 in Uhornyky, Stanyslaviv circle, Galicia, d 1935. Folklorist and translator. As I. *Franko's fiancée she collaborated with him in collecting and publishing the wedding rituals and songs of Lolin village (1886). She also translated works from German, French, and Russian into Ukrainian. Franko's correspondence with her was published by M. Vozniak in 1956. Franko dedicated some of his works to her.

Roshko, Ivan. See Irliavsky, Ivan.

Ihnatii Roshkovych: *SS Methodius and Cyril* (1876)

Roshkovych, Ihnatii [Roškovyč, Ihnatij], b 28 September 1854 in Salok, Transcarpathia, d 29 November 1915 in Budapest. Painter. After studying art in Budapest and Munich, he painted murals in Transcarpathian churches in Snyna, Prešov, Krasnoshory, and Velyka Kopania; in the Royal Palace and St Stephen's Basilica in Budapest; and in churches in Kecskemet and Cluj (Rumania). His genre paintings include *A Special Passion*, *Red Apple*, and *Only for You*.

Olha Roshkevych

Roxolana Roslak

Roslak, Roxolana [Rosljak, Roksoljana], b 11 February 1940 in Chortkiv, Galicia. Opera singer (lyric soprano). A postwar refugee, she came to Canada with her parents in 1948. She graduated from the University of Toronto's Faculty of Music in 1964. A member of the Canadian Opera Company, she has been featured on Canadian radio and television. In 1967 she created the role of Marguerite in H. Somer's *Louis Riel*. Her operatic repertoire includes principal roles in C. Gluck's *Iphigenia in Tauris*, W.A. Mozart's *Cosi fan tutte* and *Don Giovanni*, J. Offenbach's *Tales of Hoffmann*, G. Bizet's *Carmen*, R. Wagner's *Parsifal*, G. Verdi's *Don Carlos*, G. Puccini's *La Bohème*, and A. Vakhnianyn's *Kupalo* and solo parts in F.J. Haydn's *Die Schöpfung*, Verdi's *Requiem*, and I. Stravinsky's *Les Noces*. Together with pianist G. Gould she recorded P. Hindemith's *Das Marienleben* for Columbia Records in 1976.

Roslak, Yaroslav [Rosljak, Jaroslav], b 18 August 1927 in Chortkiv, Galicia. Lawyer and jurist. Roslak studied at the University of Innsbruck, emigrated to Canada in 1948, graduated from the University of Alberta (LLB, 1953), and went into private practice. He joined the Alberta attorney general's department in 1960; there he was director of criminal justice (1975–82), director of special services (1982–5), and director of appeals, research, and special projects (1985–7). In 1988 he was appointed to the Court of Queen's Bench in Alberta.

Roslavets, Petro [Roslavec'], b and d ? Cossack officer. A native of Pochep, he was the captain of Pochep company (1653–7) and colonel of Starodub regiment (intermittently in 1663–76). He participated in the 1672 uprising against D. Mnohohrishny and later became an opponent of I. Samoilovych. He secretly planned to detach his regiment from the Hetmanate and place it under the direct control of Moscow (like the Slobidska Ukraine regiments). Roslavets was tried before a military tribunal, stripped of his post, and sentenced to death. The punishment was later commuted by the hetman, and Roslavets was sent by the Russian authorities to Siberia, where he died.

Roslavsky-Petrovsky, Oleksander [Roslavs'kyj-Petrovs'kyj], b 9 April 1816 in Slabyn, Chernihiv county, d 25 December 1871 in Kharkiv. Historian, statistician, and pedagogue. After completing studies at the Bezborodko (Nizhen) Lyceum in 1834, he attended Kharkiv University (1839) and taught there (from 1837, as professor from 1839) and at the university's pedagogical institute (1844–52). He improved the study of statistics by introducing new Western techniques and approaches, headed the first separate department of statistics (from 1841), and wrote two statistics textbooks (1841, 1844). His PH D dissertation (1845) was a historical, political-economic, and statistical comparison of the population of the Russian Empire with that of other European countries. He was appointed dean of the history and philology department (1853) and rector of Kharkiv University (1859–62). In the 1850s he also carried out studies on the potential economic impact of a railway in Kharkiv gubernia. Roslavsky-Petrovsky wrote articles on the economy and trade of Kharkiv gubernia for the journals *Kharkovskie gubernskie vedomosti* and *Ekonomicheskii ukazatel'* and the series Sbornik statisticheskikh svedenii o Rossii (Collection of Statistical Data about Russia). He also wrote on the history of Kharkiv University and higher education in the Russian Empire.

Rosliak. See Roslak.

Stepan Rosokha

Metropolitan Teodosii Rostotsky

Rosokha, Stepan [Rosoxa] (Rosocha, Stefan), b 27 May 1908 in Drahove, near Khust, Transcarpathia, d 20 April 1986 in Toronto. Journalist, publisher, and political leader; member of the Shevchenko Scientific Society and the Ukrainian Academy of Arts and Sciences. While studying law at the Ukrainian Free University (LL D, 1936) and journalism at the School of Political Sciences in Prague, he was active in student organizations and the nationalist movement. He edited the student magazine *Vidrodzhennia* (1926–30) and the nationalist journal *Proboiem* in Prague (1934–44) and published the weekly *Nastup* in Uzhhorod and then in Prague (1938–44). He helped organize and then commanded the Ukrainian National Defense in Uzhhorod and from November 1938 served on the staff of the Carpathian Sich. In February 1939 he was elected to the Diet of *Carpatho-Ukraine and became its deputy speaker. After fleeing from the Hungarian invasion to Prague he was arrested there by the Gestapo in 1944 and sent to a concentration camp. In 1949 he emigrated to Canada, where he organized the Carpathian Sich Brotherhood and published its bulletin *Karpats'ka Sich* (1949–53). In 1952–60 he was editor of *Novyi shliakh*, and in 1960–86, editor and manager of the Toronto weekly *Vil'ne slovo*. He was president of the Eastern Chapter of the Ukrainian National Federation (1950–3), the Trident Sports Club (1951–3), and the Ukrainian People's Home in Toronto, and vice-president of the Ukrainian War Veterans' Association of Canada (1952). He wrote the documentary study *Soim Karpats'koï Ukraïny* (The Diet of Carpatho-Ukraine, 1949) and published a number of valuable books on Carpatho-Ukraine.

Rosokhovatsky, Ihor [Rosoxovats'kyj], b 30 August 1929 in Shpola, Cherkasy okruha. Ukrainian and Russian science fiction writer. He graduated from the Kiev Pedagogical Institute (1954) and worked as a newspaper editor. His novels and stories have been published in Ukrainian as the collections *Strilky hodynnyka* (Hands of a Clock, 1964), *Sprava komandora* (The Affair of the Commander, 1967), *Iakym ty povernehsia?* (What Will You Be

Like When You Return?, 1970), *Urahan* (Hurricane, 1977), *U pidvodnykh pecherakh* (In Underground Caves, 1979), *Zvorotnyi zv'iazok* (Reverse Connection, 1983), *Mozhlyvist' vidpovidi* (Possibility of a Reply, 1986), and *Ostannii syhnal* (The Last Signal, 1989). Rosokhovatsky cowrote, with I. Mykolaichuk, the script for the feature film *Under the Constellation Gemini* (1979). A selection of his works was published in English translation under the title *And Man Created Syhom Plus Other Sci-Fi Stories* (1990).

Rossina, Yuliia, b 24 June 1877 in Odessa, d 30 September 1960 in Kiev. Stage actress. She worked in Saksahansky's Troupe (1892–1900), O. Suslov's troupe (1900–5), various Russian operetta theaters (1906–28), and the Kharkiv (1929–35) and Kiev (1936–49) theaters of Musical Comedy.

Rostavytsia River [Rostavycja]. A left-bank tributary of the Ros River that flows eastward through Vinnytsia, Zhytomyr, and Kiev oblasts. It is 116 km long and drains a basin area of 1,460 sq km. Its water is used for irrigation and industry.

Rostavytsia Treaty. A Cossack-Polish treaty signed on 17 October 1619 on the Rostavytsia River near the town of Pavoloch, in the Zhytomyr region, by Hetman P. Sahaidachny and the Polish crown hetman S. Żółkiewski. It reduced the number of *registered Cossacks from 20,000 to 3,000, confined their movements to Zaporizhia, and prohibited Cossack campaigns in Crimean or Turkish territories. Registered Cossacks were placed under the control of the Polish government and assigned the task of defending the border of the Polish-Lithuanian Commonwealth; unregistered Cossacks and peasants were subordinated to their Polish masters. The oppressive treaty conditions gave rise to unrest that brought about Sahaidachny's replacement by Hetman Ya. Borodavka.

Rostotsky, Teodosii [Rostoc'kyj, Teodosij], b 1724, d 1805 in St Petersburg. Uniate metropolitan of Kiev. After studies at St Athanasius College in Rome, he was ordained (1754) and became a professor of philosophy and theology in Volodymyr-Volynskyi. Twice the protohegumen of the Lithuanian province of the Basilian order, he was made bishop of Kholm in 1784 and metropolitan of Kiev in 1788. He also became the first Uniate hierarch named to the Polish Senate (1790). After the third partition of Poland (1795) Rostotsky was confined by Catherine II to the city of St Petersburg. He stayed there, maintaining contact with his see through diplomatic correspondence, until his death.

Rostov oblast. An administrative territory set up on 13 September 1937 in the southwestern RSFSR. It encompasses most of the former Don Cossack province, except for the western part, which belongs to Ukraine, and a northeastern part, which belongs to Volgograd oblast. The area of Rostov oblast is 100,800 sq km, and its population in 1989 was 4,308,000, of which 71 percent was urban. The oblast has 42 raions, 22 cities, and 37 towns (smt). Its capital is Rostov-na-Donu. The western and southern regions of the oblast are Ukrainian ethnic territory. (For the history of the oblast see *Don region.)

Rostov-na-Donu. VI-20. A city (1989 pop 1,020,000) on the Don River and the administrative center of Rostov oblast in Russia. It is a major industrial and transportation center with a river harbor and an airport. Its history is linked closely with that of Ukraine and a significant portion of its population is Ukrainian.

The city originated as a settlement around a new fortress built in 1761 and named after St Dymytrii (Rostovsky) *Tuptalo. In 1797 the town became a county center of New Russia gubernia and then of Katerynoslav gubernia (1802–88). When a separate Don Cossack province was set up in 1888, Rostov-na-Donu was selected as its capital. With the building of a port and customs station in 1834 and of a railway link to Moscow in 1871 and Vladikavkaz in 1875, the town developed into a major commercial center. It exported grain and raw materials and imported tobacco and manufactured goods. By the turn of the 20th century it was, after Odessa, the second-largest city in the southern region of the Russian Empire. Its population grew from 3,000 in 1809 to 17,600 in 1860 and 119,500 in 1897.

In 1915, until 1920, many Russophiles from Galicia were evacuated to Rostov-na-Donu by the Russian authorities. There they had their own institutions, such as the Galician-Russian Committee (headed by V. Dudykevych), a gymnasium for their children, and, at the university, a student hromada, which had been transferred from Warsaw. In 1918–20 Rostov-na-Donu was a stronghold of A. Denikin's Volunteer Army. According to the Soviet census of 1926, 59,200 Ukrainians there constituted 19.2 percent of the city's population.

From 1924 Rostov-na-Donu was the capital of North Caucasus krai, in 1934–7 of the Azov-Black Sea krai, and finally, of Rostov oblast. Today the city is one of the largest agricultural-machinery manufacturing centers in Russia. It also has a large food-processing industry, light industry, and a chemical industry. Besides a university it has nine higher educational institutions. Its architectural monuments are a church from the 1780s and the city hall (1896–9).

Rostovsky, Samiilo [Rostovs'kyj, Samijlo], b and d ? Goldsmith of the latter half of the 18th century. In Kiev he produced a silver reliquary for the relics of St Barbara (1787) and a Gospel cover (1796) for St Michael's Golden-Domed Monastery, a silver chalice and disc (1795), rings, ducats, and earrings.

Rostovtsev, Mikhail [Rostovcev, Mixail] (Rostovtzeff, Michael), b 10 November 1870 in Kiev, d 20 October 1952 in New Haven, Connecticut. Russian historian and archeologist; member of the Imperial Russian Academy of Sciences. He was one of the most influential 20th-century authorities on ancient Rome, Greece, and 'South Russia,' that is, Ukraine, the Crimea, and the Kuban. He graduated from the universities of Kiev and St Petersburg and was a professor at St Petersburg University from 1901. He fled from Russia in 1918 and served as a professor at Oxford, Wisconsin in Madison (1920–5), and Yale (1925–44) universities. Among his many valuable works are *Antichnaia dekorativnaia zhivopis' na iuge Rossii* (Ancient Decorative Painting in the South of Russia, 1913), *Ellinstvo i iranstvo na iuge Rossii* (1918; pub in English as *Iranians and Greeks in South Russia*, 1922; repr 1969), *Skifiia i Bospor* (Scythia and

the Bosporus, 1925; German trans 1931), *The Social and Economic History of the Roman Empire* (1926; repr 1957, 1963), *A History of the Ancient World* (2 vols, 1926–7; repr 1928–30, 1930–3, 1945), *The Animal Style in South Russia and China* (1929; repr 1973), *The Decay of the Ancient World and Its Economic Explanations* (1930), *Caravan Cities* (1932; repr 1971), and *The Social and Economic History of the Hellenistic World* (3 vols, 1941; repr 1953, 1964).

Rostyslav Mstyslavych [Mstyslavyč], b ?, d 14 March 1167 in Zarub, on the Dnieper River. Kievan Rus' prince; son of Mstyslav I Volodymyrovych. He was appointed prince of Smolensk ca 1125–7 by his father. Rostyslav elevated the principality to what is regarded as its highest point of cultural development. He founded churches and towns, strengthened the fortifications of the capital, and established a separate Smolensk bishopric. After the death of his brother, Iziaslav, in 1154, Rostyslav was briefly grand prince of Kiev, which he later ruled (1159–67). During that period his diplomatic skills muted the internecine warfare in Rus' considerably. He died while traveling from Novgorod.

Rostyslav Mykhailovych [Myxajlovyč], b and d ? Kievan Rus' prince; son of *Mykhail Vsevolodovych of Chernihiv. Playing a supporting role for his father's ambitions, he was briefly prince of Novgorod (1229–30) and was later seated in Halych (ca 1239) and Chernihiv (1241). Danylo Romanovych retook Halych, and a protracted struggle ensued for lands in the Galician-Volhynian principality, until Danylo defeated the army formed through an alliance of Rostyslav, his father-in-law, Béla IV of Hungary, and his brother-in-law, Bolesław the Bashful of Little Poland, in the Battle of Yaroslav (1245). Rostyslav fled to Hungary, where he headed a small principality in Slavonia.

Rostyslav Volodymyrovych [Volodymyrovyč], b 1038, d 3 February 1067 in Tmutorokan. Kievan Rus' prince; grandson of Yaroslav the Wise. He is not mentioned in chronicles until 1064, but he probably governed Novgorod and Rostov-Suzdal from 1052 (after his father died) and Galicia-Volhynia from 1054 (after Yaroslav died) or 1060 (after Ihor Yaroslavych died); his sons, Volodar and Vasylko, ruled there until 1124. Rostyslav ousted Hlib Sviatoslavych from Tmutorokan in 1064 and subdued the local tribes to his authority. He was poisoned at a banquet by the Greek vicegerent of Kherson, at the bidding of Byzantine officials who feared Rostyslav's growing strength along their borders.

Rostyslav Yuriievych [Jurijevyč], b ?, d 17 April 1151. Kievan Rus' prince; son of Yurii (Volodymyrovych) Dolgorukii. A one-time prince of Novgorod (1138–41), in 1148 he allied himself with his father's major opponent, Iziaslav Mstyslavych of Kiev, ostensibly because he had been denied lands in the Suzdal region. The alliance soon deteriorated because of rumors spread by Iziaslav's boyars that Rostyslav had been seeking aid from steppe nomads in a plot against him. Rostyslav's wealth and the lands ceded to him were seized, and he was sent back to his father. In 1149 he took part in Yurii's campaign against Iziaslav, and in 1151 he was granted the Pereiaslav principality, which he ruled only briefly.

Rotar, Ivan, b 1873, d 15 March 1905 in Katerynodar, Kuban oblast. Civic leader, teacher, and writer. He worked as a lecturer at the teachers' seminary in Katerynodar. Rotar was a founding member and strong supporter of the Revolutionary Ukrainian party in the Kuban. In addition to a collection of poetry, he published a monograph about Ye. Slavynetsky in *Kievskaia starina* (1900) and left an unfinished work about A. Holovaty.

Sofiia Rotaru

Rotaru, Sofiia, b 9 August 1947 in Marshyntsi, Novoselytsia raion, Chernivtsi oblast. Ukrainian pop singer (soprano) of Moldavian descent. She graduated from the Kishinev Institute of Arts in 1974 and became very popular in Ukraine as a vocalist with the Chernivtsi-based ensemble Chervona Ruta. She won renown for her renditions of songs composed by V. *Ivasiuk. In 1977 she moved to the Crimea to sing in resort centers there. Her repertoire includes popular songs of contemporary Soviet composers (now mostly Russian) as well as modern arrangements of Ukrainian and Moldavian folk songs. She has made a number of recordings on the Melodiya label.

Rotmistrov, Volodymyr, b 16 June 1866 in Henzerivka, Pyriatyn county, Poltava gubernia, d 24 October 1941 in Kharkiv. Agronomist; full member of the All-Union Academy of Agricultural Sciences from 1935. He graduated from Kiev University (1889) and conducted research at the Debrechyn (1892–4) and Odessa (1894–1917) experimental fields and at the Ukrainian Scientific Research Institute of Plant Cultivation, Selection, and Genetics in Kharkiv (from 1928). He was one of the first advocates of cotton growing in the southern regions of Ukraine. His main publications dealt with the water regime of chernozem soils, the root systems of cultivated plants, soil melioration, and the methodology of field research. His work contributed to the improvement of agriculture in Ukraine's arid regions.

Rovno. See Rivne.

Rovynsky, Dmytro [Rovyns'kyj], b 8 November 1888 in Zinkiv, Poltava gubernia, d 3 November 1937 on Solovets Islands. Stage actor and director. He began his career in Ukrainian touring troupes and then played in Sadovsky's Theater (1916–18), the State Drama Theater (1918–19), and the Shevchenko First Theater of the Ukrainian Soviet Republic (1919–29). In 1929 he founded and directed the Leningrad Zhovten Theater. In 1933 he was arrested.

Rowing and canoeing (*vesluvannia, veslovyi sport*). Two forms of manual boat racing. In rowing, one oar per person is used to propel a shell, and two oars per person are used to propel a scull. In canoeing, a paddle is used to propel a Canadian (open) canoe or a kayak; the kayak paddle has blades on both ends. Olympic and world-championship competitions in rowing are organized by the Fédération internationale des sociétés d'aviron (FISA). Rowing events include eight-oared shell with coxswain; four-oared shell with or without cox; pair-oared shell with or without cox; and single, double, and quadruple sculls. Canoeing competitions are organized by the International Canoe Federation (ICF) and consist of Canadian singles (C-1) and pairs (C-2) events and kayak singles (K-1), pairs (K-2), and fours (K-4) events. In Olympic canoeing, women compete in the kayak events only.

In Ukraine the sport of rowing dates from the late 19th century. The first rowing competitions were held in Odessa in 1893. The first USSR competition in rowing was held in 1923, and in canoeing in 1928. In 1952 the USSR joined FISA and ICF. H. Zhylin and I. Yemchuk of the Nauka rowing club in Kiev won silver medals in double sculls at the 1952 Olympics and bronze medals at the 1956 Olympics, and captured the European championship in 1955 (a world record) and the USSR championship in 1952 and 1959.

Athletes from the Ukrainian SSR who have won Olympic gold medals in canoeing are S. Makarenko (1960, C-2 1,000 m), A. Khymych (1964, C-2 1,000 m), L. Khvedosiuk (1964 and 1968, women's K-1 500 m; 1972, K-2 500 m), V. Morozov (1964, 1972, and 1976, K-4 1,000 m; 1968, K-2 1000 m), O. Shaparenko (1968, K-2 1,000 m; 1972, K-1 1,000 m), K. Kuryshko (1972, women's K-2 500 m), Yu. Riabchynska (1972, women's K-1 500 m), Yu. Stetsenko (1972, K-4 1,000 m), Yu. Filatov (1972 and 1976, K-4 1,000 m), S. Nahorny (1976, K-2 1,000 m), S. Petrenko (1976, C-2 500 m and 1,000 m), S. Chukhrai (1976, K-4 1,000 m; 1980, K-2 500 m and 1,000 m), and S. Postriekhin (1980, C-1 500 m). Silver medalists in Olympic canoeing are V. Yurchenko (1976, C-1 1,000 m), S. Kirsanov (1988, C-4 1,000 m), O. Motuzenko (1988, K-4 1,000 m), I. Nahaiev (1988, K-2 500 m and K-4 1,000 m), and M. Slyvynsky (1988, C-1 500 m). Ukrainians from the Danube River borderlands have been part of champion Rumanian Olympic canoeing teams; and the Ukrainian G. Bossy, a top paddler in Canada during the 1950s, was on the Canadian Olympic canoeing team in 1956.

Rowers from the Ukrainian SSR on Soviet Olympic teams have included O. Huzenko, O. Kolkova, O. Puhovska, N. Rozhon, N. Tarakanova, and Ye. Zubko, members of the women's eight that won the 1976 silver medal; A. Pustoviit, a member of the women's quadruple sculls that won the 1980 silver medal; N. Frolova, M. Paziun, N. Preobrazhenska, N. Pryshchepa, O. Pyvovarova, T. Stetsenko, O. Tereshyna, N. Umanets, and V. Zhulina, members of the women's eight that won the 1980 silver medal; M. Dovhan and Yu. Shapochka, members of the men's quadruple sculls that won the 1980 silver medal; I. Frolova, I. Kalimbet, and S. Mazii, members of the women's quadruple sculls that won the 1988 silver medal; and P. Hurkovsky, M. Komarov, and V. Omelianovych, members of the men's eight that won the 1988 silver medal.

R. Senkus, T. Zakydalsky

Roxolana. See Roksoliana.

Roxolani. A nomadic tribe of *Sarmatians that ranged over the Ural foothills and Volga lowlands in the eastern Black Sea steppes during the 2nd century BC. Initially they clashed with the *Scythians, but after the 2nd century BC the Roxolani conquered the Scythians and fought together with them against the *Pontic Kingdom and Greek colonies in the Crimea. In the mid-1st century AD some of the Roxolani took to the steppes between the lower Dnieper and the Danube rivers. For nearly 70 years they settled in the Wallachian Plain and as far as Moesia province, until they were crushed by the Romans. Later, along with other Black Sea coastal tribes, they continued to fight against the Romans on the lower Danube River. In the late 2nd century AD the Roxolani were dispersed by the Goths, and in the 4th century they were annihilated by the Huns. They were last mentioned by the Gothic historian Jordan as participants in a battle against the Huns. Excavations in the steppes northwest of the Sea of Azov, between the lower Dnieper and the Molochna rivers, have uncovered a number of Middle Sarmatian barrow graves, attributed to the Roxolani. They date mostly from the 1st century BC to the 1st century AD, although some go back to the late 2nd century BC.

Royal Tribunal (*Trybunal koronnyi*). The highest appellate court in the Polish-Lithuanian Commonwealth, created in 1578 by the Great Diet in Warsaw. It limited the power of the king and heard appeals of the decisions of city, land, and *pidkomorskyi* courts. The tribunal was composed of 27 judges or deputies elected for one year at the voivodeship dietines of the gentry throughout the Commonwealth. When a case involved a church figure, it was heard by six lay judges and six clerical judges elected by church chapters. The same diet also created the *Lutske Tribunal to handle appeals from the Ukrainian territories of the Commonwealth. In 1581 the Supreme Lithuanian Tribunal was set up for Lithuanian territories. At its sessions in Piotrków and Poznań the Royal Tribunal heard appeals from Polish territories in Lublin and from Ukrainian territories in Lviv. In 1764 a special Royal Tribunal was set up in Lublin to serve the Ukrainian voivodeships of the Commonwealth.

Rozanov, Gavriil (secular name: Vasilii), b 1781, d 8 September 1858. Russian churchman and historian. He was rector of the theological seminary in Vologda (from 1814) before being consecrated bishop of Orel (1821) and then archbishop of Katerynoslav (1828–37), Kherson (1837–48), and Tver (1848–57). He was a specialist on the history of Southern Ukraine and the Zaporizhia. His publications include a history of the Samara St Nicholas's Monastery (1838), studies on early churches in the Crimea and Kherson gubernia (1848) and on the history of New Russia in *Zapiski Odesskago obshchestva istorii i drevnostei* (1853), and articles in other journals. Much of his work was based on primary sources, and he published the memoirs of M. Korzha, a Zaporozhian Cossack, in 1842.

Rozbudova derzhavy (State Building). An organ of the Zarevo Ukrainian Student Association, published quarterly in Munich (1949–50), Montreal (1951–4), Cleveland (1954), and Denver (1955–7). Edited by M. Antonovych

(1949–54) and B. Wynar (from 1954), it was ideologically aligned with the OUN Melnyk faction and devoted considerable attention to political affairs. It also published articles in Ukrainian and Soviet studies. A total of 22 issues appeared.

Rozbudova natsiï

Rozbudova natsiï (Nation Building). An ideological journal of the OUN Leadership (PUN). It was established in January 1928 and published in Prague monthly until 1931 and then bimonthly until August 1934 (a total of 79 issues appeared). The formal publisher was M. Stsiborsky and the chief editor was V. Martynets, who was assisted initially by P. Kozhevnykiv; until April 1929 the journal's editorial offices were located in Berlin, and O. Boikiv was responsible for printing it in Prague. The journal was banned in Soviet-, Polish-, and Rumanian-ruled Ukraine, but was smuggled in and widely distributed there. *Rozbudova natsiï* published articles on ideological, political, economic, military, and cultural subjects; memoirs of the period of Ukrainian statehood (1917–21); and surveys of international affairs and developments in Western and Soviet Ukraine. Regular contributors included prominent OUN leaders and other figures. The journal was closed down by the Czech authorities under Polish pressure following the assassination in Galicia of the Polish minister of the interior, B. Pieracki.

Rozdil or **Rozdol**. IV-5. A town smt (1986 pop 5,000) on the Dniester River in Mykolaiv raion, Lviv oblast. It was first mentioned in historical documents in 1569. A palace built by the Lanckoroński family, who owned the village, is used as a sanatorium today. The town has a large sewing factory, a brewery, and a forestation project.

Rozdilna [Rozdil'na]. VII-11. A city (1989 pop 17,700) and a raion center in Odessa oblast. It sprang up in 1863–5 during the construction of the Odessa–Balta railway line. In 1957 it was granted city status. Today Rozdilna is a transportation and manufacturing center. Its plants service the railway and produce metalworking machinery, dairy products, and wine.

Rozdilsky, Bohdan [Rozdil's'kyj], b 22 November 1916 in Volia Tseklynska, Jasło county, Galicia. Neurologist;

full member of the Shevchenko Scientific Society from 1968. After completing his medical studies at Poznań University (1936–9) and the Lviv Medical Institute (1941) he served in the Division Galizien (1943–5) and was a POW in Italy and Britain. Having emigrated to Canada in 1951, he specialized in neurology at McGill University (1956) and the University of Saskatchewan (PH D, 1958), where he taught until 1984. He wrote on inherited brain defects and infectious and degenerative diseases of the nervous system. He used the autoradiographic method to investigate cerebrovascular permeability.

Rozdol Sirka Manufacturing Consortium (Rozdolske vyrobnyche obiednannia Sirka). A consortium that extracts and concentrates sulfur from sulfurous ore from the *Subcarpathian Sulfur Basin. Based in Novyi Rozdol, Lviv oblast, the enterprise was set up in 1956. It consists of mines, an enrichment factory, and a distillation plant. It produces sulfur in various forms and sulfuric acid. In the 1970s the consortium employed over 5,000 workers.

Rozdol sulfur deposits. See Subcarpathian Sulfur Basin.

Rozdolne [Rozdol'ne]. VIII-14. A town smt (1986 pop 7,600) and a raion center in the Crimea. It was founded in the 1860s by German settlers, who raised sheep and later wheat. In 1944 its name was changed from Ak-Sheikh to the current name, and in 1960 it was granted smt status. The town has a food industry. A Scythian settlement and a burial ground from the 10th century AD have been discovered nearby.

Rozdolne settlement. A multi-occupational archeological site on the Kalmiius River near Rozdolne, Starobesheve raion, Donetske oblast. Excavations in 1965–7 identified five distinct occupations from the artifacts recovered. Among the items recovered were: Neolithic flint and pottery fragments; Copper Age flint knives and arrowheads; *Pit-Grave culture egg-shaped vases with corded and combed designs; *Bronze Age Multicylindrical Pottery culture stone dwellings and bronze knives; and 8th- to 9th-century *Saltiv culture tableware.

Rozdolsky, Osyp [Rozdol's'kyj], b 29 September 1872 in Dobryvody, Zbarazh county, Galicia, d 27 February 1945 in Lviv. Educator, ethnographer, and translator; full member of the VUAN from 1926 and the Shevchenko Scientific Society from 1930; father of R. *Rozdolsky. A graduate of Lviv University (1897), he taught classical languages, German, and literature at gymnasiums in Lviv, Ternopil, and Kolomyia. Under I. Franko's influence he began gathering ethnographic data in 1892. He published collections of Galician folktales (1895–9), Galician folk novellas (1900), and Galician-Ruthenian folk melodies (with S. Livokevych, 1906–7), all in *Ethnohrafichnyi zbirnyk*. He also began to record folk songs in 1900. In 1914 he was elected to the Ethnographic Commission of the Ukrainian Scientific Society in Kiev and conducted field research in the Chernihiv and Poltava regions. After returning to Galicia (1918) he continued his work and was elected to the Ethnographic Commission of the VUAN (1926). Besides collecting folklore he translated V. Stefanyk's and S. Va-

Osyp Rozdolsky   Roman Rozdolsky

sylchenko's short stories and Lesia Ukrainka's plays into German, and Plato's *Euthyphro* (1906), Euripedes' *Medea*, and Aeschylus' *Prometheus* into Ukrainian.

Rozdolsky, Roman [Rozdol's'kyj] (Rosdolsky, Rozdolski), b 18 July 1898 in Lviv, d 20 October 1967 in Detroit. Historian, interpreter of Marxism, and political activist; son of O. *Rozdolsky. He began his left-wing political activities in 1913 as an organizer of 'Drahomanov organizations,' whose *Vistnyk* he edited in 1916. In 1917 he edited the revolutionary periodical *Klychi*, and in 1918 he helped to establish the International Revolutionary Social Democratic Youth in Lviv. After serving in the Ukrainian Galician Army (1918–19) Rozdolsky became a cofounder of the Communist Party of Eastern Galicia (renamed the *Communist Party of Western Ukraine [KPZU] in 1923). He was a major theoretician of the KPZU and adhered to the faction, led by O. *Vasylkiv, that opposed Stalinist national policy in Soviet Ukraine.

From 1927 Rozdolsky lived in Vienna. His doctoral dissertation (University of Vienna 1929) concerned Engels's views on the 'nonhistorical' peoples of Austria during the Revolution of 1848; this was the first version of what later became a book on the subject (German edns 1964, 1979; English 1986). To escape a general repression against the left, in 1934 he returned to Lviv, where he worked at the university as a researcher under the Polish economic historian F. *Bujak. In the late 1930s he coedited the journal *Zhyttia i slovo* (published in Drohobych), which exposed Stalinist crimes in Soviet Ukraine while simultaneously polemicizing with the nationalist Ukrainian right. He also wrote two books on the history of the Galician peasantry in the late 18th and early 19th centuries, one on communal landholding (1936; German edn 1954), the other on serfdom. When the Soviets occupied Lviv in 1939 they destroyed all printed copies of the latter book, but Rozdolsky was able to reconstruct it after the war and publish it in Warsaw in 1962 (2 vols). To escape the Soviet authorities he moved to Cracow, where the Gestapo arrested him in 1942. He spent the rest of the war in concentration camps, including *Oświęcim, about which he published a memoir.

In 1947 Rozdolsky emigrated to the United States and settled in Detroit. His major work of the postwar period was an interpretation of Marx's economic thought, which appeared in German in 1968 and subsequently was translated into many languages, including English (*The Making of Marx's Capital*, 1977). He also wrote studies of *Joseph II's agrarian reforms (1961), the peasant deputies to the Austrian parliament in 1848–9 (1976), and revolutionary tactics in 1914–18 (1973). Although written mainly in German and Polish, Rozdolsky's works had a Ukrainian perspective and, with the exception of the book on Marxian economics, contained much material on Ukrainian themes.

BIBLIOGRAPHY
Radziejowski, J. 'Roman Rosdolsky: Man, Activist, and Scholar,' *Science & Society*, 42, no. 2 (Summer 1978)
Himka, J.-P. 'Introduction,' in R. Rosdolsky, *Engels and the 'Non-historic' Peoples: The National Question in the Revolution of 1848* (Glasgow 1986)

J.-P. Himka

Rozenbaum, Solomon, b 31 December 1885 in Poltava, d 1941 in Poltava. Painter. After graduating from the Odessa Art School (1908) and the St Petersburg Academy of Arts (1917) he worked in I. Miasoedov's studio in Poltava (1915–17) and taught in local schools. In the late 1920s he belonged to the Association of Artists of Red Ukraine. His works include genre paintings, still lifes, portraits, and landscapes, such as *Poltava's Environs* (1926), *Blast Furnaces in Makiivka* (1940), and *Winter* (1940).

Liudvyk Rozenberg   Major Teodor Rozhankovsky

Rozenberg, Liudvyk (pseuds: Chornii, Lvivsky), b ?, d 1940 in Lviv. Jewish Ukrainian political figure in Galicia. He graduated from the Ukrainian gymnasium in Rohatyn. He enlisted in the Legion of Ukrainian Sich Riflemen in 1914 and was captured by the Russians in 1916. After the Revolution of 1917 he served as a captain in the Sich Riflemen. He was a close friend of R. *Rozdolsky, and from 1920 he belonged to the Ukrainian Section of the Czech Communist party. In 1923 he was elected to the CC of the Communist Party of Western Ukraine, but he left the party in 1925. In the 1930s Rozenberg belonged to a Communist oppositionist group and contributed to the Lviv paper *Narodnia sprava*; for his activities he was imprisoned in the Polish concentration camp at Bereza Kartuzka. He was arrested by the NKVD in Lviv in September 1939 and executed in prison.

Rozhalin, Kuzma [Rožalin, Kuz'ma], b 1740 in Vovkivtsi, near Romen, d 1795 in Moscow. Physician. After being educated at the Kievan Mohyla Academy (1751–8), the Medico-Surgical School of the St Petersburg Military Hospital (1758–60), and Berlin and Leiden (PH D, 1765) universities, he taught physiology and pharmacology in the hospital schools in St Petersburg. During the Russo-Turkish War (1769–74) he directed the Yelysavethrad Hospital and supervised efforts to control the plague in Yelysavethrad, Novomyrhorod, and Kharkiv. In 1776 he was appointed chief physician for New Russia gubernia.

Rozhankovsky, Teodor [Rožankovs'kyj], b 1875 in Sokal, Galicia, d 12 April 1970 in Weehawken, New Jersey. Military officer and community leader. Under the Austrian regime he was a judge and a deputy to the Galician Diet (1908–18). In 1914 he helped organize the Legion of Sich Riflemen and served as its first commander (briefly) and as deputy commander and commander of its reserve training unit (until November 1918). In the Ukrainian Galician Army he was promoted to major and placed in command of the Stanyslaviv Military District (1918–19). He was also a member of the Ukrainian National Rada. In 1919–20 he served as military attaché in Prague; later he practiced law in Lviv. After the Second World War he emigrated to the United States.

Rozhansky, Dmytro [Rožanskij], b 1 September 1882 in Kiev, d 27 September 1936 in Leningrad. Physicist and radio engineer; corresponding member of the USSR Academy of Sciences from 1933. A graduate of St Petersburg University (1904), he worked at Göttingen University and the St Petersburg Electrotechnical Institute. In 1911 he became a professor at Kharkiv University, where he conducted extensive radio-physics research and founded what became known as the Kharkiv school of radio-physics. Rozhansky moved to Russia in 1921, first to the Radio Laboratory at Nizhnii Novgorod and in 1923 to Leningrad, where he became a professor at the polytechnical institute. His research on ultrahigh-frequency radio waves was instrumental in the early development of the Soviet pulsed radar system.

Rozhansky, Liubomyr [Rožans'kyj, Ljubomyr], b 1872 in Sukhodoly, Brody county, Galicia, d 6 February 1925 in Lviv. Community activist. After studying law at Lviv University he worked as a notary and assistant to various lawyers. Having been influenced by M. Drahomanov's ideas, he became a leader of the populist movement in Western Ukraine and a founder of the National Democratic party. In 1910 he was appointed director of the Land Mortgage Bank in Lviv. Rozhansky wrote articles for the Ukrainian press on economic and political topics, often using the pseudonym L. Seliansky or L. Sukhodolsky

Rozhavska, Yudyt [Rožavs'ka, Judyt], b 12 November 1923 in Kiev, d 10 March 1982 in Kiev. Composer, pianist, and editor. She studied composition with M. Hozenpud and piano with Y. Slivak at the Kiev Conservatory (1940–51) and then worked as a music editor for the publishers Sovetskii Kompozitor and Mystetstvo. Her works for children include the opera *Kazka pro zahublenyi chas* (The Story of Lost Time, 1968) and the ballet *Korolivstvo kryvykh dzerkal* (The Kingdom of Crooked Mirrors, 1955) as well as

Yudyt Rozhavska   Vsevolod Rozhdestvensky

songs and piano pieces. Other works include the symphonic poem *Dnipro* (1956), cantatas, concertos, chamber pieces, art songs, and music for radio and television.

Rozhdestvensky, Vsevolod [Roždestvens'kyj], b 2 July 1918 in Poltava, d 3 March 1985 in Kiev. Composer and conductor. He studied in 1936–9 with S. Bohatyrov at the Kharkiv Conservatory and in 1937–41 with L. Revutsky at the Kiev Conservatory. From 1945 he was music director and principal conductor of the Kiev Ukrainian Drama Theater. His works include the musical comedies *Za dvoma zaitsiamy* (In Pursuit of Two Hares, 1954) and *Cherevychky* (The Little Shoes, 1967), incidental music for O. Ilchenko's *Petersburg Autumn* and I. Kocherha's *Prorok* (The Prophet), *Concert Hopak* (1951) for orchestra, and cantatas, two string quartets, piano music, art songs, arrangements of folk songs, and film scores.

Ivan Rozhin

Rozhin, Ivan [Rožin] b 18 September 1897 in Kumaniv, Kamianets-Podilskyi county, Podilia gubernia, d 10 July 1972 in Detroit. Biologist; full member of the Shevchenko Scientific Society from 1947. After serving in the Army of the UNR he completed veterinary studies and worked at the All-Ukrainian Institute of Experimental Veterinary Medicine. He headed a department of the VUAN Institute of Experimental Biology in Kharkiv (1928–32) and taught pathology and hygiene in Dnipropetrovske and Bila Tserkva (1932–41). He was also a scholarly associate of the Institute of Experimental Biology and Pathology (1930–41). After the Second World War he taught at the Ukraini-

an Free University and the Ukrainian Technical and Husbandry Institute in Munich and then emigrated to the United States. Rozhin published many articles and monographs, including a survey of animal husbandry in Ukraine (1969–71).

Rozhniativ or **Rozhnitiv** [Rožnjativ, Rožnitiv]. V-5. A city (1986 pop 3,500) and a raion center in Ivano-Frankivske oblast. It was first mentioned in historical documents in the 12th century. At the end of the 14th century it came under Polish rule, and in the early 15th century the Poles built a fortress there. After it was annexed by Austria (1772), the town was granted city status, in 1785. Its fortress has been reconstructed and preserved. It has a furniture and a mixed-feed factory.

Rozhyshche [Rožyšče]. III-6. A town smt (1986 pop 14,300) on the Styr River and a raion center in Volhynia oblast. It was first mentioned in historical documents in 1377, when it was under Lithuanian rule. It was handed over to Poland in 1569, and after the partition of Poland in 1795, to Russia. In the 19th century the town became a center for woolen-cloth weaving. In the interwar period it was under Polish rule. Today the town has a reinforced-concrete plant, a canning factory, a bakery, and a cheese factory.

Rozivka. VI-18. A town smt (1986 pop 5,400) in Kuibysheve raion, Zaporizhia oblast. It was founded by German colonists in 1788. In 1901 a railway station was built in the settlement. Its main enterprises today are a footwear factory, a brickyard, and a food-processing plant. The site of the battle on the *Kalka River (1223) is nearby.

Rozner, Ionas, b 25 February 1924 in Chernivtsi, Bukovyna, d 25 March 1980 in Kiev. Soviet historian of Jewish origin. He graduated from the Kiev Pedagogical Institute (1951) and worked at the AN URSR (now ANU) Institute of History (1959–63), the Kiev Institute of the National Economy (PH D, 1969), and the ANU Institute of Economics. His works on 16th- to 19th-century Ukrainian history include *Severin Nalivaiko, rukovoditel' krest'iansko-kazatskogo vosstaniia 1594–1596 gg. na Ukraine* (Severyn Nalyvaiko, Leader of the Peasant-Cossack Uprising of 1594–6 in Ukraine, 1961) and *Kazachestvo v krest'ianskoi voine 1773–1775 gg.* (The Cossack Host in the Peasant War of 1773–5, 1966). He also wrote a work on the socioeconomic history of Russia entitled *Ekonomicheskoe razvitie Rossii v XVIII v.* (The Economic Development of Russia in the 18th Century, 1966), as well as studies on Ukrainian folk art and the history of economic thought.

Rozniichuk, Ivan [Roznijčuk] (pseud: Marko Barabolia), b 10 or 19 April 1910 in Trebushany (now Dilove), Transcarpathia, d ? Satirist. While working as a village teacher in Transcarpathia he contributed humorous sketches and biting satire on political and cultural topics to the Uzhhorod periodicals *Pchilka* (in 1928–30), *Ukraïns'ke slovo* (in 1935–6), and *Lyteraturna nedilia* (in 1943). His novel, 'Havrylo Motovylo' (1942), was never published. Rozniichuk was last heard from in 1944 after being conscripted into the Hungarian army. Editions of his works were published in Prague in 1941 and in Bratislava in 1970.

Rozov, Volodymyr, b 15 July 1876 in Kiev, d 21 May 1940 in Zagreb, Croatia. Philologist. A graduate of Kiev University (1902), he taught philological subjects (presenting the first lectures on the history of the Ukrainian language and dialectology) there (1906–16) and at the Nizhen Historical-Philological Institute (1916–18). After emigrating to Yugoslavia (1919) he taught Russian at Skopje (in the 1920s) and Zagreb (from 1930) universities. In 1928 at Ljubljana University he defended his PH D dissertation on the 15th-century Volhynian dialect. He is the author of some 100 works, including an annotated edition of 14th- and 15th-century Ukrainian charters published by the Russian Academy of Sciences (1917) and, in Ukrainian translation, by the VUAN (1928); and articles on the significance and language of the charters, on Galician and Volhynian dialects, on A. Krymsky, on Ukrainian school dramas, and on Old Bulgarian and Serbian literary monuments. His monograph on the language of the charters and his index of personal and geographical names in and lexicon to the charters have not been published.

Rozsoloda, Ivan, b ca 1771 in Slovianske (now Nykopil), d ? Storyteller; son of a Zaporozhian Cossack. In the 1880s, when he was 116, he was visited by D. *Yavornytsky, who wrote down the many tales, legends, songs, and facts about the Cossacks' folkways, customs, material culture, and economic activities Rozsoloda knew. Those materials made up a chapter of Yavornytsky's book on the Zaporizhia (1888).

Rozsosh [Rozsoš] (Russian: Rossosh). III-20. A city (1970 pop 36,000) on the Chorna Kalytva River and a raion center in Voronezh oblast, Russia. According to the census of 1926, Ukrainians represented 85.7 percent of the city's population and 95.8 percent of the county's population.

Rozsudov-Kuliabko, Vasyl [Kuljabko, Vasyl'], b 1863, d 1930. Stage actor and director. He worked in the troupes of M. Starytsky (1885–8), M. Kropyvnytsky (1888–1900), P. Saksahansky (1900–3), O. Suslov, and M. Vasyliev-Sviatoshenko and from 1927 in the Dnipropetrovske Ukrainian Music and Drama Theater.

Rozsvit (Dawn). A weekly (later semimonthly) newspaper published for Ukrainians in the Russian army interned in the POW camp in Rastatt, Germany, in 1916–18. Edited by V. Simovych, H. Petrenko, and P. Moroz, it contained articles on political developments and on Ukrainian history and culture. The newspaper was supported by the *Union for the Liberation of Ukraine and promoted the idea of Ukrainian independence.

Roztochia [Roztoččja]. A plateau that runs in a band northwest of Lviv between the Sian Lowland and the Buh Depression. It is approx 15–20 km in width and up to 400 m in height. An anticline composed largely of chalk, it constitutes a continuation of the Opilia Upland. The rivers of the region flow into the Sian (the Shklo, Liubachivka, Tanew) or Buh (the Rata, Solokiia, Huchva) systems. The region's major centers include Nesterov (Zhovkva), Rava Ruska, Belz, Uhniv, and Tomaszów.

Rozumny, Petro [Rozumnyj], b 7 March 1926 in Dnipropetrovske oblast. Philologist and dissident. During the

Petro Rozumny   Jaroslav Rozumnyj

Second World War he was deported as an *Ostarbeiter* to Germany. After graduating from the Dnipropetrovske Institute of Foreign Languages (1958) he worked as a teacher. He was persecuted in Ivano-Frankivske and then in Dnipropetrovske (1961–7) because of his contacts with the Ukrainian student movement and participation in the Ukrainian cultural revival of the 1960s. In October 1979 he joined the *Ukrainian Helsinki Group and was arrested. In December he was sentenced to three years' imprisonment for possessing a 'dangerous weapon' (a hunting knife).

Rozumnyj, Jaroslav, b 6 September 1925 in Vychilky (now Honcharivka), Buchach county, Galicia. Ukrainian-Canadian literary scholar and community figure. A postwar émigré, he graduated from the University of Ottawa (1958; PH D, 1968) and has taught Ukrainian literature at Laurentian University (1960–3) and the University of Manitoba (since 1964), where he was the head of the department of Slavic studies. He has presided over the Ukrainian Cultural and Educational Centre in Winnipeg (1968–73) and the Ukrainian Academy of Arts and Sciences in Canada (1977–80). His articles on Ukrainian literature have appeared in Ukrainian émigré and Canadian scholarly periodicals.

Rozumovsky [Rozumovs'kyj]. A Ukrainian family of Russian imperial counts and military and civic figures from the Chernihiv region. Yakiv Rozum and his son, Hryhorii (d ca 1730), were registered Cossacks in Kozelets company, Kiev regiment. Hryhorii's son, Oleksii (Aleksei, b 28 March 1709 in Lemeshi, Kozelets company, d 17 July 1771 in St Petersburg), was brought to St Petersburg to sing in the imperial court choir in 1731. There he soon became a favorite of Empress Elizabeth I, who granted him and his family many estates, secretly married him (1742), and appointed him a count (1744) and field marshal (1756). Oleksii was the first to use the name Rozumovsky. Under his influence things Ukrainian became fashionable at Elizabeth's court. He persuaded Elizabeth to restore the office of hetman in Ukraine and to appoint his brother, Kyrylo *Rozumovsky, to that position in 1750. Kyrylo appointed his brother Petro (d 1771) colonel of Nizhen regiment (1753–71) and his brother Vasyl colonel of Hadiache regiment (1755–62).

Kyrylo was married to Countess K. Naryshkina, with whom he had six sons and five daughters. The eldest son, Oleksii (Aleksei, b 23 September 1748, d 17 April 1822 in

Pochep, Mglin county, Chernihiv gubernia), was appointed a privy councillor and senator in 1786, trustee of Moscow University in 1807, and imperial minister of education (1810–16). As minister of education he oversaw the creation of more parish and county primary schools and gymnasiums (eg, in Kiev, Nizhen, and Kharkiv) and the improvement of teaching methods and school inspection. Oleksii had an abiding interest in the natural sciences. He created a large botanical garden with over 2,000 different plants and 500 orange trees on his estate in Gorenki, near Moscow, and amassed the largest private natural-science library in the empire. He was a mystic, a Freemason, and the vice-president of the Russian Bible Society. Oleksii's marriage to Countess Varvara Sheremeteva produced two sons and two daughters. He also had 10 illegitimate children, who received the surname *Perovsky. Oleksii's older son, Petro (Petr, 1775–1835), was a major general (1799–1801) and served as a state counselor to the governor of New Russia in Odessa from 1806. He was the last count of the Rozumovsky family in the Russian Empire. Petro's younger brother, Kyrylo (Kirill, 1777–1829), died insane in Kharkiv.

Hetman Rozumovsky's second son, Petro (Petr, b 26 January 1751, d 26 December 1823), was a general in the Russian army and then a senator and privy councillor. The hetman's third son was Andrii *Rozumovsky. His fourth son, Lev (b 19 January 1757, d 3 December 1818), received the rank of major general in 1790. The hetman's sixth son, Ivan (b 17 August 1761, d 1802 in Italy), served as an adjutant general to his father from 1784 and was a colonel in the Little Russian Regiment from 1789. He retired in 1796 with the rank of major general.

The hetman's fifth son, Hryhorii (Grigorii or Gregor, b 21 November 1759, d 3 June 1837 in Český Rudolec, Moravia), studied mineralogy and geology in Leiden and lived in the 1780s in Lausanne, where he published the mineralogical studies *Ouevres de M. le comte Grégoire Razoumowsky* (2 vols, 1784) and *Histoire naturelle de Jorat et de ses environs ...* (2 vols, 1789). In 1790 he was elected an honorary member of the Russian Imperial Academy of Sciences. In 1816 he published *Coup d'oeil géognostique sur le Nord de l'Europe général et en Russie en particulier*. After the death in 1818 of his second wife, Baroness Teresa-Elizabeth Schenk de Castel, Hryhorii and his sons Maximilian and Lev left St Petersburg forever, became Austrian citizens, converted to Protestantism, and lived near Vienna, in Baden bei Wien, and on their estate in Český Rudolec. They and Lev's heirs were recognized as the Austrian counts Rasumofsky. In Silesia Hryhorii discovered a new mineral that became known as Razoumowskin. He was elected a member of the royal academies of sciences in Stockholm, Turin, and Munich and of several scientific societies. Lev's son, Leo (d 28 March 1915), served in the Austrian embassy in Paris and funded the restoration of the hetman's palace in Baturyn, the tomb of the Rozumovsky family there, and churches the construction of which had been financed by Hetman Rozumovsky.

BIBLIOGRAPHY
Vasil'chikov, A. *Semeistvo Razumovskikh*, 4 vols (St Petersburg 1880, 1882, 1887, 1894)

O. Ohloblyn

Rozumovsky, Andrii [Rozumovs'kyj, Andrij] (Razoumoffsky, Andreas), b 2 November 1752 in Hlukhiv, d 23 September 1836 in Vienna. Statesman, society figure, and music patron; son of Hetman K. *Rozumovsky. His diplomatic talents were put to use through postings in Naples (1777–84), Denmark (1784–6), Sweden (1786–8), and Austria (1790–9 and 1801–7), where he played a significant role in the negotiations surrounding the Second and Third Partitions of Poland. Rozumovsky was eventually removed from his Vienna posting for maintaining a steadfast stance against Napoleon that was for a time not in line with the position of the Russian government. His views later paid him dividends, when he was appointed Russian plenipotentiary at the Congress of Vienna (1814–15) and then named prince in 1815. He was a particularly strong supporter of music and kept a kapelle of Ukrainian singers in his palace. He was also a close friend and generous patron of L. van Beethoven, who dedicated three string quartets (op 59, known as the *Razumovsky Quartets*) as well as his *Fifth* and *Sixth* symphonies to him.

Hetman Kyrylo Rozumovsky

Rozumovsky, Kyrylo [Rozumovs'kyj] (Razumovsky, Kirill), b 29 March 1728 in Lemeshi, Kozelets company, Kiev regiment, d 15 January 1803 in Baturyn, Konotip county, Chernihiv gubernia. The last hetman (1750–64) of the Hetman state. He was brought to St Petersburg as the brother of O. Rozumovsky, Empress Elizabeth's favorite, and then sent to study in Germany (1743–5). He was named a count in July 1744, and after his return to St Petersburg he was appointed president (1746–65) of the Russian Academy of Sciences. Elizabeth and the Russian government agreed to restore the office of hetman under the pressure of O. Rozumovsky and other Ukrainian nobles, and Elizabeth chose Kyrylo for the position. The choice was sanctioned by the Cossack *starshyna*'s *Hlukhiv Council of March 1750.

Rozumovsky arrived in the Hetmanate's capital of Hlukhiv in July 1751 with G. *Teplov, his adviser and the administrator of his chancellery. Under Rozumovsky the Hetmanate once again had a measure of autonomy. Elizabeth gave Rozumovsky authority over Kiev and the Zaporizhia in November 1750 and shifted supervision of Little Russian (Ukrainian) affairs from the Russian Senate to the College of Foreign Affairs, thereby signifying her treatment of the Hetmanate as a separate state rather than a Russian province.

Rozumovsky sought to rebuild the Hetmanate as an independent state. During that process two main political currents emerged within the upper echelon of the Cossack *starshyna*. The conservative current had as its spokesmen

General Chancellor A. Bezborodko and General Treasurer M. Skoropadsky, who sought to preserve the traditional Cossack order and make the Hetmanate more like the noble-dominated Polish Commonwealth. The reformist current, led by the future general chancellor V. Tumansky and his brothers, consisted primarily of young members of the *starshyna*, many of whom had studied in Western Europe. They sought models for the Hetmanate in the Western European states and proposed a system of enlightened absolutism with a hereditary monarchy (the Rozumovsky dynasty) and a constitutional parliament (general assembly). The reformists became increasingly influential in the 1760s, and in 1764 (most likely with Rozumovsky's support) they tried to present their views to the Russian government.

During Rozumovsky's hetmancy the Hetmanate was divided into 20 counties; a system of *land, *city, and *pidkomorskyi courts was established; and the position of *viit in the larger towns was occupied by members of the *starshyna*. The *starshyna*'s political rights were expanded, and they assembled to confer more frequently. At their 1763–4 general assembly in Hlukhiv they discussed major issues and projects for state reform and adopted *shliakhetstvo* (nobility) as their official name. Rozumovsky extended the possibility of becoming a *starshyna* to non-Cossack estates, such as the clergy and the burgher elite. In 1760 he restricted the mobility of the peasantry. During his frequent stays in St Petersburg the Hetmanate was ruled by the *starshyna*.

The vivification of Ukrainian political life and thought during Rozumovsky's hetmancy was due in no small measure to his own activities. He tried, in vain, to convince St Petersburg to grant the Hetmanate the right of diplomatic ties with the European states, fostered the development of trade and industry, and once again made *Baturyn the capital of the Hetmanate. He also reformed the Cossack army according to a project drawn up by Col I. Kuliabka of Lubni regiment, and planned to establish universities in Kiev and Baturyn under his patronage.

The wide-ranging program for modernizing the Hetmanate, Rozumovsky's participation in it, and the political activation of the Ukrainian nobility were completely at odds with the aims of the Russian government, and in the 1750s the government began limiting the Hetmanate's economic and political rights. In 1754 the Hetmanate's finances were brought under imperial control, and import and export duties in the Hetmanate were abolished. In 1755 the border tariffs between Russia and Ukraine were removed. In 1756 the supervision of Little Russian affairs, including control over the hetman's appointments of colonels and other officials and his distribution of hereditary estates to his relatives and supporters, was returned to the Russian Senate. In 1761 the Senate took over control of Kiev from Rozumovsky. The government of the new empress, *Catherine II, intensified Russian centralist policies with respect to Ukraine even further.

Rozumovsky's own social policies, aimed at transforming the Hetmanate into a nobility-dominated state, created greater social disparities and conflicts, and his dynastic plans met with concerted opposition from many members of the new nobility. Those difficulties were compounded by the losses Ukraine suffered as an unwilling participant in the *Seven Years' War. Catherine II used Rozumovsky's petition to make his descendants hereditary hetmans as a pretext for forcing his resignation in November 1764, and placed the Hetmanate under the control of the *Little Russian Collegium. Rozumovsky was compensated with the rank of field marshal, an enormous pension, and many estates in Ukraine, including the towns of Hadiache and Baturyn. He subsequently traveled in Germany, France, and Italy (1765–7) and led the life of an aristocrat in St Petersburg (1766–76), Baturyn (1776–85, 1794–1803), and Moscow (1784–94).

BIBLIOGRAPHY

Wassiltschikow, A. *Les comtes Alexei et Kiril Razoumovski* (Halle 1883)

Borshchak, I. *Slidamy het'mana Rozumovs'koho u Frantsiï* (Munich 1957)

Kohut, Z. *Russian Centralism and Ukrainian Autonomy: Imperial Absorption of the Hetmanate, 1760s–1830s* (Cambridge, Mass 1988)

O. Ohloblyn

Rozumovsky's Theater. A *serf theater troupe established in Hlukhiv in 1751 at the court of Hetman K. Rozumovsky. In its repertoire were operas, ballets, and comedies, such as *Iziums'kyi iarmarok* (The Fair in Izium, author unknown). Guest soloists from Italy and France were invited to participate in its productions. It also had a 40-member choir, directed by A. Rachynsky.

Viacheslav Rozvadovsky: *Moonlit Night* (oil, 1904)

Rozvadovsky, Viacheslav [Rozvadovs'kyj, Vjačeslav], b 24 September 1875 in Odessa, d 18 January 1943 in Tashkent, Uzbekistan. Painter and educator. After studying at the Odessa Art School (1890–4) and under A. Kuindzhi at the St Petersburg Academy of Arts (1894–1900) he worked in Ukraine, where he created landscapes and genre paintings, such as *Above the Dnieper* (1900), *T. Shevchenko's Grave in Kaniv* (1903), *Hutsul Girl* (1904), and *Mill* (1905), and organized the first eight traveling art exhibitions in Ukraine (1904–8). Their catalogue (*Opys kartyn narodnoho mystetstva*) was printed in Ukrainian. In 1905 he founded an art school and residence for peasant children in Kamianets-Podilskyi. The Academy of Arts sent him in 1912 to Central Asia, where he painted, taught art, and studied the local folk art.

Rozvaha (Entertainment). A weekly newspaper published for Ukrainians in the Russian army interned in the POW camp in Freistadt, Austria, in 1915–18 (a total of 134 issues). It published articles on political developments and on Ukrainian history and culture. The newspaper was supported by the *Union for the Liberation of Ukraine and promoted the idea of Ukrainian independence.

RUB. An artists' group in Lviv, formed by students and graduates of the *Novakivsky Art School. RUB held events annually starting in 1926 providing public exposure for its members. It promoted a synthesis of Eastern art with current artistic traditions of Europe, and favored works which expressed local flavor and national characteristics. In *Karby* (Notches), the first art almanac published by RUB in 1933, V. Havryliuk, V. Hrytsenko, V. Lasovsky, S. Lutsyk, M. Moroz, O. Pleshkan, H. Smolsky, and R. Chornii were listed as members.

Rubach, Mykhailo [Rubač, Myxajlo], b 2 December 1899 in Chernecha Sloboda, Romen county, Poltava gubernia, d 17 January 1980 in Kiev. Historian and archivist. From 1917 he taught and worked in Bolshevik organizations in Katerynoslav. In 1923 he was appointed deputy director of the Commission for the Study of the History of the October Revolution and the CP(B)U (Istpart), editor in chief of *Letopis' Revoliutsii*, and director of the Central Archival Administration of the Ukrainian SSR. After graduating from the Institute of Red Professorship in Moscow (1927) he served as director of the Institute of Party History of the CC CP(B)U (1929–32) and worked at the Institute of History of the Communist Academy in Moscow (1933–5). Later he headed the department of USSR history at Kharkiv University, and in 1942 he began working at the AN URSR (now ANU) Institute of History, as director of the archeography department and as senior associate of the department of history of the October Revolution and the Civil War. In 1957–69 he was a professor in the department of CPSU history at Kiev University.

Rubach was the author of *Ocherki po istorii revoliutsionnogo preobrazovaniia agrarnykh otnoshenii na Ukraine v period provedeniia Oktiabr'skoi revoliutsii* (Essays on the History of the Revolutionary Transformation of Agrarian Relations in Ukraine in the Period of the Duration of the October Revolution, 1956) and the coauthor of collective works on the Ukrainian SSR during the First World War and on the history of the Ukrainian SSR. In the 1930s he led a publicistic campaign against M. Hrushevsky (in *Chervonyi shliakh*, 1932, nos 5–12), and he was instrumental in efforts to discredit Ukrainian historiography in the 1970s.

I. Myhul

Ruban, Petro, b 1940 in Pryluka, Chernihiv oblast. Soviet political prisoner; a wood-carver by profession. For his Ukrainian pro-independence views he was imprisoned in the years 1965–73, 1976–82, and 1985–8. He was released before completing his last term and allowed to emigrate to the United States.

Ruban, Valentyna, b 30 June 1940 in Kiev. Art historian. She received her doctorate from the Institute of Art History in Moscow (1990). She is a senior researcher at the Rylski Institute of Art, Folklore, and Ethnography at the Academy of Sciences in Kiev and the author of several articles and books on the development of Ukrainian portrait painting, including *Ukraïns'kyi radians'kyi portretnyi zhyvopys* (Soviet Ukrainian Portrait Painting, 1977), *Portret v tvorchosti ukraïns'kykh zhyvopystsiv* (The Portrait in the Work of Ukrainian Painters, 1979), *Ukraïns'kyi portretnyi zhyvopys pershoï polovyny XIX stolittia* (Ukrainian Portraiture of the First Half of the 19th Century, 1984), *Ukraïns'kyi portretnyi zhyvopys druhoï polovyny XIX–pochatku XX–stolittia* (Ukrainian Portraiture of the Second Half of the 19th Century and the Beginning of the 20th Century, 1986), and *Anatol' Petryts'kyi: Portrety suchasnykiv* (Anatol Petrytsky: Portraits of Contemporaries, 1991).

Ruban, Vasyl, b 25 March 1742 in Bilhorod (Belgorod) in Slobidska Ukraine, d 5 October 1795 in St Petersburg. Publisher, historian, and Russian poet of Ukrainian descent; member of the Russian Free Economic Society. He studied at the Kievan Mohyla Academy, the Moscow Slavonic-Latin Academy (ca 1754–5), and Moscow University (1759–61). From 1784 he was head of foreign correspondence at the Imperial War College. In St Petersburg he published an anonymously written book of information about Little Russia (1773), a descriptive geography of Little Russia (1777), and *Kratkaia letopis' Malyia Rossii* (A Short Chronicle of Little Russia, 1777), thereby facilitating Russian study of Ukraine. He also published the St Petersburg journals *Ni to, ni sio* (1769), and *Trudoliubivyi muravei* (1771), Russian almanacs, the historical compendium *Starina i novizna* (Antiquity and New Times, 2 vols, 1772–3), which included materials on the history of Ukraine, V. *Hryhorovych-Barsky's account of his travels (1778), and descriptions of St Petersburg (1779) and Moscow (1782); and he wrote many panegyrics and odes in Russian and translated literature from Latin (especially Virgil), Polish, German, and French.

Ruban, Vasyl, b 1942 in Lisnyky, Kiev-Sviatoshyne raion, Kiev oblast. Writer and dissident. Ruban was arrested in 1972 while a third-year student at Kiev University. He was accused of disseminating anti-Soviet propaganda and then of 'betrayal of the fatherland' and was sentenced to 15 years' imprisonment and 5 years' internal exile. He spent six years in the Dnipropetrovske psychiatric hospital-prison before he was released and rehabilitated in 1978. Ruban published only sporadic poems before his arrest. He had prepared a novel and some short stories, which were not published. After his release he published a collection of poetry, *Khymera* (Chimera, 1988).

Rubashkin, Vladimir [Rubaškin], b 1876 in Novocherkassk, d 1932. He taught at Tartu and Kharkiv (1912–18) universities and was a professor at the Kharkiv Medical Institute (from 1922), director of the Kharkiv Institute of Protozoology (from 1923), and assistant director of the All-Ukrainian Institute of Biology, Morphology, and Experimental Medicine. He studied blood types, founded the journal *Ukraïns'kyi visnyk krov'ianykh uhrupuvan'* (1927–34), and published a histology textbook.

Rubashov, Mykhailo [Rubašov, Myxajlo], b 30 October 1912 in Chudniv, Zhytomyr county, Volhynia gubernia, d 5 January 1974 in Kiev. Writer and literary critic. He graduated from the Kiev Pedagogical Institute (1940) and after the Second World War worked for newspapers and literary journals in Kiev. He began publishing in 1940. He wrote the story collections *Sribna pidkivka* (The Little Silver Horseshoe, 1958), *Iskryste stremeno* (The Glittering Stirrup, 1961), and *Kam'iane svichado* (The Stone Mirror, 1961); the short novels *Bahriani tini* (Crimson Shadows, 1962, about T. Shevchenko as a young artist), *Plachut' berezy* (The Birches Are Crying, 1963), *Zhaha* (Thirst, 1968), and *Kopyshchans'ka trahediia* (The Kopyshche Tragedy, 1970); and several plays. Editions of his selected prose appeared in 1972 and 1982.

Bohdan Rubchak

Ivan Rubchak

Rubchak, Bohdan [Rubčak], b 6 March 1935 in Kalush, Galicia. Poet and literary scholar. In 1948, after being displaced by the Second World War, Rubchak settled in the United States. He studied comparative literature at Rutgers University in New Jersey (PH D, 1977) and since 1974 has been a professor at the University of Illinois, Chicago Circle. A member of the *New York Group, Rubchak published five collections of poetry – *Kaminnyi sad* (Stone Orchard, 1956), *Promenysta zrada* (Bright Betrayal, 1960), *Divchyni bez kraïny* (For a Girl without a Country, 1963), *Osobysta Klio* (Personal Clio, 1967), and *Marenu topyty* (To Drown Marena, 1980) – and a volume of collected works, *Krylo Ikarove* (The Wing of Icarus, 1983). Rubchak's lyrical poetry is introspective and marked by classical restraint and an intellectual atmosphere enhanced by his literary erudition. His short stories are gifted but too sporadic, and his prose consists mainly of literary criticism. Numerous essays in both English and Ukrainian have appeared in various journals and reveal that he is a knowledgeable, incisive, and eloquent critic of Ukrainian poetry, individual poets (B. Nyzhankivsky, B. Kravtsiv, V. Barka, G. Tarnawsky, P. Kylyna, V. Vovk), modernism, and émigré Ukrainian literature. Of special note are his comprehensive introduction to Ukrainian modernism in *Ostap Luts'kyi – molodomuzets'* (Ostap Lutsky, Member of the Moloda Muza, 1968), his annotations of and introduction to M. Kotsiubynsky in the translation of *Shadows of Forgotten Ancestors* (1981), and his notes to *Bohdan Ihor Antonych – Zibrani tvory* (Bohdan Ihor Antonych: Collected Works, 1967). Together with B. Boychuk he edited and wrote biographical-critical vignettes for the important two-volume anthology of contemporary Ukrainian poetry in the West, *Koordynaty* (Co ordinates, 1969).

D.H. Struk

Rubchak, Ivan [Rubčak], b 7 March 1874 in Kalush, Galicia, d 11 May 1952 in Lviv. Actor and singer (bass); husband of K. *Rubchak. He worked in the Ruska Besida Theater (1894–1914), Ternopilski Teatralni Vechory (1916), the Theater of the Legion of Ukrainian Sich Rifle-

men (1916–18), the New Lviv Theater (1921–3), V. Kossak's troupe (1920), the Ukrainska Besida Theater (1921–3), the Ruthenian Theater of the Prosvita Society (1924–6), Y. Stadnyk's touring troupe (1927–8), the Tobilevych Theater (1928–38, with interruptions), the Kotliarevsky Theater (1938–9), the Lesia Ukrainka Theater (1939–41), the Lviv Opera Theater (1941–4), and the Lviv Ukrainian Drama Theater (1944–52). During his stage career he played and sang over 500 character, comic, opera, and operetta roles, including Karas in S. Hulak-Artemovsky's *Zaporozhets' za dunaiem* (Zaporozhian Cossack beyond the Danube) and the title role in J. Strauss's *Der Zigeunerbaron*.

Kateryna Rubchak

Rubchak, Kateryna [Rubčak] (née Kossak), b 29 April 1881 in Chortkiv, Galicia, d 22 November 1919 in Zinkivtsi, near Kamianets-Podilskyi. Actress and singer (soprano); wife of I. *Rubchak. Most of her brilliant theatrical and operatic career (1896–1914) was spent in the Ruthenian People's Theater (see *Ukrainska Besida Theater). Her extensive and varied repertoire included Ukrainian and Western European dramatic roles, many of which she premiered for the Galician and Bukovynian public. She performed with L. *Kurbas and V. Yurchak in I. Franko's *Ukradene shchastia* (Stolen Happiness) to great critical acclaim. Her best theatrical roles were in T. Shevchenko's *Nazar Stodolia*, M. Starytsky's *Tsyhanka Aza* (The Gypsy Aza), *Oi ne khody, Hrytsiu ...* (Don't Go to the Party, Hryts ...), *Marusia Bohuslavka*, I. Karpenko-Kary's *Khaziaïn* (The Master), V. Vynnychenko's *Chorna pantera i bilyi vedmid'* (The Black Panther and White Bear), H. Ibsen's *Ghosts*, E. Rostand's *Les Romanesques*, A. Schnitzler's *Liebelei*, and J. Gordin's *Mirele Efros*. Her best operatic roles were in S. Hulak-Artemovsky's *Zaporozhian Cossack beyond the Danube*, M. Arkas's *Kateryna*, Ya. Lopatynsky's *Enei na mandrivtsi* (Aeneas on the Journey), C. Gounod's *Faust*, J. Offenbach's *Tales of Hoffman*, G. Puccini's *Madame Butterfly*, and S. Moniuszko's *Halka*. She also sang in operettas composed by J. Strauss, A. Sullivan, and F. Lehár. In 1916–18 she headed the Theater of the Legion of Ukrainian Sich Riflemen, and in 1919, the Chernivtsi Ukrainian Theater and the Theater of the Western Ukrainian National Republic. In 1981 UNESCO marked the centenary of her birth. A biography by P. Medvedyk was published in Kiev (1989).

V. Revutsky

Rubchak, Olha [Rubčak, Ol'ha], b 10 May 1903 in Chernivtsi, d 21 November 1981 in Kiev. Actress; daughter of I. and K. *Rubchak and wife of H. *Yura. She studied drama in Kiev (1917–18) and then worked in the New Lviv Theater (1919–20) and the Franko New Drama Theater in Kharkiv (1920–6; later the Kiev Ukrainian Drama Theater, 1926–60).

Rubenchyk, Lev [Rubenčyk], b 3 April 1896 in Odessa, d 1989. Microbiologist; corresponding member of the AN URSR (now ANU) from 1939. He graduated from the Odessa Institute of People's Education (1922) and worked there (until 1927) and at the Odessa Institute of Seed and Flour Technology (1927–31), the Ukrainian Institute of Balneology (1929–41), Odessa University (1933–41), the ANU Institute of Microbiology and Virology (from 1944), and Kiev University (1946–56). He described the role of microorganisms in the geochemical processes of saltwater environments and in the corrosion of metals and cement.

Oleksander Rubets

Rubets, Oleksander [Rubets'], b 13 October 1838 in Chuhuiv, Kharkiv gubernia, d 11 May 1913 in Starodub, Chernihiv gubernia. Musicologist, ethnographer, teacher, composer, and conductor. He studied music theory and composition with M. Zaremba at the St Petersburg Conservatory, from which he graduated in 1866, and where he later taught theory and choral singing until 1895. In 1896 Rubets lost his sight and settled in Starodub. He authored several textbooks on music theory and compiled a biographical dictionary of musicians. An enthusiastic folk song collector, he published several collections of Ukrainian folk songs (1870, 1872, and 1876). These were used as sources for musical themes by P. Tchaikovsky (*Symphony no. 2, Piano Concerto no. 1*, and the opera *Mazeppa*), N. Rimsky-Korsakov, and other composers. Rubets's musical works include an orchestral overture, several choral pieces (including a 'Hymn to Gogol'), approx 10 solo songs (such as 'Dumy moï,' the first musical arrangement of T. Shevchenko's text), and works for piano and violin. His students included A. Arensky, S. Rachmaninoff, A. Glazunov, Y. Myklashevsky, and P. Senytsia.

Rubinger, Lev, b 21 February 1890 in Horodok, Galicia, d 24 September 1983 in Rochester, New York. Military and civic activist; member of the Shevchenko Scientific Society. He served as a captain in the Ukrainian Galician Army (UHA) during the struggle for Ukrainian independence and then as a member of the Revolutionary Tribunal of the Field Staff of the Red UHA. After the First World War he remained in Soviet Ukraine, where he graduated from and then taught at the Kiev Commercial Institute. In 1926 he returned to Galicia. He practiced law in Kolomyia (to 1939), served as a prosecutor in Chortkiv (1941–3), and was elected mayor of Kolomyia (1943–4). At the end of the Second World War he fled to the West and emigrated to the United States. Rubinger wrote articles on economic, political, and military affairs for the Ukrainian press.

Rubinowicz, Wojciech, b 22 February 1889 in Sadhora (now a suburb of Chernivtsi), Bukovyna, d 13 October 1974 in Warsaw. Theoretical physicist. Rubinowicz received his doctorate from Chernivtsi University in 1914 and taught at Chernivtsi University (1918) and at the University of Ljubljana (1920–2). In 1922 he became a professor at the Lviv Polytechnical Institute, and in 1937 at Lviv University. After the Second World War he was a professor at Warsaw University (1946–60). Rubinowicz contributed substantially to the development of the quantum theory of radiation, in particular by discovering, in 1918, the selection and polarization rules for electric dipole radiation. In Lviv he gave rise to what became known as the Rubinowicz school of quantum physics.

Rubizhne [Rubižne]. IV-19, DB I-4. A city (1990 pop 75,000) in Luhanske oblast. It originated as the town of Russko-Kraska, which sprang up around the aniline dye factory built near the railway station Rubizhne in 1915. The town was renamed in 1930 and was granted city status in 1934. In addition to the Krasytel Manufacturing Consortium the city has a reinforced-concrete products plant, a metalworking plant, a baking complex, and a hosiery factory.

Rubizhne Krasytel Manufacturing Consortium (Rubizhanske vyrobnyche obiednannia Krasytel). The largest aniline dye and paint enterprise in Ukraine. Located in Rubizhne, Luhanske oblast, the consortium was established in 1974 on the basis of a chemical factory founded in 1915. It makes over 250 products, including almost all the indigo dyes produced in the former USSR from either artificial or synthetic raw materials. In the 1970s the enterprise employed over 7,000 workers.

Ruble (Russian: *rubl*; Ukrainian: *karbovanets*). The main unit of currency in the Russian Empire and then in the USSR. It was known in Muscovy from the beginning of the 14th century as a unit of both payment and weight. In Novgorod it denoted one-half of a *hryvnia*. From 1534 one ruble was worth 100 Novgorod *dengi* or 200 Muscovite *dengi*; the *dengi* were also called *kopeini dengi*, from which comes the word *kopeck*. Rubles' silver content declined steadily in the early 17th century from 68 to 48 g. Rubles began to circulate in Ukraine in the beginning of the 18th century. They began to be issued regularly in 1704 and had a silver content of 28 g, which made them equivalent to a Western European taler. The value of the ruble declined in the 18th century, and by 1764 it contained only 18 g of silver. It remained at that level until 1915, when the minting of full-value rubles from silver ceased. Gold and copper rubles were minted only briefly in the 18th century. The paper ruble came into circulation in 1841; earlier it had been used only for accounting purposes. In 1897 Russia adopted the gold standard, and the ruble was converted to a gold base. At the end of the First World War only debased paper rubles were in circulation.

The first Soviet rubles were issued in 1919 in the form of a state bank note. Silver rubles were minted in the RSFSR in 1921. In 1922 the *chervonets*, equal to 10 rubles, was introduced. In 1924, 1-, 3-, and 5-ruble notes were put into circulation, and silver rubles containing 18 g of silver were minted. In 1937 the value of the ruble was established as 0.19 of the US dollar, which contained 0.888671 g of gold. That figure was used strictly for accounting purposes and calculating import and export costs. In the major reform of 1961 the ruble was dissociated from the US dollar, and its official gold content was increased to 0.987412 g of gold.

Until 1992 rubles were printed by the USSR State Bank and State Treasury in Moscow and Leningrad in denominations of 100, 50, 25, 10, 5, 3, and 2; a 1-ruble copper-nickel coin was also minted. The notes had the Ukrainian *karbovanets'* printed on them. Since personal checks and credit cards were not used, a large number of bills were printed. The branch of the State Bank in Kiev received a supply of new bills every month and put them into circulation only on the orders of the central authorities in Moscow.

Because the ruble was a controlled currency and was not exchanged freely on the world market, its true value relative to that of other currencies was difficult to establish. The official exchange rate for trading purposes was set monthly by the State Bank. One ruble was valued at 1.11 US dollars in 1961 and 1.33 in 1973. Rubles that were traded internally on the black market or exported illegally were always worth much less. In an effort to curb black market trading in currency, in 1989 the Soviet government introduced a new exchange rate of six rubles to the dollar. The rate applied only to rubles exchanged by tourists and other visitors to the USSR and by Soviet citizens for travel abroad. All other transactions continued to be calculated on the even more unrealistic rate (in 1989 1 ruble = 2.20 US dollars). That policy meant that, in general, exports from the USSR were overvalued, and imports were undervalued; obtaining credits from abroad was much more advantageous than granting credits; and tourism and personal shipment of goods from abroad were relatively advantageous for the Soviet economy. According to many economists the inconvertibility of the ruble placed great constraints on the development of Soviet trade and the entire economy. It made it especially difficult for Western firms and individuals to make investments in Ukraine, and distorted economic performance.

B. Balan

Ruchkivsky, Serhii [Ručkivs'kyj, Serhij], b 19 January 1888 in Tarashcha, Kiev gubernia, d ? Epidemiologist; corresponding member of the USSR Academy of Medical Sciences from 1946. A graduate of Kiev University (1914), he taught at the Kiev Institute for the Upgrading of Physicians (1929–58), headed departments of the Kiev Bacteriological Institute (1929–39) and the Kiev Medical Institute (1948–58), and worked at the Kiev Scientific Research Institute of Epidemiology, Microbiology, and Parasitology. His publications deal with typhus, bacterial dysentery, botulism, and the diagnosis of infectious diseases.

Ruchko, Hnat [Ručko], b 20 January 1883 in Velyki Sorochyntsi, Myrhorod county, Poltava gubernia, d 1946. Microbiologist; corresponding member of the AN URSR (now ANU) from 1934. A graduate of the Kharkiv Medical Institute (1925), he worked at the Kharkiv Sanitation and Bacteriology Research Institute (1925–9) and the Berlin Institute of Hygiene and Immunology (1930–2) and then headed a department of the ANU Institute of Microbiology and Epidemiology (1932–7). His major research interests involved bacteriophagy and the mutability of viruses, particularly in relation to dysentery. He organized the first Soviet scientific conference in this area (1936) and initiated *Mikrobiolohichnyi zhurnal* in 1934. Ruchko was repressed in 1938 during the Yezhov terror.

Rud, Mykola [Rud'], b 9 May 1912 in Oleksandrivka, Kostiantynohrad county, Poltava gubernia. Prose writer, poet, and publicist. After graduating from the Gorky Institute of Literature (Moscow) he wrote for the Donetske press and for the periodical *Ukraïna*. He has published anthologies of poetry, such as *Naiblyzhche* (The Closest, 1936), *Slovo pislia boiu* (A Word after the Battle, 1947), and *Hrim na zelene hillia* (Thunder on the Green Boughs, 1960); books of novelettes and short stories, such as *Na Podilli* (In Podilia, 1955), *Chas klopotu i spodivan'* (A Time of Troubles and Hopes, 1956), and *Dyven'* (Wedding Bread, 1973); and the novels *I ne skazala 'liubliu'* (And She Didn't Say 'I Love,' 1964), *Z matir'iu na samoti* (Alone with Mother, 1967), and *Ne zhdy, ne klych* (Don't Wait [For Me], Don't Call, 1978).

Rudakov, Elisei, b 27 April 1929 in Tomsk, Russia. Chemist; AN URSR (now ANU) corresponding member since 1972. After graduating from the Moscow Institute of Fine Chemical Technology (1952) he worked at the Leningrad Institute of Petrochemical Processes (to 1959) and thereafter at the Novosibirsk institutes of Organic Chemistry and Catalysis and at Novosibirsk University. Since 1972 he has been a department head at the ANU Institute of Physical-Organic Chemistry and Coal Chemistry in Donetske. Rudakov developed a method to determine the thermodynamic functions of molecular interactions and a transition-state theory for heterolytic reactions. He also studied the activation of alkyl halides and alkanes by transition-metal complexes, and discovered the oxidative dehydrogenation of alkanes by means of palladium.

Rudansky, Stepan [Rudans'kyj], b 6 January 1834 in Khomutyntsi, Vinnytsia county, Podilia gubernia, d 3 May 1873 in Yalta. Poet. He studied at the St Petersburg Academy of Medicine and Surgery, and after graduation (1861) he worked for the rest of his life as a doctor in Yalta. Rudansky began to write poetry in his pre–St Petersburg days, while still a student at the Kamianets-Podilskyi Theological Seminary, and that poetry shows the influence of T. Shevchenko's work and of folklore. He began to publish his work in 1859 in St Petersburg, where he became friendly with a group of Ukrainian writers working on the journal *Osnova*. Having begun in the genre of the Romantic ballad, Rudansky then turned to poetry on social issues, using that of Shevchenko as a model. That later poetry featured a condemnation of serfdom, a rallying call to work in the field of Ukrainian culture, and a reliving of the glorious history of the Ukrainian people. Rudansky

Stepan Rudansky (portrait by V. Kovalov)   Ivan Rudchenko

Bela Rudenko   Larysa Rudenko

achieved long-lasting fame as author of *Spivomovky* (Singing Rhymes, 1880), which consisted of poems of various length, jokes, proverbs, and short anecdotes about landlords, clerics, Gypsies, Muscovites, Poles, Jews, Germans, devils, Cossacks, peasants, and so forth, derived mainly from folk literature and written in a jaunty tone with pointed humor and many witticisms. Apart from those light-hearted *spivomovky*, Rudansky wrote lyric poetry filled with an aching sadness, which reflected not only the poet's personal life but also the sufferings of all his people. Some of those poems are autobiographical, and some became popular songs (such as 'Povii vitre, na Vkraïnu' [Blow, Wind, on Ukraine]). Rudansky's works also include translations, such as of *Slovo o polku Ihorevi* (The Tale of Ihor's Campaign), of excerpts from the Králové Dvůr Manuscript, of Homer's *Iliad*, of Virgil's *Aeneid*, of a part of M. Lermontov's *Demon*, and of individual poems by H. Heine, T. Lenartowicz, and B. Radičević. Most of his significant works were published only posthumously. Rudansky's style straddles on the Romantic and the realist. His imagery and the poetics of his ballads and lyric poems are clearly of folkloric derivation. Editions of Rudansky's works have appeared in 1895–1903 (7 vols) and 1972–3 (3 vols).

I. Koshelivets

Rudchenko, Ivan [Rudčenko] (pseuds: Ivan Kyvaiholova, Ivan Ruina, I. Yakovenko, I. Bilyk), b 2 September 1845 in Myrhorod, Poltava gubernia, d 1 June 1905 in Kiev. Folklorist, literary critic, writer, and publicist; brother of P. *Myrny. His first articles and folklore materials appeared in *Osnova* in 1862. Beginning in 1867 the Lviv journal *Pravda* published many of his poems, critical articles, reviews, and translations from Russian, German, English, and Polish. His chief contributions to folklore studies were *Narodnye iuzhno-russkie skazki* (South Russian Folktales, 2 vols, 1869–70) and *Chumatskie narodnye pesni* (Folk Songs of the Chumaks, 1874). The Ems Ukase prevented him from publishing other works on folklore. With Myrny he cowrote the famous novel *Khiba revut' voly iak iasla povni?* (Do Oxen Low When Mangers Are Full?, 1880). He left a great number of manuscripts, including 1,000 folktales, which are preserved in the library of the Academy of Sciences in St Petersburg.

Rudchenko, Panas. See Myrny, Panas.

Rudenko, Bela, b 18 August 1933 in Bokovo-Antratsyt (now in Luhanske oblast). Opera singer (lyric soprano). A graduate of the Odessa Conservatory (1956), she studied singing under O. Blahovydova. She was a soloist with the Odessa Opera (1955–6), the Kiev Opera (1956–73), and, from 1973, the Bolshoi Theater in Moscow. In 1957 she won the gold medal at the Toulouse International Vocal Competition. Her operatic roles included Liudmila in M. Glinka's *Ruslan and Liudmila*, Marfa in N. Rimsky-Korsakov's *Tsar's Bride*, Yaryna in H. Maiboroda's *Maryna* and the Serf-girl in his *Arsenal*, Gilda in G. Verdi's *Rigoletto* and Violetta in his *La Traviata*, Rosina in G. Rossini's *Barber of Seville*, the Queen of the Night in W. Mozart's *Magic Flute*, and Venus in M. Lysenko's *Aeneas*. She toured abroad and from 1977 taught singing at the Moscow Conservatory. Biographies of Rudenko have been written by V. Tymofieiev and T. Shvachko (1982).

Rudenko, Larysa, b 28 January 1918 in Makiivka (now in Donetske oblast), d 19 January 1981 in Kiev. Opera singer (mezzo-soprano). A graduate of the Kiev Conservatory (1940), she studied under O. Muraviova, and then was a soloist in the Kiev Theater of Opera and Ballet (1939–70). Her nearly 50 operatic roles spanned the works of M. Lysenko, K. Dankevych, H. Maiboroda, P. Tchaikovsky, G. Bizet, and G. Verdi. She concertized abroad and from 1951 taught singing at the Kiev Conservatory. Her biography, by L. Hrysenko, was published in Kiev (1978).

Rudenko, Liudmyla, b 27 July 1904 in Lubni, Poltava gubernia. Champion swimmer and chess player. She won the 1920 Odessa championship in the women's 400-m breaststroke and won the silver medal in that event in the 1925 Ukrainian championship, and was the women's chess champion of Moscow (1928), Leningrad (1932, 1936, 1947, 1962), Uzbekistan (1955), and Ukraine (1956) and the first world women's chess champion (1950–3). In 1976 she became an international grand master.

Rudenko, Mykola, b 19 December 1920 in Yurivka, now in Lutuhyne raion, Luhanske oblast. Writer and dissident. A former managing editor of the Writers' Union of Ukraine's (SPU) journal *Dnipro* (1947–50) and secretary of the CPU organization in the SPU, beginning in 1947 he published over 10 collections of indifferent poetry and a few books of socialist-realist prose and *science fiction. Rudenko became involved in the Soviet human rights

Raisa and Mykola Rudenko

movement in the early 1970s and was consequently expelled from the CPU in 1974 and the SPU in 1975. In November 1976 he became head of the newly formed *Ukrainian Helsinki Group. He was arrested for 'anti-Soviet agitation and propaganda' in February 1977, and in July of that year he was sentenced at a closed trial to seven years in labor camps in central Russia's Perm oblast and the Mordovian ASSR, followed by five years' exile in the Altai region in Soviet Central Asia. During his incarceration, 10 of his works were smuggled to the West and published there. They include the narrative poem *Khrest* (1977; trans: *The Cross*, 1987); the poetry collection *Za gratamy* (Behind Bars, 1980); a volume of physiocratic, pantheistic philosophy, *Ekonomichni monolohy* (Economic Monologues, 1978); the play *Na dni mors'komu* (On the Sea Floor, 1981); and a novel about life in Ukraine, *Orlova balka* (The Eagle's Ravine, 1982). In December 1987 Rudenko and his wife, R. *Rudenko, were allowed to emigrate to the West. They lived in the United States until 1990, when they returned to Ukraine.

Rudenko, Raisa [Rajisa], b 1939. Dissident and political prisoner; wife of M. *Rudenko. She was arrested for disseminating Ukrainian dissident documents in April 1981, and sentenced in September to five years in a labor camp for women in the Mordovian ASSR and five years' exile in the Altai region. In 1987 she was allowed to emigrate to the West with her husband, and in 1990 she returned with him to Ukraine.

Rudenko, Roman, b 18 July 1907 in Nosivka, Nizhen county, Chernihiv gubernia, d 23 January 1981 in Moscow. Soviet jurist. He studied law at Kiev University. From 1929 he worked in the Soviet legal system, in which he advanced from the position of investigator to those of procurator of Staline (now Donetske) oblast (1938–40), deputy procurator (1942–4) and procurator (1944–53) of the Ukrainian SSR, chief Soviet prosecutor at the Nuremberg Trials (1945–6), and USSR general procurator (1953–81). He was also a candidate member (1956–9) and full member (1961–81) of the CC CPSU. In 1953 he supervised the mass execution of striking political prisoners at the Vorkuta labor camps.

Rudky. IV-4. A city (1989 pop 5,000) in Sambir raion, Lviv oblast. It was first mentioned in historical documents in 1472. Archeological evidence shows that the site was inhabited in the Bronze Age. The town was granted *Magdeburg law in the first half of the 18th century, when it was part of the Polish Commonwealth. After the partition of Poland in 1772, Rudky came under Austrian rule. In the interwar period it was under Polish rule and then part of the Ukrainian SSR. Standing on the Lviv–Sambir railway line, Rudky is an industrial and transportation center. Its factories manufacture bricks, cheese, and baked goods.

Rudky natural gas field. A gas field discovered in the western part of Lviv oblast in 1953. Two separate deposits have been found, one in a fissure of limestone at a depth of 1,200–1,450 m, and the other in a stratum of sand at a depth of 800–900 m. The gas is 96–99 percent methane. It is used for heating in Lviv, and some is exported.

Rudlovchak, Olena [Rudlovčak], b 1 February 1918 in Mukachiv, Transcarpathia. Literary scholar. She received her docent's diploma at Prague University (1967). She worked as a teacher, an editor, and a playwright and stage director of the Czechoslovak Radio's Ukrainian studio before becoming a scholarly associate (1960) and the head of research (1967) in the Šafařík University department of Ukrainian language and literature in Prešov. Rudlovchak has written articles (in *Duklia*, *Naukovyi zbirnyk* of the Svydnyk Museum of Ukrainian Culture, and other periodicals and collections) on the history of Ukrainian (especially Transcarpathian) literature, ethnography, journalism, and theater. She wrote a book-length introduction to the 1968 Prešov edition of O. Dukhnovych's works, and has edited anthologies of Ukrainian folk poetry from the Prešov region (1965) and Transcarpathian poetry to 1945 (1965, with V. Mykytas), a collection of articles on the past and present of Ukrainians in Czechoslovakia (1973, with M. Hyriak), and two anthologies of 19th-century Transcarpathian literature (1964, with Yu. Bacha; 1976). An edition of her selected literary studies, *Bilia dzherel suchasnosti* (At the Sources of the Present), was published in 1981.

Rudne. IV-4. A town smt (1986 pop 7,000) on the western outskirts of Lviv, under the administration of the Zaliznychnyi raion council. The settlement of Rudne is first mentioned in historical records in the 14th century. Today most of its residents work in Lviv.

Rudnyckyj, Jaroslav [Rudnyc'kyj], b 28 November 1910 in Peremyshl, Galicia. Slavist, linguist, and civic figure; husband of Maryna Rudnytska; member of the Shevchenko Scientific Society since 1947. After studying at Lviv University (MA, 1934; PH D, 1937) he became a research associate of the Ukrainian Scientific Institute in Berlin (1938–40), docent (1940–3) and professor (1943–80) at the Ukrainian Free University in Prague and Munich, lecturer at Prague (1941–5) and Heidelberg (1947–8) universities, and professor and first head of the department of Slavic studies at the University of Manitoba (1949–77). As a member of the Canadian Royal Commission on Bilingualism and Biculturalism (1963–71) he made an important contribution to Canada's policy of multiculturalism. He has served as president of the Ukrainian Free

Jaroslav Rudnyckyj

Milena Rudnytska

Academy of Sciences in Canada (1955–70), the Canadian Linguistic Association (1958–60), the Canadian Association of Slavists (1959), the American Name Society (1959), the Canadian Institute of Onomastic Sciences, the Canadian Comparative Literature Association, the Canadian Society for the Comparative Study of Civilizations, the Ukrainian Language Association (in Canada), and the Ukrainian Mohylo-Mazepian Academy of Arts and Sciences. He was also founding editor of *Slavistica* (1948), *Onomastica* (1951), *Ukrainica Canadiana* (1953–73), *Ukrainica Occidentalia* (1956–66), and *Slovo na storozhi* (1964–89). He was appointed member of the UNR government-in-exile in 1978, and he served as its head in 1980–9. His numerous articles and reviews on Ukrainian language, dialects, linguistics, onomastics, folklore, and literature have appeared in Ukrainian émigré and Western periodicals, and over 50 of his works have been separately published, including *Ukraïns'ka mova ta ïï hovory* (The Ukrainian Language and Its Dialects, 1937; 4th rev edn 1977), *Lehrbuch der ukrainischen Sprache* (1940; 4th edn 1964), *Lemberger ukrainische Stadtmundart* (1943), *The Term and Name 'Ukraine'* (1951), *Canadian Place Names of Ukrainian Origin* (1952), *An Etymological Dictionary of the Ukrainian Language* (2 vols [22 fascicles], 1962–82), *Geographical Names of Boikovia* (1939; repr 1962), and *Manitoba Mosaic of Place Names* (1970). He is the coauthor of *Ukrainische Mundarten: Südkarpatoukrainisch (Lemkisch, Bojkisch, Huzulisch)* (1940), *Ukrainisch-deutsches Wörterbuch* (1943), and *A Modern Ukrainian Grammar* (1949; 7th printing 1978). His papers are preserved at the National Archives of Canada in Ottawa. The most recent bibliography of his works was published in 1984.

R. Senkus

Rudnytska, Maryna [Rudnyc'ka] (née Antonovych), b 23 December 1911 in Kiev. Cultural activist; daughter of D. and K. *Antonovych and wife of J. *Rudnyckyj. She studied at Berlin (1929–31) and Prague (1931–6) universities and completed a doctorate at the Ukrainian Free University in Prague (1940). After emigrating to Canada in 1949, she taught art at St Andrew's College (1950–2, 1973–4) and Russian language and literature at the University of Manitoba (1957–8, 1963–5). For many years she worked in the Plast Ukrainian Youth Association. She has contributed articles on art and literature to the Ukrainian press,

compiled a bibliography of books on I. Franko in Canadian and American libraries (1957) and an anthology of Russian poetry (1968), and written a study on O. Stefanovych (1970).

Rudnytska, Milena [Rudnyc'ka], b 15 July 1892 in Zboriv, Galicia, d 29 March 1976 in Munich. Journalist, politician, and civic activist; wife of P. *Lysiak and mother of I.L. *Rudnytsky. After graduating from Lviv University she taught secondary school and later lectured at the Higher Pedagogical Courses in Lviv (1921–8). In the interwar period she became one of the leading activists of the *women's movement in Western Ukraine: in the 1920s she was an executive member and then president (1929–38) of the *Union of Ukrainian Women; she was one of the organizers of the First Ukrainian Women's Congress in Stanyslaviv (1934); in 1937 she was elected president of the *World Union of Ukrainian Women; and in 1938 she headed the *Druzhyna Kniahyni Olhy. She also edited the women's semimonthly *Zhinka* (1935–9) and represented Ukrainian organizations at international women's conferences. A founder and executive member of the *Ukrainian National Democratic Alliance (UNDO), she was elected to the Polish Sejm in 1928 and 1930. She was a member of the Sejm's educational and foreign affairs committees. As a member of the Ukrainian Parliamentary Representation she presented petitions from the Ukrainian people to the League of Nations, particularly on the issues of the Polish Pacification of Western Ukraine and the man-made famine in Soviet Ukraine. After emigrating in 1939, she lived in Cracow, Berlin, Prague, Geneva (where she directed the Ukrainian Relief Committee in 1945–50), New York, Rome, and Munich. Besides contributing articles on educational and women's issues to the Ukrainian press from 1919, she wrote the books *Ukraïns'ka diisnist' i zavdannia zhinochoho rukhu* (The Ukrainian Reality and the Tasks of the Women's Movement, 1934), *Don Bosko: Liudyna, pedahoh, sviatyi* (Don Bosco: Man, Pedagogue, and Saint, 1963), and *Nevydymi styhmaty* (The Invisible Stigmata, 1971).

Rudnytska, Nonna [Rudnyc'ka] (married name: Hurska), b 22 June 1934 in Vinnytsia. Actress. She completed study at the Kiev Institute of Theater Arts (1956) and then worked in the Kherson (1957–65), Chernihiv (1966–70), and Rivne (from 1971) Ukrainian Music and Drama theaters.

Rudnytsky, Antin [Rudnyc'kyj], b 7 February 1902 in Luka, Sambir county, Galicia, d 30 November 1975 in Tom's River, New Jersey. Composer, conductor, pianist, teacher, and musicologist; member of the Shevchenko Scientific Society (from 1962). He studied at the Lysenko Higher Institute of Music in Lviv, the Higher Musical School in Berlin, and Berlin University, with such teachers as E. Petri, A. Schnabel, and F. Schrecker. He subsequently conducted at opera theaters in Kharkiv (1927–30), Kiev (1930–2), Lviv, Warsaw, and Kaunas. He emigrated to the United States in 1939, where he worked as a music teacher in various institutions (including the Philadelphia Music Academy) and as a choir conductor. He was a leading organizer of Ukrainian-American musical activities and wrote the historical survey *Ukraïns'ka muzyka: Istorychno-krytychnyi ohliad* (Ukrainian Music: A Historical Critical Survey, 1963) as well as a collection of articles published

Antin Rudnytsky

Ivan Lysiak Rudnytsky

Ivan Teodor Rudnytsky

Mykhailo Rudnytsky

posthumously, *Pro muzyku i muzyk* (On Music and Musicians, 1980). His musical works were initially modernistic but gradually became more impressionistic and romantic. They include the operas *Dovbush* (1938) and *Anna Yaroslavna* (1967), three symphonies, a ballet suite and the ballet *Burï nad Zakhodom* (Storms over the West, 1932), a lyric poem, an overture, a concerto for cello and orchestra, the oratorio *Haidamaky* (1974), the cantata *Moses* (to I. Franko's poem), *Poslaniie* (The Epistle, to T. Shevchenko's poem), and works for chamber orchestra, piano, and choir, as well as approx 50 songs for voice and piano.

W. Wytwycky

Rudnytsky, Ivan. See Kedryn, Ivan.

Rudnytsky, Ivan Lysiak [Lysjak Rudnyc'kyj], b 27 October 1919 in Vienna, d 25 April 1984 in Edmonton. Historian and pedagogue; son of P. *Lysiak and M. *Rudnytska. He was educated at the University of Lviv (1937–9), the University of Berlin (1942), Charles University in Prague (PH D, 1945), the Graduate Institute of International Studies in Geneva (1951), and Columbia University (1951–3). Rudnytsky taught at La Salle College in Philadelphia (1956–67), the American University in Washington, DC (1967–71), and the University of Alberta (1971–84). He helped found the *Canadian Institute of Ukrainian Studies at the University of Alberta and was its associate director (1976–80). Rudnytsky was a prolific essayist; he published the collection *Mizh istoriieiu i politykoiu* (Between History and Politics, 1973) and edited *Drahomanov: A Symposium and Selected Writings* (1952), *Lysty Osypa Nazaruka do Viacheslava Lypyns'koho* (Letters of Osyp Nazaruk to Viacheslav Lypynsky, 1976), and *Rethinking Ukrainian History* (1981). He also contributed articles on history to *Entsyklopediia ukraïnoznavstva* and *Encyclopedia of Ukraine*. A posthumous edition of his *Essays in Modern Ukrainian History* appeared in 1987.

Rudnytsky, Ivan Teodor [Rudnyc'kyj], b 20 November 1886 in Bedrykivtsi, Zalishchyky county, Galicia, d 3 March 1951 in Hoester an der Weser, West Germany. Military officer. A graduate in law of Lviv University, during the First World War he served in the Austrian army as commander of a machine-gun company on the Italian front. He was one of the key members of the Ukrainian Military Committee, which organized the *November 1918 uprising in Lviv. In the Ukrainian Galician Army (UHA) he was promoted to captain and oversaw the training of machine gunners. Subsequently he served as a UHA

representative in Vienna and a military attaché in Prague and officer of the Ukrainian Military Organization (UVO) in Czechoslovakia. From the end of the 1920s he practiced law in Lviv and belonged to the UVO home leadership. After the Second World War he settled in West Germany.

Rudnytsky, Mykhailo [Rudnyc'kyj, Myxajlo], b 7 January 1889 in Pidhaitsi, Galicia, d 1 February 1975 in Lviv. Literary critic, literary scholar, and teacher; brother of I. Kedryn, M. Rudnytska, and A. Rudnytsky. He concluded his studies at Lviv University (PH D, 1914) and studied Western European literatures in Paris and London (1919–22). He was a professor at the Lviv (Underground) Ukrainian University (1922–5) and contributed to the newspaper *Dilo* and the journal *Nazustrich* (1934). In 1939 he became a professor of foreign literatures, and in 1948, of Ukrainian literature at Lviv University. Rudnytsky was the author of criticism and original literary work, including *Mizh ideieiu i formoiu* (Between Concept and Form, 1932), *Vid Myrnoho do Khvyl'ovoho* (From Myrny to Khvylovy, 1936), a collection of poetic prose titled *Ochi ta usta* (Eyes and Lips, 1922), collections of short stories, and literary portraits. He wrote memoirs, including *Nahody i pryhody* (Opportunities and Adventures, 1929) *Tvorchi budni Ivana Franka* (Ivan Franko's Creative Days, 1956), *Pys'mennyky zblyz'ka* (Writers at Close Range, 3 vols, 1958–64), *Zmarnovanyi siuzhet* (A Wasted Plot, 1961), *Nenapysani novely* (Unwritten Novellas, 1966), and *Neperedbacheni zustrichi* (Unforeseen Meetings, 1969). Together with V. Bieliaiev he wrote several pamphlets directed against 'bourgeois nationalists' titled 'Pid chuzhymy praporamy' (Under Foreign Flags, pub in Russian in 1954, in Ukrainian in 1956, and in Chinese in 1957). He also translated Shakespeare, H. de Balzac, P. Mérimée, and G. Flaubert into Ukrainian, and V. Stefanyk, M. Kotsiubynsky, and M. Yatskiv into French.

I. Koshelivets

Rudnytsky, Roman [Rudnyc'kyj], b 1 November 1942 in New York. Pianist; son of A. *Rudnytsky and M. *Sokil. Studying initially under his father, he graduated from the Philadelphia Conservatory and the Juilliard School of Music in New York. He has performed as a soloist and with symphony orchestras in the United States, Canada, Spain, Switzerland, Germany, Poland, and Ukraine and has taught music at the University of Indiana and Youngstown State University in Ohio. His repertoire includes the works of B. Liatoshynsky, Yu. Fiala, A. Rudnytsky, and other Ukrainian composers.

Stepan Rudnytsky

Leo Rudnytzky

Rudnytsky, Stepan [Rudnyc'kyj], b 15 December 1877 in Ternopil, Galicia, d 3 November 1937 in the Solovets Islands. Geographer; full member of the Shevchenko Scientific Society from 1901 and the VUAN (1929–34). After studying at Lviv (1895–9) and Vienna (1899–1901) universities he taught secondary school in Ternopil (1902–8) and lectured at Lviv University. During the First World War he lived in Vienna, where he was active in the Union for the Liberation of Ukraine and served as a consultant to the Ukrainian Parliamentary Representation and the government-in-exile of the Western Province of the Ukrainian National Republic. After the war he was one of the organizers of and a professor at the *Ukrainian Free University in Vienna and then Prague. In 1926 he was invited to Kharkiv by the government of Soviet Ukraine to organize geographic research. He served as a professor of geography at the Kharkiv Institute of People's Education and as director of the Ukrainian Scientific Research Institute of Geography and Cartography, which he had set up. Then he was the first holder of the chair of geography at the VUAN. In 1933 he was arrested, expelled from the VUAN as an 'outspoken propagator of fascism in geography,' and sent to a prison camp in the Soviet Arctic, where he was eventually executed.

Rudnytsky is a founder of the geography of Ukraine. He wrote comprehensive geographic surveys of Ukraine, such as *Ukraina, Land und Volk* (1916; English trans: *Ukraine: The Land and Its People*, 1918) and *Osnovy zemleznannia Ukraïny* (Foundations of the Earth Science of Ukraine, 2 vols, 1924, 1926), as well as studies of Ukrainian national territories (1923) and Ukrainian political geography (1923). He developed Ukrainian geographical terminology and published the first specialized dictionary (1908) in that field. The first wall maps of Ukraine's physical geography (1918) were prepared by Rudnytsky. His specialized monographs, such as *Osnovy morfolohiï i heolohiï Pidkarpats'koï Rusy* (Foundations of the Morphology and Geology of Subcarpathian Rus', 2 vols, 1925, 1927), dealt mainly with the morphology of Ukraine, particularly the Carpathian region. He wrote approx 70 scholarly works, including several articles on the methodology and history of geography and on 17th-century Cossack history.

V. Kubijovyč

Rudnytsky, Yaroslav. See Rudnyckyj, Jaroslav.

Rudnytsky, Yurii. See Opilsky, Yuliian.

Rudnytsky-Liubienitsky, Sylvestr [Rudnyc'kyj-Ljubjenic'kyj], b and d ? Uniate bishop. He studied at the Basilian school in Volodymyr–Volynskyi, after which he entered the Basilian order and served as hegumen of the Lavriv St Onuphrius's Monastery. He was then consecrated, as the successor to his uncle, T. Rudnytsky-Liubienitsky, as bishop of Lutske-Ostrih (1751–78). During his tenure he sought to increase discipline and educational standards in the eparchy. From 1772 he headed the Basilian chapter in Berestia.

Rudnytsky-Liubienitsky, Teodosii [Rudnyc'kyj-Ljubjenic'kyj, Teodosij], b and d ? Uniate bishop. A hegumen of the monasteries in Lutske, Hoshcha, and Pochaiv (where he funded the Pochaiv Monastery Press), he was consecrated bishop of Lutske-Ostrih in 1731. He was the crown's choice for metropolitan of Kiev in 1747 but was forced to step down in favor of F. *Hrebnytsky. He strove for friendly relations with the Orthodox in Volhynia and in the Kievan metropoly, and in 1738 wrote a book of instructions for the clergy.

Rudnytzky, Leo [Rudnyc'kyj, Leonid], b 8 September 1935 in Lviv. Literary scholar; member of the Shevchenko Scientific Society (NTSh). A postwar émigré, he studied at La Salle College in Philadelphia, the University of Pennsylvania, and the Ukrainian Free University (PH D, 1965) and has taught at the University of Pennsylvania (1958–60) and La Salle College (since 1961). He was elected president of the NTSh in the United States in 1990. He has written a book on I. Franko and German literature (1974), articles on Ukrainian literature in émigré and American scholarly periodicals, and entries for American encyclopedias. He coedited the symposium *The Ukrainian Catholic Church, 1945–1975* (1976) and has also coedited or written introductions to a number of NTSh publications.

Rudovych, Ivan [Rudovyč], b 1868, d 16 August 1929 in Lviv. Ukrainian Catholic priest and pedagogue. From 1897 a religion teacher in primary and secondary schools in Lviv, he was the longtime head of the St Paul the Apostle Society and a founding member of the Ukrainian Theological Scholarly Society. He wrote textbooks and popular works on religious themes and about church history, including *Uniia v Lvovs'koi eparkhii* (The Church Union in Lviv Eparchy, 1900) and *Korotka istoriia Halytsko-L'vovskoi eparkhii* (A Short History of Halych-Lviv Eparchy, 1901).

Rudychiv, Ivan [Rudyčiv], b 28 May 1881 in Kyshenky, Kobeliaky county, Poltava gubernia, d 28 October 1958 in Abondant, France. Lawyer and civic leader. A schoolmate of S. Petliura at the Poltava Theological Seminary, he joined the Revolutionary Ukrainian party in 1903 and was arrested shortly thereafter for political agitation. After graduating from the law faculty of Kazan University in 1912, he worked at the Mining Institute in Katerynoslav and was active in local Ukrainian organizations. During the revolutionary period he took part in the first two all-Ukrainian military congresses and in the overthrow of the Hetman government. After emigrating with the UNR government he lived in Berlin, Prague, and Paris, where he managed the Petliura Ukrainian Library (1926–50). His recollections of Petliura appeared in the collection *Symon Petliura v molodosti* (Symon Petliura in His Youth, 1936).

Rudyk, Dmytro, b 13 June 1893 in Strilche, Horodenka county, Galicia, d 30 May 1955 in Kiev. Literary scholar and critic. After the February Revolution he worked as a teacher in Uman. From 1923 he taught in Kiev and was principal of the first Ukrainian-language school there. He joined Pluh and became a founding member of the *Zakhidnia Ukraina writers' group and worked as an editor for its publishing house. His articles on Ukrainian modernist writers and reviews of literary works and translations were published in *Zhyttia i revoliutsiia, Krytyka, Zakhidnia Ukraïna, Zoria,* and *Svit*. From 1933 to 1953 Rudyk was imprisoned unjustly in concentration camps in the Soviet Arctic.

Rudyk, Paul, b 28 November 1878 in Leshniv, Brody county, Galicia, d 1 July 1936 in Edmonton. Business and community leader. Rudyk emigrated to Canada in 1898 and opened a grocery store in Edmonton in 1902, reputedly the first Ukrainian-owned business in Canada. A developer and contractor, he helped organize the National Co-operative in Vegreville, Alberta, and the General Wholesale Company. He was among the first and largest shareholders in the Trident Publishing Company, a longtime member and secretary of the Hrushevsky Institute in Edmonton (now St John's Institute), a founder of the newspaper *Ukraïns'kyi holos* (Winnipeg), and a supporter of the Presbyterian church.

Metropolitan Stefan Rudyk   Mykhailo Rudynsky

Rudyk, Stefan, b 27 December 1891 in Maidan Lypovetskyi, Peremyshliany county, Galicia, d 26 March 1969. Orthodox metropolitan. After completing theological studies in Zhytomyr and Orel in 1915, he became a village priest. In the interwar period he joined the Polish Autocephalous Orthodox church and served as a chaplain for Polish troops in Toruń, Katowice, and Cracow, until he was interned in Rumania at the outbreak of the Second World War. He was later released, and he went to Germany before being assigned to a parish in Łódź in 1943. He was consecrated bishop of Wrocław-Szczecin in 1953 and then elevated to the office of archbishop of Białystok-Gdansk in 1961. In 1965 he was made metropolitan.

Rudyk, Stepan, b 1890 in Tysmenytsia, Tovmach county, Galicia, d 1939? Political activist, member of the Communist Party of Western Ukraine (KPZU), and journalist. In 1923–31 he edited the Marxist literary and political journal *Kul'tura* in Lviv. For defending the ideas of Shumskyism and Khvylovism (see O. *Shumsky and M. *Khvylovy) he was expelled from the Party in 1927. He mustered opposition to the KPZU in Galicia and worked with the Trotskyite opposition. He was arrested by the Soviets in 1939 and was probably executed.

Rudykovsky, Andrii [Rudykovs'kyj, Andrij], b 13 October 1796 in Vilshanka, Vasylkiv county, Kiev gubernia, d 14 August 1874 in Kiev. Memoirist; brother of O. Rudykovsky. His autobiography, an unembellished, informative account of his life as an orphaned ward of the state at the Kievan Mohyla Academy in its last years, a poor laborer living with a clerical family in rural Ukraine, and a Russian cavalry officer (1815–48) in Ukraine, was published by his grandnephew, V. *Shcherbyna, in *Kievskaia starina* and separately with his brother's poetry in 1892.

Rudykovsky, Ostap [Rudykovs'kyj] (Yevstafii), b 2 October 1784 in Vilshanka, Vasylkiv county, Kiev gubernia, d 1851 in Kiev. Poet and physician. He graduated from the Kievan Mohyla Academy and the St Petersburg Medical-Surgical Academy (1806–10) and worked as an army doctor (1810–25) and a physician in hospitals in Kiev. He was a friend of Russian generals and writers and Ukrainian scholars (eg, M. Maksymovych, to whom he dedicated several of his Ukrainian poems). His large literary archive was taken by his son to St Petersburg, where it perished. Twenty-seven of his poems, Kotliarevsky-like burlesque fables in verse about the Ukrainian peasantry, Shevchenko-like Romantic ballads about the Cossacks, and (in Russian) odes and lyric poems, were published by his grandson, V. *Shcherbyna, in *Kievskaia starina* and separately in 1892.

Rudynsky, Mykhailo [Rudyns'kyj, Myxajlo], b 14 October 1887 in Okhtyrka, Kharkiv gubernia, d 23 June 1958 in Kiev. Archeologist and pedagogue. After completing studies at St Petersburg and Kharkiv universities, he worked in Putyvel, Pereiaslav, and Kiev as a gymnasium teacher (1910–17). He then worked in Poltava as a regional educational co-ordinator (1917–20), overseeing the preparation and publication of numerous children's books, textbooks, and popular works on history and art, and as the regional museum director (1920–4). In 1924 he moved to Kiev to become the academic secretary of the *All-Ukrainian Archeological Committee (VUAK). He also was active in the AN URSR (now ANU) *Cabinet of Anthropology and Ethnography and helped to edit the serial *Antropolohiia. Together with M. Makarenko, Rudynsky was one of the most prominent Ukrainian archeologists to support the idea of the independent development of a Ukrainian national culture even in prehistoric times. In 1934 he was arrested during the Stalinist terror and exiled to Siberia. He spent part of his time there (1940–4) as the director of a regional museum in Vologda. In 1944 Rudynsky returned to Kiev and resumed his scholarly work with the ANU Institute of Archeology. His major work, *Kam'iana Mohyla,* was published posthumously in 1961.

Rue (*Ruta*; Ukrainian: *ruta*). A perennial herb or shrub of the family Rutaceae. Of its approx 40 species, only the common or fragrant rue (*R. graveolens*) is found in Ukraine, where it grows wild on the rocky slopes of southern Crimea. *R. hortensis* is a popular cultivated ornamental plant that blooms in June or July. A *toxic plant, common rue contains highly aromatic essential oils and the alkaloid rutin, used as a source for vitamin preparations. In folk medicine rue was used for centuries as an antispasmodic and hypotensive agent. Many Ukrainian folk songs have been written about rue.

Rev Philip Ruh   Petro Rulin

Ruh, Philip, b 6 August 1883 in Bikenholtz, Alsace-Lorraine, d 24 October 1963 in St Boniface, Manitoba. Priest, missionary, and architect. He was ordained an Oblate priest in 1910 and went to Galicia for special training as part of a project to send celibate priests to western Canada. He arrived in Canada in 1911 and served Ukrainian Catholic parishes in Alberta and Manitoba. Although not a trained architect, Ruh designed and built over 20 Ukrainian Catholic churches in Canada, as well as the Basilian monastery in Mundare, Alberta (1922–3), and the calvary at Cook's Creek, Manitoba (1954–62). Most of his church designs have a cruciform floor plan, with a central dome and two, four, or more smaller domes, echoing the tradition of Ukrainian baroque churches. St George's Cathedral (1939–43) in Saskatoon has a cruciform plan with a central dome and six smaller ones, as has the Church of the Assumption of the Blessed Virgin Mary (1930–52) in Cook's Creek. St Josaphat's Cathedral (1936) in Edmonton is similar in style and has a classical colonnaded entrance and portico. Ruh designed and built the large wooden St Mary's Church (1924–5) in Mountain Road, Manitoba, and churches in Portage la Prairie and Dauphin (Manitoba); Kenora, St Catharines, and Grimsby (Ontario); and elsewhere. His autobiography was published in 1960.

Ruha. In the Ukrainian and Russian Orthodox churches the term designated for material assistance given, primarily by the state, for the support of the clergy and the maintenance of churches and monasteries which lacked their own landholdings or other sources of revenue. *Ruzhna tserkva* (*ruha*-supported church) was a term often used in Kiev in the 18th century. In villages the *ruha* was provided in kind by the peasant parishioners.

Ruin (*ruina*). A period in the late 17th century in the *history of Ukraine, characterized by the disintegration of Ukrainian statehood and general decline. Some historians (eg, M. Kostomarov) correlate it with the tenures of three Moscow-backed hetmans (I. Briukhovetsky, D. Mnohohrishny, and I. Samoilovych) and limit it chronologically to 1663–87 and territorially to Left-Bank Ukraine. Other historians (eg, B. Krupnytsky) consider the Ruin to apply to both Left- and Right-Bank Ukraine from the death of B. Khmelnytsky to the rise of I. Mazepa (1657–1687).

During the Ruin Ukraine became divided along the Dnieper River into Left-Bank and Right-Bank Ukraine, and the two halves became hostile to each other. Neighboring states (Poland, Muscovy, the Ottoman Empire) interfered in Ukrainian internal affairs, and Ukrainian policies were skewed by efforts to curry favor among the various occupational forces. The Ukrainian Orthodox church was subordinated to the Moscow patriarchate in 1686. Ukrainian leaders during the period were largely opportunists and men of little vision who could not muster broad popular support for their policies (Briukhovetsky, M. Khanenko, Yu. Khmelnytsky, Mnohohrishny, S. Opara, I. Sirko, Ya. Somko, P. Sukhovii, and P. Teteria). The hetmans who did their utmost to bring Ukraine out of decline were P. Doroshenko, Samoilovych, and I. Vyhovsky.

BIBLIOGRAPHY
Kostomarov, N. *Ruina: Istoricheskaia monografiia, 1663–1687*, vol 15 of *Istoricheskiia monografii i izsledovaniia Nikolaia Kostomarova* (St Petersburg–Moscow 1882)
Levitskii, O. *Ocherk narodnoi zhizni Malorossii vo 2-oi polovine* XVII *v.* (Kiev 1901)
Zerkal', S. *Ruïna kozats'ko-selians'koï Ukraïny* (New York 1968)
                                                            A. Zhukovsky

Rukh (Movement). A co-operative publishing house established in Vovchanske, Kharkiv gubernia, in 1917 and transferred to Kharkiv in December 1921. It published several book series of Ukrainian prerevolutionary literary works for general distribution to peasants, workers, and children; a library of over 100 plays; art books; editions of the collected works of I. Franko (30 vols, 1924–31), O. Kobylianska (9 vols, 1927–9), B. Hrinchenko (10 vols, 1926–30), M. Cherniavsky (10 vols, 1927–31), and H. Khotkevych (8 vols, 1928–32); and several volumes of V. Vynnychenko's works. In 1933 Rukh and its extensive network of bookstores throughout Soviet Ukraine were closed down by the Soviet authorities. In the years 1923–6 it published 128 titles with a combined pressrun of 659,500 copies.

Rukh. See Popular Movement of Ukraine.

Rukhymovych, Musii [Ruxymovyč, Musij], b October 1889 in Kagalnik, Rostov county, Don Cossack province, d 20 or 29 July 1938 or 1939. Soviet state figure. He was a political activist in Ukraine in 1911–14, a Bolshevik military leader in Kharkiv in 1917–18, and military commissar of the Donets–Kryvyi Rih Soviet Republic in 1918. In 1919–20 he held several high-ranking political and military positions in Ukraine, among them a seat in the Council of People's Commissars. After the imposition of Soviet rule Rukhymovych was a member of the Politburo of the CP(B)U, and director of the Donvuhillia coal trust

(1923–5), chairman of the Ukrainian SSR Supreme Council of the National Economy (1925–6), deputy chairman of the USSR Supreme Council of the National Economy (from 1926), and USSR people's commissar for railroad transportation (1930–4), heavy industry (1934–6), and defense production (from 1936). He perished during the Yezhov terror.

Rulikowski, Edward, b 1825 in Motovylivka, Skvyra county, Kiev gubernia, d 1900. Polish historian and ethnographer. He was the author of several valuable works describing the history and geographical features of Right-Bank Ukraine, including *Opis powiatu wasilkowskiego* (Description of Vasylkiv County, 1853), *Zapiski etnograficzne z Ukrainy* (Ethnographic Notes from Ukraine, 1879), and *Opis powiatu kijowskiego* (Description of Kiev County; pub posthumously in 1913).

Rulin, Petro, b 12 September 1892 in Kiev, d 23 July 1940? Theatrical historian, scholar, and pedagogue. He graduated from Kiev University (1916) and then taught at the Lysenko Music and Drama Institute in Kiev (1920–36; since 1934 the Kiev Institute of Theater Arts). He was director of the Kiev Theatrical Museum (1926–36) and editor of *Richnyk ukraïns'koho teatral'noho muzeiu* (Annual of the Ukrainian Theatrical Museum, 1930). Rulin was arrested in 1937, and died in prison. He wrote *Shevchenko i teatr* (Shevchenko and the Theater, 1925), *Rannia ukraïns'ka drama* (Early Ukrainian Drama, 1927), *Mariia Zan'kovets'ka* (1928), *M. Kropyvnyts'kyi* (1929), and *M. Staryts'kyi* (1931), as well as many articles on contemporary Ukrainian theater, one of which was published posthumously as *Na shliakhakh revoliutsiinoho teatru* (On the Paths of the Revolutionary Theater, 1972, abridged with a large bibliography).

Rumania or **Romania.** A country in southeastern Europe (1990 pop 23,151,514) in the lower Danube basin, situated between Hungary (west), Ukraine (north and east), Bulgaria (south, with the Danube as the border), and Serbia (southwest). Its capital is Bucharest. Its 237,500 sq km consists of sections of the eastern and southern Carpathians and Transylvanian Uplands, the Panon and Wallachian Lowlands to the west of the mountains, and the Moldavian and Dobrudja (Dobrogea) Uplands to the east. Its history is closely related to that of its historical neighbors: Bulgaria, Hungary, Austria, Austria-Hungary, Kievan Rus', the Principality of Galicia-Volhynia, Poland, the Grand Duchy of Lithuania, the Hetman state, the Russian Empire, the USSR, and Turkey. Parts of Rumania (and at certain times, the entire country) were under the control of these states or were protectorates of them.

In the past, Rumania was divided into three political formations: Moldavia (a country between the Carpathians and the Dniester; its eastern section is known as Bessarabia), Wallachia or Muntenia to the south, and Transylvania to the west. The first two came together as Rumania in 1861, and all three were united in 1918. Rumanians also constitute a majority of the inhabitants in Moldavia (at present called Moldova). Moldavians was the official name given to Rumanians living in the Russian Empire.

Ukrainians and Rumanians share an arching border which is 900 km long. Both nationalities have in common Orthodoxy, the influence of Byzantine culture, and their struggle against Turks and Crimean Tatars. They also have some similar folk traditions. Political and cultural relations between the two were active in the 16th and 17th centuries, but they subsequently tapered off because neither had its own state. In fact Ukrainians and Rumanians had virtually no direct political contact in modern times until after the First World War.

Until the creation of the Rumanian state in 1859–61, Rumanian-Ukrainian political relations were conducted mainly through *Moldavia. Contacts with Wallachia were insignificant, and even more rare with Transylvania. In the 16th and 17th centuries Cossacks assisted Moldavia and Wallachia in their struggles against Turkey. M. Viteazul's army in 1595 had 7,000 Cossacks. B. Khmelnytsky signed a treaty with Moldavia and married his son, Tymish, to Roksana, the daughter of V. Lupu, a Moldavian prince. T. Khmelnytsky led 8,000 soldiers on a campaign to defend his father-in-law, but was defeated at the Finta River on 17 May 1653 and killed on 15 September 1653 in the battle at Suceava. The increasing control of Muscovy over Ukraine and of the Ottoman Empire over Rumania that followed ended any possibility of further relations.

The Austrian annexation of *Bukovyna in 1774 and the Russian annexation of Bessarabia in 1812 brought Ukrainians and Rumanians into direct contact with one another. In Bessarabia, where the national consciousness of neither people was well developed, conflict between the two did not arise. In contrast, ethnic relations in Bukovyna became increasingly strained through the late 19th and early 20th centuries as the Ukrainians began to become politically active and demand certain national rights. The balance of power in Bukovyna shifted dramatically in 1918, when the crownland was ceded to the new Rumanian state. Ukrainians, now considered to be errant Rumanians who had forgotten how to speak their 'native' language, came under relentless attack: all schools were Rumanianized, the use of Ukrainian in the courts and in public offices was banned, the Ukrainian chairs at Chernivtsi University were abolished, and many Ukrainian societies (including *Ruska Besida) were closed down. Bukovynian Ukrainians were extremely dissatisfied with this harsh treatment. In 1940 the Rumanians withdrew from Bessarabia and North Bukovyna in response to an ultimatum from the USSR, which subsequently occupied the region.

In 1917–21 the UNR sought to establish normal relations with Rumania. In January 1918 A. Halip was sent on a public relations mission there. Subsequent representatives of Ukrainian governments included M. Halahan, V. Dashkevych-Horbatsky, and K. Matsiievych (1919–22). Rumanian diplomats in Ukraine included the generals Coanda and Concescu. Rumania recognized the Ukrainian state de facto and entered into trade agreements with it. At one point Rumania agreed to supply weapons in exchange for other goods, but the collapse of the Ukrainian front in 1919 put an end to these plans. Some conflicts arose over Rumania's military occupation of Bessarabia in March 1918 and of northern Bukovyna in November 1918, and there was a rearguard attack on the Ukrainian Galician Army in May 1919 during a brief Rumanian invasion of Pokutia.

During the interwar era the Rumanian government did not foster diplomatic or other ties with the Ukrainian SSR or the USSR as a whole. At the same time it took care not to

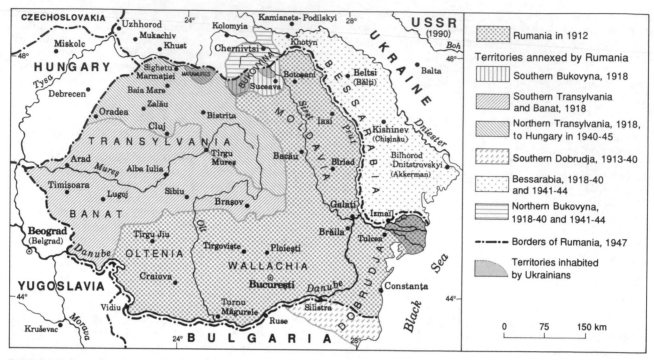

Map legend:

- Rumania in 1912
- Territories annexed by Rumania
- Southern Bukovyna, 1918
- Southern Transylvania and Banat, 1918
- Northern Transylvania, 1918, to Hungary in 1940-45
- Southern Dobrudja, 1913-40
- Bessarabia, 1918-40 and 1941-44
- Northern Bukovyna, 1918-40 and 1941-44
- Borders of Rumania, 1947
- Territories inhabited by Ukrainians

0   75   150 km

RUMANIA

antagonize the Soviets and was reluctant to grant asylum to refugees from Ukraine. In 1940 Rumania ceded North Bukovyna to the USSR. After having allied itself with Nazi Germany, Rumania invaded Bukovyna, Bessarabia, and *Transnistria in 1941 and controlled these regions until 1944, when they again came under Soviet rule. That same year Rumania was overrun by Red Army troops and became an Eastern-bloc satellite of the USSR, and closely began to follow the latter's edicts about the Ukrainian question. Rumania maintains a consulate in Kiev.

In the realm of culture, Ukraine's most significant ties to Rumania were with Moldavia, although it also had connections with Wallachia (most notably P. Mohyla's assistance with the establishment of printing presses). U. Năsturel, a scholar of the 17th century, had close relations with Kiev and imitated Ukrainian writers in his works. M. Smotrytsky's grammar was published in Snagov (1697) and Râmnic (1755), and it was influential in the preparation of the first Rumanian grammars. P. Berynda's *Leksykon slavenorosskyi* (Slavonic-Ruthenian Lexicon) was published in five editions in Rumanian translation. U. Năsturel, V. Măzăreanu (1710–90, archimandrite, writer, and reformer of Moldavian schools), G. Banulescu-Bodoni (metropolitan of Kiev, and then of Moldavia and Wallachia), M. Stefanescu (a bishop), and other Wallachian leaders studied at the Kievan Mohyla Academy. P. *Velychkovsky, who became hegumen of the Neamţ Monastery in 1779, revived Rumanian monastic life and was active in publishing and other cultural concerns. V. Costache (1768–1846), the metropolitan of Moldavia, corresponded with Ukrainian church leaders and published the Kievan *Sinopsis* in Rumanian in 1837.

In the 19th century a number of Rumanian writers and scholars focused on Ukrainian subjects. A. Hâjdău (1811–74) studied at Kharkiv University, and published a biography of H. Skovoroda in 1835. His son, B. Petriceicu Haş-

deu (1838–1907), was born in Khotyn, studied in Kharkiv, and wrote on Ukrainian themes. His *Ioan-Vodă cel Cumplit* (Ioan-Raging Prince, 1865) was based on L. Bobolynsky's chronicle. N. Gane's (1838–1916) *Domniţa Roxana* (Princess Roksana) was an original rendering of T. Khmelnytsky's marriage to Roxana Lupu. G. Asaki (1788–1869), Boleslav Hâjdeu (1812–86), and C. Stamati (1785–1869) were other writers interested in Ukraine, as were the Slavists I. Bogdan (1864–1919) and I. Bianu (1856–1935). C. Dobrogeanu-Gherea (1855–1920) studied at Kharkiv University, became the leader of the Rumanian Social Democratic party, and popularized the work of T. Shevchenko in Rumania.

Among the Rumanians interested in the Ukrainian question in the 20th century were the community leader Z. Arbore; the writers E. Bogdan, L. Fulga, M. *Sadoveanu, and M. Sorbul; the literary scholars E. Camilar and M. *Laslo-Kutsiuk; the historians B. Bezviconi, P. Constantinescu-Iaşi, M. Dan, E. Hurmuzaki, N. *Iorga, I. Nistor, S. Ciobanu, P. Panaitescu, D. Strungaru, and A. Vianu; and the linguists T. Macovei, G. Mihăila, E. Petrovici, M. Stefanescu, and G. Vrabie. Rumanian scholars have devoted most of their attention to the 17th century in particular. Many articles on Ukrainian-Rumanian relations appeared in the 17 issues of *Romanoslavica*, which were published in 1958–70 in Bucharest before a change in Rumanian government policy toward national minorities led to its demise. Emigré scholars who focused on the subject include G. Ciorănescu, G. Nandriş, and E. Turdeanu. Rumanian-Ukrainian relations have been studied in the Moldavian SSR by V. Haţak, M. Mohov, S. Popovici, and I. Varticean.

Ukrainian scholars and writers who delved into Rumanian-Ukrainian influences included the historians M. Cheredaryk, V. Hrabovetsky, O. Kaluzhniatsky, O. Karpenko, H. Koliada, N. Komarenko, M. Korduba, Ye.

Kozak, V. Mylkovych, A. Petrushevych, O. Romanets (who was interested in Ukrainian-Moldavian relations), I. Sharanevych, F. Shevchenko, and Yu. Venelin (who studied Slavic manuscripts in Rumanian libraries); the ethnographers and historians M. Drahomanov, I. Franko, I. Reboshapka, F. Vovk, and V. Zelenchuk; the musicologists K. Kvitka and S. Vorobkevych; the art critic V. Karmazyn-Kakovsky; the linguists P. Buzuk, I. Doshchivnyk, O. Horbach, Yu. Kokotailo, O. Ohiienko, M. Pavliuk, S. Semchynsky, I. Sharovolsky, D. Sheludko, V. Simovych, and R. Smal-Stotsky; and the writers Yu. Fedkovych, H. Khotkevych, M. Kotsiubynsky, A. Miastkivsky, V. Pianov, Ya. Stetsiuk, and S. Vorobkevych.

Rumanian literature is largely inaccessible to Ukrainian readers, but several translations into Ukrainian have been made. The novels translated include B. Haşdeu's *Răzvan şi Vidra*, L. Rebreanu's *Ion*, and M. Sadoveanu's *Mitrea Cocor* and *Nicoară Potcoavă*. M. Rylsky, Ya. Shporta, V. Sosiura, and M. Tereshchenko contributed to an anthology of translations of M. Eminescu's poetry, and other verse in Ukrainian translation includes that of V. Tulbure and C. Petrescu. I.L. Caragiale's drama *O scrisoare pierdută* (The Lost Letter) has also appeared in translation. A. Miastkivsky and M. Pianov have translated a number of Rumanian works into Ukrainian.

V. Tulbure translated T. Shevchenko's *Kobzar* into Rumanian, and it was published with an introduction by M. Sadoveanu in 1957. Other Ukrainian writers whose works have been rendered in Rumanian include I. Drach, V. Drozd, I. Franko, O. Honchar, Ye. Hutsalo, O. Kobylianska, M. Kotsiubynsky, Lesia Ukrainka, D. Pavlychko, V. Shevchuk, V. Stefanyk, M. Stelmakh, P. Tychyna, and Yu. Yanovsky.

In 1958 the Ukrainian Society for Friendship and Cultural Relations with Foreign Countries began staging days of Rumanian culture in Kiev and other cities of Ukraine. Various Rumanian soloist musicians and the National Theater gave performances. Rumanian films were shown, and exhibitions of Rumanian art and books were organized. There was a Ukrainian department of the Soviet-Rumanian Friendship Society (established in 1959), but it was not very active.

Economic ties. From the mid-17th century, merchants from Kiev, Nizhen, Pereiaslav, and Romen were engaged in vigorous trade with Moldavia and Wallachia. Wine was an important Rumanian export (2,769 barrels in 1759), as were nuts, salt, salted fats, and fruits. Ukrainian exports included manufactured goods, furs, agricultural produce, and various raw materials. In the 19th century imports from Moldavia included wheat, corn, and fruits; Ukrainian exports consisted mainly of sugar, coal, and livestock.

After 1918 trade between Rumania and Ukraine came to a virtual standstill; it resumed only after 1950. Ukraine has a negative trade balance with Rumania. Exports to Rumania constitute only 8 percent of its total exports, whereas Rumania sends 20 percent of its exports to Ukraine. In the 1970s Ukraine imported milled lumber (approx 260,000 cu m annually, 12 percent of the Rumanian total), petroleum products (approx 460,000 tonnes annually), steel freight cars, agricultural machinery, chemical supplies, furniture, clothing, shoes, canned goods, and fruit. Ukraine mainly exported raw materials, such as iron ore (in 1971, 50 percent of Rumania's imports), coke (29 percent), hydroelectric power (16 percent), cast iron (12 per-

cent), and coal (7 percent). Other exports included metal rollers, lathes, conducting material, and small-sized boats.

Ukrainians in Rumania. Before 1918 Ukrainians settled primarily in the northern Dobrudja region, in the Danube delta (see also *Danubian Sich). The settlements flowed directly out of the Ukrainian demographic territory in South Bessarabia and had a total population of around 20,000. About 50,000 Ukrainians also lived in northern Moldavia in the Dorohoi and Botoşani districts, where they were the predominant group until the 17th century. Today the Ukrainian language and folk customs have been only partially preserved, in villages such as Cândeşti, Rogojeşti, and Semenicea.

After the First World War Ukrainian ethnographic lands in Bukovyna, *Bessarabia, and the *Maramureş region (a small section of Transcarpathia) were ceded to Rumania, in addition to a number of Ukrainian 'oases,' such as Banat, that had previously belonged to Hungary. A total of about 1.2 million Ukrainians lived in Rumania, which figure included approx 800,000 on Ukrainian ethnographic territory. Until 1944 they were subjected to discrimination and socioeconomic exploitation.

Many Ukrainians, particularly teachers and civil servants, were transferred from Bukovyna and Bessarabia to cities in the Rumanian heartland in an effort to speed up the pace of Rumanianization. In spite of these conditions, efforts were made to maintain Ukrainian community life.

The Public Relief Committee of Ukrainian Emigrants in Rumania was established in 1923; it was headed by K. *Matsiievych, with V. Trepke as vice-president and D. Herodot as secretary. The committee co-ordinated the work of 10 émigré communities, the largest of which was the Community of Ukrainian Emigrés in Bucharest. Also active in Bucharest were the Union of Ukrainian Emigré Women (headed by N. Trepke), the Society of Ukrainian Veterans in Rumania (headed by H. Porokhivsky), and the Union of Ukrainian Farmers in Bucharest (a hetmanite group founded in 1921, headed by P. Novitsky). Ukrainian students in postsecondary schools in Bucharest established the Zoria society, which was active in 1921–6, and, later, the Ukrainian Cultural and Sports Association Bukovyna (1926–44) and the student Hromada in Iaşi.

The number of Ukrainians residing in central Rumania grew in 1940, when the Soviet annexation of Bukovyna and Bessarabia sent out waves of refugees. Before the outbreak of the Second World War the Rumanian government granted the Ukrainian minority certain cultural rights, and as a result, a Ukrainian radio station (director, M. *Kovalevsky), newspaper (*Zhyttia*, edited by I. Havryliuk), and journal (*Batava*) were established.

During the war the government once again deprived Ukrainians of their rights and began a campaign of terror to speed up assimilation, Rumanian colonization, and economic exploitation. All forms of Ukrainian organizational life were proscribed, and concentration camps were built. Ukrainian patriots, such as O. Huzar and M. Zybachynsky, were subjected to a show trial by a military tribunal in Iaşi on 26 January 1942. Prior to the invasion of Rumania by Soviet forces, some Ukrainians fled to the West, but most stayed behind. With the Soviet occupation, some Ukrainian activists (I. Hryhorovych, O. Masykevych, V. Yakubovych, and others) were arrested and deported to the USSR.

The boundaries of the Ukrainian SSR and the Rumanian

Socialist Republic established after the war did not coincide with ethnographic territories, and thus small segments of Ukrainian ethnographic territory remain part of the latter. These include southern Bukovyna (50,000 Ukrainians in 32 locales), Dobrudja (40,000 Ukrainians in 23 locales), and the Maramureş region (about 45,000 Ukrainians in 15 locales). There are about 15,000 Ukrainians living in eight villages of the Banat region (some of whom emigrated to the Ukrainian SSR in 1940) and another 15,000 dispersed throughout central Rumania. Ukrainians reside also in Baia Mare, Bucharest, Cluj, Constanţa, Iaşi, Lugoj, Ploieşti, Timişoara, Braşov, Tulcea, Suceava, Rădauţi, and other cities. The figures amount to a total of approx 165,000 Ukrainians in Rumania, although the official figure of the 1956 census was only 68,300. The Union of Ukrainians in Rumania, however, claimed in 1991 that there were 250,000 Ukrainians in Rumania (preliminary official statistics for 1992 state there are only 66,800).

Under the socialist regime in Rumania, no official Ukrainian community organizations existed even though the constitution recognized the rights of national minorities. The attitudes of the Communist party and government to local Ukrainians were variable, but usually negative. Before 1947 they did not even acknowledge the existence of a Ukrainian minority. In 1948–64 Ukrainians were afforded the opportunity for a measure of cultural and educational activity. Nevertheless, an attempt to intimidate the Ukrainian intelligentsia was made at a show trial in 1959, when V. Bilivsky, the editor of a Ukrainian publication, was charged with encouraging readers to read Ukrainian-language materials and maintain their culture, and sentenced to seven years' imprisonment. A similar trial was held in Sighetul Marmaţiei. In 1964 the Rumanian government began to close down Ukrainian cultural institutions. The adoption of a new constitution in 1965 once again enshrined minority rights, but it brought no practical gains for Ukrainians. In 1968 Ukrainians were allowed to organize district workers' councils in the Suceava and Marmureş regions. These were headed by I. Zakhariichuk and Yu. Kaniuka, but achieved little. The policies of N. Ceauşescu's regime (1965–89) thereafter became increasingly chauvinistic.

Cultural and educational life. The school reform of 1948 enabled the development of Ukrainian-language instruction at the primary, secondary, and postsecondary levels. For the next 10 years there were 120 active primary schools with Ukrainian-language courses (involving about 200 Ukrainian teachers and nearly 10,000 pupils). Ukrainian courses matching the regular school curriculum were conducted in gymnasiums in Seret, Sighetul Marmaţiei, and Suceava (with 77 graduates by 1957), and courses in Ukrainian were also offered in teachers' colleges in Seret, Sighetul Marmaţiei, and Tulcea (with 54 graduates by 1957). Textbooks were written to assist in instruction, including M. *Pavliuk's *Kurs istorychnoï hramatyky ukraïns'koï movy* (Course in the Historical Grammar of the Ukrainian Language, 1964) and Yu. Kokotailo's *Rumuns'ko-ukraïns'kyi slovnyk* (Rumanian-Ukrainian Dictionary, 1963), with 30,000 entries, and *Ukraïns'ko-rumuns'kyi slovnyk* (Ukrainian-Rumanian dictionary, 1964), with 35,000 entries.

Various reading rooms, clubs, cultural homes, self-help groups, and youth associations provided cultural amenities in Ukrainian villages. In the cities there were branches of the Asociaţia Romìna pentru legături cu Uniunea Sovietică, the Rumanian-Soviet friendship society. In general, however, the level of cultural life remained quite low, with local programs conducted in Ukrainian, Rumanian, and Russian. Outside Bucharest no notable folk art ensembles or individual artists existed.

Beginning in the mid-1960s Ukrainian cultural and educational efforts were repressed in both the city and the country. All forms of Ukrainian-language instruction were liquidated, with the exception of the titular existence of the Ukrainian department of the Sighetul Marmaţiei gymnasium and the lectureship in Ukrainian at Bucharest University. Even the use of the Ukrainian forms of place-names in publications was forbidden.

The biweekly *Novyi vik* appeared in 1949–90, under the editorship of Bilivsky and S. Zahorodny until 1959, when they were replaced by M. Bodnia and I. Kolesnyk. Its circulation was initially 10,000 but declined to 4,000 in the 1970s. By that time it consisted largely of Ukrainian translations of Rumanian content. The literary-historical bimonthly *Kulturnyi poradnyk*, edited by Bilivsky and V. Fedorovych, was published bimonthly in 1950–8 with a pressrun of 600 to 1,000.

A number of Ukrainians worked in universities and scientific institutes, including I. Robchuk and A. and K. Regush, at the Institute of Linguistics; V. Vynohradnyk (d 1973), at the Pasteur Institute in Bucharest; the Slavists K. Drapaka and I. Lemny; the pedagogue O. Antokhii; the physicist B. Pavliukh, at a polytechnical school in Iaşi; and V. Karmazyn-Kakovsky, also in Iaşi. In 1952 a department of Ukrainian language and literature was established at the Slavic department of Bucharest University. In 1963–74 the head of the chair of Slavic languages of the Institute of Foreign Languages and Literatures was M. Pavliuk, in 1974–83 M. Laslo-Kutsiuk, and from 1983 D. Horia-Mazilu and I. Robchuk.

Ukrainian literature is relatively well represented in Rumania. In the 1950s Ukrainian writers published their works in *Kul'turnyi poradnyk* and in the literary supplement to the biweekly *Novyi vik*. Departments for the publishing of works by representatives of national minorities were set up at the Literaturne Vydavnytstvo (1968–70) and Kryterion publishing houses in Bucharest. The editor of the Ukrainian section was M. Korsiuk. In the 1960s collections of poetry by H. Klempush, O. Melnychuk, D. Onyshchuk, and O. Pavlish were published in Bucharest, as were the novels and short stories of I. Fedko and S. Yatsentiuk. *Serpen'* (August, 1964), edited by S. Myhaichuk, and *Lirychni struny* (Lyrical Strings, 1968) were literary almanacs. Since 1970 the Rumanian Writers' Union's Literary Studio of Ukrainian Writers (headed by H. Mandryk) has steered through the publication of collections of verse by M. Balan, I. Fedko, K. Irod, I. Kovach, M. Korsiuk, O. Masykevych, O. Melnychuk, M. Mykhailiuk, I. Nepohoda, Yu. Pavlish, P. Romaniuk, and S. Tkachuk. I. Reboshapka transcribed and edited folk songs from southern Bukovyna, the Maramureş region, Banat, and Dobrudja, and published the anthologies *Narodni spivanky* (Folk Songs, 1969), *Oi u sadu-vynohradu* (In the Vineyard, 1971), and *Vidhomony vikiv* (The Echoes of the Ages, 1974). Other collections of folk songs include *Narod skazhe* (The People Will Tell, 1976), *Na vysokii polonyni* (In the Highlands, 1979), and *Oi Dunaiu, Dunaiu* (Oh Danube, Danube,

The Holubka Ukrainian-Rumanian music ensemble (later banned by the Ceauşescu regime) at a festival of national minorities in 1982

1980). Literary anthologies include *Nashi vesny* (Our Spring, 1972, prose, edited by M. Mykhailiuk), *Pro zemliu i khlib* (About Land and Bread, 1972, newspaper reports), *Antolohiia ukraïns'koï klasychnoï poeziï* (Anthology of Ukrainian Classic Poetry, 1970, edited by M. Laslo-Kutsiuk), *Z knyhy zhyttia: Antolohiia ukraïns'koho klasychnoho opovidannia* (From the Book of Life: An Anthology of Classic Ukrainian Short Stories, 1973), and the annual almanac *Obriï* (est 1979). M. Laslo-Kutsiuk published a study of Rumanian-Ukrainian literary relations (*Relaţiile literare româno-ucrainene în secolul XIX şi la începutul secolului al XX*, 1979), a general examination of 20th-century Ukrainian literature under the name *Shukannia formy* (In Search of Form, 1980), and other literary works. She also edited and published a two-volume collection of S. Yarychevsky's works (1977–8).

The majority of the Ukrainian population in Rumania is Orthodox, although in the Maramureş and Banat regions Greek Catholics are greater in number. After the abolition of the Greek Catholic church in Rumania in 1948, its congregation was forced to convert to Orthodoxy, the country's majority religion. In the 1980s permission was granted for Ukrainians in the Maramureş region to form a Ukrainian Orthodox church, which acts as a distinct jurisdiction within the Rumanian Transylvanian eparchy. Liturgies and sermons are almost exclusively (except in Seret) conducted in Rumanian, a practice which abets the process of assimilation. The Rumanianization of Ukrainians has also proceeded quickly because they are dispersed throughout the country and isolated from other countries with large Ukrainian populations, including Ukraine itself. Also, the intelligentsia has been intimidated to the point that it lives in the cities without any contact with the largely rural population.

After the overthrow of the Ceauşescu regime in 1989, Ukrainian life in Rumania began once more to revive. On 29 December 1989 the Union of Ukrainians of Rumania was formed and S. *Tkachuk was elected its first president. *Novyi vik was reconstituted in 1990 as *Vil'ne slovo* (under the editorship of I. Petretska-Korach and Yu. Lazarchuk) and began printing articles that were more pertinent to the interests of its readers. (See also *Moldavia.)

BIBLIOGRAPHY
Iorga, N. *Romînii de peste Nistru* (Iaşi 1918)

Panaitescu, P. *L'influence de l'oeuvre de P. Mogila dans les Principautés Roumaines* (Paris 1926)
Nistor, I. *Problema ucraineană in lumina istoriei* (Chernivtsi 1934)
Ciobanu, S. *Legăturile culturale romîno-ucrainene* (Bucharest 1938)
Nistor, I. *Ucraina în oglinda cronicelor moldoveneşti* (Bucharest 1941–2)
Constantinescu-Iaşi, P. *Relaţiile culturale romîno-ruse din trecut* (Bucharest 1954)
Tykhonov, Ie. *Derzhavnyi lad Rumuns'koï Narodnoï Respubliky* (Kiev 1959)
Studii privind relaţiile romîno-ruse şi romîno-sovietice (Bucharest 1960)
Mokhov, N. *O formakh i etapakh moldavsko-ukrainskikh sviazei v XIV–XVIII vv.* (Kishinev 1961)
Bezviconi, G. *Contribuţii la istoria relaţiilor romîno-ruse* (Bucharest 1962)
Ciorănesco, G.; et al. *Aspects des relations russo-roumaines: Rétrospective et orientations* (Paris 1967)
Marunchak, M. *Ukraïntsi v Rumuniï, Chekho-Slovachchyni, Pol'shchi, Iugoslaviï* (Winnipeg 1969)
Pavliuk, M.; Robchuk, I. 'Regional'nyi atlas ukraïns'kykh hovirok Rumuniï,' *Pratsi XII Respublikans'koï diialektolohichnoï narady* (Kiev 1971)
Romanets', O. *Dzherela braterstva: Bohdan P. Khashdeu i skhidnoromans'ko-ukraïns'ki vzaiemyny* (Lviv 1971)
Joukovsky, A. *Relations culturelles entre l'Ukraine et la Moldavie au XVIIème siècle* (Paris 1973)

A. Zhukovsky

Rumanianisms. Rumanian loanwords first penetrated into the Carpathian Ukrainian dialects adjacent to the territory of the Rumanian language during the northwestward Rumanian colonization that took place under Wallachian law in the 14th to 17th centuries and during the Rumanian domination of Bukovyna and Pokutia within the Moldavian Principality in the 14th to 18th centuries. They were introduced in southern Podilia, Bessarabia, and Dobrudja as a result of the interaction of Rumanian and Ukrainian colonists in the 16th to 19th centuries. Rumanianisms are most frequent in the Carpathian *Hutsul and *Bukovyna-Pokutia dialects, where they appear most often in the language of sheepherding, customs and rituals, public life, and lumbering, and as Carpathian toponyms and plant names. They also appear as winemaking and fishing terms in the western Steppe and southern Bessarabian dialects, and as argotisms among the Ukrainian lirnyks and in urban slang words in Odessa, Bukovyna, and Bessarabia.

Many medieval Bulgarian, Serbian, Hungarian, Turkish, and Greek loanwords, as well as modern German and French loanwords, came into the Carpathian Ukrainian dialects (eg, in Bukovyna, *šura, šušony, batoza* 'shed, winter boots, grinder' [Rumanian *şură, şoşoni, batoză*]) through Rumanian. Few dialectal Rumanianisms became part of Standard Ukrainian vocabulary, however. Those that did include *bryndza, hyrlo, gyrlyga, gryndžoly, žerep, kukurudza, mamalyga, papuša, tajstra, tyrlo, cap, caryna, rumegaty, sapaty* '(goat/ewe) cheese, estuary, shepherd's crook, sled, mountain pine, maize, cornmeal, tobacco pouch, hunting bag, corral, billy goat, sown field, to ruminate, to hoe' (from Rumanian *brînză, gîrlă, cîrlig, creangă, cucuruz, mămăligă, păpuşă, taistră, tîrlă, ţap, ţarină, a rumega, a săpa*).

Rumanianisms in the Ukrainian language have been studied by F. Miklosich, O. Kaluzhniatsky, D. Sheludko, R. Smal-Stotsky, I. Sharovolsky, I. Doshchivnyk, J. Janów, G. Pascu, D. Crânjală, D. Bogdan, O. Melnychuk, A. de Vincenz, Y. Dzendzelivsky, O. Horbach, E. Vrabie, M.

Pavliuk, I. Robchuk, J. Lobiuc, Y. Matsurek, S. Semchynsky, R. Udler, V. Prokopenko, and M. Gabinsky. Ukrainian toponyms of Rumanian origin have been studied by S. Hrabec, J. Rudnyckyj, S. Łukasik, M. Stanivsky, Yu. Karpenko, M. Bank, K. Halas, E. Petrovici, M. Korchynsky, A. Jeremia, O. Horbach, and others.

BIBLIOGRAPHY
Miklosich, F.; Kałużniacki, E. 'Über die Wanderungen der Rumunen in den Dalmatischen Alpen und Karpaten,' Denkschriften d. Phil.-Hist. Klasse. d. Wiener Akademie d. Wissenschaften, 30 (1879)
Scheludko, D. 'Rumänische Elemente im Ukrainischen,' Balkan-Archiv, 2 (Leipzig 1926)
Sharovol's'kyi, I. 'Rumuns'ki zapozycheni slova v ukraïns'kii movi,' Zbirnyk zakhodoznavstva UAN, 1 (1929)
Crânjală, D. Rumunské vlivy v Karpatech (Prague 1938)
Mel'nichuk, A. 'Moldavskie elementy v pogranichnom ukrainskom govore,' Istoricheskie zapiski Instituta istorii, iazyka i literatury Moldavskogo filiala AN SSSR, 4–5 (1955)
Vrabie, E. 'Influenţa limbii române asupra limbii ucrainene,' Romanoslavica, 14 (1967)
Horbatsch, O. 'Rumänische Lehnwörter in den ukrainischen Mundarten von drei südbukovinischen Dörfern in Rumänien,' in Festschrift für Alfred Rammelmeyer, ed H-B. Harder (Munich 1975)

O. Horbach

Rumanians or **Romanians.** The native population of *Rumania. In 1989 there were 459,350 ethnic Rumanians in Soviet Ukraine. Approx 377,000 others live in Ukrainian ethnic territory outside Ukraine's political borders.

Rumanians have historically lived in the borderlands of *Bukovyna and *Bessarabia (the Khotyn and Akkerman regions). While *Moldavia and Southern Ukraine were part of the Ottoman Empire in the 16th century, *Vlachs from Moldavia began freely colonizing the underpopulated lands between the Dniester and the Boh rivers in *Southern Ukraine. At that time entire Moldavian villages sought refuge in Ukraine, where social conditions were better. Their number rose after Ottoman-controlled territory between the Dniester and the Boh rivers was annexed by the Russian Empire in 1791. There the tsarist government granted Moldavian landowners and officials huge estates populated by Moldavian fugitives (260,000 desiatins in Ananiv and Tyraspil counties in 1792). Some Vlachs also settled east of the Boh River.

The Vlach settlers lived on good terms with their Ukrainian neighbors. They took part in the *haidamaka uprisings and were later also forced to live in the so-called *military settlements in Southern Ukraine. According to the Russian census of 1897, 185,500 Rumanians lived in the nine Ukrainian gubernias: 147,000 of them were in Kherson gubernia; 27,000, in Podilia gubernia; and 9,000, in Katerynoslav gubernia.

The Soviet regime distinguished between Rumanians and *Moldavians, although they are culturally and linguistically the same. According to the 1926 Soviet census there were 257,794 Moldavians and 1,530 Rumanians in Soviet Ukraine, 172,419 of them in the recently created Moldavian ASSR (see *Moldavian SSR). Approx 95 percent were peasants. In interwar Rumania Rumanians also lived in the ethnic Ukrainian parts of Bukovyna (32,000 in 1930) and Bessarabia (36,000 in Khotyn county and 82,000 in Akkerman county in 1930).

The number of Rumanians in Soviet Ukraine increased after parts of Rumanian ethnic territory in Bukovyna and the *Maramureş region were annexed by the USSR at the end of the Second World War. Of the 459,350 Rumanians in Ukraine according to the 1989 Soviet census, 324,525 were identified as Moldavians. In 1989, as earlier, their highest concentration was in Chernivtsi oblast (100,300 Rumanians and 84,500 Moldavians, mostly in Storozhynets, Hlyboka, Novoselytsia, and Sokyriany raions), where they made up 19.7 percent of the oblast's population, and in Odessa oblast (144,500 Moldavians and 700 Rumanians, mostly in Kotovske, Ananiv, Rozdilna, Tarutyne, and Reni raions), where they made up 5.5 percent of the population. Smaller numbers lived in the oblasts of Transcarpathia (29,500 Rumanians, in Tiachiv and Rakhiv raions), Mykolaiv (16,700 Moldavians), Donetske (13,300 Moldavians and 500 Rumanians), Kirovohrad (10,700 Moldavians, near Hruzke and Martonosha), Dnipropetrovske (6,600 Moldavians), Crimea (6,600 Moldavians), Luhanske (5,800 Moldavians), and Kherson (5,600 Moldavians). The number of Rumanians in Ukraine outside Odessa oblast has fallen substantially from what it was in the prewar period. In 1989, 62 percent of Rumanians and 78 percent of Moldavians in Ukraine gave Rumanian or Moldavian as their native tongue; only 9.8 and 6.1 percent respectively gave Ukrainian, and 3.5 and 15.5 percent, Russian.

Until the last few years of Soviet rule Ukrainian citizens of Rumanian descent were not allowed to have direct ties with Rumania. Cultural relations with Rumania were conducted through official channels by the Ukrainian Society for Friendship and Cultural Relations with Foreign Countries and the Ukrainian branch of the Rumanian-Soviet Friendship Society.

The Rumanian Ukrainians, particularly those in Chernivtsi oblast, have enjoyed a measure of cultural autonomy, however. In Chernivtsi oblast two CPU Oblast Committee newspapers, Zorile Bucovinei and Bucovina Sovietica, were published in Rumanian; Rumanian editions of the Novoselytsia, Hlyboka, and Storozhynets raion newspapers appeared from 1957; a special publishing house issued publications in Rumanian; Rumanian has been the language of instruction in some elementary and secondary schools; and Chernivtsi University has had a department of Rumanian philology. The Rumanians have had their own amateur choirs and dance groups. A number of members of the Writers' Union of Ukraine, including I. Zegria, I. Kilaru, V. Levytsky, M. Liutyk, and M. Prepelytsia, write in Rumanian and have contributed to the literary journal Nistrul, which is published in Kishinev. A Rumanian literary society headed by Levytsky has been active in Chernivtsi. In February 1990 the Social and Cultural Society of Transcarpathian Rumanians was established in Uzhhorod.

BIBLIOGRAPHY
Iorga, N. Ucraina moldovenească (Iaşi 1913)
– Romînii de peste Nistru (Iaşi 1918)
Draghicesco, D. Les Roumains d'Ukraine (Paris 1919)
Guboglo, M.; et al (eds). Ukrainsko-moldavskie etnokul'turnye vzaimosviazi v period sotsializma (Kiev 1987)

V. Kubijovyč, A. Zhukovsky

RUMChEROD. The acronym for the Central Executive Committee of the Soviets of the Rumanian Front, Black

Sea Fleet, and Odessa Military District (consisting of Kherson, Tavriia, and parts of Podilia and Volhynia gubernias). This revolutionary body was set up in May–June 1917 as a coalition of leftist parties with a Menshevik majority. It supported the Provisional Government and collaborated with the gubernia council, an organ of the Central Rada. In November–December 1917 RUMChEROD resisted the Bolshevik government. The Petrograd Soviet of People's Commissars responded to the resistance by sending agents and troops to Odessa. At the beginning of January 1918 the Bolsheviks took over RUMChEROD. The committee became opposed to the Central Rada and, with the help of Bolshevized troops from the front, took power in Odessa. RUMChEROD tried to extend its influence into Bessarabia, which was occupied by Rumanian troops. In the name of the Soviet of People's Commissars it signed a treaty with the Rumanian government on 5–9 March 1918 regarding the evacuation of Bessarabia, but the treaty was never implemented. Later that month Austrian troops occupied Odessa, and a Ukrainian government was restored. RUMChEROD was evacuated to the east and was dissolved in May.

Rumeian dialects. Dialects of the so-called Greek Hellenes, or Rumeians (*rumei*), who were forcibly resettled by the tsarist authorities from the Crimea to the northern littoral of the Sea of Azov in 1778–9 (see *Greeks). The dialects, consisting of five groups, are similar to modern Greek, but have lexical, phonetic, and morphological peculiarities. They are written in the Cyrillic alphabet. A literature based on them has been developed by writers such as D. Bhadits, L. Khonahbei, and, in the Soviet period, H. Kostoprav, A. Dimitriu, K. Pastur, A. Diamantopulo, A. Shapurma, L. Kyriakov, V. Halla, D. Telenchi, S. Kosse, P. Saravas, O. Petrenko-Ksenofontova, D. Papush, V. Bakhtarov, and H. Danchenko (Meotis). A book on the dialects spoken in the villages of Prymorske and Yalta in Pershotravneve raion in Donetske oblast was written by T. Chernysheva (1958).

Count Petr Rumiantsev (1798 engraving by John Walker based on a portrait by Dmytro Levytsky)

Rumiantsev, Petr [Rumjantsev], b 15 January 1725 in Moscow, d 19 December 1796 in Taman, Pereiaslav county, Kiev vicegerency. Russian military leader and statesman. He first distinguished himself as a general in the Seven Years' War. In November 1764, after K. Rozumovsky was forced to resign as hetman of the Left-Bank Hetmanate, Empress Catherine II appointed Rumiantsev president of the *Little Russian Collegium (1764–86) and

governor-general (1764–89) of Little Russia (ie, Left-Bank Ukraine). He also commanded the Russian army that invaded Moldavia and Wallachia during the 1769–74 Russo-Turkish War and the 'Ukrainian' army that fought in the 1787–91 war. He personally negotiated the 1774 Peace Treaty of *Küçük Kaynarca.

As Catherine's viceroy in Left-Bank Ukraine Rumiantsev implemented the centralist policies of the Russian government and eradicated the vestiges of Ukrainian autonomy, entrenching the Russian administrative and court systems. He instituted the *Rumiantsev census of Little Russia (1765–9). During the elections to the 1767 Legislative Commission he repressed Cossack *starshyna* and clergy who voiced Ukrainian autonomist demands. He initiated a series of reforms of the Hetmanate's military, tax system, and schools and in 1765 introduced a postal service. The Hetmanate's *regimental system was abolished in 1781–2; Little Russia was divided among three *vicegerencies (Kiev, Chernihiv, and Novhorod-Siverskyi) in 1782; and the *poll tax was introduced and the Cossack army transformed into Russian carabineer regiments in 1783. Rumiantsev supervised the imposition of *serfdom on the Ukrainian peasantry after Catherine's decree of May 1783, the implementation of Catherine's May 1785 charters to the nobility and the towns defining their rights and obligations, and the secularization of monastic properties in 1786.

In the 1780s Rumiantsev allied himself with noble circles (including Ukrainian autonomists) that supported the future tsar, Paul I, and were opposed to Catherine's favorite, G. *Potemkin. Rumiantsev thus incurred the wrath of Catherine, who had him removed as governor-general in 1789 and replaced with M. *Krechetnikov in 1790. Rumiantsev amassed huge estates in Ukraine. He spent his final years there and was buried in the Kievan Cave Monastery in 1797. His descendants owned the estates until the Revolution of 1917.

BIBLIOGRAPHY
Maksimovich, G. *Deiatel'nost' Rumiantseva-Zadunaiskago po upravleniiu Malorossiei* (Nizhen 1913)
Korobkov, N. *Fel'dmarshal Rumiantsev-Zadunaiskii* (Moscow 1944)
– (ed). *Fel'dmarshal Rumiantsev (1725–1796): Sbornik dokumentov* (Moscow 1947)
Fortunatov, P. (ed). *P.A. Rumiantsev: Dokumenty*, 2 vols (Moscow 1953)
Ohloblyn, O. 'Ukrainian Autonomists of the 1780's and 1790's and Count P.A. Rumyantsev-Zadunaysky,' *AUA*, 6, no. 3–4 (1958)
P.A. Rumiantsev, A.V. Suvorov, M.I. Kutuzov: Dokumenty i materialy (Kiev 1974)
Kohut, Z. *Russian Centralism and Ukrainian Autonomy: Imperial Absorption of the Hetmanate, 1760s–1830s* (Cambridge, Mass 1988)

O. Ohloblyn

Rumiantsev census (Generalnaia opis Malorossii). A comprehensive demographic and socioeconomic survey of the Left-Bank Hetman state instituted on the instruction of Empress Catherine II by Gov-Gen P. *Rumiantsev in October 1765. Its aim was to determine the legal status of persons and properties and to gather other information that would facilitate the introduction of the Russian tax, court, and military systems in the Hetmanate. It also laid the groundwork for the eradication of Ukrainian autonomy, the prevention of peasant and rank-and-file Cossack mobility, and the eventual imposition of serfdom. The census was conducted on the territory of each of the Hetmanate's 10 regiments by a special commission headed by a Russian officer. Altogether 3,500 settlements were surveyed. Family property (the *dvir*) constituted the basic unit in the census. The information gathered included population figures (age, marital status, state of health, place of birth, social status, occupation), corveé obligations, the equity and income of each family and the taxes paid, the means by which properties were acquired, the number of buildings and domestic animals on each property and their description, and the description of towns, villages, hamlets, cultivated land, forests, hayfields, and manufacturing enterprises. Copies of documents on which property ownership was based (hetmans' universals, regimental decrees, purchase and transfer records, and wills) were submitted with the data.

The census met with passive resistance from the majority of the population. Except in Kiev regiment it was not completed, because of the outbreak of the Russo-Turkish War of 1769–74. Nevertheless the data that were collected provide invaluable socioeconomic information about the Hetmanate prior to its abolition. Not all of the materials gathered have been preserved. Initially they were dispersed among the archives of the gubernial capitals of Chernihiv, Kiev, and Poltava. In the late 19th century the materials in Chernihiv were transferred to the library of the Russian Academy of Sciences in St Petersburg, those in Kiev were deposited in the Kiev University library, and those located in Poltava perished in a fire. In the 1920s all of the extant materials were deposited in the Kiev Central Archive of Ancient Documents. Now they fill 969 volumes, each with 300 to 1,000 folios; the volumes are housed in Kiev, mostly at the Central State Historical Archive but also in the Manuscript Division of the Central Scientific Library of the Academy of Sciences of Ukraine. Scholars who have studied the census include D. Bahalii, I. Boiko, V. Danylevych, P. Fedorenko, O. Hrushevsky, I. Kovalsky, T. Kruglova, O. Lazarevsky, P. Klymenko, I. Luchytsky, M. Lytvynenko, H. Maksymovych, V. Miakotin, N. Lepenko, O. Putro, M. Rklytsky, V. Romanovsky, V. Semevsky, S. Shamrai, M. Slabchenko, M. Tkachenko, and M. Vasylenko.

BIBLIOGRAPHY
Lazarevskii, A.; Konstantinovich, N. *Obozrenie Rumiantsevskoi opisi*, 4 fasc (Chernihiv 1866–85)
Bagalei, D. *General'naia opis' Malorossii* (Kiev 1883)
Miakotin, V. *Ocherki sotsial'noi istorii Ukrainy XVII–XVIII vv.*, 3 vols (Prague 1924–6)
Popova, L.; Revnyvtseva, K. *Heneral'nyi opys Livoberezhnoï Ukraïny, 1765–1769 rr.: Pokazhchyk naselenykh punktiv* (Kiev 1959)
Lytvynenko, M. *Dzherela istoriï Ukraïny XVIII st.* (Kharkiv 1970)
Kruglova, T. *Ekonomicheskaia struktura gorodskikh khoziaistv Levoberezhnoi Ukrainy v XVIII v. (po materialam General'noi opisi, 1765–1769 gg.)* (Moscow 1989)

O. Ohloblyn, A. Zhukovsky

Runkevych, Stepan [Runkevyč], b 1867, d ? Church historian. He was an employee in the chancellery of the Russian Holy Synod. He wrote histories of the Minsk archeparchy in the late 18th and early 19th centuries (1893) and of the Russian Orthodox church in the 19th century (1901) and edited *Opisanie dokumentov arkhiva zapadnorusskikh uniatskikh mitropolitov* (Description of Documents of the Archives of Western Russian Uniate Metropolitans, 2 vols, 1895).

RUP. See Revolutionary Ukrainian party.

Rural court (*sil's'kyi sud*). A local court of the Hetman state that dealt with petty criminal and civil cases in a given village. The rural courts for Cossacks were separate from those for peasants. Cossacks appealed the decisions of their courts to company courts, and peasants appealed the decisions of their rural courts to city courts. The rural courts were abolished with the introduction of serfdom in the 18th century, when their function was assumed by the landowner.

Rural soviet. See Soviet.

Anastasiia Ruryk

Ruryk, Anastasiia (née Melnyk), b 11 November 1897 in Kosiv, Chortkiv county, Galicia, d 30 October 1970 in Vancouver. Educator and civic activist. After arriving in Canada with her parents in 1898, she completed her education and became one of the first Ukrainian women to teach public school. For many years she was secretary, and in 1941–2 president, of the *Ukrainian Women's Association of Canada; later she headed its museum art committees. Her *Ukrainian Embroidery Designs and Stitches* was popular and went through four editions.

Rus'. The former name of Ukraine. In the Kiev Chronicle the term was a collective noun (ie, 'the Rus'') referring initially to the *Varangians and then to the land of the *Polianians around Kiev bounded by a triangle formed by the Dnieper, Irpin, and Ros rivers. Gradually it came to signify the entire realm of the grand prince of Kiev (Kievan Rus'). An inhabitant of Kievan Rus' and later Ukraine was called a *rusyn* – a designation that remained in use in Galicia, Bukovyna, and Transcarpathia until the 20th century (see *Ruthenians).

There are still many disputed, inconclusive hypotheses on the origin of the name. One is that its etymology is Norse, or more exactly, Swedish. This *Norman theory, first propounded by G.S. Bayer in the early 18th century, is based on the evidence of the Kiev Chronicle and 9th- and 10th-century West European, Arabic, and Byzantine sources. In *De administrando imperio* Emperor Constantine VII Porphyrogenitus provided separate 'Rus'' (Norse) and Slavic names for the Dnieper cataracts. At that time (and even now), the Finns called the Swedes *Ruotsi*. Although there is no evidence for a Swedish tribe by that name, it has been inferred that the Finns derived *Ruotsi* from the Swedish *Rōpsmenn* ('seafarers'; cf Old Swedish *rōper* 'rudder' or *rodhr* 'rowing'). One weakness of the theory is that it fails to explain why a Finnish term was adopted for a state founded by Swedes. Nor does it explain the appearance of the term *Rōs* in 8th-century Byzantine sources (and once in a 5th-century source, in connection with the Hunnic attack of 434–7), before the *Varangian route to the Byzantines had been established. Some scholars, such as E. Kunik (1875), A. Shakhmatov (1904), and A. Stender-Petersen (1953), have tried to overcome this objection by positing earlier stages of Germanic (Varangian/Gothic) colonization.

Anti-Normanists have put forth the theory of the autochthonous origin of the term 'Rus'.' Beginning with M. Maksymovych in 1837, they have proposed etymologies based on the names of the rivers Ros and Rusna and have posited that the Varangians were multiethnic, multilingual companies of mercenaries and traders consisting of Norsemen, Balts, and Slavs. This theory does not explain, however, the fact that the names of known Varangian dukes and warriors are of Swedish origin.

Supporters of a third theory, that 'Rus'' is of Iranian origin, derive the etymology of the term from the Iranian tribe of the *Roxolani (from Iranian *rokhs* 'light'). Although it suitably explains the early occurrences of the name, this theory is vitiated by historical and geographic evidence. The Roxolani lived in the Don River Basin, whereas 'Rus'' was first used in reference to the Polianian land. Interpretations of the term as being simultaneously of Iranian origin in the Don Basin and of Gothic origin along the Dnieper (eg, by V. Mavrodin), or as having been transferred from a Varangian kaganate along the Don to Kiev (eg, by G. Vernadsky), are in fact compromises with the Normanist theory.

BIBLIOGRAPHY
Brim, V. 'Proiskhozhdenie termina "Rus",' *Rossiia i Zapad*, 1 (Petrograd 1923)
Smal-Stocky, R. *The Origin of the Name 'Rus'* (Winnipeg 1949)
Simpson, G. *The Names 'Rus', 'Russia', 'Ukraine' and Their Historical Background* (Winnipeg 1951)
Stender-Petersen, A. 'Zur Rus'-Frage,' *Varangica* (Aarhus 1953)
Vernadsky, G. 'The Origin of the Name "Rus",' *Südostforschungen*, 15 (1956)
Ekblom, R. 'Roslagen-Russland,' *Zeitschrift für slavische Philologie*, 26 (1957)
Mägiste, J. 'Ruotsi, est. Rootsi m.m. i de finsk-ugriska spraaken,' *Arkiv för nordiska filologi*, 73 (1958)
Otrębski, J. 'Rus',' *Lingua Posnaniensis*, 8 (1960)
Hens'ors'kyi, A. 'Termin "Rus"' (ta pokhidni) v drevnii Rusi i v period formuvannia skhidnoslov'ians'kykh narodnostei i natsii,' *Doslidzhennia i materialy z ukraïns'koï movy*, 5 (1962)
Lehr-Spławinski, T. 'Z rozważań o pochodzeniu nazwy Rus',' in *Symbolae linguisticae in honorem Georgii Kuryłowicz* (Wrocław 1965)
Falk, K.-O. 'Kilka uwag o nazwie Ruś,' *Lingua Posnaniensis*, 12–13 (1968)
Pritsak, O. *The Origin of Rus'*, 1 (Cambridge, Mass 1981)
G.Y. Shevelov

Rus'. See Kievan Rus'.

Rus'. A newspaper published twice a week in Lviv in 1867 (75 issues in all). It was founded and financed by Count A. Gołuchowski, the Galician vicegerent, and was intended to combat Russophilism in Galicia and attract Ukrainian support for the Habsburg regime. When the newspaper's populist editor began to defend Ukrainian interests against the Poles as well as the Russians, Gołuchowski withdrew his support, and the newspaper had to close down. Its publisher was K. Horbal, and its editor was F. Zarevych. Its contributors included O. Levytsky, O. Mohylnytsky, and V. Shashkevych.

Rus'. A semimonthly journal of religious, political, and literary affairs published in Lviv from December 1885 to June 1887 (a total of 22 issues). It was published and edited by L. Bobrovych.

Rus' law (*Ruske pravo*). In a broad sense, the legal culture and system of Kievan Rus', based on Slavic and other sources, and in force in Ukrainian territories in the 9th to 14th centuries. Many aspects of this legal system were preserved in the Grand Duchy of Lithuania. The main written sources or memorials of Rus' law are *Ruskaia Pravda* and the *Lithuanian Statute.

In a narrower sense, Rus' law refers to the elements of old Ukrainian law that survived in the Kholm and Belz lands and in Galicia after their annexation by Poland in the 14th century. Rus' law continued to function in these territories, and was replaced gradually by *Polish law. Public Rus' law was completely displaced with the introduction of the Polish court system in Galicia in 1506; private law was retained longer in dealing with the Ukrainian population.

Rus' law was especially widespread among the rural population. Villages governed by Rus' law were the self-governing *hromady, which elected their own leaders and had their own courts. As serfdom spread in the 15th and 16th centuries, many villages under Rus' law were placed under Germanic and then Polish law. Nevertheless, some norms of Rus' law survived in Ukrainian *customary law.

Rus' Sea. An ancient name for the Black Sea that appears in chronicles dating from the period 858–1485. An entry in the Primary Chronicle reads, 'And the Dnieper [River] flows into the Pontic Sea as a stream, and the Sea is called the Rus' [Sea].' Arab sources of the 10th to 12th centuries (eg, al-Masudi) and some Western historians (eg, Helmold of Bosau) referred to the Rus' Sea, meaning both the Black Sea and the Sea of Azov.

Rus' voivodeship. An administrative-territorial unit in Ukraine during the 15th to 18th centuries, equivalent to a palatinate. It was established in 1434 by the Polish government on the former territories of the Principality of *Galicia-Volhynia, which was annexed by Poland in the late 14th century. Initially it was called the Rus' (Ruthenia) kingdom and ruled by a viceregent (palatine). It consisted of five territories, some of which were subdivided into counties: Lviv (Lviv and Zhydachiv counties), Sianik, Peremyshl (Peremyshl and Perevor counties), Halych (Halych, Kolomyia, and Terebovlia counties), and Kholm or Belz (Kholm and Krasnystaw counties). The territories and counties corresponded roughly to the Rus' appanage principalities and *volosti*. In 1629 the total population of the Rus' voivodeship was 943,000, and by 1770 it had risen to 1,495,000, of which the majority was Ukrainian; the urban population also included many Poles, Jews, Germans, and Armenians (for the history of the Ukrainian inhabitants of the region, see *Galicia). The administrative center was Lviv. In 1677 the voivodeship had approx 3,090 villages and 160 cities and towns. It was ruled by a voivode appointed by the Polish king, and judicial and administrative authority was exercised by castellans, city and zemstvo justices, and district reeves. A dietine of representatives of the nobility was regularly convened in Sudova Vyshnia. The voivodeship's coat of arms bore a golden lion with a golden crown on an azure field, with its forepaws on a cliff; each territory also had its own coat of arms. The Rus' voivodeship ceased to exit in 1772, when it was annexed by Austria.

A. Zhukovsky

Rusalka (Water Nymph). A publishing house of popular literature owned and operated by H. *Hanuliak in Lviv from 1921 to 1939.

Rusalka. A water nymph in Ukrainian demonology who has the appearance of a long-haired, pretty young girl and represents the soul of a drowned girl or an unbaptized dead child. According to folk belief the *rusalky* are naked, covered only by their long tresses, or dressed in a shift, or rarely in a full girl's costume. On their heads they wear wreaths of sedge. They live in groups in crystal palaces at the bottom of rivers and emerge from these only in the springtime, on Green Thursday or *rusalka* Easter. Until St Peter's day they play all night long on riverbanks, swing in the branches, run through the grass, dance, and sing. With their singing and charms they attract men, mainly bachelors, and tickle them to death. Their dancing is said to promote the growth of rye. After the first thunder they return to the rivers or rise into the sky. Sometimes *rusalky* are depicted as playful little children. In some regions not only river but also field and forest *rusalky* were believed to exist. They are capable of transforming themselves into other anthropomorphic shapes or animals. For protection against them people carry wormwood or lovage or wear a charmed shirt, kerchief, or piece of cloth. In the Chernihiv region, on the eve of Green Thursday a girl in a veil and red costume representing a *rusalka* was led about the village. The image of the *rusalka* appears frequently in Ukrainian literature, music, painting, drama, and cinema.

Rusalka (Water Nymph). A literary and scholarly populist student weekly in Lviv, edited by V. *Shashkevych; 12 issues appeared from 1 January to 2 April 1866. It published O. Konysky's critical survey of Ukrainian drama begun in *Meta*; articles on natural science and linguistics by I. Verkhratsky and O. Partytsky; works by Shaskevych, Konysky (his first poems), S. Vorobkevych, F. Zarevych, K. Klymkovych, O. Levytsky, and other writers and scholars; folk songs; criticism; and literary translations.

Rusalka (Water Nymph). A Russophile semimonthly women's newspaper published and edited by S. Shukhevych in Lviv from July 1868 to June 1869 and again in 1870 (a total of 23 issues).

Rusalka dance ensemble. A leading Ukrainian-Canadian dance company founded in Winnipeg in 1962 by P. Hladun under the auspices of the Ukrainian National Federation. The ensemble performs folk dances from all regions of Ukraine in authentic costume, as well as contemporary renditions of Ukrainian dance. It consists of about 50 amateur members between the ages of 17 and 35. Besides touring Canada and the United States, Rusalka has visited Mexico, Scotland, England, Italy, and Ukraine.

Rusalka Dnistrovaia   Vitalii Rusanivsky

Rusalka Dnistrovaia (The Dniester Nymph), subtitled *Ruthenische Volks-Lieder*. The first Ukrainian literary and folkloric miscellany published in Galicia. It was compiled by the *Ruthenian Triad (M. Shashkevych, Ya. Holovatsky, and I. Vahylevych) and printed through their efforts in the *hrazhdanka* script in Buda, Hungary, in December 1836. The miscellany consisted of folk songs recorded in various places in Galicia, with an introduction by Vahylevych; poetry and prose by the Triad's members and their translations of Serbian folk poetry and excerpts from V. Hanka's 'Králové Dvůr Manuscript'; texts of lyrical and heroic poetry from a 15th-century manuscript, with an introduction by Shashkevych; Holovatsky's note on Slavonic manuscripts in the library of St Basil's Monastery in Lviv; and Shashkevych's review of Y. Lozynsky's 1835 book of Ukrainian wedding rituals. In the manifesto-like preface Shashkevych stressed the beauty of the Ukrainian vernacular and oral folklore and provided a list of the most important contemporary publications of literature and folklore in Russian-ruled Ukraine. Of the original 1,000 copies 800 were confiscated in Lviv by the police after its sale, and distribution in Galicia was banned by Venedykt *Levytsky, the provincial censor, who did not approve of the language and orthography or of some of the contents. (The ban, which was not in effect in other provinces in the Austrian Empire, was rescinded in 1848.) Nonetheless, because of the compilers' radical Romantic orientation toward a pan-Ukrainian folk culture, literature, and history, their promotion of the vernacular as the literary language, and their pioneering use of a phonetic orthography based on the vernacular, *Rusalka Dnistrovaia* had a seminal impact on national consciousness and literature in Western Ukraine. It was republished in Ternopil in 1910, and facsimile editions of the original appeared in Kiev in 1950 and 1972 and in Philadelphia in 1961.

R. Senkus

Rusalka **songs.** Songs connected with the folk rituals of the *Rosalia feast. In time and theme they were related to the *vesnianky-hahilky*. *Rusalka* songs were sung mostly by girls during Whitsuntide, known as *rusalka, zelenyi* 'green,' or *klechalnyi* 'green-branch' week when the young unmarried people engaged in dances and games in the woods or by the rivers. In manuscripts of the 11th and 12th centuries they are described as 'demons' songs.' Despite church opposition some of the *rusalka* games survived into the 20th century. In the game of Topolia (Poplar) a girl decorated with floral wreaths was led through the village, to the accompaniment of songs with the refrain 'Stand still, O poplar, do not grow. Do not give in to the wild wind.' The ritual of *zavyvannia berizky* (wrapping the birch) was accompanied by songs about the birch tree. The ritual of *kumannia* (making friends) was also accompanied by special songs, such as 'O, godmothers and doves, we are going to the woods, we are going to make friends.' In the Pynske region of Polisia, on the second day of the Rosalia the women and girls led a *kusta*, a girl wearing a rich wreath of birch, maple, and linden leaves, various flowers, and ears of wheat, from house to house, singing a cycle of *rusalka* songs. In Svarytsevychi, Rivne oblast, this ritual was still being observed in the 1970s. The songs often mention the *rusalky* (water nymphs), who, according to folk belief, lost their power over human beings after the Rosalia. In Horodnia county, near the Desna River, girls, wearing wreaths of fragrant grasses, led the *rusalky* back to their lakes and rivers at the end of the week. In the Kharkiv region girls sang *rusalka* songs around a female scarecrow, which they finally tore apart and scattered over the fields. The *rusalka* songs are derived from ancient magical incantations that were supposed to secure a rich harvest or attract a lover to a girl. More recent songs often have a love plot in which an abandoned girl is transformed into a poplar, a young wife is poisoned by her mother-in-law, or a young bride commits suicide to escape from a repugnant husband. The *tsarynni* (from *tsaryna* 'sown field') songs are a separate group of *rusalka* songs, connected with farming, and are sung during a ritual procession through the fields. Various writers, such as T. Shevchenko, N. Gogol, P. Hulak-Artemovsky, M. Lysenko, and V. Symonenko, have drawn on *rusalka* songs in their works.

BIBLIOGRAPHY
Dei, O.; Ryl's'kyi, M. (eds). *Ihry ta pisni: Vesniano-litnia poeziia trudovoho roku* (Kiev 1963)
Voropai, O. *Zvychaï nashoho narodu*, vol 2 (Munich 1966)
Dei, O. *Narodnopisenni zhanry* (Kiev 1977; 2nd edn 1983)
Sokolova, V. *Vesenne-letnie kalendarnye obriady russkikh, ukraintsev i belorusov XIX–nachala XX v.* (Moscow 1979)
                                                    M. Mushynka

Rusalsky, Volodymyr [Rusal's'kyj] (pseud of Ivan Hevelenko), b 1911 in Uman county, Kiev gubernia, d 5 May 1957 in Adelaide, Australia. Writer. Before the Second World War he worked for newspapers and several publishing houses in Kiev. As a postwar refugee he lived in Germany and eventually settled in Australia. Rusalsky contributed to several émigré periodicals, especially *Novi dni*, and published four collections of novelettes: *Misiachni nochi* (Moonlit Nights, 1945), *Soniachni dzvony* (Sunny Bells, 1946), *Smikh Iskariota* (The Laughter of Iscariot, 1947), and *Pislia oblohy mista* (After the Siege of the City, 1951).

Rusanivsky, Vitalii [Rusanivs'kyj, Vitalij], b 25 June 1931 in Kharkiv. Linguist; corresponding (1976–82) and then full member (since 1982) of the AN URSR (now ANU). After completing his graduate studies at Kiev University (1957) he lectured there and joined the staff of the ANU Institute of Linguistics. He served as the institute's deputy director (1964–81) and then director, and has served as academic secretary of the ANU Division of Literature, Languages, and Fine Arts since 1978. He has written books on aspect and tense in 16th- and 17th-century Ukrainian (1959), the structure of the Ukrainian verb (1971), Slavic interlinguistic relations and the formation of functional styles in 16th- and 17th-century literary Ukrainian (1973), the folk vernacular as the source of development of East Slavic literary languages from the 16th to the early 18th century (1978), the origin and development of the East Slavic languages (1980), and the sources of Slavic literary languages (1985). He is also the coauthor of books on the philosophical questions of linguistics (1972), the morphology of contemporary literary Ukrainian (1969), the history of the Ukrainian language (2 vols, 1978–9), and of a Ukrainian orthographic dictionary (1974) and other works, and the editor of a collection of 15th-century Ukrainian charters (1965), several collections of articles, and secondary-school language textbooks.

Rusenko, Ivan, b 15 August 1890 in Krasna, Krosno county, Galicia, d 10 August 1960 in Korolivka, Ivano-Frankivske oblast. Writer and artist. A village teacher, he wrote in the Lemko dialect patriotic, lyrical, and satiric poetry, humorous fables, and the dramas in verse *Lemkivs'ke vesillia* (A Lemko Wedding) and *Vertep v Karpatakh* (A *Vertep* in the Carpathians), which were staged by many Lemko amateur theater groups. He also illustrated *Lemko* (the first Lemko newspaper) and D. *Vyslotsky's publications. After the Second World War he was forcibly resettled in Soviet Ukraine, where he continued teaching and writing. His postwar poems and stories about the resettled Lemkos remain unpublished.

Rush (*Luzula*; Ukrainian: *ozhyka*). Perennial herbaceous plants of the family Juncaceae, found in cold and temperate zones. Eleven species grow in Ukraine, the more common ones being the hairy (*L. pilosa*), many-headed (*L. multiflora*), and pale wood rush (*L. pallescens*). Rushes grow in wet meadows, shady forests, thickets, and grassy areas. Some, such as the snowy, the hairy, and the greater wood rushes, are cultivated as ornamental plants.

Rushnyk. An embroidered or woven towel 20–50 cm wide and 1–4 m long, used usually for a decorative or ceremonial purpose. In medieval times it was used as a basic piece of dress, covering the front and back of the body, or as a monetary unit. In Ukraine the *rushnyk* accompanied a person throughout his or her life: a newborn was placed immediately on a *rushnyk*. The *rushnyk* played a prominent role in the wedding rituals: in the engagement ceremony and the church wedding the *rushnyk* was used to tie the hands of the young couple; at the shower the bride-to-be and her bridesmaids wore the *rushnyk* across the chest; the engaged couple or their attendants carried the *rushnyk* when they invited guests to the wedding; at the wedding it was the bride's chief gift to the bridegroom, her in-laws, and the matchmakers; the *rushnyk* was worn across the

Embroidered *rushnyky*

Woven *rushnyk*

chest by the most important, if not all, wedding guests; at the departure from the bride's home and during the church service the couple stood on a *rushnyk*; and at the wedding the wedding bread was placed on a *rushnyk*. As a component of the bride's dowry the *rushnyk* represented her wealth and talents. The Hutsuls hung a *rushnyk* in the window to inform others of a death in the family. At funerals the deceased were covered with a *rushnyk*, the oxen pulling the hearse were decorated with it, the coffin was lowered into the grave with *rushnyky*, and the cross over the grave was draped with a *rushnyk*. A *rushnyk* was the most common gift made to churches. It was used in various folk rituals and celebrations – to decorate the ice cross on Epiphany and the birch tree on the Feast of the Trinity. During the Kupalo festival *rushnyky* and flower wreaths were used for decorating roadside crosses. The final sheaf of grain gathered during the harvest festival was tied with a *rushnyk*. At St Andrew's festival girls hung *rushnyky* outside their windows at night to learn whether or not they would get married. *Rushnyky* were also widely used in domestic life. When a house was constructed, the final beam was hoisted into place with *rushnyky*, which were then given to the workmen as gifts. Special *rushnyky* called *bozhnyky* or *naobraznyky* decorated icons or favorite paintings in the house. The *rushnyk* was also a symbol of the family hearth, a link between the living and the dead. A young man leaving home received a *rushnyk* from his mother or betrothed.

Rushnyky are either embroidered or woven, and each region of Ukraine has its own characteristic patterns and colors. The embroidered *rushnyky* of the Kiev, Poltava, and Chernihiv regions usually have a floral design arranged vertically in the form of a vase. A basic element of the design is the tree of life, subtended by a horizontal along the edge of the *rushnyk*. The dominant color in the Poltava *rushnyk* is bright red; in the Kiev *rushnyk* it is red and black or red and blue. A geometric pattern, embroidered in parallel stripes, is typical of Podilia. Stylized female animal and bird figures are also popular there. Volhynian *rushnyky* have geometric designs of red and blue made with a standard cross-stitch or running stitch. In Subcarpathia the dominant colors are black, red, and

yellow, and the most popular stich is the *nyz*. In Bukovyna and the Ternopil region the *rushnyky* are richly embroidered, with the horizontal and vertical stripes of black and red designs often covering one-quarter of the surface. (See also *Embroidery.)

There are two basic techniques used in *rushnyk* weaving, and they determine the nature of the design. Shuttle weaving is used to create a horizontal geometric design, in which red is the dominant color. Twill weaving is used for more elaborate designs, in which horizontal stripes are combined with stylized flowers and birds as well as squares, rhombuses, rosettes, and stars. (See also *Weaving.)

Today *rushnyky* are made mostly at specialized embroidery and weaving workshops and factories that employ hundreds of artisans. Some of them – M. Stefan from Kiev, for example, and T. Vasylieva from Kharkiv – are creative artists. Nineteen enterprises in Ukraine specialize in embroidery. The major centers are in Kiev oblast (Ivankiv, Vasylkiv, Kaharlyk, Litky), Poltava oblast (Opishnia, Velyki Sorochyntsi, Lubni), Chernihiv oblast (Nizhen, Pryluka), Vinnytsia oblast (Vinnytsia, Klembivka, Horodkivka), and Lviv oblast (Chervonohrad, Berdykhiv, Lviv). Since the 1960s much of the embroidery work has been mechanized. The recognized masters of hand embroidery include H. Herasymovych (the Hutsul region), V. Roik (Symferopil), M. Havrylo (Transcarpathia), N. Liakhova and E. Talashchenko (Kiev), A. Zaduvailo (Cherkasy), H. Hryn and O. Vasylenko (Poltava region), and Z. Chepela (Nizhen).

Woven *rushnyky* are more common. They are produced by factories in Krolevets, Bohuslav, Dihtiari, and Pereiaslav-Khmelnytskyi. Krolevets, in Sumy oblast, has been an important weaving center of high-quality *rushnyky* since the 16th century. In its products the design stands out against the plain white background and consists mostly of geometric motifs of rosettes, rhombuses, vases, flowers, and especially the tree of life. Most of the design is concentrated at the ends of the cloth. The best-known weavers in Krolevets are O. Vasylenko, Z. Cherenkova, M. Datsenko, and H. Yefimenko. Other master weavers are H. Veres (Kiev) and H. Vasylashchuk (Ivano-Frankivske oblast). In the West, K. Kolotylo in Vienna is known for her embroidered *rushnyky*.

Virtually every regional studies and ethnographic museum in Ukraine has a collection of *rushnyky*. The largest belongs to the *Ukrainian State Museum of Ethnography and Crafts in Lviv. A large collection is found in I. Honchar's private museum in Kiev.

Besides traditional designs there were also new 'artificial' designs with V. Lenin's and J. Stalin's portraits, five-point stars, hammers and sickles, and various political slogans. *Rushnyky* are a popular form of interior decoration in Ukraine and are exported to many foreign countries. The *rushnyk* often appears in folk and contemporary songs as a symbol of love, faithfulness, and patriotism.

BIBLIOGRAPHY
Ukrainskie narodnye dekorativnye rushniki (Moscow 1955)
Ukraïns'kyi vyshyvanyi rushnyk (Kiev 1980)
Zakharchuk-Chuhai, R. *Narodni khudozhni promysly URSR: Dovidnyk* (Kiev 1986)
Klid, H. 'Tradytsiia ukraïns'koho rushnyka,' *Novi dni*, June 1992
M. Mushynka

Rusin" (The Ruthenian). A weekly organ of the Greek Catholic Priests Mission Association of Pittsburgh and later of the *United Societies of Greek Catholic Religion in the USA, a fraternal organization for Carpatho-Ruthenian immigrants primarily from Transcarpathia. It appeared in Philadelphia and then Pittsburgh from June 1910 to December 1916 under the editorship of Y. Hanulia. The paper was closely allied with the Byzantine Ruthenian Greek Catholic Diocese of Pittsburgh, and defended the church against attacks by the more conservative *Amerikanskii russkii viestnik*. It was succeeded by *Prosvita* (1917).

Ruska Besida in Bukovyna. A Ukrainian community cultural-educational society which existed in Bukovyna in 1869–1940. Formed through the initiative of Ye. *Hakman, Ruska Besida was the first and (until 1918) the most active Ukrainian civic organization in Bukovyna. The organization was started as a club for the Ukrainian intelligentsia of Bukovyna, with a membership of approx 150. The group was initially headed (1869–78) by V. *Prodan and dominated by *Russophiles. In 1870–1 it published the first Ukrainian newspaper in Bukovyna, *Bukovynskaia zoria* (in *yazychiie).

During the 1880s Ruska Besida was transformed into a community-oriented educational body whose express aim was 'to spread knowledge and improve the lot of the Ruthenian [Ukrainian] people in Bukovyna.' Working through a network of village-based reading societies (*chytalni*), Ruska Besida became a regional counterpart to the Galician-based *Prosvita society. The watershed date in this process was 1884, when the organization's leadership was assumed by Ukrainian national populists (*narodovtsi*), and the group's scope of activity expanded substantially. By 1906 the Ruska Besida structure included a central office in Chernivtsi, seven regional branches, 83 village reading clubs, and a total membership of approx 6,800. By 1914 it included nine regional branches, 150 reading clubs, and a membership of approx 13,000. From 1835 Ruska Besida published the newspaper *Bukovyna* and a series of popular monthly books under the name Biblioteka dlia molodezhy, selian, i mishchanstva (with a total run of 120 titles before the undertaking ceased in 1895). Other publications issued by the society included *Lastivka* (1894–6), *Chytalnia* (1911–14), *Bukovynskyi pravo-slavnyi kalendar* (1874–1918), and individual books by authors such as Yu. Fedkovych, S. Vorobkevych, and M. Korduba. By 1918 the group had printed 270 titles.

Ruska Besida also served as the spawning ground for a host of Ukrainian institutions and organizations in Bukovyna. The first of these was the *Ruska Rada society, formed as a political body in 1870 with a membership that paralleled that of Ruska Besida. In 1875 the society was instrumental in establishing a chair of Ukrainian language and literature at the newly formed Chernivtsi University, and in 1899, a Ukrainian-language chair in the theology department of the same institution. Other groups which emerged out of Ruska Besida included Mishchanska Chytalnia (1880), the Ruthenian Dramatic and Literary Society (1884), the Chernivtsi People's Home (1884), *Ukrainska (Ruska) Shkola (1887), Bukovynskyi Boian (1895), *Ruska Kasa (1896), and the *Women's Hromada in Bukovyna (1906). These specialized affiliate organizations addressed particular sociocultural concerns while Ruska Besida took charge of its many branches and reading societies.

The activities of reading societies were banned in 1918, after the Rumanian occupation of Bukovyna, a development which effectively limited the activities of Ruska Besida to the city of Chernivtsi. Even there the local People's Home and Ukrainska Shkola society had taken on much of Ruska Besida's former activities. Only in 1938, with the banning of the Ukrainian National party by the Rumanian government, did Ruska Besida again come to life, this time as the de facto spokesbody of Ukrainian interests in Bukovyna. With the Soviet occupation of Bukovyna in 1940, Ruska Besida (along with all other Ukrainian organizations) was prohibited.

BIBLIOGRAPHY
Dmytriv, Ie. *Iliustrovana istoryia prosvitnoho tovarystva Rus'ka Besida v Chernivtsiakh, 1869–1909* (Chernivtsi 1909)

Ruska Besida in Galicia. See Ukrainska Besida.

Ruska Besida Theater. See Ukrainska Besida Theater.

Rus'ka istorychna biblioteka (Ruthenian Historical Library). A book series dealing with Ukrainian history, published in Galicia in 1886–1904 (24 volumes in all). It was edited and published by O. *Barvinsky with the assistance of O. Konysky. With V. Antonovych's help Barvinsky developed a plan to cover the full scope of Ukrainian history. Most of the books were translations from Russian of works by Ukrainian and Russian historians, such as Antonovych, D. Bahalii, M. Vladimirsky-Budanov, M. Dashkevych, M. Kostomarov, A. Yefymenko, I. Lynnychenko, F. Leontovych, I. Novytsky, and Ya. Shulhyn. At first the series was published in Ternopil. After vol 15 was released (1894), the Shevchenko Scientific Society assumed responsibility for publication of the series, and the other nine volumes came out in Lviv.

Ruska Kasa (Ruthenian Bank). A savings and loan society founded by I. Okunevsky in 1896 in Chernivtsi. By 1913 it had over 1,500 members. After the First World War the Rumanian government limited the society's activities. In 1924 it was forced to reconstitute itself as a credit bank, and it was closed by the authorities soon afterward.

Rus'ka khata (The Ruthenian House). A Bukovynian literary miscellany. It was edited by D. Mlaka (S. *Vorobkevych) in Chernivtsi and printed in 1877 in Lviv. Among the contributors were Vorobkevych (the heroic poem 'Nechai' and other works), Yu. Fedkovych (the drama 'Dovbush' and other works), N. Shram (H. Vorobkevych), P. Kulish (a libretto and a historical essay about Galicia in Cossack times), H. Barvinok, A. Shankovsky, and K. Ustyianovych.

Ruska khata (Ruthenian House [subtitled 'An Illustrated Periodical of Literature, Science, and Contemporary Life']). A semimonthly literary journal published in Lviv in 1905 (24 issues) and 1906 (1 issue) by D. Sembratovych and edited by him and Ya. Nebylovets. Among the contributors were members of the modernist group *Moloda Muza and other writers, such as V. Budzynovsky, O. Kovalenko, M. Pavlyk (who published in it the correspondence of M. Drahomanov with N. Kobrynska), and M. Mikhnovsky (the eight-part essay 'Spirillum patricianum ukrainophilicum'). Although the journal was intended for a general audience, it failed to attract many readers and was succeeded by *S'vit.

Ruska Kraina (Hungarian: Ruszka Krajna). A name for *Transcarpathia that was used briefly by the Hungarian government in 1918–19. The Hungarian government granted autonomy to Transcarpathia under that name in December 1918, and it appointed a Hungarian governor in Mukachiv and a minister of state for Ruthenia in Budapest. The Communist Hungarian government (March–August 1919) retained the use of the name Ruska Kraina. During its period in power the Ruska Kraina Commissariat, which replaced the Ministry of State, published the Ukrainian-language newspaper Rus'ka pravda in Budapest (13 issues in all). But on 8 May 1919 the representatives of Transcarpathian councils proclaimed the union of Transcarpathia with Czechoslovakia, and their proclamation was sanctioned by the Treaty of *Saint-Germain (10 September 1919). Under Czechoslovakia the region was known as Subcarpathian Ruthenia.

Rus'ka nyva (Ruthenian Field). A weekly organ of the *Ruthenian Agrarian party, published in Uzhhorod in 1920–4 and edited by M. Brashchaiko. The newspaper helped further Ukrainian national consciousness in Transcarpathia and promoted a pan-Ukrainian identity. Initially it used *etymological spelling.

Ruska Pravda. See Ruskaia Pravda.

Rus'ka pys'mennist' (Ruthenian Writing). A book series of Ukrainian literary classics published in Lviv in the years 1904–28. It was established and edited by Yu. *Romanchuk, who was succeeded in 1920 by V. Lukych (V. Levytsky) and then by M. Vozniak. The book series was renamed Ukraïns'ke pys'menstvo after the First World War. Twenty-eight volumes of works were published (23 of them by Romanchuk), including works of authors such as H. Kvitka-Osnovianenko, T. Shevchenko, P. Kulish, S. Vorobkevych, S. Rudansky, and Yu. Fedkovych.

Ruska Rada. See Ruthenian Council.

Ruska rada (Ruthenian Council). A semimonthly and, from 1900, weekly organ of the *Ruska Rada society in Chernivtsi, published from April 1898 to November 1908. It contained news; reports from village correspondents throughout Bukovyna; belles lettres; and articles on political and economic affairs and on scientific, technical, and agricultural subjects. Ruska rada played an important role in spreading Ukrainian national consciousness in Bukovyna. Its editors included I. Sozansky, I. Zakharko, and V. Stroich.

Ruska Rada society. A Bukovynian political organization founded in Chernivtsi in 1870 by members of the *Ruska Besida society. Its first president was Rev V. Prodan. The society's members informed the Ukrainian public about political matters and organized election campaigns. Until 1885 the society was dominated by Russophiles and thereafter by populists (led by I. Tyminsky, Ye. Pihuliak, O. Popovych, and I. Okunevsky), who published the organs *Ruska rada (1898–1908) and *Narodnyi holos (1909–11). From 1904 to 1914 the president was S. Smal-Stotsky. After the creation of Ukrainian parties in Bukovyna in 1906, the society's political role was diminished. In 1913 it had 842 members. The society was banned by the Rumanian regime in 1923.

Ruska Shkola. See Ukrainska Shkola.

Ruskaia Pravda (Rus' Truth [Law]). The most important collection of old Ukrainian-Rus' laws and an important source for the study of the legal and social history of Rus'-Ukraine and neighboring Slavic countries. It was compiled in the 11th and 12th centuries on the basis of customary law. The original text has never been found, but there are over 100 transcriptions in existence from the 13th to 18th centuries. There are three redactions of Ruskaia Pravda, the short, expanded, and condensed versions, and the connections between them have not been completely analyzed. V. Tatishchev found the first short redaction in 1738 in the text of a Novgorod chronicle from the 1440s. This was published by A.-L. von Schlözer in 1767. Since then some 10 more copies of the short redaction have been found, including the so-called Academic and Archeographic editions from approximately the same period. Of over 100 copies of the expanded redaction, the oldest are the Synodal edition, contained in the text of a *Kormchaia kniga from 1282, and the Troitskyi edition, found in the legal compendium Mirylo Pravednoie from the second half of the 14th century. The expanded Ruskaia Pravda was first published in 1792 by N. Boltin. The text of the condensed redaction differs somewhat from that of the two basic redactions. Its oldest version comes from a *Kormchaia kniga of the 17th century. Most historians (eg, M. Maksymeiko, A. Zimin) believe that the condensed redaction is a shortened version of the expanded redaction, and that it appeared in the 15th to 17th centuries; M. Tikhomirov and others, however, claim that the condensed redaction dates back to the mid to late 12th century, and that it served as the basis of the expanded redaction.

Noteworthy editors and publishers of the Ruskaia Pravda have been A. Musin-Pushkin, N. Kalachov, P. Mrochek-Drozdovsky, M. Vladimirsky-Budanov, V. Sergeevich, S. Yushkov, and B. Grekov. Ruskaia Pravda was published in German by G. Ewers (1814), E. Tobien (1843–4), and L. Goetz (1910–13); in French by M. Szeftel and A. Eck (1963); in Polish by I. Rakowiecki (1820–2) and A. Kucharski (1838); and in English by G. Vernadsky (1947).

Studies of the *Ruskaia Pravda* and attempts to systematize its redactions have been published by N. Kalachov, V. Kliuchevsky, V. Sergeevich, L. Goetz, and others. N. Karamzin studied its sources, particularly the influence of Byzantine canon and imperial law on the code. N. Kalachov and V. Kliuchevsky saw it as a clerical work, based on customary law and intended for church judges in civil cases. Others have detected the influence of Bulgarian law of the 9th and 10th centuries. Soviet historians (such as B. Grekov and L. Cherepnin) have used *Ruskaia Pravda* chiefly as a source of understanding social relations in Kievan Rus'; it has also been used to analyze the Kievan Rus' culture (B. Romanov) and to study the internal history and content of specific legal norms (S. Yushkov).

The 43 articles of the condensed redaction of *Ruskaia Pravda* are divided into four parts: (1) 'Pravda Iaroslava' (or 'the oldest part,' as it is called by historians [eg, V. Sergeevich, A. Presniakov, M. Tikhomirov] who do not agree that *Ruskaia Pravda* was initially promulgated by Yaroslav the Wise), consisting of articles 1–18; (2) 'Pravda Iaroslavychiv' or 'Ustav Iaroslavychiv,' consisting of articles 19–41; (3) 'Pokon vyrnyi,' which defines the penalty for murder (art 42); and (4) 'Urok mestnykam' (art 43) (see *Mest*).

'Pravda Iaroslava' dates from ca 1016 according to some historians, or from the 1030s according to others. The decrees in this section are as old as the 8th or 9th century, particularly those dealing with blood vengeance. 'Pravda Iaroslavychiv' was composed at a conference of Yaroslav's sons, Iziaslav, Vsevolod, and Sviatoslav, in Vyshhorod in 1072 (according to M. Tikhomirov, S. Yushkov, and L. Cherepnin) or in 1032–54 (according to B. Grekov and A. Zimin). The articles of this section carefully define and defend the interests of princes, government officials, and private property. The varying fines for murder (see *vyra*), depending on the victim's social rank, point to a differentiated society. Most norms of the short redaction are devoted to the protection of life, health, and property.

The expanded redaction of *Ruskaia Pravda*, consisting of 121 articles, was the most widespread. There is considerable disagreement in dating it: according to S. Yushkov and A. Zimin, it was compiled during the reign of Volodymyr Monomakh (after 1113); according to B. Rybakov, during the reign of Mstyslav I Volodymyrovych; and according to M. Tikhomirov and L. Cherepnin, before 1209.

In the criminal law of the expanded redaction blood vengeance was replaced by monetary fines and state penalties called *vyry*. If the criminal could not be identified, responsibility for murder was placed on the community in whose territory the crime occurred. Besides compensation to the victim, a state fine was imposed for assault and insult. Serious crimes, such as horse stealing, robbery, and arson, were punished by *banishment and seizure*. *Ruskaia Pravda* also contained a number of very clear laws on civil issues, such as loans, interest, land disputes, and wills, and on procedural matters, such as witness testimony, oaths, and ordeal. Most of these issues were also covered in the condensed redaction.

Ruskaia Pravda was a legal code of great importance, as can be seen from the abundance of copies that have been found. With the exception of the most privileged strata in the society, all free citizens were protected by the code. Its main purpose was to provide individuals with the power to defend their right to life, health, and property and to provide courts with the basis for a fair judgment. A characteristic feature of *Ruskaia Pravda* was its evolution toward a more humane law system.

Ruskaia Pravda is also an important source of historical information on the administration of Kievan Rus', social differentiation, financial affairs, and agricultural technology. It is an indispensable source for the study of customary law and Princely-era legislation. It had a direct influence on *Lithuanian-Ruthenian law and the *Lithuanian Statute and an indirect influence on the *Code of Laws of 1743. Some evidence of its influence can even be found in the legal codes and systems of other Slavic nations, especially in the codes of the Polish king Casimir III the Great (mid-14th century). According to the historian F. Leontovych, however, its influence on medieval Muscovite law is doubtful.

BIBLIOGRAPHY
Leontovich, F. *Russkaia Pravda i Litovskii Statut* (Kiev 1865)
Kachalov, N. *Predvaritel'nye iuridicheskie svedeniia dlia polnogo ob'iasneniia Russkoi Pravdy*, part 1 (St Petersburg 1880)
Maksimeiko, M. *Opyt kriticheskogo issledovaniia Russkoi Pravdy*, part 1 (Kharkiv 1914)
Chernov, V. *Do pytannia pro redaktsiï Rus'koï Pravdy* (Kiev 1920)
Tikhomirov, M. *Issledovanie o Russkoi Pravde* (Moscow–Leningrad 1941)
Iushkov, S. *Russkaia Pravda* (Moscow 1950)
Grekov, B. *Kievskaia Rus'* (Moscow 1953)
Kaiser, D. *The Growth of Law in Medieval Russia* (Princeton 1980)
Ya. Padokh

Ruske slovo (Ruthenian Voice). A weekly newspaper of Ukrainians in the Bačka region of Serbia. The newspaper was founded in 1945 in Ruski Krstur and then moved to Novi Sad in 1967. The Ruske Slovo press has published a monthly children's supplement (*Pyonerska zahradka*) since 1947, a monthly publication for youths (*Mak*) since 1972, and a literary-cultural quarterly (*Shvetlosts*) regularly since 1966. All of these organs appear in the local Bačka dialect, but a special literary page in *Ruske slovo* and other supplements have been published in standard Ukrainian. The press has also printed books on a regular basis.

Ruski Krstur (Kerestur Ruskyi; Hungarian: Bácz-Keresztur). A town (1981 pop 7,000) situated 50 km northwest of Novi Sad, in the *Bačka region of Serbia, that is inhabited almost exclusively by Ukrainians. Established in 1746, it was the first settlement of Bačka Ukrainians. Since 1751 a Greek Catholic parish has been active there. Published there have been the weeklies *Ruski novini* (1931–41) and *Ruske slovo* (1945–67); the children's monthlies *Nasha zahradka* (1938–41) and *Pyonerska zahradka* (from 1947); the literary and arts journals *Shvetlosts* (1952–4, and then from 1966), *Tvorchosts*, and *Visnik kulturi*; and almanacs and school texts. A gymnasium at which Ukrainian is taught was established in 1945. The town also boasts an amateur theater group, a museum, a cultural center, and a cultural and educational association named in honor of T. Shevchenko.

Ruski novini (Ruthenian News). A weekly newspaper published for the Ukrainians of the Bačka region, Serbia, by the Ruthenian People's Enlightenment Society. It began publication in December 1924 in Novi Sad under the editorship of a Croatian priest, D. Pavić. From 1927 it also published a children's supplement, *Mali novini*. Briefly suspended in 1930, *Ruski novini* renewed publication in August 1931 in Piškorevci and then Ruski Krstur under the editorship of Rev M. Firak. The newspaper was published in the local *Bačka dialect in a pressrun of 2,000. It was closed down in 1941, after the Hungarian army occupied the region.

Ruskii Sion (Ruthenian Sion). A semimonthly organ of the Ukrainian Catholic Lviv archeparchy published from 1871 to 1885 in Lviv. It was established on the initiative of Metropolitan Y. *Sembratovych and was initially called *Sion Ruskii* (1871–2). In 1880 he briefly closed the newspaper for publishing an article that offended him. It was then renamed *Halytskii Sion*, and it came out under this title until the end of 1882, when it reverted to being called *Ruskii Sion*. It published articles on theology and on church history and law, sermons, and, primarily, reports from local parishes. Its editors included Revs Yu. Pelesh, Y. Milnytsky, K. Sarnytsky, O. Toronsky, O. Bachynsky, and I. Bartoshevsky.

Rusko, Oleksii [Rus'ko, Oleksij], b 30 March 1906 in Białystok, Poland, d 25 August 1964 in Kiev. Pedagogue and government official; corresponding member of the Academy of Pedagogical Sciences of the RSFSR from 1957. He completed study at the Kiev Chemical-Technical Institute in 1932. In 1930–8 he held administrative and teaching positions at the Kiev Pedagogical Institute, and in 1938–44 he was rector of Kiev University. In 1944–58 he served as deputy minister of education of the Ukrainian SSR, and in 1958–64 as director of the *Scientific Research Institute of Pedagogy of the Ukrainian SSR. He wrote works, including textbooks, relating to the teaching of chemistry in secondary and postsecondary institutions, and on general pedagogical topics.

Ruskyi amvon (Ruthenian Pulpit). A journal containing sermons for Ukrainian Catholic priests, published in Lviv in 1896–1905.

Ruskyi Narodnyi Soiuz. See Ukrainian National Association and Ukrainian Fraternal Association.

Ruskyi selianyn (Ruthenian Peasant). A newspaper for peasants, published semimonthly from April to June 1903 and then three times a month to 1906 in Lviv. It contained articles on political affairs and popular enlightenment. It was published by Zh. Holob and edited by him and V. Demianchuk.

Ruslan. A conservative populist daily newspaper published in Lviv from 1897 to 1914. Founded by O. Barvinsky and A. Vakhnianyn, it served as the organ of the Catholic Ruthenian People's Union and then the Christian Social party (see *Christian Social Movement), supported the politics of the *New Era (co-operation with the Poles), spoke out against the Russophile movement in Western Ukraine, and advocated closer ties with the Ukrainians in Russian-ruled Ukraine. It published the works of promi-

nent writers in Russian-ruled Ukraine, such as O. Konysky, I. Nechui-Levytsky, and M. Starytsky, and contributions from Western Ukrainian writers, such as B. Lepky, O. Makovei, K. Studynsky, and V. Shchurat. The paper was especially noted for its popular-scholarly articles on Ukrainian history and the correspondence of V. Antonovych with O. Barvinsky and O. Ohonovsky, and A. Vakhnianyn with P. Kulish. *Ruslan* was edited by T. Baranovsky, S. Kulchytsky (1897–8), L. Lopatynsky (1898–1907), S. Goruk (1907–14), and V. Barvinsky (1914).

Orest Rusnak   Mykhailo Rusov

Rusnak, Orest (stage name: Rudolph Gerlach), b 24 July 1895 in Dubivtsi, Bukovyna, d 23 January 1960 in Munich. Opera and concert singer (tenor). In 1923 he graduated from the Prague Conservatory in the class of E. Fuchs; he also studied in Milan. From 1924 he appeared in Prague, Vienna, and (mainly) Germany, and from 1929 he made frequent tours in Central and Western Ukraine. Among his roles were Fernando in G. Donizetti's *La Favorita*, Arnold in G. Rossini's *William Tell*, Manrico in G. Verdi's *Il Trovatore*, Lionel in F. von Flotow's *Martha*, Chapela in A. Adam's *Le Postillon de Longjumeau*, Cavarodossi in G. Puccini's *Tosca*, and Rodolfo in his *La Bohème*. In concert he performed art songs and folk song arrangements by M. Lysenko and other Ukrainian composers. In the 1930s he recorded for the German Elektrola label. His biography, by I. Novosivsky, was published in New York (1971).

Rusnak, Vasyl, b 23 February 1899 in Nepolokivtsi, Kitsman county, Bukovyna, d 24 July 1981 in Bucharest. Bukovynian political activist. He graduated in law (1924) and history (1926) from Chernivtsi University and then established a legal practice in Chernivtsi. He headed the workers society Volia and the Ukrainian faction of the Rumanian Social Democratic party in Bukovyna, for which he edited *Borot'ba*. He was a Sovietophile and cofounder of an underground committee of communist organizations in Bukovyna. A 1928 trip to Soviet Ukraine left him largely disillusioned with radical politics, and his major activities through the 1930s were in the cultural field, particularly in theater. He is the author of a history of Ukrainian theater in Bukovyna (1975). After the Second World War he was arrested by the Soviets. Following his release in 1956, he lived in Rumania, where he helped compile Rumanian-Ukrainian and Ukrainian-Rumanian dictionaries (1963–4).

Rusov, Mykhailo (pseuds: Totsky, M. Liashenko, Mishelia), b 9 November or December 1876 in Oleshnia, Horodnia county, Chernihiv gubernia, d 24 February 1909 in St Petersburg. Political revolutionary and ethnographer; son of O. *Rusov and S. *Rusova. Like his parents, he was an adherent of M. Drahomanov's political and socialist ideas. He entered Kharkiv University in 1895, but he was expelled in 1899 for one year for his involvement in the Kharkiv Student Hromada. He initiated the creation of the *Revolutionary Ukrainian party (RUP) and its Poltava branch (1900). In 1901 he was arrested for leading a political demonstration in Poltava and spreading revolutionary propaganda, again expelled from Kharkiv University, and banned from Kharkiv and other cities with universities for two years. After emigrating in 1902, he studied at Leipzig University (1902–6), did field research for his PH D thesis on Subcarpathian buildings, and was a member of the RUP Foreign Group in Lviv. He subsidized RUP publications and activities and contributed to the party's organs *Haslo* and *Dobra novyna*. He also published several articles in *Literaturno-naukovyi vistnyk* in 1900–1 and a brochure on peasant handicrafts (1906).

Oleksander Rusov   Yurii Rusov

Rusov, Oleksander, b 7 February 1847 in Kiev, d 8 October 1915 in Saratov, Russia. Statistician, folklorist, and civic figure of Russian origin; husband of S. *Rusova and father of M. and Yu. *Rusov. A graduate of Kiev University (1868), he taught at gymnasiums in Kiev (1868–74) and belonged to the Old Hromada of Kiev. He was a founding member of the *Southwestern Branch of the Imperial Russian Geographic Society. In 1874 he helped organize the Kiev census, and in 1875–6 he prepared with F. Vovk the two-volume Prague edition of T. Shevchenko's *Kobzar*. Along with P. Chervinsky, V. Varzar, and O. Shlykevych he was one of the founders of the zemstvo statistical service in Chernihiv gubernia. He worked in the Nizhen county zemstvo (1878–80), supervised statistics-gathering in Kherson and Kharkiv gubernias (1882–92), developed an economic survey of Chernihiv gubernia (1893–8), and directed the Statistical Bureau of Poltava gubernia (1899–1902). After being banished from Poltava he worked for a few years in St Petersburg and then taught statistics at the Kiev Commercial Institute (1909–15). Rusov wrote over 40 scholarly works and many articles in statistics, history, and ethnography. His more important contributions to statistics are *Russkie trakty v kontse XVII i nachale XVIII vekov*

(Russian Highways at the End of the 17th and the Beginning of the 18th Centuries, 1876), a statistical-economic description of Nizhen county (1879), a statistical description of Kharkiv based on the 1892 census (1893), and a description of Chernihiv gubernia (2 vols, 1898–9). He also wrote studies of O. Veresai (1874), *torban* players (1892), carols (1907), and M. Lysenko (1903).

Rusov, Yurii, b 1895 in Kharkiv, d 2 August 1961 near Montreal. Biologist; member of the Shevchenko Scientific Society; son of O. *Rusov and S. *Rusova. A graduate of Kiev and Vienna universities, he represented Ukrainian students as a delegate to the Central Rada in 1917 and taught zoology and ichthyology briefly at Kamianets-Podilskyi Ukrainian State University. In the 1920s he taught in schools in Czechoslovakia and in 1930–41 he headed the ichthyology division at the National Zoological Institute in Bucharest. In Berlin (1941–6) he was a leading figure in the Ukrainian hetmanite movement. After emigrating to Canada he worked (from 1947) at the University of Montreal and the Mont-Tremblant Biological Research Station.

Sofiia Rusova

Rusova, Sofiia (née Lindfors), b 18 February 1856 in Oleshnia, Horodnia county, Chernihiv gubernia, d 5 February 1940 in Prague. Pedagogue, author, and political activist; wife of O. *Rusov and mother of M. and Yu. *Rusov; member of the Ukrainian Central Rada and a founding member and first president of the *National Council of Ukrainian Women. She headed the Department of Preschool and Adult Education in the Ministry of Education under the Hetman government, and was a professor of education at the Froebel Pedagogical Institute in Kiev before the First World War and at Kamianets-Podilskyi Ukrainian State University immediately after the war. Rusova escaped from Soviet Ukraine in 1922 and settled in Prague, where she taught at the Ukrainian Higher Pedagogical Institute between 1924 and 1939. As a member of the *Union of Ukrainian Women and honorary president of the *World Union of Ukrainian Women she frequently represented Ukrainian women at international women's conferences.

She was a vocal proponent of the left democratic wing of the Ukrainian political spectrum. She promoted daycare, adult education, and political organization of the peasants. She remained an active member of the Ukrainian Party of Socialist Revolutionaries and contributed frequently to its newspapers, especially to the Prague-based *Nova hromada*.

Her works include the memoirs *Moï spomyny* (My Memoirs, Lviv 1937) and *Nashi vyznachni zhinky* (Our Prominent Women, Kolomyia 1934; 2nd edn, Winnipeg 1945), *Persha chytanka dlia doroslykh dlia vechirnykh ta nedil'-s'kykh shkil* (First Reader for Adults for Evening and Sunday Schools, 1918), *Iedyna diial'na (trudova) shkola* (The

Unified [Labor] School, 1918), *Teoriia i praktyka doshkil'noho vykhovannia* (Theory and Practice of Preschool Education, 1924), *Suchasni techiï v novii pedahohitsi* (Contemporary Trends in Modern Pedagogy, 1932), and *Moral'ni zavdannia suchasnoï shkoly* (Moral Tasks of the Contemporary School, 1938).

M. Bohachevsky-Chomiak

Russia (Rosiia; Russian: Rossiia). The country to the north and east of Ukraine, inhabited primarily by Russians, an Eastern Slavic people, but also by numerous minorities of diverse ethnicity. The borders of the state of Russia and, to a lesser degree, of the area of compact settlement of the Russian people have expanded dramatically over the centuries. The nucleus of the Russian state was the principality of Suzdal-Vladimir in northeastern Kievan Rus'. This polity then expanded by conquest and purchase until it acquired all the other former principalities of Kievan Rus' except those of Ukraine and Belarus, which had fallen under the rule of the Polish-Lithuanian Commonwealth. Through conquest and colonization, it extended its borders to the Pacific Ocean in the mid-17th century. In the later part of the 17th century, following the *Cossack-Polish War, *Left-Bank Ukraine came under Russian suzerainty, although it was not fully integrated into the Russian state until the late 18th century. During that century the state, now formally constituted as the Russian Empire, expanded to the Black and Baltic seas by acquiring Estonia, Latvia, Lithuania, Belarus, and much of the rest of Ukraine (the *Right Bank, *Southern Ukraine, the *Crimea). In the 19th century it acquired Finland, Bessarabia, and much of Poland as well as Caucasia and more of Asia. By 1914 the Russian Empire covered an area of over 21 million sq km (about one-quarter in Europe, the rest in Asia).

The origins of Russia lay in the basin of the Oka and the

EXPANSION OF THE RUSSIAN EMPIRE IN EUROPE

upper Volga rivers, where the Slavic and Finnic areas of settlement met. There the principality of Suzdal-Vladimir emerged as part of Kievan Rus' in the late 11th century. The country's origins in the Kievan Rus' state account for both its modern name (Russia was a Latin name frequently used for Rus') and the Russian claim to the Kievan legacy. Under Prince *Yurii Dolgorukii (ca 1125–57) the principality of Suzdal-Vladimir grew in importance, and Yurii made a bid to win the Kievan throne and thus become its grand prince. His son, *Andrei Bogoliubskii (1157–74), even sought to replace Kiev as the center of the Rus' land with his own capital, Vladimir-on-the-Kliazma; to that end he waged war on Kiev in 1169, and his army plundered the city ruthlessly. Suzdal-Vladimir was involved in a second sack of Kiev in 1203.

By the beginning of the 13th century the rulers of Suzdal-Vladimir, with a territory of about 230,000 sq km and a population of about a million, were titling themselves 'grand prince.' The invasion of the *Tatars increased the importance of the principality, because Kiev was thoroughly weakened after the Tatars sacked the city in 1240, and because the Golden Horde conferred the title 'grand prince' on the rulers of Suzdal-Vladimir. Moreover there was some emigration from the Ukrainian principalities to this northern principality because of its distance from the Tatars. In 1299 the metropolitan of Kiev transferred his residence to Vladimir-on-the-Kliazma.

Nevertheless, by the end of the 13th century Vladimir was being surpassed in importance by two other cities in the principality, Moscow (first mentioned in the chronicles in 1147) and Tver. Those became the centers of two new principalities. The Muscovite principality flourished under the two grand princes Ivan Kalita (1328–41), who transferred the residence of the metropolitan of 'all Rus'' from Vladimir to Moscow (1328), had his title confirmed by the Mongol khan (1328), and extended his influence to Novgorod, Pskov, and other northern principalities, and Dmitrii Donskoi (1359–89), who conquered Tver (1375) and defeated a Mongol army at Kulikovo Pole (1380). Moscow continued to extend its influence among the other northern principalities through the early 15th century. It also exercised some attraction for Ukrainian and Belarusian boyars in Lithuania, which was falling under Polish domination.

Muscovite expansionism reached unprecedented heights during the reign of Grand Prince Ivan III (1462–1505). In that period Muscovy annexed the principalities of Yaroslavl (1463), Rostov (1474), and Tver (1485) as well as the Viatka territory (1489) and the greater part of the principality of Riazan. The greatest acquisition of Ivan III, however, was Novgorod (1471–89), a rich and huge polity that the ruler thoroughly integrated into the Muscovite state (using such methods as extensive executions and the mass deportation of the city's original population). By the early 16th century Moscow ruled over a territory approaching 3 million sq km in area and had become fully independent of Mongol suzerainty (1480).

Coinciding with the rapid expansion of Muscovy in the late 15th century was the development of an imperial ideology. Muscovy had already become an autocratic and centralist state. Ivan III, who married the niece of the last Byzantine emperor, began from time to time to call himself tsar (caesar), a title implying imperial aspirations. The Muscovites came to feel that they were superior to the Greeks, who in their view had fallen from the true faith by agreeing to the Church Union of *Florence (1439), and who moreover had fallen under Muslim Turkish rule. The Russian church asserted administrative independence from Constantinople in the 1440s (after rejecting the Florentine union), and that independence was abetted by the fall of the Byzantine capital to the Ottomans in 1453. In the early 16th century the Pskovian monk Filofei codified the theory that Muscovy had now become a *Third Rome, heir to the imperial and orthodox Christian traditions of the lapsed Roman and Byzantine empires. Moreover, in the 1450s Muscovy first began to lay official claims to Kiev and the Kievan inheritance (in the *Vita* of Dmitrii Donskoi); those claims were to be developed further in succeeding decades, as Muscovite territorial aggrandizement became represented as the 'gathering together' of the 'lands of Rus'.' In 1493 Ivan III assumed the title 'sovereign of all Rus'' (*gosudar' vseia Rusi*).

Muscovy had begun to contend with Lithuania for some lands of Rus' in the 1360s, and the conflict escalated during the reign of Grand Prince Vasilii I (1389–1425). But the conflict acquired new dimensions after Lithuania united with Poland (1385), and Muscovy had begun to perceive itself as the natural heir to the lands of the former Kievan Rus'. Muscovy and Poland-Lithuania struggled over Tver and Novgorod from 1449 to 1485, and in 1487–1537 they joined battle in a series of wars over Belarus and Ukrainian territories. In the course of the latter struggles Moscow frequently allied itself with the Crimean Tatars, who with Muscovite encouragement attacked Ukraine repeatedly and wreaked large-scale devastation. The Tatar sack of Kiev in 1482, undertaken at the instigation of Ivan III, was particularly brutal. In the course of those conflicts Muscovy managed to incorporate the Ukrainian principalities of Starodub and Novhorod-Siverskyi (1503–17).

Muscovy had avoided conflict with Poland-Lithuania during the mid- and late 16th century. But when Muscovy was plunged into a deep succession crisis during the so-called Time of Troubles (1598–1613), Poland-Lithuania seized the opportunity to intervene in Muscovy's affairs and attempted to place its own candidate on the throne of Moscow. Ukrainian Cossacks took part in Polish military campaigns against Muscovy. Although Muscovy recovered from its troubles in 1613, when the *Romanov dynasty was installed, Poland renewed hostilities in 1617 and won back Starodub and Novhorod-Siverskyi (according to the Armistice of Deulino in 1618). War broke out again in 1632 but brought no substantial change; the Polianovka Peace Treaty of 1634 essentially confirmed the agreement of 1618. The Polish-Lithuanian campaigns of the early 17th century mark the apogee of Polish eastward expansion; thereafter Poland-Lithuania went into decline, and Muscovy began to take its place as the greatest power in Eastern Europe.

In the late 16th and early 17th centuries some Ukrainians began to look to their Orthodox coreligionists in Muscovy for help in the struggle against the Catholic Poles and the Muslim Tatars. In the 1580s and 1590s Ukrainian delegations traveled to Muscovy to obtain contributions for their churches. In 1625 the Kievan metropolitan Y. Boretsky even appealed to the Muscovite tsar to take Ukraine under his protection. In 1556–9 Prince D. Vyshnevetsky and the Zaporozhian Cossacks undertook joint campaigns with Russian Cossacks, and Vyshnevetsky even formally entered Muscovite service and traveled to Muscovy. In the early 1590s Muscovy gave some material assistance to the anti-Polish Cossack uprising led by K. *Kosynsky; after the uprising was suppressed, many of the Cossacks fled to Muscovite-held Slobidska Ukraine, a pattern that was to be repeated in the early 17th century. In 1620 Hetman P. Sahaidachny sent a delegation to Moscow to try to enlist its co-operation in a campaign against the Crimean Tatars.

Beginning in the late 16th century Ukraine underwent a cultural renaissance that was to have a major impact on Muscovy by the mid-17th century. Kiev, especially after the founding of the *Kievan Mohyla College (later Academy) in 1632, became an important center of learning and the intellectual capital of the entire Orthodox world. The wide-ranging liturgical reforms of Patriarch Nikon of Moscow (1652–66) drew heavily on Kievan, as well as Greek, scholarship, and M. Smotrytsky's Slavonic grammar (1619; repub in Moscow in 1648 and 1721) influenced the development of a Russian literary language. Ukrainian influence on Russian culture became especially pronounced after 1654, when much of Ukraine came under Moscow's suzerainty.

Ukraine's entrance into the Russian sphere of political influence came as an unexpected result of the Cossack uprising against the Polish-Lithuanian Commonwealth initiated by Hetman B. *Khmelnytsky in 1648. Seeking a strong ally in his cause, Khmelnytsky began as early as 1649 to petition the Muscovite tsar for his protection. Muscovy was reluctant to renew war with the Polish-Lithuanian Commonwealth, but eventually, under the influence of Patriarch Nikon, the tsar decided to aid the Cossacks. The legal relationship between Ukraine and Muscovy was established by the *Pereiaslav Treaty of 1654, the original text of which has not survived, and the intent of which has been the subject of widely differing interpretations by Ukrainian, Russian, and Polish historians. Khmelnytsky, however, fell out with the Russians in 1656, when they made a separate peace with the Poles (but he did not formally break with them before his death in 1657). His successor, Hetman I. Vyhovsky, repudiated the relationship with Muscovy and entered into the Treaty of *Hadiache with Poland in 1658. War over Ukraine between Poland-Lithuania and Muscovy broke out anew, with Turkey also intervening. Ukrainian Cossacks joined the hostilities, often divided among themselves and often changing sides. The devastating warfare lasted until the Treaty of *Andrusovo of 1667, which in effect partitioned Ukraine between the contestants. Left-Bank Ukraine (the *Hetman state or Hetmanate) and Kiev became part of the Muscovite sphere of influence; Right-Bank Ukraine (and Galicia) remained under Polish rule. The partition was confirmed by the *Eternal Peace of 1686, signed by Muscovy and Poland.

In the course of those decades of strife (known as the *Ruin in Ukrainian historiography) the Muscovites took measures to limit the autonomy of the Hetman state. In particular Muscovy concluded several agreements (called articles) with the Cossacks, in which the terms of the Pereiaslav Treaty were restated in such a way as to restrict Ukrainian rights. Hetman I. Briukhovetsky was induced to sign the *Baturyn (1663) and *Moscow (1665) articles, which curtailed the hetman's authority and increased that of the tsar and his administration. The *Hlukhiv Articles

(1669) restored some of the Hetman state's prerogatives, but the *Konotip (1672) and *Kolomak (1687) articles again limited them. The Russian government particularly insisted on reducing and in fact eliminating the hetman's right to conduct foreign policy. In 1663 the *Little Russian Office was established as a link between the Muscovite administration and that of the Hetman state.

During the same period the Ukrainian Orthodox church was subordinated to the Muscovite church. The Kiev metropolitan S. Kosiv (1647–57), who had been reluctant to swear an oath to the tsar in 1654, favored retaining the Ukrainian church under the jurisdiction of the distant Patriarch of Constantinople. In spite of promises that Ukrainian ecclesiastical independence would be respected, the Russian authorities took advantage of internal dissension in the Ukrainian church to place it under the jurisdiction of the patriarchate of Moscow (est 1589). The formal request for that subjugation was made at a church council headed by Metropolitan H. Sviatopolk-Chetvertynsky in 1685. The Patriarch of Constantinople, faced with strong Russian political pressure, agreed to the new order in 1686.

The erosion of Ukrainian autonomy was accelerated during the reign of Tsar *Peter I, a centralizer who formally adopted for his state the name Russia (Rossiia) and proclaimed it an empire (1721). Aiming to establish access to the Baltic, he waged the Great Northern War (1701–21) against Sweden. In the course of the war he requisitioned men and provisions from Ukraine, thereby greatly burdening the country, and strove to integrate the Cossacks more completely into Russia's armed forces. Those measures prompted Hetman I. *Mazepa to turn against Peter and join forces with the Swedish king Charles XII in 1708. The Russian forces responded by destroying the Hetman state's capital of Baturyn in 1708 as well as the *Zaporozhian Sich in 1709 (both were rebuilt several decades later). Mazepa and Charles were decisively defeated at the Battle of *Poltava in 1709. To avoid a repetition of the Mazepa defection a tsarist resident was attached to the hetmancy as of 1709. After the death of Hetman I. Skoropadsky in 1722, Peter left the office of the hetman vacant. In 1722 Peter also replaced the hetmancy resident and the Little Russian Office with the *Little Russian Collegium. The Collegium assumed much greater powers than the Office had held and in fact controlled the Ukrainian administration. It even began to collect direct taxes. Acting Hetman P. Polubotok protested the activities of the Collegium (*Kolomak Petitions of 1723) and died in prison for

Gov-Gen Petr Rumiantsev's design for the new Russian state seal for relations with Ukraine

his pains (1724). In his transformation of Russia Peter initiated massive building projects; as a result thousands of Ukrainian Cossacks and peasants perished in the construction of canals and fortresses and in the building of the new capital of St Petersburg. Peter also regulated Ukrainian trade to the advantage of Russian rather than Ukrainian *merchants.

Ukrainian cultural influences were pronounced in Russia during the late 17th and early 18th centuries. Because of their relatively high level of education and their Western European cultural orientation, Ukrainians who sought careers in Russia were generally successful. They had a profound and formative influence on the emerging Russian educational system. Peter I often relied on Ukrainian intellectuals to provide leadership in various reforms. Especially prominent roles were played by the Ukrainian clergymen T. Prokopovych and S. Yavorsky in the tsar's church reform, which replaced the office of patriarch with the Holy Synod and subordinated the Russian Orthodox church to the state. Ukrainian writers, painters, directors, actors, and architects contributed to the diffusion of baroque culture in Russia.

In 1727 Tsar *Peter II (1727–30), under the influence of his adviser Prince A. *Menshikov, abolished the Little Russian Collegium and allowed a new hetman to be elected, D. Apostol. Apostol's relations with the Russian government were regulated by the Authoritative Ordinances (Reshitelnye Punkty) issued by the tsar in 1728. After the death of Apostol in 1734, Empress Anna Ivanovna (1730–40) refused to allow the election of a new hetman. Instead a *Governing Council of the Hetman Office, consisting of three Russian officials and three Cossack officers, administered Ukraine. Empress *Elizabeth I (1741–62) permitted the restoration of the hetman's office, and in 1750 the Governing Council was abolished. K. Rozumovsky was elected hetman, although he spent much of his reign fighting a rearguard action to defend Ukrainian autonomy.

The Hetman state lost its remaining autonomy when it was dismantled and Left-Bank Ukraine integrated directly into the Russian Empire during the reign of *Catherine II (1762–96). In 1764 she forced Hetman Rozumovsky to resign and abolished the office of hetman permanently. She reconstituted the Little Russian Collegium with General-Governor P. *Rumiantsev as president; it lasted until 1786, by which time Ukraine was so integrated into the imperial administrative system that a separate Little Russian administrative office was no longer necessary. In 1775 Catherine ordered the Zaporozhian Sich destroyed. In 1782 a *gubernia structure completely replaced the Ukrainian regimental system. Catherine induced the *Cossack *starshyna* to acquiesce in the eradication of Ukrainian autonomy primarily through material incentives. In 1783 she officially sanctioned serfdom in Ukraine, and in 1785 she made the Cossack *starshyna* equal to the Russian *nobility (*dvorianstvo*). Nonetheless some autonomist sentiment survived among the Cossack gentry into the 19th century.

One of the achievements of Catherine's reign was the rolling back of the Ottoman Empire through a series of successful *Russo-Turkish wars (1768–92) and the acquisition of the northern coast of the Black and Azov seas, including the Crimean Peninsula. That large territory, known as *New Russia, was sparsely inhabited, and Catherine charged its governor-general, G. *Potemkin, with the responsibility of finding colonists for it. Germans

as well as Slavs and Greeks from the Balkans were encouraged to relocate there, and numerous new settlements were established, including the major port city of Odessa (1794). Catherine also intervened in the internal affairs of neighboring Poland, as her predecessors had done throughout the century. At first her agents helped provoke and then her troops crushed the great *haidamaka uprising of 1768 (*Koliivshchyna), which plunged Right-Bank Ukraine into chaos. That episode was a prelude to the partitions of Poland (1772–95), by which Russia annexed the Right Bank up to the Zbruch River. Thus, by the end of the 18th century approx 85 percent of Ukraine had come under Russian rule; only the Western Ukrainian territories of Galicia, Transcarpathia, and Bukovyna were under the Habsburg rather than the Romanov scepter. That state of affairs was to last, with only temporary and minor changes, until 1917. At the end of the 18th century the Russian Empire had a territory of 14.5 million sq km and a population of over 36 million.

Ukrainians continued to contribute to the cultural life of Russia in the mid- and late 18th century. K. Rozumovsky presided over the Russian Academy of Sciences. Other prominent Ukrainians working in Russia in the late 18th century included the composers and directors D. Bortniansky and A. Vedel, who influenced the development of Russian choral music; the court singer and publisher of folk songs V. Trutovsky; the singer M. Poltoratsky; the painters V. Borovykovsky and A. Losenko; the portraitist D. Levytsky; the sculptor and rector of the St Petersburg Academy of Arts I. Martos; the Russian-language writer I. Bogdanovich; the editor of *Sankt-Peterburgskii vestnik* H. Braiko; the men of letters and civil servants M. Antonovsky, V. Ruban, and F. Tumansky; the jurist and professor at Moscow University S. Desnytsky; and the imperial chancellor O. Bezborodko.

By the 19th century the Russian Empire had almost wholly dismantled the political and military institutions of Ukraine, eliminated from the Right Bank the last vestige of Ukraine's separate legal code (the Lithuanian Statute) in 1840, and largely assimilated Ukraine's elite as part of the Russian nobility. Ukraine was not treated as an entity in itself; it was regarded as a region and administered as nine gubernias. Western ideas and trends no longer flowed from Ukraine to Russia, as in the 17th and 18th centuries, but from Russia to Ukraine. The most telling sign of Ukraine's subordinate status was the development of a mind-set of cultural inferiority (a common trait of colonial peoples) among many Ukrainians – *malorossiistvo* or the *Little Russian mentality.

The 'Great Russians' dealt with their Little Russian 'brothers' as subordinates. Although they regarded Ukrainians as their blood relations and rejoiced in the fact that they had become part of their body politic, they clearly did not regard Ukrainians as their social, cultural, or political equals. As Ukraine had in fact been reduced to provincial status, Ukrainians increasingly began to be seen as less sophisticated. The folk arts, foods, dance, and music of Ukraine became celebrated within the empire, but the notion that Ukrainians could sustain any serious cultural undertakings of their own was commonly dismissed as nonsense. Moreover the Russians did not differentiate between their own ethnic territory and that of Ukraine. They regarded Ukraine as part of one whole, an integral and indivisible part of the empire. Any suggestion on the part of Ukrainians that they constituted a distinct people or territory was greeted with hostility. People holding such opinions were regarded as treacherous 'Mazepists,' and the imperial authorities were always alert to signs of 'separatist' tendencies among Ukrainians.

The fondness with which Russians regarded Ukraine, and conversely their virulent attitude toward any notion of autonomy for Ukraine, were motivated by certain economic and geopolitical considerations. The total absorption of Ukraine by the Russian state had given the empire a strong agricultural base that virtually eliminated the threat of periodic famine and provided valuable products for export. In the later 19th century the development of the *Donets Basin (Donbas) provided for the growth of industry. The access to the Black Sea that followed the acquisition of Ukraine's Black Sea littoral gave the empire warmwater ports. The presence of Ukraine substantially increased the size of the empire's Slavic 'heartland' and strengthened the empire's perception of itself as a European rather than a Eurasian power.

During the reigns of Emperors *Paul I (1796–1801) and *Alexander I (1801–25) a Ukrainian national revival, similar in character to those of other East European peoples of that era, began in the Russian Empire. The vernacular Ukrainian language appeared in literature (I. *Kotliarevsky, 1798), a grammar of the language was written by A. Pavlovsky, histories of Ukraine circulated in manuscript form (*Istoriia Rusov) and appeared in print (D. Bantysh-Kamensky's Istoriia Maloi Rossii [History of Little Russia, 1822]), and a university was founded in Kharkiv (1805) with much support from local patriots (especially V. *Karazyn). A new generation of patriotic Ukrainian intelligentsia began to emerge from among the gentry of the Left Bank, largely descendants of the Cossack starshyna.

During the course of the Napoleonic Wars there were some minor territorial changes affecting Ukrainian lands under Russian rule. The Ternopil district was temporarily annexed by Russia from 1809 until 1815, when it was returned to Austria. In 1812 Russia acquired Bessarabia with its substantial Ukrainian population. In 1815 the Kholm region became part of the Congress Kingdom of Poland, which was an autonomous part of the Russian Empire.

Throughout the first half of the 19th century Ukrainians continued to contribute to Russian culture and to imperial administration. The outstanding Russian writer N. *Gogol was a Ukrainian. Other Ukrainians who wrote in the Russian language and earned a place in the history of Russian literature were N. Gnedich and V. Kapnist. Ukrainians prominent in Russia's intellectual and political life also included the minister of justice D. Troshchynsky, the minister of internal affairs V. Kochubei, the minister of education P. Zavadovsky, and the bibliographer and journalist V. Anastasevych. A number of Ukrainian emigrants from Transcarpathia also made careers in Russia in the early 19th century, including the Slavist Yu. Venelin, the philosopher P. Lodii, the economist and lawyer M. Baluhiansky, and the physician I. Orlai.

In the same period some of the more significant political developments within the Russian Empire unfolded in whole or in part on Ukrainian soil. Many Ukrainians belonged to the revolutionary *Decembrist movement, which was opposed to both tsarist absolutism and serfdom. The primary Decembrist organization in Ukraine was the *Southern Society. The *Society of United Slavs,

which unlike the Southern Society sought the establishment of a Slavic federal republic, nonetheless merged with it in the fall of 1825. Also connected with the Decembrist movement was the *Little Russian Secret Society, which had a shadowy existence; it is said to have called for the erection of an independent Ukrainian state. Another manifestation of revolutionary ferment in the Russian Empire was the unsuccessful *Polish Insurrection of 1830–1, which encompassed Right-Bank Ukraine. The suppression of the Polish insurrection had a number of repercussions for Ukrainians. Some Polish revolutionaries decided that they had been defeated because of a lack of popular support, especially among the peasantry. That conviction gave rise to an interest in and sympathy with the Ukrainian people on the part of democratically inclined representatives of the Right-Bank gentry. Also, in the aftermath of the insurrection Tsar *Nicholas I (1825–55) took measures to eliminate Polish and strengthen Russian influence in the Right Bank and Kiev: in 1835 Kiev's right of *Magdeburg law was rescinded; in 1839 the Uniate church in Belarus and Right-Bank Ukraine was abolished and replaced by the Russian Orthodox church; and in 1834 the *Kremianets Lyceum was closed and Kiev University established. Some of the government's efforts to promote Russification actually contributed to the development of the Ukrainian national movement. For example, to collect documentation showing that the Right Bank was an ancient Russian land, the government established the *Kiev Archeographic Commission in 1843; the commission, however, gave employment to some of the most outstanding representatives of the Ukrainian movement and published dozens of volumes of sources for Ukrainian history. In 1845–6 the Ukrainian movement in the Russian Empire assumed an overt political dimension with the emergence in Kiev of the *Cyril and Methodius Brotherhood, a secret society that advocated the establishment of a Slavic federal republic (with its capital in Kiev) and the abolition of serfdom.

Ukrainians participated in the military actions of the empire in the mid-19th century. In 1849 the tsar sent troops to put down the Hungarian insurrection (see the *Revolution of 1848–9 in the Habsburg monarchy); his army, which included many Ukrainian soldiers, passed through Bukovyna and Galicia and encamped for some months in Transcarpathia. In 1853–6 Russia fought Turkey and its Western European allies in the *Crimean War. The war put a great strain on the Ukrainian population and gave rise to peasant unrest, including the movement of the *Kiev Cossacks in 1855.

Defeat in the Crimean War and the growth of discontent throughout the empire forced the new tsar, *Alexander II (1855–81), to initiate a series of reforms, including the abolition of serfdom (1861) and the establishment of municipal self-government through the *zemstvo. The new, liberal atmosphere within the empire allowed the Ukrainian movement to revive; the former members of the Cyril and Methodius Brotherhood put out the journal *Osnova in St Petersburg (1861–2), and students founded the *Hromada of Kiev in 1859. The reform momentum was halted, however, after the failed *Polish Insurrection of 1863–4. The insurrection had been preceded by Polish student ferment, especially at Kiev University. Some of the Polish students there, led by V. Antonovych, began to identify with the Ukrainian people and adopted Ukrainian nationality; most of those *khlopomany (peasant-lovers) refused on principle to take part in the insurrection when it broke out in January 1863. But many members of the Right-Bank Polish gentry joined the insurgents, and the insurrection spread very quickly to the territory of Right-Bank Ukraine. The insurrection provoked reactionary and Russian nationalist sentiment in Russian society and in the tsarist government. It was alleged in the press and government circles that the Ukrainian movement was Polish-inspired, and Minister of the Interior P. *Valuev issued a secret circular in 1863 that prohibited the publication of scholarly, religious, and educational works in the Ukrainian language and limited Ukrainian publication exclusively to belles lettres. Also as a result of the insurrection, the institution of the zemstvo was excluded from Right-Bank Ukraine until 1911. The Russian government began an intensive campaign ostensibly to remove Polish influence in the last Uniate eparchy in the Russian Empire, that of Kholm; the campaign ended with the forcible liquidation of the Uniate church there in 1875.

The anti-Polish actions of the Russian government in the 1860s and 1870s favorably impressed many Ukrainians in Austrian-ruled Galicia, where the emperor had just given the Polish gentry a free hand in the political control of that crownland. Deeply embittered, many leading Galician Ukrainians looked to Russia for deliverance from the Poles. *Russophiles were also located in Transcarpathia, where the Magyar gentry was granted even more far-reaching powers in 1867, and where people well remembered that Russian troops had suppressed the Magyar insurgents in 1849. Within Russia itself a growing spirit of *Pan-Slavism encouraged a belief that in time Galicia and Transcarpathia, as lands of Rus', should be 'reunited' with Russia. The Russian government provided Russophiles in Western Ukraine with direct and indirect subsidies.

While promoting pro-Russian sympathies abroad imperial authorities were virulent about containing pro-Ukrainian sympathies at home. In 1876 the government decided to clamp down firmly on a resurgent Ukrainian movement. Tsar Alexander II issued the secret *Ems Ukase, which basically outlawed the use of the Ukrainian language in print, and the authorities simultaneously closed down the *Southwestern Branch of the Imperial Russian Geographic Society and the Ukrainophile newspaper *Kievskii telegraf and expelled M. *Drahomanov and M. *Ziber from their positions at Kiev University. The Ukrainian movement was thereafter thoroughly persecuted in the Russian Empire. The Ukrainian language was effectively banished from the school system, the courts, and even churches, and Ukrainophiles were in jeopardy of losing their positions or even their freedom. Under those conditions the center of the Ukrainian national movement shifted westward, to Galicia under Austrian rule. During the reign of *Alexander III (1881–94) the only significant achievement of the Ukrainian movement in the Russian Empire was the publication of a Russian-language journal of Ukrainian studies, Kievskaia starina (1882–1907). The intransigence of the tsarist authorities was such that when the Ukrainian movement revived at the end of the 1890s, it assumed a decidedly revolutionary character. Its major representative was in fact the *Revolutionary Ukrainian Party (RUP; est 1900), which initially called for the establishment of a Ukrainian state independent of Russia. RUP

quickly abandoned that aim and embraced a federalist program, such as had been traditional for Ukrainians in the Russian Empire since the time of the Decembrists.

A major concern of the Ukrainian movement throughout the second half of the 19th century was the problem of the relation of the Ukrainian nationality to the Russian and the relation of both to the legacy of Kievan Rus'. In the late 1850s and 1860s Ukrainian scholars, particularly M. Maksymovych, polemicized with the Pan-Slavist M. Pogodin, who claimed that Kievan Rus' had been Russian and not Ukrainian. The historian M. Kostomarov argued that the differences between the Ukrainian and Russian (in his terminology, Little Russian and Great Russian) nationalities went back to Kievan Rus'; he saw a profound divergence in national character even then, the Ukrainians being democratic and federalist and the Russians autocratic and centralist. The views of Ukrainian scholarship were codified in a 1904 essay by M. *Hrushevsky that squarely opposed the 'traditional' scheme of Russian history. Hrushevsky wrote that the Ukrainians constituted a nation distinct from the Russians and had created the Kievan Rus' state and culture; the Russians appeared on the stage of history only later, as the creators of the Suzdal-Vladimir state.

In 1897 there were over 22 million Ukrainians in the Russian Empire (17.9 percent of the total population), of whom about 20 million lived in Ukrainian ethnographic territory. The Ukrainians living in Russia proper included a large number of Ukrainian peasants who migrated into southern *Siberia in the late 19th and early 20th centuries.

The situation of Ukrainians in the Russian Empire changed dramatically as a result of the *Revolution of 1905. Under the pressure exerted by empire-wide upheaval, including tremendous peasant unrest in Ukraine, mutiny in the Black Sea Fleet, and strikes in Kharkiv, Katerynoslav, and elsewhere, Tsar *Nicholas II (1894–1917) made a number of concessions to the population. The ban on Ukrainian publication was lifted, and Ukrainian newspapers and periodicals proliferated. Branches of the *Prosvita society, co-operatives, and other Ukrainian organizations appeared. Ukrainians were elected to the limited parliament, the State *Duma (see *Ukrainian caucus in the Russian State Duma). Attempts to introduce Ukrainian into the educational system, however, were aborted by the authorities. By 1907 the revolutionary momentum had been broken, and the tsarist authorities again began to persecute the Ukrainian movement, although they were not able to return to the status quo before 1905. In particular, Ukrainian publishing continued to exist, although it was prevented from developing as dynamically as it could have in a more favorable environment. In the aftermath of the revolution the imperial court and conservative circles gave support to the extreme Russian chauvinism of the *Black Hundreds, who were also active in Ukraine.

In the late 19th and early 20th centuries Ukrainians continued to play a vital role in Russian culture and society. Drahomanov, in addition to his work in the Ukrainian sphere, was an important figure in Russian journalism and political thought; in particular, he was a founding father of Russian liberalism. Another Ukrainian proponent of Russian liberalism was M. Mohyliansky, an active constitutional democrat in St Petersburg before 1917. O. Bodiansky, a professor at Moscow University, did much to develop Slavic studies in Russia. B. Kistiakovsky was an outstanding jurist and sociologist who taught in Moscow and edited an important legal journal there. The outstanding scientist V. Vernadsky, who became the first president of the Ukrainian Academy of Sciences in 1918, had been a professor at Moscow University before the revolution.

When the First World War broke out, the tsarist government closed down many of the existing Ukrainian publications and arrested Hrushevsky, the Ukrainian movement's most prominent representative. During the course of the war Russia twice occupied Galicia and Bukovyna, where it ruthlessly persecuted the local Ukrainian movement and harassed the *Ukrainian Catholic church. The war put such a strain on the empire that in March 1917 the tsar abdicated, and power passed to the *Provisional Government. Also in March the *Central Rada was formed in Kiev, and soon it demanded autonomy for Ukraine. The Provisional Government was reluctant to recognize Ukrainian autonomy and did so only under great pressure in July 1917. In November 1917, after the Bolsheviks seized power from the Provisional Government, the Rada proclaimed the *Ukrainian National Republic (UNR), which was formally in federation with Russia. In December 1917, however, the UNR waged war on Soviet Russia. In January 1918 the UNR broke all ties with Russia and declared itself an independent state. The *Ukrainian-Soviet War that followed was largely a contest between Ukrainian independence forces and Soviet Russian armies. The contest was complicated by the presence of a large contingent of imperial loyalist troops (the Volunteer Army) headed by A. *Denikin, who viewed Russia as 'one and indivisible' and wished to restore the empire to its prerevolutionary boundaries. By 1920 most of Ukraine was under Soviet rule and factually, if not juridically, under Russian domination. In December 1922 Soviet Ukraine entered into federation with Soviet Russia and other Soviet republics as part of the Union of Soviet Socialist Republics. (For the history of Ukraine's relations with Russia since 1918 see *Union of Soviet Socialist Republics.)

Ukrainians in Russia, 19th and 20th centuries. The first indication of the number and geographic distribution of Ukrainians in Russia was provided by the census of 1897 (the surveys of 1795 did not provide a breakdown by nationality), but the data provided by that census are not accurate. Many Ukrainians were listed as Russians, and figures were given only for each county. In 1897–1914 there was a large flow of Ukrainian emigrants to beyond the Urals (about 1.5 million Ukrainians settled in Russian-ruled Asia at that time) and to eastern Subcaucasia. The number and distribution of Ukrainians in Russia just prior to the First World War were, therefore, substantially different from what the figures of 1897 would suggest. In 1915–26, emigration from Ukraine ceased almost entirely, so the prewar situation actually corresponds more closely to the situation revealed by the data gathered in the 1926 census (if substantial fatalities due to war, civil war, influenza, and typhoid are allowed for).

According to the 1897 census 22,380,000 Ukrainians lived in the Russian Empire, of whom 20,160,000 (90.1 percent) dwelt in Ukrainian ethnographic territories, 670,000 (3 percent) in regions bordering on those territories, and 1,560,000 (6.9 percent) elsewhere. Of those who dwelt elsewhere, 1,020,000 were listed as residents of European Russia, and 209,000 of Asian (not including Subcaucasian)

Russia. The actual number of Ukrainians on ethnic borderlands and on primarily Russian ethnic territory was higher.

Ukrainian-Russian ethnic borderlands included eastern Subcaucasia, the Crimea, and the northern Chernihiv region. Eastern Subcaucasia consists of the eastern section of Kuban oblast (the Batalpashinsk, Labinsk, and Maikop districts), where there were 204,800 Ukrainians (25.4 percent of the local population); Stavropol oblast, where there were 319,000 Ukrainians (36.6 percent); Black Sea gubernia, 9,300 Ukrainians (19.1 percent); Terek oblast, 42,000 Ukrainians (4.5 percent); and the Salske district of Don oblast, 22,400 Ukrainians (31 percent). According to the 1897 census there were a total of 798,000 Ukrainians (21.8 percent) in eastern Subcaucasia, and virtually all of them lived in rural settlements. (See also *Don region, *Kuban, *Stavropol region, and *Terek region.)

The 1897 figures for the Crimea suggest that only 65,000 Ukrainians (11.8 percent) resided there (with Tatars making up 35.5 percent, Russians, 31.7 percent, and others, 21 percent), but their number was probably higher. Subsequently a greater number of Ukrainians than Russians settled there and made the Crimea an ethnically mixed Ukrainian ethnographic territory. (See also *Crimea.)

The 1897 census counted only 500 Ukrainians (0.1 percent of the local population, compared to 72 percent Russian and 24 percent Belarusian) in the northern Chernihiv region (in Starodub, Mglin, Novozybkiv, and Surazh counties), on the Ukrainian-Belarus border. The actual number was probably much higher, since in 1926, 125,000 were listed as Ukrainians (14.1 percent of the total). (See also *Chernihiv region.)

The 1,020,000 Ukrainians who lived in European Russian ethnographic territories were concentrated in the Ukrainian oases near the Ukrainian ethnographic territory, northern Slobidska Ukraine (the Voronezh and Kursk regions), and the Don region; large Ukrainian settlements in the Volga Basin; and smaller outposts in the Urals. The latter two areas were situated on the eastern borders of the Russian ethnographic territory. In other sections of European Russia Ukrainians constituted less than 0.1 percent of the local population.

In northern Slobidska Ukraine the population was predominantly Russian, but 225,000 Ukrainians lived near the Ukrainian ethnographic territory. Of that number 180,000 resided in Kursk gubernia (in Belgorod, Oboian, Staryi Oskol, Putyvel, Sudzha, and Novyi Oskol counties) and 45,000 in Voronezh gubernia (in the Bobrov, Korotoiak, Novokhopersk, Valuiky, and Pavlovske districts). In those areas Ukrainians constituted 4–15 percent of the population and lived almost exclusively in rural settlements. Ukrainians were almost entirely absent from the northernmost regions of the two gubernias. (See also *Slobidska Ukraine.)

About 65,000 Ukrainians lived, primarily in villages, in the eastern end of Don oblast (in the Khoper, Ust-Medveditskaia, and Don districts and in sections of the Cherkassk, Rostov, and Donets districts), where they made up 7–12 percent of the population. There was also a substantial number of Ukrainians, however, in the major cities of the oblast, including Rostov-na-Donu (5,000, or 4.7 percent) and Novocherkassk (2,600, or 5 percent). The western section (the Sal district) of Don oblast formed part of ethnographically mixed Ukrainian-Russian eastern

Subcaucasia, where Ukrainians constituted a majority.

The largest Ukrainian colonies were in the Volga Basin. They were established mainly in the 18th century and then supplemented by additional waves of immigrants. Large oases of Ukrainians lived on both banks of the Volga, and by the late 19th century they served as a link between the Ukrainians living in Ukrainian European territories and those living in settlements in Asia. According to the census of 1897, 392,000 Ukrainians lived in the Volga Basin (7,000 of them in cities). In Astrakhan gubernia the census found 133,000 Ukrainians, or 13.3 percent of the local population. By county the distribution was as follows: Tsarev county, 75,600, or 38.2 percent; Chernyi Yar, 40,900, or 40.8 percent; and Enotaevsk, 13,700, or 18 percent. There were 149,000 Ukrainians in Samara gubernia, where they constituted 6.2 percent of the local population. By county the distribution was as follows: Novouzensk, 70,000, or 17 percent; Nikolaevsk, 18,800, or 3.5 percent; Buguruslan, 10,4000, or 2.6 percent; and Buzuluk, 9,500, or 2 percent.

A far smaller proportion of Ukrainians lived in the Urals, where Ukrainian settlements were established in the 18th and 19th centuries. Concentrations of Ukrainians lived in Orenburg gubernia (42,000, or 2.6 percent of the local population; by county: in Orenburg, 28,400, or 6 percent, and in Orsk, 8,600, or 4.5 percent) and in Ufa gubernia (5,000, or 0.2 percent of the local population, distributed in Belebei, Sterlitamak, and Ufa counties). In the Urals Ukrainians lived in regions inhabited by Russians, Finns (Mordovians), Tatars, and Bashkirs. (See also *Urals.)

According to the 1897 census there were only 34,000 Ukrainians in the rest of European Russia (central, eastern, and northern, including Belarus), where they made up less than 0.1 percent of the local population. Of that number 23,000 lived in cities, and small groups lived in villages in Elets county of Orel gubernia and in Borisoglebsk county of Tambov gubernia. The census indicated that the largest centers of Ukrainian population were St Petersburg (5,200) and Moscow (4,500). Other cities with a Ukrainian population of over 1,000 included Kursk (2,000), Kaluga (1,300), Mahiliou (1,200), Saratov (1,200), Tsaritsyn (1,100), and Tver (1,000). The actual number of Ukrainians in those regions was much higher. According to the census of 1920 there were 39,200 Ukrainians in European Russia, and according to the census of 1926, 84,000.

(For figures on Ukrainian population and distribution in Asia, see *Far East and *Siberia.)

There is little information about the life of Ukrainians in Russia, apart from the communities in *Moscow and *St Petersburg, which were important centers of Ukrainian cultural (particularly in the early 20th century), community, and political life. St Petersburg was also an important center of Ukrainian studies, as well as of literature and art.

BIBLIOGRAPHY

Kostomarov, N. 'Dve russkiia narodnosti,' in *Sobranie sochinenii*, vol 1 (St Petersburg 1903)

Kharlampovich, K. *Malorossiiskoe vliianie na velikorusskuiu tserkovnuiu zhizn'* (Kazan 1914)

Savchenko, F. *Zaborona ukraïnstva 1876 r.* (Kharkiv–Kiev 1930; repr, Munich 1970)

Myshko, D. *Ukraïns'ko-rosiis'ki zv'iazky v XIV–XVI st.* (Kiev 1959)

Shevchenko, F. *Politychni ta ekonomichni zv'iazky Ukraïny z Rosiieiu v seredyni XVII st.* (Kiev 1959)

O'Brien, C. *Muscovy and the Ukraine: From the Pereiaslavl Agreement to the Truce of Andrusovo, 1654–1667* (Berkeley 1963)

Hrushevsky, M. *The Traditional Scheme of Russian History and the Problem of a Rational Organization of the History of the East Slavs* (Winnipeg 1965)

Hunczak, T. (ed). *Russian Imperialism from Ivan the Great to the Revolution* (New Brunswick, NJ 1974)

Pelenski, J. 'The Origins of the Official Muscovite Claims to the "Kievan Inheritance," ' *HUS*, 1, no. 1 (March 1977)

Saunders, D. *The Ukrainian Impact on Russian Culture, 1750–1850* (Edmonton 1985)

Kohut, Z. *Russian Centralism and Ukrainian Autonomy: Imperial Absorption of the Hetmanate, 1760s–1830s* (Cambridge, Mass 1988)

Potichnyj, P.; Raeff M.; Pelenski, J.; Žekulin, G. (eds). *Ukraine and Russia in Their Historical Encounter* (Edmonton 1992)

J.-P. Himka, V. Kubijovyč

Russian Communist Party (Bolshevik). See Communist Party of the Soviet Union.

Russian Empire. See Russia.

Russian Executive Committee (Russian: Russkii ispolnitelnyi komitet). A political association of Galician Russophiles established in Lviv in December 1918. It supported the Hetman government in eastern Ukraine and approved of the idea of a federation with a revived Russia ruled by the Whites. The committee's organ was the renewed *Prikarpatskaia Rus'*. Its leading members were prominent Galician Russophiles, such as V. Kurylovych, D. Markov, M. Tretiak, and E. Valnytsky. It co-operated with the Ukrainian *Interparty Council and boycotted the 1922 elections to the Polish parliament. In 1923 the committee split into the socialist pro-Soviet People's Will party, which later joined the Sel-Rob party, and the conservative Galician-Russian People's Organization, which enjoyed the support of the Polish government and was given control of institutions such as the People's Home in Lviv and the Stauropegion Institute. From 1929 to 1931 the People's Organization was divided into two groups, the Russian Agrarian party and the Russian Peasants' Organization.

Russian Foreign Trade Bank (Russian: Russkii bank dlia vneshnei torgovli). One of the largest joint-stock banks in the Russian Empire, established in St Petersburg in 1871. Its major shareholders were the Deutsche Bank and several other German banks. In 1914 its assets exceeded 400 million rubles. The bank financed mainly foreign and domestic trade, although it also acquired some interests in heavy industry and sugar refining in Ukraine. In 1914, of its 66 branches 17 were located in Ukraine, where it played a major role in financing the grain and sugar trades. In 1917 its rival, the *Russian Trade and Industry Bank, gained a controlling share of it. The Soviet government of Russia nationalized it at the end of 1917, and the Soviet government of Ukraine at the beginning of 1919.

Russian language in Ukraine. The linguistic contacts involved in the political, ecclesiastical, literary, and commercial relations and population transfers between the principalities of Kiev, Chernihiv, Halych, and Volodymyr-Volynskyi and the northern Rus' principalities of Novgorod, Rostov, Suzdal, and Pereiaslavl during the medieval period have not been studied. Nor have Russian-Ukrainian relations in the Lithuanian-Ruthenian period, and particularly during Moscow's rule over the Chernihiv region (1503–1618), been examined. Discounting the Russian garrison stationed in Kiev from 1654, the first substantial Russian settlements in Ukraine (mainly of *Old Believers) arose in the northern Chernihiv region in the second half of the 17th century. From there they spread in the 18th and 19th centuries to Right-Bank and Southern Ukraine. Another branch of Old Believers, the followers of I. Nekrasov, settled in the Danube Delta in the 1770s and then migrated to Austrian-ruled Bukovyna and the Khotyn area in the 1780s. In the late 1950s V. Stolbunova and V. Kuznetsov studied their dialects in the Chernivtsi oblast villages of Bila Krynytsia, Bilousivka, and Lypovany. Because of their religious isolation from the Ukrainian milieu, their original dialects (mostly southern Russian and some central Russian) were relatively little affected, and then mostly in vocabulary, by the Ukrainian language.

Ukrainian settlers came into contact with Russian rural colonists in Slobidska Ukraine in the 17th century and in Southern Ukraine in the late 18th century. Except for those living in compact colonies, most of the Russian Old Believers, serfs, military settlers, and refugees were assimilated by the dominant Ukrainian peasantry. In the process the Ukrainian Steppe and Slobidska Ukraine dialects were influenced to varying degrees by Russian (eg, the arrested change of *o* into *i* and the transition of stressed *e* into *'o*, sporadic *akan'e*, forms such as *na ruk'í* [Russian: *na ruké*, Ukrainian: *na rucí*] 'on the arm', and dual forms of masculine nouns such as *dva hóda* (Russian: *dva góda*) 'two years'; see also *Steppe dialects). More compact Russian dialectal areas exist in Voznesenka, Vvedenka, and Pavlivka in Artsyz raion, Odessa oblast (brought by settlers from Kursk gubernia); Serhiivka and Uspenivka in Sarata raion (brought from Orel gubernia); the Old Believer village of Velykoploske in Mykhailivka raion in northern Odessa oblast (est over 200 years ago); among the Old Believers in Vinkivtsi raion in Khmelnytskyi oblast; Piatydub in Malyn raion, Zhytomyr oblast; Rakhvalivka and Krasylivka in Ivankiv raion in northern Kiev oblast; and along the northern littoral of the Sea of Azov. The Kharkiv oblast villages of Velyki Prokhody and Mali Prokhody in Derhachi raion and Ruski Tyshky, Ploske, and Lyptsi in Kharkiv raion belong to the southern group of the south Russian dialects of the Kursk region, but their stress in verbs has been influenced perceptibly by Ukrainian.

Ukraine's lower urban strata and inhabitants of suburbs and workers' settlements in the Donbas and Dnipropetrovske oblast speak a variety of Russified dialects which evolved through the Russification of local Ukrainian residents and the constant influx of Russians, who migrated or were sent to Ukraine. The slang and argot of the Russian lumpen and criminal elements in the large cities (Odessa, Kiev, Kharkiv, Dnipropetrovske, and the cities of the Donbas) became widespread in the Soviet period. They retained their Russian forms as a result of the continual seasonal influx of such elements from Leningrad and Moscow. Some features common to Ukrainian and south Russian are characteristic of this mixed Russian-Ukrainian patois (*surzhyk*): the Ukrainian pronunciation of *h* and the vowels *o, e, y*, with sporadic *akan'e*; the pronunciation of *e/'e/je* from etymological *ě*; hardened *r* and labials at the ends of words; iotized pronunciation of groups of the type *vja, bja, pja*; the hard *č, šč*; Ukrainian interword phonetics,

stress, and verbal and prepositional government (eg, *po domax* instead of Russian *po domam* 'in the homes'); lexical Ukrainianisms from everyday life; and the nondifferentiation between the predicate and attribute forms of adjectives. The *surzhyk* of Kharkiv, the Donbas, and Dnipropetrovske oblast has been studied by B. Larin, K. Nimchynov, and V. Shadura respectively. In belles lettres it has been used to depict tsarist military officers (by V. Vynnychenko), burghers (M. Starytsky), the Soviet police (O. Korniichuk), and the lumpen proletariat (V. Vynnychenko, A. Teslenko, I. Mykytenko, L. Pervomaisky, and L. Brasiuk).

Because of Russification pressures, a 'Ukrainian' provincial variant of literary Russian developed among the gentry and intelligentsia in the tsarist period, and among Party functionaries and the technical intelligentsia in the Soviet period. The imperial government attracted Russian civil servants to Ukraine by offering premiums. The Soviet government had forced Ukrainians to take seasonal or permanent jobs in other parts of the USSR and given jobs in Ukraine to non-Ukrainian immigrants. At the same time, Standard Ukrainian has been purged consistently of distinctively Ukrainian features, and the use of *surzhyk* has been tolerated. In 19th-century Galicia and Bukovyna (particularly from 1866 to the 1920s) and in Transcarpathia (until 1945) the periodicals and publications of the *Russophiles promoted a special form of literary Russian known as *yazychiie* among the clergy and, to a lesser extent, the secular intelligentsia. (See also *Russian-Ukrainian linguistic relations.)

BIBLIOGRAPHY

Zelenetskii, K. *O russkom iazyke v Novorossiiskom krae* (Odessa 1855)

Dolopchev, V. *Opyt slovaria nepravil'nostei v russkoi razgovornoi rechi (preimushchestvenno v Iuzhnoi Rossii)* (Odessa 1886; 2nd edn, Warsaw 1909)

Hnatiuk, H. *Rossiis'ko-ukraïns'ki literaturno-movni zv'iazky v druhii polovyni XVIII–pershii chetverti XIX st.* (Kiev 1957)

Miroshnik, N. *N.V. Gogol': Ego rol' v ukreplenii russko-ukrainskikh iazykovykh sviazei* (Kharkiv 1959)

Respublikans'ka naukova konferentsiia z pytan' rosiis'ko-ukraïns'kykh movnykh zv'iazkiv: Tezy dopovidei (Luhanske 1964)

Ïzhakevych, H. *Ukraïns'ko-rosiis'ki movni zv'iazky radians'koho chasu* (Kiev 1969)

Shevelov, G. 'Zum Problem des ukrainischen Anteils an der Bildung der russischen Schriftsprache Ende des 18. Jahrhunderts,' *Wiener slavistisches Jahrbuch*, 16 (1970)

Izhakevich, G. [Ïzhakevych, H.]; et al (eds). *Sopostavitel'noe issledovanie russkogo i ukrainskogo iazykov* (Kiev 1975)

Beloded [Bilodid], I.; et al (eds). *Russkii iazyk – iazyk mezhnatsional'nogo obshcheniia i edineniia narodov SSSR* (Kiev 1976)

Izhakevich, G.; et al (eds). *Kul'tura russkoi rechi na Ukraine* (Kiev 1976)

Barannik, L.; et al. *Russkie govory na Ukraine* (Kiev 1982)

Izhakevich, G.; et al (eds). *Puti povysheniia kul'tury russkoi rechi na Ukraine* (Kiev 1986)

O. Horbach

Russian Liberation Army (Russian: Russkaia osvoboditelnaia armiia [ROA]). A military formation in the German armed forces during the Second World War. It was organized in 1943 with the approval of the German High Command by Gen A. *Vlasov, a captured Red Army general, from among Soviet prisoners of war held by the Germans. In 1944 control of the ROA was transferred to the SS. In early 1945 the ROA's total strength was approx 200,000, of which about 40 percent were Ukrainians. The ROA was used by the Germans largely for propaganda purposes; its units were never committed to combat. Some ROA units participated in the anti-German uprising of early May 1945 in Czechoslovakia. At the end of the war many ROA officers and men surrendered to the Western Allies in the hope of escaping Soviet reprisal. Most of them, however, were turned over to the Soviet authorities (see *Repatriation).

Russian Music Society. Formed in St Petersburg in 1859, the society was dedicated to the development of refined musical taste and talent in the Russian Empire. It subsequently established branches in Kiev (1863), Kharkiv (1871), and Odessa (1884). These played a leading role in the music life of each center through the establishment of music schools and the sponsorship of concert programs. In 1913 the society's music schools in Kiev and Odessa were turned into full conservatories. The society was disbanded throughout the Russian Empire in 1917 with the outbreak of the revolution. The activities of the Kiev branch are described in M. Kuzmin's *Zabuti storinky muzychnoho zhyttia Kyieva* (The Forgotten Pages of the Musical Life of Kiev, 1972).

Russian Orthodox church (Russian: Russkaia Pravoslavnaia Tserkov [ROC]). The largest contemporary autocephalous Orthodox church. It is headed by the 'Patriarch of Moscow and All Rus',' who chairs the church's highest body, the Patriarchal Synod, which includes as permanent members the metropolitans of Kiev, Leningrad, and Krutitsy. In 1990 the Moscow Patriarch declared its Ukrainian and Belarusian exarchates the Ukrainian Orthodox church and the Belarusian Orthodox church. Although these new entities are granted considerable autonomy, they at present continue as components of the ROC. The synod has departments for administration, external church relations, publishing, economy, education, and other functions. The official organ of the church is the monthly *Zhurnal Moskovskoi patriarkhii* (32,000 copies in 1989). The patriarchate also publishes (since 1989) a weekly newspaper, *Moskovskii tserkovnyi vestnik*, and a monthly digest with the same name, in addition to various church and theological books and collections (eg, irregular collections put out by the theological academies, titled *Bogoslovskie trudy*) and separate journals for its exarchates abroad.

In the USSR in 1989 the ROC had 70 eparchies. Its hierarchy in 1986 comprised 82 individuals: the patriarch, 13 metropolitans, 41 archbishops, and 27 bishops (including 8 serving abroad and 6 retired hierarchs). In October 1989 there were approx 9,700 parishes, served by 8,100 priests and deacons, and 2,400 precentors. Although the number of the church's faithful is difficult to determine, it was estimated in the late 1970s at 30 to 40 million regular worshipers. In 1989 the ROC lost large numbers of believers and parishes in Ukraine to the Ukrainian Catholic, particularly in Galicia, and the Ukrainian Autocephalous Orthodox churches. From the late 1940s until the late 1980s the majority of operating Orthodox churches in the USSR (almost two-thirds) were located within the Ukrainian exarchate of the ROC, renamed the Ukrainian Orthodox church in 1990. In 1989 the ROC established an exarchate for Belarus, renamed the Belarusian Orthodox church in

1990. Outside the USSR the church has the Western European exarchate (based in London), the Central European exarchate (East Berlin), the exarchate of Central and South America (Buenos Aires), an administration for its parishes in the United States (New York) and Canada (Edmonton), spiritual missions in the Holy Land, and a permanent representation at the World Council of Churches in Geneva. Other Russian Orthodox churches outside the USSR (which often number many Ukrainians among their members) retain ties with the ROC, for example, the Autocephalous Orthodox Church in America (formerly the Russian Orthodox Greek Catholic Church in North America). The Russian Orthodox Church outside Russia, however, stands in opposition to the ROC.

The ROC maintains two theological academies (in St Petersburg and Zagorsk, near Moscow) and six seminaries (Zagorsk, St Petersburg, Odessa, and, since 1989, Kiev, Minsk [Zhirovitsky], and Tobolsk). In 1989 the academies graduated 37 full-time and 10 correspondence students; 192 full-time and 81 correspondence students completed study at the three seminaries (60 of them in Odessa). In 1988–9 the ROC was allowed to open five secondary theological schools – in Kishinev, Novosibirsk, Smolensk, Stavropol, and Chernihiv – primarily for the training of precentors. In addition the ROC operates one icon painting school and two women's choral conductor schools (in Moscow and St Petersburg). In October 1989 the ROC had 35 monasteries and convents (in 1980 there were only 16), including the Kievan Cave Monastery, reopened in 1988.

According to the Soviet constitution, the church was separate from the state. In reality, however, the latter closely controlled the former, as it did all other religious groups, through the *Council on Religious Affairs of the USSR Council of Ministers, analogous councils in the various republics, and plenipotentiaries in the individual oblasts. Prior to 1988 the activity of the ROC was limited to conducting services and performing other rites, and it was not permitted to engage in missionary, charitable, educational, or community political work (except in its officially sanctioned 'patriotic' activities). Though the ROC and other recognized religious groups acquired the rights of a juridical person, including property rights, the church did not have the right to own church buildings or their contents; they were loaned under contract by the state to a parish committee, usually composed of 20 lay people. These committees, which were officially registered with the state, were responsible for the parish's finances and activities, for hiring the priest, and so on. The state could refuse to recognize a parish, thereby making it illegal for the parishioners to gather or hold services. The state also gave permission for church synods and conferences, and for any other church function held outside the church premises. Until 1988, priests were not allowed to teach catechism to children, and organized religious instruction for people over 18 was strictly controlled. In 1988 a new all-Union law on the freedom of conscience and religious organizations was promulgated.

History. Officially the ROC traces its history to the introduction of Christianity in Rus' in the 10th century. In reality, however, the existence of the church dates only from the aftermath of the Mongol attack on Kiev in 1240 and the transfer of the seat of the Kievan metropoly to Vladimir on the Kliazma, by Metropolitan Maximos after 1283. Subsequent metropolitans of Kiev had their see in Moscow, which became the center of the new and rapidly growing Muscovite state (later Russia). With the increase in the strength and prestige of Moscow, the metropolitans began to demand their independence of the Patriarch of Constantinople, under whose jurisdiction the Kiev metropoly remained.

In 1448 Grand Prince Vasilii of Moscow appointed Bishop Iona of Riazan the new metropolitan without the consent of Constantinople, and the ROC then declared its autocephaly, which was recognized by Constantinople only in 1589. Thus, beginning in 1458, two separate and distinct Eastern Slavic metropolies came to coexist: the metropoly of Kiev, or Ukraine-Belarus, and the 'metropoly of Moscow and all Rus'.'

Having lost its links with the centers of Eastern Christianity, the Muscovite church increasingly became a tool in the state's hands. By the early 16th century, when Muscovy was freed from Mongol rule, the conviction gained currency that Moscow ('the Third Rome') was the direct descendant of Rome and Constantinople as a great Christian capital and center of Orthodoxy. This belief was buttressed after the fall of Constantinople in 1453 to the Ottoman Empire. The ROC consistently rejected closer relations with the Catholic West and opposed attempts at union (see the Church Union of *Florence).

In 1589 the ROC became a patriarchate, but this did not diminish its subservience to the tsar. After the 10th patriarch (Adriian) died in 1700, no successor was appointed to his position for over 200 years. In 1721 the patriarch was officially replaced by the *Holy Synod as the highest authority in the church. This completed the formal subjugation of the church, which became almost a governmental institution ruled by imperial fiat. The head of the Holy Synod was the *ober-prokuror*, a lay state official who was referred to as 'the tsar's eyes.' It was only in 1917 that the ROC was able to throw off briefly its state control. In November 1917 the All-Russian Local Sobor restored the patriarchate and elected Metropolitan Tikhon Beliavin as Patriarch of Moscow. After his death in 1925, the Soviet authorities prevented the election of a successor. From 1926 to 1943 the ROC was headed by patriarchal locum tenens Sergii Stragorodsky, who was elected patriarch in September 1943. After his death in 1944, he was succeeded by patriarchs Aleksei Simansky (1945–70), Pimen Izvekov (1971–90), and Aleksei Ridiger.

In its expansion the ROC relied on the political strength of the Russian state, and spread its influence to the eparchies of Kiev metropoly, especially after the Treaty of Pereiaslav in 1654. The Kievan metropolitans tried to resist this pressure and remain under the patriarchate of Constantinople, but they were unsuccessful; in 1686 the metropoly passed to the jurisdiction of Moscow. Many of the most learned clergy and hierarchy moved to Moscow and later St Petersburg, where they worked in church administration, education, missionary work, and so on. ROC missionaries established the church throughout the eastern Russian Empire, and Siberia, and even in Russian possessions in the Aleutians and Alaska, where an eparchy was established in 1870.

At its height the ROC owned vast estates and was extremely wealthy, and its affluence helped to attract many priests and monks. Increasingly, however, the state sought ways to limit its wealth, for example, by placing a ban on its acquisitions of new territories (1649). Tension between the two bodies reached its peak during the term of Patriarch Nikon (1652–8), who was removed from his position for defending too forcefully the church's prerogatives. Earlier his attempts to modernize the church had resulted in a major split, driving the *Old Believers from the ROC. The persecution of the Old Believers in Muscovy forced many of them to flee, and some established colonies in Ukraine and Belarus.

The ROC furthered Russification among the peoples conquered by the Russians and in the various churches (eg, the Georgian Orthodox church) that came under Russian domination. In particular the Kiev metropoly was prohibited from cultivating its traditional liturgical style and language (see *Church rite) and forced to conform to Russian liturgical practices and rituals.

A major shortcoming of the ROC was the low level of education that marked the clergy in the 15th and 16th centuries. To combat this problem, the church brought in numerous foreign theologians and educators, such as Maximos the Greek (in the first half of the 16th century), who translated many Greek church books. In the 17th century numerous Ukrainian churchmen – S. Yavorsky, D. Tuptalo, T. Prokopovych, and others – also rose to prominence in the church hierarchy and in theological institutions. From the 19th century the situation improved markedly. By 1913 the ROC maintained 4 theological academies (in Kiev, Moscow, St Petersburg, and Kazan), 59 seminaries, and almost 200 other schools in the Russian Empire. (See also History of the Ukrainian *Church, *Ukrainian Orthodox church, and *Kiev metropoly.)

BIBLIOGRAPHY

Ternovskii, S. *Issledovanie o podchinenii Kievskoi mitropolii Moskovskomu patriarkhatu* (Kiev 1872)
Kharlampovich, K. *Malorossiiskoe vliianie na velikorusskuiu tserkovnuiu zhizn'* (Kazan 1914)
Curtiss, J.S. *Church and State in Russia: The Last Years of the Empire* (New York 1940)
Mouravieff, A. *A History of the Church in Russia* (Oxford 1942)
Zernov, A. *The Russians and Their Church* (London 1945)
Kartashev, A. *Ocherki po istorii Russkoi tserkvi*, 2 vols (Paris 1959)
Hayward, B.; Fletcher, W. *Religion and the Soviet State: A Dilemma of Power* (New York 1969)
Pospielovsky, D. *The Russian Church under the Soviet Regime, 1917–1982* (Crestwood, NJ 1984)
Ellis, J. *The Russian Orthodox Church: A Contemporary History* (London 1986)

B. Bociurkiw, I. Korovytsky

Russian People's Council (Russian: Russkii narodnyi sovet). An organization of émigré Galician and Bukovynian Russophiles in Kiev and Rostov-na-Donu who were evacuated to the east when the Russian army retreated from Western Ukraine in 1915. The president was V. *Dudykevych.

Russian Revolution of 1905. See Revolution of 1905.

Russian Revolution of 1917. See February Revolution of 1917 and October Revolution of 1917.

Russian Social Democratic Workers' party (Russian: Rossiiskaia sotsial-demokraticheskaia rabochaia partiia, or RSDRP). The Marxist (later Communist) party of the Russian Empire. It was formed by local Marxist groups, which sprang up in the 1890s. Its founding congress was held in Minsk in March 1898 and was attended by only nine delegates, from the St Petersburg and Moscow groups, the Jewish Bund, the small Kiev newspaper *Rabochaia gazeta*, and the Kiev and Katerynoslav groups. The Minsk Congress was inconsequential, and most of the delegates were soon arrested.

An enduring controversy over goals and strategy divided the party. The so-called Economists favored legal methods of class struggle and a broadly based workers' movement that would become a political force. Their opponents, with V. Lenin in the forefront, gave priority to the political struggle and contended that the preoccupation with economic issues would lead to reforms instead of the political revolution. Lenin's rejection of 'economism' was linked closely to his effort to reorganize the RSDRP into a very different kind of party. He advocated a party with a limited membership of dedicated and tested professional revolutionaries, well trained in conspiratorial methods. Opposition to Lenin's views emerged at the Second Congress (held in Brussels and London, August 1903) and split the RSDRP into the Bolshevik (majoritarian) and *Menshevik (minoritarian) factions. Lenin's claim to the majority support in the party was untrue. His victory in 1903 was accidental, and the Stockholm Congress (April–May 1906) showed that the majority of the party supported the Mensheviks. At the May 1907 Congress in London neither faction obtained a clear majority; the balance of power was held by Jewish Bundists and Polish and Latvian delegates. After efforts to heal the breach between the factions in 1905–11 failed, Lenin held his own party conference in Prague in January 1912, elected a new Central Committee, and named his faction the RSDRP (Bolshevik). In March 1918 it changed its name to the Russian Communist Party (Bolshevik) or RCP(B).

In Ukraine the RSDRP had attracted mostly members of a minority – the Russian urban workers as well as some intellectuals and Jews. It had no appeal for the largely peasant Ukrainian population and the Ukrainian intelligentsia. The RSDRP in Ukraine was not a unified organization but reflected various divisions. Besides the Bolsheviks and Mensheviks, who were initially more numerous in Ukraine, it encompassed the Jewish Bundists, who favored national cultural (nonterritorial) autonomy and opposed Lenin's policy of assimilating Jews. The RSDRP had to contend with the emergence in 1905 of the *Ukrainian Social Democratic Workers' party (USDRP), which demanded that socialist parties be organized on the basis of nationality. The RSDRP tried to use the Ukrainian Social Democratic *Spilka against the USDRP.

Both the Bolshevik and the Menshevik factions of the RSDRP opposed Ukrainian independence. Although both factions participated in the Central Rada in 1917, they withdrew when independence was proclaimed. When the RSDRP (Bolshevik) had to give up Kiev in 1918 after signing the Peace Treaty of *Brest-Litovsk, it was confronted with an identity problem. Under the impact of defeat and retreat the party adopted the name Communist Party (Bolshevik) of Ukraine (CP[B]U) at its founding congress in Moscow on 5–12 July 1918. But it was Ukrainian only in name: its membership was mostly Russian and Jewish, and its leadership was largely non-Ukrainian and dominated by the so-called Katerynoslav group. The key Ukrainian leaders in the CP(B)U were V. Zatonsky, M.

Skrypnyk, V. Shakhrai, and Yu. Kotsiubynsky. Attempts to free the CP(B)U from the control of the Russian Communist Party (Bolshevik) were condemned by Lenin and defeated by the non-Ukrainian leaders of the party.

BIBLIOGRAPHY
Reshetar, J. *A Concise History of the Communist Party of the Soviet Union* (New York 1960)
Schapiro, L. *The Communist Party of the Soviet Union* (Cambridge 1960; 2nd rev edn 1970)
Elwood, R. *Russian Social Democracy in the Underground: A Study of the RSDRP in the Ukraine, 1907–1914* (Assen 1975)
J. Reshetar

Russian Soviet Federated Socialist Republic (Russian: Rossiiskaia Sovetskaia Federativnaia Sotsialisticheskaia Respublika, or RSFSR). The largest and most important of the 15 republics constituting the former Soviet Union. In the north it borders on the Arctic Ocean; in the east, on the Pacific Ocean; in the west, on Norway, Finland, Estonia, Latvia, Lithuania, Poland, and Belarus; and in the south, on Ukraine, Georgia, Azerbaijan, Kazakhstan, Mongolia, China, and North Korea. The Ural Mountains mark the conventional boundary between Russia's European and Asian (Siberian) parts. With an area of 17,075,400 sq km, the RSFSR accounted for 76 percent of all Soviet territory.

Because of its vast size and the diversity of its ethnic groups the RSFSR was structured as a federation. It had jurisdiction over 16 autonomous republics, 49 oblasts, and 6 krais, which themselves contain 5 autonomous national oblasts and 10 national okrugs. This division served chiefly to give the appearance of respect for national differences.

In 1989 the population of the RSFSR was 147,386,000, a figure making it the fifth most populous state in the world. Russians hold a comfortable majority of 82 percent in their own republic. They are concentrated in the European part (especially in the huge central plain around Moscow), the Volga region, southern Siberia, and the Far East. Russians constitute a majority in the Bashkir, Buriat, Kalmyk, Karelian, Komi, Mari, Mordovia, Udmurt, and Yakut autonomous republics and in most autonomous oblasts, and a significant proportion of the population in the other regions of the RSFSR.

According to the 1989 census there were 4,364,000 Ukrainians in the RSFSR. The largest and most established concentrations were in the southern regions of the European RSFSR (approx 170,000 in Krasnodar krai, 157,000 in Rostov oblast, 135,000 in Voronezh oblast, and 185,000 in Moscow oblast); in the southern Urals, (105,000 in the Orenburg oblast); and in several regions of the Asiatic RSFSR (163,000 in Primore krai, 90,000 in Khabarovsk krai). Unlike Russians who lived in Soviet Ukraine, expatriate Ukrainians in the RSFSR did not have their own schools, press, or facilities. Hence, only 43 percent of them had retained the Ukrainian language.

In economic terms the RSFSR was the backbone of the USSR. It contained three-fifths of the farmland and seven-tenths of the Union's industry. It accounted for 90 percent of the crude petroleum, 70 percent of the natural gas, 70 percent of the hard coal, 58 percent of the steel, 80 percent of the timber, and 60 percent of the cement output of the USSR; 80 percent of Soviet hard-currency exports came from the RSFSR. In 1989, 74 percent of the RSFSF's population was urban, compared with 67 percent in Soviet

Ukraine. The rate of industrialization, the level of economic development (measured by per capita industrial output), and the average per capita national income were considerably greater in the RSFSR than in other Soviet republics, with the exception of Estonia and Latvia. The average annual growth of national income per person in the 1980s (given a Soviet norm of 100) was 109 in the RSFSR and 96 in Soviet Ukraine, whose per capita output was close to the RSFSR's. Since the 1980s the RSFSR 'imported' more industrial resources, goods, and agricultural products than it 'exported' to the other USSR republics. Much of Soviet Ukraine's agricultural output, coal, iron, and steel was sent to the RSFSR. An important part of the RSFSR's investment capital was extracted from Soviet Ukraine. According to most criteria the economic development of the RSFSR was higher than that of Ukraine. But the privileged position of the Russians in the USSR could not be described in economic terms such as these.

Although neither the RSFSR nor the USSR could be described as a nation-state, they were the creations and political instruments of the Russian nation. The Russians enjoyed a special status within the USSR. Soviet ideology paid tribute to the 'great Russian people' as the 'leading nation,' with a 'special historical role' in the Soviet state. Of the 15 Union republics Russia was the only one to be mentioned in the USSR anthem. Russians were significantly overrepresented in the Soviet power structure. The central institutions and the political hierarchy were dominated by Russians. About 60 percent of the CPSU membership was Russian. In 1986, 85 percent of the 13 CC CPSU secretaries, 83 percent of the 83 USSR ministers, and 88 percent of the 17 top military commanders were Russians. By 1988 the Union leadership and elite had become more Russian than in any other period. In 1982 non-Russians constituted 38 percent of the Politburo; in 1988 they amounted to a mere 15 percent. Similarly, within the CC CPSU and the central Party bureaucracy there was a visible decline in non-Russian representation. The 16-member presidential council appointed in March 1990 included only 5 non-Russians (one Ukrainian among them). Its only non-Communist member was a Russian rightwing nationalist.

Furthermore, the Russian republic was not as distinct structurally from the USSR as were the other republics. The RSFSR had its own Supreme Soviet and Council of Ministers but did not have a separate capital, KGB branch, television and radio system, or trade-union organization. The RSFSR had no international status: in contrast to the Ukrainian SSR and the Belorussian SSR it did not even have a seat at the United Nations. From 1925 the RSFSR did not have its own Party apparatus (with a Congress, Central Committee, Politburo, and Secretariat) distinct from the all-Union structure, as had the other 14 republics, although a special Russian Bureau was set up in the CC CPSU by N. Khrushchev and M. Gorbachev. It was only in 1990 that the Russian republic got its own ministry of the interior and academy of sciences (the former USSR academy).

History. The RSFSR dates back to 7 November 1917, when the Bolsheviks overthrew the Provisional Government and established the Soviet of People's Commissars under V. Lenin's leadership as the new government of the Russian Empire. The Third All-Russian Congress of Soviets (23–31 January 1918) proclaimed the establishment of the RSFSR, and the Fifth All-Russian Congress of Soviets

adopted the First Constitution of the RSFSR on 10 July 1918. The most striking feature of the Constitution (and its revisions in 1925, 1937, and 1978) was the absence of provisions for any genuine federation. After conquering non-Russian territories the RSFSR tried to legitimize its dominance over them by proclaiming its laws to be applicable throughout the lands of the old empire and by signing bilateral treaties with the new Soviet republics, set up in the territories. By decree of the All-Russian Central Executive Committee in June 1919 Ukraine's administration of military, economic, and financial affairs, communications, railways, and labor was merged with Russia's. In the 'federation' treaty of December 1920 all the major government powers were handed over to unified Russian-Ukrainian commissariats and in reality to the RSFSR government. In later 'federative' agreements Ukraine consented to have the RSFSR represent it on the international stage. In 1920–1 similar treaties were signed by the RSFSR with other Soviet republics, which were thereby deprived, in effect, of any internal and external independence. This process of absorption of the non-Russian republics by the RSFSR led eventually to the formation of the USSR.

When the federal state of the *Union of Soviet Socialist Republics (USSR) was created on 31 December 1922, the RSFSR was reduced to the status of a republic within the Union. According to the new constitutional arrangement proposed by Lenin, the existing and future Soviet republics did not merge with the RSFSR but joined it in a state of a 'higher level,' the USSR. With the dissolution of the USSR in 1991 the RSFSR was renamed the Russian Federated Republic, and then the Russian Federation.

BIBLIOGRAPHY
Pipes, R. *The Formation of the Soviet Union: Communism and Nationalism, 1917–1923* (Cambridge 1954; rev edn, 1964)
Fitzsimmons, T. (ed). RSFSR: *Russian Soviet Federated Socialist Republic*, 2 vols (New Haven 1957)
Gregory, J. *Russian Land – Soviet People* (London 1968)
Allworth, E. (ed). *Ethnic Russia in the USSR: The Dilemma of Dominance* (New York 1980)

T. Kis

Russian Trade and Industry Bank (Russian: Russkii torgovo-promyshlennyi bank). One of the largest joint-stock banks in the Russian Empire, founded in 1890 in St Petersburg by a consortium of French banks. In the early 1900s it was saved from bankruptcy by the Ministry of Finance, and in 1912 majority control was acquired by British financiers. Of the bank's 111 branches 14 were located in Ukraine. It had assets of 360 million rubles (1917) and interests in railways, heavy industry, and sugar refining in Ukraine and elsewhere. In January 1917 controlling interest was acquired by K. Yaroshinsky, a financial magnate from Ukraine. He merged it with the *Russian Foreign Trade Bank and the International Commercial Bank, but the whole consortium was soon nationalized by the Bolshevik regime. The branches in Ukraine were nationalized by the Soviet government on 21 January 1919.

Russian Union (Russian: Russkii soiuz). A Russian political organization in Ukraine, established in May 1918 in Kiev. It represented various Russian parties and groupings, including the Constitutional Democrats, Popular Socialists, Socialist Revolutionaries, and Mensheviks. The official purpose of the union was to preserve the Russian school system and to promote Russian culture, but in practice it demanded the restoration of the privileged position of the Russian language and culture in Ukraine. Its members ultimately sought the dismantling of the Ukrainian state and the rebuilding of Russia in its prerevolutionary form.

Russianisms. See Russian-Ukrainian linguistic relations.

Russians in Ukraine. Prior to the 14th and 15th centuries an insignificant number of Russians (or more precisely, peoples of the principality of Moscow and other Russian territories) lived in Ukraine. For the most part individual Russian governmental officials or clergymen and itinerant merchants who lived for a few months at a time in the trading districts of Kiev, Chernihiv, Lutske, and other larger cities constituted the only Russian presence. In time there was also a movement of boyar families and their servants between Muscovy and Ukraine (in both directions). During the reign of Ivan IV (1533–84) the princes Pronsky, Kurbsky, and others moved into the Ukrainian territories of Lithuania, where they offered their services to the grand duke and received estates in return. Others fled to Ukraine and Belarus to escape religious or other persecution. A number of figures opposed to the official dogmas of the Russian Orthodox church, including F. Kosoi and the monks Vasiian and Artemii (a former student of Maximos the Greek), were regarded as heretics and compelled to flee from Muscovy to Ukraine. Another refugee was the printer I. Fedorov. Persecuted by Russian scribes and religious hierarchs, he left Moscow in 1566, moved to Lithuania, and then went on to Lviv and Ostrih, where he changed his name to I. *Fedorovych and became the founder of Ukrainian printing.

The first sustained Russian presence in Ukrainian lands was in the northeastern borderland regions. In the 16th century Muscovy began developing a string of fortified frontier posts in *Slobidska Ukraine as a line of defense against the Tatars. The area was then opened up to colonists, most of whom were Ukrainians, but some of whom were Russians. Muscovy's control of the Chernihiv-Siversk region in the 16th and early 17th centuries enabled Russian landowners and other Muscovite settlers to establish themselves in the region. Most of them remained there even after those territories passed under the control of the Polish-Lithuanian Commonwealth (1618–48) and then the Hetmanate. After the Time of Troubles they were joined by various Muscovite émigrés (including the Klimov, Lovshin, Griaznoi, and Saltykov families), who were granted estates by the Vasa kings Sigismund III and Władysław IV. Some of them kept their holdings throughout the Khmelnytsky period and thereafter; others intermarried with the Ukrainian nobility and Cossack officers and became assimilated.

Some Muscovites, mostly refugees, fought in the Cossack armies in the 16th and 17th centuries. Others (writers, artists, tradesmen, and the like) lived in Ukrainian monasteries, particularly in Kiev. I. Savelov, the Patriarch of Moscow after 1674, had been a monk in the Mezhyhiria Transfiguration Monastery.

Starting in the 1640s Russians studied at the Kievan Mohyla Academy, among them I. Ozerov and P. Zerkalnikov. Zerkalnikov was a merchant who subsequently brought Ye. *Slavynetsky, A. *Koretsky-Satanovsky, and other scholars to Moscow. In the 1680s the students of the academy included K. Istomin, subsequently a printer in Moscow, and K. Zotov, a naval explorer. The children of Muscovite noblemen, such as those of Prince G. Romodanovsky and the boyar P. Sheremetev, also studied in Kiev.

Mid-17th to 18th centuries. The Russian presence in Ukraine increased dramatically following the *Pereiaslav Treaty of 1654. It consisted initially of garrisons in Kiev and other Ukrainian cities and the presence of Muscovite voivodes. In Kiev the 2,000-man infantry force was increased to 5,000 in 1661. A fortress was built in the old quarter of the city, and cavalrymen and fusiliers (with their families) were accommodated next to it. Kiev's Russian population also included various administrative personnel as well as tradesmen, merchants, and traders whose extensive dealings with the troops allowed them to begin competing strongly with their local Ukrainian counterparts. The *Moscow Articles of 1665, drawn up during the tenure of Hetman I. Briukhovetsky, allowed the Muscovite force in Ukraine to increase to 11,600, with garrisons in Kiev, Chernihiv, Pereiaslav, Nizhen, Novhorod-Siverskyi, Pryluka, Poltava, and other cities. Under I. Mazepa a riflemen's regiment was stationed in the hetman's capital, Baturyn, ostensibly for his defense; the force was soon expanded to three regiments.

Wars with Turkey (until 1700) and Sweden (1700–21) and the development of the *Kievan Cave Fortress (1706–23) as a military and administrative center increased the Russian presence in Ukraine. After the Battle of *Poltava in 1709, up to 10 Russian regiments occupied the Hetmanate. Officials of the military and governmental bureaucracy, particularly of the first *Little Russian Collegium, intruded increasingly into internal Ukrainian affairs. Russian governors and military commanders were assigned to Kiev, soldiers were billeted in Hlukhiv (the new capital of the Hetmanate), and commandants were installed in all regimental towns and cities.

Beginning in the time of Peter I Russian landowners acquired increasingly larger holdings in the Hetmanate and Slobidska Ukraine. The estates of Mazepa's loyal *starshyna* and of 'Mazepist' émigrés were given to Russian aristocrats after the defeat at Poltava, most notably to Peter's favorite, A. *Menshikov. The Russian nobles often brought Russian serfs along with them to work, particularly in small-scale manufacturing enterprises. The Authoritative Ordinances imposed by the Russian government on Hetman D. Apostol in 1728 gave Russians permission to purchase land in Ukraine. The tsarist authorities also forbade the Hetmanate to trade with Western Europe as foreign commerce came to be controlled either by the government directly or by Russian merchants. The privileges thus accorded the Russians resulted in a further influx of Russian merchants or their agents into Ukraine, particularly to Kiev and other larger centers. By 1742 there were 120 major Russian merchants in Kiev, and Russians controlled much of the large-scale commerce in Left-Bank Ukraine.

Among the Russians who studied in Kiev in the early 18th century was K. Shchepin of Viatka. In 1734 M. Lomonosov began his studies at the Kievan Mohyla Academy.

There was a significant influx of Russian *Old Believers into Ukraine. Having fled persecution at the hands of the

Russian Orthodox church and the government, they established a number of settlements in the Starodub and Chernihiv regimental territories. The movement began during the tenure of Hetman D. Mnohohrishny and intensified under Mazepa and I. Skoropadsky. Despite protests from Ukrainian landowners and government officials the Russian government not only permitted the Old Believers to continue to leave Russia, but even gave them title to land on which the local Ukrainian landowners and administrators had temporarily allowed them to settle. A similarly arbitrary granting of land occurred in the northern Chernihiv region, where the ongoing settlement of Russians in the borderland reaches (in the Klintsy district) changed the region's ethnic composition. This eventually served as the rationale for excluding those lands from the Ukrainian SSR when it was being formed. (See also *Russian language in Ukraine.)

Other refugees who came to Ukraine from Russia in the 18th century included serfs and military deserters, who expected to find at least temporary shelter or freedom in the Hetmanate, the territory of the Zaporozhian Cossack state, Slobidska Ukraine, and even Right-Bank Ukraine. Some of them were forced to return, but a substantial number remained, particularly in the south, where the Zaporozhian officials and (later) the Russian administration and landowners were keen to see the area settled. They often sheltered refugees and preferred not to return them to their places of origin. In addition a number of Russian nobles to whom Catherine II granted large estates in Southern Ukraine brought their serfs with them in order to populate the region.

The exact number of Russians living in Ukrainian territories in the 18th century is unknown, but fragmentary data suggest that it was relatively small and mostly concentrated in New Russia. In 1763–4, for instance, there were 4,273 Russians and 20,505 Ukrainians in Yelysavethrad province (subsequently Kherson gubernia); the number rose to 5,851 and 57,302 respectively in 1782. In Bakhmut province there were 3,891 Russians and 12,177 Ukrainians in 1763–4, and 12,837 and 57,302 respectively in 1782.

19th and early 20th centuries. Russians were virtually absent from Right-Bank Ukraine (other than in or near Kiev) prior to the second and third partitions of Poland in 1793 and 1795. Even then only a small number of civil servants and military personnel and a still smaller number of merchants, craftsmen, and itinerant workers moved into the region. Few peasants were among the migrants. That trend continued after the unsuccessful Polish Insurrection of 1830–1 and particularly after the Polish Insurrection of 1863–4, when some of the estates confiscated from Poles were given to Russian landowners. The imperial authorities sought to de-Polonize and Russify the Right-Bank regions to the greatest extent possible, but they could not manage to dislodge the substantial Polish (and Ukrainian) presence there.

A steady stream of Russians continued to settle in the sparsely populated regions of *Southern Ukraine, in both its cities and its villages. The migrants included serfs, state peasants, military personnel, and free settlers. Some of them were subsequently assimilated by the Ukrainian population, which had grown in the region owing to mi-

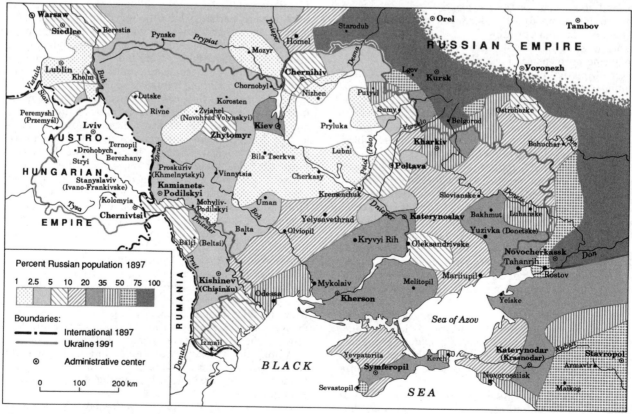

RUSSIANS IN UKRAINE, 1897

grations from the Left Bank and Right Bank as well as from Slobidska Ukraine. In areas where they constituted a large percentage or a majority of the population Russians tended to maintain their national identity. After the abolition of serfdom this became more common as emancipated Russian peasants also settled in Southern Ukraine.

The political and administrative changes that dismantled the Hetman state and Zaporizhia and imposed Russian imperial rule had cleared a wide path for Russian immigration to Left-Bank Ukraine. By the early 19th century Russian civil servants, military men of various rank, landowners (particularly from the regions of Russia bordering on Ukraine), merchants, peddlers, craftsmen, and laborers had established themselves in Ukraine. The cities in Left-Bank Ukraine lost their right of Magdeburg law, and their economies, community life, and municipal governments increasingly fell under the control of recently arrived Russians. Except in the larger port cities, such as Odessa, Russian merchants secured a firm hold on the commercial life of the Left Bank and Southern Ukraine. According to statistics for 1832, Russians controlled the most capital-intensive industries (44.6 percent; Ukrainians controlled 28.7 percent). In the commercial sector they enjoyed an absolute majority (52.6 percent; Ukrainians, 22.2 percent), particularly in the higher guilds. In 1832, Russians constituted 35.5 percent of the landed gentry in Ukraine (31.4 percent were Ukrainian). Except in the Right Bank, where Poles and Jews maintained substantial economic strength, Russians dominated the capitalist development of Ukraine. As a result the major cities of Ukraine developed an increasingly Russian character.

Another wave of Russian immigration to Ukraine came in the 1880s, when the surplus population from the central chernozem gubernias (Voronezh, Kursk, Orel, and others) began flooding into the newly established industrial centers of the Donbas and the Dnieper Industrial Region as well as (to a lesser extent) Kharkiv. In 1897, Russians made up 68 percent of the workers in heavy industry of Katerynoslav gubernia. A substantial number of them were seasonal laborers.

According to the census of 1897 there were 3.8 million Russians living in Ukraine. That figure suggests that they formed 11.7 percent of the total population of 27.8 million. There were virtually no Russians in Ukrainian territories under Austria-Hungary (apart from a settlement of 3,000 Old Believers, known as Lipovany, in Bukovyna). Russians thus made up 13.1 percent of the population in Ukrainian territories in the Russian Empire. There were 2.4 million Russians in the nine Ukrainian gubernias (10.4 percent of the local total population), 2.1 million (10 percent) within the Ukrainian SSR's 1938 boundaries, and 2.8 million (10.5 percent) within Ukraine's current boundaries.

A high proportion (42.3 percent) of the Russians in Ukraine lived in cities, particularly in comparison to the proportion (5.4 percent) of Ukrainians who lived in cities. The urban population of Ukraine made up 12.6 percent of the total population of the country (within the 1938 borders of the Ukrainian SSR). Of the urban population, Russians constituted 33.7 percent (Ukrainians, 32.5 percent). In cities of over 100,000 inhabitants they represented 53.4 percent (Ukrainians, 12.6 percent). Only 6.7 percent of the rural population in Ukraine was Russian (83 percent, Ukrainian). The largest urban concentrations of Russians in Ukraine (1897) were in Odessa, 198,200 (48.2 percent of the city's total population); Kiev, 134,300 (54.4 percent); Kharkiv, 109,000 (63 percent); Mykolaiv, 61,000 (66.3 percent); Katerynoslav, 47,100 (41.8 percent); and Kherson, 27,900 (47.9 percent).

The Russian inhabitants of Ukraine were not evenly distributed geographically. There were few of them (approx 600,000, or 3 percent of the local total) in the long-settled forested steppe regions (with the exception of Slobidska Ukraine) and northern Ukraine, and of that number 134,000 were residents of Kiev. A larger number (1.2 million) lived in Southern Ukraine and Slobidska Ukraine (approx 1 million). Another 340,000 lived in the Kuban (not including the eastern section), where they constituted about 34 percent of the population.

The Russian element in rural Ukraine tended to live either in separate villages or in separate sections of villages and only rarely with Ukrainians. Russian villages commonly differed from Ukrainian ones in appearance. They had fewer garden plots, and the structure of the farm buildings and houses was different. Their inhabitants tended to go about their daily affairs apart from Ukrainians, and there was infrequent contact between the two groups. Relations were restrained, and mixed marriages were uncommon. Russian Old Believers made up one-third of the Russian peasant population in Ukraine, but they lived completely apart from everyone else (even other Russians).

In general Russians in Ukraine considered Ukraine and Ukrainians to be an organically constituent element of the Russian state, and they assisted the imperial government in effecting its policies of centralization and Russification. They believed that Ukrainians were a Russian tribe, that their language was merely a dialect of Russian, and that their culture was a lesser variant of Russian culture, although some expressed their liking for Ukrainian nature, folklore, literature, and language and respected Ukraine's (Cossack) past.

Even those Russians in Ukraine who espoused revolutionary and internationalist ideas sought to have them realized on an 'all-Russian' scale, and believed that Ukrainian strivings for the preservation of national identity and the development of the Ukrainian language were narrow concerns that detracted from the universality of their own cause. Russian participants in the *Decembrist movement in Ukraine supported the view that all nationalities within the Russian Empire should fuse into a single (Russian) nation. The majority of the supporters of *Narodnaia Volia and liberal constitutional movements in Ukraine were either indifferent or hostile to the local national movement. The members of Russian parties active in Ukraine – the *Constitutional Democratic party (the Kadets), the *Russian Social Democratic Workers' party, and the Russian Party of Socialist Revolutionaries – supported centralist policies. Russian right-wing elements, such as the Union of the Russian People and the Kiev Club of Russian Nationalists, were openly hostile to Ukraine and Ukrainians.

The general tendency of Russians in Ukraine to subsume all features of Ukrainian identity into an overriding imperial Russian one was buttressed by Russian state policies, a thoroughly Russified educational system, the Russian Orthodox church, and the Russian press (both official and private).

As the number of Russians in Ukraine grew, so did

their influence, not only in the political, administrative, and socioeconomic spheres but also in the development of Ukrainian scholarship and culture, particularly academic life. Russian professors occupied leading positions in Ukraine's institutions of higher education, and many of them contributed significantly to the field of Ukrainian studies. Among them were the historians V. Ikonnikov and S. Golubev, the literary historians M.(N.) Petrov and V. Peretts, the philosopher A. Giliarov, the archeologist M. Rostovtsev, the chemist S. Reformatsky, the physicist Y. Kosonogov, the mathematician M. Krylov, the botanists A. Fomin and S. Navashin, the zoologist A. Severtsov, the surgeon O.(A.) Krymov, and the ophthalmologist V. Filatov.

The following Russian writers wrote about and/or lived in Ukraine: M. Artsybashev, I. Bunin, A. Chekhov, V. Garshin, N. Leskov, S. Nadson, N. Nekrasov, K. Ryleev, A. Tolstoi, K. Trenev, and A. Zhemchuzhnikov. Russian artists active in Ukraine included G. Miasoedov, M. Nesterov, V. Vasnetsov, M. Vrubel, N. Ge, I. Repin, I. Kramskoi, and L. Zhemchuzhnikov.

1917–20. The general Russian population and the revolutionary parties they supported during the period (the Kadets, the Mensheviks, the Socialist Revolutionaries [SRs], and the Bolsheviks) were largely hostile to the organization of Ukrainian national forces following the February Revolution of 1917 and to Ukrainian strivings for autonomy. They also pressured the Provisional Government in St Petersburg to institute measures inimical to Ukrainian autonomy. Shortly before the Ukrainian National Congress of April 1917 the head of the Kiev Soviet of Russian Deputies declared that demands for an autonomous Ukraine were 'a stab in the back of the revolution,' and that 'democratic forces' would reply to such demands 'with bayonets.' The Russian intelligentsia, civil servants, and influential publications, such as *Kievlianin* and *Kievskaia mysl'*, were also hostile.

The proclamation of the First Universal on 23 June 1917 and the creation of the General Secretariat were considered by most Russians in Ukraine a wrongful seizure of power. When the Ukrainian government began to exercise its legal authority, they changed their minds and urged the Provisional Government to arrive at an agreement with the Central Rada. The two governments did agree in July. After the Second Universal (16 July 1917) and the opening of the Central Rada and General Secretariat to representatives of national minorities, 54 Russian deputies (20 SRs, 20 Mensheviks, 10 Kadets, and 4 Popular Socialists) joined the two bodies. There were 8 deputies from Russian parties in the Little Rada: 3 Mensheviks (M. Balabanov and 2 Ukrainians, K. Kononenko and D. Chyzhevsky), 4 SRs (S. Saradzhiev, I. Sklovsky, K. Sukhovykh, and A. *Zarubin), and 1 Kadet (S. Krupnov). Bolshevik representatives (Yu. Piatakov and V. Zatonsky) also sat briefly in the Central Rada, but they walked out on 8 November 1917. There were two representatives of Russian parties in the General Secretariat, A. Zarubin (postal and telegraph services) and D. Odinets (secretary of Russian affairs).

Those who remained to vote on the Third Universal (20 November 1917) and the declaration of the establishment of the Ukrainian National Republic in the Little Rada included one Menshevik and two SRs, but the lone remaining Kadet walked out. The Mensheviks opposed the Fourth Universal (22 January 1918), but the SRs supported

it. Odinets continued to serve as secretary of Russian affairs in the new cabinet.

The Hetman government (April–December 1918) enjoyed the support of the majority of Russians, particularly right-wing and centrist elements. They were included in P. Skoropadsky's cabinets (they formed the majority in the administration led by S. Gerbel) and had considerable influence in the state apparatus and the army. Right-wing and extremist Russian organizations became active once again. In May 1918 the *Russian Union was established, ostensibly to unite all Russians in Ukraine in order to further Russian culture and education in the country, but in fact as an anti-Ukrainian grouping. The number of Russian refugees in Ukraine increased after the Bolshevik consolidation of power in Russia, and Russian officers used Ukraine as a base in establishing A. Denikin's loyalist Volunteer Army. Those elements left Ukraine after the seizure of power by the UNR Directory, which included no Russians in its administration.

During the course of Ukraine's independence struggle most Russians sided either with Denikin's forces (the majority of the bourgeoisie and the intelligentsia) or with the Bolsheviks (primarily the Russian proletariat). The Russian peasantry remained largely neutral.

1920–33. The establishment of Soviet power in Ukraine initially brought no change in the relations between nationalities in the country. Most Russians who held posts in the Ukrainian state, administrative, and Party apparatus believed that only the form of political system had changed, and that the 'country' (the Russian Empire and now the Soviet Union) should remain undivided and largely under central (Russian) control. The ruling party, the Communist Party (Bolshevik) of Ukraine (CP[B]U), was Ukrainian in name only. Its membership consisted primarily of Russians (53.6 percent in 1922) and other non-Ukrainian peoples (such as the Jews and Balts, and others) and was either indifferent or hostile to Ukrainian national concerns. Russian elements in the CP(B)U even attempted to separate the Donets and Kryvyi Rih regions to form the Donets–Kryvyi Rih Soviet Republic within the RSFSR. They largely ignored the development of a separate state structure for the Ukrainian SSR; they considered it and the party they belonged to as inconsequential short-term arrangements.

Change in the number of Russians in Ukraine during the first years of Soviet rule cannot be measured accurately. A substantial number of (Russian or Russified) nobles and functionaries of the tsarist regime fled from Ukraine (in fact from the USSR altogether). In Ukraine they were replaced to a certain extent by an influx of Bolsheviks from Russia. The decline of cities and industries, where Russians constituted a high percentage of the inhabitants or laborers, during the revolutionary period probably caused an out-migration to other parts of the former empire. Nevertheless the influx of Russians into the Donets Basin region continued (16,000 in 1921–3, 64,000 in 1924–5).

A more detailed picture of the Russian presence in Ukraine is provided by the Soviet census of 1926. Its figures show that there were 4.2 million Russians living in Ukrainian ethnographic territories within the USSR (12.1 percent of the total population of those regions), 2.7 million of them in the Ukrainian SSR (9.2 percent). A smaller number of Russians lived in Western Ukraine (approx 60,000) and Bessarabia (also 60,000).

RUSSIANS IN UKRAINE, 1926

A high proportion (50.4 percent) of the Russians who lived in the Ukrainian SSR lived in cities, although the figures drop if all Ukrainian ethnographic territory within the USSR (40.5 percent) is included. Russians made up 25.1 percent of the urban population of the Ukrainian SSR (Ukrainians, 47.4 percent) and 5.6 percent of its rural population (Ukrainians, 87.6 percent). Relative to the 1897 census the percentage of Russians in the Ukrainian SSR seemed to drop from 10 to 9.2, although the actual decline was probably much smaller, because the earlier census contained somewhat inflated figures.

As in 1897, the major concentrations of Russians in Ukraine (1926) were in Odessa (162,000, or 38.7 percent of the total population), Kharkiv (154,400, or 37 percent), Kiev (125,500, or 24.4 percent), Dnipropetrovske (73,400, or 31.5 percent), Donetske (59,900, or 56.3 percent), Mykolaiv (46,700, or 37 percent), Luhanske (31,300, or 43.5 percent), and Krasnodar, in the Kuban (83,400, or 51.3 percent). In general the proportion of Russians in a city increased with its size: they constituted approx 33.3 percent of the population in cities with over 100,000 inhabitants, 20.1 percent in those with between 50,000 and 100,000, and 12.2 percent in smaller cities.

The geographical distribution of Russians in Ukraine was practically the same as in 1897. There were very few in Western Ukraine (overall, 2 percent; in isolated areas, 5 percent of the local total). The larger concentrations were in four areas: Slobidska Ukraine, with an overall percentage of about 25 percent, concentrated in the Ukrainian sections of Kursk (46 percent) and Voronezh (30 percent)

gubernias; Southern Ukraine, where Russians clustered in and around seaside cities (their largest rural concentration [24 percent] was in Melitopil okruha); the Donets Basin, particularly Luhanske okruha (42.7 percent) and the Ukrainian sections of the Shakhty-Donets district (37 percent); and the Kuban (33.5 percent, particularly in the eastern areas).

Russian as a mother tongue was claimed (1926) by 98.1 percent (2,627,000) of the Russians in Ukraine as well as by 5.5 percent (1,289,000) of Ukrainians, 22.6 percent (356,000) of Jews, and 154,000 others. Linguistic Russification was particularly marked among the Ukrainian population in the cities, where 24.4 percent listed Russian as their native tongue. Of their rural counterparts only 3.2 percent did so. In contrast, barely 1.4 percent of Russians gave Ukrainian as their native tongue (1.8 percent in rural areas).

The age and gender profiles of the Russian and Ukrainian inhabitants of Ukraine in 1926 were fairly different.

Russians in Ukraine,* 1926–89

Year	Total population (Ukraine)	Russians	
		Number	% of total
1926	38,569,000	3,164,800	8.2
1959	41,869,000	7,091,300	16.9
1970	47,127,000	9,126,000	19.4
1989	51,452,000	11,356,000	22.1

*Within Ukraine's postwar borders

The ratio of men to women among Ukrainians was 100:106.1, among Russians, 100:100.2. A greater proportion of Russians (51.2 percent) than Ukrainians (43.1 percent) were aged 20 to 59 (that age-group formed 45.3 percent of the total population). Likewise there were fewer teenagers or young children among Russians (43.4 percent) than among Ukrainians (50.6 percent; that age-group represented 49 percent of the total population) and fewer old people (5.4 percent of Russians and 6.3 percent of Ukrainians; that age-group was 5.7 percent of the total).

The social/professional profile of Russians also differed from that of Ukrainians. The Ukrainians were a largely undifferentiated peasant mass, in marked contrast to the Russian community. Agriculture employed 50.6 percent of the Russians, compared to 90.7 percent of the Ukrainians. The Russians were represented more in industry (20 percent, compared to 3.8 percent for Ukrainians), the civil service (12.2 percent, compared to 2.6 percent), trade (3.3 percent, compared to 0.8 percent), and other professions (12.7 percent, compared to 2.1 percent). Russians in Ukraine were better educated than Ukrainians. In 1926, 76.5 percent of males and 51.2 percent of females over the age of five were literate, compared to figures of 66.5 percent and 32.5 percent for Ukrainians. Russian pupils made up 14.1 percent of all those enrolled in elementary schools in Ukraine, although Russian children in that age-group made up only 8.4 percent of the country's total. Russian enrollment in Ukrainian vocational schools stood at 16 percent, in technical schools, at 14.7 percent, and in workers' faculties, at 21.5 percent. That trend continued through 1936, when Russians constituted 15.4 percent of the students in postsecondary institutions, 10.3 percent of those in technical schools, and 16.2 percent of those in workers' faculties.

A substantial number of Russians in the Ukrainian SSR in 1926 had been born outside of its borders; 779,200 originated from the RSFSR (not including the Kazakh and Kirghiz ASSRs), and 112,500, from other republics. Seventy percent of the new arrivals settled in cities. Immigrants made up about one-quarter of the Russian population in Ukraine (one-third of the urban Russian population and approx 15 percent of the rural). Some 271,000 Russians had settled in the Donbas, where they constituted about one-third of the population. The constant influx of Russians into Ukraine and an emigration of Ukrainians (particularly to Siberia) account for the growing proportion of Russians in the country. That growth was not offset by the higher natural growth rate among Ukrainians.

The policy of *Ukrainization instituted in 1923–32 diminished the influence of Russians in Ukraine significantly. Some Russians returned to their country of origin, some assimilated with the Ukrainian surroundings, and some Russified Ukrainians reverted to a Ukrainian identity. The number of Russians in leading administrative and political posts was reduced as they were replaced by Ukrainians. The proportion of Russians in Ukraine's administrative apparatus in 1928–9 (given in percentages, with figures for Ukrainians in parentheses) was as follows: in rural soviets, 5.1 percent (87.9 percent); town soviets, 20.9 percent (50.9 percent); city soviets, 23.9 percent (50.4 percent); raion party conferences, 7.9 percent (82.9 percent); and okruha soviets, 14.5 percent (68.6 percent). They constituted 27.5 percent of the membership of the CP(B)U (compared to 52 percent for Ukrainians) and 17.1

percent of that of the Komsomol (compared to 64.1 percent).

After 1933. Ukrainization came to a full stop in 1933 with the tenure of P. *Postyshev. The 17th Congress of the All-Union Communist Party (Bolshevik), held from 26 January to 10 February 1934, at which J. Stalin declared that Ukrainian nationalism was 'a principal threat,' marked the formal end of the Ukrainization period. The Ukrainian position was also eroded by the man-made famine of 1932–3 (which killed millions of Ukrainian peasants), the wholesale destruction of the Ukrainian intellectual elite and religious structure in 1929–33, and the execution or deportation of between one and two million people. But the gains within the state apparatus made by Ukrainians relative to Russians during the 1920s held until the Second World War.

After 1945 the *national composition of Ukraine changed dramatically as the proportion of Russians living there more than doubled. Such a fundamental change in the *population of Ukraine did not occur spontaneously, but as part of an overall Soviet policy of Russification. The formula used for implementing the policy was systematic and straightforward. Ukrainians were moved out of their republic as often as possible on the pretext of an 'organized distribution of labor' to other parts of the USSR (particularly northern regions of the Union), where they would be bereft of Ukrainian cultural amenities and presumably assimilate with the surrounding Russian or Russian-speaking majority. Russians were brought into Ukraine on a continual basis and afforded a privileged socioeconomic status and a wide range of cultural amenities.

By 1989 the Russian population of Ukraine had grown to 11,356,000 and constituted 22.1 percent of the total population of 51,452,000. It was most concentrated in the southeastern industrial regions, in Luhanske (44.8 percent of the total oblast population), Donetske (43.6 percent), Kharkiv (33.2 percent), and Zaporizhia (32 percent) oblasts. In Crimea oblast Russians formed 67 percent of the population. They were least numerous in the western (particularly Ternopil, Ivano-Frankivske, and Transcarpathia oblasts) and northwestern (Volhynia and Rivne oblasts) regions of Ukraine. The table gives their proportional increase in the population of the Ukrainian SSR.

The influence of the Russians in Ukraine during the period increased even more than their increase in number would suggest, largely as a result of a concerted campaign of *Russification. Under the Russian Empire the efforts to Russify Ukraine were aimed largely at the cities and the middle and upper classes. In Soviet times they were extended to the countryside and to all levels of society. Consequently a Russian assigned to a rural posting in Ukraine would commonly be not only a state functionary but also an agent of cultural assimilation. Also contributing to the trend of broad Russification was the *urbanization characteristic of the 20th century, whereby millions of Ukrainians were brought to cities that had been centers of Russian (and Jewish) cultural life for over a hundred years.

The Russians in Ukraine acted as a dominant minority group by virtue of the fact that their nationality group was the controlling force in Soviet society. Their increased numbers provided them with the demographic mass to make an impact at all levels of Ukrainian society.

Socially and economically the Russians occupied a

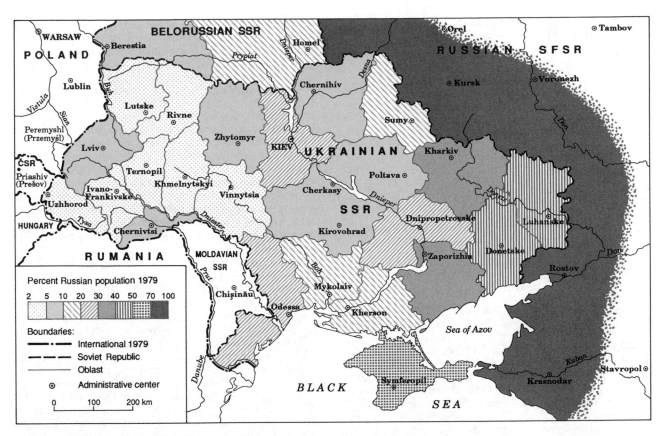

RUSSIANS IN UKRAINE, 1979

privileged position within Ukraine. They constituted a disproportionately high proportion of skilled blue-collar workers, white-collar workers, and the intelligentsia. They could obtain a full range of services in the Russian language and felt no compulsion to learn Ukrainian. Their children could be educated in Russian-language schools in every region of the republic, and the entrance requirements for higher educational institutions in Ukraine strongly favored Russians. The majority of public signs and postings on public buildings in most districts of Ukraine were unilingually Russian, as were most labels on consumer products. Official business was usually transacted in Russian. As for cultural amenities, Ukrainian publishing houses produced a disproportionately high number of Russian-language titles, translations of foreign-language literature were far more likely to be available in Russian than in Ukrainian, the theater and cinema were dominated (in quantity and often in quality) by Russian-language works, and museum and gallery services were commonly provided in Russian rather than Ukrainian.

With social pressures to adhere to Russian norms and economic mobility often linked to fluency in the Russian language, many Ukrainians became Russophones. Their number included a substantial group who became totally Russified, or who retained only a minimal ability in Ukrainian (4.5 percent in 1926, 6.5 percent in 1959, 8.5 percent in 1970, and 10.9 percent in 1979). Another linguistic phenomenon was the rise of a Ukrainian-Russian patois known as *surzhyk*. One sign of the increased Russian influence in Ukraine was a substantial rise in the number of mixed Ukrainian-Russian marriages, particularly among white-collar workers and the intelligentsia. Subtly encouraged by Soviet officials, such matches were sometimes viewed as a means of advancing one's career.

Some Russians in the Ukrainian SSR have supported the Ukrainian people and defended their interests. In the 1920s M. *Volobuiev demanded that Ukraine's economy be permitted to develop autonomously. In the 1960s and early 1970s the writer V. Nekrasov came out in defense of Ukrainian dissidents. The majority of Russian academics and writers in Ukraine, however, were simply purveyors of Russification who considered Ukrainian scholarship and culture to be elements within a Russian context. The Ukrainian dissident movement of the 1960s and 1970s gained some support among Russian circles in Ukraine, but their expressions of support for Ukrainian aspirations were sporadic and not very clear.

The sizable Russian minority in Ukraine became a significant factor in the campaign for independence in 1990–1. Some Russians were among the most vocal opponents of Ukraine's political aspirations for separation from the Soviet Union. Likewise, many Soviet and Russian political figures cited the need to 'protect' the Russian minority as an excuse for Moscow's potential intervention in Ukrainian affairs. Ultimately a substantial majority of Ukraine's Russians chose to vote for Ukrainian independence in the referendum of 1 December 1991. Observers have noted that the result reflected the Russians' belief that the Ukrainian SSR was being treated unfairly (economically and politically) within the USSR, and that they and the country would benefit by independence. At the same time the result reflected the degree to which the Russians were satisfied with the assurances of respect for minority rights that had been given by Ukrainian political leaders.

BIBLIOGRAPHY

Rittich, A. *Ethnographie des russischen Reiches* (Gotha 1878)

Lazarevskii, A. *Opisanie Staroi Malorossii*, 3 vols (Kiev 1888, 1893, 1902)

Rudnyts'kyi, S. *Ohliad natsional'noï terytoriï Ukraïny* (Berlin 1923)

Andriiashev, O. 'Narys istoriï kolonizatsiï Kyïvs'koï zemli,' in *Kyïv i ioho okolytsia v istoriï i pam'iatkakh*, ed M. Hrushevs'kyi (Kiev 1926)

Kubiiovych, V. *Terytoriia i liudnist' ukraïns'kykh zemel'* (Lviv 1935)

Itogi vsesoiuznoi perepisi naseleniia 1959 goda: Ukrainskaia SSR (Moscow 1962)

Kubiiovych, V. 'Natsional'nyi sklad naselennia Radians'koï Ukraïny v svitli soviets'kykh perepysiv z 17.12.1926 i 15.1.1959,' *ZNTSh*, 169 (1962)

Naulko, V. *Etnichnyi sklad naselennia Ukraïns'koï RSR* (Kiev 1965)

Kubiiovych, V. 'Natsional'nyi sklad naselennia URSR za perepysom 1970,' *Suchasnist'*, 1971, no. 9

Kilichenko, M. *Natsional'nye otnosheniia v SSSR i tendentsii ikh razvitiia* (Moscow 1972)

Levyts'kyi, V. 'Rosiiany u soiuznykh respublikakh,' *Ukraïns'kyi samostiinyk*, nos. 195–6 (1973)

Naulko, V. *Razvitiie mezhetnicheskikh sviazei na Ukraine* (Kiev 1975)

B. Kravtsiv, V. Kubijovyč, M. Prokop, A. Zhukovsky

Russian-Ukrainian Evangelical Baptist Union of the USA

(Rosiisko-ukrainskyi soiuz yevanhelskykh khrystiian baptystiv). An Evangelical church in the United States and Canada. Formed initially among the immigrant Baptist and Stundist communities of North Dakota by I. Kolesnykiv, the church was formally constituted in 1919 in Philadelphia. It used mostly Russian for church services in spite of the fact that a large portion of its membership was Ukrainian. This situation soon led to the formation of rival Ukrainian-language congregations, in the Ukrainian Baptist Evangelical church. Among the prominent leaders of the Russian-Ukrainian union were I. Davydiuk and I. Kmeta, author of *With Christ in America: A Story of the Russian-Ukrainian Baptists* (1948). In the 1980s the union consisted of 35 churches and missions with approx 2,000 adherents. It has official publications in Russian (*Seiatel' istiny*), Ukrainian (*Siiach pravdy*), and English (*Herald*).

Russian-Ukrainian linguistic relations.

Ukrainian influences on the Russian literary language date from the period of Kievan Rus'. They occurred mainly through literary and oral contacts within the Orthodox church. These influences grew during the so-called second period of South-Slavic influence (the end of the 14th to the 16th century, particularly under Metropolitan Cyprian) and from the mid-17th to the late 18th century, when, following Patriarch Nikon's reforms, many Ukrainians (and Belarusians) occupied important positions in the Russian church hierarchy and established religious schools in Russia. The grammars of L. Zyzanii and particularly M. Smotrytsky laid the foundations of Russian linguistic norms as they were later codified in B. Adodurov's (1738–50) and M. Lomonosov's (1755–7) grammars.

Under the impact of the Ukrainian pronunciation of Church Slavonic (CS), the Russian pronunciation of CS (and, in part, 17th- and 18th-century literary Russian) underwent archaization: (1) *akan'e* (the pronunciation of *o* as *a*), the change of unstressed *e* before hard consonants into *'o* in CS expressions (eg, *odéžda: odéža* 'clothing'), and the

mixing of etymological *ě* and *e* in pronunciation (later only in orthography, to 1917) were eliminated; (2) the spirant *h* was not pronounced *g* in religious words (eg, *Boh, Hospod'*, *blaho* 'God, Lord, grace', until the 1930s) or in Western loanwords or names (this rule later changed; *galstuk, Gejne, Gejdel'berg* 'tie, Heine, Heidelberg' with the newer pronunciation of foreign *h* as *x: Xel'sinki, Ejzenxauer* 'Helsinki, Eisenhower'). The hard pronunciation of consonants before *e* in the religious books of several northern Russian Old Believer priestless groups (later eliminated in some groups through the unified pronunciation taught at Russian theological seminaries) is most likely of Ukrainian origin. The Ukrainian CS tradition also had an archaizing influence on the morphology of literary Russian in the 18th century: it brought about the abolition of (1) earlier vernacular forms used in administrative speech (-*y*/-*i* endings in the nom pl of neut nouns, eg, *ókny, znán'i* 'windows, sciences'; sing forms without an extended stem eg, *ímja* 'name'; endings -*ov*/-*ej* in the gen pl, eg, *mestóv, púlej* 'of places, of bullets'); and (2) the unstressed ending -*oj*/-*ej* in the nominative singular of masculine adjectives (eg, *velíkoj, sínej* 'great, blue'). It was probably then that the nominal predicate in the instrumental case became widespread (eg, *on byl/budet uchitelem* 'he was/will be a teacher').

The Ukrainian language influenced Russian through Ukrainian folk songs, which became popular among the 18th-century nobility. Beginning in the 18th century Ukrainian vocabulary, syntactic constructions, and stresses were introduced into modern literary Russian. N. *Gogol almost singlehandedly 'Ukrainianized' literary Russian. Other Ukrainian authors who wrote in Russian (eg, V. Kapnist, V. Narezhny, Ye. Hrebinka, H. Kvitka-Osnovianenko, P. Kulish, T. Shevchenko, M. Vovchok, M. Kostomarov, O. Storozhenko, H. Danylevsky, D. Mordovets, V. Korolenko), Russian writers who grew up or lived for some time in Ukraine (eg, A. Chekhov, I. Babel, E. Bagritsky, I. Selvinsky, N. Ostrovsky), and Russian authors writing on Ukrainian themes (eg, A. Pushkin, K. Ryleev, A. Malyshkin, A. Serafimovich, I. Erenburg) used Ukrainianisms in their works for local color.

The penetration of Russianisms into the Ukrainian language was due to Russian political expansion into Ukraine beginning in the 17th century. Apart from the commercial and administrative-military terminology (eg, *sóbol', lazútčyk, prykáz* 'sable, scout, government department'), Russianisms began to enter literary Ukrainian of the 17th to 18th century through the elevated and chancery style of writing as common Ukrainian-Russian lexical and phraseological Church Slavonicisms (eg, *vrah, dyjável* 'enemy, devil') and loanwords from other languages (eg, *soldát* 'soldier' from the French), and replaced Ukrainian folk expressions, Polish calques, and Polonisms. The initiators of these processes were educated 17th- and 18th-century religious and secular writers who (in the tradition of 16th- and 17th-century Ukrainian-Belarusian unifying tendencies) wrote for both Ukrainian and Russian readers. Ukrainian authors who moved to Russia (Ye. Slavynetsky, S. Yavorsky, D. Tuptalo, T. Prokopovych, and others) replaced the more colorful Ukrainianisms in their language with neutral Church Slavonicisms and even Russianisms. An even more Russified literary language with a Russified phonetics and morphology was introduced at the *Kievan Mohyla Academy in the middle of the 18th century by H. Kremianetsky and S. Myslavsky and in government institutions after the abolition of the Hetmanate in Left-Bank Ukraine. H. *Skovoroda wrote in that language.

With the compulsory introduction of Russian pronunciation for the more or less orthographically, lexically, and grammatically unified 'Ukrainian-Russian' literary language in the 18th century, this language became entirely severed from its Ukrainian phonetic base. Common (Ukrainian-Russian) and Church Slavonic lexemes came to be considered Russianisms. In Orthodox church usage the Russian pronunciation of Church Slavonic texts became the norm in the 19th century.

The appearance and evolution of modern *Standard Ukrainian (SU) in the first half of the 19th century meant the rejection of the corrupted older literary language. The new language was almost devoid of Russianisms. Its journalistic and scientific style and terminology were developed under Austrian rule in 19th- and early-20th-century Galicia and Bukovyna by the borrowing of words from Polish, German, and Czech instead of Church Slavonic. In the UNR and Soviet Ukraine the normalization process of the 1920s tended to abolish unacceptable foreign elements in word formation, vocabulary, and syntax and to introduce neologisms better suited to the vernacular-folkloric style of the Ukrainian language (see *Purism).

This process was cut short by administrative interference in the 1930s and replaced by compulsory linguistic Russification (see *Language policy). In orthoepy and inflection only the Ukrainian dialectal pronunciations and morphemes that coincided with those in Russian were maintained. The most glaring Russification took place in *orthography and scientific *terminology. Recently created and already partly assimilated neologisms were replaced by new calques from the Russian, often without their being adapted to the phonetic requirements of Ukrainian; for example, the change of *o, e* into *i* was ignored (eg, the Russian calques *vzvod, pidhotovka* 'platoon, training'), while the non-Ukrainian change of *e* into *'o* (eg, *roščot, pol'ot* 'gun crew, flight') and the Russian prefix *s* (eg, *snarjad* 'cannon/bullet shell') were retained. Western loanwords that had been assimilated without the mediation of Russian and which differed phonetically from the corresponding Russian ones were replaced with the Russian forms (eg, *lampa, klub, proekt, dialekt, Hehel'* were substituted for *ljampa, kljub, projekt, dijalekt, Hegel'* 'lamp, club, project, dialect, Hegel'). Neologisms introduced in the 1920s were replaced with loanwords existing in Russian (eg, *ekvator, poljus* replaced *rivnyk, bihun* 'equator, pole'). Russian suffixes were used widely in the word formation of scientific terms: *-čyk/-sčyk* (eg, *pikirovščyk* instead of *pikuval'nyk* 'dive-bomber'); *-tel'* (eg, *začynatel'* instead of *započatkuvač* 'starter'); *-ka* (for names of actions, eg, *zakl'opka* instead of *zaklepuvannja* 'riveting'); *-o-/-e-vydnyj* (eg, *konusovydnyj* instead of *stižkuvatyj* 'cone-shaped'); *-ščyj, -a(ju)čyj, -ujučyj, -všyj* (for active participles, eg, *trudjaščyj/ služačyj, spivčuvajučyj, zaisnuvavšyj, peremihšyj* instead of *pracivnyk, spivchutlyvyj, zaisnuvalyj, peremožnyj* 'laboring/laborer, sympathizing/sympathetic, existing, conquering/triumphant'); *-myj* (for passive participles, eg, *ljubymyj* instead of *ljublenyj* 'loved'); and *-yčaty* (in verbs, eg, *važnyčaty* instead of *vdavaty važnoho* 'to feign importance').

The pressure for Russification was eased somewhat in 1939–41 (as a concession to the newly annexed Western

Ukrainians) and 1955–67. It rose again in the late 1960s, and was justified by the Party's theories on the creation of an 'areal super language' and on Russian as the 'second native language' of all the Soviet peoples. This time the offensive was directed against the language of Ukrainian belles lettres: words differing from Russian ones were rejected as 'unviable,' 'archaisms,' and 'limited dialecticisms,' and neologisms had to be borrowed from Russian.

Phonetic and lexical Russianisms are used mainly by Russified urban dwellers and workers in southern and eastern Ukraine and by army veterans in rural areas. Colloquial Russianisms are most widespread among speakers of the eastern Ukrainian dialects in the Donbas, the steppe oblasts, and the former USSR outside Ukraine. They are not as common in Slobidska and in Left-Bank and Right-Bank Ukraine. Since the Second World War they have spread to the dialects of Galicia, Bukovyna, and Transcarpathia.

There are various types of Russianisms: (1) phonetic word forms taken from Russian (eg, *fakul't'et, z vjeterkóm* 'faculty, with a breeze [ie, a fast drop in a mine shaft elevator]'); (2) grammatical categories (differentiating between predicative and attributive forms, eg, *ščaslyva junist' nam daná* 'a happy youth is given us' and *dána vymova xybna* 'the given pronunciation is wrong'); (3) inflectional morphemes (eg, *profesorá, xodimte/pidemte* instead of *profesory, xodimo* 'professors, let's go'); (4) word-forming morphemes (eg, *pokažčyk, pidšývka, bezdíl'nyčaty* instead of *pokaznyk, pidšyvannja/pidšyttja, bajdykuvaty* '[book] index, lining, to loaf'); (5) semantic forms (eg, *napravlennja, zbutysja, zakazaty* instead of *naprjamok, zdijsnytysja, zamovyty* 'direction, to be realized, to place an order'); (6) syntactic forms (eg, *ne ženysja na bahatij, narada po pytannjax* instead of *ne ženysja z bahatoju, narada z pytan'* 'don't marry a rich [woman], conference on questions of'); (7) names of places in and outside Ukraine (eg, *Rovno, Sjeverodonec'k, Buxarest* instead of *Rivne, Sivers'kodonec'ke, Bukarešt*); and, mostly, (8) phrases and words (eg, *dobro požalovaty!, pryjmaty miry, polosá, ljubýj, pryjom, daže, l'otčyk, postrojka* instead of *vitajte!, porobyty zaxody, smuha, bud'-kotryj, zasib/sposib/pidxid, navit', letun, pobudova* 'welcome!, to take measures, belt/zone, any [one], device/means/approach, even, pilot, construction'). In colloquial speech many lowbrow phonetic Russianisms, including argot and slang words, and diminutive forms of personal names (eg, *Ser'oža, Svjeta* instead of *Serhijko, Svitlanka*) are used frequently.

In the eastern Ukrainian dialects there are many common old Ukrainian-Russian lexemes and syntactic constructions that were used in 19th-century literary Ukrainian and still appear in poetry, but are not part of the normative vocabulary and syntax (eg, *hórod, hod, svád'ba, posobýty, u mene je, u mene bolyt' holova* [cf SU *misto, rik, vesillja, dopomohty, ja maju, meni bolyt' holova*] 'town, year, to help, I have, I have a headache').

Russian-Ukrainian linguistic relations have been studied by P. Zhytetsky, O. Kurylo, M. Sulyma, M. Hladky, O. Syniavsky, S. Smerechynsky, R. Smal-Stotsky, V. Chaplenko, I. Bilodid, Y. Bahmut, H. Izhakevych, F. Sereda, H. Hnatiuk, D. Miroshnyk, A. Shylovsky, B. Sharpylo, R. Boldyrev, O. Serbenska, V. Stolbunova, V. Ilienko, M. Rohal, L. Korobchynska, T. Chertorizhskaia, N. Arvat, N. Golubeva, L. Evdokimova, A. Evgrafova, B. Antonenko-Davydovych, G.Y. Shevelov, and others. In Ukrainian dialectal areas and compact colonies outside the official borders of Ukraine – in the adjacent Kursk, Belgorod, Voronezh, and Rostov oblasts of the Russian RSFSR, and in Moldavia, the Kuban, the Ural region, Siberia, and Soviet Central Asia and the Far East – Russian-Ukrainian linguistic relations have been determined by the dominant influence of Russian in all spheres of life and the absence of Ukrainian schools, institutions, press, and mass media. The Russified transitional Ukrainian-Russian dialects in Korotoiak county, Voronezh gubernia, have been studied and described by N. Grinkova; in the Voronezh, Belgorod, and Kursk regions, by A. Beskrovny, F. Medvedev, V. Sobinnikova, G. Denisevich, A. Pashkivsky, and V. Titovskaia; in the Don region, by A. Mirtov and K. Udovkina; in the Kuban, by I. Shalia, V. Chistiakov, N. Bushina, M. Sadilenko, E. Tarasenko, O. Sheinina, M. Shabalin, N. Fedorenko, and I. Cherednychenko; in the Volga region, by A. Dulzon, L. Barannik, A. Severianova, and I. Valchenko; in Kirgizia, by S. Leiferman; in the Far East, by A. Georgievsky and T. Nazarova; and in Moldavia, by L. Ermakova, Z. Riapolova, and Yu. Listrova.

(For additional information and a bibliography, see *Russian language in Ukraine.)

O. Horbach

Russification. A set of policies or processes encouraging non-Russians to adopt the Russian language and culture and thus increasing Russian political domination in Ukraine and other Eastern European countries.

The rapid expansion of Muscovy and then of the Russian Empire was connected with the Russification of the indigenous peoples of eastern Europe and northern and central Asia. The smaller nations or tribes were assimilated by the Russians. The most ambitious and talented elements of various nationalities were drawn to the administrative, industrial, and cultural centers of the empire and became Russified. Also Russified were many scholars and specialists from Western Europe who made their careers in Russia. Some figures of Balkan and even Polish and Galician (see *Russophilism) origin looked toward a powerful Russia for protection against Turkey or Germany (or Austria) and became Russified.

Ukraine came under increasing Russification pressures after the *Pereiaslav Treaty of 1654. Ukrainian autonomy was gradually restricted and finally abolished. In 1720 it was forbidden to print books in Ukrainian, and Ukrainian redactions of Church Slavonic books had to be checked against Russian redactions 'to avoid any discrepancies.' The Governing Council of the Hetman Office (est 1734) was given secret instructions to promote the merging of the two nations through intermarriage. During the reign of Catherine II a wide Russification program was implemented in Ukraine by the Second Little Russian Collegium under P. Rumiantsev. Russian became compulsory in the schools and in publications. The language of instruction at the Kievan Mohyla Academy was switched to Russian. Russian was adopted as the administrative language in the Orthodox church, and Church Slavonic, used for sermons, had to be pronounced in the Russian way. The Holy Synod in 1769 did not permit the Kievan Cave Monastery to print primers in Ukrainian. The policy of Russification was extended gradually into all spheres of social life, first in Left-Bank Ukraine, Kiev, and Slobidska Ukraine, and after the suppression of the Polish uprising (1830–1) in Right-Bank Ukraine as well.

The imperial government sharply increased its Russification efforts in the second half of the 19th century: the *Valuev circular (1863) and the *Ems Ukase (1876) blocked the development of Ukrainian literature until the Revolution of 1905. Even then some restrictions on the Ukrainian language and literature remained in force, and during the First World War Ukrainian publications were banned in Ukraine. Nevertheless, in spite of government efforts, until 1917 Russification was limited largely to the cities and industrial centers, which were inhabited by Russians and the higher strata (the intelligentsia, landowners, clergy, and burghers) of the indigenous society. Some members of these strata maintained Ukrainian traditions, language, and culture. The bulk of the Ukrainian population, the peasantry, remained Ukrainian and was not deeply affected by the Russification of education and church life. Yet long years of military service left a lasting mark on a limited segment of the common people.

The national revival and de-Russification of Ukraine that began with the 1917 Revolution was interrupted by the Soviet occupation in 1919–20. With the consolidation of Soviet power the Russians regained their dominant position in Ukraine. Russian became the language of the Party and government: most of the official press, decrees, and announcements were published in Russian. Most of the books printed in 1919–23 were Russian. The *Ukrainization of the Soviet Ukrainian government and the educational and cultural institutions met with much opposition from Russians and Russified elements. Soon after its inauguration in 1923, the process was slowed down. In 1927 the CC CP(B)U decided to 'recognize the special importance of the Russian language.' By 1930 there was active opposition to Ukrain-ization in the Party and a demand to revoke the policy. In 1932–3 the Party switched to an extreme anti-Ukrainian course: the cultural, state, and Party activists who had implemented Ukrainization were arrested and either imprisoned or shot. Ukrainization in the Kuban and other regions of the RSFSR settled by Ukrainians was replaced by intensified Russification.

In contrast to the tsarist period, under the Soviet regime Russification encompassed all Ukrainian territories, administrative and ethnic, and all social strata, including the peasantry. It was conducted by the enormous state and Party machine with the active support of the Russian minority in Ukraine and the Russian Orthodox church. Russification efforts after the Second World War, particularly in newly annexed Western Ukraine, gave rise at the beginning of the 1960s to a dissident movement among Ukrainian intellectuals and some workers. They demanded that Ukrainian be introduced as the language of instruction in higher and special secondary schools and in preschool education and as the language of administration in public institutions, enterprises, communications, and trade. They wanted the Academy of Sciences, the universities, and state publishers to issue more publications in Ukrainian. The government responded with repressions and increasing Russifi-cation pressures.

Soviet efforts at Russifying the non-Russian nationalities were based on a Soviet theory of the merging of nations. The theory tacitly assumed that the one Soviet nation being formed was Russian in language and culture. Shortly after N. Khrushchev came to power, he adopted an insidious plan to force the non-Russian languages out of elementary and secondary education. In April 1959 a new law was passed by Ukraine's Supreme Soviet giving parents the right to decide which schools, Russian-language or native-language, their children would attend. Given the state-bestowed advantages enjoyed by Russian-speakers in higher education, political and economic institutions, and cultural life, this seemingly democratic law was designed to make the non-Russian nationalities the agents of their own Russification. The Tashkent Conference of 1975 was devoted to ways of improving the teaching of Russian to non-Russian children. The Ukrainian Ministry of Education developed a plan in 1983 for upgrading Russian-language instruction in Ukraine. By 1987 only 16 percent of the schools in the national and oblast capitals were Ukrainian, 12 percent were mixed (predominantly Russian), and 72 percent were Russian. In Chernihiv, Donetske, Symferopil, and Voroshylovhrad there was no Ukrainian school at all.

Apart from pedagogical schools, vocational-technical and specialized secondary schools were almost completely Russified by the 1960s. This was true of higher education as well. Except in the departments of Ukrainian language and literature only Russian was used at the universities of Dnipropetrovske, Odessa, Kharkiv, and Donetske. At Kiev, Lviv, Uzhhorod, and Chernivtsi universities some lecturers in the social sciences used Ukrainian. All the polytechnical, medical, industrial, commercial, agricultural, and economic institutes, except for a few in the western oblasts, taught only in Russian. In 1960 only 62.5 percent of the students in Ukraine's higher educational institutions were Ukrainians (30 percent were Russians), and only 58.3 of the specialists with a higher education in Ukraine were Ukrainians (26.5 percent were Russians). In 10 years the number of higher education textbooks in Ukrainian fell from 168 titles (1970) to 38 (1980), while those in Russian rose from 263 to 422. All candidate and doctoral dissertations submitted in the academy were written in Russian.

The scientific literature published in Ukraine indicates strong discrimination in favor of Russian. Of 947 scientific titles published in Ukraine in 1970, 64.3 percent were in Russian. By 1980 Russian titles constituted 86.5 percent. Similarly, the percentage of Russian-language journals published by the AN URSR (now ANU) rose from 36.6 in 1969 to 76.2 in 1980. The production of Ukrainian books and booklets in general fell from 4,041 titles in 1961 to 2,981 in 1973, while the number of Russian titles remained unchanged at slightly above 4,400. The number of Ukrainian journals increased from 51 in 1961 to 63 in 1970 and fell to 50 in 1980, while the number of Russian journals published in Ukraine rose steadily from 26 to 41 to 50. Moreover, most of the Ukrainian journals were devoted to literature and art. According to some estimates the Ukrainian-language holdings of public libraries in Ukraine accounted for only 10 to 20 percent of the total holdings. Discrimination in favor of Russian culture was evident also in other fields; the number of museums in Ukraine, for example, fell from 174 in 1940 to 147 in 1972, while in Russia the number rose from 592 to 610. The most frequent and available radio and TV programs in Ukraine were Russian, either produced in Ukraine or beamed in from Russia.

Buttressing the efforts at Russification was a widespread attitude that the Soviet people could gain access to world culture and science only through Russian. A subtle form of Russification was practiced by linguistic institutes: their task was to make the vocabulary and grammar of literary and scientific Ukrainian increasingly similar to Russian (see *Standard Ukrainian).

The central government resettled people and manipulated migration patterns so as to promote Russification (see *National composition and *Migration). Russians were encouraged in various ways to move to Ukraine, and large numbers of them were settled there (see *Russians in Ukraine). Whereas Russians accounted for only 8.2 percent of Ukraine's population (within its postwar borders) in 1926, by 1959 they accounted for 16.9 percent, and by 1989, for 22.1 percent. The practice of resettling whole villages from the RSFSR to Ukraine continued even under Perestroika. At the same time millions of Ukrainians were resettled by force or attracted by various incentives to move to other parts of the USSR. By 1989 there were, for example, 185,000 Ukrainians in the Baltic countries, whereas before 1945 there were virtually none. In 1989 almost 6.8 million Ukrainians were scattered throughout the USSR outside Ukraine.

The success of the different Russification policies is evident to some extent in the linguistic assimilation of Ukrainians. In 1926, 4.5 percent of Ukrainians in Ukraine considered Russian their native tongue. By 1959 this figure had risen to 6.5, and by 1989, to 12.2. In 1989, 78 percent of Ukraine's population was fluent in Ukrainian, and 78.4 percent, in Russian. Russian is more prevalent in the urban areas, where only 72.1 percent of the residents are fluent in Ukrainian but 87.4 are fluent in Russian. The most Russified oblasts in Ukraine are those in which Russians constitute the highest percentage of the population: Crimea, Donetske, Luhanske, Kharkiv, Odessa, and Dnipropetrovske.

Ukrainians in other Soviet republics have been subjected to even stronger Russification pressures. They have no national rights – no Ukrainian schools and no Ukrainian publications (books and press) of their own. Likewise, access to Ukrainian materials from Ukraine is made difficult for them. Ukrainians in the RSFSR along the Ukrainian border (in Belgorod, Kursk, Voronezh, and part of Rostov oblast and Krasnodar krai) constituted 66 percent of the population there in 1926. By 1970 only 9 percent of the population in the same regions was Ukrainian. In Subcaucasia the percentage of Ukrainian inhabitants fell from 33.4 in 1926 to 2.3 in 1970. In 1926 there were 2,318,000 Ukrainians in the Asiatic part of the USSR, and in 1970 there were 2,235,000.

When M. Gorbachev's policy of Glasnost made it possible to discuss basic social problems, Russification became one of the first and central issues to be raised in the Ukrainian press. The Taras Shevchenko Ukrainian Language Society was founded in February 1989 to revive the Ukrainian language in Ukraine, and at the end of October 1989 the Supreme Soviet of the Ukrainian SSR adopted the Languages Act establishing Ukrainian as the republic's official language. The act's schedule for the conversion of state institutions, enterprises, civic organizations, and mass media to Ukrainian was based on the premise that the effects of Russification could be overcome only gradually, through patient and persistent effort.

BIBLIOGRAPHY

Dzyuba, I. *Internationalism or Russification?* (London 1968; 2nd edn, New York 1974)

Kolasky, J. *Education in Soviet Ukraine* (Toronto 1968)

Sahaydak, M. (comp). *Ethnocide of Ukrainians in the* USSR, trans O. Saciuk and B. Yasen (Baltimore–Paris–Toronto 1976)

Motyl, A.J. *Will the Non-Russians Rebel? State, Ethnicity, and Stability in the* USSR (Ithaca and London 1987)

Solchanyk, R. 'Ukraine, Belorussia, and Modavia: Imperial Integration, Russification, and the Struggle for National Survival,' in *The Nationalities Factor in Soviet Politics and Society*, ed L. Hajda and M. Belssinger (Boulder, Colo, and Oxford 1990)

B. Kravtsiv, V. Kubijovyč

Russka pravda (Ruthenian Truth). A Russophile newspaper published in Vienna in 1888–92 (68 issues appeared). It was intended for the Russophile community in Bukovyna, and published regular articles about life there and especially about the Orthodox church. It also devoted considerable attention to developments in the Russian Empire. The editors were H. Kupchanko and then K. Kozarkevych and Y. Bukhovytsky; after 1892 Kozarkevych edited and published *Pravoslavnaia Bukovina*.

Russkaia beseda (Russian Colloquy). A Russian Slavophile journal published in Moscow as a quarterly (1856–8) and bimonthly (1859–60). Among its Ukrainian contributors were P. Kulish (a Russian version of his *Chorna rada* [The Black Council], 1857), M. Vovchok (Russian peasant stories, 1858), T. Shevchenko (Russian and translated works), M. Maksymovych, and D. Mordovets (Mordovtsev).

Russkaia beseda (Russian Colloquy). A Russian Slavophile journal published monthly in St Petersburg in 1894–6. In 1894 it was called *Galitsko-russkii vestnik*. Edited by V. Dragomiretsky, it supported the Russophile movement in Western Ukraine. Contributors included the Galician Russophiles I. Hushalevych and Yu. Yavorsky.

Russkaia pravda (Ruthenian Truth). A Russophile weekly newspaper published in place of *Pravoslavnaia Rus'* in Chernivtsi from October 1910 to 1914 by A. Gerovsky. Edited by I. Tsurkanovych and, from 1912, I. Orobets, it continued the anti-Ukrainian policies of its predecessor.

Russkaia Rada. See Ruthenian Council.

Russkaia rada (Ruthenian Council). A Russophile semimonthly newspaper published in 1871–1912 in Kolomyia. It contained articles on village life, politics, economics, history, and popular enlightenment. The newspaper was published and edited by M. Bilous, initially with the assistance of Rev I. Naumovych.

Russkaia shkola (Ruthenian School). A Russophile weekly newspaper for teachers, published in Prešov by the Union of Ruthenian Teachers in Slovakia from 8 June 1926 to 1931. The four-page paper came out in *yazychiie*. It defended the interests of teachers, criticized the official Slovokization policy, and promoted a higher educational standard in the region. Its editor was I. Pieshchak, and its manager was I. Hender.

Russkaia volia (Ruthenian Will). A popular Russophile periodical published semimonthly in Ternopil (1906–7, 1910–11), Peremyshl (1908–9), and Zolochiv (1910) by F.

Protsyk and M. Matveikov. The editors were A. Stelmakh, M. Riznychok, and M. Krupa.

Russkaia zemlia (Ruthenian Land). A Russophile weekly newspaper published in Uzhhorod from June 1919 to 1938. The organ of the Carpatho-Russian Labor party, it frequently attacked the Ukrainian nationalist movement in Transcarpathia and advocated the creation of a unitary 'Russian' state encompassing Transcarpathia, Bukovyna, the rest of Ukraine, and Russia. Its editors included D. Vislotsky, V. Nichai (1919–20), A. Gagatko, and I. Tsurkanovich (1922–3, 1925–38).

Russkii golos (Ruthenian Voice). A Russophile weekly paper published in Edmonton from April 1913 to July 1916 in Russian and *yazychiie*. It tried to appeal to Orthodox Ukrainians and harshly criticized the Catholic church. It also opposed the teaching of Ukrainian in Alberta schools. The newspaper's publisher was V. Cherniak, and its editors were V. Hladyk (1913–14) and M. Ostrovsky (1914–16). In 1914 it was adopted as the organ of the Russian National Association in Canada. In total, 158 issues appeared.

Russkii golos (Russian Voice). A weekly newspaper of the Russophile right-wing community in Galicia, published in 1922–39 in Lviv. It advocated the restoration of a unitary Russian Empire and co-operation with the Russian White émigrés in Poland.

Russkii narod (Ruthenian People). A Russophile weekly newspaper published in Winnipeg from November 1914 to May 1919 (in 1918–19 on an irregular basis). Articles appeared in both Russian and *yazychiie*. The newspaper accused the organized Ukrainian community of being pro-Austrian during the First World War and opposed Ukrainian independence. *Russkii narod* also campaigned against the teaching of Ukrainian in Manitoba schools. In 1918 the paper was adopted by the newly created League for the Liberation of Carpatho-Russia, and began advocating the annexation of Transcarpathia to Russia. Its editors were V. Hladyk and P. Samilo.

Russkii solovei (The Ruthenian Nightingale). A collection of about 200 folk songs and poems in various Ukrainian dialects, published in Uzhhorod in 1890. Edited by M. *Vrabel, it contained Ukrainian folk songs from the Bačka and Prešov regions, Transcarpathia, and Galicia as well as verses by O. Dukhnovych, O. Pavlovych, and several versifiers from Bačka, such as P. Kuzmiak and H. Segedi. The book was financed partly by the Ukrainian community in Bačka; it is therefore justly claimed to be the first book published by Bačka Ukrainians. It played an important role in preserving their national identity.

Russkii vestnik (Ruthenian Herald). A weekly organ of the Autonomous Agrarian Alliance in Transcarpathia, published from 1923 to 1938 in Uzhhorod. Published in the artificial *yazychiie* by A. *Brodii and edited by him and I. Shpak, it was Russophile and pro-Hungarian in orientation and was supported by official Hungarian circles. The paper was closed down by the government of Carpatho-Ukraine in November 1938.

Russkoe slovo (Ruthenian Word). A Russophile newspaper published in Lviv weekly in 1890–1912 and semimonthly in 1913–14. It contained mostly reports on village life and articles on political and economic affairs, and also many biographies of prominent Russophiles. After the split in the Galician Russophile movement in 1909, *Russkoe slovo* became the organ of the *Old Ruthenians. Its longtime editor and publisher was V. Lutsyk. He was succeeded by Y. Markov, I. Pelekh, H. Hanuliak, and others.

Russkoe slovo (Ruthenian Word). A popular weekly (semimonthly from 1933) published in Prešov by the Greek Catholic Prešov eparchy from 8 March 1924 to 23 December 1938. Published in *yazychiie, it contained articles on educational, cultural, and political subjects. It continued the traditions of O. Dukhnovych in defending the rights of the Ruthenian (Ukrainian) population in the Prešov region, opposing Slovakization, and rejecting ties with the Soviet Union. Until 1930 local Ukrainophile populists, such as D. Zubrytsky and I. Nevytska, contributed to the paper. Its editors were S. Hoidych, S. Diulai, F. Roikovych, I. Pieshchak, A. Zubrytsky, and A. Demianchyk. The conservative religious newspaper *Da priidet tsarstviie tvoie* (1928–38), printed partly in Roman characters, came out as a supplement to *Russkoe slovo*.

Russophiles (*rusofily*, or *moskvofily*). The adherents of a sociopolitical current that appeared in the 19th century among Ukrainians in Galicia, Transcarpathia, and Bukovyna who considered themselves to be a part of the Russian nation. Russophilism covered a broad range of cultural and political attitudes and incorporated enthusiasts, sympathizers, and those looking for assistance in their national struggle. Underlying the notion of Russophilism was the implicit or explicit assumption of eventual political union with the Russian Empire. Such sympathies were encouraged by the imperial Russian authorities, who provided the Russophiles with substantial subsidies and moral encouragement.

The reasons for the emergence of Russophilism are varied. The linguistic and cultural similarities between Russians and Ukrainians at a time before the crystallization of a modern Ukrainian national consciousness represented one factor. Also important was the marked sense of inferiority many leading Ukrainians felt in the face of Polish culture. The complex was generated in part by the pseudoaristocratic aspirations of the Galician intelligentsia of the period as well as by their disdain for (and desire not to be identified with) the common people. Galician Russophiles sought to fill a cultural void in their lives by identifying with the Russian nation and the achievements of a highly developed Russian culture. Finally, social frustration came into play, as many prominent Ukrainians began looking to Russia as their savior after political changes in Austria-Hungary during the 1860s had diminished their power and prestige.

The first manifestations of Russophilism appeared in Transcarpathia in the late 18th and early 19th centuries in the use and propagation of the Russian language and the adoption of Russian etymological practices in Ukrainian; in travels by local scholars and students to Russia for study and work (Yu. Venelin, P. Lodii); in interest in Russian cultural life; and in the use of Russian by local Ukrainian authors. The harbinger of Russophilism in Galicia was the historian D. Zubrytsky, who was strongly influenced by the ideas of the Russian historian and Pan-Slavist M. *Pogodin. A professor at Moscow University, Pogodin sojourned in Lviv in 1835 and 1839–40 and developed a following among members of the Galician Ukrainian intelligentsia. The resident priest of the Russian embassy in Vienna, M. *Raevsky, was also a major figure in developing Russophile sympathies among Slavic intellectuals from the 1840s.

The Russophiles did not emerge as an identifiable group until the 1860s. Throughout the 1850s they existed in a nascent form as the secular wing of the so-called *Old Ruthenians, with whom they shared a common concern about linguistic and cultural Polonization (playing a key role in the *alphabet war) and church Latinization. Centered around the so-called Pogodin colony, the emerging movement included figures such as B. Didytsky, Ya. and I. Holovatsky, I. Hushalevych, M. Malynovsky, A. Petrushevych, S. Shekhovych, and Zubrytsky. Russophilism became particularly important in the 1860s, when the Austrian emperor granted the Polish gentry a free hand in an autonomous Galicia. (In contrast, the Russian tsar was punishing the Polish gentry in Right-Bank Ukraine for its participation in the Polish Insurrection of 1863–4.) The Russophiles split with the Old Ruthenians, who now constituted a spent force, and began to define themselves more clearly as a distinct group.

Didytsky dealt with linguistic issues in his anonymous pamphlet *V odyn chas nauchyt'sia malorusynu po velikorussky* (In One Hour a Little Russian Can Learn Great Russian) and articles in the newspaper *Slovo*, and I. Naumovych outlined the political platform of the Russophile movement in the Galician parliament and in articles in *Slovo*. The Russophiles were adherents of the notion of a common origin of the three 'Rus'' nations. They used the vernacular only for works of popular education intended for distribution among the peasantry. More commonly they employed the macaronic *yazychiie among themselves (only occasionally using Russian). *Yazychiie* was a creation of the Russophiles, who lacked fluency in Russian and were fascinated by the forms of Old Church Slavonic; the use of *yazychiie* also fed their aristocratic pretensions by differentiating them from 'common folk.' In all cases they adhered to an etymological orthography.

While maintaining a façade of loyalty to the Habsburg realm the Russophiles continued developing their pro-Russian orientation. Increasingly their Russophile sympathies brought them remuneration. The Greek Catholic clerics and teachers who emigrated to the Kholm region (within the Russian Empire) in the 1860s, ostensibly to preserve the purity of the rite in the face of Polish-inspired attempts at Latinization, secured rewarding positions. Scholarships granted by Russian institutions to students in Galicia further entrenched Russophile tendencies in the area, as did the loss of Austro-Hungarian prestige after the empire's defeat in the Austro-Prussian War of 1866. In 1867 Ya. Holovatsky and Naumovych received a stipend. In the following year V. Ploshchansky and K. Klymkovych received financial assistance. By the end of the decade a significant part of the Ukrainian intelligentsia of Galicia, secular and clerical, consisted of Russophiles. They came to control the Stauropegion Institute, the People's Home in Lviv, and the Halytsko-Ruska Matytsia society. In 1870 they gained control of the *Ruthenian

Council, which was to have continued the traditions of the Supreme Ruthenian Council of 1848.

In addition to assuming leading positions in existing structures the Russophiles established their own bodies. In 1868 a Russophile cultural organization, Russkaia Osnova, was established in Vienna. More significantly, the *Kachkovsky Society was formed in Kolomyia in 1874 (its headquarters moved to Lviv in 1876). Russophile publications included *Slovo* (1861–87), *Russkaia rada* (1871–1912), *Nauka* (1871–1939, with interruptions), *Prolom* (1880–2), *Novyi prolom* (1883–7), *Chervonaia Rus'* (1888–91), *Halytskaia Rus'* (1891–2), *Halychanyn* (1893–1913), and *Russkoe slovo* (1890–1914). *Nauka* and the reading rooms of the Kachkovsky Society were the main centers of Russophile cultural and educational work in the villages.

The principal counterbalance to the Russophiles in Galicia was the Ukrainophile populist group, which had established itself initially around the *Prosvita society in 1867. Throughout the remainder of the 1860s and through the 1870s the populists and Russophiles maintained a hostile rivalry and an ongoing struggle for control of national institutions. In 1877 a radical group of Ukrainophiles led by I. Franko and M. Pavlyk managed to wrest the students' Academic Circle from Russophile control.

The Russophiles lost their pre-eminent position in Galician Ukrainian society during the 1880s, in large measure owing to the upsurge in support for the Ukrainophile populists. The Russophiles also suffered a major setback in 1881 when a group of their prominent leaders (including O. Hrabar, A. Dobriansky, Naumovych, Ploshchansky, and Y. Markov) was tried for treason in Lviv. Although the accused were acquitted (after which a number moved to the Russian Empire), the trial tainted the movement and weakened its support. Although the Russophiles remained entrenched in the institutions they had come to dominate, and continued as a significant presence among the Galician clergy, they clearly constituted a minority party.

In the early 20th century the Russophile movement underwent some major changes. In 1900 the largely Russophile Ruthenian Council initiated a political body, the Ruthenian People's party. The Russophiles had some limited political success. In the 1906 elections to the Viennese parliament the Russophiles elected 5 deputies (compared to 27 for the populists). They managed, however, to garner support from Galician Poles, and in 1908 they elected 8 representatives to the Galician provincial diet (compared to 12 representatives of pro-Ukrainian parties).

At the same time a more radical faction of Russophiles emerged. Faced with a vigorous and politically and economically organized Ukrainian national populist movement, the younger faction called for the complete national and cultural integration of Galician Ruthenians with Russians and the adoption of the Russian language as a literary standard. The group became particularly active after the conclusion of the Russo-Japanese War and an escalation of tensions between the Russian and Austro-Hungarian empires. It allied itself with a resurgent current of *Pan-Slavism in the Russian Empire that sought to annex Galicia, Bukovyna, and Transcarpathia and thus 'reunite' all the lands of ancient Rus'.

In 1909 the Russophiles split into two factions, the *starokursnyky* (Old Liners) and the *novokursnyky* (New Liners). The leading activists of the former faction included V. Davydiak and M. Korol as well as M. Hli-

bovytsky, I. Kostetsky, V. Kurylovych, O. Monchalovsky, and Yu. Paventsky. The *starokursnyky* opposed full union with Russia, continued to use vernacular Ukrainian, and maintained their allegiance to Austria. Their official press included the newspaper *Halychanyn* and the popular weekly *Russkoe slovo*. The *novokursnyky* were led by V. Dudykevych and D. Markov. Other activists included K. and I. Cherliunchakevych, M. Hlushkevych, S. Labensky, M. Rastavetsky, K. Senyk, and O. Valnytsky. Their official organs were the daily *Prikarpatskaia Rus'* (1909–15) and the popular weekly *Golos naroda* (1909–14). The *novokursnyky* were the more active of the two groups, and they came to control most Russophile organizations, such as the Kachkovsky society, the Union of Russian Teams (sports organizations), and co-operatives. They also gained majorities in student organizations (Drug in Lviv and Bukovina in Vienna).

Russophile agitation in Galicia intensified during the years leading up to the First World War. A major reason was the material support of the Galician-Russian society. Based in St Petersburg, the group was founded in 1909 by the Russian ultranationalist V. Bobrinsky, and cultivated supporters in Galicia, which its members hoped would soon become part of the empire. Other leaders of the society were D. Verhun, E. Georgievsky (archbishop of Kholm), A. Khrapovitsky (archbishop of Volhynia), and Yu. Yavorsky (a Galician Russophile who had lived in Kiev from 1904). Galician youth were given scholarships to study in Russia, and some entered Russian Orthodox theological seminaries. Members of the Russian State Duma participated in Russophile political demonstrations. Bobrinsky conducted his pro-Russian agitation with impunity in the villages of Galicia and Bukovyna. Campaigns of conversion to Russian Orthodoxy were conducted in the Lemko region and in counties bordering the Russian empire. The religious agitation was conducted by Austrian citizens who had studied in Russia and then were sent back to Galicia as missionaries. The Austrian and Galician authorities arrested Russian Orthodox missionaries who had been sent to Galicia, or threatened to draft them into the army. In the spring of 1914 S. Bendasiuk and other missionaries were tried on changes of high treason, but were acquitted. A similar trial was held in Sighetul Marmației in 1913–14, with O. Kabaliuk and 180 peasants as defendants. Most of them were found guilty.

The shift among the *novokursnyky* to total support of Russian policies prompted the defection of such Russophiles as S. Drymaliuk, M. Korol, and I. Svientsitsky to the Ukrainian populists. The relative strength of the two movements was reflected in the size of their organizations. In 1914 the Kachkovsky Society had 300 reading rooms, and the Ukrainophile Prosvita society had 2,944; the Russophile Ruthenian Audit Union oversaw 106 co-operatives, and the Audit Union of Ukrainian Co-operatives, 909. In the elections to the Galician diet of 1913, 1 Russophile and 30 Ukrainophiles were elected.

Russophile activists living in the Russian Empire founded the Committee for the Liberation of Carpathian Ruthenia on 11 August 1914 in Kiev. They also issued a proclamation addressed to the 'long-suffering Russian people in Galicia,' which urged the people in that region to greet the Russian army and suggested that Ukrainian soldiers in the Austro-Hungarian army should defect to Russian forces. That and the committee's close collaboration with the Russian military authorities brought about repercussions in Austria-Hungary, with the massive arrest of Russophiles and Ukrainian populists alike. Thousands of Ukrainians were sent to concentration camps in Thalerhof and other locations, of whom most were freed in 1915. Thousands were also executed as the Russian army advanced, some by Austrian but most by Hungarian forces. After the capture of Lviv the committee dissolved itself in favor of the Russian People's Council, headed by Dudykevych. Russophiles sought an active role in the Russian imperial administration and attempted to liquidate all Ukrainian populist elements.

After the retreat of the Russian armies from Galicia many Russophiles followed them eastward and established several settlements near Rostov-na-Donu. A substantial number of the Russophiles, now faced with the real difference between Ukrainians and Russians, became conscious Ukrainians. Some participated in the Ukrainian Revolution of 1917 in central Ukraine, and others returned to Galicia and supported the Western Ukrainian National Republic.

In 1918 the remaining adherents of Russophilism in Galicia established the Russian Executive Committee in Lviv and revived the periodical *Prikarpatskaia Rus'* (1918–20). The Executive Committee worked with the Ukrainian Interparty Council, opposed the Polish authorities, and boycotted the elections to the Polish Sejm in 1922. Soon the Russophiles split into two groups. A left-wing faction, led by K. Valnytsky and K. Pelekhaty, established the *People's Will party, whose official press organ was *Volia narodu* (1921–8). In 1926 they joined the Sel-Soiuz group of Kholm and Volhynia to form *Sel-Rob; in the process they were compelled to drop their Russophile line and declare themselves Ukrainian-oriented. The more conservative wing of the Russophiles was based around the Russian People's Organization. Their petitions to the Polish governmental officials bore fruit when they were given control of key institutions, such as the People's Home in Lviv and the Stauropegion Institute. The Russophiles also worked closely with the Russian minority in Poland. The conservatives later split into two factions, the right-wing Russian Agrarian party and the moderate Russian Peasant Organization, but they reunited in 1931.

In the 1920s, Galician Russophiles revived the Kachkovsky society, the Ruthenian Audit Union (which in 1939 oversaw 250 co-operatives, while its Ukrainian counterpart oversaw 3,455), and other institutions. Through the 1920s and 1930s the Russophiles failed to elect a single representative to the Polish parliament, but in 1932 two of their delegates were made members of the Nonparty Bloc of Co-operation with the Government. Despite their collaboration with the Poles the Russophiles' movement went into decline, and virtually all of its members joined the Ukrainian camp.

Russophilism existed in *Transcarpathia from the second half of the 19th century, but it did not result in the establishment of a separate, distinctive group. That state of affairs reflected the uniqueness of the regional patriotism that existed there. In that period Transcarpathian Ukrainians generally considered themselves Carpatho-Ruthenians (or Rusyns). Their understanding of their national identity, however, tended to fluctuate between an uncrystallized Russophilism and a local particularism. Consequently the major patriotic Ukrainian associations or groups (specifically those that were not Magyarophile) tended to have a strong Russophile influence. That influence was reinforced by the migration of notable members of the local intelligentsia to the Russian Empire. The development of Russophilism was also influenced by the presence of imperial Russian troops in the region during the suppression of the Revolution of 1848–9 in the Habsburg monarchy. Prior to the First World War members of the Transcarpathian intelligentsia who found themselves threatened by the Hungarian authorities turned to Russia and the Pan-Slav movement for assistance. After the war there was a movement to develop Russian Orthodoxy in the region. At the same time an openly Ukrainophile movement began to develop there, which had become a major force regionally by the 1930s. A Russophile presence remained in Transcarpathia, centered largely around the *Dukhnovych society (1923–45).

Russophilism in Bukovyna developed in reaction to the Rumanianizing policies of the local authorities. Other factors included a religious affinity to Orthodox Russia and the influence of the Russian consulate in Chernivtsi. Russophilism prompted many Bukovynian youths to leave Austria and settle in Russia. Its leading activists were V. Hlibovytsky, H. Kupchanko, and V. Prodan. Like their Galician counterparts, the Bukovynian Russophiles initially dominated the nascent national cultural (Ruska Besida) and political (*Ruska Rada society) organizations in the region, but they were eclipsed by the Ukrainian populists by the end of the 19th century.

In the Lemko region Russophile activists, such as M. Hromosiak, Ya. Kachmaryk, and D. Khyliak, established, in December 1918, the Lemko Russian People's Republic. The Russophile groups did not recognize Poland's annexation of the region in 1921. They did not remain a lasting force in the region.

A Russophile current developed among Ukrainian emigrants in North America in the early part of the 20th century, largely as a result of missionary work by the Russian Orthodox church (most notably by A. *Tovt in the United States). Its activity was subsidized heavily by the Holy Synod in Moscow, which was following a policy developed by K. *Pobodenostsev. The Synod's intent, in part, was to influence indirectly the development of Russophile sentiment in Western Ukraine, the home of most of the emigrants. Russophile activity in North America waned with the fall of the Russian Empire (and the end of subsidies) in 1917.

BIBLIOGRAPHY
Didyts'kyi, B. *Svoiezhyt'ievii zapysky* (Lviv 1908)
Lozyns'kyi, M. *Ukraïnstvo i moskvofil'stvo sered ukraïns'ko-rus'koho narodu v Halychyni* (Lviv 1909)
Markov, D. *Russkaia i ukrainskaia ideia v Avstrii* (Lviv 1915)
Kushnir, V. 'Sproba kharakterystyky ideinykh pidstav ukraïns'koho politychnoho russofil'stva,' *Nova Ukraïna*, nos 7–10 (1922–3)
Andrusiak, M. *Narysy z istoriï halyts'koho moskvofil'stva* (Lviv 1935)
Mykolaievych, M. [Stakhiv, M.] *Moskvofil'stvo, ioho bat'ky i dity* (Lviv 1936)

S. Ripetsky, O. Sereda

Russo-Turkish wars. For two centuries the imperialist powers of Russia and Ottoman Turkey fought for hegemony of the Black Sea and its coastal regions. Initially Russia's goal was to gain control of the Black Sea and its straits and thereby ensure access to the Mediterranean. Russia's expansionism was disguised by its self-appointed defense of all Orthodox Christians subjugated by Turkey, liberation of the Balkan peoples from the Turkish yoke, and prevention of Turkish and Crimean Tatar raids and pillaging in Southern Ukraine and Russia. Turkey sought to protect and retain its possessions and considered Russia the aggressor. From the second half of the 18th century the Russo-Turkish wars were linked to the gradual disintegration of the Ottoman Empire.

According to the obligations enumerated in various 17th- and 18th-century treaties with Russia the Hetman state and Ukraine's inhabitants were duty-bound to participate in Russia's wars. Thousands of Ukrainian Cossacks and peasants fought and died as allies and later citizens of the Russian Empire. In the later wars many of them volunteered to help liberate their fellow Slavs and coreligionists. All of the wars involved Ukrainian strategic interests, and during each one Russian armies passed through Ukraine, inflicting various degrees of ruin and hardship.

The war of 1676–81. In 1677 a Turkish–Crimean Tatar army invaded and ravaged Right-Bank Ukraine and took the capital, Chyhyryn. The Turks' attempt to retain Chyhyryn was repelled by a Russian-Ukrainian force led by Prince G. Romodanovsky and Hetman I. Samoilovych (see *Chyhyryn campaigns, 1677–8), and the Turks were forced to retreat. In 1681 the Ottoman Porte, the Crimean Khanate, and Muscovy signed the Treaty of Bakhchesarai, according to which Muscovy had sovereignty over the Hetmanate and the Zaporizhia, both sides agreed not to colonize the Southern Ukrainian lands between the Boh and the Dniester rivers for 20 years, and Turkey retained control of the southern Kiev region, the Bratslav region, and Podilia.

The war of 1686–99. As a member of the Holy League against Turkey, Russia began the war with unsuccessful Russian-Ukrainian Cossack campaigns against the Crimean Khanate in 1687 and 1689. Hetman Samoilovych was blamed for the failure of the first campaign and was replaced by I. Mazepa. Later Peter I undertook the Azov campaigns of 1695–6, in which he captured Oziv (Azov) in 1696. By the 1699 Treaty of Carlowitz Russia consolidated its hold over the Sea of Azov and its littoral.

The war of 1710–13. During Russia's Great Northern War with Sweden the Porte, encouraged by Swedish, French, and Austrian diplomats, declared war on Russia. In early 1711 the Russian army of Peter I and Hetman I. Skoropadsky's Left-Bank Cossack regiments defeated the Crimean Tatar army and its Cossack allies, led by P. *Orlyk, and forced them to abandon Right-Bank Ukraine. The Russian offensive in Moldavia was defeated at the Prut River, however, and the *Prut Treaty of 1711 forced Russia to abandon Oziv and to destroy its fortifications on the Azov coast.

The war of 1735–9. After the Crimean Tatars invaded Ukraine in 1735, the Russian Dnieper Army (which included Ukrainian Cossack regiments) invaded the Crimea, where they captured Perekop, Yevpatoriia, and Bakhchesarai in 1736 and Ochakiv in 1737. Another Russian army recaptured Oziv and invaded the Crimea from the east. In 1739, while Turkey was occupied with its war with Austria, the Russian army captured Khotyn. The 1739 Russo-Turkish Treaty of Belgrade granted Oziv to Russia and consolidated Russia's control over the Zaporizhia but forbade Russian fleets on the Azov Sea and Black Sea.

The war of 1768–74. The theater of the war was in Moldavia and Wallachia, where Russian troops and Zaporozhian Cossacks under the supreme command of Gen P. Rumiantsev were victorious in various battles. The Russian fleet destroyed the Turkish navy in the Aegean Sea. Under the 1774 Peace Treaty of *Küçük Kaynarca Russia gained the right to have a fleet on the Black Sea and coastal fortresses in Southern Ukraine. Weakened by the war, Turkey was forced to cede *Bukovyna to Austria in 1774. Having finally gained access to the Black Sea, Catherine II no longer considered the *Zaporozhian Sich necessary for the defense of the empire and in 1775 had it destroyed.

The war of 1787–91. The new conflict erupted as a result of Turkish efforts to regain the *Crimea, which had been annexed by Russia in 1783. Under the command of A. Suvorov, Russian forces defeated the Turks at Kinburn (1787) and Focşani, in Moldavia (1789), and took Ochakiv and Izmail (1790). The 1791 Treaty of Iaşi confirmed Russia's annexation of the Crimea and granted Russia control of the lands between the Boh and the Dniester.

The war of 1806–12. After Turkey tried to regain the Black Sea's northern littoral, Russia again invaded and occupied Moldavia and Wallachia and routed the Turks near Rushchuk, on the Danube. Under the 1812 Treaty of Bucharest Turkey ceded *Bessarabia, that is, the territories between the Dniester and the Prut rivers, to Russia and guaranteed Russian access to shipping on the Danube.

The war of 1828–9. Hostilities began after Russia came out in support of the Greek revolution and sent troops to the Balkans and the Caucasus. In the early phase of the war a small force of Cossacks of the *Danubian Sich led by Otaman Y. Hladky went over to the Russian side. By the 1829 Treaty of Edirne Turkey accepted Russia's annexation of the islands at the mouth of the Danube and the Caucasian coast, including the fortress of Anapa, recognized Russia's title to Georgia and other Caucasian principalities, and guaranteed Russia access to the Danube and the Black Sea straits.

The war of 1853–6. See *Crimean War.

The war of 1877–8. In 1877 Russia declared war on Turkey in support of the Balkan rebellions. Many Ukrainian volunteers had already joined the Herzegovinian and Bulgarian uprisings and the Serbian army. Several (eg, S. Krut, A. Lysenko, V. Yanovsky) wrote memoirs about their experiences. Thousands of Ukrainians fought in Russian units during the Balkan campaign, and committees that gathered funds and medical aid for Serbian and Bulgarian soldiers were formed in Ukraine. In 1878 the Russo-Turkish Treaty of San Stefano created a 'Great Bulgaria' as Russia's satellite. At the Congress of Berlin, however, Austria-Hungary and Britain did not accept the treaty, imposed their own partition of the Balkans, and forced Russia to retreat from the Balkans.

BIBLIOGRAPHY
Chesney, F.R. *The Russo-Turkish Campaigns of 1828 and 1829 with a View of the Present State of Affairs in the East* (New York 1854)
Green F.V. *The Russian Army and Its Campaigns in Turkey in 1877–78* (New York 1879)
Petrov, V. *Vtoraia turetskaia voina v tsarstvovanie Ekateriny II, 1787–1791*, 2 vols (St Petersburg 1880)
Petrov, A. *Voina Rossii s Turtsiei, 1806–1812*, 3 vols (St Petersburg 1885–7)
Opisanie Russko-Turetskoi voiny 1877–78 g.g. na Balkanskom poluostrove, 2 vols (St Petersburg 1901)

Baiov, A. *Russkaia armiia v tsarstvovanie imp. Anny Ivanovny: Voiny Rossii s Turtsiei v 1736–1739 gg.*, 2 vols (St Petersburg 1906)

Romanovs'kyi, M. 'Viina 1735–8 rr. ta ïi naslidky dlia Ukraïny,' *Pratsi Komisiï sotsial'no-ekonomichnoï istoriï Ukraïny*, 1 (Kiev 1932)

Sumner, B.H. *Russia and the Balkans, 1870–1880* (Oxford 1937)

Smirnov, N. *Rossiia i Turtsiia v XVI–XVII vv.*, vol 1 (Moscow 1946)

Kozinets, V. *Russko-turetskie voiny XVIII i nachala XIX stoletii i ikh rol' v osvobozhdenii Moldavii ot turetskogo iga* (Kiev 1948)

Druzhinina, E. *Kiuchuk-Kainardzhiiskii mir 1774 goda (ego podgotovka i zakliuchenie)* (Moscow 1955)

A. Zhukovsky

Rustical lands. Peasant landholdings in the Austro-Hungarian Empire, including the Western Ukrainian territories, Galicia (from 1772), and Bukovyna (from 1774). The agrarian reforms introduced by Joseph II in the 1780s specified that rustical lands belonged to the peasants and guaranteed the peasantry the use of the lands in perpetuity. The peasants, however, were not permitted to sell or divide them. Nobles were legally barred from purchasing the lands, but between 1787 and 1847 nobles were able to acquire over 5 percent of all rustical lands. In 1844 rustical lands in eastern Galicia accounted for 70 percent of all the arable land, 68.5 percent of the meadows, 63.7 percent of the pastures, but only 0.7 percent of the forests (of which the nobles claimed some 98 percent). Rustical lands represented almost 49 percent of all the land, whereas over 47 percent was owned by the nobility. With the abolition of serfdom in 1848, the rustical lands were transformed into the private holdings of individual peasants.

Rustytsky, Yosyp [Rustyc'kyj, Josyp], b 12 April 1839 in Ukraine, d 26 April 1912. Surgeon. A graduate of Kiev University (1861), he worked in its surgery clinic and abroad with the leading surgeons in Berlin, Vienna, Würzburg, Strassburg, and Paris. He lectured at Kiev (from 1874) and Kazan (1889–98) universities and worked in Red Cross hospitals in Kiev. His publications dealt chiefly with treating damaged corneas, bone putrefaction, and malignant tumors and with the history of surgery.

Rusyn, Pavlo (Paulus Ruthenus; pen name of Pawel Procler), b ca 1470 in Krosno, in the Lemko region, d November 1517 in Stary Sącz, Poland. Educator and humanist poet of Ukrainian origin (see *Humanism). A graduate of Greifswald University (1499), he received his master's degree from Cracow University in 1506 and taught classical literature there (1507–8, 1511–16). Among his students were Copernicus and the Polish Latin poets Jan from Wiślica and J. Dantyszek. Collections of his Latin verse were published in Vienna in 1509, in Cracow in 1887, and in Warsaw in 1962; several poems in Ukrainian translation appeared in an anthology of 16th-century Ukrainian poetry (Kiev 1987). J. Krukierek's book about him was published in Krosno in 1935.

Rusyn (The Ruthenian). A semiweekly newspaper published in Uzhhorod in 1920–2. The semiofficial organ of H. Zhatkovych, the Czechoslovak governor of the province of Subcarpathian Ruthenia, it was published in the Transcarpathian dialect and edited by T. Zhatkovych and A. Shtefan.

Rusyn (The Ruthenian). A populist newspaper published in the Transcarpathian dialect daily in Uzhhorod in 1923.

It was supported by the Czechoslovak deputy governor of the province of Subcarpathian Ruthenia. The chief editor was a Czech, F. *Tichý; he was assisted by A. Shtefan and V. Grendzha-Donsky. *Rusyn* issued a weekly literary supplement, *Nedilia Rusyna*, and a series of popular books.

Rusynov, Yukhym, b 6 October 1905 in Odessa, d 30 November 1969 in Odessa. Composer and conductor. A graduate of the Odessa Conservatory (1936), he studied composition with P. Molchanov and M. Vilinsky and conducting with J. Přibik. He conducted the conservatory's orchestra (1934–6), and opera companies in Dnipropetrovske (1936–41), Krasnoiarske (1941–4), Kharkiv (1944–5), and Odessa (from 1945). His works include the ballets *The Three Musketeers* (1939), *Olesia* (1947), and *On the Blue Sea* (1954); character pieces for orchestra; chamber music; and art songs.

Rusyns. See Ruthenians.

Ruthenia voivodeship. See Rus' voivodeship.

Ruthenian Agrarian party (Ruska khliborobska partiia). A small Ukrainophile populist party in Czechoslovak-ruled Transcarpathia, founded in August 1920 in Uzhhorod by Rev A. Voloshyn, Rev. V. Zheltvai, M. and Yu. Brashchaiko, A. Shtefan, and A. Tovt (the party chairman). In its organ *Rus'ka nyva (1920–4) it promoted pan-Ukrainian unification, political autonomy for the Ukrainians of Transcarpathia and the Prešov region, and official use of the Transcarpathian dialect. In 1924 the party was succeeded by the *Christian People's party.

Ruthenian Audit Union (Russkii revizionnyi soiuz). The central co-ordinating body for Russophile co-operatives in Galicia, founded in 1908 in Lviv. It was analogous to the *Audit Union of Ukrainian Co-operatives (RSUK), but much smaller: the Ruthenian union had 106 co-operative branches in 1914 and 250 in 1939, whereas RSUK had 909 and 3,455 in those years.

Ruthenian Battalion of Mountain Riflemen (Ruskyi batalion hirskykh striltsiv; German: Ruthenisches Bergschützen-Corps). A pro-Austrian military formation created in January 1849 on the initiative of the *Supreme Ruthenian Council. Its purpose was to guard the Carpathian mountain passes to prevent the spread of the Hungarian insurrection into Galicia, where it found many Polish sympathizers. Of 3,460 Ukrainian volunteers, 1,410 were accepted in April. They were equipped by the Austrian government and divided into six companies stationed in Berezhany, Kolomyia, Lviv, Stanyslaviv, Stryi, and Sambir. Most of the officers were Ukrainian, but the higher command was Austrian. In May the battalion took part in the Lviv celebrations of the first anniversary of the abolition of serfdom. In September it was sent to Slovakia, where it occupied the towns of Senica and Kremnica. After the suppression of the Hungarian insurrection the battalion served as a reserve unit until January 1850, when it was demobilized in Peremyshl.

Ruthenian Congress (Sobor ruskyi). A political committee that was active in Lviv during the *Revolution of 1848. It was founded in May by Polish and Polonized nobles and intellectuals as a counterbalance to the *Supreme

Ruthenian Council. Its 64 members opposed the Polish-Ukrainian administrative partition of Galicia and collaborated with the Polish People's Council. Although it declared its loyalty to the Habsburg state, it criticized the government's liberal policies. The congress accepted the abolition of serfdom but opposed the expansion of peasant rights. Its leaders, such as L. Sapieha, A., J., and W. Dzieduszycki, and J. and L. Jabłonowski, claimed to represent the Ukrainian people simply because their ancestors had been Ruthenian nobles. Although a number of Polonophile Ukrainians, including I. *Vahylevych (who edited the congress's organ *Dnewnyk Ruskij*), M. *Popel, and O. *Krynytsky, were members of the congress, it received little Ukrainian support. On 6 October 1848 the congress was absorbed by the Polish People's Council, and ceased to exist as a separate organization.

Ruthenian Council (Ruska rada). A political organization in Lviv established in 1870 as a successor to the Supreme Ruthenian Council. It quickly became dominated by *Russophiles (V. Kovalsky, Ya. Shvedzitsky, T. Pavlykiv), who refused to co-operate with Ukrainian populists in various undertakings. The populists finally established the *People's Council in 1885 as a counterpart to it. The Ruthenian Council remained in existence until 1914. Its official publications included *Russkaia rada* (1871–1912) and *Halytskaia Rus'* (1891–2). In 1890 it helped to establish the *Ruthenian People's party.

Ruthenian National Association. See Ukrainian National Association.

Ruthenian National Union. See Ukrainian Fraternal Association.

Ruthenian Pedagogical Society. See Ridna Shkola.

Ruthenian People's Council in America. See American Ruthenian National Council.

Ruthenian People's Council in L'ubovňa, 1918. A political assembly that sought to exercise self-determination for *Transcarpathia after the collapse of the Habsburg Empire in 1918. On 8 November 1918 several hundred Transcarpathian Ukrainians under the leadership of Rev E. Nevytsky convened in Stara L'ubovňa, in the westernmost part of the *Prešov region, to discuss the future of their region in the light of the disintegration of Austria-Hungary. The council declared that the Ruthenians of Transcarpathia were of the same nationality as Ruthenians across the Carpathians, and that they no longer wanted to be united with Hungary. The council then drew up a questionnaire for distribution to the villages, asking particularly if the villagers 'want[ed] to join Rus' (Ukraine).' The original leadership of the L'ubovňa council favored union with the *Western Ukrainian National Republic and opposed union with Czechoslovakia. But when the council reconvened in Prešov on 19 November, leadership had been wrested from Nevytsky and his supporters by A. *Beskyd and other Russophiles who wanted Transcarpathia to join Czechoslovakia.

Ruthenian People's Council in Lviv. See Supreme Ruthenian Council.

Ruthenian People's Enlightenment Society (Ruske narodne prosvitne druzhstvo, or RNPD). A cultural-educational society for the Ruthenian-Ukrainians living in the *Bačka and Srem regions of Yugoslavia. Popularly known as Prosvita, it was founded 2 July 1919 in Novi Sad. Among its activists were Bishop D. Niaradi, Rev H. Kostelnyk, N. Polyvka, M. Niaradi, O. Fa, I. Kraister, M. Vynai, and O. Kostelnyk. The society had branches in all the major centers of Ruthenian-Ukrainian settlements in the Bačka and Srem regions. Their activities included providing reading rooms and organizing choirs and drama groups. The society published a variety of publications, including *Rusky kalendar* (1921–41), the weekly *Rusky novyny* (1924–41), *Ridne slovo* (1933–41), the bimonthly *Dumka* (1924–44), the children's monthly *Nasha zahradka* (1936–41), and over 100 books of the popular type. From 1936 the society had its own publishing house, in Ruski Krstur. It maintained close links with both the Lviv and the Uzhhorod *Prosvita societies. With the outbreak of the German-Yugoslav War in 1941 and the subsequent Hungarian occupation of the Bačka and Srem regions the society was suppressed. At the conclusion of the Second World War the society was not renewed.

Ruthenian People's party (Russkaia narodnaia partiia). The first *Russophile political party in Galicia. The party was formed in 1900 at the initiative of the Ruthenian Council and was supported in elections by the vicegerent and the Polish parties, who tried to use it against the growing Ukrainian populist movement. The original division in the party between the Old Ruthenians and the Russophiles eventually resulted in an open split (1909).

Ruthenian People's Theater. See Ukrainska Besida Theater.

Ruthenian Radical party. See Ukrainian Radical party.

Ruthenian Red Guard (Rusynska chervona gvardiia). A communist military formation in Transcarpathian Ukraine in 1919. At the end of March 1919 the Communist Béla Kun came to power and established a Soviet republic in Hungary, including part of Transcarpathia (the autonomous Ruska Kraina). On 24 March the Hungarian Soviet government began the organization of a Red Army, and on 9 April the Ruthenian Red Guard was formally established in Mukachiv. The 6,000 soldiers in the Ruthenian Red Guard fought against the Rumanian and Czechoslovak armies. Even after the Communists were driven from Transcarpathia in May 1919, the Ruthenian Red Guard continued to fight in the Hungarian Red Army, until August of that year.

Ruthenian Theater of the Prosvita Society (Ruskyi teatr tovarystva Prosvita). The first professional Ukrainian theater in Transcarpathia. Established in Uzhhorod in 1921 with the help of the Czechoslovakian government, it gave over 1,200 musical and dramatic performances in its eight-year history. Its first director was M. *Sadovsky (1921–3), who developed a populist-ethnographic repertoire. His successor, O. *Zaharov (1923–5), elevated the theater's artistic level with plays such as V. Vynnychenko's *Brekhnia* (Lies) and *Zakon* (The Law), G.B. Shaw's *Candida*, K. Čapek's *R.U.R.*, and others by Molière, C. Goldoni, and F. Langer. M. Lysenko's *Utoplena* (The Drowned Maiden), B. Smetana's *Bartered Bride*, S. Moniuszko's *Halka*, I. Kálmán's *Silva*, and J. Strauss's *Zigeunerbaron* were performed under Ya. Barnych's musical direction. Most successful were the productions of C. Gounod's opera *Faust* and A. Schnitzler's play *Liebelei*. Financial difficulties arose during M. Pevny's tenure as director (1926–7), and under F. Bazylevych's direction (1927–9) the theater's activities dwindled and finally ceased.

Ruthenian Training School students and faculty (1914)

Ruthenian Training School (Ruska uchytelska seminariia). An institution established in Winnipeg in 1905 by the government of Manitoba to provide bilingual teachers for Ukrainian settlements in the province. The curriculum consisted of English language, Canadian and British history, literature, mathematics, geography, botany, science, accounting, art, music, and Ukrainian language and literature, with pedagogical courses in the normal school. A Third Class Normal School Diploma was awarded to those who completed the two- to three-year program. Transferred to Brandon, Manitoba, in 1907, the school was without a Ukrainian teacher from 1910 to 1913, and in 1912 it became part of the Brandon Normal School. Faced with opposition to bilingual education, the government closed the school in 1916. J. Cressy was the school's director, and the Ukrainian teachers were Ya. Makohin, D. Pyrch, T. Ferley, and P. Karmansky. Many future Ukrainian-Canadian community leaders attended the school.

Ruthenian Triad (Ruska triitsia). A Galician literary group named after the number of the predominant members, M. *Shashkevych, Ya. *Holovatsky, and I. *Vahylevych, which existed in the late 1830s, while the three were students at the Greek Catholic Theological Seminary in Lviv. Since the group came into being during the period of *romanticism, it retained the predominant interests and features of that movement – an interest in folklore and history and a striving for Pan-Slavic unity. Its Slavophilism was noticeable in the use of Old Slavic pseudonyms: Ruslan by Shashkevych, Dalibor by Vahylevych, and Yaroslav by Holovatsky. The group united around itself other youths who were burning with a desire to work for the good of their people. Some of them (H. Ilkevych, M. Kulchytsky) were also involved in Polish revolutionary circles; most, however, were engaged in collecting oral folk literature, studying the history of Ukraine, translating the works of other Slavic authors, and writing their own verses and treatises. The members of the group maintained that the 'Ruthenians' of Galicia, Bukovyna, and Transcarpathia were all part of one Ukrainian people who had their own language, culture, and history. They emulated the Ukrainians under Russian rule, and were especially influenced by I. Kotliarevsky's *Eneïda* (Aeneid, 1789, 1809, 1820s), the collections of songs by M. Maksymovych and I. Sreznevsky, the grammar of O. Pavlovsky, and some of the early works of the *Kharkiv Romantic School. They made several attempts at publishing their own works. Their first two collections, 'Syn Rusi' [The Son of Rus', 1833] and 'Zoria' [The Star, 1834]), were not published. Their third collection, *Rusalka Dnistrovaia* (The Dniester Nymph, 1836), was published in Buda, but 800 of the original 1,000 copies printed were immediately confiscated. Although the collection was short-lived, its importance was immense, in that it was written in the spoken Ukrainian and not in the 'learned' *yazychiie*; it thus initiated the use of vernacular Ukrainian for literature in the Ukrainian lands in the Austro-Hungarian Empire. The Pan-Slavic sentiment in the miscellany makes it similar to the Slovak poet J. Kollár's collection of sonnets *Slávy dcera* ([Goddess] Slava's Daughter, 1824), which was to a great degree the inspiration for the Ruthenian Triad.

BIBLIOGRAPHY
Shakh, S. O. *Markiian Shashkevych i halyts'ke vidrodzhennia* (Paris–Munich 1961)
Humeniuk, M.; Kravchenko, Ie. (comps). *M. Shashkevych, I. Vahylevych, Ia. Holovats'kyi: Bibliohrafichnyi pokazhchyk* (Lviv 1962)
Kozik, J. *The Ukrainian National Movement in Galicia: 1815–1849* (Edmonton 1986)
Petrash, O. 'Rus'ka triitsia': *M. Shashkevych, I. Vahylevych, Ia. Holovatskyi ta ïkhni literaturni poslidovnyky*, 2nd rev edn (Kiev 1986)
Steblii, F. (ed). 'Rus'ka triitsia' v istoriï suspil'nopolitychnoho rukhu i kul'tury Ukraïny (Kiev 1987)

D.H. Struk

Ruthenians. A historic name for Ukrainians corresponding to the Ukrainian *rusyny*. The English 'Ruthenians' (sometimes 'Ruthenes') is derived from the Latin *Rutheni* (singular *Ruthenus*), which also gave rise to the German *Ruthenen* and similar words in other languages. Originally the Latin name *Rut(h)eni* was applied to a Celtic tribe of ancient Gaul (their town Segodunum later became known as Rodez). The name *Rutheni* came to be applied to the inhabitants of Kievan Rus' as a result of the medieval practice of giving newly encountered peoples the names of extinct ancient peoples. B. Unbegaun has suggested that the attested Latin *Rucenus*, a rendering of the Old Ukrainian *rusyn*, was instrumental in the selection of the name *Ruthenus*. The first use of the word *Ruteni* in reference to the inhabitants of Rus' was in the *Annales Augustiani* of 1089. For centuries thereafter *Rutheni* was used in Latin as the designation of all East Slavs, particularly Ukrainians and Belarusians. In the 16th century the word more clearly began to be associated with the Ukrainians and Belarusians of the Polish-Lithuanian Commonwealth as distinct from the Russians, who were designated *Moscovitae*.

After the partitions of Poland (1772–95) the term 'Ruthenian' underwent further restriction. It came to be associated primarily with those Ukrainians who lived under the Habsburg monarchy, in Galicia, Bukovyna, and Transcarpathia. In 1843, at the request of the Greek Catholic metropolitan of Halych, M. Levytsky, the Austrian authorities established the term *Ruthenen* as the official name of the Ukrainians within the empire. In the 1870s the central-Ukrainian political theorist M. *Drahomanov, as well as his Galician disciples I. *Franko and M. *Pavlyk, used the term *rutentsi* (a Ukrainianized version of *Ruthenen*) to denote narrow-minded, provincial, and Habsburg-true members of the Galician Ukrainian intelli-gentsia. Although the term *Ruthenen* remained in official use until the collapse of the Habsburg monarchy in 1918, Galician Ukrainians themselves began to abandon that name (from around 1900) and its Ukrainian equivalent, *rusyny*, in favor of the self-designation *ukraintsi* (Ukrainians).

In the last decades of the existence of the Habsburg monarchy there was a massive wave of Ukrainian emigration from there to the Americas. In their new countries the emigrant Ukrainians were often referred to and referred to themselves as 'Ruthenians.' In the interwar era the name 'Ruthenian' became even more restricted: it was generally used to refer to the inhabitants of Transcarpathia and to Transcarpathian emigrants in the United States. Since the Second World War the term 'Ruthenian' has been used as a self-designation almost exclusively by descendants of Transcarpathian emigrants in the United States, but since the 1970s even they have begun to abandon it in favor of the designation 'Rusyn' or 'Carpatho-Rusyn.' In official Catholic ecclesiastical language the term *Rutheni* was used in a wide sense, to denote all East Slavs of the Eastern rite (Ukrainians of Galicia and Transcarpathia as well as Belarusians) until the early 1960s. Since then the term *Rutheni* has been used to refer only to Byzantine rite Catholics of Transcarpathian origin in the United States.

J.-P. Himka

Ruthenian-Ukrainian Radical party. See Ukrainian Radical party.

Ruthenische Revue. A German-language semimonthly organ of the Lviv People's Committee and the Ukrainian caucus in the Austrian parliament, published in Vienna in 1903–5 by A. Kos and B. Yavorsky. Edited by R. Sembratovych, it informed the Western public and policymakers about the Ukrainian question in the Russian and Austro-Hungarian empires. It criticized Polish domination in Galicia and especially the prohibition of Ukrainian-language publishing in the Russian Empire. Poor translations of works by Ukrainian writers appeared in the journal. Its news articles were republished in German, French, Italian, Spanish, Swedish, Norwegian, and Japanese newspapers. After Sembratovych died, the newspaper stopped appearing. It was succeeded in 1906 by *Ukrainische Rundschau.*

Ruthenium. Ruthenium belongs to the platinum group of elements, and occurs native with other members of the group. It is hard, brittle, has a high melting point, and it forms alloys with most other metals, some of which are used for demanding applications. It possesses a plethora of co-ordination chemistry and is used in catalysis. It was identified in 1827 by G. Osann, a professor at Dorpat (Tartu) University. In 1844 C. Claus (Klaus) showed Osann's material to be quite impure, but confirmed the presence of a new element, which he named ruthenium after the Latin name for Rus' (Ruthenia [Ukraine]).

Rutka, Teofil (Bogumił), b 1623 in Kiev, d 1700 in Lviv. Polish Jesuit writer of Ukrainian descent. He entered the Jesuit order in 1647 and taught in Jesuit colleges in Poznań, Kalisz, and Lublin. He was chaplain at the court of the Lviv palatine and for the Polish crown hetman S. Jabłonowski and served as a theological instructor and adviser to Bishop Y. Shumliansky of Lviv. He devoted his attention to promoting the Church Union of *Berestia: he wrote over 30 theological and polemical works, including refutations of the writings of I. Galiatovsky (1689) and P. Mohyla (1690), and translated many Roman Catholic works from Latin into Polish.

Ivan Rutkovych: *Flight to Egypt* (fragment)

Rutkovych, Ivan [Rutkovyč], b ? in Bilyi Kamin, near Zolochiv, Galicia, d ? Icon painter of the 17th century. Most of his creative life was spent in Zhovkva (1667 to ca 1708). Some of his work has been preserved, in whole or in part, such as the iconostases of the wooden churches in Volytsia Derevlianska (1680–2) and Volia Vysotska (1688–9); the large iconostasis of the Church of Christ's Nativity in Zhovkva (1697–9, now in the National Museum in Lviv), which is considered to be the finest Ukrainian iconostasis; and separate icons, such as *Supplication* (1683) from Potylych (now in the National Museum) and *Mary's Nativity* (1683) from Vyzhliv. Rutkovych's treatment of religious subjects was realistic and almost secular in spirit. The emotive richness of his colors and the rhythm of his lines testify to the influence of contemporary European art on his style. V. Svientsitska's book about Rutkovych was published in Kiev in 1966.

Rutsky, Illia [Ruc'kyj, Illja], b 1744 in Vysoke, Pryluka regiment, d 13 October 1786 in Moscow. Physician. After being educated at the Kievan Mohyla Academy (1753–61) and the Medico-Surgical School of the St Petersburg Military Hospital (1761–6), he worked as a military doctor in the Yelysavethrad region, where he fought the plague (1770–4). Later he lectured at the St Petersburg Medico-Surgical School (1776–8) and completed a doctoral dissertation on the plague at Strasbourg University (1781). In 1782 he was appointed a professor at the Moscow Medical School.

Rutsky, Yosyf [Ruts'kyj, Josyf] (secular name: Ivan Veliamyn), b 1574 in Ruta, near Navahrudak, Belarus, d 5 February 1637 in the Derman Monastery near Dubno. Uniate churchman. He was raised as a Calvinist but came

Metropolitan Yosyf Rutsky

under the influence of Jesuits and converted to Roman Catholicism (1592) while studying in Prague. After finishing his theological training at the St Athanasius College in Rome (1603), he converted to the Uniate rite at the request of Pope Clement VII and moved to Vilnius. In 1605–6 he traveled to Moscow with a papal legate. He entered a monastery in 1607 and worked with Y. *Kuntsevych to reform monasticism in Belarus and Ukraine. In 1611 he was made an archimandrite, and in 1613 he succeeded I. Potii as metropolitan of Kiev.

As metropolitan Rutsky sought to place the Uniate educational system on a par with its Latin rite counterpart. He obtained privileges for the church, including stipends for monks to study in Rome and in Catholic academies elsewhere, and implemented measures to raise the level of teaching in Uniate schools. In 1616–17 Rutsky established a unified structure for the Basilian order which made it independent of local bishops. He also placed the Basilians in charge of a reformed school system and laid plans (discussed in 1626 at the Synod of Kobryn) for establishing a theological seminary in Minsk. Finally, Rutsky demanded (through petitions to King Sigismund III, speeches in the Diet, and discussions with Vatican officials) and obtained (1624) church legislation that prohibited Catholics from freely changing their rite.

In 1624 Rutsky started discussions with Orthodox church leaders, including Y. Boretsky, M. Smotrytsky, and P. Mohyla, about the possibility of uniting the churches under a single Patriarch of Kiev. Nothing had been realized from these negotiations by the time he died in 1637. He was buried in Vilnius, but in 1655 Muscovite soldiers removed his remains to an unknown location. A collection of Rutsky's letters, edited by A. Welykyj (Velyky), appeared in Rome in 1956.

BIBLIOGRAPHY
Nazarko, I. *Kyïvs'ki i halyts'ki mytropolyty* (Toronto 1962)
Semchuk, S. *Mytropolyt Ruts'kyi* (Toronto 1967)
Szegda, M. *Działalność prawno-organizacyjna Metropolity Józefa IV Welamina Rutskiego (1617–1637)* (Warsaw 1967)

Ruysbroeck, Willem van, b 1215 in Rubrouck, France, d ca 1295. Flemish Franciscan friar and diplomat. He was sent by King Louis XI of France in 1253–5 on an informal mission to the camp of Batu Khan on the Mongolian plain. His account of the journey, republished in 1900 as *The Journey of William of Rubruck to the Eastern Parts of the World, 1253–55*, provides a valuable description of the Mongol Empire and includes passages describing life in Kievan Rus' in this period.

Ruzhychanka burial site. A Cherniakhiv culture burial ground on the Vovk River near Ruzhychanka, Khmelnytskyi raion. Excavations in 1964–6 revealed 73 burials in which the interred were either cremated or inhumed. Among the grave goods recovered were pottery vessels, glass and carnelian jewelry, and silver and brass clasps.

Ruzhyn [Ružyn]. IV-10. A town smt (1986 pop 5,500) on the Rostavytsia River and a raion center in Zhytomyr oblast. It is first mentioned, as Shcherbiv, in historical documents at the end of the 15th century. From 1569 it was under Polish rule. In 1591 the village was acquired by the Ruzhynsky family, who changed its name to Ruzhyn and built a castle there. Its inhabitants took part in the popular revolts against the Polish nobility in 1591–3 and 1634–8. After B. Khmelnytsky's successful uprising Ruzhyn became a company center of Pavoloch regiment. In 1663 the town was destroyed by the Poles. Its inhabitants joined the anti-Polish haidamaka uprisings in 1734, 1750, and 1768. After the partition of Poland in 1793 Ruzhyn was transferred to Russia and belonged to Kiev vicegerency and then Kiev gubernia (1797–1925). Some manufacturing enterprises were set up: a woolen-cloth factory in 1811, a flour mill, a brick factory, and a distillery in 1829. Today the town is known for its agricultural output and its fish farm.

Ruzhynsky [Ružyns'kyj] (Rozhynsky). A Lithuanian princely family, with extensive estates in Volhynia and the Kiev region, that produced several Cossack leaders in the 16th century. Bohdan (Bohdanko) Ruzhynsky, known as the hetman of the Lower [Dnieper River] Cossacks and remembered in folk songs, died in 1576 during a siege by 500 Cossacks of the Tatar fortress Aslan Kermen (now Kakhivka). Ostafii Ruzhynsky (d 1587) was representative of the Polish voivode in Kiev (1575–81) and deputy starosta of Cherkasy. They were both described in *Istoriia Rusov*. Ostafii's son Mykhailo Ruzhynsky was hetman of the registered Cossacks (1585). His other son, Kyryk Ruzhynsky, was a Zaporozhian otaman and deputy starosta of Cherkasy; he commanded a Polish military detachment that suppressed the uprising led by S. Nalyvaiko, but he was defeated at Bila Tserkva in 1596.

Rvachov, Volodymyr [Rvačov], b 21 October 1926 in Chyhyryn, Kiev gubernia. Mathematician and mechanician; full member of the AN URSR (now ANU) since 1978. After graduating from Lviv University (1952) he worked and taught at the Berdianske Pedagogical Institute (1955–63) and the Kharkiv Institute of Radioelectronics (1963–7). Since 1967 he has been with the ANU Institute for Problems of Machine Building. Rvachov studied Bogoliubov R-functions and used his results to solve multidimensional problems in mathematical physics, elasticity, and the theory of plates and shells. Using R-functions, he developed a method which sped up the compiling of cumputer programs.

Rybachek, Mykhailo [Rybaček, Myxajlo], b 20 February 1874 in Orikhivets, Skalat county, Galicia, d 22 May 1926 in Lviv. Pedagogue and mathematician. He was a teacher of physics and mathematics at the gymnasium in

Kolomyia from 1898 to 1907 and then at the Academic Gymnasium of Lviv. He wrote research works and review articles in the field of mathematics and edited school textbooks. From 1916 to 1919 he was director of the branch (*filiia*) of the gymnasium. He was forced to resign from this post when he refused to sign an oath of loyalty to the Polish Republic.

Rybachuk, Ada [Rybačuk], b 27 July 1931 in Kiev. Painter, mosaicist, and graphic artist. A graduate of the Kiev State Art Institute (1951), she has created decorative mosaics, murals, and canvases; illustrated books; and made prints. Her works include several linocut series (eg, 'Seven Women from Seven Tents,' 1955–63); numerous paintings, such as *The Test* (1957) and *Hunter's Song* (1958); and woodcut and linocut illustrations for L. Pervomaisky's *Dykyi med* (Wild Honey, 1965–70) and *Opovidannia riznykh rokiv* (Stories from Different Years, 1965–70) and for her own books *Ostrov Kolguev* (Kolguev Island, 1967) and *Bab'e leto* (Indian Summer, 1969). With V. Melnychenko she created large mosaics in the Bus Station (1960–1) and Pioneer Palace (1963–9) in Kiev.

Rybak, Ihor, b 21 March 1934 in Kharkiv. Weight lifter. He won the 1956 Olympic gold medal in the lightweight class and the 1956 European championship in the middleweight class. Since the late 1950s he has been a physician.

Natan Rybak   Ivan Rybchyn

Rybak, Natan, b 3 January 1913 in Ivanivka, Yelysavethrad county, Kherson gubernia, d 11 September 1978 in Kiev. Socialist-realist writer of Jewish origin. He began publishing in 1930 and produced 3 poetry collections in the 1930s and about 20 story collections, most of them in the 1930s and 1940s. He is best known for his novels. *Harmaty zherlamy na skhid* (Cannons with Muzzles Facing East, 1934) and *Kyïv* (Kiev, 1936) idealize Stalinist industrialization and the struggle with 'counterrevolution.' *Dnipro* (The Dnieper, 2 vols, 1937–8) depicts the revolutionary period in Southern Ukraine. *Pomylka Onore de Bal'zaka* (The Mistake of Honoré de Balzac, 1940) portrays Balzac's stay in Ukraine; it was made into a film by T. Levchuk in 1969. *Zbroia z namy* (The Weapons Are with Us, 1943) is set in Ukraine during the Second World War. *Pereiaslavs'ka rada* (The Pereiaslav Council, vol 1, 1948, for which Rybak was awarded a Stalin Prize in 1950; vol 2,

1953) is a major Soviet historical epic about the Cossack-Polish War and Hetman B. Khmelnytsky. The novels *Chas spodivan' i zvershen'* (A Time of Expectations and Achievements, 1960) and *Soldaty bez mundyriv* (Soldiers without Uniforms, 1966) focus on the Cold War and Soviet nuclear physics. Editions of Rybak's works in five volumes were published in 1963–4 and 1981. Books about him by Yu. Kobyletsky (1963) and M. Lohvynenko (1972) and a collection of articles and reminiscences about him (1983) have appeared.

R. Senkus

Rybakov, Boris, b 3 June 1908 in Moscow. Russian archeologist and historian. After graduating in history from Moscow University, he worked for the Institute of Archeology of the Academy of Sciences of the USSR doing extensive fieldwork in Ukraine on Kievan Rus' sites. He became a professor of history at Moscow University (1943), director of the Institute of Archeology (1956), and director of the USSR Academy of Sciences' Institute of the History of the USSR (1968–70). A prolific writer, he has produced many scholarly and popular works about early Slavic history and Kievan Rus', including *Remeslo drevnei Rusi* (The Crafts of Old Rus', 1948), *Drevniaia Rus': Skazaniia, byliny, letopisi* (Old Rus': Tales, Epic Songs, Chronicles, 1963), *Pervye veka russkoi istorii* (1964; English translation, *The Early Centuries of Russian History*, 1965), *Iazychestvo drevnikh slavian* (The Paganism of the Early Slavs, 1981), and *Kievskaia Rus' i russkie kniazhestva XII–XIII vv.* (Kievan Rus' and the Rus' Principalities of the 12th–13th centuries, 1982). He also wrote the entries about Kievan Rus' in the multivolume *Istoriia SSSR* (History of the USSR, 1966) and edited collections on the relations between Russia, Poland, and the northern Black Sea region in the 15th to 18th centuries (1979) and on the 1073 *Izbornik* of Sviatoslav (1977). His writings have helped to establish the official Soviet interpretation that the Kievan state was the historical antecedent of 'three fraternal nations': Russia, Ukraine, and Belarus.

Rybalchenko, Vsevolod [Rybal'čenko], b 23 August 1904 in Kharkiv, d 2 February 1988 in Kiev. Composer. After graduating from the Kharkiv Institute of Music and Drama (1931), where he studied composition with S. Bohatyrov, he taught music theory at the Kharkiv Technical School of Musical Theater (1931–4). With Yu. Meitus and M. Tits he authored the operas *Perekop* (1938) and *Haidamaky* (1941). His other works include the symphonic poem *Slovo o polku Ihorevi* (Tale of Ihor's Campaign, 1968); two operas; pieces for wind instruments; and art songs to words by H. Skovoroda, T. Shevchenko, M. Rylsky, and V. Sosiura. From 1944 he worked in Kiev.

Rybalko, Pavlo, b 4 November 1894 in Malyi Istorop, Lebedyn county, Kharkiv gubernia, d 28 August 1948 in Moscow. Soviet Army marshal. He fought in the Russian Civil War. After graduating from the Frunze Military Academy (1934) he was a military attaché in Poland and China (1937–40). During the German-Soviet War he commanded the Fifth and Third tank armies and the Third Guard Army, and rose from brigadier general to marshal of tank forces. After the war he was given command of tank and mechanized forces of the Soviet Army.

Rybalske oil and gas field. One of the largest oil and gas deposits in the *Dnieper-Donets Trough. Located near Rybalske, Okhtyrka raion, Sumy oblast, it was discovered in 1962 and has been exploited since 1963. The oil and gas are found in fissures and veins at a depth of 1,500–3,450 m. Natural gas, which is up to 93 percent methane, predominates in the deposit. The oil is light and paraffinic with low sulfur content. The oil from the Rybalske field is refined at the Kremenchuk Petroleum Refinery, and the gas is piped mostly to Kiev.

Rybchyn, Ivan [Rybčyn], b 1892 in Bratyshiv, Tovmach county, Galicia, d 17 January 1970 in Sydney, Australia. Pedagogue and sociologist; full member of the Shevchenko Scientific Society from 1962. He was a longtime gymnasium teacher in Stanyslaviv (now Ivano-Frankivske) and head of the Teachers' Hromada branch there. After the Second World War he was docent of sociology and East Slavic history at the University of Graz, Austria. He emigrated to Australia in 1950. He was head of the Shevchenko Scientific Society in Australia from 1961. He wrote *Heopsykhichni reaktsiï i vdacha ukraïntsia* (Geopsychic Reactions and the Character of the Ukrainian, 1966) and many articles on social psychology and social philosophy.

Rybka. A Ukrainian folk dance performed by many couples, originally to singing and then to instrumental music in 2/4 time. The song was first written down by V. *Verkhovynets in the Kiev region in 1913.

Rybnica. VI-10. A city (1971 pop 32,000) on the left bank of the Dniester River in Moldova in a region of mixed Ukrainian-Rumanian settlement. Rybnica is a river port with a food-processing industry (sugar refinery, distillery, and creamery) and a construction materials industry (cement and steel products). Before 1917 it belonged to Balta county in Podilia gubernia. In 1926 its population of 9,400 was 33.8 percent Ukrainian, 38.0 percent Jewish, and 16.0 percent Rumanian (Moldavian). The surrounding region was 48.3 percent Ukrainian, 35.7 percent Rumanian, and 3.8 percent Russian.

Rybynsky, Volodymyr [Rybyns'kyj], b 23 February 1867 in Kozlov county, Tambov gubernia, Russia, d ? Ukrainian historian. He was a professor at the Kiev Theological Academy, an editor of *Vira ta derzhava*, a VUAN research associate (from 1920), and a member of the VUAN Hebraic Historical Archeographical Commission. He wrote many articles on ancient Hebrew history and the history of Jews in Ukraine, which appeared mostly in the academy's collection *Trudy Kievskoi dukhovnoi akademii*.

Rydz-Śmigły, Edward, b 11 March 1886 in Berezhany, Galicia, d 2 December 1941 in Warsaw. Polish military and political figure. The commander in chief of the Polish Army Organization from 1917, he saw action in Ukraine (among other places). In January 1918 he was minister of war for the Provisional Government of the Polish Republic, and he took part in the Polish-Soviet War of 1919–20 as a front commander (in Volhynia, Lithuania, and Latvia). On 7 May 1920, as commander of a combined Polish and Ukrainian army, he briefly held Kiev. From 1921 to 1935 he was an army inspector. He was a strong supporter of the Sanacja regime and the initiator of a secret military society formed to ensure the regime's continued existence even in the case of its leader's (J. Piłsudski's) death. He was also a strong supporter of the Polonization of national minorities (including forced conversion), separatism among regional Ukrainian groups, and the yeoman movement. After Piłsudski's death in 1935, he was appointed chief inspector of the armed forces (upon instructions left by Piłsudski), which position made him one of the most powerful figures in Poland.

Rye (Ukrainian: *zhyto*). A family of annual (rarely perennial) grasses that includes several wild and one cultured species (*Secale cereale*). It probably originated in southwestern Asia ca 6500 BC and has been known in Ukraine (in the Dnieper and Dniester basins and on the Kerch Peninsula) since the Hallstatt period (1000–500 BC). It is a very hardy grain and is grown chiefly in regions with a harsh climate and poor soil; it also thrives at higher altitudes.

Rye is used primarily as flour for bread, as livestock feed, and as pasture. It is a good source of albumin (protein) and vitamins, and contains many other nutrients and amino acids. On average, rye kernels are 11 percent proteins, 1.7 percent fats, 69.6 percent carbohydrates, 1.9 percent cellulose, and 1.8 percent ash. The stalks grow to 70–200 cm high and are topped by 4 to 6 ears of grain. Rye has a vegetation period of 120–150 days. Traditionally, rye straw was used for thatching roofs and stuffing mattresses. In Ukrainian folklore rye symbolized health and prosperity, to ensure which it was often buried in the corners of house foundations. Rye is also used widely in alcohol distilling, and some by-products are used in making cellulose and in starch hydrolysis.

In Ukraine 10 species of rye grow wild, and 1 (*S. cereale*) is cultivated. Except in a few small areas in the Subcarpathians, only winter rye is grown, mostly in Polisia and the Subcarpathians, some in the forest-steppe region, and a little in the steppe. Rye cultivation was fairly common in the 19th century, but its importance in Ukraine has declined in the 20th century: in 1913 some 4,517,000 ha were devoted to rye, compared to 623,000 ha in 1987 (approx 4 percent of the grain area; see *Grain production). Moreover, relatively little has been done to develop and improve rye output. Average yields have increased only marginally, from 10.1 centners per ha in 1913 to 17.8 centners per ha in 1976–80. By contrast, average yields of all the grains increased in that period from 9.4 to 26.1 centners per ha. The most common variety of rye grown in Ukraine is Kharkiv 194; others include Kharkiv 60 and 55, Polisia, Kushtro, Desnianka 2, Selected Dankivka (the most productive type), Verkhnia 32, and Belta. Most of those strains were developed in the 20th century, and displaced such traditional local strains as Turka and Hlyboka.

BIBLIOGRAPHY
Hordiienko, H. *Istoriia kul'turnykh roslyn* (Munich 1970)
Ozyme zhyto (Kiev 1977)

V. Kubijovyč

Ryegrasses. The common name for about 10 species constituting the genus *Lolium* (family Poaceae). They include annual and perennial forage and lawn grasses and darnel, a noxious weed. Ryegrasses are about 0.3–3 m high and have tough, dark green leaves. They grow wild in low-lying areas or meadows and in mountain and hilltop clearings. In Polisia, the forest-steppe, and the northern steppe regions ryegrass is sown often with other grasses, and yields 50–80 centners of hay per ha. The perennial *L. perenne* is very hardy and provides good pasturing for 7 to 10 years and longer. Ryegrasses are slowly being displaced by other fodder crops in Ukraine (see *Hayfields).

George Ryga   Maksym Rylsky

Ryga, George, b 27 July 1932 in Deep Creek, Alberta, d 18 November 1987 in Summerland, British Columbia. Dramatist. The son of Ukrainian immigrant parents, Ryga is one of Canada's most acclaimed playwrights. His best-known work is *The Ecstasy of Rita Joe* (1971), a play dealing with the plight of Canada's Indian peoples. His other plays include *Indian* (1967), *Captives of the Faceless Drummer* (1971), *Letter to My Son* (1984; on a Ukrainian theme and broadcast on Kiev State radio in 1985), and *Paracelsus* (1982). Among his novels are *Hungry Hills* (1963) and *Ballad of a Stonepicker* (1966) (both published in Ukrainian translation in Ukraine), *Night Desk* (1976), and *In the Shadow of the Vulture* (1985). Ryga wrote numerous television scripts and radio dramas, including '1927,' on Ukrainians in Canada, for the television series 'The Newcomers' (1979).

Ryhorenko, Mykola, b and d ? A kobzar of the first half of the 19th century, from Krasnyi Kut, Kharkiv gubernia. His dumas, including those about Fesko Handzha Andyber, Marusia Bohuslavka, Cossack life, and the Korsun victory, were written down by N. Nihovsky and published by P. Kulish in his *Zapiski o Iuzhnoi Rusi* (Notes on Southern Rus', 1856–7).

Ryk, Yakiv, b 6 December 1929 in Kharkiv. Sculptor. A graduate of the Kharkiv School of Applied Art (1949), he has sculpted compositions such as *Our Future* (1962–3), *Azovstal Workers* (1966–7), and *Azov Fishermen* (1969) and several public monuments in Kharkiv.

Rykhliivsky, Danylo [Ryxlijivs'kyj] (Danylo Bandurka, Maly), b ca 1738 in Kiev, d ? Banduryst. He began to play the bandura at the age of 10. As a young man he joined the Korsun kurin at the Zaporozhian Sich. In 1761 he was imprisoned for taking part in the Haidamaka uprisings. His subsequent fate is unknown.

Rykhlik, Yevhen [Ryxlik, Jevhen], b 28 November 1888 in Vilshanka, Zhytomyr county, Volhynia gubernia, d

1939. Slavist of Czech origin. A graduate of Kiev University, he taught at the Nizhen Institute of People's Education in the 1920s and was a member of the VUAN Ethnographic Commission. He published studies on the Slavophilism of the *Cyril and Methodius Brotherhood and on Ukrainian motifs in J. Słowacki's poetry (1929), articles on the lexicon of the village of Vilshanka in the Zhytomyr region, a study of Ukrainian ethnography outside Soviet Ukraine, a study of the 18th-century rebels Sava Chaly and Sawa-Caliński in Polish literature, a study of Polish translations of Ukrainian dumas, a survey of literature about Czechs in Ukraine, and reviews of Czech and Polish ethnographic journals in *Etnohrafichnyi visnyk*. He was repressed during the Stalinist terror (1930?) and most likely perished in a Soviet labor camp.

Rykhlo, Ivan [Ryxlo], b 1891, d ? Army doctor and civic leader. In 1915, while serving in the Legion of Ukrainian Sich Riflemen, he was captured by the Russians. He was one of the organizers of the Sich Riflemen in Kiev in 1917. During the next three years he served as sanitation chief of the Corps of Sich Riflemen and of the UNR Operational Army.

Rykhly Saint Nicholas's Monastery (Rykhlovskyi Pustynno-Mykolaivskyi manastyr). A men's monastery located in Rykhly, near Korop, in the Chernihiv region. It was established in 1666 on the site of a 1620 apparition of an icon of St Nicholas. Its first benefactors were Hetman D. Mnohohrishny and his brother, Vasyl. The initial wooden structures were replaced by stone ones in the 18th century. From then the monastery had four churches: the three-nave Church of St Nicholas (built in 1749–60); the Church of St John the Baptist, funded by Hetman I. Samoilovych; the Church of the Birth of Christ, built in 1749 and restored in 1847; and a small church located on the site of the reputed appearance of the icon. The monastery also had a hospice. At the turn of the 20th century the monastery was headed by a hegumen, and housed 52 monks and 100 novices. In the 1920s it was closed by the Soviet authorities, and all of its buildings were razed.

Rykhtytsky, Liubomyr. See Liubomyrsky, Stepan.

Rykov, Valerian, b 1874 in Tbilisi, Georgia, d 25 March 1942. Architect. After graduating from the St Petersburg Academy of Arts (1902) he lectured at the Kiev Polytechnic (1904–10). He was one of the founders of and a professor at the Kiev Architecture Institute (1918–23) and a lecturer at and, eventually (1934–9), the chairman of the architecture department at the Kiev State Art Institute. He designed many residential and public buildings in Kiev, including the People's Auditorium (1909), the building of the St Mary's Society of the Red Cross (1913, now the Clinical Institute), the Hippodrome (1916), and the Kiev Artistic Film Studio (1927–30). P. Makushenko's book about him was published in Kiev in 1967.

Ryleev, Kondratii, b 29 September 1795 in Batovo, near Gatchina, St Petersburg gubernia, d 25 July 1826 in St Petersburg. Russian writer and Decembrist leader. He edited the popular literary almanac *Poliarnaia zvezda*. He also became a leading figure in the Northern Society of the *Decembrist movement. For his role as a key organizer of the 1825 uprising he was arrested and later hanged in St Petersburg's Peter and Paul Fortress. While living in the Ostrohozke region Ryleev developed a considerable interest in Ukrainian history and ethnography (as documented in I. Zaslavsky's book *Rylieiev i rosiis'ko-ukraïns'ki literaturni vzaiemyny* [Ryleev and Russian-Ukrainian Literary Relations, 1958]). He incorporated Ukrainian themes into his writings, notably in the collection *Duma* (1825) and the poems 'Voinarovskii' and 'Mazepa.'

Ryllo, Maksymiliian, b 1715, d 1794. Uniate bishop and church figure. He was raised in the Vilnius region and became a Basilian priest (1742) and hegumen of the Kholm Monastery (1748–56). While bishop of Kholm (1759–84), he occasionally (1763–6 and 1773–4) had jurisdiction in areas of Right-Bank Ukraine. In 1780–4 he was the administrator and in 1784–93 bishop of Peremyshl. Ryllo founded theological seminaries in Kholm and Peremyshl, saw to the establishment of canonical chapters, and took measures to improve the quality of the clergy. He convinced Leopold II to issue a decree in 1790 establishing the equality of the Byzantine and Latin rites in the Habsburg Empire and took measures to renew Halych metropoly. Ryllo kept a diary from 1742 that provides valuable insights into church affairs.

Rylsk [Ryl'sk]. II-15. A town (1979 pop 19,000) on the Seim River and a raion center in Kursk oblast, Russia. A *Siverianian settlement probably stood at the site in the 9th century. Rylsk is first mentioned in the chronicles under the year 1152, when it was a part of Siversk principality. It was annexed by Lithuania in the 14th century and then by Russia in the 16th century. A strategic defensive point for the Russian Empire, Rylsk was attacked by the Tatars many times. From 1797 to 1926 it was a county town in Kursk gubernia. According to the Soviet census of 1926, Ukrainians represented 20.9 percent of the Rylsk county population. Most of them lived in the southern part of the county.

Rylsky, Maksym [Ryl's'kyj], b 19 March 1895 in Kiev, d 24 July 1964 in Kiev. Poet, translator, and community activist; full member of the AN URSR (now ANU) from 1943 and of the Academy of Sciences of the USSR from 1958; son of T. *Rylsky. From 1944 until the end of his life he was director of the Institute of Fine Arts, Folklore, and Ethnography of the ANU. He studied at Kiev University, initially in the medical faculty and later in the historical-philological faculty. Rylsky started to write early in life (he published his first poem in 1907), and by 1910 he had published his first youthful collection, *Na bilykh ostrovakh* (On the White Islands). The first mature collection to show his promise as an exceptional poet was *Pid osinnimy zoriamy* (Beneath the Autumn Stars, 1918). An abridged version, of half the original length, was published in 1926. The poetic talents of Rylsky reached full bloom with the publication of the collections *Synia dalechin'* (The Blue Distance, 1922), *Poemy* (Poems, 1924), *Kriz' buriu i snih* (Through Storm and Snow, 1925), *Trynadtsiata vesna* (The Thirteenth Spring, 1926), *Homin i vidhomin* (The Resonance and the Echo, 1929), and *De skhodiat'sia dorohy* (Where the Roads Meet, 1929).

Rylsky's lyric poetry grew out of the best achievements of Ukrainian poetry at his time, and out of his broad knowledge of world poetry, French writers in particular (especially the works of the Parnassians). He often used motifs and images from ancient mythology and adhered to classical forms, which practices linked him to the group of *Neoclassicists. In many other respects, however, his philosophical and contemplative lyric poetry, with its wealth of moods and motifs of nature and of the individual becoming one with nature, did not fit the narrow definition of Neoclassicism. Rylsky's apolitical poetry provoked fierce attacks from official critics. He was arrested for a brief period in 1931, and then declared himself reformed and proclaimed his acceptance of the official Soviet view of reality in his collection *Znak tereziv* (The Sign of Libra, 1932). He alone of the Neoclassicists managed to live through the Stalinist terror and become one of the main poets in the ranks of the official Soviet versifiers. He became a member of the Party in 1943. In contrast to other official poets, however, he often expressed himself ambiguously in his eulogies of the Communist party, especially in those of Stalin.

From the time he became an official poet, Rylsky published over 30 books of poetry. The major prewar works were *Kyïv* (Kiev, 1935), *Lito* (Summer, 1936), *Ukraïna* (Ukraine, 1938), and *Zbir vynohradu* (The Harvest of Grapes, 1940). During the war and the evacuation of Soviet Ukrainian leaders to Ufa he published, among others, the collections, *Za ridnu zemliu* (For the Native Land, 1941), *Slovo pro ridnu matir* (A Song about My Mother, 1942), *Zhaha* (The Thirst, 1943), and *Mandrivka v molodist'* (Journey into Youth, 1944). His numerous postwar collections include *Chasha druzhby* (The Cup of Friendship, 1946), *Virnist'* (Fidelity, 1947), *Pid zoriamy Kremlia* (Beneath the Stars of the Kremlin, 1953), *Na onovlenii zemli* (On the Reclaimed Land, 1956), *Holosiïvs'ka osin'* (Autumn in Holosiive, 1959), and *V zatinku zhaivoronka* (In the Shade of the Lark, 1961).

Throughout his literary career Rylsky also did many literary translations. An excellent example of his mastery of the art is his translation of A. Mickiewicz's *Pan Tadeusz*. His translations from French are of a similarly high standard, from the classics of the 17th century to the poetry of P. Verlaine, in particular the translations of V. Hugo's *Hernani*, E. Rostand's *Cyrano de Bergerac*, and Voltaire's *La Pucelle d'Orléans*. He also translated W. Shakespeare's *King Lear* and *Twelfth Night*, and A. Pushkin's *Evgenii Onegin*.

Like most of the Soviet poets of the interwar generation, Rylsky did not manage to revitalize his writing at the beginning of 'de-Stalinization,' and his work remained merely technically proficient versification. Rylsky achieved much, however, in his role of community activist and publicist and contributed greatly to the brief literary rebirth of the early 1960s. In his essays and articles of that period, which are collected in publications such as *Vechirni rozmovy* (Evening Conversations, 1962) and *Pro mystetstvo* (On Art, 1962), he carefully and tactfully, though unflaggingly, defended Ukrainian culture against the pressure of Russification. Rylsky was not so much an innovator in Ukrainian poetry as a practitioner of classic verse, the sonnet form in particular. He contributed more than any of his contemporaries to the development of the Ukrainian literary language. His selected works have been published as *Poeziï* (Poetry, 3 vols, 1946), *Poeziï* (Poetry, 3 vols, 1949), *Tvory* (Works, 3 vols, 1956), and *Tvory* (Works, 10 vols, 1960–2; 20 vols, 1983–).

BIBLIOGRAPHY
Novychenko, L. *Povist' pro poeta* (Kiev 1941)
Kryzhanivs'kyi, S. *Maksym Ryl's'kyi* (Kiev 1960)
Malyshko, A. *Slovo pro poeta* (Kiev 1960)
Nezabutnii Maksym Ryl's'kyi: Spohady (Kiev 1968)
Skokan, K. *M.T. Ryl's'kyi: Bibliohrafichnyi pokazhchyk: 1907–1965* (Kiev 1970)
Novychenko, L. *Poetychnyi svit Maksyma Ryl's'koho (1910–1941)* (Kiev 1980)

I. Koshelivets

Tadei Rylsky   Antin Rzhepetsky

Rylsky, Tadei [Ryl's'kyj, Tadej], b 2 January 1841 in Stavyshche, Tarashcha county, Kiev gubernia, d 7 October 1902 in Romanivka, Skvyra county, Kiev gubernia. Civic and cultural leader and ethnographer; member of the Shevchenko Scientific Society (NTSh); father of M. *Rylsky. During his student years at Kiev University (he graduated in 1862) he made the acquaintance of V. *Antonovych and was an active member of the *Hromada of Kiev. Rylsky became one of the cofounders of the *khlopoman* movement. He founded a school on his estate in Romanivka and taught there for nearly 20 years. He contributed articles to the journals *Osnova* (using the pseud Maksym Chorny), *Kievskaia starina* (*KS*), and *Zapysky NTSh* and to the Polish newspaper *Głos* on economic and social issues and on the ethnography and folklore of the Ukrainian people. Among his most important works are 'Kizucheniiu ukrainskogo narodnogo mirovozreniia' (Toward the Study of the Ukrainian Folk Weltanschauung, *KS*, 1888, no. 11; 1890, nos 9–11; 1903, nos 4–5), *O khersonskikh zarabotkakh* (About Kherson Wages, 1904), *Sil's'ki pryhody* (Village Adventures, 1905), and 'Studiï nad osnovamy rozkladu bahatstva' (Studies of the Bases of the Distribution of Wealth, *ZNTSh*, vols 1–2 [1892–3]), written in the tradition of the Austrian school of political economy.

Rymarenko, Serhii, b 11 December 1839, d 1869 in Krasnyi Yar, Astrakhan gubernia. Populist revolutionary. A medical student at Kharkiv University, he joined the Kharkiv-Kiev Secret Society in 1857 and was expelled from university for taking part in the student protests of 1858. He audited courses at the Medical-Surgical Academy in St Petersburg and organized Sunday schools. He was one of the founders of *Zemlia i Volia. Through his sister, who had married M. *Ballin, he maintained contact with clandestine circles in Kharkiv and supplied them with revolutionary literature. In 1862 he was arrested and, after a lengthy investigation, exiled to Astrakhan, where he died of consumption.

Rymaruk, Ihor, b 4 July 1958 in Miakoty, Iziaslav raion, Khmelnytskyi oblast. Poet. Rymaruk completed journalism studies at Kiev University in 1979 and has worked in the editorial offices of *Visti z Ukraïny* and the Molod publishing house and as editor of the poetry section of the Dnipro publishing house. Since 1990 he has been coeditor of the journal *Svito-vyd. A lyrical and melodious poet, he is the author of two collections of verse, *Vysoka voda* (High Water, 1984) and *Uprodovzh snihopadu* (During the Snowfall, 1988).

Rymlianyn, Pavlo. See Romanus, Paolo.

Rymsha, Andrii [Rymša, Andrij], b ca 1550 in Pianchina, near Navahrudak, Belarus, d after 1595. Ukrainian and Belarusian writer. According to some sources, he studied at the Ostrih Academy. He is the author of *Khronolohiia* (Chronology), a versified explanation of the names of the months in Church Slavonic, Hebrew, and Ukrainian, published in 1581 in Ostrih. He also composed epigrams and odes on the heraldic crests of O. Volovych (1585) and L. Sapieha (1588). Rymsha wrote prose (he wrote of the battle deeds of K. Radziwiłł in Polish, 1585) and translated from Latin. His works have been published in Kiev, in the anthology *Ukraïns'ka poeziia: Kinets' XVI – pochatok XVII st.* (Ukrainian Poetry: The End of the 16th and the Beginning of the 17th Century, 1978).

Ryndyk, Stepan, b 1887 in Dunaivtsi, Nova Ushytsia county, Podilia gubernia, d 1972 in Chicago. Satirist and mechanical engineer. He graduated from the Kiev Polytechnical Institute in 1914. In the interwar period he fled Bolshevik rule and went to Bohemia, where he taught at the Ukrainian Higher Pedagogical Institute and the Ukrainian Gymnasium. He was evacuated to Germany in 1945, and emigrated to the United States in 1951. He wrote three poetry collections, all titled *Logos* (Prague 1942; Chicago 1961, 1971), the story collections *Smilians'ka khronika* (The Smila Chronicle, 1944) and *Pryhody i liudy* (Adventures and People, 1960), and Ukrainian textbooks on the strength of materials (1924) and the elements of machines (1943).

Ryndzivky (also *rohulky*). Ukrainian Easter songs sung by boys or young men under the windows of unmarried or recently married girls during *volochinnia*, on the second or third day of Easter. They were similar to Christmas carols except for the Easter theme. The *ryndzivky* survived into the 19th century only in the Yavoriv region and the Ukrainian-Belarusian borderlands.

Ryzhenko, Yakiv [Ryženko, Jakiv], b 13 November 1892 near Pustoviitove, Kobeliaky county, Poltava gubernia, d 29 May 1974 in Astrakhan, Russia. Art scholar. A graduate of the Moscow Polytechnical Institute, in the 1920s he was deputy director of the Poltava Regional Museum. He completed postgraduate studies (1926) and worked as a researcher (from 1929) in the Department of the History of Ukrainian Culture at the Kharkiv Institute of People's Education. From 1932 he worked in Kursk and then Astrakhan. Ryzhenko wrote books on kilim weaving and the kilims of the Poltava region (1928), Ukrainian needlework (1929), and the pottery of the Poltava region (1930).

Ryzhevsky, Vasyl [Ryževs'kyj, Vasyl'], b 1886 in Strusiv, Terebovlia county, Galicia, d 4 March 1965 in Miami, Florida. Civil engineer, surveyor, and entrepreneur. During the struggle for Ukrainian independence he was a captain and technical specialist in the General Staff of the Ukrainian Galician Army. He was one of the pioneers of the budding Ukrainian industry in Galicia between the two world wars, and owned a construction company and co-owned a road construction company and cardboard factory in Lviv. He was the founding president of the Ukrainian Technical Society in Lviv and an honorary member of the Ukrainian Engineers' Society of America. He lived in the United States from 1950.

Ryznytsia (Vestry). An association for making and selling church goods, established in Sambir in 1893. It was founded by Revs T. *Ripetsky (who also served as the first director) and F. Rabii. The central office in Sambir contained a workshop, warehouse, and store. Ryznytsia also had branches in Lviv, Peremyshl, and Stanyslaviv. In 1898 the society was a founding member of the Provincial Credit Union. Ryznytsia was dissolved by the Soviet authorities in 1939.

Rzeszów voivodeship. An administrative territory in southeastern Poland, centered in Rzeszów. The voivodeship encompasses 18,658 sq km and has a population (1990) of approx 2 million. Included within its boundaries are traditionally Ukrainian regions settled by Lemkos and Boikos as well as Liubachiv county. After the Second World War the Ukrainian population was forcibly resettled from that territory in *Operation Wisła.

Rzewuski. A Polish magnate family that held large estates in Western Ukraine in the 18th and 19th centuries. It included several important figures in Polish history. Stanisław Mateusz (?–1728) was appointed field hetman (1706), voivode of Podlachia (1710), and grand hetman (1726). His son, Wacław (1706–79), was voivode of Podilia (1736–50 and 1756–62), field hetman (from 1752), grand hetman (1773–4), and starosta of Kholm, Dolyna, and Drohobych. Wacław's son, Seweryn (1743–1811), was field hetman (1774–93) and starosta of Dolyna. He defended the privileges of the magnates and the oligarchical structure of the Polish Commonwealth and played a leading role in the *Torhovytsia Confederacy. Seweryn's son, Wacław (1785–1831, also known as Emir Tadż ul-Fehr and Kozak Revukha), was an adventurer, Orientalist, and writer. In 1817–20 he traveled in Turkey and the Arab countries. Upon his return he established on his estate a Cossack order. He wrote poetry and memoirs and set T. Padura's verses to music. In 1831 he joined the Polish insurrection at the head of his own detachment and died in a skirmish.

Rzhepetska, Olena [Ržepec'ka] (née Pokrovska), b 1885 in Zhytomyr, Volhynia gubernia, d 1948 in Lviv. Writer. She published stories under the pseudonym Nichy in *Literaturno-naukovyi vistnyk* and in the Lviv calendar *Dnipro* (1934). Her prose collection *Na berehakh Horynia* (On the Banks of the Horyn) was published in 1936.

Rzhepetsky, Antin [Ržepec'kyj], b and d ? Civic and political leader. He was a bank director and a member of the Kiev Municipal Council before the Revolution of 1917. During the First World War he managed the operations of a committee for aiding refugees. As finance minister in the Hetman government (May–December 1918) he helped to develop the Ukrainian monetary system and to strengthen the *karbovanets*. In negotiations with Germany he defended Ukrainian economic interests and argued for Ukraine's right to the Crimea, but at the same time he opposed the Ukrainianization of the administrative system and favored Ukraine's federation with Russia. When the Hetman government was overthrown, he was arrested by the Directory of the UNR but was eventually released.

Rzhepetsky, Borys [Ržepec'kyj], b 22 January 1895 in Lavriv, Lutske county, Volhynia gubernia, d 3 August 1976 in New York. Economist and civic and political activist. His studies at St Petersburg University were interrupted by his military service during the First World War. After returning to Ukraine in 1917, he became a deputy gubernia commissioner for Volhynia and set up and edited the paper *Selians'ka dumka* in Berdychiv. Having been sent to Warsaw in October 1919 as a member of a UNR diplomatic mission, he remained in Poland, completed his studies in law and economics at Lublin University, and worked as an economist for the Central Union of Polish Industry and coeditor of the journal *Przegląd Gospodarczy*. During the German occupation he worked for the Ukrainian Relief Committee in Lublin and Kholm. In 1949, after spending several years in DP camps, he emigrated to the United States. He was active in the Ukrainian community in New York and served as president of the Literary-Artistic Club (1964–72).

Rzhyshchiv [Ržyščiv]. IV-12. A town smt (1986 pop 10,300) on the Dnieper River in Kaharlyk raion, Kiev oblast. In medieval times *Ivan-Horod stood at the site. After its destruction by the Mongols in 1240, the site remained uninhabited for a long time. The new settlement of Rzhyshchiv is first mentioned in historical documents in 1506. The village belonged to Kiev metropoly. After the Union of Lublin in 1569, it came under Polish rule. Its inhabitants supported the anti-Polish revolt in 1637–8 and B. Khmelnytsky's uprising. In 1648–57 Rzhyshchiv was a company center in Kaniv regiment. A monastery was built there at that time. The town tried repeatedly (in 1664, 1750, and 1768) to throw off Polish rule. In 1783 it and the entire Kiev region were acquired by Russia. In the 19th century it became a busy trading town and attracted some manufacturing – a sugar refinery in 1854 and a foundry in 1874. Today Rzhyshchiv is a river port that ships farm products and some manufactured goods. Its largest factory is a radiator plant. It is the birthplace of L. *Kostenko.

Rzhyshchiv Transfiguration Monastery (Rzhyshchivskyi Preobrazhenskyi manastyr). A monastery situated near Rzhyshchiv, on the right bank of the Dnieper River, 85 km south of Kiev. First mentioned in 1649, it belonged to the Uniate church from the early 18th century until 1794. In 1852 it was converted into a women's monastery. At the turn of the 20th century the monastery housed 70 nuns and 213 novices. It was closed by the Soviet authorities in the 1920s.

S

Sabadosh, Mykhailo [Sabadoš, Myxajlo], b 18 August 1920 in Pryborzhavske or Zadnie, near Irshava, Transcarpathia. Ukrainian writer in the Prešov region of Slovakia. A Soviet partisan during the Second World War, after the war he became a colonel in the Czechoslovak army. He has written memoirs, sketches, stories, novels, and radio plays. His major works are the wartime memoirs *Parashutystom v Karpatakh* (As a Parachutist in the Carpathians, 1966), *Frontovymy dorohamy* (Along Roads at the Front, 1970), and *Partyzans'ki Karpaty* (The Partisan Carpathians, 1973), and a trilogy about a Transcarpathian peasant family in the 1930s and 1940s, consisting of the novels *Burkhlyvi roky* (Turbulent Years, 1976), *Vidvazhni* (The Valiant, 1980), and *Peremoha* (Victory, 1984).

Sabadysh, Petro [Sabadyš], b 3 January 1909 in Oleksandrivske, Katerynoslav gubernia. Painter. In 1932 he graduated from the Kiev State Art Institute, where he studied under O. Bohomazov, V. Palmov, and M. Boichuk. He produced works such as *Apple Picking* (1929), *Pond* (1939), *Dnieper Vista* (1953), *Sunflowers* (1960), and *In the Poltava Region* (1967).

Sabal, Viktor [Sabal'], b 12 March 1919 in Ulaziv, Liubachiv county, Galicia, d 16 September 1990 in Munich. Political activist and economist. After completing study at the Ukrainian gymnasium in Peremyshl he joined the OUN. During the German occupation of Ukraine he worked in Volhynia as a member of I. Mitrynga's Ukrainian Revolutionary Democratic party and under the pseudonym Viktor Chorny wrote articles for its organ *Vpered*. After the war he settled in the United States and then moved to West Germany, where he completed his professional education and worked as an economist. He took a special interest in the Soviet economy and contributed articles on the subject to *Ukraïns'ki visti* and *Suchasnist'*.

Sabaldyr, Hryhorii, b 11 October 1883 in Pokrovska Bahachka, Khorol county, Poltava gubernia, d ? Linguist and lexicographer. He wrote a handbook of Ukrainian orthographic rules (with M. Hrunsky, 1924), a dictionary of useful words in administrative circles (1925), a Ukrainian grammar and dictionary (with M. Hrunsky, 4 edns, 1926–7), a practical Russian-Ukrainian dictionary (30,000 words, 1926), and an orthographic dictionary (with O. Kolomatska, 25,000 words, 1930). In 1934 an abusive review of books by M. Hrunsky, P. Kovaliv, and S. Smerechynsky appeared under his name in *Movoznavstvo*. He disappeared during the terror of the 1930s.

Sabaneev, Ivan, b 19 October 1856 in Moscow, d 1937 in Odessa. Russian surgeon. A graduate of Kiev University (1882), he worked in Odessa (from 1887) and helped found the municipal hospital and a residence for young doctors. In 1904–8 he lectured at Odessa University. His publications deal chiefly with plastic surgery. He designed an osteoplastic intercondylar amputation of the thigh (1890), which was widely adopted and bears his name. He studied the problems of treating tuberculosis and suturing blood vessels.

Sabanieieva, Liudmyla [Sabanjejeva, Ljudmyla], b 23 February 1922 in Korosten, Volhynia gubernia. Sculptor. In 1954 she graduated from the Kiev State Art Institute, where she studied under M. Helman. She has done realistic compositions in plaster, wood, and stone, such as *Roosters* (1957), *Metallurgists* (1960), *Little Taras* (1964), and *Father* (1967).

Mykola Sabat

Sabat, Mykola, b 1867 in Obertyn, Horodenka county, Galicia, d 1930. Pedagogue and classical philologist; director of the Ukrainian gymnasium in Stanyslaviv (now Ivano-Frankivske) in 1905–19 and 1923–7 and director of the Academic Gymnasium of Lviv in 1928–30. During the period of the Western Ukrainian National Republic he headed the secondary-school section of the State Secretariat of Education. He was a professor of Greek philology and ancient archeology at the Ukrainian Free University in Prague in 1921–3 and at the Lviv (Underground) Ukrainian University in 1924–5. He wrote on the history of Greek literature and ancient art and in 1929–30 published, in two volumes, T. Shevchenko's *Kobzar* for school-age children.

Sabat-Svirska, Mariia [Svirs'ka, Marija], b 22 March 1895 in Pomoniatyna, Rohatyn county, Galicia, d 6 April 1983 in Rivne. Opera and chamber singer (soprano). She studied at the Lysenko Higher Institute of Music in Lviv and graduated from the Lviv Conservatory (1926, class of S. Kozlovska). She appeared in Poland as a soloist of the Torun Opera (1926–9) and at the Warsaw Olimpia Theater (1929–30) and then worked in Lviv. Her main roles were Marguerite in C. Gounod's *Faust*, Tamara in A. Rubinstein's *The Demon*, and Oksana in S. Hulak-Artemovsky's

Zaporozhian Cossack beyond the Danube. She taught in music schools in Lviv (1944–50) and Rivne (1950–7).

Sabatynivka culture. A late *Bronze Age culture that existed in Southern Ukraine and the Crimea in the late 14th to 12th century BC. It was researched in the 1930s and 1940s and named after a site in Kirovohrad oblast. The culture is notable for its indigenous bronze industry and trading activity. The people lived in surface and semi-pit dwellings, often with stone walls. Burial practices included both kurhans and ground burials. Their pottery was rounded, often with a characteristic band of applied ornamentation near the crown. Some scholars regard the Sabatynivka culture as a local variant of the late *Timber-Grave culture, while others maintain that it is distinctive. There is evidence of *Multicylindrical-Pottery culture influence on this grouping and of its ties with *Noua culture tribes. Notable examples of Sabatynivka settlements include Voloske, the site of a major bronze workshop, Ushkalka, Peresadivka, and Chykalivka.

Saber. A steel sword with a curved blade and a hand guard, known in Ukrainian as a *shablia*. It first appeared in Ukraine during the 10th century. It was a primary individual weapon of the Zaporozhian Cossacks and later was adopted by the Russian cavalry. In 1918–20, sabers were used widely by the Army of the UNR and by the cavalry units of the Ukrainian Galician Army. The cavalry of the Red Army also used sabers.

Lev Sabinin   Rev Sevastiian-Stepan Sabol

Sabinin, Lev (real surname: Teplynsky), b 15 November 1874 in Poltava, d 7 December 1955 in Moscow. Actor, choreographer, and stage director. He began his theatrical career in 1890 in L. Avedikov's Russian-Ukrainian troupe and then was an actor in H. Derkach's and O. Sukhodolsky's troupes (1891–1907); director of his own Ukrainian troupe, which staged approx 100 performances of the populist-realist repertoire (1907–20); stage director of various workers' and peasants' theaters (1920–9); actor and stage director in the Ukrainian Theater of the RSFSR in Moscow (1930–4); actor in the Chernihiv Music and Drama Theater (1934–41); and artistic director of the Ukrainian Ensemble at the Novgorod Philharmonic Society (1945–50). His memoirs are titled *Sorok-p'iat' rokiv na ukraïns'kii stseni* (Forty-five Years on the Ukrainian Stage, 1937).

Sable (*Martes zibellina*; Ukrainian: *sobol*). A graceful carnivore of the family Mustelidae, 30–50 cm long (plus a 15-cm tail), and highly valued for its fine, silky fur, colored from light cinnamon to dark chestnut brown. Sables live a solitary life; they inhabit primarily the cedar and spruce forests in the taiga and northern forest zone of the former USSR. In the past sables were common in the northern forests of Ukraine; at present they are found only on animal farms, where they are bred for their fur.

Sabluchok, Ivan [Sablučok] (Sablukov), b ca 1735, d ? Portrait painter and educator. As a boy he was taken to St Petersburg to sing in the imperial court kapelle. In 1753 he began to study painting, under I. Argunov, and in 1759 he entered the Academy of Arts, where he studied under D. Levytsky and quickly rose to the rank of professor (1761) and the status of full member (1765). After moving to Kharkiv in 1767, he taught art at Kharkiv College until 1773. Only one of his paintings survives, a portrait of S. Yurev (now in the Tretiakov Gallery in Moscow).

Sabol, Sevastiian-Stepan, b 7 December 1909 in Prešov, Slovakia. Religious figure and writer. In 1924 he joined the Basilian monastic order and studied at the Chernecha Hora, Krekhiv, Lavriv, and Dobromyl monasteries. Later he studied theology at the Pontifical Gregorian University (PH D, 1950). After being ordained a Ukrainian Catholic priest in Prešov in 1934 and receiving his licentiate in theology in Rome in 1935, he was prefect for students at the Theological Seminary and a gymnasium teacher in Uzhhorod. He also edited the eparchial monthlies *Misionar* (1937–8) and *Blahovistnyk* (1939). In 1939 he was arrested by the Hungarians in Khust and then deported to the Prešov region. There he founded four new Basilian monasteries and a novitiate, on the basis of which the new Basilian province of SS Cyril and Methodius was created in 1948. In December 1948 he avoided arrest by the Czechoslovak Communist regime by escaping to Austria. A Prague court sentenced him in absentia to life imprisonment as an 'American spy, the chief leader of the Ukrainian Insurgent Army, and an enemy of the people.' After emigrating to the United States in 1951, he served as a missionary in Uniontown, Pennsylvania, and New York City and as superior of the Transcarpathian branch of the Basilian order. Sabol began writing lyrical and religious poetry in Ukrainian in 1928 under the pseudonym Zoreslav. In Uzhhorod he published the collections *Zi sertsem u rukakh* (With My Heart in My Hands, 1933) and *Sontse i blakyt'* (The Sun and the Azure [Sky], 1936). As an émigré he published the historical-dogmatic monograph *Katolytstvo i Pravoslaviie* (Catholicism and Orthodoxy, 1955), the poetry collection *Z rannikh vesen* (From Early Springtimes, 1963), and the books *Vid Uhors'koï Rusy do Karpats'koï Ukraïny* (From Hungarian Ruthenia to Carpatho-Ukraine, 1956, under the pseud Yurii Borzhava) and *Hulhota Hrekokatolyts'koï Tserkvy v Chekho-Slovachchyni* (Golgotha of the Greek Catholic Church in Czechoslovakia, 1978).

R. Senkus

Sabov, Kyrylo, b 28 August 1838 in Stavne, Transcarpathia, d 10 February 1914 in Košice, Slovakia. Priest, educator, Russophile, and cultural figure. After graduating from the Barbareum in Vienna he taught language, history, and geography at Uzhhorod Gymnasium (1862–71). He wrote two textbooks, *Grammatika pis'mennogo russkogo* *iazyka* (A Grammar of the Literary Russian Language, 1865) and the companion *Kratkii sbornik izbrannykh sochinenii v proze i stikhakh dlia uprazhneniia v russkom iazyke* (A Short Collection of Selected Works in Prose and Verse for Exercises in the Russian Language, 1868). He was also assistant editor (1867) and then chief editor (1867–9) of the first literary paper for Transcarpathian Ukrainians, *Svit*. Because of his Slavophile sympathies he was transferred to Szeged (1871–9), but later he was allowed to teach in Mukachiv and Košice.

Rev Yevmenii Sabov

Sabov, Yevmenii, b 1859 in Verbiazh, Bereg komitat, Transcarpathia, d 1934. Greek Catholic priest, educator, and Russophile leader. After his ordination (1885) he taught Ruthenian language at Uzhhorod Gymnasium (1887–98) and was active in the Society of St Basil the Great and the Uniia educational society. He cofounded the paper *Nauka* (1897–1922). After the war he served as honorary president of the Dukhnovych Society (1923–34) and edited the journal *Karpatskii svet* (1928–38). He wrote a number of grammars and anthologies, which were approved by the Hungarian authorities and used widely in schools. He advocated a distinctive literary language for Transcarpathian Ukrainians, based on *yazychiie*, Russian, and Transcarpathian dialects.

Sacerdotal Council (Dukhovna rada). A clerical committee of the *Association of Ruthenian Church Communities in the USA and Canada. Formed in 1901 as part of the effort to provide administrative order to Ukrainian Catholic church parishes in North America, the council oversaw the appointment of priests to immigrant parishes. It was headed by Rev I. *Konstankevych and continued its work until the installation of an American-based Ukrainian Catholic bishop in 1907.

Sachenko, Hryhorii [Sačenko, Hryhorij], b 6 December 1905 in Khaienky, Borzna county, Chernihiv gubernia, d 16 January 1939. Poet. He was first published in 1926, and was a member of the literary organization Pluh. His works include the collections *Zustrichnyi entuziiazm* (The Enthusiasm of Meeting, 1931) and *Zenit* (The Zenith, 1936). He also wrote literary criticism. One of his works has been published posthumously as *Na chatakh* (On Guard, 1964). He was arrested by the NKVD in 1936. After being accused of belonging to a counterrevolutionary Ukrainian organization he was sentenced in 1937 and imprisoned in concentration camps in the Far East, where he perished.

Sacher-Masoch, Leopold von, b 27 January 1836 in Lviv, d 9 March 1895 in Lindheim, Hesse. Austrian writer and historian; son of L. von Sacher-Masoch. For a brief period of time he taught at Lviv University. Some of his works are set in Galicia, and reveal his familiarity with Western Ukrainian folkways and society. They include the historical novel *Eine galizische Geschichte 1846* (1858), the short novel *Don Juan von Kolomea* (1864), and the story collections *Galizische Geschichten* (1876), *Judengeschichten* (1878), and *Polnische Geschichten* (1886). Many of his later stories have little literary value but are well known for their depiction of sexual perversion, for which R. Krafft-Ebing coined the term masochism. Translations of Sacher-Masoch's stories were published in the 1880s and 1890s in *Chervona Rus'* and *Halychanyn*.

Sacher-Masoch, Leopold von (Leopold von Sacher until 1838), b ?, d 10 September 1874 in Bruck, Lower Austria. Police director in Lviv; father of novelist L. *Sacher-Masoch. Although his duties required that he suppress peasant unrest and maintain surveillance of the budding Ukrainian movement in Galicia, his writings and some of his actions demonstrated a profound sympathy with the peasantry and Ukrainians as a whole, both of whom he felt were victimized by the Polish nobility. In both his memoiristic publications, *Polnische Revolution* (Prague 1863) and 'Memoiren eines österreichischen Polizeidirektors,' which his son published posthumously in *Auf der Höhe*, vol 2 (Leipzig 1882), he sketched the history of the Ukrainian people from the Kievan Rus' period and argued that the Ukrainians were the most gifted of the Slavic nations. Sacher had many contacts among the Ukrainian clergy and intelligentsia; he was a friend of the Galician awakener D. *Zubrytsky, whose historical researches he encouraged, and in 1835 he offered M. *Shashkevych support for the Ukrainian movement provided that it did not make an alliance with Polish revolutionaries. In 1846 Sacher-Masoch submitted a memorandum to the governor's office urging that all decrees relating to the eastern Galician peasantry be promulgated in the Ukrainian vernacular.

Sachok, Yakiv [Sačok, Jakiv], b ca 1744 in Brusyliv, Podilia, d ? Haidamaka leader. As a young man he fled to the Zaporozhian Sich and became a member of haidamaka forces under M. Zalizniak and M. Shvachka during the *Koliivshchyna rebellion (1768). After making his way to Russian-ruled Kiev he organized a haidamaka band that crossed into Polish-ruled Right-Bank Ukraine and was active in the vicinity of Kaharlyk, Bohuslav, and Smila, south of Kiev. Sachok was arrested by the Russian authorities in Kiev in May 1770; his further fate is unknown.

Sachsenhausen (aka Sachsenhausen-Oranienburg). One of the major Nazi concentration camps. It was situated near Berlin and was opened in 1936. In 1939 many Jews and political prisoners were incarcerated there; they were joined in the succeeding years of the Second World War by prisoners of war. In the fall of 1941 some 1,800 Soviet POWs, among them many Ukrainians, were executed there. Over time thousands more were either shot or killed by phenol injections. The camp supplied slave labor for the German armaments industry; several armaments factories were located at the camp. Altogether 200,000 people (about half of whom subsequently perished) were sent to Sachsenhausen, including an undetermined number of Ukrainians. Among them were the OUN leaders A. Melnyk and Ya. Stetsko, who were interned there in 1944, and O. *Olzhych, who perished there in 1944.

Saciuk, Bohdan [Sacjuk], b 12 July 1941 in Dubno, Volhynia. Educator and linguist; member of the Shevchenko Scientific Society. After emigrating to the United States with his parents he studied Romance languages at the University of Illinois (PH D, 1969) and served as vice-president and president of the *Federation of Ukrainian Student Organizations of America (1963–7). Since 1969 he has taught linguistics, Spanish, Portuguese, and English at the University of Florida. He coedited *Generative Studies in Romance Languages* (1971) and has contributed articles to scholarly journals and collections.

Sacred Congregation for Eastern Rite Catholic Churches. See Congregation for Eastern Churches.

Saddle making. Leather saddles and harnesses have been made in Ukraine since ancient times. Ornamental saddle making was well developed under the Scythians, and archeological digs have uncovered saddle remains from the Princely era. Saddles were needed for farm animals as well as for the military and for general transport. In the 15th and 16th centuries there were guilds of saddle makers in both Kiev and Lviv. The artisans often made other leather goods too, including bookbindings, belts, bags, and hats. Saddle making remained a craft until the beginning of the 20th century: at that time there were still over 1,000 small workshops in Russian-ruled Ukraine, and the work was done by hand. In the 20th century, saddles and harnesses are manufactured by the *leather industry. Saddle output has declined as the use of horses in the economy has diminished.

Sadhora (also Sadgura or Sadagura). A suburb of Chernivtsi. The town was formally established in 1770. Populated mainly by Jews (73 per cent of 4,600 inhabitants in 1910), it was a renowned market center in Bukovyna and the site of a large synagogue. In 1941–4 a Rumanian concentration camp was located there. After the Second World War the town was incorporated into Chernivtsi. Archeological excavations reveal that the Sadhora site was settled as early as Trypilian culture times, and that a Rus' center once existed there.

Sadkovsky, Viktor [Sadkovs'kyj], b ? in Kiev, d 11 November 1803 in Chernihiv. Orthodox church hierarch. A graduate of the Kievan Mohyla Academy, he was a teacher and prefect of the Mahiliou Theological Seminary from 1758 and later the chaplain of the Orthodox church for diplomats in Cracow. In 1783 he became archimandrite of the Slutsk monastery, where he founded a theology school. A diplomatic arrangement between Poland and Russia concluded in the early 1780s allowed for the formation of an Orthodox eparchy in Poland to be headed by an exarch of the metropolitan of Kiev. In 1785 Sadkovsky was elevated to this post (bishop of Pereiaslav) while retaining his position as archimandrite. His organizational efforts in the new eparchy were quite successful, and had the result that a substantial number of Uniate parishes and priests

Archbishop Viktor Sadkovsky   Mariia Sadovska-Barilotti

joined the Orthodox church. But his efforts led to his arrest in 1789 by the Polish authorities on charges of inciting the population to arms and maintaining illicit contacts with Russia. He was released in 1792, following the partitioning of Poland, and was appointed archbishop of Minsk. From 1796 he was archbishop of Chernihiv.

Sadoveanu, Mihail, b 5 November 1880 in Paşcani, Rumania, d 18 October 1961 in Bucharest. Prominent Rumanian writer. In his *Şoimii* (Falcons, 1904), *Nicoară Potcoavă* (1952), and other historical novels he depicted Ukrainian-Rumanian relations in the Cossack period. He translated a few of T. Shevchenko's poems into Rumanian and wrote the introduction to the first Rumanian edition (1952) of Shevchenko's poetry.

Sadovska-Barilotti, Mariia [Sadovs'ka, Marija] (née Tobilevych), b April 1855 in Kamiano-Kostuvate, Yelysavethrad county, Kherson gubernia, d 27 March 1891 in Odessa. Stage actress and singer (soprano); sister of I. *Karpenko-Kary, M. *Sadovsky, and P. *Saksahansky. She began her theatrical career in 1876 in a touring Russian operetta troupe and then appeared in the troupes of M. Starytsky (1883–5), M. Kropyvnytsky (1885–8), Starytsky again (1888–90), and P. Saksahansky (1890–1), in which she mostly played heroic leading-lady roles.

Sadovska-Tymkivska, Tetiana [Sadovs'ka-Tymkivs'ka, Tetjana], b 11 January 1889 in Chernihiv, d ? Actress. She began her theatrical career in the Society of Ukrainian Actors in Kiev (1915–16) and then worked in the Ukrainian National Theater (1917–18), the State Drama Theater (1918–19), the People's Theater (1919–22), and, with A. Ratmyrov, various Ukrainian theaters in Vinnytsia, Kiev, and Kirovohrad (1924–49).

Sadovsky, Ivan [Sadovs'kyj], b 6 June 1855 in Stepanivka, Sumy county, Kharkiv gubernia, d 10 August 1911 in St Petersburg. Veterinary anatomist and microbiologist. A graduate of the Kharkiv Veterinary Institute (1879), he was appointed a professor at the institute in 1890 and was the first president of the Kharkiv Society of Veterinary Physicians. He directed the Warsaw Veterinary Institute (1904–7) and the veterinary-bacteriological laboratory of the Ministry of Internal Affairs (1907–11). His publications dealt with problems of veterinary anatomy, surgery, and epizootiology. With L. Tsenkovsky he did research on anthrax and implemented vaccination against the disease.

Sadovsky, Ivan [Sadovs'kyj], b 10 July 1876 in Zhyto-myr, Volhynia gubernia, d 1 April 1948 in Vinnytsia. Character and comic stage actor. He began his theatrical career as a choir member in the Odessa Italian Opera and then worked in the troupes of P. Saksahansky and M. Sadovsky (1897–1900) and of O. Suslov, M. Yaroshenko, F. Kostenko, and V. Yavorsky (1900–18), and in various theaters in Kiev, Odessa, Kharkiv, and Vinnytsia (1919–48).

Gen Mykhailo Sadovsky   Mykola Sadovsky

Sadovsky, Mykhailo [Sadovs'kyj, Myxajlo], b 29 July 1887 in Kiev, d 29 December 1967 in Toronto. Senior UNR Army officer. Commissioned in the Russian army in 1912, he joined the UNR Army and was assigned with the rank of colonel to the General Staff and then to Supreme Headquarters. Under the UNR Directory he was chief of the field office of the defense ministry (1918–20). In the interwar period he served at the rank of brigadier general in the defense ministry of the UNR government-in-exile in Poland, and was active in community and veteran organizations. He was vice-president of the Ukrainian Military History Society and chief editor of its *Za derzhavnist'* collections and the journal *Ukraïns'kyi invalid*. After emigrating to Canada in 1950, he remained active in the UNR government-in-exile, UNR Army veterans' organizations, and the Ukrainian Orthodox church. He organized and headed the *Ukrainian Military History Institute and edited the two final volumes of *Za derzhavnist'*. He wrote many articles on the 1917–21 period in Ukrainian military history.

Sadovsky, Mykola [Sadovs'kyj] (real surname: Tobilevych), b 13 December 1856 in Kamiano-Kostuvate, Yelysavethrad county, Kherson gubernia, d 7 February 1933 in Kiev. Theater director, actor, and singer; brother of I. *Karpenko-Kary, M. *Sadovska-Barilotti, and P. *Saksahansky. In 1881 he began his theatrical career in H. Ashkarenko's, M. Kropyvnytsky's, and M. Starytsky's troupes. From 1888 he led his own troupe, which in 1898 joined Saksahansky's Troupe. Sadovsky was the artistic director of the Ruska (see *Ukrainska) Besida Theater (1905–6) and then organized the first resident Ukrainian theater in Kiev (see *Sadovsky's Theater), which was active until 1919. In 1919 he was the commissioner of people's theaters in the UNR. He was also director of the *Ruthenian Theater of the Prosvita Society (1921–3). In 1923 he worked with the émigré Ukrainian community in

Prague to organize a theater and directed several of its productions. After returning to the USSR in 1926, he performed the lead role in the film *Viter z porohiv* (English title: *The Last Pilot*, 1930) and formed a touring troupe with P. Saksahansky.

Acclaimed by Starytsky as the most talented of the *Tobilevych family, Sadovsky was an actor of the realistic-psychological school, whose best roles were profound interpretations of the heroes in historical and social dramas, such as Starytsky's *Bohdan Khmel'nyts'kyi*, Karpenko-Kary's *Sava Chalyi*, and L. Starytska-Cherniakhivska's *Het'man Doroshenko*. He also played with success as the Komandor in Lesia Ukrainka's *Kaminnyi hospodar* (The Stone Host) and was a key force behind the flowering of Ukrainian operatic theater, in which genre he staged operas by composers such as M. Lysenko, D. Sichynsky, S. Moniuszko, and P. Mascagni. He wrote *Moï teatral'ni zhadky* (My Theatrical Reminiscences, 1930; 2nd edn 1956). Biographies of him were published in Kiev in 1962, 1964, and 1982.

V. Revutsky

Valentyn Sadovsky

Sadovsky, Valentyn [Sadovs'kyj], b 27 August 1886 in Plishchyn, Iziaslav county, Volhynia gubernia, d 24 November 1947 in Kiev. Economist, political activist, and civic leader; full member of the Shevchenko Scientific Society from 1935. After graduating in law from Kiev University (1909) and in economics from St Petersburg Polytechnic (1911) he practiced law in St Petersburg. In 1915 he became an inspector of the Union of Cities of the Southwestern Front, a relief organization that worked in Russian-occupied Galicia. He joined the Revolutionary Ukrainian party in 1904 and then the Ukrainian Social Democratic Workers' party (USDRP). Having returning to Kiev after the February Revolution of 1917, he became a member of the Central and Little radas and the first secretary of justice in the General Secretariat of the Central Rada (from 28 June 1917). In 1918 he and V. Vynnychenko represented the USDRP in the Ukrainian National Union, which organized the overthrow of Hetman P. Skoropadsky. After being forced to flee Ukraine in 1920, Sadovsky lived in Tarnów, Lviv, and Czechoslovakia, where he taught at the Ukrainian Husbandry Academy in Poděbrady. He was also an associate of the Ukrainian Scientific Institute in Warsaw. In 1945 he was arrested by the NKVD in Prague and held in Lukianivka Prison in Kiev, where he died.

Sadovsky was a prolific writer who published several monographs on Ukrainian economics and demography. The most important of them were *Narys ekonomichnoï heo-*

hrafiï Ukraïny (A Survey of the Economic Geography of Ukraine, 1920), *Problemy industriializatsiï v narodnomu hospodarstvi* (Problems of Industrialization in the National Economy, 1929), *Raionizatsiia Ukraïny* (The Regionalization of Ukraine, 1931), *Pratsia v USSR* (Work in the Ukrainian SSR, 1932), *Robocha syla v sil's'komu hospodarstvi Ukraïny* (Labor Resources in Ukraine's Agriculture, 1935), and *Natsional'na polityka Sovietiv na Ukraïni* (Soviet Nationality Policies in Ukraine, 1937). He was also a regular contributor to many prerevolutionary and émigré Ukrainian newspapers and journals, such as *Rada, Ukrainskaia zhizn', Robocha hazeta, Literaturno-naukovyi vistnyk, Dzvony,* and *Tryzub.*

Sadovsky, Volodymyr [Sadovs'kyj] (pseud: Domet), b 18 August 1865 in Dovzhanka, Ternopil county, Galicia, d 1940 in Lviv. Conductor, music critic, and civic leader. As a student he belonged to the so-called *Dvanadtsiatka* (Twelve) choir group set up by Omelian *Nyzhankivsky. After graduating from the Lviv Theological Seminary (1891), he served as a priest in the Ternopil region, where he organized and conducted Ukrainian folk choirs (1891–4). In 1894 he set up a church choir at St Barbara's Church in Vienna. His last years were spent in Lviv. Sadovsky transcribed music and arranged folk songs for choir. He was one of the founders of *Artystychnyi vistnyk* in 1905 and a contributor to *Muzychnyi kalendar* (1904–7). He wrote studies in the theory and history of music and essays on composers, including M. Berezovsky, D. Bortniansky, A. Vedel, M. Lysenko, and Y. Kyshakevych.

Sadovsky, Yosyp [Sadovs'kyj, Josyp], b 10 November 1929 in Strutsivka, Zhytomyr okruha. Sculptor. A graduate of the Lviv Institute of Applied and Decorative Arts (1966), where he studied under V. Borysenko, he has taught there since 1969. He has sculpted compositions, such as *Morning* (1965), *Family of Loggers* (1967), *Highlanders* (1969), *Kozak-Mamai* (1970), *Lesia* (1971), and *Miner* (1977).

Sadovsky Ukrainian Drama Theater (Ukrainskyi dramatychnyi teatr im. M. Sadovskoho). A Galician touring theater troupe under the directorship of O. and A. Karabinevych, active in 1920–39 and then reorganized into the Ternopil Franko Ukrainian Drama Theater (see *Ternopil Ukrainian Music and Drama Theater). Its repertoire consisted mostly of ethnographical Ukrainian plays and classical operettas, as well as historical adaptations, such as *Mazepa* (based on B. Lepky's trilogy) and *Pisnia Beskydu* (The Song of the Beskyds, based on I. Lukavychenko's novel).

Sadovsky's Theater. The first Ukrainian resident theater, established by M. *Sadovsky in Poltava in 1906, with a cast drawn mostly from a young amateur drama circle in Nizhen. From 1907 it was based in Kiev. Sadovsky's Theater formed an important transitional step from the populist-ethnographic to a modern Ukrainian theater. From the modern repertoire Sadovsky's Theater staged Lesia Ukrainka's *Kaminnyi hospodar* (The Stone Host), V. Vynnychenko's *Brekhnia* (Lies) and *Moloda krov* (Young Blood), and O. Oles's études. It was most successful, however, in its productions of Ukrainian historical dramas, including M. Starytsky's *Bohdan Khmel'nyts'kyi*, L. Starytska-Cherniakhivska's *Het'man Doroshenko*, B.

Hrinchenko's *Stepovyi hist'* (The Steppe Guest), and S. Cherkasenko's *Pro shcho tyrsa shelestila* (What the Steppe Grass Murmured About). Sadovsky's Theater was also acclaimed for its staging of Ukrainian operas – M. Lysenko's *Aeneid, The Drowned Maiden,* and *Christmas Night,* D. Sichynsky's *Roksoliana,* B. Smetana's *The Bartered Bride,* S. Moniuszko's *Halka,* and P. Mascagni's *Cavaleria rusticana.* It also performed productions of plays translated into Ukrainian, including H. Heijerman's *The Good Hope,* J. Gordin's *Mirele Effros,* N. Gogol's *Revizor* (The Inspector General), A. Ostrovsky's *Dokhodnoe mesto* (Easy Money), J. Słowacki's *Mazepa,* and G. Zapolska's *Moralność pani Dulskiéj* (Madam Dulska's Moral Code). The theater was prohibited from performing E. Chirikov's *Ievreï* (The Jews) and F. Schiller's *Wilhelm Tell.* Besides Sadovsky, the directors were I. Marianenko, S. Pankivsky, F. Levytsky, and Ye. Zakharchuk. The actors were M. Zankovetska, L. Linytska, O. Korolchuk, H. Borysohlibska, H. Zatyrkevych-Karpynska, O. Polianska-Karpenko, M. Malysh-Fedorets, Ye. Khutorna, L. Kurbas, and S. Stadnyk; the soloist singers, O. Petliash-Barilotti, T. Ivliv, H. Pavlovsky, M. Lytvynenko-Volhemut, and M. Mykysha; the designers, V. Krychevsky, I. Burachok, and V. Diakiv; the conductors, H. Elinek and O. Koshyts; and the choreographer, V. Verkhovynets. In 1916 Marianenko departed with many of the leading actors to form the *Society of Ukrainian Actors. Kurbas also left, to found *Molodyi Teatr. The Sadovsky's Theater productions subsequently deteriorated, and it ceased to exist in 1919; some of the cast joined the Ukrainian Touring Theater.

BIBLIOGRAPHY
Vasyl'ko, V. *Mykola Sadovs'kyi ta ioho teatr* (Kiev 1962)
V. Revutsky

Yurii Sadylenko: *Steelworkers* (1930)

Sadylenko, Yurii, b 20 January 1903 in Zhytomyr, Volhynia gubernia, d 30 November 1967 in Kiev. Painter. After graduating from the Kiev State Art Institute (1930), where he studied under L. Kramarenko, he lectured at the Kharkiv Art Institute (1931–41) and, from 1944, at the Kiev State Art Institute. In the 1920s he was a member of the Association of Revolutionary Art of Ukraine and the Union of Contemporary Artists of Ukraine. He painted historical canvases, such as *T. Shevchenko's Arrest* (1939); genre paintings, such as *Steelworkers* (1930) and *Construction* (1930); portraits; the panel *T. Shevchenko's Grave* (1940) at the Kaniv Museum-Preserve; and illustrations for an edition of Shevchenko's *Kateryna* (1939). In 1930 he and I. Zhdanko created the large-scale frescoes of the VUAN conference hall, which were plastered over in 1940.

Šafařík, Pavel, b 13 May 1795 in Kobeliarovo, Slovakia, d 26 June 1861 in Prague. Pioneering Slavicist and leading figure in the Czech and Slovak national revivals. After graduating from Jena University (1817) he taught secondary school in Novi Sad (1819–33) and then became curator (1841) and director (1848) of the Prague University library. He was a founder of several branches of Slavic studies and the author of fundamental works in Slavic history and language, including *Geschichte der slavischen Sprache und Literatur nach allen Mundarten* (1826) and *Slovanské starožitnosti* (Slavic Antiquities, 2 vols, 1836–7). He regarded Ukrainians as a distinct people with their own language and literature. His ideas had a strong impact on the Ukrainian national awakening. He maintained close ties with the Ruthenian Triad and with other Ukrainian Slavicists, such as I. Sreznevsky, O. Bodiansky, and M. Maksymovych.

Safflower (*Carthamus tinctorius*; Ukrainian: *saflor*). A cultivated flowering annual plant of the family Asteraceae (or Compositae). It grows to 30–120 cm in height and has red, orange, yellow, or white flowers; dried flowers were once used to obtain an orange-red textile dye. Its seeds contain up to 60 percent oil, which is used in the production of margarine, soap, linoleum, and clear, nonyellowing varnish. As a *vegetable oil safflower compares in quality with sunflower oil. The meal or cake residue is used as a protein supplement for livestock.

Safonovych, Teodosii [Safonovyč, Teodosij] (Sofonovych, Feodosii), b ?, d 1676 in Kiev. Writer, church leader, and one of the first systematic Ukrainian historians. He studied at the Kievan Mohyla College and then taught there (1650–5) and served as its acting director (1653–5). From 1655 he was hegumen of St Michael's Golden-Domed Monastery. His history of Ukraine, *Kroinika z litopistsov starodavnikh ...* (Chronicle from Ancient Chroniclers ..., 1672), introduced the idea of the unity of all Ukrainian lands and set out the course by which the Cossack estate gained supremacy in Ukraine. Only a few manuscript copies of it have survived.

In the first part of the *Kroinika*, concerning history up to the end of the 13th century, Safonovych reworks the Hypatian Chronicle, and in the second part he presents a collection of accounts based mainly on Polish chroniclers, especially M. Stryjkowski. The work was often used by Ukrainian chroniclers of the 17th and 18th centuries, particularly by the author of *Sinopsis. A detailed summary of the *Kroinika* was published by E. Bolkhovitinov in his his-

Headpiece depicting the Battle of Kulikovo Pole in Teodosii Safonovych's chronicle

torical dictionary of clerical writers (vol 2, 1827). An edition of the *Kroinika* begun before the First World War by S. Golubev for the Kiev Archeographic Commission was not completed. An original manuscript of the *Kroinika* is preserved in the Västeraser Gymnasialbibliothek in Sweden, a copy of which was given to the AN URSR (now ANU) Institute of History in the 1960s; another manuscript is held by the Central State Archive in Moscow.

BIBLIOGRAPHY
Borelius, C. *Safonovičs Chronik im Codex AD 10 der Väteraser Gymnasialbibliothek, eine sprachliche Untersuchung* (Uppsala 1952)
A. Zhukovsky

Sage (*Salvia*; Ukrainian: *shavliia*). An aromatic perennial herb of the family Lamiaceae (Labiatae), native to the Mediterranean area. The leaves of the medicinal or garden sage (*S. officinalus*; Ukrainian: *shavliia likarska*) contain essential oil, alkaloids, and tanning substances. In Ukraine it is cultivated for medicinal purposes and as a food flavoring (fresh or dried). The clary sage (*S. sclarea*; Ukrainian: *shavliia muskatna*) is cultivated in southern Ukraine for its essential oil, used in the pharmaceutical, distilling, and tobacco industries.

Sago, Mitchell (né Mykhailo Saramaga), b 6 August 1914 in Winnipeg, d 15 July 1989 in Toronto. Communist leader and journalist. He joined the Young Communist League in 1930 and the Communist Party of Canada in 1932. In 1940 he was interned for two years by the Canadian government. He edited the weekly *Westerner* and then served as editor (1954–80) of the semimonthly *Ukrainian Canadian*. He was also a member of the national executive of the Association of United Ukrainian Canadians. He was a coauthor (with H. Polowy) of a book on T. Shevchenko, *The World Is My Village* (1964), and a coeditor of a history of the Workers' Benevolent Association, *Friends in Need* (1972).

Sahaidachny, Petro [Sahajdačnyj] (né Konashevych or Kononovych), b 1570? in Kulchytsi, Sambir region, Galicia, d 20 April 1622 in Kiev. Zaporozhian hetman, organizer of Ukrainian Cossack armies, and political and civic

Hetman Petro Sahaidachny (engraving, 1622)

leader. He received the appellation Sahaidachny at the Zaporozhian Sich. He was a member of the Orthodox nobility in Galicia, and he studied at the Ostrih Academy. In 1592–1600 he worked for the Kievan judge I. Aksak. He traveled to the Sich in 1601 and participated in campaigns against the Tatars and Turks. Under his leadership the Cossacks captured Ochakiv and Perekop (1607) and various towns along the Anatolian coast in Turkey (1608), including Sinop and Trabzon, where they destroyed a force of 10,000 Turks and freed many slaves. In 1618 Sahaidachny joined the anti-Turkish Holy League. Also in that year he led a 20,000-strong Cossack army in Władysław IV Vasa's Polish campaign against Muscovy. Those victories strengthened the Cossack order and captured the attention of European rulers. Sahaidachny's orientation as hetman (1614–22) was toward the conservative faction of the Cossack *starshyna*. He transformed the Cossack Host into a regular military formation and imparted a statist character to the Cossack movement.

Sahaidachny also fought for the religious and cultural rights of the Ukrainian people. Together with the entire Zaporozhian Host he registered in the Kiev Epiphany Brotherhood in 1616–19. He contributed to the establishment of a cultural center in Kiev and sought to unite Cossack military might with the Ukrainian clergy and nobility. Owing to his efforts the Orthodox hierarchy in Ukraine and Belarus was revived in 1620, and Patriarch Teophanes III of Jerusalem ordained Metropolitan Y. Boretsky and five bishops.

Sahaidachny's moderate policies regarding Poland provoked dissatisfaction among Cossack circles, and in 1620 they briefly elected Ya. Borodavka as hetman. In 1621 Sahaidachny led a force of 40,000 Cossacks alongside the Polish army in the Battle of *Khotyn, at which they routed the Turkish army. Sahaidachny died of wounds suffered in the battle; he was buried in the monastery of the Kiev Epiphany Brotherhood. He bequeathed his assets to the brotherhood schools in Kiev and Lviv and for church causes. The director of the Kiev Epiphany Brotherhood School, K. *Sakovych, wrote the panegyric *Virshi na zhalosnyi pohreb zatsnoho rytsera Petra Konashevycha Sahaidachnoho* (Verses for the Sorrowful Funeral of the Noble Knight Petro Konashevych Sahaidachny, 1622), which remains a valuable source of biographical information on Sahaidachny. Some scholars consider Sahaidachny to be the author of the tract *Poiasnennia pro uniiu* (An Explanation of the Union). He became the subject of the folk song 'Hei na hori tam zhentsi zhnut'' (Hey, on the Mountain the Harvesters Are Harvesting).

BIBLIOGRAPHY
Kamanin, I. *Ocherk getmanstva P. Sagaidachnogo* (Kiev 1901)
Chaikovs'kyi, A. *Petro Konashevych Sahaidachnyi: Istorychnyi narys* (Vienna 1917)
Kravets', M. 'Het'man Ukraïny Petro Konashevych-Sahaidachnyi,' *UIZh*, 1967, no. 4
Huslystyi, K. 'Petro Konashevych-Sahaidachnyi,' *UIZh*, 1972, no. 4

L. Wynar, A. Zhukovsky

Sahaidachny, Petro [Sahajdačnyj], b 1898 in Berezhany county, Galicia, d 12 January 1975 in New York. Journalist. A veteran officer of the Ukrainian Sich Riflemen, in the 1930s he coedited the paper *Novyi chas* and several other publications of the Ukrainska Presa publishing house in Lviv. During the Second World War he worked as an editor with *Krakivs'ki visti* in Cracow (1939–41) and managing editor of the daily *Nova Ukraïna* in German-occupied Kharkiv (late 1941 to early 1942). As a postwar refugee he worked for the Novi Dni publishing house and edited the daily *Ostanni novyny* in Salzburg. After emigrating to New York he briefly edited the journal *Novyi svit* and worked for the Ukrainian Congress Committee of America.

Yevhen Sahaidachny

Sahaidachny, Yevhen [Sahajdačnyj, Jevhen], b 22 April 1886 in Kherson, d 21 August 1961 in Kosiv, Ivano-Frankivske oblast. Painter, scenery designer, and teacher. He was educated in St Petersburg, and in 1911–18 he worked as a designer for St Petersburg and Kiev theaters. From 1917 he was a member of the Ukrainian State Academy of Arts in Kiev, and from 1922 he lectured at the Kiev State Art Institute, the Mezhyhiria Ceramics Tekhnikum, the arts and crafts school in Myrhorod, the Luhanske Workers' Faculty of Art (1932–6), the Dnipropetrovske Art Tekhnikum, and the Kosiv School of Applied Art (from 1947). His works include the decorative mural *Wedding* (1911); landscapes, such as *Lanes in Turkey* (1912) and *Gullies near Luhanske* (1930s); and many genre paintings of the Hutsuls (1940s). He amassed a large collection of folk art, particularly of the Hutsuls.

Saharda, Mykola, b 13 December 1870 in Zolotonosha, Poltava gubernia, d 1943 in Kiev. Religious scholar, librarian, and bibliographer. A graduate of the Poltava Theological Seminary (1896) and the St Petersburg Theological Academy (1904), he taught Latin at the Poltava Religious School (1897) and church history at the Poltava seminary (1899–1904) and was appointed to the chair of patristics at the St Petersburg Academy (from 1904). His articles in theology and Ukrainian church history were published in the serial *Poltavskiia eparkhial'nyia vedomosti*. Under Soviet rule he contributed bibliographic articles to *Knyhar* (1917–20), served as a presidium member in charge of the periodicals department at the National Library of Ukraine in Kiev (1925–32), coedited and contributed to *Bibliotechnyi zbirnyk* (1926–7) and the National Library's *Zhurnal bibliotekoznavstva ta bibliohrafiï* (1927–30), served as the scholarly secretary of the VUAN Bibliographic Commission (1927–32) and as an associate of the VUAN Commission for the Study of Byzantine Literature and Its Influence in Ukraine, and contributed surveys of Ucrainica in Russian journals to *Ukraïna* (1927–8). He was arrested in 1932 during the Stalinist terror.

Sahatovsky, Ivan [Sahatovs'kyj] (pseud of Mavrenko-Kotok), b 12 March 1882 in Kiev, d 13 December 1951 in Stryi, Lviv oblast. Character actor and theater director. He began his career in 1898 in the Solovtsov Russian Theater in Kiev and then worked in M. Kropyvnytsky's troupe (1900–2), led his own touring troupe in Belarus, central Russia, and the Ural region (1902–19), and worked as an actor and director in Ukrainian theaters in Kherson, Kiev, Odessa, Dnipropetrovske, and Stryi.

Oleksander Saienko: *Girl Grazing Sheep* (1922)

Saienko, Oleksander [Sajenko], b 20 August 1899 in Borzna, Chernihiv gubernia, d 5 March 1985 in Kiev. Painter and decorative artist. A graduate of the Kiev State Art Institute (1928), where he studied under V. Krychevsky, in the early 1930s he worked as an animator at the Kiev Film Factory and then as a ceramic artist in the Sci-

entific Research Institute of Mineralogy. Saienko created over 500 works. They include portraits of his wife and daughter, V. Krychevsky, M. Hrushevsky, and V. Vynnychenko; the panels *Harvest* (1922), created by means of a unique technique of straw inlay, and *Captives* (in the building of the VUAN historical section), as well as *T. Shevchenko under a Willow* (1937), and *Ivan Sirko* (1967). He also designed decorative plates, tapestries, and kilims. An album of his works was published in Kiev in 1980.

Saienko, Oleksander [Sajenko], b 25 February 1921 in Izium, Kharkiv gubernia. Writer. He is the author of the poetry collections *Oi, vydno selo* (Oh, the Village Is in Sight, 1957), *Koordynaty* (Co-ordinates, 1965), and *Obnizhok lita* (The Vestige of Summer, 1981); the novelettes for schoolchildren *Shukannia krynytsi* (The Search for the Well, 1958) and *Na chotyry brody* (The Four Crossings, 1968); and five children's books.

Saievych, Mykola [Sajevyč], b 1885, d 1944. Military officer and forester. After joining the Ukrainian Sich Riflemen Legion in 1914, he directed the legion's commissariat in Volodymyr-Volynskyi (1916–18) and developed its cultural and educational program. In 1918–19 he was the Western Ukrainian government commissioner of Kosiv county and then captain in the Ukrainian Galician Army and commander of the Guard Battalion in Kamianets-Podilskyi. In the interwar period he was a member of the leadership of the Ukrainian Military Organization. He managed Halych metropoly's forests in the Carpathians. He wrote studies of insects in Transcarpathia's forests and works on Ukrainian forestry terminology.

Saievych, Omelian [Sajevyč, Omeljan], b 1869, d 1944. Early co-operative leader. One of the first organizers of co-operatives in Galicia, he was the first director of the head office of the Audit Union of Ukrainian Co-operatives (1904–14) and its chief auditor (1904–21). For many years he was director of the Provincial Credit Union in Lviv (later Tsentrobank) and assistant to its director, K. Levytsky.

Saiga (*Saiga tatarica*; Ukrainian: *saihak*). A medium-sized mammal of the family Bovidae, similar to the antelope. It was once common in Ukraine, but its numbers were greatly reduced by hunting in the 19th century. It was given complete protection by the Soviet government in 1919 and reintroduced in the Askaniia-Nova Nature Reserve. The total saiga population now stands at about two million; it is increasing in Siberia but not in Ukraine. Since 1957 limited hunting of the saiga for its meat and skin has been allowed.

Sainfoin (*Onobrychis*; Ukrainian: *espartset*). A perennial forage herb, shrub, or annual grass of the family Leguminosae. A valuable feed crop, sainfoin grows successfully in forest-steppe and steppe regions in almost all types of soils. Three species are cultivated in Ukraine, for green feed, hay, and pasture covering respectively: *O. viciaefolia* (also known as holy clover or espareet), *O. transcaucasica* (the most productive), and *O. arenaria* (the most recent and hardy). Sainfoin is grown alone or mixed with clover, lucerne, or other grasses.

Saint Andrew (Andrii Pervozvannyi [Andrew the First-Called]), b ?, d ca 70 in Patras, Greece. Brother of St Peter and the first of the twelve disciples of Christ. Tradition has it that St Andrew was a missionary to lands surrounding the Black Sea, and that he traveled along the Dnieper River. Both the Byzantine and Ukrainian churches have, on the basis of this tradition, associated the origins of their Christianity with his name. The Kiev Church council of 1621 recognized St Andrew as the *Roskii apostol* (the apostle of Rus'), and *St Andrew's Church was later built in Kiev in his honor.

The eve of St Andrew's feast day was marked by various folk traditions and customs in the Ukrainian churches (13 December [30 November OS]). Games, often involving fortune-telling with hot wax poured in water, were played by young people throughout Ukraine. There were also many elaborate dating rituals performed at parties and village gatherings.

St Andrew's Church

Saint Andrew's Church (Andriivska tserkva). A masterpiece of rococo architecture in Kiev. It was designed for Empress Elizabeth I by B. *Rastrelli and built under the direction of I. Michurin in 1747–53. Set on a hill above the Podil district on a cruciform foundation atop a two-story building, the church has a central dome flanked by four slender towers topped with small cupolas. The exterior is decorated with Corinthian columns, pilasters, and complex cornices designed by Rastrelli and made by master craftsmen, including the Ukrainians M. Chvitka and Ya. Shevlytsky. The interior has the light and grace characteristic of the rococo style. The iconostasis is decorated with carved gilded ornaments, sculptures, and icon paintings done in 1751–4 by the Russian painter A. Antropov and

his assistant at the time, D. *Levytsky. Other paintings in the church are by P. Boryspilets, I. Romensky, and I. Chaikovsky. During the Seven Years' War the imperial court lost interest in the church, and it was unfinished when it was consecrated in 1767. Because of ground instability, the maintenance and preservation of the church have been a constant problem. Since 1958 the church has been a branch of the *Saint Sophia Museum.

St Andrew's College

Saint Andrew's College (Kolegiia sv. Andreia, or SAC). A seminary of the *Ukrainian Orthodox Church of Canada and students' residence, located in Winnipeg on the University of Manitoba campus. Incorporated in April 1946, SAC succeeded the small Orthodox seminary established in Winnipeg in 1932 to prepare candidates for the priesthood and community leadership through programs in theology, approved high school courses, and Ukrainian language and culture summer courses. In 1964 it moved to its own building on the campus and became an associate college of the university. In 1972 it was authorized to teach accredited university courses in Ukrainian and religious studies leading to a BA degree at the university. In January 1981 its humanities courses were organized into the Centre of Ukrainian Canadian Studies, which offers a BA program in Ukrainian-Canadian heritage studies. At the same time SAC was formally affiliated with the university, which provides the operating budget for the center while the college furnishes the physical facilities. The Faculty of Theology remains under the jurisdiction of the Ukrainian Orthodox church and offers a four-year B TH and M DIV degrees and a two-year diploma in theology. SAC is administered by a principal and a board of directors, and the center is headed by the director. It contains a library of 50,000 volumes, including the collection of 11,000 rare books belonging to the late Metropolitan I. *Ohiienko, a former dean of theology there. The residence can accommodate over 50 students, and regular summer and extension courses have been held there. The principals of SAC have included Rev S. Sawchuk, Rev O. Krawchenko, and P. Kondra. The current (1991) principal is R. Yereniuk; N. Aponiuk is director of the center.

O. Gerus

Saint Anthony of the Caves (Sviatyi Antonii Pecherskyi; secular name: Antyp), b ca 983 in Liubech, Chernihiv district, d 1073 in Kiev. As a youth he joined the monastery at Mt Athos, where he was tonsured and adopted the religious name Anthony. After many years he returned to Ukraine; reputedly he took up residence in a cave in which *Ilarion had lived, near the village of Berestove, on the outskirts of Kiev. Anthony's deeds and fasting attracted other monks, including *St Theodosius. This monastic community became the nucleus of the *Kievan Cave Monastery, and Anthony emerged as the founder of monasticism in Ukraine. Later, Anthony and the monks built a church and elected the first hegumen, Varlaam. When the monastic community expanded, Anthony, an adherent of hermitism and a strict ascetic, excavated for himself a new cave in an area that came to be called the Near Caves or Anthony's Caves, to distinguish them from the older caves, called the Far Caves or Theodosius's Caves. There he would cure the sick with herbs and reputedly perform miracles. Toward the end of his life Anthony was forced by Prince Iziaslav to leave Kiev briefly and settle in Chernihiv, but he soon returned to Kiev. The cult of St Anthony grew in the late 12th and early 13th centuries, and it was probably around this time that he was canonized; his feast is celebrated on 23 July (10 July OS). His life, based on an older life which has not survived, is found in the Kievan Cave Patericon.

BIBLIOGRAPHY
Heppell, M. 'The *Vita Antonii*, a Lost Source of the *Paterikon* of the Monastery of Caves,' *Byzantinoslavica* 13, no. 1 (1952)
Dublians'kyi, A. *Ukraïns'ki sviati* (Munich 1962)
Bosley, R. 'A History of the Veneration of SS Theodosij and Antonij of the Kievan Caves Monastery from the Eleventh to the Fifteenth Century,' PH D diss, Yale University, 1980
A. Zhukovsky

The iconostasis of St Barbara's Church

Saint Barbara (Sviata Varvara). Martyr, born in Nicomedia, believed to have been killed in 306, and revered in Kievan Rus'. Her life story was well known in Ukraine, and it was commonly believed that her remains were taken from Constantinople to Kiev in 1108 and held in the St Michael's Golden-Domed Monastery until its ruin. Her feast day (17 December [4 December OS]) generally marked the transition from the fall cycle to the winter cycle of activities. Folk beliefs associated with St Barbara stress her beneficial powers for pregnant women and her protection of people against skin diseases.

Saint Barbara's Church (Tserkva sv. Varvary). A Catholic church in Vienna built by the Jesuits in 1652. After the abolition of the Order of St Barbara in 1773, the church was granted to the Greek Catholics by Empress Maria Theresa, in 1775. In 1784 a parish was organized at the church, and it became a center of Ukrainian community life in Vienna. Eventually the parish became an important cultural center for the Ukrainians of the Austrian Empire, particularly when the *Barbareum seminary and a crown boarding school functioned there. Its notable curates were Ye. Striletsky (1784–1804), I. Snihursky (1813–18), I. Fogarashii (1818–34), P. Paslavsky (1834–47), S. Lytvynovych (1848–57), Y. Pelesh (1875–83), and M. Hornykevych (1923–56). The parish owns a valuable archive. In 1862 the St Barbara Brotherhood was created; it has been in existence (with small interruptions) since then.

Saint Basil the Great (Sviatyi Vasylii Velykyi), b ca 329 in Turkey, d 379 in Turkey. Archbishop of Caesarea and church father. He was an influential preacher and writer and an early organizer of Eastern monastic life. His works were widely read in Kievan Rus'. Several translations ap-

St Basil's Church

peared in the *Izbornik* of Sviatoslav (1076), including his 'Address to Young Men' and 'Hexaemeron,' nine Lenten sermons on creation. His rules for monasticism and his ascetic writings influenced Ukrainian monasticism and inspired the formation of the *Basilian monastic order, named in his honor. St Basil also wrote a Divine Liturgy that is still used by the Ukrainian Orthodox and Catholic churches on certain holidays.

Saint Basil's Church (Tserkva sv. Vasyliia). An architectural monument of the Princely era in Ovruch (now in Zhytomyr oblast). Built in the second half of the 12th century in a Byzantine style influenced strongly by the Romanesque, it was a square, three-nave structure with two towers at its western end. In 1321 the church was destroyed during the siege of Ovruch by the Lithuanian grand duke Gediminas. In 1734 a small wooden church was raised within the neglected building, and thereby saved it from complete destruction. During restoration work in 1842, the ceiling and cupolas caved in. In 1907–9 the church was restored in the pseudo-Byzantine style by A. Vesnin and V. Maksimov, using A. Shchusev's design, and many of its original features were obliterated.

ss Cyril and Methodius Ukrainian Catholic Church in St Catharines

Saint Catharines. A city (1986 pop 343,258) in Ontario on the western end of Lake Ontario in the Niagara Peninsula. It owes its development as a manufacturing (metalworking and machine-building) and shipping center to the opening of the Welland Canal (1829); it also has a winery and is a canning center for the Niagara fruit belt. According to the 1991 census, 3,245 inhabitants of St Catharines claimed Ukrainian as their only mother tongue. Ukrainians began to settle in the region in 1919. By 1931 they had set up a Prosvita society, which in 1935 became a branch of the Ukrainian National Federation. The society staged plays, ran a Ukrainian school, and sponsored public lectures. After the Second World War a number of new organizations arose: the Ukrainian Credit Union, the Plast and SUM Ukrainian youth associations, and organizations of the Canadian League for Ukraine's Liberation, which in 1962 opened the Black Sea Hall. The Ukrainian Catholics are grouped in two parishes: ss Cyril and Methodius (est 1942) and St John the Theologian (est 1979). The Ukrainian Orthodox parish of St George's was founded in 1949.

Saint Clement I, b ?, d ca 97. Apostolic church father and pope (ca 88–97). Several important early church writings, including the *Letter to the Church of Corinth* and an important collection of ecclesiastical law, have been attributed to him. It is believed that Clement I died a martyr in Chersonese Taurica in the Crimea. His reputed relics were brought to Rome in 867–8 by ss Cyril and Methodius and were deposited in the Basilica of St Clement. According to legend, some relics that remained in Chersonese were taken to Kiev by Volodymyr the Great and deposited in the Church of the Tithes. For this reason Clement was honored throughout Rus'-Ukraine on 8 December (25 November OS). Cardinal Y. Slipy named the Ukrainian Catholic University in Rome in his honor.

Saint Cyril (Sviatyi Kyrylo; secular name: Constantine), b 827 in Salonika, Greece, d 14 February 869 in Rome. Byzantine theologian, philosopher, and missionary. He learned Macedonian in Salonika, where his father was a governor. He was ordained in 848 and began his missionary work in 851. He traveled to the Arabs in the Near East (the so-called Saracen mission) and, with his brother, *St Methodius, to the Khazars (860–1); they stopped in Chersonese Taurica, where they reputedly discovered a copy of the Scriptures and Psalms in the Rus' language. There they also found what were believed to be the relics of St Clement I, which they later took to Rome. In 863 Cyril and Methodius traveled to Moravia at the invitation of Prince Rostislav and on the instructions of the Byzantine emperor Michael, in order to give the Slavic converts to Christianity a liturgy and scriptures in their vernacular. Cyril created the *Glagolitic alphabet – the oldest Slavic alphabet – and proceeded to translate church books, beginning with the Scriptures. The language that he used (and, to a large extent, created to serve the translation needs) is now known as Old *Church Slavonic; it consists of a mixture of Macedonian dialect and the language of Moravia's Slavic inhabitants. His work was acknowledged and praised by Pope Adrian II, at whose invitation the two brothers arrived in Rome in 867. There Cyril died, but his brother returned to Moravia to continue their missionary work.

St Cyril wrote a number of theological works in Greek, and possibly the *Prohlas* (Prefatory) poems to the Gospel, in which he defended the right of all peoples, Slavs in particular, to have a liturgy in their own language. The alphabet and the first Slavic literary language he created had a decisive influence on the development of Ukrainian writing, scholarship, and literature. Less attention has been paid by historians to the influence of Cyril and Methodius on Christianity in Ukraine, as their mission was restricted to the Moravian territory.

BIBLIOGRAPHY

Ohiienko, I. *Kostiantyn i Mefodii, ikh zhyttia ta diial'nist': Istorychno-literaturna monohrafiia*, 2 pts (Warsaw 1927–8)

Nahaievs'kyi, I. *Kyrylo-Metodiïvs'ke Khrystyianstvo v Rusi-Ukraïni* (Rome 1954)

Ševčenko, I. 'Three Paradoxes of the Cyrillo-Methodian Mission,' *SR*, 23, no. 2 (1964)

Dvornik, F. *Byzantine Missions among the Slavs* (New Brunswick, NJ 1970)

Piffl-Perčević, T. *Der heilige Method: Salzburg und die Slavenmission* (Innsbruck–Vienna 1987)

G.Y. Shevelov

Medieval frescoes inside the church of St Cyril's Monastery

Saint Cyril's Monastery (Kyrylivskyi manastyr). A monastery founded by Grand Prince Vsevolod Olhovych ca 1140 on the outskirts of medieval Kiev. Its church, St Cyril's, was built ca 1146; a cruciform construction with three naves and apses, six pillars, and a single dome, it served as the mausoleum of the Olhovych family of the Chernihiv branch of the Riurykide dynasty (eg, Sviatoslav III Vsevolodych, Vsevolod Sviatoslavych Chermny) in the 12th and 13th centuries. The monastery was partially destroyed by the Mongols in the 13th century. It was rebuilt under the supervision of Hegumen V. Krasovsky in 1605. In the mid-18th century a baroque pediment and four octagonal cupolas were added to the church, and in 1760 a stone campanile designed by I. Hryhorovych-Barsky, with a church on its second story, was built above the monastery's gate.

In 1786 the monastery was secularized and turned into a hospital and home for the handicapped. St Cyril's Church remained in use, however. In 1881–4 marble choir parapets and a new marble iconostasis (designed by A. Prakhov) were installed in the church; its medieval frescoes were restored, under the supervision of A. Prakhov, by M. Murashko, I. Izhakevych, I. Seleznov, Kh. Platonov, and M. Pymonenko of the Kiev Drawing School, and by M. *Vrubel, who also painted new murals in the vaults and narthex and the four icons of the iconostasis. In 1929 the monastery's grounds were classified as the St Cyril State Preserve and the church was turned into a museum. The campanile was dismantled in 1937–8. Now the church and an extant 18th-century section of the monastery's wall and corner tower constitute a branch of the *St Sophia Museum. The church's frescoes are fine examples of 12th-century Ukrainian art and the influence of Bulgarian-Byzantine painting on it. They depict the Nativity of Christ, the Presentation of Christ at the Temple, the Eucharist, the Annunciation, the Dormition, the Last Judgment and Apocalypse, an angel gathering the heavens into a scroll, the apostles, the evangelists, and various prophets and martyrs. Murals of saints – Cyril and Methodius, John the Macedonian, Euphemios – adorn its pillars, and compositions depicting St Cyril teaching the heretic, teaching in the cathedral, and teaching the emperor are found in the southern apse.

BIBLIOGRAPHY
Prakhov, A. *Otkrytie fresok Kievo-Kirillovskoi tserkvi XII v., ispolnennoe v 1881 i 1882 gg.* (St Petersburg 1883)
Sovetov, A. *Kievo-Kirillovskaia tserkov': Tserkovno-arkheologicheskoe issledovanie* (Kiev 1914)
Asieiev, Iu. 'Arkhitektura Kyrylivs'koho zapovidnyka,' in *Arkhitekturni pam'iatnyky: Zbirnyk naukovykh prats'* (Kiev 1950)
A. Zhukovsky

Saint Elijah (Sviatyi Illia). Old Testament prophet of the 9th century BC whose feast is celebrated on 2 August (20 July OS). He was particularly popular among Ukrainians, and in folk mythology took on certain roles of *Perun, the ancient god of thunder. This association was reinforced by his feast day, commonly known as 'the thundering feast day' (*hromove sviato*), which falls in a period often marked by summer storms. Folk legend attributed such unsettled conditions to God's having asked Elijah to clear the heavens of demons who had risen up against him: since that time Elijah could still be heard doing his work using thun-

St Elijah's Church

der and lightning. The feast day also marked the beginning of the harvesting season. Ukrainian iconography commonly depicted St Elijah, according to the biblical account, ascending directly to heaven in a fiery chariot.

Saint Elijah's Church (Tserkva sv. Illi). An architectural monument built at the end of the 12th century in Chernihiv as part of the *Trinity–Saint Elijah Monastery. The Romanesque stone structure consisted of a single nave and one cupola resting on a cylinder supported by internal projections of the walls. In 1649 it was rebuilt in the baroque style, and a vestibule and two smaller cupolas were added. The original interior decorations have not survived. The present iconostasis was prepared in 1774.

St George (sculpture by Johann Pinzel adorning the exterior of St George's Cathedral in Lviv)

Saint George (Sviatyi Yurii). A Christian martyr of the 3rd to 4th century whose feast is celebrated on 5 May (23 April OS). This feast day heralded the arrival of spring in the traditional Ukrainian calendar. Folk motifs note that it is St George who 'unlocks' the earth. As he was commonly regarded as a protector of agriculturists, processions to bless the fields – complete with priests, church banners, icons, and holy water – were common on his feast day. Frequently meals were eaten in the fields, and some of the food was often buried afterwards with a prayer for the fecundity of the land, or fed to animals (particularly the remains of Easter fare). St George was also regarded as a protector of animals, and on his feast day a variety of rituals were enacted to ward off 'unclean spirits' from them, particularly witches, who were believed to be doubly active during this transitional period in their efforts to 'take away' the milk of cows and leave them dry. The evening before St George 'arrived' all animals on a farmstead were rounded into outbuildings, whose entrances were then symbolically secured with a cross painted on with grease or tar. The following day the cattle were herded across embers (from fires lit the evening before as an additional protective measure) to purify and make them 'as strong as fire.' The ashes were later scattered across the sown fields.

The figure of St George in Ukrainian iconography is much in line with the general Christian image of him as the dragonslayer riding a white horse, representing the triumph of Christianity over paganism. As a symbol of chivalry St George is the patron saint of the Ukrainian scouting organization *Plast, and his feast is traditionally commemorated by Plast members as the 'Celebration of Spring' (*Sviato vesny*).

Saint George Trial (Sviatoiurskyi protses). The trial of 39 Communists accused of treason, which began its deliberations on 30 October 1921 in one of the buildings of the St George Greek Catholic Cathedral complex in Lviv. The majority (22) of the accused were Ukrainian; the remainder were Poles or Jews. Many of them were arrested when they convened for a meeting of the Communist Party of Eastern Galicia. The trial itself lasted from 22 November 1922 to 11 January 1923. Only the better known of the leaders, with a more revolutionary background, admitted they were active members of the Communist party, among them C. Grosserowa, K. Cichowski, O. Krilyk (Vasylkiv), N. Khomyn, and S. Królikowski. Most of the remaining defendants denied their membership in the Communist party and claimed only to have greater or lesser sympathies with communism. Ten of the accused were given sentences of two to three years; the rest were acquitted. The convicted defendants did not serve their sentences. They were released on bail, and never returned to prison. Abridged reports of the trial were published in 1923 in both Ukrainian and Polish. A second edition appeared in Polish in Warsaw in 1958.

St George's Cathedral

Saint George's Cathedral (Sobor sv. Yura). One of the finest examples of rococo church architecture in Europe, built in Lviv. From 1817 to 1946 it served as the seat of the Ukrainian Catholic *Halych metropoly. The cathedral's complex, consisting of the church, the campanile (its bell was made in 1341), the metropolitan's palace, office buildings, a wrought-iron fence, two gates, and a garden, stands on a high terrace overlooking the old city of Lviv. According to legend the site of the complex was originally occupied by a wooden church and a fortified monastery founded ca 1280 by Prince Lev I Danylovych and, after their destruction by King Casimir III (in 1340), by a three-apse, four-column Byzantine stone basilica (1363–1437). Under Metropolitan Atanasii Sheptytsky the basilica was dismantled and replaced by the present church, which was designed by and built under the direction of B. *Meretyn in 1744–59 and finished in 1764 by S. Fessinger, who also built the adjacent metropolitan's residence (1761–2).

Built on a cruciform ground plan, the four-column church is topped by one large cupola and four small ones. The high exterior walls are decorated with simplified Corinthian pilasters, rococo stone lanterns, and a cornice. Two stairways with delicate rococo balustrades lead to the main entrance, which is flanked by statues of Metropolitans Atanasii and L. Sheptytsky. Above the entrance is a balcony, a high window, the coat of arms of the Sheptytsky family, and an attic surmounted by a statue of St George the Dragon Slayer by J. Pinzel. The grounds in front of the church are enclosed by two rococo gates decorated with allegorical figures of Faith, Hope, and the Roman and Greek Catholic churches.

The church's interior decorations were completed only in 1790. The paintings were done by masters such as Yu. Radylovsky (*Archpriest* and *Appearance before the Apostles*), M. Smuhlevych (*Christ's Sermon*, behind the altar, and *Christ Pantocrator*, in the dome), and L. Dolynsky (local icons, oval icons of the prophets, and scenes of 16 feast days). The sculptured frame of the two entrance doors, the decorations around the entrances, and the many lanterns were done by M. Filevych. In 1942 M. Osinchuk restored the paintings and repainted the murals. With the suppression of the Ukrainian Catholic church by the Soviet regime in 1946, the cathedral was placed under the jurisdiction of the Russian Orthodox church. With renewed religious freedom in the early 1990s, the cathedral reverted to the Ukrainian (Greek) Catholic church.

BIBLIOGRAPHY
Mańkowski, T. *Lwowskie kościoły barokowe* (Lviv 1932)
Sichyns'kyi, V. *Arkhitektura katedry sv. Iura u L'vovi* (Lviv 1934)
Lohvyn, H. *Po Ukraïni* (Kiev 1968)
Ovsiichuk, V. *Arkhitekturni pam'iatky L'vova* (Lviv 1969)

S. Yaniv

St George's Church

Saint George's Church (Tserkva sv. Yura). A masterpiece of Galician wooden architecture. It was moved to Drohobych from Nadiiv in 1656, after the original church had been burned down by the Tatars in 1499. In its present form the church dates back to the beginning of the 18th century. It consists of a square central frame (7.5 by 7.5 m) flanked by two octagonal choirs, an octagonal altar frame, and a vestibule. Together the three frames are 18 m in length. They are topped by three domes without tiers. The choir tops have one tier. The oldest parts of the church are the nave and vestibule. In 1678 a 27-m-high belfry was built. The paintings in the nave were done in 1657–9 under the supervision of Stefan from Medyka; those of the octagonal upper part, in 1678; those in the choirs, in 1691; and those in the vestibule, in 1714. The iconostasis and its icons were done in 1648–50 in the Renaissance style. The latest restoration was carried out in 1974–5.

Saint George's (Dormition) Cathedral (Yuriivskyi [Uspenskyi] sobor). An architectural monument in Kaniv, built in 1144 for Prince Vsevolod Olhovych. A small, six-column church with three naves and apses and a single cupola, it was similar in structure to the church of *Saint Cyril's Monastery and the *Pyrohoshcha Church of the Mother of God in Kiev. Incorporated in its façade are rows of small niches once decorated with frescoes. Frescoes also adorned the portals. In 1805–10 the church's exterior was remodeled in the neoclassical style. The characteristic features of Kievan Rus' architecture have been relatively well preserved in the cathedral.

St George's (Dormition) Cathedral

Saint John Chrysostom (Sviatyi Ivan Zolotousty), b ca 347, d 407. An eminent preacher and church father. In 398 he was elected Patriarch of Constantinople, but in 403 he was deposed. His many sermons (and those attributed to him) circulated widely in 12th– to 17th-century Ukraine in Old Bulgarian and Old Ukrainian translations. Several manuscripts of both 'full' (138 sermons) and 'short' (67 sermons) editions of his sermons have survived. The sermons were usually didactic in tone, and exhorted people to attend church and participate in the liturgy; to observe fasts; and to revere their parents, elders, and teachers. They also encouraged believers to be generous, honest, sincere, and charitable. The Liturgy of St John Chrysostom, which is the most commonly used *liturgy in the Ukrainian church, was probably not composed by him.

Saint John's Eve. See Kupalo festival.

Saint John's Institute (Instytut sv. Ivana). A Ukrainian Orthodox students' residence established in Edmonton in 1918 as the M. Hrushevsky Ukrainian Institute on the initiative of the Adam Kotsko Student Club. The institute housed students from outside Edmonton, encouraged postsecondary education, and popularized Ukrainian culture and identity in Canada. By 1943 it had 718 alumni. In May 1944 it was renamed St John's Institute to reflect its Ukrainian Orthodox orientation. It is an integral component of the *Ukrainian Self-Reliance League. Originally located on the north side of the city, the institute was moved to a location near the University of Alberta in 1949–50. With accommodation for 60 students, a library, museum, chapel, and classrooms, it provides regular summer courses in Ukrainian studies and choir conducting. A jubilee book of the M. Hrushevsky Ukrainian Institute was printed in 1943, and of the St John's Institute in 1959.

Saint Josaphat. See Kuntsevych, Yosafat.

St Josaphat's Ukrainian Pontifical College

Saint Josaphat's Ukrainian Pontifical College (Kolegiia sv. Yosafata). A papal institution for training Ukrainian theologians, founded in 1897 by Pope Leo XIII in Rome. Since 1904 it has been run by the *Basilian monastic order. In the 1930s theology students from all Ukrainian Catholic eparchies attended St Josaphat's College. The college has produced about 350 clergymen and 5 bishops. The college's summer center is at Castelgandolfo, near Rome.

Saint Kuksha [Kukša], b ?, d 1113. A hieromonk at the Kievan Cave Monastery. Possibly of Viatichian origin, he left Kiev for (what is now) the Orel region of Russia in order to undertake pioneering missionary work among the Viatichians. He was martyred during the course of his proselytizing. Reputed to have created miracles, St Kuksha is remembered on 9 September (27 August OS). His relics are kept in the Near Caves of the Kievan Cave Monastery.

Saint Leontii. See Kunytsky, Leontii.

Saint Methodius (Sviatyi Metodii), b ?, d 885. Byzantine missionary. After joining the Byzantine imperial service, he governed a province with a large Slavic population (probably in Macedonia) before becoming hegumen of a monastery on Mt Olympus. He joined his brother *Saint Cyril in 860 for a mission to the Khazars. On their return they visited Chersonese Taurica on the Crimean Peninsula, where they acquired the reputed relics of St Clement I, which they later took to Rome. In 863 the brothers began a mission to the Slavs of Moravia. Together with Cyril, Methodius translated many liturgical texts into the early form of Church Slavonic that Cyril had developed. The brothers traveled to Rome in 867 for an audience with Pope Adrian II. Cyril died while they were in Rome, but Methodius returned to his mission as papal legate to and then bishop of Moravia. His attempts to develop a separate Slavic (vernacular) church rite were opposed by the Frankish clergy and nobility, and Methodius was imprisoned for over two years. He continued his writings, however: he completed a biography of Cyril, translated the Old Testament, and composed a code of civil and ecclesiastical law based on a Byzantine model. Although he was eventually released, his missionary work did not survive in Moravia for long. His disciples were driven out by the Franks and took refuge in Bulgaria, where they were later instrumental in the establishment of Christianity.

SS Cyril and Methodius, as the 'teachers of the Slavs,' played an important symbolic role in the Ukrainian national awakening of the 19th century. One of the first organizations dedicated to the political and national revival of Ukrainians was the *Cyril and Methodius Brotherhood.

Saint Michael the Archangel (Arkhanhel Mykhail). The supreme angel in Christian belief. Ukrainians shared many of the Christian beliefs about St Michael, particularly about his leading role in the struggle against Satan – hence, the name Arkhystratyh Mykhail 'the Supreme Commander Michael.' He was believed to have taken thunder away from Satan and handed it over to St Elijah. Ukrainians adopted St Michael as the patron saint of hunters and the city of Kiev.

Saint Michael's Golden-Domed Monastery (Mykhailivskyi Zolotoverkhyi manastyr). An Orthodox men's monastery in Kiev. Little is know about its early history. In the 1050s Prince Iziaslav Yaroslavych built St Demetrius's Monastery and Church in the old upper city of Kiev, near St Sophia Cathedral. In 1108–13 his son,

St Michael's Golden-Domed Monastery

Sviatopolk II, built a church at the monastery dedicated to the Archangel Michael. The monastery probably came under the control of the Kievan Cave Monastery ca 1128; it was mostly destroyed during the Tatar invasion of 1240 and ceased to exist.

Written records confirm that the monastery was reopened by 1496. Soon afterward it began to be known as St Michael's Golden-Domed Monastery, its name being taken from the church built by Sviatopolk (although historians are not certain which church survived the Tatar invasion, St Demetrius's or St Michael's). Restored and enlarged over the 16th century, it gradually became one of the most popular and wealthy monasteries in Ukraine. In 1620 Y. Boretsky made it the residence of the renewed Orthodox metropolitan of Kiev, and in 1633 I. *Kopynsky was named supervisor (both men were buried there). It enjoyed the patronage of hetmans and other benefactors and acquired many valuable artifacts (including the relics of St Barbara, brought to Kiev from Byzantium in the 11th century and kept in a silver sepulcher donated by Hetman I. Mazepa, and an iconostasis funded by Hetman I. Skoropadsky). Although most of the monastery's properties were secularized in the late 18th century, in the 19th and 20th centuries as many as 240 monks have lived there, and after 1800 it served as the residence of the bishop of Chernihiv (who was also vicar of Kiev). A precentors' school was located there, and many prominent composers (eg, K. Stetsenko and Ya. Yatsynevych) studied or taught at the school.

The main church of the monastery (built in either 1654–7 or 1108–13) was an important architectural and cultural monument. Originally it had three naves and three apses on the eastern side and was topped by a single large gilded cupola. It was rebuilt in a baroque style and expanded with a new façade and six additional cupolas in the 18th century. The most striking elements of the interior were the 12th-century frescoes and mosaics, probably done by Kievan artisans (including perhaps Olimpii). Although many of these were destroyed in the 13th to 16th century, some – notably the mosaics of St Demetrius of Thessalonika, the Eucharist, and Archdeacon Stephen – survived and were partially restored in the late 19th century. Seveal other frescoes were restored by A. Prakhov. Other buildings in the monastery complex included a bell tower and

three residences and refectories. Several Kievan princes were buried in the church, including Sviatopolk II.

After the Soviet seizure of power the monastery was closed, and in 1936 the main church was demolished by the authorities. Before that, some of the mosaics were hastily removed and deposited in the Tretiakov Gallery in Moscow or taken to the St Sophia Cathedral. The art scholar M. *Makarenko was repressed for protesting the destruction of St Michael's Golden-Domed Monastery and subsequently arrested and shot.

BIBLIOGRAPHY

Kievo-Zlatoverkho-Mikhailovskii monastyr: Istoricheskii ocherk ot osnovaniia ego do nastoiashchago vremeni (Kiev 1889)

Povstenko, O. 'Fresky i mozaïky Mykhailivs'koho (Dmytrivs'koho) monastyria v Kyievi,' *Ukraïns'ke mystetstvo*, no. 2 (1947)

V. Pavlovsky, A. Zhukovsky

St Nicholas (late-17th-century icon from Mykhnivka, Volhynia)

Saint Nicholas (Sviatyi Mykolai). One of the most popular saints of the Eastern and Western churches. Little is known about him except that he was bishop of Myra (now in Turkey) in the 4th century, and that he was probably born in Patara (near modern Kalamaki, Turkey). Legends of his charity, especially toward children, and of miracles associated with him, soon spread throughout Europe. In Ukraine the cult of St Nicholas was probably introduced by Metropolitan Yefrem (1089–98), to whom a popular manuscript on the miracles of St Nicholas is attributed. According to chronicles a church in St Nicholas's honor had already been built in Kiev during the reign of Prince Ihor (d 945).

In Ukrainian folk tradition there are two figures known as St Nicholas. One, 'warm Nicholas,' was celebrated in the spring, on 22 May (9 May OS), and the other 'old Nicholas,' was commemorated in the winter, on 19 December (6 December OS). The warm Nicholas was considered to be the patron saint of agriculture. He was said to walk the land, examining the freshly sown fields, 'drying places over-damp, and dampening those over-dry' after the winter. On the festival, householders would lead their horses into the fields for the first night's grazing, shear sheep, and sow buckwheat. St Nicholas was called upon to protect livestock from wolves, and his name frequently appeared in shepherds' prayers. He was also a patron of youth, particularly of orphans and poor girls. The latter he was said to assist in preserving their chastity and in seeking a husband.

In the Kiev region and Podilia a feast known as *nykol'shchyna* was held on 22 May. Ukrainian Cossacks considered Nicholas to be patron of the seas. When venturing out to sea the Cossacks would hold a church service in his honor and would carry icons with his likeness. They would pray to these icons for salvation if caught in violent storms, and there were numerous sailors' tales about their miraculous powers.

According to folk tradition the old Nicholas brought the first snow 'by shaking his beard.' He was considered the patron of spinning, and yarns and thread were often brought to church on his festival 'to add to his beard.' In Western Ukraine gifts were given to children on the eve of his feast day. The Ukrainian Catholic church encouraged the development of ritual plays and games depicting St Nicholas, an angel, and the devil (in appropriate masks and garb), which exhorted children to do good deeds. These plays, some of which were written by professional authors, were often staged by amateur theaters.

St Nicholas often appears in carols and legends. In Ukraine icons with his image were greatly cherished and found in virtually every home. His icon was also placed in an important position in iconostases, usually flanking Jesus, the Mother of God, or the patron saint of the church. In Ukraine St Nicholas was so popular that over time the 'functions' of other saints (such as Michael, Andrew, George, and Barbara) were ascribed to him.

During the Princely era, according to Ye. Onatsky, Ukrainians conducted pilgrimages to the relics of St Nicholas in Bari in southern Italy (where they had been taken in 1087 by Italian sailors). This tradition was revived in 1953 by Ukrainian émigrés on the initiative of Archbishop I. Buchko.

M. Mushynka

Saint Nicholas's Military Cathedral (Sobor sv. Mykolaia, aka Viiskovo-Mykilskyi Sobor and Velykyi Mykola). One of the finest Cossack baroque buildings financed by Hetman I. *Mazepa. It was built by Y. Starchenko in 1690–3 on one of the highest sites in Kiev, on the grounds of St Nicholas's Monastery. The cathedral consisted of three naves, five domes, an elaborately carved façade, and richly embellished portals. Inside was a unique baroque seven-tier iconostasis (15.5 m high, 22.0 m wide) donated by the Kiev burgher S. Balyka. After Mazepa's death his coat of arms was removed from the

St Nicholas's Military Cathedral

façade. A three-story baroque campanile was built in the 1750s. In 1831 the Russian military expropriated the monastery, which was then within the area of the Kiev Citadel, and began using the cathedral as the Kiev garrison church. In the 1920s, restoration of the cathedral was supervised by the VUAN. Nevertheless, the Soviet authorities dismantled the iconostasis, and in 1934 they demolished the entire cathedral.

Saint Nicholas's Monastery (Mykolaivskyi manastyr). One of the earliest monasteries in Kiev, located on a hillside later known as Askoldova Mohyla (Askold's

St Nicholas's Monastery

Tomb) in the Pecherske district. Believed to have been established in 1113 by Grand Prince Mstyslav I Volodymyrovych the Great, it was originally called the Pustynnyi Monastery because of its uninhabited location. The monastery came under the jurisdiction of the Kievan Cave Monastery in 1174. It was destroyed during the 13th-century Mongol invasion but rebuilt, and in 1497 Grand Duke Alexander Jagiellończyk of Lithuania granted it lands stretching down to Kiev's Podil district. Later the monastery enjoyed the patronage of the Zaporozhian Host. From 1696 it was called St Nicholas's Small (Malyi Mykola) Monastery to distinguish it from the nearby St Nicholas's Great (Velykyi Mykola) Monastery, whose construction that year was funded by Hetman I. Mazepa (see *St Nicholas's Military Cathedral). From 1715 the monastery was known as the Slupskyi or Slup (Pillar) Monastery, after the pillar-shaped, stone St Nicholas's Church built in the baroque style there that year (funded by Governor-General D. Golitsyn). The church was substantially remodeled in the 19th century. In 1908 the monastery housed 50 monks and novices. The monastery was secularized under Soviet rule, and the church and adjacent three-story campanile (built in 1874) were dismantled in the mid-1930s to make way for a park.

Saint Nicholas's Prytyska Church (Prytysko-Mykilska tserkva). A baroque church built at the end of the 17th century in the Podil district of Kiev. The name is derived from an icon of St Nicholas, which earlier had hung at a dock (*prytyka*) in the Kiev harbor. Its floor plan had the form of a Greek cross. Over the center of the nave a large dome rested on an octagonal drum. A campanile was built next to it in the early 18th century. In 1718 and again in 1811 the church was badly damaged by fire. It was rebuilt in the baroque style in 1750 and again in the 1820s from A. Melensky's plans. The interior was painted in 1833 by A. Sukhoveev and his assistants. In 1984, after the completion of the restoration begun in 1977, much of the building collapsed.

Saint Onuphrius's Church and Monastery (Tserkva i manastyr sv. Onufriia). A church and monastery located in Lviv. First mentioned in documents from 1292, the complex has been built and rebuilt several times – in 1453 (funded by S. Dropan), 1518 (funded by K. Ostrozky), 1655, and 1902. In 1693–8 the monastery was surrounded by defensive walls, parts of which can still be seen.

The monastery was controlled by the *Lviv Dormition Brotherhood until 1767. During this period it housed a hospital (1591–1765) and, for a time, the printing press of I. Fedorovych. In the 1630s the engraver *Illia began his work there. In 1709 the monastery (and brotherhood) accepted the Church Union of Berestia and was subordinated directly to the Vatican. In 1767 it joined the *Basilian monastic order. Expanded considerably in 1815–20, the monastery came to house a library containing, by 1939, many valuable manuscripts and over 40,000 books, the Basilian archives, and a gallery featuring icons and portraits of church and historical figures. It also served as the Basilian order's headquarters and publishing center in Galicia. Notable figures buried in the monastery's cemetery (closed after 1820) and in the church's crypts include Fedorovych and his son, Ivan; important Lviv burghers; and Basilian protohegumens such as M. Hrynevetsky and A. Radkevych.

The complex includes Saint Onuphrius's Church, a three-nave and three-apse structure built in 1680; monks' cells built in 1683; and a bell tower. The monastery was closed by the Soviet authorities following the Second World War, and the monks were exiled or killed. In 1990 the monastery was returned to the Basilian order.

St Panteleimon's Church

Saint Panteleimon's Church (Tserkva sv. Panteleimona). The only surviving example of 12th- to early-13th-century church architecture in Galicia, built near Halych in the Byzantine style with Romanesque influences. Now located in the village of Shevchenkove, in Halych raion, it has a square floor plan, four columns, three naves, and one dome. Destroyed and rebuilt several times, in the 16th century it was renovated in the late Renaissance style, expropriated by the Polish Roman Catholic church, and renamed St Stanislaus's Church. The latest renovations took place in 1965–9. Of the original structure, the walls, the western and southern portals, and three apses of the eastern façade have survived. The Romanesque decorations of the main portal and the altar apse testify to the high devel-

St Onuphrius's Church and Monastery

opment of stone carving in Galicia. Grafitti and drawings dating from the 12th to 17th centuries can be found on the interior and exterior walls.

Saint Parasceve (Sviata Paraskeviia). The name of a number of saints in the church calendar. One of the most popular saints in the Eastern church is Parasceve of Ikonia (in Asia Minor), who was martyred during the reign of Emperor Diocletian. Her feast day is 28 October, when girls used to pray to her to give them a spouse soon. Another Parasceve, who is assumed to have been of Slavic origin, lived in the 11th century and gained wide popularity in Byzantium. Her relics are found in Tirnovo (Tŭrnovo), Bulgaria. Metropolitan G. Tsamblak introduced her cult in the Ukrainian church and set her feast day as 14 October. In Belarus a Parasceve-Prakseda is honored on 28 October. She was a princess of Polatsk and a nun who made pilgrimages to many holy places. She died in Rome in 1239 and was canonized by Pope Gregory X in 1273. In Ukrainian Christian folk belief, the cult of Parasceve is associated with the cult of Fridays ('Paraska' was even used as a synonym for *piatnytsia* 'Friday,' when women did not work as hard as usual).

Saint Paul. See Minneapolis.

Saint Petersburg (Russian: Sankt-Peterburg). A city (1989 pop 5,024,000) in the delta of the Neva River in northwestern Russia. From 1712 to 1918 it was the capital of the Russian Empire. Its name was changed to Petrograd in 1914, to Leningrad in January 1924, and back to St Petersburg on 6 September 1991. Today St Petersburg is Russia's second-largest and second-most important city, with a seaport, a large industrial base, and extensive cultural, scientific, and educational facilities.

The city was founded in 1703 with the construction of the Peter and Paul Fortress and the admiralty shipyards (1704). In the 1710s Ukrainian Cossack regiments under the command of Cols P. *Polubotok, A. Markovych, and I. Charnysh took part in draining the marshes and digging the canals for ships. The development of the city was costly in human lives: the labor was backbreaking, the treatment of laborers was brutal, and the climate was harsh. In Ukraine it became common knowledge that 'St Petersburg was built on Cossack bones.' Further large-scale projects were undertaken with the labor not only of army units but also of Swedish war prisoners, Cossack convicts, and conscripted workers from all the gubernias. In Kiev gubernia alone, labor conscriptions for the St Petersburg work force raised 2,125 men in 1710, 1,365 in 1712, 1,790 in 1713, and 1,435 in 1714 and in 1715. Hired workers and skilled tradesmen were also used. Later, labor conscription was replaced by special tax levies on the gubernias.

St Petersburg was proclaimed capital of the Russian Empire in 1712, and soon became an important center of culture, learning, science, art, and education. Ukrainians summoned to the capital by Peter and his successors or attracted there by career opportunities played a prominent and sometimes a leading role in the political and cultural life of the city and empire. The city's Western atmosphere appealed to Ukrainian cultural figures. As the empire's 'window on Europe' it offered opportunities for direct contacts with the West, for foreign travel and study at foreign universities. Conditions for Ukrainian cultural and even political work were more favorable in St Petersburg than in Ukraine.

It is unknown how many Ukrainians lived in St Petersburg in different periods. Besides state officials and intellectuals there were many petty civil servants, workers, serfs, and domestic servants. Tens of thousands of Ukrainians served in military units stationed in St Petersburg and its vicinity. According to the 1897 census there were 1,500 Ukrainians in the city, but according to the estate breakdown over 11,000 peasants and over 3,000 burghers in the city came from Ukrainian gubernias. According to the 1926 census there were 10,781 Ukrainians in Leningrad, 7,392 of whom were men. In 1959 there were 68,300 Ukrainian residents, accounting for 2 percent of the total population, and 30.2 percent of them spoke Ukrainian. In 1989 there were 97,100 (2.46 percent), 31.5 percent of whom spoke Ukrainian.

18th century. During the period of the Hetman state hetmans and their plenipotentiaries or delegations came to St Petersburg for talks with the tsar or his representatives. The first hetman to visit the capital was I. *Skoropadsky. Acting hetman P. Polubotok and his officers were summoned in 1723 to St Petersburg, arrested, and imprisoned in the Peter and Paul Fortress for demanding the restoration of their former rights. Polubotok died in prison. Some of his officers, including D. Apostol, Ya. Lyzohub, V. Zhurakovsky, and M. Khanenko, were released at the beginning of 1725 after the death of Peter I but were detained in St Petersburg for several years. Ukraine's last hetman, K. Rozumovsky, often visited the capital. In 1764 his accompanying chancellery was headed by O. Tumansky, and his personal secretary was I. Martos, who stayed in St Petersburg and later became a department head at the Ministry of Justice. M. Khanenko's son, Vasyl, and S. Karnovych were personal adjutants of Grand Prince Petr Fedorovich (later Peter III), and A. Hudovych was his adjutant general. In 1775 O. *Bezborodko was appointed secretary to Catherine II, and rose steadily through the bureaucracy to become chancellor of the Russian Empire in 1797 and obtain a princely title. His circle of friends and collaborators in St Petersburg included P. Zavadovsky, Catherine's secretary, senator, and education minister (1802–10); D. Troshchynsky, Catherine's and Paul I's state secretary and then minister of appanages and minister of justice; S. Shyrai, a general and then marshal of the nobility of Chernihiv gubernia; M. Myklashevsky, eventually governor of Volhynia, Little Russia, and New Russia gubernias; O. Sudiienko, secret counsel and member of the postal authority; and Count O. Rozumovsky, senator and minister of public education. Toward the end of the 18th century the Collegium of Foreign Affairs and other state bodies were staffed by Ukrainians, such as Ya. Markovych, O. Kotlubytsky, O. Khanenko (later secretary of the Russian embassy in Britain), and I. Tumansky. V. Tomara, A. Italynsky, and, later, P. Poletyka made a career in the diplomatic service. Ukrainians such as Field Marshal I. Hudovych and Gen P. Kaptsevych attained high military rank in the imperial service.

Ukrainian scholars and educators, most of them professors or graduates of the Kievan Mohyla Academy, played a leading role in the development of Russian learning and education as well as the emergence of Ukrainian studies. Archbishop T. *Prokopovych, who supported Peter's reforms, was summoned in 1716 to St Petersburg, where he headed the Learned Council and set up an eparchial seminary. Besides Prokopovych its faculty included V. Stefanovych, V. Dmytrashko-Raicha, and I. Obydovsky. Its graduates, including H. Kozytsky and M. Motonys, became associates of the St Petersburg Academy of Sciences (est 1724) and lecturers at the academy's university and gymnasium. The two schools were attended by many Ukrainians who later distinguished themselves as scholars, such as the brothers P. and Ya. Myrovych, Ya. Kozelsky, O. Lobysevych, I. Tumansky, and S. Divovych. K. *Rozumovsky was president of the academy (1746–96), and H. Poletyka worked there as a translator. T. Yankovsky founded the Neva Seminary (1721) in St Petersburg; and many of its lecturers, including A. Zertys-Kamensky, O. Kalynovsky, and H. Kremenetsky, were Ukrainians. Besides Prokopovych some eminent leaders of the Russian Orthodox church were Ukrainians. A whole line of St Petersburg archbishops – N. Stebnytsky (1742–5), Yankovsky (1745–50), S. Kuliabka (1750–61), and V. Putsek-Hryhorovych (1761–2) – came from Ukraine.

Ukrainians were among the first organizers of medical research and training in St Petersburg, among them I. *Poletyka, N. *Ambodyk-Maksymovych, M. Terekhovsky, N. Karpynsky, Kh. Tykhorsky, S. Andriievsky, Ya. Sapolovych, and Y. Kamenetsky. Some of the original professors of the St Petersburg Medical-Surgical Academy (est 1799) were Ukrainians, such as the brothers I. and T. Smilivsky and P. Zahorsky. I. Orlai, from Transcarpathia, practiced medicine in St Petersburg. Ukrainians also taught in other schools in the capital; H. Poletyka, for example, was inspector, and L. Sichkarev a lecturer, at the Naval Cadet School. The philosopher I. Khmelnytsky and the jurist V. Zolotnytsky worked in St Petersburg.

Ukrainians in St Petersburg contributed to the development of Russian journalism. Prokopovych took part in publishing one of the first Russian newspapers, *Sankt-Peterburgskie vedomosti*. P. Bohdanovych edited that paper and published the journals *Nevinnoe uprazhnenie* (1763) and *Sobranie novostei* (1775). Editors or publishers such as M. Antonovsky, V. Ruban, F. Tumansky, and Kozytsky were of Ukrainian origin. In their journals they devoted some space to Ukrainian history, to which H. Poletyka, Bezborodko, Divovych, Ya. Markovych, and A. Rigelman devoted attention. The first work in Ukrainian ethnography, H. Kalynovsky's description of marriage rituals (1777), came out in St Petersburg, and I. Kotliarevsky's *Eneïda* (Aeneid, 1798), the first literary work in the Ukrainian vernacular, was published there.

Many Ukrainian artists studied and worked in the capital, including the architect I. Zarudny, the painters K. Holovachevsky, D. Levytsky, A. Losenko, and V. Borovykovsky, who were also professors of the St Petersburg Academy of Arts (est 1757), the engravers I. Liubetsky and H. Srebrenytsky, and the sculptor M. Kozlovsky. Ukrainian music and musicians were in great demand in St Petersburg. The court kapelle included singers and conductors such as H. Skovoroda (1741–4), M. Poltoratsky (1763–96), and D. *Bortniansky (1796–1825). Of the many singers and bandurysts employed in the capital the better known were T. Bilohradsky and O. Rozumovsky (later husband of Elizabeth I). The composer M. *Berezovsky worked in St Petersburg.

19th and early 20th centuries. After the abolition of the Hetman state Ukraine lost all attributes of autonomy and was reduced to a mere province within the empire. Individual Ukrainians continued to play a role in the imperial administration; Prince V. *Kochubei, for example, was vice-chancellor, minister for internal affairs (1802–12, 1819–25), and president of the State Council and the Committee of Ministers (1827–34), and Count M. Myloradovych was general governor of St Petersburg (1818–25). Some of the members of the clandestine revolutionary circles in St Petersburg, from which the Decembrist movement arose, were Ukrainians. O. Myklashevsky, O. Yakubovych, S. and O. Kapnist, and P. Horlenko belonged to the Union of Welfare (est 1818), and Myklashevsky and D. Iskrytsky were among the founders of the Northern Society. After the Decembrist uprising was suppressed, the Little Russian Secret Society was investigated, and its leader, V. Lukashevych, was held in the Peter and Paul Fortress.

As in the previous century Ukrainians played an important part in the development of science, scholarship, and education in the Russian Empire. The first rector of St Petersburg University (1819–21) was a Ukrainian from Transcarpathia, M. Baluhiansky, who drafted its statute. P. Lodii and V. Kukolnyk taught at the Pedagogical Institute and then at the university. In medicine D. Vellansky, Ya. Kaidanov, I. Buialsky, and O. Kalynsky, the founder of the Russian Medical Association, left their mark as researchers and educators. P. Naranovych and P. Pelekhin served on the faculty of the Medical-Surgical Academy, and F. Yavorsky was chief physician at the Admiralty Hospital (1813–21). V. Buniankovsky taught mathematics, and M. Ostrohradsky founded the St Petersburg school of mathematics. I. Sreznevsky was a professor of Slavic philology (1847–80), and M. Lazarenko was a professor of international law at the university. The director of the Mining Engineering School was Ye. Kovalevsky, who became education minister (1858–61) and permitted the printing of T. Shevchenko's *Kobzar* (1860).

At the beginning of the 19th century St Petersburg became a center for Ukrainian studies: O. Pavlovsky published a grammar of the Ukrainian vernacular (1818), and N. Tsertelev compiled a collection of old Ukrainian songs (1819). The St Petersburg Archeographic Commission, founded in 1834 under the Ministry of Public Education, published many volumes of historical documents and materials on Ukraine (see *Archeography). An impressive circle of specialists in Ukrainian studies formed around the St Petersburg journal *Osnova* (1861–2). It included V. Bilozersky, P. Kulish, M. Kostomarov, and O. Markovych. At the same time the city was one of the main centers of Ukrainian literary life. Shevchenko spent his most creative years and wrote his *Kobzar* (1840) and *Haidamaky* (1841) there. M. Markevych studied there, and from 1834 Ye. Hrebinka lectured in the city's military schools. Kulish founded the first Ukrainian printing house, which was managed by D. Kamenetsky, in St Petersburg. It printed the works of Ukrainian writers, such as M. Vovchok. Some of the Ukrainian writers or publicists who worked in the capital were V. Maslovych, B. Markovych, V. Lazarevsky, and M. Makarov. The almanacs *Molodyk* (2nd issue 1844) and *Khata* (1860) came out in St Petersburg.

Some noted Ukrainian artists studied or worked in St Petersburg in the first half of the century. I. Martos taught sculpture and served as rector (1814) of the St Petersburg Academy of Arts. D. Bezperchy, I. Buhaievsky-Blahorodny, I. Soshenko, A. Mokrytsky, H. Chestakhivsky, Shevchenko, and O. Lytovchenko were established painters. S. Hulak-Artemovsky was a leading soloist in Italian opera at the Mariinskii Theater, and Y. Petrov excelled in Russian opera.

In the second half of the century Ukrainians in St Petersburg began various organizations to meet their own needs as well as to promote larger national purposes. By staging concerts of Ukrainian music, holding commemorative services and meetings, and inviting theatrical groups from Ukraine those organizations cultivated a sense of Ukrainian identity and maintained communal unity among the inhabitants of the foreign capital. The first Ukrainian hromada was established there (see *Hromadas) and was active by the autumn of 1858. In the 1880s a large student hromada and a small populist circle arose around Kostomarov. Toward the end of the 1890s a clandestine hromada consisting mostly of civil servants was organized by activists such as O. Lototsky, P. Stebnytsky, Ye. Chykalenko, O. Borodai, V. Leontovych, and M. Slavinsky. It became known as the Old Hromada. With its support Gen M. Fedorovsky set up in 1898 the *Philanthropic Society for Publishing Generally Useful and Inexpensive Books, which devoted itself to popular education and enlightenment. In the same year the charitable *Shevchenko Society in St Petersburg was founded to give financial assistance to students from Ukraine pursuing higher education in St Petersburg. The underground *Ukrainian Student Hromada in St Petersburg (1898–1916) included students from most of the higher schools in the city. In 1903 the clandestine Northern Committee of the *Revolutionary Ukrainian party (RUP) was created in St Petersburg. Its membership included S. Tymoshenko, D. Doroshenko, P. Diatliv, and N. Shlykevych. In 1904 some of its members broke away to form the Ukrainian Social Democratic Workers' party (USDRP), and others in 1905 joined the Ukrainian Democratic Radical party, which organized the *Ukrainian caucus in the first Russian State Duma. In 1908 two branches of the *Society of Ukrainian Progressives (TUP) were set up in St Petersburg: the first consisted of the members of the Old Hromada, which had been active in the different parties during the brief liberalization period, and the second, of young members headed by M. Korchynsky. Until the Revolution of 1917 those two groups played a dominant role in the capital's Ukrainian community.

Because censorship was milder than in Ukraine, St Petersburg became the chief center for Ukrainian publishing. Over 700 titles were published there before the revolution, including the almanacs *Skladka* (The Contribution, 4th issue, 1897) and *Z nevoli* (From Captivity, 1908), a Shevchenko collection (1914), the classics of Ukrainian literature (I. Nechui-Levytsky and V. Stefanyk), the full edition of Shevchenko's *Kobzar* edited by V. Domanytsky (1907, 1908, 1910; the last one was confiscated by the censor), O. Lototsky's children's anthology *Vinok* (Garland, 1911), and the series Mal'ovani kazochky (Colored Stories). Two encyclopedic volumes of *Ukrainskii narod v ego proshlom i nastoiashchem* (The Ukrainian People in Its Past and Present, 1914–15) came out in St Petersburg. Several Ukrainian writers worked there in the late 19th century, among them I. Rudchenko, A. Kashchenko, T. Zinkivsky, S. Opatovych, D. Mordovets, and O. Dosvitny. As soon as the prohibition was lifted, the Ukrainian press began to

appear there, including the journal *Ukraïns'ke bdzhil'nytstvo* (1906–9), edited by Ye. Arkhypenko, and the official organ of the St Petersburg Committee of the USDRP *Nashe zhyttia* (1915–17). In the early 1910s P. Balytsky founded a Ukrainian bookshop. In 1917 the Drukar publishing house was founded there. When it moved to Kiev, it left a branch behind.

Many Ukrainian scholars who worked in St Petersburg were active in the Ukrainian civic and cultural organizations. The historian and sociologist M. Kovalevsky headed the Shevchenko Society for a time. The anthropologist F. *Vovk was curator of the Ukrainian section of the Ethnographic Department in the Alexander III Museum. Other scholars, such as O. Rusov and his wife, S. Rusova, A. Yefymenko, H. Zhytetsky, I. Zhytetsky, Pelekhin, O. Hrushevsky, K. Shyrotsky, V. Tymoshenko, O. Kysil, and P. Zaitsev, played an important role in the capital's Ukrainian community. In its scholarly and publishing activities the Ukrainian community found support among some eminent Russian linguists, such as A. Pypin, F. Korsh, and A. Shakhmatov, who in 1905 drafted a memorandum from the Imperial Academy of Sciences urging the lifting of all government restrictions on the Ukrainian language. Some established Ukrainian and Russian scholars and many young scholars, such as H. Holoskevych, V. Yaroshenko, V. Hantsov, L. Chykalenko, and O. Alesho, were active in the Student Circle of Ukrainian Studies, which was formed in 1906 at St Petersburg University. At the demand of the student hromada, lectures on the history of Ukrainian literature (O. Hrushevsky) and the history of Ukraine (Yefymenko) were introduced in the 1910s at the Higher Courses for Women. In 1914–17 a clandestine Ukrainian university was operated by the Hromada Ukrainian Club and the Chief Student Council. The faculty of St Petersburg University included some professors of Ukrainian origin, such as S. Bershadsky (law), I. Andriievsky (law professor and rector in 1883–7), V. Liubymenko (botany), and P. Liashchenko (economics). There were Ukrainian scholars who worked in other institutions, such as A. Markovych (law and ethnography), V. Kistiakovsky (physics and chemistry), V. Kovalevsky (economics and finance), M. Maksymovych (hydrology), B. Sreznevsky (meteorology), O. Nykolsky (zoology), and A. Marshynsky (finance). Some eminent Russian scholars, including V. Ikonnikov (history), V. Peretts (literary history), and the aforementioned linguists, specialized in Ukrainian studies.

Some members of the St Petersburg Academy of Arts were Ukrainians by descent or by place of birth, among them A. Kuindzhi, I. Repin, M. Pymonenko, K. Kostandi, and M. Bodarevsky. Among the many Ukrainian graduates of the academy were M. Murashko, S. Vasylkivsky, P. Levchenko, V. Beklemishev, M. Samokysh, I. Izhakevych, K. Trokhymenko, Yu. Bershadsky, F. Krasytsky, O. Murashko, O. Shovkunenko, G. Lukomsky, O. Hryshchenko, S. Zhuk, I. Mozalevsky, and M. Andriienko-Nechytailo. The Ukrainian graphic artists V. Masiutyn and H. Narbut (1907–8 and 1910–17) worked in St Petersburg. Ukrainians also played a prominent role in the capital's musical life. The composers M. Leontovych, Ya. Stepovy, and M. Lysenko worked there. I. Alchevsky was a star of the Imperial Opera, where another Ukrainian, M. Malko, was chief conductor until 1914. The musical scholar Y. Myklashevsky was director of the St Petersburg Institute of Music (1913–18) and editor of the journal *V mire iskusstva*. During the First World War some of the Ukrainian writers and artists in Petrograd belonged to the Ukrainian Literary and Artistic Society, founded by Zhuk.

Revolutionary and postrevolutionary period. At the outbreak of the February Revolution of 1917 the Provisional Ukrainian Revolutionary Committee of Petrograd and the Petrograd branch of the TUP issued their proclamations and organized a Ukrainian demonstration, on 12 March, in which over 30,000 people, mostly soldiers, took part. A memorandum on the Ukrainian language, Ukrainian education, and the Ukrainian church was submitted to Prince G. Lvov, the head of the Provisional Government. The *Ukrainian National Council in Petrograd, which represented 16 local organizations, was founded on 19 March 1917. Its executive committee consisted of O. Lototsky, M. Korchynsky, Stebnytsky, F. Sliusarenko, and Zaitsev. In May 1917 the functions of the council were assumed by the Ukrainian commissioner in the Provisional Government, Stebnytsky. The organizations that continued to operate set up the Council of Ukrainian Organizations in Petrograd, which was active until mid-1918. At the end of May 1917 the Central Rada sent a delegation to Petrograd for talks with the Provisional Government.

As the Ukrainian state was rebuilt, Ukrainian activists, soldiers, scholars, and artists returned in large numbers to Ukraine, and Ukrainian organizations in Petrograd were discontinued. Under the Soviet regime Ukrainian organizations were banned and dissolved. The *Leningrad Society of Researchers of Ukrainian History, Literature, and Language did some valuable work in the 1920s and was abolished in 1933. Later some Ukrainian scholars, such as Yu. Mezhenko, Ya. Aizenshtok, K. Koperzhynsky, V. Adriianova-Peretts, V. Parkhomenko, F. Pryima, M. Morenets, P. Zhur, and Yu. Margolis, found refuge and work in Leningrad. A Ukrainian drama theater operated in the city in the 1920s and was revived briefly in 1930–2 (see *Zhovten Theater in Petrograd-Leningrad). Thereafter Leningrad theaters occasionally staged Russian translations of Ukrainian prerevolutionary and Soviet plays. In the early years of Soviet rule a statue of Shevchenko was erected, and his apartment-workshop at the Academy of Arts was set aside as a memorial museum.

Some signs of organized Ukrainian activity in Lenin-

grad appeared in the 1960s. Under the auspices of the Leningrad Writers' Union P. Zhur began to stage annual concerts in honor of Shevchenko. At the end of the 1970s a circle of Ukrainian students formed around the painter V. Kalnenko, and at the beginning of the 1980s the composer I. Matsiievsky organized a folk-song ensemble, which took part in Shevchenko concerts at the Leningrad Institute of Theater, Music, and Cinema. The Ukrainian Cultural Society, which sprang up in 1988, was registered officially at the beginning of 1989 (membership, 120). It organized concerts dedicated to Hulak-Artemovsky, folk-art festivals at the Leningrad Museum of the Ethnography of the Peoples of the USSR, and commemorative evenings honoring Shevchenko, and it collected funds to construct a monument to Shevchenko. In the last 30 years a number of Ukrainian artists, such as V. Makarenko, V. Antonenko, L. Kolybaba, F. Humeniuk, M. Kovalenko, N. Pavlenko, and A. Driuchylo, have worked in St Petersburg.

BIBLIOGRAPHY

Kharlampovich, K. *Malorossiiskoe vliianie na velikorusskuiu tserkovnyiu zhizn'* (Kazan 1914)

Botsianovs'kyi, V. 'Do istorii ukraïns'koho teatru v Peterburzi za 90-ykh rokiv XIX v.,' *Naukovyi zbirnyk Leninhrads'koho tovarystva doslidnykiv ukraïns'koï istoriï, pys'menstva ta movy*, 1 (1928)

Lotots'kyi, O. *Storinky mynuloho*, 3 vols (Warsaw 1932–4)

Doroshkevych, O. *Ukraïns'ka kul'tura v dvokh stolytsiakh Rosiï* (Kiev 1945)

Bernshtein, M. *Zhurnal 'Osnova' i ukraïns'kyi literaturnyi protses kintsia 50–60kh rokiv. XIX st.* (Kiev 1959)

Morenets, N. *Shevchenko v Peterburge* (Leningrad 1960)

Kravtsiv, B. 'Ukraïnoznavstvo v Leninhradi,' *Suchasnist'*, 1961, no. 10

Zhuk, S. 'Ukraïns'ka hromada v Peterburzi i ïï rolia v buduvanni ukraïns'koï derzhavy,' *Vyzvol'nyi shliakh*, 1964, nos 2, 4

Zhur, P. *Shevchenkivs'kyi Peterburh* (Kiev 1972)

Saunders, D. *The Ukainian Impact on Russian Culture, 1750–1850* (Edmonton 1985)

B. Kravtsiv, N. Pavlenko

Saint Raphael Galician and Bukovynian Emigrant Aid Society (Tovarystvo sv. Rafaila dlia okhorony ruskykh emigrantiv z Halychyny i Bukovyny). A branch of the Austrian St Raphael Society that operated in Lviv from 1907 to 1914. Dedicated to aiding emigrants and maintaining contact with them, the Lviv society took an interest in all the countries to which Ukrainians had recently emigrated. In 1911 it began to publish *Emigrant* as a source of practical advice. The society's leading members were Rev N. Budka and M. Zaiachkivsky. After 1914 its activities ceased. From 1925 a similar purpose was served by the *Ukrainian Emigrant Aid Society.

Saint Raphael's Ukrainian Immigrants' Welfare Association of Canada (Tovarystvo opiky nad ukrainskymy poselentsiamy im. sv. Rafaila v Kanadi). A benevolent society formed in Winnipeg in January 1925 to assist Ukrainians in emigrating to Canada. The founding committee included Bishop N. Budka, A. Zahariichuk, K. Prodan, and D. Elcheshen, its longtime secretary. It published *Providnyk*, *Nove pole*, and *Preriia* and worked with its Lviv-based counterpart, the St Raphael Galician and Bukovynian Emigrant Aid Society. It ceased activities in 1938, after the Depression and restrictive government policies had brought Ukrainian immigration to Canada to a virtual halt.

Members of St Petersburg's Ukrainian Cultural Society at the unveiling of the memorial stone at the site of the future Taras Shevchenko monument (1989)

The St Sophia Cathedral

Saint Sophia Cathedral (Sofiiskyi sobor). A masterpiece of the *art and *architecture of Ukraine and Europe. It was built in Kiev at the height of Kievan Rus', in the Byzantine style, and significantly transformed during the baroque period. The cathedral was founded by Grand Prince Yaroslav the Wise and built between 1037 and 1044 (some suggest 1017–37). The original building, most of which remains at the core of the existing cathedral, is a cross-in-square plan with twelve cruciform piers marking five east–west naves intersected by five transverse aisles. Each nave springs from an apse in the east. The central nave and the main transverse aisle (transept) are barrel-vaulted and twice the width and height of the side naves. A balcony tops the north and south naves and narthex. Over the balcony, aisles, and naves rises a pyramidal arrangement of 12 smaller, peripheral domes and 1 large, central dome, all 13 of them hemispherical on tall drums. An open ambulatory girdles the north, south, and west sides, and to it a further ambulatory and exonarthex with two staircase towers were added in the late 11th century.

The centripetal plan, internal volumes, and external massing reflect the hierarchical ordering of the mosaics and frescoes inside. As the surfaces of the walls advance from the floor and the narthex, the frescoes increase in size and religious significance and culminate in the monumental mosaics *Mother of God (Orante)* in the central apse and *Christ Pantocrator* in the central dome. Among the most masterful mosaics are those of the *Church Fathers*. The more archaic *Orante* in the central apse, often referred to as the *Indestructible Wall*, is the most famous.

The cathedral's 11th-century exterior walls are of *opus mixtum*, a widely used technique of alternating courses of brick and stone. Exterior ornamentation of the original walls consists of decorative brickwork, the monochromatic painting of key architectural elements, and a number of frescoes.

The architects of earlier masonry buildings in Kiev, such as the Church of the Tithes (989–96), were from Chersonese Taurica, but those responsible for St Sophia are not documented. Despite popular speculation, the cathedral did not borrow much from the Hagia Sophia of Constantinople other than its name and some general features. Some 19th-century scholars and contemporary Byzantologists contend that all features of Kiev's St Sophia are imitations of Byzantine types created by master builders from Byzantium. Others liken certain features to German examples and suggest Romanesque influences. Some see features in the cathedral resembling churches in Armenia and Georgia, and a few even trace elements to Iran, Islam, or Bulgaria. More convincingly, a number of scholars have established an autochthonous hypothesis. They argue that by the 11th century an architectural tradition had already been established in Kievan Rus', exemplified by the 10th-century Byzantine structures and the vernacular masonry palaces and wooden structures of the Polianians from the 8th century, and that it was this hybridized tradition, not Byzantine architecture alone, that shaped St Sophia.

A number of the cathedral's features are extremely rare or do not appear at all outside of Kievan Rus' prior to its construction. Among the most notable are the number of domes and their elongation, the marked pyramidal form and overall striving for height, the fact that the width of its body is greater than its length, the combined use of mosaics and frescoes, and the styling and much of the subject matter of the frescoes.

With the sack of Kiev by the Suzdal prince Andrei Bogoliubskii in 1169, the city and the cathedral fell into a 460-year period of decline. Frequently plundered during this period, the cathedral functioned only intermittently. By 1585, its roof ruined, the cathedral had deteriorated significantly. After it had been under the Uniate church for a brief period (1610–33), the Orthodox metropolitan, P. Mohyla, took control of the cathedral. Over the following 24 years it was extensively restored, and new monastery

The iconostasis and main apse of the St Sophia Cathedral

buildings and other wooden structures were built in its precinct. After the 1654 Pereiaslav Treaty between the Hetman state and Muscovy, autocephalous control over the cathedral was lost, and after 1657, repairs became sporadic and at times deleteriously expedient.

From 1690 to 1707 Hetman I. Mazepa influenced and funded the completion of the repairs. Most significant was the exterior work: portions were heightened; the masonry was stuccoed and whitewashed; pediments and other decorative features were added throughout; all the domes, including six new ones, were covered with distinctive pear-shaped and capped cupolas; and the central cupola was gilded. A new three-story bell tower was also built in the precinct's wall. Up to that time the character of the cathedral had remained largely medieval. All the exterior work during this period, however, reflected the newly developed principles of the Ukrainian baroque. This created the current exterior appearance of the cathedral.

An 11th-century mosaic of St Mark the Evangelist on the southwestern pendentive of the St Sophia Cathedral

In the mid-18th century, largely under the patronage of Metropolitan R. Zaborovsky, another period of intense artistic activity occurred. Many silver chandeliers and finely carved and gilded wooden iconostases were installed. The three-tiered iconostasis in front of the main altar is considered to be among the most important examples of 18th-century wood carving (only the lower tier has remained). Between 1744 and 1752 the bell tower was partly rebuilt, and a fourth story and new cupola were added. The refectory (1722–30) and metropolitan's residence (1722–30, with later additions) are both fine examples of Ukrainian

baroque architecture. A wall surrounding the precinct was rebuilt in masonry, and included the flamboyantly ornamented and carefully ordered *Zaborovsky Gate (1746–8). The gate and parts of the bell tower were designed by J. *Schädel.

In the 19th century an exonarthex was added to the cathedral to replace the collapsed western gallery. In the mid-19th century the first exact survey of the cathedral was undertaken, by F. Solntsev. In the intense cultural activity unleashed by the collapse of tsarist rule in 1917, considerable research, investigations, documentation, and restoration of the cathedral took place. Much of this activity, including systematic photodocumentation, continued through the early Soviet years. In 1934, however, all religious activity was terminated, and the cathedral was turned into a museum. Many of its most important objects were confiscated by the state, and many of these were destroyed, lost, or sold abroad. In 1941–3 most of the confiscated articles preserved in Kiev's museums and the AN URSR (now ANU) Central Scientific Library were plundered by the Nazis. Currently the cathedral is part of the *St Sophia Museum.

An 11th-century fresco of the children of Grand Prince Yaroslav the Wise on the southern wall of the central nave of the St Sophia Cathedral

The art and architecture of the St Sophia Cathedral have had a wide influence. The original building's cross-in-square plan, its tall, pyramidal, domed spaces and silhouette, and its organization and stylistic treatment of mosaics and frescoes provided the model for many Kievan Rus' and later Ukrainian churches. It influenced many more, such as *Saint Volodymyr's Cathedral in Kiev (1862–82). Its clearly ordered organization, structural logic, and use of materials informed the development of the more rational and constructivist attitudes of almost all subsequent Ukrainian architecture.

Key events in Ukrainian religious, political, and cultural life have taken place in and around the cathedral. The first library in Ukraine was founded there by Yaroslav the Wise. He was eventually buried in the cathedral (his sarcophagus remains), as were other grand princes and metropolitans. Coronations were performed, foreign ambassadors were received, councils met, and many historic treaties, proclamations, and universals were announced there.

BIBLIOGRAPHY
Powstenko, O. *The Cathedral of St. Sophia in Kiev* (New York 1954)
Logvin, G. *Sofiia Kievskaia: Gosudarstvennyi arkhitekturno-isto-richeskii zapovednik* (Kiev 1971)
Tots'ka, I. (ed). *Mosaics and Frescoes of St. Sophia's Cathedral of Kiev* (Kiev 1971)
Vysotskii, S. *Sredenevekovye nadpisi Sofii Kievskoi: Po materialam graffiti XI–XVII vv.* (Kiev 1976)
Achkasova, V.; Totska, I. *St. Sophia Cathedral in Kiev: Guide* (Kiev 1986)
Vysotskii, S. *Svetskie freski Sofiiskogo sobora v Kieve* (Kiev 1989)
W. Daschko

Saint Sophia Museum (Sofiiskyi muzei). A state historical and archeological preserve established in Kiev in 1934 to protect and restore the famous *St Sophia Cathedral and other buildings and structures on the grounds (5 ha) of the former St Sophia Monastery. Its constituent monuments include the Baroque *Zaborovsky Gate, the 76-m bell tower (built 1699–1706; rebuilt 1744–8 and 1851–2), the metropolitan's residence (1722–48), the 90-m-long *bursa* (1763–7) housing the Ukrainian Archive-Museum of Literature and Art (from 1970), the brotherhood building (1750s; rebuilt 1760s and early 20th century), the 'Small' St Sophia Church opposite the cathedral (1722–30, 1760s; rebuilt 1822 and expanded 1872), and the consistory building (1722–30, 1770–83). The museum is a major European tourist attraction. The cathedral contains, in addition to its own mosaics and frescoes, those from the destroyed *St Michael's Golden-Domed Monastery, the sarcophagus of Prince Yaroslav the Wise, and exhibits dealing with the architecture of Kievan Rus' and the history of the cathedral. Kiev's famous *St Cyril's Monastery Church, *St Andrew's Church, and *Golden Gate, as well as the 14th- to 15th-century Genoese fortress in Sudak (Crimea) and the Chernihiv Architectural-Historical Preserve, are branches of the museum. In 1987 the museum received from the Hamburg Foundation the European Gold Medal for the Preservation of Historical Monuments. The Ukrainian Academy of Arts and Sciences in the US published O. Powstenko's extensive historical and architectural monograph on the subject, *The Cathedral of St Sophia in Kiev* (1954). An album about the cathedral was published in Ukrainian and English in Kiev in 1984.

Saint Theodosius of the Caves (Sviatyi Teodosii [Feodosii] Pecherskyi), b ca 1036 in Vasylkiv, in the Kiev region, d 3 May 1074 in Kiev. He studied in Kursk until 1055, when he traveled to Kiev and joined *St Anthony as one of the first monks of the Kievan Cave Monastery. A gifted leader, he became hieromonk and then hegumen of the monastery (1062), succeeding Varlaam. In 1070 he introduced a strict *Studite Typicon and reformed the monastic life. He initiated the construction of the Dormition Church in 1073 (completed in 1089) and of various buildings and catacombs, and presided over the impressive development and growth of the monastery.

Theodosius also used his authority to influence secular affairs and served as an adviser to a number of princes. He opposed Sviatoslav II Yaroslavych, who illegally seized the throne, and wrote a defense of his younger brother, Iziaslav Yaroslavych. In total, some 15 works are commonly attributed to him, including several sermons in which he chastised monks for indifference and preoccupation with personal well-being.

Theodosius was buried in the Kievan Cave Monastery catacombs, in a section known as Theodosius's Caves or the Far Caves. His relics were transferred to the Dormition Cathedral of the monastery in 1091. The major source of information on Theodosius is the life written by Nestor the Chronicler ca 1080 and included in the *Kievan Cave Patericon. Prince Sviatopolk Iziaslavych had Theodosius canonized in 1108. His feast is celebrated on 16 May.

BIBLIOGRAPHY
Dublians'kyi, A. *Ukraïns'ki sviati* (Munich 1962)
Čyževskyj, D. *A History of Ukrainian Literature (From the 11th to the End of the 19th Century)* (Littleton, Colo 1975)
Bosley, R. 'A History of the Veneration of SS Theodosij and Antonij of the Kievan Caves Monastery from the Eleventh to the Fifteenth Century,' PH D diss, Yale University, 1980
A. Zhukovsky

St Vladimir Institute

Saint Vladimir Institute (Institut im. sv. Volodymyra). A community center in Toronto. Established in 1951, the complex houses a student residence, museum, library, theater, and meeting and reception rooms as well as the offices of the *Ukrainian Canadian Research and Documentation Centre. The institute offers a variety of cultural and educational programs and makes space available for other associations to sponsor events. It is affiliated with the *Ukrainian Self-Reliance League.

Saint Vladimir University. See Kiev University.

Saint Volodymyr. See Volodymyr the Great.

St Volodymyr's Cathedral

Saint Volodymyr's Cathedral (Volodymyrskyi sobor; Sobor sv. Volodymyra). A cathedral in Kiev, built between 1862 and 1896. Its interior wall paintings and Byzantine revival architecture reflect some of the major currents in Ukrainian art and architecture of the middle and late 19th century, a period characterized by national rediscovery and the Romantic revival of historical styles.

The cathedral has an elongated cross-in-square plan. Three naves spring from apses in the east and are intersected by five transverse aisles. The apses and the first east aisle form the sanctuary. The next aisle, wider than the others and similar in dimension to the central nave, forms the transept. The westernmost aisle forms the narthex. There are balconies over the side naves and west aisles. The cathedral is topped by a series of Byzantine-like domes and barrel vaults corresponding to the plan divisions below. A large central dome on a tall drum is located over the crossing and is surrounded by four smaller domes over the adjacent side naves. Two short towers with domes are located over the narthex. The exterior walls are heavily loaded with ornamentation and marked with buttresses and three squat entry pavilions, one attached to the narthex, and the other two to each of the transepts.

In the stylistic treatment of the cathedral, its architects hoped to renew the traditions of Kievan Rus' architecture, but the result is an eclectic and Romantic rather than authentic version of the architecture of Byzantium or Kievan Rus'. In the exterior ornamentation, for example, motifs have been borrowed from many Eastern sources, most apparently from the Byzantine church architecture of early Bulgaria.

O. *Beretti is generally credited with the cathedral's final design, but because of many problems, especially shortages of funds and, later, structural defects, many other architects were involved before and after him. The first design, a wider cross-in-square plan with 13 domes, was prepared by I. Shtrom in 1859. This design was altered in 1861 by P. Sparro, who made a narrower plan with seven domes. In 1862 an essentially new design was prepared by Beretti. Full construction finally began in 1872. In 1875 R. Bernhardt made significant structural revisions to the design, and in 1876 V. Nikolaev was given the responsibility of overseeing the project to its final completion.

The paintings and decorations, executed between 1885 and 1896 by many leading Ukrainian and Russian artists, loosely follow the pictorial program of *Byzantine art and church decoration. The Russian painter V. Vasnetsov, together with teachers and pupils of the *Kiev Drawing School (eg, S. *Kostenko, O. Kurinny, M. *Pymonenko, V. Zamyrailo), is responsible for much of the work, most notably *The Baptism of Volodymyr, The Baptism of Rus', The Blessedness of Paradise*, and paintings on the columns and pilasters. By far the most striking is Vasnetsov's *Mother of God* in the central apse, a monumental mural charged with mystery, showing the influence of the new symbolist movement. Others who contributed to the interior of the cathedral include M. Nesterov, W. *Kotarbinski, P. Świedomski, A. *Prakhov, and M. *Vrubel.

Since the 1930s the cathedral has held the relics of the 4th-century Greek martyr St Barbara and the 15th-century Kievan metropolitan Makarios III. During the Second World War much of it was damaged. After the war, through donations from parishioners and state aid, it was extensively repaired and restored. Since 1943 it has been the cathedral of the Russian (from 1991, Ukrainian) Orthodox church's Kiev metropoly and the principal functioning church of Kiev.

BIBLIOGRAPHY

Beretti, A. *O stroiushchemsia sobore vo imia sv. Vladimira v Kieve* (Kiev 1884)
Dedlov, V. *Kievskii Vladimirskii sobor i ego khudozhestvennyia tvortsy* (Moscow 1901)
Kul'zhenko, S. *Sobor sviatago Vladimira v Kieve* (Kiev 1915)
Tsar'ova, M. *Kam'ianyi svidok* (Kiev 1968)

W. Daschko

Saint-Germain, Treaty of. A treaty signed between the Allies and Austria in the French town of St-Germain-en-Laye on 10 September 1919. One of the treaties ending the First World War, it recognized the dissolution of the Austro-Hungarian monarchy and the creation of the republics of Austria, Hungary, and Czechoslovakia as well as the Kingdom of Serbs, Croats, and Slovenes (from October 1929, Yugoslavia). The terms of the treaty transferred Bukovyna to Rumania and Transcarpathia to Czechoslovakia. Galicia was ceded by Austria to the Allies for their disposition. The cultural rights of all minorities living in Rumania and Czechoslovakia were to be guaranteed by Articles 10–13 of the League of Nations. The treaty recognized the autonomous status of Transcarpathia within Czechoslovakia; it was to possess its own diet, with 40 members, which would exercise jurisdiction over local matters of administration, language, education, and religion. Articles 10–13 of the St-Germain treaty were inserted into the constitution of the Czechoslovakian republic of 29 February 1920, although the territorial limits of Transcarpathia had not been defined, and the dates for the implementation of autonomy were not specified.

Saints. After the Christianization of Ukraine, the Ukrainian church initially venerated the saints of the Byzantine church. It soon began to recognize some saints of the Roman church, particularly those in the calendar of Western Slavic churches (eg, Viacheslav). The early Ukrainian church also venerated *St Cyril and *St Methodius, the original missionaries to the Slavs, who were not recognized by Byzantium. All saints were commemorated on the appropriate day, as recorded in the church calendar (*misiatseslov* or menaion). The Ukrainian church also encouraged the development of cults of its own saints.

The first native Rus' saints were *Saints Borys and Hlib, the martyred sons of Volodymyr the Great, who were canonized in the 11th century. Olha and Volodymyr were canonized by Metropolitan Ilarion ca 1037–50, although they were not assigned a feast day until later (Volodymyr's was set only in 1254 or 1263). *St Theodosius of the Caves (d 1074) was canonized in 1108, and *St Anthony of the Caves in the early 13th century. The early monks buried in the Kievan Cave Monastery (approx 118 in all), many of whom are known only by their first names, were collectively canonized by Metropolitan P. Mohyla in 1643, during services held on 28 August and 28 September. The earliest Ukrainian saints were often monks who devoted themselves to caring for the sick (eg, Ahapii, Damian of the Caves). Others were secular figures or churchmen involved in other work, eg, *St Kuksha (a missionary); *Nestor the Chronicler; *Olimpii (an icon painter, d 1114); and *Sviatoslav (Sviatosha), prince of Chernihiv (d 1143). *Iurodyvi* or 'fools for Christ,' persons who were known for their remarkable piety but also their aberrant behaviour, were rarely beatified in medieval Ukraine, although they were often venerated in Muscovy. A large number of church hierarchs became saints, beginning with Stefan, bishop of Volodymyr-Volynskyi (d 1094); *Yefrem, bishop of Pereiaslav (d 1098); Teoktyst, bishop of Chernihiv (d 1123); and *Cyril of Turiv (d 1189). Early secular saints include Prince *Mstyslav (Fedir, d 1132), son of Volodymyr Monomakh; Princess Anna (d 1113), daughter of Vsevolod I Yaroslavych; Prince Mstyslav (Yurii, d 1180), great-grandson of Volodymyr Monomakh; and *Mykhail Vsevolodovych, prince of Chernihiv, who was martyred with the boyar Teodor by the Tatars in 1246.

Later saints include *Petro (d 1326), the metropolitan of Kiev, who was born in Volhynia, and Ivan of Suceava, martyred in Akkerman (both from the 14th century); and Prince Fedir (Teodosii) of Ostrih, killed by Tatars in 1497, and Princess Yuliiana Olshanska (d 1540), whose remains are associated with a number of miracles (both from the 15th–16th centuries).

After the Church Union of *Berestia the Catholic church recognized Y. *Kuntsevych as a saint (d 1623, canonized 1867). Orthodox saints from this period include Afanasii, the hegumen of Brest, who was martyred by the Poles for his support of B. Khmelnytsky; Yov, the miracle worker of Pochaiv (d 1651); Makarii, hegumen of Ovruch and Kaniv, who was killed by the Turks in 1678; T. *Uhlytsky, archbishop of Chernihiv (d 1696); D. *Tuptalo, metropolitan of Rostov (d 1709); and Y. *Horlenko, bishop of Bilhorod (d 1754). Several Ukrainian Orthodox saints were missionaries in Siberia, among them Ioan *Maksymovych, metropolitan of Tobolsk (d 1715); I. *Kulchytsky, bishop of Irkutsk (d 1731); and S. Krystalevsky, bishop of Irkutsk (d 1771).

Most saints canonized during the Princely era, and some from afterward (eg, the Vilnius martyrs Ivan, Antin, and Evstafii), were recognized by both the Orthodox and Uniate churches (with some exceptions in the 17th–19th centuries). After the Union of Berestia the Ukrainian Catholic church was bound by the process of canonization imposed by Pope Urban VIII. Under this system, when an individual is beatified his or her cult is initially celebrated locally, and only later can full canonization occur. The recognition of a saint to be revered by the entire Catholic world is the pope's prerogative. With the absorption of the Ukrainian Orthodox church by the Russian Orthodox church in the 18th century, the right of canonization was claimed to be the special right of the Russian Holy Synod. The Orthodox church in Ukraine commemorated only those saints canonized by the Holy Synod who were of Ukrainian origin.

Today both Ukrainian churches recognize the same saints, with few exceptions. Feast days are observed for each saint, and special services are held in honor of particular saints, as well as pilgrimages to their burial places or to monasteries and churches named after them. With the imposition of Soviet rule in Ukraine, authorities forbade public celebration of saints' days, destroyed their icons and statues, and discouraged the custom of naming children after them. (See also *Hagiography.)

BIBLIOGRAPHY
Golubinskii, E. *Istoriia kanonizatsii sviatykh v Russkoi Tserkvi* (Moscow 1902)
Fedotov, G. *Sviatye drevnei Rusi (X–XVII st.)* (New York 1960)
Dublians'kyi, A. *Ukraïns'ki sviati* (Munich 1962)
Ilarion [Ohiienko, I.]. *Kanonizatsiia sviatykh v Ukraïns'kii Tserkvi* (Winnipeg 1965)

I. Korovytsky, M. Vavryk

Saints Borys and Hlib. The first saints to be canonized in Kievan Rus'. The two princes were killed in 1015 by their elder brother, Prince Sviatopolk I, during the succession struggle following the death of their father, *Volodymyr the Great. Their older brother, *Yaroslav the Wise, thereupon presented his struggle for power with Sviatopolk as a crusade to avenge the fratricide. After he came to power, Yaroslav actively sought the canonization of the princes, which was finally realized ca 1068. Meanwhile the memory of Borys and Hlib had captured the imagination of the Rus' population, in large measure because of accounts of the calmness and resignation with which they had accepted their deaths. An account of their murders, *Skazaniie i strast' i pokhvala sviatuiu muchenyku Borysa i Hliba*, is one of the oldest monuments of Ukrainian literature. The two saints have remained popular figures in Ukrainian religious thought. They are commemorated annually in both the Ukrainian Orthodox and Catholic churches on 6 August (24 July OS).

Saints Borys and Hlib Cathedral (Borysohlibskyi sobor). A cathedral built in Chernihiv in 1120–3 (or in the 1170s, according to some sources) as the family church and burial place of the Chernihiv princes. The cruciform, one-story structure had three naves, three apses, and six columns. Three burial niches were built into both the southern and northern walls of the narthex and the main circumference. Stairs to the choir balcony were built into the western wall. The façades had arching bands of ceram-

ss Borys and Hlib (late-13th-century icon)

ss Borys and Hlib Cathedral

ic decorations and a series of small decorative niches. The interior was decorated with light-colored frescoes and a colorful ceramic-tile and mosaic floor. Excavations have uncovered the remains of the gallery, fragments of two finely sculpted stone capitals, and the cornerstone of a portal with a teratological Romanesque carving depicting the pagan god Simarhlo as a dog-bird. The cathedral was rebuilt in the early 17th and again in the 19th century. From 1627 to 1659 it served as a Polish Dominican church. A campanile was added in 1672, and in the early 18th century the cathedral had five cupolas. It was heavily damaged during the Second World War and poorly restored in 1952–8 under the direction of M. Kholostenko. The ornate silver Royal Gates of the cathedral's 17th-century iconostasis are preserved in the cathedral.

Saints Peter and Paul (Sviati Petro i Pavlo). Two apostles who figure prominently in Ukrainian religious belief and whose feast day on 12 July (29 June OS) was observed as a major holiday. In Ukrainian Christian iconography Peter is portrayed as the gatekeeper of heaven, and Paul is the bearer of a sword or book. They are also regarded as plowers and protectors of fields, probably because their feast day coincides with the beginning of harvesting in Ukraine. The feast day itself was preceded by a fast (*petrivka*), during which women sang *petrivchani* songs and whitewashed and decorated their houses. The feast was celebrated with a church service, followed by a family meal and group games.

Sak, Liudmyla, b 16 September 1910 in Beirut, Lebanon, d 25 October 1985 in Kiev. Art scholar. A graduate of the Kiev State Art Institute (1930), she began teaching there in 1946. She wrote scholarly and popular articles on Ukrainian and Western European art and books on composition in sculpture (1959, with M. Helman), sculpture (1960), 17th-century Flemish painting (1970), and sculpture (1971).

Sakhalin Island [Saxalin]. An island off the Pacific coast of the Russian FR situated between the Seas of Japan and Okhotsk. With an area of 76,400 sq km it constitutes most of Sakhalin oblast (which also incorporates the Kurile Islands). Its terrain is largely mountainous and it is heavily (60 percent) forested. Temperatures range from 12 to 15°C in July and from –10 to –20°C in January. Its annual precipitation is 400–750 mm. In 1855–75 it was jointly held by the Russian Empire and Japan, and then in 1875–1905, by the Russian Empire alone. In 1905 the southern half was ceded to Japan. In 1945 the whole again came under Russian (Soviet) control; the island has been intensively colonized since then. From the mid-19th century it was used by the Russian Empire as a site for exiles and forced labor. In 1926 there were 11,000 inhabitants on the northern end of the island. In 1959 the population of Sakhalin oblast (including the sparsely inhabited Kuriles) was 649,000; it rose to 710,000 by 1989. Most (78 percent) of its inhabitants live in the city of Yuzhno-Sakhalinsk. According to the 1989 census Ukrainians made up 6.5 percent (46,000) of the island's population. Of those, 17,300 (37 percent) claimed Ukrainian as their native tongue.

Sakhnenko, Danylo [Saxnenko], b 1875 in Katerynoslav, d 1930 in Kharkiv. One of the first Ukrainian cameramen. In 1906 he operated a cinema-show booth in Katerynoslav, and in 1908 he became a chronicler for the

French firm Pater, with which he made the short documentaries *Povin' na Dnipri* (The Flood on the Dnieper) and *Katerynoslav*. He recorded the Sadovsky's Theater performances of *Natalka Poltavka* (Natalka from Poltava) and *Naimychka* (The Hired Girl) in 1911 and of *Bohdan Khmel'nyt'skyi* in 1914. In 1912 he established the cinema atelier Rodina in Katerynoslav and filmed *Obloha i oborona Zaporozhzhia* (The Siege and Defense of Zaporizhia) and *Liubov Andriia* (Andrew's Love, based on N. Gogol's *Taras Bul'ba*). In 1921 he took part in the organization of the cinema laboratory at the All-Ukrainian Photo-Cinema Administration, and from 1925 he made newsreels in Kharkiv.

Sakhnivka settlements. Multi-occupational settlements near Sakhnivka, Korsun-Shevchenkivskyi raion, Cherkasy oblast. Excavations in the early 20th century and in 1949 revealed a *Zarubyntsi culture settlement, three early Slavic (7th–8th century) settlements, and a Rus' manor-fortress, destroyed during the Mongol invasion. A cache of Kievan Rus' valuables was found in the area of the fortress in the late 19th century.

Sakhno-Ustymovych, Mykola. See Ustymovych, Mykola.

Sakhnovshchyna [Saxnovščyna]. IV-16. A town smt (1986 pop 9,400) and a raion center in Kharkiv oblast. A workers' settlement, it was named after the local landowner when the Kostiantynohrad–Lozova railway line was built in 1897–1900. Today the town has a canning factory (est 1957), a building-materials plant, and a tractor repair plant.

Olena Sakhnovska: *Witch* (woodcut)

Sakhnovska, Olena [Saxnovs'ka], b 15 May 1902 in Kiev, d 28 March 1958 in Moscow. Graphic artist. She studied at S. Nalepinska's xylography studio (1921–4) and under I. Pleshchynsky at the Kiev State Art Institute (1927–9). In 1925 she joined the *Association of Revolutionary Art of Ukraine. To escape the Stalinist terror in Ukraine she moved to Moscow in 1934. Sakhnovska specialized in printmaking and book illustrating and created mostly xylographs until 1936, after which she turned to lithographs. The influence of S. Nalepinska is evident in her early woodcuts, such as *Listening to the Radio* (1927) and *Return from the Front* (1927). She produced several series, such as 'Woman in the Revolution' (1930–2), 'T.H. Shevchenko' (1934), and 'Donbas' (1934–5). Her best-known lithographs are the cycles 'Gorky's Places in Ukraine' (1939–41), 'Kiev in 1944' (1944), and 'Old Lviv' (1946). In her book illustrations she developed her own style based on 16th- to 18th-century Ukrainian traditions. She illustrated editions of N. Gogol's works (1928–9), Lesia Ukrainka's *Lisova pisnia* (The Forest Song, 1930), and works by Soviet Ukrainian writers such as P. Panch, O. Kopylenko, and I. Mykytenko. She also designed woodcuts and etched bookplates. A catalog of a retrospective exhibition of her works was published in Kiev in 1963.

Sakhnovsky-Onykevych, Paisii [Saxnovs'kyj-Onykevyč, Pajisij], b ?, d 1626. Uniate church hierarch. As archimandrite of the Minsk monastery he signed the Church Union of *Berestia (1596). He later served as archimandrite of Kobryn and bishop of Pinsk (1603), where he defended the Uniate church against the Orthodox. He was the first head of the monastery in Byten, Volhynia (1607), and initiated a chronicle that contains valuable information about the early history of the Basilian order in Ukraine.

Sakovych, Iryna [Sakovyč], b 6 December 1926 in Slutsk, Belarus. Ceramic artist and art scholar. A graduate of the Moscow Institute of Applied and Decorative Arts (1952), she makes majolica and porcelain vases, tea sets, and cups. She has contributed articles on art to Ukrainian journals and the chapters on ceramics and artistic glass to the AN URSR (now ANU) history of Ukrainian art (vol 6, 1968) and has written a book on the ceramic folk sculpture of Soviet Ukraine (1970).

Sakovych, Kasiian [Sakovyč, Kasijan] (secular name: Kallist), b ca 1578 in Potylych, Rava Ruska district, Galicia, d 1647 in Cracow. Churchman, philosopher, and polemicist. He studied at the Zamostia and Cracow academies before being tonsured in 1620. He served as rector of the Kiev Epiphany Brotherhood School (1620–4) and then as chaplain for the local Orthodox brotherhood in Lublin. He soon joined the Uniate church and became archimandrite of the Dubno Monastery (1626–39). In 1640 he joined the Roman Catholic church and entered the Augustinian order in Cracow.

Sakovych was a gifted writer. His *Aristoteles problemata, albo Pytania o przyrodzeniu człowieczym* (Aristotle's Problem, or the Question of the Nature of Humanity, 1620) and *Tractat o Duszu* (A Tract on the Soul, 1625), both of which were published in Ukrainian translation with commentaries in *Pam'iatky bratskykh shkil na Ukraïni, kinets' XVI–pochatok XVII st.* (Monuments of the Brotherhood Schools in Ukraine, Late 16th–Early 17th Centuries, 1988), were prob-

Engraving of the capture of Kaffa in Kasiian Sakovych's *Virsh ...* (1622)

Panas Saksahansky   Oleksander Salikovsky

ably the first surveys of Western philosophy by a Ukrainian author. His *Virshi na zhalosnyi pohreb zatsnoho rytsera Petra Konashevycha Sahaidachnoho* (Poems for the Grievous Funeral of the Noble Knight Petro Konashevych Sahaidachny, 1622), written in Ukrainian in a baroque syllabic style, was recited as an elegy at Hetman P. *Sahaidachny's funeral by students of the brotherhood school. In this work he portrayed the Cossacks as knights defending Orthodoxy. After his conversion to Roman Catholicism he wrote several polemical attacks on Orthodoxy and Uniatism, including *Sobor Kiiowski schismaticki* (The Schismatic Sobor in Kiev, 1641); *Kalendarz stary ...* (The Old Calendar ..., 1642), where he criticized the retention of the Julian calendar among Ukrainians; and *Epanorthosis, albo Perspektiwa ...* (Epanorthosis, or Perspective ..., 1642), where he criticized the Byzantine church rite and described Ukrainian religious practices as superstitious. This last book drew a sharp response from both Orthodox (probably P. Mohyla) and Uniate (P. Oransky-Voina) polemicists.

Saksahan River [Saksahan']. A left-bank tributary of the Inhul River that flows through Dnipropetrovske oblast. It is 144 km long and drains a basin area of 2,025 sq km. The river is joined to the Dnieper by the Dnieper–Kryvyi Rih Canal. Kryvyi Rih is situated at its mouth. Its waters are used for industry (in the *Kryvyi Rih Iron-ore Basin) and irrigation.

Saksahansky, Panas [Saksahans'kyj] (pseud of Panas Tobilevych), b 15 May 1859 in Kamiano-Kostuvate, Yelysavethrad county, Kherson gubernia, d 17 September 1940 in Kiev. Theatrical director and actor; brother of M. *Sadovsky, I. *Karpenko-Kary, and M. *Sadovska-Barilotti. After completing his education in Yelysavethrad (1880) he worked in M. Starytsky's (from 1883), M. Kropyvnytsky's (1885), and Sadovsky's (1888) troupes; led his own *Saksahansky's Troupe (1890–1909); worked in T. Kolesnychenko's troupe (1910–15) and in the *Society of

Ukrainian Actors (1915–16); directed the *People's Theater (1918–22); worked in the Zankovetska Theater (intermittently in 1922–6); and, from 1927, led a touring troupe with Sadovsky. Saksahansky was an actor of the realistic-psychological school, gifted in gesture and mimicry, whose most famous roles were in satirical comedies, such as I. Kotliarevsky's *Natalka from Poltava*, Karpenko-Kary's *Sto tysiach* (One Hundred Thousand), *Martyn Borulia*, and *Palyvoda XVIII st* (A Rogue of the 18th Century), and Starytsky's *Za dvoma zaitsiamy* (After Two Hares). His best heroic-moralist role was Ivan in Karpenko-Kary's *Suieta* (Vanity). In Ukrainian translation he staged F. Schiller's *Die Räuber*, K. Gutzkow's *Uriel Acosta* (both in 1918), and W. Shakespeare's *Othello* (1926). He is the author of two plays, *Lytsemiry* (Hypocrites, 1908) and *Shantrapa* (Rabble, 1914), and two books of memoirs, *Po shliakhu zhyttia* (On the Path of Life, 1935) and *Iz proshlogo ukrainskogo teatra* (From the Past of the Ukrainian Theater, 1938). Biographies of him have been written by V. Chahovets (1951), B. Tobilevych (1957), L. Melnychuk-Luchko (1958), and L. Stetsenko (1959), and collections of memoirs about him were published in 1939 and 1984.

V. Revutsky

Saksahansky's Troupe. A populist-ethnographic *touring theater troupe founded in 1890 and led by P. *Saksahansky and I. *Karpenko-Kary. Originally the Society of Russian and Little Russian Actors, it changed its name many times, finally to the Society of Ukrainian Actors under the directorship of P. Saksahansky in 1907. Among the actors were M. Sadovska-Barilotti (d 1891), L. Linytska, S. Tobilevych, O. Shevchenko, D. Mova (also choir director), P. Vasylkivsky, R. Chychorsky, H. Borysohlibska, L. Rozsudov-Kuliabko, K. Pozniachenko, and S. Pankivsky. The repertoire consisted primarily of all 18 Karpenko-Kary plays, some of them premiered by the troupe. Karpenko-Kary, also an actor, was in charge of stage design, costumes, the library, and administration. Other premieres included those of M. Starytsky's *Bohdan Khmel'nyts'kyi*, I. Franko's *Ukradene shchastia* (Stolen Happiness), B. Hrinchenko's *Na hromads'kii roboti* (Doing Community Work), and L. Yanovska's *Dzvin do tserkvy sklykaie ...* (The Bell Calls to Church ...). Besides Ukraine, the troupe toured St Petersburg (1890), the Volga region (1895), the Crimea (1899), Warsaw (1903), Minsk (1908), Bessarabia, Moscow, the Don region, and the Kuban. Karpenko-Kary died in 1907, Saksahansky left the troupe in 1909, and it disbanded in 1910.

Saky. VIII-14. A city (1989 pop 34,000) on Saky Lake and a raion center in the Crimea. It sprang up at the end of the 18th century, when a salt industry, based on the salt water of Saky Lake, was established. In 1827 the first mud therapy clinic was set up. In 1952 the town was granted city status. Today Saky is a health resort and industrial center. The mud and brine from Saky Lake and local mineral water are used in treating arthritis and gastrointestinal, nervous, and gynecological disorders. The main industrial enterprises are a chemical plant, a mineral-water bottling factory, and a winery.

Saky Lake. VIII-14. A saltwater lake in western Crimea oblast. The lake is 5.5 km long, up to 3 km wide, and 1.5 m deep, with a surface area of 8.1 sq km. It has been artificially divided into two halves. Water from the eastern half (salt content, 19 percent) is used for curative baths; the water in the western half (salt content, 30 percent) serves as a source of table salt. The lake is separated from Kalamitska Bay in the Black Sea by a spit of gravel and sand 800 m wide, through which a canal has been built. The city of Saky is situated on the north shore of the lake.

Sal River. A left-bank tributary of the Don River formed by the confluence of the Dzhurak-Sal and the Kara-Sal. The river flows through Rostov oblast. It is 776 km long and drains a basin area of 21,100 sq km. It is fed by snow, and its waters are used in irrigation. The upper stretch of the river dries up seasonally.

Elia Sala: some of the sculptures adorning V. Horodetsky's residence in Kiev

Sala, Elia, b April 1864 in Milan, d 10 January 1920 in Gorla-Precotto, Italy. Italian sculptor. In the late 19th and early 20th centuries he worked in Kiev, where he carved decorative sculptures and taught at the Kiev Art School. His works include the façade composition and two lions outside the present Kiev Museum of Ukrainian Art (1897–1905), the sculptures on St Nicholas's Roman Catholic Church (1899–1909, now the Republican Building of Organ and Chamber Music), the fantastic sculptures on the façade of V. Horodetsky's residence (1902), the dragons on the State Bank building (1902–5), and portraits, such as the marble *Portrait of a Girl* (1903–5).

Salamon Shchasny, V. [Salamon Ščasnyj], b 1834, d 1900. Folklorist and publicist. While serving as a Greek Catholic priest in Galicia, he collected folk songs and published then as *Kolomyiky i shumky* (1864). These songs were reprinted by Ya. Holovatsky in his collection *Narodnye pesni Galitskoi i Ugorskoi Rusi* (Folk Songs of Galician and Hungarian Ruthenia, 4 vols, 1878). Salamon also contributed to the newspapers *Slovo*, *Novyi prolom*, and *Russkaia rada*.

Salesians (*saleziiany*). The popular name of the Society of St Francis de Sales, a Catholic religious order established in 1859 by J. Bosco for the purpose of providing a Christian education for youths. A Ukrainian branch of the Salesians was established in 1932 on the initiative of Bishop M. *Charnetsky. Shortly thereafter several Ukrainian students from the Peremyshl gymnasium went for training in Italy. After the Second World War a group of Ukrainian Salesians was sent to Argentina (Buenos Aires and Alem) for missionary work among Ukrainian emigrants there; others remained in Europe to run the St Josaphat Ukrainian Pontifical College. In 1980, 20 Ukrainian priests were members of the Salesian order, including Bishop A. Sapeliak in Argentina.

Salhyr Irrigation System. Constructed in 1952–62, it was one of the first irrigation systems in the Crimea. Its chief source of water is the Salhyr Reservoir. The water needs to be pumped at only a few points along the system; elsewhere it flows by gravity. The irrigation system serves 16 farms, which grow fruits and vegetables for the city of Symferopil, and covers an area of 8,100 ha.

Salhyr River. The largest river in the Crimea. It is 204 km long and drains a basin area of 3,750 sq km. It flows northward from a source on the northern slopes of the Crimean Mountains and empties into Syvash Lake. During the summer the upper reaches of the river dry up. A reservoir has been built on the river just outside Symferopil.

Salikovsky, Oleksander [Salikovs'kyj], b 13 March 1866 in Staryi Potik, Vinnytsia county, Podilia gubernia, d 22 November 1925 in Warsaw. Journalist and civic and political leader. Barred from university by the authorities, he worked as a rural teacher, private tutor, and gubernial civil servant. In 1904 he joined the staff of the paper *Kievskie otkliki*, and eventually he became its editor. In 1910 he moved to Moscow, where he edited *Ukrainskaia zhizn'* with S. Petliura, and later, to Rostov-na-Donu, where he edited *Priazovskii krai* (1913–15). After returning to Moscow he resumed editing *Ukrainskaia zhizn'* (1915–17) and presided over the Ukrainian Council there. In September 1917 he was appointed commissioner of Kiev gubernia. As a leading member of the Ukrainian Party of Socialists-Federalists he sat on the Central Rada and the Little Rada. Under the UNR Directory he worked in the internal affairs ministry and edited the daily *Trybuna* (1918–19) and the monthly *Literaturno-naukovyi vistnyk* (1919). In May 1920 he was appointed minister of internal affairs in V. Prokopovych's cabinet, and in October, deputy prime minister. After emigrating to Poland, he edited the daily *Ukraïns'ka trybuna* (1921–2), the monthly *Trybuna Ukraïny* (1923), and the weekly *Ukraïns'ka sprava* in Warsaw.

Saline soils. Soils with a raised content of dissolved salts (in excess of 0.25 percent). The salts are most commonly chlorides or compounds of sodium and sulfur oxides. When saline soils contain dissolved salts in excess of 1 percent, they are called solonchaks; at lower concentrations they are referred to as saline soils. Field crops grow unimpeded in soils the total salt concentration of which does not exceed 0.25 percent, or the sodium concentration of which does not rise above 0.05 percent.

Saline soils occur mostly in poorly drained lowlands of deserts, semideserts, and steppes. In Ukraine they are common on the low river terraces of the left-bank tributaries of the Dnieper River, in the Black Sea Lowland, and in the floodplains of all the steppe rivers. Together with the solonchaks the saline soils occupy 4,456,000 ha in Ukraine, or 7.4 percent of the republic's land area. In the past, saline soils occupied a smaller area in Ukraine. With the rapid expansion of irrigation in Ukraine in the 1960s, however, the level of mineralized groundwater was raised, and correspondingly, the area occupied by saline soils was increased, by the use of unlined distribution canals (which caused seepage), the lack of drainage facilities in the irrigated fields, and overwatering (there was no charge for irrigation water). A concerted effort is needed to improve or even rebuild the irrigation systems and to initiate a program of soil melioration.

Salman, Oleksandr [Sal'man], b 12 September 1914 in Petrograd, d 16 July 1971 in Lviv. Scenery designer. He studied at the Higher State Art and Technical Institute in Leningrad (1929–31) and then worked at Russian theaters until 1939; at the Odessa, Kiev, and Kharkiv opera theaters (1939–46); and at the Lviv Opera Theater (from 1946), where he became principal stage designer in 1961. He designed productions such as A. Kos-Anatolsky's *Orysia* (1964) and H. Maiboroda's *Arsenal* (1967).

Liudvyh Salo   Gen Volodymyr Salsky

Salo, Liudvyh [Sal'o, Ljudvyh], b 1853, d 1915. Pedagogue; specialist in classical philology and mathematics. He taught at the gymnasium in Kolomyia from 1893 and at the Academic Gymnasium of Lviv from 1905. In 1894–8 he headed the Shkilna Pomich society. He was a member of the Teachers' Hromada in Lviv and served as director of the Ukrainian private secondary school section of the *Provincial School Union from 1911.

Salsk [Sal'sk]. VII-22. A city (1990 pop 61,000) on the Srednii Egorlyk River and a raion center in Rostov oblast, Russia. When it was granted city status in 1926, the census showed that 38.9 percent of its population was Ukrainian. Today Salsk is a railway junction and an industrial center. Its largest plants are a foundry and brick, textile, and footwear factories.

Salsky, Volodymyr [Sal's'kyj], b 28 July 1883 in Ostrih, Volhynia gubernia, d 4 October 1940 in Warsaw. Senior staff officer. A graduate of the Nikolai Military Academy of the General Staff in St Petersburg (1912), during the First World War he served in the Russian army as division chief of staff and operations officer on corps and army staffs. In 1917, as a lieutenant colonel, he joined the UNR Army and served as chief of staff at several headquarters. In 1918–19 he was a member of the General Staff and in May 1919 became commander of the Zaporozhian Corps which liberated Kiev on 30 August. In September 1919 Salsky took command of the UNR Army, but two months later he resigned because of failing health. He served as defense minister of the UNR government-in-exile in 1920–1 and 1924–40. His highest rank was brigadier general.

Salt industry. A branch of the *food industry that extracts and processes table salt. It is one of the oldest industries in Ukraine, and for a long time it was one of the most important industries. Table salt is mined in a rock form from subterranean deposits and extracted from seawater or natural brines through evaporation. Rock salt, which is crystalline sodium chloride, occurs widely in the form of rock masses and beds and is abundant in various rocks. Natural brines are usually found in underground pools. Table salt has been an element of the human diet and a trading commodity since ancient times. It is used widely in food preservation and animal feed and as a raw material in the chemical industry (in making acids, sodas, and sodium sulfate).

In Ukraine reserves are huge: in 1969 they were estimated at over 10 billion t. Salt deposits are found in the Donets Basin, the Dnieper-Donets Trough, Subcarpathia, and Transcarpathia. Salt is also found in the waters of the Black and Azov seas, especially in their numerous estuaries and shallow bays. The largest deposits in the Donets Basin – the *Artemivske rock salt deposits, the Slovianske soda deposit (3.3 billion t), and the deposits in the Kalmiius and Kazennyi Torets valleys – were formed in the early Permian period. The salt veins are 19–220 m wide and are found at depths of 124–1,110 m. The salt is very pure, with a sodium chloride concentration of 62–98 percent. In Subcarpathia a Miocene salt seam stretches some 230 km, from near Peremyshl in the north to Bukovyna in the southeast. The seam is up to 10 km wide, and veins 0.2–70 m wide are found at depths of 14–170 m.

The salt industry in Ukraine emerged first in Subcarpathia, which for a long time was the main salt-producing area, although its reserves were not great. The salt there was extracted by boiling. Today only small deposits, near Drohobych, Bolekhiv, and Dolyna, are exploited. In Transcarpathia salt is found in a Miocene seam stretching some 300 km from Prešov in the northwest to the Maramureş Basin in the southeast. Only a part of the seam crosses Ukrainian territory; the *Solotvyna rock salt deposits are the most important part of the seam. Despite the large seawater salt reserves in southern Ukraine, especially in the Crimea, little salt is extracted from seawater. Only three sources are exploited, the *Henicheske salt lakes, Syvash Lake, and Sysak Lake.

To the end of the 18th century. Evidence of salt making and trading in Ukraine dates back to ancient times. Greek colonies on the Black Sea exported salt to Greece. The Maramureş deposits were probably mined in Roman times. Salt extraction in Subcarpathia was mentioned in the Kievan Cave Patericon under the year 1096. Some of the salt was exported to central Ukraine, which also imported salt from the east (although the eastern salt routes were vulnerable to attack by nomadic tribes). The most common salt route was the *Solianyi route. Technologically the industry was comparatively well developed. Salt brine was lifted out of shallow mines in buckets attached to a wheel turned by horses. It was boiled in large cauldrons, and the salt residue was formed in conical molds called *holovazhni* (later *tovpky* or *topky*).

After the Polish annexation of Galicia salt production became almost the exclusive preserve of the crown. Most of the larger mines (see *Zhupa*) were owned by the king, and some of them were leased out or granted to nobles or churchmen. The salt industry provided the state with considerable revenues. Beginning in the 16th century the industry became more modernized and concentrated. In the 18th century Galicia in some years produced as much as a million centners of table salt. After meeting local demand Galicia exported much salt to Lithuania and Poland.

Salt production on the Black Sea coast was much less developed, although from the 16th century it was widely practiced by the Zaporozhian Cossacks. The cost of mining was negligible, but the expense of transporting the salt to large population centers was very high. Until 1774 many of the most important deposits were under Turkish or Tatar control.

In the 17th and 18th centuries salt mining began to gain some importance in Slobidska Ukraine. Some of the deposits there had been known since 1619. Initially, peasants and Cossacks worked the salt mines on a temporary basis. After B. Khmelnytsky's revolution permanent mining settlements were established. Tor (later *Slovianske) became an early center of the salt industry in the region. In the 1660s some of the mines were acquired by the Hetman treasury. The Cossack administration of Slobidska Ukraine, especially of the Izium regiment, promoted the development of the salt industry, but progress was often hindered by Tatar attacks and the policies of the Russian authorities. In 1715 the Russian government nationalized the salt factories in Tor, Bakhmut (Artemivske), and Spivakivka and made them crown factories (sometimes in cooperation with private salt producers) under the control of the Salt Administration in St Petersburg. The labor force consisted of state peasants. In the first half of the 18th century the factories produced some 8 million kg of salt annually. It was exported to the Hetmanate, southern Russia, and even Right-Bank Ukraine. In the second half of the century the production of the Tor and Bakhmut factories began to fall, because of competition from salt enterprises in the Crimea, Astrakhan, and the Don region, the depletion of wood fuels, and the low productivity of serf labor. In 1782 the factories were closed.

Late 18th century to 1917. When Galicia became part of the Austro-Hungarian Empire, its salt industry could not compete with that of other parts of the empire, and was undercut by the salt monopoly. Most of its *zhupy* were closed. At the beginning of the 20th century Galicia produced only about 50,000 t a year. The major salt factories were in Liatske, Drohobych, Stebnyk, Bolekhiv, Dolyna, Kalush, Deliatyn, Lanchyn, and Kosiv. The only salt mine in Transcarpathia in the period was in Solotvyna.

By contrast, in central and eastern Ukraine, especially in the southern regions, the salt industry grew quickly. Until 1861 salt production was controlled completely by the state, which later leased out the deposits to private producers. Production levels fluctuated greatly from year to year (in the mid-19th century between 1.5 and 3 million centners) but tended to move upward. The salt was transported to markets by wagon (120,000 wagons and 300,000 oxen were used in 1845) or by boat along the Dnieper. In 1869–80 some 1.6 million centners of salt were produced annually in the Crimea (representing 40 percent of the output of the Russian Empire). In 1881–7 the figure reached 2.7 million. Most of that salt was made by the evaporation of natural brines. Production around Odessa was much lower than in the Crimea. Great changes in the structure of the industry followed the discovery of major rock salt deposits near Bakhmut (Artemivske) in the late 1870s. That region quickly replaced the Crimea as the most important salt-producing area, although most of the mines and processing facilities were owned by foreign syndicates. In 1910, of every 1,000 t of salt produced in Russian-ruled Ukraine, 297 were produced in the Crimea, 555 in the Donets Basin, and 11 near Odessa. In 1913 almost 1 million t of table salt was produced within the current borders of the Ukrainian SSR; that amount represented approx one-half of the total output for the Russian Empire and some 6 percent of the world output.

Since 1918. Salt production in Subcarpathia in the interwar period continued to decline, and fell to 38,000 t annually in the late 1930s. The decline was due mainly to competition from Poland. Meanwhile, production from the Solotvyna deposits in Transcarpathia increased to 200,000 t, which met almost all the demand in Czechoslovakia. In Soviet Ukraine the trend in the salt industry was to concentrate production in the larger enterprises and modernize the technology of salt processing. The trend toward salt mining (as opposed to evaporation) as the major source of salt has also continued. In 1940 the total salt output of the Ukrainian SSR was 1.9 million t.

Following an abrupt drop in production during and immediately following the Second World War the industry was rebuilt and expanded. Total production reached over 3 million t in 1960, 5 million t in 1970, 5.9 million t in 1980, and over 8 million t in 1987. In 1970 Ukraine's output accounted for 41 percent of all Soviet production and 8 percent of total world production. Some three-quarters of that production was mined in Artemivske, and another 8 percent in Solotvyna. In 1972 Holovsil, a trust under the Ukrainian SSR Ministry of the Food Industry, co-ordinated the 16 enterprises that mined and processed salt in Ukraine. Problems of the industry are studied at the Scientific Research Institute of the Salt Industry in Artemivske.

BIBLIOGRAPHY
Skal'kovskii, A. *Opyt statisticheskogo opisaniia Novorossiiskogo kraia*, vol 2 (Odessa 1853)
Denisov, V. *Russkaia solepromyshlennost'* (St Petersburg 1912)

Osuchowski, W. *Gospodarka solna na Rusi Halickiej od* XVI *do* XVIII *w.* (Lviv 1930)

Isaievych, Ia. 'Solevarna promyslovist' Pidkarpattia v epokhu feodalizmu,' *Narysy z istorii tekhniky*, no. 7 (1961)

Dzens-Litovskii, A. 'Osnovnye tipy solianykh mestorozhdenii SSSR,' *Trudy Vsesoiuznogo nauchno-issledovatel'noho instituta solianoi promyshlennosti*, no. 4 (1962)

Kuntsevych, F. 'Z istorii solianykh syndykativ Krymu i Donbasu,' *Pytannia istorii narodiv* SRSR, no. 11 (1971)

V. Kubijovyč, O. Ohloblyn

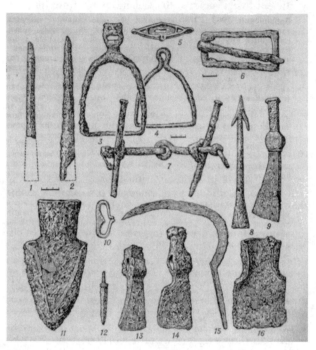

Iron artifacts of the Saltiv culture

Saltiv culture. An archeological culture of the 8th to 10th century that existed among the tribes of the Khazar kaganate along the Don and Donets Rivers and in the northern Caucasus, Azov, and middle Volga regions. It was named after a site discovered in Vovchanske county, Kharkiv gubernia, in 1900. Scholars have divided the Saltiv culture into two groups. The first lived in permanent agricultural settlements with surface dwellings, and practiced catacomb burial, including grave goods such as armor and weapons, pottery, and personal effects. The second group was composed of nomadic and seminomadic people who lived in makeshift camp sites with tentlike shelters and interred their dead without extensive grave goods. The Saltiv culture included *Alans in the forest-steppe and Bulgars in the steppe region; some members also lived in coastal centers such as Phanagoria and Sarkel. Excavations at culture sites have revealed dwellings, outbuildings, implements, pottery, and locally produced metal, stone, and wood items of high quality. Gold and silver coins as well as Byzantine and Oriental adornments testify to extensive trading activity. The onslaught of the *Pechenegs in the 10th century brought an end to the Saltiv culture. Scholars believe that after the fall of the Khazar kaganate in the latter part of that century some Saltiv culture tribes were incorporated into Kievan Rus'.

Salvini, Luigi, b 11 February 1911 in Milan, d 4 June 1957 in Rome. Italian Slavist; member of the Shevchenko Scientific Society from 1956. He graduated from Rome University and taught at the universities of Helsinki, Turku, and Ljubljana and, after the Second World War, the Higher Oriental Institute in Naples and the universities of Bari and Rome. Among his many works on Eastern European and Slavic literature and folk songs are two anthologies of Ukrainian stories in Italian translation, *Le quattro sciabole* (1940) and *L'Altopiano dei pastori* (1949). His translations of H. Kosynka, Yu. Lypa, M. Cheremshyna, V. Stefanyk, M. Khvylovy, and U. Samchuk were published in Italian journals.

Salzburg. A city (1988 pop 139,000) on the Salz River in Austria. In 1945–50, 4,000 to 8,000 Ukrainians lived in *displaced persons' camps in the city and the surrounding area. They were served by Catholic and Orthodox parishes, and maintained the weeklies *Novi dni* and *Promin'* and the daily *Ostanni novyny*. There were also a gymnasium and a number of cultural, educational, and sporting organizations, including a theatrical troupe led by H. Sovacheva. In 1951 Salzburg became the headquarters of the Ukrainian Central Relief Alliance in Austria. Today approx 265 Ukrainians live in the city and surrounding area. In Grödig, a nearby village, there is a Ukrainian cemetery, where 300 victims of the First World War (mainly evacuees from Volhynia) are buried.

Salzwedel. A city in Sachsen-Anhalt county, Germany, and the site of a German POW camp for soldiers of the Russian army in 1915–21. The camp held about 30,000 Ukrainians, for whom the *Union for the Liberation of Ukraine organized an educational and cultural program. The union's printing press in Salzwedel printed brochures and several papers: *Vil'ne slovo* (1916–19), the organ of camp organizations; *Selianyn* (1918); *Shliakh* (1919–20), the organ of the Ukrainian Military Sanitary Mission; and *Nove slovo* (1920), the organ of the Ukrainian People's party. Elementary and secondary courses were conducted in Ukrainian by interned officers, and a drama group and choir helped raise national consciousness among the soldiers.

Samara River. A left-bank tributary of the Dnieper River that flows through Donetske, Kharkiv, and Dnipropetrovske oblasts and empties into *Lenin Lake. The Samara is 311 km long and drains a basin area of 22,600 sq km. The river ices over from mid-December to mid-March and dries out in its upper reaches in the summer. It is used for industry, irrigation, and fishing. The industrial port city of Novomoskovkse is located 80 km from the mouth of the river.

Samara Saint Nicholas's Monastery (Samarskyi pustynno-mykolaivskyi manastyr). An Orthodox men's monastery on the Samara River near the settlement of Samarchuk (Novoselytsia, now part of Novomoskovske, Dnipropetrovske oblast). It was founded in 1602 as a small fortified monastery with a wooden church and a home for convalescing Cossacks on the territory of the Samara *palanka of the Zaporozhian Host. The original buildings were destroyed in the mid-17th century and then rebuilt in 1672. The Zaporozhian Host granted the monastery 18,500 ha of arable land, five mills, pasturelands, and forests to provide the Sich with food. It continued to serve as a retreat for sick and elderly Cossacks. After the destruction of the Sich in 1775, it was assigned to the Mezhyhiria Transfiguration Monastery. In 1787 it became independent once again, and in 1791 it came under the control of the eparchial bishop. Before the First World War it housed eight monks and a boys' school. The main church at the monastery, built in 1782, contained a valuable icon of the Mother of God and many church artifacts from the Zaporozhian era. The monastery was closed by the Soviet authorities in the 1920s.

Sambat. An old name of Kiev, or more precisely, of its fortress. The term is used by the Byzantine emperor Constantine VII Porphyrogenitus in his *De administrando imperio* (mid-10th century).

Sambir's town hall and market square (19th-century drawing)

Sambir. IV-4. A city (1989 pop 40,100) on the Dniester River and a raion center in Lviv oblast. When Staryi Sambir was destroyed by the Tatars in 1241, the survivors settled in the fortified settlement of Pohonych and renamed it Sambir, Novyi (New) Sambir, or Nove Misto (New Town), although the name Pohonych was used until the mid-15th century. Sambir was part of the Principality of Galicia-Volhynia (until 1349), the Polish Commonwealth (1387–1772), and the Austrian Empire (1772–1918). It was under Polish rule (1919–39) and finally became part of the Ukrainian SSR. In 1390 it was granted the rights of *Magdeburg law. In the 15th and 16th centuries it was an important trading and manufacturing town. Under Austrian and then Polish rule it was a county center. Today Sambir is an industrial and transportation center. Its factories produce radio parts, instruments, glass, furniture, clothes, and sugar and repair road-building machinery. Its chief architectural monuments are the Dominican monastery (1406), a Gothic Roman Catholic church (1530–68), Stephen Báthory's hunting lodge (16th century), the ruins of the town walls (16th–17th century), the city hall (1668) with a tall Renaissance tower, the theological seminary (1679), the Byzantine cathedral (1738, restored 1893–4), a Jesuit church (1751), an 18th-century park, and residential buildings of the 18th and 19th centuries. Recently the Les Kurbas Memorial Museum (1987) and the Boikiv-

shchyna Historical-Ethnographical Museum (1989) have been opened.

Sambir Brigade of the Ukrainian Galician Army (Sambirska [8] brygada UHA). A unit of the Third Corps of the UHA, formed in late January 1919 out of the Rudky, Hlyboka, and Krukenychi combat groups. Its first commander was Lt Col A. Kraus. In late May the Hlyboka and Krukenychi combat groups were separated from the rest of the brigade and were interned by the Czech army. In June 1919 the brigade consisted of four infantry battalions (under Lt A. Tarnavsky, Capt O. *Stanimir, Capt D. Bizanz, and Lt M. Pidhirny) and one artillery regiment (under Capt O. Bradner) from the Rudky Group and had a strength of 2,000 men. Its new commander was Maj K. Hoffman. On 31 August 1919 it was one of the first units to enter Kiev. In February 1920 the brigade was reorganized into the Eighth Galician Rifle Regiment of the Red Ukrainian Galician Army. In late April it left the Red Army, and its members were interned by the Poles.

Archbishop Volodymyr Samborsky

Samborsky, Volodymyr [Sambors'kyj], b 24 December 1882 in Kiev, d 1935 in Kiev. Archbishop of the Ukrainian Autocephalous Orthodox church (UAOC). After finishing theological studies in Uman and Kiev, he was ordained in 1902 and had become a district missionary for the Tarashcha region by 1907. He joined the UAOC in 1921 and was consecrated bishop of Lypovets (1923–5). He served as bishop of Zhytomyr (1925–6) before pressure by the Soviet authorities caused him to step down, but he resumed his duties in 1927 as bishop of Hlukhiv with responsibility for the Konotip region (to 1930) and archbishop of Vinnytsia (1930–2). After being forced once more from his post Samborsky remained under constant surveillance until 1935, when he returned to Kiev. He was arrested by the NKVD and shot.

Sambuk, Rostyslav, b 28 September 1923 in Kopatkevichy, Homel oblast, Belarus. Writer. He studied at the philological faculty of Tartu University until 1947. He is the author of many crime fiction novels in Ukrainian, such as *Iuvelir z vulytsi Kaputsyniv* (The Jeweler from Capuchin Street, 1966), *Valiza pana Vorobkevycha* (Mr Vorobkevych's Suitcase, 1970), *Seif* (The Safe, 1985), *Vybukh* (The Explosion, 1985), *Zhorstokyi lis* (The Cruel Forest, 1976), *Avtohraf dlia slidchoho* (Autograph for the Investigator, 1977), *Spe-*

kotnyi lypen' (Scorching July, 1979), and *Vel'vetovi dzhynsy* (Velvet Jeans, 1985). He has also written, in collaboration with Ye. Hutsalo, the documentary-style propaganda novels *Imeni Lenina* (Having Lenin's Name, 1974) and *Shchaslyva rodyna* (The Happy Family, 1976).

Samchevsky, Osyp [Samčevs'kyj], b 1799 in Liskonohy in the Novhorod-Siverskyi region, d 1887. Pedagogue. He taught at the Chernihiv Theological Seminary (see *Chernihiv College) and was inspector of the Novhorod-Siverskyi Gymnasium. His memoirs are published in the journal *Kievskaia starina*, vols 43–46.

Ulas Samchuk

Volodymyr Samiilenko

Samchuk, Ulas [Samčuk], b 20 February 1905 in Derman (now Ustenske), Ostrih county, Volhynia gubernia, d 9 July 1987 in Toronto. Writer and journalist. Samchuk was educated at the University of Breslau (now Wrocław, Poland) and at the Ukrainian Free University in Prague (1931). His literary career began in 1926 with short stories published in *Dukhovna besida* (Warsaw) and *Literaturno-naukovyi vistnyk*, which were later republished as the collection *Vidnaidenyi rai* (Rediscovered Paradise, 1936). He was editor of the Rivne newspaper *Volyn'* (1941–3), and he fled to Germany in 1944, where he headed the literary-artistic organization *MUR (1945–8). He emigrated to Canada after 1948 and became a longtime head of the *Slovo Association of Ukrainian Writers in Exile. Samchuk's prose is deeply rooted in the 19th-century realist tradition. His novels are broad-canvas chronicles of the Ukrainian experience in the 20th century. Themes progress from the difficult national and cultural nascence in the trilogy *Volyn'* (Volhynia, 1932, 1935, 1937), the novelette *Kulak* (1932), and the novel *Iunist' Vasylia Sheremety* (The Youth of Vasyl Sheremeta, 1946, 1947) to the Hutsul national struggle in *Hory hovoriat'* (The Hills Are Speaking, 1934), the devastating man-made famine in *Mariia* (1934), and the Second World War and forced Ukrainian labor in the trilogy *Ost* (East, 1948, 1957, 1982). He captured the struggle of the Ukrainian Insurgent Army in the novel *Choho ne hoït' vohon'* (What Fire Does Not Heal, 1959) and turned his attention to the plight of Ukrainian pioneers and later émigrés in *Na tverdii zemli* (On Solid Ground, 1967) and *Slidamy pioneriv: Epos ukraïns'koï Ameryky* (In the Footsteps of the Pioneers: The Saga of Ukrainian America, 1979). What his fiction did not encompass he captured in a series of memoirs: *Piat' po dvanadtsiatii* (Five after Twelve, 1954),

Na bilomu koni (On a White Horse, 1965), *Na koni voronomu* (On a Black Horse, 1975), and *Planeta Di-Pi* (The Planet of the DPs, 1979). An archive and museum devoted to his work was established in Toronto in 1988.

D.H. Struk

Samets, Petro [Samec'] (Sametz), b 4 June 1893 in Hleshchava, Terebovlia county, Galicia, d 6 February 1985 in Niagara Falls, Ontario. Ukrainian Orthodox priest. After emigrating to Canada in 1910, he graduated from Wesley College in Winnipeg and worked as a teacher. In 1920 he was ordained by Metropolitan Germanos and served as a missionary among Ukrainian settlers in the prairies, where he was instrumental in organizing new parishes. In 1938 he moved to Toronto, and after the war helped many new émigrés settle there.

Samiilenko, Ivan [Samijlenko], b 19 August 1914 near Poltava. Civic and political leader. Samiilenko completed a graduate degree in history at the Moscow Institute of History, Philosophy, and Literature in 1941, and taught at the Ukrainian Technical and Husbandry Institute at the DP camp in Regensburg, Germany, in 1945–9. He emigrated to the United States in 1949, completed his graduate studies at the University of New York, and taught at Long Island University in 1961–80. He was deputy premier of the *Government-in-exile of the Ukrainian National Republic from 1984 to 1988, and its premier from 1988 to 1992.

Samiilenko, Polina [Samijlenko], b 17 May 1891 in Vasylkiv, Kiev gubernia, d 1 December 1984 in Kiev. Actress. She completed study at the Lysenko Music and Drama School in Kiev (1915–17) and then joined Molodyi Teatr (1916–19) and the Franko New Drama Theater (1920–4). In 1924–33 she worked in various touring theaters in the Odessa, Podilia, and Donbas regions and in the Odessa Ukrainian Drama Theater (1928–30). In 1934–47 she was a leading actress in the Kiev Ukrainian Drama Theater. Her roles were mainly heroic-dramatic, including Yaroslavna in I. Dniprovsky's *Iablunevyi polon* (The Apple-Blossom Captivity) and the title role in G.B. Shaw's *Saint Joan*. Her memoirs are titled *Nezabutni dni horin'* (Unforgettable Days of Ardor).

Samiilenko, Stepan [Samijlenko], b 25 December 1906 in Stanislav, Kherson county, d 26 October 1977 in Zaporizhia. Linguist and educator. A graduate of the Kherson Institute of People's Education (1930), he taught at the Poltava, Luhanske, and Zaporizhia pedagogical institutes. He published over 110 works, including articles on the science of linguistics, the history of Ukrainian grammar, and the language of various writers. His most important work was *Narysy z istorychnoï morfolohiï ukraïns'koï movy* (Essays in the Historical Morphology of the Ukrainian Language, 2 vols, 1964, 1970). He coauthored the textbooks *Istorychna hramatyka ukraïns'koï movy* (A Historical Grammar of the Ukrainian Language, 1st edn 1957; 2nd edn 1962) and *Porivnial'na hramatyka ukraïns'koï ta rosiis'koï mov* (A Comparative Grammar of the Ukrainian and Russian Languages, 1961), and wrote the introduction to *Istoriia ukraïns'koï movy: Morfolohiia* (History of the Ukrainian Language: Morphology, 1978).

Samiilenko, Volodymyr [Samijlenko] (pseuds: Ivanenko, V. Poltavets, V. Syvenky, L. Sumny), b 3 February 1864 in Sorochyntsi, Myrhorod county, Poltava gubernia, d 12 August 1925 in Boiarka, Kiev oblast. Poet, dramatist, and translator. He belonged to the *Brotherhood of Taras. From 1905 he worked in Kiev for the newspapers *Hromads'ka dumka*, *Rada*, and *Shershen'*. During the period of Ukrainian statehood he served in the UNR Ministries of Education and Finance, and in 1919 he moved to Galicia with the UNR government. In 1924 he returned to Kiev, where he worked as an editor in a literary publishing house. He began to publish his verse in the Lviv *Zoria*, and from 1886 he published his poems in the almanacs *Skladka* and *Vatra* and in the journals *Pravda* and *Literaturno-naukovyi vistnyk* (LNV). His first collection, *Z poezii Volodymyra Samiilenka* (From the Poetry of Volodymyr Samiilenko), was published in Kiev in 1890; his second, *Ukraïni* (To Ukraine), which included poems written from 1884 to 1906, was published in 1906 in Lviv with an introduction by I. Franko. His unfinished poem, *Heia*, was published in part in *Literaturno-naukovyi vistnyk* (1922). In his lyric poetry Samiilenko expressed a high degree of idealism; quite a few of his poems are satirical (he wrote poems condemning ultra-patriotism, despotism, sellouts, and graphomania). He is the author of the dramatic works *Marusia Churaïvna* (1896), *U Haikhan-Beia* (At Haikan-Bey's, 1917), sections of the play *Drama bez horilky* (A Drama without Whiskey, 1895), and others. Samiilenko translated into Ukrainian Homer's *Iliad*, Dante's *Divine Comedy*, dramas by Molière, Tristan, P.-A. de Beaumarchais, and A. France, and poems by P.-J. de Béranger, G. Byron, and many others. His *Vybrani tvory* (Selected Works), which includes his autobiography, was published in Kiev in 1926; it was followed by *Vybrani poeziï* (Selected Poems, 1941, 1944, 1965) and *Tvory v dvokh tomakh* (Works in Two Volumes, 1958).

I. Koshelivets

Samizdat. See Samvydav.

Samofalov, Kostiantyn, b 12 November 1921 in Khutir Mykhailivskyi (now Druzhba), Novhorod-Siverskyi county, Chernihiv gubernia. Computer scientist. After completing his studies at the Kiev Polytechnical Institute in 1957, he taught there and in 1960 assumed Ukraine's first chair in computer technology at the institute. He has contributed to the study and the design of computer operating systems and data structures.

Samofalov, Viktor, b 31 January 1905 in Kiev, d 23 September 1973 in Kiev. Soviet historian. He graduated from the Kiev Institute of Social Education (1931) and completed courses for instructors of CP history (1932). He worked as a lecturer and CP activist in institutions of higher education in Kiev, Poltava, Cherkasy, and Tashkent until 1944. Then he worked at the Institute of Party History of the CC CPU (1945–9) and chaired the Department of CPSU History at the Higher Party School of the CC CPU (1949–73, professor from 1965). He was the author of *Komunistychna partiia Ukraïny v borot'bi za vidbudovu narodnoho hospodarstva, 1921–1925* (The CPU in the Struggle for the Rebuilding of the National Economy, 1921–5, 1963), a coauthor of *Narysy istoriï Komunistychnoï partiï Ukraïny* (Outlines of the History of the CPU, 1st–3rd edns, 1961–71), a member of the ed-

itorial board of *Ukraïns'kyi istorychnyi zhurnal* (1957–62), and head of the editorial staff of *Ukraïns'ka radians'ka entsyklopediia* (Ukrainian Soviet Encyclopedia, 1st edn, 17 vols, 1959–65).

Anatolii Samoilenko

Samoilenko, Anatolii [Samojlenko, Anatolij], b 2 January 1938 in Potiivka, Radomyshl county, Zhytomyr oblast. Mathematician; corresponding member of the AN URSR (now ANU) since 1978. Since completing his studies at Kiev University (1960), he has worked at the ANU Institute of Mathematics (as director since 1988) and at Kiev University (since 1967). Samoilenko's main contributions are to the theory of linear and nonlinear ordinary differential equations of various types and to the theory of nonlinear oscillations. In a series of papers published in the early 1960s (some jointly with M. Perestiuk) he provided a rigorous foundation for the application of asymptotic methods in solving discontinuous and impulsive systems. His most original contribution was the numeric-analytical method for the study of periodic solutions of differential equations with periodic right-hand side. A monograph on the method of accelerated convergence, written jointly by Samoilenko, N. Bogoliubov, and Yu. Mytropolsky in 1969, gives an exhaustive analysis of the speed of convergence, error estimates, stability, and applications. In the late 1960s and early 1970s Samoilenko constructed a general theory of perturbation of invariant troidal manifolds of dynamical systems. He (jointly with Mytropolsky) also made a contribution to the theory of multifrequency oscillation. In the late 1970s and early 1980s he studied aspects of the theory on systems of ordinary differential equations with impulse effects under various assumptions. His results were unified and extended in a monograph he wrote jointly with M. Perestiuk in 1987. Samoilenko, Mytropolsky, and D. Martyniuk worked together on a system of evolutionary equations with periodic and conditional periodic coefficients and published their results in a joint monograph in 1984.

W. Petryshyn

Samoilovich, Anatolii [Samojlovič, Anatolij], b 29 November 1906 in Rostov-na-Donu, Russia, d 22 October 1981 in Chernivtsi. Theoretical physicist. A graduate of Leningrad University (1929), he joined the faculty of Chernivtsi University in 1949 and became head of the department of theoretical physics there in 1962. His major contributions were in the fields of solid-state theory, where he developed a theory of surface electron states in metals, and of semiconductors, where he became a leading expert on their magnetic properties. His extensive list of publications includes a monograph on thermodynamics and statistical physics (1953).

Samoilovych [Samojlovyč]. A Cossack *starshyna* family, founded by Samuil, who was a priest in Khodorkiv, in the Skvyra region, before becoming pastor of Krasnyi Koliadyn, in Pryluka regiment. Three of his sons, Vasyl, Martyn, and Tymotei, were priests in Lebedyn and Romen, and *I. Samoilovych was hetman of Ukraine from 1672 to 1687. Ivan's son, Semen Samoilovych (b ca 1660, d 19 May 1685; buried in the Kievan Cave Monastery), served as acting hetman (1679–80) and as colonel of Starodub regiment (1680–5); he married M. Sulyma, the granddaughter of Hetman I. Sulyma. Ivan's second son, Hryhorii Samoilovych (d 11 November 1687), served as colonel of Chernihiv regiment (1685–7) and as acting hetman (1687); he married the daughter of Hetman I. Briukhovetsky. He was arrested by Muscovite forces at the Cossack General Council held near Kolomak (see *Kolomak Articles) and was beheaded in Sevsk. Hryhorii's son, Ivan Samoilovych, was a military fellow of Nizhen regiment in 1736. Ivan's youngest son, Yakiv Samoilovych (d 9 July 1695), who took over as colonel of Starodub regiment (1685–7), was subsequently arrested along with his father and exiled to Eniseisk and then Tobolsk, Siberia, where he died. Ivan's nephew, Mykhailo Samoilovych, was colonel of Hadiache regiment (1678–87) and a court functionary in Moscow from 1685; for his participation in a plot against Hetman I. Mazepa he was exiled to Tobolsk in 1692.

O. Ohloblyn

Danylo Samoilovych

Hetman Ivan Samoilovych

Samoilovych, Danylo [Samojlovyč] (real name: Sushkivsky), b 22 December 1742 in Yanivka, Chernihiv regiment, d 4 March 1804 in Mykolaiv, Kherson gubernia. Physician and founder of epidemiology in Ukraine; member of 12 foreign academies of science. After completing his studies at the Kievan Mohyla Academy (1756–61) and the Medico-Surgical School of the St Petersburg Military Hospital (1761–5) he served as chief physician of the Women's Venereological Hospital and as official doctor of Konotip regiment. He studied abroad at Strassburg and Leiden (PH D, 1780) universities and then returned to Ukraine, where he assumed the posts of physician in chief for Katerynoslav vicegerency (1784–90), quarantine chief

for Ukraine (1793–1800), and inspector for the Black Sea Medical Board (1800–4). He devoted over 30 years to the struggle against the plague in various parts of Ukraine. He showed that the disease is transmitted by contact with patients or infected objects and tried to isolate the infecting agent. He predicted the effectiveness of vaccination against the plague, which he tested on himself, and worked out a system of control methods. His selected works were published in Moscow in 1949–52.

BIBLIOGRAPHY
Borodii, M. *Danylo Samoilovych* (Kiev 1987)

Samoilovych, Ivan [Samojlovyč] (Popovych), b ? in Khodorkiv, Skvyra region, d 1690 in Tobolsk, Siberia. Cossack leader. He studied at the Kievan Mohyla College until 1648. During the tenure of Hetman D. Mnohohrishny he served as colonel of Chernihiv regiment (1668–9) and as general judge (1669–72). After Mnohohrishny was deposed, Samoilovych was elected hetman at a Cossack General Council held near Konotip in June 1672 (see *Konotip Articles). He sought to unite Left-Bank and Right-Bank Ukraine under his rule and fought against the Right-Bank hetman, P. Doroshenko. On 17 March 1674 a council of 10 senior *starshyna* of Right-Bank Ukraine recognized him as their hetman, but he could not rule de facto until Doroshenko abdicated, on 18 September 1676. Samoilovych also sought to join the regiments of Slobidska Ukraine to the Hetmanate, but that aim was decisively opposed by Moscow.

Samoilovych opposed a Muscovite-Polish alliance, which would have been detrimental to Ukraine, but he supported peaceful relations between Moscow and the Crimean Khanate and Turkey. The *Chyhyryn campaigns (1677–8) of the Turks, however, which devastated Right-Bank Ukraine and resulted in a mass forced migration to the Left Bank (1680), brought about Samoilovych's political demise. The *Eternal Peace of 1686 between Moscow and Poland (opposed vigorously by Samoilovych) officially confirmed the partition of the Hetmanate and drew it into another war against Turkey and the Crimea (campaigns in 1687 and 1689).

Samoilovych favored an authoritarian system of rule. As the self-proclaimed absolute ruler of the Little Russian State he was probably the first to formulate theoretically the hetmancy as a monarchic institution based on divine right. He wanted to secure hereditary rule of the Hetmanate for his sons, to whom he gave the best regimental governments and huge estates. Under his regime there was a significant economic resurgence in Left-Bank Ukraine. Trade with Western Europe resumed, and economic ties with Muscovy, the Balkans, the Don region, and Caucasia were strengthened. Internal trade also improved, between the Hetmanate in the north and the Zaporizhia in the south and between Slobidska Ukraine and Right-Bank Ukraine. Various trades and industries began to develop, and cultural life, which had suffered during the years of the *Ruin, was invigorated. The construction of large new churches (eg, the Mhar Transfiguration Monastery) was financed by Samoilovych and his senior *starshyna*. Under his rule, however, the Moscow patriarchate began to subvert the Ukrainian church, and subjugated it finally in 1686.

Samoilovych's despotism aroused considerable opposition among the senior Cossack *starshyna*, and they began plotting against him as his health failed. Abetted by the Muscovite government and capitalizing on the failure of the 1687 Crimean campaign, they charged him with arbitrariness and corruption and even accused him of establishing secret treasonous contacts with the Crimean khan. Samoilovych was deposed at the behest of Moscow at the Cossack General Council at Kolomak; his assets were seized, and he was exiled to Tobolsk.

O. Ohloblyn

Samoilovych, Mykola [Samojlovyč], b 1890 in Kupianka county, Kharkiv gubernia, d 1951. Civic figure and stage performer. He received his musical education in Kiev. In 1917–18 he was a member of the Ukrainian Central Rada and a delegate to the first two all-Ukrainian military congresses. An émigré from 1920, he lived in Prague, where he studied theater, performed at the Prague Opera, and received a PH D from the Ukrainian Free University. He also appeared in plays staged by the Sadovsky Ukrainian Drama Theater in Uzhhorod and the Nova Stsena theater in Khust, and he performed in Western Europe.

Samoilovych, Viktor [Samojlovyč], b 17 September 1911 in Pryluka, Poltava gubernia. Architect and art scholar. A graduate of the Kiev Civil-Engineering Institute (1940), he taught at the Kiev State Art Institute from 1941. He codesigned apartment buildings in many places in Ukraine (1951, 1955) and produced a series of plans for typical (1958, 1959, 1962) and experimental (1960) apartment buildings; wrote books on the home of the collective farmer (1951, 1956), folk creativity in the architecture of the rural dwelling (1961), the Ukrainian folk home (1972), and folk architecture (1977); and contributed to several multiauthor monographs, including one on the history of architecture in Ukraine (1957).

Samoilovych, Zakhariia [Samojlovyč, Zaxarija] (Samuilovych), b and d ? Engraver of O. *Tarasevych's school. In 1691–1706 he worked in Kiev and Moscow. The 14 copper engravings known to be done by him include the large *Adoration of the Magi* depicting Tsars Peter I and Ivan Alekseevich and the Cossack *starshyna* (dedicated to Hetman I. Mazepa), *The Resurrection* (1691), the philosophical thesis of H. Terpylovsky (1699–1706), *The Theotokos*, *St Stephen*, *St Catherine*, and *St Gregory the Great*.

Samokhvalenko, Yevhen [Samoxvalenko, Jevhen], b June 1917 in Russia, d 30 November 1984 in Dobrzyń, Poland. Ukrainian writer and community figure in postwar Poland. A pharmacist by occupation, he was a founding member of the literary and artistic association within the Ukrainian Social and Cultural Society in Poland, edited the literary-cultural supplement to the weekly *Nashe slovo* (Warsaw), and was politically active in Dobrzyń. He published hundreds of poems and articles in the Ukrainian and Polish press and wrote the poetry collections *Nad Visloiu* (At the Vistula, 1974) and *Paraleli* (Parallels, 1979).

Samokvasov, Dimitrii, b 27 May 1843 on an estate near Molotech, Novhorod-Siverskyi county, Chernihiv gubernia, d 16 August 1911 in Moscow. Russian archeologist and law historian. After studying at St Petersburg University, he taught law at Warsaw University from 1877 until he moved to Moscow in 1892 to direct the Ministry of Justice archives and teach the history of Russian law at Moscow University. He directed a number of digs in Russia and Ukraine, including the renowned *Chorna Mohyla site near Chernihiv. He published monographs and articles on early Rus' cities (including his MA dissertation in 1873), on legal history, and on early Rus' grave sites (the latter have little scholarly value). Although born in Ukraine, he opposed the Ukrainian national movement.

A drawing by Mykola Samokysh in his and Serhii Vasylkivsky's album of Ukrainian antiquities

Samokysh, Mykola [Samokyš] (Samokysha), b 25 October 1860 in Nizhen, Chernihiv gubernia, d 18 January 1944 in Symferopil. Painter and graphic artist; full member of the St Petersburg Academy of Arts (SPAA) from 1890. While studying at the SPAA (1879–85) he belonged to a group of painters, including S. Vasylkivsky, P. Martynovych, and O. Slastion, dedicated to depicting the history and folkways of the Ukrainian people. After returning from his studies in Paris (1886–9) he painted several historical canvases for the Tbilisi Museum of Military History, which established his reputation as a battle painter. In 1894–1917 he headed the SPAA battle-painting studio. He created an album of drawings and watercolors of the Russo-Japanese War with texts from his diary (1905) and the series 'The Great War in Images and Pictures' (1915). Later he painted canvases of the Russian Civil War, such as *Attack of the Budenny Cavalry* (1923) and *The Red Army Crossing the Syvash* (1935). Samokysh never lost contact with Ukraine. Around the beginning of the century he often visited Ukraine and took part in exhibitions there. He designed an album of T. Shevchenko's works (1889) and illustrated an album about Sevastopil and its past (1904). With Vasylkivsky he illustrated D. Yavornytsky's *Iz ukrainskoi stariny/La Petite Russie d'autrefois* (1900), an album which was seen as the continuation of Shevchenko's *Zhivopisnaia Ukraina. In 1912 Samokysh prepared an album of Ukrainian ornamentation. In the early 1900s he and Vasylkivsky painted the murals in the Poltava Gubernia Zemstvo building. From 1911 he spent every summer painting in Ukraine. In 1921 he moved to Symferopil, and from 1937 to 1941 he taught at the Kharkiv Art Institute.

In the Soviet period much of Samokysh's work was devoted to Cossack history, which he depicted in canvases such as *B. Khmelnytsky's Entry into Kiev in 1648* (1929), *The Battle of Zhovti Vody* (1930), *I. Bohun's Battle with Czarnecki* at Monastyryshche in 1653 (1931), *Sea Battle of the Zaporozhians with a Turkish Battleship* (1932), and *The Kharkiv Fortress in the 18th Century* (1936). A good part of his graphic work consists of battle scenes done in watercolor, ink, or pencil. Altogether Samokysh painted or drew over 10,000 works. Several thousand were book illustrations, some of them to editions of works by Ukrainian writers, such as Marko Vovchok, N. Gogol (his *Taras Bul'ba*), and I. Nechui-Levytsky (his *Mykola Dzheria*), and others for journals, such as **Ukraïns'ka khata* (1909–14), *Niva* (1910, 1912, 1914–15, 1917), *Solntse Rossii* (1914–16), and *Myslyvets' ta rybalka* (1928). Samokysh's works are distinguished by their dynamic composition, realistic rendering, vivid colors, and rich content. Books about him have been written in Ukrainian by M. Burachek (1930) and V. Yatsenko (1954, 1979), and in Russian by G. Portnov (1954), A. Polkanov (1960), and V. Tkachenko (1964).

S. Yaniv

Samokyshyn, Roman [Samokyšyn], b 1877 in Pechenizhyn, Kolomyia county, Galicia, d 1971. Partisan leader during the revolutionary period. He was a Russian POW in 1915–17 and an organizer of Free Cossack detachments in the Katerynoslav and Kherson regions after the 1917 revolution. He particularly distinguished himself in the battle for Katerynoslav against the Bolsheviks and N. Makhno's forces in January 1919.

Samooborona (Self-Defense). A military organization active in the Kholm region during the Second World War. Formed in June 1942 to defend local residents from attacks by partisans of the **Polish Home Army (AK), the group was centered in the Hrubeshiv region. Following the death of Col Ya. Halchevsky-Voinarsky in March 1943 at the hands of Polish partisans, it was led by Capt Yu. Lukashchuk. The group had up to 500 men at the height of its activity. Its most significant action was a successful encounter against a large AK detachment on 6 June 1944. Early in 1945 the force merged with the **Division Galizien.

Samoosvita (Self-Education). A correspondence school offering university-level courses in Lviv from 1930 to 1939. Major financial support was provided by the United States–based Ukrainian Workingmen's Association. In 1930–9 Samoosvita published popular encyclopedia-like fascicles, which appeared monthly under its name. A total of 117 booklets were published, with an approximate pressrun of 10,000 copies each. An additional 24 booklets were devoted to belles lettres. The editorial staff consisted of over 40 people, the chief editors being M. Stakhiv, K. Kobersky, I. Luchyshyn, and Ye. Yavorivsky. Topics covered in the periodical included social studies, world and Ukrainian history with special attention to the period 1917–20, political and current events, Ukrainian literature, science, geography, and economics.

Samoosvita (Self-Education). A journal published monthly from January 1926 and semimonthly from October 1929 to February 1933 in Kharkiv. It was sponsored by the Komsomol and the All-Ukrainian Council of Trade Unions, and was dedicated to promoting extramural education and self-education. The editor was A. Ivanivsky.

Samoosvitnyk (Self-Enlightener). A mass-circulated educational monthly (later semimonthly) journal published in Lviv in 1937–9 by the **Desheva Knyzhka publishing house. It appeared in a pressrun of 18,000 to 22,000 copies and was edited by R. Paladiichuk.

Samopomich (Self-Help). A monthly supplement to the newspaper **Ekonomist* published by the Audit Union of Ukrainian Co-operatives in Lviv in 1909–14. Edited by O. Saievych and then A. Zhuk, it contained reports on the co-operative movement in Western Ukraine and practical farming advice.

Samostiina dumka

Samostiina dumka (Independent Thought). A literary, scholarly, and political journal published in Chernivtsi monthly in 1931, semimonthly in 1932, and again monthly from January 1933 to March 1937. Edited by S. Nykorovych and O. Olzhych, the journal contained articles by prominent émigré and OUN figures (eg, M. Shapoval, N. Hryhoriiv, O. Mytsiuk, M. Stsiborsky, S. Rusova, Ye. Onatsky, and R. Sushko) and Bukovynian publicists, and scholarly and literary contributions from U. Samchuk, M. Mukhyn, O. Hrytsai, S. Smal-Stotsky, L. Biletsky, V. Simovych, S. Cherkasenko, and others.

Samostiina Ukraïna (Independent Ukraine). A monthly and, beginning in 1973, bimonthly magazine published since 1948 (except for a hiatus in 1970–1) in Chicago (and at various times and for brief periods in Winnipeg, St Paul, New York, and Toronto). The organ of the **Organization for the Rebirth of Ukraine and, since 1973, of the OUN (Melnyk faction), it contains articles on politics, history, and culture; analyses of developments in Ukraine; memoirs; and reviews. Its editors have included B. Bociurkiw, S. Kotsiuba, T. Lapychak (1950–5), Z. Knysh (1956–7), S. Kuropas (1958–9), V. Shemerdiak (1960–3), M. Panasiuk (1963–8, 1971–2), D. Kvitkovsky (1973–9), V. Nahirniak (1979–86), P. Stercho (1986–7), and P. Dorozhynsky (1987–).

Samostiinist' (Independence). A weekly pro-OUN newspaper published in Chernivtsi from January 1934 to March 1937. It did much to gain support for the nationalist cause in Bukovyna, especially among students. At its peak it had over 7,000 subscribers. The newspaper was edited by D. Kvitkovsky with the assistance of P. and I. Hryhorovych and L. Huzar. Contributors included Ukrainian activists in Bukovyna as well as OUN leaders, such as M.

Samostiinist'

Stsiborsky and Ye. Onatsky. In 1936–7 it published a humor supplement, *Chortopolokh* (ed O. Masikevych-Shypynsky), and two annual almanacs. The staff was constantly harassed, and *Samostiinist'* was censored by the Rumanian authorities, who suspended it several times and prevented its distribution in Bessarabia. The authorities finally closed it down in 1937 and sentenced the managing editor, I. Hryhorovych, to three years' hard labor for publishing 'irredentist' propaganda.

Samotos, Ivan, b 20 August 1933 in Ustia, Zhydachiv county, Galicia. Sculptor. He studied under I. Severa at the Lviv Institute of Applied and Decorative Arts (1953–9). He has done busts of I. Kotliarevsky (1966), H. Skovoroda (1969), Lesia Ukrainka (1970), and D. Yavornytsky and the portraits *Natalia* (1975) and *Oksana* (1975), and has collaborated on the victory monument in Stryi (1965–6, stone and iron), the monument to the heroes of the Second World War in Vilkhove (1967–8, marble), and other monuments.

The first edition of the Samovydets Chronicle (1846)

Samovydets Chronicle. One of the most important sources for the history of Ukraine during the years 1648–1702; it was named *Litopys samovydtsia* (Chronicle of an Eyewitness) by P. *Kulish. The introduction describes conditions in Ukraine prior to the B. *Khmelnytsky era (O. Bodiansky included it in when he published the chronicle in the journal *Chteniia v Imperatorskom obshchestve istorii i drevnostei rossiiskikh* [1846], but O. Levytsky rejected it in his edition of the chronicle [1878], believing that it had been added at a later date). Following the introduction,

the first part examines the Khmelnytsky period and the *Ruin (up to 1676); it was probably written some time after the events occurred. The second part constitutes a true chronicle of events in Left-Bank Ukraine until 1702; it was probably written in Starodub (surmised from the prevalence of local detail).

The Samovydets Chronicle was written in the Ukrainian literary language of the day, which was close to the vernacular of a dialect of Right-Bank Ukraine. The author of the chronicle is unknown, but he was likely a highly placed member of the Cossack *starshyna* and a functionary in the Ukrainian government. The investigation of his identity was carried out on the basis of autobiographical materials in the chronicle, and was greatly facilitated by V. Modzalevsky's writings (1919–22) on R. *Rakushka. In the 1920s the scholars V. Romanovsky and M. Petrovsky independently arrived at the conclusion (initially voiced by the amateur historian P. Serdiukov in 1846) that the chronicle's author was most likely Rakushka. That theory was adopted by many historians, including D. Bahalii, D. Doroshenko, M. Hrushevsky, I. Krypiakevych, and modern Soviet historiographers. Other candidates for the authorship of the chronicle were I. Bykhovets, a military chancellor (favored by L. Okinshevych), and F. Kandyba, a colonel of Korsun regiment (favored by M. Andrusiak and M. Vozniak).

The original of the Samovydets Chronicle has not been preserved; six manuscript copies, made in the 18th century or later, have survived. The oldest and most reliable are those made by P. Iskrytsky (dated 1734, closest to the original) and Ya. Kozelsky (made in the late 18th century). Those have served as the basis for scholarly research and for more recent editions, including the one published by Bodiansky (1846), who obtained the manuscript from Kulish. A more scholarly edition was issued by the Kiev Archeographic Commission (1878), edited and with an introduction by Levytsky. It was republished by the AN URSR (now ANU) Institute of History (1971, edited and with an introduction by Ya. Dzyra), and as part of the Harvard Series in Ukrainian Studies (*The Eyewitness Chronicle*, 1972).

BIBLIOGRAPHY
Levitskii, O. *Opyt issledovaniia o letopisi Samovidtsa: Letopis' Samovidtsa po novootkrytym spiskam* (Kiev 1878)
Petrovs'kyi, M. *Narysy istoriï Ukraïny XVII–pochatku XVIII stolit': Doslidy nad litopysom Samovydtsia* (Kharkiv 1930)

O. Ohloblyn

Samsonov, Grigorii, b 15 February 1918 in Detskoe Selo (now Pushkin), near Petrograd, d 22 December 1975 in Kiev. Russian physical chemist; corresponding member of the AN URSR (now ANU) from 1961. He graduated from the Moscow Institute of Chemical Technology (1940) and worked at the Moscow Institute of Nonferrous Metals and Gold (1947–56) and the ANU Institute for Problems of Materials Science. He led the Technical Sciences Division of the ANU (1961–3) and became head of the Department of Powder Metallurgy and Rare Metals at the Kiev Polytechnical Institute (in 1962). His research dealt predominantly with solid state chemistry. He developed and put into industrial production over 400 compounds (borides, nitrides, carbides, etc), including metalloceramics for atomic reactors and heat-resistant materials for machine construction. He studied the structure and properties of pyroceramics over a wide temperature range, and particle interactions during their formation. He also developed the basis for a quantum-mechanical electronic theory of particle sintering in pyroceramics.

Samus, Anatolii [Samus', Anatolij], b 17 October 1930 in Kehychivka, now in Kharkiv oblast. Sculptor. A graduate of the Voroshylovhrad Art School (1954) and Kharkiv Art Institute (1961), he has done portraits and compositions, such as *Liberation* (1965) and *Partisans* (1967), and collaborated on the monuments to the Komsomol underground in Krasnodon (1965) and the heroes of the Second World War in Luhanske (1965) and Brianka (1966).

Samus, Samiilo [Samus', Samijlo] (actual name unknown), b and d ? Cossack officer from the Pereiaslav region. He served as colonel of Bohuslav regiment (1685–1713) and as acting hetman of Right-Bank Ukraine (1692–1704), appointed by the Polish government. In 1683 he led a Cossack army in a joint engagement with Jan III Sobieski against Turkish and Tatar forces near Vienna. During the anti-Polish uprisings led by S. Palii (1702–4) Samus's army of 5,000 Cossacks defeated the Polish army near Berdychiv on 17 October 1702. Later that month, together with A. Abazyn, the colonel of Bratslav regiment, he captured Nemyriv. As a result the entire Bratslav region and large areas of Podilia fell into the hands of the rebels. Samus favored the unification of Right-Bank Ukraine with the Hetmanate, and he recognized the authority of Hetman I. *Mazepa. The advance of a superior Polish force, however, and the lack of aid from Moscow or Mazepa forced him to retreat to Bohuslav and to relinquish his title of acting hetman in January 1704. He continued as colonel of Bohuslav regiment under Mazepa, and he fought against Right-Bank Polish magnates and the Swedes (1708–9). In 1711 he joined most of the Right-Bank Cossacks in backing Hetman P. *Orlyk, and after Orlyk's capitulation Samus was captured by the Russians (along with his son, a colonel in Orlyk's army). His subsequent fate is unknown.

O. Ohloblyn

Gen Petro Samutyn

Samutyn, Petro, b 1897 in Poltava, d 14 September 1982 in Baltimore. Senior army officer. An official in the Russian army during the First World War, in 1917 he helped Ukrainianize the Sixth Russian Corps and attended as a delegate the Second and Third all-Ukrainian military congresses in Kiev. In 1920 he commanded a company of the Sixth Sich Division. In the interwar period he served on contract in the Polish army and graduated from the General Staff Academy in Warsaw. The UNR government-in-exile promoted him to brigadier general. After the Second World War he emigrated to the United States, where he was active in veterans' and community organizations. He wrote some historical articles based on his years of service in the UNR Army.

Samvydav (from *sam* 'self' and *vydannia* 'publication'; Russian: *samizdat*). Uncensored underground leaflets, monographs, serials, and other items published and distributed illegally in the USSR. Samvydav publications included a wide variety of philosophical, literary, political, scholarly, and religious studies, letters, political declarations, translations of banned foreign works, and reports on political opposition and repressions in the USSR. They provided the most detailed and accurate descriptions and criticisms of political trials, KGB actions, and conditions in labor camps and prisons. Samvydav appeared in almost all the languages of the USSR.

Generally the author of a samvydav piece typed out several copies for friends. Since access to publishing and duplicating technology was strictly controlled in the USSR, others recopied the document and distributed it further. Popular works even of book length were recopied many times and read by a large number of people. In Ukraine, as in the rest of the USSR, the first samvydav publications date from the post-Stalin period of the mid-1950s. In the early 1960s a great number of literary works, including the poetry of the *shestydesiatnyky*, appeared in samvydav. There was always a strong political current in Ukrainian underground publications, with a special interest in national and human rights and religious freedom (see *Dissident movement). The repressions of the 1970s slowed the production of samvydav materials. Many people were punished severely for writing or distributing uncensored publications.

Ukrainian samvydav materials can be found in a variety of sources: the *Chronicle of Current Events*, *Ukraïns'kyi visnyk*, and in many collections, such as *The Human Rights Movement in Ukraine: Documents of the Ukrainian Helsinki Group, 1976–1980* (1980). The most important samvydav works, by V. *Moroz, V. *Chornovil, I. *Dziuba, and M. *Osadchy, were smuggled to the West and published there, first in the original Ukrainian and then in English, French, and German translations. The largest collection of samvydav material has been amassed by Radio Liberty in Munich. *Nonconformity and Dissent in the Ukrainian SSR, 1955–1975: An Annotated Bibliography* (compiled by G. Liber and A. Mostovych, 1978) lists 1,242 separate samvydav documents smuggled to the West.

In the late 1980s political liberalization created a fertile setting for samvydav. The easing of censorship permitted more open and technically sophisticated publications to appear. Hand-copied clandestine publications were replaced by a large variety of serials, leaflets, journals, and monographs printed by numerous unofficial groups (*neformaly) and individuals.

B. Balan

San Francisco. A city (1980 pop 679,000; metropolitan pop 3,253,000) in California on the northern tip of a peninsula between the Pacific Ocean and San Francisco Bay. In

1980 about 3,600 people of Ukrainian origin lived in the metropolitan area. The first Ukrainians to arrive in the city came via Alaska along with Russian settlers in North America. In 1867 A. *Honcharenko settled in the city; later he established the Ukraina homestead nearby. The Russian Orthodox church used the city as its home base in North America in the late 19th century and launched its missionary activities among Ukrainians in Canada and the United States from there. The Prosvita society was the leading institution of the Ukrainian community in the 1910s, 1920s, and 1930s. Today Ukrainian Catholics are organized in the parish of the Immaculate Conception, and Orthodox in St Michael's parish.

Sanacja regime. The popular name for the political leadership of Poland during the years 1926–39. The Sanacja regime was founded after the armed coup of J. *Piłsudski in May 1926. The name referred to the healing (from Latin *sanatio*) of Polish social, economic, and political life Piłsudski hoped to achieve. The major political organizations under the regime were the Nonparty Bloc of Co-operation with the Government (1927–35, led by W. Sławek) and the Camp of National Unity (1936–9, led by A. Koc). The Sanacja regime's main goal was the creation of a strong executive, with restricted civil rights (April Constitution, 1935) and a stable economy. Following Piłsudski's death in 1935, the regime split into two opposing groups: the liberals, centered around President I. Mościcki, and the totalitarian nationalists, under E. *Rydz-Śmigły. The Sanacja regime was brought to an end by the German occupation in September 1939.

With regard to the Ukrainian question the regime engendered various programs (such as those drawn up by B. Miedziński and S. Srokowski) as well as strong pro-Ukrainian tendencies (L. Wasilewski, T. Hołówko, and P. Dunin-Wąsowicz). From a planned policy of state assimilation (realized essentially only in Volhynia by H. Józewski) the Sanacja regime shifted toward the Polonization ideals of the National Democrats. Despite its undertaking provisional and tactical attempts at political resolution (discussions in 1931, the *Normalization of 1935), repression was more often applied (the 1930 *Pacification, the construction of the *Bereza Kartuzka concentration camp in 1934). Toward the end of the 1930s the Sanacja regime strongly advocated the strengthening of the Polish presence in the outlying territories through forced Polonization, colonization, restricted national development, and the creation of artificial divisions among the Ukrainian population (Lemko and Hutsul separatism, the yeoman movement, and the Polish Greek Catholic and Polish Orthodox movements). The activity of pro-Ukrainian circles of the Sanacja regime was limited.

A. Zięba

Sanatoriums. See Health resorts and sanatoriums.

Sandler, Oskar, b 26 January 1910 in Kiev, d 3 May 1981 in Kiev. Composer and conductor. A graduate of the Kiev Conservatory (1937), he studied composition with V. Kosenko and conducting with H. Taranov. In 1937–40 he was a conductor at the Kiev Theater of Opera and Ballet, and in 1940–5 music director of the Kiev Russian Drama Theater. One of the creators of the Soviet musical drama in Ukraine, his works include the operas *Elsa Strauss* (1938)

and *V stepakh Ukrainy* (In the Steppes of Ukraine, 1951), the operettas *Kelykh het'mana Bohdana* (The Chalice of Hetman Bohdan, 1954) and *Kashtany Kyieva* (The Chestnut Trees of Kiev, 1972), the musical comedy *Fabryka chudes* (The Factory of Miracles, 1949), as well as nearly 40 film scores and more than 100 songs.

The fresco depicting the Dormition inside the Sandomierz cathedral

Sandomierz (Sandomyr). III-2. A Polish city (now in Tarnobrzeg voievodeship) on the left bank of the Wisła River, near the mouth of the Sian River (1989 pop 24,000). It was situated on the Kiev–Volodymyr-Volynskyi–Cracow trade route, at the junction of its branches to Peremyshl and Halych. It was destroyed in several Tatar incursions; a siege of the city by Lev Danylovych allied with the Nogay Tatars was described in the Galician-Volhynian Chronicle (1280). As Lviv and Lublin became established economic centers in the 16th century, Sandomierz declined in significance. The city has many architectural monuments. Its Gothic cathedral (built ca 1360–82) contains frescoes in the Byzantine-Ukrainian style, painted in the 1430s at the behest of Władysław II Jagiełło by Ukrainian masters of the Galician school. The main fresco depicts the Dormition of the Mother of God, and others show scenes from the life of Christ. They were discovered in 1887. An inferior restoration (1932–4) obscured the coloration and stylistic detail of the original.

Sandpiper (*Tringa*; Ukrainian: *ulit*). A small shore bird of the suborder Charadrii. With nondescript brown or gray plumage, it is long-legged and has a long, straight beak. In Ukraine the common sandpiper (*T. hypoleucos*; Ukrainian:

pereviznyk) nests on the grassy shores of lakes and rivers. Others nesting in Ukraine are the redshank (*T. totanus*; Ukrainian: *travnyk*), the green sandpiper (*T. ochropus*; Ukrainian: *chornysh*), the marsh sandpiper (*T. stagnatilis*; Ukrainian: *poruchainyk*), and the wood sandpiper (*T. glareola*; Ukrainian: *fifi*). Sandpipers migrate from Ukraine in the winter.

Sandraky settlement. A late Trypilian culture settlement near Sandraky (now incorporated into Shyroka Hreblia), Khmilnyk raion, Vinnytsia oblast. Excavations in 1949–50 revealed the remains of a surface dwelling, stone and bone tools (including a cache of flint knives), pottery (most of it decorated), the bones of domestic and wild animals, and earthenware figures of women and bulls. Artifacts from the late *Bronze Age and 17th to 18th centuries were found in the upper layer of the excavation.

Sands, Bedwin. See Raffalovich, George.

Sandstone. A type of sedimentary rock found throughout Ukraine. The highest grades of sandstone in Ukraine are located in the Dnieper region and in Kiev, Cherkasy, Kirovohrad, and Sumy oblasts. The rock is used for making grindstones and as a material in brick manufacturing. The best sandstone for the latter purpose is found in Donetske oblast and the Crimea.

Sanduliak, Ivan [Sanduljak] (Sanduliak-Lukyniv and Sanduliak-Lukych), b 1848 in Karliv near Sniatyn, Galicia, d 1926 in Karliv. Civic and political leader. A village farmer, he was active in the Ukrainian Radical party and was elected to the Galician Diet in 1908 and 1913.

Sandul-Strudza, Yakiv, b 1756 in Kozatske, Chernihiv regiment, d after 1810. Physician. A graduate of Chernihiv College (1769–77) and the medical school in Moscow (1777–9), he served as a doctor's assistant in the army and then completed his medical training in St Petersburg (1783). He worked in Southern Ukraine, where he devoted much of his time to research on leprosy. In 1792 he wrote a doctoral thesis on leprosy, the first work on the subject in the Russian Empire. From 1799 he was in charge of the gubernial medical board in Kharkiv.

Sanguszko [Sanguško]. A Lithuanian-Ukrainian princely family whose members controlled large estates in Volhynia, Podilia, and the Bratslav region from the 15th century. They held various positions in the governments of the Grand Duchy of Lithuania and the Polish Kingdom. They were initially Orthodox and later converted to Catholicism.

Although some Polish heraldists (eg, B. Paprocki) assert that the Sanguszko family line was established by *Liubartas, others (eg, M. Stryjkowski) contend that it was founded by Fedor, the son of *Algirdas. Notable members of the line included Oleksander Sanguszko (d ca 1491), the starosta of Volodymyr-Volynskyi and originator of the Koshary line (which died out in 1653); Mykhailo Sanguszko (d ca 1511), the originator of the Kovel line; Oleksander's son, Andrii Sanguszko, the starosta of Volodymyr-Volynskyi and marshal of Volhynia in the 15th century; and Oleksander's grandson, Andrii Sanguszko, the starosta of Lutske in the 16th century. Fedir Sanguszko (d 1547) was starosta of Vinnytsia, Bratslav, and Volo-dymyr-Volynskyi as well as marshal of Volhynia; he participated in campaigns against the Crimean Tatars. Dmytro Sanguszko, the starosta of Cherkasy (ca 1530–4), was murdered in Moravia as a result of family feuding. Oleksander's grandson and Dmytro's brother, Roman Sanguszko (1537–71), was the Lithuanian field hetman (from 1567), noted for his victories against Moscow and the Tatars; he opposed the Polish-Lithuanian Union of *Lublin (1569), but he was forced to sign the treaty. Adam Oleksander Sanguszko, a voivode of Volhynia, promoted the union of the Ukrainian Orthodox church with the Catholic church; he served as an emissary between Pope Urban VIII and Metropolitan P. Mohyla. Evstafii (Eustachy) Sanguszko (1768–1844) was a powerful landowner and industrialist, with textile mills and other business ventures in Volhynia and the Kiev region; his support of Napoleon in 1812 was pardoned, and his memoirs of the years 1786–1815 were published in 1876. Evstafii's son, Roman Stanyslav (Stanisław) Sanguszko (1800–81), a Polish politician, was exiled to Siberia for his part in the Polish Insurrection of 1830–1; he returned to Slavuta, where he administered the family industrial concerns (especially sugar refineries). Roman's nephew, Evstafii (Eustachy) Sanguszko (1842–1903), was a conservative politician in Galicia, marshal of the Galician Diet (1885–95), and governor of Galicia (1895–8). A selection of materials from the substantial family archive was published in *Archiwum Książąt Lubartowiczów Sanguszków w Sławucie* (Archive of the Princes Lubartowicz Sanguszko in Slavuta, 6 vols, 1887–1910).

A. Zhukovsky

Sanitary Charitable Service. See Ukrainian Medical Charitable Service.

Sanitary-epidemiological stations. Institutions created under the Soviet health care system, whose purpose is to monitor the implementation of sanitary-hygienic and epidemic-prevention measures by ministries, departments, businesses, and civil servants. These measures include steps to stop *pollution and clean the environment, to improve safety and health conditions at the workplace and in the home, and to eliminate infectious diseases. A sanitary-epidemiological station conducts research on the frequency of occurrence of infectious and work-related diseases in a given region, develops directives and methods for combating them, and monitors their implementation. It has departments of sanitary-hygiene, epidemiology, parasitology, and disinfection and is equipped with laboratories for bacteriology, virology, parasitology, and sanitary hygiene. The water-transport industry is served by special sanitary-epidemiological stations. The first station in the USSR was set up in 1927 in the Donbas. Beginning in 1931 a network of stations was developed in Ukraine. In 1983 there were 722 such stations and 24 disinfection stations in Ukraine.

BIBLIOGRAPHY
Kas'ianenko, A. *Organizatsiia sanitarno-epidemiologicheskogo obsluzhivaniia naseleniia* (Kiev 1979)

Sanitation. The promotion and maintenance of health by applying principles of *hygiene, in order to prevent disease and enhance the well-being of the environment. Sanitation in the Ukrainian SSR was governed from Moscow, with delegated authority to the republic, municipal, and rural levels. In theory *public health measures were to address separately industrial sanitation, sanitation of the home and community, radiation sanitation, food sanitation, and sanitation of schools. Some of these programs were carried out by *sanitary-epidemiological stations, but there was no identifiable government regulatory organ to take responsibility or control. In theory Soviet sanitary legislation also provided for the sanitary protection of water reservoirs, air, soil, and borders.

In reality there has been a certain amount of difficulty in obtaining an accurate assessment of the sanitation situation in Ukraine. Since the Chornobyl catastrophe and with the implementation of economic reforms, Ukraine is beginning to acknowledge that there are enormous problems in cleaning up the environment and the country's establishments. Among others the Green Party of Ukraine is putting forward as its platform an ecologically clean, nuclear-free Ukraine.

BIBLIOGRAPHY
Nikitin, A. (ed). *Sbornik rabot sanitarnoi inspektsii na Ukraine* (Kharkiv 1923)
Nikitin, A.; Pasternak, A. (eds). *Sbornik rabot sanitarnoi inspektsii na Ukraine* (Kharkiv 1924)
Medychno-sanitarna sprava v mis'kykh selyshchakh Ukraïny na 1 zhovtnia 1924 r. (Kharkiv 1925)
Materiialy sanitarnoï statystyky Ukaïny, 1876–1914 rr. (Kharkiv 1926)
Tomilin, S. *Sproba sanitarnoho opysu Ukraïny* (Kharkiv 1928)
Kaliuzhnyi, D.; Grando, A. (eds). *Materialy k istorii gigieny i sanitarii na Ukraine*, 2 vols (Kiev 1962)

P. Dzul

Sanok. See Sianik.

Santa Catarina. One of the southern states of Brazil (1990 pop 4,461,400), bordering on Paraná to the north and Rio Grande do Sul to the south, and occupying 95,318 sq km. Its capital is Florianópolis. Estimates of the number of Ukrainians in the state range from 14,000 to 35,000 and make it the second- or third-largest region of Ukrainian settlement in Brazil. Two hundred families established the state's first Ukrainian settlement, in Iracema in 1886. They were joined by additional waves of settlers, who established new communities in Itaiópolis, Papanduva, Canoinhas, Jangada, Tres Barras, Costa Carvalho, Moema, and Mafra. They faced pioneering difficulties comparable to those of Ukrainians in other areas of Brazil, with an added problem of social unrest caused by a boundary dispute with Paraná. Organized religious life started in 1897, when the Catholic priest I. Voliansky undertook missionary work in the Itaiópolis region. He was followed by Basilian priests in the early part of the century. An Orthodox church was established in Marco Cinco in Jangada. Civic institutions started with the establishment of branches of the Prosvita society in the early part of the century. (See also *Brazil.)

Santsevych, Anatolii [Sancevyč, Anatolij], b 23 June 1924 in Kostroma (now part of Kremenchuk), Poltava gubernia. Soviet historian and historiographer. He graduated from Kiev University (1952; PH D, 1969) and worked as a senior research associate at the Scientific Research Institute of Pedagogy of the Ukrainian SSR (1955–61) and the AN URSR (now ANU) Institute of History (from 1961; deputy

director in 1979–83 and professor from 1982). In 1981 he also became director of the Institute of History's Department of Bibliographic Studies and Auxiliary Historical Disciplines. He was on the editorial board of *Ukraïns'kyi istorychnyi zhurnal* (1962–88; assistant editor in 1962–4 and 1967–72). He published works in historiography, bibliographic studies, the pedagogy of history, and general history.

A Ukrainian Orthodox church in São Paulo

São Paulo. A leading industrial state and the most populous state in Brazil (1991 pop 33,069,900), occupying 248,256 sq km in the southeastern part of the country. Its capital is São Paulo. The Ukrainian community, numbering approx 30,000, is the second largest in Brazil, after Paraná. Most of the Ukrainians live in São Paulo or São Caetano do Sul, one of the four centers which form the São Paulo metropolitan region.

Ukrainian immigrants began arriving in the state in significant numbers during the 1890s, although most of them were simply passing through. One of the early settlements was the colony Ukraina in Rancharia, which was formed in 1926 by 40 Ukrainian families who had moved from Santa Catarina and Paraná. It was particularly notable for being a predominantly Catholic community that nevertheless invited an Orthodox priest to serve it in 1931, after several years of seeking a priest of its own denomination. The community later established a school and other organizations, but ultimately most of its members resettled once more in Nova Ukraína in Paraná.

The scattered pockets of Ukrainian settlement in the

state achieved a focal point only after the Second World War, when Ukrainian church and community organizations were established on a firmer footing. These were centered in the capital. The Ukrainian population of São Paulo is notable for its predominantly urban character, which is in contrast to the largely agrarian character of other Ukrainian communities in *Brazil.

N. Kerechuk

Bishop Andrii Sapeliak   Andrii Sapiehin

Sapeliak, Andrii [Sapeljak, Andrij], b 13 December 1919 in Ryshkova Volia, Jarosław county, Galicia. Ukrainian Catholic bishop of Argentina. In 1937, after schooling in Jarosław and Peremyshl, he went to Rome, where he entered the Salesian order, finished his studies, and was ordained in 1949. For several years he taught in France and Italy in the minor seminary for Ukrainian youths and served as superior of the Ukrainian Salesians. He was consecrated in 1961 and sent to Argentina as apostolic visitor (to 1968), then apostolic exarch (1968–78), and finally (since 1978) bishop. A member of the synod of the Ukrainian Catholic church since 1971, he has also served as a consultant to the Vatican commission for the codification of Eastern rite canon law.

Sapeliak, Stepan [Sapeljak], b 26 March 1951 in Rosokhach, Chortkiv raion, Ternopil oblast. Poet and dissident. He was arrested in February 1973 for raising the Ukrainian national flag in Rosokhach to mark Ukrainian independence day (22 January), and sentenced in the spring of 1974 to five years in labor camps in Perm oblast, and in Vladimir prison near Moscow, where he was active in prisoners' protests. In February 1978 he was exiled for three years to Kolyma and then the Khabarovsk territory in far eastern Siberia. After his release he was forbidden to live in Western Ukraine, and lived in Leningrad oblast and the Soviet Far East before settling in Kharkiv. In the late 1980s he cofounded the Ukrainian Association of Independent Creative Intelligentsia. In 1989 his poetry collections *Bez shabli i vitchyzny* (Without a Sword and Native Land) and *Z hirkotoiu v kameni* (With Bitterness in Stone) were published in the West.

Sapieha [Sapjeha] (Sapiha, Sopiha). A Belarusian-Lithuanian family line of magnates that owned large estates in Podlachia, around Brest, and on the Buh River. They were the second most wealthy and influential family in the

Grand Duchy of Lithuania after the *Radziwiłłs. The line probably originated among the Smolensk boyars; it was formally established by Semen Sapieha, the scribe to Prince Casimir IV Jagiellończyk. The Sapiehas held high governmental and military positions through the 16th to 18th centuries in the Grand Duchy of Lithuania, the Polish Commonwealth, and the Russian Empire. Initially they were all Orthodox, but in the late 16th and early 17th centuries they converted to Catholicism. Several members of the family line played a role in Ukrainian history.

Ivan Sapieha (ca 1450–1517) served as scribe and then marshal of the Grand Duchy of Lithuania and as voivode of Vitsebsk (1511–14) and Podlachia (from 1514); he founded the town of Koden (1511) and was the first of the family to convert to Catholicism (1514). Lev Sapieha (1557–1633) was Lithuanian chancellor (from 1589) and voivode of Vilnius (1623–33); as grand hetman of Lithuania (from 1625) he oversaw the preparation of the third *Lithuanian Statute and opposed the church union and Y. *Kuntsevych's policies. Andrii Sapieha (ca 1560–1621) held various military posts in Lithuania and was briefly voivode of Kiev (1605–9). Kazymyr Lev Sapieha (1609–56) owned estates in the Chornobyl region, served as deputy chancellor of Lithuania (from 1645), fought against B. *Khmelnytsky, halting the Cossack advance on Lithuania in 1649 and in the Battle of Berestechko (1651), and briefly captured Kiev with J. Radziwiłł's forces (1651). Paweł Jan Sapieha (ca 1610–1665) was grand hetman of Lithuania; he fought against the Cossacks near Zboriv (1649), Berestechko (1651), and Suceava (1653) and elsewhere in Galicia, Volhynia, and Polisia. Lev (Leon) Sapieha (1803–78) initially served the Russian Empire; he then participated in the Polish Insurrection of 1830–1 and had to emigrate to Galicia, where he was a political and economic leader (marshal of the Galician Diet, 1861–75) and advocated the abolition of serfdom in Galicia. Adam Sapieha (1828–1903), a Galician Polish politician, advocated Galician autonomy in the 1860s.

A. Zhukovsky

Sapiehin, Andrii [Sapjehin, Andrij] (Sapegin, Andrei), b 11 December 1883 in Voznesenske, Yelysavethrad county, Kherson gubernia, d 8 April 1946 in Kiev. Botanist and selection scientist; full member of the AN URSR (now ANU). A graduate of Odessa University (1907, professor from 1917), he organized and directed the selection department at the Odessa experimental farm (from 1912), which developed into a selection station (1918) and then the All-Union Selection and Genetics Institute (from 1928). He also was a founder and rector (1919–21) of the Odessa Agricultural Institute. He served as deputy director of the Institute of Genetics in Moscow (1933–9) and vice-president of the ANU (1939–45) and director of its Institute of Botany. Sapiehin's research dealt mainly with floristics, cytology, and genetics. He made important contributions to plant breeding and developed new varieties of spring (Odessa 3 and Odessa 4) and winter (Kooperatorka, Stepniachka, and Zemka) wheat and barley (Pallidum 32).

Sapiezhko, Kyrylo [Sapježko], b 18 March 1857, d 1928 in Kishinev, Moldavia. Surgeon. A graduate of Kiev University (1884), he taught there (1889–1901) and at Odessa University (1902–19). In 1906 he was elected chairman of the Sixth Conference of Russian Surgeons in Moscow. From 1919 he lived in Kishinev. His publications dealt with the surgical treatment of cancer and stomach ulcers and the transplantation of the mucous membrane. He proposed a new operation for umbilical hernia.

Sapitsky, Viktor [Sapic'kyj], b 1 August 1889 in the Kiev region, d 9 June 1942 in Poděbrady, Czechoslovakia. Lawyer and co-operative leader. As a student he was active in Ukrainian revolutionary organizations. During the period of Ukraine's independence he directed the Credit Bureau of the UNR Ministry of Finance. From 1922 he lectured on producer and farming co-operatives at the Ukrainian Husbandry Academy in Poděbrady. He helped edit *Ukraïns'kyi inzhener* and *Ukraïns'kyi ekonomist* and contributed articles and reviews to those journals.

Sapolovych, Yakiv [Sapolovyč, Jakiv], b 1760 in Sribne, Chernihiv regiment, d 26 August 1830 in St Petersburg. Surgeon. A graduate of the Kievan Mohyla Academy (1772–8) and of hospital schools in Kronstadt and St Petersburg (1778–83), he invented new versions of surgical instruments for army doctors. He was the first to use percussion in the Russian Empire. He was a professor of surgery at the St Petersburg Medico-Surgical School (from 1790), a member of the Medical Collegium (1795–1804), and director of the St Petersburg Medical Instruments Plant (1796–1829). He died fighting a cholera epidemic.

Sapozhnikov, Leonid [Sapožnikov], b 29 April 1906 in Pavlohrad, Katerynoslav gubernia. Fuel technologist; corresponding member of the USSR (now Russian) Academy of Science from 1946. He graduated from the Dnipropetrovske Mining Institute (1930) and headed a laboratory of the Institute of Fossil Fuels of the USSR Academy of Sciences (1937–61). Then he worked for the USSR State Planning Committee. His scientific contributions deal with coal classification and coal coking.

Sarabei, Oleh [Sarabej], b 3 October 1933 in Ordzonikidze, North Ossetia ASSR. Physicist. After graduating from Rostov University in 1955 he joined the AN URSR (now ANU) Institute of Physics in Kiev, where he subsequently became head of the Division of Solid State Electronics. His principal contributions concern the electronic structure of the solid state.

Sarafinchan, Lillian [Sarafinčan], b 17 April 1935 in Vegreville, Alberta. Painter and film production designer of Ukrainian origin. She studied at the Ontario College of

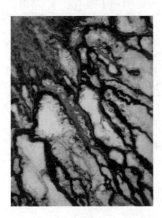

Lillian Sarafinchan: *Orchestration* (watercolor and ink, 1983)

Art in Toronto. In her swirling abstract compositions she explores the interaction of colors and properties of paint by letting the pigments run. The overall surface design is in the tradition of abstract expressionist painting, but the rhythmic patterns and dancing hues are evocative of music without lyrics (eg, her series 'Orchestration'). Sarafinchan has worked on several television and film productions as an art director, and in 1987 she received a Genie Award for best art direction in the film *Dancing in the Dark*.

Bohdan Saramaga

Saramaga, Bohdan, b 1 April 1905 in Ternopil, Galicia, d 10 April 1975 in Detroit. Conductor, violinist, teacher, and composer. In 1927 he graduated from the Lviv Conservatory in the theory and conducting class of A. Soltys. He worked as concertmaster and conductor in various theaters, including Besida in Lviv, the Tobilevych in Stanyslaviv, and the Franko in Ternopil, where he also served as artistic director in 1939–44. He subsequently emigrated to Germany, where he was a violinist in the Munich Radio Orchestra (1949). From 1950 he lived in Detroit, where he worked as a teacher at the Ukrainian Music Institute of America. His compositions include stage music, cantatas to texts by T. Shevchenko and P. Tychyna, and numerous songs.

Sarata. VII-10. A town smt (1986 pop 6,100) on the Sarata River and a raion center in Odessa oblast. It was founded in 1822 by German colonists at the site of the former Tatar settlement of Hura-Kuruder. Part of Bessarabia, it belonged to the Russian Empire in the 19th century and Rumania in 1918–40; then it became part of Ukraine. Sarata is known for its wineries.

Sarata River. A waterway that flows through Moldova and Odessa oblast into Lake Sasyk. It is 119 km long and drains a basin area of 1,250 sq km. Sections of the river are used for irrigation, although its upper course dries out in the summer.

Saratov oblast. An administrative territory set up in the RSFSR on 5 July 1936. Its area is 100,200 sq km, and its 1989 population was 2,686,000, of which 74 percent was urban. The oblast is divided into 38 raions, 17 cities, and 31 towns (smt). Its capital is Saratov. According to the 1959 census, there were 106,700 Ukrainians (4.3 percent of the population) in Saratov oblast, of whom 44,500 specified Ukrainian as their native language. The actual number of

Ukrainians in Saratov oblast is probably higher. According to the more reliable 1926 census, there were 237,000 Ukrainians (7 percent of the population) in the region, 80 percent of whom were fluent in Ukrainian.

Sarbei, Vitalii [Sarbej, Vitalij], b 30 January 1928 in Yanchekrak (now Kamianske), Zaporizhia okruha. Historian. After graduating from Kharkiv University in 1951, he taught history in secondary school. Having completing graduate studies at the AN URSR (now ANU) Institute of History (1956), he joined its staff as a research associate. Since 1978 he has chaired a department there. He has written numerous articles and 16 monographs, including *Isto-rychni pohliady O.M. Lazarevs'koho* (The Historical Views of O.M. Lazarevsky, 1961) and *Istoriia Ukraïny v dozhovtnevii bil'shovyts'kii presi* (The History of Ukraine in the Pre-October Bolshevik Press, 1986).

The building of the Shevchenko Scientific Society in Sarcelles

Sarcelles. A town (1989 pop 58,000) in the department of Val d'Oise in France, 17 km north of Paris. Since 1951 it has been the headquarters of the West European section of the *Shevchenko Scientific Society (NTSh). The society has a library of 20,000 titles and served as the editorial office of *Entsyklopediia ukraïnoznavtsva*. The Ukrainian Students' Aid Commission (1951–82), a representation of the Ukrainian Free University (until 1980), and the Ukrainian Christian Movement were also located there. The town has served as the publishing center of *Visti iz Sarseliu*, *Visti NTSh v Evropi*, and other publications. V. *Kubijovyč, O. Kulchytsky, Z. Kuzelia, O. Shulhyn, and other scholars affiliated with the NTSh are buried in a special section of the local cemetery.

Sardines (*Sardina, Sardinella, Sardinops*; Ukrainian: *sardyny*). The common name for fish of the family Clupeidae and other small (to 30 cm long) herringlike fish. Sardines are eaten fresh, salted, smoked, or canned in oil or tomato or mustard sauce; some are used as animal feed or for oil production. In Ukraine the Atlantic sardine (*Sardina pilchardus*) and *Sardinella aurita* are found in the Black Sea. (See also *Fishing industry.)

Sarkil or **Sarkel.** A fortified Khazar city built in the 830s on the lower Don River. Standing at the crossing of the major trade routes over the Don, Sarkil quickly developed into a trade center with a mixed Khazar, Bulgar, and Oghuz population. It was captured by Sviatoslav I Ihorevych in 965 and converted into an outpost of Kievan Rus' called Bila Vezha. Threatened by the Cumans, the city was abandoned by Rus' in 1117. The remains of Sarkil were studied in 1934–6 and 1949–51 by M. Artamonov.

Sarmatia. The name used by ancient and medieval writers to designate eastern and central Europe, which was occupied by Sarmatians in the later part of the 1st millennium BC. C. Ptolemy (ca 90–168 AD) distinguished between European Sarmatia (between the Don and the Vistula rivers) and Asiatic Sarmatia (east of the Don and the Sea of Azov). On M. Waldseemüller's (1513) and B. Wapowski's (1526) maps of eastern Europe, in Polish (J. Długosz, Maciej of Miechow) and Italian (O. Guanini) chronicles and travel accounts, and in humanist writings of the 16th and 17th centuries the term was used for Ukrainian and Polish territory. Polish magnates and nobles adopted the doctrine of *Sarmatyzm* in the 17th and 18th centuries, which claimed that they were descended from the ancient Sarmatians and were therefore superior to other nations. S. Velychko called the Cossacks Sarmatians, and Yu. Khmelnytsky adopted the title 'prince of Sarmatia.'

Sarmatian Sea. A sea that existed in the late Miocene epoch, around 25 million years ago. It was shallow and low in salinity, and it covered an area from the Carpathian Mountains to the Aral Sea. The sediment left by the Sarmatian Sea can still be found in southern Ukraine, Subcarpathia, and Transcarpathia.

Sarmatians (Ukrainian: *sarmaty*; Greek: *Sarmatai*; Latin: *Sarmatae*). A confederation of nomadic Iranian tribes (Aorsians, *Alans, *Roxolani, Siraces, and Iazyges) related culturally to the *Scythians. Originally, in the 7th to 4th centuries BC, they were known as *Sauromatians. In the 3rd century BC the Sarmatians conquered the Scythians in the Crimea and thenceforth dominated the steppe between the Tobol River in Siberia and the Danube. Most ancient and modern scholars (eg, Polybius, Pliny, M. Vasmer, L. Zgusta) have considered the Sauromatians and the Sarmatians to be the same people, but some (eg, Strabo, M. Rostovtsev) have viewed them as distinct. Contemporary scholars (eg, K. Smirnov, T. Sulimirski) tend to view the Sauromatians as the older ethnic substratum and culture of the Sarmatians.

Having consolidated their power in northern Caucasia and the northern Pontic steppe in the 4th to 2nd centuries BC, the Sarmatians began allying themselves with the Pontic states and helped the Scythians fight the Pontic general Diophantes. In the 1st century BC they were allies of the Pontic king Mithradates VI during his war with Rome. Thereafter the northern Pontic littoral was called *Sarmatia, and it was so designated on M.V. Agrippa's map. Some Sarmatian tribes, notably the Roxolani and Iazyges, colonized what is today southern Bulgaria and Rumania and had frequent conflicts with the Romans there.

The Sarmatians gradually became sedentary after penetrating the Hellenic colonies on the Pontic littoral and settling in the *Bosporan Kingdom. They took up agriculture and assimilated into local cultures there and in the forest-steppe region of Right-Bank Ukraine. Their political might was broken by the Ostrogoths in the 3rd century and the Huns in the 4th century. Some of the Sarmatians migrated west with the Huns and even reached as far as Spain and northern Africa. Those who remained behind intermingled with the indigenous Slavs and other peoples. The language of the Ossetians in northern Caucasia has preserved certain Sarmatian elements.

The initially matriarchal character of the Sarmatian culture (eg, women warriors before marriage) gradually disappeared as the tribes became more organized, the political power of the generals grew, and new military tactics, armor, weapons, and riding equipment (metal stirrups) were introduced. The Sarmatians' cult of the sword and fire was reflected in their art, jewelry, and metal ornamentation of armor and weapons.

BIBLIOGRAPHY
Rostovtsev, M. *Iranians and Greeks in South Russia* (Oxford 1922; repr, New York 1969)
Harmatta, J. *Studies on the History of the Sarmatians* (Budapest 1950)
Shelov, D. (ed). *Voprosy skifo-sarmatskoi arkheologii* (Moscow 1954)
Pasternak, Ia. *Arkheolohiia Ukraïny* (Toronto 1961)
Smirnov, K. *Savromaty: Rannaia istoriia i kul'tura sarmatov* (Moscow 1964)
Sulimirski, T. *The Sarmatians* (London 1970)
Khazanov, A. *Ocherki voennogo dela sarmatov* (Moscow 1971)
Terenozhkin, A.; et al (eds). *Skify i sarmaty* (Kiev 1977)
Smirnov, K. *Sarmaty i utverzhdenie ikh politicheskogo gospodstva v Skifii* (Moscow 1984)

B. Kravtsiv, A. Zhukovsky

Sarny. II-7. A city (1989 pop 34,400) on the Sluch River and a raion center in Rivne oblast. It sprang up as a workers' settlement in 1885, when the Rivne–Luninets railway line was built. Before the First World War the town belonged to Lutske county, Volhynia gubernia. In the interwar period it was under Polish rule, and in 1939 it became part of the Ukrainian SSR. Today the city is an industrial and transportation center. Its main industries are machine building and metalworking, building materials, woodworking, and flax processing.

Rev Klyment Sarnytsky

Sarnytsky, Klyment Karol [Sarnyc'kyj], b 1832, d 1909. Basilian priest and church activist. He taught biblical studies at Lviv University (from 1867) and served several terms as dean and rector of theology. In 1867 he was also appointed hegumen of St Onuphrius's Monastery in Lviv.

He oversaw the reform of the Basilian order in the Galician province by the Jesuits in 1882–1904, and in 1902 he was appointed archimandrite. Sarnytsky wrote a Hebrew grammar textbook in Polish, an elucidation of the Psalms and other biblical songs, and various other religious scholarly works.

Sartana. See Prymorske.

Sasiv. IV-5. A village (1971 pop 700) on the Buh River in Zolochiv raion, Lviv oblast. In 1615 Komarove was renamed Sasiv and granted the rights of *Magdeburg law. In 1675 the town was burned down by the Tatars, and it never recovered its former status. In the 19th century the village became known as a health resort. It is the home of the wooden St Nicholas's Church (1731), which contains a famous iconostasis painted by masters of the Zhovkva school in 1681 and an icon from 1685 depicting the transfer of St Nicholas's relics.

Saskatchewan. A prairie province (1986 pop 1,010,198) of Canada, lying between Manitoba and Alberta and covering an area of 652,330 sq km. Its capital is Regina. Its Ukrainian population in 1981 was 100,090. In the 1991 Canadian census only 28,935 inhabitants claimed Ukrainian as their mother tongue.

The first Ukrainian colony in Saskatchewan was established in 1896 in Grenfell. In subsequent years large numbers of Ukrainian immigrants moved into bloc settlements, the largest of which were in the Yorkton–Canora–Preeceville region (eastern Saskatchewan), the Rosthern–Yellow Creek–Cudworth region (north of Saskatoon), and the Radisson–Hafford–Whitkow region (east of North Battleford). The steady influx of Ukrainian settlers peaked in 1911–14.

St John the Baptist Ukrainian Catholic Church (1926) in Smuts, Saskatchewan

The urbanization of Saskatchewan's Ukrainians is a relatively recent phenomenon. In 1921 only 10 percent lived in cities. This figure jumped from 20.5 percent in 1951 to 63.3 percent in 1981. Ukrainian urban residents are mostly workers, small businessmen, public servants, and professionals. Ukrainians are the largest ethnic group in many rural localities, and in several dozen towns they constitute an absolute majority. Their influence is evident in the names of the localities, the style of the churches, the frequency with which the Ukrainian language and traditions are encountered, and the large number of municipal politicians of Ukrainian origin. The largest Ukrainian communities are in *Saskatoon, *Regina, and *Yorkton. These cities are the centers of Ukrainian religious and cultural life. Because they settled in compact groups, the Ukrainians of Saskatchewan have a higher rate of Ukrainian language-use than the Canadian average.

Holy Trinity Ukrainian Orthodox Church (1963) in Canora, Saskatchewan

St Nicholas's Ukrainian Catholic Church (1912) near Brooksby, Saskatchewan

The largest Ukrainian church in Saskatchewan is Catholic. The Redemptorist Fathers established a monastery (1913) and press in Yorkton; later the Academy of the Sacred Heart (1917), established by the Sisters Servants of Mary Immaculate for girls, and St Joseph's College (1919), established by the Christian Brothers for boys, were opened there. In 1935 the Ukrainian Catholic Brotherhood (est 1932) set up the Sheptytsky Institute in Saskatoon. The second-largest Ukrainian church is the Orthodox church, which had 21,000 faithful in the province in 1981. Saskatoon, with its Mohyla Ukrainian Institute (est 1916), has played an important role in the history of this church. It hosted the founding conferences of the church (1918) and the Ukrainian Self-Reliance League (1927). Saskatoon is the seat of both the Ukrainian Catholic and the Orthodox eparchies. In addition it is the home base of the provincial council of the Ukrainian Canadian Congress. Even though the first Ukrainian-Canadian member of the legislative as-

sembly in Saskatchewan, G. Dragan, was not elected until 1934, Ukrainians have played an important role in the province's political life. In 1952 A. Kuziak became the first Ukrainian to be appointed to a provincial cabinet. In 1956 M. Fedchuk Batten was elected to the provincial legislature, the first woman of Ukrainian origin to win a seat. S. *Worobetz served as the province's lieutenant governor in 1969–75, and S. Fedoruk has served since 1988. R. *Romanow served as deputy premier and as minister of intergovernmental affairs under A. Blakeney (1971–82), succeeded him as leader of the New Democratic party, and became premier of Saskatchewan in 1991. R. *Hnatyshyn, a Conservative MP from Saskatchewan, was a federal cabinet minister (1979–88) and was appointed Governor-General of Canada in 1990.

Ukrainians in Saskatchewan, 1911–81
(in thousands)

Year	Ukrainians	% of total population
1911	22.3	4.5
1921	28.1	3.7
1931	63.4	6.9
1941	79.8	8.9
1951	78.4	9.4
1961	78.9	8.5
1971	85.9	8.1
1981	76.8	8.0

The province passed the Multiculturalism Act in 1974, and in 1978 amended the Education Act to allow for bilingual (including Ukrainian-English) education; passage of the latter has resulted in the launching of a Ukrainian-English school program in Saskatoon.

G. Foty

Saskatoon. The second-largest city (1992 pop 186,058) in Saskatchewan, situated on the South Saskatchewan River. It is the province's chief education, food-processing, mining, and manufacturing center. Of its residents 19,825 identified themselves as of Ukrainian origin in 1981; they constitute the province's largest Ukrainian community. In 1991 only 5,245 inhabitants claimed Ukrainian as their mother tongue. The first group of Ukrainian immigrants

The first building of St George's Ukrainian Catholic Cathedral and rectory and the Prosvita hall in Saskatoon

arrived in Saskatoon in 1898. The earliest Ukrainian institutions were religious: the Ukrainian Catholic parish of St George, which in 1951 became the seat of the Saskatoon eparchy, arose in 1912, and the Orthodox Church of the Holy Theotokos's Induction into the Temple was established in 1916. The city became an important center for Ukrainian Orthodoxy: the *Ukrainian Orthodox Church of Canada (1918), the *Ukrainian Women's Association of Canada (1926), and the *Ukrainian Self-Reliance League (1927) were founded there. In 1963 the Orthodox parish of the Holy Trinity (est 1918) became the seat of Saskatoon eparchy. Since 1929 the city has been an important center of the Ukrainian Evangelical Baptist church, and since 1945 of the Ukrainian Mission and Bible Society. The *Mohyla Ukrainian Institute (est 1916) and the Catholic Shashkevych Student Residence (est 1935), which was reorganized into the *Sheptytsky Institute in 1953, have educated generations of Ukrainian community leaders. The first Ukrainian language and literature courses at a Canadian university were taught by T. Pavlychenko at the University of Saskatchewan in 1944, and the first Canadian Slavic studies department was formed at the university by C. *Andrusyshen in 1945. Since 1977 the same university has had an exchange program with the University of Chernivtsi in Ukraine. A branch of the Ukrainian National Federation was set up in 1932, and the federation's national office was located in Saskatoon (1934–40). Its paper *Novyi shliakh* was published there in 1933–41. The Ukrainian Students' National Federation (1933) and the Ukrainian National Youth Federation (1934) were founded in Saskatoon. In 1939 the first Ukrainian credit union in Canada, the New Community Savings and Credit Union, was organized there. The Ukrainian Museum of Canada (est 1936) has its main branch housed in a modern structure with several exhibition galleries. A Catholic eparchial museum is also situated in the city. Saskatoon is the home of several notable Ukrainian performing ensembles, including the Yevshan Ukrainian Folk Ballet, Pavlychenko Folklorique Ensemble, and the Vesna and Lastivka youth choruses. It also hosts a Ukrainian festival (Vesna) in the spring as well as a multiethnic festival (Folkfest) in the summer. A bilingual Ukrainian-English program has been offered at St Goretti School since 1979.

G. Foty

Sasyk Estuary (Sasyk lyman; also Kunduk Lake). VIII-10. A shoreline lake in the southern part of Odessa oblast along the Black Sea coast. Varying in width from 3 to 12 km, the lake is approx 29 km long and has a surface area of 210 sq km. Although the Kohylnyk and the Sarata rivers flow into it, the Sasyk was long a saltwater lake because of the seepage of Black Sea water into it. Its salinity commonly reached 19–20 per cent in the summer. In 1980 the Sasyk was turned into a freshwater lake with the construction of a canal from the Danube and a 14-km dam to separate it better from the Black Sea. The lake is now used for irrigation.

Sasyk Lake (Sasyk ozero). VIII-14. A salty shoreline lake in the Crimea east of Yevtaporiia. It is 14 km long, up to 9 km wide, and up to 1.2 m deep and has a surface area of 75.3 sq km. It is separated from the Black Sea by sand and gravel deposits up to 1.7 m in height. Nevertheless, since it is fed by groundwater, a certain amount of seawater seeps into the lake. The lake's water level drops in the summer, and deposits of salt are left behind.

Satanovsky, Arsenii. See Koretsky-Satanovsky, Arsenii.

Satire. A literary or artistic mode of ridicule of an individual person, a group, ideas, or society at large, through the use of hyperbole, the grotesque, parody, or irony. In art caricature is employed for the purpose of satire. Since classical times satire has existed in two major strains, the Horatian, which mildly mocks human foibles and frailties, and the Juvenalian, which expresses moral displeasure and indignation at human vices.

In Ukraine some satire appears in folk songs from the earliest times, but in literature satire developed in the 16th and 17th centuries as an effective weapon in the *polemical literature of the time, especially in that of I. *Vyshensky. Some satiric elements were present in the *intermedes of *school and *vertep dramas in the 17th and 18th centuries. In the 18th century, samples of sociopolitical satire of the Horatian tradition appeared: the carol '1764 hoda dekabria 23 dnia k. R.' (1764 Year December 23 day k. R.) by an anonymous author; the 'lampoon verses' by Ieremiia, a monk of the Kievan Cave Monastery, 'Plach kievskikh monakhov' (The Lament of Kievan Monks, 1786) and 'Pribavok k plachu kievskikh monakhov' (Addendum to the Lament of Kievan Monks, 1792); and the dialogue 'Zamysl na popa' (A Design against the Priest), ascribed to I. Nekrashevych. Some satiric elements are to be found in the tales and poems of H. Skovoroda. Likewise, I. Kotliarevsky's *Eneïda* (Aeneid, 1798) satirized contemporary mores.

Satire through irony and sarcasm is found in many of T. Shevchenko's poems, or in parts of poems ('Ieretyk' [Heretic], 'Kavkaz' [Caucasus], 'I mertvym, i zhyvym ...' [To the Dead and to the Living ...], 'Neofity' [Neophytes], 'P.S.,' 'Iurodyvyi' [The Holy Fool], 'Vo Iudeï vo dni ony' [In Judea Long Ago], 'Molytva' [A Prayer], 'Himn chernychyi' [Nuns' Hymn], and 'Saul'). His long poem 'Son' (A Dream) is a political satire, a 'comedy' bordering on the sardonic. Elements of satire can be found in Shevchenko's followers and predecessors, in the fables and proverbs of P. Hulak-Artemovsky, Ye. Hrebinka, and L. Borovykovsky and especially in the *Spivomovky* (Singing Rhymes) of S. Rudansky. Some Horatian satire can be found in works of the second half of the 19th century, such as 'Baba Paraska ta Baba Palazhka' by I. Nechui-Levytsky, 'Lovy' (The

Hunt) by P. Myrny, 'Smikh' (Laughter), 'V dorozi' (On the Way), and 'Koni ne vynni' (Horses Are Not to Blame) by M. Kotsiubynsky, some stories by S. Vasylchenko and L. Martovych, and some comedies of M. Kropyvnytsky and M. Starytsky. Political satire was often used by I. Franko ('Svyns'ka konstytutsiia' [The Swinish Constitution], *Lys Mykyta* [Fox Mykyta], and various poems).

At the beginning of the 20th century satire appeared in the poems of V. Samiilenko, O. Oles (the collection *Perezva* [The Postwedding Party, 1921]), and O. Makovei (the collection *Pryzhmurenym okom* [Through a Squinting Eye, 1923]). After the Revolution of 1917 the populist satirical traditions of the 19th century were continued by Yu. Vukhnal, Yu. Gedz (pseud of O. Savytsky), and V. Chechviansky (all repressed in the 1930s). A special place in satiric literature belongs to O. *Vyshnia (*Usmishky*, 4 vols [Smiles, 1928]). Highly satiric were some of the later stories of M. Khvylovy ('Redaktor Kark' [Editor Kark], 'Ivan Ivanovych,'); some passages of his pamphlets, in their attacks on cultural backwardness and pseudo-enlightenment (*prosvitianstvo*), took on the sarcastic, often sardonic tone of Juvenalian satire.

Satire like all other art forms was of poor quality from the 1930s to the 1960s. Most of the satiric works written, by authors such as D. Bilous, S. Voskrekasenko, P. Kliuchyna, O. Kovinka, Ye. Kravchenko, and S. Oliinyk, were tendentious in the spirit of Party decrees; those of Ya. Halan, Yu. Melnychuk, S. Tudor, and others were defamatory in their attacks on Ukrainian nationalists. True satire revived in the 1960s in some of the poetry of V. *Symonenko, I. Drach, V. Korotych, A. Kosmatenko, and even L. Kostenko. Of interest are the satiric works of the Shevchenko scholar Yu. *Ivakin through to the 1970s. Bitter satire on the realities of the Soviet world is found in the works of repressed dissident authors, such as V. Moroz ('Reportazh iz zapovidnyka imeny Berii' [Report from the Beria Reserve, 1968; trans 1974]) and M. Osadchy (*Bil'mo* [Cataract, 1971]; trans 1976), as well as in some poems of S. Karavansky, I. Kalynets, and others.

In Western Ukraine between the two world wars satire appeared in the feuilletons of T. Horobets (pseud of S. Charnetsky) and R. Kupchynsky. Among émigrés in the West, authors such as E. Kozak (*Hryts' Zozulia*, 1972), I. Kernytsky (*Budni i nedilia* [Weekdays and Sunday, 1973]), M. *Ponedilok, M. Tochylo (M. *Koliankivsky), B. Nyzhankivsky-Babai (*Virshi ironichni, satyrychni i komichni* [Poems Ironic, Satiric, and Comic, 1959]), and Z. Kohut (*Kul'turni arabesky* [Cultural Arabesques, 1969]) continue in the satiric vein, targeting the life of Ukrainians in their new countries of residence. (See also *Humoristic and satiric press.)

BIBLIOGRAPHY
Makivchuk, F. (ed). *Satyra i humor* (Kiev 1955)
Ivakin, Iu. *Satyra Shevchenka* (Kiev 1959)
Duz', I. *Ukraïns'ka radians'ka satyra 20-kh rokiv* (Kiev 1962)
Dzeverin, I. *Problema satiry v revoliutsionno-demokraticheskoi estetike* (Kiev 1962)
Minchyn, B. *Satyra na sluzhbi komunizmu* (Kiev 1964)
Honcharuk, M. *Ukraïns'ka satyra periodu revoliutsiï 1905–1907 rokiv* (Kiev 1966)

B. Kravtsiv, D.H. Struk

Satsiuk, Oleksii [Sacjuk, Oleksij], b 18 October 1909 in Volhynia, d 3 April 1960 in Chicago. Writer and community figure. After studying law at Lviv University he practiced law in Volodymyr-Volynskyi and Dubno in the 1930s. As a postwar émigré he coedited the journal *Litavry* in Salzburg, Austria, and headed the Association of Ukrainian Scholars, Writers, and Artists in Buenos Aires. He emigrated to Chicago in 1958, where he worked as an editor for the journal *Ovyd* and the M. Denysiuk publishing house. His works were published in émigré periodicals and separately as the story collection *Kolosky* (Grain Spikes, 1947), the novels *Smertonostsi* (Bearers of Death, 1947) and *Zlat-zholud'* (The Gold Acorn, 1951), and the plays *Skrypka na kameni* (A Violin on a Rock, 1952) and *U tsarstvi Okha* (In Okh's Realm, 1963).

Sauromatians. Nomadic Iranian tribes that lived in the steppes beyond the Don and the Volga rivers in the 7th to 4th centuries BC. Their origins, culture, and language were similar to those of the Scythians and Sakians. Greek historians, particularly Herodotus, remarked on the central role of women in the Sauromatian society; his observations have been supported by archeological findings. The Sauromatians allied themselves with newly arrived eastern tribes in the 3rd century BC, and from then on they were known as *Sarmatians.

Bishop Nil Savaryn   Peter Savaryn

Savaryn, Nil (Neil), b 19 May 1905 in Staryi Sambir, Galicia, d 8 January 1986 in Edmonton. Ukrainian Catholic bishop. Savaryn entered the Basilian order in 1922 and was ordained in 1931. As a missionary in Alberta he taught at the Basilian monastery at Mundare and performed parish duties until 1943, when he was consecrated as Bishop V. Ladyka's auxiliary. He was named apostolic exarch for Western Canada in 1948, and he became bishop of the newly created eparchy of Edmonton in 1956. He wrote *Rolia ottsiv Vasyliianiv u Kanadi* (The Role of the Basilian Fathers in Canada, 1939) and edited *Propam'iatna knyha z nahody zolotoho iuvileiu poselennia ukraïns'koho narodu v Kanadi* (The Commemorative Book on the Occasion of the Golden Anniversary of Ukrainian Settlement in Canada, 1941). As a participant in the Second Vatican Council Savaryn supported the Ukrainian Catholic patriarchate movement.

Savaryn, Peter (Petro), b 17 November 1926 in Zubrets, Buchach county, Galicia. Lawyer and community leader. He emigrated to Canada in 1949 and graduated from the University of Alberta in 1956. He became a stalwart supporter of the Progressive Conservative party (PC) and served as president of the Alberta PC association and Alberta vice-president for the national association. He was instrumental in the establishment of the Ukrainian-English bilingual school program in Alberta, the *Canadian Institute of Ukrainian Studies, the Canadian Foundation for Ukrainian Studies (president, 1979–83), and the Edmonton-based Heritage Savings and Trust Company. He was a member of the board of governors and of the senate at the University of Alberta (1972–8) as well as the university's chancellor (1982–6). In 1983–8 he was president of the *World Congress of Free Ukrainians. Savaryn was appointed a Queen's Counsel in 1974 and was awarded the Order of Canada in 1987.

Savchak, Demian [Savčak, Dem'jan], b 13 July 1847 in Nowa Wieś, Nowy Sącz county, Galicia, d 29 December 1912 in Lviv. Judge and civic leader. A graduate of Lviv and Cracow (LL D) universities, he was an executive member of the National Democratic party, a deputy to the Galician Diet, and a member of the Galician provincial executive for twelve years (1889–1901). He used his public office to promote the development of Raiffeisen credit co-operatives in Galicia. He was also a founding member and the first director of the *Dnister credit union and a member of the audit committee of the Provincial Audit Union. After losing his seat in the Diet he was appointed to the provincial court in Lviv. Upon retirement he opened his own law office in Borshchiv and was elected deputy marshal of the county council.

Savchak, Volodymyr [Savčak], b 25 May 1911 in Berezhany, Galicia. Painter. In the late 1930s he studied at the Vilnius Academy of Arts. A postwar refugee, since 1948 he has lived in Australia, where he worked as an art teacher. He has painted portraits of Ukrainian historical figures, Australian landscapes (eg, *Morning in Brisbane*), and icons. Ten solo shows of his work have been held in Australia, and several in North America.

Savchenko, Fedir [Savčenko] (Savtchenko, Théodore), b 1892 in the Poltava region, d ? Historian; member of the Shevchenko Scientific Society from 1927. After graduating from the Nizhen Institute of History and Philology he continued studying history, sociology, ethnology, and Romance philology in Paris (from 1914) and became a professor of Russian at the Ecole supérieure de commerce et d'industrie de Paris. In 1918, with E. Denis and A. Thomas, he founded the Cercle d'Etudes Franco-Ukrainiennes and edited its organ, *La France et l'Ucraine*. He also wrote a number of pamphlets, including *L'Ukraine et la question ukrainienne* (1918). In 1919 Savchenko was in charge of the UNR press bureau at the Paris Peace Conference. His contacts with the émigré Ukrainian Party of Socialist Revolutionaries and with M. Hrushevsky assisted him in arranging his return to Ukraine in 1925. In Kiev he worked in the historical section of the VUAN, as director of its Commission of Western and American Studies and Commission of Western Ukraine. He was also the secretary of the socioeconomic section of the VUAN Institute of the Ukrainian Scientific Language and a member of the Commissions for Cultural and Historical Songs and of Modern Ukrainian History. He was also secretary of the journal *Ukraïna* and a corresponding scholar in the Cabinet of Primitive Culture.

Savchenko wrote over 50 articles and monographs, most of which were published by the VUAN in *Ukraïna* and in *Za sto lit*. He wrote about French-Ukrainian cultural ties and the Cossackophilism of P. Mérimée (1925), H. de Balzac in Ukraine (1924), T. Shevchenko in the unpublished correspondence of O. Bodiansky (1930), and on ethnography (a collection of Ukrainian songs from 1827 to 1927, 1927–8). His monograph *Zaborona ukraïnstva 1876 r.* (1930) was republished in the Harvard Series in Ukrainian Studies as *The Suppression of the Ukrainian Activities in 1876* (1970). Savchenko was arrested and imprisoned in 1931, and perished in the Stalinist terror.

A. Zhukovsky

Ihor Savchenko

Savchenko, Ihor [Savčenko], b 11 October 1906 in Vinnytsia, d 14 December 1950 in Moscow. Film director and educator. After completing theater school in Vinnytsia (1921) he worked as an actor and director in various theaters and then studied at the Leningrad Institute of Scenery Art (1926–9). He apprenticed in the Baku Theater of Working Youth, where he acted in N. Shengelaia's film *Dvadtsat'-shest' kommisarov* (Twenty-six Commissars, 1932) and produced the agitprop film *Liude bez ruk* (People without Arms, 1931). In Moscow he directed the movie *Garmon* (The Accordion, 1934) and *Duma o kazake Golote* (Duma about the Cossack Holota, 1937). From the late 1930s Savchenko became a proponent of the heroic-romantic cinema genre. In the Kiev Artistic Film Studio he directed *Vershnyky* (Riders, 1939, based on Yu. Yanovsky's novel), *Bohdan Khmel'nyt'skyi* (1941), *Partyzany v stepakh Ukraïny* (Partisans in the Ukrainian Steppes, 1943, based on O. Korniichuk's play), and *Taras Shevchenko* (1950). He taught in the Moscow State Institute of Cinema from 1946. A biography, by I. Korniienko and M. Berezhny, was published in Kiev in 1963.

Savchenko, Ivan [Savčenko], b 2 March 1862 in Romen county, Poltava gubernia, d 3 November 1932. Pathologist and microbiologist. A graduate of Kiev University (1888), he worked there and in I. Mechnikov's laboratory at the Pasteur Institute (1895). He was a professor at Kazan University (1896–1919) and later at Kuban University (1920–32). In Kazan he also worked at the local bacteriological institute, and in Krasnodar he directed the Kuban Chemico-Bacteriological Institute. In 1905 he prepared an anti–scarlet fever serum, which was widely used in Russia and abroad. In the Kuban he organized efforts to control infectious diseases, such as scarlet fever, malaria, and typhus. He wrote scientific works on infectious diseases, immunity, phagocytosis, leprosy, cholera, anthrax, typhus, rheumatism, and pneumonia. With D. Zabolotny he performed the first enterovaccination experiment: after taking a vaccine by mouth, he swallowed a live culture of cholera.

Savchenko, Kostiantyn [Savčenko, Kostjantyn], b 27 December 1910 in Kherson, d 26 November 1956 in Odessa. Astronomer. A graduate of the Kherson Institute of People's Education (1927), he worked at Kharkiv University (1927–40) and Odessa University (from 1944) and specialized in cosmology, cosmogony, and gravitation theory.

Savchenko, Mykhailo [Savčenko, Myxajlo], b 6 June 1914 in Hlobyne, Kremenchuk county, Poltava gubernia, d 12 August 1982. Playwright and actor. He graduated from the Kharkiv Music and Drama Institute (1938). He performed at the Kharkiv (1938–41) and Kiev (1945–9) Ukrainian drama theaters and was director of the republican Building of Litterateurs. His first play, *Pravo na shchastia* (The Right to Happiness), was published in 1957. He published several collections of plays, *Rozplata za dovir'ia* (Payment for Trust, 1959), *Shliakhy do shchastia* (Roads to Happiness, 1962), *P'iesy* (Plays, 1967), *Travnevi hrozy* (May Storms, 1973), and *Hippokraty* (Hippocrateses, 1983). Published separately were his plays *Lastivka* (The Swallow, 1961), *Prohnozy* (Prognoses, 1962), *Syny Hippokrata* (Hippocrates' Sons, 1962), *Chest'* (Honor, 1963), *Mii syn* (My Son, 1969), and *Proshu vstaty!* (Please Rise!, 1971).

Savchenko, Mykola [Savčenko], b 19 December 1903 in Korsun (now Korsun-Shevchenkivskyi), Kaniv county, Kiev gubernia, d 16 March 1985 in Voroshylovhrad (now Luhanske). Plant selection scientist. A graduate of the Maslivka Institute of Selection and Seed Cultivation (1927), he worked at the Mliiv Orcharding Research Station (1927–30) and the Voroshylovhrad Agricultural Institute (1935–75, as department head; 1975–80, as professor and consultant). His research dealt mainly with the selection of fruit-bearing plants.

Savchenko, Pavlo [Savčenko], b 28 July 1887 in Zhabky (now Lutsenky), Lokhvytsia county, Poltava gubernia, d 1920 in Romen, Poltava gubernia. Symbolist poet; brother of Ya. Savchenko. A graduate of the Poltava Teachers' Seminary, he taught in Krovne (1908–10), Velyka Pysarivka (1910–12), and Derkachi (1912–14, 1918–19), in Kharkiv gubernia. From 1909 his poems and prose-poems appeared in various periodicals. He wrote the collection *Mii smikh, moia zaduma: Epilohy* (My Laughter, My Melancholy: Epilogues, 1913) and a collection in Russian, *Penie pul'* (The Singing of Bullets, 1916).

Savchenko, Stepan [Savčenko], b 28 December 1889 in Syniavka, Sosnytsia county, Chernihiv gubernia, d 16 January 1942 in Tashkent, Uzbekistan. Literary scholar and educator. A graduate of Kiev University (1913), from 1917 he taught foreign literature and Romance philology there. He wrote books in Russian on the Russian folktale (1914) and on the origin of the Romance languages (1916). In the 1920s he published articles and reviews of Western literature in *Zhyttia i revoliutsiia*. He edited, with introductions, Ukrainian editions of works by A. France (1925), R. Rolland (1927), and G. de Maupassant (10 vols, 1927–30), French 17th-century classics (1931), and other foreign works. A book of his selected writings on foreign literature was published in Kiev in 1975.

Col Volodymyr Savchenko   Yakiv Savchenko

Savchenko, Volodymyr [Savčenko], b 1882, d 18 November 1957 in the United States. Senior army officer. He served in various staff positions in the UNR Army, including chief of staff of the Katerynoslav Republican Kish and of the Eighth Zaporozhian Divisions in 1919 and acting first quartermaster general of the UNR Army in 1920. He attained the rank of colonel. During the interwar period he lived in Poland and contributed articles on recent military history to *Za derzhavnist'*, *Tabor*, and other periodicals. After the Second World War he emigrated to the United States.

Savchenko, Yakiv [Savčenko, Jakiv] (pseud: Ya. Mozheiko), b 2 April 1890 in Zhabky (now Lutsenky), Lokhvytsia county, Poltava gubernia, d 2 November 1937. Symbolist poet and literary critic. He studied at Kiev University and taught for a time in Sumy county. He began publishing poetry in Ukrainian periodicals in 1913. Published separately were his collections *Poezii* (Poems, 1918) and *Zemlia* (Earth, 1921). He evolved from *symbolism, as a member of the group Muzahet, and became a leading member of the writers' groups *Zhovten and the *All-Ukrainian Association of Proletarian Writers. From 1918 on he published literary and film criticism in *Mystetstvo*, *Zhyttia i revoliutsiia*, *Nova generatsiia*, and other Soviet Ukrainian journals; some of it was reprinted in his books *Poety i beletrysty* (Poets and Belletrists, 1927), *Doba i pys'mennyk* (The Age and the Writer, 1930), and *Narodzhennia ukraïns'koho radians'koho kino: Try fil'my O. Dovzhenka* (The Birth of Ukrainian Soviet Cinema: Three Films by O. Dovzhenko, 1930). In the *Literary Discussion of the 1920s he expounded the Party line and spoke out against the positions of M. Khvylovy and M. Zerov; his views were expressed in the polemical books *Aziiats'kyi apokalipsis* (The Asiatic Apocalypse, 1926) and *Proty restavratsiï hreko-ryms'koho mystetstva* (Against the Restoration of Greco-Roman Art, 1927). He was arrested during the Stalinist terror in 1937 and executed.

Savchenko, Yurii [Savčenko, Jurij], b 1908? in Poltava gubernia, d ? Literary scholar and critic; associate of the Taras Shevchenko Scientific Research Institute in Kharkiv in the 1920s. In the 1920s and 1930s he wrote articles about contemporary writers and a brochure on the history of T. Shevchenko's grave (1929) and edited an edition of H. Kvitka-Osnovianenko's works. He was arrested in 1934 and incarcerated in a Soviet labor camp, where he most likely perished.

Gen Volodymyr Savchenko-Bilsky   Mykola Savchuk

Savchenko-Bilsky, Volodymyr [Savčenko-Bil's'kyj], b 27 July 1867 in Olyshivka, Chernihiv county, d 21 September 1955 in Abondant, France. Senior naval officer. A commissioned officer of the Russian Black Sea Fleet, in 1917 he joined the Ukrainian armed forces and helped organize and manage the UNR Ministry of the Navy. He commanded the naval officer school in Kamianets-Podilskyi (1919) and directed the chancellery of the Ministry of the Navy (1919–20). He was promoted to rear admiral. In the interwar period he lived in Poland and then France and contributed articles to *Tabor*, *Ukraïns'kyi invalid*, and *Za derzhavnist'*.

Savchuk, Mykola [Savčuk], b 16 December 1899 in Zubivshchyna, Iziaslav county, Volhynia gubernia, d 16 February 1976 in Odessa. Zoologist; corresponding member of the AN URSR (now ANU) from 1948. A graduate of the Odessa Institute of People's Education (1930), he taught at medical, agricultural, and food-processing institutes in Odessa (1930–5) and at Odessa University (1934–48, rector from 1939). He was minister of education of the Ukrainian SSR (1948–9). His main research was in experimental biology, including regeneration, transplantation, and helminthology. He wrote *Zoolohiia bezkhrebetnykh* (The Zoology of Invertebrates, 1954).

Savchuk, Oleksii [Savčuk, Oleksij], b 30 March 1912 in Fediukivka, Zvenyhorodka county, Kiev gubernia. Writer and newpaper editor. Since 1947 he has published three books of sketches and stories, a book about O. Boichenko (1957), and the novels *Zelene sontse* (The Green Sun, 1962), *Hryhorii Ivanovych* (1967, about H. Petrovsky), *Misiats' liutyi* (The Month February, 1971), *Hostre pys'mo* (Sharp Handwriting, 1976), and *Vysoki khvyli* (Tall Waves, 1980, about V. Lenin in 1900–1).

Savchuk, Semen. See Sawchuk, Semen.

Stefaniia Savchuk

Savchuk, Stefaniia [Savčuk, Stefanija] (née Herytska), b 27 March 1899 in Zolochiv, Galicia, d 19 April 1988 in Toronto. Educator and civic leader. She graduated from the Zolochiv teachers' seminary and was a member of the Society. In 1924 she emigrated to Canada, and in 1932 she organized the Ridna Shkola Olha Basarab Women's Society in Toronto, which in 1934 became a part of the *Ukrainian Women's Organization of Canada (OUK). She was an executive member of OUK for many years, and then president (1954–72) and honorary president (1972–88). At the same time she was active in the Ukrainian National Federation as a member of its executive and presidium and in the Ukrainian Canadian Committee (now Congress). She sat on the board of directors of the Ukrainian Cultural and Educational Centre, the Ukrainian Canadian Relief Fund, the Novyi Shliakh publishing house, and the Ukrainian (Toronto) Credit Union. In 1948 she was one of the founders of the *World Federation of Ukrainian Women's Organizations, and she served as its vice-president (1956–71) and president (1971–7). As a member of the Pan-American Ukrainian Conference, she helped organize the World Congress of Free Ukrainians, served on its executive (1968–71), and headed its Welfare Council (1978–83). She was active in Canadian organizations, such as the Red Cross, the Health Council of Canada, and the National Council of Women.

Savchynsky, Hryhorii [Savčyns'kyj, Hryhorij], b 1804, d 16 February 1888 in Zvenyhorod, Galicia. Greek Catholic priest and civic activist. He contributed poems, short stories, novelettes, and articles to Galician papers, such as *Slovo*, *Nedilia*, *Lastivka*, *Zoria halytska*, *Chytanka*, *Vechernytsi*, and *Dom i shkola*. His short story 'Het! het! het!' (Away! Away! Away! 1851) is a temperance story typical of the 1850s. Some of his works were published by the Kachkovsky Society

Savchynsky, Mykola [Savčyns'kyj], b and d ? Civic activist and publicist. He was coeditor (1854–7) and then chief editor of *Zoria halytska* and its supplement *Poucheniia tserkovnyia* (Church Teachings, 1853–4). Under his editorship the journal was published in vernacular Ukrainian.

Savelov, Yoakim, b 1620, d 1690 in Moscow. Patriarch of Moscow. He entered the Mezhyhiria Tranfiguration Monastery in 1655. In 1657 he became archimandrite of a monastery in Moscow. He was consecrated metropolitan of Novgorod in 1673 and elevated to the dignity of Patriarch of Moscow in 1674. As patriarch, Savelov was particularly interested in gaining jurisdiction over Kiev metropoly from the Patriarch of Constantinople and reached an agreement on this matter with Hetman I. Samoilovych. He extended Moscow's control over the Ukrainian church by confirming the election of H. Sviatopolk-Chetvertynsky as Kievan metropolitan and establishing his authority over the metropolitan. The Patriarch of Constantinople agreed to the formal transfer of jurisdiction in 1686. Savelov repressed Westernizing Ukrainian and Belarusian churchmen and theologians in Moscow in his campaign against Western influences in church literature and education.

Savenko, Petro, b 1795, d 1843. Surgeon and ophthalmologist. A graduate of the St Petersburg Medico-Surgical Academy (1813), he specialized in surgery and ophthalmology in Germany. From 1822 he lectured at the academy on ophthalmology and surgery. His publications dealt with frostbite, burns, bladder surgery, and the mineral waters of Caucasia.

Hurii Savin   Karlo Savrych (Maksymovych)

Savin, Hurii, b 1 February 1907 in Vesegonsk, Tver gubernia, Russia, d 28 October 1975 in Kiev. Physicist, specialist in the field of mechanics; full member of the AN URSR (now ANU) from 1948. He graduated from Dnipropetrovske University (1932), became director of the ANU Institute of Mining Mechanics (1940–5), and headed various technical agencies in Lviv. He was rector of Lviv University (1945–52), vice-president of the ANU (1952–7), and chairman of the ANU Council for the Study of the Productive Resources of the Ukrainian SSR. Savin taught at Kiev University and chaired a department of the ANU Institute of Mechanics (1957–75). His main scientific contributions were in the field of the strength of materials and in the theory of elasticity, particularly as applied to mining technology. He developed equations and methods to calculate stresses and deformations in homogeneous and polymeric materials, and calculated dynamic stresses in elevator cables in mines.

Savin, Viktor, b 13 February 1907 in Zavadivka, Yelysavethrad county, Kherson gubernia, d 9 June 1971 in Lviv. Painter. He studied under S. Prokhorov and O.

Kokel at the Kharkiv Art Institute (1924–7). From 1946 he worked in Lviv. His works include portraits of U. Karmaliuk (1937), T. Shevchenko (1939) and I. Franko; genre paintings, such as *The First Tractor Column in the Village* (1930), *Class Vengeance* (1935), and *Our Girls* (1966–7); and posters and book illustrations.

Savings. Accumulated money that is not used by the population for consumption. When the money is deposited in banks, savings become one of the most important sources of capital for the economy. Prior to 1917, banks in the Russian and Austro-Hungarian empires served primarily commercial needs; their role as savings institutions was minor. (See *Banking system.) Following the 1917 Revolution, savings banks were established in the USSR and in Ukraine to absorb any excess income that was not spent by workers on their immediate needs. Because of widespread poverty and difficult living conditions in the 1920s and 1930s, savings were low and played a minor role in national finance. Fear of property confiscation discouraged people from opening savings accounts. From 1950, savings in the USSR increased at a remarkable rate. The growth was attributable mostly to the imbalance between the money supply and the consumer-goods supply. As wages and salaries rose, earners had few alternatives to depositing their unused funds into savings accounts. Thus, savings served the dual purpose of preventing inflation by absorbing the excess spending power of consumers, and channeling funds into the national economy. The growth in savings indicated a chronic shortage of consumer goods, not a higher level of affluence.

Just prior to the dissolution of the USSR depositors could open five different kinds of accounts: demand deposits, time deposits, conditional accounts, lottery accounts, and current accounts. There were four different kinds of individual savings institutions in the USSR: the central savings societies, banks of the first and second order, and savings agencies. Interest on savings was very low, 2–3 percent. Because it fell below the inflation rate, the real interest rate was negative.

Although depositing money into a savings account was relatively simple, withdrawing funds from an account (even in the case of demand deposits) was a complicated process. Depositors were allowed to withdraw only limited amounts of money at a time and had to explain what they intended to do with it. For that reason many people avoided savings banks and hoarded their savings at home, especially people involved in black market operations. With the economic reforms of 1990, a number of new co-operative savings societies have sprung up in Western Ukraine. They may be the harbinger of further changes in savings institutions.

Annual deposits in savings accounts
in Ukraine, 1940–88 (in billion rubles)

Year	Rubles
1940	0.1
1970	9.2
1980	34.3
1985	49.7
1988	65.7

By 1988 Ukraine's population had deposited a total of 65.7 billion rubles in various savings accounts. Of that amount 48.0 billion were deposited in urban areas, and 17.7 billion in rural areas. The average annual deposit amount was 1,516 rubles.

D. Goshko, B. Krawchenko

Savka, Andrii, b ca 1619 in Stebnyk, in the Prešov region, d ? Legendary leader of *opryshoks in the Prešov, Sian, and Lemko regions. During the Cossack-Polish War of 1648–57 he and V. Chepets commanded a force of 500 opryshoks that attacked Polish estates and castles (eg, in Sianik), fought units of the Polish nobility, and helped the Polish peasant rebels led by A. Napierski Kostka to fight the army of Bishop P. Gembicki of Cracow at Czorsztyn (1651). According to some sources Savka was captured and executed in Muszyna, near Nowy Sącz, in 1661.

Savoika, Teodor [Savojka], b 16 February 1866 in Liubychi Kniazi, Rava Ruska county, Galicia, d 14 July 1943 in Bircha, Dobromyl county, Galicia. He completed his theological studies in Lviv and Peremyshl and in 1901 became a parish priest in the Bereziv district. He was instrumental in the development of Ukrainian institutions in the Sian region. He also helped found the National Democratic party. Several collections of his sermons were published (1900, 1910, 1924).

Savran [Savran']. V-11. A town smt (1986 pop 7,100) at the junction of the Savranka and the Boh rivers and a raion center in Odessa oblast. It was first mentioned in historical documents at the end of the 14th century, when it was under Lithuanian rule. After 1569 it belonged to the Koniecpolski and Lubomirski magnate families. S. Koniecpolski built a fortress in the 17th century to defend the town against Turkish and Tatar attacks. After a brief period of Cossack rule (1654–67) Savran belonged to the Polish Commonwealth. In 1793 it was annexed by Russia, and later it was turned into a military settlement (1839–65). By the end of the 19th century it was a busy trading center. Today Savran is the center of a farming region and has a food industry.

Savran camp site. A Neolithic Boh-Dniester culture settlement of the 5th to early 4th millennium BC located near Savran, Odessa oblast. Excavations in 1949 and 1955 uncovered the remains of two dwellings, one of which had a stone foundation and used framing posts. Flint tools, a bone hoe, and pottery fragments were also recovered at the site.

Savranka River. A right-bank tributary of the Boh River, which it joins at Savran, that flows through Vinnytsia and Odessa oblasts. The river is 97 km long and drains a basin area of 1,770 sq km. Its waters are used for industrial and agricultural purposes as well as for irrigation and pisciculture.

Savrych, Karlo [Savryč] (pseud: Maksymovych), b 18 January 1892 in Kukilnyky, Rohatyn county, Galicia, d 1937. Western Ukrainian Communist activist. In February 1919 he chaired the conference establishing the Communist Party of Eastern Galicia (KPSH, later the *Communist Party of Western Ukraine, or KPZU) in Stanyslaviv. Savrych was elected Party secretary. To escape arrest he fled to Czechoslovakia, and then to Austria (1920). In Vienna he formed the Foreign Committee of the KPSH and founded the newspaper *Nasha pravda*. Savrych adhered to a national-communist perspective and was a leading figure in the Party's Vasylkiv faction. In 1922–4 he was secretary of the Soviet Ukrainian diplomatic mission in Warsaw. In August 1924, after being expelled from Warsaw, he took over the position of director of the Foreign Office of Aid for the Revolutionary Movement in Western Ukraine in Kharkiv and represented the interests of the KPZU before the Central Committee of the CP(B)U (to which he was elected as an alternate member and, from October 1925, a full member). On 3 March 1927 he spoke out strongly at a critical meeting of the CP(B)U Central Committee in defense of O. *Shumsky, who had come under attack for his political views. As a result he was later sent into administrative exile in Astrakhan. Subsequently he was repressed, and died in the Stalinist terror.

J. Radziejowski

Savur, Klym (nom de guerre of Dmytro Kliachkivsky), b 1914? in Galicia, d 12 February 1945 in Klevan raion, Rivne oblast. Senior UPA commander and OUN leader. After being arrested by the NKVD in 1941 for OUN activities, he was saved from execution by the outbreak of the Nazi-Soviet War. In early 1942 he was leader of the OUN (Bandera faction) in the northwestern region (Volhynia and Polisia), and in the autumn he organized combat units to fight the Germans. As the OUN combat units coalesced into the UPA in 1943, he became its commander in chief. After the reorganization and consolidation of the UPA, the Ukrainian People's Self-Defense, and other insurgent units at the end of 1943, he became, at the rank of major, commander of the UPA-North. He was killed in action by NKVD troops and promoted posthumously to colonel.

Savych [Savyč]. A family line of Cossack officers in the Chernihiv region, established by Sava *Prokopovych, who was a high-ranking *starshyna* officer, captain of Voronezh regiment (1669), and general judge (1687–1700). He traveled to Moscow with Hetman I. Mazepa on 26 July 1687. Sava's son, Semen *Savych, was the brother-in-law of P. Polubotok. He died in prison and was buried in the Aleksandr Nevsky Monastery. A branch of the Savych family relocated to Slobidska Ukraine in the early 18th century.

Other members of the Savych family line included Petro Savych (b 14 May 1729), who worked in the General Military Chancellery (1747–9 and 1751–4) and assisted Hetman K. Rozumovsky (1761); Danylo Savych (d 1763), who graduated from the Kievan Mohyla Academy (1743–9) and Moscow and Württemberg universities (1754) and became a professor of geography and physics at Moscow University (1757–61); and Oleksii *Savych, a 19th-century astronomer and mathematician.

Another Savych family line died out in the 18th century. Its members included Sava Savych, who served as captain (1671–2, 1695) and judge (1672, 1675) in Lubni regiment, and Sava's son, Vasyl Savych (d 1714), a captain (1695–1702, intermittently), osaul (1698–1700), and colonel of Lubni regiment (1709–14).

Savych, Ivan [Savyč] (pseud of Ivan Lukianenko), b 19 January 1914 in Savynky, Sosnytsia county, Chernihiv gubernia. Poet. He graduated from the Kharkiv Institute of

Journalism (1934) and Kiev University (1940) and worked as a newspaper editor in Kiev and a teacher in Kremianets and the Donbas. He was interned in German POW (1942–5) and Stalinist labor camps (1948–56). From 1957 on he published numerous poetry collections, including the representative selection *Zirko moia vechorova* (O My Evening Star, 1984), the long poem *Mariia Zan'kovets'ka* (1961), the novel *Iun' komunivs'ka* (The Commune's Youth, 1976), and the book of memoiristic narratives *Nezboryma pam'iat'* (Unfaltering Memory, 1980).

Savych, Oleksander [Savyč] (pseud: Ivan Tarasenko), 1846–1902. Writer and lawyer; member of the Lubni circuit court. He wrote the poetry collection *Na Vkraïni* (In Ukraine, 1889) and the long poems *Hanusia* (1891) and *Kyrylo: Svitova poema* (Kyrylo: A Wordly Poem, 1896). Seven poems and two stories appeared in the literary miscellany *Persha lastivka* (The First Swallow, 1905).

Savych, Oleksii [Savyč, Oleksij], b 30 March 1811 in Pushkarivka, Sumy county, Slobidska Ukraine gubernia, d 27 August 1883 in Tula gubernia, Russia. Astronomer and mathematician; member of the Russian Imperial Academy of Sciences from 1862. He studied at Kharkiv University and graduated from Moscow University (1829) and the Professorial Institute of Dorpat (Tartu) University (PH D, 1839). As a professor at St Petersburg University (1839–80) he contributed to areas such as the calculation of orbits of comets and planets, planetary science, optical refraction phenomena in astronomical observations, barometric corrections of optical observations, and gravimetric measurements. He was one of the first astronomers to use the theory of probability to interpret astronomical observations. He carried out geodesic measurements between the Black and the Caspian seas and proved that the sea levels of the two differ markedly. He wrote over 100 scientific papers; monographs on the application of practical astronomy in the geographical determination of places (1845) and on the application of the theory of probabilities in calculating observations (1857), both of which were translated into German; and an astronomy textbook (2 vols).

Savych, Semen [Savyč], b and d ? Cossack officer. Previously a registered Cossack, he was colonel of Kaniv regiment (1648–51) and an officer in charge of home front security and the mobilization of Cossack troops. He also carried out important diplomatic missions to Russia (1651) and the Crimea (1654).

Savyntsi [Savynci]. IV-18. A town smt (1986 pop 5,700) on the Dinets River in Balakliia raion, Kharkiv oblast. A Cossack settlement was established at the site in 1671. It belonged to Kharkiv and then to Izium regiment. The farming settlement was destroyed by the Tatars several times. In 1923 Savyntsi became a raion center of Izium okruha. In 1962 one of the largest sugar refineries in Ukraine was built in the town.

Savytska, Ivanna [Savyc'ka] (née Trashnevska), b 14 March 1914 in Oparivka, Krosno county, Galicia. Writer; wife of R. Savytsky. Her poems, fairy tales, stories for children, plays, songs, games, and riddles were first published in the 1930s in the Galician periodicals *Vohni*,

Ivanna Savytska

Olena Savytska

Ukraïns'kyi Beskyd, *Mii pryjatel'*, *Svit dytyny*, and *Ukraïns'ke doshkillia*. A postwar refugee in the United States since 1949, she has contributed to émigré papers and children's and women's magazines. She is the author of the verse collections *Sertse* (Heart, 1953), *Molodi pisni* (Young Songs, 1957, with music by M. Fomenko), and *Nezabud'ky* (Forget-me-nots, 1959); the story collections *Nasha khatka* (Our Little House, 1957), *Zoloti dzvinochky* (Golden Bellflowers, 1958), *Try kazochky* (Three Fairy Tales, 1961), and *Dennyk Romtsia* (Little Roman's Journal, 1963); the plays *Kazkafantaziia* (A Fairy Tale–Fantasy), *Spliacha korolivna* (The Sleeping Princess), and *Hist' iz neba* (A Guest from Heaven, 1955); and the feuilleton collection *Z ptashynoho letu* (From a Bird's-eye View, 1974).

Savytska, Olena [Savyc'ka] (née Kharechko; Helen Savitsky), b 17 February 1901 in Poltava. Geneticist and embryologist. A graduate of Leningrad University (1940), she worked in Kiev at the All-Union Scientific Research Institute of the Sugar Industry (1927–41) and the Ukrainian Scientific Research Institute of Plant Cultivation, Selection, and Genetics (1941–3). After emigrating to Germany (1944) and then to the United States she was a cytogeneticist with the US Department of Agriculture (from 1947) and the Beet Sugar Development Foundation (1947–61). Together with her husband, V. *Savytsky, she developed a monogerm sugar beet.

Savytska, Stefaniia [Savyc'ka, Stefanija], b 15 July 1891 in Peremyshl, Galicia, d 15 July 1977 in Toronto. Civic activist; wife of M. *Matchak. She was a founding member of the Union of Ukrainian Women in Lviv (1917) and the Ukrainian Women's Union in Vienna (1920). After returning from Vienna to Lviv in 1921, she worked as a bookkeeper and served on the audit committee of the Trud cooperative. She helped set up the Ukrainske Narodne Mystetstvo co-operative and then its magazine *Nova khata* (1925). After the Second World War she settled in Philadelphia, where she served as business manager of the women's magazine *Nashe zhyttia*.

Savytsky [Savyc'kyj]. A family line of Cossack officers, whose members later became landowners and community activists in the Poltava and Chernihiv regions. Stepan *Savytsky was a military clerk (1712) and the chancellor of Lubni regiment (1714–39), and a member of the codification committee that compiled the Code of Laws of 1743.

Among the descendants of the Savytsky family line were Andrii Savytsky (1811–84), a landowner in Krolevets who was an activist for peasant reform in 1861, an economist and philosopher, and the author of the work *Opyt estestvennogo bogosloviia* (Inquiry into Natural Theology, 1879–84); Andrii's nephew, Mykola *Savytsky, marshal of the nobility in Krolevets county (1896–9), head of the Chernihiv gubernia zemstvo administration (from 1906), and Chernihiv gubernial starosta in 1918; and Mykola's son, Petro *Savytsky.

Savytsky, Kostiantyn [Savyc'kyj, Kostjantyn], b 1 June 1901 in Pishchanka, Olhopil county, Podilia gubernia. Agronomist and doctor of agricultural sciences (1965). He graduated from the Faculty of Agricultural Organization at the Kiev Polytechnic Institute (1929) and worked as an experimental researcher at the farm-machinery standardization bureau of the Kiev Institute of Machine Science, and then headed the Groznyi base of the All-Union Institute of Grain Production. From 1935 to 1967 he was a senior research associate of the Ukrainian Scientific Research Institute of Land Cultivation. His most important works concern the technology of buckwheat growing.

Savytsky, Mykola [Savyc'kyj], b 1867, d 1940s? Civic and political activist. A landowner in Krolevets county, he was president of the Chernihiv gubernia zemstvo (1906–14). In the Hetman government of 1918 he served as deputy minister of internal affairs.

Savytsky, Oleksii [Savyc'kyj, Oleksij] (pseuds: Yukhym Hedz, Oles Yasny), b 30 March 1896 in Zolotonosha, Poltava gubernia, d 15 July 1937 in Kiev. Popular humorist and playwright of the 1920s and 1930s. He studied at the Lysenko Music and Drama Institute in Kiev and was a member of the Pluh peasant writers' association. His humorous and satirical stories and feuilletons of rural life in Soviet Ukraine were published in many Soviet Ukrainian papers and magazines and separately as the collections *Avtor Troiandenko* (Author Troiandenko, 1927), *Buvaie i take* (Such Things Happen, 1927), *Pryntsypiial'no* (On Principle, 1929), *Trohlodyty* (Troglodytes, 1929), *Bubna – kozyr* (Diamonds – Trump, 1930), *Zavziatyi seredniak* (The Zealous Middle Peasant, 1930), *Konkurs na hopak* (Hopak Contest, 1930), *Ti zh i Myron Hrechka* (They and Myron Hrechka, 1931), *Stolychnyi hist'* (Guest from the Capital, 1930), *Pershyi ispyt* (First Exam, 1931), and *Tykhoiu sapoiu* (With a Quiet Hoe, 1933). He also wrote several plays, and an edition of his comedies was published in 1931. Savytsky was arrested in 1936 and was executed by the NKVD.

Savytsky, Omelian [Savyc'kyj, Omeljan], b 1845 in Hrabivka, Kalush county, Galicia, d 8 August 1921 in Bolekhiv, now in Ivano-Frankivske oblast. Pedagogue. He graduated from Lviv University with a doctorate in physics and mathematics and taught at the Academic Gymnasium of Lviv from 1871 until 1907, when he became director of a gymnasium in Ternopil, a post he held until 1914. He was the author of the first textbooks in mathematics and physics published in Ukrainian for secondary school students in Galicia. He also worked on a Ukrainian terminology for mathematics and physics.

Petro Savytsky   Roman Savytsky

Savytsky, Petro [Savyc'kyj], b 29 June 1899 in Bila, Kamianets-Podilskyi county, Podilia gubernia, d 29 September 1983 in Munich. Scientist and educator. A UNR Army veteran, he completed two doctorates in Prague (in philosophy in 1924 and in natural science in 1931) and lectured at Charles University and at the Ukrainian Higher Pedagogical Institute. At the same time he undertook private research and published articles in Czech, German, and Polish scientific journals. After the Second World War he taught at the *Ukrainian Technical Husbandry Institute in Regensburg, where he served as rector in 1952–61.

Savytsky, Roman [Savyc'kyj], b 11 March 1907 in Sokal, Galicia, d 12 January 1960 in Philadelphia. Concert pianist, educator, and critic. He studied piano with V. Barvinsky at the Lysenko Higher Institute of Music in Lviv (1923–7) and with J. Herman at the Prague State Conservatory, where in 1932 he graduated from the master school for pianists in the class of V. Kurz. He performed extensively in 1932–52 as soloist with symphony orchestras and in recitals in Ukraine, Poland, Czechoslovakia, Germany, and the United States, and also performed on radio in Prague, Lviv, Kiev, and Philadelphia. In the 1930s he taught piano at the Lysenko Higher Institute of Music (Lviv, also Stryi and Sambir branches), and in 1939–41 he was assistant professor and dean of the piano department at the Lviv State Conservatory. In 1941–4 he worked as music editor and music director at Lviv Radio. He subsequently emigrated to Germany, where he founded and directed Ukrainian music schools in Karlsfeld and Berchtesgaden (1945–9). After his arrival in Philadelphia (1949) he became a faculty member of the Settlement Music School and of the Philadelphia Conservatory. From 1952 he was involved in the formation and development of the *Ukrainian Music Institute of America, of which he was the first director (1952–9). His students included V. Baley, I. Kondra-Fedoryka, Z. Krawciw-Skalsky, O. Kryshtalsky, N. Nedilsky-Slobodian, Yu. Oliinyk, J. Osinchuk, R. Savytsky Jr, M. Shlemkevych-Savytsky, and I. Zadorozhny.

R. Savytsky

Savytsky, Roman, Jr [Savyc'kyj], b 9 March 1938 in Lviv. Musicologist; son of R. *Savytsky. He studied music theory and piano (1945–60) with his father and at the Ukrainian Music Institute of America (1959). He completed a degree in library science at the Drexel Institute of Technology in Philadelphia (1962), where he specialized

Roman Savytsky, Jr   Viacheslav Savytsky   Rev Semen Sawchuk   Terry Sawchuk

in music bibliography. His writings include an English-language introduction with notes to the first volume of Z. Lysko's *Ukraïns'ki narodni melodiï* (Ukrainian Folk Melodies, 1967); bibliographies on M. Lysenko, Z. Lysko, and M. Holubets; discographies with notes on O. Myshuha, M. Menzinsky, and others; and *Ukrainian Film Guide* (1980). He has also written numerous articles and reviews in the Ukrainian periodical press and contributed entries to Ukrainian and American encyclopedias. Since 1988 he has been the music subject editor for the *Encyclopedia of Ukraine*.

Savytsky, Stepan [Savyc'kyj], b ca 1684 in the Lubni region, d 1751. Cossack officer. He served as chancellor of Lubni regiment from 1714 to 1739. In 1718 he translated into Ukrainian the first part of S. Twardowski's epic poem *Wojna domowa ...* (The Civil War ..., 1681), which was later published in the addenda to S. Velychko's Chronicle by the Kiev Archeographic Commission (vol 4, 1864). M. Hrushevsky regarded Savytsky's *Povest' o kozatskoi voine s poliakami* (The Story of the Cossack War with the Poles, 1718) as an independent historiographical work (1934). Savytsky was a member of the commission that compiled the *Code of Laws of 1743.

Savytsky, Viacheslav [Savyc'kyj, V'jačeslav] (Savitsky), b 1902 in the Kuban, d 16 April 1965 in Salinas, California. Biologist. A graduate of the Kharkiv Agricultural Institute (1924) and Leningrad University (1939), he headed the genetics laboratory at the All-Union Scientific Research Institute of the Sugar Industry (1930–41) and worked in Kiev (1941–3), Poznań (1943–5), and Halle, Germany (1945–7). After emigrating to the United States (1947) he worked for the Beet Sugar Development Foundation in Salt Lake City, Utah (1947–61), and Salinas. Savitsky and his wife, O. *Savytska, obtained productive monogerm varieties of sugar beet that enabled sugar-beet farming to be mechanized and are in use today throughout the world.

Sawchuk, Semen (Savčuk), b 14 February 1895 in Volkivtsi, Borshchiv county, Galicia, d 28 October 1983 in Winnipeg. Orthodox priest and community leader. Sawchuk emigrated to Canada with his parents in 1899. Active at the Mohyla Ukrainian Institute in Saskatoon, he took part in the founding conference of the *Ukrainian Ortho-

dox Church of Canada in 1918 and later was instrumental in establishing the *Ukrainian Self-Reliance League. He was ordained in 1920 and played a leading role in the development of the church as administrator of the consistory (1933–51) and head of its presidium (1955–63). He organized and oversaw a seminary that was attached to the consistory in 1932–45, and he helped found *St Andrew's College in 1946 and served as its rector in 1952–5. Prominent in the formation of the Ukrainian Canadian Committee (now Congress), he was its vice-president (1940–56) and an honorary president after 1980. He was president of the Ethnic Press Club of Canada (1964–7) and author of *Iak postala Ukraïns'ka pravoslavna tserkva v Kanadi* (How the Ukrainian Orthodox Church in Canada Was Formed, 1924), *Tserkovni kanony v teorii i praktytsi* (Church Canons in Theory and Practice, 1955), and *Istoriia Ukraïns'koï hreko-pravoslavnoï tserkvy v Kanadi* (History of the Ukrainian Greek Orthodox Church in Canada, 1985). His plays and short stories appeared under the pseudonym Matveiv Semen.

Sawchuk, Terry (Terrance), b 28 December 1929 in Winnipeg, d 31 May 1970 in New York. Professional hockey player. As a goaltender in 21 seasons, he recorded a goals-against-average of 2.52 with 103 regular-season and 12 play-off shutouts. He won the Calder Trophy as the National Hockey League (NHL) rookie of the year (1950–1) and the Vezina Trophy as the best goaltender in 1951–2, 1952–3, 1954–5, and 1964–5 (shared). He was a member of four Stanley Cup winners as a player with the Detroit Red Wings (1952, 1954, 1955) and Toronto Maple Leafs (1967). He was inducted into the NHL Hall of Fame in 1971.

Sazhen. See Weights and measures.

Sazhin, Mikhail [Sažin, Mixail], b 1814 in Galich, Kostroma gubernia, Russia, d ca 1885 in Omsk, Russia. Russian painter; full member of the St Petersburg Academy of Arts from 1855. In 1846 he and T. Shevchenko shared a dwelling and worked together on an album of Kiev landscapes, some of which were published as lithographs in the late 1840s by I. Laufer. Sazhin's paintings include *St Sophia Cathedral, Vydubychi Monastery, Shchekavytsia – Prince Oleh's Burial Place, At the Dnieper Crossing, Celebration of the Founding of the Chain Bridge in Kiev, Old Kiev:*

Mikhail Sazhin: *Shchekavytsia* (1840s)

Pecherske, View of Kiev from Kurenivka, Kiev University, Ruins of the Golden Gates, The Podil District, Monument to St Volodymyr, St Andrew's Church, St Nicholas's Monastery, and *St Cyril's Monastery.*

Sazhin, Viktor [Sažin], b 15 April 1917 in Yuriuzan, Ufa gubernia, Russia, d 2 October 1985 in Kiev. Technological chemist; AN URSR (now ANU) corresponding member from 1978. He graduated from the Kazakh Mining and Metallurgy (now Polytechnical) Institute in 1951. He worked there and, later, at the ANU Institute of General and Inorganic Chemistry (1961–76). He developed the theoretical foundation for industrial utilization of mineral raw materials, particularly those of low quality; introduced the upgrading of aluminum ores by autoclave treatment with acids or bases; and devised treatments for industrial wastes with high sulfur content.

Sazonov, Vitalii, b 4 April 1947 in Siberia, d 6 September 1986 in Munich. Painter. He studied archeology and history at Odessa University before devoting himself full time to painting in 1972. He participated in two exhibitions of Ukrainian nonconformist art held in a private Moscow apartment in 1975 and 1976, as well as in other unofficial exhibitions. In 1980 he was allowed to emigrate to the West, and settled in Munich. He worked in an abstract, nonobjective manner inspired by the writings of V. Kandinsky, abstract art, and the texture, color, and composition of old icons. Many of his paintings are carefully balanced, serene compositions that convey the metaphysical spirit of icons without the canonical rendering of the figures, which have been replaced by a combination of geometric and symbolic forms constituting a transformation of the visual conventions of the icon into a modern, abstract idiom (eg, *Untitled* [1979] and *Stone Baba with Angel* [1979]). The surface of his paintings is a rich overlay of colors and glazes partly stripped to reveal the layers underneath, as well as textured areas with darkened details. Solo exhibitions of his work were held in Germany, France, Spain, Australia, and Canada, and an album of his paintings was published in 1984.

Sbornik Khar'kovskogo istoriko-filologicheskogo obshchestva (Collection of the *Kharkiv Historical-Philological Society). A collection of papers and materials on

Vitalii Sazonov: untitled painting (oil, 1980)

Ukrainian literature, ethnography, history, and church history of Slobidska Ukraine, Zaporizhia, and Left-Bank Ukraine, published irregularly by the Historical-Philological Society at Kharkiv University. Between 1886 and 1914, 21 volumes appeared, edited by D. *Bahalii. The main contributors were M. Sumtsov (president of the society), M. Plokhynsky, V. Barvinsky, D. Miller, P. Korolenko, O. Vetukhiv, and V. Danylevych. Certain volumes were devoted to special subjects: volume 8 (1896), for example, to H. Skovoroda, volume 16 (1905) to the papers of the Kharkiv commission for organizing the 13th Archeological Congress in Katerynoslav (ed E. Redin), and volume 18 (1909) in honor of M. Sumtsov.

Scabious (*Scabiosa*; Ukrainian: *skabioza*). An annual and perennial herb of the teasel family Dipsacaceae, native to temperate Eurasia and the Mediterranean region, numbering about 100 species. The plants grow in steppes, in dry, sandy meadows, and occasionally in light pine forests. Yellow scabious (*S. ochroleuca*) can be found in almost all regions of Ukraine, and the Ukrainian scabious (*S. ucrainica*) grows mostly in the south. The blue *S. caucasica* and the deep purple pincushion flower or sweet scabious (*S. atropurpurea*) are used in floriculture as ornamentals. All species of scabious yield substantial amounts of nectar.

Scenery, theatrical. Elements of scenery and costume design in Ukrainian theater were present in *vertep* puppet plays and in the productions of school theaters in the 17th

In Olivia's House, Anatol Petrytsky's design for a 1936 Soviet Ukrainian production of Shakespeare's *Twelfth Night*

and 18th centuries. Painted backdrops were used in serf theaters from the late 18th century, and in amateur and professional touring theaters, from the middle of the 19th century. The Ruska Besida Theater employed K. *Ustyianovych, K. *Ploshevsky, F. *Pohlmann, and P. *Diakiv as scenery painters. The scenery for M. Starytsky's troupe was prepared under the supervision of the ethnographer F. Vovk. M. Kropyvnytsky himself was responsible for scenery in his troupe and demanded that it be made according to illustrations by the historian A. Rigelman. The designers at Sadovsky's Theater in Kiev were V. *Krychevsky Sr and I. *Buriachok, who began producing three-dimensional scenery. During the revolutionary years M. *Burachek, I. Kavaleridze, and K. *Yeleva worked for *agitprop theaters. A. *Petrytsky was the designer for a number of L. Kurbas's productions at Molodyi Theater, where he created interesting sets for the *vertep* and for Sophocles' *Oedipus Rex*. During the 1920s V. *Meller's constructivist approach to scenery and costumes at Berezil resulted in strong designs for Kurbas's productions of G. Kaiser's *Gas I* (1923) and *Jimmie Higgins* (1923, based on U. Sinclair's novel). Meller also led a design labororatory at Berezil, where he trained such designers as D. *Vlasiuk, Ye. Tovbin, V. Shkliaev, and M. *Symashkevych. *Constructivism also influenced scenery designs by M. Matkovych, Yu. *Pavlovych, H. *Tsapok, and B. *Kosariev. In opera, scenery by A. Petrytsky, O. *Khvostenko-Khvostov, and I. *Kurochka-Armashevsky was used to highlight the costumes. From the mid-1930s, with the introduction of socialist realism, painted scenery once again dominated. Designers in Western Ukraine, however (L. Borovyk and M. Radysh, for example), continued to work with more modernist techniques into the early 1940s. Notable designers of this period were F. *Nirod, Yu. *Stefanchuk, and D. *Narbut. From the late 1950s, restrictions on scenery design were lessened, and some innovation was brought in (H. Batii and M. *Kypriian) and constructivism reappeared. Ukrainian scenery designers have also worked on foreign stages – F. *Yakhymovych in the Imperial Vienna Opera (1851–71), M. *Andriienko-Nechytailo in the Royal Bucharest Opera (1923), V. *Perebyinis and M. *Krychevsky in Paris, and O. *Klymko in Buenos Aires, Washington, and New York.

BIBLIOGRAPHY
Khmuryi, V. *Anatolii Petryts'kyi: Teatral'ni kostiumy* (Kiev 1929)
Drak, A. *Ukraïns'ke teatral'ne-dekoratsiine mystetstvo* (Kiev 1961)
Verykivs'ka, I. *Khudozhnyk i stsena* (Kiev 1971)
– *Stanovlennia ukraïns'koï radians'koï stsenohrafiï* (Kiev 1981)
                                                        V. Revutsky

Schad, Johann Baptist, b 1758 in Mürsbach, Bavaria; d 1834 in Jena, Thüringen. German philosopher. Influenced by I. Kant's moral teachings, he renounced his monastic vows in 1798, wrote a PH D dissertation, and taught philosophy at Jena University (1799–1804). The author of several books, in 1805 he was invited to the chair of philosophy at the new Kharkiv University, and for the next 12 years he lectured there on logic, psychology, metaphysics, natural law, and the history of philosophy. His thought was influenced first by J. Fichte and then by F. Schelling's philosophy of nature, but formed an independent and original system and was presented in a lucid and elegant style. During his Kharkiv period he published an original book on logic, *Institutiones philosophiae universae. Tomus primus: Logicam puram et applicantam complectens* (1812), in which he distinguished formal (restricted to the understanding) and transcendental (metaphysics based on reason) logic; and a treatise on natural law, *Institutiones juris naturae* (1814), in which he argued for the harmony of law, morality, and faith and their foundation in reason. His rationalist approach to religion and praise of freedom in the lecture 'De libertate Europae vindicata' (1814) was brought to the attention of the tsarist minister of education, and in December 1816 Schad was expelled from the Russian Empire. He returned to Jena and resumed teaching there. Although his lectures in Kharkiv had attracted many students and some 10 dissertations had been written under his supervision, he left no worthy successor behind him in Kharkiv.

T. Zakydalsky

Schädel, Johann Gottfried, b 1680 in Wandsbek, near Hamburg, Germany, d 21 February 1752 in Kiev. German architect. He came to Russia in 1713 and oversaw the construction of palaces for Duke A. Menshikov on Vasilii Island, St Petersburg, in Oranienbaum, and in Kronshtadt. Later he worked with B. *Rastrelli on buildings in the Kremlin and elsewhere in Moscow (1729–31). After settling in Kiev in 1731, he designed and built an additional story to the Kievan Mohyla Academy (1732–40), the famous campanile of the Kievan Cave Monastery in transitional baroque-classicist style (1731–44), and, probably, the Zaborovsky Gate. He supervised the reconstruction of the campanile of the St Sophia Cathedral (1736–40) and the Kiev metropolitan's residence (1744–8). In his works he skillfully blended features of Western architecture with the Cossack baroque and motifs of folk ornamentation.

Schamanek, Alfred [Šamanek], b 22 May 1883 in Lviv, d 20 May 1920. Military figure. An ethnic German, he graduated from the military academy in Vienna and in 1914 was a captain on the General Staff of the Austrian army in Galicia. After serving on the Italian front he became chief of staff of the Auxiliary Corps in Syria. He returned to Galicia and in April 1919 took command of the Second Corps of the Ukrainian Galician Army (UHA) at the rank of colonel. He distinguished himself during the *Chortkiv offensive and then served as chief of the

Col Alfred Schamanek

General Staff during the UHA advance on Kiev. In 1920 he became chief of the General Staff of the Red Ukrainian Galician Army (10 February–1 March). He was killed while fighting the Bolsheviks.

Schechtman, Joseph, b 1891 in Odessa, d 1 March 1970 in New York City. Zionist leader and authority on population transfers in Europe. A graduate of Berlin University (LLD, 1914), he cofounded, with V. *Zhabotinsky, the Zionist Revisionist movement and headed it for many years. Active in Ukrainian Jewish politics, he became a member of the Central Rada, where he consistently advocated Jewish self-defense against pogroms. During the Hetman and UNR Directory regimes Schechtman collaborated with E. Tcherikower and other prominent Jews on one of the most authoritative accounts of the Jewish experience during the Ukrainian revolution, *Di idishe avtonomie un der natzionaler sekretariat in Ukraine: Materialn un dokumentn.* A shortened account of his experiences was published later in English. He also wrote a book on Jewish pogroms by A. Denikin's forces. Schechtman emigrated in 1921 and later worked with the Committee of Jewish Delegations preparing materials for the *Schwartzbard Trial.

Schelling, Friedrich Wilhelm Joseph von, b 27 January 1775 in Leonberg, Württemberg, d 20 August 1854 in Bad Ragaz, Switzerland. German idealist philosopher. His thought contains many different, sometimes contradictory, tendencies and can be divided into at least four distinct stages. In Ukraine, as elsewhere, the most influential stage was that of *Naturphilosophie*, which conceived the natural world as a self-sufficient organism of infinite variety unified by the law of identity of opposites and evolving continuously under the compulsion of internal contradiction. Emphasizing the speculative rather than the empirical method as the key to a deeper understanding of nature, Schelling pointed out various analogies between different forces, genera, and levels of evolution. In spite of their fantastic quality, these analogies had a stimulating effect on later naturalists and led to important scientific discoveries. Other parts of Schelling's thought, such as his philosophies of religion and freedom, had little influence in Ukraine.

Schelling's ideas about nature were introduced in Ukraine by J. *Schad, the first holder of the chair of philosophy at Kharkiv University (1805–16). His books and lectures acquainted students, faculty members, and the educated public with Schelling. Schad's students pro-

duced some 10 philosophical dissertations (1812–18) that borrowed freely from him and Schelling. Schad's colleagues, the medicine professors G. Koritari and Ya. Gromov, adopted Schelling's ideas in their lectures; the physics professor A. Stojković and mathematics professor T. Osipovsky criticized them as fantastic and unscientific. Schad's student and successor in the chair, A. Dudrovych (1818–30), emphasized the mystical rather than the rationalist aspects of Schelling's thought, but the interest in philosophy kindled by Schad died out gradually. Another student of Schad (or Dudrovych), N. Belousov, taught philosophy at the Nizhen Lyceum (1825–30), relying heavily on Schad's writings.

A number of Schellingians taught at the Richelieu Lyceum in Odessa in the first half of the 19th century. N. Kurliandtsev, who taught mathematics and physics (1826–35), produced the first Russian translation of Schelling – that of *Erster Entwurf eines Systems der Naturphilosophie* (1834) – and wrote a paper on the development and current state of experimental physics in which he expounded and defended Schelling's basic ideas on nature. K. Zelenetsky, who taught Russian literature (1837–58), under I. Davidov's influence combined the ideas of Schelling with those of I. Kant without having a clear idea of the differences between them. His collection of studies on some theoretical questions (4 vols, 1835–6) contained several philosophical papers on logic, the foundations of knowledge, and history. The lyceum's professor of philosophy in 1839–59, O. *Mykhnevych, was influenced mainly by Schelling's philosophy of revelation and wrote, in Russian, an exposition of Schelling's philosophy for the layman (1850).

In Kiev a Christian outlook with a Schellingian hue was propagated by P. Avsenev, who taught at the Kiev Theological Academy (1836–50) and Kiev University (1838–44). Interested in psychic phenomena, he expounded the ideas of the Schellingian school of psychology (G. von Schubert and C. Carus). Through his personal acquaintance with V. Bilozersky, M. Hulak, and O. Markovych he may have exercised a formative influence on the Romantic Christian ideology of the *Cyril and Methodius Brotherhood. The first rector of Kiev University, M. *Maksymovych, came under the influence of Schelling's *Naturphilosophie* during his study of botany at Moscow University (1821–3). In his scientific works on the chief foundations of zoology (1824) and nature (1833; 2nd edn 1847) he emphasized the unity of the natural world and its evolution. Although as a scientist he became increasingly critical of the speculative method, he rejected crude empiricism as an adequate scientific method. Schellingian ideas can be detected also in his later ethnographic works (eg, in his symbolic understanding of folk songs).

Although D. *Vellansky, the first Schellingian of Ukrainian origin, worked in St Petersburg, his writings had an influence in Ukraine as well as in Russia. His Swedish-Finnish student C. Ekeblad, the author of a biopsychological study of the capacities of the human soul (1872), served as principal of the Nizhen Lyceum for 25 years (1835–60).

Schelling's influence in Ukraine was diverse and often contradictory. His ideas aroused interest in the natural sciences, but also encouraged a contemptuous attitude toward the scientific method. Schelling glorified the creative and cognitive power of reason but diverted its energy to

Romantic musings and mystical wandering. His ideas stimulated interest in folklore and language. They were popular among members of the *Kharkiv Romantic School and may have influenced O. *Potebnia's theory of language.

BIBLIOGRAPHY

Shpet, G. *Ocherk razvitiia russkoi filosofii* (Petrograd 1922)
Čiževsky, D. 'The Influence of the Philosophy of Schelling (1775–1854) in the Ukraine,' *AUA*, 5, nos 2–3 (1956)
Ostrianyn, D.; et al (eds). *Narys istoriï filosofiï na Ukraïni* (Kiev 1966)
Kamenskii, Z. *Russkaia filosofiia nachala XIX veka i Shelling* (Moscow 1980)

T. Zakydalsky

Scherer, Jean-Benoît, b 1 September 1741 in Strasbourg, France, d 1824. Historian, geographer, and economist. After studying at Strasbourg, Jena, and Leipzig universities, he served in the Russian civil service and then at the French embassy in St Petersburg. In 1808–24 he taught French literature and Russian history at Tübingen University. He translated the Primary Chronicle with extensive annotations (1774) and wrote *Histoire raisonnée du commerce de la Russie* (1788), which contained a chapter on Ukraine, and the two-volume *Annales de la Petite-Russie ou Histoire des Cosaques-Saporogues et des Cosaques de l'Ukraine ou de la Petite-Russie* (1788), one of the earliest works in Western Europe on Ukrainian history and geography, which influenced the author of *Istoriia Rusov.*

Marie Scherrer   Ivan Schmalhausen

Scherrer, Marie, b 20 June 1902 in Rumania. French scholar of Ukrainian language and literature; member of the Shevchenko Scientific Society. She was educated in Strasbourg and Paris, and taught French in Prague until 1939. After returning to Paris she worked in the library of the Institute of Slavic Studies and taught Ukrainian literature at École des langues orientales (with E. Borschak). She wrote *Les Dumy ukrainiennes: Épopée Cosaque* (1947), translated Ukrainian literary classics into French (particularly T. Shevchenko, I. Franko, and M. Rylsky), and contributed to *Revue des études slaves* in 1959–80, notably as a longtime editor of the publication's chronicle of Ukrainian scholarship.

Schiller, Johann Christoph Friedrich von, b 10 November 1759 in Marbach, Swabia, d 9 May 1805 in Weimar. German dramatist, poet, literary theorist, and historian. Since 1839 his poems have been translated into Ukrainian by Y. Levytsky, Yu. Fedkovych, K. Bilylovsky, P. Kulish, B. Hrinchenko, I. Franko, A. Mohylnytsky, M. Markovych, O. Navrotsky, O. Levytsky, O. Konysky, O. Pchilka, I. Steshenko, O. Hrytsai, T. Piurko, S. Hordynsky, D. Zahul, and other writers. His plays (*Kabale und Liebe* and *Die Räuber)* were first staged in Ukrainian at the Ruska Besida Theater in Lviv (1881–9). In central Ukraine (because Ukrainian-language plays were banned under the tsars) the first Ukrainian performance did not take place until 1918, when *Die Räuber* was staged by P. Saksahansky at the People's Theater in Kiev. Famous Soviet Ukrainian productions of Schiller's plays include the Kiev Young Spectator's Theater's *Wilhelm Tell* in 1927, the Berezil theater's *Die Verschwörung des Fiesko zu Genua* in 1928, and the Kiev Ukrainian Drama Theater's *Don Carlos* in 1936.

Some of Schiller's dramas have been published in Ukrainian translation: *Wilhelm Tell*, trans V. Kmitsykevych (1887), B. Hrinchenko (1895, 1908), and B. Ten (1955); *Die Jungfrau von Orleans*, trans Ye. Hornytsky (1889), I. Steshenko (1906), and Ye. Drobiazko (1955); *Maria Stuart*, trans B. Hrinchenko (1896, 1911) and Yu. Koretsky (1941); *Die Räuber*, trans O. Cherniakhivsky (1911), M. Yohansen (1936), and B. Ten (1953); *Kabale und Liebe*, trans M. Yohansen (1934), A. Hozenpud (1947), and Yu. Nazarenko (1955); and *Don Carlos*, trans Iryna Steshenko (1955). Other editions of his works published in Ukrainian translation include poems (Lviv 1914, ed O. Hrytsai), ballads (Kiev 1927, trans D. Zahul), lyric poems (Kiev 1967, trans M. Lukash), selected (six) dramas (Kiev 1955), works (five poems, three dramas, Kiev 1968), and writings on esthetics (*Estetyka*, Kiev 1974, trans B. Havryshkiv).

R. Senkus

Schimser, Anton, b 16 February 1790 in Vienna, d 5 February 1836 in Lviv. Sculptor; son of the Viennese sculptor A. Schimser the Elder and brother of J.B. *Schimser. He studied at the Vienna and Paris academies of art. From 1812 he worked in Lviv, where he decorated buildings, such as No. 10 Trybunalska St, the Credit Society, and the Boworowski Library, with bas-reliefs and created many of the family monuments in the Lychakiv Cemetery. His classicist works are distinguished by their clean lines and balanced composition.

Schimser, Johann Baptist, b 30 March 1793 in Vienna, d 11 July 1856 in Lviv. Sculptor; brother of A. *Schimser. A graduate of the Vienna Academy of Art (1818), he moved to Lviv in 1826. There he worked under the supervision of his brother and, later, as an independent sculptor. He created numerous family monuments in the Lychakiv Cemetery in Lviv, the largest of which is the monument to M. Bauer, and in cemeteries in Ternopil and Stanyslaviv. He also did decorative bas-reliefs for buildings.

Schmalhausen, Ivan, b 15 April 1849 in St Petersburg, d 19 April 1894 in Kiev. Botanist of German descent; full member of the St Petersburg Academy of Sciences from 1893; father of I. *Shmalhauzen. A graduate of St Petersburg University (1871), he taught at Kiev University (from 1878) and researched the flora of central Ukraine (1886), central and southern Russia, the Crimea, and northern Caucasia (2 vols, 1895, 1897), as well as fossilized plants.

Schmalhausen was one of the founders of paleobotany in the Russian Empire.

Schmidt, Axel, b 20 October 1870 in Dorpat (now Tartu), Estonia, d 1941. German journalist. A newspaper editor in Tallinn (1896–1900) and Riga (1907–11), in 1911 he moved to Berlin, where he edited prominent journals, such as *Deutsche Politik* (1917–21) and *Der Deutsche Gedanke* (1925–8). A supporter of Ukrainian independence, during the First World War he advised the German government on its eastern policy, and he made an official visit to Kiev in 1918. That year he cofounded the *German-Ukrainian Society, and he served as the organization's general secretary and as editor of its organ *Die *Ukraine* in 1918–26. He wrote articles and several books about Eastern Europe and especially Ukraine, including *Ukraine – Land der Zukunft* (1939), which was confiscated by the Nazi authorities.

Bishop Joseph Schmondiuk

Schmondiuk, Joseph [Šmondjuk, Josyf], b 6 August 1912 in Wall, Pennsylvania, d 25 December 1978 in Philadelphia. Ukrainian Catholic church and community leader. He studied at St Josaphat's Ukrainian Pontifical College in Rome and was ordained in 1936. He was consecrated auxiliary bishop of Philadelphia in 1956. In 1961 he was appointed bishop of Stamford, Connecticut. In 1977 he was installed as metropolitan of the Ukrainian Catholic church in the United States and archbishop of Philadelphia. He played an active role in the Providence Association of Ukrainian Catholics in America and the Ukrainian Congress Committee of America and was a member of the presidium of the World Congress of Free Ukrainians. He was the first Ukrainian Catholic metropolitan born in the United States.

Schneider, Antoni (pseud: Sartorius), b 12 June 1825 in Vilshanytsia, Zolochiv circle, Galicia, d 25 February 1880. Amateur archeologist and historian. The son of German colonists, he collected materials for an archeological map and history of Galicia's towns and villages. His Polish regional studies encyclopedia of Galicia (letters A–B, 2 vols, 1868, 1874) contains ethnographic materials and information about inhabited places and Lviv's streets and buildings. He also wrote one of the first guidebooks to Lviv (1871; 2nd edn 1875). His notebooks of historical documents, compiled by place-name and topic, are preserved in the Lviv Scientific Library of the ANU and the Cracow city and voivodeship state archives.

Scholarly societies. The first learned society in Ukraine was the *Odessa Society of History and Antiquities (1839). Learned societies did not become widespread, however, until the last few decades of the 19th century. Most were associations of scholars in the humanities, law, and social sciences, such as the *Church-Archeological Society (1872) at the Kiev Theological Academy, the *Historical Society of Nestor the Chronicler (1873) at Kiev University, the *Kharkiv Historical-Philological Society (1877), the *Kiev Juridical Society (1877), the *Odessa (1889) and Nizhen (1894) historical-philological societies, the Volhynian Church-Archeological Society in Zhytomyr (1894), the Kiev Society of Antiquities and Art (1897), the *Podilia Church Historical-Archeological Society in Kamianets-Podilskyi (1903), and the *Kiev Society for the Preservation of Ancient and Artistic Monuments (1910). In regional studies the first associations were the *Society of Kuban Researchers in Katerynodar (1896), a similar one in Katerynoslav (1901), and the *Volhynia Research Society in Zhytomyr (1900).

In 1907 the *Ukrainian Scientific Society was founded in Kiev to unite all scholars in Russian-ruled Ukraine. It modeled itself on the important, multidisciplinary *Shevchenko Scientific Society (NTSh, est 1873), to which most Ukrainian scholars and scientists in Austrian-ruled Galicia belonged. Other societies in Galicia were the *Halytsko-Ruska Matytsia (1848), the *Society of Friends of Ukrainian Scholarship, Literature, and Art (1904), and the *Society of Ukrainian Lawyers (1909).

In the natural sciences the first associations were the university-affiliated *Kiev (1869), *Kharkiv (1869), and Odessa (1870) societies of naturalists; they were followed by the Kharkiv Physics and Chemistry Society (1872), the *Kharkiv Mathematics Society (1879), the *Kiev Physics and Mathematics Society (1890), and the *Kiev Physics and Chemistry Society (1910). In Galicia some Ukrainians belonged to Polish naturalists', historical, philological, and anthropological societies (see also *Naturalists' societies).

Many scholars in Russian-ruled Ukraine also belonged to imperial societies, such as the Free Economic Society (1765), the Moscow Society of History and Russian Antiquities (1805), the St Petersburg (1846) and Moscow (1864) archeological societies, the Russian Historical Society (1866), the St Petersburg Military History Society (1907, with branches in Kiev and Odessa), and the Imperial Russian Geographic Society (1845). The *Southwestern Branch of the Imperial Russian Geographic Society was a center of Ukrainian scholarship in 1873–6.

After the Revolution of 1917 most active scholarly societies were affiliated with universities or other postsecondary institutions. Under Soviet rule most of them became part of the VUAN network. In 1928 the VUAN societies were the Historical Society of Nestor the Chronicler and the Ukrainian Scientific Society in Kiev, which became affiliates in 1920; the History of Literature (1922) and Pedagogical societies in the VUAN Historical-Philological Division; the Geological (1918) and *Ukrainian Botanical (1919) societies in the VUAN Physico-Mathematical Division; and the *Society of Economists (1919) and *Society of Ukrainian Jurists (1921) at the VUAN Social-Economic Division. Outside Kiev other societies (most of them based on prerevolutionary societies) functioned as VUAN branches. They included the Poltava (1918), Lubni (1920), *Kharkiv

(1924), Dnipropetrovske (1924), Kamianets-Podilskyi (1925), *Odessa (1926), and Shepetivka (1926) scientific societies; the Oster (1924) and Nizhen (1927) scientific regional studies societies; the Cabinet for the Study of Podilia (1924) in Vinnytsia; the *Odessa Regional Studies Commission (1920); and, outside Ukraine, the *Leningrad Society of Researchers of Ukrainian History, Literature, and Language (1922). All of these societies had their own publications.

Non-VUAN societies were also active in the first years of Soviet rule, particularly in the natural, medical, and technical sciences. The Kharkiv Medical Society (1925), with its 16 sections, was prominent among them. In other areas notable associations were the Kharkiv Juridical Society (1923) and the All-Ukrainian Ethnographic Society (1924) in Kiev, the Military Sciences Society at the general staff of the Ukrainian Military District, the Donbas Scientific Society (1926) in Luhanske, and the *All-Ukrainian Learned Association of Oriental Studies (1926), All-Ukrainian Association of Physicists (1926), Ukrainian Society of World Studies (1928), and Ukrainian Physiological Society (1928) in Kharkiv. In the field of *regional studies local societies were created in Ananiv, Bila Tserkva, Berdianske, Dnipropetrovske, Konotip, Luhanske, Poltava, Proskuriv, Tulchyn, and Zinovivske. In 1930 there was a total of 44 scholarly societies in Soviet Ukraine.

In Polish-ruled interwar Western Ukraine the only new scholarly society established was the *Ukrainian Theological Scholarly Society (1923) in Lviv. The Shevchenko Scientific Society continued to unite most Western Ukrainian scholars until 1939.

During the Stalinist terror of the 1930s most societies in Soviet Ukraine were liquidated by the Soviet regime. The same fate befell the Galician societies during the Soviet occupations of 1939–41 and 1945. In Hungarian-occupied Transcarpathia (1941–4) the *Subcarpathian Scientific Society was active.

After 1945 all newly established Soviet Ukrainian societies functioned as republican branches of the all-Union geographic (see *Geographic Society of the Ukrainian SSR), botanical, microbiological, entomological, physiological, biochemical, hydrobiological, paleontological, mineralogical, chemical, medical, and other societies. The popular-scientific *Znannia Society of the Ukrainian SSR was also a branch of an all-Union counterpart. Only the Ukrainian Republican Scientific Society of Parasitologists (1945; nine branches), the Ukrainian Society for Nature Conservation (1946), the Pedagogical Society of the Ukrainian SSR (1960), and the *Ukrainian Society for the Protection of Historical and Cultural Monuments (1966) had independent republican status. Independent of all-Union and republican organizations were the Lviv Geological, Kharkiv Mathematics, and *Odessa Archeological societies.

Ukrainian émigré scholars in Bohemia during the interwar period established the *Ukrainian Historical-Philological Society, the *Ukrainian Law Society, the *Ukrainian Pedagogical Society in Prague, the *Ukrainian Physicians' Association in Czechoslovakia, the *Ukrainian Society of Bibliophiles in Prague, the *Union of Ukrainian Engineers' Organizations Abroad, the *Ukrainian Scholarly Association, and other societies. Scholars in Poland created the *Ukrainian Military History Society.

After the Second World War émigré societies functioned only in the West. They included the revived NTSh and the Ukrainian Theological Scholarly Society, the *Ukrainian Academy of Arts and Sciences in the US and Canada, the Scholarly Theological societies of the Ukrainian Orthodox Church in Canada (Winnipeg) and the USA (South Bound Brook, New Jersey), the *Ukrainian Academic Society in Paris, the *Research Institute of Volyn, and the *Ukrainian Historical Association. Scholarly work has also been conducted by the *Ukrainian Medical Association of North America, the *Ukrainian Veterinary Medical Association, the *Ukrainian Engineers' Society of America, the *Association of Ukrainian Lawyers, the *Ukrainian Library Association of America, and other professional émigré associations.

(See also *Medical scientific societies, *Pedagogical societies, *Prosvita societies, and *Scientific-technical societies.)

B. Kravtsiv, R. Senkus

School communes (*shkoly-komuny*). General education boarding schools for homeless children and youths, orphans, and juvenile delinquents, founded in the USSR in 1918. They were most prominent in the 1920s, and some schools continued to exist into the 1930s. At first the school communes provided elementary education and basic training in manufacturing processes. In the mid-1920s they became *incomplete secondary schools or institutions of *secondary education, which provided professional preparation as well as the necessary fundamentals for continued education in *tekhnikums and institutions of *higher education. Practical experience in workshops and agriculture was considered fundamental to the life of the children's collectives at the school communes. Among the best-known school communes were the Dzerzhinsky Children's Colony (founded by A. *Makarenko), the Lepeshinsky School Commune, and the Odessa School Commune.

School districts (*uchbovi okruhy*). Prerevolutionary educational administrative territorial divisions created in imperial Russia in 1803 with the educational reforms of Alexander I. The fledgling school system was to be administered from the district capital, and there was to be one university per district. By the 20th century the original 6 districts set up by Alexander I's reform had been parceled into 12 districts. According to the original legislative act only one Ukrainian city, Kharkiv, was the center of a district. Ultimately, three Ukrainian districts were created, the Kiev district (made up of Kiev, Volhynia, Podilia, Chernihiv, and Poltava gubernias), the Odessa district (encompassing Kherson, Katerynoslav, Tavriia, and Bessarabia gubernias), and the Kharkiv district (Kharkiv, Voronezh, Kursk, Penza, and Tambov gubernias and the province of the Don Cossack Host). The school districts were headed by curators.

School drama. A theatrical form of the 17th and 18th centuries, organized around the schools of that time. The playwrights were teachers of poetics, and the performers were the students, who would study the principles of drama by performing. School drama developed from the dialogic verse of the Christmas and Easter cycles, popular in Western Europe from the 12th and 13th centuries and in Ukraine from the late 16th to early 17th centuries. The earliest extant examples are P.*Berynda's *Na rozhstvo virshi ...* (Christmas Poems, 1616) and Y. Volkovych's *Rozmyshlian'ie o mutsi Khrysta Spasytela nasheho* (Reflections on the Sufferings of Christ Our Savior, 1631), printed in Lviv. The earliest dramatic works, in a more precise sense of the word, were *Prodav kota v mishku* (He Sold a Cat in a Sack) and *Naikrashchyi son* (The Best Dream), two *intermedes in J. Gawatowicz's Polish tragedy about the death of John the Baptist (1619).

In the second half of the 17th century dramatic literature saw significant developments. Following literary theories of the time, lecturers in poetics would divide dramatic works into tragedies (plays which portrayed tragic events in noble and famous families), comedies (scenes from the lives of the common people), and tragicomedies (works with elements of both). Thematically, school dramas can be divided into plays from the Christmas and Easter cycles, miracle plays (dramas based on legends about saints), morality plays (instructional dramas, in which the characters were personified abstract concepts: Truth, Love, Pride, Faith, Vanity, etc), and historical dramas. From among the extant texts the earliest is a miracle play by an anonymous author, *Aleksii, chelovik Bozhii* (Alexis, Man of God), which was staged in 1673. It was composed of a prologue, two acts, and an epilogue and was based on the legend of Alexis, the son of the Roman senator Euphimian. Influenced by Christ's teachings, Aleksii left his home and marriage and was absent for 17 years. Upon returning to his father's home he lived there for another 17 years as an unrecognized beggar. Only after his death did it become known, from a letter that he had written, that he was truly the senator's son. The repertoire of the Kievan Mohyla Academy also included, among others, the popular morality play *Tsarstvo natury liudskoi* (The Kingdom of Human Nature, 1698), from which only fragments have been preserved.

One of the most popular plays in Western Ukraine was the Easter drama, based on apocryphal tales of the descent of Jesus Christ into hell, *Slovo o zbureniu pekla* (The Tale of the Harrowing of Hell), which has been preserved in several extant manuscripts from the second half of the 17th and from the 18th century. The drama is notable in that it departs from the rules of poetics of the period; it contains witticisms and portrays folk customs, and therein lay its popularity. The play appeared in an English translation by I. Makaryk as *About the Harrowing of Hell* (1989).

The first play with a historical theme was T. *Prokopovych's tragicomedy *Vladimir*, written in 1705, when the author was beginning to lecture in poetics at the Kievan Mohyla Academy. The play glorifies Volodymyr the Great for having Christianized Rus', and for his battle against paganism, and Hetman I. Mazepa for his patronage of scholarship and the arts, painting and architecture in particular. A drama on a biblical theme, *Iosif patriarkha* (Joseph, the Patriarch, 1708), was written by L. Horka, a lecturer at the Kievan Mohyla Academy. The second play based on Ukraine's historical past, which followed Prokopovych's *Vladimir*, was the drama *Mylost' Bozhiia ...* (Divine Grace ..., 1728), written anonymously. Researchers have recognized it as one of the best dramatic works of the 18th century, the 'swan song' (O. Biletsky) of Ukrainian school drama. The well-known historical drama *Trahediia, sirich Pechal'naia povest' o smerty posledniho tsaria serbskoho Urosha v ...* (A Tragedy, or The Sad Tale of the Death of the Last Serbian Tsar, Urosh v, 1733) was written by a graduate of the Kievan Mohyla Academy, M. Kozachynsky.

In the 18th century dramas were also written on Christmas and Easter themes, namely M. Dovhalevsky's *Komicheskoe diistvie* (A Comic Play, 1736) and *Vlastotvornii obraz chelovikoliubiia Bozhiia* (The Power-Endowing Image of Divine Love for Man, 1737), H. Konysky's *Voskreseniie mertvykh* (The Resurrection of the Dead, 1746), and V. Lashchevsky's morality play *Trahedokomediia ...* (Tragicomedy, ca 1742). Altogether 20 handwritten and printed manuscripts of dramas have survived in Ukraine. The graduates of the Kievan Mohyla Academy spread the school drama to Russia as well (such as the plays staged by D. Tuptalo in Rostov). Later researchers (particularly M. Petrov, V. Riezanov) traced the origins of the Ukrainian school drama to the Western European school theater, specifically the Jesuit theater.

BIBLIOGRAPHY
Franko, I. *Iuzhno-russkaia paskhal'naia drama* (Kiev 1896)
Vozniak, M. 'Stara ukraïns'ka drama i novishi doslidy nad neiu,' *ZNTSh*, vol 112 (Lviv 1912)
– *Pochatky ukraïns'koï komediï* (Lviv 1920)
Riezanov, V. *Drama ukraïns'ka*, fasc 1, 3–6 (Kiev 1926–9)

I. Koshelivets

Schools for children of the clergy (*dukhovni uchylyshcha*). Four-year schools established in 1884 in the Russian Empire for the children of the clergy. These schools represented the first level of religious education, and their graduates could enter seminaries. Their program of study was similar to that of the first years of the *gymnasium, with the exception of the study of foreign languages. In Ukraine, in 1917 there were 30 such schools. All instruction was in Russian.

Schools for peasant youth (*shkoly selianskoi molodi*). Rural general polytechnical schools created in the USSR in 1923. These schools admitted 12- to 18-year-olds who had completed three- or four-year elementary school programs. Schools for peasant youth offered a four-year program that provided a general education with an agricultural theory and practice component. In 1928, one- and two-year evening courses were introduced, which, among other things, trained tractor operators. In the Ukrainian SSR in 1928, there were 115 schools for peasant youth. In the 108 such schools for which data exist, there were 7,018 students, of whom 1,304, or 18 percent, were women. In 1930, schools for peasant youth were renamed schools for collective-farm youth. In 1934 these schools were reorganized into *seven-year schools.

Schools for rural youth (*shkoly silskoi molodi*). Night schools for youths employed full time in the agricultural industry, established in 1944. Initially, schools for rural youth offered classes which were the equivalent of grades one to four and grades one to seven in *seven-year schools. After 1956 the schools provided courses which covered the material in grades five to ten and eight to ten in *ten-year schools. Graduates of schools for rural youth were eligible for admission to postsecondary institutions. In 1962, in the Ukrainian SSR there were 7,081 schools for rural youth, with 226,900 students. In 1958, schools for rural youth were renamed evening secondary schools for workers' and rural youth, and in 1971 they were renamed evening secondary general education schools.

Schools for workers' youth (*shkoly robitnychoi molodi*). Night schools for students who work full time, established in 1943 in the USSR. The schools offered the equivalent of grades five through seven in *seven-year schools or grades five through ten in *ten-year schools. Graduates of the schools were eligible for admission to postsecondary institutions. In 1962 there were 2,105 schools for workers' youth, with 469,000 students, in the Ukrainian SSR. In 1958 these schools were renamed evening secondary schools for workers' and rural youth, and in 1971 they were renamed evening secondary general education schools.

Schools-sanatoriums (*shkoly-sanatorii*). Special general education boarding schools for ill and physically disabled children. The curriculum and the general organization of the schools-sanatoriums are the same as those of other boarding schools. In addition the sanatoriums are responsible for supervising the students' medical conditions and treatments and for ensuring that a prescribed regime is followed under trained medical personnel. Emphasis is placed on time spent outdoors, particularly in the sunshine; students are kept on carefully regulated diets according to their conditions. Instruction is conducted at a more relaxed pace than at other schools, with a maximum of three or four classes per day. In some schools-sanatoriums – in those for children with tuberculosis, for example – students maintain a full course load of the *eight-year or even *ten-year school programs. There are schools-sanatoriums in Kiev, Odessa, Transcarpathia, Ternopil, Luhanske, and other oblasts.

Schrijvers, Joseph, b 19 December 1876 in Belgium, d 4 March 1945 in Rome. Belgian Redemptorist priest. In 1913, while he was a professor of theology and prefect at a Redemptorist seminary in Belgium, Metropolitan A. Sheptytsky asked him to establish an Eastern rite branch of the *Redemptorists in Galicia. He was protohegumen of the new province of the order until 1933. He wrote several ascetic works, a number of which appeared in Ukrainian.

Schultz, Heinrich (Shults, Henadii), b 20 December 1907 in Kiev. Hygienist. A graduate of the Kiev Medical Institute (1931), he worked as a sanitation inspector at the Donbasvodtrest in Chervonyi Promin and the Kiev Communal Sanatorium, as the Kiev oblast epidemiologist, as an associate of the Kiev Bacteriological Institute (1934–41), and as director of the Department of Public Health in the Kiev municipal government (1942–3). After the war he emigrated to Germany, where he worked as library director (1951–7) and director (1958–72) of the Institute for the Study of the USSR. He wrote numerous scientific works, including monographs on Soviet epidemiology (1951) and gerontology (1961), and medical entries for the *Entsyklopediia ukraïnoznavstva* (Encyclopedia of Ukraine, 10 vols, 1955–88) and *Encyclopedia of Ukraine* (vols 1–2, 1984, 1988).

Schulz, Bruno, b 12 July 1892 in Drohobych, Galicia, d 19 November 1942 in Drohobych. Polish writer and artist of Jewish origin. After studying architecture in Vienna and Lviv, he taught drawing at the Drohobych gymnasi-

um (1924–39). In his autobiographical prose he depicts life in Drohobych and its vicinity using both fantasy and realism. Among his works are *Sklepy cynamonowe* (1934; English trans: *Cinnamon Shops and Other Stories*, 1963), *Sanatorium pod Klepsydrą* (1937; English trans: *Sanatorium under the Sign of the Hourglass*, 1978), and a Polish translation of F. Kafka's *Trial* (1936). He was murdered by the Gestapo.

Schwartzbard Trial. The trial of S. *Petliura's assassin, Shalom Schwartzbard (b 1886 in Izmail, Bessarabia, d 1935 in Cape Town, South Africa), which took place in Paris on 18–26 October 1927. The defendant was a Jew who had participated in the Revolution of 1905 and fled to France in 1906. After serving in the French Foreign Legion during the First World War, he returned to Ukraine in 1917 and joined the Red Guards in Odessa. In 1920 he returned to Paris, where he worked as a watchmaker. After stalking his intended victim for several weeks, he shot the former head of the Ukrainian state on the Rue Racine, Paris, on 25 May 1926. His motive, he claimed, was to avenge the Jewish pogroms that Petliura had instigated in Ukraine during his term in office. There was no question that Schwartzbard had killed Petliura; the central issue of the trial was whether or not he was justified in doing so. In effect the attention of the court was focused on Petliura's actions and policies in 1918–20. The debate on Petliura's responsibility for the anti-Jewish pogroms spilled beyond the courtroom into the European press. In Petliura's defense the Ukrainian community pointed to the chaotic conditions of the revolutionary period and the serious limitations to his power. Their position was developed in *Documents sur les pogromes en Ukraine et l'assassinat de Simon Petlura à Paris* (1927). The prosecution also suggested that Schwartzbard had not acted alone but was part of a conspiracy involving the Soviet authorities. The defense, on the other hand, presented numerous witnesses of the pogroms who claimed that Petliura's sanctioning of them was common knowledge. The defense also dismissed Petliura's orders to stop the pogroms as no more than a belated attempt to win the West's support for his regime. Two books supporting the defense were published in 1927: *Les pogromes en Ukraine sous les gouvernements ukrainiens (1917–1920): Aperçu historique et documents* and B. Lecache's *Au pays des pogromes: Quand Israel meurt*.

The trial attracted much public attention in France. The press depicted Schwartzbard as a 'boyish' watchmaker-soldier who had braved the wrath of the law to slay a notorious *pogromchik*, and aroused much sympathy for him. Ultimately Schwartzbard was acquitted on grounds of justifiable homicide. After the trial he visited Jewish communities in various countries and published his memoirs, *Inem Loyf fun Yoren* (1934). Ukrainians in the West viewed the outcome as a gross miscarriage of justice. In 1958 the Committee in Defense of the Memory of Symon Petliura published *Dokument sudovoï pomylky: Protses Shvartsbarda* (A Document of a Judicial Error: The Schwarzbard Trial).

A. Makuch

Schwyz cattle. A breed of dairy and meat cattle developed from original brown shorthorn cattle in the Schwyz canton of Switzerland, introduced in Ukraine at the end of the 19th century to improve local stock. Adult males weigh 800–950 kg; females weigh 550–600 kg and yield

4,000–4,500 kg of milk annually. The animals are colored light gray to dark brown and have characteristic white patches along the upper torso and around the nose. By means of crossing with local cattle new breeds were developed in Ukraine – Lebedyn, Kostroma, and others.

Science fiction (*naukovo fantastychna literatura*). A narrative prose genre predicated on the notion that new scientific discoveries or technological innovations will have an influence on the existence of individuals or societies. Modern science fiction evolved at the end of the 19th century and appeared first in Ukrainian literature in P. Krat's utopian tale *Koly ziishlo sontse* (When the Sun Rose), published in Canada in 1918. The first major work was M. Chaikovsky's *Za sylu sontsia* (For Solar Power, 1925), which featured the development of solar cells capable of converting the sun's rays into electricity and storing it effectively to provide current for public utilities and to power automobiles, trains, and even airplanes. The next important publication was V. Vynnychenko's utopian novel *Soniashna mashyna* (Solar Machine, 1928), which also featured an invention that utilized solar energy, in a machine to produce 'solar bread' from any kind of vegetation.

Although acclaimed by readers, the aforementioned works were proscribed in Soviet Ukraine and superseded by an ideologically oriented 'science fiction of close aims,' a variant of *socialist realism aimed at juvenile readers which monopolized literary production until the late 1950s. Science fiction authors extolled Soviet science and technology and hailed the role of Party ideology in their depictions of imagined events and enterprises such as Soviet supported revolutions of American workers (eg, Yu. Smolych, V. Vladko), the invention of unbreakable glass for the building of tanks and other weapons that could not be seen by the enemy (D. Buzko), the construction of a tunnel between Moscow and Vladivostok for faster transport and military strategy (M. Trublaini), the discovery of the means to control the movement of clouds to irrigate parched areas, and the erection of a wind-driven electric power station (M. Romanivska). Such construction themes prevailed in most science fiction works, which were set in the near future on planet Earth. Only two imagined space journeys were written before the 1950s. One of them entailed a manned expedition to Mars and the discovery of extraterrestrial life (M. Kapil) and the other a flight to Venus to obtain some 'ultragold' needed by the state (Vladko). Even in works with a focus on scientific discoveries, such as an imagined cure for cancer (M. Dashkiiev) or the isolation of new metals to provide complete protection against radiation and high temperatures (V. Savchenko), the themes were meant to illustrate the primacy of socialism and to denounce its enemies.

A new era of Ukrainian science fiction began in the late 1950s with the publication of V. Berezhny's *U zoriani svity* (Into the Astral Worlds, 1956) and O. Berdnyk's *Poza chasom i prostorom* (Beyond Time and Space, 1957). Those works served as pacesetters in new depictions of cosmic journeys to other stars and galaxies and contacts with alien civilizations. In the years that followed there was an unprecedented increase in the number of science fiction themes. Authors began to feature travels to distant solar systems and galaxies, journeys through time and to a 'parallel universe' and into other extraordinary dimensions, and to dwell on notions such as interplanetary and galactic warfare, including invasions of Earth by hostile alien creatures; above all they began to write about previously prohibited subjects, such as the evolution of humans and other life forms, including robotic and humanoid creatures that gave rise to superhuman or even godlike beings. The authors also began to raise questions about the psychological, parapsychological, and sociological implications of such phenomena.

The proliferation of such themes during the 1960s and in the following decades contributed to the rise in popularity of science fiction, which soon became the most widely read genre in Soviet Ukraine. But the number of themes and the volume of publications did not ensure an overall improvement in the quality of works of science fiction. A great many of them remained simple and puerile adventure tales. A few science fiction writers, however, became the foremost contributors to the genre either by way of their extraordinary imagination, or by the number of then published items, or by the significance of the scientific, technological, philosophical, and religious notions postulated in their works. That group includes Berdnyk, Berezhny, O. Romanchuk, I. Rosokhovatsky, O. Teslenko, and V. Zaiets. Some of those writers addressed themes such as the consequences of genetic engineering for the evolution of human nature and whether it should culminate in a 'synman' (synthetic man) or an immortal and omniscient godlike being; the utilization of genetic engineering for hostile purposes, including the design and production of biological entities which could annihilate the human race and the development of techniques which would give rise to thought or mood control of entire populations; the growth, storage, and retrieval of vast volumes of knowledge in all scholarly fields; and the rise of intelligent and self-programming robotic beings and their rights and privileges in human societies.

Frequently linked and intertwined with scientific, psychological, and philosophical notions is the problem of ethics. Science fiction writers dwell not only on human ethics in the context of new developments in science and technology, but also on 'xenological ethics,' pertaining to the 'human' behavior of various creatures from space and the robotic and humanoid cultures that could evolve as a result of advancements in science.

The prevalence of complex scientific, philosophical, and even religious notions in recent Ukrainian science fiction alarmed and confused the Soviet literary authorities and Party ideologists, to such an extent that the Soviet regime harassed and prosecuted writers such as Berdnyk and M. Rudenko and eventually incarcerated them for their involvement in the Ukrainian Helsinki Group movement. But the majority of the Ukrainian science fiction writers realized that no criticism of the Soviet system would be tolerated in their popular genre, and refrained from criticizing it either overtly or obliquely. They were not reluctant, however, to censure the scientists for their professional involvements. They lampooned the role that scientists play in developments such as warfare and direct or indirect mind-control and in undertakings that benefit not the population at large but only the scientists themselves and political leaders. In addition to ridiculing severely the careerists in science, science fiction authors strove to scrutinize the general aims of science and the final results of scientific endeavors.

As a literary genre Ukrainian science fiction reached the apex of its development in the 1970s and 1980s with the rise of humorous treatments of scientific premises and of parodies of the ideas and literary forms promulgated by science fiction writers. That phenomenon does not augur the decline of science fiction in Ukrainian literature, however. Recently there has occurred a resurgence of interest in history on the part of science fiction writers, an attempt to view Ukrainian culture in the light of its contemporary and future development and place it in the context of the cosmic evolution of life. Science fiction as a result has gained an ascendancy not achieved by other genres, by dwelling on themes from the past, present, and future perspectives of Ukrainian culture in global and cosmic dimensions.

Some of the more noteworthy works of Ukrainian science fiction from 1925 to 1949 in addition to those already mentioned are Vladko's novelette *Idut' robotari* (The Robots March, 1931) and novel *Arhonavty Vsesvitu* (The Argonauts of the Universe, 1935), M. Kapii's *Kraïna blakytnykh orkhidei* (The Land of Azure Orchids, 1932), P. Lisovy's *Chervona raketa* (The Red Rocket, 1932), Buzko's *Kryshtalevyi krai: Roman* (The Crystal Land: A Novel, 1935), Smolych's *Prekrasni katastrofy* (Beautiful Catastrophes, 1935), and Trublaini's novel *Hlybynnyi shliakh* (A Profound Path, 1948); from 1950 to 1960, Dashkiiev's *Torzhestvo zhyttia* (Celebration of Life, 1952) and *Volodar vsesvitu* (Ruler of the Universe, 1955), Berdnyk's novels *Sliakhy Tytaniv* (The Paths of the Titans, 1959) and *Strila chasu* (Arrow of Time, 1960), and Savchenko's *Chorni zori* (Black Stars, 1959); and from 1960 to 1970, Berdnyk's *Sertse vsesvitu* (Heart of the Universe, 1962) and *Dity bezmezhzhia* (Children of Infinity, 1964), Berezhny's *V nebi - zemlia* (The Earth in the Heavens, 1962), *Istyna poruch* (The Truth at Hand, 1965), *Trava spivaie* (The Grass Sings, 1965), and *Koliuche ternia* (The Prickling Thornbush, 1966), Savchenko's *Pryvyd chasu* (The Apparition of Time, 1964), M. Rudenko's *Charivnyi bumeranh* (The Magic Boomerang, 1966), Yu. Lotsmanenko's collection of fantastic stories *Pravo zhyty* (The Right to Live, 1967), Rosokhovatsky's *Sprava komandora* (The Affair of the Commander, 1967), V. Bezorudko's somewhat humorous *Neitrino zalyshaetsia v sertsi* (Neutrino Remains in the Heart, 1968), and Yu. Yacheikin's *Zoriani mandry kapitana Nebrekhy* (The Stellar Wanderings of Captain Nebrekha, 1969).

Since 1970 the most prolific author of science fiction has been Berezhny (*U prominni dvokh sonts'* [In the Rays of Two Suns 1970], *Pid kryzhanym shchytom* [Under the Icy Shield, 1971], *Povitriana linza* [The Aerial Lens, 1975], *Povernennia 'Halaktyky'* [The Return of the 'Galaxy', 1978], *Kosmichnyi Hol'fstrim* [The Cosmic Gulf Stream, 1980], and *Labirynt* [The Labyrinth, 1986]); he is closely followed by Rosokhovatsky (*Iakym ty poverneshsia?* [What Will You Be Like When You Return?, 1970], *Urahan* [Hurricane, 1977], *Zvorotnyi zv'iazok* [Reverse Connection, 1983], *Mozhlyvist' vidpovidi* [Possibility of a Reply, 1986], and *Ostannii syhnal* [The Last Signal, 1989]), and Teslenko (*Dozvol'te narodytysia* [Let Me Be Born, 1979], *Koryda* [Corrida, 1983], *Vykryvlenyi prostir* [Twisted Space, 1985], and *Kam'iane iaitse* [Stone Egg, 1988]). Other notable works include Berdnyk's *Zorianyi korsar* (Stellar Corsair, 1971), Rudenko's *Narodzhennyi blyskavkoiu* (Born from Lightning, 1971), V. Hrybenko's *Fabryka heniiv* (Genius Factory, 1976), A. Dimarov's *Druha planeta* (Another Planet, 1980), Roman-

chuk's *Taiemnytsia zhovtoï valizy* (Secret of the Yellow Suitcase, 1981) and *Zorianyi krystal* (Stellar Crystal, 1986), and Zaiets's *Mashyna zabuttia* (Forgetting Machine, 1982).

W. Smyrniw

Scientific Research and Design-and-Technology Institute of the Urban Economy (Naukovo-doslidnyi i konstruktorsko-tekhnolohichnyi instytut miskoho hospodarstva). An institution established in Kiev in 1963 under the Ukrainian SSR Ministry of Communal Housing. It prepares construction plans and designs and conducts research in fields such as civil engineering, road building, electrification, and sanitation engineering. The institute is composed of over 50 specialized departments and sections.

Scientific Research and Planning Institute of the Metallurgical Industry (Naukovo-doslidnyi i proektnyi instytut metalurhiinoi promyslovosti, or Diprostal). A research institution, until 1992 under the jurisdiction of the USSR Ministry of Ferrous Metallurgy. It was founded in Kharkiv in 1928 as a branch of a state institute for planning new metallurgical plants and reconstructing existing ones in Ukraine. It was reorganized in 1930 into the State Institute of the Metallurgical and Manganese Industries and in 1965 into its present form. It has (1980) 44 departments, 11 of them on location at operating plants. Its chief areas of interest are technical and economic problems in the production of ferrous alloys and the planning of new and reconstructed metallurgical plants, plants for reprocessing secondary ferrous metals, and repair plants for metallurgical equipment. In the former USSR it was one of the main research institutes for the automation of labor-intensive processes in the production of ferrous alloys and designing machinery for pouring cast iron and ferrous alloys.

Scientific research chairs (naukovo-doslidni katedry). Soviet Ukrainian academic institutions of the 1920s and 1930s that conducted research and trained scholarly cadres. They were directly subordinated to the Ukrainian SSR Commissariat of Education. Most were attached to postsecondary schools, some were affiliated with the VUAN, and a few were completely independent. Each chair had a director and section leaders, full members, scientific co-workers, and graduate students (who became scientific co-workers after successfully defending their theses before a public meeting of the chair). Most of the chairs published their own serials and collections. In 1930 there were 104 chairs: 48 in Kharkiv, 32 in Kiev, 13 in Odessa, 7 in Dnipropetrovske, 3 in Kamianets-Podilskyi, and 1 in Nizhen. Institutions with more than one chair were the Kharkiv Technological and People's Education institutes (10 each), the Ukrainian Institute of Marxism-Leninism in Kharkiv (9), the Kiev Polytechnical Institute and the VUAN (8 each), the Kharkiv Medical Institute (7), the Kiev Agricultural Institute (6), the Kiev People's Education and Dnipropetrovske Mining institutes (5 each), the Kharkiv Agricultural Institute (4), the Kiev Medical and Odessa People's Education institutes (3 each), and the Kharkiv Veterinary, Kamianets-Podilskyi Agricultural, Odessa Polytechnical, Agricultural, and Medical, and Dnipropetrovske People's Education institutes (2 each). Some larger chairs subsequently became scientific research institutes (eg, the Scientific Research Institute of the History of Ukrainian Culture in Kharkiv). In the mid-1930s most of the chairs were liquidated and replaced by institutes at the newly reorganized universities and other postsecondary schools.

R. Senkus

Scientific Research Institute of Animal Husbandry of the Forest-Steppe and Polisia of Ukraine (Naukovo-doslidnyi instytut tvarynnytstva lisostepu i Polissia Ukrainy). Established in 1956 in Kharkiv on the basis of the Ukrainian Scientific Research Institute of Animal Husbandry (est 1935), which itself evolved from the union of the Ukrainian Scientific Research Institute of Great Horned Cattle (1932–5) and the Southern Scientific Research Institute of Milk Production of the All-Union Academy of Agricutural Sciences (1930–2). It consists of 10 divisions and 6 laboratories. Divisions are organized according to animals – great horned cattle, swine, sheep, horses, rabbits – and activities – agricultural animal breeding, the technology of animal husbandry products, mechanization, agricultural economy, and the organization and production of fodder. The six laboratories are for zoochemical analysis, the artificial insemination of agricultural animals, biochemistry, combination fodder, dairy science, and the physiology of agricultural animals. The Kiev Experimental Station of Animal Husbandry eventually became a part of the institute. Many new breeds of animals were developed there, including Myrhorod swine and Lebedyn cattle, as well as a new method of artificial insemination with cryopreserved semen.

Scientific Research Institute of Building Production (Naukovo-doslidnyi instytut budivelnoho vyrobnytstva). The chief research institution in Ukraine for the organization, technology, mechanization, and economics of construction. Set up in Kiev in 1957 under the jurisdiction of the Ukrainian SSR State Committee for Construction, it was divided into departments in Lviv and Odessa, branches in Dnipropetrovske and Luhanske, laboratories, and a building design office. A graduate program was offered.

Scientific Research Institute of Building Systems (Naukovo-doslidnyi instytut budivelnykh konstruktsii). A research institution, until 1992 under the jurisdiction of the USSR State Committee for Construction. It was founded in Kiev in 1957, with branches in Siverskodonetske, Zaporizhia, and Kremenchuk. Its departments and laboratories developed methods for determining structural demands on buildings on settling strata and filled grounds, improved building systems for industrial buildings, devised new methods of testing the quality of building systems, and studied the problems of applying precast parts in residential construction. Since 1964 it has published the technical collection *Stroitel'nye konstruktsii*.

Scientific Research Institute of Corn, All-Union (Vsesoiuznyi naukovo-doslidnyi instytut kukurudzy). Located in Dnipropetrovske, it was the main center for scientific research on the selection and cultivation of corn in the All-Union Academy of Agricultural Sciences. It was established on the basis of the Ukrainian Scientific Research Institute of Grain in 1956, at the height of N. Khrushchev's campaign to increase corn production in the USSR. With research stations in all the main corn-growing areas of the USSR, it developed new hybrids and strains of corn, offered graduate studies, and published a bulletin.

Scientific Research Institute of Dermatology and Venereology (Kharkivskyi naukovo-doslidnyi instytut dermatolohii i venerolohii). A research agency of the Ministry of Health of Ukraine. Founded as an institute by O. Fedorovsky in Kharkiv in 1924 on the basis of the Kharkiv Dermatological and Venereological Polyclinic, it is the main research center in its field in Ukraine. With its three clinical departments, five laboratories, and several auxiliary departments, it conducts research of the pathogenesis, etiology, early diagnosis, treatment, and prophylaxis of skin and venereal diseases, and publishes a serial collection of papers, *Dermatologiia i venerologiia*, in Russian.

Scientific Research Institute of Economics of the State Planning Committee of the Ukrainian SSR (Naukovo-doslidnyi ekonomichnyi instytut Derzhplanu URSR). An institution of the State Planning Committee of the former Ukrainian SSR, established in 1962 in Kiev. It prepared economic predictions and forecasts and participated in the *economic planning process in Ukraine. It also conducted research on the methodology of economic planning and capital investment. The institute was composed of 23 sections, 13 of which focused on specific sectors of the economy. It co-operated closely with other state planning bodies and the AN URSR (now ANU) Institute of Economics and published collections of articles by its researchers.

Scientific Research Institute of Land Cultivation and Animal Husbandry of the Western Regions of Ukraine (Naukovo-doslidnyi institut zemlerobstva i tvarynnytstva zakhidnykh raioniv Ukrainy). Part of the Ukrainian Academy of Agricultural Sciences, it was established in 1956 by the union of the AN URSR (now ANU) Institute of Agrobiology, the Lviv Scientific Research Station of Agriculture, and the Lviv State Farm. It is located in Obroshyne, Pustomyty raion, Lviv oblast. The Subcarpathian and Alpine-Carpathian agriculture research stations and two independent research units in Sokilnyky and Obroshyne are also components of the institute. It has 13 divisions: land cultivation, vegetation, selection and seed cultivation, meadow cultivation and fodder production, the melioration and control of ground erosion, fruit production, the organization and economy of agricultural production, plant protection, the husbandry of great horned cattle, swine, sheep and poultry, agricultural mechanization, and scientific information. Its five laboratories are for agricultural products technology, the artificial insemination of agricultural animals, agricultural animal breeding, the zoohygiene of agricultural animals, and plant nourishment, physiology, and agrochemistry. The institute offers a graduate program leading to advanced professional degrees.

Scientific Research Institute of Pedagogy of Ukraine (Naukovo-doslidnyi instytut pedahohiky Ukrainy). A research institution under the jurisdiction of the Ministry of Education of Ukraine. Founded in Kharkiv in 1926 as the Ukrainian Scientific Research Institute of Pedagogy, it opened a branch in Kiev in 1930 and was moved there in 1934. From 1955 to 1991 it was called the Scientific Research Institute of Pedagogy of the Ukrainian SSR. The institute has 17 departments. It initiates and co-ordinates research in the field of pedagogy and is the leading center of pedagogical training in Ukraine. Since 1963 it has published nine periodic compendiums, among them *Pedahohika, Doshkil'na pedahohika i psykholohiia*, and *Metodyka ukraïns'koï movy i literatury*.

Scientific Research Institute of Sugar Beets, All-Union

(Vsesoiuznyi naukovo-doslidnyi institut tsukro-vykh buriakiv). A Kiev-based center, formerly under the USSR Ministry of Agriculture, responsible for organizing and co-ordinating research on sugar beets and the selection of new beet types. The institute was established in Kiev in 1922 as the Scientific Institute of Selection, and obtained its present name in 1945. The institute (1984) consists of 20 departments, 4 laboratories, and 2 research farms. It also manages nine research and selection stations and an affiliated branch in Krasnodar krai. The institute's mandate included the development of sugar beet varieties appropriate for the varied climatic zones of the USSR. In addition to cultivating 29 sorts and hybrids, the institute was a leader in the development of the monogerm variety of sugar beet. It also offers a graduate program and publishes collections of scientific literature.

Scientific Research Institute of the History of Ukrainian Culture

(Naukovo-doslidnyi instytut istorii ukrainskoi kultury im. D. Bahaliia). An institution of higher learning, established in 1922 in Kharkiv. It was founded by D. *Bahalii as the Scientific Research Chair of the History of Ukrainian Culture, with departments of Ukrainian history, ethnography, literature, and arts, as well as a graduate department. Members of the institute included a majority of Kharkiv historians, students, and Bahalii's associates, and historians from Kiev (O. Ohloblyn, N. Polonska-Vasylenko, V. Romanovsky), Odessa (M. Slabchenko), Poltava (M. Hnip), Nizhen (M. Petrovsky, A. Yershov), and other Ukrainian cities. The institute's associates worked on subjects of general Ukrainian interest and on problems of the history of Slobidska Ukraine. The institute (and earlier the chair) published the collection *Zbirnyk* and its scientific proceedings, *Naukovi zapysky* (10 vols, 1924–30). In 1934 the institute was liquidated and many of its members were either repressed or transferred to the AN URSR (now ANU) or to the All-Ukrainian Association of Marxist-Leninist Scientific Research Institutes.

Scientific Research Institute of the Leather and Footwear Industry

(Naukovo-doslidnyi instytut shki-riano-vzuttievoi promyslovosti). One of the chief research institutions under the Ministry of Light Industry, devoted to the improvement of the technology and the quality of products in the leather and footwear industry. It was organized in Kiev in 1930 out of the Central Laboratory of the Leather and Footwear Trust. In 1983 the institute consisted of 4 departments, 12 laboratories, and an experimental factory. Its research was directed toward improving the existing technology and replacing it with a more efficient one.

Scientific Research Institute of the Organization and Mechanization of Mine Construction, All-Union

(Vsesoiuznyi naukovo-doslidnyi instytut orhani-zatsii ta mekhanizatsii shakhtnoho budivnytstva). The chief research institute for the organization and mechanization of mine shaft construction in the former Soviet Union. Founded in Kharkiv in 1947, it came under the jurisdiction of the USSR Ministry of the Coal Industry. It had (1980) 15 laboratories, 5 departments, a branch in Kryvyi Rih, an experimental mine in Donetske, and sectors in Voroshylovhrad (now Luhanske), Donetske, Karaganda in Kazakhstan, and Nizhnii Tagil, Novokuznetsk, Shakhty, and Shchekino in the RSFSR. The institute developed and refined methods for organizing the construction and reconstruction of shafts, pits, and complexes. It designed and introduced improved equipment, instruments, structural systems, and building materials and drafted safety standards and codes for mine construction. From 1949 it published the collection *Voprosy organizatsii i mekhanizatsii shakhtnogo stroitel'stva*.

Scientific Research Institute of the Organization of Production and Labor in Ferrous Metallurgy, All-Union

(Vsesoiuznyi naukovo-doslidnyi instytut orhanizatsii vyrobnytstva i pratsi chornoi metalurhii). A research institute organized in Kharkiv in 1956 out of the Research Office for the Organization and Rationalization of Ferrous Metallurgy, until 1992 under the jurisdiction of the USSR Ministry of Ferrous Metallurgy. In 1980 it had 12 departments, which dealt mainly with new production and management methods, transportation, the regulation and improvement of labor productivity, and the conservation of materials and energy. The institute published the periodic collections *Organizatsiia truda v chernoi metallurgii* and *Organizatsiia i upravlenie metallurgicheskim proizvodstvom*.

Scientific Research Institute of the Sugar Industry, All-Union

(Vsesoiuznyi naukovo-doslidnyi institut tsukrovoi promyslovosti). A research institution under the USSR Ministry of the Food Industry until 1991. It was organized in Kiev in 1927 out of the department of agricultural technology at the Kiev Polytechnical Institute. It was a key member of the Tsukor research and production conglomerate. In 1983 the institute consisted of 9 departments and 13 laboratories, a graduate school, and a branch in Kursk. Its mandate was to improve the technology of harvesting and storing sugar beets, to develop more efficient control methods and equipment for processing sugar beets and cane and for refining raw sugar, to reduce the consumption of energy in sugar refineries, to mechanize labor-intensive phases of the production process, and to automate as much of the process as possible. Attention was also devoted to labor management and work safety in the sugar industry.

Scientific Research Institute of Urban Planning

(Naukovo-doslidnyi i proektnyi instytut mistobuduvannia, aka Kiev Scientific Research Institute of Urban Planning). An architectural research institution organized in Kiev in 1963 out of the Scientific Research Institute of Urban Planning of the former Academy of Construction and Architecture of the Ukrainian SSR and several architectural planning workshops of the Ukrainian Scientific Research

Institute of Urban Planning. It deals with economic problems of city planning, population distribution, regional planning, the architectural layout of cities and settlements in Ukraine, transportation networks, landscaping, environmental upgrading, and the distribution and planning of resort areas. The institute offers full-time and correspondence graduate programs. New cities in Ukraine, such as Dniprorudne, Chervonohrad, Novovolynske, Dniprodzerzhynske, and Pivdenne, were developed according to plans prepared by the institute.

Scientific Research Institute of Virology and Epidemiology (Odeskyi naukovo-doslidnyi instytut virusolohii ta epidemiolohii im. I. Mechnikova). A research institution under the Ministry of Health of Ukraine, formed in 1920 out of the Odessa Bacteriological Station, which had been established by I. *Mechnikov in 1886. The institute has 5 departments and 10 laboratories. Among its scientists have been M. *Hamaliia and D. *Zabolotny. Its main research interest is the prevention, diagnosis, and treatment of influenza. It publishes an annual collection of papers on viruses and viral diseases titled *Virusy i virusni zakhvoriuvannia*.

Scientific Research Institute of Wheat Selection and Seed Cultivation. See Myronivka Institute of Wheat Selection and Seed Cultivation.

Scientific research institutes (*naukovo-doslidni instytuty*, or NDI). Research institutions that function independently or are part of scientific academies, scholarly societies, universities, other postsecondary schools, governmental bodies, or international agencies. In Soviet Ukraine most NDI were established in the 1920s. The overwhelming majority were located in Kharkiv (Soviet Ukrainian sources [1930] list 43, whereas émigré Ukrainian sources contend there were 93), Kiev (21 vs 69), and Odessa (7 vs 42). Others were located in Dnipropetrovske (2), Poltava (2), and Makiivka, and (according to émigré sources) Vinnytsia and Chernihiv. *Scientific research chairs and certain VUAN commissions, committees, and cabinets functioned in the same way as NDI, and most of them were reorganized into NDI in the late 1920s and early 1930s (14 in 1933, 21 in 1935).

Many NDI were established after the Second World War. By the 1980s over 60 had become part of the *Academy of Sciences of the Ukrainian SSR. Hundreds of others were subordinated to the USSR academies of Sciences, Agricultural Sciences, and Medical Sciences, various all-Union and republican ministries and agencies, the Council for Mutual Economic Assistance, UNESCO, and several international scientific organizations. (For information on individual Soviet Ukrainian institutes, see entries beginning with 'Institute ...,' 'Scientific Research Institute ...,' 'Ukrainian Institute ...,' and 'Ukrainian Scientific Research Institute ...')

In the West the role of Ukrainian NDI was performed during the interwar period by the Ukrainian Sociological Institute in Vienna (1919–24), the Ukrainian Institute of Sociology in Prague (1925–32), and the Ukrainian scientific institutes in Berlin (1926–45) and Warsaw (1930–9). In the postwar period the Shevchenko Scientific Society's Encyclopedia of Ukraine Institute in Munich and Sarcelles, France (est 1947), the Research Institute of Volyn in Winnipeg (est 1951), the Scientific Theological Institute of the Ukrainian Orthodox Church in South Bound Brook, New Jersey, the Ukrainian Military History Institute in Toronto (1952–69), the Lypynsky East European Research Institute in Philadelphia (est 1963), the Harvard Ukrainian Research Institute (est 1973), the Canadian Institute of Ukrainian Studies in Edmonton (est 1976), and the Ukrainian Canadian Research and Documentation Centre (est 1982) have functioned as NDI.

Scientific research institutes of forensic experts (*naukovo-doslidni instytuty sudovykh ekspertyz*). Institutions that conduct forensic analysis in criminal and civil cases and theoretical and practical research in forensic sciences. On order from the courts or the police they perform chemical, physical, ballistic, biological, and various technical tests for use in investigations and trials. There are two forensic research institutes in Ukraine, in Kiev (with a branch in Lviv) and in Kharkiv. Both were founded in 1923.

Scientific researcher (*naukovyi spivrobitnyk*). A term applied to persons involved in scholarly research in scientific research institutes, departments, laboratories, stations, and other institutions. The term also denotes rank.

The term 'scientific researcher' became widely used in Ukraine and in the USSR during the 1920s. Until 1922 all research was concentrated in *universities and the All-Ukrainian *Academy of Sciences. That year, however, universities were reorganized into institutes of people's education and industrial-technical institutes. Research chairs were established in those institutions, and their scholarly staff were called scientific researchers.

From the mid-1920s the term 'scientific researcher' came to denote a specific position, also known as 'scientific worker' (*naukovyi pratsivnyk*). By 1925 there were six ranked categories of scientific researchers, ranging from graduate students to renowned senior scholars. The title of scientific researcher did not necessarily imply that the person who held it had academic qualifications. Party figures (eg, V. Zatonsky and M. Skrypnyk) who had no academic degrees were listed as scientific researchers of research chairs at the *Ukrainian Institute of Marxism-Leninism.

During the 1930s the number of scientific researchers rapidly expanded to meet the Soviet state's science and technology needs. In Ukraine their number had increased from 866 in 1929 to 1,543 by 1934. As a result of the Stalinist purge of so-called bourgeois nationalists, however, the proportion of ethnic Ukrainian researchers declined from 50 percent of the total in 1929 to 30 percent in 1934. The proportion of Russians increased from 30 to 50 percent in the same period, and the proportion of Jews in the group remained stable at 16 percent. By 1940 there were 19,304 scientific researchers in Soviet Ukraine. The growth in their number was accompanied by an overall drop in the level of their professional qualifications. The ranks of senior scientific researcher and junior scientific researcher were introduced in 1934 and 1937 respectively. They remained in use until 1985.

The number of scientific researchers in Ukraine grew from 22,363 in 1950 to 46,657 in 1960 and 171,478 in 1975. With time the term came to be applied to any researcher with appropriate educational credentials. Most, however, have not had graduate degrees, and their rising number has tended to reduce the level of qualifications of the group as a whole. Between 1950 and 1975 the number of scientific researchers with doctorates dropped from just over 4 percent to 2.4 percent, and the proportion of those with candidate of sciences graduate degrees remained the same, at 27.5 percent. Most Soviet research was centralized in Russia, particularly in Moscow. In 1975 Ukraine had only 14 percent of the total number of scientific researchers in the USSR, whereas its share of the total population of the USSR was 20 percent.

In 1987 Ukraine had 215,000 scientific researchers, of whom only 3 percent had doctorates, and 33 percent, candidate of sciences degrees. Its share of the total number of scientific researchers in the USSR remained at 14 percent. Almost 17,000 scientific researchers worked in AN URSR (now ANU) institutions; 9 percent of them had doctorates, and 51 percent had candidate of sciences degrees.

In 1985 a new system of five scientific research categories was introduced: junior (*molodshyi*) scientific researcher, scientific researcher, senior (*starshyi*) scientific researcher, directing (*veduchyi*) scientific researcher, and chief (*holovnyi*) scientific researcher. The last two ranks are, as a general rule, offered only to those with a doctorate. The five categories were introduced to provide material incentive to improve research and qualifications, inasmuch as a promotion to a higher rank included a salary increase. In practice, however, because promotion has been under the control of the administration of a research institution, the new ranks have served as a bureaucratic tool for manipulating scholars.

H. Kasianov, B. Krawchenko

Scientific-technical societies (*naukovo-tekhnichni tovarystva*). Mass organizations for promoting scientific and technological development, improving economic performance, and raising labor productivity. The history of scientific-technical societies in Ukraine is linked closely with the development of such societies in Russia. Branches of the Imperial Russian Technical Society (est 1866) in St Petersburg were set up in Ukraine: in Mykolaiv (1869), Kiev (1870), Odessa (1871), Kharkiv (1879), Volhynia (1897), and Kremenchuk (1900). The Kiev branch took part in the construction of the city's water-supply and sewage systems, streetcar network, gas and electric lighting, and river transport. In 1884 it organized the empire's only secondary technical school of sugar refining, at the Smila refinery, and in 1897 it began to raise funds for building the Kiev Polytechnical Institute.

After the revolution the government called for the formation of mass organizations to promote economic development: in 1921 the Soviet of People's Commissars of the Russian SFSR issued a decree encouraging such organizations. The Ukrainian Scientific-Technical Society was established in Kharkiv in 1927 as an organization of technical-school teachers and engineers. It sponsored lectures and publications, such as *Naukovo-tekhnichnyi visnyk, Ukraïns'ki sylikaty, Sil's'ko-hospodars'ka mashyna, Tekhnika masam,* and *Problemy teplotekhniky*. It had branches in Kiev, Poltava, Dnipropetrovske, Odessa, and Artemivske and a membership of over 300. It was headed by K. Sukhomlyn and was dissolved in the mid-1930s. Its functions were taken over by the Ukrainian branches of all-Union scientific and engineering societies that were set up in the different industries starting in 1932.

Since 1954 the activities of scientific-technical societies have been directed by the trade unions. The First Ukrainian Republican Conference of Scientific-Technical Societies, held in Kiev in 1958, represented 150,000 members and elected the Ukrainian Republican Council of Scientific-Technical Societies. By 1984, societies in 24 branches of the economy represented 2,600,000 members in Ukraine. The largest (over 200,000 members) were in agriculture, machine building, and the construction industry. The work of 31,000 primary cells at the local level is co-ordinated by city and oblast councils within each society. The societies hold conferences, seminars, courses, exhibitions, and competitions on scientific and economic issues and sponsor local groups and laboratories (860,000 members) devoted to research, information gathering, and economic analysis. The societies publish 14 magazines with the help of ministries and departments of industry. The Ukrainian Republican Council of Scientific-Technical Societies was headed by I. Trefilov. Many members of the Academy of Sciences of Ukraine are active in the societies.

Scopolia (Ukrainian: *skopoliia*). A genus of large perennial herbs of the family Solanaceae. In Ukraine *S. carniolica* is found in the Carpathian Mountains and the western and Right-Bank forest-steppe, and *S. tubiflora* Kreyer is found in the western forest-steppe. The herbs are also cultivated as medicinal plants; their roots contain the alkaloids atropine, hyoscyamine, and scopolamine.

Scouting. See Plast Ukrainian Youth Association.

Scraba, Wasyl [Škraba, Vasyl'], b 1 March 1907 in Dominion City, Manitoba, d 18 April 1971 in Toronto. Businessman, politician, and community leader. He served 11 years as a trustee on the Winnipeg Board of Education, and then as alderman (1934–40) and the Liberal member of the legislative assembly for Winnipeg North (1945–9). Besides publishing the irregular *Ukrainian Canadian Review* (Winnipeg, 1936–42) he was active in the Prosvita Institute, the Ukrainian People's Home, the Ukrainian Professional and Business Club, and the Ukrainian Canadian Legion No. 141.

Scranton. A city (1980 pop 88,117) in northeastern Pennsylvania, with an estimated Ukrainian population of 2,500. The first Ukrainian census, conducted in 1909, indicated 2,000 people, a figure which rose to 4,000 in 1916. The Ukrainian population then began to diminish, so that by 1930 there were only 3,212 Ukrainians. After the Second World War an influx of displaced persons increased the Ukrainian population to approx 7,000 (1960). It has dropped rapidly since then.

Ukrainians began to arrive in Scranton during the 1880s to work in the anthracite mines, as well as on the railway and in textile industries. The community church was built in 1890 on the South Side; it later split into separate Galician (Ukrainian) and Transcarpathian parishes.

For many years the local Ukrainian Catholic church of St Volodymyr was instrumental in guiding Ukrainian social and cultural activities, including the staging of plays and the sponsoring of a Saturday school (from the 1920s). After the Second World War the church built a school (1950s) and a social hall (1960s). In the late 1920s a portion of the Ukrainian Catholic parish separated and formed the St Michael Ukrainian Orthodox church.

In 1910 Scranton hosted the founding convention of the Ruthenian National Association, and later became its headquarters. The association's name was changed to the Ukrainian Workingmen's Association in 1918 and to the *Ukrainian Fraternal Association (UFA) in 1978. In Scranton the UFA has organized a school, orchestras, and drama groups. The Ukrainian Community Center, purchased in 1957, serves as a major focal point for social and youth activities. The UFA has used Scranton as the publishing center for its newspaper *Narodna volia* (1910–) and its *English Supplement* (renamed *Fraternal Voice* in 1976); the magazine *Forum* (1967–); the almanacs *Tovarysh Emigranta* (1915–23), *Kalendar Robitnychoho Soiuzu* (1923–42, 1951), and *Almanac* (published irregularly since 1950); and other publications. Rev I. Ardan edited *Svoboda* in Scranton in the early 1900s and opened the Ruthenian Book Store, which also published books.

Chapters of the Ukrainian American Veterans, the League of Ukrainian Catholics of America, and the Ukrainian Orthodox League of the United States have been active in Scranton. In 1984 the local Ukrainian Students' Club organized Eastern Christian studies and published *Diakonia*, an English-language quarterly. In addition to branches of the UFA, Scranton has branches of the Ukrainian National Association, the Providence Association, the Ukrainian Congress Committee of America, and the Ukrainian American Citizens' Club.

A. Lushnycky

Sculpture. A general term in visual art for three-dimensional representations made by carving or modeling in a variety of materials, of which stone and clay are the most widely used. Sculpture encompasses monuments and statues, which are usually large in scale and are meant for public display; decorative or ornamental works; intimate or private pieces; and small forms. Basically it may be divided into works that are freestanding and works that are attached to a background (relief sculpture).

In Ukraine sculptural depictions dating back to the Paleolithic period have been found at the Mizyn archeological site (schematized female figures made from mammoth bones). Terra-cotta figures from the Trypilian culture and stone stelae have survived from the Bronze Age. The *Scythians left behind beautiful examples of relief sculpture. Numerous examples of Hellenic figural sculpture have been found among the ruins of the *ancient states on the northern Black Sea coast. These include heads of Aphrodite, Zeus, and Artemis, at the site of Olbia; a memorial bust (3rd–2nd century BC), at the site of Chersonese Taurica; and terra-cotta figures connected with the cults of Demeter, Aphrodite, and Astarte. Pre-Christian examples from the 1st millennium AD include the stone relief in the village of Busha, Vinnytsia oblast, of a kneeling figure, behind which stands a deer with antlers, praying to a tree with a rooster in it (1st century); stone idols, such as the one in the village of Ivankivtsi, Khmelnytskyi oblast (4th–6th century); and the *Zbruch idol, carved in low relief on all four sides of a block of stone. None of the wooden, gilded idols mentioned in the Rus' chronicles have survived. Life-size freestanding *stone babas dating from the 11th to 13th centuries AD were erected in the steppes of Ukraine by Turkic tribes. Thought to be tomb monuments of unknown function, these male and female figures in standing and sitting poses were bulky, schematized depictions differentiated by accessories of dress.

Only a few sculptures from the period of Kievan Rus' (10th–12th centuries) have been preserved. Two reliefs from St Michael's Golden-Domed Monastery in Kiev show SS Nestor and Demetrius and SS George and Theodosius (11th century). The stylized, detailed hair and armor of Nestor and Demetrius suggest Eastern prototypes; the hair and armor of George and Theodosius show a greater simplification of planes, as in Greek models. Two panel reliefs found in the catacombs of the Kievan Cave Monastery are thought to represent Hercules fighting a lion and Cybele on a chariot, themes from classical antiquity that have antecedents in sculptural reliefs found at the sites of Hellenic colonies on the northern Black Sea coast. A sarcophagus with relief carvings from the Church of the Tithes in Kiev is thought to be that of Princess Olha, and the sarcophagus from the St Sophia Cathedral in Kiev is considered to be that of Grand Prince Yaroslav the Wise, the founder of the shrine. The latter has relief carvings of crosses intertwined with plant motifs and depictions of fish and birds. The 16 stone panels in the St Sophia (11 of which are in the choir section) are carved with geometric patterns interspersed with foliage, fish, birds, and crosses. The panel above the fresco of Prince Yaroslav's family contains an eagle, an ancient symbol of Jupiter and the Roman emperors. The capitals of SS Borys and Hlib Cathedral in Chernihiv (late 12th century) contain carvings of exotic part-dog, part-bird, and part-dragon animals similar to the likeness of the pagan god Simarhlo. These have antecedents in Romanesque sculpture, as do the carvings found in the main portals of St Panteleimon's Church in Halych.

Metal icons from the 12th and 13th centuries have been found near Kiev (*Crucifixion*), and stone ones have been preserved in Kiev (*St Thomas and Christ*) and Kaniv. The relief in stone of the *Orante* (13th–14th century) in the Kievan Cave Monastery is stylized without much modeling, whereas 15th-century depictions, such as *Mother of God with SS Anthony and Theodosius of the Caves* (1470) from the Dormition Church at the monastery, have fine three-dimensional modeling. One of the most beautiful carvings is the miniature four-part, folding wood iconostasis with multifigure panels (late 15th century) from Kamianets-Podilskyi. In general the development of sculpture in Ukraine was hindered by the hostile attitude of the Eastern church to sculptural images. Sculpture was limited to relief carvings, mostly in stone or wood.

As the influence of Renaissance art spread to Ukraine, particularly Galicia, sculpture became more common. There is an attempt to convey volume and movement in the high relief in stone of *The Convincing of Thomas* (mid-16th century) from the Armenian Cathedral in Lviv, but without an understanding of anatomy and proportions. Memorial tomb sculpture appeared with depictions of reclining and semireclining figures in Renaissance architectural settings similar to those found in northern Italy (the tombs of O. Lahodovsky, A. Kysil, J. Herburt, Prince K. Ostrozky, the Syniavsky family, and K. Ramultova). The Renaissance period also engendered carved and gilded wooden iconostases with classical orders and decorative details, such as that of the Dormition Church in Lviv, now in the church of Velyki Hrybovychi, Nesterov raion, Lviv oblast. Secular buildings in the Renaissance style were lavishly decorated with carved reliefs. Architectural elements, such as the door and window frames of the Black and Korniakt buildings in Lviv, were embellished with decorative carvings on both the exterior and the interior. Relief sculptural decorations became common in church architecture. Examples may be seen in Lviv, in the exterior frieze of the Dormition Church, with carved plant motifs and figures in the metopes; the Chapel of the Three Church Fathers; and the Kampian and Boim family chapels, which have elaborately carved entablatures and a rich decoration of carved relief figures and ornaments.

During the baroque period (mid-17th to early 18th century) in Ukraine, relief carvings reached the zenith of their development in architectural decoration and in the multi-storied iconostasis, rather than, as in western Europe, in three-dimensional sculpture. Baroque profiling, s-curves, and plant motifs, including typical Ukrainian elements such as stylized sunflower heads, embellished sacred and secular architecture. Ornately carved and sumptuously gilded wooden iconostases rose to new heights of splendor in churches such as the ones in Bohorodchany (17th century, by Y. Kondzelevych) and Rohatyn (1649–51). Emphasis shifted from painted icons and architectural elements to richly carved surfaces, and these eventually dominated the structures. Plant motifs were most common, although some figures found their way into the designs. Side chapels were also adorned with smaller carved iconostases. (Many of the magnificent baroque *iconostases in Kiev and elsewhere were destroyed by the Soviet regime in the 1930s.) Nizhen, in the Chernihiv region, and Zhovkva, in Galicia, became centers of iconostasis production. Sculptors such as Yu. Shymonovych-Semyhynovsky, S. Putiatytsky, O. Kuliavsky, V. Sakovych, and H., I., and S. Stobensky worked out of Zhovkva. One of the finest baroque iconostases was in the Zhovkva Church of the Holy Trinity (ca 1720), where baroque devices such as the play of light and dark, dynamic movement, and dramatic contrasts of curved and perpendicular forms and smooth and heavily carved surfaces were used to full advantage. One of the largest surviving iconostases was installed in the Transfiguration Church in the village of Velyki Sorochyntsi, in the Poltava region, in 1732. It is 20 m wide and 17 m high, and so lavishly carved that the columns have lost their structural elements and resemble bouquets and flowering fields. The Royal Gates of the iconostasis in the St Sophia Cathedral in Kiev, commissioned by Metropolitan R. Zaborovsky in 1747, are a masterpiece of late baroque Ukrainian art. Carved entirely in silver and covered in gold, they were removed by the Soviet authorities between 1935 and 1937, as were eight chapel iconostases.

The best and most numerous examples of three-dimensional sculpture are to be found in Galicia (in the rest of Ukraine the Orthodox church continued to oppose figural carving). There sculpture was incorporated into church and secular architecture (eg, the city hall in Buchach). Figural sculptures were particularly popular in Roman Catholic churches. In the Dominican Church in Lviv, for example, 18 figures in the second story beneath the dome were carved by S. Fessinger. Sculpture in the round was incorporated into the architecture of Ukrainian Catholic churches, such as St George's Cathedral in Lviv.

These achievements resulted from efforts by talented local sculptors and imported ones, such as J. *Pfister and J. *Pinzel. In Pinzel's carved *Crucifixion with Mary and St John* (1750s) in St Martin's Church in Lviv, the polychromatic wooden figures are unequaled in the clarity of their

contrasting planes and their dramatic juxtaposing of drapery folds. In contrast the polychromatic figure of St Michael, the patron saint of Kiev, from the tower of the Town Hall in Kiev lacks sophistication. It was executed from two sheets of copper fitted over a silhouette.

The aristocracy and the rich continued to commission tomb sculptures and memorial wall plaques carved in relief. A fine example is A. Schlüter's monument to J. Sobieski and S. Danilowicz in Zhovkva, which incorporates two allegorical figures and putti with the central urn. Examples of ceramic sculpture, such as the coat of arms of Hetman I. Mazepa on the exterior of Chernihiv College, the reliefs of Mary and saints in the niches on the gates of the Novhorod-Siverskyi Transfiguration Monastery, and various decorations for secular buildings in Kiev and Pereiaslav, have survived.

Rococo sculpture in the round was characterized by elongated proportions and contrapposto poses, and it continued to be an organic part of the architectural design of buildings (eg, the statues in the Catholic cathedral of Kamianets-Podilskyi, 18th century). Decorative carvings, however, became more delicate and graceful and often appeared to float on the surface. The popularity of high, ornate iconostases did not diminish, but the carved decorations became somewhat lighter and more whimsical, and the iconostases therefore more subdued, as in the cathedral of the Mhar Transfiguration Monastery (1762–5, by S. Shalmatov), St Andrew's Church in Kiev (1760s), and the Cathedral of the Nativity of the Mother of God in Kozelets (1760s). Angel heads carved in the round were used to decorate the interior of St Andrew's Church, and shell-like forms were incorporated into asymmetrical designs. The iconostasis from the wooden Church of the Holy Protectress (carved by S. Shalmatov, 1768–73) in Romen is a rococo masterpiece, with irregular sections and carved figures in places usually reserved for painted icons. These include the central Crucifixion, the city-fortress in a cartouche below it, and the Annunciation carved in relief into the Royal Gates, which provide the architectural setting. Three-dimensional, life-size figures of Zacharius, Aaron, John the Evangelist, and John the Baptist appear in the third story. The iconostasis is topped with a beautiful composition showing the skillfully modeled figure of God carved in high relief on a background of swirling roses, putti heads, and fanciful seashell forms.

Classicism appeared in the mid-1750s and brought with it a return to the harmony, clarity, and serenity of antiquity. It did not become widely accepted, however, until the beginning of the 19th century. The Empire style was a development of classicism inspired by Greek rather than Roman prototypes and was more geometric and austere. Classicism coincided with the decline of Ukrainian autonomy and the annexation of eastern and most of central Ukraine by Russia. Russian domination brought about the loss of cultural freedom. Under tsarist rule all building designs had to be approved by the imperial government in St Petersburg. Among Ukrainian artists working in the classical style were M. Kozlovsky, I. *Martos, and K. *Klymchenko, all of whom worked mostly in Russia. Martos executed several monuments in Ukraine, including the statue of Duc de Richelieu (1823–8) in Odessa. He also designed the grave monument to Hetman K. Rozumovsky (1803–5) in Baturyn.

The unprecedented emphasis on civic architecture and

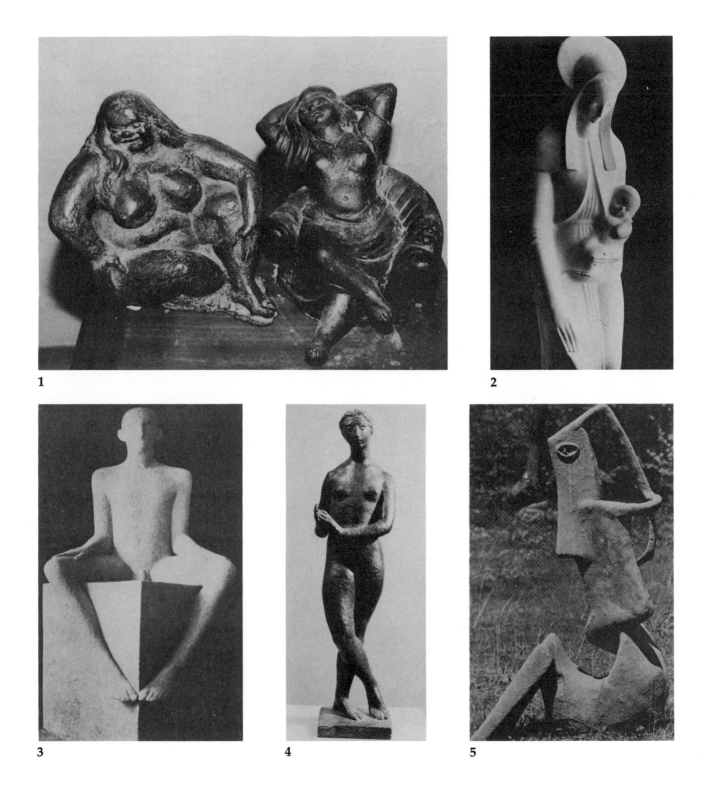

SCULPTURE 1) H. Kruk: left, *On the Beach* (bronze, 1971); right, *Girl Resting* (bronze, 1975). 2) M. Chereshnovsky: *Madonna the Rescuer* (plaster of paris, 1953; private collection). 3) O. Diachenko: *Composition with Sharp Angles* (fireclay). 4) L. Molodozhanyn: *Kore* (bronze, 1959; private collection). 5) M. Dzyndra: *Sitting Woman* (cement, 1972; artist's collection).

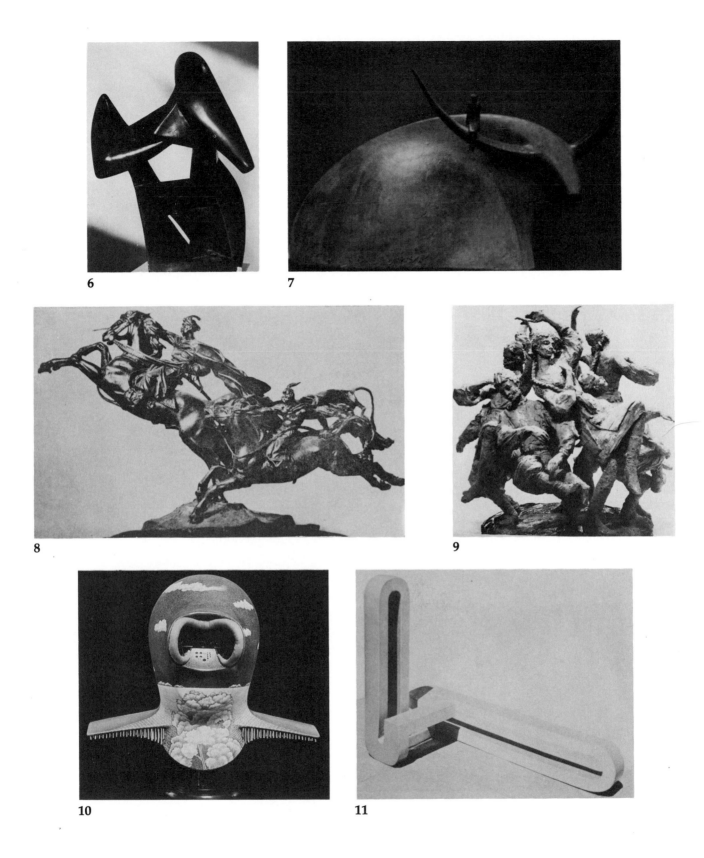

SCULPTURE 6) A. Archipenko: *Boxing* (painted plaster of paris, 1914; Saarland-Museum). 7) M. Bilyk: *Morning of the Universe* (bronze). 8) M.(B.) Mukhyn: *Glory* (wax). 9) P. Kapshuchenko: *Wreath* (terra-cotta). 10) D. Proch: *Night Landing Mask* (fiberglass, chicken bones and fiber optics, 1982; Winnipeg Art Gallery). 11) M. Urban: *Parallel Counterpoint* (painted steel, 1971; artist's collection).

town planning during the classicist period created a need for public sculpture of the type formerly unknown in Ukraine. Freestanding sculptures resembling classical models appeared as civic monuments (eg, Martos's statue of Duke A.-E. de Richelieu in Odessa) and as decorative features in city squares, parks, and gardens. The famous landmark statue of St Volodymyr by V. Demut-Malynovsky and P. Klodt (1850–3) overlooking the Dnieper River is one of the most popular examples of classical sculpture in Kiev. Most monuments, however, were dedicated to the tsars and their appointees.

In Western Ukraine under Austro-Hungarian rule, the need for civic sculpture was at first met by imported talent from Central and Western Europe, such as H. Wittwer, who was trained in Vienna, and A. *Schimser, from Bratislava, who received training in Vienna and Paris. Wittwer created the sculptures of the four fountains (1793) in Rynok Square in Lviv, which he modeled on the classical figures of Diana, Neptune, Adonis, and Amphitrite. The relief carvings of mythological and allegorical figures on the former Credit Society Building in Lviv were done by Wittwer and Schimser. Schimser also executed the Trenkle-Breyer-Venkle family monument in the Lychakiv Cemetery, composed of an angel, a grieving woman, and a youth in classical drapery carrying the symbolic vessel of sadness and tears.

In the second half of the 19th century romanticism and realism replaced classicism. The life of the peasants was depicted by H. Krasutsky in the four niches above the second story in the 'Four Seasons' Building in Lviv. In Russian-ruled Ukraine F. *Balavensky introduced ethnographic elements into his allegorical sculptures *Life* and *Charity* and created portrait busts of famous Ukrainian writers. Ukrainian themes became prevalent in the work of Ye. *Trypilska, who worked in marble and ceramic (*At the Market*, 1918). P. *Viitovych executed the figures for the Lviv Opera House, and H. *Kuznevych worked on tomb sculptures and several portrait busts of T. Shevchenko.

The monument to Hetman B. Khmelnytsky (1888) in Kiev was executed by the Russian sculptor M. *Mikeshin in a realist style. Ukrainian sculptors who worked in the realist manner were the versatile L. *Pozen, B. Eduards, and P. *Zabila, whose work was influenced by academic sculpture.

Many Ukrainian sculptors studied in Paris and were influenced by A. Rodin and the impressionists. Among them were M. *Parashchuk, who later worked in the academic style in Sofia, Bulgaria, E. *Blokh, M. *Brynsky, M. *Havrylko, and B. *Kratko.

A. *Archipenko is the most famous Ukrainian sculptor. In the 1910s he created some of the first cubist sculptures (*Walking* [1912], *Gondolier* [1914]), experimented with constructions in a variety of materials and abstraction, and revived polychromatic sculpture. His later portrait busts of T. Shevchenko and I. Franko are realistic depictions lacking the innovative approach for which he was famous. Another pioneer of modern sculpture and the father of constructivism, V. *Tatlin, spent most of his creative years working in Russia, where he was one of the leading figures of the Russian avant-garde. In Kharkiv in the 1920s, V. *Yermilov explored constructivism in his wood and metal 'experimental compositions' and 'constructions,' which were colored in an attempt to warp a continuous surface. Cubism influenced the early work of I. *Kava-

leridze, who participated in the avant-garde of the 1910s in Ukraine and in the 1920s created cubist monuments in Ukraine (monument to T. Shevchenko) before succumbing to socialist realism (eg, *Lenin and Gorky*, 1952). Other sculptors of the 1920s and 1930s were less inventive and remained loyal to realist traditions. They included I. *Severa, Ye. *Sahaidachny, M. Novoselsky, H. *Tenner, A. Pysarenko, Zh. *Dindo, and V. Klimov.

In Soviet Ukraine sculpture, like all the arts, has been subject to the dictates of *socialist realism and Party control since the 1930s. As a result most works have glorified the Bolshevik Revolution, Party leaders, workers, peasants, and Soviet heroes. Sculpture was particularly pompous during the Stalinist period, in which thousands of monuments to V. Lenin, K. Marx, J. Stalin, and M. Gorky were erected. Notable sculptors who have worked in the socialist-realist manner are M. *Lysenko, I. *Makohon, H. *Petrashevych, Ya. *Razhba, A. *Bilostotsky, H. *Pyvovarov, I. and V. *Znoba, T. *Bryzh, V. *Borodai, D. *Krvavych, Y. *Sadovsky, H. *Kalchenko, I. *Honchar, and E. *Mysko. M. Hrytsiuk, who modeled expressive figures not in keeping with socialist realism (*Artemii Vedel*), together with Yu. *Synkevych and A. *Fuzhenko executed the Shevchenko monument in Moscow (1964). H. *Sevruk, who works in ceramic relief sculpture and gets her inspiration from Ukrainian historical themes, had difficulties exhibiting her work until 1988.

The policy of Glasnost introduced in the late 1980s made it possible for many young sculptors in Ukraine to explore individual visions and experiment with new forms and materials. Several of them have worked in ceramic sculpture or terra-cotta – V. and N. Isupov, A. Ilinsky, O. Kostin, L. Krasiuk, O. Mylovzorov, M. Khusid, and R. Petruk. M. Andrushchuk and H. Drul have created abstract figures in stone, E. Kotkov has experimented with constructions in space, and M. Malyshko has worked in wood.

In the postwar years several émigré sculptors gained prominence: H. *Kruk and V. *Masiutyn in Germany; L. *Molodozhanyn in Canada; S. *Lytvynenko, V. *Simiantsev, A. *Darahan, M. *Mukhyn, A. *Pavlos, M. *Dzyndra, P. *Kapshuchenko, M. *Chereshnovsky, and the abstractionists K. *Milonadis, A. *Hunenko, and M. *Urban in the United States; F. *Yemets in Venezuela; and H. *Petsukh in Poland. Many sculptors of Ukrainian origin have worked in North America: in the United States, Ya. *Gerulak, who specializes in ceramic sculpture, M. *Bentov, who creates symbolic bronzes using geometric shapes and greatly reduced figural forms, A. Farion, who carves in stone, Ya. Harabatsch, who works with abstracted shapes, L. Koverko, and Ya. Strutynsky, who works in constructed reliefs; and in Canada, R. Kosteniuk, who creates abstract constructions based on the structure of living organisms, D. *Proch, whose work includes space-age masks, assemblages, and installations, E. *Zelenak, who creates abstract fiberglass compositions, and R. Yuristy, who constructs large-scale animal pieces for outdoor spaces.

BIBLIOGRAPHY

Nimenko, A. *Ukraïnska skul'ptura druhoï polovyny* XIX–*pochatku* XX *st.* (Kiev 1963)

Bazhan, M. (chief ed). *Istoriia ukraïns'koho mystetstva v shesty tomakh*, 6 vols (Kiev 1966–70)

Varvarets'kyi, Iu. *Stanovlennia ukraïns'koï radians'koï skul'ptury* (Kiev 1972)

Garkusha, N.; et al. *Monumental'noe i dekorativnoe iskusstvo v arkhitekture Ukrainy* (Kiev 1975)

V pam'iati narodnii (Kiev 1975)

Zapasko, Ia. (ed) *Mystetstvo onovlenoho kraiu: Naukovo-populiarnyi narys* (Kiev 1979)

Mozdyr, M. *Ukraïns'ka narodna derev'iana skul'ptura* (Kiev 1980)

Liubchenko, V. *L'vivs'ka skul'ptura XVI–XVII stolit'* (Kiev 1981)

Afanas'iev, V. *Ukraïns'ke radians'ke mystetstvo 1960–1980-kh rokiv* (Kiev 1984)

D. Zelska-Darewych

Scythia (Skytiia, Skifiia). The domain of the *Scythians. According to Herodotus Greater Scythia occupied a large rectangle of land extending nearly 700 km (20 days travel) from the Danube River in the west across the Black Sea coast and steppe region of what is today Ukraine to the lower Don Basin in the east. Individual Scythian settlements also existed in what is today the Hungarian-Rumanian borderland, probably as outposts. It is not known how far north Scythia reached into the forest-steppe zone. The Scythians were forced out of the steppe into Scythia Minor – the Crimea and the Dobrudja region south of the Danube Delta – in the 3rd century BC. The steppe of Southern Ukraine was occasionally referred to as Scythia (Skufia and Great Skuf in the Primary Chronicle) and Sarmatia until the 19th century.

Scythian art. The art of the *Scythians combined Eastern elements with influences from the Hellenic *ancient states on the northern Black Sea coast. The combination gave the art an exquisite and unique quality. The center of Scythian art can be considered *Panticapaeum, the capital of the *Bosporan Kingdom. The many Scythian artifacts found in barrows in Southern Ukraine and the Kuban were either imported from Greece or made by indigenous Hellenic and Scythian artisans. Scythian jewelery in particular attained a high level of intricacy and magnificence.

The principal feature of Scythian art is its use of a zoomorphic symbology. Objects found in Ukraine are distinguishable from their Caucasian counterparts, which reflect more the influence of Iranian, Urartian (ancient Armenian), Altaic, and, through this last, Chinese art. The Scythians fashioned gold objects depicting semirecumbent stags, deer, lions, panthers, horses and other domesticated animals, birds, and fantastic beasts (eg, griffins and sirens), as well as human faces, bodies, and groups of humans. Numerous vases, goblets, quivers, scabbards, combs, and other objects portray scenes from everyday life (eg, combat, farming, herding, taming horses, milking sheep, sewing skins) as well as motifs from Greek mythology and history. This symbology is often coupled with Greek geometric and floral ornamentation. Objects depicting griffins with lion's or eagle's heads tearing apart horses or deer personify evil forces; they were likely created as amulets.

The finest works of Scythian art have been excavated in the so-called Royal Scythian kurhans, *Kul Oba, *Haimanova Mohyla, *Melitopil, *Solokha, *Krasnokutskyi, and *Chortomlyk kurhans in Southern Ukraine, and the *Velyka Blyznytsia, Kelermes, and Kostromska kurhans in the Kuban.

In the 4th century BC, Hellenic influences began declining in the northern Black Sea littoral as a result of the in-

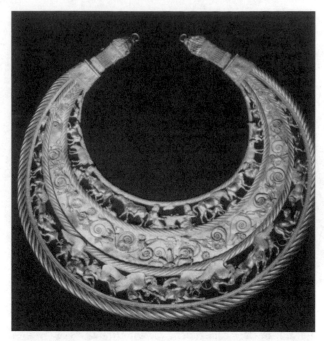

Scythian gold pectoral from the Krasnokutskyi kurhan

A detail on the pectoral

migration of the Sarmatians and other Iranian tribes. In the 3rd century BC the Sarmatians forced the Scythians out of Southern Ukraine into Crimea, where a new Scythian art developed. On the site of the new Scythian capital, *Neapolis, a mausoleum for luminaries, who were buried along with their horses, was excavated. Over 1,300 works of art were uncovered there, including frescoes with scenes of horseback riding and hunting.

During the 19th century many Scythian treasures were taken from Ukraine and Crimea to the St Petersburg Hermitage Museum. During the *Crimean War a tsarist ukase ordered the transfer of all gold artifacts found in Ukraine to the Hermitage. Only the discoveries of Scythian art made by AN URSR (now ANU) archeologists in the last few decades of the 20th century can be found in Ukraine's museums today.

BIBLIOGRAPHY
Borovka, G. *Scythian Art* (New York 1928)
Jettmar, K. *Art of the Steppes: The Eurasian Animal Style* (London 1967)

Artamonov, M. *Treasures from Scythian Tombs in the Hermitage Museum* (Leningrad 1969)

Charrière, G. *L'Art barbare scythe de la Sibérie à la Mer Noire* (Paris 1971)

Leskov, A. *Treasures from the Ukrainian Barrows: Latest Discoveries* (Leningrad 1972)

Lieskov, O. *Skarby kurhaniv Khersonshchyny* (Kiev 1974)

Vickers, M. *Scythian Treasures in Oxford* (Oxford 1979)

Mozolevs'kyi, B. *Skifs'kyi step* (Kiev 1983)

Rolle, R.; et al (eds). *Gold der Steppe: Archäologie der Ukraine* (Schleswig 1991)

S. Hordynsky

Scythians (*skyty*, *skify*). A group of Indo-European tribes that controlled the Southern Ukrainian steppe in the 7th to 3rd centuries BC. They first appeared there in the late 8th century BC after having been forced out of Central Asia. The Scythians were related to the *Sauromatians and spoke an Iranian dialect. After quickly conquering the lands of the *Cimmerians they pursued them into Asia Minor and established themselves as a power in the region. In the 670s BC they launched a successful campaign to expand into Media, Syria, and Palestine. They were forced out of Asia Minor early in the 6th century BC by the Medes, who had by then assumed control of Persia, and retreated to their lands between the lower Danube and the Don, known as *Scythia.

The bellicose Scythians were often in conflict with their neighbors, particularly the Thracians in the west and the *Sarmatians in the east. They faced their greatest military challenge around 513–512 BC, when the Persian king Darius I led an expeditionary force against them. By withdrawing and undertaking scorched-earth tactics rather than engaging in pitched battles, they forced the Persians to retreat in order to preserve their army. The event had a significant impact on subsequent Scythian development, for it confirmed their position as masters of the steppes and spurred on the political unification of the various tribes under the Royal Scythians. By the end of the 5th century BC the *Kamianka fortified settlement, near present-day Nykopil, had been established as the capital of Scythia.

The Scythians reached their apex in the 4th century BC under King Ateas, who eliminated his rivals and united all the tribal factions under his rule. He waged a successful war against the Thracians but died in 339 BC in a battle against the army of Philip II of Macedon. In 331 BC the Scythians defeated one of Alexander the Great's armies. Subsequently they began a period of decline brought about by constant Sarmatian attacks. They were forced to abandon the steppe to their rivals and re-established themselves in the 2nd century BC in the Crimea around the city of *Neapolis. There they regained part of their strength and fought several times against the *Bosporan Kingdom, and even managed to conquer Olbia and other Hellenic city-states on the northern Black Sea (Pontic) coast. Continued attacks from the Sarmatians, however, further weakened the Scythians, and an onslaught by the Germanic *Goths in the 3rd century AD finished them off completely. The Scythians subsequently disappeared as an ethnic entity through steady intermarriage with and assimilation into other cultures, particularly the Sarmatian.

The Scythians were divided into several major tribal groups. Agrarian Scythian groups lived in what is now Poltava region and between the Boh and the Dnieper riv-

A depiction of Scythians on a gold vase (4th century BC) found in the Kul-Oba kurhan near Kerch in the Crimea. The figures have combination quiver-and-bow cases that were characteristic of the Scythians.

ers. The lower Boh region near *Olbia was inhabited by Hellenized Scythians, known as Callipidae; the central Dniester region was home to the Alazones; and north of them were the Aroteres. The kingdom was dominated by the Royal Scythians, a small but bellicose minority in the lower Dnieper region and the Crimea that had established a system of dynastic succession. Their realm was divided into four districts ruled by governors who maintained justice, collected taxes, and gathered tribute from the Pontic city-states. A separate coinage, however, was not developed by the Scythians until quite late in their history. Their administrative apparatus was in fact quite loose, and the various Scythian groups handled most of their affairs through a traditional structure of tribal elders. Over time Scythian society became increasingly stratified, with the hereditary kings and their military retainers gaining an increasing amount of wealth and power. Although most Scythians were freemen, slaves were common in the kingdom.

The Scythians inhabiting the steppe were nomadic herders of horse, sheep, and cattle. Those in the forest-steppe were more sedentary cultivators of wheat, millet, barley, and other crops. (Some scholars believe that those agriculturists may have been the predecessors of the Slavs.) Scythian artisans excelled at metalworking in iron, bronze, silver, and gold. The Scythians also engaged in hunting, fishing, and extensive trade with Greece through the Pontic city-states; they provided grains, livestock, fish, furs, and slaves in exchange for luxury goods, fine ceramics, and jewelry.

The Scythians' military prowess was in large measure the result of their abilities as equestrian archers. They raised and trained horses extensively, and virtually every Scythian male had at least one mount. They lavished care and attention on their horses and dressed them in ornate trappings. Saddles and metal stirrups were not used by the Scythians, although felt or leather supports may have been. The foremost weapon of a Scythian warrior was the double-curved bow, which was used to shoot arrows over the left shoulder of a mounted horse. Warriors commonly

Kurhan (burial mound)

Horodyshche (fortified settlement)

Greek colony

Boundary of Ukraine

0   100   200 km

SCYTHIA

carried swords, daggers, knives, round shields, and spears and wore bronze helmets and chain-mail jerkins. The Scythians became a potent force not only because of their impressive array of weapons and training but also because they shared a strong underlying military ethos and belonged to a warrior society that bestowed honors and spoils on those who had distinguished themselves in battle. That ethos was reinforced by the common rite of adopting blood brothers and the use of slain foes' scalps or skulls as trophies or drinking cups.

Because of their generally nomadic or seminomadic existence the Scythians usually had relatively few possessions. Those they did have were often of exquisite quality and craftsmanship and established the Scythians' reputation in the ancient world as devotees of finery (see *Scythian art).

The Scythians never developed a written language or a literary tradition. They had a well-defined religious cosmology, however. Their deities included the fire goddess Tabiti, followed by Papeus (the 'Father'), Apia (goddess of the earth), Oetosyrus (god of the sun), Artimpasa (goddess of the moon), and Thagimasadas (god of water). The Scythians did not build temples, altars, or idols to worship their deities, but they maintained a caste of soothsayers and believed strongly in witchcraft, divination, magic, and the power of amulets. Representations of Scythians and their gold ornaments suggest that they were the first people in history to wear trousers.

Scythian burial customs were elaborate, particularly among the aristocracy. A chieftain remained unburied for 40 days after his death. During that time his internal organs were cleansed, his body cavity was stuffed with herbs, and his skin was waxed. He was then paraded through his realm accompanied by a large retinue indulging in ostentatious lamentation. After 40 days he was interred in a large *kurhan (up to 20 m high) together with his newly killed favorite wife or concubine, household servants, and horses, as well as weapons, amphoras of wine, and a large cache of goods. Lesser personages had less elaborate funerals. A common practice was the erection of anthropomorphic statues (*stone babas) as grave markers.

For many years the memory of the Scythians was best preserved by Herodotus, who included a lengthy, basically factual account of them in his *Histories*. After the last Scythians had died out in the 3rd century AD, the tribes were largely forgotten. Interest in them was revived as a result of some spectacular finds in Scythian barrows, starting with the *Melgunov kurhan in 1763. The ensuing search for richer caches impeded archeological research on the more prosaic aspects of Scythian life until Soviet archeologists undertook work in that realm in the 20th century. Scythian archeological sites in Ukraine include the *Bilske, *Kamianka, *Karavan, *Nemyriv, *Pastyrske, and *Sharpivka fortified settlements and the *Chortomlyk, *Haimanova Mohyla, *Kul Oba, *Krasnokutskyi, *Melitopil, *Oksiutyntsi, *Oleksandropil, *Solokha, *Starsha Mohyla, and *Zhabotyn kurhans.

BIBLIOGRAPHY

Minns, E. *Scythians and Greeks: A Survey of Ancient History and Archaeology on the North Coast of the Euxine from the Danube to the Caucasus* (Cambridge 1913)

Rostowzew, M. *Skythien und der Bosporus* (Berlin 1931)

Sulimirski, T. *Scytowie na Zachodniem Podolu* (Lviv 1936)

Rice, T. *The Scythians* (London 1957)

Pasternak, Ia. *Arkheolohiia Ukraïny* (Toronto 1961)

Potratz, H. *Die Skythen in Südrussland: Ein untergegangenes Volk in Südosteuropa* (Basel 1963)

Smirnov, A. *Skify* (Moscow 1966)

Kovpanenko, H. *Plemena skifs'koho chasu na Vorskli* (Kiev 1967)

Il'inskaia, V. *Skify Dneprovskogo lesostepnogo Levoberezh'ia (kurgany Posul'ia)* (Kiev 1968)

Petrov, P. *Skify: Mova i etnos* (Kiev 1968)

Vysotskaia, T. *Pozdnie skify v Iugo-Zapadnom Krymu* (Kiev 1972)

Terenozhkin, A. (ed). *Skifskie drevnosti* (Kiev 1973)

Artamanov, M. *Kimmeriitsy i skify (ot poiavleniia na istoricheskoi arene do kontsa IV v. do n.e.)* (Leningrad 1974)

Iakovenko, Ie. *Skify Skhidnoho Krymu v V–III st. do n.e.* (Kiev 1974)

Khazanov, A. *Sotsial'naia istoriia skifov: Osnovnye problemy razvitiia drevnikh kochevnikov evraziiskikh stepei* (Moscow 1975)

Chernenko, E. *Skifskie luchniki* (Kiev 1981)

Kovpanenko, G. *Kurgany ranneskifskogo vremeni v basseine r. Ros'* (Kiev 1981)

Neikhardt, A. *Skifskii rasskaz Gerodota v otechestvennoi istoriografii* (Leningrad 1982)

Il'inskaia, V.; Terenozhkin, A. *Skifiia VII–IV vv. do n.e.* (Kiev 1983)

Mozolevs'kyi, B. *Skifs'kyi step* (Kiev 1983)

Kuklina, I. *Etnogeografiia Skifii po antichnym istochnikam* (Leningrad 1985)

Rolle, R. *The World of the Scythians* (London 1989)

B. Kravtsiv, A. Makuch

Sea buckthorn (*Hippophae rhamnoides*; Ukrainian: *oblipykha, shchets*). A willowlike shrub of the family Elaeagnaceae. It grows along sea- and lakeshores and in the floodplains of rivers on gravel and sand. Sea buckthorn is used in stabilizing landslides, slopes, and ravines. Its fruit is rich in carotene, vitamin C, and vitamin E. It yields medicinal oil used to treat gastric ulcers, bedsores, and radiation injury to the skin.

Sea gull (Ukrainian: *morska chaika*). The common name given to a host of web-footed sea birds of the family Laridae (order Charadriiformes), which is composed of two subfamilies: Larinae (gull; Ukrainian: *martyn*) and Sterninae (tern; Ukrainian: *kriak* or *kriachok*). Some of the birds have a thin, straight bill; others, a powerful, curved bill. The long, pointed wings are adapted for prolonged flights over water; the legs are short. The plumage is thick and waterproof; white and black are the predominant colors. All sea gulls live close to water – seas, lakes, rivers, or marshes. They are gregarious birds that flock and nest in colonies on sandbars and cliffs, among broken reeds, and occasionally in trees and shrubs. They are scavengers; their diet includes worms and grubs, fish, marine and freshwater invertebrates, waste products of the fishing industry, and garbage. Nine species of the most common Larinae genus, *Larus*, are found in Ukraine, including the black-headed gull (*L. ridibundus*), the herring gull (*L. argentatus*), the Mediterranean gull (*L. melannocephalus*), and the slender-billed gull (*L. genei*). Nine species of Sterninae (mainly of the genus *Sterna*) are found in Ukraine, including the black tern (*S. niger*), the common tern (*S. hirundo*), and the little tern (*S. albifrons*). The image of the seagull is commonly invoked in Ukrainian folk songs and literature and the Cossacks named their seafaring boat *chaika*.

Sea transportation. A mode of transporting cargo and passengers on domestic or international seas. Sea traffic has many advantages over other modes: it uses natural waterways at the lowest cost of production, its load capacity is high, it is more fuel-efficient than other modes. Ukrainian sea traffic accounted for almost a quarter of the USSR tonnage and over half of the passenger traffic.

In Ukraine sea transportation dates back to Kievan Rus', but a steady development of the industry began in the 18th century after Russia established control of the northern shores of the Black and Azov seas. The new administration built port facilities, such as the Mykolaiv shipyard in 1775, Kherson port in 1778, Sevastopil port in 1783, and Odessa in 1794. In 1828 the Odessa steamship ran cruises on the Black Sea, and in 1833 the first steamship society was organized. Sea traffic grew rather slowly in the 19th century, because connecting railway routes began to be built only in the 1860s. The Russian government was more interested in a strong base on the Baltic Sea and an ice-free port at Murmansk than in the southern seas.

After the Second World War sea transportation became an important trade link with the West. Initially interest in sea transportation was prompted by defense requirements. Recently the growth in trade has raised the importance of Ukrainian ports.

Ukraine's sea traffic was not an autonomous industry. It was a branch of the all-Union economic system and was administered by three directorates: the Black Sea, with head office in Odessa; the Azov Sea, with an office in Mariiupil; and the Danube directorate in Izmail.

Odessa was by far the largest and most important of the directorates. It has the best facilities for internal and international cargo. Its modern equipment is capable of horizontal loading. Its ships are designed for heavy freight. Odessa's passenger traffic is also heavy. Besides having easy access to the Black Sea ports, Odessa is connected with numerous foreign ports in Asia and Europe. The Azov directorate handled mostly internal transportation, but some of its traffic flows to ports in the Near East, Northern Africa, and the Mediterranean region. Its vessels are equipped with modern devices for transporting dry cargo and timber. Container-ships are used to carry substances at high temperatures. The Danube directorate dealt with local traffic. Its physical plant consists mostly of riverboats, which carry goods along the Danube River. The directorate also served ports on the Black Sea, Soviet and foreign. More than half of its traffic is internal.

Much of the Ukrainian merchant and passenger fleet has been built in Ukraine, although some Finnish, Polish, and German ships are used (see *Shipbuilding).

Ukraine's share in the USSR freight output was approx 27.6 percent, and in the USSR shipping volume, 24.1 percent (1985). Its share of the passenger output was 54.6 percent, and of passenger volume, 59.2 percent. The reason for the high share in passenger output and volume is the climate of the Black Sea, which attracts tourists and vacationers.

Basic indexes of sea transportation, 1970–86

Category	1970	1980	1986
Freight traffic			
1. Output (in billion Tnm*)	93.0	91.1	153.0
2. Volume (in million t)	38.2	471.1	59.8
3. Average trip distance			
per t of haul (in nm)	2,434.6	1,934.2	2,558.0
Passenger traffic			
4. Output (in million m)	431.7	701.6	755.5
5. Volume (in million passengers)	19.8	28.5	28.7
6. Average trip distance per			
passenger (in nm)	21.8	24.4	26.3
7. Percentage of sea transportation			
to total transportation			
(a) freight output	28.2	21.8	28.3
(b) passenger output	1.1	0.8	0.8

*Tnm = tonnes × nautical miles.

In the last decade Odessa has become the main southern center for sea transportation. To increase its capacity, the Illichivske satellite port was developed. With its heavy cranes, Illichivske surpasses Odessa in its cargo-handling power. In 1978 the world's largest ferry began to operate between Illichivske and Varna, Bulgaria. Northeast of Odessa the new port of Yuzhnyi, specializing in chemicals, is being built. It is connected by a special railway with Horlivka, in Donetske oblast, and Togliatti, on the Volga River. Ukraine's second-largest port is Mykolaiv, which handles coal, metals, and grain. Kherson is noted for its grain shipping. Kerch is a large transit port for iron ore, coal, petroleum, and raw materials. Mariiupil, on the Sea of Azov, transports raw materials and agricultural products, particularly to Caucasia. Teodosiia and Berdianske ship mostly farm products. Ports such as Ochakiv, Yevpatoriia, Henicheske, and Skadovske are better known for their fisheries. Passenger traffic along the Crimean coast is heavy year round.

E. Bej

Seal, monk (*Monachus monachus*; Ukrainian: *tiulen bilocherevyi, monakh*). The only species of seal in Ukraine. An inhabitant of the waters of the Black Sea, this aquatic mammal belongs to the family Phocidae of true earless seals. It has been listed as an endangered species in Ukraine.

Seals. See Sphragistics.

Secession of Ukrainian students from Lviv University. In 1899 the Galician Ukrainian public began campaigning for the creation of a Ukrainian university in Lviv. Ukrainian students took an active part in the campaign. Their public rallies and demonstrations calling for the establishment of the university brought them into open conflict with the Poles, often in the form of violent street clashes. In 1901, after the administration of Lviv University expelled the Ukrainian student organizers and called on Polish students to fight the Ukrainians, 440 of the university's Ukrainian students formally withdrew in protest and registered at other universities in Vienna, Prague, Graz, and Cracow. The students had the general support of the Galician Ukrainian community, which created a 'secessional fund' to support them. The secession, which lasted from 1 December 1901 until the 1902 summer semester, had no practical results. The Ukrainian community's demands for equal status for the Ukrainian language in Lviv University's administration and the creation of Ukrainian chairs there (earlier they had demanded a separate university or the division of Lviv University into Ukrainian and Polish campuses) were ignored by the Austrian governmental bureaucracy. The secession, however, brought the issue to the attention of the Austrian parliament and of European public opinion, and the students' studies abroad widened their intellectual horizons. In the opinion of contemporary publicists and later historians the secession had negative consequences, in that it was a 'flight from the field of battle' which served only to weaken the existing Ukrainian student organizations and the campaign for a Ukrainian university in general.

B. Kravtsiv

Second World War. See World wars.

Secondary education (*serednie shkilnytstvo*). Instruction in schools for children who have completed elementary education; it provides either a general or a specialized program of study and allows students to continue their studies in institutes of *higher education.

In Ukraine, prior to the 18th century there was no significant difference among lower, middle, and higher schools. Nor was a distinction made between general and specialized programs of study. *Brotherhood schools, *college schools, and schools run by the Jesuit, Basilian, and Piarist orders provided what could be considered secondary education. Toward the end of the 18th and in the first half of the 19th century the *boarding school offered basic secondary education, as did the *gymnasium and *Realschule in the first half of the 19th century. The gymnasiums, *lyceums, and *institutes for daughters of the nobility were among the establishments offering secondary education for girls. (See *Education of women.) Secondary education was also provided by Orthodox *theological seminaries.

With the abolition of serfdom in 1861, secondary education in Russian-ruled Ukraine gradually expanded. A new development was the establishment of secondary professional schools. (See *Professional and vocational education.) The language of instruction in schools in Ukrainian territories within the Russian Empire was Russian. Only a tiny proportion of youths of school age obtained secondary education. The impoverishment of the Ukrainian peasantry and social and national discrimination resulted in a low percentage of school-age children attending secondary schools. (Two-thirds of children of school age in Ukraine in 1915 had never set foot inside a classroom.) The 1897 general population census revealed that there were only 192,582 people in the Ukrainian gubernias (out of a total population of 23.4 million) with complete secondary education, of whom 40 percent were members of the nobility or high-ranking bureaucrats.

In Western Ukraine under Austrian rule, gymnasiums and Realschulen were the principal institutions offering secondary education. There were relatively few secondary schools in Western Ukraine. In all of Galicia in 1906–7, for example, there were only 68 secondary schools, with 107,000 students, and in Bukovyna, 10 such schools, with a total enrollment of 7,300 (of which 1,800 were Ukrainians). Efforts by the Ukrainian community leadership to develop a network of Ukrainian secondary schools faced serious obstacles. The mass of the rural population was impoverished. In addition there were political barriers which were difficult to overcome. In Galicia, for example, the Polish majority in the Diet systematically blocked the development of a Ukrainian-language network of secondary schools. (The establishment of any secondary school required the passage of a resolution by the Diet.) As a result there were only six state-supported Ukrainian gymnasiums in Galicia in 1909–10.

In the course of the Ukrainian struggle for independence in 1917–20, secondary education was somewhat Ukrainianized, particularly in the gymnasiums. Wartime conditions did not permit the realization of the proposed 12-grade *unified labor schools, advocated by the Ukrainian National Republic, in which grades 9 to 12 were to have constituted general secondary education. During the period of the Western Ukrainian National Republic the Austrian system of education was retained, although efforts were undertaken to Ukrainianize secondary education.

Secondary education underwent many changes after the establishment of Soviet rule in Ukraine. In 1920 a new version of the unified labor school was introduced in the Ukrainian SSR. Grades five to seven of the *seven-year school offered secondary education. Graduates of the schools were able to continue their education in secondary professional schools, *tekhnikums, or *institutes.

In 1934 education throughout the USSR was unified, and Ukraine lost its distinctive education system. The *ten-year school was established as the basic institution of general secondary education. The seven-year school was established as the main institution offering incomplete secondary education. Since the 1930s a wide variety of other types of schools offering secondary education have been established, among them *schools for workers' youth and *schools for rural youth. *Tekhnikums have been reduced to the status of secondary schools. Parallel to the general secondary education system is a network of schools offering *secondary special education.

In the 1950s and early 1960s, under N. Khrushchev, secondary education was reformed to stress *polytechnical education. The 1966 school act downplayed this trend. More recently major reforms of the secondary school curriculum were undertaken, among them the rewriting of history and literature textbooks to rid the school program of the distortions of the past. During the recent reforms a large-scale public debate about the state of secondary education has unfolded. Among the major concerns addressed have been the scarcity of resources allocated to secondary education and the resulting shortage and inadequacy of buildings (almost 20 percent of schools operate on a two- or three-shift basis) and the absence of laboratory facilities and modern technology, such as computers.

Until the 1920s only a small number of people obtained secondary education. In 1914–15 (within the boundaries of contemporary Ukraine) there were 386 incomplete general secondary schools and 480 general secondary schools, with 49,600 and 185,800 pupils respectively. In 1927–8, incomplete general secondary schools numbered 2,420, and general secondary schools 28, with a total enrollment of 2.9 million and 231,900 respectively. By 1988–9 there were 7,984 incomplete secondary schools, with 1.1 million pu-

pils, and 9,543 secondary general-education schools, with 5.6 million pupils.

In 1958, eight years of schooling was made compulsory for all Soviet children. In 1966, universal 10-year complete secondary education was decreed and was to have been achieved by 1970. That goal, however, has not been realized.

In the 1920s the educational system underwent *Ukrainization. By 1929–30, 74 percent of all seven-year schools had Ukrainian as their language of instruction. The Russification of Ukraine's educational system, initiated in 1932–3, continued unabated until 1989. In the 1960s, for example, only 21 percent of pupils attending 10-year secondary schools in urban centers studied in Ukrainian-language establishments. Since 1989, when Ukrainian was granted state-language status, and with the rise of the Ukrainian national movement, the number of Ukrainian-language secondary schools has slowly increased.

In the 1920s and 1930s, in Ukraine under Polish rule, gymnasiums and lyceums functioned as the basic institutions offering secondary education. Technical schools were not numerous. In 1937–8 the number of students attending gymnasiums and lyceums was approximately 45,000. The number of Ukrainian students attending these schools was negligible because the transition from rural elementary to secondary schools was difficult. The Polonization of secondary education and the reluctance of the Polish authorities to allow the establishment of Ukrainian secondary schools further hindered Ukrainian access to secondary education. In 1937–8 there were only 24 Ukrainian gymnasiums, of which 19 were private institutions, and 21 lyceums, of which 16 were private schools. In Transcarpathia (under Czechoslovak rule), in 1938 there were 11 gymnasiums, of which 5 were Ukrainian institutions. In Bukovyna (under Rumanian occupation) all Ukrainian secondary schools had been Rumanianized by 1927.

In the same period Ukrainian émigrés established gymnasiums in Prague and in Kalisz, Poland. In 1945–50 many types of secondary schools operated in Ukrainian camps for displaced persons in Germany and Austria. At present the only secondary institutions outside Ukraine which use Ukrainian as the language of instruction are those located in Czechoslovakia, the Minor Seminary in Rome, and those offering *Ukrainian bilingual education, in western Canada. Ukrainian has been taught in private schools in the United States, Canada, and Brazil and in public and Catholic schools in some provinces of Canada (where numbers warrant).

BIBLIOGRAPHY
Narodna osvita, nauka i kul'tura v Ukraïns'kii RSR: *Statystychnyi zbirnyk* (Kiev 1973)
Sirka, A. *The Nationality Question in Austrian Education: The Case of Ukrainians in Galicia, 1867–1914* (Frankfurt 1980)
Matthews, M. *Education in the Soviet Union: Policies and Institutions since Stalin* (London 1982)

B. Krawchenko

Secondary general-education school (*serednia zahalno-osvitnia shkola*). A type of school established in the USSR by the 1958 school reform. Its full name was 'secondary general-education labor polytechnical school with production teaching.' The school was to offer an 11-year program of study giving pupils a complete secondary general education, as well as some vocational training in a branch of the economy. The same reform made the study of the Ukrainian language optional in the Russian-language school system in Ukraine. The vocationalization of secondary education was opposed by many education officials, and under N. Khrushchev the 11-year program was never fully implemented. The 1965 school act downplayed the vocational and polytechnical component in secondary education and restored a 10-year program (except in some non-Russian-language schools, where an 11-year program was permitted). Completion of the program gives the pupil the right to apply for entry to postsecondary institutions. Since 1986, 10-year secondary general-education schools have been gradually transformed into schools with an 11-year program. In 1988–9 there were 9,543 secondary general-education schools in Ukraine, with 5.6 million pupils. (See *Secondary education.)

Secondary special education (*serednia spetsiialna osvita*). An educational program which gives vocational or semiprofessional training as well as basic secondary education. Secondary special education in Ukraine is offered in schools under the jurisdiction of the Ukrainian Ministry of Higher and Specialized Secondary Education. Secondary special education can be obtained in some secondary schools offering training in over 400 occupations, in *tekhnikums, or in *vocational-technical schools. Full-time day study for those with 8 years of schooling (see *Eight-year school) is 3 or 4 years, and for those with completed secondary education (see *Ten-year school) 2 or 3 years (an additional year for those enrolled in evening or part-time programs). Graduates of secondary special-schools can apply to institutions of *higher education. In 1988–9 there were 737 secondary special schools in Ukraine, with 792,400 students (of whom 320,000 studied in schools offering training in industrial or construction occupations). Of the total number of students 523,400 were in full-time day programs. In 1967, secondary special education faculties were organized by some of the larger institutions of higher learning. In 1985 there were 17 such faculties in Ukraine.

The origins of secondary special education go back to the prerevolutionary period (see *Professional and vocational education). Secondary special education underwent a great expansion with industrialization. In 1914–15 there were 88 secondary special schools in Ukraine, with 88,000 students. By 1940–1 the figures were 693 and 196,300 respectively. In the 1950s secondary special schools started to attract young people with complete secondary education.

B. Krawchenko

Secretariat of the CC CPU. The top administrative and organizational body of the Communist Party of Ukraine. Similar bodies existed in the CPSU and its republican sections. The Secretariat of the CC CPU was established in 1918. It was composed of four to seven members chosen by the plenum of the CC CPU. Each member was usually responsible for a special area, such as ideology or industry. As a whole the group was responsible for managing the day-to-day affairs of the Party and enjoyed considerable influence. It was headed by the first (in 1925–34, general) secretary of the CPU. The Secretariat worked closely with the *Politburo, and there was usually some overlap in membership between the two bodies.

Sector of Government and Law of Ukraine. See Institute of State and Law of the Academy of Sciences of the Ukrainian SSR.

Sects. Religious bodies commonly formed as dissenting factions of a larger religious group and frequently regarded as extreme in their views and practices. A number of sects established religious communities in Ukraine, including various mystic and rationalist groups, offshoots of the Baptists, and groups splitting from the official Orthodox church. Although some individual groups had been active there earlier, the sects in Ukraine started becoming widespread in the 19th century.

The only indigenous Ukrainian sect to emerge was the *Malovantsi, who were active in Kiev gubernia in the late 19th and early 20th centuries. Ukraine, however, provided an attractive haven for sectarians fleeing persecution in Russia because it was outside the heartland of the empire. As early as the 1660s a significant number of *Old Believers, the first large sect to emerge from the Orthodox church in Russia, fled persecution by moving to Ukraine. Since Ukraine's southern reaches were relatively unsettled, tsarist authorities were more likely to leave sects in peace if they were out of the public eye and performing a socially useful task (ie, colonization).

The most notable sects in Ukraine – the Khlysts, Doukhobors, and Molokans – had a common origin in the Tambov region of Voronezh gubernia. The *Khlysts (also known as Khrystovoviry) arose in the mid-17th century at the same time as the Old Believer movement. Sect members started moving into Ukraine in the 1860s and established themselves in Kiev, Podilia, Poltava, and Kharkiv gubernias as well as the Kuban. The Doukhobors and Molokans had their origins in a Khlyst offshoot, the Spiritual Christians. In 1802, after a period of persecution, the Doukhobors were allowed to settle along the Molochna River in Tavriia gubernia. This region soon became their largest settlement in the Russian Empire. The Doukhobors prospered there until the early 1840s, when 4,000 of their number were relocated by tsarist authorities to the Caucasus region. The Doukhobors were subjected once again to persecution in the late 19th century, and more than 7,000 emigrated to Canada in 1897–8 under the leadership of P. Veregin. There they settled in east central Saskatchewan adjacent to an area colonized by Ukrainians. The *Molokans were formed in the 18th century in Tambov gubernia by a former Doukhobor. Because of their pacifism, members of this sect frequently came into conflict with state authorities, and throughout the 19th century groups of them were exiled to Caucasia, Siberia, and the Volga and Amur regions. By the beginning of the 20th century there were approx 1.2 million Molokans in the Russian Empire, many of whom had settled in Southern Ukraine.

Various denominations of *Evangelical Christians, most notably the *Baptists, emerged in Ukraine during the 19th century as an offshoot of German colonization in the region. Although these Protestant-based movements were regarded by tsarist authorities as sectarian, they were tolerated among the German population. When they began to emerge among Ukrainians through the *Stundists, efforts were made to eradicate what was regarded as a schismatic development.

The Soviet authorities were more openly hostile to religious sects than was the tsarist regime, particularly from the 1930s. Nevertheless, they did not eliminate sects; today a number are active in Ukraine and other parts of the former Soviet Union. The numbers of their followers are not known.

BIBLIOGRAPHY
Prugavin, A. *Raskol-sektanstvo: Materialy dla izucheniia religiozno-bytovykh dvizhenii russkogo naroda: Bibliografiia staroobriadchestva* (Moscow 1887)
Woodcock, G.; Avakumovic, I. *The Doukhobors* (Toronto–New York 1968)
Klibanov, A. *History of Religious Sectarianism in Russia, 1860s–1917*, trans E. Dunn (Oxford 1982)

Secular schools (*svitski shkoly*). Schools which operate outside of the influence of the church. They are under the jurisdiction of secular (often government) authorities, as opposed to *parochial schools, which are operated by the church.

In Ukraine before the 1917 Revolution, the distinction between secular and parochial schools was not entirely clear, since most schools combined religious and secular education, and many were jointly administered by a closely linked government and church.

This state of affairs held particularly in the Princely era. Both Volodymyr the Great and Yaroslav the Wise implemented a number of education programs focusing on literacy. Secular subjects, such as philosophy, rhetoric, grammar, and foreign languages, were taught (Vsevolod, the son of Yaroslav the Wise, for example, knew five languages). Eventually arithmetic and calendar calculation also became important at the schools.

After their reasonably independent inception, however, these schools gradually came under ecclesiastic authority, especially after the Mongol invasions, when the church was a somewhat sheltered haven. The schools remained under the church's domination until well into the 16th century, when the diffusion of Renaissance values and secular humanism to Eastern Europe resulted in many students' leaving traditional Orthodox schools. Although the alternatives were other religious schools – Catholic, particularly Jesuit, schools, and Protestant schools, the most prominent of which were Calvinist – these tended to be more modern than their Eastern Orthodox counterparts, and hence to have predominantly secular curricula and emphasis. In reaction to the increasing Western (primarily Polish) presence in Ukraine, the Orthodox schools also became more secular. This change in their nature enabled their graduates to compete with those of the Catholic and Protestant schools and thereby ensured the Orthodox schools' ability to survive. The most renowned and successful examples were the *brotherhood schools, the first of which was founded in Lviv in 1586. Throughout the 17th century the brotherhood schools provided a quasi-secular education, as did other schools established during the Hetmanate to educate the people. Religion was still a subject at these schools, but their focus was on basic education for laymen. The *Kievan Mohyla Academy, for example, had more laymen than clergy in attendance, according to 1727 data.

Under tsarist rule secularization progressed in Russian-ruled Ukraine, although the education system as a whole declined. Peter I closed monastery schools and then tried to substitute government-supported secular schools as the basic form of public education. These schools were usually poorly administered and underfunded, however; the result was that many of them closed, and that the literacy level in Ukraine dropped during Peter's reign. Catherine II tried to remedy the situation by also establishing some secular schools in Kiev, but they could not replace the widespread system of parochial schools at the village and elementary levels.

In Right-Bank Ukraine under Poland, in 1789 an education commission declared all 'Ruthenian' church schools closed, and established a new Polish secular school system in their place. Many of these schools were closed with the partition of Poland, however, and the remainder were closed after the Polish Insurrection of 1830–1 was crushed.

In the 19th century the tsarist government tried to weaken the potential for Ukrainian resistance by closing all but the most elementary-level Ukrainian schools. All new schools (two-year county schools, four-year gymnasiums, and universities) were Russian and secular. These schools had a foreign language and curriculum and were disliked by the Ukrainian population. Many people refused to attend them and were instead educated informally by the church. In the mid-1800s there were probably more Ukrainians receiving this sort of ad hoc religious education than attending the official secular schools. This state of affairs persisted, despite a decree in 1869 that officially separated the schools from the church.

The 1917 Revolution was a turning point in the secularization of schools. A resolution of the Second All-Ukrainian Teachers' Congress, held in Kiev on 10–12 August 1917, demanded that schools be secularized, and that religious instruction be allowed only with the consent of parents. In early 1918 a Ukrainian National Republic school decree based on the congress resolutions made education secular and placed it under the jurisdiction of the local organs of self-government. Only under Soviet rule was attendance at government schools enforced, and informal church instruction strictly and actively prohibited. From 19 January 1919 the church and state of the Ukrainian SSR was officially separate, and all education was secular.

In Western Ukraine Austrian- and Polish-ruled schools were separate from the church from 1863, but private religious schools were allowed. Under Soviet rule all private institutions were abolished.

(For a bibliography, see *Education.)

N. Freeland, B. Krawchenko

Sedge (*Carex*; Ukrainian: *osoka*). A perennial grassy, flowering plant of the family Cyperaceae, from a few centimeters to 4 m or more in height. The plants grow everywhere, mainly in damp places in forest zones. Many species are eaten before they bloom by grazing cattle; some are used as silage or hay. In Ukraine, of approx 100 species the most abundant are fox sedge (*C. vulpina*), elongated sedge (*C. elongata*), and early sedge (*C. praecox*). Sedge can be used in paper production and for basket or floor-mat weaving. Some sedges are cultivated as ornamental flowers.

Sedliar, Vasyl [Sedljar, Vasyl'], b 12 April 1899 in Liubech, Horodnia county, Chernihiv gubernia, d 13 July 1937. Painter and graphic artist. Sedliar studied at the Kiev Art School (1915–19) and then at the Ukrainian Academy of Arts (1919–22) under M. *Boichuk. He worked on large-scale murals, illustrated books, designed packaging, and produced ceramic works. He was part of the team

Vasyl Sedliar

Sedniv (drawing by Taras Shevchenko, 1846)

that decorated the Lutske regimental army barracks in Kiev under Boichuk's direction (1919), and he did the murals at the Kiev Institute of Plastic Arts (1924) and the Mezhyhiria Art and Ceramics Tekhnikum (1924) with O. *Pavlenko. Like Boichuk, he worked in a style combining the techniques and large simplified forms of traditional icon and folk art with formalist theory and contemporary subject matter. He used fresco in his murals and egg tempera in works such as *Portrait of the Artist O. Pavlenko* (1927) and *In the Liknep School* (1924–5). The director of the Mezhyhiria Art and Ceramics Tekhnikum (1922–30) and a teacher at the Kiev State Art Institute (1930–6), he was arrested and executed during the Stalinist terror.

Sedniv. II-12. A town smt (1982 pop 1,900) on the Snov River in Chernihiv raion, Chernihiv oblast. Known first as Snovsk, it was a well-fortified town of Kievan Rus'. According to the chronicles Prince Sviatoslav of Chernihiv defeated a Cuman army much larger than his own at Snovsk in 1068. In 1234 the town was annexed by Danylo Romanovych, and five years later it was destroyed by the Mongols. In the mid-14th century it fell under Lithuanian rule. In the 16th century it became known as Sedniv and belonged to the Polish Commonwealth. In the Hetman state established by B. Khmelnytsky Sedniv was a company center in Chernihiv regiment. From 1782 it was a volost center of Horodnia county, which was a part first of Chernihiv vicegerency and then of Chernihiv gubernia. Today it is a small agricultural town with a hydroelectric station built in 1953, a potato research station (est 1963), and a rest home of the Union of Artists. The ruins of the

old fortress and the Church of the Annunciation and Lyzohub mansion, both built by Col Ya. Lyzohub ca 1690, are tourist attractions.

Sedykh, Yurii [Sedyx, Jurij], b 11 May 1955 in Novocherkassk, Rostov oblast, Russia. Champion hammer thrower. A member of the Kiev Burevisnyk sports club, he won Olympic gold medals in the hammer throw in 1976 and in 1980 (world record), was the 1978 and 1986 European champion, won many Ukrainian SSR and USSR championships, was the 1981 world champion, set a new world record in 1984, and won the 1988 Olympic silver medal.

Seed beetles (Ukrainian: *zernoidy*). A common name for more than 900 species of the family Bruchidae. About 15 species are found in Ukraine, where they infest crops of peas, beans, beets, rice, and other seeds. The larvae develop in the seeds, thereby damaging their nutritional and sowing value.

Seed production. The branch of agriculture that produces and sorts high-quality natural and hybrid seeds for cultivation.

The first stage in seed production is seed *selection. Seeds are bred to produce plants with desirable qualities: higher yields, a shorter growing period, heat or drought resistance, and so on. Before the 20th century there was little planned seed production, and few agronomists were trained in seed sorting or selection. Peasants planted mostly unsorted seeds. In the late 19th century, however, some large landowners imported sorted seeds from abroad. The first attempts to sort seeds locally were made by landowners trying to improve the quality of sugar beets in Ukraine. Small seed-testing stations were established in Kiev in 1897 and in Katerynoslav (Dnipropetrovske) in 1907.

After the Revolution of 1917 seed sorting developed rapidly. As early as 1922 the Kharkiv Selection Station, directed later by V. *Yuriev, pioneered seed sorting in Ukraine. Several attempts to organize comprehensive seed production were made in the interwar period, but they were only partly successful because of the ravages of the famine of 1932–3. Over 30 large seed farms (covering an average of over 53,000 ha, and some covering up to 100,000 ha) were set up in Southern Ukraine and the

Crimea. They were given priority access to farm machinery and fertilizer. Nevertheless, they were underequipped and underproductive. By 1932 they had been abolished, and the entire system of seed production had been centralized under the All-Union State Seed Inspectorate of the People's Commissariat of Agriculture in Moscow. By 1940 the system was producing an adequate amount of seed for cultivation.

After the Second World War priority in seed production was given to improving strains primarily of oil-yielding, commercial, and fodder plants. Considerable attention was also given to the large-scale introduction of corn, especially after the mid-1950s. The whole matter, however, was highly politicized. T. *Lysenko's theories and practices in seed selection and production had little scientific merit but received strong support from J. Stalin and N. Khrushchev. Only in the early 1960s was a new, more rational system of seed production established.

Until the demise of the USSR in 1991, old seed varieties were improved and new hybrids developed at some 45 institutions in Ukraine, such as the *Ukrainian Scientific Research Institute of Plant Cultivation, Selection, and Genetics in Kharkiv, the All-Union Scientific Research Institute of Selection and Genetics in Odessa, and specialized institutes associated with the cultivation and processing of sugar beets, wheat, corn, and other cultures. Those institutes produced superelite and elite seeds in research nurseries. The seeds were then given to various *agricultural scientific research institutions, where they were tested and then classified and regionalized by agronomists and officials of the USSR Ministry of Agriculture. Approx 50 research stations produced elite and first-reproduction seeds that were then made available to state and collective farms for widespread cultivation.

BIBLIOGRAPHY
Haharyn, H. 'Sortove nasinnytstvo v Ukraïni,' *Naukovi zapysky UTHI*, 22 (1971–2)

Seeded area. See Crop cultivation and Land use.

Segedi, Yoakym, b 27 October 1904 in Ruski Krstur, Bačka region. He was ordained in 1927 and was a priest in the Bačka region before being consecrated auxiliary (1963–81) and then bishop (1981–3) of Križevci eparchy.

Seichter, Rudolf, b 17 October 1889 in Reichenbach, Silesia, d 19 October 1977 in Soltau, West Germany. Philatelist and a leading authority on Ukrainian stamps. A physician by profession, he graduated from Berlin University (1921) and served as a naval doctor until 1931 and during the Second World War. From 1927 he was active in the Union of Philatelists of Ukraine; he served as president in 1940–75. He studied the stamps issued by the UNR in 1918–20 and published a special catalog of them. He wrote numerous monographs and articles on Ukrainian stamps.

Seignorial court (*votchynnyi sud*). A private court established by a noble on his estate to administer justice to his peasants. The nobles had wide authority (see *domanial jurisdiction), and their decisions could not be appealed. Seignorial courts emerged in Kievan Rus' and reached their greatest power under feudalism. In Ukrainian territories of the Polish-Lithuanian Commonwealth, they sometimes heard appeals from community courts. In Rus-sian-ruled Ukraine seignorial courts were introduced along with serfdom in the late 18th century and were abolished in the reforms of 1864.

Seignorial manufacture (*votchynna promyslovist*). A term designating industry that depended upon the forced labor of enserfed peasants on patrimonial estates or service-tenure lands. The origins of this form of industry can be traced back to Kievan Rus', when it was used in light production or handicrafts. It was used for heavy manufacturing during the 17th century, and the state abetted its growth from the second half of the 18th century. Those peasants who worked in seignorial manufacturing firms often did so with a view to annulling their *quitrent. During the first half of the 19th century seignorial manufacture declined in favor of those manufacturing companies which used wage labor. It then ceased altogether with the abolition of serfdom in 1861. The first manufacturing firms of the seignorial type in Ukraine were introduced into the Left-Bank regions and were mainly geared toward tobacco, sugar, and silk processing.

Seignory (*votchyna*). Hereditary land owned outright and without any obligations to an overlord. The system of alodial landholding was practiced in Kievan Rus' as early as the 9th or 10th centuries and was the most common form of land tenure among the princes and nobles in the 11th to 15th centuries. Owners of seignories could not only dispose of their land as they wished but also administer justice and collect taxes for the state on their estates. In Ukraine the system was developed further under Lithuanian and Polish rule. In Russia the seignorial system gradually gave way to a system of service tenure.

Seim region (Posemia). A historical-geographic region along the upper Seim River contested by the Chernihiv and Pereiaslav principalities. It included such settlements as Kursk, Rylsk, and Putyvel. Its proximity to the steppe left it open to frequent attacks by nomads. Ultimately the Chernihiv principality won control over the region.

Seim River [Sejm]. The largest tributary (left-bank) of the Desna River. After originating in the uplands of Belgorod oblast the river flows for 748 km through Kursk, Sumy, and Chernihiv oblasts. It has a width of approx 80–100 m, a valley of 9–12 km, and a basin area of 27,500 sq km. It ices over from early December to late March. Its waters are used for industrial and water-supply purposes as well as for pisciculture and agriculture. Navigation is possible on its lower reaches. Some of the major centers on the river are Kursk, Lgov, Rylsk, Putyvel, and Baturyn.

Seitler. See Nyzhnohirskyi.

Sejm. See Diet and Parliament.

Sekunda, Tadei, b ca 1892, d ? Mechanical engineer and lexicographer. In 1918–19 he worked in the technological section of the Terminological Commission of the Ukrainian Academy of Sciences and then at the Institute of the Ukrainian Scientific Language. He was a specialist in Ukrainian technical terminology and edited Ukrainian technical dictionaries in the fields of statics, reinforced concrete, mining, and so forth. He also published a Ukrainian-German-Russian mechanical engineering dictionary (1925), using mostly the Ukrainian dialect from the Oster region in central Ukraine as the basis for creating new Ukrainian technical terms. He was arrested, and disappeared during the Stalinist purges in the late 1930s.

Selbud. See Village center.

Selection. The process of intentionally preferential reproduction or elimination of individual plants or animals with a certain genetic composition. It has been used from time immemorial to create new or improved species of agricultural plants and animals. Artificial selection differs from natural selection in that inherited variations are controlled by breeding. Selective breeding draws upon the sciences of anatomy, physiology, ecology, embryology, molecular biology, and *genetics. One of the early selection scientists, N. *Vavilov, formulated the homologous series law and the theory of the centers of culture in plant genesis. He defined selective breeding as a highly complex science that borrows and transforms laws dealing with plants and animals from other sciences in a discriminant way with the goal of developing a given variety; it develops its own methods and determines the phenomena which lead to the creation of new breeds.

Early successes in Ukrainian selection research were in the field of sugar beets at the end of the 19th century. Monosperm varieties were developed by I. *Buzanov and V. *Zosymovych. Other sugar beet selection scientists were L. *Sempolovsky, O. Gelmer, V. *Mykhalevych, and T. Hrynko. In 1884 the Poltava Experimental Field Station and Sugar Beet Selection Station was established; it was joined by other units in Uladivka (1880), Nemerchanka (1886), Ivanivka (1881), Verkhnia (1889), and Myronivka (1911). All of them were closed during the First World War and re-established in the 1920s. In 1911 the First Congress of Breeders and Seed Growers was held in Kharkiv.

Other scientific entities were formed: the *Ukrainian Scientific Research Institute of Plant Cultivation, Selection, and Genetics in Kharkiv, the Ukrainian Scientific Research Institute of Agriculture in Kiev, the All-Union Selection and Genetics Institute in Odessa, the All-Union *Scientific Research Institute of Corn in Dnipropetrovske, and the *Myronivka Institute of Wheat Selection and Seed Cultivation (expanded in 1968 from the original Myronivka Selection Research Station), as well as the All-Union institutes concerned with agriculture – the Institute of Sugar Beets in Kiev, the Institute of Bast Cultures in Hlukhiv, the Institute of Horticulture near Kiev, the Institute of Tobacco in Kiev, the Institute of Oil Cultures in Krasnodar, the Institute of Irrigation Agriculture in Kherson, the Institute of Land Cultivation and Animal Husbandry of the Western Regions of Ukraine in Lviv, and so on.

The short rebirth of scientific activity during the 1920s was sharply curtailed during the purges of the 1930s and the Second World War. Many leading selection scientists disappeared without a trace, including B. Panshyn, V. Kolkunov, B. Lebedynsky, I. Voitkevych, V. Rakochi, S. Nyzovy-Kysil, D. Duz-Kriatchenko, O. Filipovsky, I. Shaposhnykiv, P. Soliakov, and A. Zaporozhets.

After 1945 M. Kott, M. Bulin, A. Pozdniak, T. Hrynko, P. Hordiienko, and D. Popadiuk came to the forefront in connection with the development of the Verkhnia 020 and Uladivka 752 sugar beet varieties. The theory of distant hybridization was proposed by H. Karpechenko. Numerous grain varieties were developed with high productivity under Ukrainian climatic conditions by V. *Yuriev, director of the Kharkiv Selection Station.

Advances in Ukrianian selection also include the development of varieties of wheat – Michurin; Odessa 3, 4 (A. *Sapiehin), and 16 (F. *Kyrychenko); Durable (B. Lebedynsky); Myronivka 264 and 808 and Jubilee (V. *Remeslo); Bilotserkivska 198 and 223; Lisostepova 74 and 75 (A. Horlach); and Ukrainka (E. Zheltkevych, L. Kovalevsky, and I. Yeremeev); of winter wheat – Krymka; of millet – Myronivka 85 and 51; of Sudan grass – Myronivka 10 and 325; of spring wheat – Poltavka; of sunflower – Peredovyk (V. Pustovoit with V. Shcherbyna and H. Romanenko); of barley – Orion and Odessa 31 and 46 (P. Harkavy); and of peas – Uladivka 6 and 8 (M. Shulha), Uladivka 208 and 303 (I. Hromyk, T. Stehailo, and V. Havrylova), and Chernihivka 190 (M. Khandohin and I. Pereshkura).

A number of new corn varieties have been developed by Ukrainians: Bukovyna 1 and 3 (V. Kozubenko, at the Bukovyna Selection Station), Dnipro 56 and 90T (B. *Sokolov, at the Dnipropetrovske Selection Station), Odessa 23 and 27 (O. *Musiiko and P. Kliuchko, at the Odessa Selection Station), and Kyiv 8 (P. Oseledets, at the Kiev Selection Station). Ukrainian selection scientists in the field of orcharding and horticulture include Y. Mahomet, V. Symyrenko, I. Riabor, M. Savchenko, and L. Ro.

Because of a lack of academic freedom, and, in some cases, political persecution, many scientists emigrated from the Ukrainian SSR and continued their work in the West: O. *Arkhimovych, I. Bezpalov, H. Haharyn, I. Hromyk, O. and V. *Savitsky, S. *Symko, R. *Shekhaiev, and I. Bolsunov.

BIBLIOGRAPHY

Haharyn, H. 'Istoriia selektsiï sil's'ko-hospodars'kykh kul'tur v Ukraïni,' *Naukovi zapysky Ukraïns'koho tekhnichno-hospodars'koho instytutu*, 12 (1967)

I. Masnyk

Mykhailo Seleshko

Seleshko, Mykhailo [Seleško, Myxajlo], b 4 October 1901 in Vytvytsia, Dolyna county, Galicia, d 27 April 1981 in Toronto. Engineer, journalist, and political activist. A veteran of the Ukrainian Galician Army, he joined the Ukrainian Military Organization in 1920 and was arrested several times by the Poles. After completing a degree in chemical engineering at the Ukrainian Husbandry Academy in Poděbrady, he moved to Berlin, where he served as Col Ye. Konovalets's secretary and correspondent for several nationalist papers. He helped set up the Ukrainian Press Service in Berlin and became a member of the OUN Leadership. He was also active in the Ukrainian National Alliance in Germany. After coming to Canada in 1948, he served on the executive of the Ukrainian War Veterans' Association of Canada and the Ukrainian Liberation Fund.

Seletsky [Selec'kyj]. A family line of Cossack officers from the Chernihiv region, founded by Semen Seletsky in the 17th century. Semen's son, Vasyl Seletsky (d 1714), was a captain of the Cossack company in Divytsia (1694 and 1711–4), and his descendants retained that post until 1767. Vasyl's son, Yakiv Seletsky (d before 1762), assumed the captaincy of Divytsia company in 1714; he took part in the Derbent (1772), Polish (1733–4), and Crimean (1735, 1739) campaigns. Vasyl's grandson, Lavrentii Seletsky (b ca 1732, d 16 July 1789), was postmaster of Little Russia (1770–82); his brother, Ivan Seletsky (b 1743, d 25 July 1810), was governor of Katerynoslav and governor-general of New Russia. Lavrentii's great-grandson was Petro *Seletsky. In the 19th and early 20th centuries the Seletsky family (including Yosyp Seletsky, d 1918) held large estates in the Poltava and Katerynoslav regions.

Rev Kyrylo Seletsky   Yaroslav Selezinka

Seletsky, Kyrylo [Selec'kyj], b 29 April 1835 in Pidbuzh, Sambir circle, Galicia, d 28 April 1908 in Tsebliv, Sokal county, Galicia. Ukrainian Catholic priest and author. After being ordained in 1860, he was a priest in several villages in Galicia and authored a number of popular religious books. From 1874 he was curate of Zhuzhil and Tsebliv. There he established the first residence of the *Sisters Servants of Mary Immaculate and helped found the *Sisters of St Joseph (1894). He served as spiritual adviser to both congregations.

Seletsky, Petro [Selec'kyj], b 2 March 1821 in Maliutyntsi, Pyriatyn county, Poltava gubernia, d 5 March 1880 (buried in the Vydubychi Monastery in Kiev). After graduating in law from Kiev University he served as a functionary in the Kiev gubernial administration (from 1844) and worked for the Kiev Archeographic Commission (1845–6). He became acquainted with T. Shevchenko through N. Repnin but differed with him on the Ukrainian question. Seletsky was deputy governor of Kiev gubernia (1858–66) and marshal of the gubernial nobility (1866–80).

His notebooks were published in *Kievskaia starina* (1884, nos 2–9).

Selezinka, Yaroslav, b 1887, d July 1941 in Yertsevo, Arkhangelsk region, Russia. Army officer and community activist. After joining the Ukrainian Galician Army at the end of 1918, he served at the headquarters of the Third Corps in Stryi (January–June 1919) and then was chief logistics officer of the government of the Western Ukrainian National Republic. During the interwar period he practiced law in Radekhiv and was active in the Ukrainian National Democratic Alliance. In 1939 he was arrested by the NKVD and deported to a concentration camp, where he was executed.

Seleznov, Ivan [Selezn'ov], b 3 January 1856 in Kiev, d 31 March 1936 in Kiev. Painter. After graduating from the St Petersburg Academy of Arts (1881) he returned to Kiev, where he took part in the restoration of the 12th-century frescoes in St Cyril's Church (1884) and taught at the Kiev Drawing School (1886–90) and Kiev Art School (1901–20). He did genre paintings (eg, *The Last Chord*, 1885), historical paintings (eg, *In Pompei*, 1886), and portraits (eg, of M. Murashko and his daughter).

Self-determination. The right of every society to determine its social and political system and choose its government. Self-determination was a basic principle in 18th-century liberal thought and was one of the basic ideas of the French and American revolutions. In the 19th and 20th centuries many nations exercised this right in their constitutional acts. National self-determination, or the right of every nation to set up its own state or to associate with other nations in a larger state based on *federalism or *autonomy, is entailed by the general principle. The right of various branches of the same nation to unite in a single state is implicit in the concept of self-determination. National self-determination is accepted generally as a progressive concept in contrast to the reactionary principles of legitimacy or imperialism. During the First World War the Entente Powers supported self-determination to weaken the allegiance of the national minorities in the multinational Central Powers. In January 1917 President W. Wilson announced that the self-determination of nations was one of the aims of war. The *Paris Peace Conference applied the principle of national self-determination selectively in East-Central Europe: it recognized Poland's but not Ukraine's claim. In the interwar period many nations not satisfied with the new order in Europe pursued a revisionist policy based on the principle of self-determination. The League of Nations also applied the principle selectively: it settled several territorial disputes by means of plebiscites but ignored Western Ukraine. The charter of the United Nations refers to self-determination (in articles 1 and 2) only in a general way, but the organization's later declarations on colonialism and imperialism clearly recognize the right of self-determination.

In the 19th century the Ukrainian national movement at first alluded only vaguely to self-determination. M. *Drahomanov first defined it in political terms as self-rule and autonomy within a reorganized Russian or Austrian federation. The goal of complete independence was raised only at the end of the 19th and the beginning of the 20th centuries, by thinkers such as M. *Mikhnovsky, I. Franko, and Yu. Bachynsky. During the revolutionary period (1917–20) the idea of self-determination was expressed unequivocally in the *universals, constitutional acts, proclamations, diplomatic notes, and statements of the Ukrainian governments. The law on *national-personal autonomy, for example, granted extensive rights to the national minorities of Ukraine. The Western Ukrainian National Republic arose and united with the UNR in accordance with the idea of national self-determination.

The Soviet regime in Russia, drawing upon earlier Party declarations and V. Lenin's writings, from the very beginning actively propagated the slogan of national self-determination. The Declaration of the Rights of the Peoples of Russia, issued in November 1917, proclaimed the 'right of the peoples of Russia to free self-determination, even including secession and independent statehood.' In a note to the UNR government on 17 December 1917, the Council of People's Commissars recognized Ukraine's right to self-determination but at the same time sent an army against the republic. This behavior was based on the presupposition that only the working class, and in practice the Communist party, could exercise self-determination, if it were in the interests of the revolution. In Ukraine's case the Party decided that self-determination was detrimental to the world revolution. Nonetheless, the Soviet government often theoretically assumed Ukraine's self-determination – for example, in the 1920 agreement between the RSFSR and the Ukrainian SSR, in the Peace Treaty of Riga (1920), and in the protest notes against Poland's incorporation of Galicia. The 'self-determination' of the Ukrainian people was also the excuse for the Soviet annexation of Western Ukraine in 1939. The 1919, 1926, and 1936 constitutions of the Ukrainian SSR, however, contained no explicit reference to self-determination. In general the Party supported the self-determination of nations when doing so served Soviet foreign interests, but refused to apply it to the peoples of the USSR. Although in theory the republics had the right of self-determination insofar as they had the right to secede from the USSR, in practice they could not exercise this right. Nonetheless, the government of Ukraine executed the right to self-determination by proclaiming sovereignty on 16 July 1990 and complete independence on 24 August 1991.

V. Markus

Self-government. The authority of communities to legislate and administer their own affairs within a certain defined area, such as a province, county, or city, that is a part of a state. Self-government is closely related to *autonomy and can be bestowed also on groups, such as ethnic minorities, which do not inhabit a compact territory (see *National-personal autonomy). The modern concept of self-government should not be confused with various forms of local autonomy under feudalism or other political systems; it functions only within the framework of the modern state. Self-government is defined and granted by the sovereign state; it can take various forms and apply to different levels of government. In a federated state (see *Federalism) the constituent states or provinces enjoy a certain measure of self-government. To some degree the *Hetman state, the crownlands of *Galicia and *Bukovyna within Austria-Hungary, and the *Ukrainian SSR within the USSR enjoyed self-government. At the local level the rural *hromady and *cities and towns enjoyed a degree of self-

government under the Russian and Austrian imperial regimes, the Polish interwar regime, and the Soviet regime (see *Municipal government).

Self-heal (*Prunella*; Ukrainian: *sukhovershok*). A perennial herb of the family Labiatae. In Ukraine common self-heal (*P. vulgaris*) is found in forests, often growing as a weed; *P. grandiflora* grows in the forest-steppe and steppe zones and in the Crimea, and *P. lanciniata* is found in dry meadows and in the forest margins of Transcarpathia and the Crimea.

Self-Reliance Association of American Ukrainians (Obiednannia ukraintsiv Ameryky, or Samopomich). A social welfare organization founded in New York in 1947 by recently arrived Ukrainian immigrants. The association organized Ukrainian nurseries, schools, and homes for the elderly. It supported financially Ukrainian schools in Germany, Austria, and Poland and Ukrainian student organizations in Western countries. The original professional sections of the association (engineers, teachers, and students) eventually separated into independent societies. Most of the local branches of Self-Reliance formed credit unions bearing the same name. In 1950 the association began to publish the magazine *Novyi svit*, which in 1959 was renamed *Nash svit*. By 1962 it had 18 branches and almost 7,000 members. In 1990 it had 21 branches and 15,000 members. Its presidents have included P. Andrusiv, V. Kalyna, Yu. Revai, S. Sprynsky, and Ye. Lozynsky.

Self-Reliance federal credit unions (Samopomich). A group of Ukrainian credit unions in the United States set up since the 1950s by the larger branches of the *Self-Reliance Association of American Ukrainians. All of them are regulated and audited by the Federal Bureau of Credit Unions. By 1979 there were 16 such unions, the largest of which were in Chicago, New York, Detroit, Philadelphia, Newark, Jersey City, Passaic, and Baltimore. Along with other Ukrainian credit unions they belong to the *Ukrainian National Credit Union Association.

Selianin'' (Peasant). A monthly Russophile newspaper published in Mamaivtsi (now Novosilka) and then Chynkiv, Bukovyna, from 1895 to 1901. It was edited by G. Savchuk and then I. Biletsky.

Selianka Ukraïny. See *Kolhospnytsia Ukraïny.*

Selianska, Vira. See Vovk, Vira.

Selians'ka bidnota. See *Selians'ka pravda.*

Selians'ka dolia (Peasant Fate). A weekly organ of the Ukrainian Social Democratic party caucus in the Polish Sejm, published in Lutske in 1923 and January 1924. It was edited by Ye. Tkachuk, I. Stepaniuk, and H. Hladky. It was closed down by the Polish authorities; the weekly *Nash shliakh* (ed Kh. Prystupa) appeared in its place from March 1924 to 1925.

Selians'ka hromada (Peasant Community). A popular weekly paper published by the UNR Ministry of Education in Kamianets-Podilskyi and then Vinnytsia in 1919.

Selianska Kasa (Peasant Bank). The central association of *Raiffeisen credit co-operatives in Bukovyna, founded by S. *Smal-Stotsky and L. *Kohut in 1903 in Chernivtsi. By 1912 it represented 159 credit, 11 consumer, 2 dairy, and 2 other co-operatives, with a total membership of almost 20,000. Selianska Kasa provided loans to individuals and co-operatives, helped in the marketing of agricultural produce, organized retail stores, and ran a logging operation. It also served as the central auditing body for all types of Ukrainian co-operatives in Bukovyna. The organization experienced a major crisis after 1911. It had overextended its funds and was placed under the control of the Provincial Bank by the Austrian government and ordered to institute several reforms. It continued to function after Bukovyna was taken over by Rumania, but the authorities increasingly limited its autonomy and activities. In 1924 it was reconstituted as the Northern Bukovyna Bank. It lost its Ukrainian character and ceased to play a role in civic life. Selianska Kasa published the organ *Vistnyk soiuza* (1903–7), *Narodne bohatstvo* (semimonthly, 1908–10), and brochures and booklets on co-operative and educational topics. Its directors before the First World War were Kohut and O. Lutsky.

Selians'ka pravda (Peasant Truth). An organ of the CC CP(B)U and the Central Committee of Poor Peasants, published in Kharkiv daily in July 1921 and then three times a week to December 1925. It succeeded the daily *Selians'ka bidnota* (March 1920 to April 1921). *Selians'ka pravda* was edited by S. Pylypenko; the editorial secretary was O. Vyshnia. It published news in brief, much peasant correspondence, and advice on how and what to write about to newspapers. Members of the *Pluh writers' group were frequent contributors, and the paper did much to popularize Ukrainian literature among the peasantry. *Selians'ka pravda* had a pressrun of 7,500. It was merged with *Radians'ke selo*.

Selians'ka rada. See *Peremys'kyi vistnyk*.

Selians'kyi prapor (Peasant Flag). A popular organ of the Ukrainian People's Union, published weekly in Stanyslaviv (now Ivano-Frankivske) from July 1925 to March 1928. It was edited by I. Stovpiuk and V. Balahutrak.

Selians'kyi shliakh (Peasant Path). A weekly organ of the socialist *Sel-Soiuz peasant alliance, published in Kholm from 1927 to the end of 1928. It was published by P. Vasynchuk and edited by V. Hul.

Selianyn (Peasant). A clandestine monthly organ of the *Revolutionary Ukrainian party. It was printed in Austrian-ruled Chernivtsi in 1903 and in Lviv in 1904–5, smuggled into Russian-ruled Ukraine, and illegally distributed there among the Ukrainian peasantry. The paper was subsidized by Ye. *Chykalenko. In Chernivtsi the managing editor was L. Kohut, although D. Antonovych was the main force behind its publication. In Lviv the paper was published by M. Hankevych and edited by S. Vityk. *Selianyn* had a pressrun of some 1,000 copies. Thirty-two issues appeared.

Selianyn (Peasant). A weekly newspaper for the peasantry, published in Lviv in 1929–35. It was pro-Polish in orientation and supported the official Non-Party Bloc of Co-operation with the Government. The editors were E. Kukh, M. Chornenko, and I. Behmetiuk.

Seliava, Antonii Atanasii [Seljava, Antonij Atanasij], b ca 1583, d 1655. Uniate metropolitan. He completed his theological studies in Rome and became archimandrite of a monastery in Vilnius. In this position he engaged in polemics with M. Smotrytsky. In 1624, following the death of Archbishop Y. Kuntsevych, he became archbishop of Polatsk. He was elevated to the office of Uniate metropolitan of Kiev in 1640 and took part in delicate negotiations with Orthodox hierarchs regarding the creation of a single Uniate patriarchate for the Ruthenian (Ukrainian and Belarusian) church. These negotiations ended at the death of the Orthodox metropolitan, P. Mohyla, in 1647. The turbulent events of the Khmelnytsky uprising forced Seliava into exile to the Podlachia region, where he died.

Seliber, Valentyn, b 24 April 1920 in Tyraspil, in present-day Moldavia. Sculptor. A graduate of the Kiev State Art Institute (1953), he has created figures and compositions, such as *Female Javelin Thrower* (1951), *The Koliivshchyna Rebellion* (1954), *For Land, for Freedom* (1955), and *Snow* (1967), and collaborated on the monument to the victims of the Second World War in Petropavlivka, Cherkasy oblast (1970).

Seliuchenko, Oleksandra [Seljučenko], b 6 May 1921 in Opishnia, Zinkiv county, Poltava gubernia, d 23 June 1987 in Opishnia. Folk ceramist. She studied at the school of the Opishnia Ceramics Plant (1937–9) and then worked at the plant, where she created figurines, such as *The Vixen and Rooster* (1967), *The Sorochyntsi Fair* (1976), and *Rider* (1985), as well as decorative plates and ceramics. Her works have been exhibited at international shows in Marseille (1957, 1958), Brussels (1958), and Expo-70 in Osaka.

Ivan Selivanov: *The Golden Gate* (linocut)

Selivanov, Ivan, b 5 January 1924 in Riabkovo, now in Cheliabinsk oblast, Russia, d 2 November 1984 in Kiev. Graphic artist. After graduating from the Kiev State Art Institute in 1952, he taught there. He has produced several series of prints on Soviet themes, such as 'The Victors'

(1954) and 'The Great Working Class' (1960); linocuts, such as *Kobzar* (1961); and illustrations to editions of works by A. Holovko (1959), Yu. Yanovsky (1961), and O. Honchar (1964) and to the epic *Slovo o polku Ihorevi* (The Tale of Ihor's Campaign, 1965–73).

Selo (Village). An illustrated weekly newspaper for peasants and workers, published in Kiev from September 1909 to February 1911. It was one of the first Ukrainian-language newspapers in the Russian Empire. The official publishers were H. Yampolska and I. Malych, but the guiding force behind the newspaper was M. *Hrushevsky, who wrote most of the editorials. The managing editor and literary critic was Yu. Tyshchenko. Popular features included chronicles of developments in the Russian Empire (by M. Hekhter) and Western Ukraine and Europe (by Mykola Zalizniak and V. Doroshenko), and political and cultural commentaries by P. Stebnytsky (pseud: Smutok), Mykyta Shapoval, and others. The paper also contained articles on agriculture, hygiene, and rural economics by A. Ternychenko, V. Koroliv, and O. Mytsiuk; poetry by O. Oles, V. Samiilenko, H. Chuprynka, and Ya. Shchoholiv; and prose by V. Vynnychenko, O. Kobylianska, A. Teslenko, Modest Levytsky, L. Martovych, V. Storozhenko, V. Stefanyk, and S. Cherkasenko. At the height of its popularity, *Selo* had 4,500 to 5,000 subscribers. The publishers were constantly harassed and fined by the tsarist authorities, and the paper was finally forced to cease publication. It was succeeded by *Zasiv.

Selo (Village). A semimonthly organ of the Podilia Gubernia executive published in Kamianets-Podilskyi in 1918–19. It was edited by M. Butovsky.

Selo (Village). A semimonthly organ of the Transcarpathian branch of the Czechoslovak Agrarian party, published in Mukachiv in 1920–4. The editors were I. Pavlyk and P. Sydor. The newspaper was printed in the Transcarpathian dialect, a feature which reflected its early official support for the Ukrainian movement in Czechoslovakia. It was succeeded as the party's organ by the Russian-language *Karpatorusskii vestnik* (1923–4) and *Zemledel'skaia politika* (1927–38) and the Ukrainian-language *Zemlia i volia* (1934–8).

Selo i Misto (SiM). See Futurism and Moscow.

Sel-Rob (Ukrainian Peasants' and Workers' Socialist Alliance; Ukrainske seliansko-robitnyche sotsiialistychne obiednannia). A mass political party with pro-Soviet leanings, founded on 10 October 1926 in Lviv through a merger of *Sel-Soiuz and the People's Will party (PNV). The Communist Party of Western Ukraine (KPZU) was instrumental in the founding of Sel-Rob in that it acted as a mediator in the negotiations. The Central Committee of the new party was based on equal representation from both founding groups: M. Chuchmai, S. Makivka, and S. Kozytsky from Sel-Soiuz and K. Valnytsky, M. Zaiats, and K. Pelekhaty from the PNV. During the merger, the PNV adopted a pro-Ukrainian position (earlier it had been strongly Russophile) and issued a declaration to that effect. The directorate of the KPZU in Sel-Rob was initially represented by P. Kraikivsky. From the middle of 1927 Sel-Rob was involved in the debate among KPZU members

which ensued in the wake of the O. *Shumsky affair. On 1 September 1927 Sel-Rob was dissolved, with a return to life of both founding parties. The former PNV members now called themselves Sel-Rob Left; former Sel-Soiuz members who supported the Shumsky faction of the KPZU were called Sel-Rob Right. During the election campaign of February 1928 both sides fought bitterly against each other. The right won four seats in Volhynia and Polisia, and the left won three seats.

In May 1928 the Sel-Rob Unity, an apparently neutral organization, was established by Sel-Rob Left members. A substantial percentage of Sel-Rob Right members joined the new party. The Sel-Rob Unity had three official organs, *Nashe zhyttia*, *Nashe slovo*, and *Sel'-Rob*. Among its best-known leaders were K. Valnytsky, M. Durdella, S. Makivka, K. Pelekhaty, and M. Zaiats. Its influence was greatest in Volhynia. With the passage of time the Sel-Rob Unity became completely dominated by the KPZU and lost whatever slight independence it had had. The party organized peasant strikes and demanded the parcelation of regional and church lands for the benefit of the poorer peasants. During times of open conflict it called for the withholding of taxes. Its greatest influence was in Ukrainian rural co-operatives. Sel-Rob spoke out against any and all criticism relating to life in the USSR, collectivization, and the state of Ukrainian culture. In September 1932 the party was dissolved by the Polish authorities.

J. Radziejowski

Sel'-Rob

Sel'-Rob. A pro-Soviet weekly newspaper published in Lviv from September 1927 to September 1932 (a total of 293 issues). It was the organ of the Left faction and, from May 1928, the Unity faction of the *Sel-Rob Ukrainian Peasants' and Workers' Socialist Alliance. The editors were K. Pelekhaty, F. Yavorsky, and I. Shkvarok; they were assisted by K. Valnytsky, M. Holinaty, M. Zaiats, P. Kozlaniuk, and I. Dovhaniuk. In 1930 *Sel'-Rob* had a pressrun of 8,500. It was closed down by the Polish authorities.

Selska, Mariia [Sel's'ka, Marija] (née Reich), b 23 June 1903 in Kolomyia, Galicia, d 3 February 1980 in Lviv. Painter; wife of R. *Selsky. She studied at the Cracow (1924–5) and Vienna (1926–7) academies of art and the Académie moderne in Paris (1928–30). In the 1930s she was a member of the *Association of Independent Ukrainian Artists in Lviv. She painted landscapes, such as *Hutsul Landscape* (1956), *Bilhorod* (1964), and *Grape Gathering*

SELSKY   **581**

Mariia Selska (self-portrait, oil, 1978)

(1968); portraits, such as *Girl* (1939) and *Lesia Ukrainka* (1950); and still lifes. The influence of constructivism and cubism is evident in her works.

Sel'skii hospodar' (The Farmer). A semimonthly newspaper for peasants, published in Chernivtsi from March 1878 to March 1879 (a total of 25 issues). The publisher and editor was M. Dymytriievych.

Roman Selsky (self-portrait)

Selsky, Roman [Sel's'kyj], b 21 May 1903 in Sokal, Galicia, d 4 February 1990 in Lviv. Painter, graphic artist, and teacher; husband of M. *Selska. He studied at the Novakivsky Art School in Lviv, graduated from the Cracow Academy of Fine Arts (1927), and made several trips to Paris, where he studied with F. Léger. Upon his return to

Lviv in 1929, he was instrumental in establishing Artes, an association of left-wing artists, and taught at the Applied Arts High School (1935–47) and the Lviv Institute of Applied and Decorative Arts (1947–72). Surrealist influences are apparent in his early works, such as *Port in Hel* (1930) and *Seashore in Hel* (1932). In the late 1960s Selsky returned to painting the seashore, in works such as *At the Seashore* (1969) and *Decorative Composition* (1966), which show the influence of Léger. Selsky painted numerous landscapes, particularly of the Carpathian Mountains, such as *Fallen Spruces* (1960), *Late Flowers* (1971), the often-reproduced *Chornohora* (1972), and *Flowers in Dzembronia* (1983). The Carpathian environment is also reflected in his still lifes and compositions of interiors, such as *Dzembronia Still Life* (1965) and *Interior of a Hutsul House* (1975); many of them include views through windows and open doors, such as the impressionistic *Landscape Seen through a Window* (1938), *Winter Seen through a Window* (1970), and *Still Life by the Window* (1971) and the Matisse-like *Still Life* (1980). Except for a few realistic landscapes and somber still-life compositions from the 1940s and early 1950s, Selsky managed to avoid the narrow confines of socialist realism. His sensitive and vibrant palette and organization of flattened forms and space are in the Western European art tradition. His contribution to Ukrainian art was only partially acknowledged in the publication of a modest album of his works in 1988.

D. Zelska-Darewych

Selsky, Shchasny Feliks [Sel's'kyj, Ščasnyj], b 1852 in Kolodnytsia, Stryi county, Galicia, d 20 May 1922 in Vytvytsia, Dolyna county, Galicia. Physician and civic leader; full member of the Shevchenko Scientific Society from 1899. As a university student he was active in the Sich student society, and in 1878 he was tried with I. Franko and M. Pavlyk for being a member of a secret socialist society. After graduating from Vienna University in 1880, he specialized in gynecology, and in 1882 he became head of the gynecology department of the Lviv Polyclinic. His articles on gynecology appeared in Ukrainian and German medical journals. He also worked on Ukrainian medical terminology.

Volodymyr Selsky

Selsky, Volodymyr [Sel's'kyj], b 13 October 1883 in Vykhylivka, Proskuriv county, Podilia gubernia, d 18 February 1951 in Kiev. Geologist and geophysicist; member of the AN URSR (now ANU) from 1939. He graduated from Kiev University in 1909. He then taught at Warsaw University (1910–13), Kislovodsk gymnasium (1914–20), and the Petroleum Institute in Groznyi (1921–8). In the 1930s he worked as a geologist in state petroleum enterprises. He chaired the geophysics department of the ANU Institute of Geological Sciences (1939) and after the war organized geophysics departments at Lviv University and the Lviv Polytechnical Institute. Selsky researched the theoretical and practical problems of oil exploration, the genesis and migration of oil, and the oil reserves of Ukraine and the USSR.

Sel-Soiuz (Ukrainske sotsiialistychne obiednannia Selianskyi soiuz [The Peasant Union Ukrainian Socialist Alliance]). A Galician Ukrainian political party formed in March 1924 by members of the socialist faction of the Ukrainian Club in the Polish Sejm. The party carried out most of its activities in Volhynia and the Kholm region. Its program, ratified on 27 August 1924, asserted that it was a Ukrainian class party whose aim was to abolish the exploitation of poor Ukrainian peasants and to offer them land in the areas where they resided. It strove for national self-determination and universal, free, secular schooling in the Ukrainian language. Ultimately the party sought to eliminate capitalism and replace it with socialism. Its leaders were P. *Vasynchuk (first head), A. Bratun, S. Kozytsky, S. Nazaruk, M. Chuchmai, and S. Makivka. Its official organ was the weekly *Nashe zhyttia*. Sel-Soiuz was also involved in the development of the popular educational society Ridna Khata, and the party defended the authority of the Orthodox church from attempts to restrain it. The party's attitude toward Soviet Ukraine and the Communist Party of Western Ukraine was initially reserved and tentative, but it became more positive over time. Sel-Soiuz challenged the Polish Socialist party on its own ground, by charging that that party's policies were accommodating to the right, and its cultural activities assimilationist. On 10 October 1926 Sel-Soiuz joined forces with the People's Will party to create *Sel-Rob. A small group of Sel-Soiuz members, headed by Vasynchuk, refused to join the new organization and continued their independent activities as Sel-Soiuz until 1928. In 1927 they published the newspaper *Selians'kyi shliakh*.

J. Radziejowski

Selydove. V-18, DB III-2. A city (1989 pop 82,500) on the Solona River in Donetske oblast. It originated in 1770–3 as a settlement of Moldavian and Wallachian colonists, who were replaced within a decade by Cossacks of Myrhorod regiment. Coal deposits were discovered in the area in the 1850s. In 1956 the town was given city status, and its name changed from Selydivka to Selydove. Today it is an industrial center with two coal mines, a coal enrichment plant, a building-materials industry, and a food industry.

Semafor u maibutnie (Semaphore into the Future). A literary almanac published in Kiev by the *Association of Panfuturists in May 1922. It contained M. *Semenko's Panfuturist manifesto and articles and literary works by Semenko, G. Shkurupii, Yu. Shpol (M. Yalovy), O. Slisarenko, M. Irchan, Mykola and Marko Tereshchenko, and V. Desniak.

Semaka, Illia, b 1867 in Berehomit, Bukovyna, d 4 January 1929 in Prievidza, Slovakia. Judge and civic and political leader; brother of Ye. *Semaka. A graduate of Chernivtsi University, he served as a judge and eventually became chief judge of the provincial court. A member of the National Democratic party, he was elected to the Austrian parliament in 1907 and 1911 and to the Bukovynian Diet and its executive in 1911. In 1915–16 he was a member of the General Ukrainian Council in Vienna. As a member of the Ukrainian National Rada and its Bukovynian section, the Ukrainian Regional Committee, he played an important role in asserting Ukrainian control of Bukovyna in November 1918. In Vienna he was active in the Government-in-exile of the Western Ukrainian National Republic and then served as a judge in Slovakia.

Rev Yevhen Semaka

Semaka, Yevhen, b 1863 in Banyliv, Bukovyna, d 17 July 1912 in Chernivtsi. Church and civic leader; brother of I. *Semaka. He completed his theology training at Chernivtsi University and then was catechist in the Ukrainian gymnasium in Chernivtsi, from 1898. As a member of the Orthodox church consistory in Bukovyna, he defended the rights of the Ukrainian Orthodox believers and opposed Rumanianization of the church. He authored many religious textbooks for elementary and high schools and an illustrated history of the *Ruska Besida society in Chernivtsi (1909) under the pseudonym Yevhenii Dmytriv, and contributed articles to the newspaper *Ruska rada* (1898–1905). He also co-edited the bilingual Rumanian-Ukrainian church journal *Candela*.

Semaniuk, Ivan. See Cheremshyna, Marko.

Semantics. A branch of linguistics dealing with the meaning of morphemes, words, and phrases through time and the relationship of language, thought, and meaning. The semantics of the Ukrainian language have not been studied systematically. Semantic questions have been discussed, however, in works in lexicology and normative stylistics and in studies of the language of individual writers or literary genres, by linguists such as M. Levytsky, I. Ohiienko, V. Simovych, M. Sulyma, M. Hladky, I. Troian, B. Tkachenko, A. Kyrychenko, V. Vashchenko, I. Cherednychenko, I. Bilodid, V. Franchuk, and A. Koval. In 1982 H. Arpolenko published a book on the structural-semantic construction of the sentence in modern Ukrainian. Materials on the semantics of particular Ukrainian words and word groups have appeared in serials such as *Ridna mova* (Warsaw, 1933–9), *Pytannia movnoï kul'tury* (Kiev 1967–71), *Ridne slovo* (Kiev, 1971–4), and *Kul'tura slova* (Kiev, since 1976).

Semashko, Yosyf [Semaško, Josyf], b 5 January 1799 in Pavlivka, Lypovets county, Kiev gubernia, d 5 December 1868 in Vilnius. Church hierarch. The son of a Uniate priest, he graduated from the Catholic Theological Seminary of Vilnius University, and was ordained in 1821. In 1822 he entered the Roman Catholic College in St Petersburg. There he and members of the Holy Synod of the Russian Orthodox church prepared plans for the conversion of the *Uniates of Right-Bank Ukraine and Belarus to Orthodoxy. He helped prepare a project to establish a Uniate college, and assisted in drawing up plans to abolish the Basilian order (realized in 1832), to reorganize the eparchies, and to purge Latin elements from Uniate church rites. He was consecrated bishop of Mstsislau and head of the Belarusian consistory in 1829 and bishop of Lithuania in 1832. In 1835 he joined a secret committee working to incorporate the Uniate church into the Russian Orthodox church. Its objective was formally accomplished in February 1839. Semashko was made Orthodox archbishop of Vilnius and Lithuania, and in 1844 he moved to Zhyrovichy to assist in the conversion of Belarus. Semashko's actions were condemned by Pope Gregory XVI in 1839 and by Mykhailo Levytsky, the metropolitan of Halych and archbishop of Lviv. Semashko joined the Holy Synod in 1847 and was named a metropolitan in 1852. His autobiography and a collection of documents associated with his life were published as *Zapiski Iosifa, mitropolita Litovskogo* (The Notes of Yosyf, Metropolitan of Lithuania, 1883, 3 vols).

BIBLIOGRAPHY
Kiprianovich, G. *Zhizn' Iosifa Semashki, mitropolita Litovskago i Vilenskago i vozsoedinenie zapadno-russkikh uniatov s Pravoslavnoi tserkoviiu v 1839 g.* (2nd edn, Vilnius 1897)
Lencyk, W. *The Eastern Catholic Church and Czar Nicholas I* (Rome 1966)

W. Lencyk

Roman Sembratovych   Cardinal Sylvester Sembratovych

Sembratovych, Roman [Sembratovyč], b 6 July 1875 in Monastyrets, Lisko county, Galicia, d 8 January 1906 in Vienna. Journalist and publicist. As a law student at Vienna University he was a leading member of the Sich student society there. He became a regular contributor to various German and Austrian newspapers, for which he reported primarily on developments in Galicia (initially using the pseudonym Galizischer Slave). In 1901 he founded the weekly *X-Strahlen* to inform the German and especially the Viennese public about Ukrainian affairs. After the paper folded at the end of that year, he became the Vienna correspondent of *Frankfurter Zeitung*. In late 1902 he published the book *Polonia irredenta*, in which he severely criticized Polish chauvinism and conservatism. From 1903 to his death Sembratovych was editor of the semimonthly *Ruthenische Revue* in Vienna. In 1905 he published a second book, *Das Zarentum in dem Kampfe mit der Zivilisation*, on the tsarist repression of the Ukrainian national movement and culture.

Sembratovych, Sylvester [Sembratovyč, Syl'vester], b 3 September 1836 in Doshnytsia, Jasło circle, Galicia, d 4 August 1898 in Lviv. Ukrainian Catholic metropolitan and cardinal. He studied in Vienna and Rome and completed a PH D at the Athanasius College in 1861. He was ordained in 1860 and returned to Galicia to become a parish priest in Tylych. He served as prefect of the Greek Catholic Theological Seminary in Lviv (1863–9) and taught dogma and was dean of the theology faculty (1873–9) at Lviv University. In 1870 he founded the newspaper *Ruskii Sion*. He also helped prepare and publish popular prayer books (including the first one in Ukrainian) and church manuals. In 1879 he was consecrated bishop and named assistant to Metropolitan Y. Sembratovych, his uncle. In 1882 he became administrator of Lviv archeparchy, and in 1885 he was named metropolitan of Halych by Pope Leo XIII. Under his leadership Stanyslaviv eparchy was formed in 1885, and the *Lviv Synod held in 1891. The synod did much to reform church practices in the metropoly, and rejected attempts to introduce compulsory celibacy for Ukrainian clergymen. Sembratovych expanded the Lviv theological seminary and appointed the scholars I. Dolnytsky and O. Bachynsky to the faculty. He also helped establish St Josaphat's Ukrainian Pontifical College in Rome. During his tenure the Sisters Servants of Mary Immaculate order was established in Galicia, and the Basilian Order of Sisters was reformed. Politically, Sembratovych supported the *New Era policy of appeasement with the Poles in Galicia. In 1894 Pope Leo XIII made him a cardinal. He was buried in the crypt of St George's Cathedral in Lviv.

W. Lencyk, I. Nazarko

Sembratovych, Yosyf [Sembratovyč, Josyf], b 8 November 1821 in Krynytsia, Nowy Sącz circle, Galicia, d 23 October 1900 in Rome. Ukrainian Catholic metropolitan; uncle of S. Sembratovych. A Vienna University graduate in theology, he was ordained in 1845. After receiving a D TH degree from Vienna, he served as prefect (1850–2) at the Greek Catholic theological seminaries in Peremyshl and Lviv, vice-rector (1852–60) of the Greek Catholic seminary in Vienna, and an assistant professor (1850–2) and professor (1861–5) of New Testament studies at Lviv University. In 1865 Pope Pius IX nominated him titular bishop of Nazianzus in Rome. In 1867 he was appointed administrator of Peremyshl eparchy, a position he held until 1872. In 1870 Emperor Francis Joseph I nominated him archbishop of Lviv and metropolitan of Halych, and Pius IX made him a Roman count and assistant to the papal

Metropolitan Yosyf
Sembratovych

Rev Stefan Semchuk

throne and appointed him consultator to the Congregation for the Propagation of the Faith. Sembratovych spearheaded the temperance movement in his metropoly, thereby incurring the wrath of the local Polish nobility, which monopolized distilling and owned all the taverns. They used their influence in Vienna to try to have Sembratovych removed by accusing him of political incompetence and blaming him for the spread of Russian Orthodoxy and the Russophile movement among the peasants and clergy of Galicia. In 1882, after Rev I. *Naumovych converted to Orthodoxy and was followed by his parishioners in Hnylychky, Zbarazh county, Francis Joseph ordered Sembratovych to Vienna and demanded that he give up his metropoly. Sembratovych went to Rome, where Pope Leo XIII accepted his resignation and appointed him, instead, titular archbishop of Theodosiopolis, consultator to the Congregation for the Propagation of the Faith and to the Congregation of the Index, and chairman of the papal commission for the revision of ecclesiastical texts. During his last 18 years in Rome, Sembratovych promoted and defended the rights of the Uniate church.

W. Lencyk, I. Nazarko

Semchuk, Stefan [Semčuk], b 2 November 1899 in Lviv, Galicia, d 4 August 1984 in Winnipeg. Catholic priest and poet. Having served in the Austrian army and partisan units during the First World War, he completed his education at the Peremyshl seminary and was ordained in 1923. He served as parish priest in the Boiko and Hutsul regions before he was sent to Canada (1928) and appointed to the Holy Protectress parish in Winnipeg. He was a founder (1932) of and leading figure in the *Ukrainian Catholic Brotherhood, the editor of its publications, and its representative on the presidium of the Ukrainian Canadian Committee (now Congress). After the war he organized CARE packages for refugees in Europe and helped them to immigrate to Canada. He published several collections of verses, such as *Meteory* (Meteors, 1924), *Fanfary* (Fanfares, 1931), and *Kanads'ka rapsodiia* (Canadian Rhapsody, 1959); a collection of short stories, *Proroky* (Prophets, 1927); a history of Ukrainian literature (1965); a study of the Union of Berestia (1946); and a biography of Metropolitan Y. Rutsky (1967).

Semchyshyn, Myroslav [Semčyšyn], b 26 August 1910 in Zolochiv, Galicia. Philologist, journalist, and community figure. He studied at Lviv University (1932) and taught at the Academic Gymnasium in Lviv (1936–8) and the Lviv Pedagogical Institute (1939–41). During the German occupation he worked for the Ukrainian Relief Committee in Lviv. As a postwar refugee he worked for the Ukrainian Relief Committee in Vienna (1944–6) and taught at a Ukrainian gymnasium in Salzburg. He emigrated to England in 1947 and was the editor of *Ukraïns'ka dumka* in London (1948–50). From 1955 he lived in Chicago, where he cofounded and edited (1955–7) the paper *Ukraïns'ke zhyttia*. He was a professor of Russian, Polish, and (from 1973) Ukrainian at Northeastern Illinois State University (1961–78). He wrote articles on linguistic, literary, and pedagogical subjects, booklets in English on Ukrainians in Illinois (1976) and the Ukrainians (1977), and a book on 1,000 years of Ukrainian culture (1985). From 1981 he headed the Chicago chapter of the Shevchenko Scientific Society.

Stefan Semchyshyn

Mykola Semenenko

Semchyshyn, Stefan [Semčyšyn], b 19 August 1940 in Stara Dubrova, Bosnia, Yugoslavia. Obstetrician and maternal-fetal specialist. He emigrated to Canada in 1960 and obtained his medical training at Queen's University in Kingston, Ontario (MD, 1971) and Ohio State University in Columbus (maternal-fetal medicine, 1976–8). He has been an associate professor of obstetrics and gynecology at Seton Hall University in West Orange, New Jersey, since 1989. An advocate of education as a means of preventing pregnancy losses, he has initiated and established perinatal networks and high-risk pregnancy care centers that use his innovative programs on pregnancy literacy. He has lectured extensively and contributed numerous papers to scholarly medical journals. He is the founder of the Jacobs Institute of Women's Health, the *Perinatal Newsletter*, and the Partnership in Pregnancy Institute in New Jersey, and the author of *How to Prevent Miscarriage and Other Crises of Pregnancy* (1989; 2nd edn 1990).

Semchyshyn, Tymish [Semčyšyn, Tymiš] (nom de guerre: Richka), b 1915 in Sambir county, Galicia, d 1945? in Odessa. OUN leader. In 1941 he was deputy leader of the Southern Expeditionary Group of the OUN (Bandera faction) and organized anti-Nazi resistance in southern

Ukraine. After being arrested by the Gestapo in early 1942, he was sent to a concentration camp. He escaped in March 1943 and became OUN leader for Transnistria, where he co-ordinated resistance to the Rumanian regime. In 1944 he was a member of the OUN team that conducted negotiations with Rumanian military representatives. He was captured by the Rumanian secret police in 1945 and turned over to the NKVD, who probably killed him.

Semchyshyn, Yaroslav [Semčyšyn, Jaroslav], b 29 March 1930 in Winnipeg. Singer, actor, and community leader. A pharmacist by profession, he graduated from the University of Manitoba (1956), studied voice at the Royal Conservatory of Music in Toronto (1956–9), and sang in operas and concerts. He founded the Ukrainian Theater in Winnipeg and directed plays such as *Marusia Churai*, *Zaporozhets' za Dunaiem* (Zaporozhian Cossack beyond the Danube), and *Natalka Poltavka* (Natalka from Poltava). After serving as director of the Secretariat for Liaison with the Federal Government on Cultural Affairs (1976–83), he became director of the Department of Cultural Heritage Initiatives within the ministry and in 1984 was elected president of the Manitoba Credit Union Central.

Semdor, Semen (pseud of Symon Doroshenko), b 1888 in the Kherson region, d 12 August 1938 in Symferopil. Actor and director. He began his artistic career in Chibisov's Russian troupe in Oleksandriia (1910–13) and then worked as an actor in the Ruska Besida Theater (1913–14); led an amateur troupe in Katerynoslav (1915–17); and acted in Molodyi Teatr (1918–19), the Shevchenko First Theater of the Ukrainian Soviet Republic (1919–20), the Independent Theater in Zhytomyr (1921–2), and the Franko New Drama Theater (1923–6, with interruptions). In 1927–32 he was artistic director of a touring theatrical workshop in the Crimea. He staged H. Ibsen's *Enemy of the People*, K. Wittfogel's *Rote Soldaten*, and K. Gutzkow's *Uriel Acosta*.

Semeinaia biblioteka (Family Library). A Russophile journal of politics, history, and culture, published monthly in 1855 and then semimonthly to June 1856 in Lviv. It was edited and published by S. Shekhovych in *yazychiie. It printed two novellas by H. Kvitka-Osnovianenko and reprinted many articles and literary works from Russian journals.

Semen Olelkovych [Olel'kovyč], b ca 1420, d December 1470 in Kiev. The last appanage prince of Kiev (from 1454); son of *Olelko Volodymyrovych, brother of *Mykhailo Olelkovych, and great-grandson of the grand duke of Lithuania, Algirdas. He served as the representative of the Rus' population in the *Lithuanian-Ruthenian state and sought to expand the autonomy of the Kiev principality. He supported the Lithuanian opposition to the Polish king Casimir IV Jagiellończyk. He was backed by Lithuanian and Ruthenian boyars in an unsuccessful bid for the Lithuanian throne. After his death Kiev principality was abolished.

Semenenko, Mykola, b 16 November 1905 in Mariiupil, Katerynoslav gubernia. Geologist; full member of the AN URSR (now ANU) since 1948. He graduated from the Dnipropetrovske Mining Institute in 1927 and taught there (1937–41) and at other mining institutes. From 1944 he chaired a department at the ANU Institute of Geological Sciences and concurrently taught at Kiev University (1944–53). He organized and became director of the ANU Institute of the Geochemistry and Physics of Minerals (1969–77). Semenenko's research was in petrography, theories of metamorphism and metasomatism, Precambrian geology and geochronology, problems of ore content and the structure of metal deposits, the origin of the continental earth crust and lithosphere, and the theoretical foundations of planetary geochemistry.

Semenenko, Oleksander, b 27 August 1898 in Yelysavethrad, Kherson gubernia, d 1 June 1978 in New York. Lawyer and civic leader. During 1917–20 he was active in the Ukrainian Workers' Union in Yelysavethrad, a branch of the All-Russian Social Democratic party. After completing his law studies at the Kharkiv Institute of People's Education (1924) he joined the Kharkiv Gubernia College of Lawyers. In 1937–8 he was twice arrested by the NKVD. Under the German occupation he served as chairman of the Kharkiv Municipal Council (1942–3). As an émigré in Germany, he directed the Ukrainian Social Care Agency and was vice-president of the Ukrainian National Committee (1944–5). After living in Brazil for over 10 years, he moved to New York, where he worked at the Ukrainian Academy of Arts and Sciences and in a law firm. His memoirs, published in 1976 as *Kharkiv, Kharkiv*, provide a unique glimpse of life in the first Soviet Ukrainian capital during the 1920s and 1930s.

Semeniuk, Lidiia [Semenjuk, Lidija], b 24 March 1918 in Kiev. Architect. Since graduating from the Kiev Civil-Engineering Institute (1941) she has worked for various planning institutions in Kiev. She designed the cultural center in Zvenyhorodka (1948) and film theaters in Chernihiv and Nizhen (1949–50) and collaborated with other architects in designing the square in Pereiaslav-Khmelnytskyi (1954), residential buildings on Povitroflotskyi Prospekt in Kiev (1955–7), and the Universytet metro station in Kiev (1960).

Semenivka. I-13. A town smt (1986 pop 8,000) on the Revna River and a raion center in Chernihiv oblast. It was founded in the 1680s as a Cossack settlement in Starodub regiment by Col S. Samoilovych. After the abolition of the Hetman state it belonged to Novhorod-Siverskyi vicegerency (1782–96), Little Russia gubernia (1796–1802), and Chernihiv gubernia. In 1919, as part of Homel gubernia, Semenivka became part of Russia, but in 1926 it was reassigned to Hlukhiv and then Konotip okruhas in Ukraine. Since 1932 it has been part of Chernihiv oblast. In the 19th century the town manufactured woolen cloth and sugar. Today it has a footwear, a starch, and a brick factory.

Semenivka. IV-14. A town smt (1986 pop 8,000) and a raion center in Poltava oblast. It was established at the end of the 17th century. Under the Hetman state the village belonged to Khorol company in Myrhorod regiment. In the 19th century it was part of Khorol county in Poltava gubernia. It remains an agricultural town with a sugar refinery, a flour mill, and grain storage facilities.

Mykhailo (Mykhail) Semenko   Semen Semkovsky

Semenko, Mykhailo (Mykhail), b 31 December 1892 in Kybyntsi, Myrhorod county, Poltava gubernia, d 23 October 1937. Poet, and founder and theoretician of Ukrainian *futurism; son of the writer M. *Proskurivna. Semenko studied at the Psycho-Neurological Institute in St Petersburg. His first collection, *Préludes* (1913), shows the influence of the poets of *Ukraïns'ka khata. In the collections that followed (*Derzannia* [Excitation, 1913] and *Kverofuturyzm* [Quero-Futurism, 1914], and in the manisfesto in the latter collection, Semenko initiated Ukrainian 'querofuturism,' or the art of searching, at a time when Russian cubofuturism and egofuturism were appearing in Ukraine (in authors such as D. Burliuk, V. Kruchenykh, and V. Khliebnikov). In 1918 Semenko published in Kiev the collections *P'iero zadaiet'sia* (Pierrot Puts on Airs), *P'iero kokhaie* (Pierrot Loves), and *Deviat' poem* (Nine Long Poems). In 1919 his collections *P'iero mertvopetliie* (Pierrot Deadnooses), *Bloc-notes*, and *V sadakh bezroznykh* (In the Roseless Orchards) and the poem 'Lilit' (Lilith) were published by Fliamingo, a publishing house of the futurist writers' group of the same name, which Semenko had founded. In 1919 he proclaimed the beginning of 'revolutionary futurism' and published his 'revolutionary futurist' poems, *Tovarysh Sontse* (Comrade Sun) and *Dvi poezofil'my* (Two Poetryfilms). He was also editor of the journal *Mystetstvo*.

In 1920, together with M. Liubchenko and O. Slisarenko, Semenko published *Al'manakh tr'okh* (The Almanac of Three), and in 1921, his collection *Prominnia pohroz* (The Rays of Menace). At that time he organized the Shock Brigade of Futurist Poets, later called the *Association of Panfuturists (Aspanfut), which published its credo and manifestos in the almanac *Semafor u maibutnie* (Semaphores into the Future, 1922) and the newspaper *Katafal'k iskusstva* (1922). In response to critics Semenko altered his position to 'left-wing front-line' and changed Aspanfut to Komunkult (1924). From 1924 to 1927 he worked as editor in chief of the Odessa film studios of the All-Ukrainian Photo-Cinema Administration. In 1924 he published two collections of his works from 1910 to 1922, both titled *Kobzar*, and in 1925, the collection *V revoliutsiiu* (Into the Revolution). In 1925 he also produced the poetic film *Step* (The Steppe).

In 1927 *Zustrich na perekhresnii stantsiï* (Meeting at a Crossroad Station), which contained the works of Semen-

ko, G. Shkurupii, and M. Bazhan, was published. Also in that year Semenko founded a new futurist association called *Nova Generatsiia. After severe criticism, Semenko abandoned futurism and became a poet of the Bolshevik revolution (with poetry such as *Malyi kobzar i novi virshi* [The Little Kobzar and New Poems, 1928] and *Evropa i my* [Europe and We, 1929]). At the beginning of the 1930s he confessed to his 'erroneous' earlier position and with a 'reformed' vision wrote *Suchasni virshi* (Contemporary Poems, 1931), *Z radians'koho shchodennyka* (From a Soviet Diary, 1932), *Kytai v ohni* (China on Fire, 1932), and *Mizhnarodni dila* (International Affairs, 1933). Nevertheless Semenko was arrested in 1937 and executed with other Ukrainian writers. In the mid-1960s he was rehabilitated.

Semenko's early futurist writing abounds with urban and F. Marinetti–inspired themes and subjects, and is characterized by experimentation with form and language which attempts to shock the reader. Despite his insistence on the discarding of classical and contemporary literary achievements, especially the legacies of T. Shevchenko, O. Oles, M. Vorony, and M. Filiansky, Semenko greatly influenced the development of Ukraninian modern poetry. A complete edition of his work was published in Kharkiv in three volumes (1929–31), and there has also been a posthumous edition titled *Poeziï* (Poems, 1985).

BIBLIOGRAPHY
Nikovs'kyi, A. 'Poeziia buduchchyny,' in his *Vita Nova* (Kiev 1920)
Kachaniuk, M. 'Materiialy do istoriï futuryzmu na Ukraïni,' *Literaturnyi arkhiv*, 1930, nos 1–4
                                                                    B. Kravtsiv

Semenko, Yurii, b 30 April 1920 in Mykhailivka, now in Apostolove raion, Dnipropetrovske oblast. Journalist and political figure. He graduated from Dnipropetrovske University and the Zaporizhia Pedagogical Institute (1941). As a postwar refugee in Germany, he contributed to the newspaper *Ukraïns'ki visti* (Neu-Ulm) and its monthly Russian-language supplement, *Osvobozhdenie*. The deputy leader and, since 1971, leader of the émigré *Union of Lands of United Ukraine (SZSU), in 1955–62 he edited its organ, *Ukraïns'kyi selianyn*. He also compiled and edited collections of eyewitness accounts of the 1933 famine (1963), Soviet Ukrainian popular humor (1964), and articles on V. Dolenko and the SZSU (1975) and wrote a history of chess in Ukraine (1980) and a collection of memoirs, *Tychky* (Supports, 1991).

Semenov-Tian-Shansky, Petr [Semenov-Tjan-Šanskij], b 14 January 1827 in Urusovo, Riazan gubernia, Russia, d 11 March 1914 in St Petersburg. Russian geographer, statistician, and explorer. He graduated from St Petersburg University (1848) and studied abroad (1853–5). As director of the Central Statistical Committee at the Ministry of Internal Affairs (1864–80) and chairman of the Statistical Council (1875–97) he developed the methodology and mechanisms of data-gathering that made possible the first empire-wide census in 1897. He was one of the founders of regional geography and the inspiration behind the monumental *Rossiia – polnoe geograficheskoe opisanie nashego otechestva* (Russia – A Full Geographical Description of Our Fatherland, 19 vols, 1899–1914), which was edited by his son. Volumes 7 and 14 of that work (titled 'Little Russia' and 'New Russia') were devoted to Ukraine.

Semenov-Zuser, Semen, b 4 August 1887 in Pavlohrad, Katerynoslav gubernia, d 8 November 1951 in Kharkiv. Archeologist. A graduate of the St Petersburg Institute of Archeology, he taught at several institutions in Leningrad (1915–29) and was a curator of the USSR Academy of Sciences Museum of Anthropology and Ethnography (1929–33) before becoming professor of ancient history and archeology at Kharkiv University in 1937. From 1920 Semenov-Zuser took part in many archeological expeditions in the Black Sea area. His areas of specialization included the *Olbia settlement and the Scythian era. His doctoral dissertation, *Skifskaia problema v otechestvennoi nauke* (The Scythian Question in the Scholarship of Our Fatherland), was published as a monograph in 1948.

Sementovsky, Kostiantyn [Sementovs'kyj, Kostjantyn], b 1823 in Semenohirka, Zolotonosha county, Poltava gubernia, d 1902. Ethnographer; brother of M. and O. *Sementovsky. After graduating from the Nizhen Lyceum (1839) he worked in the civil service in Chernihiv, Poltava, Kharkiv, and Orel. He maintained friendly ties with I. Sreznevsky, A. Metlynsky, M. Kostomarov, and H. Kvitka-Osnovianenko and collected ethnographic materials and folklore. In 1843 he published several articles, on Ukrainian folk beliefs, feast days, and H. Kvitka-Osnovianenko, and in 1851, a collection of 'Little Russian' and Galician riddles.

Sementovsky, Mykola [Sementovs'kyj], b 2 March 1819 in Semenohirka (now a part of Chervonohirka, near Irkliiv), Zolotonosha county, Poltava gubernia, d 5 November 1879 in Semenohirka. Writer, historian, and ethnographer; brother of K. and O. *Sementovsky. He graduated from the Nizhen Lyceum in 1840. Among his works are the play *Nishchii* (The Pauper; pub in *Maiak*, 1843); the novels *Kochubei* (1845), *Baronessa Flagsberg* (1848), and *Potemkin* (1851); a biographical essay about I. Kotliarevsky (pub in *Severnaia pchela*, 1846); and the historical works *Starina malorossiiskaia, zaporozhskaia i donskaia* (Little Russian, Zaporozhian, and Don Antiquity, 1846), *Zaporozhskaia rukopis'* ... (Zaporozhian Manuscript ..., 1856), and *Kiev i ego sviatyni, drevnosti, dostopamiatnosti* (Kiev and Its Shrines, Antiquities, and Landmarks, 1864; 7th edn 1900).

Sementovsky, Oleksander [Sementovs'kyj], b 1820s in Semenohirky, Zolotonosha county, Poltava gubernia, d ? Forester, historian, ethnographer, and statistician; brother of M. and K. *Sementovsky. He graduated from the Nizhen Lyceum (1840), and from 1843 to 1867 he worked as a forester in Kiev and Vitsebsk gubernias. He founded a cabinet of natural resources at the Kiev Palace of State Properties and discovered lignite in Zvenyhorodka county. He wrote book-length articles in Russian on the histories of Kamianets-Podilskyi (1865), the Pochaiv Monastery (1870), and the Nizhen Lyceum (1881). He also compiled a statistical atlas.

Semianchuk, Illia [Semjančuk, Illja], b 26 March 1895 in Opryshivtsi, Stanyslaviv county, Galicia, d 28 April 1955

in Chicago. Co-operative leader. He served as an officer in the Austrian army and then in the Ukrainian Galician Army. In 1932, after studying at the Higher Trade School (1923–7) in Prague and working for an American firm, he returned to Stanyslaviv and became director of the Regional Union of Co-operatives. He also served on the board of directors of the Audit Union of Ukrainian Co-operatives, the audit committee of Tsentrobank, and the Industry and Trade Chamber in Lviv. Under the German occupation he managed the Ukrainian Co-operative Bank in Stanyslaviv and then directed Tsentrosoiuz in Lviv. After emigrating to the United States (1949) he helped found the Self-Reliance Association of American Ukrainians and the Self-Reliance Federal Credit Union in Chicago.

Semko, Mykhailo, b 1 October 1906 in Baliasne, Poltava county, d 9 September 1979 in Moscow. Mechanical engineer. He studied at the Kharkiv Polytechnical Institute and later worked there, from 1950 to 1978 as rector. He was a specialist in metal machining; he developed new methods of metal cutting utilizing superhard materials and contributed to the study of the plastic deformation of materials.

Semkovsky, Semen [Semkovskij] (né Bronshtein), b 15 March 1882 in Mahiliou, Belarus, d 18 March 1937 in Kharkiv. Philosopher and sociologist; full member of the VUAN from 1929; cousin of L. Trotsky. A graduate in law of St Petersburg University and a Menshevik, he spent 10 years in Vienna and then lectured at Kiev University (1918–20) and the Kharkiv Institute of People's Education (1920–36). In 1920 he renounced his Menshevik ties, and then advanced quickly in the academic world: he became head of the Philosophy-Sociology Division of the *Ukrainian Institute of Marxism-Leninism in Kharkiv (1922–31), chairman of the Department of European Cultural History at the Kharkiv Institute of People's Education (from 1922), chairman of the VUAN Sociology Commission (1927–36), member of the VUAN Presidium and chairman of its Association of Natural Science (1931–6), a member of the Council for the Study of the Productive Resources of the Ukrainian SSR (1934–6), and chairman of the VUAN Philosophical Commission (1934–6). He wrote many works in Russian, including books on L. Feuerbach (1922), the theory of relativity and materialism (1924), dialectical materialism and the principle of relativity (1926; Ukrainian trans, 1931), and physics and chemistry in the light of Marxism (1933). A member of the All-Ukrainian Central Executive Committee, he was arrested at the end of 1936, accused of forming a 'Trotskyist-Zinovevite terrorist organization' in Ukraine, and executed. He was posthumously rehabilitated in 1956. (See also *Philosophy.)

T. Zakydalsky

Sempolovsky, Lev [Sempolovs'kyj], b 4 April 1868 in Krerowo (now in Poznań voivodeship), Poland, d 10 October 1960 in Antonopil, Kalynivka raion, Vinnytsia oblast. Plant selection scientist. A graduate of Rostock University in Germany (1889), he worked as a chemist at selection stations in Italy and Germany (1890–7) and in 1898 became director of the sugar beet selection division at the Uladivka-Liubyntsi Selection Station (Vinnytsia county, Podilia gubernia). He developed numerous varieties of sugar beets.

Liudmyla Semykina: the stained-glass panel at Kiev University (created with Opanas Zalyvakha and Alla Horska) destroyed by the Soviet authorities in 1964

Semykina, Liudmyla, b 1924 in Odessa. Painter and designer. A graduate of the Kiev State Art Institute (1953), she painted views of Odessa, seascapes, landscapes, and still lifes. In 1963 Semykina joined the 'dissident' Club of Creative Youth in Kiev, and in 1964 she, O. *Zalyvakha, and A. *Horska created the stained-glass panel at Kiev University depicting T. Shevchenko that was destroyed by Party authorities. For her activities Semykina was expelled from the Union of Artists for one year. She was again expelled in 1968 for signing public petitions in defense of human rights and was not reinstated until 1988. In the meantime she designed original coats and outfits using Ukrainian folk-dress motifs. Her costume designs were used in the film *Zakhar Berkut*.

Senate (from Latin *senatus*, 'council of elders'). In ancient Rome and in many modern states the senate is the highest governing council. In some countries it is one of the legislative chambers of *parliament or a judicial college of the higher courts, sometimes even the supreme court (as with the *State Senate under Hetman P. Skoropadsky's regime). The ruling council in higher educational institutions is also called a senate.

In the Polish Commonwealth the Senate evolved from the royal council and in the first half of the 16th century became (along with the chamber of deputies) a part of the Parliament. After the Union of Lublin (1569) a single bicameral diet served both Poland and Lithuania. The Senate's 150 members included the Roman Catholic clergy (primate, archbishops, bishops) and secular officials (ministers, voivodes, castellans). Its sessions were held separately from those of the deputies, and its role was to approve the decisions of the lower house. Gradually that exercise became a mere formality. Neither Orthodox nor Uniate bishops were admitted to the Senate until 1791, when a new constitution guaranteed the Uniate metropolitan a Senate seat.

The Senate was introduced into Russia by Peter I in 1711 to replace the Boyar Duma, and its powers changed during the subsequent two centuries. Under Peter it served as the chief instrument of reform. For some time it was the highest governing body with administrative, judicial, and auditing powers. Collegiums and agencies of local government, represented by governors, were subordinate to it. Under Catherine II the powers of the Senate were reduced, particularly when the gubernias were placed under the control of governors general who were responsible directly to the empress. With the introduction of the State Council in 1810, the Senate was largely transformed into the empire's highest judicial body. It was abolished by the Soviet government on 5 December 1917.

In the 1920s and 1930s the Senate served as an upper house of the parliaments of Poland, Czechoslovakia, and Rumania. The Polish Senate could pass or reject bills passed by the Sejm. If the Sejm passed the bill again, it became law. The senators were elected in general elections. The 1935 constitution expanded the powers of the Senate, some of whose members were now appointed by the president. The 1920 constitution of Czechoslovakia provided for a Senate similar to the Polish one. In the 1920s its members were elected by a general vote. In Rumania some of the senators were elected by communities and counties (indirect elections), and some were appointed by the king. Deputies of the Ukrainian minorities in those three countries sat in their senates, but their numbers were disproportionately small given the size of the Ukrainian populations there.

Ivan Senchenko

Senchenko, Ivan [Senčenko], b 12 February 1901 in Natalyne, Kostiantynohrad (now Krasnohrad) county, Kharkiv gubernia, d 9 November 1975 in Kiev. Writer. He graduated from the Kharkiv Institute of People's Education in 1928. He began to publish his work in 1921 and joined the literary organizations *Pluh, *Hart, and, later, *Vaplite (1925–8). His early collections *V ohniakh vyshnevykh zaviriukh* (In the Fires of Crimson Storms) and *Opovidannia* (Stories, 1925) received positive reviews. But his subsequent prose, *Istoriia odniieï kar'iery ta inshi opovidannia* (The History of a Career and Other Stories, 1926), the novel *Parovyi mlyn* (The Steam Mill, 1926), and later prose met with criticism, and Senchenko was accused of idealizing the kulaks. His *Iz zapysok* (From Notes, 1927), also titled *Kholuievi zapysky* (A Lackey's Notes), was criticized most harshly of all, since the official critics interpreted it as a satire on the subordination of Ukrainian culture to the dictates of the Party. Senchenko continued to write many prose collections, such as *Dubovi hriady* (A Flower Bed of Oaks, 1927), *Chervonohrads'ki portrety* (Chervonohrad Portraits, 1930), *Komuna* (The Commune, 1932), *Povist' pro

Klyma (A Tale about Klym, 1933), *Za gratamy* (Behind Bars, 1934), *Rudi vovky* (Red Wolves, 1936), *Chornu bramu* (The Black Gate, 1936), *Noveli* (Novellas, 1940), *Metalisty* (The Metal Workers, 1932), *Naperedodni* (On the Eve, 1938), and *Ioho pokolinnia* (His Generation, 1947; rev edn 1965). He received a positive critical reaction only in the 1950s, with his poetry cycles on the life of the workers of Solomianka, a suburb of Kiev (1956–7), and of the Donbas (1964). The works about his native Chervonohrad (Krasnohrad) district, with which he began his literary career (especially *Chervonohrads'ki portrety*), were his best works, and he would periodically return to that subject, as in *Podorozh do Chervonohradu* (Journey to Chervonohrad, 1971) and *Savka* (1973). The autobiographical nature of those works is clearly evident. Senchenko's writing is characterized by its intimate knowledge of the life of the peasant and of folk customs, by the romanticization of the Ukrainian past, and by gentle humor. He is also the author of works for children, *Maryna* (1954), *Oi, u poli zhyto ...* (O, the Rye in the Field ..., 1957), and *Kharytonchyk-chyk* (1969). A heavily censored edition of his collected works, *Vybrani tvory* (Selected Works), was published in two volumes in 1971. Senchenko's previously banned novel *Liubov i Khreshchatyk* (Love and Khreshchatyk [Boulevard]), written in the mid-1960s, was published in 1988.

I. Koshelivets

Senchenko, Mykola [Senčenko], b 1 May 1945 in Nizhen, Chernihiv oblast. Applied mathematician, computer scientist, and librarian. A graduate of the Kharkiv Institute of Radioelectronics, he worked at the Kharkiv Engineering Institute of Public Construction; under his direction, its computing laboratory became a major computing center. As director (1985–92) of the *Central Scientific Library of the AN URSR (now ANU), he oversaw the completion of its new premises, spearheaded its computerization, and changed its status to that of a scholarly research institute. In 1989 he became chairman of the Bibliographic Commission of the International Association of Ukrainian Studies, which initiated work on a bibliography of Ucrainica. In 1989 he also became a professor of information and computational science at the Kiev Institute of Culture. A Russian-language biobibliographic catalog of his works was published in Kiev in 1990.

Sendulsky, Apollon [Sendul's'kyj], b 17 October 1830 in Sadky, Kremianets county, Volhynia gubernia, d 7 January 1882. Priest, regional historian, and educational activist. Starting in 1868 with a study of his own village, he published a series of historical and ethnographic essays about various Volhynian locations in the eparchial bulletin *Volynskie eparkhial'nye vedomosti*. His memoirs were published posthumously in *Kievskaia starina* (1896).

Seneta, Eugene, b 12 March 1941 in Staryi Sambir, Galicia. Mathematician; full member of the Shevchenko Scientific Society. A graduate of the University of Adelaide (1965) and the Australian National University in Canberra (PH D, 1968), he was appointed professor and head of the mathematics department at the University of Sydney in 1979. He has conducted research on probability and statistics as well as the demography of Ukrainian settlement in Australia. He was elected to the Australian Academy of Sciences in 1985.

Senhalevych, Fedir [Senhalevyč] (Synhalevych, Khvedir), b ca 1890, d October 1941 in Kiev. Physician, ethnographer, and civic leader. While working at the zemstvo hospital in Bohuslav (1917–18) he founded a museum and gymnasium there. Then he worked at the Lukianivka Prison in Kiev and devoted his spare time to ethnographic research. His studies on Kiev lirnyks (1927) and the spring songs, *hahilky* (1930), appeared in the periodicals of the VUAN Ethnographic Commission. He was executed by the Germans during the Second World War.

Senhalevych, Marharyta [Senhalevyč], b 1901 in Kamianets-Podilskyi, d ? Writer, translator, journalist, and librarian. She worked as an editor for *Selianka Ukraïny* (from 1928) and *Visti VUTsVK* (1934–41). From 1943 she lived in Moscow. In 1925 she published a few stories in *Hart* and *Sil's'ko-hospodars'kyi proletar*, and later, the story collections *Veleten'* (The Giant, 1930), *Nepomitna* (The Inconspicuous [Woman], 1930), and *Odnoho zymovoho vechora* (One Winter Evening, 1931) and the collection of sketches *Biitsi i budivnyky* (Fighters and Builders, 1934). She wrote, in Russian, the children's novel *Svetit vdali ogonek* (The Fire Shines from Afar, 1960).

Senin, Ivan, b 26 December 1903 in Katerynoslav gubernia, d ? Soviet government official and Party functionary. After graduating from the Kiev Polytechnical Institute in 1930, he studied at Columbia University in New York. He worked briefly as director of the Ukrainian Cable Plant in Kiev and then held various positions in the government of the Ukrainian SSR: deputy commissar and commissar of light industry (1938–46), deputy chairman of the Council of People's Commissars (1943–6), and deputy chairman of the Council of Ministers (1946–53). In the CPU he rose to the position of member of the Politburo (1949–65). Before retiring in 1965, he was elected to the USSR Supreme Soviet (1950, 1954, 1958, 1962) and Ukraine's Supreme Soviet (1951, 1955, 1963). He attended the United Nations founding conference in San Francisco in 1945 as a member of the Ukrainian delegation.

Senior elementary school (*vydilova shkola*). The name given in Austrian-ruled Galicia to the three upper classes of the seven-grade elementary urban school established by the education law of 1863. The name applied also to the two upper grades of the five-year elementary schools for girls. Instruction in these schools was in Polish, and only two private girls' schools provided instruction in Ukrainian, the Basilian order of nuns' institute in Yavoriv (1897–1906) and the Shevchenko Elementary School for Girls in Lviv. Under Polish rule senior elementary schools were abolished in favor of a seven-grade public elementary school system, introduced in the 1932 education reform. (See *Elementary schools.)

Seniutovych, Ioanykii [Senjutovyč, Ioanykij], b ? in Sosnytsia, Chernihiv regiment, d 12 November 1729 in Kiev. Orthodox churchman. He became a hieromonk in 1682 and then archimandrite and vicar of the St Sophia Monastery in Kiev. He subsequently became hegumen of St Michael's Golden-Domed Monastery (1711) and then archimandrite (1715) of the Kievan Cave Monastery. He was active in organizing the rebuilding of the monastery after a devastating fire in 1718. Seniutovych was opposed to the extension of Russian control over Ukrainian church affairs and did not abide by Peter I's decree of 1720 allowing the monastery press to print only religious books that had been censored by the Holy Synod. He was fined 1,000 rubles in 1724 for his transgression.

Seniutovych-Berezhny, Viacheslav [Senjutovyč-Berežnyj, V'jačeslav], b 15 June 1902 in Tokari, Lokhvytsia county, Poltava gubernia, d 3 February 1992 in Santa Barbara, California. Historian specializing in heraldry and genealogy; member of the Shevchenko Scientific Society from 1952. He served in A. Denikin's Volunteer Army (1919–20) and then emigrated and completed his studies at Belgrade University (1925) and the Ukrainian Free University in Munich (PH D, 1947). He moved to the United States in 1952. His publications include studies of the genealogy of P. Mohyla, I. Mazepa, N. Gogol, P. Orlyk, D. Apostol, and I. Vyhovsky and a study of the sources for medieval Ukrainian heraldry (pub in *Litopys Volyni*, 1955, no. 2).

Seniv, Ivan, b 7 October 1905 in Rohatyn, Galicia. Art historian. A graduate of the USSR Institute of Painting, Sculpture, and Architecture (1953), he has written articles on Ukrainian art and furniture and a book about the artist O. Kulchytska (1961).

Senkiw, Christina [Sen'kiv, Xrystyna] (née Welyhorsky), b 20 October 1950 in Toronto. Ukrainian-Canadian painter and graphic artist. A graduate of the University of Toronto (BFA, 1973), she has worked as an illustrator and book designer. She has designed covers for the children's magazine *Veselka* and has illustrated *The History of Ukrainian Costume* (1986) and *Timmy Kitten* (1989). Her drawings for children and paintings have been displayed in 10 solo and several group exhibitions in Toronto, Chicago, Detroit, Cleveland, and Ottawa.

Senko, Yurii [Sen'ko, Jurij], b 27 April 1913 in Burimka, Borzna county, Chernihiv gubernia, d 20 November 1957 in Trenton, New Jersey. Ethnographer. After graduating from the Kharkiv Pedagogical Institute he taught secondary school in the Poltava region and gathered materials on local ethnography, folklore, and archeology. He collaborated with the Ethnographic Commission of the VUAN. In 1943 he emigrated to Germany, and in 1950 to the United States, where he published articles on folk sayings about the liberation struggle of 1917–21 (1953) and on the destruction of the Ukrainian church under the Soviet regime (1953).

Senkovych, Fedir [Sen'kovyč], b ? in Shchyrets, Galicia, d 1631 in Lviv. Icon and portrait painter. He owned a studio in Lviv and eventually became head of the Lviv painters' guild. He painted the first iconostasis and holy shroud in the Dormition Church in Lviv (1630). The icon of the Theotokos with the prophets from Ripne (1599) and the portrait of I. Danylovych have been attributed to him. After his death his studio was inherited by his student M. Petrakhnovych.

Senkus, Murray [Sen'kus', Myroslav], b 31 August 1914 in Redberry, Saskatchewan. Organic chemist; full member of the Shevchenko Scientific Society since 1948. A graduate of the universities of Saskatchewan (M SC, 1936) and

Chicago (PH D, 1938), he was the R.J. Reynolds Tobacco Co director of chemical research (1951–60), assistant director (1960–4), and director of scientific affairs (1976–9). Since 1979 he has been a consultant in the United States and Indonesia. His research centered around organic chemistry and the chemistry of tobacco, insecticides, the recovery of fermentation products, chemotherapeutic agents, and the chemistry of flavors. He is the holder of over 60 patents.

Sentimentalism. A literary current in the literature of the late 18th century that emerged as a reaction against the rationalism of the Enlightenment and the traditions of *classicism. Its adherents stressed the importance of emotion, extolled nature, and made heroes of the common people. Early sentimentalism was influenced by the works of English writers, such as T. Gray, S. Richardson, and J. Thompson. It resulted in the development of new genres in prose and focused renewed attention on elegies, idylls, and folktales in poetry.

In Ukrainian literature sentimentalism is evident in the plays of I. Kotliarevsky (eg, *Natalka Poltavka*), in the tales of Ye. Hrebinka, and, particularly, in the stories of H. Kvitka-Osnovianenko, which were sentimental in both subject matter and motifs. O. Doroshkevych, A. Shamrai, and M. Zerov have attributed the sentimentalism of Kvitka-Osnovianenko's works (eg, *Marusia*, *Shchyra liubov* [Sincere Love], and *Serdeshna Oksana* [Poor Oksana]) to the influence of scholastic and folk poetry. D. Chyzhevsky, however, has argued that sentimentalism was not prominent in Ukrainian literature.

The influence and elements of sentimentalism are evident in the development of melodrama in Ukrainian theater of the 19th and early 20th centuries, in the works of I. Hushalevych (eg, *Pidhiriany* [Inhabitants of the Foothills, 1869]), S. Vorobkevych (eg, *Hnat Prybluda* [1875] and *Uboha Marta* [Poor Marta, 1878]), L. Manko (*Neshchasne kokhannia* [Unfortunate Love]), and O. Sukhodolsky (*Pomsta, abo Zahublena dolia* [Revenge, or the Lost Fate]). Melodrama also characterized certain plays and stagings of M. Starytsky's and M. Kropyvnytsky's productions.

B. Kravtsiv

Iryna Senyk   Omelian Senyk

Senyk, Iryna, b 8 June 1926 in Lviv. Nurse, poet, and dissident. She was arrested in December 1946 for belonging to the OUN, and served 10 years of hard labor and 13 years of exile. After settling in Ivano-Frankivske in 1969, she worked as a nurse and became acquainted with activists of the Ukrainian cultural revival. During the 1972 repressions of Ukrainian activists she was arrested again and sentenced in February 1973 to six years of strict-regime labor camp and five years of exile. At the women's labor camp in Barashevo, Mordovia, she participated in protests staged by Ukrainian inmates. After completing her exile in Kazakhstan she returned to Ukraine. Senyk's verses were published in the anthology *Invincible Spirit: Art and Poetry of Ukrainian Women Political Prisoners in the USSR* (1977) and in the collection *Suvii polotna* (Scroll of Linen, 1990).

Senyk, Oleksa (pseuds: Zaporizky, Pavlo Baida), b 25 August 1915 in Myroliubivka, Oleksandrivske county, Katerynoslav gubernia, d 20 May 1968 in Buffalo. Writer. He graduated from the Zaporizhia Pedagogical Institute in 1934. From 1936 to 1939 he was imprisoned in a Siberian labor camp. As a postwar refugee he lived in Germany (1944–9), Brazil (1949–61), and the United States (1961–8). He is the author of the fable collection *Novi baiky* (New Fables, 1953) and the plays *Maty pomyryla* (The Mother Made Peace between Them, 1946), *Shvaitsars'kyi pashport* (A Swiss Passport, 1946), and *Granit* (Granite, 1947).

Senyk, Omelian (pseuds: Hrybivsky, Kantsler, Urban), b 21 January 1891 in Yavoriv, Galicia, d 30 August 1941 in Zhytomyr, Volhynia. Political activist. During the First World War he served as a captain in the Austrian army and then in the Ukrainian Galician Army. After escaping from a Polish internment camp he returned to Lviv and helped found the Ukrainian Military Organization. He was a member of its home, and then of its supreme, command. After leaving Ukraine in 1927, he helped edit *Surma*, and in 1929 he became a member of the OUN Leadership. He visited the United States, Canada, and South America to promote the Ukrainian nationalist movement. After Ye. Konovalets's death he organized the Second Great Congress, which elected A. Melnyk as chief of the OUN. He opposed the split in the OUN in 1940. He was assassinated together with M. *Stsiborsky, allegedly by an OUN Bandera faction supporter, while leading the expeditionary groups of the Melnyk OUN faction.

Senyshyn, Ambrose [Senyšyn, Amvrozij], b 23 February 1903 in Staryi Sambir, Sambir county, Galicia, d 11 September 1976 in Philadelphia. Ukrainian Catholic metropolitan. A Basilian novice and monk from 1922 at the Krekhiv, Lavriv, Dobromyl, and Krystynopil monasteries, he was ordained in 1931 and served as a pastor in Warsaw (1931–3), hegumen of the Basilian monastery in Chicago (1933–42), and pastor at St Nicholas's Church in Chicago (1937–42). In 1942 he became auxiliary bishop of the Ukrainian Catholic exarchy in the United States. While residing in Stamford, Connecticut (at St Basil's College), he founded the Missionary Sisters of the Mother of God (1944) and the Ukrainian Catholic Committee for Refugees (1946). He also published liturgical books, edited the monthly *Kovcheh/The Ark* (1946–56), and initiated a series of recordings to standardize Ukrainian liturgical chant. Senyshyn served as apostolic exarch of Stamford (1956–8), the first bishop of Stamford eparchy (1958–61), and metropolitan of the Ukrainian Catholic church in the United

Metropolitan Ambrose Senyshyn

Pavlo Senytsia

States and archbishop of Philadelphia archeparchy (1961–76). As metropolitan he introduced the mandatory use of the Gregorian calendar in his archeparchy. He built 25 new churches and a new cathedral (in Philadelphia) and founded eight new parishes and missions and, in 1965, the Ukrainian Studies Center and Byzantine Slavic Arts Foundation at St Josaphat's Seminary in Washington, DC. In 1973 he was appointed to the Congregation for Eastern Churches.

Senyshyn, Lev [Senyšyn], b 1908 in Galicia, d 10 December 1957 in Toronto. Journalist and caricaturist. In Lviv he illustrated the humor magazines *Zhorna* (1933–4) and *Komar* (1934–9) and worked as an editor for the Ukrainska Presa publishing house. As a postwar émigré he illustrated the satirical weekly *Proty shersty* (1946–7) in Landeck, Austria. After emigrating to Canada he edited the weekly *Sport* (1955–6) in Toronto and contributed articles and illustrations to the weekly *Homin Ukraïny*.

Senytsia, Pavlo [Senycja], b 23 September 1879 in Maksymivka, Pereiaslav county, Poltava gubernia, d 3 July 1960 in Moscow. Musicologist, composer, and teacher. He studied at the Moscow Conservatory (1909) and taught in several music schools in Moscow (1905–15). He later (1921–31) worked as a research associate for the Ukrainian SSR Commissariat of Education and served as secretary of the ethnographic division of the State Institute of Music Education (1923–39). His major musicological studies include *Suchasna ukraïns'ka muzyka* (Contemporary Ukrainian Music, 1923) and *Ukraïns'ka vokal'na muzyka* (Ukrainian Vocal Music, 1925). His musical works include the operas *Life Is a Dream* (based on Calderon-Balmont) and *The Servant Girl* (based on T. Shevchenko, 1913–16); two symphonies (1905, 1912); an overture (1908); seven string quartets; approx 50 works for chorus to texts by T. Shevchenko, M. Bazhan, and others; and approx 100 solo songs to texts by T. Shevchenko, P. Tychyna, M. Rylsky, and others.

Separate Cavalry Division of the Army of the UNR (Okrema kinna dyviziia Armii UNR). Organized in May

1920 by consolidating various smaller units, it consisted of two cavalry brigades of two regiments each. The division was commanded by brigadier general I. Omelianovych-Pavlenko and had 3,000 cavalrymen. It was active until 21 November 1920, when, defending the army's rear, it crossed the Zbruch River and surrendered to the Poles.

Separate Detachment of Sich Riflemen. See Sich Riflemen.

Separate Zaporozhian Detachment. See Zaporozhian Corps.

Separation of church and state. See Church-state separation.

Sequoia (Ukrainian: *sekvoia*). A coniferous evergreen tree of the family Taxodiaceae, the tallest and probably the oldest tree known to exist, exceeding heights of 90 m and dating back some 4,000 years. The two species of sequoia are the redwood (*Sequoia sempervirens*) and the big tree, giant sequoia, or Sierra redwood (*Sequoiadendron giganteum*). In Ukraine the sequoia was introduced in the mid-19th century in the southern Crimea, in Transcaucasia, and on the Caucasian shores of the Black Sea. Ukrainian sequoias reach heights of 91 m. In the distant past sequoias were native to Ukraine. Fossils of the trees dating from the Paleogenic and Neogenic periods have been found in Dnipropetrovske, Kiev, Zhytomyr, Kirovohrad, Chernihiv, and Transcarpathia oblasts.

Seraphim [Serafym] (secular name: Stefan Ustvolsky), b and d ? Ukrainian-Canadian church figure. A Russian monk from Mount Athos and a self-proclaimed bishop, Seraphim came to Canada (after arriving in the United States in 1902) in 1903 at the request of a group of early Ukrainian-Canadian community leaders (including K. Genyk, I. Negrych, and I. Bodrug) to head the Winnipeg-based synodal 'All-Russian Patriarchal Orthodox church.' This church was intended as an independent 'democratic' Ukrainian church free of Catholic or Orthodox control. Commonly called the Seraphimite church, it quickly gained a substantial following among the immigrant Ukrainian population, which had been coping until then with sporadic religious care. Seraphim's indiscretions, however, soon raised doubts about his credibility, and the church synod persuaded him to go to Russia to seek approbation from the Holy Synod. After Seraphim's departure in January 1904 the synod assumed full control of the church, removed the bishop from his post, and reconstituted the church as the *Independent Greek church. The establishment of the Seraphimite and the Independent Greek churches caused great concern in the Ukrainian and Roman Catholic churches, which thereafter resolved to make special efforts to maintain the immigrants' traditional religious affiliations. The short-lived Seraphimite church also gave rise to the first Ukrainian-Canadian newspaper, *Kanadiis'kyi farmer* (est 1903), which had strong links to the church and its backers.

A. Makuch

Serapion of Vladimir, b ?, d 1275. Bishop and renowned preacher. An archimandrite of the Kievan Cave Monastery (from ca 1238), he was made bishop of

Vladimir in northern Rus' in 1274. Five of his sermons have survived, as well as two works that might have been written by him. In these sermons Serapion argues that certain natural disasters as well as the Tatar invasions were punishments for sins committed by the people of Rus'. His writings also refer to folk beliefs of his time regarding matters such as the existence of werewolves and witches. His biography, by E. Petukhov, and a collection of his writings appeared in 1888.

Serbia. A constituent republic (1990 pop 9,800,000) of *Yugoslavia which covers an area of 88,400 sq km and incorporates the autonomous territories of Vojvodina and Kosovo. Its population is predominantly Serbian (nearly 80 percent), with substantial Albanian, Hungarian, Rumanian, Slovak, and Ukrainian (nearly 40,000) minorities.

Up to the 16th century. Serbian-Ukrainian relations began during the Kievan Rus' period. Ukrainian writers, such as Yelysei of Kamianets-Podilskyi (15th century), Andrii of Sianik and V. Nykolsky of Transcarpathia (16th century), and S. Bakachych (17th century), influenced the development of Serbian literature through their translations of Greek and Church Slavonic texts into Serbian as well as through original works they wrote in Serbian. M. Hrushevsky speculated that Ukrainian dumas were probably influenced by Serbian heroic poetry.

17th–18th centuries. An increase in Serbo-Ukrainian contacts resulted from Serbian participation in Ukrainian Cossack armies beginning in the period preceding the Khmelnytsky revolution. In the Cossack register of 1649 there are several dozen Serbian names. Serbs acted as military leaders or were hired as mercenaries by Cossack commanders (notably under I. Vyhovsky). The *Serbyn family was a line of Cossack officers, three of whom were colonels: Ivan Yuriiovych, Ivan Fedorovych, and Voitsa. R. Dmytrashko-Raich was a colonel of the Pereiaslav regiment.

Throughout the 17th and 18th centuries Ukrainian publications were disseminated in Serbia and other southern Slavic countries, particularly those of the Kievan Cave Monastery, the sermons of Z. Kopystensky, and the works of L. Baranovych and T. Stefanovych (those of the latter in Serbian translation). Y. Raich and A. Stojković were among the many Serbs who studied at the Kievan Mohyla Academy in the 18th century. The academy's lecturers and sermonizers also traveled to Serbia, among them S. Zalutsky, who delivered sermons at the cathedral of the Belgrade metropoly. In 1733 the Serbian metropolitan, V. Joanovič, asked the Kievan metropolitan, R. Zaborovsky, to send M. Kozachynsky, T. Klymovsky, T. Levandovsky, I. Mynatsky, T. Padunovsky, and H. Shumliak to Serbia. They subsequently served as instructors of Old Church Slavonic, poetics, and rhetoric in schools in Karlovac, Vukovar, Belgrade, and Osijek. V. Kryzhanivsky, I. Lastovetsky, and P. Mykhailovsky were other graduates of the academy to teach in Serbia.

In the reign of Peter I (particularly during the Russo-Turkish War) many Serbian families, notably the Božić, Milutinović, Miloradović, and Trebinsky families, aligned themselves with the Russians. Once they became members of the Cossack *starshyna* and received estates in Ukraine, they remained there and sent their children to the Kievan Mohyla Academy. Some of their descendants became leaders in Ukrainian political and cultural life.

The number of Serbs in Southern Ukraine grew substantially in the mid-18th century as they emigrated in large numbers from the Austrian-controlled northern regions of their country. Together with Wallachian and other emigrants, they became the nucleus for new administrative and territorial units established by the Russian government, including *New Serbia (1752) and *Sloviano-Serbia (1753), both of which were incorporated into New Russia gubernia in 1764. Many of these new settlers fled to the Zaporozhian Sich. Serbs took part in the *Haidamaka uprisings and the *Koliivshchyna rebellion, but also joined the ranks of Russian armies sent to suppress them. Serbs who settled in Southern Ukraine largely became assimilated with Ukrainians.

In Serbia, Ukrainian settlements were established in the *Bačka and *Srem regions in the mid-18th century.

19th–20th centuries. V. *Karadžić, a Serbian writer, folklorist, and linguist who visited Ukraine in 1819, had a marked effect on the Ukrainian revival and the development of Ukrainian literature, and a particular influence on the members of the *Ruthenian Triad. The first Ukrainian phonetic orthography was developed on the basis of his Serbian orthography. Ya. Holovatsky, M. Kostomarov, and other Ukrainian activists maintained personal relations with their Serbian contemporaries.

In the late 19th century, committees that provided monetary, military, and voluntary assistance to the Serbian (and the general Balkan) movement for liberation from Turkey were formed in many Ukrainian cities. In Kiev such a committee was headed by M. Drahomanov, and in Odessa, by A. *Zheliabov. The poet I. *Manzhura, the actor and director M. *Sadovsky, V. Yanovsky, and other activists participated in Serbian battles against the Turks. In 1876 M. *Starytsky published *Serbs'ki narodni dumy i pisni* (Serbian Folk Dumas and Songs) in Kiev and devoted all proceeds to the Serbian Red Cross. The works of Yu. Fedkovych, I. Franko, O. Pchilka, Lesia Ukrainka, and S. Vorobkevych were influenced by events taking place in Serbia. In the late 19th and early 20th century, Serbian songs and literature were translated into Ukrainian by O. Barvinsky, M. Buchynsky, I. Franko, and O. Navrotsky. Interest in the works of M. Vovchok, T. Shevchenko, and other Ukrainian writers was also growing in Serbia. O. Barvinsky, M. Drahomanov, M. Lysenko, and other Ukrainian community activists were familiar with Serbian writers. Š. Bosković, I. Erdeljanović, B. Milojević, and other Serbian scholars were accepted as full members of the Shevchenko Scientific Society.

After the Second World War M. Rylsky published Ukrainian translations of Serbian poetry in collections, including *Serbs'ki epichni pisni* (Serbian Epic Songs, 1946) and *Serbs'ka narodnia poeziia* (Serbian Folk Poetry, 1955, with L. Pervomaisky). Serbian authors whose works appeared in Ukrainian translation include I. Andrić, B. Copić, and B. Nušić. *Slovo o polku Ihorevi* (The Tale of Ihor's Campaign) and the works of I. Franko, O. Honchar, L. Kostenko, M. Kotsiubynsky, M. Stelmakh, Yu. Yanovsky, and others appeared in Serbian translation. In 1969 the first Serbian edition of T. Shevchenko's *Kobzar* was published. In 1972 M. Kočiš published a Serbian-Croatian-Ruthenian-Ukrainian dictionary in Novi Sad.

A tendency toward Russophilism became firmly entrenched among Serbs and eventually led to an anti-Ukrainian orientation in their politics. In 1917–20 Serbia did not recognize Ukrainian independence and hindered the work of the Ukrainian Red Cross among refugees in Serbia. During the interwar period the Serbian government assistance favored Russian émigrés instead of Ukrainians. After the Second World War Ukrainian organizations were permitted to function, albeit under state supervision; the churches, however, were subject to persecution. Serbo-Ukrainian relations now occur in the context of official relations between Serbia and Ukraine. (See also *Yugoslavia.)

BIBLIOGRAPHY
Hnatiuk, V. 'Znosyny ukraïntsiv z serbamy,' in *Naukovyi zbirnyk prysviachenyi M. Hrushevs'komu* (Lviv 1906)
Shevchenko, F. 'Serby i bolhary u ukraïns'komu kozats'komu viis'ku,' in *Pytannia istoriï ta kul'tury slov'ian*, ed L. Dashkivs'ka (Kiev 1963)
Huts', M. 'Serbo-khorvats'ki narodni pisni v ukraïns'kykh perekladakh (1837–1965),' *Slovians'ke literaturoznavstvo i folkl'orystyka*, 5 (1970)

B. Kravtsiv

Serbs. See Serbia.

Oleksander Serbychenko

Serbychenko, Oleksander [Serbyčenko], b 29 November 1890 in Liubotyn, Valky county, Kharkiv gubernia, d 14 January 1938. Soviet Ukrainian leader. A Bolshevik revolutionary in Kremenchuk and Kharkiv during the First World War, after the February Revolution he was a member of the Kharkiv Council of Workers' and Soldiers' Deputies and the city's Bolshevik Committee. Under Soviet rule he headed the Kremenchuk and, from 1922, the Poltava gubernia executive committees and served as deputy chairman of the Ukrainian SSR Council of People's Commissars. Then he was a member of the All-Ukrainian Central Executive Committee, the Soviet trade representative in Austria, and a member of the CC CP(B)U (1925–33) and a candidate member of its Politburo (1930–3). He was arrested during the Yezhov terror and was most likely executed.

Serbyn. The surname of a number of officials of the Cossack Hetman state during the 17th century. It denoted their Serbian ethnic or national origins; the persons so named were probably not related. Ivan Serbyn was colonel of Lubni regiment (1668–76, with interruptions) and the father-in-law of the Kish otaman I. Sirko. Ivan Serbyn (d 11 June 1665), a Serbian nobleman from Novyi Bazar and a relative of the Serbian metropolitan Gavrilo, was colonel of Bratslav regiment (1657–8, 1663–5). He had arrived in Ukraine as a Serbian captain in 1653, and joined the Cossack armies in their struggle against Poland. A supporter of Hetman I. Vyhovsky, he assisted in the suppression of the rebellion led by M. Pushkar and participated in D. Vyhovsky's attack on Kiev (1658). He was captured and exiled to Muscovy, whence he returned in 1660. In 1664–5 he fought against Hetman P. Teteria and the Poles, and he died in battle near Uman. Voitsa (also Vuitsa, Vuk, or Vuich) Serbyn was colonel of Pereiaslav regiment (1687) and a bitter enemy of Hetman I. Samoilovych. He became general osaul in 1687, after the Kolomak mutiny. He was among the *starshyna* who opposed Hetman I. Mazepa. Mazepa denounced him to the Muscovite tsar, and in 1688 he was discharged and exiled to Sevsk.

Serbyn, Roman, b 21 March 1939 in Vyktoriv, Stanyslaviv county, Galicia. Historian and pedagogue. He studied economics, political science, and history at McGill University (PH D, 1975) and l'Université de Montréal. Since 1969 he has taught Eastern European history at l'Université du Québec à Montréal. In 1967–8 he was president of the Ukrainian Canadian Students' Union and founder and the first editor of its newspaper *Student*. He has researched and written on the 1921 famine in Ukraine, the nationality question in the Soviet Union, Ukrainian-Jewish relations, and student movements and intellectual trends in 19th-century Ukraine. He coedited *Fédéralisme et nations* (1971), *Famine in Ukraine, 1932–1933* (1986), and *Serhii Podolyns'kyi: Vybrani tvory* (Serhii Podolynsky: Selected Works, 1990).

Serbyn, Yakiv, b and d ? Printmaker of the latter half of the 18th century in Kiev. He owned his own printing shop, where he printed and sold, without the censor's approval, his own engraved texts and icons, such as *The Okhtyrka Theotokos, St Nicholas the Miracle Worker,* and *St Barbara.*

Serbyniuk, Yurii [Serbynjuk, Jurij], b 1887 in Sadhora, Bukovyna (now part of Chernivtsi), d ? in Rumania. Political and community activist and journalist. He worked for the UNR government-in-exile in Vienna (1920–1) and served as general secretary of the Ukrainian National party in Rumania (1927–38) and as a member of the Rumanian parliament (1932–3). He edited a number of newspapers in Chernivtsi, including *Hromadianyn* (1909), *Narodnyi holos* (1911–15), *Nova Bukovyna* (1914 and 1918), *Chas* (1929–32), *Narodnia syla* (1932–4), and *Rada* (1934–8). He contributed to the entry on Bukovyna in *Ukraïns'ka zahal'na entsyklopediia* (Ukrainian General Encyclopedia, vol 3, 1935). He emigrated from Chernivtsi to Rumania in 1940. He was imprisoned in the Soviet Union in 1945–54, and then returned to Rumania.

Serczyk, Władysław, b 23 July 1935. Polish historian. A professor of history at Cracow University and then at the Białystok branch of Warsaw University, he is the author of numerous essays and several books on Ukrainian history, including *Koliszczyzna* (Koliivshchyna, 1968), *Hajdamacy* (Haidamakas, 1978), *Historia Ukrainy* (History of Ukraine, 1979), *Połtawa 1709* (Poltava 1709, 1982), and *Na dalekiej Ukrainie: Dzieje Kozaczyny do 1648 r.* (In Faraway Ukraine: History of the Cossacks before 1648, 1984). His work, though sometimes following standard Soviet lines of interpretation, is significant for its attempts to understand objectively Ukrainian-Polish historical relations and its treatment of Ukraine as a distinct political entity whose interests did not necessarily coincide with those of Poland or Russia.

Serdiuk, Oleksa [Serdjuk], b 1884 in the Kuban region, d 1927 in Kiev. Orthodox priest and church activist. After graduating from St Petersburg University he continued his studies abroad. In 1921 he became a priest of the Ukrainian Autocephalous Orthodox church (UAOC) and an organizer of UAOC parishes in the Kuban region. His activities led to his arrest by the GPU. Following a lengthy incarceration and the murder of almost his entire family, he went insane and died in prison.

Oleksander Serdiuk   Antin Sereda

Serdiuk, Oleksander [Serdjuk] (Les), b 27 June 1900 in Bziv, Pereiaslav county, Poltava gubernia, d 14 December 1988 in Kiev. Actor, director, and educator. After completing studies at the Lysenko Music and Drama Institute (1919) he was a leading actor in the Shevchenko First Theater of the Ukrainian Soviet Republic in Kiev (1919–22) and in Berezil (from 1922), later (1935) the Kharkiv Ukrainian Drama Theater, of which he was also artistic director in 1957–62. His repertoire consisted of approx 200 heroic and character roles. In Berezil he played Tom Kittling in *Sekretar profspilky* (The Walking Delegate, based on L. Scott's novel, 1924), Fiesco in F. Schiller's *Die Verschwörung des Fiesco zu Genua* (1928), Mokii in M. Kulish's *Myna Mazailo* (1929), and the title role in W. Shakespeare's *Othello* (1952). He acted the title roles in the films *Prometheus* (1936) and *Nazar Stodolia* (1937). As a director he staged *Oi pidu ia v Boryslavku* (Oh, I'll Go to Boryslavka, based on I. Franko, 1956) and M. Zarudny's *Antei* (Antaeuses, 1961). He taught at the Kharkiv Theater Institute from 1945. A biography, by O. Popova, was published in Kiev in 1979.

Serdiuk, Vasyl [Serdjuk, Vasyl'], b 13 March 1900 in Chernihiv. Actor and scenery designer. He was an officer in the Army of the UNR. He acted in Ukrainian troupes in

West Volhynia (1923–32) and then acted and designed scenery in Lviv in the Zahrava Theater (1933–8), the Kotliarevsky Theater (1938–9), the Lesia Ukrainka Theater (1939–41), and Teatr u Piatnytsiu in Philadelphia (from 1963).

Serdiuk, Yurii [Serdjuk, Jurij], b 15 April 1938 in Lozova, Kharkiv oblast. He graduated from the Gorky Institute of Literature in Moscow (1965), has worked for the Molod publishing house and the Kiev Studio of Documentary-Chronicle Films, and has been a member of the editorial board of *Vitchyzna* and deputy director of the Bureau for the Promotion of Creative Literature of the Writers' Union of Ukraine. He has written the poetry collections *Surmy sertsia* (Trumpets of the Heart, 1965), *Porohy viku* (Thresholds of an Era, 1967), *Svitlytsia* (The Living Room, 1970), *Vse, shcho zi mnoiu* (All That Is with Me, 1972), *Z lirychnoï strichky* (From a Lyrical Stanza, 1976), *Okean* (The Ocean, 1979), and *Vidkrytyi okean* (The Open Ocean, 1983) and the children's storybook *Mors'kyi lev Botsmaniatko* (The Sea Lion Botsmaniatko, 1985).

Serdiuk guard divisions (*Serdiutski dyvizii*). Volunteer elite military units in the Ukrainian armed forces of 1917–18. In November 1917 two serdiuk guard divisions were formed in Kiev, one under the command of Col Yu. Kapkan and the other under Gen O. Hrekov. Together they numbered 12,000 men. Four of their regiments defended Kiev against the Bolsheviks in January 1918; the other regiments remained neutral. Toward the end of the month the two divisions were demobilized by the Central Rada, and some of their soldiers volunteered to the Separate Zaporozhian Detachment.

In July 1918 Hetman P. Skoropadsky formed a new serdiuk division, consisting mostly of volunteers from the wealthier peasantry in Left-Bank Ukraine. By October the division had 5,000 soldiers and was commanded by Col Klymenko. In the uprising against the hetman most of the division changed sides. Some of its men later joined the Siege Corps of Sich Riflemen.

Serdiuk regiments (*serdiutski polky*). Units of mercenary infantry organized by the Hetmanate in the late 17th and early 18th century for military and police duty. They were paid and outfitted by the Hetmanate. The first regiments were organized by P. Doroshenko in Right-Bank Ukraine, and they soon spread to Left-Bank Ukraine as well. Their volunteer soldiers were mainly Ukrainian peasants, Moldavians, and defecting registered Cossacks. There were three or four Serdiuk regiments, each consisting of approx 400 to 500 soldiers. They were used in frontier military campaigns, as guards for the hetman's residence, and as guards at weapons depots. They were responsible directly and only to the hetman. Serdiuk regiments were abolished by a tsarist ukase issued on 14 July 1726.

Serdiukov, Ivan [Serdjukov], b 12 November 1803 in Smilo, Romen county, Poltava gubernia, d 1886 in Mstsislau county, Belarus. Landowner and writer. After studying medicine at Kharkiv University (1822–4) he served in the chancery of N. Repnin, the governor-general of Left-Bank Ukraine, and in other government offices in Poltava. Upon retiring in 1841, he wrote articles on farming, novels, and comedies in both Ukrainian and Russian. He also

compiled a Ukrainian dictionary, which remains unpublished. His autobiographical notes, published posthumously in *Kievskaia starina* (1896, nos 11–12), are a valuable source for the social history of the Poltava region.

Serdiukova, Liudmyla [Serdjukova, Ljudmyla], b 6 May 1899 in Nemovychi, Rivne county, Volhynia gubernia, d 13 July 1984 in Trenton, New Jersey. Stage and film actress; wife of V. Serdiuk. She worked in Ukrainian troupes in western Volhynia (1923–32) and in the Zahrava, Kotliarevsky, Lesia Ukrainka, and Lviv Opera theaters (1933–44) and appeared in the film *Viter zi skhodu* (Wind from the East, 1941). In the United States she led an amateur group in Trenton.

Sereda, Antin, b 11 February 1890 in Shkarivka, Vasylkiv county, Kiev gubernia, d 11 August 1961 in Korsun-Shevchenkivskyi, Cherkasy oblast. Graphic artist, educator, and art scholar. A graduate of the Stroganov School of Applied Art in Moscow (1914), he organized many artistic handicraft workshops in Galicia and Bukovyna (1916–17) and taught at the Kiev Architectural Institute (1920–4), the Kiev State Art Institute (1924–9, 1934–41, 1944–50), and the Ukrainian Printing Institute in Kharkiv (1929–34). Sereda adapted H. *Narbut's ornamentation and lettering but used a simpler line and stronger contrast of white and black in his work. His most successful cover designs were for the journal *Siaivo* (1913), an edition of T. Shevchenko's poetry (1927), and editions of M. Kotsiubynsky's *Fata morgana* (1939), Shevchenko's *Kobzar* (1937), I. Franko's works (25 vols, 1941), and *Slovo o polku Ihorevi* (The Tale of Ihor's Campaign, 1952). He also designed a Ukrainian postage stamp (1918), commercial logos, and ornamental kilims. A retrospective show of his graphics and paintings was held in Kiev in 1969. Sereda also wrote articles on folk art and folk dress and a booklet on Narbut as a book artist (1927).

Sereda, Mykola, b 16 May 1890 in Stari Sanzhary (now Reshetnyky), Poltava county, d 16 February 1948 in Leningrad. Opera singer (lyric tenor). A graduate of the Moscow Conservatory, he was a soloist of the Kharkiv Opera (1926–33), the Sverdlovsk Opera (1933–5), and the Leningrad Opera (1935–48). His main roles included the title role in R. Wagner's *Lohengrin*, Alfred in G. Puccini's *La Traviata*, Lensky in P. Tchaikovsky's *Eugene Onegin*, Levko in N. Rimsky-Korsakov's *May Night*, and Andrii in M. Lysenko's *Taras Bulba*.

Sereda, Vasyl, b 1906 in Pohreby, Pryluka county, Poltava gubernia. Mechanical engineer. He studied and worked at the Kharkiv Institute of Railway-Transport Engineers, where he became assistant director and chaired a department from 1941. His technical contributions were in the fields of railroad machinery, the loading of granular substances, and advanced precision mechanisms. He developed vibrating feeders for loading and unloading grain and published numerous technical papers.

Sereda, Yaroslav, b 28 November 1900 in Radekhiv, Galicia, d 25 March 1981 in Lviv. Petroleum chemist; corresponding member of the AN URSR (now ANU) from 1951. He graduated from the Lviv Polytechnical Institute (1929) and taught there. He worked in Drohobych, Groznyi, Ufa,

Yaroslav Sereda   Serhii Serensen

and Lviv (1935–53) and became head of the petrochemical laboratory at the ANU Institute of the Geology and Geochemistry of Fossil Fuels (1956–63) and director of the surface-active agents laboratory at the Lviv branch of the All-Union Scientific Research and Design Applications Institute for the Petroleum-Processing and Petrochemistry Industry. His research dealt with the chemistry of petroleum processing, especially in mixtures containing sulfonic and naphthenic acids, and mineral oils. He introduced new methods of analysis for sulfur-containing crudes.

Seredenko, Mykhailo, b 21 November 1906 in Kharkiv, d 1983 in Kiev. Economist. After graduating from the Red Professors' Institute he worked in the Party apparat (1935–40) and then in the AN URSR (now ANU) Institute of Economics, where in 1947 he became head of the Department of Industrial Economics. Then he worked at the Scientific Research Institute of Economics of the State Planning Committee of the Ukrainian SSR (1964–82). Seredenko wrote over 100 works, including *Chorna metalurhiia Ukraïny, 1917–1957* (Ferrous Metallurgy of Ukraine, 1917–1957, 1957) and *Voprosy ekonomiki legkoi promyshlennosti Ukrainskoi SSR* (Questions in the Economy of Light Industry of the Ukrainian SSR, 1956, coauthor L. Gorelik), and edited *Promyslovist' Radians'koï Ukraïny za sorok rokiv* (The Industry of the Ukrainian SSR over Forty Years, 1957).

Serednii Stih culture. A Copper Age culture of the mid-4th to mid-3rd millennium BC that existed mainly along the Dnieper River and in the upper Donets River and northern Azov Sea coastal regions. It was first studied in the early 20th century and named after a site on the outskirts of Zaporizhia. Closely related to the Corded-Ware Pottery cultures of western Europe, the people of this culture made pottery with characteristic rope imprint decorations. They are also notable for being among the first people in Europe to ride on horses. Burials were in flat graves with the deceased placed in a supine position with flexed legs. Excavations at sites revealed copper adornments, earthenware figures of humans and animals, and battle axes made from antlers.

Serednytsky, Antin [Serednyc'kyj] (pseuds: Antin Verba, Antin Bilchuk), b 1 March 1916 in Verbivka, Borshchiv county, Galicia. Ukrainian writer, educator, and commu-

nity figure in postwar Poland. He graduated from Warsaw University (1948) and became a teacher in Warsaw. In 1960 he became an associate of the Warsaw University department of Ukrainian philology. He developed the curriculum for teaching Ukrainian in Poland's elementary and secondary schools, and in 1966 he was appointed deputy head of the Ukrainian Language Curriculum Commission of the Polish Ministry of Education. In the years 1969–87 he published an elementary-school Ukrainian grammar and seven Ukrainian readers. He has also played a prominent role in the *Ukrainian Social and Cultural Society (USKT [now OUP]) in Poland; for several terms he has been its vice-president and head of its literary association, and he was chief editor (1962–87) of its annual, *Ukraïns'kyi kalendar*. He is a member of the Union of Polish Writers. His works have been published in Soviet Ukrainian and OUP periodicals and separately. They include the story collections *Proidenym shliakhom* (The Road Traveled, 1976) and *Mandrivka do Chaichynets'* (A Trip to Chaichyntsi, 1984). His literary criticism and reviews have appeared in the Polish press and scholarly journals. He has received several Polish medals and citations for his contributions.

Seredyna-Buda. I-15. A city (1989 pop 9,000) on the Bobryk River and a raion center in Sumy oblast. It was founded in the 1660s by Old Believers from Muscovy. For over a hundred years the village belonged to Starodub regiment. With the abolition of the Hetman state it became part of Novhorod-Siverskyi vicegerency (1782–96), Little Russia gubernia (1796–1802), and Chernihiv gubernia (1802–1925). By the end of the 19th century soap, hempoil, leather, and milling enterprises had been established in the town. A railway link encouraged the development of lumbering at the turn of the 20th century. In 1964 the town attained city status. Today about a third of its work force is employed in industries, such as machine building, metalworking, food processing, forest products, and sewing.

Serensen, Serhii, b 29 August 1905 in Khabarovsk, Primore oblast, Far East, d 2 May 1977 in Moscow. Mechanics scientist; full member of the AN URSR (now ANU) from 1939. He graduated from the Kiev Polytechnical Institute (1926) and worked at the ANU Institute of Construction Mechanics (as director in 1934–41). He taught at aviation institutes in Kiev (1934–41) and Moscow (1934–77) and worked at the State Scientific Research Institute of Machine Science (1967–77). He calculated the load capacities of machine elements, fatigue effects, and failure modes.

Seret (Rumanian: Siret). VI-7. A town (1965 pop 6,200) on the Seret River in south Bukovyna, Rumania. According to archeological evidence the site has been inhabited since the Neolithic Period. It is first mentioned in historical documents in 1334. In 1365–88 it was the capital of Moldavia, and in 1370–1435, the seat of a Catholic diocese. Under Austrian rule (1774–1918) Seret was a county administrative center of Bukovyna crownland (1868–1918). At the beginning of the 20th century branches of the Ruska Besida and Ukrainska Shkola societies were active in Seret. Ukrainian was taught at the German gymnasium and a Ukrainian bursa was open to out-of-town students. In 1910 Ukrainians accounted for 41.8 percent of the population of Seret county. In 1918 all Bukovyna, including Seret, was occupied by Rumania. The Greek Catholic administrator, K. Zlepko, was stationed in Seret (1923–30). In 1940 Seret county was divided between Rumania and the Ukrainian SSR, and Seret, along with some 14 Ukrainian villages, remained in Rumania. In the 1950s parallel Ukrainian courses were offered at the gymnasium and teachers' college in Seret. The town's architectural monuments include the Church of the Holy Trinity (1358) and St John's Church (1377).

The Seret River

Seret River. A left-bank tributary of the Dniester River that winds along the Podolian Upland almost entirely through Ternopil oblast. It is 242 km long and drains a basin area of 3,900 sq km. The cities of Ternopil and Chortkiv and a hydroelectric station are located on the river. Its waters are used in industry and for irrigation.

Serf theater (*kripatskyi teatr*). A type of theater that appeared in eastern Ukraine in the 18th century with the imposition of serfdom in the former Hetman state. In the manner of their Russian counterparts Ukrainian landlords adopted the serf theater, themselves acting as directors; the serf theater repertoire consisted mainly of Russian, French, and Italian plays imported by the landlords from Moscow, St Petersburg, and the West, ranging from dramas and operas to ballet. The actors and musicians were illiterate peasants, and the costumes and scenery were the work of local serf craftsmen. Ukrainian plays were occasionally staged – dramas by I. Kotliarevsky and H. Kvitka-Osnovianenko and vaudevilles by V. Hohol-Yanovsky and D. Dmytrenko – particularly in the Kharkiv region. The best-known serf theater troupes were maintained in the Chernihiv region, by D. Shyrai in Spyrydonova Buda, A. Budliansky in Pantusove, and H. Tarnavsky in Kachanivka; in the Poltava region, by D. Troshchynsky in Kybyntsi; in the Zhytomyr region, by A. Ilinsky in Romanove (some actors of his troupe even received their musical education in Italy); and in the Kharkiv region, by A. Khorvat in Holovatyne. Serf theaters disappeared in the mid-19th century, but not before they had facilitated the emergence of professional theater in Ukraine and produced scores of well-trained actors.

Serfdom. A form of peasant servitude and dependence on the upper landowning classes that was characteristic of the feudal system and existed in different parts of Europe from the medieval period to the 19th century. The degree of subservience and the prevalence of the serf-lord relation differed with time and country according to natural, economic, social, and political conditions. In Ukraine serfdom developed first in the territories ruled by Poland. Under the Polish system of serfdom the peasants were bound by law to their plots of land, which were owned by the lord. The amount of obligatory labor (corvée) owed by the peasant to the lord depended on the size and quality of the peasant's plot, but the amount of labor effectively exacted was often arbitrary. The Russian system of serfdom, which was established in most Ukrainian territories under Russian rule at the end of the 18th century, was based on the principle that the lord owned the peasant under his control. He could dispose of his serfs as he wished: he could even separate them from their land. The amount of labor owed by the peasants and the size of their allotments depended on the number of adult males in their families.

Medieval period. In Kievan Rus', the Principality of Galicia-Volhynia, and the Grand Duchy of Lithuania the larger households of the princes and boyars usually produced enough to meet only their own needs, and the work was done mostly by slaves or by semifree *nepokhozhi* peasants of different types (*zakupy, izhoi, siabry,* etc). The bulk of the peasants lived on their own land and paid tribute in kind or money to the ruling prince. The free *pokhozhi* peasants sometimes had to provide unpaid labor for the construction of fortifications and roads and in emergencies were called to bear arms in a levy en masse.

Under Polish rule. As Polish rule spread throughout Ukraine in the second half of the 15th and in the 16th centuries, the position of the peasantry in Ukrainian territories changed radically. In Poland alodial land ownership was already an established privilege of the ruling class. The nobility had been exempted from any form of conditional (feudal) land tenure, and the peasants had been deprived of their former rights to land. The Polish magnates and nobles extended their serf system to Western Ukraine and, after the Union of Lublin in 1569, to Right-Bank Ukraine as well. To equalize the obligations of the different categories of peasant, the *voloka* land reform was introduced in 1557 in Ukrainian territories and was implemented gradually over the next century. Polish nobles set up *filvarky* on the better lands and began to specialize in grain farming for export. The nobles' diets of 1496, 1505, 1519, and 1520 issued decrees tying the peasants ever more closely to the land, depriving them of the right to move, subjecting them completely to the nobles' courts, and increasing their obligations to the nobles. Finally, the amount of labor owed by the serfs and all other matters affecting them were left to the decision of the nobles, their tenants, or their stewards. A uniform system of serf obligations and relations was maintained on the royal estates, where serfs received better treatment than on the private estates of the nobility.

The obligations imposed on the serfs rose steeply in cases where a tenant, not the landowner, managed the estate. Although the plots of the serfs gradually shrank, their obligations were not lowered. In 1566, 58 percent of the peasant farms in Galicia consisted of more than a half field (*pivlan*). By 1648 only 38 percent were of that size, by

1665 only 16 percent, and by 1765 only 11 percent. At the end of the 16th century the typical serf allotment was a half field. Almost 41 percent of the serf plots were of that size, and 24 percent were a quarter field. Either allotment called for draft corvée with ox or horse. The larger plots required corvée with a pair of draft animals and were therefore known as *parovi* (pair). The smaller ones were called *poiedynky* (single). Depending on the period and the locality, the amount of corvée varied from three to six days per week by one or more members of a household. The poorer serfs, such as the *horodnyky and *komornyky, with smaller or no field allotments, provided one to six days of pedestrian corvée per week. The weekly corvée quota, other seasonal or special forms of labor, and additional *quitrent varied with the territory and even the estate, as did the size of the allotments. In the 1620s, corvée on magnate estates in Volhynia came to four to six days per week per *voloka* (16.8 ha) of land, but some lords demanded labor every day of the week, including holidays. Farther eastward the serf plots became larger, the corvée became smaller, and the bond to the plot grew weaker. In the 16th and 17th centuries there were three distinct serfdom belts in Ukrainian territories. In Western Ukraine, where the *filvarky* were most developed, the peasants were exploited intensely and had the smallest allotments. In the middle belt, encompassing eastern Podilia and the northwestern Kiev region, mixed (alodial and conditional) land tenure lasted longer, and the transition to *filvarok* farming was slower. The large landowners there were usually content to receive payment in kind, and the peasants were not completely or uniformly deprived of the right to own land. In the third belt, covering the lands along the Dnieper and the Boh rivers in southwestern Ukraine, serfdom was difficult to impose: because of the proximity of the steppes and the constant danger of Tatar attack, the population was too mobile. North of the defensive line of castles many estates in the second and third belts offered 15-, 20-, or 30-year waivers from corvée or other obligations in order to attract and hold settlers.

The Hetman period. As the serfs became increasingly exploited in the western and middle belt, and as the corvée waivers expired or were foreshortened by the landowners, the peasants fled to the territories under Cossack control and joined Cossack uprisings. Those conditions contributed to the Cossack-Polish War. The peasantry participated in the war on a mass scale. Some of the peasant combatants joined the Cossack ranks and along with new Cossacks from the other estates demanded open access to land and other Cossack privileges. Former serfs who failed to gain admission to the Cossack estate first took possession of free lands in the liberated territories. But in their universals B. Khmelnytsky and his successors called upon former serfs to return in certain cases to the service of the monasteries and the nobles who recognized the Cossack state. Generally, peasant obligations in the Hetman state during the second half of the 17th and the beginning of the 18th century were light. The serf-lord relationship and the corvée depended on the kind of village and on its owner. A large number of *pospolyti, who performed corvée for the state, could own property. The Cossack *starshyna*, who received rank estates, demanded labor from their subjects. Many peasants from Western Ukraine and Right-Bank Ukraine, which were retained by Poland, fled to the Hetman state or to Slobidska Ukraine.

Most of them settled as *landless peasants on the estates of the Cossack *starshyna* or monasteries. According to the 1729–30 census of the Hetman state only 35 percent of the peasant farmers were subject to private landowners, and not all of those were required to perform corvée. Hetman I. Mazepa's universal in 1701 prohibited more than two days' corvée per week. Gradually the peasants in Hetman Ukraine lost the right to dispose of their land and, eventually, their freedom as well. In the 1740s the *pospolyti* could still move from one landowner, to another but had to leave their property (land and inventory) behind. The Cossack officers and monasteries made every effort to attach the peasants to the land, and the process was reinforced by the Russian government, which was interested in extending the imperial serf system to Ukraine.

In Right-Bank Ukraine, particularly in Volhynia, B. Khmelnytsky's uprising in 1648 brought no basic changes in the position of the peasantry. During the 18th century the *filvarok* system was restored, and the corvée demands on the serfs increased.

Under Russian rule. By the decree of 3 May 1783 Catherine II introduced the Russian serf system in the territory of the former Hetman state, and in 1785 the Cossack *starshyna* received the rights of the Russian nobility. After the Second and Third partitions of Poland the Russian serf system was extended to Right-Bank Ukraine. According to official estimates made in 1858, 60 percent of the serfs belonged to landowners, and 40 percent lived on state or appanage lands. Of the landowners' serfs only 1.2 percent paid quitrent, and the rest did corvée. State peasants usually paid quitrent. During the first half of the 19th century the land allotted to peasants diminished to the advantage of the *filvarky*, corvée increased, and the number of landless peasants rose sharply. Corvée and the poll tax rose on average to between four and six labor days per week. The norm (*urochna*) system of labor was widely adopted. Many peasants, known as *misiachnyky*, lost their land and worked only on the lord's demesne for a monthly ration of products. Others became household serfs, who worked and lived in the lord's manor. The landowners increased corvée to cover the state-imposed poll tax and tax arrears. In a separate manifesto in 1797 the Russian government proposed that the landowners limit their demands on the peasants to a three-day corvée. In 1819 it clarified some aspects of the serf-lord relationship. Those and other manifestos were largely ignored by the landowners. In 1847–8 the government issued the so-called Inventory Regulations for Right-Bank Ukraine, which diminished the personal dependence of the peasants on their masters, lowered the corvée and regulated it according to the household allotments, prohibited the transfer of corvée from one week to another, abolished certain payments, and prohibited the conversion of ordinary serfs into household serfs. Infringement of the regulations was punishable by military court, yet the position of the serfs hardly changed.

Transcarpathia. Serfdom was practiced in Transcarpathia from the 14th century. In the first half of the 16th century the serfs were bound to the land, and the corvée was greatly increased. In 1546 Stephan Werböczy codified the laws governing the serf-lord relation in the Tripartitum Code. A serf had to pay the state a household tax (*podymne*), the church a tithe (one-tenth of his grain), and his lord one-tenth of his income and perform usually three days' corvée per week. The burdens placed on the peasants, however, varied with external conditions (diminishing in wartime) and the will of the landowner.

The condition of the serfs improved after 1767, when Maria Theresa restored their right to resettle, defined their obligations, and reduced corvée by half. In 1848 the Hungarian Diet abolished corvée, but the law did not come into effect until 1853.

Bukovyna. Under Moldavian rule the peasants in Bukovyna usually performed 12 days of corvée per year and paid the lord one-tenth of their harvest. But they were free to move. The serf system introduced in 1544 was less exploitive than the Polish one, and as a result many peasants from Pokutia and Podilia escaped to Bukovyna. In 1749 the Moldavian ruler K. Mavrokordatos (Mavrocordat) abolished serfdom and imposed 24 days of corvée per year and a tax. According to the Golden Charter of Voivode G. Ghica in 1766, peasants were obliged to do 12 days of corvée and to surrender one-tenth of their harvest. That law was in effect until 1848.

Galicia and Bukovyna under Austrian rule. To increase tax revenues and improve the recruit pool for the army in the newly annexed lands, Maria Theresa and Joseph II tried to regulate serf-lord relations and to limit the dependence of the peasant on the landowner. In the 1780s a cadastre and a survey of serf obligations were carried out. The land belonging to landowners was separated from the *rustical lands reserved for the peasants, and transfers from one category to the other were prohibited. The serf's personal dependency on the lord was restricted, and he was allowed to appeal to state institutions against the lord's verdicts. Corvée was limited to a fixed number of days depending on the size of the land allotment, and additional burdens were abolished. The peasant acquired the right to sell his products freely. Village communities were given new powers of self-government. A special ombudsman (*mandator*) was appointed to look after the affairs of the peasants. Many of the reforms were ignored by the successors of Joseph II. His decree limiting serf obligations to 30 percent of the serf's total income was revoked. In spite of the law, by 1848 the landowners annexed to their *filvarky* about a million morgen of rustical land.

At the beginning of the 19th century 78 percent of the serf families in Galicia were attached to private estates, and 22 percent to state lands. The peasants were divided, according to amount of property and number of obligations, into *parovi* (pair) serfs (2.5 percent of all households, possessing 6.9 percent of the rustical lands), *poiedynky* (single) serfs (42.6 and 60.5 percent respectively), pedestrian serfs (45.9 and 32.6 percent), and the landless *komirnyky* and *khalupnyky* (9 percent of households). On the average a peasant household had to till 2 ha of the lord's land and perform 78 days of corvée per year on state lands and 133 days, and sometimes as much as 300 days, on private estates. Most (68.2 percent) of the peasant's obligations consisted of corvée, 26.6 percent of monetary payments, and 5.2 percent of other services and fees. The lord sometimes made further (illegal) exactions from the peasants by imposing various fines and by forcing them to buy a certain amount of alcohol (see *Propination).

Abolition of serfdom. The abolition of serfdom in Galicia, Bukovyna, and Transcarpathia on 16 April 1848 was speeded up by the revolutionary events in Austria. In Russia the political repercussions of the Crimean War brought about the emancipation of the serfs on 19 February 1861. But the *redemption payments and the continued social inequality of the peasants diminished the impact of those reforms and hindered the economic progress of the peasantry. (See also *Peasants.)

BIBLIOGRAPHY
Lazarevskii, A. 'Malorossiskie pospolitye krest'iane (1643–1783),' *Zapiski Chernigovskogo statisticheskogo komiteta*, 1 (1866)
Trifil'ev, E. *Ocherki iz istorii krepostnogo prava v Rossii* (Kharkiv 1904)
Franko, I. *Panshchyna ta ïi skasuvanie 1848 r. v Halychyni* (Lviv 1913)
Miakotin, V. *Ocherki siotsial'noi istorii Ukrainy XVII–XVIII st.*, 3 vols (Prague 1924)
Slabchenko, M. *Materiialy do ekonomicho-sotsial'noï istoriï Ukraïny XIX st.*, 2 vols (Odessa 1925, 1927)
Hejnosz, W. *Zagadnienie niewoli na Rusi Czerwonej pod koniec średniowiecza w świetle stosunków prawnych Polski krajów sąsiednich* (Lviv 1933)
Hurzhii, I. *Rozklad feodal'no-kriposnyts'koï systemy v sil's'komu hospodarstvi Ukraïny pershoï polovyny XIX st.* (Kiev 1954)
Blum, J. *Lord and Peasant in Russia from the Ninth to the Nineteenth Century* (Princeton 1961)
Rozdolski, R. *Stosunki poddáncze w dawnej Galicji*, 2 vols (Warsaw 1962)
Kolchin, P. *Unfree Labor: American Slavery and Russian Serfdom* (Cambridge, Mass 1987)

I. Vytanovych

Sergeev, Nikolai, b 1855 in Kharkiv, d 1919. Painter. He studied at the St Petersburg Academy of Arts and cofounded the Kuindzhi Artists' Society (1909). He painted Ukrainian landscapes, such as *Water Mill, Cossack Village,* and *Apiary in Ukraine* (1885).

Sergeevich, Vasilii [Sergeevič, Vasilij], b 1832 in Orel, Russia, d 26 November 1910 in St Petersburg. Russian legal historian. After graduating from the law faculty of Moscow University (1857) he taught state law at the universities of Moscow (1868–72) and St Petersburg, where he also served as dean (1888–97) and rector (1897–9). He wrote many valuable works on the law of Rus', including *Veche i kniaz': Russkoe gosudarstvennoe ustroistvo i upravlenie vo vremena kniazei Riurikovichei* (Assembly and Prince: The Russian State System and Government in the Era of the Riurykides, 1867), *Lektsii i issledovaniia po drevnei istorii russkogo prava* (Lectures and Research in the Ancient History of Russian Law, 1883), *Russkie iuridicheskie drevnosti* (Russian Juridical Antiquities, 3 vols, 1890–1903), and *Drevnosti russkogo prava* (Antiquities of Russian Law, 3 vols, 1908–9). He also wrote works on land ownership, serfdom, and rural life in Rus'.

Serhiienko, Hryhorii [Serhijenko, Hryhorij], b 6 April 1925 in Voronyntsi, Orzhytsia raion, Poltava oblast. Historian. He studied at Kiev University (1949–57) and worked for the Chief Archival Administration of Ukraine (1957–61). After defending his candidate's dissertation (1961) he worked for the AN URSR (now ANU) as managing editor of history, archeology, and ethnography in its publishing house, as consultant to its presidium, and as chairman of the feudal history department at its Institute of History (since 1974). He has published numerous works, among them monographs on social liberation movements in late 17th- and early 18th-century Right-Bank Ukraine (1963), society and politics in Ukraine after the Decembrist revolt

(1971), the Decembrists and their revolutionary traditions in Ukraine (1975), the Decembrists and T. Shevchenko (1980), Shevchenko and the Cyril and Methodius Brotherhood (1983), and Shevchenko in Kiev (1987). He has also coedited the institute's multivolume histories of Ukraine, of its cities and villages, and of Kiev.

Serhiienko, Ivan [Serhijenko], b 13 August 1936 in Bilotserkivtsi, near Pyriatyn, now in Poltava oblast. Cyberneticist and computer scientist; full member of the ANU (formerly AN URSR) since 1988. He graduated from Kiev University (1959) and has worked at the ANU Institute of Cybernetics (since 1952), and has taught at Kiev University (since 1970). He has contributed significant theoretical papers on cybernetics and the theory of computing. In particular he has developed new methods of numerical analysis and automated systems design.

Oleksander Serhiienko   Archbishop Teodosii Serhiiv

Serhiienko, Oleksander [Serhijenko], b 25 June 1932 in Tetkino, Kursk oblast, RSFSR. Human-rights activist and political prisoner. An art restorer by profession, he was arrested in January 1972 in Kiev for his participation in the human-rights movement, and sentenced in June to seven years in labor camps in Perm oblast and in Vladimir prison near Moscow, and three years' exile in the Khabarovsk territory in far eastern Siberia. While incarcerated, he was active in prisoners' protests and authored several appeals and declarations. His mother, O. *Meshko, wrote appeals in his defense that were circulated in Soviet samvydav and published in the West.

Serhiienko, Petro [Serhijenko], b 17 February 1902 in Vovchyk, Lubni county, Poltava gubernia, d 1 January 1984 in Kiev. Actor and pedagogue. He completed study at the Lysenko Music and Drama Institute (1931) and then worked in the Kiev Ukrainian Drama Theater (1932–75, with small interruptions), where he led the studio. He taught in the Kiev Institute of Theater Arts and the Kiev Conservatory (opera studio). He played a variety of character and morality roles, from Yarchuk in I. Mykytenko's *Sol'o na fleiti* (Solo on a Flute) to Marquis Poza in F. Schiller's *Don Carlos*, and acted in the film *V stepakh Ukraïny* (In the Steppes of Ukraine, 1952, adapted from O. Korniichuk's play).

Serhiienko, Raisa [Serhijenko, Rajisa], b 13 July 1925 in Novoukrainka, Kirovohrad okruha, d 20 March 1987 in Odessa. Opera and concert singer (lyric-dramatic soprano). After graduating from the Odessa Conservatory in 1951, she joined the Odessa Opera and Ballet Theater and appeared in roles such as Natalka in M. Lysenko's *Natalka from Poltava*, Odarka in S. Hulak-Artemovsky's *Zaporozhian Cossack beyond the Danube*, Maria in P. Tchaikovsky's *Mazeppa*, and Mariana in H. Maiboroda's *Arsenal*.

Serhiiv, Teodosii [Serhijiv, Teodosij], b 1890, d 1938? Orthodox church hierarch. He was ordained bishop of Pryluka under the jurisdiction of the Patriarchal Russian Orthodox church in 1923, and then switched to the Living (Synodal) church in 1924 and served briefly as its bishop in Poltava. Later that same year he again changed affiliations and joined the Ukrainian Autocephalous Orthodox church as a bishop of Pereiaslav (1924–8) and then Berdychiv (1928–30). From 1933 he worked as a parish priest in the Poltava region. In 1936 he was arrested and sent to a labor camp in the Kolyma region, where he died.

Serho. See Stakhanov.

Serov, Aleksandr, b 23 January 1820 in St Petersburg, d 1 February 1871 in St Petersburg. Russian composer, musicologist, and critic. A lawyer by training and initially by profession, he became one of the leading Russian musicians of the mid-19th century and perhaps the foremost music critic of his day. A strong promoter of 'Russian' music, he used also Ukrainian themes and prepared a study of Ukrainian music for the journal *Osnova in 1861. His Ukrainian works include the opera *May Night*, based on Gogol's writings (written in 1852–3 but never produced and later destroyed); several fragments ('Hopak,' 'Hrechanyky,' and 'Zaporozhian Cossack Dance') from his unrealized opera *Taras Bul'ba*; 'Little Russian Dances' for piano; and arrangements of numerous Ukrainian folk songs for chorus and orchestra. In 1861 he conducted a symphony concert in St Petersburg to raise money for the family of his deceased friend, T. Shevchenko.

Serov, Ivan, b August 1905 in Afimskaia, Vologda gubernia, Russia, d ? Stalinist functionary and general. A graduate of the Leningrad military school (1928), in the 1930s he served as a regimental commander and in Stalin's personal secretariat. Under N. Khrushchev's patronage he became a member of the CC CP(B)U Politburo and the NKVD commissar in Ukraine (1940–1) in charge of mass repressions and terror in Ukraine. As the first deputy commissar of state security (1941–5) and then internal affairs (1946–54) in Moscow, he was responsible for the mass deportation of the Volga Germans, Chechens, Ingush, Crimean Tatars, and Kalmyks. In 1945–6 he was deputy commander-in-chief of the Soviet occupational forces in Germany and oversaw *SMERSH operations, the repatriation of Soviet refugees, and the deportation of German scientists. After serving as KGB chairman (1954–8), he was put in charge of military intelligence. In 1963 he was dismissed from his job and in 1965 he was expelled from the Party for crimes committed under Stalin's regime.

Serpilin, Leonyd, b 4 April 1912 in Kiev, d 27 February 1973 in Kiev. Writer and journalist. He completed studies at the Kiev Civil-Engineering Institute in 1937. During the Second World War he was a correspondent for the newspaper *Radians'ka Ukraïna* and then became editor of *Literaturna Ukraïna*. He is the author of collections of short stories, such as *Shliakh druzhby* (The Path of Friendship, 1949) and *Ser'ozhchyna radist'* (Serozha's Joy, 1958); novels, such as *Svitanok* (Dawn, 1947), *Kliatva nad bahattiam* (Oath by the Bonfire, 1951), *Zolota osin'* (Golden Autumn, 1960), and *Vohnyk na uzlissi* (The Little Fire at the Edge of the Forest, 1967); and the romance novel *Budivnychi* (The Builders, 1955).

Serradella, common (*Ornithopus sativus*; Ukrainian: *seradelia*). An annual plant of the family Leguminosae. In Ukraine it is planted primarily in the sandy soil of Polisia for forage and green fodder.

Servetnyk, Stanyslav, b 6 October 1928 in Kurnyky, Proskuriv okruha. Muralist and stained-glass artist. A graduate of the Lviv Institute of Applied and Decorative Arts (1956), he decorated the interior of the Building of Culture in Rusiv (1964, with H. Levytska), created the stained-glass windows and decorative panels in the Dytiachyi Svit store in Lviv (1965), and painted the wall panel *Bathing* in the pavilion on Hlynna Navariia Lake, near Lviv (1966). He has also done easel paintings and book illustrations.

Service industry. A branch of the economy that provides various consumer services. In the official reporting of economic statistics in the USSR, it included such services as car repairs, tailoring, house painting and maintenance, haircutting and hairdressing, dry cleaning, photography, consumer-goods repairs (eg, televisions, radios, watches, bicycles), and some transportation services. The services were provided by state enterprises and co-operatives. In 1988 there were 892 co-operatives of the service industry in Ukraine.

In general the service industry was considered to be one of the worst developed sectors of the Soviet economy. According to official statistics the total value of such services in Ukraine in 1987 was 2.25 billion rubles, or approx 44 rubles per capita. Although the value of services increased steadily in the last years of the USSR – the respective figures for 1975 were 1.06 billion and 25, and for 1980, 1.52 billion and 31 – the supply of services still lagged considerably behind that in the developed countries. The number of service enterprises increased from 58,342 in 1980 to 63,196 in 1987. Services were especially inadequate in the countryside: per capita levels there were approx 33 rubles in 1987, compared with 49 rubles in the cities. By sector, shoe repairs accounted for approx 10.5 percent of the value produced by the industry, tailoring for 18.5 percent, housing construction and repairs for 10.3 percent, consumer-goods and vehicle repairs for 8.1 percent, and hairdressing and -cutting for 7.5 percent (1980).

The unavailability of services and their inferior quality led to the growth of a large private (black market) sector in the USSR. In recent years economic reforms have stimulated the development of a legitimate private sector in the service industry. Many private services have sprung up in Ukraine in the late 1980s and early 1990s.

Service tree. See Mountain ash.

Servitudes. Rights contained in customary or civil law to specified limited use of other people's property. In the past, peasants were allowed to use a landowner's lands for certain purposes. In Ukraine peasants usually had the right to gather wood in forests and to herd livestock in pasture and meadows owned by landowners. The 1848 land reforms in Austria granted the peasants land but did not settle the question of ownership for forests and pastures. The landowners claimed exclusive rights to these lands and demanded compensation in fees or services from the peasants for the use of them. This led to serious conflicts between landowners and peasants. In 1853 the landlords were ordered by imperial patent to compensate the peasants for the loss of servitudes with monetary payments or grants of land. Special commissions were set up to oversee the elimination of servitudes, and their work continued to 1890. Out of 30,733 claims, the commissions rejected 11,205 and settled the rest, usually by setting low indemnity payments or small transfers of forests and pasture to the peasant communities. In Galicia the peasants received altogether 1.2 million florins, 94,100 ha of forest, and 67,000 ha of grazing land for servitudes from the landowners. In some regions, particularly mountain regions, servitudes were brought under state regulation.

In Russian-ruled Ukraine, servitudes were common in Right-Bank Ukraine, which had been under Polish rule until the late 18th century, but were rare in Left-Bank Ukraine, where land was more abundant and the nobility's control over it more tenuous. Following the emancipation of the peasantry in 1861, pasture and hayfields were to be shared by landlords and peasants as before. In 1886 the Senate granted the landlords complete control over these lands, and the peasants were forced to pay for their use in fees or services.

I. Vytanovych

Seseli (Ukrainian: *zhabrytsia*). A genus of smooth perennial herbs of the family Umbelliferae, native to temperate and cold climatic regions of the Old World, with ternately compound leaves and white flowers. Eleven of its 50 species grow in Ukraine, the most common being *S. arenarium* in the steppe and forest-steppe and *S. lehmannii*, which is endemic to the Crimea.

Sevastopil or **Sevastopol** [Sevastopil' or Sevastopol']. IX-14. A city (1990 pop 361,000) and port on the Black Sea in the Crimea. The region was inhabited by the Taurians from the beginning of the 1st millennium BC. In the 5th century BC the Greek colony of *Chersonese Taurica was established at the site. In 1784, after annexing the Crimea, Catherine II ordered the fortress and naval port of Sevastopil to be built at the site of the Tatar village of Akhtiar. In 1804 it became the home of the Russian Black Sea Fleet. The city grew from 30,000 inhabitants at the beginning of the century to 47,400 in 1853. During the Crimean War (1853–6) the city was almost completely destroyed. After the war it was demilitarized. In the 1870s its naval facilities were rebuilt and expanded, and a railway connecting it with the grain-growing interior was constructed. The population of the city grew rapidly, from 11,000 in 1875 to 53,000 in 1897. Many of the residents were naval personnel. During the First World War the city was occupied by

Sevastopil

the Germans (May–November 1918), the Allied Powers (November 1918 to April 1919), and A. Denikin's forces (June 1919 to November 1920) before it was taken, finally, by the Red Army. On 29 April 1918, just before the German occupation, the Ukrainian flag was raised on the ships of the Black Sea Fleet in Sevastopil. After the war the city's port and industries were rebuilt, by 1928. Its population grew from 96,700 in 1926 to 112,000 in 1941. During the Second World War Sevastopil resisted the Germans for eight months before surrendering in July 1942. After its recapture in May 1944 the city was in ruins. In 1945–55 it was rebuilt and expanded. By 1959 its population had reached 148,000 (19 percent Ukrainian, 76 percent Russian).

Sevastopil is a picturesque city stretched out along the northern and southern shores of Sevastopil Bay. Many of its buildings are finished in white limestone, and the broad avenues are lined with trees. The port is one of the finest natural ports on the Black Sea and can accommodate the largest ships. The city is an important trading and manufacturing center in southern Ukraine. It has a significant food industry, with large fish-processing and canning plants, wineries, and meat packing plants; a machine-building industry; ship repair yards; an electric power industry; and a building-materials industry. As a commercial port in the Crimea it is second only to Teodosiia. Its chief research institutions are the Sevastopil Biological Station, the Marine Hydrophysical Institute, with its aquarium, and a branch of the Oceanography Institute. It supports two Russian theaters and four major museums: the *Khersones Historical-Archeological Museum, the Sevastopil Art Museum, the Museum of the Black Sea Fleet (est 1869), and the Museum of the Defense of Sevastopil. The main architectural monuments are the Doric Cathedral of ss Peter and Paul (1843–8), the quay Grafska Prystan (1846), and the Sevastopil Panorama (1905).

Sevastopil Art Museum (Sevastopilskyi khudozhnii muzei). A museum in Sevastopil, founded as the Sevastopil Picture Gallery in 1927. It replaced the People's Art Museum in Yalta (est 1922), which consisted of nationalized private collections from the summer homes and palaces of Crimea. The gallery was renamed in 1965. Housed in a turn-of-the-century four-story building in the eclectic

style, it contains over 4,000 works of painting, graphic art, sculpture, and applied art in its departments of Russian and Ukrainian prerevolutionary art, Soviet art, and Western European art, including works by M. Samokysh, S. Vasylkivsky, V. Orlovsky, V. Tropinin, I. Aivazovsky, I. Kramskoi, O. Murashko, P. Levchenko, M. Hlushchenko, T. Yablonska, V. Kasiian, I. Kavaleridze, P. Slota, A. Kashshai, P. Sulymenko, S. Shyshko, and V. Zaretsky. An album of paintings in the museum was published in Kiev in 1986.

Sevastopil Biological Station. See Institute of the Biology of Southern Seas of the Academy of Sciences of the Ukrainian SSR.

Ihor Ševčenko

Ševčenko, Ihor, b 10 February 1922 in Radość, Poland. Byzantine scholar and pedagogue; foreign member of the AN URSR (now ANU) since 1991. A graduate of Charles University in Prague (1945) and the University of Leuven in Belgium (1949), from 1949 he taught in the United States at the universities of California and Michigan, Columbia University, and (from 1965) Harvard. In 1973 he became an associate director of the Harvard Ukrainian Research Institute. His essays have been published in the collections *Society and Intellectual Life in Late Byzantium* (1981), *Ideology, Letters, and Culture in the Byzantine World* (1982), and *Byzantium and the Slavs in Letters and Culture* (1991). He has written articles about relations between Byzantium and Kievan Rus'. His translation of G. Orwell's *Animal Farm* into Ukrainian (1947) was the first foreign-language translation of that work. A festschrift in Ševčenko's honor, titled *Okeanos*, was published in 1983.

Seven Years' War. In the years 1756–63 England and Prussia fought against a coalition of France, Austria, Russia, and other nations seeking political influence, some of whom were desirous of maintaining their colonial systems. The war spread beyond Europe to the French and English colonies in North America and the Indies. As a result of the conflict Prussia emerged as a powerful force in Europe.

Despite Hetman K. *Rozumovsky's efforts to have Ukraine remain neutral he was forced to provide troops for the Russian army's invasion of East Prussia. In 1757 he sent 8,000 Ukrainian peasants into the war, most of whom died. The regular Cossack forces, including the Chernihiv, Chuhuiv, Kiev, and Nizhen regiments, took part in various campaigns; they were a deciding factor in the victory at Gross-Jägersdorf on 30 August 1757. On 9 October 1760

Berlin was captured by Cossack divisions serving in the Russian army.

H. *Orlyk participated in the war as a French general. He died in 1759 from wounds received at the Battle of Bergen.

Seven-year school (*semyrichna shkola*). In Soviet Ukraine, a seven-grade incomplete-secondary school, established in 1920 and in existence until 1958 (see *Unified labor school). In 1925–8 some of the seven-year schools in urban areas were transformed into *factory seven-year schools, and some rural seven-year schools were turned into schools for collective-farm youth (see *Schools for peasant youth). In 1934 a unified general-education school system was introduced. Seven-year schools were reorganized into incomplete-secondary schools of seven grades. Graduates of seven-year schools could continue to complete their secondary education or gain admission to institutions offering *secondary special education. In 1958 the seven-year school was transformed into the *eight-year school.

Ivan Severa: *Portrait of Ivan Franko* (plaster, 1955)

Severa, Ivan, b 21 May 1891 in Novosilky, Yavoriv county, Galicia, d 20 December 1971 in Lviv. Sculptor and educator. He studied at the wood carving school in Yavoriv (1904–7), the Lviv Handicrafts School (1910–14), and the St Petersburg (1915–17), Prague (1919–20), and Rome (1921–4) academies of art. In 1926 he emigrated from Prague to Soviet Ukraine, where he lectured at the Kiev (1926–9) and Kharkiv (1929–33) art institutes. To escape the Stalinist terror in Ukraine he moved to Frunze, Kirgizia. In 1935 he settled in Moscow, and in 1941 he returned to Lviv. From 1945 he taught at the Lviv Institute of Applied and Deco-

rative Arts. In his early sculptures, such as *Wave* (1921) and *Self-Portrait* (1925), modernist influences are evident. Later he created realist busts of T. Shevchenko (1927), V. Lenin (1929), I. Franko (1947), and V. Stefanyk (1949); sculptures of I. Gonta and Lesia Ukrainka; and the composition *Rebellious Egypt*. D. Krvavych's book about Severa was published in Kiev in 1958.

Severtsov, Aleksei [Sjevercov, Aleksej], b 23 September 1866 in Moscow, d 19 December 1936 in Moscow. Russian zoologist; full member of the USSR Academy of Sciences (AN SSSR) from 1920 and the VUAN/AN URSR (now ANU) from 1925. A graduate of Moscow University (1890), he worked at Yurev (1899–1902), Kiev (1902–11), and Moscow (1911–30) universities. One of the pioneers of evolutionary morphology, while in Kiev he proposed a theory of 'phylembriogenesis' and documented the relation between phylogenesis and ontogenesis. In 1930 he founded the AN SSSR laboratory of evolutionary morphology. Severtsov wrote *Etiudy po teorii evoliutsii* (Studies on the Theory of Evolution, 1912) and *Morphologische Gesetzmässigkeiten der Evolution* (1931). His collected works were published by V. Kasianenko (1951) and E. Veselov (1975).

Ivan Severyn: *Hutsul Girl from Dovhopole* (pastel, 1908)

Severyn, Ivan, b 5 October 1881 in Ostapivka, Myrhorod county, Poltava gubernia, d 20 February 1964 in Kiev. Landscape painter. He studied under O. Slastion at the Myrhorod Handicrafts School and the Kharkiv City School of Drawing and Painting (1903–5) and then at the Cracow Academy of Arts (1905–7) and in Rome (1907) and Paris (1908, 1912–13). He painted many landscapes while he was a member of a geological expedition to Tian Shan and Tibet (1915–17). After living in Kirgizia for several years, he returned to Ukraine and taught at an art tekhnikum (1925–7) and the Kharkiv Art Institute (1927–33). A member of the *Association of Revolutionary Art of Ukraine, in the mid-1930s he was arrested and sent to a labor camp. His early works, such as *Zakopane* (1907), *Environs of Rome* (1907), *Kuban Cossack* (1909), and the cycle 'Hutsul Region' (1905–11), are impressionist in style. The few works he produced during the Soviet period include the cycle 'Dnieper Hydroelectric Station' (1930–2).

Severyn, Yurii, b 12 October 1927 in Kharkiv. Graphic artist. A graduate of the Kharkiv Art Institute (1952), he has done satirical prints and book illustrations, using mostly lithography. He has produced several series, such as '1905' (1955), 'From the Time of the Civil War in Ukraine' (1957), and 'History Lesson' (1965), in collaboration with V. Chernukha, and has illustrated the collection *Smiites' na zdorov'ia* (Laugh for Good Health, 1960), S. Rudansky's *Spivomovky* (Sung Sayings, 1966), and O. Vyshnia's *Myslyvs'ki usmishky* (Hunting Humor, 1969). A catalog of his works was published in 1964.

Sevliush or **Sevluš.** See Vynohradiv.

Oleksander Sevriuk

Sevriuk, Oleksander [Sevrjuk], b 1893, d 26 or 27 December 1941 near Frankfurt an der Oder. Political leader and diplomat. In 1917–18 he represented the Ukrainian Party of Socialist Revolutionaries in the Central Rada. In November 1917 he was elected to the Rada's Committee for the Defense of the Revolution in Ukraine and drafted the law creating the Constituent Assembly of Ukraine. In early 1918 he headed the UNR delegation that negotiated the Peace Treaty of *Brest-Litovsk with the Central Powers and served as UNR emissary in Berlin. From April 1919 he was a member of the Ukrainian delegation at the Paris Peace Conference, and later he worked with the UNR mission in Rome for the repatriation of Ukrainian prisoners of war. In 1920–31 he lived as an émigré in France and then in Germany and was involved in Ukrainian Sovietophile circles. His recollections of the negotiations in Brest-Litovsk appeared in the Paris Sovietophile paper *Ukraïns'ki visty* (1927). Sevriuk died in a railway accident. There were allegations that he was a Soviet-Nazi double agent and that he was assassinated by the Gestapo.

Halyna Sevruk: *Olimpii* (1975)

Sevruk, Halyna, b 18 May 1929 in Samarkand, Uzbekistan. Ceramist. After graduating from the Kiev State Art Institute (1959) she worked for the Art Fund as a decorator of buildings; she created mosaics (*The Forest Song*, 1963) and large-scale ceramic panels (eg, for the Khmilnyk Sanatorium, the Chorne More Hotel in Odessa, the Kiev Hotel in Kiev, the Hradetskyi Hotel in Chernihiv, and School 204 in Kiev). For speaking out against the political persecution of her friends she was expelled from the Union of Artists of Ukraine in 1968. In 1970–5 she produced several relief sculptures of Slavic pagan gods for the Cinema Building and the Kievan Cave Monastery Preserve in Kiev. Sevruk has won recognition for her many small ceramic reliefs depicting historical figures from Ukrainian history, mythology, folklore, and famous historical buildings. She has also done over 20 paintings (mostly in tempera) and over 30 ink drawings. The first solo exhibition of her works was held in Kiev in 1984, and in 1991 she had a solo exhibition in Toronto.

Sexual life. Ethnographic and anthropological studies of ancient cultures in Ukraine present a complex image of customs, rituals, norms, and traditions that celebrated and regulated sexual activity. The permissive pagan norms that regulated sexual relations and customs were universally accepted as manifestations of the will of the gods, the laws of nature, and the interests of society. The idea of individual love had not yet emerged; instead the human body was perceived as an integral part of nature, and sexuality as a general generative force. Although sexual activity was closely tied to the need to perpetuate the clan and was regulated by the institutions of marriage and family, it was not limited simply to the procreative function, but was practiced in a broad context of cultural phenomena. The juxtaposition of the spiritual and the physical and of 'pure' love and 'impure' sensuality that is characteristic of later repressive morality was absent.

Sexuality was openly discussed and was incorporated into songs, dances, and other celebratory elements of folk culture. Group amusements, games, and rituals were given special import, and the entire population – children, youths, and adults – participated in them. Those mechanisms of sexual socialization combined the reproductive and the erotic functions of sexuality. Some relicts of ancient customs and traditions were even orgiastic in nature, but they in no way prove there was total sexual freedom at the time of their inception. All sexual activity in ancient Ukrainian society was strictly regulated by particular norms, customs, traditions, and other elements of the folk culture.

After the Christianization of Rus' the sexual customs and mores of the population became subject to the regulation of the church and the strictures of Christian morality. The church condemned carnality and limited sexual relations to their basic procreative function. All manifestations of eroticism, sensuality, and even attraction were discouraged, sometimes by force. The new morality effected considerable changes in many spheres of everyday life, where sexuality and eroticism had not been segregated from other elements of human and social interaction. Folk customs, rituals, songs, dances, and other elements of popular culture with erotic content were banned, and the nature of married life changed through its subordination exclusively to reproduction and its strict regulation by the church. Because the church's impositions on sexual and other accepted folkways and social behavior were foreign in origin, they elicited widespread dissatisfaction and opposition, even on the part of princes.

The church sanctioned only conjugal sexual relations and punished extramarital ones. In accordance with the Fifth Book of Moses (or Deuteronomy, chapter 22, verse 22) adultery with a married woman was a capital offense. In Byzantine law adultery was punishable by amputation of the nose; the marriage of the adultress was then annulled, but the adulterer was forbidden to leave his wife. The *ustav* of laws issued by Grand Prince Volodymyr the Great made no mention of church and Byzantine regulation of sexual activity, with the implication that customary norms were still in force. In the *ustav* of Yaroslav the Wise, however, the norms of church and customary law were merged. Thereafter women who gave birth to illegitimate children were imprisoned in convents, marriage dissolutions were banned, and monetary fines were levied on rapists. An important norm was introduced that contributed much to the liberalization of gender relations: the strict prohibition of forcibly arranged marriages of children by their parents, under church penalty.

Under Christianity in the Ukrainian lands of Kievan Rus' and after its disintegration, there was a tendency to combine Byzantine and customary law. Some Byzantine norms were adopted by the population wholeheartedly or as compromises, but the majority were rejected altogether, and sexual relations continued to be regulated by customs, traditions, and customary law. Later, in the Lithuanian-Ruthenian state, the Lithuanian Statute prohibited nonconsensual betrothals and marriages, but all other aspects of sexual life remained under the regulation of customary law.

After the fall of Kievan Rus' a different tendency manifested itself in the Russian lands, particularly during the rise of the Muscovite centralized state: an increasing reliance on Byzantine legal norms, which later served as the foundations of Russian legislation. In the Hetman state, even after the Pereiaslav Treaty of 1654 and subsequent

encroachments of tsarist rule, Russian legislation had a limited application, and in the lower courts the norms of customary law were applied almost exclusively. Even under tsarist rule sexuality in Ukraine, as opposed to Russia proper, continued to be subject to the more liberal norms of customary law. Although Christian morality had a certain impact, it was interpreted by the population in a manner that blended it with the norms and customs of pagan times. Thus, for example, the *Kupalo festival remained a folk tradition until recently, and the custom of rolling couples across a sown field was still practiced in the 19th century. Folk oral literature, folk dances, and folk songs composed at the height of the influence of the Orthodox church retained erotic and romantic motifs. Certain forms of sexual relations proscribed by Christianity did not so much disappear as become disguised. One could say that under Christianity there was a separation of folkways and official culture, although the latter predominated. Such was the case in the sphere of sexuality, where a dual morality was established and has persisted to this day, though with a different content.

The gulf between official and actually practiced sexual morality widened in the 19th and early 20th centuries under the impact of the concept of the individual and his or her rights and the rise of secularism and the secular state. Changes occurred in both sexual attitudes and the means of controlling sexual relations. 'External' controls and prohibitions were largely replaced by 'internal' norms emphasizing the intimacy of sexual relations and their significance in emotional development. New biological, physiological, and psychological studies enhanced the scientific study of sexuality and substantiated the positions of those who polemicized with the still dominant Christian ideology.

Under Soviet rule the domination of the church was forcibly ended, and an entirely new situation emerged. Contradictory processes were unleashed: on the one hand, a progressive individualization of sexuality not regulated by external taboos but by internal moral factors, and on the other, the threat of the dehumanization of gender relations, the growth in sexual alienation, and the increasing instability of relationships. New mechanisms of socialization and the control of sexuality had not yet replaced the old religious ones, and people lost their points of reference for sexual conduct and had to face their problems alone. A significant proportion of peasants abandoned their villages and folkways and resettled in the cities, thereby altering the traditional pattern of life, destroying customary attitudes, relations, and socialization patterns, and affecting sexual relations. For many sexuality became the last refuge in the face of economic hardships and complex social and psychological problems. The transformations spawned various psychiatric, psychological, and sociological studies of sexuality, which replaced the earlier, prerevolutionary, biological and physiological focus on sexual life and examined problems in a wider social, political, and cultural context.

Soviet sociological studies of sexual behavior conducted in Ukraine and Russia in the 1920s were distinctive in their methodology and depth and the variety of problems they addressed. The sociological studies conducted by Z. Hurevych, F. Grosser, M. Glezer, A. Vorozhbyt, O. Furmanov, and D. Las deserve attention. Some, including Hurevych and Grosser's study of contemporary sexual life (1928), were published later in the German periodical *Zeitschrift für Sexualwissenschaft* and reprinted in other countries. Those studies were the first to show the complex and contradictory picture of the simultaneous demise of old sexual mores and the creation of and search for new social norms of sexual conduct.

Hurevych's studies indicated that 94.7 percent of married men and 61.7 percent of married women had had premarital sex. Comparison of other data for Ukraine and Russia indicates that premarital sex was widespread. Eleven percent had had intercourse before the age of 17, and 40 percent married and had sex at 17. The average age of sexual initiation was 17.2 for males and 19.3 for females. A comparison of data from the early and mid-1920s reveals that the average age of sexual initiation dropped among women, and that the age range for maximal sexual activity expanded. Studies conducted in the 1920s indicated significant tendencies: on the one hand, the traditional pattern whereby women's first sexual experience was with their husbands and men's was with casual acquaintances, and on the other, the novel phenomenon whereby women were widening their circle of sexual partners to include casual acquaintances and men were decreasing their contacts with prostitutes.

Forty-five percent of married men and 18 percent of married women had had extramarital relations. The reasons given by men were marital breakup (38 percent), 'infatuation' (25 percent), and dissatisfaction with married life (14 percent), and by women, marital breakup (38 percent), dissatisfaction with married life (21 percent), and the inadequacy of their sexual relations with their spouses (17 percent).

The data thus indicated a breakdown of traditional norms and sexual values and not the establishment of new ones. Premarital sex was engaged in not only by men, as was considered natural, but also by women. Both men and women allowed extramarital affairs, an attitude which indicates a certain dissociation of sex from marriage. On the one hand, the freedom to remain married in spite of such affairs had spread to include both genders, which change was a positive development. On the other hand, women had begun to adopt traditionally 'male' values, the implication being an imminent loss of moral direction in sexual conduct and, ultimately, a consumerist attitude vis-à-vis sex.

The sociological studies of sexual problems conducted in the 1920s and 1930s tended not to be objective in their conclusions, however. Just as Christian morality had sanctioned only the reproductive function and deemed all other sexual activity sinful, many of the studies were biologically biased in their conclusions, and approved only of sexual activity resulting in procreation. Masturbation was considered a physically and mentally debilitating disease that hampered normal development, or a perversion. Premarital celibacy was deemed healthy. Sexual activity was deemed to require a great amount of energy which 'could be better expended in more valuable areas.' One could consider those conclusions to be an ideological justification of the principles of the new sexual morality that was subsequently imposed by the totalitarian Soviet state. Its principles were essentially identical to those of Christianity. Only sex within marriage that served the reproductive needs of the family was approved of. All other sexual activity was considered an unhealthy distraction that prevented people from engaging in more important activities, such as the construction of the new communist society.

*Abortion, which had been allowed in 1920, was banned in Soviet Ukraine in 1936. Thereafter discussion of sexual matters was not allowed in the press or in any public forum. Only the mention of sexual deviants or perpetrators of sex crimes was allowed, and only to highlight their severe punishment. Further studies of sexuality were prohibited, and existing publications dealing with sex were removed from stores and libraries. Even folk customs and rituals with erotic undertones that had been tolerated by the Orthodox church were suppressed.

Given that prior to the clampdown sexual matters had been freely discussed by scholars, in the press, and by society at large, the state's about-face produced a conspicuous gulf between official attitudes and actual sexual mores.

The sociological studies of the 1920s had convincingly proved that under Christian morality society had maintained a certain sexual culture and corresponding mechanisms of socializing new generations. The fairly disparate picture of the sexual life of the time, which portrayed a pursuit of simple human gratification and an absence of spiritual values, indicated not a 'sexual bacchanalia' but a search for new moral directions, the rupture of the old system of double standards, and the transition to liberalized and more egalitarian sexual norms.

The destructive influence of the totalitarian state, begun in the 1930s, continued into the 1980s. The various prohibitions and punishments, the censorship, and the dearth of information about sexuality and its importance resulted in the imposition of an antisexual, repressive morality. The consequences became manifest only when the totalitarian system began crumbling after 1985.

It became obvious that there were practically no mechanisms of socializing youth, in society at large or within the family. Not only sexual education but any information concerning sexuality had been effectively suppressed for decades. Recent sociological sample studies indicate that 33 percent of young people first learn about sex from their peers; 19 percent, from their parents; 17 percent, from literature; 12 percent, from their teachers and doctors; 7 percent, from older siblings; and 3 percent, from casual acquaintances.

In 1983 a course on the 'ethics and psychology of family life' was introduced in Ukraine's primary schools. Similar courses were introduced in pedagogical institutes. Both in content and intent, however, they promoted only a slightly more liberal perspective on the existing repressive morality. The total information ban on sexuality has been replaced by information about gender differences, psychophysiology, and hygiene with the aim of dissuading youth from engaging in adolescent and premarital sex. Homosexuality, pornography, group sex, and contraception are still not discussed. Only information about venereal diseases and the harmful consequences of adolescent sex, abortion, and masturbation has been presented, and sexual restraint and sex solely within the parameters of marriage have been condoned. Sexual love as an important component of human life has been completely ignored, as has a positive attitude toward sexuality.

It is not surprising that such forms of sex education have not attracted or been useful to the young. Adolescent sexuality, which is now manifested at an early age and much earlier than the capacity or need to form a family, has had no place in recent sex education in Ukraine. The attitudes of young people have consequently been shaped by varied and not always positive information and personal experiences. Their problems and interests have not corresponded to their knowledge and understanding of ethical and psychological issues. Most parents and teachers have approached sexuality from a biological perspective and have had little knowledge about it themselves. They have not recognized that sexuality is more than just relief of physical tension, that it is also an important avenue of self-realization, emotional bonding, and sharing of experiences.

As a consequence the number of adolescent abortions, extramarital births, and abandoned babies has grown, and the average age of those who contract venereal diseases and those forced into marriage by pregnancy has dropped. The repressive model of sexual morality still dominates and has resulted in marital crises. In recent years there have been a marked increase in divorce rates (now almost one in three marriages end after the first year), a reduction in birthrates, greater incidence of marital discord, sexually contracted illnesses, and sterility, and one of the highest abortion rates in the world. In 1925–7 there was an average of 5 abortions per 1,000 women aged 15 to 49. In 1980–8 the average rose to 90 per 1,000.

General attitudes toward sexuality have changed. The taboo of the 'sacredness' of intimacy has been removed. Sex has become the subject of study, therapy, education, and recreation and is now exploited in advertising and business. Sexuality has become a preoccupation of writers and artists. Most of the literature produced, however, has been of little merit and has bordered on the pornographic, because a society that has been saddled with a repressive morality is not immune to fascination with pornography.

A certain breakdown of the stereotypes of sexual conduct generated by totalitarianism has occurred. Social changes and the disintegration of existing forms of social relations have brought about changes in the family and have affected spousal intimacy. Such changes become more acute with the increase in social and psychological tensions and the accelerated deterioration of socioeconomic conditions to be found in a society ridding itself of its totalitarian legacy.

Alongside the detrimental changes the progressive historical process of the liberation of women has begun. Monogamy for men was and continues to be only nominal. The secret impetus in the rupture of traditional norms is women's need for sexual equality. That does not mean a blurring of gender roles, but an equality in sexual gratification and the removal of constraints imposed by Christian and communist morality. Whereas previously the fidelity of a wife was viewed as the sine qua non of marital life, now the perception is forming that the wife owes fidelity only if her husband is satisfactory in all respects. Most recent divorces and separations have been initiated by women, and societal opinion has just begun rejecting the condemnation of women who are unfaithful as a result of their dissatisfaction with their husbands.

The new tendencies in heterosexual relations indicate that new principles of sexual morality are being established, which increasingly contradict the prevailing systems of sex education, official morality, and laws governing sexual relations. Today the article of Ukraine's criminal code that has prohibited male homosexuality since 1934 is widely considered an anachronism. Also inconsistent with 'civilized' views on sexual relations is another article of the code, that which stipulates punishment for 'perversions,' such as the intentional prolongation of the sexual act, coitus interruptus, the watching of erotica, erotic fantasies, and other 'morally and socially unacceptable forms of sexual gratification.'

In Ukraine not only the legal aspects of the regulation of sexual relations but also scientific views about the nature of sexuality, its norms, and pathology are out of step with progressive attitudes toward sexual morality and current practices. Although the medico-biological aspects of sexuality were studied during the Soviet period, sexual relations in a wider social and cultural context have essentially been ignored since the 1920s.

(See also *Marriage and *Prostitution.)

BIBLIOGRAPHY
Hurevych, Z.; Grosser, F. *Suchasne polove zhyttia* (Kharkiv 1928) – *Problemy polovoi zhizni* (Kharkiv 1930)
Hurevych, Z.; Vorozhbyt, A. *Stateve zhyttia selianky* (Kharkiv 1931)
Stern, M.; with Stern, A. *Sex in the USSR* (New York 1980)
Shlapentokh, V. *Love, Marriage, and Friendship in the Soviet Union: Ideals and Practices* (New York 1984)
Levin, E. *Sex and Society in the World of the Orthodox Slavs, 900–1700* (Ithaca, NY and London 1989)
Worobec, C. 'Temptress or Virgin?: The Precarious Sexual Position of Women in Postemancipation Ukrainian Peasant Society,' *SR*, 49, no. 2 (Summer 1990)

I. Voitovych

Sexually transmitted diseases. See Venereal diseases.

SFUZhO. See World Federation of Ukrainian Women's Organizations.

Shabatura, Stefaniia [Šabatura, Stefanija], b 6 November 1938 in Ivanie Zolote, Zalishchyky county, Galicia. Textile artist and political prisoner. A graduate of the Lviv Institute of Applied and Decorative Arts, she gained prominence in the 1960s as a tapestry and kilim maker. Her work was displayed at many group exhibitions. Her participation in public campaigns in defense of V. Moroz and other Ukrainian political prisoners resulted in her expulsion from the Union of Artists of Ukraine and her own arrest, imprisonment in a Mordovian labor camp (1972–6), and exile in a Tadzhik village (1976–9). In the camp she produced over 100 bookplates and over 150 drawings, which were confiscated and destroyed. Toward the end of her exile she joined the *Ukrainian Helsinki Group. In December 1979 she was allowed to return to Lviv, but she was not permitted to exhibit her works until the late 1980s. In 1990 she was elected a member of the Lviv City Council.

Shablenko, Antin [Šablenko], b 17 January 1872 in Sumy, Kharkiv gubernia, d 24 May 1930. Writer. From 1893 he published his work in *Zoria* (1893), *Vil'na Ukraïna* (1906), *Ukraïns'ka khata*, and *Literaturno-naukovyi vistnyk* (1910). His short stories and prose were also published as separate collections, such as *Likhtarnyk* (Lamplighter, 1899), *Nova khatyna* (The New Cottage, 1900), and *Za pivdnia* (In Half a Day, 1906). During the Soviet period he belonged to the literary organization *Pluh and contributed to the current press.

Stefaniia Shabatura: *Cassandra* (tapestry)

Yevhen Shabliovsky

Shabliovsky, Yevhen [Šabliovs'kyj, Jevhen], b 27 April 1906 in Kamin-Koshyrskyi, Kovel county, Volhynia gubernia, d 10 January 1983 in Kiev. Literary scholar and critic; corresponding member of the AN URSR (now ANU) from 1934. He studied at the Kiev Institute of People's Education until 1931. He specialized in the works of T.

Shevchenko and in 1932 published his first study, *Proletars'ka revoliutsiia i Shevchenko* (The Proletarian Revolution and Shevchenko), which was the first attempt to treat Shevchenko according to official ideology, as a revolutionary democrat and student of the Russian literary critics V. Belinsky and N. Chernyshevsky. For his loyalty to Party policy Shabliovsky was appointed director of the *Taras Shevchenko Scientific Research Institute (1933–5). His other works on Shevchenko were written in a similar official vein – *T.H. Shevchenko, ioho zhyttia ta tvorchist'* (T.H. Shevchenko: His Life and Works, 1934) and *Shevchenko i rosiis'ka revoliutsiina demokratiia* (Shevchenko and Russian Revolutionary Democracy, 1934). Shortly after his appointment Shabliovsky was arrested and sent to a prison camp. In 1954 he was released and was rehabilitated, and in 1956 he was reinstated as a corresponding member of the ANU and worked at the Institute of Literature of the ANU. He published several more works on Shevchenko: *Narod i slovo Shevchenka* (The People and the Poetry of Shevchenko, 1961), *Humanizm Shevchenka i nasha suchasnist'* (Shevcheko's Humanism and Our Times, 1964), *Poetychnyi svit Tarasa Shevchenka* (The Poetic World of Taras Shevchenko, 1976), *T.G. Shevchenko i russkie revoliutsionnye demokraty* (T.H. Shevchenko and the Russian Revolutionary Democrats, 1962; in Russian), and others. Shabliovsky also wrote some works on the theory of *socialist realism, including *Sotsialistychnyi realizm i svitova kul'tura* (Socialist Realism and World Culture, 1973) and *Na peredovykh rubezhakh suchasnosti* (On the Front Line of Contemporaneity, 1975). His literary scholarship is marked by an adherence to official Party policy and an emphasis on the guiding role of Russian literature in the development of Ukrainian literature (as in *Estetyka Chernyshevs'koho i nasha suchasnist'* [The Esthetics of Chernyshevsky and Our Times, 1978] and, in Russian, *Chernyshevskii i Ukraina* [Chernyshevsky and Ukraine, 1978]).

I. Koshelivets

Shad (*Caspialosa*; Ukrainian: *puzanok, ploskun*). A fish of the family Clupeidae, it is among the largest of the herrings, reaching 75 cm in length and 5.5 to 6 kg in weight. In Ukraine shad is found in the Black Sea; it swims up rivers to spawn. It is a valuable commercial fish with good-quality, though bony, meat. Water pollution and damming of rivers have caused the shad population to decrease in recent years.

Shadlun, Mykola [Šadlun], b 6 December 1883 in Vesele, Melitopil county, Tavriia gubernia, d ? Geologist and civic figure. A professor at the St Petersburg Mining Institute, in 1919 he served as UNR minister of the national economy. An émigré in Czechoslovakia, he lectured at the Ukrainian Husbandry Academy in Poděbrady (1922–3) and then returned to the Soviet Union. In the late 1920s he lectured in the mining faculty of the Urals Polytechnical Institute in Sverdlovsk. In Poděbrady he wrote two textbooks, one on crystallography (1922) and the other on mineralogy (1923).

Shafonsky, Opanas [Šafons'kyj], b 13 December 1740 in Sosnytsia, Chernihiv region, d 27 March 1811 in Yaklychi, Sosnytsia county, Chernihiv gubernia. Historian, medical doctor, and government official. From 1750 he studied abroad in Halle (LL D), Leiden (PH D), and Strasbourg (MD,

1763). In 1770 he moved to Moscow, where together with D. Samoilovych and K. Yahelsky he took measures to combat the bubonic plague. With the publication of his description of plagues in Moscow (1774) and his medical typological description of Moscow, Shafonsky established the foundation for the development of *epidemiology in the Russian Empire. In 1781 he returned to Chernihiv, where he served as a court prosecutor, a civil servant, and a general judge. He is best known for his *Chernigovskogo namestnichestva topograficheskoe opisanie* (A Topographical Description of Chernihiv Vicegerency, 1851), published in Kiev after his death. It contains a wealth of information (based on materials and documents compiled by D. Pashchenko) concerning the history, natural science, economics, demographics, and socioeconomic and sanitary conditions in Left-Bank Ukraine in the late 18th century.

Shafran, Oleksa [Šafran], b and d ? Cossack officer. As a Zaporozhian colonel Shafran distinguished himself in numerous raids against the Turks and Tatars in Turkey and the Crimea. In particular he led a Cossack escape from Balaklava after a seven-year captivity. In 1626 he commanded 400 Cossacks in a successful action against Trabzon and other fortified locations.

Shah. A minor silver coin used in the Polish Commonwealth in the 16th to 18th centuries. It was introduced in 1528; the largest quantity of *shahy* was minted in 1618–24 under Sigismund III. In value the *shah* was equivalent to two kopecks; hence, the two-kopeck copper coin minted in Russia was called a *shah* in Ukraine. In the 19th century the *shah* was devalued to the equivalent of half a kopeck; hence, the half-kopeck silver coin was popularly known as a *shah* in Ukraine. In 1918 the Central Rada established the *shah* as one of its main units of currency: its value was set at a hundredth of a *hryvnia* (or one two-hundredth of a *karbovanets*). It was printed on paper and issued in denominations of 10, 20, 30, 40, and 50.

Stepan Shahaida   Hryhorii Shain

Shahaida, Stepan [Šahajda] (real surname: Shahadyn), b 9 January 1896 in Biloholovy, Zboriv county, Galicia, d 12 January 1938. Stage and film actor. He first performed in an army drama circle. Then he became a pupil of L. Kurbas and a leading actor in Berezil (1922–8), particularly in its productions of G. Kaiser's *Gas I* and P. Mérimée's *La*

Jacquerie. Simultaneously he began acting in the Odessa Artistic Film Studio, and from 1928 he worked only in cinema, in which genre he appeared in O. Dovzhenko's *Ivan* and *Aerograd*, F. Lopatynsky's *Karmeliuk*, and other films. He was arrested in late 1937 and executed.

Shain, Hryhorii [Šajn, Hryhorij], b 19 April 1892 in Odessa, d 4 August 1956 in Moscow, buried near Simeiz, in the Crimea. Astrophysicist; full member of the USSR Academy of Sciences from 1939. He served as director of the Crimean Astronomical Observatory from 1942 to 1952. His main areas of interest were astrospectroscopy and the physical processes in nebulae. He is credited with the discovery of the correlation between very fast star rotations and a certain class of spectral characteristics. He discovered over 150 gas nebulae and studied carbon spectral lines in stellar atmospheres, as well as binary stars, comets, stellar corona, and other astronomical phenomena.

Shaitan-Koba. Paleolithic camp site in a grotto on the Bodrak River near Skalyste, Crimea. Excavations in 1929–30 uncovered flint tools, the bones of various wild animals, and other objects.

The Ukrainian edition of William Shakespeare's complete works

Shakespeare, William, baptized 26 April 1564 in Stratford-upon-Avon, d 3 May 1616 in Stratford. His works were first translated into Ukrainian by P. Kulish and M. Starytsky. Other translators of Shakespeare's plays include I. Franko, Yu. Fedkovych, P. Hrabovsky, Ya. Hordynsky, M. Rylsky, I. Kocherha, Yu. Klen, and L. Taniuk. Among the more outstanding translations are T. Osmachka's rendering of *Macbeth* and *Henry IV*, I. Steshenko's *Othello*, H. Kochur's *Hamlet*, M. Lukash's *Two Gentlemen of Verona*, and M. Bazhan's *The Tempest*. Emigré writers who have translated Shakespeare's works include V. Barka, M. Slavinsky, I. Kostetsky, S. Hordynsky, O. Tarnavsky, Ya. Slavutych, and O. Zuievsky.

The first staging of a Shakespeare play in Ukraine was L. Kurbas's production of *Macbeth* by Kyidramte in 1920, in which Kurbas both directed the play and played the lead role. *Othello* was first staged in 1923 by the Ukrainska Besida Theater in Lviv under the direction of O. Zaharov, who also played the title role. It was staged again in 1925–6 in Dnipropetrovske, directed by P. Saksahansky, with the lead role played by B. Romanytsky. The Ukrainian premiere of *Hamlet* was staged in Lviv in 1943, directed by Y. Hirniak with V. Blavatsky in the title role. It was subsequently staged in 1956 in Kharkiv with Ya. Helias in the title role. M. Krushelnytsky played the role of King Lear in a production of *King Lear* staged in Kiev in 1959. Of all his plays Shakespeare's comedies *Taming of the Shrew, The Merry Wives of Windsor,* and *Much Ado About Nothing* have become most popular in Ukraine and are staged most often.

In addition to individual editions of Shakespeare's works, the following collections of his works in Ukrainian translation have been published: *Vybrani tvory* (Selected Works, 2 vols, 1950, 1952), *Tvory* (Works, 3 vols, 1964, 1969), and the complete *Tvory* (Works, 6 vols, 1983–6). His sonnets were translated and published as a complete collection by I. Kostetsky in 1958 and by D. Palamarchuk in 1964.

I. Koshelivets

Stepan Shakh

Shakh, Stepan [Šax], b 3 January 1891 in Kulykiv, Zhovkva county, Galicia, d 16 September 1978 in Sydney, Australia. Teacher, civic leader, and writer; member of the Shevchenko Scientific Society from 1954. After graduating from Lviv University (1915) he served in the Austrian army and the Ukrainian Galician Army. He taught at the Academic Gymnasium (1920–5 and 1929–32) and served as secretary of the Prosvita society's main branch (1920–32, with interruptions) in Lviv, and directed the gymnasium in Peremyshl (from 1932). A postwar refugee in Germany, he taught in Bavaria (1946–56) and retired before moving to Australia (1978), where he died after his arrival. He wrote a popular history of the Prosvita society (1932), the reminiscences *Lviv, misto moieï molodosty* (Lviv, the City of My Youth, 3 vols, 1955–6) and *Mizh Sianom i Dunaitsem* (Between the Sian and the Dunajec, 1960), and three studies about M. Shashkevych.

Shakhbazian, Haik [Šaxbazjan, Hajk], b 21 January 1896 in Panik, Surmalinskii county, Yerevan gubernia (now in Turkey), d 10 September 1982 in Kiev. Hygienist; corresponding member of the USSR Academy of Medical Sciences from 1957. A graduate of the Kiev Medical Institute (1925), he worked at the Ukrainian Scientific Research Institute of Occupational Hygiene and Diseases in Kiev as a research associate (1939–41) and as its director (1946–52),

and at the Kiev Medical Stomatological Institute (1932–52). From 1952 he was a professor at the Kiev Medical Institute. His publications deal with the effects of low-concentration pollutants on workers and the reclamation of microclimates.

Boris Shakhlin

Shakhlin, Boris [Šaxlin], b 27 January 1937 in Ishim, Tiumen oblast, Russia. Champion gymnast. A member of the Kiev Burevisnyk sports club, he was the overall 1960 Olympic, 1958 world, and 1955 European champion in gymnastics. In 1956 he won Olympic gold medals in the pommel horse and team exercises. In 1960 he captured four Olympic gold medals (combined exercises, horse vault, pommel horse, parallel bars), two silver (rings team), and one bronze (horizontal bar). In 1964 he took one gold (horizontal bar), one silver (combined exercises), and one bronze (rings) Olympic medal. He was also a world champion in 1954 (team exercises) and 1958 (team exercises, combined exercises, pommel horse, parallel bars, horizontal bar) and a European champion in 1955 (combined exercises, horizontal bar, parallel bars, pommel horse) and 1963 (rings and horizontal bar), and he won a total of 19 medals in the USSR championships of 1954, 1957–60, and 1962–4. Since leaving competition he has taught at the Kiev Institute of Physical Culture. He wrote the books *Narodzhennia peremoh* (The Birth of Victories, 1962) and *Moia himnastyka* (My Gymnastics, [1964]).

Shakhmatov, Aleksei [Šaxmatov, Aleksej], b 17 June 1864 in Narva, d 16 August 1920 in Petrograd. Russian Slavist and linguist; from 1897 member of the Russian Academy of Sciences (RAS). After receiving his doctorate from Moscow University (1894) he worked in the Division of Russian Language and Literature of RAS, as head of the division in 1906–20, and as editor of the academy's Russian dictionary in 1897–1907. From 1908 he was a professor at St Petersburg University. He was basically a neogrammarian, although he combined the neogrammarian and philological methods in his historical-linguistic studies. He viewed Ukrainian and Belarusian as the major north and south Russian dialectal groups and examined their origins within the historical framework of the Russian language. Finding little historical evidence for his theories, Shakhmatov repeatedly changed his views and rejected his previous works.

His views on the origins of Ukrainian changed least: he consistently held that it developed out of the autochthonous 'southern dialect' of the 'common ancient Russian' language. But, he situated its source sometimes between the Prut and lower Dnieper rivers, and at other times farther north, in the middle Dnieper Basin. During the first half of the 20th century, the Shakhmatov school was the most influential linguistic school in Russia and the USSR. It included some Ukrainian linguists, such as V. *Hantsov and, to a degree, L. *Bulakhovsky. Also significant for Ukrainian studies was Shakhmatov's textual criticism of the medieval Rus' chronicles, particularly of the Primary Chronicle, which is known today only from copies from 1377 onwards. He presented a synthesizing survey and a reconstruction of these chronicles in *Razyskaniia o drevneishikh russkikh letopisnykh svodakh* (Research on the Oldest Rus' Chronicle Compilations, 1905–8), *Povest' vremennykh let* (The Tale of Bygone Years, 1916), and *Obozrenie russkikh letopisnykh svodov XIV–XVI vv.* (Survey of 14th- to 16th-Century Rus' Chronicle Compilations, 1938).

His most important publications on the Ukrainian language consist of an article on the dispalatalization of consonants before *e* and *i* (1903), a short survey of the history of Ukrainian in the encyclopedic compendium *Ukrainskii narod v ego proshlom i nastoiashchem* (The Ukrainian People in Its Past and Present, 1916), and detailed reviews of A. Krymsky's and S. Smal-Stotsky's grammars and of the manuscript of B. Hrinchenko's four-volume Ukrainian-Russian dictionary (which made possible its publication). He sat on the RAS committee that recommended the abolition of tsarist restrictions on Ukrainian publications (in 1905–6) and on the commission that verified P. Morachevsky's Ukrainian translation of the Gospel. Shakhmatov's attitude toward Ukrainian was in keeping with his liberal politics and his support of the cultural rights of all the peoples in the Russian Empire. He opposed the empire's dismemberment, however, and after the February Revolution he was a vocal opponent of the Ukrainian independence movement.

BIBLIOGRAPHY
Izvestiia Otdeleniia russkogo iazyka i slovesnosti Rossiiskoi akademii nauk, 25 (1922) [collection of articles about Shakhmatov]
Obnorskii, S. (ed). *A.A. Shakhmatov, 1864–1920: Sbornik statei i materialov* (Moscow–Leningrad 1947)
Tymoshenko, P. 'O.O. Shakhmatov i ukraïns'ka mova,' *Ukraïns'ka mova v shkoli*, 1956, no. 4

G.Y. Shevelov

Shakhovskoi, Aleksandr [Šaxovskoj], b 5 May 1777 on the Bezzabota estate in the Smolensk district, Russia, d 3 February 1846 in Moscow. Russian writer, playwright, and theatrical activist. He is the author of over 100 works for theater, including vaudeville pieces of little artistic value based on Ukrainian life, such as *Aktor u sebia na rodine* (The Actor at Home in His Native Land), *Ukrainskaia nevesta* (The Ukrainian Bride), and, the most widely known, *Kazak-stikhotvorets* (The Cossack Poet), which remained in the repertoire of theaters for over 50 years. P. Hulak-Artemovsky derided the play for its distortion of the Ukrainian language and Ukrainian life, and customs. The journal *Ukrainskii vestnik* published similar criticisms. I. *Kotliarevsky wrote his vaudeville *Moskal'-charivnyk*

(The Muscovite-Sorcerer) as a 'retort' to *Kozak-stikhotvorets*.

Shakhovskoi, Aleksei [Šaxovskoj, Aleksej], b ca 1690, d 1737. Russian imperial official in Ukraine. After being assigned to Hetman D. Apostol (1729–31) Shakhovskoi became head of the *Governing Council of the Hetman Office, which in 1734 appropriated the functions of the hetman. He was ordered secretly by Empress Anna Ivanovna to encourage mixed marriages between Ukrainians and Russians and to prevent contacts of Hetmanate officers with Right-Bank or Belarusian nobles. After reporting conflicts that had arisen with Cossack officers in the governing council Shakhovskoi received further instructions to start a rumor campaign blaming the hetman and his supporters for the taxes, abuses, and sundry ills in the land. He was replaced in 1736 by Prince I. Bariatinsky.

Semen Shakhovsky   Vasyl Shakhrai

Shakhovsky, Semen [Šaxovs'kyj], b 20 May 1909 in Syniakivshchyna (now Bilousivka), Lokhvytsia county, Poltava gubernia, d 16 June 1984 in Lviv. Literary scholar and critic. He graduated from the Kharkiv Institute of People's Education in 1932 and completed postgraduate studies at the Taras Shevchenko Scientific Research Institute in Kharkiv. He was a lecturer in Ukrainian literary history at the Universities of Kharkiv and Lviv and, in his last years, a professor at the Ukrainian Printing Institute in Lviv. He is the author of texts in Ukrainian literary history, including *Istoriia ukraïns'koï literatury* (History of Ukrainian Literature, 1951), and a number of monographs about individual writers, such as M. Kotsiubynsky, P. Tychyna, V. Stefanyk, Yu. Smolych, and Lesia Ukrainka. He also wrote books on literary theory, including *Literaturni rody i vydy* (Literary Genres and Aspects, 1963), and published numerous critical articles.

Shakhrai, Vasyl [Šaxrai, Vasyl'], b 11 February 1888 in Kharkivtsi, Pyriatyn county, Poltava gubernia, d fall 1919 in Katerynodar, Kuban oblast. Bolshevik leader. Upon the outbreak of the 1917 Revolution he quickly established himself as a revolutionary leader in Poltava gubernia. With the other Bolshevik deputies he left the All-Ukrainian Congress of Workers', Soldiers', and Peasants' Deputies in December 1917 to participate in the First All-

Ukrainian Congress of Soviets, at which he defended Ukraine's right to self-determination and was elected to the Central Executive Committee of Ukraine's Soviets. As people's commissar for military affairs he helped disarm the Haidamaka units supporting the Central Rada and organize Red Cossack detachments in the gubernia. In January 1918 he represented the Soviet government of Ukraine in the Russian delegation to the Brest-Litovsk peace conference. On 16–19 March, at the Second All-Ukrainian Congress of Soviets, Shakhrai was chosen people's commissar for agrarian affairs. He took part in the *Tahanrih Bolshevik Conference of 19–20 April. Under the pseudonym of V. Skorostansky he wrote the booklet *Revolutsiia na Ukraïni* (Revolution in Ukraine, 1918) and, with S. *Mazlakh, *Do khvyli! Shcho diiet'sia na Ukraïni i z Ukraïnoiu?* (1919; trans, *On the Current Situation in the Ukraine*, 1970). In March both authors were expelled from the Party for criticizing V. Lenin's nationality policy and advocating an independent Ukrainian communist party and state. Shakhrai continued to serve in the Bolshevik underground in Ukraine and Kuban, where he was executed by A. Denikin's troops.

J. Koshiw

Shakhtarske [Šaxtars'ke]. V-19, DB III-4. A city (1989 pop 88,400) and a raion center in Donetske oblast. It was established in 1953 by the amalgamation of the towns of Oleksiieve-Orlivka (founded 1764), Katyk (founded 1905), and Olkhivchyk (founded 1784). In 1958 Shakhtarske was granted city status. The city has seven coal mines and three coal enrichment plants as well as concrete, asphalt, sewing, and knitwear factories.

Shakhty [Šaxty]. VI-21. A city (1986 pop 223,000) in Rostov oblast, Russia. It originated as the mining settlement of Gornoe Grushevskoe in 1867. In 1881 it became the town of Aleksandrovsk-Grushevskii, and in 1920 it was renamed Shakhty. According to the 1926 census, Ukrainians represented 13.5 percent of the city's and 13.1 percent of the raion's population. In 1928 it was the site of the *Shakhty Trial. Today Shakhty is an industrial and transportation center. Its main industries are cotton-fabrics manufacturing, sewing, and coal mining.

Shakhty Trial. The first major show trial in the USSR. In March 1928, in the raion center of Shakhty in the Donbas, 53 mining engineers and technicians were arrested by the Unified State Political Administration (OGPU) and accused of organizing mine accidents, engaging in industrial wrecking and sabotage, maintaining criminal links with former mine proprietors in the West, and belonging from 1922 to a counterrevolutionary organization funded and directed by a 'Paris center.' They were tried at the USSR Supreme Court in Moscow between 18 May and 6 July 1928. The presiding judge was the future USSR general procurator and foreign minister A. Vyshinsky, and the prosecutor was the future RSFSR and USSR people's commissar of justice, N. Krylenko. The court gave 4 acquittals, 4 suspended sentences, 34 imprisonment sentences of 1 to 10 years, and 11 death sentences. To demonstrate the 'humaneness' of Soviet justice 6 death sentences were commuted to imprisonment from 6 to 10 years. The Stalinist regime used the trial to lay the blame for the failure of its industrialization policies on 'bourgeois specialists' and foreign-capitalist-inspired conspiracies. The trial opened the Party's general

offensive against internal opponents, both real and imagined, particularly in Soviet Ukraine (see *Purges and *Terror). The methods of extracting false confessions that proved effective in this case were used in subsequent show trials.

B. Krawchenko

Shalaputy. See Khlysts.

Shalashnikov, Aleksandr [Šalašnikov], b 1857 in Berezovo, Tobolsk gubernia, Russia, d 11 March 1890 in Kharkiv. Microbiologist and parasitologist. A graduate of the Kharkiv Veterinary Institute (1882, 1886), he worked with V. Danylevsky in its physiology department and as head of its bacteriology laboratory (from 1887). Together with L. Tsenkovsky he developed the first anthrax vaccine in the Russian Empire and distributed it in Ukraine.

Shalia, Ivan [Šalja], b 9 April 1893 in Baryshivka, Pereiaslav county, Poltava gubernia, d ? Linguist. A graduate of Petrograd University (1916), he was a school inspector in Pereiaslav and Kiev and a lecturer at the Kiev (1920–6) and Kuban (1926–33) pedagogical institutes. With P. Horetsky he cowrote the best and most widely used Ukrainian language textbook of the 1920s (8 edns, 1926–9). When Ukrainian institutions in the Kuban were shut down in 1933, he was arrested; he probably perished in a concentration camp.

Oleksander Shalimov

Shalimov, Oleksander [Šalimov], 20 January 1918 in Vvedenka, Lipetsk county, Tambov gubernia, Russia. Surgeon; full member of the AN URSR (now ANU) from 1978. A graduate of the Kuban Medical Institute (1941), from 1959 to 1970 he worked in Kharkiv as a leading surgeon in hospitals and research institutions. He was appointed a department head at the Kiev Institute for the Upgrading of Physicians (1970) and director of the Kiev Scientific Research Institute of Clinical and Experimental Surgery (1972). He introduced new surgical procedures in the treatment of gastroenterological and vascular diseases. The first pancreas transplants in Ukraine were performed under his supervision.

Shalmatov, Sysoi [Šalmatov, Sysoj], b ? in Ostashkov, Tver gubernia, Russia, d ? Wood carver and sculptor. In 1752 he moved to Okhtyrka, in Slobidska Ukraine, and set up his own workshop, at which he carved iconostases for

Sysoi Shalmatov: the iconostasis in the cathedral of the Mhar Transfiguration Monastery

the churches of the Okhtyrka (1755–60), Mhar (1762–5), Lokhvytsia (1765–70), and Poltava (1772) monasteries. His finest works were the iconostasis and wooden statues commissioned by Otaman P. Kalnyshevsky for the Church of the Holy Protectress in Romen (1768–75). The statues for the Catholic church in Chopovychi, near Malyn, in the Kiev region, were also carved by Shalmatov, in 1774–5.

Shamo, Ihor [Šamo], b 21 February 1925 in Kiev, d 16 August 1982 in Kiev. Composer. He studied composition with B. Liatoshynsky and graduated from the Kiev Con-

Ihor Shamo

Ahapii Shamrai

servatory in 1951. His works include the cantatas *Duma pro tr'okh vitriv* (Duma about Three Winds, 1948) and *Spiva Ukraïna* (Ukraine Is Singing, 1961); 3 symphonies (1964, 1967, 1975); concertos for flute with orchestra; chamber pieces; film scores; and more than 300 solo songs, including 'Kyieve mii' (My Kiev), 'Ne shumy kalynon'ko' (Don't Rustle, Vibernum), and 'Try porady' (Three Admonitions). He has a lyrical style and is best known for his popular songs.

Shamota, Mykola [Šamota], b 17 December 1916 in Poltava, d 4 January 1984 in Kiev. Literary scholar, publicist, and Communist party functionary. He graduated from the Nizhen Pedagogical Institute in 1939 and studied at the Academy of Social Sciences of the Central Committee of the CPSU. He was a full member of the AN URSR (now ANU) and director of its Institute of Literature (1961–78). He specialized in the theory of *socialist realism. His works include *Ideinist' i maisternist'* (Idealism and Mastery, 1953), *Pro khudozhnist'* (About Artistic Work, 1957), *Talant i narod* (Talent and the People, 1958), *Pro svobodu tvorchosti* (About Creative Freedom, 1973), and *Humanizm i sotsialistychnyi realizm* (Humanism and Socialist Realism, 1976). Shamota was the spokesman of L. Brezhnev's policy of Russification. After N. Khrushchev's thaw he used his position as director of the Institute of Literature to suppress the renaissance in literature engendered by the *shestydesiatnyky. He vociferously opposed deviations from the Party line and rehabilitations of proscribed authors. After the announcement of the new policy of Glasnost Shamota's works were harshly criticized as examples of ideological dogmatism.

Shamov, Vladimir [Šamov], b 3 June 1882 in Menzelinsk, Ufa gubernia, Russia, d 30 March 1962 in Leningrad. Russian surgeon; full member of the USSR Academy of Medical Sciences from 1945. A graduate of the St Petersburg Military-Medical Academy (1908), he worked in Kharkiv as director of the surgery department at the Kharkiv Medical Institute (1923–39), the surgical clinic at the All-Ukrainian Institute of Experimental Medicine, the Kharkiv Oblast Clinical Hospital, and the Ukrainian Central Institute for Blood Transfusion (1930–9). He wrote numerous scientific works on blood transfusion, anesthesia, tissue and organ transplantation, neurosurgery, urology, and oncology.

Shamrai, Ahapii [Šamraj, Ahapij], b 2 October 1896 in Myropillia, Sudzha county, Kursk gubernia, d 7 April 1952 in Kiev. Literary scholar and critic. He graduated from Kharkiv University in 1921 and then taught Ukrainian literary history at the Kharkiv Institute of People's Education and contributed to the work of the Taras Shevchenko Scientific Research Institute in Kharkiv. He lived in internal exile in 1933–44 and headed chairs of Western European literature in Izhevsk, Ferhan, and Perm. In 1944 he returned to Ukraine and was a professor at Kiev University. He was one of the leading representatives of the new school in literary studies. He wrote a study of Ukrainian literary history, *Ukraïns'ka literatura: Styslyi ohliad* (Ukrainian Literature: A Concise Survey, 1927, 1928); edited *Kharkivs'ki poety 30–40-ykh rokiv XIX stolittia* (Kharkiv Poets of the 1830s and 1840s, 1930); and wrote a study of Ukrainian romanticism, *Pershyi tvir novoï ukraïns'koï literatury* (The First Work of the New Ukrainian

Literature, 1951), and the posthumously published *Natalka Poltavka I. Kotliarevs'koho* (I. Kotliarevsky's 'Natalka Poltavka,' 1955). He also wrote studies of the works of H. Kvitka-Osnovianenko, M. Kotsiubynsky, T. Shevchenko, O. Storozhenko, and S. Vasylchenko. Western writers whose works he examined include W. Shakespeare, V. Hugo, and E.T.A. Hoffman. A selection of his works was published posthumously, *Vybrani statti i doslidzhennia* (Selected Articles and Studies, 1963).

I. Koshelivets

Shamrai, Hanna [Šamraj], b 4 April 1869, d 7 August 1943 in Kiev. Historian and translator; mother of S. Shamrai and sister of M. and O. Hrushevsky. Until the early 1930s she was an associate of the VUAN and published in its collections and periodicals (1924–9) studies dealing with the urban history of Left-Bank Ukraine in the 17th and 18th centuries and articles on A. Soltanovsky's stories and on P. Kulish's literary plans in the 1870s.

Serhii Shamrai   Gen Pavlo Shandruk

Shamrai, Serhii [Šamraj, Serhij] (Shamraiev), b 30 August 1900 in Vladikavkaz, Terek oblast, d 27 January 1939. Historian. He graduated from the Kiev Institute of People's Education. From 1924 he worked for the VUAN Historical-Geographical Commission and the Kiev Scientific Research Chair of Ukraine's History. He specialized in the socioeconomic history of 18th- and 19th-century Ukraine; his major work was *Kyïvs'ka kozachchyna 1855 r.* (The Kiev Cossacks of 1855, 1928). Many of his studies were published in the *Zapysky* of the historical-philological division of the VUAN and in the journal *Ukraïna*. He was arrested in 1932 and 1937 for his association with M. *Hrushevsky, his uncle, and died in a labor camp. A bibliography of Shamrai's works was compiled by S. Bilokin (1985).

Shandor, Vikentii [Šandor, Vikentij], b 12 October 1907 in Baranyntsi, Transcarpathia. Civic and political activist. After graduating from the Mukachiv Trade Academy (1927) he worked at the Subcarpathian Bank, studied law at Prague University (1930–5), and served at the Land Bank in Bratislava (1935–45). In 1938–9 he was the official representative of the government of Carpatho-Ukraine to the Czechoslovak government in Prague. After emigrating to the United States in 1947, he helped found the Carpathian Alliance, which he headed for many years, and worked as executive director of the secretariat of the Pan-

American Ukrainian Conference. In 1985 he was elected vice-chairman of the executive of the Ukrainian National Council. He has written many articles on legal and political issues, particularly in relation to Transcarpathia.

Shandro, Andrew [Šandro, Andrij], b 3 April 1886 in Ruskyi Banyliv, Vyzhnytsia county, Bukovyna, d 14 January 1942 in Edmonton. Politician and community leader. Shandro came to Canada with his parents in 1898. He was elected to the Alberta legislature in 1913 as a Liberal in the Whitford constituency, the first Ukrainian to occupy such a post in Canada. His first election was overturned by the courts, but he won the subsequent by-election. A Russophile in ideology, he supported the Alberta Liberal party's anti-Ukrainian position on the bilingual school question in 1913–14.

Shandruk, Pavlo [Šandruk], b 28 February 1889 in Borsuky, Kremianets county, Volhynia, d 15 February 1979 in Trenton, New Jersey. Senior UNR Army officer; full member of the Shevchenko Scientific Society from 1948. A graduate of the Aleksei Military School in Moscow (1913), he was commissioned in the Russian army and commanded a company and a battalion during the First World War. He joined the UNR Army in February 1918 and held a variety of positions: commander of an armored train of the Zaporozhian Corps (1918), battalion commander (1919), commander of the Ninth Infantry Regiment of the Third Iron Rifle Division (1919), commander of the First Recruit Regiment (1919), and commander of the Seventh Infantry Brigade of the Third Iron Rifle Division (1920). While serving under contract in the Polish army (1936–9) he graduated from the General Staff Academy (1938) and was promoted to lieutenant colonel and to colonel.

After being released from a German POW camp at the end of 1944, he chaired the *Ukrainian National Committee. In March 1945 the UNR government-in-exile appointed him commander in chief of the Ukrainian National Army (UNA). At the end of the war, during May 1945, he tried to save UNA units from capture by the Red Army. After the war he emigrated from Germany to the United States, where he continued to be active in veterans' organizations and in the UNR government-in-exile. He was promoted to major general and elected honorary commander of the Free Cossacks. Shandruk was the editor of *Ukraïns'ko-moskovska viina v 1920 r. v dokumentakh* (The Ukrainian-Russian War in 1920 in Documents, 1933) and the author of *Arms of Valor* (1959).

P. Sodol

Shanghai. A major city (1988 pop 7,220,000) in eastern *China, on the East China Sea coast along the Yangtze River. It is a major industrial and commercial center, a seaport, and a railway and truck terminal. In the 1930s and 1940s about 4,000 Ukrainians lived in Shanghai; it was the second-largest center of Ukrainian life in China after *Harbin.

Ukrainians began to settle in Shanghai in the early part of the century. A Ukrainian Hromada, consisting of merchants and office workers of local Russian institutions, was soon established, and in 1905 it donated 400 rubles to a fund in St Petersburg for publishing the Gospel in Ukrainian. In the 1920s refugees from the Far East and Siberia and, eventually, Manchuria settled in Shanghai. They formed the Shanghai Hromada, which had about 250 members in 1938 and was active until 1949. Its leading members were M. Kvashenko, B. Vobly, and M. Milko. On its initiative the Ukrainian Emigration Committee was founded in Shanghai in 1939. The committee was recognized by the Japanese military mission, which governed Shanghai under the Japanese occupation in 1937–45, as an official institution for aiding Ukrainians (as well as Georgians and Turko-Tatars). On its initiative the Ukrainian National Colony in Shanghai was set up in 1941. The colony's leading members were P. Boiko-Sokolsky, O. Vitkovsky, H. Totsky, H. Snizhny, and O. Drobiazko. In 1942 the committee was renamed the Ukrainian Representative Committee. That same year a Ukrainian National Committee headed by Drobiazko became active.

The Ukrainians in Shanghai had their own press: in 1937 two issues of *Shankhais'ka hromada* appeared, followed by the paper *Ukraïns'kyi holos na Dalekomu Skhodi* (1941–4, ed Milko, Drobiazko, and I. Svit). At the same time S. Vasyliiv and Svit edited *Call of the Ukraine* (1941–2, seven issues), to which Milko and R. Korda contributed articles. In 1941–2 a Ukrainian radio program served the residents of Shanghai.

Before Communist troops took Shanghai in 1949, most of its Ukrainian residents managed to emigrate to Argentina, the United States, or Canada.

A. Zhukovsky

Shan-Koba. A Mesolithic–Neolithic cave site near the Chorna River in southwestern Crimea. Excavations in 1928 and in 1935–6 revealed six distinct occupations. Items from the lower strata consisted of flint tools and wild animal bones. Thick-walled pottery fragments were discovered in the uppermost strata.

Shankovsky, Amvrosii [Šankovs'kyj, Amvrosij] (pen names: Perekonos, Hermohen, Ponomarev Hermohen, Starshyi sviashchenyk), b December 1832 in Lopatyn, Zolochiv circle, Galicia, d 7 May 1906 in Chernivtsi, Bukovyna. Greek Catholic priest, civic leader, and publicist. After completing his theological education in Vienna and Lviv (1856) he taught secondary school in Stanyslaviv, Kolomyia, and Chernivtsi and contributed numerous poems, short stories, humorous sketches, and articles under various initials and pseudonyms to papers such as *Holos narodnyi* (1866), *Hazeta shkol'na* (1875), *Rodimyi listok* (1880), and *Halytskaia Rus'* (1891–2). He translated German-language textbooks and revised them for the use of Ukrainian students (1879–86). His recollections, published in *Rodimyi listok* (1880–3), are a valuable source for Galician history of the 1840s.

Shankovsky, Lev [Šankovs'kyj], b 9 September 1903 in Duliby, Stryi county, Galicia. Military historian; member of the Shevchenko Scientific Society. After completing studies in Lviv and Warsaw he taught commerce in secondary schools in Western Ukraine and Poland. A veteran of the Ukrainian Galician Army and the UNR army, he was a sergeant in the UPA (1942–5) and a founding member of the Ukrainian Supreme Liberation Council. As a postwar refugee in Germany he taught at the Ukrainian Economic Institute in Munich (1946–9); he then moved to the United States, where he worked as a librarian and edited the English-language quarterly *Prologue* (1957–61) and the

Lev Shankovsky   Vladimir Shaposhnikov

newspaper *Ameryka* (1968–76). Many of Shankovsky's writings have dealt with the Ukrainian struggle for independence, in particular the role of military forces in those efforts. He has written *Ukraïns'ka armiia v borot'bi za derzhavnist'* (The Ukrainian Army in the Struggle for Statehood, 1958) and *Pokhidni hrupy OUN* (The OUN Expeditionary Groups, 1958) and contributed to *Istoriia ukraïns'koho viis'ka* (History of the Ukrainian Army, 1936; 2nd rev edn 1953), *Entsyklopediia ukraïnoznavstva*, and *Encyclopedia of Ukraine*.

Shaparenko, Oleksandr [Šaparenko], b 16 February 1946 in Stepanivka, now in Sumy raion. Champion canoeist. As a member of USSR teams he was the 1966 world champion in the men's 1,000-m kayak singles and pairs (with Yu. Stetsenko), the 1967 European championship in the 1,000-m kayak singles, the Olympic gold medalist in the 1968 1,000-m kayak pairs (with V. Morozov) and the 1972 1,000-m kayak singles, the 1969 European champion in the 1,000-m kayak singles and pairs, the world champion in the 1,000-m singles in 1970 and 1973 and 10,000-m kayak fours in 1977 and 1978, and the USSR champion 18 times in the years 1967–9 and 1971–9.

Shaposhnikov, Vladimir [Šapošnikov], b 6 June 1870 in Volsk, Saratov gubernia, Russia, d 3 October 1952 in Kiev. Organic chemist and technologist; VUAN/AN URSR (now ANU) full member from 1922. A graduate of the St Petersburg Technological Institute (1893), he worked there (to 1900), taught and directed a department at the Kiev Polytechnical Institute (1900–22), directed a department and the technological laboratory at the Kiev Commercial Institute (1913–20) and Institute of the National Economy (1920–34), and directed the ANU Institute of Chemical Technology (1934–8) and a department at the ANU Institute of Organic Chemistry (1938–41). His research dealt mainly with the technology of fibrous materials and the chemistry of dyes. He studied the problems of color, structure, and tautomerism in dyes and introduced a new method of azophenine synthesis. He wrote over 150 works, including a six-volume study of Soviet cotton (1932–3), and edited *Zbirnyk Instytutu khimichnoï tekhnolohiï* (12 issues, 1936–41).

Shaposhnykov, Volodymyr [Šapošnykov], b 1949 in Kharkiv. Architect and painter. A graduate of the Kharkiv Civil-Engineering Institute (1976), he worked as an architect for two years and then turned to 'magic realist' painting. In his large and ambitious *Small Kharkiv Poliptych* (1987) Shaposhnykov attempted to paint a secular iconostasis. His painting *Night* (1986), created after the Chornobyl nuclear accident, depicts a frontal figure with radiation streaming from its darkened body. Shaposhnykov has exhibited in Kharkiv (1988) and Leningrad.

Shapoval, Ivan [Šapoval], b 4 January 1905 in Harazhivka, now in Blyzniuky raion, Kharkiv oblast. Writer and pedagogue. He completed studies at the Dnipropetrovske Metallurgical Institute (1938) and until 1970 was a docent at the Dnipropetrovske Mining Institute. He achieved great popularity as a writer with his fictionalized biography of D. Yavornytsky, *V poshukakh skarbiv* (In Search of Treasures, 1963; repub 1983), after the publication of which he became active in the movement to revive Ukrainian culture. His other works include *Stezhkamy nezvidanymy* (Along Unfamiliar Paths, 1966), *Shyroki kryla* (Broad Wings, 1969), *Akademik O.P. Chekmar'ov* (Academician Chekmarov, 1971), *Volodymyr Maiakovs'kyi* (1974), and *Prydniprovs'ki dzherela* (Dnieper Springs, 1982).

Shapoval, Ivan [Šapoval], b 26 January 1909 in Pavlivshchyna, Zolotonosha county, Poltava gubernia. Sculptor. A graduate of the Odessa (1934) and Kiev State (1941) art institutes, he taught at the latter from 1944. He has done marble portraits of Soviet figures, such as M. Strazhesko (1946) and P. Tychyna (1949), and several monuments, including one to V. Chubar in Kiev (1967–70).

Gen Mykola Shapoval

Mykyta Shapoval

Shapoval, Mykola [Šapoval], b 17 December 1886 in Sriblianka, Bakhmut county, Katerynoslav gubernia, d 25 June 1948 in Seloncourt, Doubs, France. Military and political figure; brother and political supporter of Mykyta *Shapoval. A Russian army officer from 1910, in 1915 he was wounded and captured at the East Prussian front. In a POW camp at Rastatt he founded the Zaporizka Sich cultural and educational society. After his release he organized and headed the Ukrainian Hromada in Biała Podlaska (1916–17), published the paper *Ridne slovo* there, and worked for the *Union for the Liberation of Ukraine. In 1918 he helped organize the *Bluecoats division of the UNR Army and was colonel of its First Zaporozhian Regi-

ment until late April. Under the UNR Directory, in 1919 he commanded the Seventh Infantry Division and the Podilian Group, which later became part of the Third Iron Rifle Division. He then commanded the UNR cadet schools in Kamianets-Podilskyi, Jasło, and Stanyslaviv, where he was promoted to the rank of general. In November 1920 Shapoval and his cadets were demobilized and sent to Polish internment camps in Łańcut and Kalisz. In 1923 he fled Polish persecution to Prague, and from September 1924 he lived in Paris. From 1929 he headed the 2,000-member *Ukrainian Hromada in France and edited its organs, *Vistnyk* (1929–37) and *Ukraïns'ka volia* (1938–40), in Paris. A committed democratic-socialist and antifascist publicist, he was imprisoned by the Gestapo in 1940–1, and from October 1942 until the Allied liberation of France he was forbidden to live in Paris or to have contact with Ukrainians. Shapoval wrote many political articles and a book on the problems of democracy in T. Masaryk's works, in addition to translating R. Rolland's *Le Jeu de l'amour et de la mort* into Ukrainian. He is buried in Sochaux, France.

Shapoval, Mykola [Šapoval], b 15 June 1919 in Persha Bahachka, Myrhorod county, Poltava gubernia, d 22 March 1982 in Kharkiv. Writer and journalist. He graduated from Uzhhorod University (1950) and from 1947 on published nine poetry collections, several children's poetry books, the novels *Idu do liudei* (I Am Going to the People, 1967) and *Ostannii postril* (The Last Shot, 1977), and the prose collections *Oliana* (1958), *Movchazna liubov* (Silent Love, 1960), *Nad Pslom nebo vysoke* (Over the Psol the Heavens Are High, 1962), *Vesna pochynalas' u veresni* (Spring Began in September, 1963), *Nichna vtecha* (Night Escape, 1963), *Troie, de vy?* (Threesome, Where Are You?, 1964), *Iasnyi khlib* (Light Bread, 1969), *Neimovirna pravda* (Unbelievable Truth, 1972), *Veresnevi zlyvy* (September Downpours, 1973), *Hulkyi step* (The Humming Steppe, 1974), *Moieï radosti teplo* (The Warmth of My Happiness, 1976), and *Pole v obiimakh* (The Field in an Embrace, 1977).

Shapoval, Mykyta [Šapoval] (pseuds: M. Sribliansky, M. Butenko), b 8 June 1882 in Sriblianka, Bakhmut county, Katerynoslav gubernia, d 25 February 1932 in Řževnyca, near Prague. Political and civic leader and publicist; brother of Mykola *Shapoval. He was a forester by profession. He joined the Revolutionary Ukrainian party in 1901 and became coeditor of the journal *Ukraïns'ka khata* (1909–14), as well as a co-organizer of the Ukrainian Party of Socialist Revolutionaries (UPSR) and leader of its CC. He was a member of the Central Rada and Little Rada (1917–18) and became the postal and telegraph minister after the Third Universal (November 1917). He assisted in the drafting of the Fourth Universal and served as the commissioner of Kiev county. After the fourth congress of the UPSR (12 May 1918) he became a member of its 'central current' faction. During the rule of the Hetman government Shapoval was general secretary and then head of the *Ukrainian National Union (14 November 1918 to January 1919). He was a co-organizer of the rebellion against the Hetman government (November 1918) and then minister of lands in the Directory (December 1918 to February 1919). In February 1919 he moved to Galicia, but the Western Ukrainian National Republic would not grant him residency owing to his revolutionary political views.

Shapoval then lived in Budapest, where he was secretary of the UNR diplomatic mission (1919–20), and in Prague, where (with the support of T. Masaryk) he came to play an important role in Ukrainian community life. He headed the *Ukrainian Civic Committee (1921–5) and was instrumental in founding Ukrainian institutions of higher education in Prague and the Ukrainian Husbandry Academy in Poděbrady, the Ukrainian Higher Pedagogical Institute, and the All-Ukrainian Workers' Union in Czechoslovakia. He headed the *Ukrainian Institute of Sociology in Prague and the affiliated Ukrainian Workers' University, and he published and edited the monthly *Nova Ukraïna (1922–8). He also headed the émigré UPSR, which criticized the actions of the UPSR Foreign Delegation in Vienna, and strongly opposed the Government-in-exile of the UNR.

Shapoval wrote over 50 publicistic works, including *Revoliutsiinyi sotsiializm na Ukraïni* (Revolutionary Socialism in Ukraine, 1921), *Misto i selo* (The Town and the Village, 1926), *Mizhnatsional'ne stanovyshche ukraïns'koho narodu* (The International Status of the Ukrainian People, 1934), *Velyka revoliutsiia i ukraïns'ka vyzvol'na prohrama* (The Great Revolution and the Ukrainian Liberation Agenda, 1927), *Liakhomaniia* (Polonophilism, 1931), *Shchodennyk* (Diary [from 22 January 1919 to 22 February 1932], 2 vols, 1958), and *Het'manshchyna i Dyrektoriia* (The Hetman Government and the Directory, 1958); much of his work remained unpublished. He also wrote the poetry collections *Sny viry* (Dreams of Faith, 1908) and *Samotnist'* (Loneliness, 1910) and the short prose works *Zhertvy hromads'koï baiduzhosty* (The Victims of Community Apathy, 1910), *Shevchenko i samostiinist' Ukraïny* (Shevchenko and the Independence of Ukraine, 1917), and *Lysty z lisu* (Letters from the Wood, 1918). A biography of Shapoval was written by B. Homzyn (1932), and his autobiography was edited by S. Zerkal (1956).

A. Zhukovsky

Col Oleksander Shapoval   Archbishop Nestor Sharaievsky

Shapoval, Oleksander [Šapoval], b 1888, d 1972 in Chicago. Military leader. He served as an officer in the UNR Army, in which he commanded the Khmelnytsky Regiment (1917), and took part in the overthrow of the Hetman government in 1918. Under the Directory he commanded the UNR Army's Right-Bank front against the Bolsheviks,

and on 13 February 1919 he became defense minister in S. Ostapenko's cabinet. Eventually he left the Ukrainian Party of Socialists-Independentists and joined the hetmanite movement. After emigrating to Prague he managed the library of the Ukrainian Higher Pedagogical Institute. In 1927 he settled in the United States, where he was appointed supreme otaman of the United Hetman Organization and editor of its organ *Nash stiah.

Shapovalenko, Ivan [Šapovalenko], b 1820 in Mykolaivka, Hadiache county, Poltava gubernia, d 15 July 1890 in Duvan, Trans-Baikal oblast, Russia. Painter. A serf owned by P. Kapnist, he was granted freedom in 1836 while serving Kapnist in Naples. Having received a stipend from the Russian Committee for the Support of Artists he studied under R. Dauria in Naples and A. Ivanov in Rome. With the support of N. Gogol and H. Galagan he was able to remain in Rome. There he copied works by Raphael and other Italian masters. From 1845 he worked in the mosaic workshop of St Luke's Academy in Rome, which trained mosaicists for St Isaac's Cathedral in St Petersburg. From 1851 to 1862 he worked as a master in the mosaic department of the St Petersburg Academy of Arts. His extant works include *Portrait of a Neapolitan Woman* (1851) and copies of two mosaic floors from the ancient baths of Otricoli, near Rome.

Sharaievsky, Nestor [Šarajevs'kyj], b 1865 in the Chyhyryn region, d 29 October 1929 in Kiev. Archbishop of the Ukrainian Autocephalous Orthodox church (UAOC). A graduate of the Kiev Theological Academy (1890), he was ordained in 1891 and then taught law in gymnasiums in Vinnytsia. During the period of Ukrainian statehood he was delegate from the Ukrainian clergy to the Central Rada. With V. Lypkivsky he campaigned for the Ukrainianization of the Orthodox church in Ukraine and the creation of the UAOC. In 1921 he was consecrated archbishop of Kiev and elected vice-metropolitan. He also served on the presidium of the All-Ukrainian Orthodox Church Council and headed the UAOC commission for translating liturgical texts into Ukrainian. He is the only bishop of the UAOC who died a natural death. He is buried in Kiev.

Isydor Sharanevych

Sharanevych, Isydor [Šaranevyč], b 16 February 1829 in Kozara, Stryi circle, Galicia, d 4 December 1901 in Lviv. Historian and civic leader. After being educated in Lviv and Vienna he taught at gymnasiums in Peremyshl and Lviv and at Lviv University (from 1871). His valuable work in the field of Galician history was published in *Is-*

toriia Galitsko-Volodimirskoi Rusi (History of Galician-Volodymyrian Rus', 1863), *Rys wewnętrznych stosunków Galicji Wschodniej w drugiej połowie XV w.* (Outline of the Internal Conditions of Eastern Galicia in the Second Half of the 15th Century, 1869), and *Die Hypatios-Chronik als Quellen-Beitrag zur österreichischen Geschichte* (1872, based on his doctoral dissertation). In the field of church history he wrote *Rzut oka na beneficja Kościoła ruskiego za czasów Rzeczypospolitej Polskiej* (A Glance at the Benefices of the Ruthenian Church during the Time of the Polish Commonwealth, 1875; rev edn 1902 under a different title) and works on the Stauropegion brotherhood and Ukrainian church figures. He also undertook archeological expeditions and worked to preserve historical monuments in Galicia. Sharanevych was a longtime elder of the Stauropegion Institute and the only lay participant in the Lviv Synod of 1891. Somewhat Russophile in his orientation, he wrote many of his studies in the artificial **yazychiie*. Biographies of him were written by M. Hrushevsky (*ZNTSh*, 1902) and M. Kravets (*Arkhivy Ukraïny*, 1969).

Sharhei, Oleksander. See Kondratiuk, Yurii.

St Nicholas's Monastery in Sharhorod

Sharhorod [Šarhorod]. V-9. A town smt (1986 pop 5,000) on the Murashka River and a raion center in Vinnytsia oblast. In 1383 Grand Duke Vytautas granted the site to his servant V. Karachevsky, who established the settlement of Kniazhna Luka. In 1497 it was renamed Karacheva Pustynia. In 1579 J. Zamoyski renamed it Sharhorod and built a fortress there. In 1588 the town obtained the rights of **Magdeburg law. It participated in the anti-Polish revolts led by K. Kosynsky and S. Nalyvaiko. In 1626 an Orthodox brotherhood was founded there. During B. Khmelnytsky's uprising Sharhorod was captured by M. Kryvonis and assigned to Bratslav regiment. It was surrendered to Poland under the Treaty of Andrusovo in 1667. In 1672–99 the town was occupied by the Turks, who called it Küçük Stambul (Little Stambul). In 1734 Capt Verlan led a haidamaka revolt from Sharhorod. After the partition of Poland in 1793, Sharhorod was transferred to Russia and became part of Mohyliv county in Podilia gubernia. Its Basilian monastery (est 1717) was converted to an Orthodox one. Today the town has a food industry. Its

architectural monuments include the ruins of the old fortress, a synagogue (1589), a church (1595), and some residential buildings from the 18th and 19th centuries.

Sharko, Vadym [Šarko], b 14 April 1882 in Kiev, d 1930 ? Political activist. A mathematician by profession, he lectured at the Kiev Co-operative Institute and worked at the VUAN Institute of the Ukrainian Scientific Language on the development of mathematical terminology. He was arrested and imprisoned in 1930 as a member of the **Union for the Liberation of Ukraine; his further fate is unknown.

Oleksander Sharkovsky   Yelysaveta Shasharovska-Chepil

Sharkovsky, Oleksander [Šarkovs'kyj], b 7 December 1936 in Kiev. Mathematician; corresponding member of the AN URSR (now ANU) since 1978. A graduate of Kiev University (1958), he has worked at the ANU Institute of Mathematics since 1961 and at Kiev University since 1967. His main publications deal with the theory of dynamical systems, theories of stability and oscillations, and the development of qualitative and analytical methods in the theory of functional and functional-differential equations (and the same equations with delay). He developed a celebrated theorem on continuous functions in 1964, which attracted attention in the mid-1970s after a new and surprising theorem proven by S. Lie and J. Yorke was shown to be a special case of Sharkovsky's general scheme. He has also made contributions to difference equations and their application.

Sharleman, Mykola [Šarleman'] (Charlemagne), b 12 February 1887 in Kremenchuk, Poltava gubernia, d 1970. Zoologist; member of the Shevchenko Scientific Society from 1929. He worked at the AN URSR (now ANU) Institute of Zoology (1919–41) and was one of the founders of its museum. A specialist in zoogeography and ornithology, he wrote *Slovnyk zoolohichnoï nomenkliatury* (A Dictionary of Zoological Nomenclature, 2 vols, 1927), *Ptakhy Ukraïny* (The Birds of Ukraine, 1938), and a monograph about **Slovo o polku Ihorevi* as a source for the natural history of Kievan Rus'.

Sharonov, Mikhail [Šaronov, Mixail], b 30 October 1881 in Belgorod, Kursk gubernia, Russia, d 30 December

1957 in Kiev. Painter. A graduate of the Moscow School of Painting, Sculpture, and Architecture (1910), he studied at the St Petersburg Academy of Arts (1911–15). In the Soviet period he taught at the Kharkiv (1925–35) and Kiev State (1935–57) art institutes. He painted socialist-realist canvases, such as *Red Army Commander* (1928) and *On Patrol* (1930), and portraits of writers such as M. Rylsky, I. Kocherha, and M. Stelmakh (all in 1942–3).

Sharovolsky, Ivan [Šarovol's'kyj], b 16 June 1876 in Prokhorivka, Zolotonosha county, Poltava gubernia, d 9 July 1954 in Prokhorivka. Philologist and translator. A graduate of Kiev University (1900), he became a professor there in 1908. The author of a Russian history of Western European medieval literature (1909), in the late 1920s he wrote articles on German and Rumanian loanwords in the Ukrainian language and on the Rumanian origin of the Ukrainian future-tense verb ending -*mu*. He was also chief editor of two German-Ukrainian dictionaries (1929; 1948, 2nd edn 1955) and translated into Ukrainian T. More's *Utopia*.

Sharpivka fortified settlement. A Scythian town of the 6th to 4th century BC near Pastyrske, Smila raion Cherkasy oblast. The settlement was protected by its location on a ravine and by walls and moats. Excavations in 1938–40 and 1945–7 uncovered the remains of wood-frame surface dwellings, local and Greek pottery, iron-smelting furnaces, tools, jewelry, and zoomorphic and anthropomorphic cult statues. The town's inhabitants were agriculturalists who also hunted and traded with other centers in the Black Sea region.

Sharukan. A Cuman town of the 11th to 13th centuries, believed to have been located along the lower Donets River. Sharukan was formed around an Alan settlement. It had a mixed population and served as a winter haven for the Cumans. It was captured by Volodymyr Monomakh's army in 1111, and then gradually declined over two centuries.

Sharvarok (Polish: *szarwark*, from German *Scharwerk*). The labor obligations of serfs in addition to corvée under Polish rule. Also called *mostovshchyna* (from *mist* 'bridge'), *sharvarok* consisted of constructing roads, bridges, dams, and buildings for the nobles. A form of *daremshchyna* (literally, 'unpaid' labor), it was abolished in Left-Bank Ukraine by Hetman B. Khmelnytsky, but it persisted in the Right-Bank latifundia until the mid-19th century. It was abolished in Austrian-ruled Western Ukraine in 1848. In Russian-ruled Ukraine it was limited in 1847 to eight days per peasant household per year and abolished in 1861. Thereafter the term was used in Ukraine to refer to road maintenance, which was the responsibility of the village *hromady* until the Revolution of 1917 in Right-Bank Ukraine and the Soviet occupation of 1939 in Western Ukraine.

Shary, Ivan [Šaryj], b 1894 in Veremiivka, Zolotonosha county, Poltava gubernia, d 1930. Political activist. He graduated from Kiev University (1917), and took part in the Battle of Kruty in 1918 and published an account of it in the Kiev newspaper *Narodnia sprava*. He was a Socialist Revolutionary delegate to the 1919 Labor Congress, a pro-UNR partisan in the Kholodnyi Yar region (1920–3) under the assumed name Ivan Chorny, and a Ukrainian teacher

in institutions of higher education (until 1929). He was arrested by the GPU for organizing resistance to collectivization and for being a member of the *Union for the Liberation of Ukraine, sentenced to death, and shot.

Shasharovska-Chepil, Yelysaveta [Šašarovs'ka-Čepil', Jelysaveta] (Liza), b 4 October 1916 in Hannover, Germany. Stage actress. She worked in the Tobilevych Theater and Y. Stadnyk's troupe in Lviv (1929–39), the Lesia Ukrainka Theater and the Lviv Opera Theater (1939–44), and the Ensemble of Ukrainian Actors in West Germany and the United States (1945–57). In 1943 she played Ophelia in the first Ukrainian production of W. Shakespeare's *Hamlet*.

Volodymyr Shasharovsky   Otaman Bohuslav
                           Shashkevych

Shasharovsky, Volodymyr [Šašarovs'kyj], b 11 January 1905 in Peremyshl, Galicia, d 15 December 1992 in Philadelphia. Actor and stage director. He began his theatrical career in 1925 in Polish theaters and then worked in various Ukrainian troupes in Western Ukraine (1926–39) and in the Lesia Ukrainka Theater (1939–41), the Lviv Opera Theater (1941–4), and the émigré Ensemble of Ukrainian Actors (1946–53). In the United States he was artistic director of the Rozvaha Theater, the Ukrainian Theater in Philadelphia, and Teatr u Piatnytsiu (1953–74).

Shashkevych, Bohuslav [Šaškevyč], b 1 July 1888 in Lolyn, Dolyna county, Galicia, d 23 June 1935 in Edmonton. Military figure; great-grandson of M. Shashkevych. An officer in the Austrian army on the eastern front, he was captured by Russian forces in 1915 and sent to a POW camp in Turkestan. He escaped and led an Iranian rebel unit against the British and Russians. In 1916 he returned via Baghdad and Istanbul to Austria and rejoined the Austrian army on the northern and eastern fronts. He received six military decorations. During the Ukrainian-Polish War in Galicia (1918–19) he was a major commanding the Uhniv Brigade and, in May 1919, the First Division of the Ukrainian Galician Army. In June and July 1919 he organized and commanded the Zbarazh Brigade and then the Zolochiv Brigade. In February 1920, instead of joining the Red Ukrainian Galician Army, his brigade fought the Bolsheviks and joined with the UNR Army under Col O. Udovychenko in Mohyliv-Podilskyi. After being released from an internment camp in Czechoslovakia he moved to Germany (1922) and then to Canada.

Rev Hryhorii Shashkevych

Shashkevych, Hryhorii [Šaškevyč, Hryhorij], b 1809, d 30 August 1888 in Peremyshl, Galicia. Greek Catholic priest and civic and political leader. In 1848 he was elected president of the Regional Ruthenian Council in Stanyslaviv (a branch of the Supreme Ruthenian Council in Lviv) and deputy to the Austrian parliament. In Vienna he served as adviser to the education ministry (1848–65) and head of its Galician school department as well as rector of the Greek Catholic Theological Seminary. After returning to Galicia he was elected to the Galician Diet (1867). He wrote one of the first Ukrainian grammar textbooks for public schools (1862) and collaborated with Ya. Holovatsky and Yu. Vyslobotsky on a German-Ukrainian legal dictionary (1851).

Monument to Rev Markiian Shashkevych at the new Rusalka Dnistrovaia Museum in Lviv (sculptors Dmytro Krvavych and Mykola Posikira, 1990)

Shashkevych, Markiian [Šaškevyč, Markijan] (pseud: Ruslan), b 6 November 1811 in Pidlyssia, Zolochiv circle, Galicia, d 7 June 1843 in Novosilky Lisni, now in Buzke raion, Lviv oblast. Poet and leader of the literary revival in Western Ukraine based on the vernacular. He graduated from the Greek Catholic Theological Seminary in Lviv in 1838 and worked as a priest in the rural Lviv region. During his studies he met Ya. Holovatsky and I. Vahylevych, with whom he formed the *Ruthenian Triad. He also organized nationally conscious Ukrainian young people (H. Il-

kevych, I. Bilynsky, F. Minchakevych, M. Kozlovsky, A. Velychkovsky, and others) to work for national and cultural revival in Western Ukrainian lands, particularly to reintroduce the use of spoken Ukrainian in writing and sermons. Their efforts resulted in the preparation of collections of folklore, *Syn Rusy* (Son of Rus', 1833) and *Zoria* (The Star, 1834), and the publication of the almanac **Rusalka Dnistrovaia* (1836). The almanac had a decisive effect on the revival and development of Ukrainian literature in Galicia.

Shashkevych's first published poem appeared in 1835. His literary canon, however, is fairly small. Apart from a few personal lyric verses, he largely wrote patriotic poems. In 1836 he published the brochure *Azbuka i Abecadlo* (The Alphabet and the Abecedarium), written against attempts to Latinize the Ukrainian alphabet. He relayed into spoken Ukrainian selections of *Slovo o polku Ihorevi* (The Tale of Ihor's Campaign) and translated the New Testament into the vernacular (1842). His *Chytanka dlia malykh ditei* (Reader for Small Children, 1850) was published posthumously by Holovatsky.

His fame as a reviver of national consciousness and initiator of a new Ukrainian literature in Galicia began growing after his death. In 1911 a large celebration of the centenary of his birth was staged, and a monument was erected in his memory on Bila Hora (near Pidlyssia). In 1959 a literary memorial museum was opened in Pidlyssia. In recent times Shashkevych has been invoked in reaction to the Russification of Ukraine and the assimilation of Ukrainians in the diaspora. The Shashkevych Institute was established in 1961 in Winnipeg; it publishes the periodical *Shashkevychiiana* (edited by M. *Marunchak).

BIBLIOGRAPHY
Tershakovets', M. 'Do zhyttiepysu Markiiana Shashkevycha z dodatkom: Materiialy, dokumenty ...,' *NTSh*, 105–6 (1906)
Lepkyi, B. *Markiian Shashkevych* (Kolomyia 1912)
Popovych, D. *Markiian Shashkevych na tli vidrodzhennia Halyts'koï Ukraïny* (1943)
Bilets'kyi, O. *Slovo pro Markiiana Shashkevycha* (Lviv 1961)
Shakh, S. *Markiian Shashkevych i halyts'ke vidrodzhennia* (Paris–Munich 1961)
Lutsiv, L. *Markiian Shashkevych* (Jersey City 1962)
Marunchak, M. *Markiian Shashkevych na tli doby* (Winnipeg 1962)
Shalata, M. *Markiian Shashkevych: Chyttia i tvorchist' i hromads'ka diial'nist'* (Kiev 1969)

M. Marunchak

Shashkevych, Volodymyr [Šaškevyč], b 7 April 1839 in Nestanychi, Zolochiv circle, Galicia, d 16 February 1885 in Lviv. Writer; son of M. Shashkevych. He studied at Lviv and Vienna universities and worked as a civil servant in Galician towns from 1869. His poetry, influenced by folklore and T. Shevchenko, was published in the literary miscellanies *Zoria halytskaia* (Galician Star, 1860) and *Antolohiia ruska* (Ruthenian Anthology, 1881) and in the periodicals *Vistnyk* (1865), *Pravda* (1867), and *Osnova* (1872). His collection *Zil'nyk* (Herbarium) was published in 1863. He also wrote the play *Syla liubovy* (The Power of Love, 1864), edited the Lviv periodicals *Vechernytsi* (1862–3) and *Rusalka* (1866) and two readers for peasants (*Zoria* [The Star], 1871, 1872), and translated a few of H. Heine's poems into Ukrainian.

Shatalin, Viktor [Šatalin], b 15 November 1926 in Zemlianye Khutory, now in Saratov oblast, Russia. Painter;

corresponding member of the USSR (now Russian) Academy of Arts since 1978. A graduate of the Kiev State Art Institute (1953), in 1968 he began teaching there. He is known for his socialist-realist paintings, such as *Combat Assignment* (1960), *Land* (1964), *Detachments of Young Fighters Gathered* (1969–70), *Comrades in Arms* (1971–2), and *Battle for the Dnieper* (1983). He has also painted portraits, including one of H. Maiboroda (1977), and landscapes. An album of his works came out in 1974.

A lake in Shatsk National Park

Oleksa Shatkivsky: *Callas* (oil, 1967–70)

Shatkivsky, Oleksa [Šatkivs'kyj], b 28 May 1908 in Pochaiv, Kremianets county, Volhynia gubernia, d 28 June 1979 in Lviv. Painter and printmaker. While studying at the Warsaw Academy of Arts (1931–9) he belonged to the *Spokii group of Ukrainian artists. After the Second World War he taught at the Lviv Institute of Applied and Decorative Arts (1948–56) and the Ukrainian Printing Institute in Lviv (1950–6). He painted many landscapes of Volhynia, the Carpathians, and Lviv, including *Apiary* (1951), *Lenin Avenue in Lviv* (1967), and *Carpathian Landscape* (1968), and created many lithographs and engravings. Expressionist influences are evident in his work. Catalogs of retrospective and posthumous exhibitions of his works were published in 1969 and 1981.

Shatsk National Park. The second national park to be created in Ukraine, after the Carpathian National Park. It was proposed in the 1970s and set up in 1983. The park covers 32,500 ha in the northwestern part of Volhynia oblast, near the Belarusian and Polish borders. Its vegetation consists mainly of mixed forests and peat marshes on the upper watershed of the Prypiat River. More than 25 lakes dot the area, the largest of which is Svytiaz Lake. The intermittent forests are predominantly pine and hornbeam. Numerous organizations have established recreational bases in the area, particularly around Svytiaz Lake. Besides providing camping and hiking facilities the park conserves the natural landscape and its forest and wetland ecosystems, and supports scientific research.

Shatulsky, Matthew [Šatul's'kyj, Matvij], b 16 November 1883 in Bazaliia, Starokostiantyniv county, Volhynia gubernia, d 20 December 1952 in Winnipeg. Communist activist and journalist. He emigrated to the United States (1909) and then to Canada (1911), where he became active in the workers' organization Samoobrazovanie. He joined the staff of *Ukraïns'ki robitnychi visti* in 1920 and helped organize the Workers' Benevolent Association. Together with M. Popovich and I. Navizivsky, he was a leading member of the *Ukrainian Labour-Farmer Temple Association. In 1940–2 he was arrested under Defence of Canada regulations and kept in a detention camp. His articles, short stories, and feuilletons were collected by P. Krawchuk and published with a biographical introduction in *Siiach slova pravdy* (Sower of the Word of Truth, 1983).

Shatunovsky, Samuil [Šatunovs'kyj, Samujil], b 25 March 1859 in Velyka Znamianka, Melitopil county, Tavriia gubernia, d 27 March 1929 in Odessa. Mathematician. He studied and then taught at technological and engineering institutes in St Petersburg. In 1905 he joined the faculty of Odessa University and in 1917 became a professor. In his works he deals with various problems in mathematical analysis and algebra, particularly in group theory, theory of numbers, and geometry. Shatunovsky was one of the founders of the constructive approach in contemporary mathematics. He used the axiomatic method to lay the logical foundations of geometry, algebraic fields and Galois group theories, and analysis.

Shatylov, Petro [Šatylov], b 1869 in Kozatska *sloboda*, Staryi Oskol county, Kursk gubernia, d 13 May 1921. Internal medicine specialist. After graduating from Kharkiv University in 1895, he lectured there and in 1909 was appointed a professor of diagnostics and propaedeutics of internal medicine. In 1914 he also became a professor at the Kharkiv Women's Institute. Shatylov was the founder of the Kharkiv school of internal medicine and an innovator in diagnostics. In 1912 in the Kharkiv Military Hospital he performed the first vaccination against typhoid fever in the Russian Empire. His writings include medical textbooks and monographs on microbiology, epidemiology, immunology, anthropology, and hematology. He tested vaccines against epidemic typhus on himself, and died of the disease.

Shaula, Matvii [Šaula, Matvij], b ?, d 1596 in Warsaw. Zaporozhian Cossack leader. A supporter of S. Nalyvaiko's uprising, in 1595 he took Kiev with a detachment of Zaporozhian Cossacks and advanced into Belarus against Polish forces. In March 1596, after returning to Right-Bank Ukraine, Shaula was elected by the Cossacks to replace the deposed hetman H. Loboda. Later that year he was injured in the Battle of Solonytsia, turned over to S. Żółkiewski by traitors, and executed.

Dmitrii Shavykin: *For Steam Travel* (poster, 1930)

Shavykin, Dmitrii [Šavykin, Dmitrij], b 3 April 1902 in Aleksandrov, Vladimir gubernia, Russia, d 29 March 1965 in Kiev. Painter and graphic artist. From 1915 he lived in Kiev, where he studied at the Kiev State Art Institute (1922–8) under M. Burachek, F. Krychevsky, and L. Kramarenko. In 1927 he joined the *Union of Contemporary Artists of Ukraine. His series of Donbas landscapes (1931–4) and *Evening on the Dnieper* (1957) show expressionist influences. M. *Boichuk's influence is evident in Shavykin's murals at the Children's Village in Kiev (1924, destroyed)

and the Kaniv Museum-Preserve (1940). He also painted portraits of writers, such as his wife, N. Zabila, and L. Pervomaisky, and created kilims, posters, and illustrations for children's magazines (*Zhovtenia* and *Tuk-tuk*) and books, including Zabila's retelling of the tale of Ihor's campaign (*Slovo pro Ihoriv pokhid*, 1940) and A. Holovko's *Maty* (Mother, 1936). B. Lobanovsky's book about him was published in Kiev in 1962.

Shchaslyvy, Pavlo [Ščaslyvyj], b ?, d 1610 in Lviv. Builder in Lviv of Italian origin. From 1582 he presided over the masons' guild in Lviv. He constructed a number of buildings in Lviv, including the Golden Rose Synagogue (1580–2), the Jesuit school, and the residential buildings of M. Nakhmanovych and I. Siuskiundovych. In 1592 he moved to Zhovkva, where he began building the local castle (from 1596), designed the model of the Roman Catholic cathedral (1604–9), and served as mayor from 1601.

Shchasny, Serhii [Ščasnyj, Serhij], b 7 September 1875 in St Petersburg, d 19 March 1943. Microbiologist and epidemiologist. A graduate of Kiev University (1899, pupil of V. Pidvysotsky), he worked at Odessa University (from 1901, from 1919 as a professor), directed the Odessa Bacteriological Station (1919–28), taught at the Odessa Medical Institute (1921–8), and worked at the Crimean Institute of Epidemiology and Microbiology (from 1928) and the Crimean Medical Institute (1928–38). A specialist in immunology, epidemiology, and anaphylaxis, he played an active role in combating an outbreak of plague in Odessa (1910–11).

Shchastia [Ščastja]. V-20, DB II-6. A city (1989 pop 14,300) on the Dinets River in Luhanske oblast. In the mid-18th century a village was established at the site by runaway serfs. A workers' settlement was built in 1953 during the construction of the Luhanske Raion Electric Power Station. In 1963 Shchastia attained city status. It is administered by a municipal raion council of Luhanske city. Its chief industries are coal mining and power generation.

Shchavnytsky, Mykhailo [Ščavnyc'kyj, Myxajlo], b 1754, d 1819. Uniate priest and pedagogue. He was raised in Transcarpathia and he finished his studies in Vienna in 1780, after which he became vice-rector of the Barbareum. In 1784–7 he was the first rector of the Greek Catholic Theological Seminary in Lviv. He was the organizer and briefly rector of the Studium Ruthenum at Lviv University. From 1787 he was vice-director of the Uzhhorod Theological Seminary.

Shchavynsky, Vasyl [Ščavyns'kyj, Vasyl'], b 1868 in the Kiev region, d 27 December 1924 in Leningrad. Art historian, collector, and restorer; member of the *Leningrad Society of Researchers of Ukrainian History, Literature, and Language from 1922. He studied chemistry at the St Petersburg Technological Institute and the Riga and Zürich polytechnical institutes. In 1917 he organized the Society for the Study and Preservation of Monuments of Ukrainian Antiquity in Petrograd. From 1918 he worked as a restorer at the Hermitage Museum, and in 1919 he became director of the Department of Painting Techniques at the Russian Academy of Material Culture and a professor at the Petrograd Institute of Photography and Photo-technology. He wrote articles on Dutch painting, art restoration, and T. Shevchenko and Rembrandt (*Ukraïnu*, 1925, nos 1–2). His valuable collections of Dutch paintings, Mezhyhiria ceramics, Ukrainian kilims, and Shevchenko's self-portrait are preserved at the Kiev Museum of Western and Eastern Art and the Hermitage Museum. His Russian monograph on the history of painting techniques and color technology in Kievan Rus' was published posthumously in 1935.

Shchedrivky. See Carols.

Shchedrova, Valentyna (Ščedrova], b 10 January 1930 in Sursko-Lytovske, Katerynoslav okruha. Sculptor. A graduate of the Dnipropetrovske Art School (1952) and the Kharkiv Art Institute (1961), she has created plaster statues, such as *Builders* (1963), *A Mother's Dream* (1964), and *Youth* (1965). She collaborated on memorial monuments to the students of the Dnipropetrovske Transport Institute (1967) and to medics (1970) who died in Dnipropetrovske in the Second World War.

Shchekariv. See Krasnystaw.

Shchekavytsia (19th-century engraving)

Shchekavytsia [Ščekavycja] (also Olehivka, Olehova hora, or Skavyka). A landmark hill in Kiev overlooking the old town district of Podil. Named after Shchek, one of the legendary founders of Kiev, the hill is mentioned in medieval chronicles as early as 1151. By the 15th or 16th century it had been fortified, and in 1619 it was designated a residential area for the burghers of Kiev. A renowned cemetery was established on the hill in the later 18th century, which became the burial site of figures such as A. Vedel, A. Melensky, and V. Ikonnikov. In 1782 the famous All Saints' Church was built there, and a stone bell tower was added in 1809. Neither structure is still standing. The hill is also occasionally called after the Kievan prince Oleh, who was reputed to have been buried there.

Shchelkov, Ivan [Ščelkov], b 1833 in Kharkiv, d 1909. Physiologist. He completed medical studies at Kharkiv University (1855) and later was a professor (1863–86) and rector (1884–90) there. From 1890 he was rector of Warsaw University.

Mikhail Shchepkin (portrait by Taras Shevchenko, 1858)

Fedor Shchepotev

Shchepkin, Mikhail [Ščepkin, Mixail], b 17 November 1788 in Krasne, Slobidska Ukraine gubernia, d 23 August 1863 in Yalta, Tavriia gubernia (buried in Moscow). Actor and one of the founders of theatrical realism on Ukrainian and Russian stages. A serf until 1822, he began his career in P. Barsov's troupe in Kursk (1805) and then acted in Y. Kalynovsky and I. Shtein's troupe in Kharkiv (1816–18) and in the Poltava Free Theater (1818–21), led his own troupe in Kiev (1822), and worked in the Moscow Malyi Theater (from 1823). He toured frequently in Ukraine; his repertoire included Chuprun in I. Kotliarevsky's *Moskal'-charivnyk* (The Muscovite-Sorcerer) and the title role in H. Kvitka-Osnovianenko's *Shel'menko-denshchyk* (Shelmenko the Orderly). He was a friend of T. *Shevchenko.

Shchepotev, Fedor [Ščepotev], b 19 July 1906 in Alforovka, Novokhopersk county, Voronezh gubernia. Forester, dendrologist, and selection scientist; corresponding member of the ANU (formerly AN URSR) since 1965. A graduate of the Voronezh Forest Technology Institute, he worked at the Ukrainian Scientific Research Institute of Forest Management and Agroforest Amelioration in Kharkiv (1933–41, 1946–66) and headed a department of Donetske University (from 1966). He published over 125 works on the introduction, selection, and mutation of tree species and the influence of different chemical and physical stimulants on tree growth and development. By crossing distant breeds he developed hybrid forms of the walnut and poplar that are fast-growing and cold-resistant.

Shchepotiev, Volodymyr [Ščepot'jev], b 6 November 1880 in Poltava, d 29 November 1937. Ethnographer and literary historian. Before the Revolution of 1917 he was a member of the Archival Commission of Poltava (ACP). In the Soviet period he was a professor at the Poltava Institute of People's Education, head of the Poltava Scholarly Society of the VUAN, an associate of the Kharkiv Chair of the History of Ukrainian Culture, and a member of the Ethnographic Commission of the VUAN. One of the compilers of the systematic index to *Kievskaia starina* (published by the ACP in 1911), he wrote a booklet about M. Lysenko (Poltava 1913, under the pseud Budyshanets) and a book about Ukrainian writers from the earliest times to the 1860s (published by the Poltava Prosvita society in

Volodymyr Shchepotiev   Mykola Shcherbak

Yurii Shcherbak   Danylo Shcherbakivsky

1918; 2nd edn 1919), and contributed articles on Ukrainian folklore and writers (I. Kotliarevsky, T. Shevchenko, O. Storozhenko) to *Trudy Poltavskoi uchenoi arkhivnoi komissii*, *Etnohrafichnyi visnyk*, *Ukraïna*, and *Zapysky Poltavs'koho INO*. He was arrested in 1930 and sentenced at the show trial of the *Union for the Liberation of Ukraine to three years in a Siberian labor camp. He was released in 1936 but was rearrested in 1937, tortured, and shot by the NKVD.

Shcherbak, Mykola [Ščerbak], b 16 September 1924 in Savinka, Saratov oblast, Russia. Geologist; full member of the AN URSR (now ANU) since 1979. A graduate of the Donetske Polytechnical Institute, he was a scholarly associate and department head with the ANU Institute of Geological Sciences (1955–69) and then the ANU Institute of the Geochemistry and Physics of Minerals (1969–83, as director from 1977). His main scholarly interest is the origin and development of crystalline rock formations in Ukraine. He is particularly noted for developing an isotopic method of dating rocks and for establishing a stratigraphic scheme of the Ukrainian Crystalline Shield.

Shcherbak, Oleksander [Ščerbak], b 25 June 1863 in Chernihiv gubernia, d 23 April 1934 in Sevastopil. Neurologist, psychiatrist, and physiotherapist. A graduate of the St Petersburg Military Medical Academy (1887), he upgraded his knowledge abroad and was a professor of psychiatry at Warsaw University (1894–1911). He organized and directed the Institute of Physiotherapy in Sevastopil (1914–34, from 1955 the Yalta Scientific Research Institute of Physiotherapy and Medical Climatology). He wrote on myopathies, hysteria, migraine, the classification of mental diseases, and the effect of medicines on blood circulation in the brain.

Shcherbak, Yurii [Ščerbak, Jurij], b 12 October 1934 in Kiev. Prose writer, dramatist, and publicist; physician by profession. Having obtained a degree from the Medical Institute of Kiev in 1958, he worked in the Scientific Research Institute of Epidemiology, Microbiology, and Parasitology in Kiev until the late 1980s, when he devoted himself exclusively to writing. In the early 1950s he began publishing so-called *mal'ovani retsenziï* (painted reviews). His published works include the collections of stories *Iak na viini!* (Just as at War, 1966) and *Malen'ka futbol'na komanda* (A Small Soccer Team, 1973), and the novel *Bar'ier*

nesumisnosti (The Barrier of Incongruity, 1971). His novelistic account of medical struggles with rabies, *Prychyny i naslidky* (Causes and Effects, 1987), is among the best examples of contemporary Soviet literature. Equally notable are his popular publicistic articles in the Ukrainian and Russian press concerning the Chornobyl disaster, and his documentary account of the events, *Chornobyl'* (1988), which has been translated into several languages. Upon the accession of M. Gorbachev to power Shcherbak played an active role in the Ukrainian cultural renaissance, by contributing to enunciations of opposition to Russification, voicing ecological concerns, researching the man-made famine of 1932–3, and serving other causes. Since 1987 he has been president of the *Zelenyi Svit ecological society. In 1989 he was elected in Kiev as member of the new Congress of People's Deputies. He headed the Green party of Ukraine, was Ukraine's environment minister (1991–2), and is Ukraine's ambassador to Israel (since October 1992).

I. Koshelivets

Shcherbakivsky, Danylo [Ščerbakivs'kyj], b 17 December 1877 in Shpychyntsi, Skvyra county, Kiev gubernia, d 6 June 1927 in Kiev. Ethnographer, art scholar, archeologist, and museologist; brother of V. *Shcherbakivsky. After studying at Kiev University (1897–1901) he taught history at the Uman Gymnasium (1906–10), collected articles of folk art and handicrafts for museums in Kiev and Poltava, and conducted archeological digs in Right-Bank Ukraine. As head of the historical folkways and folk art departments of the Kiev City Museum of Antiquities and Art (later the All-Ukrainian Historical Museum and now the *Historical Museum of Ukraine) from 1910, he enriched its holdings with about 30,000 new objects and proposed for the first time to treat works of folk art as art objects in their own right. In 1923 he traveled to Moscow to save 5,000 'nationalized' gold and silver objects that had been removed from Ukrainian churches. He was one of the founders and the scientific secretary of the Ukrainian State Academy of Arts, chairman of its Department of Folk Art, a cofounder and a member of the VUAN Ethnographic Commission (from 1920), scientific secretary of the arts section of the Ukrainian Scientific Society in Kiev (from 1921), vice-chairman of the All-Ukrainian

Archeological Committee (from 1922), and founder of the Kiev Ethnographic Society (est 1924). He also lectured on folk art and the history of Ukrainian art at the Academy of Arts and the new Kiev Archeological, Pedagogical, Architectural, and State Art institutes and conducted art seminars at the Historical Museum. Devastated by the removal of many objects from the Historical Museum and their secret sale, and by his persecution and the undermining of his work at the museum by the Communist authorities, he committed suicide by jumping off a bridge into the Dnieper.

Over 40 of Shcherbakivsky's works have been published. Several dozen of his manuscripts still await publication. His chief works are a study of the *Kozak-Mamai theme in Ukrainian painting in *Siaivo* (1913); studies of Ukrainian wooden churches and symbolism in Ukrainian art in the collection of the arts section of the Ukrainian Scientific Society (1921); and books on serf orchestras, choirs, and Kapellen in Ukraine (1924), Ukrainian portraiture (1925, with F. Ernst), book covers by 17th- and 18th-century Kievan goldsmiths (1926), Galician and Bukovynian wooden churches, chapels, crosses, and figures (*L'Art d'Ukraine*, 1926), and the Ukrainian kilim (1927).

V. Pavlovsky

Shcherbakivsky wrote important works about wooden churches in Ukraine (*ZNTSh*, vol 74 [1906]), the architecture of various peoples in Ukraine (1910), churches in the Boiko region (*ZNTSh*, vol 114 [1913]), Ukrainian art (1913; 2nd edn 1925), the principal elements of Ukrainian Easter egg ornamentation (1925), the prehistoric formation of the Ukrainian nation (1937; 3rd edn 1958), and the Stone Age in Ukraine (1947). A biography of him, by P. Kurinny, was published in Geneva in 1947.

V. Pavlovsky

Shcherban, Oleksander [Ščerban'], b 2 March 1906 in Dykanka, Poltava county, Poltava gubernia, d 7 January 1992 in Kiev. Scientist in the field of mining technology and thermodynamics; full member of the ANU (formerly AN URSR) since 1957. He graduated from the Dnipropetrovske Mining Institute (1933). He served as assistant director of the ANU Institute of Mining (1946–53), the first scientific secretary of the presidium of the ANU (1953–7), and vice-president of the ANU (1957–61). He became assistant chairman of the Council of Ministers (1961–5) and headed a department at the AN URSR Institute of Thermoenergetics (now the ANU Institute of Technical Thermophysics). He has made scientific contributions in the fields of thermal flow in mines, the automated control of air purification, and geothermal energy utilization.

Vadym Shcherbakivsky   Oleksander Shcherban

Shcherbakivsky, Vadym [Ščerbakivs'kyj], b 17 March 1876 in Shpychyntsi, Skvyra county, Kiev gubernia, d 18 January 1957 in London. Ethnographer and archeologist; member of the Shevchenko Scientific Society (from 1930), the Ukrainian Academy of Arts and Sciences, the Slovak Scientific Society, the Czechoslovak Academy of Sciences, and the International Anthropological Institute (France). He studied at the Universities of St Petersburg, Moscow, and Kiev (1902) and participated in Ukrainian social-democratic political activities, for which he was arrested several times. In 1907 he moved to Galicia, where he worked in the National Museum in Lviv (1908–10). He later participated in excavations in Bilhorod, near Kiev (1910–12), and worked as curator of the archeological section of the Poltava Zemstvo Museum (1912–22). During the existence of the Ukrainian State Shcherbakivsky was a professor at the Ukrainian University in Poltava (1918). As an émigré he was a professor at the Ukrainian Free University (1922–45 in Prague and 1945–51 in Munich). In 1951 he moved to England, where he did research on ancient Ukrainian history, in London.

Yurii Shcherbatenko: *Window* (oil, 1968)

Shcherbatenko, Yurii [Ščerbatenko, Jurij], b 29 December 1915 in Sochi, Black Sea gubernia. Painter. He graduated from the Donetske Art Tekhnikum (1935) and the Kiev State Art Institute (1942), where he studied under F. Krychevsky, S. Hryhoriev, and K. Yeleva. He has painted works such as *Lesia Ukrainka* (1957), *Physicists* (1967), *Bowels of the Earth* (1968), and *Soccer* (1971).

Shcherbatsky, Heorhii [Ščerbac'kyj, Heorhij], b ?, d 18 August 1754 in Moscow. Churchman and teacher. A monk of the Transfiguration–St Sophia Monastery in Kiev, he served as a professor of poetics (1749–50) and philosophy (1751–2) and as prefect (1752–3) at the Kievan Mohyla Academy. In 1753–4 he taught at the Slavonic-Greek-Latin Academy in Moscow. He wrote the play *Tragedokomediia naritsaemaia Fotii* (A Tragicomedy Called Photius, 1749) and two Latin recensions of his philosophy courses, which were deeply influenced by the Cartesian method and doctrines.

Shcherbatsky, Tymofii [Ščerbac'kyj, Tymofij] (secular name: Tykhon Shcherbak), b 1698 in Trypilia, Kiev regiment, d 18 April 1767 in Moscow. Orthodox church hierarch. After graduating from the Kievan Mohyla Academy and working in church administration he was hegumen of the Mhar Transfiguration, Vydubychi, and St Michael's Golden-Domed monasteries, and then archimandrite of the Kievan Cave Monastery (1740–8). In 1748 he became metropolitan of Kiev. He entered into conflict with the Kievan academy, which he attempted to place fully under his own authority. He claimed for the Kiev metropolitan the right to name professors to the academy, and issued a statute in 1752 reforming the organization and curriculum of the school. His attempt to establish a printing press for the metropoly brought him into conflict with the Kievan Cave Monastery Press, and his efforts to take over Pereiaslav eparchy were opposed by the Russian Holy Synod. Throughout his tenure in Kiev, Shcherbatsky was embroiled in disputes with S. Liaskoronsky, the rector of the Kievan academy, and with N. Solonyna and M. Stefanovsky, the archimandrites of the Kiev Epiphany Brotherhood Monastery. The constant conflict resulted in the weakening of Kiev metropoly and contributed to its eventual subjugation by the Russian Orthodox church. Shcherbatsky moved to Moscow, where he was metropolitan (1757–67) and a member of the Holy Synod. He is the subject of a biography by I. Graevsky (1910).

Fedir Shcherbyna

Shcherbyna, Fedir [Ščerbyna], b 13 February 1849 in Novodereviankivka *stanytsia*, Kuban oblast, d 28 October 1936 in Prague. Statistician, economic historian, and teacher; corresponding member of the Russian Academy of Sciences from 1904 and full member of the Shevchenko Scientific Society from 1924. Shcherbyna studied at the Petrovskoe Agricultural Academy near Moscow (1872–4) and at Odessa University (1874–7); in Odessa he was a member of the city's Hromada. He was exiled to Vologda gubernia in 1877–81 for his political agitation among Odessa workers. In 1884–1901 he was director of the statistical bureau of the Voronezh gubernia zemstvo and helped edit 66 volumes of statistical information. In addition he published 16 volumes of statistics dealing with Voronezh gubernia (1887) as well as a history of the Voronezh zemstvo (1891).

Shcherbyna was placed under house arrest in 1901 for his public demands for the establishment of a constitutional system within the Russian Empire, and exiled to the Kuban. There he did research and wrote about the history of the Kuban, particularly the Cossacks. In 1906 he headed the revived Kuban Cossack council (dormant since the end of the 18th century), and in 1907 he became a socialist representative to the Second Duma. After the February Revolution of 1917 he was elected a member of the Kuban Legislative Council (1917–20), and headed the supreme court of the Kuban Cossack Host. Shcherbyna emigrated to Yugoslavia (1920) and then to Prague (1921), where he became a professor (1922–36) and rector (1924–5) of the *Ukrainian Free University. He also taught statistics at the Ukrainian Husbandry Academy in Poděbrady (from 1922).

Shcherbyna is most noted for his statistical work. His first work in the field, *Ocherki iuzhno-russkikh artelei i obshchinno-artel'nikh form* (An Outline of Southern Russian Artels and *Obshchina*-Artel Forms, 1881), was based on research he had undertaken in Odessa from 1875, and had a significant impact on the development of the co-operative movement in Ukraine. He wrote many studies about zemstvo communities, and notable works such as *Krest'ianskoe khoziaistvo v ostrogoskom uezde* (Peasant Agriculture in Ostrohozke County, 1885) and *Krest'ianskie biudzhety* (Peasant Budgets, 1900). He also wrote many works about the Kuban, including *Istoriia Kubanskogo Kazach'ego Voiska* (A History of the Kuban Cossack Host, 2 vols, 1910, 1913).

BIBLIOGRAPHY
Mytsiuk, O. *Naukova diial'nist' statystyka F.A. Shcherbyny* (Poděbrady 1931)

A. Zhukovsky

Shcherbyna, Nykyfor [Ščerbyna], b 22 February 1900 in the Cossack settlement of Starokorsunska, Kuban, d 21 March 1977 in New York. Poet. He was active in the Prosvita society (1919–20) and the Ukrainian Literary Society (1920–3) in the Kuban and was secretary of the literary journal *Zoria* (1920–3) in Krasnodar. He contributed poems and stories to the major Soviet Ukrainian literary periodicals as a member of Hart (1923) and the Association of Panfuturists (1924–6) in Kiev and Vaplite (1927–30) and the All-Ukrainian Association of Proletarian Writers (1930–2) in Kharkiv. Published separately were his poetry collections *Ranok* (Morning, 1929) and *Homin budniv* (The Echo of Workdays, 1930). In 1931 he was accused of 'nationalism,' and his work was not published again until 1941. In the 1930s he translated 12 books of Russian literature into Ukrainian. An associate of the Taras Shevchenko Scientific Research Institute (1935–6), he graduated from Kharkiv University in 1936 and then worked as a teacher in Novoselivka (1936–7) and a lecturer in world literature at the Kharkiv Pedagogical Institute (1937–8). As a postwar refugee he lived in Germany and, from 1950, the United States, where he contributed to émigré periodicals and published a collection of poems for children, *Prolisky* (Clearings, 1969).

Volodymyr Shcherbyna   Volodymyr Shcherbytsky

Shcherbyna, Volodymyr [Ščerbyna], b 28 May 1850 in Kiev, d 1936 in Kiev. Historian, pedagogue, and community activist; corresponding member of the VUAN. He studied at Kiev University (1868–73) under V. Antonovych and M. Drahomanov and wrote his dissertation on Hetman K. Rozumovsky. He studied pedagogy in St Petersburg (1876) and then taught history and literature in gymnasiums there and in Kiev (1879–1920). He was a member of the Kievan Historical Archives Group (headed by Antonovych in the 1880s and 1890s), the Kiev Archeographic Commission, and the Historical Society of Nestor the Chronicler. He published his studies in *Arkhiv Iugo-Zapadnoi Rossii*, *Chteniia v Istoricheskom obshchestve Nestora-letopistsa*, and *Kievskaia starina* (mostly in 1891–9), as well as in ZNTSh (under the cryptonym 'V.I.'), *Ukraïna*, and ZIFV. In 1901 he traveled through Right-Bank Ukraine to collect ancient documents and art.

Together with Ya. Shulhyn, V. Naumenko, and O. Levytsky Shcherbyna was active in many Kievan community and cultural organizations. From 1920 he devoted himself to scholarly work in the National Library of Ukraine and the VUAN Archival Administration and Archeographic Commission, directed (from 1925) the VUAN Commission on the History of Kiev and Right-Bank Ukraine, and was a member of the VUAN Chair of Ukrainian History (later the *Institute of History of the AN URSR). He was an acclaimed specialist on the history of Kiev (particularly the 17th and 18th centuries), and he also wrote about the haidamaka uprisings and the Cossack period and compiled memoirs of Antonovych (1909) and Shulhyn (1912).

In 1926, on the 50th anniversary of the beginning of Shcherbyna's scholarly activity, the VUAN published *Novi studiï z istoriï Kyieva V.I. Shcherbyny* (New Studies of the History of Kiev by V. Shcherbyna); the publication also contained biographical and bibliographical information.

A. Zhukovsky

Shcherbytsky, Volodymyr [Ščerbyc'kyj], b 17 February 1918 in Verkhnodniprovske, Katerynoslav gubernia, d 16 February in 1990 in Kiev. Communist party and Soviet government leader. A graduate of the Dnipropetrovske Chemical Technology Institute (1941), after the Second World War he worked as an engineer in Dniprodzerzhynske. From 1948 he was a Party functionary; he rose through the ranks to the positions of first secretary of the Dniprodzerzhynske City Committee (1952–4), CC CPU candidate (1954–6) and full member (1956–89), second (1954–5) and first (1955–7, 1963–5) secretary of the Dnipropetrovske Oblast Committee, CPSU Central Auditing Commission member (1956–61), CC CPU Presidium member (1957–66), CC CPU secretary (1957–61), chairman of the Ukrainian Council of Ministers (1961–3, 1965–72), CC CPSU member (1961–89), CC CPSU Presidium candidate (1961–3, 1965–6), CC CPSU Politburo candidate (1966–71) and member (1971–89), CC CPU Politburo member (1966–89), and CPU first secretary (1972–89) and member of the USSR and Ukrainian SSR Supreme Soviet presidia (1972–89).

A protégé of L. Brezhnev and a Moscow loyalist, Shcherbytsky replaced P. *Shelest as CPU first secretary and purged Shelest's supporters from the Party and government apparatus and cultural and academic institutions. From 1972 to approx 1986 his neo-Stalinist rule in Ukraine was marked by intensified *Russification, repression of the *dissident movement, ideological conservatism (especially in *nationality policy), and economic and cultural stagnation. On Shcherbytsky's initiative all Party work and all CPU congresses were conducted in Russian. A recognized opponent of M. Gorbachev's policies, he was one of the last three Brezhnevites to be dropped from the CC CPSU Politburo, in September 1989. A few days later he was replaced as CPU first secretary by V. Ivashko.

R. Senkus

Shchirbiavy, Ivan [Ščirbjavyj], b and d ? Carpenter from Husakiv, Galicia. In 1641 he built a wooden church in Dusivtsi, near Peremyshl. It is the oldest extant wooden church in Ukraine with three domes and small side choirs near the nave.

Shchoholiv, Irynarkh [Ščoholiv, Irynarx], b 1873 in the Katerynoslav region, d 1943. Entomologist. A graduate of the Kiev Polytechnical Institute and a member of the Agricultural Scientific Committee of Ukraine (1919–24), he was a professor at the Kiev Agricultural Institute (from 1923). He compiled *Slovnyk ukraïns'kyi entomologychnoï nomenklatury* (A Ukrainian Dictionary of Entomological Terms, 1918) and coauthored *Slovnyk zoolohychnoï nomenklatury* (Dictionary of Zoological Terms, 1928).

Shchoholiv, Ivan [Ščoholiv] (Shchoholev; pseud: Ivan Tohobichny), b 1862 in Horodyshche, Cherkasy county, Kiev gubernia, d 1933. Dramatist and stage actor, director, and entrepreneur. He headed the *Society of Ukrainian Actors (1907–10) and was an actor at the theater in the People's Home in the Kiev suburb of Lukianivka (from 1910). He wrote melodramatic 'ethnographic' plays, several of which were staged in prerevolutionary central Ukraine and Galicia. They include *Zahublenyi rai* (Lost Paradise, 1896), *Zhydivka – vykhrestka* (The Jewess – Convert, 1896, pub 1909), *Dushohuby* (The Murderers, 1898, pub 1910, based on E. Zola's *Thérèse Raquin*), *Maty – nai-*

Ivan Shchoholiv (portrait by Vitalii Kravchenko)   Yakiv Shchoholiv

Mykola Shchors   Vasyl Shchurat

mychka (The Mother – Hired Woman, 1899, pub 1909, based on T. Shevchenko's 'Naimychka'), *Kokhaitesia, chornobrovi!* (Love Each Other, Dark-browed Ones!, 1901, based on Shevchenko's 'Kateryna'), *Bortsi za mrii* (Fighters for [Their] Dreams, 1903, pub 1924), and *Chernytsia* (The Nun, 1906, with H. Ashkarenko). An edition of Shchoholiv's plays was published in Kiev in 1972.

Shchoholiv, Yakiv [Ščoholiv, Jakiv] (Shchoholev), b 6 November 1823 in Okhtyrka, Kharkiv gubernia, d 8 June 1898 in Kharkiv. Romantic poet. He studied at Kharkiv University until 1848 and worked in clerical-bureaucratic positions in various institutions. He began to publish in 1840 in *Literaturnaia gazeta*, *Otechestvennye zapiski*, and the almanac *Molodyk*. In 1883 he published the poetry collection *Vorsklo*, and in 1898, *Slobozhanshchyna* (Slobidska Ukraine). His main poetic inspiration was the poetry of T. Shevchenko and folklore. Shchoholiv was associated with the *Kharkiv Romantic School, and a great deal of his poetry is a Romantic representation of Ukrainian history, in particular of the Cossack era and the Zaporozhian Cossacks. His Cossackophile romanticism expresses a longing for the past and for the 'lost Sich.' Quite a number of his poems depict images of Ukrainian nature; others deal with social concerns. Many of his poems have been set to music and have become part of the popular repertoire; they include 'Priakha' (The Spinner), 'Cherevychky' (Shoes), and 'Zymovyi vechir' (A Winter's Evening). Shchoholiv's works have also been published posthumously: *Tvory: Povnyi zbirnyk* (Works: The Complete Collection, 1919), *Poezii* (Poems, 1926), *Tvory* (Works, 2 vols, 1930), *Poezii* (Poems, 1958), and *Tvory* (Works, 1961).

BIBLIOGRAPHY
Kaspruk, A. *Iakiv Shchoholiv: Narys zhyttia i tvorchosty* (Kiev 1958)
I. Koshelivets

Shchors, Mykola [Ščors], b 25 May 1895 in Snovske (now Shchors), Horodnia county, Chernihiv gubernia, d 30 August 1919 in Biloshytsia (now Shchorsivka), Ovruch county, Volhynia gubernia. Bolshevik military leader. He graduated from military schools in Kiev (1914) and Vilnius and served as a captain in the Russian imperial army. From 1918 he commanded Bolshevik military units, including the Bohun Regiment, the 2nd Brigade, the 1st

Ukrainian Soviet Division, and the 44th Riflemen's Division, that fought the Army of the UNR in 1919. He died in battle against the Seventh Brigade of the Ukrainian Galician Army near Korosten. Shchors became a cult hero in the Ukrainian SSR and the USSR, and on J. Stalin's orders he was proclaimed the 'Ukrainian Chapaev.' Monuments to him were erected, and a museum in his honor was opened. He was the subject of a novel by S. Skliarenko, a film by O. Dovzhenko, and an opera by B. Liatoshynsky. In the late 1980s, Soviet historiographers began to re-examine his history in a more objective light (*Arkhivy Ukraïny*, 1985, no. 5; *Kyïv*, 1988, no. 11; *Literaturna Ukraïna*, 1989, no. 33).

Shchors [Ščors]. II-12. A city (1989 pop 12,600) on the Snov River and a raion center in Chernihiv oblast. A *khutir* established at the site in the 1860s developed into a settlement after the Homel–Bakhmach railway line was constructed (1874), and adopted the name of the nearest railway station, Snovske. In 1924 the settlement was granted city status, and in 1935 it was renamed Shchors. Today it is an industrial and transportation center. It has a furniture factory and railway servicing shops.

Shchotove [Ščotove]. V-20, DB III-6. A town smt (1986 pop 6,300) in Luhanske oblast. It originated in 1783 and attained smt status in 1938. The town is administered by the Antratsyt municipal council. Its coal mine has been working since 1918. It also has a tractor-parts factory.

Shchupak, Samiilo [Ščupak, Samijlo] b 16 March 1894 or 10 April 1895 in Lypovets, Kiev gubernia, d 10 March 1937. Literary critic and political activist. He joined the Communist party in 1919 and was editor of the journal *Hlobus* and the newspapers *Bil'shovyk* and *Proletars'ka pravda* in the 1920s. His first published work appeared in 1920. In 1930 he moved to Kharkiv and became editor of *Literaturna hazeta* (1930–6) and the journal *Krytyka*. He was one of the leaders of the All-Ukrainian Association of Proletarian Writers and an organizer of the Writers' Union of Ukraine. His articles of literary criticism adhered to the Party line, and in the *Literary Discussion of 1925–8 he came out against M. Khvylovy. Collections of his writings include *Krytyka i proza* (Criticism and Prose, 1930),

Borot'ba za metodolohiiu (The Struggle for Methodology, 1933), and *Sotsiialistychnyi realizm u khudozhnii literaturi* (Socialist Realism in Literature, 1934). He was arrested on 10 November 1936, accused of being a member of a Trotskyite counterrevolutionary group, and sentenced to death by shooting. He was posthumously rehabilitated.

Shchurat, Vasyl [Ščurat, Vasyl'] (pseuds: V. Boronchynsky, V. Iskra, I. Khmaryn, Komon, V. Konin, Omega, Omikron, V. Sava, V. Sigma, Vin, V. Vyslobotsky, Zyzyk), b 24 August 1871 in Vysloboky, Lviv county, Galicia, d 27 April 1948 in Lviv. Literary scholar, community leader, writer, and translator; member of the *Shevchenko Scientific Society (NTSh) from 1914. Shchurat entered literary and public life as a protégé of I. Franko, under whose influence he remained until 1896. He studied at Vienna University (1892–4), graduated from Lviv University (1895), and received a PH D in Slavic philology from Vienna University (1896). He worked as a state gymnasium teacher in Stanyslaviv (1897), Peremyshl (1898–1901), Brody (1901–7), and Lviv (1907–18) and was active in the Prosvita society and the NTSh. He was coeditor of the Chernivtsi newspaper *Bukovyna* (1896, 1904–6), helped edit the modernist journal *S'vit* (Lviv 1906–7), and was chief editor of the pedagogical journal *Uchytel'* (1908–9) and the weekly *Nedilia* (1911).

Shchurat contributed much to the revival of the NTSh after the First World War as its president (1919–25). He was also at the forefront of the campaign for the creation of a Ukrainian university in Lviv. After the failure of that campaign he initiated the idea of establishing the *Lviv (Underground) Ukrainian University and served as its first rector (1921–3), for which involvement he was imprisoned for three months in 1921 by the Polish authorities. He refused to swear allegiance to the new Polish republic. In 1928 he became president of the Society of Writers and Journalists in Galicia. In 1929 he was elected a full member of the VUAN, but in 1930 he renounced his membership in protest against the Soviet show trial of the *Union for the Liberation of Ukraine and the Stalinist repression of Ukrainian intellectuals. After the Soviet occupation of Galicia in 1939, he was elected full member of the AN URSR (now ANU). He was director of the ANU Lviv Scientific Library (1939–41 and 1944–8) and was a professor at Lviv University.

Shchurat published scholarly articles and literary criticism in Austrian, Polish, Czech, and Western Ukrainian periodicals (mainly in *Zapysky NTSh*). His many poems, stories, translations, and literary and political articles were published from 1890 on in *Zoria, Dilo, Narod, Radykal, Pravda, Zhytie i slovo, Hromads'kyi holos, Bukovyna, Ruslan, S'vit, Uchytel', Dzvinok, Nedilia, Zerkalo,* and *Zyz.* His scholarly purview ranged from medieval Ukrainian literature (eg, *Moleniie Danyla Zatochnyka*) to that of the 19th century (especially T. Shevchenko, M. Shashkevych, P. Kulish, I. Kotliarevsky, Yu. Fedkovych, Franko, V. Samiilenko, and H. Kvitka-Osnovianenko). Shchurat devoted much attention to Ukrainian-Polish relations, particularly in literature. Among his many publications were booklets on the Bible in Shevchenko's poetry (1904), the Grünwald Song (1906), the Peregrination of Danylo of Korsun (1906), the Pochaiv *Bohohlasnyk* (1908), J. Słowacki in Ukrainian literature (1909), and the Koliivshchyna rebellion in Polish literature to 1841 (1910); an anthology of 19th-century po-

etry in translation (1903); a book of literary essays (1913); a collection of articles about Shevchenko (1914); a book on Shevchenko and the Poles (1917); a collection of articles on the Ukrainian revival in early 19th-century Galicia (1919); and a monograph on the philosophical foundations of Kulish's works (1922).

Shchurat wrote the poetry collections *Lux in tenebris* (1895), *Moï lysty* (My Letters, 1898), *Raz do mene molodist' pryishla* (One Time Youth Came to Me, 1904), *Na trymbiti* [sic] (On the Trembita, 1904), *Istorychni pisni* (Historical Songs, 1907; expanded posthumous edn 1937), and *Vybir pisen'* (A Selection of Songs, 1909) and the narrative poem *V suzdal's'kii tiurmi* (In a Suzdal Prison, 1916). He also wrote the versified prayer book *Iz hlybyny vozzvakh* (From the Depths [He] Called Forth, 1900, 1905) and the religious narrative poem *Zarvanytsia* (1902). He translated into Ukrainian poetry and prose from classical Greek (a book of Horace's odes [1901]), French (eg, *Chanson de Roland* [1895], V. Hugo, G. Flaubert, G. de Maupassant), German (eg, H. Heine, J.W. von Goethe, D. von Liliencron, P. Lindau), Polish, Russian, Bulgarian, and other languages. Until 1914 his 1907 contemporary Ukrainian *Slovo o polku Ihorevi* (The Tale of Ihor's Campaign) was the best Ukrainian poetic rendition of the Rus' epic. Large editions of Shchurat's poetry were published in Lviv in 1957 and 1962, and a book of his selected scholarly works (with his bibliography) appeared in Kiev in 1963.

I. Koshelivets

Platonida Shchurovska

Shchurovska, Platonida [Ščurovs'ka] (married name: Rossinevich), b 1893 in the Cherkasy region, d 1973 in Prague. Educator and conductor. After studying music under O. Koshyts in Kiev, she was assistant conductor of the *Ukrainian Republican Kapelle during its tour of Europe (1919). She lectured at the Ukrainian Higher Pedagogical Institute in Prague and conducted its choir (1923–33). While she taught singing at a secondary school in Uzhhorod, she conducted the Banduryst choir (1934–6). Returning to Prague, she taught at the state conservatory.

Shchurovsky, Petro [Ščurovs'kyj], b 1850 in Poltava, d 1908 in Kursk, Russia. Pianist, conductor, and composer. After graduating from the Moscow Conservatory he served as choirmaster at the Moscow Opera (1878–82) and then worked in smaller centers in the empire. He wrote piano pieces, vocal solos, two orchestral suites, and the operas *Bohdan Khmelnytsky* (1883) and *Vakula the Blacksmith* (unfinished).

Shchurovsky, Tymofii [Ščurovs'kyj, Tymofij], b 1740 in Volhynia, d 15 April 1812. Basilian missionary and church figure. After graduating from a Basilian school and completing his theology training in Rome with a doctorate in canon law, he was apostolic protonotary and then head of the Basilian novitiate in Byten, Volhynia, and hegumen of the monastery in Biała Podlaska. He later administered monasteries throughout the eparchies of Berestia, Volodymyr-Volynskyi, and Kiev. He published several spiritual poems in Latin and Polish, a collection of religous sayings and slogans (1780), an introduction to canon law and the decrees and decisions (1792), and four volumes of catechism and simple theological instruction (1792). Shchurovsky was especially noted as an orator.

Volodymyr Shchurovsky   Mykola Shchyrba

Shchurovsky, Volodymyr [Ščurovs'kyj], b 23 February 1890 in Nyzhnii Strutyn, Dolyna county, Galicia, d 4 May 1969 in Dresden, Germany. Physician; member of the Shevchenko Scientific Society. A graduate of Lviv University (1914), he joined the Ukrainian Sich Riflemen (USS) and served at the rank of captain as chief physician of the Eastern Group of the Ukrainian Galician Army and of the First Brigade of the USS. He attended to I. Franko in 1916, while working in the USS hospital in Lviv. After the war he lectured at the Lviv (Underground) Ukrainian University. In 1939 he emigrated and settled in Dresden, where he worked as a hospital physician. His war recollections were published in *Kalendar Chervonoï Kalyny* (1924, 1935) and *Ukraïns'ka Halyts'ka Armiia* (Ukrainian Galician Army, vol 1, 1958).

Shchurovsky, Yurii [Ščurovs'kyj, Jurij], b 28 April 1927 in Kiev. Composer and educator. He graduated from the Kiev Conservatory in 1951 and studied composition with B. Liatoshynsky in 1954. He lectured at the conservatory on musical theory in 1952–5 and then taught music until 1960. He was an editor for the Mystetstvo publishing house from 1951, and in 1973 was appointed editor of the Muzychna Ukraina publishing house. His compositions include two symphonies (1962, 1966), a string quartet (1949), a piano sonata (1951) and trio (1949), several cello quartets (1966), and some radio and film music.

Shchusev, Aleksei [Ščusev, Aleksej], b 8 October 1873 in Kishinev, Bessarabia gubernia, d 24 May 1949 in Moscow. Russian architect; full member of the St Petersburg (later USSR) Academy of Arts from 1910 and the USSR Academy of Sciences from 1943. A graduate of the St Petersburg Academy of Arts (1897), from 1913 he lectured in various art institutes and designed important buildings in Moscow, including the Lenin Mausoleum (1924), and other Russian and Soviet cities. In Ukraine he oversaw the construction of the Trinity Cathedral at the Pochaiv Monastery (1905–12) and the church on I. Kharytonenko's estate in Nativka (1908–12), and the restoration of St Basil's Church in Ovruch (1904–11). He drew up plans for the iconostasis of the Dormition Cathedral and the murals in the refectory at the Kievan Cave Monastery (1902–10). After the Second World War he helped plan the reconstruction of Kiev's Khreshchatyk Blvd and the AN URSR (now ANU) Main Astronomical Observatory (1949). N. Sokolov's book about him was published in Moscow in 1952.

Shchutska, Marusia [Ščuc'ka, Marusja], b 1941 in Vereshyna, Hrubeshiv county, Kholm region (now in Poland). Opera singer (soprano). After graduating from the Higher Music School in Łódź in 1970, she sang with the Polish National Philharmonic Orchestra in Warsaw and toured Czechoslovakia, Denmark, Italy, Yugoslavia, and Hungary with the Capella Bydgostiensis. In 1972 she joined the Łódź Opera as a soloist and appeared in roles such as Papagena in W. Mozart's *The Magic Flute*, Olympia in J. Offenbach's *Tales of Hoffmann*, the Priestess in G. Verdi's *Aida*, and Eurydice in C. Monteverdi's *The Legend of Orpheus*.

Shchyrba, Mykola [Ščyrba] (pseud: M. Kholmsky), b 6 December 1902 in Lotiv, Hrubeshiv county, Lublin gubernia, d 28 August 1984 in Yalta. Communist activist and publicist. In the 1920s he was a member of the Ukrainian Social Democratic party and then joined the Communist Party of Western Ukraine. In 1944 he was imprisoned in a Nazi concentration camp. Having returned to Poland in 1948, he worked in a publishing house in Warsaw. In 1955 he appealed to the Polish Party leader, E. Ochab, to establish *Nashe slovo, the Ukrainian newspaper in Poland, and the next year he became its first editor. He was one of the founding members of the *Ukrainian Social and Cultural Society in Poland and served for many years as its vice-president. He wrote poetry, stories, and a novel, which were published in *Nasha kul'tura*, the literary supplement to *Nashe slovo*.

Shchyrsky, Ivan [Ščyrs'kyj] (monastic name: Inokentii), b ca 1650, most likely in the Chernihiv region, d 1714 in Liubech, Chernihiv regiment. Baroque engraver. He studied engraving under O. *Tarasevych at the Vilnius Academy Press (1677–80) and theology and literature at the academy. He worked as a master engraver in Vilnius (1680–3) and then in Chernihiv and Kiev, where he also taught poetics at the Kievan Mohyla College. In 1686 he took monastic vows at the Kievan Cave Monastery, and soon afterward he cofounded the St Anthony of the Caves Monastery in Liubech. Shchyrsky created over 100 copper engravings. Those from his Vilnius period included copies of the Częstochowa and other miraculous icons, coats

Ivan Shchyrsky: *Sailing of the Nymphs* (copper-engraving illustration to Stefan Yavorsky's poem *Echo głosu* [The Voice's Echo, 1689] dedicated to Hetman Ivan Mazepa)

Ivan Shchyrsky: *Teza* in honor of Prokip Kalachynsky (1690s)

of arms (eg, for A. Kysil), and pictures of Christ carrying the cross and SS Dominic, Thomas Aquinas, John Chrysostom, and Michael Gedroyc. During his time in Ukraine he created many fine, detailed engravings: illustrations for religious and panegyrical books, such as L. Baranovych's *Blahodat' i istyna* (Grace and Truth, 1683), L. Krzczonowicz's *Redivivus Phoenix* (1683) and *Ilias oratoria* (1698), S. Yavorsky's *Echo głosu wołającego na puszczy* (Echo of a Voice of One Calling in the Wilderness, 1689), P. Orlyk's *Hippomenes Sarmacki ...* (The Sarmatian Hippomenes ..., 1698), and J. Ornowski's *Bogaty ... wirydarz Zacharzewskich ...* (The Rich ... Orchard of the Zacharzhewskis ..., 1705); L. Baranovych's coat of arms (1683); a depiction of the Dormition (1686); antimensia for Patriarch Adrian of Moscow (1694, with L. Tarasevych and Fedir), Archbishop I. Maksymovych of Chernihiv (1697), and Metropolitan I. Krokovsky of Kiev (1708); the famous engraving *Labarum triumphale ...* (1698) for the poetic *teza* honoring P. Kalachynsky, the rector of the Mohyla College; a portrait of Metropolitan V. Yasynsky (1707); and two large, complex illustrations to poetic theses of scholarly disputes at the Kievan Mohyla Academy in 1708, dedicated to Yasynsky and Field Marshal B. Sheremetev. D. Stepovyk's book about Shchyrsky and the poetic image in Ukrainian baroque engraving was published in Kiev in 1988.

D. Stepovyk

Sheatfish (*Silurus glanis*; Ukrainian: *som zvychainyi*). A large, scaleless, freshwater catfish of the family Siluridae, reaching 5 m in length and up to 300 kg in weight. It is a valuable commercial fish. In Ukraine sheatfish inhabit the Black Sea basin. In Western Ukraine a pygmy sheatfish of a different family (*Amiurus nebulosus*) has been acclimatized; its body length is about 30 cm, and its weight, 500 g.

Shebelynka gas field. One of the largest deposits of natural gas in the former USSR, covering almost 250 sq km in Balakliia and Pervomaiske raions, in Kharkiv oblast.

Located in the *Dnieper-Donets Trough, it was discovered in 1950 and has been exploited since 1956. The gas is found at depths of 1,300–2,500 m, primarily in the Carboniferous and Permian strata. It is high in methane (up to 93 percent) and contains some ethane (up to 4 percent), butane, propane, and coal gas. In 1970, 340 wells pumped 31 billion cu m of gas (almost 16 percent of the USSR total and over one-half the total for Ukraine) from the field. The gas is processed by the *Shebelynka Gas Industry Authority and used in industry and for heating in Kiev, Odessa, Mykolaiv, and Dnipropetrovske.

Shebelynka Gas Industry Authority (Shebelynske hazopromyslove upravlinnia, or Shebelynkahazprom). A major gas-processing complex located in Chervonyi Donets, Balakliia raion, Kharkiv oblast. It was established in 1956 to refine and process gas from the Shebelynka gas field. Most of the gas is processed by low-temperature separation plants. The complex includes four gas condensers and five compressor stations.

Shebelynka Rebellion. A peasant uprising in 1829 in Shebelynka *sloboda* and the surrounding villages and *slobody* in Slobidska Ukraine gubernia. It was provoked by the imperial Russian government's implementation of *military settlements in the gubernia and the conversion of the peasants into military settlers. Beginning on 6 June 1829 approx 3,000 peasants joined the rebellion, which was led by S. Demin (Domin) and K. Vedernikov. The revolt was mercilessly and brutally crushed on 11 June 1829; 109 people were killed, and 143 were tried by military court. The two leaders were sentenced to hard labor for life, and 48 men were deported to military settlements in Kherson gubernia.

Bohdan Shebunchak

Shebunchak, Bohdan [Šebunčak], b 26 December 1921 in Solotvyna, Nadvirna county, Galicia. Physician and civic leader. After completing his medical studies at the universities of Lviv (1942–4) and Erlangen (1948) he settled in the United States, where he opened a private practice in Bloomfield, New Jersey. He has been president of the *Ukrainian Medical Association of North America (1969–71) and the *Organization for the Rebirth of Ukraine (1970–8), as well as an executive member of the Ukrainian Congress Committee of America, the World Congress of Free Ukrainians, and the Ukrainian American Coordinating Council.

Sheep farming. A branch of *animal husbandry that breeds and raises sheep for meat, milk, wool, and hides. Sheep are a domestic ruminant artiodactyl of the genus *Ovis* and the family Bovidae. They were domesticated some 8,000 years ago. They grow to 100 cm high at the shoulder and can reach weights of 180 kg (ewes are smaller, up to 100 kg). Sheep are classified by the shape of their tails. Their principal feeds are cultivated and natural grasses, hay, spring straw, silage, and concentrates. Under favorable conditions sheep live 14 to 15 years and produce good wool for 6 to 8 years. The quality of fleece ranges from fine to coarse. The average annual clip from fine-wooled sheep is 5–6 kg of wool; coarse-wooled sheep produce 1–4 kg. The yield of pure wool after washing is 30–50 percent from fine-wooled animals and up to 75 percent from coarse-wooled animals.

Sheep have been raised in Ukraine since the Neolithic period. Sheep farming was widespread in Ukraine, especially in the steppes (before the land was tilled), the Carpathian Mountains (particularly in the high meadows or *polonyny*), and forested areas (where there were extensive

Askaniia sheep

hayfields). Sheep farming declined in importance in the forest-steppe regions of the Right Bank and Galicia as more land was brought under cultivation. Peasant households raised long-haired sheep primarily for domestic needs – for wool, which was used to make blankets and clothing (see *Weaving), as well as for meat and milk. Sheep manure was used as fertilizer. Popular local breeds of sheep included the Gray Sokil and Black Reshetylivka, both of which provided good wool. Wallachian sheep were common in the Carpathians, the Kherson region, and Bukovyna. The Hutsuls made *bryndza* cheese from their milk.

Sheep raising acquired commercial importance in the early- to mid-19th century, when large numbers of Merino sheep were imported and raised on the steppes. The virgin land provided plenty of pasture. The number of fine-wooled Merino sheep in the three steppe gubernias of Ukraine (Kherson, Katerynoslav, and Tavriia) increased from 400,000 in 1823 to 1.9 million in 1837, 3 million in 1848, and 7.1 million in 1866. Most sheep belonged to large landowners, some of whom raised as many as 100,000 sheep at a time. Ukrainian wool became an important export commodity (see *Wool industry). After peaking in the 1870s, sheep raising began to decline in importance. On the world market Ukrainian wool was displaced by cheaper Argentinian and Australian wool. At the same time, the steppes were brought under extensive cultivation. The number of fine-wooled sheep in the steppe gubernias decreased to 1.2 million in 1911–12, and the total number of sheep fell from 9 million in 1883 to 2 million in 1912. The decline in sheep raising in the other six Ukrainian gubernias was not as dramatic: from 6 million sheep in 1883 to 4 million sheep in 1911. Most of the sheep in those areas were coarse-wooled and were kept for strictly domestic use; even there, however, domestic wool was slowly displaced by manufactured textiles, and the area devoted to pasturing sheep was reduced. In Galicia the number of sheep decreased from 650,000 in the 1860s to 300,000 in 1910. The total number of sheep in Ukraine (within the current borders) was approximately 16 million (approx 12 percent of the total livestock) in 1883; by 1912 the figure was down to 7 million (approx 4 percent of all livestock). In the Kuban region at that time there were some 8 million sheep.

The sheep population declined even more during the First World War and especially in the revolutionary period. It began a rapid increase in the 1920s, however, partially owing to the unavailability of manufactured textiles. By 1928, there were 10 million sheep (approx 4 percent of all livestock) within the contemporary borders of Ukraine, and another 3.5 million on other Ukrainian territories. As before the war, the major regions for sheep farming were the Carpathians, Polisia (especially the Chernihiv region), the Crimea, and the Kuban.

The collectivization of agriculture and the man-made famine of 1932–3 again resulted in a dramatic decrease in the sheep population. Many animals were slaughtered by their owners instead of being turned over to the collective farms; others died because of neglect and feed shortages on the new farms. Their number in the Ukrainian SSR fell from 8.1 million in 1928 to 2 million in 1933, but rebounded to 4.7 million in 1940. After the Second World War the number of sheep increased steadily for several years and reached 5.8 million in 1950 and 11.1 million in 1960. Since then sheep farming has stagnated. The number of sheep in Ukraine in recent years has been 8.3 million (1970), 9 million (1980), and 8.8 million (1988).

Today most sheep in Ukraine are raised on collective farms (6.3 million in 1988). The commercial importance of wool has prompted the concentration of sheep farming especially in the traditional regions of commercial wool production (southern Ukraine). Relatively few private households keep sheep for domestic needs. Much breeding has been done in the 20th century to improve the quality of Ukrainian sheep, and particularly their wool production. The Askaniia sheep was bred by M. Ivanov at the Askaniia-Nova Nature Reserve in the 1920s, and several strains have been improved by crossbreeding. Merino sheep are an important source for much crossbreeding, and most Ukrainian sheep now are fine-wooled. Other common breeds are the Précoce (in Polisia and the forest-steppe region), Tsigai (in Donetske, Crimea, and Odessa oblasts), Karakul (in Poltava, Odessa, and Chernivtsi oblasts), and Sokil (in Poltava oblast). Relatively few sheep are raised primarily for meat or milk: annual production of mutton and lamb (together with some goat meat) was 73,000 t in 1960 but only 42,000 t in 1987. Problems of sheep breeding and raising are studied at the Scientific Research Institute of Animal Husbandry of the Forest-Steppe and Polisia of Ukraine, at the Ukrainian Scientific Research Institute of Animal Husbandry of the Steppe Regions, and at various oblast agricultural research stations.

BIBLIOGRAPHY
Vivcharstvo (Kiev 1971)
Krotov, A. *Vivcharstvo* (Kiev 1978)

V. Kubijovyč

Sheffer, Tamara [Šeffer], b 23 April 1909 in Poltava. Musicologist. She graduated from the Kiev Conservatory in 1938 and later lectured there (1945–53). She was a coauthor of *Muzykal'naia kul'tura Ukrainskoi SSR* (The Musical Culture of the Ukrainian SSR, 1957, repub 1961), *Narysy z istoriï ukraïns'koï muzyky* (Essays in the History of Ukrainian Music, 2 vols, 1964), and *Ryl's'kyi i muzyka* (Rylsky and Music, 1969) and the author of a monograph on L. Revutsky (1958).

Sheikovsky, Kalenyk [Šejkovs'kyj], b 1835 in Kamianets-Podilskyi, d 1903 in Menzelinsk, Ufa gubernia, Russia. Writer, linguist, educator, and ethnographer. As a student at Kiev University (1858–61) he helped organize Ukrainian Sunday schools in Kiev and published for them a book on domestic science (2 parts, 1860). He also wrote an ethnographic study on Podilian folkways (two parts, 1859–60). In 1876 he was exiled to Ufa gubernia for printing a Ukrainian translation of Ovid's *Metamorphoses*. His most important work was a Russian dictionary of vernacular Ukrainian, which contained many little-known dialectal words and his own neologisms. The first fascicle (*A–Byjak*) appeared in 1861. Because of the ban on Ukrainian-language publications (1863), financial difficulties, and the loss of materials in a fire, he managed to publish only two more fascicles (*T–Xlivec'*, 1884, 1886).

Sheka, Ivan [Šeka], b 16 October 1907 in Haichul (now Novoukrainka), Oleksandrivske county, Katerynoslav gubernia. Chemist; AN URSR (now ANU) corresponding member since 1967. A graduate of the Mykolaiv Institute of People's Education (1929), in 1933 he joined the ANU Institute of Chemistry (renamed General and Inorganic Chemistry). Sheka's research dealt with the physical chemistry of nonaqueous solutions, co-ordination chemistry, and the technology of rare elements. He introduced into industry several novel processes for obtaining indium, zirconium, and hafnium in various forms (pure powders, oxides, etc). He is the coauthor of *The Chemistry of Gallium* (English trans 1966).

Shekera, Anatolii [Šekera, Anatolij], b 17 May 1935 in Vladivostok. Ballet dancer and choreographer. In 1956 he completed study at the Perm Choreography School, and in 1964, the ballet studio at the Moscow State Theater Institute. He danced in the Lviv (1964–7) and the Kiev (1967–77; from 1974 as principal ballet master) theaters of opera and ballet; since 1977 he has been the choreographer in the latter theater.

Petro Shekeryk-Donykiv

Shekeryk-Donykiv, Petro [Šekeryk-Donykiv], b 20 April 1889 in Holove, Kosiv county, Galicia, d ? in Siberia. Hutsul civic and political leader. He was active in the Sich movement, H. Khotkevych's theater, and the Ukrainian Radical party. He was a member of the Ukrainian National Rada in Stanyslaviv in 1918–19 and a delegate to the Labor Congress in Kiev. An effective speaker, he was elected deputy to the Polish Sejm (1928–30) and mayor of Zhabie (1933–9). He was arrested by the Soviets in 1939 and deported to Siberia, where he disappeared. He collected ethnographic materials on the Hutsuls and wrote short stories about the opryshoks.

Shekhaiev, Roman [Šexajev] (Shekhai), b ?, d 4 July 1977 in Argentina. Ukrainian plant selection scientist. A specialist in the selection of potatoes and beans in Ukraine (1923–43), he headed the agronomy department of the Institute of the Fermentation Industry in Kiev and organized the Ukrainian Scientific Research Station for Potato Cultivation. Shekhaiev moved to Germany in 1943 and to San Miguel, Argentina, in 1950, where he worked at Tucumán University, directed a research station that he established in Catamarca, and developed potato varieties suitable for the subtropical climates of northern Argentina, Bolivia, and Peru.

Shekhonin, Mykola [Šexonin], b 1882, d 1970 in Argentina. Architect. A graduate of the St Petersburg Institute of Civil Engineering, from 1909 he lived in Kiev and taught architecture in various technical schools there, such as the Kiev Building Tekhnikum, the Kiev Polytechnical Institute, and the Kiev State Art Institute. From 1932 he headed the Second Architectural Art Workshop in Kiev. He created the plans for the façade of the Kiev Public Library (1909), the Kiev Military Engineering School (1913–17, 1918–20), the Ukrainian Printing Pavilion at the Agricultural Exhibition in Kiev (1913), the tobacco factory in Romen (1925), the Building of State Institutions on Khreshchatyk Blvd in Kiev (1929–31), the Food Workers' Club in Kiev's Podil district (1929–32), and the residential building of employees of the grain delivery department on Lysenko St in Kiev (1933–5). A postwar refugee, from 1950 he lived in Argentina.

Shekhovych, Severyn [Šexovyč], 1829–72. Galician journalist and writer. In the 1840s he was a member of a Russophile literary and civic circle known as the Pogodin Colony. He edited and published the first women's magazines in Galicia, *Lada* (1853) and *Rusalka* (1868–70), and served as editor or coeditor of many newspapers: *Zoria halytska* (1854), *Semeinaia biblioteka* (1855–6), *Pys'mo do hromady* (1864–5), *Shkola* (1865), *Hospodar* (1869), *Pravotar'* (1868–9), and *Chytanka* (1879, 1886). He also wrote verses and novelettes in the *yazychiie, including *Pavlyna Petrovna* (1855) and *Popadianka i popadehrafiianka* (The Priest's Daughter and the Priest-Count's Daughter, 1862).

Shekhtman, Manuil [Šextman, Manuïl], b 2 February 1900 in Lypnyky, Ovruch county, Volhynia gubernia, d 1941. Painter. He studied at the Kiev Art School (1913–20) and under M. Boichuk at the Kiev State Art Institute (1922–7). In the 1920s he belonged to the *Association of Revolutionary Art of Ukraine. From 1934 he worked in Moscow. His easel paintings include *Dina* (1926), *Expulsion of the Jews* (1927), *Refugees* (1929), and *Horrors of War* (1938). Under Boichuk's supervision he painted the frescoes *Corvée* and *Harvest Festival* at the Peasant Sanatorium in Odessa. They were condemned as 'nationalist formalist' and destroyed.

Manuil Shekhtman: *Refugees* (tempera, 1929)

Shelduck (*Tadorna tadorna*; Ukrainian: *halahaz, pehanka*). A large, short-billed, Old World duck of the family Anatidae, with white, black, and red plumage. In Ukraine it is found in the steppe zone, from the Danube River east to the shores of the Sea of Azov. It winters in western Europe. The down of shelducks is of commercial value.

Petro Shelest

Shelest, Petro [Šelest], b 14 February 1908 in Andriivka, Zmiiv county, Kharkiv gubernia. Communist party and Soviet government leader. A graduate of the Mariiupil Metallurgical Institute (1935), from 1940 he worked as a Party official in defense industries in Kharkiv, Cheliabinsk, and Saratov, and from 1948 as a plant director in Leningrad and Kiev. A protégé of N. Khrushchev and M. Pidhirny, he rose in the Party to the positions of second secretary of the Kiev City Committee (1954), second (1954) and first (1957) secretary of the Kiev Oblast Committee, CC CPU candidate (1954) and member (1956), CC CPU Presidium candidate (1960) and member (1961), CC CPSU member (1961), CC CPU secretary and chief of the CC CPU Bureau for Industry and Construction (1962), CPU first secretary and member of the Presidium of the Ukrainian Supreme Soviet (1963), CC CPSU Presidium candidate (1963) and member (1964), and CC CPSU and CC CPU Politburo member and member of the Presidium of the USSR Supreme Soviet (1966).

As the CPU first secretary Shelest pursued domestic policies that fostered renewed, though limited, forms of cultural and educational Ukrainization and a measure of autonomous administration and economic development. To some extent he tolerated the *dissident movement and the activities and patriotic writings of the nationally conscious intelligentsia in Ukraine. Consequently he came into conflict with L. Brezhnev and others in the CPSU Politburo. In 1970 Shelest published *Ukraïno nasha Radians'ka* (O Ukraine, Our Soviet [Land]), a popular book that mentioned Ukraine's glorious Cossack past and cultural achievements. In January 1972 the Moscow leadership attacked the 'national deviations' in Ukraine by launching a wave of arrests of Ukrainian dissidents. In May Shelest was abruptly replaced as first secretary by V. *Shcherbytsky and transferred to Moscow, where he served in the largely symbolic post of Soviet deputy premier for 11 months. His book was harshly denounced (May 1973) for its ideological and factual 'errors,' including 'nationalism,' 'idealization of the past,' 'economic autarchism,' and 'national narrow-mindedness,' and he was rebuked by Shcherbytsky for Party failures in Ukraine. Soon after his removal from the CPSU Politburo his many supporters in the CPU were purged. A collection of his speeches, *Ideï Lenina peremahaiut'* (Lenin's Ideas Triumph, 1971), came out just before his downfall.

BIBLIOGRAPHY
Bilinsky, Ya. 'The Communist Party of Ukraine after 1966,' in *Ukraine in the Seventies*, ed P.J. Potichnyj (Oakville, Ont 1975)
Pelenski, Ja. 'Shelest and His Period in Soviet Ukraine (1963–1972): A Revival of Controlled Ukrainian Autonomism,' ibid.
Tillett, L. 'Ukrainian Nationalism and the Fall of Shelest,' *SR*, December 1975
Hodnett, G. 'The Views of Petro Shelest,' *AUA*, 14 (1978–80)
V. Markus, R. Senkus

Shelest, Vasyl [Šelest, Vasyl'], b ?, d 1768 in Kodnia, near Zhytomyr. Zaporozhian Cossack and haidamaka leader. In the spring of 1768 he organized a rebel detachment in Kholodnyi Yar, near Chyhyryn, consisting of peasants, Zaporozhians, and Left-Bank Cossacks. During the Koliivshchyna rebellion he led them through the Cherkasy region. He was captured by a Polish punitive expedition and executed.

Shelest, Vitalii [Šelest, Vitalij], b 15 October 1940 in Kharkiv. Theoretical physicist; AN URSR (now ANU) corresponding member since 1969; son of P. *Shelest. A graduate of Kiev University (1962), he received a doctorate in 1968 for his work under N. *Bogoliubov (M. Boholiubov) on hadronic models. He was head of the Department of Theoretical Particle Physics at the ANU Institute of Theoretical Physics in 1969–74; since 1976 he has worked at institutions of the USSR State Standards Committee in Moscow. Shelest has made several significant contributions in the fields of particle theory and statistical physics. His book *Fizyky sperechaiut'sia* (Physicists Argue, 1973), written with O. Rozhen, reveals him to be a perspicacious observer of the international physics community and a gifted popularizer of physics.

Sheliah (also *sheleh, sheliuh*). The Ukrainianized name of the Polish-Lithuanian 16th- and 17th-century currency known as the *szeląg* or solidus, of the schillings used in Polish-ruled Prussian and Brandenburg towns, and of the solidi used in Swedish-ruled Baltic towns in the 17th century. The *szeliąg* or solidus of the Polish-Lithuanian Commonwealth was at first a silver coin and then a paper note. Use of the Swedish Baltic coins, issued by Queen Christina, Charles X Gustav, and Charles XII, and the Polish copper *boratynki* (designed by T. Boratini) was particularly widespread. A *sheliah* was worth one-third of a Polish-Lithuanian grosz. It was equal to two-ninths of a Russian kopeck.

Sheliah-Sosonko, Yurii [Šeljah-Sosonko, Jurij], b 10 January 1933 in Kiev. Botanist; full member of the AN URSR (now ANU) since 1990. A graduate of Chernivtsi University (1956), he became an associate of the ANU Institute of Botany in 1962 and one of its department heads in 1972. His major research interest is theoretical and applied geobotany. He has prepared guides to several nature reserves outside Ukraine and was the editor and an author of *Rastitel'nyi mir* (The Plant World, 1985), in the series Priroda Ukrainskoi SSR (Nature in the Ukrainian SSR).

Sheliushko, Mykola [Šeljuško], b 18 October 1912 in Kamianske (now Dniprodzerzhynske), Katerynoslav county, d 6 February 1983 in Lviv. Opera singer (tenor). After graduating from the Lviv Conservatory in 1950, he taught there and sang as a soloist with the Lviv Theater of Opera and Ballet, with which he appeared as Bohun in K. Dankevych's *Bohdan Khmelnytsky*, the False Dmitri in M. Mussorgsky's *Boris Godunov*, and Jontek in S. Moniuszko's *Halka*.

Sheliuzhko, Lev [Šeljužko], b 26 March 1890 in Kiev, d 23 August 1969 in Munich. Entomologist. A graduate of Kiev University (1912), he worked at the AN URSR (now ANU) Zoological Museum (1920–33), to which he donated his butterfly collection, at the lepidoptera museum at Kiev University (1939–43), and at the Bavarian zoological collection in Munich (1945–69).

A shelterbelt in Ukraine

Shelterbelt. A barrier of trees and shrubs cultivated to protect crops from wind, reduce soil erosion on fields, and maintain higher water levels. Shelterbelts are located in Ukraine primarily in the steppe and forest-steppe regions. They first came into use in 1809, when V. Lomykovsky planted tall trees around the fields of his Poltava gubernia estate. In the 1890s V. Dokuchaev and Yu. Vysotsky undertook ground-breaking research in Ukraine on the use of shelterbelts for drought control. Shelterbelts started coming into common use in Ukraine early in the 20th century and were developed systematically around mid-century as part of a state afforestation program, particularly in 1938–9 and 1948–52. Oaks, pines, birches, and poplars commonly make up higher-elevation windbreaks; lindens, maples, and apple and pear trees often form the lower shelterbelts.

Shelton, Ian (Shevchuk), b 30 March 1957 in Winnipeg. Ukrainian-Canadian astronomer. He studied at the universities of Manitoba and Toronto (M SC, 1990). As resident astronomer at the University of Toronto observatory on Las Campanas Mountain in Chile, he discovered a supernova on 23 February 1987, the first since 1604. It was officially named the Supernova Shelton 1987A.

Sheludko, Dmytro [Šelud'ko], b 21 September 1892 in Irkliiv, Zolotonosha county, Poltava gubernia, d 8 May 1954 in Sofia, Bulgaria. Linguist and literary scholar. He studied at Kiev, St Petersburg, and Halle universities and worked for some time in Germany, Italy, and Spain. From 1930 he taught at Köln University. In 1931 he published a 60-page article on Germanisms in the Ukrainian language with a dictionary of approx 700 loanwords. From 1933 he lived in Bulgaria. He also wrote articles on the Old French epics, Provençal literature, Bulgarian-Ukrainian literary relations, and T. Shevchenko and Bulgarian literature.

Serhii Shelukhyn

Shelukhyn, Serhii [Šeluxyn, Serhij] (Šeluchyn; pseud: S. Pavlenko), b 1864 in Poltava gubernia, d 25 December 1938 in Prague. Lawyer, civic activist, and state figure. A judge in various centers, he was active in the Ukrainian movement from 1905, as head of the Revolutionary Committee in Odessa and a member of the Ukrainian Party of Socialists-Federalists. In 1917–18 he was a member of the Central Rada, a general judge in the UNR, minister of justice in the governments of V. Holubovych and V. Chekhivsky, and a state senator in the Hetman government. He also headed the Ukrainian State delegation in peace negotiations with the RSFSR (1918) and participated in the Paris Peace Conference (1919) as a legal adviser. He emigrated to Czechoslovakia (via Vienna) in 1921 and taught criminal law at the Ukrainian Free University and the Ukrainian Higher Pedagogical Institute (1924–5), headed the Ukrainian Law Society and the Ukrainian Committee in Czechoslovakia, was vice-president of the People's Ukrainian Council, and wrote about the law code *Ruskaia Pravda*, the Celtic origin of Rus', the history of Ukrainian law, and international politics in Ukraine.

The first *shematyzm* of the Ukrainian Catholic eparchy of Toronto (1948–63) and the 1938 Lviv *shematyzm*

Shematyzm (from Latin *schematismus*; German: *Schematismus*; Polish: *szematyzm*). An annual handbook of institutions and officeholders. In the Austrian Empire the government published one in German for the entire empire and one in German (1785–1869) or Polish (1780–1, 1870–1914) for Galicia and Lodomeria. It listed all dignitaries, functionaries, bishops, schools, teachers, and officers of community organizations.

The Ukrainian Catholic church published eparchial *shematyzmy* containing a historical survey of the eparchy and information about all clerics, other persons active in church life, parishes, church organizations, and church property. They came out annually (with occasional interruptions) from the early 19th century until the Second World War, first only in Latin, then in both Latin and Ukrainian, and finally only in Ukrainian. Directories for Mukachiv eparchy were published from 1814, for Peremyshl eparchy from 1828, for Lviv archeparchy and Križevci eparchy from 1832, for Prešov eparchy from 1848, and for Stanyslaviv eparchy from 1886. The last ones appeared in Lviv in 1944 and in Prešov in 1948. The Roman Catholic church published *schematismi* for Lviv archdiocese (1814–1915, 1917–39) and Peremyshl diocese (1819–1914, 1916–35), and the Armenian Catholic church for its Lviv archdiocese (1843–1939). The Orthodox archeparchy of Bukovyna issued a *schematismus* from 1841 until 1914, and the Apostolic Administration in the Lemko region published one from 1936 until the Second World War. The Ukrainian Basilian Fathers published a *shematyzm* of their order in 1867 and have issued a *catalogus* from Rome every few years since the First World War. The fullest collections of such ecclesiastical directories are preserved in the libraries of Rome, Vienna, and Warsaw. They have not been published in Soviet Ukraine.

In the West only a few such directories have been compiled by the Ukrainian Catholic church. In 1951 an annual English-language directory of Philadelphia archeparchy was first published. Jubilee *shematyzmy* were published by Toronto eparchy in 1963, by Saskatoon eparchy in 1961, and by the Byzantine Ruthenian metropolitan province in Pittsburgh in 1984. In addition, annual Ukrainian Catholic and Orthodox almanacs published in Toronto, Yorkton, and South Bound Brook, New Jersey, have listed the names and addresses of Ukrainian clergy outside the USSR.

BIBLIOGRAPHY
Kramarz, H. 'Schematyzmy galicyjskie jako źródło historyczne,' *Studia Historyczne*, 25, no. 1 (1982)

I. Patrylo

Serhii Shemet

Volodymyr Shemet

Edmund Sheparovych

Ivan Sheparovych

Shemet, Serhii [Šemet, Serhij], b 1875 in Poltava gubernia, d 1957 in Australia. Engineer and civic and political activist; brother of V. *Shemet. A landowner in the Poltava region, he was a founding member of the *Ukrainian Democratic Agrarian party in Lubni (1917). He favored the Ukrainianization of the Hetman government and opposed its overthrow in November 1918. After emigrating to Tarnów in 1919 and then to Vienna, Berlin, and Paris he became active, with V. Lypynsky, in the monarchist movement: he was a member of the *Ukrainian Union of Agrarians-Statists (USKhD), a contributor to the journal *Khliborobs'ka Ukraïna* and other hetmanite publications, personal secretary to Hetman P. Skoropadsky, and a member of the USKhD Central Council.

Shemet, Volodymyr [Šemet], b 1873, d 14 May 1933. Civic and political activist; brother of S. *Shemet. A landowner in the Poltava region, he was a member of the *Brotherhood of Taras, a deputy to the First Russian State Duma in 1905, and publisher of the paper *Khliborob* in Lubni (1905). During the First World War he helped organize a private Ukrainian gymnasium in Kiev (1915–16). He was a founding member of the *Ukrainian Democratic Agrarian party (1917) and a deputy from Poltava gubernia to the Central Rada. From 1919 he was a research associate of the Ukrainian Academy of Sciences. Under the Soviet regime he suffered political persecution and died of starvation.

Shepa, Antin [Šepa], b 17 April 1928 in Pidhirne, Transcarpathia. Painter. In 1954 he graduated from the Lviv Institute of Applied and Decorative Arts, where he studied under R. Selsky, Y. Bokshai, and A. Erdeli. His canvases are mostly landscapes, such as *The Carpathian Region* (1966), *The Hutsul Region* (1968), and *Old Transcarpathia* (1969). He has also painted murals in various public buildings, such as *Carpathian Opryshoks*, in the trade center in Bushtyna, Transcarpathia (1968), and *Highland Wedding* and *The Severe Beskyds*, in the restaurant at Nyzhni Vorota, Transcarpathia (1969).

Sheparovych, Edmund [Šeparovyč], b 1889 in Galicia, d 1967 in Vienna. Military officer. During the First World War he was a cavalry officer in the Austrian army. In 1919 he joined the Ukrainian Galician Army and commanded a reserve cavalry regiment in Stryi. From June 1919 he commanded the First Cavalry Brigade. In Vinnytsia he organized the First Reserve Cavalry Regiment. In 1920 he commanded the Third Cavalry Regiment of the Red Ukrainian Galician Army, which rebelled against the Bolsheviks in April and conducted partisan warfare against H. *Kotovsky in Kherson and Kiev gubernias before joining up with the UNR Army. In late 1920 Sheparovych emigrated to Vienna, where he worked as a banker and businessman.

Sheparovych, Ivan [Šeparovyč], b 1889 in Kolodiivka, Stanyslaviv county, Galicia, d 3 December 1969 in New York. Co-operative and civic leader; brother of Yu. *Sheparovych. In the 1920s he organized and headed the Stanyslaviv branch of Silskyi Hospodar. Then he served on the society's board of directors in Lviv and represented the society in the Agricultural Chamber, over which he presided in 1941–4. After emigrating to the United States he organized Ukrainian co-operatives and engaged in émigré political activity. From its inception he presided over the Ukrainian Economic Advisory Association (1957–63). As the US president of the *Ukrainian National Democratic Alliance he was a key member of the émigré Ukrainian National Council.

Sheparovych, Lev [Šeparovyč], b 4 March 1888 in Kolodiivka, Stanyslaviv county, Galicia, d 1 June 1941 in Cracow. Military officer. A student of electrical engineering at the Karlsruhe Polytechnic, during the First World War he was a captain in the Austrian army. When the November Uprising broke out in 1918, he took part in occupying the central postal and telegraph building in Lviv and broadcasting the proclamation of the Western Ukrainian National Republic. A captain in the Ukrainian Galician Army (UHA), he organized and commanded the Communications Regiment in Stanyslaviv. From July 1919 he was chief of telegraph services at the Supreme Command. In April 1920, while serving in the UHA Technical Battalion in Balta, he established contact with Ukrainian partisan units and helped persuade the battalion to join Gen M. Omelianovych-Pavlenko's UNR Army against the Red Army. In

Lev Sheparovych   Yuliian Sheparovych

the interwar period he headed the Lviv office of the German Siemens company.

Sheparovych, Olena. See Fedak-Sheparovych, Olena.

Sheparovych, Yuliian [Šeparovyč, Julijan], b 16 February 1886 in Kolodiivka, Stanyslaviv county, Galicia, d 28 July 1949 in Munich. Military and community figure; brother of I. *Sheparovych. He studied law at Lviv University. During the First World War he was an artillery officer in the Austrian army. As a major in the Ukrainian Galician Army (UHA), in January 1919 he commanded the Stanyslaviv Battery during battles with the Poles near Lviv and then the Third Artillery Regiment in the Third Berezhany Brigade. After the disintegration of the UHA in 1920, he was chief of staff in the anti-Bolshevik partisan force commanded by A. Volynets in Volhynia. After returning to Galicia in the summer of 1920, he founded and then directed the Co-operative Union in Stanyslaviv. From 1925 he sat on the board of directors of *Tsentrosoiuz, and from 1930 chaired the board. He also headed the *Moloda Hromada society in Lviv. During the German occupation of Galicia he was an official of the Landwirtschaftliche Zentralstelle in Lublin and defended the interests of Ukrainian farmers and co-operatives. After the war he emigrated to Germany.

Gen Volodymyr Shepel

Shepel, Volodymyr [Šepel'], b 1888, d ? Military officer. He was lieutenant colonel in the UNR Army. During the Ukrainian-Polish War he commanded the Krukenychi Group of the Ukrainian Galician Army (to June 1919). Later he was a training officer of the First Recruit Regiment of the UNR Army in Kamianets-Podilskyi. In 1920 he commanded a brigade of the Fourth Gray Division and of the Second Volhynian Division. Eventually he was promoted to brigadier general.

Shepetivka [Šepetivka]. III-8. A city (1990 pop 51,000) on the Huska River and a raion center in Khmelnytskyi oblast. It was first mentioned in historical documents in 1594. At the end of the 16th century it was granted the rights of Magdeburg law. It belonged to the Polish Commonwealth until 1793. Under Russian rule Shepetivka was part of Iziaslav county in Volhynia gubernia. The town's owners, the Sanguszko family, introduced some manufacturing in the town: they built a woolen-cloth factory in 1816 and a sugar refinery in 1843. The Kiev–Brest railway line built through Shepetivka in 1873 stimulated further economic growth. In 1919 the town was the site of battles between the Sich Riflemen and Bolshevik forces. In 1923 Shepetivka was granted city status and was chosen as the administrative center of an okruha. In 1930 it became a raion center of Vinnytsia and in 1937 of Khmelnytskyi oblast. The city is an industrial and transportation center. It is the junction of several trunk lines and highways. It has metalworking shops servicing the railway industry, a farm machinery plant, building-materials plants, and a food industry.

Shepitko, Larysa [Šepitko], b 6 January 1938, d 2 July 1979. Film director and actress. She acted in the film *Tavriia* (1959, Kiev Artistic Film Studio) and completed study at the State Institute of Cinematography in Moscow (1963, pupil of O. Dovzhenko). Her thesis film, *The Heat*, 1964, received an award at the Karlovy Vary film festival in Czechoslovakia, and *The Ascent*, 1972 was awarded the Golden Bear at the Berlin Festival. She made three other films; the last one, *Farewell*, 1979, was completed after her tragic death in an automobile accident.

Sheptytsky, Andrei [Šeptyc'kyj, Andrej] (Szeptycki; secular name: Roman Oleksander), b 29 July 1865 in Prylbychi, Yavoriv county, Galicia, d 1 November 1944 in Lviv. Church, cultural, and civic figure; metropolitan of Halych, archbishop of Lviv, and bishop of Kamianets-Podilskyi. He was a member of a prominent Ukrainian-Polish noble family, which included several influential Ukrainian (Uniate) churchmen, on his father's side, and the Fredros, a prominent Polish family, on his mother's side. Although baptized in the Roman Catholic church, he petitioned the Vatican to change his rite and in May 1888 entered the Basilian Greek Catholic monastery in Dobromyl. In August 1892, after finishing his primary theological training, he was ordained by Bishop Yu. Pelesh. He then completed his studies at the University of Cracow (PH D in law, 1894) and, in theology and philosophy, at the Jesuit seminary in Cracow.

Sheptytsky quickly rose through the Greek Catholic church ranks: he served as master of novices in Dobromyl (1893–6), hegumen of St Onuphrius's Monastery in Lviv (1896–7), and hegumen and professor of theology at the

Metropolitan Andrei Sheptytsky

Krystynopil Monastery. He also founded the journal *Misionar* (1897). He was consecrated as bishop of Stanyslaviv in September 1899 and was enthroned as metropolitan of Halych, archbishop of Lviv, and bishop of Kamianets-Podilskyi in January 1901. He was also a member and vice-marshal of the Galician Diet (from 1901) and a member of the Austrian House of Lords and the Imperial Ministerial Council (from 1903). In these capacities he often spoke in support of Ukrainian rights in Galicia and agitated for the establishment of Ukrainian schools and a university. Although his proposals were initially met with skepticism by many Ukrainians in Galicia, who feared his conservatism and believed he had been placed at the head of the Greek Catholic church to help Latinize and Polonize it, his forceful defense of Eastern church traditions and rights and of the Ukrainian movement soon won him great support and admiration (his condemnation of M. Sichynsky's 1908 assassination of Vicegerent A. Potocki, however, conflicted with wide popular support for the act).

During the Russian occupation of Galicia in the First World War, Sheptytsky was arrested (September 1914) and deported. Distrusted by the tsarist government for his Austro-Hungarian loyalties, missionary Catholic zeal, and high standing among Ukrainians, he was detained, first in Kiev and then in Nizhnii Novgorod, Kursk, Suzdal, and Yaroslavl, before being released after the February Revolution of 1917. He then traveled briefly to Petrograd and Kiev, where he met with members of the *Central Rada.

After his return to Lviv in September 1917, Sheptytsky quickly engaged in church affairs and the struggle for Ukrainian independence. In his last speech in the Austrian House of Lords (February 1918), concerned with the Brest-Litovsk Peace Treaty, he supported the transfer of the Kholm region to the Central Rada and the general principle of national self-determination. As a member of the Ukrainian National Rada he supported the creation of the Western Ukrainian National Republic and lobbied for recognition of the new state. For this stance he was put under virtual house arrest by the Polish government and confined to Lviv from November 1918 to December 1919. When he was allowed to leave the city, he traveled extensively for over two years throughout Western Europe and North and South America, visiting Ukrainian emigrants and rallying support for the Ukrainian movement in Galicia. He lobbied Western political leaders and Catholic officials, stressing the humanitarian aspects of the Ukrainian movement. When, during his return in September 1923, he entered Poland, he was detained in Poznań for his anti-Polish activities before being permitted to proceed to Lviv in January 1924.

Sheptytsky's political influence among Galician Ukrainians was greatly enhanced by his activities during the struggle for Ukrainian independence and after. He maintained good relations with a variety of political leaders and organizations, particularly the influential Ukrainian National Democratic Alliance, and he spoke out against the *Pacification campaign in 1930 and interceded with the Polish government both directly and through the Vatican. He also did much to reinforce the Ukrainian character of his church (although this caused a negative reaction from the Polish Roman Catholic church) and to strengthen its ties to the laity. In 1931 he sponsored the creation of the *Ukrainian Catholic Union to further the church's teachings and social-political influence. He was denounced by the Ukrainian pro-Soviet groups in Galicia, especially after his strong criticism of the man-made famine of 1932–3 in Soviet Ukraine and his condemnation of communism. His relations with the radical nationalist camp were also often strained, particularly when he criticized the terrorism and assassinations of Polish officials carried out by the Organization of Ukrainian Nationalists.

Sheptytsky was an active and dynamic pastor who frequently issued pastoral letters commenting on a variety of religious and social issues. He convoked eparchial synods in 1905 and during the Soviet and German occupations of Western Ukraine (annually in 1941–3), and convened large meetings of Greek Catholic bishops (including bishops from Poland, Czechoslovakia, Yugoslavia, and North America) in Lviv in 1927 and in Rome in 1929. He also hosted the first synod of Eastern eparchs in Lviv (1940). In 1904 he established the *Studite Fathers in Galicia; in 1906 he prepared the order's rules (the *Typicon*) with his brother, Klymentii; and in 1913 he introduced the congregation of the *Redemptorist Fathers into Galicia. He dispatched many priests to minister to Ukrainian immigrants in the Americas, and arranged the nomination of the first Greek Catholic bishops for both the United States (S. Ortynsky in 1907) and Canada (N. Budka in 1912). While attending the Eucharistic Congress in Montreal in 1910 he made his first visitation to Ukrainian settlers throughout the continent. In the interwar period Sheptytsky actively supported the *Catholic Action movement and provided funds and other assistance for its various organizations and projects, and the Ukrainian Youth for Christ festival in 1933. In

1928 he founded the *Greek Catholic Theological Academy, which soon became a leading center for the study of Eastern Catholicism.

Sheptytsky was a generous patron of the arts, education, and various charitable causes. A church museum founded by him in 1905 grew to be one of the most important Ukrainian museums of its time (see *National Museum). Later renamed the Ukrainian National Museum and the Lviv Museum of Ukrainian Art, from 1913 it occupied its own impressive premises in Lviv. The museum acquired a large collection of icons, church artifacts, textiles, folk art, documents and books, and contemporary Ukrainian art, and published its own books and catalogues. Sheptytsky was a benefactor of the Novakivsky Art School and provided financial support to such artists as V. Diadyniuk, M. Sosenko, M. Boichuk, O. Kurylas, and P. Kholodny, Sr. In 1902 he founded the *Narodnia Lichnytsia society, which later established and maintained a large modern hospital in Lviv. He also donated land for an agricultural school run by the Prosvita society in Myluvannia; cofounded the Land Mortgage Bank (1910); provided funds for the Prosvita, Ridna Shkola, and other societies; and donated land in Pidliute to the Ukrainian scouting organization *Plast, for a camp.

Throughout his life Sheptytsky was especially concerned with expanding the role and prestige of the Uniate church. He first traveled to the Russian Empire in 1887 to meet with intellectuals (eg, the Russian philosopher V. Solovev and the prominent Ukrainian historian V. Antonovych) who were favorably disposed toward the church union. Under the strong influence of the Jesuits, who were actively proselytizing in Russia, he maintained many contacts with individual Catholics there. His title of bishop of Kamianets-Podilskyi, an eparchy located in the Russian Empire but in fact inactive, gave him the right to claim responsibility for all Eastern rite Catholics in the empire. Pope Pius x acknowledged this right in 1907–8, and subsequent popes reaffirmed it. In 1907 Sheptytsky formally organized the Russian (Eastern rite) Catholic church and appointed the Russian A. Zerchaninov as his administrator of Eastern rite Catholics throughout the empire, and the next year he traveled incognito to Russia and Ukraine to make contact with Catholic and Uniate supporters. Later, during his brief detention in Kiev in 1914, he managed secretly to appoint Y. Botsian as Uniate bishop of Lutske and D. Yaremko as bishop of Ostrih. Before leaving the Russian Empire in 1917, he convoked a synod of the Russian Catholic church in Petrograd and appointed the Studite L. Fedorov as his exarch for Russia. He also briefly visited Kiev, where he appointed M. Tsehelsky as his administrator for Ukrainian Catholics in eastern Ukraine.

In practice, however, Sheptytsky's efforts to establish a Uniate presence in the Russian Empire, especially eastern Ukraine, met with little success. The Russian Catholic church never attracted more than a few thousand adherents, and most Orthodox Ukrainians rejected the overtures, despite their great personal regard for the metropolitan (who always maintained good relations with such leaders as Hetman P. Skoropadsky, S. Petliura, and D. Doroshenko). Metropolitan Sheptytsky's prestige was enhanced in 1938 when he condemned the Polish government's persecution of Orthodox believers and destruction of Orthodox churches in Kholm and Volhynia. Sheptytsky was somewhat more successful in improving relations with Western churches. From 1907 to 1927 he was a leading participant in a series of ecumenical congresses held in Velehrad, Czechoslovakia. He helped establish pro-union organizations in the Netherlands, Belgium, and even England, and he attracted several prominent converts to Eastern Catholicism.

The Second World War was a difficult time for Sheptytsky and the entire Ukrainian Catholic church. During the first Soviet occupation of Western Ukraine (1939–41) he remained in Lviv and tried to defend his church; he issued several pastoral letters exhorting his faithful to resist the atheism imposed by the regime. Although much church property was confiscated and most religious schools and other institutions were closed down, the authorities did not harm the metropolitan because of his prominence and their still precarious hold over Western Ukraine. Fearing for the future of the church, in December 1939 he secretly consecrated Y. *Slipy as his coadjutor with the right of succession. He also introduced several reforms intended to permit the church to function despite official restrictions. At the same time, however, Sheptytsky believed that the occupation of Western Ukraine presented great opportunities for his ecumenical work and the possible reunification of the Orthodox and Catholic churches. He appointed exarchs for Volhynia and Polisia (M. Charnetsky), eastern Ukraine (Y. Slipy), Belarus (A. Nemantsevich), and Russia and Siberia (his brother, K. Sheptytsky) and began to make plans to establish the Uniate church throughout the USSR.

Although Sheptytsky did not sympathize with Nazi ideology, when the Germans occupied Western Ukraine he initially believed that German rule would be better than Soviet rule, and that it could provide for the establishment of an independent Ukrainian state (earlier, in 1938, he had welcomed the declaration of an independent *Carpatho-Ukraine). In June 1941, as honorary head of the Ukrainian National Council in Lviv, he supported the creation of the Ukrainian State Administration and appealed to the German authorities to permit the establishment of a united Ukraine including all of eastern Ukraine. His optimism waned, however, when he realized that this would not be permitted, and when he witnessed the cruelty of the Nazis toward the local population and the Jews in particular. In early 1942 he sent a letter to H. Himmler protesting Nazi treatment of the Jews and the use of Ukrainians in anti-Jewish repressions. He also began to provide refuge to Jews hiding from the Nazis and instructed his monasteries and convents to do the same. In November 1942 he issued a strong pastoral letter denouncing all killing, including the politically motivated assassinations carried out by competing Ukrainian parties. He remained active in Ukrainian political life throughout the war despite his failing health, and attempted to mediate between competing factions and to come to an understanding with Ukrainian Orthodox church leaders. He also supported the creation of the *Division Galizien and assigned military chaplains to it. After the Soviets occupied Western Ukraine in 1939 and again in 1944, he remained in Lviv in order to preserve the church. Soviet attacks on the church were moderate until his death because of the recognition of his great authority. His public funeral demonstrated the continuing respect for him, but his death greatly weakened the position of the Greek Catholic church.

Sheptytsky was a prolific writer on issues of church organization and history, theology, spirituality, ecumenism, and philosophy. As background for his proposed beatification, 22 volumes of his works were collected, 6 of which had been published or republished by 1989. These were primarily Sheptytsky's pastoral letters and articles in newspapers, journals, and other publications, in Ukrainian, Polish, Latin, German, and other languages. The first volume of his pastoral letters, *Tvory Sluhy Bozhoho Mytropolyta Andreia Sheptyts'koho: Pastyrs'ki lysty* (The Works of the Servant of God Metropolitan Andrei Sheptytsky: Pastoral Letters, 1965), contains a comprehensive bibliography of his publications by A. Bazylevych. Two volumes of his pastoral letters from the period of the Second World War were published in Yorkton, Saskatchewan (1961, 1969), and three of his theological works were republished in Rome in 1978. His and his brother's study of Studite monastic rule, *Typicon*, appeared in French in 1964. In recognition of his scholarly work he was made a full member of the Shevchenko Scientific Society (1925) and of the Ukrainian Theological Scholarly Society.

In response to Sheptytsky's great accomplishments as metropolitan, his work for church unity, his readiness to die for Christ, his fearless stand against Nazi and Soviet regimes, and his death *in odore sanctitatis*, a popular movement for his beatification arose in the 1950s, spearheaded by Archbishop I. *Buchko, who appointed M. *Hrynchyshyn as official postulator. The first phase of the process was completed in 1968, when Pope Paul VI gave Sheptytsky the title 'Servant of God.' Since then, leaders of the Ukrainian Catholic church have continued their efforts to have him recognized as a saint, often in the face of opposition from leaders of the Polish Catholic church. Sheptytsky was also vilified by Soviet propaganda. This vilification did not diminish his status in Ukrainian historiography, especially among Ukrainian Catholic scholars, and with the triumph of democratic groups in Ukraine in 1990 and the re-emergence of the Ukrainian Catholic church, he has attained great popularity in contemporary Ukraine. He has been the subject of numerous biographies, articles, dissertations, and collections published in interwar Western Ukraine, Poland, North America, Rome, and elsewhere.

BIBLIOGRAPHY
Hrynchyshyn, M. *Dlia informatyvnoho protsesu beatyfikatsiï i kanonizatsiï Sluhy Bozhoho Andreia Sheptyts'koho ...* (Rome 1958)
Schuver, U. *De reus op de Sint-Jorisberg* (Rotterdam 1959)
Hryn'okh, I. *Sluha Bozhyi Andrei: Blahovisnyk iednosty* (Munich 1961)
Kravcheniuk, O. *Veleten' zo Sviatoiurs'koï hory: Prychynky do biohrafiï sluhy Bozhoho Andreia Sheptyts'koho na pidstavi chuzhomovnykh dzherel* (Yorkton 1963)
Korolevskij, C. *Métropolite André Szeptyckyj, 1865–1944* (Rome 1964)
Laba, V. *Mytropolyt Andrei Sheptyts'kyi: Ioho zhyttia i zasluhy* (Rome 1965)
Prokoptschuk, G. *Der Metropolit: Leben und Wirken des grossen Förderers der Kirchenunion: Graf Andreas Scheptytzkyj* (Munich 1955; 2nd edn, 1967)
Marunchak, M. (ed). *Two Documents of the Ukrainian Catholic Church 1911–1976* (Winnipeg 1977)
Magocsi, P.R. (ed). *Morality and Reality: The Life and Times of Andrei Sheptyts'kyi* (Edmonton 1989)

W. Lencyk

Metropolitan Atanasii Sheptytsky

Archimandrite Klymentii Sheptytsky

Sheptytsky, Atanasii [Šeptyc'kyj, Atanasij (Antonij)], b 1686 in Voshchantsi, near Rudky, Galicia, d 22 December 1746 in Lviv. Uniate metropolitan. He entered ca 1703 the Basilian monastery in Univ, where his uncle, V. Sheptytsky, was archimandrite. In 1710 he was ordained and in 1713 appointed archimandrite of the Univ monastery and coadjutor to his uncle, who was then bishop of Lviv, Halych, and Kamianets-Podilskyi. He succeeded his uncle as bishop in 1715. Sheptytsky founded the brotherhood at St George's Church in Lviv and played a key role in organizing and conducting the 1720 Synod of *Zamostia. On L. Kyshka's recommendation he succeeded him as the Uniate metropolitan of Kiev and all Rus' in 1729. His election was not supported by the Basilian superiors and all the bishops. As bishop and metropolitan, Sheptytsky led the struggle against the Polish clergy's drive to convert Uniates to Roman Catholicism, the nobles' exploitation of the clergy and peasantry, and Polonization in general. In 1732 he founded the *Univ Monastery Press to publish standardized liturgical books in accordance with the Zamostia Synod's decisions, and in 1739 he oversaw the reform of the Basilian order.

Sheptytsky, Klymentii [Šeptyc'kyj, Klymentij], b 17 November 1869 in Prylbychi, Yavoriv county, Galicia, d 1 May 1958. Studite monk; brother of A. *Sheptytsky. After entering the Studite order he studied theology in Innsbruck (1913–17). He was later (1939) secretly named exarch for Russia and Siberia. In 1944 he succeeded his brother as archimandrite of the Studite order. That year he led a Ukrainian Catholic delegation that went to Moscow for discussion of the future of the church following the occupation of Galicia. His arrest in 1947 was accompanied by a 25-year prison sentence, which he served in a number of concentration camps until his death.

Sheptytsky, Lev [Šeptyc'kyj] (Ludwig), b 23 August 1717 in Peremyshl, d 25 May 1779 in Radomyshl, in Right-Bank Ukraine. Uniate metropolitan. He studied at the Theatine papal college in Lviv, received a doctorate in civil and canon law from the Ecclesiastical Academy in Rome, graduated from the diplomatic academy there, and then entered the Basilian order. In 1743 he was elected archimandrite of St Nicholas's Monastery in Myltsi, near Kovel, Volhynia. In 1749 he succeeded his late uncle, A.

Metropolitan Lev Sheptytsky   Bishop Varlaam Sheptytsky

Sheptytsky, as bishop of Lviv, Halych, and Kamianets-Podilskyi. During his 30-year episcopate he created the cathedral chapters in those cities and oversaw the completion of the new St George's Cathedral (its construction was initiated and funded by his uncle) and episcopal residence in Lviv, and the compilation of a descriptive register of all Uniate parishes, buildings, and landholdings. In 1762 Sheptytsky was named coadjutor to F. Volodkovych, the ailing metropolitan of Kiev and all Rus', and thereafter he supervised the day-to-day affairs of the metropoly. After the 1772 partition of Poland, Uniate faithful under both Russian and Austrian rule were under his jurisdiction. He used his influence at the papal and Viennese courts to defend his faithful from Polish oppression and from attempts to convert them to Roman Catholicism and to Polonize them. In 1778 he succeeded Volodkovych as metropolitan. He died 15 months later. Sheptytsky convinced Empress Maria Theresa to found the *Barbareum Greek Catholic seminary in Vienna and laid the groundwork for the creation of the Greek Catholic Theological Seminary in Lviv.

Sheptytsky, Varlaam [Šeptyc'kyj] (secular name: Vasilii), b 3 February 1647 in Voshchantsi, near Sambir, Galicia, d 5 April 1715 in Univ. Uniate bishop. He entered the Orthodox monastery at Univ and in 1668 was elected archimandrite. In 1669 he established the Univ Monastery Press, which published many important monographs and religious texts. Together with Bishop Y. Shumliansky of Lviv he soon began working toward extending church union to the Lviv eparchy. He participated in the Colloquium of Lublin of 1680, led by the Uniate metropolitan of Kiev, K. Zhokhovsky. After converting to Catholicism in March 1681, he defended the Uniate position at the eparchial sobor of 1694, and in July 1700 he participated in the proclamation of the union in Lviv eparchy. After Shumliansky's death (1708) Sheptytsky was nominated as bishop of Lviv by King August II Frederick. He was elected bishop in January 1710 at a congress attended by the Kievan metropolitan, A. Vynnytsky, and representatives of the Ukrainian nobility, the Stauropegion Brotherhood, and the clergy; he was consecrated in June 1710.

Sheptytsky Institute (Instytut im. A. Sheptytskoho). A Ukrainian Catholic student residence located in *Saska-

toon. Run by the Redemptorist Fathers, it was established in 1953 as a successor to the M. Shashkevych Institute (est 1935 by the Ukrainian Catholic Brotherhood of Canada). The facility accommodates approx 100 students, houses a library, hosts community activities, and occasionally sponsors Ukrainian studies courses.

Sherehii, Yevhen [Šerehjij, Jevhen], b 1910 in Dusyna, Bereg county, Transcarpathia, d 1985. Composer; brother of Yu. *Sherehii. He was director of the Transcarpathian Ukrainian Music and Drama Theater in Uzhhorod in 1946–64. He wrote the music to V. Grendzha-Donsky's opera *When the Orchards Are Blooming* (1937) and composed the operettas *Tango for Oneself* (1936) and *Children of the 20th Century* (1937, both librettos by Yu. Sherehii), as well as music for dramatic works, such as O. Oles's *At the Dnieper* (1938), T. Shevchenko's *Haidamakas* (1939), and H. Kupchenko's *The Quiet Ukrainian Night*.

Yurii Sherehii   Irodion Sheremetynsky

Sherehii, Yurii [Šerehij, Jurij], b 18 January 1907 in Dusyna, Bereg Svaliava county, Transcarpathia, d 25 May 1990 in Bratislava. Theater director, actor, and playwright. He began his theatrical career in the Ruthenian Theater of the Prosvita Society in Uzhhorod (1923–7). In 1934–8 he was founder (with his brother Ye. Sherehii) and artistic director of the *Nova Stsena theater in Khust. He worked with amateur theaters in Yugoslavia (1939–40), as administrative director of the Ukrainian Theater in Drohobych (1942–4), and as stage director in the Prešov Ukrainian National Theater (1945–7 and 1954–6) and the People's Opera in Košice (1947–54). He wrote numerous dramas, including *Chasy mynaiut'* (Times Pass, 1938), and taught drama in Bratislava (1963–9).

Sherekh, Yurii. See Shevelov, George.

Sheremet, Mykola [Šeremet], b 23 December 1906 in Mahiliou, Belarus, d 28 October 1986 in Kiev. Poet and prose writer. He graduated from the Kiev Institute of People's Education in 1929. His first published work, the collection of poetry *U pokhid* (Into Battle), was published in 1929. He belonged to the literary organization *Molodniak. He published many poetry collections, all of which adhered to the Party line. His collections of essays, which are similar to his poetry in spirit, include *Krov ïkh ne proishla daremno* (Their Blood Was Not Spilled in Vain, 1938),

V lisakh Ukrainy (In the Forests of Ukraine, 1944), *V partyzans'kykh zahonakh* (In the Partisan Detachments, 1947), and *Molodi mesnyky* (The Young Avengers, 1949); he also wrote the novel *Vartovi myru* (Guardians of Peace, 1936). In the early 1960s he harshly criticized the *shestydesiatnyky.

Sheremeta, Andrii [Šeremeta, Andrij], b 13 December 1871 in Birche, Rudky county, Galicia, d 5 February 1946 in Lviv. Actor and singer. He worked in the Ruska Besida Theater (1889–1914 and 1922–4), in Ternopilski Teatralni Vechory (1916–18), in the New Lviv Theater (1919–20), in V. Kossak's troupe (1920–2), in various troupes in Galicia (1925–39), in the Lesia Ukrainka Theater (1939–41), and in the Lviv Opera Theater (1941–4).

Sheremetev, Vasilii [Šeremetev, Vasilij], b ca 1622, d 3 November 1682. Russian military and state figure. A commander of Russian troops in Ukraine in 1654–6, he was under B. Khmelnytsky's command in the Battle of Okhmativ (1655). A voivode of Kiev in 1658–60, he was captured during a battle near Chudniv by Polish forces, who turned him over to the Crimean khan. His freedom was purchased by Muscovy in 1681.

Sheremetynsky, Irodion [Šeremetyns'kyj], b 9 November 1873 in Pliakhova, Berdychiv county, Kiev gubernia, d 5 March 1937 in Sevliush, Transcarpathia. Veterinarian and agronomist. He graduated from the Kharkiv Veterinary Institute (1896) and the Kiev Polytechnical Institute (1914). He worked as a veterinarian in Nikolaevsk-na-Amure, in the Far East, and in Kharkiv gubernia, as an agronomist for the Odessa zemstvo administration (1913–14), and as assistant head of the animal husbandry department at the Katerynoslav Agricultural Research Station (from 1915). In December 1918 he was appointed director of the animal husbandry department of the UNR Ministry of Land Affairs. From February 1919 he was also director of the ministry's veterinary department, and from May 1920 he taught animal husbandry at the Kamianets-Podilskyi Ukrainian State University. He emigrated to Tarnów, Poland, in late 1920, and in 1922 he became a professor and chairman of the general and special animal husbandry departments at the Ukrainian Husbandry Academy in Poděbrady, Bohemia. He taught at the academy until 1935 and was also its first secretary, the dean of its Faculty of Agronomy and Forestry, and prorector (1927–8). He presided over the Association of Ukrainian Agricultural Technologists. Sheremetynsky wrote the academy's animal husbandry (3 vols) and special zootechny (2 vols, 1927) textbooks.

Shershen' (Hornet). An illustrated socialist weekly eight-page magazine of humor and satire, edited and published by V. Lozynsky in Kiev from mid-January to late July 1906 (a total of 26 issues). It was the only Ukrainian-language periodical of its kind in Russian-ruled Ukraine in its day. Contributors included many of the most prominent writers and cultural figures of the time. Its cartoons and political caricatures were drawn by F. Krasytsky, I. Buriachok, V. Maslianykov, P. Naumov, V. Riznychenko, and O. Slastion. *Shershen'* primarily satirized Russian conservatism and chauvinism, but also criticized Ukrainian political parties and newspapers. The publisher was constantly ha-

Cover of the first issue of *Shershen'* (drawing by Fotii Krasytsky)

rassed by the tsarist authorities, and two issues of the journal were confiscated.

A biweekly with the same name and masthead appeared in New York City (March–November 1908) and then Scranton, Pennsylvania (to June 1911). From October 1910 it was published by the Ukrainian Workingmen's Association. The editors were A. Kichak, M. Mykytyshyn (1909), and V. Hryshko.

Sherstiuk, Hryhorii [Šerstjuk, Hryhorij] (pseuds: Ya. Hetmanchuk, H. Chubrii), b 26 November 1882 in Sherstiukivka (now Novyi Tahamlyk), Poltava county, d 6 November 1911. Pedagogue, writer, and publisher. He worked briefly for the paper *Poltavskaia mysl'* in Poltava and became secretary of *Ridnyi krai*, in which he published book reviews and articles on civic life, education, and literature. He contributed articles to *Rada* and in 1907 founded in Kiev the Ukrainskyi Uchytel publishing house, which issued his Ukrainian school grammar (1907, 1912, 1917) and syntax (1909, 1917), translations and original works for children, and *Svitlo* (1910–14), the first Ukrainian educational journal in the Russian Empire. Sherstiuk also published and edited *Svitlo* (Light, 1908), a miscellany for children, and contributed poems and stories to almanacs and *Literaturno-naukovyi vistnyk* in Lviv.

Sherstobytov, Yevhen [Šerstobytov, Jevhen], b 19 June 1928 in Verkhnoudinsk (now Ulan-Ude), Buriat AR. Film director and screenwriter. In 1960 he completed study in the director's faculty of the State Institute of Cinema Art in Moscow, and in 1962 he began working in the Kiev Artistic Film Studio. He has written or cowritten and produced over a dozen children's films, including *Tumannist' Andromedy* (The Nebula of Andromeda, 1967) and *Beremo vse dlia sebe* (We Take Everything for Ourselves, 1980).

Viktor Shestopalov

Shestopalov, Viktor [Šestopalov], b 23 January 1923 in Slovianske, Izium county, Kharkiv gubernia. Theoretical physicist; AN URSR (now ANU) full member since 1979. A graduate of Kharkiv University (1949), he taught at postsecondary schools in Kharkiv (1952–71) and worked from 1965 at the ANU Institute of Radio Physics and Electronics, where he became director in 1973. His major contributions are in the field of the generation, propagation, and diffraction of electomagnetic submillimeter waves. Among his many publications is a monograph on sum equations in the contemporary theory of diffraction (1983).

Shestovytsia fortified settlement and burial site. A Rus' settlement of the 9th to 12th century near Shestovytsia, Chernihiv raion. Excavations from 1925 to 1958 identified the remains of an earthen wall and moat, semi-pit dwellings with clay ovens, millstones, pottery, and jewelry. Excavation of the burial ground yielded several hundred kurhans of the 10th to 12th centuries. Three types of burial traditions were encountered at the site: cremation, primary inhumation, and cenotaph (empty tomb for persons buried elsewhere). The remains of slaves and war horses buried with their masters, armor, weapons, jewelry, clothing, and items of daily use (some of which were of Scandinavian origin) were found in several kurhans.

Shestydesiatnyky (The Sixtiers). The literary generation that began to publish in the second half of the 1950s, during N. Khrushchev's 'de-Stalinization,' and reached their literary peak in the early 1960s; hence, their name. The first representatives were L. *Kostenko and V. *Symonenko. Following their lead came a veritable proliferation of poets: I. *Drach, M. *Vinhranovsky, H. Kyrychenko, V. Holoborodko, I. Kalynets, B. Mamaisur, and others. At first V. *Korotych was close to the group. The more prominent prose writers were Valerii *Shevchuk, Hryhir *Tiutiunnyk, V. *Drozd, Ye. *Hutsalo, and Ya. Stupak, and literary critics, I. *Dziuba, I. *Svitlychny, Ye. *Sverstiuk,

and I. Boichak. The *shestydesiatnyky* held their 'literary parents' responsible for Stalinist crimes, for adapting to a despotic regime, and for creative impotence (eg, Dziuba in 'Oda chesnomu boiahuzovi' [Ode to an Honest Coward]). In turn, some of the older writers, such as P. Tychyna, P. Voronko, M. Sheremet, and M. Chabanivsky, exhibited a hostile attitude to the experimentation and innovation of the *shestydesiatnyky*. Characteristic of *shestydesiatnyky* poetry was the renewal of poetic forms and subjects, which had been stamped out by the dogma of *socialist realism. The prose of the group was characterized by realistic descriptions free of the constraints of socialist realism, witty humor (as in the short stories of Tiutiunnyk) or sharp satire (as in Drozd's 'Katastrofa' [Catastrophe] and 'Maslyny' [Olives]), subtle delineation of the motives of protagonists, and an interest in historical subjects (as in the works of Shevchuk).

The *shestydesiatnyky* movement lasted barely a decade. The writers concerned were harshly criticized at a special meeting of the creative intelligentsia as early as 1963, and they were completely silenced by the arrests of 1965–72. During the course of those repressions some individual writers went over to the official position without having offered particular resistance (eg, Korotych, Drozd, and Hutsalo). Some of them were denied permission to publish, or refused to do so for some time (Kostenko); others were not published again until the changes after 1985 (Mamaisur, Holoborodko, Stupak). Others, who continued to opposed national discrimination and Russification, were arrested and punished with long sentences (Svitlychny, Sverstiuk, V. Stus, Kalynets, and V. Marchenko), whereupon some died in labor camps (Stus, Marchenko). Only Dziuba recanted, and after his release he was permitted to continue his literary work. The *shestydesiatnyky* movement completely died out at the beginning of the 1970s. Elements of the literary rebirth that it had initiated remained only in the works of certain poets and prose writers (Kostenko, Shevchuk). Apart from that, the *shestydesiatnyky* movement played an important role in popularizing samvydav literature and, most of all, in strengthening the opposition movement against Russian state chauvinism and Russification (as in Dziuba's book *Internatsionalizm chy rusyfikatsiia?* [Internationalism or Russification?, 1965], the essays of Sverstiuk, the samvydav poetry of many authors, especially Symonenko and M. Kholodny, the accusatory leaflets and protest letters of Stus, Marchenko, and others). With the declaration of glasnost and perestroika in 1985, the *shestydesiatnyky* once again became active both in their own creative work and in publicistic writings in defense of the Ukrainian language and the autonomy of Ukrainian culture. Some of them, like Drach and Dziuba, became active politically.

BIBLIOGRAPHY

Koshelivets', I. *Suchasna literatura v URSR* (Munich 1964)
Kravtsiv, B. (ed). *Shistdesiat poetiv shistdesiatykh rokiv* (Munich 1967)
Koshelivets', I. *Panorama nainovishoï literatury v URSR* (Munich 1963; 2nd edn, 1974)
Luckyj, G.S.N. (ed). *Discordant Voices: The Non-Russian Soviet Literatures* (Oakville, Ont 1975)

I. Koshelivets

Aleksandr Shevchenko: *Girl with Pears* (1933)

Shevchenko, Aleksandr (Oleksandr) [Ševčenko], b 7 July 1883 in Kharkiv, d 28 August 1948 in Moscow. Artist and theorist. He began his studies in Kharkiv and continued them in Paris (1905–6) and at the Moscow School of Painting, Sculpture, and Architecture (1907–9). In March 1912 he participated in the avant-garde Donkey's Tail Exhibition in Moscow together with V. Tatlin, M. Larionov, N. Goncharova, K. Malevich, and M. Chagall. Their Neoprimitivist work was based on folk art and rural culture. In 1913 Shevchenko published, in Russian, booklets on Neoprimitivism, in which he expounded on his theory of the Eastern origins of Slavic art and its alienation from Western art, and on the principles of cubism and other modern art trends. In 1914 he took part in Exhibition No. 14: Futurists, Rayonists, Primitives, organized by Larionov. In 1919 he, O. Hryshchenko, and their students organized in Moscow the 12th State Exhibition of 182 works by 38 artists. Its catalog contained Shevchenko's and Hryshchenko's manifesto and articles on 'color dynamics' and 'tectonic primitivism.' In 1920–30 Shevchenko was an instructor in the painting division of the Moscow Higher Artistic and Technical Workshops and participated in many large group exhibitions in Moscow and abroad. He later taught at the Higher Artistic and Technical Institute in Moscow. An album of his paintings and graphics was published in Moscow in 1966, and a collection of materials by and about him appeared there in 1980.

N. Mykytyn

Shevchenko, Arkady [Ševčenko, Arkadij], b 11 October 1930 in Horlivka, Donetske oblast. The highest-ranking Soviet official to defect from the USSR. A graduate of the Moscow Institute of International Relations (1954), in 1956

he was posted to the Department of United Nations and Disarmament Affairs of the USSR Foreign Ministry. In 1963 he was appointed chief of the Security Council and Political Affairs Division at the Soviet UN mission in New York. In December 1972 he was appointed undersecretary-general of the UN. Disillusioned with the Soviet system, he began supplying information to the CIA in 1975, and three years later he asked for asylum in the United States. He resided in Washington, DC, where he was a consultant and lecturer on Soviet affairs. In 1985 he published his memoirs, *Breaking with Moscow*.

Fedir Shevchenko

Shevchenko, Fedir [Ševčenko], b 24 August 1914 in Dunaivtsi, Nova Ushytsia county, Podilia gubernia. Historian; corresponding member of the AN URSR (now ANU) since 1969. He graduated from the Moscow Historical Archives Institute (1937), and from 1940 he worked in state archives in Chernivtsi, Krasnodar, and Uzbekistan. From 1945 to 1949 he was deputy head of the ANU commission on the history of the Great Patriotic War, and from 1949 to 1968 he worked at the ANU Institute of History (assistant director in 1964–7; PH D, 1963). He was editor in chief of *Ukraïns'kyi istorychnyi zhurnal* (*UIZh*, 1957–72), editor of the collections *Selians'kyi rukh na Bukovyni v 40-ykh rokakh XIX st.* (The Peasant Movement in Bukovyna in the 1840s) and *Narysy z istoriï Pivnichnoï Bukovyny* (Essays in the History of Northern Bukovyna, 1980), editor in chief of the annual *Istoriohrafichni doslidzhennia v Ukraïns'kii RSR* in 1968, and a member of the editorial board of *Istoriografiia istorii Ukrainskoi SSR* (The Historiography of the History of the Ukrainian SSR, 1987), in which he wrote on the 1648–54 period.

From 1968 to 1972 Shevchenko was director of the ANU Institute of Archeology, whence he returned to the ANU Institute of History; from 1982 he headed the Section of Historical Geography and Cartography, which compiled an atlas of the history of the Ukrainian SSR. His research has centered on the Middle Ages, the Second World War, historiography, and problems of Slavic studies. He has published works on the political and economic ties of Ukraine with Russia in the mid-17th century (1959), the international significance of the 1768 uprising in Right-Bank Ukraine (*UIZh*, 1968, no. 9), and the use of film documentaries in history education (*UIZh*, 1976, no. 6). He presented M. Hrushevsky in a positive light in 'Na chasi – vsebichnyi analiz' (It Is Time for an All-Round Analysis, *Kyïv*, 1988, no. 9).

A. Zhukovsky

Shevchenko, Ihor. See Ševčenko, Ihor.

Shevchenko, Ivan [Ševčenko] b 21 September 1902 in Pavlysh, Oleksandriia county, Kherson gubernia, d 23 April 1977 in Pavlysh. Poet, journalist, and editor of provincial newspapers. He belonged to the *Molodniak literary organization. His first published work was the poem *Porohy* (The Rapids, 1920). Subsequently he published the collection *Komsomol'tsi* (The Komsomol Members, 1925). Thereafter he wrote little and worked on a collective farm in Pavlysh. His song 'Dvanadtsiat' kosariv' (The Twelve Mowers) was popular in the 1920s. A revised edition of Shevchenko's verse appeared as *Poezii* (Poems) in 1962.

Shevchenko, Ivan [Ševčenko], b 18 March 1903 in Borovytsia, Chyhyryn county, Kiev gubernia. Soviet Ukrainian party historian. A graduate of the Cherkasy Pedagogical Institute (1935), he worked in the CP (1929–39) and headed the department of CPSU history at Kiev University (from 1943, as professor from 1962). A specialist in the history of the CPU during the First World War, he wrote *Z istorii sotsial-demokratychnykh orhanizatsii na Ukraïni* (From the History of Social-Democratic Organizations in Ukraine, 1956) and *Kommunisticheskaia partiia Ukrainy v bor'be za ukreplenie soiuza rabochikh i krest'ian (1919–1920 gg.)* (The Communist Party of Ukraine in the Struggle to Strengthen the Union of Workers and Peasants [1919–20], 1968).

Shevchenko, Ivan [Ševčenko], b 22 March 1905 in Novyi Starodub, Oleksandriia county, Kherson gubernia. Surgeon. A graduate of the Kharkiv Medical Institute (1930), he worked as a physician and surgeon in the Kharkiv region. He was director of the Kiev Roentgeno-Radiological and Oncological Scientific Research Institute (1945–71) and department head at the Kiev Institute for the Upgrading of Physicians (1971–6). He introduced new methods of diagnosing and treating malignant tumors and cancer of the esophagus. His publications deal with premalignant disorders and the prevention, diagnosis, and rehabilitation of oncological patients.

Shevchenko, Ivan [Ševčenko], b 19 August 1913 in Preobrazhenka, near Tomakivka, Katerynoslav county. Scenery designer. A pupil of O. Khvostenko-Khvostov, he completed study at the Kharkiv Art College (1941) and the Kharkiv Art Institute (1951). In 1951 he became principal designer in the Zhytomyr Ukrainian Music and Drama Theater.

Shevchenko, Lazar [Ševčenko], b 1884 in Hnidyn, near Boryspil, Pereiaslav county, Poltava gubernia, d 1936. Heroic and character actor; brother of Y. *Shevchenko. He worked in the Ruska Besida Theater in Lviv (1907–14) and the State People's Theater in Kiev (1918–19) and then became an adviser in Donbas workers' theaters. In 1934 he was an art director of programs broadcast in Kiev. In 1935 he was arrested. He was poisoned in prison.

Shevchenko, Liudmyla [Ševčenko, Ljudmyla], b 9 November 1895 in Kyrylivka (now Shevchenkove), Zvenyhorodka county, Kiev gubernia, d 22 October 1969 in Kiev. Ethnographer and folklorist; daughter of T. Shevchenko's nephew, Prokop. After graduating from the Archeological Institute (1923) she worked at the All-Ukrainian Academy of Sciences and then in various Kiev museums (1934–47). As department head at the Kiev Museum of Ukrainian Art she helped in its evacuation in 1941. From 1947 she worked at the AN URSR (now ANU) Institute of Fine Arts, Folklore, and Ethnography. She published over 20 articles in ethnography and folklore, including recollections of V. Hnatiuk (1927), the autobiography of the kobzar P. Kulyk (1929), and works on the rites associated with the beginning of a building (1926), the family and social status of women in Ukraine, T. Shevchenko's homeland, and the art of Ukrainian highlanders.

Shevchenko, Mykhailo [Ševčenko, Myxajlo], b 26 March 1923 in Oleksiivka, Yelysavethrad county. Opera singer (baritone). A graduate of the Kiev Conservatory (1956), he studied singing under D. Yevtushenko and performed in the Red Army Chorus. In 1955–78 he was a soloist of the Kiev Theater of Opera and Ballet. He taught at the Kiev Conservatory (1974–9).

Shevchenko, Oleksander [Ševčenko], b 29 October 1908 in Katerynoslav (now Dnipropetrovske), d 20 November 1984 in Dnipropetrovske. Metallurgist and specialist in metal-coining processes; corresponding member of the AN URSR (now ANU) from 1972. He studied and taught at the Dnipropetrovske Metallurgical Institute. He worked in the All-Union Scientific Research and Design-and-Technology Institute of Pipe Production (from 1945) and taught at the Dnipropetrovske Institute of Chemical Technology (1954–60). He made contributions in the fields of refractory-metals processing, continuous pipe manufacturing processes, and bimetallic and layered pipes design.

Shevchenko, Oleksander [Ševčenko], b 1940. Journalist and political prisoner. He was arrested in March 1980 and sentenced, for editing the samvydav journal *Ukraïns'kyi visnyk*, to five years in labor camps in Perm oblast and three years' exile in Kazakhstan. During his imprisonment he wrote numerous petitions and open letters of protest on behalf of political prisoners. After his release in the spring of 1987, he returned to Kiev, where he has been active in the national movement, the Ukrainian Helsinki Union, and the Ukrainian Culturological Club and worked as the scholarly editor of *Ukrainskii biokhimicheskii zhurnal*. In March 1990 he was elected to the Ukrainian Supreme Council as a deputy from a Kiev district.

Shevchenko, Semen [Ševčenko], b ? in Novi Petrivtsi, Kiev county, d ca 1868. Potter. In 1799 he was sent to work as an apprentice at the *Mezhyhiria Faience Factory. In 1802 he became assistant to the master modeler I. Sambirsky, and in 1811, a worker at Kh. Vimert's secret laboratory. He made vases, table sets, decorative plates (including ones with applied clay portraits of T. Shevchenko, M. Kostomarov, P. Kulish, and G. Garibaldi), and figurines, such as *Winter* (1852) and *Girl with Grapes* (1852). His works are in the classicist style, enlivened with decorative folk motifs.

Shevchenko, Taras [Ševčenko], b 9 March 1814 in Moryntsi, Kiev gubernia, d 10 March 1861 in St Petersburg, Russia. Artist, poet, and national bard of Ukraine.

Born a serf, Shevchenko was orphaned in his early teens and grew up in poverty and misery. He was taught to read by the village precentor and was often beaten for 'wasting time' on drawing, for which he had an innate talent. At the age of 14 he was taken by his owner, P. Engelhardt, to serve as houseboy, and traveled extensively with him, first to Vilnius (1828–31) and then to St Petersburg. Engelhardt noticed Shevchenko's artistic talent and apprenticed him to the painter V. Shiriaev for four years. During that period Shevchenko spent his free time sketching the statues in the imperial summer gardens. There he met the Ukrainian artist I. *Soshenko, who introduced him to other compatriots in St Petersburg, Ye. *Hrebinka, V. *Hryhorovych, and O. Venetsianov. Through them he met the Russian painter K. *Briullov, whose portrait of the Russian poet V. *Zhukovsky was disposed of in a lottery, the proceeds of which were used to buy Shevchenko's freedom from Engelhardt on 22 April (OS, 5 May NS) 1838.

Shevchenko enrolled in the Academy of Fine Arts in St Petersburg and pursued his art studies as well as his general education. In 1840 he published his first collection of poems, *Kobzar. That collection of eight Romantic poems was followed by the epic poem 'Haidamaky' (Haidamakas, 1841) and the ballad 'Hamaliia' (1844). In the 1840s Shevchenko visited Ukraine three times (1843, 1845, and 1846). Those visits made a profound impact on him. He visited his serf family, met some of the more prominent Ukrainians (P. *Kulish, M. *Maksymovych), and was befriended by the Repnin family (esp V. *Repnina). He was, furthermore, struck by the ravaged state of Ukraine. He decided to capture some of the old historical ruins and cultural monuments of Ukraine by preparing an album of etchings, which he called Zhivopisnaia Ukraina (Picturesque Ukraine, 1844). After graduating from the academy (1845) he became a member of the *Kiev Archeographic Commission. That position gave rise to his second visit to Ukraine and to extensive travels during which he sketched historical and architectural monuments and collected folkloric and other ethnographic materials. During those travels he wrote some of his most satirical and politically subversive poems ('Son' [Dream], 'Velykyi l'okh' [The Great Dungeon], 'Kavkaz' [Caucasus], and others), which he transcribed into the collection 'Try lita' (Three Years). The collection, however, was not published.

In 1846 Shevchenko came to Kiev and joined the secret *Cyril and Methodius Brotherhood. A denunciation resulted in the arrest of the members of the brotherhood; Shevchenko was arrested on 5 April 1847. The discovery of the satirical poems, highly critical of the tsar, in the Try lita manuscript collection brought him a particularly severe sentence, to military duty as a private in the Orenburg special corps in a remote area of the Caspian Sea. Tsar Nicholas I himself initiated the sentencing order with the admonition that the prisoner be prevented from writing and painting. At Orenburg and at Orsk fortresses, however, Shevchenko managed to continue doing both. He hid his poetry, written secretly in several notebooks (1847, 1848, 1849, 1850) known as zakhaliavni knyzhechky (bootleg booklets). Many of his sketches from that period have as their theme the life of the Kazakhs. Owing to his skill as a painter Shevchenko was included in a military expedition to survey and describe the Aral Sea (1848–9). After 1850 the terms of his imprisonment were more harshly enforced, and he was sent to the fortress in Novo-

petrovskoe (now *Fort-Shevchenko), where he stayed until his release in 1857, two years after the death of Tsar Nicholas. Shevchenko was not allowed to live in Ukraine. He waited for half a year in Nizhnii-Novgorod and then moved to St Petersburg. He was permitted to visit Ukraine in 1859 but was once again arrested and sent back to St Petersburg, where he remained under police surveillance until his death. Shevchenko was buried in St Petersburg, but two months afterward his remains were transferred to the Chernecha Hill near Kaniv, in Ukraine.

Taras Shevchenko (photograph, 1858)

Shevchenko has a uniquely important place in Ukrainian history. He created the conditions that allowed the transformation of Ukrainian literature into a fully functional modern literature. His influence on Ukrainian political thought and his role as an inspirer of a modern democratic ideal of renewed Ukrainian statehood are without parallel. His poetry contributed greatly to the evolution of national consciousness among the Ukrainian intelligentsia and people, and his influence on various facets of cultural and national life is felt to this day.

Shevchenko's literary output consists of one middle-sized collection of poetry (Kobzar); the drama Nazar Stodolia; two dramatic fragments; nine novelettes, a diary, and an autobiography in Russian; and over 250 letters. Even in the first period of his literary development (1837–43) Shevchenko wrote highly sophisticated poetical works. He adopted the stylistic and versificatory elements of the Ukrainian folk song for his verse; the poems are also remarkable for their formal originality. A complex and shifting metric structure, assonance and internal rhyme, masterfully applied caesuras and enjambments, and sophisticated alliterations are grafted onto a 4 + 4 + 6 syllable unit derived from the *kolomyika* song structure. The regular strophe is abandoned. Innovations can also be found in Shevchenko's use of epithets, similes, metaphors, symbols, and personifications. A man of his time and influenced in his world outlook by the current of *romanticism, Shevchenko managed to find his own manner of Romantic poetic expression, which encompassed the themes and ideas germane to Ukraine and to his personal vision of its past and future.

The early period contains the ballads 'Prychynna' (The Deranged [Girl], 1837), 'Topolia' (The Poplar, 1839), and 'Utoplena' (The Drowned Maiden, 1841). Romantic in their style and outlook on the world, those works have an affinity with Ukrainian folk ballads that is evident in their plot and their use of supernatural motifs. Of special note is the early ballad 'Kateryna,' dedicated to Zhukovsky in memory of the purchase of Shevchenko's freedom. Although the proceeds of the sale of the Russian poet's portrait helped secure Shevchenko's freedom, he chooses a tale in which a Ukrainian girl is seduced by a Russian soldier and left with child – a memento of the fact that it was the Russian tsars who had introduced serfdom to Ukraine. Several poems besides 'Kateryna' treat the theme of the seduced woman and abandoned mother ('Vid'ma' [Witch, 1847], 'Maryna' [1848], and the ballads 'Lileia' [Lily, 1846] and 'Rusalka' [Mermaid, 1846]). The oblique reference to Ukraine's history and fate in 'Kateryna' is echoed in other early poems, such as 'Tarasova nich' (Taras's Night, 1838), 'Ivan Pidkova' (1839), 'Haidamaky' (Haidamakas, 1841), and 'Hamaliia' (1842). Cossack raids against the Turks are recalled in 'Ivan Pidkova' and 'Hamaliia'; 'Tarasova nich' and, especially, 'Haidamaky' draw on the struggle against Polish oppression. Shevchenko wrote the Romantic drama *Nazar Stodolia* at the end of the early period of his creativity. Its action takes place near Chyhyryn, the Cossack capital, during the 17th century.

Taras Shevchenko (self-portrait, pencil, 1845)

Although Shevchenko's poetic achievements were evident to his contemporaries in the early period of his creativity, it was not until the second period (1843–5) that his poetry assured him the stature of a national bard. Having spent eight months in Ukraine, Shevchenko realized the full extent of his country's misfortune under Russian rule

Taras Shevchenko (self-portrait, sepia, 1849)

Taras Shevchenko (self-portrait, etching, 1860)

and progressively identified his own role as that of a poet-spokesman for his nation's aspirations. The poems 'Rozryta mohyla' (The Plundered Grave, 1843), 'Chyhyryne, Chyhyryne' (1844), and 'Son' (Dream, 1844) were written as a reaction to what Shevchenko saw happening in Ukraine. In 'Son' he portrayed with bitter sarcasm the lawlessness of tsarist rule. Satire is also apparent in 'Velykyi l'okh' (The Great Dungeon), 'Kavkaz' (Caucasus), 'Kholodnyi iar,' and 'I mertvym, i zhyvym ...' (To the Dead and to the Living ...), all written in 1845. 'Velykyi l'okh,' called a 'mystery,' consists of three parts and allegorically summarizes Ukraine's passage from freedom to captivity. In 'Kavkaz' Shevchenko universalized Ukraine's fate by turning his attention to the myth of Prometheus, the eternal free spirit, terribly punished for rebellion against the gods yet eternally reborn. He localized the action in the Caucasus, whose inhabitants suffered a fate similar to that of Ukrainians at the hands of the Russian tsars. Finally, in his poetic epistle 'To the Dead and to the Living ...' Shevchenko turned his bitter satire against the Ukrainians themselves. He reminded them that only in 'one's own house' is there 'one's own truth' and entreated them to realize their national potential, to stop serving foreign masters, to become honorable and free people, worthy of their history and heritage, in their own free land.

Similarly, in the poem 'Try lita' (Three Years), which gave its name to the whole second period and to the body of work written at that time, Shevchenko presented his own 'awakening' to the shame around him. He wept for his lost innocence and scorned the coming new year swaddled in one more 'ukase.' His scorn for the inactivity of his compatriots is echoed also in the poem 'Mynaiut' dni, mynaiut' nochi' (The Days Pass, the Nights Pass), in which somnolent inactivity is seen as far worse than death in chains. In December 1845 Shevchenko composed a cycle of poems titled 'Davydovi psalmy' (Psalms of David). He chose the psalms that had resonance for him (1, 12, 43, 52, 53, 81, 93, 132, 136, 149) and imbued the biblical texts with contemporary political relevance. He ends the *Try lita* collection with his famous 'Zapovit' (Testament). That 24-line poem has been translated into more than 60 languages, has been set to music by H. Hladky, and has achieved a stature among Ukrainians similar to that of a national anthem. 'Zapovit' merges his own requests with exhortations to 'break the chains and christen freedom with drops of blood.' With 'Zapovit' Shevchenko firmly laid claim to the title of national bard.

Along with other works of the *Try lita* period 'Ivan Hus' or 'Ieretyk' (Jan Hus or Heretic, 1845) introduces another of Shevchenko's major themes. Dedicated to P. Šafařík, the poem uses a historical theme (the trial and burning of Hus in Costanza in 1415) as a vehicle for the Pan-Slavic ideas of the Cyril and Methodius Brotherhood, of which Shevchenko had become a member.

The cycle 'V kazemati' (In the Casemate) was written in the spring of 1847 at the time of Shevchenko's arrest and interrogation. It marks the beginning of the hardest period of his life (1847–57). The 13 poems of the cycle contain reminiscences (the famous lyrical poem 'Sadok vyshnevyi kolo khaty' [The Cherry Orchard by the House]), reflections on the fate of the poet and of his fellow members of the brotherhood, and poignant reassertions of his beliefs and his commitment to Ukraine. Shevchenko's stand was unequivocal, and he exhorted his fellow Cyrillo-Methodians as well as all compatriots, 'Love your Ukraine / Love her ... in the harshest time / In the very last harsh minute / Pray to God for her.' Through his exile Shevchenko's views did not change, although his poems grew more contemplative and reflective. He continued in his 'bootleg' poetry to write autobiographic, landscape, and narrative as well as historical, political, religious, and philosophical poems. Of special interest is the long poem 'Moskaleva krynytsia' (A Soldier's Well), written in two variants, 1847 and 1857, which reveals Shevchenko's preoccupation with the theme of human inhumanity to fellow human beings and of the human capacity to accept and forgive. A comparison of the two variants provides an insight into the maturation process of Shevchenko as poet and thinker.

The autobiographical poems embrace such lyrics as 'Meni trynadtsiatyi mynalo' (I Was Turning 14), 'A.O. Kozachkovs'komu' (To A.O. Kozachkovsky), 'I vyris ia na chuzhyni' (I Grew Up in a Foreign Land), 'Khiba samomu napysat'' (Should I Then Myself Write?), 'I zolotoï i dorohoï' (Both Golden and Dear), and 'Lichu v nevoli dni i nochi' (I Count Both Days and Nights in Captivity). But personal reflection also occurs in some of the landscape poems, especially where Shevchenko describes the *paysage* of his captivity ('Sontse zakhodyt', hory chorniiut'' [The Sun Is Setting, the Hills Turn Dark], 'I nebo nevmyte,

Soldiers guarding Taras Shevchenko's grave on Chernecha Hill in Kaniv in 1861

i zaspani khvyli' [The Sky Is Unwashed and the Waves Are Not Yet Awake], and the like). Varied and rich are the poems devoted to narratives and description motivated by the memory of the village way of life. Elements of folk songs are used in depicting sadness, parting, loneliness, aspects of the daily life of Ukrainian peasants, motherhood, the harsh fate of women, and the longing for happiness. The poetic style of the poems is marked by a simplicity of vocabulary, concrete description, and metaphors. There is frequent use of personification (the wind whispers, fate wanders, thoughts sleep, evil laughs). Shevchenko consistently refined his use of folkloric material. He expanded the use of ancient folkloric symbolism and made full use of the expressivity of folk songs (typical earthiness, repetition to insinuate emotional gradation, poetical alogism, psychological parallelism, fixed imagery). The ingestion and transformation of folkloric elements was so successful that many original poems have become folk songs in their own right.

Shevchenko continued sporadically to reiterate his political convictions and to point to the enslavement of individuals (serfdom) and nations by the tsarist regime. In the

Taras Shevchenko's relatives and friends by his casket in Kiev (7 May 1861): 1, Taras's brother Mykyta; 2, Taras's brother Yosyp; 3, Mykyta's son Petro; 4, Yosyp's wife; 5, Taras's sister Yaryna; 6, Yosyp's son; 7, Taras's second cousin Varfolomii; 8 and 9, Varfolomii's daughters; 10, Varfolomii's son; 11, Varfolomii's wife; 12, Ivan Soshenko

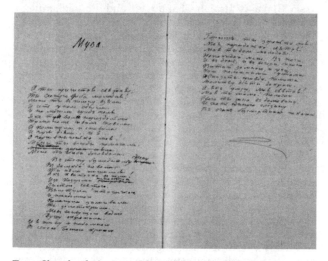

Taras Shevchenko's poem 'Muza' (Muse, 1858) in his own handwriting

poem 'Poliakam' (To the Poles, 1847), he continued his Pan-Slavic call for brotherhood between the Poles and the Ukrainians, who were set against each other by religious difference. Shevchenko used a Kazakh legend in the short poem 'U Boha za dveryma lezhala sokyra' (God Had an Ax Lying behind the Door, 1848) to describe, in allegorical terms, the misfortunes of the Kazakhs, who were also under tsarist Russian domination. Satire did not leave Shevchenko's arsenal. In the satiric 'Tsari' (Tsars, 1848) he gave glimpses of the killing, sexual debauchery, incest, and adultery which he saw as typical of royal courts, from that of the biblical King David to that of St Volodymyr of Rus'. The successful combination of an offhand burlesque style with bitter invective gave Shevchenko a powerful though somewhat veiled weapon in his attack on tsarism in general and on the Russian tsar in particular. Much more direct are his accusations against the Russian tsars in 'Irzhavets'' (1847).

Parallel to the motifs of the seduced girl and the unwed mother, which occur frequently in Shevchenko's poems, is the motif of incest. It appears in 'Tsari' and in 'Vid'ma' and forms the basis for 'Kniazhna' (Princess, 1847). Although in many of his poems Shevchenko harshly attacks the hypocrisy of the church and the clergy, he remains steadfast in his belief that divine justice will one day triumph for Ukraine and for all of humanity. His millenarian vision appears in many of his poems but is perhaps best encapsuled in the following lines from 'I Arkhimed i Halilei' (Both Archimedes and Galileo, 1860): 'And on the reborn earth / There will be no enemy, no tyrant / There will be a son, and there will be a mother, / And there will be human beings on the earth.'

The last period of Shevchenko's creativity begins after his return from exile (1857–61) and is marked in his works by more frequent allusion to the Bible and to classical literature and by the increasingly dominant role of contemplative lyricism. The period contains such longer poems as 'Neofity' (Neophytes, 1857), 'Iurodyvyi' (God's Fool, 1857), the second redaction of 'Vid'ma' (1858), 'Nevol'nyk' (The Captive, begun in 1845 and finished in 1859), and 'Mariia' (1859). There are also renditions of biblical texts ('Podrazhaniie Iiezekiiliu Hlava 19' [Imitation of Ezekiel Chapter 19], 'Osii Hlava 14' [Esau Chapter 14], 'Isaia Hlava 35' [Isaiah Chapter 35], and 'Podrazhaniie 11 Psalmu' [Imitation of the 11th Psalm]), in which Shevchenko turns to the Scriptures for analogies to the contemporary situation. In the '11th Psalm' he proclaims what might be the motto of his creativity: 'I will glorify / Those small mute slaves! / On guard by them / I will place the word.' The last period also contains some of the most profound contemplative lyrics written by Shevchenko. The period ends with a reflective poem addressed to his muse: 'Chy ne pokynut' nam, neboho' (Should We Not Call It Quits, [My] Friend), written in two parts on 26 and 27 February, eleven days before his death. Like many of Shevchenko's last poems it is full of allusions to classical mythology, including a reference to the river Styx, which he was preparing to cross.

The novelettes which Shevchenko wrote in exile were unpublished during his life. They are connected with the tradition of the satiric-exposé prose of N. Gogol but contain many asides (excursions into the past, inserted episodes, authorial comments, reminiscences, and commentaries). Although written in Russian, they contain many Ukrainianisms. The first of the novelettes ('Nai-

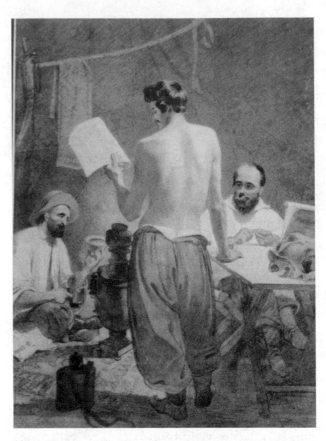

Taras Shevchenko: *Shevchenko Among Friends* (sepia, 1851)

michka' [The Servant Girl, 1844] and 'Varnak' [The Convict, 1845]) share the antiserfdom themes of Shevchenko's like-named poems. 'Kniaginia' (Princess, 1853) is similar in theme to the poem 'Kniazhna.' The remaining six ('Muzykant' [The Musician, 1854–5], 'Neschastnyi' [The Unfortunate, 1855], 'Kapitansha' [The Captain-Woman, 1855], 'Khudozhnik' [The Artist, 1856], 'Blizentsy' [The Twins, 1855–6], and 'Progulka s udovol'stviiem i ne bez morali' [A Stroll with Pleasure and Not without a Moral, 1858]) are not thematically similar to any particular poems. Shevchenko's diary ('Zhurnal'), also written in Russian, consists of daily notations from his life along with comments and observations. It is of great value to the interpretation of his poetic works and also important in its revelation of his erudition and breadth of thought.

In the intellectual history of Ukraine Shevchenko has a unique position, and the importance of his poetry for Ukrainian culture cannot be underestimated. His *Kobzar* marks the beginning of a new era in the development of Ukrainian literature and language. By blending in his poetic works the vernacular Ukrainian together with elements of the bookish language drawn from Old Church Slavonic as well as from the *chronicles, Shevchenko firmly established the literary Ukrainian language and made it serviceable for any future literary work or genre. Furthermore he played the main role in the national awakening and drive for national liberation of the Ukrainian people. The revolutionary and ideological content of Shevchenko's political poems found resonance among other enslaved peoples. The earliest translations of his poems – mainly into Polish, Russian, Czech, and German – appeared while he was still alive. By the 1990s parts of the *Kobzar* had been translated into more than 100 languages. Shevchenko's poetry has also become a source for various other works in literature, music, and art.

Some of the more important translations have been the following: (1) into Russian, *Sobranie sochinenii v 5 tt.* (Collected Works, 5 vols, 1948–9, 1955–6, 1964–5), *Kobzar'* (1972), and a four-volume collected works in 1977; (2) into Polish, *Wiersze wybrane* (Selected Poems, 1913), *Zbiorek wybranych poezij* (A Collection of Selected Poems, 1921), *Utwory wybrane* (Selected Works, 1955), and two other selected collections in 1972 and 1974; (3) into Czech, *Výbor básní* (Selected Poems, 1900), *Výbor z dila největšiho básnika a buditele Ukrajiny* (Selection from the Works of the Greatest Poet and Awakener of Ukraine, 1951), *Kobzar* (1953), *Nazar Stodola* (1958), and *Hajdamáci* (Haidamakas, 1961); (4) into Hungarian, *Kobzos* (1953); (5) into Rumanian, *Cobzarul* (1957); (6) into Serbo-Croatian, *Kobzar* (1969); (7) into Bulgarian, *Izbrani proizvedeniia* (Selected Works, 2 vols, 1960) and *Kobzar* (1964); (8) into German, *Ausgewählte Gedichte von Taras Schewtschenko* (1911), *Der Kobzar* (2 vols, 1951), *Die Haidamaken und andere Dichtungen* (1951), and *Der Kobzar* (1962); (9) into English, *The Kobzar of Ukraine* (1922), *Selected Poems* (1945), *Song out of Darkness – Selected Poems* (1961), *The Poetical Works of Taras Shevchenko: The Kobzar* (1964, 1967), and *Selected Works: Poetry and Prose* (1979); (10) into French, *Poésies* (1964); (11) into Italian, *Liriche scelte del 'Cobzar'* (1927) and *Liriche Ucraine* (1942); and (12) into Spanish, *Obras escogidas* (1964).

Although Shevchenko is seen mainly as a poet, he was also a highly accomplished artist. There are 835 works extant from that domain of his creativity. Another 270 are known but have been lost. Although trained in the academic classicist style in St Petersburg, Shevchenko was able to move beyond stereotypical historical and mythological subjects to realistic renderings of ethnographic themes and genre scenes expressing veiled criticism of the absence of personal, social, and national freedom under tsarist domination. Shevchenko's portraits have a broad social range of subjects, from peasants (*The Kazakh Girl*, 1856) to members of the nobility (*Princess E. Keikuatova*, 1847). They are remarkable for their use of light to achieve sensitive three-dimensional modeling. Shevchenko painted over 150 portraits, 43 of them self-portraits. He also painted numerous landscapes which recorded the archi-

Taras Shevchenko: *Gifts in Chyhyryn (Foreign Emissaries at Hetman Bohdan Khmelnytsky's Residence)* (etching, 1844)

tectural monuments of Ukraine. While in exile he depicted Kirghiz folkways and the surrounding countryside, as well as the misery of life in tsarist prisons and in the Russian army. Shevchenko was also very proficient in watercolor, aquatint, and etching. On 2 September 1860 the Academy of Arts recognized his mastery of engraving by declaring him an academician engraver. Yet Shevchenko's contributions to the development of Ukrainian painting have long been overshadowed by his fame as the bard of Ukraine.

Shevchenko studies. The importance of Shevchenko and his work in the Ukrainian intellectual, literary, cultural, and political spheres has given rise to multifaceted studies of the poet and his work. The studies reflect different approaches: the biographic, bibliographic, literary, textological, linguistic, lexicographic, esthetic, psychological, pedagogical, ethical, religious, philosophical, political, sociological, and art-historical. Of prime importance to all of the studies are the poetic and artistic works of the poet. The manuscripts and originals of a majority of them are housed in the ANU Institute of Literature. A unique collection of Shevchenkiana can also be found in the ANU Central Scientific Library – over 15,000 items collected by Yu. Mezhenko. The largest collection of publications of the works of Shevchenko and documents about his life and works has been amassed in the Shevchenko Museum in Kiev. Some autographs and papers of the poet are to be found in other archives, libraries, and museums throughout Ukraine, as well as in libraries in St Petersburg, Moscow, Cracow, Geneva, and elsewhere. There is no complete register of all archival Shevchenkiana.

Although bibliographic studies of Shevchenko play a paramount role in the study of the poet and his work, and although that aspect of Shevchenko studies has been highly developed, a complete bibliography of Shevchenko's works and of works about him and his work does not exist. Especially needed is a bibliography of the Shevchenkiana of the 1970s and 1980s, in foreign languages.

The first known published works concerning Shevchenko date from 1839. During the poet's life various reviews of his works appeared in the Ukrainian, Russian, Polish, Czech, German, French, and Italian press. The first publication of Shevchenko's poems outside of the Russian Empire was *Novye stikhotvoreniia Pushkina i Shavchenki* [sic]

An edition (1961) of foreign translations of Taras Shevchenko's 'Zapovit' (Testament) and the monument to Shevchenko in Kiev (sculptor Matvii Manizer, 1939)

(The New Poems of Pushkin and Shevchenko), which appeared in Leipzig in 1859 at the initiative of Kulish. A full *Kobzar* appeared in St Petersburg in 1860 (see also **Kobzar*), and a Russian translation of the *Kobzar*, with a bibliography listing Shevchenko's published works and other Russian translations, appeared in 1860. The last book published before the poet's death was his *Bukvar' iuzhnorusskii* (A South Russian [Ukrainian] Primer, 1861), which Shevchenko prepared for Ukrainian Sunday schools and published at his own cost.

At the beginning of the 1860s most materials about Shevchenko appeared in the journal **Osnova*. The first article about Shevchenko in German, by H.-L. Zunk, appeared in *Die Gartenlaube* in 1862 in Leipzig. The first study of Shevchenko's life and work to appear separately was in Polish: *Taras Szewczenko* by L. Sowiński with a translation of 'Haidamaky' as an addendum (1861). *Przekłady pisarzów małorossyjskich: Taras Szewczenko* (Translations of Little Russian Writers: Taras Shevchenko) was published in 1862 (repub 1863) by A. Gorzałczyński. A biographical and critical study of Shevchenko by G. Battaglia, *Taras Szewczenko, życie i pisma jego* (Taras Shevchenko, His Life and Letters, 1865), did much to popularize Shevchenko among Polish readers. J.-G. Obrist, the first translator of Shevchenko into German, used Battaglia's work when he wrote his *T.G. Szewczenko, ein kleinrussischer Dichter* (1870).

V. Maslov's *T.G. Shevchenko – Biograficheskii ocherk* (T.G. Shevchenko, A Biographic Sketch, 1874, 1887) was the first relatively full biography of Shevchenko to appear in Russia and was also based on Battaglia's work. The Valuev circular (1863) and the Ems Ukase (1876) put an effective stop to the publication of works in Ukrainian in the Russian Empire. Publications of Shevchenko's works and works about him thenceforth were issued primarily in Galicia and abroad. *Poeziï Tarasa Shevchenka* (The Poems of Taras Shevchenko), which appeared in Lviv in 1867 in two volumes, contained mainly Shevchenko's political poems; in Ukraine under Russian rule they either were prohibited or were published after being altered by censorship. Following the appearance of the two-volume Prague edition of *Kobzar* (1876) the French literary scholar E.-A. Durand published a large promotional article in *Revue des deux mondes* (15 June 1876), 'Le poète national de la Petite-Russie, T.G. Chevtchenko,' which produced echo articles, one by J.A. Stevens in the New York monthly *The Galaxy* (June 1876) and one by C. Dickens, Jr, in the London weekly *All the Year Round* (5 May 1877). At about the same time, V. Lesevych published an article, 'Taras Shevchenko, el gran poeta de Ucraina,' and translations of some poems in the Madrid journal *La Ilustración española y americana* (1877, no. 4). A more thorough article, 'Die Kleinrussen und ihr Sänger' by K. Franzos, appeared in *Augsburger Allgemeine Zeitung* (1877, nos 164–5). It was expanded into a booklet, *Vom Don zur Donau* (1878), in which the author emphasizes the universality of Shevchenko's works. Of importance in making Shevchenko accessible to the world at large was the work done by M. Drahomanov while he was an exile from Ukraine under Russian rule. Of special note is his brochure *La littérature oukrainienne proscrite par le gouvernement russe* (which was distributed at the Literary Congress in Paris in 1878). In Geneva Drahomanov published the *Kobzar* (1881), the poem 'Maria' (*Marija Maty Isusowa* [Maria Mother of Jesus, 1882]), and *Poeziï T. Shevchenka*,

zaboroneni v Rosiï (Poems of T. Shevchenko Forbidden in Russia, 1890).

The main promoter of Shevchenko in the 1880s was I. Franko. Beginning with his youthful study 'Prychynky do otsinennia poezii Tarasa Shevchenka' (Contributions to the Evaluation of Taras Shevchenko's Poetry, *S'vit* [1881, nos 8–12, and 1882, no. 1]), Franko continued throughout his creative life to write on various aspects of Shevchenko's creativity. His study of the poem 'Perebendia' (1889) is both perceptive and objective; it considers Shevchenko's unique brand of romanticism in the context of European romanticism and Ukrainian folk traditions. Insights into Shevchenko's use of the ballad genre are to be found in Franko's study '"Topolia" T. Shevchenka' (T. Shevchenko's 'Topolia,' 1890). The cult of Shevchenko was becoming widespread in Ukraine, and epigones of Shevchenko were appearing among Ukrainian writers; Franko cautioned against both phenomena. He published a popular sketch of Shevchenko in the newspaper *Zoria* (1891, no. 5) giving a synthetic view of Shevchenko's life and works against the background of his era. With some variations the same article appeared in Polish (*Kurier Lwowski*, 1893, nos. 62–4, 66–8), German (*Die Zeit*, no. 4136, 1914), and, after Franko's death, English (*Slavonic Review*, vol 3, 1924). The last work by Franko on Shevchenko was his study of the poem 'Mariia,' published after Franko's death in *ZNTSh* (vols 119–20, 1917). Franko considered 'Mariia' to be one of Shevchenko's best works and used it as proof that exile had not daunted the poet's creative spirit.

Interest in Shevchenko continued to grow in the late 19th century. O. Konysky collected the articles on Shevchenko which he had published in *Zoria* and expanded them into a two-volume monograph, *Taras Shevchenko-Hrushivs'kyi: Khronika ioho zhyttia* (Taras Shevchenko-Hrushivsky: A Chronicle of His Life, 1898, 1901), which also appeared in an abridged version in Russian in Odessa in 1898. Basing his work on the sources available, Konysky corrected many errors in previous biographies of Shevchenko and presented the first scholarly biography of the poet. S. Liudkevych's 'Pro osnovu i znachennia spivnosty v poeziï Tarasa Shevchenka' (On the Origin and Meaning of Musicality in the Poetry of T. Shevchenko, *Moloda Ukraïna*, 1901, nos 5–6, 8–9, and 1902, no. 4) was the first in a long line of works dealing with Shevchenko's poetics. The foundation for a bibliography of Shevchenkiana was laid by M. Komarov with his *Shevchenko v literature i iskusstve: Bibliograficheskii ukazatel' materialov dlia izucheniia zhizni i proizvedenii T. Shevchenko* (Shevchenko in Literature and Art: A Bibliographic Guide to the Materials for the Study of the Life and Works of T. Shevchenko, 1903).

Textological problems connected with Shevchenko's *Kobzar* were studied by V. *Domanytsky, who based his findings on autographs and various publications of Shevchenko's works. He published his work in *Kievskaia starina* (1906, nos 9–12), 'Krytychnyi rozslid nad tekstom *Kobzaria*' (A Critical Study of the Text of the *Kobzar*), and as a separate monograph in 1907. The first 'full' edition of the *Kobzar* appeared under Domanytsky's editorship in St Petersburg in 1907 (repub in 1908). The historian of the Zaporozhian Sich D. Yavornytsky published valuable archival materials in 1909 as *Materialy do biohrafiï T. Shevchenka* (Materials Pertaining to the Biography of T. Shevchenko). Also of interest was his study 'Zaporozhtsy v poezii T. Shevchenko' (Zaporozhians in the Poetry of

TARAS SHEVCHENKO 1) *Self-Portrait* (oil, 1840; Kiev Shevchenko Museum). 2) *Gypsy Fortune-Teller* (watercolor on paper, 1841; Kiev Shevchenko Museum). 3) *Kateryna* (oil, 1842; Kiev Shevchenko Museum). 4) *Gifts in Chyhyryn in 1649* (etching, 1844; Kiev Shevchenko Museum). 5) *Pochaiv Monastery from the South* (watercolor on paper, 1846; Taras Shevchenko Gallery, Kharkiv). 6) *Portrait of E. Keikuatova* (oil, 1847; Kiev Shevchenko Museum). 7) *Portrait of Horlenko* (oil, 1846–7; Kharkiv Art Museum). 8) *Running the Gauntlet*, from the series 'Parable of the Prodigal Son' (India ink and bister on paper, 1856–7; Kiev Shevchenko Museum). 9) *Turkmenian Sepulchers at Kara-Tau* (watercolor on paper, 1851–7; Kiev Shevchenko Museum).

Shevchenko), published in *Letopis' Ekaterinoslavskoi uchenoi arkhivnoi komissii* (no. 8, 1912).

Several works appeared on Shevchenko in connection with the centenary of his birth: V. Shchurat collected his articles on Shevchenko in *Z zhyttia i tvorchosty Tarasa Shevchenka* (From the Life and Works of T. Shevchenko, 1914); O. Novytsky published a monograph *T. Shevchenko iak maliar* (T. Shevchenko as an Artist, 1914), the first major study on Shevchenko the artist; and Ya. Yarema wrote *Uiava Shevchenka* (The Imagination of Shevchenko, 1914), focusing on metaphor in Shevchenko's poetry.

A major contribution to Shevchenko studies outside of Ukraine came from the Swedish Slavist A. Jensen, whose monograph *Taras Schewtschenko: Ein ukrainisches Dichterleben* (1916) pointed to the universal themes and concerns of Shevchenko's poetry. Of interest as the first attempt at a psychological approach to Shevchenko's work was S. Balei's *Z psykholohiï tvorchosty Shevchenka* (On the Psychology of Shevchenko's Creativity, 1916).

Shevchenko studies continued to develop during the struggle for Ukraine's independence and under the new Soviet regime. The All-Ukrainian Academy of Sciences (VUAN), established in 1918, embraced several scholars working on Shevchenko and using various approaches, such as factual research and documentation (S. Yefremov, M. Novytsky, V. Miiakovsky, Ye. Markovsky), the sociology of literature (D. Bahalii, Y. Hermaize, O. Doroshkevych, M. Plevako, V. Koriak), esthetic criticism (P. Fylypovych, V. Petrov, P. Rulin, B. Varneke), and formalism (B. Yakubsky, A. Shamrai, Ya. Aizenshtok, B. Navrotsky). Soviet Ukrainian Shevchenko studies begin with the publication of the collection of essays *Taras Shevchenko*, edited by Ye. Hryhoruk and Fylypovych, which was published in 1921 to mark the 60th anniversary of the poet's death. Most Shevchenko studies in the 1920s were published as articles collected in jubilee editions (*Shevchenkivs'kyi zbirnyk* [The Shevchenko Miscellany, 1924], *Shevchenko ta ioho doba* [Shevchenko and His Era, 2 vols, 1925–6]), but separate studies also appeared, notably Aizenshtok's *Shevchenkoznavstvo – suchasna problema* (Shevchenko Studies: A Current Problem, 1922), Plevako's *Shevchenko i krytyka* (Shevchenko and Criticism, 1924), Bahalii's *T.H. Shevchenko i Kyrylo-Metodiïvtsi* (T. Shevchenko and the Cyrillo-Methodians, 1925), and O. Bahrii's *T.G. Shevchenko v literaturnoi obstanovke* (T. Shevchenko in a Literary Setting, 1925). In Galicia, under Polish rule, two works of importance appeared, I. Svientsitsky's *Shevchenko v svitli krytyky i diisnosty* (Shevchenko in the Light of Criticism and Reality, 1922) and M. Vozniak's *Shevchenko i kniazhna Repnina* (Shevchenko and Princess Repnina, 1925).

In 1926 the Taras Shevchenko Scientific Research Institute was established in Kharkiv, with a branch in Kiev. It was devoted to the collection of Shevchenko's autographs and artworks, to the study of his biography, and to textological studies of his poems. The results of those efforts were published in annual collections of the institute (*Shevchenko*, 1928, 1930) as well as in the institute's organ *Literaturnyi arkhiv*, which appeared bimonthly in 1930–1. The Kiev branch of the institute prepared for publication a dictionary of Shevchenko's language and a dictionary of Shevchenko's acquaintances, but neither was published owing to the political repressions of the 1930s.

One of the foremost Shevchenko scholars of the first quarter of the 20th century was Yefremov. His many articles, written over a period of more than 15 years, were collected in a single volume, *Taras Shevchenko* (1914). In 1921 Yefremov became head of the VUAN Commission for the Publication of Monuments of Modern Literature. One of the objectives was the preparation of an academic edition of Shevchenko's works. Only two volumes appeared, vol 4, *Shchodenni zapysky* (Daily Notes, 1927), and vol 3, *Lystuvannia* (Correspondence, 1929). The volumes were edited by Yefremov and annotated by the scholars A. Loboda, Miiakovsky, M. Novytsky, O. Novytsky, D. Revutsky, Rulin, and Fylypovych. The remaining volumes, as well as O. Novytsky's volume devoted to the artistic works of Shevchenko, were never published, because most of the scholars perished in the wake of the trial of the *Union for the Liberation of Ukraine.

The terror of the 1930s put a stop to meaningful study of Shevchenko. The VUAN was closed, and the scholars at the institute were arrested. Most perished. Those who remained were placed under the control of Party officials, not necessarily connected with Shevchenko scholarship, whose main role was to liquidate all expression of true scholarship. The era of systematic falsification of Shevchenko's works began, and it lasted, to a greater or lesser degree, throughout the remainder of the Soviet regime. Although works on Shevchenko did not cease to be written, most of them, by such Party scholars as V. Zatonsky, A. Khvylia, and Ye. Shabliovsky, merit little discussion.

Meanwhile Shevchenko studies continued outside of Soviet Ukraine. D. Doroshenko prepared a popular scholarly work, *Schewtschenko, der grosse ukrainische Nationaldichter*, and published it in Berlin in 1929. The work was republished in French (Prague 1931), English (Prague, Winnipeg, and New York 1936, and Augsburg 1946), and Italian (Prague 1939). Doroshenko also presented a concise survey of Shevchenko studies in the 1920s in 'Die Forschung über T. Ševčenko in der Nachkriegszeit,' published in *Zeitschrift für slavische Philologie* (vol 9, 1932). E. Borschak pointed to Shevchenko's role in the struggle for Ukrainian self-determination in the study 'Le mouvement national ukrainien au XIXe siècle,' which appeared in *Le monde Slave* (November 1930). The Shevchenko Scientific Society (NTSh) in Lviv published Borschak's study *Shevchenko u Frantsiï: Narys iz istoriï franko-ukraïns'kykh*

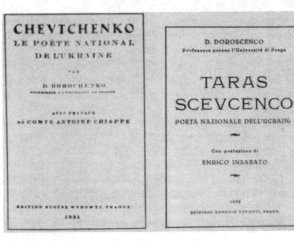

Books about Taras Shevchenko in French and Italian

vzaiemyn (Shevchenko in France: Sketch of the History of French-Ukrainian Relations, 1933). P. *Zaitsev prepared *Szewczenko a Polacy* (Shevchenko and the Poles, 1934), in which he studied Shevchenko against the background of Ukrainian-Polish relations in the mid-19th century. V. Simovych's popular study *Taras Shevchenko: Ioho zhyttia i tvorchist'* (T. Shevchenko: His Life and Works) was published in several editions (1934, 1941, 1944). Simovych also prepared an annotated *Kobzar* in 1921. S. Smal-Stotsky's study *Taras Shevchenko: Interpretatsiï* (T. Shevchenko: Interpretations, 1934) emphasized Shevchenko's critical attitude to Russia and his contention that Ukraine's greatest misfortune lay in its domination by Russia. In 1937 the Ukrainian Scientific Institute in Berlin published the collection *Taras Schewtschenko, der ukrainische Nationaldichter (1814–1861)*, which contained articles and some translations. Of note was the publication *Studiï nad poetychnoiu tvorchistiu T. Shevchenka* (Studies on the Poetic Creation of T. Shevchenko, 1939) by F. Kolessa, which consisted of two monographs, 'Folkl'ornyi element u poeziï T. Shevchenka' (The Folkloric Element in the Poetry of T. Shevchenko) and 'Virshova forma poezii T. Shevchenka' (The Verse Forms in the Poetry of T. Shevchenko), which remains a basic work in the field.

The main center of Shevchenko studies in the 1930s was the Ukrainian Scientific Institute in Warsaw, which published 13 volumes of a 16–volume set of the complete works of Shevchenko (1934–8). The Soviet occupation of Poland put an end to the edition. A biography of Shevchenko by Zaitsev, which had been planned for the first volume, did not appear until 1955 in the United States. Vols 2–4 and 6–12 were edited by Zaitsev, vol 14 by B. Lepky, vol 15 by R. Smal-Stotsky; vol 16, which consisted of a bibliography, was compiled by V. Doroshenko. That incomplete full edition of Shevchenko's works was the greatest achievement of prewar Shevchenko scholarship. The volumes contained commentaries and annotations by the editors and such Shevchenko scholars as L. Biletsky, I. Bryk, Doroshenko, O. Lototsky, Ye. Malaniuk, S. Siropolko, and D.Chyzhevsky.

Works which appeared during the Second World War were Aizenshtok's *Iak pratsiuvav Shevchenko* (How Shevchenko Worked, 1940), O. Borshchahivsky and M. Yosypenko's *Shevchenko i teatr* (Shevchenko and the The-

Books in Shevchenko studies by Western authors

ater, 1941), M. Hrinchenko's *Shevchenko i muzyka* (Shevchenko and Music, 1941), S. Hordynsky's *Shevchenko – maliar* (Shevchenko the Painter, 1942), Ye.Yu. Pelensky's *Shevchenko – kliasyk* (Shevchenko: A Classic, 1942), and some articles by L. Bulakhovsky and O. Doroshkevych.

The first postwar work on Shevchenko, which appeared in English in the United States, was *Taras Shevchenko: The Poet of Ukraine* (1945) by C.A. Manning, who provided the translations and annotations. In Soviet Ukraine the AN URSR (now ANU) Institute of Literature was re-established after the war, but the Shevchenko section was slow to produce any studies. Its main work centered on the completion of a 10-volume full collection of Shevchenko's works, begun before the war: vols 3–4 (dramatic works) appeared in 1949, and vol 5 (the diary and autobiography) in 1951; vols 1–2 (the poems) were republished from the 1939 edition in 1951–3, and vol 6 (letters, notes) in 1957; finally, vols 7–10 (the artistic works) appeared in 1961–4. Unfortunately the 10-volume 'full academic' edition was not free of the standard censorship and the falsifications which marred Shevchenko scholarship in Soviet Ukraine. Some of those deficiencies were removed from the subsequent full edition in six volumes, which appeared in 1963–4. Shevchenko's artistic oeuvre was republished in a separate four-volume edition in 1961–4. Beginning in 1952 the institute held annual conferences on Shevchenko, the proceedings of which were published in collections. Their content on the whole reflected the Party line in Shevchenko studies and the want of scholarly rigor. Somewhat more scholarly were the works of S. Chavdarov (*Pedahohichni ideï Tarasa Hryhorovycha Shevchenka* [Pedagogical Ideas of T. Shevchenko, 1953]), V. Shubravsky (*Dramaturhiia Shevchenka* [Shevchenko's Dramaturgy, 1957, 1959, 1961]), Yu. *Ivakin (*Satyra Shevchenka* [Satire of Shevchenko, 1959, 1964]), Ye. Nenadkevych (*Z tvorchoï laboratoriï T.H. Shevchenka* [From the Creative Laboratory of Shevchenko, 1959]), and D. Iofanov (*Materialy pro zhyttia i tvorchist' Tarasa Shevchenka* [Material on the Life and Works of T. Shevchenko, 1957]).

Many works appeared to mark the 1961 and 1964 anniversaries, some of which reflected the political 'thaw.' Among the more notable were Ivakin's *Styl' politychnoï poeziï Shevchenka* (The Style of Shevchenko's Political Poetry, 1961) and his two-volume commentary on the *Kobzar* (1964–8), V. Vashchenko's *Mova Tarasa Shevchenka* (The Language of T. Shevchenko, 1963), P. Prykhodko's *Shevchenko i ukraïns'kyi romantyzm* (Shevchenko and Ukrainian Romanticism, 1963), H. Verves's *T.H. Shevchenko i Pol'shcha* (Shevchenko and Poland, 1964), and a two-volume dictionary of Shevchenko's language (1964). A two-volume bibliography of Shevchenko's life and works (1963) contains information only about works written in the territory of the former USSR in the years 1839–1959. It was augmented in 1968 by F. Sarana's bibliography of the jubilee literature of 1960–4, but that bibliography also excluded works written outside of the USSR. Some work in presenting a bibliography of Shevchenko translations and foreign-language criticism was done by H. Hresko, N. Andriianova, M. Zanichkovsky, and V. Kulyk in 1967–8 in Lviv. Their works had too small pressruns, however, and are not readily available.

An attempt at summarizing the work done on Shevchenko studies in Soviet Ukraine was the institute's compendium *Shevchenkoznavstvo: Pidsumky i problemy* (Shevchenko Studies: Summations and Problems, 1975) and the two-volume *Shevchenkivs'kyi slovnyk* (A Shevchenko Dictionary, 1978). Also notable for its breadth was the collective volume *Tvorchyi metod i poetyku T.H. Shevchenka* (The Creative Method and the Poetics of T. Shevchenko, 1980).

In the emigration after the Second World War Shevchenko studies have been continued in the publications of the Ukrainian Free Academy of Sciences (UVAN) in Canada and the United States. The UVAN in Canada republished the four-volume *Kobzar*, edited and annotated by Biletsky, and the UVAN in the United States prepared the English-language volume *Taras Ševčenko, 1814–1861: A Symposium* (1962), edited by G.Y. Shevelov and Miiakovsky. The NTSh established the Shevchenko Studies Commission, headed by Zaitsev, which published Zaitsev's biography of Shevchenko (1955) as well as Yu. Boiko's *Ševčenko: Sein Leben und sein Werk* (1965). Studies on Shevchenko were published in ZNTSh (vols 161 [1953], 167 [1958], 176 [1962], 179–80 [1965]), and 214 [1991]. The NTSh also prepared guides to Shevchenkiana in the libraries of Paris (1961) and Munich (1964). The Ukrainian Free University (UVU) published Boiko's *Shevchenko i Moskva* (Shevchenko and Moscow, 1952), *Tvorchist' Tarasa Shevchenka na tli zakhidn'o-evropeis'koï literatury* (The Creativity of Shevchenko in Relation to Western European Literature, 1956), and, in conjunction with the University of Munich, the collection *Taras Ševčenko, 1814–1861* (1964). The UVU published a four-language collection of Shevchenko's poems (Ukrainian, English, French, and German) in 1961. Hordynsky's book on Shevchenko as an artist was translated into German as *Taras Schewtschenko als Maler* (1964), and a new work on Shevchenko the artist by I. Keivan and Hordynsky, *Taras Shevchenko, obrazotvorchyi mystets'* (Taras Shevchenko the Painter Artist), appeared in 1964.

The M. Denysiuk publishing firm in Chicago republished the Warsaw edition of the works of Shevchenko in 1959–63 (14 volumes). Vol 13, edited by B. Kravtsiv, was devoted to Shevchenko scholarship and contained articles by Kulish, Franko, Shchurat, M. Hrushevsky, Yefremov, O. Novytsky, S. Smal-Stotsky, Navrotsky, and Kolessa. In 1961 V. Barka published his *Pravda Kobzaria* (The Truth of the Kobzar). L. Lutsiv published *T. Shevchenko, spivets' ukraïns'koï slavy i voli* (T. Shevchenko, the Singer of Ukrainian Glory and Freedom, 1964), and K. Uhryn and A. Zhukovsky edited a collection of articles and translations, *Taras Chevtchenko, 1814–1861: Sa vie et son oeuvre* (1964). G. Luckyj edited a compendium, *Shevchenko and the Critics, 1861–1980* (1980), which contained original essays and translations from Ukrainian.

In response to the paucity of such studies in Soviet Ukraine, some monographs appeared dealing with Shevchenko's religious beliefs, such as Biletsky's *Viruiuchyi Shevchenko* (Shevchenko the Believer, 1949), V. Yashchun's *Relihiine i moral'no-etychne oblychchia Tarasa Shevchenka* (The Religious and Moral-Ethical Aspect of T. Shevchenko, 1959), I. Vlasovsky's *Obraz Tarasa Shevchenka v svitli relihiinoï dumky* (A View of Shevchenko in the Light of Religious Thought, 1961), D. Buchynsky's *Khrystians'ko-filosofichna dumka Tarasa Shevchenka* (The Christian-Philosophic Thinking of T. Shevchenko, 1962), and Metropolitan Ilarion's (I. Ohiienko) *Relihiinist' Tarasa Shevchenka* (T. Shevchenko's Religiosity, 1964).

A new mythopoeic and psychoanalytic approach to the study of Shevchenko was proposed by G. Grabowicz in *The Poet as Mythmaker: A Study of Symbolic Meaning in Taras Ševčenko* (1982; Ukrainian trans 1991) and by L. Pliushch in *Ekzod Tarasa Shevchenka ...* (The Exodus of Taras Shevchenko, 1986).

BIBLIOGRAPHY
1. Bibliographic Guides:
Iashek, M. *T. Shevchenko: Materiialy do bibliohrafiï (rr. 1903–21)* (Kharkiv 1921)
Bilets'kyi, O. (ed). *Opys rukopysiv T.H. Shevchenka* (Kiev 1961)
Kyryliuk, Ie. (ed). *T.H. Shevchenko: Bibliohrafiia bibliohrafii 1840–1960* (Kiev 1961)
Velinská, E.; Zilynskyj, O. *Taras Ševčenko v české kultuře: Bibliografie* (Prague 1962)
Kyryliuk, Ie. (ed). *T.H. Shevchenko: Bibliohrafiia literatury pro zhyttia i tvorchist', 1839–1959*, 2 vols (Kiev 1963)
Bahrych, M. *T.H. Shevchenko: Bibliohrafichnyi pokazhchyk (1917–1963)* (Kiev 1964)
Kaspert, A. *Shevchenko i muzyka: Notohrafichni ta bibliohrafichni materiialy (1861–1961)* (Kiev 1964)
Hres'ko, M. *T. Shevchenko frantsuz'koiu movoiu (1847–1967): Bibliohrafichnyi pokazhchyk* (Lviv 1967)
Hres'ko, M.; Andrianova, N. *T.H. Shevchenko movamy italiis'koiu, espans'koiu, portuhal's'koiu, ta esperanto: Bibliohrafichnyi pokazhchyk* (Lviv 1968)
Hres'ko, M.; Zanichkovs'kyi, M.; Kulyk V. *T.H. Shevchenko v nimets'kykh perekladakh ta krytytsi (1843–1917): Bibliohrafichnyi pokazhchyk* (Lviv 1968)
Borodin, V. (ed). *T.H. Shevchenko: Bibliohrafichnyi pokazhchyk (1965–1988)* (Kiev 1989)
2. Dictionaries:
Nestor Litopysets' [N. Malecha]. *Slovnychok Shevchenkovoï movy* (Mykolaiv 1916)
Vashchenko, V., Petrova, P. *Shevchenkova leksyka: Slovopokazhchyk do poeziï T.H. Shevchenka* (Kiev 1951)
Mytropolyt Ilarion [I. Ohiienko]. *Hramatychno-stylistychnyi slovnyk Shevchenkovoï movy* (Winnipeg 1961)
Vashchenko, V. (ed). *Slovnyk movy Shevchenka*, 2 vols (Kiev 1964)
Marakhov, H. *T.H. Shevchenko v koli suchasnykiv: Slovnyk personalii* (Kiev 1976)
Kyryliuk, Ie. (ed). *Shevchenkivs'kyi slovnyk*, 2 vols (Kiev 1978)
Slovar iazyka russkikh proizvedenii T.G. Shevchenko v dvokh tt. (Kiev 1985–6)
3. Collections:
Zbirnyk pam'iati T. Shevchenka (Kiev 1915)
Pam'iati T.H. Shevchenka: Zbirnyk filolohichnoho fakul'tetu Kyïvs'koho universytetu (Kiev 1939)
Shevchenko ta ioho doba: Zbirnyk UVAN (Augsburg 1947)
T.H. Shevchenko v krytytsi (Kiev 1953)
Zbirnyk prats' naukovykh shevchenkivs'kykh konferentsii, vols 1–27 (Kiev 1954–86)
Pytannia Shevchenkoznavstva (Kiev 1958)
Stetsiuk, V.; Kravtsiv, B. (eds). *T. Shevchenko: Zbirnyk dopovidei Svitovoho kongresu ukraïns'koï vil'noï nauky dlia vshanuvannia storichchia smerty patrona NTSh*, vol 176 of ZNTSh (New York–Paris 1962)
T.H. Shevchenko v vospominaniiakh sovremennikov (Moscow 1962)
T.H. Shevchenko: Dokumenty i materialy, 1814–1963 (Kiev 1963)
Dzherela movnoï maisternosti T.H. Shevchenka (Kiev 1964)
Shevchenko i mirovaia kul'tura (Moscow 1964)
Sbornik Ševčenkovsý (Bratislava 1965)
T.H. Shevchenko: Dokumenty ta materiialy do biohrafiï (1814–1861) (Kiev 1975)
Der Revolutionäre Demokrat Taras Ševčenko, 1814–1861 (Berlin 1976)
T.H. Shevchenko v internatsional'nykh literaturnykh zv'iazkakh (Kiev 1981)
Spohady pro Tarasa Shevchenka (Kiev 1982)
4. Monographs:
Iefremov, S. *Taras Shevchenko, zhyttia ioho ta dila* (Kiev 1908, 1917)
Ievshan, M. *Taras Shevchenko* (Kiev 1911)
Jensen, A. *Taras Schewtschenko: Ein ukrainisches Dichterleben* (Vienna 1916)
Hrushevs'kyi, O. *Zhyttia i tvorchist' T.H. Shevchenka* (Kiev 1918)

Koriak, V. *Borot'ba za Shevchenka* (Kharkiv 1925)

Smal'-Stots'kyi, S. *Rytmika Shevchenkovoï poeziï* (Prague 1925)

Bilets'kyi, L. *Poetychna evoliutsiia naiholovnishykh obraziv ta idei Tarasa Shevchenka* (Prague 1926)

Navrots'kyi, B. *Haidamaky Tarasa Shevchenka: Dzherela, styl', kompozytsiia* (Kharkiv 1928)

Doroshkevych, O. *Etiudy z shevchenkoznavstva* (Kharkiv–Kiev 1930)

Navrots'kyi, B. *Shevchenkova tvorchist'* (Kharkiv–Kiev 1931)

Revuts'kyi, D. *Shevchenko i narodna pisnia* (Kiev 1939)

Shaginian, M. *Taras Shevchenko* (Moscow 1941, 1946, 1957, 1964)

Matthews, W.K. *Taras Shevchenko: The Man and the Symbol* (London 1951, Winnipeg 1961)

Pil'huk, I. *T.H. Shevchenko – Osnovopolozhnyk novoï ukraïns'koï literatury* (Kiev 1954)

Khinkulov, L. *Taras Grigor'evich Shevchenko, 1814–1861* (Moscow 1957, 1960, 1966)

Kyryliuk, Ye. *T.H. Shevchenko: Zhyttia i tvorchist'* (Kiev 1959, 1964, 1979)

Nenadkevych, Ye. *Z tvorchoï laboratoriï T.H. Shevchenka* (Kiev 1959)

Nevrlý, M. *T. Ševčenko – Revolučný básnik Ukrajiny* (Bratislava 1960)

Domanyts'kyi, V. *Taras Shevchenko: Syntetychno-natsiolohichni studiï ioho zhyttia i tvorchosty* (Chicago 1961)

Mol'nar, M. *T. Shevchenko u chekhiv ta slovakiv* (Prešov 1961)

Ryl's'kyi, M. *Poetyka Shevchenka* (Kiev 1961)

Solovei D. *Shevchenko i samostiinist' Ukraïny* (Munich 1962)

Pil'huk, I. *Tradytsiï T.H. Shevchenka v ukraïns'kii literaturi (dozhovtnevyi period)* (Kiev 1963)

Shubravs'kyi, V. *Shevchenko i literatury narodiv SRSR* (Kiev 1964)

Kodats'ka, L. *Odnoimenni tvory T.H Shevchenka* (Kiev 1968)

Palamarchuk, H. *Neskorenyi Prometei: Tvorchist' Shevchenka-khudozhnyka 1850–1857 rr.* (Kiev 1968)

Borodin, V. *T.H. Shevchenko i tsars'ka tsenzura* (Kiev 1969)

Zhur, P. *Tretia zustrich: Khronika ostann'oï mandrivky T. Shevchenka na Ukraïnu* (Kiev 1970)

Borodin, V. *Nad tekstamy T.H. Shevchenka* (Kiev 1971)

Zhur, P. *Shevchenkivs'kyi Peterburg* (Kiev 1972)

Chamata, N. *Rytmika T.H.Shevchenka* (Kiev 1974)

Zhur, P. *Lito pershe: Z khroniky zhyttia i tvorchosti T. Shevchenka* (Kiev 1979)

Smilians'ka, V. *Styl' poeziï Shevchenka* (Kiev 1981)

Grabowicz, G. *The Poet as Mythmaker: A Study of Symbolic Meaning in Taras Ševčenko* (Cambridge, Mass 1982)

Serhiienko, H. *T.H. Shevchenko i Kyrylo-Mefodiïvs'ke tovarystvo* (Kiev 1983)

Chub, D. *Shevchenko the Man: The Intimate Life of a Poet* (Melbourne 1985)

Tarakhan-Bereza, Z. *Shevchenko – poet i khudozhnyk* (Kiev 1985)

Borodin, V. *Tekstolohiia poetychnykh tvoriv T.H. Shevchenka* (Kiev 1986)

Pliushch, L. *Ekzod Tarasa Shevchenka* (Edmonton 1986)

Fedchenko, P. *Taras Hryhorovych Shevchenko* (Kiev 1989)

M. Antokhii, D.H. Struk, D. Zelska-Darewych

Shevchenko, Valentyna [Ševčenko], b 2 March 1935 in Kryvyi Rih, Dnipropetrovske oblast. Soviet government leader and Party functionary. A graduate of Kiev University (1960), she taught secondary school and advanced through the Party hierarchy to membership in the CC CPU (by 1976), the CPU Politburo (by 1985), and the CC CPSU (by 1986). In Ukraine's government she served as deputy minister of education (1969–75) and deputy chairman (1975–85) and then chairman (1985–90) of the Presidium of the Supreme Soviet. Identified with Brezhnev's regime in Ukraine, she was criticized in the late 1980s by the Ukrainian democratic opposition. She withdrew her candidacy in the 1990 elections to the Ukrainian Supreme Soviet and disappeared from public life.

Shevchenko, Volodymyr [Ševčenko], b 23 December 1929 in Balta (now in Odessa oblast), d 30 March 1987 in Kiev. Cinematographer and director. He graduated from the State Institute of Cinema Arts in Moscow (1967) and in 1971 became a director in the Ukrainian Studio of Chronicle-Documentary Films. Among his films are *Drevnyi horod L'va* (The Ancient City of the Lion [Lviv], 1970), *Bytva za Kyïv* (The Battle for Kiev, 1973), the trilogy *Radians'ka Ukraïna: Roky borot'by i peremoh* (Soviet Ukraine: The Years of Struggle and Victory, 1974–7), *Poïzd nadzvychainoho pryznachennia* (The Train with a Singular Assignment, 1980), all propaganda films, and a documentary about Chornobyl (1986).

Yona Shevchenko

Shevchenko, Yona [Ševčenko, Jona], b 26 April 1887 in Hnidyn, near Boryspil, Pereiaslav county, Poltava gubernia, d 1940. Actor and drama critic. After completing study at the Lysenko Music and Drama School he worked in Molodyi Teatr (1917–19) and Berezil (1922–4). He is the author of *Ukraïns'kyi suchasnyi teatr* (Ukrainian Contemporary Theater, 1929) and *Ukraïns'ki dramaturhy* (Ukrainian Playwrights, 1929). In 1936 he was arrested. He died in prison.

Shevchenko, Yurii [Ševčenko, Jurij], b 8 July 1926 in Kiev. Scientist in mechanics; corresponding member of the ANU (formerly AN URSR) since 1982. He graduated from Kiev University (1951) and taught at the Kiev Polytechnical Institute (1956–61). He has worked at the ANU Institute of Mechanics since 1961 (as a department head since 1972). He has developed methods of calculating loading stresses in machine components and a theory of thermoplasticity, including numerical methods of calculation that are widely used today in various types of machine design.

Shevchenko Company (Rota im. Tarasa Shevchenka). A unit of the 13th International Brigade that fought in the *Spanish Civil War. Organized in June 1937, it was composed of Ukrainians, Belarusians, Poles, and Spaniards and was staffed mostly by communists. The commander was a Belarusian communist, S. Tomashevych. The company was dissolved in the autumn of 1938.

Shevchenko First Theater of the Ukrainian Soviet Republic (Pershyi teatr Ukrainskoi Radianskoi Respubliky im. T. Shevchenka). A theater established in March

1919 in Kiev on the basis of the forced unification of the *State Drama Theater and *Molodyi Teatr (and later joined by the First Youth Theater of the Kiev Soviet of Workers' Deputies). Among its actors were H. Borysohlibska, V. Vasylko, L. Hakkebush, P. Samiilenko, M. Tereshchenko, and H. Yura. The theater's repertoire consisted mostly of Soviet and classical dramas. Its artistic directorship consisted of an artificial union (O. Zaharov from the school of realistic-psychological theater and the experimentalist stage director L. Kurbas) and did not have positive results. The only exception was Kurbas's adaptation of T. Shevchenko's *The Haidamakas* in 1920. In early 1920 Yura departed with his conservative Molodyi Teatr group to form the touring Franko New Drama Theater (see *Kiev Ukrainian Drama Theater), and Tereshchenko's radical Molodyi Teatr group formed Tsentrostudiia (later the *Mykhailychenko Theater). In the summer of 1920 Kurbas left the theater to form *Kyidramte, and in 1921 Zaharov also left. Financial difficulties and demands for service in many Ukrainian cities resulted in the regrouping of the remaining ensemble as a touring theater until 1927, when it became the *Dnipropetrovske Ukrainian Music and Drama Theater.

V. Revutsky

Shevchenko Gallery (Halereia kartyn T.H. Shevchenka). A collection of T. Shevchenko's paintings established in Kharkiv in 1933 on the basis of the Literary Museum at the Taras Shevchenko Scientific Research Institute. Its original holdings consisted of 137 canvases, most of them donated by the Russian Museum and Hermitage in Leningrad and the Tretiakov Gallery, the Pushkin Museum, and the Historical Museum in Moscow. In 1933 the Chernihiv and Kiev historical museums transferred most of the literary and artistic works by Shevchenko in their collections to the gallery, and on the 125th anniversary of Shevchenko's birthday almost all of his artistic works were displayed there. During the Second World War the collection was evacuated. In 1944 it was returned intact, and in 1948 it was transferred to the *Kiev Shevchenko Museum.

Shevchenko Museum. See Kiev Shevchenko Museum.

Shevchenko Peak [Ševčenka pik]. A mountain peak (elevation, 4,200 m) in the Great Caucasus Range. The peak is covered with snow and ice. It was first scaled in 1938 by an expedition of Ukrainian mountaineers, who named it in honor of T. *Shevchenko.

Shevchenko prizes. See Prizes and awards.

Shevchenko Scientific Society (Naukove tovarystvo im. Shevchenka, or NTSh). The oldest, and for a long time the only, prominent Ukrainian scholarly society. It was founded on 11 December 1873 in Austrian-ruled Lviv as the Shevchenko Society (Tovarytsvo im. Shevchenka) with the aim of fostering the development of Ukrainian literature. The society's initiators were leading Ukrainian community and cultural figures on both sides of the Austrian-Russian border, headed by O. *Konysky. Its benefactors included Ye. *Myloradovych, D. *Pylchykov, M. *Zhuchenko, and Rev S. *Kachala. The Shevchenko Society's first act was the purchase of a press and the establishment of its own publishing house in 1874. By 1891 it had

The building of the Shevchenko Scientific Society in Lviv

published 20 books, including O. Ohonovsky's pioneering three-volume history of Ukrainian literature and the periodicals *Pravda* (1878–9) and *Zoria* (from 1885). The society's first presidents were K. *Sushkevych (1874–85), S. *Hromnytsky (1885–6, 1887–90), D. *Hladylovych (1886–7, 1890–2), and Yu. *Tselevych (1892).

1893–1914. Because the publication of Ukrainian literature and scholarship in Russian-ruled Ukraine was severely restricted after the imposition of the 1876 *Ems Ukase and subsequent tsarist edicts, in 1893 the Shevchenko Society was reorganized on the initiative of Konysky and V. *Antonovych 'to foster and develop science and art in the Ukrainian-Ruthenian language [and] to preserve and collect ... the monuments of antiquity [and] the scientific objects of Ukraine-Rus'.' Renamed the Shevchenko Scientific Society and modeled on Western European scientific institutions, the NTSh pursued the aim of becoming 'the progenitor of a future Ukrainian-Ruthenian academy of sciences.' Under the leadership of O. *Barvinsky (1893–7) a library (70,000 cataloged volumes and 500 manuscripts in 1914 – the fullest and most systematic collection of Ucrainica in the world), museum (15,047 artifacts in 1920), and bookstore were established in Lviv. The NTSh's 137 members were divided among three sections – Philological (directed by O. Ohonovsky), Historical-Philosophical (A. Vakhnianyn), and Mathematical–Natural Sciences–Medical (I. Verkhratsky).

The NTSh acquired a pan-Ukrainian importance and scholarly prestige under the presidency (1897–1913) of M. *Hrushevsky, who was also director of the Historical-Philosophical Section from 1894. Assisted by V. *Hnatiuk as NTSh secretary (1898–1926) and head of the Ethnographic Commission, and I. Franko as director (1898–1908) of the Philological Section, Hrushevsky turned the NTSh into a de facto academy of sciences to which virtually all Ukrainian scholars belonged. On his suggestion, in 1899 the NTSh was divided into 32 prominent full members, who represented the sections, and many regular members, who could not vote on scholarly matters at section meetings. As a result Lviv acquired the status of a Ukrainian cultural and scholarly capital. Seminars were created within the various NTSh commissions and other bodies, and younger scholars were gainfully employed, the NTSh thereby being given a quasi-university function. Under Hrushevsky and Franko the Historical-Philosophical and Philological sections grouped together all the major Ukrainian historians and philologists. Contacts with foreign learned institutions were established by the participation of NTSh members in international congresses and conferences, and by an exchange of publications with nearly 250 foreign institutions.

The primary NTSh organ, *Zapysky NTSh (est 1892), became a quarterly (1895) and then a bimonthly (1896) under Hrushevsky's editorship (1895–1913). A second periodical, the quarterly Khronika NTSh, was founded in 1900 to provide information about NTSh activities. Pioneering and fundamental research was also published in the NTSh Legal Commission's *Chasopys' pravnycha (from 1893); the Archeographic Commission's *Zherela do istoriï Ukraïny-Rusy (from 1895) and *Pam'iatky ukraïns'ko-rus'koï movy i literatury (from 1896); the Ethnographic Commission's *Etnohrafichnyi zbirnyk (from 1895) and *Materiialy do ukraïns'koï etnolohiï (from 1899); the Mathematical–Natural Science–Medical Section's series *Zbirnyk Matematychno-pryrodopysno-likarskoi sektsii NTSh (from 1897); the Historical-Philosophical Section's series *Rus'-ka istorychna biblioteka (from 1894) and *Zbirnyk Istorychno-filosofichnoi sektsii NTSh (from 1898), and an annual monograph series, Ukraïns'ko-rus'kyi arkhiv (from 1905); the Philological Section's series *Zbirnyk Filolohichnoi sektsi NTSh (from 1898); and the Bibliographic Commission's *Materiialy do ukraïns'koï bibliohrafiï (from 1909). In addition the NTSh published the *Ukrainska biblioteka series of annotated Ukrainian literary classics (24 vols, 1901–4) and the prominent cultural-political monthly *Literaturno-naukovyi vistnyk (1898–1906).

Changes occurred in the NTSh's role and scope after tsarist restrictions on Ukrainian writing and scholarship were lifted in the wake of the Revolution of 1905. The *Ukrainian Scientific Society in Kiev (est 1907), for example, took over publication of Literaturno-naukovyi vistnyk. Nonetheless, the NTSh retained its importance in the Ukrainian scholarly world, even after Hrushevsky resigned as president in 1913 and his functions were assumed by the vice-president, S. *Tomashivsky (1913–18).

1915–44. The First World War interrupted all NTSh activities, including plans to transform the NTSh into an academy of sciences in 1916. During the occupation of Galicia in 1914–15, the NTSh was outlawed, and its buildings and presses were confiscated. Many of its members died at the front or were civilian casualties, and many of its valuable library, archival, and museum holdings and scholarly acquisitions, as well as its student residence, were destroyed.

The NTSh was revived during the interwar Polish occupation of Western Ukraine, but it functioned on a lesser scale. Many of its members became political émigrés in the West, some emigrated to Soviet Ukraine, and the influx of new scholarly cadres declined (in 1923 the NTSh had 106 full members, 30 of them foreign scholars). Polish interference and taxation, the slashing of government subsidies, the withdrawal of rights to print schoolbooks, and the confiscation of most Ukrainian-American and Soviet Ukrainian publications addressed to its library also impinged on the NTSh's activities, income, and ability to publish. With the establishment of the All-Ukrainian *Academy of Sciences in Kiev and Ukrainian scholarly institutions in Poland and Bohemia in the 1920s, the NTSh was no longer the primary Ukrainian scholarly center.

The NTSh continued its activities under the presidency of V. *Shchurat (1919–25), K. *Studynsky (1925–31), V. *Levytsky (1931–5), and I. *Rakovsky (1935–49). The NTSh Museum's collections were divided up to form the new NTSh museums of Culture and History (1920, with departments of archeology, ethnography, art, numismatics, and historical monuments [75,000 artifacts in 1927]), Natural Science (1920), and the Ukrainian Military (1937). The NTSh Library was rebuilt and expanded (over 300,000 vols in 1939) under the directors I. Krevetsky and V. Doroshenko. In 1921 the Institute of Normal and Pathological Psychology (directed by S. Balei) and the Bacteriological-Chemical Institute (directed by M. Muzyka) were created as part of the NTSh. In the early 1920s the NTSh organized the *Lviv (Underground) Ukrainian University and *Lviv (Underground) Ukrainian Higher Polytechnical School. It established relations with the VUAN in Kiev and co-operated with it in many matters, particularly *orthography. An outstanding example of such collaboration was a Ukrainian mathematical dictionary (1926), which was prepared jointly by the academy's Institute of the Ukrainian Scientific Language and the NTSh. The NTSh's three scholarly sections and Legal, Statistical, Classic Philology, Linguistic, Archeological, Ethnographic, Art History, Physiographic, Bibliographic, and Publishing commissions remained active. The Shevchenko Studies Commission, with its own Serial, Terminological, Scientific-Technical, and Scientific-Agronomical commissions, and two other journals, *Stara Ukraïna (1924–5) and *S'ohochasne i mynule (1939), were established. In the 1930s the NTSh sponsored the preparation of an atlas of Ukraine (ed by V. *Kubijovyč) and copublished the serials *Ukraïns'ka knyha, *Ukraïns'ka muzyka, and *Likars'kyi vistnyk. With the Stalinist suppression of Soviet Ukrainian culture in the 1930s, the NTSh partly regained its earlier status in the Ukrainian scholarly world. Its international prestige remained high, as attested by the acceptance of membership in the NTSh by M. Planck (in 1923), D. Hilbert (in 1924), and A. Einstein (in 1929).

From its founding in 1873 until 1939 the NTSh issued 591 serial volumes (including 155 vols of Zapysky NTSh, 121 of them in 1891–1914), 352 individual scholarly publications, textbooks, and maps, 103 books of literary journalism, 95 belletristic works, and 31 informational publications.

During the first Soviet occupation of Galicia (1939–41) the NTSh was shut down. In 1940 it was forced by the Soviet authorities to dissolve, and its properties were expropriated by the state. Many of its members disappeared or were repressed, and others fled to German-occupied Poland. During the German occupation of Galicia (1941–4) the Nazi regime did not allow the NTSh to be publicly active. Before the Soviet reoccupation of Lviv in 1944, most remaining NTSh members fled to the West.

After 1947. On the initiative of Kubijovyč and Rakovsky, the NTSh was revived in Munich in June 1947 by members who had sought refuge in postwar Germany. Rakovsky was re-elected president (1947–9) and was succeeded by Z. *Kuzelia (1949–52); Kubijovyč was elected general secretary. New full members, particularly postwar émigré scholars from Soviet Ukraine, were elected, and the sections and several commissions resumed their work. New Nationality Research, Encyclopedia, Bibliological, and Ukrainian Language institutes were estab-

Some of the members of the first émigré executive of the Shevchenko Scientific Society (Mittenwald, 1947). Sitting, from left: Yevhen Khraplyvy, Volodymyr Kubijovyč, Zenon Kuzelia, Leonyd Biletsky; standing: Yaroslav Padokh, Ivan Rozhin, Bohdan Lonchyna, Ivan Mirchuk, Rev Vasyl Laba, Yuliian Pavlykovsky

lished, and the journal *S'ohochasne i mynule* (1948–9) was revived. After the mass emigration of Ukrainian refugees from Germany and Austria to countries of the New World in 1947–9, chapters of the NTSh were established in the United States (1947), Canada (1949), and Australia (1950). In 1951 the NTSh executive center, library, and archives were transferred from Munich to *Sarcelles, near Paris. In 1952 the American chapter purchased its own building in New York City and established a library and archives there.

In 1953 the NTSh had 126 full members and 226 regular members; in 1964 it had 139 full members and 485 regular members, over half of them in the United States. In 1955 the European, American, Canadian, and Australian chapters became autonomous NTSh societies, headed by Kubijovyč, V. Yaniv, and A. Zhukovsky in Sarcelles, by M. Chubaty, R. Smal-Stotsky, M. Stakhiv, O. Andrushkiv, Ya. Padokh, and L. Rudnytzky in New York City, by Ye. Vertyporokh and B. Stebelsky in Toronto, and by Ye. Pelensky, P. Shulezhko, I. Rybchyn, T. Liakhovych, I. Vashchyshyn, and R. Mykytovych in Melbourne. The NTSh General Council was established in 1978. Consisting of representatives from the four societies and the three sections, it was successively headed by Smal-Stotsky, Vertyporokh, Andrushkiv, V. Mackiw, and Padokh, with Rudnytzky as scientific secretary, W. Lencyk as general secretary, and I. Sierant as secretary-treasurer.

The four NTSh societies co-operated in the work of the NTSh sections and 16 commissions. The Historical-Philosophical Section (70 members in 1985) was based in Sarcelles and New York City and directed by I. Mirchuk, Kubijovyč, and V. Markus; the Philological Section (59 members) was based in New York City and directed by Z. Kuzelia, K. Kysilevsky, and V. Lev; and the Medical–

Natural Sciences–Mathematical Section (54 members) was based in New York City and directed by M. Zaitsev, W. Petryshyn (mathematics and physics), and R. Osinchuk (chemistry, biology, and medicine).

The NTSh has continued publishing *Zapysky NTSh* (vols 156–220, 1948–91); many of the volumes have doubled as collections of the various sections and as festschriften, and others have been monographs. It has also published 13 volumes (1949–89) of *encyclopedias of Ukraine, which have served as the basis of *Ukraine: A Concise Encyclopaedia* and *Encyclopedia of Ukraine*; 57 monographs in its Biblioteka ukrainoznavstva series (since 1951); and over 40 valuable collections of historical and memoiristic articles about regions and vicinities of Galicia in its Ukrainskyi arkhiv series (since 1960). Beginning in 1949 it renewed the publication of its chronicle, *Khronika NTSh*, of which nos 75–81 have been issued. In addition the American NTSh has published 14 volumes of *Proceedings* (since 1951), over 40 issues of scholarly *Papers* (since 1958), several literary works, and a few dozen other books and brochures. It has also copublished several books with the Ukrainian Academy of Arts and Sciences in the US and the periodicals *Ukraïns'ka knyha* (since 1971) and *Nationalities Papers* (since 1973). The Canadian NTSh has published over 20 volumes of conference materials, collections of articles, and monographs. Of special interest are two volumes of *Zakhidn'okanads'kyi zbirnyk* (1973, 1975), which describe the history of Ukrainian settlement, schools, and churches in western Canada, the works of I. Kiriak and O. Luhovy, and Ukrainian place-names in Canada.

In Lviv the Shevchenko Scientific Society was reactivated on 21 October 1989. It adopted the original NTSh statutes (from 4 July 1874, modified in 1904, 1909, and 1949) as well as the statutes of the NTSh General Council (from 27 October 1978). It is headed by O. *Romaniv (also head of the Natural Sciences Section), with Yu. Babei as vice-president in charge of the scientific sections, Ya. Isaievych as vice-president in charge of the humanities sections, and O. Kupchynsky as scientific secretary; other members of the presidium (and heads of sections) are Ya. Burak (Physical-Mathematical), M. Ilnytsky (Philological), R. Kyrchiv (Ethnography and Folkloristics), V. Ovsiichuk (Art Studies), and Yu. Slyvka (Historical-Philo-sophical). In addition to the six sections the Lviv NTSh established ecological (M. Holubets), medical (Ya. Hanitkevych), Slavic studies (V. Chornii), Oriental studies (Ya. Dashkevych), bibliographic and bibliological (M. Lizanets), publishing and printing (R. Mashtalir), and economic (S. Zlupko) commissions. It also took over the publishing of *Zapysky NTSh* (from vol 221), began issuing the proceedings of the medical section, *Likars'kyi zbirnyk*, and in 1991 started an international edition of the NTSh *Visnyk*.

BIBLIOGRAPHY
Khronika Naukovoho tovarystva im. Shevchenka, nos 1–80 (1900–66)
Hnatiuk, V. *Naukove tovarystvo imeny Shevchenka u L'vovi (Istorychnyi narys pershoho 50-richchia–1873–1923)* (Lviv 1923; 2nd edn, Munich–Paris 1984)
– 'Naukove tovarystvo imeny Shevchenka u L'vovi,' *LNV*, nos 1–9 (1925)
Istoriia Naukovo tovarystva im. Shevchenka z nahody 75-richchia ioho zasnuvannia, 1873–1948 (New York–Munich 1949)
Doroshenko, V. *Ohnyshche ukraïns'koï nauky – Naukove tovarystvo im. Shevchenka* (New York–Philadelphia 1951)

- *Biblioteka Naukovoho tovarystva im. Shevchenka u L'vovi* (New York 1961)
Naukove tovarystvo im. Shevchenka v ZDA (New York 1963)
Vynar, L. *Mykhailo Hrushevs'kyi i Naukove tovarystvo im. Tarasa Shevchenka 1892–1930* (Munich 1970)
Kubiiovych, V. 'Naukove tovarystvo im. Shevchenka u 1939–1952 rr.,' *UI*, 10, nos 1–2 (1973)
Lew, W. *A Century of Dedicated Work for Scholarship and Nation: A Brief History of the Shevchenko Scientific Society* (New York 1973)
Vertyporokh, L. '25-richchia Kanads'koho NTSh,' in *Iuvileinyi zbirnyk naukovykh prats' z nahody 100-richchia NTSh i 25-richchia NTSh u Kanadi* (Toronto 1977)
Publications of the Shevchenko Scientific Society, 1945–1980 (New York 1980; Munich 1983; Lviv 1991)
Boiko, M. *Index to the Memoirs of the Shevchenko Scientific Society, 1892–1982* (Bloomington, Ind 1984)
Romaniv, O. *Rozvytok pryrodnycho-tekhnichnykh nauk na zakhidnii Ukraïni v NTSh* (Lviv 1989)

B. Kravtsiv, V. Kubijovyč

Shevchenko Society in Saint Petersburg (Tovarystvo im. T.H. Shevchenka v Peterburzi). A charitable organization founded in St Petersburg in 1898 to aid needy students from Ukraine enrolled in the city's higher schools. The society covered school fees, the cost of books and equipment, and the medical costs of sick students. It helped students find jobs and living accommodation. To raise funds it collected membership dues and donations and organized concerts, public lectures, and bazaars. By 1900 its membership was over 200, and by 1907, almost 550. Of the 280 members in 1902, only half lived in St Petersburg; the others belonged to branches of the society in Kiev, Kharkiv, Odessa, Vilnius, Sukhumi, Baku, Irkutsk, Ashkhabad, Katerynodar, and Tbilisi. In 1905 a proposal to merge with the Philanthropic Society for Publishing Generally Useful and Inexpensive Books was rejected by the general meeting, but the two societies worked closely together. They collaborated in publishing T. Shevchenko's *Kobzar* under V. Domanytsky's editorship (1907; 2nd edn 1908). The first president of the society was A. *Markovych, and the first board of directors included prominent cultural figures, such as D. Mordovets, V. Lesevych, I. Repin, and V. Korolenko. With the outbreak of the First World War the number of students in St Petersburg declined, and membership fell to 67. The society decided to discontinue its activities.

Shevchenko Ukrainian Drama Theater. See Shevchenko First Theater of the Ukrainian Soviet Republic.

Shevchenkove [Ševčenkove]. IV-18. A town smt (1986 pop 6,500) and raion center in Kharkiv oblast. It was established at the beginning of the 20th century as a railway settlement called Bulatselivka on the Kupianka–Kharkiv–Belgorod line. In 1922 it was renamed, and in 1935 it became a raion center. Shevchenkove has a food and a building-materials industry.

Shevchenkove [Ševčenkove]. IV-12. A village (1972 pop 3,800) in Zvenyhorodka raion, Cherkasy oblast. Until 1929 its name was Kyrylivka. Its significance lies in the fact that T. *Shevchenko grew up there (1816–28). He also visited the village in 1843, 1845, and 1859. Today an obelisk marks the site of his home. The graves of his parents and the 18th-century cottage in which Shevchenko attended his first school lessons have been preserved. His parents' cottage has been converted into a literary memorial museum.

Shevchuk, Anatolii [Ševčuk, Anatolij] (pseud: Ivan Yavtushenko), b 6 February 1937 in Zhytomyr. Writer and political prisoner; brother of Valerii *Shevchuk. A typesetter by profession, he published 10 stories and a few poems in Soviet Ukrainian periodicals (1962–4). He was arrested by the KGB in Zhytomyr in May 1966 and sentenced at a closed trial in September to five years' imprisonment in a Mordovian strict-regime labor camp. A collection of prose he had prepared for publication was confiscated and never published. Three of his stories and excerpts of letters to his brother were first published in V. Chornovil's *Lykho z rozumu* (Woe from Wit, Paris 1967). In the late 1980s he began publishing stories again in periodicals.

Shevchuk, Hryhorii [Ševčuk, Hryhorij], b 8 February 1916 in Krasnohirka, Skvyra county, Kiev gubernia. Historian. A graduate of the Kiev Pedagogical Institute (1938), he worked at the AN URSR (now ANU) Institute of History (1946–67) and the Kiev Institute of Culture (from 1968). He contributed to the collective works *Istoriia Ukraïns'koï RSR* (History of the Ukrainian SSR, 2 vols, 1967) and *Rozvytok ukraïns'koï kul'tury za roky Radians'koï vlady* (The Development of Ukrainian Culture during the Years of Soviet Rule, 1967) and wrote *Borot'ba trudiashchykh Radians'koï Ukraïny proty kontrrevoliutsiï na Pivdni v 1920 r.* (The Struggle of the Workers of Soviet Ukraine against the Counterrevolution in the South in 1920, 1956) and *Kul'turne budivnytstvo na Ukraïni u 1921–1925 rokakh* (Cultural Construction in Ukraine in 1921–5, 1963).

Valerii Shevchuk

Shevchuk, Valerii [Ševčuk, Valerij], b 20 August 1939 in Zhytomyr. Writer. He is a master of psychological prose on contemporary themes. His collections include *Sered tyzhnia* (Midweek, 1967), *Naberezhna, 12* (12 Naberezhna Street, 1968), *Seredokhrestia* (The Intersection, 1968), *Vechir sviatoï oseny* (An Evening of the Sacred Autumn, 1969), *Kryk pivnia na svitanku* (Cock's Crow at Dawn, 1979), *Dolyna dzherel* (The Valley of Springs, 1981), *Tepla osin'* (The Warm Autumn, 1981), and *Dzygar odvichnyi* (The Eternal Clock, 1987). He is adept at perceiving the extraordinary in the ordinary and at exalting simple humanity to greatness. His masterful construction of themes serves as a backdrop for wide-ranging portraits of life, from concise realistic descriptions to those bordering on the fantastic (particularly in 'Zhyttia ta pryhody Vitaliia Voloshyns'koho' [The Life and Adventures of Vitalii Voloshynsky]). His terse expression, the sophisticated psychological motivation of his characters (departures from the officially sanctioned divisions between 'positive' and 'negative' ones), and his bold unwillingness to adhere to the dogmas of *socialist realism and official ideology set him apart from other writers of Soviet prose but also attracted the hostility of the Soviet literary hierarchy. His works were not fully recognized for their merit until the late 1980s. In such works as his novelette-preamble *Dim na hori* (The House on the Hill, 1983) Shevchuk has combined the native folkloric tradition of the fantastic, as in N. Gogol, with historical themes and a philosophical quest for the meaning of life and self, in multilevel prose which some critics call *khymerna proza* (chimerical prose – somewhat reminiscent of the magic realism of Latin American prose).

Shevchuk has also drawn on the medieval Kievan period for his novels *Na poli smyrennomu* (On the Peaceful Field, 1982) and *Petro uteklyi* (Peter the Fugitive, 1985), the novelistic essay *Myslenne derevo* (The Thinking Tree, 1986), and the trilogy tracing the secularization of Ukraine through the 17th, 18th, and 19th centuries, *Try lystky za viknom* (Three Leaves outside the Window, 1986). He has also translated *Litopys Samiila Velychka* (The Chronicle of Samiilo Velychko, 1986–7) and love lyrics of the 16th to 19th centuries (in *Pisni Kupidona* [Cupid's Songs] 1984) into contemporary Ukrainian.

I. Koshelivets, D.H. Struk

Shevchuk, Vasyl [Ševčuk, Vasyl'], b 30 April 1932 in Barashi, Yemilchyne raion, Zhytomyr oblast. Writer of historical fiction. He graduated from Kiev University (1955) and worked as an editor for *Pioneriia, Literaturna Ukraïna,* the Dnipro publishing house, and the Kiev Artistic Film Studio. From 1953 to 1959 he published four children's poetry books and a collection of lyrical poetry (1958). He then switched to prose and wrote the novelettes *Horobynoï nochi* (A Stormy Summer Night, 1960), *Zelenyi shum* (The Green Murmur, 1963), *Vitryla* (Sails, 1964, about T. Shevchenko), and *Trubliat' lebedi nad Slavutychem* (The Swans Are Trumpeting above the Slavutych, 1967); a story collection for children (1965); a novel about H. Skovoroda, *Hryhorii Skovoroda* (1969; rev edn: *Predtecha* [The Precursor, 1972]); the Cossack novel *Pobratymy ...* (1972; English trans: *Bloodbrothers,* 1980); the novelle collection *Den' – iak zhyttia* (A Day Is like a Lifetime, 1979); *Veselych* (1980), a novel about the medieval author of *Slovo o polku Ihorevi;* the contemporary novelette 'Tepla osin'' (A Warm Autumn, 1981); a reinterpretation of the *Slovo ...* titled *Slovo pro Ihoriv pokhid* (1982); the novel *Zlam* (The Break, 1982); two critically acclaimed novels about T. Shevchenko, *Syn voli* (The Son of Liberty, 1984) and *Ternovyi svit* (The Thorny World, 1986); and the historical fantasy novel *Feniks* (The Phoenix, 1988).

Shevchukevych, Opanas [Ševčukevyč], b 17 March 1902 in Vyzhenka, Chernivtsi county, Bukovyna, d ? Sculptor; physician by profession. A graduate of the medical faculty of Freiburg University (1929), he studied sculpture under K. Kollwitz at the Berlin Academy of Arts. The first exhibitions of his works in Germany and Chernivtsi in the late 1920s were favorably received by the critics. He did portraits of K. Kollwitz (1928), M. Ivasiuk (1957–8), O. Kobylianska (1962–3), T. Shevchenko (1963), and M. Drahomanov (1970) and compositions such as *Beggar* (1925) and *Death over the Dancer.*

Shevchyky. A folk dance performed by one or two people to instrumental music in 2/3 time. It mimics the movements of a shoemaker (*shvets*) through pantomime.

Shevel, Heorhii [Ševel', Heorhij], b 9 May 1919 in Kharkiv, d 16 November 1988 in Kiev. Party and Soviet government leader. A graduate of Kharkiv University (1941), he served as a secretary and first secretary of the Lviv Oblast Komsomol Committee (1944–6), a secretary (1946–50) and first secretary (1950–4) of the Ukrainian Komsomol CC, a CC CPU member (1952–80), second secretary of the CPU Kiev City Committee and agitation and propaganda secretary of the CPU Kiev Oblast Committee (1954–61), and CC CPU chief of agitation and propaganda (1961–70). As the Ukrainian minister of foreign affairs (1970–80) he headed the Ukrainian delegation at the United Nations General Assembly.

Shevelev, Arnold [Ševelev, Arnol'd], b 28 November 1928 in Balakliia (now in Kharkiv oblast). Soviet historian and CPSU functionary; corresponding member of the ANU (formerly AN URSR) since 1972. He graduated from Kiev University (1948) and taught in institutions of higher education from 1954 (from 1968 as a professor). He served as secretary (1969–72) and assistant director (from 1972) of the Kiev branch of the CPU. As director of the ANU *Institute of History (1973–8) he was instrumental in curtailing its autonomous research and eliminating most of its pre-1917 publications. He wrote many works on the history of the CPSU and the CPU and a collection of essays on the development of research in Soviet and foreign history in the Ukrainian SSR (1975). He was editor in chief of *Istoriia Ukraïns'koï RSR* (History of the Ukrainian SSR, 8 vols in 10 books, 1977–9).

Sheveliv, Borys [Ševeliv], b 2 April 1893 in Chernihiv, d ? Literary scholar. In the 1920s and early 1930s he was a member of the VUAN Chernihiv Scientific Society and an associate of the VUAN Commission for the Study of Left-Bank Ukraine. He published articles on L. Hlibov, P. Kulish, S. Nis, A. Svydnytsky, O. Lazarevsky, and the Chernihiv Hromada in VUAN serials (*Za sto lit, Ukraïna*) and compendiums, and edited an edition of Hlibov's works (1927). He stopped publishing during the Stalinist terror, and his fate is unknown.

Shevelov, George Yurii [Ševel'ov, Jurij] (pseuds: Yurii Sherekh, Hryhorii Shevchuk, Yur. Sher., Yu. Sh., Hr. Sh.,

George Shevelov

et al), b 17 December 1908 in Łomża, Poland. Slavic linguist, philologist, essayist, literary historian, and critic; full member of the Shevchenko Scientific Society since 1949 and of the Ukrainian Academy of Arts and Sciences since 1945. After studying under L. Bulakhovsky at Kharkiv University (candidate 1939) he lectured there in Slavic linguistics (1939–43). Having emigrated to Germany, he taught at the Ukrainian Free University in Munich (1946–9) and obtained a doctorate there (1949). He was also vice-president of the *MUR literary association (1945–9). After settling in the United States he served as lecturer in Russian and Ukrainian at Harvard University (1952–4), associate professor (1954–8) and professor of Slavic philology at Columbia University (1958–77), and president of the *Ukrainian Academy of Arts and Sciences (1959–61, 1981–6). He was a founding member of the *Slovo Association of Ukrainian Writers in Exile.

Shevelov is the author of some 500 articles, reviews, and books on Slavic philology and linguistics and the history of literature. In Slavic linguistics he has contributed to such areas as phonology, morphology, syntax, lexicology, etymology, literary languages, and onomastics. He has devoted special attention to Old Church Slavonic, Belarusian, Polish, Russian, Slovak, Serbo-Croation, Macedonian, and above all Ukrainian. In his most important work, *A Historical Phonology of the Ukrainian Language* (1979), Shevelov demonstrated the historical continuity of the language. His other important publications in linguistics are *Do henezy nazyvnoho rechennia* (On the Genesis of the Nominal Sentence, 1947), *Halychyna v formuvanni novoï ukraïns'koï literaturnoï movy* (Galicia in the Formation of the Modern Ukrainian Literary Language, 1949, 1975), *Narys suchasnoï ukraïns'koï literaturnoï movy* (An Outline of the Contemporary Ukrainian Literary Language, 1951), *The Syntax of Modern Literary Ukrainian: The Simple Sentence* (1963; Ukrainian version 1951), *A Prehistory of Slavic: The Historical Phonology of Common Slavic* (1964, 1965), *Die ukrainische Schriftsprache, 1798–1965* (1966), *Teasers and Appeasers: Essays and Studies on Themes of Slavic Philology* (1971), and *The Ukrainian Language in the First Half of the Twentieth Century, 1900–1941: Its State and Status* (1989; Ukrainian version 1987).

His numerous articles in the field of literature, literary criticism, and theater were collected in *Ne dlia ditei* (Not for Children, 1964), *Druha cherha: literatura, teatr, ideolohiï* (The Second Round: Literature, Theater, Ideologies, 1978), and *Tretia storozha* (The Third Watch, 1991). He was one of the organizers of émigré literary life in Germany after the Second World War. Shevelov was editor or coeditor of many scholarly and literary journals, serials, books, and other publications, including *Arka* (1947–8), *The Annals of the Ukrainian Academy of Arts and Sciences in the US* (1960–1), *Historical Phonology of the Slavic Languages* (5 vols, 1973–83), and *Suchasnist'* (1978–87). He was also linguistics subject editor for *Entsyklopediia ukraïnoznavstva* (Encyclopedia of Ukraine, 1949–52, 1955–89), *Ukraine: A Concise Encyclopaedia* (vol 1, 1963), and *Encyclopedia of Ukraine* (vols 1–2, 1984, 1988), to which he contributed numerous articles.

A bibliography of his works by J. Hursky appeared in *Symbolae in honorem Georgii Y. Shevelov* (1971) and *Studies in Ukrainian Linguistics in Honor of George Y. Shevelov* (1985).

J. Hursky

Shiller, Nikolai [Šiller, Nikolaj], b 13 March 1848 in Moscow, d 23 November 1910 in St Petersburg. Physicist. A graduate of Moscow University (1868), he did postgraduate work at Berlin University (1871–4). In 1876 he was appointed a professor at Kiev University, and there in 1884 he assumed the first chair of theoretical physics in Ukraine. His major contributions were in the fields of thermodynamics and electromagnetism. He showed that the differential equations describing the second law of thermodynamics contain an integrating factor that is a universal function of temperature, and developed what became known as the Shiller (1900)–Carathéodory (1909) formulation of the second law of thermodynamics. His work on dielectric susceptibility and displacement currents was highly regarded by J. Maxwell. Shiller was the founder of the *Kiev Physics and Mathematics Society (1890) and served as its president until 1904. In 1903 he became the rector of the Kharkiv Applied Technology Institute.

Shilov, Evgenii [Šilov, Jevgenij], b 10 August 1893 in Serpukhov, Moscow gubernia, d 22 July 1970 in Kiev. Organic chemist; AN URSR (now ANU) full member from 1951. A graduate of Moscow University (1917), he taught at the Ivanovo-Voznesensk Polytechnical (1919–30) and Chemical-Technical institutes. From 1947 he directed the Laboratory of Organic Reaction Mechanisms at the ANU Institute of Organic Chemistry. Shilov's research was devoted to organic reaction mechanisms and analytical chemistry. He introduced (jointly with Ya. Syrkin) the concept of cyclic four- and six-center transition states in bimolecular reactions, and contributed to the theory and practice of bleaching natural fibers by processes involving chlorine or peroxides.

Shimanovsky, Yulii [Šimanovskij, Julij], b 8 February 1829 in Riga, d 25 April 1868 in Kiev. Russian surgeon. A graduate of Tartu University (1856), he taught surgery at Helsinki University. In 1861 he was appointed a professor of operative surgery at Kiev University and director of the surgery department at the Kiev Military Hospital. He invented about 80 surgical instruments and a number of new surgical methods. He wrote a large number of articles and books, including the monographs *Operativnaia khirurgiia* (Operative Surgery, 3 vols, 1864–9) and *Voenno-khirurgicheskie pis'ma* (Military-Surgical Letters, 1868).

Shipbuilding. A branch of the *machine-building industry that builds and repairs cargo, passenger, fishing, military, and other ships, as well as barges and floating docks, cranes, derricks, and other equipment. In Ukraine the first shipbuilding facilities were constructed in Mykolaiv in 1788 by the Russian Admiralty to build sailing ships for the Russian Imperial Black Sea Fleet. Later they became the *Mykolaiv Shipyard. The first steamships were produced in the Russian Empire in 1815. A machine-building plant built in Kiev in 1862 changed to shipbuilding later in the 19th century. Two other shipyards built in Mykolaiv in the 1890s merged in 1907 to form the *Black Sea Shipyard. By 1913 in Russian-ruled Ukraine there were seven dockyards that built and repaired ships (in Odessa, Mykolaiv, Kherson, and elsewhere) and several smaller facilities that built river craft, barges, and so on. Ukraine accounted for about 13 percent of all shipbuilding in the Russian Empire.

The shipbuilding industry developed more rapidly after the Revolution of 1917. In the interwar period most of the existing factories were reconstructed, and several new ones were built. By 1928–9 shipbuilding accounted for 14 percent of all machine building in Ukraine, and Ukrainian output constituted a major share of Soviet production. The industry built ships for river and sea transportation and the fishing fleet. It was devastated during the Second World War and reconstructed after the war.

Today many different types of ships are built in Ukraine, including transport ships, tankers, whaling ships, research ships, trawlers, passenger ships, and dredges. Some of the ships weigh up to 150,000 t. In general, however, Soviet sources provided little information about the shipbuilding industry, especially about its military sector. It is known that until 1941 Ukrainian shipyards produced 15 to 20 warships annually.

Shirokov, Aleksandr [Širokov], b 18 September 1905 in Ivanovo, Russia. Geologist; corresponding member of the AN URSR (now ANU) since 1957. He graduated from (1930) and taught at (from 1946) the Dnipropetrovske Mining Institute. His major fields of interest include mining geology and estimations of the extent and quality of coal deposits in Ukraine and the European section of Russia, particularly the Donets Basin. He served as deputy head of the Supreme Soviet of the Ukrainian SSR in 1963–6.

Shishmanov, Dimitar [Šišmanov], b 1889 in Sofia, Bulgaria, d 1945. Writer and literary scholar; son of I. Shishmanov and M. Drahomanov's daughter, Lidiia. Besides contributing short stories, novels, and plays to Bulgarian literature, he acquainted the Bulgarian reader with the history of Ukraine and its literature. He accompanied his father to Kiev in 1918, where he became familiar with contemporary Ukrainian literature and translated a shortened version of S. Yefremov's history of Ukrainian literature (published in Sofia in 1919). He contributed articles on Ukrainian writers and on M. Hrushevsky (1935) to *Ukrains'ko-bolhars'kyi ohliad* and edited some of the Bulgarian translations of writers such as M. Kotsiubynsky, I. Franko, O. Oles, and Yu. Fedkovych, which appeared in the journal. In 1945 he was executed by Bulgarian Communists.

Shishmanov, Ivan [Šišmanov], b 4 July 1862 in Svishtov, Bulgaria, d 22 July 1928 in Oslo. Bulgarian literary scholar, folklorist, and civic figure; full member of the Bul-

garian Academy of Sciences and the Shevchenko Scientific Society. After studying at Jena, Geneva, and Leipzig universities he was a professor at Sofia University (from 1894). Through his father-in-law, M. *Drahomanov, and his wife's cousin, Lesia Ukrainka, he developed friendships with other Ukrainian writers (I. Franko) and scholars (V. Hnatiuk). He later became Bulgaria's minister of education (1903–7) and Bulgarian emissary to the Central Rada in Kiev (1918–19). In 1920 he initiated the creation of the Bulgarian-Ukrainian Society. Among his many works are articles on Ukrainian literature (particularly on T. Shevchenko) and its influence on the Bulgarian revival. His collected works were published in two volumes (1965–6).

Shkandrij, Myroslav [Škandrij], b 17 March 1950 in Leeds, England. Literary scholar. A graduate of the University of Toronto (PH D, 1980), he has taught at the universities of Calgary (1978–83), Manitoba (1983–5), Ottawa (1985–7), and, since 1987, Manitoba again, where beginning in 1990 he has served as a department head. Shkandrij is the author of articles on contemporary Ukrainian literature. He has translated and edited *Mykola Khvylovy, The Cultural Renaissance in Ukraine: Polemical Pamphlets, 1926–1927* (1985) and written the monograph *Modernists, Marxists, and the Nation: The Ukrainian Literary Discussion of the 1920s* (1992).

Shkarivka settlement. A Middle *Trypilian culture (late 4th to early 3rd millennium BC) settlement located near Shkarivka, Bila Tserkva raion, Kiev oblast. Excavations in 1967–73 uncovered the remains of rectangular and L-shaped houses with domed ovens, imprinted pottery, and ritual hearths.

Shkavrytko, Myroslav [Škavrytko], b 18 October 1922 in Galicia, d 16 September 1984 in Winnipeg. Journalist and religious leader. In Galicia he studied at Lviv University and then worked as a teacher. As a postwar refugee he organized Ukrainian theaters in Italy and worked with the Ukrainian press service in Great Britain. He emigrated to Canada in 1953; in 1963–73 he was chief editor of *Kanadi-is'kyi farmer* in Winnipeg. From the 1970s Shkavrytko was one of the leaders of the Ukrainian Native Faith church. He wrote the church's creed and many of its prayers.

Shkilnyk, Mykhailo [Škil'nyk, Myxajlo], b 19 September 1891 in Surokhiv, Jarosław county, Galicia, d 14 November 1972 in Toronto. Jurist and political activist. He completed his law studies in Lviv, Cracow, and Kiev. In 1918–20 he worked in the UNR Ministry of Trade and Industry and headed the consular department at the Ministry of Foreign Affairs. After returning to Galicia, from 1921 he worked as a judge in Peremyshliany. In 1945 he left for Germany and then emigrated to Canada. In the 1960s he served as president of the Association of Ukrainian Lawyers. In addition to numerous articles on the revolutionary period, he wrote *Ukraïna u borot'bi za derzhavnist' v 1917–1921 rokakh* (Ukraine in the Struggle for Statehood in 1917–1921, 1971).

Shkliarevsky, Oleksii [Škljarevs'kyj, Oleksij], b 3 April 1839 in Krasnopillia, Krolevets county, Chernihiv gubernia, d 5 July 1906 in Kiev. Pathologist and biophysicist. A graduate of Moscow University (1862), he taught general

Ivan Shishmanov   Mykhailo Shkilnyk

pathology at Kiev University (from 1869) and hygiene at the Higher Courses for Women (1878–80). His publications deal with the inflammation process and blood diseases. His lectures on medical physics were published in the university's *Izvestiia* (1881–2).

Shkol'na chasopys' (School Periodical). A semimonthly paper of pedagogical and scholarly affairs, published in Lviv from September 1880 to May 1889. In 1882–3 it was the organ of the Ruthenian Pedagogical Society (later *Ridna Shkola). Shkol'na chasopys'* published articles on pedagogy, extracurricular education, and educational policies; literary works; ethnographic studies; and professional news for teachers. The editor and publisher was H. Vretsona. The journal was succeeded by *Uchytel'*.

Shkolnyk, Arkadii [Škol'nyk, Arkadij], b 22 February 1916 in Kharkiv, d 28 October 1986 in Kharkiv. Dramatist. From 1942 on he wrote a number of plays, including *Liudyna shukaie shchastia* (A Person Seeks Happiness, 1955), *Iunist' moia* (My Youth, 1959), *Za tse ne sudiat'* (For This They Don't Judge, 1967), and *Pereval* (The Mountain Pass, 1969). He also wrote several plays for children. A collection of his selected plays was published in 1985.

Shkraba, Orest [Škraba], b 1898, d ? Civic and political leader in Bukovyna. In the 1920s he was active in the Zaporozhe student organization. After opening a law office in Kitsman he became active in politics and joined the Ukrainian National party. In 1930 and 1932 he was elected to the Rumanian parliament.

A sugar container by Vasyl Shkribliak, jug by Mykola Shkribliak, and plate by Yurii Shkribliak

Shkribliak [Škribljaky]. The family name of a group of Hutsul folk artists from Yavoriv, Kosiv county, Galicia (now Kosiv raion, Ivano-Frankivske oblast), who have specialized in wood carving and inlay. Yurii Shkribliak (b 28 April 1822, d 1884) was the founder of the family tradition. He made wooden flasks, miniature barrels, goblets, plates, spoons, crosses, cups, axes, pistols, rifles, and powder horns decorated with geometrical carvings and copper-wire or sheep-horn inlay. Noted for their original forms and fine technical execution, they were displayed at agricultural fairs in Vienna (1872), Lviv (1877), Trieste (1878), Stanyslaviv (1879), and Kolomyia (1880). Yurii taught his craft to his sons, Vasyl (1856–1928), Mykola (1858–1920), and Fedir (1859–1942). Vasyl specialized in flat carving and inlay of variously colored wood, beads, metal, and mother-of-pearl. His best works are plates, shelves, and furniture. In 1905–15 he taught at the provincial wood carving school in Vyzhnytsia. His works were

shown at exhibitions in Ternopil (1884), Cracow (1887), Lviv (1894, 1905), and Kolomyia (1880, 1912). Mykola introduced a pitted background to heighten the contrast with the carved design. His favorite motif was the rosette. Mykola taught the family craft to his sons, Fedir (b 28 April 1893, d 10 November 1960) and Vasyl (b 1900), and Fedir passed it on to his son, Dmytro (b 20 October 1925). Similar work has been done by the *Korpaniuk brothers (the sons of Kateryna, the daughter of Yurii Shkribliak) and their descendants. An album of works by the Shkribliak family was published in Kiev in 1979.

Yurii Shkrumeliak

Shkrumeliak, Yurii [Škrumeljak, Jurij] (pseuds: Ivan Sorokaty, Yu. Ihorkiv, O. Pidhirsky, Smyk], b 18 April 1895 in Lanchyn, Nadvirna county, Galicia, d 20 October 1965 in Lviv. Writer and journalist. A veteran of the Ukrainian Sich Riflemen, in the 1920s he studied at Lviv and Prague universities and the Ukrainian Higher Pedagogical Institute in Prague. In Lviv he worked as a coeditor for the Svit Dytyny (1920–30) and I. Tyktor (1928–9) publishers and was chief editor of the popular weekly *Narodnia sprava* (from 1928) and the children's monthly *Dzvinochok* (1931–9). He began publishing in 1915. In the interwar years he wrote many children's books, notably *Iurza-Murza, Zapysky Ivasia Krilyka* (The Notes of Ivas Bunny), *Strilets' Nevmyrakha* (The Rifleman Nevmyrakha), *Mova vikiv* (The Language of Ages), and a four-part history of Ukraine for children. He also translated into Ukrainian stories for children from *The Thousand and One Nights* (tales of Aladdin, Ali Baba, and Sinbad the Sailor). His poems, stories, feuilletons, and belletristic reminiscences appeared in *Mytusa, Students'kyi visnyk, Svit dytyny*, and *Narodnia sprava* and in the Chervona Kalyna publishing house annual *Istorychnyi kalendar-al'manakh Chervonoï kalyny*. Published separately were his long poem *Son Halycha* (The Dream of Halych, 1920), the memoirs *Poïzd mertsiv* (The Train of the Dead, 1922), the poetry collection *Aveleva zhertva* (Abel's Sacrifice, 1926), and the novels *Cheta Krylatykh* (The Squadron of the Winged Ones, 1928), *Vohni z polonyn* (Fires from the Mountain Pastures, 1930), and *Vysoki hory i nyz'ki dolyny* (High Mountains and Low Valleys, 1939). Although he had published a pro-Soviet poetry collection in 1941, from 1946 to 1955 Shkrumeliak was a Soviet political prisoner in Siberia. He was rehabilitated in 1956, and the regime published his poetry collection *Sopilka spivaie* (The *Sopilka* Is Singing, 1957) and a book of selected works, *Pryvit Hoverli* (Greeting to Hoverlia, 1964).

R. Senkus

Shkurat, Stepan [Škurat], b 8 January 1886 in Kobeliaky, Poltava gubernia, d 26 February 1973 in Romen, Sumy oblast. Stage and film actor and singer. He began his acting career in an amateur troupe in Romen (1910–28). In 1918 the troupe came under the direction of I. Kavaleridze, who invited Shkurat to act in his film *Zlyva* (A Downpour, 1929). Shkurat later became a leading heroic and character actor in O. Dovzhenko's films, including *Zemlia* (The Earth, 1930); he also appeared in I. Savchenko's *Vershnyky* (The Riders, 1939) and I. Kavaleridze's *Poviia* (The Strumpet, 1961, based on P. Myrny's novel). A biography, by V. Oleksenko, was published in Kiev in 1983.

Geo Shkurupii   Mykola Shlemkevych

Shkurupii, Geo [Škurupij] (Yurii), b 20 April 1903 in Bendery, now in Moldova, d 8 December 1937. Writer of poetry and prose. His first published work appeared in the almanac *Hrono* in 1920. He was an active member of the Association of Panfuturists, and his works were published in *Vyr revoliutsiï*, *Shliakhy mystetstva*, *Hlobus*, *Hrono*, *Semafor u maibutnie*, *Zhyttia i revoliutsiia*, *Nova generatsiia*, *Chervonyi shliakh*, and *Literaturna hazeta*. His collections of poetry include *Psykhotezy* (Psychotheses, 1922), *Baraban* (The Drum, 1923), *Zharyny sliv* (The Embers of Words, 1925), *More* (The Sea, 1927), and *Dlia druziv poetiv – suchasnykiv vichnosty* (To My Friends the Poets, Contemporaries of Eternity, 1929). His short stories include 'Peremozhets' drakona' (The Slayer of the Dragon, 1925), 'Pryhody mashynista Khorpa' (The Adventures of Khorp the Machinist, 1925), 'Shtab smerty' (Death Staff, 1926), 'Sichneve povstannia' (The January Uprising, 1928), 'Zruinovanyi polon' (Ruined Captivity, 1930), 'Strashna myt'' (A Terrible Moment, 1930), and those collected in *Monhol's'ki opovidannia* (Mongolian Stories, 1930). His novellas and novels include *Dveri v den'* (The Door to the Day, 1929), *Zhanna batal'ionerka* (Zhanna the Battalion Member, 1930), and *Mis Andriiena* (Miss Andriena, 1934). He was arrested in 1934, sentenced to 10 years in concentration camps, resentenced by a special NKVD tribunal, and shot.

I. Koshelivets

Shkval (Squall). A political and literary journal in Odessa, published by the CP(B)U semimonthly in Russian (1924–5), weekly in Russian (1926–9) and Ukrainian (1929), and three times a month in Ukrainian (1930–3). From mid-1929 it was a supplement to the Odessa newspaper *Chornomors'ka komuna*. The journal issued supplements devoted to science and technology (1926), sports (1926), women's affairs (1926–7), and science and art (1927). After three issues in 1933, *Shkval* was merged with the journal *Metalevi dni* (1930–3) to form the monthly journal *Literaturnyi zhovten'*, six issues of which appeared in 1934–5. In 1929 *Shkval* had a pressrun of 33,439 copies.

Shlapak, Dmytro [Šlapak] (pseuds: D. Lisovy, D. Pidhainy, D. Yakovenko), b 5 May 1923 in Yasynuvate, now in Borova raion, Kharkiv oblast. Literary scholar and critic. He graduated from the CC CPU Higher Party School (1949) and worked as deputy chief editor of *Molod' Ukraïny* and editor of **Vechirnii Kyïv* in 1945–52, a lecturer at Kiev and Lviv universities and a department head and dean at the Ukrainian Printing Institute in Lviv in 1953–63, an officer of the Ministry of Culture, and a docent at the Ukrainian Institute of Theater Arts in Kiev. He is the author of many articles and books on Soviet Ukrainian literature, including studies of Soviet Ukrainian publicism during the Second World War (1955), Yu. Zbanatsky (1963), O. Dov-zhenko (1964), Soviet Ukrainian dramaturgy (1970, 1981), M. Zarudny (1981), and A. Malyshko (1982), and *Literatura heroïky i krasy* (A Literature of Heroics and Beauty, 1972).

Shleifer, Georgii [Šlejfer, Georgij], b 16 June 1855 in Kiev, d 9 April 1913 in Kiev. Architect; son of P. *Shleifer. After graduating from the St Petersburg Institute of Civil Engineering he worked in the Kiev Department of Public Works and developed the city's water-supply and sewage systems. He also designed apartment buildings and the building that is now the Kiev Ukrainian Drama Theater.

Shleifer, Pavel [Šlejfer], b 20 June 1814 in Kiev, d 24 April 1879 in Kiev. Portrait painter and architect. In 1836–40 he audited lectures at the St Petersburg Academy of Arts. He taught painting at the Kiev Institute for Daughters of the Nobility (1846–9) and then served as architect of the Kiev School District (1852–79). He designed the Kiev Stock Exchange (destroyed in 1875) and painted portraits of a woman (1836), man (1842), and his wife (late 1840s).

Shlemkevych, Mykola [Šlemkevyč] (pseuds: M. Ivaneiko, S. Vilshyna, R. Sribny), b 27 January 1894 in Pyliava, Buchach county, Galicia, d 14 February 1966 in Passaic, New Jersey. Philosopher, publicist, and political figure; full member of the Shevchenko Scientific Society from 1941 and the Ukrainian Academy of Arts and Sciences in the US. His studies at Vienna University were interrupted by the First World War, and in 1915 he was deported by the Russian occupational authorities from Galicia to Siberia. As editorial secretary of the paper *Robitnycha hazeta* in Kiev (1917–19) he witnessed the rebirth and defeat of Ukrainian independence. While completing his studies at Vienna University (PH D, 1926) he began contributing to *Literaturno-naukovyi vistnyk*. After studying at the Sorbonne (1928–9) he returned to Lviv, became an ideologue of the *Front of National Unity, and edited its journal **Peremoha* (1933–9) and paper *Ukraïns'ki visty* (1935–9). During the Second World War he headed the publishing department of the Ukrainske Vydavnytstvo publishing house in Cracow and Lviv (1941–4). As a postwar refugee in Vienna and then Munich, he was a founding member of the *Ukrainian National State Union, the deputy chairman of its executive council, a founding member of the *Ukrainian National Council, and a member of *MUR. After emigrating to New Jersey in 1949, he cofounded the *Union of Ukrainian National Democrats (1950), founded and edited *Lysty do pryiateliv (1953–66), and founded the Kliuchi publishing house (1956) and *Ukrainian Research and Information Institute (1961). Besides many articles in the Galician and émigré press, he wrote several books on Ukrainian culture and political thought, including Ukraïns'ka synteza chy ukraïns'ka hromadians'ka viina (A Ukrainian Synthesis or a Ukrainian Civil War, 1946; 2nd edn, 1949), Zahublena ukraïns'ka liudyna (The Lost Ukrainian Person, 1954), and Halychanstvo (Galicianness, 1956). His chief philosophical work, Filosofiia (Philosophy, 1934; 2nd edn: Sutnist' filosofiï [The Essence of Philosophy], 1981), a revised translation of his PH D dissertation, criticizes absolutist (W. Windelband, H. Rickert, W. Wundt, G. Fechner, M. Schlick, A. Comte, and E. Mach), relativist (K. Fischer and W. Dilthey), and classical (Plato and I. Kant) definitions of philosophy and argues from the historical evidence that philosophy has three tasks: to criticize the existing spiritual culture (science, art, and religion), to articulate problems to the point at which they can be handled by science, and to unify the different spheres of spiritual culture in a coherent worldview.

T. Zakydalsky

Arnold Shlepakov

Shlepakov, Arnold [Šlepakov, Arnol'd], b 16 June 1930 in Vinnytsia. Historian; full member of the ANU (formerly AN URSR) since 1982. After graduating in international relations from Kiev University (1952; PH D, 1966) he worked for the ANU (from 1955), directed the Department of Contemporary History in its Institute of History (from 1969), served as director of the ANU Institute of Social and Economic Problems of Foreign Countries (until 1991), and taught at the Kiev Institute of Culture (1968–70) and Kiev University (from 1970). He wrote Ukraïns'ka trudova emihratsiia v SShA i Kanadi (kinets' XIX–pochatok XX st.) (Ukrainian Labor Emigrants in the United States and Canada [Late 19th to Early 20th Century], 1960), worked with UNESCO as an expert on international migration (1967), and was a member of the editorial board of Ukraïns'kyi istorychnyi zhurnal and Istoriia Ukraïns'koï RSR (History of the Ukrainian SSR, 8 vols, 1977–9).

Shliakh (Path). A monthly journal of literature, the arts, and politics, established in Moscow in March 1917 by Mykyta Shapoval and O. Mytsiuk. In August 1917 the journal was transferred to Kiev, where it appeared until 1919. The publisher and editor was F. Kolomyichenko.

Shliakh continued the traditions of Shapoval's earlier journal, *Ukraïns'ka khata. Among its contributors were some of the most distinguished cultural figures of the time, such as M. Vorony, O. Oles, H. Chuprynka, Ya. Mamontov, Khrystia Alchevska, O. Kobylianska, P. Tychyna, M. Rylsky, and Mykyta Shapoval (pseud: Sribliansky). The journal also contained translations of Western European literature, a cultural chronicle, and reviews. A total of 25 issues appeared.

Shliakh (Path). A monthly and later semimonthly journal published by the Orthodox Petro Mohyla Society in Lutske from May 1937 to September 1939. Shliakh printed articles on religious, cultural, and historical topics. The editor was Ye. Bohuslavsky.

Shliakh (The Way). A weekly organ of the Ukrainian Catholic metropoly in the United States, published in Philadelphia since 1940. Since 1946 a parallel English-language version has been published as The Way. Both papers contain articles on church history, popular theology, news, and belles lettres, mostly on religious themes. The editors of Shliakh have been V. Fedash (1946–9), P. Isaiv (1949–54), L. Mydlovsky (1954–75), M. Dolnytsky, and I. Skochylias. The Way has been edited by Revs M. Fedorovych, R. Moskal, R. Popivchak, and others.

Shliakh do zdorov'ia (Way to Health). A magazine published in Kharkiv (1925–36) and then in Kiev (1937–41) by the People's Commissariat of Health of the Ukrainian SSR. It appeared monthly in 1925–8, semimonthly in 1929–30, every 10 days in 1931–2, and again monthly in 1933–41. It published the supplements Za tverezist' (1929–32), Za zdorove kharchuvannia (1931–2), and Zdorova zmina (1931–3). The editor of the magazine was D. Yefymov.

Shliakh osvity (Path of Education). A monthly organ of the People's Commissariat of Education. It first appeared in Kharkiv in 1922 as the Russian-language Put' prosveshcheniia, which in 1923–6 was published in Russian and Ukrainian. From 1926 Shliakh osvity appeared only in Ukrainian. In 1931 it was renamed Komunistychna osvita, and from 1936 to June 1941 it was published in Kiev. After the Second World War it was revived as *Radians'ka shkola. Shliakh osvity published articles on pedagogy, educational theory and practice, and the organization and administration of education; preschool, professional, political, and social education; education in Western Europe; and book reviews, sample curricula, and news of the teaching profession in Ukraine. The journal, which advocated the creation of a distinct Ukrainian educational system, was an important achievement of the *Ukrainization policy directed by the people's commissar of education, M. Skrypnyk. For most of the 1920s it was edited by Ya. *Riappo. In 1927 it had 7,000 subscribers.

Shliakh peremohy (Way to Victory). A weekly newspaper of the OUN (Bandera faction), published in Munich since February 1954. It supports the Anti-Bolshevik Bloc of Nations and publicizes the history of the OUN, Ukrainian Insurgent Army, and Ukrainian Supreme Liberation Council, stressing the anti-Soviet and anti-Nazi activities of these organizations during the Second World War. It has devoted separate pages to music, the Ukrainian Youth Association, the Mikhnovsky Student Association, and

Shliakh peremohy

women. The chief editors have been P. Kizko, D. Shtykalo, D. Chaikovsky, M. Styranka, B. Vitoshynsky, S. Lenkavsky, H. Drabat, V. Kosyk, A. Bedrii, S. Halamai, A. Haidamakha, I. Kashuba, and V. Panchuk. Contributors have included prominent émigré publicists and activists associated with the Bandera faction.

Shliakh vykhovannia i navchannia (Path of Upbringing and Teaching). An educational journal published monthly in 1927–31 and then quarterly to 1939 in Lviv. Until 1930 it was called *Shliakh navchannia i vykhovannia*, and appeared as a supplement to *Uchytel's'ke slovo*. It published articles on educational theory and practice and sample elementary-school curricula and lessons. The journal's editors and regular contributors included distinguished pedagogues in Western Ukraine, such as P. Bilaniuk, M. Vozniak, A. Zeleny, D. Kozii, Ye. Pelensky, D. and I. Petriv, S. Rusova, V. Simovych, S. Siropolko, I. Stronsky, M. Taranko, and I. Fylypchak.

Shliakhta. See Nobility.

Shliakhy (Paths). An illustrated biweekly journal of literature and community affairs, published in Lviv from 1913 to 1918; from April 1913 to March 1914 it was the organ of the Ukrainian Student Union, and from December 1915 to August 1916 it was funded by the Press Committee of the Ukrainian Sich Riflemen. Among its editors were R. Zaklynsky, M. Strutynsky, O. Kohut, Yu. Okhrymovych, F. Fedortsiv, and D. Dontsov. It published literary contributions by V. Atamaniuk, P. Karmansky, R. Kupchynsky, V. Birchak, M. Pidhirianka, Yu. Shkrumeliak, and M. Yatskiv; Ye. Olesnytsky's memoirs; translations of works by R. Tagore, G. Hauptmann, M. Konopnicka, and D. Merezhkovsky; publicism by D. Dontsov, V. Zalizniak, V. Starosolsky, O. Nazaruk, and F. Fedortsiv; S. Balei's long work on the psychology of T. Shevchenko's works; M. Holubets's and I. Krypiakevych's articles on art; O. Zalesky's articles on music; and news and reviews.

Shliakhy mystetstva

Shliakhy mystetstva (Paths of Art). A literary and art journal, five issues of which were published in Kharkiv in 1921–3 by the art sector of the Ukrainian SSR Chief Political Education Committee. It was edited by V. Blakytny and H. Kotsiuba and then V. Koriak, and its aim was to become the main forum for pro-communist writers and artists in Ukraine. It promoted several styles that became characteristic of Soviet Ukrainian art of the 1920s, such as monumentalism, constructivism, revolutionary realism, and anti-impressionism. Some of the major figures involved with the journal were former *Borotbists. Since it appeared before the fragmentation of the Ukrainian literary community into several competing groups, it published works by almost every prominent Soviet Ukrainian writer and critic of the time. After the dissolution of *Shliakhy mystetstva*, most of its supporters joined the *Hart literary group.

Oleksander Shlikhter

Shlikhter, Oleksander [Šlixter] (Aleksandr), b 1 November 1868 in Lubni, Poltava gubernia, d 2 December 1940 in Kiev. Bolshevik revolutionary, economist, diplomat, and functionary; full member of the VUAN from 1929. After studying at Kharkiv and Bern universities (1889–91) he worked in the Russian Social Democratic Workers' party underground in Kiev and Zlatopil and was arrested and exiled several times. He joined the Bolsheviks and helped organize a general strike in Kiev in 1903. During the Revolution of 1905–6 he organized railway workers' strikes in Ukraine, the Kiev general strike, and other revolutionary actions. In November 1917 he took part in the Bolshevik coup in Petrograd, and in 1918–19 he was V. Lenin's commissar of requisitions in Russia and Siberia (1918) and Ukraine (1919).

Under Soviet rule Shlikhter served as chairman of the Tambov Gubernia Executive Committee (1920); member of the All-Russian, USSR, and All-Ukrainian central executive committees; plenipotentiary of the USSR People's Commissariat of Foreign Affairs in Ukraine and member of its collegium (1923–7); head of the Ukrainian Association of Consumer Co-operative Societies (1923); member of the Presidium of the All-Ukrainian Central Executive Committee (1923–37); a CP(B)U Organizational Bureau member (1924–6); rector of the Artem Communist University in Kharkiv (1924–7); a CC CP(B)U member (1925–37) and Politburo candidate member (1926–37); commissar of agriculture in Ukraine (1927–30); director of the VUAN Institute for the Socialist Reconstruction of Agriculture (1928–34); director of the Ukrainian Institute of Marxism-Leninism (1930–1) and president of the All-Ukrainian Association of Marxist-Leninist Scientific Research Institutes

(1931–3); VUAN and AN URSR (now ANU) vice-president (1931–8); and chairman of the Council for the Study of the Productive Resources of the Ukrainian SSR (1934–7). Even though he was an opponent of M. Skrypnyk's views on the national question, Shlikhter was arrested in 1937, but he survived the Stalinist terror. He wrote articles on economic, historical, and political subjects. Editions of his selected works were published in Kharkiv (4 vols, 1930–2) and Kiev (1959), and a volume of his writings on the agrarian question and early Soviet requisitioning policy appeared in Moscow in 1975.

R. Senkus

Shlopak, Tetiana [Šlopak, Tetjana], b 18 September 1918 in Kiev. Ophthalmologist. After graduating from the Odessa Medical Institute in 1946, she worked at the institute until 1953. Then she headed the ophthalmology department of the Ivano-Frankivske (1954–66) and Kiev medical institutes. Her publications deal with the pathogenesis and treatment of myopia, glaucoma, and eye tuberculosis, the theory of elastotonometry, and the biochemistry of a normal and a diseased eye.

Shlykevych, Oleksander [Šlykevyč], b 1849, d 1909. Statistician and zemstvo activist. He was president of the Kozelets county zemstvo and an executive member of the Chernihiv gubernia zemstvo. In the 1880s he studied the economy of each county of Chernihiv gubernia and then worked on a synthetic description of the gubernia and a comprehensive map of its soils. His invention of the so-called combinatorial tables was an important contribution to statistical methodology. An advocate of converting marshes into farmland, he oversaw the construction of a drainage canal from Zavorychi (northeast of Kiev) to the Poltava gubernia border in 1895–8.

Shmaida, Mykhailo [Šmajda, Myxajlo], b 2 November 1920 in Krásny Brod, near Medzilaborce, in the Prešov region. Writer and ethnographer. He began publishing stories, poems, and plays in Prešov periodicals in 1948. He wrote the first two Ukrainian novels published in postwar Slovakia, *Parazyty* (Parasites, 1955) and *Trishchat' kryhy* (The Ice Floes Are Breaking Up, 1957), the story collection *V'iazka kliuchiv* (Chain of Keys, 1956), and the novels *Lemky* (Lemkos, 1965) and *Rozizdy* (Travels, 1970). His works, which have served to reinforce the national identity of the Prešov region's Ukrainians, depict their society in the interwar, wartime, and postwar years. Since 1960 Shmaida has worked as an ethnographer at the *Svydnyk Museum of Ukrainian Culture; he has published transcriptions of Transcarpathian Christmas carols and oral folklore in *Duklia* and *Nove zhyttia* and has drawn on that folklore in his literary works.

Shmalhauzen, Ivan [Šmal'hauzen] (Schmalhausen) b 23 April 1884 in Kiev, d 7 October 1963 in Moscow. Biologist, zoologist, and theorist in evolutionary studies; full member of the VUAN and AN URSR (now ANU) from 1922 and the USSR Academy of Sciences (AN SSSR) from 1935; son of I. *Schmalhausen. A graduate of Kiev University (1907), he was a professor at the university (1921–41) and director of the ANU Institute of Zoology (1930–41) and the AN SSSR Institute of Animal Morphology in Moscow (1935–48). He wrote *Osnovy sravnitel'noi anatomii pozvonochnykh* (Foun-

Ivan Shmalhauzen   Andrii Shmigelsky

dations of Comparative Vertebrate Anatomy, 1923) and conducted innovative embryological studies of the dynamics of growth. In 1938 he became a professor of Darwinism at Moscow University, and in the next decade he developed a modern evolutionary theory that integrated systematics, morphology, embryology, and population genetics. His four major publications in this field were *Organizm kak tseloe v individual'nom i istoricheskom razvitii* (The Organism as a Whole in Individual and Historical Development, 1938; repr 1982), *Puti i zakonomernosti evoliutsionnogo protsessa* (Trends and Laws of the Evolutionary Process, 1939), *Faktory evoliutsii* (Factors of Evolution, 1946; English edn 1949), and the innovative textbook of evolutionary biology *Problemy darvinizma* (Problems of Darwinism, 1946). Shmalhauzen was an outspoken critic of T. *Lysenko's 'creative Darwinism' and was removed from his appointments in 1948. For the remainder of his career he worked at the AN SSSR Institute of Zoology on the origin of terrestrial vertebrates and on cybernetic approaches to evolutionary theory.

M. Adams

Shmidt, Otto [Šmidt], b 30 September 1891 in Mahiliou, Belarus, d 7 September 1956 in Moscow. Mathematician, astronomer, and geophysicist; full member of the AN URSR (now ANU) from 1934 and of the USSR Academy of Sciences from 1935. A student of D. Grave, he completed his studies at Kiev University in 1913. He continued to work with Grave and taught at Kiev University (1917–20) before moving to Moscow. His main interest in mathematics was the abstract theory of groups. His first monograph on the subject was published in Kiev in 1916. In the 1930s he showed how the theory of groups can be applied to topology, theoretical physics, and quantum physics.

Shmigelsky, Andrii [Šmigel's'kyj, Andrij], b 1866 in Zaluzhe, Zbarazh county, Galicia, d 1920 in Proskuriv (now Khmelnytskyi). Civic and political activist. A farmer by vocation, he was active in the Ukrainian Radical party and, from 1899, in the Ukrainian Social Democratic party. He was a leading organizer of Ukrainian economic and civic institutions in Zbarazh county and a contributor to *Narod* and *Zemlia i volia*. In 1907 he was elected for a brief term to the Galician Diet. In December 1918 he was delegated to the Ukrainian National Rada and was appointed to its executive. In 1919 he attended the Labor Congress in

Kiev. After retreating west across the Zbruch River with the Ukrainian Galician Army he died of typhus.

Fedir Shmit

Shmit, Fedir [Šmit], b 3 May 1877 in St Petersburg, d 10 November 1942 in Tashkent, Uzbekistan. Art historian of German origin; VUAN/AN URSR (now ANU) full member from 1921. A graduate of St Petersburg University (1900), he researched the architecture and painting of Byzantium, the Balkans, the Near East, and Kievan Rus'. In 1912 he became chairman of the department of art history at Kharkiv University; later he chaired the museum section of the All-Ukrainian Committee for the Protection of Monuments of Antiquity (1919–20). In 1921 he moved to Kiev. There he chaired the St Sophia Cathedral Commission, served as the first head of the All-Ukrainian Archeological Committee, was a professor at the Architectural Institute and the Lysenko Music and Drama Institute, and became rector (in 1922) of the Archeological Institute and director (in 1923) of the Museum of Religious Cults and the Museum of the St Sophia Cathedral. In December 1924 he was appointed a professor at Leningrad University and the director of the Russian Institute of Art History. Shmit published a book in Russian on art, its psychology, its stylistics, and its evolution (1919) and books in Ukrainian on the art of ancient Rus'-Ukraine (1919), the psychology of painting (1921), monuments of Rus' art (1922), and art as a subject of study (1923).

Shmorhun, Petro [Šmorhun], b 1 January 1921 in Oslamiv, near Vinkivtsi, Nova Ushytsia county, Podilia gubernia. Historian. A graduate of the Kiev Pedagogical Institute (1948), he worked at the Institute of Party History of the CC CPU (1951–68) and as deputy chief editor of *Ukraïns'kyi istorychnyi zhurnal* (1962–5, 1967–8). From 1970 he was director of the Department of CPSU History in the Institute for the Upgrading of Social Science Instructors at Kiev University. He is the author of *Rady robitnychykh deputativ na Ukraïni v 1905 r.* (Councils of Workers' Deputies in Ukraine in 1905, 1955) and *Lenin i bil'shovyts'ki orhanizatsiï na Ukraïni (1907–1917 rr.)* (Lenin and Bolshevik Organizations in Ukraine [1907–17], 1960) and a contributor to *Narysy istoriï Komunistychnoï partiï Ukraïny* (Outlines of the History of the Communist Party of Ukraine, 1970).

Shmyhelsky, Anton [Šmyhel's'kyj], b 23 July 1901 in Pluhiv, Zolochiv county, Galicia, d 4 November 1972 in Lviv. Poet. After the February Revolution of 1917 he lived in Kiev. There he headed the council of L. Kurbas's literary study group (1922) and was a founding member and secretary in charge of the Kiev branch of the writers' group Pluh (1923). After moving to Kharkiv he worked as an editor of *Narodnyi uchytel'* and *Hart*. From 1927 to 1933 he belonged to the writers' groups Zakhidnia Ukraina and the All-Ukrainian Association of Proletarian Writers. After the Second World War he lived in Lviv. He began publishing in 1923 and wrote 11 poetry collections, including *Pamolod'* (The Young Generation, 1927), *Pokhid* (The Military Expedition, 1933), *Vokzaly* (Train Stations, 1939), *Velinnia sertsia* (The Heart's Command, 1955), *Povnolittia* (Adulthood, 1958 [selected poetry]), *Stiahy nad Karpatamy* (Banners above the Carpathians, 1962), *Zemli okrasa* (The Earth's Adornment, 1964), and *Veresneve polum'ia* (September's Glow, 1973). He also translated Russian, Belarusian, Polish, and Armenian poetry into Ukrainian.

Shniukov, Yevhen [Šnjukov, Jevhen], b 26 March 1930 in Arkhangelsk, Russia. Geologist; member of the AN URSR (now ANU) since 1982. He graduated from Kiev University (1953) and worked at the Institute of the Geochemistry and Physics of Minerals (1967–77) and the ANU Institute of Geological Sciences (as director from 1977). His scientific contributions are devoted to problems of the genesis and distribution patterns of manganese and other ores, to the impact of mud volcanoes upon ore formation, and to the geological structure and mineral resources of the oceans (particularly the Azov and Black seas). He discovered several deposits of iron ore in the Kerch area.

Shock-worker movement. See Socialist competition.

Memorial plaque on the building in Lviv where Sholom Aleichem lived in 1906

Sholom Aleichem [Šolom Alejxem] (pseud of Sholom Rabinovich), b 2 March 1859 in Pereiaslav (now Pereiaslav-Khmelnytskyi), Poltava gubernia, d 13 May 1916 in New York. Yiddish writer. He became a rabbi in Lubni (1880–3) and later moved to Kiev and then Odessa, where he devoted his time to writing. Beginning in 1905 he traveled to England, the United States, Switzerland, Germany, and Italy. He settled in New York City in 1914. From 1883 on he published novels, stories (including the first Yiddish stories for children), and plays. Most of them depict *shtetl* life in Ukraine and include Ukrainian proverbs, folk songs, and folklore and Ukrainian characters (children, workers, and revolutionaries). Over 30 editions of Aleichem's works have been published in Ukrainian translation. In Ukraine his plays have been staged (eg, by L. Kurbas), and films based on his works have been made. A. Kahan's Ukrainian novel about him was published in Kiev in 1963. A memorial museum was founded in Sholom Aleichem's honor in Pereiaslav-Khmelnytskyi in 1978, and a monument was erected there in 1984.

Zoltan Sholtes: *After the Rain* (1958)

Sholtes, Zoltan [Šoltes], b 21 July 1909 in Prykopa, Prešov region, d 16 December 1990 in Uzhhorod. Painter. He studied under Y. Bokshai and A. Erdeli at the Uzhhorod Art School (1930–3). A resident of Uzhhorod, he has painted many Transcarpathian landscapes, such as *Spring* (1945), *Winter Evening* (1956), *Highland* (1958), *Storm above the Beskyds* (1968), and *View of Rivna Meadow* (1979), and portraits.

Sholudko, Panas [Šolud'ko], b and d ? Master carpenter from Nizhen. In 1759–61 he built the Assumption Church in Berezna, in the Chernihiv region. This masterpiece of Ukrainian wooden architecture had five domes and two additional domed towers at the entrance. Measuring 27.5 by 19.6 m and 35 m in height, it was one of the largest wooden buildings in Ukraine in the 18th century. The church was destroyed by the Soviet authorities in the 1930s.

Shonk-Rusych, Konstantyn [Šonk-Rusyč] (Szonk-Rusych), b 3 June 1915 in Zhytomyr, Volhynia gubernia, d 3 July 1983 in New York. Enamelist and editor. He studied cinematography in Kiev and then worked as a scenery designer. A postwar émigré in the United States from 1949, he developed his own technique of enameling on copper and silver and created colorful portraits of historical figures, miniatures of animals and plants, linocuts, and mosaics. His book *Lino-Block Prints* was published in 1966. He edited the magazines *Dnipro* (1958–62) and *Nash litopys* (1980–1), wrote an illustrated history of Ukrainian art (1978) and a book on wood carving in Ukraine, and compiled *Ukraine in Postcards* (1981).

Panas Sholudko: the Assumption Church in Berezna

Shooting (*striletskyi sport*). The sport of firing at targets with rifles, shotguns, handguns (pistols or revolvers), and air guns. In Ukraine the sport dates from the late medieval period, when rifle brotherhoods appeared in towns of Western Ukraine, and members competed each year for the title of Rifle King. In the early 20th century, small-caliber competitions were first held in Galicia, by the *Sokil sports society. The first shooting competition in the Russian Empire took place in 1898. In Soviet Ukraine shooting competitions were first held in Zaporizhia in 1925, and then in other cities. The first all-Union meet was held in Kharkiv in 1927. Since 1952 Soviet marksmen have competed in the Olympic Games and in world and European championships; Ukrainians have been part of USSR teams. H. Kupko, D. Dobruk, M. Prozorovsky, N. Kalenychenko, V. Zemenko, V. *Romanenko, Ya. *Zheliezniak, and S. Tiahnii have won world or European championships. Olympic gold medals have been won by V. Borisov (1956, free rifle, three positions OR [prone WR]), Romanenko (1956, running-deer shooting OR), Zheliezniak (1972, moving-target WR), and D. Monakov (1988, trapshooting). Borisov also won Olympic silver (1956, small-bore rifle, prone) and bronze (1960, free rifle) medals.

Shopinsky, Vasyl [Šopins'kyj, Vasyl'] (né Zhonochyn), b 22 July 1887 in Tereshivtsi, Letychiv county, Podilia gubernia, d 26 August 1967 in New York. Communist activist and writer in the United States. After emigrating to the United States in 1908, he worked at various jobs and in

1919 began to contribute to the paper *Robitnyk,* the Soviet journals *Chervonyi shliakh* and *Pluzhanyn,* and the Galician Sovietophile journal *Nova kul'tura.* His collection of short stories, *Fabrychna nevolia* (Factory Slavery, 1925), and three plays, *Zhebrats'ka Ameryka* (Beggar's America, 1930), *Peony* (Peons, 1930), and *Zmova pinkertontsiv* (Conspiracy of the Pinkerton Guards, 1931), were published in the Ukrainian SSR.

Short story. See Prose.

Short-fallow system (*parova systema*). A system of farming that divides the arable land into two parts, a sown part and a fallow part. Under a two-field fallow system, which developed out of the long-fallow (*perelohova*) system, half of the farmland lies fallow, whereas under a three-field system the farmland is divided into three parts – the winter field (in Ukraine usually sown with winter rye), the spring field (devoted to barley, oats, and wheat), and the fallow field. The three-field system predominated in central and eastern Ukraine as late as the 1920s. The main shortcoming of the system was that soil fertility was not restored. The fallow field was usually used as cattle pasture; hence, it became less porous and lost moisture. The cultivation of the same cereal crops year after year increased weed contamination. The shortage of fodder held back the growth of animal husbandry. For those reasons the fallow-field system was replaced by *crop rotation. In Western Ukraine the change took place in the mid-19th century, but in central and eastern Ukraine it occurred mostly in the 1920s. At the same time the amount of land that was left fallow was sharply reduced.

With the development of agrotechnology the fallow field becomes a part of the system of crop rotation. Fallow land is plowed and harrowed to destroy weeds, preserve moisture, and accumulate plant nourishment. There are two types of fallow, true fallow and occupied fallow. True fallow land is plowed in the fall (bare fallow) or in the spring (early fallow). This type of fallow is common in Ukraine in the forest-steppe and steppe belts. Its total area was about 5,000 ha in 1913, 3,900,000 ha in 1940, 2,200,000 ha in 1958, 700,000 ha in 1960, and 200,000 ha in 1962 (as a result of N. Khrushchev's agrarian policy). Occupied fallow is an important advance in agriculture. Under this system the fallow land is not only tilled, as under true fallow, but planted with fast-growing crops that ripen during the first half of the summer, mostly feed crops that restore nitrogen to the soil (peas, vetch, esparcet, lupine, etc) or corn for silage or early potatoes. Occupied fallow is more common in moist regions, such as Polisia and the forest-steppe belt. Lupine is grown on the fallow land in Polisia, where the soil is sandy. In dry regions tall plants, such as corn and sunflowers, are grown in strips to protect other plants from the sun and wind and to hold the snow in place. When the fallow crops are gathered, the occupied fallow land is plowed, fertilized, and seeded with winter crops.

Shostak, Peter [Šostak, Petro], b 30 January 1943 in Bonnyville, Alberta. Artist and teacher. A graduate of the University of Alberta (1965; M ED 1970), Shostak taught curriculum development at the University of Victoria, British Columbia (1969–79), before embarking upon a full-time artistic career. His oils and serigraphs depict scenes

A 1985 painting by Peter Shostak reproduced on a Christmas card

from his childhood in the Ukrainian bloc-settlements in east central Alberta. He has published three collections of his work, *When Nights Were Long* (1982), *Saturday Came But Once a Week* (1984), and *For Our Children* (1992). Shostak is active in the Ukrainian community in Victoria and is one of the most popular Ukrainian-Canadian artists today. His works have been exhibited across Canada.

Shostakivska, Yuliia [Šostakivs'ka, Julija], b 31 May 1871 in Poltava, d 12 July 1939 in Dnipropetrovske. Stage actress. She worked in the troupes of M. Starytsky (1888–91), M. Kropyvnytsky (1892–3 and 1895–7), H. Derkach (1893–4), and her husband, D. Haidamaka (1898–1919). She later toured with Haidamaka in various troupes (1918–26) and worked in the Donetske (1927–34) and Dnipropetrovske (1934–9) Ukrainian Music and Drama theaters.

Shostka [Šostka]. II-14. A city (1990 pop 94,000) on the Shostka River and a raion center in Sumy oblast. It originated as a workers' settlement that sprang up around a gunpowder factory built in 1739. From 1782 it belonged to Novhorod-Siverskyi vicegerency, from 1796, to Little Russia gubernia, and from 1802 to 1925, to Chernihiv gubernia. A railway built in 1893 linked Shostka with other industrial centers and stimulated its growth. In 1924 it attained city status. It has several large chemical plants, including the Svema Manufacturing Consortium, a number of building-materials factories, and a large food industry.

Shovheniv, Ivan [Šovheniv], b 25 September 1874 in Kamianka, Kupianka county, Kharkiv gubernia, d 13 April 1943 in Danzig (now Gdańsk, Poland). Hydraulic engi-

Ivan Shovheniv

neer; father of O. *Teliha. He graduated from the St Petersburg Institute of Communications (1899) and directed engineering projects on the Volga, Oka, and Moskva rivers. He then studied in Germany (1910–12), was director of an irrigation project in Turkestan, taught at the St Petersburg Polytechnical Institute, and was deputy director of the melioration department of the Imperial Russian Ministry of Agriculture. He returned to Ukraine in 1918 and became director of the Hetman government's Department of Water Communications. He worked in the VUAN melioration section, and was a professor at the Kiev Polytechnical Institute (1918–20). He emigrated in 1920 and helped found the Ukrainian Husbandry Academy in Poděbrady, Bohemia (1922–8), of which he was the first rector (1922–6). From 1929 he worked in Warsaw for the Ministry of Agriculture and the Ukrainian Scientific Institute and headed the Ukrainian Black Sea Institute (1941–2). He wrote numerous articles and larger works, including ones on water management in Ukraine (1923) and in the Dnieper Basin (1936), the hydraulics of groundwaters (1929), floods in Ukraine (1936), Ukraine's energy resources (1940) and water management (1941), and the Black Sea (1941). He also wrote textbooks on plane analytic geometry (1923), hydraulics (2 vols, 1923, 1927), hydrology (1924), and hydraulic engineering (1924, 1925).

Shovkoplias, Ivan [Šovkopljas], b 8 April 1921 in Lazirky, Lubni county, Poltava gubernia. Archeologist. A graduate of Kiev University (1945), he worked in the Historical Museum of Ukraine (1945–9) and then at the AN URSR (now ANU) Institute of Archeology (since 1949). A specialist in the Late Paleolithic and the history of archeology in Ukraine, he is best known for his survey work *Arkheolohichni doslidzhennia na Ukraïni, 1917–1957* (Archeological Studies in Ukraine, 1917–57) and the bibliographical *Rozvytok radians'koï arkheolohiï na Ukraïni, 1917–1966* (The Development of Soviet Archeology in Ukraine, 1917–66, 1969). He also wrote a monograph on the Stone Age in Ukraine (1962) and a general survey of archeology (1964), and served as a member of the editorial committee for the three-volume *Arkheolohiia Ukraïns'koï RSR* (The Archeology of the Ukrainian SSR, 1971–5).

Shovkoplias, Yurii [Šovkopljas, Jurij], b 6 February 1903 in Kharkiv, d 12 October 1978 in Kharkiv. Writer and teacher. In Kharkiv he worked as a teacher (1923–30), be-

longed to the writers' group *Prolitfront (1930), and headed Kharkiv University's department of journalism (1949–51), the literature and art department of the CP(B)U city committee (1951–3), and the Kharkiv branch of the Writers' Union of Ukraine (1953–6). Later he was editor in chief of the literary journal *Prapor*. He began publishing stories in 1926 and wrote the novels *Vesna nad morem* (Spring at the Seashore, 1929), *Proiekt elektryfikatsiï* (The Project of Electrification, 1929), *Zavtra* (Tomorrow, 1931), *Zemlianyi pokhid* (The Land March, 1933), *Inzhenery* (Engineers, 2 vols, 1934, 1937; rev edn 1964), *Pochynaietsia iunist'* (Youth Begins, 1938), and, a trilogy, *Liudyna zhyve dvichi* (A Person Lives Twice, 1964); the story collections *Henii* (A Genius, 1929), *Pronyklyvist' doktora Piddubnoho* (The Insight of Doctor Piddubny, 1930), *Profesor* (1930), and *Studenty* (Students, 1930); the essay collections *Elektrychnyi SRSR* (The Electrical USSR, 1932) and *Narodzhennia elektrychnoho strumu* (The Birth of the Electrical Current, 1936); and a few children's books. An edition of his selected works (2 vols) appeared in 1973.

Oleksii Shovkunenko and his *Old Oak* (oil, 1955)

Shovkunenko, Oleksii [Šovkunenko, Oleksij], b 21 March 1884 in Kherson, d 12 March 1974 in Kiev. Painter and educator; full member of the USSR Academy of Arts from 1947. A graduate of the Odessa Art School (1908) and the St Petersburg Academy of Arts (1917), he took part in the exhibitions of the *Society of South Russian Artists (1913–19) and was a member of the Kostandi Society of Artists (1924–9). He taught at the Odessa Art Polytechnic (1926–9) and Art Institute (1929–35) and at the Kiev State Art Institute (1936–63). He painted portraits, including ones of prominent Ukrainian cultural figures, such as Yu. Yanovsky, P. Tychyna, M. Rylsky, I. Le, L. Pervomaisky, M. Lytvynenko-Volgemut, V. Zabolotny, N. Uzhvii, M. Lysenko, and O. Bohomolets, and many natural, urban, and industrial landscapes of Ukraine, Caucasia, Moscow, the Urals, Moldavia, and Bashkiria, including series depicting the Odessa shipyard (1925–35) and the construction of the Dnieper Hydroelectric Station (1930–2). For the latter series he was awarded the grand prize at the Art and Technology in Contemporary Life Exhibition in Paris

Yurii Shovkoplias

Marat Shpak

(1937). A volume of recollections about Shovkunenko was published in 1980, and L. Vladych's books about him appeared in 1960 and 1983.

Shpak, Marat [Špak], b 13 April 1926 in Chupakhivka, now in Okhtyrka raion, Sumy oblast. Experimental physicist; AN URSR (now ANU) corresponding member since 1969 and full member since 1990. A graduate of Chernivtsi University (1951), he joined the ANU Institute of Physics in 1955 and served as its director in 1970–87. His major contributions are in solid-state physics, where he discovered the exciton luminescence of molecular crystals, and in quantum optics, where he contributed to the development of highly stabilized lasers.

Shpak, Mykola [Špak] (pseud of Mykola Shpakovsky), b 23 February 1909 in Lypky, Skvyra county, Kiev gubernia, d 19 July 1942 in Kiev. Poet. He was a member of the literary organization *Molodniak and the Literary Union of the Red Army and Navy. In the 1920s and early 1930s he worked for provincial newspapers, in which he began to publish his poetry in 1928. During the Second World War he was imprisoned by the Germans, escaped, and organized a partisan group. He was captured in Kiev and shot to death. During the German occupation he wrote patriotic Soviet verse under the pseudonym Pylyp Komashka. He wrote collections in the official Soviet patriotic manner: *Narkomu raport* (Report to the People's Commissar, 1933), *V dorozi* (On the Road, 1934), *Moia liubov* (My Love, 1936), *Bahatstvo* (Riches, 1938), and *Syla zemna* (Earthly Strength, 1940). Some posthumous editions of his works have been published: *Poeziï* (Poems, 1946), *Zhyttia krasuiet'sia* (Life Parades Itself, 1947), *Vybrani poeziï* (Selected Poems, 1950, and a few revised editions), and *Kazky* (Tales, 1960).

Shpakov, Anatolii [Špakov, Anatolij], b 8 June 1926 in Novohradkivka, Odessa okruha. Art scholar. A graduate of Leningrad University (1951), he has written articles on Ukrainian art and monographs on the artists O. Murashko (1959), V. Kasiian (1960), and M. Hlushchenko (1962), on Soviet Ukrainian painting (coauthor, 1957), and on Soviet Ukrainian book graphics (1973).

Shpol, Yuliian. See Yalovy, Mykhailo.

Shpola [Špola]. IV-12. A city (1989 pop 22,400) on the Shpolka River and a raion center in Cherkasy oblast. The village was first mentioned in the 18th century, when it was under Polish rule. In 1768 it participated in the Koliivshchyna rebellion. After the partition of Poland in 1793, it became part of Bratslav vicegerency, Voznesenske vicegerency (1795–7), and then Kiev gubernia. A sugar refinery was built there in 1851, and a railway station in 1874. In 1938 the town attained city status. Most of its inhabitants are employed in light industry and the food industry.

Shpyhotsky, Opanas [Špyhoc'kyj], b and d ? Writer and folklorist of the early 19th century. He studied at Kharkiv University and belonged to the *Kharkiv Romantic School. He began publishing his works in *Ukrainskii al'-manakh* (1831). His works include 'Malorosiis'ka balada' (Little Russian Ballad, 1831), which initiated the form of

the folkloric ballad in Ukrainian literature. He also wrote sonnets (eg, 'Til'ky tebe vbachyla' [I (female) Only Noticed You] and 'Znaiesh, Saniu-serden'ko' [You Know, Sania Dearest Heart]). His works were republished in H. Nedilko's *Ukraïns'ki poety-romantyky 20–40-ykh rokiv XIX st.* (Ukrainian Romantic Poets of the 1820s to 1840s, 1968).

Archbishop Bohdan Shpylka   Osyp Shpytko

Shpylka, Bohdan [Špyl'ka], b 1892, d 1 November 1965 in Ottawa. Archbishop of the Ukrainian Orthodox Church of America in 1937–65. Originally from Galicia, he emigrated to the United States in 1936 to assume church duties. He wrote Orthodox catechisms in both Ukrainian and English and published a variety of propagandistic brochures.

Shpytko, Osyp [Špytko] (pseud: Hryts Shchypavka), b 1869 in Horodnytsia, Husiatyn county, Galicia, d 1942 in Brazil. Writer. He edited the newspaper *Bukovyna* (1899) and satirical periodical *Antsykhryst* (1906) in Chernivtsi, the literary paper *Dzvin* (1906) in Lviv, and the newspaper *Pidhirs'kyi dzvin* (1912) in Sianik. A member of the Lviv modernist writers' group Moloda Muza in the 1900s, he wrote stories, the autobiographical novella *Vyrid* (The Degenerate), humor and satire, the poetic parody collection *Novomodnyi spivannyk* (A New-fashioned Songbook, 1901), and the lyric poetry collection *Osinni kvity* (Autumn Flowers, 1910). After emigrating to Brazil in 1912, he continued writing and published in Portuguese the collection *No túmulo da vida* (1930) under the pseudonym Ossep Stefanovetch.

Shrah, Illia [Šrah, Illja], b 23 August 1847 in Sedniv, Horodnia county, Chernihiv gubernia, d 11 April 1919 in Chernihiv. Civic and political activist; son of a Saxon German who worked for the Lyzohub family. Shrah studied law at St Petersburg University, from which he was expelled in 1869 for participating in a student demonstration. Later he was admitted to Kiev University. From 1869 he was a councillor in the Chernihiv gubernia zemstvo administration, and in 1906 he was elected to the First Russian State *Duma, where he headed the 40-member Ukrainian caucus. He was also vice-president of the Autonomists' Union (1905–6) and the Society of Ukrainian Progressives. He belonged to the Radical Democratic party, out of which the Ukrainian Party of Socialists-Federalists was formed in 1917. He was a representative of

Illia Shrah

Chernihiv gubernia in the Central Rada. Shrah contributed articles to the periodicals *Zapysky Naukovoho tovarystva im. Shevchenka*, *Pravda* in Lviv, *Rada* and *Iuzhnye zapiski* in Kiev, *Ukrainskii vestnik* in St Petersburg, and *Literaturno-naukovyi vistnyk*. His autobiography (annotated by S. Yefremov) was published in *Nashe mynule* (1919, nos 1–2).

Mykola Shrah (portrait by Mykhailo Zhuk, 1915)

Shrah, Mykola [Šrah], b 4 May 1894, d 1 February 1970. Economist and political leader; son of I. *Shrah. He studied in Moscow. He was vice-president of the Central Rada from 28 June 1917 to 29 March 1918 and a member of the CC of the Ukrainian Party of Socialist Revolutionaries (UPSR). After the 4th congress of his party (May 1918) he joined the 'center current.' In 1919 he was a consul for the Ukrainian diplomatic mission in Budapest, and from 1920 to 1924 he was a member of the Foreign Delegation of the UPSR in Vienna and a coeditor of *Boritesia – poborete!*, in which he published 'Slova i dila sotsiialistiv v natsional'-nii spravi' (Words and Deeds of Socialists in the National Cause, 1920, no. 2) and 'Vidrodzhennia Zakordonnoï hrupy Ukraïns'koï komunistychnoï partiï' (The Rebirth of the Foreign Group of the Ukrainian Communist Party, 1920, no. 4). In 1924 he returned with M. Hrushevsky to Ukraine, where he worked in Kharkiv with the Society of Technical and Scientific Workers (1928–31). He was imprisoned during the Stalinist terror. From 1952 he was a lecturer at the Kharkiv Institute of the National Economy,

and from 1966 he was a professor at the Lviv Polytechnical Institute. He published various articles on economics and socialist politics, as well as a book of translations of G. de Maupassant's stories called *Na vodi* (On Water, 1923).

Leontii Shramchenko   Mykola Shramchenko

Shramchenko, Leontii [Šramčenko, Leontij], b 17 November 1877 in Oleshivka, Chernihiv county, Chernihiv gubernia, d 21 June 1954 in Geneva. Economist, political activist, and educator. After graduating in law from Moscow University (1907) he worked as a zemstvo statistician in Chernihiv and Tbilisi (1910–17). In 1918 he was delegated by the Ukrainian Transcaucasian Territorial Council to the Ukrainian National Union. In the following year he served in the UNR government as deputy economics minister during B. Martos's premiership and as state secretary under Prime Minister I. Mazepa. He taught statistics at the Ukrainian Husbandry Academy in Poděbrady from 1922 and at the Ukrainian Free University in Prague from 1930. After being promoted to the rank of full professor in 1934, he served as dean of the law and social sciences faculty at the Ukrainian Free University (1937–45), dean of the economics department at the Ukrainian Technical and Husbandry Institute (1947), and director of the Ukrainian Institute of Sociology (1935–40). He wrote two statistics textbooks (1936) and studies of several Ukrainian statisticians, among them F. Shcherbyna (1929) and O. Rusov (1938).

Shramchenko, Mykola [Šramčenko], b 24 April 1909 in Chernihiv, d 26 September 1968 in Washington, DC. Painter. In 1933 he graduated from the Kiev State Art Institute, where he studied under M. Boichuk. A postwar émigré in the United States from 1949, he taught painting at the National Academy of Arts in Washington and took part in Ukrainian-American art exhibitions. Evolving in his style from realism to expressionism, he specialized in portraits, among them ones of Ye. Malaniuk and M. Omelianovych-Pavlenko. He also painted several series depicting the atrocities of the Soviet regime ('Prodigal Son,' 'The Power of Darkness,' and 'Messiah') and illustrated a Department of State publication about the NKVD massacre of Polish officers at Katyn.

Shramchenko, Oleksander [Šramčenko], b 26 March 1859 in Voronezh, Russia, d 29 April 1921 in Kiev. Ethnographer. After graduating from Kiev University in 1887, he taught school in Caucasia and the Kholm region and collected ethnographic materials. From 1909 he worked in

Kiev as an associate and longtime treasurer of the Ukrainian Scientific Society, editor of its journal *Ukraïna* and its *Ukraïns'kyi etnohrafichnyi zbirnyk*, and scientific secretary of the Committee of the National Library of Ukraine. Some of his ethnographic materials collected in the Kholm region were published in the *zbirnyk*. He also translated many of V. Antonovych's works from Russian into Ukrainian.

Sviatoslav Shramchenko   Avhustyn Shtefan

Shramchenko, Sviatoslav [Šramčenko, Svjatoslav], b 3 May 1893 in Baku, Transcaucasian krai, d 24 June 1958 in Philadelphia. Naval officer. A graduate of the Alexander Military Law Academy in St Petersburg, in 1917 he was a member of the Ukrainian Military Revolutionary Staff of the Baltic Fleet. Later he served as senior adjutant to the UNR minister for naval affairs (1918), deputy minister for naval affairs (1919), deputy commander of the UNR naval school (1919), and chief of the organizational department of the Naval General Staff (1920). He was promoted to the rank of naval commander. During the Second World War he chaired the Ukrainian Relief Committee in Kholm (1941–4). He wrote over 200 articles on naval history, which appeared in journals such as *Za derzhavnist'* and *Tabor*, and books, including *Istoriia ukraïns'koho viis'ka* (History of the Ukrainian Armed Forces, 1936). After the Second World War he emigrated to the United States.

Shramenko, Mykola [Šramenko], b 9 May 1891, d 14 August 1974 in Dornstadt, West Germany. Military and political figure. During the Ukrainian-Soviet War he was a colonel in the UNR Army. In 1919–20 he commanded the Kiev Division and took part in two Winter campaigns (1919–20, 1921). After emigrating to Poland and Germany he headed the Breslau (Wrocław) chapter of the Ukrainian National Alliance (1941–4). A postwar refugee in Germany, he was secretary of the Ukrainian National Council and a member of the UNR government-in-exile in charge of military affairs.

Shramko, Borys [Šramko], b 17 January 1921 in Homel, Belarus. Archeologist and ancient historian. He graduated from Kharkiv University (1949) and taught there in 1950 (as a professor of ancient history and archeology from 1966). In the 1960s he became a member of UNESCO international committees and studied the history of agricultur-

al implements and the history of ancient iron metallurgy. Shramko has written works on the prehistory and ancient peoples of the Donets Basin (1962), the economy of the prehistoric tribes inhabiting Ukraine's forest-steppe (1971), excavations of early Iron Age kurhans in Kharkiv oblast (1983), the archeology of the early Iron Age in Eastern Europe (1983), and the *Bilske fortified settlement (the city Helon, 1987).

Shreier-Tkachenko, Onysia [Šrejer-Tkačenko, Onysja], b 10 January 1905 in Krasnostavtsi, Kamianets-Podilskyi county, Podilia gubernia, d 16 October 1985 in Kiev. Musicologist. She completed her undergraduate (1940) and graduate (1947) degrees at the Kiev Conservatory. She lectured at the Kiev Conservatory from 1944, and in 1960 was appointed head of the department of music history. She edited and contributed chapters to *Istoriia ukraïns'koï dozhovtnevoï muzyky* (History of Pre-Soviet Ukrainian Music, 1969), was a coauthor of the two-volume *Narysy z istoriï ukraïns'koï muzyky* (Essays in the History of Ukrainian Music, 1964), and wrote *Istoriia ukraïns'koï muzyky* (History of Ukrainian Music, 1980) as well as numerous articles and brochures on musicians and the history of music in Ukraine.

Shrew (Ukrainian: *zemleryika, bilozubka, burozubka*). An insectivorous, mouselike mammal of the family Soricidae, including the genera *Sorex* and *Crocidura*. Shrews are chiefly terrestrial animals; some are burrowers, some arboreal, and some semiaquatic. They feed on invertebrates and worms and are helpful in controlling noxious insects. In Ukraine the common shrew (*S. araneus*) is the smallest mammal. Musk shrews (*C. suaveolens* and *C. leucodon*) have few enemies because they emit an extremely unpleasant scent.

Shtaierman, Illia [Štajerman, Illja], b 10 April 1891 in Kamianets-Podilskyi, Podilia gubernia, d 24 July 1962 in Moscow. Mathematician; corresponding member of the AN URSR (now ANU) from 1939. After completing his studies at Kiev University (1914) and the Kiev Polytechnical Institute (1918), he taught at the institute (1920–41) and the university (1930–41) and worked at the ANU Institute of Mathematics (1934–41). From 1943 he was a professor at the Moscow Institute of Civil Engineering. His works deal with applied mathematics, particularly the theory of elasticity and mechanics.

Shtanhei, Volodymyr [Štanhej], b 1895 in Moshuriv, Uman county, Kiev gubernia, d 1937. Writer. He published his first stories as a German POW in 1916–17 in the Union for the Liberation of Ukraine newspapers *Prosvitnyi lystok* and *Hromads'ka dumka*. After returning to Ukraine following the Revolution of 1917, he worked as a teacher and functionary in Uman county. Until 1932 he belonged to the writers' group Pluh. From 1927 to 1933 he published many story collections, including *Batrachka* (The Female Farmhand, 1927), *Obraza* (The Insult, 1929), *Udruhe narodzheni* (Born Again, 1931), and *Tom novel* (A Volume of Novellas, 1932). He was arrested during the Stalinist terror in 1934 and was imprisoned on the Solovets Islands, where he was shot by the NKVD.

Shtefan, Avhustyn [Štefan], b 11 January 1893 in Poroshkove, Transcarpathia, d 4 September 1986 in Philadelphia. Teacher, civic activist, and Transcarpathian state figure; member of the Shevchenko Scientific Society. After completing studies in theology in Uzhhorod and in philosophy in Budapest he became a teacher in Uzhhorod (1917). A founding member of the Ruthenian People's party (1920–4), in 1922 he established and directed the State Commercial Academy in Uzhhorod (moved to Mukachiv in 1926), an institution which trained and educated an entire generation of Ukrainophile students in that region. He retained that post until 1938, after which he served as minister of educational and religious affairs in the republic of Carpatho-Ukraine. With the fall of the state to the Hungarians he fled to Bratislava, where he was director of the Ukrainian Academy of Commerce (1939–40) and the Ukrainian Gymnasium in Prague (1940–5). He oversaw the evacuation of the school to Augsburg, Germany, where he directed it in 1945–9, and then emigrated to the United States, where he taught at a Ukrainian Catholic academy for girls until 1969.

Shtefan was a leading Ukrainophile community figure in Transcarpathia. He was a cofounder of the Prosvita and Teachers' Hromada societies in the region, head of a municipal cultural-educational council for the town of Mukachiv, editor of the newspaper *Rusyn* (1921–3), and coeditor of the journals *Pidkarpats'ka Rus'* (1924–38), *Uchytel's'kyi holos* (1930–9), and *Zemlia i volia* (1934–8), the organ of the Ukrainian wing of the Czechoslovak Agrarian party. He was a long-standing member of the presidium of the Ukrainian (Ruthenian) National Council of Transcarpathia and (in addition to his ministerial duties) president of the Carpatho-Ukrainian Diet. He took an active role in émigré politics and served as deputy premier of the Government-in-exile of the UNR. He also wrote extensively; his major works include *From Carpatho-Ruthenia to Carpatho-Ukraine* (1969), *Avhustyn Voloshyn, prezydent Karpats'koï Ukraïny* (Avhustyn Voloshyn, President of Carpatho-Ukraine, 1977), and *Za pravdu i voliu: Spomyny i deshcho z istoriï Karpats'koï Ukraïny* (For Justice and Freedom: Memoirs and Some of the History of Carpatho-Ukraine, 2 vols, 1973, 1981).

Shtein, Leonid [Štejn], b 12 November 1934 in Kamianets-Podilskyi, d 4 July 1973 in Lviv. Chess grand master. After settling in Lviv following the Second World War, he joined the city's new chess club and studied the game with O. Sokolsky. In 1960 and 1962 he won the chess championship of Ukraine, and in 1964 and 1965, the USSR championship. He took second place at international tournaments in Mar del Plata in 1966 and Kislovodsk in 1967, first and second place at Sarajevo in 1967 and Las Palmas in 1972, and first place at the grand master tournament in Moscow in 1967, Pärnu in 1971, and Zagreb in 1972. E. Lazarev wrote a biography about him in 1980.

Shteingel, Teodor [Štejngel'], b 1870 in Horodok, Rivne county, Volhynia gubernia, d 1946 in Dresden. Political and cultural leader and diplomat. A graduate of Kiev University, he set up a school, hospital, co-operative, and reading room in Horodok, as well as a museum (1902) to house his valuable archeological, historical, and ethnographic collections. He excavated burial sites of the medieval period in Rivne county. Although he was a Russian baron, he supported the Ukrainian national movement. In

Teodor Shteingel

Vasilii Shternberg (self-portrait)

1906 he served as deputy from Kiev to the First State Duma, where he joined the Ukrainian caucus. He was a member of the Society of Ukrainian Progressives and vice-president of the Kiev Scientific Society. After the February Revolution of 1917 he chaired the executive committee of the Kiev City Duma, the precursor of the Central Rada. In 1918 the Hetman government sent him as a diplomatic envoy to Berlin. He returned to live in Western Ukraine during the interwar era but left for Germany in 1939.

Shtendera, Yevhen [Štendera, Jevhen] (nom de guerre: Prirva), b 2 January 1924 in Galicia. Librarian and journalist. From 1943 he fought in the ranks of the UPA as captain of the Danyliv Tactical Sector (1945–7) and commander of the raid into Eastern Prussia (1948). After making his way to West Germany he studied at the Ukrainian Free University (1949) and was coeditor of *Do zbroï* (1950–6), *Suchasna Ukraïna* (1951–6), *Ukraïns'kyi samostiinyk* (1953–6), and *Rozbudova* (1956–7). He emigrated to Canada in 1956, where he studied library science at the University of Alberta (1959–73) and coedited *Ukraïns'ki visti* (1957–64). Since 1976 he has been managing editor of the multivolume *Litopys UPA* (Chronicle of the UPA).

Shtepa, Anton [Štepa], b 22 September 1903 in Svarychivka, Borzna county, Chernihiv gubernia. Wood carver. He made liras and banduras and carved thematic sculptures, such as *The Kobzar Was Going to Kiev and Sat Down to Rest* (1966), *Lirnyk* (1968), and *Partisans* (1974), and bas-reliefs, including some inspired by T. Shevchenko's poetry. A catalog of his work was published in 1976.

Shtepa, Kostiantyn [Štepa, Kostjantyn] (Shteppa, Konstantin), b 15 December 1896 in Lokhvytsia, Poltava gubernia, d 19 November 1958 in New York. Ancient and medieval historian. He studied at the Poltava Theological Seminary (1910–14), Petrograd University (1914–16), and the Nizhen Historical-Philological Institute and received a doctorate in 1927. He was a professor at the Nizhen Institute of People's Education (1922–30) and Kiev University (1930–8). In the 1930s he was also the chairman of the VUAN Byzantological Commission. He was imprisoned by the NKVD in 1938–9. During the German occupation he was briefly rector of Kiev University and then editor of Kiev's *Novoe russkoe slovo* (1941–3). A postwar refugee, he taught Russian at the US Army school in Oberammergau (1950–2) and served on the Council of the Institute for the Study of the USSR in Munich. In 1952 he emigrated to the United States, where he worked as an analyst for the American Committee for Liberation. Shtepa wrote books in Ukrainian on ancient and Christian demonology (2 vols, 1926–7) and peasant revolts in the Roman Empire (1934); in Russian on slave revolutions in the ancient world (1941) and the Soviet system of governing the masses and its psychological consequences (pseud: V. Lagodin, 1951); and in English, titled *Russian Purge and the Extraction of Confession* (pseud: W. Godin, with F. Beck, 1951) and *Russian Historians and the Soviet State* (1962). He also wrote articles in Ukrainian on ancient religious syncretism in relation to early Ukrainian folk motifs (1927), the persecution of witches in Ukraine (1928), and Ukrainian legends about the creation of the first people (1928).

Shtepa, Pavlo [Štepa], b 12 September 1897 in Novodmytriivska Stanytsia, Kuban region, d 2 March 1980 in Toronto. Engineer and political activist; full member of the Shevchenko Scientific Society. A graduate of the Kuban Technical School (1919), he took part in the liberation struggle in the Kuban and then emigrated to Prague. After specializing in agronomy at the Ukrainian Husbandry Institute (1925–7) he emigrated to Canada in 1927. There he contributed to *Novyi shliakh* and served as vice-president of the Ukrainian War Veterans' Association of Canada. He wrote a number of publicistic works, including *Ukraïnets' a moskvyn* (What's a Ukrainian and What's a Muscovite, 1959), *Moskovstvo* (Muscoviteness, 1968), and *Mafiia* (Mafia, 1971), as well as two specialized Ukrainian dictionaries.

Shternberg, Vasilii [Šternberg, Vasilij], b 12 February 1818 in St Petersburg, d 8 November 1845 in Rome. Russian painter. A graduate of the St Petersburg Academy of Arts, during a three-year stay in Ukraine (1836–9) he did many Ukrainian landscapes and genre scenes (eg, the lithograph *Market in Ichnia*, 1836; the painting *Windmills in the Steppe*, 1836). A friend of T. *Shevchenko, he made the frontispiece etching to the poet's *Kobzar* (1840) and drew several portraits of him. Shevchenko dedicated his poems 'Ivan Pidkova' and 'Na nezabud'' (Don't Forget) to Shternberg.

Shtets, Mykola [Štec'], b 16 March 1932 in Habura, Humenné county, Slovakia. Ukrainian linguist in the Prešov region. A graduate of Kiev University (candidate's diss, 1964), he has taught Ukrainian phonetics and historical grammar in the department of Ukrainian language and literature at the Prešov Philosophical Faculty of Košice University since 1959. He became department head in 1968 and faculty dean in 1976. He has written several articles on the Ukrainian dialects in the Prešov region and Transcarpathia, the local literary language, and Ukrainian-Slovak comparative grammar and linguistic relations; a popular booklet (with Yu. Bacha and A. Kovach) on Ukrainians in Czechoslovakia (1967); and a monograph on the post-1918 literary language of the Ukrainians in Transcarpathia and eastern Slovakia (1969).

Shtilman, Illia [Štil'man, Illja], b 3 December 1902 in Kiev, d 11 August 1966 in Kiev. Painter and educator. In 1927 he graduated from the Kiev State Art Institute, where he studied under F. Krychevsky and M. Burachek. He subsequently taught there (1933–64) and served as its director (1940–4). He painted landscapes and genre paintings, such as *Seamstresses* (1927), the series 'The Dnieper Dresses in Granite' (1936–7), *Collective-Farm Field* (1950), *The Storm Approaches* (1951), and *Sedniv Vistas* (1966).

Andrii Shtoharenko   Dmytro Shtohryn

Shtoharenko, Andrii [Štoharenko, Andrij], b 15 October 1902 in Novi Kaidaky, now part of Dnipropetrovske. Composer and pedagogue. In 1912 he entered the Russian Musical Society's music school in Katerynoslav. He organized his own orchestra in Dnipropetrovske during the 1920s and taught singing in high schools. Shtoharenko was recruited in 1930 to study composition with S. Bohatyrov at the Kharkiv Conservatory. He graduated in 1936 and gained immediate recognition with the symphonic cantata *Pro kanal's'ki roboty* (About the Canal Work, 1936). He occupied several key administrative positions in the musical hierarchy of the Ukrainian SSR. In 1944 he became vice-chairman of the Union of Composers of Ukraine, and in 1948–54 he was vice-chairman of the USSR Union of Composers. In 1954–68 he was a teacher of composition and rector of the Kiev Conservatory. In 1968 he became head of the Faculty of Composition there and head of the Union of Composers of Ukraine. Shtoharenko's works include the symphonic cantata *Ukraïno moia* (My Ukraine, 1943), the *Kiev Symphony* (1972), symphonic suites, a violin concerto, chamber and choral pieces, songs, incidental music, and film scores. His biography, by M. Borovyk, was published in Kiev in 1965.

Shtohryn, Dmytro [Štohryn], b 9 November 1923 in Zvyniach, Chortkiv county, Galicia. Librarian and educator; full member of the Shevchenko Scientific Society. After emigrating to the United States in 1950, he completed his studies in Ukrainian literature and library science at the University of Ottawa (PH D, 1970). From 1960 he served as the Slavic cataloger at the library of the University of Illinois at Urbana–Champaign. In 1961 he was appointed associate of the university's Russian and East European Center, where he has organized annual Ukrainian studies conferences. He has lectured on Ukrainian literature since 1970 and served as president of the Ukrainian Librarians' Association of America in 1970–8. He reprinted *Kataloh vydan' Ukraïns'koï akademiï nauk, 1918–1930* (Catalog of Publications of the Ukrainian Academy of Sciences, 1918–30, 1966), wrote *Svitla i tini ukraïns'kykh studii v Harvardi* (Lights and Shadows of Ukrainian Studies at Harvard, 1973), and edited the biographical guide *Ukrainians in North America* (1975).

Zinovii Shtokalko   Yosyp Shtokalo

Shtokalko, Zinovii [Štokalko, Zinovij], b 25 May 1920 in Berezhany, Galicia, d 28 June 1968 in New York. Bandura virtuoso, composer, and writer. A medical doctor by profession, he studied music with the bandurysts B. Klevchutsky and Yu. Singalevych (Lviv). He improved bandura playing techniques and developed his own distinct style of interpretation. He also acquired one of the most valuable collections of *dumas outside Ukraine. Shtokalko's legacy includes independent works for bandura ('Atonal Etude' and others); a large methodological study of the instrument, published posthumously as *A Kobzar Handbook* (1989); and a definitive recording of dumas and other Ukrainian songs (recorded for M. Surmach in New York, 1952). His literary works appeared under the pen name Zinovii Berezhan in the posthumous collection *Na okraïnakh nochi* (On the Edges of Night, 1977).

Shtokalo, Yosyp [Štokalo, Josyp], b 16 November 1897 in Skomorokhy, Sokal county, Galicia, d 5 January 1987 in Kiev. Mathematician and science historian; full member of the AN URSR (now ANU) since 1951. After graduating from the Dnipropetrovske Institute of People's Education in 1931, he taught at Kharkiv University and other higher schools. He worked in Kiev at the ANU Institute of Mathematics (1942–9, 1956–63) and Kiev University (1944–51, 1956–72), chaired the presidium of the Lviv branch of the ANU (1949–56), and headed the natural sciences and technology section of the ANU Institute of History (from 1963). Shtokalo's works deal with differential equations, operational calculus, the history of mathematics, and Ukrainian terminology in various sciences. After 1945 he became particularly interested in the qualitative and stability theory of solutions of systems of linear ordinary differential equations in the Liapunov sense and in the 1940s and 1950s published a series of articles and three monographs in these areas. He is regarded as one of the founders of the history of Soviet mathematics, and particularly of the his-

tory of Ukrainian mathematics. In addition to articles on mathematics in Ukraine and articles about M. Ostrohradsky and H. Vorony, he edited the three-volume collections of Vorony's (1952–3) and Ostrohradsky's (1959–61) works, a Russian-Ukrainian mathematical dictionary (1960), and approx 18 other Russian-Ukrainian terminology dictionaries. He was the editor (with O. Boholiubov and A. Yushkevych as associates) of the four-volume *Istoriia otechestvennoi matematiki* (A History of the Fatherland's Mathematics, 1966–70), for which he and his associates received the prestigious A. Koyré award from the International Academy of the History of Sciences in 1970.

W. Petryshyn

Shtoliuk, Myron [Štoljuk] (aka Shtola), b ? in Roztoky, near Kolomyia, Galicia, d 2 June 1830 in Vyzhnytsia, Bukovyna. Rebel leader. After deserting the Austrian army in 1817, Shtoliuk led a band of Hutsul *opryshoks that attacked noble estates in Pokutia and Bukovyna. He was captured in 1829, tortured in prison, and then tried and hanged. Folk songs and legends about him were collected and published by I. Franko and others.

Shtolko, Valentyn [Štol'ko], b 14 November 1931 in Viknyna, now in Haisyn raion, Kirovohrad oblast. Architect. A graduate of the Kiev State Art Institute (1956), he collaborated in designing the Tarasova Hora Hotel in Kaniv (1962), the Turyst Hotel in Cherkasy (1967), the Hradetskyi Hotel in Chernihiv (1980), pavilions at the Exhibition of the Achievements of the National Economy in Kiev (1977, 1979), the Podil Covered Market in Kiev (1980), and the covered market in Chernivtsi (1981). He has written articles on architectural problems and a book on the architecture of constructions with hanging roofs (1979).

Oleh Shtul   Dmytro Shtykalo

Shtul, Oleh [Štul'] (pseuds: O. Zhdanovych, O. Shuliak), b 1 July 1917 in Lopatychi, Ovruch county, Volhynia gubernia, d 4 November 1977 in Toronto. Political activist, publicist, and editor. He studied philology and history at Warsaw University (1934–9). From 1939 he was active in the cultural arm of the Leadership of Ukrainian Nationalists (PUN), in which he collaborated closely with O. Olzhych, served as cultural representative for the OUN executive in the Generalgouvernement, and represented central Ukrainian territories in the Central Executive of the OUN (1941–3). From 1941 he participated in the OUN expeditionary groups, and in 1942 he began training partisan cadres in Volhynia. In 1943 he was proxy for the OUN colonel A. Melnyk at the UPA Polisian Sich under T. Borovets (later the Ukrainian People's Revolutionary Army) and coeditor of its organ *Oborona Ukraïny*. Shtul was imprisoned by the Germans in the Sachsenhausen concentration camp in 1943–4. He remained as an émigré in Germany and Austria after 1945. Continuing his activities as a journalist and publicist, he contributed to several OUN publications, *Za samostiinist'*, *Orlyk*, and the weekly *Promin'*. In 1948 he moved to Paris, where he edited the weekly *Ukraïns'ke slovo* until 1977. He was also press and information secretary for PUN (member from 1955) and later became its vice-president (1964) and president (until his death). Shtul was an active member of the Ukrainian National Alliance in France and the Ukrainian Orthodox parish in Paris, as well as head of the controlling commission of the Shevchenko Scientific Society in Europe in 1966–77.

Apart from his many articles he wrote the surveys of Ukrainian history *Viky hovoriat'* (The Ages Speak, 1940, 1941, 1954), *V im'ia pravdy* (In the Name of Truth, 1947, 1948, 1991), about the origins and actions of the UPA, and *Na zov Kyieva* (Heeding the Call of Kiev, 1977), about the life and works of O. Teliha, and edited the anthology *Olena Teliha* (1977). Shtul was buried in South Bound Brook, New Jersey. Memoirs about him and a selection of his articles were published by the Shevchenko Scientific Society in Europe under the title *Paryzh Olehovi Shtulevi* (Paris to Oleh Shtul, 1986).

A. Zhukovsky

Shtykalo, Dmytro [Štykalo], b 7 November 1909 in Ilkovychi, Sokal county, Galicia, d 4 November 1963 in Munich. Journalist and political activist. As a law student at Lviv University he was active in student organizations and the OUN: he headed the Union of Ukrainian Student Organizations under Poland (1932–3) and contributed articles on ideological and political issues to nationalist periodicals, such as *Students'kyi shliakh* and *Nash klych*. He was arrested several times and imprisoned in *Bereza Kartuzka for two years (1934–6). After joining the Bandera faction of the OUN, during the Second World War he edited its underground publications and the broadcasts of the OUN-UPA radio station in the Carpathian Mountains. After the war he directed a Ukrainian radio program in Madrid and coedited the nationalist periodicals *Ukraïnets'-Chas* in Paris, *Vyzvol'nyi shliakh* in London, and *Ukraïns'kyi samostiinyk* and *Shliakh peremohy* in Munich. Of his poems, the duma on Bereza Kartuzka (1938) was the most popular.

Shubenko-Shubin, Leonid [Šubenko-Šubin], b 7 August 1907 in Kars, Turkey. Specialist in energetics; full member of the ANU (formerly AN URSR) since 1967. He graduated from Leningrad University (1930) and the Leningrad Boiler Turbine Institute (1931). He became director of the Central Boiler Turbine Scientific Research Institute in Leningrad (1944–50) and worked as chief designer at the Kharkiv Turbine Plant (1950–67) and the ANU Institute for Problems of Machine Building (from 1968). He contributed to the fields of steam and gas turbines, the optimization of processes and construction, and automated design.

Lev Shubnikov

Shubnikov, Lev [Šubnikov], b 29 September 1901 in St Petersburg, d 8 November 1945 in a Gulag labor camp. Experimental low-temperature physicist. A graduate of the Leningrad Polytechnical Institute (1926), from 1926 to 1930 he worked at the Cryogenic Laboratory in Leiden, Holland, where he distinguished himself as a crystal grower. Using his high-purity bismuth monocrystals, the low-temperature quantum oscillation of electrical magnetoresistance (now known as the Shubnikov–de Haas effect) was discovered in 1930. In 1930 he joined the Ukrainian Physical-Technical Institute in Kharkiv, and in 1931 he became director of its cryogenic laboratory, the first such laboratory in the USSR. From 1934 to 1937 a number of breakthrough discoveries were made by Shubnikov and his collaborators: the full diamagnetism of superconductors, the transition from the paramagnetic to the antiferromagnetic state (1934), the existence of two critical fields in superconducting alloys (1935), and the detailed conditions for the breakdown of superconductivity (1936). In 1935 Shubnikov also assumed the chair of solid-state physics at Kharkiv University. After L. *Landau was dismissed from Kharkiv University on trumped-up political charges in December 1936 and subsequently arrested, Shubnikov wrote a letter of protest to the university rector and resigned. He was arrested by the NKVD in August 1937 on fabricated charges of espionage and sentenced to 10 years' imprisonment. Attempts by the Soviet physicist P. Kapitsa to obtain his release (he succeeded in obtaining a release for Landau) remained fruitless, and Shubnikov died in a labor camp. He was posthumously rehabilitated in 1957. A book containing his selected works and memoirs about him was published in Kiev in 1989.

O. Bilaniuk

Shuhaievsky, Valentyn [Šuhajevs'kyj], b 15 April 1884 in Kiev, d 2 November 1966 in the United States. Historian, numismatist, and archeologist. He graduated from the St Petersburg Archeological Institute (1908) and was appointed to the position of department director at the Chernihiv Museum of Ukrainian Antiquities (1917, now the Chernihiv Historical Museum). He became director of the numismatic collections at the All-Ukrainian Museum Quarter on the grounds of the Kievan Cave Monastery (1919) and the Kiev Historical Museum. He was a professor of numismatics at Kiev University and a senior associate of the Kiev Institute of Archeology. During the Second World War he worked in museums in Lviv, Sambir, and Prague. He emigrated from Germany to the United States in 1949, where he became an assistant director of the Ukrainian desk at the Voice of America. Shuhaievsky's brochures describe coins discovered in Chernihiv gubernia (1915), coins and currency in 17th-century Left-Bank Ukraine (1918), the collection and preservation of monuments of antiquity (1920), coins and currency in 17th-century Ukraine (1924, 1926, 1928, 1951 1952), 18th-century Chernihiv (1927), and the Cossack figure Yu. Dunin-Borkovsky (1925, 1928).

Hermina Shukhevych

Iryna Shukhevych: *Portrait of Marta Rozhankovska* (oil)

Shukhevych, Hermina [Šukhevyč] (née Liubovych), b 1852 in Peremyshl, d 1939 in Lviv. Women's leader and civic activist; wife of V. *Shukhevych. She was a founder of a number of women's organizations in Lviv: the *Club of Ruthenian Women (which she also headed), the *Trud women's co-operative, and the *Ukrainska Zakhoronka society. She also served as director of the St Olha Institute for Girls. She helped her husband organize the ethnographic march to the Vysokyi Zamok in 1887 and the Ukrainian ethnographic section at the Lviv Exhibition of 1894.

Shukhevych, Iryna [Šuxevyč] (née Velychkovska), b 21 November 1885 in Vyshniv, Rohatyn county, Galicia, d 17 February 1979 in Stamford, Connecticut. Portrait and icon painter. She studied painting in Lviv and Cracow (1911–12) and painted the murals of village churches in Galicia, first with M. *Sosenko and then alone. She was a member of the Zarevo art society in Cracow and the Ukrainian Association of Artists in Lviv. A postwar émigré, from 1950 she lived in the United States. Her icons can be found in churches in Galicia, Bukovyna, Rome, and the United States.

Shukhevych, Osyp [Šuxevyč], b 4 January 1816 in Rakiv, Stryi circle, d 1870 in Tyshkivtsi, Horodenka county, Galicia. Priest, writer, and translator; father of V. *Shukhevych. As a student at the Greek Catholic Theological Seminary in Lviv (1835–8) he became a member of the circle headed by the *Ruthenian Triad. From 1848 he was parish priest in Tyshkivtsi. In the years 1848–9 he translated into the Galician dialect of Ukrainian works by W. Scott, Virgil, and J.G. von Herder. An edition of Shukhevych's translations, with an introduction by I. Franko, was published in 1883 by his son.

Gen Roman Shukhevych (portrait)

Shukhevych, Roman [Šuxevyč] (noms de guerre: Dzvin, Shchuka, Tur, Taras Chuprynka, R. Lozovsky), b 17 July 1907 in Krakovets, Yavoriv county, Galicia, d 5 March 1950 in Bilohorshcha, near Lviv. Supreme commander of the *Ukrainian Insurgent Army, head of the OUN Home Leadership, chairman of the General Secretariat of the *Ukrainian Supreme Liberation Council (UHVR), and its general secretary for military affairs. He joined the Ukrainian Military Organization in 1923 and the OUN in 1929; he was active in their combat branches and known as Dzvin. In 1926 he took part in the political assassination of the Lviv school superintendent S. Sobiński. In 1930–4 he headed the OUN combat branch in Galicia and Poland. After being arrested in connection with B. *Pieracki's assassination, he was held for six months in the Bereza Kartuzka concentration camp and sentenced in 1936 to four years' imprisonment, which was reduced by an amnesty to two years'. During 1938–9 he was staff officer in the Carpathian Sich. In 1941 Shukhevych was briefly chief of the OUN (Bandera faction) in Ukrainian territories within the Generalgouvernement. He joined the Nachtigall Battalion (see *Legion of Ukrainian Nationalists) in April 1941 and became its top OUN liaison and political officer. When the Nachtigall and Roland battalions were merged in October 1941 to form Schutzmannschaftbataillon 201, Shukhevych was appointed deputy battalion commander and commander of its first company with the rank of captain. The battalion was disarmed and demobilized, and its officers were arrested in January 1943. Shukhevych, however, managed to escape and join the UPA. At the Third OUN Congress on 25 August, he was confirmed as head of the OUN Home Leadership, and in November he was appointed supreme commander of the UPA in the rank of lieutenant colonel. The UHVR elected him on 15 July 1944 to head its General Secretariat and to hold the portfolio of military affairs, and confirmed his appointment to the top post in the UPA. In 1946 he was promoted to brigadier general.

Shukhevych died in combat with special units of the MVD. Posthumously, he was awarded the UPA's highest decorations: the Gold Cross of Combat Merit First Class and the Cross of Merit in gold.

BIBLIOGRAPHY
Ianiv, V. *Shukhevych-Chuprynka: Liudyna i symvol* (Munich 1950)
Kravtsiv, B. *Liudyna i voiak* (New York 1952)
Mirchuk, P. *Roman Shukhevych* (New York 1970)

P. Sodol

Stepan Shukhevych

Volodymyr Shukhevych

Shukhevych, Stepan [Šuxevyč], b 1 January 1877 in Serafyntsi, Horodenka county, Galicia, d 6 June 1945 in Amberg, Germany. Lawyer and civic activist. During the First World War he commanded a regiment of the Ukrainian Sich Riflemen (1914–15) and then (1919) the Fourth (Zolochiv) Brigade and was in the Supreme Command of the Ukrainian Galician Army. In 1920 he returned to Lviv and opened a law office, and thenceforth often defended members of the *Ukrainian Military Organization and the OUN. For many years he chaired the audit committee of the *Chervona Kalyna publishing house, which he helped organize. He wrote short stories and a book of memoirs (1919).

Shukhevych, Volodymyr [Šuxevyč], b 15 March 1849 in Tyshkivtsi, Kolomyia circle, Galicia, d 10 April 1915 in Lviv. Ethnographer, civic leader, educator, and publicist; full member of the Shevchenko Scientific Society from 1908. After graduating from Lviv University he taught secondary school in Lviv. He founded several educational societies, such as Ruska (*Ukrainska) Besida, which he headed in 1895–1910, the *Boian society (1891), and the *Lysenko Music Society in Lviv, which he headed in 1903–15. He served on the executive of the Prosvita society. He founded and edited the journals *Dzvinok* (1890–5) and *Uchytel'* (1893–1905) and edited the newspaper *Zerkalo*. Many of his articles appeared in *Zoria* and *Dilo*. He wrote a chemistry textbook (1884) and compiled several anthologies for school use. On his expeditions to the Hutsul and other regions he collected ethnographic materials and also

valuable museum pieces, which he donated to the National Museum in Lviv. In 1902–8 he was custodian of the Dzieduszycki Museum, at which he set up a natural science and ethnographic section. In 1894 he organized an ethnographic section at the Provincial Exhibition in Lviv. Shukhevych's major work, which is unsurpassed to this day, is his five-volume ethnographic and folkloric study *Huculszczyzna* (The Hutsul Region, 1899–1908; in Polish, 4 vols, 1902–8), which propagated knowledge about the Hutsul folk life.

M. Mushynka

Yurii Shukhevych

Shukhevych, Yurii [Šuxevyč, Jurij], b 28 March 1933 in Lviv county, Galicia. Soviet political prisoner; son of R. *Shukhevych. In 1945, after his mother had been sentenced to 10 years in labor camps, he and his sister were sent to orphanages in Chornobyl and then Staline (now Donetske). He was first arrested in August 1948, simply because he was his father's son, and was sentenced to 10 years in the Vladimir prison near Moscow. In April 1956 he was officially recognized as unjustly persecuted and released, but intervention by the Soviet procurator general, R. Rudenko, resulted in his rearrest in the fall of that year and his return to Vladimir prison. The day his 10-year term ended in 1958, he was again arrested on fabricated charges of spreading 'anti-Soviet agitation and propaganda' among his fellow inmates; he was tried in Lviv, and sentenced in December of that year to 10 years in labor camps in the Mordovian ASSR. There he participated in hunger strikes to protest the unlawful acts of the camp authorities, and in July 1967 he wrote a letter of protest to the chairman of the Presidium of the Ukrainian Supreme Soviet. When he was released in August 1968, he was forbidden to live in Ukraine for five years, and he settled in Nalchik in the Kabardino-Balkar ASSR, where he worked as an electrician. In March 1972, during the wave of arrests among the intelligentsia in Ukraine, he was arrested a third time, for compiling his prison memoirs, and sentenced to nine years in labor camps and five years' exile. In 1973, while in a Mordovian camp, he was arrested a fourth time, for writing a document in his own defense, and resentenced to 10 years in prison and 5 years' exile. Until 1978 he served his term in Vladimir, and then he was transferred to the prison in Chistopol, in the Tatar ASSR.

During his imprisonment Shukhevych demanded reviews of his case, participated in campaigns for the official recognition of political-prisoner status, and sought the right to leave the USSR. In 1979 he renounced his Soviet citizenship and joined the *Ukrainian Helsinki Group. In March 1982 he was exiled to Tomsk oblast, in Siberia. Altogether Shukhevych was subjected to 35 years of incarceration and exile for refusing to denounce his father and the Ukrainian liberation movement. As a result he was often seriously ill; in 1982 he completely lost his sight. In 1981 the US Congress passed a resolution calling for his release and for permission for him to emigrate, and about 200 Canadian mayors and members of Parliament also spoke out on his behalf. In February 1982 he was declared 'prisoner of the month' by Amnesty International, and in August 1986, 40 US senators signed a petition to M. Gorbachev calling for his release. In 1989 he was finally allowed to return to Ukraine, where he has remained politically active.

BIBLIOGRAPHY
Shukhevych, Iu. 'Holovi Prezydiï VR URSR,' *U pivstolittia radians'koï vlady* (Paris 1968)
Iurii Shukhevych: Son of a Ukrainian General (Smoloskyp 1973)
Sorokowski, A. 'Guilty by Birth,' *Barrister*, 7, no. 1 (1980)
                                                        O. Zinkevych

Shul, Andrii [Šul', Andrij] (Szul, Andrij), b 21 August 1944 in Neutitschein, Germany. Musicologist, educator, and conductor; son of R. *Smerechynska-Shul. He studied piano in New York with R. Savytsky (1952–4) and at the Juilliard School of Music (1954–62). He obtained a PH D in musicology at the Ukrainian Free University in 1971 with a dissertation on the choral style of D. Bortniansky's 35 sacred concertos. Shul's writings include *Tvorchist' Dmytra Bortnian's'koho: Krytychnyi ohliad* (The Works of Dmytro Bortniansky: A Critical Survey, 1980), and miscellaneous articles and reviews. In 1972 he was appointed staff editor of Ukrainian studies for the *Repértoire International de Littérature Musicale* (RILM Abstracts) in Pennsylvania. He has also appeared as a pianist and entertainer on American radio, television, and stage.

Shulaivskyi camp site. A multi-occupational Neolithic Surskyi-Dnieper culture settlement (6th millennium BC) on Shulaivskyi Island in the Dnieper River near Zvonetske, Solone raion, Dnipropetrovske oblast. Excavations in 1946 revealed the remains of pit-houses, stone tools (including some for woodworking), microlithic flint pieces, wild and domestic animal bones, and pottery fragments.

Shulezhko, Pavlo [Šuležko] (Shuleshko, Paul), b 28 June 1902 in Zolotonosha, Poltava gubernia, d 8 July 1984 in San Francisco. Mechanical engineer, physicist, and mathematician; full member of the Shevchenko Scientific Society from 1960. He studied in Poltava and Kharkiv, worked as an engineer in Kharkiv (1928–38), and taught at Kharkiv University (1938–42). As a postwar émigré he was a professor at the Ukrainian Technical and Husbandry Institute in Regensburg, Germany (1945–9), the University of New South Wales in Australia (1953–9), and the Rochester Institute of Technology in Rochester, New York (1960–73). His main contributions were in the areas of the strength of materials and boundary-value problems. He wrote over 100 technical papers and several books, including books in Ukrainian on theoretical mechanics (1947) and the strength of materials (1947). In 1958–9 he headed the Australian chapter of the Shevchenko Scientific Society.

Pavlo Shulezhko   Illia Shulha

Shulgin, Vasilii [Šul'gin, Vasilij], b 13 January 1878 in Kiev, d 15 February 1976 in Vladimir, RSFSR. Russian conservative political leader and publicist. A graduate of the law faculty at Kiev University (1900), he was a deputy from Volhynia to the Second and Fourth Russian State Dumas. Before the First World War he was a leading member of the Ukrainophobic *Kiev Club of Russian Nationalists and editor (1913–19) of the reactionary newspaper *Kievlianin. An opponent of the UNR, during the Russian Civil War he was an ideologue of the White forces and one of the founders of the Russian Volunteer Army in the Don region and the Kuban. In 1920 he fled abroad, and in the 1920s, while living in Yugoslavia, France, and Poland, he was a leading figure among the White émigrés. He published several books in the West, including the anti-Ukrainian diatribes *Ukrainstvuiushchie i my!* (The Ukrainianizers and We!, 1929) and *Le plus grand mensonge du XXe siècle: L'Ukraine* (1939), as well as several anti-Semitic tracts.

His strong sense of Russian nationalism led him to accept the Soviet state as the continuation of the Russian Empire, and he appreciated the Soviet leadership's ability to control the various nationalities, especially the Ukrainians. In 1961 he published an open letter urging Russian émigrés to stop criticizing the Soviet Union. His memoirs of the 1917 Revolution (1925), of the year 1920 (1927), and of his time in the State Duma (1979) were published in Moscow; the last appeared in English translation as *The Years: Memoirs of a Member of the Russian Duma, 1906–1917* (1984).

Shulgin, Vitalii [Šul'gin, Vitalij], b 1822 in Kaluga, Russia, d 1878 in Kiev. Publicist and pedagogue. He grew up in Nizhen and studied (1838) and taught history at Kiev University (1849–62). In 1863 he founded the ultraconservative, anti-Ukrainian newspaper *Kievlianin (which he edited until his death). His writings include the monograph *Iugo-Zapadnyi krai v poslednee 25-letie (1838–1863)* (The Southwestern Land [Ukraine] in the Past 25 Years [1838–63], 1863), numerous publicistic works, and a series of history textbooks. They are characterized by a strong pro-Russian bias.

Shulha, Illia [Šul'ha, Illja], b 20 July 1878 in Kropyvna, Zolotonosha county, Poltava gubernia, d 19 December

1938 in Petropavlovsk, Kazakhstan. Realist painter. He graduated from the Kiev Drawing School (1899), the Moscow School of Painting, Sculpture, and Architecture (1903), and the St Petersburg Academy of Arts (1909), where he studied under I. Repin. He taught art in Vinnytsia (1910–19), Zolotonosha, and Kiev (1928–38; from 1934 at the Kiev State Art Institute). He produced over 1,000 impressionist and realist works. They included historical paintings, such as *Col Dzhedzhalii and His Regiment Entering Kropyvna* (1913) and *Cossack Scouts* (1916); genre scenes, such as *Young Women at Home* (1918), *Blessing of the Water* (1914); landscapes, such as *Church in Vinnytsia* (1913) and *Winter in the Woods* (1937); and portraits, including ones of his wife (1906) and T. Shevchenko (1926) and self-portraits (1928, 1936). He was arrested by the NKVD in March 1938 and died after a few months of imprisonment. His life is documented in an article by Yu. Slastion in *Vyzvol'nyi shliakh* (1961, nos 9–10).

Ivan Shulha: *Portrait of a Girl in a Green Kerchief* (oil, 1917)

Shulha, Ivan [Šul'ha], b 31 October 1889 in Mykhailivka, Oleshky county, Tavriia gubernia, d 23 April 1956 in Kiev. Painter. He studied at the Odessa Art School (1906–11) under K. Kostandi and at the St Petersburg Academy of Arts (1911–17). From 1922 he lived in Kharkiv, and in the 1920s he was a member of the *Association of Artists of Red Ukraine. During the period 1919–21 he painted propaganda posters and wall panels. His work consists mainly of historical and genre paintings, such as *The Cossacks Are Leaving* (1909), *Cossack Campaign* (1915–17), *The Lena Executions* (1926), *Collective Fish Farm* (1932), *T. Shevchenko's Meeting with I. Soshenko* (1938), *Cossack Song* (1945), and *The Pereiaslav Council* (1951). A catalog of his posthumous exhibition was published in 1962.

Shulha, Pelaheia [Šul'ha, Pelaheja], b 30 October 1899 in Viazivok, Cherkasy county, Kiev gubernia, d 7 September 1986 in Kiev. Geologist. She graduated from the Kiev Institute of People's Education (1929) and was a scholarly associate of the AN URSR (now ANU) Institute of Geological Sciences in 1930–76 (department head, 1950–62). Her main research interest was sediment formations in Ukraine. She wrote *Paleontologiia i stratigrafiia verkhnego dokembriia i nizhnego paleozoia iugo-zapada Vostochno-Evropeiskoi platformy* (The Paleontology and Stratigraphy of the Late Precambrian and Early Paleozoic in the Southwestern Part of the East European Platform, 1976).

Oleksander Shulhyn

Shulhyn, Oleksander [Šul'hyn] (Choulguine, Alexandre), b 30 July 1889 in Sokhvyne, Poltava gubernia, d 4 March 1960 in Paris. Political leader, community and cultural activist, historian, and sociologist; full member of the Shevchenko Scientific Society from 1948 and of the Ukrainian Academy of Arts and Sciences; son of Ya. *Shulhyn. He studied history and philosophy at St Petersburg University (1908–15) and worked there until 1917. He joined the St Petersburg branch of the Society of Ukrainian Progressives and became a member of the CC of the Ukrainian Democratic Radical party (UDRP) and a delegate to the Soviet of Workers' and Soldiers' Deputies.

Returning to Kiev after the February Revolution, Shulhyn was elected to the Central Rada and its Little Rada. From July 1917 to 30 January 1918 he served as general secretary for nationality (later international) affairs. He was a coauthor of the *Statute of the Higher Administration of Ukraine and a co-organizer of the Congress of the Peoples of Russia in Kiev (held September 1917). During his tenure as director of foreign policy Great Britain and France officially recognized the UNR, and Ukraine began peace negotiations with the Central Powers in Brest. Under the Hetman government he worked in the Ministry of External Affairs of the Ukrainian State, and from July 1918 to the end of the year he was Ukrainian ambassador to Bulgaria. In 1919 the Directory of the UNR appointed him as a delegate to the Paris Peace Conference, and in 1920 he was head of the Ukrainian delegation to the first assembly of the *League of Nations in Geneva. From 1921 he headed the UNR extraordinary diplomatic mission in Paris.

From 1923 to 1927 Shulhyn lived in Prague, where he was a professor of history and the philosophy of history at the Ukrainian Free University and the Ukrainian Higher Pedagogical Institute, and head of the Prague committee of the renewed UDRP. In 1926 he became minister of external affairs of the *Government-in-exile of the UNR and director of its foreign policy (1926–36, 1939–40, and 1945–6).

In 1927 Shulhyn moved to Paris. There he served as head of the *Supreme Emigration Council (1929–39), head of the UNR government-in-exile (1939–40), and coeditor of the weekly *Tryzub* (editor in 1940). From 1933 to 1938 he protested against the Bolshevik terror, forced labor, and man-made famine in the Ukrainian SSR. In an open letter to F. Nansen, published as the brochure *La Société des Nations et les réfugiés ukrainiens* (1929), he petitioned for the official recognition of Ukrainian refugees. During the German occupation Shulhyn was arrested in Paris (1940–1) as a Ukrainian pro-French political activist. After 1945 he devoted himself to scholarly work. He founded and headed the *Ukrainian Academic Society in Paris (1946–60) and initiated the *International Free Academy of Arts and Sciences (vice-president in 1952–60). He was also the Ukrainian representative in the International Refugee Organization (1948–52) and a consultant to French organizations for the protection of refugees and stateless persons (1952–60).

Shulhyn wrote a number of studies about Ukraine's struggle for *independence (1917–20) and the activities of the UNR government-in-exile, including *Polityka* (Politics, 1918), *L'Ukraine, la Russie, et les puissances de l'Entente* (1918), *Les problèmes de l'Ukraine* (1919; also in English, Dutch, and Hungarian [1920] edns), *Chronologie des principaux événements en Ukraine, 1917–19* (1919), *L'Ukraine et le cauchemar rouge: Les massacres en Ukraine* (1927), *Derzhavnist' chy Haidamachchyna?* (Statehood or Haidamaka Insurgency?, 1931), *Bez terytoriï* (Without a Territory, 1934), and *L'Ukraine contre Moscou, 1917* (1935; English trans 1959). Among his sociological and historiographic works are *Narysy z novoï istoriï Evropy* (Essays on Modern European History, 1925), *Uvahy do istoriï rozvytku ranishn'oho kapitalizmu* (Remarks on the History of the Development of Early Capitalism, 1928), *Les origines de l'esprit national moderne et J.-J. Rousseau* (1938), *L'histoire et la vie: Les lois, le hasard, la volonté humaine* (1957), and *Michel Hrouchevskyj et sa conception de l'histoire de l'Est Européen* (1959). He also contributed to émigré encyclopedias of Ukraine (*Ukraïns'ka zahal'na entsyklopediia* and *Entsyklopediia ukraïnoznavstva*) and various journals and anthologies, including *Tryzub*, *Prométhée* (1926–38), *La Revue de Prométhée* (1938–40), and *Ukraïns'ka literaturna hazeta* (1956–60). A biography of Shulhyn, in French, was edited by O. Perrin (1961), and a festschrift in his honor was edited by V. Yaniv (*ZNTSh*, no. 186 [1969]).

A. Zhukovsky

Shulhyn, Yakiv [Šul'hyn, Jakiv], b 19 February 1851 in Kiev, d 28 November 1911 in Kiev. Community activist, pedagogue, and historian; member of the Shevchenko Scientific Society. He graduated from Kiev University (1874), where he studied under V. Antonovych and M. Drahomanov. Shulhyn was an important figure in the Ukrainian cultural renaissance of the late 19th and early 20th centuries. He belonged to the Old Hromada of Kiev, and in 1876

Yakiv Shulhyn   Nadiia Shulhyna-Ishchuk

he donated his inheritance of 12,000 rubles to fund Drahomanov's emigration and the publication of *Hromada in Geneva. He continued his studies abroad (1876–7) and then taught in gymnasiums in Kiev and Odessa. Shulhyn was arrested in 1879 because of his national and cultural activities and for importing a printing press for the Old Hromada. He was exiled to Siberia for four years, and upon his return he worked in a bank in Yelysavethrad. In 1899 he returned to Kiev, where he resumed teaching, contributed to the work of the Southwestern Branch of the Imperial Russian Geographic Society, wrote articles for *Kievskaia starina*, and assisted the Vik publishing house. He was a member of the Historical Society of Nestor the Chronicler and a founding member and secretary of the Ukrainian Scientific Society in Kiev.

Later in life Shulhyn wrote articles on the history of 17th- and 18th-century Left-Bank Ukraine (1899; pub under the cryptonym 'L.Ch.'), the Koliivshchyna rebellion (1890), Right-Bank Ukraine in the mid-18th century (1891), and P. Polubotok (1890). Memoirs of him were published by M. Hrushevsky (*ZNTSh*, vol 107 [1912]) and V. Shcherbyna (*ZNTK*, vol 10 [1912]).

A. Zhukovsky

Shulhyna-Ishchuk, Nadiia [Šul'hyna-Iščuk, Nadija], b 1888 in Kiev, d 10 April 1979 in Philadelphia. Pedagogue, mathematician, and women's activist; daughter of Ya. *Shulhyn. After graduating from the Bestuzhev Courses in St Petersburg and Kiev University, she taught mathematics in secondary schools in Kiev (1913–23). Emigrating from Soviet Ukraine, she taught at the Ukrainian Higher Pedagogical Institute in Prague (1926–7) and at the Ukrainian gymnasium in Rivne (1928–44). As a postwar displaced person she emigrated to the United States in 1950. Before the First World War Shulhyna-Ishchuk was a member of the Society of School Education and contributed to the development of Ukrainian mathematical terminology and wrote the first Ukrainian-language mathematics primer in Russian-ruled Ukraine. She wrote articles on the methodology of teaching mathematics, which appeared in journals such as *Ukraïns'ka shkola*. In the United States she served as a member of the Education Commission of the World Federation of Ukrainian Women's Organizations.

Shuliar, Andrii [Šuljar, Andrij], b 15 December 1918 in Maidan, Stanyslaviv county, Galicia. Architect. A graduate of the Lviv Polytechnical Institute (1947), he took part in drawing up the general city plans for Lviv, Sokal, Chervonohrad, and Truskavets, and in the restoration of architectural monuments in Lviv and other cities. He designed the Staryi Dub restaurant in Truskavets (1979) and the village center of Vuzlove, in Lviv oblast (1982), and prepared the architectural design for over 50 monuments. He is the author of articles and books on urban planning and architectural history.

Shulte, Yurii [Šul'te, Jurij], b 30 July 1910 in Debaltseve, Bakhmut county, Katerynoslav gubernia. Metallurgist; corresponding member of the ANU (formerly AN URSR) since 1969. He graduated from the Dnipropetrovske Metallurgical Institute (1931) and worked at the Zaporizhia Dniprospetsstal Electrometallurgical Plant and the Zaporizhia Machine-Building Institute (from 1947). His main technical work is in the area of improving steel manufacturing productivity and increasing the quality of cast and forged steels.

Shumborsky, Felitsiian [Šumbors'kyj, Felicijan] (secular name: Pylyp), b 14 October 1771 in Ostrih, Volhynia, d 1851. Uniate bishop of Kholm. In 1811 he became secretary to the bishop of Kholm, F. Tsikhovsky, his first appointment in a steady rise in the ecclesiastic administration until his consecration as bishop of Kholm in 1830. Under his administration, jurisdiction over Kholm eparchy was transferred from the metropolitan of Halych to the Vatican, and the eparchy's ties to the rest of the Ukrainian Catholic church were thereby cut. At the same time Shumborsky was pressured to convert to Orthodoxy by the Russian church and authorities, and he was summoned to St Petersburg in 1840 by Tsar Nicholas I. He resisted these pressures, but the eparchy was finally converted in 1875. A biography of him was published in Polish by A. Kossowski (1937), and the journal of his 1840 trip to St Petersburg appeared in *Bohosloviia*, no. 45 (1981).

Shumelda, Yakiv [Šumelda, Jakiv], b 1914 in Bushkovychi, Peremyshl county, Galicia, d 3 February 1993 in San Francisco. Political figure, economist, and lawyer. In the 1930s he was active in Ukrainian student organizations in Prague and Berlin and became a member of the Leadership of Ukrainian Nationalists. During the Second World War he was a leading member of the OUN Melnyk faction's expeditionary groups in central Ukraine and a member of the Kiev city administration (1941). A postwar émigré, he taught in San Francisco and wrote *Vid Marksa do Malenkova* (From Marx to Malenkov, 1955), works on changes in the USSR after Stalin (1957) and the strategy and tactics of the Ukrainian liberation movement (1966), the memoirs *Na polovyni dorohy* (Halfway, 1985), and a biography of M. Kapustiansky (1985). He also wrote articles on Ukrainian historiography and the history of Ukrainian nationalism.

Shumeyko, Stephen [Šumejko, Stepan], b 17 January 1908 in Newark, New Jersey, d 12 August 1962 in New York. Editor and community leader. After graduating in law (1931) he joined the staff of *Svoboda* and served as the first editor (1933–58) of the Ukrainian National Association's *Ukrainian Weekly*. He was a founder and the first

Stephen Shumeyko

president of the *Ukrainian Youth League of North America (1933–6). As president of the Ukrainian Congress Committee of America (1944–9) he promoted the cause of Ukraine's independence at the founding conference of the United Nations in San Francisco. He also served as general secretary of the Pan-American Ukrainian Conference. His writings include *Ukrainian National Movement* (1939) and translations of P. Kulish's *Chorna rada* (The Black Council) and other works of Ukrainian literature.

Shumka. A Ukrainian dance company founded in Edmonton in 1959 by C. Kuc. Consisting of approx 50 nonprofessional dancers, the troupe has developed an international reputation for the quality of its dancing and the staging of its productions. In addition to touring extensively (Tunisia, Japan, Hong Kong, Ukraine), the group held a command performance for Queen Elizabeth II in Edmonton (1978), was featured at a gala for President R. Reagan in Ottawa (1981), and performed at the opening ceremonies of the 1988 Calgary Winter Olympics. The ensemble's artistic directors have included C. Kuc, O. Semchuk, and J. Pichlyh; G. Zwozdesky has served as its longtime musical director.

Shumka. A Ukrainian folk song and dance. With its 2/4 time the *shumka* is similar to the *kolomyika. The dance is accompanied by the song. A. Kotsipynsky published a collection of *shumka* songs.

Shumliansky, Oleksander [Šumljans'kyj], b 1748 in Yakivtsi, near Poltava, d 6 July 1795 in Moscow. Physician; brother of P. *Shumliansky. After being educated at the Kievan Mohyla Academy (1758–71) and the medical school at the St Petersburg Military Hospital (1773–6), he wrote a doctoral dissertation at Strasbourg University on the structure of the kidney (1782), in which he gave the first scientific description of Bowman's capsule (Shumliansky's capsula and loop). From 1786 he served as a professor of internal medicine and obstetrics in Moscow's medical schools. The founder of histology in the Russian Empire, he translated medical books into Russian and wrote *Mnenie odnogo istinoliubtsa o popravlenii naipolezneishei dlia liudei nauki* (The Opinion of a Lover of Truth on the Improvement of the Science Most Useful to Man, 1787).

Shumliansky, Pavlo [Šumljans'kyj], b 1752 in Mali Budyshcha, near Poltava, d 1821 in Kharkiv. Physician;

brother of O. *Shumliansky. He was educated at the Kievan Mohyla Academy (1763–70), the St Petersburg Medical School (1773–4), and Strasbourg University (1784–9), where he wrote a doctoral dissertation on local inflammation. He lectured at the St Petersburg Medical School and in 1795 became a professor of surgery and pharmacology at the Moscow Medical School. In 1805–17 he served as a professor of surgery at and the dean of the medical faculty of Kharkiv University. His publications deal with the medicinal properties of water, mineral waters in Poltava gubernia, and bone dislocations. He contributed to the reorganization of medical education in the Russian Empire.

Shumliansky, Yosyf [Šumljans'kyj, Josyf] (secular name: Ivan), b 1643, d 1708. Bishop of Lviv. The scion of an Orthodox noble family, he grew up with close ties to the court of Jan III Sobieski and even joined him in defending Vienna from a Turkish onslaught in 1683. In spite of strong opposition from church authorities, Shumliansky was made Orthodox bishop of Lviv in 1676. A year later he secretly converted to Catholicism and then used his position to steer the eparchy to a union with Rome. His secret negotiations with the Vatican and preparatory work among the eparchy's clergy culminated in 1700 in the conversion of the entire eparchy (with the exception of the Lviv Dormition Brotherhood, which accepted the union in 1708, and the Maniava Hermitage). M. Andrusiak published a biography of Shumliansky in Lviv in 1934.

Shumovska-Horain, Oleksandra [Šumovs'ka], b 1896 in Volhynia gubernia, d 1985 in Paris. Music teacher and composer. She studied music at the Warsaw and Paris conservatories. From the 1920s she lived in Paris and taught music. In 1927 she organized a female quartet known as Lel and for 12 years she toured with it through France, Belgium, Spain, and Holland. Its repertoire included Ukrainian works. She wrote music for female voice and for children, piano pieces (for four hands), and church music.

Pavlo Shumovsky

Oleksander Shumsky

Shumovsky, Pavlo [Šumovs'kyj], b 1899 in Myrohoshcha, Dubno county, Volhynia gubernia, d 27 January 1983 in Paris. Biologist, agronomist, and political and civic figure; full member of the Shevchenko Scientific Society from 1950. He studied agronomy at Kiev (1918–19), Berlin (1921–4), and Cracow (1925–6) universities and taught at the Higher Agricultural School of Warsaw University (1927–39) and the Lviv Polytechnic Institute (1939–41). During the war he served as director of the Department of Animal Husbandry at the Chamber of Agriculture in Lviv, and, as a founding member of the *Ukrainian Supreme Liberation Council (UHVR), took part in the resistance movement. After emigrating to France he became a research associate and then head of the biochemistry and physiology laboratory of the State Veterinary School in Maisons-Alfort (1945–65). He did research on animal hybridization, artificial insemination, and sperm storage and published numerous scientific papers in various languages. He was active in the External Representation of the UHVR. He was a professor at the Ukrainian Technical and Husbandry Institute and president of the board of directors of the Petliura Ukrainian Library in Paris (1968–81).

Shumske [Šums'ke]. III-7. A town smt (1986 pop 4,700) on the Viliia River and a raion center in Ternopil oblast. It was first mentioned, as the fortress of Shumsk, in the Hypatian Chronicle under the year 1149. In 1224 it was briefly an independent principality. Then it became part of the Principality of Galicia-Volhynia. On Burundai's demand the town's fortifications were dismantled in 1261. From the mid-14th century Shumske was ruled by the Lithuanian dynasty. Under Polish rule (1569–1793) a Basilian monastery was built in 1637 but was transferred to the Franciscan order in 1676. In 1715 a Roman Catholic church was built. In the 19th century Shumske belonged to Kremianets county of Volhynia gubernia. By mid-century it had a distillery, a brewery, a brick factory, tanneries, and weaving factories. In the interwar period (1919–39) Shumske was ruled by Poland. Today it is an agricultural town, with a farm machinery repair plant and a consumer-goods plant. An old Slavic settlement has been discovered in its vicinity.

Shumsky, Oleksander [Šums'kyj], b 2 December 1890 in Zhytomyr county, Volhynia gubernia, d 18 September 1946 in the Solovets Islands. Revolutionary and national-communist leader. He joined the Ukrainian Social Democratic Spilka in 1908. After the February Revolution he worked for the Kiev Gubernia zemstvo administration and became a leading member of the *Ukrainian Party of Socialist Revolutionaries (UPSR), which he represented in the Central Rada. In January 1918 a UPSR group including Shumsky conspired to overthrow the Rada. At the Fourth UPSR Congress in May 1918, he was a leader of the left faction of the *Borotbists, and in the autumn he was a member of the Borotbist Chief Revolutionary Committee that took part in the popular insurrection against the Hetman government. In January 1919, together with the Russian Bolsheviks, he organized a rebellion in Left-Bank Ukraine against the UNR Directory. During the second Soviet occupation of Ukraine the Borotbists entered into an entente with the CP(B)U, and Shumsky was appointed commissar of education in Kh. Rakovsky's Soviet Ukrainian government. He introduced policies to combat Russification and foster a Ukrainian cultural rebirth. In March 1920 Shumsky merged the Borotbists with the CP(B)U, and in April he was appointed to the CC CP(B)U Politburo and Organizational Bureau and the Comintern Executive Committee. That same year he became commissar of internal affairs in

Ukraine and chairman of Poltava okruha's executive committee. After participating in negotiations on the Peace Treaty of Riga he served as the first and only Soviet Ukrainian ambassador to Poland. After returning to Ukraine in February 1923, Shumsky edited the monthly *Chervonyi shliakh* (until November 1926) and directed the CP(B)U Department of Agitation and Propaganda (May–September 1924). He replaced V. Zatonsky as Ukraine's commissar of education (September 1924 to February 1927) and actively implemented social and cultural *Ukrainization policies. In 1925 he protested to J. Stalin against the appointment of the new CP(B)U general secretary, L. *Kaganovich, and urged that he be replaced by a Ukrainian, V. Chubar. Shumsky called for accelerated Ukrainization and recruitment of Ukrainians to leadership positions in the CP(B)U and the trade unions in order to facilitate the de-Russification of Ukraine's working class. As a result of his conflicts with Kaganovich in 1925–6, a national-communist oppositional current, popularly known as Shumskyism, developed within the CP(B)U. Shumsky's ideas were echoed in the writings of M. *Khvylovy, whom Shumsky refused to condemn at a CP(B)U Politburo meeting. Shumsky's line was supported by the CC of the *Communist Party of Western Ukraine (KPZU) until Moscow, acting through the Comintern, managed to split the CC.

In February 1927 Shumsky was relieved of all his posts in Ukraine (he was replaced by M. *Skrypnyk) and transferred to Moscow. Thereafter the Party officially referred to Shumskyism as a 'nationalist deviation.' Shumsky was appointed rector of the Leningrad Institute of the National Economy and the Polytechnical Institute (September 1927), deputy head of the mass-agitation department of the All-Union Party CC (February 1930), chairman of the Trade Union of Educational Workers, and a member of the All-Union Central Council of Trade Unions (February 1931). In May 1933 he was arrested and accused of leading an anti-Party, counterrevolutionary, nationalist struggle in the CP(B)U and KPZU, of belonging to the Ukrainian Military Organization, and of preparing an armed uprising in Ukraine. He was imprisoned in a concentration camp in the Solovets Islands, where he committed suicide to protest his unlawful incarceration.

BIBLIOGRAPHY

Majstrenko, I. *Borot'bism: A Chapter in the History of Ukrainian Communism* (New York 1954)

Mace, J. *Communism and the Dilemmas of National Liberation: National Communism in Soviet Ukraine, 1918–1933* (Cambridge, Mass 1983)

Panchuk, M. 'Zhyttia i smert' Oleksandra Shums'koho,' *Literaturna Ukraïna*, 26 January 1989

R. Senkus, A. Zhukovsky

Shumsky, Yurii [Šums'kyj, Jurij] (real surname: Shomin), b 17 November 1887 in Tyraspil, Kherson gubernia, d 7 June 1954 in Kiev. Actor. He first appeared on stage in an amateur circle in Kherson (1907). Later he organized an amateur theater (1917) and a theatrical studio (1919–21), and did agitprop theater work (1921–4) for the People's Commissariat of Education. His professional career was spent in the Odessa Ukrainian Drama Theater (1925–34) and the Kiev Ukrainian Drama Theater (1934–54). Shumsky's repertoire (Ukrainian and non-Ukrainian) included such characters as Bzhostovsky in I. Kocherha's *Feia hirkoho myhdaliu* (The Fairy of the Bitter Almond, 1926), the title

Yurii Shumsky   Danylo Shumuk

character in O. Korniichuk's *Bohdan Khmel'nyts'kyi* (1939) and P. Beaumarchais's *Le mariage de Figaro* (1927), and Philip II in F. Schiller's *Don Carlos* (1936). In silent cinema he played the title role in *Benia Krik* (1927), Benedio Synytsia in *Boryslav smiiet'sia* (1927, based on I. Franko), and Sylin in *Maiak na Chornomu mori* (The Lighthouse on the Black Sea, 1928). A biography, by B. Stepanov, was published in Kiev in 1971.

Shumuk, Danylo [Šumuk], b 30 December 1914 in Boremshchyna, Volodymyr-Volynskyi county, Volhynia gubernia. Longest-serving prisoner of conscience in the USSR. He spent 44 years of his life in prison or exile, 38 of them under Soviet rule. He was arrested in January 1934, and in 1935 he was sentenced by the Polish court in Kovel to eight years' imprisonment for his role in the underground Communist Party of Western Ukraine in Volhynia. After being amnestied by the Polish government in May 1939, he was conscripted into a Red Army penal battalion in May 1941, was captured by the Germans, and spent several months in a concentration camp holding Soviet prisoners of war, near Poltava. After managing to escape he returned to Volhynia. There he joined the anti-Soviet, anti-German *Ukrainian Insurgent Army in 1943. In February 1945 he was captured in Kiev oblast and sentenced to death by a secret military court in Rivne; the sentence was commuted to 20 years in Norilsk, Taishet, and other labor camps in Siberia, and in the Vladimir prison near Moscow. In August 1956, after a review of his case, he was freed before completing his term, and returned home. In November 1957 he was rearrested. Having refused to become a KGB informer, he was accused of 'anti-Soviet propaganda and agitation,' and in May 1958 he was tried in Lutske and sentenced to 10 years in labor camps in Siberia. After his release in 1967 he lived in Bohuslav and Kiev. In January 1972 he was again arrested, for writing memoirs, and in July he was sentenced in Lviv to 10 years in special-regime camps in Mordovia and Perm oblast, followed by five years' exile in Kazakhstan.

In the camps Shumuk renounced his Soviet citizenship (in 1972) and participated in campaigns for the acknowledgment of political-prisoner status, in strikes, and in other political protests. In 1979 he cofounded a Helsinki Accords monitoring group in the camp and joined the *Ukrainian Helsinki Group. For many years he demanded the right to join his relatives in Canada. Amnesty International and Ukrainian community campaigns for his release took place in many Western countries, and the Canadian government repeatedly appealed on his behalf to the USSR government. As a result he was finally allowed to emigrate, in April 1987, to Canada, after he had completed his term of exile. Shumuk's memoirs were smuggled out and published in the West in Ukrainian (1974; rev edn 1983) and English (*Life Sentence*, 1984). Selections of essays and reminiscences by Shumuk, *Perezhyte i peredumane* (My Life and Thoughts in Retrospect) and *Iz Gulagu u vil'nyi svit* (From the Gulag into a Free World), appeared in Detroit in 1983 and in Toronto in 1991, respectively.

O. Zinkevych

Shumylo, Mykyta [Šumylo], b 10 June 1903 in Mykhailivka, Cherkasy county, Kiev gubernia, d 8 March 1982 in Kiev. Writer and teacher. He concluded his studies at the Institute of Cinematography in Moscow in 1938 and taught in schools until the outbreak of the Second World War. He published collections of short stories: *Vada* (The Defect, 1934), *Urozhai* (The Harvest, 1934), *Holubyi zenit* (The Azure Zenith, 1948), *Shchedri sertsem* (Generous of Heart, 1952), and *Ia – tvii brat* (I Am Your Brother, 1961). He also wrote the novel *Prokuror respubliky* (Prosecutor of the Republic, 1958), a collection of stories for children *De ty, moia chaiechko?* (Where Are You, My Little Seagull?, 1979), a volume of literary criticism titled *Oles' Honchar* (1950, 1951), and literary scenarios, and translated works of Russian and Belarusian writers.

Shumytsky, Mykola [Šumyc'kyj], b 30 April 1889 in Chernihiv, d February 1982 in Paris. Architect and civic leader. A graduate of the Kiev Polytechnical Institute, he was active in the revolutionary events of 1917–19 as chairman of the Council of Railways of Ukraine (1917), deputy of the railway workers to the Central Rada, and member of the Ukrainian Military Council. In September 1919 he was sent as a member of the UNR delegation to the Paris Peace Conference. In 1921 he was appointed head of the Ukrainian diplomatic mission in Paris. He worked closely with S. Petliura. He was the sole president of the *Union of Ukrainian Emigré Organizations in France (1925–42) and its representative in the Advisory Council on Refugees of the League of Nations. His publications include articles on Ukrainian architecture and wooden churches and recollections of the revolutionary period.

Shut, Andrii [Šut, Andrij], b ?, d 1873. The most talented kobzar of the Chernihiv region. After losing his sight at 17 as a result of smallpox, he learned to play the kobza from P. Kozel. His repertoire included the dumas about the Widow and Her Three Sons, the Cossack Fesko Handzha Andyber, Khmelnytsky and Barabash, Khmelnytsky and Vasile of Moldavia, the death of Bohdan Khmelnytsky, Ivan Konovchenko, the Bila Tserkva peace treaty, the Flight of the Three Brothers from Azov, Oleksii Popovych, Samiilo Kishka, and the Oppression of Ukraine by the Polish Gentry. He also sang historical and lyrical songs and psalms. Shut's songs were transcribed and published by P. Kulish, H. Bazylevych, and A. Metlynsky.

Shut, Vasyl [Šut', Vasyl'], b 26 April 1899 in Zolotonosha, Poltava gubernia, d 23 August 1982 in Chicago. Composer, conductor, and teacher. He graduated from

Vasyl Shut

the Lysenko Drama and Music Institute in Kiev in the composition class of V. Zolotarev (1930). In the 1930s he was composer-conductor in music-drama theaters in Kiev and the Donbas region, and he wrote music for nearly 30 plays. In 1950 he settled in Chicago, where he taught piano and conducted the St Nicholas Cathedral choir. His compositions include four symphonies; piano and violin concertos and sonatas; seven string quartets; three piano trios and a piano sextet; and 34 published solo songs to texts by T. Shevchenko, I. Franko, Lesia Ukrainka, O. Oles, O. Teliha, T. Kurpita, and others.

Shutenko, Taisiia [Šutenko, Taïsija], b 5 October 1905 in Kharkiv, d 14 September 1975 in Kiev. Composer and educator. A graduate of the Kharkiv Music and Drama Institute (1930) and the Moscow Conservatory (1937), she taught in vocational music schools and secondary music schools in Kharkiv. In 1956 she moved to Kiev. She wrote orchestral works, such as the symphony *Karmeliuk* (1937), an overture, and a string quartet; works for folk instruments (including 16 pieces for bandura); and musical scores for plays, such as *Marusia Bohuslavka*, *Princess Victoria*, *Macbeth*, and *Puss in Boots*.

Shutko, Mykola [Šut'ko], b 19 December 1927 in Kryvyi Rih (now in Dnipropetrovske oblast). Stage and film actor. He completed study at the Dnipropetrovske Theater school in 1948 and then worked in the Chernivtsi Oblast Ukrainian Music and Drama Theater (1950–63), the Kiev Ukrainian Drama Theater (1963–82), and the Kiev Artistic Film Studio (1982). He acted in the films *Vony bylysia za bat'kivshchynu* (They Fought for the Fatherland, 1975) and *Vavilon XX* (Babylon XX, 1979).

Shvachka, Mykyta [Švačka], b ca 1728, d after 1768 in Nerchinsk, Siberia. Zaporozhian Cossack and haidamaka leader. At the outbreak of the *Koliivshchyna rebellion (1768) he joined forces with M. Zalizniak. Together with a detachment led by A. Zhurba he took the town of Khvastiv and established it as a rebel operations center. In the summer of 1768 he was captured by tsarist troops near Bohuslav and sentenced to hard labor in Siberia, where he died. Shvachka became a folk hero and the subject of a poem by T. Shevchenko.

Shvachko, Oleksii [Švačko, Oleksij], b 18 January 1901 in Chopylky, near Pereiaslav, Poltava gubernia, d 28 March 1988 in Kiev. Film director and stage actor. He was a student at the Lysenko Music and Drama Institute in

Kiev (1920–2) and completed his studies at the Kiev Institute of People's Education (1925). He acted in Berezil (1922–5) and in the Odessa (1925–8) and Kiev (from 1928) artistic film studios. He directed the film productions of I. Karpenko-Kary's *Martyn Borulia* (1953) and *Zemlia* (Land, based on O. Kobylianska, 1954) and the documentaries *Daleko vid batkivshchyny* (Far from the Fatherland, 1965) and *Rozvidnyky* (The Scouts, 1968).

Shvarno Danylovych [Švarno Danylovyč] (Lithuanian: Švarnas), b ca 1230, d 1269. Kievan Rus' prince and grand duke of Lithuania (from 1267); younger son of Danylo Romanovych. He married the daughter of Grand Duke Mindaugas in 1254 to strengthen a treaty between Lithuania and Galicia-Volhynia, and was given rule over Chorna Rus'. After Danylo's death in 1264 he also ruled the Halych, Kholm, and Dorohychyn principalities. When Mindaugas was assassinated (1263), Shvarno assisted his son, *Vaišvilkas, in securing the Lithuanian throne. Vaišvilkas, a monk, abdicated in 1267 in favor of Shvarno, who ruled as grand duke until his death.

Shvetlosts (Enlightenment). A literary and art quarterly published for the Ruthenians of Yugoslavia by *Ruske slovo* in Ruski Krstur in 1952–4 and 1966–7 and since 1967 in Novi Sad. It contains poetry, prose, and popular and scholarly articles on the language, history, and folklore of the Ruthenians, and it serves as a bridge between Yugoslavian culture and the culture of other countries, particularly Ukraine and Czechoslovakia. The centerpiece of the journal consists of the literary works of Ruthenian writers, such as Ya. Feisa, M. Vinai, M. Kovach, Ye. Kochish, and H. Nad (of the older generation); M. Kochish, V. Mudry, V. Kostelnyk, M. Koloshniai, M. Budynsky, L. Budynsky Falts, and M. Skuban (of the middle generation); and D. Paparhai, H. Hafich, A. Prokop, M. Striber, B. Vesermini, I. Hardy, and D. Hrubenia (of the younger generation).

Fedir Shvets   Ivan Shvets

Shvets, Fedir [Švec'], b 1882 in Cherkasy county, Kiev gubernia, d 20 June 1940 in Prague. Geologist and political activist. He graduated from Dorpat University (1910) and taught as a professor of geology at Kiev University (1917–18). He was a member of the CC of the Peasant Association and of the 'central current' of the Ukrainian Party of Socialist Revolutionaries. He was also a member of the Directory of the UNR (1918–19). He emigrated to Prague, where he served as a professor at the Ukrainian Free University (from 1923) and the Ukrainian Higher Pedagogical Institute (1924–9). He published numerous geological studies.

Shvets, Ivan [Švec'], b 25 May 1901 in Khutir Mykhailivskyi (now Druzhba), Hlukhiv county, Chernihiv gubernia, d 5 September 1983 in Kiev. Energy research scientist; full member of the AN URSR (now ANU) from 1950. He studied and taught at the Kiev Industrial (now Polytechnical) Institute and became director of the ANU Institute of Thermoenergetics (1942–54). He was rector of Kiev University (1952–72), and worked at the ANU Institute of Technical Thermophysics (from 1975). He developed new steam and gas turbines, served on various energy and electrification committees, and was active in energy administration and energy politics in the USSR.

Shvets, Vasyl [Švec', Vasyl'], b 17 January 1918 in Ivankiv, Radomyshl county, Kiev gubernia. Writer. He began publishing in the 1930s and has published many poetry collections, the most recent being *Spodivannia* (Expectations, 1984), and one novel, *Lysty v okopy* (Letters to the Trenches, 1985). The Second World War is a constant theme in his works. In 1982 he became the first recipient of the V. Sosiura Prize.

Anatolii Shydlovsky

Shydlovsky, Anatolii [Šydlovs'kyj, Anatolij] (Shidlovsky, Anatol), b 10 October 1933 in Vepryk, Bobrovytsia raion, Chernihiv oblast. Electrical and electric power engineer; full member of the ANU (formerly AN URSR) since 1985. He studied at the Kiev Polytechnical Institute and has worked since 1959 at the ANU Institute of Electrodynamics, where he has been director since 1973. He also served as secretary of the ANU Division of the Physical-Technical Problems of Energetics. He has made contributions in the areas of multiphase electric circuitry and the stabilization of electric power networks.

Shydlovsky, Andrii [Šydlovs'kyj, Andrij] (Shidlovsky, Andrei), b 17 November 1818 in Voronezh gubernia, Russia, d 7 May 1892 in Karabachyn, Radomyshl county, Kiev gubernia. Astronomer and geodesist. A graduate of Kharkiv (PH D, 1837) and Dorpat (M PHIL, 1841) universities, he worked as an astronomer at the Pulkovo Observatory (1841–3) and was a professor at Kharkiv University (1843–56) and Kiev University (1856–68), where he also directed the Kiev Astronomical Laboratory. Shydlovsky took part in a major geodesic survey under the leadership of V. Struve; as part of this effort, he measured the exact geographic co-ordinates of a number of locations in Ukraine. He also took part in other surveys and expeditions.

Shyian, Anatolii [Šyjan, Anatolij], b 5 April 1906 in Borysivka, now in Belgorod oblast, Russia, d 11 May 1989 in Kiev. Writer. He completed studies at the Kiev Institute of Forest Technology in 1929. He is the author of many novels and short stories, such as *Balanda* (Prison Soup, 1930), *Na kryzhyni* (On the Ice Floe, 1930), *Opovidannia* (Stories, 1931), *Kateryna Kozhushana* (1938), *Magistral'* (The Highway, 1934), and *Khurtovyna* (The Storm, 1979, 1984). His stories for children include *Ivasyk-Telesyk* (1947), *Kotyhoroshko* (1947), *Ialynka* (The Christmas Tree, 1947), *P'iesy-kazky* (Plays – Fairy Tales, 1951), *Pro khloptsiv-iuntsiv, dobrykh molodtsiv* (About the Boys – Good Fellows All, 1955), and *Ivan – muzhyts'kyi syn* (Ivan, the Peasant's Son, 1959, 1982).

Shyian, Kyr [Šyjan], b 21 June 1902 in Berezova Luka, Myrhorod county, Poltava gubernia, d 1974. Historian. He graduated from the Nizhen Institute of People's Education (1930) and taught in Kharkiv at the Scientific Research Institute of the History of Ukrainian Culture (1930–4), the Pedagogical Institute (1939–56), and the university (from 1956; director of the department of the history of the USSR from 1963). He wrote *Borot'ba robitnychoho klasu Ukraïny za vidbudovu promyslovosti (1921–1926 rr.)* (The Struggle of the Working Class of Ukraine for the Rebuilding of Industry [1921–6], 1959), coauthored *Mynule i suchasne sela* (The Past and Present of the Village, 1963), and contributed to the collective works *Istoriia robitnychoho klasu Ukraïns'koï RSR* (History of the Working Class of the Ukrainian SSR, vol 2, 1967) and *Rozvytok narodnoho hospodarstva Ukraïns'koï RSR, 1917–1967* (Development of the National Economy of the Ukrainian SSR, 1917–67, 1967).

Shyianiv, Hryhorii [Šyjaniv, Hryhorij], b 30 November 1874 in the Chernihiv region, d 23 December 1955 near Poděbrady, Czechoslovakia. Lawyer, judge, and civic figure. In 1918 he was a member of the UNR General Court and the Hetman government's State Senate (supreme court). An émigré in Bohemia from 1920, he taught law at the Ukrainian Husbandry Academy in Poděbrady and was a member of its last senate. He wrote for the academy the first Ukrainian textbook about automobiles and a textbook on private law.

Shylo, Havrylo [Šylo], b 26 March 1910 in Dereviane, Rivne county, Volhynia gubernia, d 17 January 1988 in Lviv. Linguist. A graduate of Warsaw University (1937), he defended his candidate's dissertation on the palatography and phonemic system of Ukrainian at the University of Lviv (1947) and taught at pedagogical institutes in Lviv (1947–59) and Drohobych (from 1959). He wrote a monograph on the southwestern Ukrainian dialects (1957) and articles on their lexicon, phonetics, syntax, and toponyms and on Slavic prothesis. He also prepared a linguistic atlas and dictionary of the dialects of the Dniester Basin, which remain unpublished.

Kostiantyn Shylo   Yurii Shymko

Shylo, Kostiantyn [Šylo, Kostjantyn], b 11 June 1879 in Orlovskoe, Primore oblast in the Far East, d 1933. Civic and cultural activist; father of M. *Shylo. The commissioner of education in Kiev gubernia under the Central Rada, in the 1920s he headed the editorial department at the Kiev branch of the All-Ukrainian Academy of Sciences and lectured at the Kiev Agricultural Institute. He was arrested in 1929, tried for belonging to the *Union for the Liberation of Ukraine, and given a suspended three-year sentence. After the trial he worked briefly in the laboratory of a veterinary institute.

Shylo, Mykola [Šylo], b 6 September 1913 in Kiev, d 22 April 1982 in Kiev. Architect; son of K. Shylo. A graduate of the Kiev Civil-Engineering Institute (1939), in 1953 he was appointed director of the Kiev Planning Institute of Residential-Civil and Communal Construction. In Kiev he designed the building of the Ministry of Agriculture (1955–6) and residential buildings. He also helped to plan the expansion of the city center (1970).

Shymanovsky, Oleksander [Šymanovs'kyj], b 16 July 1860 in Ukraine, d 3 January 1918 in Kiev. Ophthalmologist. A graduate of Kiev University (1884), he worked there from 1891 and taught at the Higher Courses for Women (1910–11). His publications deal with conjunctivitis, eye traumas, tuberculous infections of the eye, and the transplantation of the anterior part of the eye.

Shymanovsky, Vitalii [Šymanovs'kyj, Vitalij], b 12 November 1928 in Antonivka, Bila Tserkva okruha. Specialist in construction mechanics and design; corresponding member of the ANU (formerly AN URSR) since 1982. He graduated from the Kiev Hydromelioration Institute (1954). From 1962 to 1980 he worked at the USSR Institute of Building Constructs as assistant director, and in 1980 he became director of the Ukrainian Scientific Research and Development Institute of Steel Construction. He has developed new methods of constructing and calculating loading and stresses in suspension bridge structures.

Shymanovsky, Vsevolod [Šymanovs'kyj], b 1866 in Kiev, d 1934 in Krymske, Krasnodar krai. Apiarist. He completed military training and served on the general staff of the Russian army, and then taught in rural schools in Kiev and Volhynia gubernias. In 1910–26 he taught at the Boiarka Apiarian School. He wrote *Metody pchelovozhe-niia* (Methods of Beekeeping, 1926).

Shymchuk, Mykola [Šymčuk], b 9 January 1949 in Ko-pytkove, Zdolbuniv raion, Rivne oblast. Artist. He completed study at the Lviv Institute of Applied and Decorative Arts (1973), where he specialized in decorative glass. Since 1975 he has participated in international, local, and all-Union group exhibitions. He has shown his stained glass at solo exhibitions in Lviv (1980, 1983, and 1987).

Shymko, Yurii [Šymko, Jurij], b 6 September 1940 in Koźle, Silesia, Poland. Community leader and politician leader. After emigrating to Canada with his parents (1953) he graduated from the University of Toronto (1961) and the Ontario College of Education (1963). He taught secondary school and was active in the Progressive Conservative party. In 1978 he was elected in the High Park electoral district to the Canadian House of Commons, and in 1981 and 1985 as a member of the provincial parliament in Ontario. He has been active in a number of Ukrainian organizations, particularly the Canadian League for Ukraine's Liberation. In 1973–8 he served as general secretary of the *World Congress of Free Ukrainians, and in 1988 he was elected its president.

Ioanikii Shymonovych   Volodymyr Shynkaruk

Shymonovych, Ioanikii [Šymonovyč, Ioanikij], b 16 November 1885 in Husiatyn, Kamianets-Podilskyi county, Podilia gubernia, d 1938? Economist and statistician. He studied at St Petersburg University and was active in the Ukrainian Hromada there. In 1917 he was elected to the Ukrainian Central Rada in Kiev and appointed to the position of aide to the UNR minister of postal and telegraph services. Later he taught political economy at the Kamianets-Podilskyi Ukrainian State University (1920–1) and in Lviv. In 1926 he emigrated to Soviet Ukraine. He was a member of the Scientific Research Department of Agricultural Economics in Kiev. He taught at the Kiev Agricultural Institute and in Kazan, Russia, and Staline (Donetske). He was imprisoned in Stalinist concentration camps in the 1930s, and his fate after 1938 is unknown. Shymonovych wrote works on Ukrainian industry (1920), Ukrainians in the Soviet Far East (1923), Galicia (1928), and agricultural co-operatives in Ukraine, and a history of political economy (1923).

Shymonovych-Semyhynovsky, Yurii [Šymonovyč-Semyhynovs'kyj, Jurij] (Polish: Jerzy Eleuter Szymono-wicz Semiginowski), b ca 1660 in Lviv, d 1711. Galician painter and engraver. After studying at St Luke's Academy in Rome he was appointed painter to the court of King Jan III Sobieski in 1687. He painted allegorical presentations of the four seasons on the plafonds in the Wilanów royal castle in Warsaw and portraits of the royal family and of the royal couple on horses. The icons of St Anne at St Anne's Church in Cracow and of St Sebastian at the Holy Cross Church in Warsaw, as well as the pictures of Bacchus, Ariadne, and the Holy Family now in the Lviv Art Gallery, are attributed to him.

Shynkaruk, Volodymyr [Šynkaruk], b 22 April 1928 in Haivoron, Bila Tserkva okruha. Philosopher; full member of the ANU (formerly AN URSR) since 1978 and corresponding member of the USSR (now Russian) Academy of Sciences since 1981. Since graduating from Kiev University (1950; candidate of sciences, 1954) he has lectured there on the history of philosophy. He was appointed dean of the philosophy faculty in 1965 and head of the department of ethics, esthetics, and logic in 1967. Since 1968 he has directed the ANU Institute of Philosophy, and he was the first editor of its journal *Filosofs'ka dumka* (1969–71, 1979–88). He served three terms (1972–86) as president of the Ukrainian Branch of the Philosophical Society of the USSR and vice-president of the society. His numerous (over 250) publications deal chiefly with the history of dialectical materialism, the relationship between the dialectic in its ontological, logical, and epistemological sense, and the role of Marxism-Leninism, the Soviet worldview, and Soviet culture. His chief works are books in Russian on the logic, dialectic, and theory of knowledge of G. Hegel (1964) and I. Kant (1974); on the unity of the dialectic, logic, and theory of knowledge (1977); and on the humanism of the dialectico-materialistic worldview (coauthor, 1984). As chief editor of complete editions of the works of H. Skovoroda (2 vols, 1973) and T. Prokopovych (3 vols, 1979–81) and the ANU history of philosophy in Ukraine (2 vols, 1987), he has contributed to the study of Ukrainian intellectual history. In 1989 he was elected to the USSR Congress of People's Deputies as the head of the *Znannia Society of the Ukrainian SSR, and chaired the Ukrainian Supreme Soviet's working group on drafting new language legislation.

T. Zakydalsky

Shypyntsi [Šypynci]. V-6. A village (1989 pop 3,160) in Kitsman raion, Chernivtsi oblast. It is a historical site on the left bank of the Sovytsia River (a tributary of the Prut River), first mentioned in documentary sources in 1433. Its name probably derived from the hissing (*shypinnia*) of water flowing into a nearby hollow known as Kruhle Boloto. In the 13th to 15th centuries Shypyntsi was the center of the *Shypyntsi land. Many Neolithic artifacts of the Trypilian culture have been found there, including painted ceramics and figurines. A bracelet and a hatchet date from the Bronze Age, and Roman coins have also been found. Archeological digs were conducted by J. Szombathy (1893) and E. Kostin (1904–14), and their findings were transferred to the Chernivtsi Museum and the Vienna Museum of Natural History. Some of the earliest immigrants to Canada came from Shypyntsi; they established a like-named settlement near Smoky Lake, Alberta (1896).

Shypyntsi land (Shypynska zemlia; Terra Sepinecensis). The historical name of a territory in *Bukovyna from the time of the Principality of Galicia-Volhynia to the establishment of the Principality of *Moldavia (from the late 13th to the mid-15th centuries). The beginning of its existence has been variously fixed at after the Tatar invasion in the mid-13th century (M. Korduba), after the dissolution of the Galician-Volhynian principality in the mid-14th century (B. Tymoshchuk), and during the migration of Rumanian peoples from Transylvania in the mid-14th century (T. Balan). The first mention of the Shypyntsi land occurs in J. Długosz's account of Casimir III the Great's campaign against Moldavia in 1359; the last extant document to mention it is from 1444 (in E. Hurmuzaki [ed], *Documente privitoare la istoria Românilor*, vol 1, no. 2 [1874]).

The Shypyntsi land was made up of sections of northern Bukovyna and Bessarabia, covering approx the same area as present-day *Chernivtsi oblast; its capital was *Shypyntsi. The land was divided into three *volosti*, Tsetsyn (east of Chernivtsi), Khotyn, and Khmeliv (near Karapchiv, in the Cheremosh River valley). The *volost* centers were fortified settlements known in various documents as *hrady*. The Shypyntsi land developed successfully because of its relative isolation from Tatar nomads and its position on the Lviv–Suceava trade route; Shypyntsi was particularly known for its large livestock markets. In the 14th and 15th centuries there were more than 100 villages in the land, some of which had existed since the Princely era (Kitsman, Kuchuriv, Onut, Repuzhyntsi, Vasyliv); others had been established at the end of the 13th and the beginning of the 14th centuries (Hlyboka, Luzhany, Vashkivtsi). Among the few that arose after the arrival of the Rumanians in the 14th century were Rokytna and Tarasivtsi.

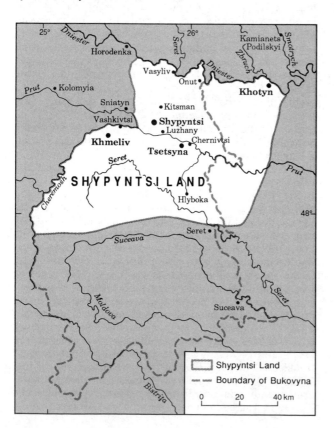

Because it was essentially a borderland between Moldavia and Poland, the Shypyntsi land was in most respects autonomous and sovereign until the Moldavian principality extended its control over it. The territory was then settled by *Ukrainians, who continue to make up the population.

BIBLIOGRAPHY
Korduba, M. 'Moldavs'ko-pol's'ka hranytsia na Pokutti do smerty Stefana Velykoho,' *Zbirnyk NTSh* (Lviv 1906)
Balan, T. *Ţara Şipeniţului* (Chernivtsi 1926)
Tymoshchuk, B. *Shypyns'ka zemlia za arkheolohichnymy danymy: Mynule i suchasne Pivnichnoï Bukovyny* (Kiev 1973)

A. Zhukovsky

Shyriaieve [Šyrjajeve]. VI-11. A town smt (1986 pop 7,400) on the Velykyi Kuialnyk River and a raion center in Odessa oblast. It was founded at the end of the 18th century by Bulgarian settlers and runaway Ukrainian serfs, and was called Stepanivka until 1918. It is an agricultural town with several food-processing plants.

Shyroke [Šyroke]. VI-14. A town smt (1986 pop 11,700) on the Inhulets River and a raion center in Dnipropetrovske oblast. It originated in the second half of the 18th century as a Cossack wintering settlement in Inhulets palanka of the New Sich territory. In the 19th century it belonged to Kherson gubernia and developed as a farming and trading town. In 1938 it attained smt status. Today the town has a brewery and a chicken incubating station.

Shyroke burial site. A *Cimmerian burial ground of the 9th to early 8th century BC near Shyroke, Skadovske raion, Kherson oblast. Excavations in 1961–3 uncovered approx 130 flexed burials pointing south. Grave goods recovered included pottery, adornments, and stone tools.

Shyrokov, Oleksander [Šyrokov] (Shirokov, Aleksandr), b 5 September 1905 in Ivanovo, Russia. Geologist; corresponding member of the AN URSR (now ANU) since 1957. He graduated from the Dnipropetrovske Mining Institute in 1930 and worked there from 1946, becoming professor and department head in 1979. His research involved the elucidation of patterns of coal-vein formation in the major basins of the European part of the USSR, with particular emphasis on the Donetske Basin. His numerous publications include *Bol'shoi Donbass* (The Great Donbas, 1957).

Shyrotsky, Kostiantyn [Šyroc'kyj, Kostjantyn] (Sherotsky; pseuds: Kost, K. Ladyzhenko, K. Sushchynsky), b 7 June 1886 in Vilshanka, Olhopil county, Podilia gubernia, d 13 September 1919 in Bilousivka, Bratslav county, Podilia gubernia. Art historian and community figure. A graduate of the St Petersburg Archeological Institute (1911) and St Petersburg University (1912), he lectured in the university's department of art history and was active in the Ukrainian Hromada in St Petersburg. He devoted himself to the study of Ukrainian and Russian art and architecture and collected Western Ukrainian folk art. He contributed to *Rada*, *Ukrainskaia zhizn'*, and *Zapysky NTSh*. After the February Revolution he was appointed commissioner of Horodenka county in Galicia by the Russian Provisional Government, and in 1918 he organized the UNR Secretariat of Education. He wrote 16 articles

Kostiantyn Shyrotsky

much information about Ukrainian folklore and ethnography. His own works include a historical and ethnographic study of Olyshivka (1854), a collection of 'Little Russian' sayings and proverbs (1857), and a two-volume collection of poetry (1856–7).

Serhii Shyshko: *Kiev: Khreshchatyk* (oil, 1973)

on T. Shevchenko's artworks (1911–14), books on H. Levytsky (1914), the first volume of a history of Ukraine's decorative art (1914, dealing with interior home decoration), and an illustrated guide to Kiev (1917). Under the pseudonym K. Baladyzhenko he and P. Balytsky wrote, in Russian, an illustrated history of Galicia (1915), a book on Bukovyna and its past (1915), and a brief history of the Principality of Galicia (1915).

Shyshaky [Šyšaky]. IV-15. A town smt (1986 pop 5,100) on the Psol River and a raion center in Poltava oblast. The village probably originated in the 14th century. It was first mentioned in historical documents in the 17th century. Under the Hetman state it was a company center of Myrhorod regiment. In the 19th century it belonged to Myrhorod county in Poltava gubernia. Today the town has a cheese, a brick, and a mineral-water bottling factory.

Shyshatsky, Varlaam [Šyšac'kyj], b 1751 in Shyshaky, Poltava region, d 23 July 1820 in Novhorod-Siverskyi. Orthodox churchman. He probably studied at the Kievan Mohyla Academy before taking his monastic vows in 1776. He was prefect and rector of the Pereiaslav College. At the same time he served as hegumen of the Moshnohorskyi and Pereiaslav–St Michael's monasteries. He served as rector of the Novhorod-Siverskyi Seminary (1785–7), overseer of the Holy Spirit Monastery in Vilnius (1787–9), and head of several other monasteries in the Novhorod-Siverskyi region before being consecrated bishop of Zhytomyr in 1795. Subsequently he was bishop of Volhynia and of Mahiliou and Belarus (1805) and archbishop of Mahiliou and Vitsebsk (1808). In these positions he often supported the principle of an autocephalous Ukrainian-Belarusian Orthodox church, independent of the Moscow Patriarchate. During the French army's occupation of Mahiliou in 1812, he became a supporter of Napoleon Bonaparte and praised him in sermons. After the Russian army recaptured the town in 1813, Shyshatsky was defrocked and sentenced to life imprisonment in the Novhorod-Siverskyi Transfiguration Monastery.

Shyshatsky-Illich, Oleksander [Šyšac'kyj-Illič], b 1828 in Krasylivka, Kozelets county, Chernihiv gubernia, d 1859 in Chernihiv. Poet and ethnographer. A graduate of the Chernihiv Theological Seminary, he edited the *Chernigovskie gubernskie vedomosti* (1854–9), which printed

Shyshko, Serhii [Šhyško, Serhij], b 25 June 1911 in Nosivka, Nizhen county, Chernihiv gubernia. Painter. He studied at the Kiev State Art Institute (1929–33) under F. Krychevsky and at the Leningrad Institute of Painting, Sculpture, and Architecture (1936–43). Athough he paints portraits and still lifes, he is best known for his landscapes, many of which constitute the 'Kiev Suite' begun in 1944. He has also painted series depicting the landscapes of Samarkand (1942), the Carpathians (1947), Crimea (1956), and places connected with T. Shevchenko's life. His work has been shown in numerous exhibitions in Ukraine and abroad and reproduced in three albums (1971, 1977, 1987).

Siabry. A class of peasants in Kievan Rus' and later in the Lithuanian-Ruthenian state who communally farmed land or engaged in other production, such as beekeeping, fishing, or the salt trade. The *siabr* system of ownership and economy is interpreted in different ways by historians. It is mentioned in the missive of Metropolitan K. Smoliatych, who equates the status of *siabry* to that of **izhoi*. In the laws of the Grand Duchy of Lithuania (the Lithuanian Statute of 1529) they are described as participants in peasant husbandry who do not necessarily have the same rights as **landless* peasants. The *siabr* economy expanded rapidly in central and eastern Ukraine in the 16th and 17th centuries, when those regions were colonized, but it was gradually displaced by the rule of hereditary nobles. Vestiges, such as community use of pastures and fields, remained until the early 20th century.

Siadrysty, Mykola [Sjadrystyj], b 1 September 1937 in Kolisnykivka, Kupianka raion, Kharkiv oblast. Master of microscopic miniatures. A graduate of the Kharkiv Agricultural Institute (1960) and the Kharkiv Art School (1961), he has created microscopic bas-relief portraits of T.

Mykola Siadrysty

Shevchenko, S. Krushelnytska, and Dante in cherrystones or thorn-berry stones and watercolor portraits of I. Franko, V. Symonenko, Michelangelo, and E. Hemingway on pear or apple seed sections. He has also produced some of the world's smallest books, including a 0.6-sq-mm version of Shevchenko's *Kobzar*, a synchronous motor 200 times smaller than a poppy seed, and a 3.5-mm-long frigate with 337 details. He is the author of two books, *Chy varto pidkuvaty blokhu?* (Is It Worth Shoeing a Flea?, 1966) and *Tainy mikrotekhniki* (Secrets of Microtechnology, 1969). His unbelievable works have been exhibited around the world.

Siaivo (Aura). A publishing house in Kiev, established in 1913 to publish the journal *Siaivo*. Its first book was M. Vorony's poetry collection *V siaivi mrii* (In the Aura of Dreams, 1913). In 1914 Siaivo was closed down in the tsarist crackdown on Ukrainian-language publications after the outbreak of the First World War. Revived in 1918 by P. Kovzhun and M. Semenko, it published several important books of poetry and prose: P. Tychyna's *Soniashni klarnety* (Sunny Clarinets, 1918), O. Slisarenko's *Na berezi kastal'-s'komu* (On the Castalian Shore, 1918), V. Yaroshenko's *Svitotin'* (Lightshadow, 1918), M. Semenko's *Deviat' poem* (Nine Poems, 1918) and *P'iero kokhaie* (Pierrot Loves, 1918), M. Ivchenko's *Shumy vesniani* (Murmurs of Spring, 1919), and H. Zhurba's *Pokhid zhyttia* (The March of Life, 1919). Siaivo ceased publishing in 1919, but it was again renewed during the period of the Ukrainization policy (1926–9). In that period it published a series of classic Ukrainian novels, a library of world literature (translations of V. Hugo, U. Sinclair, S. Zweig, and others), a Desheva biblioteka (Inexpensive Library) of Ukrainian literature, a two-volume edition of T. Shevchenko's works, L. Hlibov's poetry, and a 12-volume edition of J. London's works in Ukrainian translation.

Siaivo (Aura). A monthly journal of literature and the arts published in Kiev from January 1913 to September 1914 (a total of 21 issues). It was established on the initiative of its illustrator, P. Kovzhun. The formal editor and publisher was the actor O. Korolchuk, but the actual editor was I. Steshenko. *Siaivo* published articles by prominent cultural figures: V. Krychevsky wrote on architecture; P. Chaika, Ye. Kuzmin, A. Sereda, and O. Sudomora on art; M. Biliashivsky and D. Shcherbakivsky on folk art and ethnography; V. O'Connor-Vilinska, V. Boretsky, and V. Verkhovynets on music; and M. Vorony, M. Sadovsky, I. Steshenko, S. Rusova, and K. Shyrotsky on theater. It also published original literary works by I.

Franko, O. Oles, M. Vorony, M. Rylsky, and others; literary criticism (eg, about the works of V. Vynnychenko, Yu. Fedkovych, and M. Kotsiubynsky); and reproductions of the works of T. Shevchenko, M. Burachek, F. Krasytsky, M. Pymonenko, O. Sudomora, M. Paraschuk, F. Balavensky, and other artists. The journal was closed down by the Russian government following the outbreak of the First World War.

Sian dialects. Ukrainian dialects spoken in a narrow belt running along the Sian River from the upper Sian in the south to the Polish dialectal zone in the north and west. Except for a small northeastern section, the Sian dialectal area remained after 1945 within the political borders of Poland. Its speakers were dispersed as a result of postwar 'repatriation' to Soviet Ukraine and the forced resettlement of those left behind in 1947 in western and northern Poland. It is likely that the Sian dialects (and part of the contiguous *Lemko dialects) constituted a prehistoric transitional Ukrainian-Polish dialect, whose speakers in the west (between the Wisłok [Vyslik] and Sian rivers) became Polonized during the 14th to 19th centuries.

The dialects had the following phonetic traits: (1) retention of the distinction between the ancient *i* and *ы*, though not in the groups *k'i, h'i, x'i* and *čы, žы, šы, rы* (eg, *žыti* [Standard Ukrainian (SU) *žyty*] 'to live'); retention of the groups *kы, hы, xы* in the south and north, but their change into *k'e, h'e, x'e* when stressed, and into *k'i, h'i, x'i* when unstressed in the center; (2) evolution of the groups *pě, bě, vě, mě* into *pji, bji, vji, mn'i* (eg, *bjílyj, mn'íra* [SU *bílyj, míra*] 'white, measure'); (3) tense pronunciation of stressed *e* and raised pronunciation of unstressed *e, o* as *i, u* (eg, *vêrx, muludíc'i* [SU *verx, molodýcja*] 'top, young woman'), and lowered pronunciation of stressed *y, i* (eg, *bek* [SU *byk*] 'bull'); (4) lowered pronunciation of *e* as *a* before and after *r* and after *č, ž, š, j* (eg, *saradína, šastyj* [SU *seredýna, šostyj*] 'middle, sixth'); (5) retention in certain dialects of *'u* from *ē* (eg, *t'útka* [SU *títka*] 'aunt'), and of *o, ou, ы, y* from *ō* (eg, *myst* [SU *mist*] 'bridge'); (6) retention of *'a* in the north and south, but its alteration into *'e* in the middle of the zone (and *'i* when unstressed [eg, *muludic'i* (SU *molodýci*) 'young women']); (7) labialization of the group *av* into *oŭ* (eg, *stoŭ* [SU *stav*] 'he stood'); (8) semisoft *l* before *e, i* (eg, *bыli* [SU *buly*] 'they were'); (9) change of *l* into *ŭ* after a vowel at the end of a syllable (eg, *viŭ* [SU *vil*] 'ox'); (10) absence of epenthetic *l'* after labials in verb forms (eg, *lómju* [SU *lomljú*] 'am breaking', but *ziml'ê* [SU *zemlja*] 'land'); (11) hardening of the group *r'u* (and sporadically *r'e* from *r'a*) (eg, *žúrus'i, purédok* [SU *žurjusja, porjadok*] 'I worry, order'); (12) hardening of *-t', -s', -c'* at the ends of words and of the suffixes *-s'k-, -c'k-, -ycju* (eg, *xódit, vês* [fs'on in the north], *xlópic, rubítnicu* [SU *xódyt', ves', xlópec', robitnýcju*] 'he walks, entire, boy, worker [fem acc]'); (13) absence of lengthened consonants in nouns of the type *vis'il'ê* (SU *vesillja*) 'wedding'; (14) prothetic *v-/ŭ-, j-*, and (rarely) *h-* before initial vowels (eg, *vóku, hós'in, jíncыj* [SU *óko, ósin', ínšyj*] 'eye, autumn, other'); (15) the changes *vn, bn > mn, st' > s'c', n'k > jk* (eg, *mnuk, drimnыj, s'c'iná, malêjk'ij* [SU *vnuk, dribnyj, stina, malen'kyj*] 'grandson, petty, wall, little'); (16) postpalatal *ŋ* in the groups *ŋk, ŋg* (eg, *rыŋka* 'skillet'); (17) progressive assimilation of the groups *žk, žc* as *žg, ždz* (eg, *knížga, kníždz'i* [SU *knyžka, knyžci*] 'book' nom and loc); (18) palatalization of consonantal groups before *i* (eg, *z'l'is, d'vi* [SU *zliz, dvi*] 'he got off, two'); and (19) phonetics between words of the type *d'it, malízmu* [SU *did, my* *maly*] 'grandfather, we had', with changes of the preposition/prefix *v* into *f/x* before unvoiced consonants and into *h* before voiced consonants (eg, *hdóma, xpaй* [SU *vdóma, vpav*] 'at home, he fell').

In declension, the dialects had features such as endings of the type *kós'c'om, tom mom rukóm/toй moй rukóй, f silú, pal'c'íma, pu pul'óx* [SU *kístju, cijéju, mojéju rukóju, v selí, pál'cjamy, po poljáx*] 'with a bone, with my hand, in the village, with the fingers, on fields'); separate dual forms (eg, *d'vi ruc'í* [SU *dvi ruký*] 'two hands'); use of nominative instead of vocative singular forms, except in personal names with zero endings (eg, *mam* [SU *mamo*] 'mother!'); uncontracted adjectival forms (eg, *ládnuji póli* [SU *harne pole*] 'fine field') and widespread use of soft-type adjectives (eg, *ríd'-n'ij* [SU *ridnyj*] 'native'); and enclitic pronominal forms (eg, *mi, t'i, ti, s'i, si, ji, ju/n'u* [SU *mene/meni, tebe, tobi, sebe, sobi, jiji/jij, jiji*] 'myself/to me, you, to you, oneself, to oneself, her/to her, her [acc]').

In conjugation, the dialects had infinitive forms such as *mučý, pičý* (SU *mohtý, pektý*) 'to be able, to bake'; present-tense forms such as *hádam, -aš, -at* (SU *hovorju, -ryš, -rjat'*) 'I/you/they speak'; past-tense forms such as *pisáйjim, -is, -álam, -álas, -álizmu, -álisti* (SU *ia pysáv, ty pysáv, ja pysála, ty pysála, my pysály, vy pysály*) 'I/you/I (fem)/you (fem)/we/you (pl) wrote'; future-tense forms such as *búdu pisáй, búdu pisála* (SU *budu pysaty*) 'I (masc, fem) will write'; conditional forms such as *xudíй bыm, xudíй bыs, xudíli bыzmu, xudíli bыsti* (SU *ja b xodýv, ty b xodýv, my b xodýly, vy b xodý-ly*) 'I/you sing/we/you (pl) would go'; and imperative forms such as *xot', xód'mu, xót'ti* (SU *xodý, xodímo, xodít'*) 'you/let us/you (pl) go'.

Other traits included adverbs ending in -*'i* (eg, *lad'n'i* [SU *harno*] 'nicely'); the suffix -*isku* (eg, *žýtnisku* [SU *žytnycja*] 'rye store'); the suffixes -*'ê, -'êti* added to the surnames of unmarried girls (eg, *Kuval'ê* [SU *Kovalivna*] 'Koval's daughter'); the prefixes *na-* (in superlatives, eg, *nalad'-n'ššыj* [SU *najharnišyj*] 'most beautiful') and *pry-* (instead of *pro-*, eg, *pryrok* [SU *prorok*] 'prophet'); prepositions and conjunctions such as *biz, bêstu, žy, žyby* (SU *bez/kriz', prote, ščo, ščob*) 'without/through, however, that, so that'; and characteristic stresses and lexemes, many of which are Polonisms, particularly calques and, along the linguistic border, phonetic substitutions.

BIBLIOGRAPHY
Verkhrats'kyi, I. 'Pro hovor dolivs'kyi,' *ZNTSh*, 35–6 (1900)
Pshep'iurs'ka, M. *Nadsians'kyi hovir* (Warsaw 1938)
Pshepiurs'ka-Ovcharenko, M. 'Na pohranychchiakh nadsians'koho hovoru,' *ZNTSh*, 162 (1954)

O. Horbach

Sian Lowland (Nadsianska kotlovyna). A triangle-shaped lowland along the Sian River situated between the Little Polish Upland, the Carpathian foothills, and the Opilia Upland and Roztochia. It merges with the Dniester Lowland in the southeast. With the exception of its southeastern tip, located in Ukraine, the lowland is situated in present-day Poland. The western section of the formation, including the Sian region and the southern Kholm region, has historically been inhabited by Ukrainians.

The Sian Lowland is a tectonic depression along the Carpathian foothills filled in by Miocene strata (up to 300 m thick) covered with glacial and alluvial deposits. It consists of elevated plateaus (the tallest being Tarnohorod) dissected by the valleys of rivers, such as the Tanev, the Liubachivka, the Shklo, and the Vyshnia. Loess can be found in parts of the plateaus, and dunes are situated in some of its sandy reaches. A large proportion of the lowland's forests have been cleared out, although pine forests mixed with firs and birches occur in the region's sandy areas, and fir forests mixed with hornbeams and maples grow in its heavier soils. The lowland has a population density of 80 persons/sq km; the population is predominantly (75 percent) rural.

Sian River [Sjan] (Polish: San). The largest (right-bank) Carpathian tributary of the Vistula River. It is 444 km long and drains a basin area of 16,730 sq km. It flows quickly near its headwaters in the Beskyds. The cities of Peremyshl and Jarosław are situated on it. Although only the source of the river is located in Ukraine itself, the Sian runs for 50 km along the Polish-Ukrainian border and then continues through a large section of Ukrainian ethnic territory in Poland, notably the *Sian region.

Sian region [Sjan] (Posiannia, also Zasiannia). A name occasionally used to designate the area situated approx along both sides of the Sian River north of the Lemko region and the city of Sianik along the border between Ukrainian and Polish ethnic territory. The Sian region includes sections of the Low and Middle Beskyds, the Carpathian foothills, and the Sian Lowland. Its major centers include the cities of *Peremyshl, *Jarosław, and *Sianik as well as Brzozów (Bereziv), Radymno, Przeworsk (Perevorsk), and Leżajsk. It was part of the Kievan Rus' state and the Galician-Volhynian principality before coming under Polish control, as part of the Rus' voivodeship, in 1340–1772. In 1772–1918 the Sian region was part of the Austrian Empire, in 1918–19, part of the Western Ukrainian National Republic, and in 1923–39, part of the Polish state. In 1939 the region was divided between Germany (in the Generalgouvernement) and the Soviet Union along the Sian River, and then in 1941 occupied totally by the Germans. It was subsequently taken over by the Soviet Union and then ceded once more to Poland in a treaty signed on 16 August 1945. Only a tiny corner of the region, around Peremyshl, was incorporated into the Ukrainian SSR.

Starting in the 15th century the Sian region was subjected to extensive Polonization with the colonization of lands by Polish settlers, the Polonization of incoming German settlers, and the common switch of religious and linguistic affiliation among the local population to the Roman Catholic rite and the Polish language. Over time the area's Ukrainian population became a definite minority, and the boundary between Polish and Ukrainian ethnic territory was rolled back approx 50 km to the east, from near the Vistula River to the Sian. Only a few pockets of Ukrainians remain in those easternmost reaches, the furthest afield being in the village of Ternavka, in the Przeworsk region. Other villages in those eastern areas generally had an ethnically mixed population in which the Ukrainians (commonly known as *zamishantsi*) generally spoke Polish even though they understood the Ukrainian language and were adherents of the Greek Catholic church. It is estimated that in 1939 approx 40,000 Ukrainians lived in the Sian region west of the Polish-Ukrainian border. That number included about 50 per cent of the Ukrainian population that used Polish as its home language, but not the *zamishantsi*.

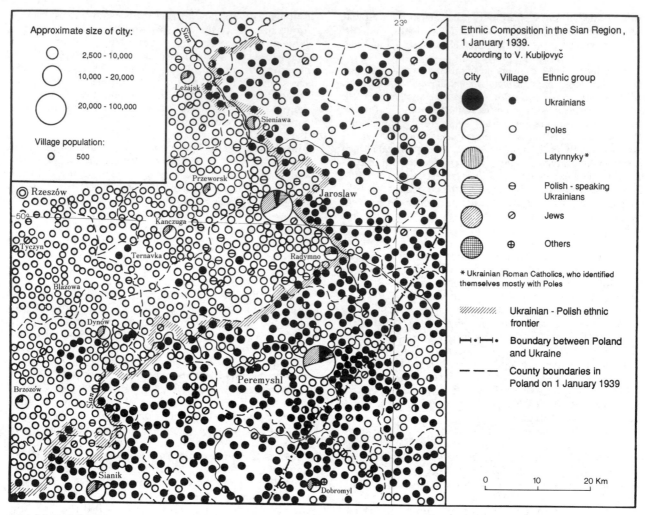

SIAN REGION

After the establishment of postwar boundaries in 1945–6, most of the Ukrainian population in the Sian region was resettled in the Ukrainian SSR. A smaller proportion was resettled in western or northern Poland, and only a tiny rump of Ukrainians was left in and around Peremyshl. The only completely Ukrainian settlement remaining in the region was the village of Kalnykiv, east of Radymno.

V. Kubijovyč

Sianik or **Sianok** [Sjanik or Sjanok] (Polish: Sanok). IV-3. A city (1989 pop 39,400) on the Sian River and a county center in Krosno voivodeship, Poland. It was first mentioned, as a fortified town of Kievan Rus', in the Hypatian Chronicle under the year 1150. Later it was part of Peremyshl and then Galicia principalities. It was granted the rights of *Magdeburg law by Yurii II Boleslav in 1339, and developed into an important trade center. In the mid-14th century Sianik was annexed by Poland and turned into the capital of Sianik land in Rus' voivodeship. In 1550, during the course of Catholic persecution of the Orthodox, St Demetrius's Church was closed. Toward the end of the 16th century the town declined. With the partition of Poland in 1772, it was transferred to Austria, and became a county center of the Galician crownland. In the

second half of the 19th century the town grew as a railway link and attracted industry. Its population increased from 2,500 at mid-century to 5,100 in 1880, 9,000 in 1900, and 12,100 in 1921. At the same time Ukrainian residents of Sianik were subjected to strong Polonization pressures.

Ukrainian peasant homes in the open-air museum in Sianik

From 1880 to 1900 the Ukrainian population fell from 18 percent to 13.5 percent. In the interwar period the town remained a center of Ukrainian cultural life in the eastern Lemko region. In 1930 the *Lemkivshchyna Museum was established there, and in 1936 Sianik was chosen as the seat of the *Lemko Apostolic Administration. At the beginning of 1939, 1,800 (11.5 percent) of the town's residents were Ukrainian, 8,700 (56 percent) were Polish, and 5,100 (32.5 percent) were Jewish. Under the German occupation (1939–44) the Ukrainian population increased to 3,000, and Ukrainian cultural life revived. A Ukrainian secondary school was set up, and the Ukrainian Relief Committee, under P. Bilaniuk, was active. In 1946–7, during *Operation Wisła, Ukrainians were deported from the town, and all signs of community life died out.

Today Sianik is an industrial city. Its regional museum contains many Ukrainian monuments, including some icons from the former Lemkivshchyna Museum. The open-air Museum of Folk Architecture (est 1958) contains many exhibits by Boiko, Lemko, and other Ukrainian folk artists. Its periodical (published from 1969) often deals with Ukrainian folklore. The city's chief architectural monuments are the castle (built in 1523–48, renovated in 1672–7 and 1952–3), the Franciscan church and monastery (17th and 19th centuries), and a church in the classical style (1784–9). An Orthodox parish and a branch of the Ukrainian Social and Cultural Society have been set up.

BIBLIOGRAPHY
Tarnovych, Iu. *Kniazhe misto Sianik* (Cracow 1941)

V. Kubijovyč

Siberia

Siberia. A large portion of Russia's territory in Asia, stretching from the Arctic Ocean south to Kazakhstan and Mongolia (3,500 km), and from the Urals east to the Pacific watershed (7,000 km). The region has an area of about 10 million sq km and a 1989 population of 26 million. In pre-Soviet usage Siberia included the *Far East and had an area of 12.5 million sq km. Its southern border with the so-called Steppe krai coincided largely with the present border, except that Omsk county belonged to the Steppe krai.

Physical features. The main geomorphological regions of Siberia are the West Siberian Lowland (a huge plain of about 2 million sq km) and its southern continuation, the South Siberian Lowland; the Central Siberian Plateau, between the Yenisei and Lena rivers (average altitude 500–700 m); the mountains of southern Siberia (Altai, Saian, Yablonovyi, and Stanovoi ranges); and the mountains of northeastern Siberia (Verkhoiansk, Cherskii, and Momskii ranges). Siberia is rich in natural resources: it had 75 percent of the former USSR coal deposits, petroleum and natural gas, iron ore, rare (gold) and nonferrous metals, and diamonds.

The climate of Siberia is continental and for the most part moderately cold: subpolar and polar in the north and moderately warm and dry in the southwest. The average annual temperature is almost everywhere below 0°C (–15 to –18°C in the northeast); the average July temperature is 2 to 5°C in the extreme north and 22°C in the southwest; and the average January temperature is –16°C in the southwest and –50°C in the northeast. The world's lowest temperatures, adjusted for elevation, were recorded at Verkhoiansk (–68°C) and Oimiakon (–71°C). Precipitation (coming mostly in the summer) ranges from 150–250 mm in the northeast to 500–530 mm in the west and reaches 2 m in the mountains. Snow cover lasts 5 to 10 months; much of the area is covered by permafrost. The dense river network empties mostly into the Arctic Ocean. The largest rivers are the Ob, Yenisei, and Lena. Ice-free for 5 to 8 months of the year, they are important transportation routes and sources of power.

Ukrainians in Siberia. Information about Ukrainians in Siberia before the close of the 19th century, which marks the onset of mass peasant colonization, is rather incidental and inaccurate. Ukrainians made a significant contribution to the economic and cultural development of the region. There were Ukrainians among the Russian traders and state servitors who colonized Siberia and the Far East in the 17th and 18th centuries and then Kamchatka and Alaska. There were many Ukrainians among the exiles from various social strata who were banished by the authorities to Siberia. In 1642 'Cherkes' (as Ukrainians were known in Muscovy in the 17th century) families from *Slobidska Ukraine (188 people altogether) were deported to the Lena River, where they arrived only in 1646–7. This deportation was followed by others in 1646 and 1649. Even more Ukrainians were deported in the second half of the 17th century. Most of them were political exiles – opponents of Moscow's policy in Ukraine or persons suspected of 'vacillation' or treason. Among them were the relatives and supporters of Hetman I. *Vyhovsky, the opponents of the Moscow appointee I. Briukhovetsky (1660s), Hetman D. *Mnohohrishny and his relatives (1670s), and Hetman I. *Samoilovych, with his son Yakiv and nephew Mykhailo (1680s). After I. Mazepa's defeat at Poltava (1709) many 'Mazepists,' such as General Judge V. Chuikevych, Col H. Novytsky, and the Myrovych family, ended up in Siberia. In 1723 Mazepa's nephew, A. *Voinarovsky, was exiled to Yakutsk. In the 1760s participants in the Koliivshchyna rebellion were condemned to Siberian penal colonies, and in the 1770s, after the destruction of the Zaporozhian Sich, some of its officers were exiled to Siberia. In the 19th century Ukrainian revolutionaries (the *Decembrists), populists (A. Krasovsky, S. Bohomolets, S. Kovalyk, Ye. Kovalsky, and Ya. Stefanovych), Social Democrats, and Bolsheviks (H. Petrovsky and M. Skrypnyk) were exiled there by court sentence or administrative order. Participants in peasant uprisings, such as U. *Karmaliuk, were deported there as convicts or so-called free settlers. Some Ukrainian civic and cultural figures suspected of 'scparatism' by the authorities were transferred to government positions in Siberia. Many Ukrainians served in the Siberian Cossack hosts.

Ukrainians played an important role in the economic, administrative, and cultural life of Siberia. They were found also in the higher administrative ranks: Gen M. Sulyma, the governor general of East (1833–4) and West (1834–6) Siberia, Gen P. Kaptsevych, the governor general of Tobolsk and Tomsk gubernias (1822–6), and several other governors of Siberian gubernias were of Ukrainian origin. They were also prominent in the church hierarchy of Siberia: F. *Leshchynsky (1702–21), I. *Maksymovych (1711–15), A. Stakhovsky (1721–40), A. *Matsiievych (1741–2), and P. Koniuskevych (1758–68) were metropolitans of Tobolsk and Siberia, and I. Kulchytsky (1727–31), I. Nerunovych (1732–47), and S. Krystalsky (1753–71) were bishops of Irkutsk. They surrounded themselves with clergy, mostly of Ukrainian origin, who contributed significantly to the cultural development of Siberia. Some of them (notably H. Novytsky) did research on Siberia and the Far East.

The mass immigration of Ukrainian peasants to Siberia began in the late 1880s. In 1885–1914, 1,742,000 people (almost all of them Ukrainians) from nine Ukrainian gubernias and over 2,000,000 from all Ukrainian territories emigrated beyond the Urals. Of these, almost 35 percent settled in Siberia; the remaining settled mostly in the Steppe krai (now Kazakhstan) and the Far East. According to the 1897 census there were 142,000 Ukrainians in Siberia, 120,000 of them in the western regions. The real figure was unquestionably much higher. The proportion of Ukrainians in the population was highest in the southwestern part of Tomsk and Tobolsk gubernias. This sort of concentration reflected a desire by the Ukrainians to settle near their own people and in a forest-steppe or steppe environment with which they were familiar. During and immediately after the First World War there was little immigration to Siberia from Ukraine. Hence, the Ukrainian population of Siberia in 1914 was only slightly lower than in the 1926 census. This figure was about 1 million, or 12 percent of the total population. Since in fact about 19 percent of the inhabitants of Siberia originated from Ukraine, the actual figure was probably higher.

1917–20. The February Revolution in Russia sparked a vigorous political movement in Siberia. Ukrainians created various organizations: the Ukrainian Free Community in Omsk, the Regional Council in Tomsk, the Altai Gubernia Council in Kainsk, and other associations in Slavgorod, Kurgan, and Biisk. Branches of Kievan relief institutions for deportees from Galicia and Bukovyna and captured Ukrainian soldiers of the Austrian army were set up in Omsk and other towns. Some Ukrainian POWs became active in Ukrainian communities in Siberia. Ukrainian papers appeared, among them *Ukraïns'kyi holos* in Omsk and *Ukraïns'ke slovo* in Tomsk. At the same time military organizations were formed, and at the end of 1917 several separate Ukrainian units were set up, including the Sahaidachny Battalion in Omsk and a battalion in Irkutsk. At the beginning of August 1917 the First Ukrainian Congress of Siberia took place in Omsk and established the Supreme Ukrainian Council of Siberia. Headed by H. Kontsevych (vice-president, M. Novoselsky), the council sent a delegate to the Central Rada in Kiev.

In early October 1917 the democratic parties of Siberia held a conference which proclaimed Siberia's autonomy and convened the Extraordinary Congress of Siberia in Tomsk on 6–15 December 1917. The congress set up a provisional government consisting of the Siberian Provisional Oblast Duma (which included five Ukrainian deputies), an oblast council (responsible to the Duma), and an executive body (which included a Ukrainian member named Sulyma). The congress greeted the Central Rada in Kiev on the proclamation of the Third Universal, and the oblast soviet refused (7 January 1918) to recognize the Bolshevik government in Petrograd. At the end of January 1918 the Tomsk soviet of workers and soldiers disbanded the Siberian oblast council, but the provisional government continued to operate. Thus, there were two governments in Siberia. The position of the oblast council and the Provisional Autonomous Government was bolstered by the landing of Japanese and British troops at Vladivostok in April, the offensive of the Czechoslovak Corps against the

Bolsheviks in May, and the landing of American troops in August 1918.

The Second Siberian All-Ukrainian Conference took place in Omsk on 11–13 August 1918 while these events unfolded. It was an important milestone in the history of Ukrainians in Siberia. It demanded that the Siberian oblast duma proclaim the independence of Siberia, give self-government to the various nationalities (including Ukrainians), and form a Siberian army for the country's defense. These hopes were quickly dashed. The Whites had entered the military contest in Siberia and had forced the abdication of the democratic Provisional Autonomous Government in November 1918 to the central Russian Provisional Government (later headed by Admiral A. *Kolchak). This development represented a major setback to the Ukrainian movement in Siberia. A second major blow for the Ukrainians occurred in late 1919, when the Sahaidachny Battalion was dissolved after suffering heavy casualties against the Bolsheviks on the Ural front. This disaster was followed in January 1920 by the defeat of Kolchak's forces by Bolshevik forces, who then advanced and had taken control of the entire Far East by November 1920.

1920s. The population of Siberia remained fairly stable during and after the war, with relatively few casualties during the revolution but little influx, since the flow of immigrants from west of the Urals was interrupted until the end of the civil war. Immigration increased somewhat after 1924, with a planned resettlement program. As a result the population of Siberia grew only modestly, from about 10 million at the beginning of 1915 to about 11 million (including Ishim and Kurgan okrugs, which belonged officially to Ural krai) by the end of 1926. The percentage of Russians, Ukrainians, and Belarusians together was practically the same (86.9) as in 1911 (86.7); the indigenous population declined from 10.6 to 7.5 percent.

Ukrainians lived mainly in large groups on the arable lands of southwestern Siberia, which was part of the so-called Central Asian Steppe krai. In the Siberian part of this Steppe krai, consisting of almost the entire Slavgorod and parts of Omsk and Kamensk okrugs, Ukrainians formed a majority of the population: of 580,000 inhabitants, 310,000 (53.4 percent) were Ukrainians, 200,000 (34 percent) were Russians, and 25,000 (4.3 percent) were indigenous peoples. In the 17 raions of the Siberian part of the Central Asian Steppe krai Ukrainians formed a majority in 12. Another 400,000 Ukrainians lived in the part of west Siberia where Russians formed a majority. There they accounted for 10 to 40 percent of the population and lived usually in separate villages.

Most of the 115,000 Ukrainians in east Siberia settled on pockets of fertile chernozem soils. According to the 1926 census they constituted 8.8 percent of the total rural population. Their largest urban concentrations in Siberia were in Omsk (9,700), Slavgorod (4,100), Krasnoiarsk (1,600), Irkutsk (1,300) and Tomsk (1,200). Ukrainians accounted for a notably high percentage of the population in Slavgorod and Omsk okrugs.

Since the 1930s. Siberian development played a key role in the long-range economic planning of the Soviet Union with the institution of *five-year plans. The region was to be developed for the exploitation of its industrial natural resources. Starting in the 1930s a number of measures were taken to facilitate these changes: new energy

Political and administrative boundaries of former USSR, 1990

— International boundary
—— Boundary between Kazakh SSR and RSFSR
— Boundaries of oblasts, krais and autonomous SSRs
--- Boundaries of autonomous oblasts and autonomous okrugs
═══ Present boundaries of West Siberia and East Siberia

◦—◦ Gas pipeline   ▲ Gas field
•—• Oil pipeline   ▲ Oil field
▨ Territories settled by Ukrainians

Large economic regions
········· Eastern boundary of the East Siberia large
economic region, 1938-57, 1960-63 and
northwestern boundary of the West Siberia
large economic region, 1963-71

*Exept where noted, names
of administrative units are the
same as those of their centers

▨ Autonomous SSRs
▥ Autonomous oblasts
▨ Autonomous okrugs
⋰ Krais
☐ Oblasts
Tomsk Administrative centers*

SIBERIA

sources (such as the Kuznetsk Coal Basin) were developed; a second Siberian railway line was built; and mining and metallurgical facilities were built in Norilsk in order to obtain the strategic nickel and stimulate development in the far north. Millions of victims of Stalin's terror, imprisoned in Siberian forced-labor camps, worked and died in the process. Some impressive gains were made in industry; they are reflected in the growth of the urban population from 1.0 to 4.4 million (from 9.2 to 31.3 percent of the total). In the same period agriculture declined, largely as a result of the collectivization campaign.

During the Second World War Siberia's economy grew at a tremendous pace as a massive effort was made to supply the Soviet Union's military demands. About one million people and hundreds of industrial plants (mainly from Ukraine) were evacuated there; hundreds of new factories were built; and coal mining (to replace the Donets Basin deposits), heavy industry, and the chemical industry were expanded. Gross industrial production

almost doubled in 1940–5. In the postwar period the region has continued to grow, with special emphasis placed on heavy industry, machine building, coal and oil extraction, the chemical industry, and hydroelectric power. Agricultural production has also grown, mostly as a result of an increase in the area sown.

As the Siberian economy expanded, its population grew through natural increase and as a result of immigration from the western regions of the Union. In the 1950s, because of hydroelectric power dam construction and the development of resource-based industries, population growth was more rapid in east than in west Siberia. By 1960–73 the emigration of people from Siberia, particularly west Siberia, was greater than the immigration thereto. In the 1960s the population exchange between Ukraine and Siberia proved to be in Ukraine's favor for the first time: in 1968–9, 50,000 Ukrainians emigrated to Siberia, and 68,000 Siberians came to Ukraine (most of them returnees). Ukrainian workers continue to take temporary (two- to three-year) jobs in Siberia, particularly on major projects in east Siberia (the Baikal-Amur Mainline) and the northern districts of west Siberia (the oil and gas fields), because wages in Siberia are two to three times higher than in Ukraine.

The national composition of Siberia has changed considerably in the last 50 years. From the end of the 1920s there has been a steady flow of Ukrainians into Siberia: deportees and prisoners of concentration camps (where Ukrainians constituted a majority), settlers of virgin steppes in the 1950s, and voluntary workers attracted by better living conditions and a more open political atmosphere. In the 1940s between 300,000 and 400,000 Germans from the Volga region and Ukraine were resettled in Siberia. The 1959 and 1970 censuses provide nationality figures only for separate oblasts and not for Siberia as a whole, and tend to underestimate the number of Ukrainians and other non-Russian Europeans. Siberia's national composition according to the 1979 census is shown in table 1.

TABLE 1
National composition of Siberia (1979 census)

Nationality	Population (in 1,000s)	Percent
Ukrainian	682	2.9
Russian	19,972	84.8
German	460	2.0
Tatar	445	1.9
Buriat	128	0.5
Yakut	314	1.3
Other	1,558	6.6
Total	23,559	100.0

Between 1926 and 1959 the number of Ukrainians and indigenous peoples declined in absolute and relative terms, and the number of Russians increased. The group called 'others' grew, mainly because of the influx of Germans. In the 1960s the number of Ukrainians and other European non-Russian people continued to decline (in part because of the Soviet regime's policy of Russification), but the absolute and relative numbers of indigenous people increased, mostly because of their high birth rate (table 2).

The distribution of Ukrainians in Siberia has undergone great changes, according to the Soviet censuses. Their numbers in west Siberia fell dramatically, from 738,000 (9.8 percent of the population) in 1926 to 463,000 (3.8

TABLE 2
Changes in national composition of Siberia, 1926–1970

Nationality	1926		1959		1970	
	1,000s	%	1,000s	%	1,000s	%
Ukrainian	853	7.8	692	3.6	580	2.7
Russian	8,304	76.2	16,075	83.6	18,121	85.1
Belarusian	323	3.0	139	0.7	141	0.6
Indigenous	841	7.7	1,062	5.6	1,455	6.8
Other	586	5.3	1,244	6.5	1,027	4.8
Total	10,907	100.0	19,212	100.0	21,324	100.0

percent) in 1959 and 360,000 (2.7 percent) in 1970, and then rose, with new immigrants, to 387,000 (3.0 percent) in 1979; the number of Ukrainians in east Siberia grew from 115,000 (3.4 percent) in 1926 to 229,000 (3.3 percent) in 1959, then fell to 220,000 (2.7 percent) in 1970, and rose again to 227,000 (2.8 percent) in 1979. The number of Ukrainians declined mainly in southwestern Siberia, where in the 1920s they accounted for one-third or more of the population (in the part that belonged to the Central Asian Steppe krai). Their numbers increased in east Siberia, however, particularly in the far north. In the Yakutsk ASSR, for example, Ukrainians increased from 100 (0.03 percent) in 1926 to 1,200 (0.2 percent) in 1959, 20,300 (3.1 percent) in 1970, and 46,300 (5.4 percent) in 1979. By contrast, the number and proportion of Ukrainians in Omsk oblast in 1979 was only 103,800 (5.3 percent), a decline from 104,600 (5.8 percent) in 1970, 128,000 (7.8 percent) in 1959, and 166,000 (22.2 percent) in 1926 (within the present Omsk oblast borders).

The figures on national composition do not coincide with the figures on language use, because increasingly the non-Russian immigrants and their descendants have adopted Russian. In the 1959 census 54 percent of Ukrainians in Siberia listed Ukrainian as their mother tongue, compared with 49.3 percent in 1979. In 1979 only 85,000 Ukrainians (12 percent) spoke Ukrainian fluently. Linguistic Russification is higher in those regions where Ukrainians settled at the turn of the century, and lower in areas of recent settlement, such as east Siberia and the far north. Soviet statistics on nationality and language were not entirely reliable. It is probable that there are over 2 million Siberian inhabitants of Ukrainian origin. The long-term Russification of Ukrainians in Siberia has been facilitated by urbanization and the mixing of different nationalities in the state farms. A high percentage of Ukrainians have intermarried. At the same time there are no Ukrainian schools (at the beginning of the 1930s they operated briefly in west Siberia) and no local Ukrainian press or books. The other peoples of European origin (except for the Germans) have been subjected to the same kind of Russification. Russification, however, has made little headway among the more numerous of the indigenous peoples who have had their own autonomous republics or oblasts.

BIBLIOGRAPHY
Kiselev, S. *Drevniaia istoriia Iuzhnoi Sibiri*, 2nd edn (Moscow 1951)
Pokshishevskii, V. *Zaselenie Sibiri* (Irkutsk 1951)
Problemy izucheniia natsional'nykh otnoshenii v Sibiri na sovremennom etape (Novosibirsk 1967)
Istoriia Sibiri s drevneishikh vremen do nashykh dnei, 5 vols (Leningrad 1968–9)
Zapadnaia Sibir' (Moscow 1971)
Morozova, T. *Ekonomicheskaia geografiia Sibiri* (Moscow 1975)
Krestianstvo Sibiri v epokhu feodalizma (Novosibirsk 1982)
Krestianstvo Sibiri v epokhu kapitalizma (Novosibirsk 1983)
Obshchestvennyi byt i kul'tura russkogo naselenniia Sibiri, XVIII–nachalo XX v. (Novosibirsk 1983)
Stebelsky, I. 'Ukrainian Peasant Colonization East of the Urals, 1896–1914,' *Soviet Geography*, 1984, no. 9
Kul'turno-bytovye protsessy u russkikh Sibiri (Novosibirsk 1985)
                                   V. Kubijovyč, O. Ohloblyn, I. Svit

Sich. A mass physical-education and fire-fighting organization that was active in Galicia from 1900 to 1930 and spread from there to Bukovyna, Transcarpathia, and

Officers of the Sich society in Lviv county

Ukrainian communities abroad. Beyond its immediate practical purpose, it strove to promote national consciousness and to raise the educational and cultural level of the peasantry and working class. Organized by leading members of the *Ukrainian Radical party, its ideology was secular and somewhat anticlerical.

The first Sich society was founded by K. *Trylovsky in Zavallia, Sniatyn county, in May 1900. In the next few years similar societies arose in Kolomyia and Horodenka counties, and then in other counties of Galicia and Bukovyna. Local village and town societies were grouped first into county organizations. A central association for all of Galicia was formed in Stanyslaviv in 1908. Its head office was located in Kolomyia. The chief executive body, the Supreme Sich Committee, consisted of Trylovsky (president), I. Sanduliak (vice-president), I. Chuprei (secretary), and M. Lahodynsky (treasurer). In 1912 it was renamed the Ukrainian Sich Union (USU), and its office was moved to Lviv. USU executive members were Trylovsky (general otaman), Ya. Vesolovsky (general *osaul*), M. Balytsky (secretary), S. Vynnykiv (general treasurer), D. Katamai (general quartermaster), and F. Kalynovych (general *chetar*). In addition to those already named, the key organizers were A. Kuzmych, Yu. Solomiichuk-Yuzenchuk, P. Shekeryk-Donykiv, A. Chaikovsky, R. Stavnychy, L. Lepky, R. Dashkevych, H. Nychka, V. Hurkevych, V. Lysy, V. Bemko, D. Vitovsky, S. Ripetsky, M. Uhryn-Bezhrishny, O. Demchuk, M. Khrobak, and O. Semeniuk. The number of local societies increased steadily; by 1913 there were over 900 branches, with a combined membership of 80,000. Sich members wore the local folk costume, a crimson sash over the shoulder inscribed with the wearer's place-name, and a hat decorated with a red feather and a star-shaped badge. From 1910 a special uniform was worn by members of urban and some rural branches. Each member carried a long-handled wooden Hutsul ax. Village and county branches had their own flags.

The Sich societies held annual county and, later, province-wide congresses. Their program included a parade, choreographed exercises, and a concert. The first congress was held in Kolomyia in 1902. Larger ones took place in Stanyslaviv in 1911 and Sniatyn in 1912. The largest, known as the Shevchenko assembly, was held in June 1914 in Lviv. Approx 12,000 members of the Sich, Sokil,

and Ukrainian Sich Riflemen's societies, the Plast scouting association, and sports clubs took part, and Czech, Croatian, and Slovenian Sokol and other physical education organizations sent observers.

After Trylovsky founded the *Ukrainian Sich Riflemen (USS) society in March 1913, a riflemen's section, chaired by D. Katamai, was set up in the USU to train young men in the military arts. Eventually the section broke away from the USU and formed separate Sich Riflemen's units (96 in 1914). Their field exercises were conducted according to O. Demchuk and O. Semeniuk's infantryman's manual (1914). In August 1914 the USS Legion within the Austrian army was formed out of volunteers belonging to the USS, USU, and Sokil societies.

To popularize and promote the Sich movement, Trylovsky and Chuprei edited and published songbooks; annual almanacs (11 by 1914); magazines, such as the monthly *Zoria (1902–3) and the biweekly *Khlops'ka pravda* (1903, 1909) in Kolomyia; and the official Sich organ *Sichovi visty (1912–14, 1922–4) in Lviv.

After the First World War, the Sich societies resumed their activities in many localities of Galicia, until the Polish authorities prohibited them, in 1924 (the last local society, in Horbachi near Lviv, was closed down in 1930). Their restricted physical-education and sports program was continued by branches of the *Luh society.

In Bukovyna the first Sich society was founded in 1903 in Kitsman by S. Yarychevsky and O. Popovych. The central body, the Union of Siches, was set up in 1904 in Chernivtsi. The presidents were Ye. Pihuliak, T. Halip, and R. Siretsky; other leading members were I. Popovych, H. Hordy, Yu. Lysan, L. Yasinchuk, and D. Rusnak. A pan-Bukovynian Sich assembly took place in Chernivtsi in 1912. By then there were 112 local branches, with a combined membership of 9,000. Under the interwar Rumanian occupation the societies were banned.

In Russian-ruled Ukraine, community leaders followed the development of the Sich movement in Galicia with great interest, but were not permitted to set up similar societies. After the 1917 Revolution they established a Sich society in Kiev, and its statute was approved in 1918 by the Ukrainian government. In February 1919 Trylovsky and O. Andriievsky organized the Supreme Sich Committee in Vinnytsia, and in October 1919 P. Shekeryk-Donykiv and A. Shmigelsky formed a Sich society in Kamianets-Podilskyi. Its membership grew to 300, but the Soviet occupation of Podilia ended all efforts to build a Sich network in the region.

In Transcarpathia a Sich Committee was formed in 1920 in Uzhhorod at the initiative of Trylovsky. That year, D. and V. Klempush founded the first Transcarpathian Sich society in Yasinia. In 1938–9 the *Carpathian Sich grew out of the Transcarpathian Sich movement.

In the United States and Canada, the Sich movement began with the founding of the physical education and rifle society of the First Branch of the Ukrainian Sich Riflemen in New York in July 1915. A central organization, the Sitch Ukrainian American Athletic Association, was set up in November 1916 under the leadership of P. Zadoretsky. By 1920 it had approx 60 branches and over 3,000 members. Besides physical education, the association was involved in various sports and in paramilitary training. It ran a commercial firm called the Sitch Bazaar, which included a publishing house and bookstore, and published physical education manuals and the magazine

American officials preparing to review a parade of Sich (Sitch) guards in Chicago in the 1930s

Sichovi visty (1918–24). In 1924–5, as the Ukrainian community became politically more differentiated, some Sich societies joined the hetmanite Sitch organization, others formed the *Chornomorska Sich athletic society, and the rest remained independent organizations. In Canada the Sitch Organization was founded in 1924. In 1927 it had 21 branches, and in 1928 it was renamed the Canadian Sitch Organization. At first it was connected with the Sitch Ukrainian American Athletic Association, and in 1934 it became part of the *United Hetman Organization, with 50 branches in Ontario and the prairie provinces.

In Western Europe the first Sich society was organized in 1912 by Ukrainian workers in Hamburg. In 1921 in Vienna, Trylovsky set up a workers' physical education society, which eventually evolved into the External Committee of Siches, consisting of former members of the Sich societies in Galicia. Emigrés in Czechoslovakia founded Sich societies in Poděbrady (1926), Prague (1927), and other cities. In 1927 they held their first congress and formed the Ukrainian Sich Union. Its members belonged to local workers' gymnastics clubs and took part in international workers' olympiads in Prague in 1927 and 1934 and in Vienna in 1931. The leaders of the union were V. Petrov, I. Sokalsky (1933–8), and O. Bezpalko.

BIBLIOGRAPHY
Tryl'ovs'kyi, P. (ed). *Hei, tam na hori 'Sich' ide! Propam'iatna knyha 'Sichei'* (Edmonton 1965)

P. Trylovsky, E. Zharsky

Sich. See Zaporozhian Sich.

Sich. A semimonthly organ of the hetmanite *Sich society in the United States, published in Chicago from July 1924 to May 1934. It succeeded *Sichovi visty*. The newspaper published memoirs, political commentaries, ideological articles, reports on the activities of Sich locals, and national and international news of interest to the Ukrainian community. The editors were O. Nazaruk and, from 1926, M. Bodrug. In 1934 it was succeeded by *Nash stiah*.

Sich Council (Sichova Rada). The highest governing body in the Zaporozhian Sich from the 16th to 18th centuries; also called the Military Council. It was empowered to decide legislative, executive, and judicial matters, as well as the participation of the army in war and the settlement of peace. It elected and summoned the officer staff (*starshyna*), with the kish otaman at its head. The Sich Council also received foreign diplomats and determined the course of diplomatic relations. It fulfilled certain economic functions, such as the distribution of the communal agricultural and fishing districts among the kurins of the Sich. As an organ of direct self-government the Sich Council upheld the right of every Cossack to participate in its meetings, but the poor Cossacks (*siromy*) and *holota were excluded from deliberations. The council met irregularly on the central square of the Sich; in the 18th century, it met twice a year. Measures were adopted by a majority vote, which was estimated visually with no exact count of hands. Before the demise of Zaporozhian Sich the authority of the Sich Council was supplanted by that of the Sich *Council of Officers.

Sich Riflemen (Sichovi Striltsi, Kyivski Sichovi Striltsi [KSS]). A leading regular unit of the *Army of the UNR which operated from 1917 to 1919 under different organizational forms: as the Galician-Bukovynian Kurin of Sich Riflemen, the First Kurin of Sich Riflemen, the Regiment of Sich Riflemen, the Separate Detachment of Sich Riflemen, the Division of Sich Riflemen, the Siege Corps of Sich Riflemen, the Corps of Sich Riflemen, and the Group of Sich Riflemen. Its name was derived from the Ukrainian Sich Riflemen in Galicia.

The Galician-Bukovynian Kurin of the KSS was established in Kiev on 13 November 1917 by the *Galician-Bukovynian Committee. Its first recruits were former soldiers of the Austro-Hungarian army who had escaped from Russian POW camps and come to Kiev to participate in the building of a Ukrainian state. By the end of January 1918 the kurin had about 500 men organized in three companies, commanded by Capts R. Sushko, I. Chmola, and V. Kuchabsky. Under Col Ye. Konovalets's command it defended Kiev against a Bolshevik insurrection and, later, the invading Bolshevik forces, and then secured the UNR government's retreat to Zhytomyr. After recapturing Kiev on 1 March 1918, the First Kurin of the KSS was assigned the task of guarding government institutions and preserving public order in the city. It expanded into the Regiment of KSS, consisting of two infantry kurins and a reserve kurin, a cavalry recognizance unit, and an artillery battery. A third of its approx 3,000 men were from the Dnieper region of Ukraine.

When P. Skoropadsky came to power on 29 April 1918, the KSS declined to serve under him and were disarmed by German troops. The regiment's soldiers joined other military or militia units. Many of them transferred to the Second Zaporozhian Regiment (commanded by P. Bolbochan), where they formed the Third Kurin under R. Sushko's command. With the hetman's consent to a partial regrouping of the KSS, the Separate Detachment was formed at the end of August 1918 in Bila Tserkva. Its ap-

Officers of the Sich Riflemen and representatives of the Ukrainian Sich Riflemen in Kiev in 1918. First row, from left: Ivan Rykhlo (1st), Yevhen Konovalets (5th), Teodor Rozhankovsky (6th), Andrii Melnyk (8th), Roman Sushko (9th); second row: Ivan Chmola (5th), Mykhailo Matchak (6th); third row: Ivan Andrukh (3rd), Vasyl Kuchabsky (4th), Hryts Hladky (6th); fourth row: Ivan Rogulsky (3rd), Ostap Hrytsai (4th)

prox 1,200 men were divided into an infantry regiment consisting of a machine-gun company, a reconnaissance troop, an artillery battery, and a technical unit. The detachment played a key role in overthrowing the Hetman: it began the revolt in Bila Tserkva and scored a decisive victory over his guard on 18 November at *Motovylivka. During the siege of Kiev the detachment grew into the Division of KSS (11,000 men) and in early December into the Siege Corps of KSS (approx 25,000 men) by incorporating two Dnieper and the Black Sea divisions. After taking Kiev on 14–15 December 1918, the Siege Corps was dissolved into its constituent units.

Sich Riflemen listening to a kobzar in Kiev

At the beginning of the second phase of the Ukrainian-Soviet War, in January 1919, the Division of KSS was divided into three combat groups, which set out in different directions to block the Bolshevik offensive in Kiev. Having suffered heavy losses, the KSS fell back at the end of February and regrouped as the Corps of KSS (approx 7,000 men). Despite a severe setback at Berdychiv (29–30 March) the corps continued to fight in the Shepetivka and Kremianets region. In July it was renamed the Group of KSS and was

assigned to Col A. Wolf's army group for the Kiev offensive. The KSS Group (approx 8,600 men) consisted of six infantry regiments, six artillery regiments, a cavalry regiment, an automobile unit, and four or five armored trains. After fighting its way toward Korosten the group had to fall back to Shepetivka when a new front with A. Denikin opened up. In mid-October the Riflemen were transferred to the Denikin front. The group suffered heavy battle losses and was racked by disease. Pinned down near Starokostiantyniv on 6 December 1919, the KSS decided to demobilize. Some of the members joined partisan units; others were interned by the Poles until the spring of 1920.

The Sich Riflemen was one of the chief regular units of the UNR Army. As the driving force behind the anti-Het-

Members of the last supreme command of the Sich Riflemen (Lutske, January 1920). Sitting, from left: Capt Mykhailo Matchak, Col Andrii Melnyk, Col Yevhen Konovalets, Col Roman Sushko, Capt Ivan Dankiv; standing: Capt Ivan Andrukh, Col Roman Dashkevych, Capt Vasyl Kuchabsky, Capt Yaroslav Chyzh man coup, it was very influential with the Directory. After the war some of the KSS officers founded and led the *Ukrainian Military Organization.

BIBLIOGRAPHY
Konovalets', Ie. *Prychynky do istoriï ukraïns'koï revoliutsiï* (Prague 1928)
Bezruchko, M. *Sichovi stril'tsi v borot'bi za derzhavnist'* (Kalisz 1932)
Zoloti vorota: Istoriia Sichovykh stril'tsiv 1917–1919 (London 1937)
Ripets'kyi, S. *Ukraïns'ke sichove striletstvo* (New York 1956)
Dashkevych, R. *Artyleriia Sichovykh stril'tsiv u borot'bi za Zoloti kyïvs'ki vorota* (New York 1965)
Babii, O. (ed). *Korpus sichovykh stril'tsiv* (Chicago 1969)
Ievhen Konovalets' ta ioho doba (Munich 1974)

L. Shankovsky

Sich student societies. The name of Ukrainian student societies active in Lviv, Chernivtsi, Vienna, and Graz from the late 19th to the mid-20th century. The first society of this type was formed in Lviv (1861–3). In Chernivtsi a Sich student society was formed in 1902 by members of the *Soiuz (est 1875) and *Moloda Ukraina (est 1900) Ukrainian student associations. The group was active in Ukrainian life throughout Bukovyna, in helping establish Sich societies in villages, publishing occasional brochures and journals, and sponsoring a drama group and choir. It was disbanded by the Rumanian government in 1923. The Rus' student society of Graz changed its name to Sich in 1910. It remained active until the end of the 1940s. The longest-lasting and most active of these organizations was the *Sich student society of Vienna (1868–1947).

Sich student society of Vienna (Ukrainske akademichne tovarystvo 'Sich' u Vidni). One of the oldest and most active of Ukrainian student associations. The society was formed in 1868 by A. *Vakhnianyn and Yu. *Tselevych. It was the first Ukrainian student organization to adopt an openly populist approach to Ukrainian affairs. Over the years the society lent its support to leading Ukrainian causes, and many community leaders emerged from its ranks. Thus it played a significant role in the national revival in Ukrainian lands under Austro-Hungarian rule.

In the 1870s the Sich society was active in popularizing the political ideas of M. *Drahomanov and, under the leadership of O. *Terletsky, in promoting the development of a socialist movement among Ukrainians. Such activity caused it to be temporarily disbanded (1877). After its reconstitution the group tended to maintain more mainstream Ukrainian positions. In 1901–2 it supported the movement for the *secession of Ukrainian students from Lviv University; in the early 1900s it engaged in the struggle for a Ukrainian university in Lviv; in 1913 it organized riflemen detachments in anticipation of the war, and in 1914–18 assisted the *Union for the Liberation of Ukraine; in 1917 it called for the union of all Ukrainian lands into one state (for which it was again temporarily disbanded); and in 1930 it sharply protested the *Pacification of Ukrainians in Galicia. The society also engaged in a certain amount of publishing activity. In the 1870s it prepared booklets for general distribution among the population. In 1920–4 it published the journal *Molode zhyttia*. Other publications included *Nash svit* (prepared by the Drahomanov Hromada, affiliated with the society), the humor journal *Ieretyk*, and several anniversary almanacs

(1898, 1908, and 1932). The society was also active in cultural, educational, and intellectual work among Ukrainians in Vienna. Sich members also maintained active ties with non-Ukrainian individuals and groups and had a significant impact in establishing a profile for Ukrainians in such circles. During the wars society members provided assistance to injured Ukrainian soldiers and deported workers.

Sich actively promoted co-operation among various student groups. It initiated the first meeting between Galician and Bukovynian students, which took place in Kolomyia in 1881. It provided the earliest call for a central body for Ukrainian student groups outside the Ukrainian SSR (leading eventually to the formation of the *Central Union of Ukrainian Students in 1922).

The vitality of the Sich society in Vienna reflected the fact that for many years Vienna was the major European center of study for Ukrainians outside of Ukraine. In the early 1920s Prague overtook Vienna in this respect, and Sich, although remaining active, was somewhat diminished in status. In 1941 the association became a branch of the *Nationalist Organization of Ukrainian Students in Germany (while retaining its own name). In 1947, after the Soviet occupation of Vienna, almost all of the members of Sich left Vienna, and the last president of Sich, S. Naklovych, was arrested and sent to Siberia by the Soviet authorities.

Z. Kokhanovsky

Sicheslav. See Dnipropetrovske.

Sichko, Petro [Sičko], b 18 August 1926 in Vytvytsia, Dolyna county, Galicia. Freedom fighter and political prisoner; husband of S. *Sichko and father of V. *Sichko. An officer in the Ukrainian Insurgent Army, he studied at Chernivtsi University, where he founded the underground organization Fighters for a Free Ukraine. It was uncovered by the Stalinist authorities, and in January 1947 Sichko was arrested. A few months later he was sentenced to death; his sentence was commuted to 25 years in labor camps. Sichko was amnestied in January 1957, settled in Dolyna, and worked as an economist and engineer. He was subjected to ongoing KGB persecution. In February 1978 he joined the *Ukrainian Helsinki Group. He was arrested in July 1979, and in December he was sentenced in Lviv to three years in a strict-regime camp near Brianka, Luhanske oblast. In May 1982, 40 days before his term ended, he was rearrested for writing letters of protest; in July he was sentenced on fabricated charges to three more years in a camp near Kherson. He was released in 1985.

Sichko, Stefaniia [Sičko, Stefanija] (née Petrash), b 1 April 1925 in Zalukva, Stanyslaviv county, Galicia. Freedom fighter and political prisoner; wife of P. *Sichko and mother of V. *Sichko. She was imprisoned in 1947–57 in a labor camp near Magadan, in far eastern Siberia, for involvement in the Ukrainian Insurgent Army. After her release she lived in Dolyna, Ivano-Frankivske oblast, and wrote appeals for the release of her husband and sons after they were arrested in 1979–80. She joined the Initiative Group for the Defense of Rights of the Believers and the Church in Ukraine in 1982, and was active in the underground Ukrainian Catholic church.

Petro and Stefaniia Sichko and their children (standing, from left) Volodymyr, Oksana, and Vasyl

Sichko, Vasyl [Sičko, Vasyl'], b 22 December 1956 in Magadan, Soviet Far East. Dissident; son of P. and S. *Sichko. He was expelled from Kiev University in 1977 for refusing to become a KGB informer, and joined the *Ukrainian Helsinki Group in February 1978. In July 1979, after renouncing his Soviet citizenship while making a speech at V. *Ivasiuk's grave, he was arrested and sentenced to three years' imprisonment. In 1982 he received another three years for allegedly possessing drugs. Since his release (1985) he has been active in the Ukrainian Catholic movement. In November 1988 he was elected president of the Ukrainian Christian Democratic Front.

Sichovi visty (Sich News). Monthly organ of the Galician *Sich society, first published in Lviv in 1912–14 as a monthly supplement to *Hromads'kyi holos*. It contained articles on sports and other subjects of popular interest, and reports of Sich activities. The editor was D. *Katamai. The paper was renewed in 1922 and published separately until 1924 under the editorship of R. Dashkevych.

Sichovi visty (Sich News). A biweekly organ of the *Sich societies in the United States, published in 1918–23 in New York and in 1924 in Chicago. In 1920–3 the editor was S. Musiichuk. The paper was succeeded by *Sich*.

Sichulski, Kazimierz, b 17 January 1879 in Lviv, d November 1942 in Lviv. Polish painter. A graduate of the Cracow Academy of Fine Arts (1904) and the Vienna Kunstgewerbeschule (1908), he taught at the State Applied

Arts and Crafts School in Lviv (1920–30) and the Cracow academy (1930–9). With genre painting his specialty, he devoted much of his work to the life of the Hutsuls. Some of his better-known works are *Black Lamb* (1904), *Procession from the Mountain Meadow* (1925), *Hutsul Wedding*, and *Old Woman with Rooster* (1926). He also created mosaics and stained-glass windows and designed furniture.

Denys Sichynsky   Myroslav Sichynsky

Sichynsky, Denys [Sičyns'kyj], b 2 October 1865 in Kliuvyntsi, Husiatyn county, Galicia, d 6 June 1909 in Stanyslaviv. Composer, conductor, and teacher. He received his musical training in Ternopil and at the Lviv Conservatory (1888–91) and then organized and conducted the choral association *Boian in Lviv, Kolomyia, Stanyslaviv, and Peremyshl. From 1899 he lived in Stanyslaviv, where he founded a music school and organized the Muzychna Biblioteka music publishing association, which printed numerous works by Ukrainian composers. He was also active in establishing the Union of Song and Music Societies. Sichynsky is considered to be the first professionally trained Western Ukrainian composer. His compositions include the opera *Roksoliana* (libretto by V. Lutsyk and S. Charnetsky, 1908); works for symphony and chamber orchestras; piano solos; choral works, including the cantata *Lichu v nevoli* (I Count the Days and Nights in Bondage; text by T. Shevchenko); a score for a liturgy; approx 20 songs for solo voice to texts by T. Shevchenko, I. Franko, Lesia Ukrainka, B. Lepky, U. Kravchenko, and H. Heine; and folk song arrangements. His biography, by S. Pavlyshyn, was published in Kiev in 1956 (2nd edn, 1980).

Sichynsky, Mykola [Sičyns'kyj], b 1850, d 1894. Greek Catholic priest and civic activist. An organizer of the Ukrainian community in Husiatyn county, he was elected to the Galician Diet in 1883. In 1884 he was appointed to a parish in Chernivtsi. He opposed the Russophile movement and helped found the populist People's Council. In politics he supported the *New Era policy.

Sichynsky, Myroslav [Sičyns'kyj], b 11 October 1886 in Chernykhivtsi, Zbarazh county, Galicia, d 16 March 1979 in Westland, Michigan. Civic and political activist; son of Rev M. *Sichynsky. On 12 April 1908 he assassinated the viceroy of Galicia, A. Potocki, in protest against Polish violence and fraud in the 1908 election. After his death sentence was commuted to life imprisonment by the Austrian emperor, he escaped (1911) and eventually (1915) was accepted as a political refugee by the United States. He then immersed himself in Ukrainian-American community activity as a founder of the Ukrainian Federation of the Socialist Party and editor of its weeklies *Robitnyk (1914–17) and *Narod* (1917). As a leading activist of the Federation of Ukrainians in the United States, he was appointed editor of its *Ukraïns'ka hazeta*. In 1920 he helped found the *Oborona Ukrainy organization and edited its paper *Ukraïns'ka hromada*. He was president of the *Ukrainian Fraternal Association in 1933–41. During the 1940s Sichynsky adopted an increasingly pro-Soviet stance, which helped precipitate the crisis that led to Oborona Ukrainy's dissolution. His recollections were published by M. Shapoval in 1928.

Sichynsky, Teodosii [Sičyns'kyj, Teodosij], b and d ? Church painter and sculptor at the beginning of the 18th century. He painted the iconostasis of the Krasnopushcha monastery church and served as hegumen of the Basilian monastery in Vyspa, near Bibrka.

Volodymyr Sichynsky and his drawing of the ruins of Hetman Kyrylo Rozumovsky's palace

Sichynsky, Volodymyr [Sičyns'kyj], b 24 June 1894 in Kamianets-Podilskyi, d 25 June 1962 in Paterson, New Jersey. Architect, graphic artist, and art scholar; son of Ye. *Sitsinsky; full member of the Shevchenko Scientific Society from 1930. Having interrupted his studies at the St Petersburg Institute of Civil Engineers (1912–17) he helped organize the Architectural Institute in Kiev (1918–19) and served as director of the construction department of Podilia gubernia. After fleeing from Soviet rule to Lviv, he taught at the Academic Gymnasium there (1921–3) and then moved to Prague to study at Charles University (PH D, 1927) and teach at the Ukrainian Higher Pedagogical Institute (1923–33). He chaired the Library and Bibliographic Commission of the *Ukrainian Society of Bibliophiles in Prague from 1927 and served as the society's president (1934–43). In 1930 he cofounded the *Association of Independent Ukrainian Artists in Lviv. In 1942 he was appointed an associate professor of art history at the Ukrainian Free University. In 1944–5 he was imprisoned

and tortured by the Gestapo in Prague. A postwar refugee in Germany, in 1949 he emigrated to the United States.

As an architect he adapted the styles of Kievan Rus' and the Cossack baroque to modern techniques and materials. He designed the Redemptorist Church of the Holy Spirit in Michalovce (1933–4) and the Boiko-style wooden Church of the Nativity of the Mother of God in Komarnyky (1937), both in the Prešov region; the Ukrainian churches in Whippany, New Jersey (1949), and Pôrto União, Brazil (1951); and the Orthodox cathedral in Montreal (1957). He also designed many private and public buildings and a number of grave monuments, in which he employed folk forms of the many-armed cross, and the covers of over 70 books and journals.

Sichynsky systematically researched Ukrainian architecture and art, and he wrote over 500 articles and reviews. He is the author of books on 10th- to 13th-century Ukrainian architecture (1926); the history of world art to the Renaissance (a textbook, 1926, 1928); Ukrainian publishing logos (1926, 1938); the architecture of Potylych (1928), Bardejov (1931), Lavriv (1936), and the Korniakt Tower and Residence (1932), St George's Cathedral (1934), and St Nicholas's Church (1936) in Lviv; Ukrainian wooden architecture and carving (1936); and the history of 16th- to 18th-century Ukrainian engraving (1937). He also wrote essays on the history of Ukrainian industry (1937), an introduction to Ukrainian regional studies (1937), *Ukraine in Foreign Comments and Descriptions from the Sixth to the Twentieth Century* (1938; English trans 1953), and books on wooden architecture in Transcarpathia (1940, in Czech) and Hetman I. Mazepa (1951). He compiled and illustrated the albums *Monumenta Architecturae Ukrainae* (1940, 1946; 300 illustrations) and albums of ornaments in historical styles (1940), Ukrainian historical (1943) and folk (1943, 1946) ornaments, applied art (1943), folk furniture (1945), and embroidery (1947). He also wrote booklets on artists, such as O. Tarasevych (1934), H. Levytsky (1936), T. Shevchenko (1937), and H. Narbut (1943), and on the towns of Zboriv (1939), Bardejov (1939), and Kholm (1941). His magnum opus, on the history of Ukrainian architecture, was published in 1956. A biobibliography of Sichynsky by I. Keivan was published in Toronto in 1958.

S. Hordynsky

Sichynsky, Yukhym. See Sitsinsky, Yevtym.

Siderite. A common mineral, iron carbonate ($FeCO_3$); member of the calcite group. Siderite ores contain iron used in the manufacture of iron and steel. They usually lie in thin beds with shale, clay, or coal seams, and in hydrothermal metallic veins. The largest concentration of siderite ores in Ukraine is found in the *Kerch Iron-ore Basin. Smaller deposits, which are not mined, are located in the Donets Basin and the Carpathian Mountains near Rakhiv.

Sidorov, Aleksei, b 13 June 1891 in Mykolaivka, Putyvl county, Kursk gubernia (now in Sumy oblast), d 30 June 1978 in Moscow. Russian art scholar and bibliologist; corresponding member of the USSR Academy of Sciences from 1946. He is the author of studies on the history of Russian drawing and on book art, and of articles on I. Hrabar, O. Shovkunenko, H. Narbut, I. Fedorych, and T. Shevchenko.

Siechkin, Vitalii [Sječkin, Vitalij], b 5 September 1927 in Kharkiv, d 3 May 1988 in Kishinev. Composer, pianist, and teacher. After obtaining undergraduate degrees from the Kharkiv State Conservatory in piano (1947) and composition (class of M. Tits, 1950) he completed graduate studies at the Moscow Conservatory (1954). From 1955 to 1984 he was affiliated with the Kiev Conservatory, as instructor, assistant professor (1965), head of the piano department (from 1971), and full professor (1976). His works include the overture *Mii kokhanyi kraiu* (My Beloved Country, 1951) for symphony orchestra, a concerto for piano and orchestra (1962), 'Andante cantabile' for string quartet (1951), sonatas and other works for solo piano, the suite *Estonian Impressions* (1967) for cello and piano, and works for chorus and for solo voice.

Siedin, Mytrofan [Sjedin], b 1861 in the Kuban, d 1918. Writer. He wrote *Shcho posiiesh, te i pozhnesh* (What You Sow, That You Will Reap, 1899), *Na Chornomor'ï* (At the Black Sea, 1910), and other Ukrainian plays, and poetry and prose in Russian. From 1915 to 1917 he published the Katerynodar journal *Prikubanskiia step'*. He was killed by soldiers of A. Denikin's army. A biography of him by his daughter appeared in Krasnodar in 1965.

Siedlce. I-3. A city (1989 pop 70,500) and a voivodeship center in Poland. It was first mentioned in the chronicles in 1448, and it received the rights of Magdeburg law in 1547. Under Russian rule, in 1837–45 and 1867–1912 Siedlce was the center of gubernias that included Ukrainian-populated regions of Podlachia. In the 1860s the Russian authorities established a Russian gymnasium in Siedlce, which attracted many Ukrainian students from Podlachia. I. *Nechui-Levytsky taught at the school in 1861–72. Siedlce was one of the centers of Russophilism in Podlachia. In 1874, during the forcible conversion of Greek Catholic Podlachians to Russian Orthodoxy, many of them were imprisoned in Siedlce jails.

Siege Corps of Sich Riflemen (Osadnyi korpus Sichovykh striltsiv). An operational grouping of units of the Army of the UNR formed on 3 December 1918 for the purpose of capturing Kiev. Its principal combat units were the Division of Sich Riflemen, the Black Sea Division, and the Dnieper Division. It was augmented with partisan detachments, and at its peak reached a strength of 50,000 soldiers. On 15 December 1918 its units entered Kiev, and in early 1919 the corps was deactivated. Its commander was Otaman Ye. *Konovalets.

Siemiatycze (Ukrainian: Semiatychi or Simiatychi). I-3. A town (1989 pop 13,900) in northern Podlachia and a county center in Białystok voivodeship, Poland. Over one-third of the county's population is Ukrainian. The Ukrainians are regarded as Belarusians. Many of them accept the classification; others call themselves simply 'locals' or 'Orthodox.'

Siemieński, Lucjan, b 13 August 1807 in Kamiana Hora, near Rava Ruska, Galicia, d 27 November 1877 in Cracow. Polish revolutionary, writer, and ethnographer. After the Polish Insurrection of 1830–1 he lived in Lviv, where he was close to S. Goszczyński and other writers of the Ukrainian school in Polish literature. He lived as a po-litical émigré in Strasbourg, Poznań, and Brussels from 1837 to 1848 and then settled in Cracow. Among his literary works are *Dumki* (Little Dumas, 1838), a poetry collection based on Ukrainian folk and historical songs, and a Polish translation of fragments of *Slovo o polku Ihorevi* (The Tale of Ihor's Campaign). In Poznań he published a book of Polish, Ukrainian, and Lithuanian legends (1845). Ukrainian historical themes are found in some of his stories and other writings, and the Ukrainian legendary figure *Vernyhora appears in his long poem *Trzy wieszczby* (Three Prophecies, 1843).

Sieniawski. A Polish magnate family which was influential in Polish political and military affairs in the 16th to 18th centuries and had extensive landholdings in Galicia (around Sieniawa) and Podilia. Some of its members played a significant role in Ukrainian history. Mikołaj (ca 1489–1569) was a royal field hetman (from 1539), voivode of Rus' (from 1553), and royal grand hetman (from 1561). He defended Poland's southeastern frontier against the Tatars. His son, also Mikołaj (?–1587), was a royal field hetman (from 1569) and castellan of Kamianets-Podilskyi (from 1576). Mikołaj Hieronim (1645–83) was voivode of Volhynia (from 1680) and royal field hetman (from 1682). He fought against the Cossacks, Tatars, and Turks (in 1683 at Vienna). He was the father of A. *Sieniawski.

Sieniawski, Adam, b ca 1666, d 1726. Polish magnate; last of the Sieniawski dynasty. He was the voivode of Belz (from 1692), royal field hetman (from 1702), royal grand hetman (from 1706), and castellan of Cracow (from 1710). He fought against the Cossack forces led by S. Palii (1703–4) and was supported by Muscovy in his (unsuccessful) candidacy to the Polish throne (1706). His correspondence in 1704–8 with Hetman I. Mazepa, who hoped to bring him into a coalition against Muscovy, was published by the Ukrainian Academy of Arts and Sciences (ed O. Subtelny). As a consequence of the marriage of his daughter, Zofia, Sieniawski's considerable properties were transferred to the Czartoryski family after his death.

Sienkiewicz, Henryk, b 5 May 1846 in Wola Okrzejska, Podlachia, d 15 November 1916 in Vevey, Switzerland. Polish writer. His first novel, *Na marne* (In Vain, 1872), was set in Kiev. In *Ogniem i mieczem* (With Fire and Sword, 1884), the first part of his famous historical trilogy, he depicted in a crude, chauvinistic manner the Cossack-Polish War, Hetman B. Khmelnytsky, and the Ukrainian Cossacks. His approach was condemned by both Ukrainian (I. Franko) and Polish (Z. Kaczkowski, A. Świętochowski, B. Prus, E. Orzeszkowa) contemporary writers, and the novel's historical distortions have been criticized in books by the Polish historians O. Górka (1934) and Z. Wójcik (1960), and in an essay by V. Antonovych.

Sierkov, Pylyp [Sjerkov] (Serkov, Filipp), b 9 October 1908 in Forpost, Smolensk gubernia, Russia. Physiologist; full member of the AN URSR (now ANU) since 1978. A graduate of the Smolensk Medical Institute (1931), he was an associate of the Kiev Medical Institute (1935–41), a department head and prorector of Vinnytsia (1944–53) and Odessa (1953–66) universities, and assistant director of the ANU Institute of Physiology. His research concerns the physiology of skeletal muscles, the myoneural transmissions and electrical activity in the brain, and epilepsy, as well as the history of physiology in Ukraine.

Sieverodonetsk. See Siverskodonetske.

Sighetul Marmaţiei (Ukrainian: Syhit Marmaroskyi; Hungarian: Máramoros Sziget). VI-4. A city (1971 population, 39,300) in northern Rumania near the Ukrainian border. Situated on the Maramureş Basin along the Tysa River, the city has a diverse population of Ukrainians (15–20 percent), Rumanians, Hungarians, and Jews. Its major economic activities include construction, textile manufacturing, lumbering, and the food industry. A number of Ukrainian villages surround the city in the *Maramureş region.

The earliest references to the settlement are from the 13th century. By 1394 it had become the principal city of Máramoros komitat. In the 19th and 20th centuries the Greek Catholic church and a Ruthenian student residence were active there. The city was the site of notorious show trials early in the 20th century when the Hungarian government, fearing pro-Russian sentiment in its borderland regions, tried recent converts to Orthodoxy for treason. In 1904–6, 9 people were sentenced to varying terms of imprisonment, and in 1913 a total of 94 people from the region were tried, of whom 32 were convicted and sentenced to fines and prison terms. The trials became a cause célèbre in both the Slavic world and Western Europe. The city was also the site of a meeting of representatives from the Maramureş region on 8 December 1918, who voted to unite Transcarpathia and Ukraine, as well as the site of a battle between the Ukrainian Galician Army and Rumanian troops on 15–17 January 1919.

Sigillography. See Sphragistics.

Sigismund I the Old (Polish: Zygmunt Stary), b 1 January 1467 in Cracow, d 1 April 1548 in Cracow. King of Poland and grand duke of Lithuania; son of Casimir IV. After obtaining Lithuanian territories in 1506 as an inheritance from his brother, Alexander Jagiellończyk, he was elected king of Poland in 1507. He brought in fiscal and monetary reforms, but his extensions of royal power resulted in clashes with the nobility. In Galicia, Volhynia, and Podilia his reign was marked by increased Polish control over Ukrainian lands and a growing Polonization of the Ukrainian nobility. In 1535 he defeated the invading forces of Muscovy.

Sigismund II Augustus (Polish: Zygmunt), b 1 August 1520 in Cracow, d 7 July 1572 at a private estate in Knyszyn (near the Polish-Lithuanian border). King of Poland and grand duke of Lithuania; son of Sigismund I the Old. The last of the Jagiellon dynasty, he became grand duke of Lithuania while still a minor and was crowned king (and coruler) of Poland in 1530. In 1548 he assumed full control of both domains. His reign continued the *voloka land reforms (1557) and the promotion of Renaissance culture initiated during his father's era. It also saw the incorporation of the Ukrainian provinces of Podlachia, Volhynia, and Kiev directly into the Polish realm, shortly before the formal merger of Poland and Lithuania by the Union of *Lublin in 1569.

Sigismund III Vasa (Polish: Zygmunt III Waza; Lithuanian: Žygimantas), b 20 June 1566 in Gripsholm, Sweden, d 30 April 1632 in Warsaw. Grand duke of Lithuania and king of Poland (1587–1632) and king of Sweden (1592–9); son of the Swedish king John III Vasa and Katarzyna, the daughter of Sigismund I. He was a zealous Catholic, and during his rule the pivotal Church Union of *Berestia was signed (1596). He transferred the capital of Poland from Cracow to Warsaw. He supported the Jesuits and tried to suppress the Orthodox church in Ukraine. The restrictions placed by Sigismund on the Cossacks sparked rebellions led by K. Kosynsky (1591–3), S. Nalyvaiko (1595–6), and T. Fedorovych (1630). The strength of the Cossack armies grew and resulted in the first clashes of the Polish-Cossack wars. Sigismund briefly held Moscow during the Time of Troubles (1610–12). In his wars against Turkey, particularly in the Battle of *Khotyn (1621), Sigismund enlisted the aid of the Cossacks, led by P. Sahaidachny.

Sihorsky, Vitalii [Sihors'kyj, Vitalij], b 19 November 1922 in Bubnivska Slobidka, Zolotonosha county, Poltava gubernia. Electrical and electronic engineer. A graduate of the Lviv Polytechnical Institute (1949), he taught there and then served as assistant director of the AN URSR (now ANU) Institute of Machine Science and Automation (1953–9). From 1959 to 1964 he headed departments at the Automation and Mathematics institutes in Novosibirsk and taught at the Electric Technology Institute and university there. Since 1964 he has held the chair of technical electronics at the Kiev Polytechnical Institute. A specialist in circuit theory, he developed powerful mathematical methods of analysis and synthesis of complex electronic circuits. He has written over 150 works, including textbooks and monographs.

Siiach (Sower). A publishing house in Cherkasy in 1917–18. It republished new editions of works by P. Hulak-Artemovsky, Ye. Hrebinka, B. Hrinchenko, A. Kashchenko, H. Kovalenko, I. Nechui-Levytsky, I. Franko, P. Kulish, M. Levytsky, I. Manzhura, and S. Cherkasenko, and textbooks for elementary schools.

Siiach (Sower). Monthly organ of the Ukrainian Evangelical Reformed church, published in Kolomyia in 1932–3. It was edited by T. Dovhaliuk and V. Borovsky. After 1933 *Siiach* appeared as a supplement to *Vira i nauka.

Siiach. See Dnipro.

Siiak, Ivan [Sijak], b 8 April 1887 in Liashky Murovani, Lviv county, Galicia, d after 1939? in the Far East (Soviet sources cite December 1937 with no location). Civic, military, and political figure. A lawyer by training, by 1914 he was a leading member of the Ukrainian Social Democratic party. During the First World War he fought for the Sich Riflemen and led the Railway Engineering Corps of the Ukrainian Galician Army. After being captured by Bolshevik forces near Stavyshche in 1919, he joined the Red Army and directed the activities of the Galician Revolutionary Committee (1920). During the 1920s he taught at educational institutions in Kiev and Kharkiv, held a position with the Soviet embassy in Warsaw, and became a member of the CC CP(B)U. From 1930 he directed the Ukrainian Institute of Linguistic Education in Kharkiv. He was

Ivan Siiak   Gen Volodymyr Sikevych

arrested in 1933 during the Stalinist terror, sent to a labor camp, and later shot.

Sikalo, Ivan, b 6 June 1909 in Sosnytsia, Chernihiv gubernia, d 24 March 1975 in Vinnytsia. Stage actor and director. He studied drama in Donetske (1930–5) and worked in the Donetske Ukrainian Drama Theater (1935–41) and the Izmail Ukrainian Music and Drama Theater (1945–8), and from 1949 at the Vinnytsia Ukrainian Music and Drama Theater.

Sikevych, Volodymyr [Sikevyč], b 5 September 1870 in Tarashcha, Kiev gubernia, d 27 July 1952 in Toronto. Military and political leader. He served as a colonel in the general staff of the Russian army. During the Ukrainian struggle for independence he served as brigadier general of the Army of the UNR and head of the Repatriation Commission of the UNR consulates in Hungary and Austria (1919–20). From 1924 he lived in Canada (Winnipeg and Toronto) and was active in Ukrainian veterans' organizations. He wrote *Storinky iz zapysnoï knyzhky* (Pages from a Notebook, 7 vols, 1943–51).

Sikorski, Władysław, b 20 May 1881 in Tuszów Narodowy, Poland, d 4 July 1943 near Gibraltar. Polish general and statesman. From 1908 he was one of the leaders of the clandestine Polish Union of Active Struggle and its paramilitary organizations in Galicia. After the creation of the Polish Republic in November 1918, Sikorski commanded the Peremyshl Military District. During the Ukrainian-Polish War of 1918–19 he commanded Polish divisions that fought the Ukrainians for Lviv and fought at Horodok and Chortkiv; and during the Polish-Soviet War of 1919–20 he commanded the Polisian Group and the Polish Third and Fifth armies. After the war he served as Poland's chief of general staff (1921–2), prime minister (1922–3), minister of military affairs (1922–3, 1924–5), inspector general of the infantry (1923–4), and commander of the Lviv Military District (1925–8). An opponent of J. Piłsudski's 1926 coup, in 1928 he was forced into retirement. In 1936 he was a leader of the Front Morges, the centrist opposition to the Sanacja government. After the German invasion of Poland in September 1939, Sikorski fled to France; he served as prime minister of the Polish government-in-exile in France (from June 1940 in Eng-

land) and commander in chief of the Polish forces and *Polish Home Army. In July 1941 he negotiated an agreement with the USSR and the creation of Gen W. *Anders's army from among Polish soldiers (including some 2,000 Ukrainians) who had been deported and interned in the USSR. His request that the International Red Cross investigate the Katyn Massacre of Polish officers resulted in J. Stalin's severing diplomatic relations with the Polish government-in-exile in April 1943. Sikorski died in an airplane crash.

Ihor Sikorsky

Sikorsky, Ihor (Igor) [Sikors'kyj], b 25 May 1889 in Kiev, d 26 October 1972 in Easton, Connecticut. Aeronautical engineer and designer and pioneer of aviation technology; son of I. *Sikorsky. While studying at the Kiev Polytechnical Institute (1908–12) he designed two helicopters, among the first such designs in the world, as well as a series of biplanes. He was a member of the pioneering Kiev Aeronautical Society. On 29 December 1911 he established the world speed record (111 km/hr) for a loaded plane (three passengers) in a plane of his own design, the C-6. From 1912 to 1917 he worked as chief designer of a Russian-Baltic aviation company, where he designed and built the first airplanes with multiple engines, including the *Illia Muromets* and the *Vytiaz*. In 1918 he emigrated to France, and in 1919 to the United States, where he founded a number of aviation companies and headed several design teams which constructed various airplanes and hydroplanes. In 1939 he perfected the design of the first successful helicopter in the world. His Sikorsky Helicopter Co developed military and civilian helicopters and was considered the world leader in its field.

Sikorsky, Ivan [Sikors'kyj], b 7 June 1842 in Antoniv, Skvyra county, Kiev gubernia, d 14 February 1919 in Kiev. Psychiatrist and psychologist; father of I. *Sikorsky. A graduate of Kiev University (1869), he worked there and (from 1873) at I. Balinsky's clinic in St Petersburg. In 1885 he became head of the department of psychiatry and nervous diseases at Kiev University. He founded and edited the journal *Voprosy nervno-psikhologicheskoi meditsiny* (1896–1905). He was the founder of the Medical-Pedagogical Institute for Pediatric Anomalies in Kiev and president of the Scientific Society of Psychiatrists and the Kiev Froebel Society. One of the founders of child psychology, he set up the world's first institute of child psychology, in

Kiev (1912). He wrote numerous works (approx 20 in child psychology), including *Vseobshchaia psikhologiia s fiziognomikoi v illiustrirovannom izlozhenii* (General Psychology with Physiognomy in an Illustrated Presentation, 1912). He also published a collection of his scholarly articles (5 vols, 1899–1900).

Mykhailo Sikorsky

Metropolitan Polikarp Sikorsky

Sikorsky, Mykhailo [Sikors'kyj, Myxajlo], b 1923 in Chyhyryn, Cherkasy okruha. Museologist and historian. He graduated from Kiev University in 1951 and was appointed director of the *Pereiaslav-Khmelnytskyi Historical Museum. He founded most of the city's 17 museums and personally collected a large proportion of their holdings. His accomplishments include the Museum of Folk Architecture and Folkways, the Archeological Museum, the Museum of Kobza Playing, and the Folk-Art Museum of the Kiev Region, as well as memorial museums dedicated to A. Kozachkovsky (est 1954), H. Skovoroda (est 1972), V. Zabolotny, and Sholom Aleichem. Sikorsky also helped organize regional museums in Brovary, Tarashcha, Berezan, and Chyhyryn. He wrote numerous scholarly works, including *Na zemli pereiaslavs'kii* (In Pereiaslav Land, 1983, coauthor). A documentary novel about Sikorsky was written by M. Makhinchuk (1989).

Sikorsky, Polikarp [Sikors'kyj] (secular name: Petro), b 20 June 1875 in Zelenky, Kaniv county, Kiev gubernia, d 22 October 1953 in Aulnay-sous-Bois, near Paris. Metropolitan of the Ukrainian Autocephalous Orthodox church (UAOC). A graduate of the Kiev Theological Seminary (1898) and the law faculty of Kiev University (1910), he was a member of the *Hromada of Kiev and worked as an official of the Orthodox consistory office in Kiev (1908–18); a section head in the UNR government-in-exile's Ministry of Religious Faiths (1918–19); and deputy director of that government's Department of General Affairs in Tarnów, Poland (1919–21). He also served as a member of the All-Ukrainian Church Council and Sobor in 1917–18. An émigré in the interwar Polish Republic, he became a hieromonk in 1922 and served as superior of Orthodox monasteries in Derman, Myltsi, and Zahaitsi Mali in Volhynia and Vilnius in Lithuania; dean of the Volodymyr-Volynskyi Cathedral (1925–7); and superior of the monas-

tery in Zhyrovichy, Belarus (1927–32). In April 1932 he was consecrated Orthodox bishop of Lutske and vicar of Volhynia eparchy by Metropolitan D. Valedinsky of the Polish Autocephalous Orthodox church, but he was unable to function fully because of Polish administrative sanctions. A member of the Commission for the Translation of the Bible and Liturgical Books (1932–9) of the Ukrainian Scientific Institute in Warsaw, he organized and headed its section in Lutske from 1937. During the 1939–41 Soviet occupation of Western Ukraine, Sikorsky refused to recognize the authority of the Patriarch of Moscow. In August 1941, during the German occupation, Metropolitan Valedinsky elevated him to the office of archbishop of Lutske and Kovel, and in December appointed him provisional administrator of the revived UAOC in Reichskommissariat Ukraine. In February 1942 Sikorsky consecrated the first two bishops of the UAOC on Ukrainian territory (N. Abramovych and I. Huba), and in May 1942 the Kiev sobor of UAOC bishops elected him their head and a metropolitan. In January 1944 he fled from the Soviet reoccupation of Volhynia to Warsaw, and thence, in July, to Germany. From 1945 he headed the UAOC abroad from Gronau, near Hannover; from Heidenau, near Hamburg; and, from April 1950 to his death, from Paris. He is buried at the Pères-Lachaise cemetery in Paris.

BIBLIOGRAPHY
Vlasovs'kyi, I. *Arkhypastyrs'kyi iuvilei Vysokopreosviashchenishoho Mytropolyta Polikarpa, 1932–1952* (London 1952)

Sikorsky, Yakiv [Sikors'kyj, Jakiv], b 8 November 1904 in Dzhuryntsi, Bratslav county, Podilia gubernia, 2 November 1980. Writer. He is the author of books of prose, including *Matrosova topolia* (The Sailor's Poplar, 1956), *Narodzhennia* (Birth, 1957), *Shturm* (The Storming, 1958), *Maiak u stepu* (The Lighthouse in the Steppe, 1961), *Ne khody manivtsiamy* (Don't Lose Your Way, 1963), *Tak pochalasia vesna* (Thus Spring Began, 1964), *Aistry* (Asters, 1966), *Suvora pam'iat'* (A Grim Memory, 1973), and *Smertiu khorobrykh* (With the Death of the Brave, 1980), and a few books in Russian.

Silberfarb, Moisei. See Zilberfarb, Moyshe.

Silicosis. See Pneumoconiosis.

Silk industry. A branch of the *textile industry that produces silk thread and cloth from natural and synthetic silk and related fibers. The main raw materials for the industry are natural and synthetic silk fibers.

Silk cloth has been known in Ukraine since the time of Kievan Rus'. In the 14th to 16th centuries artisans producing clothes from silk, especially women's clothes and men's shirts, formed separate guilds. Natural silk was not produced in Ukraine, but imported from Asia and sometimes Western Europe. In the 17th century the first workshops for making silk cloth appeared. A state-owned silk enterprise was established in Kiev in 1725. V. Ivanov and R. Smorazin operated small weaving shops in Kiev in the 1750s and 1760s. The Nova Vodolaha silk manufactory was opened in 1774. No silk factories were set up in the 19th century, and the silk industry in Ukraine was poorly developed until the 20th century.

Silk production began to grow after 1930. That year 88 t of silk cocoons were produced in the Ukrainian SSR. By 1940 production had reached 412 t. The real development of the industry, however, began only after the Second World War. Several large factories were established, including the Darnytsia Silk Manufacturing Complex in Kiev, which produces synthetic silk, the *Kiev Silk Manufacturing Complex, and the Cherkasy and Lutske silk complexes, both of which have produced synthetic silk since 1969. In addition silk cloth for industrial purposes is produced in Kiev, Lysychanske, and some cotton factories. In 1960, 110,000 t of synthetic and natural silk thread were produced, and by 1970 the output had reached 167,000 t. Silk production peaked in the mid-1970s. It dropped to 151,000 t in 1980, 137,000 t in 1985, and 109,000 t in 1987. The decrease is probably owing to the lack of commitment on the part of economic planners and managers to producing expensive silk cloth and clothing: the number of silk dresses produced in Ukraine, for example, increased from 1.7 million in 1970 to 2.8 million in 1980 and then dropped to 1.5 million (1987). Of the 159.2 million sq m of silk cloth produced in 1975, 89 percent was made from synthetic silk fibers, 9 percent from staple fiber, and the rest from natural silk. Overall, silk cloth accounts for 16 percent of all textiles produced in Ukraine (1982).

B. Wynar

Silkor. See *Robselkor.*

Silkworm breeding. A branch of agriculture that breeds and raises silkworms for use in the *silk industry. Silkworms of the genus *Bombyx* are an important source of commercial silk. The native Chinese silkworm was introduced in Ukraine in the 18th century with the encouragement of the Russian government, which hoped to develop a source of inexpensive domestic silk. Silkworm breeding spread slowly because of inhospitable conditions and the reluctance of the population to experiment. Some silk was produced in Kiev gubernia and Slobidska Ukraine. At the beginning of the 19th century some 1,000 kg of raw silk was produced in Russian-ruled Ukraine, much of it in the southern steppe gubernias.

At the end of the 1920s the Soviet government began to encourage silkworm breeding in Ukraine. In 1930, 88 t of cocoons were produced. The figure increased to 347 t in 1945, 1,400 t in 1970, and 33,200 t in 1984. In 1984 almost 50,000 ha of land were devoted to mulberry trees, on which silkworms feed. In 1991, silkworms were bred in 18 oblasts of Ukraine and on over 2,700 collective and state farms. The most productive areas were Crimea, Dnipropetrovske, Zaporizhia, and Odessa oblasts. Many silkworm cocoons were produced on private plots. Research in silkworm breeding was conducted at the *Ukrainian Research Station for Silk Production in Merefa, Kharkiv oblast, and at the department of general entomology at the Ukrainian Academy of Agricultural Sciences in Kiev.

BIBLIOGRAPHY
Shovkivnytstvo (Kiev 1956)
Dovidnyk po shovkivnytstvu (Kiev 1962)
Ponomar'ov, O. 'Do istorii shovkovoho vyrobnytstva na Ukraïni v XVIII stolitti,' *Istoriia narodnoho hospodarstva ta ekonomichnoï dumky Ukraïns'koï RSR*, 1970, nos 3–4

B. Wynar

Sil's'ke budivnytstvo (Rural Construction). A monthly magazine of the Ministry of Rural Construction and Ukrainian Inter–Collective Farm Construction Alliance, published from 1951 in Kiev. It published articles on rural housing construction, architecture, planning, and engineering. Its pressrun declined from 22,900 in 1970 to 16,500 in 1975.

Sil's'ki visti (Village News). A daily organ of the CC CPU and the Ukrainian SSR Ministry of Agriculture until 1991, published in Kiev since 1939. It was originally called *Kolhospnyk Ukraïny*. In 1949 this paper was merged with *Tvarynnytstvo Ukraïny* and *Radians'kyi selianyn* to form *Kolhospne selo*, which was renamed *Sil's'ki visti* in 1965. The paper reported on rural life in Soviet Ukraine and promoted labor productivity and socialist values among the peasantry. In 1975 the paper's pressrun was 649,000; by 1980 it had increased to 834,000. After the Ukrainian declaration of independence the newspaper continued to appear as a government publication. In 1992 its pressrun was 2,268,000.

Members of the supreme council of the Silskyi Hospodar society in 1900. Sitting, from left: Rev Yosyp Folys, Rev T. Dutkevych, Yevhen Olesnytsky (chairman), Ivan Kyveliuk, Rev Stepan Onyshkevych; standing: Oleksander Harasevych, Hryn Tershakovets, Kyrylo Kakhnykevych, Mykhailo Kotsiuba, Andrii Kornelia, Hryhorii Velychko, Andrii Zhuk

Silskyi Hospodar (Farmer). The most important Ukrainian agricultural organization in Galicia. In was founded in 1899 in the town of Olesko, Zolochiv county, by Revs T. and Yu. *Dutkevych with the goal of raising the living standard of the peasantry by improving agriculture and education. Initially the organization limited its activities to the Zolochiv region (Brody county and Olesko judicial district). In 1903 its headquarters was transferred to Lviv, and in 1904 it was reorganized into the Silskyi Hospodar Provincial Agricultural Society with a mandate to organize branches throughout Galicia. The organization grew slowly: in early 1909 it had only five branches and 700 members.

The rapid development of Silskyi Hospodar (SH) began with the first agricultural exhibition, organized in 1909 in Stryi by the *Prosvita society. At the annual meeting of SH held during the exhibition, its statute was amended to expand its range of activities and restructure it into a three-tiered organization, with a central office, county branches, and village locals. At the same time Ye. *Olesnytsky replaced T. Dutkevych as president of SH. Assisted by S.

Onyshkevych and H. Velychko, he extended the organization's activities to all parts of Galicia and took over almost all agricultural work formerly done by the Prosvita society and by various co-operatives. In 1910 SH had 85 branches, 317 locals, and 12,500 members.

SH acted as the legal representative of Ukrainian peasants before the government. It organized courses and lectures for agricultural instructors and farmers; established research stations and model farms, orchards, apiaries, and livestock and poultry farms; instructed peasants about agricultural machinery and equipment, the collective use of machines, and effective land management; and organized a school of orcharding and farming. It published the journal *Hospodars'ka chasopys'* (1910–18, 1920) and 27 brochures in its book series. In 1911 it established a syndicate for the distribution and sale of farm products (see *Tsentrosoiuz) and the Provincial Union for the Breeding and Raising of Livestock. Profits from those two organizations were used to fund SH's other activities.

The First World War interrupted the operations of SH. In 1915 it began to rebuild its facilities. The effort was assisted financially by the Austrian government, which recognized the organization as the central union of Ukrainian peasants. From the end of 1918 until May 1919 it functioned in the areas controlled by the Western Ukrainian National Republic, which granted it official recognition. After the consolidation of Polish rule in Galicia, SH operations were suspended for a brief period.

Directors and administrators of the Silskyi Hospodar society in 1938. Sitting, from left: Ivan Lapchuk, Illia Lysy, Mykhailo Kholievchuk, Myron Lutsky (chief administrator), Yevhen Khraplyvy (chairman of the board of directors), Antin Romanenko, unidentified person; standing: I. Rybak, Roman Holod, Mykhailo Borovsky, N. Onyshkevych, I. Kiliar, Petro Zeleny, Kharytia Kononenko, I. Myhul, M. Kliufas, M. Lokshynsky, V. Dzerovych-Sobolta, R. Doberchak, Olha Duchyminska-Myhul

SH resumed its activities in 1920, but on a very limited scale. The number of branches fell drastically (in 1924 there were only 10), and its new organ, *Hospodars'ko-kooperatyvnyi chasopys*, was taken over by the Audit Union of Ukrainian Co-operatives (RSUK). From 1927 it increased its activity quickly, supported by the Association of Ukrainian Agronomists and various Ukrainian co-operatives, which provided funds. In 1929 SH was reorganized. A board of directors, headed by Yu. Pavlykovsky (1924–9), T. Voinarovsky-Stolobut (1929–36), and M. Lutsky (1936–9), was responsible for its general policy. The administration was left to the chairman, Ye. *Khraplyvy (1928–39),

and his executive, which included M. Kholievchuk, I. Lapchuk, I. Lysy, B. Hnatevych, and A. Romanenko. The primary goal of the organization was to provide peasants with theoretical and practical training in agriculture. The most significant development in that area was the introduction of the *Khliborobskyi Vyshkil Molodi program in 1932. A section of SH organized courses in home economics for peasant women. Formed in 1936, the section was headed by O. Kysilevska, assisted by I. Pavlykovska. Its organizers included Kh. Kononenko and I. Dombchevska.

SH published several periodicals: *Sil's'kyi hospodar, *Ukraïns'kyi pasichnyk, Praktychne sadivnytstvo (1933–8, edited by M. Borovsky), *Khliborobs'ka molod', and Sad i horod (1939). During its history it published almost 180 textbooks and popular manuals on all aspects of agriculture, almost 120 of them in the interwar period. From 1928 SH issued an annual calendar, and just before the outbreak of the Second World War it began to publish an agricultural encyclopedia, edited by Khraplyvy. SH also printed hundreds of pamphlets, leaflets, and posters. In the interwar period it operated eight model farms, an agricultural school in Korshiv, and an advanced school in Yanchyn, where instructors and assistant agronomists were trained. The growth of SH is summarized in the table below.

Growth of Silskyi Hospodar, 1910–44

	Branches	Locals	Members	Professional staff
1910	85	317	12,500	4
1918	88	1,815	83,400	5
1927	52	112	18,400	15
1932	73	1,928	45,400	25
1939	60	2,040	160,000	167
1944	66	2,040	250,000	250

SH attempted to extend its activities to Volhynia during the interwar period, and from 1928 it operated a branch in Lutske, directed by V. Ostrovsky and then R. Klos, but the branch was closed by the Polish authorities in 1937. For a short period SH also maintained a branch in Kremianets, directed by B. Kozubsky. Throughout the period SH worked closely with RSUK, sometimes sharing personnel and facilities.

In 1939 the Soviet authorities liquidated SH. It continued its work in the German-occupied Generalgouvernement and established a headquarters in Jarosław (directed by L. Bachynsky and M. Kaplysty). In practice its work was limited to the peasants of the region. That office published 17 issues of the monthly Sil's'kyi hospodar, several booklets, and a calendar. A regional SH organization was established in Cracow in 1940–1 and was affiliated with the Ukrainian Central Committee. It included 130 locals in the Lemko and Sian regions.

When all of Galicia was occupied by the Germans in 1941, SH renewed its activity in Lviv under the presidency of Khraplyvy and the directorship of Ya. Zaishly. It worked closely with the Lviv Agricultural Chamber, which was directed by Khraplyvy, and was recognized as the main professional association of Ukrainian farmers. It renewed the publication of Sil's'kyi hospodar and Ukraïns'kyi pasichnyk and issued a few booklets and calendars. With the second Soviet occupation of Galicia in 1944, SH was dissolved.

SH not only improved the economic standing of the Ukrainian peasantry but also did much to raise their national consciousness. Among its prominent activists, in addition to ones already mentioned, were O. Duchyminska, P. Zeleny, M. Khronoviat, M. Tvorydlo, and V. Vakulovsky.

BIBLIOGRAPHY
Dubrivnyi, P. (ed). *Kraiove hospodars'ke tovarystvo 'Sil's'kyi hospodar' u L'vovi, 1899–1944* (New York 1970)

P. Zeleny

Silskyi Hospodar (Farmer). The central organization of agricultural co-operatives in the Ukrainian SSR, founded by the government at the beginning of the New Economic Policy in 1922 in place of the *Tsentral union. By 1928 it represented over 22,000 co-operatives and had over 2.9 million members. Its turnover that year was 169 million rubles; the turnover of its member co-operatives was 448 million rubles. In 1927 3,594 general and 8,606 specialized agricultural co-operatives belonged to the organization. Of the specialized co-operatives, 582 specialized in dairy and livestock, 615 in sugar beets, 209 in fruit and vegetables, and 189 in beekeeping. There were also 3,119 machine and tractor co-operatives. The primary co-operatives were organized into 24 general, 46 specialized, and 18 credit associations. They included Dobrobut, a livestock and dairy co-operative that marketed over 16 million kg of meat and 1.6 million kg of dairy products in 1925–6; Plodospilka, an association of orcharding, gardening, grape-growing, and beekeeping co-operatives established in 1925; Buriakspilka, an association of sugar-beet producers; and Ukrkooptakh, an association of poultry farmers. All of these associations ran their own processing and distribution facilities, and many published books and brochures on the co-operative movement. Silskyi Hospodar also published **Sil's'kyi hospodar* (1923–7), which later became *Kooperovane selo* (1927–8) and then *Kooperovana hromada* (1928–30). The organization and almost the entire *co-operative movement were dissolved in the early 1930s with the introduction of collectivization.

Sil's'kyi hospodar (Farmer). A semimonthly organ of the *Tsentral union of agricultural co-operatives, published in Kiev from July 1918 to the end of 1919 (a total of 35 issues). It contained articles on farming and the co-operative movement in Ukraine.

Sil's'kyi hospodar (Farmer). A semimonthly organ of the *Silskyi Hospodar agricultural co-operative union, published in Kharkiv from 1923. In 1927 it was renamed *Kooperovane selo*, and in mid-1928 it was merged with *Radians'kyi kredyt* to form *Kooperovana hromada*, which appeared semimonthly until January 1930.

Sil's'kyi hospodar (Farmer). A popular farming journal published by the *Silskyi Hospodar society semimonthly in Lviv (1926–39, 1942–4) and monthly in Jarosław (1940–1). The editors were Ye. Khraplyvy (1928–34, 1938–42), V. Sozansky (1925–9), P. Dubrivny, M. Borovsky (1932–6), P. Zeleny, L. Bachynsky (1940–1), and I. Drabaty. *Sil'sk'kyi hospodar* appeared in a pressrun of 5,000 to 10,000 in the interwar period and up to 50,000 during the Second World War. The monthly supplement *Ukraïns'kyi pasichnyk* was published in 1928–39 and 1941–4.

Sil's'kyi hospodar (1926–44)

Sil's'kyi svit (Rural World). A popular agricultural monthly and, from 1926, semimonthly published in Peremyshl (1923–4) by S. Dmokhovsky and in Lviv (1925–8) and Lutske (1928–31) by Ye. Arkhypenko (from November 1924). It issued the supplements *Supriaha, Ukraïns'ke molocharstvo*, and *Ukraïns'ke pasichnytstvo*.

Sil's'kyi teatr. See *Masovyi teatr*.

Ivan Silvai

Silvai, Ivan [Sil'vaj] (pseud: Uriil Meteor), b 15 March 1838 in Suskove, d 13 February 1904 in Nove Davydkove, Bereg komitat, Transcarpathia. Priest and Russophile writer. He began writing in 1855 in the *yazychiie but later switched to Russian. His lyric poems, epic ballads ('Fedor Kor'iatovich,' 'L'voborets'), satirical stories and novelettes ('Kraitsarovaia komediia' [The Kreutzer Comedy], 'Millioner') about the Magyarone clergy and Transcarpathian rural society, and anecdotal and historical tales appeared in *Tserkovnaia gazeta* (Budapest), *Svit'', Novyi svit'', Sova, Karpat'', Lystok''*, and *Misiatseslov* (Uzhhorod), and *Slovo* (Lviv). He also wrote two volumes of sermons, a short autobiography, articles on Ruthenian life under Hungarian rule and on his enemy, Bishop S. Pankovych (I. Pankovics) of Mukachiv, and a study of Transcarpathian miracle-working icons. A book of his religious poems was published in 1903, and a Russian edition of his collected works appeared in Prešov in 1957.

Silvansky, Mykola [Sil'vans'kyj], b 5 January 1916 in Kharkiv, d 5 March 1985 in Kiev. Composer, pianist, and pedagogue. A graduate of the Moscow Conservatory (1944), he studied composition with V. Barabashov in Kharkiv and, in 1944–53, was a soloist with the Kharkiv Philharmonic. In 1947 he began teaching at Kharkiv music schools, and from 1955 at the Kiev Conservatory. His works include the ballets *Nezvychainyi den'* (Unusual Day, 1964) and *Mal'chysh-Kybal'chysh* (1981), the musical *The Magical Power of Tsar Dobrylo* (1982), the symphonic tale *Ivasyk-Telesyk* (to the words of P. Tychyna, 1965), five piano concertos, chamber works, pieces for piano and bandura, art songs, arrangements of Ukrainian folk songs, and music for radio.

Tiberii Silvashi: *Summer in Mukachiv* (oil, 1985)

Silvashi, Tiberii [Sil'vashi, Tiberij], b 13 July 1947 in Mukachiv, Transcarpathia oblast. Painter. A graduate of the Kiev State Art Institute (1971) and a secretary of the Union of Artists of Ukraine in Kiev, he has worked within the representational framework. His brush stroke is gesturally abstract, however, with drips of paint and an expressionist palette; his compositions are sometimes unusual or off-balance; and the subject matter may be somewhat enigmatic (eg, *There, beyond the Window*, 1984). At the Young Ukrainian Artists Exhibition in Moscow in 1985, his works attracted international recognition (eg, *Dedication to My Daughter*, 1983; *Weekend*, 1983).

Silvestrov, Valentin. See Sylvestrov, Valentyn.

Sim Brativ fortified settlement. A Black Sea trading center of the 6th to 2nd century BC on the lower Kuban River near Varenykivska, Krasnodar krai, RF. The site was first excavated in 1878 and again in 1938–40 and 1949–50 by N. Anfimov. It originated as one of the major settlements of the Sindians, a Maeotan tribe eventually assimilated by the Sarmatians. It was fortified in the 5th century BC with walls, towers, and a moat. The inhabitants engaged in agriculture, fishing, handicraft production, and trade. Archeological excavations uncovered the remains of a large (420 sq m) 3rd-century BC stone house with an inner court. The site's archeological name is derived from its proximity to the *Sim Brativ kurhans.

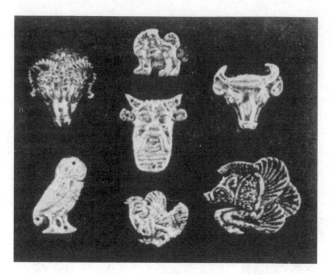

Gold ornaments found in the Sim Brativ kurhans

Sim Brativ kurhans. A group of seven (hence the name 'Seven Brothers') 5th- to 4th-century BC Sindian kurhans located by the mouth of the Kuban River to the west of the *Sim Brativ fortified settlement. Excavations in 1875–8 by V. Tisenhausen revealed tombs made from stone and unfired brick, in which the remains of humans and horses, weapons, vases, gold ornaments, and harnesses were found.

The Simeiz sanatorium

Simeiz [Simejiz]. IX-15. A town smt (1986 pop 4,700) on the southern shore of the Crimea, administered by the Yalta city council. Sheltered from northern winds by the Crimean Mountains, it is a health resort area. Its sanatoriums employ climatotherapy and baths to treat pulmonary tuberculosis. A branch of the Crimean Astrophysical Observatory is located there.

Simenovych, Volodymyr [Simenovyč], b 14 January 1858 in Filvarky, Buchach county, Galicia, d 13 June 1932 in Chicago. Physician, journalist, and community leader; brother of O. *Kysilevska. After graduating in law from Lviv University (1884) he emigrated to the United States and settled in Shenandoah, Pennsylvania, in 1887. He edited the weekly *Ameryka, organized co-operative stores in Pennsylvania, obtained a medical degree (1892), and moved to Chicago, where he taught obstetrics at the National Medical University (1905–7). An active member of the Ukrainian community, he founded the Brotherhood of the Ukrainian National Association and the Ukrainian So-

Volodymyr Simenovych   Myroslav Simenovych-Simens

cial Club, chaired the education commission of the Ukrainian National Association (1912–14), and edited the weekly *Ukraïna* (1930–2).

Simenovych-Simens, Myroslav [Simenovyč-Simens], b 16 February 1885 in Chernivtsi, Bukovyna, d 14 March 1967 in Chicago. Physician and community leader. After emigrating to the United States in 1907, he graduated from Loyola University (1912) and practiced medicine in Chicago. In 1920 he served in the mission of the Western Ukrainian National Republic to London. In the interwar period he organized the hetmanite movement in the United States and served as chief otaman of the *Sich societies in the United States and Canada (1927–40). In 1933 he chaired the exhibition committee which set up the Ukrainian pavilion at the Chicago World's Fair. He was one of the founders of the Ukrainian Congress Committee of America in 1940 and then the United Ukrainian American Relief Committee. After the war he revived the United Hetman Organization and served as its president (1952–9), and helped establish the League of Americans of Ukrainian Descent and the Ukrainian Medical Association of North America. He was elected the first president of the Ukrainian Museum in Chicago, which he helped found in 1953. In recognition of his contributions to the Ukrainian cause he was awarded an honorary doctorate by the Ukrainian Free University (1959).

Valentyn Simiantsev: *Portrait of Gen Mykhailo Omelianovych-Pavlenko* (1948)

Simferopol. See Symferopil.

Simiantsev, Valentyn [Simjantsev], b 23 April 1899 in Velykyi Burluk, Vovchanske county, Kharkiv gubernia, d ? Sculptor and writer. An engineer by training, during the Ukrainian-Soviet War he served in the cavalry of the Khmelnytsky Regiment (1917–20). As an interwar émigré in Czechoslovakia, he studied art at the Ukrainian Husbandry Academy in Poděbrady (to 1929) and worked as an engineer. A postwar refugee, in 1949 he settled in the United States and worked as sculptor for the US Military Institute of Pathology in Washington. He has sculpted busts and medallions and has written four volumes of memoirs (1963, 1973, 1976, 1978).

Ludwyk Simiginowicz-   Kostiantyn Siminsky
Staufe

Simiginowicz-Staufe, Ludwyk Adolph [Symyhynovyč] (pseuds: Adolph Sand, Adolph Staufe), b 28 May 1832 in Suceava, Rumania, d 19 May 1897 in Chernivtsi. German writer and ethnographer; the first German poet in Bukovyna. The son of a Ukrainian father and a German mother, he was educated in Chernivtsi and Vienna. After debuting as a poet in Chernivtsi (1848) he worked as a teacher there (1849–52, 1857–8, 1876–97) and in Kronstadt (Braşov), Transylvania (1858–71), and as a journalist and critic in Vienna (1852–6). His literary and theater reviews, stories, poems, and translations of Ukrainian, Rumanian, and Polish fairy tales were published in German periodicals in Vienna, Chernivtsi, Lviv, and elsewhere. He wrote poetry collections and compiled the first album of German poetry published in Bukovyna (1852). He also compiled and translated *Märchen aus der Bukowina* (2 vols, 1853, 1855), *Ruthenische Sagen und Märchen aus der Bukowina* (1880), and *Kleinrussische Volkslieder* (1888).

Siminsky, Kostiantyn [Simins'kyj] (Syminsky), b 6 March 1879 in Myleichytsi, Brest county, Hrodna gubernia, d 13 June 1932 in Kiev. Civil and construction mechanics engineer; full member of the VUAN from 1926. He studied at the Kiev Polytechnical Institute and in 1914 became a professor there. He taught and conducted research at various institutions in Kiev. He became director of the VUAN Institute of Technical Mechanics (in 1921) and the Kiev branch of the Scientific Research Institute of Structures of the VUAN (in 1929) and was vice-president of the VUAN (1931–2). He studied fatigue effects in metals and wood, particularly in bridges, and developed the method of determining fatigue effects by drilling holes in materials. He also studied the strength of other building materials (eg, granite) and developed new equations and measuring methodology for structures. Among his numerous works are monographs, including textbooks on the statics of structures (1930), technical mechanics (1931), and spatial forms (1934).

Alex Simirenko   Roman Simovych

Simirenko, Alex [Symyrenko, Oleksa], b 6 September 1931 in Kiev, d 27 April 1979 in Philadelphia. Sociologist; son of V. *Symyrenko. He and his mother fled from Soviet Ukraine in the late 1930s and lived as refugees in Prague and postwar Bavaria. In 1950 they emigrated to the United States. Simirenko graduated from the University of Minnesota (PH D, 1961) and was a professor of sociology at the University of Nevada (1960–9), California State University (Northridge, 1968–71), and Pennsylvania State University (from 1969). A specialist in American ethnic studies and Soviet sociology, he wrote *Pilgrims, Colonists, and Frontiersmen: An Ethnic Community in Transition* (1964), about the Transcarpathian community in Minneapolis, and edited, with introductions, the collections *Soviet Sociology: Historical Antecedents and Current Appraisals* (1966) and *Social Thought in the Soviet Union* (1969). An edition of his selected articles, *The Professionalization of Soviet Society*, was published posthumously in 1982.

Simon (Symon), b ca 1166, d 22 May 1226. Churchman and literary figure. A monk of the Kievan Cave Monastery, he became bishop of Vladimir-Suzdal in 1215. His correspondence with the monk Polikarp provided the basis for the redaction of the *Kievan Cave Patericon. He was buried at the Cave Monastery, where he lived as an ascetic before his death. He was later canonized by the Orthodox church.

Simovych, Oksana [Simovyč] (née Boiko), b 18 August 1914 in Ternopil, Galicia, d 15 January 1986 in Philadelphia. Violinist and teacher; wife of R. *Simovych. A graduate of the Chopin School of Music in Stanyslaviv (1938), she also studied at conservatories in Warsaw, Vienna, and Philadelphia. From 1930 she performed as a solo violinist or in ensemble in Ukraine, Western Europe, and the United States. She was a member of the Munich Symphony Orchestra (1940s), the Settlement Music School

orchestra (Philadelphia, 1950s), and the orchestra of the Ukrainian Music Institute of America (Philadelphia, 1961–73).

Simovych, Roman [Simovyč], b 28 February 1901 in Sniatyn, Galicia, d 30 July 1984 in Lviv. Composer and teacher. He graduated in composition and piano from the Prague Conservatory in 1933 and completed its Master School in 1936 in the composition class of V. Novak. From 1936 he taught at the Lysenko Higher Institute of Music in Drohobych and Stanyslaviv. From 1951 he lectured at the Lviv Conservatory (professor in 1963). His compositions include the ballet *Dovbush's Sopilka* (1948), seven symphonies (including the *Hutsul* [no. 1] and the *Lemko* [no. 2]); the symphonic poems *Maksym Kryvonis* (1954), *Dovbush* (1955), and *In Memory of Ivan Franko* (1956); overtures for symphony orchestra; a string quartet; numerous works for piano (two trios and two sonatas, three suites, a sonatina, and a fantasia); and works for choir with orchestra and for choir a cappella.

Vasyl Simovych

Simovych, Vasyl [Simovyč, Vasyl'] (pseud: V. Vernyvolia), b 9 March 1880 in Hadynkivtsi, Husiatyn county, Galicia, d 13 March 1944 in Lviv. Linguist, philologist, and cultural figure; member of the Shevchenko Scientific Society (NTSh) from 1923. As a student at Chernivtsi University (1899–1904), where his mentor was S. *Smal-Stotsky, he joined the *Revolutionary Ukrainian party and in 1902–3 was a coeditor of its journals *Haslo* and *Selianyn* and of the newspaper *Bukovyna*. He defended his PH D dissertation on the verb in I. Galiatovsky's works in 1913. During the First World War he worked with the *Union for the Liberation of Ukraine as a cultural organizer and teacher in German and Austrian POW camps holding 40,000 Ukrainian soldiers of the Russian Army. He produced for them a synchronic grammar of Ukrainian (1918); its expanded 2nd edition (1921) incorporated elements of scholarly grammar. In 1919–20 he headed the Cultural-Educational Department of the Ukrainian Military Mission for Ukrainian Prisoners in Germany, edited its periodical, *Shliakh* (Salzwedel), and wrote a popular booklet on how to become literate. In Berlin (1920–3) he worked as an editor and translator for the Ukrainska Nakladnia publishing house and prepared annotated editions of T. Shevchenko's *Kobzar* (1921) and of works by I. Franko and B. Lepky (1922). Then, while serving as a professor (1923–33; and rector, 1926–30) at the *Ukrainian

Higher Pedagogical Institute in Prague and at the Higher Trade School in Prague, he played an active role in Ukrainian life in Czechoslovakia. He was a member of the Prague Linguistic Circle, and produced a textbook of Old Church Slavonic grammar (1926), an anthology of Old Ukrainian literature (1932), and articles in Ukrainian historical morphology (eg, on the pronoun *ščo* 'what, that', masculine nouns and male names ending in -*o*, and adjectives) and phonology (the interplay of *e* and *o*) and the history of Ukrainian linguistics and orthography (I. Galiatovsky's translations of the Bible, M. Luchkai's grammar, the *drahomanivka* script, J. Jireček's proposal for a Ukrainian Latin alphabet).

After 1933, in Lviv, Simovych worked as an editor of the Prosvita society's publications (including the journal *Zhyttia i znannia*, in which he published articles on the Ukrainian language), *Ukraïns'ka zahal'na entsyklopediia* (The Ukrainian General Encyclopedia), the cultural-literary journal *Nazustrich* (1934–8), and the scholarly journal *S'ohochasne i mynule* (1939). He was a member of the NTSh board of directors and the NTSh Language Commission. He devoted his attention to Ukrainian modern and historical phonology and morphology, the history of Ukrainian orthography, and the practical problems of the normative language. The first and most prominent Ukrainian phonologist of the 'Prague structuralist school,' he combined its ideas with the approaches of W. Humboldt and O. *Potebnia.

During the first Soviet occupation of Galicia (1939–41), Simovych served as professor, dean of philology, and rector (1941) at Lviv University. Under the German occupation (1941–4) he was briefly imprisoned, and then worked as an editor for the Lviv branch of the Ukrainske Vydavnytstvo publishing house and played an active role in the Ukrainian Central Committee's Scholarly Fund and Relief Committee for Eastern Ukrainian Refugees. A detailed evaluation of his scholarly contributions is found in the two-volume collection of his works *Ukraïns'ke movoznavstvo* (Ukrainian Linguistics, 1981, 1984), edited by G.Y. Shevelov.

G.Y. Shevelov

Simpson, George, b 24 March 1893 in Chatsworth, Ontario, d 6 March 1969 in Saskatoon. Historian and civic figure; full member of the Shevchenko Scientific Society from 1948 and of the Ukrainian Academy of Arts and Sciences in Canada. After studying at the University of Saskatchewan (1919), the University of Toronto (1920), and the University of London he became a lecturer in history at the University of Saskatchewan in Saskatoon in 1922 (professor in 1928, department head in 1940). Simpson developed a considerable empathy for Ukrainians, through his contacts with them in the 1920s, which led him to learn the Ukrainian language and to organize the first department of Slavic studies at a Canadian university, in Saskatoon in 1945. He edited an English translation of D. Doroshenko's *History of the Ukraine* (1939), prepared a series of radio broadcasts in 1939 on the Ukrainian question, and wrote several items about Ukrainian history, including a historical atlas of Ukraine (1941). He was an adviser to public officials in Canada on Ukrainian matters and a participant in the negotiations leading to the formation of the Ukrainian Canadian Committee (now Congress).

Sindians (*syndy*). A Maeotian tribe which inhabited the Taman Peninsula, the Black Sea coastal region adjacent to it, and a portion of the Kuban during the 1st millennium BC. The Sindians practiced agriculture, fishing, manufacturing, and trade. They formed a state in the 5th century BC, and a century later they became part of the Bosporan Kingdom. The Greeks exerted a major influence on the Sindians, particularly with respect to language and religion. In the 1st to 2nd century AD they were assimilated by the Sarmatians. Many archeological remains in the Taman and Kuban regions can be traced to the Sindians. The most noted among them are the *Sim Brativ fortified settlement and the *Sim Brativ kurhans.

Volodymyr Singalevych   Gen Volodymyr Sinkler

Singalevych, Volodymyr [Singalevyč] (originally Schilling), b 1880 in Galicia, d 1945 in Austria. Politician and civic figure of German heritage. A lawyer by training, he was a member of the National Democratic party, an elected representative to the Austrian parliament from the Peremyshl region (1911–18), and a member of the Galician Diet (1913–14). From 1914 he was in Vienna as deputy chief for the military administration of the Ukrainian Sich Riflemen and as a member of the National Council of the Western Ukrainian National Republic (1919–23, responsible for finances and, later, internal affairs). In 1930–9 he was director of the Land Mortgage Bank in Lviv.

Sinkevych, Dionisii [Sinkevyč, Dionisij], b ? Rozdilie, Galicia, d ? Engraver. The hegumen of the Krekhiv (1690–1700) and St George's (Lviv) monasteries, he did a large wood engraving of the Krekhiv monastery (1699), which is of interest to historians of wooden architecture, and illustrated the Akathist (1699), Hiermologion (1700), and Triodion for Eastertide (1701) published in Lviv. Western influences are evident in his work.

Sinkler, Volodymyr, b 12 January 1879 in Novoi Margelan, Fergana oblast, Turkestan, d 1945 in Kiev. UNR Army general. A graduate of the General Staff Academy in St Petersburg, during the First World War he reached the rank of brigadier general in the Russian army. In 1918 he joined the Ukrainian State army and served as general quartermaster on the General Staff. In 1919 he was chief of staff of the UNR Army, and in 1920 he became chief of the General Staff and a member of the Higher Military Council. He was promoted to major general by the UNR government-in-exile. When the Red Army occupied Poland in 1945, he was arrested by the NKVD. He died in prison.

Title page of *Sinopsis* (1674)

Sinopsis (Synopsis). One of the first synthetic surveys of Ukrainian and East European history. It was first published by the Kievan Cave Monastery Press in 1674, and some 30 more printings had appeared by 1836, 21 of them in St Petersburg. The author is believed to have been I. *Gizel or a monk at the Kievan Cave Monastery, P. Kokhanovsky. *Sinopsis* covers events from the time of the early Slavs (relating an account of them as descendants of Mosoch, the son of Japheth) to the mid-17th century. The third Kiev edition (1680) includes an account of the Chyhyryn campaigns of 1677–9 and the reign of Tsar Fedor Alekseevich. Based on historical works by M. Stryjkowski, M. Bielski, M. Kromer, and A. Guagnini, as well as the Primary, Hustynia, and other Rus' and Cossack chronicles, it attempts to justify historically the unification of Ukraine and Russia. It devotes particular attention to the political history of Kievan Rus' and includes lists of Rus' princes, Polish palatines, Cossack hetmans, Russian tsars, and metropolitans of Kiev. The *Sinopsis* was for many years the standard text on the history of Kievan Rus'. It gained great popularity throughout Ukraine and Russia and was translated into Latin, Greek, and Rumanian.

Sioło (Hamlet). A bilingual Polish-Ukrainian miscellany, four volumes of which were published in the Polish alphabet in Lviv in 1866–7. The editor and publisher was P. *Svientsitsky (Święcicki), who had as his aim the strengthening of Ukrainian-Polish understanding and the combating of Galician Russophilism and Russian imperialism. *Sioło* contained articles on Ukrainian Cossack history and T. Shevchenko; prose and poetry by Svientsitsky, Shevchenko, Yu. Fedkovych, H. Kvitka-Osnovianenko, and M. Vovchok; a Ukrainian translation of the Primary Chronicle; poems dedicated to Shevchenko by Polish émigré authors; and bibliographic surveys of Ukrainian publications.

Sion, tserkov', shkola (Zion, Church, School). A semimonthly supplement to *Vistnyk*, the official newspaper for Ukrainians in the Austrian Empire, published in Vienna in 1858–9 (a total of 53 issues). It contained belles lettres, news, sermons, and articles on current affairs, culture, and education. The editor and publisher was V. Zborovsky (pseud of Yu. Vyslobotsky).

Sion ruskii. See *Ruskii Sion.*

Siret. See Seret.

Siretsky, Bohdan [Sirec'kyj], b 1907, d 1941 in Mykolaiv. Civic figure. A secondary school teacher in Bukovyna, he was one of the leading members of the Chornomore student society. In the 1930s he revived the Plast Ukrainian Youth Association in Bukovyna and served as its leader (1933–4). During the Second World War he joined the *OUN expeditionary groups and was arrested and shot by the Germans.

Ivan Sirko's gravestone

Sirko, Ivan, b ca 1605–10 in Merefa, Kharkiv region, d 11 August 1680 in Hrushivka, (now Illinka, Tomakivka raion, Dnipropetrovske oblast). Zaporozhian Cossack military leader. He served as colonel of Vinnytsia regiment (1658–60) and was elected Kish otaman of the Zaporozhian Host eight times in the 1660s and 1670s. Sirko participated in the Cossack-Polish War (1648–57), campaigned against the Tatars in the lower Dnieper region and the Perekop Isthmus in the late 1650s, and joined the Varenytsia Uprising (1664–5). He led Cossack campaigns against the Crimean Tatars (1668) and against Turkish fortifications in Ochakiv and Islamkermen (1670–1). In 1678, together with the army of Hetman I. Samoilovych and the Russian army of G. Romodanovsky, he halted the advance of Turkish and Tatar forces on Right-Bank Ukraine.

Sirko often changed his political orientation. He opposed I. *Vyhovsky, Yu. Khmelnytsky (whom he had previously supported against Vyhovsky), and P. Teteria for their pro-Polish policies, and during their hetmancies he was not hostile toward Muscovy. After the Treaty of *Andrusovo (1667), however, he became openly anti-Muscovite. Disregarding his own animosity toward the Turks and Tatars, Sirko supported Hetman P. *Doroshenko for a lengthy period before severing ties with him.

Sirko's military exploits against the Turks and Tatars became the subject of folk legends and dumas. His letters to Doroshenko (of 1 October 1673) and the Crimean khan (of 1679) have been preserved (by S. Velychko, A. Rigelman, and N. Markevych). He is associated with a famous letter written by the Zaporozhian Cossacks in reply to the demands of the Turkish sultan to surrender voluntarily (depicted in a painting by I. Repin, 1891). The historian D. Yavornytsky composed two dumas about Sirko and published a biography in 1894.

O. Ohloblyn

Vasyl Sirko   Stepan Siropolko

Sirko, Vasyl, b 5 March 1899 in Kinashiv, Rohatyn county, Galicia, d 3 November 1937. Galician Communist leader. In 1919 he was active in the communist underground in Stanyslaviv and took part in the founding conference of the Communist Party of Eastern Galicia. In 1920 he conducted agitation and propaganda within the Ukrainian Galician Army (UHA), helped organize Red UHA units, and, in the summer, headed the Terebovlia county Revolutionary Committee of the *Galician Socialist Soviet Republic. In 1921 he taught at the Second Kiev Red Officers School until April and then supervised CP(B)U agitation and propaganda work in Galicia. He served as a CP(B)U functionary in Kiev, Donetske, Makiivka, and Kryvyi Rih until he was arrested during the Stalinist terror in 1933. He either died in a Soviet concentration camp or was executed by the NKVD.

Siromantsi. See Graywolves Company of the Ukrainian Insurgent Army.

Siropolko, Stepan, b 1872 in Pryluka, Poltava gubernia, d 21 February 1959 in Prague. Pedagogue and bibliographer. He graduated from Moscow University, where he was an active member of the Ukrainian Hromada and co-editor of the periodical *Ukrainskaia zhizn'*. In 1917 he became director of public education in Kiev. While in Kiev he lectured at the Froebel Pedagogical Institute. He also acted as consultant to the General Secretariat of the Central Rada on educational matters. After 1921 he emigrated, first to Poland and then to Czechoslovakia. He was an active member of the Ukrainian community, in Prague in particular: he taught at the Ukrainian Higher Pedagogical Institute (1925–32), he organized and was head of the *Ukrainian Society of Bibliophiles in Prague and edited its journal *Knyholiub*, and he headed the Ukrainian Pedagogical Society in Prague and the Union of Ukrainian Journalists and Writers Abroad. He was also a member of the Ukrainian Historical-Philological Society and became an honorary member of the *Prosvita society in Lviv. He wrote articles on pedagogical topics for Ukrainian- and foreign-language periodicals. His published works include *Vzirtsevyi katalog shkilnoï i narodn'oï biblioteky* (A Model Catalog for the School and Public Library, 1918), *Narodni biblioteky* (People's Libraries, 1919), *Zavdannia shkoly* (The Task of the School, 1919), *Korotkyi kurs bibliotekoznavstva* (A Short Library Science Course, 1924),

Shkoloznavstvo (Pedagogy, 1926), *Narodnia osvita na Soviets'kii Ukraïni* (Public Education in Soviet Ukraine, 1934), and *Istoriia osvity na Ukraïni* (The History of Education in Ukraine, 1937).

Sirozhupannyky. See Graycoats.

Siry, Yurii. See Tyshchenko, Yurii.

Sisters of Saint Josaphat (Sestry Sviatoho Sviashchenomuchenyka Yosafata, or Yosafatky). A Ukrainian Catholic order of nuns founded in 1911 by Rev O. Dyky of St George's Cathedral in Lviv with the assistance of Rev I. Zhygal. Its members ran orphanages, homes for the aged, and nurseries; provided religious guidance to young female domestics and workers; and assiduously disseminated the Catholic press. Its rule (388 regulations) was confirmed by Metropolitan A. Sheptytsky and reconfirmed in 1943 by Bishop H. Khomyshyn and in 1975 by Cardinal Y. Slipy. In 1939 the order had 40 members and 16 novices, who lived in eight houses in Lviv archeparchy and two in Stanyslaviv eparchy. It was abolished after the 1944 Soviet reoccupation of Galicia and has since been inactive.

Sisters of Saint Joseph (Sestry Sviatoho Yosyfa, or Yosyfitky). A Ukrainian Catholic order of nuns founded in 1894 by Rev K. *Seletsky, the curate of Zhuzhil, Sokal county, Galicia. Its first convent was opened in 1909 in nearby Tsebliv. After Seletsky's death in 1918, Bishop Y. Kotsylovsky, the order's new guardian, modified and approved the order's rule. The sisters promoted the veneration of St Joseph; performed acts of charity; ran nurseries; and cared for orphans, the infirm, and the aged. They received spiritual guidance from the *Redemptorist Fathers. Before the order was abolished by the Soviet regime in 1945, it had 25 houses and approx 100 sisters in Galicia. Today the order exists in Poland (12 houses and approx 25 members in 1990), Brazil (4 houses and approx 30 members in 1990), and Canada (2 houses in Saskatoon and 1 in Winnipeg and 10 members in 1990). It has operated St Joseph's Home for the Aged in Saskatoon since 1964.

The first home and chapel of the Sisters Servants of Mary Immaculate in Mundare, Alberta (1903)

Sisters Servants of Mary Immaculate (Sestry sluzhebnytsi Neporochnoi Divy Marii). A congregation of Ukrainian Catholic nuns established in 1892 in Zhuzhil, Sokal county, Galicia, by the local priest, K. *Seletsky, under the spiritual guidance of Y. Lomnytsky of the Basilian order. The first charter was approved by Metropolitan S. Sembratovych in May 1892, and in September of that year a novitiate was opened in Zhuzhil, with nine novices. The first prioress was Sister Y. Hordashevska. In 1894 the novitiate was moved to Krystynopil.

The congregation's aims were to educate children; to perform acts of charity; and to run nurseries, orphanages, schools, hospitals, and homes for the aged and infirm. Members of the order also assisted in various church work. Convents of the congregation were established in Canada (1902), Yugoslavia (1906), Brazil (1911), Czechoslovakia (1928), the United States (1935), and Argentina (1965).

The constitution of the Sisters Servants was revised at its first congress, held in 1907 in Galicia, and again in 1929. In 1932 the Congregation for Eastern Churches raised the status of the Sisters Servants of Mary Immaculate to that of a congregation of papal law, thereby standardizing its rules and administration, and in 1934 divided it into three provinces (Europe, Canada, and Brazil). Each province was to govern itself but accepted a common constitution and the authority of the general curia, which was initially in Zhuzhil, then in Krystynopil, and after 1934 in Lviv. After the Second World War the general curia was moved to Rome. At the same time the congregation was suppressed in Galicia by the Soviet authorities, and many of its members who did not flee the Red Army were imprisoned or exiled.

The novitiate of the Sisters Servants of Mary Immaculate in Ancaster, Ontario

Before the war the Sisters Servants had 107 houses in Ukraine, all of which were closed after its abolition by the Soviets. They also maintained 15 orphanages for approx 380 orphans (1938) and provided religious instruction for over 4,200 children. The next largest province was Canada, where by the end of the First World War there were 100 members in 20 houses. Today the Sisters Servants are organized into five provinces (Ukraine, Canada, Brazil, United States, and Poland), two vice-provinces (Czechoslovakia and Yugoslavia), and one delegature (Argentina) and have over 1,000 members in approx 120 houses. The liberalization in Ukraine since the late 1980s has permitted the congregation to re-establish itself there after almost 50 years.

BIBLIOGRAPHY
Velykyi, A. *Narys istoriï zhromadzhennia ss Sluzhebnyts'*, PNDM (Rome 1968)

I. Khoma

Sitch. See Sich.

Sitnytsky, Mykola [Sitnyc'kyj], b 1884, d 1934. Galician pedagogue. He taught German and Ukrainian language in the Zalishchyky Seminary and, from 1924 to 1932, in the Ukrainian Girls' Institute in Peremyshl, where for a time he was director. In the period of the Western Ukrainian National Republic he was director of the radio station of the Ukrainian Galician Army.

Yevtym Sitsinsky

Sitsinsky, Yevtym (Yukhym) [Sicins'kyj, Jevtym (Juxym)] (Sichynsky, Sitsynsky), b 1 October 1859 in Maznyky, Letychiv county, Podilia gubernia, d 7 December 1937 in Kamianets-Podilskyi. Historian, archeologist, teacher, and civic activist; member of the Shevchenko Scientific Society from 1894; father of V. *Sichynsky. A graduate of the Kiev Theological Academy (1885), he taught in the Kuban and then was ordained and stationed in Kamianets-Podilskyi (1889), where later he became archpriest of the cathedral parish. He established an eparchial historical-archeological museum in 1890 and directed it until 1922, headed the eparchial historical society (1903–21) and edited its publications *Podol'skie eparkhial'nye vedomosti* and *Trudy* (vols 6, 8–12), helped establish the Prosvita society in Podilia (1905), and carried out extensive field research throughout the region, during the course of which he studied architecture and collected museum pieces. His magnum opus was *Istoricheskie svedeniia o prikhodakh i tserkvakh Podol'skoi eparkhii* (Historical Information about the Parishes and Churches of Podilia Eparchy, 7 vols, 1895–1911), and his other works included *Arkheologicheskaia karta Podol'skoi gubernii* (Archeological Map of Podilia gubernia, 1901), *Ischezaiushchii tip dereviannykh tserkvei Podolii* (The Vanishing Type of Wooden Churches in Podilia, 1904), *Oboronni zamky Zakhidn'oho Podillia* (Defensive Castles of Western Podilia, 1928), and *Narysy z istoriï Podillia* (Studies of the History of Podilia, 2 vols, 1928). His most popular monograph was *Gorod Kamenets Podol'skii: Istoricheskoe opisanie* (The City of Kamianets-Podilskyi: A Historical Description, 1895).

In 1918 he helped establish a state university in Kamianets-Podilskyi, at which he taught archeology and Podilian history (1918–20). Under Soviet rule he was given a lowly teaching position at the Institute of People's Education (1920–6) and eventually dismissed. Sitsinsky was arrested in 1929, and spent 10 months in prison. Upon his release he worked for a short time at the museum of the Kievan Cave Monastery. He returned to Kamianets-Podilskyi, where, forbidden to teach, he lived out his days in poverty.

Siuren camp sites. Two Stone Age cave sites near the village of Tankove (formerly Siuren), Bakhchesarai raion, the Crimea. Siuren was excavated in 1879–80, in 1924–29 by G. Bonch-Osmolovsky, and in 1954–5 by E. Vekilova. Siuren I revealed three Upper Paleolithic occupations containing the remains of hearths, flint and bone tools, and wild animal bones. Of particular interest was the discovery of a piece of a deer antler inscribed with crooked lines and notches. Siuren II contained two Mesolithic occupations in which geometrically shaped flints pieces, arrowheads, and stone and flint tools were found.

Sivach (Sower). A monthly religious journal published in Lviv in 1936–9. The contributors were Revs H. Kubai, O. Gorchynsky, P. Dzedzyk, O. Hodunko, V. Rabii, I. Myroniuk, M. Mosora, and V. Popadiuk. It contained sermons and catechismal materials.

Sivach/The Sower. The semimonthly organ of the Stamford Ukrainian Catholic eparchy. It was founded by Bishop B. Losten in February 1986 and is published in English and Ukrainian. The editor of the English section is Msgr L. Mosko, and the editors of the Ukrainian section are B. Tarnavsky, O. Roshka, and W. Lencyk. The newspaper reports on religious life in the eparchy and on developments in the Ukrainian Catholic church, and includes articles on cultural and historical issues.

Siverianians (*siveriany*).An East Slavic tribe that lived in the Desna Basin and the upper reaches of the Seim, the Sula, the Psol, and the Vorskla rivers late in the 1st millennium AD. Their main settlements included *Chernihiv, Novhorod-Siverskyi, Putyvl, Kursk, and Liubech. The Siverianian territories bordered on those of the Polianians and Drehovichians in the west and the Radimichians, Krivichians, and Viatichians in the north. They settled the uninhabited southern steppes. The Siverianians were primarily farmers, herders, hunters, fishermen, and artisans. In the 8th and early 9th centuries they paid *tribute to the Khazars. Later, together with other East Slavic *tribes, they belonged to the Kievan Rus' state. According to the Primary Chronicle Oleh conquered the Siverianians in 884, and imposed a light tribute upon them and forbade them to give the Khazars any further payments. In 907 they took part in Oleh's campaign against Byzantium. The Siverianians lost their distinctive tribal features, and after 1024 they are not mentioned in the chronicles. A vestige of their name remained in *Siversk principality: the Siversk land was known as such until the 16th or 17th century. Many Siverianian settlements of the 8th to 10th centuries have been discovered near Romen (Monastyryshche, Petrivske, and Novotroitske), as well as kurhan burial sites (with evidence of the tribe's practice of cremation) and valuable treasures.

BIBLIOGRAPHY
Samokvasov, D. *Severianskaia zemlia i severiane po gorodishcham i mogilam* (Moscow 1908)

A. Zhukovsky

Siversk principality. One of the appanage principalities of the Chernihiv-Siversk land. It was founded in 1097 and was also known as Novhorod-Siverskyi principality (after its capital). Initially its territory extended along the Snov and the middle Desna rivers, and after the mid-1130s it expanded along the Seim River as far as Kursk. The region around the upper Desna and the Oka rivers, settled by the *Viatichians, also came under its control.

The first ruler of the Siversk principality was *Oleh Sviatoslavych; his successors, the Olhovych dynasty, frequently also controlled *Chernihiv principality and often contended for the Kievan throne. In the 1140s and 1150s Siversk principality separated from the Chernihiv region, and by the end of the 12th century it had been divided into several small principalities around Kursk, Putyvl, and other cities. Princes of Siversk clashed with the Cumans, particularly in the late 12th century. One of those campaigns, led by *Ihor Sviatoslavych in 1185, was celebrated in the epic poem *Slovo o polku Ihorevi* (The Tale of Ihor's Campaign).

When Batu Khan attacked Eastern Europe in the 1240s, Siversk principality was ravaged, but it continued to exist under Tatar hegemony. In the mid-14th century it came under the Grand Duchy of Lithuania; the first Lithuanian prince of Siversk was Dmytro Olgierdovych (son of Algirdas). Muscovy controlled Siversk principality from 1503 and liquidated it in 1523. The territory was later briefly held by Poland (1618–48).

BIBLIOGRAPHY
Golubovskii, P. *Istoriia Severskoi zemli do poloviny XIV st.* (Kiev 1881)
Bagalei, D. *Istoriia Severskoi zemli do poloviny XIV st.* (Kiev 1882)
Hrushevs'kyi, M. 'Chernyhiv i Siovershchyna v ukraïns'kii istoriï,' in *Chernyhiv i pivnichne livoberezhzhia* (Kiev 1928)
Rymut, K. 'Nazwy miejscowe dawnego księstwa Siewierskiego,' *Onomastica*, 1970, nos 1–2
Drevnerusskie kniazhestva X–XIII vv. (Moscow 1975)
Rybakov, B. 'Chernigovskoe i Severskoe kniazhestva,' in *Kievskaia Rus' i russkie kniazhestva XII–XIII vv.* (Moscow 1982)

A. Zhukovsky

Siverske [Sivers'ke]. V-19, DB II-4. A city (1989 pop 15,000) on the Bakhmutka River in Artemivske raion, Donetske oblast. It originated as a workers' settlement around the dolomite-processing plant built in 1913. In 1961 it attained city status. Its original name, Yama, was changed to Siverske in 1973. Today, besides the dolomite-processing complex, it has a brick factory. A literary memorial museum dedicated to V. *Sosiura is located in the city.

Siverskodonetske [Sivers'kodonec'ke]. V-19, DB II-4. A city (1990 pop 132,000) on the Donets River in Luhanske oblast. It was founded in 1934 as the Lyskhimbud builders' settlement during the construction of a nitrogen-fertilizer manufacturing complex in the suburbs of Lysychanske. In 1950 the settlement was renamed, and in 1958 it was granted city status. Today the city is the largest center of the chemical industry in Ukraine. It is the home of the Azot and the Skloplastyk manufacturing consortiums, the Impuls Research and Manufacturing Consortium, a chemical-metallurgical plant, building-materials plants, construction enterprises, and woodworking factories.

Siverskodonetske Azot Manufacturing Consortium (Siverskodonetske vyrobnyche obiednannia Azot). A chemical manufacturing enterprise located in Siverskodonetske, Luhanske oblast. It is based on a chemical manufacturing complex which came into operation in 1951. The consortium produces over 100 items, including ammonium and potassium nitrate, carbamide, ammonium sulfate, ammonia water, ammonium, methanol, formalin, glues, paints, polyethelene, and adipic and sebacic acids.

Siverskodonetske Skloplastyk Manufacturing Consortium (Siverskodonetske vyrobnyche obiednannia Skloplastyk). A fiberglass manufacturing consortium located in Siverskodonetske, Luhanske oblast. It was founded in 1977 on the basis of the first specialized fiberglass factory in the USSR, which came into operation in 1963. It produces over 160 items, including pipes and tubes, noncorroding machine parts, fiberglass sheets, and thermal plastics.

Siverskyi Donets River. See Donets River.

Siverskyi Donets–Donbas Canal. See Donets-Donbas Canal.

Sixth Sich Division of the Army of the UNR (Shosta sichova dyviziia Armii UNR). A military force recruited in the spring of 1920 from among Ukrainian POWs (soldiers of the UNR Army and the Russian Volunteer Army) in Polish internment camps at Łańcut and Brest-Litovsk. Its commander, Col M. Bezruchko, and chief of staff, Col V. Zmiienko, had been senior officers in the demobilized Sich Riflemen Group of the UNR Army. Its 250 officers and 1,770 soldiers were organized into the 16th Infantry Brigade (under Col R. Sushko), the 17th Infantry Brigade (Col O. Voroniv), the 6th Sich Cavalry Battalion (Lt V. Herasymenko), the 6th Light Artillery Brigade (Col Nasoniv), the 6th Sich Technical Battalion (Capt V. Bokitko), and several reserve units. As part of the Third Polish Army, the division advanced in early May 1920 from Brest-Litovsk through the Soviet rear to Berdychiv. From 8 May to 9 June it held Kiev, and then if fought the Red Army at Ihnatpil, Perha, Kovel, and Kholm. In late August it distinguished itself in the defense of Zamość. After being transferred to Galicia with the remainder of the UNR Army in September, the division suffered many casualties in the final battles with the Red Army at Popivtsi in November. After the Polish-Soviet armistice in October, most of the remaining soldiers retreated into Poland and were interned in camps at Aleksandrów Kujawski and Szczepiórno. A reserve brigade commanded by Gen Fedyniuk-Bilynsky remained on active duty at Brest-Litovsk until the Second Winter Campaign.

L. Shankovsky

Sixtus Erasmus (Sykst Erazm), b ca 1570 in Lviv, d ca 1635 in Zamostia. Philosopher and physician. After graduating from Cracow University (PH D, 1596) he taught there until 1600 and then studied medicine in Padua (MD, 1602). He worked at the Lviv Catholic Hospital and taught medicine at the Zamostia Academy (1614–29). He wrote a number of scientific books, including an analysis of the mineral waters of the Shklo resort, a study of the curative benefits of mud baths, and a medical commentary on Seneca.

Skaba, Andrii, b 12 December 1905 in Khorishky, Kobeliaky county, Poltava gubernia, d 26 June 1986 in Kiev. Soviet Party and state activist and historian; member of the AN URSR (now ANU) from 1967. After graduating from Kharkiv University (1934) he worked at the Kharkiv Pedagogical Institute and Kharkiv University (1936–40) and headed the departments of contemporary history at the universities of Lviv (1940–1) and Kharkiv (1946–9). He served as director of the Central State Archive of the October Revolution of the Ukrainian SSR in Kharkiv (1946–9) and as editor of the oblast newspaper, *Sotsialistychna Kharkivshchyna*. He was secretary of the Kharkiv oblast committee of the CPU (1951–9), minister of higher and secondary special education of the Ukrainian SSR (1959), and secretary of the CC CPU (1959–68). From 1968 to 1973 he was director of the ANU *Institute of History. Skaba published works on the history of Soviet society and of the Communist party, including a monograph on the Paris Peace Conference and foreign intervention in Soviet territory in 1919 (1971). He was editor in chief of *Radians'ka entsyklopediia istoriï Ukraïny* (The Soviet Encyclopedia of the History of Ukraine, 4 vols, 1969–72). Skaba was a hardline ideologue of the CPSU, particularly regarding *nationality policy, and a proponent of Russification. He persecuted the *shestydesiatnyky and supported the repression of opposition groups.

A. Zhukovsky

Skadovske [Skadovs'ke]. VII-13. A city (1989 pop 22,900) on Dzharylhach Bay and a raion center in Kherson oblast. It was founded in 1894 as a seaport on the site of the fishing village of Ali-Ahok. In 1961 it attained city status. Skadovske is an industrial, transportation, and health resort center. It has a building-materials and a food industry.

Mykola Skadovsky: *Along Volodymyrka* (oil, 1891)

Skadovsky, Mykola [Skadovs'kyj], b 16 November 1846 in Bilozerka, near Kherson, d 10 June 1892 in Bilozerka. After graduating from the Moscow School of Painting, Sculpture, and Architecture (1869) he studied at the Düsseldorf Academy of Arts. He was a founder of the *Society of South Russian Artists and specialized in genre painting. His works include *Hunting* (1879), *Before the Storm* (1881), *Tavern Orator* (1881), *The Homeless* (1886), *Hunting by His Excellency* (1886), and *Along Volodymyrka* (1891). He also painted some landscapes and portraits.

Bishop Yov Skakalsky

Skakalsky, Yov [Skakal's'kyj, Jov], b 1 January 1914 in Kremianets, Volhynia, d 18 February 1974 in Curitiba, Brazil. Orthodox bishop. He graduated from the theological seminary in Kremianets and was ordained a hieromonk of the Pochaiv Monastery in 1938. During the Second World War he worked in the theological consistory in Kholm and, later, as a chaplain for Orthodox soldiers of the *Division Galizien. In 1951 he emigrated to Canada, where he served as secretary to Metropolitan I. Ohiienko (1953–64) and then as chaplain of St Andrew's College. In 1967 he moved to the United States, and in 1968 he was consecrated a bishop of the Ukrainian Orthodox Church in the USA and vicar for South America. In 1971 he was elevated to the rank of archbishop. He is the author of *Palomnytstvo po sviatykh mistsiakh skhodu* (Pilgrimages to Holy Places in the East, 1966).

Skakandii, Vasyl [Skakandij, Vasyl'], b 4 March 1941 in Serednie, Transcarpathia. Graphic artist. A graduate of the Kiev State Art Insitute (1965), he has made prints and illustrated books. He has produced the linocut series 'Oleksa Borkaniuk' and 'Legends of the Carpathians' (1967) and a portrait of V. Stefanyk (1970); illustrated S. Petőfi's poem *Az Apostol* (Apostle, 1968) and a collection of Transcarpathian folk songs (1968); and designed the jacket for P. Skunts's *Na hrani epokh* (At the Turn of Epochs, 1968).

Skala (The Rock). A Ukrainian Catholic reading-room society organized in the Stanyslaviv eparchy of Galicia by Bishop H. Khomyshyn in 1931 as part of *Catholic Action. Skala reading rooms were similar to those of the *Prosvita society. They were normally under the jurisdiction of the local parish priest. In 1936 there were 187 branches of Skala, with some 5,500 members, and by 1939 there were some 3,075 branches, with a membership of 360,000. With the Soviet occupation of Western Ukraine in 1939, Skala was banned by the authorities.

Skala-Podilska [Skala-Podil's'ka]. V-7. A town smt (1986 pop 5,200) on the Zbruch River in Borshchiv raion, Ternopil oblast. Until 1940 it was known as Skala or Skala-nad-Zbruchem (Skala-on-the Zbruch). It is first mentioned in historical documents in the early 14th century. In 1518 it was granted the rights of *Magdeburg law, and in 1538 S. Lanckoroński built a fortress to defend the town from the Tatars and Turks. Nevertheless they destroyed the fortress and town in 1539 and 1615. In 1648 M. Kryvonis captured Skala, but the Poles soon recovered it. The town declined under Turkish rule (1672–99). In the 18th century the Poles tried to Polonize it, and in 1719 they built a Roman Catholic church there. In 1770 half the population

The castle ruins in Skala-Podilska

perished from the plague. The town prospered under Austrian rule (1772–1918). In the interwar period it was under the rule of Poland. Today it has an asphalt, a fruit-canning, and a food-processing plant. Its monuments include the ruins of a castle, a baroque palace, a Roman Catholic church (1719), and one of Ukraine's finest parks (34 ha).

Skala-Starytsky, Myroslav. See Starytsky, Myroslav.

Remnants of the castle in Skalat

Skalat. IV-6. A town (1989 pop 5,100) on the Hnyla River in Pidvolochyske raion, Ternopil oblast. The village was first mentioned in a historical document in 1564. In 1600 it was granted the rights of *Magdeburg law, and in 1630 its Polish landlord built a castle there. In 1648 the castle was captured by the Cossacks, and in 1672 it was destroyed by the Turks. At the partition of Poland in 1772, Skalat was annexed by Austria, and in 1867 it became a county center of Galicia crownland. In the interwar period (1919–39) the town was under Polish rule. Today it is an industrial center with a radio factory, a chemical products plant, an asphalt factory, and a mixed-feed factory. The old castle was renovated at the end of the 19th century and is a tourist attraction.

Skalii, Raisa [Skalij, Rajisa], b 11 December 1938 in Bilashky, Pohrebyshche raion, Vinnytsia oblast. Theater and cinema critic. She completed study at the Kiev Institute of Theater Arts (1967) and since 1971 has headed the art section of *Literaturna Ukraïna*. She is the author of many articles about L. Kurbas and established the date of his death from her research in the Solovets Islands.

Skalkovsky, Apolon [Skal'kovs'kyj], b 13 January 1808 in Zhytomyr, Volhynia gubernia, d 9 January 1899 in Odessa, Kherson gubernia. Economist and historian; corresponding member of the Russian Academy of Sciences from 1856. He studied law at the universities of Vilnius and Moscow. He was one of the founders of the *Odessa Society of History and Antiquities and an active participant in the *Society of Agriculture of Southern Russia. During the preparations for the peasant reforms of 1861 he defended the serfs.

Skalkovsky wrote numerous works on the history and economics of 18th- and 19th-century Southern Ukraine, including *Khronologicheskoe obozrenie istorii Novorossiiskogo kraia, 1730–1823* (A Chronological Survey of the History of New Russia Land, 1730–1823, 2 vols, 1836, 1838), *Opyt statisticheskogo opisaniia Novorossiiskogo kraia* (An Attempt at a Statistical Description of New Russia Land, 2 vols, 1850, 1853; vol 3 remained in manuscript), and *Pervoe tridtsatiletie Odessy, 1795–1825* (The First Thirty Years of Odessa, 1795–1825, 1837). He discovered and preserved the archives of the 18th-century Zaporozhian Sich (now in Kiev) and published a number of studies based on them, particularly *Istoriia Novoi Sechi ili posledniago Kosha Zaporozhskogo* (History of the New Sich or the Last Zaporozhian Kish, 3 vols, 1840; 2nd edn 1846; 3rd edn 1885–6). He also published documentary studies on the history of the 18th-century Zaporizhia and Right-Bank Ukraine (mostly in *Kievskaia starina*). His historical works were written from a Romantic perspective and are imbued with an idealized view of the Zaporizhia. His interpretation of the haidamaka uprisings is from the point of view of the Polish gentry. His works are a valuable historical source because of the scope of their documentation. Skalkovsky also wrote publicistic articles and several novels. His archives, including an unpublished journal (begun in Polish during his student days and later written in Russian), are preserved in St Petersburg and Odessa.

O. Ohloblyn, A. Zhukovsky

Skansens. See Museums of folk architecture and folkways.

Skarga, Piotr, b February 1536, d 27 September 1612 in Cracow. Polish Jesuit Counter-Reformation polemicist. He taught at the Jesuit academy in Vilnius and then served as an adviser on religious affairs to King Sigismund III Vasa. He engaged in polemics with both Protestants and Orthodox in the Polish-Lithuanian Commonwealth. An early proponent of the union of the Orthodox church with Rome, in 1577 he wrote *O jedności Kościoła Bożego pod jednym pasterzem* (On the Unity of God's Church under One Shepherd), one of the first examples of *polemical literature involving the Ukrainian church. Dedicated to Prince K. *Ostrozky, the most influential Ukrainian Orthodox leader, the tract outlined the ideological basis for a church union. In 1595–6 Skarga participated in the synods and discussions that culminated in the Church Union of *Berestia; he delivered the closing speech at the synod, in October 1596, and wrote the treatise 'Synod brzeski i jego obrona' (The Berestia Synod and Its Defense), translated and published in Ukrainian in 1597. His other polemical works include *O rządzie y jedności Kościola Bożego pod jednym pasterzem* (On the Order and Unity of God's Church under One Shepherd, 1590) and *Na treny i lament Theofila Ortologa do Rusi greckiego nabożeństwa przestroga* (On the Threnos and Lament of Theofilus Ortologion, a Warning to the Greek Faithful of Rus', 1610).

BIBLIOGRAPHY
Tretiak, J. *Piotr Skarga w dziejach i literaturze uniji brzeskiej* (Cracow 1912)
Tazbir, J. *Piotr Skarga: Szermierz kontrreformacji* (Warsaw 1978)
W. Lencyk

Skarzhynsky [Skaržyns'kyj]. A family line of nobility and Cossack officers of Belarusian origin. Oleksander-Mykhailo Skarzhynsky (d ca 1753) graduated from Orsha College and in the 1730s served as a translator from Latin and Polish in the Russian army. He resettled in Ukraine and became captain of Lubni regiment (1737–50). His sons were Ivan, the flag-bearer of Lubni regiment (1773) and later a marshal of the nobility in Zolotonosha county; Mykhailo, captain of Lubni regiment (1765–73) and marshal of the nobility in Lubni county; and Petro. Three branches of the Skarzhynsky family originated from them and intermarried with many Ukrainian *starshyna* families in the 18th and 19th centuries (the Skoropadsky, Zakrevsky, Znachko-Yavorsky, Myloradovych, Myklashevsky, and Sudiienko families). The Lubni branch included Kateryna Skarzhynska (1853–1924), who founded the Museum of Ukrainian Antiquities of Lubni (in Kruhlyk village, 1874). The Chernihiv branch included the brothers Matvii (b 1830) and Ivan (1836–97) Skarzhynsky, who were noted activists in Chernihiv gubernia in the later 19th century. They assisted O. Lazarevsky in gathering archival materials on the history of the Hetmanate. The Kherson branch included a number of noted military and zemstvo administration officials in the 19th and 20th centuries, such as Viktor *Skarzhynsky.

O. Ohloblyn

Skarzhynsky, Viktor [Skaržyns'kyj], b October 1787 in Trykraty, Yelysavethrad county, Katerynoslav vicegerency, d 1861. Landowner and developer of new farming methods. He graduated from Moscow University (1805) and worked with the Department of Public Education. He returned to his family's estate and introduced crop rotation and modern methods of land cultivation in Southern Ukraine. In addition to breeding fine horses, he acclimatized a breed of Caucasian sheep and a breed of Hungarian cattle. He also acclimatized various tree and bush varieties, from Western Europe and North America, to Ukrainian conditions and developed a fruit orchard with

221 varieties, a dendrological park with 281 varieties, a mulberry plantation of 150 ha, and a vineyard (100 ha). He was a strong promoter of steppe forestation and planted about 400 ha of forest on his estate. To share his experience and encourage others to follow his example, Skarzhynsky published many articles on farming and forestation, most of them in *Zapiski Imperatorskogo obshchestva sel'skogo khoziaistva Iuzhnoi Rossii.*

Skating (*kovzaniarskyi sport*). Figure skating and speed skating were introduced in Ukraine in the 19th century. They have become well developed under Soviet rule. The Skating Federation of the USSR joined the International Skating Union in 1947, and Soviet skaters have competed in world and European competitions since 1948 and in Olympic speed skating since 1956. Medals in world skating championships have been captured by the Ukrainian athletes O. Honcharenko (1953, 1956, 1958), V. Bryndzei (1977), and T. Tarasova (1981). In 1983 N. Horbenko won the gold medal at the 1984 world junior championships. In 1984 V. Huk won two men's gold medals (500 m, 1,500 m) and one silver (3,000 m) in the world junior speed skating championships and was chosen the overall world champion. In 1987 R. Popadchuk set a world junior record in the men's 500-m (37.58). V. Petrenko won a bronze medal in men's figure skating at the 1988 Winter Olympics, a silver at the 1990 and 1991 world championships, and a gold at the 1992 Winter Olympics. O. Baiul won the world championship in women's figure skating in Prague in 1993.

Skazaniie i strast' i pokhvala sviatuiu muchenyku Borysa i Hliba (The Tale and Passion and Glorification of the Holy Martyrs Borys and Hlib). One of the oldest monuments of Ukrainian literature. It describes the murder of *SS Borys and Hlib by their brother, Prince Sviatopolk I, after the death of their father, Volodymyr the Great, in 1015. The oldest extant manuscript of the tale dates from the late 11th century and is found in the *Uspenskii sbornik* of the 12th century. More than 170 manuscript copies of the tale have survived, in six redactions, many of them with different titles. They all deal with the same central issues and use a rhythmical prose, stylized laments, and complex literary devices, based in part on the Bible and other liturgical books. The tale was used to promote the cult of Borys and Hlib and their canonization and to condemn the fratricidal struggle among the Rus' princes.

Skehar, Hryhorii, b 30 August 1891 in Pohorylivka, Kitsman county, Bukovyna, d 31 August 1957 in Los Angeles. Civic activist and journalist. After emigrating to

Hryhorii Skehar

Canada in 1908 and then to the United States in 1919, he graduated from Northwestern University (DDS, 1923) and practiced dentistry in Chicago. He was active in the Organization for the Rebirth of Ukraine and a contributor to many Ukrainian papers in Canada and the United States. From 1938 he reviewed books on Ukrainian history and literature for *Books Abroad*. For many years he served as secretary of the Ukrainian Center in Los Angeles. In 1940 he published his recollections, titled *Po Amerytsi* (Through America).

Skhidnii svit (Oriental World). A scholarly journal of the *All-Ukrainian Learned Association of Oriental Studies (VUNAS), published bimonthly in Kharkiv in 1927–31 (a total of 17 issues). It succeeded *Biuleten' VUNAS* (5 issues, 1926). After the first issue the articles appeared in Ukrainian with Russian, English, French, and German résumés. The journal published articles on the history, archeology, culture, economy, literature, and contemporary politics of the Near, Middle, and Far East; Soviet Central Asia; the Crimea; and Caucasia. Many articles focused specifically on Ukraine's relations with these areas. Attention was also devoted to contemporary political and economic developments. The journal also contained book reviews and notices and reports on VUNAS activities and Oriental studies in Ukraine and abroad. Among its 180 contributors were prominent scholars, such as A. Krymsky, V. Dubrovsky, A. Kovalivsky, V. Buzeskul, P. Ritter, M. Horban, O. Hrushevsky, V. Parkhomenko, and Ya. Riappo. In 1929 *Skhidnii svit* had a pressrun of 600. In late 1930 it was renamed *Chervonyi skhid*; under its new name it ceased publication after its third issue. An index to it was published in Kharkiv in 1964.

The skiing team of Peremyshl's Berkut sports society in the Carpathian Mountains (1931)

Skiing (*lyzhnyi sport, leshchetarstvo*). Skiing was introduced in Western Ukraine in the 1890s and was promoted there by A. Budzynovsky and I. Bobersky in the early 20th century. The sport became popular in the 1920s, thanks to the efforts of the *Carpathian Ski Club in Lviv, which organized Alpine and Nordic competitions in Lviv and the Carpathian Mountains, and the Sokil and Luh athletic societies and Plast scouting organization. Because of central and eastern Ukraine's flatness, skiing was less popular there. In the 1920s it began developing in the Donbas, and a Soviet Winter Spartakiad was held there in 1927. In time Alpine and Nordic skiing became a significant part of Soviet military training in various regions of Soviet Ukraine. After the Second World War, the Carpathian region, particularly the resorts of Vorokhta and Slavske, became Ukraine's main skiing center. Skiing was part of the school and Ready for Labor and Defense of the USSR physical education programs. Republican and USSR skiing championships were held annually. The Carpathian Ski Club was revived in the United States and since 1955 has cosponsored annual skiing competitions with the Ukrainian Sports Federation of the USA and Canada.

Skirgaila (Skyrhailo, Ivan), b 1354, d 1397 in Kiev. Lithuanian prince and ruler of Kiev in 1395–7; son of Algirdas. A strong supporter of his brother, Władysław II *Jagiełło, he was his vicegerent from 1386 until 1392, and, being Orthodox, encouraged Ruthenian activity in the Grand Duchy of Lithuania. He lost his influence when Jagiełło relinquished Lithuania to their cousin, Vytautas. In 1395 he was granted Kiev after the death of Volodymyr, the son of Algirdas. Skirgaila died under mysterious circumstances, probably from poison.

Skivsky, Ivan [Skivs'kyj], b 1777, d 1850. Basilian priest and professor. He was raised in the Volhynia region, and studied at Vilnius University and then taught at Basilian schools in Uman, Bar, and Liubar. In 1824 he became archimandrite of the Pochaiv Monastery. In 1831 he was arrested by tsarist authorities during the suppression of the Uniate church in the Russian Empire and exiled to the Kostroma region. Upon his return to Kiev in 1848, he served as a priest in a Latin rite church.

Skladka (no. 1, 1887)

Skladka (The Contribution). The title of four literary almanacs edited by V. Aleksandrov (Kharkiv 1887, 1893) and K. Bilylovsky (Kharkiv 1896, St Petersburg 1897). Published in them were poems by Aleksandrov, Bilylovsky, V. Samiilenko, B. Hrinchenko, Ya. Shchoholev, P. Hrabovsky, I. Franko, M. Vorony, V. Shchurat, I. Steshenko, L. Starytska-Cherniakhivska, P. Richytsky, S. Shelukhyn, H. Kerner, F. Korsh, and N. Shamraiev; prose by Bilylovsky, H. Barvinok, M. Hrinchenko, Starytska-Cherniakhivska, Lesia Ukrainka, D. Mordovets, I. Nechui-Levytsky, S. Nis, and A. Krymsky; V. Samiilenko's drama *Marusia Churaïvna* and M. Kropyvnytsky's opera *Vii*

(based on N. Gogol's story); Bilylovsky's memoirs and bibliography of Aleksandrov; and oral folklore transcriptions and ethnographic articles by D. Yavornytsky.

Składkowski, Felicjan, b 9 June 1885 in Gąbin, Warsaw gubernia, d 31 August 1962 in London. Polish military and state figure; a doctor by training. He was a close associate of J. Piłsudski, and as minister of internal affairs (1926–31) he implemented the *Pacification operation aimed against Ukrainians. He was appointed premier of Poland by E. Rydz-Śmigły (1936–9); as such he was also partly responsible for the harsh anti-Ukrainian policies of the Polish government in the prewar period. He emigrated after the Second World War. His writings were published in *Nie ostatnie słowo oskarżonego: Wspomnienia i artykuły* (Not the Last Word of the Accused: Memoirs and Articles, 1964).

Sklavenes (*sklaviny*). The Greek name for West Slavs, used by Byzantine writers of the 6th to 8th centuries AD. The term was used to distinguish the Slavic tribes inhabiting the territory between the Dniester and the Danube rivers, including southern Poland, Slovakia, and Transylvania, from the *Antes to the east. The Sklavenes practiced agriculture, animal husbandry, craft manufacturing, and trade. They formed a strong tribal confederation, which was destroyed by the *Avars in the second half of the 6th century.

Skliar, Ivan [Skljar], b 21 February 1906 in Myrhorod, Poltava gubernia, d 26 October 1970 in Myrhorod. Banduryst. He joined the Myrhorod Banduryst Ensemble in 1927 and served as its director in 1933–43. From 1943 he sang as a soloist with the Verovka State Chorus. He composed many songs and pieces for folk instruments and made technical improvements to the bandura and other instruments that allowed them to be played in a broader range of keys.

Skliarenko, Semen [Skljarenko], b 26 September 1901 in Keleberda, Zolotonosha county, Poltava gubernia, d 8 March 1962 in Kiev. Writer. In the 1920s he worked as a journalist, first in Chernihiv and then at the Kiev newspaper *Proletars'ka pravda*. He began to publish his poetry in 1918 and was coeditor of one of the first Soviet literary journals, *Vyr revoliutsiï* (1921), and, later, of the journal *Zhyttia i revoliutsiia*. Skliarenko published prose works from 1930; he wrote over 60 books of stories, novelettes, and novels. During the 1930s he wrote a series of major prose works on the subject of construction, including a novel about the construction of the Dnieper Hydroelectric Station, *Burun* (The Billow, 1932). The novel-trilogy *Shliakh na Kyïv* (The Road to Kiev, 1937–40), an attack aimed at 'Ukrainian bourgeois nationalism,' distorts, according to the official Soviet interpretation, the historical events of the Ukrainian liberation struggle. During the Second World War, Skliarenko was a war correspondent and wrote the war novels *Ukraïna klyche* (Ukraine Calls, 1943) and *Podarunok z Ukraïny* (Gift from Ukraine, 1944). Critics noted the formulaic nature of Skliarenko's postwar novel *Khaziaïn* (Farmer, 1948), about the rebuilding of the co-operative farms, and, similarly, his adherence to a fixed formula and his lack of knowledge of pre-Soviet Transcarpathian life in *Karpaty* (The Carpathians, 1952). Skliarenko's greatest achievements are the historical

Semen Skliarenko   Volodymyr Skliarenko

novels *Sviatoslav* (1959) and *Volodymyr* (1962). Editions of his works have been published in five (1965) and three (1981) volumes.

I. Koshelivets

Skliarenko, Volodymyr [Skljarenko], b 7 June 1907 in Kiev, d 8 May 1984 in Kiev. Theater director; pupil of L. *Kurbas. He completed study at the Lysenko Music and Drama Institute in Kiev and worked in *Berezil (director's workshop, 1926) until 1933. He was artistic director of the Kharkiv Young Spectator's Theater (1935–44), the Lviv Young Spectator's Theater (1944–7), the Lviv Opera Theater (simultaneously he taught in the Lviv Conservatory, 1947–52), the Kharkiv Opera Theater (1952–4), the Kiev Opera Theater (1954–62), and the Kiev Ukrainian Drama Theater (1962–7). He taught at the Kiev Institute of Theater Arts (1967–75) and the Kiev Institute of Culture (1967–84). He produced approx 200 dramas, operas, and operettas, including M. Zarudny's *Maryna*, M. Lysenko's *Taras Bul'ba*, and H. Maiboroda's *Mylana*.

Skliarenko, Yevhen [Skljarenko, Jevhen], b 18 January 1924 in Baitsury, Belgorod region, Russia. Historian. He graduated from the Kiev Pedagogical Institute (1951), and in 1956 he began working at the AN URSR (now ANU) Institute of History. From 1966 to 1970 he headed its Department of Scientific Information and Propaganda. He published works on the CPU and on the history of the working class.

Skliar-Otava, Polina. See Otava, Polina.

Sklifosovsky, Nikolai (Sklifasovsky), b 6 April 1836 in Dubossary, Tyraspil county, Kherson gubernia (now Moldova), d 13 December 1904 in Yakivtsi (now part of Poltava). Russian surgeon. A graduate of Moscow University (1859), he practiced medicine in Odessa and defended a doctoral dissertation at Kharkiv University (1863). He was a professor of surgical pathology at Kiev University (1870) and the St Petersburg Medico-Surgical Academy (1871), head of the surgical clinic of Moscow University and consultant to the surgical department of the Moscow Military Hospital (1880), and director of the St Petersburg Institute for the Upgrading of Physicians (1893–1900). One of the leading military surgeons in Russia, he pioneered the use of anesthetics and aseptic methods in operations and promoted medical education for women. He

initiated the Pirogov medical conferences and edited a number of medical journals. His publications dealt with the improvement of medical services in the military, bone surgery, and abdominal operations.

Sklovsky, Yevhen [Sklovs'kyj, Jevhen], b 13 April 1869 in Kiev, d 10 October 1930. Pediatrician. A graduate of Kiev University (1891), he worked as a zemstvo doctor (1892–6) and at the university (from 1896), where he organized the first neonatal consultation service (1906) and the first nursery (1911) in Ukraine. He directed the maternity and childhood care section of the Kiev Regional Health Department (1918–20) and the Department of Children's Diseases at the Kiev Clinical Institute (1920–8). From 1929 he worked at the Kiev Scientific Research Institute of Maternity and Childhood Care. His publications dealt with child tuberculosis, diphtheria, and infant mortality.

Skoba, Antin, b 1856 in Bahachka, Myrhorod county, Poltava gubernia, d after 1908 in Bahachka. Lirnyk. His repertoire included dumas, humorous and historical songs, and psalms. F. Kolessa and O. Slastion transcribed many of the songs he performed. Some of them were recorded by phonograph, and some were published in 1910 in *Materiialy do ukraïns'koï etnolohiï* (Materials in Ukrainian Ethnology).

Skobelsky, Petro [Skobel's'kyj], 1849–1912. Teacher and historian. A graduate of the theological seminary in Lviv, he started out on a promising career as a historian until material circumstances forced him to become a teacher. He then taught at the Academic Gymnasium in Lviv (1879–90), a gymnasium in Brody (1890–1902), and several gymnasiums in Lviv (from 1902). While in Lviv he wrote several essays, edited the literary journal *Zoria* (1889–90), and published collections of historical documents about the Sanguszko family (1886) and the Stauropegion Institute (1887). He also translated several works by T. Shevchenko into German and several German works into Ukrainian.

Skoblykov, Oleksander, b 25 February 1929 in Druzhkivka, Staline okruha. Sculptor. In 1954 he graduated from the Kiev State Art Institute, where he studied under M. Lysenko. He has sculpted genre compositions, such as *On Virgin Land* (1960); portraits, such as *Yuliia* (1958), T. *Shevchenko* (1964), and B. *Paton* (1980); and monuments, such as those to T. Shevchenko in Châlette-sur-Loing, France (1974), V. Vernadsky in Kiev (1981), the unification of Ukraine and Russia in Kiev (1982), and A. Tsereteli in Batumi (1984).

Skocen, Alexander. See Skotsen, Oleksander.

Skochok, Pavlo [Skočok], b 5 May 1935 in Ostriv, Rokytne raion, Kiev oblast. Journalist and political prisoner. In the 1960s he published articles concerning the ecology of Ukraine and contributed to the literary section of *Radians'ka Ukraïna*. Several of his articles were circulated in samvydav form. He was arrested in December 1978 in Kiev and sentenced to an indefinite term in the Dnipropetrovske psychiatric prison. He was released in the spring of 1987. Since that time he has been a member of the editorial board of *Ukraïns'kyi visnyk*.

Skok, Volodymyr, b 4 June 1932 in Kiev. Physiologist; full member of the AN URSR (now ANU) since 1979 and its vice-president since 1988; full member of the USSR Academy of Sciences since 1987. He graduated from Kiev University (1955) and worked at its Institute of Physiology (1956–62), and then became an associate (1962), department head (1970), and assistant director (1980) at the ANU Institute of Physiology. His main research is on the physiology of the autonomic nervous system.

Skole. IV-4. A city (1989 pop 6,700) on the Opir River in the High Beskyd and a raion center in Lviv oblast. It was first mentioned in historical documents in 1397. Under Polish rule the village was destroyed by the Tatars (1594) and by the Hungarians (1610, 1657). In the 17th and 18th centuries *opryshoks were active in the area. After the partition of Poland in 1772, the town belonged to Austria, and in 1912 it was granted city status. In the interwar period it was held by Poland (1919–39). Today its main industries are lumbering, woodworking, building materials, and handicrafts. Its most valuable monument is the tripartite wooden Church of St Panteleimon (17th century), which contains a unique baroque iconostasis.

Skolozdra, Volodymyr, b 20 August 1912 in Drohovyzhe, Zhydachiv county, Galicia, d 7 August 1980 in

Volodymyr Skolozdra: the monument to Vasyl Stefanyk in Lviv (granite, 1971)

Lviv. Sculptor. He studied at the Lviv Arts and Crafts School (1939–41) and sculpted mostly portraits and monuments. His works include busts of V. Stefanyk (1953), Lesia Ukrainka (1958), I. Franko (1972), and L. van Beethoven (1954); statues of O. Dovbush (with M. Riabinin, 1951) and T. Shevchenko as a soldier (1963); and monuments to V. Stefanyk in Lviv (1971) and Edmonton (1971). An album of his works was published in 1990.

Skomorokhov, Oleksander [Skomoroxov], b 6 March 1874 in Stavropol, d 22 August 1946 in Kiev. Electrical engineer. He studied in St Petersburg and from 1911 taught at the Kiev Polytechnical Institute. In 1933–41 he taught at the Kharkiv Electrotechnical Institute, and from 1944 he held the chair of electrical engineering at the Kiev Polytechnical Institute. He was the author of one of the first textbooks on electrical machinery and transformers in the Russian Empire (1914).

11th-century fresco depicting *skomorokhy* in Kiev's St Sophia Cathedral

Skomorokhy. Itinerant minstrels in Kievan Rus'. The first written reference to them dates back to 1068, but they were active in Rus' long before then. They are depicted in the frescoes of the St Sophia Cathedral in Kiev. According to some scholars the *skomorokhy* developed under the influence of foreign models. Others suggest that they evolved from pagan priests in the rural areas of Rus'. The latter hypothesis is supported by the recorded condemnation by the church authorities of the *skomorokhy* as representatives of paganism. By the 11th century the *skomorokhy* had become professional entertainers who performed songs, dances, mime shows, acrobatics, games, puppet shows, short dramatic scenes, and animal tricks for the common people as well as for nobles and court dignitaries. By the 12th century, when court singers started joining their troupes, the *skomorokhy* added **bylyny* to their repertoire. As Kievan Rus' began to decline in the 12th and 13th centuries, many *skomorokhy* moved to safer principalities in the north and particularly to Novgorod. There they survived as a social group until 1572, when they were forcibly moved to Moscow by Ivan IV. In 1648 they were proscribed by Aleksei I, a blow from which they never recovered. The influence of the *skomorokhy* in Ukraine can be seen in Ukrainian theatrical productions of the 16th century.

BIBLIOGRAPHY
Zguta, Russell. *Russian Minstrels: A History of the* Skomorokhi (New York 1978)

Skomorovsky, Kelestyn [Skomorovs'kyj] (pseud: Kelestyn Dolynianenko), b 16 April 1820 in Dolyniany, Berezhany circle, d 16 April 1866 in Ostapie, Ternopil circle, Galicia. Poet and priest. In the years 1840–9 he studied at the Greek Catholic Theological Seminary in Lviv, during which time he became a sympathizer with the Polish revolutionary movement. Inspired by the Romantic poetry of M. Shashkevych, T. Shevchenko, and K. Ujejski, he wrote poems in the Galician dialect of Ukrainian. Only three are extant: 'Ptytsi-posly' (Birds-Envoys), in the literary miscellany **Vinok rusynam na obzhynky* (Vienna 1847), *Na czest' bratej powernuwszych z newoli* (In Honor of Brothers Who Have Returned from Imprisonment, 1848), and a translation of A. Khomiakov's *Ermak* (1849). From the early 1850s he was parish priest in Ostapie, where he wrote poems and translated the Epistles; none of those works has ever been published. The manuscripts were analyzed by Ya. Hordynsky in *Zapysky NTSh* (vol 128). The materials Skomorovsky collected for a German-Ukrainian dictionary were supplemented and published by O. Partytsky in 1867.

Viktor Skopenko

Anatolii Skorokhod

Skopenko, Viktor, b 18 December 1935 in Novhorodka, now in Kirovohrad oblast. Chemist; AN URSR (now ANU) corresponding member since 1978 and full member since 1987. After graduating from Kiev University (1958) he taught there and became a professor in 1971, prorector in

1975, and chairman of the inorganic chemistry department in 1977. He is currently rector of Kiev University. His research deals predominantly with co-ordination chemistry in nonaqueous solvents and on the surface of various support matrices. He developed extensively the co-ordination chemistry of linear and particularly nonlinear pseudohalide ligands, and he contributed to and, with A. Golub and H. Kohler, edited the definitive monograph *Chemie der Pseudohalogenide* (1979; English trans: *Chemistry of Pseudohalides*, 1986). He also introduced new catalysts based on metal complexes adsorbed on silica gel and modified with organic additives.

Skoreyko, William [Skorejko, Vasyl'], b 8 December 1922 in Edmonton. Businessman and politician. After studying commerce and opening his own business, he served as member of parliament for Edmonton East in 1958–74.

Skorobohatko, Vitalii [Skorobohat'ko, Vitalij], b 18 July 1927 in Kiev. Mathematician. After graduating from Lviv University in 1951, he taught there and then worked at different institutes of the AN URSR (now ANU): the Institute of Mathematics (1961–6), the Physical Mechanical-Institute (1967–73), and the Institute of Applied Mathematics and Mechanics (since 1973). His studies deal mostly with partial differential equations, mathematical physics, computational mathematics, and geometry.

Skorodynsky, Andrii [Skorodyns'kyj, Andrij], b 1850, d 1912 in Lviv. Educator. He was director of the Prosvita society's head office (1882–1908), a founder of the society's Lviv branch, and the founder of the first Prosvita reading room in Lviv. He was also active in the Zoria society.

Skorokhod, Anatolii [Skoroxod, Anatolij], b 10 September 1930 in Nykopil, Kryvyi Rih okruha. Mathematician; full member of the AN URSR (now ANU) since 1985. After graduating from Kiev University in 1953 he worked at the ANU Institute of Mathematics and taught at Kiev University. His monograph on the theory of random processes (1961) developed certain probabilistic methods in the field of stochastic differential equations and limit theorems of Markov processes and substantially extended the existence, uniqueness, and other results for stochastic differential equations obtained independently by Y. Hikhman in Kiev and K. Ito in Japan. These were the first results in the field to be obtained by probabilistic methods. Skorokhod explored a number of new notions which became known as the Skorokhod space, Skorokhod topology, and the Skorokhod version of weak convergence. In the theory of Markov processes, one of the major fields of study at the Institute of Mathematics, he demonstrated that (under weak additional conditions and manipulation) a continuous, homogeneous, and strongly Markov process in a finite-dimensional space becomes quasi-diffusive. In the early 1970s Skorokhod and Hikhman wrote a three-volume treatise on the theory of stochastic processes. In another series of monographs Skorokhod made fundamental contributions to the theory of random processes with independent increments (1964), intequation in Hilbert space (1974), random linear operators (1978), stochastic equations for complex systems (1983), processes with independent increments (1986), and asymptotic methods in the theory of stochastic differential equations (1987). Many of these works have been translated into English. The work of Skorokhod, Hikhman, B. Hniedenko, and V. Koroliuk has established the reputation of the Kiev school of probability theory.

W. Petryshyn

Skorokhodko, Antin [Skoroxod'ko], b 13 March 1883 in Kaniv, Kiev gubernia, d 26 February 1954 in Kiev. Veterinarian and specialist in zoohygiene. A graduate of the Kharkiv Veterinary Institute (1909), he worked as a zemstvo veterinarian, chaired the department of zoohygiene at the Kiev Veterinary-Zootechnical Institute (1922–9), and served as rector of the institute (1924–6). From 1947 he was a professor at the Kiev Veterinary Institute (now the veterinary faculty of the Ukrainian Agricultural Academy). His publications dealt with the hygiene, care, and feeding of farm animals.

Yelysaveta Skoropadska

Skoropadska, Yelysaveta [Skoropads'ka, Jelysaveta] (married name: Kuzhim), b 27 November 1899 in St Petersburg, d 16 February 1976 in Obertsdorf, near Bremen, Germany. Civic leader and sculptor; daughter of Hetman P. *Skoropadsky. She studied sculpture in St Petersburg before the Revolution of 1917. She continued her studies in the 1920s in Berlin and Florence. Her works were exhibited in Germany, Holland, Finland, and the United States. She assisted her father in his political activities as his pri-

vate secretary, and in 1959 she assumed the leadership of the hetmanite movement from her recently deceased sister, Mariia, who had succeeded their brother, D. *Skoropadsky.

Coat of arms of the
Skoropadsky family

Skoropadsky [Skoropads'kyj]. A family line of state, military, and community leaders, known since the 17th century. It was founded by Fedir Skoropadsky, who was reportedly slain in the Battle of Zhovti Vody (1648). His grandson, Ivan *Skoropadsky, was hetman of Ukraine from 1708 to 1722. Ivan had no sons; his brothers, Vasyl (d 1727) and Pavlo (d before 1739), continued the Skoropadsky line. Vasyl served as a military chancellor (1676), captain of Berezna company (1697–1709), quartermaster of Chernihiv regiment (1713–21), and a fellow of the standard (1726); his branch of the Skoropadsky family line continued into the 20th century. Pavlo Skoropadsky served as a fellow of the standard (1712); his branch of the line died out in the late 18th century.

Vasyl's more distinguished descendants included his son, Mykhailo (b ca 1697, d 2 January 1758 in Hlukhiv), a graduate of the Kievan Mohyla Academy and a political activist in the Hetmanate. He served as a fellow of the standard (1715; honored as 'first among fellows' in 1733) and as general treasurer (1741–58), and he participated in the Persian and Caucasian campaigns (1720–30), the Polish campaign (1733–4), and the Russo-Turkish War (1735–9). Mykhailo's older son, Ivan (b 9 August 1727 in Sorochyntsi, d 1782), was a noted Ukrainian autonomist and a candidate for hetman. He studied at the Kievan Mohyla Academy and in Germany and served as general osaul (1762–81) and as deputy of the nobility of Hlukhiv county (1767). Ivan's great-great-grandson, Heorhii (b 11 October 1873 in Avdiivka, Chernihiv gubernia, d ?), served as head of the Sosnytsia county zemstvo administration (1905–7) and was elected to the Third (1907) and Fourth (1912) Russian State Dumas.

Mykhailo Skoropadsky's younger son, Yakiv (b 1730, d ca 1785), served as major of a cuirassier regiment (1764). Yakiv's grandson, Ivan (b 30 January 1805, d 8 February 1887), served as marshal of Pryluka county (1844–7) and Poltava gubernia (1847–52); he supported the 1861 agrarian reforms, and he built one of the finest palaces and gardens in Left-Bank Ukraine (see *Trostianets Dendrological Park). Ivan's son, Petro (b 6 March 1834, d 30 June 1885), was a colonel of the Cavalry Guard and a veteran of the Caucasian wars (1863); he served as marshal of Starodub county (1869–85) and was a local zemstvo activist. Ivan's daughter and Petro's sister, Ye. *Myloradovych, was a noted Ukrainian activist. Petro's son, P. *Skoropadsky, was hetman of the Ukrainian State in 1918. Pavlo's son, D. *Skoropadsky, succeeded his father as head of the émigré hetmanite movement. After his death his sister, Mariia Skoropadska-Montresor (d 11 February 1959), headed the movement.

Danylo Skoropadsky   Hetman Ivan Skoropadsky

Skoropadsky, Danylo [Skoropads'kyj], b 13 February 1904 in St Petersburg, d 22 February 1957 in London. Political and civic figure; son of Hetman P. Skoropadsky. He was heir apparent (announced in 1938) to P. Skoropadsky as leader of the hetmanite movement, and he assumed that role from his mother in 1948. He traveled to Canada and the United States in 1937–8 and 1953 in order to meet with hetmanite supporters. He moved to England in 1938, where he published (with V. Korostovets) an English-language journal about the Ukrainian question, took an active role in the Scottish League for the Liberation of Europe, and was honorary head of the Association of Ukrainians in Great Britain.

Skoropadsky, Ivan [Skoropads'kyj], b 1646 in Uman, d 14 July 1722 in Hlukhiv. Cossack leader and hetman of Ukraine (1708–22). After the Turks leveled Uman in 1674, he moved to Left-Bank Ukraine, where he served under Hetman I. Samoilovych as military chancellor (1675–6), secretary of Chernihiv regiment (1681–94), general standard-bearer (1698), and second general osaul (1701). He was sent on many diplomatic missions: on behalf of Samoilovych he went to Moscow (1675 and 1676) and the Crimea (1681), and on behalf of Hetman I. Mazepa he went to Poland (1690), Moscow (1693 and 1696), and the Zaporozhian Sich (1703). In 1706 Mazepa appointed him colonel of Starodub regiment.

Skoropadsky was elected hetman at the Council of Officers in Hlukhiv on 6 November 1708. Peter I never fully trusted him, however; he refused to ratify the *Reshetylivka Articles (1709) drawn up by Skoropadsky for a new agreement between Ukraine and Russia, and he held up the official documents confirming Skoropadsky as hetman until 1710. Skoropadsky nevertheless fought alongside Russian troops in the Battle of Poltava.

The Russian victory freed Peter from any further restraint in his policy toward Ukraine. Devastated by war, Russian repressions, and a plague epidemic, Left-Bank Ukraine became a military colony. Not only did Peter sta-

tion 10 dragoon regiments on Ukrainian territory at the expense of the local population, he also interfered increasingly in Ukraine's internal affairs, which previously came under the jurisdiction of the hetman. The Cossack army was put under Russian command, and the general artillery was deported to Russia. The capital of the Hetmanate was moved to Hlukhiv in 1709, and the hetman became subject to constant supervision by Russian residents of the tsar. The Russian tsar reserved the right to appoint higher-echelon officers (the general *starshyna*, colonels, and even captains), and he replaced Ukrainians with Russians, Moldavians, Serbs, and Poles.

On 27 May 1722 Peter set up the *Little Russian Collegium, which sharply reduced the powers of the hetman and the Ukrainian government. Cultural and religious life was also subjected to restrictions: Ukrainian printing was proscribed in 1720, and the Kievan Mohyla Academy was repressed. The terrorized Ukrainian people began to turn against the hetman and his government. Skoropadsky's protests against Russian actions had little influence on the tsar, who had already decided to limit Ukrainian autonomy and abolish the Hetman state when Mazepa allied with Sweden. Skoropadsky was buried in the Hamaliivka Monastery near Hlukhiv.

BIBLIOGRAPHY
Kostruba, T. *Het'man Ivan Skoropads'kyi 1709–1722* (Lviv 1932)
Ohloblyn, O. *Ukraïna za chasiv Skoropads'koho i Polubotka* (Kiev 1941)

O. Ohloblyn

Hetman Pavlo Skoropadsky

Skoropadsky, Pavlo [Skoropads'kyj], b 15 May 1873 in Wiesbaden, Germany, d 26 April 1945 in Metten, Bavaria. Ukrainian noble, general, and statesman; scion of the *Skoropadsky family. He grew up on his father's estate in Trostianets (Pryluka county, Poltava gubernia), studied at the Starodub gymnasium, and graduated from the elite Page Corps cadet school in St Petersburg. He served in a cavalry guard Regiment and commanded a company of the Chita Cossack Regiment in the Russo-Japanese War. He was appointed aide-de-camp to Emperor Nicholas II in 1905, a colonel in 1906, commander of the 20th Finnish Dragoon Regiment in 1910, and a major general and commander of a cavalry regiment in the emperor's House Guard in 1911. During the First World War he commanded the 1st Brigade of the 1st Cavalry Guard Division, then the 5th Cavalry and 1st Cavalry Guard divisions, and the 34th Army Corps (at the rank of lieutenant general).

After the February Revolution of 1917 Skoropadsky oversaw the Ukrainization of the 34th Corps as the 1st Ukrainian Corps. He was elected honorary otaman of the Ukrainian *Free Cossacks at their first congress in October 1917. In October–November of that year the disciplined 60,000-man First Corps and the Free Cossacks under his command controlled the Vapniarka–Zhmerynka–Koziatyn–Shepetivka railway corridor. It disarmed and demobilized pro-Bolshevik military units returning from the southwestern and Rumanian fronts and thereby prevented them from attacking Kiev and plundering Ukraine. As an opponent of the Central Rada's socialist policies (especially its agrarian reforms) Skoropadsky initiated a rightwing conspiracy known as the Ukrainian People's Hromada, consisting of his fellow noble landowners and loyal officers. Its plans to overthrow the Rada and establish an authoritarian state ruled by the Skoropadsky dynasty gained the support of the *Ukrainian Democratic Agrarian party and the *All-Ukrainian Union of Landowners. On 24 April 1918 Skoropadsky was assured by Gen W. Groener, the German chief of staff, that the German army would support a coup d'état.

On 29 April 1918 the German-backed coup proved successful. Skoropadsky was proclaimed hetman of the Ukrainian State (as the UNR was renamed) at an agrarian congress convened by the Union of Landowners. The Central Rada and all land committees were dissolved, all UNR ministers were removed, the Rada's laws and reforms were revoked, and censorship of the press was introduced. The *Hetman government appointed by Skoropadsky included members of the Russian *Constitutional Democratic party and even anti-Ukrainian Russian monarchists (who were major figures in S. Gerbel's November–December cabinet). The government's social and economic policies were subject to and shaped by Germany's imperialistic aims, as well as the interests of Ukraine's large landowners, industrialists, and capitalists. The Hetman government also allowed Russian anti-Bolshevik political leaders and military organizations to turn Kiev into one of their staging areas. Ukrainian democrats refused to take part in the government, and in late May 1918 they formed the *Ukrainian National-State Union (later renamed the *Ukrainian National Union [UNS]) to co-ordinate political opposition. The left (including the Bolsheviks) exploited the dissatisfaction, and it soon erupted in the form of agrarian uprisings (see *Partisan movement), railway and other strikes, sabotage (bombings and arson in Kiev, Odessa, and elsewhere), and assassinations (eg, of the German field marshal H. von *Eichhorn). The government and the German and Austrian military responded with repressive measures.

Skoropadsky's attempts in October 1918 to diffuse opposition to his regime by entering into negotiations with the UNS and asserting his support for Ukraine's independence from the Central Powers proved unsuccessful, and his November manifesto of federation with a future non-Bolshevik Russia only accelerated the momentum of the UNS-led popular rebellion against his regime. On 14 December 1918, after German troops abandoned Kiev, Skoropadsky abdicated and fled to Germany by way of Switzerland, and his government surrendered power to the *Directory of the UNR.

For most of the interwar years Skoropadsky lived in Wannsee, near Berlin, and received German financial support. From there he headed the hetmanite movement, consisting of monarchist émigré organizations such as the *Ukrainian Union of Agrarians-Statists in Europe, the *United Hetman Organization in Canada and the United States, and the Ukrainian Hetman Organization of America. He was also honorary president of the Ukrainska Hromada society in Berlin. Because of his links with governing Junker circles, in 1926 he was able to initiate the creation of the *Ukrainian Scientific Institute in Berlin. Skoropadsky never relinquished his claim to Ukraine. During the Second World War he lobbied the Nazi government for the release of OUN leaders imprisoned in German concentration camps. He was mortally wounded during an Allied air raid on the railway station at Plattling, in Bavaria, and was buried in Wiesbaden. Excerpts from his memoirs appeared in *Khliborobs'ka Ukraïna* (vols 4 and 5 [1922–3, 1924–5]).

O. Ohloblyn, A. Zhukovsky

Oleksander Skoropys-Yoltukhovsky

Skoropys-Yoltukhovsky, Oleksander [Skoropys-Joltuxovs'kyj] (pseuds: H. Budiak, L. Halin, O. Vyshnevsky), b 1880 in Podilia gubernia, d 1950. Revolutionary figure and civic leader; son-in-law of Ye. *Chykalenko. He joined the *Revolutionary Ukrainian party (RUP) in 1901, became a member of its editorial committee in Lviv in 1903, and wrote one of its pamphlets (pub 1904). After the 1904–5 split in RUP he became one of the leaders of the Ukrainian Social Democratic *Spilka. During the Revolution of 1905 he established a strong Spilka network that organized peasant disturbances in Kherson and Kiev gubernias. He was arrested in September 1906 and imprisoned. In 1909 he escaped from exile in Siberia to Central Europe. After the outbreak of the First World War he became a member of the presidia of the émigré *Union for the Liberation of Ukraine (SVU, 1914–18) and the *General Ukrainian Council in Vienna (1915–16). In 1915 he established the SVU Central Bureau in Berlin and became the leading SVU organizer in German prisoner-of-war camps. In February 1918 he negotiated at Brest-Litovsk the prisoners' release and formation as the UNR Army's *Bluecoats divisions. From March 1918 he served as the UNR commissioner and Hetman government's starosta in the Entente-occupied Kholm region and Podlachia. He was arrested by the Poles in Brest and interned at Kalisz in December 1918. He was released in 1920 and lived thereafter in Berlin, where he became a leading member of the conservative monarchist *Ukrainian Union of Agrarians-Statists. In 1926 he helped P. Skoropadsky establish the *Ukrainian Scientific Institute in Berlin and was appointed vice-chairman of its board of governors. Skoropys-Yoltukhovsky was arrested in 1945 after the Soviet occupation of Berlin, and perished in a Soviet concentration camp. He wrote political works, such as *Na perelomi: Uvahy pro suchasni vidnosyny Rosiï* (At the Turning Point: Observations on Contemporary Russian Relations, 1905) and *Znachinnia samostiinoï Ukraïny dlia evropeis'koï rivnovahy* (The Significance of an Independent Ukraine for European Stability, 1913); the afterword to the SVU 1917 edition of the first RUP pamphlet, M. Mikhnovsky's *Samostiina Ukraïna* (Independent Ukraine); a booklet about Ukrainians in the POW camps (1918); and memoiristic articles about the RUP, the Spilka, and the SVU.

R. Senkus

Skorulska, Nataliia [Skorul's'ka, Natalija], b 20 February 1915 in Zhytomyr, d August 1982 in Kiev. Ballerina, ballet master, and scenarist. In 1930 she completed study at the Zhytomyr ballet school, and in 1934, the Kiev Music and Choreography College. In 1934–56 she was a soloist in the Kiev Theater of Opera and Ballet (from 1957 its ballet master). She is the scenarist of A. Svechnikov's ballet *Marusia Bohuslavka* and H. Zhukovsky's ballet *The Forest Song*. From 1972 she taught at the Kiev Institute of Culture.

Mykhailo Skorulsky   Myroslav Skoryk

Skorulsky, Mykhailo [Skorul's'kyj, Myxajlo], b 6 September 1887 in Kiev, d 21 February 1950 in Kiev. Composer, pedagogue, and music critic. A graduate in composition from the St Petersburg Conservatory (1914), he taught music theory in Zhytomyr (1915–33) and at the Kiev Conservatory (1933–50). His works include the opera *Svichchyne vesillia* (Svichka's Wedding, 1948); the ballets *Bondarivna* (The Barrelmaker's Daughter, 1939) and *Lisova pisnia* (Forest Song, 1946); the oratorio *Holos materi* (Mother's Voice, 1943); two symphonies (1923, 1932); the symphonic poem *Mykyta Kozhumiaka* (1949); choral and chamber pieces; incidental music; songs to works by Lesia Ukrainka, P. Tychyna, and V. Sosiura; and arrangements of Ukrainian folk songs. A monograph on him has been written by M. Mykhailiv (1960).

Skorupsky, Volodymyr [Skorups'kyj], b 29 November 1912 in Kopychyntsi, Husiatyn county, Galicia, d 11 December 1985 in Toronto. Poet. His law studies at the University of Lviv (1935–9) were interrupted by the Second World War. He emigrated to Austria in 1945 and to Canada in 1948. From 1977 to 1984 he was editor of the weekly *Novyi shliakh* in Toronto. He began his literary career with lyrical poems, which were published in the semimonthly *Nazustrich* in 1938; his first separate collections, *Vesnianyi homin* (Spring Din, 1946) and *Zhyttia* (Life, 1947), were published in Austria. While in Canada Skorupsky continued writing lyrical poetry with a contemplative mood and national consciousness expressed in rather classical stanzas. Seven more collections appeared during his life: the nostalgic *Moia oselia* (My Homestead, 1954), *U dorozi* (Along the Way, 1957), and *Bez ridnoho poroha* (Without a Native Threshold, 1958); the reflective *Iz dzherela* (From the Source, 1961), *Aistry nevidtsvili* (Asters Still Blooming, 1972), and *Spokonvichni luny: Legendy i mity* (Eternal Echoes: Legends and Myths, 1977); and *Nad mohyloiu: Vinok sonetiv* (At the Grave: A Wreath of Sonnets, 1963), commemorating his mother's death.

Skoryk, Myroslav, b 13 July 1938 in Lviv. Composer and musicologist. He graduated (1960) from the Lviv Conservatory in the classes of A. Soltys and S. Liudkevych and then completed graduate studies (1964) at the Moscow Conservatory in the composition class of D. Kabalevsky. He subsequently lectured in composition at the Lviv Conservatory (1964–6) and the Kiev Conservatory (1966–88), returning to Lviv in 1988. One of the most notable contemporary Ukrainian composers, Skoryk has written the ballet score *Stonecutters* (1967), the symphonic *Waltz* (1960), the symphonic poem *Stronger than Death* (1963), *Hutsul Triptych* (1965, based on his film score to *Tini zabutykh predkiv* [Shadows of Forgotten Ancestors]), *Carpathian Concero* (1972), and the cantatas for voice and orchestra *Spring* (1960, text by I. Franko) and *The Person* (1964). He has also written concertos for violin (1969), for piano (1977 and 1982), and for violoncello (1983); *Suite* (1961) and *Partita* (1966) for string orchestra; *Partita* II (1970) for chamber orchestra; film scores; and music for theater. Skoryk also completed M. Leontovych's opera *Na rusalchyn velykden'* (On Rusalka Easter) in 1978 and published a study of S. Prokofiev's system of harmonics in 1969. A biobibliographic work on Skoryk has been prepared by Yu. Shyrytsia (1979).

Skoryna (Skaryna), Frantsisk or **Georgii,** b ca 1485–90 in Polatsk, Belarus, d before 1552. Pioneering Belarusian printer, physician, writer, and translator. He studied humanities at Cracow University (1504–6), and received a medical degree from Padua University in 1512. He then settled in Prague, where he established a press and published a Church Slavonic Psalter (1517) and his translations of 22 books of the Old Testament in *Bibliia ruska* (Ruthenian Bible, 1517–20). This achievement marked the beginning of publishing among the East Slavs. Ca 1520 he founded a press in Vilnius, and printed in Church Slavonic the prayer book *Malaia podorozhnaia knizhnitsa* (Small Travel Book, 1522) and an *Apostol* (1525). Skoryna's books were noted for their ornamentation, engravings, and high technical quality. The first East Slavic books with title pages, they contained extensive introductions, notes, glosses, and postscripts in the 'Ruthenian' (Belarusian-Ukrainian) literary language of the time, which feature makes them an invaluable source for the study of East Slavic linguistic history. The books were widely distributed and copied throughout Ukraine and may have influenced early printing in Lviv and Ostrih (I. *Fedorovych and his successors), as well as Moscow, and even the language of Ukrainian manuscripts (eg, the *Peresopnytsia Gospel).

Skotsen, Oleksander [Skocen'] (Skocen, Alexander), b 28 July 1918 in Lviv. Soccer star. In 1935–9 he distinguished himself as the center forward of Lviv's Ukraina team. During the Soviet occupation of Galicia he played on Kiev's Dynamo team (1940–1), and under German rule he played again for Ukraina (1941–3) and coached Kolomyia's Dovbush team (1943–4). As a postwar émigré, he played on Ukrainian DP teams, both named Ukraina, in Salzburg, Austria (1945), and Ulm, Germany (1946–7). After turning professional he played for two years (1948–50) on Nice's team in France's highest soccer league and was recognized as the best center forward in France. After emigrating to Canada in 1950, he served as captain of the teams Ukraina in Edmonton and Ukraina (1951) and Trident (1951–4) in Toronto. In 1953 the Toronto and District Football Association awarded him the Holland Cup as best player. He then coached the Ontario All-Star team in 1956 and was a referee and sports commentator for the Ukrainian-Canadian press and radio. His memoirs, *Z futbolom u svit* (With Soccer into the World, 1985), are a valuable source on soccer and sports in Ukraine and in the postwar émigré community.

Hryhorii Skovoroda (lithograph by Mykhailo Zhuk, 1925)

Skovoroda, Hryhorii, b 3 December 1722 in Chornukhy, Lubni regiment, d 9 November 1794 in Pan-Ivanivka, Kharkiv vicegerency (now Skovorodynivka, Zolochiv raion, Kharkiv oblast). Philosopher and poet. He was educated at the Kievan Mohyla Academy (1734–53, with two interruptions). He sang in Empress Elizabeth's court Kapelle in St Petersburg (1741–4), served as music director at the Russian imperial mission in Tokai, Hungary (1745–50), and taught poetics at Pereiaslav College (1751). He resumed his studies at the Kievan academy, but left after completing only two years of the four-year theology course to serve as tutor to V. Tomara (1753–9). He spent the next 10 years in Kharkiv, teaching poetics (1759–60), syntax and Greek (1762–4), and ethics (1768–9) at Kharkiv College. After his dismissal from the college he abandoned any hope of securing a regular position and spent the rest of his life wandering about eastern Ukraine, particularly Slobidska Ukraine. Material support from friends enabled him to devote himself to reflection and writing. Most of his works were dedicated to his friends and circulated among them in manuscript copies.

Although there is no sharp distinction between Skovoroda's literary and philosophical works, his collection of 30 verses (composed from 1753 to 1785) titled *Sad bozhestvennykh pesnei* (Garden of Divine Songs), his dozen or so songs, his collection of 30 fables (composed between 1760 and 1770) titled *Basni Khar'kovskiia* (Kharkiv Fables), his translations of Cicero, Plutarch, Horace, Ovid, and Muretus, and his letters, written mostly in Latin, are generally grouped under the former category. Some of his songs and poems became widely known and became part of Ukrainian folklore. His philosophical works consist of a treatise on Christian morality and 12 dialogues.

Skovoroda's thought has been interpreted in different ways: as an eclectic, loose collection of ideas (F. Kudrinsky); as a strict, rationalist system (A. Efimenko, H. Tysiachenko); as a form of Christian mysticism (V. Ern, D. Chyzhevsky); as a version of Christian Platonism in the patristic tradition (D. Bahalii); and as a moral philosophy (F. Zelenohorsky, I. Mirchuk, I. Ivano, V. Shynkaruk). There have been disagreements about the character of his metaphysical doctrine (dualism vs monism, idealism vs 'semi-materialism'). The debates about its nature to a large extent have arisen because of Skovoroda's style of writing, which is literary rather than philosophical. His ideas are not organized and presented in a systematic way, but are scattered throughout his dialogues, fables, letters, and poetry. Skovoroda preferred to use symbols, metaphors, or emblems instead of well-defined philosophical concepts to convey his meaning. Moreover, he delighted in contradiction and often left it to readers to find their way out of an apparent one. In the absence of explicit statements of doctrine and expected solutions to obvious problems, it is sometimes uncertain what exactly Skovoroda had in mind.

For Skovoroda the purpose of philosophy is practical – to show the way to happiness. Hence, the two central questions for him are what happiness is and how it can be attained. For him happiness is an inner state of peace, gaiety, and confidence which is attainable by all. To reach this state, some understanding of the world and oneself and an appropriate way of life are necessary. Skovoroda approaches metaphysics and anthropology not as a speculative thinker, but as a moralist: he does no more than outline those truths that are necessary for happiness. His basic metaphysical doctrine is that there are two natures in everything: the ideal, inner, invisible, eternal, and immutable; and the material, outer, sensible, temporal, and mutable. The first is higher, for it imparts being to the second. This dualism extends through all reality – the macrocosm or universe, and the two microcosms of humanity and the Bible. In the macrocosm the inner nature is God, and the outer is the physical world. Skovoroda's view on God's relation to the world is panentheist rather than pantheist. In man the inner nature is the soul; the outer, the body. In the Bible the inner truth is the symbolical meaning; the outer, the literal meaning.

From this metaphysical scheme Skovoroda drew a number of fundamental conclusions for practical life. Since the universe is ordered by a provident God, every being has been provided with all that is necessary for happiness. The assurance that what is necessary is easy and what is difficult is unnecessary (for happiness) brings peace of mind. It also serves as a criterion for the material conditions of happiness: we need only those goods that are necessary to health and are available to all people. But to dispel anxiety about material security is not enough for happiness. Active by nature, humans must also fulfill themselves in action by assuming the congenial task or vocation assigned to them by God. To pursue one's task regardless of external rewards is to be happy, while to pursue wealth, glory, or pleasure through uncongenial work is to be in despair. Furthermore, since vocations are distributed by God in such a way as to ensure a harmonious social order, to adopt an uncongenial task leads to social discord and unhappiness for others.

The doctrine of congenial work is the central doctrine in Skovoroda's moral system. Although it is not metaphysically plausible, it expresses his faith in the creative potential of human beings and the possibility of self-fulfillment in this life for everyone. Although they were never presented in a systematic fashion, Skovoroda's ideas form a remarkably coherent system. His chief authorities are the ancient philosophers (the Stoics, the Cynics, Epicurus, Plato, and Aristotle), from whom he selects the basic elements of his own teaching. Following the patristic tradition, he treats the Bible allegorically: he holds that its literal meaning (anthropomorphic God and miracles) is external and false, and that its inner, symbolic meaning coincides with the truth known to the ancient philosophers. In this way he reconciles secular learning with Christian faith.

Skovoroda's influence in the 19th century on writers such as I. Kotliarevsky, H. Kvitka-Osnovianenko, T. Shevchenko, and P. Kulish was minimal. But his poetic style, ideas, and moral example have played an important role in the rebirth of Ukrainian culture in the 20th century. Poets such as M. Filiansky, P. Tychyna, V. Barka, V. Stus, H. Chubai, I. Kalynets, and I. Drach have found inspiration in him. The fullest editions of Skovoroda's works were published in Kharkiv in 1894 (ed D. Bahalii), in St Petersburg in 1912 (ed V. Bonch-Bruevich), in Kiev in 1961 (2 vols) and 1973 (2 vols), and in Moscow in 1973 (2 vols). An English translation of Skovoroda's fables and aphorisms, together with a biography and an analysis of the works, was published by D.B. Chopyk in 1990.

BIBLIOGRAPHY
Ern, V. *Grigorii Savvich Skovoroda: Zhizn' i uchenie* (Moscow 1912)
Bahalii, D. *Ukraïns'kyi mandrovanyi filosof Hryhorii Savych Skovoroda* (Kharkiv 1926)
Chyzhevs'kyi, D. *Filosofiia H.S. Skovorody* (Warsaw 1934)
Red'ko, M. *Svitohliad H.S. Skovorody* (Lviv 1967)
Berkovych, E.; Stavyns'ka, R.; Shtraimysh, R. (comps). *Hryhorii Skovoroda: Biobibliohrafiia* (Kharkiv 1968)
Popov, P. *Hryhorii Skovoroda* (Kiev 1969)
Nizhynets', A. *Na zlami dvokh svitiv* (Kharkiv 1970)
Kovalivs'kyi, A. (ed). *Hryhorii Skovoroda: Biobibliohrafiia* (Kiev 1972)
Makhnovets', L. *Hryhorii Skovoroda: Biohrafiia* (Kiev 1972)
Shynkaruk, V. (ed). *Filosofiia Hryhoriia Skovorody* (Kiev 1972)
Tschizewsky, D. *Skoworoda: Dichter, Denker, Mystiker* (Munich 1974)
Myshanych, O. *Hryhorii Skovoroda i usna narodna tvorchist'* (Kiev 1976)
Ivan'o, I. *Filosofiia i styl' myslennia H. Skovorody* (Kiev 1983)
                                                        T. Zakydalsky

Skovoroda Society of Higher School Teachers (Tovarystvo vchyteliv vyshchykh shkil im. H. Skovorody). An organization of Ukrainian secondary-school teachers, founded in 1908 in Bukovyna and centered in Chernivtsi. In 1913 it had 80 members. Its goal was to organize teachers in Bukovyna, to improve the general level of Ukrainian schooling and instruction, and to publish school hand-books and textbooks. Together with the Teacher's Hromada in Lviv it published, from 1911, the pedagogical journal *Nasha shkola*. The leaders of the organization were I. Pryima, A. Artymovych, M. Korduba, and V. Kmitsykevych. It ceased operation in 1914.

Skovoroda-Zachyniaiev, Oleksander [Skovoroda-Začynjajev] (real name: Zachyniaiev], b 22 August 1877 in Voskresenka, Zadonsk county, Voronezh gubernia, Russia, d ? Educator and psychophysiologist. He was a gymnasium principal in Kiev (until 1919) and (in the 1920s) a research associate of the VUAN Scientific-Pedagogical Commission, the director of the reflexology laboratory of the VUAN, a lecturer at the Kiev Veterinary-Zootechnical, Art, and Music and Drama institutes, and a docent of the Kiev Medical Institute. He was arrested in the 1930s, and his further fate is unknown.

Skriaha, Prokip [Skrjaha], b ? in Ostapy, near Luhyny, in the Zhytomyr region, d 13 January 1770 in Kodnia, near Zhytomyr. Banduryst. He accompanied detachments of haidamakas and Don Cossacks during the Koliivshchyna rebellion of 1768 and provided them with songs and entertainment. He was captured and executed by Polish forces. His exploits were chronicled in *Kievskaia starina* (1882, no. 4).

Rev Yosafat Skruten

Skruten, Yosafat [Skruten', Josafat] (secular name: Ivan), b 24 February 1894 in Parkhach, Sokal county, Galicia, d 12 October 1951 in Rome. Basilian priest, church historian, and journalist; full member of the Shevchenko Scientific Society from 1930. He studied at the Gregorian University in Rome and at Lviv University and was ordained in 1918. He edited the journal *Postup* (1921–4) and coedited the newspaper *Nyva* and the theological journal *Bohosloviia*. He also founded and edited *Analecta Ordinis S. Basilii Magni* (1924–39), the theological journal of the Basilian Fathers, and contributed to *Dilo*, *Nova zoria*, *Novyi chas*, *Khrystyians'kyi holos*, *Krakivs'ki visti*, and other periodicals. In 1923 he cofounded the *Ukrainian Theological Scholarly Society, and in 1929 he became a professor of philosophy at the Greek Catholic Theological Academy in Lviv. He emigrated to Bavaria in 1939 and then to Rome in 1949, where he was chaplain of St Josaphat's Ukrainian Pontifical College. Skruten published several articles and reviews on the history of the Basilian order, on Y. Kuntsevych, and on other subjects in church history, mostly in the *Analecta*.

Skrutok, Oleksa (Skrutka), b 1861 in Peremyshl, Galicia, d 1914. Painter. After graduating from the Cracow School of Fine Arts (1891) he studied in Munich and then worked in Lviv and Peremyshl. From 1898 he belonged to the *Society for the Advancement of Ruthenian Art in Lviv and took part in its exhibitions. He painted portraits (eg, of V. Nahirny [1912]); landscapes, such as *Evening* (1893), *In the Meadow* (1893), *Silence* (1894), and *Landscape with a Pond* (1895); genre paintings, such as *Dutch Fisherman* (1892) and *Old Woman in a Window* (1898); iconostases; religious paintings, such as *Resurrection of Lazarus* (1900); and historical paintings depicting the Cossack period.

Yosyp Skrypa   Ihor Skrypnyk

Skrypa, Yosyp (pseud: Vronsky) b 1 March 1894 in Siedliska, Zamość county, Poland, d 12 February 1929 in Prague. Civic and political activist in the Kholm region. After being evacuated to Baku during the First World War, he completed a pedagogical course and then returned to his home village to work as a teacher and organizer of farmers and youth groups. He was also vice-president of the Kholm National Committee. In 1922 he was elected to the Polish Sejm, where he belonged to the Ukrainian caucus, then to a faction of the Ukrainian Social Democrats, and finally to the Communist Party of Western Ukraine.

Skrypchynska, Eleonora [Skrypčyns'ka], b 11 October 1899 in Dubno, Volhynia gubernia. Choir conductor and pedagogue; wife of H. *Verovka. A student of B. Yavorsky and V. Pukhalsky, she taught music in Kiev from 1919. She was affiliated mainly with the Lysenko Music and Drama Institute (1923–34) and its successor, the Kiev Conservatory (from 1934). She also conducted numerous professional and amateur choirs in 1920–44, and the *Verovka State Chorus in 1944–66, serving as its artistic director and principal conductor in 1964–6.

Skrypetsky, Samson [Skrypec'kyj] (secular name: Stepan), b 1723 in Khyriv (near Sambir), Galicia, d after 1784. Basilian priest and church painter. After entering the

Basilian monastery in Dobromyl and training as a church painter (1750–4), he painted at St Onuphrius's Monastery in Lviv and the Zhovkva and Univ monasteries.

Skrypnyk, Ihor, b 13 November 1940 in Zhmerynka, Vinnytsia oblast. Mathematician, full member of the AN URSR (now ANU) since 1985. After completing his graduate studies at Lviv University in 1965, he taught there and in 1967 moved to Donetske, where he has worked at the ANU Institute of Applied Mathematics and Mechanics (director from 1977) and at Donetske University. Skrypnyk's main works are in nonlinear functional analysis, nonlinear partial differential equations (PDEs) of mathematical physics, and function theory. In the early 1970s he introduced the notion of the topological degree for a wide class of nonlinear maps type (α) and developed the complete theory for a single-valued degree analogous to that for the Brouwer degree. He used the latter to extend many classical theorems to his general class of mappings. The topological degree theory developed by the American mathematician F. Browder in the 1980s for maps of type (S_+) is essentially the same as Skrypnyk's for type (α). Skrypnyk used his topological results to obtain weak solutions of boundary value problems in physics, elasticity, and mechanics. He also obtained important results in his study of the regularity theory of these solutions and summarized them in a monograph on nonlinear elliptic equations of higher order (1973). He extended many of his results to nonelliptic PDEs and to elliptic PDEs that are not in divergent form. He also studied the solutions of Monge-Ampère equations and wrote a study of investigation methods for nonlinear elliptic boundary value problems (1990).

W. Petryshyn

Skrypnyk, Leonid (pseuds: Leonid Lain, M. Lansky), b 1893, d 23 February 1929 in Kharkiv. Futurist writer and theorist. He graduated from the Kiev Polytechnical Institute and was involved in flying experiments at N. Zhukovsky's Aerodynamics Institute near Moscow before the First World War. In the Soviet period he worked in Kiev in the administration of the Southwestern Railway and then operated the film laboratory at the Odessa factory of the All-Ukrainian Photo-Cinema Administration. He published prose, reviews, and criticism in the journals *Chervonyi shliakh* (the novelette 'Ivan Petrovych i Feliks,' 1928, no. 11), *Zhyttia i revoliutsiia, Nova generatsiia*, and *Vsesvit* (as its associate editor) and in *Kul'tura i pobut*, the supplement to *Visti VUTsVK*. From 1928 he belonged to the futurist writers' group Nova Generatsiia. He wrote the first Ukrainian reference book for the photographer (1927), the first Ukrainian book of essays on the history of cinematic art (1928), and the experimental 'screen novel' *Inteligent* (The Intellectual, 1929; repr in *Suchasnist'* in 1984), and translated into Ukrainian U. Sinclair's *100 Percent, the Story of a Patriot* (1928). His book on art and social culture and his novel 'Epizod z zhyttia chudnoï liudyny' (Episode from the Life of a Strange Person) were not completed.

Skrypnyk, Lev, b 1903 in Yasynuvata, Bakhmut county, Katerynoslav gubernia, d 1939 in Poltava. Writer. While working as a miner in the Donbas in the 1920s, he became a member of the Zaboi writers' group and the All-Ukrainian Association of Proletarian Writers. He wrote *Vybukh* (Explosion, 1928), *Dvisti p'iatdesiat persha verstva* (The

251st Verst, 1929), *Za vse* (For Everything, 1930), *Malen'ka stepova rudnia* (The Little Steppe Mine, 1930), *Smertna kamera* (Death Cell, 1931), and other 'proletarian' prose collections; *Budynok prymusovykh prats'* (The Forced Labor Building, 1930), the first novel set in a Soviet Ukrainian prison; and the novels *Rudnia* (The Mine, 1930) and *Novosmolianka* (1930). Skrypnyk died in a hospital for the mentally ill (according to Soviet sources) or was a victim of the Stalinist terror.

Skrypnyk, Mary, b 11 December 1915 near Timmins, Ontario. Editor, translator, and community leader; a Communist party member since 1932. From 1960 she was an editor of the **Ukrainian Canadian.* In this capacity she began translating works of Ukrainian literature into English; these were published by the Dnipro publishing house in the Ukrainian SSR. She is best known for her translations of works by T. Shevchenko, I. Franko, Lesia Ukrainka, H. Kvitka-Osnovianenko, and O. Kobylianska. Skrypnyk was awarded the Maxim Gorky Prize by the Writers' Union of the USSR in 1976. She has also translated several Ukrainian-Canadian historical works by P. Krawchuk.

Patriarch Mstyslav Skrypnyk   Mykola Skrypnyk

Skrypnyk, Mstyslav (secular name: Stepan), b 10 April 1898 in Poltava. Orthodox patriarch. A nephew of S. **Petliura, in 1917–21 he served in the UNR Army. When the army retreated to Poland, he was interned in a camp in Kalusz. After his release he lived in Galicia and then Volhynia, where from 1926 he worked with the local government. In 1930 he completed a degree in political science in Warsaw. In the 1930s Skrypnyk was a leading member of the **Volhynian Ukrainian Alliance. He served as a member of the Polish Sejm (1930–9), where he was especially active in defending the Ukrainian Orthodox church. He participated in church life, as a delegate to various church councils and a permanent executive member. He was ordained a priest and made bishop of Pereiaslav in 1942 (he received his chirotonium in Kiev), but was persecuted by the Gestapo in 1942–3. He emigrated to Germany in 1944 and was active in organizing émigré church life in Western Europe. In 1947–9 he was acting bishop of the Ukrainian Greek Orthodox Church of Canada. In 1950 he

became head of the consistory and deputy metropolitan of the Ukrainian Orthodox Church in the USA. In 1969 he became metropolitan of the **Ukrainian Autocephalous Orthodox church (UAOC) in Western Europe, and in 1971, metropolitan of the church in the United States. In 1990, after the revival and legalization of the UAOC in Ukraine, Skrypnyk was installed as its patriarch. He was the founder of the religious and cultural center in South Bound Brook, New Jersey, and a supporter of the unification of all Orthodox jurisdictions. He was given an honorary doctorate from St Andrew's College in Winnipeg and made an honorary member of the Shevchenko Scientific Society in the USA. He has published a number of articles and served as editor of various periodicals and collections of works.

I. Korovytsky

Skrypnyk, Mykola, b 25 January 1872 in Yasynuvata, Bakhmut county, Katerynoslav gubernia, d 7 July 1933 in Kharkiv. Bolshevik leader and Soviet Ukrainian statesman; VUAN full member from 1929. After his first arrest in 1901, Skrypnyk abandoned his studies at the St Petersburg Technological Institute and became a full-time Marxist revolutionary in St Petersburg, Odessa, Katerynoslav, Riga, and Moscow. By 1917 he had been arrested 15 times and exiled 7 times to places such as Yakutia (1909–13) and Tambov gubernia (1914–17). During the Bolshevik coup in Petrograd in November 1917, he was a member of the supreme command of the military-revolutionary committee. In December 1917 he was elected in absentia to the **People's Secretariat, the first Soviet government in Ukraine, and in March 1918 he was appointed its chairman by V. Lenin. At the **Tahanrih Bolshevik Conference Skrypnyk was chosen chief of the bureau that was to set up the CP(B)U. Although he delivered the keynote address at the Party's first congress (July 1918), he was not elected to the CP(B)U leadership. Until January 1919 he was a member of the All-Russian Cheka collegium in charge of the section for combating counterrevolution. He returned as a Bolshevik commissar to Ukraine, where he served as people's commissar of worker-peasant inspection (1920–1), internal affairs (1921–2), justice (1922–7), and education (1927–33); general procurator (1922–7); and, briefly (February–July 1933), head of the Ukrainian State Planning Commission and deputy premier of the Ukrainian Council of People's Commissars. At the same time he rose in the CP(B)U to the positions of CC member (April 1920) and Politburo candidate (1923–5) and member (1925–33), and in the All-Union Communist Party (Bolshevik), CC candidate (1923–5) and member (1927–33). He also took part in organizing the **Communist International, was a member of its Executive Committee, and headed its CP(B)U delegation. As a leading Party scholar he directed the All-Ukrainian Commission for the History of the October Revolution and the CP(B)U, the **Ukrainian Institute of Marxism-Leninism (1928–30), and its chair of the national question (1926–31), and presided over the Ukrainian Society of Marxist Historians (from 1928).

Among the non-Ukrainian members and leaders of the CP(B)U (eg, E. Kviring and D. Lebid) he encountered Russian chauvinism and a rejection of all things Ukrainian as counterrevolutionary. To overcome this attitude Skrypnyk persuaded the CC CP(B)U to introduce **Ukrainization policies and actively advocated the development of a Ukrainian 'proletarian' culture and literature and Ukraine's political and economic autonomy. As people's commissar of education he Ukrainized the press and publishing, elementary and secondary education, and, to a significant extent, higher education. In 1927 he convened an all-Ukrainian conference (attended also by Western Ukrainian specialists) to standardize Ukrainian *orthography. Its so-called Skrypnykivka spelling system was officially adopted in 1928.

A dogmatic Leninist, he remained a determined enemy of the opponents of Soviet rule, including the Ukrainian 'nationalists.' He participated in the military and ideological struggle that led to the physical destruction of the postrevolutionary Ukrainian intelligentsia and the Party supporters of *national communism. At the same time he saw Russian great-power chauvinism and centralism as the chief threats to Ukrainian culture and fought against them. Convinced of the need to unite all Ukrainian ethnic territories within one Soviet Ukrainian state, he opposed Russian Bolshevik plans to establish a separate *Donets–Kryvyi Rih Soviet Republic in 1918. Later he demanded that the Ukrainian parts of adjacent Russian gubernias and the regions of compact Ukrainian settlement in Central Asia and the Far East be incorporated in the Ukrainian SSR. Throughout the 1920s he devoted much attention to the cultural needs of Ukrainians in these regions as well as in Polish, Czech, Hungarian, and Rumanian territories.

Skrypnyk's activities contradicted the imperialistic plans of the central leadership in Moscow. In January 1933 J. Stalin sent P. *Postyshev to Ukraine to take control of the CP(B)U. Skrypnyk's policies and theories were condemned, and he was removed as education commissar. Foreseeing the reversal of Ukrainization and his inevitable liquidation as an old opponent of Stalin, he committed suicide.

Skrypnyk's undeniable contributions to and defense of Ukrainian culture made him a symbol of Ukraine's struggle for sovereignty. He was rehabilitated in the mid-1950s. His policies, views, speeches, brochures (partly collected in 4 vols in 1929–30), and over 800 articles have been republished in Ukraine in a selected edition (1991).

BIBLIOGRAPHY
Babko, Iu.; Bilokobyl's'kyi, I. *Mykola Oleksiiovych Skrypnyk* (Kiev 1967)
Koshelivets', I. *Mykola Skrypnyk* (Munich 1972)
Skrypnyk, M. *Statti i promovy z natsional'noho pytannia*, ed I. Koshelivets' (Munich 1974)
Mace, J. *Communism and the Dilemmas of National Liberation: National Communism in Soviet Ukraine, 1918–1933* (Cambridge, Mass 1983)

I. Koshelivets

Skuba, Mykola, b 6 December 1907 in Horbove, Novhorod-Siverskyi county, Chernihiv gubernia, d 24 October 1937 in Kiev. Writer. A member of the writers' groups Molodniak and Nova Generatsiia, he began publishing in the Kharkiv press in 1927 and wrote the poetry collections *Perehony* (Races, 1930), *Demonstratsiia* (The Demonstration, 1931), *Pisni* (Songs, 1934), and *Novi pisni* (New Songs, 1935). He was arrested during the Stalinist terror in 1937, and executed by the NKVD. He was posthumously rehabilitated, and a book of his poems was published in Kiev in 1965.

Skubii, Ivan [Skubij], b 1858 in Leliukhivka, Kobeliaky county, Poltava gubernia, d after 1909 in Leliukhivka. Lirnyk. Blind from the age of 10, he became a well-known performer of dumas. His style of playing was closer to the kobzar style. His dumas were written down by F. Kolessa and O. Slastion and published in *Materiialy do ukraïns'koï etnolohiï*, 14 (1913).

Skubova, Mariia, b 1880 in Ivanivka, Skalat county, Galicia, d 11 April 1952 in New York. Civic activist. After emigrating to the United States in 1907, she founded the Ukrainian Besida society, which helped young emigrant girls. During the First World War she served as a nurse in the Austrian army and, upon being captured, in a hospital in Kiev. She returned to Lviv in 1916 through a prisoner exchange and continued to work in Ukrainian hospitals. In 1921 she returned to the United States, where she collected funds for the needy in Ukraine, organized exhibits of Ukrainian art and customs, set up women's organizations, and (after visiting Galicia in 1930) rallied public support to protest the 1930 Polish Pacification. After the Second World War she organized aid for Ukrainian refugees in DP camps. She supported the Ukrainian Academy of Arts and Sciences in the US financially and was a member of its executive board.

Skulsky, Andrii [Skul's'kyj, Andrij] (Skolsky), b in the late 16th century in Lviv, d ca 1655 in Lviv. Printer and writer. He studied at the Lviv Dormition Brotherhood School and then worked at and directed (1630–3, 1641–3) the brotherhood's press. He also co-owned, with M. Slozka, a press in Lviv (1638–40); worked as a printer in Moldavia; and directed the press established by Bishop A. Zhelyborsky at St George's Church in Lviv (1643–6) and the Univ Monastery (from 1646). In 1651 Skulsky was arrested near Sokal by the Poles, accused of spying for the Cossacks, and tortured, but he was eventually released. Skulsky wrote and published *Virshi z trahodii Khristos paskhon Hryhoriia Bohoslova* (Verses from the Tragedy of the Paschal Christ by Gregory the Theologian, 1630).

Skunts, Petro [Skunc'], b 20 May 1942 in Mizhhiria, Transcarpathia. Poet of the *shestydesiatnyky* generation. He graduated from Uzhhorod University (1963) and has worked as a newspaper and book editor in Uzhhorod. He is the author of the collections *Sontse v rosi* (Sun in the Dew, 1961), *Verkhovyns'ka pisnia* (Highland Song, 1962), *Poliusy zemli* (The Earth's Axis, 1964), *Pohliad* (A Look, 1967), *Na hranytsi epokh* (On the Threshold of Epochs, 1968), *Vsesvit, hory i ia* (The Universe, Mountains, and I, 1970), *Rozryv-trava* (Impatiens, 1979), and *Seismichna zona* (The Seismic Zone, 1983). He has also edited a book of Transcarpathian legends (1972).

Skurykhin, Volodymyr [Skuryxin], b 17 April 1926 in Viatka (now Kirov), Russia. Systems theoretist; full member of the AN URSR (now ANU) since 1978. He studied in Ivanovo and since 1958 has worked at the ANU Institute of Cybernetics. His main contributions are in applying cybernetics and computers to the automation of manufacturing processes. He was instrumental in creating the first automated and computerized industrial control system in the USSR. He also designed and put into operation some early CAD/CAM systems and other automated design and data-processing systems.

Skvarko, Zakhar, b 27 September 1870 in Kormanychi, Peremyshl county, Galicia, d 2 August 1925 in Kolomyia, Galicia. Co-operative and civic leader. After graduating from Lviv University he practiced law in Mostyska and organized a People's Home credit union and a branch of the Prosvita society. A member of the National Democratic party, in 1907 he was elected to the Galician Diet. In 1910 he was appointed director of the Pokutia credit union in Kolomyia. During the First World War he left for Vienna (1914–15), where he organized relief for Ukrainian office workers and edited the popular National Democratic organ *Svoboda*. In 1919, after returning to Kolomyia, he was elected county president of the Ukrainian National Rada.

SKVU. See World Congress of Free Ukrainians.

Skvyra. IV-10. A city (1989 pop 18,900) on the Skvyrka River and a raion center in Kiev oblast. It was first mentioned in historical documents in 1390, when it was a frontier settlement of the Grand Duchy of Lithuania. In 1482 it was destroyed by the Tatars. From 1569 it was under Polish rule. In 1616 it was granted the rights of *Magdeburg law. Under the Hetman state Skvyra was a company center of Bila Tserkva (1648–51) and Pavoloch (1651–74) regiments. It was recaptured by Poland in 1686, and supported the haidamaka rebellions of 1736 and 1768. It was acquired by Russia in 1793, and from 1797 it was a county center in Kiev gubernia. In 1938 it attained city status. Today it is an industrial and agricultural town. Its main industries are food processing, clothing, and sanitary technology. It is the home of the Selection and Seed Research Station of the Ukrainian Scientific Research Institute of Orcharding.

Skybenko, Anatolii, b 10 October 1924 in Kiev, d 17 July 1981 in Kiev. Stage director, actor, and pedagogue. He completed study at the Kiev Institute of Theater Arts (1949) and then worked in theaters in Drohobych and Vinnytsia (1950–4) and in the Kiev Ukrainian Drama Theater (1954–81). In 1956–81 he taught in the Kiev Institute of Theater Arts.

Skybynsky, Hryhorii [Skybyns'kyj, Hryhorij], b in the 1660s in Western Ukraine, d 1716 in Moscow. Theologian. In the 1670s he lived in Moscow. Then he moved, for eight years, to Rome, where in 1688 he converted from Orthodoxy to the Uniate faith. After living in France and Germany and studying Calvinism and Lutheranism for several more years, he returned to Moscow and re-embraced the Orthodox faith (although he remained labeled a 'heretic' and 'Latinizer'). He left several unpublished manuscripts, including 'Brevis poetica cum prosodia conscripta'; 'Perechnevoe skazaniie o myri' (A Listing of the Story of the World); and 'Kratkoe skazanie i opisanie ... o grade Ryme' (A Brief Story and Description ... of the City of Rome, 4 parts), a polemical work criticizing the papacy and attacking Catholicism. A biography, by A. Sobolevsky, and two of his works were published in *Chteniia v Imperatorskom obshchestve istorii i drevnostei rossiskikh* (1914, no. 2).

Skydan, Karpo, b ?, d 1638. Cossack officer. He was a colonel of unregistered Zaporozhian Cossacks and a lead-

ing figure in Cossack uprisings against the Poles, including one in 1637 led by P. Pavliuk and one in 1638 with Ya. Ostrianyn. Skydan was recruiting in Cherkasy later in 1638 and, returning to the aid of D. Hunia, was seriously injured in a battle near Zhovnyn, captured by Polish forces, and presumably executed.

Skyrda, Liudmyla, b 15 September 1945 in Kirovohrad. Writer and literary scholar. She graduated from Kiev University (1968), where she has lectured in the department of the history of Ukrainian literature since 1972. She has written the poetry collections *Chekannia* (Waiting, 1965), *Skhody* (Stairs, 1976), *Kryla* (Wings, 1979), *Elehiia vechirn'oho sadu* (Elegy of the Evening Garden, 1983), *Muzyka dlia dvokh* (Music for Two, 1986), and *Dni i nochi* (Days and Nights, 1987). Her scholarly publications include books about contemporary Ukrainian poetry (1983), Ye. Pluzhnyk (1989), and the contemporary Ukrainian narrative poem (1990).

Skytsiuk, Ivan [Skycjuk], b 12 August 1907 in Chornyi Ostriv, Proskuriv county, Podilia gubernia. Decorative artist; husband of M. *Tymchenko. In 1941 he graduated from the Kiev School of Applied Art. He painted dishes with floral motifs; plates, such as *Firebird* (1967) and *Red Bird* (1967); decorative panels, such as *Fishes among Flowers* (1963) and *May Bugs Hum above the Cherry Trees* (1964); and the murals in the Kazka toy store in Kiev (1978–9, with M. Tymchenko).

Mykhailo Slabchenko

Slabchenko, Mykhailo [Slabčenko, Myxajlo], b 21 July 1882 in Moldavanka, outside Odessa, d 29 November 1952 in Pervomaiske, Mykolaiv oblast. Historian; full member of the AN URSR (now ANU) in 1926–30. A graduate of Odessa University and the St Petersburg Military-Juridical Academy, he completed his studies in Germany. He took an active part in the Ukrainian national movement as a member of student organizations, the Revolutionary Ukrainian party (1903), and the Ukrainian Social Democratic Workers' party (1906–18). In the 1920s he served as a professor at the Odessa Institute of People's Education (in the chair of Ukrainian history), headed the social-historical section of the Odessa Scientific Society, and directed the Odessa branch of the (Kharkiv-based) Scientific Research Chair of Ukrainian History. He also coedited several publications of the Odessa Scientific Society's historical-philological section (three volumes, 1928–9) and social-historical section (five volumes, 1927–30).

The main body of his work was devoted to the history of the law and economy of the Hetmanate and the Zaporizhia in the 17th and 18th centuries. His important early studies include *Malorusskii polk v administrativnom otnoshenii* (The Little Russian Regiment in Its Administrative Aspect, 1909), *Opyty po istorii prava Malorossii XVII–XVIII st.* (Studies of the Legal History of Little Russia in the 17th and 18th Centuries, 1911), *Protokol otpusknykh pisem za getmana D. Apostola 1728 g.* (Record of Release Letters under Hetman D. Apostol in 1728, 1913), *Tsentral'nye uchrezhdeniia Ukrainy XVII–XVIII st.* (Central Institutions of Ukraine in the 17th and 18th Centuries, 1918), and *Pro sudivnytstvo na Ukraïni* (On the Judicial System in Ukraine, 1920). In the early 1920s Slabchenko began working on a large project dealing with the organization of the Ukrainian economy from the Khmelnytsky period to the First World War. The first part of the undertaking, a series titled Khoziaistvo Getmanshchiny v XVII–XVIII stoletiiakh (The Economy of the Hetmanate in the 17th and 18th Centuries), was completed in four Russian-language books; they dealt with land tenure and forms of agriculture (vol 1, 1922), the development of factories and industry (vol 2, 1922), the growth of commerce and commercial capitalism (vol 3, 1923), and the state economy of the Hetmanate (vol 4, 1925). The first and fourth books in the series also appeared in Ukrainian. Slabchenko produced the groundbreaking studies *Sotsiial'no-pravova orhanizatsiia Sichi Zaporoz'koï* (The Social and Legal Organization of the Zaporozhian Sich, 1927) and *Palankova orhanizatsiia Zaporoz'kykh Vol'nostiv* (The Palanka Organization of Zaporozhian Free Settlements, 1929). Those works tied in with his other studies, a monograph on feudalism in Ukraine (1929) and a collection of materials on the economic and social history of Ukraine in the 19th century (2 vols, 1925, 1927).

Slabchenko was instrumental in developing Odessa as a center of Ukrainian historical studies. His work was cut short when he was arrested in 1929 in the first major Soviet assault on the Ukrainian intelligentsia and tried for membership in the so-called *Union for the Liberation of Ukraine (SVU). He served his six-year sentence in the Solovets Islands. After the Second World War he worked in Pervomaiske (he was not allowed to return to Odessa) as a school teacher and then foreign language inspector. He was denounced by a colleague, and died in poverty and obscurity. In 1989 the Supreme Court of the Ukrainian SSR rehabilitated him along with other defendants in the SVU trial. In 1990 his name was restored to the membership list of the AN URSR (now ANU), which had expelled him in 1930.

I. Myhul, O. Ohloblyn

Slabchenko, Taras [Slabčenko], b 1904 in Odessa, d 1937 ? Historian; son of M. *Slabchenko. He worked as a lecturer in the workers' faculty of the Odessa Medical Institute and the Odessa Workers' University. In the 1920s he was a member of the VUAN social-historical section and the secretary of the Odessa Scientific Society affiliated with the VUAN. He wrote many works on general and cultural history, including the monograph *Z lystuvannia M.L. Kropyvnyts'koho* (From the Correspondence of M.L. Kropyvnytsky, 1927). He was arrested on 20 December 1929 in connection with the show trial of the Union for the Liberation of Ukraine, and sentenced on 19 April 1930 to

Taras Slabchenko   Yevhen Slabchenko

three years' confinement. Further details of his life are unknown, except that on 27 October 1937 he was sentenced to be shot by the military collegium of the USSR Supreme Court. Slabchenko was posthumously rehabilitated in 1959.

Slabchenko, Yevhen [Slabčenko, Jevhen], b 8 December 1898 in Kiev, d 10 September 1966 in Nice, France. Filmmaker and journalist. He studied at the universities of Prague and Berlin and at the Sorbonne in Paris. He organized the first Plast scouting group in central Ukraine (1917). From the mid-1920s he lived in France under the name Eugène Deslaw. There he was the official representative of the All-Ukrainian Photo-Cinema Administration and film correspondent for the Kharkiv futurist journal *Nova generatsiia*. In the 1930s he made pioneering short experimental sound films and worked on many French film productions. In 1936 he codirected (with J. Darroy) *La Guerre des gosses*, which received an award as best European film at a 1939 New York film festival. During the Second World War he worked in Spain and Switzerland, and after the war he worked in French television. His *Vision fantastique*, the first film with solarized images, received an honorable mention at the 1956 Venice Film Festival.

Slaboshpytsky, Mykhailo [Slabošpyts'kyj, Myxajlo], b 28 July 1946 in Marianivka, Shpola raion, Cherkasy oblast. Literary critic and writer. He graduated from Kiev University (1971), and from 1975 to 1983 he worked as editor in charge of literary criticism at the newspaper *Literaturna Ukraïna*. Since 1991 he has been executive secretary of the Kiev branch of the Writers' Union of Ukraine. He has written many articles about the works of contemporary Ukrainian writers, and introductions to various literary editions, surveys, and reviews. Published separately have been his book in Russian and English on contemporary Ukrainian literature (coauthor, A. Shevchenko, 1981, 1983, 1985, 1987, 1989), a collection of literary profiles (1984), books of stories for children, the novel-essay *Mariia Bashkyrtseva* (1986), a study of R. Ivanychuk (1989), and the novel *Dushi na vitrakh* (Souls in the Winds, 1981). He has edited a collection of articles by Russian and other non-Ukrainian Soviet critics on Ukrainian writers (1987) and a book of O. Vlyzko's selected works (1988). In August 1992 he was elected head of the newly created Ukrainian World Co-ordinating Council.

Slang. Unconventional, nonstandard words and phrases used in colloquial speech, particularly in urban environments. Such words and phrases are generally used by various occupational groups (eg, merchants, craftsmen, students, and soldiers) and subcultural groups (criminals, prisoners, and drug users) before they become accepted in the dominant culture. They give new emphasis to certain attitudes or express new shades of meaning, and they can be derogatory, satirical, shocking, or euphemistic. Slang terms in Ukrainian (many of them borrowed from Polish, Russian, and Yiddish) have not been systematically studied. They have been used to achieve special effects by writers such as I. Franko, V. Vynnychenko, M. Khvylovy, Yu. Yanovsky, O. Korniichuk, L. Pervomaisky, I. Mykytenko, and O. Berdnyk.

Slanské Mountains (Ukrainian: Soloni hory). Volcanic mountains located in eastern Czechoslovakia between the Košice-Prešov Basin and the Tysa Lowland. A number of Ukrainian villages, including Banske, are situated along the ridge. The highest peak is Mount Šimonka, at 1,092 m.

Slastenenko, Yefym, b 1902 in the Far East. Zoologist and ichthyologist; full member of the Shevchenko Scientific Society since 1955. He worked at the Ukrainian Scientific Research Institute of Fish Management in Kiev (1930–3), the USSR Academy of Sciences in Leningrad (1932–8), and Rostov University (1938–42). He emigrated to Canada in 1950. He specialized in the fish of the Black and Azov seas.

Slastion, Opanas [Slast'on] (Slaston, pseud: Opishnianskyi Honchar), b 14 January 1855 in Berdianske, Tavriia gubernia, d 24 September 1933 in Myrhorod, Poltava ok-

Opanas Slastion: illustration in the 1886 edition of Taras Shevchenko's *Haidamaky*

ruha. Painter, illustrator, architect, art scholar, ethnographer, and kobzar. After graduating from the St Petersburg Academy of Arts (1882) he worked as an artist for the Ministry of Defense in St Petersburg (1887–1900), where he was able to study materials on the Ukrainian Cossacks, and presided over the Ukrainian Club in the capital (1897–1900). In 1883–5 he did 55 pen drawings for the 1886 St Petersburg edition of T. Shevchenko's epic poem 'Haidamaky.' His genre paintings and landscapes were reproduced frequently in the journals *Niva* and *Zhivopisnoe obozrenie*, and he contributed sketches to *Zoria* (Lviv) and to satirical magazines, such as *Shershen'*, *Oskolki*, *Strekoza*, and *Shut*. From 1900 to 1928 he taught at the Myrhorod Arts and Crafts School and created illustrations for more of Shevchenko's poems. Slastion's articles were published in periodicals such as *Kievskaia starina*, *Ridnyi krai*, *Rada*, and *Siaivo*. For many years he wandered about Ukraine, painting landscapes, such as *Myrhorod* (1901) and *Evening: Village* (1904), drawing architectural monuments, collecting folklore and folk art, and writing down the songs performed by kobzars (later used by F. Kolessa in his two volumes of materials on Ukrainian ethnology, 1913). He became a skilled performer of Cossack dumas on the bandura. His gallery of kobzars in Left-Bank Ukraine, drawn from 1875 to 1928, was not published until 1961. From the ethnographic materials Slastion collected he prepared albums on Ukrainian and Zaporozhian antiquities (his lithographs of the mid-1890s perished in a flood in 1900), folk dress, folk ornaments, embroidery, wood carvings, ceramics, and architecture. He supported F. *Krychevsky's architectural design of the Poltava Zemstvo Building in the Ukrainian 'folk' style, and in 1910–13 he designed dozens of village public buildings in that style (eg, in Velyki Sorochyntsi). Slastion prepared the materials for a book of Ukrainian folk dumas (1927) and wrote recollections about his friend P. Martynovych (1931). In 1920 Slastion founded the Myrhorod Regional Studies Museum, to which he donated his valuable collection of historical and ethnographic materials, and in 1928 he organized the first peasant banduryst chorus. A biography of Slastion by A. Abbasov was published in Kiev in 1973, and a catalog of a retrospective exhibition of his works appeared in 1975.

Slastion, Yurii, b 1903 in Myrhorod, Poltava gubernia. Architect, painter, and composer; son of O. *Slastion; full member of the Ukrainian Academy of Arts and Sciences in the US. A postwar émigré in the United States since 1949, he painted portraits and landscapes, composed choral music to the Liturgy of St John Chrysostom (1956), designed Hetman P. Skoropadsky's burial chamber in Wiesbaden, Germany, and painted the iconostases of the Ukrainian Orthodox churches in Minneapolis and Denver.

Slavechna River. See Slovechna River.

Slavery. Slavery existed in Ukrainian territory from ancient times. The first references to it appear in Arab historical sources of the 9th century, which speak of Magyar hordes moving from the Volga to the Pannonian Lowland and enslaving some of the local Slavs and selling them in Black Sea coastal towns to Greek buyers. The accounts of Arab and Jewish travelers attest that from the 10th to 13th centuries many slaves were shipped from Kievan Rus' through the Black Sea towns to Byzantium, Spain, Turkestan, and Arab countries. The Greek colonies, in particular Chersonese Taurica, acted as middlemen in the slave trade. There was a particular square in Constantinople where Rus' merchants sold slaves (known then as *cheliad*). The trade in slaves is also mentioned in chronicles and other Ukrainian sources.

Slaves were taken mainly from among prisoners of war, people born in captivity or married to slaves, and those guilty of certain crimes (arson, horse theft) or of deliberately defaulting on loans. *Ruskaia Pravda* specified that slaves were not afforded the protection of the law, and treated them instead as the personal (hereditary) possessions of their owners. Nevertheless slavery in Ukraine remained relatively humane, particularly under the influence of Christianity and the church. The humaneness was already apparent in the Princely era, when (under certain circumstances) slaves could be freed, and sometimes they owned property. (See also *Kholop* and *Zakup*.)

The institution of slavery continued to exist (under various categories and names) in Ukraine although in increasingly milder forms. It disappeared in the 15th century in the Ukrainian lands controlled by Poland and in the 16th century in the Ukrainian lands controlled by the Grand Duchy of Lithuania. In the late 16th century it was completely replaced by *serfdom. By the time Ukraine began to fall under the rule of Muscovy (from the mid-17th century), slavery had largely disappeared as an institution. For Ukrainians in the 15th and 16th centuries the greatest threat of slavery was being captured by Crimean Tatars for sale in the slave markets of *Turkey.

BIBLIOGRAPHY
Zimin, A. *Kholopy na Rusi* (Moscow 1973)

M. Zhdan

Slavia. A leading Czech journal of Slavic philology, published since 1922 (except in 1941–6) by the *Slavic Institute in Prague. Ukrainian contributors before the Second World War included S. and R. Smal-Stotsky, V. Simovych, I. Pankevych, D. Chyzhevsky, I. Ohiienko, D. Doroshenko, F. Kolessa, L. Biletsky, and K. Chekhovych; after the war, only scholars from Soviet Ukraine and the satellite countries were published, among them O. Melnychuk, M. Onyshkevych, Ya. Dashkevych, B. Struminsky, T. Holynska-Baranova, O. Zilynsky, and H. Koliada.

Slavia Orientalis. A quarterly scholarly journal devoted to Slavic studies, published in Warsaw by the Polish Academy of Sciences since 1952. Until 1957 the journal was called *Kwartalnik Instytutu Polsko-Radzieckiego* and included articles on political topics. Most of the articles are published in Polish, although some appear in Ukrainian, Russian, and other languages. Contributors are primarily from Poland, republics of the former USSR, and other Slavic countries. The articles on Ukrainian subjects have usually dealt with 19th-century literature and history, early Ukrainian culture, or Western Ukrainian dialects. Books on Ukrainian topics by Soviet Ukrainian and Western scholars have been reviewed. An index to the journal up to 1986 was published in vol 36 (1987).

Slavic Congress in Prague, 1848. A congress of representatives of the Slavic peoples of the Austrian Empire,

called at the initiative of P. Šafařík and J. Jelačić and organized by Czech activists, such as F. Palacký, K. Zap, K. Havlíček-Borovský, and F. Rieger. The assembly was convened to consolidate the forces of the Slavs in response to calls for the unification of all German lands (including Austria with Czech-inhabited Bohemia) by the German parliament in Frankfurt; its formal sessions began on 2 June 1848. A number of Galician Ukrainians participated in the congress, including delegates from the *Supreme Ruthenian Council (I. *Borysykevych, H. *Hynylevych, and O. *Zaklynsky); none were present from Transcarpathia. A delegation from the pro-Polish *Ruthenian Congress led by J. Lubomirski and including L. Sapieha, K. Cięglewicz, and L. Stecki participated in the assembly. A total of 363 delegates attended the congress, of whom 61 belonged to the Polish-Ukrainian contingent from Galicia. Three working commissions were struck: Czecho-Slovak, Polish-Ukrainian, and Southern Slav. As a result of talks held in the Polish-Ukrainian commission, formed at the initiative of Palacký and M. Bakunin and headed by Sapieha, an agreement was reached concerning the political, cultural, and national equality of Poles and Ukrainians. A majority of the commission accepted a proposal put forward by the Supreme Ruthenian Council to divide Galicia into eastern and western sections, but under Polish pressure the matter was referred to the Galician Diet and the State Council.

The congress dealt with other issues, including a formula for the restructuring of the Habsburg empire as a federation of autonomous peoples. The congress also sent a special petition to Emperor Ferdinand I demanding equal rights for all Slavic peoples of the Austrian Empire, which included a call for Ukrainian language rights in Galicia. None of the proposals discussed at the congress was ever officially adopted. Because of an uprising that broke out in Prague, the proceedings of the congress were halted on 12 June 1848. The congress produced no concrete results for Galician Ukrainians.

BIBLIOGRAPHY
Sozans'kyi, I. 'Do istorii uchasty halyts'kykh rusyniv u Slov'ians'komu kongresi v Prazi 1848 r.,' *ZNTSh*, 72 (Lviv 1906)
Navalovs'kyi, M. *Ukraïntsi i Slov'ians'kyi kongres u Prazi 1848 r.* (Kharkiv 1930)
Začek, B. (ed). *Slovanský sjezd v Praze* (Prague 1958)
Orton, L. *The Prague Slav Congress of 1848* (Boulder, Colo 1978)
Kozik, J. *The Ukrainian National Movement in Galicia, 1815–1849* (Edmonton 1986)

B. Kravtsiv

Slavic Institute (Slovanský ústav). A Czechoslovak state-funded research institution, founded in Prague on the initiative (1920) of President T. Masaryk. It was legally constituted in 1922 to study and develop Czechoslovakia's cultural and economic relations with other Slavic countries. Under the directors L. Niederle (1928–32) and M. Murko (1932–40) the institute was active in the field of *Slavic studies. During that time it published many serials, over 70 monographs, and over 50 annual volumes of *Byzantinoslavica*, *Germanoslavica*, *Slavia*, and *Slavische Rundschau*. Its Slavic Library (Slovanská knihovna, est 1924) was one of the largest Slavic libraries outside the USSR; in 1946 it contained 244,000 monographs and 150,000 annual periodical runs. The institute supported scholarly institutions and individual scholars engaged in Ukrainian studies. Ukrainian émigré scholars who were members of the institute included L. Biletsky, D. Chyzhevsky, F. and O. Kolessa, O. Lototsky, O. Mytsiuk, I. Ohiienko, S. Smal-Stotsky, F. Steshko, and V. Timoshenko; they worked on its numerous commissions, particularly on its autonomous Research Board on Slovakia and Subcarpathian Ruthenia. From 1931 to 1940 the Ukrainian Historical Cabinet functioned within the institute. The institute's activities were restricted during the German occupation, and it was closed down in 1943. It was reactivated in 1945, but Soviet repression forced it to suspend its activities in 1948. In 1953 it was revived as part of the Czechoslovak Academy of Sciences.

Slavic languages. A group of languages within the Indo-European language family. They developed out of the dialects of Proto-Slavic, an ancestral language that arose between the Oder and Dnieper rivers. Today there are 12 Slavic languages: Belarusian, Russian, Ukrainian, Czech, Lower Sorbian, Polish, Slovak, Slovenian, Upper Sorbian, Bulgarian, Macedonian, and Serbo-Croatian. Of the historically recorded languages Polabian is extinct. In the period of its disintegration, Proto-Slavic consisted of a continuum of dialects. The contemporary Slavic languages were formed as a result of the unification of particular dialects around political and cultural centers.

The traditional conception of the history of language as constant disintegration is false: the theory that Proto-Slavic split first into Proto–East Slavic, Proto–West Slavic, and Proto–South Slavic is not supported by historical or linguistic facts. The widely accepted division of the Slavic languages into three groups – East, West, and South (or, less accepted, North, Central, and South) – is merely conventional and can be justified only from a geographic perspective. In reality, with the exception of regions of later colonization, the boundaries between the Slavic languages have been fluid. There are transitional dialects between them, and even between the literary languages the transitions are gradual.

The principle according to which the Slavic languages have been grouped is primarily a genetic one. Structurally they have much in common if one compares them in geographically contiguous pairs. There are, however, few traits common to all of them. For example, in prosody, phonemically relevant intonation in stressed vowels exists only in Slovene and Serbo-Croatian; lengthened vowels exist in Slovak and Czech; and stress is fixed in Polish, Slovak, Upper and Lower Sorbian, Czech, and Macedonian. In phonetics, Polish has nasal vowels, Czech and Slovak have diphthongs, and Slovenian and Macedonian have no opposition in the palatalization of consonants. In morphology, nouns are indeclinable only in Bulgarian and Macedonian, and conjugation is split only in Serbo-Croatian, Bulgarian, and Macedonian.

Traits common to all the Slavic languages are synchronically evident partly in the principles of their construction and partly in their material elements. Traits of the first type are, for example, the alternation of particular vowels with a zero morpheme (although which vowel alternates varies by language; cf Ukrainian *son : snu*, Polish *sen : snu*, Serbo-Croatian *san : sna* 'dream' nom : gen), similarities in the root structure, the existence of two stems in the verb versus one usually in the noun, and agreement of the adjective with the noun. The most obvious material similarities are in vocabulary and, even more, in the repertoire of word roots (often, however, with a semantic shift; eg, Ukrainian *hora* 'mountain' vs Bulgarian *gora* 'forest', Ukrainian *šum* 'din' vs Serbo-Croatian *šuma* 'forest'), particularly in the set of prepositions and prefixes (with partial differences) and, less often, of suffixes.

Slavic studies (*slavistyka, slovianoznavstvo*). A branch of the humanities and social sciences dealing with the archeology, history, language, literature, culture, folklore, and ethnography of the various Slavic nations and the Slavs as a whole. Until the beginning of the 19th century knowledge about the Slavs was provided by missionaries (eg, SS Cyril and Methodius, J. Križanić), travelers, Byzantine, Arab, German, and other chroniclers, and early philologists (in Ukraine, primarily 16th- and 17th-century grammarians and lexicographers, such as L. Zyzanii, M. Smotrytsky, I. Uzhevych, P. Berynda, and Ye. Slavynetsky). The groundwork for modern Slavic studies was prepared by various pre-Romantic archeographers and collectors of Slavic ancient manuscripts, antiquities, and ethnography, as well as by the South and West Slavic liberation struggles. The biblical-textual research of the Czech scholar J. Dobrovský and his *Institutiones linguae Slavicae dialecti veteris ...* (1822) provided the basis for including the Slavic languages in the study of comparative Indo-European philology. P.J. Šafařík's two epoch-making works, *Slovanske starožitnosti* (Slavic Antiquities, 1837) and *Slovanský národopis* (Slavic Ethnography, 1842), placed the study of the origins and history of the Slavs on a scientific basis and thus served as a turning point in the history of Slavic studies.

In the early 19th-century Russian Empire the ideological influence of *Pan-Slavism engendered widespread intellectual interest in Slavic history and ethnography (by V. Lamansky and others) in addition to philology and archeology. In 1811 a Chair of Slavic Literature, held by M. Kachenovsky, was created in Moscow University. In 1835 the minister of education, S. Uvarov, established chairs of the 'history and literature of Slavic dialects' at all of the empire's universities. The first generation of Slavists (young university graduates, including the Ukrainians O. Bodiansky, I. Sreznevsky, and V. Hryhorovych) were sent abroad to study and do research in various Slavic countries and Western and Central European universities.

With the establishment of the Russian chairs, a Slavic chair at the Collège de France in Paris (1840, first held by A. Mickiewicz), and chairs of Slavic philology at Vienna University (1849, held by the pioneering Slavists F. Miklosich, V. Jagić, and N. Trubetskoi) and other universities in Austria-Hungary and Germany, Slavic studies entered their modern stage of development. Until 1918 Vienna, with its university, academy of sciences, and institutes of Slavic philology (est 1886) and Eastern European history (est 1907), was a major center, where many Western Ukrainian and other European Slavists were trained. In the interwar period Prague (with its Slavic Institute), Cracow, Warsaw, Berlin, Breslau, and Leipzig filled the same role. St Petersburg (Leningrad), Moscow, and Kiev have remained important research centers.

Large-scale development and specialization in Slavic studies has occurred during the 20th century. Since the end of the First World War, and particularly after the Second World War, Slavic studies institutes, departments, and chairs have been created at many Western universities. The most prominent centers in the English-speaking world have been the University of London, with its School of Slavonic Studies (est 1915), Columbia University, Harvard University, and the University of California at Berkeley.

Major books on comparative Slavic grammar have been written by F. Miklosich (4 vols, 1852–75), V. Vondrák (1906, 1908), J. Mikkola (3 vols, 1913–50), V. Porzhezinsky (1916), G. Ilinsky (1916), A. Meillet (1924; 2nd edn 1934), A. Vaillant (5 vols, 1950–77), S. Bernshtein (2 vols, 1961, 1974), the Ukrainian linguists G.Y. Shevelov (1964) and O. Melnychuk (1966), Z. Stieber (1969), and S. Ivšić (1970). Comparative Slavic etymological dictionaries have been compiled by Miklosich (1886), E. Berneker (1908, 1914), L. Sadnik and R. Aitzetmüller (1963–), F. Koneczny (1973–), F. Sławski (1974–), and O. Trubachev (1974–). T. Lehr and A. Brückner (1929), M. Weingart-Spławiński (1937), R. Trautmann (1947), R. de Bray (1951; 3rd expanded edn 1980), T. Lehr-Spławiński, W. Kuraszkiewicz, F. Sławski (1954), and K. Horálek (1955) have written survey histories of the Slavic languages. Survey histories of Slavic cultures have been produced by T. Florinsky (1895), L. Niederle (1909), the Ukrainian historian D. Doroshenko (1922), and P. Diehls (1963). With the exception of the synthetic comparative histories of A. Pypin and V. Spasovich (1880–4), J. Karásek (1906), J. Máchal (1922–9), F. Wollman (1928), E. Georgiev (1958–63), and the Ukrainian scholar D. Chyzhevsky (1952, 1968), the study of Slavic literatures has been limited to national histories or the history of general developments and literary currents in relation to the non-Slavic world. Synthetic studies have been written on Slavic folk culture by K. Moszyński (3 vols, 1929–39) and on Slavic archeology by Niederle (11 vols, 1902–25) and members of the Polish archeological-linguistic (Lehr-Spławiński [1946], G. Labuda [2 vols, 1960, 1964]) and anthropological (J. Czekanowski [1957]) schools.

Thousands of Slavic studies monographs have been published around the world. Research has also been published in a multitude of scholarly serials and journals, such as *Archiv für slavische Philologie* (Berlin, 42 vols, 1876–1929), *Russkii filologicheskii vestnik* (Warsaw, 78 vols, 1879–1918), *Zhurnal Ministerstva narodnago prosveshcheniia* (St Petersburg, 1834–1917), *Prace filologiczne* (Warsaw, since 1885), *Izvestiia Otdeleniia russkogo iazyka i slovesnosti Akademii nauk* (St Petersburg, 1896–1927) and its *Sbornik* (101 vols, 1867–1928), **Slovanský přehled* (Prague, since 1899), *Rocznik slawistyczny* (Cracow, since 1908), *Južnoslovenski filolog* (Belgrade, since 1913), *Slavia occidentalis* (Poznań, since 1921), **Revue des études slaves* (Paris, since 1921), **Slavia* (Prague, since 1922), *The Slavonic and East European Review* (London, since 1922), *Zeitschrift für slavische Philologie* (Heidelberg, since 1925), **Slavische Rundschau* (Prague, Berlin, and Vienna, 17 vols, 1929–40), *Byzantinoslavica* (Prague, since 1929), *Slavic Review* (United States, since 1941), *Slavia antiqua* (Poznań, since 1948), *Pamiętnik słowiański* (Warsaw, since 1949), *Uchenye zapiski Instituta slavianovedeniia* (Moscow, since 1949), *Oxford Slavonic Papers* (since 1950), *Wiener slavistisches Jahrbuch* (Vienna, since 1950), *Osteuropa* (Stuttgart, since 1951), *Richerche slavistiche* (Rome, since 1952), **Slavia Orientalis* (Warsaw, since 1952), *Scando-Slavica* (Copenhagen, since 1954), *Studia slavica* (Budapest, since 1955), *Canadian Slavonic Papers* (since

1956), *Die Welt der Slaven* (Wiesbaden, Köln–Vienna, and Munich, since 1956), *l'Etudes slaves et est-européenes / Slavic and East European Studies* (Montreal, 1956–76), *Zeitschrift für Slawistik* (East Berlin, since 1956), *Slovo* (Zagreb, since 1957), *Slovanské štúdie* (Bratislava, since 1957), *The Slavic and East European Journal* (United States, since 1957), *Romanoslavica* (Bucharest, since 1958), *International Journal of Slavic Linguistics and Poetics* (The Hague, Lisse, and Columbus, Ohio, since 1959), *Slavica Pragensia* (Prague, since 1959), *Slavica* (Debrecen, since 1961), *Voprosy istorii slavian* (Voronezh, since 1963), *Acta Baltico-Slavica* (Białystok, since 1964), *Sovetskoe slavianovedenie* (Moscow, since 1965), *Anzeiger für slavische Philologie* (Wiesbaden and Graz, since 1966), *Slavica Slovaca* (Bratislava, since 1966), *Canadian-American Slavic Studies* (since 1967), *Slavica Wratislaviensia* (Wrocław, since 1969), *Zbornik za slavistiku* (Novi Sad, since 1970), *Folia Slavica* (Columbus, Ohio, since 1977), *International Review of Slavic Linguistics* (Edmonton, since 1979), and *Die Slawischen Sprachen* (Salzburg, since 1982).

In Ukraine. For practical reasons and because of political circumstances, Slavic studies in Ukraine have not focused on the Slavs in general, but on individual Slavic languages and literatures, especially Old Church Slavonic, Russian, and Polish. Until the Soviet period many leading Slavists at universities in Ukraine were Russian (eg, A. Sobolevsky, N. Durnovo) or Polish (eg, Lehr-Spławiński and Stieber in interwar Lviv). Among Ukrainian scholars, pioneering contributions to the study of comparative Slavic linguistics were made by O. Potebnia in the 19th century and M. Hrunsky and L. Bulakhovsky in the 20th century. After 1946 Bulakhovsky and his colleagues in Kiev (eg, O. Melnychuk, V. Kolomiiets, I. Bilodid, V. Skliarenko, V. Rusanivsky, Z. Veselovska) created a major center of Slavic accentological and syntactic research. A former student of Bulakhovsky, G.Y. Shevelov of Columbia University, made significant contributions to Slavic phonology.

From 1957 Slavic studies in Ukraine were co-ordinated by the AN URSR (now ANU) Presidium's Ukrainian Committee of Slavists, headed by Bulakhovsky (1957–61), M. Rylsky (1961–4), Bilodid (1964–81), and Rusanivsky (from 1981). In addition to the many scholars of Slavic languages and literatures in Ukraine, in 1980 there were 124 professional Slavic historians (including many not specializing in Russian history): 34 in Kiev, 25 in Lviv, 13 in Kharkiv, 13 in Uzhhorod, 8 in Odessa, 5 in Donetske, and 5 in Lutske.

Ukrainian Slavists have published in many Ukrainian, Russian, and foreign periodicals and collections and participated in many national and international Slavic studies conferences. The Ninth International Congress of Slavists was held in Kiev in 1983. The Ukrainian-language serials devoted to Slavic studies have been **Slovo* (Lviv, 1936–9), *Pytannia slov'ians'koho movoznavstva* (Lviv, 8 issues, 1948–63), *Slov'ians'ke movoznavstvo* (Kiev, 4 vols, 1958–62), *Mizhslov'ians'ki literaturni vzaiemyny* (Kiev, 3 vols, 1958–63), *Slov'ians'ke literaturoznavstvo i fol'klorystyka* (Kiev, since 1965), and *Problemy slov'ianoznavstva* (formerly *Ukraïns'ke slov'ianoznavstvo*, Lviv, since 1976 [no. 39 in 1989]).

Old Church Slavonic studies. Until the Revolution of 1917 textbooks of Old *Church Slavonic (OCS) were available only in Russian in Russian-ruled Ukraine. In Soviet Ukraine in the 1920s, such scholars as Hrunsky, P. Buzuk, and H. Holoskevych produced studies of OCS writing and grammar in Ukrainian. In the 1930s the Stalinist suppression of Ukrainian culture and the exclusion of OCS as a subject of study in postsecondary schools brought about a decline in the area. Conditions improved significantly in the postwar period, particularly after Stalin's death. Textbooks of OCS have been written by Hrunsky (1941, 1946), K. Trofymovych (1958), V. Besedina-Nevzorova (1962), M. Stanivsky (1964), and A. Maiboroda (1975). Studies in OCS morphology have been produced by M. Boichuk (1952), Trofymovych (1958), and others.

In Austrian- and interwar Polish-ruled Western Ukraine, studies of OCS texts and language were produced by O. Kaluzhniatsky, P. Kopko, I. Svientsitsky, I. Ohiienko, O. Kolessa, I. Pankevych, and Ya. Hordynsky. OCS grammars for Ukrainian gymnasiums and theological seminaries were written by M. Vozniak (1925), S. Karkhut (1931), A. Hryhoriev (1938), and N. Rusnak (1943) in Western Ukraine, and by the émigré scholars J. Rudnyckyj (1947) and V. Lev (1956).

Russian studies. Before the Revolution of 1917 many prominent Russian specialists (eg, I. Rizhsky, Sreznevsky, M. Maksymovych, N. Lavrovsky, Potebnia, M. Khalansky, A. Sobolevsky, D. Ovsianiko-Kulikovsky, P. Vladimirov, D. Zelenin, Durnovo, M. Dashkevych, S. Kulbakin, M. Sumtsov, V. Peretts, Hrunsky, M. Gudzii, B. Liapunov, and V. Mochulsky) taught at universities in Russian-ruled Ukraine and influenced the development of Ukrainian studies. After the revolution many Russian specialists emigrated to the West (eg, Chyzhevsky) or to Russia. Others were repressed during the Stalinist terror. In interwar Lviv Svientsitsky and V. Vavryk were Russian specialists.

Because of the Stalinist nationality policy (the promotion of Russian as the second native language in Ukraine), from the 1930s Russian studies had a preferred status in Soviet Ukraine. University departments of the Russian language also doubled as departments of general linguistics, especially after 1945, and Russian subjects were allotted increasingly more space in journals devoted to Ukrainian philology, such as *Ukraïns'ka mova i literatura v shkoli*, *Movoznavstvo*, and *Radians'ke literaturoznavstvo*, in addition to having their own Russian-language serials (eg, *Voprosy russkoi literatury*, *Voprosy russkogo iazykoznaniia*). The main centers of Russian studies were in Kiev and Kharkiv (and, to a lesser extent, Odessa), which trained the Russian specialists teaching in Dnipropetrovske and (after 1945) in Lviv and Chernivtsi.

In the Soviet period efforts were initially applied to the writing of postsecondary textbooks, some of which have been used outside Ukraine. Among the many books published were ones on the history of the Russian language by Bulakhovsky (1929, 1931, 1935; 2 vols, 1941, 1948), O. Finkel and M. Bazhenov (1941), and F. Huzhva (1967); on Russian historical grammar by Bulakhovsky (1921–31, 1935) and N. Bukatevich, S. Savitskaia, and L. Usacheva (1974); on Russian historical syntax by Ya. Sprynchak (2 vols, 1960, 1964); on the history of standard Russian by V. Brodskaia and S. Tsalenchuk (1951) and G. Shkliarevsky (1959, 1967, 1968); on Ukrainian and Russian comparative grammar by T. Baimut, Boichuk, M. Volynsky, M. Zhovtobriukh, T. Malyna, and S. Samiilenko (1957, 1961), and by M. Britsyn, Zhovtobriukh, and Maiboroda (1978); and on East Slavic comparative grammar by Bukatevich, I. Hrytsiutenko, H. Mizhevska, M. Pavliuk, Savitskaia, and

F. Smahlenko (1958). A Russian etymological dictionary was compiled by H. Tsyhanenko (1970).

Russianists in Ukraine studied various aspects of the Russian language, such as phonetics (P. Kryvoruchko, N. Yakovenko, L. Skalozub, L. Tsyptsiura), morphology (H. Kyrychenko, A. Hermanovych, N. Vakulenko), word formation (I. Markovsky, E. Okhomush, V. Franchuk), lexicology (I. Sydorenko, V. Syrotina, M. Muravytska, A. Matveev), intonation (Yakovenko), stylistics (V. Masalsky, L. Loseva, L. Rikhter, S. Puhach), dialectology (M. Tikhomirova, Usacheva, Loseva, V. Stolbunova, L. Buznik, Britsyn), and especially syntax (V. Borkovsky, L. Kirina, V. Rinberg, E. Kuzmicheva, H. Pavlovska, H. Chumakov, R. Shvets, A. Akishyna, N. Arvat, M. Karpenko, Finkel, Huzhva, L. Boldyrev, Loseva, Kryvoruchko, M. Ionina, V. Kononenko).

Ukrainian specialists on Russian literature wrote about many writers, particularly N. Gogol (H. Izhakevych, N. Krutikova, D. Miroshnyk, Zaslavsky), M. Lermontov (D. Iofanov, I. Zaslavsky), A. Pushkin (Bulakhovsky, Gudzii, Rylsky, O. Biletsky, Krutikova), A. Chekhov (V. Kapustin, Krutikova, M. Levchenko), N. Nekrasov (V. Malkin, Ye. Shabliovsky, D. Chaly), L. Tolstoi (A. Chicherin, Krutikova), M. Gorky (Shkliarevsky, O. Burmistrenko, Karpenko, Syrotina, N. Zhuk), V. Maiakovsky (A. Trostianetsky, H. Makarov), M. Sholokhov (S. Koltakov), A. Tolstoi (T. Chertorizhskaia, V. Verbytska, L. Zvereva), K. Fedin (H. Sodol, V. Oleshkevych), A. Fadeev (Izhakevych, S. Tsypin, Tsalenchuk, I. Kruk, H. Samiilenko), L. Leonov (V. Ruban, Kruk, M. Malynovska), V. Shishkov (M. Sydorenko), and A. Tvardovsky (A. Khvylia), as well as the Russian works of H. Kvitka-Osnovianenko (T. Velychko), T. Shevchenko (P. Petrova, Chertorizhskaia, L. Kodatska, and others), and other Ukrainian writers. A two-volume multiauthor monograph on Ukrainian-Russian literary relations (ed Krutikova et al) appeared in Kiev in 1987.

Polish studies. Until 1939 Lviv University, the Ossolineum Institute, and numerous Polish scholarly journals and learned societies made Lviv a major center of Polish scholarship, with specialists in the fields of Polish language (A. Małecki, W. Taszycki, S. Rospond, S. Hrabec), literature (R. Pilat, E. Kucharski, J. Kleiner, S. Kolbuszewski, R. Ingarden), and ethnography (A. Kalina, A. Fiszer). Lviv's Ukrainian philologists (eg, O. Ohonovsky, P. Kopko, K. Studynsky, V. Shchurat, I. Franko) also wrote frequently on Polish subjects. In the 1920s and early 1930s the Soviet Ukrainian scholar S. Rodzevych wrote about Polish literature. After the Second World War Galicia's Polish scholars were repatriated, and only a few Ukrainian specialists in the Polish language (eg, L. Humetska, M. Onyshkevych) and literature (eg, T. Pachovsky, R. Kyrchiv) remained active in Lviv. Kiev became a major postwar center of studies in Polish literature (Rylsky, V. Vedina, H. Verves, Yu. Bulakhovska, O. Tsybenko, S. Levinska, P. Verbytsky, I. Lozynsky, V. Radyshevsky) and language (O. Tkachenko, M. Pavliuk, Levinska, M. Pylynsky, V. Rusanivsky). A few Polonists were active in Chernivtsi (eg, V. Fedorishchev). Postwar émigré scholars who wrote on Polish linguistic subjects included Shevelov and O. Horbach.

Belarusian studies. Belarusian studies were less developed in Ukraine. Until 1939 they were cultivated in Lviv by scholars such as Svientsitsky and L. Ossowski. In Soviet Ukraine scholars such as P. Buzuk in the 1920s and L. Humetska, Z. Veselovska, V. Kupriienko, H. Pivtorak,

I. Vykhovanets, and A. Nepokupny in the postwar period studied Belarusian linguistic problems. In the West, Shevelov also contributed to Belarusian linguistic studies.

Slovak, Czech, and Sorbian studies. In the early 20th century, Slovak ethnography and history were studied in Lviv by scholars such as V. Hnatiuk and S. Tomashivsky. In the interwar period Slovak linguistic subjects were studied at Lviv University by Stieber. In the postwar period scholars such as Onyshkevych and V. Andel (author of a textbook on the Slovak language [1972]) in Lviv, Y. Dzendzelivsky and M. Symulyk in Uzhhorod, and V. Kolomiiets-Melnychuk, V. Skrypka, and M. Haidai in Kiev wrote on the Slovak language. Slovak literature was studied by H. Syvachenko and others. Scholars living in Slovakia, such as M. Molnar and M. Nevrlý in Bratislava and I. Matsynsky in Prešov, also wrote on Slovak literature and Slovak-Ukrainian literary relations.

In the prerevolutionary period and the 1920s the main centers of Czech philological studies were Kharkiv (Bulakhovsky) and Kiev (Florinsky, A. Stepovych, Ye. Rykhlik). In the postwar period Kiev remained the main research center of Czech linguistics (Bulakhovsky, Melnychuk, Kolomiiets-Melnychuk, R. Kravchuk, V. Pitinov, V. Tsviakh, Y. Andersh), literature (P. Hontar, V. Shevchuk, F. Pohrebennyk, I. Zhuravska, V. Motorny, Syvachenko, and others), and folklore (Skrypka, Haidai). The Czech language was also studied by Lviv scholars, such as Trofymovych, H. Lastovetska, Andel, and M. Pushkar (author of textbooks on modern Czech [1963], historical phonetics [1965], and historical morphology [1970, 1972]).

In the interwar period the Sorbian languages were researched by the Lviv Polish linguists Taszycki and Stieber. In the postwar period they were studied in Drohobych by I. Kovalyk and in Lviv by Trofymovych (author of a textbook on the Upper Sorbian language [1964] and coauthor, with Motorny, of books on the history of Sorbian literature [1970, 1987]).

Bulgarian and Serbo-Croatian studies. In central Ukraine the Southern Slavic languages were studied in the context of Old Church Slavonic at Kharkiv, Odessa, and Kiev universities by scholars such as P. Biliarsky, Hryhorovych, A. Kochubinsky, B. Liapunov, Jagić, and M. Popruzhenko. M. Drinov of Kharkiv University wrote pioneering works on Bulgarian and South Slavic history. Bulgarian studies were later pursued in Kharkiv by Kulbakin and Bulakhovsky, and in Kiev by Florinsky, K. Radchenko, and Stepovych. In the 1930s D. Sheludko wrote on Bulgarian literature. In the postwar period modern Bulgarian was studied by Bernshtein (author of an atlas of Bulgarian dialects in the USSR [1958]), Pavliuk, N. Kossek, S. Ovcharuk, T. Nikolaevskaia, I. Stoianov, and others. Studies of Bulgarian literature were written by V. Zakharzhevska, N. Shumada, O. Shpylova, M. Golberg, O. Hrybovska, M. Maliarchuk, and others. O. Mordvintsev studied Bulgarian folklore and ethnography.

Serbo-Croatian studies were pursued in the prerevolutionary period by Kulbakin, Florinsky, Radchenko, Stepovych, and Hnatiuk. In the postwar period I. Zheliezniak in Kharkiv and Z. Rozova in Lviv specialized in the Serbo-Croatian language. Serbian and Croatian literatures were studied by Ye. Kyryliuk, V. Hrymych, P. Rudiakov, I. Yushchuk, and others. Serbo-Croatian folk songs in Ukraine were studied by M. Huts.

(See also *Linguistics, *Literature studies, *Polish language in Ukraine, *Russian language in Ukraine, and *Slovak-Ukrainian linguistic relations.)

BIBLIOGRAPHY

Iagich, I. [Jagić, V.]. *Istoriia slavianskoi filologii* (St Petersburg 1910; repr, Leipzig 1967)
Lehr-Spławiński, T. *Zarys dziejów słowianoznawstwa polskiego* (Cracow 1948)
Manning, C.A. *A History of Slavic Studies in the United States* (Milwaukee 1957)
Kravchuk, R. *Z istoriï slov'ians'koho movoznavstva (vydatni slavisty-movoznavtsi)* (Kiev 1961)
Kurz, J.; et al (eds). *Slovanská filologie na Univerzitě Karlove* (Prague 1968)
Izhakevich, G.; Romanova, N.; Franchuk, V. (eds). *Traditsii russkogo iazykoznaniia na Ukraine* (Kiev 1977)
Kudělka, M.; Šimeček, Z.; Šťastný, V.; Večerka, R. *Československá slavistika v letech 1918–1939* (Prague 1977)
Hrozienčik, J. (ed). *Štúdie z dejín svetovej slavistiky do polovice 19. storočia* (Bratislava 1978)
D'iakov, V.; et al (eds). *Issledovaniia po istoriografii slavianovedeniia i balkanistiki* (Moscow 1981)
– *Istoriki-slavisty SSSR: Biobibliograficheskii slovar'-spravochnik* (Moscow 1981)
Gerhardt, D.; Harder, H.B.; et al (eds). *Materialen zur Geschichte der Slavistik in Deutschland*, 2 vols (Wiesbaden 1982, 1987)
Myl'nikov, A.; et al (eds). *Slavianovedenie i balkanistika v zarubezhnykh stranakh* (Moscow 1983)
Slavistyka (Kiev 1983)
D'iakov, V. (ed). *Istoriograficheskie issledovaniia po slavianovedeniiu i balkanistike* (Moscow 1984)
Hamm, J.; Wytrzens, G. (eds). *Beiträge zur Geschichte der Slawistik in nichtslawischen Ländern* (Vienna 1985)
Markov, D.; D'iakov, V. (eds). *Slavianovedenie v dorevoliutsionnoi Rossii: Izuchenie iuzhnykh i zapadnykh slavian* (Moscow 1988)

O. Horbach, R. Senkus

Slavin, Lazar, b 11 June 1906 in Vitsebsk, Belarus, d 30 November 1971 in Kiev. Archeologist of Jewish origin; corresponding member of the AN URSR (now ANU) from 1939. He studied at Leningrad University (1923–6) before working at the USSR Academy of Sciences Institute of the History of Material Culture (1929–38). He was sent from Leningrad to Kiev in 1938 as the deputy director of the ANU Institute of Archeology, and soon became its director (1939–41 and 1944–6). Slavin was a gifted organizer and he quickly rebuilt the institute, which had been thoroughly savaged by two purges of Ukrainian archeologists (1933 and 1937); however, this was done using mainly Russian archeologists. He remained with the institute as deputy director (1946–9), then as a scholarly associate (1949–71). From 1945 to 1970 he also headed the University of Kiev's Department of Archeology and Museum Studies. His specialization was the archeology of the northern Black Sea region, particularly the *Olbia settlement. He published over 70 scholarly articles and monographs, including *Ol'viia* (1938) and *Drevnii gorod Ol'viia* (The Ancient City of Olbia, 1951).

Slavinsky, Maksym [Slavins'kyj] (Slavynsky; pseuds: M. Holovaty, S. Lavynsky, Obozrevatel, Observator), b 12 August 1868 in Stavyshche, Tarashcha county, Kiev gubernia, d November 1945 in Kiev. Civic and political leader, publicist, and poet. After graduating from the law faculty of Kiev University he lived in Katerynoslav, where he edited the newspaper *Pridneprovskii krai*. From 1898 he lived in St Petersburg, where he was a coeditor of the pro-

Maksym Slavinsky

gressive newspaper *Severnyi kur'er* and the journal *Vestnik Evropy*. He was editor of *Ukrainskii vestnik* (1906), the organ of the Ukrainian caucus of the First State Duma, and then official publisher and technical editor of *Ukrainskii narod v ego proshlom i nastoiashchem* (The Ukrainian People in the Past and Present, 2 vols, 1914, 1916). He became a member of the Ukrainian Party of Socialists-Federalists (1917–18), and in 1917 he was a representative of the Central Rada to the Provisional Government in St Petersburg. He was elected head of the commission to develop proposals for the restructuring of the Russian Empire as a federation.

Slavinsky returned to Ukraine in 1918. Under the Hetman government he was a member of the council of the foreign affairs ministry, ambassador to the Don region, and a participant in the talks with Soviet Russia (May–June 1918). In the second government of F. Lyzohub (1918) he was minister of labor. Under the Directory he headed the diplomatic mission of the UNR in Prague (1919). From 1923 Slavinsky taught modern history at the Ukrainian Husbandry Academy and the history of Western European literature at the Ukrainian Higher Pedagogical Institute in Prague. He was arrested by the Soviet authorities in Prague in 1945, and died in a Kiev prison.

Slavinsky wrote many historical, literary, and publicistic articles on nationhood, including 'Shcho take natsiia?' (What Is a Nation?), 'Natsiia i inteligentsiia' (The Nation and the Intelligentsia), and 'Natsional'na struktura Rosiï' (The National Structure of Russia), as well as a popular textbook on the history of Ukraine (pub in 1947). He also wrote lyric poetry. Together with Lesia Ukrainka Slavinsky translated and published H. Heine's *Buch der Lieder* as *Knyha pisen'* (1892); some of the songs became immensely popular, particularly 'Koly rozluchaiut'sia dvoie' (When Two [People] Part; music by M. Lysenko). Slavinsky also translated the works of J. Goethe, A. Mickiewicz, and R. Rolland and works from Czech literature. His memoirs were published in the newspaper *Ameryka* during the 1950s.

A. Zhukovsky

Slavische Rundschau. A German-language journal of Slavic studies, published by the German Society for Slavic Studies in Prague in 1929–40 (a total of 17 volumes). Edited by F. Spina, G. Gesemann, and others, it contained regular chronicles of cultural and scholarly developments in Slavic countries, as well as bibliographies and book reviews, and included separate sections devoted to Ukrainian affairs and publications.

Slavistica. A series of booklets and monographs in Slavic and Ukrainian studies, primarily philology and linguistics, published in Ukrainian and English by the Ukrainian Free Academy of Sciences (now *Ukrainian Academy of Arts and Sciences), initially in Augsburg (3 issues in 1948), then in Winnipeg, and since 1977 in Montreal. Edited until 1973 by J.B. Rudnyckyj, it has published works by Rudnyckyj, V. Chaplenko, R. Smal-Stotsky, G.Y. Shevelov, P. Kovaliv, I. Ohiienko, G. Simpson, W. Kirkconnell, P. Fylypovych, M. Mandryka, C. Manning, S. Hordynsky, M. Ovcharenko, O. Woycenko, O. Baran, P. Odarchenko, and others. Its 87th title appeared in 1986.

Slavonic-Ruthenian language. The bookish language used in 15th- to 18th-century Ukrainian and Belarusian scholarly, publicistic, and literary works. The term *slavenorosskii* (Slavonic-Ruthenian [SR]) was introduced in the late 15th century and was popularized by P. *Zhytetsky (1889). SR evolved out of the Ukrainian redaction of 11th- to 14th-century Church Slavonic, which became archaized and came under the influence of Middle Bulgarian and Serbian in the 14th century as a result of the grammatical and stylistic reforms of the Bulgarian patriarch Euthymius (see *Orthography). From the mid-17th century it influenced the norms of literary Russian. From the mid-18th century its Left-Bank Ukrainian variant became so much like the Russian variant that the latter took precedence. In the 1720s and 1730s, SR was introduced in Srem and Bačka (now in Yugoslavia) by Russians and Ukrainians teaching there; it remained the foundation of the archaized Serbian bookish language for over a century. In Galicia, Bukovyna, and Transcarpathia, SR survived in the form of a lexically Russified bookish language (*yazychiie) until the first half of the 20th century.

SR differs from the Old Ukrainian bookish language in its lexicon and style (Latinisms, Polonisms, calques, hypotactic and periodic sentence construction, and periphrasis). Its norms were laid out in the grammar *Adelphotes (Lviv 1591) and in the grammars of L. *Zyzanii (1596) and M. *Smotrytsky (1619). Its vocabulary was codified in the lexicons of L. Zyzanii (1596) and P. *Berynda (1627, 1653), the dictionary *Synonima slavenorosskaia, Ye. *Slavynetsky's Latin-Slavonic (1642) and Slavonic-Latin (1649, with A. Koretsky-Satanovsky) dictionaries, and in smaller Slavonic-Polish dictionaries (anon, Suprasl 1722, repr Pochaiv 1751, 1756, 1804; Y. Levytsky, 1830).

SR avoided clearly Ukrainian and Belarusian phonetic traits (*ikan'je*), retained etymological spellings (the letters ы and ѣ), did not mark the secondary doubling of consonants, introduced the hardened *c* in suffixes, and retained the Church Slavonic cases and their endings in declension and conjugation. The meanings of obsolete verb forms (the aorist and imperfective), artificially created moods based on Greek grammar (the optative and subjunctive), and word-formation devices (eg, -*tel'nыj* [cf -*abilis*, -*andus*], *xlebotvorec* 'baker') were taken from the Greek and Latin. The system of conjunctions and the wide use of active participles and the 'dative absolute' were taken from Old Slavonic syntax (oriented on the language of the Ostrih Bible and liturgical books). The vocabulary was based on borrowings from the Bible, Greek, Latin, and, to the 18th century, Polish; the use of vernacular dialectal expressions was avoided. The synthetic character of SR resulted in a varied application by authors, depending on their erudition and themes. The syntax of SR had a discernible impact on the chancery language.

BIBLIOGRAPHY
Hrushevs'kyi, M. *Istoriia ukraïns'koï literatury*, 5 (Kiev 1926–7; repr, New York 1960)
Zhytets'kyi, P. 'Narys literaturnoï istoriï ukraïns'koï movy v XVII st.,' in *Vybrani pratsi: Filolohiia*, ed L. Masenko (Kiev 1987)
O. Horbach

Slavophiles. Adherents of a philosophical, ideological, social, and political movement in Russia in 1840–70 that idealized everything Russian; their outlook was opposed to that of the Westerners, who advocated a broad adoption of Western ways in Russia. The Slavophiles celebrated the difference between Russia and the West; they contrasted Orthodoxy ('the only true Christian religion') with Catholicism and Protestantism and Muscovite traditions with Western ones, and advocated a pan-Slavic unity under Russia's hegemony. They praised the old way of life and the social system of Muscovy, particularly of the pre-Petrine period, including the commune, artel, and village council. The chief spokesmen of Slavophilism – A. Khomiakov, I. Kireevsky, I. and K. Aksakov, Yu. Samarin,

and I. Belaev – advocated the abolition of serfdom and the introduction of some democratic rights, but they also favored a centralized Russian Empire and Russia's leadership among the Slavic nations. They opposed independence for Ukraine and even for Poland. Among Ukrainians the Slavophiles had little influence. Some ethnographic and historical works of M. Maksymovych and O. Bodiansky (both worked in Moscow) reflect Slavophile ideas. The attempts of the Aksakov brothers to gain the co-operation of T. Shevchenko, M. Kostomarov, and P. Kulish with the Slavophiles proved unsuccessful.

Slavs (*sloviany*). The largest group of ethnically and linguistically related peoples in Europe. They belong to the Indo-European linguistic family and are descended from the ancient Slavs mentioned in Greco-Roman and Byzantine sources. Occupying eastern and southeastern Europe, they are usually divided into the East Slavs (Ukrainians, Russians, and Belarusians), West Slavs (Poles, Czechs, Slovaks, and Wends), and South Slavs (Bulgarians, Serbs, Croats, Slovenes, and Macedonians).

The original homeland of the ancient Slavs has not been identified, but by the beginning of the 1st millennium BC

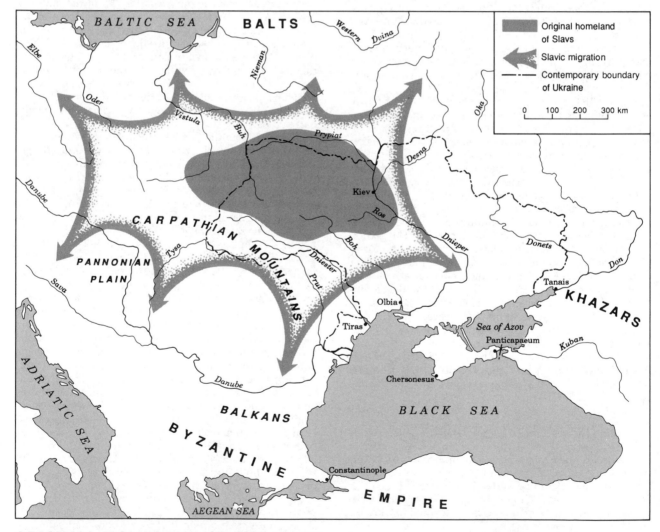

ORIGINAL HOMELAND OF THE SLAVS

they were the dominant population in the region extending from the Elbe and the Oder rivers in the west to the upper Dnieper in the east. They were a peaceful people who practiced farming and animal husbandry and developed handicrafts and trade. Their religion was animistic: they worshiped ancestors and various spirits in nature and a pantheon of heavenly deities, such as Perun, Dazhboh, and Svaroh.

The division of the ancient Slavs into various branches and tribes began in the 2nd to 4th centuries AD, when the Germanic tribes, such as the Goths, moved south and split the Slavs into eastern and western groups. Then, at the end of the 5th century, when the Huns had been overcome, the Slavs expanded southward. In the south they formed two tribal confederations, of the *Antes and the *Sklavenes. Soon those disintegrated into separate tribes, including the Polianians, Siverianians, Derevlianians, and Volhynians. Some of those tribes were later brought together under Kievan Rus'.

In the 19th century the idea of Slavic cultural and political unity (see *Pan-Slavism) became influential among Slavic peoples who were undergoing a national revival. Some movements, such as the Slavophile one in Russia, tried to harness that idea to the imperial ambitions of Russia.

BIBLIOGRAPHY
Niederle, L. *Slovanské starožitnosti*, 4 vols (Prague 1902–24)
Lehr-Spławiński, T. *O pochodzeniu i praojczyźnie Słowian* (Poznań 1946)
Tretiakov, P. *Vostochnoslavianskie plemena* (Moscow 1953)
Dvornik, F. *The Slavs: Their Early History and Civilization* (Boston 1956)
Baran, V. *Ranni slov'iany mizh Dnistrom i Pryp'iattiu* (Kiev 1972)
Petrov, V. *Etnohenez slovian* (Kiev 1972)
Pasternak, Ia. *Ranni slov'iany v istorychnykh, arkheolohichnykh ta lingvistychnykh doslidzhenniakh* (Toronto–New York 1976)
Váňa, Z. *The World of the Ancient Slavs* (London 1983)
Conte, F. *Les Slaves: Aux origines des civilisations d'Europe centrale et orientale* (Paris 1986)

Slavuta. III-7. A city (1989 pop 35,100) on the Horyn River and a raion center in Khmelnytskyi oblast. In 1634 the town of Slavutyna arose by the amalgamation of two villages, Derazhnia and Volia. Later it was renamed Slavuta. In 1754 the town was granted the rights of *Magdeburg law. After the second partition of Poland in 1793, Slavuta was annexed by Russia and became part of Iziaslav county in Volhynia gubernia. Its owners, the Sanguszko family, established their residence there and built a horse-breeding stable (1803), a woolen-cloth factory (1818), a paper factory, and a machine factory. Those enterprises grew during the 19th century, particularly after the construction of the Shepetivka–Zdolbuniv railway line. In 1923 Slavuta became a raion center of Volhynia gubernia, and in 1938 it attained city status. Today its chief industries are building-materials manufacturing, woodworking, and metalworking.

Slavutych, Yar [Slavutyč, Jar] (né Hryhorii Zhuchenko), b 11 January 1918 in Blahodatne, Oleksandriia county, Kherson gubernia. Poet and literary scholar; president of the Shevchenko Scientific Society in western Canada since 1976. A graduate of the Zaporizhia Pedagogical Institute (1940) and the University of Pennsylvania (PH D, 1955), he taught Ukrainian at the United States Army Language

Yar Slavutych

School in Monterey, California (1955–60), and the University of Alberta (1960–83). Since 1945 he has published 12 books of poetry, including two volumes of collected works (1963, 1978) and, the most recent collection, *Zhyvi smoloskypy* (Living Torches, 1983). His poems have appeared in Ukrainian émigré periodicals and anthologies and in Canadian English-language anthologies, and some have been translated into English (*Oasis* [1959], *The Conquerors of the Prairies* [trilingual edn 1984]), French (*L'Oiseau de feu* [1976]), German, Hungarian, Russian, and other European languages. They have also been set to music (by S. Yaremenko, H. Kytasty, and E. Wolf) and have been recorded by the Ukrainian Bandurist Chorus of Detroit. Slavutych has also written a book of memoiristic sketches (1957; 3rd rev edn 1985), the booklets *The Muse in Prison* (1956) and *Modern Ukrainian Poetry* (1957), the textbooks *Conversational Ukrainian* (1959; 4th edn 1973) and *Ukrainian for Beginners* (1962; 5th edn 1975), a survey of Ukrainian poetry in Canada (1976), and literary and onomastic articles and reviews in émigré and Canadian scholarly periodicals and collections. The editor of the literary almanac *Pivnichne siaivo* (5 vols, 1964–71), two volumes of papers on Ukrainian settlers in western Canada (1973, 1975), and an anthology of Ukrainian poetry in Canada (1975), he also compiled an annotated bibliography of books of Ukrainian literature published in Canada (1984; 2nd rev edn 1986) and translated into Ukrainian a book of selected poems by J. Keats (1958). A collection of articles and reviews about his poetic works (1978, ed W. Zyla) and a bibliography of his writings (1985; rev edn 1986) have appeared.

R. Senkus

Slavutych [Slavutyč]. A city (1989 pop 15,900) on the left bank of the Dnieper River at the mouth of the Desna River, 50 km from Chornobyl, in Chernihiv oblast. It was founded in 1987 for the workers of the Chornobyl Nuclear Power Station, who had been evacuated from Prypiat and Chornobyl after the accident at the station. In 1988 it was granted city status.

Slavynetsky, Yepifanii [Slavynec'kyj, Jepifanij], b ?, d 19 November 1675 in Moscow. Churchman, theologian, philologist, and translator. He studied Greek, Latin, Polish, and theology at the Kiev Epiphany Brotherhood School (until 1632) and then at various European academies. Upon his return to Kiev he took monastic vows and became a hieromonk of the Kievan Cave Monastery (1642–9) and a professor at the Kievan Mohyla College

(Academy). In 1649 he was summoned by Tsar Aleksei Mikhailovich to Moscow to teach at the monastery school and translate and prepare liturgical books, including a translation of the Bible. While still in Kiev, he compiled a Latin-Slavonic (Ukrainian) lexicon (1642) based on the Polish-Latin lexicons of A. Calepino and G. Knapski. He revised this dictionary with A. Koretsky-Satanovsky in Moscow (1650). He also prepared a Greek-Slavonic-Latin lexicon (before 1675) and compiled a dictionary of religious terms for use in translating church books, and authored over 50 sermons. Although none of these works were published in his lifetime, they circulated widely throughout Muscovy, Ukraine, and Eastern Europe and greatly influenced early Slavic philology. In Moscow, Slavynetsky supported the church reforms introduced by Patriarch Nikon; he drafted many reforms himself and revised numerous church books to bring them into line with the new policies.

BIBLIOGRAPHY
Rotar, I. *Epifanii Slavinetskii, literaturnyi deiatel' XVII veka* (Kiev 1901)

A. Zhukovsky

Sławek, Walery, b 2 November 1879 in Ukraine, d 2 May 1939 in Warsaw. Polish politician. A leading figure in the Polish Socialist party (PPS), he was a close associate of J. Piłsudski. As a representative of the Polish Ministry of Military Affairs he was a signatory to the Polish-Ukrainian army convention of 24 April 1920. After 1926 he emerged as one of the leaders of the *Sanacja regime. He was a cofounder and chairman of the Nonpartisan Bloc of Co-operation with the Government (1927–35), a delegate to the Polish Sejm (1928–38), marshal of the Polish Sejm (1938), and premier of Poland (1930–1 and 1935). Sławek was a moderate in Ukrainian matters, who distanced himself from certain actions of the Polish Roman Catholic church and tried to reach an understanding with the Galician Ukrainian political mainstream (the Ukrainian National Democratic Alliance) following the *Pacification in 1930.

Sleshynsky, Ivan [Slešyns'kyj], b 23 July 1854 in Lysianka, Cherkasy county, Kiev gubernia, d 9 March 1931 in Cracow, Poland. Ukrainian-Polish mathematician. He graduated from Odessa University in 1875 and continued his studies under the great German mathematician K. Weierstrass at Berlin University (PH D, 1882). He was professor at Odessa (1883–1909) and Cracow (1911–24) universities and did research on continued fractions, the least squares method, and the axiomatic proof theory based on mathematical logic. He was one of the first promoters of mathematical logic in the Russian Empire.

Slidamy maloï sviatoï (In the Footsteps of the Little Saint). A popular Ukrainian Catholic journal published quarterly, bimonthly, and again quarterly in Bois-Colombes, France (1948–52), Edmonton (1952–66), and, since 1966, Amiens, France. The editors have been S. Saprun and, since 1952, Rev Yu. Prokopiv.

Slipansky, Andrii [Slipans'kyj, Andrij], b 5 October 1896 in Nenadykha, Tarashcha county, Kiev gubernia, d ? Agronomist. Upon graduating he worked in different research institutions in Kharkiv and was appointed a professor at the Ukrainian Scientific Research Institute of Economics and Agricultural Organization. In the 1930s he served as vice-president of the All-Ukrainian Academy of Agricultural Sciences. His publications dealt with agronomy and agricultural economics. He was arrested in the Stalinist terror of the 1930s and sent to a prison camp, where he perished.

Slipchenko, Pavlo [Slipčenko], b 12 July 1904 in Synivka, Hadiache county, Poltava gubernia. Specialist in the field of hydro-technology. He studied in Kharkiv and worked on many major hydro-constructions in Ukraine. In 1959–61 he served as director of the Institute of the Organization and Mechanization of Construction of the Ukrainian SSR Academy of Construction and Architecture, from 1960 as a member of the academy's presidium, and in 1962–3 as its vice-president. His main technical contributions concerned the mechanization of construction technology for hydro-structures.

Slipchuk, Petro [Slipčuk], b 19 January 1914 in Minyne, Radomyshl county, Kiev gubernia, d 5 November 1979 in Kiev. Poet and humorist. He is the author of collections of humor and satire, among them *Baiky* (Fables, 1944), *Liudozhery* (Cannibals, 1945), *Iak dbaiesh, tak i maiesh* (What You Work At Is What You Get, 1955), *Otaki dila* (That's the Way It Is, 1961), *Iushka z pertsem* (Broth with Pepper, 1967), and *Vinok baiok* (A Garland of Fables, 1973).

Slipko, Yurii, b 26 May 1912 in Slipky (now Vynnyky), Kobeliaky county, Poltava gubernia, d 4 October 1969. Poet. In the early 1930s he worked as a teacher and newspaper editor. He began publishing in 1930 in *Nova generatsiia* and other journals. He was arrested during the Stalinist terror (1934–5) and imprisoned in a labor camp in the Kolyma region. After being released in 1947, he worked as a miner in the Donbas. During the post-Stalin thaw he began writing again and published the collections *Proloh do pisni* (Prologue to a Song, 1966) and *Zelena fantaziia* (The Green Fantasy, 1968). Published posthumously was the collection *Na liudnim vichi* (At the Crowded Public Assembly, 1971).

Slipko-Moskaltsiv, Kostiantyn [Slipko-Moskal'civ, Kostjantyn], b 3 June 1901 in Warsaw, d ? Painter and art scholar. He taught at the Kharkiv Institute of People's Education (from 1925 to the early 1930s) and researched children's art. He published articles on art in *Chervonyi shliakh* and wrote the books *M. Boichuk* (1930), *S. Vasyl'kivs'kyi* (1930), and *O. Murashko* (1931). He was arrested during the Stalinist terror, and his fate is unknown.

Sliporid River. A right-bank tributary of the Sula River that flows for 83 km through the Dnieper Lowland in Poltava oblast and drains a basin area of 560 sq km. The river has a width of 4–10 m and is used for irrigation. Five sluices are located on it.

Slipy, Yosyf [Slipyj, Josyf] (Slipy-Kobernytsky-Dychkovsky), b 17 February 1892 in Zazdrist, Terebovlia county, Galicia, d 7 September 1984 in Rome. Head of the Ukrainian Catholic church, major archbishop, metropolitan of Halych, archbishop of Lviv and bishop of Kamianets-Podilskyi, cardinal (from 1965), and theologian; full member of the Shevchenko Scientific Society from 1930.
    Slipy began studying theology in Lviv at the Greek

Cardinal Yosyf Slipy

Catholic Theological Seminary and at the university (1911–12). He was ordained by Metropolitan A. *Sheptytsky in October 1917, continued his studies at the Jesuit theological faculty in Innsbruck (TH D, 1918), and then defended his habilitation at Innsbruck University (1920). He completed his studies in Rome at the Gregorianum with a *magister agregatus* in dogmatics and a second habilitation (1924). In 1922 Slipy began to teach dogmatics at the Lviv Theological Seminary. He soon showed his abilities as an organizer of Ukrainian theological studies, in helping to found the quarterly *Bohosloviia* (which he also edited) and the *Ukrainian Theological Scholarly Society, whose *Pratsi* he also edited. In late 1925 he was appointed rector of the theological seminary, where he established the Asketychna biblioteka (Ascetic Library) monograph series. In 1928 he was named the first rector of the *Greek Catholic Theological Academy. This institution soon emerged as the most important center of Ukrainian Catholic theological study and training; it published numerous works on religious topics, developed a large museum of church objects and icons, and trained many priests and theologians. In 1935 Metropolitan Sheptytsky named Slipy canon of St George's Cathedral and archdean of Lviv archeparchy. In October 1939, after the outbreak of the Second World War and the Soviet occupation of Western Ukraine, Sheptytsky nominated Slipy as his coadjutor. The nomination was ratified by Pope Pius XII in November 1939, and in December Slipy was secretly consecrated and given the title Archbishop of Serrei. After Sheptytsky's death on 1 November 1944, Slipy succeeded him as metropolitan of Halych, archbishop of Lviv, and bishop of Kamianets-Podilskyi.

On 11 April 1945, after the consolidation of Soviet rule in Western Ukraine, Slipy, together with all the other Greek Catholic bishops, was arrested. He was sentenced at a secret trial in 1946 to eight years of hard labor for treason. After the completion of his sentence he was taken to Kiev and told to endorse the liquidation of the Greek Catholic church and renounce his ecclesiastical rights and titles in favor of the Patriarch of Moscow. When he refused, he was again deported to a labor camp. He spent a total of over 18 years in the gulag, but he steadfastly refused to break allegiance with Rome and denounce the pope. In 1963, upon the intervention of Pope John XXIII and the American president J.F. Kennedy, N. Khrushchev finally agreed to his release from a labor camp in Mordovia and permitted him to emigrate. Slipy arrived in Rome on

9 February 1963, where he was greeted as a true Christian martyr and a Ukrainian national hero. The Vatican recognized Slipy as the Ukrainian Catholic major archbishop with expanded powers and authority, and in December 1963 Pope Paul VI named him a member of the Sacred Congregation for Eastern Rite Catholic Churches. In January 1965 he was honored with the title and dignity of cardinal.

Slipy was especially concerned with improving the organization and prestige of his church. In a 11 October 1963 speech at the Second Vatican Council, he proposed the creation of a Ukrainian Catholic patriarchate (see *Patriarch). He also convoked a *synod of Ukrainian bishops, which the Vatican Congregation for the Eastern Churches refused to sanction. In 1969, at the fourth synod of Ukrainian bishops, Slipy declared that the Ukrainian Catholic church 'is now organized as a patriarchate,' and in 1975 he accepted the title of patriarch; this too was opposed by the Vatican. Slipy's efforts toward realizing the separate identity of the Ukrainian Catholic church did meet with success toward the end of his life, however, when Pope John Paul II, in a 1980 letter to him, recognized the legal role of the synod in the Ukrainian Catholic church. The first officially recognized synod of Ukrainian bishops was then called by the pope in March 1980 and presided over by Slipy. The second synod (January–February 1983), also under Slipy, accepted the Statute of the Synod of the Ukrainian Catholic church.

After his 1963 release Slipy also turned his attention to reviving Ukrainian Catholic scholarship. In November 1963 he founded the *Ukrainian Catholic University and an associated publishing house, library, and archive, and revived *Bohosloviia* as the organ of the Ukrainian Theological Scholarly Society (which had been renewed just prior to Slipy's release). He also renewed publication of *Dzvony*, a literary and popular-scientific journal, and *Nyva*, a religious journal. Slipy built the St Sophia Cathedral in Rome, modeled on the St Sophia Cathedral in Kiev, and initiated the publication of *Blahovisnyk Verkhovnoho arkhyiepyskopa vizantiis'ko-ukraïns'koho obriadu*. He purchased a former procurator general's office for his official abode, and established there the Ukrainian Catholic parish of SS Sergius and Bacchus in Rome. He revitalized the Studite Fathers and acquired a monastery for them in Castel Gandolfo, near Rome. He organized branches of the Ukrainian Catholic University in Washington, London, Chicago, and Philadelphia.

As a theologian Slipy was an authority on dogmatic theology and scholastic philosophy. His earliest theological works, including his habilitation theses *Die Trinitätslehre des byzantinischen Patriarchen Photios* (1921) and *De principio spirationis in SS Trinitate* (published in 1926), were concerned with the Holy Trinity and attempted to reconcile Eastern and Western Christian differences over the nature of the Trinity and the procession of the Holy Spirit. A series of his works on the Sacraments was smuggled out of Ukraine in manuscript during the war and published in Yorkton, Saskatchewan (5 books in 3 vols, 1953–60). Slipy also published articles on the Church Union of Berestia, the history of the Ukrainian Catholic church, the influence of St Thomas Aquinas on Ukrainian theology, and other subjects; these have been collected and published in Rome in thirteen volumes (1968–84). In recognition of his scholarly work he was made full (1930) and honorary (1964) member of the Shevchenko Scientific

Society, full member of the Tiberian Academy in Rome (1965), and a member of the Papal Academy of St Thomas (1981). He also received honorary doctorates from the Ukrainian Free University in Munich and from several universities in the United States and Canada. Slipy's remains have been transferred, in accordance with his wishes, to a crypt at St George's Cathedral in Lviv. The ceremony was conducted on 28 August 1992 with more than a million faithful in attendance.

BIBLIOGRAPHY
Bilaniuk, P. 'The Father of Modern Ecumenism: Patriarch Joseph Cardinal Slipyj (1892–1984): A Biblio-Biographical Sketch,' *Bohosloviia*, no. 48 (1984)
Choma, I.; Muzychka, I. (eds). *Intrepido Pastori: Naukovyi zbirnyk na poshanu Patriiarkha Iosyfa v soroklittia vstuplennia na Halyts'kyi prestil* (Rome 1984)
Pelikan, J. *Confessor between East and West: A Portrait of Ukrainian Cardinal Josyf Slipyj* (Grand Rapids, Mich 1990)

W. Lencyk

Slisarenko, Anatolii, b 30 March 1923 in Kiev. Film director and screenwriter. He completed study in the actor's (1948) and director's (1949) faculties at the Kiev Institute of Theater Arts. He has worked in the Ukrainian Studio of Chronicle-Documentary Films (1950–6 and since 1963) and the Kiev Artistic Film Studio (1956–61). He has directed four feature films and many documentaries and written two collections of prose (1979, 1985).

Oleksa Slisarenko   Fedir Sliusarenko

Slisarenko, Oleksa (pseud of Oleksa Snisar), b 28 March 1891 in Konivtsov *khutir* (now Shyputove), Vovchanske county, Kharkiv gubernia, d 3 November 1937. Poet and prose writer. In the 1920s he moved to Kharkiv, where he became editor at the Knyhospilka publishing house. He was also coeditor of *Universal'nyi zhurnal* (1928–9). His first published poems appeared in 1910–11, in the student journal *Do pratsi* and in *Rillia*. In Kiev he joined the Bila Studiia group of Ukrainian symbolists and met with members of the Muzahet group. His first anthology of symbolist poetry, *Na berezi Kastal's'komu* (On the Kastal Coast, 1919), was marked by the influence of P. Tychyna, O. Oles, and K. Balmont and other Russian symbolists. It also evinced some elements of expressionism. He subsequently joined the Panfuturist organizations Aspanfut and Komunkult and published the collections of

futurist poems *Poemy* (Poems, 1923) and *Baida* (1928). His attention to form and to poetic expression is evident. He began writing prose in 1924 and published over 20 collections of English- and American-style crime-adventure stories, including *Bunt* (The Revolt, 1928), *Zlamanyi gvynt* (The Broken Bolt, 1929), *Chornyi Anhel* (Black Angel, 1929), *Khlibna rika* (The River of Bread, 1932), and *Straik* (Strike, 1932). His prose deals mainly with the period immediately preceding and during the revolution, and his protagonists are antiheroes, people who are thrust into collisions with the revolution. Slisarenko also wrote poetry for children. In 1931 he published a collection of stories under the pseudonym Omelko Buts, *Posmertna zbirka tvoriv* (Posthumous Collection of Works). A selection of his works appeared in 1930, and a complete six-volume edition was published in 1931–3. Slisarenko was repressed during the Stalinist terror because of his ties to the symbolists and Panfuturists, his membership in Hart and Vaplite, and, particularly, his sharp rebuke of M. Gorky in 1927, after Gorky refused to permit the publication of a translation of *Mat'* (Mother) into Ukrainian. He was arrested in 1934 and sent to the Solovets Islands, where he was shot. In the late 1950s he was rehabilitated, and his novels *Bunt* and *Chornyi Anhel* were republished in 1965 and 1990.

B. Kravtsiv

Sliusarchuk, Kostiantyn [Sljusarčuk, Kostjantyn], b 1869 in Stanyslaviv county, Galicia, d autumn 1919 in Hrushky, near Kamianets-Podilskyi. Senior army officer. During the First World War he was an officer in the Austrian army; he supervised the training of the Legion of Sich Riflemen in 1917. Upon joining the Ukrainian Galician Army in November 1918 he was given command of the Southern Group, which was re-formed in January 1919 into the Lviv Brigade. He was promoted to colonel in January 1919 and was assigned to a diplomatic mission for negotiating a permanent armistice with Poland. In August 1919 Sliusarchuk was put in charge of military training. He died of typhus in the so-called Quadrangle of Death.

Sliusarenko, Fedir [Sljusarenko], b 1886 in Cherkasy, d 9 May 1958 in Prague. Classical philologist, historian, and educator. A graduate of the St Petersburg Historical-Philological Institute, he was active in the St Petersburg Ukrainian Hromada and read public lectures on Ukrainian history and literature. In 1918 he worked for the UNR government in Kiev. He emigrated to Vienna and then Prague and taught classical philology and archeology at the Ukrainian Free University (UVU, 1924–39), where he also served as dean of the philosophy faculty (1936–9). He also taught Slavic history at the Ukrainian Higher Pedagogical Institute, classical archeology at the Ukrainian Studio of Plastic Arts in Prague, and Latin at the Ukrainian Gymnasium in Modržany. His studies and articles on the history of ancient Greece and Ukraine (the Greek colonies on the Black Sea littoral) were published in the serials of the UVU and the Ukrainian Historical-Philological Society in Prague.

Sliusarivna, Mariia [Sljusarivna, Marija], b 31 August 1912 in Kosiv, Galicia. Stage actress. She acted in the Tobilevych Theater (1932–8), the Kotliarevsky Theater and the Lesia Ukrainka Theater (1938–41), the Stanyslaviv Franko Ukrainian Drama Theater (1941–4), and the Ukrainian theater in Austria under H. Sovacheva (1945–8). From 1948 she appeared sporadically with Ukrainian troupes in Canada.

Sliusarsky, Anton [Sljusars'kyj], b 12 January 1901 in Syniukhy, Volodymyr-Volynskyi county, Volhynia gubernia, d 2 March 1980 in Kharkiv. Historian. He graduated from the Institute of People's Education in Kiev in 1929, assumed a lectureship at Kharkiv University in 1934, and served as dean of its Faculty of History in 1947–62. He received his doctorate in history in 1964 and was made a full professor in 1965. He studied the history of the peasantry in central and Slobidska Ukraine, in which field he published *Slobids'ka Ukraïna* (Slobidska Ukraine, 1954), *V.N. Karazin, ego nauchnaia i obshchestvennaia deiatel'nost'* (V.N. Karazyn, His Scientific and Social Activities, 1955), and *Sotsial'no-ekonomicheskoe razvitie Slobozhanshchiny XVII–XVIII vv.* (The Socioeconomic Development of Slobidska Ukraine in the 17th–18th Centuries, 1964). He was coeditor of the volume on Kharkiv oblast (1967) in the series Istoriia mist i sil URSR (History of the Cities and Villages of the Ukrainian SSR).

Sliuzar, Volodymyr [Sljuzar], b 20 January 1895 in Chunkiv, Zastavna county, Bukovyna, d 26 December 1976 in Montreal. Ukrainian Orthodox priest and community leader. After serving as a commander in the 14th Brigade of the Ukrainian Galician Army he completed his theological and law studies at Chernivtsi University. He arrived in Canada in 1923, where he was ordained (1924) and appointed pastor of St Sophia Cathedral in Montreal (1926). He subsequently helped organize parishes in Lachine, Ottawa, Oshawa, Hamilton, and Toronto. After the Second World War he was appointed assistant to Archbishop M. Khoroshy.

Slobidska Ukraine (Slobozhanshchyna). A historical-geographic region in northeastern Ukraine that corresponds closely to the area of the Ostrohozke, Izium, Kharkiv, Okhtyrka, and Sumy Cossack regiments. Its name, derived from the *sloboda* settlements founded there, came into use in the early 17th century and continued until the early 19th century. Slobidska Ukraine bordered on the Hetmanate to the west, the borderlands of the Crimean Khanate and the Zaporizhia to the south, the Don River to the east, and Muscovy to the north. It included sections of the Central Upland and the adjacent Donets Lowland as well as the southeastern section of the Dnieper Lowland and a small area of the Donets Ridge.

Pre–17th century. The oldest evidence of settlement in the territory dates from the Upper Paleolithic. The territory was subsequently settled by *Siverianians. After being incorporated into the Kievan Rus' state in the late 9th century, it was, in succession, part of the Chernihiv, Pereiaslav, and Novhorod-Siverskyi principalities. After its devastation during the Tatar invasions of the 13th century it remained uninhabited. In the early 16th century it came under the control of Muscovy. At that time it was essentially an expanse of wild steppe through which Tatars passed during their raids into Muscovy – usually along the *Murava Road or the Izium and Kalmiius roads. The empty steppes of the region also attracted Ukrainian *ukhodnyky or dobychnyky, who engaged primarily in beekeeping, fishing, and hunting. They developed a regional

*salt industry (primarily in the Bakhmut region and near Tor [later Slovianske]).

From the later 16th century there were two contending streams of colonizers in Slobidska Ukraine: from the north came Muscovite service personnel for the construction of defense lines and fortifications (against invaders from the Crimea to the south as well as the Polish-Lithuanian Commonwealth to the southwest); from the west came Ukrainian agricultural settlers. Some of the latter group were attracted specifically by the resources of the region, and others simply sought to escape the increasingly harsh conditions under Polish rule. There were also some refugees to Slobidska Ukraine and the Don region from exploitative landowners in Muscovy. The Ukrainian migration, however, was much larger than the two sources of Russian colonization.

In the late 16th century the Muscovite government established a number of advance garrisons in the wild steppe: Orel, Livny, and Voronezh (1585); Yelets (1592); Belgorod, Oskol, and Kursk (1596); and Valuiky (1599). During Muscovy's Time of Trouble (1605–13) that expansion came to a halt, but Vilnyi, Khotmyzsk, Userd, and other centers were built (largely on the ruins of medieval towns) soon thereafter. In the 1630s and 1640s the so-called Belgorod Line was constructed, stretching from Okhtyrka (1653) in the west to Ostrohozke (1653) in the east. A string of other settlements was also founded, including Chuhuiv (1627) and Oboian (1649). In the late 17th century the Izium Line (from the Kolomak River to Valuiky) was constructed. In the early 18th century the Belgorod Line lost its strategic significance owing to the increasingly dense settlement of Slobidska Ukraine and the establishment of the *Ukrainian Line (1731–3), which drew upon the resources of Slobidska Ukraine to its south.

17th and 18th centuries. The Ukrainian colonization of Slobidska Ukraine proceeded in a number of waves. Immigration was particularly substantial in the 1630s in the wake of unsuccessful Cossack insurrections. A contingent of about 1,000 migrants led by Hetman Ya. *Ostrianyn settled near Chuhuiv in 1638. Migration increased as a result of the Khmelnytsky uprising, particularly after the Treaty of *Bila Tserkva in 1651. In 1652 some 2,000 Cossacks of Chernihiv and Nizhen regiments, led by Col I. *Dzykovsky, established Ostrohozke. Another detachment, led by H. Kondratiev, moved from Stavyshche, in Bila Tserkva regiment, to Sumy. A similar influx founded Kharkiv in 1654. The *Ruin also resulted in a wave of colonization, primarily from Right-Bank Ukraine, in the 1670s and 1680s. Vovcha (Vovchanske) was founded in 1674, and Izium in 1681. The suppression of the rebellion led by S. *Palii prompted another wave of settlement in the early 18th century. The last major surge of colonization occurred in the 1720 and 1730s, after the restoration of Polish control in Right-Bank Ukraine, the defeat of the haidamaka uprising of 1734, and the entrenchment of the Cossack *starshyna* as landowners in the Hetmanate. The influx of Ukrainians into Slobidska Ukraine pushed Russian colonists (as well as some Ukrainians) toward the east and southeast, in the direction of the Don and the Volga rivers.

In the late 17th century the population of Slobidska Ukraine was about 120,000. The 1732 census indicated a population of 400,000, and that of 1773, over 660,000. The settling of the region added approx 100,000 sq km to Ukrainian ethnographic territory as its border moved

Boundary of Ukraine
Boundary of Slobidska Ukraine
Ukrainian ethnic boundary
Boundary of regiment
The Ukrainian line
The Belgorod line
Regimental towns
Other towns

0   50   100 Km

SLOBIDSKA UKRAINE

120–200 km eastward. In the mid-18th century Slobidska Ukraine constituted 25 percent of Ukrainian ethnographic territory and was inhabited by 10 percent of its population.

The Muscovite government initially encouraged Ukrainian immigration to Slobidska Ukraine. Moscow sought to benefit from the resulting economic development of its unpopulated frontier and from a capable military force that could defend its southern borders. The settlement of Slobidska Ukraine also helped to stem the flow of Russian serfs escaping to the Don region. Ukrainian colonists therefore were supplied with weapons and granted the right to establish *sloboda* settlements with title to the lands, traditional Cossack privileges, and a regimental form of administration.

In the 1650s Ostrohozke, Sumy, Okhtyrka, and Kharkiv regiments were established, and in 1685 Izium regiment was partitioned from the Kharkiv structure. In 1734 those regiments were divided into 98 companies. The regiments and their colonels were granted official recognition in a tsar's charter. In the 18th century a more concerted effort was made to centralize the administration of the region in the hands of a higher military official. That official was usually chosen from among the local colonels or from the

ranks of Russian generals. F. Shydlovsky (a colonel of Kharkiv regiment), F. Osypov (a colonel of Okhtyrka regiment), O. Lesevytsky (a colonel of Okhtyrka regiment), V. Kapnist (brigadier general), and others served in that position.

In contrast to the Hetmanate, Slobidska Ukraine possessed no territorial autonomy. It was subject directly to Muscovite state authority. Initially it was under the voivode of Belgorod (who in turn was responsible to the War Office [Razriadnyi prikaz]). In 1688 it was placed under Muscovy's Foreign Office (Posolskii prikaz), and in 1708 under the military governor of Azov. In 1711 the administration of Sumy and Okhtyrka regiments was placed in the jurisdiction of the Kiev governor, and Kharkiv regiment followed suit in 1718. That same year the administration of Izium and Ostrohozke regiments was transferred to the Voronezh governor. From 1726 the regiments came under the authority of the War College.

The administration of Slobidska Ukraine and the posts therein were similar, with some exceptions, to those of the *regimental system of the Hetmanate. In the later 17th century the members of the general staff were elected at Cossack (officers') councils and confirmed by Muscovite officials. In the 18th century the positions became Russian appointments, the *starshyna* usually coming from the Cossack elite, and regimental colonels and company captains occasionally being foreigners. A number of leading Cossack families filled regimental and other positions in an almost hereditary manner. Such 'dynasties' included the Kondratiev family in Sumy regiment, the Perekrestov-Osypov and Lesevytsky families in Okhtyrka, the Donets-Zakharzhevskys and Danylevskys in Izium, the Shydlovskys, Kulykovskys, and Kvitkas in Kharkiv, and the Teviashovs in Ostrohozke.

Social organization and economy. Slobidska Ukraine was similar socially and economically to the Hetmanate. The first Ukrainian settlers in the region were divided along social lines into Cossacks, clergymen, burghers (merchants and craftsmen), and common peasants (*pospolyti*). There was no nobility in the region in the 17th century. The majority of the population consisted of Cossacks, who constituted half of the region's population until the mid-18th century. The Cossacks themselves were divided into *Cossack helpers, *elect Cossacks, and the *Cossack *starshyna*. In 1732 there were 23,565 elect Cossacks and 72,226 helpers in the four regiments (in 1763, there were 58,231 and 108,301 respectively). *Landless peasants, mainly former Cossacks and free peasants who had lost their households and land, worked on the estates of wealthier Cossack estate owners. In 1732 there were 12,978 of them in the four regiments. The elect Cossacks gradually became a closed class of freemen, and the landless peasants became enserfed to the *starshyna* landowners. The common peasants became divided into those working their own land and those on the estates of the *starshyna*, Russian service personnel, and monasteries. The burghers were few in number.

Russians in Slobidska Ukraine formed a separate, socially heterogeneous group. Initially they came in various official capacities, but by the 18th century they had become local landowners, small independent farmers (*odnodvirtsi*), or common peasants. One estimate put the number of Russians in the four regiments at 1,650, concentrated mainly in the Kharkiv region. As in the Hetmanate the Cossack *starshyna* amassed progressively larger estates, and the local peasantry was increasingly impoverished. By 1768, 196,336 of 381,745 male peasants in the region were virtual serfs.

The largest Cossack landowner families in Slobidska Ukraine were the Danylevsky, Donets-Zakharzhevsky, Kvitka, Kovalevsky, Kondratiev, Kulykovsky, Lesevytsky, Nadarzhynsky, Osypov, Perekrestov, Teviashov, and Shydlovsky. The Kapnist, Myklashevsky, Myloradovych, and Polubotok families from the Hetmanate also had large estates in the region. The Russian landowners included the Dunin, Gendrikov, Golitsyn, Kropotkin, and Yusupov families. Among other foreign landowners was the Moldavian Kantemir family.

The local economy was also similar to that of the Hetmanate, with agriculture and animal husbandry the primary occupations. The prevalent form of farming was the rotating field system. In the late 18th century the three-field system came into use. Apart from Cossack and small peasant landholdings, large estates were also established by Cossack officeholders, the Russian aristocracy, and various monasteries. Those grew in size to approach the latifundia of Right-Bank Ukraine.

Sheepherding, beekeeping, orchard keeping, fishing,

milling, distilling, and the production of various handicrafts were also significant contributors to the region's economy. Toward the end of the 18th century there were about 34,000 craftsmen in Slobidska Ukraine. The salt industry was another significant undertaking, with plants in Tor, Bakhmut, and Spivakivka; saltpeter was a particularly important product. In the 18th century, manufacturing plants were established, which concentrated on cloth and clothing manufacture as well as serving the region's agricultural economy. Of specific note was a tobacco-processing plant established in Okhtyrka, the first in Ukraine and in the Russian Empire.

The focal points of trade were the local markets, of which there were 271 in 1779. In addition there were 10 middle-sized and 2 large markets (Sumy and Kharkiv). The transit trade with Russia, the Hetmanate, Zaporizhia, Southern Ukraine, the Crimea and the Don region, Caucasia, and Iran was also important. Trade between Slobidska Ukraine and the Hetmanate was particularly significant: the Hetmanate exported manufactured goods (such as glass and steel products) in exchange for salt.

Political life. Slobidska Ukraine's political life was conducted within the framework of the Russian (later imperial Russian) state, although its frontier location initially offered it semiautonomy. Moreover, the region's geographic location, between Russia and the Crimean Khanate, the Hetmanate, and the Don region, often placed it in the midst of controversies. Slobidska Ukraine was the object of ruinous Tatar attacks from the south that continued until the Russo-Turkish wars of 1768–74 secured its borders by the Peace Treaty of *Küçük-Kaynarca (1774). Slobidska Ukraine's westernmost regions (Sumy and Okhtyrka) suffered extensive damage during the Russo-Swedish conflict of 1708–9. The Russo-Turkish War of 1735–9 was also very damaging.

The marked difference in social order between Slobidska Ukraine and Russia gave rise to repeated conflicts and even open rebellion. In 1670 a revolt began in Ostrohozke regiment in support of the peasant rebellion led by S. Razin. The colonel of the regiment, I. Dzykovsky, led the insurgency and briefly expelled all Russian officials from the eastern reaches of the territory. The uprising was suppressed, however, and Dzykovsky was executed along with many of his supporters. The inhabitants of Slobidska Ukraine also participated in the Bulavin rebellion that erupted in 1707. When the Crimean khan Devlet Girei attacked the region in 1711, some of the local population (from Nova and Stara Vodolaha) rose to assist him. Subsequently Peter I had a tenth of the captured rebels executed and the rest exiled along with their families. The Right-Bank haidamaka uprisings also spread to Slobidska Ukraine, but these resulted only in limited local disturbances.

Relations between Slobidska Ukraine and the Hetmanate were strengthened during the tenures of Hetmans I. *Samoilovych and I. *Mazepa. Both sought to expand their jurisdictions to the territory, where a large portion of the Right Bank's population had resettled. Petitions to that end were presented in Moscow in 1680 and 1681 by the hetman's emissaries, M. Samoilovych (colonel of Hadiache) and I. Mazepa (at that time a notable military fellow). They were rebuffed. Mazepa repeated the request once he became hetman, and was again refused.

A treaty concluded by P. *Petryk with the Crimean

Khanate in 1692 provided for the joining of the western regiments (Sumy and Okhtyrka) to the Hetmanate, and a transfer of population from the eastern regiments (Kharkiv, Izium, and Ostrohozke) to Right-Bank Ukraine. The territory's *starshyna* was ambivalent about such plans. The upper echelons of Sumy and Okhtyrka regiments were more closely connected (even related) to their counterparts in the Hetmanate and were therefore positively inclined. The leadership of the eastern regiments preferred the direct rule of the tsar, albeit with greater autonomy for the territory as a whole. Union with the Hetmanate ceased to be an issue after the Battle of *Poltava in 1709, when the Russian government embarked upon an intensified anti-Ukrainian policy.

That development, however, did not affect other relations between the Hetmanate and Slobidska Ukraine. Apart from economic and cultural ties, there were family connections between the leading families of the *starshyna*. Among those in the Hetmanate with kin in Slobidska Ukraine were the Apostol, Charnysh, Cherniakh, Chetvertynsky, Hamaliia, Horlenko, Hrechany, Ivanenko, Kapnist, Lisnytsky, Lyzohub, Maksymovych, Markovych, Myklashevsky, Myloradovych, Polubotok, Rodzianko, Savych, Samoilovych, Skoropadsky, Sulyma, Zabila, Zarudny, and Zhurakovsky families. Highly placed people usually did not sever their connections when moving from one territory to another. Conversely, leaders from Slobidska Ukraine often played a part in the political affairs of the Hetmanate. Slobidska Ukraine also offered a refuge for Hetmanate officials and their families during political or military crises (particularly during 1708–9).

Church relations also served to bring the two territories together. Although the church hierarchy of Slobidska Ukraine was directly tied to the Moscow patriarchate (later to the Russian Synod), religious life in the region had a distinctly Ukrainian character. The main institution was the Belgorod eparchy, whose bishops (particularly in the 18th century) tended to come from the Hetmanate and were graduates of the Kievan Mohyla Academy or Chernihiv College. Ostrohozke regiment belonged to the Voronezh eparchy, whose hierarchy and clergy also included many Ukrainians educated in Kiev, Chernihiv, or (later) Kharkiv College.

The more notable bishops of Belgorod were Ye. Tykhorsky (1722–31), who founded Kharkiv College; Y. *Horlenko (1748–54); Y. Mytkevych (1758–63); S. *Myslavsky (1769–75), a scholar, former rector of the Kievan Mohyla Academy, and future metropolitan of Kiev; and T. Mochulsky (1787–99), a member of the Russian Academy. In 1799 Slobidska Ukraine's religious center moved to the Kharkiv eparchy, whose first bishop (1799–1813) was Kh. Sulyma, a member of a notable family of Cossack leaders.

*Kharkiv College became the main institution of higher learning in Slobidska Ukraine in the 18th century. It was modeled on the Kievan Mohyla Academy, and its curriculum was mostly theological. Its professors included scholars educated at the Kievan Academy or Chernihiv and Pereiaslav colleges, as well as some who studied at German universities. The college's students were not only local but from the whole of Left-Bank Ukraine and neighboring districts of Russia. Another major educational center in Slobidska Ukraine was a Latin-Slavic school in Ostrohozke (est 1733, moved to Voronezh in 1737, and then returned to Ostrohozke in 1742). It also had a complement of Ukrainian instructors educated in the Hetmanate, Galicia, and Germany. H. *Skovoroda taught at the colleges in Pereiaslav and Kharkiv. His activities and writings were closely tied to Slobidska Ukraine.

Loss of autonomy. Beginning with the reign of Peter I the imperial Russian government intervened increasingly in the internal affairs of Slobidska Ukraine's regiments. Under the empress Anna Ivanovna the territory's autonomy was abolished outright in 1732, but it was renewed by Elizabeth I in 1743. Finally, on 8 August (28 July OS) 1765, Empress Catherine II issued a decree abolishing the Cossack order and the regimental system in Slobidska Ukraine. The Slobidska Ukraine military formations were transformed into the Kharkiv uhlan and the Sumy, Okhtyrka, Izium, and Ostrohozke hussar regiments. The rank-and-file Cossacks and helpers were ranked at a status comparable to that of state peasants, and the officer class was absorbed into the Russian nobility. The territory itself was governed as Slobidska Ukraine gubernia, with its capital in Kharkiv.

The abolition of the regimental order caused dissatisfaction among the Cossack *starshyna* of Slobidska Ukraine. F. Krasnokutsky, the colonel of Izium regiment, together with members of Kharkiv regiment's *starshyna*, protested openly. This action resulted in a series of arrests and the institution of measures designed to curb a wider movement. Krasnokutsky was divested of his holdings and titles and exiled to the Kuban. Others were sentenced to flogging. Further protests were made during the election of representatives to the Legislative Commission of 1767–8, including a call for the restoration of the regimental system from the Sumy region. But the Russian government managed to suppress the dissent.

In 1835, after a number of administrative changes, the gubernia itself was dissolved. Most of it (the southern section) was reorganized as Kharkiv gubernia, and the rest was assigned to Voronezh and Kursk gubernias. That pattern was continued during the formation of the USSR. Northern Slobidska Ukraine became part of the RSFSR, and the southern section, of the Ukrainian SSR.

BIBLIOGRAPHY

Gumilevskii, F. *Istoriko-statisticheskoe opisanie Khar'kovskoi eparkhii* (Kharkiv 1857–9)
Golovinskii, P. *Slobodskie kozachie polki* (St Petersburg 1864)
Bagalei, D. *Ocherki iz istorii kolonizatsii i byta stepnoi okrainy Moskovskogo gosudarstva* (Moscow 1887)
Miklashevskii, I. *K istorii khoziaistvennogo byta Moskovskogo gosudarstva: Zaselenie i sel'skoe khoziaistvo slobodskoi okrainy XVII v.* (Moscow 1894)
Bahalii, D. *Istoriia Slobods'koï Ukraïny* (Kharkiv 1918; 2nd edn, 1990)
Sumtsov, M. *Slobozhane* (Kharkiv 1918)
Iurkevych, V. *Emigratsiia na skhid i zaliudnennia Slobozhanshchyny za B. Khmel'nyts'koho* (Kiev 1932)
Sliusars'kyi, A. *Slobids'ka Ukraïna: Istorychnyi narys XVII–XVIII st.* (Kharkiv 1954)
Sliusarskii, A. *Sotsial'no-ekonomicheskoe razvitie Slobozhanshchiny XVII–XVIII vv.* (Kharkiv 1964)
Diachenko, M. 'Etapy zaselennia Slobids'koï Ukraïny v XVII i pershii polovyni XVIII st.,' *UIZh*, 1970, no. 8

V. Kubijovyč, O. Ohloblyn

Slobidska Ukraine dialects. Dialects of the northern part of eastern Ukraine, spoken mainly in the southeastern districts of Sumy oblast, Kharkiv oblast, the northern areas of Luhanske oblast, the southern parts of Kursk, Belgorod, and Voronezh oblasts, and the northwestern part of Rostov oblast. Their boundaries cannot be defined precisely. These dialects arose from the intermingling in 16th- to 17th-century Slobidska Ukraine of settlers from the middle Dnieper region, particularly from the northeastern Poltava area, the Chernihiv region, and the Right Bank. There are fewer local variations among these dialects than among the Middle Dnieper dialects. The distinctive phonetic features are the following: the consonants *d, t, n, l, z, s* are softened before the *i* that had evolved from the old *ō* (eg, *s't'il, pod'il* 'table, division'); the pronunciation of unstressed *e* is close to *y* (eg, *vᵉ/ysna* 'spring'), of unstressed *y* to *e* (eg, *žʸ/ₑve* 'lives'), and of unstressed *o* to *u* (eg, *tᵒ/ᵤbi* 'to you'); *r* tends to be softened (eg, *bazar', komar', r'ama* 'market, mosquito, frame') and the alveolar *l* appears in parallel with the ordinary *l* (eg, *ložka–ļožka* 'spoon'). The distinctive morphological features are the following: the unstressed endings of the soft noun group are modified toward the hard group (eg, *z'at'ov'i, z'at'om* [Standard Ukrainian (SU) *z'atevi, z'atem*] 'son-in-law' dat, instr); there is no change of *d, t, z, s* into the corresponding sibilants *ž̧, č, ž, š* in the conjugation of the first person singular (eg, *xod'u, nos'u* [SU *xodžu, nošu*] 'I go, I carry'; the third person of second conjugation verbs (if the ending is unstressed) takes the form *xode, nose* [SU *xodyt', nosyt'*] 'he walks, he carries'); and the third person plural of the second conjugation has the same ending as the first conjugation (eg, *nos'ut'–nos'ut* [SU *nos'at'*] 'they carry'). These dialects also have a distinctive vocabulary; eg, *hyr'avyj* 'sickly', *blahyj* 'sick', and *burta* 'pile'.

Slobidskyi Kish. See Haidamaka Battalion of Slobidska Ukraine.

Slobidskyi Regiment (Slobidskyi polk). A military formation organized in the mid-18th century by the tsarist government on the frontier of *New Serbia and the Zaporizhia, in southwestern Ukraine, for the purpose of checking the Zaporozhian Cossacks. Its main base was the St Elizabeth Fortress (now the city of Kirovohrad). Like the five Cossack regiments in Slobidska Ukraine, the regiment enjoyed a measure of autonomy. In 1760 it had 6,536 men, of which 213 were officers. In 1764 its troops were reorganized into a lancer regiment.

Sloboda. A self-governing settlement in 16th- to 18th-century Ukraine. The inhabitants of a *sloboda* were exempted by the owner (usually a magnate, also the state or the church) from obligations, such as fees and taxes, for an extended period (15 to 25 years). The privileges were offered by owners to attract peasants and skilled workers from other regions. The largest number of *slobody* sprang up in the first half of the 17th century in Right-Bank and Left-Bank Ukraine. In the 1630s and 1640s hundreds of *slobody* were created in the border regions of Muscovy, and they attracted peasants from Left-Bank and Right-Bank Ukraine. By the end of the 18th century there were 523 *slobody* in that territory, which was called *Slobidska Ukraine, and over 100 *slobody* on the lands of the New Sich.

In the 19th and early 20th centuries the term was sometimes used in central and eastern Ukraine to refer to larger villages as well as to industrial or factory settlements which did not have the status of cities or towns. About 100 places in Ukraine still retain *sloboda* or *slobidka* in their name, usually with an adjective referring to the larger town or territory where the settlement sprang up, among them Sharhorod (Shahorodska *sloboda*) and Krasyliv (Krasylivska *slobidka*) in eastern Podilia.

Slobodian, Nataliia [Slobodjan, Natalija], b 27 February 1923 in Kiev. Ballerina. In 1941 she completed study at the Kiev Choreography School (pupil of K. Vasina). In 1944–68 she was a soloist in the Lviv Theater of Opera and Ballet, and from 1968 she was the ballet master there. She was the first performer of the heroic roles in A. Kos-Anatolsky's ballets *Orysia*, *Khustka Dovbusha* (Dovbush's Shawl), and *Soichyne krylo* (The Jay's Wing).

Roman Slobodian

Slobodian, Roman [Slobodjan], b 17 October 1889 in Nastasiv, Ternopil county, Galicia, d 20 May 1982 in Elizabeth, New Jersey. Community leader. After emigrating to the United States in 1906, he joined the *Ukrainian National Association and, eventually, served as its financial secretary (1920–33) and supreme treasurer (1933–66). He was a founding and leading member of the United Ukrainian Organizations in America and the Ukrainian Congress Committee of America. In the interwar period he organized financial aid for Ukrainian institutions in Galicia, and after the war he was chairman of the audit committee and vice-president of the *United Ukrainian American Relief Committee.

Slobodianiuk-Podolian, Stepan [Slobodjanjuk-Podoljan], b 2 August 1876 in Lityn, Podilia gubernia, d 15 September 1932 in Leningrad. Painter. He studied at the Odessa Art School (1899–1901) and audited courses at the St Petersburg Academy of Arts (1905–12). From 1925 he lived in Katerynoslav. He painted portraits, such as *Woman's Portrait* (1915), *Ukrainian Woman* (1916), *Sailor from the Cruiser* Aurora (1917), *Ukrainian Girl* (1926), and *Moldavian Woman* (1928), and canvases on historical subjects, such as *Karmaliuk's Funeral* (1912), *Lenin's Arrival at the Finland Station* (1924), and *Karmaliuk* (1926).

Slobodianyk, Hnat [Slobodjanyk], b 1902 in Lysivka, Proskuriv county, Podilia gubernia. Civil engineer. He studied at the Kiev Polytechnical Institute and worked at the Mezhyhiria Ceramics Institute. From 1934 he held the chair of construction materials at the Kiev Civil-Engineering Institute and served as assistant director of the Scientific Research Institute of Building Materials. He specialized in the field of building materials, particularly concrete and bricks, and developed a new method of manufacturing high-grade cement. He published numerous technical papers.

Oleksander Slobodianyk

Slobodianyk, Oleksander [Slobodjanyk] (Slobodyanik, Alexander), b 5 September 1941 in Lviv. Pianist. His initial musical education took place in Lviv, where at 6 he appeared on radio and by 14 played with the orchestra of the Lviv Philharmonic. From 1956 he studied at the Moscow Conservatory with H. Neuhaus, and in 1964 he graduated from that school in the class of V. Gornostaeva. He made his debut tour of the United States in 1968 and subsequently appeared in recitals and with orchestras throughout Europe, the Americas, and the Far East. Since 1969 he has made recordings (mainly on the Melodiya and Angel labels) of works by J. Haydn, L. van Beethoven, F. Chopin, F. Liszt, M. Mussorgsky, S. Prokofiev, I. Stravinsky, and B. Liatoshynsky.

Slobodivna, Mariia, b 8 December 1876 in Ulhivok, Rava Ruska county, Galicia, d 28 August 1935 in Kharkiv. Stage actress and writer. She worked in the Ruska Besida Theater (1893–1902) and wrote the collection of stories *I khto vona bula?* (And Who Was She?, 1901) and the drama *Vona* (She, 1911). After moving to Soviet Ukraine in 1934, she and her husband, A. *Krushelnytsky, were arrested.

Slobodnik, Włodzimierz, b 19 September 1900 in Novoukrainka, Yelysavethrad county, Kherson gubernia. Polish poet and translator. Since 1927 he has produced numerous poetry collections and several books of satire and poetry for children. Some of his poems are on Ukrainian themes. In the years 1939–41 he lived in Lviv and Kiev and belonged to the Writers' Union of Ukraine. Since 1958 he has lived in Warsaw, where he has had links with the Ukrainian Social and Cultural Society and contributed to its organs *Nashe slovo* and *Ukraïns'kyi kalendar*. He has translated into Polish poems by T. Shevchenko, I. Franko, Yu. Fedkovych, Ya. Shchoholev, P. Tychyna, M. Rylsky, M. Bazhan, M. Tereshchenko, L. Pervomaisky, I. Drach, and A. Malyshko; edited Polish editions of Shevchenko's (1955) and Rylsky's (1965) selected poems; and written about Shevchenko. His poems have been translated into Ukrainian by M. Marfiievych, D. Pavlychko, and Pervomaisky.

Slobodyshche, Treaty of (aka Treaty of Chudniv). A pact signed in Slobodyshche, near Chudniv, in eastern Volhynia, on 27 October 1660 by Yu. Khmelnytsky and Poland. It followed Khmelnytsky's shift to the Poles and the defeat of Russian forces near Liubar. The treaty abolished the Pereiaslav Articles of 1659 and re-established formal ties between Ukraine and Poland. Although the Ukrainians insisted on the full reinstatement of the terms of the Treaty of *Hadiache of 1658, the Poles, represented by S. Potocki and J. Lubomirski, did not agree to a provision for a separate Ukrainian state structure. The treaty thus granted Ukraine a limited autonomy under hetman rule, with obligations to ally with Poland against Muscovy and to refrain from attacking Crimean Tatar territories. It was approved by a Cossack council in Korsun, but Left-Bank regiments headed by Ya. Somko and V. Zolotarenko maintained their allegiance to Muscovy. That split marked the beginning of the division of Ukraine into the Left- and Right-Bank zones.

Slota, Petro [Sl'ota], b 16 October 1911 in Paniutyne, Pavlohrad county, Katerynoslav gubernia, d 25 June 1974 in Kiev. Painter. In 1940 he graduated from the Kiev State Art Institute, where he studied under F. Krychevsky. He painted rural and urban landscapes, such as *Kiev: Khreshchatyk* (1957), *Notre Dame in Paris* (1960), *First Spring* (1964–5), and *Azure Morning* (1969). An album of his works was published in 1972.

Slovakia (Slovensko). A republic in the southwestern Carpathian region, at around the midpoint of the Danube Valley, bordering on Poland to the north, Hungary to the south, the Czech Republic to the west, and Ukraine to the east. Slovakia covers an area of 49,000 sq km and has a population of 5,400,000 (1985), of whom nearly 86 percent are Slovaks, 12 percent are Hungarians, and just over 1 percent are Czechs. Official figures indicate that 42,000 Ukrainians live in the republic, although the actual number is probably somewhere between 130,000 and 145,000. The capital is Bratislava (1990 pop 440,421).

Ukrainians and Slovaks share a 200-km border in the *Prešov region, and both peoples have had similar social structures, daily life, language, and folk art. Both Slovaks and Ukrainians, especially those living in Transcarpathia and a small area of Galicia, also lived for a long period of time under Hungarian rule.

Important trade routes that tied Ukraine to eastern, central, and western Europe have passed through Slovakia since the Middle Ages. Itinerant Slovak merchants and tradesmen traveled to Kievan Rus'. A number of leading Transcarpathian clergymen, who later became bishops or professors at theological seminaries, studied in the 18th century at the theological seminary in Trnava. That city was also a publishing center for Transcarpathian Ukrainians and produced works such as *Katekhyzys* (Catechism, 1698), *Bukvar* (Primer, 1699), and *Kratkoe prypadkov moral'nykh sobraniie* (A Short Collection of Moral Parables, 1727).

The first Slovak scholars to develop a serious interest in Ukraine were J. Kollár (1793–1852) and P. Šafařík (1795–1861). They maintained direct contact with Ukrainian activists and supported the development of the Ukrainian national revival. Šafařík was one of the first Europeans to come out in defense of Ukrainian national, linguistic, and cultural autonomy. In the 1840s L. Štúr began studying

SLOVAKIA

Ukrainian folk poetry. The most notable exponent of Ukrainian-Slovak relations in the 19th century was B. Nósak-Nezabudov (1818–77), whose Slovak translation of the Duma about the Escape of the Three Brothers from Oziv (1848) was the first Ukrainian work to be published in Slovakia. J. Hurban, A. Radlinský, P. Kellner, and others also devoted much attention to Transcarpathian Ukrainians. At the Slavic Congress in Prague in 1848, Slovaks supported Galician and Transcarpathian Ukrainian motions. In 1850 the first Ukrainian (Ruthenian) literary association was formed, in Prešov; it included four Slovaks. A. *Dobriansky, the Transcarpathian Ukrainian who contributed most to Slovak culture, was one of the cofounders (in 1863) of the Matica Slovenská cultural-educational association. In the late 19th century P. Hrabovsky published several of his translations of Slovak classics in the Galician press.

In the late 19th century Slovak interest in Ukraine waned as the Slovakian intelligentsia grew increasingly Russophilie in orientation. In the early 20th century F. Votruba, a Czech, translated selections of works by I. Franko (collected for a single volume in 1914), B. Hrinchenko, B. Lepky, Lesia Ukrainka, and V. Stefanyk into Slovak, and published a number of articles about the Ukrainian language and Ukrainian literature. T. Shevchenko's works became widely known in Slovakia in 1911–14 because of translations and articles by J. Slavík, S. Vajanský, and I. Lach. Meanwhile V. Hnatiuk, I. Franko, and S. Tomashivsky published articles on Slovak community affairs in the Galician press. Nevertheless, Ukrainian-Slovak relations deteriorated significantly in the Prešov region after the Slovak national movement began to display an expansionist attitude toward Ukrainians. Many Ukrainians still preferred to identify with the Slovaks rather than the non-Slavic Hungarians, and many Ukrainian settlements subsequently were Slovakized.

Pressure on Ukrainians in Slovakia to assimilate increased after 1919, when a section of Ukrainian Transcarpathia west of the Uzh River was included in the Slovak republic. The leaders of the Slovak People's party followed a policy of Slovakization toward Ukrainians and declined to enter into a working relationship with Ukrainian politicians from Transcarpathia (although they did work with the Magyarone A. Brodii). In response, Ukrainians cultivated ties with Czech political parties that were either neutral toward or supportive of Ukrainian concerns.

Understandably, Ukrainian-Slovak cultural ties were minimal at the time. A club of friends of Transcarpathia in Bratislava published *Podkarpatská Revue*; a few books about Transcarpathia were published; and a few works by Transcarpathian authors were translated. The other Ukrainian territories and their cultural characteristics remained totally outside the sphere of Slovak interest. Ukraine was similarly uninterested in Slovakia.

In 1938–9 there were official contacts between the governments of Carpatho-Ukraine and Slovakia which led them to issue joint declarations against Hungarian and Czech aggression. The regime of the Slovak People's Republic (1939–44) did not tolerate any manifestations of local Ukrainian national activity, and in 1942 President J. Tiso even declared that the Ukrainian-Ruthenian question no longer existed. This action led some of the Ukrainian population to sympathize with the USSR and to support the partisan movement. During the German-Soviet conflict in Ukraine, there were two divisions of the Slovak army on Ukrainian territory, but they did not participate directly in battle. Many Slovaks, along with Transcarpathian Ukrainians, joined in the Czechoslovak army corps led by Gen L. Svoboda. In 1944 they fought alongside the Soviet army in Ukraine. In 1944 and early 1945 the Ukrainian Division Galizien was stationed in western Slovakia. In 1945–6 detachments of the Ukrainian Insurgent Army crossed into Slovak territory.

The lot of Ukrainians improved dramatically after 1945, in no small measure owing to their influence in the Czechoslovakian Communist party. The Ukrainian minority did not manage to secure any political autonomy in Slovakia, but it did make some cultural gains. Ukrainian culture was popularized in Slovakia, and Slovak in Ukraine. In 1948–89 more than 150 titles in Ukrainian literature were translated (by J. Andrejčuk, J. Kokavec, M. Krno, P. and M. Ličko, A. Pestremenko, I. Rusanka, R. Skukalko, and others) and published. A number of scholars specializing in Ukrainian (including F. Gondor, P. Hapak, D. Haraksim, J. Hrozienčik, V. Khoma, V. Latta, M. Molnar, and M.

Nevrlý) were given positions at the Slovak Academy of Sciences and Bratislava University. They have published monographs on the works of I. Franko and T. Shevchenko, on Ukrainian history, and on numerous other subjects. Bratislava and Kiev were proclaimed twin cities, and exchanges of writers, artists, exhibitions, and theater productions between them take place frequently. A Ukrainian cultural society (named after T. Shevchenko) with its own dramatic collective operates freely in Bratislava. In 1988–9 a telebridge program was broadcast between Kiev and Bratislava.

Another center of Ukrainian studies in Slovakia is Prešov, where, at Šafařík University, there is a chair of Ukrainian language and literature and a research department of Ukrainian studies. Ukrainian plays and operas have also been staged in Slovakia, notably those of I. Kotliarevsky, S. Hulak-Artemovsky, I. Franko, L. Dmyterko, O. Korniichuk, Yu. Meitus, T. Shevchenko, V. Sobko, M. Starytsky, and M. Tsehlynsky, many of which have also been broadcast on radio and television. Concert tours of the Verovka State Chorus, the State Dance Ensemble of Ukraine, the State Banduryst Kapelle of Ukraine of Kiev, the Transcarpathian Folk Chorus, the Kiev Ukrainian Drama Theater, the Duklia Ukrainian Folk Ensemble, and the Ukrainian National Theater in Prešov have served to popularize Ukrainian culture. Official ties were established between the Kiev Ukrainian Drama Theater and the Zabrosky Theater of Prešov, which has resulted in yearly exchanges of productions. A similar affiliation exists with the Ukrainian theater in Uzhorod. There have also been a number of exhibits of Ukrainian books and paintings in Slovakia. Official 'Days of Ukrainian Culture in Slovakia' and 'Days of Slovak Culture in Ukraine' have also been important, as have annual festivals of song and dance held by Ukrainians in Czechoslovakia. The Ukrainian branch of the Slovak Writers' Union and the Ukrainian department of the Slovak Educational Publishing House (which has issued more than 430 Ukrainian publications) also strengthen Ukrainian-Slovak literary ties.

The equating of Slovak and Czech culture has made the popularization of Slovak culture in Ukraine more difficult. Of 152 titles of Czech and Slovak authors published in Ukraine before 1968, only 8 were by Slovaks (the first translation appeared in 1951). In order to compensate for this inequality the department of Ukrainian literature of the Slovak publishing house in Prešov printed 15 translations of Slovak works in 1958–62, the Cultural Association of Ukrainian Workers published 6 Slovak plays in Ukrainian translation, and the literary journal *Duklia published translations of contemporary Slovak literature. Few of these publications reached Ukraine, however, and eventually such editions were halted. In 1964 an anthology of Slovak poetry was published, which included the verse of 51 Slovak authors translated by I. Drach, H. Kucher, V. Luchuk, A. Malyshko, M. Rylsky, D. Pavlychko, I. Svitlychny, V. Symonenko, B. Ten, V. Zhytnyk, and others.

Despite improvements in Ukrainian-Slovak cultural relations, Slovakia has maintained a systematic policy of Slovakization of its Ukrainian population in the Prešov region in political, cultural (by closing Ukrainian schools), and religious matters (a Slovak was appointed as administrator of the Prešov eparchy in 1968). National hostility to Ukrainians was most openly expressed in 1968–9, during the Dubček administration, when calls were made for the deportation of all Ukrainians from the Prešov region

to the Ukrainian SSR. The other Ukrainian settlements in Slovakia are found mainly around Košice, a large industrial center that draws many Ukrainians from the Prešov region. Every year there is a Ukrainian folk festival at *Svydnyk. Ukrainians are organized in the *Cultural Association of Ukrainian Workers (renamed in 1990 the Union of Ukrainian-Ruthenians of Czechoslovakia), which has its own choir (Karpaty) and a theater group (Dumka). Ukrainians also live in Bratislava.

The difficulties between Ukrainians and Slovaks have been carried over into émigré affairs, particularly in the United States. Attempts have been made to Slovakize Ukrainian emigrants from the Prešov region on the grounds that there are no longer any 'Ukrainians' there and that all Greek Catholics are Slovaks. As well, the Vatican has appointed Slovak administrators to a number of Transcarpathian Greek Catholic communities in Canada.

BIBLIOGRAPHY
Shevchuk, S. Suchasni ukraïns'ko-slovats'ki literaturni zv'iazky 1945–1960 (Kiev 1963)
Mol'nar, M. Slovaky i ukraïntsi (Bratislava–Prešov 1965)
Nevrlý, M. Bibliografia ukrajiniky v slovenskej reči 1945–1964 (Bratislava 1965)
Pazhur, O. Ukraïntsi Chekhoslovachchyny 1945–1964 (Prešov 1967)
Chuma, A. Bondar; A. Ukraïns'ka shkola na Zakarpatti ta Skhidnii Slovachchyni (Prešov 1969)
Sirka, J. The Development of Ukrainian Literature in Czechoslovakia, 1945–1975: A Survey of Social, Cultural an[d] Historical Aspects (Frankfurt am Main 1978)
Sirka, I. Rozvytok natsional'noï svidomosty lemkiv Priashivshchyny u svitli ukraïns'koï khudozhnoï literatury Chekhoslovachchyny (Munich 1980)

O. Zilynsky

Slovaks. A people belonging to the West Slavs. Linguistically Slovaks are closely related to the Czechs. Since the dispersal of the Slavic tribes in the 6th and 7th centuries from their original homeland between the upper Vistula and middle Dnieper regions, the Slovaks have inhabited the southern slopes of the Carpathian Mountains, especially its western ranges. In 1985 about 5,400,000 Slovaks lived in Slovakia (area, 49,000 sq km), where they made up nearly 86 percent of the population. Another 308,000 Slovaks lived in the Czech lands of Czechoslovakia, and an estimated 600,000 lived abroad, mostly in the United States. A small minority of 12,000 Slovaks lives in Ukraine in the lowlands of Transcarpathia oblast near the border with Slovakia.

Slovak-Ukrainian relations. Slovak relations with Ukraine, which date from medieval times, have been limited. Slovaks have maintained strong ties, however, with Ukrainians (Ruthenians) living south of the Carpathians, especially those living in the *Prešov region (since 1918, within the boundaries of *Slovakia).

In medieval times trade routes from Halych and later Lviv to Hungary passed through Slovak towns, such as Bardejov, Prešov, and Košice. But not until the Slavic national revivals of the 19th century was a mutual awareness of the distinctness of the Slovak and Ukrainian peoples developed. The influential Slovak Pan-Slavist P. Šafařík was one of the first in Europe to argue that Ukrainians were a people distinct from both the Russians and the Poles. Relations throughout the rest of the 19th century took the form primarily of translation of Ukrainian writers for publication in Slovak periodicals. The most active translator was B. Nósak-Nezabudov (1818–77). Both I. *Franko and P. *Hrabovsky translated the Slovak poet S. Chalupka.

After 1918 Slovak-Ukrainian relations were basically limited to ties with Ukrainians living in the Prešov region and *Transcarpathia. Beginning in 1948, however, when Communist Czechoslovakia became part of the Soviet bloc, Slovak-Ukrainian relations expanded. Communist Ukrainian and Slovak governments encouraged the publication of translations of the other people's classic and contemporary writers, the exchange of folk ensembles, the twinning of cities (Bratislava and Kiev), and the holding of annual festivities, such as the 'Days of Ukrainian Culture in Slovakia' and 'Days of Slovak Culture in Ukraine.' There were also unofficial links between dissidents in Ukraine and the Ukrainian minority in Slovakia. Of particular importance in that regard was the publication program of the Ukrainian Branch of the Slovak Pedagogical Publishing House, based in Prešov. The opportunity enjoyed by banned Soviet Ukrainian authors of being published in Prešov, as well as the existence of a liberal Ukrainian-language media (radio and newspapers) in Czechoslovakia during the 1960s, contributed to the Soviet decision to intervene militarily in Czechoslovakia in 1968.

Slovak-Ukrainian relations in the Prešov region. Because of geographic proximity Slovak-Ukrainian relations have historically been most intense south of the Carpathians, in particular in the Prešov region. In that region Slovak-Ukrainian linguistic contacts are closest, since East Slovak dialects (Šariš, Zemplín) form part of a linguistic transition zone with Transcarpathian Ukrainian dialects and Ukrainian dialects of the Prešov region.

For centuries Slovaks and Ukrainians south of the Carpathians shared the same political, social, and cultural fate within the Hungarian kingdom. In an attempt to improve their status, Slovaks and Ukrainians of the Prešov region worked together closely during each group's 19th-century national revival. A. *Dobriansky was elected to the Hungarian parliament from a Slovak-inhabited district and was a founding member of Slovakia's first cultural organization, the Matica Slovenska (1863). Analogously, four Slovaks were among the founding members of the first Ruthenian (Ukrainian) cultural organization, the Prešov Literary Society, founded by the national leader O. *Dukhnovych in 1850.

Relations between the two national groups have not been completely harmonious in the 20th century. Throughout the whole interwar period Ukrainians living in the historical counties of Spiš (Szepes), Šariš (Sáros), and Zemplín (Zemplén) – the so-called Prešov region – remained under a Slovak administration. All efforts to unite the Prešov region with Transcarpathian Ukraine during the short-lived era of post-Munich federal Czechoslovakia were blocked by the Slovak autonomist government; then, under the Slovak state during the Second World War, Ukrainians experienced various degrees of discrimination.

Since the establishment of Communist rule in Czechoslovakia in 1948, Slovak-Ukrainian relations in the Prešov region have varied. The Czechoslovak and later Slovak Communist authorities have provided educational and cultural facilities for the national minorities living within their borders.

Some antagonism between the two groups has been evident also within the Greek Catholic church (forcibly liquidated in 1950, restored in 1968). Traditionally headed by bishops of Ukrainian ethnic background, since 1969 the church has been headed by a Slovak administrator (J. Hirka), who in 1991 was consecrated bishop. He has allowed services in the vast majority of churches to switch from Church Slavonic to Slovak as the liturgical language. The efforts to Slovakize the Greek Catholic church and to claim that all 'Rusnaks' living in Slovakia are by ethnicity Slovak are strongly supported by Slovak Catholic circles in the West, particularly Canada, where a distinct Slovak Byzantine (Greek Catholic) church was established in 1981.

Since the Velvet Revolution of 1989, which brought profound political, social, and economic changes to Czechoslovakia, Slovak-Ukrainian relations in the Prešov region have at times been difficult. The local Ukrainian intelligentsia is, in particular, critical of several decisions by the Slovak republic government to support that portion of the Ukrainian population which promotes the idea that Ruthenians (Rusyns) form a separate nationality. Whereas Slovakia has welcomed Ukraine's regained independence, relations between the two states have at times been strained because of differing interpretations regarding the divisions (Ruthenian vs Ukrainian) among the Ukrainians in the Prešov region.

BIBLIOGRAPHY
Hnatiuk, V. 'Slovaky chy rusyny: Prychynok do vyiasnennia sporu pro natsional'nist' zakhidnykh rusyniv,' *ZNTSh*, 42, no.4 (1901)
Húsek, J. *Národopisná hranice mezi Slováky a Karpatorusy* (Bratislava 1925)
Mol'nar, M. *Slovaky i ukraïntsi* (Bratislava and Prešov 1965)
P. Magocsi

Slovak-Ukrainian linguistic relations. Historically, the linguistic contacts between Ukrainians and Slovaks took place in the western Transcarpathian Prešov region. There they have affected the (southern) Lemko and contiguous Ukrainian Carpathian and eastern Slovak dialects and the local variants of the literary languages. Contemporary eastern Slovak dialects reveal several ancient Lechitic traits, and the eastern Zemplín dialects are under the influence of Ukrainian. Their expansion into the Lemko and Middle-Carpathian regions resulted in the development of the so-called Sotak dialect in the Snina (Snyna) vicinity of the Prešov region and of the mixed Ukrainian-Slovak dialects west of Uzhhorod. Among the oldest traits common to western Ukrainian, southern Polish, and Slovak are the endings -*ox* in the locative plural of masculine and neuter nouns (eg, Ukrainian Dniester dialect *u pal'c'ox* 'in the fingers', Ukrainian western Transcarpathian dialect *u l'isox* 'in forests', 16th-century Polish *w ogrodoch* 'in the gardens', Slovak *o chłapoch* 'about men') and -*me* in first-person plural verbs (eg, Ukrainian *dame*, Slovak *dáme* 'we will give'). Remnants of early Ukrainian-Slovak contacts are the Slovak forms *čerieslo* (cf Ukrainian *čereslo*) 'plowshare' and the reflex *o* < *ъ* in the eastern Slovak, and perhaps middle Slovak, dialects (eg, *moch, voš, piesok* [cf Ukrainian *mox, voša, pisok*] 'moss, louse, sand'). Greek Catholic eastern Slovaks were also influenced by the Ukrainian variant of Church Slavonic. As a result of 19th- and 20th-century Slovakization pressures, many syntactic and phraseological Slovakisms and Slovak calques entered the local literary language of the Ukrainians of the Prešov region.

The influence of Slovak (as that of Polish) on the Ukrainian language was strongest and most enduring in the Lemko dialects. In those dialects (1) the labialization *CelC > ColC > ColoC* in the word *pelevnyk* 'grain husk' is absent; (2) sonorous *r, l* in weak positions of the groups *Cr(l)ъ(ь)C* retained longer their sonant character after the disappearance of the weak *jer*, and therefore the vowel *ы* appeared before them instead of, as in other Ukrainian dialects, after them (eg, *кырvavыj* [SU *kryvavyj*] 'bloody', *hыrmity* [SU *hrymity*] 'to thunder', *sыíza* [SU *sl'oza*] 'tear', *bыйxa* [SU *bloxa*] 'flea'); (3) the palatalization of *s, z* has a dorsal character, *n* before *g, k* becomes ŋ, and *l'* after labials in fourth-class verbs is replaced by *j* (eg, *robju* [SU *roblju*] 'I make'); (4) contracted verbal endings of the type *trymam, -aš, -at, -ame, -ate* (SU *trymaju, -aješ, -aje, -ajemo, -ajete*) 'I/you (sing)/he/we/you(pl) hold', sporadic forms with *ča < če* (eg, *časaty, čalo, čapiha* [SU *česaty, čolo, čepiha*] 'to comb, forehead, plow handle'), and syntactic and aspectual peculiarities (eg, the atemporal use of the present tense of perfective verbs [eg, *kvočka vыl'ahne kur'jata* 'the hen broods chicks']) appeared; and (5) numerous Slovakisms entered the southern Lemko (and, to a lesser extent, the northern Lemko, Boiko, and western and middle Transcarpathian) lexicon; eg, words such as *bratranec'* 'cousin', *pec* 'stove', *bradlo* 'haystack', *draha* 'road', *blanar* 'glassmaker', *l'adnyk* 'vetch', *bodak* 'bayonet', *rixlyk* 'fast train', semantic creations and calques such as *pas'ika* 'clearing', *poros'ačka* 'sow', and lexical parallels such as *rebryna* 'ladder', *lyška* 'vixen'. Hungarian, German, and other European loanwords entered the dialects partly also via Slovak.

Slovak-Ukrainian linguistic relations have been studied by scholars such as O. Broch, V. Hnatiuk, S. Tomashivsky, S. Czambel, A. Petrov, F. Pastrnek, Z. Stieber, O. Halaga, V. Latta, M. Onyshkevych, and Y. Dzendzelivsky.

BIBLIOGRAPHY

Onyshkevych, M. 'Slovats'ko-ukraïns'ki movni zv'iazky,' in *Pytannia slov'ianoznavstva* (Lviv 1962)

Dzendzelivs'kyi, I. *Ukraïns'ko-zakhidnoslov'ians'ki leksychni paraleli* (Kiev 1969)

Horbach, O. *Pivdennolemkivs'ka hovirka i diialektnyi slovnyk sela Krasnyi Brid bl. Medzhylaborets' (Priashivshchyna)* (Munich 1973)

O. Horbach

Slovanský přehled (Slavonic Survey). The leading Czech journal of Slavic studies, literature, culture, and affairs, published in Prague since 1898, except during the Second World War. After the war it was the bimonthly organ of the Institute of the History of European Socialist Countries of the Czechoslovak Academy of Sciences. Founded and edited until 1931 by A. Černý, *Slovanský přehled* from the beginning was sympathetic toward Ukrainian concerns and issues. It has published translations of Ukrainian writers (I. Franko, T. Shevchenko, Lesia Ukrainka, B. Hrinchenko, B. Lepky, O. Vyshnia, I. Mykytenko, O. Korniichuk, L. Pervomaisky, and others) as well as articles by Ukrainian scholars and publicists, such as V. Hnatiuk, S. Yefremov, O. Hrushevsky, B. Lepky, D. Doroshenko, O. Mytsiuk, Ye. Vyrovy, H. Bochkovsky, I. Bryk, A. Zhyvotko, O. Zilynsky, and M. Molnar. The journal initially contained much information about Ukrainian-Czech relations and Ukrainian life in general,

but since the Second World War it has published works by Ukrainians mainly from Soviet Ukraine or the Soviet-bloc countries and has not devoted attention to Ukrainian émigré affairs.

Slovechna River [Slovečna] (also Slavechna). A right-bank tributary of the Prypiat River that flows for 158 km through Polisia, Zhytomyr, and Homel (Belarus) oblasts and drains a basin area of 2,670 sq km. The river is 4–10 m wide, and its valley is approx 2.5 km wide. Its source is in the Ovruch Ridge. The river is used for water-supply purposes, irrigation, and, in its lower reaches, log rafting.

Slovechne-Ovruch Ridge. See Ovruch Ridge.

The 17th-century limestone church in Slovianohirske

Slovianohirske [Slovjanohirs'ke]. IV-18, DB I-3. A city (1989 pop 5,600) on the Donets River in Donetske oblast, administered by the Slovianske city council. Its origins can be traced to the village of Banne (or Banivske), which was established by Prince G. Potemkin near his palace and baths at the end of the 18th century. Under the Soviet regime it was converted into a health resort. In 1964 the town was granted city status and renamed Slovianohirske. It has three sanatoriums, a recreational base, and a campsite. A 17th-century limestone church and the *Sviati Hory Dormition Monastery stand within the city limits.

Sloviano-Serbia. An administrative-territorial region of the mid-18th century in Ukraine. The region was created by the Russian government in 1753 to protect the southern borders of the empire against Turko-Tatar attacks and to colonize sparsely inhabited territory; it was situated south of the Donets River in the area between the Bakhmut and the Luhanka rivers. It bordered on the Don Cossack lands to the east and partially to the south, on the Zaporizhia to the west, on Slobidska Ukraine to the north, and on the Crimean Khanate to the south. Bakhmut (now Artemivske) became its administrative center. As in the case of *New Serbia, Serbian military units were moved in from Hungary (as well as Bulgarians, Greeks, Wallachians, and other Orthodox peoples from the Ottoman Empire). Some of the military formations, however, consisted of Ukrainian peasants and Cossacks, and the majority of new settlers were Ukrainians. The Serbs, who were granted a certain degree of autonomy, were organized into two regiments (1,300 soldiers), under R. Preradovich and I. Shevich, and placed along the *Ukrainian Line; their presence gave the region a semimilitary character. According to the census of 1760 there were 112 settlements, with a total population of 26,000, in the new territory. Frequent conflicts arose between the foreign military units and the local Ukrainian population as well as with the Ukrainians of neighboring Zaporizhia. In 1764 the territory was liquidated and included in the Catherinian province of New Russia gubernia. The foreign population eventually assimilated with local Ukrainians.

BIBLIOGRAPHY
Bahalii, D. *Zaselennia Pivdennoï Ukraïny* (Kharkiv 1920)
Polons'ka-Vasylenko, N. *The Settlement of the Southern Ukraine (1750–1775)* (New York 1955)

A. Zhukovsky

Slovianoserbske [Slov'janoserbs'ke]. V-19, DB II-5. A town smt (1986 pop 8,000) on the Donets River and a raion center in Luhanske oblast. To protect its southern frontier from the Tatars, the Russian government attracted colonists from Serbia, Croatia, Bulgaria, and Poland and in 1753 set up the military settlement of Pidhirne. In 1784 it was granted town status and renamed Donetske. Because of frequent flooding the town was moved in 1817 and renamed Slovianoserbske. Until 1882 it served as a county center of Katerynoslav gubernia. Many of its residents made their living as chumaks, carrying grain to Azov ports and bringing back salt and fish. In 1964 the settlement attained smt status, and in 1966 it became a raion center. It has a dairy, a bakery, and a fruit-canning factory.

Sloviansk [Slov'jans'k] (Russian: Slaviansk-na-Kubani). VIII-19. A city (1990 pop 58,000) on the Protoka River and a raion center in Krasnodar krai, RF. Until 1958 it was named Stanitsa Slavianskaia. The city is a highway junction and a river port. It has a large food industry. According to the census of 1926, Ukrainians accounted for 69.1 percent of the Sloviansk raion population.

Slovianske [Slov'jans'ke]. V-18, DB I-3. A city (1989 pop 143,000) on the Kazennyi Torets River and a raion center in Donetske oblast. It originated as the fortified settlement Tor (est 1645), which developed into a salt manufacturing and trading center. In 1685–1764 it was a company center of Izium regiment. Then it became a county center in Katerynoslav vicegerency. In 1784 Tor was reclassified as a town and renamed Slovenske. A decade later it was renamed Slovianske and became a part of Slobidska Ukraine (from 1835, Kharkiv) gubernia. With the construction of a railway line (1869) nearby, the town grew

rapidly. Its greatest industrial expansion occurred during the industrialization drive of the 1930s. Today the city is an important industrial and health resort center. It has machine-building plants, an electric power station, a soda and a chemicals manufacturing consortium, a salt and a ceramics manufacturing complex, and oil- and meat-processing complexes.

Slovianske Heavy-Machine-Building Plant (Slovianskyi zavod vazhkoho mashynobuduvannia). A factory of the heavy-machine-building industry, located in Slovianske, Donetske oblast. A soda factory was built on the site of the present factory in 1912 by the South Russian Joint-Stock Company. In 1923 the factory began to assemble and repair agricultural machinery. In 1927 it began to repair mining equipment. Since the 1930s it has built primarily spare parts and equipment for the coke and chemical industries. Its machinery was evacuated at the outset of the Second World War, and the facilities were rebuilt after the war. In the early 1970s over 1,300 workers were employed at the plant.

Slovianske Pedagogical Institute (Slovianskyi derzhavnyi pedahohichnyi instytut). An institution of higher learning, under the jurisdiction of the Ministry of Education, located in the city of Slovianske, Donetske oblast. It was founded in 1954 on the basis of the Teacher's Institute (1939). In 1982 the institute had five faculties: physics-mathematics, industrial and technical teacher training, elementary-school teacher training, pedagogy with specialization in preschool pedagogy and psychology, and handicapped child education. There was a correspondence and a preparatory section. The institute is fully equipped with study facilities, laboratories, and workshops. The library has 306,500 volumes in its collection. The student enrollment in 1986–7 was 5,100.

Slovo (Word). A privately owned publishing house in Kiev that operated from 1922 to 1926. Its shareholders were primarily writers, activists in the Ukrainian co-operative movement, and workers in Kiev's publishing industry. The directors were H. Holoskevych, P. Fylypovych, and S. Tytarenko. Slovo published several poetry collections by the *Neoclassicists M. Zerov, P. Fylypovych, M. Drai-Khmara, and M. Rylsky; H. Kosynka's first story collection (1922); T. Osmachka's first poetry collection (1922); two books of Zerov's essays on Ukrainian literature (1924, 1926); the poetry anthology *Siaivo* (The Aura, 1922), edited by Zerov; and a collection dedicated to the memory of P. Stebnytsky.

Slovo (Word). A newspaper of politics, literature, and current affairs, published in Lviv semiweekly in 1861–72 and then three times a week until 1887. The editor was B. Didytsky (1861–71) and then V. Ploshchansky. Initially *Slovo* published articles and literary works in the Galician vernacular and was funded by M. *Kachkovsky and Metropolitan H. Yakhymovych. From the mid-1860s, however, it was the main organ of the Russophile movement in Galicia, and published only in the artificial *yazychiie. From 1867 to 1870 it issued a biweekly journal, *Halychanyn. From 1876 it was subsidized by the tsarist government, which it openly supported. *Slovo* published political commentaries and literary and historical works. It remains a valuable source for the study of 19th-century Galicia, especially the Russophile movement. Frequent censorship and confiscations by the Austrian authorities and a steady loss of subscribers forced the paper's eventual closure.

The editorial board of *Slovo* (Kiev, 1907–9): from left: Valentyn Sadovsky, Symon Petliura, Yakym Mikhura, Mykola Porsh

Slovo (Word). A weekly newspaper of the *Ukrainian Social Democratic Workers' party, legally published in Kiev from May 1907 to July 1909 (a total of 105 issues) by O. Koroleva (1907–8) and S. Petliura (1909). The editors were M. Porsh, V. Sadovsky, Ya. Mikhura, and Petliura. The newspaper concentrated on raising the political and social consciousness of its working-class readers, but over time it began devoting more attention to the struggle for Ukrainian political and cultural rights. In addition to the editors, who wrote mostly on political (Porsh), cultural (Petliura), and economic (Sadovsky, Mikhura) topics, regular contributors included A. Zhuk, D. Dontsov, H. Kovalenko, V. and D. Doroshenko, Isaak Mazepa, L. Yurkevych, V. Chekhivsky, and V. Stepankivsky. The newspaper also published prose and poetry by S. Cherkasenko, H. Chuprynka, Dniprova Chaika, and other writers.

Slovo (Word). The organ of the *Ukrainian Social Democratic Workers' party. Its aim was to promote national consciousness among Ukraine's working class. Only one issue was published, in Kharkiv in November 1915, before the publication was closed down by the tsarist authorities. It was printed by the Dzvin publishing house (directed by Yu. Tyshchenko) and edited by V. Vynnychenko. Contributors included V. Sadovsky and S. Petliura.

Slovo (Word). A daily newspaper published in Kamianets-Podilskyi in 1920. It was edited by Kotliarenko with the assistance of N. Hryhoriiv and P. Bohatsky.

Slovo (Word). A semiannual journal of Slavic studies published by the Greek Catholic Theological Academy in Lviv in 1936–8 (a total of six issues). The journal published several articles on Ukrainian philology. The editor was K. Chekhovych.

Slovo (Word). A weekly newspaper published in Regensburg from November 1945 to December 1946. It was one of the first papers established by Ukrainian refugees in Germany after the Second World War. The editor was S. Dovhal.

Slovo (Word). A Ukrainian-Canadian evangelical publication. It appeared in 1950 as a bimonthly tabloid in Toronto and then moved in 1951 to Saskatoon, where it became a quarterly journal. Publication soon became less regular, and ceased altogether in 1955. *Slovo* was the publication of the Independent Ukrainian Evangelical church, a faction of the Ukrainian Evangelical Alliance of North America that hoped to restore a church structure comparable to that of the *Independent Greek church in Canada in 1903–12. The main figures involved with the publication included L. Standret, P. Bodnar, M. Korak, and I. Kudryn; P. Krat and I. Bodrug served as its spiritual mentors.

Slovo, the organ of the Slovo Association of Ukrainian Writers in Exile

Slovo (The Word). A nonperiodic almanac published by the *Slovo Association of Ukrainian Writers in Exile. The almanac includes poetry, fiction, criticism, memoirs, and documents. The first almanac appeared in 1962 with H. *Kostiuk as editor in chief. The editorial note promised a continuation of the publishing tradition of *MUR and guaranteed publication access to various literary groups, movements, and generations.The editorial promise has held for the 12 issues that have appeared so far, and the almanac has reflected the various literary endeavors of Ukrainian émigré writers. Kostiuk remained editor in chief for vols 2 (1964) and 3 (1968). Vols 4 (1970) and 5 (1973) were under the editorship of S. *Hordynsky, and vol 6 (without a date), of U. *Samchuk. Vols 7–12 (1978, 1980, 1981, 1983, 1987, and 1990) did not indicate who among the editorial committee was the responsible editor. The editorial committee of the almanac consisted of the following: Yu. Boiko–Blokhyn (vols 10–12), O. Chernenko (vol 10), Hordynsky (vols 1–12), S. Hrybinska (Kuzmenko) (vols 9–12), Yu. Klynovy (Stefanyk) (vols 4–11), O. Kopach (vols 8–12), I. Korovytsky (vols 1, 3), Kostiuk (vols 1–3, 6–

12), B. Kravtsiv (vols 1–2), V. Lesych (vol 1), D. Nytchenko (vols 10–12), P. Odarchenko (vols 3, 12), B. Oleksandriv (vols 6–8), B. Rubchak (vols 2–3, 12), Samchuk (vols 6–11), Yu. Shevelov (vols 6–12), M. Shlemkevych (vols 1–2), O. Tarnavsky (vols 2–12), H. Zhurba (vol 1), O. Zinkevych (vol 12), and O. Zuievsky (vols 5–12).

Slovo Association of Ukrainian Writers in Exile (Obiednannia ukrainskykh pysmennykiv v emigratsii Slovo). An association initiated in New York on 26 June 1954 to continue and develop the ideology and activities of its European predecessor, *MUR, and to embrace within its membership all Ukrainian writers outside of Ukraine, the Soviet Union, and its former satellite countries. There were 13 initiating members: O. Burevii, D. Humenna, I. Kernytsky, H. *Kostiuk, B. Kravtsiv, Yu. Lavrinenko, V. Lesych, L. Lyman, Ye. Malaniuk, O. *Tarnavsky, Yu. Sherekh [Shevelov], M. Shlemkevych, and H. Zhurba. Officially the association came into existence on 19 January 1957, when the bylaws of the association were signed by 22 writers in attendance and accepted by proxy by an additional 34 writers. Slovo holds periodic conventions (seven to date: 1958, 1964, 1968, 1970, 1975, 1982, and 1990) attended by delegates from the various national affiliates (the United States, Canada, England, Argentina, Brazil, Australia, Germany, and France). The presidents of the association have been Kostiuk (1954–75), Tarnavsky (1975–92), and D.H. Struk (since 1992). Since 1962 Slovo has published an irregular literary almanac, *Slovo, which includes contributions by its members. The association also fulfills the function of a publisher by allowing its authors to publish their works under the auspices and name of Slovo. There are two ongoing committees in the association, a biobibliographic one and an archival one, the latter of which also is charged with the preservation and publication of works and papers of deceased authors. In 1964 the association established a financial assistance fund for its members. At the time of the seventh convention in 1990 there were 128 members, of which 63 were in the United States, 46 in Canada, 7 in Germany, 5 in Australia, 3 each in England and France, and 1 in Brazil.

BIBLIOGRAPHY
Kostiuk, H. Z litopysu literaturnoho zhyttia v diiaspori (Munich 1971)
Tarnavs'kyi, O. 'Ob'iednannia ukraïns'kykh pys'mennykiv "Slovo",' Slovo, no. 12 (1990)

D.H. Struk

Slovo Bozhe (Word of God). A popular monthly religious supplement to the Russophile newspaper *Nauka, published in Lviv from January 1879 to December 1881. It was edited by Rev O. Shcherban.

Slovo Dobroho Pastyria (Word of the Good Shepherd). A Basilian publishing house in New York City. From 1950 to 1962 it issued popular-educational bimonthly booklets on religious and social subjects, including the history of the Ukrainian Catholic church and the Basilian order. The editors-in-chief were Revs V. Gavlich (1950–1), S. Sabol (1951–3), M. Vavryk (1953–4), V. Vavryk (1954–61), and M. Solovii. Among the authors were M. Wojnar, A. Velyky, A. Pekar, H. Luzhnytsky, I. Nazarko, and the editors.

Slovo i chas

Slovo i chas (Word and Time). A scholarly journal of literary theory, history, and criticism; an organ of the Institute of Literature of the AN URSR (now ANU) and of the Writers' Union of Ukraine. The journal was established in Kiev in 1957 as *Radians'ke literaturoznavstvo*, and was published first as a bimonthly and from January 1965 as a monthly periodical. It was renamed *Slovo i chas* in 1990. The first editor in chief was O. *Biletsky (1957–61), who was succeeded by I. Dzeverin. As a result of the change in editors the quality of the journal noticeably deteriorated. Its large section on literary theory became limited to fatuous theorizing on the issues of *socialist realism. In addition to traces of a propagandistic Party-minded tone in the articles on literary history and literary criticism, there is a marked absence of papers on current trends in world literature and on the relationship of Ukrainian literature with foreign literature. The journal further deteriorated with the intensified persecution of the early 1960s, which resulted in a narrowing of the issues permitted for discussion and in many authors' being prohibited from publishing their work in the journal (eg, I. Dziuba, I. Svitlychny, Ye. Sverstiuk, V. Ivanysenko). The quality of *Slovo i chas*, in fact, is indicative of the general deterioration in Ukrainian literary scholarship caused by the gradual loss of scholars of the old school (eg, S. Maslov, Biletsky, P. Popov, Ye. Nenadkevych), who were gradually replaced by scholars educated in the Soviet system. Among the latter group there were few who could be considered authorities in Old Ukrainian literature, and for that reason the scope of the journal was reduced to studies of 19th- and 20th-century literature; typical contributors were those who specialized in the relationship between Ukrainian and Russian literature (N. Krutikova) or in the theory of socialist realism (M. Shamota). The democratization and policy of glasnost announced in 1985, which improved the quality of many other literary journals, have also had some effect on *Slovo i chas*.

I. Koshelivets

Slovo istyny (The Word of Truth). An Orthodox monthly journal published from November 1947 to October 1951 in Winnipeg. Edited by Bishop I. Ohiienko, it contained articles on the history of Ukrainian Orthodoxy, theological, cultural, and historical topics, and the Ukrainian language. It was succeeded by *Nasha kul'tura*.

Slovo na storozhi (The Word on Guard). An annual publication of the Ukrainian Language Association, published from 1964 to 1988, first in Winnipeg and then in

Montreal (a total of 25 issues). It contained original and re-printed articles on the Ukrainian language and the teaching of it, on the use of Ukrainian in Canada, and on language policies and Russification in the Ukrainian SSR. Its editor was J. *Rudnyckyj.

Slovo naroda (The Word of the People). The first and, until 1946, only Ukrainian-language newspaper in the Prešov region, published from December 1931 to August 1932 (a total of 15 issues). Edited by I. Nevytska, it was the unofficial organ of the local Prosvita society. Its contributors were local populists and émigrés from Soviet Ukraine. The paper spoke out against both the Russophile and regional 'Ruthenian' political orientations in Transcarpathia; demanded the introduction of teaching in Ukrainian in elementary schools; and promoted Ukrainian culture, a pan-Ukrainian national identity, and the use of Standard Ukrainian.

'Slovo o kniaz'iakh' (Sermon on Princes). A 12th-century monument of homiletic literature. It was delivered as a eulogy in the Chernihiv cathedral ca 1175 by an unidentified cleric during the feast day of the transfer of the relics of SS Borys and Hlib. In it the author spoke of the warring princes Sviatoslav III Vsevolodovych of Chernihiv and Oleh Sviatoslavych of Novhorod-Siverskyi. He invoked the lives of Borys and Hlib and the peace-loving Davyd Sviatoslavych of Chernihiv to exhort the princes to pursue peaceful coexistence, to respect the princely hierarchy, and to present a united front against the Cumans for the welfare of Rus'. A structurally and stylistically simple but moving sermon, it is thematically reminiscent of the epic *Slovo o polku Ihorevi* (The Tale of Ihor's Campaign).

Slovo o polku Ihorevi (full title: *Slovo o polku Ihorevi, Ihoria syna Sviatoslavlia, vnuka Ol'hova* [The Tale of Ihor's Campaign, Ihor the Son of Sviatoslav, Grandson of Oleh]). An epic poem of the late 12th century written by an anonymous author.

History of the work. The original was discovered in 1795 by Graf A. Musin-Pushkin, *ober-prokuror* of the *Holy Synod (1791–6), in the archives of Yoil, the archimandrite of the Transfiguration Monastery in Yaroslavl, Russia, and was published in St Petersburg in 1800 with the assistance of the paleographers M. Malynovsky and M. *Bantysh-Kamensky. The original manuscript and many printed copies perished in the Moscow fire of 1812. The want of an original allowed a number of skeptical critics in the early 19th century (I. Belikov, I. Davydov, M. Kachenovsky, O. Senkovsky, and others) to consider the work a falsification of a later date. Subsequent skeptics included the French Slavists L. Léger and A. *Mazon (who believed that either Yoil or Bantysh-Kamensky wrote the work) and the Russian A. Zimin. The majority of scholars, however, believe it to be authentic. In 1818 K. Kalaidovich noticed an epigraph taken from the *Slovo* in the Pskov *Apostol* of 1307. In 1829 R. Tymkovsky published a 15th-century manuscript, *Zadonshchina* (Past the Don [River]), that was modeled on the *Slovo* (plagiarized, according to M. Speransky).

A wide range of scholars, particularly M. *Maksymovych, demonstrated connections between the *Slovo* and Ukrainian folk poetry. In the 19th century the poem served as the subject of studies by the Russians E. Barsov, V. *Miller, M. Tikhonov, A. *Veselovsky, and P. Viazem-

Pages from the 1974 Kiev edition of *Slovo o polku Ihorevi* (translation by Maksym Rylsky, linocuts by Ivan Selivanov)

sky. Ukrainian academics, apart from Maksymovych, who published works on the *Slovo* included O. *Ohonovsky, O. *Potebnia, and P. *Zhytetsky. In the 20th century more than 700 major studies of the *Slovo* have been published in a variety of languages, including works by D. *Chyzhevsky, M. *Hrunsky, V. *Peretts, and O. *Pritsak. In the late 1930s work on the subject was halted in the Ukrainian SSR and was limited to Russian-language studies commissioned by the Academy of Sciences of the USSR. Owing to political circumstances Russian scholars were the leaders in the field; nonetheless, Ukrainians, Belarusians, and Russians all considered the *Slovo* as belonging to their own literature, because it is a literary monument of Kievan Rus', to which all three East Slavic nations lay claim. But no serious scholar has disputed that it was written in Ukraine, and that much of its semantic and poetic usage is characteristically Ukrainian. In the 1920s M. *Skrypnyk sought to have the *Slovo* recognized as an exclusively Ukrainian work.

Historical basis and content. The subject of the poem is the unsuccessful campaign mounted in the spring of 1185 by Ihor Sviatoslavych, prince of Novhorod-Siverskyi, against the Cumans. Its central theme is the fate of the territories of Rus'. In addressing that theme the author condemns the various princes for their feuding and their selfishness at the expense of the general good.

The poem was written in an epic lyrical style. The historical subject matter is interspersed with dreams, laments, nature's reaction to the hero's fate, monologues of princes, and other motifs and devices.

The poem begins with an invocation of Boian, who sang the praises of princes of the 11th century. The author of the *Slovo* promises to emulate Boian's style and to join the glories of the past with those of the present. After a description of preparations for the campaign, of the three-day battle, and of Ihor's defeat the author proceeds to analyze the reasons for the decline of the Rus' land. After a description of Ihor's escape from captivity the work concludes with praise of the 'ancient princes' Ihor and Vsevolod and of the 'younger ones,' represented by Volodymyr Ihorevych.

Language and poetics. The language of the work is the contemporary Rus' literary language, similar to that of the chronicles, but with a marked increase in the incidence of the vernacular. Most scholars believe that the author was from either Kiev or Chernihiv, but others (A. Orlov, A. Yugov) contend that he was from Galicia. Some have surmised that the copy discovered by Musin-Pushkin had already been modified by succeeding generations of copyists and changed to adhere more closely to the Bulgarian orthography that was in use in the 16th century, or that even Musin-Pushkin's copy may not have been a copy of the original but a copy of other copies. Such multicopying could explain a number of obscure passages in the epic.

The vocabulary is relatively limited; it consists of slightly more than 900 words, combining literary Church-Slavonic with contemporary Rus' terms and archaisms preserved in various old dialects. There are also some influences from other languages.

The poem is particularly rich in epithets, similes, metaphors, the use of metonymy, and hyperbole. The author frequently personifies nature and represents it as a conscious being that either aids or harms humans. The rhythmic structure of the *Slovo* is a matter of considerable debate. All efforts to define its rhythmic structure, including those of R. Abicht in 1901 (syllabic verse), F. Korsh in 1909 (4/4 rhythm), V. *Birchak in 1910 (Byzantine church canonic rhythm), E. Sievers in 1926 (theory of random stress), and Metropolitan I. *Ohiienko in 1946 (rhythmic elements from ancient Hebraic verse), have been unsuccessful. Maksymovych sought to prove that the rhythm of the *Slovo* was a point of departure for the subsequent evolution of the *duma. Zhytetsky underscored the recitative character of the *Slovo* and claimed that each verse-sentence, regardless of the number of syllables, formed a poetic whole with a distinctive pattern of stresses. F. *Kolessa demonstrated a connection between the poem and the laments that developed into dumas. The *Slovo*'s poetic form lends itself to a wide scope of expression and can incorporate many different rhythms depending on the theme and mood.

Translations. Translations and adaptations of the *Slovo* have appeared in many languages, but most are in Ukrainian and Russian. Ukrainian verse and prose adaptations have been done by I. Vahylevych (completed in 1836, published 1884), B. Didytsky (in the *yazychiie*, 1849), Maksymovych (1857), S. Rudansky (completed 1860, published 1896), Yu. Fedkovych (1866, 1902), I. *Franko (1873, 1952), Ohonovsky (1876), P. Myrny (1883, 1896), O. Partytsky (1884), M. Cherniavsky (1894), I. Steshenko (1899, 1967), K. Zinkivsky (1907, 1967), V. Shchurat (1907, 1912), M. Hrushevsky (1923), P. Kostruba (1928), M. Hrunsky (1931), M. Matviiv-Melnyk (1936), S. Hordynsky (1936, 1950, 1989), N. Zabila (1938), V. Svidzinsky (1938), M. Rylsky (1939), Ohiienko (1949), M. Arkas (1951), L. Makhnovets (1953), O. Kovalenko (1954), and M. Kravchuk (1968).

Ukrainian adaptations of fragments of the poem have also been published, including those of the 'Lament of Yaroslavna,' by M. Shashkevych (1833), T. Shevchenko (1860), V. Mova (Lymansky, 1893), B. Lepky (1915), and others. Ya. Kupala translated it into Belarusian (prose, 1919; verse, 1921).

The first verse translation of the *Slovo* into Russian was I. Seriakov's (1803); it was followed by those of V. Kapnist (1809), V. Zhukovsky (1817–19), M. Delarue (1839), L. Mei

(1850), N. Gerbel (1854), A. Maikov (1869), Barsov (1887), K. Balmont (1929), S. Shervinsky (1934), G. Shtorm (1934), I. Novikov (1938), V. Stelletsky (1938), M. Zabolotsky (1946), A. Yugov (1950), S. Botvinnik (1957), and M. Rilenkov (1962).

The first edition of 'Slovo' evoked great interest in Germany's literary world. In 1803 J. Richter published one of the first translations of the poem, followed by J. Miller (1811), A. Bolz (1854), F. Bodenstedt (1861), R. Abicht, R.M. Rilke (1904, printed 1930), A. Luther (1923), E. Sievers (1926), K.H. Meyer (1933), H. Raal (1963), H. Baumann (1968), S. Hordynsky and L. Kaczurowskyj-Kriukow (1985). The poem was translated into English by L. Wiener (1902), L.A. Magnus (1905), H. de Vere Beauclerk (1918), B.A. Guerney (1943), S.H. Cross (1948), V. Nabokov (1961), C.H. Andrushyshen and W. Kirkconnell (1963), I. Petrova (1981), D. Ward (1985), and others. French translations have been published by N. Blanchard and N. Ekstein (1823), F. de Bargon (1878), N. Koulman and M. Behagel (1937), and A. Grégoire (1945).

Polish translations of the *Slovo* include those of C. Godebski (1821), S. Krasiński (1856), Lepky (1899), and J. Tuwim (1927, 1944). Czech translations include those of V. Hanka (1921) and F. Kubka (1946). Other languages into which the epic has been translated are Serbian (I. Khadzhevic, 1842; I. Sankovic; and others), Slovene (M. Pletershnik, 1865), Bulgarian (R. Zinzifov, 1863; L. Stoianov, 1954), Italian (D. Ciampolli, 1911; E. Gatto, 1928), Spanish (J. and R. Maikiel, 1949), Danish (T. Lange, 1888), Hungarian (S. Ridl, 1858; H. Strypsky), Hebrew and Yiddish (S. Mendelssohn, 1875; D. Hofstein and I. Feffer, 1938), Abkhaz, Bashkir, Armenian, Georgian, Kazakh, Tatar, Uzbek, Rumelian-Greek, and many other languages.

H. Khotkevych wrote a historical play based on the *Slovo* in 1926. H. Luzhnytsky also adapted it for the stage. I. Borodin used motifs from the poem in his opera *Prince Igor*, as did M. Lysenko in his *Plach Yaroslavny* (Yaroslavna's Grief). Painters and graphic artists, such as H. Narbut, P. Kholodny, Sr, O. Kulchytska, P. Andrusiv, J. Hnizdovsky, P. Lopata, as well the Russians V. Vasnetsov and V. Favorsky, drew inspiration from the epic. It is also reflected in the sculpture of M.(B). Mukhyn and A. Pavlos and in the stained-glass compositions of L. Molodozhanyn.

BIBLIOGRAPHY

Maksymovych, M. *Pesn' o polku Igoreve* (Kiev 1837)

Ohonov'kyi, O. *Slovo o polku Ihorevi* (Lviv 1876)

Barsov, E. *Slovo o polku Igoreve kak khudozhestvennyi pamiatnik Kievskoi druzhinnoi Rusi*, 2 vols (Moscow 1887, 1889)

Potebnia, A. *Slovo o polku Igoreve: Tekst i primechaniia*, 2nd edn (Kharkiv 1914)

Peretts', V. *Slovo o polku Ihorevim: Pam'iatka feodal'noï Ukraïny-Rusy XII v.* (Kiev 1926)

Hruns'kyi, M. *Slovo o polku Ihorevim* (Kharkiv 1931)

Orlov, A. *Slovo o polku Igoreve* (Leningrad 1938, 1946)

Mazon, A. 'Le Slovo d'Igor,' *Revue des Études Slaves*, 18–19, 21 (1938–9, 1944)

Dmitriev, L. *Slovo o polku Igoreve: Bibliografiia izdanii, perevodov, i issledovanii* (Moscow–Leningrad 1938–54)

Adrianova-Peretts, V. (ed). *Slovo o polku Igoreve: Bibliografiia izdanii, perevodov, i issledovanii* (Moscow 1940)

Davidova, O.; Poplavskaia, I.; Romanchenko, I.; Sostavila, O. (eds). *Slovo o polku Igoreve: Bibliograficheskii ukazatel'* (Moscow 1940)

Grégoire, H.; Jakobson, R.; Szeftel, M. (eds). *La Geste du Prince Igor* (New York 1948)

Adrianova-Peretts, V. (ed). *Slovo o polku Igoreve* (Moscow–Leningrad 1950)

Likhachev, D. *Slovo o polku Igoreve* (Moscow–Leningrad 1950)

Maslov, S. (ed). *Slovo o polku Ihorevi v ukraïns'kykh khudozhnikh perekladakh i perespivakh XIX–XX st.* (Kiev 1953)

Slovo o polku Ihorevim (Kiev 1955)

Makhnovets', L. '*Slovo o polku Ihorevi*' ta ioho poetychni pereklady i perespivy (Kiev 1967)

Dmitriev, L. *Istoriia pervogo izdaniia 'Slova o polku Igoreve'* (Moscow–Leningrad 1960)

Hordyns'kyi, S. '*Slovo o polku Ihorevi*' i ukraïns'ka narodnia poeziia (Winnipeg 1963)

Slovo o polku Igoreve (Moscow 1961, 1967)

Pritsak, O. 'The Igor Tale as a Historical Document,' *AUA*, 12 (1969–72)

Mann, R. *Lances Sing: A Study of the Igor Tale* (Columbus, Ohio 1990)

S. Hordynsky

'Slovo o zakoni i blahodati' (Sermon on Law and Grace). A prominent monument of medieval Ukrainian oratorical and political literature. It was written in Kiev between 1037 and 1050, most likely by *Ilarion. In it the politically astute and erudite author affirms the independence of the Kievan Rus' state and its church and denies Constantinople's assumption of ascendancy over Kiev. Using metaphor and antithesis the author contrasts the 'law' of the Old Testament (cold, darkness, and enslavement) with the 'grace' of the New Testament (warmth, light, and freedom) and eloquently describes and praises the benefits of the Christianization of Kievan Rus'. The work's central part, a patriotic eulogy to Grand Princes Volodymyr the Great and Yaroslav the Wise, describes Volodymyr's conversion as the result of divine inspiration rather than of Byzantine influence. It ends with a prayer on behalf of 'our entire land' for deliverance from those who would conquer it. Although the sermon was intended for a select audience, its popularity was wide, and its structure and stylistic and rhetorical devices were copied by others (eg, the author of the eulogy to Prince Volodymyr Vasylkovych in the Volhynian Chronicle, and Domentijan, the Serbian author of the lives of SS Simeon and Sava [1253]). An English translation of the *Slovo* by N.L. Ickler appeared in the journal *Comitatus* (vol 9, 1978). It has been analyzed by many scholars, notably I. Zhdanov, N. Rozov, L. Müller, and A. Moldavan.

R. Senkus

Slovo o zburenniu pekla (The Tale of the Harrowing of Hell). An Easter drama dating back to the late 17th and early 18th centuries. It is based on apocryphal tales of Jesus's descent into hell, whence he led all the sinners. It is the only example of 17th-century drama that was not written according to the scholastic edicts of poetics. It has neither prologue nor epilogue and does not follow the usual three-to-five-act structure. It is written in syllabically uneven lines of richly rhyming verse and is reminiscent of contemporary Cossack dumas. The language is close to the vernacular of the day, and its robust humor and depiction of everyday life account for its popularity and its influence on contemporary verse. It has been translated into English by I. Makaryk (*About the Harrowing of Hell*, 1989). (See also *School drama.)

Słowacki, Juliusz, b 4 November 1809 in Kremianets, Volhynia gubernia, d 2 April 1849 in Paris. Polish Roman-

tic poet and dramatist; member of the *Ukrainian school in Polish literature. He spent parts of his childhood and youth in Kremianets and knew the Ukrainian language and Ukrainian folk songs and folklore. In the summer of 1827 he visited Odessa, Tulchyn, and Uman. Ukrainian linguistic and folkloric elements and themes are found in his first poem, 'Duma ukraińska' (Ukrainian Duma, 1826), in his narrative poem 'Żmija' (The Snake, 1832), and in other poems. He depicted Ukrainian historical events in his narrative poems 'Jan Kazimierz' (1839), 'Bienowski' (1841), and 'Sen srebrny Salomei' (Salome's Silver Dream, 1843) and in the dramatic romance 'Ksiądz Marek' (The Priest Marek, 1843). He also utilized Ukrainian settings and folklore in his plays 'Balladyna' (1834), 'Mazepa' (1839), and 'Lilla Weneda' (1840). Słowacki's works have been translated into Ukrainian by I. Verkhratsky, M. Starytsky, O. Pchilka, V. Shchurat, P. Stebnytsky, S. Tverdokhlib, M. Zerov, M. Rylsky, M. Bazhan, V. Gzhytsky, A. Malyshko, M. Tereshchenko, M. Zisman, B. Ten, Ye. Drobiazko, and others. Ukrainian editions of his works appeared in Kiev in 1959 (2 vols) and in 1969. Books about him have been written by the Soviet Ukrainian scholars Ye. Rykhlik (1929), H. Verves (1959), S. Levinska (1973), and R. Radyshevsky (1985), and a Ukrainian biobibliographic guide was published by V. Stefanovych (1959).

R. Senkus

Slozka, Mykhailo [Sl'ozka, Myxajlo] (Sliozka), b ? in Belarus, d 1667 in Lviv. Printer and bookseller. He worked at (1633) and directed (1634–7, 1643–51) the Lviv Dormition Brotherhood Press. From 1638 he also ran his own press in Lviv. Slozka printed over 50 books in Church Slavonic, Latin, and Polish. Among his most important publications were the *Apostol* (1639), with illustrations by the renowned engraver *Illia; I. Galiatovsky's *Kliuch razumieniia* (The Key of Understanding, 1659) and *Nebo novoie* (The New Heaven, 1665); Latin works by S. Okolski; and T. Prokopovych's panygeric in honor of Bishop A. Zhelyborsky. Slozka often clashed with the Lviv Brotherhood, who tried to maintain their publishing monopoly; in the prefaces to some of his publications he defended his independence as a publisher. In 1646 Metropolitan P. Mohyla forbade him to print church books, but Slozka disregarded the ban and was anathematized by Mohyla. Only 14 days after Slozka's death was the anathema lifted and his burial allowed.

The Sluch River in Volhynian Polisia

Engraving of St John the Evangelist in the 1639 Lviv *Apostol* printed by Mykhailo Slozka

Sluch River [Sluč]. A right-bank tributary of the Horyn River that flows northward for 451 km through Khmelnytskyi, Zhytomyr, and Rivne oblasts and drains a basin area of 13,900 sq km. Its valley is between 0.2 and 0.8 km wide in its upper reaches and up to 5 km wide downstream. The river itself is 5–50 m wide for most of its course and 110 m at its widest point. The Sluch is used for industrial and water-supply purposes as well as for irrigation, fishing, and water transportion (it is navigable for 290 km). Its main tributaries include (right) the Tnia and (left) the Korchyk, the Smolka, and the Khomora. A small hydroelectric station exists in its upper reaches. The main centers along the river include Novohrad-Volynskyi and Sarny.

Slutsk Chronicle. A short redaction of West Ruthenian chronicles. It was compiled in the 15th century at the court of the Slutsk princes, about whom it also contains some information. The Slutsk Chronicle consists of two parts. The first part describes events in the Grand Duchy of Lithuania from the mid-14th century to 1446. The second part de-scribes events in Kievan Rus' from 970 to 1237. The Slutsk Chronicle is a major source for the history of Belarus and Lithuania, and a source for Ukrainian history to the mid-15th century. It was published in vol 17 of *Polnoe sobranie russkikh letopisei* (Complete Collection of Russian Chronicles, 1907). Its language contains Belarusian influences.

Slutsk principality. A principality of Kievan Rus', with Slutsk as capital. It was formed out of a portion of Turiv-Pinske principality in the 1190s and was for a period a dependency of the Principality of Galicia-Volhynia. In 1326 it became a vassal of the Grand Duchy of Lithuania, and it was ruled by the descendants of Algirdas until 1612, when it was inherited by the Radziwiłłs. The principality was abolished in 1791.

Abram Slutskin

Slutskin, Abram [Sluc'kin], b 5 July 1881 in Borisoglebsk, Voronezh gubernia, Russia, d 13 July 1950 in Kharkiv. Microradiowave physicist; full AN URSR (now ANU) member from 1948. A graduate of Kharkiv University (1916), he conducted breakthrough research on the magnetron generation of centimeter waves there and at the ANU Physical-Technical Institute in Kharkiv, where from 1930 he headed the electromagnetic waves research section. Slutskin is credited with decisive contributions to the creation, in 1939, of the first Soviet decimeter radiolocation system.

Slutsky, Hryhorii [Sluc'kyj, Hryhorij], b 8 October 1916 in Kiev, d 1 March 1990 in Kiev. Architect. A graduate of the Kiev Civil-Engineering Institute (1940), he directed the group that prepared the plan for the general development of Kiev (1964–7) and the plan of development of Kiev's Vidradnyi and Obolon raions, designed residential buildings on Kiev's Bessarabska Square (1948–50) and Engels St (1950–3), collaborated on the design for Kiev's Main Post Office (1952–6) and River Station (1959–60), and wrote articles on architecture.

Slutsky, Mykhailo [Sluc'kyj, Myxajlo], b 19 July 1907 in Kiev, d 23 June 1959 in Moscow. Film director. He completed cinematography courses in the Kiev State Institute of Cinema (1932) and then worked as a director of documentary films in 1947–56 at the Ukrainian Studio of Chronicle-Documentary Films. Among his films are *Radians'ka Ukraïna* (Soviet Ukraine, 1947) and *Kvitucha Ukraïna* (Flowering Ukraine, 1951).

Slutsky, Oleksander [Sluc'kyj], b 20 June 1915 in Kiev, d 9 June 1967. Historian. A graduate of Kiev University (1935), he worked at the AN URSR (now ANU) Institute of History (from 1938) and taught at various institutions of higher education in Kiev. He wrote *Radians'ke i kul'turne budivnytstvo na Ukraïni v pershi roky borot'by za sotsialistychnu industrializatsiiu kraïny (1926–1929 rr.)* (Soviet and Cultural Construction in Ukraine in the First Years of the Struggle for the Socialist Industrialization of the Country [1926–9], 1957) and *Rabochii klass Ukrainy v bor'be za sozdanie fundamenta sotsialisticheskoi ekonomiki (1926–1932 gg.)* (The Working Class of Ukraine in the Struggle to Lay the Foundation of a Socialist Economy [1926–32], 1963).

Yevhen Slutsky   Gen Oleksander Slyvynsky

Slutsky, Yevhen [Sluc'kyj, Jevhen], b 19 April 1880 in Novoe, Yaroslavl gubernia, Russia, d 10 March 1948 in Moscow. Economist, mathematician, and statistician. After graduating in economics from Kiev University (MA, 1911) he taught economics and statistics at the Kiev Commercial Institute (1913–26). Then he worked in Moscow at the Institute for the Study of Business Cycles (1926–30), the Central Institute of Meteorology (1930–8), and the Mathematics Institute of the USSR Academy of Sciences (1938–48). Slutsky made fundamental contributions to economics and mathematics: he built the basis for modern indifference-curve analysis with its income and substitution effects (1915), developed the theory of stochastic processes and applied it to economic cycles (1927), and reformulated the fundamental concept of economics as part of the general theory of purposive action on praxeology (1925). His work in economics influenced O. Lange and the Polish praxeologist T. Kotarbiński. In mathematics he made an important contribution to probability theory.

Sluzhbovets' (The Civil Servant). A weekly organ of the Central Administration and Kharkiv branch of the Union of Soviet Trade Employees, published in Kharkiv in 1925–31 (a total of 269 issues). It contained trade union news, political and economic articles, prose, and poetry.

Sluzhbovyk (The Employee). A monthly organ of the *Union of Ukrainian Private Office Employees, published in Lviv in 1919–39. Its editors included V. Tsmailo-Kulchytsky, P. Podlevsky, V. Poliansky, O. Navrotsky, and A. Nyvynsky.

Sluzhebnyk. See Liturgicon.

Sluzhka, Ivan [Služka], b and d ? Ukrainian civil and military engineer during the 16th century. He is mentioned in chronicles of the period as the designer and builder of five churches and the Kyselivka fortifications in Kiev in 1542–8.

Slynko, Ivan [Slyn'ko], b 25 November 1902 in Vasylkivka, Pavlohrad county, Katerynoslav gubernia. Historian and civic figure. A graduate of the Dnipropetrovske Metallurgical Institute (1935), he worked as a CP(B)U propagandist (1938), as head of the AN URSR (now ANU) presidium's Commission on the History of the Great Fatherland War (1946–50), and as department director (1950–2) and senior research associate (from 1952) at the ANU Institute of History. His published works are about the popular struggle in Ukraine during the Second World War (coauthor, 1957), socialist reconstruction and the technical rebuilding of agriculture in Ukraine (1961), and the under-ground and the partisan movement in Ukraine in 1944 (1970).

Slyvynsky, Andrii [Slyvyns'kyj, Andrij], b 1908 in Dubosari, Tyraspil county, Kherson gubernia. Civil engineer; member of the Ukrainian SSR Academy of Construction and Architecture from 1956. He designed metallurgical and chemical factories in the Donbas, the Urals, and Siberia. He contributed to theoretical foundations in the fields of the organization and mechanization of the construction industry. In 1956–7 he served as assistant minister of the metallurgical and chemical industry of the Ukrainian SSR.

Slyvynsky, Oleksander [Slyvyns'kyj], b 1886 in Poltava gubernia, d 1953 in Canada. Senior UNR Army officer. During the First World War he served as chief of staff of a division and a cavalry corps in the Russian army, and received the highest decoration for bravery in combat. In June 1917 he became a member of the General Military Committee of the Central Rada, and in November he was appointed deputy chief and then chief of the General Staff of the UNR Army. During the Hetman government he continued to serve, at the rank of colonel, as chief of the General Staff. He drafted a comprehensive organizational plan for a regular Ukrainian army. In the interwar period he lived in Germany and then emigrated to Canada.

Smakula, Oleksander (Alexander), b 9 September 1900 in Dobrovody, Zbarazh county, Galicia, d 17 May 1983 in Auburndale, Massachusetts. Physicist, crystallographer, inventor; full member of the Shevchenko Scientific Society from 1930 and the American Physical Society and fellow of the American Optical Society. A graduate of Göttingen University (PH D, 1927), he taught there and then headed the optical laboratory at the Kaiser Wilhelm Institute in Heidelberg (1930–4) and the research laboratory at the Carl Zeiss Optical Co in Jena, Germany (1934–45). From 1951 to 1966 he was a professor at the Massachusetts Institute of Technology, where he organized in 1964 and headed until 1975 the Laboratory of Crystal Physics. Smakula wrote over 100 works, among them important contributions on color centers in crystals (his formulae are basic in the field), the optical properties of solids, the measurement of dielectric properties of materials, and interactions be-

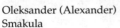
Oleksander (Alexander)   Roman Smal-Stotsky
Smakula

tween radiation and crystal lattices. He undertook important studies of the optical properties of organic crystals (his crystallographic measurements contributed to the discovery of vitamins A, B_2, and D); contributed to the development of quantum theory; and discovered and perfected the standard antireflection coating for lenses, universally used today in photographic cameras, microscopes, telescopes, and other optical lenses and apparatuses.

L. Onyshkevych

Smallpox (Ukrainian: *vispa*). An acute infectious disease caused by a virus (pox virus), for which there is no known cure. Escalating to epidemics and then leveling off through the centuries, smallpox has been known to exist and ravage nations from ancient times. In the Russian Empire 100,000 to 150,000 people succumbed to the disease every year. After the imposition of Soviet rule smallpox was controlled through isolation and vaccination, and it had been eliminated in the USSR by 1936. The campaign of the World Health Organization, begun in 1950, brought smallpox under control throughout the world; the disease was pronounced eradicated in 1977.

Smal-Stotsky, Ivan [Smal'-Stoc'kyj], b 1905 in Poltava gubernia. Writer. As a postwar refugee in Australia he published the prose collection *Potolocheni khliba* (Trampled Grain, 1954), the novel *Klepachivskyi reid* (The Klepachi Raid, 1968), and the reportage *Kinofil'mova ekspedytsiia* (The Filming Expedition, 1970). He has contributed to many émigré periodicals.

Smal-Stotsky, Roman [Smal'-Stoc'kyj] (Smal-Stocki), b 8 January 1893 in Chernivtsi, d 27 April 1969 in Washington, DC. Scholar and political figure; member of the Shevchenko Scientific Society (NTSh) from 1934; son of S. *Smal-Stotsky. He studied at Vienna, Leipzig, and Munich (PH D, 1914) universities. During the First World War he was an emissary of the *Union for the Liberation of Ukraine (SVU) in Munich and worked as an SVU organizer and teacher among the Ukrainians from the Russian army held in POW camps in Germany. After the war he was a representative of the Western Ukrainian National Republic (1918–19) in Berlin and an adviser (1919–21) and extraordinary envoy and plenipotentiary minister (1921–3) of the UNR in Berlin, a professor of comparative Slavic linguistics at the Ukrainian Free University in Prague (1923–

6), a visiting professor (and unofficial UNR envoy) in London and Cambridge (1924–5), and a professor at Warsaw University (1926–39). In Warsaw he was also the UNR government-in-exile's deputy minister of foreign affairs, minister of culture, deputy premier (1926–44), and minister of foreign affairs; he was a member of the UNR delegation to the League of Nations, secretary of the Ukrainian Scientific Institute in Warsaw (1929–39) and editor of its *Pratsi*, a leading figure in the *Promethean movement, and co-publisher (with I. Ohiienko) of the series Studiï do ukraïns'koï hramatyky (Studies in Ukrainian Grammar, 7 vols, 1926–9). During the Second World War he lived under Gestapo house arrest in Prague. A postwar refugee in Germany, in 1947 he emigrated to the United States. Until 1965 he was a professor of East European history at Marquette University in Milwaukee, founding director of its Slavic Institute, and editor of the institute's publications. From 1951 he was president of the American NTSh, and from 1955 head of its Supreme Council and a member of the Political Council of the Ukrainian Congress Committee of America.

Smal-Stotsky produced studies on Ukrainian word formation (particularly of adjectives); on Rumanianisms, Hungarianisms, and Germanisms in the Ukrainian language; on etymology; and on Soviet (Russian) language policy in Ukraine. His more important works are *Abriss der ukrainischen Substantivbildung* (1915), *Narys slovotvoru prykmetnykiv ukraïns'koï movy* (A Study of the Word Formation of Ukrainian Adjectives, 1925), *Znachennia ukraïns'kykh prykmetnykiv* (The Significance of Ukrainian Adjectives, 1926), *Prymityvnyi slovotvir* (Primitive Word Formation, 1929), *Ukraïns'ka mova v Soviets'kii Ukraïni* (The Ukrainian Language in Soviet Ukraine, 1936; 2nd expanded edn 1969), *Die germanisch-deutschen Kultureinflüsse im Spiegel der ukrainischen Sprache* (1942), *The Origin of the Word 'Rus''* (1949), *The Nationality Problem of the Soviet Union and Russian Communist Imperialism* (1952), *The Captive Nations: Nationalism of the Non-Russian Nations in the Soviet Union* (1960), and *The History of Modern Bulgarian Literature* (with C. Manning, 1960). In the United States he published political articles in American newspapers, the *Ukrainian Weekly*, and the *Ukrainian Quarterly*, and contributed the chapter on the history of the Ukrainian language to *Ukraine: A Concise Encyclopaedia* (vol 1, 1963). Articles about him and a select bibliography of his works can be found in *ZNTSh* (vol 177, 1963).

O. Horbach

Smal-Stotsky, Stepan [Smal'-Stoc'kyj], b 8 January 1859 in Nemyliv, Kamenetsky county, Galicia, d 17 August 1938 in Prague. Philologist, pedagogue, and cultural, economic, and political figure; member of the Shevchenko Scientific Society from 1899 and the VUAN from 1918; father of R. *Smal-Stotsky. He studied at the universities of Chernivtsi (1879–83) and Vienna (PH D, 1884), where he became a disciple of F. *Miklosich. While serving as a professor of Ukrainian language and literature at Chernivtsi University (1885–1918), he played a key role in the national and cultural revival of Bukovyna's Ukrainians: he headed the *Soiuz (1879–82), *Ukrainska Shkola (1887–91), and *Ruska Rada (1904–14) societies and was a founding member of the People's Home, a leading member of the Ruska Besida society, a deputy from the National Democratic party in the Bukovynian Provincial Diet

Stepan Smal-Stotsky   Mark Smerchanski

(1892–1911) and the Diet's deputy marshal (1904–10), a long-term coeditor of the daily *Bukovyna*, and a member of the Provincial Executive Board and Provincial School Council. He organized over 100 village reading houses and, together with M. Vasylko and other Bukovynian leaders, fought for and attained equality for Ukrainians in Bukovyna's civil service and political life. As the head of the Ruska Kasa savings and loan society and *Selianska Kasa union of agricultural credit co-operatives, he helped build the Ukrainian co-operative movement in Bukovyna.

From 1911 to 1918 Smal-Stotsky was a member of the Austrian Parliament in Vienna. During the First World War he played a leading role in the *Union for the Liberation of Ukraine. He was a cofounder of the *Graycoats division and represented the Western Ukrainian National Republic's (ZUNR) Ministry of Military Affairs in Vienna. In 1917 he was in charge of the Ukrainian Sich Riflemen's charity work, propaganda, and publishing. From 1919 he lived in Prague, where he served as an envoy of the ZUNR, a professor at the Ukrainian Free University (1921–38), and director of the Museum of Ukraine's Struggle for Independence (1935–8). He was buried in Cracow.

Smal-Stotsky was a precursor of the phonological method in Ukrainian linguists. In his works on Ukrainian linguistics and literature he combined positivist language with a national-romantic weltanschauung. He wrote *Über die Wirkungen der Analogie in der Deklination des Kleinrussischen* (1886, PH D dissertation) and, with T. Gartner, the influential *Grammatik der ruthenischen (ukrainischen) Sprache* (4 edns, 1893, 1907, 1914, 1928). In it he proved that Ukrainian sprang directly from Proto-Slavic, and vitiated the theory of a Proto-East Slavic language. He propounded the same view in his later works, particularly in his book on the development of views concerning the relatedness of the Slavic languages and their common origin (1925; rev edn 1927). He unequivocally opposed V. *Hantsov's view that Standard Ukrainian developed out of the northern and southern Ukrainian dialects. His obvious exaggerations (eg, regarding the particular closeness of Ukrainian and Serbian and the absence of diphthongs in the northern Ukrainian dialects), however, hindered the acceptance of his many valid views by other linguists. In literature, from 1913 Smal-Stotsky focused his attention on T. Shevchenko's works. His studies were published as

one book, *Taras Shevchenko: Interpretatsiï* (Taras Shevchenko: Interpretations, 1934; repr 1965). He also wrote a book on the culture and history of Bukovynian Rus' (1897) and articles on the Hankenstein Codex; Ukrainian orthography and etymology; Ukrainian writers, such as I. Kotliarevsky, M. Shashkevych, Yu. Fedkovych, V. Stefanyk (the preface to his first novella collection, 1897), I. Franko, and O. Kobylianska; and his recollections of Nemyliv (1933).

BIBLIOGRAPHY
Na poshanu storichchia narodyn Stepana Smal'-Stots'koho, vol 172 of ZNTSh, ed K. Kysilevs'kyi (New York–Paris–Sydney–Toronto 1960)
Simovych, V. *Ukraïns'ke movoznavstvo: Rozvidky i statti*, vol 2, ed G.Y. Shevelov (Ottawa 1984)

Smerchanski, Mark [Smerčans'kyj], b 1 November 1914 in Malonton, Manitoba. Mining and metallurgical engineer, and politician. After being educated at the University of Manitoba (1937) and Virginia Polytechnical Institute (1938) Smerchanski managed mines in British Guiana (now Guyana) during the Second World War and then established several mining and manufacturing enterprises in Canada. He sat in the provincial legislature as a Liberal for the constituency of Burrows (1962–6) and in the federal House of Commons as Liberal member for Provencher (1968–72). Smerchanski played an important role in the establishment of the department of Slavic studies at the University of Manitoba, as the head of the Ukrainian Studies Fund, and in the building of the Holy Family nursing home in Winnipeg.

Smerd. The name given to a member of a class of peasantry of the Kievan state in the 11th and 12th centuries. The delineation of the group is somewhat imprecise and a subject of historical debate. Most scholars (M. Braichevsky, B. Grekov, M. Hrushevsky in his early writings, M. Maksymeiko, M. Vladimirsky-Budanov, and others) contend the name was given to two categories of peasants: the free, who gradually lost their freedom with the development of the feudal order, and the dependent peasantry. Others (V. Kliuchevsky, M. Hrushevsky in his later writings, S. Chernov, and A. Presniakov) maintain that only the free peasants, including both those who lived on their own land and those who settled on the estates of princes, were thus designated.

The name disappeared from use in the 12th century but resurfaced in the 13th and 14th centuries as a designation of dependent peasants of the Galician-Volhynian state. It sometimes surfaces in documents of the 15th and 16th centuries concerning Ukrainian territories under Poland and Lithuania as a term for people of low station. From the 13th century the name was increasingly replaced by *kmet. The designation was also used by West Slavs, including Serbs (*smardi*) and Poles (*smardowie, smurdowie*).

BIBLIOGRAPHY
Maksymeiko, M. *Pro smerdiv Rus'koï Pravdy* (Kiev 1927)
Grekov, B.D. *Krest'iane na Rusi*, vol 1 (Moscow 1952)
                                                            A. Zhukovsky

Smerechynska-Shul, Rozha [Smerečyns'ka-Šul', Roža] (née Smereczynska von Dindorf), b 23 April 1914 in Lviv, d 27 October 1986 in Philadelphia. Educator, musicologist, music and art critic. After graduating from the

Szymanowski Conservatory in Lviv in the theory class of S. Barbag and Z. Lissa (1934) she studied musicology at Lviv University (1935–7) with A. Chybinski. She then taught piano and theory at the Lysenko Higher Institute of Music (1937–9) and the Lviv State Conservatory (1939–41). Emigrating to the United States in the 1950s, she taught piano at the Ukrainian Music Institute of America in New York, Jersey City, and other cities. Her writings include the handbook *Osnovy muzychnoho mystetstva: Teoriia i istoriia* (Principles of the Art of Music: Theory and History, 1973), articles, and reviews.

Smerechynsky, Serhii [Smerečyns'kyj, Serhij], b 21 September 1892 in Mechetna, Balta county, Podilia gubernia, d ? Archivist and linguist. As director of the Vinnytsia Archives, he published articles on the predicative instrumental and nominative (1928), on relative clauses in Ukrainian (1929) and a book of essays on Ukrainian syntax in relation to phraseology and stylistics (1932), in which he advocated the use of vernacular constructions in all fields of speech and writing, including science and journalism. He was assailed for this stance by Party critics, such as H. Sabaldyr and O. Matviienko. During the terror in the 1930s he was arrested, and his further fate is unknown.

Smerek, Myroslav, b 1935 in Manastyr, Jarosław county, Galicia. Modernist painter and educator. In 1962 he graduated from the art faculty of Toruń University. He painted the urban landscape series 'Birth of a Factory' and, from his travels in Ukraine, series of paintings of Ukrainian churches and Crimean landscapes (1964). The influence of the icon tradition is evident in his work.

Smereka, Antonina (real surname: Bahlii), b 14 March 1892 in Kiev, d 29 June 1981 in Kharkiv. Actress. She was one of the founders of *Molodyi Teatr (1916–19) and an actress in the Theater of the Western Ukrainian National Republic (1919), Kyidramte (1920–1), Berezil (1922–34), and the Kharkiv Ukrainian Drama Theater (1935–51).

SMERSH (Russian acronym for *smert shpionam* 'death to the spies'). A special division of the *NKVD. Active between 1942–6 under the direction of V. Abakumov and I. Serov, SMERSH acted inside the USSR and among the Russian occupational troops in Europe. Its task was to eliminate alleged opponents of the Soviet regime among Soviet citizens who during the Second World War had spent time outside of the control of Soviet authorities (prisoners of war, *Ostarbeiter, and war refugees). It terrorized its victims outside of the USSR through *repatriation and within the country by mass arrests, executions, or deportations to the gulag.

Smiach camp sites. A group of Mesolithic and Neolithic sites near Smiach, Novhorod-Siverskyi raion, Chernihiv oblast. Excavations in 1925–7 uncovered 18 separate camps and work areas. *Swiderian and *Pitted-Comb Pottery Culture artifacts have been recovered at the site.

Smidovych, Antin [Smidovyč], b 10 June 1872 in Kamianets-Podilskyi, Podilia gubernia, d 1 February 1916 in the Katerynoslav region. Sanitary physician and civic leader. After graduating from Kiev University (1898) he worked as a physician for the Odessa (1899–1904), Voronezh (1904–6), and Kherson (1906–8) zemstvos. As director of the sanitation bureau of the Katerynoslav zemstvo (1908–16) he helped reorganize the zemstvo's sanitary system, encouraged technological applications, promoted sanitary education, and edited a zemstvo sanitary magazine. He died taking part in an organized effort to control a cholera epidemic.

Smiian, Petro [Smijan], b 13 January 1918 in Borzna, Chernihiv gubernia. Historian. A graduate of the Kiev Pedagogical Institute (1938), he taught and worked in Nizhen, Kiev, Uzhhorod, and Lviv, and from 1955 he taught history at the Lutske Pedagogical Institute. In addition to articles on the history of Volhynia he has written the monographs *Revoliutsiinyi ta natsional'no-vyzvol'nyi rukh na Zakarpatti kintsia XIX–pochatku XX st.* (The Revolutionary and National Liberation Movement in Transcarpathia of the Late 19th to Early 20th Century, 1968) and *Zhovtneva revoliutsiia i Zakarpattia: 1917–1919 rr.* (The October Revolution and Transcarpathia: 1917–19, 1972).

Smiian, Serhii [Smijan, Serhij], b 17 May 1925 in Kiev. Theater director. He completed study at the Kiev Institute of Theater Arts (1948) and then worked as an artistic director in Ukrainian drama theaters in Poltava (1951–6), Dnipropetrovske (1956–9), Lviv (1959–66), Zaporizhia (1966–70), and Kiev (1970–8); as stage director in the Kiev Theater of Opera and Ballet (1978–81); and as artistic director of the Kiev Theater of Musical Comedy (1981–7). He has taught at the Kiev Institute of Theater Arts since 1970.

Smila. IV-12. A city (1989 pop 77,500) on the Tiasmyn River and a raion center in Cherkasy oblast. At the end of the 16th century a Cossack settlement named Tiasmyne arose at the site of a former *khutir.* In 1633 it became the estate of S. Koniecpolski, and a few years later it was renamed Smila. Under the Hetman state (1648–67) it was a company center in Chyhyryn regiment. Under Polish rule the town suffered from frequent Tatar raids and feudal oppression. Its inhabitants joined the haidamaka revolts in 1734, 1750, and 1769–70. To appease its residents the Polish king granted Smila the rights of *Magdeburg law in 1773. The town was annexed by Russia in 1793, and became part of Cherkasy county in Kiev gubernia. In 1838 it was purchased by the Bobrinsky family, who built two sugar refineries nearby. Industrial development was stimulated by the construction of the Fastiv–Znamianka railway line in 1876. By 1910 there were 23 factories in Smila, and its population had reached 29,000. In 1921, under the Soviet regime, the Institute of the Sugar Industry was established in Smila. The town was granted city status and promoted to the status of a raion center in 1926. Today it is an industrial and transportation center. It has a large machine-building plant, a sugar refinery, a brewery, and a sewing factory.

Smila Machine-Building Plant (Smilianskyi mashynobudivnyi zavod). A factory of the machine-building industry in Smila, Cherkasy oblast. It was established in 1930 as a machinery repair plant and began to produce new machines in 1957. Initially it specialized in machinery and equipment for the sugar industry, but now it makes a larger assortment of products for use in the food, transportation, and other industries, including salt mills, molasses boilers, dough kneaders, distillers, and filters. In 1972 the plant employed some 1,600 workers.

Leonid Smiliansky   Adrian Smirnov

Smiliansky, Leonid [Smilians'kyj], b 27 February 1904 in Konotip, Chernihiv gubernia, d 11 November 1966 in Kiev. Writer and journalist. In 1928 he concluded his studies at the Kiev Institute of People's Education. He belonged to the literary organizations Hart, Molodniak, and the All-Ukrainian Association of Proletarian Writers and was first published in 1925. For some time he worked as a journalist and literary critic for various publications. He also showed talent in the genres of narrative prose, dramaturgy, and the film scenario (in 1956 he worked on the film *Ivan Franko*, and in 1959 he wrote a film version of the novel *Sashko*). Smiliansky's first novels were written in the constructivist style, among them *Novi oseli* (New Settlements, 1928) and *Zlochyn brygadyra* (The Crime of the Brigadier, 1930). During the Second World War he began writing psychological short stories, such as *Na zastavi* (At the Outpost, 1941), *Topky pohasheni* (The Stoves Are Out, 1941), *Pidslukhani noveli* (Overheard Novellas, 1942), and *Sertse* (Heart, 1943). Smiliansky's historical and biographical works, marred by the tendency to distort historical fact, consist of *Mykhailo Kotsiubyns'kyi* (1940), *Zoloti vorota* (The Golden Gates, 1942), *Ievshan-zillia* (Wormwood, 1943), the two-volume novel about T. Shevchenko *Poetova molodist'* (The Poet's Youth, 1960–2), the drama about Lesia Ukrainka *Chervona troianda* (The Red Rose, 1955), the drama about I. Franko *Muzhyts'kyi posol* (The Peasant Delegate, 1956), and others. An edition of his works in four volumes was published in 1970.

I. Koshelivets

Smilivsky, Ivan [Smilivs'kyj], b 1762, d 1808. Pathologist and internal medicine specialist. A graduate of the Kievan Mohyla Academy and the St Petersburg Medico-Surgical School (1790), in 1796 he was appointed an adjunct professor of pathology and internal medicine and in 1805 a professor of hygiene, physiology, and pathology at the St Petersburg Medico-Surgical Academy. He translated a number of German medical textbooks into Russian and wrote several works on diseases such as tuberculosis.

Smirnov, Adrian, b 16 November 1908 in Novgorod, Russia. Theoretical physicist; AN URSR (now ANU) full member since 1967. A graduate of Leningrad University (1932), he has worked at the Ural Physical-Technical Institute in Sverdlovsk (1932–9), the Ural branch of the USSR Academy of Sciences (1939–49), and the ANU Institute of Physics (1949–50) and Institute of Metal Physics (since 1950). He served as scientific secretary of the ANU Physics Division (1963–6), ANU vice-president (1970–4), and editor of *Ukrainskii fizicheskii zhurnal*. Smirnov has contributed to the development of the theory of imperfect metallic crystals, the theory of the electronic energy spectrum of ordered alloys, the quantum theory of electric resistance in metals and alloys, and the molecular-kinetic theory of order and diffusion in metals and alloys. He developed the theory of phase transitions in alloys with several superstructures under high pressures and the theory of the scattering of slow neutrons in ordered alloys.

Smirnov, Boris, b 26 March 1881 in Vladikavkaz, North Ossetian region, d 4 December 1954 in Moscow. Painter and graphic artist. A lecturer at the Moscow Art Institute, he prepared illustrations for the 1914 Katerynoslav edition of T. Shevchenko's complete works and for illustrated editions of Shevchenko's *Prychynna* (The Insane Girl, 1945) and *Dumy moï* (My Thoughts, 1945). He also painted landscapes, the canvases *Shevchenko's Burial on Chernecha Hill, near Kaniv* (1944), *Raftsmen Singing* [Shevchenko's] *'The Dnieper Is Roaring and Groaning'* (1945), and *Shevchenko's Final Road* (1946), and the album *Na Vkraïni mylii* (In Dear Ukraine, 1945–7).

Smirnov, Mikhail, 1833–77. Historian. His master's dissertation at the Odessa Pedagogical Institute was among the first works to deal with the history of Galicia and Volhynia in the 14th and 15th centuries. It was published as *Sud'ba Chervonnoi ili Galitskoi Rusi* (The Destiny of Red or Galician Rus', 1860; Ukrainian trans pub in vol 5 of the Ruska istorychna biblioteka series [1886]). Smirnov taught at the Richelieu Lyceum (from 1861) and Odessa University (from 1868).

Smirnov, Pavel, b 21 September 1882 in Simbirsk (now Ulianovsk), d 2 April 1947 in Moscow. Russian historian. He studied history at Kiev University under M. Dovnar-Zapolsky and taught there (1912–20, as professor from 1919) and at the Kiev Institute of People's Education (1921–3). He was arrested and sent to Tashkent, where subsequently he taught at the state university (1927–34). After returning to Moscow he was a professor at the Historical-Archival Institute from 1938 (PH D, 1942). A specialist in the socioeconomic and urban history of Russia (16th–19th centuries), he also wrote a monograph about Kievan Rus', published by the VUAN as *Volz'kyi shliakh i starodavni rusy: Narysy z rus'koï istoriï VI–IX vv.* (The Volga Route and the Ancient Rus': Studies of Rus' History of the 6th–9th Centuries, ZIFV, no. 75 [1928]), which challenged the notion that the Russian state descended from Kievan Rus'.

Smirnov, Valerii, b 7 March 1937 in Tahanrih, Rostov oblast. Microbiologist and virologist; full member of the AN URSR (now ANU) since 1985. A graduate of the Dnipropetrovske Medical Institute (1961), he worked for the Scientific Research Institute of Epidemiology, Microbiology, and Hygiene of the Ukrainian Ministry of Health (1961–

Valerii Smirnov   Oleksander Smohorzhevsky

74, assistant director from 1963) and directed the Lviv Scientific Research Institute of Epidemiology and Microbiology (1974–7) and the ANU Institute of Microbiology and Virology (from 1977). In 1978 he became head of the Ukrainian Microbiology Society and editor of *Mikrobiologicheskii zhurnal*.

Smishko, Markiian [Smiško, Markijan], b 7 November 1900 in Lviv, d 20 March 1987 in Lviv. Archeologist. A graduate of the University of Lviv (1931), he taught archeology there (1932–41), then directed the Lviv branch of the AN URSR (now ANU) Institute of Archeology (1940–1 and 1944–51) before joining the ANU Institute of Social Sciences (from 1970 as a senior associate). Smishko wrote several articles about archeological research in Western Ukraine after its annexation by the USSR. A specialist in the formative period of the Eastern Slavs, he wrote several monographs, including *Karpats'ki kurhany pershoï polovyny I tysiacholittia nashoï ery* (Carpathian Kurhans of the First Millennium AD, 1960).

Smohorzhevsky, Oleksander [Smohorževs'kyj], b 23 February 1896 in Lisovi Berlyntsi (now Lisove), Mohyliv-Podilskyi county, Podilia gubernia, d 7 May 1969 in Kiev. Mathematician. After completing his studies at the Kiev Institute of People's Education in 1929, he worked at the Kiev Polytechnical Institute (professor from 1938). He made important contributions to geometry, particularly to the theory of geometric construction in Lobachevsky space, solved a number of construction problems in hyperbolic geometry, and constructed a two-dimensional metric geometry. He also made contributions to analysis, particularly to the theory of differential equations and orthogonal polynomials.

Smohozhevsky, Yason [Smohoževs'kyj, Jason] (Smogorzhevsky), b 1714 in Smorohov, Belarus, d 1788 in Radomyshl, in Right-Bank Ukraine. Uniate metropolitan. He joined the Basilian order and left in 1734 for Rome, where he studied at the St Athanasius College and was ordained (1740). He returned to Polatsk to serve as a preacher and then vicar to Bishop F. Hrebnytsky. In 1762–80 he was archbishop of Polatsk, and in 1780–8 he was Uniate metropolitan of Kiev. Although the 1772 partition of Poland had divided the metropoly among three powers, he at-

tempted to maintain control over all its eparchies from his see in Radomyshl. He ordained P. Biliansky as bishop of Lviv and defended the rights of the Kievan metropolitan to appoint bishops, against Roman Catholic encroachments.

Smola, Parfenii. See Kuts, Valentyn.

Smolensk nobility. The ruling class of the Smolensk region. Largely of Belarusian origin, it defended its rights as a local aristocracy from the encroachments of Muscovy after the territory's annexation by the Muscovite state in the mid-17th century. Beginning with Peter I Russian authorities incrementally limited the Smolensk nobility's rights despite numerous petitions and protests. In 1764–5 the Smolensk military organization was abolished outright, the territory was reconstituted as a Russian gubernia, and the nobility was incorporated into the Russian nobility.

Geographic proximity, historical ties and a similarity of traditions, and an autonomous legal status as well as a distaste for the centralizing tendencies of Moscow helped to develop relations between the Smolensk nobility and Cossack *starshyna*. Hetmans I. Samoilovych and D. Apostol and a number of officers' families (Dunin-Borkovsky, Hamaliia, Lyzohub, Myklashevsky, and others) were directly related to Smolensk aristocratic lines (Engelhardt, Khrapovitsky, Korsak, Krasno-Mylashevich, Likoshin, Paseka, Rachinsky, Ridvansky, Savitsky, Voevodsky, and others). Such family, cultural, and economic ties brought about frequent bilateral resettlement, the sale and exchange of estates, and the introduction of Smolensk peasants into Ukraine. A regiment of Smolensk nobility participated in the Chyhyryn, Crimean, and Azov campaigns led by the Cossacks.

The ties between the two areas also developed a political dimension. In the 18th century the Smolensk nobility was so impoverished and weakened by Russian policies that it sought even closer ties with Ukrainians. The extent of its effort was great enough to alarm the imperial officials, and Anna Ivanovna noted in a secret ukase to Prince A. Shakhovskoi, dated 31 January 1734, that it was necessary 'to pull the Little Russians away from relations with the Smolenskians.' The Russian government was particularly disturbed by Smolensk ties to the Hetmanate government. The autonomist aspirations of the Smolensk territory, also supported by the Polish Commonwealth, had a certain impact on Ukrainian affairs, particularly in the 1730s. The abolition of the autonomy of the Smolensk nobility was part of a broader process of centralization of power within the Russian Empire; it was followed closely by similar moves against the Ukrainian Hetmanate. The last significant episode of Ukrainian-Smolensk relations occurred in the late 18th century, when the Russian government (under Paul I) uncovered the so-called Smolensk conspiracy of 1798; among the participants were several Ukrainian officers of the Russian army (Gen P. Bilukha-Kokhanovsky, Capt F. Lukashevych, the brother of V. Lukashevych, and others).

O. Ohloblyn

Smoliak, Vitalii [Smoljak, Vitalij], b 25 April 1915 in Ivankivtsi, Proskuriv county, Podilia gubernia, d 29 November 1982 in Ivano-Frankivske. Stage director and actor. He acted in the Kharkiv Oblast Touring Theater and the Kiev Theater of Transport Workers (1935–47), directed in the Ivano-Frankivske Ukrainian Music and Drama Theater (1947–55 and 1968–75), and led the Poltava Ukrainian Music and Drama Theater (1955–68).

Smoliatych, Klym. See Klym Smoliatych.

Ivan Smolii

Dmytro Smolych

Smolii, Ivan [Smolij], b 14 August 1915 in Mykhnivets, Turka county, Galicia, d 24 February 1984 in Utica, New York. Writer and journalist; vice-president of the Ukrainian Journalists' Association of America. He debuted as a poet and story writer in Lviv periodicals in 1937, and in 1939 he published the play *Zhyttia na vazi* (Life in the Balance). As a postwar refugee in Germany and, from 1947, the United States he published the story collections *Divchyna z Vinnytsi* (The Girl from Vinnytsia, 1947), *Manekeny* (Mannequins, 1956), and *Zrada* (Betrayal, 1959), the play *Nich nad pshenychnoiu zemleiu* (Night over the Wheaten Land, 1954), the fairy tale *Sontsebory* (The Sun Fighters, 1960), and the novels *Kordony padut'* (The Borders Are Falling, 1951), *U zelenomu Pidhir'i* (In the Green Pidhiria, 1960), and *Nespokiina osin'* (Turbulent Autumn, 1981). Most of his prose works are set in wartime Galicia. He also published poems, publicistic articles, and book reviews in the Ukrainian-American press. From 1979 to his death he was chief editor of the Ukrainian Fraternal Association weekly, **Narodna volia.*

Smoloskyp (Torch). A journal, a publishing house, an information service, and an organization in defense of human rights in Ukraine. O. **Zinkevych is the founder, director, and chief editor. The journal began as a youth supplement to the newspaper *Ukraïns'ke slovo* in Paris (1952–6) under the name *Smoloskyp* before appearing as an independent journal (1956–68; a total of 130 issues). It devoted attention to émigré student issues and popularized and republished the works of the **shestydesiatnyky.*

The V. Symonenko Smoloskyp Publishers (named in honor of a prominent *shestydesiatnyk*) was founded in Baltimore in 1967. It has published works of Ukrainian **samvydav and literature banned in the USSR, such as poetry collections by L. Kostenko, V. Holoborodko, O. Teliha, I. Kalynets, M. Rudenko, M. Kholodny, S. Karavansky, T. Melnychuk, A. Pashko, and O. Berdnyk; novels by O.

Smoloskyp, a magazine published by Smoloskyp

Honchar, M. Osadchy, M. Rudenko, B. Antonenko-Davydovych, and O. Berdnyk; publicism by V. Moroz, O. Berdnyk, M. Rudenko, V. Stus, and Ye. Sverstiuk; the collected works of M. Khvylovy (5 vols, 1982–5); a book about L. Kurbas (1989); *Martyrolohiia ukraïns'kykh tserkov* (Martyrology of the Ukrainian Churches, 2 vols, 1985, 1987); collections of documents of the Ukrainian Helsinki Group; the samvydav journal **Ukraïns'kyi visnyk*; the memoirs of D. Shumuk, Ye. Hrytsiak, and Dokia Humenna; and other collections and anthologies. It has also published works in English, such as the pamphlet series Documents of Ukrainian Samvydav, a collection of O. Teliha's poetry (1977), *Women's Voices from Soviet Labor Camps* (1976), *Dissent in Ukraine* (1977), *The Human Rights Movement in Ukraine: Documents of the Ukrainian Helsinki Group, 1976–1980* (1980), *Ethnocide of Ukrainians in the USSR* (1980), and *A Thousand Years of Christianity in Ukraine: An Encyclopedic Chronology* (1988).

The Smoloskyp Ukrainian Information Service was founded in 1967. It has informed the émigré Ukrainian and Western media and public about developments in Ukraine, particularly political repression and the arrest and imprisonment of dissidents. To inform better the Western media and governments, an English-language service was established in 1974 (directed by B. Yasen), a Spanish-language service was established in Buenos Aires in 1975 (directed by O. Yakhno), and the English-language quarterly *Smoloskyp* has been published.

The Smoloskyp Organization for the Defense of Human Rights in Ukraine was founded in 1970 (directed by A. Zwarun and A. Fedynsky). It has distributed leaflets and brochures in English about Ukrainian political prisoners, collected thousands of signatures on petitions protesting their treatment, and submitted them to the United Nations and other international bodies. The organization was a member of Amnesty International and has participated in international conferences on human rights.

O. Zinkevych

Smoloskypy (Torches). A monthly organ of the **Union of Ukrainian Nationalist Youth (SUNM), published in Lviv in 1927–9. It was edited by O. Bodnarovych, and supported the SUNM faction that advocated co-operation with legal Ukrainian political parties in Western Ukraine (particularly the Ukrainian National Democratic Alliance) and open political activity.

Yurii Smolych (part of a portrait by Anatol Petrytsky, watercolor and gouache, 1931)

Hryhorii Smolsky: *Betrothed Hutsul Woman* (1957)

Smolsky, Hryhorii [Smol's'kyj, Hryhorij], b 2 December 1893 in Pidhirky, Kalush county, Galicia, d 1 February 1985 in Lviv. Painter. He studied at the Novakivsky Art School in Lviv (1923–30) and the Académie Colarossi in Paris (1934–5). He participated in the interwar exhibitions of the Association of Independent Ukrainian Artists, the Ukrainian Art Alliance, and the Lviv Artists' Association. He painted landscapes, particularly of the Hutsul region and Paris (eg, *Notre Dame* [1934] and *Bridge on the Seine* [1935]); portraits, such as *Self-Portrait* (1923), *My Father* (1925), *S. Liudkevych* (1953), *Betrothed Hutsul Woman* (1957), and *V. Stefanyk* (1959); and many Hutsul genre paintings and still lifes. He wrote accounts of his stays in Rome and Paris and the novel *Oleksa Dovbush* (1935).

Smolych, Dmytro [Smolyč], b 11 April 1919 in Petrograd, d 28 April 1987 in Kiev. Opera director. After graduating from the Stanislavsky Opera and Drama Studio in Moscow (1941), he served as an opera director (1941–53) and the chief director (1970–87) of the Kiev Theater of Opera and Ballet, a founder and the chief director of the Cheliabinsk Opera and Ballet Theater (1955–8), chief director of the Odessa Opera and Ballet Theater (1958–62), artistic director of the Minsk Opera and Ballet Theater (1962–9), and chief director of the Lviv Theater of Opera and Ballet (1969–70). He staged many Ukrainian, Russian, and other European operas, including G. Bizet's *Carmen* (1947), S. Moniuszko's *Halka* (1949), K. Dankevych's *Bohdan Khmelnytsky* (1954) and *Nazar Stodolia* (1961), Yu. Meitus's *Young Guard* (1955), and O. Sandler's *In the Steppes of Ukraine* (1962).

Smolych, Yurii [Smolyč, Jurij], b 7 July 1900 in Uman, Kiev gubernia, d 16 August 1976 in Kiev. Writer and Soviet community activist. He was editor of the journals *Sil's'kyi teatr* (1926–9) and *Universal'nyi zhurnal* 1928–9), a member of the literary organizations *Hart and *Vaplite, and one of the organizers of the Techno-Artistic Group A. Upon the formation of the Writers' Union of Ukraine, he became editor of *Literaturnyi zhurnal* (1934) and headed the Kharkiv branch of the Writers' Union until the Second World War. After the war he lived in Kiev and for some time was editor of the periodical *Ukraïna*.

Smolych is known as one of the founders of Soviet Ukrainian prose. His first collection of short stories, *Kinets' mista za bazarom* (The City End beyond the Bazaar, 1924), was followed by the collections *Nedili i ponedilky* (Sundays and Mondays, 1927) and *Pivtory liudyny* (One and a Half Persons, 1927). His prose from the 1920s is characterized by searching and experimentation with form, by originality and strong plots. Smolych pioneered the Soviet Ukrainian fantasy novel with *Ostannii Eidzhevud* (The Last of the Edgewoods, 1926), and continued to develop this genre in the trilogy *Hospodarstvo doktora Hal'vanesku* (The Property of Doctor Galvanescu, 1929), *Shche odna prekrasna katastrofa* (Another Beautiful Catastrophe, 1932), and *Shcho bulo potim* (What Happened Next, 1934).

From the late 1920s, the satirical novel, which was mainly directed against the Ukrainian liberation struggle and the Ukrainian national-minded intelligentsia, began to be an important genre in Smolych's work (*Fal'shyva Mel'pomena* [The False Melpomene, 1928], *Po toi bik sertsia* [On the Other Side of the Heart, 1930]). His satirical novels were also directed against people of the capitalist world and their reactions upon coming into contact with the Soviet regime, portrayed according to the image of them projected in the Soviet press (*Sorok visim hodyn* [Forty-Eight Hours, 1933]). Among Smolych's better works from the second half of the 1930s is an autobiographical trilogy, set in the era of the childhood and youth of his generation: *Nashi tainy* (Our Secrets, 1936), *Dytynstvo* (Childhood, 1937), *Visimnadtsiatylitni* (The Eighteen-year-olds, 1938). During the Second World War, Smolych published several collections of short stories (*Narod voiuie* [The People are Fighting, 1941], *Noveli* [Novellas, 1942], and others). The novel *Vony ne proishly* (They Did Not Get Through, 1946) is also on the subject of war.

In the 1950s, Smolych turned to the events of the Ukrainian-Soviet War in *Svitanok nad morem* (Dawn by the Sea, 1956) and in the two-part novel *Myr khatam, viina palatam*

(Peace to [Peasant] Houses, War on Palaces, 1958) and *Reve ta stohne Dnipr shyrokyi* (The Broad Dnieper Roars and Groans, 1960). These latter works are publicistic novels or political pamphlets on the history of the UNR and its activists, and their literary merit is overshadowed by the grotesque style of political propaganda.

One of Smolych's greatest literary achievements is the memoir trilogy *Rozpovid' pro nespokii* (A Tale of Unrest, 1968), *Rozpovid' pro nespokii tryvaie* (The Tale of Unrest Continues, 1969), and *Rozpovidi pro nespokii nemaie kintsia* (The Tale of Unrest Has No End, 1970), in which he described literary life in Kharkiv in the 1920s and 1930s. Smolych also wrote publicistic political pamphlets directed against Ukrainian nationalism (*Vorohy liudstva ta ikh naimantsi* [The Enemies of the Human Race and their Hirelings, 1953]) and popular literary criticism: *Persha knyha* (The First Book, 1951) and *Rozmova z chytachem* (Conversation with the Reader, 1953). His collected works have been published in six volumes twice (1958–9 and 1971–3), and in seven volumes (1984). In the role of community activist, Smolych participated in the activities of the Writers' Union of Ukraine, and for many years he headed the *Ukraina Society. In 1970, Smolych was decorated with the highest award of the USSR, Hero of the Soviet Union, mainly for his activities in the society, whose work was directed against Ukrainian émigré groups.

BIBLIOGRAPHY
Piskunov, V. *Tvorchist' Iu. Smolycha* (Kiev 1962)
Shakhovs'kyi, S. *Iurii Smolych* (Kiev 1970)
– *Pro Iu. Smolycha* (Kiev 1980)
Holubieva, Z. *Iurii Smolych: Narys zhyttia i tvorchosti* (Kiev 1990)

I. Koshelivets

Smorhachova, Liudmyla [Smorhačova, Ljudmyla], b 29 November 1950 in Kiev. Ballet dancer. In 1968 she completed study at the Kiev Choreography School and joined the Kiev Theater of Opera and Ballet as leading ballerina. In 1978 she won the first prize gold medal at the Second International Ballet Competition in Tokyo.

Smotrych, Oleksander [Smotryč] (pen name of Oleksander Floruk), b 28 April 1922 in Kamianets-Podilskyi. Writer. During the Second World War he worked as a journalist for the nationalist papers *Ukraïns'ke slovo* (Kiev) and *Holos* (Berlin). As a postwar refugee in Germany and, since the late 1940s, Toronto he wrote the story collections *Nochi* (Nights, 1947), *Vony ne zhyvut' bil'she* (They Are No Longer Alive, 1948), *Vybrane* (Selections, 1952), and *Buttia: 16 nikomu nepotribnykh opovidan'* (Being: 16 Stories Nobody Needs, 1973). Having switched to poetry, he published on his own nine booklets of satirical and provocative poems titled *Virshi* (Verses, 1974–5) and the collections *20 korotkykh virshiv* (20 Short Verses, 1975) and *1933* (1975). A lyrical collection, *Uzhynok* (The Reaping, 1985), was published by Suchasnist. His stories and poems have appeared in *Novi dni*, *Suchasnist'*, and other émigré periodicals.

Smotrych [Smotryč]. V-7. A town smt (1986 pop 3,000) on the Smotrych River in Dunaivtsi raion, Khmelnytskyi oblast. It was first mentioned in historical documents in the 1370s. In 1448 it was granted the rights of *Magdeburg law. Since the 18th century Smotrych has developed a rep-

utation for ceramic art. On 22 July 1919 a battle between the UNR and the Bolshevik armies took place there. In 1923–62 the town served as a raion center.

The Smotrych River

Smotrych River [Smotryč]. A left-bank tributary of the Dniester River that flows southward for 168 km through Khmelnytskyi oblast and drains a basin area of 1,800 sq km. With a width of 10–15 m (40 m at its widest point), the river is particularly notable for its tall banks, which give it a ravinelike appearance. It is used for water supply, irrigation, and fishing. A small hydroelectric station is situated on it, as well as the city of Kamianets-Podilskyi and the town of Horodok.

Smotrytsky, Herasym [Smotryc'kyj], b ? in Smotrych (now in Dunaivtsi raion, Khmelnytskyi oblast), d October 1594. Writer and teacher. He was secretary at the Kamianets-Podilskyi county office and in 1576 was invited by Prince K. *Ostrozky to Ostrih, where he became one of the leading activist members of the Ostrih intellectual circle. In 1580 Smotrytsky became the first rector of the Ostrih Academy. He was one of the publishers of the Ostrih Bible, to which he wrote the foreword and the verse dedication to Prince K. Ostrozky. The dedication is one of the earliest examples of Ukrainian versification (nonsyllabic) and is somewhat reminiscent of Ukrainian dumas. Smotrytsky's polemical works against those betraying the Orthodox faith and a satire on the clergy have been lost. Only his book, *Kliuch tsarstva nebesnoho* (Key to the Heavenly Kingdom, 1587), which is the first printed example of Ukrainian polemical literature, has survived. It is composed of a dedication to the prince of Ostrih, the appeal 'Do narodov ruskykh ...' (To the Rus' Peoples ...), and two polemical treatises, 'Kliuch tsarstva nebesnoho ...' (Key to the Heavenly Kingdom ...) and 'Kalendar rymskyi novyi' (The New Roman Calendar). In the last-named Smotrytsky calls for the independence of 'the Rus' faith,' polemicizes with the Jesuit B. Herbest, criticizes the Catholic teaching on the divine origin of the pope's authority, and rejects the Gregorian calendar. Smotrytsky did not always use theological arguments in his work; instead he often used folk humor with anecdotes and proverbs, and he wrote in a language close to the vernacular, which made his work accessible to the broad masses.

I. Koshelivets

Smotrytsky, Meletii [Smotryc'kyj, Meletij] (secular name: Maksym), b 1577 in Smotrych (now in Dunaivtsi raion, Khmelnytskyi oblast), d 27 December 1633 at the

Archbishop Meletii Smo-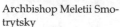trytsky

Gen Kost Smovsky

Derman Monastery, Volhynia. Philologist, churchman, and polemicist; son of H. Smotrytsky. He studied at the Ostrih Academy; the Jesuit college in Vilnius; and, from 1605, in Leipzig, Nuremberg, and Wittenberg. In 1608, he returned to Vilnius to teach at the Orthodox brotherhood school. There he wrote (in Polish) his famous defense of the Orthodox church, *Trenos, to iest lament iedyney ś. powszechnej apostolskiey wschodniey cerkwie* (Threnos, or the Lament for the One Holy Universal Apostolic Eastern Church, 1610). He entered the Holy Spirit Monastery in Vilnius in 1617 and published a *didactic gospel. He is believed to have served as a professor and rector of the Kiev Epiphany Brotherhood School in 1618–20. In 1620 he was consecrated archbishop of Polatsk by Patriarch Theophanes of Jerusalem. During the next three years he wrote several polemical tracts, including *Verificacia niewinności* (A Verification of Innocence, 1620) and *Oborona verificaciey* (A Defense by Verification, 1621), justifying the re-establishment of the Orthodox hierarchy by Theophanes and defending the Orthodox against charges of collusion with the Moslems and Muscovites (see also *polemical literature). Smotrytsky travelled to Constantinople and the Holy Land, and after his return he joined the Uniate church, in 1627, and entered the Derman Monastery (some scholars believe he may have converted secretly earlier). In 1627–8 he negotiated with Y. Boretsky and P. Mohyla in an attempt to re-create a united Ruthenian church in union with Rome but under its own patriarch. In preparation for the discussions, he wrote *Apologia peregrinatiey do kraiów wschodnych* (Apology for the Peregrination to Eastern Lands, 1628). When the negotiations failed, Smotrytsky was condemned at the Orthodox church synod in Kiev in 1628 and forced to recant his conversion to Catholicism. Subsequently he returned to the Derman Monastery.

Smotrytsky's most significant contribution to philology was *Gramatiki slavenskiia pravilnoe syntagma* (The Correct Syntax of Slavonic Grammar, 1619; reprinted in 1974 with an introduction by O. Horbach [Horbatsch]). This work influenced the form of the Church Slavonic used in Ukraine, Russia, Rumania, Serbia, and Croatia, and several subsequent editions were published. A shortened version, for use as a school textbook, appeared in Kremianets in 1638. Smotrytsky's grammar has been extensively studied by Ukrainian, Russian, and German linguists. Facsim-

ile reprints of most of his collected works were published in 1987 in two volumes introduced and edited by D. Frick.

BIBLIOGRAPHY
Solovii, M. *Meletii Smotryts'skyi iak pys'mennyk*, 2 vols (Rome–Toronto 1977–8)
Frick, D. 'Meletij Smotryc'kyj and the Ruthenian Question in the Early Seventeenth Century,' *HUS*, 8 (1984)
– 'Meletij Smotryc'kyj and the Ruthenian Language Question,' *HUS*, 9 (1985)

O. Horbach

Smovsky, Kost [Smovs'kyj, Kost'], b 21 May 1892 in Poltavska *stanytsia*, Kuban, d 8 February 1960 in Minneapolis. UNR Army officer. After joining the UNR Army in 1917, he commanded a number of its best units: an artillery battery of the Haidamaka Battalion, which distinguished itself in suppressing the Bolshevik insurrection in Kiev (January 1918); the Black Sea Artillery Regiment (1919); the Lubni Cavalry Regiment; the Tenth Artillery Regiment of the Graycoats, during the First Winter Campaign (1919–20); and the First Cavalry Brigade of the Separate Cavalry Division (1920). He was promoted to the rank of brigadier general. His recollections about the wars for Ukraine's independence were published in *Svoboda* in 1958.

Smt. See Urban-type settlement.

Smyk, Oleksander, b 1900 in Nekhvoroshcha, Konstantynohrad county, Poltava gubernia, d 1942 in Kiev. Architect. After graduating from the Kiev State Art Institute in 1928, he worked for various planning and construction agencies in Kiev and taught architecture at the Kiev State Art and Civil-Engineering institutes (1929–41). He designed (with A. Dobrovolsky) the Roads Administration building in Luhanske in 1935 and residential buildings in Kiev. His style displayed elements of classical architectural forms as well as distinctively Ukrainian features.

Peter Smylski

Smylski, Peter [Smyl's'kyj, Petro], b 15 April 1915 in Dauphin, Manitoba. Stomatologist and community activist. A graduate in dentistry from the University of Alberta (1940), he served in the Dental Corps of the Canadian army (1943–6), specialized in dental surgery, and was a professor at the University of Toronto (1965–80) and head of the oral surgery division at the Toronto General Hospital. He has been president of the Ukrainian Canadian Veterans' Association and chairman of the board of directors of the St Vladimir Institute in Toronto.

Smyrnov, Mykola, b 21 January 1912 in Kharkiv, d 4 October 1963 in Donetske. Stage director and actor. He completed study at the Kharkiv Music and Drama Institute (1933) and then worked in the Donetske Ukrainian Music and Drama Theater (1933–41, and 1949–63 as principal stage director).

Oleksandra Smyrnova-Zamkova

Smyrnova-Zamkova, Oleksandra, b 31 May 1880 in Pereiaslav, Poltava gubernia, d 22 September 1962 in Kiev. Pathologist and anatomist; full member of the AN URSR (now ANU) from 1951. A graduate of Montpellier University in France (1905), she taught at the Higher Medical Courses for Women (1908–20), the Kiev Medical Institute (1920–30), and the ANU Institute of Clinical Physiology (1931–53, department head from 1938). She also headed the Department of Pathological Anatomy at the Second Kiev Medical Institute (1933–41) and the morphology laboratory at the ANU Institute of Physiology (1953–62). She published numerous works, of which the most important dealt with the pathological anatomy of infectious diseases, radiation sickness, and the origins of tumors. She wrote *Osnovnoe argirofil'noe veshchestvo i ego funktsional'noe znachenie* (The Basic Argyrophilic Substance and Its Functional Significance, 1955).

Snake (Ukrainian: *zmiia, hadiuka, vuzh*). Any of numerous limbless, scaled reptiles of the order Squamata, related to *lizards, divided into the suborders Serpentes and Ophidia and, further, into the poisonous family Viperidae and the harmless family Colubridae. In Ukraine there are only two species of poisonous snakes, the common viper (*Vipera berus*), found in Polisia and the forest-steppe, and the steppe viper (*V. ursini*). A subspecies of the steppe viper is also found in the Carpathians. Viper bites incapacitate but are not life-threatening to adult humans. The nonpoisonous snakes include the common or grass snake (*Natrix natrix*) and the water snake (*N. tessellata*).

Snapdragon (*Antirrhinum*; Ukrainian: *rotyky, l'vyni pashchi*). A herbaceous plant of the family Scrophulariaceae. Two species are known in Ukraine, wild snapdragons (*A. oronthium*), which grow as weeds in the fields and occasionally in brushwood, and multicolored garden snapdragons (*A. majus*), which are cultivated as decorative flowers.

Snapweed (*Impatiens*; Ukrainian: *rozryv-trava, balzamin*). A herbaceous plant of the family Balsaminaceae, of which there are about 400 species worldwide. In Ukraine *I. parviflora* (introduced from Mongolia) and *I. nolitangere* (touch-me-not) grow naturally in shady forests and ravines and near springs and orchards in Polisia, in the forest-steppe, and in the Carpathian Mountains. Orchard snapweed or garden balsam (*I. balsamina*) and *I. roylei* are cultivated as ornamentals. In folklore snapweed figures as a magic herb with powers to break chains, open locks, and so on.

The main street in Sniatyn

Sniatyn [Snjatyn]. V-6. A city (1989 pop 10,300) on the Prut River and a raion center in Ivano-Frankivske oblast. It was first mentioned in a historical document in 1158, as a fortified town in Halych principality. From 1387 it was under Polish rule. In 1448 it was granted the rights of *Magdeburg law, and by the 16th century it had developed into an important trade center. After the partition of Poland in 1772, it was annexed by Austria, and in 1919 it fell under Polish rule. In 1939 it became part of the Ukrainian SSR. Today Sniatyn manufactures furniture, cheese, bricks, and reinforced concrete. It has two literary memorial museums, one dedicated to M. Cheremshyna and the other to V. Kasiian.

Sniehirov, Yevhen [Snjehir'ov, Jevhen] (Helii), b 14 October 1927 in Kharkiv, d 28 December 1978 in Kiev. Writer and dissident. He graduated from the Kharkiv Theater Institute and worked as an actor, a lecturer in Ukrainian literature in secondary schools and at the institute, a member of the editorial board of *Literaturna Ukraïna*, and director at the Kiev Studio of Chronicle-Documentary Films. His first published work appeared in 1954, when he began working as a prose writer and critic. He published a collection of stories, *Lito vernet'sia* (Summer Will Return, 1957), a novel, *Chy ia mav pravo?* (Did I Have the Right?, 1962), and a satire cowritten with Yu. Lubotsky, *Zolotyi buts* (The Golden Boot, 1963). Continued repressions and Russification in Ukraine prompted him to join the Ukrainian dissident movement in the 1970s. For doing so he was expelled from the Party and the Writers' Union of Ukraine in 1974. He then began writing letters of protest to the leaders of the USSR, in which he renounced his Soviet citizenship. He also wrote a work circulated by samvydav (1974–7), alternately titled *Naboï dlia rozstrilu* (Bullets

Yevhen Sniehirov   Bishop Ivan Snihursky

for Execution) and *Nen'ko moia, nen'ko* (Oh, Mother of Mine, Mother). In it he denounces the show-trial of the so-called *Union for the Liberation of Ukraine in Kharkiv as a state provocation which brought about the destruction of the Ukrainian intelligentsia in the 1930s. On 22 September 1977 he was arrested. On 31 March 1978 he fell gravely ill and was taken from prison to a hospital, where he died.

The most complete collection of his samvydav writings was published as *Naboï dlia rozstrilu* (New York–Toronto 1983). It includes the aforementioned work, the satirical story *I choho oto ia liapaiu* (And Why Am I Babbling?, 1977), an account of his prison experiences, fragments of prose and verse, and recollections about him written by others. In 1990 *Naboi dlia rozstrilu* was republished in Ukraine, and Sniehirov was posthumously reinstated as a member of the Writers' Union of Ukraine.

I. Koshelivets

Snihur, Luka, b 1846 in Pohar, Stryi circle, Galicia, d 1928. Builder and wood carver. He built about 35 wooden village churches in Galicia, including those in Rosokhach (1882), Oriava (1882), Husne Vyzhne (1890), Matkiv (1899), Kryve (1922), and Klymets (1925). They are distinguished by their fine construction and original form. He also carved the iconostases in the churches of Kryve, Radych, and Dovzhky.

Snihurivka. VI-13. A city (1989 pop 18,000) on the Inhulets River and a raion center in Mykolaiv oblast. It was founded in 1812 and granted city status in 1961. Today it is an administrative and agricultural city. Its plants manufacture reinforced-concrete products and dairy products, bottle mineral water, and repair machinery. The main pumping stations of the Inhulets and the Yavkyne irrigation systems are located in Snihurivka.

Snihursky, Ivan [Snihurs'kyj], b 8 May 1784 in Berestiany, Sambir circle, Galicia, d 24 April 1847 in Peremyshl. Church and cultural leader. He studied theology in Vienna (to 1808) and then was pastor at St Barbara's Church there (1808–13) and a professor of theology and dean of the faculty (1817–18) at the University of Vienna. In 1818 he was consecrated bishop of Peremyshl. As bishop he revived the eparchial theological seminary and founded a valuable library and a publishing house. Under his patronage I. Lavrivsky and I. Mohylnytsky organized a comprehensive educational system that by 1832 included almost 400 schools. From 1824 to 1833 Snihursky also

served as principal of the Peremyshl Polish gymnasium. Yu. Zhelakhovsky published a biography of Snihursky in 1894 in Lviv.

Snip (The Sheaf). A literary almanac published in Kharkiv in 1841. Edited by O. Korsun, it contained M. Kostomarov's play *Pereiaslavs'ka nich* (Pereiaslav Night) and his translation of five of Byron's *Hebrew Melodies*; poems by M. Petrenko; poetry and fables by S. and P. Pysarevsky and O. Korsun (including his translations of five Czech poems); P. Korenytsky's satirical poem 'Vechernytsi' (Evening Parties); and the first Ukrainian translation of a poem by Petrarch, by M. Pysarevska.

Snip (1912–13)

Snip (The Sheaf). A weekly newspaper published by M. Mikhnovsky in Kharkiv from January 1912 to January 1913 (a total of 52 issues). Edited by M. Bilenky, it promoted Ukrainian patriotism among the intelligentsia and was one of the first newspapers to advocate separation of Ukraine from Russia. Among the contributors were I. Franko, L. Pakharevsky, M. Kononenko, and T. Zhoralsky.

Snitko, Oleh, b 30 April 1928 in Kiev, d 14 April 1990 in Kiev. Solid-state physicist; AN URSR (now ANU) corresponding member from 1968 and full member from 1985. After graduating from Kiev University (1951) he investigated the properties of semiconductors at the ANU Institute of Physics in Kiev. He joined the ANU Institute of Semiconductors in 1961 and served as a department head (from 1962), a deputy director (1967–70), and director (from 1970). Snitko's primary contribution comes from his investigation of electronic processes on hyperpure semiconductor surfaces. He is author of 250 publications (5 monographs) and has a number of inventions.

Snizhne [Snižne]. V-19, DB III-5. A city (1990 pop 69,000) under oblast jurisdiction in Donetske oblast. It was founded in 1784 and was known as Vasylivka village until 1864. It belonged to the Don Cossack province. In 1900 anthracite coal began to be mined there, and thereafter the town grew quickly (1939 pop 16,200). In 1938 it attained city status. Today it has seven coal mines, a chemical machinery building plant, a machine repair factory, and several enterprises of light industry.

Snov River. A right-bank tributary of the Desna River that flows for 253 km through Briansk oblast (RF) and Chernihiv oblast and drains a basin area of 8,700 sq km. The river is 4–14 m wide in its upper reaches and 20–40 m wide downstream (at one point reaching 200 m). The Snov is frozen over from late November to early April. It is used for water supply and irrigation. Its lower reaches are navigable.

Snovske. See Shchors.

Snowberry (*Symphoricarpos*; Ukrainian: *snizhnoiahidnyk*). A shrub belonging to the family Caprifoliaceae, with bell-shaped, pinkish or white flowers and two-seeded berries. Three species are cultivated in Ukraine as ornamentals in parks and orchards, snowberry or waxberry (*S. albus*), Indian currant or coralberry (*S. orbiculatus*), and wolfberry (*S. occidentalis*).

Snowdrop (*Galanthus*; Ukrainian: *pidsnizhnyk*). Bulbous, white-flowered plants of the family Amaryllidaceae. Two species are found in Ukraine, common snowdrop (*G. nivalis*), which grows in deciduous forests, in brushwoods on the right bank of the Dnieper River, and in Carpathian meadows and is listed as an endangered species in Ukraine, and the folded snowdrop (*G. plicatus*), native to Crimean forests. The name *pidsnizhnyk* is also commonly used for *Scilla sibirica*, *Hepatica nobilis*, and *Anemone nemorosa*.

Zenon Snylyk

Snylyk, Zenon, b 14 November 1933 in Putiatyntsi, Rohatyn county, Galicia. Journalist and athlete. A graduate of the universities of Rochester and Chicago (MA, 1958), Snylyk was a member of the US soccer team in the 1956, 1960, and 1964 Olympic Games – the only player in US soccer history to appear on three Olympic teams – and served as team captain in 1956 and 1960. He also played on and/or captained US teams in three Pan-American games and one World Cup series. He taught political science briefly at McGill University in Montreal before becoming chief editor of The *Ukrainian Weekly* in 1962. He served in that capacity until becoming chief editor of the newspaper *Svoboda* in 1980. Snylyk was also an assistant editor of *Ukraine: A Concise Encyclopaedia*, vol 2.

Snyna (Slovak: Snina). V-3. A town (1970 pop 10,000) in the Chirokha River Valley in the Prešov region of Czechoslovakia. It is on the border of Ukrainian ethnic territory. In 1961 there were 44 Ukrainian villages, with a total population of 25,000, in its vicinity.

Soaring or **gliding** (*shyriannia*). The sport of soaring in Ukraine began with the pioneering efforts of K. Arzeulov, Yu. *Tereverko, and M. Delone. Arzeulov, who was of Armenian descent, built and flew a glider in the Crimea in 1906, and in 1916 he made aviation history by being the first pilot to master the intentional spin. In 1908–9 Delone, a mechanics professor at the Kiev Polytechnical Institute, directed the construction of several versions of the Chanute glider, which were successfully flown near the village of Dzvinkove in Kiev county. In 1910 he published a pamphlet on how to build and fly a glider. Tereverko was the first to fly with a passenger.

By the early 1920s glider building and flying had attracted many enthusiasts, among them S. *Korolov, the chief designer of the Soviet space program, and the aircraft designer O. *Antonov. Antonov's record-setting glider A-9 and his all-metal gliders A-11, A-13, and A-15 played an important role in the development of gliding in the USSR. Dozens of glider clubs sprang up throughout Ukraine. The most prominent were at the Kiev Polytechnical Institute, the Kiev School for Glider Instructors, the Kharkiv Aviation School, and the Odessa branch of the Aviation Society of Ukraine and the Crimea, at which S. Korolov designed and built his K-5 glider in 1924. From 1923, annual gliding competitions were held near the village of Koktebel, in the Crimea; in 1944 Koktebel was renamed Planerske (from *planer* 'glider'), and in 1970 a soaring museum was founded there. In 1925, Soviet Ukrainian pilots participated in the sixth international competition on the Wasserkuppe, a hill in the Rhön Mountains of Germany; one of them (V. Yakovchuk) placed third in the duration category, with a flight of 91 minutes. As a sport, gliding gained great popularity in the USSR in the 1930s, and Soviet pilots established several world records.

Interwar Western Ukraine. S. Chervinsky of Volhynia designed and built a biplane glider and made successful flights in 1917 in the Crimea. After the First World War he returned to Kovel and built an open-frame monoplane glider in which he made several flights in 1927. In the late 1920s, groups of enthusiasts in Dubno, Volhynia, and Zbarazh, Galicia, designed and built gliders. The first true soaring flight in Galicia was made at the Lysa Hora site, near Zolochiv, in 1928 by S. Grzeszczyk.

The most active gliding center in Galicia was the Aviation Association of Students at the Lviv Polytechnical Institute. Founded under Austrian rule in 1903, it was revived under Polish rule in 1923, and contributed significantly to advances in glider design and flight in interwar Galicia. Over 400 gliders and sailplanes were built in its government-supported workshops in the 1930s; many were exported, and several were used in Polish- and world-record flights. The last ISTUS (International Study Commission for Motorless Flight) conference and glider competition before the Second World War was held in Lviv in May 1939.

Postwar Ukraine. After the Second World War, gliding in Ukraine flourished for about two decades. In 1952 the Ukrainian pilot V. Yefymenko established a new world flight record of 636 km (it has since been surpassed) in the glider A-9. In the 1972 world championships in Yugoslavia, the Ukrainian pilot Ye. Rudensky placed second in the standard class. Ukrainians who placed high in Soviet championships are V. Honcharenko, Z. Solovei, and M.

Verytennykov. Gliding in Ukraine, and in the USSR as a whole, has been conducted under the patronage of various paramilitary defense organizations; in 1951 they were amalgamated into the *Voluntary Society for Assistance to the Army, Air Force, and Navy (DOSAAF). Because gliding could not be practiced in the USSR outside the framework of the DOSAAF, it was wholly contingent on government support. Since the 1970s, when relatively expensive fiberglass construction became the norm for high-performance sailplanes, Soviet metal-and-wood gliders ceased to be competitive on the world level. At the world championships in Austria in 1989, Soviet pilots flew sailplanes built in the West, but did not do well. Inside the USSR gliding, as a paramilitary sport, remained as popular as ever. From the 1970s it relied heavily on Czech, Polish, and Lithuanian gliders and sailplanes. Some of the more active soaring centers in Ukraine are Buzova (30 km W of Kiev), Borodianka (55 km NW of Kiev), Kamenka (10 km NW of Dnipropetrovske), Sutysky (45 km S of Vinnytsia), and Voronovo (55 km W of Rivne).

BIBLIOGRAPHY
Sheremetev, B. *Planery* (Moscow 1959)
Cynk, J. *Polish Aircraft, 1893–1939* (London 1971)
Antonov, O. *Desiat' raziv spochatku* (Kiev 1973)
Vetrov, G. *S.P. Korolev v aviatsii* (Moscow 1988)

O. Bilaniuk

Sob River. A left-bank tributary of the Boh River that flows southward for 115 km through Vinnytsia oblast and drains a basin area of 2,840 sq km. The river originates in the Dnieper Upland; it is 3–5 m wide near its source and 60–80 m wide downstream. It supplies water for industrial and agricultural purposes and feeds a hydroelectric station. It is also used for pisciculture. The city of Haisyn is situated on it.

Hanna Sobachko-Shostak: *Whirlwind* (wall decoration in gouache and watercolor, 1920)

Sobachko-Shostak, Hanna [Sobačko-Šostak], b 15 December 1883 in Skoptsi (now Veselynivka), Pereiaslav county, Poltava gubernia, d 3 December 1965 in Cherkizovo, Moscow oblast. Master of folk decorative painting. In 1910 she began painting embroidery and kilim patterns in A. Semigradova and E. Pribilskaia's folk-art workshop in Skoptsi. From 1932 she lived in exile in Cherkizovo and designed embroidery patterns for the local cloth factory. Her decorative paintings, with floral and faunal motifs, are distinguished by their dynamic composition, asymmetry, and use of intense colors. Sobachko's work was exhibited in Kiev (1913, 1919, 1963, 1965), St Petersburg (1913), Moscow (1915, 1927, 1936), Paris (1913, 1937), Berlin (1914, 1922), and New York (1939). A book about her by H. Miestiechkin was published in Kiev in 1965.

Sobachky archeological site. A Neolithic settlement near Zaporizhia. The site was excavated in 1928–9, then flooded by the Kakhivka Reservoir. Uncovered in the course of excavations were dwellings with stone hearths, stone and bone tools, handmade pottery with imprinted geometric designs, and granite polishing stones. The inhabitants engaged primarily in fishing.

Sobkivka settlement. A late Bronze Age *Bilohrudivka culture settlement near Sobkivka, Uman raion, Cherkasy oblast. Excavations in 1951–2 revealed dwellings, a large number of ash pits, handmade pottery (with some imprinted designs), flint tools, and bronze adornments. The settlement's inhabitants engaged in agriculture, animal hus-bandry, hunting, and fishing.

Sobko, Petro, b 30 May 1819 in Kiev, d 26 November 1870 in St Petersburg. Civil engineer. He studied and taught at the Engineers' Corps Institute in St Petersburg. He designed (1839–40) a suspension bridge over the Neva River and introduced steel components in wooden bridge trusses. He initiated the first course on building mechanics in the Russian Empire and set up one of the first laboratories in that field. He was a specialist in railroad construction and held an important position in the St Petersburg–Warsaw Railroad Co. He wrote a number of handbooks and textbooks on structural mechanics and railroad engineering.

Vadym Sobko

Sobko, Vadym, b 18 May 1912 in Moscow, d 12 September 1981 in Kiev. Prose writer and playwright. He graduated from the philological faculty of Kiev University in 1939. He began to publish his work in 1930. He published the poetry collections *Pohliad vpered* (Looking Ahead, 1932), *Traktorobudni* (Tractor Days, 1932), and *Mii tovarysh* (My Friend, 1933), and the narrative poem *Mikron* (Micron, 1934), among others. Sobko published collections of short stories, including *Montazhnyky* (The Assemblers, 1931) and *Liudy ryshtovan'* (People of Scaffolding, 1933). He achieved some measure of popularity with his adventure novels *Hranit* (Granite, 1937) and *Kreizer* (Cruiser, 1940). He wrote the novel trilogy *Shliakh zori* (Path of the Star), with the parts titled *Krov Ukraïny* (The Blood of Ukraine, 1943), *Kavkaz* (The Caucasus, 1946), and *Vohon' Stalinhradu* (The Fire of Stalingrad, 1947), which was based on the events of the Second World War. The play *Zhyttia pochynaiet'sia znovu* (Life Begins Anew, 1950) and the novel *Zaporuka myru* (Guarantee of Peace, 1950) deal with postwar life in Germany. Sobko's various other works discuss reconstruction and moral issues; among them are *Bile polum'ia* (White Flames, 1952), *Zvychaine zhyttia* (Ordinary Life, 1957), the play *Kyïvs'kyi zoshyt* (A Kievan Notebook, 1964), and works on youth issues and sports themes, such as the novel *Stadion* (Stadium, 1954). His selected works have been published as *Vybrani tvory v dvokh tomakh* (Selected Works in Two Volumes, 1954) and *Tvory* (Works, vols 1–4, 1979–81).

I. Koshelivets

Sobol, Mykola [Sobol'], b 19 February 1910 in Velyka Rublivka, Okhtyrka county, Kharkiv gubernia. CPU and Soviet government leader and mechanical engineer. A graduate of the Kharkiv Mechanical and Machine-Building Institute (1936), he directed the Kharkiv Machine-Building Plant (1954–8), headed the Kharkiv Economic Region's Council of the National Economy (1958–60) and the Ukrainian Council of the National Economy (1960–1), and served as first secretary of the Kharkiv Oblast Party Committee (1961–3), second secretary and member of the CPU Politburo (1963–6), first deputy premier of the Ukrainian SSR (1966–72), and a CC CPSU member (1961–71).

Sobol, Naum [Sobol'], b April 1898 in Kodyma, Balta county, Podilia gubernia, d 10 October 1967 in Kharkiv. Scenery designer. He studied in Yu. Bershadsky's private school in Odessa (1916–20). A member of the Association of Revolutionary Art in Ukraine, he created scenery for the Kharkiv Theater of Musical Comedy, the Kharkiv Russian Drama Theater, and the Lviv Theater of Opera and Ballet (eg, L. Minkus's *Don Quixote*, 1939).

Sobol, Oleksander [Sobol'], b 13 January 1909 in Białystok, Poland. Ballet dancer and pedagogue. In 1925 he completed study in the ballet studio at the Kharkiv Theater of Opera and Ballet, and in 1933 at the Moscow Choreography School. He was a soloist in the Kharkiv Theater of Opera and Ballet (1933–5), the Moscow Bolshoi Theater (1935–9), and the Moscow and Warsaw musical theaters (1945–61). In 1960–77 he taught in the choreography schools in Moscow, Warsaw, Łódź, and Szczecin.

Sobolev, Feliks, b 25 July 1931, d 20 April 1984 in Kiev. He completed study in the actor's (1953) and director's (1959) faculties in the Kiev Institute of Theater Arts and then worked for the Kiev Studio of Scientific-Popular Films. His film *Mova tvaryn* (The Language of the Animals, 1967) won a prize at an international film festival in Leipzig in 1969. Other films are *Ia i druhyi* (I and Another, 1971), *Biosphere* (1973), *Koly shchezaiut' bar'iery* (When Bar-

riers Disappear, 1980), and *Kyïvs'ka symfoniia* (Kievan Symphony, 1982).

Sobolevsky, Aleksei [Sobolevskij, Aleksej], b 7 January 1857 in Moscow, d 24 May 1929 in Moscow. Russian Slavist, linguist, paleographer, and folklorist; member of the Russian (later USSR) Academy of Sciences from 1893. A graduate of Moscow (1878, 1881) and Kharkiv (PH D, 1884) universities, he taught at the universities of Kiev (1882–8) and St Petersburg (1888–1908). A specialist in Old Church Slavonic and the history of the Russian language, he defended the Russian chauvinist concept of a single Russian language divided into a 'Great Russian' (including Belarusian) and a 'Little Russian' (ie, Ukrainian) dialect. In his books of essays (1884) and lectures (1888, 1891, 1903, 1907) on the history of the Russian language, he described the phonetic features of numerous 12th- to 15th-century manuscripts written in Ukraine. He described them tendentiously as 'Galician-Volhynian' and maintained that 'Great Russian' was spoken at that time in Kiev and Chernihiv. In an article on the 'ancient Kievan dialect' (1905) he explained the presence of Galician-Volhynian features in those manuscripts, as well as in the modern northeastern Ukrainian dialects, as the result of 'in-migration' of Galicians and Volhynians after the Mongol invasion and the northward 'out-migration' of the indigenous 'Russian' population. Sobolevsky's revival of the theories of M. *Pogodin led to a polemic with P. Zhytetsky, K. Mykhalchuk, A. Pypin, A. Shakhmatov, V. Jagić, and A. Krymsky, who wrote a detailed response (five articles in *Kievskaia starina*, 1898–9). He was the most important contributor to the historical dialectology of the East Slavic languages. In his books on Russian dialectology (1890, 1911) and in an article on the 'Little Russian dialect' (1892), he divided the Ukrainian dialects into archaic northern (including archaic Carpathian) and southern groups. In his etymologies of ethnonyms, hydronyms, toponyms, anthroponyms, and contemporary place-names and surnames in Ukraine and Eastern Europe, he often suggested uncritically a derivation from the Scythian and Sarmatian languages.

O. Horbach

Sobolevsky, Hryhorii [Sobolevs'kyj, Hryhorij], b 1741 in Hlukhiv, Nizhen regiment, d 16 January 1807. Medical botanist and pharmacologist. A graduate of the school of the St Petersburg General Army Hospital in 1761, he studied in Paris and Leiden, and completed a doctoral dissertation in 1775. He practiced medicine and taught botany in St Petersburg and was director of the botanical garden (from 1779) and a professor of botany (from 1796) at the medical college there. He built a large botanical, mineralogical, and zoological collection and a sizable library. His most important work was a catalog of plants in the St Petersburg region (1796–9).

Soboliev, Dmytro [Soboljev] (Sobolev, Dmitrii), b 6 August 1872 in Khripeli, Kostroma gubernia, Russia, d 16 March 1949 in Kharkiv. Geologist. He graduated from Warsaw University in 1899. He then became a professor at Kharkiv University (1914) and chaired its geology department (1922). He conducted research on the Devonian deposits of the East European Platform and the geological structure, paleontology, tectonics, and geomorphology of Ukraine. He was one of the first to assert, in 1933, the presence of petroleum deposits in the Dnieper-Donets Trough.

Participants of the first sobor of the Ukrainian Autocephalous Orthodox church (October 1921)

Sobor. A formal gathering or council of bishops, church officials, and monastic and lay representatives morally representing the whole particular church and dealing with matters of faith, morality, rite, and canonical and cultural life. The term is derived from the Church Slavonic word for an assembly. The sobor is distinguished from the *synod, which is usually an assembly of bishops. From the earliest days of the Christian church, councils were convened as a means of deciding matters related to church life and policy. The development of a full church infrastructure led eventually to the existence of several types of sobors reflecting different ecclesiastical jurisdictions. These include ecumenical (*vselenskyi*), particular (*pomisnyi*), provincial (*provintsiinyi*), eparchial (*eparkhiialnyi*), and minor (*soborchyk*) sobors.

The ecumenical sobor is a general council of the whole church; it brings together the church hierarchy of the whole Christian world to resolve fundamental matters of faith, morality, and ecclesiastical discipline. According to the Orthodox teaching, only seven ecumenical sobors of the Christian church have been convoked (between 325 and 787). Since the split into the Catholic and Orthodox churches, Catholics have continued to hold ecumenical sobors (8th–21st), convoked by the pope, which are not recognized but are occasionally attended by the representatives of the Orthodox church. The particular sobor brings together the clergy (occasionally the laity as well) of a particular church; it is presided over by the head of the particular or autocephalous church (ie, a patriarch, major archbishop, or metropolitan). The decisions of the sobor are binding on all the members of the particular church, although in the case of Ukrainian Catholics the decisions must first be approved by the pope.

Sobors are also held within specific ecclesiastical jurisdictions. Provincial sobors take place in metropolies not headed by a patriarch or major archbishop. In many respects they resemble particular sobors. Eparchial sobors bring together representatives of the clergy and frequently lay church leaders from within the jurisdiction of a single bishop. Minor sobors are assemblies of representatives from a deanery under the authority of a protopresbyter.

Chronicles record the first known Ukrainian church sobor as having taken place in Kiev in 1051. Sobors were convened periodically from then on; one notable assembly held in 1415 formed a separate metropoly for the church in Lithuanian lands. Once established in 1596, the Ukrainian Catholic church convened sobors and synods of its own. A particularly notable sobor, held in 1640 under the leadership of Metropolitan P. Mohyla, involved a considerable body of lay people and approved a new profession of faith for the Orthodox church. Ukrainian Orthodox sobors ceased to be held for several hundred years following the church's absorption into the Russian Orthodox church in 1685. Assemblies of this sort were convened once more only in 1918 and 1921, in conjunction with the restoration of the *Ukrainian Autocephalous Orthodox church. A major tenet of this church was the primacy of the sobor, with the full participation of the laity, in church affairs (see *Sobor rule). Since the Second World War various jurisdictions of the Ukrainian Orthodox church have held a number of major sobors in the West. On 5–6 June 1990 an all-Ukrainian sobor was held in Kiev which revived the Ukrainian Autocephalous Orthodox church and elected Metropolitan M. *Skrypnyk the patriarch of Kiev and all Ukraine.

BIBLIOGRAPHY
Diiannia i postanovy L'vivs'kykh arkhyeparkhiial'nykh soboriv 1940– 43 pid provodom Sluhy Bozhoho Mytropolyta Andreia Sheptyts'koho (Winnipeg 1984)
I. Korovytsky, I. Patrylo

Sobor of the Greek Catholic church in 1946. See Lviv Sobor of 1946.

Sobor rule (*sobornopravnist'*). The principle under which church policy or decisions affecting a church are made by its lay membership together with the ecclesiastical hierarchy. The concept of sobor rule in Ukraine was adhered to until the absorption of the Ukrainian Orthodox by the Russian Orthodox church and its subjugation to the decrees of the Holy Synod. The principle was revived in the 20th century with the re-establishment of the Ukrainian Autocephalous Orthodox church in Ukraine and the creation of Ukrainian jurisdictions in the West.

Soborna Ukraïna (United Ukraine). A nationalist paper published in Vienna from October 1921 to May 1922. Financed by W. Habsburg-Lothringen (V. Vyshyvany) and edited by V. Andriievsky, it was antisocialist, anti-Russian, anti-Polish, and anti-hetmanite. It advocated the primacy of national over class or party interests, the creation of a national church, absolute reliance on 'our own [Ukrainian] forces,' and an 'aristocratic democracy' (later changed to a 'peasant national democracy').

Sobor-Ruled Episcopal church (Soborno-iepyskopska tserkva). A Ukrainian Orthodox church (officially called the Fraternal Association of Ukrainian Autocephalous Churches or simply the Ukrainian Autocephalous church) formed in 1925 by a group of Ukrainian Orthodox bishops led by T. Buldovsky of Lubni. These clerics had not joined the Ukrainian Autocephalous Orthodox church (UAOC) because of misgivings about its canonicity. At the same time they had become increasingly frustrated with attempts to reform the Russian Orthodox church in Ukraine, which rejected Ukrainianization of church life, autocephaly for the Ukrainian church, and sobor rule. It was initially supported by the Soviet government, which hoped to discredit both the Russian church and the UAOC. Although it never attracted a large following, the Sobor-Ruled church did gain adherents, particularly in the Poltava, Katerynoslav, Vinnytsia, and Kherson regions. It went into decline following the normalization of relations between the regime and the Russian church in 1927 and the start of intensive religious persecutions in 1929. Its last church was closed in 1937. Buldovsky himself survived the Stalinist terror and during the Second World War joined the UAOC as bishop of Kharkiv.

Montreal's Ukraina soccer team in 1957

Soccer or **football** (*futbol, kopanyi m'iach*). The most popular team and spectator sport in the world. Soccer was introduced in Ukraine in 1878 by employees of British enterprises in Odessa. In the 1880s and 1890s other British, German, and Czechoslovak workers introduced it in the Donbas and Kiev. The first soccer clubs in Ukraine were organized during the early 1900s: Pivden (Russian: Iug; Kiev 1904), Tekhnika (Mykolaiv 1906), Politekhnika (Kiev 1906), Ukrainskyi Sportyvnyi Kliub (Lviv 1906), Sianova Chaika (Peremyshl 1907), Feniks (Kharkiv 1908), Yuzivka (Kharkiv 1909), Kramatorske (Kharkiv 1909), Ukraina (Lviv 1911), and others in the Donbas region. By the eve of the First World War, soccer was played throughout Ukraine. Various clubs held intercity matches and tournaments; leagues were established in Kiev (1911), Kharkiv (1912), and the Donbas (1913); referee colleges were created; and soccer manuals were published. Odessa, Kiev, and Kharkiv teams participated in the first Russian soccer championship in 1912, and Odessa won the second championship in 1913.

Under early Soviet rule, soccer teams were formed within the many sanctioned workers' sports clubs. In 1921 the first republican competition among Soviet Ukrainian city clubs was won by Kharkiv. In 1924 Kharkiv won the USSR championship, and Mykolaiv placed second and Odessa third. The first children's soccer clubs were organized in 1933, and an advanced school for soccer coaches was established in 1935. Beginning in 1936 the republican championships were no longer competed for by city clubs

but by collectives of sport clubs affiliated with various trade unions. That year the USSR league championships and playoffs for the USSR Cup first took place. In 1937 a competition for the Ukrainian Cup was introduced. Today the best-known Ukrainian clubs are Dynamo in Kiev (est 1927), Shakhtar in Donetske (1935), Dnipro in Dnipropetrovske (1936), and Chornomorets in Odessa (1958).

In 1961 Dynamo broke the 25-year hold on the USSR championship enjoyed by Moscow teams. It then became the most successful club in Soviet soccer; it won the USSR championship a record 12 times (1961, 1966–8, 1971, 1974–5, 1977, 1980–1, 1985–6), the USSR Cup 8 times (1954, 1964, 1966, 1974, 1978, 1982, 1985, 1987), the European Cup-Winners' Cup in 1975 and 1986, and the European Supercup in 1975. In 1976 the entire team represented the USSR at the Montreal Olympics and won the bronze medal. Two Dynamo players have been named European Footballer of the Year, O. Blokhin in 1975 and I. Belanov in 1986.

Following Dynamo's lead, other Ukrainian clubs claimed Soviet championships. League titles were won by Zoria of Luhanske (1972) and Dnipro of Dnipropetrovske (1983, 1989), and the USSR Cup was won by Shakhtar of Donetske (1961–2, 1980, 1983), Karpaty of Lviv (1969), and Dnipro (1989). Five Ukrainians (O. Cherednyk, V. Liuty, O. Mykhailychenko, V. Tatarchuk, and V. Tyshchenko) were on the USSR soccer team that won the 1988 Olympic gold medal. In 1979 the Ukrainian SSR had 954,000 registered soccer players in 27,000 collective sport clubs, 20,000 soccer fields, and 900 stadiums. Information and statistics about soccer in Ukraine and the USSR and about international competitions appeared in *Futbol*, an annual Ukrainian calendar–reference book, issued in a pressrun of approx 100,000 copies.

In Western Ukraine under Polish rule, Ukrainian clubs formed a soccer union in 1921 in Lviv, under the aegis of the *Sokil society and then the *Ukrainian Sports Union. Beginning in 1928 many clubs played in the Polish state league. Soccer also developed successfully in Transcarpathia and Bukovyna, and clubs from Lviv, Chernivtsi, and Uzhhorod participated in competitions against each other. After the Soviet occupation of Western Ukraine all interwar clubs and leagues were disbanded, and new clubs were organized according to the Soviet trade-union model.

Postwar Ukrainian refugees organized their own soccer teams, leagues, and competitions in German and Austrian DP camps between 1945 and 1949, and then in Canada, the United States, England, and Australia. O. *Skotsen gained prominence as a professional soccer player in France. With the founding of the *Ukrainian Sports Federation of the USA and Canada, championship competitions were organized. As members of the semiprofessional American Soccer League, the Ukrainian Nationals of Philadelphia won six championships (1961, 1962, 1963–4, 1968, 1970), more than any other club in the league's history. The US National Open Challenge Cup has been captured by two Ukrainian teams: the Ukrainian Nationals (1960–1, 1963, 1966) and the New York Ukrainians (1965). The Ukraina club of Montreal won the Canadian soccer championship in 1957, and the Newark Ukrainian Sitch captured the Professional American Soccer League's Lewis Cup in 1963.

BIBLIOGRAPHY
Al'manakh Rady fizychnoï kul'tury (Munich 1951)

Mykhailov, M. *Futbol Ukraïny* (Kiev 1968)
Riordan, J. *Soviet Sport: Background to the Olympics* (Oxford 1980)
Skotsen', O. *Z futbolom u svit: Spomyny* (Toronto 1985)

I. Kuzych-Berezovsky, E. Zharsky

Sochi [Soči]. X-20. A city (1989 pop 337,000) on the Black Sea in Krasnodar krai, RF. It was founded in 1896 at the site of Dakhivskyi outpost. Sochi is the center of the largest tourist and health resort area (350,000 ha) in the RF. The climate is subtropical, and the water is suitable for bathing between June and October. According to the census of 1926, Ukrainians accounted for 16.9 percent of the population of Sochi raion.

Sochynsky, Rostyslav [Sočyns'kyj], b 10 February 1916 in Vinnytsia, Podilia gubernia, d 17 September 1985 in New York. Physician and journalist. He completed his medical studies at Warsaw and Berlin universities. An active member of the OUN, he was arrested by the Gestapo in 1942, and spent three years in the Sachsenhausen concentration camp. After working as a doctor in DP camps he emigrated to the United States (1950) and opened a private practice in New York. He was president of the Ukrainian Medical Association of North America (1961–3) and sat on the board of directors of the Ukrainian Institute of America (from 1979). He contributed scientific articles to *Likars'kyi visnyk* and popular articles on medicine and cultural affairs to the Ukrainian press.

Sochyvets, Ivan [Sočyvec'], b 9 May 1917 in Lebedivka, Kozelets county, Chernihiv gubernia. Writer. He graduated from the CC CPU Higher Party School (1958) and has worked as a teacher, journalist, section editor of *Radians'ke Podillia* and *Radians'ka osvita*, and secretary responsible for the journal *Perets'*. Since 1958 he has published 20 collections of humorous and satirical prose, the most recent in 1987. He has published in *Perets'* under the pseudonyms I. Yosypenko and I. Lebidko.

Social insurance. In the USSR and its successor states, public programs that offer financial assistance to people whose income had been reduced because of old age, pregnancy, illness, disability, or temporary unemployment. Social insurance funds are also used to maintain health resorts and sanatoriums. Social insurance is funded directly from the state budget and from contributions by enterprises, collective farms, institutions, and organizations. There have been no deductions for the purpose from employees' wages. Until the mid-1960s, collective farmers were excluded from most social insurance schemes. In Ukraine social insurance has been administered by the Ukrainian Republican Council of Trade Unions. State expenditures on social insurance grew from 1.7 billion rubles in 1970 (12.8 percent of total state expenditures) to 6.1 billion rubles in 1988 (18.6 percent). (See also *Pension and *Social security.)

Social mobility. The movement of individuals and groups from one social level and status to another. Under Soviet rule Ukrainian society was transformed from a primarily agrarian society into an industrial one within the span of one generation. In 1940, 47 percent of Ukraine's working population were peasants, but by 1990 only 14 percent of the population still worked in agriculture. The status of peasant is, in practice, no longer inherited. The scale of social change has been so immense that one can speak of the mobility of an entire social class and its imminent disappearance as a result of the massive rural out-migration and the catastrophically declining, and now negative, natural *population growth.

*Migration for purposes of social mobility has generally been one-directional. There has been practically no rural in-migration, because the quality of rural life has been inferior. Young unmarried women in search of a higher social status and better life have been the most active and numerous group involved in rural out-migration to the large cities and oblast centers. After completing their obligatory military service many young unmarried peasant men have followed the same route. Peasant parents have usually encouraged such out-migration, wishing the best for their children, and have provided indispensable financial support to their children while they have studied and established roots and families in the urban environment.

Such mobility was intensive even in the Stalinist 1930s, 1940s, and 1950s, despite stringent limitations on the freedom of movement (ie, the internal *passport system). The most fortunate were the many young peasant men and women who, until the mid-1950s, were brought into the cities as part of ongoing labor mobilizations and organized recruitment to study in vocational and technical schools. The peasantry was considered an inexhaustible source of renewal of the urban working class, and the state fostered the creation of such 'labor reserves.' Upon completion of their compulsory military service young men had the right to choose where they wanted to work, and most chose the city. They circumvented any remaining restrictions by obtaining the documents necessary for relocation through purchase, bribery, or the help of friends or relatives.

Most of the young people who have migrated into the cities chose vocations that guaranteed them material well-being though not a particularly high social status. Women have been attracted to the teaching profession in particular; men have found work in industry and transportation, where they have constituted two-thirds of the skilled workers. Former peasants, however, have also constituted three-quarters of the low-status manual laborers. Existing limitations on establishing residence in the city and the need to have a document of registered residency have forced young rural out-migrants to seek less attractive, physically demanding jobs at enterprises allowed to hire workers by municipal authorities. Rural out-migrants have not, in fact, had the same employment advantages as urban youths.

Because of their upbringing most urban inhabitants aspire to be more educated than their parents. The tendency increases with the level of education the parents have attained. According to a survey of young workers in Ukraine conducted in the late 1980s, getting a higher education was a goal for 48 percent of male respondents whose parents had not completed secondary school and were manual laborers, for 54 percent of male respondents whose parents had finished secondary school and were manual laborers, and for 79 percent of male and 83 percent of female respondents whose parents had higher educations.

Many urban dwellers begin their adult working lives at the bottom of the social ladder. A mobility study of working people living in Kiev conducted by the recently created Institute of Sociology of the Academy of Sciences of Ukraine indicates that the first job of every third man or woman is an unskilled, physically demanding one. Family status (ie, of the parents) does not play a role there. Only 1 of every 4 children of skilled workers finishes vocational school and becomes a skilled worker, and only 1 of 20 manages to enter a postsecondary institution immediately after finishing secondary school, compared to 39 percent of children whose parents have higher educations. Even within the latter group, however, 1 of 5 begins independent life as a manual laborer.

By the time they have reached the age of 30, most children have attained the same educational level and qualifications as their parents. By that time only 5 percent of working-class children are still unskilled manual laborers. Among sons of skilled blue-collar workers, only 16 percent have not attained the same qualifications as their fathers, 24 percent have attained the same qualifications, and the remainder have finished secondary-specialized or postsecondary school and become white-collar workers. By the age of 30 only 20 percent of children whose parents do not have higher educations and have simple white-collar jobs have followed in their parents' footsteps; 30 percent are skilled workers, and 50 percent are specialists with higher educations. Only 10 percent of children whose parents have higher educations become manual laborers; 75 percent finish postsecondary school and become part of the same social stratum their parents belong to. Among that group (in contrast to peasant children) there is a high probability that the parents' social status will be inherited through occupational mobility, though in an entirely different occupation.

A number of objective factors have influenced young people's choices of what social-mobility route to follow. Skilled blue-collar workers, for example, receive much higher wages than those who begin working only after finishing postsecondary school. The former attain material independence relatively quickly, whereas the latter spend years attaining it. The profession one chooses and the type of educational institution one attends determine the level of one's material and financial well-being basically for life. Until the early 1990s the reality was such that those involved in creative, substantive labor after many years of secondary and postgraduate studies were in effect penalized: they were not able to satisfy basic everyday needs, lagged behind their peers in terms of social status and material well-being, and were forced to prolong their material dependence on their parents and other family members.

The principal direction of inter- and intragenerational mobility has been upward. The opposite phenomenon, downward social mobility, has also occurred, however. Today it cannot be said that unattractive, physically demanding jobs are performed solely by any particular group or stratum. Occupational research has shown that the formation of the category of unskilled laborers has been gradual and that it constitutes only 6 or 7 percent of those studied. Jobs not requiring skill were performed by people who earlier had jobs requiring certain qualifications; 40–67 percent of them had vocational training and even higher educations. For them mobility has been a process of self-demotion, of the avoidance of using acquired knowledge and skills, and of descent to the bottom of the social pyramid.

Under Soviet rule upward mobility into the stratum of the Party, state, and economic leadership was different from the mobility experienced by most people. Members of all social strata were recruited, but in a strictly regulated fashion that placed tough demands on them. Candidates were expected to have a higher education, to have graduated as well from a higher Party, trade-union, or economic school that trained leading cadres, and to have practical experience in Komsomol, Party, government, or economic organs. Official cadre policy demanded of candidates work experience in all possible agencies before allowing them into the exclusive *nomenklatura. Once part of that elite, they remained in it for life. Those involved in scandals or mismanagement were simply transferred, for it was in the best interests of the elite as a whole to protect its corporate status and its individual members. The elite's mechanism of self-preservation functioned accurately until the late 1980s.

BIBLIOGRAPHY
Matthews, M. *Class and Society in Soviet Russia* (London 1972)
Yanowitch, M. *Social and Economic Inequality in the Soviet Union: Six Studies* (White Plains, NY 1977)
Lane, D. *The End of Social Inequality?: Class, Status, and Power under State Socialism* (London 1982)
Yanowitch, M. (ed). *The Social Structure of the USSR: Recent Soviet Studies* (Armonk, NY 1986)
Clark, W.M. *Soviet Regional Elite Mobility after Khrushchev* (New York, Westport, Conn, and London 1989)

S. Makeev

Social security (*sotsiialne zabezpechennia*). Publicly financed and administered programs intended to maintain, protect, and raise basic living standards. The term covers programs that replace income lost because of pregnancy, illness, accident, disability, the death or absence of a family's breadwinner, unemployment, old age, retirement, and other factors.

In the past the provision of social security for the infirm, the ill, and the aged was a family responsibility. Later, community organizations, such as churches and guilds, assumed some of the responsibility. With the development of industry in the second half of the 19th century the state, especially the local authorities, began to play a role in social assistance. Comprehensive social security policies, however, are a 20th-century phenomenon.

In Soviet Ukraine social security consisted of programs such as *social insurance, *pensions, benefits for single mothers, family income supplements, benefits for the permanently disabled, health care for old age pensioners, invalids, and war veterans, social and medical rehabilitation, and student stipends. According to Soviet convention holiday pay was classified as a social security benefit. The social security program was funded in part from an earmarked payroll tax (differentiated by sector) and in part from general budgetary revenue derived from indirect and profit taxes. The absolute value of benefits increased with the income of the recipient household.

Before 1917 in Russian-ruled Ukraine, social security as a state program was virtually nonexistent. Churches, zemstvo and municipal councils, benevolent associations, and various aid committees and charities provided some relief to the destitute. In 1888 a workmen's compensation scheme for victims of industrial accidents was introduced in some of the larger factories. In 1912 a factory insurance fund providing social security payments in the case of illness was established. That benefit, however, was offered only in the Donbas and in some of the larger cities.

In interwar Western Ukraine under Polish rule, social security provisions provided support to victims of accidents. A 1927 law established pensions and disability payments for civil servants and rudimentary unemployment insurance benefits. A 1933 law unified social security benefits for workers and civil servants. Interwar Transcarpathia under Czechoslovak rule was covered by relatively advanced social security legislation from 1924 on. In 1929, pensions were extended to all civil servants. In all of interwar Western Ukraine, apart from Polish, Czechoslovak, and Rumanian state programs, there existed many privately run social insurance schemes based on the contributions of earners. Employee-contribution-based unemployment insurance programs also received subsidies from the various states.

Demands for basic social security benefits were articulated in Ukraine during the Revolution of 1917. Although the various Ukrainian governments of 1917–20 had plans to implement such programs, the conditions of war did not allow their realization. Social security (old age, disability, and survivor pensions) in Ukraine was introduced in 1922 for the urban population. All employed persons, students, and servicemen were covered by the scheme. With the adoption of the First Five-Year Plan (1928–32), the social security system was modified to make it less egalitarian and to reinforce the incentives thought necessary for industrialization. It was remodified in 1956, and from then on benefit levels were raised more or less in line with the growth in average earnings. Not until 1965, however, were state pensions provided for the collective-farm population. Other programs were extended to that social group over the next five years.

Most Soviet social security payments were related to employment in some way. There were, however, three more general programs available to the population: child allowances, family income supplements, and student stipends. Provisions were also made for burial grants. Nonmilitary and noncooperative state employees were entitled to an old age pension on reaching the age of 60 if they were men or 55 if they were women, provided they had a record of 25 or 20 years of employment respectively. There were lower retirement ages with correspondingly reduced employment requirements for underground workers and certain other designated categories. From 1967, collective farmers were entitled to pensions at the same age and with the same employment record as state employees. The value of a pension was determined by the level of earnings either during the last 12 months before retirement or during the last consecutive five-year period of employment in the last 10 years before retirement. Certain categories of white-collar employees (eg, teachers and physicians) received long-service pensions rather than those just described, and there existed a scheme of retirement pensions for members of the Party elite at more than double the normal maximum rate.

In Ukraine between 1970 and 1990 the number of pensioners grew from 8.9 to 13.1 million. Almost 40 percent of retired state employees and 89 percent of collective farmers received less than 60 rubles a month. In 1989 the old age pension was set at a minimum of 70 rubles and a maximum of 120. Because the poverty line was a monthly per capita income of 75 rubles or less, almost 40 percent of all pensioners were forced to continue working to supplement their pension incomes. In addition there was and still is an acute shortage of homes for the aged and disabled. In 1988 only 1 in 80 of that group received accommodation, compared to 1 in 16 in the United States.

A survivors' benefit program offered entitlements to a deceased state employee's or collective farmer's dependent children, grandchildren, siblings under the age of 16, parents, and surviving spouse (if above working age). The value of the benefit varied according to the number of dependents and the earnings of the deceased. In 1989 the maximum benefit was 60 rubles a month for a single dependent and 120 rubles for two or more dependents.

Disability pensions varied, distinctions being made between incapacity resulting from industrial accidents or occupational diseases on the one hand and general loss of working capacity on the other. In 1970 disability pensions were extended to collective farmers. Sickness benefits, including benefits for seven days to those (mainly mothers) who had to remain at home to care for sick children, depended upon earnings, type of employment, and union membership. Those benefits also were extended to collective farmers, in 1970.

From 1968 women state employees were entitled to a period of 56 days prenatal and 56 days postnatal paid leave, and they could then take further unpaid leave until their child's first birthday without loss of their jobs or seniority. Maternity benefits were extended to collective farmers in the 1960s.

Child allowances were paid to single mothers (in 1989, 20 rubles a month per child); mothers with four or more children received payments ranging from 4 to 15 rubles per child from the child's first to fifth birthdays. Single payments were also made on the birth of a child (from 50 rubles in 1989 for the first child to 100 rubles for additional children). Family income supplements of 12 rubles a month per child until the child's eighth birthday were given to families with a per capita income of less than 50 rubles a month.

Despite attempts to improve the social security system, social welfare has been and continues to be a major problem in Ukraine. Social security payments have been low. The amount paid to assist large families, for example, remained unchanged from 1944 until December 1990, when the rate was finally increased. In 1988 approx 9 percent of the average income of blue- and white-collar workers and collective farmers came from various social security payments. Yet that same year almost 40 percent of Ukraine's population lived in impoverished circumstances. The situation of the disabled has been particularly critical, because they have had few adequate facilities and programs. According to a 1989 survey, for the majority of old age pensioners and the disabled their families were still the main source of assistance. A major problem with the social security system has been the fact that many benefits have been based on employment instead of need. Because regulations governing entitlements to various benefits have been so complex, some eligible applicants have failed to qualify for assistance. The absence of protection for the unemployed has been a serious flaw remedied only by the unemployment legislation of March 1991. Because of recent economic difficulties, however, it is unlikely that social security benefits will improve. Although Ukrainian state expenditures on pensions and social security benefits grew from 11.8 billion rubles in 1970 to 39.3 billion in 1988, inflation offset the real value of those increases.

BIBLIOGRAPHY

A Report on Social Security Programs in the Soviet Union Prepared by the u.s. Team That Visited the u.s.s.r. under the East-West Exchange Program in August–September 1958 (Washington 1960)

Fedorov, O. *Sotsial'ne zabezpechennia v Ukraïns'kii RSR* (Kiev 1969)

Lantsev, M. *The Economic Aspects of Social Security in the USSR* (Moscow 1979)

Batygin, K. (ed). *Sovetskoe sotsial'noe strakhovanie: Uchebnoe posobie dlia vysshikh profsoiuznykh shkol,* 2nd rev edn (Moscow 1985)

Pronina, L. *Povyshenie eftektivnosti sotsial'nogo obespecheniia* (Moscow 1990)

D. Goshko, B. Krawchenko

Social stratification. Social ranking based on differences in age, sex, race, religion, ancestry, class, occupation, wages, material well-being, and social and political status. Because society is structured hierarchically, the ranking, and hence social inequality, is constantly maintained and replicated.

In Soviet Ukraine the process of social stratification had four main tendencies. First, certain categories of the population were forcibly excluded from the officially defined social structure and deprived of their basic civil rights and liberties. In the 1920s and 1930s (and in the 1940s and 1950s in newly annexed Western Ukraine) such discrimination affected the so-called socially foreign social strata, that is, the 'bourgeois' intelligentsia, clergy, nobility, landowners, and prosperous farmers (*kulaks). In 1953, 167,000 'socially foreign' Ukrainians were living in the Arctic and Asian parts of the USSR, where they had been deported as 'special settlers.' That social division into those who are and those who are not officially discriminated against was maintained into the 1980s. People were persecuted not only because of their social origins but for the way they thought. Also outside the official social structure were vagrants; 36,000 people were registered as such in Ukraine in 1989 (0.15 percent of the employable population).

The second tendency was the prevalent one from the 1930s to the mid-1980s. Its distinguishing trait was the Soviet state's monopoly on the right to create social inequality wherever and whenever it chose, with the aim of subordinating individuals and making them totally dependent on the state. To that end all surplus production and a significant part of essential production were taken by the state for its own use before being returned to the producers (workers and peasants) in quantities sufficient only for satisfying their basic needs. The state's view of social equality meant in practice the equalization of wages, regardless of qualifications. Thus, for example, in the late 1970s a professor's salary was no higher than a skilled worker's. The differences in wage incomes that remained were illusory, because there was a permanent shortage of basic goods and services. Wages did not reflect differences in living standards because most people were unable to buy anything with the money they earned. The state was forced, however, to create better conditions for certain groups in order to encourage their loyalty and active support and their enthusiasm for current and prospective goals and tasks. As a rule the privileges and benefits such groups received from the state were not made public.

The third tendency consisted of attempts by most individuals and groups to counter the state's efforts to subordinate them by participating in an illegal or semilegal system of trading and bartering goods and services (see *Underground economy). In order to attain an adequate standard of living, many people moonlighted, worked overtime, became seasonal *migrant workers at higher-paying construction projects in the Soviet Arctic and Asia, or did mechanical or house repairs in addition to their official jobs. Often materials stolen from state enterprises and offices and official vehicles were used to generate additional incomes. Such unsanctioned economic activity supplemented the official Soviet system of social stratification (ie, inequality between the rulers and the ruled) by creating widespread, partly latent social inequality. It was latent because Soviet ideology stated that rich people should not exist, and the state did not allow personal accumulation of wealth.

In a condition of permanent shortages of goods and services only the members of the state and Party elite (see *Nomenklatura) had full access to limited resources and were able to satisfy all of their basic and more sophisticated needs. A special system of goods and services was created for their exclusive use, and the purchase value of every ruble they earned was guaranteed (unlike the rubles paid to ordinary people). A system of symbols reflecting the inequality that rapidly developed was introduced, and even certain colors became symbols of power (eg, the white stone used for the façades of Party buildings, the black limousines available only to the elite). Prestige and its symbolic trappings became the marks of success. Those in power were credited by their peers with primary responsibility in attaining various goals and rewarded with *prizes and awards and *orders, medals, and honorific titles; some even had towns, squares, and streets named after them.

The dichotomy between the ruling elite and the rest of society generally characterized the stratification process. The power structure was not homogeneous, however, and its various participants did not enjoy the same privileges. Closest to the ruling elite were those functionaries, ideologists, writers, artists, and scientists who catered to it and consequently received certain benefits and status.

The most oppressed and impoverished class consisted of the collective-farm peasants, who relied on their small *private plots to eke out a subsistence. In the 1930s, 1940s, and 1950s they were not even paid in money for their labor. In the mid-1950s wage labor was introduced, but in 1960 the collective farmer still received a monthly wage that was less than a third that of an urban worker (in the late 1980s it was 15 percent lower). In the last few decades in rural areas homemade spirits served as the universal form of exchange and were used instead of money as payment for services. Although work absenteeism was not characteristic of the rural population, the number of work-related accidents in agriculture was higher than in industry and twice as high as in construction. The retirement pensions of collective farmers were always minimal (eg, 51 percent lower than those of urban blue- and white-collar workers in 1980). Whereas urban workers received housing from the state, rural inhabitants had to build homes at their own expense and without government support.

Practically all agricultural production was until recently shipped to urban centers, and the peasants sold the products of their private plots at markets to earn money. In the late 1980s, rural inhabitants still consumed 30 percent less meat, 25 percent less sugar, 19 percent less milk, but nearly twice as much bread as urban inhabitants. In rural areas services virtually did not exist, qualified medical aid was in chronic short supply, and the quality of elementary education was much worse than in urban schools. Such rural-urban inequality was the primary stimulus of rural out-migration; 130,000 rural homes in Ukraine were uninhabited by 1990.

In urban areas inequality also flourished. The material and social status of individuals was determined by ministries, state agencies, and enterprises, which themselves were stratified. Employees in heavy industries received higher wages than those in light or food industries, and wages at different plants, factories, and research institutes varied. Defense-industry employees had better working conditions and wages, the newest technology and equipment, easier access to housing, and more perquisites than employees of civil industries.

The goods, services, and benefits people had access to were not determined by what they earned and could afford but by their access to the Party and state functionaries, warehouse managers, and black marketeers who controlled and distributed goods and services. Those in control and those who had access to them constituted an economically privileged stratum (approx 3 to 10 percent of the employed population). Urban housing, which was in chronic short supply, illustrates the state of affairs well. In 1989, for example, of 245,000 families in Ukraine who received new apartments, 89 percent had been on the waiting list for an average of 11 years, whereas 11 percent were not on the list, and received apartments out of turn because they knew the right people. Such privileges were far from available to everyone and were most accessible to denizens of large cities (eg, Kiev, Moscow, Leningrad) where power, goods, and services were concentrated.

In 1991 the Ukrainian Branch of the USSR Center for the Study of Public Opinion conducted a sample survey. Of the respondents 0.5 percent defined themselves as upper class; 12 percent, as higher middle class; 57 percent, as lower middle class; and 18 percent, as lower class. Fifty-six percent of the respondents stated that the material well-being of the middle class (the class of 75 percent of the respondents) had worsened, and 68 percent stated that the lot of the 'entrepreneurs' (those involved in co-operative ventures or running their own businesses) had improved.

The fourth tendency is one that became pronounced in the late 1980s, after the production of goods and provision of services outside the state-controlled sector was officially allowed: a new stratum of people owning private property individually or collectively (through co-operatives). The stratum grew rapidly, from 249,000 persons in 1989 to 779,000 (3 percent of the employed population) in 1990. By 1990 the wages of employees of co-operatives were three times those of blue and white-collar employees of the state. The new stratum was considered 'alien' and inimical to the organizational principles of a socialist society by a large part of the Soviet Ukrainian public, particularly by older people. In a State Statistics Committee public opinion survey of people aged 45 and over, only 33 percent of the respondents stated that employees of co-operatives and self-employed entrepreneurs should receive the same old age security as state-employed blue- and white-collar workers; 50 percent stated they should not. The co-operatives' relatively high profits at a time when everyone else's material well-being had worsened created much distrust and dislike of the new stratum.

(For a bibliography, see *Class.)

S. Makeev

Social welfare departments (Russian: Prikazy obshchestvennogo prizreniia). Agencies set up in 1775 within gubernia administrations of the Russian Empire to oversee primary schools, hospitals, almshouses, orphanages, poorhouses, insane asylums, and homes for the aged. They also distributed welfare funds provided by the state and private contributions. Most of the welfare institutions were supported by the church and private charity. Each department in a gubernia was run by a board chaired by the provincial governor and was provided with a budget of 15,000 rubles. When zemstvos were introduced in the 1860s, the social welfare departments were abolished in most of the gubernias, including Left-Bank and Southern Ukraine, and their functions were taken over by the zemstvos. They continued to operate in Right-Bank Ukraine until the early 20th century.

Socialism. A political movement calling for collective ownership of the means of production or an egalitarian distribution of wealth.

Socialist ideas first appeared in Ukrainian territory in the 1830s and 1840s, but they were limited to the most radical factions of the Polish conspiratorial movement in Galicia and Right-Bank Ukraine, such as the Association for the Polish People. Although individual Ukrainians participated in those vaguely socialist groups, a Ukrainian socialist movement as such did not emerge until the 1870s. The most influential Ukrainian socialist thinker was M. *Drahomanov, who adapted Western European socialist theories to the particular situation of the Ukrainian nation; his peasant-oriented, decentralist brand of socialism eventually came to be known as *radicalism. Other Ukrainian socialist theorists of the 1870s were Drahomanov's close associates M. *Ziber, an interpreter and proponent of *Marxism, and S. *Podolynsky, who was influenced by Drahomanov's radicalism, Marxism, and Russian *populism. Drahomanov, Ziber, and Podolynsky were first active in Kiev, but at the end of the 1870s they emigrated to Western Europe in order to carry on political work without the interference of the tsarist police and censors. Under their influence and also under the influence of Polish socialists Ukrainian university students in Vienna and Lviv were converted to socialism, including I. *Franko, M. *Pavlyk, and O. *Terletsky. Pavlyk and especially Franko participated in the Polish socialist movement in Lviv in the late 1870s and early 1880s as well as in carrying on socialist propaganda among Ukrainians. Independently of the rest of the Ukrainian socialist movement, the socialist *South Russian Union of Workers was founded in Odessa in 1875.

The first Ukrainian political party was a socialist party, the *Ukrainian Radical party (est 1890 in Lviv). In 1899 the left wing of that party broke off to form the *Ukrainian Social Democratic party (USDP), which espoused Marxist socialism. Branches of both parties also appeared in Bukovyna in the decade before the First World War. In Russian-ruled Ukraine a Marxist group calling itself Ukrainian Social Democracy was formed in 1897; although it was small and isolated from the mainstream of Ukrainian politics, its membership included the prominent writers M. *Kotsiubynsky and Lesia *Ukrainka. Another small group, consisting of left-wing Poles who embraced Ukrainian nationality, founded the *Ukrainian Socialist party in Kiev in 1900. Much more substantial was the socialist *Revolutionary Ukrainian party (RUP), founded in Kharkiv in 1900. In the process of clarifying its ideology, RUP changed its name and split into two groups at the end of 1904. Those who remained in RUP rechristened it the *Ukrainian Social Democratic Workers' party (USDRP). Most of those who left formed the Ukrainian Social Democratic *Spilka, which became an autonomous group within the Russian Social Democratic Workers' party (RSDRP) (Mensheviks). Both parties were Marxist, but they disagreed over the national question.

National minorities in Ukraine also had their own socialist parties. The Marxist RSDRP existed in Ukraine, both its Bolshevik and Menshevik factions, with the latter having by far the larger membership before 1917. The other major Russian socialist party in Ukraine was the non-Marxist, populist Russian Socialist Revolutionary party. Polish socialists in Dnieper Ukraine belonged primarily to the Polish Socialist party, but also to the Social Democracy of the Kingdom of Poland and Lithuania; in Galicia Polish socialists belonged to the Galician (after 1897, Polish) Social Democratic party. Jewish socialists in Dnieper Ukraine belonged to the *Bund (affiliated with the Mensheviks) and to several parties that combined socialism with Zionism: Poale Zion, the Jewish Socialist Labor party, and the Zionist Socialist Labor party (the latter two joined in 1917 to form the United Jewish Workers' party). Jewish socialists in Galicia founded the Jewish Social Democratic party, which had links with the Bund.

The revolutionary events of 1917 brought socialism into greater prominence. In April 1917, after tsarism was overthrown, a *Ukrainian Party of Socialist Revolutionaries (SRs) was formed. That agrarian socialist party grew rapidly; it received the greatest number of votes in the Ukrainian elections to the *All-Russian Constituent Assembly in December 1917. Together with the USDRP it dominated the *Central Rada and the government of the *Ukrainian National Republic (UNR). In November 1917, as a result of the *October Revolution, the Bolsheviks seized power in Russia and attempted to initiate an all-European socialist revolution. The revolutionary Marxist socialism of the Bolsheviks attracted the left wings of the Ukrainian SRs (the *Borotbists) and the USDRP (Independentists), even though the UNR had been at war with the Bolsheviks since December 1917. In 1920 the majority of the Borotbists merged with the Ukrainian branch of the Bolsheviks, the *Communist Party (Bolsheviks) of Ukraine (CP[B]U), and the Independentists and a minority of the Borotbists formed the *Ukrainian Communist party (Ukapisty). The revolutionary period 1917–20 also gave rise to the *Communist Party of Western Ukraine and the *Communist Party of Transcarpathian Ukraine.

By the late 1920s the only political party left in the Ukrainian Soviet Socialist Republic was the CP(B)U; the rest had been liquidated or, like the Ukapisty in 1925, had liquidated themselves. In Western Ukraine other socialist parties continued to exist alongside the Communist par-

ties. The Ukrainian Radical party in Galicia and the Ukrainian Party of Socialist Revolutionaries in Volhynia merged in 1926 to form the moderate Ukrainian Socialist Radical party (USRP). In both Galicia and Bukovyna the USDP continued to exist, wavering between pro- and anti-communist platforms. An affiliate of the Czechoslovak Social Democratic party was established in Transcarpathia in 1920. Socialist organizations and periodicals also flourished among Ukrainian immigrants in Canada and the United States, especially in the first three decades of the 20th century. After the Revolution of 1917 most of the Ukrainian socialists in Canada regrouped around the pro-communist *Ukrainian Labour-Farmer Temple Association. In the United States they became associated with either the pro-Communist United Ukrainian Toilers Organization or the Ukrainian Workingmen's Association (which maintained connections with the Ukrainian Socialist Radical party in Galicia). With the consolidation of Stalinism in the 1930s, which brought with it forced collectivization, the man-made famine, and the annihilation of the Ukrainian intelligentsia, socialism lost much of its popularity among Ukrainians, particularly in Galicia and Bukovyna and in the emigration. During the Second World War no socialist groups were active in Ukraine, except for the thoroughly Stalinist CP(B)U.

In the postwar Ukrainian diaspora the traditional moderate Ukrainian socialist parties were revived – the USDRP, the USDP, and the USRP. In 1950 they joined together to form the Ukrainian Socialist party. The *Ukrainian Revolutionary Democratic party, a new creation composed largely of émigrés from Soviet Ukraine, was also socialist; the socialist perspective was particularly pronounced in the party's left wing, which published the newspaper *Vpered*. Under the impact of the new left movement of the 1960s and 1970s a sector of Ukrainian youth in the diaspora, primarily in Canada, adopted a revolutionary socialist and anti-Stalinist ideology; their periodicals were *Meta* and *Diialoh*.

BIBLIOGRAPHY
Borys, J. 'Political Parties in the Ukraine,' in *The Ukraine, 1917–1921: A Study in Revolution*, ed T. Hunczak (Cambridge, Mass 1977)
Himka, J.-P. *Socialism in Galicia: The Emergence of Polish Social Democracy and Ukrainian Radicalism (1860–1890)* (Cambridge, Mass 1983)

J.-P. Himka

Socialist competition. Various measures used in the Soviet Union to increase worker productivity. They included both noneconomic incentives, or appeals to the 'socialist consciousness' of the workers, and material incentives or rewards. Their use led to the characterization of socialist competition as 'the principal form of the socialist organization of labor' (J. Stalin, 1929) or 'the economic standard of socialism.' In the beginning of the 1970s, socialist competition was recognized officially as one of the most important methods for building socialism and communism and one of the moving forces behind the growth of labor productivity. It was even given juridical status in 1977, when the new Soviet constitution declared that 'working collectives develop socialist competition' (Article 8).

Soviet sources describe the 'Communist Saturdays' instituted in 1919 as precursors of socialist competition. V.

Lenin, who himself took part in the exercises, ascribed great significance to these Saturdays of 'voluntary' work for the state, and in 1920 a special law was passed defining them. They were abandoned after a few years, however, when the New Economic Policy was adopted, and a more market-based economic system was introduced. Although the Communist Saturdays did not involve competition among workers, they were the first of the extra-economic measures used to increase production and labor discipline.

Real socialist competition was introduced in the workplace in 1926, when the shock-worker movement began. In that movement individuals, groups of workers (the so-called brigades), or whole factories pledged to increase the quantity and quality of production and challenged others to emulate their initiative. One of the first factories to take part in the movement was the Odessa Factory of Industrial Textiles. The movement acquired a mass character after the First Five-Year Plan (1928–33) was approved, and J. Stalin's plan of rapid industrialization was adopted. Shock workers and shock-worker enterprises were strongly favored: they were given better machinery and equipment and more raw materials and resources so that they could meet their announced production goals. Such favorable treatment was especially significant in the 1930s, when many goods were in short supply. The first all-Union congress of shock-worker brigades, held in Moscow in December 1929, appealed to all workers to complete the goals of the First Five-Year Plan in four years. Similar congresses of collective-farm shock workers were held in 1934 and 1935.

The next stage in the development of socialist competition was competition among workers, brigades, and enterprises with respect to increases in production goals. In 1932 the Donets miner N. Izotov became the model for a campaign that stressed not only overfulfillment of plans but also the idea that workers should assist other, less productive, workers in the completion of their jobs, and that shock workers should oversee the work of others. 'Izotov schools' were even set up, and Izotovites trained novice workers in their techniques. Socialist competition reached its highest stage in 1935 with the emergence of the Stakhanovite movement. The purpose of that movement was to establish extremely high quotas and standards of production. The campaign was initiated by another Donbas miner, A. *Stakhanov, who set a record for coal mining in a single shift by overfulfilling his quota by a factor of 14. His accomplishments were publicized by the Soviet propaganda machine, and he was held up as an example to other workers. Within weeks hundreds of other workers and work brigades were following his lead and announcing their attainment of much higher production goals. The movement was especially popular among miners and metalworkers, although it spread to almost all branches of the economy. Many of the Stakhanovites were semiskilled workers. Ukraine's prominent Stakhanovites included M. Demchenko, a woman in Cherkasy oblast who harvested 523 centners of sugar beets from a single hectare, and P. Kryvonis, a locomotive engineer who raised his average speed on the Slovianske–Lozova line. Many Stakhanovites became '200ers' or '500ers,' by overfulfilling their production quotas by 200 or 500 percent. Many of the Stakhanovite achievements were spurious: they were usually attained with the help of other workers, better tools and equipment, or reduced job requirements.

Socialist competition was widely used after the Second World War, mostly to rationalize production and improve the use and effectiveness of machinery and equipment. Since the late 1950s the main slogan of the movement was 'Learn, Work, and Live in a Communist Manner.' A major innovation was the use of model workers to fight alcoholism and low morale in the workplace, both common problems in Soviet industry.

Formally, socialist competition was defined as a voluntary expression of working-class initiative. In reality, however, it was organized from above: resolutions of Party plenums, conferences, and congresses were often filled with directives to organize and conduct worker competitions. The competitions involved most of the working population (58.1 percent in 1930 and 85 percent in 1957). In 1976 some 87 million people in the USSR and 21 million in Ukraine took part in some form of competition. Over the years many different approaches were developed to encourage participation. On the eve of the demise of the USSR, popular programs included various *prizes and awards, often financial ones made by the Party, the Communist Youth League, government, or trade unions. Most of the campaigns were organized by the *trade unions. Despite all of these efforts, socialist competition was only partially successful. Soviet production in both industry and agriculture continued to lag considerably behind that of the West in both volume and quality of goods. Worker productivity in the USSR was less than half that in the United States. Only a very small number of model workers or record setters benefited from the material incentives provided by socialist competition. In many cases their achievements resulted in higher quotas and goals for other workers, an outcome that often caused animosity among workers.

Besides those main forms of socialist competition there were others. Soviet sources have counted as many as 300 different campaigns. The vast majority of them, however, were short-lived and had little impact. Imposed by bureaucratic orders from above, the competitions often degenerated into mere formalities, deception, and record falsification. For that reason other ways to stimulate worker interest and initiative, such as *production conferences, were tried, but those measures too were only partially successful.

BIBLIOGRAPHY

Sotsialisticheskoe sorevnovanie: Voprosy teorii i praktiki organizatsii (Moscow 1978)

Siegelbaum, L. *Stakhanovism and the Politics of Productivity in the USSR, 1935–41* (Cambridge, Mass 1988)

F. Haienko

Socialist International. The name of several different international associations and organizations of socialist or Communist parties. The First International, known as the International Workingmen's Association, was founded on 28 September 1864 in London by some of the most influential British and French trade-union leaders of the time.

The Second Socialist International was founded in Paris in 1889. Unlike the First International, it was a loose federation of national parties and trade unions without individual membership.

After the Bolsheviks seized power in Russia, they established the Third or *Communist International (Comintern) in Moscow, in 1919. It was totally dominated by the

Russian Communist Party (Bolshevik) (RKP[B]) and was used as an instrument of Moscow's foreign policy. The Fourth International was a coalition of parties loyal to L. Trotsky and opposed to the Stalinist Third International. It was founded at a congress in France in 1938. Racked by internal dissent, it split into two factions in 1953. Now, only a few small groups declare allegiance to the Fourth International.

In 1951 the Committee of the International Socialist Conference called a congress in Frankfurt at which the Socialist International was reconstituted. Its headquarters are in London. The membership consists of parties: each has one vote, regardless of size, and unanimity is required for a resolution to be passed. Stressing democracy and civil rights, this international was decidedly anti-Soviet in orientation.

From the 1870s some prominent Ukrainians, such as M. Drahomanov, M. Ziber, and S. Podolynsky, maintained close ties with Western European socialists and socialist organizations. In 1904 the Revolutionary Ukrainian party informed the executive of the Second International about its history and platform. In 1913 delegates of the Ukrainian Social Democratic party (of Western Ukraine) and the Ukrainian Social Democratic Workers' party (USDRP) attended the extraordinary congress of the Second International in Basel. After 1919 the CP(B)U was a member of the Comintern, even though it formed only a section of the RKP(B). The *Communist Party of Western Ukraine was also a member; the *Communist Party of Transcarpathian Ukraine belonged to the Comintern through the Czechoslovak Communist party. In the 1920s Ukrainian issues were raised and discussed frequently in the Comintern. J. Stalin's despotic centralism eventually destroyed the autonomy of Ukrainian Communists.

In the interwar period delegates from the émigré USDRP attended congresses and conferences of the Labor and Socialist International, and one of the party's leaders, P. Fedenko, served on the association's executive committee. The Ukrainian Socialist Radical party and the Ukrainian Socialist party also belonged to this international. These Ukrainian parties consistently attacked Soviet Communism and advocated Ukrainian independence at the international forum.

BIBLIOGRAPHY
Fedenko, P. *Sotsiializm davnii i novochasnii* (London–Paris–Munich 1968)

B. Balan

Socialist realism. The only officially sanctioned so-called 'creative method' in Soviet literature and art from the early 1930s. The revolutionary poets of the late 19th century (H.L. Veier, E. Potier) and the Russian revolutionary democrats (V. Belinsky, M. Chernyshevsky, M. Dobroliubov) were considered its forerunners. To a certain extent the title 'revolutionary democrat' was also applied, artificially, to I. Franko, Lesia Ukrainka, and M. Kotsiubynsky. M. Gorky is acknowledged as the writer who laid down the principles of socialist realism before 1917, and who was its leading practitioner in the early years of Soviet rule. Before its official adoption as the prescribed style the *All-Ukrainian Association of Proletarian Writers promoted their version of the form, 'proletarian realism.' The term socialist realism and its theoretical underpinnings were officially adopted by the First Congress of Writers of

the USSR in August 1934, when the Soviet Writers' Union was established. Those active in other fields (theater, painting, sculpture, cinema, music) were also organized into single artistic unions, and also adopted socialist realism as the basic creative method.

According to the resolution of the first Writers' Union congress: 'socialist realism demands a true, historical, and concrete depiction of reality in its revolutionary development. The realism and historical concreteness of the artistic rendering of reality must be tied to the ideological re-education and training of workers in the spirit of socialism. Socialist realism guarantees the artist exclusive control over creative initiative, and choice of form, style, and genre.' As applied, however, those principles had a very narrow meaning. The 'true depiction of reality in its revolutionary development' meant that literature and art were to serve as glorifying illustrations of the CPSU's policies, and to portray what was hoped for in such a way that it seemed real. Deviations into truly realistic portrayals of Soviet reality and its deficiencies were attacked as 'slavishness to facts' or 'anti-Soviet agitation and propaganda.' That response resulted in the formulation of such theoretical conceptions as the 'varnishing of reality' and the 'theory of no conflict,' that is, painting reality with a rosy hue.

Socialist realism's need to hide falsity of content gave rise to certain characteristics of style in all Soviet literature and art. In literature it was responsible for the presence of compendiums of useless information and statistical data, the use of artificial verbal ornamentation, the overuse of epithets and similes (even in the works of superior writers, such as O. Honchar and P. Zahrebelny), a decline in the lexicon to the level of journalistic vocabulary, a reliance on artificial pathos that dipped into sentimentality (in the novels of M. Stelmakh, the biographical narratives of Yu. Martych), and a preponderance of didacticism and moralizing. In painting it resulted in excessive pathos, photographism (with gestures and motion depicted as if frozen by photographs), and the tendency to dwell on luxurious uniforms and interiors.

Changes in socialist realism occurred in step with changes in the regime. The initial programmatic resolution that guaranteed choice of form, style, and genre had no practical application. In its first period (1934–41) socialist realism's range in prose and painting was restricted to depictions of industrialization and collectivization (in painting, the focus was mainly on portraits and monuments to J. Stalin). Poetry was reduced to stilted odes to the Party and its leaders (eg, P. Tychyna's *Partiia vede* [The Party Leads the Way] and M. Rylsky's *Pisnia pro Stalina* [Song about Stalin]). Music consisted of cantatas dedicated to the Party. During the Second World War art was mainly the patriotic poster and the satirical caricature, and literature was dominated by patriotic themes and publicistic style (eg, narratives and articles of O. Dovzhenko). Gradually the theme of glorification of the Russian 'big brother' crept in, and it was intensified after the war. The theme reached a climax in the 'unification celebrations' of 1954. It was reflected in various genres and media: in prose, in works such as N. Rybak's *Pereiaslavs'ka rada* (The Pereiaslav Council, 2 vols, 1948, 1953), and in painting, in M. Derehus's *Pereiaslav Council* (1952) and M. Khmelko's *Forever with Moscow, Forever with the Russian People* (1951–4). The theme remained constant in Ukrainian socialist-realist literature and art; only its intensity varied.

Socialist realism was enforced in literature and the other arts by means of repressions. In the 1930s over 300 writers were executed or otherwise prevented from publishing. Some painters, such as A. Petrytsky, survived the terror, but their works were destroyed (an extensive series of Petrytsky's portraits). Many others, including M. Boichuk, S. Nalepinska, V. Sedliar, and I. Padalka, were shot. Theater was also decimated in the name of the new form. The Berezil theater was liquidated, and its founder and director, L. Kurbas, died in a prison camp, as did its principal playwright, M. Kulish. Its major actors, such as Y. Hirniak, were imprisoned. Writers of the brief literary renaissance of the 1950s and 1960s were persecuted because of their deviations from the officially sanctioned method. Departures from the norm were labeled 'formalism,' 'abstractionism,' or 'modernism' and proscribed. In its last stage socialist realism was praised for its Party orientation and its 'populism' (*narodnist*). Those terms continued to be used as synonyms for devoted service to the interests of the Party. Socialist realism also demanded isolation from the literature and art of the West, with particular emphasis on the 'revisionism' of Western Communist critics (eg, R. Garaudy, *Réalisme sans rivages*).

Theoreticians of socialist realism based their writings on those of K. Marx, F. Engels, and V. Lenin, various resolutions of the CPSU, and the speeches of various Party leaders. A large body of writings created in the last few decades consists entirely of dogmatic pronouncements and tendentious interpretations of artificially chosen quotes from officially accepted works.

Since the announcement of Perestroika and Glasnost in 1985, there have been signs that the dogmatic constraints of socialist realism have been widened. Indeed, reference to socialist realism has largely been avoided, especially since the breakup of the Soviet Union.

BIBLIOGRAPHY
Kryzhanivs'kyi, S. *Sotsialistychnyi realizm – tvorchyi metod radians'koï literatury* (Kiev 1961)
Pytannia sotsialistychnoho realizmu, 5 vols (1961–75)
Ovcharenko, O. *Sotsialistychnyi realizm i suchasnyi literaturnyi protses* (Kiev 1971)
Shamota, M. *Humanizm i sotsialistychnyi realizm* (Kiev 1976)
I. Koshelivets

Socialist Revolutionaries.

Representatives of a current within the Russian Empire's revolutionary movement that tried to create a synthesis of *populism and *Marxism to appeal to peasants as well as workers and the radical intelligentsia. Socialist revolutionary (SR) groups first emerged in the late 1890s. Among the earliest SR formations was the Party of Socialist Revolutionaries, founded in 1897 and known as the Southern party because it had branches primarily in the cities of Ukraine (including Kharkiv and Odessa) and southern Russia. At the end of 1901 the Southern party joined with other SR groups to form the Socialist Revolutionary party. The SRs became particularly interested in the peasantry as a result of the peasant unrest that broke out in Poltava and Kharkiv gubernias in 1902. They formed a Peasant Union in 1902, and in the program adopted at their first party congress in 1905 they called for the socialization of the land. The 1905 congress also created a regional party organization for Ukraine, uniting the pre-existing Kharkiv, Kiev, Poltava, Volhynia, and Voronezh party committees.

The SR movement in Ukraine was primarily connected with the Russian revolutionary movement, but groups of Ukrainian SRs also appeared between 1905 and 1917. Not until revolution broke out in the spring of 1917, however, was the *Ukrainian Party of Socialist Revolutionaries (UPSR) formally founded in Kiev. The UPSR played a large role in the revolutionary events in Ukraine during the next few years.

The Russian SRs had included federalism in their program prior to the revolution, but in the spring of 1917 they generally adopted a hostile attitude to the Central Rada's strivings for Ukrainian autonomy. Only when the Russian Provisional Government finally made concessions to Ukrainian autonomy in July 1917 did Russian SRs co-operate with the Rada, but they completely opposed the proclamation of Ukrainian independence in January 1918. Prominent Russian SRs in Ukraine during the revolutionary era included A. Zarubin (post and telegraph minister in the autonomous Ukrainian government) and P. Nezlobin (chairman of the Kiev soviet). Although divided over the national question, Russian and Ukrainian SRs ran joint lists in the Kharkiv, Kherson, and Poltava districts during the elections to the all-Russian constituent assembly conducted in late 1917 and early 1918. The election results demonstrated the great popularity of the SRs in Ukraine, where Russian and especially Ukrainian SRs received about two-thirds of the votes cast.

Both the Russian and the Ukrainian SRs split into left and right factions after the October Revolution of 1917, with the left SRs supporting the Bolsheviks. After the Bolsheviks solidified their power, SR influence was eliminated in Soviet Ukraine, as right SRs emigrated abroad, and left SRs merged with the Bolsheviks. The Russian SRs disappeared in late 1919, and the Ukrainian SRs (including the pro-Bolshevik *Borotbists), in 1920–1. Ukrainian SRs in western Volhynia, which came under Polish rule in 1920, joined with the Galician-based *Ukrainian Radical party in 1926 to form the Ukrainian Socialist Radical party. The UPSR also continued to exist in the emigration, although it was riven by factional divisions in 1921.

J.-P. Himka

Sociedade dos Amigos da Cultura Ucraniana.
See Society of Friends of Ukrainian Culture.

Society for the Advancement of Ruthenian Art
(Tovarystvo dlia rozvoiu ruskoi shtuky). The first Ukrainian organization in Galicia concerned with the development of 'Ruthenian art in general, and painting, sculpture, and jewelry-making in particular,' the financial well-being of its members, and the organization of exhibitions. The society was founded in 1898 in Lviv. Its board of directors was headed by V. *Nahirny, and Yu. *Pankevych headed its executive. The artists who participated in its first exhibition (1899) were Pankevych, I. Trush, A. Pylykhovsky, O. Skrutok, and K. Ustyianovych. The participants in the society's second exhibition (1900) included the aforementioned and O. Novakivsky, O. Kurylas, T. Kopystynsky, A. Manastyrsky, M. Ivasiuk, Ye. Turbatsky, Ya. Pstrak, O. Kosanovsky, and the wood sculptor A. Kavka. The third exhibition was held in 1903. The society continued to function until the First World War, but after it began accepting folk artisans as members, many of its original members left to join the *Society of Friends of Ukrainian Scholarship, Literature, and Art.

Society for the Advancement of Ukrainian Scholarship. See Association for the Advancement of Ukrainian Studies.

Society for the Preservation of Soldiers' Graves (Tovarystvo okhorony voiennykh mohyl). An organization set up in Lviv in 1927 to care for the graves of Ukrainian soldiers who were killed or died during 1914–20. Headed by B. Yaniv, the society ensured that each grave was marked by a military stone cross and kept in good order. It had 32 chapters in Galicia and was active until 1939.

Society for the Promotion of the Arts (Obshchestvo pooshchreniia khudozhestv). A philanthropic society of art patrons, established in 1821 in St Petersburg. It organized art exhibitions, lotteries, competitions, and sales of artworks; financed trips abroad for artists; and published art textbooks and journals, such as *Iskusstvo i khudozhestvennaia promyshlennost'* (1898–1902) and *Khudozhestvennyia sokrovishcha Rossii* (1901–7). It also maintained a museum of applied art and a drawing school (from 1857). The society supported many Ukrainian artists, including T. Shevchenko, I. Soshenko, A. Mokrytsky, H. Lapchenko, P. Boryspolets, K. Trutovsky, S. Vasylkivsky, and M. Samokysh. It was active until 1929.

Society of Agriculture of Southern Russia (Obshchestvo selskogo khoziaistva iuzhnoi Rossii). The first agricultural society in Ukraine and one of the first in the Russian Empire. Founded on the initiative of Prince M. *Vorontsov in 1828, it made its head office in Odessa and extended its operations throughout Kherson, Katerynoslav, Tavriia, and Bessarabia gubernias. To improve farming in the region the society supported scientific research, disseminated agricultural information, and promoted various enterprises related to farming. Besides funding experiments on local and foreign grains, feed crops, and industrial crops, the society ran an experimental fruit farm, helped to introduce meteorological monitoring, prepared soil maps of the southern gubernias, provided financial assistance to university students, held agricultural exhibitions, contests, and conferences, and encouraged railroad construction, the digging of artesian wells, farm-machine building and distribution, and forestation. From its inception the society published its own journal, titled at first *Listki* and then *Zapiski*. Its efforts at improving viticulture, sheep raising, and orcharding were particularly important in the economic development of Southern Ukraine.

Society of Antiquities and Art (Kyivske tovarystvo starozhytnostei i mystetstva). A society founded in 1897 on the basis of the Kiev Society of Art Promoters and an organizing committee for the creation of a museum in Kiev. It was led by B. Khanenko and numbered about 200 members. The artifacts collected by the society were kept in the Kiev Municipal Museum of Antiquities and Art (later the Kiev Museum of Ukrainian Art). The society existed until 1908. Its historical collections formed the basis of the Historical Museum of the Ukrainian SSR in 1936, and its folk-art collections formed the basis of the Kiev Museum of Ukrainian Decorative Folk Art (1964).

Society of Argentinian-Ukrainian Graduates (Tovarystvo ukrainskykh vysokoshkilnykiv Argentiny, or TUVA; Spanish: La Unión de Graduados Ucranios de la República Argentina). An association of professional men and women established in 1971 in Buenos Aires to promote the development of the Ukrainian community and the growth of Ukrainian culture in Latin America. Its leading founders were O. Yakhno and V. Pokhyliak. Its two professional sections, medical and engineering, maintain contacts with Ukrainian professional associations in North America. The society organizes lectures and panel discussions by Argentinian and Ukrainian scholars and political figures as well as national conferences of Ukrainian graduates in Argentina (1984, 1987). The presidents of the society have included Yakhno and Yu. Ivanyk.

Society of Contributors to the Fine Arts in Transcarpathian Ruthenia (Tovarystvo deiatelei zobrazhaiuchikh iskustv na Podkarpatskoi Rusi). A society of artists, established in 1931 in Uzhhorod and headed by A. Erdeli. It had 40 non-Ukrainian and Ukrainian members, including Y. Bokshai, A. Boretsky, A. Dobosh, and E. Kontratovych. The society held annual exhibitions, and its members received government travel grants. After the imposition of Hungarian rule in 1939, the society was renamed the Union of Subcarpathian Artists.

Society of Economists (Tovarystvo ekonomistiv pry VUAN). An association formed in 1919 to support research and publications on the economic history and current economic conditions of Ukraine. It consisted of three sections: statistics (headed by M. Ptukha), the study of the Ukrainian economy (headed by K. Vobly), and the study of the cooperative movement (headed by P. Pozharsky). The society was headed by Vobly (president), H. Kryvchenko (vice-president), and A. Laponohov (academic secretary). In 1929–30 it had 135 members. The society sponsored several VUAN publications. In the early 1930s it was abolished along with many other VUAN institutes and societies.

Society of Former Combatants of the Ukrainian Republican Democratic Army in France (Tovarystvo buvshykh voiakiv Armiï UNR u Frantsiï). A veterans' organization established in Paris in 1927 for the furthering of traditions of armed struggle for Ukrainian statehood. In 1939 it had 22 branches in France (the number declined to 12 in 1945) with nearly 1,000 members. It published various educational and informative materials until 1939 and worked with the Union of Ukrainian Emigré Organizations in France as well as French veterans' groups and other Ukrainian combatants' organizations. In 1961 the society split into two groups of the same name; they were reunited in 1977. The society has been headed by Gen O. *Udovychenko (1927–75), V. Kalinichenko (1975–9), Ya. Musianovych (1979–82), and (since 1982) Yu. Yeremiiv. Its long-standing secretary was M. Kovalsky. Members included V. Lazarkevych, K. Mytrovych, V. Nedaikaska, M. Panasiuk, A. Polovyk, V. Solonar, L. Vasyliv, P. Verzhbitsky, and P. Yosypyshyn. In 1928–9 the society published the journal *Viis'kova sprava* (edited by I. Rudychiv), and later, a bulletin, which continues to appear.

Society of Friends of Education (Tovarystvo prykhyl-nykiv osvity). A students' aid society founded in Lviv in 1927 by the Shevchenko Scientific Society. Its aim was to assist needy Ukrainian students attending institutions of higher learning. The society was the guardian of the Academic Students' Home in Lviv; it also helped run the refectory, gave loans to students, and so on. Its heads were V. Detsykevych and, from 1933, O. Kulchytsky. The society was dissolved in 1934 by the Polish authorities.

Society of Friends of Ukrainian Culture (Tovarystvo prykhylnykiv ukrainskoi kultury; Portuguese: Sociedade dos Amigos da Cultura Ucraniana). An organization established at the General Congress of Brazilian Ukrainians in Curitiba in 1947. It was based in the country's larger settlements, and it published the *Boletim Informativo* in Portuguese in 1950–61 and broadcast a radio program during approximately the same period. With an out-migration of active supporters to North America in 1960–5, the society lost much of its dynamism. In 1975 it had three branches in Paraná and one in Rio Grande do Sul. Leading figures in the group included Rev M. Ivaniv, Rev M. Kaminsky, O. Dilai, R. Kupchynsky, and M. Hets.

Society of Friends of Ukrainian Scholarship, Literature, and Art (Tovarystvo prykhylnykiv ukrainskoi nauky, literatury i shtuky). A society founded on the initiative of M. *Hrushevsky and I. *Trush in Lviv in 1904. It united scholars, writers, and artists from Russian-ruled and Western Ukraine and popularized their work. In 1904 it organized a summer school for students from Russian-ruled Ukraine, where were offered courses in Ukrainian literature (taught by I. Franko), history (Hrushevsky), anthropology (F. Vovk), language (I. Bryk), the history of socialism (M. Hankevych), and the history of Galicia (K. Studynsky). In 1905 it sponsored the All-Ukrainian Exhibition of Art and Crafts in Lviv. The society also published several books. Although its activities slowly waned, the society continued to exist until the First World War. Its long-time president was Hrushevsky, and its secretaries were Trush and M. Mochulsky. Among its more prominent members were Franko, M. Arkas, M. Lysenko, V. Hnatiuk, F. Krasytsky, Yu. Pankevych, and M. Boichuk.

Society of Kiev Physicians. See Kiev Medical Society.

Society of Kuban Researchers (Russian: Obshchestvo liubitelei izucheniia Kubanskoi oblasti). A regional studies society in Katerynodar that was active in the years 1896–1917. Works on the Kuban's natural environment, history, ethnology, and statistics were published in its *Izvestiia* (6 vols, 1899–1913).

Society of Researchers of Ukrainian History, Literature, and Language. See Leningrad Society of Researchers of Ukrainian History, Literature, and Language.

Society of Ruthenian Church Communities in the USA and Canada. See Association of Ruthenian Church Communities in the USA and Canada.

Society of Ruthenian Ladies (Obshchestvo ruskykh [russkykh] dam). A Russophile women's organization.

Founded in Lviv in 1878, the society was the first organization of Ukrainian women. Its original aims were to decorate the altar of the Dormition Church in Lviv, to provide educational scholarships for needy Ukrainian girls, and to engage in general philanthropic work. In the mid-1880s it had about a hundred members. It published the children's fortnightly *Vinochek* (1904–8).

Society of Saint Andrew (Tovarystvo sviatoho Andreia). An association of Ukrainian Catholic priests in Galicia founded in 1930 in Stryi deanery. Its statute, which was confirmed by Metropolitan A. Sheptytsky in May 1931, stated that the society's members were to provide moral and material support to each other, their families, and the community at large. The society's chief organizer was Rev Y. Savytsky, a catechist in Stryi and later the director of its central office in Lviv. Its president was Rev Yu. Dzerovych. Deanery chapters were headed by protopresbyters. The society organized religious retreats for priests and missions, published the church statute and a religious almanac, and ran a sanatorium in Hrebeniv, Stryi county. It was forcibly abolished after the 1939 Soviet occupation of Galicia.

Society of Saint Basil the Great (Obshchestvo sv. Vasiliia Velikogo). A Russophile cultural-educational society established in Uzhhorod in 1864 by O. Dukhnovych for the purpose of spreading education and preserving the religious and national traditions of the Ruthenian people of Transcarpathia. Headed by I. Rakovsky (president), A. Dobriansky (honorary president), and I. Mondok (secretary) and supported by bishops V. Popovych and Y. Gaganets, the society grew quickly to about 500 members, mostly clerical and secular intelligentsia. It published school texts, literary works, and periodicals, such as *Svit* (1867–71), *Novyi svit* (1871–2), *Karpat"* (1873–86), *Uchytel'* (1867), and *Nauka* (1897–1902). The language of its publication was an artificial mixture of Russian, Church Slavonic, and the vernacular. Owing to the intervention of the Hungarian authorities and pressure from Bishop S. Pankovych, the society changed its orientation in the 1870s to a pro-Hungarian one and began to decline. In 1895 a group of young populist-minded priests, including A. Voloshyn, V. Hadzhega, and P. Gebei, tried to revitalize it, but without success. In 1902 the society was dissolved, and its assets were transferred to the new commercial publishing venture *Uniia.

Society of Saint John the Baptist (Tovarystvo sv. Ioana Khrystytelia; also Obshchestvo sv. Ioana Krestitelia). An educational society founded in September 1862 in Prešov by O. *Dukhnovych and A. *Dobriansky. Its purpose was to promote a national renaissance by providing financial aid in the form of loans and bursaries to poor students as well as peasants and even whole organizations. The society maintained a student residence in Prešov under Dukhnovych's management (1863–5). Headed by A. Dobriansky and supported by Bishop Y. Gaganets, the society had a membership of over 400. After Dukhnovych's death in 1865 the society declined, and by the end of the decade it had ceased to exist.

Society of Saint Paul the Apostle (Tovarystvo sv. apostola Pavla u Lvovi). A Ukrainian Catholic religious society founded in Lviv in 1897. It was formed under the influence of the social action ideas espoused by Pope *Leo XIII. Until the First World War it sought mainly to infuse a (Catholic) religious consciousness into Galician national populism, which had been marked by a spirit of secular liberalism or even radicalism. Indirectly it also promoted a sense of Ukrainophilism among the often Russophile Galician clergy. After the war the society promoted charitable work, particularly among orphans and other war victims. It published a series of nearly 50 popular booklets and the journal *Nyva* and led a campaign against attempts to enforce celibacy among the clergy in Stanyslaviv and Peremyshl eparchies. After sending a memorandum to the League of Nations in 1925 regarding the persecution of the Ukrainian clergy by Polish authorities, the society was forcibly liquidated.

Society of School Education (Tovarystvo shkilnoi osvity; full name: Society for the Dissemination of School Education in Ukraine [Tovarystvo rozpovsiudzhennia shkilnoi osvity na Ukraini]). A Ukrainian educational and pedagogical society founded in March 1917 in Kiev by Ukrainian teachers. Its goal was to organize Ukrainian education. The ruling body of the society was the Council of the Society, the first head of which was I. Steshenko. The society organized the first all-Ukrainian conference of teachers, held on 5–6 April 1917, and the first Ukrainian gymnasium in Kiev. It set up a string of practical courses in Ukrainian studies for teachers. The society published textbooks and developed a Ukrainian educational terminology. It took part in the operations of the General Secretariat of the Ukrainian Central Rada. During the occupation of Ukraine by General A. Denikin's Volunteer Army, in the second half of 1919, the society assumed complete responsibility for maintaining Ukrainian-language education, for defending it against the administration, and for establishing a financial base to ensure its continuation. It ran its operations on generous donations from the Ukrainian community and the Ukrainian co-operative movement.

Society of South Russian Artists (Obshchestvo iuzhnorusskikh khudozhnikov). An association of artists who lived in Southern Ukraine, established in Odessa in 1890. Among its founders were K. Kostandi (its president from 1902 to 1921), M. Kuznetsov, H. Ladyzhensky, M. Skadovsky, M. Kravchenko, V. Edvards, A. Popov, and A. Rozmaritsyn. Later members included I. Aivazovsky, Yu. Bershadsky, Ye. Bukovetsky, P. Volokidin, D. Krainiev, P. Levchenko, M. Pymonenko, V. Zauze, and P. Nilus. The society organized annual general exhibitions and more frequent solo shows of works by its members. It participated in the work of the Odessa Art School and helped found the Odessa City Museum of Art. Its activities ceased in 1922 after the death of Kostandi. A book about the society by V. Afanasiev was published in Kiev in 1961.

Society of Teachers in Higher Schools. See Skovoroda Society of Higher School Teachers.

Society of Ukrainian Actors (Tovarystvo ukrainskykh artystiv pid orudoiu I. Marianenka). A theater under I.

Marianenko, created in Kiev in January 1915 with some actors who had left *Sadovsky's Theater, among them M. Zankovetska, P. Saksahansky, O. Polianska, T. Sadovska-Tymkivska, V. Vasylko, L. Linytska, M. Petlishenko, and S. Butovsky; the young actors B. *Romanytsky and I. Kozlovsky began their theatrical careers in this troupe. It successfully toured Kamianets-Podilskyi and Yelysavethrad in the summer of 1915 and spent the winter in Odessa. Its repertoire consisted of Ukrainian classical populist-realistic plays directed by Saksahansky, and O. Koshyts's student choir participated in some productions. The troupe was active until 1916. Marianenko became director of the *Ukrainian National Theater; Zankovetska and Saksahansky continued working with a group of young actors until early 1918.

Society of Ukrainian Co-operators (Tovarystvo ukrainskykh kooperatoriv). An organization of co-operative leaders and theoreticians, established in June 1936 in Lviv by the Audit Union of Ukrainian Co-operatives. In 1937 it had 2,285 members. The president was Yu. Pavlykovsky, and the secretary A. Zhuk. The society organized three co-operative festivals (in 1936, 1937, and 1938) with lectures, discussions, and displays of co-operative literature and periodicals. In 1938 it produced *Do dobra i krasy* (To Goodness and Beauty), a film on the co-operative movement by Yu. Dorosh, written by R. Kupchynsky and V. Levytsky-Sofroniv. The society ceased to exist after the Soviet occupation of Western Ukraine in 1939.

Society of Ukrainian Engineers and Associates in Canada (Tovarystvo ukrainskykh inzheneriv u Kanadi, or TUIK). A professional association established in Toronto in 1950 to cultivate social contacts among Ukrainian engineers, further their professional development, and maintain relations with similar non-Ukrainian associations. As branches sprang up in Montreal, Sarnia, Windsor, Winnipeg, Montreal, and Edmonton, a national executive distinct from the Toronto society was set up (1954). From 1953 to 1975 the society was known as the Ukrainian Technical Society of Canada. TUIK organizes scientific lectures, symposia, and conferences; contributes financial aid to Ukrainian academic institutions; and publishes an annual bulletin (since 1984) and the quarterly *Visti ukraïns'kykh inzheneriv* (in partnership with the Ukrainian Engineers' Society of America). Since 1955 it has held eight international conferences with its American counterpart. A brief history of the society was prepared by Yu. Kurys in 1987, and in 1992 the society published a book on Ukrainian engineers in the diaspora.

Society of Ukrainian Engineers in Prague (Tovarystvo ukrainskykh inzheneriv u Prazi, or TUI). A professional organization set up in 1930 in Prague. During the next nine years it helped members with employment and legal problems, maintained contacts with Czech professional associations and the Ukrainian Technical Society in Lviv, and organized lectures for the Ukrainian community. It was a founding member of the Union of Ukrainian Engineers' Organizations Abroad, from which it seceded in 1932. The society's membership grew from 53 in 1930 to 150 in 1938. Its leading members included A. Halka, V. Domanytsky, P. Stetskiv, M. Hlavach, O. Dolny, F. Serbyn, P. Zeleny, A. Keivan, and R. Karatnytsky.

Society of Ukrainian Jurists (Tovarystvo ukrainskykh pravnykiv). A society of legal scholars established in Kiev in 1921 within the All-Ukrainian Academy of Sciences to conduct legal research and disseminate legal knowledge. Its members, varying from 35 to 70 in number, were active in various commissions and sections of the academy. The society's presidents were O. Levytsky, O. Huliaiev, and O. Malynovsky; its secretary was B. Yazlovsky. In the late 1920s the society was suppressed by the Soviet government.

Society of Ukrainian Lawyers (Tovarystvo ukrainskykh pravnykiv). An association of various legal specialists, including scholars, in Galicia, founded in Lviv in 1909. Its purpose was to promote the participation of Ukrainian lawyers in public life and to improve their professional qualifications. S. Dnistriansky was the first president. The more notable presidents in the interwar period were V. Detsykevych and Z. Lukavetsky. The society published *Pravnychyi vistnyk* (1910–13), and in 1914 it organized a national congress in Lviv. Its members collaborated with the Union of Ukrainian Lawyers in publishing the review *Zhyttia i pravo* (1928–39). After the Soviet occupation of Western Ukraine in 1939, the society was dissolved.

Society of Ukrainian Lawyers in New York. See Association of Ukrainian Lawyers.

Society of Ukrainian Progressives (Tovarystvo ukrainskykh postupovtsiv, or TUP). A clandestine, nonpartisan political and civic organization of Ukrainians in the Russian Empire. It was founded in 1908 at the instigation of former members of the Ukrainian Democratic Radical party to co-ordinate the Ukrainian national movement and to protect it from the rising wave of reaction by the Russian government and Russian nationalism after the dissolution of the Second State Duma (June 1907). In addition to Democratic Radicals, some Social Democrats and politically unaffiliated people belonged to TUP. Its highest governing body, the annually elected council, included figures such as M. Hrushevsky, Ye. Chykalenko, I. Shrah, S. Yefremov, P. Stebnytsky, S. Petliura, V. Vynnychenko, N. Hryhoriiv, F. Matushevsky, D. Doroshenko, V. Prokopovych, A. Viazlov, T. Shteingel, and L. Starytska-Cherniakhivska.

The central office of TUP in Kiev, where there were also several branches (hromadas), co-ordinated the activities of about 60 TUP hromadas in Ukraine as well as 2 in St Petersburg and 1 in Moscow. The group's main aim was to defend the gains of the Ukrainian movement and to demand further rights. Its minimal program was the Ukrainization of elementary education, the introduction of the Ukrainian language and of Ukrainian literature and history instruction in secondary and higher schools, and permission for the use of Ukrainian in public institutions, the courts, and the church. Its political platform demanded constitutional parliamentarism and autonomy for Ukraine. Until 1917 TUP, in effect, directed the Ukrainian movement in central Ukraine, in that it co-ordinated the work of the Prosvita societies and various cultural and educational clubs and collaborated closely with the Ukrainian Scientific Society in Kiev. It owned the Ukrainian bookstore in Kiev (the former publisher of *Kievskaia stari-*

na). The Kiev daily **Rada* and the Moscow journal **Ukrainskaia zhizn'* were its unofficial publications.

Through its hromada in St Petersburg TUP maintained friendly contacts with the opposition in the Third and Fourth state dumas, particularly with the Constitutional Democratic party (P. Miliukov and N. Nekrasov) and a group of autonomists-federalists (V. Obninsky), who recognized Ukraine's right to national and cultural development, and with Russian scholars, such as A. Shakhmatov, F. Korsh, and S. Melgunov.

In September 1914 TUP adopted a neutral position on the war and the belligerents: it disapproved of the pro-Russian declaration of *Ukrainskaia zhizn'* and was critical (November 1914) of the activities of the Union for the Liberation of Ukraine in Austria. At the end of 1914, members of TUP (beginning with Hrushevsky) were taken into custody. In December 1914 the society issued the declaration 'Our Position,' in which it supported 'the democratic autonomy of Ukraine, guaranteed also by the federation of equal nations.' In January 1917 it responded favorably to American president W. Wilson's peace efforts and expressed 'the will of the Ukrainian people for independent development.'

On 17 March 1917, after the February Revolution, TUP convened a conference of Ukrainian organizations and parties in Kiev and set up the Central Rada. At its final conference on 7 April in Kiev, TUP decided to fight for Ukraine's autonomy by legal means and changed its name to the Union of Ukrainian Autonomists-Federalists, which in June of that year turned into the Ukrainian Party of Socialists-Federalists.

BIBLIOGRAPHY
Doroshenko, V. *Ukraïnstvo v Rosiï: Noviishi chasy* (Vienna 1916)
Doroshenko, D. *Istoriia Ukraïny 1917–23. rr.*, vol 1, *Doba Tsentral'-noï Rady* (Uzhhorod 1932; repr, New York 1954)
                                                                A. Zhukovsky

Society of Ukrainian Writers and Journalists (Tovarystvo ukrainskykh pysmennykiv i zhurnalistiv). An organization uniting nationally conscious Ukrainian writers and journalists in Transcarpathia, based from 1930 to 1938 in Uzhhorod and in 1938–9 in Khust. Leading members were V. Grendzha-Donsky, S. Sabol, D. Popovych, A. Voron, and Yu. Borshosh-Kumiatsky. The society published several literary works and two almanacs.

Society of United Slavs (Tovarystvo ziednanykh slovian). A clandestine revolutionary organization founded at the beginning of 1823 in Zviahel by the brothers and officers P. and A. Borysov and the Polish revolutionary J. Lubliński. It had several dozen members, mostly lower-rank officers of troops stationed in Volhynia and the Kiev region as well as local petty civil servants. Most members were Ukrainian: the Borysov brothers, I. Horbachevsky, Ya. Andriievych, P. Hromnytsky, Ya. Drahomanov, M. Lisovsky, and I. Sukhyniv. The head of the society was P. Borysov, and its ideologists were J. Lubliński and I. *Horbachevsky.

The main aims of the society were to liberate the Slavs from foreign rule, abolish the monarchical system, reconcile the Slavic nations, and set up a federation of democratic Slavic republics, each with its own legislature and executive. The federation was to include Russians (embracing also Ukrainians and Belarusians), Poles, Hungarians (together with Slavs in Hungary), Bohemians, Croatians, Dalmatians, Serbs, and Moravians. The social program of the society proposed to abolish serfdom and to diminish class inequalities. The society believed that the people, not just the army, had to be prepared for the revolution. The ideological principles and political program of the society were formulated in its oath and catechism (consisting of 17 rules).

In September 1825 the Society of United Slavs joined with the Southern Society (of *Decembrists) but retained its own program and separate executive. The society's members were the most active participants in the uprising of Chernihiv Regiment in Trylisy on 10–15 January 1826. Most of them were sentenced to hard labor in Siberia. The society's ideas influenced the program of the *Cyril and Methodius Brotherhood.

BIBLIOGRAPHY
Bahalii, D. *Povstannia dekabrystiv na Ukraïni* (Kharkiv 1926)
Nechkina, M. *Obshchestvo soedinennykh slavian* (Moscow–Leningrad 1927)
Luciani, G. *La Société des Slaves Unis, 1823–25 (Panslavisme et solidarité slave au XIXe siècle)* (Bordeaux 1963)
Gorbachevskii, I. *Zapiski i pis'ma* (Moscow 1966)

Society of UNR Army Soldiers (Tovarystvo voiakiv Armii UNR). An organization of UNR Army veterans formed in 1924 in Kalisz, Poland. Its purpose was to help members cope as political émigrés in Poland, and thus to preserve cadres for a future Ukrainian army. Its head office was eventually moved to Warsaw, where it published a bulletin to maintain contact among its four chapters. Its presidents were V. Kushch and M. Bezruchko. In 1939 the society was dissolved by the German authorities.

Society of Veterans of the Ukrainian Insurgent Army (UPA) in Canada (Tovarystvo kolyshnikh voiakiv UPA v Kanadi). A veterans' association established in Toronto in 1951 by former UPA members. With a membership based largely in Toronto, Montreal, Winnipeg, and Edmonton, the society has consistently supported the Ukrainian independence movement. It has published or cosponsored a number of brochures and books (including its own commemorative issue in 1982) and has prepared an irregular section for the newspaper *Homin Ukraïny* under the title 'Voiats'ka vatra' (The Soldier's Campfire) since 1957. It maintains cordial relations with other Ukrainian veterans' associations. Its presidents have included S. Kotelets, M. Koshyk, I. Kozak, V. Kozak, and M. Kulyk.

Society of Volyn (Tovarystvo Volyn). An association of Volhynians founded by M. Dzivak in New York in 1951 to maintain contacts among former inhabitants of Volhynia, to provide aid and moral support to needy members, and to publish materials on Volhynia. Branches of the New York society sprang up in Cleveland and Buffalo (1953), and similar societies appeared in Winnipeg (1950) and Toronto (1951). Two issues of the quarterly *Volyn'* came out in New York in 1951, edited by A. Trachuk. Since 1953 the society has collaborated with the *Research Institute of Volyn in Winnipeg in publishing the popular chronicle of Volhynian studies *Litopys Volyni* and various monographs and collections.

Society of Writers and Journalists (Tovarystvo pys'mennykiv i zhurnalistiv im. Ivana Franka). A professional

The executive of the Society of Writers and Journalists. Sitting, from left: Ivan Kvasnytsia, Konstantyna Malytska, Vasyl Stefanyk (president), Mykhailo Rudnytsky (vice-president), Kyrylo Valzhetsky; standing: Ivan Nimchuk, Dmytro Paliiv, Lev Hankevych, Vasyl Mudry, Lev Lepky

association of Western Ukrainian litterateurs, which existed from 1925 to 1939. It was based in Lviv, and had about 60 full and candidate members. From 1933 on it held competitions and gave annual awards for the best literary works. The society was headed by A. Chaikovsky, V. Stefanyk, V. Shchurat, B. Lepky, and, from 1934, R. Kupchynsky.

Socinian schools (*sotsyniianski shkoly*). Educational institutions founded in Ukraine by the *Socinians. The schools existed from the end of the 16th to the first half of the 17th century. The most significant of the schools was in Kyselyn ([Kysylyn] now in Volhynia oblast); it was founded in 1612. Attempts were made to have it reorganized as an academy. Other well-known schools were in *Hoshcha, Liakhivtsi, and Cherniakhiv. The program of study placed great emphasis on the development of rational thought, mathematics, philosophy, rhetoric, Latin, and anti-Catholic polemics. Protestant scholars and publicists, such as O. Kysil, M. Tverdokhlib, P. Stehman, and S. Nemyrych, taught in these schools. The schools were closed in 1658 after the Socinian sect was banned by the Polish parliament.

Socinians (*sotsyniiany*). A Protestant sect whose name is derived from that of its Italian founders, F. and L. Socinius (Sozzini). The Socinians were Unitarians; they believed that Christ was a man whose divinity arose from his office and not his nature. They rejected communion and prayers for the dead, but respected the Sabbath and condemned war. Elders and deacons were their community leaders, and only their pastors had the right to conduct services and deliver sermons. The emphasis they placed on education led them to establish schools and publishing houses with high standards.

F. Socinius moved to Cracow in 1579 and assumed the leadership of the previously established Minor Reformed Church (Polish Brethren). Many existing Protestant communities throughout the Polish-Lithuanian Commonwealth adopted Socinianism. The movement also attracted adherents throughout Belarus and Ukraine (particularly in Volhynia and the Kiev region), including such leading noble families as the Hoisky, Nemyrych, Seniuta, Pronsky, Peresidsky, Chaplych, and Shpanovsky families, many of whom established Socinian schools and communities on their estates. Settlements were also founded in Kyselyn, Hoshcha, Khmilnyk, Liakhivtsi, Cherniakhiv (near Zhytomyr), Berestechko, and elsewhere. Repressions against the Socinians began in 1644 and intensified after the members of the sect showed support for Charles X Gustav of Sweden in the Polish-Swedish War (1655–7). In 1658 the Polish parliament ordered the Socinians either to convert to Catholicism or to face expulsion and the confiscation of their schools and shrines.

The Socinians were active in producing *polemical literature; some examples, as well as some anti-Socinian versified works of the late 16th century, have been preserved. Among Ukrainian translations of Socinian texts of that period, the most notable is the *Nehalevsky Gospel, published in 1581.

BIBLIOGRAPHY
Wilbur, E. *The History of Unitarianism: Socinianism and Its Antecedents* (Cambridge 1945)
Levytsky, O. 'Socinianism in Poland and South-West Rus'',' *AUAAS*, 3, no.1 (1953)
Kot, S. *Socinianism in Poland: The Social and Political Ideas of the Polish Anti-Trinitarians in the Sixteenth and Seventeenth Centuries* (Boston 1957)

I. Korovytsky

Sociology. The study of human relationships, the rules and norms that guide them, and the development of institutions and movements that conserve and change society. Sociological methodology includes the analysis of data obtained through questionnaires and surveys, the analysis of official statistics, the observation of human interaction, and the study of historical records. Within the discipline of sociology there are numerous specializations and subdivisions, such as the sociology of the family, of work, of political organizations and behavior, of ethnic and race relations, of sex roles, and of aging, and criminology and statistics.

Although sociology as a distinct discipline arose relatively recently, in Ukraine as in other countries elements of sociological thought can be found in earlier periods of history. Sermons and didactic works of the Kievan Rus' period and some of the polemical literature of the Renaissance and baroque periods can be considered forerunners of sociological thought in Ukraine. Ukrainian folklore also provides rich materials for sociological research, with its accurate descriptions of human relations, the nature of kinship ties, and community mores and standards, and Ukrainian ethnographers have contributed significantly to the development of sociology. The works of 19th- and early 20th-century Ukrainian writers and publicists are another important source of sociological information, especially on the behavior of various social groups.

The origins of sociology as a separate discipline in Ukraine can be traced to M. Drahomanov and his circle of scholars, who worked in Geneva in the 1880s. Members of the group included S. Podolynsky, F. Vovk, and V. Navrotsky. Their works appeared in the periodical *Hromada* (Geneva, 1878–82) and in separate monographs. Because sociology became established as a separate discipline later than other branches of the social sciences, however, the precursors of Ukrainian sociological thought

have to be sought in disciplines such as philosophy, historiography, geography, law, economics, and statistics. Scholars in those disciplines played an instrumental role in establishing various sociological schools of thought.

Philosophers such as P. Yurkevych, V. Lesevych, K. Hankevych, I. Fedorovych, and O.(A.) Stronin played significant roles in the development of sociology in Ukraine. Bold conceptions of the development of Ukrainian society and analyses of the relationship among various social groups in Ukraine were advanced by the 18th-century author of *Istoriia Rusov*, by 19th-century historians, such as M. Kostomarov, O. Lazarevsky, V. Antonovych, P. Kulish, Drahomanov, and M. Hrushevsky, and by early 20th-century political thinkers of the state school, such as V. Lypynsky and S. Tomashivsky. Rich sociological material can be found in early 20th-century works on the socioeconomic history of Ukraine by D. Bahalii and members of his school, such as M. Slabchenko and O. Hermaize, and in the anthropological-geographical works of S. Rudnytsky and V. Kubijovyč. Economic theorists such as M. Ziber (who stressed the economic factor in the development of society), Maksym *Kovalevsky (who related the early development of the Slavic tribes to a general schema of human social development), and M. Tuhan-Baranovsky (who developed ethical conceptions of understanding social problems) provided many new ideas for the development of Ukrainian sociology. Legal scholars such as B. *Kistiakovsky (who was the first to explore methodological questions) and S. Dnistriansky (who viewed law as a social construct and thus hastened a sociological analysis of law) occupy an important place in the history of sociology in Ukraine, as do the Ukrainian statisticians O. Rusov and V. and F. Shcherbyna.

The series Studiï z polia suspil'nykh nauk i statystyky (Studies from the Field of Social Sciences and Statistics), published in Lviv in 1902–12 by the Shevchenko Scientific Society (NTSh), can be considered a turning point in the history of sociological thought in Ukraine. It provided a forum for researchers in social problems and social theory, such as V. Okhrymovych, V. Starosolsky, V. Levynsky, V. Paneiko, M. Lozynsky, M. Hekhter, Mykola Zalizniak, S. Baran, Yu. Okhrymovych, and Yu. Bachynsky. Works with substantial sociological content by that group were also published in the NTSh serials *Chasopys' pravnycha* (1889–1900), *Chasopys' pravnycha i ekonomichna* (1900–6, 1912), and *Zbirnyk Pravnychoï komisiï* (1925–9). After the First World War the study of social problems and social thought in Ukraine was centered in the NTSh Economic, Sociological, and Statistical Commission in Lviv.

None of the works by the aforementioned authors, however, were grounded on the principles and methodology of modern sociological theory, and none advanced a novel theory of the development of society. Only after the cataclysms of the First World War, the Revolution of 1917, and the ensuing Ukrainian-Soviet and Ukrainian-Polish wars shook the foundations of the established social order did the need to study new social phenomena become apparent. Ukrainian social and political thought underwent great development in that period, and its authors began to understand that sociology can offer much in the attempt to understand the dynamics of Ukrainian national development.

In the 1920s in the Ukrainian SSR, sociological research was almost entirely conducted by scholars of the VUAN. The VUAN Socioeconomic Division had a department of sociology, first headed, in 1918–20, by B. Kistiakovsky. After his death the department was headed by the Marxist S. Semkovsky, under whom, however, it did not leave much of a legacy. A Sociological Commission was also founded within the Socioeconomic Division.

After his return to Ukraine in 1924, Hrushevsky devoted much energy to the organization of sociological research in the VUAN. His closest collaborators in that undertaking were Y. Hermaize, P. Klymenko, and K. *Hrushevska. The VUAN Cabinet for the Study of Primitive Culture, headed by Hrushevska, focused on genetic sociology. Its members published their contributions in the journal *Pervisne hromadianstvo ta ioho perezhytky na Ukraïni (1926–9). F. *Savchenko was a major contributor to the field.

Institutes in disciplines close to sociology, most notably the VUAN Demographic Institute headed by M. *Ptukha, provided valuable, pioneering analyses of biosociological processes. They include studies by Ptukha on Ukraine's population, its sex and age structure, and its mortality; by Yu. *Korchak-Chepurkivsky on mortality in Ukraine; by P. Pustokhod on Ukraine's demographic characteristics; by M. *Tratsevsky on natality in Ukraine; and by I. Kovalenko on suicide in Kharkiv.

Ukraïns'kyi visnyk eksperymental'noï pedagohiky i refleksolohiï (1925–30), published by the Ukrainian Scientific Research Institute of Pedagogy in Kharkiv, carried a number of articles in educational sociology. Research on sociopsychology and collective reflexology was also done by the Ukrainian State Psychoneurological Institute in Kharkiv and the Kiev Psychoneurological Institute.

The Ethnographic Society, the Geographic Society, and especially the Anthropological Society in Ukraine also contributed to the development of sociology. Significant were L. Nikolaev's three volumes of materials on Ukraine's anthropology (1926–7) and the three-volume compendium Kryminal'na antropolohiia i sudova medytsyna (Criminal Anthropology and Forensic Medicine, 1926–8).

The Ukrainian Institute of Marxism-Leninism (1922–30) in Kharkiv, despite its partisan approach to problems, published in its journal Prapor marksyzmu (1927–30) considerable descriptive sociological material. The institute also had a philosophical-sociological research section and a sociology department, as did its successor, the All-Ukrainian Association of Marxist-Leninist Institutes (1931–6).

The Stalinist reorganization of scholarship in Ukraine in the late 1920s and early 1930s resulted in serious restrictions on academic freedom in sociology. The authorities now allowed only a Marxist approach, and 'sociology' and 'historical materialism' were regarded as synonyms. After 1930 the terror and the repression of Ukrainian scholars put an end to serious sociological research. Most of the pre-Soviet generation of scholars were liquidated, and their replacements avoided sensitive, politically dangerous issues and limited themselves to promoting Marxist-Leninist-Stalinist dogmas and Soviet propaganda. Sociology lost its independent status and was condemned as a 'bourgeois science.' Empirical microsociological and sociometric research was unable to develop, because the use of mathematical statistics, the theory of probability, and structural-functional analysis was banned in the study of Soviet society.

With the Great Terror of 1936–8 sociology disappeared in Ukraine for some 30 years. The first hint that it was being revived came in the early 1960s, when the AN URSR Institute of Philosophy's Department of Atheism carried out field research in Western Ukraine. The results, however, were never published. After the reorganization of the Institute of Philosophy in 1963 sociological research was conducted by its departments of the Methodology of Sociological Inquiry, of the History of Philosophical and Sociological Thought in Ukraine, and of Philosophical Questions of the Construction of Communism. In 1969 the institute began publishing the journal Filosofs'ka dumka, which contained some quasi-sociological articles. Because Ukraine did not have a separate scholarly journal devoted to sociology, however, articles on methodological questions and the results of empirical sociological research were never published. The compendium Sotsiolohiia na Ukraïni (Sociology in Ukraine, 1968) carried some research results and was heralded as the first issue of a Ukrainian annual review of sociology, but subsequent volumes never appeared.

From the 1960s on, sociological research in Ukraine was carried out by special sociological groups affilliated with various CPU republican, raion, and city committees; by departments of the AN URSR (now ANU) Institute of Philosophy; by sociological laboratories at postsecondary institutes and universities; and by laboratories of the sociology of labor, applied sociology, and the scientific organization of labor at Ukraine's large industrial enterprises. Most Ukrainian sociologists belonged to the USSR Sociological Association, which was founded in 1958 as a professional but not scholarly organization. It had five regional branches in Ukraine. With the establishment of the Moscow journal Sotsiologicheskie issledovaniia in 1974, Ukrainian sociologists had a forum for the publication of their studies. Most of the research done in Ukraine focused on the socioeconomic problems of regional, urban, and industrial-enterprise development, economic administration, demographic trends, inter-nationality and religious relations, the sociology of science and culture, industrial relations, and child socialization. Applied sociology was the norm. Scholars with unorthodox views, or those who sought to show the true sorry state of Soviet society, were not tolerated.

In the postwar period sociology was one of the most underdeveloped scholarly disciplines in Ukraine and in the USSR as a whole. Several factors account for that state of affairs: virtual total Party control over the topics and methodology of research; the fact that sociology was not considered a separate discipline but part of the study of historical materialism; the significant political risk in carrying out innovative research; stagnation in the development of alternative theoretical principles and models and the paucity of sources for independent analysis; severe restrictions on the publication of social data collected by the state; a shortage of equipment essential for research, such as computers; inadequate conditions for the training of qualified sociologists in Ukraine and the inability to study abroad; and isolation from the international sociological community. Prohibitions on the publication of sociological research potentially embarrassing to the authorities and their unwillingness to listen to, let alone implement, practical recommendations by sociologists also contributed to the degradation of sociology in Ukraine.

During the 1960s and 1970s the most significant sociological work was done by ethnographers who studied ethno-sociological processes in Ukraine, notably V. Naulko and A. Orlov. Non-Ukrainian sociologists also made important contributions. Yu. Arutiunian's Russian monograph on the sociological study of the village (1968), a politically daring study of a Ukrainian village in Zaporizhia, was widely considered one of the best Soviet sociological studies in the period. Works by dissidents, such as I. Dziuba and V. Chornovil, which circulated in *samvydav form, and articles published in the 1970s samvydav journal *Ukraïns'kyi visnyk* discussed many interesting sociological questions.

The processes of democratization and openness in the late 1980s brought to the fore the need for objective and comprehensive knowledge about society, and a veritable boom of sociological research has taken place. The reorganization of the USSR Institute of Concrete Sociological Research into the Institute of Sociology and the establishment in 1988 of the All-Union Center for the Study of Public Opinion are manifestations of the new trend. In Ukraine, within the framework of the ANU Institute of Philosophy, the Department of Sociology, the Subdepartment of the Sociology of Mass Media and Public Opinion, the Sector of the Social and Psychological Problems of Public Opinion, and the Sector of the Sociology of Youth have been established. In Kiev there now also exists the Republican Sociological Center of the Sociological Association of Ukraine. Centers in Kiev, Lviv, and Dnipropetrovske now study *public opinion. In 1990, plans were announced for establishment of sociology faculties at Kiev and Kharkiv universities, and the ANU Institute of Sociology, headed by Yu. Pakhomov, was founded in Kiev. Sociological research is being done in the Center of Political Psychology established in 1990 at Kiev University, and the ANU presidium is also engaged in work in the field. Sociological research is published in the journal *Filosofs'ka i sotsiolohichna dumka*, which replaced *Filosofs'ka dumka* in 1989, and in separate monographs.

Among the leading sociologists in Ukraine today are L. Sokhan, V. Chornovolenko, O. Yakuba, V. Ossovsky, V. Tykhonovych, A. Ruchka, L. Aza, K. Hryshchenko, Ye. Suimenko, M. Honcharenko, V. Piddubny, and V. Paniotto. Some of the more significant books published in Ukraine in recent years are by V. Voitovych, on the dynamics of prestige and the appeal of professions (1989); by Ye. Holovakha, on young people's life perspectives and professional self-definition (1989); by L. Kravchenko and B. Moroz, on the guarantee of societal renewal (1990); by V. Kusherets and V. Poltorak, on elections to soviets and public opinion (1990); by Paniotto and Yu. Yakovenko, on mail surveys in sociological research (1988); by Paniotto, on experience from models of social processes (1989); and by Ruchka, on the value approach in sociological knowledge (1989). Also published have been the collection *Profesiine samovyzhachennia i trudovyi shliakh molodi* (Professional Self-Definition and the Working Life of Young People, 1987), V. Picha's *After Hours: Soviet Worker at Leisure* (1989), and a multiauthor collection of sociological research on the consequences of the Chornobyl nuclear accident (1990).

Emigré sociology. In the 1920s, Ukrainian émigrés began organizing sociological research. The first significant initiatives were taken by M. Hrushevsky, who had a firm grasp of the interrelationships among the various social sciences. The *Ukrainian Sociological Institute (1919–24), established in Vienna under his aegis, published M. Shrah's book on the state and socialist society (1923) and V. Starosolsky's book on the theory of the nation (1922).

Ukrainian sociological studies were also continued in Prague, where the Ukrainian Sociological Society was founded in 1923 on the initiative of Mykyta *Shapoval. In 1924 the *Ukrainian Institute of Sociology was established in Prague; it was headed, until his death in 1932, by Shapoval. That institute published the first and only Ukrainian sociological journal, *Suspil'stvo* (6 issues, 1925–7), and works such as an edition of M. Drahomanov's selected works (vol 1, 1937), V. Koval's booklet on the socioeconomic nature of agricultural co-operation (1925), M. Mandryka's booklet on national minorities in international law (1926), V. Petriv's booklet on society and the military (1924), and Shapoval's booklet on Ukrainian sociology (1927), and books on general sociology (1929) and the sociography of Ukraine (1933). Shapoval not only brought together established and young Ukrainian social scientists but also maintained ties with Western sociologists and ensured the institute's participation in international sociological congresses. Under him *Suspil'stvo* reviewed the latest Western sociological works and published a chronicle of the profession and bibliographies.

A real attempt was made at that time to propagate sociological education and studies through the establishment of chairs of sociology at the *Ukrainian Technical and Husbandry Institute in Poděbrady (headed by O. Bochkovsky), the Ukrainian Higher Pedagogical Institute in Prague (headed by S. Ripetsky), and the Ukrainian Free University in Prague (headed by O. Eikhelman and later V. Domanytsky). Works published by the interwar Prague circle included articles by O. Bochkovsky on 'nationology' and 'nationography' as branches of a special sociological discipline for scientific study of the nation (1927), by V. Domanytsky on 'rurbanism,' by M. Mandryka on sociology and problems of public education in the United States (1925), and by V. Starosolsky on the internal form of the word in sociological terminology (nd); and booklets by M. Shapoval on the army and the revolution (nd) and the city and the village (1926), and his book on the system of the social sciences and sociography (nd). Contributions were also made by S. Goldelman, O. Eikhelman, T. Olesevych, I. Ivasiuk, V. Sadovsky, and O. Mytsiuk.

Postwar émigré sociologists and those born in the West have not had the institutional base that existed in interwar Prague, and their research has not been systematic. Much of it has focused on the study of social processes in Ukraine (W. Isajiw, B. Levytsky, A. Simirenko, B. Krawchenko, and S. Protsiuk) and the study of Ukrainian communities in Canada and the United States (Isajiw, V. Nahirny, W. R. Petryshyn, O. Wolowyna, I. Zielyk, W. Darcovich, B. Tsymbalisty), Germany (V. Maruniak), and Brazil (O. Borushenko). Sociological studies about Ukrainians in North America have also been written by non-Ukrainian scholars. The *Ukrainian Center for Social Research in New York and the *Ukrainian Free University in Munich have been the most important community-based institutions involved in sociological research. Most sociological research about Ukrainians undertaken in the West, however, has been carried out in universities and colleges.

BIBLIOGRAPHY

Simirenko, A. (ed). *Soviet Sociology: Historical Antecedents and Current Appraisals* (Chicago 1966)

Vytanovych, I. 'Kharakter i orhanizatsiia sotsiolohichnykh doslidzhen' na Ukraïni,' *Suchasnist'*, 1972, nos 7–8

Weinberg, E.A. *The Development of Sociology in the Soviet Union* (London and Boston 1974)

Vucinich, A. *Social Thought in Tsarist Russia: The Quest for a General Science of Society, 1861–1917* (Chicago and London 1976)

Matthews, M.; Jones, T.A. *Soviet Sociology, 1964–75: A Bibliography* (New York and London 1978)

N. Chernysh

Soda industry. A branch of the chemical industry that processes soda, chiefly sodium carbonate as well as sodium hydroxide (caustic soda), crystal carbonate, and sodium bicarbonate decahydrate. Soda is widely used in the making of cleansers, detergents, drying agents, paper, glass, bicarbonate of soda, and other household and industrial products. The first soda factory in Ukraine was established in Lysychanske, in the Donets Basin, in 1890. The second and largest soda plant was founded in Slovianske in 1898. In 1966 a third plant was built in Crimea oblast. Total production of sodium carbonate in the Ukraine increased from 413,000 t in 1940 to 773,000 t in 1960, 1,077,000 t in 1980, and 1,325,000 t in 1987, and production of caustic soda increased from 77,600 t in 1940 to 104,400 t in 1960, 396,400 t in 1980, and 488,800 t in 1987.

Sodomora, Andrii, b 1 December 1937 in Vyriv, Kamianka Strumylova county, Galicia. Translator and writer. A graduate of Lviv University (1959), he is an award-winning Ukrainian translator of classical literature. Published separately have been his translations of Menander's *Misanthrope* (1962), Aristophanes' comedies (1980), Horace's works (1982), and Ovid's *Metamorphoses* (1985). He has also written a novel about Horace, *Nache te lystia derev* (As If Those Leaves of Trees, 1982), a book of portraits of classical writers, *Zhyva antychnist'* (Live Antiquity, 1983), and many articles.

Sofia. The capital of *Bulgaria (1989 pop 1,217,024). In 1889–95 M. Drahomanov lived and worked in Sofia. In 1918–21 the UNR maintained an embassy there, headed by O. Shulhyn and then F. Shulha. P. Sikora and Yu. Nalysnyk edited the journal *Ukrainsko-bolgarski pregled* (1919–20) in Sofia. After the First World War a small Ukrainian colony, consisting mostly of veterans of the UNR Army, sprang up in Sofia. The sculptor M. Parashchuk worked there from 1921. The head offices of the Ukrainian Hromada in Bulgaria, the Ukrainian Alliance in Bulgaria, and the Union of Ukrainian Organizations in Bulgaria (from 1934) were located in the city. The Bulgarian-Ukrainian Society (headed by I. Shishmanov), the small Ukrainian Student Association, and the Sich physical-education society were also active between the wars. All Ukrainian associations were dissolved after the Second World War, although an extensive cultural exchange between Kiev and Sofia is conducted by official institutions.

Sofiia Alekseevna, b 17 September 1657 in Moscow, d 3 July 1704 in Moscow. Regent of Russia; older sister of Peter I. After the death of her brother Fedor Alekseevich in 1682, she assumed power of regency on behalf of her physically and mentally disabled brother Ivan and her half-brother, Peter. During her time in power she brought the Ukrainian Orthodox church under the control of the patriarch of Moscow, concluded an 'eternal peace' with Poland (1686) which secured Russian control over Kiev and its vicinity, replaced Hetman I. Samoilovych with I. Mazepa (1687), entrenched Russian supremacy in the affairs of the Hetmanate through the signing of the Kolomak Articles (1687), and undertook two unsuccessful campaigns against the Crimean Tatars (1687 and 1689). She was deposed by Peter in 1689 and kept in a convent for the rest of her life.

Sofiivka [Sofijivka]. V-14. A town smt (1986 pop 8,200) on the Kamianka River and a raion center in Dnipropetrovske oblast. The region began to be settled at the end of the 18th century, and the village of Sofiivka was founded in 1793 by Gen I. Dunin, who was granted large tracts of land along the Kamianka River. The village developed but remained an agricultural settlement. Today it has a food industry, the administration of an irrigation system, and a regional museum.

Sofiivka burial site. A Copper Age burial ground of the mid-3rd millennium BC near Sofiivka, Baryshivka raion, Kiev oblast. Excavated by I. Samoilovsky and Yu. Zakharuk in 1948, the site yielded approx 150 graves with cremated remains either placed in earthenware urns or wrapped in cloth. Imprinted pottery and tools and weapons made of rock, flint, and copper were interred in the graves. Sofiivka and similar *Middle-Dnieper culture sites constituted a regional variation of the *Trypilian culture.

Sofiivka Park

Sofiivka Park [Sofijivka]. A dendrological park in Uman, Cherkasy oblast. The park was built by L. Metzel for the Polish count S. Potocki, the voivode of Rus' voivodeship in 1782–8, who named it after his second wife. It is situated on a picturesque site featuring many ravines and gullies that straddle both sides of the Kamianka River along the outskirts of the city. Construction began in 1796, and by the summer of 1800 the park was ready for public viewing, although work continued on it until 1805. Sofiivka included extensive landscaping to create or enhance grottoes, rock faces, waterfalls, and a system of waterways and lakes. Footbridges, sluice-gates, fountains, sculptures, and buildings were erected throughout the site. As well, a large number of trees – silver spruces, poplars, white pine – were planted in what had previously been a barren area to create the Dubnyk, Hrybok, and Zvirynets forests within the complex.

After Potocki died in 1805, possession of the property passed to his brother, who took no interest in its development or maintenance. In 1831, following the Polish uprising, the estate and its park were confiscated, and given by the Russian tsar Nicholas I to his wife. The site then became commonly known as the Empress's Park (Tsarytsyn sad) until 1859, when it was turned into a school for orchard growing. At that time a host of new architectural features were added. In 1899 the park was put under the administration of V. Pashkevych, who introduced foreign tree varieties and developed the site as an arboretum. The park was declared a state nature preserve in 1929, and its historic name was restored in 1946. In 1955 Sofiivka was put under the jurisdiction of the AN URSR (now ANU). It houses nearly 500 local and imported varieties of trees and shrubs and is an important center of the Central Republican Botanical Garden for introduction and acclimatization research.

Sofroniv-Levytsky, Vasyl. See Levytsky-Sofroniv, Vasyl.

Soft-drink industry. In Ukrainian economic planning the soft-drink industry formally includes all plants making and bottling soft drinks, fruit drinks, soda water, kvass (a sour drink made from bread or malt), and powdered and concentrated drinks. It also includes beer brewers and bottlers, which are treated separately under *brewing industry.

Initially, most soft drinks were made from essences and artificial flavors, but since the 1960s drinks from natural flavors have predominated. Over 50 types of nonalcoholic drinks were produced in the USSR, including some soft drinks produced under license from Western companies. Kvass is especially popular: it accounted for 17 percent of all production in 1987. In Ukaine in 1980 there were almost 900 plants producing nonalcoholic beverages. The plants were distributed throughout the country, but the largest were in Kiev, Zaporizhia, Odessa, Dnipropetrovske, and Vinnytsia. Total production of soft drinks in Ukraine increased from 413 million L in 1940 to 659 million L in 1970, 906 million L in 1980, and 1,253 million L in 1987. In general the development of the industry was not given great priority in Soviet economic planning. Most of the bottling was automated, but packaging and handling were usually not. Kvass is sold on street corners from small tanks; customers drink from the same glass, which is rinsed after each use.

S'ohochasne i mynule (The Present and the Past). A scholarly journal of Ukrainian studies, published by the Shevchenko Scientific Society. The first four issues of the journal appeared in Lviv in 1939 under the formal editorship of I. Rakovsky, with V. *Simovych as the de facto editor. The third and fourth issues were devoted to T. Shevchenko. The journal was renewed after the Second World War in Munich. Two more issues appeared there in 1948–9, one under the editorship of Z. Kuzelia and the

other of O. Kulchytsky. Both were devoted to matters concerning Ukrainian life in displaced persons camps.

Soil. See Soil classification.

Soil classification. The grouping of thousands of different soils on the basis of their common characteristics. Soil classification contributes to the organization and communication of information about soils and enhances the understanding of their genesis, the processes within them, their relationships with the physical environment, and their place in the landscape.

Despite more than a century of soil science research and international communication, there is no universal soil classification system accepted by all countries. Soil classification in Ukraine follows the Russian system. In that system the broadest soil groups (called 'soil types') are based on the properties of the soil profile (ie, horizons and other phenomena observed in a vertical cross-section of a soil body down to two meters). The old US soil classification system, which recognized three orders ('zonal soils,' 'intrazonal soils,' and 'azonal soils'), employed nomenclature for the 'great soil groups' of the 'zonal soils' and conceptually differentiated them in a way that corresponded to the 'soil types' of the Russian system. Since that classification system is also familiar to many in North America, the terminology from the old US soil classification system is employed here to describe the soils of Ukraine and their distribution.

Location and environmental relationship. In Ukraine three broad belts of soils corresponding to the belts of natural vegetation dominate most of the territory. First is the podzols of forested Polisia, formed on outwash sandy plains or on clayey till plains, which contain pockets of bog soils and ribbons of meadow soils on floodplains. The southern boundary of this belt follows along the line Lutske–Rivne–Zhytomyr–Kiev–Chernhiv–Novhorod-Siverskyi. Second is the belt of soils associated with the forest-steppe, consisting of the gray forest soils (formed under the broad-leaved deciduous forest), the deep chernozems (formed under the prairie), and the transitional podzolized chernozems or degraded chernozems (so modified under conditions of encroaching forest), all of which evolved on calcium-rich loess deposits. This belt also contains some bog soils in depressions and meadow soils in river valleys. The southern boundary of the belt follows along the line Chişinău–Pervomaiske–Kirovohrad–Kremenchuk–Krasnohrad–Kupianka–Valuiky. Third is a belt of soils associated with the steppe, consisting of common chernozems in the northern part and southern chernozems to the south. This belt arches around the Sea of Azov into the Kuban Lowland and part of the Stavropol Upland and contains chernozems particularly rich in available carbonates. Along the north coast of the Black Sea and along both sides of Syvash Lake are the chestnut soils. Interspersed among the southern chernozems and the chestnut soils, especially between the Inhul River in the west and the Molochna River in the east, are many shallow depressions consisting of leached meadow gley soils (known in Russian as *solod* and in German as *Wiesenboden*), and along the coast, solonetz soils (including the salt-laden solonchak soils).

In the Crimea there is an analogous, although inverse, sequence of soil belts associated with rising elevation from north to south: in the north, chestnut soils with associated solonetz and solonchak soils; in the middle, southern chernozems, followed by a carbonate-rich, shallow variant of the common chernozems and small areas of chernozems on heavy clays (Kerch Peninsula); and in the mountains, stony brown mountain forest soils interspersed with small pockets of mountain meadow soils at the highest elevations. On the warm south slopes the soil is transitional into the reddish brown soils typical in a Mediterranean climate.

A similar sequence occurs in Subcaucasia, with carbonate-rich variants of the common chernozems and the deep chernozems at low elevations in the north, carbonate-rich brown mountain forest soils on the mountain slopes, and mountain meadow soils at the highest elevations. On the southern slopes to the Black Sea coast are reddish brown soils. Only the broad alluvial plain of the Kuban River is dominated by 'azonal' alluvial soils; its delta contains 'intrazonal' bog soils.

In the Carpathian region one can observe both a vertical zonation and a transition to the Central European brown forest soils. With rising elevation the degraded chernozems and the gray forest soils of the Subcarpathian Basin give way to increasingly podzolized meadow gley soils. On higher slopes appear gray mountain forest podzols in areas covered by fir trees and brown mountain forest soils in areas of beech forests. The highest elevations have mountain meadow soils. On the Transcarpathian side of the Carpathians brown forest soils cover the foothills and meadow gley soils prevail in the lowland.

Characteristics. The major representatives of the great soils groups in Ukraine include, in order of importance, the chernozems and their related chestnut soils, the various podzolized chernozems of the forest-steppe, and the podzols of the forest.

Chernozems occupy 41 percent of Ukraine's surface area and even more of its agricultural land (54 percent) and plowland (58 percent).

Chestnut soils, related to the chernozems, occupy only 3.3 percent of the area of Ukraine and 3.4 percent of its agricultural land but account for 3.9 percent of its plowland. Whereas in the chernozems the zone of calcium carbonate accumulation occurs about a meter below the surface, that mineral concentration is characterized in chestnut soils by the presence of sodium cations. Their presence causes the chestnut soils to change gradually into salinized chestnut soils and solonetz.

The solonetz is low both in humus (1–3 percent) and in available plant nutrients. In the solonetz the salts are leached to a certain depth, which allows for a broader range of plants to grow. The solonchak, by contrast, is salinized right to the surface, and only salt-loving species of plants (halophytes) can survive. The process of salinization can be reversed only with expensive meliorative measures, such as subsurface drainage, deep plowing, the application of gypsum, or other agronomic techniques.

The podzolized soils of the forest-steppe developed with the encroachment of deciduous forest into the domain of the steppe. One-third of the soils in the forest-steppe are podzolized; their area represents 12 percent of the area of Ukraine but 18 percent of its agricultural land and 21 percent of its plowland.

Degraded chernozems still retain the chernozem habitus. Chemical analyses of degraded chernozems, compared with analyses of chernozems, reveal some decline in the proportion of absorbed calcium and magnesium and the presence of hydrogen in the absorbing complex of the soil. Inherent soil fertility is diminished as a result but can be enhanced with the application of chemical fertilizers and manure. Podzolized chernozem is more severely leached than degraded chernozem, as is apparent by the presence of a narrow leached zone at the bottom of the topsoil layer. Gray forest soils, by contrast, have a thinner (20 cm) dark gray layer of topsoil with a lower (1.5 to 3.5 percent) concentration of humus.

Podzols of the forest and associated soils are found in northern and northwestern Ukraine. The prevalent soils are the podzols, formed on the fluvioglacial deposits under conditions of humid continental climate and under the cover of coniferous and mixed forests. The podzols occupy about 13.5 percent of the area of Ukraine; another 1 percent, the remaining part of the region, consists of alluvial and organic soils. Known for their infertility, the podzols account for only 7.8 percent of the agricultural land and 6.8 percent of the plowland of Ukraine.

Bog soils, formed under poor drainage conditions, are representative of the hydromorphic suborder of the intrazonal soils. In Ukraine bog soils are abundant in the wet regions of Polisia (the Prypiat River Basin), in Chernihiv Polisia, and in the shallow troughs of small river valleys of the forest-steppe. Because of their high organic content, bog soils can be agriculturally productive, but first they must be drained and then treated with fertilizer. Bog soils occupy about 5.5 percent of the area of Ukraine and 4.5 percent of its agricultural land but only 0.24 percent of the plowland.

Meadow soils are formed on the floodplains of streams and rivers, where occasional floods and imperfect drainage provide for increased moisture. Excluding the solonetz, meadow soils occupy 4.3 percent of the area of Ukraine and 4.4 percent of its agricultural land but only 2.1 percent of the plowland.

Rendzina soils are thin, stony, dark-colored soils developed from soft limestones, chalk, or marls. Small areas of rendzina soil are found in the Volhynia-Kholm Upland. Soviet classification referred to them as carbonate-rich turfy soils formed on marls, chalk, or limestone, and considered them a subcategory of the chernozems.

Azonal soils are determined neither by climate nor by any particular soil-forming process associated with a topographic feature, but by the nature of the parent material. Commonly found on steep slopes, azonal soils show scant soil development and are generally of little significance to agriculture.

Mountain soils, developed on weathered solid rocks, are shallow and full of rock fragments. In the Carpathian Mountains, for example, are found gray mountain forest podzols, brown mountain forest soils, and mountain meadow soils. The mountain forest soils scarcely resemble the podzols. The mountain meadow soils developed under alpine meadows (sometimes overgrown with peat moss) are shallow. They usually undergo podzolization and develop a gley horizon.

In the Caucasus Mountains the main soils at higher elevations where coniferous forests grow are gray mountain forest podzols. At lower elevations, under deciduous forests, are the brown mountain forest podzolized soils. The latter soils, also found in the Crimean Mountains, are darker than those of the Carpathian Mountains because of the warmer climate and higher concentrations of calcium carbonate; they are also less acidic (pH 5–6).

BIBLIOGRAPHY
Nabokikh, A. *Sostav i proiskhozhdenie razlichnykh gorizontov nekotorykh iuzhno-russkikh pochv i gruntov* (St Petersburg 1911)
Krokos, V. *Les i fosyl'ni grunty Pivdenno – Zakhidn'oï Ukraïny* (Kharkiv 1924)
Materiialy doslidzhennia gruntiv Ukraïny, 1–7 (Kharkiv–Kiev 1924–8)
Makhov, H. *Grunty Ukraïny* (Kharkiv 1930)
Miklaszewski, S. *Gleby Polski* (Warsaw 1930)
Makhov, G. 'A New Soil Map of the Ukraine,' *Annals of the Ukrainian Academy of Arts and Sciences in the us*, 1, no. 1 (1951)
Vernander, N.; et al. *Pochvy USSR* (Kiev–Kharkiv 1951)
Harkusha, I. *Hruntoznavstvo* (Kiev 1954)
Agrogidrologicheskie svoistva osnovnykh tipov pochv Ukrainskoi SSR (Kiev 1955)
Ahrokhimiia i hruntoznavstvo, 1 (Kiev 1966)
Agrokhimicheskaia kharakteristika pochv SSSR: Ukrainskaia SSR (Moscow 1973)
Atlas pochv Ukrainskoi SSR (Kiev 1979)
Priroda Ukrainskoi SSR: Pochvy (Kiev 1986)
Krikunov, V.; Polupan, N. *Pochvy USSR i ikh plodorodie* (Kiev 1987)
G. Makhov, I. Stebelsky

Soil conservation.

A system of management and land-use methods which safeguard the soil against depletion or deterioration by natural or by man-induced (anthropogenic) factors. Soil conservation methods are usually designed by agronomists, soil scientists, or other specialists in agricultural or earth sciences and are promoted by means of education, extension services, incentives, and laws. The socioeconomic characteristics of the farmers, the organizational structure of agriculture, and the land tenure system usually influence the adoption of soil conservation practices. Since soil is the basic resource for agricultural production, the sustained development of agriculture in Ukraine depends on the maintenance of good soil quality and the retention of land area with good soils for crop production.

When it was a constituent part of the USSR, Ukraine played a disproportionately important role in Soviet agriculture. Endowed with relatively excellent climatic and land resources, Ukraine occupied only 2.7 percent of what was the USSR's land area but accounted for 7.5 percent of Soviet agricultural land, 15 percent of cultivated land, 15.6 percent of the sown area, and 22.5 percent of the value of agricultural production (1987). Of certain heat-loving but soil-demanding crops Ukraine contributed an even larger share of the sown area: 30 percent of the vegetables, 37 percent of the sunflowers, 49 percent of the sugar beets, and 53 percent of the corn for grain (1987). Under the pressure of Soviet five-year plans that compelled the republic to maximize the use of its land for agricultural output, the land uses of Ukraine were highly committed to agricultural production (see the table).

Over one-half (56.9 percent in 1984) of the total land area of Ukraine is cultivated and thus exposed for at least part of the year to wind and water erosion. Other agricultural lands too are cultivated occasionally, or grazed and trampled by livestock, and thus become susceptible to degradation. Nearly half a million hectares of formerly agricultural land is classified as loose sands and gullies. Only forested lands (16.6 percent of the land area) and wetlands (1.3 percent) provide some ecological protection. Some wetlands and forests, but mostly agricultural lands, have been lost to water reservoirs (especially the very large ones on the Dnieper Cascade, which account for most of the 3.9 percent), to roads (1.6 percent), and to

Land uses of Ukraine, 1 November 1984 (in 1,000 ha; percentage of total in parentheses)

All agricultural land	42,558.1	(70.5)		
Cultivated land			34,356.9	(56.9)
Orchards, vineyards, and perennial plantings			1,157.7	(1.9)
Hayfields, pastures, and fallow			7,043.5	(11.7)
All non-agricultural land	17,796.9	(29.5)		
Forests, scrublands, and shelterbelts			9,993.5	(16.6)
Wetlands			759.6	(1.3)
Water reservoirs			2,359.5	(3.9)
Sands and gullies			487.5	(0.8)
Roads and trails			982.8	(1.6)
Other land uses			3,214.0	(5.3)
Total	60,355.0	(100.0)	60,355.0	(100.0)

rural settlements, cities, industrial construction, and open-pit mining (the remaining 5.3 percent).

The implementation of soil conservation has several prerequisites: (1) awareness on the part of the agricultural decision-makers (farmers, landlords, government officials) that there is a soil degradation problem; (2) knowledge about soil degradation processes; (3) recognition of their underlying causes (including socioeconomic relations and political institutions); (4) the development of methods that may be employed or the restructuring of systems that may be needed to rectify or prevent soil degradation; and (5) willingness on the part of the decision-makers to co-operate in the implementation of soil conservation. The prerequisites gradually became present in response to the very severe soil degradation that became evident in Ukraine toward the end of the 19th century (see *Soil erosion).

Before the Revolution of 1917, soil scientists, who described and mapped soil erosion in Ukraine, had conducted studies to understand the processes of degradation and worked out methods to combat soil erosion. V. *Dokuchaev (1892) proposed a variety of agronomic measures and established test plots in Ukraine for trials. P. Kostychev (1893) devised special crop rotations for dry farming. O. Izmailsky (1894) recommended snow retention and plowing perpendicular to the slope to conserve soil moisture and reduce the occurrence of dust storms. H. Vysotsky studied soil protective afforestation (1895) and devised effective blow-through *shelterbelts (1898). Cognizant of the problem and aware of local research in soil science, a few landlords and colonists (often German Mennonites) implemented afforestation, shelterbelts, and the retention of gully erosion on their own properties with some success. By contrast the peasantry appeared to be ignorant and, in any case, were economically helpless. The tsarist government neglected agricultural development. Only after pressure was applied by naturalists and physicians, who were appalled by the poverty, the soil erosion, the famines, and the cholera epidemics, did the government commission three exhaustive studies, on gullies, on rural poverty, and on land tenure. Even so, nothing more was done until the peasant revolts of 1905 shocked the Russian imperial autocracy enough to implement land reforms.

The Stolypin agrarian reforms (1906–11) began to

change the socioeconomic relations so as to allow agronomic improvement on peasant farms and the implementation of soil conservation methods. Imperial policy, however, opposed the use of the Ukrainian language in schools and publications and thus hampered the development of literacy among the Ukrainian peasantry and the improvement of agronomic practices. Consequently, efforts to curtail gully erosion by means of ridging, trenching, and the afforestation of gullies became more common on the large estates than on private plots. That whole period of agronomic improvement was curtailed by the First World War and the 1917 revolution.

Most of the estate land partitioned among the peasantry during the revolution was kept by the farmers, but it was declared nationalized by the Bolshevik government. Small portions of the estates were retained by the government as state farms, and peasants were encouraged to join into several forms of collective farms. Rural extension service, begun before the revolution, was continued, often by the same specialists who advocated the measures that would facilitate the introduction of improved crop rotation and soil conservation measures – the consolidation of land and the enclosure of land into individual family farms. Basic research was encouraged by the Agricultural Scientific Committee of Ukraine (1920–7), affiliated with the People's Commissariat of Agricultural Affairs of the Ukrainian SSR. The policy of Ukrainization broadened the base from which trained personnel could be drawn, and enhanced the dissemination of proper agronomic practices and soil conservation techniques among the rural population of Ukraine.

The mass collectivization of agriculture (1930–4), coupled with the repression of Ukrainian patriots, initiated a new phase in the history of soil conservation. Research was centralized and geared to the implementation of agronomic improvements and soil conservation practices on collective and state farms. The All-Union (soon renamed Ukrainian) Scientific Research Institute of Forest Management and Agroforest Amelioration had developed by 1941 a grandiose shelterbelt scheme for the European steppe and forest-steppe, including the selection of tree species and the planting techniques to be used. Following the Second World War a massive campaign for planting and pond construction in the steppe and forest-steppe culminated with a decree (1948) that became known as 'Stalin's plan for the transformation of nature.' The grass-field crop rotation developed by V. Viliams was touted as a means for improving soil productivity and was propagated for widespread adoption. Boasting about those measures as well as the tempo of mechanization and motorization that enabled deep plowing, the Party generated a sense of euphoria. Subsequent studies of the soil conservation efforts revealed (1954), in fact, severe soil erosion. The problems, commonly associated with large-scale mechanized farming, were aggravated either because the recommended soil conservation measures were not implemented properly or because the fragmented responsibility and narrow incentives in socialized agriculture (such as bonuses paid to achieve specific job targets or production quotas) negated the application of recommended agronomic practices. Disregard for communal land now became a basic problem.

Under N. Khrushchev priorities were placed on increasing the output of agricultural production rather than on soil conservation. Reforms in agriculture (such as disbanding the *machine-tractor stations and making the tractor drivers directly responsible to collective farms) could have provided the means for implementing improved agronomic practices, but the ambitious programs and erratic 'campaigns' to sow more corn at the expense of small grains or pastures relegated soil conservation to a position of low priority. Severe soil degradation was the result. Much farmland was lost to the creation of water reservoirs on the Dnieper, open-pit mining, and urban growth (for land was considered a free commodity, and the Ministries of Energy and Electrification and of Mining carried more weight than that of Agriculture). In 1963, when the leadership realized that soil conservation was imperative, it commissioned the Ukrainian Planning Institute for Land Organization (Uzkrzemproekt) to devise comprehensive soil protection measures for each watershed in Ukraine. Although Khrushchev was deposed the following year, the project continued its work.

L. Brezhnev's agricultural policy involved the adoption of long-term planning and increased capital investment in the agricultural sector. So that agricultural output from the same land area would be increased, more chemical fertilizers, herbicides, and pesticides were made available, and massive drainage and irrigation projects were undertaken. In 1967, in an effort to counteract past soil degradation, a decree was issued 'Concerning the Undeferable Measures to Protect the Soils against Wind and Water Erosion.' Responsibilities for conservation practices were identified, and fines for violations were specified. A land cadastre, designed to serve as a benchmark on soil conditions, was commissioned. In 1970 the land codex of the Ukrainian SSR was prepared, to restrict the allocation of good agricultural land to other uses. Basic research on regional systems of soil conservation practice was undertaken, and its results published, presumably as a guide for central decision-making. In areas susceptible to water erosion, soil-conserving crop rotations with more cover crops were recommended along with the use of terraces and contour strip cropping (perpendicular to upland slopes). In areas susceptible to wind erosion (mostly in the steppe) the alignment of shelterbelts and fields perpendicular to the prevailing direction of the wind was recommended, along with the use of blade cultivators (or sweep plows – to avoid the turning of the sod), the retention of stubble cover, and the use of curtains of tall crops to reduce wind velocity.

Contour strip cropping was not widely used because it would have necessitated a major reorganization of fields and a greater use of small maneuverable tractors (which, together with skilled operators, were in short supply). Instead, less effective methods, such as trenching, pitting, and other field techniques, were more commonly applied in the areas prone to water erosion. High priority was given to combating wind erosion in the steppe. Machinery for conservation tillage (such as blade cultivators or sweep plows) was pressed into production. By 1983 the plowless tillage had been expanded to 7 million ha in Ukraine. Fertilizers were provided to invigorate overgrazed pastures and treat deficient soils. Earth-moving machinery was supplied to terrace slopes and fill in the gullies. A concerted effort was made at the filling in of gullies and at afforestation to stabilize loose sands. According to official reports, between 1965 and 1983 the area in gullies was reduced from 324.1 thousand to 258 thousand ha, and the area of loose sands was reduced from 293.7 thousand to 177.7 thousand ha.

Despite well-publicized soil conservation efforts during the Brezhnev period, erosion continued to grow. The area suffering from soil erosion in Ukraine increased from 1961 to 1980 by 1.4 million ha on plowland alone and by more than 2 million ha on all agricultural land. The trend was related to increased soil compaction from heavy machinery, increased mineralization from heavier use of chemicals, greater quantities of industrial emissions, acid rain, and water erosion from sprinkler irrigation on sloping, clayey chernozems.

(See also *Land use.)

BIBLIOGRAPHY

Muntian, V. *Pravova okhorona hruntiv URSR* (Kiev 1965)

Dolhilevych, M. *Zakhyst hruntiv vid vitrovoï eroziï na Ukraïni* (Lviv 1967)

Vedenichev, P. *Zemel'nye resursy Ukrainskoi SSR i ikh khoziaistvennoe ispol'zovanie* (Kiev 1972)

Tsemko, V. *Pravo sil's'kohospodars'koho vykorystannia zemli v Ukraïns'kii RSR* (Kiev 1975)

Ekonomicheskie problemy ispol'zovaniia zemel'nykh i vodnykh resursov v sel'skom khoziaistve (Kiev 1978)

Ekologo-ekonomicheskie aspekty okhrany pochv Ukrainskoi SSR (Kiev 1980)

Morgun, F.; Shikula, N.; Tarariko, A. *Pochvozashchitnoe zemledelie* (Kiev 1983; 2nd edn 1988)

Mikhailiuchenko, M.; Teleshek, Iu. *Zaslon erozii* (Kiev 1987)

I. Stebelsky

Soil erosion. The process by which unprotected soil is washed away by meltwater or rainwater (water erosion) or blown away (wind erosion). In Ukraine soil erosion occurs in regions of enhanced relief, mostly on the high right banks of rivers (as in the Kaniv region along the Dnieper), on the more elevated parts of the Dnieper Lowland, on the strips between the Dnieper and the Boh rivers, between the Dniester and the Prut, in Slobidska Ukraine, on the Donets Ridge, on the Azov Upland, and in the Carpathian Mountains. East and southeast winds (dry winds known as black storms) cause soil loss in the eastern parts of Ukraine. About 12.5 million ha of arable land in Ukraine are affected by water erosion. Erosion has increased as a result of deforestation, the tilling of slopes, and backward agrotechnology. Erosion eventually results in the formation of ravines, an increase in the amount of unusable land, and a loss of soil fertility.

The severity of soil erosion in Ukraine varies from place to place, according to natural conditions, land uses, and cultural practices. The forest zone in the northwest of Ukraine is the least susceptible to erosion. The forest-steppe zone suffers much more from water erosion, although the problem varies considerably with topography. The steppe zone, suffering from both wind and water erosion, has some of the most severely eroded soils in Ukraine. The mountain zones, despite their protective forest cover, suffer from high values of soil erosion.

BIBLIOGRAPHY

Borot'ba z eroziieiu hruntiv (Kiev 1968)

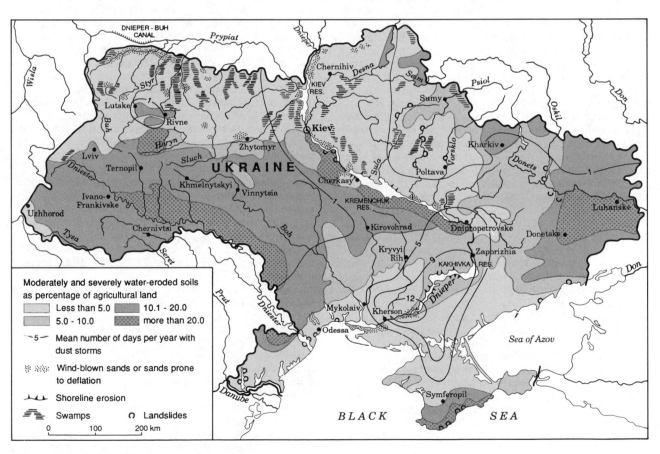

SOIL EROSION

Ekologo-ekonomicheskie aspekty okhrany pochv Ukrainskoi SSR (Kiev 1980)

Gensiruk, S.; Gaidarova, L.; Babich, A. *Ovragi i peski: Lesorazvedenie, ekologiia, ekonomika* (Kiev 1986)

Stebelsky, I. 'Agricultural Development and Soil Degradation in the Soviet Union: Policies, Patterns, and Trends,' in *Environmental Problems in the Soviet Union and Eastern Europe* (Boulder, Colo, and London 1987)

I. Stebelsky

Soil science. The systematized study of soils as an evolving natural resource influenced by living organisms and physical factors. It deals with the origin and formation of soils, their chemical, physical, and biological properties, their classification and geographical distribution, and their fertility. Soil science as a distinct discipline emerged only at the end of the 19th century, largely as a result of the contributions of V. *Dokuchaev.

The earliest scientific studies of soils in Ukraine, especially the first soil maps, resulted from the surveys of the country's agricultural potential conducted in the 1880s by the zemstvos. In 1888–94 Dokuchaev studied the soils of Poltava gubernia and published a detailed (1:420,000) soil map of the region. Previously he had published his research on the chernozem and the genesis of the steppes. In the prerevolutionary period the soils of Ukraine were studied by both Ukrainian scientists and specialists from St Petersburg and Moscow. A. Nabokikh, who polemicized with the Russian soil scientists in Moscow and St Petersburg, researched the soils of Podilia and Kharkiv gubernias and founded a distinct school of soil scientists in Ukraine. F. *Levchenko studied the soils of Volhynia, N. Frolov, those of Kiev gubernia, B. Polynov, those of Chernihiv gubernia, and S. Zakharov, those of Subcaucasia and Caucasia. Methods to combat drought in the steppes were explored not only by Dokuchaev but also by the prominent Russian soil scientist P. Kostychev, the Ukrainian agronomist O. Izmailsky, and the Ukrainian forester–soil scientist Yu. *Vysotsky. K. *Gedroits was director (1922–30) of the agrochemical department of the Nosivka Agricultural Research Station near Nizhen and did research on soil colloids and soil cation-exchange capacity. His laboratory analysis of the chernozems was based mostly on samples collected in Ukraine. The contributors to soil research in Ukraine included the Ukrainian geologist P. *Tutkovsky and the botanist and geographer G. *Tanfilev.

Before the 1917 revolution Ukraine was not viewed as a separate country, so integrated studies of Ukraine's soils did not begin until the 1920s. They were undertaken mostly by the *Agricultural Scientific Committee of Ukraine and its soil science section (1920–7), which was directed by H. *Makhiv (1923–7). It compiled 10 volumes of *Materiialy doslidzhennia gruntiv Ukraïny* (Research Materials on the Soils of Ukraine) and published a large (1:1,000,000) soils map of Ukraine. Soil research in Ukraine was conducted also by scientific research stations (35 in 1927), the Ukrainian Scientific Research Institute of Soil Science in Kiev, and the Ukrainian Scientific Research Institute of Fertilizers in Kiev. Soil science departments were active in postsecondary institutions, particularly at agricultural institutes. When the Agricultural Scientific Committee was abolished and many of its associates were purged during the collectivization, soil science in Ukraine suffered a grave setback.

In the 1920s and 1930s the outstanding soil scientists in Ukraine, besides those already mentioned, were D. *Vilensky, V. *Krokos, and O. *Sokolovsky. Some important contributions were made by I. Bandura, O. *Dushechkin, O. *Hrinchenko, H. Hrin, M. Krupsky, and T. *Taranets.

A new phase of soil research in Ukraine began in the second half of the 1930s. Its purpose was practical – to raise soil fertility, as promised by the leading Soviet soil scientist, V. Viliams. In the post-Stalin period soil mismanagement on collective and state farms was admitted, and research was diversified in an attempt to aid in the regional application of agronomic practices and the intensification of agriculture. With the full-scale mechanization and motorization of agriculture, the use of chemicals, and the implementation of large-scale drainage and irrigation projects, the assessment of the human impact on soil assumed primary importance. A detailed survey and inventory of soils was commissioned, to be used as a standard for rating soil management. Basic research concerning soil characteristics and soil genesis continued to be closely related to certain branches of geology (mineralogy), geography (climatology, geomorphology), biology (plant physiology), and chemistry. At the same time soil science emerged as the basis of other related applied disciplines, such as agronomy, agrochemistry, and soil mapping, and the development and testing of agrotechnical, agrochemical, and melioration techniques.

The major achievements of the post-Stalin period included a comprehensive, detailed, large-scale inventory mapping of the soils of Ukraine. Spearheaded by the Ministry of Agriculture of the Ukrainian SSR and the *Ukrainian Scientific Research Institute of Soil Science and Agrochemistry, the project involved research institutes, universities, and agricultural stations and produced maps to the scale of 1:10,000 or 1:25,000 for each farm and 1:50,000 for each raion, together with soil descriptions and agronomic recommendations (1956–62). Subsequently (1969–72), generalized soil maps were produced for each oblast (1:200,000) and for the entire republic (1:750,000). After numerous studies, such as soil-water characteristics, water-air regimes in the soil, water-salt interactions, the impact of tillage, soil erosion, and soil fertility, a comprehensive soil evaluation and mapping of the distribution of soil quality was undertaken. Some of the findings were generalized in the soils atlas of the Ukrainian SSR. The major contributors to soil science after the Second World War have been Hrinchenko, Hrin, Krupsky, H. Andrushchenko, M. Godlin, I. Hoholiv, O. Mozheiko, G. Sambur, N. Sereda, M. Shykula, S. Skorina, M. Veklich, and especially N. Vernander.

Today soil research is conducted principally at the Ukrainian Scientific Research Institute of Soil Science in Kiev, which is affiliated with the Ministry of Agriculture of Ukraine, and the Ukrainian Scientific Research Institute of Soil Science and Agrochemistry in Kharkiv, which was (until 1991) affiliated with the All-Union Academy of Agricultural Sciences in Moscow. Applied research is conducted at numerous agricultural research stations and even at agricultural laboratories on state farms and large collective farms. There are soil science departments in the geology faculties of the universities, agricultural academies, and agricultural and polytechnical institutes. Publications in soil science have been almost exclusively in the

Russian language. The main periodical, *Ahrokhimiia i hruntoznavstvo* (Kiev 1966–), published by the Ministry of Agriculture of Ukraine and the Ukrainian Scientific Research Institute of Soil Science and Agrochemistry, changed to Russian in the 1980s.

BIBLIOGRAPHY
Vilenskii, D. *Istoriia pochvovedeniia v Rossii* (Moscow 1958)
Kovda, V.; Iegorov, V. (eds). *100 let geneticheskogo pochvovedeniia* (Moscow 1986)

I. Bandura, I. Stebelsky

Soiuz (Union). The first Ukrainian student association in Chernivtsi. It was founded in 1875, and existed, except for 1903–5, until 1922, when it was dissolved by the Rumanian authorities. Membership varied from 50 to 100 students. The association took part in political and cultural-educational work and published *Bukovyns'kyi al'manakh* (Bukovynian Almanac, 1885) and the almanac *Soiuz* (1875–1903, 1905–10). The association's heads were D. *Vintskovsky (1875–9), S. *Smal-Stotsky (1879–83), O. *Kolessa (1891–4), P. Klym, T. *Halip, Yu. Tevtul, and V. Butsura, among others. When the association was dissolved, its members joined the academic associations *Sich and *Chornomore.

Soiuz (Union). A weekly organ of the Ukrainian Presbyterian Mission, published in New York (1908–11) and Pittsburgh (1912–21). It contained articles on religious themes, reports on the activities of Ukrainian Presbyterian and Evangelical congregations, and news relating to Ukraine and Ukrainian communities in North America. *Soiuz* was especially critical of the Catholic church. The editor was Z. Bychynsky.

The town hall in Sokal

Sokal [Sokal']. III-5. A city (1989 pop 22,400) on the Buh River and a raion center in Lviv oblast. It was first mentioned in historical documents in 1411, when it belonged to Belz principality. It obtained the rights of *Magdeburg law in 1424, and from 1462 it was a county center of Belz voivodeship. It developed slowly during the 15th and 16th centuries because of frequent Tatar attacks. In 1524 the town was rebuilt on the other side of the river, and its fortress was reinforced. During the next century it became an important center for the production of shoes, gold arti-

facts, and weapons. The Roman Catholics established two monasteries in the town. The Cossacks captured the town in 1648 and 1655, during B. Khmelnytsky's uprising. After the partition of Poland in 1772, Sokal was annexed by Austria and became a county center of the Galician crownland. It prospered as a manufacturing and trading town and by the end of the 19th century had a population of 8,000. In February 1919 the Ukrainian Galician Army successfully resisted the Polish forces, but by the summer the Poles had captured Sokal. The Polish government established the *Sokal border between Galicia and Volhynia. In 1939 the city was occupied by the Soviet army. Today Sokal is an industrial center specializing in the manufacture of synthetic fibers, reinforced concrete, bricks, hosiery, and foodstuffs. Its main architectural monuments are an Orthodox chapel (15th century), St Nicholas's Church (16th century), the remnants of the town walls and a tower (16th century), a Bernardine nunnery (1604), a Brigittine nunnery (1624), a Roman Catholic church in the Renaissance style (17th century), and St Michael's Church, in the baroque style (1778–1835). Archeologists have discovered artifacts from the Mesolithic, Neolithic, Bronze Age, and Hellenic and Celtic periods in the Sokal region.

Sokal border (Sokalskyi kordon). An administrative division separating the Ukrainian territories of interwar Poland. Its name was derived from the town of Sokal, on the Buh River. The division line ran along the former Austro-Russian border and the dividing line between the Lviv-Ternopil and Volhynia voivodeships. It effectively isolated Volhynia and other Ukrainian areas in the interwar Polish state from eastern Galicia. In that respect the Sokal border was regarded as a symbol of the desire of the Polish government to keep Ukrainians regionally fragmented (and thus limit their potential for co-ordinated political, cultural, and economic action). The Sokal border came into existence because of the signing of a Polish-Vatican *concordat (1925) which restricted the jurisdiction of Ukrainian Catholic bishops to eastern Galicia, and which supported (particularly after 1928) the Ukrainization of the Orthodox Church in Volhynia, the abolition by the Polish government of major Ukrainian co-operative and popular-education societies (Prosvita, the Audit Union of Ukrainian Co-operatives, and the like) north of the border (so that the area of their activities was restricted largely to Galicia), and the sanctioning by the Polish administration of the creation of regional Ukrainian political and economic organizations in Volhynia (such as the Volhynian Ukrainian Alliance). The main architect of the Sokal border was the Volhynia voivode, H. *Józewski. Its existence exacerbated the regional differences (political, social, and religious) in Ukrainian society in interwar Poland. The impact of the Sokal border began to lessen over time as a result of increased economic integration (through the building of railway lines connecting the regions directly) and the activities of illegal Ukrainian organizations, such as the OUN and the Communist Party of Western Ukraine.

A. Zięba

Sokal Brigade of the Ukrainian Galician Army (Sokalska [5] brygada UHA). A unit of the First Corps of the UHA formed in January 1919 from units of the Northern Group. The brigade had about 6,000 soldiers, organized into three infantry battalions, a cavalry troop, an engineering company, and an artillery regiment. During the winter and spring it operated on the Polish-Ukrainian front around Sokal and in June 1919 it took part in the Chortkiv offensive, in which it distinguished itself in battles around Terebovlia. Its commanders were Capts P. Petryk and V. Kossar. In February 1920 the brigade was reorganized into the Second Cavalry Regiment of the Red Ukrainian Galician Army, which on 28 April surrendered to the Poles.

Sokalsky, Ivan [Sokal's'kyj], b 13 May 1830 in Kharkiv, d 12 May 1896 in Kharkiv, d ? Economist and statistician. A graduate of Kharkiv (1850) and Kiev (PH D, 1872) universities, he taught at the Richelieu Lyceum in Odessa and then at Kharkiv University (from 1858), where he offered the first course in the Russian Empire on the history of economic schools. In 1862–4 he traveled and studied industry, finance, and agriculture in Western Europe. After his return to Kharkiv Sokalsky organized and directed the first one-day censuses in Kharkiv (1866, 1873, and 1879) and studied the cottage industry in Slobidska Ukraine. He also edited the monthly journal of the Kharkiv gubernia statistical committee, *Statisticheskii listok* (1882–5). He wrote many articles and the monograph *Reforma na ocheredi* (The Coming Reform, 1895), in which he advocated bimetallism.

Petro Sokalsky   Volodymyr Sokalsky
                        (1863–1919)

Sokalsky, Petro [Sokal's'kyj] (Sokolsky), b 26 September 1832 in Kharkiv, d 14 April 1887 in Odessa. Composer, folklorist, and music critic; brother of I. *Sokalsky. He graduated in 1852 from the Faculty of Natural Sciences at Kharkiv University and settled in 1858 in Odessa, where he worked as assistant editor of the newspaper *Odesskii vestnik*. He was active in the city's musical life as a critic in the newspaper and a promoter for the development of musical institutions. His works include the operas *Mazepa* (1859), *May Night* (1876), and *The Siege of Dubno* (1878); 14 choruses; piano music; and art songs to words by T. Shevchenko, L. Hlibov, and others. He also collected and studied Ukrainian folk songs. His research was published posthumously as *Russkaia narodnaia muzyka, velikorusskaia i malorusskaia v ee stroenii melodicheskom i ritmicheskom i otlichiia ee ot osnov sovremennoi garmonicheskoi muzyki* (Russian Folk Music, Great Russian and Ukrainian, Its Melodic and Rhythmic Structure, and Its Differentiation from the Principles of Contemporary Harmonic Music, 1888). A

Ukrainian translation of this work, and a biography, by T. Karysheva, were published in Kiev in 1959. A collection of his essays and reviews was published in Kiev in 1977.

Sokalsky, Volodymyr [Sokal's'kyj] (secular name: Vasyl), b ca 1725, d ca 1790. After studying at the Kievan Mohyla Academy and serving as hegumen of the Samara St Nicholas's Monastery, he became (from 1762) the last pastor at the church of the Zaporozhian Sich and the last archimandrite of the monastery (1774–5). He later became archimandrite of St Nicholas's Monastery near Baturyn (1776–90).

Sokalsky, Volodymyr [Sokal's'kyj] (pseud: Don Diese), b 6 May 1863 in Heidelberg, Germany, d 1919 in Sevastopil. Composer and music critic; son of I. *Sokalsky. He graduated in 1885 from the Faculty of Law at Kharkiv University while also studying piano at the Russian Music Society school. In the fields of music history and theory he was self-taught. He was active as both a pianist and a conductor. His works include the *Symphony in G Minor* (1892); the children's opera *Ripka* (The Turnip, 1900), based on a Ukrainian folk tale; choruses; piano pieces; and art songs.

Sokha. A unit of land taxation used in Rus' from the 13th to the 17th centuries. Until the mid-16th century it was defined by the size of the work force: in the 13th to 15th centuries it consisted of an area that could be worked by two or three peasants; the size of the unit varied with the region. In the mid-16th century the great *sokha*, defined by a spatial unit, the *chetvert*, was introduced throughout Muscovy. Its size varied according to the quality of the land and the social position of the owner. In 1679 the *sokha* was replaced by the *household tax.

Pavlo Sokhan   Rev Isydor Sokhotsky

Sokhan, Pavlo [Soxan'], b 18 November 1926 in Novoivanivka, now in Bilopillia raion, Sumy oblast. Historian; corresponding member of the AN URSR (now ANU) since 1985. A graduate of the Kharkiv Pedagogical Institute (1953), he joined the ANU Institute of History in 1964 and became assistant director in 1974 and head of the revived Archeographic Commission in 1988 (since 1991, the Institute of Ukrainian Archeography). His specializations include Ukraine's historical ties with East European nations and the history of Bulgaria.

Sokhanivsky, Mykhailo [Soxanivs'kyj, Myxajlo], b 13 June 1915 in Zhyznomyr, Buchach county, Galicia. Stage actor and singer (baritone). He began his theatrical career in Lviv in the Bohema Theater (1936) and then was a member of D. Kotko's choir (1937) and an actor and singer in the Ternopil Ukrainian Music and Drama Theater (1939–44) and the Ukrainian Theater in Austria under H. Sovacheva (1945–8). After 1948 he appeared sporadically with Ukrainian troupes in Canada.

Sokhotsky, Isydor [Soxoc'kyj] (pseud: Sydir Yaroslavyn), b 4 April 1895 in Lany, Bibrka county, Galicia, d 22 May 1977 in Philadelphia. Church and community activist; member of the Shevchenko Scientific Society from 1965. He studied theology at Lviv University and philosophy at the Lviv (Underground) Ukrainian University before being ordained in 1923 and serving as a village priest. In 1944 he emigrated to Germany, and in 1950 to the United States, where he was pastor in Shamokin, Pennsylvania. He published popular studies on the role of the Ukrainian Catholic clergy (1951) and the Western Ukrainian struggle for independence in 1918–23 (1956), and coedited a history of the Ukrainian Catholic church in the United States (1959). Sokhotsky also wrote *Istorychni postati Halychyny XIX–XX st.* (Historical Figures of Galicia in the 19th–20th Centuries, 1961).

Mariia Sokil   Vasyl Sokil

Sokil, Mariia, b 18 October 1902 in Zherebets (now Kirove), Oleksandrivske county, Katerynoslav gubernia. Operatic soprano; wife of A. *Rudnytsky. She graduated from the Dnipropetrovske Music Conservatory and performed as a soloist in opera theaters in Kharkiv (from 1927) and Kiev (from 1930). In 1932–7 she performed in Lviv, Warsaw, Prague, Vienna, and Berlin, and in 1937–8 she gave concerts in the United States and Canada. From 1958 she lectured at the Philadelphia Music Conservatory and Music Academy. Her notable roles were Marguerite in C. Gounod's *Faust*, Tatiana in P. Tchaikovsky's *Eugene Onegin*, Desdemona in G. Verdi's *Othello*, Elsa in R. Wagner's *Lohengrin*, Maryltsia in M. Lysenko's *Taras Bulba*, and Mimi in G. Puccini's *La Bohème*.

Sokil, Vasyl, b 5 March 1905 in Husarka, Oleksandrivske county, Katerynoslav gubernia. Writer and journalist. He graduated from Kharkiv University in 1932 and began publishing his poems and short stories during the 1920s. His published works include the short stories 'Nadry' (Bowels of the Earth, 1932) and 'Potoky syl' (Stream of Forces, 1932); the plays *Mariia* (1947), *Dim na hori* (The House on the Hill, 1950, coauthored with D. Vyshensky), and *Chervona kalyna* (Red Viburnum, 1954); the comedy *Doroha mamochka* (Dear Mother, 1953, coauthored with I. Bahmut); and librettos for the operas *Pavel Korchagin* (1962), *Vasilii Gubanov* (1970), and *Lieutenant Schmidt* (1971). Sokil also translated into Ukrainian works of Russian, Belarusian, Polish, and Kirghiz authors. In 1978 he emigrated from Ukraine to the United States, and in 1986 he moved to Australia. While in the United States he published the satirical novelette *Taka dovha nich* (Such a Long Night, 1984). In addition to his memoirs, *Zdaleka do blyz'koho* (From Far Away to Close at Hand, 1987), Sokil has published articles in émigré literary journals and newspapers.

Sokil, Yurii (Sokol), b 21 September 1937 in Dnipropetrovske. Film producer and cinematographer. He graduated from the Moscow Film Institute in 1961 and then worked at the Mosfilm Studio with directors such as D. Khzhabzovitsky, A. Mitta, and G. Chukry. In 1979 he emigrated to Australia, first to Melbourne, where he shot a number of award-winning films with the director Paul Cox (*Lonely Hearts*, *Man of Flowers*, *Cactus*), and then to Sydney, where he continued to work with such film directors as John Duigan, Lex Marinos, and Bob Ellis. In 1987 he established and developed Waterloo Studios, one of the largest film complexes in Sydney. In 1989 he received a Milli Award, one of the highest Australian professional honors, as cinematographer of the year.

The officers of Sokil-Batko with Ivan Bobersky in Lviv in 1928. Sitting, from left: Ya. Vintskovsky, N. Yatsiv, O. Sopotnytsky, S. Lavriv, Bobersky, D. Navrotska, M. Levytsky, T. Franko, S. Lototsky; standing: L. Ohonovsky, O. Liubinetsky, I. Mryts, M. Halibei, S. Haiduchok, T. Bilostotsky, B. Makarushka, I. Panchak, S. Kotsiuba, O. Verkhola, M. Tril

Sokil (Falcon; Czech: Sokol). A mass physical-education movement that played an important role in the national rebirth of several Slavic peoples, particularly the Czechs. The first Sokol society was founded in Prague in 1862. Other Slavic peoples followed the Czechs' example and established their own counterparts. In 1907 the national societies came together to form the Sokol Union, which organized international meets and congresses. After the Soviet occupation of Eastern Europe, the Sokol movement was suppressed. Some societies are still active in the various Slavic émigré communities.

The Polish Sokół society was founded in Lviv in 1867, and the Ukrainian Sokil society was founded there in February 1894. The latter's statute was based on that of the Czech society, and its activity extended to all of Galicia and Bukovyna. There it propagated national unity, self-confidence, and dignity through physical education. The first president was V. *Nahirny (1894–1900), and the first director was V. Lavrivsky. A. Budzynovsky initiated the expansion of the society's program to encompass fire fighting (practiced until 1932), hiking, fencing, cycling, and shooting (from 1912). Besides physical activities and sports, the society also encouraged amateur choral, orchestral, and theatrical activities. In 1912 rifle units were organized by S. *Goruk; thenceforth the society was often known as the Sokil Physical Activity and Riflemen's Society. I. *Bobersky, who headed the Sokil teachers' circle from 1901 and presided over Sokil in 1908–12, contributed greatly to Sokil's growth in the decade before the First World War. In Galicia's towns, beginning with Stanyslaviv (1902), branches concentrating primarily on physical education were set up, while those founded in rural areas usually combined physical education and fire fighting. The local branches, which were free to call themselves Sich or Sokil, grew in number from 6 in 1902 to 70 in 1903, 243 in 1905, 373 in 1907, 601 in 1910, and 974 in 1914. They were concentrated mostly in Lviv county and Galician Podilia. In Pokutia and Bukovyna, where the *Sich societies attracted most of their followers, only a few Sokil branches existed. The combined Sokil membership grew to approx 33,000. The parent organization in Lviv served as the central office of the movement; from 1909 it was called Sokil-Batko ('Sokil-Father').

Like the rival Sich movement, Sokil organized regional (in 1906 in Stryi and in 1910 in Ternopil) and then provincial assemblies (in 1911 in Lviv) of its constituent organizations. In June 1914 the so-called Shevchenko assembly was attended by 12,000 members of Sich, Sokil, and the scouting organization Plast. It was held at the Ukrainskyi Horod, the sports field owned by Sokil-Batko in Lviv. In 1912 Sokil representatives took part in the All-Slavic Sokol congress and games in Prague celebrating the 50th anniversary of the Czech society.

Before the First World War the more important figures in the Sokil movement were K. Gutkovsky, V. Shukhevych, Yu. Vintskovsky (head of the photography and cycling sections), Ya. Yaroslavenko (composer of the Sokil anthem and other Sokil songs), M. Voloshyn, Y. Domanyk, L. Lepky, and P. Dyhdalevych.

In Russian-ruled Ukraine several dozen Russian Sokol gymnastics societies were founded in the early 20th century. The largest society was in Kiev. It hosted the 1913 Russian Sokol congress attended by 250 members from Katerynoslav, Odessa, Kharkiv, Chernihiv, Tahanrih, and Kursk.

The First World War interrupted the activities of the Sokil society in Galicia. After the war the Polish authorities obstructed the revival of the movement and prohibited its expansion into Volhynia, Podlachia, and the Kholm and Lemko regions. In 1918–20 only Sokil-Batko was able to function, and the 1933 law on associations precipitated the further decline of Sokil. In 1938 the Polish government seized, under the pretext of military need, Sokil-Batko's sports field in Lviv. The number of Sokil branches varied from 6 in 1921 to 37 in 1923, 586 in 1928, 493 in 1930, 370 in 1934, 233 in 1936 (23,000 members), and 300 in 1939 (approx 35,000 members). From 1933 Sokil devoted more attention to athletics and sports (volleyball, basketball, track-and-field sports, and boxing); its sports section was headed by O. Navrotsky. Before the *Ukrainian Sports Union was founded in 1925, and after it was abolished by the Polish authorities in 1937, Sokil-Batko functioned as the central office for the many sports clubs in Galicia. It organized the so-called Zaporozhian Games in 1923 and the third provincial Sokil assembly in 1934. It continued holding various regional Sokil public gatherings and events and conducting courses for physical-education instructors.

Prominent figures in Sokil in the 1920s and 1930s, in addition to those who had already been important before the war, were M. Zaiachkivsky (president, 1922–33), M. Khronoviat (president, 1934–9), S. Haiduchok, M. Tril, I. Mryts (head of the skiing section), M. Halibei, Ya. and E. Blahitka, T. Bilostotsky, E. Zharsky, and A. Palii.

Sokil published the monthly magazines *Visty z Zaporozha (1910–14) and *Sokil's'ki visty (1928–39); annual almanacs from 1894; and many sports, physical education, and organizational booklets by authors such as V. Lavrivsky, A. Budzynovsky, I. Bobersky, S. Haiduchok, M. Tril, O. Verkhola, E. Zharsky, Ya. Blahitka, T. and P. Franko, D. Navrotska, D. Siiak, K. Sukhoverska, and I. Mryts.

Outside Ukraine the most active Ukrainian Sokil societies were founded by émigrés in interwar Czechoslovakia. There, beginning in 1922, Sokil branches sprang up in Poděbrady, Prague, Příbram, Liberec, Brno, and other towns. Together they formed the Union of the Ukrainian Sokil Movement Abroad in 1932; in 1934 it had 460 members. The societies took part in Czech Sokol events, sometimes as representatives of the Galician Sokil movement, and maintained contacts with Sokil-Batko and I. Bobersky in Canada and then Yugoslavia. The German occupation of Czechoslovakia brought an end to the Sokil movement in Czechoslovakia. Elsewhere, small Sokil groups existed in Zagreb, Riga, Harbin, Bucharest, Brazil, Paris, and Shanghai. A Sokil society was set up in Buenos Aires in 1931, and several smaller branches were organized in Argentina. In the United States, a small Sokil society was founded in New York in 1913. Unlike Sich, however, the Sokil movement did not take root in North America.

E. Zharsky

Sokilka sheep (sokilska poroda ovets). A breed of sheep developed in Ukraine in the village of Sokilka (now in Kobeliaky raion, Poltava oblast) during the 19th century from local sheep and Karakuls imported from the Crimea, selecting for high-quality pelts. These sturdy animals have high-quality pelts, strong bodies, and coarse wool and are highly productive (115–120 lambs per 100 ewes). They are raised principally for lamb pelts, the fine fur of which is usually a gray with a distinctly steel bluish tint. The sheep are now also raised on various farms in Dnipropetrovske oblast (see *Sheep farming).

Sokil's'ki visty (Sokil News). Monthly organ of the Galician *Sokil society published in Lviv in 1928–39. It contained articles on physical education, sports, and recreation. The editors of the journal included S. Koretsky, S. Haiduchok, and I. Mryts. In 1930 it had a pressrun of 1,000.

Ivan Sokoliansky

Sokoliansky, Ivan [Sokoljans'kyj], b 6 April 1889 in Dinska *stanytsia*, Katerynodar division, Kuban oblast, d 27 November 1960 in Moscow. Specialist in vision and hearing impairment. He worked at the school for deaf-mutes in Oleksandrivske before completing his studies at the St Petersburg Psychoneurological Institute (1913). He taught at the Kiev (1920–3) and Kharkiv (1923–6) institutes of People's Education. In 1925 he organized a school-clinic for deaf and blind mutes and was one of the founders of the Scientific Research Institute of Pedagogy, which he directed from 1926 to 1929. Then he was director of the Scientific Research Institute of Defectology of the Ukrainian SSR. Arrested in 1934, he was soon exonerated and given a position at the Institute of Defectology in Moscow. He introduced a new method of teaching blind and deaf mutes and invented various devices for deaf and blind people.

Sokolov, Borys, b 12 September 1897 in Kharkiv, d 1 September 1984 in Dnipropetrovske. Agronomist and selection scientist; member of the All-Union Academy of Agricultural Sciences from 1956. A graduate of the Kharkiv Agricultural Institute (1923), he worked for the Dnipropetrovske Selection and Research Station (1924–30), where he organized the first maize selection laboratory in the USSR, and the Ukrainian Scientific Research Institute of Seed Cultivation (from 1956 the All-Union Scientific Research Institute of Corn). He demonstrated the effectiveness of heterosis in Soviet selection practices and developed 18 hybrid and 4 new sorts of corn.

Sokolov, Ivan, b 10 June 1823 in Astrakhan, Russia, d 12 November 1910 in Kharkiv. Russian painter. After graduating from the St Petersburg Academy of Arts (1855) he was elected a member (1857) and appointed a professor (1864) there. He visited Ukraine often, and in 1860 he settled in Kharkiv, where he was elected vice-president of the Kharkiv Society of Friends of the Fine Arts. He was acquainted with T. Shevchenko, who did an etching based on Sokolov's *Friends* (1858). Sokolov painted many Ukrainian genre scenes and portraits of Ukrainian peasants. They include *Kobzar* (1857), *From the Market* (1859), *Girls Telling Fortunes on St John's Eve* (1859), *Seeing Off the Recruits* (1860), *Ukrainian Woman* (1860), and *Morning after a Wedding in Little Russia*. L. Zhemchuzhnikov made 17 etchings of Sokolov's paintings for the album **Zhivopisnaia Ukraina* (Picturesque Ukraine). P. Hovdia's book on Sokolov was published in 1980.

Ivan Sokolov: *Girls Telling Fortunes on St John's Eve* (oil, 1859)

Sokolov, Teodosii, b 23 January 1870 in Kahul, Bessarabia gubernia, d 1941 in Kiev. Gynecologist and obstetrician. A graduate of Kiev University (1897), he worked at the university, the Kiev Bacteriological Institute, and the Kiev Medical Institute (professor from 1921). His publications dealt with severe blood loss in women, septic abortions, and myomas. He was one of the early organizers of the system of maternity and childhood care in Ukraine.

Sokolov, Viktor, b 17 April 1919 in Taburyshche, Oleksandriia county, Kherson gubernia. Writer. A former steelworker, he headed the Donetske branch of the Writers' Union of Ukraine (1958–66) and later was chief editor of the literary journal *Donbas*. Since 1949 he has published 19 books of poetry (most recently *Chekannia* [The Wait, 1984]), the novels in verse *Na berehakh Ishymu* (On the Banks of the Ishim, 1956) and *Moie sertse v Donbasi* (I Left My Heart in the Donbas, 1960), and the documentary novels *Volodia* (1967) and *Sertse syl'nishe vohniu* (The Heart Is Stronger Than Fire, 1973).

Yurii Sokolov (1889–1941)

Sokolov, Yurii, b 20 April 1889 in Nizhen, Chernihiv gubernia, d 15 January 1941 in Kiev. Folklorist and literary scholar; from 1939 full member of the AN URSR (now ANU). After graduating from Moscow University (1911) he worked as a teacher and collected Russian and, later,

Ukrainian folklore. With his brother, Borys, he founded the journal *Khudozhestvennyi fol'klor* (1922) and published the anthology *Poeziia derevni* (The Poetry of the Village, 1926). He helped uproot 'bourgeois' approaches to folklore and encouraged the growth of 'Soviet folklore' based on the principles of class consciousness and socialist realism. In 1939 he was appointed director of the ANU Institute of Ukrainian Folklore in Kiev and ordered to rid Ukrainian folklore of 'bourgeois nationalism.' At his initiative a folk creativity section was founded at the Writers' Union of Ukraine. He published over 150 works, including the textbook *Russkii fol'klor* (Russian Folklore, 1938).

Yurii Sokolov (1896–1971)   Oleksander Sokolovsky

Sokolov, Yurii, b 26 May 1896 in Labinska *stanytsia* in the Kuban, d 2 February 1971 in Kiev. Mathematician and mechanician; corresponding member of the AN URSR (now ANU) from 1939. After graduating from the Kiev Institute of People's Education (1921) he worked in the Division of Applied Mathematics of the VUAN and then at the ANU Institute of Mathematics (1934–71). He also taught at various institutions of higher learning in Kiev. Sokolov made significant contributions to celestial mechanics, hydromechanics, differential equations, and the theory of filtration. He is especially known for his work on the n-body problem and for practical solutions to various problems in the filtration of groundwater. He introduced and rigorously studied a new and effective method for the approximate solution of differential and integral equations, known as the averaging method with functional corrections or the Sokolov method. As shown by Sokolov, the method was useful in various applications to physical sciences.

Sokolovska, Kateryna [Sokolovs'ka], b 1840 in Paskivka, Vovchanske county, Kharkiv gubernia, d 24 October 1883. Poet. In the 1860s, while working as a teacher in Husynka, near Kupianka, she began writing poetry and plays. An epigone of T. Shevchenko, she published a collection of poetry about peasant life, *Zirka* (The Star, 1871). An edition of her poems was published in Kharkiv in 1931.

Sokolovska, Mariia [Sokolovs'ka, Marija] (Marusia), b 1894 in Radomyshl county, Kiev gubernia, d 1919 (some sources cite 20 November 1921), near Bazar. Military figure in the anti-Bolshevik uprising of 1919. A teacher by profession, she joined a partisan military force led by her brothers Omelko and Dmytro in March. After their death in June, she assumed leadership of the 300 cavalry and 700 infantry troops. In August her force was associated with the First Corps of the Ukrainian Galician Army. It was defeated and interned in September by a Hungarian regiment of the 58th Soviet Division, and the injured Sokolovska was captured and tortured to death.

Sokolovsky, Oleksander [Sokolovs'kyj], b 8 September 1895 in Konotip, Chernihiv gubernia, d 29 August 1938. Writer. In 1914 he began his studies at the law faculty of Kiev University, but he was arrested in 1915 for circulating antiwar declarations and sentenced to six years of hard labor. After the February Revolution of 1917 he returned to Ukraine. Sokolovsky's first novel, which was immensely popular, was 'Narodovol'tsi' (Members of Narodnaia Volia), printed in 1925 in the periodical *Zhyttia i revoliutsiia*. The next-published novels were *Pershi khorobri* (The First Brave Ones, 1928), *Bohun* (1931), *Nova zbroia* (The New Weapon, 1932), *Rokovani na smert'* (Destined for Death, 1933), and *Buntari* (The Rebels, 1934). Sokolovsky was arrested in 1937 and shot. He was rehabilitated in the 1950s. His novels *Buntari* and *Rokovani na smert'* were republished posthumously in 1960. The historical novel *Bohun* was republished in 1957 in Munich and in 1964 in Kiev, and a two-volume collection of Sokolovsky's works was published in 1971.

Oleksii Sokolovsky

Sokolovsky, Oleksii [Sokolovs'kyj, Oleksij], b 13 March 1884 in Velyka Burimka, Zolotonosha county, Poltava gubernia, d 25 April 1959 in Kharkiv. Agronomist and soil scientist; full member of the VUAN and AN URSR (now ANU) from 1929, the All-Ukrainian Academy of Agricultural Sciences from 1926, the All-Union Academy of Agricultural Sciences from 1935, and the Ukrainian Academy of Agricultural Sciences from 1956. He graduated from Kiev University (1908) and the Moscow Agricultural Institute (1910) and worked in the laboratories of the soil scientists D. Prianishnikov and V. Viliams. In 1924 he was appointed a professor, and in 1944 director, of the Kharkiv Agricultural Institute. He was the first president of the All-Ukrainian Academy of Agricultural Sciences. In the mid-1930s he was arrested, and spent several years in prison camps. From 1945 he headed the Laboratory of Soil Science at the ANU and then the Ukrainian Scientific Research Institute of Soil Science and Agrochemistry (1956–

9), into which the laboratory was reorganized. Sokolovsky introduced a new approach in soil colloids research, made important contributions to the theory of the soil's colloidal complex, and proposed a genetic system of soil classification. He discovered new colloidal soil technology and developed a chemical method of improving saline soils and an alkalinization method of dealing with water filtration in irrigation canals. In his numerous publications he dealt with the physical and chemical properties of soil, the effect of cation exchange on the mechanical and hydroscopic properties of the soil, the melioration of podzolic and saline soils, and the role of calcium in the fixation of mineral colloids and humus in the soil. He wrote a textbook on soil science, *Kurs sil's'kohospodars'koho hruntoznavstva* (A Course in Agricultural Soil Science, 1951), which appeared in Ukrainian and Russian and was reprinted several times. An edition of his selected works came out in 1971.

Sokolovsky, Volodymyr [Sokolovs'kyj], b 1916 in Nymburk, Bohemia. Veterinary surgeon; full member of the Shevchenko Scientific Society from 1954. After completing his education in Berlin (1943) and Vienna (DVM, 1945) he worked in Bavaria. He emigrated to the United States in 1951 and settled in Chicago. He published scientific papers on small-animal surgery and artificial insemination and was a coauthor of the handbook *Management of Trauma in Dogs and Cats* (1981).

Sokolovsky, Yurii [Sokolovs'kyj, Jurij], b ? in Poltava, d 1922 in Belgrade, Serbia. Zemstvo activist and political leader. He directed the agronomy department of the Poltava gubernia zemstvo and was one of the founders of an association that helped peasants to resettle in Siberia. He was also a member of the Russian Constitutional Democratic party. Under the Hetman government of 1918 he served as minister of food supplies in F. Lyzohub's first cabinet. At the end of 1918 the UNR Directory sent him, along with V. Prokopovych and K. Matsiievych, on a diplomatic mission to Rumania and Serbia. He remained in Belgrade as an émigré.

Sokołowski, Marian, b 1839 in Czyżew Łomżyński, Poland, d 25 March 1911 in Cracow. Polish art historian; full member of the Polish Academy of Sciences. A professor at Cracow University from 1882, he wrote a book on archeological study in Galician Ruthenia (1883) and books on 'Ruthenian' painting (1885), Byzantine and Rus' medieval culture (1888), and church art (1889).

Sokolyshyn, Oleksander [Sokolyšyn] (Sokolyszyn, Alexander), b 8 September 1914 in Chernivtsi, Bukovyna. Librarian; member of the Shevchenko Scientific Society. After graduating in law from Chernivtsi (1938) and Lviv (1941) universities he obtained a doctorate in political science from Innsbruck University (1947) and an MLS from Columbia University (1958). He emigrated to the United States in 1955 and worked in the United Nations library and the New York and Brooklyn public libraries as well as the law library at Yale University. He compiled *Ukrainian Selected and Classified Bibliography in English* (1972) and *Ukrainians in Canada and the United States: A Guide to Information Sources* (1981).

Yevhen Sokovych   Ivan Sokulsky

Sokovych, Yevhen [Sokovyč, Jevhen], b 1864, d 1946 in Potsdam, Germany. Civil engineer and politician. He served as minister of communications in the UNR Council of National Ministers headed by V. Holubovych (January–April 1918) and later as Ukrainian consul in Lausanne, Switzerland. He was a specialist in highway construction, and from 1922 he taught at the Ukrainian Husbandry Academy in Poděbrady, Czechoslovakia, where he prepared textbooks on geometry (1922) and melioration (1925).

Sokulsky, Ivan [Sokul's'kyj], b 7 July 1940 in Dnipropetrovske oblast, d 22 June 1992 in Dnipropetrovske. Poet, journalist, and dissident. He was expelled from Dnipropetrovske University, and worked as a journalist. In June 1969 he was arrested for composing a letter from 'the creative youth of Dnipropetrovske' protesting the suppression of Ukrainian culture. After serving over four years in a Mordovian labor camp and in the Vladimir prison he returned to Ukraine. In October 1979 he joined the Ukrainian Helsinki Group. He was arrested in April 1980 and sentenced in January 1981 to 10 years in prison and 3 years of exile for 'anti-Soviet agitation and propaganda.' He was released in 1988. His poems were published in the underground *Ukraïns'kyi visnyk* (nos 1–2, 1971).

Sokyriany [Sokyrjany]. V-8. A city (1989 pop 11,700) on the Sokyrianka River and a raion center in Chernivtsi oblast. It was first mentioned in historical documents in 1666, as Sekuriany. At that time it belonged to the Moldavian principality. It was annexed by Russia in 1812, occupied by Rumania in 1918–40, and then incorporated into the Ukrainian SSR. In 1966 it was granted city status. Sokyriany is an administrative and agricultural center. Its industry includes a beverage and a cheese factory and a stone quarry.

Sokyrko, Volodymyr, b 14 January 1892 in Bilohorodka, Iziaslav county, Volhynia gubernia, d 14 October 1983 in Chernivtsi. Stage and film actor. He began his theatrical career in the Odessa Theater of Miniatures (1910) and in D. Haidamaka's troupe, and then was an actor in the Franko New Drama Theater (1921–31), the Kharkiv Theater of the Revolution (1931–41), the Kharkiv Ukrainian Drama Theater (1941–3), and the Chernivtsi Oblast Ukrainian Music and Drama Theater (1944–76). He played Ivonika in O. Kobylianska's *Zemlia* (The Land) and the title role in W.

Shakespeare's *Othello* and acted in the films *Mirabeau* (1930) and *Nad Cheremoshem* (On the Banks of the Cheremosh River, 1956).

The palace of the Galagan family in Sokyryntsi (architect Pavlo Dubrovsky, 1829)

Sokyryntsi [Sokyrynci]. A village (1976 pop 2,000) in Sribne raion, Chernihiv oblast. It was first mentioned in the chronicles under the year 1092. As the estate of the Galagan family the locality was developed into a cultural center. A dendrological park was set up in 1763 and redesigned as a landscape park in 1825–35, a *vertep* puppet theater was established in 1781, and a palace was built by the architect P. Dubrovsky in 1829. The kobzar O. *Veresai lived in Sokyryntsi in the 19th century. One of the first cooperatives in Ukraine, an agricultural credit union, was organized in Sokyryntsi by Hryhorii *Galagan in 1871. Today the Galagan palace and park are used by an agricultural tekhnikum.

Solchanyk, Roman [Sol'čanyk], b 24 September 1944 in Uzhok, Transcarpathia. Historian and political analyst. He graduated from Rutgers University and the University of Michigan (PH D, 1973), and wrote his PH D dissertation on the Communist Party of Western Ukraine. He taught Eastern European, Russian, and Soviet history at Michigan (1972–3) and Rutgers (1973–5) universities. Since 1977 he has been a research analyst specializing in Ukraine and nationality issues at Radio Liberty in Munich, and in 1988 he became director of program research and development there. His articles have appeared in *Radio Liberty Research, The Ukrainian Weekly,* and British and North American scholarly journals and collections. He compiled and edited, with T. Hunczak, a collection of documents and materials pertaining to 20th-century Ukrainian socio-political thought (3 vols, 1983).

Solenyk, Karpo, b 26 May 1811 in Lepel, Vitsebsk gubernia, Belarus, d 19 October 1851 in Kharkiv. Actor and one of the pioneers of Ukrainian professional theater. He studied at Vilnius University (1829–31) and first appeared on stage in 1832 as part of I. Shtein's troupe in Kharkiv. He worked with L. Mlotkovsky's troupe (1833–42) in Kursk, Kiev, and Kharkiv and then continued acting in Kharkiv, from which he toured extensively as a guest actor

throughout Russian-ruled Ukraine. He twice refused an invitation to join the Imperial Theater in St Petersburg. Solenyk's creative mastery was most evident in comic roles from the Ukrainian repertoire, including I. Kotliarevsky's *Natalka Poltavka* (Natalka from Poltava) and *Moskal'-charivnyk* (The Muscovite-Sorcerer), H. Kvitka-Osnovianenko's *Svatannia na Honcharivtsi* (Matchmaking at Honcharivka) and *Shel'menko-denshchyk* (Shelmenko the Orderly), V. Dmytrenko's *Kum-miroshnyk* (The Godfather-Miller), and *Vechir na khutori* (Evening on a *Khutir*), based on N. Gogol. He also played over 60 roles (in Russian) from works by Gogol, W. Shakespeare, Molière, F. von Schiller, and D. Lensky. Biographies of Solenyk have been written by O. Kysil (1928), M. Dibrovenko (1951) and A. Hrim (1963).

Solianych, Dmytro [Soljanyč], b 1876 in Ustia, Sniatyn county, Galicia, d 1941 in Edmonton. Early Ukrainian-Canadian writer and community figure. As a young man he organized village reading houses and branches of the Sich society in Pokutia. After emigrating to Alberta in 1903, he contributed stories about Pokutian peasant and immigrant life to the Ukrainian press in Canada and the United States. A collection, *Khto vynuvatyi ta inshi opovidannia* (Who Is to Blame and Other Stories), was published in Edmonton in 1932.

Solianyi route (Solianyi shliakh). The overland trade route (mentioned in an 1170 chronicle) by which salt was transported from the Crimea to Kievan Rus'. It began along the left bank of the Dnieper River in the region of Kiev. Near the mouth of the Vorskla River it was met by branches from Pereiaslav and Romen. There the route crossed to the right bank of the Dnieper River and continued southward, avoiding the elbow in the Dnieper and crossing again to the left bank near the mouth of the Konka River, at Kamianka Crossing. From there (near present-day Kakhivka) the route turned toward Perekop and continued farther on to the Crimea, Chersonese Taurica, Sudak, and Teodosiia. The Solianyi route was the most common but not the only route used to transport salt from the Black Sea estuaries to Kievan Rus'. Salt was also brought to Rus' from Kalush and Stryi, in Galicia.

Solntsev, Volodymyr [Solncev], b 23 July 1892 in Kiev, d 1973 in Germany. Internal medicine specialist. A graduate of Kiev University (1917), he worked at the internal medicine clinic of the Kiev Medical Institute (docent from 1928, professor from 1937). In 1939 he became chairman of functional diagnostics at the Ukrainian Institute of Clinical Medicine. In 1943 he settled in Germany. His publications, dealing with internal medicine, balneology, and geriatrics, appeared in Ukrainian, Russian, German, and English.

Solntseva, Yuliia [Solnceva, Julija], b 7 August 1901 in Moscow, d 29 October 1989 in Moscow. Film director, actress, and producer; wife of O. *Dovzhenko. Using Dovzhenko's scripts she produced the films *Poema pro more* (A Poem about the Sea, 1958), *Povist' polum'ianykh lit* (A Chronicle of Flaming Years, 1961), and *Zacharovana Desna* (The Enchanted Desna [River], 1965), as well as *Nezabutnie* (The Unforgettable, 1968) and *Zoloti vorota* (The Golden Gate, 1969), about Dovzhenko. She also edited a five-volume collection of his works (1983–5).

Andrii Solohub at his easel (Paris, 1981)

Solohub, Andrii, b 8 December 1922 in Konotip, Chernihiv gubernia. Sculptor and painter. A postwar émigré, he studied sculpting in Salzburg (1947–9) under F. Yemets and painting at the Ecole nationale des beaux arts in Paris. He has created busts (eg, of S. Petliura) and small sculptures and has painted modernist portraits (*Self-Portrait, Daria Siiak, Emma Andiievska, Irena Zhukovska, Oksana and Danylo Struk*), still lifes (*Still Life with Violin*), and landscapes (*Toledo, Paris, Istanbul, Venice*) and the iconostasis of St Simon's Ukrainian Orthodox Church in Paris (1973). Recently he has devoted himself to landscape aquarelles of Venice, southern France, and Paris. An album of his drawings was published in 1974.

Solohub, Vasyl, b 8 September 1928 near Priadivka, now is Tsarychanka raion, Dnipropetrovske oblast. Writer. He has written the poetry collections *Students'ki lita* (Student Years, 1957) and *Trudne shchastia* (Hard Luck, 1959); the children's poetry book *Ia vzhe pidris* (I've Already Grown Up, 1960); the prose collections *Stezhka vyvodyt' na shliakh* (The Path Leads Out to the Road, 1958), *U kraplyni vidbylosia sontse* (In a Droplet the Sun Was Reflected, 1960), *Vohniana spadshchyna* (A Fiery Legacy, 1962), *Polynove prychastia* (Wormwood Communion, 1972), and *Osviachennia liubov'iu* (Sanctification by Love, 1978); and the novels *Chesnist'* (Integrity, 1967) and *Sotvory sebe* (Create Yourself, 1980).

Solohub-Bocconi, Iryna, b May 1885 in Neslykhiv, Kamianka Strumylova county, Galicia, d 1972 in Milan. Opera singer (soprano). A graduate of the Lviv Conservatory (1905; pupil of C. Zaremba and O. Myshuha), she made her debut in the Lviv Opera Theater in the name-part in S.

Moniuszko's *Halka*. In 1906–14 she performed in Poznań and Milan, notably in the name-parts in G. Puccini's *Madame Butterfly* and G. Verdi's *Aida* and *La Traviata*. She was also well known as a chamber singer in Lviv, Vienna, and a number of Italian cities, where she performed songs by M. Lysenko, A. Vakhnianyn, and O. Nyzhankivsky; folk songs; and operatic arias. She retired from the stage in 1923.

Excavation of the Solokha kurhan

Solokha kurhan. A Royal Scythian burial mound of the late 5th to early 4th century BC near Velyka Znamianka, now in Kamianka-Dniprovska raion, Zaporizhia oblast. Excavations by N. *Veselovsky in 1912–13 uncovered two burial vaults – a looted central chamber and an intact side chamber, under an 18 m mound. Among the items recovered in the course of excavations were the remains of five horses and their handler, a masterfully executed gold comb with figures of warring Scythians, a Greek helmet, a bronze mace, and domestic items. Solokha was one of the richest of the Royal Scythian kurhans found in Ukraine; the collection is housed in the Hermitage in St Petersburg.

Solomarsky, Oleksandr [Solomars'kyj], b 12 July 1897 in Yeiske, Kuban gubernia, d 12 June 1980 in Kiev. Stage director, actor, pedagogue, and public figure. He began his theatrical career in Kiev (1922) and in 1924 organized (with I. Deieva) the *Kiev Young Spectator's Theater, where he worked as actor and director until 1931. He led the Odessa Russian Drama Theater (1944–53) and, again, the Kiev Young Spectator's Theater (1953–61) and taught at the Kiev Institute of Theater Arts (1954–78).

Solomon, John, b 24 May 1910 in Zoria, Manitoba, d 25 June 1985 in Winnipeg. Judge, politician, and community leader. After graduating from the University of Manitoba (LLB, 1934) Solomon practiced law. He was elected to the Manitoba legislature as a Liberal-Progressive for Emerson constituency (1941–57) and served as deputy speaker (1953–7). He was appointed county court judge for Winnipeg in 1957 and a member of the Manitoba Court of Queen's Bench in 1970. He was president of the *Ukrainian Self-Reliance League (1941–9), president of the board of directors of St Andrew's College in Winnipeg (1957–85), and a longtime member of the consistory of the Ukrainian Orthodox Church of Canada.

John Solomon

Solomonik, Ella, b 11 June 1917 in Ekaterinburg, Perm gubernia. Historian. A graduate of Leningrad University (1941), she taught history in high schools and pedagogical institutes in 1941–5. From 1948 she worked in the archeological department of the Crimean branch of the USSR Academy of Sciences (now the Academy of Sciences of Ukraine Institute of Archeology). Among her scholarly works are *Sarmatskie znaki Severnogo Prichernomor'ia* (Sarmatian Inscriptions of the Northern Black Sea Coast, 1959), *Novye epigraficheskie pamiatniki Khersonesa* (New Epigraphic Monuments of Chersonesus, 1964), and *Graffiti s khory Khersonesa* (Graffiti from the Gallery of Chersonesus, 1984).

Anton Solomukha in his Paris studio

Solomukha, Anton [Solomuxa], b 2 November 1945 in Kiev. Painter. A graduate of the Kiev State Art Institute (1975), he worked as a muralist. He was allowed to emigrate to France in 1978, after which he participated in exhibitions of Ukrainian nonconformist art held in Munich, London, and New York in 1979 and in a group exhibition (together with V. Makarenko, V. Sazonov, and V. Strelnikov) in Toronto, Winnipeg, Chicago, Detroit, Cleveland, and New York in 1982–3. A versatile artist, in the 1970s he created surrealist compositions, such as *Ukrainian Folk Songs No. 3*, and experimented with abstraction, in which style he painted intricate compositions of interlocking shapes, such as *Symphony* (1979) and *Conversation* (1979). Solomukha has been inspired by his Ukrainian heritage to create series of works – 'Forgotten Ancestors,' 'Cossack

Dreams,' and 'Ukrainian Folk Songs and Tales' – filled with elements of the fantastic and grotesque (eg, *Old Woman and Dog* [1982], *Hey, Hryts* [1983], and *Rendezvous in the Steppe* [1984]). Solomukha's more recent works are painted in a neoexpressionist manner and make use of signs and symbols as part of an overall painterly surface (eg, *Homage to My Chair* [1986] and *Snail Climbing to Heaven* [1986]). He has had numerous solo exhibitions, including Chicago (1990), New York (1991), and annual ones in Paris and Köln.

D. Zelska-Darewych

Solona River. A right-bank tributary of the Vovcha River. It flows for 81 km through Donetske and Dnipropetrovske oblasts and drains a basin area of 946 sq km. The river is used, in parts, for irrigation. Its upper course dries out in the summer.

Solonchak soils. See Soil classification.

Solone. V-15. A town smt (1986 pop 6,400) and raion center in Dnipropetrovske oblast. It was founded at the beginning of the 18th century and named Engelhardtivka after its founder and owner. After being sold to another landowner in the 1780s, the village was renamed Solonenke. At the end of the 19th century it had just under 1,800 inhabitants and was known as Solone. In 1960 it attained smt status. Its economy rests on agriculture and food processing.

Solonetz soils. See Soil classification.

Solonyna, Kostiantyn, b ?, d 1696. Colonel of Kiev regiment in 1669–78 and 1687–8. He was Hetman I. Mnohohrishny's emissary to Muscovy and his representative at a 1671 conference of Polish and Russian deputies in Myhnovychi. In 1672 he was a candidate for hetman, and in 1676 he represented Hetman I. Samoilovych in Moscow. He lost his office because of his opposition to Hetman I. Mazepa. His nephew, Serhii (b ca 1660, d 1737), became the first in a line of Solonyna captains of Oster company in Kiev regiment (1709–76).

Solonynka, Mariia, b 7 January 1909 in Birky Velyki, Ternopil county, Galicia, d 26 February 1982 in Toronto. Community figure; wife of V. Solonynka. A Maslosoiuz employee, she was jailed by the Polish authorities in 1937 for her membership in the OUN. In 1948 she arrived in Canada, where she headed the Women's Association of the Canadian League for Ukraine's Liberation in 1952–75 and edited the women's section of *Homin Ukraïny* for many years.

Solonynka, Vasyl, b 20 October 1912 in Dovzhanka, Ternopil county, Galicia, d 25 September 1990 in Toronto. Journalist and political figure. He was arrested in 1933 by the Polish authorities for his involvement in the OUN and sentenced in 1934 to eight years' imprisonment. After his release in May 1939, he joined an OUN (Bandera faction) expeditionary group. From July 1941 to May 1943 he was imprisoned in Lviv by the Gestapo. A postwar refugee in Austria, he emigrated to Canada in 1948. There he was a leading member of the *Canadian League for Ukraine's Liberation, served as editor in chief (1954–78) of its paper,

Vasyl Solonynka

Homin Ukraïny, headed the Ukrainian Journalists' Association of Canada (1970–2), and was a member of the executive of the Ethnic Press Club.

Solonytsia, Battle of. The culmination of the uprising led by S. *Nalyvaiko and H. *Loboda in 1594–6. After losing a battle near the landmark Hostryi Kamin, the rebels retreated to Left-Bank Ukraine with their families (altogether nearly 10,000 refugees) and made camp at Solonytsia, near Lubni. Polish forces, led by Crown Hetman S. Żółkiewski, began a siege of the encampment on 26 May 1596. In secret negotiations with Loboda the Poles promised amnesty for the registered Cossacks. That offer prompted an armed conflict among the Cossacks, in which Loboda was killed. As the Poles prepared for their decisive attack, the registered Cossacks seized Nalyvaiko and the other rebel leaders and turned them over to Żółkiewski (7 June 1596). The Poles attacked anyway and slaughtered everyone in the camp, including the women and children. Only a small contingent of Cossacks broke through and escaped to the Zaporozhian Sich.

Solonytsivka [Solonycivka]. IV-17. A town smt (1986 pop 11,000) on the Udy River in Derhachi raion, Kharkiv oblast. It was founded in the 17th century. It attained smt status in 1938. The town has a furniture and a silicate brick factory. It is the home of a juvenile labor colony.

Solotvyn or Solotvyna. V-5. A town smt (1986 pop 4,100) on the Bystrytsia Solotvynska River in Bohorodchany raion, Ivano-Frankivske oblast. It was first mentioned, as Krasnopol, in the 12th-century Halych Chronicle, and it has been known as Solotvyn since the second half of the 16th century. It came under Polish rule in the second half of the 14th century. By the mid-18th century it was an important center for the manufacture and sale of salt, honey, leather, and lumber. At that time its inhabitants participated in the opryshok movement. After the partition of Poland in 1772, Solotvyn was annexed by Austria, and in 1918 it fell under Polish rule. In 1939 it was incorporated into the Ukrainian SSR. Today it manufactures forest products and has a regional museum.

Solotvyna. VI-4. A town smt (1986 pop 9,200) on the Tysa River in Tiachiv raion, Transcarpathia oblast. It was first mentioned in 14th-century sources and has been known as Aknaslatyna, Maramoroska Solotvyna, and Slatynski Doly. The town was under Hungarian rule until 1919, was ceded to Czechoslovakia in 1920, and was reoccupied by Hungary in 1939. Since 1945 it has been part of Ukraine. In 1947 it was promoted to smt status. Its main industry is salt mining. Two abandoned shafts have been converted into allergy hospitals.

One of the Solotvyna rock salt mines

Solotvyna rock salt deposits. Large salt reserves located in Tiachiv raion, Transcarpathia oblast. The salt is of a high quality. The deposit, which is 1,800 m long and 400–760 m wide, has been known since the 8th century. Industrial mining began at the end of the 18th century, and by the 20th century eight mines had been opened, and seven of them exhausted. In 1982 two underground mines were active. The salt is processed locally for domestic use and for use as feed. In 1981 total recoverable reserves were estimated at 222 million t. In 1970 the deposit yielded 451,000 t. In 1960 the 326,000 t mined there accounted for 10 percent of all Soviet salt production.

Dmytro Solovei

Solovei, Dmytro [Solovej], b 4 November 1888 in Sribne, Pryluka county, Poltava gubernia, d 9 July 1966 in St Paul, Minnesota. Historian, statistician, pedagogue, and publicist; member of the Ukrainian Academy of Arts and Sciences in the US. He entered Kharkiv University in 1910, but was suspended in 1914 for organizing a commemoration of T. Shevchenko and then exiled to Poltava. In 1920 he was arrested by Soviet security forces and sentenced to death. His sentence was commuted, and he was allowed to move to Kharkiv to work as a statistician for a government bulletin. In 1926 he undertook graduate studies at the Scientific Research Chair of Ukrainian Culture and established himself there as a research associate. In 1943 he moved to Lviv; subsequently he emigrated to the West. He eventually settled in the United States.

Many of Solovei's writings dealt with political issues after the Second World War, and he served as an associate of the Institute for the Study of the USSR. His works include *Holhota Ukraïny* (The Golgotha of Ukraine, 1953), *Ukraïns'ke selo v rokakh 1931–1933* (The Ukrainian Village in 1931–3, 1955), *Ukraïna v systemi soviets'koho koloniializmu* (Ukraine in the Soviet Colonial System, 1959), *Holod u systemi koloniial'noho panuvannia v Ukraïni* (Famine in the System of Colonial Domination in Ukraine, 1959–60), *Polityka TsK KPRS u plianuvanni rozvytku promyslovosty ta promyslovykh kadriv na Ukraïni* (The Policies of the CC of the CPSU for Developing Industry and Industrial Cadres in Ukraine, 1960), *Ukraïns'ka nauka v koloniial'nykh putakh* (Ukrainian Scholarship in Colonial Chains, 1963), and *Rozhrom Poltavy* (The Destruction of Poltava, 1974).

A. Zhukovsky

Solovei, Oksana (Solovej), b 2 July 1919 in Poltava. Translator and journalist; member of the Ukrainian Academy of Arts and Sciences in the US; daughter of D. Solovei. A postwar refugee in Germany and Minneapolis, she has contributed literary and cultural articles and reviews and Ukrainian translations of English, French, German, and Russian literature to periodicals such as *Suchasnist'*, *Moloda Ukraïna*, and *Ukraïns'ki visti*. Published separately have been her translations of H.W. Longfellow's *Song of Hiawatha* (1965), A. Camus's *Les justes* (1968), Vercors's *Le silence de la mer* (1970), V. Shalamov's *Kolyma Tales* (1972), and J. Cocteau's *La voix humaine* (1974).

Solovets Islands. A penal colony in the White Sea, Arkhangelsk oblast, Russia. With an area of 347 sq km, the islands are largely covered with forest and many lakes and swamps. The climate is cold and damp.

In the 1420s and 1430s monks settled on the islands; they had become a major outpost of Russian monastic life in the far north by the end of the 16th century. A strategic frontier fortress was built there. Until 1903 the islands were used by the tsars as a prison or place of banishment for political and religious offenders, but there were seldom more than a few dozen prisoners at one time. Among them were Ukrainians: some confederates of V. *Kochubei and I. *Iskra, who had denounced Hetman I. Mazepa to the tsar, and who were interned there in 1708–12; some of Mazepa's supporters after 1709, including the general osaul D. *Maksymovych and the colonel Y. Pokotylo of the serdiuk regiment; the archimandrite H. *Odorsky and the protopriest (of Lokhvytsia) I. *Rohachevsky, in 1712; P. *Kalnyshevsky, the last Kish otaman of the New Sich, in 1776–1801; and Yu. *Andruzky, a member of the Cyril and Methodius Brotherhood, in 1850–4.

Most of the monks evacuated the islands after the Russian Revolution, and in 1923 the Bolsheviks established the Solovets Special Purpose Camp there, modeled on prisoner-of-war camps. Later it became part of the Northern Special Purpose camp complex, and still later, Section Eight of the White Sea–Baltic camp complex. In 1937 the camp in the Solovets Islands was renamed the Solovets Special Purpose Prison of the Main Administration of State Security of the USSR. For most of the 1920s the regime in the camp was relatively mild, and the number of prisoners relatively small. With the onset of the Stalinist terror, however, the Solovets Islands were packed with prisoners living in severe conditions, subjected to cold, hunger, punishment cells, and beatings. In 1931–3 many prisoners were sent to work on the *White Sea Canal. Late in 1938 the prisoners were evacuated from the Solovets Islands to other camps, and the islands became a naval base.

Ukrainians in the camp in the mid-1920s were primarily Petliurists, anti-Bolshevik insurgents, and clergymen. During dekulakization and *collectivization in 1928–33 masses of Ukrainian peasants were exiled to the islands; among them were 325 peasants arrested for cannibalism during the man-made *famine of 1932–3. Arrests in the early 1930s, following the trial of the *Union for the Liberation of Ukraine, brought much of the non-Communist Ukrainian intellectual elite to the camp, as well as thousands of activists of the *Ukrainian Autocephalous Orthodox church. In 1933 Ukrainian Communists also began to fill the camps.

Among prominent Ukrainians who were interned in the Solovets Islands were the physician and political activist A. Barbar; the Communist poet V. Bobynsky; V. Chekhivsky, leader of the Ukrainian Social Democratic Workers' party and later of the Ukrainian Autocephalous Orthodox church; the writer and critic H. Epik; the poet P. Fylypovych; the historian Y. Hermaize; the writer and Communist activist M. Irchan; the Socialist Revolutionary P. Khrystiuk; the Futurist poet H. Koliada; L. Kurbas, the director of the Berezil theater; the writer and political figure A. Krushelnytsky; the playwright M. Kulish; the writer M. Liubchenko; the writer V. Mysyk; the literary historian M. Novytsky; M. Pavlushkov (arrested as head of the Association of Ukrainian Youth); S. Pidhainy, who later did much to document the history of the Solovets camps; the writers V. Pidmohylny, Ye. Pluzhnyk, and K. Polishchuk; M. Poloz, former commissar of finances of Soviet Ukraine; the geographer S. Rudnytsky; the writer M. Semenko a leading exponent of futurism; S. Semko former rector of the Kiev Institute of People's Education; the literary historian Ye. Shabliovsky; the writer G. Shkurupii; O. Shumsky, whose name became synonymous with Ukrainian national communism; the historian M. Slabchenko; the writer O. Slisarenko; the prominent CP(B)U activist P. Solodub; the hygienist V. Udovenko; the poet and journalist M. Vorony; the writer V. Vrazhlyvy; the Marxist historian M. Yavorsky; the memoirist V. Yurchenko; and the Neoclassicist poet and critic M. Zerov.

From 1924 until 1930 (perhaps longer) the Solovets camp had its own journal, *Solovetskie ostrova*. After conditions in the Solovets camp became known in the West, the Soviets released a propaganda film, *Solovki*, which mendaciously depicted life in the prison camp.

BIBLIOGRAPHY
Efimenko, P. 'Ssyl'nye malorossiiane v Arkhangel'skoi gubernii 1708–1802 g.,' *KS*, 1882, no. 9
Kol'chin, M. *Ssyl'nye i zatochennye v ostrog Solovetskogo monastyria v XVI–XIX vv: Istoricheskii ocherk* (Moscow 1908)
Chykalenko, L. (ed). *Solovets'ka katorha (dokumenty)* (Warsaw 1931)

Pidhainy, S. *Ukraïns'ka inteligentsiia na Solovkakh: Spohady 1933–1941* (Neu-Ulm 1947)
– *Islands of Death* (Toronto 1953)
– 'Solowky Concentration Camp' and 'Portraits of Solowky Exiles,' in *Black Deeds of the Kremlin: A White Book*, ed S. Pidhainy et al (Toronto 1953)
Solzhenitsyn, A. *The Gulag Archipelago, 1918–1956: An Experiment in Literary Investigation*, vol 2 (New York 1975)
Frumenkov, G. *Uzniki Solovetskogo monastyria*, 4th edn (Arkhangelsk 1979)

A. Zhukovsky

Solovev, Sergei (Soloviev), b 17 May 1820 in Moscow, d 16 October 1879 in Moscow. Russian historian and historiographer; member of the Imperial Russian Academy of Sciences from 1872. A graduate of Moscow University (1842; PH D, 1848), he was a professor there (1847–77) and served as dean of history and philology (1855–69) and rector (1871–7). He was a leading representative of the statist school of Russian history. Among his many works are a monumental history of Russia and its empire to 1775 (29 vols, 1851–79; 10th edn, 15 vols, 1959–66), which contains valuable information on medieval Rus' and the Hetman state (English trans ed E. Graham and pub as *History of Russia*, 1976–); a history of relations among the Riurykide princes of Rus' (PH D diss, 1847); a history of the fall of Poland (1863); and articles on Prince Danylo of Galicia (1847), Little Russia up to its subjugation by Tsar Aleksei Mikhailovich (3 pts, 1848–9), Princess Olha (1850), the grandsons of Grand Prince Yaroslav the Wise (1851), Hetman I. Vyhovsky (1859), the Cossacks up to the time of Hetman B. Khmelnytsky (1859), and L. Baranovych (1862). An edition of his selected works was published in 1983.

Anatolii Solovianenko   Rev Meletii Solovii
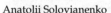

Solovianenko, Anatolii [Solov'janenko, Anatolij], b 25 September 1932 in Donetske. Opera singer (lyric-dramatic tenor). A graduate of the Donetske Polytechnical Institute (1954), he studied singing under O. Korobeichenko (1952–62), obtained a scholarship to Milan's La Scala, and completed study at the Kiev Conservatory (1978). Since 1965 he has been a soloist of the Kiev Theater of Opera and Ballet. His operatic roles include Andrii in S. Hulak-Artemovsky's *Zaporozhian Cossack beyond the Danube*, Petro in M. Lysenko's *Natalka from Poltava*, Lensky in P. Tchaikovsky's *Eugene Onegin*, Edgar in G. Donizetti's *Lucia di Lammermoor*, Alfredo in G. Verdi's *La Traviata*, and Ro-

dolfo in Puccini's *La Bohème*. He has concertized abroad, including with the New York Metropolitan Opera (1977–8). In recital he often performs Ukrainian folk songs.

Solovii, Meletii [Solovij, Meletij] (Solovey, Meletius), b 29 April 1918 in Perevoloka, Buchach county, Galicia, d 27 December 1984 in Edmonton. Basilian priest, church historian, and journalist. He entered the Basilian order in 1932 and was ordained in 1941. He studied theology in Olomouc, Czechoslovakia, at the University of Vienna (D TH, 1944), and at the Pontifical Oriental Institute in Rome (D TH, 1950). In 1950 he emigrated to Canada, where he helped edit the Basilian journal *Svitlo* (1957–64) and other publications and worked as a parish priest. In 1968–71 he was a professor at the University of Ottawa. A specialist in liturgics, he wrote *Bozhestvenna liturhiia* (1964; English trans *The Byzantine Divine Liturgy*, 1972), *Introduction to Eastern Liturgical Theology* (1972), *Meletii Smotryts'kyi iak pys'mennyk* (Meletii Smotrytsky as a Writer, 2 vols, 1977–8), and numerous articles, and coauthored (with A. Velyky) a biography of Y. Kuntsevych (1967).

Solovii, Tadei [Solovij, Tadej], b 1857 in Potorytsia, Sokal county, Galicia, d 31 August 1912 in Lviv. Lawyer and civic activist. A law graduate of Vienna University, he opened his own office in Lviv in 1888. He served as legal counsel of the Galician Provincial Bank (1901–12) and of the Greek Catholic metropoly of Halych. He avoided politics and was active in various Ukrainian economic and cultural organizations, as a founding member of the *Land Mortgage Bank, an executive member of Silskyi Hospodar, and a trustee of the National Museum. Many societies, students, and artists enjoyed his generous financial support.

Archbishop Varlaam Solovii

Solovii, Varlaam [Solovij] (secular name: Viktor), b 29 November 1891 in Kyryiivka, Sosnytsia county, Chernihiv gubernia, d 31 January 1966 in Sydney, Australia. Community and church activist and bishop of the Ukrainian Autocephalous Orthodox church. He studied at the theological seminaries in Novhorod-Siverskyi and Chernihiv and the law faculty at Warsaw University (1914). During the struggle for Ukrainian independence he served in the Sich Riflemen and then as a legal adviser to the government of the UNR and the Directory. In the interwar period he lived in Poland and was involved in the Ukrainianization of church life in Volhynia and Polisia as an adviser to Metropolitan D. Valedinsky. A postwar émigré in Germany, he moved in 1950 to Australia, where he was president of the Association of Ukrainians in Australia (1951–2). He was ordained in 1954 and consecrated bishop of Australia and New Zealand in 1958, with his see in Sydney.

Solovii, Volodymyr [Solovij], b 1891 in the Lemko region, d 15 November 1958 in Montreal. Political activist; son of T. *Solovii. In 1918–20 he served as secretary of the UNR mission to Switzerland. In the interwar period he was active in the Ukrainian National Democratic Alliance and, in the election of 1930, ran for a seat in the Polish Sejm. In 1939 he left for Paris, and in the following year was sent to London by O. Shulhyn as a representative of the *Government-in-exile of the UNR. In 1948 he emigrated to Canada.

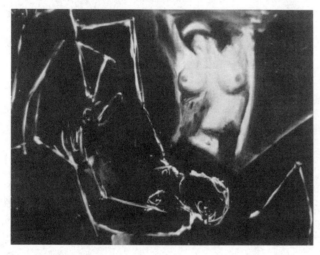

Jurij Solovij: *Lovers* (oil, 1967)

Solovij, Jurij, b 6 June 1921 in Lviv. Painter, sculptor, and art critic. A graduate of the Lviv Arts and Crafts School (1944) and a postwar refugee in Germany and then the United States, he has experimented with several styles (postimpressionism, expressionism, abstract expressionism). Since the 1970s he has used mixed media in unusual combinations. Since the 1950s he has been preoccupied with the themes of birth and death. His later works deal with the universality of pain in human life. Some of his characteristic works are *Motherhood* (1947), *Astral* (1948), *Crucifixion* (1950, 1969), and the series '1,000 Heads.' Solo exhibitions of his works have been held in New York (1959, 1965, 1970, 1972), Chicago (1960, 1972, 1980), Toronto (1963, 1972, 1973), Munich (1971), and Winnipeg (1973). His art criticism has been published in the émigré press and separately as *Pro rechi bil'shi nizh zori* (About Things Greater than Stars, 1978).

Soloviov, Mykhailo [Solovjov, Myxajlo] (Solovev, Mikhail), b 29 May 1886 in Elets, Orel gubernia, Russia, d 3 March 1980 in Kharkiv. Epidemiologist; full member of the USSR Academy of Medical Sciences from 1945. A graduate of Moscow University (1911), he worked at the Odessa Military Hospital and in the municipal sanitation organization (1914–20), and at the Odessa Medical Institute (1920–5), the Kharkiv Institute of Microbiology and Epidemiology (1925–31), and the Kharkiv Medical Insti-

tute (professor from 1930). His publications dealt with the prevention of infectious diseases, particularly cholera, malaria, diphtheria, anthrax, and scarlet fever.

Soltan, Yosyf II, b ?, d 1522 in Smolensk, Russia. Orthodox metropolitan of Kiev. A Belarusian noble, he took monastic vows and served as an archimandrite in Slutsk and as bishop of Smolensk (1498–1507) before his elevation to the office of metropolitan of Kiev in 1507. Soltan rejected the Church Union of *Florence. He assiduously defended the rights of the Orthodox church in Ukraine and Belarus, rid it of administrative faults and abuses, and improved discipline within it. He convoked three sobors, of which the first, in Vilnius in January 1509, was the most important, and he was the author of the regulations adopted at the sobor. In 1511 King Sigismund I granted Soltan a royal privilege reaffirming the authority of Sol-tan and his bishops over all the Orthodox faithful and churches in the Polish Kingdom and the Grand Duchy of Lithuania, and forbade individuals of the Catholic faith to interfere in matters of the Eastern church. Soltan traveled throughout the Orthodox East and maintained good relations with the patriarch of Constantinople. His description of the Slutsk monastery was published in *Akty Zapadnoi Rossii* (vol 1).

Soltanovsky, Avtonom [Soltanovs'kyj], b 1826 in eastern Podilia, d 1886. Pedagogue. He wrote a valuable series of articles dealing with Right-Bank Ukraine during the years 1846–67, entitled 'Zapysky,' serialized in *Kievskaia starina* (1892–4). The series is an important source for the history of the region in the 19th century, in particular for the state of secondary education.

Soltys, Adam (Sołtys), b 4 July 1890 in Lviv, d 6 July 1968 in Lviv. Composer, conductor, and teacher. The son of a well-known Polish conductor and composer, M. Sołtys, he studied at the Lviv Conservatory (1903–11), the Berlin State Academy of Music (1911–14), the Berlin State Academy of the Arts (1914–16), and the musicological department of Berlin University (PH D, 1921). He was a professor at the Lviv State Conservatory during 1930–9 and 1945–68. His main works include the ballet *Levyne sertse* (The Lion's Heart, 1930), music for the play *Kaminnyi hospodar* (Stone Host, by Lesia Ukrainka, 1941), two symphonies (1922 and 1946), works for chorus, solo songs, and arrangements of Ukrainian and Polish folk songs.

Soltys (Polish: *sołtys*, from German *Schultheiss* and Latin *scultetus*). An official appointed by the feudal owner of a village to act as his deputy in matters of local administration and justice. The office, based on Germanic law, was introduced in Western Ukrainian territories that were acquired by Poland in the 14th century. Until the 16th century the office was hereditary. It was not fixed to a specific class: a *soltys* could be a nobleman, a burgher, or a wealthy peasant. A military figure could be rewarded for service by becoming a *soltys* and receiving a *soltystvo* (a manor estate). In the 14th and 15th centuries those officials came to constitute an influential socioeconomic group. In 1923–39 in Western Ukrainian villages under Polish rule, the *soltys* was the chief of the local administration and of the territorial government overseen by the village council.

Solukha, Kost [Soluxa, Kost'], b 1869 in Podilia gubernia, d 1922. Civic and cultural activist and philanthropist. A graduate of Kiev University, he worked as a zemstvo physician in Kamianets-Podilskyi. He was active in the Podilia Prosvita society and served as its president from 1907 to 1914. In 1918 he was one of the founders of the *Kamianets-Podilskyi Ukrainian State University.

Solutrean culture. An Upper Paleolithic culture named after the La Solutré settlement site in France. Initially regarded as a separate epoch, it was reclassified (by Soviet Ukrainian archeologists) in the 1950s in conjunction with the Aurignacian culture to form a single Aurignacian-Solutrean culture. A significant discrepancy exists in the dating of this period, with starting dates ranging from 40,000 to 35,000 BC, and finishing dates from 25,000 to 15,000 BC. Major developments during this time included the appearance of Cro-Magnon man and the development of stable settlement sites and more permanent forms of shelter (specifically pit dwellings). Significant sites of this period in Ukraine include *Pekari and *Molodove. (See also *Paleolithic Period.)

Som, Mykola, b 5 January 1935 in Trebukhiv, Brovary raion, Kiev oblast. Poet of the *shestydesiatnyky generation. He has written the poetry collections *Idu na pobachennia* (I'm Going for a Rendezvous, 1957), *Viknamy do sontsia* (With Windows Facing the Sun, 1960), *Sviatyi khlib* (Sacred Bread, 1961), *Mriia* (A Dream, 1963), *Vyshyvanka* (An Embroidery, 1964), *Duma nad vohnem* (A Duma over a Fire, 1968), *Stezhka do okeanu* (The Path to the Ocean, 1973), *B'iu cholom* (I Kowtow, 1978), *Tovarystvo* (Company, 1979), and *Prysviaty i poslannia* (Dedications and Epistles, 1983), and many songs. He edited a collection of V. *Symonenko's poems and reminiscences about him, *Z matiriu na samoti* (Alone with Mother, 1990). He was awarded the annual V. Sosiura Prize in 1983.

Somko, Nadiia, b 15 January 1916 in Konotip, Chernihiv gubernia. Painter and sculptor; wife of S. *Makarenko. From 1934 to 1941 she studied at the Kharkiv and then Kiev State art institutes. As a refugee she has lived in Italy (1943–8), Argentina (1948–60), and the United States (since 1960). She has painted Ukrainian and American landscapes, genre scenes, still lifes, portraits, and historical battle scenes. They include *Glory to the Victors* (depicting George Washington, donated on the occasion of the US bicentennial to the City of Los Angeles), *Prince Ihor's Battle with the Polovtsians, Hetman Bohdan Khmelnytsky, Battle near Kaffa,* and *Hetman Vyhovsky's Victory.* In the 1970s she created 23 bronze and terra-cotta sculptures, among them *Victory, Prince Oleh, Prince Sviatoslav's Battle with a Khazar, Hetman Bohdan Khmelnytsky, Jubilant Cossack, Farewell, Buffalo Bill,* and *Don Quixote and Sancho Panza.* Solo exhibitions of her works have been held in New York, Los Angeles, Boston, Chicago, Detroit, Cleveland, and Philadelphia. A book about Somko and Makarenko (1971) and an album of her works (1981) have been published.

Somko, Yakym, b ? in Pereiaslav, d 28 September 1663 in Borzna. Cossack leader and acting hetman of Left-Bank Ukraine (1660–3); first father-in-law of B. Khmelnytsky. He was a captain of Pereiaslav regiment in 1654, and in 1658 he became its acting colonel. At the Pereiaslav Coun-

Nadiia Somko: *Dreams* (oil)

cil of 1660 that followed the conclusion of the Treaty of *Slobodyshche (to which Somko was opposed) he was again elected colonel of Pereiaslav regiment and acting hetman of Left-Bank Ukraine. In 1660–2 he fought against both the Poles and the Tatars, who sought to occupy his territory. He initially supported Muscovy but gradually became disenchanted with its policies (particularly since they hindered his efforts at uniting all of the Cossack state under his command). His withdrawal of support caused Muscovy to distrust him. Bishop M. Fylymonovych, a stalwart Moscow loyalist and supporter of I. Briukhovetsky, was also ill-disposed toward him. Somko, however, had the backing of the anti-Muscovite Kievan clergy led by I. Gizel and I. Galiatovsky.

Somko's opponents accused him of secret dealings with Yu. Khmelnytsky and P. Teteria and with Poland and the Crimea. Moscow took advantage of the accusation – and of the fact that it had not yet approved the decision of the Cossack *starshyna* council at Kozelets in 1662 to recognize Somko's tenure as hetman – to instigate a *chorna rada in Nizhen (27–28 June 1663). The general gathering of Cossacks was convened to choose a new hetman. V. Zolotarenko chose to support Somko, but a majority opted for I. Briukhovetsky, who was elected hetman. As the event became increasingly hostile, Somko, Zolotarenko, and their supporters sought the protection of the Muscovite officials who were present as observers. But the officials imprisoned them and then handed them over to Briukhovetsky, who had them executed in Borzna. Somko is depicted by P. Kulish in his historical novel *Chorna rada* (The Black Council, 1857).

A. Zhukovsky

Somov, Orest (pseud: Porfirii Baisky), b 21? December 1793 in Vovcha, Kharkiv gubernia, d 8 June 1833 in St Petersburg. Russian Romantic prose writer and critic of Ukrainian origin. As a student at Kharkiv University he collected Ukrainian folklore and contributed poems and fables to *Khar'kovskii Demokrit"* (1816) and *Ukrainskii vestnik* (1817). From 1817 he lived in St Petersburg, where he was close to Decembrist circles and A. Pushkin and belonged to the Free Society of Devotees of Russian Literature and the Free Society of Devotees of Literature, Sciences, and Arts. He promoted and influenced N. *Gogol as a writer and corresponded with I. Kotliarevsky and M. Maksymovych. His poems (one on B. Khmelnytsky), prose, translations, polemical and literary articles, and reviews appeared in the periodicals *Blagonamerennyi, Nevskii zritel', Sorevnovatel', Severnaia pchela, Syn otechestva, Literaturnaia gazeta* (of which he was editor, 1830–1), and *Utrenniaia zvezda* and in literary almanacs. Some of his belletristic works, such as an unfinished novel about S. Harkusha, 'Gaidamak' (The Haidamaka, fragments published in 1827, 1829, and 1830), and the tales 'Gaidamak' (1825), 'Iurodivyi' (The Holy Fool, 1827), 'Rusalka' (The Water Nymph, 1829), 'Oboroten'' (The Werewolf, 1829), 'Svatovstvo' (Matchmaking, 1831), 'Videnie na iavu' (An Apparition While Awake, 1831),'Nedobryi glaz' (The Evil Eye, 1833), and 'Kievskiia ved'my' (Kievan Witches, 1833), were based on Ukrainian folktales and legends. Editions of his works were published only recently, in Ann Arbor, Michigan (1974), and Moscow (1984). Z. Kyryliuk's monograph about Somov (Kiev 1965) contains a bibliography of his works.

R. Senkus

Sonata. An instrumental composition for one or two instruments, usually in several movements. The first sonatas written by Ukrainian composers were by M. Berezovsky (for violin and cembalo) and D. Bortniansky (for piano). Among M. Lysenko's many instrumental works there is a three-part piano sonata. At the beginning of the 20th century, V. Barvinsky, Ya. Stepovy, and L. Revutsky wrote sonatas for piano; in later periods, V. Kosenko, B. Liatoshynsky, M. Tits, R. Simovych, Yu. Shurovsky, and M. Skoryk were some of the most notable Ukrainian composers to use the sonata form.

Sonechko (Little Sun). An illustrated children's magazine published semimonthly by the Ukrainska Shkola society in Rivne in 1936–9. It was edited by P. Zinchenko and A. Vivcharuk.

Sonevytsky, Ihor [Sonevyc'kyj], b 2 January 1926 in Hadynkivtsi, Kopychyntsi county, Galicia. Composer, musicologist, conductor, and teacher; member of the Shevchenko Scientific Society since 1977. He studied at the Staatliche Hochschule für Musik in Munich (diploma, 1950) and the Ukrainian Free University (PH D, 1961). Emigrating to the United States after the Second World War, he became a cofounder of the *Ukrainian Music Institute of America as well as president and artistic director of the Music and Art Center of Greene County, New York. His compositions include the opera *Star*, the ballet *Cinderella*, incidental music for numerous theater plays, a *Piano Concerto in G Major*, variations and miniatures for piano, approx 60 art songs for voice and piano (including cycles to

Ihor Sonevytsky   Leonid Sonevytsky

texts by T. Shevchenko, I. Franko, and V. Symonenko), the cantata *Love Ukraine*, and liturgical music. He wrote musicological works, such as *Artem Vedel' i ioho muzychna spadshchyna* (Artem Vedel and His Musical Legacy, 1966), *Kompozytors'ka spadshchyna Nestora Nyzhankivs'koho* (Compositional Legacy of Nestor Nyzhankivsky, 1973), and *Muzykolohichni pratsi Zinoviia Lys'ka* (Ethnomusicological Works of Zinovii Lysko, 1976), and edited the second edition of M. Hrinchenko's *Istoriia ukraïns'koï muzyky* (History of Ukrainian Music, 1961).

Sonevytsky, Leonid [Sonevyc'kyj], b 25 April 1922 in Chortkiv, Galicia, d 6 August 1966 in New York. Historian; son of M. *Sonevytsky. He studied at the universities of Lviv (1940–1), Vienna (1945–6), and Munich (1946–8) and at the Ukrainian Free University (PH D, 1948). He served as secretary of the Historical Commission of the Shevchenko Scientific Society in Europe (1949–50). After emigrating to the United States Sonevytsky studied at Columbia University (1952–3, 1957–9), lectured at Seton Hall University, and worked as a librarian at Brooklyn College (from 1960). He served as secretary of the Ukrainian Academy of Arts and Sciences in the US (1954) and editor of its publication, *Annals* (from 1959), and as editorial co-ordinator (1958–60) of *Entsyklopediia ukraïnoznavstva* (EU) and *Ukraine: A Concise Encyclopaedia*.

Sonevytsky researched the history of the Ukrainian church and studied Ukrainian diplomatic history of the 20th century. Of note is his *Istoriia Ukraïny: Synkronistychno-khronolohichna tablytsia* (The History of Ukraine: A Synchronic and Chronological Table), published in vol 3 of EU and separately (1960). Most of Sonevytsky's works appeared in the monograph *Leonid Sonevyts'kyi: Studiï z istoriï Ukraïny* (Leonid Sonevytsky: Studies of the History of Ukraine, vol 202 [1982] of *Zapysky NTSh*).

A. Zhukovsky

Sonevytsky, Mykhailo [Sonevyc'kyj, Myxajlo], b 22 April 1892 in Hadynkivtsi, Husiatyn county, Galicia, d 30 November 1975 in New York. Classical philologist; full member of the Shevchenko Scientific Society from 1954; father of I. and L. Sonevytsky. After studying at Chernivtsi (1910–11) and Vienna (1911–14; PH D, 1923) universities he taught Latin, Greek, and classical literature at Ukrainian gymnasiums. A DP after the Second World War, he em-

Mykhailo Sonevytsky

igrated to the United States in 1950, and from 1963 was a professor at the Ukrainian Catholic University in Rome. He is the author of the children's books *Pryhody Odysseia* (Odysseus' Adventures, 1918), *Myrmidons'kyi lytsar* (The Mirmidonian Knight, 2 parts, 1936), and *Homin davnomy-nulykh dniv* (The Echo of Days Long Past, 1938; repr 1955); a history of classical Greek literature (2 vols, Rome 1970, 1977); a Ukrainian translation of Xenophon's *Anabasis* (1986); and popular articles on classical culture and pedagogical subjects in *Zhyttia i znannia* and *Ukraïns'ka shkola* (1936–9).

Song. The solo song with piano accompaniment is one of the most popular genres for Ukrainian composers. M. Lysenko wrote a wide variety of pieces for solo voice. At the turn of the 20th century, D. Sichynsky, K. Stetsenko, Ya. Stepovy, and S. Liudkevych were notable composers of songs. During the 20th century songs have had a prominent place in the works of B. Liatoshynsky, V. Kosenko, Yu. Meitus, F. Nadenenko, H. Maiboroda, M. Dremliuha, and others.

Songbirds. Nearly half of all birds are songbirds; they represent 35–55 families and more than 4,000 species in the suborder Oscines, order Passeriformes. In Ukraine the following families can be heard: larks (Alaudidae), *swallows, *wagtails, wrens (Troglodytidae), *thrushes, *warblers, *titmice, waxwings, treecreepers (Certhiidae), hedge *sparrows, finches (Fringillidae), *starlings, orioles (Oriolidae), and *crows. Some songbirds are kept as pets for their melodious tones. Most songbirds living in the wild are valuable because they control various agricultural pests.

Songs of the Ukrainian Sich Riflemen. Songs created by the Legion of Ukrainian Sich Riflemen (USS) during the First World War (1914–18). They included marching songs, love songs, laments, and humorous songs. The chief creators of these songs were M. *Haivoronsky (conductor of the USS orchestra), R. *Kupchynsky, and L. *Lepky. Many of the songs of the USS have been arranged for choir or for solo voice, by composers such as S. Liudkevych, L. Revutsky, O. Koshyts, A. Rudnytsky, and N. Nyzhankivsky. Labeled as 'nationalistic' and banned in Soviet Ukraine, this genre of song soared in popularity in Ukraine during the late 1980s with the liberalization following glasnost.

Sonnet. A 14-line poem (usually in iambic pentameter) consisting of two sections of two quatrains and two tercets. The rhyme scheme of the quatrains is either a regular abba, abba or (less frequently) an alternating abab, abab. The tercets are less restricted, following a cdc, cdc; cde, cde; cde, edc; or other pattern (M. Zerov's tercets followed a ccd, ede tercet scheme). It is believed that sonnets were devised by Provençal troubadours, but they first appear in written form in Italy. F. da Barberini and A. da Tempo are considered to be the first poets to have mastered them. Petrarch (1304–74) set the number of lines and rhyme scheme. There are other forms of the sonnet extant in Italy, some ranging up to 20 or 22 lines with a short coda of 1 or 2 lines ending the poem.

In Ukrainian poetry the first sonnets were O. Shpyhotsky's translations-adaptations of a poem by Sappho and the sonnets of A. Mickiewicz. Sonnets were subsequently written by L. Borovykovsky, M. Shashkevych, Yu. Fedkovych, U. Kravchenko, and S. Charnetsky. The form became particularly common in the late 19th and early 20th centuries. I. Franko played an important role in developing sonnets, in his *Sonety* (Sonnets, 1882) and the cycles *Vil'ni sonety* (Free Sonnets) and *Tiuremni sonety* (Prison Sonnets). Lesia Ukrainka and M. Cherniavsky published *Donets'ki sonety* (The Don Sonnets) in 1898. The zenith of the Ukrainian form of sonnet was attained by the *Neoclassicists M. *Zerov (his *Sonnetarium*, published in 1948, contains 85 original sonnets and 28 in translation) and M. Rylsky. Others continued this efflorescence into the 1930s, and their products were complemented by the contributions from Galicia of B.I. Antonych (with the cycle *Zryvy i kryla* [Rises and Wings] and others). In Soviet Ukraine wholesale repressions sent all of literature into decline, and sonnets did not reappear until the mid-1950s. In the 1970s and 1980s they became popular once again. D. *Pavlychko has been particularly productive, largely in translating sonnets from other languages.

In émigré literature the form has also been popular, and in some cases the sonnets have been of high quality. E. *Andiievska, S. Hordynsky, I. Kachurovsky, Yu. Klen, B. Kravtsiv, M. Orest, O. Tarnavsky, and O. Zuievsky are among the form's practitioners.

Departures from the canonical scheme of the sonnet are known as sonnetoids (examples of which abound in Zerov's *Catalepton*, 1951). A wreath of sonnets is a complex composition that consists of 14 sonnets, of which the last line of a sonnet is repeated as the first line of the next, followed by a 15th sonnet that consists of the 14 first lines of the preceding sonnets. V. Bobynsky, B. Hrinchenko, Kravtsiv, V. Malyskho, L. Mosendz, O. Tarnavsky, O. Vedmitsky, M. Zhuk, and I. Kalynets are among those who have published wreaths.

BIBLIOGRAPHY
Chaplia, V. *Sonet v ukraïns'kii poeziï* (Odessa 1930)
Koshelivets', I. *Narysy z teoriï literatury* (Munich 1954)
Kachurovs'kyi, I. *Strofika* (Munich 1967)
Moroz, O. *Etiud pro sonet* (Kiev 1973)
Ukraïns'kyi sonet, intro by A. Dobrians'kyi (Kiev 1976)
                                                    I. Koshelivets

Sontsetsvit (Rockrose). An almanac published in 1922 in Tarnów, Poland. It contained works by writers and artists who had fled Soviet-occupied Ukraine, such as the graphic artists P. Kovzhun and P. Kholodny, Jr, and the symbolist poets Yu. Lypa, N. Livytska-Kholodna, M. Obidny, P. Tenianko, and Ye. Ivanenko.

Myroslava Sopilka   John Sopinka

Sopilka, Myroslava (pseud of Yuliia Mysko-Pastushenko), b 29 August 1897 in Vynnyky, now a district of Lviv, d 28 November 1937 near Kiev. Poet. She was a member of the radical group Luch in Vynnyky, and in 1928 she began to publish her poems, such as 'V tserkvi' (In the Church) and 'Son chornoï nochi' (Dream of a Black Night) in the Sovietophile journal *Vikna. She was a member of the literary group *Horno, which was made up of writers dedicated to propagating communism. In 1930 Sopilka moved to the Ukrainian SSR and became a member of the literary organization *Zakhidna Ukraina. In 1931 she published the collection of poetry *Robotiashchymy rukamy* (With Working Hands). She was arrested in 1937, and shot by the NKVD. *Do sontsia: Vybrane* (Toward the Sun: Selected Works) was published posthumously in 1973.

Sopilka (fipple flute). A wind instrument of varied construction made of wood or bark. Generally cylindrical, blocked at one end, and with 6 to 8 finger holes (up to 10 since 1970), its related forms include the *telenka, floiara,* and *dentsivka*. The earliest-known example found in Ukraine is a mammoth-bone flute from the Paleolithic period. The flute is known from the Princely period of the Kievan state and is depicted on an 11th-century fresco in Kiev's St Sophia Cathedral. In folk tradition it was commonly the instrument of shepherds or part of trio ensembles (*troisti myzyky). Today it is featured mainly in folk instrumental ensembles. Prominent *sopilka* performers include I. *Skliar, Y. Bobrovnykov, D. Demenchuk, and V. Zuliak.

Sopilnyk, Petro [Sopil'nyk], b 14 February 1922 in Sokolove, Katerynoslav gubernia. Painter and decorative artist. In 1961 he graduated from the Institute of Painting, Sculpture, and Architecture of the USSR Academy of Arts. His work consists of decorative wall panels, such as *Hutsul Wedding* (1963), *Kiev Legend* (at the Kiev Hotel in Ivano-Frankivske, 1965), and *Dniester* (at the Dnister Café in Ivano-Frankivske, 1966); and relief sculptures, such as the steel *Eternal Revolutionary* (1967), at the Ivano-

Frankivske Cinema, and the bronze *Danko* (1968) and a copper portrait of V. Stefanyk (1971), at the Ivano-Frankivske Pedagogical Institute. He has also designed docorative plates and a carved vase commemorating Yu. Fedkovych (1956).

Sopinka, John, b 19 March 1933 in Broderick, Saskatchewan. Lawyer and Canadian Supreme Court judge of Ukrainian origin. A graduate of the University of Toronto (LLB, 1958), he became one of the most successful civil litigation lawyers in Canada. He was involved in a number of difficult and controversial trials and served as counsel for several royal commissions. He represented the Ukrainian Canadian Committee before the Royal (Deschênes) Commission of Inquiry on War Criminals in Canada (1985–7). In 1988 Sopinka was appointed a justice of the Supreme Court of Canada.

Sopolyha, Myroslav, b 26 March 1946 in Svydnyk (Svidník), in the Prešov region of Slovakia. Ethnographer and museologist; associate of the Slovak Academy of Sciences. A graduate of the Prešov Faculty of Košice University, since 1967 he has worked at the Svydnyk Museum of Ukrainian Culture (now the Dukhnovych Museum). He acquired many of the museum's folk artifacts, organized the creation of its open-air museum, and became deputy director of its scholarly section. In 1979 he received a PH D from Bratislava University. He has published numerous articles on the material culture and folk architecture of the Prešov region in the museum's *Naukovyi zbirnyk*, Slovak scholarly periodicals, and *Nashe slovo* (Warsaw). He has also written monographs on the region's Ukrainian folk architecture (1976) and peasant dwellings (1983).

Sorghum (*Sorghum vulgare*; Ukrainian: *sorho*). A strong and hardy cereal grass of the family Gramineae (Poaceae), raised chiefly for grain. The species includes the grain sorghums – durra, milo, and millet – as well as broom corn and Sudan grass (*S. sudanense*; Ukrainian: *sudanska trava*), grown for hay and fodder. Introduced in Ukraine in 1912, sorghum is raised primarily in southern areas. The grain is rich in carbohydrates (12–18 percent sugars) and proteins (10 percent); it also contains calcium, iron, vitamin B, and nicotinic acid. It is usually ground into a meal used in porridge, flatbreads, and cakes; it is also used in making edible oil, starch, dextrose, and alcoholic beverages. Sweet sorghums, or sorgos, are used for syrup manufacture.

Sorochynsky, Lev [Soročyns'kyj], b 1895 in Haisyn, Podilia gubernia, d 31 January 1963 in Olyphant, Pennsylvania. Conductor, singer, and teacher. He studied under O. Koshyts and then in 1919 became a member of the Ukrainian Republican Kapelle. In 1921–6 he served as an assistant to Koshyts in the Ukrainian Republican Kapelle when it toured Europe and North and South America. From 1926 he conducted Ukrainian choruses in the United States, most notably in Rochester (New York), Chicago, and Olyphant.

Sorochynsky, Petro [Soročyns'kyj], b and d ? Zaporozhian Cossack leader. A representative of the older, more conservative Cossack forces, he was elected Kish otaman in 1701–2, 1796–7, and 1709. He favored an alliance with the Crimean Khanate against Muscovy rather than with

Poland or Sweden (as promoted by K. Hordiienko). The Muscovite authorities hoped that Sorochynsky's views would reverse the anti-Muscovy policies of the Zaporozhians, but he fought against them in 1709, with the assistance of the Crimea. Hordiienko was re-elected otaman and led the Zaporozhians from the Sich into exile (eventually to establish the Oleshky Sich). Sorochynsky's further fate is unknown.

Sorochyntsi. See Velyki Sorochyntsi.

Bohdan Soroka: *Carolers* (woodcut, 1991)

Soroka, Bohdan, b 2 September 1940 in Lviv. Graphic artist and painter; son of M. *Soroka and K. *Zarytska. A graduate of the Lviv Institute of Applied and Decorative Arts (1964), since the 1960s he has created imaginative, often expressionistic, line engravings and bookplates. His print series 'Folkloric Motifs' (1969), 'Slavic Mythology' (1970–2), 'Children's Games' (1974), 'Kupalo Festival Games' (1974), 'Proverbs' (1976), and 'March of the Gnomes' (1979–84) reveal his fascination with Ukrainian folklore. Soroka has also engraved prints depicting the old architecture (particularly churches) of Lviv, Drohobych, and Zhovkva (now Nesterov), and the series 'Symbols of Hryhorii Skovoroda' (1975), 'Travels in Uzbekistan' (1981–2), and 'Stations of the Cross' (1990); created graphic illustrations to works by I. Kalynets, Lesia Ukrainka, R. Ivanychuk, V. Stefanyk, and T. Shevchenko; and painted large-scale decorative murals in Lviv, including one inside the Quality Building and the large composition *Musicians*, on the ceiling of the former Carmelite Sisters' church. Solo exhibitions of his works have been held in Lviv (1983, 1989), Kiev (1987, 1990), and Toronto, Ottawa, and Edmonton (1991).

Mykhailo Soroka

Soroka, Mykhailo [Myxajlo], b 27 March 1911 in Koshliaky, Zbarazh county, Galicia, d 16 June 1971 in the Mordovian ASSR. Political prisoner; husband of K. *Zarytska and father of B. *Soroka. In 1938 he was imprisoned by the Polish authorities for his involvement in the OUN. In 1940 he was arrested in Lviv by the NKVD and sentenced to eight years in labor camps in Arctic Russia. After his release he returned to Lviv, but he was rearrested in 1949 and exiled to the Krasnoiarsk territory, in northern Siberia. In 1952 he was again arrested, for allegedly forming an underground organization of Ukrainian political prisoners in a Vorkuta camp, and in September 1953 he was sentenced to 25 years in labor camps in Kazakhstan, Siberia, and Mordovia.

Soroka, Oleksander, b 21 April 1900 in Khlypnivka, Zvenyhorod county, Kiev gubernia, d 28 December 1963 in Kiev. Choir conductor. He graduated in conducting from the Kiev Institute of Music and Drama (1930). In 1923 he joined the *DUMKA choral ensemble, and in 1935 he became its conductor and from 1937 its principal conductor. In 1940–6 he was artistic director of the Trembita choir in Lviv, after which he returned to DUMKA as principal conductor. He is best known as an interpreter of large-scale choral works, such as M. Lysenko's *Biut' porohy* (The Rapids Roar), S. Liudkevych's *Kavkaz* (The Caucasus), and A. Shtoharenko's *Ukraïno moia* (My Ukraine).

Soroka, Oleksander, b 19 December 1901 in Baryshivka, Pereiaslav county, Poltava gubernia, d 12 October 1941. Poet, prose writer, and translator. He was first published in 1925 in the almanac *Kyïv – Hart*, and he continued to publish his poetry and prose in periodicals. His poetry was also published in the collections *Kymak* (1929), *Na reikakh* (On the Rails, 1931), *Zhyttia v rusi* (Life in Action, 1936), *Horno* (The Forge, 1941), and *Vybrane* (Selected Works, 1959, 1966). He was arrested by the NKVD in 1941 and killed on the way to prison in Irkutsk, Siberia.

Soroka, Petro, b 3 April 1891 in Lviv, d 1948 in Lviv. Stage actor and director. He began his theatrical career in an amateur group at the Sokil society (1908) and then acted in the Ruska Besida (1912–14) and the Ternopilski Teatralni Vechory and New Lviv theaters (1917–20), led his own troupe (1921–38), and worked in the Lesia Ukrainka Theater, Lviv Opera Theater, and Lviv Ukrainian Drama Theater (1939–46).

Osyp Sorokhtei (self-portrait, oil, 1937)

Sorokhtei, Osyp [Soroxtej], b 28 February 1890 in Baranchychi, Sambir county, Galicia, d 27 November 1941 in Stanyslaviv, Galicia. Painter and graphic artist. He studied at the Cracow Academy of Arts (1911–14, 1919–20) and taught drawing at the Ukrainian gymnasiums in Stanyslaviv (1920–6, 1929–39) and Sniatyn (1926–9). Sorokhtei worked mostly in pencil, pen, and watercolor. He drew expressionistic portraits of T. Shevchenko (1922), I. Kotliarevsky (1922), Ye. Hrebinka, and M. Menzinsky and 50 drawings on biblical themes and 42 on Christ's Passion; painted Subcarpathian landscapes and genre scenes, religious paintings, and still lifes; did caricatures of Ukrainian Sich Riflemen, public figures, church leaders, and intellectuals; and illustrated A. Lototsky's *Zhyttia i pryhody Tsiapky Skoropada* (The Life and Adventures of Tsiapka Skoropad, 1926). He took part in exhibitions organized by the Circle of Contributors to Ukrainian Art and the Association of Independent Ukrainian Artists in Lviv and in two international shows of graphic art in Warsaw (1931). Retrospective exhibitions of his works were held in Stanyslaviv (1942) and Lviv (1970).

The Soroky fortress

Soroky. V-9. A city (1975 pop 29,500) on the right bank of the Dniester River in Moldova. It was first mentioned in 1499. Today the city lies on the Ukrainian ethnic border. It manufactures electric appliances, metal goods, and clothing. The old fortress and a cave monastery are tourist attractions.

Sorrel (*Rumex acetosa*; Ukrainian: *shchavel*). A hardy perennial herb of the buckwheat family Polygonaceae. There are many species common in the temperate zone of the Northern Hemisphere; in Ukraine about 20 are known, of which *R. acetosa* (Ukrainian: *shchavel kyslyi*) is widely cultivated. Its leaves contain oxalic acid, vitamin B complex, iron, and minerals. Young leaves are used to make sorrel soup (Ukrainian green borshch), in salads, and as flavoring in omelets and sauces. Extracts from *R. confertus* (Ukrainian: *shchavel kinskyi*) roots were used in folk medicine as an astringent and as purgative agents in treating colitis.

Sosenko, Ksenofont, b 9 February 1861 in Mezhyhirka, Halych circle, Galicia, d 17 April 1941 in Koniukhy, Kozova raion, Ternopil oblast. Ethnographer. While serving as a parish priest in a number of Galician villages, he gathered ethnographic materials and wrote several insightful studies, on the spring songs, *hahilky* (1922); the Ukrainian religious worldview (1923); and the traditional Ukrainian Christmas (1928). A memorial regional museum was established in Koniukhy in 1991 in the building where Sosenko lived.

Modest Sosenko (self-portrait, oil, 1915)

Sosenko, Modest, b 23 April 1875 in Porohy, Stanyslaviv county, Galicia, d 4 February 1920 in Lviv. Painter. He studied at the Cracow (1896–1900) and Munich (1901–2) academies of art and the Ecole nationale des beaux arts in Paris (1902–5). From 1906 he lived in Lviv but traveled often, to Italy (1908–13), Russian-ruled Ukraine (1913), and Egypt and Palestine (1914). He painted portraits, such as *Portrait of a Girl* (1913), *Metropolitan Andrei Sheptytsky*, and *Self-Portrait* (1915); Hutsul genre scenes, such as *Boys on a Fence* (1912), *Trembita Players* (1914), *Dance* (1915), and *Musicians*; landscapes of Paris, the Carpathian Mountains, and southern Dalmatia; and large-scale murals, in the Lysenko Music Institute in Lviv (1915), the Wallachian (Dormition) Church in Lviv, and the Galician village churches of Pidbereztsi, Pechenizhyn, Rykiv, Bilche Zolote, Zolochiv, Tovmach, Slavsko, Puzhnyky, Deviatnyky, and Yabloniv. Together with Yu. Makarevych he painted the iconostases in the church in Zolochiv and the cathedral in Stanyslaviv. In his church paintings he combined the traditions of Byzantine painting with modern artistic approaches. He compiled a book of ornaments in 16th- and 17th-century Galician manuscripts from the Stauropegion Museum (1923). A catalog of his memorial exhibition was published in 1960.

Sosenko, Petro, b 25 September 1900 in Duliby, Galicia, d ? Legal historian; son of K. Sosenko. In the 1920s he emigrated to Soviet Ukraine, where he was a research associate of the Commission for the Study of the History of Western-Ruthenian and Ukrainian Law of the VUAN. He wrote articles on contemporary Soviet law (1924) and the importance of church registers for the history of law (1929). He was arrested during the terror in 1933, and disappeared in prison.

Ivan Soshenko: *Hay Selling by the Dnieper* (oil, before 1850)

Soshenko, Ivan [Sošenko], b 2 June 1807 in Bohuslav, Kaniv county, Kiev gubernia, d 18 July 1876 in Korsun, Kaniv county. Painter. After studying at the St Petersburg Academy of Arts (1834–8) he taught painting in gymnasiums in Nizhen (1839–46), Nemyriv (1846–56), and Kiev. He painted portraits, such as *Portrait of M. Chaly's Grandmother* and *Woman's Portrait*; genre scenes, such as *Hay Selling by the Dnieper* and *Boys Fishing* (1857); landscapes; and icons. In 1835 he introduced T. *Shevchenko to Ye. Hrebinka, V. Zhukovsky, K. Briullov, and A. Venetsianov, and in 1838 he helped to purchase Shevchenko's freedom and to place him in the St Petersburg Academy. M. Chaly's biography of Soshenko was published in Kiev in 1876.

Sosiura, Volodymyr [Sosjura], b 6 January 1898 in Debaltseve, Katerynoslav gubernia, d 8 January 1965 in Kiev. Poet. During the Ukrainian-Soviet War he fought in the UNR Army and then in the Red Army. After the war ended, he studied at the Artem Communist University in Kharkiv (1922–3) and at the workers' faculty of the Kharkiv Institute of People's Education (1923–5). He was a member of the literary organizations *Pluh, Hart, Vaplite, and the All-Ukrainian Association of Proletarian Writers. His first poem to be published appeared in 1917. His first collection, *Poeziï* (Poems), published in 1921, was followed by his Romantic revolutionary poem *Chervona zyma* (The Red Winter, 1922), which was acclaimed as the best example of epic poetry from the period of the struggle for independence in Ukraine, and brought him fame overnight. Sosiura was to write many other works thematically based on that struggle, in which he united intimate, community, and universal concerns, such as in the collec-

Volodymyr Sosiura

tions *Misto* (The City, 1924), *Snihy* (The Snows, 1925), and *Zoloti shuliky* (The Golden Hawks, 1927).

His poems, filled with an organic lyricism, leave an impression of sincerity, revolutionary enthusiasm, and passionate feeling. Sosiura drew his unique lyrical style from the wellspring of folk literature. His style leaned toward classically simple verse, a songlike quality, and a Romantic, uplifted mood. Even in his early period Sosiura's poetry reflected his era and its contradictions, such as the impossibility of uniting loyalty to the Bolshevik revolution with feelings of duty toward one's country, a dilemma faced by all the Ukrainian intelligentsia of the 1920s. It can be seen in the poem about internal strife (between communard and nationalist) *Dva Volod'ky* (The Two Volodias, 1930) and in the collection *Sertse* (The Heart, 1931), which was banned immediately after its release.

Although Sosiura had been a Party member since 1920, until the early 1930s his poetry brought him into conflict with the Communist party. That, together with the deaths of millions of Ukrainian peasants as a result of the man-made famine and the persecution and shootings of Ukrainian cultural activists during the 1930s, brought Sosiura near to a mental breakdown. Despite those difficult circumstances he was virtually the only poet in Ukraine in the 1930s who continued to work on lyric love poetry, such as in the collections *Chervoni troiandy* (Red Roses, 1932), *Novi poeziï* (New Poems, 1937), *Liubliu* (I Love, 1939), and *Zhuravli pryletily* (The Cranes Have Returned, 1940). From 1942 to 1944 Sosiura was a war correspondent. During that period he produced the collections *Pid hul kryvavyi* (During the Bloody Rumblings of War, 1942) and *V hodynu hnivu* (In the Hour of Anger, 1942) and the poem 'Oleh Koshovyi' (1943), among others. The most noteworthy of his postwar collections are *Zelenyi svit* (Green World, 1949), *Solov'ïni dali* (The Nightingale Distances, 1956), and *Tak nikhto ne kokhav* (No One Has Loved like This, 1960).

An important part of Sosiura's works are his poems written on a grander epic scale, such as the poems '1871' (1923) and 'Zaliznytsia' (The Railway, 1924) and the versified novel *Taras Triasylo* (1926). In 1948 Sosiura was awarded the highest prize at that time, the Stalin Prize, but beginning in 1951 he was again harshly attacked. He was accused of bourgeois nationalism for his patriotic poem 'Liubit' Ukraïnu' (Love Ukraine), written in 1944. Although he was productive, Sosiura's poetic achievements were much less than his talents promised. His collected works have been published in 3-volume editions (1929–30 and 1957–8) and in 10 volumes (1970–2). In 1988 the poem 'Mazepa,' only excerpts of which had previously been published (1929), and the autobiographical novel *Tretia rota* (The Third Company) were published.

BIBLIOGRAPHY
Dolengo, O. *Tvorchist' V. Sosiury* (Kharkiv 1931)
Stebun, I. *Volodymyr Sosiura* (Kiev 1948)
Burliai, Iu. *Volodymyr Sosiura: Zhyttia i tvorchist'* (Kiev 1959)
Kudin, O. *Volodymyr Sosiura* (Kiev 1959)
Radchenko, Iu. *Volodymyr Sosiura: Literaturno-krytychnyi narys* (Kiev 1967)
Morenets', V. *Volodymyr Sosiura* (Kiev 1990)

I. Koshelivets

Soskin, Marat, b 8 April 1929 in Kiev. Physicist; AN URSR (now ANU) corresponding member since 1988. A graduate of Kiev University (1952), he joined the ANU Institute of Physics in 1956. Soskin has made substantive contributions in the fields of exciton spectroscopy of molecular crystals, quantum electronics, laser spectroscopy, and dynamic holography.

Sosnivka. III-5. A city (1975 pop 11,200) on the left bank of the Buh River in Lviv oblast, administered by the Chervonohrad city council. It was founded in 1955 in connection with the development of the Lviv-Volhynia Coal Basin. In 1968 it attained city status. Sosnivka has three coal mines and an enrichment plant.

Mykhailo Sosnovsky

Sosnovsky, Mykhailo [Sosnovs'kyj, Myxajlo], b 1 December 1919 in Hai, Ternopil county, Galicia, d 25 July 1975 in Jersey City, New Jersey. Journalist, scholar, and community leader. As a refugee in postwar Germany he served on the executive of the Central Union of Ukrainian Students, edited its organs *Visti TseSUSu* and *Students'kyi visnyk*, contributed articles to the Fürth newspaper *Chas* and journal *Samostiinyk*, and studied law at Erlangen University. In late 1948 he emigrated to Canada. In Toronto he cofounded the *Canadian League for Ukraine's Liberation, served as a member of its executive (1949–68), cofounded its newspaper *Homin Ukraïny, was the newspaper's first chief editor in 1948–9, and was its editor again in 1951–4. After breaking with the OUN Bandera faction, he served as executive director of the World Congress of Free Ukrainians in Winnipeg and New York (1969–72). From 1972 he coedited the daily *Svoboda in Jersey City.

Sosnovsky wrote widely on Soviet politics, émigré issues, and international affairs. He also published books in

Ukrainian on Ukraine in the international arena in 1945–65 (1966; his PH D diss at the Ukrainian Free University) and Dmytro Dontsov (1974), and wrote a brief survey history of Ukrainian political thought (1976). A large posthumous collection of his selected essays and articles appeared in 1979.

The Oleksander Dovzhenko Literary Memorial Museum in Sosnytsia. Bronze statue of Dovzhenko by Anatolii Fuzhenko

Sosnytsia [Sosnycja]. II-13. A town smt (1986 pop 8,000) on the Ubid River and a raion center in Chernihiv oblast. It was first mentioned in the Hypatian Chronicle under the year 1234. From 1340 it was under Lithuanian rule, and from 1618, under Polish rule. In 1637 one of its residents, K. *Skydan, raised a rebellion against the Polish nobles. In 1648 the town was captured by the Cossacks, and thereafter became a company center of Nizhen and then Chernihiv regiment. After the abolition of the Hetman state Sosnytsia belonged to Novhorod-Siverskyi vicegerency (1782–96) and then became a county center of Little Russia and Chernihiv (1802–1923) gubernias. Under the Soviet regime it was a raion center of Snov (1923–5) and Konotip okruhas and Chernihiv oblast (since 1935). Today its main industries are food processing and clothes manufacturing. The birthplace of O. *Dovzhenko, it has a literary memorial museum dedicated to him. It also has a rich regional museum founded by Yu. Vynohradsky. The wooden Church of the Holy Protectress (17th century, reconstructed in 1724) and its bell tower (19th century) remain neglected and in disrepair.

Soton, Spyrydon, b ? in Tver (now Kalinin), d 1503 in the Ferapont monastery, in Moscow. Orthodox metropolitan. He was bishop of Tver until 1474, when the patriarch of Constantinople appointed him metropolitan of Kiev and all Rus', with his jurisdiction in the Grand Duchy of Lithuania and the Kingdom of Poland. Since this was done without consultation with the local bishops or King Casimir IV Jagiellończyk (who had appointed his own candidate), Soton was not recognized as metropolitan, and was imprisoned when he arrived in Lithuania in 1476. After his release he fled to Moscow. There he was opposed by the metropolitan of Moscow, who also claimed jurisdiction over most of the Rus' eparchies, and he was imprisoned in the Ferapont-Belozerskii monastery. He remained in the monastery, where he wrote theological works and a hagiography of two monks of the monastery, until his death.

Sotsialisticheskii Donbass (Socialist Donbas). A Russian-language organ of Donetske oblast's CPU Committee and Soviet, published five times a week in Donetske. It first appeared in July 1917 as *Izvestiia* of the Yuzivka Revolutionary and Party committees. From 1920 the newspaper appeared as *Diktatura truda*, and in 1932 it acquired its *Sotsiialisticheskii Donbass* name and became the oblast paper. From July 1944, a parallel Ukrainian-language paper, *Sotsialistychnyi Donbas*, renamed in December 1945 **Radians'ka Donechchyna*, appeared. In 1975 *Sotsialisticheskii Donbass* had the largest pressrun (373,000) of any oblast-level newspaper in Ukraine.

Sotsialistychna hromada. See *Nova hromada*.

Sotsialistychna Kharkivshchyna (Socialist Kharkiv Region). An organ of Kharkiv oblast's CPU Committee and Soviet, published five times a week in Kharkiv. It began publication in Russian in 1917 and changed names several times before becoming *Proletarii* (1920–4) and then *Khar'kovskii proletarii* (1924–30). From March 1930 it appeared in Ukrainian as *Kharkivs'kyi proletar*, and in 1934 it acquired its last name. A parallel Russian-language edition, *Krasnoe znamia*, was established in 1938. In 1980 the latter had a pressrun of 131,000; that of *Sotsialistychna Kharkivshchyna* was only 62,000.

Sotsialistychna kul'tura (Socialist Culture). A popular monthly journal of cultural, political, educational, and scientific affairs, published in Kiev in 1937–41 and since 1955. It was preceded by several journals with similar profiles, such as *Kul'turno-osvitnia robota* (1947–54) and *Kolbud* (1936–7) in Kiev, and, in Kharkiv, *Kul'tfront* (1931–5), *Za masovu komunistychnu osvitu* (1931–3), *Kul'trobitnyk* (1928–30), *Selians'kyi budynok* (1924–30), and the Russian-language *Kul'trabotnik* (1927), *Rabochii klub* (1925–6), and *Put' k kommunizmu* (1921–4). Until 1970 the journal was intended for village cultural workers and librarians. From 1970 to 1990 it was an organ of the Ministry of Culture and Council of Trade Unions of the Ukrainian SSR, and dealt also with urban and working-class issues. In 1975 *Sotsialistychna kul'tura* had a pressrun of 65,000. In 1991 the journal's name was changed to *Ukraïns'ka kul'tura* to reflect its new orientation. It is now published by the Ministry of Culture, the Ukrainian Cultural Fund, and the Council of the Federation of Independent Trade Unions of Ukraine, and has a pressrun of 31,000. The chief editor is V. Burban.

Sotsialistychne tvarynnytstvo. See *Tvarynnytstvo Ukraïny*.

Sotsiial-Demokrat (Social Democrat). An organ of the Ukrainian Social Democratic Workers' party, published in Poltava in 1907 and edited by P. Diatliv. After the fifth issue the newspaper was closed down by the tsarist authorities.

Sotskyi. A term denoting a certain type of low-ranking official. It has feudal origins, and its meaning varies. In Kievan Rus' a *sotskyi* was a levy captain, although the word was used to refer to certain representatives of princes in accounts of the looting of *sotskyi* homes in 1113. During the Lithuanian-Polish period in Galicia and Podlachia, suburban craftsmen and farmers were said to be part of *sotni* or under the jurisdiction of a *sotskyi*. The term disappeared in Lithuania in the 14th century. In the 17th and 18th centuries, in Left- and Right-Bank Ukraine and in Western Ukrainian territories, a *sotskyi* was a young messenger or minor official, particularly in municipal governments. Such officials were sometimes known as *sotnychky* or *osavul'chyky*. In the Russian Empire a *sotskyi* was a police officer of low rank in a village, chosen at a village council. Each one oversaw 100 to 200 households. In 1837 such officers were made a part of local police forces.

South Russia Consumer Society (Russian: Potrebitelskoe obshchestvo Yuga Rossii). An association of consumer co-operatives, established in Kharkiv in 1912 on the initiative of the Moscow Union of Consumer Co-operatives. It attempted to impose central Russian control over the Ukrainian co-operative movement, but such control was resisted by the Ukrainian leaders. Its activities were limited to Kharkiv and Katerynoslav gubernias. With the emergence of the **Dniprosoiuz union in 1917, the South Russian Consumer Society lost its importance, and it was dissolved by 1919. It was headed by V. Tsellarius and M. Kuznetsov.

South Russian Union of Workers (Pivdennorosiiskyi soiuz robitnykiv). The first revolutionary organization among workingmen in the Russian Empire. It was established in Odessa in October 1875 on the basis of existing workers' clubs or groups and was dedicated specifically to improving labor conditions and generally to changing the political situation in the empire. It had approx 60 members and was headed by E. Zaslavsky. It organized two strikes in Odessa, and it was in the process of attempting to establish comparable groups in other cities (Kharkiv, Tahanrih, Kerch, Sevastopil, and others) when it was shut down by the police late in 1875. Fifteen of its leading members were arrested.

South Russian Workers' Union (Pivdennorosiiskyi robitnychyi soiuz). A revolutionary workers' organization in Kiev in 1880–1. Its membership consisted of several hundred workers, including Russians, Poles, Jews, and a majority of Ukrainians. The union was organized in the spring of 1880 by Ye. Kovalska and N. Shchedrin, two members of the Black Repartition (Chernyi Peredel) organization that had formed in the split of **Zemlia i Volia. The union demanded sweeping economic changes, including collective ownership of land and factories, the recognition of all basic liberties, and the satisfaction of more immediate labor demands (including shorter working days and safer conditions). Tactically, the union advocated the use of terror in order to achieve its aims. Sabotage and the murder of factory managers and owners were common threats made by the union leadership. Those tactics met with some success in the Kiev Arsenal, where Shchedrin concentrated his efforts.

With the arrest of Shchedrin and Kovalska in October 1880, the union came under new leadership. The change signaled a substantial moderation in tactics, with individual acts of terror being rejected in favor of long-term propaganda and strike activity. The union was liquidated in April 1881 upon the arrest of its remaining leaders and the seizure of its printing press. Its leaders were sentenced by military tribunal to various terms of hard labor or exile to Siberia.

South Volhynian dialects. The northeastern group of the *southwestern dialects, spoken in the territory of what are today the southern parts of Volhynia, Rivne, and Zhytomyr oblasts and the northern parts of Lviv, Khmelnytskyi, and Vinnytsia oblasts. The dialects are bounded by the *Polisian dialects to the north, the *southeastern dialects to the east, and the *Podilian and *Dniester dialects, to which they are most similar, to the south. The phonetic features of the South Volhynian dialects are (1) raised pronunciation of unstressed *o* as *u*, particularly after labials and velars (eg, *xulódna* [Standard Ukrainian (SU) *xolódna*] 'cool'); (2) lowered pronunciation of *y* as *é* and, after *k, g, h,* and *x,* as *i* (eg, *réba, rúk'i* [SU *rýba, rúky*] 'fish, hands'); (3) prothetic *h-* before initial vowels (eg, *horáty, húlyc'a, hínšyj* [SU *oráty, vúlycja, ínšyj*] 'to plow, street, other'); (4) hardened *r'* (eg, *búra* [SU *búrja*] 'storm'); (5) *s'c'* instead of *st'* (eg, *vús'c'ilka* [SU *výstilka*] 'padding'); (6) *xv/kv* instead of *f* (eg, *xvósa* [SU *fósa*] 'ditch'); (7) *mn'* instead of *mj* (eg, *xomn'ák* [SU *xomják*] 'hamster'); (8) coronal (eastern Ukrainian) pronunciation of palatal dentals *s', z', c', dz'* (also in the suffixes *-ec', -ys'ko, -s'kij*); (9) bilabial or labiodental pronunciation of postvocalic *v* in the northeast (eg, *dav* [SU *daŭ*] 'he gave'); (10) doubled soft consonants in forms such as *z'íl'l'e, s'm'ijéc'c'a* [SU *zíllja, smijetsja*] 'herbs, he is laughing'.

In nominal declension, dual forms have been retained (eg, *dvi pól'i* [SU *dva pólja*] 'two fields'). In adjectives, soft-type endings (eg, *hárn'ij, hírk'ij* [SU *hárnyj, hirkýj*] 'nice, bitter') and long forms (eg, *muludája* [SU *molodá*] 'young') have been retained. Third-person pronouns after prepositions omit *n-* (eg, *do jóho, z jéju, do jíx, z jímy* [SU *do n'óho, z néju, do nýx, z nýmy*] 'to him, with her, to them, with them'). Endings of the pronominal soft declension have influenced the hard (eg, *téji, méji* [SU *tijéji, mojéji*] 'of that, of my'). Sometimes such endings are also used in adjectives. Verbs have endings and forms of the type *xód'at', dasýš* [SU *xódjat', dasý*] 'they walk, you (sing) will give' and, in the east, *pytát', búdu robýt'* [SU *pytáty, búdu robýty*] 'to ask, I will make'.

Certain features of the Sian and Dniester dialects are evident in the group of so-called Buh dialects west of the upper Styr River. There the stressed *'a* after palatal sibilants and *r* has changed to *'e* (eg, *loš'ét'a* [SU *lošáta*] 'foals') and, in the southern Kholm region, also to *'i* (eg, *t'íško* [SU *tjážko*] 'heavily'); *ky, gy, xy* have changed to *k'e, g'e, x'e* when stressed and to *k'i, g'i, x'i* when unstressed (eg, *k'énuŭ, rúk'i* [SU *kýnuv, rúky*] 'he threw, hands'); stressed *e* is lowered to *a* (eg, *dan'* [SU *den'*] 'day', and unstressed *e, o* is raised to *i, u* (eg, *pirihórujut, rubývim* [SU *perehorjújut', robýv*] 'they will endure, I made').

The dialects have been studied by linguists such as V. Kaminsky, S. Haievsky, P. Hladky, L. Rak, K. Dejna, H. Shylo, P. Lysenko, M. Peretiatko, L. Bova (Kovalchuk), T. Baimut, M. Kravchuk, L. Baranovska, Ya. Pura, F. Babii, H. Kozachuk, O. Horbach, and M. Korzoniuk.

O. Horbach

Southeastern dialects. A dialectal group consisting of the Middle Dnieper, Slobidska Ukrainian, and Steppe dialects. They have the same type of phonetics as the

Podilian and South Volhynian dialects of the southwestern group, and a type of simplified morphology, syntax, and, to a certain extent, vocabulary similar to that of the Polisian dialects. V. Hantsov and, later, O. Kurylo expressed the view that the southeastern dialects developed as a result of the intermingling of speakers of the southwestern and Polisian dialects who colonized southeastern Ukraine. L. Bulakhovsky and F. Zhylko maintained that they are one of the three primeval, fundamental Ukrainian dialects spoken by the ancient Polianians of the Ros River basin and the Pereiaslav region; they did not, however, point out any distinctive ancient traits, and their hypothesis is unconvincing. Modern Standard Ukrainian is based on the northern belt of the southeastern dialects.

Southern Branch of the All-Union Academy of Agricultural Sciences (Pivdenne viddilennia Vsesoiuznoi akademii silskohospodarskykh nauk). Until the demise of the USSR in 1991, a regional center for agricultural research in the Ukrainian SSR and the Moldavian SSR. In 1991 it became the Ukrainian Academy of Agrarian Sciences. It was set up in Kiev under the jurisdiction of the presidium of the All-Union Academy of Agricultural Sciences and the Council of Ministers of the Ukrainian SSR in 1969. The branch had various sections, such as agronomy, animal husbandry and veterinary medicine, the mechanization and electrification of farming, hydrotechnology and melioration, and farm economics and organization. It had a publishing department and the Central Republican Agricultural Research Library. It oversaw the work of 19 scientific research institutes and their experimental stations and seed farms. The branch planned and co-ordinated agricultural research at scientific and higher educational institutions in Ukraine and Moldavia.

Southern Buh River. See Boh River.

Southern Economic Region of the USSR. See Regional economics.

Southern Mineral Enrichment Complex (Pivdennyi hirnycho-zbahachuvalnyi kombinat). A large mineral enrichment plant located in Kryvyi Rih, Dnipropetrovske oblast. The first plant opened in 1955, and a second plant in 1961. The complex, which consists of an open-pit mine, two crushing mills, two wet magnetic separation plants, and two agglomeration plants, processes ore from the *Kryvyi Rih Iron-ore Basin. In 1969 it processed 33.2 million t of ore to produce 15.7 million t of concentrate (with an iron content of 64.6 percent) and 8.1 million of agglomerates (with an iron content of 56.4 percent). In the 1970s it employed over 4,000 workers.

Southern Railroad. See Railroad transportation.

Southern Rebels (Pivdenni buntari). An association of populist revolutionaries active in Ukraine in the mid-1870s. Formed in 1875 in Odessa by V. *Debohorii-Mokriievych and Ya. *Stefanovych, the group was among the first to express disenchantment with the tactics adopted by the 'going to the people' movement and the populist organization Zemlia i Volia. The role of the intelligentsia in the countryside, the rebels believed, was to provoke the peasantry to revolution by any means possible. To that end the group's 20 or more members, based originally in Kiev and later in Yelysavethrad, disguised themselves as peasants and tradespeople while spreading revolutionary propaganda. Stefanovych attempted his most audacious scheme in November 1876 in Chyhyryn county. Disguising himself as an 'imperial commissioner,' he claimed to be bearing documents from the tsar which urged the peasants to rise up in revolution against the nobles and imperial officials. He managed to organize a clandestine force of approx 1,000 people before the plot was discovered and the people responsible arrested in September 1877. By 1878 the remaining members of the Southern Rebels either had been arrested or had joined other revolutionary organizations.

Southern Society (Russian: Yuzhnoe obshchestvo). A conspiratorial organization of Russian military officers stationed in Ukraine that was part of what became known as the *Decembrist movement. The society was founded by Col P. *Pestel in March 1821 in place of the Tulchyn council of the *Union of Welfare. It was headed by a Fundamental Council and a Directory and, from the fall of 1825, Lt Col S. *Muravev-Apostol. Its leaders (called boyars) met secretly each year during the January contract fair in Kiev to debate the program and tactics for the military overthrow of tsarist absolutism, the abolition of serfdom, and the creation of a unitary Russian democratic state and constitutional monarchy. In 1823 the society was divided into three branches, Tulchyn, Kamianka, and Vasylkiv. In September 1825 the *Society of United Slavs, which had Ukrainians among its members, merged with the Vasylkiv branch. After the suppression of the uprising of the Chernihiv Regiment led by Muravev-Apostol and the Vasylkiv branch in January 1826, the members of the Southern Society were arrested. Pestel, Muravev-Apostol, and M. Bestuzhev-Riumin were hanged in St Petersburg in July, the other members were sentenced to long terms of hard labor and exile in Siberia, and the soldiers of the Chernihiv Regiment were punished and transferred to penal regiments in the Caucasus.

Southern Ukraine. The largest (250,000 sq km) historical-geographic region of Ukraine, stretching from the Black Sea and the Azov Sea in the south to the forest-steppe in the north. Also known as Steppe Ukraine, it was permanently and conclusively settled by Ukrainians only in the second half of the 18th century. From the end of the 18th century until 1917 Southern Ukraine, as part of the Russian Empire, was known as *New Russia.

 Location and boundaries. The history of Southern Ukraine and the ethnic composition of its population were influenced by its location on the littoral of the Black Sea (into which flow all the major rivers of Ukraine) adjacent to the Asiatic steppes (the steppes of Southern Ukraine are their western extension). Throughout its history the region was repeatedly invaded by hordes of nomads from Asia, who severed the main territory of Ukraine and its inhabitants from the Black Sea. At the same time the Mediterranean seafaring powers tried to establish colonies and extend their influence on the northern littoral of the Black Sea, and the peoples inhabiting the main territory of Ukraine also tried to reach the Black Sea shore. Those three directions of expansion intersected on the territory of Southern Ukraine and resulted in conflicts that endured for millennia.

In antiquity the Greeks established *ancient states on the northern Black Sea coast, some of which were subsequently united into the *Bosporan Kingdom and later incorporated into the Roman Empire and its successor, the Byzantine Empire. The influences of the highly developed Mediterranean cultures extended from them deep into the interior. Trade with them and Byzantium contributed to the growth of the Kievan Rus' state. The latter state's link with the south became tenuous in the 10th to 12th centuries, when the *Pechenegs and then the *Cumans invaded Southern Ukraine, and was almost completely severed in the 13th century after the Mongol (*Tatar) invasion. The collapse of Byzantium and the occupation of Southern Ukraine at the end of the 15th century by Turkey through its vassal, the Crimean Khanate, converted Southern Ukraine into a depopulated steppe controlled by the nomads. The emergence of the Cossacks around the *Zaporozhian Sich in the mid-16th century resulted in a protracted struggle for control of the steppes. The matter was resolved only in the late 18th century, after Turkey's defeats in the Russo-Turkish wars created the conditions for permanent Ukrainian settlement in the steppes and their unification with the rest of Ukraine. Southern Ukraine thus joined Ukraine, which by that time had been incorporated within the Russian Empire.

The northern boundaries of Southern Ukraine are not precise. From the geographical standpoint they consist of a transition zone between the steppe and the forest-steppe. From the historical standpoint they correspond to the southern frontiers of the Kievan, Lithuanian, and Polish states, which together with the Ukrainian farming settlement fluctuated southward deep into the steppe or northward into the forest-steppe. From the end of the 18th century the northern boundary of Southern Ukraine corresponded to the northern limit of the new possessions of the Russian Empire. That limit followed the old frontiers between Poland and Turkey (from the Dniester to the Boh), Poland and Zaporizhia (to the Dnieper), and the Left Bank or Hetman Ukraine and the Zaporizhia (along the Dnieper and its left-bank tributary, the Orel). It was also the northern boundary of the three gubernias that succeeded New Russia: Kherson, Katerynoslav, and Tavriia. The other boundaries of Southern Ukraine included the southern part of Bessarabia in the west and the western part of the Don region in the east, both of which were peopled by Ukrainians.

With the rise of industry in the Donets Basin and the Dnieper Industrial Region from the 1880s, Southern Ukraine underwent economic differentiation. Over time the division became pronounced, and today Southern Ukraine consists of the agricultural steppe (Odessa, Mykolaiv, Kirovohrad, and Kherson oblasts and the Crimea), the Donets Basin (Donetske and Luhanske oblasts), and the Dnieper Industrial Region (Dnipropetrovske and Zaporizhia oblasts).

 Physical geography. With the exception of southern Crimea, Southern Ukraine presents a monotonous, flat, predominantly low-lying landscape, with its particular steppe climate, vegetation, and fauna. All those characteristics vary over the great distances of Southern Ukraine, particularly on the fringe of the forest-steppe and in the east.

The largest part of Southern Ukraine is occupied by the *Black Sea Lowland and its extension: to the south, the

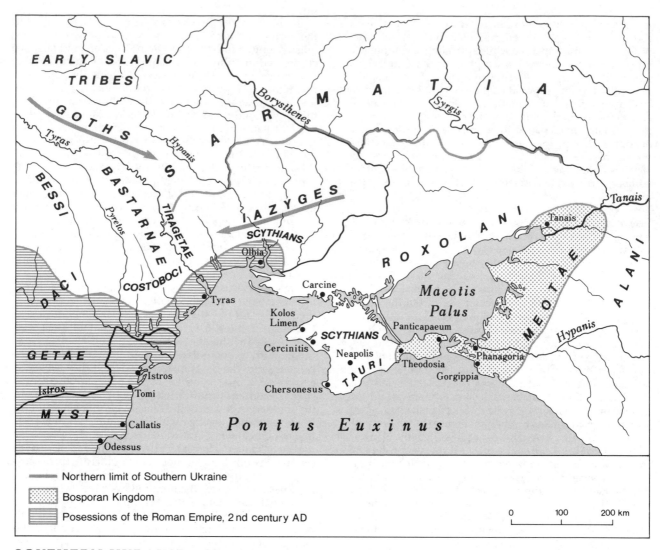

Legend:
- Northern limit of Southern Ukraine
- Bosporan Kingdom
- Posessions of the Roman Empire, 2nd century AD

0   100   200 km

SOUTHERN UKRAINE, 2ND CENTURY BC TO 2ND CENTURY AD

Crimean Lowland, and to the east, the narrow Azov Low-land, which widens eastward into the broad Lower-Don Lowland. The northwestern part of Southern Ukraine is occupied by the southern extremities of the undulating *Pokutian-Bessarabian Upland between the Danube and the Dniester, and the severely dissected *Podolian Upland. A considerably larger area is occupied by the southern part of the *Dnieper Upland, the *Zaporozhian Ridge, and the *Azov Upland. The northeastern part of Southern Ukraine is occupied by the extensions of the *Dnieper Lowland and the *Central Upland, the Donets Lowland, and the highest part of Southern Ukraine, the *Donets Ridge (reaching 367 m). The southern part of the Crimea is occupied by the Crimean Mountains.

The climate of Southern Ukraine differs from that of the rest of Ukraine. Influenced to a greater extent by the easterly winds, it is moderately continental and dry. The mean annual temperature ranges from 7°C to 10°C. The coldest winters occur in the northeast (mean January temperature, –7°C); the warmest are recorded in the southwest (–2°C). Absolute minimum temperatures range from –42°C to –28°C. Summer temperatures are nearly the same

throughout Southern Ukraine (July means range from 21°C to 23°C). The frost-free period increases from 150 days in the northeast to 210 days in the southwest; the growing period, from 200 to 230 days. The mean annual precipitation is highest along the border with the forest steppe (475 mm) and lowest over the sea (250–300 mm); from year to year, however, it varies widely (from 200 to 800 mm). Maximum precipitation is obtained in May, June, and July, when downpours prevail. The snow cover is uneven and may last from 30 to 100 days per year. Strong winds often include hurricanes, desiccating winds or *sukhovii*, and dust storms. Long, warm summers are conducive to the production of heat-loving crops, but frequent droughts and *sukhovii* cause wide fluctuations in yields.

The river network of Southern Ukraine is not dense, but the region is crossed by several large rivers: the Danube, the Dniester, the Boh, the Inhul, the Dnieper and its tributaries (the Inhulets, the Orel, the Samara, and others), and the Don and its tributary, the Donets. A number of small rivers flow toward the Black Sea (such as the Kohylnyk, the Velykyi Kuialnyk, the Malyi Kuialnyk, and the Tyli-

SOUTHERN UKRAINE IN THE SECOND HALF OF THE 18TH CENTURY

hul) and the Azov Sea (the Salhyr, the Molochna, the Oby- tochna, the Berda, the Kalmiius, the Miius, and others), most of which empty into coastal lakes or limans. In the summer the small rivers of Southern Ukraine are shallow or dry up completely. Between the Dnieper and the Molochna and on much of the Crimean Lowland there are no rivers at all. Along the coast there are many lakes, formed out of former inlets cut off from the sea by bars.

The soils and vegetation of Southern Ukraine reveal a zonal distribution reflecting the availability of moisture.

Southern Ukraine, especially the Donets Basin and the Dnieper Industrial Region, is the richest part of Ukraine for mineral resources. Here one finds almost all the bitu-

minous coal (the Donets Basin, with total proven reserves of coal of 55.6 billion t in 1977) and iron ore (the Kryvyi Rih basin deposits, with proven reserves of 15.9 billion t in 1975) of Ukraine, all the manganese ore (the Nykopil basin deposits, with reserves of approximately 2 billion t), most of the common salt (the Artemivske rock salt deposits), and all the nonferrous metal ores (mercury at Mykytivka, northwest of Horlivka, in the Donets Basin, bauxite de- posits in Dnipropetrovske oblast, chromite and nickel near Zavallia, on the Boh River). Refractory and flux ma- terials, lignite coals, limestones, marls, gypsum, kaolin, graphite, marble, and all kinds of building materials are abundant.

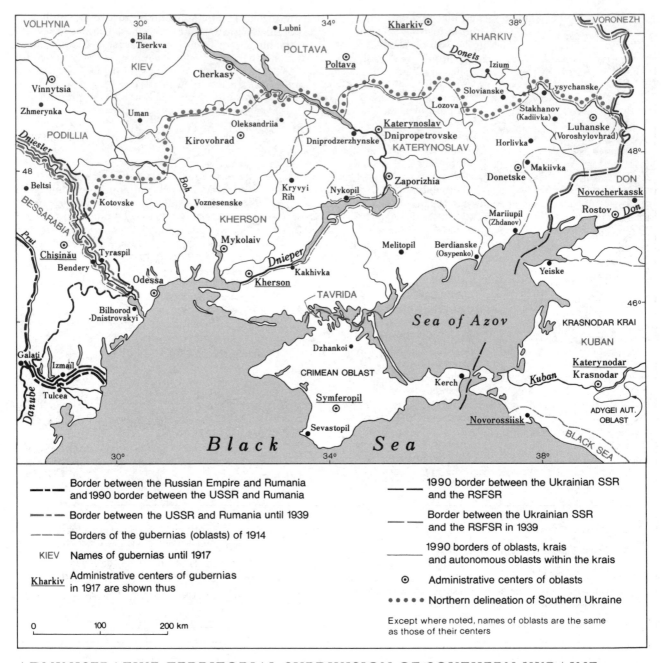

Border between the Russian Empire and Rumania and 1990 border between the USSR and Rumania

1990 border between the Ukrainian SSR and the RSFSR

Border between the USSR and Rumania until 1939

Border between the Ukrainian SSR and the RSFSR in 1939

Borders of the gubernias (oblasts) of 1914

1990 borders of oblasts, krais and autonomous oblasts within the krais

KIEV Names of gubernias until 1917

Kharkiv Administrative centers of gubernias in 1917 are shown thus

⊙ Administrative centers of oblasts

• • • • Northern delineation of Southern Ukraine

0   100   200 km

Except where noted, names of oblasts are the same as those of their centers

ADMINISTRATIVE-TERRITORIAL SUBDIVISION OF SOUTHERN UKRAINE DURING THE 19TH AND 20TH CENTURIES

Economy and demography. In the 1860s and 1870s, great changes occurred in the economy and demography of Southern Ukraine in conjunction with the abolition of serfdom (1861), the construction of railroads (1865 to the 1880s), which provided an all-season connection between the interior and the sea, and the beginnings of heavy industry. Large-scale industrial development of Southern Ukraine began at the end of the 1870s in conjunction with the exploitation of the Donets Basin coal (the output of which increased from 1.3 million t in 1880 to 23.5 million t in 1913), Kryvyi Rih iron ore (0.1 million t in 1881, but 6.4 million t in 1913), and Nykopil manganese ore (beginning in 1886 and reaching 276,000 t in 1913) as well as the con-

struction of a dense network of railroads connecting the Donets Basin with seaports and with Kryvyi Rih (the railroad to Katerynoslav was completed in 1884). Industrial development was favored by the convenient geographical location of the coal and iron-ore deposits, not far from one another or from the sea, and stimulated by a rapid influx of foreign capital. Within a short period of time on the territory of Southern Ukraine arose two of the largest centers of heavy industry in Eastern Europe, the *Donets Basin (bituminous coal mining, metal smelting, and chemical industries) and the *Dnieper Industrial Region (including the cities of Katerynoslav, Oleksandrivske, Kryvyi Rih, and Nykopil and specializing in the mining of iron and manganese ores, metal smelting, and machine building). Of secondary significance were the industrial cities of Mariiupil and Kerch. Meanwhile the seaports, notably Odessa, Mykolaiv, Kherson, and Sevastopil, grew in industrial importance as they became sites of shipbuilding, food processing, machine building (especially for agriculture), and other branches of industry that used imported raw materials. As ports they were important centers of trade and commerce.

The ethnic composition of the population in Southern Ukraine, the most varied in all Ukrainian lands, changed over time. Until 1820 the influx of Ukrainians was by far the strongest. Later the inflow of Jews and, especially after 1880, of Russians markedly increased (see table 1).

Odessa and Katerynoslav emerged as the main cultural centers in Southern Ukraine. Lower on the scale of significance were Yelysavethrad, Kherson, and other towns.

The First World War and especially the Revolution of 1917 brought about an economic decline in Southern Ukraine. Foreign trade came to a standstill, and the port cities declined. During 1918–20 Southern Ukraine was a battleground for the armies of the Ukrainian National Republic, the Bolsheviks, the French, the Whites led by A. *Denikin and later P. *Wrangel, and the detachments of the anarchist N. *Makhno, as well as other insurgent forces. Ukraine incorporated Kherson, Katerynoslav, and Tavriia gubernias, although the Crimean Peninsula became an autonomous republic within the RSFSR. The western part of the former Don Cossack lands also went to Ukraine, but by 1924 Tahanrih and Shakhty counties had been transferred to the RSFSR. In the west, part of Bessarabia was occupied by Rumania.

During 1919–20 the heavy industry of Southern Ukraine collapsed. The sown area had declined to one-half its prewar levels by 1921–2, and the grain harvest to one-quarter by 1921, a drought year; the result was famine. Livestock declined to two-thirds of its 1916 level.

The national composition of the population changed between 1910 and the 1920s, with an increased number of Ukrainians and a decreased number of Germans, Jews, and Russians. The Ukrainian presence grew most markedly in the agricultural steppe but diminished in the Donets Basin, which continued to register an in-migration of Russians.

The development of Southern Ukraine was interrupted once more by the Second World War. Political borders again underwent change. In 1940 the southern part of Bessarabia was annexed by Ukraine, and until 1954 it formed Izmail oblast (subsequently it became part of Odessa oblast). The western portion of the Moldavian ASSR, settled by Rumanians, was ceded by the Ukrainian SSR to the newly formed Moldavian SSR. In 1946 the Crimean ASSR was transformed into an ordinary oblast which, in 1954, was transferred from the RSFSR to the Ukrainian SSR. After frequent changes in the economic regionalization of the USSR, stabilization was achieved in 1962, and Southern Ukraine was defined to include all of the South region (Crimea, Kherson, Mykolaiv, and Odessa oblasts) and most of the Donets-Dnieper region (Dnipropetrovske, Donetske, Kirovohrad, Luhanske, and Zaporizhia oblasts).

The population of Southern Ukraine as just defined reached 23.2 million on 1 January 1990. (At the end of the 18th century it was about 1 million, and in the mid-19th century 2.5 million, but by 1897 it had grown to 6.7 million, by 1926 to 11.4 million, and by 1959 to 17.2 million.) The population growth rate of Southern Ukraine has been considerably higher than that of the rest of Ukraine, and the region's share of Ukraine's population has grown continually: from 23 percent in 1897 (still within the Russian Empire) to 30 percent in 1926, 41 percent in 1959, and 45 percent in 1990. Fully 78 percent of the people in Southern Ukraine live in cities or urban-type settlements, compared to only 22 percent in 1926.

The distribution of the population is not uniform. Population densities are highest in the two industrial regions, around Odessa, and along the southwestern coast of the Crimea, where dense clusters of cities, urban-type settlements, and suburbs abound. Rural population densities are related to natural conditions (soil fertility and moisture availability) and have not changed much since 1897, except for an increase in northern Crimea, where irrigation has been introduced. The distribution of population as of 1 January 1987 is shown in table 2. The growth of population has also been uneven. Since the 1930s the urban population has increased rapidly, and the rural population has generally declined (see table 3). As in all of Ukraine, the ethnic composition of the urban population differs from that of the rural population. Notably, Ukrainians are largely overrepresented (75.3 percent in 1970) in the rural population category.

TABLE 1
Ethnic composition of Southern Ukraine, 1897

Ethnic group	1,000s	%
Ukrainians	3,535	59.0
Russians	1,196	20.0
Jews	372	6.2
Germans	290	4.8
Rumanians (Moldavians)	198	3.3
Bulgarians	113	1.9
Greeks	57	0.9
Others	232	3.9
Total	5,993	100.0

TABLE 2
Population of Southern Ukraine by region, 1987

Region	Total 1,000s	Total per sq km	Urban 1,000s	Urban % of total	Rural 1,000s	Rural per sq km
Donets Basin	8,217	154.5	7,350	89.4	867	16.3
Dnieper Industrial	5,921	100.2	4,782	80.8	1,139	20.2
Southwest Steppe	6,392	57.6	4,076	63.8	2,316	20.9
Crimea	2,397	88.8	1,671	69.7	726	26.9
Total	22,927	91.6	17,879	78.0	5,048	20.2

TABLE 3
Rural and urban population of Southern Ukraine (in thousands), 1926–87

Year	Total	Urban	Rural
1926	11,440	2,840	8,600
1959	17,186	11,195	5,991
1987	22,927	17,879	5,048

The present distribution of population (density of settlement) is shown on the map. The ethnic composition of the population is shown in table 4.

In the 1880s the steppes of Southern Ukraine became completely plowed. Since then land use has not changed significantly. The present land uses are shown in table 5. Lands held by agricultural enterprises, which account for 85 percent of the entire land area, are mostly devoted to agricultural land uses, as shown in table 7.

The sown area of Southern Ukraine represents 45 percent of the sown area of Ukraine. The structure of the sown area in Southern Ukraine is indicated in table 6. The main grain crops of Southern Ukraine, their significance among all the grains of the region, and their share of the sown areas in Ukraine are illustrated in table 8. The number of livestock (as of 1 January 1976) and the livestock

TABLE 4
Ethnic composition of the population of Southern Ukraine, 1926–79 (total population in thousands; percentage of total in parentheses)

Ethnic group	1979		1970		1926	
Ukrainians	12,852	(58.8)	12,377	(60.7)	–	(65.5)
Russians	7,587	(34.7)	6,633	(32.5)	–	(17.8)
Jews	275	(1.3)	321	(1.6)	–	(5.4)
Belarusians	269	(1.2)	263	(1.3)	–	(0.5)
Bulgarians	222	(1.0)	219	(1.1)	–	(1.3)
Rumanians	172	(0.8)	170	(0.8)	–	(1.7)
Greeks	93	(0.4)	96	(0.5)	–	(0.9)
Tatars	61	(0.3)	53	(0.3)	–	(1.9)
Poles	35	(0.2)	40	(0.2)	–	(0.5)
Gagauzy	27	(0.1)	24	(0.1)	–	(0.1)
Others	248	(1.1)	204	(1.0)	–	(4.4)
Total	21,841	(100.0)	20,400	(100.0)	–	(100.0)

TABLE 5
Land uses of Southern Ukraine, 1 November 1982

	Million ha	%
Agricultural land uses	19.4	77.6
Plowland	15.9	63.6
Hayfields and pastures	2.9	11.6
Orchards, vineyards, and berry plantings	0.6	2.4
Forests and woodlots	1.7	6.8
Other	3.9	15.6
Total land area	25.0	100.0

TABLE 7
Land uses of agricultural enterprises in Southern Ukraine, 1 November 1982

	Million ha	%
Agricultural land uses	19.1	89.7
Plowland	15.9	74.7
Pastures	2.5	11.7
Hayfields	0.1	0.5
Orchards, vineyards, and berry plantings	0.6	2.8
Forests and woodlots (estimate)	1.2	5.6
Other (estimate)	1.0	4.7
Total held by agricultural enterprises	21.3	100.0

TABLE 8
Main grain crops of Southern Ukraine (sown areas in 1965 and 1975)

	1,000 ha		% of all grain		Share of Ukraine	
	1965	1975	1965	1975	1965	1975
Winter wheat	3,609	4,405	46.9	56.2	49.1	55.4
Spring barley	1,703	1,422	22.1	18.1	65.5	39.9
Corn for grain	1,030	667	13.4	8.5	56.7	53.5
All grain	7,701	7,843	100.0	100.0	46.7	47.4

density per 100 ha of agricultural land, with comparisons to the Ukrainian averages, are given in table 9. The annual output of animal products (the mean for 1971–5, inclusive) is given in table 10.

Southern Ukraine may be divided into several agricultural zones: (1) grain-oil seed, with the production of sugar beets and milk-meat animal husbandry, in the northern part of the steppe; (2) grain-oil seed, milk-meat animal husbandry, poultry farming, and fruit and vegetable gardening in the middle zone of the steppe; (3) grain-oil seed, fruit and vegetable gardening, melon growing, vineyard keeping, and milk-meat animal husbandry in the southern and Crimean steppe; (4) vineyard-orchard, tobacco, and vegetable growing, milk-meat animal husbandry, and sheep raising in the foothills of the Crimea and southern Crimea; and (5) milk production and fruit and vegetable growing in suburban areas in the Donets Basin, the Dnieper Industrial Region, and around large cities.

Industry. Possessing the largest supply of conveniently

TABLE 6
Sown area structure in Southern Ukraine, 1986

	Donets Basin		Dnieper Industrial Region		Southwest Steppe		Crimea		Total Southern Ukraine	
	1,000 ha	%	1,000 ha	%	1,000 ha	%	1,000 ha	%	1,000 ha	%
Grain	1,451	50.4	1,969	52.8	3,735	54.0	587	48.5	7,742	52.5
Technical crops	291	10.1	441	11.8	837	12.1	78	6.4	1,647	11.2
Potatoes and vegetables	156	5.4	172	4.6	300	4.3	43	3.6	671	4.6
Feed crops	980	34.1	1,149	30.8	2,046	29.6	503	41.5	4,678	31.7
Total sown	2,878	100.0	3,731	100.0	6,918	100.0	1,211	100.0	14,738	100.0

TABLE 9
Livestock in Southern Ukraine, 1976

	1,000s	As % of Ukraine	Units/100 ha of agricultural land	
			South Ukr	Ukraine
Cattle	9,065	37.5	47.2	57.3
Cows	3,188	35.5	16.6	21.3
Pigs	7,168	42.5	37.3	39.9
Sheep and goats	5,682	62.3	29.6	21.6

TABLE 10
Farm output of animal products (mean production; thousand tonnes), 1971–5

	1,000 t	As % of Ukraine	T/100 ha agricultural land	
			South Ukr	Ukraine
Meat and fat	1,219	37.2	6.3	7.8
Pork	560	37.1	2.9	3.6
Milk	7,543	37.0	39.3	48.2
Wool	17.99	67.6	0.09	0.06

located extractable mineral reserves in Eastern Europe, and having developed both heavy industry and other derivative, more complex branches of industry on the basis of those reserves, Southern Ukraine is the most industrialized part of Ukraine and one of the most highly industrialized regions in what was the Soviet Union. In 1968 it produced 185.2 million t of bituminous coal in the Donets Basin (93 percent of the Ukrainian output, 31 percent of the USSR output), 8 million t of lignite (from part of the Dnieper Lignite Coal Basin), 87.8 million t of iron ore (from Kryvyi Rih and Kerch, accounting for all of the republic's production and 55 percent of the USSR's), and 4.8 million t of manganese ore (from the Nykopil Manganese-ore Basin, contributing all of the republic's and 56 percent of the USSR's output). Ferrous metallurgy in the Donets Basin, Mariiupil (formerly Zhdanov), and the Dnieper Industrial Region contributed 36.7 million t of pig iron (all of the republic's and 49 percent of the USSR's output), 42.8 million t of steel (all of the republic's and 42 percent of the USSR's output), and 30.6 million t of rolled metal (all of the republic's and 43 percent of the USSR's output). Southern Ukraine also provided all the nonferrous metallurgy of Ukraine (notably aluminum smelting in Zaporizhia), almost all its heavy-machine building (Donets Basin, Dnieper Industrial Region), and almost all the shipbuilding (in the seaports). Agricultural-machine building also was important. The region led Ukraine in the production of chemicals, especially coke-chemicals (100 percent of the country's production), sulfuric acid, caustic soda, mineral fertilizers, paints, synthetic tars, and plastics (all in the Donets Basin, the Dnieper Industrial Region, and Odessa). Southern Ukraine also produced about two-thirds of the electric power in Ukraine. The largest generating stations are found in the Donets Basin (thermal), the Dnieper (hydro as well as thermal), and Odessa (thermal). In addition four nuclear reactor complexes were to be built: near Zaporizhia, on the Boh River (the South Ukrainian), near Odessa, and in the Crimea (the plans for the Odessa and

the Crimea nuclear plants have been canceled). Of considerable significance is the preparation of building materials (Donets Basin, Dnieper Industrial Region, Crimea, Odessa), especially cement. The food-processing and textile industries are also important, particularly in the southwest steppe.

BIBLIOGRAPHY
Lebedintsev, A. *Khanskaia Ukraina* (Odessa 1913)
Bahalii, D. *Zaselennia Pivdennoï Ukraïny* (Kharkiv 1920)
Stepova Ukraïna: Ekonomichno-heohrafichni narysy (Kharkiv 1929)
Ohloblyn, O. *Narysy z istoriï kapitalizmu na Ukraïni*, 1 (Kiev–Kharkiv 1931)
Polons'ka-Vasylenko, N. *The Settlement of the Southern Ukraine (1750–1775)* (New York 1955)
Khizhniak, A. *Nizhnee Pridneprov'e* (Moscow 1956)
Druzhinina, E. *Severnoe Prichernomor'e v 1775–1800 gg.* (Moscow 1959)
Polons'ka-Vasylenko, N. *Zaselennia Pivdennoï Ukraïny v polovyni XVIII st. (1734–1775)*, 2 vols (Munich 1960)
— *Zaporizhzhia XVIII stolittia ta ioho spadshchyna*, 2 vols (Munich 1965, 1967)
Druzhinina, E. *Iuzhnaia Ukraina v 1800–1825 gg.* (Moscow 1970)
Kabuzan, V. *Narodonaselenie Bessarabskoi oblasti i levoberezhnykh raionov Pridnestrov'ia (konets XVIII–pervaia polovina XIX v.)* (Kishinev 1974)
— *Zaselenie Novorossii (Ekaterinoslavskoi i Khersonskoi gubernii) v XVIII–pervoi polovine XIX veka (1719–1858 gg.)* (Moscow 1976)
Zelenchuk, V. *Naselenie Bessarabii i Podnestrov'ia v XIX v. (Etnicheskie i sotsial'no-demograficheskie protsessy)* (Kishinev 1979)
      V. Kubijovyč, Ya. Pasternak, M. Arkas, M. Zhdan, N. Polonska-Vasylenko, O. Ohloblyn, I. Stebelsky

Southwestern Branch of the Imperial Russian Geographic Society (Russian: Yugo-zapadnyi otdel Imperatorskogo russkogo geograficheskogo obshchestva). A virtually independent learned association established in Kiev on 13 February 1873 to conduct geographic, ethnographic, economic, and statistical research in Ukraine. Unlike other regional branches of the imperial Russian society, such as the East Siberian, West Siberian, and Caucasian, the Southwestern branch left archeological and historical research to other, already-established learned societies in Kiev. Most of the founders and key members of the association were members of the Old *Hromada of Kiev, including V. Antonovych, V. Berenshtam, F. Vovk, M. Drahomanov, P. Zhytetsky, O. Lashkevych, M. Lysenko, and O. Rusov. The first president was Hryhorii *Galagan, and the managing director was P. *Chubynsky.

The scholarly output of the association over the brief period of its existence is impressive. It published two volumes of *Zapiski* (1874–5) containing studies by O. Klosovsky, M. Yasnopolsky, O. Rohovych, and M. Levchenko as well as the aforementioned members. As supplements to the periodical, it published a collection of O. Veresai's dumas and songs, Rohovych's bibliography of naturalist studies of the Kiev school district (1874), H. Kupchanko's materials on Bukovyna, and a folk-song collection. It supported the publication of I. Rudchenko's collection of chumak songs (1874), Drahomanov and Antonovych's collection of historical songs (1874–5), and the preparation for print of Drahomanov's collection of folk legends and stories (1876) and of M. Maksymovych's collected works (1876–80). The society conducted a voluntary census of Kiev in March 1874 and published an analysis with its results (1875). In August 1874 it participated in the Third Archeological Congress, which it had helped organize in

Kiev, and in March 1875, in a geographic congress and exhibition in Paris. The society set up a library and museum that displayed artifacts collected during field expeditions by its members and sponsored a public lecture series on various aspects of Ukrainian life. Finally, some of its members gained editorial control over the newspaper *Kievskii telegraf* and often ran articles on Ukrainian themes.

The accomplishments of the society and its success in generating interest in Ukrainian studies aroused the suspicion of Russian chauvinists. Starting in 1874, denunciations of the society arrived in the Third Section of the police in St Petersburg. The denunciations became more numerous and extreme when Antonovych was elected president and Chubynsky vice-president of the society, in May 1875. In his memorandum the curator of the Kiev school district, M. *Yuzefovych, who at first had been a strong supporter and an influential member of the association, accused the members of the society of political sedition and separatism. As a result an imperial commission was established in September 1875 to study the whole Ukrainian situation. Its recommendation of further repressive measures was approved by Alexander II and is known as the *Ems Ukase. The Southwestern Branch was dissolved in June 1876, and Chubynsky was forced to leave Kiev. According to the secret ukase, the society could be renewed if all the former members were excluded from it.

In spite of its short life the Southwestern Branch made an important contribution to the Ukrainian national revival. Not only did it publish some valuable scholarly works and monuments of the oral tradition, it also brought together a group of Ukrainian scholars and civic leaders who spearheaded the national movement until the end of the century.

BIBLIOGRAPHY

Zhytets'kyi, I. 'Pivdenno-zakhidnyi viddil Heohrafichnoho tovarystva u Kyievi,' *Ukraïna*, 1927, no. 5
Savchenko, F. *Zaborona ukraïnstva 1876* (Kiev–Kharkiv 1930; repr, Munich 1970)

B. Kravtsiv

Southwestern dialects. A group consisting of the Podilian, South Volhynian, Dniester, Sian, Lemko, Transcarpathian, Hutsul, and Bukovyna-Pokutia dialects. Together with the group of *southeastern dialects (the boundary between the two groups runs along the line Khvastiv–Pervomaiske–Tyraspil), they form the basic southern group of Ukrainian dialects. The dialects differ from the *northern dialects in the change, independently of stress, of the ancient vowels $\bar{o}$, $\bar{e}$ into i (u, $\ddot{u}$, 'u, '$\ddot{u}$ in the subdialects of the Carpathian region), $\check{e}$ into 'i, and $ę$ into 'a ('e ['y], 'i in the subdialects of Bukovyna and central Galicia), and in morphological, syntactic, and lexical peculiarities. They differ from the southeastern dialects in retaining many phonetic and morphological archaisms and allowing fewer phonetic innovations.

Southwestern Economic Region of the USSR. See Regional economics.

Southwestern land (Russian: Yugo-zapadnyi krai). An administrative territory set up by the Russian government in Right-Bank Ukraine in 1832. Known officially as Kiev general gubernia, it consisted of Kiev, Podilia, and Volhynia gubernias and existed until 1917. The designation 'southwestern' was in the context of the territory of the Russian Empire, and 'Yugo-Zapadnaia Rossiia' (Southwestern Russia) was also frequently used to refer to Russian-ruled Ukraine (eg, *Arkhiv Iugo-Zapadnoi Rossii*). That

centralist Russian viewpoint remained in the terminology of the Soviet administration, wherein names such as 'Pivdenno-zakhidnyi ekonomichnyi raion SSSR' (Southwestern Economic Region of the USSR) were used to refer to Ukraine.

Southwestern Railroad. See Railroad transportation.

Sova, Andrii, b 30 December 1912 in Odessa. Film actor and reciter. He completed study at the Odessa Theater College (1938) and then worked in the Odessa (1938–41) and Kiev (1944–50) artistic film studios and the Kiev Philharmonic Society Ukrconcert (1951–9) and became known as a reciter in the genre of satirical miniature (1959–79). He acted in the films *Taiemnychyi ostriv* (The Mysterious Island, 1940) and *V dalekomu plavanni* (On a Distant Sea Voyage, 1945).

Sova, Petro, b 1894 in Nové Zamky, Komárno county, Slovakia, d ? Russophile Transcarpathian historian and civic figure. After graduating from the Law Academy in Prešov he worked for the Czechoslovakian civil service as a department head in the Uzhhorod regional branch of the Ministry of Education and as a cultural attaché in the governor's office. He was also a city council member and vice-mayor (1924–7) of Uzhhorod and a founding member of the Russian National Autonomist party. As deputy head of the People's Council of Transcarpathian Ukraine (1944–5) he led a campaign to support the Soviet annexation of Transcarpathia after the Second World War. Sova wrote a number of regional studies, including *Proshloe Uzhgoroda* (Uzhhorod's Past, 1937) and *Arkhitekturnye pamiatniki Zakarpat'ia* (Architectural Monuments of Transcarpathia, 1958). He also translated *Slovo o polku Ihorevi* (The Tale of Ihor's Campaign) into Hungarian.

Sova (Owl). A Russophile satirical paper published in 1871 in Uzhhorod (three issues) and Budapest (two issues). The journal was founded by the prominent Transcarpathian Russophile E. Hrabar. Edited by V. Kimak, it satirized the *Magyarone clergy in Transcarpathia.

Sovacheva, Hanna [Sovačeva], b 7 December 1877 in Pryluka, Poltava gubernia, d 7 July 1954 in Abondant, near Paris. Character and comic actress, singer (mezzo-soprano), and stage director. After completing study at the Lysenko Music and Drama School in Kiev, she worked in the Kiev Opera House and was active in the drama circle of the Kiev Hromada. She joined the State Drama Theater in 1918 and then worked in the Ruska Besida Theater in Lviv (1921–3), the Ruthenian Theater of the Prosvita Society in Uzhhorod (1923–31), the Tobilevych Theater (1932–3), the Zahrava and Kotliarevsky theaters (1934–9), the Lesia Ukrainka Drama Theater (1939–41), and the Lviv Opera House (1941–4). After the Second World War she lived in Austria and, from 1949, in France. She led a Ukrainian troupe in Salzburg in 1945–9.

Sovachiv, Vasyl [Sovačiv, Vasyl'], b 1876 in Pryluka, Poltava gubernia, d 3 May 1924 in Slyvky, Kalush county, Galicia. Army physician and civic activist. As a medical student in Kiev he was president of the Young Hromada for five years. He served as an army doctor in the Russo-Japanese War and in the First World War. After returning to Kiev in 1917, he worked in the local hospitals and was active in the Ukrainian Democratic Agrarian party. With the UNR Directory's evacuation from Kiev to Vinnytsia, he was appointed chief of the Sanitary Administration of the UNR Army. Later he was a member of the chief executive of the Ukrainian Red Cross. In the 1920s he worked as a physician in the health resort of Pidliute, near Kalush.

Cover of the publication of the 1990 declaration of Ukraine's sovereignty, signed by members of Ukraine's parliament

Sovereignty. The legal and political concept that deals with ultimate authority in the decision-making process of the state. In international law it is the freedom of a state from outside interference in administering its internal and external affairs. Sovereignty is a fundamental principle of international legal relations and the essential property of a modern state. The source and locus of sovereignty may be a monarch or dictator or, as in democratic states, the people. In totalitarian regimes a single political party exercises sovereign powers. Relations of vassalage, protection, or union between states entail a limitation or loss of sovereignty.

The Ukrainian Hetman state of the 17th to 18th century enjoyed only partial sovereignty. The new states of the 19th to 20th centuries gained sovereignty by claiming the right to *self-determination. The Central Rada, acting as a sovereign power, proclaimed the establishment of the UNR

Hanna Sovacheva

Vasyl Sovachiv

in the Third Universal (20 November 1917) and the republic's complete sovereignty in the Fourth Universal (22 January 1918). According to the latter, full sovereignty belongs to the Ukrainian people. The unilateral declaration of sovereignty gave Ukraine the right to enter into international relations. Its sovereignty was recognized by several states: the Central Powers in the Peace Treaty of Brest-Litovsk, Soviet Russia in the same treaty and in the peace agreement of 12 June 1918, and Poland in the Treaty of Warsaw.

The state organs of the Ukrainian SSR claimed sovereignty, beginning with the Declaration of the Rights of the Nations of Russia (15 November 1917) and continuing to the union agreement between the Ukrainian SSR and the Russian SSR (28 December 1920). Ukraine's agreements with Poland, the Baltic states, and others also presupposed this principle. In reality, however, the Ukrainian SSR had only nominal sovereignty, for it remained under the control of Soviet Russia and was used as a tool of Soviet foreign policy. In a formal sense Ukraine continued to exist as a separate state, but real sovereignty belonged to the central government in Moscow and the Russian Communist party.

The declaration and agreement on the establishment of the USSR in 1922 stressed the sovereignty of the new Union republics, but this sovereignty was even more fictitious than before. The powers of the republics were minimal, and control over international relations was completely assumed by the USSR. The only attribute that could support the theoretical sovereignty of the republics was their right of secession from the USSR, which was guaranteed in all Soviet constitutions. As further proofs of sovereignty, Soviet jurists pointed to the 'voluntary' entry of the republics into the USSR, the impossibility that the territory of the republics could be altered without their consent, and the restoration of some prerogatives in foreign affairs to the republics in 1944. According to the Soviet view the most important sovereign rights of the Ukrainian SSR were the right to enter into international treaties and agreements and the right to exchange diplomatic and consular envoys with other countries. As a result of these changes, the Ukrainian SSR and the Belorussian SSR acquired a partial international status, but not sovereignty. (See *International legal status of Ukraine.)

The Soviet doctrine of sovereignty was complex and eclectic. In the international arena the USSR defended sovereignty as a hard and inalienable principle which included noninterference in the domestic affairs of the USSR and the members of the Soviet bloc, their equality, and their territorial integrity, but the USSR regarded anticolonial and national liberation movements as expressions of popular sovereignty, and therefore claimed the right to support them. Limiting of the state powers of the Union republics was interpreted as the joint exercise of the sovereign rights of the Union and the republics. Soviet theory described sovereignty as 'one whole' in which there could be no conflict between Union and republican sovereignty. The theory of the 'unity of sovereignty' had replaced the doctrine of 'dual sovereignty' only in the latter years of the USSR. A modified version of this doctrine applied to members of the Soviet bloc, which were said to exercise sovereignty vis-à-vis foreign states in solidarity and with the assistance of the USSR. The so-called Brezhnev doctrine, which was invoked to justify Soviet intervention in Czechoslovakia in 1968, rested on this definition of limited sovereignty. Matters were further complicated by the unilateral declaration of Ukraine's sovereignty on 16 July 1990 by the elected government of the republic. Up to its dissolution in 1991 the Union government had ignored such declarations in most of the republics.

BIBLIOGRAPHY
Paliienko, M. *Problema suverenitetu suchasnoï derzhavy* (Kharkiv 1929)
Deklaratsiia pro derzhavnyi suverenitet Ukraïny (Kiev 1990)

V. Markus

Sovetskaia Ukraina. See *Pravda Ukrainy* and *Raduga*.

Soviet (Russian: *sovet*; Ukrainian: *rada* 'council'). The basic institution of government, with both legislative and executive functions, in the USSR. Soviets controlled all other government institutions at every administrative-territorial level.

The first soviets in the Russian Empire arose spontaneously during the Revolution of 1905 as workers' strike councils. They appeared in the larger industrial cities, including Kiev, Katerynoslav, and Mykolaiv in Ukraine. The method for choosing their delegates, their internal rules of order, and their powers differed greatly from soviet to soviet. Most leftist political parties were represented in the soviets. Formally the bodies were usually called soviets of workers' deputies.

Within a month after the February Revolution of 1917 about 600 soviets sprang up in the gubernia cities and industrial centers of the empire. Initially they included representatives from a wide range of leftist parties and were usually dominated by Socialist Revolutionaries (especially in rural areas) or Mensheviks. In many instances the soviets acted as alternative parliaments or forums and won considerable popular support. At first the Bolsheviks were a small minority in most soviets and advocated 'all power to the soviets.' At the First All-Russian Congress of Soviets, held in June 1917, only 10 percent of the delegates were Bolsheviks. The second congress, held after the Bolshevik coup in November 1917, was taken over by the Bolsheviks after most of the other parties withdrew in protest. This body elected the Bolshevik-dominated All-Russian Central Executive Commitee, which in January 1918 dispersed the *All-Russian Constituent Assembly and proclaimed the transfer of all power to the soviets.

In Ukraine the *All-Ukrainian Congress of Workers', Soldiers', and Peasants' Deputies, which convened in Kiev on 17–19 December 1917, endorsed the Central Rada. The Bolshevik delegates rejected this action, however, and left Kiev for Kharkiv to join an alternate congress of soviets from the Kryvyi Rih and Donets Basin. Calling itself the *All-Ukrainian Congress of Soviets, this body proclaimed Soviet rule in Ukraine and established the *All-Ukrainian Central Executive Committee (VUTsVK). Ukrainian democratic and nationalist parties generally rejected the soviet system of government on the grounds that it gave too much power to Russian or Russified workers and soldiers at the expense of the peasantry; they advocated a single parliament elected on the basis of universal suffrage. Eventually the Bolsheviks, with the support of the *Borotbists and then the *Ukrainian Communist party, were able to establish soviet power throughout the cities and towns of Ukraine. At the same time they were able to assert their authority over rural soviets, most of which had been organized and controlled by the Ukrainian Party of Socialist Revolutionaries.

Beginning in 1919–20 an entire system of soviets was constructed in Ukraine. At the base of the pyramid, rural, town, and city soviets were elected by local inhabitants. In 1925 there were 10,314 rural, 155 town, and 70 city soviets. At the higher levels elections were indirect: local soviets sent delegates to raion soviets, which in turn sent delegates to gubernia (to 1925), okruha, and oblast (from 1932) soviets. Even the All-Ukrainian Congress of Soviets, the highest legislative body in Ukraine, was elected on an indirect basis by the okruha (later oblast) soviets. Soviet elections were closely controlled by the Party and dominated by workers and soldiers, who were disproportionately represented (in 1920, for every 1,000 soldiers, 10,000 urban workers, and 50,000 peasants the gubernia and city congresses of soviets sent one delegate to the All-Ukrainian Congress). The soviets were required by law to meet for a certain length of time a set number of times a year (usually two). They elected their own executive committees, which had executive authority between sessions of the soviet. Central control over the soviets was assured by the subordination of local soviets and executive committees to their higher counterparts all the way up to the VUTsVK and the All-Ukrainian Congress of Soviets. Decisions of lower bodies which were deemed unconstitutional or contradictory could be overturned by higher bodies, and the instructions-circulars and orders of higher bodies were mandatory for lower ones. In the 1920s a degree of decentralization was preserved: the administrative personnel of the soviets was elected (although the Party in practice controlled the process); within their territory and competency local soviets were the highest authority; and the soviets controlled their own assets and budgets, which were set by them and only ratified by the higher bodies.

The 1936 Constitution abolished the indirect electoral system and the unequal vote (although the 'dictatorship of the proletariat' remained a feature of Soviet political theory for many years) and introduced a system of direct elections to soviets at all levels. It also established the *Supreme Soviet of the Ukrainian SSR as the republic's highest legislative body. In 1985 there were 9,431 rural, 121 urban district, 421 town, 479 raion, and 25 oblast soviets in Ukraine, with a total of over 526,000 deputies. Elections to local soviets were held every two and a half years (formerly every two years); the Supreme Soviet was elected every five (formerly four) years. All citizens over the age of 18 were eligible and expected to vote. Candidates were usually nominated by the Party or some allied organization to ensure communist domination. Until the reforms initiated by M. Gorbachev, only one candidate per electoral district was permitted.

At every level soviets elected their own executive committees to exercise executive power between sessions of the soviet. In theory the soviets were responsible for certain services in their districts, including housing, social security, public works, food distribution, cultural affairs, and the police. In reality they had very little authority. They were severely restricted by plans and budgets set by the central planners and authorities. Although they could make reports and recommendations to the higher authorities, they had little influence on the planning. Many enterprises and institutions within a local district were directly subordinated to central (Union, Union-republi-

can, and republican) ministries and were beyond the control of the local soviet. In the last few years of the USSR there was a strong demand for decentralization.

BIBLIOGRAPHY
Hazard, J.N. *The Soviet System of Government* (Chicago 1957)
Scott, D.J.R. *Russian Political Institutions* (London 1958)

B. Balan

Soviet Army (Russian: Sovetskaia Armiia; Ukrainian: Radianska Armiia). The regular army of the USSR, known until September 1946 as the Workers' and Peasants' Red Army or simply the Red Army. It was established by decree of the Soviet government on 28 January 1918 out of Red Guard Detachments. The Bolshevik troops that brought Ukraine under Soviet control in 1918–20 were generally Russian in national composition. They received support from Ukrainian or partly Ukrainian units, such as the *Red Cossacks, the *Tarashcha Division, and the Bohun Regiment, and occasional help from partisan groups led by N. Makhno, N. Hryhoriiv, and D. Zeleny. For a while (January–April 1920) Galicians formed their own unit, the *Red Ukrainian Galician Army, within the Red Army. The Communist commander of the Ukrainian front, V. Antonov-Ovsiienko, was responsible to Moscow, not to the Bolshevik government of Ukraine in Kharkiv. The People's Commissariat for Military Affairs in Kharkiv had no real power and was abolished in 1919.

The Ukrainian SSR never had its own army. In the 1920s, territorial divisions consisting of Ukrainians and using Ukrainian as the language of command constituted a militia and were stationed in the larger cities. Except for the Red Cossacks, stationed near Proskuriv, Starokostiantyniv, and Berdychiv, regular army units in Ukraine were of mixed national composition, and used Russian. Most Ukrainians in the regular forces were stationed outside Ukraine. The commander of the Ukrainian-Crimean Military District was responsible not to the government of the Ukrainian SSR, but to Moscow. With the abolition of the territorial units (1934) and the division of Ukraine into three military districts (1938), Ukraine was integrated even more closely into the all-Union military system. By 1937 Russian became the language of command in all military units. Also, the military traditions of the imperial Russian army (eg, officer ranks, uniforms, insignia) were gradually reintroduced.

During the Second World War, 4.5 million Ukrainians served in the Red Army. Except for the First Ukrainian Partisan Division (est 1943) under Col P. *Vershigora, there were no separate Ukrainian units in the Soviet armed forces. Because of national discrimination, non-Russians refused at first to fight the German invaders: of 3.6 million Soviet prisoners of war by March 1943, 2 million were non-Russian. The harsh treatment of the population and POWs by the Germans eventually persuaded non-Russians to fight. Approx 1.7 million Ukrainians were decorated for bravery in the war. In 1943 the Bohdan Khmelnytsky Medal was introduced, and in 1944 a People's Commissariat of Defense was established for Ukraine (with Gen S. Kovpak as the first commissar), but this was only a symbolic gesture.

After the war the Soviet Army remained an integrated multinational force. The territory of Ukraine was reorganized into three military districts (Kiev, Odessa, and Subcarpathia), and Donetske and Luhanske oblasts were assigned to the Northern Caucasia Military District. Because of its geographic location along the western border of the USSR and on the Black Sea, Ukraine was strategically important. It was the home of the Black Sea Fleet, major air-fields near Zhytomyr, and missile bases in the Carpathians.

The Soviet Army was an instrument of Russification. Its medium of communication was exclusively Russian; all of its recreational, cultural, and press activities were in Russian as well. Conscripts spent their term of service outside their own republics, and demobilized servicemen were encouraged to live and work in new settlements, mostly in the east. Political education in the army promoted Russian chauvinism and glorified Russian military heroes. Besides national discrimination, the army suffered from a rigid caste system similar to that of the tsarist army. The officers were separated sharply from the common soldiers by material privileges, uniforms, honors, and statutes.

In its Declaration on State Sovereignty (16 July 1990) the Supreme Soviet of the Ukrainian SSR stated its intention to nationalize the army in Ukraine. As the first step toward implementing this proclamation it demanded that all Ukrainians serving in the Soviet armed forces be stationed in Ukraine by 1 December 1990.

BIBLIOGRAPHY
Zakharov, V. (ed). 50 let vooruzhennykh sil SSSR (Moscow 1968)
Avidar, Y. The Party and the Army in the Soviet Union (Jerusalem 1983)
Seaton, A; Seaton, J. The Soviet Army, 1918 to the Present (London 1986)
Hagen, M. von Soldiers in the Proletarian Dictatorship (Ithaca, NY 1990)

L. Shankovsky

Soviet partisans in Ukraine, 1941–5.

In Ukraine, Soviet partisans played a less important role in the Soviet war effort against the Germans than they did in other parts of the Soviet Union. Recruited from Party cadres left behind the German lines, escapees from German POW camps, and refugees from the German terror, they found little support among the population and, except for the northeastern region, no suitable terrain for their operations.

At the end of June 1941, immediately after the Germans crossed the Soviet border, the Central Committee of the All-Union Communist Party (Bolshevik) ordered Party members to organize an underground on occupied territories. In 1941 underground cells sprang up in a few Ukrainian cities, but most Party members ignored the order. The first partisan detachments appeared in Chernihiv and Sumy oblasts. They developed out of M. Popudrenko's and S. *Kovpak's underground groups, which were joined by small army units that broke through the German encirclement of the Soviet forces east of Kiev. It was only in the spring of 1942, when these partisans established a radio link with Moscow and received special reinforcements dropped by parachute, that they began to show some activity. Apart from two other partisan detachments, which sprang up at the end of 1941 and were quickly wiped out by the Germans, one (500 men) in the Nykopil and Kryvyi Rih regions and the other (400 men) in the eastern Dnipropetrovske region, there were no other Soviet partisans in Ukraine at the time. A significant partisan movement developed by the spring of 1942 in oc-cupied Belarusian and southwestern Russian territories, where 80 percent of the Soviet partisan activity was concentrated. In Ukraine, Soviet partisans achieved a significant strength only in mid-1943.

Soviet partisans came under the Ministry of State Security, not under the defense ministry. On 30 May 1942 the Central Staff of the USSR Partisan Movement was set up in Moscow, and on 20 June the CC CP(B)U established the Ukrainian Staff of the Partisan Movement in Voroshylovhrad. The nominal chief of the Ukrainian Staff was N. *Khrushchev, but its actual chief was T. Strokach, deputy commissar of the NKVD of the Ukrainian SSR. On its orders S. Kovpak and A. Saburov conducted an extended raid in October 1942 to March 1943 from the Briansk forests into northern Ukraine. German troops in the region were sparse; hence, they encountered little resistance. Then, in May 1943, Kovpak was sent on a long raid from Putyvl across Volhynia to the Carpathian Mountains to cut German supply lines and to demonstrate Soviet power in Volhynia and Galicia, where UPA forces were forming. His force was crushed by the Germans at Deliatyn on 1 August, and some of its surviving bands were wiped out by the UPA. In spite of the losses, the raid had an important psychological effect on the Ukrainian population: it destroyed its belief in German invincibility. The returning survivors were assigned to the First Ukrainian Partisan Division under the command of P. *Vershigora, which in January–July 1944 conducted a raid from Volhynia through northwestern Galicia, the Kholm region, Podlachia, and Belarus. The other partisan raids in 1943 – led by M. Naumov in southern Ukraine and Ya. Melnyk and A. Fedorov in Right-Bank Ukraine and Volhynia – were less significant. V. Behma's and Col D. Medvedev's Soviet units were based in Volhynia, but their operations extended into adjacent regions. As the Red Army advanced through Ukraine the partisan movement grew rapidly. According to Soviet sources there were 13,300 partisans in Ukraine at the beginning and 43,500 at the end of 1943.

Small partisan units and Komsomol underground groups that arose spontaneously and had a distinctly national profile constituted a special branch of the Soviet partisan movement in Ukraine. They had no contact with the Ukrainian Staff and often were treated as hostile forces by the Soviets. For many years after the war, they were not recognized as Soviet partisans by Soviet authorities. The Young Guards in the Donbas, an underground group in Vinnytsia (arrested by the NKVD in 1944), a unit in the Chernihiv region (wiped out by Fedorov in March 1942), and Capt I. Kudria's group in the Dykanka forests are some examples of such groups.

At the beginning of 1944 the number of Soviet partisans in Ukraine rose to 47,800, or about 10 percent of the USSR total. Moving west in advance of the Red Army, the partisans assumed the role of a vanguard. The leading Soviet partisan units in Ukraine were under Vershigora, Naumov, I. Artiukhov, V. Shangin, and M. Shukaev. The last unit was defeated by the UPA in the Carpathians. The partisans pursued the Germans into Poland, where Vershigora's division distinguished itself, and into Czechoslovakia. The Ukrainian Staff directed the Soviet partisan movement until it was abolished on 1 June 1945.

BIBLIOGRAPHY
Klokov, V; Kulyk, I; Slynko, I. Narodna borot'ba na Ukraïni u roky Velykoï Vitchyznianoï viiny (Kiev 1957)

Armstrong, J. (ed). *Soviet Partisans in World War* II (Madison 1964)
Ukraïns'ka RSR u Velykii Vitchyznianii viini Radians'koho soiuzu 1941–1945, 3 vols (Kiev 1967–9)
Kucher, V. *Partyzans'ki kraï i zony na Ukraïni v roky Velykoï Vitchyznianoï viiny, 1941–1944* (Kiev 1974)
Cooper, M. *The Phantom War: The German Struggle against Soviet Partisans, 1941–1944* (London 1979)

A. Makuch, L. Shankovsky, Ye. Stakhiv

Soviet people (*radianskyi narod*). A concept of official Soviet *nationality policy which implied a total or near-total integration of the various nations and ethnic groups in the USSR. Concomitantly it implied their linguistic and cultural *Russification. Less often, in casual usage, 'Soviet people' was the synonym of *sovetskie liudi* (the Soviet population). The political and scholarly concept of the Soviet people was adumbrated under N. Khrushchev and was more fully developed under L. Brezhnev.

In an emotive, nonanalytical sense V. Lenin used *sovetskie liudi* in 1919, and J. Stalin spoke of the *sovetskii narod* in his patriotic appeals during the Second World War. It was N. Khrushchev, however, who first used 'Soviet people' in a more precise sense. At the 22nd CPSU Congress in 1961 he claimed that the Soviet people were a new historical multinational community sharing a common economic base, socialist fatherland, social-class structure, worldview (Marxism-Leninism), and goal (the building of communism) and many common mental traits. Khrushchev, however, soon stopped using the concept altogether.

For a number of internal political and external diplomatic-ideological reasons (such as competing pressures from non-Russians and Russian nationalist dissidents, the frontier war with China, and the competition with the Chinese leadership for influence in the world Communist movement), Brezhnev formally adopted the concept of the Soviet people, defined in terms similar to those used by Khrushchev, at the 24th CPSU Congress in 1971 and emphasized it during the 50th anniversary of the USSR in 1972. After the political and diplomatic-ideological crises ended in the mid-1970s, Brezhnev virtually dropped the use of the concept, in 1976 and 1977. An implicit reason for his caution was the opposition to the term 'Soviet people' in 1971 by republican leaders, including P. Shelest from Ukraine. The concept was also rejected by many Soviet scholars and was never fully defined. In the face of mounting pressure from the various national movements in the USSR, M. Gorbachev suspended use of the concept in September 1989, although he later made casual references to it on occasion.

Ya. Bilinsky

Soviet Progress in Chemistry. See *Ukraïns'kyi khimichnyi zhurnal*.

Sovietology. The interdisciplinary study of the Soviet Union, particularly of its political life, combining the methods of political science, history, economics, sociology, linguistics, and other sciences. Some Sovietologists have insisted that the field is sui generis, that it differs from French, German, or Italian studies because of the pervasiveness of politics in Soviet life and because of Soviet hostility to Western democracies. Others have questioned this claim. As recent events following Perestroika have shown, Sovietology has been too Russocentric and has not devoted sufficient attention to the non-Russian nationalities of the USSR.

The study of Soviet Ukraine, or 'Ukrainology,' is a branch of Sovietology. The coverage of Ukrainian affairs has been uneven: some periods, such as the period of the struggle for independence (1917–20) and the period since the outbreak of the Second World War, have received more attention than the important interwar years. The first comprehensive and up-to-date studies of the development of Soviet Ukraine were by C.A. Manning (*Ukraine under the Soviets*, 1953), B. Dmytryshyn (*Moscow and the Ukraine 1918–1953: A Study of Russian Bolshevik Nationality Policy*, 1956), and R. Sullivant (*Soviet Politics and the Ukraine, 1917–1957*, 1962). Yu. Lavrynenko's annotated bibliography (*Ukrainian Communism and Soviet Russian Policy toward the Ukraine: An Annotated Bibliography, 1917–1953*, 1953) can be described as a protohistory of Soviet Ukraine up to 1953. R. Szporluk's brief popular history of Ukraine (1979) and O. Subtelny's college textbook in Ukrainian history (1988) cover the Soviet period to the year of their publication. A social history of Ukraine spanning over 60 years of Soviet rule and focusing on the development of national consciousness has been written by B. Krawchenko (*Social Change and Consciousness in Twentieth-Century Ukraine*, 1985).

The revolutionary period of 1917–20 has been comprehensively dealt with by J.S. Reshetar, Jr (*The Ukrainian Revolution, 1917–1920: A Study in Nationalism*, 1952), J. Borys (*The Russian Communist Party and the Sovietization of Ukraine: A Study in the Communist Doctrine of the Self-Determination of Nations*, 1960; 2nd rev edn: *The Sovietization of Ukraine, 1917–1923*, 1980), and T. Hunczak, ed. (*The Ukraine, 1917–1921: A Study in Revolution*, 1977). It has also given rise to more specialized monographs by A.E. Adams (*Bolsheviks in the Ukraine: The Second Campaign*, 1963), O.S. Fedyshyn (*Germany's Drive to the East and the Ukrainian Revolution, 1917–1918*, 1971), I. Majstrenko (*Borot'bism: A Chapter in the History of Ukrainian Communism*, 1954), and M. Palij (*The Anarchism of Nestor Makhno, 1917–1921: An Aspect of the Ukrainian Revolution*, 1976). The first 15 years of Soviet rule have been analyzed by J.E. Mace (*Communism and the Dilemmas of National Liberation: National Communism in Soviet Ukraine, 1918–1933*, 1983).

The most important specialized studies about the 1930s are R. Conquest's monograph (*The Harvest of Sorrow: Soviet Collectivization and the Terror-Famine*, 1986) and R. Serbyn and B. Krawchenko's (eds) collection on the famine (*Famine in Ukraine, 1932–1933*, 1986), G.S.N. Luckyj's study of literary politics (*Literary Politics in the Soviet Ukraine, 1917–1934*, 1956), and H. Kostiuk's book on the terror (*Stalinist Rule in the Ukraine: A Study of the Decade of Mass Terror, 1929–39*, 1960). On Western Ukraine there is an older study by V. Kuchabsky [W. Kutschabsky] (*Die Westukraine im Kampfe mit Polen und dem Bolshewismus*, 1934) and a recent one by J. Radziejowski (*The Communist Party of Western Ukraine, 1919–1929*, trans A. Rutkowski, 1983).

Ukrainian political life during the Second World War has been examined by J.A. Armstrong (*Ukrainian Nationalism, 1939–1945*, 1955; 2nd edn 1963; 3rd edn 1990). On the postwar period the coverage is more extensive. The Ukrainian Party apparatus has been studied briefly by Armstrong (*The Soviet Bureaucratic Elite: A Case Study of the Ukrainian Apparatus*, 1959) and B. Harasymiw (*Political Elite Recruitment in the Soviet Union*, 1984). Ya. Bilinsky's thorough study of political developments in Ukraine (*The Second Soviet Republic: The Ukraine after World War II*, 1964) does not deal with the dissidents of the 1960s. Two wide surveys of different areas of national life, with some attention to methodology, have been edited by P. Potichnyj (*Ukraine in the Seventies*, 1975) and B. Krawchenko (*Ukraine after Shelest*, 1983). B. Lewytzkyj has written an analytical study of the main changes in Ukraine in the postwar period (*Politics and Society in Soviet Ukraine, 1953–1980*, 1984). The Ukrainian dissident movement has been analyzed by K. Farmer (*Ukrainian Nationalism in the Post-Stalin Era: Myth, Symbol, and Ideology in Soviet Nationalities Policy*, 1980) and J. Bilocerkowycz (*Soviet Ukrainian Dissent: A Study of Political Alienation*, 1988). The Chornobyl disaster has been described by D.R. Marples (*Chernobyl and Nuclear Power in the USSR*, 1986; *The Social Impact of the Chernobyl Disaster*, 1988) and M. Bojcun and V. Haynes (*The Chernobyl Disaster: The True Story of a Catastrophe*, 1988). The developments of the last few years under perestroika have been examined by Marples (*Ukraine under Perestroika*, 1991).

The Ukrainian economy and Party history have been researched by V. Holubnychy, a selection of whose works came out posthumously under I. Koropeckyj's editorship (*Soviet Regional Economics: Selected Works of Vsevolod Holubnychy*, 1982). Koropeckyj has also edited three collections of articles on Ukrainian economics (*Ukraine within the USSR: An Economic Balance Sheet*, 1977; *Integration Processes in the Ukrainian Economy: A Historical Perspective*, 1988; *Studies in Ukrainian Economics*, 1988), and V. Bandera and Z. Melnyk have edited a book on the Soviet economy touching on Ukraine (*The Soviet Economy in Regional Perspective*, 1973).

Ya. Bilinsky

Sovietophilism. A political disposition among people outside the Soviet Union to support or sympathize with the USSR. The policy was justified by various theories and was adopted out of different motives, from the idealistic to the mercenary.

The left factions of the Ukrainian Party of Socialist Revolutionaries and the Ukrainian Social Democratic Workers' party, who, even before the Bolsheviks seized power in Ukraine, propagated an alliance with the Russian Communist party and the creation of a Soviet Ukraine, can be considered the first Sovietophiles. In 1919–21 these groups coalesced into the Borotbists and Ukrainian Communist party.

In the early 1920s Sovietophile tendencies arose among Ukrainian émigrés in Prague and Vienna, especially the left Socialist Revolutionaries, led by M. Hrushevsky and grouped around the journal *Boritesia-Poborete!*; the Galician Social Democrats, under S. Vityk and grouped around his journal, *Nova hromada*; and followers of V. Vynnychenko, with his journal, *Nova doba*. In France in the 1920s, the *Union of Ukrainian Citizens in France, led by E. Borschak, and its newspaper, *Ukraïns'ki visty*, were Sovietophile. Some circles of the Government-in-exile of the Western Ukrainian National Republic (those of Ye. Petrushevych and V. Paneiko) also favored rapprochement with the Soviet Ukrainian regime, especially after eastern Galicia had been awarded to Poland in 1923 by the Conference of Ambassadors in Paris. This stance was a tactical measure to gain political support from the USSR against Poland.

In the 1920s Sovietophilism became increasingly popular also in Galicia, primarily as a reaction to the colonial policies of Poland. Cultural Sovietophilism, or the belief that Ukrainian culture could develop only with the support of the Soviet Ukrainian state, was widespread. The Ukrainization policy of the early 1920s in Soviet Ukraine fed expectations of a national revival. Many soldiers and officers of the Ukrainian Galician Army who had served in central or eastern Ukraine stayed there or returned there later. Galician organizations, such as the Shevchenko Scientific Society and some Ukrainian co-operatives, worked with their Soviet counterparts but without supporting the Soviet regime. Several Western Ukrainian political parties adopted a pro-Soviet platform – the *Ukrainian Party of Labor, headed by M. Zakhidny, the *Communist Party of Western Ukraine, and the *Sel-Rob party. A section of the student movement represented by the *Working Alliance of Progressive Students in Prague was Sovietophile. Many pro-Soviet groups and organizations in Galicia were supported and sometimes even funded by the Soviet consulate in Lviv. The collectivization, the man-made famine, and the widespread repressions of the 1930s greatly undermined the strength of Sovietophilism in Western Ukraine and abroad.

Among Ukrainian immigrant communities in North and South America, Sovietophilism spread through the so-called progressive movement. It rested on many of the same hopes and expectations as those of the political émigrés in Europe. Moreover, many Ukrainian workers and farmers were influenced by leftist parties in their new homelands. The Soviet government encouraged Sovietophilism, especially during and immediately after the Second World War, when it enjoyed much sympathy in the West as an ally. The main pro-Soviet Ukrainian organizations in North America were the *League of American Ukrainians, the *Ukrainian Labour-Farmer Temple Association, and the *Association of United Ukrainian Canadians. Soviet agents and provocateurs encouraged Sovietophilism among the post–Second World War émigrés. Some effort was made to convince emigrants (especially in France and Argentina) to return to the Soviet Union. No Sovietophile organizations were established by the postwar refugees, however, and only a few people, such as Yu. *Kosach, supported the USSR openly. In the post-Stalin period Sovietophilism declined rapidly among Ukrainians in the West. Official Soviet attempts to encourage more contacts with the West often backfired: instead of attracting support for the Soviet regime they exposed its repressive and Russian-chauvinist nature. J. *Kolasky's denunciation of Russification in education, for example, made a strong impression in Canada. The arguments of advocates of accommodation and compromise with the Soviet regime, such as M. *Koliankivsky and T. *Lapychak, found no response in the Ukrainian community. Sovietophilism among Western political and trade-union circles was criticized frequently by Ukrainian human rights activists.

B. Balan

Sovietskyi [Sovjets'kyj]. VIII-15. A town smt (1986 pop 9,400) in the southeastern Crimean Lowland and a raion center in the Crimea. The village was first mentioned in historical documents in 1798, as Ichky. After the Crimean War many Tatar inhabitants of the area emigrated to Turkey, and Russian and German colonists came in. In the 1890s Ichky became a station on a railway line. It was renamed in 1950. The town has a food industry and a winery.

Sovnarkom. See Council of People's Commissars.

Sowa, Antoni. See Żeligowski, Edward.

Sowiński, Leonard, b 7 November 1831 in Berezivka, Novohrad-Volynskyi county, d 23 December 1887 in Stetkivtsi, Zhytomyr county, Volhynia gubernia. Polish writer and translator. The son of a Polish noble and a Ukrainian peasant woman, he studied at Kiev University (1847–55), where he was a leading student radical. In his allegorical narrative poem *Z życia* (From Life, 1860) he wrote about contemporary events in Ukraine. An early Polish popularizer of T. Shevchenko, from the beginning of the 1860s on he translated and published several of Shevchenko's narrative poems and ballads and many of his lyrical verses in *Kurier Wileński* and Warsaw periodicals. He also wrote a book of studies of Ukrainian literature (1860) and a study of Shevchenko (1861), which included his translation of 'Haidamaky' (The Haidamakas). His translation of Shevchenko's 'Naimychka' (The Servant Girl) was published separately in Lviv in 1871. In his five-act tragedy in verse *Na Ukrainie* (In Ukraine, 1875) he depicted the conflicts between the Polish gentry and Ukrainian peasantry during the Polish Insurrection of 1863–4, and in his novel *Na rozstajnych drogach* (At the Crossroads, 1887) he portrayed critically the Polish gentry in Ukraine. Sowiński's familiarity with Ukrainian history, folkways, and literature is evident in his school and university memoirs (1st edn 1961). Translations of some of his poems have appeared in a Ukrainian anthology of Polish poetry (1979).

R. Senkus

Soybean (*Glycine soja* or *max*; Ukrainian: *soia*). An annual leguminous plant of the family Fabaceae, economically the most important bean in the world. It ranges from one to more than seven feet in height. The plant was introduced in Ukraine late in the 19th century. The seeds contain 24–45 percent protein, 20–32 percent carbohydrates, and 13–37 percent fat along with vitamins D, B, and E. Soybean occupies the leading place in the world's *vegetable-oil industry. Soybean oil is used for margarine and shortening, in food preparation, and, industrially, in the manufacturing of fibers, plastics, glue, paints, and soap.

Sozh River [Sož]. A left-bank tributary of the Dnieper River that flows for 648 km through Smolensk oblast (RF) and Mahiliou and Homel oblasts (Belarus) and drains a basin area of 42,100 sq km. The river is navigable for 373 km. For approx 20 km from its mouth the Sozh demarcates the border between Ukraine and Belarus along the northern edge of Chernihiv oblast.

Sozontiv, Symon, b 20 July 1898 in Lahery, Zmiiv county, Kharkiv gubernia, d 17 March 1980 in Dammartin-sur-Tigeaux, France. Political and community activist in France. He served as a captain in the Army of the UNR, was interned in Poland, and in 1923 emigrated to Czechoslovakia. He graduated with a degree in engineering from

the Ukrainian Husbandry Academy in Poděbrady in 1927 and then moved to France, where he set up a rubber factory. He headed the UNR government-in-exile (1954–5) and several Ukrainian organizations in France, including the Ukrainian Community Aid Society (1946–54), the Ukrainian Central Civic Committee (1948–69), and the executive branch of the Ukrainian National Council (1948–54). He founded the Franco-Ukrainian Hromada publishing house, which was active in 1948–56, and was the publisher of *Vil'na Ukraïna* and *L'Ukraine libre* (1953–4) in Paris.

Space travel. Along with the United States, the USSR was a world leader in exploring space as the final frontier. Scientists from Ukraine played a key role in the Soviet space program from its inception. Ukrainian scientists throughout the world have also contributed to planetary *astronomy and other space sciences. A number of Ukrainian scientists made important contributions to the development of jet engines and *rockets. The first world exhibition devoted to problems of outer space was held in Kiev from 19 June to 1 September 1925.

The era of space travel was inaugurated by the successful Soviet launching of the first satellite, Sputnik, into orbit in 1957. Its designer, and the 'invisible scientist' who actually controlled the Soviet space program, was the Ukrainian S. *Korolov, whose Luna-3 satellite brought back the first photographs of the far side of the moon (1959). Korolov put the first man in space (1961) and the first man-made object on the moon and planned the first walk of a man in space. His work was continued by another scientist of Ukrainian descent, M. *Yanhel, who headed manned and unmanned Soviet spaceflights after Korolov's death. Yu. *Kondratiuk (real name: O. Sharhei) analyzed ways to ensure the safety of the crew during space travel. As early as 1929 he proposed a manned lunar module and solved the problems of re-entry and landing on the earth. His Lunar Orbit Rendezvous technique of 1929 was used to land all US astronauts on the moon, and his works were translated and published by NASA.

A number of Ukrainian astronauts have orbited the earth. In August 1962 P. *Popovych on Vostok-4 was the fourth person and the first Ukrainian in space. In October 1968 H. *Berehovy spent four days in orbit around the earth on Soiuz-3, doing geophysical, astronomical, and medical experiments. Other Ukrainian astronauts include H. Dobrovolsky (who died tragically in the explosion of Soiuz-11), A. Fylypenko, V. Horbatko, H. Hrechko, Yu. *Romanenko, L. *Kyzym, and I. *Volk.

Besides B. *Paton and D. *Dudko, Ukrainian contributors to space technology include V. Bernadsky, V. Paton, V. Stesyn, V. Lapchynsky, A. Zahrebelny, E. Ternovy, S. Havrysh, M. Huzhva, N. Kovalenko, V. Pylypenko, V. Lakyza, A. Tsapenko, A. Bily, V. Dolodarenko, H. Tretiachenko, K. Herasymenko, A. Pidhorily, E. Oleksiienko, I. Taranenko, H. Volokyta, L. Korniienko, A. Mykolaienko, V. Fedchuk, A. Markus, V. Udovenko, N. Velychko, V. Shevchenko, E. Ivchenko, and V. Semenenko.

Spain. According to Arabic chronicles Slavs, the ancestors of Ukrainians from the Black Sea coast, served as slaves, soldiers, and scholars to the Arab rulers of Spain. In the 17th century, as the exploits of the Zaporozhian Cossacks against the Turks became widely known throughout Europe, a number of books on Ukraine and the Cossacks appeared in Spain. Occasionally Cossacks served as mercenaries in the Spanish armies. During the Napoleonic Wars some Ukrainians served in the French forces in Spain.

During the period of Ukrainian independence Ye. Kulisher was appointed ambassador of the UNR to Spain, but he had no opportunity to serve in this capacity. Ukrainians fought on both sides in the Spanish Civil War (1936–9). A separate Ukrainian unit, the Shevchenko Company, was active on the republican side and published its own paper, *Borot'ba*. During the Second World War Yu. Karmanin served as an OUN information officer in Spain.

After the war a small Ukrainian community established itself in Spain, chiefly in Madrid. From 1947 a group of 25 or 30 young Ukrainian refugees supported by Obra Católica de Asistencia Universitaria studied in Spain. The students formed a chorus and dance group, the Obnova Society of Ukrainian Catholic Students (1947), and the Ukrainian Student Hromada (1956). A few Ukrainian families also settled in Madrid. By 1953 the Ukrainian community numbered 68 members. The Association of Ukrainian Friends of Spain, headed by A. Kishka, was set up in 1957. A Ukrainian program was broadcast three times per week (1951–5) and then daily on the national radio. In 1952 a Ukrainian section was established at the Centro de Estudios Orientales under its director, Rev S. Morillo. The center's journal, *Oriente* (renamed *Oriente europeo* in 1956), published many articles on Ukrainian questions. The monthly *Las cartas de Espania* came out in Ukrainian, English, Polish, Czech, Slovak, Rumanian, Hungarian, and Croatian (1950–1). Concerts and other performances by Ukrainian students have popularized Ukrainian culture among the wider public. Two Ukrainian political institutions were established in Spain: a representation of the executive board of the Ukrainian National Council and a delegation of the Anti-Bolshevik Bloc of Nations.

Spanish themes have an important place in Ukrainian literature. They are at the heart of masterpieces such as Lesia Ukrainka's *Kaminnyi hospodar* (The Stone Host), N. Koroleva's *Predok* (Ancestor), and B.I. Antonych's *Al'kazar* (Alcazar). D. Mordovets and Koroleva (a Ukrainian writer of Spanish origin) have written travel accounts of Spain. Translations of Spanish literature into Ukrainian have been done by M. Ivanov, M. Lukash, and D. Buchynsky.

Spanish Civil War. A military struggle in 1936–9 between the Popular Front coalition government of the Spanish Republic and the Falange movement and its allies led by Gen F. Franco.

In the USSR the International Organization to Assist the Fighters for the Spanish Revolution (IOAFSR) was set up; in it was a section for the Ukrainian SSR. By September 1936 the Ukrainian SSR had contributed 548,500 rubles to the IOAFSR fund. During the course of the war much material assistance to the Spanish Republic came from Ukraine. As well, a number of Ukrainians were among the 2,000 to 3,000 Soviet military and other specialists dispatched to Spain. Some 5,000 Spanish children were brought to the USSR to study in Soviet schools, a considerable number of them to Ukraine.

Many Ukrainians from Western Ukraine and the diaspora (Canada, Argentina, France, the United States, Belgium) fought in the ranks of the International Brigades,

Ukrainian-Canadian volunteers in the Mackenzie-Papineau Battalion and Shevchenko Company of the 13th International Brigade during the Spanish Civil War

which were formed of people from 54 states. Some 400 Ukrainians came from Canada alone (accounting for 30–40 percent of the total Canadian contingent), at least 200 from Galicia and Volhynia, 58 from Transcarpathia, and an undetermined number from Bukovyna and the diaspora outside Canada. Estimates of the total number of Poles and Ukrainians in the brigades run as high as 5,000, representing between 12 and 20 percent of the total International Brigade force. Ukrainians were dispersed among all the brigades, but fought mainly with the 13th and 15th. In the 13th International Brigade there was the Taras Shevchenko Company, while in the 15th International Brigade Ukrainian volunteers served in the Canadian Mackenzie-Papineau Battalion (which contained a unit informally named after Maksym *Kryvonis) and in the American Abraham Lincoln Battalion. In December 1937 the Taras Shevchenko Company began publishing its own newspaper, *Borot'ba* (The Struggle), edited by V. Krys.

In addition to participating directly in military operations, Ukrainians in Western Ukraine and the diaspora established several solidarity committees which supported the Republican efforts morally and materially. An insignificant number of Ukrainians also fought on Franco's side.

BIBLIOGRAPHY
Shevchenko, F. 'Rota im. Tarasa Shevchenka v boiakh proty fashyzmu v Ispanii,' *UIZh*, 1961, no. 1
Kravchuk, P. *Za vashu i nashu svobodu* (Toronto 1976)
Momryk, M. '"For Your Freedom and Ours": Konstantin (Mike) Olynyk, A Ukrainian Volunteer in the International Brigades,' *Canadian Ethnic Studies*, 20, no. 2 (1988)
Lial'ka, Ia.; et al. *Internatsional'na solidarnist' trudiashchykh zakhidnoukrains'kykh zemel' z respublikans'koiu Ispaniieiu* (Kiev 1988)

S. Cipko

Sparrow (*Passer*; Ukrainian: *horobets*). Small, chiefly seed-eating birds with conical bills in the Old World family Ploceidae, the most common being the house sparrow (*P. domesticus*). Sparrows nest in tree hollows, burrows, and buildings and often inhabit populated areas. In Ukraine the tree or field sparrow (*P. montanus*), which nests in the wild, is also common. Sparrows may be useful or harmful in that they consume the seeds of both important crops and noxious weeds.

Spartak (Spartacus). A USSR-wide sports society for white-collar employees in the state commerce, civil aviation, road transportation, culture, and health care sectors. It was founded in 1935 out of sports circles organized in 1925–6 by industrial co-operative artels. In 1960 Spartak was reorganized into a voluntary trade-union sports organization. About 50 forms of sport were cultivated by the society. In Ukraine, Spartak had over 2 million members. The Spartak Kiev women's handball team won 19 USSR and 12 European championships. Thirteen of its members were on the USSR teams that won gold medals at the 1976 and 1980 Olympic Games.

Spartak (Spartacus). An organ of the central committee of the youth wing of the Communist Party of Western Ukraine. It was published in Berlin from November 1926 to May 1928 and distributed illegally in Western Ukraine. It was succeeded in Lviv by the monthly *Molodyi Spartak* (1931–4) and the Polish-language journal *Spartak* (1933).

Spartakiad. The name applied to athletic contests in the USSR. Soviet Ukrainian republican Spartakiads were held from 1923. In 1928 the first USSR-wide Spartakiad took place as a counterpart to the Olympic Games, in which the USSR did not participate at the time. The Ukrainian SSR teams took second place overall and won gold medals in volleyball, handball, gymnastics, shooting, and motorcycling. In 1932–3 separate USSR Spartakiads for trade-union athletes and the Dynamo sports society were introduced. In the 1950s Spartakiads for the Peoples of the USSR, for the Voluntary Society for Assistance to the Army, Air Force, and Navy of the USSR, for schoolchildren, for secondary and postsecondary students, and for the military forces of the Warsaw Pact were added. The Spartakiad of the Peoples of the USSR, in which winners of republican Spartakiads competed, was the largest among them. From 1956 it took place every four years, usually a year or two before each Olympic Games, and its winners were sent as the USSR representatives to the Olympics. In the eighth such Spartakiad, held in 1983, 654 Ukrainian athletes participated and won 102 gold, 92 silver, and 91 bronze individual or team medals.

Spas. IV-3. A village on the Dniester River in Staryi Sambir raion, Lviv oblast. Until the 18th century a monastery, which was said to be the burial place of Lev I Danylovych, stood there. In the 17th century Spas was the seat of the Orthodox Peremyshl eparchy. Today the ruins of a fortress and Queen Bona's palace remain.

Spaska, Yevheniia [Spas'ka, Jevhenija], b 1 January 1892 in Nizhen, Chernihiv gubernia, d 12 September 1980 in Alma-Ata, Kazakh SSR. Art scholar. A graduate of the Moscow Higher Courses for Women (1914), she studied Ukrainian folk art under D. Shcherbakivsky at the All-Ukrainian Historical Museum in Kiev and headed the handicrafts department at the Kiev Agricultural Museum (1925–6). Then she worked as production manager in the Kiev textile firm Tekstylkhudozheksport (1926–31), which had 6,000 employees. She studied old Chernihiv pottery and wrote *Hanchars'ki kakhli Chernihivshchyny XVIII–XIX st.* (Ceramic Tiles of the Chernihiv Region in the 18th–19th Centuries, 1928) and articles on the potters of Silesia (1929), the ornamentation of Bubnivtsi pottery (1929), P.

Yevheniia Spaska

Lytvynova's life and work (1928), and the porcelain factory of A. Miklashevsky (1959). In the 1930s she was arrested and exiled to Kazkhstan, where she worked in Uralsk, Semipalatinsk, and Alma-Ata and studied the copper pots of the nomads. Her memoirs remain unpublished.

Spasky, Vasyl [Spas'kyj, Vasyl'] (Spassky, Vasilii), b 1831 in Shchigry, Kursk gubernia, Russia, d 30 January 1884 in Kharkiv. Pedagogue and statistician. As an educational worker in Kharkiv he was active in educational organizations, associations, and the first Sunday school for men in Kharkiv. In March 1873 he organized a one-day census of Kharkiv. His major work was *Kharakteristika Kharkova v otnoshenii gramotnosti i prosveshcheniia* (The Characteristics of Kharkiv with Respect to Literacy and Education, 1875).

Special boards (*osoblyvi narady*; Russian: *osobye soveshchaniia* or OSO). Soviet internal police courts under the *GPU, *NKVD, and *MVD which played a key role from 1928 to 1953 in the system of mass terror. Composed of members of the secret police, they reached their verdicts on the basis of materials provided by the investigative organs and in the absence of the accused. Often the accused did not see the text of the charges before the sentence was put into effect. Until 1936 the boards had the power to sentence political prisoners ('counterrevolutionaries') to a maximum of five years in concentration camp, and to exile 'socially unsafe elements' (kulaks, priests, and criminals). After 1936, and especially in 1937–8 and 1947–8, the boards sentenced vast numbers of people to 10, 15, and 25 years in concentration camp, and even to death.

Under the secret police chief N. Yezhov (see *Yezhov terror), special boards were established at the oblast and raion levels. Three-member committees called troikas, composed of the local NKVD chief, the secretary of the Party committee, and the local militia chief, prepared lists of suspects to be arrested and passed them to the boards for approval. In some cases the troikas simply carried out arrests in the name of the boards without waiting for their approval.

Special Broadcasting Service (SBS). An independent state-funded body established in 1977 to oversee ethnic broadcasting in Australia. Its mandate includes the Ukrainian radio programs produced in Adelaide (since 1975), Canberra (1976–), Newcastle (1978–), Perth (1976–), Melbourne (1975–), and Sydney (1976–). Initially all the broadcasts were prepared and aired by volunteers, with production costs funded by the Ukrainian community. More recently the Melbourne and Sydney broadcasts have received direct SBS assistance.

Special Detachments (Russian: *osobye otdely*). Soviet security forces established in 1918 to deal with espionage within the Soviet armed forces, military districts, arms factories, and institutions connected with defense. In wartime (1918–22, 1941–2) they were granted extralegal powers to carry out secret executions and terrorize the population. Recruited among the secret police, they were subordinate to the Cheka, then the GPU, and finally the NKVD. In 1943 the Special Detachments were replaced by the independent counterespionage agency *SMERSH, which combated the Ukrainian Insurgent Army and the OUN underground. They were revived in 1946 and abolished after eight years of operation.

Special schools (*spetsiialni shkoly*). Schools for children with physical and mental disabilities, until 1991 under the jurisdiction of the USSR Ministry of Education. There are nine types of special schools organized for students with various disabilities, among them schools for the deaf and schools for the blind. Special schools are boarding schools which offer vocational, incomplete, and complete secondary education. In Ukraine special schools were organized after 1917. In 1927 there were 101 special schools, with 4,600 pupils, and in 1987–8, 406 schools, with a total enrollment of 86,000. In addition, there are special schools for adults with visual and learning disabilities, which offer evening and part-time courses.

Speedwell (*Veronica*; Ukrainian: *veronika*). Small herbs of the family Scrophulariaceae, with small white, purple, or pink blossoms, often cultivated as ornamentals. They grow in Ukraine in the natural state in forests, meadows, and marshes (43 of 300 species). Medicinal veronica (*V. officinalis*) is used as herbal tea and in folk medicine.

Spendiarov, Aleksandr (Spendiarian), b 1 November 1871 in Kakhivka, d 7 May 1928 in Yerevan, Armenia. Armenian composer and conductor. For more than 40 years he lived and worked in the Crimea, where he was exposed to Ukrainian folk music influences. His works include *Crimean Sketches* for orchestra (two cycles: 1903, 1912); *Ukrainian Suite* for chorus and orchestra; the ballad 'Song of the Dnieper Sprite' (text by A. Podolynsky) for solo voice; 'Testament' (text by T. Shevchenko) for male chorus a cappella; and arrangements of Ukrainian folk songs for chorus, duet, and solo voice.

Speransky, Aleksandr [Speranskij], b 25 July 1865 in Moscow, d 26 August 1919 in Kiev. Chemist. A graduate of Moscow University (1886), he did postgraduate work in Leipzig and taught at Moscow University. A professor at Kiev University from 1907, he established the department of physical chemistry there. His research centered on solid solutions and the thermodynamics of concentrated and saturated solutions.

Speransky, Mikhail [Speranskij, Mixail], b 1 May 1863 in Moscow, d 12 April 1938 in Moscow. Russian Slavist, Byzantinist, and archeographer; corresponding member of the Russian Academy of Sciences (from 1902) and full member of the USSR Academy of Sciences (from 1921). He graduated from Moscow University (PH D, 1899) and taught at the Bezborodko Historical-Philological Institute (1896–1906; see *Nizhen Lyceum) and Moscow University (1907–23). He wrote numerous articles and reviews in the field of medieval East Slavic literature; book-length articles on Slavic apocryphal Gospels (his MA thesis, 1895), manuscripts at the Bezborodko institute (1901), the South Russian (Ukrainian) song (1904), and cryptography in South Slavic and Rus' literary monuments (1929); books on East Slavic translated collections of apothegms (1904) and Slavic relations in Russian literature (2 vols, 1903, 1905); numerous lithographed textbooks on the history of Russian literature (1896–1917); a history of old Rus' literature (1914; 3rd edn 1921); and a university textbook of Rus' oral literature (1917; repr 1969). He also wrote several articles about N. Gogol, one on I. Kotliarevsky's *Eneïda* (Aeneid, 1902), and one on I. Kulzhynsky (1907).

Sperkach, Valentyn [Sperkač], b 7 November 1939 in Kiev. Film director. He completed the director's course at the Kiev Institute of Theater Arts (1967) and has worked at the Kiev Studio of Chronicle-Documentary Films, where he has produced the propagandistic *Znaiomtes', Radians'ka Ukraïna* (Introducing Soviet Ukraine, 1982), *Zemlia moïkh predkiv* (The Land of My Ancestors, 1982), and other films.

Spetsfondy. Special depositories in Soviet libraries and archives consisting of materials confiscated or prohibited by the authorities. They were established in 1931, although in prerevolutionary imperial Russia and Austria-Hungary political, pornographic, anti-Semitic, and anti-Christian literature was also widely censored (see *Censorship).

During the *terror 'provocative' books were taken directly out of stores and state publishing houses. Publications of political émigrés and foreign publications with an ideology contrary to the official line were also banned. Lists of such materials were published by the People's Commissariat of Education (Narkomos, only until the Second World War) and the government censorship agency *Glavlit. The names of certain prolific authors were often followed by the directive 'all titles, for all years, in all languages.'

Spetsfondy were established at research libraries, particularly those of scientific institutes, and in museums and state archives. A maximum of two copies of each banned publication were preserved, and the rest were destroyed. Libraries with unrestricted public access were forbidden to hold the works, which were thus effectively taken completely out of circulation.

In Ukraine in the 1930s, all endeavors in Ukrainian studies that were at variance with Party directives were prohibited, as were all forms of art that departed from officially sanctioned *socialist realism and some works of the Ukrainian canon, such as Lesia Ukrainka's *Boiarynia* (Noblewoman) and T. Shevchenko's works critical of B. Khmelnytsky. In the postwar period there was no consistent formula for the proscription of Russian or Ukrainian works, and censors were largely simple functionaries adhering to the latest inclinations of the Party. Numerous lists were compiled chaotically by various institutions and agencies, such as the Book Chamber of the Ukrainian SSR. The materials held in *spetsfondy* could be accessed only by

Party officials and scholars at postsecondary institutions, scientific institutes, and museums, who had to present a letter, signed by the president of the institution they represented, in which the topic of their research was outlined. *Libraries did not make available catalogs of their *spetsfond* holdings to the general readership.

In 1989, as a result of Perestroika, substantial portions of the *spetsfondy* were transferred back to the open collections of libraries, and émigré publications were also made accessible to readers. But literature deemed to be subversive, ethnically, racially, or nationally inflammatory (particularly anti-Semitic items), pornography, and certain works by authors such as V. Vynnychenko and M. Khvylovy continued to be banned and collected. With the dissolution of the USSR, *spetsfondy* in newly independent Ukraine have been merged with other library holdings.

BIBLIOGRAPHY
Bilokin', S. 'Na polytsiakh spetsfondiv u rizni roky,' *Slovo i chas*, 1990, no. 1

S. Bilokin

Sphragistics (from the Greek *sphragis* 'seal'), also known as sigillography (from the Latin *sigillum*). A scholarly discipline with three branches, the art of making seals, the law of seals (legal norms in the use of seals), and the study of seals. Seals first appeared in the early civilizations (Egypt, Babylon) and were adopted by the Greeks and Romans. The use of seals was brought into Ukraine by the Scythians, the Antes, the Goths, and others. The law of seals (initially customary, then state, law) was codified in the early stages of the Kievan Rus' state. The study of seals as an academic discipline was initiated in the 13th century in Germany and in the mid-18th century in Ukraine.

Ukrainian seal making was categorized (as in Western Europe) according to the various materials in which impressions were made, such as metals (gold, silver, lead, etc) and various waxes. The use of seals engendered titles for persons whose duty it was to affix them, such as the *pechatnyk* (head of the prince's chancellery) during the Princely era, or the general chancellor during the Hetmanate. Ukrainian seals had their own national style (the octagonal seal was used almost exclusively in Ukraine) and were of high artistic quality. Early craftsmen included D. Galakhovsky, I. Shchyrsky, and I. Myhura; the best-known modern craftsmen were H. *Narbut and L. *Terletsky.

There were three basic types of state seal in the Kievan Rus' state. The oldest was the archaic or Old Rus' seal, which was used until the 10th century. Its distinguishing feature was the dynastic mark of the Kievan rulers, the *trident or bident. The exact shape and characteristics of the archaic seal depended on the station of the bearer. A two-sided seal belonging to Sviatoslav I Ihorevych is among the oldest surviving examples of the art; it has a bident on one side and a rosette on the other.

After the adoption of Christianity by the Kievan Rus' state the so-called Greco-Rus' seal was used until the late 11th century. The face bore the likeness of the saint after whom the grand prince was named, and the reverse was marked with the Greek legend God Help Your Servant (name of the bearer of the seal), Archon of Rus'. The seal used by Yaroslav the Wise, with St George on the face and the legend God Help Your Servant Georgos, Archon of Rus', was of the Greco-Rus' type.

From the left: the seals of the Kievan grand princes Sviatoslav I Ihorevych, Iziaslav Volodymyrovych, and Iziaslav Yaroslavych

In the 12th century a new form of seal emerged that was used until the late 13th or early 14th century. Its five types were as follows: (1) face with the likeness of the saint namesake of the ruler, reverse with a trident-bident; (2) face with the likeness of the saint namesake of the ruler, reverse with the likeness of the saint namesake of the ruler's father or overlord; (3) face with the likeness of the saint namesake of the ruler, reverse with the likeness of Christ; (4) face with the likeness of the saint namesake of the ruler, reverse with the Church Slavonic initials 'IC XC'; (5) face with the likeness of one of various persons, reverse with a legend in Greek or Church Slavonic and some vestigial features of the older Greco-Rus' seal. An example of the last is the seal of Volodymyr Monomakh, the face of which has a likeness of St Basil, and the reverse, the Greek legend Seal of Basileus, the Most Venerable Archon of Rus' Monomakh.

The seal of Prince Yurii Lvovych of Galicia

Seals underwent a fundamental change beginning in the 13th century in the Principality of Galicia-Volhynia. They became heavily influenced by Western European heraldic and Gothic themes, and their legends were written in Latin. The new type of seal was subsequently adopted by the Lithuanian-Ruthenian state. The face of the seal of Yurii I Lvovych bears the likeness of the king seated on a throne and the annular legend (*sigillum*) *Domini Georgi Regis Rusie*. The reverse shows a likeness of a knight cavalryman who carries a shield on his left shoulder and a standard in his right hand. The shield is marked with the dynastic symbol of a lion, which is circumscribed by the legend *S. Domini Georgi Ducis Ladimerie*. Prince Władysław Opolczyk ruled Galicia as a vice-regent of the Hungarian king Louis I; the face of his seal bears a seated monarch, holding a sword in his right hand, positioned between two coats of arms (Silesia and Rus'), circumscribed by a Latin legend.

The seals of the Grand Duchy of Lithuania bore a likeness of the seated ruler or a Lithuanian-Ruthenian *pohon'* (a heraldic horseman, with a sword in the right hand and a shield with an Orthodox cross on the left shoulder), surrounded by the heraldic arms of the larger constituent principalities (Lithuania, Samogitia, Volhynia, Kiev, Belarus). It also showed the title of the prince as a legend.

Beginning in 1648 new military, state, and national seals were introduced for the hetmans. They bore the likeness of a Cossack musketeer, a practice adopted from Zaporozhian Host seals, starting with Hetman B. Khmelnytsky's seals. These showed the Middle Ukrainian annular inscription Seal of the Army of His Royal Grace of the Zaporizhia. Hetman I. Vyhovsky's seal bore his coat of arms, his name, and the inscription Great Hetman of the Principality of Rus' and Starosta of Chyhyryn. On Hetman I. Mazepa's seal the traditional likeness of a Cossack warrior was circumscribed by the inscription Seal of the Little Russian Army of His Royal Illustrious Majesty of the Zaporizhia. The inscription on P. Orlyk's seal, Seal of Little Russia and of the Glorious Zaporozhian Army, reflected the schism between Ukraine and Russia. Hetman K. Rozumovsky reverted to the traditional form of seal.

The seal of Hetman Ivan Mazepa

The seal of the Zaporozhian Cossack Host

In 1766, after the abolition of the Hetmanate, a new seal was issued by the Little Russian Collegium, depicting the imperial eagle with a five-field shield on its breast (representing the five Ukrainian principalities of Kiev, Chernihiv, Pereiaslav, Novhorod-Siverskyi, and Starodub). Less important documents were frequently stamped with personal seals which bore family or personal coats of arms. In the 19th century, emblems of Ukraine's former statehood appeared on the seals of the occupying foreign monarchies. They included the archangel of Kiev principality on the seal of the Russian Empire and the coats of arms of Galicia and Lodomeria (later also the seal of Bukovyna) on the seal of Austria-Hungary.

The first seals of the independent Ukrainian state were adopted by the Ukrainian Central Rada on 22 March 1918. V. *Krychevsky designed both the Great and the Lesser seals. The Great Seal bore a trident (the heraldic emblem of the UNR) framed by a laurel ornament. The Lesser Seal showed a trident framed by a rhomboid ornament. Both seals had the annular Ukrainian inscription *Ukraïns'ka Narodnia Respublika* (Ukrainian National Republic), with three rings dividing the words. Both seals had elements of Ukrainian folk art, but their design was very different

The great seal of the 1918 Ukrainian State

The oldest municipal seal of Lviv

from that of the traditional seals of ancient Ukrainian states and those of European states.

The seal of the Hetman government bore a traditional likeness of a Cossack warrior, framed by a floral ornament, placed under a trident, and circumscribed by the legend *Ukraïns'ka Derzhava* (Ukrainian State). It adhered to heraldic conventions of European sphragistics, and its artistic style was closely modeled on 17th- and 18th-century Ukrainian seals.

The seal of the Directory of the UNR, used by S. Petliura, was fairly modest, consisting of a trident and the Ukrainian initials 'UNR' in annular arrangement along with the legend *Holovnyi Otaman Respublikans'kykh Ukraïns'kykh Zbroinykh Syl* (Supreme Otaman of the Ukrainian Republican Armed Forces), the title of the head of state. Other seals were adopted by bodies that had jurisdiction over regions of Ukraine, including the Western Ukrainian National Republic, the Kuban, the Crimea, the Galician SSR (briefly), and Carpatho-Ukraine (in 1939). With the exception of that of the Ukrainian SSR they also all bore regional coats of arms.

The use of the seal of the Ukrainian SSR (which bore the republic's coat of arms) was established by the Central Executive Committee (CEC) of the USSR on 17 June 1925. It was used only by higher central and local government institutions and some of their autonomous departments. Lesser state agencies used seals without the arms, and their inscriptions indicated their jurisdiction. Community, co-operative, and other organizations followed suit in their use of seals. The state seal of the Ukrainian SSR underwent numerous changes, as did its coat of arms. Initially it showed a crossed hammer and sickle, illuminated by the sun's rays and framed by sheaves of wheat, with the legend *Proletari vsikh kraïn iednaitesia* (Proletarians of All Countries Unite) and the name of the republic in Ukrainian and Russian (as adopted by the CEC of the Ukrainian SSR on 14 March 1919). When the republic's new constitution was ratified in 1929, the seal was changed to have only a Ukrainian legend, and the Ukrainian initials 'USRR' were placed above the hammer and sickle. The adoption of yet another constitution on 30 January 1937 meant replacement of the initials USRR with URSR. A law passed on 5 June 1950 placed a five-point star above the coat of arms, replaced the initials with *Ukraïns'ka RSR*, and restored the bilingual legend. The Moldavian ASSR, part of the Ukrainian SSR until 1941, had the Ukrainian seal with a bilingual legend in Ukrainian and Moldavian. In 1992 Ukraine, once again independent, declared the trident its seal.

Territorial seals. These were official marks used in the appanage principalities and *volosti* of the Lithuanian principality; Ukrainian voivodeships and their subdivisions in the Polish kingdom; the regiments and palankas of the Cossack Hetmanate and the Zaporizhia; vicegerencies, gubernias, and other subdivisions of the Russian Empire; the crown territories of the Austro-Hungarian Empire; and all zemstvos until 1918.

The seals of the appanage principalities of Kievan Rus' were identical to the state seal. The oldest such seal to have been preserved (11th century) belonged to Iziaslav Volodymyrovych. The face shows a trident framed by a legend, and the reverse has a legend only. The seals of princes of the Lithuanian states are of a transitional stage in Ukrainian territorial sphragistics.

In the Polish kingdom all seals of voivodeships, territories, and districts bore the coat of arms framed by a Latin inscription (eg, Seal of Rus' Voivodeship). The seal of the Zaporizhia (mid-16th century) had a likeness of a Cossack musketeer with the inscription, in Middle Ukrainian, Seal of the Zaporozhian Army. The oldest extant examples date from 1576, 1596, and 1608.

In 1648 seals for the regiments and companies of the Hetmanate were introduced. They bore the family or personal coat of arms of their commanding officer and an appropriate legend. The Zaporizhia, as an autonomous constituent of the Cossack state, had three types of its own seals, the territorial army seal, palanka seals, and kurin seals. The highest seal of the Zaporizhia had to be changed after 1648, when it was adopted as the Great Seal of the Hetmanate. A spear was added, thrust into the ground before the musketeer, and the annular inscription, in Middle Ukrainian, Seal of the Glorious Zaporozhian Host. In 1763 the words 'of Little Russia' and 'Imperial Majesty' were added.

*Palanka seals showed the likeness of an animal (lion, horse, eagle, deer, etc) alongside the coat of arms of the regiment, and an appropriate legend. The seal of the Samara palanka, for example, bore a lion, the regimental arms, and the inscription Regimental Seal of the Samara Palanka. The seal of the Kodak palanka had a likeness of a horse, flanked by the regimental seal and the initials 'P.P.K.P.'

The seals of Zaporozhian kurins had various figures and inscriptions and followed no set pattern. The last form of Cossack territorial seal was the seal for Cossack armies established in the late 18th and early 19th centuries, namely the Boh, Black Sea, Budzhak, Kuban, and other armies.

Ukrainian territorial seals under the Russian Empire (for vicegerencies, gubernias, oblasts, etc) and Austria-Hungary (the crownlands of Galicia, Lodomeria, Bukovyna, Transcarpathia, etc) were heraldic, and their inscriptions were in foreign languages.

Local seals. Seals of cities, towns, and villages had many forms. City seals were already in use in the mid-13th century in Western Ukraine. The oldest extant seal is from Volodymyr-Volynskyi (late 13th century), affixed to a document from 1324. It has a likeness of St George, the patron saint of the city, and a Latin legend identifying the seal. At the beginning of the 14th century seals began appearing in Lviv, Peremyshl, and other Galician and some Volhynian cities.

The subsequent rapid development of city seals was influenced by the establishment of autonomous German urban communities. All of these seals bear the city's coat of arms (designed with considerable thematic imagination and variety) and a Latin or early Middle Ukrainian annular inscription (some in the contemporary Western Ukrainian dialect). Larger cities, such as Kiev, had a lesser and a greater seal. During the Hetmanate in the 17th and 18th centuries, seals were dominated by Cossack symbols (maces, Cossacks, weaponry, various types of crosses, heavenly lights, etc).

Rural communities in Ukraine had various seals the origins of which are difficult to trace. They have not been adequately studied, and most of them have been lost. Inscriptions on such seals were in Ukrainian, and they were adorned with emblems of everyday life, such as trees, animals, farm implements (scythes, sickles, rakes, hoes, etc), fruits, trees, and farm buildings. They were often of high artistic quality, and their style was characteristically Ukrainian.

The Russian Empire's ascendancy arrested the development of Ukrainian local seals. Established traditional seals were replaced by new ones that had no historical relevance, on which the dominant image was the imperial eagle (eg, on the seal of Poltava). The seals of newly established cities had mundane designs, and rarely did they have historical themes. Cossack sphragistic traditions were maintained in the city seals of the Kuban. The Austrian authorities rarely made changes to city seals, and then only minor ones to adapt them to Austrian forms.

In 1917–20 the independent Ukrainian government did not have sufficient time to address the issue of city seals, and after the Bolsheviks took power city seals disappeared completely. The use of city seals continued in Western Ukraine in the 1920s and 1930s but was discontinued in 1939. In the postwar Soviet period a new form of sphragistics and *heraldry emerged, most of it far removed from Ukrainian and Western European traditions. A new seal for Kiev, for example, was created with a maple leaf (allegedly the floral emblem of the city) and a drawn bow (an imperfect reference to the crossbow that once appeared on the city's seal).

Seals of lineage. In the early years of the Kiev principality leading families used their own seals or amulets, marked by emblems or runes, to denote their ancestral or personal holdings. The seals were of various provenance, including Slavic, Greek, Gothic, and Oriental sources. After the adoption of Christianity as the official religion a cross or a line perpendicular to the design was usually added. The designs of these seals of lineage provide the oldest images preserved on Rus' seals. Under the Galician-Volhynian state they became heraldic.

Western European heraldry appeared in Ukrainian territories at the beginning of the 14th century. Leading families began displaying their emblems on their coats of arms, which had to be confirmed by monarchs and grand princes. The practice led to the creation of heraldic seals. In the Middle Ages they were widely used, particularly by princesses, boyars, members of the prince's host, merchants, and other classes. The peasantry also used emblems (eg, beekeepers for the marking of their hives), but their emblems did not come to be used as seals. The revival of the Ukrainian state in the 17th century resulted in further developments in family and personal seals. They were used by the nobility, Cossack officers, the clergy, burghers, and Cossacks of lower rank. Families and individuals who did not have coats of arms created them in styles of their own choosing. Cossack traditions generated a new set of images used in seals, including those of weapons (swords, sabers, arrows, bows), heavenly bodies (the sun, half-moons, stars), and various crosses, hearts, towers, and so on. The seals provided the basis for the coats of arms of the descendants of Cossack officers and the Left-Bank nobility. In some cases Cossack officers ignored the emblems of their ancestors and created their own, based on Cossack motifs. V. Dunin-Borkovsky, a general quartermaster, for example, replaced his family emblem of a swan with a saber and cross. Ukrainian octagonal coats of arms emerged in the seals of that time, and initials denoting the bearer's name and status were also added.

In the 19th century the creation of Ukrainian family seals came to an end, since only the Russian or Austro-Hungarian imperial government conferred coats of arms and titles. Ukrainian family seals were reduced to two formats, a coat of arms without initials, or initials under the crown of a knight of the nobility, a baron, or a count. They were small, so-called signet or ring seals that served to seal letters and other missives. In the 20th century seals of lineage fell into complete disuse.

Church seals. By the mid-20th century 18 impressions of the seal of the metropolitan of Kiev had been found. The oldest belonged to Metropolitan Theopemptos, who arrived in Kiev in 1037. On the face is a likeness of John the Baptist, and on the reverse the legend, in Greek, God Help Theopemptos, the Metropolitan of Rus'. Two other extant impressions from the 11th century belonged to the metropolitans Yefrem and Georgios.

In the 12th century the standard face image of the seal of the metropolitan showed Mary with the Holy Child. The legend on the reverse went through various minor variations. Exceptions to the standard format included the seal of Nicephorus II (from 1182), which bore a legend on both sides that read O Christ, Watch Over Me, the Archpastor of All of Rus', and Keep Me in Your Thoughts, and that of Ioan II (1189–1190), which bore a likeness of St John Chrysostom and the legend Watch over Your Servant Ioan, Metropolitan of Rus'.

The seals of bishops were similar. Three impressions of the seal of Cosma, the bishop of Halych (from 1157), are extant. The face shows the traditional likeness of Mary, and the verso bears the legend Mother of God, Watch over Me, Cosma of Halych. Seals of old Ukrainian monasteries usually had only appropriate inscriptions and no images.

As heraldry developed in Ukraine in the 14th century, church seals increasingly began using heraldic images. The seals of Ukrainian clerical hierarchs of the 16th century were single-sided and had annular inscriptions. They usually had two sections for images. One section bore a likeness of Christ, Mary, a saint, or other religious figure; the other showed the family emblems of the hierarch and an appropriate symbol of his office (miter, crozier, or cross). The heraldic elements gradually became more prominent, as did elements of Western European church heraldry, such as ecclesiastical headgear, emblems, or Latin annular inscriptions. The lower orders of clergy used heraldic seals almost exclusively.

In the 15th century the seals of monasteries, monastic orders, cathedral assemblies, brotherhoods, and parishes became increasingly sophisticated and of high artistic quality. The seal of the Lviv Dormition Brotherhood bore a likeness of its church's bell tower (16th century). The seal of Kiev metropoly and of the assembly of the St Sophia Cathedral in Kiev showed the Kievan Cave Monastery and a symbolic representation of God's wisdom (17th century). The Mezhyhiria Transfiguration Monastery's seal bore a representation of a valley, a river, and mountains (18th century). Other parishes adopted images of three-domed churches or likenesses of their patron saints. In the 20th century Ukrainian Catholic hierarchs adopted a new seal (influenced by Western European churches) that bears a two-field heraldic shield. The right field usually shows the emblem of the eparchy or exarchate (the unchanging symbol of the particular position); the left field shows the family or personal emblem of the person holding the post, accompanied by the appropriate symbol for the position.

Governmental and institutional seals. Seals were already being used by diplomatic, trade, boyar, and military officials in the 10th century, under Ihor I and Sviatoslav I Ihorevych. The oldest that have been preserved belonged to Ratybor, a vice-regent of Tmutorokan and *tysiatskyi* of Kiev in the late 11th century (the face with the likeness of St Clement, the Roman Pope [Ratybor was his Christian name], and the verso with the legend From Ratybor). The legend on the seal used by D. Dedko, vice-regent of Halych in the early 14th century, was similar to those used in Western Europe at the time (Guardian and Overseer of Rus' Lands). Seals designed for municipal governments and institutions underwent accelerated development under the Hetman state in the 17th and 18th centuries (eg, seals of the General Chancellery, the General Court, and regimental and company administrations). One of the best examples of institutional seals of the era belonged to the Kievan Mohyla Academy. It had an annular Latin inscription (*Kiioviensis Sigillum Academia*) and an image of the academy in sunlight and cloud. After the abolition of the Hetmanate this Ukrainian sphragistical style was lost as seals became copies of the Russian and Austro-Hungarian imperial models. In the mid-19th century it was revived by various community organizations in Galicia and Bukovyna, and in 1917–18 there was a brief efflorescence in the design of governmental seals, such as postal seals and the *postage stamps of the government of the Western Ukrainian National Republic (in the form of a trident) and of the military. After the Bolshevik takeover this form of seal was maintained only in Galician organizations and, partially, in émigré circles. In the first decades after the Second World War a number of émigré Ukrainian graphic artists produced seals in traditional styles for Ukrainian community institutions.

The study of seals. Ukrainian sphragistics was one of the disciplines Hetman K. Rozumovsky planned to have taught at his university in Baturyn (along with heraldry, diplomacy, and related subjects), but the university was never established. Academic study in sphragistics did not begin until the mid-19th century. Scholars and hobbyists in the field have included K. Antypovych, B. Barvinsky, K. Bolsunovsky, M. Bytynsky, M. Hrushevsky, P. Klymenko, P. Klymkevych, I. Krypiakevych, O. Lazarevsky, Ye. Liutsenko, I. Lutsky, V. Modzalevsky, H. Myloradovych, H. Narbut, Ya. Pasternak, V. Prokopovych, M. Petrov, V. Seniutovych-Berezhny, M. and M. Slabchenko, A. Storozhenko, and P. Yefymenko (Sr), as well as the Russians A. Barsukov, E. Kamentseva, A. Lappo-Danilevsky, N.

Likhachev, V. Lukomsky, B. Rybakov, and V. Yanin, the Poles A. Darowski-Weryha, M. Gumowski, F. Piekosiński, W. Semkowicz, and W. Wittig, the German W. Ewald, and the Rumanian N. Banescu. In Soviet Ukraine in the 1970s, D. Blifeld, V. Fomenko, V. Havrylenko, O. Markevych, V. Strelsky, and others published related works.

Artifacts of Ukrainian sphragistics are held in various archives and museums of Ukraine and Russia, particularly the State Hermitage in St Petersburg, state museums of history in Moscow and Kiev, the ANU Institute of Archeology, the National Museum and the ANU Institute of Social Sciences in Lviv, and in the hands of private collectors. Other Ukrainian sphragistic collections are found in Belarus, France, Germany, Greece, Hungary, Latvia, Lithuania, Poland, Turkey, and the United States.

BIBLIOGRAPHY
Ivanov, P. Sbornik snimkov s drevneishikh russkikh pechatei (Moscow 1858)
Weryga-Darowski, O. 'Znaki pieczętne ruskie,' in Noty heraldyczne (Paris 1862)
Snimki drevneishikh russkikh pechatei (Moscow 1882)
Barsukov, A. 'Pravitel'stvennye pechati v Malorossii,' KS, 1887, no. 9
Bolsunovskii, K. Sfragisticheskie i geral'dicheskie pamiatniki Iugo-Zapadnogo kraia, 3 vols (Kiev 1899–1914)
Hrushevs'kyi, M. 'Pechati z okolytsi Halycha,' ZNTSh, 38 (1900)
Likhachev, N. Russkaia sfragistika (St Petersburg 1900)
Lappo-Danilevskii, A. Pechati poslednikh galitsko-vladimirskikh kniazei i ikh sovetniki: Boleslav Iurii II, kniaz' Vsei Maloi Rossii (St Petersburg 1906)
Slabchenko, M. Materialy po malorusskoi sfragistike (Odessa 1912)
Kryp'iakevych, I. 'Z kozats'koï sfragistyky,' ZNTSh, 122, 124 (1918)
Antypovych, K. 'Kyïvs'ka mis'ka pechatka,' in Iubileinyi zbirnyk na poshanu akademika Dmytra Ivanovycha Bahaliia (Kiev 1927)
Kornylovych, M. 'Pechatky 16-ty kyïvs'kykh tsekhiv,' in Iuvileinyi zbirnyk na poshanu akademika Mykhaila Serhiievycha Hrushevs'koho (Kiev 1928)
Slabchenko, M. 'Zaporiz'ki pechatky XVII v.,' ZIFV, 19 (1928)
Prokopovych, V. 'Pechat' malorossiiskaia: Sfragistychni etiudy,' ZNTSh, 163 (Paris–New York 1954)
Klymkevych, R. 'Naidavnishi pechati ukraïns'kykh mist,' Kyïv, 1963, nos 1–2
Ianin, V. Aktovye pechati drevnei Rusi X–XV vv. (Moscow 1970)
Havrylenko, V. Ukraïns'ka sfrahistyka (Kiev 1977)

R. Klymkevych

Spilka, A. The collective pseudonym for Spilka Adeska (Odessa Association), a group of compilers of a Russian-Ukrainian dictionary published in Lviv (1893–1900) under the direction of M. Umanets (M. Komar). Members of the group included T. Desiatyn-Lukianiv, T. Zinkivsky, O. Kosach (O. Pchilka), V. Nazarevsky, M. Starytsky, and K. Ukhach-Okhorovych.

Spilka, V. The collective pseudonym of the compilers (Yu. *Kobyliansky, L. *Kohut, Z. *Kuzelia, V. *Simovych, and Ye. Tsapler) who, together with V. *Kmitsykevych, published a German-Ukrainian dictionary in Chernivtsi in 1912.

Spilka, Ukrainian Social Democratic (Ukrainska sotsiial-demokratychna spilka). A party formed by M. *Melenevsky and other orthodox Marxists who left the *Revolutionary Ukrainian party (RUP) in December 1904.

They rejected as bourgeois and nationalist the program of the RUP majority. They saw as their primary goal social revolution and fusion with the Russian Social Democratic Workers' party (RSDWP) as the unitary, centralized workers' party of all nationalities in the Russian Empire. In January 1905 the Spilka (the Ukrainian word for 'association' or 'union') was constituted as the autonomous, territorial section in Ukraine of the *Menshevik wing of the RSDWP to do political work on its behalf among the Ukrainian-speaking rural proletariat. Because the Spilka worked closely with the Russian and Jewish Mensheviks and the Jewish Workers' *Bund, in 1905–7 it built a mass-based organization in Ukraine's villages and small towns that was stronger and had more influence than RUP and its successor, the *Ukrainian Social Democratic Workers' party (USDWP). The Spilka had within its ranks not only nationally conscious Ukrainians (eg, H. Dovzhenko, M. Halahan, P. Kanivets, M. Korenetsky, P. Krat, V. Mazurenko, Melenevsky, O. Skoropys-Yoltukhovsky, H. and M. Tkachenko) and nationally indifferent ones (P. Tuchapsky), but also ethnic Ukrainians who were hostile to the Ukrainian national movement (I. Kyriienko) and non-Ukrainians (Yu. Larin, V. Perekrestov, A. Podolsky [Hoikhberg], R. Rabinovich, A. Rish, L. Slutsky, S. Sokolov, Y. Soroker, S. Zavadsky).

During the Revolution of 1905–6 the Spilka's 3,000 to 7,000 members organized and led many strikes and other disturbances in Chernihiv, Kiev, Kherson, Podilia, Poltava, and Volhynia gubernias. At the same time, through its organ *Pravda (1905) and its propagandistic brochures in Ukrainian and Russian, the Spilka waged a fierce ideological struggle against the USDWP and thus gained the support of many former RUP cells. From December 1905 the Spilka published Pravda and most of its literature in Russian. The Spilka's gains were the greatest during the elections to the First and Second Russian state dumas, and in the Second Duma it had 14 delegates (the USDWP had 1). At the Fifth RSDWP Congress in London in May 1907, the 10 Spilka delegates constituted 25 percent of all delegates from Ukraine.

During the tsarist reaction of 1907, mass arrests brought the Spilka to nearly total collapse, and several of its leaders (eg, Rabinovich, Rish, Soroker, H. Tkachenko) were exiled to Siberia. Thereafter the Spilka had little impact in Ukraine. In 1908 Melenevsky moved the Spilka center from Kiev abroad and formed small fraternal groups in Lviv, Vienna, Paris, Geneva, and Zurich linked by L. Trotsky's Menshevik paper, Pravda (1908–12), published in Lviv (nos 1–4 in Ukrainian) and then Vienna (in Russian). Because its leaders increasingly compromised with the centralist, Russian chauvinist tendencies within the RSDWP at a time when national consciousness was on the rise within the Ukrainian peasantry, many of its remaining Ukrainian members left the party and joined the USDWP, and the 'internationalists' joined the RSDWP or the Bund. The Spilka held its last conference in 1909, and its last document, an appeal by Melenevsky, appeared in 1912. By 1913 the Spilka was defunct.

BIBLIOGRAPHY
Rish, A. Ocherki po istorii ukrainskoi sotsial-demokraticheskoi 'Spilki' (Kharkiv 1926)
Halahan, M. Z moïkh spomyniv (80-ti roky do svitovoï viiny), 1 (Lviv 1930)

R. Senkus

Spinach (*Spinacia oleracea*; Ukrainian: *shpinat, shpynat*). A hardy, leafy annual vegetable of the goosefoot family Chenopodiaceae that grows wild in Central Asia and in Transcaucasia. It contains high levels of iron, calcium, and iodine, vitamins A, B complex, and C, proteins, and fat. In Ukraine garden spinach grows in a cool climate on rich soil. Sowing can be repeated several times a summer. Spinach is consumed fresh or cooked and is preserved frozen or canned.

Spirea (*Spiraea*; Ukrainian: *tavolha*). Deciduous shrubs of the family Rosaceae, popularly cultivated for their attractive white, pink, or red flowers. In Ukraine seven species of spirea grow as underbrush on forest outskirts, on the slopes of ravines, in brushwood, and on steppes; they form dense ground covers. Ten other species are used as decorative hedges and ornamental borders in gardens and parks.

Spiro, Petr, b 1844 in Moscow, d 1894. Physiologist. A graduate of Moscow University (1867), he worked at Odessa University (from 1871), where he obtained a medical degree (1874) and became a professor (from 1885). He researched the physiology of respiration, digestion, and hypnosis and participated in the work of the first experimental psychology laboratory in the Russian Empire (est 1882 in Odessa).

Spiš (German: Zips, Hungarian: Szepes). A region of northeastern Slovakia, located in the central Carpathian and the western Beskyd mountains. It includes the basins of the upper Poprad and Hornád rivers, the Spišská Magura massif, a small part of the Tatra Mountains, and the Slovenské Rudohorie Mountains. It covers an area of approx 3,700 sq km, with a population (1965) of 255,000. It constitutes part of the historical *Prešov region of Ukrainian settlement. The territory was settled fairly late, initially by Slovaks in the south, Poles in the north, and Germans (13th century). In 1270 the German settlers formed a union of 24 Spiš towns. Of those, the Hungarian king Sigismund ceded 13 to Poland in 1412 (which Poland held until the 18th century). Otherwise, the region was controlled by Hungary and administered as Szepes komitat until 1919. It now belongs to Slovakia and Poland. In the 14th and 15th centuries Ukrainians (Lemkos) began settling there; they now live in the northern and eastern sections of the region, in the Stará L'ubovňa district. They are divided between a compact settlement of approx 230 sq km and a number of small pockets (the westernmost Ukrainian outpost being Osturnia). There are about 15,000 Ukrainians living in the Spiš area.

Spiš, Treaty of. An agreement concluded in 1214 between the Hungarian king Andrew II and the Polish prince Leszek the White to divide the principality of Prince Roman Mstyslavych of Halych upon that prince's death. Andrew's son, Kálmán, who was married to Leszek's daughter, Salome, was to assume the throne of Halych, and Leszek was to annex western Galicia, including Peremyshl. Soon after the plan was implemented, the Halych boyars overthrew their new master and called Mstyslav Mstyslavych to the throne.

Spišská Magura. A mountain massif in the western Beskyds in Czechoslovakia, on the border of Ukrainian and Slovak ethnic territory. The massif consists of lightly folded flysch formations with ridges reaching 1,156 m. The ridges are mostly covered with woods and meadows and are sparsely populated.

Spivak, Borys, b 12 March 1925 in Shpola (now in Cherkasy oblast), d 4 June 1971. Historian. He graduated in history from Odessa University (1951) and taught at Uzhhorod University (from 1954, as professor from 1966). He wrote *Narysy istoriï revoliutsiinoï borot'by trudiashchykh Zakarpattia 1930–1945 rr.* (Essays on the History of the Revolutionary Struggle of the Workers of Transcarpathia in 1930–45, 1961), *Storinky istoriï* (The Pages of History, 1962), and *Revoliutsiinyi rukh na Zakarpatti v 1924–1929 rokakh* (The Revolutionary Movement in Transcarpathia in 1924–9, 1964).

Spivak, Eliahu (Illia), b 22 October 1890 in Vasylkiv, Kiev gubernia, d 12 August 1952 in Moscow. Jewish-Ukrainian philologist; AN URSR (now ANU) corresponding member from 1939. A graduate of the Hlukhiv Teachers' Institute (1919), he taught in Yiddish secondary schools in Kiev, Kharkiv, and Odessa in the 1920s; at the Odessa Institute of People's Education (1927–30); and at the Kiev Institute of Professional Education (1930–2). In the early 1930s he was head of the philological section of the VUAN *Institute of Jewish Culture in Kiev and then director of the ANU Cabinet of Jewish Culture (1936–48). He was arrested during the Zhdanov purge of Jewish intellectuals in 1949 and condemned to death with 25 other Yiddish cultural figures by a secret Military Collegium tribunal. He was executed in Lubianka Prison. Spivak wrote a Yiddish textbook (1923) and articles on the history of the Yiddish language, on Yiddish lexicology and lexicography, and on the language and style of Sholom Aleichem and Mendele Mocher Seforim. In 1935 he initiated the academic Russian-Yiddish dictionary project. The manuscript of the dictionary was confiscated after his arrest, and was not published until 1984, in Moscow.

Spivomovky. Short verses generally based on folk anecdotes, jokes, sayings, or tales. They can be found in literary works, such as L. Borovykovsky's and Ye. Hrebinka's fables. S. Rudansky wrote three collections of *spivomovky* (1851–60), and I. Franko wrote a cycle titled *Novi spivomovky* (New *Spivomovky*).

Spokii (Tranquility). An art circle established in 1927 by Ukrainian students at the Warsaw Academy of Arts. Among its founding members were P. Andrusiv, V. Vaskivsky, N. Khasevych, and P. *Mehyk (its president). By the time it was dissolved in 1939, it had organized 13 exhibitions, including two traveling exhibitions in Volhynia, and published albums of woodcuts (1936) and N. Khasevych's bookplates (1939) and 13 catalogues of its shows. Its members also participated in the exhibitions of the Association of Independent Ukrainian Artists in Lviv and the exhibitions of Ukrainian graphic art in Berlin and Prague. In 1939 Spokii had 33 members.

Spolitakevych, Volodymyr [Spolitakevyč], b 6 January 1882 in Vytkiv Staryi, Radekhiv county, Galicia, d 6 December 1932 in Yonkers, New York. Greek Catholic priest and civic activist. After being ordained (1906) he came to the United States (1907) and served in several parishes in Pennsylvania and New York. In 1914 he was elected chairman of the education committee of the Ukrainian National Association. He also served as president of the United Ukrainian Organizations in America in 1924–6.

Spomahateli. Wealthy elect Cossacks in 18th-century Left-Bank Ukraine who hired and equipped poor Cossacks to perform their military duty. The term was also applied to Cossacks who could not serve because of old age, illness, or a handicap. Such Cossacks were excused from service but were required to pay part of the cost of equipping a substitute.

Sport (Sport). A monthly sports journal published in Kiev in 1936–41 by the Communist Youth League of Ukraine and the Committee on Physical Culture and Sports of the Council of People's Commissars of the Ukrainian SSR. *Sport* succeeded the Russian-language *Vestnik fizicheskoi kul'tury* (Kharkiv, 1922–9) and Ukrainian-language *Visnyk fizychnoï kul'tury* (Kharkiv, 1929–30) and *Fizkul'turnyk Ukraïny* (Kharkiv, 1931–4; Kiev, 1934–6).

Sportfishing (*rybalskyi sport*). The first fishing clubs were established in the larger towns of Ukraine before the 1917 Revolution. Under Soviet rule fishermen belonged to the Ukrainian Hunting and Fishing Society (est 1921); in 1984 it had over 500,000 members in its 25 oblast and 514 raion collectives. Sportfishing in the USSR as a whole was under the control of the All-Union Federation of Sportfishing in Moscow.

Sports. Organized athletic games and competitions. In medieval Ukraine, certain sporting activities were engaged in as part of military training or religious ceremonies, or for entertainment. The chronicles mention that the upper classes engaged in bear hunting; capturing wild horses; fighting; and games involving running, dancing, singing, and wrestling. During funeral feasts duels and primitive boxing matches took place.

Little is known about competitions among the Cossacks, but their reputation for marksmanship, swordsmanship, and horsemanship suggests that they trained to develop their skills and physical endurance.

Western Ukraine. Sports in the modern sense were introduced in Ukraine in the latter half of the 19th century from Western Europe. The first organized Ukrainian competitions occurred only after the founding of the *Sokil (1894) and *Sich (1900) physical education societies in Galicia. The first sports circles sprang up at Ukrainian gymnasiums. In 1907–8 a soccer team was organized by I. *Bobersky at the Ukrainian Academic Gymnasium in Lviv. By 1911 its membership and activities had expanded so much that the Ukraina sports club was established. The club organized soccer matches with Polish, Czech, Hungarian, and German teams; track-and-field meets; and wrestling, tennis, and cycling competitions. So-called Zaporozhian Games were held in Lviv in 1911 and 1914. In Peremyshl the Sianova Chaika club was organized by

local gymnasium teachers in 1912. Another club was organized in Ternopil.

After the hiatus of the First World War, the Sokil, Sich, and Ukraina societies resumed their sports activities, and new sports clubs were formed. In Lviv, the Carpathian Ski Club, the Lviv Tennis Club, the Ukrainian Student Sports Club, *Plai, Bohun, Burevii, Chornomortsi, Meta, Tryzub, Strila, and the Tur hunting society appeared; in Peremyshl, Sian, Berkut, Spartanky, and Sianova Chaika; in Stanyslaviv, the Ukrainian Sports Club and Prolom; in Sambir, Dnister; in Stryi, Skala; in Ternopil, Podilia; and in Drohobych, Vatra. The Orly Catholic youth association and the Kameniari Union of Ukrainian Progressive Youth formed sports sections within their organizations. About a dozen clubs competed in the Zaporozhian Games, which were revived by the central Sokil branch in 1923 and held annually in either Lviv or Peremyshl. Outstanding female athletes were O. Sekela and M. Husar from Berkut, and O. Kobziar and N. Nyzhankivska from Sokil in Lviv; outstanding male athletes were R. Shukhevych, Yu. Hnateiko, R. Rak, and V. Kobziar from Lviv, and Berkut's T. Kozak, M. Romanets, I. Medvid, and Yu. Semeniuk. The most popular sport was soccer; the Ukraina, Prolom, Podilia, Dnister, and Skala clubs had the best teams. In 1925 the *Ukrainian Sports Union was founded in Lviv to co-ordinate the sports activities of the various societies and clubs. The rapid rise in the popularity of soccer led clubs such as Ukraina, Prolom, and Sian to join the Polish Soccer Association. Attempts by Polish authorities to obstruct the growth of the Western Ukrainian sports movement did not succeed. In 1939 there were over 200 Ukrainian clubs and sports sections within the Sokil and *Luh societies, with a combined total of over 3,000 participants. The Zaporozhian Games of 1934 and 1939 demonstrated the vitality of Ukrainian organized sports in Galicia.

In Czechoslovak-ruled Transcarpathia, the Sich societies and the Plast scouting organization continued the sports activities they had begun before the war. The Rus' Ukrainian sports society of Uzhhorod became part of the Czechoslovak Soccer League. In interwar Bukovyna, the Rumanian authorities abolished the Sich societies that had been established there before the war. Most of the extant Ukrainian sports clubs were devoted to soccer. R. Petrushenko of the Dovbush club in Chernivtsi was a member of the Rumanian skating team in the 1936 Olympic Games.

Ukraine under tsarist rule. Before the 1917 Revolution there were no Ukrainian organized sports activities. The upper classes, however, had access to yachting, tennis, and gymnastics clubs. Workers and students organized their own unofficial sports groups, and the Russian Sokol and Boy Scout organizations promoted gymnastics. Ukrainian athletes, such as the wrestlers I. Piddubny and O. Harkavenko, the fencers Klimov and Zakharov, and the equestrians Boboshko and Rodzianko, participated in competitions throughout Europe. Some Ukrainians represented Russia at the 1908 and 1912 Olympic Games. In 1913 the first All-Russian Olympiad took place in Kiev.

Soviet Ukraine. Under Soviet rule, organized sports were well developed as a result of the Soviet state's emphasis on *physical education for the entire population. In 1922 the Spartak organization was founded by the Komsomol to unite all existing sports circles and to control their activities. In 1923 the first All-Ukrainian *Spartakiad took place in Kharkiv, and the Higher Council on Physical Culture of Ukraine was created to co-ordinate all physical education and organized sports in Ukraine. Thenceforth all sports clubs were part of Komsomol or trade-union organizations. At the 1928 All-Union Spartakiad, the collective Ukrainian team placed second overall and first in volleyball, handball, gymnastics, shooting, and motorcycling. In 1930 the first All-Ukrainian Rural Spartakiad took place in Kiev; competitors were the victors in 300 raion and 25 okruha Spartakiads. Prominent Ukrainian athletes who participated in republican, all-Union, and Red Sport International competitions in the 1920s and 1930s were V. Kalyna, H. Raievsky, M. Pidhaietsky, and Z. Synytska in track-and-field sports; M. Dmytriiev, Ye. Bokova, and T. Demydenko in gymnastics; V. Furmaniuk in swimming; H. Popov, H. Novak, Ya. Kutsenko, and M. Kasianyk in weight lifting; and P. Makhnytsky, M. Sazhko, and I. Mykhilovsky in Greco-Roman wrestling.

Sports contacts with the West increased after the Second World War, and Soviet physical education and sports training were improved. In 1959 the Committee on Physical Culture and Sports of Ukraine's Council of Ministers was reorganized into the Union of Sports Societies and Organizations of the Ukrainian SSR; like its predecessors, it was subordinated to its all-Union counterpart in Moscow. Oblast, city, raion, and local councils of physical culture oversaw the work of all voluntary sports societies, physical culture collectives at industrial enterprises and collective and state farms, and sports clubs. Until August 1991 there were nine republican branches of all-Union *sports societies in Ukraine – *Avanhard (over 3 million members), *Burevisnyk (approx 560,000 members), *Dynamo, Kolos (formerly Kolhospnyk; 4.7 million members), Lokomotyv (approx 470,000 members), *Spartak (over 2.6 million members), Trudovi Rezervy (approx 690,000 members), Vodnyk (approx 90,000 members), and Zenit – with a combined membership of over 17 million. Military reservists were trained in paramilitary sports such as fly-ing, skydiving, gliding, car racing, motorcycling, skin diving, motorboating, and shooting by clubs of the *Voluntary Society for Assistance to the Army, Air Force, and Navy.

Ukraine was deprived of its own representation in international sports, but Ukrainian athletes participated in the *Olympic Games as members of USSR teams from 1952. Since the 1950s over 80 world records and many European and Soviet records have been set by athletes from Ukraine. Kiev's Dynamo soccer team won the 1975 and 1986 European Cup-Winners' Cup and over a dozen USSR championships and cups. Many international competitions have taken place in Kiev: European equestrian championships (1973–5); international women's handball championships; European track-and-field, boxing, and judo championships (1975); the Golden Ring floor-exercises tournament (1976); a world wrestling championship (1983); and USSR–West Germany and USSR–United States track-and-field competitions (1983). Odessa hosted an international swimming and track-and-field competition in 1974; USSR–United States boxing competitions took place in Donetske in 1979 and 1982; and a USSR–East Germany boxing competition was held in Zaporizhia in 1981. Today over 50 dif-

ferent sports are practiced in Ukraine. The 10 most popular are (in descending order) track-and-field sports, soccer, volleyball, shooting, basketball, table tennis, skiing, handball, swimming, and gymnastics.

Recognizing the political importance of sports in fostering national pride and international recognition, the Soviet central authorities ruled out separate representations from the Soviet national republics at international competitions. Like any other colonial power, the USSR exploited the athletic potential of its constituent nations to build up the central sports organizations, which were Russian. Unofficial data show a staggering mortality rate among Soviet Olympic medal winners, which suggests that Soviet athletes were forced to ingest steroids and other dangerous drugs, and to undergo physiological experiments.

Sports periodicals published in Ukraine include *Vestnik fizicheskoi kul'tury* (1922–9), *Visnyk fizychnoï kul'tury* (1929–30), *Fizkul'turnyk Ukraïny* (1930–5), *Sport* (1936–41), *Radians'kyi sport* (1934–9, 1950–64), *Fizkul'tura i sport* (1957–64), *Sportyvna hazeta* (since 1964), and *Start* (since 1965).

Abroad. In Canada, the Canadian Ukrainian Athletic Clubs (CUAC) in Winnipeg (1925) and in Oshawa (1927) were the earliest manifestations of organized sports activity by Ukrainians. Over 60 Ukrainian sports clubs, leagues, and teams have been active in Canada. The CUAC is still in existence; its women's softball team won the national championship in 1965. The other Ukraina teams have also won national championships – Montreal's soccer team in 1957 and Toronto's volleyball team in 1975.

In the interwar period Sich societies in the United States and Canada established their own track-and-field, swimming, volleyball, soccer, softball, basketball, bowling, and tennis clubs and competitions. Ukrainian youth athletic competitions were held in Philadelphia in 1935 and 1936. Young athletes from the United States and Canada competed in the first Ukrainian-American Olympiad held in Philadelphia in 1936. In 1938 the Ukrainian National Association founded a baseball league; by 1940 it had 28 teams.

Ukrainian refugees in postwar Germany set up the *Ukrainian Council for Physical Culture in November 1945 to co-ordinate the 51 sports clubs (with a combined membership of 3,700) that arose in the DP camps. The most popular sport was soccer, with 29 clubs in the US zone of Germany alone. In volleyball there were 29 men's and 16 women's teams. There were 15 basketball teams. The council's hockey team scored a victory over the best American army team. Track-and-field sports, skiing, swimming, table tennis, tennis, mountain climbing, boxing, and weight lifting were practiced also. The council organized games and athletic competitions among Ukrainian teams and between Ukrainian and non-Ukrainian teams, as well as courses for trainers and coaches (1946–7). At the 1948 DP Olympiad in Nuremberg, Ukrainian teams took first place in soccer, men's volleyball, the 400-m men's relay, and heavyweight boxing. After the mass emigration of refugees to the New World in the late 1940s, new Ukrainian sports clubs were founded in the host countries. Soccer, tennis, volleyball, and swimming have been particularly popular. The *Ukrainian Sports Federation of the USA and Canada was founded in 1953–4. In 1980 it organized, with other émigré communities of the captive nations of the USSR, the Free Olympiad in Toronto. The Ukrainian delegation won 11 gold, 8 silver, and 7 bronze medals and took second place overall. At the second such Olympiad, in 1984, the Ukrainian women's team placed first overall, the men's team second overall.

(See also *Acrobatics, *Basketball, *Boxing, *Cycling, *Fencing, *Gymnastics, *Hockey, *Mountaineering, *Parachuting, *Rowing and canoeing, *Shooting, *Skating, *Skiing, *Soaring, *Soccer, *Sportfishing, *Swimming, *Tennis, *Track-and-field sports, *Volleyball, *Water polo, *Weight lifting, *Wrestling, and *Yachting.)

BIBLIOGRAPHY
Al'manakh Rady fizychnoï kul'tury (Munich 1951)
Chernova, Ie. Rozvytok fizychnoï kul'tury i sportu v Ukraïns'kii RSR (Kiev 1959)
Sport na Ukraïni, 1957–1960: Dovidnyk (Kiev 1961)
Sport na Ukraïni, 1960–1964: Dovidnyk (Kiev 1966)
Sport na Ukraïni, 1965–1967: Dovidnyk (Kiev 1969)
Kizchenko, V. 'Z istorii rozvytku sportu na Ukraïni (kinets' XIX–pochatok XX st.),' UIZh, 1980, no. 7
Riordan, J. Soviet Sport: Background to the Olympics (Oxford 1980)
Sportyvni vysoty Ukraïny (Kiev 1980)
Rymarenko, P. Sports in Ukraine (Kiev 1988)

E. Zharsky

Sports palaces (*palatsy sportu*). Covered buildings for sports competitions and other mass events. Most such palaces have ice rinks and movable stands seating from 3,000 to 14,000 spectators. The largest sports palaces in Ukraine are the Kiev Sports Palace, built in 1960 by M. Hrechyna, O. Zavarov, and others; the Labor Reserve Palace in Lviv, built in 1970 by S. Sokolov; and the Youth Palace in Zaporizhia, built in 1972.

Sports societies. In the USSR, the first all-Union mass voluntary societies providing the population with athletic and sports facilities, training, and activities were the Komsomol organization Spartak (est 1922) and the paramilitary Dynamo (Russian: Dinamo; est 1924). From 1926 on sports clubs were founded by various USSR trade unions, and in 1936–8 the All-Union Central Council of Trade Unions united them in 64 sports societies. By 1957 most of these societies had been amalgamated.

In Soviet Ukraine there were republican branches of nine all-Union societies: Dynamo, for employees of the MVD, KGB, and other police and security forces; Spartak (est 1935; over 2 million members in 1986), for white-collar employees in state trade, civil aviation, culture, and public health; Lokomotyv (Russian: Lokomotiv, est 1936; 462,000 members in 1985), for railway workers; Zenit (est 1936; part of the Trud society in 1957–66), for employees of the machine-building industry; Vodnyk (Russian: Vodnik, est 1938; over 100,000 members in 1985), for river and sea transportation workers; Kolos (est 1950; 4.7 million members in 1984), formerly Kolhospnyk (1950–70), the republican equivalent of the all-Union Urozhai society for collective farmers and other rural-based employees; Avanhard (est 1957; over 3 million members in 1985), the republican equivalent of the all-Union Trud society for industrial and construction workers; Burevisnyk (Russian: Burevestnik, est 1957; 525,000 members in 1985), for postsecondary students; and Trudovi Rezervy (Russian: Trudovye Rezervy, est 1943; 686,000 members in 1986), for students and employees of vocational and technical schools.

The Ukrainian societies were composed of athletic collectives (47,900 in Ukraine in 1987) and sports clubs, with a combined membership of over 17 million in 1984. All of them were governed by councils elected at society conferences held every four years and were supervised by the All-Union Council of Voluntary Sports Societies. The societies funded and trained their own individuals and teams participating in intersociety, republican, USSR, and international competitions. In the years 1952–80 Burevisnyk's athletes won 36 Olympic gold medals; Spartak's, 22; Avanhard's, 21; Dynamo's, 15; Lokomotyv's, 10; Kolos's, 5; Zenit's, 4; Trudovi Rezervy's, 1; and Vodnyk's, 1. Teams that have won Soviet and/or international cups are the Kiev Dynamo *soccer team; Avanhard's soccer teams Shakhtar in Donetske and Dnipro in Dnipropetrovske, and its Budivelnyk basketball team in Kiev; Burevisnyk's Medin women's volleyball team in Odessa; the Kharkiv Lokomotyv men's volleyball team; Spartak's women's volleyball team, Aviator rugby team, and Sokil ice hockey-team in Kiev; and Kolos's women's field-hockey team in Boryspil.

R. Senkus

Sportyvna hazeta (Sports Gazette). The only Soviet Ukrainian newspaper devoted solely to sports, founded in April 1934. It is published three times a week in Kiev as the official organ of the Committee on Physical Culture and Sports of the Ukrainian Supreme Soviet and Republican Council of Trade Unions. It was called *Radians'kyi sport* until 1964 and did not come out in 1940–9. In 1980 it had a circulation of 450,000.

Sprat (Ukrainian: *shprot, tiulka*). A valuable commercial food-fish of the herring family Clupeidae (genus *Clupea*) that is usually less than 12 cm long, lives in vast schools, and feeds on plankton. Sprats (*C. sprattus*) are sold fresh, smoked, salted, spiced, or canned in oil. Some are used as bait or are processed for fish meal and oil. In Ukraine the Black Sea sprat (*C. sprattusphalerius*) and the *tiulka* (*C. delicatula*) are found in Black Sea waters, from which they migrate in the spring toward the Danube, Dnieper, Buh, Tylihul, and Berezan estuaries.

Spravnyk (Russian: *spravnik*). A county police and court official in the Russian Empire. The office was created by Catherine II's 1775 law on gubernial administration and was introduced in Ukraine in the 1780s. The *spravnyk* was elected for a three-year term by the nobility of a county. In 1862 his powers were restricted to policing, and thenceforth he was appointed by the gubernial governor. The post existed until the Revolution of 1917.

Sprawy Narodowościowe (Nationality Issues). A bimonthly organ of the Polish *Institute for Nationalities Research, published in Warsaw in 1927–39. Edited by S. Paprocki, it printed articles and information on Polish communities outside Poland, on the various minorities within Poland, and on nationality and ethnic issues in general. It devoted attention to the League of Nations and the national question in the USSR and throughout the world, and featured an extensive book review section, bibliography, and chronicle of events. The journal remains an important source of information on interwar Ukraine. Indexes to it appeared in 1933 and 1937.

Spring of Nations. See Revolution of 1848–9 in the Habsburg monarchy.

Spring rituals. Traditional folk rituals practiced in the spring, from the equinox (20–21 March) to the summer solstice (21–22 June). Originally these rituals were believed to possess magical powers that ensured a bountiful harvest and fertility in domestic animals. The ritual cycle began with the rite of *provody (bidding winter farewell and welcoming spring), just before the beginning of Lent. Winter was usually personified by minor deities (Kostrub, Morena, Smertka, or Masliana), effigies of which were burned or drowned ceremonially. Spring was personified by a young girl crowned with a wreath and holding a green branch in her hand. She was the central figure in the ritual games, dances, and songs (see *Vesnianky-hahilky). The arrival of migratory birds signaled the beginning of the spring festival called *stricha* (from 'greeting'). On the Feast of the 40 Martyrs (22 March [9 March OS]) bird-shaped buns called *zhaivoronky* (larks) were baked and tossed into the air by children and told to bring spring with them. The largest number of agrarian rituals was designated for the Lenten period and *Easter. Their magical meaning is clearest in the ritual first sowing, the first release of livestock to pasture (on St George's feast), and the decorating of fields and farmhouses with green branches (see *Rosalia).

BIBLIOGRAPHY
Voropai, O. *Zvychaï nashoho narodu*, vol 1 (Munich 1958)
Krut', Iu. *Khliborobs'ka obriadova poeziia slov'ian* (Kiev 1973)
Sokolova, V. *Vesene-letnie kalendarnye obriady russkikh, ukraintsev i belorusov XIX–nachalo XX v.* (Moscow 1979)

M. Mushynka

Spruce (*Picea*; Ukrainian: *smereka, yalyna*). A coniferous, evergreen ornamental and timber tree of the family Pinaceae, with a straight trunk and thick conical crown, reaching heights of 20–80 m. Its wood is valuable in the production of construction lumber, paper, and musical instruments and as a source of tar, turpentine, and tanning substances. Two species grow naturally in Ukraine, Norway spruce (*P. abies* or *P. excelsa*) and mountain spruce (*P. montana*). Spruce trees cover an area of about 850,000 ha, or 12.5 percent of all forests in Ukraine (third most common after pine and oak trees), principally in the Carpathian Mountains, where pure spruce forests are also to be found. Smaller islands of spruce exist in the Roztochia, Podlachia, Podilia, and Chernihiv regions. Eastern spruce (*P. orientalis*) is found in Caucasia, and Engelmann spruce (*P. engelmanni*) and blue spruce (*P. pungens*) are cultivated as ornamentals.

Spurry (*Spergula*; Ukrainian: *steliushok*). A small, white-flowered herb of the family Caryophyllaceae. Three species are found in Ukraine (*S. arvenis* is the most common) growing as weeds in sandy soils, in solonchaks, along roads, and in wastelands. Spurry green is a feed suitable for silage.

Spynul, Mykola, 1867–1928. Bukovynian political and pedagogical activist. He published articles on education in the daily *Bukovyna*. He was a member of the Austrian parliament (1907–18) and the Bukovynian Diet (1911–18) from the National Democratic party, and he served as sec-

retary of the Bukovynian Ukrainian Club. He was deported to Siberia by the Russian occupational authorities in 1914 (released in 1915). Spynul participated in setting up the Ukrainian government in Bukovyna (November 1918). He served as consul for the Western Ukrainian National Republic in Vienna in 1919 and remained there until his death.

Squash (*Cucurbita pepo* or *C. maxima*; Ukrainian: *harbuz, kabachok*). An annual vegetable of the gourd family Cucurbitaceae. Summer squash is a quick-growing, small-fruited bush, the young fruit of which (7 to 12 days old) is cooked as a vegetable. Pumpkin squash (*C. pepo* var.) is a round, hollow, deep yellow fruit of a vine plant; its seeds are used to produce cooking oil or dried as a popular snack food. Ukrainian folk custom held that if a girl rejected a marriage proposal she gave the unlucky suitor a large pumpkin, which he had to carry home in view of the whole village. Overripe squash is used as livestock feed. In Ukraine squash is grown predominantly in the steppe and forest-steppe regions.

Squill (*Scilla*; Ukrainian: *proliska*). A grassy, perennial, bulbous herb of the family Liliaceae, with small white, blue, or purple flowers. Of its nearly 60 species, Ukraine has 4, including *S. autumnalis*, common in the southern steppes and the Crimea, *S. bifolia*, and *S. sibirica*, which grows naturally in forests and thickets and is also cultivated for decoration.

Squirrel, Eurasian red (*Sciurus vulgaris*; Ukrainian: *bilka, vyvirka*). A bushy-tailed, tufted, arboreal mammal of the rodent family Sciuridae. Also known as the common or pine squirrel, in Ukraine it is found in the forest and forest-steppe zones, where it lives in tree hollows or in nests of leaves and twigs. Squirrels are hunted in Ukraine for their fur.

Sreblo (aka *serebro* 'silver'). Silver coins minted in the 10th and 11th centuries by Volodymyr the Great and his sons Sviatopolk I and Yaroslav the Wise. Weighing between 1.73 and 4.68 g, they bore on one side an image of the prince and the Slavonic inscription Volodymyr (or Sviatopolk) Is on the Throne and on the other side the dynastic symbol, a trident, and This Is His Silver, or Yaroslav's Silver. The only other silver coins of the period were minted by Prince Oleh-Mykhailo of Tmutorokan in 1078. Beginning in the 13th century the word *sreblo* was used to denote any kind of coin and was interchangeable with the term *kuna*. Approx 300 silver coins of Kievan Rus' have been discovered, most of them in a hoard found in Nizhen in 1852.

Srebrenytsky, Hryhorii [Srebrenyc'kyj, Hryhorij], b 1741 in Chernechyna, Okhtyrka region, d 1773. Copper engraver. He learned engraving at the Kievan Cave Monastery Press (to 1758) and the St Petersburg Academy of Arts, where he studied under E. Chemesov. From 1767 he taught at the academy.

Srem. A historical region of what used to be northeastern Yugoslavia, lying between the Sava and Danube rivers and covering an area of 6,870 sq km. Its population is over 500,000 and includes Serbs, Croats, Hungarians, Slovaks, and Ukrainians (about 10,000). The larger, eastern part of Srem belongs to the Autonomous Region of Vojvodina within *Serbia; the smaller, western part belongs to *Croatia. Ukrainians began to migrate into Srem from *Bačka, just north of Srem, at the end of the 18th century. After the Second World War some Ukrainians from Bosnia moved to Srem. Ukrainian communities are found in cities such as Sremska Mitrovica, Indjia, Šid, Vukovar, and Vinkovci and in villages such as Bačinci, Berkasovo, Petrovci, Andrijevci, and Mikloševci.

Sreznevsky, Borys [Sreznevs'kyj], b 31 March 1857 in St Petersburg, d 24 March 1934 in Kiev. Meteorologist and climatologist; full member of the VUAN from 1920. He graduated from St Petersburg University (1879) and was a professor at Tartu University (1894–1918). From 1919 he headed the Kiev Meteorological Observatory. He did fundamental work on storms in the Black Sea region and wrote the monograph *O vlazhnosti* (On Humidity, 1915) and others on cyclonic atmospheric disturbances. He studied the effect of weather on people and developed several meteorological instruments. He also organized the publication of a number of Ukrainian meteorological periodicals.

Izmail Sreznevsky

Sreznevsky, Izmail [Sreznevskij], b 13 June 1812 in Yaroslavl, Russia, d 21 February 1880 in St Petersburg. Russian philologist and Slavist; full member of the Imperial Academy of Sciences from 1854. A graduate in political science at Kharkiv University (MA 1837), he lectured in Slavic philology at Kharkiv (1842–6) and St Petersburg (1847–80) universities. He collected and published songs of wandering Slovak tradesmen (1832) and of Ukrainian peasants in Kharkiv, Poltava, and Katerynoslav gubernias (*Zaporozhskaia starina* [Zaporozhian Antiquity, 1833–8]). With I. Roskovshenko he published *Ukrainskii al'manakh* (Ukrainian Almanac, 1831), where his own verses in Ukrainian Romantic style and narratives in Russian appeared. He was a founder and editor of *Izvestiia Imperatorskoi akademii nauk po otdeleniiu russkogo iazyka i slovesnosti*, where he published many linguistic and historical monuments of the medieval period in Old Church Slavonic and Eastern Slavic. As a linguist Sreznevsky belonged to the Romantic school of philology. In his *Mysli ob istorii russkogo iazyka* (Reflections on the History of the Russian Language, 1849) he gave a synthetic survey of the comparative phonetics and morphology of the Slavic languages and then of the East Slavic languages, including Russian.

Treating Ukrainian as a dialect of one Russian language, he held that the 'southern' (ie, Ukrainian) dialect, as distinct from the 'northern' (Russian and Belarusian) dialect, arose only in the 13th to 14th century, and that in the 15th to 16th century the former divided into the western (Transcarpathian and Ruthenian) and the eastern ('Ukrainian') dialects, while the latter divided into the Belarusian and Great Russian dialects. He believed wrongly that until the 13th century there was no distinction between the religious and secular styles of the literary language, that the structure of the vernacular changed in the 13th to 14th century, and that elements of the popular language began to enter the literary language in the 15th to 16th century. These views and Sreznevsky's authority paved the way for the theory of the Proto-Russian and Old Russian language of the Eastern Slavs. Following A. Vostokov's example, he turned to grammatical and lexicographic studies and the publishing (not always very accurate) of medieval manuscripts. He systematically collected lexical data from old Eastern Slavic manuscripts, which his daughter edited and published posthumously as *Materialy dlia slovaria drevne-russkogo iazyka po pis'mennym pamiatnikam* (Materials for a Dictionary of the Old Russian Language of Literary Monuments, 3 vols, 1893–1912; 4th edn 1989). It is a unique lexicographic collection, based partly on monuments of Old Ukrainian.

O. Horbach

Sribliansky, M. See Shapoval, Mykyta.

Sribna Zemlia (Silver Land). A promotional and poetic name for Transcarpathia. Historically it referred to the Spiš region of western Transcarpathia.

Sribne. III-13. A town smt (1986 pop 3,600) on the Lysohir River and a raion center in Chernihiv oblast. In the medieval period the town of Serebriane, which was first mentioned in the chronicles under the year 1174, stood near the site of Sribne. In the 13th century it was destroyed by the Mongols. From the 1340s Sribne village was under Lithuanian rule, and from 1569, under Polish rule. In the 1640s an Orthodox brotherhood arose there, and it set up a school and hospital. Under the Hetman state (1648–1782) the town was a company center in Pryluka regiment. In the 19th century it belonged to Pryluka county in Poltava gubernia. A sugar refinery and a soap factory were added in the 1840s to its woolen-cloth weaving shops. In 1965 Sribne was granted smt status. Today its main industry is food processing.

Sribny, Fedir [Sribnyj], b 1881 in Nadvirna, Galicia, d 1950. Historian; member of the Shevchenko Scientific Society (NTSh) from 1917. He taught in gymnasiums in Stanyslaviv and Lviv and worked at the Lviv branch of the AN URSR (now ANU) Institute of History (1940–1). In 1943–4 he participated in the academic meetings of the historical section of the NTSh. Among his works was an important series of studies of the organization of the Lviv Stauropegion Institute from the late 16th to the mid-18th centuries (*Zapysky NTSh*, vols 106, 108, 111–15 [1911–13]).

Sribny, Viacheslav [Sribnyj, Vjačeslav] (pseud of V. Sribnytsky), b 17 September 1911 in Myhiia, Yelysavethrad county, Kherson gubernia. Writer. He wrote the story collections *Liudyna zalyshylas' zhyty* (A Person Stayed to Live, 1958), *Ty potribnyi liudiam* (You Are Needed by People, 1970), and *Ostannii litak* (The Last Plane, 1976) and the novel *Sosny na kameni* (Pines on a Rock, 1958).

Srochynsky, Kornylo [Sročyns'kyj], b 17 November 1731 in Peremyshl, Galicia, d 21 March 1790. Basilian priest, writer, and noted preacher. He entered the Basilian order in 1754 and, after serving as a missionary in the Za-

mostia region, became hegumen of the Krystynopil Monastery (1766–76). Later he served as consultator for the order in the Galician province and then hegumen of the Lavriv St Onuphrius's Monastery. He prepared a handbook of sermons for Basilian missionaries that was published in 1790 as *Methodus peragendi missiones*. Srochynsky also left histories of the Lavriv monastery and an account of the 1768 haidamaka uprising in Uman, which were published posthumously.